*Selected Works of the Brontë Sisters*

# Selected Works of the
# Brontë Sisters

**CHARLOTTE BRONTË**

*Jane Eyre & Villette*

**EMILY BRONTË**

*Wuthering Heights*

**ANNE BRONTË**

*Agnes Grey &
The Tenant of Wildfell Hall*

*Wordsworth Editions*

2

Readers who are interested in other titles from
Wordsworth Editions are invited to visit out website at
www.wordsworth-editions.com

For our latest list and a full mail-order service contact
Bibliophile Books, 5 Thomas Road, London E14 7BN
Tel: +44 0207 515 9222   Fax: +44 0207 538 4115
e-mail: orders@bibliophilebooks.com

This edition published 2005 by Wordsworth Editions Limited
8B East Street, Ware, Hertfordshire SG12 9HJ

ISBN 1 84022 060 0

Typeset in Great Britain by Antony Gray
Printed and bound by Clays Ltd, St Ives plc

# CONTENTS

# CONTENTS

# *Biographical Notice*

It has been thought that all the works published under the names of Currer, Ellis, and Acton Bell, were, in reality, the production of one person. This mistake I endeavoured to rectify by a few words of disclaimer prefixed to the third edition of *Jane Eyre*. These, too, it appears, failed to gain general credence, and now, on the occasion of a reprint of *Wuthering Heights* and *Agnes Grey*, I am advised distinctly to state how the case really stands.

Indeed, I feel myself that it is time the obscurity attending those two names – Ellis and Acton – was done away. The little mystery, which formerly yielded some harmless pleasure, has lost its interest; circumstances are changed. It becomes, then, my duty to explain briefly the origin and authorship of the books written by Currer, Ellis, and Acton Bell.

About five years ago, my two sisters and myself, after a somewhat prolonged period of separation, found ourselves reunited, and at home. Resident in a remote district where education had made little progress, and where, consequently, there was no inducement to seek social intercourse beyond our own domestic circle, we were wholly dependent on ourselves and each other, on books and study, for the enjoyments and occupations of life. The highest stimulus, as well as the liveliest pleasure we had known from childhood upwards, lay in attempts at literary composition; formerly we used to show each other what we wrote, but of late years this habit of communication and consultation had been discontinued; hence it ensued, that we were mutually ignorant of the progress we might respectively have made.

One day, in the autumn of 1845, I accidentally lighted on a manuscript volume of verse in my sister Emily's handwriting. Of course, I was not surprised, knowing that she could and did write verse: I looked it over, and something more than surprise seized me – a deep conviction that these were not common effusions, nor at all like the poetry women generally write. I thought them condensed and terse, vigorous and genuine. To my ear, they had also a peculiar music – wild, melancholy, and elevating.

My sister Emily was not a person of demonstrative character, nor one, on the recesses of whose mind and feelings, even those nearest and dearest to her could, with impunity, intrude unlicensed; it took hours to reconcile her to the discovery I had made, and days to persuade her that such poems merited publication. I knew, however, that a mind like hers could not be without some latent spark of honourable ambition, and refused to be discouraged in my attempts to fan that spark to flame.

Meantime, my younger sister quietly produced some of her own compositions, intimating that since Emily's had given me pleasure, I might like

to look at hers. I could not but be a partial judge, yet I thought that these verses too had a sweet sincere pathos of their own.

We had very early cherished the dream of one day becoming authors. This dream, never relinquished even when distance divided and absorbing tasks occupied us, now suddenly acquired strength and consistency: it took the character of a resolve. We agreed to arrange a small selection of our poems, and, if possible, get them printed. Averse to personal publicity, we veiled our own names under those of Currer, Ellis, and Acton Bell; the ambiguous choice being dictated by a sort of conscientious scruple at assuming Christian names positively masculine, while we did not like to declare ourselves women, because – without at that time suspecting that our mode of writing and thinking was not what is called 'feminine' – we had a vague impression that authoresses are liable to be looked on with prejudice; we had noticed how critics sometimes use for their chastisement the weapon of personality, and for their reward, a flattery, which is not true praise.

The bringing out of our little book was hard work. As was to be expected, neither we nor our poems were at all wanted; but for this we had been prepared at the outset; though inexperienced ourselves, we had read the experience of others. The great puzzle lay in the difficulty of getting answers of any kind from the publishers to whom we applied. Being greatly harassed by this obstacle, I ventured to apply to the Messrs Chambers, of Edinburgh, for a word of advice; *they* may have forgotten the circumstance, but *I* have not, for from them I received a brief and businesslike, but civil and sensible reply, on which we acted, and at last made a way.

The book was printed: it is scarcely known, and all of it that merits to be known are the poems of Ellis Bell. The fixed conviction I held, and hold, of the worth of these poems has not indeed received the confirmation of much favourable criticism; but I must retain it notwithstanding.

Ill-success failed to crush us: the mere effort to succeed had given a wonderful zest to existence; it must be pursued. We each set to work on a prose tale: Ellis Bell produced *Wuthering Heights*, Acton Bell, *Agnes Grey*, and Currer Bell also wrote a narrative in one volume. These manuscripts were perseveringly obtruded upon various publishers for the space of a year and a half; usually, their fate was an ignominious and abrupt dismissal.

At last *Wuthering Heights* and *Agnes Grey* were accepted on terms somewhat impoverishing to the two authors; Currer Bell's book found acceptance nowhere, nor any acknowledgment of merit, so that something like the chill of despair began to invade his heart. As a forlorn hope, he tried one publishing house more – Messrs Smith and Elder. Ere long, in a much shorter space than that on which experience had taught him to calculate – there came a letter, which he opened in the dreary expectation of finding two hard hopeless lines, intimating that Messrs Smith and Elder 'were not disposed to publish the manuscript', and, instead, he took out of the envelope a letter of two pages. He read it trembling. It declined, indeed, to

publish that tale, for business reasons, but it discussed its merits and demerits so courteously, so considerately, in a spirit so rational, with a discrimination so enlightened, that this very refusal cheered the author better than a vulgarly-expressed acceptance would have done. It was added, that a work in three volumes would meet with careful attention.

I was then just completing *Jane Eyre*, at which I had been working while the one volume tale was plodding its weary round in London: in three weeks I sent it off; friendly and skilful hands took it in. This was in the commencement of September 1847; it came out before the close of October following, while *Wuthering Heights* and *Agnes Grey*, my sisters' works, which had already been in the press for months, still lingered under a different management.

They appeared at last. Critics failed to do them justice. The immature but very real powers revealed in *Wuthering Heights* were scarcely recognised; its import and nature were misunderstood; the identity of its author was misrepresented; it was said that this was an earlier and ruder attempt of the same pen which had produced *Jane Eyre*. Unjust and grievous error! We laughed at it at first, but I deeply lament it now. Hence, I fear, arose a prejudice against the book. That writer who could attempt to palm off an inferior and immature production under cover of one successful effort, must indeed be unduly eager after the secondary and sordid result of authorship, and pitiably indifferent to its true and honourable meed. If reviewers and the public truly believed this, no wonder that they looked darkly on the cheat.

Yet I must not be understood to make these things subject for reproach or complaint; I dare not do so; respect for my sister's memory forbids me. By her any such querulous manifestation would have been regarded as an unworthy, and offensive weakness.

It is my duty, as well as my pleasure, to acknowledge one exception to the general rule of criticism. One writer [Sidney Dobell], endowed with the keen vision and fine sympathies of genius, has discerned the real nature of *Wuthering Heights*, and has, with equal accuracy, noted its beauties and touched on its faults. Too often do reviewers remind us of the mob of Astrologers, Chaldeans, and Soothsayers gathered before the 'writing on the wall,' and unable to read the characters or make known the interpretation. We have a right to rejoice when a true seer comes at last, some man in whom is an excellent spirit, to whom have been given light, wisdom, and understanding; who can accurately read the 'Mene, Mene, Tekel, Upharsin' of an original mind (however unripe, however inefficiently cultured and partially expanded that mind may be); and who can say with confidence, 'This is the interpretation thereof.'

Yet even the writer to whom I allude shares the mistake about the authorship, and does me the injustice to suppose that there was equivoque in my former rejection of this honour (as an honour, I regard it). May I assure him that I would scorn in this and in every case to deal in equivoque;

I believe language to have been given us to make our meaning clear, and not to wrap it in dishonest doubt.

*The Tenant of Wildfell Hall* by Acton Bell, had likewise an unfavourable reception. At this I cannot wonder. The choice of subject was an entire mistake. Nothing less congruous with the writer's nature could be conceived. The motives which dictated this choice were pure, but, I think, slightly morbid. She had, in the course of her life, been called on to contemplate, near at hand and for a long time, the terrible effects of talents misused and faculties abused; hers was naturally a sensitive, reserved, and dejected nature; what she saw sank very deeply into her mind; it did her harm. She brooded over it till she believed it to be a duty to reproduce every detail (of course with fictitious characters, incidents, and situations) as a warning to others. She hated her work, but would pursue it. When reasoned with on the subject, she regarded such reasonings as a temptation to self-indulgence. She must be honest; she must not varnish, soften, or conceal. This well-meant resolution brought on her misconstruction and some abuse, which she bore, as it was her custom to bear whatever was unpleasant, with mild, steady patience. She was a very sincere and practical Christian, but the tinge of religious melancholy communicated a sad shade to her brief, blameless life.

Neither Ellis nor Acton allowed herself for one moment to sink under want of encouragement; energy nerved the one, and endurance upheld the other. They were both prepared to try again; I would fain think that hope and the sense of power was yet strong within them. But a great change approached: affliction came in that shape which to anticipate is dread; to look back on, grief. In the very heat and burden of the day, the labourers failed over their work.

My sister Emily first declined. The details of her illness are deep-branded in my memory, but to dwell on them, either in thought or narrative, is not in my power. Never in all her life had she lingered over any task that lay before her, and she did not linger now. She sank rapidly. She made haste to leave us. Yet, while physically she perished, mentally, she grew stronger than we had yet known her. Day by day, when I saw with what a front she met suffering, I looked on her with an anguish of wonder and love. I have seen nothing like it; but, indeed, I have never seen her parallel in anything. Stronger than a man, simpler than a child, her nature stood alone. The awful point was, that, while full of ruth for others, on herself she had no pity; the spirit was inexorable to the flesh; from the trembling hand, the unnerved limbs, the faded eyes, the same service was exacted as they had rendered in health. To stand by and witness this, and not dare to remonstrate, was a pain no words can render.

Two cruel months of hope and fear passed painfully by, and the day came at last when the terrors and pains of death were to be undergone by this treasure, which had grown dearer and dearer to our hearts as it wasted before our eyes. Towards the decline of that day, we had nothing left of

Emily but her mortal remains as consumption left them. She died December 19, 1848.

We thought this enough: but we were utterly and presumptuously wrong. She was not buried ere Anne fell ill. She had not been committed to the grave a fortnight, before we received distinct intimation that it was necessary to prepare our minds to see the younger sister go after the elder. Accordingly, she followed in the same path with slower step, and with a patience that equalled the other's fortitude. I have said that she was religious, and it was by leaning on those Christian doctrines in which she firmly believed, that she found support through her most painful journey. I witnessed their efficacy in her latest hour and greatest trial, and must bear my testimony to the calm triumph with which they brought her through. She died May 28, 1849.

What more shall I say about them? I cannot and need not say much more. In externals, they were two unobtrusive women; a perfectly secluded life gave them retiring manners and habits. In Emily's nature the extremes of vigour and simplicity seemed to meet. Under an unsophisticated culture, inartificial tastes, and an unpretending outside, lay a secret power and fire that might have informed the brain and kindled the veins of a hero; but she had no worldly wisdom; her powers were unadapted to the practical business of life; she would fail to defend her most manifest rights, to consult her most legitimate advantage. An interpreter ought always to have stood between her and the world. Her will was not very flexible, and it generally opposed her interest. Her temper was magnanimous, but warm and sudden; her spirit altogether unbending.

Anne's character was milder and more subdued; she wanted the power, the fire, the originality of her sister, but was well-endowed with quiet virtues of her own. Long-suffering, self-denying, reflective, and intelligent, a constitutional reserve and taciturnity placed and kept her in the shade, and covered her mind, and especially her feelings, with a sort of nun-like veil, which was rarely lifted. Neither Emily nor Anne was learned; they had no thought of filling their pitchers at the well-spring of other minds; they always wrote from the impulse of nature, the dictates of intuition, and from such stores of observation as their limited experience had enabled them to amass. I may sum up all by saying, that for strangers they were nothing, for superficial observers less than nothing; but for those who had known them all their lives in the intimacy of close relationship, they were genuinely good and truly great.

This notice has been written, because I felt it a sacred duty to wipe the dust off their gravestones, and leave their dear names free from soil.

CURRER BELL
*September 19, 1850*

# JANE EYRE

# Jane Eyre

## CHARLOTTE BRONTË

TO

# W. M. THACKERAY, ESQ.

THIS WORK IS

RESPECTFULLY INSCRIBED

BY THE AUTHOR

## Preface to the Second Edition

A preface to the first edition of *Jane Eyre* being unnecessary, I gave none: this second edition demands a few words both of acknowledgment and miscellaneous remark.

My thanks are due in three quarters.

To the Public, for the indulgent ear it has inclined to a plain tale with few pretensions.

To the Press, for the fair field its honest suffrage has opened to an obscure aspirant.

To my Publishers, for the aid their tact, their energy, their practical sense and frank liberality have afforded an unknown and unrecommended Author.

The Press and the Public are but vague personifications for me, and I must thank them in vague terms; but my Publishers are definite: so are certain generous critics who have encouraged me as only large-hearted and high-minded men know how to encourage a struggling stranger; to them, i.e., to my Publishers and the select Reviewers, I say cordially, Gentlemen, I thank you from my heart.

Having thus acknowledged what I owe those who have aided and approved me, I turn to another class; a small one, so far as I know, but not, therefore, to be overlooked. I mean the timorous or carping few who doubt the tendency of such books as *Jane Eyre*: in whose eyes whatever is unusual is wrong; whose ears detect in each protest against bigotry – that parent of crime – an insult to piety, that regent of God on earth. I would suggest to such doubters certain obvious distinctions; I would remind them of certain simple truths.

Conventionality is not morality. Self-righteousness is not religion. To attack the first is not to assail the last. To pluck the mask from the face of the Pharisee, is not to lift an impious hand to the Crown of Thorns.

These things and deeds are diametrically opposed: they are as distinct as is vice from virtue. Men too often confound them: they should not be confounded: appearance should not be mistaken for truth; narrow human doctrines, that only tend to elate and magnify a few, should not be substituted for the world-redeeming creed of Christ. There is – I repeat it – a difference; and it is a good, and not a bad action to mark broadly and clearly the line of separation between them.

The world may not like to see these ideas dissevered, for it has been accustomed to blend them; finding it convenient to make external show pass for sterling worth – to let whitewashed walls vouch for clean shrines. It may hate him who dares to scrutinise and expose – to rase the gilding, and show base metal under it – to penetrate the sepulchre, and reveal charnel relics: but hate as it will, it is indebted to him.

Ahab did not like Micaiah, because he never prophesied good concerning him, but evil; probably he liked the sycophant son of Chenaanah better; yet might Ahab have escaped a bloody death, had he but stopped his ears to flattery, and opened them to faithful counsel.

There is a man in our own days whose words are not framed to tickle delicate ears: who, to my thinking, comes before the great ones of society, much as the son of Imlah came before the throned Kings of Judah and Israel; and who speaks truth as deep, with a power as prophet-like and as vital – a mien as dauntless and as daring. Is the satirist of *Vanity Fair* admired in high places? I cannot tell; but I think if some of those amongst whom he hurls the Greek fire of his sarcasm, and over whom he flashes the levin-brand of his denunciation, were to take his warnings in time – they or their seed might yet escape a fatal Ramoth-Gilead.

Why have I alluded to this man? I have alluded to him, Reader, because I think I see in him an intellect profounder and more unique than his contemporaries have yet recognised; because I regard him as the first social regenerator of the day – as the very master of that working corps who would restore to rectitude the warped system of things; because I think no commentator on his writings has yet found the comparison that suits him, the terms which rightly characterise his talent. They say he is like Fielding: they talk of his wit, humour, comic powers. He resembles Fielding as an eagle does a vulture: Fielding could stoop on carrion, but Thackeray never does. His wit is bright, his humour attractive, but both bear the same relation to his serious genius that the mere lambent sheet-lightning playing under the edge of the summer-cloud does to the electric death-spark hid in its womb. Finally, I have alluded to Mr Thackeray, because to him – if he will accept the tribute of a total stranger – I have dedicated this second edition of *Jane Eyre*.

CURRER BELL
*December 21st, 1847*

## Note to the Third Edition

I avail myself of the opportunity which a third edition of *Jane Eyre* affords me, of again addressing a word to the Public, to explain that my claim to the title of novelist rests on this one work alone. If, therefore, the authorship of other works of fiction has been attributed to me, an honour is awarded where it is not merited; and consequently, denied where it is justly due.

This explanation will serve to rectify mistakes which may already have been made, and to prevent future errors.

CURRER BELL
*April 13th, 1848*

## Chapter 1

There was no possibility of taking a walk that day. We had been wandering, indeed, in the leafless shrubbery an hour in the morning; but since dinner (Mrs Reed, when there was no company, dined early) the cold winter wind had brought with it clouds so sombre, and a rain so penetrating, that further outdoor exercise was now out of the question.

I was glad of it: I never liked long walks, especially on chilly afternoons: dreadful to me was the coming home in the raw twilight, with nipped fingers and toes, and a heart saddened by the chidings of Bessie, the nurse, and humbled by the consciousness of my physical inferiority to Eliza, John, and Georgiana Reed.

The said Eliza, John, and Georgiana were now clustered round their mama in the drawing-room: she lay reclined on a sofa by the fireside, and with her darlings about her (for the time neither quarrelling nor crying) looked perfectly happy. Me, she had dispensed from joining the group; saying, 'She regretted to be under the necessity of keeping me at a distance; but that until she heard from Bessie, and could discover by her own observation, that I was endeavouring in good earnest to acquire a more sociable and childlike disposition, a more attractive and sprightly manner – something lighter, franker, more natural, as it were – she really must exclude me from privileges intended only for contented, happy, little children.'

'What does Bessie say I have done?' I asked.

'Jane, I don't like cavillers or questioners; besides, there is something truly forbidding in a child taking up her elders in that manner. Be seated somewhere; and until you can speak pleasantly, remain silent.'

A small breakfast-room adjoined the drawing-room, I slipped in there. It contained a bookcase: I soon possessed myself of a volume, taking care that it should be one stored with pictures. I mounted into the window-seat: gathering up my feet, I sat cross-legged, like a Turk; and, having drawn the red moreen curtain nearly close, I was shrined in double retirement.

Folds of scarlet drapery shut in my view to the right hand; to the left were the clear panes of glass, protecting, but not separating me from the drear November day. At intervals, while turning over the leaves of my book, I studied the aspect of that winter afternoon. Afar, it offered a pale blank of mist and cloud; near a scene of wet lawn and storm-beat shrub, with ceaseless rain sweeping away wildly before a long and lamentable blast.

I returned to my book – Bewick's *History of British Birds*: the letterpress thereof I cared little for, generally speaking; and yet there were certain introductory pages that, child as I was, I could not pass quite as a blank. They were those which treat of the haunts of sea-fowl; of 'the solitary rocks and promontories' by them only inhabited; of the coast of Norway, studded with

isles from its southern extremity, the Lindeness, or Naze, to the North Cape –

> Where the Northern Ocean, in vast whirls,
> Boils round the naked, melancholy isles
> Of farthest Thule; and the Atlantic surge
> Pours in among the stormy Hebrides.

Nor could I pass unnoticed the suggestion of the bleak shores of Lapland, Siberia, Spitzbergen, Nova Zembla, Iceland, Greenland, with 'the vast sweep of the Arctic Zone, and those forlorn regions of dreary space, that reservoir of frost and snow, where firm fields of ice, the accumulation of centuries of winters, glazed in Alpine heights above heights, surround the pole and concentre the multiplied rigours of extreme cold.' Of these death-white realms I formed an idea of my own: shadowy, like all the half-comprehended notions that float dim through children's brains, but strangely impressive. The words in these introductory pages connected themselves with the succeeding vignettes, and gave significance to the rock standing up alone in a sea of billow and spray; to the broken boat stranded on a desolate coast; to the cold and ghastly moon glancing through bars of cloud at a wreck just sinking.

I cannot tell what sentiment haunted the quite solitary churchyard, with its inscribed headstone; its gate, its two trees, its low horizon, girdled by a broken wall, and its newly-risen crescent, attesting the hour of eventide.

The two ships becalmed on a torpid sea, I believed to be marine phantoms.

The fiend pinning down the thief's pack behind him, I passed over quickly: it was an object of terror.

So was the black horned thing seated aloof on a rock, surveying a distant crowd surrounding a gallows.

Each picture told a story; mysterious often to my undeveloped understanding and imperfect feelings, yet ever profoundly interesting: as interesting as the tales Bessie sometimes narrated on winter evenings, when she chanced to be in good humour; and when, having brought her ironing-table to the nursery hearth, she allowed us to sit about it, and while she got up Mrs Reed's lace frills, and crimped her nightcap borders, fed our eager attention with passages of love and adventure taken from old fairy tales and other ballads; or (as at a later period I discovered) from the pages of *Pamela*, and *Henry, Earl of Moreland*.

With Bewick on my knee, I was then happy: happy at least in my way. I feared nothing but interruption, and that came too soon. The breakfast-room door opened.

'Boh! Madam Mope!' cried the voice of John Reed; then he paused: he found the room apparently empty.

'Where the dickens is she!' he continued. 'Lizzy! Georgy!' (calling to his sisters) 'Joan is not here: tell mama she is run out into the rain – bad animal!'

'It is well I drew the curtain,' thought I; and I wished fervently he might not discover my hiding place: nor would John Reed have found it out himself; he was not quick either of vision or conception; but Eliza just put her head in at the door, and said at once – 'She is in the window-seat, to be sure, Jack.'

And I came out immediately, for I trembled at the idea of being dragged forth by the said Jack.

'What do you want?' I asked, with awkward diffidence.

'Say, "What do you want, Master Reed?"' was the answer. 'I want you to come here;' and seating himself in an armchair, he intimated by a gesture that I was to approach and stand before him.

John Reed was a schoolboy of fourteen years old; four years older than I, for I was but ten: large and stout for his age, with a dingy and unwholesome skin; thick lineaments in a spacious visage, heavy limbs and large extremities. He gorged himself habitually at table, which made him bilious, and gave him a dim and bleared eye and flabby cheeks. He ought now to have been at school; but his mama had taken him home for a month or two, 'on account of his delicate health.' Mr Miles, the master, affirmed that he would do very well if he had fewer cakes and sweetmeats sent him from home; but the mother's heart turned from an opinion so harsh, and inclined rather to the more refined idea that John's sallowness was owing to over-application and, perhaps, to pining after home.

John had not much affection for his mother and sisters, and an antipathy to me. He bullied and punished me; not two or three times in the week, nor once or twice in the day, but continually: every nerve I had feared him, and every morsel of flesh in my bones shrank when he came near. There were moments when I was bewildered by the terror he inspired, because I had no appeal whatever against either his menaces or his inflictions; the servants did not like to offend their young master by taking my part against him, and Mrs Reed was blind and deaf on the subject: she never saw him strike or heard him abuse me, though he did both now and then in her very presence, more frequently, however, behind her back.

Habitually obedient to John, I came up to his chair: he spent some three minutes in thrusting out his tongue at me as far as he could without damaging the roots: I knew he would soon strike, and while dreading the blow, I mused on the disgusting and ugly appearance of him who would presently deal it. I wonder if he read that notion in my face; for, all at once, without speaking, he struck suddenly and strongly. I tottered, and on regaining my equilibrium retired back a step or two from his chair.

'That is for your impudence in answering mama awhile since,' said he, 'and for your sneaking way of getting behind curtains, and for the look you had in your eyes two minutes since, you rat!'

Accustomed to John Reed's abuse, I never had an idea of replying to it; my care was how to endure the blow which would certainly follow the insult.

'What were you doing behind the curtain?' he asked.

'I was reading.'

'Show the book.'

I returned to the window and fetched it thence.

'You have no business to take our books; you are a dependant, mama says; you have no money; your father left you none; you ought to beg, and not to live here with gentlemen's children like us, and eat the same meals we do, and wear

clothes at our mama's expense. Now, I'll teach you to rummage my bookshelves: for they *are* mine; all the house belongs to me, or will do in a few years. Go and stand by the door, out of the way of the mirror and the windows.'

I did so, not at first aware what was his intention; but when I saw him lift and poise the book and stand in act to hurl it, I instinctively started aside with a cry of alarm: not soon enough, however; the volume was flung, it hit me, and I fell, striking my head against the door and cutting it. The cut bled, the pain was sharp: my terror had passed its climax; other feelings succeeded.

'Wicked and cruel boy!' I said. 'You are like a murderer – you are like a slave-driver – you are like the Roman emperors!'

I had read Goldsmith's *History of Rome*, and had formed my opinion of Nero, Caligula, etc. Also I had drawn parallels in silence, which I never thought thus to have declared aloud.

'What! what!' he cried. 'Did she say that to me? Did you hear her, Eliza and Georgiana? Won't I tell mama? but first –'

He ran headlong at me: I felt him grasp my hair and my shoulder: he had closed with a desperate thing. I really saw in him a tyrant, a murderer. I felt a drop or two of blood from my head trickle down my neck, and was sensible of somewhat pungent suffering: these sensations for the time predominated over fear, and I received him in frantic sort. I don't very well know what I did with my hands, but he called me 'Rat! Rat!' and bellowed out aloud. Aid was near him: Eliza and Georgiana had run for Mrs Reed, who was gone upstairs: she now came upon the scene, followed by Bessie and her maid Abbot. We were parted: I heard the words – 'Dear! dear! What a fury to fly at Master John!'

'Did ever anybody see such a picture of passion!'

Then Mrs Reed subjoined – 'Take her away to the red-room, and lock her in there.' Four hands were immediately laid upon me, and I was borne upstairs.

## *Chapter 2*

I resisted all the way: a new thing for me, and a circumstance which greatly strengthened the bad opinion Bessie and Miss Abbot were disposed to entertain of me. The fact is, I was a trifle beside myself; or rather *out* of myself, as the French would say: I was conscious that a moment's mutiny had already rendered me liable to strange penalties, and, like any other rebel slave, I felt resolved, in my desperation, to go all lengths.

'Hold her arms, Miss Abbot: she's like a mad cat.'

'For shame! for shame!' cried the lady's-maid. 'What shocking conduct, Miss Eyre, to strike a young gentleman, your benefactress's son! Your young master.'

'Master! How is he my master? Am I a servant?'

'No; you are less than a servant, for you do nothing for your keep. There, sit down, and think over your wickedness.'

They had got me by this time into the apartment indicated by Mrs Reed, and

had thrust me upon a stool: my impulse was to rise from it like a spring; their two pair of hands arrested me instantly.

'If you don't sit still, you must be tied down,' said Bessie. 'Miss Abbot, lend me your garters; she would break mine directly.'

Miss Abbot turned to divest a stout leg of the necessary ligature. This preparation for bonds, and the additional ignominy it inferred, took a little of the excitement out of me.

'Don't take them off,' I cried; 'I will not stir.'

In guarantee whereof, I attached myself to my seat by my hands.

'Mind you don't,' said Bessie; and when she had ascertained that I was really subsiding, she loosened her hold of me; then she and Miss Abbot stood with folded arms, looking darkly and doubtfully on my face, as incredulous of my sanity.

'She never did so before,' at last said Bessie, turning to the Abigail.

'But it was always in her,' was the reply. 'I've told Missis often my opinion about the child, and Missis agreed with me. She's an underhand little thing: I never saw a girl of her age with so much cover.'

Bessie answered not; but ere long, addressing me, she said – 'You ought to be aware, Miss, that you are under obligations to Mrs Reed: she keeps you: if she were to turn you off, you would have to go to the poor-house.'

I had nothing to say to these words: they were not new to me: my very first recollections of existence included hints of the same kind. This reproach of my dependence had become a vague singsong in my ear: very painful and crushing, but only half intelligible. Miss Abbot joined in – 'And you ought not to think yourself on an equality with the Misses Reed and Master Reed, because Missis kindly allows you to be brought up with them. They will have a great deal of money, and you will have none: it is your place to be humble, and to try to make yourself agreeable to them.'

'What we tell you is for your good,' added Bessie, in no harsh voice; 'you should try to be useful and pleasant, then, perhaps, you would have a home here; but if you become passionate and rude, Missis will send you away, I am sure.'

'Besides,' said Miss Abbot, 'God will punish her: He might strike her dead in the midst of her tantrums, and then where would she go? Come, Bessie, we will leave her: I wouldn't have her heart for anything. Say your prayers, Miss Eyre, when you are by yourself; for if you don't repent, something bad might be permitted to come down the chimney and fetch you away.'

They went, shutting the door, and locking it behind them.

The red-room was a square chamber, very seldom slept in, I might say never, indeed, unless when a chance influx of visitors at Gateshead Hall rendered it necessary to turn to account all the accommodation it contained: yet it was one of the largest and stateliest chambers in the mansion. A bed supported on massive pillars of mahogany, hung with curtains of deep red damask, stood out like a tabernacle in the centre; the two large windows, with their blinds always drawn down, were half shrouded in festoons and falls of similar drapery; the carpet was red; the table at the foot of the bed was covered with a crimson cloth;

the walls were a soft fawn colour with a blush of pink in it; the wardrobe, the toilet-table, the chairs were of darkly polished old mahogany. Out of these deep surrounding shades rose high, and glared white, the piled-up mattresses and pillows of the bed, spread with a snowy Marseilles counterpane. Scarcely less prominent was an ample cushioned easy-chair near the head of the bed, also white, with a footstool before it; and looking, as I thought, like a pale throne.

This room was chill, because it seldom had a fire; it was silent, because remote from the nursery and kitchen; solemn, because it was known to be so seldom entered. The housemaid alone came here on Saturdays, to wipe from the mirrors and the furniture a week's quiet dust: and Mrs Reed herself, at far intervals, visited it to review the contents of a certain secret drawer in the wardrobe, where were stored divers parchments, her jewel-casket, and a miniature of her deceased husband; and in those last words lies the secret of the red-room – the spell which kept it so lonely in spite of its grandeur.

Mr Reed had been dead nine years: it was in this chamber he breathed his last; here he lay in state; hence his coffin was borne by the undertaker's men; and, since that day, a sense of dreary consecration had guarded it from frequent intrusion.

My seat, to which Bessie and the bitter Miss Abbot had left me riveted, was a low ottoman near the marble chimney-piece; the bed rose before me; to my right hand there was the high, dark wardrobe, with subdued, broken reflections varying the gloss of its panels; to my left were the muffled windows; a great looking-glass between them repeated the vacant majesty of the bed and room. I was not quite sure whether they had locked the door; and when I dared move, I got up and went to see. Alas! yes: no jail was ever more secure. Returning, I had to cross before the looking-glass; my fascinated glance involuntarily explored the depth it revealed. All looked colder and darker in that visionary hollow than in reality: and the strange little figure there gazing at me, with a white face and arms specking the gloom, and glittering eyes of fear moving where all else was still, had the effect of a real spirit: I thought it like one of the tiny phantoms, half fairy, half imp, Bessie's evening stories represented as coming out of lone, ferny dells in moors, and appearing before the eyes of belated travellers. I returned to my stool.

Superstition was with me at that moment; but it was not yet her hour for complete victory: my blood was still warm; the mood of the revolted slave was still bracing me with its bitter vigour; I had to stem a rapid rush of retrospective thought before I quailed to the dismal present.

All John Reed's violent tyrannies, all his sisters' proud indifference, all his mother's aversion, all the servants' partiality, turned up in my disturbed mind like a dark deposit in a turbid well. Why was I always suffering, always browbeaten, always accused, for ever condemned? Why could I never please? Why was it useless to try to win anyone's favour? Eliza, who was headstrong and selfish, was respected. Georgiana, who had a spoiled temper, a very acrid spite, a captious and insolent carriage, was universally indulged. Her beauty, her pink cheeks and golden curls, seemed to give delight to all who looked at her, and to

purchase indemnity for every fault. John no one thwarted, much less punished; though he twisted the necks of the pigeons, killed the little pea-chicks, set the dogs at the sheep, stripped the hothouse vines of their fruit, and broke the buds off the choicest plants in the conservatory: he called his mother "old girl", too; sometimes reviled her for her dark skin, similar to his own; bluntly disregarded her wishes; not unfrequently tore and spoiled her silk attire; and he was still 'her own darling'. I dared commit no fault: I strove to fulfil every duty; and I was termed naughty and tiresome, sullen and sneaking, from morning to noon, and from noon to night.

My head still ached and bled with the blow and fall I had received: no one had reproved John for wantonly striking me; and because I had turned against him to avert farther irrational violence, I was loaded with general opprobrium.

'Unjust! – unjust!' said my reason, forced by the agonising stimulus into precocious though transitory power: and Resolve, equally wrought up, instigated some strange expedient to achieve escape from insupportable oppression – as running away, or, if that could not be effected, never eating or drinking more, and letting myself die.

What a consternation of soul was mine that dreary afternoon! How all my brain was in tumult, and all my heart in insurrection! Yet in what darkness, what dense ignorance, was the mental battle fought! I could not answer the ceaseless inward question – *why* I thus suffered; now, at the distance of – I will not say how many years, I see it clearly.

I was a discord in Gateshead Hall: I was like nobody there; I had nothing in harmony with Mrs Reed or her children, or her chosen vassalage. If they did not love me, in fact, as little did I love them. They were not bound to regard with affection a thing that could not sympathise with one amongst them; a heterogeneous thing, opposed to them in temperament, in capacity, in propensities; a useless thing, incapable of serving their interest, or adding to their pleasure; a noxious thing, cherishing the germs of indignation at their treatment, of contempt of their judgement. I know that had I been a sanguine, brilliant, careless, exacting, handsome, romping child – though equally dependent and friendless – Mrs Reed would have endured my presence more complacently; her children would have entertained for me more of the cordiality of fellow-feeling; the servants would have been less prone to make me the scapegoat of the nursery.

Daylight began to forsake the red-room; it was past four o'clock, and the beclouded afternoon was tending to drear twilight. I heard the rain still beating continuously on the staircase window, and the wind howling in the grove behind the hall; I grew by degrees cold as a stone, and then my courage sank. My habitual mood of humiliation, self-doubt, forlorn depression, fell damp on the embers of my decaying ire. All said I was wicked, and perhaps I might be so; what thought had I been but just conceiving of starving myself to death? That certainly was a crime: and was I fit to die? Or was the vault under the chancel of Gateshead Church an inviting bourne? In such vault I had been told did Mr Reed lie buried; and led by this thought to recall his idea, I dwelt on it with gathering dread. I

could not remember him; but I knew that he was my own uncle – my mother's brother – that he had taken me when a parentless infant to his house; and that in his last moments he had required a promise of Mrs Reed that she would rear and maintain me as one of her own children. Mrs Reed probably considered she had kept this promise; and so she had, I dare say, as well as her nature would permit her; but how could she really like an interloper not of her race, and unconnected with her, after her husband's death, by any tie? It must have been most irksome to find herself bound by a hard-wrung pledge to stand in the stead of a parent to a strange child she could not love, and to see an uncongenial alien permanently intruded on her own family group.

A singular notion dawned upon me. I doubted not – never doubted – that if Mr Reed had been alive he would have treated me kindly; and now, as I sat looking at the white bed and overshadowed walls – occasionally also turning a fascinated eye towards the dimly gleaming mirror – I began to recall what I had heard of dead men, troubled in their graves by the violation of their last wishes, revisiting the earth to punish the perjured and avenge the oppressed; and I thought Mr Reed's spirit, harassed by the wrongs of his sister's child, might quit its abode – whether in the church vault or in the unknown world of the departed – and rise before me in this chamber. I wiped my tears and hushed my sobs, fearful lest any sign of violent grief might waken a preternatural voice to comfort me, or elicit from the gloom some haloed face, bending over me with strange pity. This idea, consolatory in theory, I felt would be terrible if realised: with all my might I endeavoured to stifle it – I endeavoured to be firm. Shaking my hair from my eyes, I lifted my head and tried to look boldly round the dark room; at this moment a light gleamed on the wall. Was it, I asked myself, a ray from the moon penetrating some aperture in the blind? No; moonlight was still, and this stirred; while I gazed, it glided up to the ceiling and quivered over my head. I can now conjecture readily that this streak of light was, in all likelihood, a gleam from a lantern carried by someone across the lawn: but then, prepared as my mind was for horror, shaken as my nerves were by agitation, I thought the swift darting beam was a herald of some coming vision from another world. My heart beat thick, my head grew hot; a sound filled my ears, which I deemed the rushing of wings; something seemed near me; I was oppressed, suffocated: endurance broke down; I rushed to the door and shook the lock in desperate effort. Steps came running along the outer passage; the key turned, Bessie and Abbot entered.

'Miss Eyre, are you ill?' said Bessie.

'What a dreadful noise! it went quite through me!' exclaimed Abbot.

'Take me out! Let me go into the nursery!' was my cry.

'What for? Are you hurt? Have you seen something?' again demanded Bessie.

'Oh! I saw a light, and I thought a ghost would come.' I had now got hold of Bessie's hand, and she did not snatch it from me.

'She has screamed out on purpose,' declared Abbot, in some disgust. 'And what a scream! If she had been in great pain one would have excused it, but she only wanted to bring us all here: I know her naughty tricks.'

'What is all this?' demanded another voice peremptorily; and Mrs Reed came along the corridor, her cap flying wide, her gown rustling stormily. 'Abbot and Bessie, I believe I gave orders that Jane Eyre should be left in the red-room till I came to her myself.'

'Miss Jane screamed so loud, ma'am,' pleaded Bessie.

'Let her go,' was the only answer. 'Loose Bessie's hand, child: you cannot succeed in getting out by these means, be assured. I abhor artifice, particularly in children; it is my duty to show you that tricks will not answer: you will now stay here an hour longer, and it is only on condition of perfect submission and stillness that I shall liberate you then.'

'O aunt! have pity! Forgive me! I cannot endure it – let me be punished some other way! I shall be killed if – '

'Silence! This violence is all most repulsive:' and so, no doubt, she felt it. I was a precocious actress in her eyes; she sincerely looked on me as a compound of virulent passions, mean spirit, and dangerous duplicity.

Bessie and Abbot having retreated, Mrs Reed, impatient of my now frantic anguish and wild sobs, abruptly thrust me back and locked me in, without farther parley. I heard her sweeping away; and soon after she was gone, I suppose I had a species of fit: unconsciousness closed the scene.

## *Chapter 3*

The next thing I remember is, waking up with a feeling as if I had had a frightful nightmare, and seeing before me a terrible red glare, crossed with thick black bars. I heard voices, too, speaking with a hollow sound, and as if muffled by a rush of wind or water: agitation, uncertainty, and an all-predominating sense of terror confused my faculties. Ere long, I became aware that someone was handling me; lifting me up and supporting me in a sitting posture, and that more tenderly than I had ever been raised or upheld before. I rested my head against a pillow or an arm, and felt easy.

In five minutes more the cloud of bewilderment dissolved: I knew quite well that I was in my own bed, and that the red glare was the nursery fire. It was night: a candle burnt on the table; Bessie stood at the bed-foot with a basin in her hand, and a gentleman sat in a chair near my pillow, leaning over me.

I felt an inexpressible relief, a soothing conviction of protection and security, when I knew that there was a stranger in the room, an individual not belonging to Gateshead, and not related to Mrs Reed. Turning from Bessie (though her presence was far less obnoxious to me than that of Abbot, for instance, would have been), I scrutinised the face of the gentleman: I knew him; it was Mr Lloyd, an apothecary, sometimes called in by Mrs Reed when the servants were ailing: for herself and the children she employed a physician.

'Well, who am I?' he asked.

I pronounced his name, offering him at the same time my hand: he took it,

smiling and saying, 'We shall do very well by and by.' Then he laid me down, and addressing Bessie, charged her to be very careful that I was not disturbed during the night. Having given some further directions, and intimated that he should call again the next day, he departed; to my grief. I felt so sheltered and befriended while he sat in the chair near my pillow; and as he closed the door after him, all the room darkened and my heart again sank: inexpressible sadness weighed it down.

'Do you feel as if you should sleep, Miss?' asked Bessie, rather softly.

Scarcely dared I answer her; for I feared the next sentence might be rough. 'I will try.'

'Would you like to drink, or could you eat anything?'

'No, thank you; Bessie.'

'Then I think I shall go to bed, for it is past twelve o'clock; but you may call me if you want anything in the night.'

Wonderful civility this! It emboldened me to ask a question.

'Bessie, what is the matter with me? Am I ill?'

'You fell sick, I suppose, in the red-room with crying; you'll be better soon, no doubt.'

Bessie went into the housemaid's apartment, which was near. I heard her say – 'Sarah, come and sleep with me in the nursery; I daren't for my life be alone with that poor child tonight: she might die; it's such a strange thing she should have that fit: I wonder if she saw anything. Missis was rather too hard.'

Sarah came back with her; they both went to bed; they were whispering together for half an hour before they fell asleep. I caught scraps of their conversation, from which I was able only too distinctly to infer the main subject discussed.

'Something passed her, all dressed in white, and vanished' – 'A great black dog behind him' – 'Three loud raps on the chamber door' – 'A light in the churchyard just over his grave,' etc., etc.

At last both slept: the fire and the candle went out. For me, the watches of that long night passed in ghastly wakefulness; ear, eye, and mind were alike strained by dread: such dread as children only can feel.

No severe or prolonged bodily illness followed this incident of the red-room; it only gave my nerves a shock of which I feel the reverberation to this day. Yes, Mrs Reed, to you I owe some fearful pangs of mental suffering, but I ought to forgive you, for you knew not what you did: while rending my heartstrings, you thought you were only uprooting my bad propensities.

Next day, by noon, I was up and dressed, and sat wrapped in a shawl by the nursery hearth. I felt physically weak and broken down: but my worse ailment was an unutterable wretchedness of mind: a wretchedness which kept drawing from me silent tears; no sooner had I wiped one salt drop from my cheek than another followed. Yet, I thought, I ought to have been happy, for none of the Reeds were there, they were all gone out in the carriage with their mama. Abbot, too, was sewing in another room, and Bessie, as she moved hither and thither, putting away toys and arranging drawers, addressed to me every now

and then a word of unwonted kindness. This state of things should have been to me a paradise of peace, accustomed as I was to a life of ceaseless reprimand and thankless fagging; but, in fact, my racked nerves were now in such a state that no calm could soothe, and no pleasure excite them agreeably.

Bessie had been down into the kitchen, and she brought up with her a tart on a certain brightly painted china plate, whose bird of paradise, nestling in a wreath of convolvuli and rosebuds, had been wont to stir in me a most enthusiastic sense of admiration; and which plate I had often petitioned to be allowed to take in my hand in order to examine it more closely, but had always hitherto been deemed unworthy of such a privilege. This precious vessel was now placed on my knee, and I was cordially invited to eat the circlet of delicate pastry upon it. Vain favour! coming, like most other favours long deferred and often wished for too late! I could not eat the tart; and the plumage of the bird, the tints of the flowers, seemed strangely faded: I put both plate and tart away. Bessie asked if I would have a book: the word *book* acted as a transient stimulus, and I begged her to fetch *Gulliver's Travels* from the library. This book I had again and again perused with delight. I considered it a narrative of facts, and discovered in it a vein of interest deeper than what I found in fairy tales: for as to the elves, having sought them in vain among foxglove leaves and bells, under mushrooms and beneath the ground-ivy mantling old wall-nooks, I had at length made up my mind to the sad truth, that they were all gone out of England to some savage country where the woods were wilder and thicker, and the population more scant; whereas, Lilliput and Brobdingnag being, in my creed, solid parts of the earth's surface, I doubted not that I might one day, by taking a long voyage, see with my own eyes the little fields, houses, and trees, the diminutive people, the tiny cows, sheep, and birds of the one realm; and the cornfields, forest-high, the mighty mastiffs, the monster cats, the tower-like men and women, of the other. Yet, when this cherished volume was now placed in my hand – when I turned over its leaves, and sought in its marvellous pictures the charm I had, till now, never failed to find – all was eerie and dreary; the giants were gaunt goblins, the pigmies malevolent and fearful imps, Gulliver a most desolate wanderer in most dread and dangerous regions. I closed the book, which I dared no longer peruse, and put it on the table, beside the untasted tart.

Bessie had now finished dusting and tidying the room, and having washed her hands, she opened a certain little drawer, full of splendid shreds of silk and satin, and began making a new bonnet for Georgiana's doll. Meantime she sang: her song was –

> 'In the days when we went gypsying,
> A long time ago.'

I had often heard the song before, and always with lively delight; for Bessie had a sweet voice, at least, I thought so. But now, though her voice was still sweet, I found in its melody an indescribable sadness. Sometimes, preoccupied with her work, she sang the refrain very low, very lingeringly; 'A long time ago'

came out like the saddest cadence of a funeral hymn. She passed into another ballad, this time a really doleful one.

> 'My feet they are sore, and my limbs they are weary;
>   Long is the way, and the mountains are wild;
> Soon will the twilight close moonless and dreary
>   Over the path of the poor orphan child.
>
> Why did they send me so far and so lonely,
>   Up where the moors spread and grey rocks are piled?
> Men are hard-hearted, and kind angels only
>   Watch o'er the steps of a poor orphan child.
>
> Yet distant and soft the night breeze is blowing,
>   Clouds there are none, and clear stars beam mild,
> God, in His mercy, protection is showing,
>   Comfort and hope to the poor orphan child.
>
> Ev'n should I fall o'er the broken bridge passing,
>   Or stray in the marshes, by false lights beguiled,
> Still will my Father, with promise and blessing,
>   Take to His bosom the poor orphan child.
>
> There is a thought that for strength should avail me,
>   Though both of shelter and kindred despoiled;
> Heaven is a home, and a rest will not fail me;
>   God is a friend to the poor orphan child.'

'Come, Miss Jane, don't cry,' said Bessie as she finished. She might as well have said to the fire, 'don't burn!' but how could she divine the morbid suffering to which I was a prey? In the course of the morning Mr Lloyd came again.

'What, already up!' said he, as he entered the nursery. 'Well, nurse, how is she?'

Bessie answered that I was doing very well.

'Then she ought to look more cheerful. Come here, Miss Jane: your name is Jane, is it not?'

'Yes, sir, Jane Eyre.'

'Well, you have been crying, Miss Jane Eyre; can you tell me what about? Have you any pain?'

'No, sir.'

'Oh! I dare say she is crying because she could not go out with Missis in the carriage,' interposed Bessie.

'Surely not! why, she is too old for such pettishness.'

I thought so too; and my self-esteem being wounded by the false charge, I answered promptly, 'I never cried for such a thing in my life: I hate going out in the carriage. I cry because I am miserable.'

'Oh fie, Miss!' said Bessie.

The good apothecary appeared a little puzzled. I was standing before him;

he fixed his eyes on me very steadily: his eyes were small and grey; not very bright, but I dare say I should think them shrewd now: he had a hard-featured yet good-natured looking face. Having considered me at leisure, he said – 'What made you ill yesterday?'

'She had a fall,' said Bessie, again putting in her word.

'Fall! why, that is like a baby again! Can't she manage to walk at her age? She must be eight or nine years old.'

'I was knocked down,' was the blunt explanation, jerked out of me by another pang of mortified pride; 'but that did not make me ill,' I added; while Mr Lloyd helped himself to a pinch of snuff.

As he was returning the box to his waistcoat pocket, a loud bell rang for the servants' dinner; he knew what it was. 'That's for you, nurse,' said he; 'you can go down; I'll give Miss Jane a lecture till you come back.'

Bessie would rather have stayed, but she was obliged to go, because punctuality at meals was rigidly enforced at Gateshead Hall.

'The fall did not make you ill; what did, then?' pursued Mr Lloyd when Bessie was gone.

'I was shut up in a room where there is a ghost till after dark.'

I saw Mr Lloyd smile and frown at the same time. 'Ghost! What, you are a baby after all! You are afraid of ghosts?'

'Of Mr Reed's ghost I am: he died in that room, and was laid out there. Neither Bessie nor anyone else will go into it at night, if they can help it; and it was cruel to shut me up alone without a candle, so cruel that I think I shall never forget it.'

'Nonsense! And is it that makes you so miserable? Are you afraid now in daylight?'

'No: but night will come again before long: and besides, I am unhappy, very unhappy, for other things.'

'What other things? Can you tell me some of them?'

How much I wished to reply fully to this question! How difficult it was to frame any answer! Children can feel, but they cannot analyse their feelings; and if the analysis is partially effected in thought, they know not how to express the result of the process in words. Fearful, however, of losing this first and only opportunity of relieving my grief by imparting it, I, after a disturbed pause, contrived to frame a meagre, though, as far as it went, true response.

'For one thing, I have no father or mother, brothers or sisters.'

'You have a kind aunt and cousins.'

Again I paused; then bunglingly enounced – 'But John Reed knocked me down, and my aunt shut me up in the red-room.'

Mr Lloyd a second time produced his snuff-box.

'Don't you think Gateshead Hall a very beautiful house?' asked he. 'Are you not very thankful to have such a fine place to live at?'

'It is not my house, sir; and Abbot says I have less right to be here than a servant.'

'Pooh! you can't be silly enough to wish to leave such a splendid place?'

'If I had anywhere else to go, I should be glad to leave it; but I can never get away from Gateshead till I am a woman.'

'Perhaps you may – who knows? Have you any relations besides Mrs Reed?'

'I think not, sir.'

'None belonging to your father?'

'I don't know: I asked Aunt Reed once, and she said possibly I might have some poor, low relations called Eyre, but she knew nothing about them.'

'If you had such, would you like to go to them?'

I reflected. Poverty looks grim to grown people; still more so to children: they have not much idea of industrious, working, respectable poverty; they think of the word only as connected with ragged clothes, scanty food, fireless grates, rude manners, and debasing vices: poverty for me was synonymous with degradation.

'No; I should not like to belong to poor people,' was my reply.

'Not even if they were kind to you?'

I shook my head: I could not see how poor people had the means of being kind; and then to learn to speak like them, to adopt their manners, to be uneducated, to grow up like one of the poor women I saw sometimes nursing their children or washing their clothes at the cottage doors of the village of Gateshead: no, I was not heroic enough to purchase liberty at the price of caste.

'But are your relatives so very poor? Are they working people?'

'I cannot tell; Aunt Reed says if I have any, they must be a beggarly set: I should not like to go a-begging.'

'Would you like to go to school?'

Again I reflected: I scarcely knew what school was: Bessie sometimes spoke of it as a place where young ladies sat in the stocks, wore backboards, and were expected to be exceedingly genteel and precise: John Reed hated his school, and abused his master; but John Reed's tastes were no rule for mine, and if Bessie's accounts of school-discipline (gathered from the young ladies of a family where she had lived before coming to Gateshead) were somewhat appalling, her details of certain accomplishments attained by these same young ladies were, I thought, equally attractive. She boasted of beautiful paintings of landscapes and flowers by them executed; of songs they could sing and pieces they could play, of purses they could net, of French books they could translate; till my spirit was moved to emulation as I listened. Besides, school would be a complete change: it implied a long journey, an entire separation from Gateshead, an entrance into a new life.

'I should indeed like to go to school,' was the audible conclusion of my musings.

'Well, well! who knows what may happen?' said Mr Lloyd, as he got up. 'The child ought to have change of air and scene,' he added, speaking to himself; 'nerves not in a good state.'

Bessie now returned; at the same moment the carriage was heard rolling up the gravel-walk.

'Is that your mistress, nurse?' asked Mr Lloyd. 'I should like to speak to her before I go.'

Bessie invited him to walk into the breakfast-room, and led the way out. In

the interview which followed between him and Mrs Reed, I presume, from after-occurrences, that the apothecary ventured to recommend my being sent to school; and the recommendation was no doubt readily enough adopted; for as Abbot said, in discussing the subject with Bessie when both sat sewing in the nursery one night, after I was in bed, and, as they thought, asleep, 'Missis was, she dared say, glad enough to get rid of such a tiresome, ill-conditioned child, who always looked as if she were watching everybody, and scheming plots underhand.' Abbot, I think, gave me credit for being a sort of infantine Guy Fawkes.

On that same occasion I learned, for the first time, from Miss Abbot's communications to Bessie, that my father had been a poor clergyman; that my mother had married him against the wishes of her friends, who considered the match beneath her; that my grandfather Reed was so irritated at her disobedience, he cut her off without a shilling; that after my mother and father had been married a year, the latter caught the typhus fever while visiting among the poor of a large manufacturing town where his curacy was situated, and where that disease was then prevalent: that my mother took the infection from him, and both died within a month of each other.

Bessie, when she heard this narrative, sighed and said, 'Poor Miss Jane is to be pitied too, Abbot.'

'Yes,' responded Abbot; 'if she were a nice, pretty child, one might compassionate her forlornness; but one really cannot care for such a little toad as that.'

'Not a great deal, to be sure,' agreed Bessie: 'at any rate, a beauty like Miss Georgiana would be more moving in the same condition.'

'Yes, I dote on Miss Georgiana!' cried the fervent Abbot. 'Little darling! – with her long curls and her blue eyes, and such a sweet colour as she has; just as if she were painted! – Bessie, I could fancy a Welsh rabbit for supper.'

'So could I – with a roast onion. Come, we'll go down.' They went.

## Chapter 4

From my discourse with Mr Lloyd, and from the above reported conference between Bessie and Abbot, I gathered enough of hope to suffice as a motive for wishing to get well: a change seemed near, I desired and waited it in silence. It tarried, however: days and weeks passed: I had regained my normal state of health, but no new allusion was made to the subject over which I brooded. Mrs Reed surveyed me at times with a severe eye, but seldom addressed me: since my illness, she had drawn a more marked line of separation than ever between me and her own children; appointing me a small closet to sleep in by myself, condemning me to take my meals alone, and pass all my time in the nursery, while my cousins were constantly in the drawing-room. Not a hint, however, did she drop about sending me to school: still I felt an instinctive certainty that she would not long endure me under the same roof with her; for her glance,

now more than ever, when turned on me, expressed an insuperable and rooted aversion.

Eliza and Georgiana, evidently acting according to orders, spoke to me as little as possible: John thrust his tongue in his cheek whenever he saw me, and once attempted chastisement; but as I instantly turned against him, roused by the same sentiment of deep ire and desperate revolt which had stirred my corruption before, he thought it better to desist, and ran from me uttering execrations, and vowing I had burst his nose. I had indeed levelled at that prominent feature as hard a blow as my knuckles could inflict; and when I saw that either that or my look daunted him, I had the greatest inclination to follow up my advantage to purpose; but he was already with his mama. I heard him in a blubbering tone commence the tale of how 'that nasty Jane Eyre' had flown at him like a mad cat: he was stopped rather harshly – 'Don't talk to me about her, John: I told you not to go near her; she is not worthy of notice; I do not choose that either you or your sisters should associate with her.'

Here, leaning over the banister, I cried out suddenly, and without at all deliberating on my words – 'They are not fit to associate with me.'

Mrs Reed was rather a stout woman; but, on hearing this strange and audacious declaration, she ran nimbly up the stair, swept me like a whirlwind into the nursery, and crushing me down on the edge of my crib, dared me in an emphatic voice to rise from that place, or utter one syllable during the remainder of the day.

'What would Uncle Reed say to you, if he were alive?' was my scarcely voluntary demand. I say scarcely voluntary, for it seemed as if my tongue pronounced words without my will consenting to their utterance: something spoke out of me over which I had no control.

'What?' said Mrs Reed under her breath: her usually cold composed grey eye became troubled with a look like fear; she took her hand from my arm, and gazed at me as if she really did not know whether I were child or fiend. I was now in for it.

'My Uncle Reed is in heaven, and can see all you do and think; and so can papa and mama: they know how you shut me up all day long, and how you wish me dead.'

Mrs Reed soon rallied her spirits: she shook me most soundly, she boxed both my ears, and then left me without a word. Bessie supplied the hiatus by a homily of an hour's length, in which she proved beyond a doubt that I was the most wicked and abandoned child ever reared under a roof. I half believed her; for I felt indeed only bad feelings surging in my breast.

November, December, and half of January passed away. Christmas and the New Year had been celebrated at Gateshead with the usual festive cheer; presents had been interchanged, dinners and evening parties given. From every enjoyment I was, of course excluded: my share of the gaiety consisted in witnessing the daily apparelling of Eliza and Georgiana, and seeing them descend to the drawing-room, dressed out in thin muslin frocks and scarlet sashes, with hair elaborately ringleted; and afterwards, in listening to the sound of the piano or the harp played below, to the passing to and fro of the butler and footman, to

the jingling of glass and china as refreshments were handed, to the broken hum of conversation as the drawing-room door opened and closed. When tired of this occupation, I would retire from the stairhead to the solitary and silent nursery: there, though somewhat sad, I was not miserable. To speak truth, I had not the least wish to go into company, for in company I was very rarely noticed; and if Bessie had but been kind and companionable, I should have deemed it a treat to spend the evenings quietly with her, instead of passing them under the formidable eye of Mrs Reed, in a room full of ladies and gentlemen. But Bessie, as soon as she had dressed her young ladies, used to take herself off to the lively regions of the kitchen and housekeeper's room, generally bearing the candle along with her. I then sat with my doll on my knee till the fire got low, glancing round occasionally to make sure that nothing worse than myself haunted the shadowy room; and when the embers sank to a dull red, I undressed hastily, tugging at knots and strings as I best might, and sought shelter from cold and darkness in my crib. To this crib I always took my doll; human beings must love something, and, in the dearth of worthier objects of affection, I contrived to find a pleasure in loving and cherishing a faded graven image, shabby as a miniature scarecrow. It puzzles me now to remember with what absurd sincerity I doted on this little toy, half fancying it alive and capable of sensation. I could not sleep unless it was folded in my night-gown; and when it lay there safe and warm, I was comparatively happy, believing it to be happy likewise.

Long did the hours seem while I waited the departure of the company, and listened for the sound of Bessie's step on the stairs: sometimes she would come up in the interval to seek her thimble or her scissors, or perhaps to bring me something by way of supper – a bun or a cheesecake – then she would sit on the bed while I ate it, and when I had finished, she would tuck the clothes round me, and twice she kissed me, and said, 'Good-night, Miss Jane.' When thus gentle, Bessie seemed to me the best, prettiest, kindest being in the world; and I wished most intensely that she would always be so pleasant and amiable, and never push me about, or scold, or task me unreasonably, as she was too often wont to do. Bessie Lee must, I think, have been a girl of good natural capacity, for she was smart in all she did, and had a remarkable knack of narrative; so, at least, I judge from the impression made on me by her nursery tales. She was pretty too, if my recollections of her face and person are correct. I remember her as a slim young woman, with black hair, dark eyes, very nice features, and good, clear complexion; but she had a capricious and hasty temper, and indifferent ideas of principle or justice: still, such as she was, I preferred her to anyone else at Gateshead Hall.

It was the fifteenth of January, about nine o'clock in the morning: Bessie was gone down to breakfast; my cousins had not yet been summoned to their mama; Eliza was putting on her bonnet and warm garden-coat to go and feed her poultry, an occupation of which she was fond: and not less so of selling the eggs to the housekeeper and hoarding up the money she thus obtained. She had a turn for traffic, and a marked propensity for saving; shown not only in the vending of eggs and chickens, but also in driving hard bargains with the gardener about flower-roots, seeds, and slips of plants; that functionary having

orders from Mrs Reed to buy of his young lady all the products of her parterre she wished to sell: and Eliza would have sold the hair off her head if she could have made a handsome profit thereby. As to her money, she first secreted it in odd corners, wrapped in a rag or an old curl-paper; but some of these hoards having been discovered by the housemaid, Eliza, fearful of one day losing her valued treasure, consented to entrust it to her mother, at a usurious rate of interest – fifty or sixty per cent.; which interest she exacted every quarter, keeping her accounts in a little book with anxious accuracy.

Georgiana sat on a high stool, dressing her hair at the glass, and interweaving her curls with artificial flowers and faded feathers, of which she had found a store in a drawer in the attic. I was making my bed, having received strict orders from Bessie to get it arranged before she returned (for Bessie now frequently employed me as a sort of under-nurserymaid, to tidy the room, dust the chairs, etc.). Having spread the quilt and folded my night-dress, I went to the window-seat to put in order some picture-books and doll's house furniture scattered there; an abrupt command from Georgiana to let her playthings alone (for the tiny chairs and mirrors, the fairy plates and cups, were her property) stopped my proceedings; and then, for lack of other occupation, I fell to breathing on the frost-flowers with which the window was fretted, and thus clearing a space in the glass through which I might look out on the grounds, where all was still and petrified under the influence of a hard frost.

From this window were visible the porter's lodge and the carriage-road, and just as I had dissolved so much of the silver-white foliage veiling the panes as left room to look out, I saw the gates thrown open and a carriage roll through. I watched it ascending the drive with indifference; carriages often came to Gateshead, but none ever brought visitors in whom I was interested; it stopped in front of the house, the doorbell rang loudly, the newcomer was admitted. All this being nothing to me, my vacant attention soon found livelier attraction in the spectacle of a little hungry robin, which came and chirruped on the twigs of the leafless cherry-tree nailed against the wall near the casement. The remains of my breakfast of bread and milk stood on the table, and having crumbled a morsel of roll, I was tugging at the sash to put out the crumbs on the window-sill, when Bessie came running upstairs into the nursery.

'Miss Jane, take off your pinafore; what are you doing there? Have you washed your hands and face this morning?' I gave another tug before I answered, for I wanted the bird to be secure of its bread: the sash yielded; I scattered the crumbs, some on the stone sill, some on the cherry-tree bough, then, closing the window, I replied – 'No, Bessie; I have only just finished dusting.'

'Troublesome, careless child! and what are you doing now? You look quite red, as if you have been about some mischief: what were you opening the window for?'

I was spared the trouble of answering, for Bessie seemed in too great a hurry to listen to explanations; she hauled me to the washstand, inflicted a merciless, but happily brief scrub on my face and hands with soap, water, and a coarse towel; disciplined my head with a bristly brush, denuded me of my pinafore, and

then hurrying me to the top of the stairs, bid me go down directly, as I was wanted in the breakfast-room.

I would have asked who wanted me: I would have demanded if Mrs Reed was there; but Bessie was already gone, and had closed the nursery-door upon me. I slowly descended. For nearly three months, I had never been called to Mrs Reed's presence; restricted so long to the nursery, the breakfast, dining, and drawing-rooms were become for me awful regions, on which it dismayed me to intrude.

I now stood in the empty hall; before me was the breakfast-room door, and I stopped, intimidated and trembling. What a miserable little poltroon had fear, engendered of unjust punishment, made of me in those days! I feared to return to the nursery, and feared to go forward to the parlour; ten minutes I stood in agitated hesitation; the vehement ringing of the breakfast-room bell decided me; I *must* enter.

'Who could want me?' I asked inwardly, as with both hands I turned the stiff door-handle, which, for a second or two, resisted my efforts. 'What should I see besides Aunt Reed in the apartment? – a man or a woman?' The handle turned, the door unclosed, and passing through and curtseying low, I looked up at – a black pillar! – such, at least, appeared to me, at first sight, the straight, narrow, sable-clad shape standing erect on the rug: the grim face at the top was like a carved mask, placed above the shaft by way of capital.

Mrs Reed occupied her usual seat by the fireside; she made a signal to me to approach; I did so, and she introduced me to the stony stranger with the words: 'This is the little girl respecting whom I applied to you.'

*He*, for it was a man, turned his head slowly towards where I stood, and having examined me with the two inquisitive-looking grey eyes which twinkled under a pair of bushy brows, said solemnly, and in a bass voice, 'Her size is small: what is her age?'

'Ten years.'

'So much?' was the doubtful answer; and he prolonged his scrutiny for some minutes. Presently he addressed me – 'Your name, little girl?'

'Jane Eyre, sir.'

In uttering these words I looked up: he seemed to me a tall gentleman; but then I was very little; his features were large, and they and all the lines of his frame were equally harsh and prim.

'Well, Jane Eyre, and are you a good child?'

Impossible to reply to this in the affirmative: my little world held a contrary opinion: I was silent. Mrs Reed answered for me by an expressive shake of the head, adding soon, 'Perhaps the less said on that subject the better, Mr Brocklehurst.'

'Sorry indeed to hear it! she and I must have some talk;' and bending from the perpendicular, he installed his person in the armchair opposite Mrs Reed's. 'Come here,' he said.

I stepped across the rug; he placed me square and straight before him. What a face he had, now that it was almost on a level with mine! what a great nose! and what a mouth! and what large prominent teeth!

'No sight so sad as that of a naughty child,' he began, 'especially a naughty little girl. Do you know where the wicked go after death?'

'They go to hell,' was my ready and orthodox answer.

'And what is hell? Can you tell me that?'

'A pit full of fire.'

'And should you like to fall into that pit, and to be burning there for ever?'

'No, sir.'

'What must you do to avoid it?'

I deliberated a moment; my answer, when it did come, was objectionable: 'I must keep in good health, and not die.'

'How can you keep in good health? Children younger than you die daily. I buried a little child of five years old only a day or two since, a good little child, whose soul is now in heaven. It is to be feared the same could not be said of you were you to be called hence.'

Not being in a condition to remove his doubt, I only cast my eyes down on the two large feet planted on the rug, and sighed, wishing myself far enough away.

'I hope that sigh is from the heart, and that you repent of ever having been the occasion of discomfort to your excellent benefactress.'

'Benefactress! benefactress!' said I inwardly: 'they all call Mrs Reed my benefactress; if so, a benefactress is a disagreeable thing.'

'Do you say your prayers night and morning?' continued my interrogator.

'Yes, sir.'

'Do you read your Bible?'

'Sometimes.'

'With pleasure? Are you fond of it?

'I like Revelations, and the book of Daniel, and Genesis and Samuel, and a little bit of Exodus, and some parts of Kings and Chronicles, and Job and Jonah.'

'And the Psalms? I hope you like them?'

'No, sir.'

'No? oh, shocking! I have a little boy, younger than you, who knows six Psalms by heart: and when you ask him which he would rather have, a gingerbread-nut to eat or a verse of a Psalm to learn, he says: "Oh! the verse of a Psalm! angels sing Psalms;" says he, "I wish to be a little angel here below;" he then gets two nuts in recompense for his infant piety.'

'Psalms are not interesting,' I remarked.

'That proves you have a wicked heart; and you must pray to God to change it: to give you a new and clean one: to take away your heart of stone and give you a heart of flesh.'

I was about to propound a question, touching the manner in which that operation of changing my heart was to be performed, when Mrs Reed interposed, telling me to sit down; she then proceeded to carry on the conversation herself.

'Mr Brocklehurst, I believe I intimated in the letter which I wrote to you three weeks ago, that this little girl has not quite the character and disposition I could wish: should you admit her into Lowood School I should be glad if the

superintendent and teachers were requested to keep a strict eye on her, and, above all, to guard against her worst fault, a tendency to deceit. I mention this in your hearing, Jane, that you may not attempt to impose on Mr Brocklehurst.'

Well might I dread, well might I dislike Mrs Reed; for it was her nature to wound me cruelly; never was I happy in her presence; however carefully I obeyed, however strenuously I strove to please her, my efforts were still repulsed and repaid by such sentences as the above. Now, uttered before a stranger, the accusation cut me to the heart; I dimly perceived that she was already obliterating hope from the new phase of existence which she destined me to enter; I felt, though I could not have expressed the feeling, that she was sowing aversion and unkindness along my future path; I saw myself transformed under Mr Brocklehurst's eye into an artful, noxious child, and what could I do to remedy the injury?

'Nothing, indeed,' thought I, as I struggled to repress a sob, and hastily wiped away some tears, the impotent evidences of my anguish.

'Deceit is, indeed, a sad fault in a child,' said Mr Brocklehurst; 'it is akin to falsehood, and all liars will have their portion in the lake burning with fire and brimstone; she shall, however, be watched, Mrs Reed. I will speak to Miss Temple and the teachers.'

'I should wish her to be brought up in a manner suiting her prospects,' continued my benefactress; 'to be made useful, to be kept humble: as for the vacations, she will, with your permission, spend them always at Lowood.'

'Your decisions are perfectly judicious, madam,' returned Mr Brocklehurst. 'Humility is a Christian grace, and one peculiarly appropriate to the pupils of Lowood; I, therefore, direct that especial care shall be bestowed on its cultivation amongst them. I have studied how best to mortify in them the worldly sentiment of pride; and, only the other day, I had a pleasing proof of my success. My second daughter, Augusta, went with her mama to visit the school, and on her return she exclaimed: "Oh, dear papa, how quiet and plain all the girls at Lowood look, with their hair combed behind their ears, and their long pinafores, and those little holland pockets outside their frocks – they are almost like poor people's children! and," said she, "they looked at my dress and mama's, as if they had never seen a silk gown before." '

'This is the state of things I quite approve,' returned Mrs Reed; 'had I sought all England over, I could scarcely have found a system more exactly fitting a child like Jane Eyre. Consistency, my dear Mr Brocklehurst; I advocate consistency in all things.'

'Consistency, madam, is the first of Christian duties; and it has been observed in every arrangement connected with the establishment of Lowood: plain fare, simple attire, unsophisticated accommodations, hardy and active habits; such is the order of the day in the house and its inhabitants.'

'Quite right, sir. I may then depend upon this child being received as a pupil at Lowood, and there being trained in conformity to her position and prospects?'

'Madam, you may: she shall be placed in that nursery of chosen plants, and I trust she will show herself grateful for the inestimable privilege of her election.'

'I will send her, then, as soon as possible, Mr Brocklehurst; for, I assure you, I feel anxious to be relieved of a responsibility that was becoming too irksome.'

'No doubt, no doubt, madam; and now I wish you good-morning. I shall return to Brocklehurst Hall in the course of a week or two: my good friend, the Archdeacon, will not permit me to leave him sooner. I shall send Miss Temple notice that she is to expect a new girl, so that there will be no difficulty about receiving her. Goodbye.'

'Goodbye, Mr Brocklehurst; remember me to Mrs and Miss Brocklehurst, and to Augusta and Theodore, and Master Broughton Brocklehurst.'

'I will, madam. Little girl, here is a book entitled the *Child's Guide;* read it with prayer, especially that part containing "An account of the awfully sudden death of Martha G—, a naughty child addicted to falsehood and deceit." '

With these words Mr Brocklehurst put into my hand a thin pamphlet sewn in a cover, and having rung for his carriage, he departed.

Mrs Reed and I were left alone: some minutes passed in silence; she was sewing, I was watching her. Mrs Reed might be at that time some six or seven and thirty; she was a woman of robust frame, square-shouldered and strong-limbed, not tall, and, though stout, not obese: she had a somewhat large face, the under jaw being much developed and very solid; her brow was low, her chin large and prominent, mouth and nose sufficiently regular; under her light eyebrows glimmered an eye devoid of ruth; her skin was dark and opaque, her hair nearly flaxen; her constitution was sound as a bell – illness never came near her; she was an exact, clever manager; her household and tenantry were thoroughly under her control; her children only at times defied her authority and laughed it to scorn; she dressed well, and had a presence and port calculated to set off handsome attire.

Sitting on a low stool, a few yards from her armchair, I examined her figure; I perused her features. In my hand I held the tract containing the sudden death of the Liar, to which narrative my attention had been pointed as to an appropriate warning. What had just passed; what Mrs Reed had said concerning me to Mr Brocklehurst; the whole tenor of their conversation, was recent, raw, and stinging in my mind; I had felt every word as acutely as I had heard it plainly, and a passion of resentment fomented now within me.

Mrs Reed looked up from her work; her eye settled on mine, her fingers at the same time suspended their nimble movements.

'Go out of the room; return to the nursery,' was her mandate. My look or something else must have struck her as offensive, for she spoke with extreme though suppressed irritation. I got up, I went to the door; I came back again; I walked to the window, across the room, then close up to her.

*Speak* I must: I had been trodden on severely, and *must* turn: but how? What strength had I to dart retaliation at my antagonist? I gathered my energies and launched them in this blunt sentence – 'I am not deceitful: if I were, I should say I loved *you*; but I declare I do not love you: I dislike you the worst of anybody in the world except John Reed; and this book about the liar, you may give to your girl, Georgiana, for it is she who tells lies, and not I.'

Mrs Reed's hands still lay on her work inactive: her eye of ice continued to dwell freezingly on mine.

'What more have you to say?' she asked, rather in the tone in which a person might address an opponent of adult age than such as is ordinarily used to a child.

That eye of hers, that voice stirred every antipathy I had. Shaking from head to foot, thrilled with ungovernable excitement, I continued – 'I am glad you are no relation of mine: I will never call you aunt again so long as I live. I will never come to see you when I am grown up; and if anyone asks me how I liked you, and how you treated me, I will say the very thought of you makes me sick, and that you treated me with miserable cruelty.'

'How dare you affirm that, Jane Eyre?'

'How dare I, Mrs Reed? How dare I? Because it is the *truth*. You think I have no feelings, and that I can do without one bit of love or kindness; but I cannot live so: and you have no pity. I shall remember how you thrust me back – roughly and violently thrust me back – into the red-room, and locked me up there, to my dying day; though I was in agony; though I cried out, while suffocating with distress, "Have mercy! Have mercy, Aunt Reed!" And that punishment you made me suffer because your wicked boy struck me – knocked me down for nothing. I will tell anybody who asks me questions, this exact tale. People think you a good woman, but you are bad, hardhearted. *You* are deceitful!'

Ere I had finished this reply, my soul began to expand, to exult, with the strangest sense of freedom, of triumph, I ever felt. It seemed as if an invisible bond had burst, and that I had struggled out into unhoped-for liberty. Not without cause was this sentiment: Mrs Reed looked frightened; her work had slipped from her knee; she was lifting up her hands, rocking herself to and fro, and even twisting her face as if she would cry.

'Jane, you are under a mistake: what is the matter with you? Why do you tremble so violently? Would you like to drink some water?'

'No, Mrs Reed.'

'Is there anything else you wish for, Jane? I assure you, I desire to be your friend.'

'Not you. You told Mr Brocklehurst I had a bad character, a deceitful disposition; and I'll let everybody at Lowood know what you are, and what you have done.'

'Jane, you don't understand these things: children must be corrected for their faults.'

'Deceit is not my fault!' I cried out in a savage, high voice.

'But you are passionate, Jane, that you must allow: and now return to the nursery – there's a dear – and lie down a little.'

'I am not your dear; I cannot lie down: send me to school soon, Mrs Reed, for I hate to live here.'

'I will indeed send her to school soon,' murmured Mrs Reed *sotto voce*; and gathering up her work, she abruptly quitted the apartment.

I was left there alone – winner of the field. It was the hardest battle I had fought, and the first victory I had gained: I stood awhile on the rug, where Mr

Brocklehurst had stood, and I enjoyed my conqueror's solitude. First, I smiled to myself and felt elate; but this fierce pleasure subsided in me as fast as did the accelerated throb of my pulses. A child cannot quarrel with its elders, as I had done; cannot give its furious feelings uncontrolled play, as I had given mine, without experiencing afterwards the pang of remorse and the chill of reaction. A ridge of lighted heath, alive, glancing, devouring, would have been a meet emblem of my mind when I accused and menaced Mrs Reed: the same ridge, black and blasted after the flames are dead, would have represented as meetly my subsequent condition, when half an hour's silence and reflection had shown me the madness of my conduct, and the dreariness of my hated and hating position.

Something of vengeance I had tasted for the first time; as aromatic wine it seemed, on swallowing, warm and racy: its after-flavour, metallic and corroding, gave me a sensation as if I had been poisoned. Willingly would I now have gone and asked Mrs Reed's pardon; but I knew, partly from experience and partly from instinct, that was the way to make her repulse me with double scorn, thereby re-exciting every turbulent impulse of my nature.

I would fain exercise some better faculty than that of fierce speaking; fain find nourishment for some less fiendish feeling than that of sombre indignation. I took a book – some Arabian tales; I sat down and endeavoured to read. I could make no sense of the subject; my own thoughts swam always between me and the page I had usually found fascinating. I opened the glass-door in the breakfast-room: the shrubbery was quite still: the black frost reigned, unbroken by sun or breeze, through the grounds. I covered my head and arms with the skirt of my frock, and went out to walk in a part of the plantation which was quite sequestered; but I found no pleasure in the silent trees, the falling fir-cones, the congealed relics of autumn, russet leaves, swept by past winds in heaps, and now stiffened together. I leaned against a gate, and looked into an empty field where no sheep were feeding, where the short grass was nipped and blanched. It was a very grey day; a most opaque sky, 'onding on snaw', canopied all; thence flakes fell at intervals, which settled on the hard path and on the hoary lea without melting. I stood, a wretched child enough, whispering to myself over and over again, 'What shall I do? – what shall I do?'

All at once I heard a clear voice call, 'Miss Jane! where are you? Come to lunch!'

It was Bessie, I knew well enough; but I did not stir; her light step came tripping down the path.

'You naughty little thing!' she said. 'Why don't you come when you are called?'

Bessie's presence, compared with the thoughts over which I had been brooding, seemed cheerful; even though, as usual, she was somewhat cross. The fact is, after my conflict with and victory over Mrs Reed, I was not disposed to care much for the nursemaid's transitory anger; and I *was* disposed to bask in her youthful lightness of heart. I just put my two arms round her and said, 'Come, Bessie! don't scold.'

The action was more frank and fearless than any I was habituated to indulge in: somehow it pleased her.

'You are a strange child, Miss Jane,' she said, as she looked down at me; 'a little roving, solitary thing: and you are going to school, I suppose?'

I nodded.

'And won't you be sorry to leave poor Bessie?'

'What does Bessie care for me? She is always scolding me.'

'Because you're such a queer, frightened, shy little thing. You should be bolder.'

'What! to get more knocks?'

'Nonsense! But you are rather put upon, that's certain. My mother said, when she came to see me last week, that she would not like a little one of her own to be in your place. Now, come in, and I've some good news for you.'

'I don't think you have, Bessie.'

'Child! what do you mean? What sorrowful eyes you fix on me! Well, but Missis and the young ladies and Master John are going out to tea this afternoon, and you shall have tea with me. I'll ask cook to bake you a little cake, and then you shall help me to look over your drawers; for I am soon to pack your trunk. Missis intends you to leave Gateshead in a day or two, and you shall choose what toys you like to take with you.'

'Bessie, you must promise not to scold me any more till I go.'

'Well, I will; but mind you are a very good girl, and don't be afraid of me. Don't start when I chance to speak rather sharply; it's so provoking.'

'I don't think I shall ever be afraid of you again Bessie, because I have got used to you, and I shall soon have another set of people to dread.'

'If you dread them they'll dislike you.'

'As you do, Bessie?'

'I don't dislike you, Miss: I believe I am fonder of you than of all the others.'

'You don't show it.'

'You little sharp thing! you've got quite a new way of talking. What makes you so venturesome and hardy?'

'Why, I shall soon be away from you, and besides' – I was going to say something about what had passed between me and Mrs Reed, but on second thoughts I considered it better to remain silent on that head.

'And so you're glad to leave me?'

'Not at all, Bessie; indeed, just now I'm rather sorry.'

'Just now! and rather! How coolly my little lady says it! I dare say now if I were to ask you for a kiss you wouldn't give it me: you'd say you'd *rather* not.'

'I'll kiss you and welcome: bend your head down.' Bessie stooped; we mutually embraced, and I followed her into the house quite comforted. That afternoon lapsed in peace and harmony; and in the evening Bessie told me some of her most enchanting stories, and sang me some of her sweetest songs. Even for me life had its gleams of sunshine.

## Chapter 5

Five o'clock had hardly struck on the morning of the 19th of January, when Bessie brought a candle into my closet and found me already up and nearly dressed. I had risen half an hour before her entrance, and had washed my face, and put on my clothes by the light of a half-moon just setting, whose rays streamed through the narrow window near my crib. I was to leave Gateshead that day by a coach which passed the lodge gates at six a.m. Bessie was the only person yet risen; she had lit a fire in the nursery, where she now proceeded to make my breakfast. Few children can eat when excited with the thoughts of a journey; nor could I. Bessie, having pressed me in vain to take a few spoonfuls of the boiled milk and bread she had prepared for me, wrapped up some biscuits in a paper and put them into my bag; then she helped me on with my pelisse and bonnet, and wrapping herself in a shawl, she and I left the nursery. As we passed Mrs Reed's bedroom, she said, 'Will you go in and bid Missis goodbye?'

'No, Bessie: she came to my crib last night when you were gone down to supper, and said I need not disturb her in the morning, or my cousins either; and she told me to remember that she had always been my best friend, and to speak of her and be grateful to her accordingly.'

'What did you say, Miss?'

'Nothing: I covered my face with the bedclothes, and turned from her to the wall.'

'That was wrong, Miss Jane.'

'It was quite right, Bessie. Your Missis has not been my friend: she has been my foe.'

'O Miss Jane! don't say so!'

'Goodbye to Gateshead!' cried I, as we passed through the hall and went out at the front door.

The moon was set, and it was very dark; Bessie carried a lantern, whose light glanced on wet steps and gravel road sodden by a recent thaw. Raw and chill was the winter morning: my teeth chattered as I hastened down the drive. There was a light in the porter's lodge: when we reached it, we found the porter's wife just kindling her fire: my trunk, which had been carried down the evening before, stood corded at the door. It wanted but a few minutes of six, and shortly after that hour had struck, the distant roll of wheels announced the coming coach; I went to the door and watched its lamps approach rapidly through the gloom.

'Is she going by herself?' asked the porter's wife.

'Yes.'

'And how far is it?'

'Fifty miles.'

'What a long way! I wonder Mrs Reed is not afraid to trust her so far alone.'

The coach drew up; there it was at the gates with its four horses and its top

laden with passengers: the guard and coachman loudly urged haste; my trunk was hoisted up; I was taken from Bessie's neck, to which I clung with kisses.

'Be sure and take good care of her,' cried she to the guard, as he lifted me into the inside.

'Ay, ay!' was the answer: the door was slapped to, a voice exclaimed 'All right,' and on we drove. Thus was I severed from Bessie and Gateshead; thus whirled away to unknown, and, as I then deemed, remote and mysterious regions.

I remember but little of the journey; I only know that the day seemed to me of a preternatural length, and that we appeared to travel over hundreds of miles of road. We passed through several towns, and in one, a very large one, the coach stopped; the horses were taken out, and the passengers alighted to dine. I was carried into an inn, where the guard wanted me to have some dinner; but, as I had no appetite, he left me in an immense room with a fireplace at each end, a chandelier pendent from the ceiling, and a little red gallery high up against the wall filled with musical instruments. Here I walked about for a long time, feeling very strange and mortally apprehensive of someone coming in and kidnapping me; for I believed in kidnappers, their exploits having frequently figured in Bessie's fireside chronicles. At last the guard returned; once more I was stowed away in the coach, my protector mounted his own seat, sounded his hollow horn, and away we rattled over the 'stony street' of L—.

The afternoon came on wet and somewhat misty: as it waned into dusk, I began to feel that we were getting very far indeed from Gateshead: we ceased to pass through towns; the country changed; great grey hills heaved up round the horizon: as twilight deepened, we descended a valley, dark with wood, and long after night had overclouded the prospect, I heard a wild wind rushing amongst trees.

Lulled by the sound, I at last dropped asleep; I had not long slumbered when the sudden cessation of motion awoke me; the coach-door was open, and a person like a servant was standing at it: I saw her face and dress by the light of the lamps.

'Is there a little girl called Jane Eyre here?' she asked. I answered 'Yes', and was then lifted out; my trunk was handed down, and the coach instantly drove away.

I was stiff with long sitting, and bewildered with the noise and motion of the coach: gathering my faculties, I looked about me. Rain, wind, and darkness filled the air; nevertheless, I dimly discerned a wall before me and a door open in it; through this door I passed with my new guide: she shut and locked it behind her. There was now visible a house or houses – for the building spread far – with many windows, and lights burning in some; we went up a broad pebbly path, splashing wet, and were admitted at a door; then the servant led me through a passage into a room with a fire, where she left me alone.

I stood and warmed my numbed fingers over the blaze, then I looked round; there was no candle, but the uncertain light from the hearth showed, by intervals, papered walls, carpet, curtains, shining mahogany furniture: it was a parlour, not so spacious or splendid as the drawing-room at Gateshead, but comfortable enough. I was puzzling to make out the subject of a picture on the

wall, when the door opened, and an individual carrying a light entered; another followed close behind.

The first was a tall lady with dark hair, dark eyes, and a pale and large forehead; her figure was partly enveloped in a shawl, her countenance was grave, her bearing erect.

'The child is very young to be sent alone,' said she, putting her candle down on the table. She considered me attentively for a minute or two, then further added – 'She had better be put to bed soon; she looks tired: are you tired?' she asked, placing her hand on my shoulder.

'A little, ma'am.'

'And hungry too, no doubt: let her have some supper before she goes to bed, Miss Miller. Is this the first time you have left your parents to come to school, my little girl?'

I explained to her that I had no parents. She enquired how long they had been dead: then how old I was, what was my name, whether I could read, write, and sew a little: then she touched my cheek gently with her forefinger, and saying, 'She hoped I should be a good child,' dismissed me along with Miss Miller.

The lady I had left might be about twenty-nine; the one who went with me appeared some years younger: the first impressed me by her voice, look, and air. Miss Miller was more ordinary; ruddy in complexion, though of a careworn countenance; hurried in gait and action, like one who had always a multiplicity of tasks on hand: she looked, indeed, what I afterwards found she really was, an under-teacher. Led by her, I passed from compartment to compartment, from passage to passage, of a large and irregular building; till, emerging from the total and somewhat dreary silence pervading that portion of the house we had traversed, we came upon the hum of many voices, and presently entered a wide, long room, with great deal tables, two at each end, on each of which burnt a pair of candles, and seated all round on benches, a congregation of girls of every age, from nine or ten to twenty. Seen by the dim light of the dips, their number to me appeared countless, though not in reality exceeding eighty; they were uniformly dressed in brown stuff frocks of quaint fashion, and long holland pinafores. It was the hour of study; they were engaged in conning over their tomorrow's task, and the hum I had heard was the combined result of their whispered repetitions.

Miss Miller signed to me to sit on a bench near the door, then walking up to the top of the long room she cried out – 'Monitors, collect the lesson-books and put them away!'

Four tall girls arose from different tables, and going round, gathered the books and removed them. Miss Miller again gave the word of command – 'Monitors, fetch the supper-trays!'

The tall girls went out and returned presently, each bearing a tray, with portions of something, I knew not what, arranged thereon, and a pitcher of water and mug in the middle of each tray. The portions were handed round; those who liked took a draught of the water, the mug being common to all. When it came to my turn, I drank, for I was thirsty, but did not touch the food,

excitement and fatigue rendering me incapable of eating; I now saw, however, that it was a thin oaten cake shared into fragments.

The meal over, prayers were read by Miss Miller, and the classes filed off, two and two, upstairs. Overpowered by this time with weariness, I scarcely noticed what sort of a place the bedroom was, except that, like the schoolroom, I saw it was very long. Tonight I was to be Miss Miller's bedfellow; she helped me to undress: when laid down I glanced at the long rows of beds, each of which was quickly filled with two occupants; in ten minutes the single light was extinguished, and amidst silence and complete darkness I fell asleep.

The night passed rapidly: I was too tired even to dream; I only once awoke to hear the wind rave in furious gusts, and the rain fall in torrents, and to be sensible that Miss Miller had taken her place by my side. When I again unclosed my eyes, a loud bell was ringing; the girls were up and dressing; day had not yet begun to dawn, and a rushlight or two burned in the room. I too rose reluctantly; it was bitter cold, and I dressed as well as I could for shivering, and washed when there was a basin at liberty, which did not occur soon, as there was but one basin to six girls, on the stands down the middle of the room. Again the bell rang; all formed in file, two and two, and in that order descended the stairs and entered the cold and dimly lit schoolroom: here prayers were read by Miss Miller; afterwards she called out – 'Form classes!'

A great tumult succeeded for some minutes, during which Miss Miller repeatedly exclaimed, 'Silence!' and 'Order!' When it subsided, I saw them all drawn up in four semicircles, before four chairs, placed at the four tables; all held books in their hands, and a great book, like a Bible, lay on each table, before the vacant seat. A pause of some seconds succeeded, filled up by the low, vague hum of numbers; Miss Miller walked from class to class, hushing this indefinite sound.

A distant bell tinkled: immediately three ladies entered the room, each walked to a table and took her seat; Miss Miller assumed the fourth vacant chair, which was that nearest the door, and around which the smallest of the children were assembled: to this inferior class I was called, and placed at the bottom of it.

Business now began: the day's Collect was repeated, then certain texts of Scripture were said, and to these succeeded a protracted reading of chapters in the Bible, which lasted an hour. By the time that exercise was terminated, day had fully dawned. The indefatigable bell now sounded for the fourth time: the classes were marshalled and marched into another room to breakfast: how glad I was to behold a prospect of getting something to eat! I was now nearly sick from inanition, having taken so little the day before.

The refectory was a great, low-ceiled, gloomy room; on two long tables smoked basins of something hot, which, however, to my dismay, sent forth an odour far from inviting. I saw a universal manifestation of discontent when the fumes of the repast met the nostrils of those destined to swallow it; from the van of the procession, the tall girls of the first class, rose the whispered words – 'Disgusting! The porridge is burnt again!'

'Silence!' ejaculated a voice; not that of Miss Miller, but one of the upper teachers, a little and dark personage, smartly dressed, but of somewhat morose

aspect, who installed herself at the top of one table, while a more buxom lady presided at the other. I looked in vain for her I had first seen the night before; she was not visible: Miss Miller occupied the foot of the table where I sat, and a strange, foreign-looking, elderly lady, the French teacher, as I afterwards found, took the corresponding seat at the other board. A long grace was said and a hymn sung; then a servant brought in some tea for the teachers, and the meal began.

Ravenous, and now very faint, I devoured a spoonful or two of my portion without thinking of its taste; but the first edge of hunger blunted, I perceived I had got in hand a nauseous mess; burnt porridge is almost as bad as rotten potatoes; famine itself soon sickens over it. The spoons were moved slowly: I saw each girl taste her food and try to swallow it; but in most cases the effort was soon relinquished. Breakfast was over, and none had breakfasted. Thanks being returned for what we had not got, and a second hymn chanted, the refectory was evacuated for the schoolroom. I was one of the last to go out, and in passing the tables, I saw one teacher take a basin of the porridge and taste it; she looked at the others; all their countenances expressed displeasure, and one of them, the stout one, whispered – 'Abominable stuff! How shameful!'

A quarter of an hour passed before lessons again began, during which the schoolroom was in a glorious tumult; for that space of time it seemed to be permitted to talk loud and more freely, and they used their privilege. The whole conversation ran on the breakfast, which one and all abused roundly. Poor things! it was the sole consolation they had; Miss Miller was now the only teacher in the room: a group of great girls standing about her spoke with serious and sullen gestures. I heard the name of Mr Brocklehurst pronounced by some lips; at which Miss Miller shook her head disapprovingly; but she made no great effort to check the general wrath; doubtless she shared in it.

A clock in the schoolroom struck nine; Miss Miller left her circle, and standing in the middle of the room, cried – 'Silence! To your seats!'

Discipline prevailed: in five minutes the confused throng was resolved into order, and comparative silence quelled the Babel clamour of tongues. The upper teachers now punctually resumed their posts: but still, all seemed to wait. Ranged on benches down the sides of the room, the eighty girls sat motionless and erect; a quaint assemblage they appeared, all with plain locks combed from their faces, not a curl visible; in brown dresses, made high and surrounded by a narrow tucker about the throat, with little pockets of holland (shaped something like a Highlander's purse) tied in front of their frocks, and destined to serve the purpose of a work-bag: all, too, wearing woollen stockings and country-made shoes, fastened with brass buckles. Above twenty of those clad in this costume were full-grown girls, or rather young women; it suited them ill, and gave an air of oddity even to the prettiest.

I was still looking at them, and also at intervals examining the teachers – none of whom precisely pleased me; for the stout one was a little coarse, the dark one not a little fierce, the foreigner harsh and grotesque, and Miss Miller, poor thing! looked purple, weather-beaten, and overworked – when, as my eye

wandered from face to face, the whole school rose simultaneously, as if moved by a common spring.

What was the matter? I had heard no order given: I was puzzled. Ere I had gathered my wits, the classes were again seated: but as all eyes were now turned to one point, mine followed the general direction, and encountered the personage who had received me last night. She stood at the bottom of the long room, on the hearth; for there was a fire at each end; she surveyed the two rows of girls silently and gravely. Miss Miller, approaching, seemed to ask her a question, and having received her answer, went back to her place, and said aloud – 'Monitor of the first class, fetch the globes!'

While the direction was being executed, the lady consulted moved slowly up the room. I suppose I have a considerable organ of veneration, for I retain yet the sense of admiring awe with which my eyes traced her steps. Seen now, in broad daylight, she looked tall, fair, and shapely; brown eyes with a benignant light in their irids, and a fine pencilling of long lashes round, relieved the whiteness of her large front; on each of her temples her hair, of a very dark brown, was clustered in round curls, according to the fashion of those times, when neither smooth bands nor long ringlets were in vogue; her dress, also in the mode of the day, was of purple cloth, relieved by a sort of Spanish trimming of black velvet; a gold watch (watches were not so common then as now) shone at her girdle. Let the reader add, to complete the picture, refined features; a complexion, if pale, clear; and a stately air and carriage, and he will have, at least, as clearly as words can give it, a correct idea of the exterior of Miss Temple – Maria Temple, as I afterwards saw the name written in a prayer-book entrusted to me to carry to church.

The superintendent of Lowood (for such was this lady) having taken her seat before a pair of globes placed on one of the tables, summoned the first class round her, and commenced giving a lesson on geography; the lower classes were called by the teachers: repetitions in history, grammar, etc., went on for an hour; writing and arithmetic succeeded, and music lessons were given by Miss Temple to some of the elder girls. The duration of each lesson was measured by the clock, which at last struck twelve. The superintendent rose – 'I have a word to address to the pupils,' said she.

The tumult of cessation from lessons was already breaking forth, but it sank at her voice. She went on – 'You had this morning a breakfast which you could not eat; you must be hungry: I have ordered that a lunch of bread and cheese shall be served to all.'

The teachers looked at her with a sort of surprise.

'It is to be done on my responsibility,' she added, in an explanatory tone to them, and immediately afterwards left the room.

The bread and cheese was presently brought in and distributed, to the high delight and refreshment of the whole school. The order was now given 'To the garden!' Each put on a coarse straw bonnet, with strings of coloured calico, and a cloak of grey frieze, I was similarly equipped, and, following the stream, I made my way into the open air.

The garden was a wide enclosure, surrounded with walls so high as to exclude every glimpse of prospect; a covered verandah ran down one side, and broad walks bordered a middle space divided into scores of little beds: these beds were assigned as gardens for the pupils to cultivate, and each bed had an owner. When full of flowers they would doubtless look pretty; but now, at the latter end of January, all was wintry blight and brown decay. I shuddered as I stood and looked round me: it was an inclement day for outdoor exercise; not positively rainy, but darkened by a drizzling yellow fog; all under foot was still soaking wet with the floods of yesterday. The stronger among the girls ran about and engaged in active games, but sundry pale and thin ones herded together for shelter and warmth in the verandah; and amongst these, as the dense mist penetrated to their shivering frames, I heard frequently the sound of a hollow cough.

As yet I had spoken to no one, nor did anybody seem to take notice of me; I stood lonely enough: but to that feeling of isolation I was accustomed; it did not oppress me much. I leant against a pillar of the verandah, drew my grey mantle close about me, and, trying to forget the cold which nipped me without, and the unsatisfied hunger which gnawed me within, delivered myself up to the employment of watching and thinking. My reflections were too undefined and fragmentary to merit record: I hardly yet knew where I was; Gateshead and my past life seemed floated away to an immeasurable distance; the present was vague and strange, and of the future I could form no conjecture. I looked round the convent-like garden, and then up at the house – a large building, half of which seemed grey and old, the other half quite new. The new part, containing the schoolroom and dormitory, was lit by mullioned and latticed windows, which gave it a church-like aspect; a stone tablet over the door bore this inscription: 'Lowood Institution. This portion was rebuilt AD—, by Naomi Brocklehurst, of Brocklehurst Hall, in this county. "Let your light so shine before men, that they may see your good works, and glorify your Father which is in heaven." – St Matt. v. 16.'

I read these words over and over again: I felt that an explanation belonged to them, and was unable fully to penetrate their import. I was still pondering the signification of 'Institution', and endeavouring to make out a connection between the first words and the verse of Scripture, when the sound of a cough close behind me made me turn my head. I saw a girl sitting on a stone bench near; she was bent over a book, on the perusal of which she seemed intent: from where I stood I could see the title – it was *Rasselas*; a name that struck me as strange, and consequently attractive. In turning a leaf she happened to look up, and I said to her directly – 'Is your book interesting?' I had already formed the intention of asking her to lend it to me someday. 'I like it,' she answered, after a pause of a second or two, during which she examined me.

'What is it about?' I continued. I hardly know where I found the hardihood thus to open a conversation with a stranger; the step was contrary to my nature and habits: but I think her occupation touched a chord of sympathy somewhere; for I too liked reading, though of a frivolous and childish kind; I could not digest or comprehend the serious or substantial.

'You may look at it,' replied the girl, offering me the book.

I did so; a brief examination convinced me that the contents were less taking than the title: *Rasselas* looked dull to my trifling taste; I saw nothing about fairies, nothing about genii; no bright variety seemed spread over the closely-printed pages. I returned it to her; she received it quietly, and without saying anything she was about to relapse into her former studious mood: again I ventured to disturb her – 'Can you tell me what the writing on that stone over the door means? What is Lowood Institution?'

'This house where you are come to live.'

'And why do they call it Institution? Is it in any way different from other schools?'

'It is partly a charity-school: you and I, and all the rest of us, are charity children. I suppose you are an orphan: are not either your father or your mother dead?'

'Both died before I can remember.'

'Well, all the girls here have lost either one or both parents, and this is called an institution for educating orphans.'

'Do we pay no money? Do they keep us for nothing?'

'We pay, or our friends pay, fifteen pounds a year for each.'

'Then why do they call us charity-children?'

'Because fifteen pounds is not enough for board and teaching, and the deficiency is supplied by subscription.'

'Who subscribes?'

'Different benevolent-minded ladies and gentlemen in this neighbourhood and in London.'

'Who was Naomi Brocklehurst?'

'The lady who built the new part of this house as that tablet records, and whose son overlooks and directs everything here.'

'Why?'

'Because he is treasurer and manager of the establishment.'

'Then this house does not belong to that tall lady who wears a watch, and who said we were to have some bread and cheese?'

'To Miss Temple? Oh, no! I wish it did: she has to answer to Mr Brocklehurst for all she does. Mr Brocklehurst buys all our food and all our clothes.'

'Does he live here?'

'No – two miles off, at a large hall.'

'Is he a good man?'

'He is a clergyman, and is said to do a great deal of good.'

'Did you say that tall lady was called Miss Temple?'

'Yes.'

'And what are the other teachers called?'

'The one with red cheeks is called Miss Smith; she attends to the work, and cuts out – for we make our own clothes, our frocks, and pelisses, and everything; the little one with black hair is Miss Scatcherd; she teaches history and grammar,

and hears the second class repetitions; and the one who wears a shawl, and has a pocket-handkerchief tied to her side with a yellow ribband, is Mme Pierrot: she comes from Lisle, in France, and teaches French.'

'Do you like the teachers?'

'Well enough.'

'Do you like the little black one, and the Madame — ? I cannot pronounce her name as you do.'

'Miss Scatcherd is hasty – you must take care not to offend her; Mme Pierrot is not a bad sort of person.'

'But Miss Temple is the best – isn't she?'

'Miss Temple is very good and very clever; she is above the rest, because she knows far more than they do.'

'Have you been long here?'

'Two years.'

'Are you an orphan?'

'My mother is dead.'

'Are you happy here?'

'You ask rather too many questions. I have given you answers enough for the present: now I want to read.'

But at that moment the summons sounded for dinner; all re-entered the house. The odour which now filled the refectory was scarcely more appetising than that which had regaled our nostrils at breakfast: the dinner was served in two huge tin-plated vessels, whence rose a strong steam redolent of rancid fat. I found the mess to consist of indifferent potatoes and strange shreds of rusty meat, mixed and cooked together. Of this preparation a tolerably abundant plateful was apportioned to each pupil. I ate what I could, and wondered within myself whether every day's fare would be like this.

After dinner, we immediately adjourned to the schoolroom: lessons recommenced, and were continued till five o'clock.

The only marked event of the afternoon was, that I saw the girl with whom I had conversed in the verandah dismissed in disgrace by Miss Scatcherd from a history class, and sent to stand in the middle of the large schoolroom. The punishment seemed to me in a high degree ignominious, especially for so great a girl – she looked thirteen or upwards. I expected she would show signs of great distress and shame; but to my surprise she neither wept nor blushed: composed, though grave, she stood, the central mark of all eyes. 'How can she bear it so quietly – so firmly?' I asked of myself. 'Were I in her place, it seems to me I should wish the earth to open and swallow me up. She looks as if she were thinking of something beyond her punishment – beyond her situation: of something not round her nor before her. I have heard of day-dreams – is she in a day-dream now? Her eyes are fixed on the floor, but I am sure they do not see it – her sight seems turned in, gone down into her heart: she is looking at what she can remember, I believe; not at what is really present. I wonder what sort of a girl she is – whether good or naughty.'

Soon after five p.m. we had another meal, consisting of a small mug of coffee,

and half a slice of brown bread. I devoured my bread and drank my coffee with relish; but I should have been glad of as much more – I was still hungry. Half an hour's recreation succeeded, then study; then the glass of water and the piece of oatcake, prayers, and bed. Such was my first day at Lowood.

## Chapter 6

The next day commenced as before, getting up and dressing by rushlight; but this morning we were obliged to dispense with the ceremony of washing; the water in the pitchers was frozen. A change had taken place in the weather the preceding evening, and a keen north-east wind, whistling through the crevices of our bedroom windows all night long, had made us shiver in our beds, and turned the contents of the ewers to ice.

Before the long hour and a half of prayers and Bible-reading was over, I felt ready to perish with cold. Breakfast-time came at last, and this morning the porridge was not burnt; the quality was eatable, the quantity small. How small my portion seemed! I wished it had been doubled.

In the course of the day I was enrolled a member of the fourth class, and regular tasks and occupations were assigned me: hitherto, I had only been a spectator of the proceedings at Lowood; I was now to become an actor therein. At first, being little accustomed to learn by heart, the lessons appeared to me both long and difficult; the frequent change from task to task, too, bewildered me; and I was glad when, about three o'clock in the afternoon, Miss Smith put into my hands a border of muslin two yards long, together with needle, thimble, etc., and sent me to sit in a quiet corner of the schoolroom, with directions to hem the same. At that hour most of the others were sewing likewise; but one class still stood round Miss Scatcherd's chair reading, and as all was quiet, the subject of their lessons could be heard, together with the manner in which each girl acquitted herself, and the animadversions or commendations of Miss Scatcherd on the performance. It was English history; among the readers I observed my acquaintance of the verandah: at the commencement of the lesson, her place had been at the top of the class, but for some error of pronunciation, or some inattention to stops, she was suddenly sent to the very bottom. Even in that obscure position, Miss Scatcherd continued to make her an object of constant notice; she was continually addressing to her such phrases as the following: 'Burns' (such it seems was her name: the girls here were all called by their surnames, as boys are elsewhere), 'Burns, you are standing on the side of your shoe; turn your toes out immediately.' 'Burns, you poke your chin most unpleasantly; draw it in.' 'Burns, I insist on your holding your head up; I will not have you before me in that attitude,' etc. etc.

A chapter having been read through twice, the books were closed and the girls examined. The lesson had comprised part of the reign of Charles I, and there were sundry questions about tonnage and poundage and ship-money,

which most of them appeared unable to answer; still, every little difficulty was
solved instantly when it reached Burns: her memory seemed to have retained
the substance of the whole lesson, and she was ready with answers on every
point. I kept expecting that Miss Scatcherd would praise her attention; but,
instead of that, she suddenly cried out – 'You dirty, disagreeable girl! you have
never cleaned your nails this morning!'

Burns made no answer: I wondered at her silence.

'Why,' thought I, 'does she not explain that she could neither clean her nails
nor wash her face, as the water was frozen?'

My attention was now called off by Miss Smith desiring me to hold a skein of
thread: while she was winding it, she talked to me from time to time, asking
whether I had ever been at school before, whether I could mark, stitch, knit,
etc.; till she dismissed me, I could not pursue my observations on Miss
Scatcherd's movements. When I returned to my seat, that lady was just delivering
an order of which I did not catch the import; but Burns immediately left the
class, and going into the small inner room where the books were kept, returned
in half a minute, carrying in her hand a bundle of twigs tied together at one end.
This ominous tool she presented to Miss Scatcherd with a respectful curtsey;
then she quietly, and without being told, unloosed her pinafore, and the teacher
instantly and sharply inflicted on her neck a dozen strokes with the bunch of
twigs. Not a tear rose to Burns' eye; and, while I paused from my sewing,
because my fingers quivered at this spectacle with a sentiment of unavailing and
impotent anger, not a feature of her pensive face altered its ordinary expression.

'Hardened girl!' exclaimed Miss Scatcherd; 'nothing can correct you of your
slatternly habits: carry the rod away.'

Burns obeyed: I looked at her narrowly as she emerged from the book-closet;
she was just putting back her handkerchief into her pocket, and the trace of a
tear glistened on her thin cheek.

The play-hour in the evening I thought the pleasantest fraction of the day at
Lowood: the bit of bread, the draught of coffee swallowed at five o'clock had
revived vitality, if it had not satisfied hunger: the long restraint of the day was
slackened; the schoolroom felt warmer than in the morning – its fires being
allowed to burn a little more brightly, to supply, in some measure, the place of
candles, not yet introduced: the ruddy gloaming, the licensed uproar, the
confusion of many voices gave one a welcome sense of liberty.

On the evening of the day on which I had seen Miss Scatcherd flog her pupil,
Burns, I wandered as usual among the forms and tables and laughing groups
without a companion, yet not feeling lonely: when I passed the windows, I now
and then lifted a blind, and looked out; it snowed fast, a drift was already forming
against the lower panes; putting my ear close to the window, I could distinguish
from the gleeful tumult within, the disconsolate moan of the wind outside.

Probably, if I had lately left a good home and kind parents, this would have
been the hour when I should most keenly have regretted the separation; that
wind would then have saddened my heart; this obscure chaos would have
disturbed my peace! as it was, I derived from both a strange excitement, and

reckless and feverish, I wished the wind to howl more wildly, the gloom to deepen to darkness, and the confusion to rise to clamour.

Jumping over forms, and creeping under tables, I made my way to one of the fireplaces; there, kneeling by the high wire fender, I found Burns, absorbed, silent, abstracted from all round her by the companionship of a book, which she read by the dim glare of the embers.

'Is it still *Rasselas*?' I asked, coming behind her.

'Yes,' she said, 'and I have just finished it.'

And in five minutes more she shut it up. I was glad of this.

'Now,' thought I, 'I can perhaps get her to talk.' I sat down by her on the floor.

'What is your name besides Burns?'

'Helen.'

'Do you come a long way from here?'

'I come from a place farther north, quite on the borders of Scotland.'

'Will you ever go back?'

'I hope so; but nobody can be sure of the future.'

'You must wish to leave Lowood?'

'No! why should I? I was sent to Lowood to get an education; and it would be of no use going away until I have attained that object.'

'But that teacher, Miss Scatcherd, is so cruel to you?'

'Cruel? Not at all! She is severe: she dislikes my faults.'

'And if I were in your place I should dislike her; I should resist her. If she struck me with that rod, I should get it from her hand; I should break it under her nose.'

'Probably you would do nothing of the sort: but if you did, Mr Brocklehurst would expel you from the school; that would be a great grief to your relations. It is far better to endure patiently a smart which nobody feels but yourself, than to commit a hasty action whose evil consequences will extend to all connected with you; and besides, the Bible bids us return good for evil.'

'But then it seems disgraceful to be flogged, and to be sent to stand in the middle of a room full of people; and you are such a great girl: I am far younger than you, and I could not bear it.'

'Yet it would be your duty to bear it, if you could not avoid it: it is weak and silly to say you *cannot bear* what it is your fate to be required to bear.'

I heard her with wonder: I could not comprehend this doctrine of endurance; and still less could I understand or sympathise with the forbearance she expressed for her chastiser. Still I felt that Helen Burns considered things by a light invisible to my eyes. I suspected she might be right and I wrong; but I would not ponder the matter deeply; like Felix, I put it off to a more convenient season.

'You say you have faults, Helen: what are they? To me you seem very good.'

'Then learn from me, not to judge by appearances: I am, as Miss Scatcherd said, slatternly; I seldom put, and never keep, things in order; I am careless; I forget rules; I read when I should learn my lessons; I have no method; and sometimes I say, like you, I cannot *bear* to be subjected to systematic arrangements. This is all

very provoking to Miss Scatcherd, who is naturally neat, punctual, and particular.'

'And cross and cruel,' I added; but Helen Burns would not admit my addition: she kept silence.

'Is Miss Temple as severe to you as Miss Scatcherd?'

At the utterance of Miss Temple's name, a soft smile flitted over her grave face.

'Miss Temple is full of goodness; it pains her to be severe to anyone, even the worst in the school: she sees my errors, and tells me of them gently; and if I do anything worthy of praise, she gives me my meed liberally. One strong proof of my wretchedly defective nature is, that even her expostulations, so mild, so rational, have not influence to cure me of my faults; and even her praise, though I value it most highly, cannot stimulate me to continued care and foresight.'

'That is curious,' said I, 'it is so easy to be careful.'

'For you I have no doubt it is. I observed you in your class this morning, and saw you were closely attentive: your thoughts never seemed to wander while Miss Miller explained the lesson and questioned you. Now, mine continually rove away; when I should be listening to Miss Scatcherd, and collecting all she says with assiduity, often I lose the very sound of her voice; I fall into a sort of dream. Sometimes I think I am in Northumberland, and that the noises I hear round me are the bubbling of a little brook which runs through Deepden, near our house; then, when it comes to my turn to reply, I have to be awakened; and having heard nothing of what was read for listening to the visionary brook, I have no answer ready.'

'Yet how well you replied this afternoon.'

'It was mere chance; the subject on which we had been reading had interested me. This afternoon, instead of dreaming of Deepden, I was wondering how a man who wished to do right could act so unjustly and unwisely as Charles the First sometimes did; and I thought what a pity it was that, with his integrity and conscientiousness, he could see no farther than the prerogatives of the crown. If he had but been able to look to a distance, and see how what they call the spirit of the age was tending! Still, I like Charles – I respect him – I pity him, poor murdered king! Yes, his enemies were the worst: they shed blood they had no right to shed. How dared they kill him!'

Helen was talking to herself now: she had forgotten I could not very well understand her – that I was ignorant, or nearly so, of the subject she discussed. I recalled her to my level.

'And when Miss Temple teaches you, do your thoughts wander then?'

'No, certainly, not often: because Miss Temple has generally something to say which is newer than my own reflections; her language is singularly agreeable to me, and the information she communicates is often just what I wished to gain.'

'Well, then, with Miss Temple you are good?'

'Yes, in a passive way: I make no effort, I follow as inclination guides me. There is no merit in such goodness.'

'A great deal: you are good to those who are good to you. It is all I ever desire to be. If people were always kind and obedient to those who are cruel and unjust,

the wicked people would have it all their own way: they would never feel afraid, and so they would never alter, but would grow worse and worse. When we are struck at without a reason, we should strike back again very hard; I am sure we should – so hard as to teach the person who struck us never to do it again.'

'You will change your mind, I hope, when you grow older: as yet you are but a little untaught girl.'

'But I feel this, Helen; I must dislike those who whatever I do to please them, persist in disliking me, I must resist those who punish me unjustly. It is as natural as that I should love those who show me affection, or submit to punishment when I feel it is deserved.'

'Heathens and savage tribes hold that doctrine, but Christians and civilised nations disown it.'

'How? I don't understand.'

'It is not violence that best overcomes hate – nor vengeance that most certainly heals injury.'

'What then?'

'Read the New Testament, and observe what Christ says, and how He acts; make His word your rule, and His conduct your example.'

'What does He say?'

'Love your enemies; bless them that curse you; do good to them that hate you and despitefully use you.'

'Then I should love Mrs Reed, which I cannot do; I should bless her son John, which is impossible.'

In her turn, Helen Burns asked me to explain, and I proceeded forthwith to pour out, in my own way, the tale of my sufferings and resentments. Bitter and truculent when excited, I spoke as I felt, without reserve or softening.

Helen heard me patiently to the end: I expected she would then make a remark, but she said nothing.

'Well,' I asked impatiently, 'is not Mrs Reed a hard-hearted, bad woman?'

'She has been unkind to you, no doubt; because you see, she dislikes your cast of character, as Miss Scatcherd does mine; but how minutely you remember all she has done and said to you! What a singularly deep impression her injustice seems to have made on your heart! No ill-usage so brands its record on my feelings. Would you not be happier if you tried to forget her severity, together with the passionate emotions it excited? Life appears to me too short to be spent in nursing animosity or registering wrongs. We are, and must be, one and all, burdened with faults in this world: but the time will soon come when, I trust, we shall put them off in putting off our corruptible bodies; when debasement and sin will fall from us with this cumbrous frame of flesh, and only the spark of the spirit will remain, the impalpable principle of light and thought, pure as when it left the Creator to inspire the creature: whence it came it will return; perhaps again to be communicated to some being higher than man – perhaps to pass through gradations of glory, from the pale human soul to brighten to the seraph! Surely it will never, on the contrary, be suffered to degenerate from man to fiend? No; I cannot believe that: I hold another creed: which no one ever

taught me, and which I seldom mention; but in which I delight, and to which I cling: for it extends hope to all: it makes Eternity a rest – a mighty home, not a terror and an abyss. Besides, with this creed, I can so clearly distinguish between the criminal and his crime; I can so sincerely forgive the first while I abhor the last: with this creed revenge never worries my heart, degradation never too deeply disgusts me, injustice never crushes me too low: I live in calm, looking to the end.'

Helen's head, always drooping, sank a little lower as she finished this sentence. I saw by her look she wished no longer to talk to me, but rather to converse with her own thoughts. She was not allowed much time for meditation: a monitor, a great rough girl presently came up, exclaiming in a strong Cumberland accent – 'Helen Burns, if you don't go and put your drawer in order, and fold up your work this minute, I'll tell Miss Scatcherd to come and look at it!'

Helen sighed as her reverie fled, and getting up, obeyed the monitor without reply as without delay.

## Chapter 7

My first quarter at Lowood seemed an age; and not the golden age either; it comprised an irksome struggle with difficulties in habituating myself to new rules and unwonted tasks. The fear of failure in these points harassed me worse than the physical hardships of my lot; though these were no trifles.

During January, February, and part of March, the deep snows, and, after their melting, the almost impassable roads, prevented our stirring beyond the garden walls, except to go to church; but within these limits we had to pass an hour every day in the open air. Our clothing was insufficient to protect us from the severe cold: we had no boots, the snow got into our shoes and melted there: our ungloved hands became numbed and covered with chilblains, as were our feet: I remember well the distracting irritation I endured from this cause every evening, when my feet inflamed; and the torture of thrusting the swelled, raw, and stiff toes into my shoes in the morning. Then the scanty supply of food was distressing: with the keen appetites of growing children, we had scarcely sufficient to keep alive a delicate invalid. From this deficiency of nourishment resulted an abuse, which pressed hardly on the younger pupils: whenever the famished great girls had an opportunity, they would coax or menace the little ones out of their portion. Many a time I have shared between two claimants the precious morsel of brown bread distributed at teatime; and after relinquishing to a third half the contents of my mug of coffee, I have swallowed the remainder with an accompaniment of secret tears, forced from me by the exigency of hunger.

Sundays were dreary days in that wintry season. We had to walk two miles to Brocklebridge Church, where our patron officiated. We set out cold, we arrived at church colder: during the morning service we became almost paralysed. It

was too far to return to dinner, and an allowance of cold meat and bread, in the same penurious proportion observed in our ordinary meals, was served round between the services.

At the close of the afternoon service we returned by an exposed and hilly road, where the bitter winter wind, blowing over a range of snowy summits to the north, almost flayed the skin from our faces.

I can remember Miss Temple walking lightly and rapidly along our drooping line, her plaid cloak, which the frosty wind fluttered, gathered close about her, and encouraging us, by precept and example, to keep up our spirits, and march forward, as she said, 'like stalwart soldiers.' The other teachers, poor things, were generally themselves too much dejected to attempt the task of cheering others.

How we longed for the light and heat of a blazing fire when we got back! But, to the little ones at least, this was denied: each hearth in the schoolroom was immediately surrounded by a double row of great girls, and behind them the younger children crouched in groups, wrapping their starved arms in their pinafores.

A little solace came at tea-time, in the shape of a double ration of bread – a whole, instead of a half, slice – with the delicious addition of a thin scrape of butter: it was the hebdomadal treat to which we all looked forward from Sabbath to Sabbath. I generally contrived to reserve a moiety of this bounteous repast for myself; but the remainder I was invariably obliged to part with.

The Sunday evening was spent in repeating, by heart, the Church Catechism, and the fifth, sixth, and seventh chapters of St Matthew; and in listening to a long sermon, read by Miss Miller, whose irrepressible yawns attested her weariness. A frequent interlude of these performances was the enactment of the part of Eutychus by some half-dozen of little girls, who, overpowered with sleep, would fall down, if not out of the third loft, yet off the fourth form, and be taken up half dead. The remedy was, to thrust them forward into the centre of the schoolroom, and oblige them to stand there till the sermon was finished. Sometimes their feet failed them, and they sank together in a heap; they were then propped up with the monitors' high stools.

I have not yet alluded to the visits of Mr Brocklehurst; and indeed that gentleman was from home during the greater part of the first month after my arrival; perhaps prolonging his stay with his friend the archdeacon: his absence was a relief to me. I need not say that I had my own reasons for dreading his coming: but come he did at last.

One afternoon (I had then been three weeks at Lowood), as I was sitting with a slate in my hand, puzzling over a sum in long division, my eyes, raised in abstraction to the window, caught sight of a figure just passing: I recognised almost instinctively that gaunt outline; and when, two minutes after, all the school, teachers included, rose *en masse*, it was not necessary for me to look up in order to ascertain whose entrance they thus greeted. A long stride measured the schoolroom, and presently beside Miss Temple, who herself had risen, stood the same black column which had frowned on me so ominously from the

hearthrug of Gateshead. I now glanced sideways at this piece of architecture. Yes, I was right: it was Mr Brocklehurst, buttoned up in a surtout, and looking longer, narrower, and more rigid than ever.

I had my own reasons for being dismayed at this apparition; too well I remembered the perfidious hints given by Mrs Reed about my disposition, etc.; the promise pledged by Mr Brocklehurst to apprise Miss Temple and the teachers of my vicious nature. All along I had been dreading the fulfilment of this promise, I had been looking out daily for the 'Coming Man', whose information respecting my past life and conversation was to brand me as a bad child for ever: now there he was.

He stood at Miss Temple's side; he was speaking low in her ear: I did not doubt he was making disclosures of my villainy; and I watched her eye with painful anxiety, expecting every moment to see its dark orb turn on me a glance of repugnance and contempt. I listened too; and as I happened to be seated quite at the top of the room, I caught most of what he said: its import relieved me from immediate apprehension.

'I suppose, Miss Temple, the thread I bought at Lowton will do; it struck me that it would be just of the quality for the calico chemises, and I sorted the needles to match. You may tell Miss Smith that I forgot to make a memorandum of the darning needles, but she shall have some papers sent in next week; and she is not, on any account, to give out more than one at a time to each pupil: if they have more, they are apt to be careless and lose them. And, O ma'am! I wish the woollen stockings were better looked to! – when I was here last, I went into the kitchen-garden and examined the clothes drying on the line; there was a quantity of black hose in a very bad state of repair: from the size of the holes in them I was sure they had not been well mended from time to time.'

He paused.

'Your directions shall be attended to, sir,' said Miss Temple.

'And, ma'am,' he continued, 'the laundress tells me some of the girls have two clean tuckers in the week: it is too much; the rules limit them to one.'

'I think I can explain that circumstance, sir. Agnes and Catherine Johnstone were invited to take tea with some friends at Lowton last Thursday, and I gave them leave to put on clean tuckers for the occasion.'

Mr Brocklehurst nodded.

'Well, for once it may pass; but please not to let the circumstance occur too often. And there is another thing which surprised me; I find, in settling accounts with the housekeeper, that a lunch, consisting of bread and cheese, has twice been served out to the girls during the past fortnight. How is this? I looked over the regulations, and I find no such meal as lunch mentioned. Who introduced this innovation? and by what authority?'

'I must be responsible for the circumstance, sir,' replied Miss Temple: 'the breakfast was so ill prepared that the pupils could not possibly eat it; and I dared not allow them to remain fasting till dinner-time.'

'Madam, allow me an instant. You are aware that my plan in bringing up these girls is, not to accustom them to habits of luxury and indulgence, but to render

them hardy, patient, self-denying. Should any little accidental disappointment of the appetite occur, such as the spoiling of a meal, the under or the over dressing of a dish, the incident ought not to be neutralised by replacing with something more delicate the comfort lost, thus pampering the body and obviating the aim of this institution; it ought to be improved to the spiritual edification of the pupils, by encouraging them to evince fortitude under the temporary privation. A brief address on those occasions would not be mistimed, wherein a judicious instructor would take the opportunity of referring to the sufferings of the primitive Christians; to the torments of martyrs; to the exhortations of our blessed Lord Himself, calling upon His disciples to take up their cross and follow Him; to His warnings that man shall not live by bread alone, but by every word that proceedeth out of the mouth of God; to His divine consolations, "If ye suffer hunger or thirst for My sake, happy are ye." Oh, madam, when you put bread and cheese, instead of burnt porridge, into these children's mouths, you may indeed feed their vile bodies, but you little think how you starve their immortal souls!'

Mr Brocklehurst again paused – perhaps overcome by his feelings. Miss Temple had looked down when he first began to speak to her; but she now gazed straight before her, and her face, naturally pale as marble, appeared to be assuming also the coldness and fixity of that material; especially her mouth, closed as if it would have required a sculptor's chisel to open it, and her brow settled gradually into petrified severity.

Meantime, Mr Brocklehurst, standing on the hearth with his hands behind his back, majestically surveyed the whole school. Suddenly his eye gave a blink, as if it had met something that either dazzled or shocked its pupil; turning, he said in more rapid accents than he had hitherto used – 'Miss Temple, Miss Temple, what – *what* is that girl with curled hair? Red hair, ma'am, curled – curled all over?' And extending his cane he pointed to the awful object, his hand shaking as he did so.

'It is Julia Severn,' replied Miss Temple, very quietly.

'Julia Severn, ma'am! And why has she, or any other, curled hair? Why, in defiance of every precept and principle of this house, does she conform to the world so openly – here in an evangelical, charitable establishment – as to wear her hair one mass of curls?'

'Julia's hair curls naturally,' returned Miss Temple, still more quietly.

'Naturally! Yes, but we are not to conform to nature; I wish these girls to be the children of Grace: and why that abundance? I have again and again intimated that I desire the hair to be arranged closely, modestly, plainly. Miss Temple, that girl's hair must be cut off entirely; I will send a barber tomorrow: and I see others who have far too much of the excrescence – that tall girl, tell her to turn round. Tell all the first form to rise up and direct their faces to the wall.'

Miss Temple passed her handkerchief over her lips, as if to smooth away the involuntary smile that curled them; she gave the order, however, and when the first class could take in what was required of them, they obeyed. Leaning a little back on my bench, I could see the looks and grimaces with

which they commented on this manœuvre: it was a pity Mr Brocklehurst could not see them too; he would perhaps have felt that, whatever he might do with the outside of the cup and platter, the inside was further beyond his interference than he imagined.

He scrutinised the reverse of these living medals some five minutes, then pronounced sentence. These words fell like the knell of doom – 'All those topknots must be cut off.'

Miss Temple seemed to remonstrate.

'Madam,' he pursued, 'I have a Master to serve whose kingdom is not of this world: my mission is to mortify in these girls the lusts of the flesh; to teach them to clothe themselves with shamefacedness and sobriety, not with braided hair and costly apparel; and each of the young persons before us has a string of hair twisted in plaits which vanity itself might have woven; these, I repeat, must be cut off; think of the time wasted, of – '

Mr Brocklehurst was here interrupted: three other visitors, ladies, now entered the room. They ought to have come a little sooner to have heard his lecture on dress, for they were splendidly attired in velvet, silk, and furs. The two younger of the trio (fine girls of sixteen and seventeen) had grey beaver hats, then in fashion, shaded with ostrich plumes, and from under the brim of this graceful head-dress fell a profusion of light tresses, elaborately curled; the elder lady was enveloped in a costly velvet shawl, trimmed with ermine, and she wore a false front of French curls.

These ladies were deferentially received by Miss Temple, as Mrs and the Misses Brocklehurst, and conducted to seats of honour at the top of the room. It seems they had come in the carriage with their reverend relative, and had been conducting a rummaging scrutiny of the room upstairs, while he transacted business with the housekeeper, questioned the laundress, and lectured the superintendent. They now proceeded to address divers remarks and reproofs to Miss Smith, who was charged with the care of the linen and the inspection of the dormitories: but I had no time to listen to what they said; other matters called off and enchained my attention.

Hitherto, while gathering up the discourse of Mr Brocklehurst and Miss Temple, I had not, at the same time, neglected precautions to secure my personal safety; which I thought would be effected, if I could only elude observation. To this end, I had sat well back on the form, and while seeming to be busy with my sum, had held my slate in such a manner as to conceal my face: I might have escaped notice, had not my treacherous slate somehow happened to slip from my hand, and falling with an obtrusive crash, directly drawn every eye upon me; I knew it was all over now, and, as I stooped to pick up the two fragments of slate, I rallied my forces for the worst. It came.

'A careless girl!' said Mr Brocklehurst, and immediately after – 'It is the new pupil, I perceive.' And before I could draw breath, 'I must not forget I have a word to say respecting her.' Then aloud: how loud it seemed to me! 'Let the child who broke her slate come forward!'

Of my own accord I could not have stirred; I was paralysed: but the two great

girls who sat on each side of me, set me on my legs and pushed me towards the dread judge, and then Miss Temple gently assisted me to his very feet, and I caught her whispered counsel – 'Don't be afraid, Jane, I saw it was an accident; you shall not be punished.'

The kind whisper went to my heart like a dagger. 'Another minute, and she will despise me for a hypocrite,' thought I; and an impulse of fury against Reed, Brocklehurst, and Co. bounded in my pulses at the conviction. I was no Helen Burns.

'Fetch that stool,' said Mr Brocklehurst, pointing to a very high one from which a monitor had just risen: it was brought.

'Place the child upon it.'

And I was placed there, by whom I don't know: I was in no condition to note particulars; I was only aware that they had hoisted me up to the height of Mr Brocklehurst's nose, that he was within a yard of me, and that a spread of shot orange and purple silk pelisses and a cloud of silvery plumage extended and waved below me.

Mr Brocklehurst hemmed.

'Ladies,' said he, turning to his family, 'Miss Temple, teachers, and children, you all see this girl?' Of course they did; for I felt their eyes directed like burning-glasses against my scorched skin.

'You see she is yet young; you observe she possesses the ordinary form of childhood; God has graciously given her the shape that He has given to all of us; no signal deformity points her out as a marked character. Who would think that the Evil One had already found a servant and agent in her? Yet such, I grieve to say, is the case.'

A pause – in which I began to steady the palsy of my nerves, and to feel that the Rubicon was passed; and that the trial, no longer to be shirked, must be firmly sustained.

'My dear children,' pursued the black marble clergyman, with pathos, 'this is a sad, a melancholy occasion; for it becomes my duty to warn you, that this girl, who might be one of God's own lambs, is a little castaway: not a member of the true flock, but evidently an interloper and an alien. You must be on your guard against her; you must shun her example; if necessary, avoid her company, exclude her from your sports, and shut her out from your converse. Teachers, you must watch her: keep your eyes on her movements, weigh well her words, scrutinise her actions, punish her body to save her soul: if, indeed, such salvation be possible, for (my tongue falters while I tell it) this girl, this child, the native of a Christian land, worse than many a little heathen who says its prayers to Brahma and kneels before Juggernaut – this girl is – a liar!'

Now came a pause of ten minutes, during which I, by this time in perfect possession of my wits, observed all the female Brocklehursts produce their pocket-handkerchiefs and apply them to their optics, while the elderly lady swayed herself to and fro, and the two younger ones whispered, 'How shocking!'

Mr Brocklehurst resumed.

'This I learned from her benefactress; from the pious and charitable lady

who adopted her in her orphan state, reared her as her own daughter, and whose kindness, whose generosity the unhappy girl repaid by an ingratitude so bad, so dreadful, that at last her excellent patroness was obliged to separate her from her own young ones, fearful lest her vicious example should contaminate their purity: she has sent her here to be healed, even as the Jews of old sent their diseased to the troubled pool of Bethesda; and, teachers, superintendent, I beg of you not to allow the waters to stagnate round her.'

With this sublime conclusion, Mr Brocklehurst adjusted the top button of his surtout, muttered something to his family, who rose, bowed to Miss Temple, and then all the great people sailed in state from the room. Turning at the door, my judge said – 'Let her stand half an hour longer on that stool, and let no one speak to her during the remainder of the day.'

There was I, then, mounted aloft; I, who had said I could not bear the shame of standing on my natural feet in the middle of the room, was now exposed to general view on a pedestal of infamy. What my sensations were, no language can describe; but just as they all rose, stifling my breath and constricting my throat, a girl came up and passed me: in passing, she lifted her eyes. What a strange light inspired them! What an extraordinary sensation that ray sent through me! How the new feeling bore me up! It was as if a martyr, a hero, had passed a slave or victim, and imparted strength in the transit. I mastered the rising hysteria, lifted up my head, and took a firm stand on the stool. Helen Burns asked some slight question about her work of Miss Smith, was chidden for the triviality of the enquiry, returned to her place, and smiled at me as she again went by. What a smile! I remember it now, and I know that it was the effluence of fine intellect, of true courage; it lit up her marked lineaments, her thin face, her sunken grey eye, like a reflection from the aspect of an angel. Yet at that moment Helen Burns wore on her arm 'the untidy badge;' scarcely an hour ago I had heard her condemned by Miss Scatcherd to a dinner of bread and water on the morrow because she had blotted an exercise in copying it out. Such is the imperfect nature of man! such spots are there on the disc of the dearest planet; and eyes like Miss Scatcherd's can only see those minute defects, and are blind to the full brightness of the orb.

## Chapter 8

Ere the half-hour ended, five o'clock struck; school was dismissed, and all were gone into the refectory to tea. I now ventured to descend: it was deep dusk; I retired into a corner and sat down on the floor. The spell by which I had been so far supported began to dissolve; reaction took place, and soon, so overwhelming was the grief that seized me, I sank prostrate with my face to the ground. Now I wept: Helen Burns was not here; nothing sustained me; left to myself I abandoned myself, and my tears watered the boards. I had meant to be so good, and to do so much at Lowood: to make so many friends, to earn respect and win

affection. Already I had made visible progress: that very morning I had reached the head of my class; Miss Miller had praised me warmly; Miss Temple had smiled approbation; she had promised to teach me drawing, and to let me learn French, if I continued to make similar improvement two months longer: and then I was well received by my fellow-pupils; treated as an equal by those of my own age, and not molested by any; now, here I lay again crushed and trodden on; and could I ever rise more?

'Never,' I thought; and ardently I wished to die. While sobbing out this wish in broken accents, someone approached: I started up – again Helen Burns was near me; the fading fires just showed her coming up the long, vacant room; she brought my coffee and bread.

'Come, eat something,' she said; but I put both away from me, feeling as if a drop or a crumb would have choked me in my present condition. Helen regarded me, probably with surprise: I could not now abate my agitation, though I tried hard; I continued to weep aloud. She sat down on the ground near me, embraced her knees with her arms, and rested her head upon them; in that attitude she remained silent as an Indian. I was the first who spoke – 'Helen, why do you stay with a girl whom everybody believes to be a liar?'

'Everybody, Jane? Why, there are only eighty people who have heard you called so, and the world contains hundreds of millions.'

'But what have I to do with millions? The eighty, I know, despise me.'

'Jane, you are mistaken: probably not one in the school either despises or dislikes you: many, I am sure, pity you much.'

'How can they pity me after what Mr Brocklehurst has said?'

'Mr Brocklehurst is not a god: nor is he even a great and admired man; he is little liked here; he never took steps to make himself liked. Had he treated you as an especial favourite, you would have found enemies, declared or covert, all around you; as it is, the greater number would offer you sympathy if they dared. Teachers and pupils may look coldly on you for a day or two, but friendly feelings are concealed in their hearts; and if you persevere in doing well, these feelings will ere long appear so much the more evidently for their temporary suppression. Besides, Jane' – she paused.

'Well, Helen?' said I, putting my hand into hers: she chafed my fingers gently to warm them, and went on – 'If all the world hated you, and believed you wicked, while your own conscience approved you, and absolved you from guilt, you would not be without friends.'

'No; I know I should think well of myself; but that is not enough: if others don't love me I would rather die than live – I cannot bear to be solitary and hated, Helen. Look here; to gain some real affection from you, or Miss Temple, or any other whom I truly love, I would willingly submit to have the bone of my arm broken, or to let a bull toss me, or to stand behind a kicking horse, and let it dash its hoof at my chest –'

'Hush, Jane! you think too much of the love of human beings; you are too impulsive, too vehement; the sovereign hand that created your frame, and put life into it, has provided you with other resources than your feeble self, or than

creatures feeble as you. Besides this earth, and besides the race of men, there is an invisible world and a kingdom of spirits: that world is round us, for it is everywhere; and those spirits watch us, for they are commissioned to guard us; and if we were dying in pain and shame, if scorn smote us on all sides, and hatred crushed us, angels see our tortures, recognise our innocence (if innocent we be: as I know you are of this charge which Mr Brocklehurst has weakly and pompously repeated at second-hand from Mrs Reed; for I read a sincere nature in your ardent eyes and on your clear front), and God waits only the separation of spirit from flesh to crown us with a full reward. Why, then, should we ever sink overwhelmed with distress, when life is so soon over, and death is so certain an entrance to happiness – to glory?'

I was silent; Helen had calmed me; but in the tranquillity she imparted there was an alloy of inexpressible sadness. I felt the impression of woe as she spoke, but I could not tell whence it came; and when, having done speaking, she breathed a little fast and coughed a short cough, I momentarily forgot my own sorrows to yield to a vague concern for her.

Resting my head on Helen's shoulder, I put my arms round her waist; she drew me to her, and we reposed in silence. We had not sat long thus, when another person came in. Some heavy clouds, swept from the sky by a rising wind, had left the moon bare; and her light, streaming in through a window near, shone full both on us and on the approaching figure, which we at once recognised as Miss Temple.

'I came on purpose to find you, Jane Eyre,' said she; 'I want you in my room; and as Helen Burns is with you, she may come too.'

We went; following the superintendent's guidance, we had to thread some intricate passages, and mount a staircase before we reached her apartment; it contained a good fire, and looked cheerful. Miss Temple told Helen Burns to be seated in a low armchair on one side of the hearth, and herself taking another, she called me to her side.

'Is it all over?' she asked, looking down at my face. 'Have you cried your grief away?'

'I am afraid I never shall do that.'

'Why?'

'Because I have been wrongly accused; and you, ma'am, and everybody else, will now think me wicked.'

'We shall think you what you prove yourself to be, my child. Continue to act as a good girl, and you will satisfy us.'

'Shall I, Miss Temple?'

'You will,' said she, passing her arm round me. 'And now tell me who is the lady whom Mr Brocklehurst called your benefactress?'

'Mrs Reed, my uncle's wife. My uncle is dead, and he left me to her care.'

'Did she not, then, adopt you of her own accord?'

'No, ma'am; she was sorry to have to do it: but my uncle, as I have often heard the servants say, got her to promise before he died that she would always keep me.'

'Well now, Jane, you know, or at least I will tell you, that when a criminal is accused, he is always allowed to speak in his own defence. You have been charged with falsehood; defend yourself to me as well as you can. Say whatever your memory suggests as true; but add nothing and exaggerate nothing.'

I resolved, in the depth of my heart, that I would be most moderate – most correct; and, having reflected a few minutes in order to arrange coherently what I had to say, I told her all the story of my sad childhood. Exhausted by emotion, my language was more subdued than it generally was when it developed that sad theme; and mindful of Helen's warnings against the indulgence of resentment, I infused into the narrative far less of gall and wormwood than ordinary. Thus restrained and simplified, it sounded more credible: I felt as I went on that Miss Temple fully believed me.

In the course of the tale I had mentioned Mr Lloyd as having come to see me after the fit: for I never forgot the, to me, frightful episode of the red-room: in detailing which, my excitement was sure, in some degree, to break bounds; for nothing could soften in my recollection the spasm of agony which clutched my heart when Mrs Reed spurned my wild supplication for pardon, and locked me a second time in the dark and haunted chamber.

I had finished: Miss Temple regarded me a few minutes in silence; she then said – 'I know something of Mr Lloyd; I shall write to him; if his reply agrees with your statement, you shall be publicly cleared from every imputation; to me, Jane, you are clear now.'

She kissed me, and still keeping me at her side (where I was well contented to stand, for I derived a child's pleasure from the contemplation of her face, her dress, her one or two ornaments, her white forehead, her clustered and shining curls, and beaming dark eyes), she proceeded to address Helen Burns.

'How are you tonight, Helen? Have you coughed much today?'

'Not quite so much, I think, ma'am.'

'And the pain in your chest?'

'It is a little better.

Miss Temple got up, took her hand and examined her pulse; then she returned to her own seat: as she resumed it, I heard her sigh low. She was pensive a few minutes, then rousing herself, she said cheerfully – 'But you two are my visitors tonight; I must treat you as such.' She rang her bell.

'Barbara,' she said to the servant who answered it, 'I have not yet had tea; bring the tray and place cups for these two young ladies.'

And a tray was soon brought. How pretty, to my eyes, did the china cups and bright teapot look, placed on the little round table near the fire! How fragrant was the steam of the beverage, and the scent of the toast! of which, however, I, to my dismay (for I was beginning to be hungry), discerned only a very small portion: Miss Temple discerned it too.

'Barbara,' said she, 'can you not bring a little more bread and butter? There is not enough for three.'

Barbara went out: she returned soon – 'Madam, Mrs Harden says she has sent up the usual quantity.'

Mrs Harden, be it observed, was the housekeeper: a woman after Mr Brocklehurst's own heart, made up of equal parts of whalebone and iron.

'Oh, very well!' returned Miss Temple; 'we must make it do, Barbara, I suppose.' And as the girl withdrew she added, smiling, 'Fortunately, I have it in my power to supply deficiencies for this once.'

Having invited Helen and me to approach the table and placed before each of us a cup of tea with one delicious but thin morsel of toast, she got up, unlocked a drawer, and taking from it a parcel wrapped in paper, disclosed presently to our eyes a good-sized seed-cake.

'I meant to give each of you some of this to take with you,' said she, 'but as there is so little toast, you must have it now,' and she proceeded to cut slices with a generous hand.

We feasted that evening as on nectar and ambrosia; and not the least delight of the entertainment was the smile of gratification with which our hostess regarded us, as we satisfied our famished appetites on the delicate fare she liberally supplied.

Tea over and the tray removed, she again summoned us to the fire; we sat one on each side of her, and now a conversation followed between her and Helen, which it was indeed a privilege to be admitted to hear.

Miss Temple had always something of serenity in her air, of state in her mien, of refined propriety in her language, which precluded deviation into the ardent, the excited, the eager: something which chastened the pleasure of those who looked on her and listened to her, by a controlling sense of awe; and such was my feeling now: but as to Helen Burns, I was struck with wonder.

The refreshing meal, the brilliant fire, the presence and kindness of her beloved instructress, or, perhaps, more than all these, something in her own unique mind, had roused her powers within her. They woke, they kindled: first, they glowed in the bright tint of her cheek, which till this hour I had never seen but pale and bloodless; then they shone in the liquid lustre of her eyes, which had suddenly acquired a beauty more singular than that of Miss Temple's – a beauty neither of fine colour nor long eyelash, nor pencilled brow, but of meaning, of movement, of radiance. Then her soul sat on her lips, and language flowed, from what source I cannot tell. Has a girl of fourteen a heart large enough, vigorous enough, to hold the swelling spring of pure, full, fervid eloquence? Such was the characteristic of Helen's discourse on that, to me, memorable evening; her spirit seemed hastening to live within a very brief span as much as many live during a protracted existence.

They conversed of things I had never heard of; of nations and times past; of countries far away; of secrets of nature discovered or guessed at: they spoke of books: how many they had read! What stores of knowledge they possessed! Then they seemed so familiar with French names and French authors: but my amazement reached its climax when Miss Temple asked Helen if she sometimes snatched a moment to recall the Latin her father had taught her, and taking a book from a shelf, bade her read and construe a page of Virgil; and Helen obeyed, my organ of veneration expanding at every sounding line. She had

scarcely finished ere the bell announced bedtime! no delay could be admitted; Miss Temple embraced us both, saying, as she drew us to her heart – 'God bless you, my children!'

Helen she held a little longer than me: she let her go more reluctantly; it was Helen her eye followed to the door; it was for her she a second time breathed a sad sigh; for her she wiped a tear from her cheek.

On reaching the bedroom, we heard the voice of Miss Scatcherd: she was examining drawers; she had just pulled out Helen Burns's, and when we entered Helen was greeted with a sharp reprimand, and told that tomorrow she should have half a dozen of untidily folded articles pinned to her shoulder.

'My things were indeed in shameful disorder,' murmured Helen to me, in a low voice: 'I intended to have arranged them, but I forgot.'

Next morning, Miss Scatcherd wrote in conspicuous characters on a piece of pasteboard the word 'Slattern,' and bound it like a phylactery round Helen's large, mild, intelligent, and benign-looking forehead. She wore it till evening, patient, unresentful, regarding it as a deserved punishment. The moment Miss Scatcherd withdrew after afternoon school, I ran to Helen, tore it off, and thrust it into the fire: the fury of which she was incapable had been burning in my soul all day, and tears, hot and large, had continually been scalding my cheek; for the spectacle of her sad resignation gave me an intolerable pain at the heart.

About a week subsequently to the incidents above narrated, Miss Temple, who had written to Mr Lloyd, received his answer: it appeared that what he said went to corroborate my account. Miss Temple, having assembled the whole school, announced that enquiry had been made into the charges alleged against Jane Eyre, and that she was most happy to be able to pronounce her completely cleared from every imputation. The teachers then shook hands with me and kissed me, and a murmur of pleasure ran through the ranks of my companions.

Thus relieved of a grievous load, I from that hour set to work afresh, resolved to pioneer my way through every difficulty: I toiled hard, and my success was proportionate to my efforts; my memory, not naturally tenacious, improved with practice; exercise sharpened my wits; in a few weeks I was promoted to a higher class; in less than two months I was allowed to commence French and drawing. I learned the first two tenses of the verb *Etre*, and sketched my first cottage (whose walls, by the bye, outrivalled in slope those of the leaning tower of Pisa), on the same day. That night, on going to bed, I forgot to prepare in imagination the Barmecide supper of hot roast potatoes, or white bread and new milk, with which I was wont to amuse my inward cravings: I feasted instead on the spectacle of ideal drawings, which I saw in the dark; all the work of my own hands: freely pencilled houses and trees, picturesque rocks and ruins, Cuyp-like groups of cattle, sweet paintings of butterflies hovering over unblown roses, of birds picking at ripe cherries, of wrens' nests enclosing pearl-like eggs, wreathed about with young ivy sprays. I examined, too, in thought, the possibility of my ever being able to translate currently a certain little French story which Mme Pierrot had that day shown me; nor was that problem solved to my satisfaction ere I fell sweetly asleep.

Well has Solomon said – 'Better is a dinner of herbs where love is, than a stalled ox and hatred therewith.'

I would not now have exchanged Lowood with all its privations for Gateshead and its daily luxuries.

## *Chapter 9*

But the privations, or rather the hardships, of Lowood lessened. Spring drew on: she was indeed already come; the frosts of winter had ceased; its snows were melted, its cutting winds ameliorated. My wretched feet, flayed and swollen to lameness by the sharp air of January, began to heal and subside under the gentler breathings of April; the nights and mornings no longer by their Canadian temperature froze the very blood in our veins; we could now endure the play-hour passed in the garden: sometimes on a sunny day it began even to be pleasant and genial, and a greenness grew over those brown beds, which, freshening daily, suggested the thought that Hope traversed them at night, and left each morning brighter traces of her steps. Flowers peeped out amongst the leaves; snowdrops, crocuses, purple auriculas, and golden-eyed pansies. On Thursday afternoons (half-holidays) we now took walks, and found still sweeter flowers opening by the wayside, under the hedges.

I discovered, too, that a great pleasure, an enjoyment which the horizon only bounded, lay all outside the high and spike-guarded walls of our garden: this pleasure consisted in prospect of noble summits girdling a great hill-hollow, rich in verdure and shadow; in a bright beck, full of dark stones and sparkling eddies. How different had this scene looked when I viewed it laid out beneath the iron sky of winter, stiffened in frost, shrouded with snow! – when mists as chill as death wandered to the impulse of east winds along those purple peaks, and rolled down 'ing' and holm till they blended with the frozen fog of the beck! That beck itself was then a torrent, turbid and curbless: it tore asunder the wood, and sent a raving sound through the air, often thickened with wild rain or whirling sleet; and for the forest on its banks, *that* showed only ranks of skeletons.

April advanced to May: a bright, serene May it was; days of blue sky, placid sunshine, and soft western or southern gales filled up its duration. And now vegetation matured with vigour; Lowood shook loose its tresses; it became all green, all flowery; its great elm, ash, and oak skeletons were restored to majestic life; woodland plants sprang up profusely in its recesses; unnumbered varieties of moss filled its hollows, and it made a strange ground-sunshine out of the wealth of its wild primrose plants: I have seen their pale gold gleam in overshadowed spots like scatterings of the sweetest lustre. All this I enjoyed often and fully, free, unwatched, and almost alone: for this unwonted liberty and pleasure there was a cause, to which it now becomes my task to advert.

Have I not described a pleasant site for a dwelling, when I speak of it as

bosomed in hill and wood, and rising from the verge of a stream? Assuredly, pleasant enough: but whether healthy or not is another question.

That forest-dell, where Lowood lay, was the cradle of fog and fog-bred pestilence; which, quickening with the quickening spring, crept into the Orphan Asylum, breathed typhus through its crowded schoolroom and dormitory, and, ere May arrived, transformed the seminary into an hospital.

Semi-starvation and neglected colds had predisposed most of the pupils to receive infection: forty-five out of the eighty girls lay ill at one time. Classes were broken up, rules relaxed. The few who continued well were allowed almost unlimited license; because the medical attendant insisted on the necessity of frequent exercise to keep them in health: and had it been otherwise, no one had leisure to watch or restrain them. Miss Temple's whole attention was absorbed by the patients: she lived in the sick-room, never quitting it except to snatch a few hours' rest at night. The teachers were fully occupied with packing up and making other necessary preparations for the departure of those girls who were fortunate enough to have friends and relations able and willing to remove them from the seat of contagion. Many, already smitten, went home only to die: some died at the school, and were buried quietly and quickly, the nature of the malady forbidding delay.

While disease had thus become an inhabitant of Lowood, and death its frequent visitor; while there was gloom and fear within its walls; while its rooms and passages steamed with hospital smells, the drug and the pastille striving vainly to overcome the effluvia of mortality, that bright May shone unclouded over the bold hills and beautiful woodland out of doors. Its garden, too, glowed with flowers: hollyhocks had sprung up tall as trees, lilies had opened, tulips and roses were in bloom; the borders of the little beds were gay with pink thrift and crimson double daisies; the sweetbriars gave out, morning and evening, their scent of spice and apples; and these fragrant treasures were all useless for most of the inmates of Lowood, except to furnish now and then a handful of herbs and blossoms to put in a coffin.

But I, and the rest who continued well, enjoyed fully the beauties of the scene and season; they let us ramble in the wood, like gypsies, from morning till night; we did what we liked, went where we liked: we lived better too. Mr Brocklehurst and his family never came near Lowood now: household matters were not scrutinised into; the cross housekeeper was gone, driven away by the fear of infection; her successor, who had been matron at the Lowton Dispensary, unused to the ways of her new abode, provided with comparative liberality. Besides, there were fewer to feed; the sick could eat little; our breakfast-basins were better filled; when there was no time to prepare a regular dinner, which often happened, she would give us a large piece of cold pie, or a thick slice of bread and cheese, and this we carried away with us to the wood, where we each chose the spot we liked best, and dined sumptuously.

My favourite seat was a smooth and broad stone, rising white and dry from the very middle of the beck, and only to be got at by wading through the water; a feat I accomplished barefoot. The stone was just broad enough to accommodate,

comfortably, another girl and me, at that time my chosen comrade – one Mary Ann Wilson; a shrewd, observant personage, whose society I took pleasure in, partly because she was witty and original, and partly because she had a manner which set me at my ease. Some years older than I, she knew more of the world, and could tell me many things I liked to hear: with her my curiosity found gratification: to my faults also she gave ample indulgence, never imposing curb or rein on anything I said. She had a turn for narrative, I for analysis; she liked to inform, I to question; so we got on swimmingly together, deriving much entertainment, if not much improvement, from our mutual intercourse.

And where, meantime, was Helen Burns? Why did I not spend these sweet days of liberty with her? Had I forgotten her? or was I so worthless as to have grown tired of her pure society? Surely the Mary Ann Wilson I have mentioned was inferior to my first acquaintance: she could only tell me amusing stories, and reciprocate any racy and pungent gossip I chose to indulge in; while, if I have spoken truth of Helen, she was qualified to give those who enjoyed the privilege of her converse a taste of far higher things.

True, reader; and I knew and felt this: and though I am a defective being, with many faults and few redeeming points, yet I never tired of Helen Burns; nor ever ceased to cherish for her a sentiment of attachment, as strong, tender, and respectful as any that ever animated my heart. How could it be otherwise, when Helen, at all times and under all circumstances, evinced for me a quiet and faithful friendship, which ill-humour never soured, nor irritation never troubled? But Helen was ill at present: for some weeks she had been removed from my sight to I knew not what room upstairs. She was not, I was told, in the hospital portion of the house with the fever patients; for her complaint was consumption, not typhus: and by consumption I, in my ignorance, understood something mild, which time and care would be sure to alleviate.

I was confirmed in this idea by the fact of her once or twice coming downstairs on very warm sunny afternoons, and being taken by Miss Temple into the garden; but, on these occasions, I was not allowed to go and speak to her; I only saw her from the schoolroom window, and then not distinctly; for she was much wrapped up, and sat at a distance under the verandah.

One evening, in the beginning of June, I had stayed out very late with Mary Ann in the wood; we had, as usual, separated ourselves from the others, and had wandered far; so far that we lost our way, and had to ask it at a lonely cottage, where a man and woman lived, who looked after a herd of half-wild swine that fed on the mast in the wood. When we got back, it was after moonrise: a pony, which we knew to be the surgeon's, was standing at the garden door. Mary Ann remarked that she supposed someone must be very ill, as Mr Bates had been sent for at that time of the evening. She went into the house; I stayed behind a few minutes to plant in my garden a handful of roots I had dug up in the forest, and which I feared would wither if I left them till the morning. This done, I lingered yet a little longer: the flowers smelt so sweet as the dew fell; it was such a pleasant evening, so serene, so warm; the still glowing west promised so fairly another fine day on the morrow; the moon rose with such majesty in the grave

east. I was noting these things and enjoying them as a child might, when it entered my mind as it had never done before: 'How sad to be lying now on a sick bed, and to be in danger of dying! This world is pleasant – it would be dreary to be called from it, and to have to go who knows where?'

And then my mind made its first earnest effort to comprehend what had been infused into it concerning heaven and hell; and for the first time it recoiled, baffled; and for the first time glancing behind, on each side, and before it, it saw all round an unfathomed gulf: it felt the one point where it stood – the present; all the rest was formless cloud and vacant depth; and it shuddered at the thought of tottering, and plunging amid that chaos. While pondering this new idea, I heard the front door open; Mr Bates came out, and with him was a nurse. After she had seen him mount his horse and depart, she was about to close the door, but I ran up to her.

'How is Helen Burns?'

'Very poorly,' was the answer.

'Is it her Mr Bates has been to see?'

'Yes.'

'And what does he say about her?'

'He says she'll not be here long.'

This phrase, uttered in my hearing yesterday, would have only conveyed the notion that she was about to be removed to Northumberland, to her own home. I should not have suspected that it meant she was dying; but I knew instantly now! It opened clear on my comprehension that Helen Burns was numbering her last days in this world, and that she was going to be taken to the region of spirits, if such region there were. I experienced a shock of horror, then a strong thrill of grief, then a desire – a necessity to see her; and I asked in what room she lay.

'She is in Miss Temple's room,' said the nurse.

'May I go up and speak to her?'

'Oh no, child! It is not likely; and now it is time for you to come in; you'll catch the fever if you stop out when the dew is falling.'

The nurse closed the front door; I went in by the side entrance which led to the schoolroom: I was just in time; it was nine o'clock, and Miss Miller was calling the pupils to go to bed.

It might be two hours later, probably near eleven, when I – not having been able to fall asleep, and deeming, from the perfect silence of the dormitory, that my companions were all wrapt in profound repose – rose softly, put on my frock over my night-dress, and, without shoes, crept from the apartment, and set off in quest of Miss Temple's room. It was quite at the other end of the house; but I knew my way; and the light of the unclouded summer moon, entering here and there at passage windows, enabled me to find it without difficulty. An odour of camphor and burnt vinegar warned me when I came near the fever room: and I passed its door quickly, fearful lest the nurse who sat up all night should hear me. I dreaded being discovered and sent back; for I *must* see Helen, I must embrace her before she died, I must give her one last kiss, exchange with her one last word.

Having descended a staircase, traversed a portion of the house below, and succeeded in opening and shutting, without noise, two doors, I reached another flight of steps; these I mounted, and then just opposite to me was Miss Temple's room. A light shone through the keyhole and from under the door; a profound stillness pervaded the vicinity. Coming near, I found the door slightly ajar; probably to admit some fresh air into the close abode of sickness. Indisposed to hesitate, and full of impatient impulses – soul and senses quivering with keen throes – I put it back and looked in. My eye sought Helen, and feared to find death.

Close by Miss Temple's bed, and half covered with its white curtains, there stood a little crib. I saw the outline of a form under the clothes, but the face was hid by the hangings: the nurse I had spoken to in the garden sat in an easy-chair asleep; an unsnuffed candle burnt dimly on the table. Miss Temple was not to be seen: I knew afterwards that she had been called to a delirious patient in the fever-room. I advanced; then paused by the crib side: my hand was on the curtain, but I preferred speaking before I withdrew it. I still recoiled at the dread of seeing a corpse.

'Helen!' I whispered softly, 'are you awake?'

She stirred herself, put back the curtain, and I saw her face, pale, wasted, but quite composed: she looked so little changed that my fear was instantly dissipated.

'Can it be you, Jane?' she asked, in her own gentle voice.

'Oh!' I thought, 'she is not going to die; they are mistaken: she could not speak and look so calmly if she were.'

I got on to her crib and kissed her: her forehead was cold, and her cheek both cold and thin, and so were her hand and wrist; but she smiled as of old.

'Why are you come here, Jane? It is past eleven o'clock: I heard it strike some minutes since.'

'I came to see you, Helen: I heard you were very ill, and I could not sleep till I had spoken to you.'

'You came to bid me goodbye, then: you are just in time probably.'

'Are you going somewhere, Helen? Are you going home?'

'Yes; to my long home – my last home.'

'No, no, Helen!' I stopped, distressed. While I tried to devour my tears, a fit of coughing seized Helen; it did not, however, wake the nurse; when it was over, she lay some minutes exhausted; then she whispered – 'Jane, your little feet are bare; lie down and cover yourself with my quilt.'

I did so: she put her arm over me, and I nestled close to her. After a long silence, she resumed, still whispering – 'I am very happy, Jane; and when you hear that I am dead, you must be sure and not grieve: there is nothing to grieve about. We all must die one day, and the illness which is removing me is not painful; it is gentle and gradual: my mind is at rest. I leave no one to regret me much; I have only a father; and he is lately married, and will not miss me. By dying young, I shall escape great sufferings. I had not qualities or talents to make my way very well in the world: I should have been continually at fault.'

'But where are you going to, Helen? Can you see? Do you know?'

'I believe; I have faith: I am going to God.'

'Where is God? What is God?'

'My Maker and yours, who will never destroy what He created. I rely implicitly on His power, and confide wholly in His goodness: I count the hours till that eventful one arrives which shall restore me to Him, reveal Him to me.'

'You are sure, then, Helen, that there is such a place as heaven, and that our souls can get to it when we die?'

'I am sure there is a future state; I believe God is good; I can resign my immortal part to Him without any misgiving. God is my father; God is my friend: I love Him; I believe He loves me.'

'And shall I see you again, Helen, when I die?'

'You will come to the same region of happiness: be received by the same mighty, universal Parent, no doubt, dear Jane.'

Again I questioned, but this time only in thought. 'Where is that region? Does it exist?' And I clasped my arms closer round Helen; she seemed dearer to me than ever; I felt as if I could not let her go; I lay with my face hidden on her neck. Presently she said, in the sweetest tone – 'How comfortable I am! That last fit of coughing has tired me a little; I feel as if I could sleep: but don't leave me, Jane; I like to have you near me.'

'I'll stay with you, *dear* Helen: no one shall take me away.'

'Are you warm, darling?'

'Yes.'

'Good-night, Jane.'

'Good-night, Helen.'

She kissed me, and I her, and we both soon slumbered.

When I awoke it was day: an unusual movement roused me; I looked up; I was in somebody's arms; the nurse held me; she was carrying me through the passage back to the dormitory. I was not reprimanded for leaving my bed; people had something else to think about; no explanation was afforded then to my many questions; but a day or two afterwards I learned that Miss Temple, on returning to her own room at dawn, had found me laid in the little crib; my face against Helen Burns's shoulder, my arms round her neck. I was asleep, and Helen was – dead.

Her grave is in Brocklebridge churchyard: for fifteen years after her death it was only covered by a grassy mound; but now a grey marble tablet marks the spot, inscribed with her name, and the word 'Resurgam'.

## Chapter 10

Hitherto I have recorded in detail the events of my insignificant existence: to the first ten years of my life I have given almost as many chapters. But this is not to be a regular autobiography: I am only bound to invoke Memory where I know her responses will possess some degree of interest; therefore I now pass a space

of eight years almost in silence: a few lines only are necessary to keep up the links of connection.

When the typhus fever had fulfilled its mission of devastation at Lowood, it gradually disappeared from thence; but not till its virulence and the number of its victims had drawn public attention on the school. Enquiry was made into the origin of the scourge, and by degrees various facts came out which excited public indignation in a high degree. The unhealthy nature of the site; the quantity and quality of the children's food; the brackish, fetid water used in its preparation; the pupils' wretched clothing and accommodations – all these things were discovered, and the discovery produced a result mortifying to Mr Brocklehurst, but beneficial to the institution.

Several wealthy and benevolent individuals in the county subscribed largely for the erection of a more convenient building in a better situation; new regulations were made; improvements in diet and clothing introduced; the funds of the school were entrusted to the management of a committee. Mr Brocklehurst, who, from his wealth and family connections, could not be overlooked, still retained the post of treasurer; but he was aided in the discharge of his duties by gentlemen of rather more enlarged and sympathising minds: his office of inspector, too, was shared by those who knew how to combine reason with strictness, comfort with economy, compassion with uprightness. The school, thus improved, became in time a truly useful and noble institution. I remained an inmate of its walls, after its regeneration, for eight years: six as pupil, and two as teacher; and in both capacities I bear my testimony to its value and importance.

During these eight years my life was uniform: but not unhappy, because it was not inactive. I had the means of an excellent education placed within my reach; a fondness for some of my studies, and a desire to excel in all, together with a great delight in pleasing my teachers, especially such as I loved, urged me on: I availed myself fully of the advantages offered me. In time I rose to be the first girl of the first class; then I was invested with the office of teacher; which I discharged with zeal for two years: but at the end of that time I altered.

Miss Temple, through all changes, had thus far continued superintendent of the seminary: to her instruction I owed the best part of my acquirements; her friendship and society had been my continual solace; she had stood me in the stead of mother, governess, and, latterly, companion. At this period she married, removed with her husband (a clergyman, an excellent man, almost worthy of such a wife) to a distant county, and consequently was lost to me.

From the day she left I was no longer the same: with her was gone every settled feeling, every association that had made Lowood in some degree a home to me. I had imbibed from her something of her nature and much of her habits: more harmonious thoughts: what seemed better regulated feelings had become the inmates of my mind. I had given in allegiance to duty and order; I was quiet; I believed I was content: to the eyes of others, usually even to my own, I appeared a disciplined and subdued character.

But destiny, in the shape of the Revd Mr Nasmyth, came between me and Miss Temple: I saw her in her travelling dress step into a post-chaise, shortly

after the marriage ceremony; I watched the chaise mount the hill and disappear beyond its brow; and then retired to my own room, and there spent in solitude the greatest part of the half-holiday granted in honour of the occasion.

I walked about the chamber most of the time. I imagined myself only to be regretting my loss, and thinking how to repair it; but when my reflections were concluded, and I looked up and found that the afternoon was gone, and evening far advanced, another discovery dawned on me, namely, that in the interval I had undergone a transforming process; that my mind had put off all it had borrowed of Miss Temple – or rather that she had taken with her the serene atmosphere I had been breathing in her vicinity – and that now I was left in my natural element, and beginning to feel the stirring of old emotions. It did not seem as if a prop were withdrawn, but rather as if a motive were gone: it was not the power to be tranquil which had failed me, but the reason for tranquillity was no more. My world had for some years been in Lowood: my experience had been of its rules and systems; now I remembered that the real world was wide, and that a varied field of hopes and fears, of sensations and excitements, awaited those who had courage to go forth into its expanse, to seek real knowledge of life amidst its perils.

I went to my window, opened it, and looked out. There were the two wings of the building; there was the garden; there were the skirts of Lowood; there was the hilly horizon. My eye passed all other objects to rest on those most remote, the blue peaks; it was those I longed to surmount; all within their boundary of rock and heath seemed prison-ground, exile limits. I traced the white road winding round the base of one mountain, and vanishing in a gorge between two; how I longed to follow it farther! I recalled the time when I had travelled that very road in a coach; I remembered descending that hill at twilight; an age seemed to have elapsed since the day which brought me first to Lowood, and I had never quitted it since. My vacations had all been spent at school: Mrs Reed had never sent for me to Gateshead; neither she nor any of her family had ever been to visit me. I had had no communication by letter or message with the outer world: school-rules, school-duties, school-habits and notions, and voices, and faces, and phrases, and costumes, and preferences, and antipathies – such was what I knew of existence. And now I felt that it was not enough; I tired of the routine of eight years in one afternoon. I desired liberty; for liberty I gasped; for liberty I uttered a prayer; it seemed scattered on the wind then faintly blowing. I abandoned it and framed a humbler supplication; for change, stimulus: that petition, too, seemed swept off into vague space: 'Then,' I cried, half desperate, 'grant me at least a new servitude!'

Here a bell, ringing the hour of supper, called me downstairs.

I was not free to resume the interrupted chain of my reflections till bedtime: even then a teacher who occupied the same room with me kept me from the subject to which I longed to recur, by a prolonged effusion of small talk. How I wished sleep would silence her. It seemed as if, could I but go back to the idea which had last entered my mind as I stood at the window, some inventive suggestion would rise for my relief.

Miss Gryce snored at last; she was a heavy Welshwoman, and till now her habitual nasal strains had never been regarded by me in any other light than as a nuisance; tonight I hailed the first deep notes with satisfaction; I was debarrassed of interruption; my half-effaced thought instantly revived.

'A new servitude! There is something in that,' I soliloquised (mentally, be it understood; I did not talk aloud). 'I know there is, because it does not sound too sweet; it is not like such words as Liberty, Excitement, Enjoyment: delightful sounds truly; but no more than sounds for me; and so hollow and fleeting that it is mere waste of time to listen to them. But Servitude! That must be matter of fact. Anyone may serve: I have served here eight years; now all I want is to serve elsewhere. Can I not get so much of my own will? Is not the thing feasible? Yes – yes – the end is not so difficult; if I had only a brain active enough to ferret out the means of attaining it.'

I sat up in bed by way of arousing this said brain: it was a chilly night; I covered my shoulders with a shawl, and then I proceeded *to think* again with all my might.

'What do I want? A new place, in a new house, amongst new faces, under new circumstances: I want this because it is of no use wanting anything better. How do people do to get a new place? They apply to friends, I suppose: I have no friends. There are many others who have no friends, who must look about for themselves and be their own helpers; and what is their resource?'

I could not tell: nothing answered me; I then ordered my brain to find a response, and quickly. It worked and worked faster: I felt the pulses throb in my head and temples; but for nearly an hour it worked in chaos; and no result came of its efforts. Feverish with vain labour, I got up and took a turn in the room; undrew the curtain, noted a star or two, shivered with cold, and again crept to bed.

A kind fairy, in my absence, had surely dropped the required suggestion on my pillow; for as I lay down, it came quietly and naturally to my mind: 'Those who want situations advertise; you must advertise in the *—shire Herald*.'

'How? I know nothing about advertising.'

Replies rose smooth and prompt now: 'You must enclose the advertisement and the money to pay for it under a cover directed to the editor of the *Herald*; you must put it, the first opportunity you have, into the post at Lowton; answers must be addressed to J. E., at the post-office there; you can go and enquire in about a week after you send your letter, if any are come, and act accordingly.'

This scheme I went over twice, thrice; it was then digested in my mind; I had it in a clear practical form: I felt satisfied, and fell asleep.

With earliest day, I was up: I had my advertisement written, enclosed, and directed before the bell rang to rouse the school; it ran thus: 'A young lady accustomed to tuition' (had I not been a teacher two years?) 'is desirous of meeting with a situation in a private family where the children are under fourteen (I thought that as I was barely eighteen, it would not do to undertake the guidance of pupils nearer my own age). She is qualified to teach the usual branches of a good English education, together with French, Drawing, and Music' (in those days, reader, this now narrow catalogue of accomplishments

would have been held tolerably comprehensive). 'Address, J. E., Post-office, Lowton, —shire.' This document remained locked in my drawer all day: after tea, I asked leave of the new superintendent to go to Lowton, in order to perform some small commissions for myself and one or two of my fellow-teachers; permission was readily granted; I went. It was a walk of two miles, and the evening was wet, but the days were still long; I visited a shop or two, slipped the letter into the post-office, and came back through heavy rain, with stream-ing garments, but with a relieved heart.

The succeeding week seemed long: it came to an end at last, however, like all sublunary things, and once more, towards the close of a pleasant autumn day, I found myself afoot on the road to Lowton. A picturesque track it was, by the way; lying along the side of the beck and through the sweetest curves of the dale: but that day I thought more of the letters, that might or might not be awaiting me at the little burgh whither I was bound, than of the charms of lea and water.

My ostensible errand on this occasion was to get measured for a pair of shoes; so I discharged that business first, and when it was done, I stepped across the clean and quiet little street from the shoemaker's to the post-office: it was kept by an old dame, who wore horn spectacles on her nose, and black mittens on her hands.

'Are there any letters for J. E.?' I asked.

She peered at me over her spectacles, and then she opened a drawer and fumbled among its contents for a long time, so long that my hopes began to falter. At last, having held a document before her glasses for nearly five minutes, she presented it across the counter, accompanying the act by another inquisitive and mistrustful glance – it was for J. E.

'Is there only one?' I demanded.

'There are no more,' said she; and I put it in my pocket and turned my face homeward: I could not open it then; rules obliged me to be back by eight, and it was already half-past seven.

Various duties awaited me on my arrival: I had to sit with the girls during their hour of study; then it was my turn to read prayers; to see them to bed: afterwards I supped with the other teachers. Even when we finally retired for the night, the inevitable Miss Gryce was still my companion: we had only a short end of candle in our candlestick, and I dreaded lest she should talk till it was all burnt out; fortunately, however, the heavy supper she had eaten produced a soporific effect: she was already snoring before I had finished undressing. There still remained an inch of candle: I now took out my letter; the seal was an initial F.; I broke it; the contents were brief.

If J. E., who advertised in the —shire Herald of last Thursday, possesses the acquirements mentioned, and if she is in a position to give satisfactory references as to character and competency, a situation can be offered her where there is but one pupil, a little girl, under ten years of age; and where the salary is thirty pounds per annum. J. E. is requested to send references, name, address, and all particulars to the direction: 'Mrs Fairfax, Thornfield, near Millcote, —shire.'

I examined the document long: the writing was old-fashioned and rather uncertain, like that of an elderly lady. This circumstance was satisfactory: a private fear had haunted me, that in thus acting for myself, and by my own guidance, I ran the risk of getting into some scrape; and, above all things, I wished the result of my endeavours to be respectable, proper, *en règle*. I now felt that an elderly lady was no bad ingredient in the business I had on hand. Mrs Fairfax! I saw her in a black gown and widow's cap; frigid, perhaps, but not uncivil: a model of elderly English respectability. Thornfield! that, doubtless, was the name of her house: a neat orderly spot, I was sure; though I failed in my efforts to conceive a correct plan of the premises. Millcote, —shire; I brushed up my recollections of the map of England; yes, I saw it; both the shire and the town. —shire was seventy miles nearer London than the remote county where I now resided: that was a recommendation to me. I longed to go where there was life and movement: Millcote was a large manufacturing town on the banks of the A—; a busy place enough, doubtless: so much the better; it would be a complete change at least. Not that my fancy was much captivated by the idea of long chimneys and clouds of smoke – 'but,' I argued, 'Thornfield will, probably, be a good way from the town.'

Here the socket of the candle dropped, and the wick went out.

Next day new steps were to be taken; my plans could no longer be confined to my own breast; I must impart them in order to achieve their success. Having sought and obtained an audience of the superintendent during the noontide recreation, I told her I had a prospect of getting a new situation where the salary would be double what I now received (for at Lowood I only got £15 per annum); and requested she would break the matter for me to Mr Brocklehurst, or some of the committee, and ascertain whether they would permit me to mention them as references. She obligingly consented to act as mediatrix in the matter. The next day she laid the affair before Mr Brocklehurst, who said that Mrs Reed must be written to, as she was my natural guardian. A note was accordingly addressed to that lady, who returned for answer, that 'I might do as I pleased: she had long relinquished all interference in my affairs.' This note went the round of the committee, and at last, after what appeared to me most tedious delay, formal leave was given me to better my condition if I could; and an assurance added, that as I had always conducted myself well, both as teacher and pupil, at Lowood, a testimonial of character and capacity, signed by the inspectors of that institution, should forthwith be furnished me.

This testimonial I accordingly received in about a month, forwarded a copy of it to Mrs Fairfax, and got that lady's reply, stating that she was satisfied, and fixing that day fortnight as the period for my assuming the post of governess in her house.

I now busied myself in preparations: the fortnight passed rapidly. I had not a very large wardrobe, though it was adequate to my wants; and the last day sufficed to pack my trunk, the same I had brought with me eight years ago from Gateshead.

The box was corded, the card nailed on. In half an hour the carrier was to call

for it to take it to Lowton, whither I myself was to repair at an early hour the next morning to meet the coach. I had brushed my black stuff travelling-dress, prepared my bonnet, gloves, and muff; sought in all my drawers to see that no article was left behind; and now having nothing more to do, I sat down and tried to rest. I could not; though I had been on foot all day, I could not now repose an instant; I was too much excited. A phase of my life was closing tonight, a new one opening tomorrow: impossible to slumber in the interval; I must watch feverishly while the change was being accomplished.

'Miss,' said a servant who met me in the lobby, where I was wandering like a troubled spirit, 'a person below wishes to see you.'

'The carrier, no doubt,' I thought, and ran downstairs without enquiry. I was passing the back-parlour or teachers' sitting-room, the door of which was half open, to go to the kitchen, when someone ran out – 'It's her, I am sure! – I could have told her anywhere!' cried the individual who stopped my progress and took my hand.

I looked: I saw a woman attired like a well-dressed servant, matronly, yet still young; very good-looking, with black hair and eyes, and lively complexion.

'Well, who is it?' she asked, in a voice and with a smile I half recognised; 'you've not quite forgotten me, I think, Miss Jane?'

In another second I was embracing and kissing her rapturously: 'Bessie! Bessie! Bessie!' that was all I said; whereat she half laughed, half cried, and we both went into the parlour. By the fire stood a little fellow of three years old, in plaid frock and trousers.

'That is my little boy,' said Bessie directly.

'Then you are married, Bessie?'

'Yes; nearly five years since to Robert Leaven, the coachman; and I've a little girl besides Bobby there, that I've christened Jane.'

'And you don't live at Gateshead?'

'I live at the lodge: the old porter has left.'

'Well, and how do they all get on? Tell me everything about them, Bessie: but sit down first; and, Bobby, come and sit on my knee, will you?' but Bobby preferred sidling over to his mother.

'You're not grown so very tall, Miss Jane, nor so very stout,' continued Mrs Leaven. 'I dare say they've not kept you too well at school: Miss Reed is the head and shoulders taller than you are; and Miss Georgiana would make two of you in breadth.'

'Georgiana is handsome, I suppose, Bessie?'

'Very. She went up to London last winter with her mama, and there everybody admired her, and a young lord fell in love with her: but his relations were against the match; and – what do you think? – he and Miss Georgiana made it up to run away; but they were found out and stopped. It was Miss Reed that found them out: I believe she was envious; and now she and her sister lead a cat and dog life together; they are always quarrelling.'

'Well, and what of John Reed?'

'Oh, he is not doing so well as his mama could wish. He went to college, and

he got – plucked, I think they call it: and then his uncles wanted him to be a barrister, and study the law: but he is such a dissipated young man, they will never make much of him, I think.'

'What does he look like?'

'He is very tall: some people call him a fine-looking young man; but he has such thick lips.'

'And Mrs Reed?'

'Missis looks stout and well enough in the face, but I think she's not quite easy in her mind: Mr John's conduct does not please her – he spends a deal of money.'

'Did she send you here, Bessie?'

'No, indeed: but I have long wanted to see you, and when I heard that there had been a letter from you, and that you were going to another part of the country, I thought I'd just set off, and get a look at you before you were quite out of my reach.'

'I am afraid you are disappointed in me, Bessie.' I said this laughing: I perceived that Bessie's glance, though it expressed regard, did in no shape denote admiration.

'No, Miss Jane, not exactly: you are genteel enough; you look like a lady, and it is as much as ever I expected of you: you were no beauty as a child.'

I smiled at Bessie's frank answer: I felt that it was correct, but I confess I was not quite indifferent to its import: at eighteen most people wish to please, and the conviction that they have not an exterior likely to second that desire brings anything but gratification.

'I dare say you are clever, though,' continued Bessie, by way of solace. 'What can you do? Can you play on the piano?'

'A little.'

There was one in the room; Bessie went and opened it, and then asked me to sit down and give her a tune: I played a waltz or two, and she was charmed.

'The Miss Reeds could not play as well!' said she exultingly. 'I always said you would surpass them in learning: and can you draw?'

'That is one of my paintings over the chimney-piece.' It was a landscape in water colours, of which I had made a present to the superintendent, in acknowledgement of her obliging mediation with the committee on my behalf, and which she had framed and glazed.

'Well, that is beautiful. Miss Jane! It is as fine a picture as any Miss Reed's drawing-master could paint, let alone the young ladies themselves, who could not come near it: and have you learnt French?'

'Yes, Bessie, I can both read it and speak it.'

'And you can work on muslin and canvas?'

'I can.'

'Oh, you are quite a lady, Miss Jane! I knew you would be: you will get on whether your relations notice you or not. There was something I wanted to ask you. Have you ever heard anything from your father's kinsfolk, the Eyres?'

'Never in my life.'

'Well, you know Missis always said they were poor and quite despicable: and they may be poor; but I believe they are as much gentry as the Reeds are; for one day, nearly seven years ago, a Mr Eyre came to Gateshead and wanted to see you; Missis said you were at school fifty miles off; he seemed so much disappointed, for he could not stay: he was going on a voyage to a foreign country, and the ship was to sail from London in a day or two. He looked quite a gentleman, and I believe he was your father's brother.'

'What foreign country was he going to, Bessie?'

'An island thousands of miles off, where they make wine – the butler did tell me – '

'Madeira?' I suggested.

'Yes, that is it – that is the very word.'

'So he went?'

'Yes; he did not stay many minutes in the house: Missis was very high with him; she called him afterwards a "sneaking tradesman". My Robert believes he was a wine-merchant.'

'Very likely,' I returned; 'or perhaps clerk or agent to a wine-merchant.'

Bessie and I conversed about old times an hour longer, and then she was obliged to leave me: I saw her again for a few minutes the next morning at Lowton, while I was waiting for the coach. We parted finally at the door of the Brocklehurst Arms there; each went her separate way; she set off for the brow of Lowood Fell to meet the conveyance which was to take her back to Gateshead, I mounted the vehicle which was to bear me to new duties and a new life in the unknown environs of Millcote.

## Chapter 11

A new chapter in a novel is something like a new scene in a play; and when I draw up the curtain this time, reader, you must fancy you see a room in the George Inn at Millcote, with such large figured papering on the walls as inn rooms have; such a carpet, such furniture, such ornaments on the mantelpiece, such prints, including a portrait of George the Third, and another of the Prince of Wales, and a representation of the death of Wolfe. All this is visible to you by the light of an oil lamp hanging from the ceiling, and by that of an excellent fire, near which I sit in my cloak and bonnet; my muff and umbrella lie on the table, and I am warming away the numbness and chill contracted by sixteen hours' exposure to the rawness of an October day: I left Lowton at four o'clock p.m., and the Millcote town clock is now just striking eight.

Reader, though I look comfortably accommodated, I am not very tranquil in my mind. I thought when the coach stopped here there would be someone to meet me; I looked anxiously round as I descended the wooden steps the 'boots' placed for my convenience, expecting to hear my name pronounced, and to see some description of carriage waiting to convey me to Thornfield. Nothing of

the sort was visible; and when I asked a waiter if anyone had been to enquire after a Miss Eyre, I was answered in the negative: so I had no resource but to request to be shown into a private room: and here I am waiting, while all sorts of doubts and fears are troubling my thoughts.

It is a very strange sensation to inexperienced youth to feel itself quite alone in the world, cut adrift from every connection, uncertain whether the port to which it is bound can be reached, and prevented by many impediments from returning to that it has quitted. The charm of adventure sweetens that sensation, the glow of pride warms it; but then the throb of fear disturbs it; and fear with me became predominant when half an hour elapsed and still I was alone. I bethought myself to ring the bell.

'Is there a place in this neighbourhood called Thornfield?' I asked of the waiter who answered the summons.

'Thornfield? I don't know, ma'am; I'll enquire at the bar.' He vanished, but reappeared instantly – 'Is your name Eyre, Miss?'

'Yes.'

'Person here waiting for you.'

I jumped up, took my muff and umbrella, and hastened into the inn-passage: a man was standing by the open door, and in the lamp-lit street I dimly saw a one-horse conveyance.

'This will be your luggage, I suppose?' said the man rather abruptly when he saw me, pointing to my trunk in the passage.

'Yes.' He hoisted it on to the vehicle, which was a sort of car, and then I got in; before he shut me up, I asked him how far it was to Thornfield.

'A matter of six miles.'

'How long shall we be before we get there?'

'Happen an hour and a half.'

He fastened the car door, climbed to his own seat outside, and we set off. Our progress was leisurely, and gave me ample time to reflect; I was content to be at length so near the end of my journey; and as I leaned back in the comfortable though not elegant conveyance, I meditated much at my ease.

'I suppose,' thought I, 'judging from the plainness of the servant and carriage, Mrs Fairfax is not a very dashing person: so much the better; I never lived amongst fine people but once, and I was very miserable with them. I wonder if she lives alone except this little girl; if so, and if she is in any degree amiable, I shall surely be able to get on with her; I will do my best; it is a pity that doing one's best does not always answer. At Lowood, indeed, I took that resolution, kept it, and succeeded in pleasing; but with Mrs Reed, I remember my best was always spurned with scorn. I pray God Mrs Fairfax may not turn out a second Mrs Reed; but if she does, I am not bound to stay with her! let the worst come to the worst, I can advertise again. How far are we on our road now, I wonder?'

I let down the window and looked out; Millcote was behind us; judging by the number of its lights, it seemed a place of considerable magnitude, much larger than Lowton. We were now, as far as I could see, on a sort of common; but there

were houses scattered all over the district; I felt we were in a different region to Lowood, more populous, less picturesque; more stirring, less romantic.

The roads were heavy, the night misty; my conductor let his horse walk all the way, and the hour and a half extended, I verily believe, to two hours; at last he turned in his seat and said – 'You're noan so far fro' Thornfield now.'

Again I looked out: we were passing a church; I saw its low broad tower against the sky, and its bell was tolling a quarter; I saw a narrow galaxy of lights too, on a hillside, marking a village or hamlet. About ten minutes after, the driver got down and opened a pair of gates: we passed through, and they clashed to behind us. We now slowly ascended a drive, and came upon the long front of a house: candlelight gleamed from one curtained bow-window; all the rest were dark. The car stopped at the front door; it was opened by a maidservant; I alighted and went in.

'Will you walk this way, ma'am?' said the girl; and I followed her across a square hall with high doors all round: she ushered me into a room whose double illumination of fire and candle at first dazzled me, contrasting as it did with the darkness to which my eyes had been for two hours inured; when I could see, however, a cosy and agreeable picture presented itself to my view.

A snug small room; a round table by a cheerful fire; an armchair high-backed and old-fashioned, wherein sat the neatest imaginable little elderly lady, in widow's cap, black silk gown, and snowy muslin apron; exactly like what I had fancied Mrs Fairfax, only less stately and milder looking. She was occupied in knitting; a large cat sat demurely at her feet; nothing in short was wanting to complete the beau-ideal of domestic comfort. A more reassuring introduction for a new governess could scarcely be conceived; there was no grandeur to overwhelm, no stateliness to embarrass; and then, as I entered, the old lady got up and promptly and kindly came forward to meet me.

'How do you do, my dear? I am afraid you have had a tedious ride; John drives so slowly; you must be cold, come to the fire.'

'Mrs Fairfax, I suppose?' said I.

'Yes, you are right: do sit down.'

She conducted me to her own chair, and then began to remove my shawl and untie my bonnet-strings; I begged she would not give herself so much trouble.

'Oh, it is no trouble; I dare say your own hands are almost numbed with cold. Leah, make a little hot negus and cut a sandwich or two: here are the keys of the storeroom.'

And she produced from her pocket a most housewifely bunch of keys, and delivered them to the servant.

'Now, then, draw nearer to the fire,' she continued. 'You've brought your luggage with you, haven't you, my dear?'

'Yes, ma'am.'

'I'll see it carried into your room,' she said, and bustled out.

'She treats me like a visitor,' thought I. 'I little expected such a reception; I anticipated only coldness and stiffness: this is not like what I have heard of the treatment of governesses; but I must not exult too soon.'

She returned; with her own hands cleared her knitting apparatus and a book or two from the table, to make room for the tray which Leah now brought, and then herself handed me the refreshments. I felt rather confused at being the object of more attention than I had ever before received, and, that too, shown by my employer and superior; but as she did not herself seem to consider she was doing anything out of her place, I thought it better to take her civilities quietly.

'Shall I have the pleasure of seeing Miss Fairfax tonight?' I asked, when I had partaken of what she offered me.

'What did you say, my dear? I am a little deaf,' returned the good lady, approaching her ear to my mouth.

I repeated the question more distinctly.

'Miss Fairfax? Oh, you mean Miss Varens! Varens is the name of your future pupil.'

'Indeed! Then she is not your daughter?'

'No, I have no family.'

I should have followed up my first enquiry, by asking in what way Miss Varens was connected with her; but I recollected it was not polite to ask too many questions: besides, I was sure to hear in time.

'I am so glad,' she continued, as she sat down opposite to me, and took the cat on her knee; 'I am so glad you are come; it will be quite pleasant living here now with a companion. To be sure it is pleasant at any time; for Thornfield is a fine old hall, rather neglected of late years perhaps, but still it is a respectable place; yet you know in winter-time one feels dreary quite alone in the best quarters. I say alone – Leah is a nice girl to be sure, and John and his wife are very decent people; but then you see they are only servants, and one can't converse with them on terms of equality: one must keep them at due distance, for fear of losing one's authority. I'm sure last winter (it was a very severe one, if you recollect, and when it did not snow, it rained and blew), not a creature but the butcher and postman came to the house, from November till February; and I really got quite melancholy with sitting night after night alone; I had Leah in to read to me sometimes; but I don't think the poor girl liked the task much: she felt it confining. In spring and summer one got on better: sunshine and long days make such a difference; and then, just at the commencement of this autumn, little Adela Varens came and her nurse: a child makes a house alive all at once; and now you are here I shall be quite gay.'

My heart really warmed to the worthy lady as I heard her talk; and I drew my chair a little nearer to her, and expressed my sincere wish that she might find my company as agreeable as she anticipated.

'But I'll not keep you sitting up late tonight,' said she; 'it is on the stroke of twelve now, and you have been travelling all day: you must feel tired. If you have got your feet well warmed, I'll show you your bedroom. I've had the room next to mine prepared for you; it is only a small apartment, but I thought you would like it better than one of the large front chambers: to be sure they have finer furniture, but they are so dreary and solitary, I never sleep in them myself.'

I thanked her for her considerate choice, and as I really felt fatigued with my

long journey, expressed my readiness to retire. She took her candle, and I followed her from the room. First she went to see if the hall-door was fastened; having taken the key from the lock, she led the way upstairs. The steps and banisters were of oak; the staircase window was high and latticed; both it and the long gallery into which the bedroom doors opened looked as if they belonged to a church rather than a house. A very chill and vaultlike air pervaded the stairs and gallery, suggesting cheerless ideas of space and solitude; and I was glad, when finally ushered into my chamber, to find it of small dimensions, and furnished in ordinary, modern style.

When Mrs Fairfax had bidden me a kind good-night, and I had fastened my door, gazed leisurely round, and in some measure effaced the eerie impression made by that wide hall, that dark and spacious staircase, and that long, cold gallery, by the livelier aspect of my little room, I remembered that, after a day of bodily fatigue and mental anxiety, I was now at last in safe haven. The impulse of gratitude swelled my heart, and I knelt down at the bedside, and offered up thanks where thanks were due; not forgetting, ere I rose, to implore aid on my further path, and the power of meriting the kindness which seemed so frankly offered me before it was earned. My couch had no thorns in it that night; my solitary room no fears. At once weary and content, I slept soon and soundly: when I awoke it was broad day.

The chamber looked such a bright little place to me as the sun shone in between the gay blue chintz window curtains, showing papered walls and a carpeted floor, so unlike the bare planks and stained plaster of Lowood, that my spirits rose at the view. Externals have a great effect on the young: I thought that a fairer era of life was beginning for me – one that was to have its flowers and pleasures, as well as its thorns and toils. My faculties, roused by the change of scene, the new field offered to hope, seemed all astir. I cannot precisely define what they expected, but it was something pleasant: not perhaps that day or that month, but at an indefinite future period.

I rose; I dressed myself with care: obliged to be plain – for I had no article of attire that was not made with extreme simplicity – I was still by nature solicitous to be neat. It was not my habit to be disregardful of appearance or careless of the impression I made: on the contrary, I ever wished to look as well as I could, and to please as much as my want of beauty would permit. I sometimes regretted that I was not handsomer; I sometimes wished to have rosy cheeks, a straight nose, and small cherry mouth; I desired to be tall, stately, and finely developed in figure; I felt it a misfortune that I was so little, so pale, and had features so irregular and so marked. And why had I these aspirations and these regrets? It would be difficult to say: I could not then distinctly say it to myself; yet I had a reason, and a logical, natural reason too. However, when I had brushed my hair very smooth, and put on my black frock – which, Quakerlike as it was, at least had the merit of fitting to a nicety – and adjusted my clean white tucker, I thought I should do respectably enough to appear before Mrs Fairfax, and that my new pupil would not at least recoil from me with antipathy. Having opened my chamber window, and seen that I left all things straight and neat on the toilet table, I ventured forth.

Traversing the long and matted gallery, I descended the slippery steps of oak; then I gained the hall: I halted there a minute; I looked at some pictures on the walls (one, I remember, represented a grim man in a cuirass, and one a lady with powdered hair and a pearl necklace), at a bronze lamp pendent from the ceiling, at a great clock whose case was of oak curiously carved, and ebon black with time and rubbing. Everything appeared very stately and imposing to me; but then I was so little accustomed to grandeur. The hall-door, which was half of glass, stood open; I stepped over the threshold. It was a fine autumn morning; the early sun shone serenely on embrowned groves and still green fields; advancing on to the lawn, I looked up and surveyed the front of the mansion. It was three storeys high, of proportions not vast, though considerable: a gentleman's manor-house, not a nobleman's seat: battlements round the top gave it a picturesque look. Its grey front stood out well from the background of a rookery, whose cawing tenants were now on the wing: they flew over the lawn and grounds to alight in a great meadow, from which these were separated by a sunk fence, and where an array of mighty old thorn trees, strong, knotty, and broad as oaks, at once explained the etymology of the mansion's designation. Farther off were hills: not so lofty as those round Lowood, nor so craggy, nor so like barriers of separation from the living world; but yet quiet and lonely hills enough, and seeming to embrace Thornfield with a seclusion I had not expected to find existent so near the stirring locality of Millcote. A little hamlet, whose roofs, were blent with trees, straggled up the side of one of these hills; the church of the district stood nearer Thornfield: its old tower-top looked over a knoll between the house and gates.

I was yet enjoying the calm prospect and pleasant fresh air, yet listening with delight to the cawing of the rooks, yet surveying the wide, hoary front of the hall, and thinking what a great place it was for one lonely little dame like Mrs Fairfax to inhabit, when that lady appeared at the door.

'What! out already?' said she. 'I see you are an early riser.' I went up to her, and was received with an affable kiss and shake of the hand.

'How do you like Thornfield?' she asked. I told her I liked it very much.

'Yes,' she said, 'it is a pretty place; but I fear it will be getting out of order, unless Mr Rochester should take it into his head to come and reside here permanently; or, at least, visit it rather oftener: great houses and fine grounds require the presence of the proprietor.'

'Mr Rochester!' I exclaimed. 'Who is he?'

'The owner of Thornfield,' she responded quietly. 'Did you not know he was called Rochester?'

Of course I did not – I had never heard of him before; but the old lady seemed to regard his existence as a universally understood fact, with which everybody must be acquainted by instinct.

'I thought,' I continued, 'Thornfield belonged to you.'

'To me? Bless you, child; what an idea! To me! I am only the housekeeper – the manager. To be sure I am distantly related to the Rochesters by the mother's side, or at least my husband was; he was a clergyman, incumbent of Hay – that little village yonder on the hill – and that church near the gates was his. The

present Mr Rochester's mother was a Fairfax, and second cousin to my husband: but I never presume on the connection – in fact, it is nothing to me; I consider myself quite in the light of an ordinary housekeeper: my employer is always civil, and I expect nothing more.'

'And the little girl – my pupil!'

'She is Mr Rochester's ward; he commissioned me to find a governess for her. He intended to have her brought up in —shire, I believe. Here she comes, with her "bonne", as she calls her nurse.' The enigma then was explained: this affable and kind little widow was no great dame; but a dependant like myself. I did not like her the worse for that; on the contrary, I felt better pleased than ever. The equality between her and me was real; not the mere result of condescension on her part: so much the better – my position was all the freer.

As I was meditating on this discovery, a little girl, followed by her attendant, came running up the lawn. I looked at my pupil, who did not at first appear to notice me: she was quite a child, perhaps seven or eight years old, slightly built, with a pale, small-featured face, and a redundancy of hair falling in curls to her waist.

'Good-morning, Miss Adela,' said Mrs Fairfax. 'Come and speak to the lady who is to teach you, and to make you a clever woman someday.' She approached.

'C'est là ma gouvernante?' said she, pointing to me, and addressing her nurse; who answered – 'Mais oui, certainement.'

'Are they foreigners?' I enquired, amazed at hearing the French language.

'The nurse is a foreigner, and Adela was born on the Continent; and, I believe, never left it till within six months ago. When she first came here she could speak no English; now she can make shift to talk it a little: I don't understand her, she mixes it so with French; but you will make out her meaning very well, I dare say.'

Fortunately I had had the advantage of being taught French by a French lady; and as I had always made a point of conversing with Mme Pierrot as often as I could, and had besides, during the last seven years, learnt a portion of French by heart daily – applying myself to take pains with my accent, and imitating as closely as possible the pronunciation of my teacher, I had acquired a certain degree of readiness and correctness in the language, and was not likely to be much at a loss with Mlle Adela. She came and shook hands with me when she heard that I was her governess; and as I led her in to breakfast, I addressed some phrases to her in her own tongue: she replied briefly at first, but after we were seated at the table, and she had examined me some ten minutes with her large hazel eyes, she suddenly commenced chattering fluently.

'Ah!' cried she, in French, 'you speak my language as well as Mr Rochester does: I can talk to you as I can to him, and so can Sophie. She will be glad: nobody here understands her: Mme Fairfax is all English. Sophie is my nurse; she came with me over the sea in a great ship with a chimney that smoked – how it did smoke! – and I was sick, and so was Sophie, and so was Mr Rochester. Mr Rochester lay down on a sofa in a pretty room called the salon, and Sophie and I had little beds in another place. I nearly fell out of mine; it was like a shelf. And Mademoiselle what is your name?'

'Eyre – Jane Eyre.'

'Aire? Bah! I cannot say it. Well, our ship stopped in the morning, before it was quite daylight, at a great city – a huge city, with very dark houses and all smoky; not at all like the pretty clean town I came from; and Mr Rochester carried me in his arms over a plank to the land, and Sophie came after, and we all got into a coach, which took us to a beautiful large house, larger than this and finer, called an hotel. We stayed there nearly a week: I and Sophie used to walk every day in a great green place full of trees, called the Park; and there were many children there besides me, and a pond with beautiful birds in it, that I fed with crumbs.'

'Can you understand her when she runs on so fast?' asked Mrs Fairfax.

I understood her very well, for I had been accustomed to the fluent tongue of Mme Pierrot.

'I wish,' continued the good lady, 'you would ask her a question or two about her parents: I wonder if she remembers them?'

'Adèle,' I enquired, 'with whom did you live when you were in that pretty clean town you spoke of?'

'I lived long ago with mama; but she is gone to the Holy Virgin. Mama used to teach me to dance and sing, and to say verses. A great many gentlemen and ladies came to see mama, and I used to dance before them, or to sit on their knees and sing to them: I liked it. Shall I let you hear me sing now?'

She had finished her breakfast, so I permitted her to give a specimen of her accomplishments. Descending from her chair, she came and placed herself on my knee; then, folding her little hands demurely before her, shaking back her curls and lifting her eyes to the ceiling, she commenced singing a song from some opera. It was the strain of a forsaken lady, who, after bewailing the perfidy of her lover, calls pride to her aid; desires her attendant to deck her in her brightest jewels and richest robes, and resolves to meet the false one that night at a ball, and prove to him, by the gaiety of her demeanour, how little his desertion has affected her.

The subject seemed strangely chosen for an infant singer; but I suppose the point of the exhibition lay in hearing the notes of love and jealousy warbled with the lisp of childhood; and in very bad taste that point was: at least I thought so.

Adèle sang the canzonette tunefully enough, and with the *naïveté* of her age. This achieved, she jumped from my knee and said, 'Now, Mademoiselle, I will repeat you some poetry.'

Assuming an attitude, she began 'La Ligue des Rats: fable de La Fontaine.' She then declaimed the little piece with an attention to punctuation and emphasis, a flexibility of voice and an appropriateness of gesture, very unusual indeed at her age, and which proved she had been carefully trained.

'Was it your mama who taught you that piece?' I asked.

'Yes, and she just used to say it in this way: "Qu'avez vous donc? lui dit un de ces rats; parlez!"; She made me lift my hand – so – to remind me to raise my voice at the question. Now shall I dance for you?'

'No, that will do: but after your mama went to the Holy Virgin, as you say, with whom did you live then?'

'With Mme Frédéric and her husband: she took care of me, but she is nothing related to me. I think she is poor, for she had not so fine a house as mama. I was not long there. Mr Rochester asked me if I would like to go and live with him in England, and I said yes; for I knew Mr Rochester before I knew Mme Frédéric, and he was always kind to me and gave me pretty dresses and toys: but you see he has not kept his word, for he has brought me to England, and now he is gone back again himself, and I never see him.'

After breakfast, Adèle and I withdrew to the library, which room, it appears, Mr Rochester had directed should be used as the schoolroom. Most of the books were locked up behind glass doors; but there was one bookcase left open containing everything that could be needed in the way of elementary works, and several volumes of light literature, poetry, biography, travels, a few romances, etc. I suppose he had considered that these were all the governess would require for her private perusal; and, indeed, they contented me amply for the present; compared with the scanty pickings I had now and then been able to glean at Lowood, they seemed to offer an abundant harvest of entertainment and information. In this room, too, there was a cabinet piano, quite new and of superior tone; also an easel for painting and a pair of globes.

I found my pupil sufficiently docile, though disinclined to apply: she had not been used to regular occupation of any kind. I felt it would be injudicious to confine her too much at first; so, when I had talked to her a great deal, and got her to learn a little, and when the morning had advanced to noon, I allowed her to return to her nurse. I then proposed to occupy myself till dinner-time in drawing some little sketches for her use.

As I was going upstairs to fetch my portfolio and pencils, Mrs Fairfax called to me: 'Your morning school-hours are over now, I suppose,' said she. She was in a room the folding-doors of which stood open: I went in when she addressed me. It was a large, stately apartment, with purple chairs and curtains, a Turkey carpet, walnut-panelled walls, one vast window rich in stained glass, and a lofty ceiling, nobly moulded. Mrs Fairfax was dusting some vases of fine purple spar, which stood on a sideboard.

'What a beautiful room!' I exclaimed, as I looked round; for I had never before seen any half so imposing.

'Yes; this is the dining-room. I have just opened the window, to let in a little air and sunshine; for everything gets so damp in apartments that are seldom inhabited; the drawing-room yonder feels like a vault.'

She pointed to a wide arch corresponding to the window, and hung like it with a Tyrian-dyed curtain, now looped up. Mounting to it by two broad steps, and looking through, I thought I caught a glimpse of a fairy place, so bright to my novice-eyes appeared the view beyond. Yet it was merely a very pretty drawing-room, and within it a boudoir, both spread with white carpets, on which seemed laid brilliant garlands of flowers; both ceiled with snowy mouldings of white grapes and vine-leaves, beneath which glowed in rich contrast crimson couches and ottomans; while the ornaments on the pale Parian mantelpiece were of sparkling Bohemian glass, ruby red; and between the windows large mirrors repeated the general blending of snow and fire.

'In what order you keep these rooms, Mrs Fairfax!' said I. 'No dust, no canvas coverings: except that the air feels chilly, one would think they were inhabited daily.'

'Why, Miss Eyre, though Mr Rochester's visits here are rare, they are always sudden and unexpected; and as I observed that it put him out to find everything swathed up, and to have a bustle of arrangement on his arrival, I thought it best to keep the rooms in readiness.'

'Is Mr Rochester an exacting, fastidious sort of man?'

'Not particularly so; but he has a gentleman's tastes and habits, and he expects to have things managed in conformity to them.'

'Do you like him? Is he generally liked?'

'Oh, yes; the family have always been respected here. Almost all the land in this neighbourhood, as far as you can see, has belonged to the Rochesters time out of mind.'

'Well, but, leaving his land out of the question, do you like him? Is he liked for himself?'

'*I* have no cause to do otherwise than like him; and I believe he is considered a just and liberal landlord by his tenants: but he has never lived much amongst them.'

'But has he no peculiarities? What, in short, is his character?'

'Oh! his character is unimpeachable, I suppose. He is rather peculiar, perhaps: he has travelled a great deal, and seen a great deal of the world, I should think. I dare say he is clever, but I never had much conversation with him.'

'In what way is he peculiar?'

'I don't know – it is not easy to describe – nothing striking, but you feel it when he speaks to you; you cannot be always sure whether he is in jest or earnest, whether he is pleased or the contrary; you don't thoroughly understand him, in short – at least, I don't: but it is of no consequence, he is a very good master.'

This was all the account I got from Mrs Fairfax of her employer and mine. There are people who seem to have no notion of sketching a character, or observing and describing salient points, either in persons or things: the good lady evidently belonged to this class; my queries puzzled, but did not draw her out. Mr Rochester was Mr Rochester in her eyes; a gentleman, a landed proprietor – nothing more: she enquired and searched no further, and evidently wondered at my wish to gain a more definite notion of his identity.

When we left the dining-room, she proposed to show me over the rest of the house; and I followed her upstairs and downstairs, admiring as I went; for all was well arranged and handsome. The large front chambers I thought especially grand: and some of the third-storey rooms, though dark and low, were interesting from their air of antiquity. The furniture once appropriated to the lower apartments had from time to time been removed here, as fashions changed: and the imperfect light entering by their narrow casement showed bedsteads of a hundred years old; chests in oak or walnut, looking, with their strange carvings of palm branches and cherubs' heads, like types of the Hebrew ark; rows of

venerable chairs, high-backed and narrow; stools still more antiquated, on whose cushioned tops were yet apparent traces of half-effaced embroideries, wrought by fingers that for two generations had been coffin-dust. All these relics gave to the third storey of Thornfield Hall the aspect of a home of the past: a shrine of memory. I liked the hush, the gloom, the quaintness of these retreats in the day; but I by no means coveted a night's repose on one of those wide and heavy beds: shut in, some of them, with doors of oak; shaded, others, with wrought old English hangings crusted with thick work, portraying effigies of strange flowers, and stranger birds, and strangest human beings, all which would have looked strange, indeed, by the pallid gleam of moonlight.

'Do the servants sleep in these rooms?' I asked.

'No; they occupy a range of smaller apartments to the back; no one ever sleeps here: one would almost say that, if there were a ghost at Thornfield Hall, this would be its haunt.'

'So I think: you have no ghost, then?'

'None that I ever heard of,' returned Mrs Fairfax, smiling.

'Nor any traditions of one? no legends or ghost stories?'

'I believe not. And yet it is said the Rochesters have been rather a violent than a quiet race in their time: perhaps, though, that is the reason they rest tranquilly in their graves now.'

'Yes – "after life's fitful fever they sleep well," ' I muttered. 'Where are you going now, Mrs Fairfax?' for she was moving away.

'On to the leads; will you come and see the view from thence?' I followed still, up a very narrow staircase to the attics, and thence by a ladder and through a trap-door to the roof of the hall. I was now on a level with the crow colony, and could see into their nests. Leaning over the battlements and looking far down, I surveyed the grounds laid out like a map: the bright and velvet lawn closely girdling the grey base of the mansion; the field, wide as a park, dotted with its ancient timber; the wood, dun and sere, divided by a path visibly overgrown, greener with moss than the trees were with foliage; the church at the gates, the road, the tranquil hills, all reposing in the autumn day's sun; the horizon bounded by a propitious sky, azure, marbled with pearly white. No feature in the scene was extraordinary, but all was pleasing. When I turned from it and repassed the trap-door, I could scarcely see my way down the ladder; the attic seemed black as a vault compared with that arch of blue air to which I had been looking up, and to that sunlit scene of grove, pasture, and green hill, of which the hall was the centre, and over which I had been gazing with delight.

Mrs Fairfax stayed behind a moment to fasten the trap-door; I, by dint of groping, found the outlet from the attic, and proceeded to descend the narrow garret staircase. I lingered in the long passage to which this led, separating the front and back rooms of the third storey: narrow, low, and dim, with only one little window at the far end, and looking, with its two rows of small black doors all shut, like a corridor in some Bluebeard's castle.

While I paced softly on, the last sound I expected to hear in so still a region, a laugh, struck my ear. It was a curious laugh; distinct, formal, mirthless. I stopped:

the sound ceased, only for an instant; it began again, louder: for at first, though distinct, it was very low. It passed off in a clamorous peal that seemed to wake an echo in every lonely chamber; though it originated but in one, and I could have pointed out the door whence the accents issued.

'Mrs Fairfax!' I called out: for I now heard her descending the great stairs. 'Did you hear that loud laugh? Who is it?'

'Some of the servants, very likely,' she answered: 'perhaps Grace Poole.'

'Did you hear it?' I again enquired.

'Yes, plainly: I often hear her: she sews in one of these rooms. Sometimes Leah is with her; they are frequently noisy together.'

The laugh was repeated in its low, syllabic tone, and terminated in an odd murmur.

'Grace!' exclaimed Mrs Fairfax.

I really did not expect any Grace to answer; for the laugh was as tragic, as preternatural a laugh as any I ever heard; and, but that it was high noon, and that no circumstance of ghostliness accompanied the curious cachinnation; but that neither scene nor season favoured fear, I should have been superstitiously afraid. However, the event showed me I was a fool for entertaining a sense even of surprise.

The door nearest me opened, and a servant came out, a woman of between thirty and forty; a set, square-made figure, red-haired, and with a hard, plain face: any apparition less romantic or less ghostly could scarcely be conceived.

'Too much noise, Grace,' said Mrs Fairfax. 'Remember directions!' Grace curtseyed silently and went in.

'She is a person we have to sew and assist Leah in her housemaid's work,' continued the widow; 'not altogether unobjectionable in some points, but she does well enough. By the bye, how have you got on with your new pupil this morning?'

The conversation, thus turned on Adèle, continued till we reached the light and cheerful region below. Adèle came running to meet us in the hall, exclaiming – 'Mesdames, vous êtes servies!' adding, 'J'ai bien faim, moi!'

We found dinner ready, and waiting for us in Mrs Fairfax's room.

## Chapter 12

The promise of a smooth career, which my first calm introduction to Thornfield Hall seemed to pledge, was not belied on a longer acquaintance with the place and its inmates. Mrs Fairfax turned out to be what she appeared, a placid-tempered, kind-natured woman, of competent education and average intelligence. My pupil was a lively child, who had been spoilt and indulged, and therefore was sometimes wayward; but as she was committed entirely to my care, and no injudicious interference from any quarter ever thwarted my plans for her improvement, she soon forgot her little freaks, and became obedient and

teachable. She had no great talents, no marked traits of character, no peculiar development of feeling or taste which raised her one inch above the ordinary level of childhood; but neither had she any deficiency or vice which sunk her below it. She made reasonable progress, entertained for me a vivacious, though perhaps not very profound, affection; and by her simplicity, gay prattle, and efforts to please, inspired me, in return, with a degree of attachment sufficient to make us both content in each other's society.

This, *par parenthèse*, will be thought cool language by persons who entertain solemn doctrines about the angelic nature of children, and the duty of those charged with their education to conceive for them an idolatrous devotion: but I am not writing to flatter parental egotism, to echo cant, or prop up humbug; I am merely telling the truth. I felt a conscientious solicitude for Adèle's welfare and progress, and a quiet liking for her little self: just as I cherished towards Mrs Fairfax a thankfulness for her kindness, and a pleasure in her society proportionate to the tranquil regard she had for me, and the moderation of her mind and character.

Anybody may blame me who likes, when I add further, that, now and then, when I took a walk by myself in the grounds; when I went down to the gates and looked through them along the road; or when, while Adèle played with her nurse, and Mrs Fairfax made jellies in the storeroom, I climbed the three staircases, raised the trap-door of the attic, and having reached the leads, looked out afar over sequestered field and hill, and along dim skyline – that then I longed for a power of vision which might overpass that limit; which might reach the busy world, towns, regions full of life I had heard of but never seen – that then I desired more of practical experience than I possessed; more of intercourse with my kind, of acquaintance with variety of character, than was here within my reach. I valued what was good in Mrs Fairfax, and what was good in Adèle; but I believed in the existence of other and more vivid kinds of goodness, and what I believed in I wished to behold.

Who blames me? Many, no doubt; and I shall be called discontented. I could not help it: the restlessness was in my nature; it agitated me to pain sometimes. Then my sole relief was to walk along the corridor of the third storey, backwards and forwards, safe in the silence and solitude of the spot, and allow my mind's eye to dwell on whatever bright visions rose before it – and, certainly, they were many and glowing; to let my heart be heaved by the exultant movement, which, while it swelled it in trouble, expanded it with life; and, best of all, to open my inward ear to a tale that was never ended – a tale my imagination created, and narrated continuously; quickened with all of incident, life, fire, feeling, that I desired and had not in my actual existence.

It is in vain to say human beings ought to be satisfied with tranquillity: they must have action; and they will make it if they cannot find it. Millions are condemned to a stiller doom than mine, and millions are in silent revolt against their lot. Nobody knows how many rebellions besides political rebellions ferment in the masses of life which people earth. Women are supposed to be very calm generally: but women feel just as men feel; they need exercise for their faculties,

and a field for their efforts, as much as their brothers do; they suffer from too rigid a restraint, too absolute a stagnation, precisely as men would suffer; and it is narrow-minded in their more privileged fellow-creatures to say that they ought to confine themselves to making puddings and knitting stockings, to playing on the piano and embroidering bags. It is thoughtless to condemn them, or laugh at them, if they seek to do more or learn more than custom has pronounced necessary for their sex.

When thus alone, I not unfrequently heard Grace Poole's laugh: the same peal, the same low, slow ha! ha! which, when first heard, had thrilled me: I heard, too, her eccentric murmurs; stranger than her laugh. There were days when she was quite silent; but there were others when I could not account for the sounds she made. Sometimes I saw her: she would come out of her room with a basin, or a plate, or a tray in her hand, go down to the kitchen and shortly return, generally (oh, romantic reader, forgive me for telling the plain truth!) bearing a pot of porter. Her appearance always acted as a damper to the curiosity raised by her oral oddities: hard-featured and staid, she had no point to which interest could attach. I made some attempts to draw her into conversation, but she seemed a person of few words: a monosyllabic reply usually cut short every effort of that sort.

The other members of the household, viz., John and his wife, Leah the housemaid, and Sophie the French nurse, were decent people; but in no respect remarkable; with Sophie I used to talk French, and sometimes I asked her questions about her native country; but she was not of a descriptive or narrative turn, and generally gave such vapid and confused answers as were calculated rather to check than encourage enquiry.

October, November, December passed away. One afternoon in January, Mrs Fairfax had begged a holiday for Adèle, because she had a cold; and, as Adèle seconded the request with an ardour that reminded me how precious occasional holidays had been to me in my own childhood, I accorded it, deeming that I did well in showing pliability on the point. It was a fine, calm day, though very cold; I was tired of sitting still in the library through a whole long morning: Mrs Fairfax had just written a letter which was waiting to be posted, so I put on my bonnet and cloak and volunteered to carry it to Hay; the distance, two miles, would be a pleasant winter afternoon walk. Having seen Adèle comfortably seated in her little chair by Mrs Fairfax's parlour fireside, and given her her best wax doll (which I usually kept enveloped in silver paper in a drawer) to play with, and a storybook for change of amusement; and having replied to her 'Revenez bientôt, ma bonne amie, ma chère Mlle Jeannette,' with a kiss I set out.

The ground was hard, the air was still, my road was lonely; I walked fast till I got warm, and then I walked slowly to enjoy and analyse the species of pleasure brooding for me in the hour and situation. It was three o'clock; the church bell tolled as I passed under the belfry: the charm of the hour lay in its approaching dimness, in the low-gliding and pale-beaming sun. I was a mile from Thornfield, in a lane noted for wild roses in summer, for nuts and blackberries in autumn, and even now possessing a few coral treasures in hips and haws, but

whose best winter delight lay in its utter solitude and leafless repose. If a breath of air stirred, it made no sound here; for there was not a holly, not an evergreen to rustle, and the stripped hawthorn and hazel bushes were as still as the white, worn stones which causewayed the middle of the path. Far and wide, on each side, there were only fields, where no cattle now browsed; and the little brown birds, which stirred occasionally in the hedge, looked like single russet leaves that had forgotten to drop.

This lane inclined uphill all the way to Hay; having reached the middle, I sat down on a stile which led thence into a field. Gathering my mantle about me, and sheltering my hands in my muff, I did not feel the cold, though it froze keenly; as was attested by a sheet of ice covering the causeway, where a little brooklet, now congealed, had overflowed after a rapid thaw some days since. From my seat I could look down on Thornfield: the grey and battlemented hall was the principal object in the vale below me; its woods and dark rookery rose against the west. I lingered till the sun went down amongst the trees, and sank crimson and clear behind them. I then turned eastward.

On the hilltop above me sat the rising moon; pale yet as a cloud, but brightening momentarily, she looked over Hay, which, half lost in trees, sent up a blue smoke from its few chimneys: it was yet a mile distant, but in the absolute hush I could hear plainly its thin murmurs of life. My ear, too, felt the flow of currents; in what dales and depths I could not tell: but there were many hills beyond Hay, and doubtless many becks threading their passes. That evening calm betrayed alike the tinkle of the nearest streams, the sough of the most remote.

A rude noise broke on these fine ripplings and whisperings, at once so far away and so clear: a positive tramp, tramp, a metallic clatter, which effaced the soft wave-wanderings; as, in a picture, the solid mass of a crag, or the rough boles of a great oak, drawn in dark and strong on the foreground, efface the aerial distance of azure hill, sunny horizon, and blended clouds where tint melts into tint.

The din was on the causeway: a horse was coming; the windings of the lane yet hid it, but it approached. I was just leaving the stile; yet, as the path was narrow, I sat still to let it go by. In those days I was young, and all sorts of fancies bright and dark tenanted my mind: the memories of nursery stories were there amongst other rubbish; and when they recurred, maturing youth added to them a vigour and vividness beyond what childhood could give. As this horse approached, and as I watched for it to appear through the dusk, I remembered certain of Bessie's tales, wherein figured a North-of-England spirit called a 'Gytrash', which, in the form of horse, mule, or large dog, haunted solitary ways, and sometimes came upon belated travellers, as this horse was now coming upon me.

It was very near, but not yet in sight; when, in addition to the tramp, tramp, I heard a rush under the hedge, and close down by the hazel stems glided a great dog, whose black and white colour made him a distinct object against the trees. It was exactly one form of Bessie's Gytrash – a lion-like creature with long hair

and a huge head: it passed me, however, quietly enough; not staying to look up, with strange pretercanine eyes, in my face, as I half expected it would. The horse followed, a tall steed, and on its back a rider. The man, the human being, broke the spell at once. Nothing ever rode the Gytrash: it was always alone; and goblins, to my notions, though they might tenant the dumb carcasses of beasts, could scarce covet shelter in the commonplace human form. No Gytrash was this, only a traveller taking the short cut to Millcote. He passed, and I went on; a few steps, and I turned: a sliding sound and an exclamation of 'What the deuce is to do now?' and a clattering tumble, arrested my attention. Man and horse were down; they had slipped on the sheet of ice which glazed the causeway. The dog came bounding back, and seeing his master in a predicament, and hearing the horse groan, barked till the evening hills echoed the sound, which was deep in proportion to his magnitude. He snuffed round the prostrate group, and then he ran up to me; it was all he could do, there was no other help at hand to summon. I obeyed him, and walked down to the traveller, by this time struggling himself free of his steed. His efforts were so vigorous, I thought he could not be much hurt; but I asked him the question – 'Are you injured, sir?'

I think he was swearing, but am not certain; however, he was pronouncing some formula which prevented him from replying to me directly.

'Can I do anything?' I asked again.

'You must just stand on one side,' he answered as he rose, first to his knees, and then to his feet. I did; whereupon began a heaving, stamping, clattering process, accompanied by a barking and baying which removed me effectually some yards' distance; but I would not be driven quite away till I saw the event. This was finally fortunate; the horse was re-established, and the dog was silenced with a 'Down, Pilot!' The traveller now, stooping, felt his foot and leg, as if trying whether they were sound; apparently something ailed them, for he halted to the stile whence I had just risen, and sat down.

I was in the mood for being useful, or at least officious, I think, for I now drew near him again.

'If you are hurt, and want help, sir, I can fetch someone either from Thornfield Hall or from Hay.'

'Thank you: I shall do: I have no broken bones, only a sprain;' and again he stood up and tried his foot, but the result extorted an involuntary 'Ugh!'

Something of daylight still lingered, and the moon was waxing bright: I could see him plainly. His figure was enveloped in a riding cloak, fur collared and steel clasped; its details were not apparent, but I traced the general points of middle height and considerable breadth of chest. He had a dark face, with stern features and a heavy brow; his eyes and gathered eyebrows looked ireful and thwarted just now; he was past youth, but had not reached middle-age; perhaps he might be thirty-five. I felt no fear of him and but little shyness. Had he been a handsome, heroic-looking young gentleman, I should not have dared to stand thus questioning him against his will, and offering my services unasked. I had hardly ever seen a handsome youth; never in my life spoken to one. I had a theoretical reverence and homage for beauty, elegance, gallantry, fascination;

but had I met those qualities incarnate in masculine shape, I should have known instinctively that they neither had nor could have sympathy with anything in me, and should have shunned them as one would fire, lightning, or anything else that is bright but antipathetic.

If even this stranger had smiled and been good-humoured to me when I addressed him; if he had put off my offer of assistance gaily and with thanks, I should have gone on my way and not felt any vocation to renew enquiries: but the frown, the roughness of the traveller, set me at my ease: I retained my station when he waved to me to go, and announced – 'I cannot think of leaving you, sir, at so late an hour, in this solitary lane, till I see you are fit to mount your horse.'

He looked at me when I said this; he had hardly turned his eyes in my direction before.

'I should think you ought to be at home yourself,' said he, 'if you have a home in this neighbourhood: where do you come from?'

'From just below; and I am not at all afraid of being out late when it is moonlight: I will run over to Hay for you with pleasure, if you wish it: indeed, I am going there to post a letter.'

'You live just below – do you mean at that house with the battlements?' pointing to Thornfield Hall, on which the moon cast a hoary gleam, bringing it out distinct and pale from the woods, that, by contrast with the western sky, now seemed one mass of shadow.

'Yes, sir.'

'Whose house is it?'

'Mr Rochester's.'

'Do you know Mr Rochester?'

'No, I have never seen him.'

'He is not resident, then?'

'No.'

'Can you tell me where he is?'

'I cannot.'

'You are not a servant at the hall, of course. You are – ' He stopped, ran his eye over my dress, which, as usual, was quite simple: a black merino cloak, a black beaver bonnet; neither of them half fine enough for a lady's-maid. He seemed puzzled to decide what I was; I helped him.

'I am the governess.'

'Ah, the governess!' he repeated; 'deuce take me, if I had not forgotten! The governess!' and again my raiment underwent scrutiny. In two minutes he rose from the stile: his face expressed pain when he tried to move.

'I cannot commission you to fetch help,' he said; 'but you may help me a little yourself, if you will be so kind.'

'Yes, sir.'

'You have not an umbrella that I can use as a stick?'

'No.'

'Try to get hold of my horse's bridle and lead him to me: you are not afraid?'

I should have been afraid to touch a horse when alone, but when told to do it,

I was disposed to obey. I put down my muff on the stile, and went up to the tall steed; I endeavoured to catch the bridle, but it was a spirited thing, and would not let me come near its head; I made effort on effort, though in vain: meantime, I was mortally afraid of its trampling forefeet. The traveller waited and watched for some time, and at last he laughed.

'I see,' he said, 'the mountain will never be brought to Muhammad, so all you can do is to aid Muhammad to go to the mountain; I must beg of you to come here.'

I came. 'Excuse me,' he continued: 'necessity compels me to make you useful.' He laid a heavy hand on my shoulder, and leaning on me with some stress, limped to his horse. Having once caught the bridle, he mastered it directly and sprang to his saddle; grimacing grimly as he made the effort, for it wrenched his sprain.

'Now,' said he, releasing his under lip from a hard bite, 'just hand me my whip; it lies there under the hedge.'

I sought it and found it.

'Thank you; now make haste with the letter to Hay, and return as fast as you can.'

A touch of a spurred heel made his horse first start and rear, and then bound away; the dog rushed in his traces; all three vanished,

> Like heath that, in the wilderness,
> The wild wind whirls away.

I took up my muff and walked on. The incident had occurred and was gone for me: it was an incident of no moment, no romance, no interest in a sense; yet it marked with change one single hour of a monotonous life. My help had been needed and claimed; I had given it: I was pleased to have done something; trivial, transitory though the deed was, it was yet an active thing, and I was weary of an existence all passive. The new face, too, was like a new picture introduced to the gallery of memory; and it was dissimilar to all the others hanging there: firstly, because it was masculine; and, secondly, because it was dark, strong, and stern. I had it still before me when I entered Hay, and slipped the letter into the post-office; I saw it as I walked fast downhill all the way home. When I came to the stile, I stopped a minute, looked round and listened, with an idea that a horse's hoofs might ring on the causeway again, and that a rider in a cloak, and a Gytrash-like Newfoundland dog, might be again apparent: I saw only the hedge and a pollard willow before me, rising up still and straight to meet the moonbeams; I heard only the faintest waft of wind roaming fitful among the trees round Thornfield, a mile distant; and when I glanced down in the direction of the murmur, my eye, traversing the hall-front, caught a light kindling in a window: it reminded me that I was late, and I hurried on.

I did not like re-entering Thornfield. To pass its threshold was to return to stagnation; to cross the silent hall, to ascend the darksome staircase, to seek my own lonely little room, and then to meet tranquil Mrs Fairfax, and spend the long winter evening with her, and her only, was to quell wholly the faint excitement

wakened by my walk, to slip again over my faculties the viewless fetters of an uniform and too still existence; of an existence whose very privileges of security and ease I was becoming incapable of appreciating. What good it would have done me at that time to have been tossed in the storms of an uncertain struggling life, and to have been taught by rough and bitter experience to long for the calm amidst which I now repined! Yes, just as much good as it would do a man tired of sitting still in a 'too easy chair' to take a long walk: and just as natural was the wish to stir, under my circumstances, as it would be under his.

I lingered at the gates; I lingered on the lawn; I paced backwards and forwards on the pavement; the shutters of the glass door were closed; I could not see into the interior; and both my eyes and spirit seemed drawn from the gloomy house – from the grey hollow filled with rayless cells, as it appeared to me – to that sky expanded before me, a blue sea absolved from taint of cloud; the moon ascending it in solemn march; her orb seeming to look up as she left the hilltops, from behind which she had come, far and farther below her, and aspired to the zenith, midnight dark in its fathomless depth and measureless distance; and for those trembling stars that followed her course; they made my heart tremble, my veins glow when I viewed them. Little things recall us to earth; the clock struck in the hall; that sufficed; I turned from moon and stars, opened a side-door, and went in.

The hall was not dark, nor yet was it lit, only by the high-hung bronze lamp; a warm glow suffused both it and the lower steps of the oak staircase. This ruddy shine issued from the great dining-room, whose two-leaved door stood open, and showed a genial fire in the grate, glancing on marble hearth and brass fire-irons, and revealing purple draperies and polished furniture, in the most pleasant radiance. It revealed, too, a group near the mantelpiece: I had scarcely caught it, and scarcely become aware of a cheerful mingling of voices, amongst which I seemed to distinguish the tones of Adèle, when the door closed.

I hastened to Mrs Fairfax's room; there was a fire there too, but no candle, and no Mrs Fairfax. Instead, all alone, sitting upright on the rug, and gazing with gravity at the blaze, I beheld a great black and white long-haired dog, just like the Gytrash of the lane. It was so like it that I went forward and said – 'Pilot,' and the thing got up and came to me and snuffed me. I caressed him, and he wagged his great tail; but he looked an eerie creature to be alone with, and I could not tell whence he had come. I rang the bell, for I wanted a candle; and I wanted, too, to get an account of this visitant. Leah entered.

'What dog is this?'

'He came with master.'

'With whom?'

'With master – Mr Rochester – he is just arrived.'

'Indeed! and is Mrs Fairfax with him?'

'Yes, and Miss Adèle; they are in the dining-room, and John is gone for a surgeon; for master has had an accident; his horse fell and his ankle is sprained.'

'Did the horse fall in Hay Lane?'

'Yes, coming downhill; it slipped on some ice.'

'Ah! Bring me a candle, will you, Leah?'

Leah brought it; she entered, followed by Mrs Fairfax, who repeated the news; adding that Mr Carter the surgeon was come, and was now with Mr Rochester: then she hurried out to give orders about tea, and I went upstairs to take off my things.

## *Chapter 13*

Mr Rochester, it seems, by the surgeon's orders, went to bed early that night; nor did he rise soon next morning. When he did come down, it was to attend to business: his agent and some of his tenants were arrived, and waiting to speak with him.

Adèle and I had now to vacate the library: it would be in daily requisition as a reception-room for callers. A fire was lit in an apartment upstairs, and there I carried our books, and arranged it for the future schoolroom. I discerned in the course of the morning that Thornfield Hall was a changed place: no longer silent as a church, it echoed every hour or two to a knock at the door, or a clang of the bell: steps, too, often traversed the hall, and new voices spoke in different keys below; a rill from the outer world was flowing through it; it had a master: for my part, I liked it better.

Adèle was not easy to teach that day; she could not apply: she kept running to the door and looking over the banisters to see if she could get a glimpse of Mr Rochester; then she coined pretexts to go downstairs, in order, as I shrewdly suspected, to visit the library, where I knew she was not wanted; then, when I got a little angry, and made her sit still, she continued to talk incessantly of her 'ami, M. Edouard Fairfax *de* Rochester', as she dubbed him (I had not before heard his prenomens), and to conjecture what presents he had brought her: for it appears he had intimated the night before, that when his luggage came from Millcote, there would be found amongst it a little box in whose contents she had an interest.

'Et cela doit signifier,' said she, 'qu'il y aura là dedans un cadeau pour moi, et peut-être pour vous aussi, mademoiselle. Monsieur a parlé de vous: il m'a demandé le nom de ma gouvernante, et si elle n'était pas une petite personne, assez mince et un peu pâle. J'ai dit qu'oui: car c'est vrai, n'est-ce pas, mademoiselle?'

I and my pupil dined as usual in Mrs Fairfax's parlour; the afternoon was wild and snowy, and we passed it in the schoolroom. At dark I allowed Adèle to put away books and work, and to run downstairs; for, from the comparative silence below, and from the cessation of appeals to the doorbell, I conjectured that Mr Rochester was now at liberty. Left alone, I walked to the window; but nothing was to be seen thence: twilight and snowflakes together thickened the air, and hid the very shrubs on the lawn. I let down the curtain and went back to the fireside.

In the clear embers I was tracing a view, not unlike a picture I remembered

to have seen of the castle of Heidelberg, on the Rhine, when Mrs Fairfax came in, breaking up by her entrance the fiery mosaic I had been piecing together, and scattering too some heavy unwelcome thoughts that were beginning to throng on my solitude.

'Mr Rochester would be glad if you and your pupil would take tea with him in the drawing-room this evening,' said she: 'he has been so much engaged all day that he could not ask to see you before.'

'When is his tea-time?' I enquired.

'Oh, at six o'clock: he keeps early hours in the country. You had better change your frock now; I will go with you and fasten it. Here is a candle.'

'Is it necessary to change my frock?'

'Yes, you had better: I always dress for the evening when Mr Rochester is here.'

This additional ceremony seemed somewhat stately; however, I repaired to my room, and, with Mrs Fairfax's aid, replaced my black stuff dress by one of black silk; the best and the only additional one I had, except one of light grey, which, in my Lowood notions of the toilette, I thought too fine to be worn, except on first-rate occasions.

'You want a brooch,' said Mrs Fairfax. I had a single little pearl ornament which Miss Temple gave me as a parting keepsake: I put it on, and then we went downstairs. Unused as I was to strangers, it was rather a trial to appear thus formally summoned in Mr Rochester's presence. I let Mrs Fairfax precede me into the dining-room, and kept in her shade as we crossed that apartment; and, passing the arch, whose curtain was now dropped, entered the elegant recess beyond.

Two wax candles stood lighted on the table, and two on the mantelpiece; basking in the light and heat of a superb fire, lay Pilot – Adèle knelt near him. Half reclined on a couch appeared Mr Rochester, his foot supported by the cushion; he was looking at Adèle and the dog: the fire shone full on his face. I knew my traveller with his broad and jetty eyebrows; his square forehead, made squarer by the horizontal sweep of his black hair. I recognised his decisive nose, more remarkable for character than beauty; his full nostrils, denoting, I thought, choler; his grim mouth, chin, and jaw – yes, all three were very grim, and no mistake. His shape, now divested of cloak, I perceived harmonised in squareness with his physiognomy: I suppose it was a good figure in the athletic sense of the term – broad chested and thin flanked, though neither tall nor graceful.

Mr Rochester must have been aware of the entrance of Mrs Fairfax and myself; but it appeared he was not in the mood to notice us, for he never lifted his head as we approached.

'Here is Miss Eyre, sir,' said Mrs Fairfax, in her quiet way. He bowed, still not taking his eyes from the group of the dog and child.

'Let Miss Eyre be seated,' said he: and there was something in the forced stiff bow, in the impatient yet formal tone, which seemed further to express, 'What the deuce is it to me whether Miss Eyre be there or not? At this moment I am not disposed to accost her.'

I sat down quite disembarrassed. A reception of finished politeness would

probably have confused me: I could not have returned or repaid it by answering grace and elegance on my part; but harsh caprice laid me under no obligation; on the contrary, a decent quiescence, under the freak of manner, gave me the advantage. Besides, the eccentricity of the proceeding was piquant: I felt interested to see how he would go on.

He went on as a statue would, that is, he neither spoke nor moved. Mrs Fairfax seemed to think it necessary that someone should be amiable, and she began to talk. Kindly, as usual – and, as usual, rather trite – she condoled with him on the pressure of business he had had all day; on the annoyance it must have been to him with that painful sprain: then she commended his patience and perseverance in going through with it.

'Madam, I should like some tea,' was the sole rejoinder she got. She hastened to ring the bell; and when the tray came, she proceeded to arrange the cups, spoons, etc., with assiduous celerity. I and Adèle went to the table; but the master did not leave his couch.

'Will you hand Mr Rochester's cup?' said Mrs Fairfax to me; 'Adèle might perhaps spill it.'

I did as requested. As he took the cup from my hand, Adèle, thinking the moment propitious for making a request in my favour, cried out – 'N'est-ce pas, monsieur, qu'il y a un cadeau pour Mlle Eyre dans votre petit coffre?'

'Who talks of cadeaux?' said he gruffly. 'Did you expect a present, Miss Eyre? Are you fond of presents?' and he searched my face with eyes that I saw were dark, irate, and piercing.

'I hardly know, sir; I have little experience of them: they are generally thought pleasant things.'

'Generally thought? But what do *you* think?'

'I should be obliged to take time, sir, before I could give you an answer worthy of your acceptance: a present has many faces to it, has it not? and one should consider all, before pronouncing an opinion as to its nature.'

'Miss Eyre, you are not so unsophisticated as Adèle: she demands a "cadeau", clamorously, the moment she sees me: you beat about the bush.'

'Because I have less confidence in my deserts than Adèle has: she can prefer the claim of old acquaintance, and the right too of custom; for she says you have always been in the habit of giving her playthings; but if I had to make out a case I should be puzzled, since I am a stranger, and have done nothing to entitle me to an acknowledgement.'

'Oh, don't fall back on over-modesty! I have examined Adèle, and find you have taken great pains with her: she is not bright, she has no talents; yet in a short time she has made much improvement.'

'Sir, you have now given me my "cadeau"; I am obliged to you: it is the meed teachers most covet – praise of their pupils' progress.'

'Humph!' said Mr Rochester, and he took his tea in silence.

'Come to the fire,' said the master, when the tray was taken away, and Mrs Fairfax had settled into a corner with her knitting; while Adèle was leading me by the hand round the room, showing me the beautiful books and ornaments on

the consoles and chiffonnières. We obeyed, as in duty bound; Adèle wanted to take a seat on my knee, but she was ordered to amuse herself with Pilot.

'You have been resident in my house three months?'

'Yes, sir.'

'And you came from?'

'From Lowood School, in —shire.'

'Ah! a charitable concern. How long were you there?'

'Eight years.'

'Eight years! you must be tenacious of life. I thought half the time in such a place would have done up any constitution! No wonder you have rather the look of another world. I marvelled where you had got that sort of face. When you came on me in Hay Lane last night, I thought unaccountably of fairy tales, and had half a mind to demand whether you had bewitched my horse: I am not sure yet. Who are your parents?'

'I have none.'

'Nor ever had, I suppose: do you remember them?'

'No.'

'I thought not. And so you were waiting for your people when you sat on that stile?'

'For whom, sir?'

'For the men in green: it was a proper moonlight evening for them. Did I break through one of your rings, that you spread that damned ice on the causeway?'

I shook my head. 'The men in green all forsook England a hundred years ago,' said I, speaking as seriously as he had done. 'And not even in Hay Lane, or the fields about it, could you find a trace of them. I don't think either summer or harvest, or winter moon, will ever shine on their revels more.'

Mrs Fairfax had dropped her knitting, and, with raised eyebrows, seemed wondering what sort of talk this was.

'Well,' resumed Mr Rochester, 'if you disown parents, you must have some sort of kinsfolk: uncles and aunts?'

'No; none that I ever saw.'

'And your home?'

'I have none.'

'Where do your brothers and sisters live?'

'I have no brothers or sisters.'

'Who recommended you to come here?'

'I advertised, and Mrs Fairfax answered my advertisement.'

'Yes,' said the good lady, who now knew what ground we were upon, 'and I am daily thankful for the choice Providence led me to make. Miss Eyre has been an invaluable companion to me, and a kind and careful teacher to Adèle.'

'Don't trouble yourself to give her a character,' returned Mr Rochester: 'eulogiums will not bias me; I shall judge for myself. She began by felling my horse.'

'Sir?' said Mrs Fairfax.

'I have to thank her for this sprain.'

The widow looked bewildered.

'Miss Eyre, have you ever lived in a town?'

'No, sir.'

'Have you seen much society?'

'None but the pupils and teachers of Lowood, and now the inmates of Thornfield.'

'Have you read much?'

'Only such books as came in my way; and they have not been numerous or very learned.'

'You have lived the life of a nun: no doubt you are well drilled in religious forms; Brocklehurst, who I understand directs Lowood, is a parson, is he not?'

'Yes, sir.'

'And you girls probably worshipped him, as a convent full of *religieuses* would worship their director.'

'Oh, no.'

'You are very cool! No! What! a novice not worship her priest! That sounds blasphemous.'

'I disliked Mr Brocklehurst; and I was not alone in the feeling. He is a harsh man; at once pompous and meddling; he cut off our hair; and for economy's sake bought us bad needles and thread, with which we could hardly sew.'

'That was very false economy,' remarked Mrs Fairfax, who now again caught the drift of the dialogue.

'And was that the head and front of his offending?' demanded Mr Rochester.

'He starved us when he had the sole superintendence of the provision department, before the committee was appointed; and he bored us with long lectures once a week, and with evening readings from books of his own inditing, about sudden deaths and judgements, which made us afraid to go to bed.'

'What age were you when you went to Lowood?'

'About ten.'

'And you stayed there eight years: you are now, then, eighteen?'

I assented.

'Arithmetic, you see, is useful; without its aid, I should hardly have been able to guess your age. It is a point difficult to fix where the features and countenance are so much at variance as in your case. And now what did you learn at Lowood? Can you play?'

'A little.'

'Of course: that is the established answer. Go into the library – I mean, if you please. (Excuse my tone of command; I am used to say, "Do this," and it is done: I cannot alter my customary habits for one new inmate.) – Go, then, into the library; take a candle with you; leave the door open; sit down to the piano, and play a tune.'

I departed, obeying his directions.

'Enough!' he called out in a few minutes. 'You play *a little*, I see; like any other English schoolgirl; perhaps rather better than some, but not well.'

I closed the piano and returned. Mr Rochester continued – 'Adèle showed me some sketches this morning, which she said were yours. I don't know whether they were entirely of your doing; probably a master aided you?'

'No, indeed!' I interjected.

'Ah! that pricks pride. Well, fetch me your portfolio, if you can vouch for its contents being original; but don't pass your word unless you are certain: I can recognise patchwork.'

'Then I will say nothing, and you shall judge for yourself, sir.'

I brought the portfolio from the library.

'Approach the table,' said he; and I wheeled it to his couch. Adèle and Mrs Fairfax drew near to see the pictures.

'No crowding,' said Mr Rochester: 'take the drawings from my hand as I finish with them; but don't push your faces up to mine.'

He deliberately scrutinised each sketch and painting. Three he laid aside; the others, when he had examined them, he swept from him.

'Take them off to the other table, Mrs Fairfax,' said he, 'and look at them with Adèle; you' (glancing at me) 'resume your seat, and answer my questions. I perceive those pictures were done by one hand: was that hand yours?'

'Yes.'

'And when did you find time to do them? They have taken much time, and some thought.'

'I did them in the last two vacations I spent at Lowood, when I had no other occupation.'

'Where did you get your copies?'

'Out of my head.'

'That head I see now on your shoulders?'

'Yes, sir.'

'Has it other furniture of the same kind within?'

'I should think it may have: I should hope – better.'

He spread the pictures before him, and again surveyed them alternately.

While he is so occupied, I will tell you, reader, what they are: and first, I must premise that they are nothing wonderful. The subjects had, indeed, risen vividly on my mind. As I saw them with the spiritual eye, before I attempted to embody them, they were striking; but my hand would not second my fancy, and in each case it had wrought out but a pale portrait of the thing I had conceived.

These pictures were in water-colours. The first represented clouds low and livid, rolling over a swollen sea: all the distance was in eclipse; so, too, was the foreground; or rather, the nearest billows, for there was no land. One gleam of light lifted into relief a half-submerged mast, on which sat a cormorant, dark and large, with wings flecked with foam; its beak held a gold bracelet set with gems, that I had touched with as brilliant tints as my palette could yield, and as glittering distinctness as my pencil could impart. Sinking below the bird and mast, a drowned corpse glanced through the green water; a fair arm was the only limb clearly visible, whence the bracelet had been washed or torn.

The second picture contained for foreground only the dim peak of a hill, with

grass and some leaves slanting as if by a breeze. Beyond and above spread an expanse of sky, dark blue as at twilight: rising into the sky was a woman's shape to the bust, portrayed in tints as dusk and soft as I could combine. The dim forehead was crowned with a star; the lineaments below were seen as through the suffusion of vapour; the eyes shone dark and wild; the hair streamed shadowy, like a beamless cloud torn by storm or by electric travail. On the neck lay a pale reflection like moonlight; the same faint lustre touched the train of thin clouds from which rose and bowed this vision of the Evening Star.

The third showed the pinnacle of an iceberg piercing a polar winter sky: a muster of northern lights reared their dim lances, close serried, along the horizon. Throwing these into distance, rose, in the foreground, a head, a colossal head, inclined towards the iceberg, and resting against it. Two thin hands, joined under the forehead, and supporting it, drew up before the lower features a sable veil; a brow quite bloodless, white as bone, and an eye hollow and fixed, blank of meaning but for the glassiness of despair, alone were visible. Above the temples, amidst wreathed turban folds of black drapery, vague in its character and consistency as cloud, gleamed a ring of white flame, gemmed with sparkles of a more lurid tinge. This pale crescent was 'the likeness of a kingly crown'; what it diademed was 'the shape which shape had none.'

'Were you happy when you painted these pictures?' asked Mr Rochester presently.

'I was absorbed, sir: yes, and I was happy. To paint them, in short, was to enjoy one of the keenest pleasures I have ever known.'

'That is not saying much. Your pleasures, by your own account, have been few; but I dare say you did exist in a kind of artist's dreamland while you blent and arranged these strange tints. Did you sit at them long each day?'

'I had nothing else to do, because it was the vacation, and I sat at them from morning till noon, and from noon till night: the length of the midsummer days favoured my inclination to apply.'

'And you felt self-satisfied with the result of your ardent labours?'

'Far from it. I was tormented by the contrast between my idea and my handiwork: in each case I had imagined something which I was quite powerless to realise.'

'Not quite: you have secured the shadow of your thought; but no more, probably. You had not enough of the artist's skill and science to give it full being: yet the drawings are, for a schoolgirl, peculiar. As to the thoughts, they are elfish. These eyes in the Evening Star you must have seen in a dream. How could you make them look so clear, and yet not at all brilliant? for the planet above quells their rays. And what meaning is that in their solemn depth? And who taught you to paint wind. There is a high gale in that sky, and on this hilltop. Where did you see Latmos? For that is Latmos. There! put the drawings away!'

I had scarce tied the strings of the portfolio, when, looking at his watch, he said abruptly – 'It is nine o'clock: what are you about, Miss Eyre, to let Adèle sit up so long? Take her to bed.'

Adèle went to kiss him before quitting the room: he endured the caress, but scarcely seemed to relish it more than Pilot would have done, nor so much.

'I wish you all good-night, now,' said he, making a movement of the hand towards the door, in token that he was tired of our company, and wished to dismiss us. Mrs Fairfax folded up her knitting: I took my portfolio: we curtseyed to him, received a frigid bow in return, and so withdrew.

'You said Mr Rochester was not strikingly peculiar, Mrs Fairfax,' I observed, when I rejoined her in her room, after putting Adèle to bed.

'Well, is he?'

'I think so: he is very changeful and abrupt.'

'True: no doubt he may appear so to a stranger, but I am so accustomed to his manner, I never think of it; and then, if he has peculiarities of temper, allowance should be made.'

'Why?'

'Partly because it is his nature – and we can none of us help our nature; and partly because he has painful thoughts, no doubt, to harass him, and make his spirits unequal.'

'What about?'

'Family troubles, for one thing.'

'But he has no family.'

'Not now, but he has had – or, at least, relatives. He lost his elder brother a few years since.'

'His *elder* brother?'

'Yes. The present Mr Rochester has not been very long in possession of the property; only about nine years.'

'Nine years is a tolerable time. Was he so very fond of his brother as to be still inconsolable for his loss?'

'Why, no – perhaps not. I believe there were some misunderstandings between them. Mr Rowland Rochester was not quite just to Mr Edward; and perhaps he prejudiced his father against him. The old gentleman was fond of money, and anxious to keep the family estate together. He did not like to diminish the property by division, and yet he was anxious that Mr Edward should have wealth, too, to keep up the consequence of the name; and, soon after he was of age, some steps were taken that were not quite fair, and made a great deal of mischief. Old Mr Rochester and Mr Rowland combined to bring Mr Edward into what he considered a painful position, for the sake of making his fortune: what the precise nature of that position was I never clearly knew, but his spirit could not brook what he had to suffer in it. He is not very forgiving: he broke with his family, and now for many years he has led an unsettled kind of life. I don't think he has ever been resident at Thornfield for a fortnight together, since the death of his brother without a will left him master of the estate; and, indeed, no wonder he shuns the old place.'

'Why should he shun it?'

'Perhaps he thinks it gloomy.'

The answer was evasive. I should have liked something clearer; but Mrs

Fairfax either could not, or would not, give me more explicit information of the origin and nature of Mr Rochester's trials. She averred they were a mystery to herself, and that what she knew was chiefly from conjecture. It was evident, indeed, that she wished me to drop the subject, which I did accordingly.

## Chapter 14

For several subsequent days I saw little of Mr Rochester. In the mornings he seemed much engaged with business, and, in the afternoon, gentlemen from Millcote or the neighbourhood called, and sometimes stayed to dine with him. When his sprain was well enough to admit of horse exercise, he rode out a good deal; probably to return these visits, as he generally did not come back till late at night.

During this interval, even Adèle was seldom sent for to his presence, and all my acquaintance with him was confined to an occasional *rencontre* in the hall, on the stairs, or in the gallery, when he would sometimes pass me haughtily and coldly, just acknowledging my presence by a distant nod or a cool glance, and sometimes bow and smile with gentlemanlike affability. His changes of mood did not offend me, because I saw that I had nothing to do with their alternation; the ebb and flow depended on causes quite disconnected with me.

One day he had had company to dinner, and had sent for my portfolio; in order, doubtless, to exhibit its contents: the gentlemen went away early, to attend a public meeting at Millcote, as Mrs Fairfax informed me; but the night being wet and inclement, Mr Rochester did not accompany them. Soon after they were gone he rang the bell: a message came that I and Adèle were to go downstairs. I brushed Adèle's hair and made her neat, and having ascertained that I was myself in my usual Quaker trim, where there was nothing to retouch – all being too close and plain, braided locks included, to admit of disarrangement – we descended, Adèle wondering whether the *petit coffre* was at length come; for, owing to some mistake, its arrival had hitherto been delayed. She was gratified: there it stood, a little carton, on the table when we entered the dining-room. She appeared to know it by instinct.

'Ma boîte! ma boîte!' exclaimed she, running towards it.

'Yes, there is your "boîte" at last: take it into a corner, you genuine daughter of Paris, and amuse yourself with disembowelling it,' said the deep and rather sarcastic voice of Mr Rochester, proceeding from the depths of an immense easy-chair at the fireside. 'And mind,' he continued, 'don't bother me with any details of the anatomical process, or any notice of the condition of the entrails: let your operation be conducted in silence: tiens-toi tranquille, enfant; comprends-tu?'

Adèle seemed scarcely to need the warning; she had already retired to a sofa with her treasure, and was busy untying the cord which secured the lid. Having removed this impediment, and lifted certain silvery envelopes of tissue paper,

she merely exclaimed – 'Oh ciel! Que c'est beau!' and then remained absorbed in ecstatic contemplation.

'Is Miss Eyre there?' now demanded the master, half rising from his seat to look round to the door, near which I still stood.

'Ah! well, come forward; be seated here.' He drew a chair near his own. 'I am not fond of the prattle of children,' he continued; 'for, old bachelor as I am, I have no pleasant associations connected with their lisp. It would be intolerable to me to pass a whole evening *tête-à-tête* with a brat. Don't draw that chair farther off, Miss Eyre; sit down exactly where I placed it – if you please, that is. Confound these civilities! I continually forget them. Nor do I particularly affect simple-minded old ladies. By the bye, I must have mine in mind; it won't do to neglect her; she is a Fairfax, or wed to one; and blood is said to be thicker than water.'

He rang, and despatched an invitation to Mrs Fairfax, who soon arrived, knitting-basket in hand.

'Good-evening, madam; I sent to you for a charitable purpose. I have forbidden Adèle to talk to me about her presents, and she is bursting with repletion; have the goodness to serve her as auditress and interlocutrice; it will be one of the most benevolent acts you ever performed.'

Adèle, indeed, no sooner saw Mrs Fairfax, than she summoned her to her sofa, and there quickly filled her lap with the porcelain, the ivory, the waxen contents of her 'boîte'; pouring out, meantime, explanations and raptures in such broken English as she was mistress of.

'Now I have performed the part of a good host,' pursued Mr Rochester, 'put my guests into the way of amusing each other, I ought to be at liberty to attend to my own pleasure. Miss Eyre, draw your chair still a little farther forward: you are yet too far back; I cannot see you without disturbing my position in this comfortable chair, which I have no mind to do.'

I did as I was bid, though I would much rather have remained somewhat in the shade; but Mr Rochester had such a direct way of giving orders, it seemed a matter of course to obey him promptly.

We were, as I have said, in the dining-room: the lustre, which had been lit for dinner, filled the room with a festal breadth of light; the large fire was all red and clear; the purple curtains hung rich and ample before the lofty window and loftier arch; everything was still, save the subdued chat of Adèle (she dared not speak loud), and, filling up each pause, the beating of winter rain against the panes.

Mr Rochester, as he sat in his damask-covered chair, looked different to what I had seen him look before; not quite so stern – much less gloomy. There was a smile on his lips, and his eyes sparkled, whether with wine or not, I am not sure; but I think it very probable. He was, in short, in his after-dinner mood; more expanded and genial, and also more self-indulgent than the frigid and rigid temper of the morning; still he looked preciously grim, cushioning his massive head against the swelling back of his chair, and receiving the light of the fire on his granite-hewn features, and in his great, dark eyes; for he had great, dark eyes, and very fine eyes, too – not without a certain change in their depths sometimes, which, if it was not softness, reminded you, at least, of that feeling.

He had been looking two minutes at the fire, and I had been looking the same length of time at him, when, turning suddenly, he caught my gaze fastened on his physiognomy.

'You examine me, Miss Eyre,' said he: 'do you think me handsome?'

I should, if I had deliberated, have replied to this question by something conventionally vague and polite; but the answer somehow slipped from my tongue before I was aware – 'No, sir.'

'Ah! By my word! there is something singular about you,' said he: 'you have the air of a little *nonnette*; quaint, quiet, grave, and simple, as you sit with your hands before you, and your eyes generally bent on the carpet (except, by the bye, when they are directed piercingly to my face; as just now, for instance); and when one asks you a question, or makes a remark to which you are obliged to reply, you rap out a round rejoinder, which, if not blunt, is at least brusque. What do you mean by it?'

'Sir, I was too plain; I beg your pardon. I ought to have replied that it was not easy to give an impromptu answer to a question about appearances; that tastes mostly differ; and that beauty is of little consequence, or something of that sort.'

'You ought to have replied no such thing. Beauty of little consequence, indeed! And so, under pretence of softening the previous outrage, of stroking and soothing me into placidity, you stick a sly penknife under my ear! Go on: what fault do you find with me, pray? I suppose I have all my limbs and all my features like any other man?'

'Mr Rochester, allow me to disown my first answer: I intended no pointed repartee: it was only a blunder.'

'Just so: I think so: and you shall be answerable for it. Criticise me: does my forehead not please you?'

He lifted up the sable waves of hair which lay horizontally over his brow, and showed a solid enough mass of intellectual organs, but an abrupt deficiency where the suave sign of benevolence should have risen.

'Now, ma'am, am I a fool?'

'Far from it, sir. You would, perhaps, think me rude if I enquired in return whether you are a philanthropist?'

'There again! Another stick of the penknife, when she pretended to pat my head: and that is because I said I did not like the society of children and old women (low be it spoken!). No, young lady, I am not a general philanthropist; but I bear a conscience'; and he pointed to the prominences which are said to indicate that faculty, and which, fortunately for him, were sufficiently conspicuous; giving, indeed, a marked breadth to the upper part of his head: 'and, besides, I once had a kind of rude tenderness of heart. When I was as old as you, I was a feeling fellow enough; partial to the unfledged, unfostered, and unlucky; but Fortune has knocked me about since: she has even kneaded me with her knuckles, and now I flatter myself I am hard and tough as an India-rubber ball; pervious, though, through a chink or two still, and with one sentient point in the middle of the lump. Yes: does that leave hope for me?'

'Hope of what, sir?'

'Of my final re-transformation from India-rubber back to flesh?'

'Decidedly he has had too much wine,' I thought; and I did not know what answer to make to his queer question: how could I tell whether he was capable of being re-transformed?

'You looked very much puzzled, Miss Eyre; and though you are not pretty any more than I am handsome, yet a puzzled air becomes you; besides, it is convenient, for it keeps those searching eyes of yours away from my physiognomy, and busies them with the worsted flowers of the rug; so puzzle on. Young lady, I am disposed to be gregarious and communicative tonight.'

With this announcement he rose from his chair, and stood, leaning his arm on the marble mantelpiece: in that attitude his shape was seen plainly as well as his face; his unusual breadth of chest, disproportionate almost to his length of limb. I am sure most people would have thought him an ugly man; yet there was so much unconscious pride in his port; so much ease in his demeanour; such a look of complete indifference to his own external appearance; so haughty a reliance on the power of other qualities, intrinsic or adventitious, to atone for the lack of mere personal attractiveness, that, in looking at him, one inevitably shared the indifference, and, even in a blind, imperfect sense, put faith in the confidence.

'I am disposed to be gregarious and communicative tonight,' he repeated, 'and that is why I sent for you: the fire and the chandelier were not sufficient company for me; nor would Pilot have been, for none of these can talk. Adèle is a degree better, but still far below the mark; Mrs Fairfax ditto; you, I am persuaded, can suit me if you will: you puzzled me the first evening I invited you down here. I have almost forgotten you since: other ideas have driven yours from my head; but tonight I am resolved to be at ease; to dismiss what importunes, and recall what pleases. It would please me now to draw you out – to learn more of you – therefore speak.'

Instead of speaking, I smiled; and not a very complacent or submissive smile either.

'Speak,' he urged.

'What about, sir?'

'Whatever you like. I leave both the choice of subject and the manner of treating it entirely to yourself.'

Accordingly I sat and said nothing: 'If he expects me to talk for the mere sake of talking and showing off, he will find he has addressed himself to the wrong person,' I thought.

'You are dumb, Miss Eyre.'

I was dumb still. He bent his head a little towards me, and with a single hasty glance seemed to dive into my eyes.

'Stubborn?' he said, 'and annoyed. Ah! it is consistent. I put my request in an absurd, almost insolent form. Miss Eyre, I beg your pardon. The fact is, once for all, I don't wish to treat you like an inferior: that is' (correcting himself), 'I claim only such superiority as must result from twenty years' difference in age and a century's advance in experience. This is legitimate, *et j'y tiens*, as Adèle would say; and it is by virtue of this superiority, and this alone, that I desire you to have

the goodness to talk to me a little now, and divert my thoughts, which are galled with dwelling on one point – cankering as a rusty nail.'

He had deigned an explanation, almost an apology, and I did not feel insensible to his condescension, and would not seem so.

'I am willing to amuse you, if I can, sir – quite willing; but I cannot introduce a topic, because how do I know what will interest you? Ask me questions, and I will do my best to answer them.'

'Then, in the first place, do you agree with me that I have a right to be a little masterful, abrupt, perhaps exacting, sometimes, on the grounds I stated, namely, that I am old enough to be your father, and that I have battled through a varied experience with many men of many nations, and roamed over half the globe, while you have lived quietly with one set of people in one house?'

'Do as you please, sir.'

'That is no answer; or rather it is a very irritating, because a very evasive one. Reply clearly.'

'I don't think, sir, you have a right to command me, merely because you are older than I, or because you have seen more of the world than I have; your claim to superiority depends on the use you have made of your time and experience.'

'Humph! Promptly spoken. But I won't allow that, seeing that it would never suit my case, as I have made an indifferent, not to say a bad, use of both advantages. Leaving superiority out of the question, then, you must still agree to receive my orders now and then, without being piqued or hurt by the tone of command. Will you?'

I smiled: I thought to myself Mr Rochester is peculiar – he seems to forget that he pays me £30 per annum for receiving his orders.

'The smile is very well,' said he, catching instantly the passing expression; 'but speak too.'

'I was thinking, sir, that very few masters would trouble themselves to enquire whether or not their paid subordinates were piqued and hurt by their orders.'

'Paid subordinates! What! you are my paid subordinate, are you? Oh yes, I had forgotten the salary! Well then, on that mercenary ground, will you agree to let me hector a little?'

'No, sir, not on that ground; but, on the ground that you did forget it, and that you care whether or not a dependant is comfortable in his dependency, I agree heartily.'

'And will you consent to dispense with a great many conventional forms and phrases, without thinking that the omission arises from insolence?'

'I am sure, sir, I should never mistake informality for insolence: one I rather like, the other nothing free-born would submit to, even for a salary.'

'Humbug! Most things free-born will submit to anything for a salary; therefore, keep to yourself, and don't venture on generalities of which you are intensely ignorant. However, I mentally shake hands with you for your answer, despite its inaccuracy; and as much for the manner in which it was said, as for the substance of the speech; the manner was frank and sincere; one does not

often see such a manner: no, on the contrary, affectation, or coldness, or stupid, coarse-minded misapprehension of one's meaning are the usual rewards of candour. Not three in three thousand raw school-girl-governesses would have answered me as you have just done. But I don't mean to flatter you: if you are cast in a different mould to the majority, it is no merit of yours: Nature did it. And then, after all, I go too fast in my conclusions: for what I yet know, you may be no better than the rest; you may have intolerable defects to counterbalance your few good points.'

'And so may you,' I thought. My eye met his as the idea crossed my mind: he seemed to read the glance, answering as if its import had been spoken as well as imagined – 'Yes, yes, you are right,' said he; 'I have plenty of faults of my own: I know it, and I don't wish to palliate them, I assure you. God wot I need not be too severe about others; I have a past existence, a series of deeds, a colour of life to contemplate within my own breast, which might well call my sneers and censures from my neighbours to myself. I started, or rather (for like other defaulters, I like to lay half the blame on ill fortune and adverse circumstances) was thrust on to a wrong tack at the age of one-and-twenty, and have never recovered the right course since: but I might have been very different; I might have been as good as you – wiser – almost as stainless. I envy you your peace of mind, your clean conscience, your unpolluted memory. Little girl, a memory without blot or contamination must be an exquisite treasure – an inexhaustible source of pure refreshment: is it not?'

'How was your memory when you were eighteen, sir?'

'All right then; limpid, salubrious: no gush of bilge water had turned it to fetid puddle. I was your equal at eighteen – quite your equal. Nature meant me to be, on the whole, a good man, Miss Eyre; one of the better kind, and you see I am not so. You would say you don't see it; at least I flatter myself I read as much in your eye (beware, by the bye, what you express with that organ; I am quick at interpreting its language). Then take my word for it, I am not a villain: you are not to suppose that – not to attribute to me any such bad eminence; but, owing, I verily believe, rather to circumstances than to my natural bent, I am a trite commonplace sinner, hackneyed in all the poor petty dissipations with which the rich and worthless try to put on life. Do you wonder that I avow this to you? Know, that in the course of your future life you will often find yourself elected the involuntary confidant of your acquaintances' secrets: people will instinctively find out, as I have done, that it is not your forte to tell of yourself, but to listen while others talk of themselves; they will feel, too, that you listen with no malevolent scorn of their indiscretion, but with a kind of innate sympathy; not the less comforting and encouraging because it is very unobtrusive in its manifestations.'

'How do you know? – how can you guess all this, sir?'

'I know it well; therefore I proceed almost as freely as if I were writing my thoughts in a diary. You would say, I should have been superior to circumstances; so I should – so I should; but you see I was not. When fate wronged me, I had not the wisdom to remain cool: I turned desperate; then I degenerated. Now, when

any vicious simpleton excites my disgust by his paltry ribaldry, I cannot flatter myself that I am better than he: I am forced to confess that he and I are on a level. I wish I had stood firm – God knows I do! Dread remorse when you are tempted to err, Miss Eyre; remorse is the poison of life.'

'Repentance is said to be its cure, sir.'

'It is not its cure. Reformation may be its cure; and I could reform – I have strength yet for that – if – but where is the use of thinking of it, hampered, burdened, cursed as I am? Besides, since happiness is irrevocably denied me, I have a right to get pleasure out of life: and I *will* get it, cost what it may.'

'Then you will degenerate still more, sir.'

'Possibly: yet why should I, if I can get sweet, fresh pleasure? And I may get it as sweet and fresh as the wild honey the bee gathers on the moor.'

'It will sting – it will taste bitter, sir.'

'How do you know? – you never tried it. How very serious – how very solemn you look: and you are as ignorant of the matter as this cameo head' (taking one from the mantelpiece). 'You have no right to preach to me, you neophyte, that have not passed the porch of life, and are absolutely unacquainted with its mysteries.'

'I only remind you of your own words, sir: you said error brought remorse, and you pronounced remorse the poison of existence.'

'And who talks of error now? I scarcely think the notion that flittered across my brain was an error. I believe it was an inspiration rather than a temptation: it was very genial, very soothing – I know that. Here it comes again! It is no devil, I assure you; or if it be, it has put on the robes of an angel of light. I think I must admit so fair a guest when it asks entrance to my heart.'

'Distrust it, sir; it is not a true angel.'

'Once more, how do you know? By what instinct do you pretend to distinguish between a fallen seraph of the abyss and a messenger from the eternal throne – between a guide and a seducer?'

'I judged by your countenance, sir, which was troubled when you said the suggestion had returned upon you. I feel sure it will work you more misery if you listen to it.'

'Not at all – it bears the most gracious message in the world: for the rest, you are not my conscience-keeper, so don't make yourself uneasy. Here, come in, bonny wanderer!'

He said this as if he spoke to a vision, viewless to any eye but his own; then, folding his arms, which he had half extended, on his chest, he seemed to enclose in their embrace the invisible being.

'Now,' he continued, again addressing me, 'I have received the pilgrim – a disguised deity, as I verily believe. Already it has done me good: my heart was a sort of charnel; it will now be a shrine.'

'To speak truth, sir, I don't understand you at all: I cannot keep up the conversation, because it has got out of my depth. Only one thing, I know: you said you were not as good as you should like to be, and that you regretted your own imperfection; one thing I can comprehend: you intimated that to have a sullied

memory was a perpetual bane. It seems to me, that if you tried hard, you would in time find it possible to become what you yourself would approve; and that if from this day you began with resolution to correct your thoughts and actions, you would in a few years have laid up a new and stainless store of recollections, to which you might revert with pleasure.'

'Justly thought; rightly said, Miss Eyre; and, at this moment, I am paving hell with energy.'

'Sir?'

'I am laying down good intentions, which I believe durable as flint. Certainly, my associates and pursuits shall be other than they have been.'

'And better?'

'And better – so much better as pure ore is than foul dross. You seem to doubt me; I don't doubt myself: I know what my aim is, what my motives are; and at this moment I pass a law, unalterable as that of the Medes and Persians, that both are right.'

'They cannot be, sir, if they require a new statute to legalise them.'

'They are, Miss Eyre, though they absolutely require a new statute: unheard-of combinations or circumstances demand unheard-of rules.'

'That sounds a dangerous maxim, sir; because one can see at once that it is liable to abuse.'

'Sententious sage! so it is: but I swear by my household gods not to abuse it.'

'You are human and fallible.'

'I am: so are you – what then?'

'The human and fallible should not arrogate a power with which the divine and perfect alone can be safely entrusted.'

'What power?'

'That of saying of any strange, unsanctioned line of action, "Let it be right." '

' "Let it be right" – the very words: you have pronounced them.'

'*May* it be right then,' I said, as I rose, deeming it useless to continue a discourse which was all darkness to me; and, besides, sensible that the character of my interlocutor was beyond my penetration; at least, beyond its present reach; and feeling the uncertainty, the vague sense of insecurity, which accompanies a conviction of ignorance.

'Where are you going?'

'To put Adèle to bed: it is past her bedtime.'

'You are afraid of me, because I talk like a Sphynx.'

'Your language is enigmatical, sir: but though I am bewildered, I am certainly not afraid.'

'You *are* afraid – your self-love dreads a blunder.'

'In that sense I do feel apprehensive – I have no wish to talk nonsense.'

'If you did, it would be in such a grave, quiet manner, I should mistake it for sense. Do you never laugh, Miss Eyre? Don't trouble yourself to answer – I see you laugh rarely; but you can laugh very merrily: believe me, you are not naturally austere, any more than I am naturally vicious. The Lowood constraint still clings to you somewhat; controlling your features, muffling your voice, and

restricting your limbs; and you fear in the presence of a man and a brother – or father, or master, or what you will – to smile too gaily, speak too freely, or move too quickly: but, in time, I think you will learn to be natural with me, as I find it impossible to be conventional with you; and then your looks and movements will have more vivacity and variety than they dare offer now. I see at intervals the glance of a curious sort of bird through the close-set bars of a cage: a vivid, restless, resolute captive is there; were it but free, it would soar cloud-high. You are still bent on going?'

'It has struck nine, sir.'

'Never mind, wait a minute: Adèle is not ready to go to bed yet. My position, Miss Eyre, with my back to the fire, and my face to the room, favours observation. While talking to you, I have also occasionally watched Adèle (I have my own reasons for thinking her a curious study, reasons that I may, nay, that I shall, impart to you someday). She pulled out of her box, about ten minutes ago, a little pink silk frock; rapture lit her face as she unfolded it; coquetry runs in her blood, blends with her brains, and seasons the marrow of her bones. "Il faut que je l'essaie!" cried she, "et à l'instant même!" and she rushed out of the room. She is now with Sophie, undergoing a robing process: in a few minutes she will re-enter; and I know what I shall see, a miniature of Céline Varens, as she used to appear on the boards at the rising of – . But never mind that. However, my tenderest feelings are about to receive a shock: such is my presentiment; stay now, to see whether it will be realised.'

Ere long, Adèle's little foot was heard tripping across the hall. She entered, transformed as her guardian had predicted. A dress of rose-coloured satin, very short, and as full in the skirt as it could be gathered, replaced the brown frock she had previously worn; a wreath of rosebuds circled her forehead; her feet were dressed in silk stockings and small white satin sandals.

'Est-ce que ma robe va bien?' cried she, bounding forwards; 'et mes souliers? et mes bas? Tenez, je crois que je vais danser!'

And spreading out her dress, she chasséed across the room; till, having reached Mr Rochester, she wheeled lightly round before him on tiptoe, then dropped on one knee at his feet, exclaiming – 'Monsieur, je vous remercie mille fois de votre bonté'; then rising, she added, 'C'est comme cela que maman faisait, n'est-ce pas, monsieur?'

'Pre-cise-ly!' was the answer; 'and, "comme cela," she charmed my English gold out of my British breeches' pocket. I have been green, too, Miss Eyre, ay, grass green: not a more vernal tint freshens you now than once freshened me. My Spring is gone, however, but it has left me that French floweret on my hands, which, in some moods, I would fain be rid of. Not valuing now the root whence it sprang; having found that it was of a sort which nothing but gold dust could manure, I have but half a liking to the blossom, especially when it looks so artificial as just now. I keep it and rear it rather on the Roman Catholic principle of expiating numerous sins, great or small, by one good work. I'll explain all this someday. Good-night.'

Mr Rochester did, on a future occasion, explain it. It was one afternoon, when he chanced to meet me and Adèle in the grounds: and while she played with Pilot and her shuttlecock, he asked me to walk up and down a long beech avenue within sight of her.

He then said that she was the daughter of a French opera-dancer, Céline Varens, towards whom he had once cherished what he called a '*grande passion*'. This passion Céline had professed to return with even superior ardour. He thought himself her idol, ugly as he was: he believed, as he said, that she preferred his '*taille d'athlète*' to the elegance of the Apollo Belvidere.

'And, Miss Eyre, so much was I flattered by this preference of the Gallic sylph for her British gnome, that I installed her in an hotel; gave her a complete establishment of servants, a carriage, cashmeres, diamonds, dentelles, etc. In short, I began the process of ruining myself in the received style, like any other spoony. I had not, it seems, the originality to chalk out a new road to shame and destruction, but trod  the old track with stupid exactness not to deviate an inch from the beaten centre. I had – as I deserved to have – the fate of all other spoonies. Happening to call one evening when Céline did not expect me, I found her out; but it was a warm night, and I was tired with strolling through Paris, so I sat down in her boudoir; happy to breathe the air consecrated so lately by her presence. No, I exaggerate; I never thought there was any consecrating virtue about her: it was rather a sort of pastille perfume she had left; a scent of musk and amber, than an odour of sanctity. I was just beginning to stifle with the fumes of conservatory flowers and sprinkled essences, when I bethought myself to open the window and step out on to the balcony. It was moonlight and gaslight besides, and very still and serene. The balcony was furnished with a chair or two; I sat down, and took out a cigar, I will take one now, if you will excuse me.'

Here ensued a pause, filled up by the producing and lighting of a cigar; having placed it to his lips and breathed a trail of Havannah incense on the freezing and sunless air, he went on – 'I liked bonbons too in those days, Miss Eyre, and I was *croquant* – (overlook the barbarism) – *croquant* chocolate comfits, and smoking alternately, watching meantime the equipages that rolled along the fashionable streets towards the neighbouring opera-house, when in an elegant close carriage drawn by a beautiful pair of English horses, and distinctly seen in the brilliant city-night, I recognised the "voiture" I had given Céline. She was returning: of course my heart thumped with impatience against the iron rails I leant upon. The carriage stopped, as I had expected, at the hotel door; my flame (that is the very word for an opera inamorata) alighted: though muffled in a cloak – an unnecessary encumbrance, by the bye, on so warm a June evening – I knew her instantly by her little foot, seen peeping from the skirt of her dress, as

she skipped from the carriage step. Bending over the balcony, I was about to murmur "Mon ange" – in a tone, of course, which should be audible to the ear of love alone – when a figure jumped from the carriage after her; cloaked also; but that was a spurred heel which had rung on the pavement, and that was a hatted head which now passed under the arched *porte cochère* of the hotel.

'You never felt jealousy, did you, Miss Eyre? Of course not: I need not ask you; because you never felt love. You have both sentiments yet to experience: your soul sleeps; the shock is yet to be given which shall waken it. You think all existence lapses in as quiet a flow as that in which your youth has hitherto slid away. Floating on with closed eyes and muffled ears, you neither see the rocks bristling not far off in the bed of the flood, nor hear the breakers boil at their base. But I tell you – and you may mark my words – you will come someday to a craggy pass in the channel, where the whole of life's stream will be broken up into whirl and tumult, foam and noise: either you will be dashed to atoms on crag points, or lifted up and borne on by some master-wave into a calmer current – as I am now.

'I like this day; I like that sky of steel; I like the sternness and stillness of the world under this frost. I like Thornfield, its antiquity, its retirement, its old crow trees and thorn trees, its grey facade, and lines of dark windows reflecting that metal welkin: and yet how long have I abhorred the very thought of it, shunned it like a great plague-house? How I do still abhor –'

He ground his teeth and was silent: he arrested his step and struck his boot against the hard ground. Some hated thought seemed to have him in its grip, and to hold him so tightly that he could not advance.

We were ascending the avenue when he thus paused; the hall was before us. Lifting his eye to its battlements, he cast over them a glare such as I never saw before or since. Pain, shame, ire, impatience, disgust, detestation, seemed momentarily to hold a quivering conflict in the large pupil dilating under his ebon eyebrow. Wild was the wrestle which should be paramount; but another feeling rose and triumphed: something hard and cynical: self-willed and resolute: it settled his passion and petrified his countenance: he went on – 'During the moment I was silent, Miss Eyre, I was arranging a point with my destiny. She stood there, by that beech-trunk – a hag like one of those who appeared to Macbeth on the heath of Forres. "You like Thornfield?" she said, lifting her finger; and then she wrote in the air a memento, which ran in lurid hieroglyphics all along the house-front, between the upper and lower row of windows, "Like it if you can! Like it if you dare!"

' "I will like it," said I; "I dare like it;" and' (he subjoined moodily) 'I will keep my word; I will break obstacles to happiness, to goodness – yes, goodness. I wish to be a better man than I have been, than I am; as Job's leviathan broke the spear, the dart, and the habergeon, hindrances which others count as iron and brass, I will esteem but straw and rotten wood.'

Adèle here ran before him with her shuttlecock. 'Away!' he cried harshly; 'keep at a distance, child; or go in to Sophie!' Continuing then to pursue his walk in silence, I ventured to recall him to the point whence he had abruptly

diverged – 'Did you leave the balcony, sir,' I asked, 'when Mlle Varens entered?'

I almost expected a rebuff for this hardly well-timed question, but, on the contrary, waking out of his scowling abstraction, he turned his eyes towards me, and the shade seemed to clear off his brow. 'Oh, I had forgotten Céline! Well, to resume. When I saw my charmer thus come in accompanied by a cavalier, I seemed to hear a hiss, and the green snake of jealousy, rising on undulating coils from the moonlit balcony, glided within my waistcoat, and ate its way in two minutes to my heart's core. Strange!' he exclaimed, suddenly starting again from the point. 'Strange that I should choose you for the confidant of all this, young lady; passing strange that you should listen to me quietly, as if it were the most usual thing in the world for a man like me to tell stories of his opera-mistresses to a quaint, inexperienced girl like you! But the last singularity explains the first, as I intimated once before: you, with your gravity, considerateness, and caution were made to be the recipient of secrets. Besides, I know what sort of a mind I have placed in communication with my own: I know it is one not liable to take infection: it is a peculiar mind: it is a unique one. Happily I do not mean to harm it: but, if I did, it would not take harm from me. The more you and I converse, the better; for while I cannot blight you, you may refresh me.' After this digression he proceeded – 'I remained in the balcony. "They will come to her boudoir, no doubt," thought I: "let me prepare an ambush." So putting my hand in through the open window, I drew the curtain over it, leaving only an opening through which I could take observations; then I closed the casement, all but a chink just wide enough to furnish an outlet to lovers' whispered vows: then I stole back to my chair; and as I resumed it the pair came in. My eye was quickly at the aperture. Céline's chambermaid entered, lit a lamp, left it on the table, and withdrew. The couple were thus revealed to me clearly: both removed their cloaks, and there was "the Varens", shining in satin and jewels, my gifts of course, and there was her companion in an officer's uniform; and I knew him for a young roué of a vicomte – a brainless and vicious youth whom I had sometimes met in society, and had never thought of hating because I despised him so absolutely. On recognising him, the fang of the snake Jealousy was instantly broken; because at the same moment my love for Céline sank under an extinguisher. A woman who could betray me for such a rival was not worth contending for; she deserved only scorn; less, however, than I, who had been her dupe.

'They began to talk; their conversation eased me completely: frivolous, mercenary, heartless, and senseless, it was rather calculated to weary than enrage a listener. A card of mine lay on the table; this being perceived, brought my name under discussion. Neither of them possessed energy or wit to belabour me soundly, but they insulted me as coarsely as they could in their little way: especially Céline, who even waxed rather brilliant on my personal defects – deformities she termed them. Now it had been her custom to launch out into fervent admiration of what she called my "*beauté mâle*": wherein she differed diametrically from you, who told me point-blank, at the second interview, that you did not think me handsome. The contrast struck me at the time and –'

Adèle here came running up again.

'Monsieur, John has just been to say that your agent has called and wishes to see you.'

'Ah! in that case I must abridge. Opening the window, I walked in upon them; liberated Céline from my protection; gave her notice to vacate her hotel; offered her a purse for immediate exigencies; disregarded screams, hysterics, prayers, protestations, convulsions; made an appointment with the vicomte for a meeting at the Bois de Boulogne. Next morning I had the pleasure of encountering him; left a bullet in one of his poor etiolated arms, feeble as the wing of a chicken in the pip, and then thought I had done with the whole crew. But unluckily the Varens, six months before, had given me this filette Adèle, who, she affirmed, was my daughter; and perhaps she may be, though I see no proofs of such grim paternity written in her countenance: Pilot is more like me than she. Some years after I had broken with the mother, she abandoned her child, and ran away to Italy with a musician or singer. I acknowledged no natural claim on Adèle's part to be supported by me, nor do I now acknowledge any, for I am not her father; but hearing that she was quite destitute, I e'en took the poor thing out of the slime and mud of Paris, and transplanted it here, to grow up clean in the wholesome soil of an English country garden. Mrs Fairfax found you to train it; but now you know that it is the illegitimate offspring of a French opera-girl, you will perhaps think differently of your post and protégée: you will be coming to me someday with notice that you have found another place – that you beg me to look out for a new governess, etc. – Eh?'

'No: Adèle is not answerable for either her mother's faults or yours: I have a regard for her; and now that I know she is, in a sense, parentless – forsaken by her mother and disowned by you, sir – I shall cling closer to her than before. How could I possibly prefer the spoilt pet of a wealthy family, who would hate her governess as a nuisance, to a lonely little orphan, who leans towards her as a friend?'

'Oh, that is the light in which you view it! Well, I must go in now; and you too: it darkens.'

But I stayed out a few minutes longer with Adèle and Pilot – ran a race with her, and played a game of battledore and shuttlecock. When we went in, and I had removed her bonnet and coat, I took her on my knee; kept her there an hour, allowing her to prattle as she liked: not rebuking even some little freedoms and trivialities into which she was apt to stray when much noticed, and which betrayed in her a superficiality of character, inherited probably from her mother, hardly congenial to an English mind. Still she had her merits; and I was disposed to appreciate all that was good in her to the utmost. I sought in her countenance and features a likeness to Mr Rochester, but found none: no trait, no turn of expression announced relationship. It was a pity: if she could but have been proved to resemble him, he would have thought more of her.

It was not till after I had withdrawn to my own chamber for the night, that I steadily reviewed the tale Mr Rochester had told me. As he had said, there was probably nothing at all extraordinary in the substance of the narrative itself: a

wealthy Englishman's passion for a French dancer, and her treachery to him, were everyday matters enough, no doubt, in society; but there was something decidedly strange in the paroxysm of emotion which had suddenly seized him when he was in the act of expressing the present contentment of his mood, and his newly revived pleasure in the old hall and its environs. I meditated wonderingly on this incident; but gradually quitting it, as I found it for the present inexplicable, I turned to the consideration of my master's manner to myself. The confidence he had thought fit to repose in me seemed a tribute to my discretion: I regarded and accepted it as such. His deportment had now for some weeks been more uniform towards me than at the first. I never seemed in his way; he did not take fits of chilling hauteur: when he met me unexpectedly, the encounter seemed welcome; he had always a word and sometimes a smile for me: when summoned by formal invitation to his presence, I was honoured by a cordiality of reception that made me feel I really possessed the power to amuse him, and that these evening conferences were sought as much for his pleasure as for my benefit.

I, indeed, talked comparatively little, but I heard him talk with relish. It was his nature to be communicative; he liked to open to a mind unacquainted with the world glimpses of its scenes and ways (I do not mean its corrupt scenes and wicked ways, but such as derived their interest from the great scale on which they were acted, the strange novelty by which they were characterised); and I had a keen delight in receiving the new ideas he offered, in imagining the new pictures he portrayed, and following him in thought through the new regions he disclosed, never startled or troubled by one noxious allusion.

The ease of his manner freed me from painful restraint: the friendly frankness, as correct as cordial, with which he treated me, drew me to him. I felt at times as if he were my relation rather than my master: yet he was imperious sometimes still; but I did not mind that; I saw it was his way. So happy, so gratified did I become with this new interest added to life, that I ceased to pine after kindred: my thin crescent-destiny seemed to enlarge; the blanks of existence were filled up; my bodily health improved; I gathered flesh and strength.

And was Mr Rochester now ugly in my eyes? No, reader: gratitude, and many associations, all pleasurable and genial, made his face the object I best liked to see; his presence in a room was more cheering than the brightest fire. Yet I had not forgotten his faults; indeed, I could not, for he brought them frequently before me. He was proud, sardonic, harsh to inferiority of every description: in my secret soul I knew that his great kindness to me was balanced by unjust severity to many others. He was moody, too; unaccountably so; I more than once, when sent for to read to him, found him sitting in his library alone, with his head bent on his folded arms; and, when he looked up, a morose, almost a malignant, scowl blackened his features. But I believed that his moodiness, his harshness, and his former faults of morality (I say *former*, for now he seemed corrected of them) had their source in some cruel cross of fate. I believed he was naturally a man of better tendencies, higher principles, and purer tastes than such as circumstances had developed, education instilled, or destiny encouraged. I thought there were excellent materials in him; though for the present they hung

together somewhat spoiled and tangled. I cannot deny that I grieved for his grief, whatever that was, and would have given much to assuage it.

Though I had now extinguished my candle and was laid down in bed, I could not sleep for thinking of his look when he paused in the avenue, and told how his destiny had risen up before him, and dared him to be happy at Thornfield.

'Why not?' I asked myself. 'What alienates him from the house? Will he leave it again soon? Mrs Fairfax said he seldom stayed here longer than a fortnight at a time; and he has now been resident eight weeks. If he does go, the change will be doleful. Suppose he should be absent spring, summer, and autumn: how joyless sunshine and fine days will seem!'

I hardly know whether I had slept or not after this musing; at any rate, I started wide awake on hearing a vague murmur, peculiar and lugubrious, which sounded, I thought, just above me. I wished I had kept my candle burning: the night was drearily dark; my spirits were depressed. I rose and sat up in bed, listening. The sound was hushed.

I tried again to sleep; but my heart beat anxiously: my inward tranquillity was broken. The clock, far down in the hall, struck two. Just then it seemed my chamber-door was touched; as if fingers had swept the panels in groping a way along the dark gallery outside. I said, 'Who is there?' Nothing answered. I was chilled with fear.

All at once I remembered that it might be Pilot, who, when the kitchen-door chanced to be left open, not unfrequently found his way up to the threshold of Mr Rochester's chamber: I had seen him lying there myself in the mornings. The idea calmed me somewhat: I lay down. Silence composes the nerves; and as an unbroken hush now reigned again through the whole house, I began to feel the return of slumber. But it was not fated that I should sleep that night. A dream had scarcely approached my ear, when it fled affrighted, scared by a marrow-freezing incident enough.

This was a demoniac laugh – low, suppressed, and deep – uttered, as it seemed, at the very keyhole of my chamber door. The head of my bed was near the door, and I thought at first the goblin-laugher stood at my bedside – or rather, crouched by my pillow: but I rose, looked round, and could see nothing; while, as I still gazed, the unnatural sound was reiterated: and I knew it came from behind the panels. My first impulse was to rise and fasten the bolt; my next, again to cry out, 'Who is there?'

Something gurgled and moaned. Ere long, steps retreated up the gallery towards the third-storey staircase: a door had lately been made to shut in that staircase; I heard it open and close, and all was still.

'Was that Grace Poole? and is she possessed with a devil?' thought I. Impossible now to remain longer by myself: I must go to Mrs Fairfax. I hurried on my frock and a shawl; I withdrew the bolt and opened the door with a trembling hand. There was a candle burning just outside, and on the matting in the gallery. I was surprised at this circumstance: but still more was I amazed to perceive the air quite dim, as if filled with smoke; and, while looking to the right hand and left, to find whence these blue wreaths issued, I became further aware of a strong smell of burning.

Something creaked: it was a door ajar; and that door was Mr Rochester's, and the smoke rushed in a cloud from thence. I thought no more of Mrs Fairfax; I thought no more of Grace Poole, or the laugh: in an instant, I was within the chamber. Tongues of flame darted round the bed: the curtains were on fire. In the midst of blaze and vapour, Mr Rochester lay stretched motionless, in deep sleep.

'Wake! wake!' I cried. I shook him, but he only murmured and turned: the smoke had stupefied him. Not a moment could be lost: the very sheets were kindling, I rushed to his basin and ewer; fortunately, one was wide and the other deep, and both were filled with water. I heaved them up, deluged the bed and its occupant, flew back to my own room, brought my own water-jug, baptised the couch afresh, and, by God's aid, succeeded in extinguishing the flames which were devouring it.

The hiss of the quenched element, the breakage of a pitcher which I flung from my hand when I had emptied it, and, above all, the splash of the shower-bath I had liberally bestowed, roused Mr Rochester at last. Though it was now dark, I knew he was awake; because I heard him fulminating strange anathemas at finding himself lying in a pool of water.

'Is there a flood?' he cried.

'No, sir,' I answered; 'but there has been a fire: get up, do; you are quenched now; I will fetch you a candle.'

'In the name of all the elves in Christendom, is that Jane Eyre?' he demanded. 'What have you done with me, witch, sorceress? Who is in the room besides you? Have you plotted to drown me?'

'I will fetch you a candle, sir; and, in Heaven's name, get up. Somebody has plotted something: you cannot too soon find out who and what it is.'

'There! I am up now; but at your peril you fetch a candle yet: wait two minutes till I get into some dry garments, if any dry there be – yes, here is my dressing-gown. Now run!'

I did run; I brought the candle which still remained in the gallery. He took it from my hand, held it up, and surveyed the bed, all blackened and scorched, the sheets drenched, the carpet round swimming in water.

'What is it? and who did it?' he asked.

I briefly related to him what had transpired: the strange laugh I had heard in the gallery; the step ascending to the third storey; the smoke, the smell of fire which had conducted me to his room; in what state I had found matters there, and how I had deluged him with all the water I could lay hands on.

He listened very gravely; his face, as I went on, expressed more concern than astonishment; he did not immediately speak when I had concluded.

'Shall I call Mrs Fairfax?' I asked.

'Mrs Fairfax? No; what the deuce would you call her for? What can she do? Let her sleep unmolested.'

'Then I will fetch Leah, and wake John and his wife.'

'Not at all: just be still. You have a shawl on. If you are not warm enough, you may take my cloak yonder; wrap it about you, and sit down in the armchair:

there, I will put it on. Now place your feet on the stool, to keep them out of the wet. I am going to leave you a few minutes. I shall take the candle. Remain where you are till I return; be as still as a mouse. I must pay a visit to the second storey. Don't move, remember, or call anyone.'

He went: I watched the light withdraw. He passed up the gallery very softly, unclosed the staircase door with as little noise as possible, shut it after him, and the last ray vanished. I was left in total darkness. I listened for some noise, but heard nothing. A very long time elapsed. I grew weary: it was cold, in spite of the cloak; and then I did not see the use of staying, as I was not to rouse the house. I was on the point of risking Mr Rochester's displeasure by disobeying his orders, when the light once more gleamed dimly on the gallery wall, and I heard his unshod feet tread the matting. 'I hope it is he,' thought I, 'and not something worse.'

He re-entered, pale and very gloomy. 'I have found it all out,' said he, setting his candle down on the washstand; 'it is as I thought.'

'How, sir?'

He made no reply, but stood with his arms folded, looking on the ground. At the end of a few minutes he enquired in rather a peculiar tone – 'I forget whether you said you saw anything when you opened your chamber door.'

'No, sir, only the candlestick on the ground.'

'But you heard an odd laugh? You have heard that laugh before, I should think, or something like it?'

'Yes, sir: there is a woman who sews here, called Grace Poole, she laughs in that way. She is a singular person.'

'Just so. Grace Poole – you have guessed it. She is, as you say, singular – very. Well, I shall reflect on the subject. Meantime, I am glad that you are the only person, besides myself, acquainted with the precise details of tonight's incident. You are no talking fool: say nothing about it. I will account for this state of affairs' (pointing to the bed): 'and now return to your own room. I shall do very well on the sofa in the library for the rest of the night. It is near four: in two hours the servants will be up.'

'Good-night, then, sir,' said I, departing.

He seemed surprised – very inconsistently so, as he had just told me to go.

'What!' he exclaimed, 'are you quitting me already, and in that way?'

'You said I might go, sir.'

'But not without taking leave; not without a word or two of acknowledgement and goodwill: not, in short, in that brief, dry fashion. Why, you have saved my life! – snatched me from a horrible and excruciating death! and you walk past me as if we were mutual strangers! At least shake hands.'

He held out his hand; I gave him mine: he took it first in one, then in both his own.

'You have saved my life: I have a pleasure in owing you so immense a debt. I cannot say more. Nothing else that has being would have been tolerable to me in the character of creditor for such an obligation: but you: it is different; I feel your benefits no burden, Jane.'

He paused; gazed at me: words almost visible trembled on his lips, but his voice was checked.

'Good-night again, sir. There is no debt, benefit, burden, obligation, in the case.'

'I knew,' he continued, 'you would do me good in some way, at some time; I saw it in your eyes when I first beheld you: their expression and smile did not' – (again he stopped) – 'did not' (he proceeded hastily) 'strike delight to my very inmost heart so for nothing. People talk of natural sympathies; I have heard of good genii: there are grains of truth in the wildest fable. My cherished preserver, good-night!'

Strange energy was in his voice, strange fire in his look.

'I am glad I happened to be awake,' I said: and then I was going.

'What! you *will* go?'

'I am cold, sir.'

'Cold? Yes, and standing in a pool! Go, then, Jane; go!' But he still retained my hand, and I could not free it. I bethought myself of an expedient.

'I think I hear Mrs Fairfax move, sir,' said I.

'Well, leave me': he relaxed his fingers, and I was gone.

I regained my couch, but never thought of sleep. Till morning dawned I was tossed on a buoyant but unquiet sea, where billows of trouble rolled under surges of joy. I thought sometimes I saw beyond its wild waters a shore, sweet as the hills of Beulah; and now and then a freshening gale, wakened by hope, bore my spirit triumphantly towards the bourne: but I could not reach it, even in fancy – a counteracting breeze blew off land, and continually drove me back. Sense would resist delirium: judgement would warn passion. Too feverish to rest, I rose as soon as day dawned.

## Chapter 16

I both wished and feared to see Mr Rochester on the day which followed this sleepless night: I wanted to hear his voice again, yet feared to meet his eye. During the early part of the morning, I momentarily expected his coming; he was not in the frequent habit of entering the schoolroom, but he did step in for a few minutes sometimes, and I had the impression that he was sure to visit it that day.

But the morning passed just as usual: nothing happened to interrupt the quiet course of Adèle's studies; only soon after breakfast, I heard some bustle in the neighbourhood of Mr Rochester's chamber, Mrs Fairfax's voice, and Leah's, and the cook's – that is, John's wife – and even John's own gruff tones. There were exclamations of 'What a mercy master was not burnt in his bed!' 'It is always dangerous to keep a candle lit at night.' 'How providential that he had presence of mind to think of the water-jug!' 'I wonder he waked nobody!' 'It is to be hoped he will not take cold with sleeping on the library sofa,' etc.

To much confabulation succeeded a sound of scrubbing and setting to rights; and when I passed the room, in going downstairs to dinner, I saw through the open door that all was again restored to complete order; only the bed was stripped of its hangings. Leah stood up in the window-seat, rubbing the panes of glass dimmed with smoke. I was about to address her, for I wished to know what account had been given of the affair: but, on advancing, I saw a second person in the chamber – a woman sitting on a chair by the bedside, and sewing rings to new curtains. That woman was no other than Grace Poole.

There she sat, staid and taciturn-looking, as usual, in her brown stuff gown, her check apron, white handkerchief, and cap. She was intent on her work, in which her whole thoughts seemed absorbed: on her hard forehead, and in her commonplace features, was nothing either of the paleness or desperation one would have expected to see marking the countenance of a woman who had attempted murder, and whose intended victim had followed her last night to her lair, and (as I believed), charged her with the crime she wished to perpetrate. I was amazed – confounded. She looked up, while I still gazed at her: no start, no increase or failure of colour betrayed emotion, consciousness of guilt, or fear of detection. She said 'Good-morning, Miss,' in her usual phlegmatic and brief manner; and taking up another ring and more tape, went on with her sewing.

'I will put her to some test,' thought I: 'such absolute impenetrability is past comprehension.'

'Good-morning, Grace,' I said. 'Has anything happened here? I thought I heard the servants all talking together a while ago.'

'Only master had been reading in his bed last night; he fell asleep with his candle lit, and the curtains got on fire; but, fortunately, he awoke before the bedclothes or the woodwork caught, and contrived to quench the flames with the water in the ewer.'

'A strange affair!' I said, in a low voice: then looking at her fixedly – 'Did Mr Rochester wake nobody? Did no one hear him move?'

She again raised her eyes to me, and this time there was something of consciousness in their expression. She seemed to examine me warily; then she answered – 'The servants sleep so far off, you know, Miss, they would not be likely to hear. Mrs Fairfax's room and yours are the nearest to master's; but Mrs Fairfax said she heard nothing: when people get elderly, they often sleep heavy.' She paused, and then added, with a sort of assumed indifference, but still in a marked and significant tone – 'But you are young, Miss, and I should say a light sleeper: perhaps you may have heard a noise?'

'I did,' said I, dropping my voice, so that Leah, who was still polishing the panes, could not hear me, 'and at first I thought it was Pilot: but Pilot cannot laugh; and I am certain I heard a laugh, and a strange one.'

She took a new needleful of thread, waxed it carefully, threaded her needle with a steady hand, and then observed, with perfect composure – 'It is hardly likely master would laugh, I should think, Miss, when he was in such danger: you must have been dreaming.'

'I was not dreaming,' I said, with some warmth, for her brazen coolness

provoked me. Again she looked at me; and with the same scrutinising and conscious eye.

'Have you told master that you heard a laugh?' she enquired.

'I have not had the opportunity of speaking to him this morning.'

'You did not think of opening your door and looking out into the gallery?' she further asked.

She appeared to be cross-questioning me, attempting to draw from me information unawares. The idea struck me that if she discovered I knew or suspected her guilt, she would be playing off some of her malignant pranks on me; I thought it advisable to be on my guard.

'On the contrary,' said I, 'I bolted my door.'

'Then you are not in the habit of bolting your door every night before you get into bed?'

'Fiend! she wants to know my habits, that she may lay her plans accordingly!' Indignation again prevailed over prudence: I replied sharply, 'Hitherto I have often omitted to fasten the bolt: I did not think it necessary. I was not aware any danger or annoyance was to be dreaded at Thornfield Hall: but in future' (and I laid marked stress on the words) 'I shall take good care to make all secure before I venture to lie down.'

'It will be wise so to do,' was her answer: 'this neighbourhood is as quiet as any I know, and I never heard of the hall being attempted by robbers since it was a house; though there are hundreds of pounds' worth of plate in the plate-closet, as is well known. And you see, for such a large house, there are very few servants, because master has never lived here much; and when he does come, being a bachelor, he needs little waiting on: but I always think it best to err on the safe side; a door is soon fastened, and it is as well to have a drawn bolt between one and any mischief that may be about. A deal of people, Miss, are for trusting all to Providence; but I say Providence will not dispense with the means, though He often blesses them when they are used discreetly.' And here she closed her harangue: a long one for her, and uttered with the demureness of a Quakeress.

I still stood absolutely dumfoundered at what appeared to me her miraculous self-possession, and most inscrutable hypocrisy, when the cook entered.

'Mrs Poole,' said she, addressing Grace, 'the servants' dinner will soon be ready: will you come down?'

'No; just put my pint of porter and bit of pudding on a tray, and I'll carry it upstairs.'

'You'll have some meat?'

'Just a morsel, and a taste of cheese, that's all.'

'And the sago?'

'Never mind it at present: I shall be coming down before tea-time: I'll make it myself.'

The cook here turned to me, saying that Mrs Fairfax was waiting for me: so I departed.

I hardly heard Mrs Fairfax's account of the curtain conflagration during dinner, so much was I occupied in puzzling my brains over the enigmatical

character of Grace Poole, and still more in pondering the problem of her position at Thornfield and questioning why she had not been given into custody that morning, or, at the very least, dismissed from her master's service. He had almost as much as declared his conviction of her criminality last night: what mysterious cause withheld him from accusing her? Why had he enjoined me, too, to secrecy? It was strange: a bold, vindictive, and haughty gentleman seemed somehow in the power of one of the meanest of his dependants; so much in her power, that even when she lifted her hand against his life, he dared not openly charge her with the attempt, much less punish her for it.

Had Grace been young and handsome, I should have been tempted to think that tenderer feelings than prudence or fear influenced Mr Rochester in her behalf; but, hard-favoured and matronly as she was, the idea could not be admitted. 'Yet,' I reflected, 'she has been young once; her youth would be contemporary with her master's: Mrs Fairfax told me once, she had lived here many years. I don't think she can ever have been pretty; but, for aught I know, she may possess originality and strength of character to compensate for the want of personal advantages. Mr Rochester is an amateur of the decided and eccentric: Grace is eccentric at least. What if a former caprice (a freak very possible to a nature so sudden and headstrong as his) has delivered him into her power, and she now exercises over his actions a secret influence, the result of his own indiscretion, which he cannot shake off, and dare not disregard?' But, having reached this point of conjecture, Mrs Poole's square, flat figure, and uncomely, dry, even coarse face, recurred so distinctly to my mind's eye, that I thought, 'No; impossible! my supposition cannot be correct. Yet,' suggested the secret voice which talks to us in our own hearts, '*you* are not beautiful either, and perhaps Mr Rochester approves you: at any rate, you have often felt as if he did; and last night – remember his words; remember his look; remember his voice!'

I well remembered all; language, glance, and tone seemed at the moment vividly renewed. I was now in the schoolroom; Adèle was drawing; I bent over her and directed her pencil. She looked up with a sort of start.

'Qu'avez-vous, mademoiselle?' said she. 'Vos doigts tremblent comme la feuille, et vos joues sont rouges: mais, rouges comme des cerises!'

'I am hot, Adèle, with stooping!' She went on sketching; I went on thinking.

I hastened to drive from my mind the hateful notion I had been conceiving respecting Grace Poole; it disgusted me. I compared myself with her, and found we were different. Bessie Leaven had said I was quite a lady; and she spoke truth – I was a lady. And now I looked much better than I did when Bessie saw me; I had more colour and more flesh, more life, more vivacity, because I had brighter hopes and keener enjoyments.

'Evening approaches,' said I, as I looked towards the window. 'I have never heard Mr Rochester's voice or step in the house today; but surely I shall see him before night: I feared the meeting in the morning; now I desire it, because expectation has been so long baffled that it is grown impatient.'

When dusk actually closed, and when Adèle left me to go and play in the nursery with Sophie, I did most keenly desire it. I listened for the bell to ring

below; I listened for Leah coming up with a message; I fancied sometimes I heard Mr Rochester's own tread, and I turned to the door, expecting it to open and admit him. The door remained shut; darkness only came in through the window. Still it was not late; he often sent for me at seven and eight o'clock, and it was yet but six. Surely I should not be wholly disappointed tonight, when I had so many things to say to him! I wanted again to introduce the subject of Grace Poole, and to hear what he would answer; I wanted to ask him plainly if he really believed it was she who had made last night's hideous attempt; and if so, why he kept her wickedness a secret. It little mattered whether my curiosity irritated him; I knew the pleasure of vexing and soothing him by turns; it was one I chiefly delighted in, and a sure instinct always prevented me from going too far; beyond the verge of provocation I never ventured; on the extreme brink I liked well to try my skill. Retaining every minute form of respect, every propriety of my station, I could still meet him in argument without fear or uneasy restraint; this suited both him and me.

A tread creaked on the stairs at last. Leah made her appearance; but it was only to intimate that tea was ready in Mrs Fairfax's room. Thither I repaired, glad at least to go downstairs; for that brought me, I imagined, nearer to Mr Rochester's presence.

'You must want your tea,' said the good lady, as I joined her; 'you ate so little at dinner. I am afraid,' she continued, 'you are not well today: you look flushed and feverish.'

'Oh, quite well! I never felt better.'

'Then you must prove it by evincing a good appetite; will you fill the teapot while I knit off this needle?' Having completed her task, she rose to draw down the blind, which she had hitherto kept up, by way, I suppose, of making the most of daylight, though dusk was now fast deepening into total obscurity.

'It is fair tonight,' said she, as she looked through the panes, 'though not starlight; Mr Rochester has, on the whole, had a favourable day for his journey.'

'Journey! – Is Mr Rochester gone anywhere? I did not know he was out.'

'Oh, he set off the moment he had breakfasted! He is gone to the Leas, Mr Eshton's place, ten miles on the other side Millcote. I believe there is quite a party assembled there; Lord Ingram, Sir George Lynn, Colonel Dent, and others.'

'Do you expect him back tonight?'

'No – nor tomorrow either; I should think he is very likely to stay a week or more: when these fine, fashionable people get together, they are so surrounded by elegance and gaiety, so well provided with all that can please and entertain, they are in no hurry to separate. Gentlemen especially are often in request on such occasions; and Mr Rochester is so talented and so lively in society, that I believe he is a general favourite: the ladies are very fond of him; though you would not think his appearance calculated to recommend him particularly in their eyes: but I suppose his acquirements and abilities, perhaps his wealth and good blood, make amends for any little fault of look.'

'Are there ladies at the Leas?'

'There are Mrs Eshton and her three daughters – very elegant young ladies indeed; and there are the Honourable Blanche and Mary Ingram, most beautiful women, I suppose: indeed I have seen Blanche, six or seven years since, when she was a girl of eighteen. She came here to a Christmas ball and party Mr Rochester gave. You should have seen the dining-room that day – how richly it was decorated, how brilliantly lit up! I should think there were fifty ladies and gentlemen present – all of the first county families; and Miss Ingram was considered the belle of the evening.'

'You saw her, you say, Mrs Fairfax: what was she like?'

'Yes, I saw her. The dining-room doors were thrown open; and, as it was Christmas-time, the servants were allowed to assemble in the hall, to hear some of the ladies sing and play. Mr Rochester would have me to come in, and I sat down in a quiet corner and watched them. I never saw a more splendid scene: the ladies were magnificently dressed; most of them – at least most of the younger ones – looked handsome; but Miss Ingram was certainly the queen.'

'And what was she like?'

'Tall, fine bust, sloping shoulders; long, graceful neck: olive complexion, dark and clear; noble features; eyes rather like Mr Rochester's: large and black, and as brilliant as her jewels. And then she had such a fine head of hair; raven-black and so becomingly arranged: a crown of thick plaits behind, and in front the longest, the glossiest curls I ever saw. She was dressed in pure white; an amber-coloured scarf was passed over her shoulder and across her breast tied at the side, and descending in long, fringed ends below her knee. She wore an amber-coloured flower, too, in her hair: it contrasted well with the jetty mass of her curls.'

'She was greatly admired, of course?'

'Yes, indeed: and not only for her beauty, but for her accomplishments. She was one of the ladies who sang: a gentleman accompanied her on the piano. She and Mr Rochester sang a duet.'

'Mr Rochester? I was not aware he could sing.'

'Oh! he has a fine bass voice, and an excellent taste for music.'

'And Miss Ingram: what sort of a voice had she?'

'A very rich and powerful one: she sang delightfully; it was a treat to listen to her; and she played afterwards. I am no judge of music, but Mr Rochester is; and I heard him say her execution was remarkably good.'

'And this beautiful and accomplished lady, she is not yet married.'

'It appears not: I fancy neither she nor her sister have very large fortunes. Old Lord Ingram's estates were chiefly entailed, and the eldest son came in for everything almost.'

'But I wonder no wealthy nobleman or gentleman has taken a fancy to her: Mr Rochester, for instance. He is rich, is he not?'

'Oh! yes. But you see there is a considerable difference in age: Mr Rochester is nearly forty; she is but twenty-five.'

'What of that? More unequal matches are made every day.'

'True: yet I should scarcely fancy Mr Rochester would entertain an idea of the sort. But you eat nothing: you have scarcely tasted since you began tea.'

'No: I am too thirsty to eat. Will you let me have another cup?'

I was about again to revert to the probability of a union between Mr Rochester and the beautiful Blanche; but Adèle came in, and the conversation was turned into another channel.

When once more alone, I reviewed the information I had got; looked into my heart, examined its thoughts and feelings, and endeavoured to bring back with a strict hand such as had been straying through imagination's boundless and trackless waste, into the safe fold of common sense.

Arraigned at my own bar, Memory having given her evidence of the hopes, wishes, sentiments I had been cherishing since last night – of the general state of mind in which I had indulged for nearly a fortnight past; Reason having come forward and told, in her own quiet way, a plain, unvarnished tale, showing how I had rejected the real, and rabidly devoured the ideal – I pronounced judgement to this effect: That a greater fool than Jane Eyre had never breathed the breath of life; that a more fantastic idiot had never surfeited herself on sweet lies, and swallowed poison as if it were nectar.

'*You*,' I said, 'a favourite with Mr Rochester? *You* gifted with the power of pleasing him? *You* of importance to him in any way? Go! your folly sickens me. And you have derived pleasure from occasional tokens of preference – equivocal tokens shown by a gentleman of family and a man of the world to a dependant and a novice. How dared you? Poor stupid dupe! – Could not even self-interest make you wiser? You repeated to yourself this morning the brief scene of last night? – Cover your face and be ashamed! He said something in praise of your eyes, did he? Blind puppy! Open their bleared lids and look on your own accursed senselessness! It does good to no woman to be flattered by her superior, who cannot possibly intend to marry her; and it is madness in all women to let a secret love kindle within them, which, if unreturned and unknown, must devour the life that feeds it; and, if discovered and responded to, must lead, *ignis-fatuus*-like, into miry wilds whence there is no extrication.

'Listen, then, Jane Eyre, to your sentence: tomorrow, place the glass before you, and draw in chalk your own picture, faithfully, without softening one defect; omit no harsh line, smooth away no displeasing irregularity; write under it, "Portrait of a Governess, disconnected, poor, and plain".

'Afterwards, take a piece of smooth ivory – you have one prepared in your drawing-box: take your palette, mix your freshest, finest, clearest tints; choose your most delicate camel-hair pencils; delineate carefully the loveliest face you can imagine; paint it in your softest shades and sweetest hues, according to the description given by Mrs Fairfax of Blanche Ingram; remember the raven ringlets, the oriental eye; What! you revert to Mr Rochester as a model! Order! No snivel! – no sentiment! – no regret! I will endure only sense and resolution. Recall the august yet harmonious lineaments, the Grecian neck and bust; let the round and dazzling arm be visible, and the delicate hand; omit neither diamond ring nor gold bracelet; portray faithfully the attire, aerial lace and glistening satin, graceful scarf and golden rose; call it "Blanche, an accomplished lady of rank".

'Whenever, in future, you should chance to fancy Mr Rochester thinks well of you, take out these two pictures and compare them: say, "Mr Rochester might probably win that noble lady's love, if he chose to strive for it; is it likely he would waste a serious thought on this indigent and insignificant plebeian?"'

'I'll do it,' I resolved: and having framed this determination, I grew calm, and fell asleep.

I kept my word. An hour or two sufficed to sketch my own portrait in crayons; and in less than a fortnight I had completed an ivory miniature of an imaginary Blanche Ingram. It looked a lovely face enough, and when compared with the real head in chalk, the contrast was as great as self-control could desire. I derived benefit from the task: it had kept my head and hands employed, and had given force and fixedness to the new impressions I wished to stamp indelibly on my heart.

Ere long, I had reason to congratulate myself on the course of wholesome discipline to which I had thus forced my feelings to submit. Thanks to it, I was able to meet subsequent occurrences with a decent calm, which, had they found me unprepared, I should probably have been unequal to maintain, even externally.

## Chapter 17

A week passed, and no news arrived of Mr Rochester: ten days, and still he did not come. Mrs Fairfax said she should not be surprised if he were to go straight from the Leas to London, and thence to the Continent, and not show his face again at Thornfield for a year to come; he had not unfrequently quitted it in a manner quite as abrupt and unexpected. When I heard this, I was beginning to feel a strange chill and failing at the heart. I was actually permitting myself to experience a sickening sense of disappointment; but rallying my wits, and recollecting my principles, I at once called my sensations to order; and it was wonderful how I got over the temporary blunder – how I cleared up the mistake of supposing Mr Rochester's movements a matter in which I had any cause to take a vital interest. Not that I humbled myself by a slavish notion of inferiority: on the contrary, I just said – 'You have nothing to do with the master of Thornfield, further than to receive the salary he gives you for teaching his protégée, and to be grateful for such respectful and kind treatment as, if you do your duty, you have a right to expect at his hands. Be sure that is the only tie he seriously acknowledges between you and him; so don't make him the object of your fine feelings, your raptures, agonies, and so forth. He is not of your order: keep to your caste, and be too self-respecting to lavish the love of the whole heart, soul, and strength, where such a gift is not wanted and would be despised.'

I went on with my day's business tranquilly; but ever and anon vague suggestions kept wandering across my brain of reasons why I should quit Thornfield; and I kept involuntarily framing advertisements and pondering

conjectures about new situations: these thoughts I did not think it necessary to check; they might germinate and bear fruit if they could.

Mr Rochester had been absent upwards of a fortnight, when the post brought Mrs Fairfax a letter.

'It is from the master,' said she, as she looked at the direction. 'Now I suppose we shall know whether we are to expect his return or not.'

And while she broke the seal and perused the document, I went on taking my coffee (we were at breakfast): it was hot, and I attributed to that circumstance a fiery glow which suddenly rose to my face. Why my hand shook, and why I involuntarily spilt half the contents of my cup into my saucer, I did not choose to consider.

'Well, I sometimes think we are too quiet; but we run a chance of being busy enough now: for a little while at least,' said Mrs Fairfax, still holding the note before her spectacles.

Ere I permitted myself to request an explanation, I tied the string of Adèle's pinafore, which happened to be loose: having helped her also to another bun and refilled her mug with milk, I said, nonchalantly – 'Mr Rochester is not likely to return soon, I suppose?'

'Indeed he is – in three days, he says: that will be next Thursday; and not alone either. I don't know how many of the fine people at the Leas are coming with him: he sends directions for all the best bedrooms to be prepared; and the library and drawing-rooms are to be cleaned out; and I am to get more kitchen hands from the George Inn, at Millcote, and from wherever else I can; and the ladies will bring their maids and the gentlemen their valets: so we shall have a full house of it.' And Mrs Fairfax swallowed her breakfast and hastened away to commence operations.

The three days were, as she had foretold, busy enough. I had thought all the rooms at Thornfield beautifully clean and well arranged; but it appears I was mistaken. Three women were got to help; and such scrubbing, such brushing, such washing of paint and beating of carpets, such taking down and putting up of pictures, such polishing of mirrors and lustres, such lighting of fires in bedrooms, such airing of sheets and feather-beds on hearths, I never beheld, either before or since. Adèle ran quite wild in the midst of it: the preparations for company and the prospect of their arrival, seemed to throw her into ecstasies. She would have Sophie to look over all her 'toilettes', as she called frocks; to furbish up any that were '*passées*', and to air and arrange the new. For herself, she did nothing but caper about in the front chambers, jump on and off the bedsteads, and lie on the mattresses and piled-up bolsters and pillows before the enormous fires roaring in the chimneys. From school duties she was exonerated: Mrs Fairfax had pressed me into her service, and I was all day in the storeroom, helping (or hindering) her and the cook; learning to make custards and cheese-cakes and French pastry, to truss game and garnish dessert-dishes.

The party were expected to arrive on Thursday afternoon, in time for dinner at six. During the intervening period I had no time to nurse chimeras; and I believe I was as active and gay as anybody – Adèle excepted. Still, now and then, I received

a damping check to my cheerfulness; and was, in spite of myself, thrown back on the region of doubts and portents, and dark conjectures. This was when I chanced to see the third-storey staircase door (which of late had always been kept locked) open slowly, and give passage to the form of Grace Poole, in prim cap, white apron, and handkerchief; when I watched her glide along the gallery, her quiet tread muffled in a list slipper; when I saw her look into the bustling, topsy-turvy bedrooms, just say a word, perhaps, to the charwoman about the proper way to polish a grate, or clean a marble mantelpiece, or take stains from papered walls, and then pass on. She would thus descend to the kitchen once a day, eat her dinner, smoke a moderate pipe on the hearth, and go back, carrying her pot of porter with her, for her private solace, in her own gloomy, upper haunt. Only one hour in the twenty-four did she pass with her fellow-servants below; all the rest of her time was spent in some low-ceiled, oaken chamber of the second storey: there she sat and sewed – and probably laughed drearily to herself, as companionless as a prisoner in his dungeon.

The strangest thing of all was, that not a soul in the house, except me, noticed her habits, or seemed to marvel at them: no one discussed her position or employment; no one pitied her solitude or isolation. I once, indeed, overheard part of a dialogue between Leah and one of the charwomen, of which Grace formed the subject. Leah had been saying something I had not caught, and the charwoman remarked – 'She gets good wages, I guess?'

'Yes,' said Leah; 'I wish I had as good; not that mine are to complain of, there's no stinginess at Thornfield; but they're not one fifth of the sum Mrs Poole receives. And she is laying by: she goes every quarter to the bank at Millcote. I should not wonder but she has saved enough to keep her independent if she liked to leave; but I suppose she's got used to the place; and then she's not forty yet, and strong and able for anything. It is too soon for her to give up business.'

'She is a good hand, I dare say,' said the charwoman.

'Ah! – she understands what she has to do, nobody better,' rejoined Leah significantly; 'and it is not everyone could fill her shoes – not for all the money she gets.'

'That it is not!' was the reply. 'I wonder whether the master –'

The charwoman was going on; but here Leah turned and perceived me, and she instantly gave her companion a nudge.

'Doesn't she know?' I heard the woman whisper.

Leah shook her head, and the conversation was of course dropped. All I had gathered from it amounted to this, that there was a mystery at Thornfield; and that from participation in that mystery I was purposely excluded.

Thursday came: all work had been completed the previous evening; carpets were laid down, bed-hangings festooned, radiant white counterpanes spread, toilet tables arranged, furniture rubbed, flowers piled in vases: both chambers and saloons looked as fresh and bright as hands could make them. The hall, too, was scoured; and the great carved clock, as well as the steps and banisters of the staircase, were polished to the brightness of glass; in the dining-room,

the sideboard flashed resplendent with plate; in the drawing-room and boudoir, vases of exotics bloomed on all sides. Afternoon arrived: Mrs Fairfax assumed her best black satin gown, her gloves, and her gold watch; for it was her part to receive the company, to conduct the ladies to their rooms, etc. Adèle, too, would be dressed: though I thought she had little chance of being introduced to the party that day at least. However, to please her, I allowed Sophie to apparel her in one of her short, full muslin frocks. For myself, I had no need to make any change; I should not be called upon to quit my sanctum of the schoolroom; for a sanctum it was now become to me, 'a very pleasant refuge in time of trouble.'

It had been a mild, serene spring day – one of those days which, towards the end of March or the beginning of April, rise shining over the earth as heralds of summer. It was drawing to an end now; but the evening was even warm, and I sat at work in the schoolroom with the window open.

'It gets late,' said Mrs Fairfax, entering in rustling state. 'I am glad I ordered dinner an hour after the time Mr Rochester mentioned; for it is past six now. I have sent John down to the gates to see if there is anything on the road: one can see a long way from thence in the direction of Millcote.' She went to the window. 'Here he is!' said she. 'Well, John' (leaning out), 'any news?'

'They're coming, ma'am,' was the answer. 'They'll be here in ten minutes.'

Adèle flew to the window. I followed, taking care to stand on one side, so that, screened by the curtain, I could see without being seen.

The ten minutes John had given seemed very long, but at last wheels were heard; four equestrians galloped up the drive, and after them came two open carriages. Fluttering veils and waving plumes filled the vehicles; two of the cavaliers were young, dashing-looking gentlemen; the third was Mr Rochester, on his black horse, Mesrour, Pilot bounding before him; at his side rode a lady, and he and she were the first of the party. Her purple riding-habit almost swept the ground, her veil streamed long on the breeze; mingling with its transparent folds, and gleaming through them, shone rich raven ringlets.

'Miss Ingram!' exclaimed Mrs Fairfax, and away she hurried to her post below.

The cavalcade, following the sweep of the drive, quickly turned the angle of the house, and I lost sight of it. Adèle now petitioned to go down; but I took her on my knee, and gave her to understand that she must not on any account think of venturing in sight of the ladies, either now or at any other time, unless expressly sent for: that Mr Rochester would be very angry, etc. Some natural tears she shed on being told this; but as I began to look very grave, she consented at last to wipe them.

A joyous stir was now audible in the hall: gentlemen's deep tones and ladies' silvery accents blent harmoniously together, and distinguishable above all, though not loud, was the sonorous voice of the master of Thornfield Hall, welcoming his fair and gallant guests under its roof. Then light steps ascended the stairs; and there was a tripping through the gallery, and soft cheerful laughs, and opening and closing doors, and, for a time, a hush.

'Elles changent de toilettes,' said Adèle; who, listening attentively, had followed every movement; and she sighed.

'Chez maman,' said she, 'quand il y avait du monde, je le suivais partout, au salon et à leurs chambres; souvent je regardais les femmes de chambre coiffer et habiller les dames, et c'était si amusant: comme cela on apprend.'

'Don't you feel hungry, Adèle?'

'Mais oui, mademoiselle: voilà cinq ou six heures que nous n'avons pas mangé.'

'Well now, while the ladies are in their rooms, I will venture down and get you something to eat.'

And issuing from my asylum with precaution, I sought a back-stairs which conducted directly to the kitchen. All in that region was fire and commotion; the soup and fish were in the last stage of projection, and the cook hung over her crucibles in a frame of mind and body threatening spontaneous combustion. In the servants' hall two coachmen and three gentlemen's gentlemen stood or sat round the fire; the abigails, I suppose, were upstairs with their mistresses; the new servants, that had been hired from Millcote, were bustling about everywhere. Threading this chaos, I at last reached the larder; there I took possession of a cold chicken, a roll of bread, some tarts, a plate or two and a knife and fork: with this booty I made a hasty retreat. I had regained the gallery, and was just shutting the back-door behind me, when an accelerated hum warned me that the ladies were about to issue from their chambers. I could not proceed to the schoolroom without passing some of their doors, and running the risk of being surprised with my cargo of victualage; so I stood still at this end, which, being windowless, was dark: quite dark now, for the sun was set and twilight gathering.

Presently the chambers gave up their fair tenants one after another: each came out gaily and airily, with dress that gleamed lustrous through the dusk. For a moment they stood grouped together at the other extremity of the gallery, conversing in a key of sweet subdued vivacity: they then descended the staircase almost as noiselessly as a bright mist rolls down a hill. Their collective appearance had left on me an impression of high-born elegance, such as I had never before received.

I found Adèle peeping through the schoolroom door, which she held ajar. 'What beautiful ladies!' cried she in English. 'Oh, I wish I might go to them! Do you think Mr Rochester will send for us by and by, after dinner?'

'No, indeed, I don't; Mr Rochester has something else to think about. Never mind the ladies tonight; perhaps you will see them tomorrow: here is your dinner.'

She was really hungry, so the chicken and tarts served to divert her attention for a time. It was well I secured this forage, or both she, I, and Sophie, to whom I conveyed a share of our repast, would have run a chance of getting no dinner at all: everyone downstairs was too much engaged to think of us. The dessert was not carried out till after nine, and at ten footmen were still running to and fro with trays and coffee-cups. I allowed Adèle to sit up much later than usual; for she declared she could not possibly go to sleep while the doors kept

opening and shutting below and people bustling about. Besides, she added, a message might possibly come from Mr Rochester when she was undressed; 'et alors quel dommage!'

I told her stories as long as she would listen to them; and then for a change I took her out into the gallery. The hall lamp was now lit, and it amused her to look over the balustrade and watch the servants passing backwards and forwards. When the evening was far advanced, a sound of music issued from the drawing-room, whither the piano had been removed; Adèle and I sat down on the top step of the stairs to listen. Presently a voice blent with the rich tones of the instrument; it was a lady who sang, and very sweet her notes were. The solo over, a duet followed, and then a glee: a joyous conversational murmur filled up the intervals. I listened long: suddenly I discovered that my ear was wholly intent on analysing the mingled sounds, and trying to discriminate amidst the confusion of accents those of Mr Rochester; and when it caught them, which it soon did, it found a further task in framing the tones, rendered by distance inarticulate, into words.

The clock struck eleven. I looked at Adèle, whose head leant against my shoulder; her eyes were waxing heavy, so I took her up in my arms and carried her off to bed. It was near one before the gentlemen and ladies sought their chambers.

The next day was as fine as its predecessor: it was devoted by the party to an excursion to some site in the neighbourhood. They set out early in the forenoon, some on horseback, the rest in carriages; I witnessed both the departure and the return. Miss Ingram, as before, was the only lady equestrian; and, as before, Mr Rochester galloped at her side; the two rode a little apart from the rest. I pointed out this circumstance to Mrs Fairfax, who was standing at the window with me –

'You said it was not likely they should think of being married,' said I, 'but you see Mr Rochester evidently prefers her to any of the other ladies.'

'Yes, I dare say: no doubt he admires her.'

'And she him,' I added; 'look how she leans her head towards him as if she were conversing confidentially; I wish I could see her face; I have never had a glimpse of it yet.'

'You will see her this evening,' answered Mrs Fairfax. 'I happened to remark to Mr Rochester how much Adèle wished to be introduced to the ladies, and he said: "Oh! let her come into the drawing-room after dinner; and request Miss Eyre to accompany her." '

'Yes; he said that from mere politeness: I need not go, I am sure,' I answered.

'Well, I observed to him that as you were unused to company, I did not think you would like appearing before so gay a party – all strangers; and he replied, in his quick way – "Nonsense! If she objects, tell her it is my particular wish; and if she resists, say I shall come and fetch her in case of contumacy." '

'I will not give him that trouble,' I answered. 'I will go, if no better may be; but I don't like it. Shall you be there, Mrs Fairfax?'

'No; I pleaded off, and he admitted my plea. I'll tell you how to manage so as to avoid the embarrassment of making a formal entrance, which is the most

disagreeable part of the business. You must go into the drawing-room while it is empty, before the ladies leave the dinner-table; choose your seat in any quiet nook you like; you need not stay long after the gentlemen come in, unless you please: just let Mr Rochester see you are there and then slip away – nobody will notice you.'

'Will these people remain long, do you think?'

'Perhaps two or three weeks, certainly not more. After the Easter recess, Sir George Lynn, who was lately elected member for Millcote, will have to go up to town and take his seat; I dare say Mr Rochester will accompany him: it surprises me that he has already made so protracted a stay at Thornfield.'

It was with some trepidation that I perceived the hour approach when I was to repair with my charge to the drawing-room. Adèle had been in a state of ecstasy all day, after hearing she was to be presented to the ladies in the evening; and it was not till Sophie commenced the operation of dressing her that she sobered down. Then the importance of the process quickly steadied her, and by the time she had her curls arranged in well-smoothed, drooping clusters, her pink satin frock put on, her long sash tied, and her lace mittens adjusted, she looked as grave as any judge. No need to warn her not to disarrange her attire: when she was dressed, she sat demurely down in her little chair, taking care previously to lift up the satin skirt for fear she should crease it, and assured me she would not stir thence till I was ready. This I quickly was: my best dress (the silver-grey one, purchased for Miss Temple's wedding, and never worn since) was soon put on; my hair was soon smoothed; my sole ornament, the pearl brooch, soon assumed. We descended.

Fortunately there was another entrance to the drawing-room than that through the saloon where they were all seated at dinner. We found the apartment vacant; a large fire burning silently on the marble hearth, and wax candles shining in bright solitude, amid the exquisite flowers with which the tables were adorned. The crimson curtain hung before the arch: slight as was the separation this drapery formed from the party in the adjoining saloon, they spoke in so low a key that nothing of their conversation could be distinguished beyond a soothing murmur.

Adèle, who appeared to be still under the influence of a most solemnising impression, sat down, without a word, on the footstool I pointed out to her. I retired to a window-seat, and taking a book from a table near, endeavoured to read. Adèle brought her stool to my feet; ere long she touched my knee.

'What is it, Adèle?'

'Est-ce que je ne puis pas prendre une seule de ces fleurs magnifiques, mademoiselle? Seulement pour compléter ma toilette.'

'You think too much of your "toilette", Adèle: but you may have a flower.' And I took a rose from a vase and fastened it in her sash. She sighed a sigh of ineffable satisfaction, as if her cup of happiness were now full. I turned my face away to conceal a smile I could not suppress: there was something ludicrous as well as painful in the little Parisienne's earnest and innate devotion to matters of dress.

A soft sound of rising now became audible; the curtain was swept back from

the arch; through it appeared the dining-room, with its lit lustre pouring down light on the silver and glass of a magnificent dessert-service covering a long table; a band of ladies stood in the opening; they entered, and the curtain fell behind them.

There were but eight; yet, somehow, as they flocked in, they gave the impression of a much larger number. Some of them were very tall; many were dressed in white; and all had a sweeping amplitude of array that seemed to magnify their persons as a mist magnifies the moon. I rose and curtseyed to them: one or two bent their heads in return, the others only stared at me.

They dispersed about the room, reminding me, by the lightness and buoyancy of their movements, of a flock of white plumy birds. Some of them threw themselves in half-reclining positions on the sofas and ottomans: some bent over the tables and examined the flowers and books: the rest gathered in a group round the fire: all talked in a low but clear tone which seemed habitual to them. I knew their names afterwards, and may as well mention them now.

First, there was Mrs Eshton and two of her daughters. She had evidently been a handsome woman, and was well preserved still. Of her daughters, the eldest, Amy, was rather little: naïve, and childlike in face and manner, and piquant in form; her white muslin dress and blue sash became her well. The second, Louisa, was taller and more elegant in figure; with a very pretty face, of that order the French term *minois chiffoné*: both sisters were fair as lilies.

Lady Lynn was a large and stout personage of about forty, very erect, very haughty-looking, richly dressed in a satin robe of changeful sheen: her dark hair shone glossily under the shade of an azure plume, and within the circlet of a band of gems.

Mrs Colonel Dent was less showy; but, I thought, more lady-like. She had a slight figure, a pale, gentle face, and fair hair. Her black satin dress, her scarf of rich foreign lace, and her pearl ornaments, pleased me better than the rainbow radiance of the titled dame.

But the three most distinguished – partly, perhaps, because the tallest figures of the band – were the Dowager Lady Ingram and her daughters, Blanche and Mary. They were all three of the loftiest stature of women. The Dowager might be between forty and fifty: her shape was still fine; her hair (by candlelight at least) still black; her teeth, too, were still apparently perfect. Most people would have termed her a splendid woman of her age: and so she was, no doubt, physically speaking; but then there was an expression of almost insupportable haughtiness in her bearing and countenance. She had Roman features and a double chin, disappearing into a throat like a pillar: these features appeared to me not only inflated and darkened, but even furrowed with pride; and the chin was sustained by the same principle, in a position of almost preternatural erectness. She had, likewise, a fierce and a hard eye: it reminded me of Mrs Reed's; she mouthed her words in speaking; her voice was deep, its inflections very pompous, very dogmatical, very intolerable, in short. A crimson velvet robe, and a shawl turban of some gold-wrought Indian fabric, invested her (I suppose she thought) with a truly imperial dignity.

Blanche and Mary were of equal stature, straight and tall as poplars. Mary was too slim for her height, but Blanche was moulded like a Dian. I regarded her, of course, with special interest. First, I wished to see whether her appearance accorded with Mrs Fairfax's description; secondly, whether it at all resembled the fancy miniature I had painted of her; and thirdly – it will out! – whether it were such as I should fancy likely to suit Mr Rochester's taste.

As far as person went, she answered point for point, both to my picture and Mrs Fairfax's description. The noble bust, the sloping shoulders, the graceful neck, the dark eyes and black ringlets were all there; but her face? Her face was like her mother's; a youthful unfurrowed likeness: the same low brow, the same high features, the same pride. It was not, however, so saturnine a pride! she laughed continually; her laugh was satirical, and so was the habitual expression of her arched and haughty lip.

Genius is said to be self-conscious. I cannot tell whether Miss Ingram was a genius, but she was self-conscious – remarkably self-conscious indeed. She entered into a discourse on botany with the gentle Mrs Dent. It seemed Mrs Dent had not studied that science: though, as she said, she liked flowers, 'especially wild ones'; Miss Ingram had, and she ran over its vocabulary with an air. I presently perceived she was (what is vernacularly termed) *trailing* Mrs Dent; that is, playing on her ignorance: her *trail* might be clever, but it was decidedly not good-natured. She played: her execution was brilliant; she sang, her voice was fine; she talked French apart to her mama; and she talked it well, with fluency and with a good accent.

Mary had a milder and more open countenance than Blanche; softer features too, and a skin some shades fairer (Miss Ingram was dark as a Spaniard) – but Mary was deficient in life: her face lacked expression, her eye lustre; she had nothing to say, and having once taken her seat, remained fixed like a statue in its niche. The sisters were both attired in spotless white.

And did I now think Miss Ingram such a choice as Mr Rochester would be likely to make? I could not tell – I did not know his taste in female beauty. If he liked the majestic, she was the very type of majesty: then she was accomplished, sprightly. Most gentlemen would admire her, I thought; and that he *did* admire her, I already seemed to have obtained proof: to remove the last shade of doubt, it remained but to see them together.

You are not to suppose, reader, that Adèle has all this time been sitting motionless on the stool at my feet: no; when the ladies entered, she rose, advanced to meet them, made a stately reverence, and said with gravity – 'Bon jour, mesdames.'

And Miss Ingram had looked down at her with a mocking air, and exclaimed, 'Oh, what a little puppet!'

Lady Lynn had remarked, 'It is Mr Rochester's ward, I suppose – the little French girl he was speaking of.'

Mrs Dent had kindly taken her hand, and given her a kiss. Amy and Louisa Eshton had cried out simultaneously – 'What a love of a child!'

And then they had called her to a sofa, where she now sat, ensconced between

them, chattering alternately in French and broken English; absorbing not only the young ladies' attention, but that of Mrs Eshton and Lady Lynn, and getting spoilt to her heart's content.

At last coffee is brought in, and the gentlemen are summoned. I sit in the shade – if any shade there be in this brilliantly-lit apartment; the window-curtain half hides me. Again the arch yawns; they come. The collective appearance of the gentlemen, like that of the ladies, is very imposing: they are all costumed in black; most of them are tall, some young. Henry and Frederick Lynn are very dashing sparks indeed; and Colonel Dent is a fine soldierly man. Mr Eshton, the magistrate of the district, is gentleman-like: his hair is quite white, his eyebrows and whiskers still dark, which gives him something of the appearance of a 'père noble de théâtre'. Lord Ingram, like his sisters, is very tall; like them, also, he is handsome; but he shares Mary's apathetic and listless look: he seems to have more length of limb than vivacity of blood or vigour of brain.

And where is Mr Rochester?

He comes in last: I am not looking at the arch, yet I see him enter. I try to concentrate my attention on those netting-needles, on the meshes of the purse I am forming – I wish to think only of the work I have in my hands, to see only the silver beads and silk threads that lie in my lap; whereas, I distinctly behold his figure, and I inevitably recall the moment when I last saw it; just after I had rendered him, what he deemed, an essential service, and he, holding my hand, and looking down on my face, surveyed me with eyes that revealed a heart full and eager to overflow; in whose emotions I had a part. How near had I approached him at that moment! What had occurred since, calculated to change his and my relative positions? Yet now, how distant, how far estranged we were! So far estranged, that I did not expect him to come and speak to me. I did not wonder, when, without looking at me, he took a seat at the other side of the room, and began conversing with some of the ladies.

No sooner did I see that his attention was riveted on them, and that I might gaze without being observed, than my eyes were drawn involuntarily to his face; I could not keep their lids under control: they would rise, and the irids would fix on him. I looked, and had an acute pleasure in looking, a precious yet poignant pleasure; pure gold, with a steely point of agony: a pleasure like what the thirst-perishing man might feel who knows the well to which he has crept is poisoned, yet stoops and drinks divine draughts nevertheless.

Most true is it that 'beauty is in the eye of the gazer'. My master's colourless, olive face, square, massive brow, broad and jetty eyebrows, deep eyes, strong features, firm, grim mouth, all energy, decision, will, were not beautiful, according to rule; but they were more than beautiful to me; they were full of an interest, an influence that quite mastered me, that took my feelings from my own power and fettered them in his. I had not intended to love him; the reader knows I had wrought hard to extirpate from my soul the germs of love there detected; and now, at the first renewed view of him, they spontaneously arrived, green and strong! He made me love him without looking at me.

I compared him with his guests. What was the gallant grace of the Lynns,

the languid elegance of Lord Ingram, even the military distinction of Colonel Dent, contrasted with his look of native pith and genuine power? I had no sympathy in their appearance, their expression: yet I could imagine that most observers would call them attractive, handsome, imposing; while they would pronounce Mr Rochester at once harsh-featured and melancholy-looking. I saw them smile, laugh – it was nothing; the light of the candles had as much soul in it as their smile; the tinkle of the bell as much significance as their laugh. I saw Mr Rochester smile: his stern features softened; his eye grew both brilliant and gentle, its ray both searching and sweet. He was talking, at the moment, to Louisa and Amy Eshton. I wondered to see them receive with calm that look which seemed to me so penetrating: I expected their eyes to fall, their colour to rise under it; yet I was glad when I found they were in no sense moved. 'He is not to them what he is to me,' I thought: 'he is not of their kind. I believe he is of mine; I am sure he is – I feel akin to him – I understand the language of his countenance and movements: though rank and wealth sever us widely, I have something in my brain and heart, in my blood and nerves, that assimilates me mentally to him. Did I say, a few days since, that I had nothing to do with him but to receive my salary at his hands? Did I forbid myself to think of him in any other light than as a paymaster? Blasphemy against nature! Every good, true, vigorous feeling I have gathers impulsively round him. I know I must conceal my sentiments: I must smother hope; I must remember that he cannot care much for me. For when I say that I am of his kind, I do not mean that I have his force to influence, and his spell to attract; I mean only that I have certain tastes and feelings in common with him. I must, then, repeat continually that we are for ever sundered: and yet, while I breathe and think, I must love him.'

Coffee is handed. The ladies, since the gentlemen entered, have become lively as larks; conversation waxes brisk and merry. Colonel Dent and Mr Eshton argue on politics; their wives listen. The two proud dowagers, Lady Lynn and Lady Ingram, confabulate together. Sir George – whom, by the bye, I have forgotten to describe, a very big, and very fresh-looking country gentleman, stands before their sofa, coffee-cup in hand, and occasionally puts in a word. Mr Frederick Lynn has taken a seat beside Mary Ingram, and is showing her the engravings of a splendid volume: she looks, smiles now and then, but apparently says little. The tall and phlegmatic Lord Ingram leans with folded arms on the chair-back of the little and lively Amy Eshton; she glances up at him, and chatters like a wren: she likes him better than she does Mr Rochester. Henry Lynn has taken possession of an ottoman at the feet of Louisa: Adèle shares it with him: he is trying to talk French with her, and Louisa laughs at his blunders. With whom will Blanche Ingram pair? She is standing alone at the table, bending gracefully over an album. She seems waiting to be sought; but she will not wait too long: she herself selects a mate.

Mr Rochester, having quitted the Eshtons, stands on the hearth as solitary as she stands by the table: she confronts him, taking her station on the opposite side of the mantelpiece.

'Mr Rochester, I thought you were not fond of children?'

'Nor am I.'

'Then, what induced you to take charge of such a little doll as that?' (pointing to Adèle). 'Where did you pick her up?'

'I did not pick her up; she was left on my hands.'

'You should have sent her to school.'

'I could not afford it: schools are so dear.'

'Why, I suppose you have a governess for her: I saw a person with her just now – is she gone? Oh, no! there she is still, behind the window-curtain. You pay her, of course; I should think it quite as expensive, more so; for you have them both to keep in addition.'

I feared – or should I say, hoped? – the allusion to me would make Mr Rochester glance my way; and I involuntarily shrank farther into the shade: but he never turned his eyes.

'I have not considered the subject,' said he indifferently, looking straight before him.

'No, you men never do consider economy and common sense. You should hear mama on the chapter of governesses: Mary and I have had, I should think, a dozen at least in our day; half of them detestable and the rest ridiculous, and all incubi – were they not, mama?'

'Did you speak, my own?'

The young lady thus claimed as the dowager's special property, reiterated her question with an explanation.

'My dearest, don't mention governesses; the word makes me nervous. I have suffered a martyrdom from their incompetency and caprice. I thank Heaven I have now done with them!'

Mrs Dent here bent over to the pious lady, and whispered something in her ear; I suppose, from the answer elicited, it was a reminder that one of the anathematised race was present.

'Tant pis!' said her ladyship, 'I hope it may do her good!' Then, in a lower tone, but still loud enough for me to hear, 'I noticed her; I am a judge of physiognomy, and in hers I see all the faults of her class.'

'What are they, madam?' enquired Mr Rochester aloud.

'I will tell you in your private ear,' replied she, wagging her turban three times with portentous significancy.

'But my curiosity will be past its appetite; it craves food now.'

'Ask Blanche; she is nearer you than I.'

'Oh, don't refer him to me, mama! I have just one word to say of the whole tribe; they are a nuisance. Not that I ever suffered much from them; I took care to turn the tables. What tricks Theodore and I used to play on our Miss Wilsons, and Mrs Greys, and Mme Jouberts! Mary was always too sleepy to join in a plot with spirit. The best fun was with Mme Joubert: Miss Wilson was a poor sickly thing, lachrymose and low-spirited, not worth the trouble of vanquishing, in short; and Mrs Grey was coarse and insensible; no blow took effect on her. But poor Mme Joubert! I see her yet in her raging passions, when

we had driven her to extremities – spilt our tea, crumbled our bread and butter, tossed our books up to the ceiling, and played a charivari with the ruler and desk, the fender and fire-irons. Theodore, do you remember those merry days?'

'Yaas, to be sure I do,' drawled Lord Ingram; 'and the poor old stick used to cry out "Oh you villains childs!" – and then we sermonised her on the presumption of attempting to teach such clever blades as we were, when she was herself so ignorant.'

'We did; and, Tedo, you know, I helped you in prosecuting (or persecuting) your tutor, whey-faced Mr Vining – the parson in the pip, as we used to call him. He and Miss Wilson took the liberty of falling in love with each other – at least Tedo and I thought so; we surprised sundry tender glances and sighs which we interpreted as tokens of "la belle passion", and I promise you the public soon had the benefit of our discovery; we employed it as a sort of lever to hoist our dead-weights from the house. Dear mama, there, as soon as she got an inkling of the business, found out that it was of an immoral tendency. Did you not, my lady-mother?'

'Certainly, my best. And I was quite right: depend on that: there are a thousand reasons why liaisons between governesses and tutors should never be tolerated a moment in any well-regulated house; firstly – '

'Oh, gracious, mama! Spare us the enumeration! *Au reste*, we all know them: danger of bad example to innocence of childhood; distractions and consequent neglect of duty on the part of the attached – mutual alliance and reliance; confidence thence resulting – insolence accompanying – mutiny and general blow-up. Am I right, Baroness Ingram, of Ingram Park?'

'My lily-flower, you are right now, as always.'

'Then no more need be said: change the subject.'

Amy Eshton, not hearing or not heeding this dictum, joined in with her soft, infantine tone: 'Louisa and I used to quiz our governess too; but she was such a good creature, she would bear anything: nothing put her out. She was never cross with us; was she, Louisa?'

'No, never: we might do what we pleased; ransack her desk and her workbox, and turn her drawers inside out; and she was so good-natured, she would give us anything we asked for.'

'I suppose, now,' said Miss Ingram, curling her lip sarcastically, 'we shall have an abstract of the memoirs of all the governesses extant: in order to avert such a visitation, I again move the introduction of a new topic. Mr Rochester, do you second my motion?'

'Madam, I support you on this point, as on every other.'

'Then on me be the onus of bringing it forward. Signior Eduardo, are you in voice tonight?'

'Donna Bianca, if you command it, I will be.'

'Then, signior, I lay on you my sovereign behest to furbish up your lungs and other vocal organs, as they will be wanted on my royal service.'

'Who would not be the Rizzio of so divine a Mary?'

'A fig for Rizzio!' cried she, tossing her head with all its curls, as she moved to

the piano. 'It is my opinion the fiddler David must have been an insipid sort of fellow; I like black Bothwell better: to my mind a man is nothing without a spice of the devil in him; and history may say what it will of James Hepburn, but I have a notion, he was just the sort of wild, fierce, bandit hero whom I could have consented to gift with my hand.'

'Gentlemen, you hear! Now which of you most resembles Bothwell?' cried Mr Rochester.

'I should say the preference lies with you,' responded Colonel Dent.

'On my honour, I am much obliged to you,' was the reply.

Miss Ingram, who had now seated herself with proud grace at the piano, spreading out her snowy robes in queenly amplitude, commenced a brilliant prelude; talking meantime. She appeared to be on her high horse tonight; both her words and her air seemed intended to excite not only the admiration, but the amazement of her auditors: she was evidently bent on striking them as something very dashing and daring indeed.

'Oh, I am so sick of the young men of the present day!' exclaimed she, rattling away at the instrument. 'Poor, puny things, not fit to stir a step beyond papa's park gates: nor to go even so far without mama's permission and guardianship! Creatures so absorbed in care about their pretty faces, and their white hands, and their small feet; as if a man had anything to do with beauty! As if loveliness were not the special prerogative of woman – her legitimate appanage and heritage! I grant an ugly *woman* is a blot on the fair face of creation; but as to the *gentlemen*, let them be solicitous to possess only strength and valour: let their motto be: Hunt, shoot, and fight: the rest is not worth a fillip. Such should be my device, were I a man.'

'Whenever I marry,' she continued after a pause which none interrupted, 'I am resolved my husband shall not be a rival, but a foil to me. I will suffer no competitor near the throne; I shall exact an undivided homage: his devotions shall not be shared between me and the shape he sees in his mirror. Mr Rochester, now sing, and I will play for you.'

'I am all obedience,' was the response.

'Here then is a Corsair-song. Know that I dote on Corsairs; and for that reason, sing it *con spirito*.'

'Commands from Miss Ingram's lips would put spirit into a mug of milk and water.'

'Take care, then: if you don't please me, I will shame you by showing how such things *should* be done.'

'That is offering a premium on incapacity: I shall now endeavour to fail.'

'Gardez-vous en bien! If you err wilfully, I shall devise a proportionate punishment.'

'Miss Ingram ought to be clement, for she has it in her power to inflict a chastisement beyond mortal endurance.'

'Ha! explain!' commanded the lady.

'Pardon me, madam: no need of explanation; your own fine sense must inform you that one of your frowns would be a sufficient substitute for capital punishment.'

'Sing!' said she, and again touching the piano, she commenced an accompaniment in spirited style.

'Now is my time to slip away,' thought I: but the tones that then severed the air arrested me. Mrs Fairfax had said Mr Rochester possessed a fine voice: he did – a mellow, powerful bass, into which he threw his own feeling, his own force: finding a way through the ear to the heart, and there waking sensation strangely. I waited till the last deep and full vibration had expired – till the tide of talk, checked an instant, had resumed its flow; I then quitted my sheltered corner and made my exit by the side-door, which was fortunately near. Thence a narrow passage led into the hall: in crossing it, I perceived my sandal was loose; I stopped to tie it, kneeling down for that purpose on the mat at the foot of the staircase. I heard the dining-room door unclose; a gentleman came out; rising hastily, I stood face to face with him: it was Mr Rochester.

'How do you do?' he asked.

'I am very well, sir.'

'Why did you not come and speak to me in the room?'

I thought I might have retorted the question on him who put it: but I would not take that freedom. I answered – 'I did not wish to disturb you, as you seemed engaged, sir.'

'What have you been doing during my absence?'

'Nothing particular; teaching Adèle as usual.'

'And getting a good deal paler than you were – as I saw at first sight. What is the matter?'

'Nothing at all, sir.'

'Did you take any cold that night you half drowned me?'

'Not the least.'

'Return to the drawing-room: you are deserting too early.'

'I am tired, sir.'

He looked at me for a minute.

'And a little depressed,' he said. 'What about? Tell me.'

'Nothing – nothing, sir. I am not depressed.'

'But I affirm that you are: so much depressed that a few more words would bring tears to your eyes – indeed, they are there now, shining and swimming; and a bead has slipped from the lash and fallen on to the flag. If I had time, and was not in mortal dread of some prating prig of a servant passing, I would know what all this means. Well, tonight I excuse you; but understand that so long as my visitors stay, I expect you to appear in the drawing-room every evening; it is my wish; don't neglect it. Now go, and send Sophie for Adèle. Good-night, my – ' He stopped, bit his lip, and abruptly left me.

Merry days were these at Thornfield Hall; and busy days too: how different from the first three months of stillness, monotony, and solitude I had passed beneath its roof! All sad feelings seemed now driven from the house, all gloomy associations forgotten: there was life everywhere, movement all day long. You could not now traverse the gallery, once so hushed, nor enter the front chambers, once so tenantless, without encountering a smart lady's-maid or a dandy valet.

The kitchen, the butler's pantry, the servants' hall, the entrance hall, were equally alive; and the saloons were only left void and still when the blue sky and halcyon sunshine of the genial spring weather called their occupants out into the grounds. Even when that weather was broken, and continuous rain set in for some days, no damp seemed cast over enjoyment: indoor amusements only became more lively and varied, in consequence of the stop put to outdoor gaiety.

I wondered what they were going to do the first evening a change of entertainment was proposed: they spoke of 'playing charades,' but in my ignorance I did not understand the term. The servants were called in, the dining-room tables wheeled away, the lights otherwise disposed, the chairs placed in a semicircle opposite the arch. While Mr Rochester and the other gentlemen directed these alterations, the ladies were running up and down stairs ringing for their maids. Mrs Fairfax was summoned to give information respecting the resources of the house in shawls, dresses, draperies of any kind; and certain wardrobes of the third storey were ransacked, and their contents, in the shape of brocaded and hooped petticoats, satin sacques, black modes, lace lappets, etc., were brought down in armfuls by the abigails; then a selection was made, and such things as were chosen were carried to the boudoir within the drawing-room.

Meantime, Mr Rochester had again summoned the ladies round him, and was selecting certain of their number to be of his party. 'Miss Ingram is mine, of course,' said he: afterwards he named the two Misses Eshton, and Mrs Dent. He looked at me: I happened to be near him, as I had been fastening the clasp of Mrs Dent's bracelet, which had got loose.

'Will you play?' he asked. I shook my head. He did not insist, which I rather feared he would have done; he allowed me to return quietly to my usual seat.

He and his aids now withdrew behind the curtain: the other party, which was headed by Colonel Dent, sat down on the crescent of chairs. One of the gentlemen, Mr Eshton, observing me, seemed to propose that I should be asked to join them; but Lady Ingram instantly negatived the notion.

'No,' I heard her say: 'she looks too stupid for any game of the sort.'

Ere long a bell tinkled, and the curtain drew up. Within the arch, the bulky figure of Sir George Lynn, whom Mr Rochester had likewise chosen, was seen enveloped in a white sheet: before him, on a table, lay open a large book; and at

his side stood Amy Eshton, draped in Mr Rochester's cloak, and holding a book in her hand. Somebody, unseen, rang the bell merrily; then Adèle (who had insisted on being one of her guardian's party), bounded forward, scattering round her the contents of a basket of flowers she carried on her arm. Then appeared the magnificent figure of Miss Ingram, clad in white, a long veil on her head, and a wreath of roses round her brow; by her side walked Mr Rochester, and together they drew near the table. They knelt; while Mrs Dent and Louisa Eshton, dressed also in white, took up their stations behind them. A ceremony followed, in dumb show, in which it was easy to recognise the pantomime of a marriage. At its termination, Colonel Dent, and his party consulted in whispers for two minutes, then the Colonel called out – 'Bride!' Mr Rochester bowed, and the curtain fell.

A considerable interval elapsed before it again rose. Its second rising displayed a more elaborately prepared scene than the last. The drawing-room, as I have before observed, was raised two steps above the dining-room, and on the top of the upper step, placed a yard or two back within the room, appeared a large marble basin, which I recognised as an ornament of the conservatory – where it usually stood, surrounded by exotics, and tenanted by gold fish – and whence it must have been transported with some trouble, on account of its size and weight.

Seated on the carpet, by the side of this basin, was seen Mr Rochester, costumed in shawls, with a turban on his head. His dark eyes and swarthy skin and Paynim features suited the costume exactly: he looked the very model of an Eastern emir, an agent or a victim of the bowstring. Presently advanced into view Miss Ingram. She, too, was attired in oriental fashion: a crimson scarf tied sash-like round the waist; an embroidered handkerchief knotted about her temples; her beautifully moulded arms bare, one of them upraised in the act of supporting a pitcher, poised gracefully on her head. Both her cast of form and feature, her complexion and her general air, suggested the idea of some Israelitish princess of the patriarchal days; and such was doubtless the character she intended to represent.

She approached the basin, and bent over it as if to fill her pitcher; she again lifted it to her head. The personage on the well-brink now seemed to accost her; to make some request: 'She hasted, let down her pitcher on her hand, and gave him to drink.' From the bosom of his robe he then produced a casket, opened it and showed magnificent bracelets and earrings; she acted astonishment and admiration; kneeling, he laid the treasure at her feet; incredulity and delight were expressed by her looks and gestures; the stranger fastened the bracelets on her arms and the rings in her ears. It was Eliezer and Rebecca: the camels only were wanting.

The divining party again laid their heads together: apparently they could not agree about the word or syllable the scene illustrated. Colonel Dent, their spokesman, demanded 'the tableau of the whole'; whereupon the curtain again descended.

On its third rising only a portion of the drawing-room was disclosed; the rest being concealed by a screen, hung with some sort of dark and coarse drapery.

The marble basin was removed; in its place stood a deal table and a kitchen chair: these objects were visible by a very dim light proceeding from a horn lantern, the wax candles being all extinguished.

Amidst this sordid scene, sat a man with his clenched hands resting on his knees, and his eyes bent on the ground. I knew Mr Rochester; though the begrimed face, the disordered dress (his coat hanging loose from one arm, as if it had been almost torn from his back in a scuffle), the desperate and scowling countenance, the rough, bristling hair might well have disguised him. As he moved, a chain clanked; to his wrists were attached fetters.

'Bridewell!' exclaimed Colonel Dent, and the charade was solved.

A sufficient interval having elapsed for the performers to resume their ordinary costume, they re-entered the dining-room. Mr Rochester led in Miss Ingram; she was complimenting him on his acting.

'Do you know,' said she, 'that, of the three characters, I liked you in the last best? Oh, had you but lived a few years earlier, what a gallant gentleman-highwayman you would have made!'

'Is all the soot washed from my face?' he asked, turning it towards her.

'Alas! yes: the more's the pity! Nothing could be more becoming to your complexion than that ruffian's rouge.'

'You would like a hero of the road then?'

'An English hero of the road would be the next best thing to an Italian bandit; and that could only be surpassed by a Levantine pirate.'

'Well, whatever I am, remember you are my wife; we were married an hour since, in the presence of all these witnesses.' She giggled, and her colour rose.

'Now, Dent,' continued Mr Rochester, 'it is your turn.' And as the other party withdrew, he and his band took the vacated seats. Miss Ingram placed herself at her leader's right hand; the other diviners filled the chairs on each side of him and her. I did not now watch the actors; I no longer waited with interest for the curtain to rise; my attention was absorbed by the spectators; my eyes, erewhile fixed on the arch, were now irresistibly attracted to the semicircle of chairs. What charade Colonel Dent and his party played, what word they chose, how they acquitted themselves, I no longer remember; but I still see the consultation which followed each scene: I see Mr Rochester turn to Miss Ingram, and Miss Ingram to him; I see her incline her head towards him, till the jetty curls almost touch his shoulder and wave against his cheek; I hear their mutual whisperings; I recall their interchanged glances; and something even of the feeling roused by the spectacle returns in memory at this moment.

I have told you, reader, that I had learnt to love Mr Rochester: I could not unlove him now, merely because I found that he had ceased to notice me – because I might pass hours in his presence, and he would never once turn his eyes in my direction – because I saw all his attentions appropriated by a great lady, who scorned to touch me with the hem of her robes as she passed; who, if ever her dark and imperious eye fell on me by chance, would withdraw it instantly as from an object too mean to merit observation. I could not unlove him, because I felt sure he would soon marry this very lady – because I read daily

in her a proud security in his intentions respecting her – because I witnessed hourly in him a style of courtship which, if careless and choosing rather to be sought than to seek, was yet, in its very carelessness, captivating, and in its very pride, irresistible.

There was nothing to cool or banish love in these circumstances, though much to create despair. Much too, you will think, reader, to engender jealousy: if a woman, in my position, could presume to be jealous of a woman in Miss Ingram's. But I was not jealous: or very rarely; the nature of the pain I suffered could not be explained by that word. Miss Ingram was a mark beneath jealousy: she was too inferior to excite the feeling. Pardon the seeming paradox; I mean what I say. She was very showy, but she was not genuine: she had a fine person, many brilliant attainments; but her mind was poor, her heart barren by nature: nothing bloomed spontaneously on that soil; no unforced natural fruit delighted by its freshness. She was not good; she was not original: she used to repeat sounding phrases from books: she never offered, nor had, an opinion of her own. She advocated a high tone of sentiment; but she did not know the sensations of sympathy and pity; tenderness and truth were not in her. Too often she betrayed this, by the undue vent she gave to a spiteful antipathy she had conceived against little Adèle: pushing her away with some contumelious epithet if she happened to approach her; sometimes ordering her from the room, and always treating her with coldness and acrimony. Other eyes besides mine watched these manifestations of character – watched them closely, keenly, shrewdly. Yes; the future bridegroom, Mr Rochester himself, exercised over his intended a ceaseless surveillance; and it was from this sagacity – this guardedness of his – this perfect, clear consciousness of his fair one's defects – this obvious absence of passion in his sentiments towards her, that my ever-torturing pain arose.

I saw he was going to marry her, for family, perhaps political reasons, because her rank and connections suited him; I felt he had not given her his love, and that her qualifications were ill adapted to win from him that treasure. This was the point – this was where the nerve was touched and teased – this was where the fever was sustained and fed: *she could not charm him.*

If she had managed the victory at once, and he had yielded and sincerely laid his heart at her feet, I should have covered my face, turned to the wall, and (figuratively) have died to them. If Miss Ingram had been a good and noble woman, endowed with force, fervour, kindness, sense, I should have had one vital struggle with two tigers – jealousy and despair: then, my heart torn out and devoured, I should have admired her – acknowledged her excellence, and been quiet for the rest of my days: and the more absolute her superiority, the deeper would have been my admiration – the more truly tranquil my quiescence. But as matters really stood, to watch Miss Ingram's efforts at fascinating Mr Rochester, to witness their repeated failure – herself unconscious that they did fail; vainly fancying that each shaft launched hit the mark, and infatuatedly pluming herself on success, when her pride and self-complacency repelled further and further what she wished to allure – to witness *this*, was to be at once under ceaseless excitation and ruthless restraint.

Because, when she failed, I saw how she might have succeeded. Arrows that continually glanced off from Mr Rochester's breast and fell harmless at his feet, might, I knew, if shot by a surer hand, have quivered keen in his proud heart – have called love into his stern eye, and softness into his sardonic face; or, better still, without weapons a silent conquest might have been won.

'Why can she not influence him more, when she is privileged to draw so near to him?' I asked myself. 'Surely she cannot truly like him, or not like him with true affection! If she did, she need not coin her smiles so lavishly, flash her glances so unremittingly, manufacture airs so elaborate, graces so multitudinous. It seems to me that she might, by merely sitting quietly at his side, saying little and looking less, get nigher his heart. I have seen in his face a far different expression from that which hardens it now while she is so vivaciously accosting him; but then it came of itself: it was not elicited by meretricious arts and calculated manœuvres; and one had but to accept it – to answer what he asked without pretension, to address him when needful without grimace – and it increased and grew kinder and more genial, and warmed one like a fostering sunbeam. How will she manage to please him when they are married? I do not think she will manage it; and yet it might be managed; and his wife might, I verily believe, be the very happiest woman the sun shines on.'

I have not yet said anything condemnatory of Mr Rochester's project of marrying for interest and connections. It surprised me when I first discovered that such was his intention: I had thought him a man unlikely to be influenced by motives so commonplace in his choice of a wife; but the longer I considered the position, education, etc., of the parties, the less I felt justified in judging and blaming either him or Miss Ingram for acting in conformity to ideas and principles instilled into them, doubtless, from their childhood. All their class held these principles: I supposed, then, they had reasons for holding them such as I could not fathom. It seemed to me that, were I a gentleman like him, I would take to my bosom only such a wife as I could love; but the very obviousness of the advantages to the husband's own happiness offered by this plan convinced me that there must be arguments against its general adoption of which I was quite ignorant: otherwise I felt sure all the world would act as I wished to act.

But in other points, as well as this, I was growing very lenient to my master: I was forgetting all his faults, for which I had once kept a sharp look-out. It had formerly been my endeavour to study all sides of his character: to take the bad with the good; and from the just weighing of both, to form an equitable judgement. Now I saw no bad. The sarcasm that had repelled, the harshness that had startled me once, were only like keen condiments in a choice dish: their presence was pungent, but their absence would be felt as comparatively insipid. And as for the vague something – was it a sinister or a sorrowful, a designing or a desponding expression? – that opened upon a careful observer, now and then, in his eye, and closed again before one could fathom the strange depth partially disclosed; that something which used to make me fear and shrink, as if I had been wandering amongst volcanic-looking hills, and had suddenly felt the ground quiver and seen it gape: that something, I, at intervals, beheld still; and

with throbbing heart, but not with palsied nerves. Instead of wishing to shun, I longed only to dare – to divine it; and I thought Miss Ingram happy, because one day she might look into the abyss at her leisure, explore its secrets and analyse their nature.

Meantime, while I thought only of my master and his future bride – saw only them, heard only their discourse, and considered only their movements of importance – the rest of the party were occupied with their own separate interests and pleasures. The Ladies Lynn and Ingram continued to consort in solemn conferences, where they nodded their two turbans at each other, and held up their four hands in confronting gestures of surprise, or mystery, or horror, according to the theme on which their gossip ran, like a pair of magnified puppets. Mild Mrs Dent talked with good-natured Mrs Eshton; and the two sometimes bestowed a courteous word or smile on me. Sir George Lynn, Colonel Dent, and Mr Eshton discussed politics, or county affairs, or justice business. Lord Ingram flirted with Amy Eshton; Louisa played and sang to and with one of the Messrs Lynn; and Mary Ingram listened languidly to the gallant speeches of the other. Sometimes all, as with one consent, suspended their by-play to observe and listen to the principal actors: for, after all, Mr Rochester and – because closely connected with him – Miss Ingram were the life and soul of the party. If he was absent from the room an hour, a perceptible dullness seemed to steal over the spirits of his guests; and his re-entrance was sure to give a fresh impulse to the vivacity of conversation.

The want of his animating influence appeared to be peculiarly felt one day that he had been summoned to Millcote on business, and was not likely to return till late. The afternoon was wet: a walk the party had proposed to take to see a gypsy camp, lately pitched on a common beyond Hay, was consequently deferred. Some of the gentlemen were gone to the stables: the younger ones, together with the younger ladies, were playing billiards in the billiard-room. The dowagers Ingram and Lynn sought solace in a quiet game at cards. Blanche Ingram, after having repelled, by supercilious taciturnity, some efforts of Mrs Dent and Mrs Eshton to draw her into conversation, had first murmured over some sentimental tunes and airs on the piano, and then, having fetched a novel from the library, had flung herself in haughty listlessness on a sofa, and prepared to beguile, by the spell of fiction the tedious hours of absence. The room and the house were silent: only now and then the merriment of the billiard-players was heard from above.

It was verging on dusk, and the clock had already given warning of the hour to dress for dinner, when little Adèle, who knelt by me in the drawing-room window-seat, suddenly exclaimed – 'Voilà M. Rochester, qui revient!'

I turned, and Miss Ingram darted forwards from her sofa: the others, too, looked up from their several occupations; for at the same time a crunching of wheels and a splashing tramp of horse-hoofs became audible on the wet gravel. A post-chaise was approaching.

'What can possess him to come home in that style?' said Miss Ingram. 'He rode Mesrour (the black horse), did he not, when he went out? and Pilot was with him: what has he done with the animals?'

As she said this, she approached her tall person and ample garments so near the window, that I was obliged to bend back almost to the breaking of my spine: in her eagerness she did not observe me at first, but when she did, she curled her lip and moved to another casement. The post-chaise stopped; the driver rang the doorbell, and a gentleman alighted attired in travelling garb; but it was not Mr Rochester; it was a tall, fashionable-looking man, a stranger.

'How provoking!' exclaimed Miss Ingram: 'you tiresome monkey!' (apostrophising Adèle), 'who perched you up in the window to give false intelligence?' and she cast on me an angry glance, as if I were in fault.

Some parleying was audible in the hall, and soon the newcomer entered. He bowed to Lady Ingram, as deeming her the eldest lady present.

'It appears I come at an inopportune time, madam,' said he, 'when my friend, Mr Rochester, is from home; but I arrive from a very long journey, and I think I may presume so far on old and intimate acquaintance as to instal myself here till he returns.'

His manner was polite; his accent, in speaking, struck me as being somewhat unusual, not precisely foreign, but still not altogether English: his age might be about Mr Rochester's, between thirty and forty; his complexion was singularly sallow: otherwise he was a fine-looking man, at first sight especially. On closer examination, you detected something in his face that displeased, or rather that failed to please. His features were regular, but too relaxed: his eye was large and well cut, but the life looking out of it was a tame, vacant life – at least so I thought.

The sound of the dressing-bell dispersed the party. It was not till after dinner that I saw him again: he then seemed quite at his ease. But I liked his physiognomy even less than before: it struck me as being at the same time unsettled and inanimate. His eye wandered, and had no meaning in its wandering: this gave him an odd look, such as I never remembered to have seen. For a handsome and not an unamiable-looking man, he repelled me exceedingly: there was no power in that smooth-skinned face of a full oval shape: no firmness in that aquiline nose and small cherry mouth; there was no thought on the low, even forehead; no command in that blank, brown eye.

As I sat in my usual nook, and looked at him with the light of the girandoles on the mantelpiece beaming full over him – for he occupied an armchair drawn close to the fire, and kept shrinking still nearer, as if he were cold – I compared him with Mr Rochester. I think (with deference be it spoken) the contrast could not be much greater between a sleek gander and a fierce falcon: between a meek sheep and the rough-coated keen-eyed dog, its guardian.

He had spoken of Mr Rochester as an old friend. A curious friendship theirs must have been: a pointed illustration, indeed, of the old adage that 'extremes meet.'

Two or three of the gentlemen sat near him, and I caught at times scraps of their conversation across the room. At first I could not make much sense of what I heard; for the discourse of Louisa Eshton and Mary Ingram, who sat nearer to me, confused the fragmentary sentences that reached me at intervals. These last were discussing the stranger; they both called him 'a beautiful man'. Louisa said

he was 'a love of a creature', and she 'adored him'; and Mary instanced his 'pretty little mouth, and nice nose', as her ideal of the charming.

'And what a sweet-tempered forehead he has!' cried Louisa, 'so smooth – none of those frowning irregularities I dislike so much; and such a placid eye and smile!'

And then, to my great relief, Mr Henry Lynn summoned them to the other side of the room, to settle some point about the deferred excursion to Hay Common.

I was now able to concentrate my attention on the group by the fire, and I presently gathered that the newcomer was called Mr Mason; then I learned that he was but just arrived in England, and that he came from some hot country: which was the reason, doubtless, his face was so sallow, and that he sat so near the hearth, and wore a surtout in the house. Presently the words Jamaica, Kingston, Spanish Town, indicated the West Indies as his residence; and it was with no little surprise I gathered, ere long, that he had there first seen and become acquainted with Mr Rochester. He spoke of his friend's dislike of the burning heats, the hurricanes, and rainy seasons of that region. I knew Mr Rochester had been a traveller: Mrs Fairfax had said so; but I thought the continent of Europe had bounded his wanderings; till now I had never heard a hint given of visits to more distant shores.

I was pondering these things, when an incident, and a somewhat unexpected one, broke the thread of my musings. Mr Mason, shivering as someone chanced to open the door, asked for more coal to be put on the fire, which had burnt out its flame, though its mass of cinder still shone hot and red. The footman who brought the coal, in going out, stopped near Mr Eshton's chair, and said something to him in a low voice, of which I heard only the words, 'old woman' – 'quite troublesome.'

'Tell her she shall be put in the stocks if she does not take herself off,' replied the magistrate.

'No – stop!' interrupted Colonel Dent. 'Don't send her away, Eshton; we might turn the thing to account; better consult the ladies.' And speaking aloud, he continued – 'Ladies, you talked of going to Hay Common to visit the gypsy camp; Sam here says that one of the old Mother Bunches is in the servants' hall at this moment, and insists upon being brought in before "the quality", to tell them their fortunes. Would you like to see her?'

'Surely, colonel,' cried Lady Ingram, 'you would not encourage such a low impostor? Dismiss her, by all means, at once!'

'But I cannot persuade her to go away, my lady,' said the footman; 'nor can any of the servants: Mrs Fairfax is with her just now, entreating her to be gone; but she has taken a chair in the chimney-corner, and says nothing shall stir her from it till she gets leave to come in here.'

'What does she want?' asked Mrs Eshton.

' "To tell the gentry their fortunes," she says, ma'am; and she swears she must and will do it.'

'What is she like?' enquired the Misses Eshton, in a breath.

'A shockingly ugly old creature, miss; almost as black as a crock.'

'Why, she's a real sorceress!' cried Frederick Lynn. 'Let us have her in, of course.'

'To be sure,' rejoined his brother; 'it would be a thousand pities to throw away such a chance of fun.'

'My dear boys, what are you thinking about?' exclaimed Mrs Lynn.

'I cannot possibly countenance any such inconsistent proceeding,' chimed in the Dowager Ingram.

'Indeed, mama, but you can – and will,' pronounced the haughty voice of Blanche, as she turned round on the piano-stool; where till now she had sat silent, apparently examining sundry sheets of music. 'I have a curiosity to hear my fortune told: therefore, Sam, order the beldame forward.'

'My darling Blanche! recollect –'

'I do – I recollect all you can suggest; and I must have my will – quick, Sam!'

'Yes – yes – yes!' cried all the juveniles, both ladies and gentlemen. 'Let her come – it will be excellent sport!'

The footman still lingered. 'She looks such a rough one,' said he.

'Go!' ejaculated Miss Ingram, and the man went.

Excitement instantly seized the whole party: a running fire of raillery and jests was proceeding when Sam returned.

'She won't come now,' said he. 'She says it's not her mission to appear before the "vulgar herd" (them's her words). I must show her into a room by herself, and then those who wish to consult her must go to her one by one.'

'You see now, my queenly Blanche,' began Lady Ingram, 'she encroaches. Be advised, my angel girl – and –'

'Show her into the library, of course,' cut in the 'angel girl.' 'It is not my mission to listen to her before the vulgar herd either: I mean to have her all to myself. Is there a fire in the library?'

'Yes, ma'am – but she looks such a tinker.'

'Cease that chatter, blockhead! and do my bidding.'

Again Sam vanished; and mystery, animation, expectation rose to full flow once more.

'She's ready now,' said the footman, as he reappeared. 'She wishes to know who will be her first visitor.'

'I think I had better just look in upon her before any of the ladies go,' said Colonel Dent.

'Tell her, Sam, a gentleman is coming.'

Sam went and returned.

'She says, sir, that she'll have no gentlemen; they need not trouble themselves to come near her; nor,' he added, with difficulty suppressing a titter, 'any ladies either, except the young and single.'

'By Jove, she has taste!' exclaimed Henry Lynn.

Miss Ingram rose solemnly: 'I go first,' she said, in a tone which might have befitted the leader of a forlorn hope, mounting a breach in the van of his men.

'Oh, my best! oh, my dearest! pause – reflect!' was her mama's cry; but she

swept past her in stately silence, passed through the door which Colonel Dent held open, and we heard her enter the library.

A comparative silence ensued. Lady Ingram thought it 'le cas' to wring her hands: which she did accordingly. Miss Mary declared she felt, for her part, she never dared venture. Amy and Louisa Eshton tittered under their breath, and looked a little frightened.

The minutes passed very slowly: fifteen were counted before the library-door again opened. Miss Ingram returned to us through the arch.

Would she laugh? Would she take it as a joke? All eyes met her with a glance of eager curiosity, and she met all eyes with one of rebuff and coldness; she looked neither flurried nor merry: she walked stiffly to her seat, and took it in silence.

'Well, Blanche?' said Lord Ingram.

'What did she say, sister?' asked Mary.

'What did you think? How do you feel? Is she a real fortune-teller?' demanded the Misses Eshton.

'Now, now, good people,' returned Miss Ingram, 'don't press upon me. Really your organs of wonder and credulity are easily excited: you seem, by the importance you all – my good mama included – ascribe to this matter, absolutely to believe we have a genuine witch in the house, who is in close alliance with the old gentleman. I have seen a gypsy vagabond; she has practised in hackneyed fashion the science of palmistry and told me what such people usually tell. My whim is gratified; and now I think Mr Eshton will do well to put the hag in the stocks tomorrow morning, as he threatened.'

Miss Ingram took a book, leant back in her chair, and so declined further conversation. I watched her for nearly half an hour: during all that time she never turned a page, and her face grew momently darker, more dissatisfied, and more sourly expressive of disappointment. She had obviously not heard anything to her advantage: and it seemed to me, from her prolonged fit of gloom and taciturnity, that she herself, notwithstanding her professed indifference, attached undue importance to whatever revelations had been made her.

Meantime, Mary Ingram, Amy and Louisa Eshton, declared they dared not go alone; and yet they all wished to go. A negotiation was opened through the medium of the ambassador, Sam; and after much pacing to and fro, till, I think, the said Sam's calves must have ached with the exercise, permission was at last, with great difficulty, extorted from the rigorous Sibyl, for the three to wait upon her in a body.

Their visit was not so still as Miss Ingram's had been: we heard hysterical giggling and little shrieks proceeding from the library; and at the end of about twenty minutes they burst the door open, and came running across the hall, as if they were half-scared out of their wits.

'I am sure she is something not right!' they cried, one and all. 'She told us such things! She knows all about us!' and they sank breathless into the various seats the gentlemen hastened to bring them.

Pressed for further explanation, they declared she had told them of things

they had said and done when they were mere children; described books and ornaments they had in their boudoirs at home: keepsakes that different relations had presented to them. They affirmed that she had even divined their thoughts, and had whispered in the ear of each the name of the person she liked best in the world, and informed them of what they most wished for.

Here the gentlemen interposed with earnest petitions to be further enlightened on these two last-named points; but they got only blushes, ejaculations, tremors, and titters, in return for their importunity. The matrons, meantime, offered vinaigrettes and wielded fans; and again and again reiterated the expression of their concern that their warning had not been taken in time; and the elder gentlemen laughed, and the younger urged their services on the agitated fair ones.

In the midst of the tumult, and while my eyes and ears were fully engaged in the scene before me, I heard a hem close at my elbow: I turned, and saw Sam.

'If you please, miss, the gypsy declares that there is another young single lady in the room who has not been to her yet, and she swears she will not go till she has seen all. I thought it must be you: there is no one else for it. What shall I tell her?'

'Oh, I will go by all means,' I answered: and I was glad of the unexpected opportunity to gratify my much-excited curiosity. I slipped out of the room, unobserved by any eye – for the company were gathered in one mass about the trembling trio just returned – and I closed the door quietly behind me.

'If you like, miss,' said Sam, 'I'll wait in the hall for you; and if she frightens you, just call and I'll come in.'

'No, Sam, return to the kitchen: I am not in the least afraid.' Nor was I; but I was a good deal interested and excited.

## Chapter 19

The library looked tranquil enough as I entered it, and the Sibyl – if Sibyl she were – was seated snugly enough in an easy-chair at the chimney-corner. She had on a red cloak and a black bonnet: or rather, a broad-brimmed gypsy hat, tied down with a striped handkerchief under her chin. An extinguished candle stood on the table; she was bending over the fire, and seemed reading in a little black book, like a prayer-book, by the light of the blaze: she muttered the words to herself, as most old women do, while she read; she did not desist immediately on my entrance: it appeared she wished to finish a paragraph.

I stood on the rug and warmed my hands, which were rather cold with sitting at a distance from the drawing-room fire. I felt now as composed as ever I did in my life: there was nothing indeed in the gypsy's appearance to trouble one's calm. She shut her book and slowly looked up; her hat-brim partially shaded her face, yet I could see, as she raised it, that it was a strange one. It looked all brown and black: elf-locks bristled out from beneath a white band which passed under her chin, and came half over her cheeks, or rather jaws: her eye confronted me at once, with a bold and direct gaze.

'Well, and you want your fortune told?' she said, in a voice as decided as her glance, as harsh as her features.

'I don't care about it, mother; you may please yourself: but I ought to warn you, I have no faith.'

'It's like your impudence to say so: I expected it of you; I heard it in your step as you crossed the threshold.'

'Did you? You've a quick ear.'

'I have; and a quick eye and a quick brain.'

'You need them all in your trade.'

'I do; especially when I've customers like you to deal with. Why don't you tremble?'

'I'm not cold.'

'Why don't you turn pale?'

'I am not sick.'

'Why don't you consult my art?'

'I'm not silly.'

The old crone 'nichered' a laugh under her bonnet and bandage; she then drew out a short black pipe, and lighting it began to smoke. Having indulged a while in this sedative, she raised her bent body, took the pipe from her lips, and while gazing steadily at the fire, said very deliberately – 'You are cold; you are sick; and you are silly.'

'Prove it,' I rejoined.

'I will, in few words. You are cold, because you are alone: no contact strikes the fire from you that is in you. You are sick; because the best of feelings, the highest and the sweetest given to man, keeps far away from you. You are silly, because, suffer as you may, you will not beckon it to approach, nor will you stir one step to meet it where it waits you.'

She again put her short black pipe to her lips, and renewed her smoking with vigour.

'You might say all that to almost anyone who you knew lived as a solitary dependent in a great house.'

'I might say it to almost anyone: but would it be true of almost anyone?'

'In my circumstances.'

'Yes; just so, in *your* circumstances: but find me another precisely placed as you are.'

'It would be easy to find you thousands.'

'You could scarcely find me one. If you knew it, you are peculiarly situated: very near happiness; yes, within reach of it. The materials are all prepared; there only wants a movement to combine them. Chance laid them somewhat apart; let them be once approached and bliss results.'

'I don't understand enigmas. I never could guess a riddle in my life.'

'If you wish me to speak more plainly, show me your palm.'

'And I must cross it with silver, I suppose?'

'To be sure.'

I gave her a shilling: she put it into an old stocking-foot which she took out of

her pocket, and having tied it round and returned it, she told me to hold out my hand. I did. She approached her face to the palm, and pored over it without touching it.

'It is too fine,' said she. 'I can make nothing of such a hand as that; almost without lines: besides, what is in a palm? Destiny is not written there.'

'I believe you,' said I.

'No,' she continued, 'it is in the face: on the forehead, about the eyes, in the eyes themselves, in the lines of the mouth. Kneel, and lift up your head.'

'Ah! now you are coming to reality,' I said, as I obeyed her. 'I shall begin to put some faith in you presently.'

I knelt within half a yard of her. She stirred the fire, so that a ripple of light broke from the disturbed coal: the glare, however, as she sat, only threw her face into deeper shadow: mine, it illumined.

'I wonder with what feelings you came to me tonight,' she said, when she had examined me a while. 'I wonder what thoughts are busy in your heart during all the hours you sit in yonder room with the fine people flitting before you like shapes in a magic-lantern: just as little sympathetic communion passing between you and them as if they were really mere shadows of human forms, and not the actual substance.'

'I feel tired often, sleepy sometimes, but seldom sad.'

'Then you have some secret hope to buoy you up and please you with whispers of the future?'

'Not I. The utmost I hope is, to save money enough out of my earnings to set up a school someday in a little house rented by myself.'

'A mean nutriment for the spirit to exist on: and sitting in that window-seat (you see I know your habits) – '

'You have learned them from the servants.'

'Ah! you think yourself sharp. Well, perhaps I have: to speak truth, I have an acquaintance with one of them, Mrs Poole – '

I started to my feet when I heard the name.

'You have – have you?' thought I; 'there is diablerie in the business after all, then!'

'Don't be alarmed,' continued the strange being; 'she's a safe hand is Mrs Poole: close and quiet; anyone may repose confidence in her. But, as I was saying: sitting in that window-seat, do you think of nothing but your future school? Have you no present interest in any of the company who occupy the sofas and chairs before you? Is there not one face you study? One figure whose movements you follow with at least curiosity?'

'I like to observe all the faces and all the figures.'

'But do you never single one from the rest – or it may be, two?'

'I do frequently; when the gestures or looks of a pair seem telling a tale: it amuses me to watch them.'

'What tale do you like best to hear?'

'Oh, I have not much choice! They generally run on the same theme – courtship; and promise to end in the same catastrophe – marriage.'

'And do you like that monotonous theme?'

'Positively, I don't care about it: it is nothing to me.'

'Nothing to you? When a lady, young and full of life and health, charming with beauty and endowed with the gifts of rank and fortune, sits and smiles in the eyes of a gentleman you –'

'I what?'

'You know – and perhaps think well of.'

'I don't know the gentlemen here. I have scarcely interchanged a syllable with one of them; and as to thinking well of them, I consider some respectable, and stately, and middle-aged, and others young, dashing, handsome, and lively: but certainly they are all at liberty to be the recipients of whose smiles they please, without my feeling disposed to consider the transaction of any moment to me.'

'You don't know the gentlemen here? You have not exchanged a syllable with one of them? Will you say that of the master of the house!'

'He is not at home.'

'A profound remark! A most ingenious quibble! He went to Millcote this morning, and will be back here tonight or tomorrow: does that circumstance exclude him from the list of your acquaintance – blot him, as it were, out of existence?'

'No; but I can scarcely see what Mr Rochester has to do with the theme you had introduced.

'I was talking of ladies smiling in the eyes of gentlemen; and of late so many smiles have been shed into Mr Rochester's eyes that they overflow like two cups filled above the brim: have you never remarked that?'

'Mr Rochester has a right to enjoy the society of his guests.'

'No question about his right: but have you never observed that, of all the tales told here about matrimony, Mr Rochester has been favoured with the most lively and the most continuous?'

'The eagerness of a listener quickens the tongue of a narrator.' I said this rather to myself than to the gypsy, whose strange talk, voice, manner, had by this time wrapped me in a kind of dream. One unexpected sentence came from her lips after another, till I got involved in a web of mystification; and wondered what unseen spirit had been sitting for weeks by my heart watching its workings and taking record of every pulse.

'Eagerness of a listener!' repeated she: 'yes; Mr Rochester has sat by the hour, his ear inclined to the fascinating lips that took such delight in their task of communicating; and Mr Rochester was so willing to receive and looked so grateful for the pastime given him; you have noticed this?'

'Grateful! I cannot remember detecting gratitude in his face.'

'Detecting! You have analysed, then. And what did you detect, if not gratitude?'

I said nothing.

'You have seen love: have you not? – and, looking forward, you have seen him married, and beheld his bride happy?'

'Humph! Not exactly. Your witch's skill is rather at fault sometimes.'

'What the devil have you seen, then?'

'Never mind: I came here to enquire, not to confess. Is it known that Mr Rochester is to be married?'

'Yes; and to the beautiful Miss Ingram.'

'Shortly?'

'Appearances would warrant that conclusion: and, no doubt (though, with an audacity that wants chastising out of you, you seem to question it), they will be a superlatively happy pair. He must love such a handsome, noble, witty, accomplished lady; and probably she loves him, or, if not his person, at least his purse. I know she considers the Rochester estate eligible to the last degree; though (God pardon me!) I told her something on that point about an hour ago which made her look wondrous grave: the corners of her mouth fell half an inch. I would advise her black-aviced suitor to look out: if another comes, with a longer or clearer rent-roll, he's dished – '

'But, mother, I did not come to hear Mr Rochester's fortune: I came to hear my own; and you have told me nothing of it.'

'Your fortune is yet doubtful: when I examined your face, one trait contradicted another. Chance has meted you a measure of happiness: that I know. I knew it before I came here this evening. She has laid it carefully on one side for you. I saw her do it. It depends on yourself to stretch out your hand, and take it up: but whether you will do so, is the problem I study. Kneel again on the rug.'

'Don't keep me long; the fire scorches me.'

I knelt. She did not stoop towards me, but only gazed, leaning back in her chair. She began muttering, 'The flame flickers in the eye; the eye shines like dew; it looks soft and full of feeling; it smiles at my jargon: it is susceptible; impression follows impression through its clear sphere; where it ceases to smile, it is sad; an unconscious lassitude weighs on the lid: that signifies melancholy resulting from loneliness. It turns from me; it will not suffer further scrutiny; it seems to deny, by a mocking glance, the truth of the discoveries I have already made, to disown the charge both of sensibility and chagrin: its pride and reserve only confirm me in my opinion. The eye is favourable.

'As to the mouth, it delights at times in laughter; it is disposed to impart all that the brain conceives; though I dare say it would be silent on much the heart experiences. Mobile and flexible, it was never intended to be compressed in the eternal silence of solitude; it is a mouth which should speak much and smile often, and have human affection for its interlocutor. That feature too is propitious.

'I see no enemy to a fortunate issue but in the brow; and that brow professes to say, "I can live alone, if self-respect and circumstances require me so to do. I need not sell my soul to buy bliss. I have an inward treasure born with me, which can keep me alive if all extraneous delights should be withheld, or offered only at a price I cannot afford to give." The forehead declares, "Reason sits firm and holds the reins, and she will not let the feelings burst away and hurry her to wild chasms. The passions may rage furiously, like true heathens, as they are; and the desires may imagine all sorts of vain things: but judgement shall still have the last word in every argument, and the casting vote in every

decision. Strong wind, earthquake-shock, and fire may pass by: but I shall follow the guiding of that still small voice which interprets the dictates of conscience."

'Well said, forehead; your declaration shall be respected. I have formed my plans – right plans I deem them – and in them I have attended to the claims of conscience, the counsels of reason. I know how soon youth would fade and bloom perish, if, in the cup of bliss offered, but one dreg of shame, or one flavour of remorse were detected; and I do not want sacrifice, sorrow, dissolution – such is not my taste. I wish to foster, not to blight – to earn gratitude, not to wring tears of blood – no, nor of brine: my harvest must be in smiles, in endearments, in sweet – That will do. I think I rave in a kind of exquisite delirium. I should wish now to protract this moment *ad infinitum*; but I dare not. So far I have governed myself thoroughly. I have acted as I inwardly swore I would act; but further might try me beyond my strength. Rise, Miss Eyre: leave me; "the play is played out." '

Where was I? Did I wake or sleep? Had I been dreaming? Did I dream still? The old woman's voice had changed: her accent, her gesture, and all were familiar to me as my own face in a glass – as the speech of my own tongue. I got up, but did not go. I looked; I stirred the fire, and I looked again: but she drew her bonnet and her bandage closer about her face, and again beckoned me to depart. The flame illuminated her hand stretched out: roused now, and on the alert for discoveries, I at once noticed that hand. It was no more the withered limb of eld than my own; it was a rounded supple member, with smooth fingers, symmetrically turned; a broad ring flashed on the little finger, and stooping forward, I looked at it, and saw a gem I had seen a hundred times before. Again I looked at the face; which was no longer turned from me – on the contrary, the bonnet was doffed, the bandage displaced, the head advanced.

'Well, Jane, do you know me?' asked the familiar voice.

'Only take off the red cloak, sir, and then – '

'But the string is in a knot – help me.'

'Break it, sir.'

'There, then – "Off, ye lendings!" ' And Mr Rochester stepped out of his disguise.

'Now, sir, what a strange idea!'

'But well carried out, eh? Don't you think so?'

'With the ladies you must have managed well.'

'But not with you?'

'You did not act the character of a gypsy with me.'

'What character did I act? My own?'

'No; some unaccountable one. In short, I believe you have been trying to draw me out – or in; you have been talking nonsense to make me talk nonsense. It is scarcely fair, sir.'

'Do you forgive me, Jane?'

'I cannot tell till I have thought it all over. If, on reflection, I find I have fallen into no great absurdity, I shall try to forgive you; but it was not right.'

'Oh, you have been very correct – very careful, very sensible.'

I reflected, and thought, on the whole, I had. It was a comfort; but, indeed, I had been on my guard almost from the beginning of the interview. Something of masquerade I suspected. I knew gypsies and fortune-tellers did not express themselves as this seeming old woman had expressed herself; besides I had noted her feigned voice, her anxiety to conceal her features. But my mind had been running on Grace Poole – that living enigma, that mystery of mysteries, as I considered her. I had never thought of Mr Rochester.

'Well,' said he, 'what are you musing about? What does that grave smile signify?'

'Wonder and self-congratulation, sir. I have your permission to retire now, I suppose?'

'No; stay a moment; and tell me what the people in the drawing-room yonder are doing.'

'Discussing the gypsy, I dare say.'

'Sit down! – Let me hear what they said about me.'

'I had better not stay long, sir; it must be near eleven o'clock. Oh, are you aware, Mr Rochester that a stranger has arrived here since you left this morning?'

'A stranger! – no; who can it be? I expected no one; is he gone?'

'No; he said he had known you long, and that he could take the liberty of installing himself here till you returned.'

'The devil he did! Did he give his name?'

'His name is Mason, sir; and he comes from the West Indies; from Spanish Town, in Jamaica, I think.'

Mr Rochester was standing near me; he had taken my hand, as if to lead me to a chair. As I spoke he gave my wrist a convulsive grip; the smile on his lips froze: apparently a spasm caught his breath.

'Mason! – the West Indies!' he said, in the tone one might fancy a speaking automaton to enounce its single words; 'Mason! – the West Indies!' he reiterated; and he went over the syllables three times, growing in the intervals of speaking, whiter than ashes: he hardly seemed to know what he was doing.

'Do you feel ill, sir?' I enquired.

'Jane, I've got a blow; I've got a blow, Jane!' He staggered.

'Oh, lean on me, sir.'

'Jane, you offered me your shoulder once before; let me have it now.'

'Yes, sir, yes; and my arm.'

He sat down, and made me sit beside him. Holding my hand in both his own, he chafed it; gazing on me, at the same time, with the most troubled and dreary look.

'My little friend!' said he, 'I wish I were in a quiet island with only you; and trouble, and danger, and hideous recollections removed from me.'

'Can I help you, sir? – I'd give my life to serve you.'

'Jane, if aid is wanted, I'll seek it at your hands; I promise you that.'

'Thank you, sir. Tell me what to do, I'll try, at least, to do it.'

'Fetch me now, Jane, a glass of wine from the dining-room: they will be at supper there; and tell me if Mason is with them, and what he is doing.'

I went. I found all the party in the dining-room at supper, as Mr Rochester had said; they were not seated at table, the supper was arranged on the sideboard; each had taken what he chose, and they stood about here and there in groups, their plates and glasses in their hands. Everyone seemed in high glee; laughter and conversation were general and animated. Mr Mason stood near the fire, talking to Colonel and Mrs Dent, and appeared as merry as any of them. I filled a wineglass (I saw Miss Ingram watch me frowningly as I did so: she thought I was taking a liberty, I dare say), and I returned to the library.

Mr Rochester's extreme pallor had disappeared, and he looked once more firm and stern. He took the glass from my hand.

'Here is to your health, ministrant spirit!' he said. He swallowed the contents and returned it to me. 'What are they doing, Jane?'

'Laughing and talking, sir.'

'They don't look grave and mysterious, as if they had heard something strange?'

'Not at all: they are full of jests and gaiety.'

'And Mason?'

'He was laughing too.'

'If all these people came in a body and spat at me, what would you do, Jane?'

'Turn them out of the room, sir, if I could.'

He half smiled. 'But if I were to go to them, and they only looked at me coldly, and whispered sneeringly amongst each other, and then dropped off and left me one by one, what then? Would you go with them?'

'I rather think not, sir: I should have more pleasure in staying with you.'

'To comfort me?'

'Yes, sir, to comfort you, as well as I could.'

'And if they laid you under a ban for adhering to me?'

'I, probably, should know nothing about their ban; and if I did, I should care nothing about it.'

'Then, you could dare censure for my sake?'

'I could dare it for the sake of any friend who deserved my adherence; as you, I am sure, do.'

'Go back now into the room; step quietly up to Mason, and whisper in his ear that Mr Rochester is come and wishes to see him: show him in here and then leave me.'

'Yes, sir.'

I did his behest. The company all stared at me as I passed straight among them. I sought Mr Mason, delivered the message, and preceded him from the room: I ushered him into the library, and then I went upstairs.

At a late hour, after I had been in bed some time, I heard the visitors repair to their chambers: I distinguished Mr Rochester's voice, and heard him say, 'This way, Mason; this is your room.'

He spoke cheerfully: the gay tones set my heart at ease. I was soon asleep.

I had forgotten to draw my curtain, which I usually did, and also to let down my window-blind. The consequence was, that when the moon, which was full and bright (for the night was fine), came in her course to that space in the sky opposite my casement, and looked in at me through the unveiled panes, her glorious gaze roused me. Awaking in the dead of night, I opened my eyes on her disk – silver-white and crystal clear. It was beautiful, but too solemn: I half rose, and stretched my arm to draw the curtain.

Good God! What a cry!

The night – its silence – its rest, was rent in twain by a savage, a sharp, a shrilly sound that ran from end to end of Thornfield Hall.

My pulse stopped: my heart stood still; my stretched arm was paralysed. The cry died, and was not renewed. Indeed, whatever being uttered that fearful shriek could not soon repeat it: not the widest-winged condor on the Andes could, twice in succession, send out such a yell from the cloud shrouding his eyrie. The thing delivering such utterance must rest ere it could repeat the effort.

It came out of the third storey; for it passed overhead. And overhead – yes, in the room just above my chamber-ceiling – I now heard a struggle: a deadly one it seemed from the noise; and a half-smothered voice shouted – 'Help! help! help!' three times rapidly.

'Will no one come?' it cried; and then, while the staggering and stamping went on wildly, I distinguished through plank and plaster: 'Rochester! Rochester! for God's sake, come!'

A chamber-door opened: someone ran, or rushed, along the gallery. Another step stamped on the flooring above and something fell; and there was silence.

I had put on some clothes, though horror shook all my limbs; I issued from my apartment. The sleepers were all aroused: ejaculations, terrified murmurs sounded in every room; door after door unclosed; one looked out and another looked out; the gallery filled. Gentlemen and ladies alike had quitted their beds; and 'Oh! what is it?' – 'Who is hurt?' – 'What has happened?' – 'Fetch a light!' – 'Is it fire?' – 'Are there robbers?' – 'Where shall we run?' was demanded confusedly on all hands. But for the moonlight they would have been in complete darkness. They ran to and fro; they crowded together: some sobbed, some stumbled: the confusion was inextricable.

'Where the devil is Rochester?' cried Colonel Dent. 'I cannot find him in his bed.'

'Here! here!' was shouted in return. 'Be composed, all of you: I'm coming.'

And the door at the end of the gallery opened, and Mr Rochester advanced with a candle: he had just descended from the upper storey. One of the ladies ran to him directly; she seized his arm: it was Miss Ingram.

'What awful event has taken place?' said she. 'Speak! let us know the worst at once!'

'But don't pull me down or strangle me,' he replied: for the Misses Eshton were clinging about him now; and the two dowagers, in vast white wrappers, were bearing down on him like ships in full sail.

'All's right! – all's right!' he cried. 'It's a mere rehearsal of *Much Ado about Nothing*. Ladies, keep off, or I shall wax dangerous.'

And dangerous he looked: his black eyes darted sparks. Calming himself by an effort, he added – 'A servant has had the nightmare; that is all. She's an excitable, nervous person: she construed her dream into an apparition, or something of that sort, no doubt; and has taken a fit with fright. Now, then, I must see you all back into your rooms; for, till the house is settled, she cannot be looked after. Gentlemen, have the goodness to set the ladies the example. Miss Ingram, I am sure you will not fail in evincing superiority to idle terrors. Amy and Louisa, return to your nests like a pair of doves, as you are. Mesdames' (to the dowagers), 'you will take cold to a dead certainty, if you stay in this chill gallery any longer.'

And so, by dint of alternate coaxing and commanding, he contrived to get them all once more enclosed in their separate dormitories. I did not wait to be ordered back to mine, but retreated unnoticed, as unnoticed I had left it.

Not, however, to go to bed: on the contrary, I began and dressed myself carefully. The sounds I had heard after the scream, and the words that had been uttered, had probably been heard only by me; for they had proceeded from the room above mine: but they assured me that it was not a servant's dream which had thus struck horror through the house; and that the explanation Mr Rochester had given was merely an invention framed to pacify his guests. I dressed, then, to be ready for emergencies. When dressed, I sat a long time by the window looking out over the silent grounds and silvered fields and waiting for I knew not what. It seemed to me that some event must follow the strange cry, struggle, and call.

No: stillness returned: each murmur and movement ceased gradually, and in about an hour Thornfield Hall was again as hushed as a desert. It seemed that sleep and night had resumed their empire. Meantime the moon declined: she was about to set. Not liking to sit in the cold and darkness, I thought I would lie down on my bed, dressed as I was. I left the window, and moved with little noise across the carpet; as I stooped to take off my shoes, a cautious hand tapped low at the door.

'Am I wanted?' I asked.

'Are you up?' asked the voice I expected to hear viz., my master's.

'Yes, sir.'

'And dressed?'

'Yes.'

'Come out, then, quietly.'

I obeyed. Mr Rochester stood in the gallery holding a light.

'I want you,' he said: 'come this way: take your time, and make no noise.'

My slippers were thin: I could walk the matted floor as softly as a cat. He

glided up the gallery and up the stairs, and stopped in the dark, low corridor of the fateful third storey: I had followed and stood at his side.

'Have you a sponge in your room?' he asked in a whisper.

'Yes, sir.'

'Have you any salts – volatile salts?'

'Yes.'

'Go back and fetch both.'

I returned, sought the sponge on the washstand, the salts in my drawer, and once more retraced my steps. He still waited; he held a key in his hand: approaching one of the small, black doors, he put it in the lock; he paused, and addressed me again.

'You don't turn sick at the sight of blood?'

'I think I shall not: I have never been tried yet.'

I felt a thrill while I answered him; but no coldness, and no faintness.

'Just give me your hand,' he said: 'it will not do to risk a fainting fit.'

I put my fingers into his. 'Warm and steady,' was his remark: he turned the key and opened the door.

I saw a room I remembered to have seen before, the day Mrs Fairfax showed me over the house: it was hung with tapestry; but the tapestry was now looped up in one part, and there was a door apparent, which had then been concealed. This door was open; a light shone out of the room within: I heard thence a snarling, snatching sound, almost like a dog quarrelling. Mr Rochester, putting down his candle, said to me, 'Wait a minute,' and he went forward to the inner apartment. A shout of laughter greeted his entrance; noisy at first, and terminating in Grace Poole's own goblin ha! ha! *She* then was there. He made some sort of arrangement without speaking, though I heard a low voice address him: he came out and closed the door behind him.

'Here, Jane!' he said; and I walked round to the other side of a large bed, which with its drawn curtains concealed a considerable portion of the chamber. An easy-chair was near the bed-head: a man sat in it, dressed with the exception of his coat; he was still; his head leant back; his eyes were closed. Mr Rochester held the candle over him; I recognised in his pale and seemingly lifeless face – the stranger, Mason: I saw too that his linen on one side and one arm was almost soaked in blood.

'Hold the candle,' said Mr Rochester, and I took it: he fetched a basin of water from the washstand: 'Hold that,' said he. I obeyed. He took the sponge; dipped it in, and moistened the corpse-like face; he asked for my smelling-bottle, and applied it to the nostrils. Mr Mason shortly unclosed his eyes; he groaned. Mr Rochester opened the shirt of the wounded man, whose arm and shoulder were bandaged: he sponged away blood, trickling fast down.

'Is there immediate danger?' murmured Mr Mason.

'Pooh! No – a mere scratch. Don't be so overcome, man: bear up! I'll fetch a surgeon for you now, myself: you'll be able to be removed by morning, I hope. Jane,' he continued.

'Sir?'

'I shall have to leave you in this room with this gentleman, for an hour, or perhaps two hours: you will sponge the blood as I do when it returns: if he feels faint, you will put the glass of water on that stand to his lips, and your salts to his nose. You will not speak to him on any pretext – and – Richard, it will be at the peril of your life if you speak to her: open your lips – agitate yourself – and I'll not answer for the consequences.'

Again the poor man groaned; he looked as if he dared not move; fear, either of death or of something else, appeared almost to paralyse him. Mr Rochester put the now bloody sponge into my hand, and I proceeded to use it as he had done. He watched me a second, then saying, 'Remember! – No conversation,' he left the room. I experienced a strange feeling as the key grated in the lock, and the sound of his retreating step ceased to be heard.

Here then I was in the third storey, fastened into one of its mystic cells; night around me; a pale and bloody spectacle under my eyes and hands; a murderess hardly separated from me by a single door: yes – that was appalling – the rest I could bear; but I shuddered at the thought of Grace Poole bursting out upon me.

I must keep to my post, however. I must watch this ghastly countenance – these blue, still lips forbidden to unclose – these eyes now shut, now opening, now wandering through the room, now fixing on me, and ever glazed with the dullness of horror. I must dip my hand again and again in the basin of blood and water, and wipe away the trickling gore. I must see the light of the unsnuffed candle wane on my employment; the shadows darken on the wrought, antique tapestry round me, and grow black under the hangings of the vast old bed, and quiver strangely over the doors of a great cabinet opposite – whose front, divided into twelve panels, bore, in grim design, the heads of the twelve apostles, each enclosed in its separate panel as in a frame; while above them at the top rose an ebon crucifix and a dying Christ.

According as the shifting obscurity and flickering gleam hovered here or glanced there, it was now the bearded physician, Luke, that bent his brow; now St John's long hair that waved; and anon the devilish face of Judas, that grew out of the panel, and seemed gathering life and threatening a revelation of the arch-traitor – of Satan himself – in his subordinate's form.

Amidst all this, I had to listen as well as watch: to listen for the movements of the wild beast or the fiend in yonder side den. But since Mr Rochester's visit it seemed spellbound: all the night I heard but three sounds at three long intervals, a step creak, a momentary renewal of the snarling, canine noise, and a deep human groan.

Then my own thoughts worried me. What crime was this, that lived incarnate in this sequestered mansion, and could neither be expelled nor subdued by the owner? – what mystery, that broke out now in fire and now in blood, at the deadest hours of night? What creature was it, that, masked in an ordinary woman's face and shape, uttered the voice, now of a mocking demon, and anon of a carrion-seeking bird of prey?

And this man I bent over – this commonplace, quiet stranger – how had he become involved in the web of horror? and why had the Fury flown at him?

What made him seek this quarter of the house at an untimely season, when he should have been asleep in bed? I had heard Mr Rochester assign him an apartment below – what brought him here? And why, now, was he so tame under the violence or treachery done him? Why did he so quietly submit to the concealment Mr Rochester enforced? Why *did* Mr Rochester enforce this concealment? His guest had been outraged, his own life on a former occasion had been hideously plotted against; and both attempts he smothered in secrecy and sank in oblivion! Lastly, I saw Mr Mason was submissive to Mr Rochester; that the impetuous will of the latter held complete sway over the inertness of the former: the few words which had passed between them assured me of this. It was evident that in their former intercourse, the passive disposition of the one had been habitually influenced by the active energy of the other: whence then had arisen Mr Rochester's dismay when he heard of Mr Mason's arrival? Why had the mere name of this unresisting individual – whom his word now sufficed to control like a child – fallen on him, a few hours since, as a thunderbolt might fall on an oak?

Oh! I could not forget his look and his paleness when he whispered: 'Jane, I have got a blow – I have got a blow, Jane.' I could not forget how the arm had trembled which he rested on my shoulder: and it was no light matter which could thus bow the resolute spirit and thrill the vigorous frame of Fairfax Rochester.

'When will he come? When will he come?' I cried inwardly, as the night lingered and lingered – as my bleeding patient drooped, moaned, sickened: and neither day nor aid arrived. I had, again and again, held the water to Mason's white lips; again and again offered him the stimulating salts: my efforts seemed ineffectual: either bodily or mental suffering, or loss of blood, or all three combined, were fast prostrating his strength. He moaned so, and looked so weak, wild, and lost, I feared he was dying; and I might not even speak to him.

The candle, wasted at last, went out; as it expired, I perceived streaks of grey light edging the window curtains: dawn was then approaching. Presently I heard Pilot bark far below, out of his distant kennel in the courtyard: hope revived. Nor was it unwarranted: in five minutes more the grating key, the yielding lock, warned me my watch was relieved. It could not have lasted more than two hours: many a week has seemed shorter.

Mr Rochester entered, and with him the surgeon he had been to fetch.

'Now, Carter, be on the alert,' he said to this last: 'I give you but half an hour for dressing the wound, fastening the bandages, getting the patient downstairs and all.'

'But is he fit to move, sir?'

'No doubt of it; it is nothing serious; he is nervous, his spirits must be kept up. Come, set to work.'

Mr Rochester drew back the thick curtain, drew up the holland blind, let in all the daylight he could; and I was surprised and cheered to see how far dawn was advanced: what rosy streaks were beginning to brighten the east. Then he approached Mason, whom the surgeon was already handling.

'Now, my good fellow, how are you?' he asked.

'She's done for me, I fear,' was the faint reply.

'Not a whit! – courage! This day fortnight you'll hardly be a pin the worse of it: you've lost a little blood; that's all. Carter, assure him there's no danger.'

'I can do that conscientiously,' said Carter, who had now undone the bandages; 'only I wish I could have got here sooner: he would not have bled so much – but how is this? The flesh on the shoulder is torn as well as cut. This wound was not done with a knife: there have been teeth here!'

'She bit me,' he murmured. 'She worried me like a tigress, when Rochester got the knife from her.'

'You should not have yielded: you should have grappled with her at once,' said Mr Rochester.

'But under such circumstances, what could one do?' returned Mason. 'Oh, it was frightful!' he added, shuddering. 'And I did not expect it: she looked so quiet at first.'

'I warned you,' was his friend's answer; 'I said – be on your guard when you go near her. Besides, you might have waited till tomorrow, and had me with you: it was mere folly to attempt the interview tonight, and alone.'

'I thought I could have done some good.'

'You thought! you thought! Yes, it makes me impatient to hear you: but, however, you have suffered, and are likely to suffer enough for not taking my advice; so I'll say no more. Carter – hurry! – hurry! The sun will soon rise, and I must have him off.'

'Directly, sir; the shoulder is just bandaged. I must look to this other wound in the arm: she has had her teeth here too, I think.'

'She sucked the blood: she said she'd drain my heart,' said Mason.

I saw Mr Rochester shudder: a singularly marked expression of disgust, horror, hatred, warped his countenance almost to distortion, but he only said – 'Come, be silent, Richard, and never mind her gibberish: don't repeat it.'

'I wish I could forget it,' was the answer.

'You will when you are out of the country: when you get back to Spanish Town, you may think of her as dead and buried – or rather, you need not think of her at all.'

'Impossible to forget this night!'

'It is not impossible: have some energy, man. You thought you were as dead as a herring two hours since, and you are all alive and talking now. There! – Carter has done with you or nearly so; I'll make you decent in a trice. Jane' (he turned to me for the first time since his re-entrance), 'take this key: go down into my bedroom, and walk straight forward into my dressing-room: open the top drawer of the wardrobe and take out a clean shirt and neck-handkerchief: bring them here; and be nimble.'

I went; sought the repository he had mentioned, found the articles named, and returned with them.

'Now,' said he, 'go to the other side of the bed while I order his toilet; but don't leave the room: you may be wanted again.'

I retired as directed.

'Was anybody stirring below when you went down, Jane?' enquired Mr Rochester presently.

'No, sir; all was very still.'

'We shall get you off cannily, Dick: and it will be better, both for your sake, and for that of the poor creature in yonder. I have striven long to avoid exposure, and I should not like it to come at last. Here, Carter, help him on with his waistcoat. Where did you leave your furred cloak? You can't travel a mile without that, I know, in this damned cold climate. In your room? – Jane, run down to Mr Mason's room, the one next mine, and fetch a cloak you will see there.'

Again I ran, and again returned, bearing an immense mantle lined and edged with fur.

'Now, I've another errand for you,' said my untiring master; 'you must away to my room again. What a mercy you are shod with velvet, Jane! – a clod-hopping messenger would never do at this juncture. You must open the middle drawer of my toilet-table and take out a little phial and a little glass you will find there, quick!'

I flew thither and back, bringing the desired vessels.

'That's well! Now, doctor, I shall take the liberty of administering a dose myself, on my own responsibility. I got this cordial at Rome, of an Italian charlatan – a fellow you would have kicked, Carter. It is no a thing to be used indiscriminately, but it is good upon occasion: as now, for instance. Jane, a little water.'

He held out the tiny glass, and I half-filled it from the water-bottle on the washstand.

'That will do; now wet the lip of the phial.'

I did so; he measured twelve drops of a crimson liquid, and presented it to Mason.

'Drink, Richard: it will give you the heart you lack for an hour or so.'

'But will it hurt me? – is it inflammatory?'

'Drink! drink! drink!'

Mr Mason obeyed, because it was evidently useless to resist. He was dressed now: he still looked pale, but he was no longer gory and sullied. Mr Rochester let him sit three minutes after he had swallowed the liquid; he then took his arm – 'Now I am sure you can get on your feet,' he said – 'try.'

The patient rose.

'Carter, take him under the other shoulder. Be of good cheer, Richard; step out – that's it!'

'I do feel better,' remarked Mr Mason.

'I am sure you do. Now, Jane, trip on before us away to the backstairs; unbolt the side-passage door, and tell the driver of the post-chaise you will see in the yard – or just outside, for I told him not to drive his rattling wheels over the pavement – to be ready; we are coming: and, Jane, if anyone is about, come to the foot of the stairs and hem.'

It was by this time half-past five, and the sun was on the point of rising; but I

found the kitchen still dark and silent. The side-passage door was fastened; I opened it with as little noise as possible: all the yard was quiet; but the gates stood wide open, and there was a post-chaise, with horses ready harnessed, and driver seated on the box, stationed outside. I approached him, and said the gentlemen were coming; he nodded: then I looked carefully round and listened. The stillness of early morning slumbered everywhere; the curtains were yet drawn over the servants' chamber windows; little birds were just twittering in the blossom-blanched orchard trees, whose boughs drooped like white garlands over the wall enclosing one side of the yard; the carriage horses stamped from time to time in their closed stables: all else was still.

The gentlemen now appeared. Mason, supported by Mr Rochester and the surgeon, seemed to walk with tolerable ease: they assisted him into the chaise; Carter followed.

'Take care of him,' said Mr Rochester to the latter, 'and keep him at your house till he is quite well: I shall ride over in a day or two to see how he gets on. Richard, how is it with you?'

'The fresh air revives me, Fairfax.'

'Leave the window open on his side, Carter; there is no wind – goodbye, Dick.'

'Fairfax – '

'Well, what is it?'

'Let her be taken care of; let her be treated as tenderly as may be: let her – ' he stopped and burst into tears.

'I do my best; and have done it, and will do it,' was the answer: he shut up the chaise door, and the vehicle drove away.

'Yet would to God there was an end of all this!' added Mr Rochester, as he closed and barred the heavy yard-gates.

This done, he moved with slow step and abstracted air towards a door in the wall bordering the orchard. I, supposing he had done with me, prepared to return to the house; again, however, I heard him call 'Jane!' He had opened the portal and stood at it, waiting for me.

'Come where there is some freshness, for a few moments,' he said; 'that house is a mere dungeon: don't you feel it so?'

'It seems to me a splendid mansion, sir.'

'The glamour of inexperience is over your eyes,' he answered; 'and you see it through a charmed medium: you cannot discern that the gilding is slime and the silk draperies cobwebs; that the marble is sordid slate, and the polished woods mere refuse chips and scaly bark. Now *here*' (he pointed to the leafy enclosure we had entered) 'all is real, sweet, and pure.'

He strayed down a walk edged with box, with apple trees, pear trees, and cherry trees on one side, and a border on the other full of all sorts of old-fashioned flowers, stocks, sweet-williams, primroses, pansies, mingled with southernwood, sweet-briar, and various fragrant herbs. They were fresh now as a succession of April showers and gleams, followed by a lovely spring morning, could make them: the sun was just entering the dappled east, and his light

illumined the wreathed and dewy orchard trees and shone down the quiet walks
under them.

'Jane, will you have a flower?'

He gathered a half-blown rose, the first on the bush, and offered it to me.

'Thank you, sir.'

'Do you like this sunrise, Jane? That sky with its high and light clouds which
are sure to melt away as the day waxes warm – this placid and balmy atmosphere?'

'I do, very much.'

'You have passed a strange night, Jane.'

'Yes, sir.'

'And it has made you look pale – were you afraid when I left you alone with
Mason?'

'I was afraid of someone coming out of the inner room.'

'But I had fastened the door – I had the key in my pocket: I should have been
a careless shepherd if I had left a lamb – my pet lamb – so near a wolf's den,
unguarded: you were safe.'

'Will Grace Poole live here still, sir?'

'Oh yes! don't trouble your head about her – put the thing out of your
thoughts.'

'Yet it seems to me your life is hardly secure while she stays.'

'Never fear – I will take care of myself.'

'Is the danger you apprehended last night gone by now, sir?'

'I cannot vouch for that till Mason is out of England: nor even then. To live,
for me, Jane, is to stand on a crater-crust which may crack and spew fire any day.'

'But Mr Mason seems a man easily led. Your influence, sir, is evidently potent
with him: he will never set you at defiance or wilfully injure you.'

'Oh no! Mason will not defy me; nor, knowing it, will he hurt me – but,
unintentionally, he might in a moment, by one careless word, deprive me, if not
of life, yet for ever of happiness.'

'Tell him to be cautious, sir: let him know what you fear, and show him how
to avert the danger.'

He laughed sardonically, hastily took my hand, and as hastily threw it from
him.

'If I could do that, simpleton, where would the danger be? Annihilated in a
moment. Ever since I have known Mason, I have only had to say to him "Do
that," and the thing has been done. But I cannot give him orders in this case: I
cannot say "Beware of harming me, Richard"; for it is imperative that I should
keep him ignorant that harm to me is possible. Now you look puzzled; and I will
puzzle you further. You are my little friend, are you not?'

'I like to serve you, sir, and to obey you in all that is right.'

'Precisely: I see you do. I see genuine contentment in your gait and mien, your
eye and face, when you are helping me and pleasing me – working for me, and
with me, in, as you characteristically say, "*all that is right*": for if I bid you do what
you thought wrong, there would be no light-footed running, no neat-handed
alacrity, no lively glance and animated complexion. My friend would then turn to

me, quiet and pale, and would say, "No, sir; that is impossible: I cannot do it, because it is wrong"; and would become immutable as a fixed star. Well, you too have power over me, and may injure me: yet I dare not show you where I am vulnerable, lest, faithful and friendly as you are, you should transfix me at once.'

'If you have no more to fear from Mr Mason than you have from me, sir, you are very safe.'

'God grant it may be so! Here, Jane, is an arbour; sit down.'

The arbour was an arch in the wall, lined with ivy; it contained a rustic seat. Mr Rochester took it, leaving room, however, for me: but I stood before him.

'Sit,' he said; 'the bench is long enough for two. You don't hesitate to take a place at my side, do you? Is that wrong, Jane?'

I answered him by assuming it: to refuse would, I felt, have been unwise.

'Now, my little friend, while the sun drinks the dew – while all the flowers in this old garden awake and expand, and the birds fetch their young ones' breakfast out of the Thornfield, and the early bees do their first spell of work – I'll put a case to you, which you must endeavour to suppose your own: but first, look at me, and tell me you are at ease, and not fearing that I err in detaining you, or that you err in staying.'

'No, sir; I am content.'

'Well then, Jane, call to aid your fancy: suppose you were no longer a girl well reared and disciplined, but a wild boy indulged from childhood upwards; imagine yourself in a remote foreign land; conceive that you there commit a capital error, no matter of what nature or from what motives, but one whose consequences must follow you through life and taint all your existence. Mind, I don't say a *crime*; I am not speaking of shedding of blood or any other guilty act, which might make the perpetrator amenable to the law: my word is *error*. The results of what you have done become in time to you utterly insupportable; you take measures to obtain relief: unusual measures, but neither unlawful nor culpable. Still you are miserable; for hope has quitted you on the very confines of life: your sun at noon darkens in an eclipse, which you feel will not leave it till the time of setting. Bitter and base associations have become the sole food of your memory: you wander here and there, seeking rest in exile: happiness in pleasure – I mean in heartless, sensual pleasure such as dulls intellect and blights feeling. Heart-weary and soul-withered, you come home after years of voluntary banishment: you make a new acquaintance – how or where no matter: you find in this stranger much of the good and bright qualities which you have sought for twenty years, and never before encountered; and they are all fresh, healthy, without soil and without taint. Such society revives, regenerates: you feel better days come back – higher wishes, purer feelings; you desire to recommence your life, and to spend what remains to you of days in a way more worthy of an immortal being. To attain this end, are you justified in overleaping an obstacle of custom – a mere conventional impediment which neither your conscience sanctifies nor your judgement approves?'

He paused for an answer: and what was I to say? Oh, for some good spirit to suggest a judicious and satisfactory response! Vain aspiration! The west wind

whispered in the ivy round me; but no gentle Ariel borrowed its breath as a medium of speech: the birds sang in the tree-tops; but their song, however sweet, was inarticulate.

Again Mr Rochester propounded his query: 'Is the wandering and sinful, but now rest-seeking and repentant, man justified in daring the world's opinion, in order to attach to him for ever this gentle, gracious, genial stranger, thereby securing his own peace of mind and regeneration of life?'

'Sir,' I answered, 'a wanderer's repose or a sinner's reformation should never depend on a fellow-creature. Men and women die; philosophers falter in wisdom, and Christians in goodness: if anyone you know has suffered and erred, let him look higher than his equals for strength to amend and solace to heal.'

'But the instrument – the instrument! God, who does the work, ordains the instrument. I have myself – I tell it you without parable – been a worldly, dissipated, restless man; and I believe I have found the instrument for my cure in –'

He paused: the birds went on carolling, the leaves lightly rustling. I almost wondered they did not check their songs and whispers to catch the suspended revelation; but they would have had to wait many minutes – so long was the silence protracted. At last I looked up at the tardy speaker: he was looking eagerly at me.

'Little friend,' said he, in quite a changed tone – while his face changed too, losing all its softness and gravity, and becoming harsh and sarcastic – 'you have noticed my tender penchant for Miss Ingram: don't you think if I married her she would regenerate me with a vengeance?'

He got up instantly, went quite to the other end of the walk, and when he came back he was humming a tune.

'Jane, Jane,' said he, stopping before me, 'you are quite pale with your vigils: don't you curse me for disturbing your rest?'

'Curse you? No, sir.'

'Shake hands in confirmation of the word. What cold fingers! They were warmer last night when I touched them at the door of the mysterious chamber. Jane, when will you watch with me again?'

'Whenever I can be useful, sir.'

'For instance, the night before I am married! I am sure I shall not be able to sleep. Will you promise to sit up with me to bear me company? To you I can talk of my lovely one: for now you have seen her and know her.'

'Yes, sir.'

'She's a rare one, is she not, Jane?'

'Yes, sir.'

'A strapper – a real strapper, Jane: big, brown, and buxom; with hair just such as the ladies of Carthage must have had. Bless me! there's Dent and Lynn in the stables! Go in by the shrubbery, through that wicket.'

As I went one way, he went another, and I heard him in the yard, saying cheerfully – 'Mason got the start of you all this morning; he was gone before sunrise: I rose at four to see him off.'

## Chapter 21

Presentiments are strange things! and so are sympathies; and so are signs; and the three combined make one mystery to which humanity has not yet found the key. I never laughed at presentiments in my life, because I have had strange ones of my own. Sympathies, I believe, exist (for instance, between far-distant, long-absent, wholly estranged relatives asserting, notwithstanding their alienation, the unity of the source to which each traces his origin) whose workings baffle mortal comprehension. And signs, for aught we know, may be but the sympathies of Nature with man.

When I was a little girl, only six years old, I one night heard Bessie Leaven say to Martha Abbot that she had been dreaming about a little child; and that to dream of children was a sure sign of trouble, either to oneself or one's kin. The saying might have worn out of my memory, had not a circumstance immediately followed which served indelibly to fix it there. The next day Bessie was sent for home to the deathbed of her little sister.

Of late I had often recalled this saying and this incident; for during the past week scarcely a night had gone over my couch that had not brought with it a dream of an infant, which I sometimes hushed in my arms, sometimes dandled on my knee, sometimes watched playing with daisies on a lawn, or again, dabbling its hands in running water. It was a wailing child this night, and a laughing one the next: now it nestled close to me, and now it ran from me; but whatever mood the apparition evinced, whatever aspect it wore, it failed not for seven successive nights to meet me the moment I entered the land of slumber.

I did not like this iteration of one idea – this strange recurrence of one image, and I grew nervous as bedtime approached and the hour of the vision drew near. It was from companionship with this baby-phantom I had been roused on that moonlight night when I heard the cry; and it was on the afternoon of the day following I was summoned downstairs by a message that someone wanted me in Mrs Fairfax's room. On repairing thither, I found a man waiting for me, having the appearance of a gentleman's servant: he was dressed in deep mourning, and the hat he held in his hand was surrounded with a crape band.

'I dare say you hardly remember me, Miss,' he said, rising as I entered; 'but my name is Leaven: I lived coachman with Mrs Reed when you were at Gateshead, eight or nine years since, and I live there still.'

'Oh, Robert! how do you do? I remember you very well: you used to give me a ride sometimes on Miss Georgiana's bay pony. And how is Bessie? You are married to Bessie?'

'Yes, Miss: my wife is very hearty, thank you; she brought me another little one about two months since – we have three now – and both mother and child are thriving.'

'And are the family well at the house, Robert?'

'I am sorry I can't give you better news of them, Miss: they are very badly at present – in great trouble.'

'I hope no one is dead,' I said, glancing at his black dress. He too looked down at the crape round his hat and replied – 'Mr John died yesterday was a week, at his chambers in London.'

'Mr John?'

'Yes.'

'And how does his mother bear it?'

'Why, you see, Miss Eyre, it is not a common mishap: his life has been very wild: these last three years he gave himself up to strange ways, and his death was shocking.'

'I heard from Bessie he was not doing well.'

'Doing well! He could not do worse: he ruined his health and his estate amongst the worst men and the worst women. He got into debt and into jail: his mother helped him out twice, but as soon as he was free he returned to his old companions and habits. His head was not strong: the knaves he lived amongst fooled him beyond anything I ever heard. He came down to Gateshead about three weeks ago and wanted missis to give up all to him. Missis refused: her means have long been much reduced by his extravagance; so he went back again, and the next news was that he was dead. How he died, God knows! – they say he killed himself.'

I was silent: the tidings were frightful. Robert Leaven resumed – 'Missis had been out of health herself for some time: she had got very stout, but was not strong with it; and the loss of money and fear of poverty were quite breaking her down. The information about Mr John's death and the manner of it came too suddenly: it brought on a stroke. She was three days without speaking; but last Tuesday she seemed rather better: she appeared as if she wanted to say something, and kept making signs to my wife and mumbling. It was only yesterday morning, however, that Bessie understood she was pronouncing your name; and at last she made out the words, "Bring Jane – fetch Jane Eyre: I want to speak to her." Bessie is not sure whether she is in her right mind, or means anything by the words; but she told Miss Reed and Miss Georgiana, and advised them to send for you. The young ladies put it off at first; but their mother grew so restless, and said, "Jane, Jane," so many times, that at last they consented. I left Gateshead yesterday: and if you can get ready, Miss, I should like to take you back with me early tomorrow morning.'

'Yes, Robert, I shall be ready: it seems to me that I ought to go.'

'I think so too, Miss. Bessie said she was sure you would not refuse: but I suppose you will have to ask leave before you can get off?'

'Yes; and I will do it now'; and having directed him to the servants' hall, and recommended him to the care of John's wife, and the attentions of John himself, I went in search of Mr Rochester.

He was not in any of the lower rooms; he was not in the yard, the stables, or the grounds. I asked Mrs Fairfax if she had seen him; yes: she believed he was playing billiards with Miss Ingram. To the billiard-room I hastened: the click of balls and the hum of voices resounded thence; Mr Rochester, Miss Ingram, the

two Misses Eshton, and their admirers, were all busied in the game. It required some courage to disturb so interesting a party; my errand, however, was one I could not defer, so I approached the master where he stood at Miss Ingram's side. She turned as I drew near, and looked at me haughtily: her eyes seemed to demand, 'What can the creeping creature want now?' and when I said, in a low voice, 'Mr Rochester,' she made a movement as if tempted to order me away. I remember her appearance at the moment – it was very graceful and very striking: she wore a morning robe of sky-blue crape; a gauzy azure scarf was twisted in her hair. She had been all animation with the game, and irritated pride did not lower the expression of her haughty lineaments.

'Does that person want you?' she enquired of Mr Rochester; and Mr Rochester turned to see who the 'person' was. He made a curious grimace – one of his strange and equivocal demonstrations – threw down his cue and followed me from the room.

'Well, Jane?' he said, as he rested his back against the schoolroom door, which he had shut.

'If you please, sir, I want leave of absence for a week or two.'

'What to do? – where to go?'

'To see a sick lady who has sent for me.'

'What sick lady? – where does she live?'

'At Gateshead, in —shire.'

'—shire? That is a hundred miles off! Who may she be that sends for people to see her that distance?'

'Her name is Reed, sir – Mrs Reed.'

'Reed of Gateshead? There was a Reed of Gateshead, a magistrate.'

'It is his widow, sir.'

'And what have you to do with her? How do you know her?'

'Mr Reed was my uncle – my mother's brother.'

'The deuce he was! You never told me that before: you always said you had no relations.'

'None that would own me, sir. Mr Reed is dead, and his wife cast me off.'

'Why?'

'Because I was poor, and burdensome, and she disliked me.'

'But Reed left children? – you must have cousins? Sir George Lynn was talking of a Reed of Gateshead yesterday, who, he said, was one of the veriest rascals on town; and Ingram was mentioning a Georgiana Reed of the same place, who was much admired for her beauty a season or two ago in London.'

'John Reed is dead, too, sir: he ruined himself and half-ruined his family, and is supposed to have committed suicide. The news so shocked his mother that it brought on an apoplectic attack.'

'And what good can you do her? Nonsense, Jane! I would never think of running a hundred miles to see an old lady who will, perhaps, be dead before you reach her: besides, you say she cast you off.'

'Yes, sir, but that is long ago; and when her circumstances were very different: I could not be easy to neglect her wishes now.'

'How long will you stay?'

'As short a time as possible, sir.'

'Promise me only to stay a week – '

'I had better not pass my word: I might be obliged to break it.'

'At all events you *will* come back: you will not be induced under any pretext to take up a permanent residence with her?'

'Oh, no! I shall certainly return if all be well.'

'And who goes with you? You don't travel a hundred miles alone.'

'No, sir, she has sent her coachman.'

'A person to be trusted?'

'Yes, sir, he has lived ten years in the family.'

Mr Rochester meditated. 'When do you wish to go?'

'Early tomorrow morning, sir.'

'Well, you must have some money; you can't travel without money, and I dare say you have not much: I have given you no salary yet. How much have you in the world, Jane?' he asked, smiling.

I drew out my purse; a meagre thing it was. 'Five shillings, sir.' He took the purse, poured the hoard into his palm, and chuckled over it as if its scantiness amused him. Soon he produced his pocket-book: 'Here,' said he, offering me a note; it was fifty pounds, and he owed me but fifteen. I told him I had no change.

'I don't want change; you know that. Take your wages.'

I declined accepting more than was my due. He scowled at first; then, as if recollecting something, he said – 'Right, right! Better not give you all now: you would, perhaps, stay away three months if you had fifty pounds. There are ten; is it not plenty?'

'Yes, sir, but now you owe me five.'

'Come back for it, then; I am your banker for forty pounds.'

'Mr Rochester, I may as well mention another matter of business to you while I have the opportunity.'

'Matter of business? I am curious to hear it.'

'You have as good as informed me, sir, that you are going shortly to be married?'

'Yes; what then?'

'In that case, sir, Adèle ought to go to school: I am sure you will perceive the necessity of it.'

'To get her out of my bride's way, who might otherwise walk over her rather too emphatically? There's sense in the suggestion; not a doubt of it. Adèle, as you say, must go to school; and you, of course, must march straight to – the devil?'

'I hope not, sir; but I must seek another situation somewhere.'

'In course!' he exclaimed, with a twang of voice and a distortion of features equally fantastic and ludicrous. He looked at me some minutes.

'And old Madam Reed, or the Misses, her daughters, will be solicited by you to seek a place, I suppose?'

'No, sir; I am not on such terms with my relatives as would justify me in asking favours of them – but I shall advertise.'

'You shall walk up the pyramids of Egypt!' he growled. 'At your peril you advertise! I wish I had only offered you a sovereign instead of ten pounds. Give me back nine pounds, Jane; I've a use for it.'

'And so have I, sir,' I returned, putting my hands and my purse behind me. 'I could not spare the money on any account.'

'Little niggard!' said he, 'refusing me a pecuniary request! Give me five pounds, Jane.'

'Not five shillings, sir; nor five pence.'

'Just let me look at the cash.'

'No, sir; you are not to be trusted.'

'Jane!'

'Sir?'

'Promise me one thing.'

'I'll promise you anything, sir, that I think I am likely to perform.'

'Not to advertise: and to trust this quest of a situation to me. I'll find you one in time.'

'I shall be glad so to do, sir, if you, in your turn, will promise that I and Adèle shall be both safe out of the house before your bride enters it.'

'Very well! very well! I'll pledge my word on it. You go tomorrow, then?'

'Yes, sir; early.'

'Shall you come down to the drawing-room after dinner?'

'No, sir, I must prepare for the journey.'

'Then you and I must bid goodbye for a little while?'

'I suppose so, sir.'

'And how do people perform that ceremony of parting, Jane? Teach me; I'm not quite up to it.'

'They say, Farewell, or any other form they prefer.'

'Then say it.'

'Farewell, Mr Rochester, for the present.'

'What must I say?'

'The same, if you like, sir.'

'Farewell, Miss Eyre, for the present; is that all?'

'Yes?'

'It seems stingy, to my notions, and dry, and unfriendly. I should like something else: a little addition to the rite. If one shook hands, for instance; but no – that would not content me either. So you'll do no more than say Farewell, Jane?'

'It is enough, sir: as much goodwill may be conveyed in one hearty word as in many.'

'Very likely; but it is blank and cool – "Farewell." '

'How long is he going to stand with his back against that door?' I asked myself; 'I want to commence my packing.' The dinner-bell rang, and suddenly away he bolted, without another syllable: I saw him no more during the day, and was off before he had risen in the morning.

I reached the lodge at Gateshead about five o'clock in the afternoon of the first of May: I stepped in there before going up to the hall. It was very clean and

neat: the ornamental windows were hung with little white curtains; the floor was spotless; the grate and fire-irons were burnished bright, and the fire burnt clear. Bessie sat on the hearth, nursing her last-born, and Robert and his sister played quietly in a corner.

'Bless you! – I knew you would come!' exclaimed Mrs Leaven, as I entered.

'Yes, Bessie,' said I, after I had kissed her; 'and I trust I am not too late. How is Mrs Reed? – Alive still, I hope.'

'Yes, she is alive; and more sensible and collected than she was. The doctor says she may linger a week or two yet; but he hardly thinks she will finally recover.'

'Has she mentioned me lately?'

'She was talking of you only this morning, and wishing you would come: but she is sleeping now, or was ten minutes ago, when I was up at the house. She generally lies in a kind of lethargy all the afternoon, and wakes up about six or seven. Will you rest yourself here an hour, Miss, and then I will go up with you?'

Robert here entered, and Bessie laid her sleeping child in the cradle and went to welcome him: afterwards she insisted on my taking off my bonnet and having some tea; for she said I looked pale and tired. I was glad to accept her hospitality; and I submitted to be relieved of my travelling garb just as passively as I used to let her undress me when a child.

Old times crowded fast back on me as I watched her bustling about – setting out the tea-tray with her best china, cutting bread and butter, toasting a teacake, and, between whiles, giving little Robert or Jane an occasional tap or push, just as she used to give me in former days. Bessie had retained her quick temper as well as her light foot and good looks.

Tea ready, I was going to approach the table; but she desired me to sit still, quite in her old peremptory tones. I must be served at the fireside, she said; and she placed before me a little round stand with my cup and a plate of toast, absolutely as she used to accommodate me with some privately purloined dainty on a nursery chair: and I smiled and obeyed her as in bygone days.

She wanted to know if I was happy at Thornfield Hall, and what sort of a person the mistress was; and when I told her there was only a master, whether he was a nice gentleman, and if I liked him. I told her he was rather an ugly man, but quite a gentleman; and that he treated me kindly, and I was content. Then I went on to describe to her the gay company that had lately been staying at the house; and to these details Bessie listened with interest: they were precisely of the kind she relished.

In such conversation an hour was soon gone: Bessie restored to me my bonnet, etc., and, accompanied by her, I quitted the lodge for the hall. It was also accompanied by her that I had, nearly nine years ago, walked down the path I was now ascending. On a dark, misty, raw morning in January, I had left a hostile roof with a desperate and embittered heart – a sense of outlawry and almost of reprobation – to seek the chilly harbourage of Lowood: that bourne so far away and unexplored. The same hostile roof now again rose before me: my prospects were doubtful yet; and I had yet an aching heart. I still felt as a wanderer on the

face of the earth; but I experienced firmer trust in myself and my own powers, and less withering dread of oppression. The gaping wound of my wrongs, too, was now quite healed; and the flame of resentment extinguished.

'You shall go into the breakfast-room first,' said Bessie, as she preceded me through the hall; 'the young ladies will be there.'

In another moment I was within that apartment. There was every article of furniture looking just as it did on the morning I was first introduced to Mr Brocklehurst: the very rug he had stood upon still covered the hearth. Glancing at the bookcases, I thought I could distinguish the two volumes of Bewick's *British Birds* occupying their old place on the third shelf, and *Gulliver's Travels* and the *Arabian Nights* ranged just above. The inanimate objects were not changed; but the living things had altered past recognition.

Two young ladies appeared before me; one very tall, almost as tall as Miss Ingram – very thin too, with a sallow face and severe mien. There was something ascetic in her look, which was augmented by the extreme plainness of a straight-skirted, black, stuff dress, a starched linen collar, hair combed away from the temples, and the nun-like ornament of a string of ebony beads and a crucifix. This I felt sure was Eliza, though I could trace little resemblance to her former self in that elongated and colourless visage.

The other was as certainly Georgiana: but not the Georgiana I remembered – the slim and fairy-like girl of eleven. This was a full-blown, very plump damsel, fair as waxwork, with handsome and regular features, languishing blue eyes, and ringleted yellow hair. The hue of her dress was black too; but its fashion was so different from her sister's – so much more flowing and becoming – it looked as stylish as the other's looked puritanical.

In each of the sisters there was one trait of the mother – and only one; the thin and pallid elder daughter had her parent's Cairngorm eye: the blooming and luxuriant younger girl had her contour of jaw and chin – perhaps a little softened, but still imparting an indescribable hardness to the countenance, otherwise so voluptuous and buxom.

Both ladies, as I advanced, rose to welcome me, and both addressed me by the name of 'Miss Eyre'. Eliza's greeting was delivered in a short, abrupt voice, without a smile; and then she sat down again, fixed her eyes on the fire, and seemed to forget me. Georgiana added to her 'How d'ye do?' several commonplaces about my journey, the weather, and so on, uttered in rather a drawling tone: and accompanied by sundry side-glances that measured me from head to foot – now traversing the folds of my drab merino pelisse, and now lingering on the plain trimming of my cottage bonnet. Young ladies have a remarkable way of letting you know that they think you a 'quiz' without actually saying the words. A certain superciliousness of look, coolness of manner, nonchalance of tone, express fully their sentiments on the point, without committing them by any positive rudeness in word or deed.

A sneer, however, whether covert or open, had now no longer that power over me it once possessed: as I sat between my cousins, I was surprised to find how easy I felt under the total neglect of the one and the semi-sarcastic

attentions of the other – Eliza did not mortify, nor Georgiana ruffle me. The fact was, I had other things to think about; within the last few months feelings had been stirred in me so much more potent than any they could raise – pains and pleasures so much more acute and exquisite had been excited than any it was in their power to inflict or bestow – that their airs gave me no concern either for good or bad.

'How is Mrs Reed?' I asked soon, looking calmly at Georgiana, who thought fit to bridle at the direct address, as if it were an unexpected liberty.

'Mrs Reed? Ah! mama, you mean; she is extremely poorly: I doubt if you can see her tonight.'

'If,' said I, 'you would just step upstairs and tell her I am come, I should be much obliged to you.'

Georgiana almost started, and she opened her blue eyes wild and wide. 'I know she had a particular wish to see me,' I added, 'and I would not defer attending to her desire longer than is absolutely necessary.'

'Mama dislikes being disturbed in an evening,' remarked Eliza. I soon rose, quietly took off my bonnet and gloves, uninvited, and said I would just step out to Bessie – who was, I dared say, in the kitchen – and ask her to ascertain whether Mrs Reed was disposed to receive me or not tonight. I went, and having found Bessie and despatched her on my errand, I proceeded to take further measures. It had heretofore been my habit always to shrink from arrogance: received as I had been today, I should, a year ago, have resolved to quit Gateshead the very next morning; now, it was disclosed to me all at once that that would be a foolish plan. I had taken a journey of a hundred miles to see my aunt, and I must stay with her till she was better – or dead: as to her daughters' pride or folly, I must put it on one side, make myself independent of it. So I addressed the housekeeper; asked her to show me a room, told her I should probably be a visitor here for a week or two, had my trunk conveyed to my chamber, and followed it thither my self: I met Bessie on the landing.

'Missis is awake,' said she; 'I have told her you are here: come and let us see if she will know you.'

I did not need to be guided to the well-known room, to which I had so often been summoned for chastisement or reprimand in former days. I hastened before Bessie; I softly opened the door: a shaded light stood on the table, for it was now getting dark. There was the great four-post bed with amber hangings as of old; there the toilet-table, the armchair, and the footstool, at which I had a hundred times been sentenced to kneel, to ask pardon for offences by me uncommitted. I looked into a certain corner near, half expecting to see the slim outline of a once dreaded switch which used to lurk there, waiting to leap out imp-like and lace my quivering palm or shrinking neck. I approached the bed; I opened the curtains and leant over the high-piled pillows.

Well did I remember Mrs Reed's face, and I eagerly sought the familiar image. It is a happy thing that time quells the longings of vengeance and hushes the promptings of rage and aversion. I had left this woman in bitterness and hate, and I came back to her now with no other emotion than a sort of ruth for her

great sufferings, and a strong yearning to forget and forgive all injuries – to be reconciled and clasp hands in amity.

The well-known face was there: stern, relentless as ever – there was that peculiar eye which nothing could melt, and the somewhat raised, imperious, despotic eyebrow. How often had it lowered on me menace and hate! and how the recollection of childhood's terrors and sorrows revived as I traced its harsh line now! And yet I stooped down and kissed her: she looked at me.

'Is this Jane Eyre?' she said.

'Yes, Aunt Reed. How are you, dear aunt?'

I had once vowed that I would never call her aunt again: I thought it no sin to forget and break that vow now. My fingers had fastened on her hand which lay outside the sheet: had she pressed mine kindly, I should at that moment have experienced true pleasure. But unimpressionable natures are not so soon softened, nor are natural antipathies so readily eradicated. Mrs Reed took her hand away, and, turning her face rather from me, she remarked that the night was warm. Again she regarded me so icily, I felt at once that her opinion of me – her feeling towards me – was unchanged and unchangeable. I knew by her stony eye – opaque to tenderness, indissoluble to tears – that she was resolved to consider me bad to the last; because to believe me good would give her no generous pleasure: only a sense of mortification.

I felt pain, and then I felt ire; and then I felt a determination to subdue her – to be her mistress in spite both of her nature and her will. My tears had risen, just as in childhood: I ordered them back to their source. I brought a chair to the bed-head: I sat down and leaned over the pillow.

'You sent for me,' I said, 'and I am here; and it is my intention to stay till I see how you get on.'

'Oh, of course! You have seen my daughters?'

'Yes.'

'Well, you may tell them I wish you to stay till I can talk some things over with you I have on my mind: tonight it is too late, and I have a difficulty in recalling them. But there was something I wished to say – let me see – '

The wandering look and changed utterance told what wreck had taken place in her once vigorous frame. Turning restlessly, she drew the bedclothes round her; my elbow, resting on a corner of the quilt, fixed it down: she was at once irritated.

'Sit up!' said she; 'don't annoy me with holding the clothes fast. Are you Jane Eyre?'

'I am Jane Eyre.'

'I have had more trouble with that child than anyone would believe. Such a burden to be left on my hands – and so much annoyance as she caused me, daily and hourly, with her incomprehensible disposition, and her sudden starts of temper, and her continual, unnatural watchings of one's movements! I declare she talked to me once like something mad, or like a fiend – no child ever spoke or looked as she did; I was glad to get her away from the house. What did they do with her at Lowood? The fever broke out there, and many of the pupils died. She, however, did not die: but I said she did – I wish she had died!'

'A strange wish, Mrs Reed; why do you hate her so?'

'I had a dislike to her mother always; for she was my husband's only sister, and a great favourite with him: he opposed the family's disowning her when she made her low marriage; and when news came of her death, he wept like a simpleton. He would send for the baby; though I entreated him rather to put it out to nurse and pay for its maintenance. I hated it the first time I set my eyes on it – a sickly, whining pining thing! It would wail in its cradle all night long – not screaming heartily like any other child, but whimpering and moaning. Reed pitied it; and he used to nurse it and notice it as if it had been his own: more, indeed, than he ever noticed his own at that age. He would try to make my children friendly to the little beggar: the darlings could not bear it, and he was angry with them when they showed their dislike. In his last illness, he had it brought continually to his bedside; and but an hour before he died, he bound me by vow to keep the creature. I would as soon have been charged with a pauper brat out of a workhouse: but he was weak, naturally weak. John does not at all resemble his father, and I am glad of it: John is like me and like my brothers – he is quite a Gibson. Oh, I wish he would cease tormenting me with letters for money? I have no more money to give him: we are getting poor. I must send away half the servants and shut up part of the house; or let it off. I can never submit to do that – yet how are we to get on? Two-thirds of my income goes in paying the interest of mortgages. John gambles dreadfully, and always loses – poor boy! He is beset by sharpers: John is sunk and degraded – his look is frightful – I feel ashamed for him when I see him.'

She was getting much excited. 'I think I had better leave her now,' said I to Bessie, who stood on the other side of the bed.

'Perhaps you had, Miss: but she often talks in this way towards night – in the morning she is calmer.'

I rose. 'Stop!' exclaimed Mrs Reed, 'there is another thing I wished to say. He threatens me – he continually threatens me with his own death, or mine: and I dream sometimes that I see him laid out with a great wound in his throat, or with a swollen and blackened face. I am come to a strange pass: I have heavy troubles. What is to be done? How is the money to be had?'

Bessie now endeavoured to persuade her to take a sedative draught: she succeeded with difficulty. Soon after, Mrs Reed grew more composed, and sank into a dozing state. I then left her.

More than ten days elapsed before I had again any conversation with her. She continued either delirious or lethargic; and the doctor forbade everything which could painfully excite her. Meantime, I got on as well as I could with Georgiana and Eliza. They were very cold, indeed, at first. Eliza would sit half the day sewing, reading, or writing, and scarcely utter a word either to me or her sister. Georgiana would chatter nonsense to her canary bird by the hour, and take no notice of me. But I was determined not to seem at a loss for occupation or amusement: I had brought my drawing materials with me, and they served me for both.

Provided with a case of pencils, and some sheets of paper, I used to take a seat

apart from them, near the window, and busy myself in sketching fancy vignettes, representing any scene that happened momentarily to shape itself in the ever-shifting kaleidoscope of imagination: a glimpse of sea between two rocks; the rising moon, and a ship crossing its disk; a group of reeds and water-flags, and a naiad's head, crowned with lotus-flowers, rising out of them; an elf sitting in a hedge-sparrow's nest, under a wreath of hawthorn-bloom.

One morning I fell to sketching a face: what sort of a face it was to be, I did not care or know. I took a soft black pencil, gave it a broad point, and worked away. Soon I had traced on the paper a broad and prominent forehead and a square lower outline of visage: that contour gave me pleasure; my fingers proceeded actively to fill it with features. Strongly-marked horizontal eyebrows must be traced under that brow; then followed, naturally, a well-defined nose, with a straight ridge and full nostrils; then a flexible-looking mouth, by no means narrow; then a firm chin, with a decided cleft down the middle of it: of course, some black whiskers were wanted, and some jetty hair, tufted on the temples, and waved above the forehead. Now for the eyes: I had left them to the last, because they required the most careful working. I drew them large; I shaped them well: the eyelashes I traced long and sombre; the irids lustrous and large. 'Good! but not quite the thing,' I thought, as I surveyed the effect: 'they want more force and spirit'; and I wrought the shades blacker, that the lights might flash more brilliantly – a happy touch or two secured success. There, I had a friend's face under my gaze; and what did it signify that those young ladies turned their backs on me? I looked at it; I smiled at the speaking likeness: I was absorbed and content.

'Is that a portrait of someone you know?' asked Eliza, who had approached me unnoticed. I responded that it was merely a fancy head, and hurried it beneath the other sheets. Of course, I lied: it was, in fact, a very faithful representation of Mr Rochester. But what was that to her, or to anyone but myself? Georgiana also advanced to look. The other drawings pleased her much, but she called that 'an ugly man.' They both seemed surprised at my skill. I offered to sketch their portraits; and each, in turn, sat for a pencil outline. Then Georgiana produced her album. I promised to contribute a water-colour drawing: this put her at once into good humour. She proposed a walk in the grounds. Before we had been out two hours, we were deep in a confidential conversation: she had favoured me with a description of the brilliant winter she had spent in London two seasons ago – of the admiration she had there excited – the attention she had received; and I even got hints of the titled conquest she had made. In the course of the afternoon and evening these hints were enlarged on: various soft conversations were reported, and sentimental scenes represented; and, in short, a volume of a novel of fashionable life was that day improvised by her for my benefit. The communications were renewed from day to day: they always ran on the same theme – herself, her loves, and woes. It was strange she never once adverted either to her mother's illness, or her brother's death, or the present gloomy state of the family prospects. Her mind seemed wholly taken up with reminiscences of past gaiety, and aspirations after dissipations to come. She passed about five minutes each day in her mother's sick-room, and no more.

Eliza still spoke little: she had evidently no time to talk. I never saw a busier person than she seemed to be; yet it was difficult to say what she did: or rather, to discover any result of her diligence. She had an alarm to call her up early. I know not how she occupied herself before breakfast, but after that meal she divided her time into regular portions, and each hour had its allotted task. Three times a day she studied a little book, which I found, on inspection, was a Common Prayer Book. I asked her once what was the great attraction of that volume, and she said, 'The Rubric.' Three hours she gave to stitching, with gold thread, the border of a square crimson cloth, almost large enough for a carpet. In answer to my enquiries after the use of this article, she informed me it was a covering for the altar of a new church lately erected near Gateshead. Two hours she devoted to her diary; two to working by herself in the kitchen-garden; and one to the regulation of her accounts. She seemed to want no company; no conversation. I believe she was happy in her way: this routine sufficed for her; and nothing annoyed her so much as the occurrence of any incident which forced her to vary its clockwork regularity.

She told me one evening, when more disposed to be communicative than usual, that John's conduct, and the threatened ruin of the family, had been a source of profound affliction to her: but she had now, she said, settled her mind, and formed her resolution. Her own fortune she had taken care to secure; and when her mother died – and it was wholly improbable, she tranquilly remarked, that she should either recover or linger long – she would execute a long-cherished project: seek a retirement where punctual habits would be permanently secured from disturbance, and place safe barriers between herself and a frivolous world. I asked if Georgiana would accompany her.

'Of course not. Georgiana and she had nothing in common: they never had had. She would not be burdened with her society for any consideration. Georgiana should take her own course; and she, Eliza, would take hers.'

Georgiana, when not unburdening her heart to me, spent most of her time in lying on the sofa, fretting about the dullness of the house, and wishing over and over again that her aunt Gibson would send her an invitation up to town. 'It would be so much better,' she said, 'if she could only get out of the way for a month or two, till all was over.' I did not ask what she meant by 'all being over', but I suppose she referred to the expected decease of her mother and the gloomy sequel of funeral rites. Eliza generally took no more notice of her sister's indolence and complaints than if no such murmuring, lounging object had been before her. One day, however, as she put away her account-book and unfolded her embroidery, she suddenly took her up thus – 'Georgiana, a more vain and absurd animal than you was certainly never allowed to cumber the earth. You had no right to be born, for you make no use of life. Instead of living for, in, and with yourself, as a reasonable being ought, you seek only to fasten your feebleness on some other person's strength: if no one can be found willing to burden her or himself with such a fat, weak, puffy, useless thing, you cry out that you are ill-treated, neglected, miserable. Then, too, existence for you must be a scene of continual change and excitement, or else the world is a dungeon:

you must be admired, you must be courted, you must be flattered – you must have music, dancing, and society – or you languish, you die away. Have you no sense to devise a system which will make you independent of all efforts, and all wills, but your own? Take one day; share it into sections; to each section apportion its task: leave no stray unemployed quarters of an hour, ten minutes, five minutes – include all; do each piece of business in its turn with method, with rigid regularity. The day will close almost before you are aware it has begun; and you are indebted to no one for helping you to get rid of one vacant moment: you have had to seek no one's company, conversation, sympathy, forbearance; you have lived, in short, as an independent being ought to do. Take this advice: the first and last I shall offer you; then you will not want me or anyone else, happen what may. Neglect it – go on as heretofore, craving, whining, and idling – and suffer the results of your idiocy, however bad and insufferable they may be. I tell you this plainly; and listen: for though I shall no more repeat what I am now about to say, I shall steadily act on it. After my mother's death, I wash my hands of you: from the day her coffin is carried to the vault in Gateshead Church, you and I will be as separate as if we had never known each other. You need not think that because we chanced to be born of the same parents, I shall suffer you to fasten me down by even the feeblest claim: I can tell you this – if the whole human race, ourselves excepted, were swept away, and we two stood alone on the earth, I would leave you in the old world, and betake myself to the new.'

She closed her lips.

'You might have spared yourself the trouble of delivering that tirade,' answered Georgiana. 'Everybody knows you are the most selfish, heartless creature in existence: and I know your spiteful hatred towards me: I have had a specimen of it before in the trick you played me about Lord Edwin Vere: you could not bear me to be raised above you, to have a title, to be received into circles where you dare not show your face, and so you acted the spy and informer, and ruined my prospects for ever.' Georgiana took out her handkerchief and blew her nose for an hour afterwards; Eliza sat cold, impassible, and assiduously industrious.

True, generous feeling is made small account of by some, but here were two natures rendered, the one intolerably acrid, the other despicably savourless for the want of it. Feeling without judgement is a washy draught indeed; but judgement untempered by feeling is too bitter and husky a morsel for human deglutition.

It was a wet and windy afternoon: Georgiana had fallen asleep on the sofa over the perusal of a novel; Eliza was gone to attend a saint's-day service at the new church – for in matters of religion she was a rigid formalist: no weather ever prevented the punctual discharge of what she considered her devotional duties; fair or foul, she went to church thrice every Sunday, and as often on weekdays as there were prayers.

I bethought myself to go upstairs and see how the dying woman sped, who lay there almost unheeded: the very servants paid her but a remittent attention: the hired nurse, being little looked after, would slip out of the room whenever

she could. Bessie was faithful; but she had her own family to mind, and could only come occasionally to the hall. I found the sickroom unwatched, as I had expected: no nurse was there; the patient lay still, and seemingly lethargic; her livid face sunk in the pillows: the fire was dying in the grate. I renewed the fuel, rearranged the bedclothes, gazed awhile on her who could not now gaze on me, and then I moved away to the window.

The rain beat strongly against the panes, the wind blew tempestuously: 'One lies there,' I thought, 'who will soon be beyond the war of earthly elements. Whither will that spirit – now struggling to quit its material tenement – flit when at length released?'

In pondering the great mystery, I thought of Helen Burns, recalled her dying words – her faith – her doctrine of the equality of disembodied souls. I was still listening in thought to her well-remembered tones – still picturing her pale and spiritual aspect, her wasted face and sublime gaze, as she lay on her placid deathbed, and whispered her longing to be restored to her divine Father's bosom – when a feeble voice murmured from the couch behind: 'Who is that?'

I knew Mrs Reed had not spoken for days: was she reviving? I went up to her.

'It is I, Aunt Reed.'

'Who – I?' was her answer. 'Who are you?' looking at me with surprise and a sort of alarm, but still not wildly. 'You are quite a stranger to me – where is Bessie?'

'She is at the lodge, aunt.'

'Aunt,' she repeated. 'Who calls me aunt? You are not one of the Gibsons; and yet I know you – that face, and the eyes and forehead, are quite familiar to me: you are like – why, you are like Jane Eyre!'

I said nothing: I was afraid of occasioning some shock by declaring my identity.

'Yet,' said she, 'I am afraid it is a mistake: my thoughts deceive me. I wished to see Jane Eyre, and I fancy a likeness where none exists: besides, in eight years she must be so changed.' I now gently assured her that I was the person she supposed and desired me to be: and seeing that I was understood, and that her senses were quite collected, I explained how Bessie had sent her husband to fetch me from Thornfield.

'I am very ill, I know,' she said ere long. 'I was trying to turn myself a few minutes since, and find I cannot move a limb. It is as well I should ease my mind before I die: what we think little of in health, burdens us at such an hour as the present is to me. Is the nurse here? or is there no one in the room but you?'

I assured her we were alone.

'Well, I have twice done you a wrong which I regret now. One was in breaking the promise which I gave my husband to bring you up as my own child; the other – ' she stopped. 'After all, it is of no great importance, perhaps,' she murmured to herself: 'and then I may get better; and to humble myself so to her is painful.'

She made an effort to alter her position, but failed: her face changed; she seemed to experience some inward sensation – the precursor, perhaps, of the last pang.

'Well, I must get it over. Eternity is before me: I had better tell her. Go to my dressing-case, open it, and take out a letter you will see there.'

I obeyed her directions. 'Read the letter,' she said.

It was short, and thus conceived:

Madam,

Will you have the goodness to send me the address of my niece, Jane Eyre, and to tell me how she is? It is my intention to write shortly and desire her to come to me at Madeira. Providence has blessed my endeavours to secure a competency; and as I am unmarried and childless, I wish to adopt her during my life, and bequeath her at my death whatever I may have to leave.

I am, Madam, etc., etc.,

JOHN EYRE
MADEIRA

It was dated three years back.

'Why did I never hear of this?' I asked.

'Because I disliked you too fixedly and thoroughly ever to lend a hand in lifting you to prosperity. I could not forget your conduct to me, Jane – the fury with which you once turned on me; the tone in which you declared you abhorred me the worst of anybody in the world; the unchildlike look and voice with which you affirmed that the very thought of me made you sick, and asserted that I had treated you with miserable cruelty. I could not forget my own sensations when you thus started up and poured out the venom of your mind: I felt fear as if an animal that I had struck or pushed had looked up at me with human eyes and cursed me in a man's voice. Bring me some water! Oh, make haste!'

'Dear Mrs Reed,' said I, as I offered her the draught she required, 'think no more of all this, let it pass away from your mind. Forgive me for my passionate language: I was a child then; eight, nine years have passed since that day.'

She heeded nothing of what I said; but when she had tasted the water and drawn breath, she went on thus – 'I tell you I could not forget it; and I took my revenge: for you to be adopted by your uncle, and placed in a state of ease and comfort, was what I could not endure. I wrote to him; I said I was sorry for his disappointment, but Jane Eyre was dead: she had died of typhus fever at Lowood. Now act as you please: write and contradict my assertion – expose my falsehood as soon as you like. You were born, I think, to be my torment: my last hour is racked by the recollection of a deed which, but for you, I should never have been tempted to commit.'

'If you could but be persuaded to think no more of it, aunt, and to regard me with kindness and forgiveness – '

'You have a very bad disposition,' said she, 'and one to this day I feel it impossible to understand: how for nine years you could be patient and quiescent under any treatment, and in the tenth break out all fire and violence, I can never comprehend.'

'My disposition is not so bad as you think: I am passionate, but not vindictive.

Many a time, as a little child, I should have been glad to love you if you would have let me; and I long earnestly to be reconciled to you now: kiss me, aunt.'

I approached my cheek to her lips: she would not touch it. She said I oppressed her by leaning over the bed, and again demanded water. As I laid her down – for I raised her and supported her on my arm while she drank – I covered her ice-cold and clammy hand with mine: the feeble fingers shrank from my touch – the glazing eyes shunned my gaze.

'Love me, then, or hate me, as you will,' I said at last, 'you have my full and free forgiveness: ask now for God's, and be at peace.'

Poor, suffering woman! it was too late for her to make now the effort to change her habitual frame of mind: living, she had ever hated me – dying, she must hate me still.

The nurse now entered, and Bessie followed. I yet lingered half an hour longer, hoping to see some sign of amity: but she gave none. She was fast relapsing into stupor; nor did her mind again rally: at twelve o'clock that night she died. I was not present to close her eyes, nor were either of her daughters. They came to tell us the next morning that all was over. She was by that time laid out. Eliza and I went to look at her: Georgiana, who had burst out into loud weeping, said she dared not go. There was stretched Sarah Reed's once robust and active frame, rigid and still: her eye of flint was covered with its cold lid; her brow and strong traits wore yet the impress of her inexorable soul. A strange and solemn object was that corpse to me. I gazed on it with gloom and pain: nothing soft, nothing sweet, nothing pitying, or hopeful, or subduing did it inspire; only a grating anguish for *her* woes – not *my* loss – and a sombre tearless dismay at the fearfulness of death in such a form.

Eliza surveyed her parent calmly. After a silence of some minutes she observed – 'With her constitution she should have lived to a good old age: her life was shortened by trouble.' And then a spasm constricted her mouth for an instant: as it passed away she turned and left the room, and so did I. Neither of us had dropt a tear.

## Chapter 22

Mr Rochester had given me but one week's leave of absence: yet a month elapsed before I quitted Gateshead. I wished to leave immediately after the funeral, but Georgiana entreated me to stay till she could get off to London, whither she was now at last invited by her uncle, Mr Gibson, who had come down to direct his sister's interment and settle the family affairs. Georgiana said she dreaded being left alone with Eliza; from her she got neither sympathy in her dejection, support in her fears, nor aid in her preparations; so I bore with her feeble-minded wailings and selfish lamentations as well as I could, and did my best in sewing for her and packing her dresses. It is true, that while I worked, she would idle; and I thought to myself, 'If you and I were destined to live always together, cousin, we

would commence matters on a different footing. I should not settle tamely down into being the forbearing party; I should assign you your share of labour, and compel you to accomplish it, or else it should be left undone: I should insist, also, on your keeping some of those drawling, half-insincere complaints hushed in your own breast. It is only because our connection happens to be very transitory, and comes at a peculiarly mournful season, that I consent thus to render it so patient and compliant on my part.'

At last I saw Georgiana off; but now it was Eliza's turn to request me to stay another week. Her plans required all her time and attention, she said; she was about to depart for some unknown bourne; and all day long she stayed in her own room, her door bolted within, filling trunks, emptying drawers, burning papers, and holding no communication with anyone. She wished me to look after the house, to see callers, and answer notes of condolence.

One morning she told me I was at liberty. 'And,' she added, 'I am obliged to you for your valuable services and discreet conduct! There is some difference between living with such an one as you and with Georgiana: you perform your own part in life and burden no one. Tomorrow,' she continued, 'I set out for the Continent. I shall take up my abode in a religious house near Lisle – a nunnery you would call it; there I shall be quiet and unmolested. I shall devote myself for a time to the examination of the Roman Catholic dogmas, and to a careful study of the workings of their system: if I find it to be, as I half suspect it is, the one best calculated to ensure the doing of all things decently and in order, I shall embrace the tenets of Rome and probably take the veil.'

I neither expressed surprise at this resolution nor attempted to dissuade her from it. 'The vocation will fit you to a hair,' I thought: 'much good may it do you!'

When we parted, she said: 'Goodbye, cousin Jane Eyre; I wish you well: you have some sense.'

I then returned: 'You are not without sense, cousin Eliza; but what you have, I suppose, in another year will be walled up alive in a French convent. However, it is not my business, and so it suits you, I don't much care.'

'You are in the right,' said she; and with these words we each went our separate way. As I shall not have occasion to refer either to her or her sister again, I may as well mention here, that Georgiana made an advantageous match with a wealthy worn-out man of fashion, and that Eliza actually took the veil, and is at this day superior of the convent where she passed the period of her novitiate, and which she endowed with her fortune.

How people feel when they are returning home from an absence, long or short, I did not know: I had never experienced the sensation. I had known what it was to come back to Gateshead when a child after a long walk, to be scolded for looking cold or gloomy; and later, what it was to come back from church to Lowood, to long for a plenteous meal and a good fire, and to be unable to get either. Neither of these returnings was very pleasant or desirable: no magnet drew me to a given point, increasing in its strength of attraction the nearer I came. The return to Thornfield was yet to be tried.

My journey seemed tedious – very tedious: fifty miles one day, a night spent at an inn; fifty miles the next day. During the first twelve hours I thought of Mrs Reed in her last moments; I saw her disfigured and discoloured face, and heard her strangely altered voice. I mused on the funeral day, the coffin, the hearse, the black train of tenants and servants – few was the number of relatives – the gaping vault, the silent church, the solemn service. Then I thought of Eliza and Georgiana; I beheld one the cynosure of a ballroom, the other the inmate of a convent cell; and I dwelt on and analysed their separate peculiarities of person and character. The evening arrival at the great town of — scattered these thoughts; night gave them quite another turn: laid down on my traveller's bed, I left reminiscence for anticipation.

I was going back to Thornfield: but how long was I to stay there? Not long; of that I was sure. I had heard from Mrs Fairfax in the interim of my absence: the party at the hall was dispersed; Mr Rochester had left for London three weeks ago, but he was then expected to return in a fortnight. Mrs Fairfax surmised that he was gone to make arrangements for his wedding, as he had talked of purchasing a new carriage: she said the idea of his marrying Miss Ingram still seemed strange to her; but from what everybody said, and from what she had herself seen, she could no longer doubt that the event would shortly take place. 'You would be strangely incredulous if you did doubt it,' was my mental comment. 'I don't doubt it.'

The question followed, 'Where was I to go?' I dreamt of Miss Ingram all the night: in a vivid morning dream I saw her closing the gates of Thornfield against me and pointing me out another road; and Mr Rochester looked on with his arms folded – smiling sardonically, as it seemed, at both her and me.

I had not notified to Mrs Fairfax the exact day of my return; for I did not wish either car or carriage to meet me at Millcote. I proposed to walk the distance quietly by myself; and very quietly, after leaving my box in the ostler's care, did I slip away from the George Inn, about six o'clock of a June evening, and take the old road to Thornfield: a road which lay chiefly through fields, and was now little frequented.

It was not a bright or splendid summer evening, though fair and soft: the haymakers were at work all along the road; and the sky, though far from cloudless, was such as promised well for the future: its blue – where blue was visible – was mild and settled, and its cloud strata high and thin. The west, too, was warm: no watery gleam chilled it – it seemed as if there was a fire lit, an altar burning behind its screen of marbled vapour, and out of apertures shone a golden redness.

I felt glad as the road shortened before me: so glad that I stopped once to ask myself what that joy meant: and to remind reason that it was not to my home I was going, or to a permanent resting-place, or to a place where fond friends looked out for me and waited my arrival. 'Mrs Fairfax will smile you a calm welcome, to be sure,' said I; 'and little Adèle will clap her hands and jump to see you: but you know very well you are thinking of another than they, and that he is not thinking of you.'

But what is so headstrong as youth? What so blind as inexperience? These affirmed that it was pleasure enough to have the privilege of again looking on Mr Rochester, whether he looked on me or not; and they added – 'Hasten! hasten! be with him while you may: but a few more days or weeks, at most, and you are parted from him for ever!' And then I strangled a new-born agony – a deformed thing which I could not persuade myself to own and rear – and ran on.

They are making hay, too, in Thornfield meadows: or rather, the labourers are just quitting their work, and returning home with their rakes on their shoulders, now, at the hour I arrive. I have but a field or two to traverse, and then I shall cross the road and reach the gates. How full the hedges are of roses! But I have no time to gather any; I want to be at the house. I passed a tall briar, shooting leafy and flowery branches across the path; I see the narrow stile with stone steps; and I see – Mr Rochester sitting there, a book and a pencil in his hand; he is writing.

Well, he is not a ghost; yet every nerve I have is unstrung: for a moment I am beyond my own mastery. What does it mean? I did not think I should tremble in this way when I saw him, or lose my voice or the power of motion in his presence. I will go back as soon as I can stir: I need not make an absolute fool of myself. I know another way to the house. It does not signify if I knew twenty ways; for he has seen me.

'Hillo!' he cries; and he puts up his book and his pencil. 'There you are! Come on, if you please.'

I suppose I do come on; though in what fashion I know not; being scarcely cognisant of my movements, and solicitous only to appear calm; and, above all, to control the working muscles of my face – which I feel rebel insolently against my will, and struggle to express what I had resolved to conceal. But I have a veil – it is down: I may make shift yet to behave with decent composure.

'And this is Jane Eyre? Are you coming from Millcote, and on foot? Yes – just one of your tricks: not to send for a carriage, and come clattering over street and road like a common mortal, but to steal into the vicinage of your home along with twilight, just as if you were a dream or a shade. What the deuce have you done with yourself this last month?'

'I have been with my aunt, sir, who is dead.'

'A true Janian reply! Good angels be my guard. She comes from the other world – from the abode of people who are dead; and tells me so when she meets me alone here in the gloaming! If I dared, I'd touch you, to see if you are substance or shadow, you elf! – but I'd as soon offer to take hold of a blue *ignis fatuus* light in a marsh. Truant! truant!' he added, when he had paused an instant. 'Absent from me a whole month, and forgetting me quite, I'll be sworn!'

I knew there would be pleasure in meeting my master again, even though broken by the fear that he was so soon to cease to be my master, and by the knowledge that I was nothing to him: but there was ever in Mr Rochester (so at least I thought) such a wealth of the power of communicating happiness, that to taste but of the crumbs he scattered to stray and stranger birds like me, was to feast genially. His last words were balm: they seemed to imply that it

imported something to him whether I forgot him or not. And he had spoken of Thornfield as my home – would that it were my home!

He did not leave the stile, and I hardly liked to ask to go by. I enquired soon if he had not been to London.

'Yes; I suppose you found that out by second-sight.'

'Mrs Fairfax told me in a letter.'

'And did she inform you what I went to do?'

'Oh, yes, sir! Everybody knew your errand.'

'You must see the carriage, Jane, and tell me if you don't think it will suit Mrs Rochester exactly; and whether she won't look like Queen Boadicea, leaning back against those purple cushions. I wish, Jane, I were a trifle better adapted to match with her externally. Tell me now, fairy as you are – can't you give me a charm, or a philtre, or something of that sort, to make me a handsome man?'

'It would be past the power of magic, sir'; and, in thought, I added, 'A loving eye is all the charm needed: to such you are handsome enough; or rather your sternness has a power beyond beauty.'

Mr Rochester had sometimes read my unspoken thoughts with an acumen to me incomprehensible: in the present instance he took no notice of my abrupt vocal response; but he smiled at me with a certain smile he had of his own, and which he used but on rare occasions. He seemed to think it too good for common purposes: it was the real sunshine of feeling – he shed it over me now.

'Pass, Janet,' said he, making room for me to cross the stile: 'go up home, and stay your weary little wandering feet at a friend's threshold.'

All I had now to do was to obey him in silence: no need for me to colloquise further. I got over the stile without a word, and meant to leave him calmly. An impulse held me fast – a force turned me round. I said – or something in me said for me, and in spite of me – 'Thank you, Mr Rochester, for your great kindness. I am strangely glad to get back again to you: and wherever you are is my home – my only home.'

I walked on so fast that even he could hardly have overtaken me had he tried. Little Adèle was half wild with delight when she saw me. Mrs Fairfax received me with her usual plain friendliness. Leah smiled, and even Sophie bid me 'bon soir' with glee. This was very pleasant; there is no happiness like that of being loved by your fellow-creatures, and feeling that your presence is an addition to their comfort.

I that evening shut my eyes resolutely against the future: I stopped my ears against the voice that kept warning me of near separation and coming grief. When tea was over and Mrs Fairfax had taken her knitting, and I had assumed a low seat near her, and Adèle, kneeling on the carpet, had nestled close up to me, and a sense of mutual affection seemed to surround us with a ring of golden peace, I uttered a silent prayer that we might not be parted far or soon; but when, as we thus sat, Mr Rochester entered, unannounced, and looking at us, seemed to take pleasure in the spectacle of a group so amicable – when he said he supposed the old lady was all right now that she had got her adopted daughter back again, and added that he saw Adèle was 'prête à croquer sa petite

maman Anglaise' – I half ventured to hope that he would, even after his marriage, keep us together somewhere under the shelter of his protection, and not quite exiled from the sunshine of his presence.

A fortnight of dubious calm succeeded my return to Thornfield Hall. Nothing was said of the master's marriage, and I saw no preparation going on for such an event. Almost every day I asked Mrs Fairfax if she had yet heard anything decided: her answer was always in the negative. Once she said she had actually put the question to Mr Rochester as to when he was going to bring his bride home; but he had answered her only by a joke and one of his queer looks, and she could not tell what to make of him.

One thing specially surprised me, and that was, there were no journeyings backward and forward, no visits to Ingram Park: to be sure it was twenty miles off, on the borders of another county; but what was that distance to an ardent lover? To so practised and indefatigable a horseman as Mr Rochester, it would be but a morning's ride. I began to cherish hopes I had no right to conceive: that the match was broken off; that rumour had been mistaken; that one or both parties had changed their minds. I used to look at my master's face to see if it were sad or fierce; but I could not remember the time when it had been so uniformly clear of clouds or evil feelings. If, in the moments I and my pupil spent with him, I lacked spirits and sank into inevitable dejection, he became even gay. Never had he called me more frequently to his presence; never been kinder to me when there – and, alas! never had I loved him so well.

## Chapter 23

A splendid Midsummer shone over England: skies so pure, suns so radiant as were then seen in long succession, seldom favour even singly, our wave-girt land. It was as if a band of Italian days had come from the South, like a flock of glorious passenger birds, and lighted to rest them on the cliffs of Albion. The hay was all got in; the fields round Thornfield were green and shorn; the roads white and baked; the trees were in their dark prime; hedge and wood, full-leaved and deeply tinted, contrasted well with the sunny hue of the cleared meadows between.

On Midsummer-eve, Adèle, weary with gathering wild strawberries in Hay Lane half the day, had gone to bed with the sun. I watched her drop asleep, and when I left her, I sought the garden.

It was now the sweetest hour of the twenty-four: 'Day its fervid fires had wasted,' and dew fell cool on panting plain and scorched summit. Where the sun had gone down in simple state – pure of the pomp of clouds – spread a solemn purple, burning with the light of red jewel and furnace flame at one point, on one hill-peak, and extending high and wide, soft and still softer, over half heaven. The east had its own charm of fine deep blue, and its own modest gem, a rising and solitary star: soon it would boast the moon; but she was yet beneath the horizon.

I walked a while on the pavement; but a subtle, well-known scent – that of a cigar – stole from some window; I saw the library casement open a hand-breadth; I knew I might be watched thence; so I went apart into the orchard. No nook in the grounds more sheltered and more Eden-like; it was full of trees, it bloomed with flowers: a very high wall shut it out from the court, on one side; on the other, a beech avenue screened it from the lawn. At the bottom was a sunk fence; its sole separation from lonely fields: a winding walk, bordered with laurels and terminating in a giant horse-chestnut, circled at the base by a seat, led down to the fence. Here one could wander unseen. While such honey-dew fell, such silence reigned, such gloaming gathered, I felt as if I could haunt such shade for ever; but in threading the flower and fruit parterres at the upper part of the enclosure, enticed there by the light the now rising moon cast on this more open quarter, my step is stayed – not by sound, not by sight, but once more by a warning fragrance.

Sweet-briar and southernwood, jasmine, pink, and rose have long been yielding their evening sacrifice of incense: this new scent is neither of shrub nor flower; it is – I know it well – it is Mr Rochester's cigar. I look round and I listen. I see trees laden with ripening fruit. I hear a nightingale warbling in a wood half a mile off; no moving form is visible, no coming step audible; but that perfume increases: I must flee. I make for the wicket leading to the shrubbery, and I see Mr Rochester entering. I step aside into the ivy recess; he will not stay long: he will soon return whence he came, and if I sit still he will never see me.

But no – eventide is as pleasant to him as to me, and this antique garden as attractive; and he strolls on, now lifting the gooseberry-tree branches to look at the fruit, large as plums, with which they are laden; now taking a ripe cherry from the wall; now stooping towards a knot of flowers, either to inhale their fragrance or to admire the dew-beads on their petals. A great moth goes humming by me; it alights on a plant at Mr Rochester's foot: he sees it, and bends to examine it.

'Now, he has his back towards me,' thought I, 'and he is occupied too; perhaps, if I walk softly, I can slip away unnoticed.'

I trode on an edging of turf that the crackle of the pebbly gravel might not betray me: he was standing among the beds at a yard or two distant from where I had to pass; the moth apparently engaged him. 'I shall get by very well,' I meditated. As I crossed his shadow, thrown long over the garden by the moon, not yet risen high, he said quietly, without turning – 'Jane, come and look at this fellow.'

I had made no noise: he had not eyes behind – could his shadow feel? I started at first, and then I approached him.

'Look at his wings,' said he, 'he reminds me rather of a West Indian insect; one does not often see so large and gay a night-rover in England; there! he is flown.'

The moth roamed away. I was sheepishly retreating also; but Mr Rochester followed me, and when we reached the wicket, he said – 'Turn back: on so lovely

a night it is a shame to sit in the house; and surely no one can wish to go to bed while sunset is thus at meeting with moonrise.'

It is one of my faults, that though my tongue is sometimes prompt enough at an answer, there are times when it sadly fails me in framing an excuse; and always the lapse occurs at some crisis, when a facile word or plausible pretext is specially wanted to get me out of painful embarrassment. I did not like to walk at this hour alone with Mr Rochester in the shadowy orchard; but I could not find a reason to allege for leaving him. I followed with lagging step, and thoughts busily bent on discovering a means of extrication; but he himself looked so composed and so grave also, I became ashamed of feeling any confusion: the evil – if evil existent or prospective there was – seemed to lie with me only; his mind was unconscious and quiet.

'Jane,' he recommenced, as we entered the laurel walk, and slowly strayed down in the direction of the sunk fence and the horse-chestnut, 'Thornfield is a pleasant place in summer, is it not?'

'Yes, sir.'

'You must have become in some degree attached to the house, you, who have an eye for natural beauties, and a good deal of the organ of Adhesiveness?'

'I am attached to it, indeed.'

'And though I don't comprehend how it is, I perceive you have acquired a degree of regard for that foolish little child Adèle, too; and even for simple dame Fairfax?'

'Yes, sir; in different ways, I have an affection for both.'

'And would be sorry to part with them?'

'Yes.'

'Pity!' he said, and sighed and paused. 'It is always the way of events in this life,' he continued presently: 'no sooner have you got settled in a pleasant resting-place, than a voice calls out to you to rise and move on, for the hour of repose is expired.'

'Must I move on, sir?' I asked. 'Must I leave Thornfield?'

'I believe you must, Jane. I am sorry, Janet, but I believe indeed you must.'

This was a blow: but I did not let it prostrate me.

'Well, sir, I shall be ready when the order to march comes.'

'It is come now – I must give it tonight.'

'Then you *are* going to be married, sir?'

'Ex-act-ly – pre-cise-ly: with your usual acuteness, you have hit the nail straight on the head.'

'Soon, sir?'

'Very soon, my – that is, Miss Eyre: and you'll remember, Jane, the first time I, or Rumour, plainly intimated to you that it was my intention to put my old bachelor's neck into the sacred noose, to enter into the holy estate of matrimony – to take Miss Ingram to my bosom, in short (she's an extensive armful: but that's not to the point – one can't have too much of such a very excellent thing as my beautiful Blanche): well, as I was saying – listen to me, Jane! You're not turning your head to look after more moths, are you? That was only a lady-clock, child,

"flying away home". I wish to remind you that it was you who first said to me, with that discretion I respect in you – with that foresight, prudence, and humility which befit your responsible and dependent position – that in case I married Miss Ingram, both you and little Adèle had better trot forthwith. I pass over the sort of slur conveyed in this suggestion on the character of my beloved; indeed, when you are far away, Janet, I'll try to forget it: I shall notice only its wisdom; which is such that I have made it my law of action. Adèle must go to school; and you, Miss Eyre, must get a new situation.'

'Yes, sir, I will advertise immediately: and meantime, I suppose – ' I was going to say, 'I suppose I may stay here, till I find another shelter to betake myself to': but I stopped, feeling it would not do to risk a long sentence, for my voice was not quite under command.

'In about a month I hope to be a bridegroom,' continued Mr Rochester; 'and in the interim, I shall myself look out for employment and an asylum for you.'

'Thank you, sir; I am sorry to give – '

'Oh, no need to apologise! I consider that when a dependent does her duty as well as you have done yours, she has a sort of claim upon her employer for any little assistance he can conveniently render her; indeed I have already, through my future mother-in-law, heard of a place that I think will suit: it is to undertake the education of the five daughters of Mrs Dionysius O'Gall of Bitternutt Lodge, Connaught, Ireland. You'll like Ireland, I think: they're such warm-hearted people there, they say.'

'It is a long way off, sir.'

'No matter – a girl of your sense will not object to the voyage or the distance.'

'Not the voyage, but the distance: and then the sea is a barrier – '

'From what, Jane?'

'From England and from Thornfield: and – '

'Well?'

'From *you*, sir.'

I said this almost involuntarily, and, with as little sanction of free will, my tears gushed out. I did not cry so as to be heard, however; I avoided sobbing. The thought of Mrs O'Gall and Bitternutt Lodge struck cold to my heart; and colder the thought of all the brine and foam, destined, as it seemed, to rush between me and the master at whose side I now walked, and coldest the remembrance of the wider ocean – wealth, caste, custom intervened between me and what I naturally and inevitably loved.

'It is a long way,' I again said.

'It is, to be sure; and when you get to Bitternutt Lodge, Connaught, Ireland, I shall never see you again, Jane: that's morally certain. I never go over to Ireland, not having myself much of a fancy for the country. We have been good friends, Jane; have we not?'

'Yes, sir.'

'And when friends are on the eve of separation, they like to spend the little time that remains to them close to each other. Come! we'll talk over the voyage and the parting quietly half an hour or so, while the stars enter into their shining

life up in heaven yonder: here is the chestnut tree: here is the bench at its old roots. Come, we will sit there in peace tonight, though we should never more be destined to sit there together.' He seated me and himself.

'It is a long way to Ireland, Janet; and I am sorry to send my little friend on such weary travels: but if I can't do better, how is it to be helped? Are you anything akin to me, do you think, Jane?'

I could risk no sort of answer by this time: my heart was still.

'Because,' he said, 'I sometimes have a queer feeling with regard to you – especially when you are near me, as now: it is as if I had a string somewhere under my left ribs, tightly and inextricably knotted to a similar string situated in the corresponding quarter of your little frame. And if that boisterous Channel, and two hundred miles or so of land come broad between us, I am afraid that cord of communion will be snapt; and then I've a nervous notion I should take to bleeding inwardly. As for you, you'd forget me.'

'That I *never* should, sir: you know – ' Impossible to proceed.

'Jane, do you hear that nightingale singing in the wood? Listen!'

In listening, I sobbed convulsively; for I could repress what I endured no longer; I was obliged to yield, and I was shaken from head to foot with acute distress. When I did speak, it was only to express an impetuous wish that I had never been born, or never come to Thornfield.

'Because you are sorry to leave it?'

The vehemence of emotion, stirred by grief and love within me, was claiming mastery, and struggling for full sway, and asserting a right to predominate, to overcome, to live, rise, and reign at last: yes, and to speak.

'I grieve to leave Thornfield: I love Thornfield: I love it, because I have lived in it a full and delightful life, momentarily at least. I have not been trampled on. I have not been petrified. I have not been buried with inferior minds, and excluded from every glimpse of communion with what is bright and energetic and high. I have talked, face to face, with what I reverence, with what I delight in, with an original, a vigorous, an expanded mind. I have known you, Mr Rochester; and it strikes me with terror and anguish to feel I absolutely must be torn from you for ever. I see the necessity of departure; and it is like looking on the necessity of death.'

'Where do you see the necessity?' he asked suddenly.

'Where? You, sir, have placed it before me.'

'In what shape?'

'In the shape of Miss Ingram; a noble and beautiful woman, your bride.'

'My bride! What bride? I have no bride!'

'But you will have.'

'Yes; I will! – I will!' He set his teeth.

'Then I must go: you have said it yourself.'

'No: you must stay! I swear it – and the oath shall be kept.'

'I tell you I must go!' I retorted, roused to something like passion. 'Do you think I can stay to become nothing to you? Do you think I am an automaton? – a machine without feelings? and can bear to have my morsel of bread snatched from my lips, and my drop of living water dashed from my cup? Do you think,

because I am poor, obscure, plain, and little, I am soulless and heartless? You think wrong! – I have as much soul as you, and full as much heart! And if God had gifted me with some beauty and much wealth, I should have made it as hard for you to leave me, as it is now for me to leave you. I am not talking to you now through the medium of custom, conventionalities, nor even of mortal flesh; it is my spirit that addresses your spirit; just as if both had passed through the grave, and we stood at God's feet, equal, as we are!'

'As we are!' repeated Mr Rochester – 'so,' he added, enclosing me in his arms, gathering me to his breast, pressing his lips on my lips: 'so, Jane!'

'Yes, so, sir,' I rejoined: 'and yet not so; for you are a married man – or as good as a married man, and wed to one inferior to you – to one with whom you have no sympathy – whom I do not believe you truly love; for I have seen and heard you sneer at her. I would scorn such a union: therefore I am better than you – let me go!'

'Where, Jane? To Ireland?'

'Yes – to Ireland. I have spoken my mind, and can go anywhere now.'

'Jane, be still; don't struggle so, like a wild frantic bird that is rending its own plumage in its desperation.'

'I am no bird; and no net ensnares me; I am a free human being with an independent will, which I now exert to leave you.'

Another effort set me at liberty, and I stood erect before him.

'And your will shall decide your destiny,' he said: 'I offer you my hand, my heart, and a share of all my possessions.'

'You play a farce, which I merely laugh at.'

'I ask you to pass through life at my side – to be my second self, and best earthly companion.'

'For that fate you have already made your choice, and must abide by it.'

'Jane, be still a few moments: you are over-excited: I will be still too.'

A waft of wind came sweeping down the laurel-walk and trembled through the boughs of the chestnut: it wandered away – away – to an indefinite distance – it died. The nightingale's song was then the only voice of the hour: in listening to it, I again wept. Mr Rochester sat quiet, looking at me gently and seriously. Some time passed before he spoke; he at last said – 'Come to my side, Jane, and let us explain and understand one another.'

'I will never again come to your side: I am torn away now, and cannot return.'

'But, Jane, I summon you as my wife: it is you only I intend to marry.'

I was silent: I thought he mocked me.

'Come, Jane – come hither.'

'Your bride stands between us.'

He rose, and with a stride reached me.

'My bride is here,' he said, again drawing me to him, 'because my equal is here, and my likeness. Jane, will you marry me?'

Still I did not answer, and still I writhed myself from grasp: for I was still incredulous.

'Do you doubt me, Jane?'

'Entirely.'

'You have no faith in me?'

'Not a whit.'

'Am I a liar in your eyes?' he asked passionately. 'Little sceptic, you *shall* be convinced. What love have I for Miss Ingram? None: and that you know. What love has she for me? None: as I have taken pains to prove: I caused a rumour to reach her that my fortune was not a third of what was supposed, and after that I presented myself to see the result; it was coldness both from her and her mother. I would not – I could not – marry Miss Ingram. You – you strange, you almost unearthly thing! – I love as my own flesh. You – poor and obscure, and small and plain as you are – I entreat to accept me as a husband.'

'What, me!' I ejaculated, beginning in his earnestness – and especially in his incivility – to credit his sincerity: 'me who have not a friend in the world but you – if you are my friend: not a shilling but what you have given me?'

'You, Jane, I must have you for my own – entirely my own. Will you be mine? Say yes, quickly.'

'Mr Rochester, let me look at your face: turn to the moonlight.'

'Why?'

'Because I want to read your countenance – turn!'

'There! you will find it scarcely more legible than a crumpled, scratched page. Read on: only make haste, for I suffer.'

His face was very much agitated and very much flushed, and there were strong workings in the features, and strange gleams in the eyes.

'Oh, Jane, you torture me!' he exclaimed. 'With that searching and yet faithful and generous look, you torture me!'

'How can I do that? If you are true, and your offer real, my only feelings to you must be gratitude and devotion – they cannot torture.'

'Gratitude!' he ejaculated; and added wildly – 'Jane, accept me quickly. Say, Edward – give me my name – Edward – I will marry you.'

'Are you in earnest? Do you truly love me? Do you sincerely wish me to be your wife?'

'I do; and if an oath is necessary to satisfy you, I swear it.'

'Then, sir, I will marry you.'

'Edward – my little wife!'

'Dear Edward!'

'Come to me – come to me entirely now,' said he; and added, in his deepest tone, speaking in my ear as his cheek was laid on mine, 'Make my happiness – I will make yours.'

'God pardon me!' he subjoined ere long; 'and man meddle not with me: I have her, and will hold her.'

'There is no one to meddle, sir. I have no kindred to interfere.'

'No – that is the best of it,' he said. And if I had loved him less I should have thought his accent and look of exultation savage; but, sitting by him, roused from the nightmare of parting – called to the paradise of union – I thought only of the bliss given me to drink in so abundant a flow. Again and again he said,

'Are you happy, Jane?' And again and again I answered, 'Yes.' After which he murmured, 'It will atone – it will atone. Have I not found her friendless, and cold, and comfortless? Will I not guard, and cherish, and solace her? Is there not love in my heart, and constancy in my resolves? It will expiate at God's tribunal. I know my Maker sanctions what I do. For the world's judgement – I wash my hands thereof. For man's opinion – I defy it.'

But what had befallen the night? The moon was not yet set, and we were all in shadow: I could scarcely see my master's face, near as I was. And what ailed the chestnut tree? it writhed and groaned; while wind roared in the laurel walk, and came sweeping over us.

'We must go in,' said Mr Rochester: 'the weather changes. I could have sat with thee till morning, Jane.'

'And so,' thought I, 'could I with you.' I should have said so, perhaps, but a livid, vivid spark leapt out of a cloud at which I was looking, and there was a crack, a crash, and a close rattling peal; and I thought only of hiding my dazzled eyes against Mr Rochester's shoulder.

The rain rushed down. He hurried me up the walk, through the grounds, and into the house; but we were quite wet before we could pass the threshold. He was taking off my shawl in the hall, and shaking the water out of my loosened hair, when Mrs Fairfax emerged from her room. I did not observe her at first, nor did Mr Rochester. The lamp was lit. The clock was on the stroke of twelve.

'Hasten to take off your wet things,' said he; 'and before you go, good-night – good-night, my darling!'

He kissed me repeatedly. When I looked up, on leaving his arms, there stood the widow, pale, grave, and amazed. I only smiled at her, and ran upstairs. 'Explanation will do for another time,' thought I. Still, when I reached my chamber, I felt a pang at the idea she should even temporarily misconstrue what she had seen. But joy soon effaced every other feeling, and loud as the wind blew, near and deep as the thunder crashed, fierce and frequent as the lightning gleamed, cataract-like as the rain fell during a storm of two hours' duration, I experienced no fear and little awe. Mr Rochester came thrice to my door in the course of it, to ask if I was safe and tranquil: and that was comfort, that was strength for anything.

Before I left my bed in the morning, little Adèle came running in to tell me that the great horse-chestnut at the bottom of the orchard had been struck by lightning in the night, and half of it split away.

## Chapter 24

As I rose and dressed, I thought over what had happened, and wondered if it were a dream. I could not be certain of the reality till I had seen Mr Rochester again, and heard him renew his words of love and promise.

While arranging my hair, I looked at my face in the glass, and felt it was no

longer plain: there was hope in its aspect and life in its colour; and my eyes seemed as if they had beheld the fount of fruition, and borrowed beams from the lustrous ripple. I had often been unwilling to look at my master, because I feared he could not be pleased at my look; but I was sure I might lift my face to his now, and not cool his affection by its expression. I took a plain but clean and light summer dress from my drawer and put it on: it seemed no attire had ever so well become me, because none had I ever worn in so blissful a mood.

I was not surprised, when I ran down into the hall, to see that a brilliant June morning had succeeded to the tempest of the night; and to feel, through the open glass door, the breathing of a fresh and fragrant breeze. Nature must be gladsome when I was so happy. A beggar-woman and her little boy – pale, ragged objects both – were coming up the walk, and I ran down and gave them all the money I happened to have in my purse – some three or four shillings: good or bad, they must partake of my jubilee. The rooks cawed, and blither birds sang; but nothing was so merry or so musical as my own rejoicing heart.

Mrs Fairfax surprised me by looking out of the window with a sad countenance, and saying gravely – 'Miss Eyre, will you come to breakfast?' During the meal she was quiet and cool: but I could not undeceive her then. I must wait for my master to give explanations; and so must she. I ate what I could, and then I hastened upstairs. I met Adèle leaving the schoolroom.

'Where are you going? It is time for lessons.'

'Mr Rochester has sent me away to the nursery.'

'Where is he?'

'In there,' pointing to the apartment she had left; and I went in, and there he stood.

'Come and bid me good-morning,' said he. I gladly advanced; and it was not merely a cold word now, or even a shake of the hand that I received, but an embrace and a kiss. It seemed natural: it seemed genial to be so well loved, so caressed by him.

'Jane, you look blooming, and smiling, and pretty,' said he: 'truly pretty this morning. Is this my pale, little elf? Is this my mustard-seed? This little sunny-faced girl with the dimpled cheek and rosy lips; the satin-smooth hazel hair, and the radiant hazel eyes?' (I had green eyes, reader; but you must excuse the mistake: for him they were new-dyed, I suppose.)

'It is Jane Eyre, sir.'

'Soon to be Jane Rochester,' he added: 'in four weeks, Janet; not a day more. Do you hear that?'

I did, and I could not quite comprehend it: it made me giddy. The feeling, the announcement sent through me, was something stronger than was consistent with joy – something that smote and stunned: it was, I think almost fear.

'You blushed, and now you are white, Jane: what is that for?'

'Because you gave me a new name – Jane Rochester; and it seems so strange.'

'Yes, Mrs Rochester,' said he; 'young Mrs Rochester – Fairfax Rochester's girl-bride.'

'It can never be, sir; it does not sound likely. Human beings never enjoy

complete happiness in this world. I was not born for a different destiny to the rest of my species: to imagine such a lot befalling me is a fairy tale – a day-dream.'

'Which I can and will realise. I shall begin today. This morning I wrote to my banker in London to send me certain jewels he has in his keeping, heirlooms for the ladies of Thornfield. In a day or two I hope to pour them into your lap: for every privilege, every attention shall be yours that I would accord a peer's daughter, if about to marry her.'

'Oh, sir! – never mind jewels! I don't like to hear them spoken of. Jewels for Jane Eyre sounds unnatural and strange: I would rather not have them.'

'I will myself put the diamond chain round your neck, and the circlet on your forehead, which it will become: for nature, at least, has stamped her patent of nobility on this brow, Jane; and I will clasp the bracelets on these fine wrists, and load these fairy-like fingers with rings.'

'No, no, sir! think of other subjects, and speak of other things, and in another strain. Don't address me as if I were a beauty; I am your plain, Quakerish governess.'

'You are a beauty in my eyes, and a beauty just after the desire of my heart, delicate and aërial.'

'Puny and insignificant, you mean. You are dreaming, sir, or you are sneering. For God's sake, don't be ironical!'

'I will make the world acknowledge you a beauty, too,' he went on, while I really became uneasy at the strain he had adopted, because I felt he was either deluding himself or trying to delude me. 'I will attire my Jane in satin and lace, and she shall have roses in her hair; and I will cover the head I love best with a priceless veil.'

'And then you won't know me, sir; and I shall not be your Jane Eyre any longer, but an ape in a harlequin's jacket – a jay in borrowed plumes. I would as soon see you, Mr Rochester, tricked out in stage-trappings, as myself clad in a court-lady's robe; and I don't call you handsome, sir, though I love you most dearly: far too dearly to flatter you. Don't flatter me.'

He pursued his theme, however, without noticing my deprecation. 'This very day I shall take you in the carriage to Millcote, and you must choose some dresses for yourself. I told you we shall be married in four weeks. The wedding is to take place quietly, in the church down below yonder; and then I shall waft you away at once to town. After a brief stay there, I shall bear my treasure to regions nearer the sun: to French vineyards and Italian plains; and she shall see whatever is famous in old story and in modern record: she shall taste, too, of the life of cities; and she shall learn to value herself by just comparison with others.'

'Shall I travel? – and with you, sir?'

'You shall sojourn at Paris, Rome, and Naples: at Florence, Venice, and Vienna: all the ground I have wandered over shall be re-trodden by you: wherever I stamped my hoof, your sylph's foot shall step also. Ten years since, I flew through Europe half mad; with disgust, hate, and rage as my companions: now I shall revisit it healed and cleansed, with a very angel as my comforter.'

I laughed at him as he said this. 'I am not an angel,' I asserted; 'and I will not

be one till I die: I will be myself. Mr Rochester, you must neither expect nor
exact anything celestial of me – for you will not get it, any more than I shall get it
of you: which I do not at all anticipate.'

'What do you anticipate of me?'

'For a little while you will perhaps be as you are now, a very little while; and
then you will turn cool; and then you will be capricious; and then you will be
stern, and I shall have much ado to please you: but when you get well used to
me, you will perhaps like me again, *like* me, I say, not *love* me. I suppose your
love will effervesce in six months, or less. I have observed in books written by
men, that period assigned as the farthest to which a husband's ardour extends.
Yet, after all, as a friend and companion, I hope never to become quite
distasteful to my dear master.'

'Distasteful! and like you again! I think I shall like you again, and yet again:
and I will make you confess I do not only *like*, but *love* you – with truth, fervour,
constancy.'

'Yet are you not capricious, sir?'

'To women who please me only by their faces, I am the very devil when I find
out they have neither souls nor hearts – when they open to me a perspective of
flatness, triviality, and perhaps imbecility, coarseness, and ill-temper: but to the
clear eye and eloquent tongue, to the soul made of fire, and the character that
bends but does not break – at once supple and stable, tractable and consistent – I
am ever tender and true.'

'Had you ever experience of such a character, sir? Did you ever love such an
one?'

'I love it now.'

'But before me: if I, indeed, in any respect come up to your difficult standard?'

'I never met your likeness. Jane, you please me, and you master me – you seem
to submit, and I like the sense of pliancy you impart; and while I am twining the
soft, silken skein round my finger, it sends a thrill up my arm to my heart. I am
influenced – conquered; and the influence is sweeter than I can express; and the
conquest I undergo has a witchery beyond any triumph I can win. Why do you
smile, Jane? What does that inexplicable, that uncanny turn of countenance mean?'

'I was thinking, sir (you will excuse the idea; it was involuntary), I was
thinking of Hercules and Samson with their charmers –'

'You were, you little elfish –'

'Hush, sir! You don't talk very wisely just now; any more than those gentle-
men acted very wisely. However, had they been married, they would no doubt
by their severity as husbands have made up for their softness as suitors; and so
will you, I fear. I wonder how you will answer me a year hence, should I ask a
favour it does not suit your convenience or pleasure to grant.'

'Ask me something now, Janet – the least thing; I desire to be entreated –'

'Indeed I will, sir; I have my petition all ready.'

'Speak! But if you look up and smile with that countenance, I shall swear
concession before I know to what, and that will make a fool of me.'

'Not at all, sir; I ask only this: don't send for the jewels, and don't crown me

with roses: you might as well put a border of gold lace round that plain pocket-handkerchief you have there.'

'I might as well "gild refined gold." I know it: your request is granted then – for the time. I will remand the order I despatched to my banker. But you have not yet asked for anything; you have prayed a gift to be withdrawn: try again.'

'Well then, sir, have the goodness to gratify my curiosity, which is much piqued on one point.'

He looked disturbed. 'What? what?' he said hastily. 'Curiosity is a dangerous petition: it is well I have not taken a vow to accord every request – '

'But there can be no danger in complying with this, sir.'

'Utter it, Jane: but I wish that instead of a mere enquiry into, perhaps, a secret, it was a wish for half my estate.'

'Now, King Ahasuerus! What do I want with half your estate? Do you think I am a Jew-usurer, seeking good investment in land? I would much rather have all your confidence. You will not exclude me from your confidence if you admit me to your heart?'

'You are welcome to all my confidence that is worth having, Jane; but for God's sake, don't desire a useless burden! Don't long for poison – don't turn out a downright Eve on my hands!'

'Why not, sir? You have just been telling me how much you liked to be conquered, and how pleasant over-persuasion is to you. Don't you think I had better take advantage of the confession, and begin and coax and entreat – even cry and be sulky if necessary – for the sake of a mere essay of my power?'

'I dare you to any such experiment. Encroach, presume, and the game is up.'

'Is it, sir? You soon give in. How stern you look now! Your eyebrows have become as thick as my finger, and your forehead resembles what, in some very astonishing poetry, I once saw styled, "a blue-piled thunderloft." That will be your married look, sir, I suppose?'

'If that will be *your* married look, I, as a Christian, will soon give up the notion of consorting with a mere sprite or salamander. But what had you to ask, thing, out with it?'

'There, you are less than civil now; and I like rudeness a great deal better than flattery. I had rather be a *thing* than an angel. This is what I have to ask, Why did you take such pains to make me believe you wished to marry Miss Ingram?'

'Is that all? Thank God it is no worse!' And now he unknit his black brows; looked down, smiling at me, and stroked my hair, as if well pleased at seeing a danger averted. 'I think I may confess,' he continued, 'even although I should make you a little indignant, Jane – and I have seen what a fire-spirit you can be when you are indignant. You glowed in the cool moonlight last night, when you mutinied against fate, and claimed your rank as my equal. Janet, by the bye, it was you who made me the offer.'

'Of course I did. But to the point if you please, sir – Miss Ingram?'

'Well, I feigned courtship of Miss Ingram, because I wished to render you as madly in love with me as I was with you; and I knew jealousy would be the best ally I could call in for the furtherance of that end.'

'Excellent! Now you are small – not one whit bigger than the end of my little finger. It was a burning shame and a scandalous disgrace to act in that way. Did you think nothing of Miss Ingram's feelings, sir?'

'Her feelings are concentrated in one – pride; and that needs humbling. Were you jealous, Jane?'

'Never mind, Mr Rochester: it is in no way interesting to you to know that. Answer me truly once more. Do you think Miss Ingram will not suffer from your dishonest coquetry? Won't she feel forsaken and deserted?'

'Impossible! – when I told you how she, on the contrary, deserted me: the idea of my insolvency cooled, or rather extinguished, her flame in a moment.'

'You have a curious, designing mind, Mr Rochester. I am afraid your principles on some points are eccentric.'

'My principles were never trained, Jane: they may have grown a little awry for want of attention.'

'Once again, seriously; may I enjoy the great good that has been vouchsafed to me, without fearing that anyone else is suffering the bitter pain I myself felt a while ago?'

'That you may, my good little girl: there is not another being in the world has the same pure love for me as yourself – for I lay that pleasant unction to my soul, Jane, a belief in your affection.'

I turned my lips to the hand that lay on my shoulder. I loved him very much – more than I could trust myself to say – more than words had power to express. 'Ask something more,' he said presently; 'it is my delight to be entreated, and to yield.'

I was again ready with my request. 'Communicate your intentions to Mrs Fairfax, sir: she saw me with you last night in the hall, and she was shocked. Give her some explanation before I see her again. It pains me to be misjudged by so good a woman.'

'Go to your room, and put on your bonnet,' he replied. 'I mean you to accompany me to Millcote this morning; and while you prepare for the drive, I will enlighten the old lady's understanding. Did she think, Janet, you had given the world for love, and considered it well lost?'

'I believe she thought I had forgotten my station, and yours, sir.'

'Station! station! – your station is in my heart, and on the necks of those who would insult you, now or hereafter. Go.'

I was soon dressed; and when I heard Mr Rochester quit Mrs Fairfax's parlour, I hurried down to it. The old lady had been reading her morning portion of Scripture – the Lesson for the day; her Bible lay open before her, and her spectacles were upon it. Her occupation, suspended by Mr Rochester's announcement, seemed now forgotten: her eyes, fixed on the blank wall opposite, expressed the surprise of a quiet mind stirred by unwonted tidings. Seeing me, she roused herself: she made a sort of effort to smile, and framed a few words of congratulation; but the smile expired, and the sentence was abandoned unfinished. She put up her spectacles, shut the Bible, and pushed her chair back from the table.

'I feel so astonished,' she began, 'I hardly know what to say to you, Miss Eyre. I have surely not been dreaming, have I? Sometimes I half fall asleep when I am sitting alone and fancy things that have never happened. It has seemed to me more than once when I have been in a doze, that my dear husband, who died fifteen years since, has come in and sat down beside me; and that I have even heard him call me by my name, Alice, as he used to do. Now, can you tell me whether it is actually true that Mr Rochester has asked you to marry him? Don't laugh at me. But I really thought he came in here five minutes ago, and said that in a month you would be his wife.'

'He has said the same thing to me,' I replied.

'He has! Do you believe him? Have you accepted him?'

'Yes.'

She looked at me bewildered.

'I could never have thought it. He is a proud man: all the Rochesters were proud: and his father, at least, liked money. He, too, has always been called careful. He means to marry you?'

'He tells me so.'

She surveyed my whole person: in her eyes I read that they had there found no charm powerful enough to solve the enigma.

'It passes me!' she continued; 'but no doubt it is true since you say so. How it will answer, I cannot tell: I really don't know. Equality of position and fortune is often advisable in such cases; and there are twenty years of difference in your ages. He might almost be your father.'

'No, indeed, Mrs Fairfax!' exclaimed I, nettled; 'he is nothing like my father! No one, who saw us together, would suppose it for an instant. Mr Rochester looks as young, and is as young, as some men at five-and-twenty.'

'Is it really for love he is going to marry you?' she asked.

I was so hurt by her coldness and scepticism, that the tears rose to my eyes.

'I am sorry to grieve you,' pursued the widow; 'but you are so young, and so little acquainted with men, I wished to put you on your guard. It is an old saying that "all is not gold that glitters"; and in this case I do fear there will be something found to be different to what either you or I expect.'

'Why? – am I a monster?' I said: 'is it impossible that Mr Rochester should have a sincere affection for me?'

'No: you are very well; and much improved of late; and Mr Rochester, I dare say, is fond of you. I have always noticed that you were a sort of pet of his. There are times when, for your sake, I have been a little uneasy at his marked preference, and have wished to put you on your guard: but I did not like to suggest even the possibility of wrong. I knew such an idea would shock, perhaps offend you; and you were so discreet, and so thoroughly modest and sensible, I hoped you might be trusted to protect yourself. Last night I cannot tell you what I suffered when I sought all over the house, and could find you nowhere, nor the master either; and then, at twelve o'clock, saw you come in with him.'

'Well, never mind that now,' I interrupted impatiently; 'it is enough that all was right.'

'I hope all will be right in the end,' she said: 'but believe me, you cannot be too careful. Try and keep Mr Rochester at a distance: distrust yourself as well as him. Gentlemen in his station are not accustomed to marry their governesses.'

I was growing truly irritated: happily, Adèle ran in.

'Let me go, let me go to Millcote too!' she cried. 'Mr Rochester won't: though there is so much room in the new carriage. Beg him to let me go, mademoiselle.'

'That I will, Adèle'; and I hastened away with her, glad to quit my gloomy monitress. The carriage was ready: they were bringing it round to the front, and my master was pacing the pavement, Pilot following him backwards and forwards.

'Adèle may accompany us, may she not, sir?'

'I told her no. I'll have no brats! – I'll have only you.'

'Do let her go, Mr Rochester, if you please: it would be better.'

'Not it: she will be a restraint.'

He was quite peremptory, both in look and voice. The chill of Mrs Fairfax's warnings, and the damp of her doubts were upon me: something of unsubstantiality and uncertainty had beset my hopes. I half lost the sense of power over him. I was about mechanically to obey him, without further remonstrance; but as he helped me into the carriage, he looked at my face.

'What is the matter?' he asked; 'all the sunshine is gone. Do you really wish the bairn to go? Will it annoy you if she is left behind?'

'I would far rather she went, sir.'

'Then off for your bonnet, and back like a flash of lightning!' cried he to Adèle. She obeyed him with what speed she might.

'After all, a single morning's interruption will not matter much,' said he, 'when I mean shortly to claim you – your thoughts, conversation, and company – for life.'

Adèle, when lifted in, commenced kissing me, by way of expressing her gratitude for my intercession: she was instantly stowed away into a corner on the other side of him. She then peeped round to where I sat; so stern a neighbour was too restrictive; to him, in his present fractious mood, she dared whisper no observations, nor ask of him any information.

'Let her come to me,' I entreated: 'she will, perhaps, trouble you, sir: there is plenty of room on this side.' He handed her over as if she had been a lapdog. 'I'll send her to school yet,' he said, but now he was smiling.

Adèle heard him, and asked if she was to go to school 'sans mademoiselle?'

'Yes,' he replied, 'absolutely sans mademoiselle; for I am to take mademoiselle to the moon, and there I shall seek a cave in one of the white valleys among the volcano-tops, and mademoiselle shall live with me there, and only me.'

'She will have nothing to eat: you will starve her,' observed Adèle.

'I shall gather manna for her morning and night: the plains and hillsides in the moon are bleached with manna, Adèle.'

'She will want to warm herself: what will she do for a fire?'

'Fire rises out of the lunar mountains: when she is cold, I'll carry her up to a peak, and lay her down on the edge of a crater.'

'Oh, qu'elle y sera mal – peu comfortable! And her clothes, they will wear out: how can she get new ones?'

Mr Rochester professed to be puzzled. 'Hem!' said he. 'What would you do, Adèle? Cudgel your brains for an expedient. How would a white or a pink cloud answer for a gown, do you think? And one could cut a pretty enough scarf out of a rainbow.'

'She is far better as she is,' concluded Adèle, after musing some time: 'besides, she would get tired of living with only you in the moon. If I were mademoiselle, I would never consent to go with you.'

'She has consented: she has pledged her word.'

'But you can't get her there; there is no road to the moon: it is all air; and neither you nor she can fly.'

'Adèle, look at that field.' We were now outside Thornfield gates, and bowling lightly along the smooth road to Millcote, where the dust was well laid by the thunderstorm, and where the low hedges and lofty timber trees on each side glistened green and rain-refreshed.

'In that field, Adèle, I was walking late one evening about a fortnight since – the evening of the day you helped me to make hay in the orchard meadows; and as I was tired with raking swaths, I sat down to rest me on a stile; and there I took out a little book and a pencil, and began to write about a misfortune that befell me long ago, and a wish I had for happy days to come: I was writing away very fast, though daylight was fading from the leaf, when something came up the path and stopped two yards off me. I looked at it. It was a little thing with a veil of gossamer on its head. I beckoned it to come near me; it stood soon at my knee. I never spoke to it, and it never spoke to me, in words; but I read its eyes, and it read mine; and our speechless colloquy was to this effect – 'It was a fairy, and come from Elf-land, it said; and its errand was to make me happy: I must go with it out of the common world to a lonely place – such as the moon, for instance – and it nodded its head towards her horn, rising over Hayhill: it told me of the alabaster cave and silver vale where we might live. I said I should like to go; but reminded it, as you did me, that I had no wings to fly.

' "Oh," returned the fairy, "that does not signify! Here is a talisman will remove all difficulties"; and she held out a pretty gold ring. "Put it," she said, "on the fourth finger of my left hand, and I am yours, and you are mine; and we shall leave earth, and make our own heaven yonder." She nodded again at the moon. The ring, Adèle, is in my breeches-pocket, under the disguise of a sovereign: but I mean soon to change it to a ring again.'

'But what has mademoiselle to do with it? I don't care for the fairy: you said it was mademoiselle you would take to the moon?'

'Mademoiselle is a fairy,' he said, whispering mysteriously. Whereupon I told her not to mind his badinage; and she, on her part, evinced a fund of genuine French scepticism: denominating Mr Rochester 'un vrai menteur', and assuring him that she made no account whatever of his 'contes de fée', and that 'du reste, il n'y avait pas de fées, et quand même il y en avait': she was sure they would never appear to him, nor ever give him rings, or offer to live with him in the moon.

The hour spent at Millcote was a somewhat harassing one to me. Mr Rochester obliged me to go to a certain silk warehouse: there I was ordered to choose half a dozen dresses. I hated the business, I begged leave to defer it: no – it should be gone through with now. By dint of entreaties expressed- in energetic whispers, I reduced the half-dozen to two: these, however, he vowed he would select himself. With anxiety I watched his eye rove over the gay stores: he fixed on a rich silk of the most brilliant amethyst dye, and a superb pink satin. I told him in a new series of whispers, that he might as well buy me a gold gown and a silver bonnet at once: I should certainly never venture to wear his choice. With infinite difficulty, for he was stubborn as a stone, I persuaded him to make an exchange in favour of a sober black satin and pearl-grey silk. 'It might pass for the present,' he said; 'but he would yet see me glittering like a parterre.'

Glad was I to get him out of the silk warehouse, and then out of a jeweller's shop: the more he bought me, the more my cheek burned with a sense of annoyance and degradation. As we re-entered the carriage, and I sat back feverish and fagged, I remembered what, in the hurry of events, dark and bright, I had wholly forgotten – the letter of my uncle, John Eyre, to Mrs Reed: his intention to adopt me and make me his legatee. 'It would, indeed, be a relief,' I thought, 'if I had ever so small an independency; I never can bear being dressed like a doll by Mr Rochester, or sitting like a second Danae with the golden shower falling daily round me. I will write to Madeira the moment I get home, and tell my uncle John I am going to be married, and to whom: if I had but a prospect of one day bringing Mr Rochester an accession of fortune, I could better endure to be kept by him now.' And somewhat relieved by this idea (which I failed not to execute that day), I ventured once more to meet my master's and lover's eye, which most pertinaciously sought mine, though I averted both face and gaze. He smiled; and I thought his smile was such as a sultan might, in a blissful and fond moment, bestow on a slave his gold and gems had enriched: I crushed his hand, which was ever hunting mine, vigorously, and thrust it back to him red with the passionate pressure.

'You need not look in that way,' I said; 'if you do, I'll wear nothing but my old Lowood frocks to the end of the chapter. I'll be married in this lilac gingham: you may make a dressing-gown for yourself out of the pearl-grey silk, and an infinite series of waistcoats out of the black satin.'

He chuckled; he rubbed his hands. 'Oh, it is rich to see and hear her?' he exclaimed. 'Is she original? Is she piquant? I would not exchange this one little English girl for the Grand Turk's whole seraglio, gazelle-eyes, houri forms, and all!'

The Eastern allusion bit me again. 'I'll not stand you an inch in the stead of a seraglio,' I said; 'so don't consider me an equivalent for one. If you have a fancy for anything in that line, away with you, sir, to the bazaars of Stamboul without delay, and lay out in extensive slave-purchases some of that spare cash you seem at a loss to spend satisfactorily here.'

'And what will you do, Janet, while I am bargaining for so many tons of flesh and such an assortment of black eyes?'

'I'll be preparing myself to go out as a missionary to preach liberty to them that are enslaved – your harem inmates amongst the rest. I'll get admitted there, and I'll stir up mutiny; and you, three-tailed bashaw as you are, sir, shall in a trice find yourself fettered amongst our hands: nor will I, for one, consent to cut your bonds till you have signed a charter, the most liberal that despot ever yet conferred.'

'I would consent to be at your mercy, Jane.'

'I would have no mercy, Mr Rochester, if you supplicated for it with an eye like that. While you looked so, I should be certain that whatever charter you might grant under coercion, your first act, when released, would be to violate its conditions.'

'Why, Jane, what would you have? I fear you will compel me to go through a private marriage ceremony, besides that performed at the altar. You will stipulate, I see, for peculiar terms – what will they be?'

'I only want an easy mind, sir; not crushed by crowded obligations. Do you remember what you said of Céline Varens? – of the diamonds, the cashmeres you gave her? I will not be your English Céline Varens. I shall continue to act as Adèle's governess; by that I shall earn my board and lodging, and thirty pounds a year besides. I'll furnish my own wardrobe out of that money, and you shall give me nothing but – '

'Well, but what?'

'Your regard; and if I give you mine in return, that debt will be quit.'

'Well, for cool native impudence and pure innate pride, you haven't your equal,' said he. We were now approaching Thornfield. 'Will it please you to dine with me today?' he asked, as we re-entered the gates.

'No, thank you, sir.'

'And what for, "no, thank you?" if one may enquire.'

'I never have dined with you, sir: and I see no reason why I should now: till – '

'Till what? You delight in half-phrases.'

'Till I can't help it.'

'Do you suppose I eat like an ogre or a ghoul, that you dread being the companion of my repast?'

'I have formed no supposition on the subject, sir; but I want to go on as usual for another month.'

'You will give up your governessing slavery at once.'

'Indeed, begging your pardon, sir, I shall not. I shall just go on with it as usual. I shall keep out of your way all day, as I have been accustomed to do: you may send for me in the evening, when you feel disposed to see me, and I'll come then; but at no other time.'

'I want a smoke, Jane, or a pinch of snuff, to comfort me under all this, "pour me donner une contenance," as Adèle would say; and unfortunately I have neither my cigar-case nor my snuff-box. But listen – whisper. It is your time now, little tyrant, but it will be mine presently; and when once I have fairly seized you, to have and to hold, I'll just – figuratively speaking – attach you to a chain like this' (touching his watch-guard). 'Yes, bonny wee thing, I'll wear you in my bosom, lest my jewel I should tyne.'

He said this as he helped me to alight from the carriage, and while he afterwards lifted out Adèle, I entered the house, and made good my retreat upstairs.

He duly summoned me to his presence in the evening. I had prepared an occupation for him; for I was determined not to spend the whole time in a *tête-à-tête* conversation. I remembered his fine voice; I knew he liked to sing – good singers generally do. I was no vocalist myself, and, in his fastidious judgement, no musician, either; but I delighted in listening when the performance was good. No sooner had twilight, that hour of romance, began to lower her blue and starry banner over the lattice, than I rose, opened the piano, and entreated him, for the love of heaven, to give me a song. He said I was a capricious witch, and that he would rather sing another time; but I averred that no time like the present.

'Did I like his voice?' he asked.

'Very much.' I was not fond of pampering that susceptible vanity of his; but for once, and from motives of expediency, I would e'en soothe and stimulate it.

'Then, Jane, you must play the accompaniment.'

'Very well, sir, I will try.'

I did try, but was presently swept off the stool and denominated 'a little bungler.' Being pushed unceremoniously to one side – which was precisely what I wished – he usurped my place, and proceeded to accompany himself: for he could play as well as sing. I hied me to the window-recess. And while I sat there and looked out on the still trees and dim lawn, to a sweet air was sung in mellow tones the following strain:

The truest love that ever heart
    Felt at its kindled core,
Did through each vein, in quickened start,
    The tide of being pour.

Her coming was my hope each day,
    Her parting was my pain;
The chance that did her steps delay
    Was ice in every vein.

I dreamed it would be nameless bliss,
    As I loved, loved to be;
And to this object did I press
    As blind as eagerly.

But wide as pathless was the space
    That lay our lives between,
And dangerous as the foamy race
    Of ocean-surges green.

And haunted as a robber-path
    Through wilderness or wood;
For Might and Right, and Woe and Wrath,
    Between our spirits stood.

I dangers dared; I hindrance scorned;
   I omens did defy:
Whatever menaced, harassed, warned,
   I passed impetuous by.

On sped my rainbow, fast as light;
   I flew as in a dream;
For glorious rose upon my sight
   That child of Shower and Gleam.

Still bright on clouds of suffering dim
   Shines that soft, solemn joy;
Nor care I now, how dense and grim
   Disasters gather nigh.

I care not in this moment sweet,
   Though all I have rushed o'er
Should come on pinion, strong and fleet,
   Proclaiming vengeance sore:

Though haughty Hate should strike me down,
   Right, bar approach to me,
And grinding Might, with furious frown,
   Swear endless enmity.

My love has placed her little hand
   With noble faith in mine,
And vowed that wedlock's sacred band
   Our nature shall entwine.

My love has sworn, with sealing kiss,
   With me to live – to die;
I have at last my nameless bliss:
   As I love – loved am I!

He rose and came towards me, and I saw his face all kindled, and his full falcon-eye flashing, and tenderness and passion in every lineament. I quailed momentarily – then I rallied. Soft scene, daring demonstration, I would not have; and I stood in peril of both: a weapon of defence must be prepared – I whetted my tongue: as he reached me, I asked with asperity, 'whom he was going to marry now?'

'That was a strange question to be put by his darling Jane.'

'Indeed! I considered it a very natural and necessary one: he had talked of his future wife dying with him. What did he mean by such a pagan idea? *I* had no intention of dying with him – he might depend on that.'

'Oh, all he longed, all he prayed for, was that I might live with him! Death was not for such as I.'

'Indeed it was: I had as good a right to die when my time came as he had: but I should bide that time, and not be hurried away in a suttee.'

'Would I forgive him for the selfish idea, and prove my pardon by a reconciling kiss?'

'No: I would rather be excused.'

Here I heard myself apostrophised as a 'hard little thing'; and it was added, 'any other woman would have been melted to marrow at hearing such stanzas crooned in her praise.'

I assured him I was naturally hard – very flinty, and that he would often find me so; and that, moreover, I was determined to show him divers rugged points in my character before the ensuing four weeks elapsed: he should know fully what sort of a bargain he had made, while there was yet time to rescind it.

'Would I be quiet and talk rationally?'

'I would be quiet if he liked, and as to talking rationally, I flattered myself I was doing that now.'

He fretted, pished, and pshawed. 'Very good,' I thought; 'you may fume and fidget as you please: but this is the best plan to pursue with you, I am certain. I like you more than I can say; but I'll not sink into a bathos of sentiment: and with this needle of repartee I'll keep you from the edge of the gulf too; and, moreover, maintain by its pungent aid that distance between you and myself most conducive to our real mutual advantage.'

From less to more, I worked him up to considerable irritation; then, after he had retired, in dudgeon, quite to the other end of the room, I got up, and saying, 'I wish you good-night, sir,' in my natural and wonted respectful manner, I slipped out by the side-door and got away.

The system thus entered on, I pursued during the whole season of probation; and with the best success. He was kept, to be sure, rather cross and crusty; but on the whole I could see he was excellently entertained, and that a lamb-like submission and turtle-dove sensibility, while fostering his despotism more, would have pleased his judgement, satisfied his common-sense, and even suited his taste less.

In other people's presence I was, as formerly, deferential and quiet; any other line of conduct being uncalled for: it was only in the evening conferences I thus thwarted and afflicted him. He continued to send for me punctually the moment the clock struck seven; though when I appeared before him now, he had no such honeyed terms as 'love' and 'darling' on his lips: the best words at my service were 'provoking puppet', 'malicious elf', 'sprite', 'changeling', etc. For caresses, too, I now got grimaces; for a pressure of the hand, a pinch on the arm; for a kiss on the cheek, a severe tweak of the ear. It was all right: at present I decidedly preferred these fierce favours to anything more tender. Mrs Fairfax, I saw, approved me: her anxiety on my account vanished; therefore I was certain I did well. Meantime, Mr Rochester affirmed I was wearing him to skin and bone, and threatened awful vengeance for my present conduct at some period fast coming. I laughed in my sleeve at his menaces. 'I can keep you in reasonable check now,' I reflected; 'and I don't doubt to be able to do it hereafter: if one expedient loses its virtue, another must be devised.'

Yet after all my task was not an easy one; often I would rather have pleased

than teased him. My future husband was becoming to me my whole world; and more than the world: almost my hope of heaven. He stood between me and every thought of religion, as an eclipse intervenes between man and the broad sun. I could not, in those days, see God for His creature: of whom I had made an idol.

## Chapter 25

The month of courtship had wasted: its very last hours were being numbered. There was no putting off the day that advanced – the bridal day; and all preparations for its arrival were complete. *I*, at least, had nothing more to do: there were my trunks, packed, locked, corded, ranged in a row along the wall of my little chamber; tomorrow, at this time, they would be far on their road to London: and so should I (d.v.), or rather, not I, but one Jane Rochester, a person whom as yet I knew not. The cards of address alone remained to nail on: they lay, four little squares, in the drawer. Mr Rochester had himself written the direction, 'Mrs Rochester, — Hotel, London', on each: I could not persuade myself to affix them, or to have them affixed. Mrs Rochester! She did not exist: she would not be born till tomorrow, sometime after eight o'clock a.m.; and I would wait to be assured she had come into the world alive before I assigned to her all that property. It was enough that in yonder closet, opposite my dressing-table, garments said to be hers had already displaced my black stuff Lowood frock and straw bonnet: for not to me appertained that suit of wedding raiment; the pearl-coloured robe, the vapoury veil pendent from the usurped portmanteau. I shut the closet to conceal the strange, wraith-like apparel it contained; which, at this evening hour – nine o'clock – gave out certainly a most ghostly shimmer through the shadow of my apartment. 'I will leave you by yourself, white dream,' I said. 'I am feverish: I hear the wind blowing: I will go out of doors and feel it.'

It was not only the hurry of preparation that made me feverish; not only the anticipation of the great change – the new life which was to commence tomorrow: both these circumstances had their share, doubtless, in producing that restless, excited mood which hurried me forth at this late hour into the darkening grounds: but a third cause influenced my mind more than they.

I had at heart a strange and anxious thought. Something had happened which I could not comprehend; no one knew of or had seen the event but myself: it had taken place the preceding night. Mr Rochester that night was absent from home; nor was he yet returned: business had called him to a small estate of two or three farms he possessed thirty miles off – business it was requisite he should settle in person, previous to his meditated departure from England. I waited now his return; eager to disburden my mind, and to seek of him the solution of the enigma that perplexed me. Stay till he comes, reader: and, when I disclose my secret to him, you shall share the confidence.

I sought the orchard, driven to its shelter by the wind, which all day had blown

strong and full from the south, without, however, bringing a speck of rain. Instead of subsiding as night drew on, it seemed to augment its rush and deepen its roar: the trees blew steadfastly one way, never writhing round, and scarcely tossing back their boughs once in an hour; so continuous was the strain bending their branchy heads northward – the clouds drifted from pole to pole, fast following, mass on mass: no glimpse of blue sky had been visible that July day.

It was not without a certain wild pleasure I ran before the wind, delivering my trouble of mind to the measureless air-torrent thundering through space. Descending the laurel walk, I faced the wreck of the chestnut-tree; it stood up black and riven: the trunk, split down the centre, gaped ghastly. The cloven halves were not broken from each other, for the firm base and strong roots kept them unsundered below; though community of vitality was destroyed – the sap could flow no more: their great boughs on each side were dead, and next winter's tempests would be sure to fell one or both to earth: as yet, however, they might be said to form one tree – a ruin, but an entire ruin.

'You did right to hold fast to each other,' I said: as if the monster-splinters were living things, and could hear me. 'I think, scathed as you look, and charred and scorched, there must be a little sense of life in you yet, rising out of that adhesion at the faithful, honest roots: you will never have green leaves more – never more see birds making nests and singing idylls in your boughs; the time of pleasure and love is over with you: but you are not desolate: each of you has a comrade to sympathise with him in his decay.' As I looked up at them, the moon appeared momentarily in that part of the sky which filled their fissure; her disk was blood-red and half overcast; she seemed to throw on me one bewildered, dreary glance, and buried herself again instantly in the deep drift of cloud. The wind fell, for a second, round Thornfield; but far away over wood and water, poured a wild, melancholy wail: it was sad to listen to, and I ran off again.

Here and there I strayed through the orchard, gathered up the apples with which the grass round the tree roots was thickly strewn; then I employed myself in dividing the ripe from the unripe; I carried them into the house and put them away in the storeroom. Then I repaired to the library to ascertain whether the fire was lit, for, though summer, I knew on such a gloomy evening Mr Rochester would like to see a cheerful hearth when he came in: yes, the fire had been kindled sometime, and burnt well. I placed his armchair by the chimney-corner: I wheeled the table near it: I let down the curtain, and had the candles brought in ready for lighting. More restless than ever, when I had completed these arrangements I could not sit still, nor even remain in the house: a little timepiece in the room and the old clock in the hall simultaneously struck ten.

'How late it grows!' I said. 'I will run down to the gates: it is moonlight at intervals; I can see a good way on the road. He may be coming now, and to meet him will save some minutes of suspense.'

The wind roared high in the great trees which embowered the gates; but the road as far as I could see, to the right hand and the left, was all still and solitary: save for the shadows of clouds crossing it at intervals as the moon looked out, it was but a long pale line, unvaried by one moving speck.

A puerile tear dimmed my eye while I looked – a tear of disappointment and impatience; ashamed of it, I wiped it away. I lingered; the moon shut herself wholly within her chamber, and drew close her curtain of dense cloud: the night grew dark; rain came driving fast on the gale.

'I wish he would come! I wish he would come!' I exclaimed, seized with hypochondriac foreboding. I had expected his arrival before tea; now it was dark: what could keep him? Had an accident happened? The event of last night again recurred to me. I interpreted it as a warning of disaster. I feared my hopes were too bright to be realised; and I had enjoyed so much bliss lately that I imagined my fortune had passed its meridian, and must now decline.

'Well, I cannot return to the house,' I thought; 'I cannot sit by the fireside, while he is abroad in inclement weather: better tire my limbs than strain my heart; I will go forward and meet him.'

I set out; I walked fast, but not far: ere I had measured a quarter of a mile, I heard the tramp of hoofs; a horseman came on, full gallop; a dog ran by his side. Away with evil presentiment! It was he: here he was, mounted on Mesrour, followed by Pilot. He saw me; for the moon had opened a blue field in the sky, and rode in it watery bright: he took his hat off, and waved it round his head. I now ran to meet him.

'There!' he exclaimed, as he stretched out his hand and bent from the saddle: 'you can't do without me, that is evident. Step on my boot-toe; give me both hands: mount!'

I obeyed: joy made me agile: I sprang up before him. A hearty kissing I got for a welcome, and some boastful triumph, which I swallowed as well as I could. He checked himself in his exultation to demand, 'But is there anything the matter, Janet, that you come to meet me at such an hour? Is there anything wrong?'

'No, but I thought you would never come. I could not bear to wait in the house for you, especially with this rain and wind.'

'Rain and wind, indeed! Yes, you are dripping like a mermaid; pull my cloak round you: but I think you are feverish, Jane: both your cheek and hand are burning hot. I ask again, is there anything the matter?'

'Nothing now; I am neither afraid nor unhappy.'

'Then you have been both?'

'Rather: but I'll tell you all about it by and by, sir, and I dare say you will only laugh at me for my pains.'

'I'll laugh at you heartily when tomorrow is past; till then I dare not: my prize is not certain. This is you, who have been as slippery as an eel this last month, and as thorny as a briar-rose? I could not lay a finger anywhere but I was pricked; and now I seem to have gathered up a stray lamb in my arms. You wandered out of the fold to seek your shepherd, did you, Jane?'

'I wanted you: but don't boast. Here we are at Thornfield: now let me get down.'

He landed me on the pavement. As John took his horse, and he followed me into the hall, he told me to make haste and put something dry on, and then return to him in the library; and he stopped me, as I made for the staircase, to

extort a promise that I would not be long: nor was I long; in five minutes I rejoined him. I found him at supper.

'Take a seat and bear me company, Jane: please God, it is the last meal but one you will eat at Thornfield Hall for a long time.'

I sat down near him, but told him I could not eat.

'Is it because you have the prospect of a journey before you, Jane? Is it the thoughts of going to London that takes away your appetite?'

'I cannot see my prospects clearly tonight, sir; and I hardly know what thoughts I have in my head. Everything in life seems unreal.'

'Except me: I am substantial enough – touch me.'

'You, sir, are the most phantom-like of all: you are a mere dream.'

He held out his hand, laughing. 'Is that a dream?' said he, placing it close to my eyes. He had a rounded, muscular, and vigorous hand, as well as a long, strong arm.

'Yes; though I touch it, it is a dream,' said I, as I put it down from before my face. 'Sir, have you finished supper?'

'Yes, Jane.'

I rang the bell and ordered away the tray. When we were again alone, I stirred the fire, and then took a low seat at my master's knee.

'It is near midnight,' I said.

'Yes: but remember, Jane, you promised to wake with me the night before my wedding.'

'I did; and I will keep my promise, for an hour or two at least: I have no wish to go to bed.'

'Are all your arrangements complete?'

'All, sir.'

'And on my part likewise,' he returned, 'I have settled everything; and we shall leave Thornfield tomorrow, within half an hour after our return from church.'

'Very well, sir.'

'With what an extraordinary smile you uttered that word – "very well", Jane! What a bright spot of colour you have on each cheek! and how strangely your eyes glitter! Are you well?'

'I believe I am.'

'Believe! What is the matter? Tell me what you feel.'

'I could not, sir: no words could tell you what I feel. I wish this present hour would never end: who knows with what fate the next may come charged?'

'This is hypochondria, Jane. You have been overexcited, or over-fatigued.'

'Do you, sir, feel calm and happy?'

'Calm? – no: but happy – to the heart's core.'

I looked up at him to read the signs of bliss in his face: it was ardent and flushed.

'Give me your confidence, Jane,' he said: 'relieve your mind of any weight that oppresses it, by imparting it to me. What do you fear? – that I shall not prove a good husband?'

'It is the idea farthest from my thoughts.'

'Are you apprehensive of the new sphere you are about to enter? – of the new life into which you are passing?'

'No.'

'You puzzle me, Jane: your look and tone of sorrowful audacity perplex and pain me. I want an explanation.'

'Then, sir, listen. You were from home last night?'

'I was: I know that; and you hinted a while ago at something which had happened in my absence: nothing, probably, of consequence; but, in short, it has disturbed you. Let me hear it. Mrs Fairfax has said something, perhaps? or you have overheard the servants talk? – your sensitive self-respect has been wounded?'

'No, sir.' It struck twelve – I waited till the timepiece had concluded its silver chime, and the clock its hoarse, vibrating stroke, and then I proceeded.

'All day yesterday I was very busy, and very happy in my ceaseless bustle; for I am not, as you seem to think, troubled by any haunting fears about the new sphere, et cetera: I think it a glorious thing to have the hope of living with you, because I love you. No, sir, don't caress me now – let me talk undisturbed. Yesterday I trusted well in Providence, and believed that events were working together for your good and mine: it was a fine day, if you recollect – the calmness of the air and sky forbade apprehensions respecting your safety or comfort on your journey. I walked a little while on the pavement after tea, thinking of you; and I beheld you in imagination so near me, I scarcely missed your actual presence. I thought of the life that lay before me – *your* life, sir – an existence more expansive and stirring than my own: as much more so as the depths of the sea to which the brook runs are than the shallows of its own strait channel. I wondered why moralists call this world a dreary wilderness: for me it blossomed like a rose. Just at sunset, the air turned cold and the sky cloudy: I went in, Sophie called me upstairs to look at my wedding-dress, which they had just brought; and under it in the box I found your present – the veil which, in your princely extravagance, you sent for from London: resolved, I suppose, since I would not have jewels, to cheat me into accepting something as costly. I smiled as I unfolded it, and devised how I would tease you about your aristocratic tastes, and your efforts to masque your plebeian bride in the attributes of a peeress. I thought how I would carry down to you the square of unembroidered blond I had myself prepared as a covering for my low-born head, and ask if that was not good enough for a woman who could bring her husband neither fortune, beauty, nor connections. I saw plainly how you would look; and heard your impetuous republican answers, and your haughty disavowal of any necessity on your part to augment your wealth, or elevate your standing, by marrying either a purse or a coronet.'

'How well you read me, you witch!' interposed Mr Rochester: 'but what did you find in the veil besides its embroidery? Did you find poison, or a dagger, that you look so mournful now?'

'No, no, sir; besides the delicacy and richness of the fabric, I found nothing save Fairfax Rochester's pride; and that did not scare me, because I am used to

the sight of the demon. But, sir, as it grew dark, the wind rose: it blew yesterday evening, not as it blows now – wild and high – but "with a sullen, moaning sound" far more eerie. I wished you were at home. I came into this room, and the sight of the empty chair and fireless hearth chilled me. For some time after I went to bed, I could not sleep – a sense of anxious excitement distressed me. The gale still rising, seemed to my ear to muffle a mournful under-sound; whether in the house or abroad I could not at first tell, but it recurred, doubtful yet doleful at every lull; at last I made out it must be some dog howling at a distance. I was glad when it ceased. On sleeping, I continued in dreams the idea of a dark and gusty night. I continued also the wish to be with you, and experienced a strange, regretful consciousness of some barrier dividing us. During all my first sleep, I was following the windings of an unknown road; total obscurity environed me; rain pelted me; I was burdened with the charge of a little child: a very small creature, too young and feeble to walk, and which shivered in my cold arms, and wailed piteously in my ear. I thought, sir, that you were on the road a long way before me; and I strained every nerve to overtake you, and made effort on effort to utter your name and entreat you to stop – but my movements were fettered, and my voice still died away inarticulate; while you, I felt, withdrew farther and farther every moment.'

'And these dreams weigh on your spirits now, Jane, when I am close to you? Little nervous subject! Forget visionary woe, and think only of real happiness! You say you love me, Janet: yes – I will not forget that; and you cannot deny it. *Those* words did not die inarticulate on your lips. I heard them clear and soft: a thought too solemn perhaps, but sweet as music – "I think it is a glorious thing to have the hope of living with you, Edward, because I love you." Do you love me, Jane? – repeat it.'

'I do, sir – I do, with my whole heart.'

'Well,' he said, after some minutes' silence, 'it is strange; but that sentence has penetrated my breast painfully. Why? I think because you said it with such an earnest, religious energy, and because your upward gaze at me now is the very sublime of faith, truth, and devotion: it is too much as if some spirit were near me. Look wicked, Jane: as you know well how to look: coin one of your wild, shy, provoking smiles, tell me you hate me – tease me, vex me; do anything but move me: I would rather be incensed than saddened.'

'I will tease you and vex you to your heart's content, when I have finished my tale: but hear me to the end.'

'I thought, Jane, you had told me all. I thought I had found the source of your melancholy in a dream.'

I shook my head. 'What! is there more? But I will not believe it to be anything important. I warn you of incredulity beforehand. Go on.'

The disquietude of his air, the somewhat apprehensive impatience of his manner, surprised me: but I proceeded.

'I dreamt another dream, sir: that Thornfield Hall was a dreary ruin, the retreat of bats and owls. I thought that of all the stately front nothing remained but a shell-like wall, very high and very fragile-looking. I wandered, on a

moonlight night, through the grass-grown enclosure within: here I stumbled over a marble hearth, and there over a fallen fragment of cornice. Wrapped up in a shawl, I still carried the unknown little child: I might not lay it down anywhere, however tired were my arms – however much its weight impeded my progress, I must retain it. I heard the gallop of a horse at a distance on the road; I was sure it was you; and you were departing for many years and for a distant country. I climbed the thin wall with frantic perilous haste, eager to catch one glimpse of you from the top: the stones rolled from under my feet, the ivy branches I grasped gave way, the child clung round my neck in terror, and almost strangled me; at last I gained the summit. I saw you like a speck on a white track, lessening every moment. The blast blew so strong I could not stand. I sat down on the narrow ledge; I hushed the scared infant in my lap: you turned an angle of the road: I bent forward to take a last look; the wall crumbled; I was shaken; the child rolled from my knee, I lost my balance, fell, and woke.'

'Now, Jane, that is all.'

'All the preface, sir; the tale is yet to come. On waking, a gleam dazzled my eyes; I thought – Oh, it is daylight! But I was mistaken; it was only candlelight. Sophie, I supposed, had come in. There was a light in the dressing-table, and the door of the closet, where, before going to bed, I had hung my wedding-dress and veil, stood open; I heard a rustling there. I asked, "Sophie, what are you doing?" No one answered; but a form emerged from the closet; it took the light, held it aloft, and surveyed the garments pendent from the portmanteau. "Sophie! Sophie!" I again cried: and still it was silent. I had risen up in bed, I bent forward: first surprise, then bewilderment, came over me; and then my blood crept cold through my veins. Mr Rochester, this was not Sophie, it was not Leah, it was not Mrs Fairfax: it was not – no, I was sure of it, and am still – it was not even that strange woman, Grace Poole.'

'It must have been one of them,' interrupted my master.

'No, sir, I solemnly assure you to the contrary. The shape standing before me had never crossed my eyes within the precincts of Thornfield Hall before; the height, the contour were new to me.'

'Describe it, Jane.'

'It seemed, sir, a woman, tall and large, with thick and dark hair hanging long down her back. I know not what dress she had on: it was white and straight; but whether gown, sheet, or shroud, I cannot tell.'

'Did you see her face?'

'Not at first. But presently she took my veil from its place; she held it up, gazed at it long, and then she threw it over her own head, and turned to the mirror. At that moment I saw the reflection of the visage and features quite distinctly in the dark oblong glass.'

'And how were they?'

'Fearful and ghastly to me – oh, sir, I never saw a face like it! It was a discoloured face – it was a savage face. I wish I could forget the roll of the red eyes and the fearful blackened inflation of the lineaments!'

'Ghosts are usually pale, Jane.'

'This, sir, was purple: the lips were swelled and dark; the brow furrowed: the black eyebrows widely raised over the bloodshot eyes. Shall I tell you of what it reminded me?'

'You may.'

'Of the foul German spectre – the Vampyre.'

'Ah! – what did it do?'

'Sir, it removed my veil from its gaunt head, rent it in two parts, and flinging both on the floor, trampled on them.'

'Afterwards?'

'It drew aside the window-curtain and looked out; perhaps it saw dawn approaching, for, taking the candle, it retreated to the door. Just at my bedside, the figure stopped: the fiery eyes glared upon me – she thrust up her candle close to my face, and extinguished it under my eyes. I was aware her lurid visage flamed over mine, and I lost consciousness: for the second time in my life – only the second time – I became insensible from terror.'

'Who was with you when you revived?'

'No one, sir, but the broad day. I rose, bathed my head and face in water, drank a long draught; felt that though enfeebled I was not ill, and determined that to none but you would I impart this vision. Now sir, tell me who and what that woman was?'

'The creature of an over-stimulated brain; that is certain. I must be careful of you, my treasure: nerves like yours were not made for rough handling.'

'Sir, depend on it, my nerves were not in fault; the thing was real: the transaction actually took place.'

'And your previous dreams, were they real too? Is Thornfield Hall a ruin? Am I severed from you by insuperable obstacles? Am I leaving you without a tear – without a kiss – without a word?'

'Not yet.'

'Am I about to do it? Why, the day is already commenced which is to bind us indissolubly; and when we are once united, there shall be no recurrence of these mental terrors: I guarantee that.'

'Mental terrors, sir! I wish I could believe them to be only such: I wish it more now than ever; since even you cannot explain to me the mystery of that awful visitant.'

'And since I cannot do it, Jane, it must have been unreal.'

'But, sir, when I said so to myself on rising this morning, and when I looked round the room to gather courage and comfort from the cheerful aspect of each familiar object in full daylight, there – on the carpet – I saw what gave the distinct lie to my hypothesis, the veil, torn from top to bottom in two halves!'

I felt Mr Rochester start and shudder; he hastily flung his arms round me. 'Thank God!' he exclaimed, 'that if anything malignant did come near you last night, it was only the veil that was harmed. Oh, to think what might have happened!'

He drew his breath short, and strained me so close to him, I could scarcely pant. After some minutes' silence, he continued, cheerily – 'Now, Janet, I'll

explain to you all about it. It was half dream, half reality. A woman did, I doubt not, enter your room: and that woman was – must have been – Grace Poole. You call her a strange being yourself: from all you know, you have reason so to call her – what did she do to me? what to Mason? In a state between sleeping and waking, you noticed her entrance and her actions; but feverish, almost delirious as you were, you ascribed to her a goblin appearance different from her own: the long dishevelled hair, the swelled black face, the exaggerated stature, were figments of imagination; results of nightmare: the spiteful tearing of the veil was real: and it is like her. I see you would ask why I keep such a woman in my house: when we have been married a year and a day, I will tell you; but not now. Are you satisfied, Jane? Do you accept my solution of the mystery?'

I reflected, and in truth it appeared to me the only possible one: satisfied I was not, but to please him I endeavoured to appear so – relieved, I certainly did feel; so I answered him with a contented smile. And now, as it was long past one, I prepared to leave him.

'Does not Sophie sleep with Adèle in the nursery?' he asked, as I lit my candle.

'Yes, sir.'

'And there is room enough in Adèle's little bed for you. You must share it with her tonight, Jane: it is no wonder that the incident you have related should make you nervous, and I would rather you did not sleep alone: promise me to go to the nursery.'

'I shall be very glad to do so, sir.'

'And fasten the door securely on the inside. Wake Sophie when you go upstairs, under pretence of requesting her to rouse you in good time tomorrow; for you must be dressed and have finished breakfast before eight. And now, no more sombre thoughts: chase dull care away, Janet. Don't you hear to what soft whispers the wind has fallen? and there is no more beating of rain against the window-panes: look here' (he lifted up the curtain) – 'it is a lovely night!'

It was. Half heaven was pure and stainless: the clouds, now trooping before the wind, which had shifted to the west, were filing off eastward in long, silvered columns. The moon shone peacefully.

'Well,' said Mr Rochester, gazing enquiringly into my eyes, 'how is my Janet now?'

'The night is serene, sir; and so am I.'

'And you will not dream of separation and sorrow tonight; but of happy love and blissful union.'

This prediction was but half fulfilled: I did not indeed dream of sorrow, but as little did I dream of Joy; for I never slept at all. With little Adèle in my arms, I watched the slumber of childhood – so tranquil so passionless, so innocent – and waited for the coming day: all my life was awake and astir in my frame: and as soon as the sun rose I rose too. I remember Adèle clung to me as I left her: I remember I kissed her as I loosened her little hands from my neck; and I cried over her with strange emotion, and quitted her because I feared my sobs would break her still sound repose. She seemed the emblem of my past life; and he I was now to array myself to meet, the dread, but adored, type of my unknown future day.

# *Chapter 26*

Sophie came at seven to dress me: she was very long indeed in accomplishing her task; so long that Mr Rochester, grown, I suppose, impatient of my delay, sent up to ask why I did not come. She was just fastening my veil (the plain square of blond after all) to my hair with a brooch; I hurried from under her hands as soon as I could.

'Stop!' she cried in French. 'Look at yourself in the mirror: you have not taken one peep.'

So I turned at the door: I saw a robed and veiled figure, so unlike my usual self that it seemed almost the image of a stranger. 'Jane!' called a voice, and I hastened down. I was received at the foot of the stairs by Mr Rochester.

'Lingerer!' he said, 'my brain is on fire with impatience, and you tarry so long!'

He took me into the dining-room, surveyed me keenly all over, pronounced me 'fair as a lily, and not only the pride of his life, but the desire of his eyes,' and then telling me he would give me but ten minutes to eat some breakfast, he rang the bell. One of his lately hired servants, a footman, answered it.

'Is John getting the carriage ready?'

'Yes, sir.'

'Is the luggage brought down?'

'They are bringing it down, sir.'

'Go you to the church: see if Mr Wood (the clergyman) and the clerk are there: return and tell me.'

The church, as the reader knows, was but just beyond the gates; the footman soon returned.

'Mr Wood is in the vestry, sir, putting on his surplice.'

'And the carriage?'

'The horses are harnessing.'

'We shall not want it to go to church; but it must be ready the moment we return: all the boxes and luggage arranged and strapped on, and the coachman in his seat.'

'Yes, sir.'

'Jane, are you ready?'

I rose. There were no groomsmen, no bridesmaids, no relatives to wait for or marshal: none but Mr Rochester and I. Mrs Fairfax stood in the hall as we passed. I would fain have spoken to her, but my hand was held by a grasp of iron: I was hurried along by a stride I could hardly follow; and to look at Mr Rochester's face was to feel that not a second of delay would be tolerated for any purpose. I wonder what other bridegroom ever looked as he did – so bent up to a purpose, so grimly resolute: or who, under such steadfast brows, ever revealed such flaming and flashing eyes.

I know not whether the day was fair or foul; in descending the drive, I gazed neither on sky nor earth: my heart was with my eyes; and both seemed migrated into Mr Rochester's frame. I wanted to see the invisible thing on which, as we went along, he appeared to fasten a glance fierce and fell. I wanted to feel the thoughts whose force he seemed breasting and resisting.

At the churchyard wicket he stopped: he discovered I was quite out of breath. 'Am I cruel in my love?' he said. 'Delay an instant: lean on me, Jane.'

And now I can recall the picture of the grey old house of God rising calm before me, of a rook wheeling round the steeple, of a ruddy morning sky beyond. I remember something, too, of the green grave-mounds; and I have not forgotten, either, two figures of strangers straying amongst the low hillocks and reading the mementoes graven on the few mossy headstones. I noticed them, because, as they saw us, they passed round to the back of the church; and I doubted not they were going to enter by the side-aisle door and witness the ceremony. By Mr Rochester they were not observed; he was earnestly looking at my face, from which the blood had, I dare say, momentarily fled: for I felt my forehead dewy, and my cheeks and lips cold. When I rallied, which I soon did, he walked gently with me up the path to the porch.

We entered the quiet and humble temple; the priest waited in his white surplice at the lowly altar, the clerk beside him. All was still: two shadows only moved in a remote corner. My conjecture had been correct: the strangers had slipped in before us, and they now stood by the vault of the Rochesters, their backs towards us, viewing through the rails the old time-stained marble tomb, where a kneeling angel guarded the remains of Damer de Rochester, slain at Marston Moor in the time of the civil wars, and of Elizabeth, his wife.

Our place was taken at the communion rails. Hearing a cautious step behind me, I glanced over my shoulder: one of the strangers – a gentleman, evidently – was advancing up the chancel. The service began. The explanation of the intent of matrimony was gone through; and then the clergyman came a step farther forward, and, bending slightly towards Mr Rochester, went on.

'I require and charge you both (as ye will answer at the dreadful day of judgement, when the secrets of all hearts shall be disclosed), that if either of you know any impediment why ye may not lawfully be joined together in matrimony, ye do now confess it; for be ye well assured that so many as are coupled together otherwise than God's Word doth allow, are not joined together by God, neither is their matrimony lawful.'

He paused, as the custom is. When is the pause after that sentence ever broken by reply? Not, perhaps, once in a hundred years. And the clergyman, who had not lifted his eyes from his book, and had held his breath but for a moment, was proceeding: his hand was already stretched towards Mr Rochester, as his lips unclosed to ask, 'Wilt thou have this woman for thy wedded wife? – ' when a distinct and near voice said – 'The marriage cannot go on: I declare the existence of an impediment.'

The clergyman looked up at the speaker and stood mute; the clerk did the same; Mr Rochester moved slightly, as if an earthquake had rolled under his

feet: taking a firmer footing, and not turning his head or eyes, he said, 'Proceed.'

Profound silence fell when he had uttered that word, with deep but low intonation. Presently Mr Wood said – 'I cannot proceed without some investigation into what has been asserted, and evidence of its truth or falsehood.'

'The ceremony is quite broken off,' subjoined the voice behind us. 'I am in a condition to prove my allegation: an insuperable impediment to this marriage exists.'

Mr Rochester heard, but heeded not: he stood stubborn and rigid, making no movement but to possess himself of my hand. What a hot and strong grasp he had! and how like quarried marble was his pale, firm, massive front at this moment! How his eye shone, still watchful, and yet wild beneath!

Mr Wood seemed at a loss. 'What is the nature of the impediment?' he asked. 'Perhaps it may be got over – explained away?'

'Hardly,' was the answer. 'I have called it insuperable, and I speak advisedly.'

The speaker came forward and leaned on the rails. He continued, uttering each word distinctly, calmly, steadily, but not loudly – 'It simply consists in the existence of a previous marriage. Mr Rochester has a wife now living.'

My nerves vibrated to those low-spoken words as they had never vibrated to thunder – my blood felt their subtle violence as it had never felt frost or fire; but I was collected, and in no danger of swooning. I looked at Mr Rochester: I made him look at me. His whole face was colourless rock: his eye was both spark and flint. He disavowed nothing: he seemed as if he would defy all things. Without speaking, without smiling, without seeming to recognise in me a human being, he only twined my waist with his arm and riveted me to his side.

'Who are you?' he asked of the intruder.

'My name is Briggs, a solicitor of — Street, London.'

'And you would thrust on me a wife?'

'I would remind you of your lady's existence, sir, which the law recognises, if you do not.'

'Favour me with an account of her – with her name, her parentage, her place of abode.'

'Certainly.' Mr Briggs calmly took a paper from his pocket, and read out in a sort of official, nasal voice: ' "I affirm and can prove that on the 20th of October AD (a date of fifteen years back), Edward Fairfax Rochester, of Thornfield Hall, in the county of —, and of Ferndean Manor, in —shire, England, was married to my sister, Bertha Antoinetta Mason, daughter of Jonas Mason, merchant, and of Antoinetta his wife, a Creole, at — church, Spanish Town, Jamaica. The record of the marriage will be found in the register of that church – a copy of it is now in my possession. Signed, Richard Mason." '

'That – if a genuine document – may prove I have been married, but it does not prove that the woman mentioned therein as my wife is still living.'

'She was living three months ago,' returned the lawyer.

'How do you know?'

'I have a witness to the fact, whose testimony even you, sir, will scarcely controvert.'

'Produce him – or go to hell.'

'I will produce him first – he is on the spot. Mr Mason, have the goodness to step forward.'

Mr Rochester, on hearing the name, set his teeth; he experienced, too, a sort of strong convulsive quiver; near to him as I was, I felt the spasmodic movement of fury or despair run through his frame. The second stranger, who had hitherto lingered in the background, now drew near; a pale face looked over the solicitor's shoulder – yes, it was Mason himself. Mr Rochester turned and glared at him. His eye, as I have often said, was a black eye: it had now a tawny, nay, a bloody light in its gloom; and his face flushed – olive cheek and hueless forehead received a glow as from spreading, ascending heart-fire: and he stirred, lifted his strong arm – he could have struck Mason, dashed him on the church-floor, shocked by ruthless blow the breath from his body – but Mason shrank away, and cried faintly, 'Good God!' Contempt fell cool on Mr Rochester – his passion died as if a blight had shrivelled it up: he only asked – 'What have *you* to say?'

An inaudible reply escaped Mason's white lips.

'The devil is in it if you cannot answer distinctly. I again demand, what have *you* to say?'

'Sir – sir,' interrupted the clergyman, 'do not forget you are in a sacred place.' Then addressing Mason, he enquired gently, 'Are you aware, sir, whether or not this gentleman's wife is still living?'

'Courage,' urged the lawyer, 'speak out.'

'She is now living at Thornfield Hall,' said Mason, in more articulate tones: 'I saw her there last April. I am her brother.'

'At Thornfield Hall!' ejaculated the clergyman. 'Impossible! I am an old resident in this neighbourhood, sir, and I never heard of a Mrs Rochester at Thornfield Hall.'

I saw a grim smile contort Mr Rochester's lips, and he muttered – 'No, by God! I took care that none should hear of it – or of her under that name.' He mused – for ten minutes he held counsel with himself: he formed his resolve, and announced it – 'Enough! all shall bolt out at once, like the bullet from the barrel. Wood, close your book and take off your surplice; John Green (to the clerk), leave the church: there will be no wedding today.' The man obeyed.

Mr Rochester continued, hardily and recklessly: 'Bigamy is an ugly word! – I meant, however, to be a bigamist; but fate has out-manœuvred me, or Providence has checked me, perhaps the last. I am little better than a devil at this moment; and, as my pastor there would tell me, deserve no doubt the sternest judgements of God, even to the quenchless fire and deathless worm. Gentlemen, my plan is broken up: what this lawyer and his client say is true: I have been married, and the woman to whom I was married lives! You say you never heard of a Mrs Rochester at the house up yonder, Wood; but I dare say you have many a time inclined your ear to gossip about the mysterious lunatic kept there under watch and ward. Some have whispered to you that she is my bastard half-sister: some, my cast-off mistress. I now inform you that she is my wife, whom I married fifteen years ago, Bertha Mason by name; sister of this resolute personage, who is now, with his

quivering limbs and white cheeks, showing you what a stout heart men may bear. Cheer up, Dick! – never fear me! – I'd almost as soon strike a woman as you. Bertha Mason is mad; and she came of a mad family; idiots and maniacs through three generations! Her mother, the Creole, was both a madwoman and a drunkard! – as I found out after I had wed the daughter: for they were silent on family secrets before. Bertha, like a dutiful child, copied her parent in both points. I had a charming partner – pure, wise, modest: you can fancy I was a happy man. I went through rich scenes! Oh! my experience has been heavenly, if you only knew it! But I owe you no further explanation. Briggs, Wood, Mason, I invite you all to come up to the house and visit Mrs Poole's patient, and *my wife*! You shall see what sort of a being I was cheated into espousing, and judge whether or not I had a right to break the compact, and seek sympathy with something at least human. This girl,' he continued, looking at me, 'knew no more than you, Wood, of the disgusting secret: she thought all was fair and legal, and never dreamt she was going to be entrapped into a feigned union with a defrauded wretch, already bound to a bad, mad, and embruted partner! Come all of you – follow!'

Still holding me fast, he left the church: the three gentlemen came after. At the front door of the hall we found the carriage.

'Take it back to the coach-house, John,' said Mr Rochester coolly: 'it will not be wanted today.'

At our entrance, Mrs Fairfax, Adèle, Sophie, Leah, advanced to meet and greet us.

'To the right-about – every soul!' cried the master; 'away with your congratulations! Who wants them? Not I! – they are fifteen years too late!'

He passed on and ascended the stairs, still holding my hand, and still beckoning the gentlemen to follow him, which they did. We mounted the first staircase, passed up the gallery, proceeded to the third storey: the low, black door, opened by Mr Rochester's master-key, admitted us to the tapestried room, with its great bed and its pictorial cabinet.

'You know this place, Mason,' said our guide; 'she bit and stabbed you here.'

He lifted the hangings from the wall, uncovering the second door: this, too, he opened. In a room without a window, there burnt a fire guarded by a high and strong fender, and a lamp suspended from the ceiling by a chain. Grace Poole bent over the fire, apparently cooking something in a saucepan. In the deep shade, at the farther end of the room, a figure ran backwards and forwards. What it was, whether beast or human being, one could not, at first sight, tell: it grovelled, seemingly, on all fours; it snatched and growled like some strange wild animal: but it was covered with clothing, and a quantity of dark, grizzled hair, wild as a mane, hid its head and face.

'Good-morrow, Mrs Poole!' said Mr Rochester. 'How are you? and how is your charge today?'

'We're tolerable, sir, I thank you,' replied Grace, lifting the boiling mess carefully on to the hob: 'rather snappish, but not 'rageous.'

A fierce cry seemed to give the lie to her favourable report: the clothed hyena rose up, and stood tall on its hind-feet.

'Ah! sir, she sees you!' exclaimed Grace: 'you'd better not stay.'

'Only a few moments, Grace: you must allow me a few moments.'

'Take care then, sir! – for God's sake, take care!'

The maniac bellowed: she parted her shaggy locks from her visage, and gazed wildly at her visitors. I recognised well that purple face, those bloated features. Mrs Poole advanced.

'Keep out of the way,' said Mr Rochester, thrusting her aside: 'she has no knife now, I suppose, and I'm on my guard.'

'One never knows what she has, sir: she is so cunning: it is not in mortal discretion to fathom her craft.'

'We had better leave her,' whispered Mason.

'Go to the devil!' was his brother-in-law's recommendation.

' 'Ware!' cried Grace. The three gentlemen retreated simultaneously. Mr Rochester flung me behind him; the lunatic sprang and grappled his throat viciously, and laid her teeth to his cheek: they struggled. She was a big woman, in stature almost equalling her husband, and corpulent besides: she showed virile force in the contest – more than once she almost throttled him, athletic as he was. He could have settled her with a well-planted blow: but he would not strike: he would only wrestle. At last he mastered her arms; Grace Poole gave him a cord, and he pinioned them behind her: with more rope, which was at hand, he bound her to a chair. The operation was performed amidst the fiercest yells and the most convulsive plunges. Mr Rochester then turned to the spectators: he looked at them with a smile both acrid and desolate.

'That is *my wife*,' said he. 'Such is the sole conjugal embrace I am ever to know – such are the endearments which are to solace my leisure hours! And *this* is what I wished to have' (laying his hand on my shoulder): 'this young girl, who stands so grave and quiet at the mouth of hell, looking collectedly at the gambols of a demon. I wanted her just as a change after that fierce ragout. Wood and Briggs, look at the difference! Compare these clear eyes with the red balls yonder – this face with that mask – this form with that bulk; then judge me, priest of the gospel and man of the law, and remember with what judgement ye judge ye shall be judged! Off with you now. I must shut up my prize.'

We all withdrew. Mr Rochester stayed a moment behind us, to give some further order to Grace Poole. The solicitor addressed me as he descended the stair.

'You, madam,' said he, 'are cleared from all blame: your uncle will be glad to hear it – if, indeed, he should be still living – when Mr Mason returns to Madeira.'

'My uncle! What of him? Do you know him?'

'Mr Mason does. Mr Eyre has been the Funchal correspondent of his house for some years. When your uncle received your letter intimating the contemplated union between yourself and Mr Rochester, Mr Mason, who was staying at Madeira to recruit his health, on his way back to Jamaica, happened to be with him. Mr Eyre mentioned the intelligence; for he knew that my client here was acquainted with a gentleman of the name of Rochester. Mr Mason, astonished

and distressed as you may suppose, revealed the real state of matters. Your uncle, I am sorry to say, is now on a sick-bed; from which, considering the nature of his disease – decline – and the stage it has reached, it is unlikely he will ever rise. He could not then hasten to England himself, to extricate you from the snare into which you had fallen, but he implored Mr Mason to lose no time in taking steps to prevent the false marriage. He referred him to me for assistance. I used all despatch, and am thankful I was not too late: as you, doubtless, must be also. Were I not morally certain that your uncle will be dead ere you reach Madeira, I would advise you to accompany Mr Mason back; but as it is, I think you had better remain in England till you can hear further, either from or of Mr Eyre. Have we anything else to stay for?' he enquired of Mr Mason.

'No, no – let us be gone,' was the anxious reply; and without waiting to take leave of Mr Rochester, they made their exit at the hall door. The clergyman stayed to exchange a few sentences, either of admonition or reproof, with his haughty parishioner; this duty done, he too departed.

I heard him go as I stood at the half-open door of my own room, to which I had now withdrawn. The house cleared, I shut myself in, fastened the bolt that none might intrude, and proceeded – not to weep, not to mourn, I was yet too calm for that, but – mechanically to take off the wedding-dress, and replace it by the stuff gown I had worn yesterday, as I thought, for the last time. I then sat down: I felt weak and tired. I leaned my arms on a table, and my head dropped on them. And now I thought: till now I had only heard, seen, moved – followed up and down where I was led or dragged – watched event rush on event, disclosure open beyond disclosure: but *now, I thought*.

The morning had been a quiet morning enough – all except the brief scene with the lunatic: the transaction in the church had not been noisy; there was no explosion of passion, no loud altercation, no dispute, no defiance or challenge, no tears, no sobs: a few words had been spoken, a calmly pronounced objection to the marriage made; some stern, short questions put by Mr Rochester; answers, explanations given, evidence adduced; an open admission of the truth had been uttered by my master; then the living proof had been seen; the intruders were gone, and all was over. I was in my own room as usual – just myself, without obvious change: nothing had smitten me, or scathed me, or maimed me. And yet where was the Jane Eyre of yesterday? – where was her life? – where were her prospects?

Jane Eyre, who had been an ardent, expectant woman – almost a bride, was a cold, solitary girl again: her life was pale; her prospects were desolate. A Christmas frost had come at midsummer; a white December storm had whirled over June; ice glazed the ripe apples, drifts crushed the blowing roses; on hayfield and cornfield lay a frozen shroud: lanes which last night blushed full of flowers, today were pathless with untrodden snow; and the woods, which twelve hours since waved leafy and fragrant as groves between the tropics, now spread, waste, wild, and white as pine-forests in wintry Norway. My hopes were all dead – struck with a subtle doom, such as, in one night, fell on all the first-born in the land of Egypt. I looked on my cherished wishes,

yesterday so blooming and glowing; they lay stark, chill, livid corpses that could never revive. I looked at my love: that feeling which was my master's – which he had created; it shivered in my heart, like a suffering child in a cold cradle; sickness and anguish had seized it; it could not seek Mr Rochester's arms – it could not derive warmth from his breast. Oh, never more could it turn to him; for faith was blighted – confidence destroyed! Mr Rochester was not to me what he had been; for he was not what I had thought him. I would not ascribe vice to him; I would not say he had betrayed me; but the attribute of stainless truth was gone from his idea, and from his presence I must go: that I perceived well. When – how – whither, I could not yet discern; but he himself, I doubted not, would hurry me from Thornfield. Real affection, it seemed, he could not have for me; it had been only fitful passion: that was balked; he would want me no more. I should fear even to cross his path now: my view must be hateful to him. Oh, how blind had been my eyes! How weak my conduct!

My eyes were covered and closed: eddying darkness seemed to swim round me, and reflection came in as black and confused a flow. Self-abandoned, relaxed, and effortless, I seemed to have laid me down in the dried-up bed of a great river; I heard a flood loosened in remote mountains, and felt the torrent come: to rise I had no will, to flee I had no strength. I lay faint, longing to be dead. One idea only still throbbed lifelike within me – a remembrance of God: it begot an unuttered prayer: these words went wandering up and down in my rayless mind, as something that should be whispered, but no energy was found to express them – 'Be not far from me, for trouble is near: there is none to help.'

It was near: and as I had lifted no petition to Heaven to avert it – as I had neither joined my hands, nor bent my knees, nor moved my lips – it came: in full heavy swing the torrent poured over me. The whole consciousness of my life lorn, my love lost, my hope quenched, my faith death-struck, swayed full and mighty above me in one sullen mass. That bitter hour cannot be described: in truth, 'the waters came into my soul; I sank in deep mire: I felt no standing; I came into deep waters; the floods overflowed me.'

## *Chapter* 27

Sometime in the afternoon I raised my head, and looking round and seeing the western sun gilding the sign of its decline on the wall, I asked, 'What am I to do?'

But the answer my mind gave – 'Leave Thornfield at once' – was so prompt, so dread, that I stopped my ears. I said I could not bear such words now. 'That I am not Edward Rochester's bride is the least part of my woe,' I alleged: 'that I have wakened out of most glorious dreams, and found them all void and vain, as a horror I could bear and master; but that I must leave him decidedly, instantly, entirely, is intolerable. I cannot do it.'

But, then, a voice within me averred that I could do it and foretold that I

should do it. I wrestled with my own resolution: I wanted to be weak that I might avoid the awful passage of further suffering I saw laid out for me; and Conscience, turned tyrant, held Passion by the throat, told her tauntingly, she had yet but dipped her dainty foot in the slough, and swore that with that arm of iron he would thrust her down to unsounded depths of agony.

'Let me be torn away, then!' I cried. 'Let another help me!'

'No; you shall tear yourself away, none shall help you: you shall yourself pluck out your right eye; yourself cut off your right hand: your heart shall be the victim, and you the priest to transfix it.'

I rose up suddenly, terror-struck at the solitude which so ruthless a judge haunted, at the silence which so awful a voice filled. My head swam as I stood erect. I perceived that I was sickening from excitement and inanition; neither meat nor drink had passed my lips that day, for I had taken no breakfast. And, with a strange pang, I now reflected that, long as I had been shut up here, no message had been sent to ask how I was, or to invite me to come down: not even little Adèle had tapped at the door; not even Mrs Fairfax had sought me. 'Friends always forget those whom fortune forsakes,' I murmured, as I undrew the bolt and passed out. I stumbled over an obstacle: my head was still dizzy, my sight was dim, and my limbs were feeble. I could not soon recover myself. I fell, but not on to the ground; an outstretched arm caught me. I looked up – I was supported by Mr Rochester, who sat in a chair across my chamber threshold.

'You come out at last,' he said. 'Well, I have been waiting for you long, and listening: yet not one movement have I heard, nor one sob: five minutes more of that death-like hush, and I should have forced the lock like a burglar. So you shun me? – you shut yourself up and grieve alone! I would rather you had come and upbraided me with vehemence. You are passionate: I expected a scene of some kind. I was prepared for the hot rain of tears; only I wanted them to be shed on my breast: now a senseless floor has received them, or your drenched handkerchief. But I err: you have not wept at all! I see a white cheek and a faded eye, but no trace of tears. I suppose, then, your heart has been weeping blood?

'Well, Jane! not a word of reproach? Nothing bitter – nothing poignant? Nothing to cut a feeling or sting a passion? You sit quietly where I have placed you, and regard me with a weary, passive look.

'Jane, I never meant to wound you thus. If the man who had but one little ewe lamb that was dear to him as a daughter, that ate of his bread and drank of his cup, and lay in his bosom, had by some mistake slaughtered it at the shambles, he would not have rued his bloody blunder more than I now rue mine. Will you ever forgive me?'

Reader, I forgave him at the moment and on the spot. There was such deep remorse in his eye, such true pity in his tone, such manly energy in his manner; and besides, there was such unchanged love in his whole look and mien – I forgave him all: yet not in words, not outwardly; only at my heart's core.

'You know I am a scoundrel, Jane?' ere long he enquired wistfully – wondering, I suppose, at my continued silence and tameness, the result rather of weakness than of will.

'Yes, sir.'

'Then tell me so roundly and sharply – don't spare me.'

'I cannot: I am tired and sick. I want some water.' He heaved a sort of shuddering sigh, and taking me in his arms, carried me downstairs. At first I did not know to what room he had borne me- all was cloudy to my glazed sight: presently I felt the reviving warmth of a fire; for, summer as it was, I had become icy cold in my chamber. He put wine to my lips; I tasted it and revived; then I ate something he offered me, and was soon myself. I was in the library – sitting in his chair – he was quite near. 'If I could go out of life now, without too sharp a pang, it would be well for me,' I thought; 'then I should not have to make the effort of cracking my heart-strings in rending them from among Mr Rochester's. I must leave him, it appears. I do not want to leave him – I cannot leave him.'

'How are you now, Jane?'

'Much better, sir; I shall be well soon.'

'Taste the wine again, Jane.'

I obeyed him; then he put the glass on the table, stood before me, and looked at me attentively. Suddenly he turned away, with an inarticulate exclamation, full of passionate emotion of some kind; he walked fast through the room and came back; he stooped towards me as if to kiss me; but I remembered caresses were now forbidden. I turned my face away and put his aside.

'What! – How is this?' he exclaimed hastily. 'Oh, I know! you won't kiss the husband of Bertha Mason? You consider my arms filled and my embraces appropriated?'

'At any rate, there is neither room nor claim for me, sir.'

'Why, Jane? I will spare you the trouble of much talking; I will answer for you – Because I have a wife already, you would reply. I guess rightly?'

'Yes.'

'If you think so, you must have a strange opinion of me; you must regard me as a plotting profligate – a base and low rake who has been simulating disinterested love in order to draw you into a snare deliberately laid, and strip you of honour and rob you of self-respect. What do you say to that? I see you can say nothing: in the first place, you are faint still, and have enough to do to draw your breath; in the second place, you cannot yet accustom yourself to accuse and revile me, and besides, the floodgates of tears are opened, and they would rush out if you spoke much; and you have no desire to expostulate, to upbraid, to make a scene: you are thinking how *to act* – *talking* you consider is of no use. I know you – I am on my guard.'

'Sir, I do not wish to act against you,' I said; and my unsteady voice warned me to curtail my sentence.

'Not in *your* sense of the word, but in *mine* you are scheming to destroy me. You have as good as said that I am a married man – as a married man you will shun me, keep out of my way: just now you have refused to kiss me. You intend to make yourself a complete stranger to me: to live under this roof only as Adèle's governess; if ever I say a friendly word to you, if ever a friendly feeling

inclines you again to me, you will say, "That man had nearly made me his mistress: I must be ice and rock to him"; and ice and rock you will accordingly become.'

I cleared and steadied my voice to reply: 'All is changed about me, sir; I must change too – there is no doubt of that; and to avoid fluctuations of feeling, and continual combats with recollections and associations, there is only one way – Adèle must have a new governess, sir.'

'Oh, Adèle will go to school – I have settled that already; nor do I mean to torment you with the hideous associations and recollections of Thornfield Hall – this accursed place – this tent of Achan – this insolent vault, offering the ghastliness of living death to the light of the open sky – this narrow stone hell, with its one real fiend, worse than a legion of such as we imagine. Jane, you shall not stay here, nor will I. I was wrong ever to bring you to Thornfield Hall, knowing as I did how it was haunted. I charged them to conceal from you, before I ever saw you, all knowledge of the curse of the place; merely because I feared Adèle never would have a governess to stay if she knew with what inmate she was housed, and my plans would not permit me to remove the maniac elsewhere – though I possess an old house, Ferndean Manor, even more retired and hidden than this, where I could have lodged her safely enough, had not a scruple about the unhealthiness of the situation, in the heart of a wood, made my conscience recoil from the arrangement. Probably those damp walls would soon have eased me of her charge: but to each villain his own vice; and mine is not a tendency to indirect assassination, even of what I most hate.

'Concealing the madwoman's neighbourhood from you, however, was something like covering a child with a cloak and laying it down near a upas-tree: that demon's vicinage is poisoned, and always was. But I'll shut up Thornfield Hall: I'll nail up the front door and board the lower windows: I'll give Mrs Poole two hundred a year to live here with *my wife*, as you term that fearful hag: Grace will do much for money, and she shall have her son, the keeper at Grimsby Retreat, to bear her company and be at hand to give her aid in the paroxysms, when *my wife* is prompted by her familiar to burn people in their beds at night, to stab them, to bite their flesh from their bones, and so on –'

'Sir,' I interrupted him, 'you are inexorable for that unfortunate lady: you speak of her with hate – with vindictive antipathy. It is cruel – she cannot help being mad.'

'Jane, my little darling (so I will call you, for so you are), you don't know what you are talking about; you misjudge me again: it is not because she is mad I hate her. If you were mad, do you think I should hate you?'

'I do indeed, sir.'

'Then you are mistaken, and you know nothing about me, and nothing about the sort of love of which I am capable. Every atom of your flesh is as dear to me as my own: in pain and sickness it would still be dear. Your mind is my treasure, and if it were broken, it would be my treasure still: if you raved, my arms should confine you, and not a strait waistcoat – your grasp, even in fury, would have a charm for me: if you flew at me as wildly as that woman did this morning, I should

receive you in an embrace, at least as fond as it would be restrictive. I should not shrink from you with disgust as I did from her: in your quiet moments you should have no watcher and no nurse but me; and I could hang over you with untiring tenderness, though you gave me no smile in return; and never weary of gazing into your eyes, though they had no longer a ray of recognition for me. But why do I follow that train of ideas? I was talking of removing you from Thornfield. All, you know, is prepared for prompt departure: tomorrow you shall go. I only ask you to endure one more night under this roof, Jane; and then, farewell to its miseries and terrors for ever! I have a place to repair to, which will be a secure sanctuary from hateful reminiscences, from unwelcome intrusion – even from falsehood and slander.'

'And take Adèle with you, sir,' I interrupted; 'she will be a companion for you.'

'What do you mean, Jane? I told you I would send Adèle to school; and what do I want with a child for a companion, and not my own child, a French dancer's bastard? Why do you importune me about her! I say, why do you assign Adèle to me for a companion?'

'You spoke of a retirement, sir; and retirement and solitude are dull: too dull for you.'

'Solitude! solitude!' he reiterated with irritation. 'I see I must come to an explanation. I don't know what sphinx-like expression is forming in your countenance. *You* are to share my solitude. Do you understand?'

I shook my head: it required a degree of courage, excited as he was becoming, even to risk that mute sign of dissent. He had been walking fast about the room, and he stopped, as if suddenly rooted to one spot. He looked at me long and hard: I turned my eyes from him, fixed them on the fire, and tried to assume and maintain a quiet, collected aspect.

'Now for the hitch in Jane's character,' he said at last, speaking more calmly than from his look I had expected him to speak. 'The reel of silk has run smoothly enough so far; but I always knew there would come a knot and a puzzle: here it is. Now for vexation, and exasperation, and endless trouble! By God! I long to exert a fraction of Samson's strength, and break the entanglement like tow!'

He recommenced his walk, but soon again stopped, and this time just before me. 'Jane! will you hear reason?' (he stooped and approached his lips to my ear); 'because, if you won't, I'll try violence.' His voice was hoarse; his look that of a man who is just about to burst an insufferable bond and plunge headlong into wild license. I saw that in another moment, and with one impetus of frenzy more, I should be able to do nothing with him. The present – the passing second of time – was all I had in which to control and restrain him: a movement of repulsion, flight, fear would have sealed my doom, and his. But I was not afraid: not in the least. I felt an inward power; a sense of influence, which supported me. The crisis was perilous; but not without its charm: such as the Indian, perhaps, feels when he slips over the rapid in his canoe. I took hold of his clenched hand, loosened the contorted fingers, and said to him, soothingly – 'Sit down; I'll talk to you as long as you like, and hear all you have to say, whether reasonable or unreasonable.'

He sat down: but he did not get leave to speak directly. I had been struggling

with tears for some time: I had taken great pains to repress them, because I knew he would not like to see me weep. Now, however, I considered it well to let them flow as freely and as long as they liked. If the flood annoyed him, so much the better. So I gave way and cried heartily.

Soon I heard him earnestly entreating me to be composed. I said I could not while he was in such a passion.

'But I am not angry, Jane: I only love you too well; and you had steeled your little pale face with such a resolute, frozen look, I could not endure it. Hush, now, and wipe your eyes.'

His softened voice announced that he was subdued; so I, in my turn, became calm. Now he made an effort to rest his head on my shoulder, but I would not permit it. Then he would draw me to him: no.

'Jane! Jane!' he said, in such an accent of bitter sadness it thrilled along every nerve I had; 'you don't love me, then? It was only my station, and the rank of my wife, that you valued? Now that you think me disqualified to become your husband, you recoil from my touch as if I were some toad or ape.'

These words cut me: yet what could I do or say? I ought probably to have done or said nothing; but I was so tortured by a sense of remorse at thus hurting his feelings, I could not control the wish to drop balm where I had wounded.

'I *do* love you,' I said, 'more than ever: but I must not show or indulge the feeling: and this is the last time I must express it.'

'The last time, Jane! What! do you think you can live with me, and see me daily, and yet, if you still love me, be always cold and distant?'

'No, sir; that I am certain I could not; and therefore I see there is but one way: but you will be furious if I mention it.'

'Oh, mention it! If I storm, you have the art of weeping.'

'Mr Rochester, I must leave you.'

'For how long, Jane? For a few minutes, while you smooth your hair – which is somewhat dishevelled; and bathe your face – which looks feverish?'

'I must leave Adèle and Thornfield. I must part with you for my whole life: I must begin a new existence among strange faces and strange scenes.'

'Of course: I told you you should. I pass over the madness about parting from me. You mean you must become a part of me. As to the new existence, it is all right: you shall yet be my wife: I am not married. You shall be Mrs Rochester – both virtually and nominally. I shall keep only to you so long as you and I live. You shall go to a place I have in the south of France: a whitewashed villa on the shores of the Mediterranean. There you shall live a happy, and guarded, and most innocent life. Never fear that I wish to lure you into error – to make you my mistress. Why did you shake your head? Jane, you must be reasonable, or in truth I shall again become frantic.'

His voice and hand quivered: his large nostrils dilated; his eye blazed: still I dared to speak.

'Sir, your wife is living: that is a fact acknowledged this morning by yourself. If I lived with you as you desire, I should then be your mistress: to say otherwise is sophistical – is false.'

'Jane, I am not a gentle-tempered man – you forget that: I am not long-enduring; I am not cool and dispassionate. Out of pity to me and yourself, put your finger on my pulse, feel how it throbs, and – beware!'

He bared his wrist, and offered it to me: the blood was forsaking his cheek and lips, they were growing livid; I was distressed on all hands. To agitate him thus deeply, by a resistance he so abhorred, was cruel: to yield was out of the question. I did what human beings do instinctively when they are driven to utter extremity – looked for aid to one higher than man: the words 'God help me!' burst involuntarily from my lips.

'I am a fool!' cried Mr Rochester suddenly. 'I keep telling her I am not married, and do not explain to her why. I forget she knows nothing of the character of that woman, or of the circumstances attending my infernal union with her. Oh, I am certain Jane will agree with me in opinion, when she knows all that I know! Just put your hand in mine, Janet – that I may have the evidence of touch as well as sight, to prove you are near me – and I will in a few words show you the real state of the case. Can you listen to me?'

'Yes, sir; for hours if you will.'

'I ask only minutes. Jane, did you ever hear or know that I was not the eldest son of my house: that I had once a brother older than I?'

'I remember Mrs Fairfax told me so once.'

'And did you ever hear that my father was an avaricious, grasping man?'

'I have understood something to that effect.'

'Well, Jane, being so, it was his resolution to keep the property together; he could not bear the idea of dividing his estate and leaving me a fair portion: all, he resolved, should go to my brother, Rowland. Yet as little could he endure that a son of his should be a poor man. I must be provided for by a wealthy marriage. He sought me a partner betimes. Mr Mason, a West India planter and merchant, was his old acquaintance. He was certain his possessions were real and vast: he made enquiries. Mr Mason, he found, had a son and daughter; and he learned from him that he could and would give the latter a fortune of thirty thousand pounds: that sufficed. When I left college, I was sent out to Jamaica, to espouse a bride already courted for me. My father said nothing about her money; but he told me Miss Mason was the boast of Spanish Town for her beauty: and this was no lie. I found her a fine woman, in the style of Blanche Ingram: tall, dark, and majestic. Her family wished to secure me because I was of a good race; and so did she. They showed her to me in parties, splendidly dressed. I seldom saw her alone, and had very little private conversation with her. She flattered me, and lavishly displayed for my pleasure her charms and accomplishments. All the men in her circle seemed to admire her and envy me. I was dazzled, stimulated: my senses were excited; and being ignorant, raw, and inexperienced, I thought I loved her. There is no folly so besotted that the idiotic rivalries of society, the prurience, the rashness, the blindness of youth, will not hurry a man to its commission. Her relatives encouraged me; competitors piqued me; she allured me: a marriage was achieved almost before I knew where I was. Oh, I have no respect for myself when I think of that act! – an agony of inward contempt

masters me. I never loved, I never esteemed, I did not even know her. I was not sure of the existence of one virtue in her nature: I had marked neither modesty, nor benevolence, nor candour, nor refinement in her mind or manners – and, I married her: gross, grovelling, mole-eyed blockhead that I was! With less sin I might have – But let me remember to whom I am speaking.

'My bride's mother I had never seen: I understood she was dead. The honeymoon over, I learned my mistake; she was only mad, and shut up in a lunatic asylum. There was a younger brother, too – a complete dumb idiot. The elder one, whom you have seen (and whom I cannot hate, whilst I abhor all his kindred, because he has some grains of affection in his feeble mind, shown in the continued interest he takes in his wretched sister, and also in a dog-like attachment he once bore me), will probably be in the same state one day. My father and my brother Rowland knew all this; but they thought only of the thirty thousand pounds, and joined in the plot against me.

'These were vile discoveries; but except for the treachery of concealment, I should have made them no subject of reproach to my wife, even when I found her nature wholly alien to mine, her tastes obnoxious to me, her cast of mind common, low, narrow, and singularly incapable of being led to anything higher, expanded to anything larger – when I found that I could not pass a single evening, nor even a single hour of the day with her in comfort; that kindly conversation could not be sustained between us, because whatever topic I started, immediately received from her a turn at once coarse and trite, perverse and imbecile – when I perceived that I should never have a quiet or settled household, because no servant would bear the continued outbreaks of her violent and unreasonable temper, or the vexations of her absurd, contradictory, exacting orders – even then I restrained myself: I eschewed upbraiding, I curtailed remonstrance; I tried to devour my repentance and disgust in secret; I repressed the deep antipathy I felt.

'Jane, I will not trouble you with abominable details: some strong words shall express what I have to say. I lived with that woman upstairs four years, and before that time she had tried me indeed: her character ripened and developed with frightful rapidity; her vices sprang up fast and rank: they were so strong, only cruelty could check them, and I would not use cruelty. What a pigmy intellect she had, and what giant propensities! How fearful were the curses those propensities entailed on me! Bertha Mason, the true daughter of an infamous mother, dragged me through all the hideous and degrading agonies which must attend a man bound to a wife at once intemperate and unchaste.

'My brother in the interval was dead, and at the end of the four years my father died too. I was rich enough now – yet poor to hideous indigence: a nature the most gross, impure, depraved I ever saw, was associated with mine, and called by the law and by society a part of me. And I could not rid myself of it by any legal proceedings: for the doctors now discovered that *my wife* was mad – her excesses had prematurely developed the germs of insanity. Jane, you don't like my narrative; you look almost sick – shall I defer the rest to another day?'

'No, sir, finish it now; I pity you – I do earnestly pity you.'

'Pity, Jane, from some people is a noxious and insulting sort of tribute, which

one is justified in hurling back in the teeth of those who offer it; but that is the sort of pity native to callous, selfish hearts; it is a hybrid, egotistical pain at hearing of woes, crossed with ignorant contempt for those who have endured them. But that is not your pity, Jane; it is not the feeling of which your whole face is full at this moment – with which your eyes are now almost overflowing – with which your heart is heaving – with which your hand is trembling in mine. Your pity, my darling, is the suffering mother of love: its anguish is the very natal pang of the divine passion. I accept it, Jane; let the daughter have free advent – my arms wait to receive her.'

'Now, sir, proceed; what did you do when you found she was mad?'

'Jane, I approached the verge of despair; a remnant of self-respect was all that intervened between me and the gulf. In the eyes of the world, I was doubtless covered with grimy dishonour; but I resolved to be clean in my own sight – and to the last I repudiated the contamination of her crimes, and wrenched myself from connection with her mental defects. Still, society associated my name and person with hers; I yet saw her and heard her daily: something of her breath (faugh!) mixed with the air I breathed; and besides, I remembered I had once been her husband – that recollection was then, and is now, inexpressibly odious to me; moreover, I knew that while she lived I could never be the husband of another and better wife; and, though five years my senior (her family and her father had lied to me even in the particular of her age), she was likely to live as long as I, being as robust in frame as she was infirm in mind. Thus, at the age of twenty-six, I was hopeless.

'One night I had been awakened by her yells – (since the medical men had pronounced her mad, she had, of course, been shut up) – it was a fiery West Indian night; one of the description that frequently precede the hurricanes of those climates. Being unable to sleep in bed, I got up and opened the window. The air was like sulphur-steams – I could find no refreshment anywhere. Mosquitoes came buzzing in and hummed sullenly round the room; the sea, which I could hear from thence, rumbled dull like an earthquake – black clouds were casting up over it; the moon was setting in the waves, broad and red, like a hot cannon-ball – she threw her last bloody glance over a world quivering with the ferment of tempest. I was physically influenced by the atmosphere and scene, and my ears were filled with the curses the maniac still shrieked out; wherein she momentarily mingled my name with such a tone of demon-hate, with such language! – no professed harlot ever had a fouler vocabulary than she: though two rooms off, I heard every word – the thin partitions of the West India house opposing but slight obstruction to her wolfish cries.

' "This life," said I at last, "is hell: this is the air – those are the sounds of the bottomless pit! I have a right to deliver myself from it if I can. The sufferings of this mortal state will leave me with the heavy flesh that now cumbers my soul. Of the fanatic's burning eternity I have no fear: there is not a future state worse than this present one – let me break away, and go home to God!"

'I said this whilst I knelt down at, and unlocked a trunk which contained a brace of loaded pistols: I meant to shoot myself. I only entertained the intention

for a moment; for, not being insane, the crisis of exquisite and unalloyed despair, which had originated the wish and design of self-destruction, was past in a second.

'A wind fresh from Europe blew over the ocean and rushed through the open casement: the storm broke, streamed, thundered, blazed, and the air grew pure. I then framed and fixed a resolution. While I walked under the dripping orange trees of my wet garden, and amongst its drenched pomegranates and pineapples, and while the refulgent dawn of the tropics kindled round me – I reasoned thus, Jane – and now listen; for it was true Wisdom that consoled me in that hour, and showed me the right path to follow.

'The sweet wind from Europe was still whispering in the refreshed leaves, and the Atlantic was thundering in glorious liberty; my heart, dried up and scorched for a long time, swelled to the tone, and filled with living blood – my being longed for renewal – my soul thirsted for a pure draught. I saw hope revive – and felt regeneration possible. From a flowery arch at the bottom of my garden I gazed over the sea – bluer than the sky: the old world was beyond; clear prospects opened thus: ' "Go," said Hope, "and live again in Europe: there it is not known what a sullied name you bear, nor what a filthy burden is bound to you. You may take the maniac with you to England; confine her with due attendance and precautions at Thornfield: then travel yourself to what clime you will, and form what new tie you like. That woman, who has so abused your long-suffering, so sullied your name, so outraged your honour, so blighted your youth, is not your wife, nor are you her husband. See that she is cared for as her condition demands, and you have done all that God and humanity require of you. Let her identity, her connection with yourself, be buried in oblivion: you are bound to impart them to no living being. Place her in safety and comfort: shelter her degradation with secrecy, and leave her."

'I acted precisely on this suggestion. My father and brother had not made my marriage known to their acquaintance; because, in the very first letter I wrote to apprise them of the union – having already begun to experience extreme disgust of its consequences, and, from the family character and constitution, seeing a hideous future opening to me – I added an urgent charge to keep it secret: and very soon the infamous conduct of the wife my father had selected for me was such as to make him blush to own her as his daughter-in-law. Far from desiring to publish the connection, he became as anxious to conceal it as myself.

'To England, then, I conveyed her; a fearful voyage I had with such a monster in the vessel. Glad was I when I at last got her to Thornfield, and saw her safely lodged in that third-storey room, of whose secret inner cabinet she has now for ten years made a wild beast's den – a goblin's cell. I had some trouble in finding an attendant for her, as it was necessary to select one on whose fidelity dependence could be placed; for her ravings would inevitably betray my secret: besides, she had lucid intervals of days – sometimes weeks – which she filled up with abuse of me. At last I hired Grace Poole from the Grimsby Retreat. She and the surgeon, Carter (who dressed Mason's wounds that night he was stabbed and worried), are the only two I have ever admitted to my confidence. Mrs Fairfax may indeed have suspected something, but she

could have gained no precise knowledge as to facts. Grace has, on the whole, proved a good keeper; though, owing partly to a fault of her own, of which it appears nothing can cure her, and which is incident to her harassing profession, her vigilance has been more than once lulled and baffled. The lunatic is both cunning and malignant; she has never failed to take advantage of her guardian's temporary lapses; once to secrete the knife with which she stabbed her brother, and twice to possess herself of the key of her cell, and issue therefrom in the night-time. On the first of these occasions, she perpetrated the attempt to burn me in my bed; on the second, she paid that ghastly visit to you. I thank Providence, who watched over you, that she then spent her fury on your wedding apparel, which perhaps brought back vague reminiscences of her own bridal days: but on what might have happened, I cannot endure to reflect. When I think of the thing which flew at my throat this morning, hanging its black and scarlet visage over the nest of my dove, my blood curdles – '

'And what, sir,' I asked, while he paused, 'did you do when you had settled her here? Where did you go?'

'What did I do, Jane? I transformed myself into a will-o'-the-wisp. Where did I go? I pursued wanderings as wild as those of the March-spirit. I sought the Continent, and went devious through all its lands. My fixed desire was to seek and find a good and intelligent woman, whom I could love: a contrast to the fury I left at Thornfield – '

'But you could not marry, sir.'

'I had determined and was convinced that I could and ought. It was not my original intention to deceive, as I have deceived you. I meant to tell my tale plainly, and make my proposals openly: and it appeared to me so absolutely rational that I should be considered free to love and be loved, I never doubted some woman might be found willing and able to understand my case and accept me, in spite of the curse with which I was burdened.'

'Well, sir?'

'When you are inquisitive, Jane, you always make me smile. You open your eyes like an eager bird, and make every now and then a restless movement, as if answers in speech did not flow fast enough for you, and you wanted to read the tablet of one's heart. But before I go on, tell me what you mean by your "Well, sir?" It is a small phrase very frequent with you; and which many a time has drawn me on and on through interminable talk: I don't very well know why.'

'I mean, What next? How did you proceed? What came of such an event?'

'Precisely! and what do you wish to know now?'

'Whether you found anyone you liked: whether you asked her to marry you; and what she said.'

'I can tell you whether I found anyone I liked, and whether I asked her to marry me: but what she said is yet to be recorded in the book of Fate. For ten long years I roved about, living first in one capital, then another: sometimes in St Petersburg; oftener in Paris; occasionally in Rome, Naples, and Florence. Provided with plenty of money and the passport of an old name, I could choose my own society: no circles were closed against me. I sought my ideal of a woman

amongst English ladies, French countesses, Italian signoras, and German gräfinnen. I could not find her. Sometimes, for a fleeting moment, I thought I caught a glance, heard a tone, beheld a form, which announced the realisation of my dream: but I was presently undeceived. You are not to suppose that I desired perfection, either of mind or person. I longed only for what suited me – for the antipodes of the Creole: and I longed vainly. Amongst them all I found not one whom, had I been ever so free, I – warned as I was of the risks, the horrors, the loathings of incongruous unions – would have asked to marry me. Disappointment made me reckless. I tried dissipation – never debauchery: that I hated, and hate. That was my Indian Messalina's attribute: rooted disgust at it and her restrained me much, even in pleasure. Any enjoyment that bordered on riot seemed to approach me to her and her vices, and I eschewed it.

'Yet I could not live alone; so I tried the companionship of mistresses. The first I chose was Céline Varens – another of those steps which make a man spurn himself when he recalls them. You already know what she was, and how my liaison with her terminated. She had two successors: an Italian, Giacinta, and a German, Clara; both considered singularly handsome. What was their beauty to me in a few weeks? Giacinta was unprincipled and violent: I tired of her in three months. Clara was honest and quiet; but heavy, mindless, and unimpressible: not one whit to my taste. I was glad to give her a sufficient sum to set her up in a good line of business, and so get decently rid of her. But, Jane, I see by your face you are not forming a very favourable opinion of me just now. You think me an unfeeling, loose-principled rake: don't you?'

'I don't like you so well as I have done sometimes, indeed, sir. Did it not seem to you in the least wrong to live in that way, first with one mistress and then another? You talk of it as a mere matter of course.'

'It was with me; and I did not like it. It was a grovelling fashion of existence: I should never like to return to it. Hiring a mistress is the next worse thing to buying a slave: both are often by nature, and always by position, inferior: and to live familiarly with inferiors is degrading. I now hate the recollection of the time I passed with Céline, Giacinta, and Clara.'

I felt the truth of these words; and I drew from them the certain inference, that if I were so far to forget myself and all the teaching that had ever been instilled into me, as – under any pretext – with any justification – through any temptation – to become the successor of these poor girls, he would one day regard me with the same feeling which now in his mind desecrated their memory. I did not give utterance to this conviction: it was enough to feel it. I impressed it on my heart, that it might remain there to serve me as aid in the time of trial.

'Now, Jane, why don't you say "Well, sir?" I have not done. You are looking grave. You disapprove of me still, I see. But let me come to the point. Last January, rid of all mistresses – in a harsh, bitter frame of mind, the result of a useless, roving, lonely life – corroded with disappointment, sourly disposed against all men, and especially against all *woman*kind (for I began to regard the notion of an intellectual, faithful, loving woman as a mere dream), recalled by business, I came back to England.

'On a frosty winter afternoon, I rode in sight of Thornfield Hall. Abhorred spot! I expected no peace – no pleasure there. On a stile in Hay Lane I saw a quiet little figure sitting by itself. I passed it as negligently as I did the pollard willow opposite to it: I had no presentiment of what it would be to me; no inward warning that the arbitress of my life – my genius for good or evil – waited there in humble guise. I did not know it, even when, on the occasion of Mesrour's accident, it came up and gravely offered me help. Childish and slender creature! It seemed as if a linnet had hopped to my foot and proposed to bear me on its tiny wing. I was surly; but the thing would not go: it stood by me with strange perseverance, and looked and spoke with a sort of authority. I must be aided, and by that hand: and aided I was.

'When once I had pressed the frail shoulder, something new – a fresh sap and sense – stole into my frame. It was well I had learnt that this elf must return to me – that it belonged to my house down below – or I could not have felt it pass away from under my hand, and seen it vanish behind the dim hedge, without singular regret. I heard you come home that night, Jane, though probably you were not aware that I thought of you or watched for you. The next day I observed you – myself unseen – for half an hour, while you played with Adèle in the gallery. It was a snowy day, I recollect, and you could not go out of doors. I was in my room; the door was ajar: I could both listen and watch. Adèle claimed your outward attention for a while; yet I fancied your thoughts were elsewhere: but you were very patient with her, my little Jane; you talked to her and amused her a long time. When at last she left you, you lapsed at once into deep reverie: you betook yourself slowly to pace the gallery. Now and then, in passing a casement, you glanced out at the thick-falling snow; you listened to the sobbing wind, and again you paced gently on and dreamed. I think those day visions were not dark: there was a pleasurable illumination in your eye occasionally, a soft excitement in your aspect, which told of no bitter, bilious, hypochondriac brood-ing: your look revealed rather the sweet musings of youth when its spirit follows on willing wings the flight of Hope up and on to an ideal heaven. The voice of Mrs Fairfax, speaking to a servant in the hall, wakened you: and how curiously you smiled to and at yourself, Janet! There was much sense in your smile: it was very shrewd, and seemed to make light of your own abstraction. It seemed to say – "My fine visions are all very well, but I must not forget they are absolutely unreal. I have a rosy sky and a green flowery Eden in my brain; but without, I am perfectly aware, lies at my feet a rough tract to travel, and around me gather black tempests to encounter." You ran downstairs and demanded of Mrs Fairfax some occupation: the weekly house accounts to make up, or something of that sort, I think it was. I was vexed with you for getting out of my sight.

'Impatiently I waited for evening, when I might summon you to my presence. An unusual – to me – a perfectly new character I suspected was yours: I desired to search it deeper and know it better. You entered the room with a look and air at once shy and independent: you were quaintly dressed – much as you are now. I made you talk: ere long I found you full of strange contrasts. Your garb and manner were restricted by rule; your air was often diffident, and altogether that

of one refined by nature, but absolutely unused to society, and a good deal afraid of making herself disadvantageously conspicuous by some solecism or blunder; yet when addressed, you lifted a keen, a daring, and a glowing eye to your interlocutor's face: there was penetration and power in each glance you gave; when plied by close questions, you found ready and round answers. Very soon you seemed to get used to me: I believe you felt the existence of sympathy between you and your grim and cross master, Jane; for it was astonishing to see how quickly a certain pleasant ease tranquillised your manner: snarl as I would, you showed no surprise, fear, annoyance, or displeasure at my moroseness; you watched me, and now and then smiled at me with a simple yet sagacious grace I cannot describe. I was at once content and stimulated with what I saw: I liked what I had seen, and wished to see more. Yet, for a long time, I treated you distantly, and sought your company rarely. I was an intellectual epicure, and wished to prolong the gratification of making this novel and piquant acquaintance: besides, I was for a while troubled with a haunting fear that if I handled the flower freely its bloom would fade – the sweet charm of freshness would leave it. I did not then know that it was no transitory blossom, but rather the radiant resemblance of one, cut in an indestructible gem. Moreover, I wished to see whether you would seek me if I shunned you – but you did not; you kept in the schoolroom as still as your own desk and easel; if by chance I met you, you passed me as soon, and with as little token of recognition, as was consistent with respect. Your habitual expression in those days, Jane, was a thoughtful look; not despondent, for you were not sickly; but not buoyant, for you had little hope, and no actual pleasure. I wondered what you thought of me, or if you ever thought of me, and resolved to find this out.

'I resumed my notice of you. There was something glad in your glance, and genial in your manner, when you conversed: I saw you had a social heart; it was the silent schoolroom – it was the tedium of your life – that made you mournful. I permitted myself the delight of being kind to you; kindness stirred emotion soon: your face became soft in expression, your tones gentle; I liked my name pronounced by your lips in a grateful happy accent. I used to enjoy a chance meeting with you, Jane, at this time: there was a curious hesitation in your manner: you glanced at me with a slight trouble – a hovering doubt: you did not know what my caprice might be – whether I was going to play the master and be stern, or the friend and be benignant. I was now too fond of you often to simulate the first whim; and, when I stretched my hand out cordially, such bloom and light and bliss rose to your young, wistful features, I had much ado often to avoid straining you then and there to my heart.'

'Don't talk any more of those days, sir,' I interrupted, furtively dashing away some tears from my eyes; his language was torture to me; for I knew what I must do – and do soon – and all these reminiscences, and these revelations of his feelings, only made my work more difficult.

'No, Jane,' he returned: 'what necessity is there to dwell on the Past, when the Present is so much surer – the Future so much brighter?'

I shuddered to hear the infatuated assertion.

'You see now how the case stands – do you not?' he continued. 'After a youth and manhood passed half in unutterable misery and half in dreary solitude, I have for the first time found what I can truly love – I have found *you*. You are my sympathy – my better self – my good angel. I am bound to you with a strong attachment. I think you good, gifted, lovely: a fervent, a solemn passion is conceived in my heart; it leans to you, draws you to my centre and spring of life, wraps my existence about you, and, kindling in pure, powerful flame, fuses you and me in one.

'It was because I felt and knew this, that I resolved to marry you. To tell me that I had already a wife is empty mockery: you know now that I had but a hideous demon. I was wrong to attempt to deceive you; but I feared a stubbornness that exists in your character. I feared early instilled prejudice: I wanted to have you safe before hazarding confidences. This was cowardly: I should have appealed to your nobleness and magnanimity at first, as I do now – opened to you plainly my life of agony – described to you my hunger and thirst after a higher and worthier existence – shown to you, not my *resolution* (that word is weak), but my resistless *bent* to love faithfully and well, where I am faithfully and well loved in return. Then I should have asked you to accept my pledge of fidelity and to give me yours. Jane – give it me now.'

A pause.

'Why are you silent, Jane?'

I was experiencing an ordeal: a hand of fiery iron grasped my vitals. Terrible moment: full of struggle, blackness, burning! Not a human being that ever lived could wish to be loved better than I was loved; and him who thus loved me I absolutely worshipped: and I must renounce love and idol. One drear word comprised my intolerable duty – 'Depart!'

'Jane, you understand what I want of you? Just this promise – "I will be yours, Mr Rochester."'

'Mr Rochester, I will *not* be yours.'

Another long silence.

'Jane!' recommenced he, with a gentleness that broke me down with grief, and turned me stone-cold with ominous terror – for this still voice was the pant of a lion rising – 'Jane, do you mean to go one way in the world, and to let me go another?'

'I do.'

'Jane' (bending towards and embracing me), 'do you mean it now?'

'I do.'

'And now?' softly kissing my forehead and cheek.

'I do,' extricating myself from restraint rapidly and completely.

'Oh, Jane, this is bitter! This – this is wicked. It would not be wicked to love me.'

'It would to obey you.'

A wild look raised his brows – crossed his features: he rose; but he forbore yet. I laid my hand on the back of a chair for support: I shook, I feared – but I resolved.

'One instant, Jane. Give one glance to my horrible life when you are gone. All happiness will be torn away with you. What then is left? For a wife I have but the maniac upstairs: as well might you refer me to some corpse in yonder churchyard. What shall I do, Jane? Where turn for a companion and for some hope?'

'Do as I do: trust in God and yourself. Believe in heaven. Hope to meet again there.'

'Then you will not yield?'

'No.'

'Then you condemn me to live wretched and to die accursed?' His voice rose.

'I advise you to live sinless, and I wish you to die tranquil.'

'Then you snatch love and innocence from me? You fling me back on lust for a passion – vice for an occupation?'

'Mr Rochester, I no more assign this fate to you than I grasp at it for myself. We were born to strive and endure – you as well as I: do so. You will forget me before I forget you.'

'You make me a liar by such language: you sully my honour. I declared I could not change: you tell me to my face I shall change soon. And what a distortion in your judgement, what a perversity in your ideas, is proved by your conduct! Is it better to drive a fellow-creature to despair than to transgress a mere human law, no man being injured by the breach? for you have neither relatives nor acquaintances whom you need fear to offend by living with me?'

This was true: and while he spoke my very conscience and reason turned traitors against me, and charged me with crime in resisting him. They spoke almost as loud as Feeling: and that clamoured wildly. 'Oh, comply!' it said. 'Think of his misery; think of his danger – look at his state when left alone; remember his headlong nature; consider the recklessness following on despair – soothe him; save him; love him; tell him you love him and will be his. Who in the world cares for *you*? or who will be injured by what you do?'

Still indomitable was the reply – '*I* care for myself. The more solitary, the more friendless, the more unsustained I am, the more I will respect myself. I will keep the law given by God; sanctioned by man. I will hold to the principles received by me when I was sane, and not mad – as I am now. Laws and principles are not for the times when there is no temptation: they are for such moments as this, when body and soul rise in mutiny against their rigour; stringent are they; inviolate they shall be. If at my individual convenience I might break them, what would be their worth? They have a worth – so I have always believed; and if I cannot believe it now, it is because I am insane – quite insane: with my veins running fire, and my heart beating faster than I can count its throbs. Preconceived opinions, foregone determinations, are all I have at this hour to stand by: there I plant my foot.'

I did. Mr Rochester, reading my countenance, saw I had done so. His fury was wrought to the highest: he must yield to it for a moment, whatever followed; he crossed the floor and seized my arm and grasped my waist. He seemed to devour me with his flaming glance: physically, I felt, at the moment, powerless as stubble exposed to the draught and glow of a furnace: mentally, I

still possessed my soul, and with it the certainty of ultimate safety. The soul, fortunately, has an Interpreter – often an unconscious, but still truthful inter-preter – in the eye. My eye rose to his; and while I looked in his fierce face I gave an involuntary sigh; his grip was painful, and my overtaxed strength almost exhausted.

'Never,' said he, as he ground his teeth, 'never was anything at once so frail and so indomitable. A mere reed she feels in my hand!' (And he shook me with the force of his hold.) 'I could bend her with my finger and thumb: and what good would it do if I bent, if I uptore, if I crushed her? Consider that eye: consider the resolute, wild, free thing looking out of it, defying me, with more than courage – with a stern triumph. Whatever I do with its cage, I cannot get at it – the savage, beautiful creature! If I tear, if I rend the slight prison, my outrage will only let the captive loose. Conqueror I might be of the house; but the inmate would escape to heaven before I could call myself possessor of its clay dwelling-place. And it is you, spirit – with will and energy, and virtue and purity – that I want: not alone your brittle frame. Of yourself you could come with soft flight and nestle against my heart, if you would: seized against your will, you will elude the grasp like an essence – you will vanish ere I inhale your fragrance. Oh! come, Jane, come!'

As he said this, he released me from his clutch, and only looked at me. The look was far worse to resist than the frantic strain: only an idiot, however, would have succumbed now. I had dared and baffled his fury; I must elude his sorrow: I retired to the door.

'You are going, Jane?'

'I am going, sir.'

'You are leaving me?'

'Yes.'

'You will not come? You will not be my comforter, my rescuer? My deep love, my wild woe, my frantic prayer, are all nothing to you?'

What unutterable pathos was in his voice! How hard it was to reiterate firmly, 'I am going.'

'Jane!'

'Mr Rochester!'

'Withdraw, then, I consent; but remember, you leave me here in anguish. Go up to your own room; think over all I have said, and, Jane, cast a glance on my sufferings – think of me.'

He turned away; he threw himself on his face on the sofa. 'Oh, Jane! my hope – my love – my life!' broke in anguish from his lips. Then came a deep, strong sob.

I had already gained the door; but, reader, I walked back – walked back as determinedly as I had retreated. I knelt down by him; I turned his face from the cushion to me; I kissed his cheek; I smoothed his hair with my hand.

'God bless you, my dear master!' I said. 'God keep you from harm and wrong – direct you, solace you – reward you well for your past kindness to me.'

'Little Jane's love would have been my best reward,' he answered; 'without it, my heart is broken. But Jane will give me her love: yes – nobly, generously.'

Up the blood rushed to his face; forth flashed the fire from his eyes; erect he sprang; he held his arms out; but I evaded the embrace, and at once quitted the room.

'Farewell!' was the cry of my heart as I left him. Despair added, 'Farewell for ever!'

That night I never thought to sleep; but a slumber fell on me as soon as I lay down in bed. I was transported in thought to the scenes of childhood: I dreamt I lay in the red-room at Gateshead; that the night was dark, and my mind impressed with strange fears. The light that long ago had struck me into syncope, recalled in this vision, seemed glidingly to mount the wall, and tremblingly to pause in the centre of the obscured ceiling. I lifted up my head to look: the roof resolved to clouds, high and dim; the gleam was such as the moon imparts to vapours she is about to sever. I watched her come – watched with the strangest anticipation; as though some word of doom were to be written on her disk. She broke forth as never moon yet burst from cloud: a hand first penetrated the sable folds and waved them away; then, not a moon, but a white human form shone in the azure, inclining a glorious brow earthward. It gazed and gazed on me. It spoke to my spirit: immeasurably distant was the tone, yet so near, it whispered in my heart – 'My daughter, flee temptation.'

'Mother, I will.'

So I answered after I had waked from the trance-like dream. It was yet night, but July nights are short: soon after midnight, dawn comes. 'It cannot be too early to commence the task I have to fulfil,' thought I. I rose: I was dressed; for I had taken off nothing but my shoes. I knew where to find in my drawers some linen, a locket, a ring. In seeking these articles, I encountered the beads of a pearl necklace Mr Rochester had forced me to accept a few days ago. I left that; it was not mine: it was the visionary bride's who had melted in air. The other articles I made up in a parcel; my purse, containing twenty shillings (it was all I had), I put in my pocket: I tied on my straw bonnet, pinned my shawl, took the parcel and my slippers, which I would not put on yet, and stole from my room.

'Farewell, kind Mrs Fairfax!' I whispered, as glided past her door. 'Farewell, my darling Adèle!' I said, as I glanced towards the nursery. No thought could be admitted of entering to embrace her. I had to deceive a fine ear: for aught I knew it might now be listening.

I would have got past Mr Rochester's chamber without a pause; but my heart momentarily stopping its beat at that threshold, my foot was forced to stop also. No sleep was there: the inmate was walking restlessly from wall to wall; and again and again he sighed while I listened. There was a heaven – a temporary heaven – in this room for me, if I chose: I had but to go in and to say – 'Mr Rochester, I will love you and live with you through life till death,' and a fount of rapture would spring to my lips. I thought of this.

That kind master, who could not sleep now, was waiting with impatience for day. He would send for me in the morning; I should be gone. He would have me sought for: vainly. He would feel himself forsaken; his love rejected: he would

suffer; perhaps grow desperate. I thought of this too. My hand moved towards the lock: I caught it back, and glided on.

Drearily I wound my way downstairs: I knew what I had to do, and I did it mechanically. I sought the key of the side-door in the kitchen; I sought, too, a phial of oil and a feather; I oiled the key and the lock. I got some water, I got some bread: for perhaps I should have to walk far; and my strength, sorely shaken of late, must not break down. All this I did without one sound. I opened the door, passed out, shut it softly. Dim dawn glimmered in the yard. The great gates were closed and locked; but a wicket in one of them was only latched. Through that I departed, it, too, I shut; and now I was out of Thornfield.

A mile off, beyond the fields, lay a road which stretched in the contrary direction to Millcote; a road I had never travelled, but often noticed, and wondered where it led: thither I bent my steps. No reflection was to be allowed now: not one glance was to be cast back; not even one forward. Not one thought was to be given either to the past or the future. The first was a page so heavenly sweet – so deadly sad – that to read one line of it would dissolve my courage and break down my energy. The last was an awful blank: something like the world when the deluge was gone by.

I skirted fields, and hedges, and lanes till after sunrise. I believe it was a lovely summer morning: I know my shoes, which I had put on when I left the house, were soon wet with dew. But I looked neither to rising sun, nor smiling sky, nor wakening nature. He who is taken out to pass through a fair scene to the scaffold, thinks not of the flowers that smile on his road, but of the block and axe-edge; of the disseverment of bone and vein; of the grave gaping at the end: and I thought of drear flight and homeless wandering – and oh! with agony I thought of what I left. I could not help it. I thought of him now – in his room – watching the sunrise; hoping I should soon come to say I would stay with him and be his. I longed to be his; I panted to return: it was not too late; I could yet spare him the bitter pang of bereavement. As yet my flight, I was sure, was undiscovered. I could go back and be his comforter – his pride; his redeemer from misery, perhaps from ruin. Oh, that fear of his self-abandonment – far worse than my abandonment – how it goaded me! It was a barbed arrowhead in my breast; it tore me when I tried to extract it; it sickened me when remembrance thrust it farther in. Birds began singing in brake and copse: birds were faithful to their mates; birds were emblems of love What was I? In the midst of my pain of heart and frantic effort of principle, I abhorred myself. I had no solace from self-approbation: none even from self-respect. I had injured – wounded – left my master. I was hateful in my own eyes. Still I could not turn, nor retrace one step. God must have led me on. As to my own will or conscience, impassioned grief had trampled one and stifled the other. I was weeping wildly as I walked along my solitary way: fast, fast I went like one delirious. A weakness, beginning inwardly, extending to the limbs, seized me, and I fell: I lay on the ground some minutes, pressing my face to the wet turf. I had some fear – or hope – that here I should die: but I was soon up; crawling forwards on my hands and knees, and then again raised to my feet – as eager and as determined as ever to reach the road.

When I got there, I was forced to sit to rest me under the hedge; and while I sat, I heard wheels, and saw a coach come on. I stood up and lifted my hand; it stopped. I asked where it was going: the driver named a place a long way off, and where I was sure Mr Rochester had no connections. I asked for what sum he would take me there; he said thirty shillings; I answered I had but twenty; well, he would try to make it do. He further gave me leave to get into the inside, as the vehicle was empty: I entered, was shut in, and it rolled on its way.

Gentle reader, may you never feel what I then felt! May your eyes never shed such stormy, scalding, heart-wrung tears as poured from mine. May you never appeal to Heaven in prayers so hopeless and so agonised as in that hour left my lips; for never may you, like me, dread to be the instrument of evil to what you wholly love.

### *Chapter 28*

Two days are passed. It is a summer evening; the coachman has set me down at a place called Whitcross; he could take me no farther for the sum I had given, and I was not possessed of another shilling in the world. The coach is a mile off by this time; I am alone. At this moment I discover that I forgot to take my parcel out of the pocket of the coach, where I had placed it for safety; there it remains, there it must remain; and now, I am absolutely destitute.

Whitcross is no town, nor even a hamlet; it is but a stone pillar set up where four roads meet: whitewashed, I suppose, to be more obvious at a distance and in darkness. Four arms spring from its summit: the nearest town to which these point is, according to the inscription, distant ten miles; the farthest, above twenty. From the well-known names of these towns I learn in what county I have lighted; a north-midland shire, dusk with moorland, ridged with mountain: this I see. There are great moors behind and on each hand of me; there are waves of mountains far beyond that deep valley at my feet. The population here must be thin, and I see no passengers on these roads: they stretch out east, west, north, and south – white, broad, lonely; they are all cut in the moor, and the heather grows deep and wild to their very verge. Yet a chance traveller might pass by; and I wish no eye to see me now: strangers would wonder what I am doing, lingering here at the signpost, evidently objectless and lost. I might be questioned: I could give no answer but what would sound incredible and excite suspicion. Not a tie holds me to human society at this moment – not a charm or hope calls me where my fellow-creatures are – none that saw me would have a kind thought or a good wish for me. I have no relative but the universal mother, Nature: I will seek her breast and ask repose.

I struck straight into the heath; I held on to a hollow I saw deeply furrowing the brown moorside; I waded knee-deep in its dark growth; I turned with its turnings, and finding a moss-blackened granite crag in a hidden angle, I sat

down under it. High banks of moor were about me; the crag protected my head: the sky was over that.

Some time passed before I felt tranquil even here: I had a vague dread that wild cattle might be near, or that some sportsman or poacher might discover me. If a gust of wind swept the waste, I looked up, fearing it was the rush of a bull; if a plover whistled, I imagined it a man. Finding my apprehensions unfounded, however, and calmed by the deep silence that reigned as evening declined at nightfall, I took confidence. As yet I had not thought; I had only listened, watched, dreaded; now I regained the faculty of reflection.

What was I to do? Where to go? Oh, intolerable questions, when I could do nothing and go nowhere! – when a long way must yet be measured by my weary, trembling limbs before I could reach human habitation – when cold charity must be entreated before I could get a lodging: reluctant sympathy importuned, almost certain repulse incurred, before my tale could be listened to, or one of my wants relieved!

I touched the heath: it was dry, and yet warm with the heat of the summer day. I looked at the sky; it was pure: a kindly star twinkled just above the chasm ridge. The day fell, but with propitious softness; no breeze whispered. Nature seemed to me benign and good; I thought she loved me, outcast as I was; and I, who from man could anticipate only mistrust, rejection, insult, clung to her with filial fondness. Tonight, at least, I would be her guest, as I was her child: my mother would lodge me without money and without price. I had one morsel of bread yet: the remnant of a roll I had bought in a town we passed through at noon with a stray penny – my last coin. I saw ripe bilberries gleaming here and there, like jet beads in the heath: I gathered a handful and ate them with the bread. My hunger, sharp before, was, if not satisfied, appeased by this hermit's meal. I said my evening prayers at its conclusion, and then chose my couch.

Beside the crag the heath was very deep: when I lay down my feet were buried in it; rising high on each side, it left only a narrow space for the night-air to invade. I folded my shawl double, and spread it over me for a coverlet; a low, mossy swell was my pillow. Thus lodged, I was not, at least at the commencement of the night, cold.

My rest might have been blissful enough, only a sad heart broke it. It plained of its gaping wounds, its inward bleeding, its riven chords. It trembled for Mr Rochester and his doom; it bemoaned him with bitter pity; it demanded him with ceaseless longing; and, impotent as a bird with both wings broken, it still quivered its shattered pinions in vain attempts to seek him.

Worn out with this torture of thought, I rose to my knees. Night was come, and her planets were risen: a safe, still night: too serene for the companionship of fear. We know that God is everywhere; but certainly we feel His presence most when His works are on the grandest scale spread before us; and it is in the unclouded night-sky, where His worlds wheel their silent course, that we read clearest His infinitude, His omnipotence, His omnipresence. I had risen to my knees to pray for Mr Rochester. Looking up, I, with tear-dimmed eyes, saw the mighty Milky Way. Remembering what it was – what countless systems there

swept space like a soft trace of light – I felt the might and strength of God. Sure was I of His efficiency to save what He had made: convinced I grew that neither earth should perish, nor one of the souls it treasured. I turned my prayer to thanksgiving: the Source of Life was also the Saviour of spirits. Mr Rochester was safe: he was God's, and by God would he be guarded. I again nestled to the breast of the hill and ere long in sleep forgot sorrow.

But next day, Want came to me pale and bare. Long after the little birds had left their nests; long after bees had come in the sweet prime of day to gather the heath honey before the dew was dried – when the long morning shadows were curtailed, and the sun filled earth and sky – I got up, and I looked round me.

What a still, hot, perfect day! What a golden desert this spreading moor! Everywhere sunshine. I wished I could live in it and on it. I saw a lizard run over the crag; I saw a bee busy among the sweet bilberries. I would fain at the moment have become bee or lizard, that I might have found fitting nutriment, permanent shelter here. But I was a human being, and had a human being's wants: I must not linger where there was nothing to supply them. I rose; I looked back at the bed I had left. Hopeless of the future, I wished but this – that my Maker had that night thought good to require my soul of me while I slept; and that this weary frame, absolved by death from further conflict with fate, had now but to decay quietly, and mingle in peace with the soil of this wilderness. Life, however, was yet in my possession, with all its requirements, and pains, and responsibilities. The burden must be carried; the want provided for; the suffering endured; the responsibility fulfilled. I set out.

Whitcross regained, I followed a road which led from the sun, now fervent and high. By no other circumstance had I will to decide my choice. I walked a long time, and when I thought I had nearly done enough, and might conscientiously yield to the fatigue that almost overpowered me – might relax this forced action, and, sitting down on a stone I saw near, submit resistlessly to the apathy that clogged heart and limb – I heard a bell chime – a church bell.

I turned in the direction of the sound, and there, amongst the romantic hills, whose changes and aspect I had ceased to note an hour ago, I saw a hamlet and a spire. All the valley at my right hand was full of pasture-fields, and cornfields, and wood; and a glittering stream ran zigzag through the varied shades of green, the mellowing grain, the sombre woodland, the clear and sunny lea. Recalled by the rumbling of wheels to the road before me, I saw a heavily-laden waggon labouring up the hill, and not far beyond were two cows and their drover. Human life and human labour were near. I must struggle on: strive to live and bend to toil like the rest.

About two o'clock p.m. I entered the village. At the bottom of its one street there was a little shop with some cakes of bread in the window. I coveted a cake of bread. With that refreshment I could perhaps regain a degree of energy: without it, it would be difficult to proceed. The wish to have some strength and some vigour returned to me as soon as I was amongst my fellow-beings. I felt it would be degrading to faint with hunger on the causeway of a hamlet. Had I nothing about me I could offer in exchange for one of these rolls? I considered.

I had a small silk handkerchief tied round my throat; I had my gloves. I could hardly tell how men and women in extremities of destitution proceeded. I did not know whether either of these articles would be accepted: probably they would not; but I must try.

I entered the shop: a woman was there. Seeing a respectably-dressed person, a lady as she supposed, she came forward with civility. How could she serve me? I was seized with shame: my tongue would not utter the request I had prepared. I dared not offer her the half-worn gloves, the creased handkerchief: besides, I felt it would be absurd. I only begged permission to sit down a moment, as I was tired. Disappointed in the expectation of a customer, she coolly acceded to my request. She pointed to a seat; I sank into it. I felt sorely urged to weep; but conscious how unseasonable such a manifestation would be, I restrained it. Soon I asked her 'if there were any dressmaker or plain-workwoman in the village?'

'Yes; two or three. Quite as many as there was employment for.'

I reflected. I was driven to the point now. I was brought face to face with Necessity. I stood in the position of one without a resource, without a friend, without a coin. I must do something. What? I must apply somewhere. Where?

'Did she know of any place in the neighbourhood where a servant was wanted?'

'Nay; she couldn't say.'

'What was the chief trade in this place? What did most of the people do?'

'Some were farm labourers; a good deal worked at Mr Oliver's needle-factory, and at the foundry.'

'Did Mr Oliver employ women?'

'Nay; it was men's work.'

'And what do the women do?'

'I knawn't,' was the answer. 'Some does one thing, and some another. Poor folk mun get on as they can.'

She seemed to be tired of my questions: and, indeed, what claim had I to importune her? A neighbour or two came in; my chair was evidently wanted. I took leave.

I passed up the street, looking as I went at all the houses to the right hand and to the left; but I could discover no pretext, nor see an inducement to enter any. I rambled round the hamlet, going sometimes to a little distance and returning again, for an hour or more. Much exhausted, and suffering greatly now for want of food, I turned aside into a lane and sat down under the hedge. Ere many minutes had elapsed, I was again on my feet, however, and again searching something – a resource, or at least an informant. A pretty little house stood at the top of the lane, with a garden before it, exquisitely neat and brilliantly blooming. I stopped at it. What business had I to approach the white door or touch the glittering knocker? In what way could it possibly be the interest of the inhabitants of that dwelling to serve me? Yet I drew near and knocked. A mild-looking, cleanly-attired young woman opened the door. In such a voice as might be expected from a hopeless heart and fainting frame – a voice wretchedly low and faltering – I asked if a servant was wanted here?

'No,' said she; 'we do not keep a servant.'

'Can you tell me where I could get employment of any kind?' I continued. 'I am a stranger, without acquaintance in this place. I want some work: no matter what.'

But it was not her business to think for me, or to seek a place for me: besides, in her eyes, how doubtful must have appeared my character, position, tale. She shook her head, she 'was sorry she could give me no information,' and the white door closed, quite gently and civilly: but it shut me out. If she had held it open a little longer, I believe I should have begged a piece of bread; for I was now brought low.

I could not bear to return to the sordid village, where, besides, no prospect of aid was visible. I should have longed rather to deviate to a wood I saw not far off, which appeared in its thick shade to offer inviting shelter; but I was so sick, so weak, so gnawed with nature's cravings, instinct kept me roaming round abodes where there was a chance of food. Solitude would be no solitude – rest no rest – while the vulture, hunger, thus sank beak and talons in my side.

I drew near houses; I left them, and came back again, and again I wandered away: always repelled by the consciousness of having no claim to ask – no right to expect interest in my isolated lot. Meantime, the afternoon advanced, while I thus wandered about like a lost and starving dog. In crossing a field, I saw the church spire before me: I hastened towards it. Near the churchyard, and in the middle of a garden, stood a well-built though small house, which I had no doubt was the parsonage. I remembered that strangers who arrive at a place where they have no friends, and who want employment, sometimes apply to the clergyman for introduction and aid. It is the clergyman's function to help – at least with advice – those who wished to help themselves. I seemed to have something like a right to seek counsel here. Renewing then my courage, and gathering my feeble remains of strength, I pushed on. I reached the house, and knocked at the kitchen-door. An old woman opened: I asked was this the parsonage?

'Yes.'

'Was the clergyman in?'

'No.'

'Would he be in soon?'

'No, he was gone from home.'

'To a distance?'

'Not so far – happen three mile. He had been called away by the sudden death of his father: he was at Marsh End now, and would very likely stay there a fortnight longer.'

'Was there any lady of the house?'

'Nay, there was naught but her, and she was housekeeper'; and of her, reader, I could not bear to ask the relief for want of which I was sinking; I could not yet beg; and again I crawled away.

Once more I took off my handkerchief – once more I thought of the cakes of bread in the little shop. Oh, for but a crust! for but one mouthful to allay the pang of famine! Instinctively I turned my face again to the village; I found the

shop again, and I went in; and though others were there besides the woman I ventured the request – 'Would she give me a roll for this handkerchief?'

She looked at me with evident suspicion: 'Nay, she never sold stuff i' that way.'

Almost desperate, I asked for half a cake; she again refused. 'How could she tell where I had got the handkerchief?' she said.

'Would she take my gloves?'

'No! what could she do with them?'

Reader, it is not pleasant to dwell on these details. Some say there is enjoyment in looking back to painful experience past; but at this day I can scarcely bear to review the times to which I allude: the moral degradation, blent with the physical suffering, form too distressing a recollection ever to be willingly dwelt on. I blamed none of those who repulsed me. I felt it was what was to be expected, and what could not be helped: an ordinary beggar is frequently an object of suspicion; a well-dressed beggar inevitably so. To be sure, what I begged was employment; but whose business was it to provide me with employment? Not, certainly, that of persons who saw me then for the first time, and who knew nothing about my character. And as to the woman who would not take my handkerchief in exchange for her bread, why, she was right, if the offer appeared to her sinister or the exchange unprofitable. Let me condense now. I am sick of the subject.

A little before dark I passed a farmhouse, at the open door of which the farmer was sitting, eating his supper of bread and cheese. I stopped and said – 'Will you give me a piece of bread? for I am very hungry.' He cast on me a glance of surprise; but without answering, he cut a thick slice from his loaf, and gave it to me. I imagine he did not think I was a beggar, but only an eccentric sort of lady, who had taken a fancy to his brown loaf. As soon as I was out of sight of his house, I sat down and ate it.

I could not hope to get a lodging under a roof, and sought it in the wood I have before alluded to. But my night was wretched, my rest broken: the ground was damp, the air cold: besides, intruders passed near me more than once, and I had again and again to change my quarters: no sense of safety or tranquillity befriended me. Towards morning it rained; the whole of the following day was wet. Do not ask me, reader, to give a minute account of that day; as before, I sought work; as before, I was repulsed; as before, I starved; but once did food pass my lips. At the door of a cottage I saw a little girl about to throw a mess of cold porridge into a pig trough. 'Will you give me that?' I asked.

She stared at me. 'Mother!' she exclaimed, 'there is a woman wants me to give her this porridge.'

'Well, lass,' replied a voice within, 'give it her if she's a beggar. T' pig doesn't want it.'

The girl emptied the stiffened mould into my hands and I devoured it ravenously.

As the wet twilight deepened, I stopped in a solitary bridle-path, which I had been pursuing an hour or more.

'My strength is quite failing me,' I said in a soliloquy. 'I feel I cannot go much farther. Shall I be an outcast again this night? While the rain descends so, must I

lay my head on the cold, drenched ground? I fear I cannot do otherwise: for who will receive me? But it will be very dreadful, with this feeling of hunger, faintness, chill, and this sense of desolation – this total prostration of hope. In all likelihood, though, I should die before morning. And why cannot I reconcile myself to the prospect of death? Why do I struggle to retain a valueless life? Because I know, or believe, Mr Rochester is living: and then, to die of want and cold is a fate to which nature cannot submit passively. Oh, Providence! sustain me a little longer! Aid! – direct me!'

My glazed eye wandered over the dim and misty landscape. I saw I had strayed far from the village: it was quite out of sight. The very cultivation surrounding it had disappeared. I had, by cross-ways and by-paths, once more drawn near the tract of moorland; and now, only a few fields, almost as wild and unproductive as the heath from which they were scarcely reclaimed, lay between me and the dusky hill.

'Well, I would rather die yonder than in a street or on a frequented road,' I reflected. 'And far better that crows and ravens – if any ravens there be in these regions – should pick my flesh from my bones, than that they should be prisoned in a workhouse coffin and moulder in a pauper's grave.'

To the hill, then, I turned. I reached it. It remained now only to find a hollow where I could lie down, and feel at least hidden, if not secure. But all the surface of the waste looked level. It showed no variation but of tint: green, where rush and moss overgrew the marshes; black, where the dry soil bore only heath. Dark as it was getting, I could still see these changes, though but as mere alternations of light and shade; for colour had faded with the daylight.

My eye still roved over the sullen swell and along the moor-edge, vanishing amidst the wildest scenery, when at one dim point, far in among the marshes and the ridges, a light sprang up. 'That is an *ignis fatuus*,' was my first thought; and I expected it would soon vanish. It burnt on, however, quite steadily, neither receding nor advancing. 'Is it, then, a bonfire just kindled?' I questioned. I watched to see whether it would spread: but no; as it did not diminish, so it did not enlarge. 'It may be a candle in a house,' I then conjectured; 'but if so, I can never reach it. It is much too far away: and were it within a yard of me, what would it avail? I should but knock at the door to have it shut in my face.'

And I sank down where I stood, and hid my face against the ground. I lay still a while: the night-wind swept over the hill and over me, and died moaning in the distance; the rain fell fast, wetting me afresh to the skin. Could I but have stiffened to the still frost – the friendly numbness of death – it might have pelted on; I should not have felt it; but my yet living flesh shuddered at its chilling influence. I rose ere long.

The light was yet there, shining dim but constant through the rain. I tried to walk again: I dragged my exhausted limbs slowly towards it. It led me aslant over the hill, through a wide bog, which would have been impassable in winter, and was splashy and shaking even now, in the height of summer. Here I fell twice; but as often I rose and rallied my faculties. This light was my forlorn hope: I must gain it.

Having crossed the marsh, I saw a trace of white over the moor. I approached it; it was a road or a track: it led straight up to the light, which now beamed from a sort of knoll, amidst a clump of trees – firs, apparently, from what I could distinguish of the character of their forms and foliage through the gloom. My star vanished as I drew near: some obstacle had intervened between me and it. I put out my hand to feel the dark mass before me: I discriminated the rough stones of a low wall – above it, something like palisades, and within, a high and prickly hedge. I groped on. Again a whitish object gleamed before me: it was a gate – a wicket; it moved on its hinges as I touched it. On each side stood a sable bush – holly or yew.

Entering the gate and passing the shrubs, the silhouette of a house rose to view, black, low, and rather long; but the guiding light shone nowhere. All was obscurity. Were the inmates retired to rest? I feared it must be so. In seeking the door, I turned an angle: there shot out the friendly gleam again, from the lozenged panes of a very small latticed window, within a foot of the ground, made still smaller by the growth of ivy or some other creeping plant, whose leaves clustered thick over the portion of the house wall in which it was set. The aperture was so screened and narrow, that curtain or shutter had been deemed unnecessary; and when I stooped down and put aside the spray of foliage shooting over it, I could see all within. I could see clearly a room with a sanded floor, clean scoured; a dresser of walnut, with pewter plates ranged in rows, reflecting the redness and radiance of a glowing peat-fire. I could see a clock, a white deal table, some chairs. The candle, whose ray had been my beacon, burnt on the table; and by its light an elderly woman, somewhat rough-looking, but scrupulously clean, like all about her, was knitting a stocking.

I noticed these objects cursorily only – in them there was nothing extraordinary. A group of more interest appeared near the hearth, sitting still amidst the rosy peace and warmth suffusing it. Two young, graceful women – ladies in every point – sat, one in a low rocking-chair, the other on a lower stool; both wore deep mourning of crape and bombazeen, which sombre garb singularly set off very fair necks and faces: a large old pointer dog rested its massive head on the knee of one girl – in the lap of the other was cushioned a black cat.

A strange place was this humble kitchen for such occupants! Who were they? They could not be the daughters of the elderly person at the table; for she looked like a rustic, and they were all delicacy and cultivation. I had nowhere seen such faces as theirs: and yet, as I gazed on them, I seemed intimate with every lineament. I cannot call them handsome – they were too pale and grave for the word: as they each bent over a book, they looked thoughtful almost to severity. A stand between them supported a second candle and two great volumes, to which they frequently referred, comparing them, seemingly, with the smaller books they held in their hands, like people consulting a dictionary to aid them in the task of translation. This scene was as silent as if all the figures had been shadows and the firelit apartment a picture: so hushed was it, I could hear the cinders fall from the grate, the clock tick in its obscure corner; and I even fancied I could distinguish the click-click of the woman's knitting-needles.

When, therefore, a voice broke the strange stillness at last, it was audible enough to me.

'Listen, Diana,' said one of the absorbed students; 'Franz and old Daniel are together in the night-time, and Franz is telling a dream from which he has awakened in terror – listen!' And in a low voice she read something, of which not one word was intelligible to me; for it was in an unknown tongue – neither French nor Latin. Whether it were Greek or German I could not tell.

'That is strong,' she said, when she had finished: 'I relish it.' The other girl, who had lifted her head to listen to her sister, repeated, while she gazed at the fire, a line of what had been read. At a later day, I knew the language and the book; therefore, I will here quote the line: though, when I first heard it, it was only like a stroke on sounding brass to me – conveying no meaning: ' "Da trat hervor Einer, anzusehen wie die Sternen Nacht." Good! good!' she exclaimed, while her dark and deep eye sparkled. 'There you have a dim and mighty archangel fitly set before you! The line is worth a hundred pages of fustian. "Ich wäge die Gedanken in der Schale meines Zornes und die Werke mit dem Gewichte meines Grimms." I like it!'

Both were again silent.

'Is there ony country where they talk i' that way?' asked the old woman, looking up from her knitting.

'Yes, Hannah – a far larger country than England, where they talk in no other way.'

'Well, for sure case, I knawn't how they can understand t'one t'other: and if either o' ye went there, ye could tell what they said, I guess?'

'We could probably tell something of what they said, but not all – for we are not as clever as you think us, Hannah. We don't speak German, and we cannot read it without a dictionary to help us.'

'And what good does it do you?'

'We mean to teach it sometime – or at least the elements, as they say; and then we shall get more money than we do now.'

'Varry like: but give ower studying; ye've done enough for tonight.'

'I think we have: at least I'm tired. Mary, are you?'

'Mortally: after all, it's tough work fagging away at a language with no master but a lexicon.'

'It is, especially such a language as this crabbed but glorious Deutsch. I wonder when St John will come home.'

'Surely he will not be long now: it is just ten' (looking at a little gold watch she drew from her girdle). 'It rains fast, Hannah: will you have the goodness to look at the fire in the parlour?'

The woman rose: she opened a door, through which I dimly saw a passage: soon I heard her stir a fire in an inner room; she presently came back.

'Ah, childer!' said she, 'it fair troubles me to go into yond' room now: it looks so lonesome wi' the chair empty and set back in a corner.'

She wiped her eyes with her apron: the two girls, grave before, looked sad now.

'But he is in a better place,' continued Hannah: 'we shouldn't wish him here again. And then, nobody need to have a quieter death nor he had.'

'You say he never mentioned us?' enquired one of the ladies.

'He hadn't time, bairn: he was gone in a minute, was your father. He had been a bit ailing like the day before, but naught to signify; and when Mr St John asked if he would like either o' ye to be sent for, he fair laughed at him. He began again with a bit of a heaviness in his head the next day – that is, a fortnight sin' – and he went to sleep and niver wakened: he wor a'most stark when your brother went into t' chamber and fand him. Ah, childer! that's t' last o' t' old stock – for ye and Mr St John is like of different soart to them 'at's gone; for all your mother wor mich i' your way, and a'most as book-learned. She wor the pictur' o' ye, Mary: Diana is more like your father.'

I thought them so similar I could not tell where the old servant (for such I now concluded her to be) saw the difference. Both were fair complexioned and slenderly made; both possessed faces full of distinction and intelligence. One, to be sure, had hair a shade darker than the other, and there was a difference in their style of wearing it; Mary's pale brown locks were parted and braided smooth: Diana's duskier tresses covered her neck with thick curls. The clock struck ten.

'Ye'll want your supper, I am sure,' observed Hannah; 'and so will Mr St John when he comes in.'

And she proceeded to prepare the meal. The ladies rose; they seemed about to withdraw to the parlour.

Till this moment, I had been so intent on watching them, their appearance and conversation had excited in me so keen an interest, I had half-forgotten my own wretched position: now it recurred to me. More desolate, more desperate than ever, it seemed from contrast. And how impossible did it appear to touch the inmates of this house with concern on my behalf; to make them believe in the truth of my wants and woes – to induce them to vouchsafe a rest for my wanderings! As I groped out the door, and knocked at it hesitatingly, I felt that last idea to be a mere chimera. Hannah opened.

'What do you want?' she enquired, in a voice of surprise, as she surveyed me by the light of the candle she held.

'May I speak to your mistresses?' I said.

'You had better tell me what you have to say to them. Where do you come from?'

'I am a stranger.'

'What is your business here at this hour?'

'I want a night's shelter in an out-house or anywhere, and a morsel of bread to eat.'

Distrust, the very feeling I dreaded, appeared in Hannah's face. 'I'll give you a piece of bread,' she said, after a pause; 'but we can't take in a vagrant to lodge. It isn't likely.'

'Do let me speak to your mistresses.'

'No, not I. What can they do for you? You should not be roving about now; it looks very ill.'

'But where shall I go if you drive me away? What shall I do?'

'Oh, I'll warrant you know where to go and what to do. Mind you don't do wrong, that's all. Here is a penny; now go –'

'A penny cannot feed me, and I have no strength to go farther. Don't shut the door: oh, don't, for God's sake!'

'I must; the rain is driving in –'

'Tell the young ladies. Let me see them –'

'Indeed, I will not. You are not what you ought to be, or you wouldn't make such a noise. Move off.'

'But I must die if I am turned away.'

'Not you. I'm fear'd you have some ill plans agate that bring you about folk's houses at this time o' night. If you've any followers – housebreakers or suchlike – anywhere near, you may tell them we are not by ourselves in the house; we have a gentleman, and dogs, and guns.' Here the honest but inflexible servant clapped the door to and bolted it within.

This was the climax. A pang of exquisite suffering – a throe of true despair – rent and heaved my heart. Worn out, indeed, I was; not another step could I stir. I sank on the wet doorstep: I groaned – I wrung my hands – I wept in utter anguish. Oh, this spectre of death! Oh, this last hour, approaching in such horror! Alas, this isolation – this banishment from my kind! Not only the anchor of hope, but the footing of fortitude was gone – at least for a moment; but the last I soon endeavoured to regain.

'I can but die,' I said, 'and I believe in God. Let me try to wait His will in silence.'

These words I not only thought, but uttered; and thrusting back all my misery into my heart, I made an effort to compel it to remain there dumb and still.

'All men must die,' said a voice quite close at hand; 'but all are not condemned to meet a lingering and premature doom, such as yours would be if you perished here of want.'

'Who or what speaks?' I asked, terrified at the unexpected sound, and incapable now of deriving from any occurrence a hope of aid. A form was near – what form, the pitch-dark night and my enfeebled vision prevented me from distinguishing. With a loud long knock, the newcomer appealed to the door.

'Is it you, Mr St John?' cried Hannah.

'Yes – yes; open quickly.'

'Well, how wet and cold you must be, such a wild night as it is! Come in – your sisters are quite uneasy about you, and I believe there are bad folks about. There has been a beggar-woman – I declare she is not gone yet! – laid down there. Get up! for shame! Move off, I say!'

'Hush, Hannah! I have a word to say to the woman. You have done your duty in excluding, now let me do mine in admitting her. I was near, and listened to both you and her. I think this is a peculiar case – I must at least examine into it. Young woman, rise, and pass before me into the house.'

With difficulty I obeyed him. Presently I stood within that clean, bright kitchen – on the very hearth – trembling, sickening; conscious of an aspect in

the last degree ghastly, wild, and weather-beaten. The two ladies, their brother, Mr St John, the old servant, were all gazing at me.

'St John, who is it?' I heard one ask.

'I cannot tell: I found her at the door,' was the reply.

'She does look white,' said Hannah.

'As white as clay or death,' was responded. 'She will fall: let her sit.'

And indeed my head swam: I dropped, but a chair received me. I still possessed my senses, though just now I could not speak.

'Perhaps a little water would restore her. Hannah, fetch some. But she is worn to nothing. How very thin, and how very bloodless!'

'A mere spectre!'

'Is she ill, or only famished?'

'Famished, I think. Hannah, is that milk? Give it me, and a piece of bread.'

Diana (I knew her by the long curls which I saw drooping between me and the fire as she bent over me) broke some bread, dipped it in milk, and put it to my lips. Her face was near mine: I saw there was pity in it, and I felt sympathy in her hurried breathing. In her simple words, too, the same balm-like emotion spoke: 'Try to eat.'

'Yes – try,' repeated Mary gently; and Mary's hand removed my sodden bonnet and lifted my head. I tasted what they offered me: feebly at first, eagerly soon.

'Not too much at first – restrain her,' said the brother; 'she has had enough.' And he withdrew the cup of milk and the plate of bread.

'A little more, St John – look at the avidity in her eyes.'

'No more at present, sister. Try if she can speak now – ask her her name.'

I felt I could speak, and I answered – 'My name is Jane Elliott.' Anxious as ever to avoid discovery, I had before resolved to assume an *alias*.

'And where do you live? Where are your friends?'

I was silent.

'Can we send for anyone you know?'

I shook my head.

'What account can you give of yourself?'

Somehow, now that I had once crossed the threshold of this house, and once was brought face to face with its owners, I felt no longer outcast, vagrant, and disowned by the wide world. I dared to put off the mendicant – to resume my natural manner and character. I began once more to know myself; and when Mr St John demanded an account – which at present I was far too weak to render – I said after a brief pause – 'Sir, I can give you no details tonight.'

'But what, then,' said he, 'do you expect me to do for you?'

'Nothing,' I replied. My strength sufficed for but short answers. Diana took the word – 'Do you mean,' she asked, 'that we have now given you what aid you require? and that we may dismiss you to the moor and the rainy night?'

I looked at her. She had, I thought, a remarkable countenance, instinct both with power and goodness. I took sudden courage. Answering her compassionate gaze with a smile, I said – 'I will trust you. If I were a masterless and stray dog, I

know that you would not turn me from your hearth tonight: as it is, I really have no fear. Do with me and for me as you like; but excuse me from much discourse – my breath is short – I feel a spasm when I speak.' All three surveyed me, and all three were silent.

'Hannah,' said Mr St John, at last, 'let her sit there at present, and ask her no questions; in ten minutes more, give her the remainder of that milk and bread. Mary and Diana, let us go into the parlour and talk the matter over.'

They withdrew. Very soon one of the ladies returned – I could not tell which. A kind of pleasant stupor was stealing over me as I sat by the genial fire. In an undertone she gave some directions to Hannah. Ere long, with the servant's aid, I contrived to mount a staircase; my dripping clothes were removed; soon a warm, dry bed received me. I thanked God – experienced amidst unutterable exhaustion a glow of grateful joy – and slept.

## Chapter 29

The recollection of about three days and nights succeeding this is very dim in my mind. I can recall some sensations felt in that interval; but few thoughts framed, and no actions performed. I knew I was in a small room and in a narrow bed. To that bed I seemed to have grown; I lay on it motionless as a stone; and to have torn me from it would have been almost to kill me. I took no note of the lapse of time – of the change from morning to noon, from noon to evening. I observed when anyone entered or left the apartment: I could even tell who they were; I could understand what was said when the speaker stood near to me; but I could not answer; to open my lips or move my limbs was equally impossible. Hannah, the servant, was my most frequent visitor. Her coming disturbed me. I had a feeling that she wished me away: that she did not understand me or my circumstances; that she was prejudiced against me. Diana and Mary appeared in the chamber once or twice a day. They would whisper sentences of this sort at my bedside – 'It is very well we took her in.'

'Yes; she would certainly have been found dead at the door in the morning had she been left out all night. I wonder what she has gone through?'

'Strange hardships, I imagine – poor, emaciated, pallid wanderer!'

'She is not an uneducated person, I should think, by her manner of speaking; her accent was quite pure; and the clothes she took off, though splashed and wet, were little worn and fine.'

'She has a peculiar face; fleshless and haggard as it is, I rather like it; and when in good health and animated, I can fancy her physiognomy would be agreeable.'

Never once in their dialogues did I hear a syllable of regret at the hospitality they had extended to me, or of suspicion of, or aversion to, myself. I was comforted.

Mr St John came but once: he looked at me, and said my state of lethargy was the result of reaction from excessive and protracted fatigue. He pronounced it

needless to send for a doctor: nature, he was sure, would manage best, left to herself. He said every nerve had been overstrained in some way, and the whole system must sleep torpid a while. There was no disease. He imagined my recovery would be rapid enough when once commenced. These opinions he delivered in a few words, in a quiet, low voice; and added, after a pause, in the tone of a man little accustomed to expansive comment, 'Rather an unusual physiognomy; certainly, not indicative of vulgarity or degradation.'

'Far otherwise,' responded Diana. 'To speak truth, St John, my heart rather warms to the poor little soul. I wish we may be able to benefit her permanently.'

'That is hardly likely,' was the reply. 'You will find she is some young lady who has had a misunderstanding with her friends, and has probably injudiciously left them. We may, perhaps, succeed in restoring her to them, if she is not obstinate: but I trace lines of force in her face which make me sceptical of her tractability.' He stood considering me some minutes; then added, 'She looks sensible, but not at all handsome.'

'She is so ill, St John.'

'Ill or well, she would always be plain. The grace and harmony of beauty are quite wanting in those features.'

On the third day I was better; on the fourth, I could speak, move, rise in bed, and turn. Hannah had brought me some gruel and dry toast, about, as I supposed, the dinner-hour. I had eaten with relish: the food was good – void of the feverish flavour which had hitherto poisoned what I had swallowed. When she left me, I felt comparatively strong and revived: ere long satiety of repose and desire for action stirred me. I wished to rise; but what could I put on? Only my damp and bemired apparel; in which I had slept on the ground and fallen in the marsh. I felt ashamed to appear before my benefactors so clad. I was spared the humiliation.

On a chair by the bedside were all my own things, clean and dry. My black silk frock hung against the wall. The traces of the bog were removed from it; the creases left by the wet smoothed out: it was quite decent. My very shoes and stockings were purified and rendered presentable. There were the means of washing in the room, and a comb and brush to smooth my hair. After a weary process, and resting every five minutes, I succeeded in dressing myself. My clothes hung loose on me; for I was much wasted, but I covered deficiencies with a shawl, and once more, clean and respectable looking – no speck of the dirt, no trace of the disorder I so hated, and which seemed so to degrade me, left – I crept down a stone staircase with the aid of the banisters, to a narrow low passage, and found my way presently to the kitchen.

It was full of the fragrance of new bread and the warmth of a generous fire. Hannah was baking. Prejudices, it is well known, are most difficult to eradicate from the heart whose soil has never been loosened or fertilised by education: they grow there, firm as weeds among stones. Hannah had been cold and stiff, indeed, at the first: latterly she had begun to relent a little; and when she saw me come in tidy and well-dressed, she even smiled.

'What, you have got up!' she said. 'You are better, then. You may sit you down in my chair on the hearthstone, if you will.'

She pointed to the rocking-chair: I took it. She bustled about, examining me every now and then with the corner of her eye. Turning to me, as she took some loaves from the oven, she asked bluntly – 'Did you ever go a-begging afore you came here?'

I was indignant for a moment; but remembering that anger was out of the question, and that I had indeed appeared as a beggar to her, I answered quietly, but still not without a certain marked firmness – 'You are mistaken in supposing me a beggar. I am no beggar; any more than yourself or your young ladies.'

After a pause she said, 'I dunnut understand that: you've like no house, nor no brass, I guess?'

'The want of house or brass (by which I suppose you mean money) does not make a beggar in your sense of the word.'

'Are you book-learned?' she enquired presently.

'Yes, very.'

'But you've never been to a boarding-school?'

'I was at a boarding-school eight years.'

She opened her eyes wide. 'Whatever cannot ye keep yourself for, then?'

'I have kept myself; and, I trust, shall keep myself again. What are you going to do with these gooseberries?' I enquired, as she brought out a basket of the fruit.

'Mak' 'em into pies.'

'Give them to me and I'll pick them.'

'Nay; I dunnut want ye to do nought.'

'But I must do something. Let me have them.'

She consented; and she even brought me a clean towel to spread over my dress, 'lest,' as she said, 'I should mucky it.'

'Ye've not been used to sarvant's wark, I see by your hands,' she remarked. 'Happen ye've been a dressmaker?'

'No, you are wrong. And now, never mind what I have been: don't trouble your head further about me; but tell me the name of the house where we are.'

'Some calls it Marsh End, and some calls it Moor House.'

'And the gentleman who lives here is called Mr St John?'

'Nay; he doesn't live here: he is only staying a while. When he is at home, he is in his own parish at Morton.'

'That village a few miles off?'

'Aye.'

'And what is he?'

'He is a parson.'

I remembered the answer of the old housekeeper at the parsonage, when I had asked to see the clergyman. 'This, then, was his father's residence?'

'Aye; old Mr Rivers lived here, and his father, and grandfather, and gurt [great] grandfather afore him.'

'The name, then, of that gentleman, is Mr St John Rivers?'

'Aye; St John is like his kirstened name.'

'And his sisters are called Diana and Mary Rivers?'

'Yes.'

'Their father is dead?'

'Dead three weeks sin' of a stroke.'

'They have no mother?'

'The mistress has been dead this mony a year.'

'Have you lived with the family long?'

'I've lived here thirty year. I nursed them all three.'

'That proves you must have been an honest and faithful servant. I will say so much for you, though you have had the incivility to call me a beggar.'

She again regarded me with a surprised stare. 'I believe,' she said, 'I was quite mista'en in my thoughts of you: but there is so mony cheats goes about, you mun forgie me.'

'And though,' I continued, rather severely, 'you wished to turn me from the door, on a night when you should not have shut out a dog.'

'Well, it was hard: but what can a body do? I thought more o' th' childer nor of mysel: poor things! They've like nobody to tak' care on 'em but me. I'm like to look sharpish.'

I maintained a grave silence for some minutes.

'You munnut think too hardly of me,' she again remarked.

'But I do think hardly of you,' I said; 'and I'll tell you why – not so much because you refused to give me shelter, or regarded me as an impostor, as because you just now made it a species of reproach that I had no "brass" and no house. Some of the best people that ever lived have been as destitute as I am; and if you are a Christian, you ought not to consider poverty a crime.'

'No more I ought,' said she: 'Mr St John tells me so too; and I see I wor wrang – but I've clear a different notion on you now to what I had. You look a raight down dacent little crater.'

'That will do – I forgive you now. Shake hands.'

She put her floury and horny hand into mine; another and heartier smile illumined her rough face, and from that moment we were friends.

Hannah was evidently fond of talking. While I picked the fruit, and she made the paste for the pies, she proceeded to give me sundry details about her deceased master and mistress, and 'the childer', as she called the young people.

Old Mr Rivers, she said, was a plain man enough, but a gentleman, and of as ancient a family as could be found. Marsh End had belonged to the Rivers ever since it was a house: and it was, she affirmed, 'aboon two hundred year old – for all it looked but a small, humble place, naught to compare wi' Mr Oliver's grand hall down i' Morton Vale. But she could remember Bill Oliver's father a journeyman needlemaker; and th' Rivers wor gentry i' th' owd days o' th' Henrys, as onybody might see by looking into th' registers i' Morton Church vestry.' Still, she allowed, 'the owd maister was like other folk – naught mich out o' th' common way: stark mad o' shooting, and farming, and sichlike'. The mistress was different. She was a great reader, and studied a deal; and the 'bairns' had taken after her. There was nothing like them in these parts, nor ever had been; they had liked learning, all three, almost from the time they could speak; and they had always been 'of a mak' of their own'. Mr St John,

when he grew up, would go to college and be a parson; and the girls, as soon as they left school, would seek places as governesses: for they had told her their father had some years ago lost a great deal of money by a man he had trusted turning bankrupt; and as he was now not rich enough to give them fortunes, they must provide for themselves. They had lived very little at home for a long while, and were only come now to stay a few weeks on account of their father's death; but they did so like Marsh End and Morton, and all these moors and hills about. They had been in London, and many other grand towns; but they always said there was no place like home; and then they were so agreeable with each other – never fell out nor 'threaped'. She did not know where there was such a family for being united.

Having finished my task of gooseberry picking, I asked where the two ladies and their brother were now.

'Gone over to Morton for a walk; but they would be back in half an hour to tea.'

They returned within the time Hannah had allotted them: they entered by the kitchen door. Mr St John, when he saw me, merely bowed and passed through; the two ladies stopped: Mary, in a few words, kindly and calmly expressed the pleasure she felt in seeing me well enough to be able to come down; Diana took my hand: she shook her head at me.

'You should have waited for my leave to descend,' she said. 'You still look very pale – and so thin! Poor child! – poor girl!'

Diana had a voice toned, to my ear, like the cooing of a dove. She possessed eyes whose gaze I delighted to encounter. Her whole face seemed to me full of charm. Mary's countenance was equally intelligent – her features equally pretty; but her expression was more reserved, and her manners, though gentle, more distant. Diana looked and spoke with a certain authority: she had a will, evidently. It was my nature to feel pleasure in yielding to an authority supported like hers, and to bend, where my conscience and self-respect permitted, to an active will.

'And what business have you here?' she continued. 'It is not your place. Mary and I sit in the kitchen sometimes, because at home we like to be free, even to license – but you are a visitor, and must go into the parlour.'

'I am very well here.'

'Not at all, with Hannah bustling about and covering you with flour.'

'Besides, the fire is too hot for you,' interposed Mary.

'To be sure,' added her sister. 'Come, you must be obedient.' And still holding my hand she made me rise, and led me into the inner room.

'Sit there,' she said, placing me on the sofa, 'while we take our things off and get the tea ready; it is another privilege we exercise in our little moorland home – to prepare our own meals when we are so inclined, or when Hannah is baking, brewing, washing, or ironing.'

She closed the door, leaving me solus with Mr St John, who sat opposite, a book or newspaper in his hand. I examined first, the parlour, and then its occupant.

The parlour was rather a small room, very plainly furnished, yet comfortable,

because clean and neat. The old-fashioned chairs were very bright, and the walnut-wood table was like a looking-glass. A few strange, antique portraits of the men and women of other days decorated the stained walls; a cupboard with glass doors contained some books and an ancient set of china. There was no superfluous ornament in the room – not one modern piece of furniture, save a brace of workboxes and a lady's desk in rosewood, which stood on a side-table: everything – including the carpet and curtains – looked at once well worn and well saved.

Mr St John – sitting as still as one of the dusty pictures on the walls, keeping his eyes fixed on the page he perused, and his lips mutely sealed – was easy enough to examine. Had he been a statue instead of a man, he could not have been easier. He was young – perhaps from twenty-eight to thirty – tall, slender; his face riveted the eye; it was like a Greek face, very pure in outline: quite a straight, classic nose; quite an Athenian mouth and chin. It is seldom, indeed, an English face comes so near the antique models as did his. He might well be a little shocked at the irregularity of my lineaments, his own being so harmonious. His eyes were large and blue, with brown lashes; his high forehead, colourless as ivory, was partially streaked over by careless locks of fair hair.

This is a gentle delineation, is it not, reader? Yet he whom it describes scarcely impressed one with the idea of a gentle, a yielding, an impressible, or even of a placid nature. Quiescent as he now sat, there was something about his nostril, his mouth, his brow, which, to my perceptions, indicated elements within either restless, or hard, or eager. He did not speak to me one word, nor even direct to me one glance, till his sisters returned. Diana, as she passed in and out, in the course of preparing tea, brought me a little cake, baked on the top of the oven.

'Eat that now,' she said: 'you must be hungry. Hannah says you have had nothing but some gruel since breakfast.'

I did not refuse it, for my appetite was awakened and keen. Mr Rivers now closed his book, approached the table, and, as he took a seat, fixed his blue pictorial-looking eyes full on me. There was an unceremonious directness, a searching, decided steadfastness in his gaze now, which told that intention, and not diffidence, had hitherto kept it averted from the stranger. 'You are very hungry,' he said.

'I am, sir.' It is my way – it always was my way, by instinct – ever to meet the brief with brevity, the direct with plainness.

'It is well for you that a low fever has forced you to abstain for the last three days: there would have been danger in yielding to the cravings of your appetite at first. Now you may eat, though still not immoderately.'

'I trust I shall not eat long at your expense, sir,' was my very clumsily-contrived, unpolished answer.

'No,' he said coolly: 'when you have indicated to us the residence of your friends, we can write to them, and you may be restored to home.'

'That, I must plainly tell you, is out of my power to do; being absolutely without home and friends.'

The three looked at me, but not distrustfully; I felt there was no suspicion in their glances: there was more of curiosity. I speak particularly of the young ladies. St John's eyes, though clear enough in a literal sense, in a figurative one were difficult to fathom. He seemed to use them rather as instruments to search other people's thoughts, than as agents to reveal his own: the which combination of keenness and reserve was considerably more calculated to embarrass than to encourage.

'Do you mean to say,' he asked, 'that you are completely isolated from every connection?'

'I do. Not a tie links me to any living thing: not a claim do I possess to admittance under any roof in England.'

'A most singular position at your age!'

Here I saw his glance directed to my hands, which were folded on the table before me. I wondered what he sought there: his words soon explained the quest.

'You have never been married? You are a spinster?'

Diana laughed. 'Why, she can't be above seventeen or eighteen years old, St John,' said she.

'I am near nineteen: but I am not married. No.'

I felt a burning glow mount to my face; for bitter and agitating recollections were awakened by the allusion to marriage. They all saw the embarrassment and the emotion. Diana and Mary relieved me by turning their eyes elsewhere than to my crimsoned visage; but the colder and sterner brother continued to gaze, till the trouble he had excited forced out tears as well as colour.

'Where did you last reside?' he now asked.

'You are too inquisitive, St John,' murmured Mary in a low voice; but he leaned over the table and required an answer by a second firm and piercing look.

'The name of the place where, and of the person with whom I lived, is my secret,' I replied concisely.

'Which, if you like, you have, in my opinion, a right to keep, both from St John and every other questioner,' remarked Diana.

'Yet if I know nothing about you or your history, I cannot help you,' he said. 'And you need help, do you not?'

'I need it, and I seek it so far, sir, that some true philanthropist will put me in the way of getting work which I can do, and the remuneration for which will keep me, if but in the barest necessaries of life.'

'I know not whether I am a true philanthropist; yet I am willing to aid you to the utmost of my power in a purpose so honest. First, then, tell me what you have been accustomed to do, and what you *can* do.'

I had now swallowed my tea. I was mightily refreshed by the beverage; as much so as a giant with wine: it gave new tone to my unstrung nerves, and enabled me to address this penetrating young judge steadily.

'Mr Rivers,' I said, turning to him, and looking at him, as he looked at me, openly and without diffidence, 'you and your sisters have done me a great service – the greatest man can do his fellow-being; you have rescued me, by your

noble hospitality, from death. This benefit conferred gives you an unlimited claim on my gratitude, and a claim, to a certain extent, on my confidence. I will tell you as much of the history of the wanderer you have harboured, as I can tell without compromising my own peace of mind – my own security, moral and physical, and that of others.

'I am an orphan, the daughter of a clergyman. My parents died before I could know them. I was brought up a dependant; educated in a charitable institution. I will even tell you the name of the establishment, where I passed six years as a pupil, and two as a teacher – Lowood Orphan Asylum, —shire: you will have heard of it, Mr Rivers? – the Revd Robert Brocklehurst is the treasurer.'

'I have heard of Mr Brocklehurst, and I have seen the school.'

'I left Lowood nearly a year since to become a private governess. I obtained a good situation, and was happy. This place I was obliged to leave four days before I came here. The reason of my departure I cannot and ought not to explain: it would be useless, dangerous, and would sound incredible. No blame attached to me: I am as free from culpability as any one of you three. Miserable I am, and must be for a time; for the catastrophe which drove me from a house I had found a paradise was of a strange and direful nature. I observed but two points in planning my departure – speed, secrecy: to secure these, I had to leave behind me everything I possessed except a small parcel; which, in my hurry and trouble of mind, I forgot to take out of the coach that brought me to Whitcross. To this neighbourhood, then, I came, quite destitute. I slept two nights in the open air, and wandered about two days without crossing a threshold: but twice in that space of time did I taste food; and it was when brought by hunger, exhaustion, and despair almost to the last gasp, that you, Mr Rivers, forbade me to perish of want at your door, and took me under the shelter of your roof. I know all your sisters have done for me since – for I have not been insensible during my seeming torpor – and I owe to their spontaneous, genuine, genial compassion as large a debt as to your evangelical charity.'

'Don't make her talk any more now, St John,' said Diana, as I paused; 'she is evidently not yet fit for excitement. Come to the sofa and sit down now, Miss Elliott.'

I gave an involuntary half start at hearing the *alias:* I had forgotten my new name. Mr Rivers, whom nothing seemed to escape, noticed it at once.

'You said your name was Jane Elliott?' he observed.

'I did say so; and it is the name by which I think it expedient to be called at present, but it is not my real name, and when I hear it, it sounds strange to me.'

'Your real name you will not give?'

'No: I fear discovery above all things; and whatever disclosure would lead to it, I avoid.'

'You are quite right, I am sure,' said Diana. 'Now do, brother, let her be at peace a while.'

But when St John had mused a few moments he recommenced as imperturbably and with as much acumen as ever.

'You would not like to be long dependent on our hospitality – you would

wish, I see, to dispense as soon as may be with my sisters' compassion, and, above all with my *charity* (I am quite sensible of the distinction drawn, nor do I resent it – it is just): you desire to be independent of us?'

'I do: I have already said so. Show me how to work, or how to seek work: that is all I now ask; then let me go, if it be but to the meanest cottage; but till then, allow me to stay here: I dread another essay of the horrors of homeless destitution.'

'Indeed you *shall* stay here,' said Diana, putting her white hand on my head. 'You *shall*,' repeated Mary, in the tone of undemonstrative sincerity which seemed natural to her.

'My sisters, you see, have a pleasure in keeping you,' said Mr St John, 'as they would have a pleasure in keeping and cherishing a half-frozen bird, some wintry wind might have driven through their casement. I feel more inclination to put you in the way of keeping yourself, and shall endeavour to do so; but observe, my sphere is narrow. I am but the incumbent of a poor country parish: my aid must be of the humblest sort. And if you are inclined to despise the day of small things, seek some more efficient succour than such as I can offer.'

'She has already said that she is willing to do anything honest she *can* do,' answered Diana for me; 'and you know, St John, she has no choice of helpers: she is forced to put up with such crusty people as you.'

'I will be a dressmaker; I will be a plain-workwoman; I will be a servant, a nurse-girl, if I can be no better,' I answered.

'Right,' said Mr St John, quite coolly. 'If such is your spirit, I promise to aid you, in my own time and way.'

He now resumed the book with which he had been occupied before tea. I soon withdrew, for I had talked as much, and sat up as long, as my present strength would permit.

## *Chapter 30*

The more I knew of the inmates of Moor House, the better I liked them. In a few days I had so far recovered my health that I could sit up all day, and walk out sometimes. I could join with Diana and Mary in all their occupations; converse with them as much as they wished, and aid them when and where they would allow me. There was a reviving pleasure in this intercourse, of a kind now tasted by me for the first time – the pleasure arising from perfect congeniality of tastes, sentiments, and principles.

I liked to read what they liked to read: what they enjoyed, delighted me; what they approved, I reverenced. They loved their sequestered home. I, too, in the grey, small, antique structure, with its low roof, its latticed casements, its mouldering walls, its avenue of aged firs – all grown aslant under the stress of mountain winds; its garden, dark with yew and holly – and where no flowers but of the hardiest species would bloom – found a charm both potent and permanent. They clung to the purple moors behind and around their dwelling – to the

hollow vale into which the pebbly bridle-path leading from their gate descended, and which wound between fern-banks first, and then amongst a few of the wildest little pasture-fields that ever bordered a wilderness of heath, or gave sustenance to a flock of grey moorland sheep, with their little mossy-faced lambs: they clung to this scene, I say, with a perfect enthusiasm of attachment. I could comprehend the feeling, and share both its strength and truth. I saw the fascination of the locality. I felt the consecration of its loneliness: my eye feasted on the outline of swell and sweep – on the wild colouring communicated to ridge and dell by moss, by heath-bell, by flower-sprinkled turf, by brilliant bracken, and mellow granite crag. These details were just to me what they were to them – so many pure and sweet sources of pleasure. The strong blast and the soft breeze; the rough and the halcyon day; the hours of sunrise and sunset; the moonlight and the clouded night, developed for me, in these regions, the same attraction as for them – wound round my faculties the same spell that entranced theirs.

Indoors we agreed equally well. They were both more accomplished and better read than I was; but with eagerness I followed in the path of knowledge they had trodden before me. I devoured the books they lent me: then it was full satisfaction to discuss with them in the evening what I had perused during the day. Thought fitted thought; opinion met opinion: we coincided, in short, perfectly.

If in our trio there was a superior and a leader, it was Diana. Physically, she far excelled me: she was handsome; she was vigorous. In her animal spirits there was an affluence of life and certainty of flow, such as excited my wonder, while it baffled my comprehension. I could talk a while when the evening commenced, but the first gush of vivacity and fluency gone, I was fain to sit on a stool at Diana's feet, to rest my head on her knee, and listen alternately to her and Mary, while they sounded thoroughly the topic on which I had but touched. Diana offered to teach me German. I liked to learn of her: I saw the part of instructress pleased and suited her; that of scholar pleased and suited me no less. Our natures dovetailed: mutual affection – of the strongest kind – was the result. They discovered I could draw: their pencils and colour-boxes were immediately at my service. My skill, greater in this one point than theirs, surprised and charmed them. Mary would sit and watch me by the hour together: then she would take lessons; and a docile, intelligent, assiduous pupil she made. Thus occupied, and mutually entertained, days passed like hours, and weeks like days.

As to Mr St John, the intimacy which had arisen so naturally and rapidly between me and his sisters did not extend to him. One reason of the distance yet observed between us was, that he was comparatively seldom at home: a large proportion of his time appeared devoted to visiting the sick and poor among the scattered population of his parish.

No weather seemed to hinder him in these pastoral excursions: rain or fair, he would, when his hours of morning study were over, take his hat, and, followed by his father's old pointer, Carlo, go out on his mission of love or duty – I scarcely know in which light he regarded it. Sometimes, when the day was very unfavourable, his sisters would expostulate. He would then say, with a

peculiar smile, more solemn than cheerful – 'And if I let a gust of wind or a sprinkling of rain turn me aside from these easy tasks, what preparation would such sloth be for the future I propose to myself?'

Diana and Mary's general answer to this question was a sigh, and some minutes of apparently mournful meditation.

But besides his frequent absences, there was another barrier to friendship with him: he seemed of a reserved, an abstracted, and even of a brooding nature. Zealous in his ministerial labours, blameless in his life and habits, he yet did not appear to enjoy that mental serenity, that inward content, which should be the reward of every sincere Christian and practical philanthropist. Often, of an evening, when he sat at the window, his desk and papers before him, he would cease reading or writing, rest his chin on his hand, and deliver himself up to I know not what course of thought; but that it was perturbed and exciting might be seen in the frequent flash and changeful dilation of his eye.

I think, moreover, that Nature was not to him that treasury of delight it was to his sisters. He expressed once, and but once in my hearing, a strong sense of the rugged charm of the hills, and an inborn affection for the dark roof and hoary walls he called his home; but there was more of gloom than pleasure in the tone and words in which the sentiment was manifested; and never did he seem to roam the moors for the sake of their soothing silence – never seek out or dwell upon the thousand peaceful delights they could yield.

Incommunicative as he was, some time elapsed before I had an opportunity of gauging his mind. I first got an idea of its calibre when I heard him preach in his own church at Morton. I wish I could describe that sermon: but it is past my power. I cannot even render faithfully the effect it produced on me.

It began calm – and indeed, as far as delivery and pitch of voice went, it was calm to the end: an earnestly felt, yet strictly restrained zeal breathed soon in the distinct accents, and prompted the nervous language. This grew to force – compressed, condensed, controlled. The heart was thrilled, the mind astonished, by the power of the preacher: neither were softened. Throughout there was a strange bitterness; an absence of consolatory gentleness; stern allusions to Calvinistic doctrines – election, predestination, reprobation – were frequent; and each reference to these points sounded like a sentence pronounced for doom. When he had done, instead of feeling better, calmer, more enlightened by his discourse, I experienced an expressible sadness; for it seemed to me – I know not whether equally so to others – that the eloquence to which I had been listening had sprung from a depth where lay turbid dregs of disappointment – where moved troubling impulses of insatiate yearnings and disquieting aspirations. I was sure St John Rivers – pure-lived, conscientious, zealous as he was – had not yet found that peace of God which passeth all understanding: he had no more found it, I thought, than had I with my concealed and racking regrets for my broken idol and lost elysium – regrets to which I have latterly avoided referring, but which possessed me and tyrannised over me ruthlessly.

Meantime a month was gone. Diana and Mary were soon to leave Moor House, and return to the far different life and scene which awaited them, as

governesses in a large, fashionable, south-of-England city, where each held a situation in families by whose wealthy and haughty members they were regarded only as humble dependants, and who neither knew nor sought out their innate excellences, and appreciated only their acquired accomplishments as they appreciated the skill of their cook or the taste of their waiting-woman. Mr St John had said nothing to me yet about the employment he had promised to obtain for me; yet it became urgent that I should have a vocation of some kind. One morning, being left alone with him a few minutes in the parlour, I ventured to approach the window-recess – which his table, chair, and desk consecrated as a kind of study – and I was going to speak, though not very well knowing in what words to frame my enquiry – for it is at all times difficult to break the ice of reserve glassing over such natures as his – when he saved me the trouble by being the first to commence a dialogue.

Looking up as I drew near – 'You have a question to ask of me?' he said.

'Yes; I wish to know whether you have heard of any service I can offer myself to undertake?'

'I found or devised something for you three weeks ago; but as you seemed both useful and happy here – as my sisters had evidently become attached to you, and your society gave them unusual pleasure – I deemed it inexpedient to break in on your mutual comfort till their approaching departure from Marsh End should render yours necessary.'

'And they will go in three days now?' I said.

'Yes; and when they go, I shall return to the parsonage at Morton: Hannah will accompany me; and this old house will be shut up.'

I waited a few moments, expecting he would go on with the subject first broached: but he seemed to have entered another train of reflection: his look denoted abstraction from me and my business. I was obliged to recall him to a theme which was of necessity one of close and anxious interest to me.

'What is the employment you had in view, Mr Rivers? I hope this delay will not have increased the difficulty of securing it.'

'Oh, no; since it is an employment which depends only on me to give, and you to accept.'

He again paused: there seemed a reluctance to continue. I grew impatient: a restless movement or two, and an eager and exacting glance fastened on his face, conveyed the feeling to him as effectually as words could have done, and with less trouble.

'You need be in no hurry to hear,' he said: 'let me frankly tell you, I have nothing eligible or profitable to suggest. Before I explain, recall, if you please, my notice, clearly given, that if I helped you, it must be as the blind man would help the lame. I am poor; for I find that, when I have paid my father's debts, all the patrimony remaining to me will be this crumbling grange, the row of scathed firs behind, and the patch of moorish soil, with the yew trees and holly bushes in front. I am obscure: Rivers is an old name; but of the three sole descendants of the race, two earn the dependant's crust among strangers, and the third considers himself an alien from his native country – not only for life,

but in death. Yes, and deems, and is bound to deem, himself honoured by the lot, and aspires but after the day when the cross of separation from fleshly ties shall be laid on his shoulders, and when the Head of that church-militant of whose humblest members he is one, shall give the word, "Rise, follow Me!"'

St John said these words as he pronounced his sermons, with a quiet, deep voice; with an unflushed cheek, and a coruscating radiance of glance. He resumed – 'And since I am myself poor and obscure, I can offer you but a service of poverty and obscurity. *You* may even think it degrading – for I see now your habits have been what the world calls refined: your tastes lean to the ideal, and your society has at least been amongst the educated; but *I* consider that no service degrades which can better our race. I hold that the more arid and unreclaimed the soil where the Christian labourer's task of tillage is appointed him – the scantier the meed his toil brings – the higher the honour. His, under such circumstances, is the destiny of the pioneer; and the first pioneers of the Gospel were the Apostles – their captain was Jesus, the Redeemer, Himself.'

'Well?' I said, as he again paused – 'proceed.'

He looked at me before he proceeded: indeed, he seemed leisurely to read my face, as if its features and lines were characters on a page. The conclusions drawn from this scrutiny he partially expressed in his succeeding observations.

'I believe you will accept the post I offer you,' said he, 'and hold it for a while: not permanently, though: any more than I could permanently keep the narrow and narrowing – the tranquil, hidden office of English country incumbent; for in your nature is an alloy as detrimental to repose as that in mine, though of a different kind.'

'Do explain,' I urged, when he halted once more.

'I will; and you shall hear how poor the proposal is, how trivial – how cramping. I shall not stay long at Morton, now that my father is dead, and that I am my own master. I shall leave the place probably in the course of a twelvemonth; but while I do stay, I will exert myself to the utmost for its improvement. Morton, when I came to it two years ago, had no school: the children of the poor were excluded from every hope of progress. I established one for boys: I mean now to open a second school for girls. I have hired a building for the purpose, with a cottage of two rooms attached to it for the mistress's house. Her salary will be thirty pounds a year: her house is already furnished, very simply, but sufficiently, by the kindness of a lady, Miss Oliver; the only daughter of the sole rich man in my parish – Mr Oliver, the proprietor of a needle-factory and iron-foundry in the valley. The same lady pays for the education and clothing of an orphan from the workhouse, on condition that she shall aid the mistress in such menial offices connected with her own house and the school as her occupation of teaching will prevent her having time to discharge in person. Will you be this mistress?'

He put the question rather hurriedly; he seemed half to expect an indignant, or at least a disdainful rejection of the offer: not knowing all my thoughts and feelings, though guessing some, he could not tell in what light the lot would appear to me. In truth it was humble – but then it was sheltered, and I wanted a

safe asylum: it was plodding – but then, compared with that of a governess in a rich house, it was independent; and the fear of servitude with strangers entered my soul like iron: it was not ignoble – not unworthy – not mentally degrading. I made my decision.

'I thank you for the proposal, Mr Rivers, and I accept it with all my heart.'

'But you comprehend me?' he said. 'It is a village school: your scholars will be only poor girls – cottagers' children – at the best, farmers' daughters. Knitting, sewing, reading, writing, ciphering, will be all you will have to teach. What will you do with your accomplishments? What, with the largest portion of your mind – sentiments – tastes?'

'Save them till they are wanted. They will keep.'

'You know what you undertake, then?'

'I do.'

He now smiled: and not a bitter or a sad smile, but one well pleased and deeply gratified.

'And when will you commence the exercise of your function?'

'I will go to my house tomorrow, and open the school, if you like, next week.'

'Very well: so be it.'

He rose and walked through the room. Standing still, he again looked at me. He shook his head.

'What do you disapprove of, Mr Rivers?' I asked.

'You will not stay at Morton long: no, no!'

'Why? What is your reason for saying so?'

'I read it in your eye; it is not of that description which promises the maintenance of an even tenor in life.'

'I am not ambitious.'

He started at the word 'ambitious.' He repeated, 'No. What made you think of ambition? Who is ambitious? I know I am: but how did you find it out?'

'I was speaking of myself.'

'Well, if you are not ambitious, you are – ' He paused.

'What?'

'I was going to say, impassioned: but perhaps you would have misunderstood the word, and been displeased. I mean, that human affections and sympathies have a most powerful hold on you. I am sure you cannot long be content to pass your leisure in solitude, and to devote your working hours to a monotonous labour wholly void of stimulus: any more than I can be content,' he added, with emphasis, 'to live here buried in morass, pent in with mountains – my nature, that God gave me, contravened; my faculties, heaven-bestowed, paralysed – made useless. You hear now how I contradict myself. I, who preached contentment with a humble lot, and justified the vocation even of hewers of wood and drawers of water in God's service – I, His ordained minister, almost rave in my restlessness. Well, propensities and principles must be reconciled by some means.'

He left the room. In this brief hour I had learnt more of him than in the whole previous month: yet still he puzzled me.

Diana and Mary Rivers became more sad and silent as the day approached for

leaving their brother and their home. They both tried to appear as usual; but the sorrow they had to struggle against was one that could not be entirely conquered or concealed. Diana intimated that this would be a different parting from any they had ever yet known. It would probably, as far as St John was concerned, be a parting for years: it might be a parting for life.

'He will sacrifice all to his long-framed resolves,' she said: 'natural affection and feelings more potent still. St John looks quiet, Jane; but he hides a fever in his vitals. You would think him gentle, yet in some things he is inexorable as death; and the worst of it is, my conscience will hardly permit me to dissuade him from his severe decision: certainly, I cannot for a moment blame him for it. It is right, noble, Christian: yet it breaks my heart!' And the tears gushed to her fine eyes. Mary bent her head low over her work.

'We are now without father: we shall soon be without home and brother,' she murmured.

At that moment a little accident supervened, which seemed decreed by fate purposely to prove the truth of the adage, that 'misfortunes never come singly,' and to add to their distresses the vexing one of the slip between the cup and the lip. St John passed the window reading a letter. He entered.

'Our uncle John is dead,' said he.

Both the sisters seemed struck: not shocked or appalled; the tidings appeared in their eyes rather momentous than afflicting.

'Dead?' repeated Diana.

'Yes.'

She riveted a searching gaze on her brother's face. 'And what then?' she demanded, in a low voice.

'What then, Die?' he replied, maintaining a marble immobility of feature. 'What then? Why – nothing. Read.'

He threw the letter into her lap. She glanced over it, and handed it to Mary. Mary perused it in silence, and returned it to her brother. All three looked at each other, and all three smiled – a dreary, pensive smile enough.

'Amen! We can yet live,' said Diana at last.

'At any rate, it makes us no worse off than we were before,' remarked Mary.

'Only it forces rather strongly on the mind the picture of what *might have been*,' said Mr Rivers, 'and contrasts it somewhat too vividly with what *is*.'

He folded the letter, locked it in his desk, and again went out.

For some minutes no one spoke. Diana then turned to me.

'Jane, you will wonder at us and our mysteries,' she said, 'and think us hard-hearted beings not to be more moved at the death of so near a relation as an uncle; but we have never seen him or known him. He was my mother's brother. My father and he quarrelled long ago. It was by his advice that my father risked most of his property in the speculation that ruined him. Mutual recrimination passed between them: they parted in anger, and were never reconciled. My uncle engaged afterwards in more prosperous undertakings: it appears he realised a fortune of twenty thousand pounds. He was never married, and had no near kindred but ourselves and one other person, not more closely related than we.

My father always cherished the idea that he would atone for his error by leaving his possessions to us; that letter informs us that he has bequeathed every penny to the other relation, with the exception of thirty guineas, to be divided between St John, Diana, and Mary Rivers, for the purchase of three mourning rings. He had a right, of course, to do as he pleased: and yet a momentary damp is cast on the spirits by the receipt of such news. Mary and I would have esteemed ourselves rich with a thousand pounds each; and to St John such a sum would have been valuable, for the good it would have enabled him to do.'

This explanation given, the subject was dropped, and no further reference made to it by either Mr Rivers or his sisters. The next day I left Marsh End for Morton. The day after, Diana and Mary quitted it for distant B——. In a week, Mr Rivers and Hannah repaired to the parsonage: and so the old grange was abandoned.

## *Chapter 31*

My home, then, when I at last find a home, is a cottage; a little room with whitewashed walls and a sanded floor, containing four painted chairs and a table, a clock, a cupboard, with two or three plates and dishes, and a set of tea-things in delf. Above, a chamber of the same dimensions as the kitchen, with a deal bedstead and chest of drawers; small, yet too large to be filled with my scanty wardrobe: though the kindness of my gentle and generous friends has increased that, by a modest stock of such things as are necessary.

It is evening. I have dismissed, with the fee of an orange, the little orphan who serves me as a hand-maid. I am sitting alone on the hearth. This morning, the village school opened. I had twenty scholars. But three of the number can read: none write or cipher. Several knit, and a few sew a little. They speak with the broadest accent of the district. At present, they and I have a difficulty in understanding each other's language. Some of them are unmannered, rough, intractable, as well as ignorant; but others are docile, have a wish to learn, and evince a disposition that pleases me. I must not forget that these coarsely-clad little peasants are of flesh and blood as good as the scions of gentlest genealogy; and that the germs of native excellence, refinement, intelligence, kind feeling, are as likely to exist in their hearts as in those of the best-born. My duty will be to develop these germs: surely I shall find some happiness in discharging that office. Much enjoyment I do not expect in the life opening before me: yet it will, doubtless, if I regulate my mind, and exert my powers as I ought, yield me enough to live on from day to day.

Was I very gleeful, settled, content, during the hours I passed in yonder bare, humble schoolroom this morning and afternoon? Not to deceive myself, I must reply – No: I felt desolate to a degree. I felt – yes, idiot that I am – I felt degraded. I doubted I had taken a step which sank instead of raising me in the scale of social existence. I was weakly dismayed at the ignorance, the poverty,

the coarseness of all I heard and saw round me. But let me not hate and despise myself too much for these feelings; I know them to be wrong – that is a great step gained; I shall strive to overcome them. Tomorrow, I trust, I shall get the better of them partially; and in a few weeks, perhaps, they will be quite subdued. In a few months, it is possible, the happiness of seeing progress, and a change for the better in my scholars may substitute gratification for disgust.

Meantime, let me ask myself one question – Which is better? – To have surrendered to temptation; listened to passion; made no painful effort – no struggle; but to have sunk down in the silken snare; fallen asleep on the flowers covering it; wakened in a southern clime, amongst the luxuries of a pleasure villa: to have been now living in France, Mr Rochester's mistress; delirious with his love half my time – for he would – oh, yes, he would have loved me well for a while. He *did* love me – no one will ever love me so again. I shall never more know the sweet homage given to beauty, youth, and grace – for never to anyone else shall I seem to possess these charms. He was fond and proud of me – it is what no man besides will ever be. But where am I wandering, and what am I saying, and above all, feeling? Whether is it better, I ask, to be a slave in a fool's paradise at Marseilles – fevered with delusive bliss one hour – suffocating with the bitterest tears of remorse and shame the next – or to be a village-schoolmistress, free and honest, in a breezy mountain nook in the healthy heart of England?

Yes; I feel now that I was right when I adhered to principle and law, and scorned and crushed the insane promptings of a frenzied moment. God directed me to a correct choice: I thank His providence for the guidance!

Having brought my eventide musings to this point, I rose, went to my door, and looked at the sunset of the harvest-day, and at the quiet fields before my cottage, which, with the school, was distant half a mile from the village. The birds were singing their last strains –

The air was mild, the dew was balm.

While I looked, I thought myself happy, and was surprised to find myself ere long weeping – and why? For the doom which had reft me from adhesion to my master: for him I was no more to see; for the desperate grief and fatal fury – consequences of my departure – which might now, perhaps, be dragging him from the path of right, too far to leave hope of ultimate restoration thither. At this thought, I turned my face aside from the lovely sky of eve and lonely vale of Morton – I say *lonely*, for in that bend of it visible to me there was no building apparent save the church and the parsonage, half-hid in trees, and, quite at the extremity, the roof of Vale Hall, where the rich Mr Oliver and his daughter lived. I hid my eyes, and leant my head against the stone frame of my door; but soon a slight noise near the wicket which shut in my tiny garden from the meadow beyond it made me look up. A dog – old Carlo, Mr Rivers' pointer, as I saw in a moment – was pushing the gate with his nose, and St John himself leant upon it with folded arms; his brow knit, his gaze, grave almost to displeasure, fixed on me. I asked him to come in.

'No, I cannot stay; I have only brought you a little parcel my sisters left for you. I think it contains a colour-box, pencils, and paper.'

I approached to take it: a welcome gift it was. He examined my face, I thought, with austerity, as I came near: the traces of tears were doubtless very visible upon it.

'Have you found your first day's work harder than you expected?' he asked.

'Oh, no! On the contrary, I think in time I shall get on with my scholars very well.'

'But perhaps your accommodations – your cottage – your furniture – have disappointed your expectations? They are, in truth, scanty enough; but – ' I interrupted – 'My cottage is clean and weather-proof; my furniture sufficient and commodious. All I see has made me thankful, not despondent. I am not absolutely such a fool and sensualist as to regret the absence of a carpet, a sofa, and silver plate; besides, five weeks ago I had nothing – I was an outcast, a beggar, a vagrant; now I have acquaintance, a home, a business. I wonder at the goodness of God; the generosity of my friends; the bounty of my lot. I do not repine.'

'But you feel solitude an oppression? The little house there behind you is dark and empty.'

'I have hardly had time yet to enjoy a sense of tranquillity, much less to grow impatient under one of loneliness.'

'Very well; I hope you feel the content you express: at any rate, your good sense will tell you that it is too soon yet to yield to the vacillating fears of Lot's wife. What you had left before I saw you, of course I do not know; but I counsel you to resist firmly every temptation which would incline you to look back: pursue your present career steadily, for some months at least.'

'It is what I mean to do,' I answered. St John continued – 'It is hard work to control the workings of inclination and turn the bent of nature; but that it may be done, I know from experience. God has given us, in a measure, the power to make our own fate; and when our energies seem to demand a sustenance they cannot get – when our will strains after a path we may not follow – we need neither starve from inanition, nor stand still in despair: we have but to seek another nourishment for the mind, as strong as the forbidden food it longed to taste – and perhaps purer; and to hew out for the adventurous foot a road as direct and broad as the one Fortune has blocked up against us, if rougher than it.

'A year ago I was myself intensely miserable, because I thought I had made a mistake in entering the ministry: its uniform duties wearied me to death. I burnt for the more active life of the world – for the more exciting toils of a literary career – for the destiny of an artist, author, orator; anything rather than that of a priest: yes, the heart of a politician, of a soldier, of a votary of glory, a lover of renown, a luster after power, beat under my curate's surplice. I considered; my life was so wretched, it must be changed, or I must die. After a season of darkness and struggling, light broke and relief fell: my cramped existence all at once spread out to a plain without bounds – my powers heard a call from heaven to rise, gather their full strength, spread their wings, and mount beyond ken. God had an errand for me; to bear which afar, to deliver it well, skill and

strength, courage and eloquence, the best qualifications of soldier, statesman, and orator, were all needed: for these all centre in the good missionary.

'A missionary I resolved to be. From that moment my state of mind changed; the fetters dissolved and dropped from every faculty, leaving nothing of bondage but its galling soreness – which time only can heal. My father, indeed, opposed the determination, but since his death, I have not a legitimate obstacle to contend with; some affairs settled, a successor for Morton provided, an entanglement or two of the feelings broken through or cut asunder – a last conflict with human weakness, in which I know I shall overcome, because I have vowed that I *will* overcome – and I leave Europe for the East.'

He said this, in his peculiar, subdued, yet emphatic voice; looking, when he had ceased speaking, not at me, but at the setting sun, at which I looked too. Both he and I had our backs towards the path leading up the field to the wicket. We had heard no step on that grass-grown track; the water running in the vale was the one lulling sound of the hour and scene; we might well then start when a gay voice, sweet as a silver bell, exclaimed – 'Good-evening, Mr Rivers. And good-evening, old Carlo. Your dog is quicker to recognise his friends than you are, sir; he pricked his ears and wagged his tail when I was at the bottom of the field, and you have your back towards me now.'

It was true. Though Mr Rivers had started at the first of those musical accents, as if a thunderbolt had split a cloud over his head, he stood yet, at the close of the sentence, in the same attitude in which the speaker had surprised him – his arm resting on the gate, his face directed towards the west. He turned at last, with measured deliberation. A vision, as it seemed to me, had risen at his side. There appeared, within three feet of him, a form clad in pure white – a youthful, graceful form: full, yet fine in contour; and when, after bending to caress Carlo, it lifted up its head, and threw back a long veil, there bloomed under his glance a face of perfect beauty. Perfect beauty is a strong expression; but I do not retrace or qualify it: as sweet features as ever the temperate clime of Albion moulded; as pure hues of rose and lily as ever her humid gales and vapoury skies generated and screened, justified, in this instance, the term. No charm was wanting, no defect was perceptible; the young girl had regular and delicate lineaments; eyes shaped and coloured as we see them in lovely pictures, large, and dark, and full; the long and shadowy eyelash which encircles a fine eye with so soft a fascination; the pencilled brow which gives such clearness; the white smooth forehead, which adds such repose to the livelier beauties of tint and ray; the cheek oval, fresh, and smooth; the lips, fresh too, ruddy, healthy, sweetly formed; the even and gleaming teeth without flaw; the small dimpled chin; the ornament of rich, plenteous tresses – all advantages, in short, which, combined, realise the ideal of beauty, were fully hers. I wondered, as I looked at this fair creature: I admired her with my whole heart. Nature had surely formed her in a partial mood; and, forgetting her usual stinted stepmother dole of gifts, had endowed this, her darling, with a grand-dame's bounty.

What did St John Rivers think of this earthly angel? I naturally asked myself that question as I saw him turn to her and look at her; and, as naturally, I sought

the answer to the enquiry in his countenance. He had already withdrawn his eye from the Peri, and was looking at a humble tuft of daisies which grew by the wicket.

'A lovely evening, but late for you to be out alone,' he said, as he crushed the snowy heads of the closed flowers with his foot.

'Oh, I only came home from S——' (she mentioned the name of a large town some twenty miles distant) 'this afternoon. Papa told me you had opened your school, and that the new mistress was come; and so I put on my bonnet after tea, and ran up the valley to see her: this is she?' pointing to me.

'It is,' said St John.

'Do you think you shall like Morton?' she asked of me, with a direct and naïve simplicity of tone and manner, pleasing, if childlike.

'I hope I shall. I have many inducements to do so.'

'Did you find your scholars as attentive as you expected?'

'Quite.'

'Do you like your house?'

'Very much.'

'Have I furnished it nicely?'

'Very nicely, indeed.'

'And made a good choice of an attendant for you in Alice Wood?'

'You have indeed. She is teachable and handy.' (This then, I thought, is Miss Oliver, the heiress; favoured, it seems, in the gifts of fortune, as well as in those of nature! What happy combination of the planets presided over her birth, I wonder?)

'I shall come up and help you to teach sometimes,' she added. 'It will be a change for me to visit you now and then; and I like a change. Mr Rivers, I have been *so* gay during my stay at S——. Last night, or rather this morning, I was dancing till two o'clock. The ——th regiment are stationed there since the riots; and the officers are the most agreeable men in the world: they put all our young knife-grinders and scissor merchants to shame.'

It seemed to me that Mr St John's under lip protruded, and his upper lip curled a moment. His mouth certainly looked a good deal compressed, and the lower part of his face unusually stern and square, as the laughing girl gave him this information. He lifted his gaze, too, from the daisies, and turned it on her. An unsmiling, a searching, a meaning gaze it was. She answered it with a second laugh, and laughter well became her youth, her roses, her dimples, her bright eyes.

As he stood, mute and grave, she again fell to caressing Carlo. 'Poor Carlo loves me,' said she. '*He* is not stern and distant to his friends; and if he could speak, he would not be silent.'

As she patted the dog's head, bending with native grace before his young and austere master, I saw a glow rise to that master's face. I saw his solemn eye melt with sudden fire, and flicker with resistless emotion. Flushed and kindled thus, he looked nearly as beautiful for a man as she for a woman. His chest heaved once, as if his large heart, weary of despotic constriction, had expanded, despite

the will, and made a vigorous bound for the attainment of liberty. But he curbed it, I think, as a resolute rider would curb a rearing steed. He responded neither by word nor movement to the gentle advances made him.

'Papa says you never come to see us now,' continued Miss Oliver, looking up. 'You are quite a stranger at Vale Hall. He is alone this evening, and not very well: will you return with me and visit him?'

'It is not a seasonable hour to intrude on Mr Oliver,' answered St John.

'Not a seasonable hour! But I declare it is. It is just the hour when papa most wants company: when the works are closed and he has no business to occupy him. Now, Mr Rivers, *do* come. Why are you so very shy, and so very sombre?' She filled up the hiatus his silence left by a reply of her own.

'I forgot!' she exclaimed, shaking her beautiful curled head, as if shocked at herself. 'I am so giddy and thoughtless! *Do* excuse me. It had slipped my memory that you have good reasons to be indisposed for joining in my chatter. Diana and Mary have left you, and Moor House is shut up, and you are so lonely. I am sure I pity you. Do come and see papa.'

'Not tonight, Miss Rosamond, not tonight.'

Mr St John spoke almost like an automaton: himself only knew the effort it cost him thus to refuse.

'Well, if you are so obstinate, I will leave you; for I dare not stay any longer: the dew begins to fall. Good-evening!'

She held out her hand. He just touched it. 'Good-evening!' he repeated, in a voice low and hollow as an echo. She turned, but in a moment returned.

'Are you well?' she asked. Well might she put the question: his face was blanched as her gown.

'Quite well,' he enunciated; and, with a bow, he left the gate. She went one way; he another. She turned twice to gaze after him as she tripped fairy-like down the field; he, as he strode firmly across, never turned at all.

This spectacle of another's suffering and sacrifice rapt my thoughts from exclusive meditation on my own. Diana Rivers had designated her brother 'inexorable as death.' She had not exaggerated.

## *Chapter 32*

I continued the labours of the village-school as actively and faithfully as I could. It was truly hard work at first. Some time elapsed before, with all my efforts, I could comprehend my scholars and their nature. Wholly untaught, with faculties quite torpid, they seemed to me hopelessly dull; and, at first sight, all dull alike: but I soon found I was mistaken. There was a difference amongst them as amongst the educated; and when I got to know them, and they me, this difference rapidly developed itself. Their amazement at me, my language, my rules, and ways, once subsided, I found some of these heavy-looking, gaping rustics wake up into sharp-witted girls enough. Many showed themselves obliging, and

amiable too; and I discovered amongst them not a few examples of natural politeness, and innate self-respect, as well as of excellent capacity, that won both my goodwill and my admiration. These soon took a pleasure in doing their work well, in keeping their persons neat, in learning their tasks regularly, in acquiring quiet and orderly manners. The rapidity of their progress, in some instances, was even surprising; and an honest and happy pride I took in it: besides, I began personally to like some of the best girls; and they liked me. I had amongst my scholars several farmers' daughters: young women grown, almost. These could already read, write, and sew; and to them I taught the elements of grammar, geography, history, and the finer kinds of needlework. I found estimable characters amongst them – characters desirous of information and disposed for improvement – with whom I passed many a pleasant evening hour in their own homes. Their parents then (the farmer and his wife) loaded me with attentions. There was an enjoyment in accepting their simple kindness, and in repaying it by a consideration – a scrupulous regard to their feelings – to which they were not, perhaps, at all times accustomed, and which both charmed and benefited them; because, while it elevated them in their own eyes, it made them emulous to merit the deferential treatment they received.

I felt I became a favourite in the neighbourhood. Whenever I went out, I heard on all sides cordial salutations, and was welcomed with friendly smiles. To live amidst general regard, though it be but the regard of working people, is like 'sitting in sunshine, calm and sweet'; serene inward feelings bud and bloom under the ray. At this period of my life, my heart far oftener swelled with thankfulness than sank with dejection: and yet, reader, to tell you all, in the midst of this calm, this useful existence – after a day passed in honourable exertion amongst my scholars, an evening spent in drawing or reading contentedly alone – I used to rush into strange dreams at night: dreams many-coloured, agitated, full of the ideal, the stirring, the stormy – dreams where, amidst unusual scenes, charged with adventure, with agitating risk and romantic chance, I still again and again met Mr Rochester, always at some exciting crisis; and then the sense of being in his arms, hearing his voice, meeting his eye, touching his hand and cheek, loving him, being loved by him – the hope of passing a lifetime at his side, would be renewed, with all its first force and fire. Then I awoke. Then I recalled where I was, and how situated. Then I rose up on my curtainless bed, trembling and quivering; and then the still, dark night witnessed the convulsion of despair, and heard the burst of passion. By nine o'clock the next morning I was punctually opening the school; tranquil, settled, prepared for the steady duties of the day.

Rosamond Oliver kept her word in coming to visit me. Her call at the school was generally made in the course of her morning ride. She would canter up to the door on her pony, followed by a mounted livery servant. Anything more exquisite than her appearance, in her purple habit, with her Amazon's cap of black velvet placed gracefully above the long curls that kissed her cheek and floated to her shoulders, can scarcely be imagined: and it was thus she would enter the rustic building, and glide through the dazzled ranks of the village children. She generally came at the hour when Mr Rivers was engaged in giving

his daily catechising lesson. Keenly, I fear, did the eye of the visitress pierce the young pastor's heart. A sort of instinct seemed to warn him of her entrance, even when he did not see it; and when he was looking quite away from the door, if she appeared at it, his cheek would glow, and his marble-seeming features, though they refused to relax, changed indescribably, and in their very quiescence became expressive of a repressed fervour, stronger than working muscle or darting glance could indicate.

Of course, she knew her power: indeed, he did not, because he could not, conceal it from her. In spite of his Christian stoicism, when she went up and addressed him, and smiled gaily, encouragingly, even fondly in his face, his hand would tremble and his eye burn. He seemed to say, with his sad and resolute look, if he did not say it with his lips, 'I love you, and I know you prefer me. It is not despair of success that keeps me dumb. If I offered my heart, I believe you would accept it. But that heart is already laid on a sacred altar: the fire is arranged round it. It will soon be no more than a sacrifice consumed.'

And then she would pout like a disappointed child; a pensive cloud would soften her radiant vivacity; she would withdraw her hand hastily from his, and turn in transient petulance from his aspect, at once so heroic and so martyr-like. St John, no doubt, would have given the world to follow, recall, retain her, when she thus left him; but he would not give one chance of heaven, nor relinquish, for the elysium of her love, one hope of the true, eternal Paradise. Besides, he could not bind all that he had in his nature – the rover, the aspirant, the poet, the priest – in the limits of a single passion. He could not – he would not – renounce his wild field of mission warfare for the parlours and the peace of Vale Hall. I learnt so much from himself in an inroad I once, despite his reserve, had the daring to make on his confidence.

Miss Oliver already honoured me with frequent visits to my cottage. I had learnt her whole character, which was without mystery or disguise: she was coquettish, but not heartless; exacting, but not worthlessly selfish. She had been indulged from her birth, but was not absolutely spoilt. She was hasty, but good-humoured; vain (she could not help it, when every glance in the glass showed her such a flush of loveliness), but not affected; liberal-handed; innocent of the pride of wealth; ingenuous; sufficiently intelligent; gay, lively, and unthinking: she was very charming, in short, even to a cool observer of her own sex like me; but she was not profoundly interesting or thoroughly impressive. A very different sort of mind was hers from that, for instance, of the sisters of St John. Still, I liked her almost as I liked my pupil Adèle; except that, for a child whom we have watched over and taught, a closer affection is engendered than we can give an equally attractive adult acquaintance.

She had taken an amiable caprice to me. She said I was like Mr Rivers, only, certainly, she allowed, 'not one-tenth so handsome, though I was a nice neat little soul enough, but he was an angel'. I was, however, good, clever, composed, and firm, like him. I was a *lusus naturæ*, she affirmed, as a village schoolmistress: she was sure my previous history, if known, would make a delightful romance.

One evening, while, with her usual childlike activity, and thoughtless yet not

offensive inquisitiveness, she was rummaging the cupboard and the table-drawer of my little kitchen, she discovered first two French books, a volume of Schiller, a German grammar and dictionary, and then my drawing-materials and some sketches, including a pencil-head of a pretty little cherub-like girl, one of my scholars, and sundry views from nature, taken in the Vale of Morton and on the surrounding moors. She was first transfixed with surprise, and then electrified with delight.

'Had I done these pictures? Did I know French and German? What a love – what a miracle I was! I drew better than her master in the first school in S—. Would I sketch a portrait of her, to show to papa?'

'With pleasure,' I replied; and I felt a thrill of artist-delight at the idea of copying from so perfect and radiant a model. She had then on a dark-blue silk dress; her arms and her neck were bare; her only ornament was her chestnut tresses, which waved over her shoulders with all the wild grace of natural curls. I took a sheet of fine cardboard, and drew a careful outline. I promised myself the pleasure of colouring it; and, as it was getting late then, I told her she must come and sit another day.

She made such a report of me to her father, that Mr Oliver himself accompanied her next evening – a tall, massive-featured, middle-aged, and grey-headed man, at whose side his lovely daughter looked like a bright flower near a hoary turret. He appeared a taciturn, and perhaps a proud personage; but he was very kind to me. The sketch of Rosamond's portrait pleased him highly: he said I must make a finished picture of it. He insisted, too, on my coming the next day to spend the evening at Vale Hall.

I went. I found it a large, handsome residence, showing abundant evidences of wealth in the proprietor. Rosamond was full of glee and pleasure all the time I stayed. Her father was affable; and when he entered into conversation with me after tea, he expressed in strong terms his approbation of what I had done in Morton school, and said he only feared, from what he saw and heard, I was too good for the place, and would soon quit it for one more suitable.

'Indeed,' cried Rosamond, 'she is clever enough to be a governess in a high family, papa.'

I thought I would far rather be where I am than in any high family in the land. Mr Oliver spoke of Mr Rivers – of the Rivers family – with great respect. He said it was a very old name in that neighbourhood; that the ancestors of the house were wealthy; that all Morton had once belonged to them; that even now he considered the representative of that house might, if he liked, make an alliance with the best. He accounted it a pity that so fine and talented a young man should have formed the design of going out as a missionary; it was quite throwing a valuable life away. It appeared, then, that her father would throw no obstacle in the way of Rosamond's union with St John. Mr Oliver evidently regarded the young clergyman's good birth, old name, and sacred profession as sufficient compensation for the want of fortune.

It was the 5th of November, and a holiday. My little servant, after helping me to clean my house, was gone, well satisfied with the fee of a penny for her aid. All

about me was spotless and bright – scoured floor, polished grate, and well-rubbed chairs. I had also made myself neat, and had now the afternoon before me to spend as I would.

The translation of a few pages of German occupied an hour; then I got my palette and pencils, and fell to the more soothing, because easier occupation, of completing Rosamond Oliver's miniature. The head was finished already: there was but the background to tint and the drapery to shade off; a touch of carmine, too, to add to the ripe lips – a soft curl here and there to the tresses – a deeper tinge to the shadow of the lash under the azured eyelid. I was absorbed in the execution of these nice details, when, after one rapid tap, my door unclosed, admitting St John Rivers.

'I am come to see how you are spending your holiday,' he said. 'Not, I hope, in thought? No, that is well: while you draw you will not feel lonely. You see, I mistrust you still, though you have borne up wonderfully so far. I have brought you a book for evening solace,' and he laid on the table a new publication – a poem: one of those genuine productions so often vouchsafed to the fortunate public of those days – the golden age of modern literature. Alas! the readers of our era are less favoured. But courage! I will not pause either to accuse or repine. I know poetry is not dead, nor genius lost; nor has Mammon gained power over either, to bind or slay: they will both assert their existence, their presence, their liberty and strength again one day. Powerful angels, safe in heaven! they smile when sordid souls triumph, and feeble ones weep over their destruction. Poetry destroyed? Genius banished? No! Mediocrity, no: do not let envy prompt you to the thought. No; they not only live, but reign and redeem: and without their divine influence spread everywhere, you would be in hell – the hell of your own meanness.

While I was eagerly glancing at the bright pages of *Marmion* (for *Marmion* it was), St John stooped to examine my drawing. His tall figure sprang erect again with a start: he said nothing. I looked up at him: he shunned my eye. I knew his thoughts well, and could read his heart plainly; at the moment I felt calmer and cooler than he: I had then temporarily the advantage of him, and I conceived an inclination to do him some good, if I could.

'With all his firmness and self-control,' thought I, 'he tasks himself too far: locks every feeling and pang within – expresses, confesses, imparts nothing. I am sure it would benefit him to talk a little about this sweet Rosamond, whom he thinks he ought not to marry: I will make him talk.'

I said first, 'Take a chair, Mr Rivers.' But he answered, as he always did, that he could not stay. 'Very well,' I responded, mentally, 'stand if you like; but you shall not go just yet, I am determined: solitude is at least as bad for you as it is for me. I'll try if I cannot discover the secret spring of your confidence, and find an aperture in that marble breast through which I can shed one drop of the balm of sympathy.'

'Is this portrait like?' I asked bluntly.

'Like! Like whom? I did not observe it closely.'

'You did, Mr Rivers.'

He almost started at my sudden and strange abruptness: he looked at me astonished. 'Oh, that is nothing yet,' I muttered within. 'I don't mean to be baffled by a little stiffness on your part; I'm prepared to go to considerable lengths.' I continued, 'You observed it closely and distinctly; but I have no objection to your looking at it again,' and I rose and placed it in his hand.

'A well-executed picture,' he said; 'very soft, clear colouring; very graceful and correct drawing.'

'Yes, yes; I know all that. But what of the resemblance? Who is it like?'

Mastering some hesitation, he answered, 'Miss Oliver, I presume.'

'Of course. And now, sir, to reward you for the accurate guess, I will promise to paint you a careful and faithful duplicate of this very picture, provided you admit that the gift would be acceptable to you. I don't wish to throw away my time and trouble on an offering you would deem worthless.'

He continued to gaze at the picture: the longer he looked, the firmer he held it, the more he seemed to covet it. 'It is like!' he murmured; 'the eye is well managed: the colour, light, expression, are perfect. It smiles!'

'Would it comfort, or would it wound you to have a similar painting? Tell me that. When you are at Madagascar, or at the Cape, or in India, would it be a consolation to have that memento in your possession? or would the sight of it bring recollections calculated to enervate and distress?'

He now furtively raised his eyes: he glanced at me, irresolute, disturbed: he again surveyed the picture.

'That I should like to have it is certain: whether it would be judicious or wise is another question.'

Since I had ascertained that Rosamond really preferred him, and that her father was not likely to oppose the match, I – less exalted in my views than St John – had been strongly disposed in my own heart to advocate their union. It seemed to me that, should he become the possessor of Mr Oliver's large fortune, he might do as much good with it as if he went and laid his genius out to wither, and his strength to waste, under a tropical sun. With this persuasion I now answered – 'As far as I can see, it would be wiser and more judicious if you were to take to yourself the original at once.'

By this time he had sat down: he had laid the picture on the table before him, and with his brow supported on both hands, hung fondly over it. I discerned he was now neither angry nor shocked at my audacity. I saw even that to be thus frankly addressed on a subject he had deemed unapproachable – to hear it thus freely handled – was beginning to be felt by him as a new pleasure – an unhoped-for relief. Reserved people often really need the frank discussion of their sentiments and griefs more than the expansive. The sternest-seeming stoic is human after all; and to 'burst' with boldness and goodwill into 'the silent sea' of their souls is often to confer on them the first of obligations.

'She likes you, I am sure,' said I, as I stood behind his chair, 'and her father respects you. Moreover, she is a sweet girl – rather thoughtless; but you would have sufficient thought for both yourself and her. You ought to marry her.'

'*Does* she like me?' he asked.

'Certainly; better than she likes anyone else. She talks of you continually: there is no subject she enjoys so much or touches upon so often.'

'It is very pleasant to hear this,' he said – 'very: go on for another quarter of an hour.' And he actually took out his watch and laid it upon the table to measure the time.

'But where is the use of going on,' I asked, 'when you are probably preparing some iron blow of contradiction, or forging a fresh chain to fetter your heart?'

'Don't imagine such hard things. Fancy me yielding and melting, as I am doing: human love rising like a freshly opened fountain in my mind and overflowing with sweet inundation all the field I have so carefully and with such labour prepared – so assiduously sown with the seeds of good intentions, of self-denying plans. And now it is deluged with a nectarous flood – the young germs swamped – delicious poison cankering them: now I see myself stretched on an ottoman in the drawing-room at Vale Hall at my bride Rosamond Oliver's feet: she is talking to me with her sweet voice – gazing down on me with those eyes your skilful hand has copied so well – smiling at me with these coral lips. She is mine – I am hers – this present life and passing world suffice to me. Hush! say nothing – my heart is full of delight – my senses are entranced – let the time I marked pass in peace.'

I humoured him: the watch ticked on: he breathed fast and low: I stood silent. Amidst this hush the quarter sped; he replaced the watch, laid the picture down, rose, and stood on the hearth.

'Now,' said he, 'that little space was given to delirium and delusion. I rested my temples on the breast of temptation, and put my neck voluntarily under her yoke of flowers; I tasted her cup. The pillow was burning: there is an asp in the garland: the wine has a bitter taste: her promises are hollow – her offers false: I see and know all this.'

I gazed at him in wonder.

'It is strange,' pursued he, 'that while I love Rosamond Oliver so wildly – with all the intensity, indeed, of a first passion, the object of which is exquisitely beautiful, graceful, and fascinating – I experience at the same time a calm, unwarped consciousness that she would not make me a good wife; that she is not the partner suited to me; that I should discover this within a year after marriage; and that to twelve months' rapture would succeed a lifetime of regret. This I know.'

'Strange indeed!' I could not help ejaculating.

'While something in me,' he went on, 'is acutely sensible to her charms, something else is as deeply impressed with her defects: they are such that she could sympathise in nothing I aspired to – co-operate in nothing I undertook. Rosamond a sufferer, a labourer, a female apostle? Rosamond a missionary's wife? No!'

'But you need not be a missionary. You might relinquish that scheme.'

'Relinquish! What! my vocation? My great work? My foundation laid on earth for a mansion in heaven? My hopes of being numbered in the band who have merged all ambitions in the glorious one of bettering their race – of carrying

knowledge into the realms of ignorance – of substituting peace for war – freedom for bondage – religion for superstition – the hope of heaven for the fear of hell? Must I relinquish that? It is dearer than the blood in my veins. It is what I have to look forward to, and to live for.'

After a considerable pause, I said – 'And Miss Oliver? Are her disappointment and sorrow of no interest to you?'

'Miss Oliver is ever surrounded by suitors and flatterers: in less than a month, my image will be effaced from her heart. She will forget me; and will marry, probably, someone who will make her far happier than I should do.'

'You speak coolly enough; but you suffer in the conflict. You are wasting away.'

'No. If I get a little thin, it is with anxiety about my prospects, yet unsettled – my departure, continually procrastinated. Only this morning, I received intelligence that the successor, whose arrival I have been so long expecting, cannot be ready to replace me for three months to come yet; and perhaps the three months may extend to six.'

'You tremble and become flushed whenever Miss Oliver enters the schoolroom.'

Again the surprised expression crossed his face. He had not imagined that a woman would dare to speak so to a man. For me, I felt at home in this sort of discourse. I could never rest in communication with strong, discreet, and refined minds, whether male or female, till I had passed the outworks of conventional reserve, and crossed the threshold of confidence, and won a place by their heart's very hearthstone.

'You *are* original,' said he, 'and not timid. There is something brave in your spirit, as well as penetrating in your eye; but allow me to assure you that you partially misinterpret my emotions. You think them more profound and potent than they are. You give me a larger allowance of sympathy than I have a just claim to. When I colour, and when I shake before Miss Oliver, I do not pity myself. I scorn the weakness. I know it is ignoble: a mere fever of the flesh: not, I declare, the convulsion of the soul. *That* is just as fixed as a rock, firm set in the depths of a restless sea. Know me to be what I am – a cold, hard man.'

I smiled incredulously.

'You have taken my confidence by storm,' he continued, 'and now it is much at your service. I am simply, in my original state – stripped of that blood-bleached robe with which Christianity covers human deformity – a cold, hard, ambitious man. Natural affection only, of all the sentiments, has permanent power over me. Reason, and not feeling, is my guide; my ambition is unlimited: my desire to rise higher, to do more than others, insatiable. I honour endurance, perseverance, industry, talent; because these are the means by which men achieve great ends and mount to lofty eminence. I watch your career with interest, because I consider you a specimen of a diligent, orderly, energetic woman: not because I deeply compassionate what you have gone through, or what you still suffer.'

'You would describe yourself as a mere pagan philosopher,' I said.

'No. There is this difference between me and deistic philosophers: I believe;

and I believe the Gospel. You missed your epithet. I am not a pagan, but a Christian philosopher – a follower of the sect of Jesus. As His disciple I adopt His pure, His merciful, His benignant doctrines. I advocate them: I am sworn to spread them. Won in youth to religion, she has cultivated my original qualities thus: From the minute germ, natural affection, she has developed the over-shadowing tree, philanthropy. From the wild stringy root of human uprightness, she has reared a due sense of the Divine justice. Of the ambition to win power and renown for my wretched self, she has formed the ambition to spread my Master's kingdom; to achieve victories for the standard of the cross. So much has religion done for me; turning the original materials to the best account; pruning and training nature. But she could not eradicate nature: nor will it be eradicated "till this mortal shall put on immortality".'

Having said this, he took his hat, which lay on the table beside my palette. Once more he looked at the portrait.

'She *is* lovely,' he murmured. 'She is well named the Rose of the World, indeed!'

'And may I not paint one like it for you?'

'*Cui bono?* No.'

He drew over the picture the sheet of thin paper on which I was accustomed to rest my hand in painting, to prevent the cardboard from being sullied. What he suddenly saw on this blank paper, it was impossible for me to tell; but something had caught his eye. He took it up with a snatch; he looked at the edge; then shot a glance at me, inexpressibly peculiar, and quite incomprehensible: a glance that seemed to take and make note of every point in my shape, face, and dress; for it traversed all, quick, keen as lightning. His lips parted, as if to speak: but he checked the coming sentence, whatever it was.

'What is the matter?' I asked.

'Nothing in the world,' was the reply; and, replacing the paper, I saw him dexterously tear a narrow slip from the margin. It disappeared in his glove; and, with one hasty nod and 'good-afternoon', he vanished.

'Well!' I exclaimed, using an expression of the district, 'that caps the globe, however!'

I, in my turn, scrutinised the paper; but saw nothing on it save a few dingy stains of paint where I had tried the tint in my pencil. I pondered the mystery a minute or two; but finding it insolvable, and being certain it could not be of much moment, I dismissed, and soon forgot it.

## Chapter 33

When Mr St John went, it was beginning to snow; the whirling storm continued all night. The next day a keen wind brought fresh and blinding falls; by twilight the valley was drifted up and almost impassable. I had closed my shutter, laid a mat to the door to prevent the snow from blowing in under it, trimmed my fire,

and after sitting nearly an hour on the hearth listening to the muffled fury of the tempest, I lit a candle, took down *Marmion*, and beginning –

> Day set on Norham's castled steep,
> And Tweed's fair river broad and deep
> And Cheviot's mountains lone;
> The massive towers, the donjon keep
> The flanking walls that round them sweep,
> In yellow lustre shone –

I soon forgot storm in music.

I heard a noise: the wind, I thought, shook the door. No; it was St John Rivers, who, lifting the latch, came in out of the frozen hurricane – the howling darkness – and stood before me: the cloak that covered his tall figure all white as a glacier. I was almost in consternation, so little had I expected any guest from the blocked-up vale that night.

'Any ill news?' I demanded. 'Has anything happened?'

'No. How very easily alarmed you are?' he answered, removing his cloak and hanging it up against the door, towards which he again coolly pushed the mat which his entrance had deranged. He stamped the snow from his boots.

'I shall sully the purity of your floor,' said he, 'but you must excuse me for once.' Then he approached the fire. 'I have had hard work to get here, I assure you,' he observed, as he warmed his hands over the flame. 'One drift took me up to the waist; happily the snow is quite soft yet.'

'But why are you come?' I could not forbear saying.

'Rather an inhospitable question to put to a visitor; but since you ask it, I answer simply to have a little talk with you; I got tired of my mute books and empty rooms. Besides, since yesterday I have experienced the excitement of a person to whom a tale has been half-told, and who is impatient to hear the sequel.'

He sat down. I recalled his singular conduct of yesterday, and really I began to fear his wits were touched. If he were insane, however, his was a very cool and collected insanity: I had never seen that handsome-featured face of his look more like chiselled marble than it did just now, as he put aside his snow-wet hair from his forehead and let the firelight shine free on his pale brow and cheek as pale, where it grieved me to discover the hollow trace of care or sorrow now so plainly graved. I waited, expecting he would say something I could at least comprehend; but his hand was now at his chin, his finger on his lip: he was thinking. It struck me that his hand looked wasted like his face. A perhaps uncalled-for gush of pity came over my heart: I was moved to say – 'I wish Diana or Mary would come and live with you: it is too bad that you should be quite alone; and you are recklessly rash about your own health.'

'Not at all,' said he: 'I care for myself when necessary. I am well now. What do you see amiss in me?'

This was said with a careless, abstracted indifference which showed that my solicitude was, at least in his opinion, wholly superfluous. I was silenced.

He still slowly moved his finger over his upper lip, and still his eye dwelt dreamily on the glowing grate; thinking it urgent to say something, I asked him presently if he felt any cold draught from the door, which was behind him.

'No, no!' he responded shortly and somewhat testily.

'Well,' I reflected, 'if you won't talk, you may be still; I'll let you alone now, and return to my book.'

So I snuffed the candle and resumed the perusal of *Marmion*. He soon stirred; my eye was instantly drawn to his movements; he only took out a morocco pocketbook, thence produced a letter, which he read in silence, folded it, put it back, relapsed into meditation. It was vain to try to read with such an inscrutable fixture before me; nor could I, in my impatience, consent to be dumb; he might rebuff me if he liked, but talk I would.

'Have you heard from Diana and Mary lately?'

'Not since the letter I showed you a week ago.'

'There has not been any change made about your own arrangements? You will not be summoned to leave England sooner than you expected?'

'I fear not, indeed: such chance is too good to befall me.' Baffled so far, I changed my ground. I bethought myself to talk about the school and my scholars.

'Mary Garrett's mother is better, and Mary came back to the school this morning, and I shall have four new girls next week from the Foundry Close – they would have come today but for the snow.'

'Indeed!'

'Mr Oliver pays for two.'

'Does he?'

'He means to give the whole school a treat at Christmas.'

'I know.'

'Was it your suggestion?'

'No.'

'Whose, then?'

'His daughter's, I think.'

'It is like her: she is so good-natured.'

'Yes.'

Again came the blank of a pause: the clock struck eight strokes. It aroused him; he uncrossed his legs, sat erect, turned to me.

'Leave your book a moment, and come a little nearer the fire,' he said.

Wondering, and of my wonder finding no end, I complied.

'Half an hour ago,' he pursued, 'I spoke of my impatience to hear the sequel of a tale: on reflection, I find the matter will be better managed by my assuming the narrator's part, and converting you into a listener. Before commencing, it is but fair to warn you that the story will sound somewhat hackneyed in your ears; but stale details often regain a degree of freshness when they pass through new lips. For the rest, whether trite or novel, it is short.

'Twenty years ago, a poor curate – never mind his name at this moment – fell in love with a rich man's daughter; she fell in love with him, and married him,

against the advice of all her friends, who consequently disowned her immediately after the wedding. Before two years passed, the rash pair were both dead, and laid quietly side by side under one slab. (I have seen their grave; it formed part of the pavement of a huge churchyard surrounding the grim, soot-black old cathedral of an overgrown manufacturing town in —shire.) They left a daughter, which, at its very birth, Charity received in her lap – cold as that of the snow-drift I almost stuck fast in tonight. Charity carried the friendless thing to the house of its rich maternal relations; it was reared by an aunt-in-law, called (I come to names now) Mrs Reed of Gateshead. You start – did you hear a noise? I dare say it is only a rat scrambling along the rafters of the adjoining schoolroom: it was a barn before I had it repaired and altered, and barns are generally haunted by rats. To proceed. Mrs Reed kept the orphan ten years: whether it was happy or not with her, I cannot say, never having been told; but at the end of that time she transferred it to a place you know – being no other than Lowood School, where you so long resided yourself. It seems her career there was very honourable: from a pupil, she became a teacher, like yourself – really it strikes me there are parallel points in her history and yours – she left it to be a governess: there, again, your fates were analogous; she undertook the education of the ward of a certain Mr Rochester.'

'Mr Rivers!' I interrupted.

'I can guess your feelings,' he said, 'but restrain them for a while: I have nearly finished; hear me to the end. Of Mr Rochester's character I know nothing, but the one fact that he professed to offer honourable marriage to this young girl, and that at the very altar she discovered he had a wife yet alive, though a lunatic. What his subsequent conduct and proposals were is a matter of pure conjecture; but when an event transpired which rendered enquiry after the governess necessary, it was discovered she was gone – no one could tell when, where, or how. She had left Thornfield Hall in the night; every research after her course had been vain: the country had been scoured far and wide; no vestige of information could be gathered respecting her. Yet that she should be found is become a matter of serious urgency: advertisements have been put in all the papers; I myself have received a letter from one Mr Briggs, a solicitor, communicating the details I have just imparted. Is it not an odd tale?'

'Just tell me this,' said I, 'and since you know so much, you surely *can* tell it me – what of Mr Rochester? How and where is he? What is he doing? Is he well?'

'I am ignorant of all concerning Mr Rochester: the letter never mentions him but to narrate the fraudulent and illegal attempt I have adverted to. You should rather ask the name of the governess – the nature of the event which requires her appearance.'

'Did no one go to Thornfield Hall, then? Did no one see Mr Rochester?'

'I suppose not.'

'But they wrote to him?'

'Of course.'

'And what did he say? Who has his letters?'

'Mr Briggs intimates that the answer to his application was not from Mr Rochester, but from a lady: it is signed "Alice Fairfax".'

I felt cold and dismayed: my worst fears then were probably true: he had in all probability left England and rushed in reckless desperation to some former haunt on the Continent. And what opiate for his severe sufferings – what object for his strong passions – had he sought there? I dared not answer the question. Oh, my poor master – once almost my husband – whom I had often called 'my dear Edward!'

'He must have been a bad man,' observed Mr Rivers.

'You don't know him – don't pronounce an opinion upon him,' I said, with warmth.

'Very well,' he answered quietly: 'and indeed my head is otherwise occupied than with him: I have my tale to finish. Since you won't ask the governess's name, I must tell it of my own accord. Stay! I have it here – it is always more satisfactory to see important points written down, fairly committed to black and white.'

And the pocket-book was again deliberately produced, opened, sought through; from one of its compartments was extracted a shabby slip of paper, hastily torn off: I recognised in its texture and its stains of ultramarine, and lake, and vermilion, the ravished margin of the portrait-cover. He got up, held it close to my eyes: and I read, traced in Indian ink, in my own handwriting, the words 'Jane Eyre' – the work doubtless of some moment of abstraction.

'Briggs wrote to me of a Jane Eyre:' he said, 'the advertisements demanded a Jane Eyre: I knew a Jane Elliott. I confess I had my suspicions, but it was only yesterday afternoon they were at once resolved into certainty. You own the name and renounce the *alias*?'

'Yes – yes; but where is Mr Briggs? He perhaps knows more of Mr Rochester than you do.'

'Briggs is in London. I should doubt his knowing anything at all about Mr Rochester; it is not in Mr Rochester he is interested. Meantime, you forget essential points in pursuing trifles: you do not enquire why Mr Briggs sought after you – what he wanted with you.'

'Well, what did he want?'

'Merely to tell you that your uncle, Mr Eyre of Madeira, is dead; that he has left you all his property, and that you are now rich – merely that – nothing more.'

'I! – rich?'

'Yes, you, rich – quite an heiress.'

Silence succeeded.

'You must prove your identity of course,' resumed St John presently: 'a step which will offer no difficulties; you can then enter on immediate possession. Your fortune is vested in the English funds; Briggs has the will and the necessary documents.'

Here was a new card turned up! It is a fine thing, reader, to be lifted in a moment from indigence to wealth – a very fine thing; but not a matter one can comprehend or consequently enjoy, all at once. And then there are other chances in life far more thrilling and rapture-giving: *this* is solid, an affair of the actual world, nothing ideal about it: all its associations are solid and sober, and its manifestations are the same. One does not jump, and spring, and shout

hurrah! at hearing one has got a fortune; one begins to consider responsibilities, and to ponder business; on a base of steady satisfaction rise certain grave cares, and we contain ourselves, and brood over our bliss with a solemn brow.

Besides, the words Legacy, Bequest, go side by side with the words, Death, Funeral. My uncle I had heard was dead – my only relative; ever since being made aware of his existence, I had cherished the hope of one day seeing him: now, I never should. And then this money came only to me: not to me and a rejoicing family, but to my isolated self. It was a grand boon doubtless; and independence would be glorious – yes, I felt that – *that* thought swelled my heart.

'You unbend your forehead at last,' said Mr Rivers. 'I thought Medusa had looked at you, and that you were turning to stone. Perhaps now you will ask how much you are worth?'

'How much am I worth?'

'Oh, a trifle! Nothing of course to speak of – twenty thousand pounds, I think they say – but what is that?'

'Twenty thousand pounds?'

Here was a new stunner – I had been calculating on four or five thousand. This news actually took my breath for a moment: Mr St John, whom I had never heard laugh before, laughed now.

'Well,' said he, 'if you had committed a murder, and I had told you your crime was discovered, you could scarcely look more aghast.'

'It is a large sum – don't you think there is a mistake?'

'No mistake at all.'

'Perhaps you have read the figures wrong – it may be two thousand!'

'It is written in letters, not figures, twenty thousand.'

I again felt rather like an individual of but average gastronomical powers sitting down to feast alone at a table spread with provisions for a hundred. Mr Rivers rose now and put his cloak on.

'If it were not such a very wild night,' he said, 'I would send Hannah down to keep you company: you look too desperately miserable to be left alone. But Hannah, poor woman! could not stride the drifts so well as I: her legs are not quite so long: so I must e'en leave you to your sorrows. Good-night.'

He was lifting the latch: a sudden thought occurred to me.

'Stop one minute!' I cried.

'Well?'

'It puzzles me to know why Mr Briggs wrote to you about me; or how he knew you, or could fancy that you, living in such an out-of-the-way place, had the power to aid in my discovery.'

'Oh! I am a clergyman,' he said; 'and the clergy are often appealed to about odd matters.' Again the latch rattled.

'No; that does not satisfy me!' I exclaimed: and indeed there was something in the hasty and unexplanatory reply which, instead of allaying, piqued my curiosity more than ever.

'It is a very strange piece of business,' I added; 'I must know more about it.'

'Another time.'

'No; tonight! – tonight!' and as he turned from the door, I placed myself between it and him. He looked rather embarrassed.

'You certainly shall not go till you have told me all,' I said.

'I would rather not just now.'

'You shall! – you must!'

'I would rather Diana or Mary informed you.'

Of course these objections wrought my eagerness to a climax: gratified it must be, and that without delay; and I told him so.

'But I apprised you that I was a hard man,' said he, 'difficult to persuade.'

'And I am a hard woman, impossible to put off.'

'And then,' he pursued, 'I am cold: no fervour infects me.'

'Whereas I am hot, and fire dissolves ice. The blaze there has thawed all the snow from your cloak; by the same token, it has streamed on to my floor, and made it like a trampled street. As you hope ever to be forgiven, Mr Rivers, the high crime and misdemeanour of spoiling a sanded kitchen, tell me what I wish to know.'

'Well, then,' he said, 'I yield; if not to your earnestness, to your perseverance: as stone is worn by continual dropping. Besides, you must know someday, as well now as later. Your name is Jane Eyre?'

'Of course: that was all settled before.'

'You are not, perhaps, aware that I am your namesake? – that I was christened St John Eyre Rivers?'

'No, indeed! I remember now seeing the letter E. comprised in your initials written in books you have at different times lent me; but I never asked for what name it stood. But what then? Surely –'

I stopped: I could not trust myself to entertain, much less to express, the thought that rushed upon me – that embodied itself, that, in a second, stood out a strong, solid probability. Circumstances knit themselves, fitted themselves, shot into order: the chain that had been lying hitherto a formless lump of links was drawn out straight, every ring was perfect, the connection complete. I knew, by instinct, how the matter stood, before St John had said another word; but I cannot expect the reader to have the same intuitive perception, so I must repeat his explanation.

'My mother's name was Eyre; she had two brothers; one a clergyman, who married Miss Jane Reed, of Gateshead; the other, John Eyre, Esq., merchant, late of Funchal, Madeira. Mr Briggs, being Mr Eyre's solicitor, wrote to us last August to inform us of our uncle's death, and to say that he had left his property to his brother the clergyman's orphan daughter, overlooking us, in consequence of a quarrel, never forgiven, between him and my father. He wrote again a few weeks since, to intimate that the heiress was lost, and asking if we knew anything of her. A name casually written on a slip of paper has enabled me to find her out. You know the rest.' Again he was going, but I set my back against the door.

'Do let me speak,' I said; 'let me have one moment to draw breath and reflect.' I paused – he stood before me, hat in hand, looking composed enough. I resumed – 'Your mother was my father's sister?'

'Yes.'

'My aunt, consequently?'

He bowed.

'My uncle John was your uncle John? You, Diana, and Mary are his sister's children, as I am his brother's child?'

'Undeniably.'

'You three, then, are my cousins; half our blood on each side flows from the same source?'

'We are cousins; yes.'

I surveyed him. It seemed I had found a brother: one I could be proud of, one I could love; and two sisters, whose qualities were such, that, when I knew them but as mere strangers, they had inspired me with genuine affection and admiration. The two girls, on whom, kneeling down on the wet ground, and looking through the low, latticed window of Moor House kitchen, I had gazed with so bitter a mixture of interest and despair, were my near kinswomen; and the young and stately gentleman who had found me almost dying at his threshold was my blood relation. Glorious discovery to a lonely wretch! This was wealth indeed! – wealth to the heart! – a mine of pure, genial affections. This was a blessing, bright, vivid, and exhilarating; not like the ponderous gift of gold: rich and welcome enough in its way, but sobering from its weight. I now clapped my hands in sudden joy – my pulse bounded, my veins thrilled.

'Oh, I am glad! – I am glad!' I exclaimed.

St John smiled. 'Did I not say you neglected essential points to pursue trifles?' he asked. 'You were serious when I told you you had got a fortune; and now, for a matter of no moment, you are excited.'

'What *can* you mean? It may be of no moment to you; you have sisters and don't care for a cousin; but I had nobody; and now three relations, or two, if you don't choose to be counted, are born into my world full-grown. I say again, I am glad!'

I walked fast through the room: I stopped, half suffocated with the thoughts that rose faster than I could receive, comprehend, settle them: thoughts of what might, could, would, and should be, and that ere long. I looked at the blank wall: it seemed a sky thick with ascending stars, every one lit me to a purpose or delight. Those who had saved my life, whom, till this hour, I had loved barrenly, I could now benefit. They were under a yoke, I could free them: they were scattered, I could reunite them: the independence the affluence which was mine, might be theirs too. Were we not four? Twenty thousand pounds shared equally, would be five thousand each, enough and to spare: justice would be done, mutual happiness secured. Now the wealth did not weigh on me: now it was not a mere bequest of coin, it was a legacy of life, hope, enjoyment.

How I looked while these ideas were taking my spirit by storm, I cannot tell; but I perceived soon that Mr Rivers had placed a chair behind me, and was gently attempting to make me sit down on it. He also advised me to be composed; I scorned the insinuation of helplessness and distraction, shook off his hand, and began to walk about again.

'Write to Diana and Mary tomorrow,' I said, 'and tell them to come home directly. Diana said they would both consider themselves rich with a thousand pounds, so with five thousand they will do very well.'

'Tell me where I can get you a glass of water,' said St John; 'you must really make an effort to tranquillise your feelings.'

'Nonsense! and what sort of an effect will the bequest have on you? Will it keep you in England, induce you to marry Miss Oliver, and settle down like an ordinary mortal?'

'You wander: your head becomes confused. I have been too abrupt in communicating the news; it has excited you beyond your strength.'

'Mr Rivers! you quite put me out of patience: I am rational enough; it is you who misunderstand, or rather who affect to misunderstand.'

'Perhaps, if you explained yourself a little more fully, I should comprehend better.'

'Explain! What is there to explain? You cannot fail to see that twenty thousand pounds, the sum in question, divided equally between the nephew and three nieces of our uncle, will give five thousand to each? What I want is, that you should write to your sisters and tell them of the fortune that has accrued to them.'

'To you, you mean.'

'I have intimated my view of the case: I am incapable of taking any other. I am not brutally selfish, blindly unjust, or fiendishly ungrateful. Besides, I am resolved I will have a home and connections. I like Moor House, and I will live at Moor House; I like Diana and Mary, and I will attach myself for life to Diana and Mary. It would please and benefit me to have five thousand pounds; it would torment and oppress me to have twenty thousand; which, moreover, could never be mine in justice, though it might in law. I abandon to you, then, what is absolutely superfluous to me. Let there be no opposition, and no discussion about it; let us agree amongst each other, and decide the point at once.'

'This is acting on first impulses; you must take days to consider such a matter, ere your word can be regarded as valid.'

'Oh! if all you doubt is my sincerity, I am easy: you see the justice of the case?'

'I *do* see a certain justice; but it is contrary to all custom. Besides, the entire fortune is your right: my uncle gained it by his own efforts; he was free to leave it to whom he would: he left it to you. After all, justice permits you to keep it: you may, with a clear conscience, consider it absolutely your own.'

'With me,' said I, 'it is fully as much a matter of feeling as of conscience: I must indulge my feelings; I so seldom have had an opportunity of doing so. Were you to argue, object, and annoy me for a year, I could not forego the delicious pleasure of which I have caught a glimpse – that of repaying, in part, a mighty obligation, and winning to myself lifelong friends.'

'You think so now,' rejoined St John, 'because you do not know what it is to possess, nor consequently to enjoy wealth: you cannot form a notion of the importance twenty thousand pounds would give you; of the place it would enable you to take in society; of the prospects it would open to you: you cannot – '

'And you,' I interrupted, 'cannot at all imagine the craving I have for fraternal and sisterly love. I never had a home, I never had brothers or sisters; I must and will have them now: you are not reluctant to admit me and own me, are you?'

'Jane, I will be your brother – my sisters will be your sisters – without stipulating for this sacrifice of your just rights.'

'Brother? Yes; at the distance of a thousand leagues! Sisters? Yes; slaving amongst strangers! I, wealthy – gorged with gold I never earned and do not merit! You, penniless! Famous equality and fraternisation! Close union! Intimate attachment!'

'But, Jane, your aspirations after family ties and domestic happiness may be realised otherwise than by the means you contemplate: you may marry.'

'Nonsense, again! Marry! I don't want to marry, and never shall marry.'

'That is saying too much: such hazardous affirmations are a proof of the excitement under which you labour.'

'It is not saying too much: I know what I feel, and how averse are my inclinations to the bare thought of marriage. No one would take me for love; and I will not be regarded in the light of a mere money speculation. And I do not want a stranger – unsympathising, alien, different from me; I want my kindred: those with whom I have full fellow-feeling. Say again you will be my brother: when you uttered the words I was satisfied, happy; repeat them, if you can, repeat them sincerely.'

'I think I can. I know I have always loved my own sisters; and I know on what my affection for them is grounded, respect for their worth and admiration of their talents. You too have principle and mind: your tastes and habits resemble Diana's and Mary's; your presence is always agreeable to me; in your conversation I have already for some time found a salutary solace. I feel I can easily and naturally make room in my heart for you, as my third and youngest sister.'

'Thank you: that contents me for tonight. Now you had better go; for if you stay longer, you will perhaps irritate me afresh by some mistrustful scruple.'

'And the school, Miss Eyre? It must now be shut up, I suppose?'

'No. I will retain my post of mistress till you get a substitute.'

He smiled approbation: we shook hands, and he took leave.

I need not narrate in detail the further struggles I had, and arguments I used, to get matters regarding the legacy settled as I wished. My task was a very hard one; but, as I was absolutely resolved – as my cousins saw at length that my mind was really and immutably fixed on making a just division of the property – as they must in their own hearts have felt the equity of the intention; and must, besides, have been innately conscious that in my place they would have done precisely what I wished to do – they yielded at length so far as to consent to put the affair to arbitration. The judges chosen were Mr Oliver and an able lawyer: both coincided in my opinion: I carried my point. The instruments of transfer were drawn out: St John, Diana, Mary, and I, each became possessed of a competency.

## Chapter 34

It was near Christmas by the time all was settled: the season of general holiday approached. I now closed Morton school, taking care that the parting should not be barren on my side. Good fortune opens the hand as well as the heart wonderfully; and to give somewhat when we have largely received, is but to afford a vent to the unusual ebullition of the sensations. I had long felt with pleasure that many of my rustic scholars liked me, and when we parted, that consciousness was confirmed: they manifested their affection plainly and strongly. Deep was my gratification to find I had really a place in their unsophisticated hearts: I promised them that never a week should pass in future that I did not visit them, and give them an hour's teaching in their school.

Mr Rivers came up as, having seen the classes, now numbering sixty girls, file out before me, and locked the door, I stood with the key in my hand, exchanging a few words of special farewell with some half-dozen of my best scholars: as decent, respectable, modest, and well-informed young women as could be found in the ranks of the British peasantry. And that is saying a great deal; for after all, the British peasantry are the best taught, best mannered, most self-respecting of any in Europe: since those days I have seen paysannes and Bäuerinnen; and the best of them seemed to me ignorant, coarse, and besotted, compared with my Morton girls.

'Do you consider you have got your reward for a season of exertion?' asked Mr Rivers, when they were gone. 'Does not the consciousness of having done some real good in your day and generation give pleasure?'

'Doubtless.'

'And you have only toiled a few months! Would not a life devoted to the task of regenerating your race be well spent?'

'Yes,' I said; 'but I could not go on for ever so: I want to enjoy my own faculties as well as to cultivate those of other people. I must enjoy them now; don't recall either my mind or body to the school; I am out of it and disposed for full holiday.'

He looked grave. 'What now? What sudden eagerness is this you evince? What are you going to do?'

'To be active: as active as I can. And first I must beg you to set Hannah at liberty, and get somebody else to wait on you.'

'Do you want her?'

'Yes, to go with me to Moor House. Diana and Mary will be at home in a week, and I want to have everything in order against their arrival.'

'I understand. I thought you were for flying off on some excursion. It is better so: Hannah shall go with you.'

'Tell her to be ready by tomorrow then; and here is the schoolroom key: I will give you the key of my cottage in the morning.'

He took it. 'You give it up very gleefully,' said he; 'I don't quite understand your light-heartedness, because I cannot tell what employment you propose to yourself as a substitute for the one you are relinquishing. What aim, what purpose, what ambition in life have you now?'

'My first aim will be to *clean down* (do you comprehend the full force of the expression?) – to *clean down* Moor House from chamber to cellar; my next to rub it up with bees-wax, oil, and an indefinite number of cloths, till it glitters again; my third, to arrange every chair, table, bed, carpet, with mathematical precision; afterwards I shall go near to ruin you in coals and peat to keep up good fires in every room; and lastly, the two days preceding that on which your sisters are expected will be devoted by Hannah and me to such a beating of eggs, sorting of currants, grating of spices, compounding of Christmas cakes, chopping up of materials for mince-pies, and solemnising of other culinary rites, as words can convey but an inadequate notion of to the uninitiated like you. My purpose, in short, is to have all things in an absolutely perfect state of readiness for Diana and Mary before next Thursday; and my ambition is to give them a beau-ideal of a welcome when they come.'

St John smiled slightly: still he was dissatisfied.

'It is all very well for the present,' said he; 'but seriously, I trust that when the first flush of vivacity is over, you will look a little higher than domestic endearments and household joys.'

'The best things the world has!' I interrupted.

'No, Jane, no: this world is not the scene of fruition; do not attempt to make it so: nor of rest; do not turn slothful.'

'I mean, on the contrary, to be busy.'

'Jane, I excuse you for the present: two months' grace I allow you for the full enjoyment of your new position, and for pleasing yourself with this late-found charm of relationship; but *then*, I hope you will begin to look beyond Moor House and Morton, and sisterly society, and the selfish calm and sensual comfort of civilised affluence. I hope your energies will then once more trouble you with their strength.'

I looked at him with surprise. 'St John,' I said, 'I think you are almost wicked to talk so. I am disposed to be as content as a queen, and you try to stir me up to restlessness! To what end?'

'To the end of turning to profit the talents which God has committed to your keeping; and of which He will surely one day demand a strict account. Jane, I shall watch you closely and anxiously – I warn you of that. And try to restrain the disproportionate fervour with which you throw yourself into commonplace home pleasures. Don't cling so tenaciously to ties of the flesh; save your constancy and ardour for an adequate cause; forbear to waste them on trite transient objects. Do you hear, Jane?'

'Yes; just as if you were speaking Greek. I feel I have adequate cause to be happy, and I *will* be happy. Goodbye!'

Happy at Moor House I was, and hard I worked; and so did Hannah: she was charmed to see how jovial I could be amidst the bustle of a house turned

topsy-turvy – how I could brush, and dust, and clean, and cook. And really, after a day or two of confusion worse confounded, it was delightful by degrees to invoke order from the chaos ourselves had made. I had previously taken a journey to S— to purchase some new furniture: my cousins having given me *carte blanche* to effect what alterations I pleased, and a sum having been set aside for that purpose. The ordinary sitting-room and bedrooms I left much as they were: for I knew Diana and Mary would derive more pleasure from seeing again the old homely tables, and chairs, and beds, than from the spectacle of the smartest innovations. Still some novelty was necessary, to give to their return the piquancy with which I wished it to be invested. Dark handsome new carpets and curtains, an arrangement of some carefully selected antique ornaments in porcelain and bronze, new coverings, and mirrors, and dressing-cases, for the toilet tables, answered the end: they looked fresh without being glaring. A spare parlour and bedroom I refurnished entirely, with old mahogany and crimson upholstery: I laid canvas on the passage, and carpets on the stairs. When all was finished, I thought Moor House as complete a model of bright modest snugness within, as it was, at this season, a specimen of wintry waste and desert dreariness without.

The eventful Thursday at length came. They were expected about dark, and ere dusk fires were lit upstairs and below; the kitchen was in perfect trim; Hannah and I were dressed, and all was in readiness.

St John arrived first. I had entreated him to keep quite clear of the house till everything was arranged: and, indeed, the bare idea of the commotion, at once sordid and trivial, going on within its walls sufficed to scare him to estrangement. He found me in the kitchen, watching the progress of certain cakes for tea, then baking. Approaching the hearth, he asked, 'If I was at last satisfied with housemaid's work?' I answered by inviting him to accompany me on a general inspection of the result of my labours. With some difficulty, I got him to make the tour of the house. He just looked in at the doors I opened; and when he had wandered upstairs and downstairs, he said I must have gone through a great deal of fatigue and trouble to have effected such considerable changes in so short a time: but not a syllable did he utter indicating pleasure in the improved aspect of his abode.

This silence damped me. I thought perhaps the alterations had disturbed some old associations he valued. I enquired whether this was the case: no doubt in a somewhat crestfallen tone.

'Not at all; he had, on the contrary, remarked that I had scrupulously respected every association: he feared, indeed, I must have bestowed more thought on the matter than it was worth. How many minutes, for instance, had I devoted to studying the arrangement of this very room? – By the bye, could I tell him where such a book was?'

I showed him the volume on the shelf: he took it down, and withdrawing to his accustomed window recess, he began to read it.

Now, I did not like this, reader. St John was a good man; but I began to feel he had spoken truth of himself when he said he was hard and cold. The humanities and amenities of life had no attraction for him – its peaceful enjoyments no charm. Literally, he lived only to aspire – after what was good and great, certainly;

but still he would never rest, nor approve of others resting round him. As I looked at his lofty forehead, still and pale as a white stone – at his fine lineaments fixed in study – I comprehended all at once that he would hardly make a good husband: that it would be a trying thing to be his wife. I understood, as by inspiration, the nature of his love for Miss Oliver; I agreed with him that it was but a love of the senses. I comprehended how he should despise himself for the feverish influence it exercised over him; how he should wish to stifle and destroy it; how he should mistrust its ever conducing permanently to his happiness or hers. I saw he was of the material from which nature hews her heroes – Christian and Pagan – her lawgivers, her statesmen, her conquerors: a steadfast bulwark for great interests to rest upon; but, at the fireside, too often a cold cumbrous column, gloomy and out of place.

'This parlour is not his sphere,' I reflected: 'the Himalayan ridge or Caffre bush, even the plague-cursed Guinea Coast swamp would suit him better. Well may he eschew the calm of domestic life; it is not his element: there his faculties stagnate – they cannot develop or appear to advantage. It is in scenes of strife and danger – where courage is proved, and energy exercised, and fortitude tasked – that he will speak and move, the leader and superior. A merry child would have the advantage of him on this hearth. He is right to choose a missionary's career – I see it now.'

'They are coming! they are coming!' cried Hannah, throwing open the parlour door. At the same moment old Carlo barked joyfully. Out I ran. It was now dark; but a rumbling of wheels was audible. Hannah soon had a lantern lit. The vehicle had stopped at the wicket; the driver opened the door: first one well-known form, then another, stepped out. In a minute I had my face under their bonnets, in contact first with Mary's soft cheek, then with Diana's flowing curls. They laughed – kissed me – then Hannah: patted Carlo, who was half wild with delight; asked eagerly if all was well; and being assured in the affirmative, hastened into the house.

They were stiff with their long and jolting drive from Whitcross, and chilled with the frosty night air; but their pleasant countenances expanded to the cheerful firelight. While the driver and Hannah brought in the boxes, they demanded St John. At this moment he advanced from the parlour. They both threw their arms round his neck at once. He gave each one quiet kiss, said in a low tone a few words of welcome, stood a while to be talked to, and then, intimating that he supposed they would soon rejoin him in the parlour, withdrew there as to a place of refuge.

I had lit their candles to go upstairs, but Diana had first to give hospitable orders respecting the driver; this done, both followed me. They were delighted with the renovation and decorations of their rooms; with the new drapery, and fresh carpets, and rich tinted china vases: they expressed their gratification ungrudgingly. I had the pleasure of feeling that my arrangements met their wishes exactly, and that what I had done added a vivid charm to their joyous return home.

Sweet was that evening. My cousins, full of exhilaration, were so eloquent in

narrative and comment, that their fluency covered St John's taciturnity: he was sincerely glad to see his sisters; but in their glow of fervour and flow of joy he could not sympathise. The event of the day – that is, the return of Diana and Mary – pleased him; but the accompaniments of that event, the glad tumult, the garrulous glee of reception irked him: I saw he wished the calmer morrow was come. In the very meridian of the night's enjoyment, about an hour after tea, a rap was heard at the door. Hannah entered with the intimation that 'a poor lad was come, at that unlikely time, to fetch Mr Rivers to see his mother, who was drawing away.'

'Where does she live, Hannah?'

'Clear up at Whitcross Brow, almost four miles off, and moor and moss all the way.'

'Tell him I will go.'

'I'm sure, sir, you had better not. It's the worst road to travel after dark that can be: there's no track at all over the bog. And then it is such a bitter night – the keenest wind you ever felt. You had better send word, sir, that you will be there in the morning.'

But he was already in the passage, putting on his cloak; and without one objection, one murmur, he departed. It was then nine o'clock: he did not return till midnight. Starved and tired enough he was: but he looked happier than when he set out. He had performed an act of duty; made an exertion; felt his own strength to do and deny, and was on better terms with himself.

I am afraid the whole of the ensuing week tried his patience. It was Christmas week: we took to no settled employment, but spent it in a sort of merry domestic dissipation. The air of the moors, the freedom of home, the dawn of prosperity, acted on Diana and Mary's spirits like some life-giving elixir: they were gay from morning till noon, and from noon till night. They could always talk; and their discourse, witty, pithy, original, had such charms for me, that I preferred listening to, and sharing in it, to doing anything else. St John did not rebuke our vivacity; but he escaped from it: he was seldom in the house; his parish was large, the population scattered, and he found daily business in visiting the sick and poor in its different districts.

One morning at breakfast, Diana, after looking a little pensive for some minutes, asked him, 'If his plans were yet unchanged.'

'Unchanged and unchangeable,' was the reply. And he proceeded to inform us that his departure from England was now definitely fixed for the ensuing year.

'And Rosamond Oliver?' suggested Mary, the words seeming to escape her lips involuntarily: for no sooner had she uttered them, than she made a gesture as if wishing to recall them. St John had a book in his hand – it was his unsocial custom to read at meals – he closed it, and looked up.

'Rosamond Oliver,' said he, 'is about to be married to Mr Granby, one of the best connected and most estimable residents in S—, grandson and heir to Sir Frederic Granby: I had the intelligence from her father yesterday.'

His sisters looked at each other and at me; we all three looked at him: he was serene as glass.

'The match must have been got up hastily,' said Diana: 'they cannot have known each other long.'

'But two months: they met in October at the county ball at S—. But where there are no obstacles to a union, as in the present case, where the connection is in every point desirable, delays are unnecessary: they will be married as soon as S— Place, which Sir Frederic gives up to them, can be refitted for their reception.'

The first time I found St John alone after this communication, I felt tempted to enquire if the event distressed him: but he seemed so little to need sympathy, that, so far from venturing to offer him more, I experienced some shame at the recollection of what I had already hazarded. Besides, I was out of practice in talking to him: his reserve was again frozen over, and my frankness was congealed beneath it. He had not kept his promise of treating me like his sisters; he continually made little, chilling differences between us, which did not at all tend to the development of cordiality: in short, now that I was acknowledged his kinswoman, and lived under the same roof with him, I felt the distance between us to be far greater than when he had known me only as the village schoolmistress. When I remembered how far I had once been admitted to his confidence, I could hardly comprehend his present frigidity.

Such being the case, I felt not a little surprised when he raised his head suddenly from the desk over which he was stooping, and said – 'You see, Jane, the battle is fought and the victory won.'

Startled at being thus addressed, I did not immediately reply: after a moment's hesitation I answered – 'But are you sure you are not in the position of those conquerors whose triumphs have cost them too dear? Would not such another ruin you?'

'I think not; and if I were, it does not much signify; I shall never be called upon to contend for such another. The event of the conflict is decisive: my way is now clear; I thank God for it!' So saying, he returned to his papers and his silence.

As our mutual happiness (i.e., Diana's, Mary's, and mine) settled into a quieter character, and we resumed our usual habits and regular studies, St John stayed more at home: he sat with us in the same room, sometimes for hours together. While Mary drew, Diana pursued a course of encyclopædic reading she had (to my awe and amazement) undertaken, and I fagged away at German, he pondered a mystic lore of his own: that of some Eastern tongue, the acquisition of which he thought necessary to his plans.

Thus engaged, he appeared, sitting in his own recess, quiet and absorbed enough; but that blue eye of his had a habit of leaving the outlandish-looking grammar, and wandering over, and sometimes fixing upon us, his fellow-students, with a curious intensity of observation: if caught, it would be instantly withdrawn; yet ever and anon, it returned searchingly to our table. I wondered what it meant: I wondered, too, at the punctual satisfaction he never failed to exhibit on an occasion that seemed to me of small moment, namely, my weekly visit to Morton school; and still more was I puzzled when, if the day was unfavourable, if there

was snow, or rain, or high wind, and his sisters urged me not to go, he would invariably make light of their solicitude, and encourage me to accomplish the task without regard to the elements.

'Jane is not such a weakling as you would make her,' he would say: 'she can bear a mountain blast, or a shower, or a few flakes of snow, as well as any of us. Her constitution is both sound and elastic; better calculated to endure variations of climate than many more robust.'

And when I returned, sometimes a good deal tired, and not a little weather-beaten, I never dared complain, because I saw that to murmur would be to vex him: on all occasions fortitude pleased him; the reverse was a special annoyance.

One afternoon, however, I got leave to stay at home, because I really had a cold. His sisters were gone to Morton in my stead: I sat reading Schiller; he, deciphering his crabbed Oriental scrolls. As I exchanged a translation for an exercise, I happened to look his way: there I found myself under the influence of the ever-watchful blue eye. How long it had been searching me through and through, and over and over, I cannot tell: so keen was it, and yet so cold, I felt for the moment superstitious – as if I were sitting in the room with something uncanny.

'Jane, what are you doing?'

'Learning German.'

'I want you to give up German and learn Hindustani.'

'You are not in earnest?'

'In such earnest that I must have it so: and I will tell you why.'

He then went on to explain that Hindustani was the language he was himself at present studying; that, as he advanced, he was apt to forget the commencement; that it would assist him greatly to have a pupil with whom he might again and again go over the elements, and so fix them thoroughly in his mind; that his choice had hovered for some time between me and his sisters; but that he had fixed on me because he saw I could sit at a task the longest of the three. Would I do him this favour? I should not, perhaps, have to make the sacrifice long, as it wanted now barely three months to his departure.

St John was not a man to be lightly refused: you felt that every impression made on him, either for pain or pleasure, was deep-graved and permanent. I consented. When Diana and Mary returned, the former found her scholar transferred from her to her brother: she laughed, and both she and Mary agreed that St John should never have persuaded them to such a step. He answered quietly – 'I know it.'

I found him a very patient, very forbearing, and yet an exacting master: he expected me to do a great deal; and when I fulfilled his expectations, he, in his own way, fully testified his approbation. By degrees, he acquired a certain influence over me that took away my liberty of mind: his praise and notice were more restraining than his indifference. I could no longer talk or laugh freely when he was by, because a tiresomely importunate instinct reminded me that vivacity (at least in me) was distasteful to him. I was so fully aware that only

serious moods and occupations were acceptable, that in his presence every effort to sustain or follow any other became vain: I fell under a freezing spell. When he said 'go,' I went; 'come,' I came; 'do this,' I did it. But I did not love my servitude: I wished, many a time, he had continued to neglect me.

One evening when, at bedtime, his sisters and I stood round him, bidding him good-night, he kissed each of them, as was his custom; and, as was equally his custom, he gave me his hand. Diana, who chanced to be in a frolicsome humour (*she* was not painfully controlled by his will; for hers, in another way, was as strong), exclaimed – 'St John! you used to call Jane your third sister, but you don't treat her as such: you should kiss her too.'

She pushed me towards him. I thought Diana very provoking, and felt uncomfortably confused; and while I was thus thinking and feeling, St John bent his head; his Greek face was brought to a level with mine, his eyes questioned my eyes piercingly – he kissed me. There are no such things as marble kisses or ice kisses, or I should say my ecclesiastical cousin's salute belonged to one of these classes; but there may be experiment kisses, and his was an experiment kiss. When given, he viewed me to learn the result; it was not striking: I am sure I did not blush; perhaps I might have turned a little pale, for I felt as if this kiss were a seal affixed to my fetters. He never omitted the ceremony afterwards, and the gravity and quiescence with which I underwent it, seemed to invest it for him with a certain charm.

As for me, I daily wished more to please him; but to do so, I felt daily more and more that I must disown half my nature, stifle half my faculties, wrest my tastes from their original bent, force myself to the adoption of pursuits for which I had no natural vocation. He wanted to train me to an elevation I could never reach; it racked me hourly to aspire to the standard he uplifted. The thing was as impossible as to mould my irregular features to his correct and classic pattern, to give to my changeable green eyes the sea-blue tint and solemn lustre of his own.

Not his ascendancy alone, however, held me in thrall at present. Of late it had been easy enough for me to look sad: a cankering evil sat at my heart and drained my happiness at its source – the evil of suspense.

Perhaps you think I had forgotten Mr Rochester, reader, amidst these changes of place and fortune. Not for a moment. His idea was still with me, because it was not a vapour sunshine could disperse, nor a sand-traced effigy storms could wash away; it was a name graven on a tablet, fated to last as long as the marble it inscribed. The craving to know what had become of him followed me everywhere; when I was at Morton, I re-entered my cottage every evening to think of that; and now at Moor House, I sought my bedroom each night to brood over it.

In the course of my necessary correspondence with Mr Briggs about the will, I had enquired if he knew anything of Mr Rochester's present residence and state of health; but, as St John had conjectured, he was quite ignorant of all concerning him. I then wrote to Mrs Fairfax, entreating information on the subject. I had calculated with certainty on this step answering my end: I felt sure it would elicit an early answer. I was astonished when a fortnight passed without

reply; but when two months wore away, and day after day the post arrived and brought nothing for me, I fell a prey to the keenest anxiety.

I wrote again: there was a chance of my first letter having missed. Renewed hope followed renewed effort: it shone like the former for some weeks, then, like it, it faded, flickered: not a line, not a word reached me. When half a year wasted in vain expectancy, my hope died out, and then I felt dark indeed.

A fine spring shone round me, which I could not enjoy. Summer approached; Diana tried to cheer me: she said I looked ill, and wished to accompany me to the seaside. This St John opposed; he said I did not want dissipation, I wanted employment; my present life was too purposeless, I required an aim; and, I suppose, by way of supplying deficiencies, he prolonged still further my lessons in Hindostanee, and grew more urgent in requiring their accomplishment: and I, like a fool, never thought of resisting him – I could not resist him.

One day I had come to my studies in lower spirits than usual; the ebb was occasioned by a poignantly felt disappointment. Hannah had told me in the morning there was a letter for me, and when I went down to take it, almost certain that the long-looked-for tidings were vouchsafed me at last, I found only an unimportant note from Mr Briggs on business. The bitter check had wrung from me some tears; and now, as I sat poring over the crabbed characters and flourishing tropes of an Indian scribe, my eyes filled again.

St John called me to his side to read; in attempting to do this my voice failed me: words were lost in sobs. He and I were the only occupants of the parlour: Diana was practising her music in the drawing-room, Mary was gardening – it was a very fine May day, clear, sunny, and breezy. My companion expressed no surprise at this emotion, nor did he question me as to its cause; he only said – 'We will wait a few minutes, Jane, till you are more composed.' And while I smothered the paroxysm with all haste, he sat calm and patient, leaning on his desk, and looking like a physician watching with the eye of science an expected and fully understood crisis in a patient's malady. Having stifled my sobs, wiped my eyes, and muttered something about not being very well that morning, I resumed my task, and succeeded in completing it. St John put away my books and his, locked his desk, and said – 'Now, Jane, you shall take a walk; and with me.'

'I will call Diana and Mary.'

'No; I want only one companion this morning, and that must be you. Put on your things, go out by the kitchen-door: take the road towards the head of Marsh Glen: I will join you in a moment.'

I know no medium: I never in my life have known any medium in my dealings with positive, hard characters, antagonistic to my own, between absolute submission and determined revolt. I have always faithfully observed the one, up to the very moment of bursting, sometimes with volcanic vehemence, into the other; and as neither present circumstances warranted, nor my present mood inclined me to mutiny, I observed careful obedience to St John's directions; and in ten minutes I was treading the wild track of the glen, side by side with him.

The breeze was from the west: it came over the hills, sweet with scents of heath and rush; the sky was of stainless blue; the stream descending the ravine,

swelled with past spring rains, poured along plentiful and clear, catching golden gleams from the sun, and sapphire tints from the firmament. As we advanced and left the track, we trod a soft turf, mossy fine and emerald green, minutely enamelled with a tiny white flower, and spangled with a star-like yellow blossom: the hills, meantime, shut us quite in; for the glen, towards its head, wound to their very core.

'Let us rest here,' said St John, as we reached the first stragglers of a battalion of rocks, guarding a sort of pass, beyond which the beck rushed down a waterfall; and where, still a little farther, the mountain shook off turf and flower, had only heath for raiment and crag for gem – where it exaggerated the wild to the savage, and exchanged the fresh for the frowning – where it guarded the forlorn hope of solitude, and a last refuge for silence.

I took a seat: St John stood near me. He looked up the pass and down the hollow; his glance wandered away with the stream, and returned to traverse the unclouded heaven which coloured it: he removed his hat, let the breeze stir his hair and kiss his brow. He seemed in communion with the genius of the haunt: with his eye he bade farewell to something.

'And I shall see it again,' he said aloud, 'in dreams when I sleep by the Ganges: and again in a more remote hour – when another slumber overcomes me – on the shore of a darker stream!'

Strange words of a strange love! An austere patriot's passion for his fatherland! He sat down; for half an hour we never spoke; neither he to me nor I to him: that interval past, he recommenced – 'Jane, I go in six weeks; I have taken my berth in an East Indiaman which sails on the 20th of June.'

'God will protect you; for you have undertaken His work,' I answered.

'Yes,' said he, 'there is my glory and joy. I am the servant of an infallible Master. I am not going out under human guidance, subject to the defective laws and erring control of my feeble fellow-worms: my king, my lawgiver, my captain, is the All-perfect. It seems strange to me that all round me do not burn to enlist under the same banner, to join in the same enterprise.'

'All have not your powers, and it would be folly for the feeble to wish to march with the strong.'

'I do not speak to the feeble, or think of them: I address only such as are worthy of the work, and competent to accomplish it.'

'Those are few in number, and difficult to discover.'

'You say truly; but when found, it is right to stir them up – to urge and exhort them to the effort – to show them what their gifts are, and why they were given – to speak Heaven's message in their ear, to offer them, direct from God, a place in the ranks of His chosen.'

'If they are really qualified for the task, will not their own hearts be the first to inform them of it?'

I felt as if an awful charm was framing round and gathering over me: I trembled to hear some fatal word spoken which would at once declare and rivet the spell.

'And what does *your* heart say?' demanded St John.

'My heart is mute – my heart is mute,' I answered struck and thrilled.

'Then I must speak for it,' continued the deep relentless voice. 'Jane, come with me to India: come as my helpmeet and fellow-labourer.'

The glen and sky spun round: the hills heaved! It was as if I had heard a summons from Heaven – as if a visionary messenger, like him of Macedonia, had enounced, 'Come over and help us!' But I was no apostle, I could not behold the herald, I could not receive his call.

'Oh, St John!' I cried, 'have some mercy!'

I appealed to one who, in the discharge of what he believed his duty, knew neither mercy nor remorse. He continued – 'God and nature intended you for a missionary's wife. It is not personal, but mental endowments they have given you: you are formed for labour, not for love. A missionary's wife you must – shall be. You shall be mine: I claim you – not for my pleasure, but for my Sovereign's service.'

'I am not fit for it: I have no vocation,' I said.

He had calculated on these first objections: he was not irritated by them. Indeed, as he leaned back against the crag behind him, folded his arms on his chest, and fixed his countenance, I saw he was prepared for a long and trying opposition, and had taken in a stock of patience to last him to its close – resolved, however, that that close should be conquest for him.

'Humility, Jane,' said he, 'is the groundwork of Christian virtues: you say right that you are not fit for the work. Who is fit for it? Or who, that ever was truly called, believed himself worthy of the summons? I, for instance, am but dust and ashes. With St Paul, I acknowledge myself the chiefest of sinners; but I do not suffer this sense of my personal vileness to daunt me. I know my Leader: that He is just as well as mighty; and while He has chosen a feeble instrument to perform a great task, He will, from the boundless stores of His providence, supply the inadequacy of the means to the end. Think like me, Jane – trust like me. It is the Rock of Ages I ask you to lean on: do not doubt but it will bear the weight of your human weakness.'

'I do not understand a missionary life: I have never studied missionary labours.'

'There I, humble as I am, can give you the aid you want: I can set you your task from hour to hour; stand by you always; help you from moment to moment. This I could do in the beginning: soon (for I know your powers) you would be as strong and apt as myself, and would not require my help.'

'But my powers – where are they for this undertaking? I do not feel them. Nothing speaks or stirs in me while you talk. I am sensible of no light kindling – no life quickening – no voice counselling or cheering. Oh, I wish I could make you see how much my mind is at this moment like a rayless dungeon, with one shrinking fear fettered in its depths – the fear of being persuaded by you to attempt what I cannot accomplish!'

'I have an answer for you – hear it. I have watched you ever since we first met: I have made you my study for ten months. I have proved you in that time by sundry tests: and what have I seen and elicited? In the village school I found you could

perform well, punctually, uprightly, labour uncongenial to your habits and inclinations; I saw you could perform it with capacity and tact: you could win while you controlled. In the calm with which you learnt you had become suddenly rich, I read a mind clear of the vice of Demas: lucre had no undue power over you. In the resolute readiness with which you cut your wealth into four shares, keeping but one to yourself, and relinquishing the three others to the claim of abstract justice, I recognised a soul that revelled in the flame and excitement of sacrifice. In the tractability with which, at my wish, you forsook a study in which you were interested, and adopted another because it interested me; in the untiring assiduity with which you have since persevered in it – in the unflagging energy and unshaken temper with which you have met its difficulties – I acknowledge the complement of the qualities I seek. Jane, you are docile, diligent, disinterested, faithful, constant, and courageous; very gentle, and very heroic: cease to mistrust yourself – I can trust you unreservedly. As a conductress of Indian schools, and a helper amongst Indian women, your assistance will be to me invaluable.'

My iron shroud contracted round me; persuasion advanced with slow, sure step. Shut my eyes as I would, these last words of his succeeded in making the way, which had seemed blocked up, comparatively clear. My work, which had appeared so vague, so hopelessly diffuse, condensed itself as he proceeded, and assumed a definite form under his shaping hand. He waited for an answer. I demanded a quarter of an hour to think, before I again hazarded a reply.

'Very willingly,' he rejoined; and rising, he strode a little distance up the pass, threw himself down on a swell of heath, and there lay still.

'I *can* do what he wants me to do: I am forced to see and acknowledge that,' I meditated, 'that is, if life be spared me. But I feel mine is not the existence to be long protracted under an Indian sun. What then? He does not care for that: when my time came to die, he would resign me, in all serenity and sanctity, to the God who gave me. The case is very plain before me. In leaving England, I should leave a loved but empty land – Mr Rochester is not there; and if he were, what is, what can that ever be to me? My business is to live without him now: nothing so absurd, so weak as to drag on from day to day, as if I were waiting some impossible change in circumstances, which might reunite me to him. Of course (as St John once said) I must seek another interest in life to replace the one lost: is not the occupation he now offers me truly the most glorious man can adopt or God assign? Is it not, by its noble cares and sublime results, the one best calculated to fill the void left by uptorn affections and demolished hopes? I believe I must say, Yes – and yet I shudder. Alas! If I join St John, I abandon half myself: if I go to India, I go to premature death. And how will the interval between leaving England for India, and India for the grave, be filled? Oh, I know well! That, too, is very clear to my vision. By straining to satisfy St John till my sinews ache, I *shall* satisfy him – to the finest central point and farthest outward circle of his expectations. If I *do* go with him – if I *do* make the sacrifice he urges I will make it absolutely: I will throw all on the altar – heart, vitals, the entire victim. He will never love me; but he shall approve me; I will show him energies he has not yet seen, resources he has never suspected. Yes, I can work as

hard as he can, and with as little grudging.

'Consent, then, to his demand is possible: but for one item – one dreadful item. It is – that he asks me to be his wife, and has no more of a husband's heart for me than that frowning giant of a rock, down which the stream is foaming in yonder gorge. He prizes me as a soldier would a good weapon, and that is all. Unmarried to him, this would never grieve me; but can I let him complete his calculations – coolly put into practice his plans – go through the wedding ceremony? Can I receive from him the bridal ring, endure all the forms of love (which I doubt not he would scrupulously observe) and know that the spirit was quite absent? Can I bear the consciousness that every endearment he bestows is a sacrifice made on principle? No: such a martyrdom would be monstrous. I will never undergo it. As his sister, I might accompany him – not as his wife: I will tell him so.'

I looked towards the knoll: there he lay, still as a prostrate column; his face turned to me: his eye beaming watchful and keen. He started to his feet and approached me.

'I am ready to go to India, if I may go free.'

'Your answer requires a commentary,' he said; 'it is not clear.'

'You have hitherto been my adopted brother – I, your adopted sister: let us continue as such: you and I had better not marry.'

He shook his head. 'Adopted fraternity will not do in this case. If you were my real sister it would be different: I should take you, and seek no wife. But as it is, either our union must be consecrated and sealed by marriage, or it cannot exist: practical obstacles oppose themselves to any other plan. Do you not see it, Jane? Consider a moment – your strong sense will guide you.'

I did consider; and still my sense, such as it was, directed me only to the fact that we did not love each other as man and wife should: and therefore it inferred we ought not to marry. I said so. 'St John,' I returned, 'I regard you as a brother – you, me as a sister: so let us continue.'

'We cannot – we cannot,' he answered, with short, sharp determination: 'it would not do. You have said you will go with me to India: remember – you have said that.'

'Conditionally.'

'Well – well. To the main point – the departure with me from England, the co-operation with me in my future labours – you do not object. You have already as good as put your hand to the plough: you are too consistent to withdraw it. You have but one end to keep in view – how the work you have undertaken can best be done. Simplify your complicated interests, feelings, thoughts, wishes, aims; merge all considerations in one purpose: that of fulfilling with effect – with power – the mission of your great Master. To do so, you must have a coadjutor: not a brother – that is a loose tie – but a husband. I, too, do not want a sister: a sister might any day be taken from me. I want a wife: the sole helpmeet I can influence efficiently in life, and retain absolutely till death.'

I shuddered as he spoke: I felt his influence in my marrow – his hold on my limbs.

'Seek one elsewhere than in me, St John: seek one fitted to you.'

'One fitted to my purpose, you mean – fitted to my vocation. Again I tell you it is not the insignificant private individual – the mere man, with the man's selfish senses – I wish to mate: it is the missionary.'

'And I will give the missionary my energies – it is all he wants – but not myself: that would be only adding the husk and shell to the kernel. For them he has no use: I retain them.'

'You cannot – you ought not. Do you think God will be satisfied with half an oblation? Will He accept a mutilated sacrifice? It is the cause of God I advocate: it is under His standard I enlist you. I cannot accept on His behalf a divided allegiance: it must be entire.'

'Oh! I will give my heart to God,' I said. '*You* do not want it.'

I will not swear, reader, that there was not something of repressed sarcasm both in the tone in which I uttered this sentence, and in the feeling that accompanied it. I had silently feared St John till now, because I had not understood him. He had held me in awe, because he had held me in doubt. How much of him was saint, how much mortal, I could not heretofore tell: but revelations were being made in this conference: the analysis of his nature was proceeding before my eyes. I saw his fallibilities: I comprehended them. I understood that, sitting there where I did, on the bank of heath, and with that handsome form before me, I sat at the feet of a man, erring as I. The veil fell from his hardness and despotism. Having felt in him the presence of these qualities, I felt his imperfection and took courage. I was with an equal – one with whom I might argue – one whom, if I saw good, I might resist.

He was silent after I had uttered the last sentence, and I presently risked an upward glance at his countenance. His eye, bent on me, expressed at once stern surprise and keen enquiry. 'Is she sarcastic, and sarcastic to *me*!' it seemed to say. 'What does this signify?'

'Do not let us forget that this is a solemn matter,' he said ere long; 'one of which we may neither think nor talk lightly without sin. I trust, Jane, you are in earnest when you say you will give your heart to God: it is all I want. Once wrench your heart from man, and fix it on your Maker, the advancement of that Maker's spiritual kingdom on earth will be your chief delight and endeavour; you will be ready to do at once whatever furthers that end. You will see what impetus would be given to your efforts and mine by our physical and mental union in marriage: the only union that gives a character of permanent conformity to the destinies and designs of human beings; and, passing over all minor caprices – all trivial difficulties and delicacies of feeling – all scruple about the degree, kind, strength or tenderness of mere personal inclination – you will hasten to enter into that union at once.'

'Shall I?' I said briefly; and I looked at his features, beautiful in their harmony, but strangely formidable in their still severity; at his brow, commanding but not open; at his eyes, bright and deep and searching, but never soft; at his tall imposing figure; and fancied myself in idea *his wife*. Oh! it would never do! As his curate, his comrade, all would be right: I would cross oceans with him in that capacity; toil under Eastern suns, in Asian deserts with him in that office; admire

and emulate his courage and devotion and vigour; accommodate quietly to his masterhood; smile undisturbed at his ineradicable ambition; discriminate the Christian from the man: profoundly esteem the one, and freely forgive the other. I should suffer often, no doubt, attached to him only in this capacity: my body would be under rather a stringent yoke, but my heart and mind would be free. I should still have my unblighted self to turn to: my natural unenslaved feelings with which to communicate in moments of loneliness. There would be recesses in my mind which would be only mine, to which he never came, and sentiments growing there fresh and sheltered which his austerity could never blight, nor his measured warrior-march trample down: but as his wife – at his side always, and always restrained, and always checked – forced to keep the fire of my nature continually low, to compel it to burn inwardly and never utter a cry, though the imprisoned flame consumed vital after vital – *this* would be unendurable.

'St John!' I exclaimed, when I had got so far in my meditation.

'Well?' he answered icily.

'I repeat I freely consent to go with you as your fellow-missionary, but not as your wife; I cannot marry you and become part of you.'

'A part of me you must become,' he answered steadily: 'otherwise the whole bargain is void. How can I, a man not yet thirty, take out with me to India a girl of nineteen, unless she be married to me? How can we be for ever together – sometimes in solitudes, sometimes amidst savage tribes – and unwed?'

'Very well,' I said shortly; 'under the circumstances, quite as well as if I were either your real sister, or a man and a clergyman like yourself.'

'It is known that you are not my sister; I cannot introduce you as such: to attempt it would be to fasten injurious suspicions on us both. And for the rest, though you have a man's vigorous brain, you have a woman's heart and – it would not do.'

'It would do,' I affirmed with some disdain, 'perfectly well. I have a woman's heart, but not where you are concerned; for you I have only a comrade's constancy; a fellow-soldier's frankness, fidelity, fraternity, if you like; a neophyte's respect and submission to his hierophant: nothing more – don't fear.'

'It is what I want,' he said, speaking to himself; 'it is just what I want. And there are obstacles in the way: they must be hewn down. Jane, you would not repent marrying me – be certain of that; we *must* be married. I repeat it: there is no other way; and undoubtedly enough of love would follow upon marriage to render the union right even in your eyes.'

'I scorn your idea of love,' I could not help saying, as I rose up and stood before him, leaning my back against the rock. 'I scorn the counterfeit sentiment you offer: yes, St John, and I scorn you when you offer it.'

He looked at me fixedly, compressing his well-cut lips while he did so. Whether he was incensed or surprised, or what, it was not easy to tell: he could command his countenance thoroughly.

'I scarcely expected to hear that expression from you,' he said: 'I think I have done and uttered nothing to deserve scorn.'

I was touched by his gentle tone, and overawed by his high, calm mien.

'Forgive me the words, St John; but it is your own fault that I have been roused

to speak so unguardedly. You have introduced a topic on which our natures are at variance – a topic we should never discuss: the very name of love is an apple of discord between us. If the reality were required, what should we do? How should we feel? My dear cousin, abandon your scheme of marriage – forget it.'

'No,' said he; 'it is a long-cherished scheme, and the only one which can secure my great end: but I shall urge you no further at present. Tomorrow, I leave home for Cambridge: I have many friends there to whom I should wish to say farewell. I shall be absent a fortnight – take that space of time to consider my offer: and do not forget that if you reject it, it is not me you deny, but God. Through my means, He opens to you a noble career; as my wife only can you enter upon it. Refuse to be my wife, and you limit yourself for ever to a track of selfish ease and barren obscurity. Tremble lest in that case you should be numbered with those who have denied the faith, and are worse than infidels!'

He had done. Turning from me, he once more

> Looked to river, looked to hill.

But this time his feelings were all pent in his heart: I was not worthy to hear them uttered. As I walked by his side homeward, I read well in his iron silence all he felt towards me: the disappointment of an austere and despotic nature, which has met resistance where it expected submission – the disapprobation of a cool, inflexible judgement, which has detected in another feelings and views in which it has no power to sympathise: in short, as a man, he would have wished to coerce me into obedience: it was only as a sincere Christian he bore so patiently with my perversity, and allowed so long a space for reflection and repentance.

That night, after he had kissed his sisters, he thought proper to forget even to shake hands with me, but left the room in silence. I – who, though I had no love, had much friendship for him – was hurt by the marked omission: so much hurt that tears started to my eyes.

'I see you and St John have been quarrelling, Jane,' said Diana, 'during your walk on the moor. But go after him; he is now lingering in the passage expecting you – he will make it up.'

I have not much pride under such circumstances: I would always rather be happy than dignified; and I ran after him – he stood at the foot of the stairs.

'Good-night, St John,' said I.

'Good-night, Jane,' he replied calmly.

'Then shake hands,' I added.

What a cold, loose touch he impressed on my fingers! He was deeply displeased by what had occurred that day; cordiality would not warm, nor tears move him. No happy reconciliation was to be had with him – no cheering smile or generous word: but still the Christian was patient and placid; and when I asked him if he forgave me, he answered that he was not in the habit of cherishing the remembrance of vexation; that he had nothing to forgive, not having been offended.

And with that answer he left me. I would much rather he had knocked me down.

## Chapter 35

He did not leave for Cambridge the next day, as he had said he would. He deferred his departure a whole week, and during that time he made me feel what severe punishment a good yet stern, a conscientious yet implacable man can inflict on one who has offended him. Without one overt act of hostility, one upbraiding word he contrived to impress me momently with the conviction that I was put beyond the pale of his favour.

Not that St John harboured a spirit of unchristian vindictiveness – not that he would have injured a hair of my head, if it had been fully in his power to do so. Both by nature and principle, he was superior to the mean gratification of vengeance: he had forgiven me for saying I scorned him and his love, but he had not forgotten the words; and as long as he and I lived he never would forget them. I saw by his look, when he turned to me, that they were always written on the air between me and him; whenever I spoke, they sounded in my voice to his ear, and their echo toned every answer he gave me.

He did not abstain from conversing with me: he even called me as usual each morning to join him at his desk; and I fear the corrupt man within him had a pleasure unimparted to, and unshared by, the pure Christian, in evincing with what skill he could, while acting and speaking apparently just as usual, extract from every deed and every phrase the spirit of interest and approval which had formerly communicated a certain austere charm to his language and manner. To me, he was in reality become no longer flesh, but marble; his eye was a cold, bright, blue gem; his tongue a speaking instrument – nothing more.

All this was torture to me – refined, lingering torture. It kept up a slow fire of indignation and a trembling trouble of grief, which harassed and crushed me altogether. I felt how – if I were his wife, this good man, pure as the deep sunless source, could soon kill me, without drawing from my veins a single drop of blood, or receiving on his own crystal conscience the faintest stain of crime. Especially I felt this when I made any attempt to propitiate him. No ruth met my ruth. *He* experienced no suffering from estrangement – no yearning after reconciliation; and though, more than once, my fast falling tears blistered the page over which we both bent, they produced no more effect on him than if his heart had been really a matter of stone or metal. To his sisters, meantime, he was somewhat kinder than usual: as if afraid that mere coldness would not sufficiently convince me how completely I was banished and banned, he added the force of contrast; and this I am sure he did not by malice, but on principle.

The night before he left home, happening to see him walking in the garden about sunset, and remembering, as I looked at him, that this man, alienated as he now was, had once saved my life, and that we were near relations, I was moved to make a last attempt to regain his friendship. I went out and approached him as he stood leaning over the little gate; I spoke to the point at once:

'St John, I am unhappy because you are still angry with me. Let us be friends.'

'I hope we are friends,' was the unmoved reply; while he still watched the rising of the moon, which he had been contemplating as I approached.

'No, St John, we are not friends as we were. You know that.'

'Are we not? That is wrong. For my part, I wish you no ill and all good.'

'I believe you, St John; for I am sure you are incapable of wishing anyone ill; but, as I am your kinswoman, I should desire somewhat more of affection than that sort of general philanthropy you extend to mere strangers.'

'Of course,' he said. 'Your wish is reasonable, and I am far from regarding you as a stranger.'

This, spoken in a cool, tranquil tone, was mortifying and baffling enough. Had I attended to the suggestions of pride and ire, I should immediately have left him; but something worked within me more strongly than those feelings could. I deeply venerated my cousin's talent and principle. His friendship was of value to me: to lose it tried me severely. I would not so soon relinquish the attempt to reconquer it.

'Must we part in this way, St John? And when you go to India, will you leave me so, without a kinder word than you have yet spoken?'

He now turned quite from the moon and faced me. 'When I go to India, Jane, will I leave you! What! do you not go to India?'

'You said I could not unless I married you.'

'And you will not marry me! You adhere to that resolution?'

Reader, do you know, as I do, what terror those cold people can put into the ice of their questions? How much of the fall of the avalanche is in their anger? of the breaking up of the frozen sea in their displeasure?

'No, St John, I will not marry you. I adhere to my resolution.'

The avalanche had shaken and slid a little forward but it did not yet crash down.

'Once more, why this refusal?' he asked.

'Formerly,' I answered, 'because you did not love me; now, I reply, because you almost hate me. If I were to marry you, you would kill me. You are killing me now.'

His lips and cheeks turned white – quite white.

'*I should kill you – I am killing you?* Your words are such as ought not to be used: violent, unfeminine, and untrue. They betray an unfortunate state of mind: they merit severe reproof: they would seem inexcusable, but that it is the duty of man to forgive his fellow even until seventy-and-seven times.'

I had finished the business now. While earnestly wishing to erase from his mind the trace of my former offence, I had stamped on that tenacious surface another and far deeper impression: I had burnt it in.

'Now you will indeed hate me,' I said. 'It is useless to attempt to conciliate you: I see I have made an eternal enemy of you.'

A fresh wrong did these words inflict: the worse, because they touched on the truth. That bloodless lip quivered to a temporary spasm. I knew the steely ire I had whetted. I was heart-wrung.

'You utterly misinterpret my words,' I said, at once seizing his hand: 'I have no intention to grieve or pain you – indeed, I have not.'

Most bitterly he smiled – most decidedly he withdrew his hand from mine. 'And now you recall your promise, and will not go to India at all, I presume?' said he, after a considerable pause.

'Yes, I will, as your assistant,' I answered.

A very long silence succeeded. What struggle there was in him between Nature and Grace in this interval, I cannot tell: only singular gleams scintillated in his eyes, and strange shadows passed over his face. He spoke at last.

'I before proved to you the absurdity of a single woman of your age proposing to accompany abroad a single man of mine. I proved it to you in such terms as, I should have thought, would have prevented your ever again alluding to the plan. That you have done so, I regret – for your sake.'

I interrupted him. Anything like a tangible reproach gave me courage at once. 'Keep to common sense, St John: you are verging on nonsense. You pretend to be shocked by what I have said. You are not really shocked: for, with your superior mind, you cannot be either so dull or so conceited as to misunderstand my meaning. I say again, I will be your curate, if you like, but never your wife.'

Again he turned lividly pale; but, as before, controlled his passion perfectly. He answered emphatically but calmly – 'A female curate, who is not my wife, would never suit me. With me, then, it seems, you cannot go: but if you are sincere in your offer, I will, while in town, speak to a married missionary, whose wife needs a coadjutor. Your own fortune will make you independent of the Society's aid; and thus you may still be spared the dishonour of breaking your promise and deserting the band you engaged to join.'

Now I never had, as the reader knows, either given any formal promise or entered into any engagement; and this language was all much too hard and much too despotic for the occasion. I replied – 'There is no dishonour, no breach of promise, no desertion in the case. I am not under the slightest obligation to go to India, especially with strangers. With you I would have ventured much, because I admire, confide in, and, as a sister, I love you; but I am convinced that, go when and with whom I would, I should not live long in that climate.'

'Ah! you are afraid of yourself,' he said, curling his lip.

'I am. God did not give me my life to throw away; and to do as you wish me would, I begin to think, be almost equivalent to committing suicide. Moreover, before I definitively resolve on quitting England, I will know for certain whether I cannot be of greater use by remaining in it than by leaving it.'

'What do you mean?'

'It would be fruitless to attempt to explain; but there is a point on which I have long endured painful doubt, and I can go nowhere till by some means that doubt is removed.'

'I know where your heart turns and to what it clings. The interest you cherish is lawless and unconsecrated. Long since you ought to have crushed it: now you should blush to allude to it. You think of Mr Rochester?'

It was true. I confessed it by silence.

'Are you going to seek Mr Rochester?'

'I must find out what is become of him.'

'It remains for me, then,' he said, 'to remember you in my prayers, and to entreat God for you, in all earnestness, that you may not indeed become a castaway. I had thought I recognised in you one of the chosen. But God sees not as man sees: *His* will be done.'

He opened the gate, passed through it, and strayed away down the glen. He was soon out of sight.

On re-entering the parlour, I found Diana standing at the window, looking very thoughtful. Diana was a great deal taller than I: she put her hand on my shoulder, and, stooping, examined my face.

'Jane,' she said, 'you are always agitated and pale now. I am sure there is something the matter. Tell me what business St John and you have on hands. I have watched you this half hour from the window; you must forgive my being such a spy, but for a long time I have fancied I hardly know what. St John is a strange being – '

She paused – I did not speak: soon she resumed – 'That brother of mine cherishes peculiar views of some sort respecting you, I am sure: he has long distinguished you by a notice and interest he never showed to anyone else – to what end? I wish he loved you – does he, Jane?'

I put her cool hand to my hot forehead; 'No, Die, not one whit.'

'Then why does he follow you so with his eyes, and get you so frequently alone with him, and keep you so continually at his side? Mary and I had both concluded he wished you to marry him.'

'He does – he has asked me to be his wife.'

Diana clapped her hands. 'That is just what we hoped and thought! And you will marry him, Jane, won't you? And then he will stay in England.'

'Far from that, Diana; his sole idea in proposing to me is to procure a fitting fellow-labourer in his Indian toils.'

'What! He wishes you to go to India?'

'Yes.'

'Madness!' she exclaimed. 'You would not live three months there, I am certain. You never shall go: you have not consented, have you, Jane?'

'I have refused to marry him – '

'And have consequently displeased him?' she suggested.

'Deeply: he will never forgive me, I fear: yet I offered to accompany him as his sister.'

'It was frantic folly to do so, Jane. Think of the task you undertook – one of incessant fatigue, where fatigue kills even the strong, and you are weak. St John – you know him – would urge you to impossibilities: with him there would be no permission to rest during the hot hours; and unfortunately, I have noticed, whatever he exacts, you force yourself to perform. I am astonished you found courage to refuse his hand. You do not love him then, Jane?'

'Not as a husband.'

'Yet he is a handsome fellow.'

'And I am so plain, you see, Die. We should never suit.'

'Plain! You? Not at all. You are much too pretty, as well as too good, to be grilled alive in Calcutta.' And again she earnestly conjured me to give up all thoughts of going out with her brother.

'I must indeed,' I said; 'for when just now I repeated the offer of serving him for a deacon, he expressed himself shocked at my want of decency. He seemed to think I had committed an impropriety in proposing to accompany him unmarried: as if I had not from the first hoped to find in him a brother, and habitually regarded him as such.'

'What makes you say he does not love you, Jane?'

'You should hear himself on the subject. He has again and again explained that it is not himself, but his office he wishes to mate. He has told me I am formed for labour – not for love: which is true, no doubt. But, in my opinion, if I am not formed for love, it follows that I am not formed for marriage. Would it not be strange, Die, to be chained for life to a man who regarded one but as a useful tool?'

'Insupportable – unnatural – out of the question!'

'And then,' I continued, 'though I have only sisterly affection for him now, yet, if forced to be his wife, I can imagine the possibility of conceiving an inevitable, strange, torturing kind of love for him, because he is so talented; and there is often a certain heroic grandeur in his look, manner, and conversation. In that case, my lot would become unspeakably wretched. He would not want me to love him; and if I showed the feeling, he would make me sensible that it was a superfluity, unrequired by him, unbecoming in me. I know he would.'

'And yet St John is a good man,' said Diana.

'He is a good and a great man; but he forgets, pitilessly, the feelings and claims of little people, in pursuing his own large views. It is better, therefore, for the insignificant to keep out of his way, lest, in his progress, he should trample them down. Here he comes! I will leave you, Diana.' And I hastened upstairs as I saw him entering the garden.

But I was forced to meet him again at supper. During that meal he appeared just as composed as usual. I had thought he would hardly speak to me, and I was certain he had given up the pursuit of his matrimonial scheme: the sequel showed I was mistaken on both points. He addressed me precisely in his ordinary manner, or what had, of late, been his ordinary manner – one scrupulously polite. No doubt he had invoked the help of the Holy Spirit to subdue the anger I had roused in him, and now believed he had forgiven me once more.

For the evening reading before prayers, he selected the twenty-first chapter of Revelation. It was at all times pleasant to listen while from his lips fell the words of the Bible: never did his fine voice sound at once so sweet and full – never did his manner become so impressive in its noble simplicity, as when he delivered the oracles of God: and tonight that voice took a more solemn tone – that manner a more thrilling meaning – as he sat in the midst of his household circle (the May moon shining in through the uncurtained window, and rendering almost

unnecessary the light of the candle on the table): as he sat there, bending over the great old Bible, and described from its page the vision of the new heaven and the new earth – told how God would come to dwell with men, how He would wipe away all tears from their eyes, and promised that there should be no more death, neither sorrow nor crying, nor any more pain, because the former things were passed away.

The succeeding words thrilled me strangely as he spoke them: especially as I felt, by the slight, indescribable alteration in sound, that in uttering them, his eye had turned on me.

'He that overcometh shall inherit all things; and I will be his God, and he shall be my son. But,' was slowly, distinctly read, 'the fearful, the unbelieving, etc., shall have their part in the lake which burneth with fire and brimstone, which is the second death.'

Henceforward, I knew what fate St John feared for me.

A calm, subdued triumph, blent with a longing earnestness, marked his enunciation of the last glorious verses of that chapter. The reader believed his name was already written in the Lamb's book of life, and he yearned after the hour which should admit him to the city to which the kings of the earth bring their glory and honour; which has no need of sun or moon to shine in it, because the glory of God lightens it, and the Lamb is the light thereof.

In the prayer following the chapter, all his energy gathered – all his stern zeal woke: he was in deep earnest, wrestling with God, and resolved on a conquest. He supplicated strength for the weak-hearted; guidance for wanderers from the fold: a return, even at the eleventh hour, for those whom the temptations of the world and the flesh were luring from the narrow path. He asked, he urged, he claimed the boon of a brand snatched from the burning. Earnestness is ever deeply solemn: first, as I listened to that prayer, I wondered at his; then, when it continued and rose, I was touched by it, and at last awed. He felt the greatness and goodness of his purpose so sincerely: others who heard him plead for it, could not but feel it too.

The prayer over, we took leave of him: he was to go at a very early hour in the morning. Diana and Mary having kissed him, left the room – in compliance, I think, with a whispered hint from him: I tendered my hand, and wished him a pleasant journey.

'Thank you, Jane. As I said, I shall return from Cambridge in a fortnight: that space, then, is yet left you for reflection. If I listened to human pride, I should say no more to you of marriage with me; but I listen to my duty, and keep steadily in view my first aim – to do all things to the glory of God. My Master was long-suffering: so will I be. I cannot give you up to perdition as a vessel of wrath: repent – resolve, while there is yet time. Remember, we are bid to work while it is day – warned that "the night cometh when no man shall work." Remember the fate of Dives, who had his good things in this life. God give you strength to choose that better part which shall not be taken from you!'

He laid his hand on my head as he uttered the last words. He had spoken earnestly, mildly: his look was not, indeed, that of a lover beholding his mistress,

but it was that of a pastor recalling his wandering sheep – or better, of a guardian angel watching the soul for which he is responsible. All men of talent, whether they be men of feeling or not; whether they be zealots, or aspirants, or despots – provided only they be sincere – have their sublime moments, when they subdue and rule. I felt veneration for St John – veneration so strong that its impetus thrust me at once to the point I had so long shunned. I was tempted to cease struggling with him – to rush down the torrent of his will into the gulf of his existence, and there lose my own. I was almost as hard beset by him now as I had been once before, in a different way, by another. I was a fool both times. To have yielded then would have been an error of principle; to have yielded now would have been an error of judgement. So I think at this hour, when I look back to the crisis through the quiet medium of time: I was unconscious of folly at the instant.

I stood motionless under my hierophant's touch. My refusals were forgotten – my fears overcome – my wrestlings paralysed. The Impossible – i.e., my marriage with St John – was fast becoming the Possible. All was changing utterly with a sudden sweep. Religion called – Angels beckoned – God commanded – life rolled together like a scroll – death's gates opening, showed eternity beyond: it seemed, that for safety and bliss there, all here might be sacrificed in a second. The dim room was full of visions.

'Could you decide now?' asked the missionary. The enquiry was put in gentle tones: he drew me to him as gently. Oh, that gentleness! how far more potent is it than force! I could resist St John's wrath: I grew pliant as a reed under his kindness. Yet I knew all the time, if I yielded now, I should not the less be made to repent, someday, of my former rebellion. His nature was not changed by one hour of solemn prayer: it was only elevated.

'I could decide if I were but certain,' I answered: 'were I but convinced that it is God's will I should marry you, I could vow to marry you here and now – come afterwards what would!'

'My prayers are heard!' ejaculated St John. He pressed his hand firmer on my head, as if he claimed me: he surrounded me with his arm, *almost* as if he loved me (I say *almost* – I knew the difference – for I had felt what it was to be loved; but, like him, I had now put love out of the question, and thought only of duty). I contended with my inward dimness of vision, before which clouds yet rolled. I sincerely, deeply, fervently longed to do what was right; and only that. 'Show me, show me the path!' I entreated of Heaven. I was excited more than I had ever been; and whether what followed was the effect of excitement the reader shall judge.

All the house was still; for I believe all, except St John and myself, were now retired to rest. The one candle was dying out: the room was full of moonlight. My heart beat fast and thick: I heard its throb. Suddenly it stood still to an inexpressible feeling that thrilled it through, and passed at once to my head and extremities. The feeling was not like - an electric shock, but it was quite as sharp, as strange, as startling: it acted on my senses as if their utmost activity hitherto had been but torpor, from which they were now summoned and forced to wake. They rose expectant: eye and ear waited while the flesh quivered on my bones.

'What have you heard? What do you see?' asked St John. I saw nothing, but I heard a voice somewhere cry – 'Jane! Jane! Jane!' – nothing more.

'O God! what is it?' I gasped.

I might have said, 'Where is it?' for it did not seem in the room – nor in the house – nor in the garden; it did not come out of the air – nor from under the earth – nor from overhead. I had heard it – where, or whence, for ever impossible to know! And it was the voice of a human being – a known, loved, well-remembered voice – that of Edward Fairfax Rochester; and it spoke in pain and woe, wildly, eerily, urgently.

'I am coming!' I cried. 'Wait for me! Oh, I will come!' I flew to the door and looked into the passage: it was dark. I ran out into the garden: it was void.

'Where are you?' I exclaimed.

The hills beyond Marsh Glen sent the answer faintly back – 'Where are you?' I listened. The wind sighed low in the firs: all was moorland loneliness and midnight hush.

'Down superstition!' I commented, as that spectre rose up black by the black yew at the gate. 'This is not thy deception, nor thy witchcraft: it is the work of nature. She was roused, and did – no miracle – but her best.'

I broke from St John, who had followed, and would have detained me. It was *my* time to assume ascendency. *My* powers were in-play and in force. I told him to forbear question or remark; I desired him to leave me: I must and would be alone. He obeyed at once. Where there is energy to command well enough, obedience never fails. I mounted to my chamber; locked myself in; fell on my knees; and prayed in my way – a different way to St John's, but effective in its own fashion. I seemed to penetrate very near a Mighty Spirit; and my soul rushed out in gratitude at His feet. I rose from the thanksgiving – took a resolve – and lay down, unscared, enlightened – eager but for the daylight.

## Chapter 36

The daylight came. I rose at dawn. I busied myself for an hour or two with arranging my things in my chamber, drawers, and wardrobe, in the order wherein I should wish to leave them during a brief absence. Meantime, I heard St John quit his room.

He stopped at my door: I feared he would knock – no, but a slip of paper was passed under the door. I took it up. It bore these words –

You left me too suddenly last night. Had you stayed but a little longer, you would have laid your hand on the Christian's cross and the angel's crown. I shall expect your clear decision when I return this day fortnight. Meantime, watch and pray that you enter not into temptation: the spirit, I trust, is willing, but the flesh, I see, is weak. I shall pray for you hourly.

    Yours,
                                                              St John

'My spirit,' I answered mentally, 'is willing to do what is right; and my flesh, I hope, is strong enough to accomplish the will of Heaven, when once that will is distinctly known to me. At any rate, it shall be strong enough to search – enquire – to grope an outlet from this cloud of doubt, and find the open day of certainty.'

It was the first of June; yet the morning was overcast and chilly: rain beat fast on my casement. I heard the front-door open, and St John pass out. Looking through the window, I saw him traverse the garden. He took the way over the misty moors in the direction of Whitcross – there he would meet the coach.

'In a few more hours I shall succeed you in that track, cousin,' thought I: 'I too have a coach to meet at Whitcross. I too have some to see and ask after in England, before I depart for ever.'

It wanted yet two hours of breakfast-time. I filled the interval in walking softly about my room, and pondering the visitation which had given my plans their present bent. I recalled that inward sensation I had experienced: for I could recall it, with all its unspeakable strangeness. I recalled the voice I had heard; again I questioned whence it came, as vainly as before: it seemed in *me* – not in the external world. I asked was it a mere nervous impression – a delusion? I could not conceive or believe: it was more like an inspiration. The wondrous shock of feeling had come like the earthquake which shook the foundations of Paul and Silas's prison; it had opened the doors of the soul's cell and loosed its bands – it had wakened it out of its sleep, whence it sprang trembling, listening, aghast; then vibrated thrice a cry on my startled ear, and in my quaking heart and through my spirit, which neither feared nor shook, but exulted as if in joy over the success of one effort it had been privileged to make, independent of the cumbrous body.

'Ere many days,' I said, as I terminated my musings, 'I will know something of him whose voice seemed last night to summon me. Letters have proved of no avail – personal enquiry shall replace them.'

At breakfast I announced to Diana and Mary that I was going a journey, and should be absent at least four days.

'Alone, Jane?' they asked.

'Yes; it was to see or hear news of a friend about whom I had for some time been uneasy.'

They might have said, as I have no doubt they thought, that they had believed me to be without any friends save them: for, indeed, I had often said so; but, with their true natural delicacy, they abstained from comment, except that Diana asked me if I was sure I was well enough to travel. I looked very pale, she observed. I replied, that nothing ailed me save anxiety of mind, which I hoped soon to alleviate.

It was easy to make my further arrangements; for I was troubled with no enquiries – no surmises. Having once explained to them that I could not now be explicit about my plans, they kindly and wisely acquiesced in the silence with which I pursued them, according to me the privilege of free action I should under similar circumstances have accorded them.

I left Moor House at three o'clock p.m., and soon after four I stood at the foot

of the signpost of Whitcross, waiting the arrival of the coach which was to take me to distant Thornfield. Amidst the silence of those solitary roads and desert hills, I heard it approach from a great distance. It was the same vehicle whence, a year ago, I had alighted one summer evening on this very spot – how desolate, and hopeless, and objectless! It stopped as I beckoned. I entered – not now obliged to part with my whole fortune as the price of its accommodation. Once more on the road to Thornfield, I felt like the messenger-pigeon flying home.

It was a journey of six-and-thirty hours. I had set out from Whitcross on a Tuesday afternoon, and early on the succeeding Thursday morning the coach stopped to water the horses at a wayside inn, situated in the midst of scenery whose green hedges and large fields and low pastoral hills (how mild of feature and verdant of hue compared with the stern North-Midland moors of Morton!) met my eye like the lineaments of a once familiar face. Yes, I knew the character of this landscape: I was sure we were near my bourne.

'How far is Thornfield Hall from here?' I asked of the ostler.

'Just two miles, ma'am, across the fields.'

'My journey is closed,' I thought to myself. I got out of the coach, gave a box I had into the ostler's charge, to be kept till I called for it; paid my fare; satisfied the coachman, and was going: the brightening day gleamed on the sign of the inn, and I read in gilt letters, 'The Rochester Arms'. My heart leapt up: I was already on my master's very lands. It fell again: the thought struck it: 'Your master himself may be beyond the British Channel, for aught you know: and then, if he is at Thornfield Hall, towards which you hasten, who besides him is there? His lunatic wife: and you have nothing to do with him: you dare not speak to him or seek his presence. You have lost your labour – you had better go no farther,' urged the monitor. 'Ask information of the people at the inn; they can give you all you seek: they can solve your doubts at once. Go up to that man, and enquire if Mr Rochester be at home.'

The suggestion was sensible, and yet I could not force myself to act on it. I so dreaded a reply that would crush me with despair. To prolong doubt was to prolong hope. I might yet once more see the Hall under the ray of her star. There was the stile before me – the very fields through which I had hurried, blind, deaf, distracted with a revengeful fury tracking and scourging me, on the morning I fled from Thornfield: ere I well knew what course I had resolved to take, I was in the midst of them. How fast I walked! How I ran sometimes! How I looked forward to catch the first view of the well-known woods! With what feelings I welcomed single trees I knew, and familiar glimpses of meadow and hill between them!

At last the woods rose; the rookery clustered dark; a loud cawing broke the morning stillness. Strange delight inspired me: on I hastened. Another field crossed – a lane threaded – and there were the courtyard walls – the back offices: the house itself, the rookery still hid. 'My first view of it shall be in front,' I determined, 'where its bold battlements will strike the eye nobly at once, and where I can single out my master's very window: perhaps he will be standing at it – he rises early: perhaps he is now walking in the orchard, or on

the pavement in front. Could I but see him! – but a moment! Surely, in that case, I should not be so mad as to run to him? I cannot tell – I am not certain. And if I did – what then? God bless him! What then? Who would be hurt by my once more tasting the life his glance can give me? I rave: perhaps at this moment he is watching the sun rise over the Pyrenees, or on the tideless sea of the south.'

I had coasted along the lower wall of the orchard – turned its angle: there was a gate just there, opening into the meadow, between two stone pillars crowned by stone balls. From behind one pillar I could peep round quietly at the full front of the mansion. I advanced my head with precaution, desirous to ascertain if any bedroom window-blinds were yet drawn up: battlements, windows, long front – all from this sheltered station were at my command.

The crows sailing overhead perhaps watched me while I took this survey. I wonder what they thought. They must have considered I was very careful and timid at first, and that gradually I grew very bold and reckless. A peep, and then a long stare; and then a departure from my niche and a straying out into the meadow; and a sudden stop full in front of the great mansion, and a protracted, hardy gaze towards it. 'What affectation of diffidence was this at first?' they might have demanded; 'what stupid regardlessness now?'

Hear an illustration, reader.

A lover finds his mistress asleep on a mossy bank; he wishes to catch a glimpse of her fair face without waking her. He steals softly over the grass, careful to make no sound; he pauses – fancying she has stirred: he withdraws: not for worlds would he be seen. All is still: he again advances: he bends above her; a light veil rests on her features: he lifts it, bends lower; now his eyes anticipate the vision of beauty – warm, and blooming, and lovely, in rest. How hurried was their first glance! But how they fix! How he starts! How he suddenly and vehemently clasps in both arms the form he dared not, a moment since, touch with his finger! How he calls aloud a name, and drops his burden, and gazes on it wildly! He thus grasps and cries, and gazes, because he no longer fears to waken by any sound he can utter – by any movement he can make. He thought his love slept sweetly: he finds she is stone dead.

I looked with timorous joy towards a stately house: I saw a blackened ruin.

No need to cower behind a gatepost, indeed! – to peep up at chamber lattices, fearing life was astir behind them! No need to listen for doors opening – to fancy steps on the pavement or the gravel-walk! The lawn, the grounds were trodden and waste: the portal yawned void. The front was, as I had once seen it in a dream, but a shell-like wall, very high and very fragile-looking, perforated with paneless windows: no roof, no battlements, no chimneys – all had crashed in.

And there was the silence of death about it: the solitude of a lonesome wild. No wonder that letters addressed to people here had never received an answer: as well despatch epistles to a vault in a church aisle. The grim blackness of the stones told by what fate the Hall had fallen – by conflagration: but how kindled? What story belonged to this disaster? What loss, besides mortar and marble and woodwork had followed upon it? Had life been wrecked as well as property? If

so, whose? Dreadful question: there was no one here to answer it – not even dumb sign, mute token.

In wandering round the shattered walls and through the devastated interior, I gathered evidence that the calamity was not of late occurrence. Winter snows, I thought, had drifted through that void arch, winter rains beaten in at those hollow casements; for, amidst the drenched piles of rubbish, spring had cherished vegetation: grass and weed grew here and there between the stones and fallen rafters. And oh! where meantime was the hapless owner of this wreck? In what land? Under what auspices? My eye involuntarily wandered to the grey church tower near the gates, and I asked, 'Is he with Damer de Rochester, sharing the shelter of his narrow marble house?'

Some answer must be had to these questions. I could find it nowhere but at the inn, and thither, ere long, I returned. The host himself brought my breakfast into the parlour. I requested him to shut the door and sit down: I had some questions to ask him. But when he complied, I scarcely knew how to begin, such horror had I of the possible answers. And yet the spectacle of desolation I had just left prepared me in a measure for a tale of misery. The host was a respectable-looking, middle-aged man.

'You know Thornfield Hall, of course?' I managed to say at last.

'Yes, ma'am; I lived there once.'

'Did you?' Not in my time, I thought: you are a stranger to me.

'I was the late Mr Rochester's butler,' he added.

The late! I seem to have received, with full force, the blow I had been trying to evade.

'The late!' I gasped. 'Is he dead?'

'I mean the present gentleman, Mr Edward's father,' he explained. I breathed again: my blood resumed its flow. Fully assured by these words that Mr Edward – *my* Mr Rochester (God bless him, wherever he was!) – was at least alive: was, in short, 'the present gentleman'. Gladdening words! It seemed I could hear all that was to come – whatever the disclosures might be – with comparative tranquillity. Since he was not in the grave, I could bear, I thought, to learn that he was at the Antipodes.

'Is Mr Rochester living at Thornfield Hall now?' I asked, knowing, of course, what the answer would be, but yet desirous of deferring the direct question as to where he really was.

'No, ma'am – oh, no! No one is living there. I suppose you are a stranger in these parts, or you would have heard what happened last autumn, Thornfield Hall is quite a ruin: it was burnt down just about harvest-time. A dreadful calamity! such an immense quantity of valuable property destroyed: hardly any of the furniture could be saved. The fire broke out at dead of night, and before the engines arrived from Millcote, the building was one mass of flame. It was a terrible spectacle: I witnessed it myself.'

'At dead of night!' I muttered. Yes, that was ever the hour of fatality at Thornfield. 'Was it known how it originated?' I demanded.

'They guessed, ma'am: they guessed. Indeed, I should say it was ascertained

beyond a doubt. You are not perhaps aware,' he continued, edging his chair a little nearer the table, and speaking low, 'that there was a lady – a – a lunatic, kept in the house?'

'I have heard something of it.'

'She was kept in very close confinement, ma'am; people even for some years was not absolutely certain of her existence. No one saw her: they only knew by rumour that such a person was at the Hall; and who or what she was it was difficult to conjecture. They said Mr Edward had brought her from abroad, and some believed she had been his mistress. But a queer thing happened a year since – a very queer thing.'

I feared now to hear my own story. I endeavoured to recall him to the main fact.

'And this lady?'

'This lady, ma'am,' he answered, 'turned out to be Mr Rochester's wife! The discovery was brought about in the strangest way. There was a young lady, a governess at the Hall, that Mr Rochester fell in – '

'But the fire,' I suggested.

'I'm coming to that, ma'am – that Mr Edward fell in love with. The servants say they never saw anybody so much in love as he was: he was after her continually. They used to watch him – servants will, you know, ma'am – and he set store on her past everything: for all, nobody but him thought her so very handsome. She was a little small thing, they say, almost like a child. I never saw her myself; but I've heard Leah the housemaid, tell of her. Leah liked her well enough. Mr Rochester was about forty, and this governess not twenty; and you see, when gentlemen of his age fall in love with girls, they are often like as if they were bewitched. Well, he would marry her.'

'You shall tell me this part of the story another time,' I said; 'but now I have a particular reason for wishing to hear all about the fire. Was it suspected that this lunatic, Mrs Rochester, had any hand in it?'

'You've hit it, ma'am: it's quite certain that it was her, and nobody but her, that set it going. She had a woman to take care of her called Mrs Poole – an able woman in her line, and very trustworthy, but for one fault – a fault common to a deal of them nurses and matrons – *she kept a private bottle of gin by her*, and now and then took a drop over-much. It is excusable, for she had a hard life of it: but still it was dangerous; for when Mrs Poole was fast asleep after the gin and water, the mad lady, who was as cunning as a witch, would take the keys out of her pocket, let herself out of her chamber, and go roaming about the house, doing any wild mischief that came into her head. They say she had nearly burnt her husband in his bed once: but I don't know about that. However, on this night, she set fire first to the hangings of the room next her own, and then she got down to a lower storey, and made her way to the chamber that had been the governess's – (she was like as if she knew somehow how matters had gone on, and had a spite at her) – and she kindled the bed there; but there was nobody sleeping in it, fortunately. The governess had run away two months before; and for all Mr Rochester sought her as if she had been the most precious thing he

had in the world, he never could hear a word of her; and he grew savage – quite savage on his disappointment: he never was a wild man, but he got dangerous after he lost her. He would be alone, too. He sent Mrs Fairfax, the housekeeper, away to her friends at a distance; but he did it handsomely, for he settled an annuity on her for life: and she deserved it – she was a very good woman. Miss Adèle, a ward he had, was put to school. He broke off acquaintance with all the gentry, and shut himself up like a hermit at the Hall.'

'What! did he not leave England?'

'Leave England? Bless you, no! He would not cross the door-stones of the house, except at night, when he walked just like a ghost about the grounds and in the orchard as if he had lost his senses – which it is my opinion he had; for a more spirited, bolder, keener gentleman than he was before that midge of a governess crossed him, you never saw, ma'am. He was not a man given to wine, or cards, or racing, as some are, and he was not so very handsome; but he had a courage and a will of his own, if ever man had. I knew him from a boy, you see: and for my part, I have often wished that Miss Eyre had been sunk in the sea before she came to Thornfield Hall.'

'Then Mr Rochester was at home when the fire broke out?'

'Yes, indeed was he; and he went up to the attics when all was burning above and below, and got the servants out of their beds and helped them down himself, and went back to get his mad wife out of her cell. And then they called out to him that she was on the roof, where she was standing, waving her arms, above the battlements, and shouting out till they could hear her a mile off: I saw her and heard her with my own eyes. She was a big woman, and had long black hair: we could see it streaming against the flames as she stood. I witnessed, and several more witnessed, Mr Rochester ascend through the skylight on to the roof; we heard him call "Bertha!" We saw him approach her; and then, ma'am, she yelled and gave a spring, and the next minute she lay smashed on the pavement.'

'Dead?'

'Dead! Ay, dead as the stones on which her brains and blood were scattered.'

'Good God!'

'You may well say so, ma'am: it was frightful!'

He shuddered.

'And afterwards?' I urged.

'Well, ma'am, afterwards the house was burnt to the ground: there are only some bits of walls standing now.'

'Were any other lives lost?'

'No – perhaps it would have been better if there had.'

'What do you mean?'

'Poor Mr Edward!' he ejaculated, 'I little thought ever to have seen it! Some say it was a just judgement on him for keeping his first marriage secret, and wanting to take another wife while he had one living: but I pity him, for my part.'

'You said he was alive?' I exclaimed.

'Yes, yes: he is alive; but many think he had better be dead.'

'Why? How?' My blood was again running cold. 'Where is he?' I demanded. 'Is he in England?'

'Ay – ay – he's in England; he can't get out of England, I fancy – he's a fixture now.'

What agony was this! And the man seemed resolved to protract it.

'He is stone-blind,' he said at last. 'Yes, he is stone-blind, is Mr Edward.'

I had dreaded worse. I had dreaded he was mad. I summoned strength to ask what had caused this calamity.

'It was all his own courage, and a body may say, his kindness, in a way, ma'am: he wouldn't leave the house till everyone else was out before him. As he came down the great staircase at last, after Mrs Rochester had flung herself from the battlements, there was a great crash – all fell. He was taken out from under the ruins, alive, but sadly hurt: a beam had fallen in such a way as to protect him partly; but one eye was knocked out, and one hand so crushed that Mr Carter, the surgeon, had to amputate it directly. The other eye inflamed: he lost the sight of that also. He is now helpless, indeed – blind and a cripple.'

'Where is he? Where does he now live?'

'At Ferndean, a manor-house on a farm he has, about thirty miles off: quite a desolate spot.'

'Who is with him?'

'Old John and his wife: he would have none else. He is quite broken down, they say.'

'Have you any sort of conveyance?'

'We have a chaise, ma'am, a very handsome chaise.'

'Let it be got ready instantly; and if your post-boy can drive me to Ferndean before dark this day, I'll pay both you and him twice the hire you usually demand.'

## *Chapter 37*

The manor-house of Ferndean was a building of considerable antiquity, moderate size, and no architectural pretensions, deep buried in a wood. I had heard of it before. Mr Rochester often spoke of it, and sometimes went there. His father had purchased the estate for the sake of the game covers. He would have let the house, but could find no tenant, in consequence of its ineligible and insalubrious site. Ferndean then remained uninhabited and unfurnished, with the exception of some two or three rooms fitted up for the accommodation of the squire when he went there in the season to shoot.

To this house I came just ere dark on an evening marked by the characteristics of sad sky, cold gale, and continued small penetrating rain. The last mile I performed on foot, having dismissed the chaise and driver with the double remuneration I had promised. Even when within a very short distance of the manor-house, you could see nothing of it, so thick and dark grew the timber of the gloomy wood about it. Iron gates between granite pillars showed me where

to enter, and passing through them, I found myself at once in the twilight of close-ranked trees. There was a grass-grown track descending the forest aisle between hoar and knotty shafts and under branched arches. I followed it, expecting soon to reach the dwelling; but it stretched on and on, it wound far and farther: no sign of habitation or grounds was visible.

I thought I had taken a wrong direction and lost my way. The darkness of natural as well as of sylvan dusk gathered over me. I looked round in search of another road. There was none: all was interwoven stem, columnar trunk, dense summer foliage – no opening anywhere.

I proceeded: at last my way opened, the trees thinned a little; presently I beheld a railing, then the house scarce, by this dim light, distinguishable from the trees, so dank and green were its decaying walls. Entering a portal, fastened only by a latch, I stood amidst a space of enclosed ground, from which the wood swept away in a semicircle. There were no flowers, no garden-beds; only a broad gravel-walk girdling a grass-plat, and this set in the heavy frame of the forest. The house presented two pointed gables in its front; the windows were latticed and narrow: the front door was narrow too, one step led up to it. The whole looked, as the host of the Rochester Arms had said, 'quite a desolate spot.' It was as still as a church on a weekday: the pattering rain on the forest leaves was the only sound audible in its vicinage.

'Can there be life here?' I asked.

Yes, life of some kind there was; for I heard a movement – that narrow front-door was unclosing, and some shape was about to issue from the grange.

It opened slowly: a figure came out into the twilight and stood on the step; a man without a hat: he stretched forth his hand as if to feel whether it rained. Dusk as it was, I had recognised him – it was my master, Edward Fairfax Rochester, and no other.

I stayed my step, almost my breath, and stood to watch him – to examine him, myself unseen, and alas! to him invisible. It was a sudden meeting, and one in which rapture was kept well in check by pain. I had no difficulty in restraining my voice from exclamation, my step from hasty advance.

His form was of the same strong and stalwart contour as ever: his port was still erect, his hair was still raven black; nor were his features altered or sunk: not in one year's space, by any sorrow, could his athletic strength be quelled or his vigorous prime blighted. But in his countenance I saw a change: that looked desperate and brooding – that reminded me of some wronged and fettered wild beast or bird, dangerous to approach in his sullen woe. The caged eagle, whose gold-ringed eyes cruelty has extinguished, might look as looked that sightless Samson.

And, reader, do you think I feared him in his blind ferocity? – if you do, you little know me. A soft hope blent with my sorrow that soon I should dare to drop a kiss on that brow of rock, and on those lips so sternly sealed beneath it: but not yet. I would not accost him yet.

He descended the one step, and advanced slowly and gropingly towards the grass-plat. Where was his daring stride now? Then he paused, as if he knew not

which way to turn. He lifted his hand and opened his eyelids; gazed blank, and with a straining effort, on the sky, and toward the amphitheatre of trees: one saw that all to him was void darkness. He stretched his right hand (the left arm, the mutilated one, he kept hidden in his bosom); he seemed to wish by touch to gain an idea of what lay around him: he met but vacancy still; for the trees were some yards off where he stood. He relinquished the endeavour, folded his arms, and stood quiet and mute in the rain, now falling fast on his uncovered head. At this moment John approached him from some quarter.

'Will you take my arm, sir?' he said; 'there is a heavy shower coming on: had you not better go in?'

'Let me alone,' was the answer.

John withdrew without having observed me. Mr Rochester now tried to walk about: vainly, all was too uncertain. He groped his way back to the house, and, re-entering it, closed the door.

I now drew near and knocked: John's wife opened for me. 'Mary,' I said, 'how are you?'

She started as if she had seen a ghost: I calmed her. To her hurried 'Is it really you, miss, come at this late hour to this lonely place?' I answered by taking her hand; and then I followed her into the kitchen, where John now sat by a good fire. I explained to them, in a few words, that I had heard all which had happened since I left Thornfield, and that I was come to see Mr Rochester. I asked John to go down to the turnpike-house, where I had dismissed the chaise, and bring my trunk, which I had left there: and then, while I removed my bonnet and shawl, I questioned Mary as to whether I could be accommodated at the Manor House for the night; and finding that arrangements to that effect, though difficult, would not be impossible, I informed her I should stay. Just at this moment the parlour-bell rang.

'When you go in,' said I, 'tell your master that a person wishes to speak to him, but do not give my name.'

'I don't think he will see you,' she answered; 'he refuses everybody.'

When she returned, I enquired what he had said.

'You are to send in your name and your business,' she replied. She then proceeded to fill a glass with water, and place it on a tray, together with candles.

'Is that what he rang for?' I asked.

'Yes: he always has candles brought in at dark, though he is blind.'

'Give the tray to me; I will carry it in.'

I took it from her hand: she pointed me out the parlour door. The tray shook as I held it; the water spilt from the glass; my heart struck my ribs loud and fast. Mary opened the door for me, and shut it behind me.

This parlour looked gloomy: a neglected handful of fire burnt low in the grate; and, leaning over it, with his head supported against the high, old-fashioned mantelpiece, appeared the blind tenant of the room. His old dog, Pilot, lay on one side, removed out of the way, and coiled up as if afraid of being inadvertently trodden upon. Pilot pricked up his ears when I came in: then he jumped up with a yelp and a whine, and bounded towards me: he almost knocked the tray from my

hands. I set it on the table; then patted him, and said softly, 'Lie down!' Mr Rochester turned mechanically to *see* what the commotion was: but as he *saw* nothing, he returned and sighed.

'Give me the water, Mary,' he said.

I approached him with the now only half-filled glass; Pilot followed me, still excited.

'What is the matter?' he enquired.

'Down, Pilot!' I again said. He checked the water on its way to his lips, and seemed to listen: he drank, and put the glass down. 'This is you, Mary, is it not?'

'Mary is in the kitchen,' I answered.

He put out his hand with a quick gesture, but not seeing where I stood, he did not touch me. 'Who is this? Who is this?' he demanded, trying, as it seemed, to *see* with those sightless eyes – unavailing and distressing attempt! 'Answer me – speak again!' he ordered, imperiously and aloud.

'Will you have a little more water, sir? I spilt half of what was in the glass,' I said.

'*Who* is it? *What* is it? Who speaks?'

'Pilot knows me, and John and Mary know I am here. I came only this evening,' I answered.

'Great God! – what delusion has come over me? What sweet madness has seized me?'

'No delusion – no madness: your mind, sir, is too strong for delusion, your health too sound for frenzy.'

'And where is the speaker? Is it only a voice? Oh! I *cannot* see, but I must feel, or my heart will stop and my brain burst. Whatever – whoever you are – be perceptible to the touch or I cannot live!'

He groped; I arrested his wandering hand, and prisoned it in both mine.

'Her very fingers!' he cried; 'her small, slight fingers! If so there must be more of her.'

The muscular hand broke from my custody; my arm was seized, my shoulder – neck – waist – I was entwined and gathered to him.

'Is it Jane? *What* is it? This is her shape – this her size – '

'And this her voice,' I added. 'She is all here: her heart, too. God bless you, sir! I am glad to be so near you again.'

'Jane Eyre! – Jane Eyre,' was all he said.

'My dear master,' I answered, 'I am Jane Eyre: I have found you out – I am come back to you.'

'In truth? – in the flesh? My living Jane?'

'You touch me, sir, you hold me, and fast enough: I am not cold like a corpse, nor vacant like air, am I?'

'My living darling! These are certainly her limbs, and these her features; but I cannot be so blest, after all my misery. It is a dream; such dreams as I have had at night when I have clasped her once more to my heart, as I do now; and kissed her, as thus – and felt that she loved me, and trusted that she would not leave me.'

'Which I never will, sir, from this day.'

'Never will, says the vision? But I always woke and found it an empty mockery; and I was desolate and abandoned – my life dark, lonely, hopeless – my soul athirst and forbidden to drink – my heart famished and never to be fed. Gentle, soft dream, nestling in my arms now, you will fly, too, as your sisters have all fled before you: but kiss me before you go – embrace me, Jane.'

'There, sir – and there!'

I pressed my lips to his once brilliant and now rayless eyes – I swept his hair from his brow, and kissed that too. He suddenly seemed to arouse himself: the conviction of the reality of all this seized him.

'It is you – is it, Jane? You are come back to me then?'

'I am.'

'And you do not lie dead in some ditch under some stream? And you are not a pining outcast amongst strangers?'

'No, sir! I am an independent woman now.'

'Independent! What do you mean, Jane?'

'My uncle in Madeira is dead, and he left me five thousand pounds.'

'Ah! this is practical – this is real!' he cried: 'I should never dream that. Besides, there is that peculiar voice of hers, so animating and piquant, as well as soft: it cheers my withered heart; it puts life into it. What, Janet! Are you an independent woman? A rich woman?'

'Quite rich, sir. If you won't let me live with you, I can build a house of my own close up to your door, and you may come and sit in my parlour when you want company of an evening.'

'But as you are rich, Jane, you have now, no doubt, friends who will look after you, and not suffer you to devote yourself to a blind lameter like me?'

'I told you I am independent, sir, as well as rich: I am my own mistress.'

'And you will stay with me?'

'Certainly – unless you object. I will be your neighbour, your nurse, your housekeeper. I find you lonely: I will be your companion – to read to you, to walk with you, to sit with you, to wait on you, to be eyes and hands to you. Cease to look so melancholy, my dear master; you shall not be left desolate, so long as I live.'

He replied not: he seemed serious – abstracted; he sighed; he half-opened his lips as if to speak: he closed them again. I felt a little embarrassed. Perhaps I had too rashly overleaped conventionalities; and he, like St John, saw impropriety in my inconsiderateness. I had indeed made my proposal from the idea that he wished and would ask me to be his wife: an expectation, not the less certain because unexpressed, had buoyed me up, that he would claim me at once as his own. But no hint to that effect escaping him and his countenance becoming more overcast, I suddenly remembered that I might have been all wrong, and was perhaps playing the fool unwittingly; and I began gently to withdraw myself from his arms – but he eagerly snatched me closer.

'No – no – Jane; you must not go. No – I have touched you, heard you, felt the comfort of your presence – the sweetness of your consolation: I cannot give up these joys. I have little left in myself – I must have you. The world may laugh – may call me absurd, selfish – but it does not signify. My very soul

demands you: it will be satisfied, or it will take deadly vengeance on its frame.'

'Well, sir, I will stay with you: I have said so.'

'Yes – but you understand one thing by staying with me; and I understand another. You, perhaps, could make up your mind to be about my hand and chair – to wait on me as a kind little nurse (for you have an affectionate heart and a generous spirit, which prompt you to make sacrifices for those you pity), and that ought to suffice for me no doubt. I suppose I should now entertain none but fatherly feelings for you: do you think so? Come – tell me.'

'I will think what you like, sir: I am content to be only your nurse, if you think it better.'

'But you cannot always be my nurse, Janet: you are young – you must marry one day.'

'I don't care about being married.'

'You should care, Janet: if I were what I once was, I would try to make you care – but – a sightless block!'

He relapsed again into gloom. I, on the contrary, became more cheerful, and took fresh courage: these last words gave me an insight as to where the difficulty lay; and as it was no difficulty with me, I felt quite relieved from my previous embarrassment. I resumed a livelier vein of conversation.

'It is time someone undertook to rehumanise you,' said I, parting his thick and long uncut locks; 'for I see you are being metamorphosed into a lion, or something of that sort. You have a "faux air" of Nebuchadnezzar in the fields about you, that is certain: your hair reminds me of eagles' feathers; whether your nails are grown like birds' claws or not, I have not yet noticed.'

'On this arm, I have neither hand nor nails,' he said, drawing the mutilated limb from his breast, and showing it to me. 'It is a mere stump – a ghastly sight! Don't you think so, Jane?'

'It is a pity to see it; and a pity to see your eyes – and the scar of fire on your forehead: and the worst of it is, one is in danger of loving you too well for all this; and making too much of you.'

'I thought you would be revolted, Jane, when you saw my arm, and my cicatrised visage.'

'Did you? Don't tell me so – lest I should say something disparaging to your judgement. Now, let me leave you an instant, to make a better fire, and have the hearth swept up. Can you tell when there is a good fire?'

'Yes; with the right eye I see a glow – a ruddy haze.'

'And you see the candles?'

'Very dimly – each is a luminous cloud.'

'Can you see me?'

'No, my fairy: but I am only too thankful to hear and feel you.'

'When do you take supper?'

'I never take supper.'

'But you shall have some tonight. I am hungry: so are you, I dare say, only you forget.'

Summoning Mary, I soon had the room in more cheerful order: I prepared

him, likewise, a comfortable repast. My spirits were excited, and with pleasure and ease I talked to him during supper, and for a long time after. There was no harassing restraint, no repressing of glee and vivacity with him; for with him I was at perfect ease, because I knew I suited him; all I said or did seemed either to console or revive him. Delightful consciousness! It brought to life and light my whole nature: in his presence I thoroughly lived; and he lived in mine. Blind as he was, smiles played over his face, Joy dawned on his forehead: his lineaments softened and warmed.

After supper, he began to ask me many questions, of where I had been, what I had been doing, how I had found him out; but I gave him only very partial replies: it was too late to enter into particulars that night. Besides, I wished to touch no deep-thrilling chord – to open no fresh well of emotion in his heart: my sole present aim was to cheer him. Cheered, as I have said, he was: and yet but by fits. If a moment's silence broke the conversation, he would turn restless, touch me, then say, 'Jane.'

'You are altogether a human being, Jane? You are certain of that?'

'I conscientiously believe so, Mr Rochester.'

'Yet how, on this dark and doleful evening, could you so suddenly rise on my lone hearth? I stretched my hand to take a glass of water from a hireling, and it was given me by you: I asked a question, expecting John's wife to answer me, and your voice spoke at my ear.'

'Because I had come in, in Mary's stead, with the tray.'

'And there is enchantment in the very hour I am now spending with you. Who can tell what a dark, dreary, hopeless life I have dragged on for months past? Doing nothing, expecting nothing; merging night in day; feeling but the sensation of cold when I let the fire go out, of hunger when I forgot to eat: and then a ceaseless sorrow, and, at times, a very delirium of desire to behold my Jane again. Yes: for her restoration I longed, far more than for that of my lost sight. How can it be that Jane is with me, and says she loves me? Will she not depart as suddenly as she came? Tomorrow, I fear I shall find her no more.'

A commonplace, practical reply, out of the train of his own disturbed ideas, was, I was sure, the best and most reassuring for him in this frame of mind. I passed my finger over his eyebrows, and remarked that they were scorched, and that I would apply something which would make them grow as broad and black as ever.

'Where is the use of doing me good in any way, beneficent spirit, when, at some fatal moment, you will again desert me – passing like a shadow, whither and how to me unknown, and for me remaining afterwards undiscoverable?'

'Have you a pocket-comb about you, sir?'

'What for, Jane?'

'Just to comb out this shaggy black mane. I find you rather alarming, when I examine you close at hand: you talk of my being a fairy, but I am sure, you are more like a brownie.'

'Am I hideous, Jane?'

'Very, sir: you always were, you know.'

'Humph! The wickedness has not been taken out of you, wherever you have sojourned.'

'Yet I have been with good people; far better than you: a hundred times better people; possessed of ideas and views you never entertained in your life: quite more refined and exalted.'

'Who the deuce have you been with?'

'If you twist in that way you will make me pull the hair out of your head; and then I think you will cease to entertain doubts of my substantiality.'

'Who have you been with, Jane?'

'You shall not get it out of me tonight, sir; you must wait till tomorrow; to leave my tale half told, will, you know, be a sort of security that I shall appear at your breakfast table to finish it. By the bye, I must mind not to rise on your hearth with only a glass of water then: I must bring an egg at the least, to say nothing of fried ham.'

'You mocking changeling – fairy-born and human-bred! You make me feel as I have not felt these twelve months. If Saul could have had you for his David, the evil spirit would have been exorcised without the aid of the harp.'

'There, sir, you are redd up and made decent. Now I'll leave you: I have been travelling these last three days, and I believe I am tired. Good-night.'

'Just one word, Jane: were there only ladies in the house where you have been?'

I laughed and made my escape, still laughing as I ran upstairs. 'A good idea!' I thought with glee. 'I see I have the means of fretting him out of his melancholy for some time to come.'

Very early the next morning I heard him up and astir, wandering from one room to another. As soon as Mary came down I heard the question: 'Is Miss Eyre here?' Then: 'Which room did you put her into? Was it dry? Is she up? Go and ask if she wants anything; and when she will come down.'

I came down as soon as I thought there was a prospect of breakfast. Entering the room very softly, I had a view of him before he discovered my presence. It was mournful, indeed, to witness the subjugation of that vigorous spirit to a corporeal infirmity. He sat in his chair – still, but not at rest: expectant evidently; the lines of now habitual sadness marking his strong features. His countenance reminded one of a lamp quenched, waiting to be re-lit – and alas! it was not himself that could now kindle the lustre of animated expression: he was dependent on another for that office! I had meant to be gay and careless, but the powerlessness of the strong man touched my heart to the quick: still I accosted him with what vivacity I could.

'It is a bright, sunny morning, sir,' I said. 'The rain is over and gone, and there is a tender shining after it: you shall have a walk soon.'

I had wakened the glow: his features beamed.

'Oh, you are indeed there, my skylark! Come to me. You are not gone: not vanished? I heard one of your kind an hour ago, singing high over the wood: but its song had no music for me, any more than the rising sun had rays. All the melody on earth is concentrated in my Jane's tongue to my ear (I am glad it is not naturally a silent one): all the sunshine I can feel is in her presence.'

The water stood in my eyes to hear this avowal of his dependence; just as if a royal eagle, chained to a perch, should be forced to entreat a sparrow to become its purveyor. But I would not be lachrymose: I dashed off the salt drops, and busied myself with preparing breakfast.

Most of the morning was spent in the open air. I led him out of the wet and wild wood into some cheerful fields: I described to him how brilliantly green they were; how the flowers and hedges looked refreshed; how sparklingly blue was the sky. I sought a seat for him in a hidden and lovely spot, a dry stump of a tree; nor did I refuse to let him, when seated, place me on his knee. Why should I, when both he and I were happier near than apart? Pilot lay beside us: all was quiet. He broke out suddenly while clasping me in his arms – 'Cruel, cruel deserter! Oh, Jane, what did I feel when I discovered you had fled from Thornfield, and when I could nowhere find you; and, after examining your apartment, ascertained that you had taken no money, nor anything which could serve as an equivalent! A pearl necklace I had given you lay untouched in its little casket; your trunks were left corded and locked as they had been prepared for the bridal tour. What could my darling do, I asked, left destitute and penniless? And what did she do? Let me hear now.' Thus urged, I began the narrative of my experience for the last year. I softened considerably what related to the three days of wandering and starvation, because to have told him all would have been to inflict unnecessary pain: the little I did say lacerated his faithful heart deeper than I wished.

I should not have left him thus, he said, without any means of making my way: I should have told him my intention. I should have confided in him: he would never have forced me to be his mistress. Violent as he had seemed in his despair, he, in truth, loved me far too well and too tenderly to constitute himself my tyrant: he would have given me half his fortune, without demanding so much as a kiss in return, rather that I should have flung myself friendless on the wide world. I had endured, he was certain, more than I had confessed to him.

'Well, whatever my sufferings had been, they were very short,' I answered: and then I proceeded to tell him how I had been received at Moor House; how I had obtained the office of schoolmistress, etc. The accession of fortune, the discovery of my relations, followed in due order. Of course, St John Rivers' name came in frequently in the progress of my tale. When I had done, that name was immediately taken up.

'This St John, then, is your cousin?'

'Yes.'

'You have spoken of him often: do you like him?'

'He was a very good man, sir; I could not help liking him.'

'A good man. Does that mean a respectable well-conducted man of fifty? Or what does it mean?'

'St John was only twenty-nine, sir.'

' "*Jeune encore*", as the French say. Is he a person of low stature, phlegmatic, and plain. A person whose goodness consists rather in his guiltlessness of vice, than in his prowess in virtue.'

'He is untiringly active. Great and exalted deeds are what he lives to perform.'

'But his brain? That is probably rather soft? He means well: but you shrug your shoulders to hear him talk?'

'He talks little, sir: what he does say is ever to the point. His brain is first-rate, I should think not impressible, but vigorous.'

'Is he an able man, then?'

'Truly able.'

'A thoroughly educated man?'

'St John is an accomplished and profound scholar.'

'His manners, I think, you said are not to your taste? – priggish and parsonic?'

'I never mentioned his manners; but, unless I had a very bad taste, they must suit it; they are polished, calm, and gentlemanlike.'

'His appearance, I forget what description you gave of his appearance; a sort of raw curate, half strangled with his white neckcloth, and stilted up on his thick-soled high-lows, eh?'

'St John dresses well. He is a handsome man: tall, fair, with blue eyes, and a Grecian profile.'

(Aside.) 'Damn him!' – (To me.) 'Did you like him, Jane?'

'Yes, Mr Rochester, I liked him: but you asked me that before.'

I perceived, of course, the drift of my interlocutor. Jealousy had got hold of him: she stung him; but the sting was salutary: it gave him respite from the gnawing fang of melancholy. I would not, therefore, immediately charm the snake.

'Perhaps you would rather not sit any longer on my knee, Miss Eyre?' was the next somewhat unexpected observation.

'Why not, Mr Rochester?'

'The picture you have just drawn is suggestive of a rather too overwhelming contrast. Your words have delineated very prettily a graceful Apollo: he is present to your imagination, tall, fair, blue-eyed, and with a Grecian profile. Your eyes dwell on a Vulcan, a real blacksmith, brown, broad-shouldered: and blind and lame into the bargain.'

'I never thought of it, before; but you certainly are rather like Vulcan, sir.'

'Well, you can leave me, ma'am: but before you go' (and he retained me by a firmer grasp than ever), 'you will be pleased just to answer me a question or two.' He paused.

'What questions, Mr Rochester?'

Then followed this cross examination.

'St John made you schoolmistress of Morton before he knew you were his cousin?'

'Yes.'

'You would often see him? He would visit the school sometimes?'

'Daily.'

'He would approve of your plans, Jane? I know they would be clever, for you are a talented creature!'

'He approved of them – yes.'

'He would discover many things in you he could not have expected to find? Some of your accomplishments are not ordinary.'

'I don't know about that.'

'You had a little cottage near the school, you say: did he ever come there to see you?'

'Now and then.'

'Of an evening?'

'Once or twice.'

A pause.

'How long did you reside with him and his sisters after the cousinship was discovered?'

'Five months.'

'Did Rivers spend much time with the ladies of his family?'

'Yes; the back parlour was both his study and ours: he sat near the window, and we by the table.'

'Did he study much?'

'A good deal.'

'What?'

'Hindustani.'

'And what did you do meantime?'

'I learnt German, at first.'

'Did he teach you?'

'He did not understand German.'

'Did he teach you nothing?'

'A little Hindustani.'

'Rivers taught you Hindustani?'

'Yes, sir.'

'And his sisters also?'

'No.'

'Only you?'

'Only me.'

'Did you ask to learn?'

'No.'

'He wished to teach you?'

'Yes.'

A second pause.

'Why did he wish it? Of what use could Hindustani be to you?'

'He intended me to go with him to India.'

'Ah! here I reach the root of the matter. He wanted you to marry him?'

'He asked me to marry him.'

'That is a fiction – an impudent invention to vex me.'

'I beg your pardon, it is the literal truth: he asked me more than once, and was as stiff about urging his point as ever you could be.'

'Miss Eyre, I repeat it, you can leave me. How often am I to say the same

thing? Why do you remain pertinaciously perched on my knee, when I have given you notice to quit?'

'Because I am comfortable there.'

'No, Jane, you are not comfortable there, because your heart is not with me: it is with this cousin – this St John. Oh, till this moment, I thought my little Jane was all mine! I had a belief she loved me even when she left me: that was an atom of sweet in much bitter. Long as we have been parted, hot tears as I have wept over our separation, I never thought that while I was mourning her, she was loving another! But it is useless grieving. Jane, leave me: go and marry Rivers.'

'Shake me off, then, sir, push me away, for I'll not leave you of my own accord.'

'Jane, I ever like your tone of voice: it still renews hope, it sounds so truthful. When I hear it, it carries me back a year. I forget that you have formed a new tie, But I am not a fool – go – '

'Where must I go, sir?'

'Your own way – with the husband you have chosen.'

'Who is that?'

'You know – this St John Rivers.'

'He is not my husband, nor ever will be. He does not love me: I do not love him. He loves (as he *can* love, and that is not as you love) a beautiful young lady called Rosamond. He wanted to marry me only because he thought I should make a suitable missionary's wife, which she would not have done. He is good and great, but severe; and, for me, cold as an iceberg. He is not like you, sir: I am not happy at his side, nor near him, nor with him. He has no indulgence for me – no fondness. He sees nothing attractive in me; not even youth only a few useful mental points – Then I must leave you, sir, to go to him?'

I shuddered involuntarily, and clung instinctively closer to my blind but beloved master. He smiled.

'What, Jane! Is this true? Is such really the state of matters between you and Rivers?'

'Absolutely, sir! Oh, you need not be jealous! I wanted to tease you a little to make you less sad: I thought anger would be better than grief. But if you wish me to love you, could you but see how much I *do* love you, you would be proud and content. All my heart is yours, sir: it belongs to you; and with you it would remain, were fate to exile the rest of me from your presence for ever.'

Again, as he kissed me, painful thoughts darkened his aspect.

'My seared vision! My crippled strength!' he murmured regretfully.

I caressed, in order to soothe him. I knew of what he was thinking, and wanted to speak for him, but dared not. As he turned aside his face a minute, I saw a tear slide from under the sealed eyelid, and trickle down the manly cheek. My heart swelled.

'I am no better than the old lightning-struck chestnut-tree in Thornfield orchard,' he remarked ere long. 'And what right would that ruin have to bid a budding woodbine cover its decay with freshness?'

'You are no ruin, sir – no lightning-struck tree: you are green and vigorous. Plants will grow about your roots, whether you ask them or not, because they take delight in your bountiful shadow, and as they grow they will lean towards you, and wind round you, because your strength offers them so safe a prop.'

Again he smiled: I gave him comfort.

'You speak of friends, Jane?' he asked.

'Yes, of friends,' I answered rather hesitatingly: for I knew I meant more than friends, but could not tell what other word to employ. He helped me.

'Ah! Jane. But I want a wife.'

'Do you, sir?'

'Yes: is it news to you?'

'Of course: you said nothing about it before.'

'Is it unwelcome news?'

'That depends on circumstances, sir – on your choice.'

'Which you shall make for me, Jane. I will abide by your decision.'

'Choose then, sir – her *who loves you best.*'

'I will at least choose – *her I love best.* Jane, will you marry me?'

'Yes, sir.'

'A poor blind man, whom you will have to lead about by the hand?'

'Yes, sir.'

'A crippled man, twenty years older than you, whom you will have to wait on?'

'Yes, sir.'

'Truly, Jane?'

'Most truly, sir.'

'Oh! my darling! God bless you and reward you!'

'Mr Rochester, if ever I did a good deed in my life – if ever I thought a good thought – if ever I prayed a sincere and blameless prayer – if ever I wished a righteous wish, I am rewarded now. To be your wife is, for me, to be as happy as I can be on earth.'

'Because you delight in sacrifice.'

'Sacrifice! What do I sacrifice? Famine for food, expectation for content. To be privileged to put my arms round what I value – to press my lips to what I love – to repose on what I trust: is that to make a sacrifice? If so, then certainly I delight in sacrifice.'

'And to bear with my infirmities, Jane: to overlook my deficiencies.'

'Which are none, sir, to me. I love you better now, when I can really be useful, to you, than I did in your state of proud independence, when you disdained every part but that of the giver and protector.'

'Hitherto I have hated to be helped – to be led: henceforth, I feel I shall hate it no more. I did not like to put my hand into a hireling's, but it is pleasant to feel it circled by Jane's little fingers. I preferred utter loneliness to the constant attendance of servants; but Jane's soft ministry will be a perpetual joy. Jane suits me: do I suit her?'

'To the finest fibre of my nature, sir.'

'The case being so, we have nothing in the world to wait for: we must be married instantly.'

He looked and spoke with eagerness: his old impetuosity was rising.

'We must become one flesh without any delay, Jane: there is but the licence to get – then we marry.'

'Mr Rochester, I have just discovered the sun is far declined from its meridian, and Pilot is actually gone home to his dinner. Let me look at your watch.'

'Fasten it into your girdle, Janet, and keep it henceforward: I have no use for it.'

'It is nearly four o'clock in the afternoon, sir. Don't you feel hungry?'

'The third day from this must be our wedding-day, Jane. Never mind fine clothes and jewels, now: all that is not worth a fillip.'

'The sun has dried up all the raindrops, sir. The breeze is still: it is quite hot.'

'Do you know, Jane, I have your little pearl necklace at this moment fastened round my bronze scrag under my cravat? I have worn it since the day I lost my only treasure, as a memento of her.'

'We will go home through the wood: that will be the shadiest way.'

He pursued his own thoughts without heeding me.

'Jane! you think me, I dare say, an irreligious dog: but my heart swells with gratitude to the beneficent God of this earth just now. He sees not as man sees, but far clearer: judges not as man judges, but far more wisely. I did wrong: I would have sullied my innocent flower – breathed guilt on its purity: the Omnipotent snatched it from me. I, in my stiff-necked rebellion, almost cursed the dispensation: instead of bending to the decree, I defied it. Divine justice pursued its course; disasters came thick on me: I was forced to pass through the valley of the shadow of death. *His* chastisements are mighty; and one smote me which has humbled me for ever. You know I was proud of my strength: but what is it now, when I must give it over to foreign guidance, as a child does its weakness? Of late, Jane – only – only of late – I began to see and acknowledge the hand of God in my doom. I began to experience remorse, repentance; the wish for reconcilement to my Maker. I began sometimes to pray: very brief prayers they were, but very sincere.

'Some days since: nay, I can number them – four; it was last Monday night, a singular mood came over me: one in which grief replaced frenzy – sorrow, sullenness. I had long had the impression that since I could nowhere find you, you must be dead. Late that night – perhaps it might be between eleven and twelve o'clock – ere I retired to my dreary rest, I supplicated God, that, if it seemed good to Him, I might soon be taken from this life, and admitted to that world to come, where there was still hope of rejoining Jane.

'I was in my own room, and sitting by the window, which was open: it soothed me to feel the balmy night-air; though I could see no stars, and only by a vague, luminous haze, knew the presence of a moon. I longed for thee, Janet! Oh, I longed for thee both with soul and flesh! I asked of God, at once in anguish and humility, if I had not been long enough desolate, afflicted, tormented; and might not soon taste bliss and peace once more. That I merited all I endured, I acknowledged – that I could scarcely endure more, I pleaded; and the alpha and

omega of my heart's wishes broke involuntarily from my lips in the words –
"Jane! Jane! Jane!" '

'Did you speak these words aloud?'

'I did, Jane. If any listener had heard me, he would have thought me mad: I
pronounced them with such frantic energy.'

'And it was last Monday night, somewhere near midnight?'

'Yes; but the time is of no consequence: what followed is the strange point.
You will think me superstitious – some superstition I have in my blood, and
always had: nevertheless, this is true – true at least it is that I heard what I now
relate.

'As I exclaimed "Jane! Jane! Jane!" a voice – I cannot tell whence the voice
came, but I know whose voice it was – replied, "I am coming: wait for me;" and a
moment after, went whispering on the wind the words – "Where are you?"

'I'll tell you, if I can, the idea, the picture these words opened to my mind:
yet it is difficult to express what I want to express. Ferndean is buried, as you
see, in a heavy wood, where sound falls dull, and dies unreverberating. "Where
are you?" seemed spoken amongst mountains; for I heard a hill-sent echo
repeat the words. Cooler and fresher at the moment the gale seemed to visit my
brow: I could have deemed that in some wild, lone scene, I and Jane were
meeting. In spirit, I believe we must have met. You no doubt were, at that hour,
in unconscious sleep, Jane: perhaps your soul wandered from its cell to comfort
mine; for those were your accents – as certain as I live – they were yours!'

Reader, it was on Monday night – near midnight – that I too had received the
mysterious summons: those were the very words by which I replied to it. I
listened to Mr Rochester's narrative, but made no disclosure in return. The
coincidence struck me as too awful and inexplicable to be communicated or
discussed. If I told anything, my tale would be such as must necessarily make a
profound impression on the mind of my hearer: and that mind, yet from its
sufferings too prone to gloom, needed not the deeper shade of the supernatural.
I kept these things then, and pondered them in my heart.

'You cannot now wonder,' continued my master, 'that when you rose upon
me so unexpectedly last night, I had difficulty in believing you any other than a
mere voice and vision, something that would melt to silence and annihilation, as
the midnight whisper and mountain echo had melted before. Now, I thank
God! I know it to be otherwise. Yes, I thank God!'

He put me off his knee, rose, and reverently lifting his hat from his brow, and
bending his sightless eyes to the earth, he stood in mute devotion. Only the last
words of the worship were audible.

'I thank my Maker, that, in the midst of judgement, he has remembered
mercy. I humbly entreat my Redeemer to give me strength to lead henceforth a
purer life than I have done hitherto!'

Then he stretched his hand out to be led. I took that dear hand, held it a
moment to my lips, then let it pass round my shoulder: being so much lower of
stature than he, I served both for his prop and guide. We entered the wood, and
wended homeward.

## Chapter 38

### CONCLUSION

Reader, I married him. A quiet wedding we had: he and I, the parson and clerk, were alone present. When we got back from church, I went into the kitchen of the manor-house, where Mary was cooking the dinner and John cleaning the knives, and I said – 'Mary, I have been married to Mr Rochester this morning.' The housekeeper and her husband were both of that decent phlegmatic order of people to whom one may at any time safely communicate a remarkable piece of news without incurring the danger of having one's ears pierced by some shrill ejaculation, and subsequently stunned by a torrent of wordy wonderment. Mary did look up, and she did stare at me: the ladle with which she was basting a pair of chickens roasting at the fire, did for some three minutes hang suspended in air; and for the same space of time John's knives also had rest from the polishing process: but Mary, bending again over the roast, said only – 'Have you, Miss? Well, for sure!'

A short time after she pursued – 'I seed you go out with the master, but I didn't know you were gone to church to be wed;' and she basted away. John, when I turned to him, was grinning from ear to ear.

'I told Mary how it would be,' he said: 'I knew what Mr Edward' (John was an old servant, and had known his master when he was the cadet of the house, therefore, he often gave him his Christian name) – 'I knew what Mr Edward would do; and I was certain he would not wait long neither: and he's done right, for aught I know. I wish you joy, Miss!' and he politely pulled his forelock.

'Thank you, John. Mr Rochester told me to give you and Mary this.' I put into his hand a five-pound note. Without waiting to hear more, I left the kitchen. In passing the door of that sanctum some time after, I caught the words – 'She'll happen do better for him nor ony o' t' grand ladies.' And again, 'If she ben't one o' th' handsomest, she's noan faâl and varry good-natured; and i' his een she's fair beautiful, onybody may see that.'

I wrote to Moor House and to Cambridge immediately, to say what I had done: fully explaining also why I had thus acted. Diana and Mary approved the step unreservedly. Diana announced that she would just give me time to get over the honeymoon, and then she would come and see me.

'She had better not wait till then, Jane,' said Mr Rochester, when I read her letter to him; 'if she does; she will be too late, for our honeymoon will shine our life long: its beams will only fade over your grave or mine.'

How St John received the news, I don't know: he never answered the letter in which I communicated it: yet six months after he wrote to me, without, however, mentioning Mr Rochester's name or alluding to my marriage. His letter was then calm, and, though very serious, kind. He has maintained a regular, though

not frequent, correspondence ever since: he hopes I am happy, and trusts I am not of those who live without God in the world, and only mind earthly things.

You have not quite forgotten little Adèle, have you, reader? I had not; I soon asked and obtained leave of Mr Rochester, to go and see her at the school where he had placed her. Her frantic joy at beholding me again moved me much. She looked pale and thin: she said she was not happy. I found the rules of the establishment were too strict, its course of study too severe for a child of her age: I took her home with me. I meant to become her governess once more, but I soon found this impracticable; my time and cares were now required by another – my husband needed them all. So I sought out a school conducted on a more indulgent system, and near enough to permit of my visiting her often, and bringing her home sometimes. I took care she should never want for anything that could contribute to her comfort: she soon settled in her new abode, became very happy there, and made fair progress in her studies. As she grew up, a sound English education corrected in a great measure her French defects; and when she left school, I found in her a pleasing and obliging companion: docile, good-tempered, and well-principled. By her grateful attention to me and mine, she has long since well repaid any little kindness I ever had it in my power to offer her.

My tale draws to its close: one word respecting my experience of married life, and one brief glance at the fortunes of those whose names have most frequently recurred in this narrative, and I have done.

I have now been married ten years. I know what it is to live entirely for and with what I love best on earth. I hold myself supremely blest – blest beyond what language can express; because I am my husband's life as fully as he is mine. No woman was ever nearer to her mate than I am: ever more absolutely bone of his bone and flesh of his flesh. I know no weariness of my Edward's society: he knows none of mine, any more than we each do of the pulsation of the heart that beats in our separate bosoms; consequently, we are ever together. To be together is for us to be at once as free as in solitude, as gay as in company. We talk, I believe, all day long: to talk to each other is but a more animated and an audible thinking. All my confidence is bestowed on him, all his confidence is devoted to me; we are precisely suited in character – perfect concord is the result.

Mr Rochester continued blind the first two years of our union: perhaps it was that circumstance that drew us so very near – that knit us so very close: for I was then his vision, as I am still his right hand. Literally, I was (what he often called me) the apple of his eye. He saw nature – he saw books through me; and never did I weary of gazing for his behalf, and of putting into words the effect of field, tree, town, river, cloud, sunbeam – of the landscape before us; of the weather round us and impressing by sound on his ear what light could no longer stamp on his eye. Never did I weary of reading to him; never did I weary of conducting him where he wished to go: of doing for him what he wished to be done. And there was a pleasure in my services, most full, most exquisite, even though sad – because he claimed these services without painful shame or damping humiliation. He loved me so truly, that he knew no reluctance in profiting by my attendance: he felt I loved him so fondly, that to yield that attendance was to indulge my sweetest wishes.

One morning at the end of the two years, as I was writing a letter to his dictation, he came and bent over me, and said – 'Jane, have you a glittering ornament round your neck?'

I had a gold watch-chain: I answered 'Yes.'

'And have you a pale-blue dress on?'

I had. He informed me then, that for some time he had fancied the obscurity clouding one eye was becoming less dense; and that now he was sure of it.

He and I went up to London. He had the advice of an eminent oculist; and he eventually recovered the sight of that one eye. He cannot now see very distinctly: he cannot read or write much; but he can find his way without being led by the hand: the sky is no longer a blank to him – the earth no longer a void. When his first-born was put into his arms, he could see that the boy had inherited his own eyes, as they once were – large, brilliant, and black. On that occasion, he again, with a full heart, acknowledged that God had tempered judgement with mercy.

My Edward and I, then, are happy: and the more so, because those we most love are happy likewise. Diana and Mary Rivers are both married: alternately, once every year, they come to see us, and we go to see them. Diana's husband is a captain in the navy, a gallant officer and a good man. Mary's is a clergyman, a college friend of her brother's, and, from his attainments and principles, worthy of the connection. Both Captain Fitzjames and Mr Wharton love their wives, and are loved by them.

As to St John Rivers, he left England: he went to India. He entered on the path he had marked for himself; he pursues it still. A more resolute, indefatigable pioneer never wrought amidst rocks and dangers. Firm, faithful, and devoted, full of energy, and zeal, and truth, he labours for his race; he clears their painful way to improvement; he hews down like a giant the prejudices of creed and caste that encumber it. He may be stern; he may be exacting; he may be ambitious yet; but his is the sternness of the warrior Greatheart, who guards his pilgrim convoy from the onslaught of Apollyon. His is the exaction of the apostle, who speaks but for Christ, when he says – 'Whosoever will come after me, let him deny himself, and take up his cross and follow me.' His is the ambition of the high master-spirit, which aims to fill a place in the first rank of those who are redeemed from the earth – who stand without fault before the throne of God, who share the last mighty victories of the Lamb, who are called, and chosen, and faithful.

St John is unmarried: he never will marry now. Himself has hitherto sufficed to the toil, and the toil draws near its close: his glorious sun hastens to its setting. The last letter I received from him drew from my eyes human tears, and yet filled my heart with divine joy: he anticipated his sure reward, his incorruptible crown. I know that a stranger's hand will write to me next, to say that the good and faithful servant has been called at length into the joy of his Lord. And why weep for this? No fear of death will darken St John's last hour: his mind will be unclouded, his heart will be undaunted, his hope will be sure, his faith steadfast. His own words are a pledge of this – 'My Master,' he says, 'has forewarned me. Daily He announces more distinctly, "Surely I come quickly!" and hourly I more eagerly respond, "Amen; even so come, Lord Jesus!" '

# VILLETTE

# Villette

## CHARLOTTE BRONTË

# Contents

## CHAPTER I

# *Bretton*

My godmother lived in a handsome house in the clean and ancient town of Bretton. Her husband's family had been residents there for generations, and bore, indeed, the name of their birthplace – Bretton of Bretton: whether by coincidence, or because some remote ancestor had been a personage of sufficient importance to leave his name to his neighbourhood, I know not.

When I was a girl I went to Bretton about twice a year, and well I liked the visit. The house and its inmates specially suited me. The large peaceful rooms, the well-arranged furniture, the clear wide windows, the balcony outside, looking down on a fine antique street, where Sundays and holidays seemed always to abide – so quiet was its atmosphere, so clean its pavement – these things pleased me well.

One child in a household of grown people is usually made very much of, and in a quiet way I was a good deal taken notice of by Mrs Bretton, who had been left a widow, with one son, before I knew her; her husband, a physician, having died while she was yet a young and handsome woman.

She was not young, as I remember her, but she was still handsome, tall, well-made, and though dark for an Englishwoman, yet wearing always the clearness of health in her brunette cheeks, and its vivacity in a pair of fine, cheerful black eyes. People esteemed it a grievous pity that she had not conferred her complexion on her son, whose eyes were blue – though, even in boyhood, very piercing – and the colour of his long hair such as friends did not venture to specify, except as the sun shone on it, when they called it golden. He inherited the lines of his mother's features, however; also her good teeth, her stature (or the promise of her stature, for he was not yet full-grown), and, what was better, her health without flaw, and her spirits of that tone and equality which are better than a fortune to the possessor.

In the autumn of the year – I was staying at Bretton; my godmother having come in person to claim me of the kinsfolk with whom was at that time fixed my permanent residence. I believe she then plainly saw events coming, whose very shadow I scarce guessed; yet of which the faint suspicion sufficed to impart unsettled sadness, and made me glad to change scene and society.

Time always flowed smoothly for me at my godmother's side; not with tumultuous swiftness, but blandly, like the gliding of a full river through a plain. My visits to her resembled the sojourn of Christian and Hopeful beside a certain pleasant stream, with 'green trees on each bank, and meadows beautified with lilies all the year round.' The charm of variety there was not, nor the excitement of incident; but I liked peace so well, and sought stimulus so little, that when the latter came I almost felt it a disturbance, and wished rather it had still held aloof.

One day a letter was received of which the contents evidently caused Mrs Bretton surprise and some concern. I thought at first it was from home, and trembled, expecting I knew not what disastrous communication; to me, however, no reference was made, and the cloud seemed to pass.

The next day, on my return from a long walk, I found, as I entered my bedroom, an unexpected change. In addition to my own French bed in its shady recess, appeared in a corner a small crib, draped with white; and in addition to my mahogany chest of drawers, I saw a tiny rosewood chest. I stood still, gazed, and considered.

'Of what are these things the signs and tokens?' I asked. The answer was obvious. 'A second guest is coming: Mrs Bretton expects other visitors.'

On descending to dinner, explanations ensued. A little girl, I was told, would shortly be my companion: the daughter of a friend and distant relation of the late Dr Bretton's. This little girl, it was added, had recently lost her mother; though indeed, Mrs Bretton ere long subjoined, the loss was not so great as might at first appear. Mrs Home (Home it seems was the name) had been a very pretty, but a giddy, careless woman, who had neglected her child, and disappointed and disheartened her husband. So far from congenial had the union proved, that separation at last ensued – separation by mutual consent, not after any legal process. Soon after this event, the lady having over-exerted herself at a ball, caught cold, took a fever, and died after a very brief illness. Her husband, naturally a man of very sensitive feelings, and shocked inexpressibly by too sudden communication of the news, could hardly, it seems, now be persuaded but that some over-severity on his part – some deficiency in patience and indulgence – had contributed to hasten her end. He had brooded over this idea till his spirits were seriously affected; the medical men insisted on travelling being tried as a remedy, and meanwhile Mrs Bretton had offered to take charge of his little girl. 'And I hope,' added my godmother in conclusion, 'the child will not be like her mama; as silly and frivolous a little flirt as ever sensible man was weak enough to marry. For,' said she, 'Mr Home *is* a sensible man in his way, though not very practical: he is fond of science, and lives half his life in a laboratory trying experiments – a thing his butterfly wife could neither comprehend nor endure; and indeed,' confessed my godmother, 'I should not have liked it myself.'

In answer to a question of mine, she further informed me that her late husband used to say, Mr Home had derived this scientific turn from a maternal uncle, a French savant; for he came, it seems, of mixed French and Scottish origin, and had connections now living in France, of whom more than one wrote *de* before his name, and called himself noble.

That same evening at nine o'clock, a servant was despatched to meet the coach by which our little visitor was expected. Mrs Bretton and I sat alone in the drawing-room waiting her coming; John Graham Bretton being absent on a visit to one of his schoolfellows who lived in the country. My godmother read the evening paper while she waited; I sewed. It was a wet night; the rain lashed the panes, and the wind sounded angry and restless.

'Poor child!' said Mrs Bretton from time to time. 'What weather for her journey! I wish she were safe here.'

A little before ten the doorbell announced Warren's return. No sooner was the door opened than I ran down into the hall: there lay a trunk and some band-boxes, beside them stood a person like a nurse-girl, and at the foot of the staircase was Warren with a shawled bundle in his arms.

'Is that the child?' I asked.

'Yes, miss.'

I would have opened the shawl, and tried to get a peep at the face, but it was hastily turned from me to Warren's shoulder.

'Put me down, please,' said a small voice when Warren opened the drawing-room door, 'and take off this shawl,' continued the speaker, extracting with its minute hand the pin, and with a sort of fastidious haste doffing the clumsy wrapping. The creature which now appeared made a deft attempt to fold the shawl; but the drapery was much too heavy and large to be sustained or wielded by those hands and arms. 'Give it to Harriet, please,' was then the direction, 'and she can put it away.' This said, it turned and fixed its eyes on Mrs Bretton.

'Come here, little dear,' said that lady. 'Come and let me see if you are cold and damp: come and let me warm you at the fire.'

The child advanced promptly. Relieved of her wrapping, she appeared exceedingly tiny; but was a neat, completely-fashioned little figure, light, slight, and straight. Seated on my godmother's ample lap, she looked a mere doll; her neck, delicate as wax, her head of silky curls, increased, I thought, the resemblance.

Mrs Bretton talked in little fond phrases as she chafed the child's hands, arms, and feet; first she was considered with a wistful gaze, but soon a smile answered her. Mrs Bretton was not generally a caressing woman: even with her deeply-cherished son, her manner was rarely sentimental, often the reverse; but when this small stranger smiled at her, she kissed it, asking – 'What is my little one's name?'

'Missy.'

'But besides Missy?'

'Polly, papa calls her.'

'Will Polly be content to live with me?'

'Not *always*; but till papa comes home. Papa is gone away.' She shook her head expressively.

'He will return to Polly, or send for her.'

'Will he, ma'am? Do you know he will?'

'I think so.'

'But Harriet thinks not: at least not for a long while. He is ill.'

Her eyes filled. She drew her hand from Mrs Bretton's, and made a movement to leave her lap; it was at first resisted, but she said – 'Please, I wish to go: I can sit on a stool.'

She was allowed to slip down from the knee, and taking a footstool, she carried it to a corner where the shade was deep, and there seated herself. Mrs Bretton,

though a commanding, and in grave matters even a peremptory woman, was often passive in trifles: she allowed the child her way. She said to me, 'Take no notice at present.' But I did take notice: I watched Polly rest her small elbow on her small knee, her head on her hand; I observed her draw a square-inch or two of pocket handkerchief from the doll-pocket of her doll-skirt, and then I heard her weep. Other children in grief or pain cry aloud, without shame or restraint; but this being wept: the tiniest occasional sniff testified to her emotion. Mrs Bretton did not hear it: which was quite as well. Ere long, a voice, issuing from the corner, demanded – 'May the bell be rung for Harriet?'

I rang; the nurse was summoned and came.

'Harriet, I must be put to bed,' said her little mistress. 'You must ask where my bed is.'

Harriet signified that she had already made that enquiry.

'Ask if you sleep with me, Harriet.'

'No, missy,' said the nurse: 'You are to share this young lady's room,' designating me.

Missy did not leave her seat, but I saw her eyes seek me. After some minutes' silent scrutiny, she emerged from her corner.

'I wish you, ma'am, good-night,' said she to Mrs Bretton; but she passed me mute.

'Good-night, Polly,' I said.

'No need to say good-night, since we sleep in the same chamber;' was the reply with which she vanished from the drawing-room. We heard Harriet propose to carry her upstairs. 'No need,' was again her answer –' No need, no need:' and her small step toiled wearily up the staircase.

On going to bed an hour afterwards, I found her still wide awake. She had arranged her pillows so as to support her little person in a sitting posture; her hands, placed one within the other, rested quietly on the sheet, with an old-fashioned calm most unchildlike. I abstained from speaking to her for some time, but just before extinguishing the light, I recommended her to lie down.

'By and by,' was the answer.

'But you will take cold, missy.'

She took some tiny article of raiment from the chair at her crib side, and with it covered her shoulders. I suffered her to do as she pleased. Listening awhile in the darkness, I was aware that she still wept – wept under restraint, quietly and cautiously.

On awaking with daylight, a trickling of water caught my ear. Behold! there she was risen and mounted on a stool near the washstand, with pains and difficulty inclining the ewer (which she could not lift) so as to pour its contents into the basin. It was curious to watch her as she washed and dressed, so small, busy, and noiseless. Evidently she was little accustomed to perform her own toilet; and the buttons, strings, hooks and eyes, offered difficulties which she encountered with a perseverance good to witness. She folded her nightdress, she smoothed the drapery of her couch quite neatly; withdrawing into a corner, where the sweep of the white curtain concealed her, she became still. I half rose,

and advanced my head to see how she was occupied. On her knees, with her forehead bent on her hands, I perceived that she was praying.

Her nurse tapped at the door. She started up.

'I am dressed, Harriet,' said she: 'I have dressed myself, but I do not feel neat. Make me neat!'

'Why did you dress yourself, missy?'

'Hush! speak low, Harriet, for fear of waking *the girl*' (meaning me, who now lay with my eyes shut). 'I dressed myself to learn, against the time you leave me.'

'Do you want me to go?'

'When you are cross, I have many a time wanted you to go, but not now. Tie my sash straight; make my hair smooth, please.'

'Your sash is straight enough. What a particular little body you are!'

'It must be tied again. Please to tie it.'

'There, then. When I am gone you must get that young lady to dress you.'

'On no account.'

'Why? She is a very nice young lady. I hope you mean to behave prettily to her, missy, and not show your airs.'

'She shall dress me on no account.'

'Comical little thing!'

'You are not passing the comb straight through my hair, Harriet: the line will be crooked.'

'Ay, you are ill to please. Does that suit?'

'Pretty well. Where should I go now that I am dressed?'

'I will take you into the breakfast-room.'

'Come, then.'

They proceeded to the door. She stopped.

'Oh! Harriet, I wish this was papa's house! I don't know these people.'

'Be a good child, missy.'

'I am good, but I ache here;' putting her hand to her heart, and moaning while she reiterated 'Papa! papa!'

I roused myself and started up, to check this scene while it was yet within bounds.

'Say good-morning to the young lady,' dictated Harriet.

She said 'good-morning,' and then followed her nurse from the room. Harriet temporarily left that same day, to go to her own friends, who lived in the neighbourhood.

On descending, I found Paulina (the child called herself Polly, but her full name was Paulina Mary) seated at the breakfast table, by Mrs Bretton's side; a mug of milk stood before her, a morsel of bread filled her hand, which lay passive on the table-cloth: she was not eating.

'How we shall conciliate this little creature,' said Mrs Bretton to me, 'I don't know: she tastes nothing, and, by her looks, she has not slept.'

I expressed my confidence in the effects of time and kindness.

'If she were to take a fancy to anybody in the house, she would soon settle; but not till then,' replied Mrs Bretton.

## CHAPTER 2

### *Paulina*

Some days elapsed, and it appeared she was not likely to take much of a fancy to anybody in the house. She was not exactly naughty or wilful: she was far from disobedient; but an object less conducive to comfort – to tranquillity even – than she presented, it was scarcely possible to have before one's eyes. She moped: no grown person could have performed that uncheering business better; no furrowed face of adult exile, longing for Europe at Europe's antipodes, ever bore more legibly the signs of home sickness than did her infant visage. She seemed growing old and unearthly. I, Lucy Snowe, plead guiltless of that curse, an overheated and discursive imagination; but whenever, opening a room-door, I found her seated in a corner alone, her head on her pigmy hand, that room seemed to me not inhabited, but haunted.

And again, when of moonlight nights, on waking, I beheld her figure, white and conspicuous in its night-dress, kneeling upright in bed, and praying like some Catholic or Methodist enthusiast – some precocious fanatic or untimely saint – I scarcely know what thoughts I had; but they ran risk of being hardly more rational and healthy than that child's mind must have been.

I seldom caught a word of her prayers, for they were whispered low: sometimes, indeed, they were not whispered at all, but put up unuttered; such rare sentences as reached my ear still bore the burden, 'Papa; my dear papa!' This, I perceived, was a one-idead nature; betraying that monomaniac tendency I have ever thought the most unfortunate with which man or woman can be cursed.

What might have been the end of this fretting, had it continued unchecked, can only be conjectured: it received, however, a sudden turn.

One afternoon Mrs Bretton, coaxing her from her usual station in a corner, had lifted her into the window-seat, and, by way of occupying her attention, told her to watch the passengers and count how many ladies should go down the street in a given time. She had sat listlessly, hardly looking, and not counting, when – my eye being fixed on hers – I witnessed in its irid and pupil a startling transfiguration. These sudden, dangerous natures – *sensitive* as they are called – offer many a curious spectacle to those whom a cooler temperament has secured from participation in their angular vagaries. The fixed and heavy gaze swum, trembled, then glittered in fire; the small overcast brow cleared; the trivial and dejected features lit up; the sad countenance vanished, and in its place appeared a sudden eagerness, an intense expectancy.

'It *is*!' were her words.

Like a bird or a shaft, or any other swift thing, she was gone from the room. How she got the house-door open I cannot tell; probably it might be ajar;

perhaps Warren was in the way and obeyed her behest, which would be impetus enough. I – watching calmly from the window – saw her, in her black frock and tiny braided apron (to pinafores she had an antipathy), dart half the length of the street; and, as I was on the point of turning, and quietly announcing to Mrs Bretton that the child was run out mad, and ought instantly to be pursued, I saw her caught up, and rapt at once from my cool observation, and from the wondering stare of the passengers. A gentleman had done this good turn, and now, covering her with his cloak, advanced to restore her to the house whence he had seen her issue.

I concluded he would leave her in a servant's charge and withdraw; but he entered: having tarried a little while below, he came upstairs.

His reception immediately explained that he was known to Mrs Bretton. She recognised him; she greeted him, and yet she was fluttered, surprised, taken unawares. Her look and manner were even expostulatory; and in reply to these, rather than her words, he said – 'I could not help it, madam: I found it impossible to leave the country without seeing with my own eyes how she settled.'

'But you will unsettle her.'

'I hope not. And how is papa's little Polly?'

This question he addressed to Paulina, as he sat down and placed her gently on the ground before him.

'How is Polly's papa?' was the reply, as she leaned on his knee, and gazed up into his face.

It was not a noisy, not a wordy scene: for that I was thankful; but it was a scene of feeling too brimful, and which, because the cup did not foam up high or furiously overflow, only oppressed one the more. On all occasions of vehement, unrestrained expansion, a sense of disdain or ridicule comes to the weary spectator's relief; whereas I have ever felt most burdensome that sort of sensibility which bends of its own will, a giant slave under the sway of good sense.

Mr Home was a stern-featured – perhaps I should rather say, a hard-featured man: his forehead was knotty, and his cheek-bones were marked and prominent. The character of his face was quite Scotch; but there was feeling in his eye, and emotion in his now agitated countenance. His northern accent in speaking harmonised with his physiognomy. He was at once proud-looking and homely-looking.

He laid his hand on the child's uplifted head. She said – 'Kiss Polly.'

He kissed her. I wished she would utter some hysterical cry, so that I might get relief and be at ease. She made wonderfully little noise: she seemed to have got what she wanted – *all* she wanted, and to be in a trance of content. Neither in mien nor features was this creature like her sire, and yet she was of his strain: her mind had been filled from his, as the cup from the flagon.

Indisputably Mr Home owned manly self-control, however he might secretly feel on some matters. 'Polly,' he said, looking down on this little girl, 'go into the hall; you will see papa's greatcoat lying on a chair; put your hand into the pockets, you will find a pocket-handkerchief; bring it to me.'

She obeyed; went and returned deftly and nimbly. He was talking to Mrs

Bretton when she came back, and she waited with the handkerchief in her hand. It was a picture, in its way, to see her, with her tiny stature and trim, neat shape, standing at his knee. Seeing that he continued to talk, apparently unconscious of her return, she took his hand, opened the unresisting fingers, insinuated into them the handkerchief, and closed them upon it one by one. He still seemed not to see or feel her; but by and by, he lifted her to his knee; she nestled against him, and though neither looked at or spoke to the other for an hour following, I suppose both were satisfied.

During tea, the minute thing's movements and behaviour gave, as usual, full occupation to the eye. First she directed Warren, as he placed the chairs.

'Put papa's chair here, and mine near it, between papa and Mrs Bretton: *I* must hand his tea.'

She took her own seat, and beckoned with her hand to her father.

'Be near me, as if we were at home, papa.'

And again, as she intercepted his cup in passing, and would stir the sugar and put in the cream herself, 'I always did it for you at home, papa: nobody could do it as well, not even your own self.'

Throughout the meal she continued her attentions: rather absurd they were. The sugar-tongs were too wide for one of her hands, and she had to use both in wielding them; the weight of the silver cream-ewer, the bread and butter plates, the very cup and saucer tasked her insufficient strength and dexterity; but she would lift this, hand that, and luckily contrived through it all to break nothing. Candidly speaking, I thought her a little busybody; but her father, blind like other parents, seemed perfectly content to let her wait on him, and even wonderfully soothed by her offices.

'She is my comfort!' he could not help saying to Mrs Bretton. That lady had her own 'comfort' and nonpareil on a much larger scale, and for the moment, absent; so she sympathised with his foible.

This second 'comfort' came on the stage in the course of the evening. I knew this day had been fixed for his return, and was aware that Mrs Bretton had been expecting him through all its hours. We were seated round the fire, after tea, when Graham joined our circle: I should rather say, broke it up – for, of course, his arrival made a bustle; and then, as Mr Graham was fasting, there was refreshment to be provided. He and Mr Home met as old acquaintance; of the little girl he took no notice for a time.

His meal over, and numerous questions from his mother answered, he turned from the table to the hearth. Opposite where he had placed himself was seated Mr Home, and at his elbow, the child. When I say *child* I use an inappropriate and undescriptive term – a term suggesting any picture rather than that of the demure little person in a mourning frock and white chemisette, that might just have fitted a good-sized doll – perched now on a high chair beside a stand, whereon was her toy workbox of white varnished wood, and holding in her hands a shred of a handkerchief, which she was professing to hem, and at which she bored perseveringly with a needle, that in her fingers seemed almost a skewer, pricking herself ever and anon, marking the cambric with a track of

minute red dots; occasionally starting when the perverse weapon – swerving from her control – inflicted a deeper stab than usual; but still silent, diligent, absorbed, womanly.

Graham was at that time a handsome, faithless-looking youth of sixteen. I say faithless-looking, not because he was really of a very perfidious disposition, but because the epithet strikes me as proper to describe the fair, Celtic (not Saxon) character of his good looks; his waved light auburn hair, his supple symmetry, his smile frequent, and destitute neither of fascination nor of subtlety, (in no bad sense.) A spoiled, whimsical boy he was in those days.

'Mother,' he said, after eyeing the little figure before him in silence for some time, and when the temporary absence of Mr Home from the room relieved him from the half-laughing bashfulness, which was all he knew of timidity – 'Mother, I see a young lady in the present society to whom I have not been introduced.'

'Mr Home's little girl, I suppose you mean,' said his mother.

'Indeed, ma'am,' replied her son, 'I consider your expression of the least ceremonious: Miss Home *I* should certainly have said, in venturing to speak of the gentlewoman to whom I allude.'

'Now, Graham, I will not have that child teased. Don't flatter yourself that I shall suffer you to make her your butt.'

'Miss Home,' pursued Graham, undeterred by his mother's remonstrance, 'might I have the honour to introduce myself, since no one else seems willing to render you and me that service? Your slave, John Graham Bretton.'

She looked at him; he rose and bowed quite gravely. She deliberately put down thimble, scissors, work; descended with precaution from her perch, and curtsying with unspeakable seriousness, said, 'How do you do?'

'I have the honour to be in fair health, only in some measure fatigued with a hurried journey. I hope, ma'am, I see you well.'

'Tor-rer-ably well,' was the ambitious reply of the little woman; and she now essayed to regain her former elevation, but finding this could not be done without some climbing and straining – a sacrifice of decorum not to be thought of – and being utterly disdainful of aid in the presence of a strange young gentleman, she relinquished the high chair for a low stool: towards that low stool Graham drew in his chair.

'I hope, ma'am, the present residence, my mother's house, appears to you a convenient place of abode?'

'Not par-tic-er-er-ly: I want to go home.'

'A natural and laudable desire, ma'am; but one which, notwithstanding, I shall do my best to oppose. I reckon on being able to get out of you a little of that precious commodity called amusement, which mama and Mistress Snowe there fail to yield me.'

'I shall have to go with papa soon: I shall not stay long at your mother's.'

'Yes, yes; you will stay with me I am sure. I have a pony on which you shall ride, and no end of books with pictures to show you.'

'Are *you* going to live here now?'

'I am. Does that please you? Do you like me?'

'No.'

'Why?'

'I think you queer.'

'My face, ma'am?'

'Your face and all about you. You have long red hair.'

'Auburn hair, if you please: mama calls it auburn, or golden, and so do all her friends. But even with my "long red hair", (and he waved his mane with a sort of triumph – tawny he himself well knew that it was, and he was proud of the leonine hue) 'I cannot possibly be queerer than is your ladyship.'

'You call me queer?'

'Certainly.'

(After a pause) 'I think I shall go to bed.'

'A little thing like you ought to have been in bed many hours since; but you probably sat up in the expectation of seeing me?'

'No, indeed.'

'You certainly wished to enjoy the pleasure of my society. You knew I was coming home, and would wait to have a look at me.'

'I sat up for papa, and not for you.'

'Very good, Miss Home. I am going to be a favourite: preferred before papa soon, I dare say.'

She wished Mrs Bretton and myself good-night; she seemed hesitating whether Graham's deserts entitled him to the same attention, when he caught her up with one hand, and with that one hand held her poised aloft above his head. She saw herself thus lifted up on high, in the glass over the fireplace. The suddenness, the freedom, the disrespect of the action were too much.

'For shame, Mr Graham!' was her indignant cry, 'put me down!' – and when again on her feet, 'I wonder what you would think of me if I were to treat you in that way, lifting you with my hand' (raising that mighty member) 'as Warren lifts the little cat?'

So saying, she departed.

## CHAPTER 3

### The Playmates

Mr Home stayed two days. During his visit he could not be prevailed on to go out: he sat all day long by the fireside, sometimes silent, sometimes receiving and answering Mrs Bretton's chat, which was just of the proper sort for a man in his morbid mood – not over-sympathetic, yet not too uncongenial; sensible, and even with a touch of the motherly – she was sufficiently his senior to be permitted this touch.

As to Paulina, the child was at once happy and mute, busy and watchful. Her

father frequently lifted her to his knee; she would sit there till she felt or fancied he grew restless; then it was – 'Papa, put me down; I shall tire you with my weight.'

And the mighty burden slid to the rug, and establishing itself on carpet or stool just at 'papa's' feet, the white workbox and the scarlet-speckled handkerchief came into play. This handkerchief it seems was intended as a keepsake for 'papa,' and must be finished before his departure; consequently the demand on the sempstress's industry (she accomplished about a score of stitches in half an hour) was stringent.

The evening, by restoring Graham to the maternal roof (his days were passed at school), brought us an accession of animation – a quality not diminished by the nature of the scenes pretty sure to be enacted between him and Miss Paulina.

A distant and haughty demeanour had been the result of the indignity put upon her the first evening of his arrival: her usual answer, when he addressed her, was – 'I can't attend to you; I have other things to think about.' Being implored to state *what* things: 'Business.'

Graham would endeavour to seduce her attention by opening his desk and displaying its multifarious contents: seals, bright sticks of wax, penknives, with a miscellany of engravings – some of them gaily coloured – which he had amassed from time to time. Nor was this powerful temptation wholly unavailing: her eyes, furtively raised from her work, cast many a peep towards the writing-table, rich in scattered pictures. An etching of a child playing with a Blenheim spaniel happened to flutter to the floor.

'Pretty little dog!' said she, delighted.

Graham prudently took no notice. Ere long, stealing from her corner, she approached to examine the treasure more closely. The dog's great eyes and long ears, and the child's hat and feathers, were irresistible.

'Nice picture!' was her favourite criticism.

'Well – you may have it,' said Graham.

She seemed to hesitate. The wish to possess was strong, but to accept would be a compromise of dignity. No. She put it down and turned away.

'You won't have it then, Polly?'

'I would rather not, thank you.'

'Shall I tell you what I will do with the picture if you refuse it?'

She half turned to listen.

'Cut it into strips for lighting the taper.'

'No!'

'But I shall.'

'Please – don't.'

Graham waxed inexorable on hearing the pleading tone; he took the scissors from his mother's work-casket.

'Here goes!' said he, making a menacing flourish. 'Right through Fido's head, and splitting little Harry's nose.'

'No! *No*! NO!'

'Then come to me. Come quickly, or it is done.'

She hesitated, lingered, but complied.

'Now, will you have it?' he asked, as she stood before him.

'Please.'

'But I shall want payment.'

'How much?'

'A kiss.'

'Give the picture first into my hand.'

Polly, as she said this, looked rather faithless in her turn. Graham gave it. She absconded a debtor, darted to her father, and took refuge on his knee. Graham rose in mimic wrath and followed. She buried her face in Mr Home's waistcoat.

'Papa – papa – send him away!'

'I'll not be sent away,' said Graham.

With face still averted, she held out her hand to keep him off.

'Then, I shall kiss the hand,' said he; but that moment it became a miniature fist, and dealt him payment in a small coin that was not kisses.

Graham – not failing in his way to be as wily as his little playmate – retreated apparently quite discomfited; he flung himself on a sofa, and resting his head against the cushion, lay like one in pain. Polly, finding him silent, presently peeped at him. His eyes and face were covered with his hands. She turned on her father's knee, and gazed at her foe anxiously and long. Graham groaned.

'Papa, what is the matter?' she whispered.

'You had better ask him, Polly.'

'Is he hurt?' (groan second.)

'He makes a noise as if he were,' said Mr Home.

'Mother,' suggested Graham, feebly, 'I think you had better send for the doctor. Oh my eye!' (Renewed silence broken only by sighs from Graham.)

'If I were to become blind – ?' suggested this last.

His chastiser could not bear the suggestion. She was beside him directly.

'Let me see your eye: I did not mean to touch it, only your mouth; and I did not think I hit so *very* hard.'

Silence answered her. Her features worked, 'I am sorry; I am sorry!'

Then succeeded emotion, faltering, weeping.

'Have done trying that child, Graham,' said Mrs Bretton.

'It is all nonsense, my pet,' cried Mr Home.

And Graham once more snatched her aloft, and she again punished him; and while she pulled his lion's locks, termed him – 'The naughtiest, rudest, worst, untruest person that ever was.'

On the morning of Mr Home's departure, he and his daughter had some conversation in a window-recess by themselves; I heard part of it.

'Couldn't I pack my box and go with you, papa?' she whispered earnestly.

He shook his head.

'Should I be a trouble to you?'

'Yes, Polly.'

'Because I am little?'

'Because you are little and tender. It is only great, strong people that should travel. But don't look sad, my little girl; it breaks my heart. Papa will soon come back to his Polly.'

'Indeed, indeed, I am not sad, scarcely at all.'

'Polly would be sorry to give papa pain; would she not?'

'Sorrier than sorry.'

'Then Polly must be cheerful: not cry at parting; not fret afterwards. She must look forward to meeting again, and try to be happy meanwhile. Can she do this?'

'She will try.'

'I see she will. Farewell, then. It is time to go.'

'*Now*? – just *now*?'

'Just now.'

She held up quivering lips. Her father sobbed, but she, I remarked, did not. Having put her down, he shook hands with the rest present, and departed.

When the street-door closed, she dropped on her knees at a chair with a cry – 'Papa!'

It was low and long; a sort of 'Why hast thou forsaken me?' During an ensuing space of some minutes, I perceived she endured agony. She went through, in that brief interval of her infant life, emotions such as some never feel; it was in her constitution: she would have more of such instants if she lived. Nobody spoke. Mrs Bretton, being a mother, shed a tear or two. Graham, who was writing, lifted up his eyes and gazed at her. I, Lucy Snowe, was calm.

The little creature, thus left unharassed, did for herself what none other could do – contended with an intolerable feeling; and, ere long, in some degree, repressed it. That day she would accept solace from none; nor the next day: she grew more passive afterwards.

On the third evening, as she sat on the floor, worn and quiet, Graham, coming in, took her up gently, without a word. She did not resist: she rather nestled in his arms, as if weary. When he sat down, she laid her head against him; in a few minutes she slept; he carried her upstairs to bed. I was not surprised that, the next morning, the first thing she demanded was, 'Where is Mr Graham?'

It happened that Graham was not coming to the breakfast-table; he had some exercises to write for that morning's class, and had requested his mother to send a cup of tea into the study. Polly volunteered to carry it: she must be busy about something, look after somebody. The cup was entrusted to her: for, if restless, she was also careful. As the study was opposite the breakfast-room, the doors facing across the passage, my eye followed her.

'What are you doing?' she asked, pausing on the threshold.

'Writing,' said Graham.

'Why don't you come to take breakfast with your mama?'

'Too busy.'

'Do you want any breakfast?'

'Of course.'

'There then.'

And she deposited the cup on the carpet, like a jailer putting a prisoner's pitcher of water through his cell-door, and retreated. Presently she returned.

'What will you have besides tea – what to eat?'

'Anything good. Bring me something particularly nice; that's a kind little woman.'

She came back to Mrs Bretton.

'Please, ma'am, send your boy something good.'

'You shall choose for him, Polly; what shall my boy have?'

She selected a portion of whatever was best on the table, and, ere long, came back with a whispered request for some marmalade, which was not there. Having got it, however (for Mrs Bretton refused the pair nothing), Graham was shortly after heard lauding her to the skies; promising that, when he had a house of his own, she should be his housekeeper, and perhaps – if she showed any culinary genius – his cook; and, as she did not return, and I went to look after her, I found Graham and her breakfasting *tête-à-tête* – she standing at his elbow, and sharing his fare: excepting the marmalade, which she delicately refused to touch; lest, I suppose, it should appear that she had procured it as much on her own account as his. She constantly evinced these nice perceptions and delicate instincts.

The league of acquaintanceship thus struck up was not hastily dissolved; on the contrary, it appeared that time and circumstances served rather to cement than loosen it. Ill-assimilated as the two were in age, sex, pursuits, etc., they somehow found a great deal to say to each other. As to Paulina, I observed that her little character never properly came out, except with young Bretton. As she got settled, and accustomed to the house, she proved tractable enough with Mrs Bretton; but she would sit on a stool at that lady's feet all day long, learning her task, or sewing, or drawing figures with a pencil on a slate, and never kindling once to originality, or showing a single gleam of the peculiarities of her nature. I ceased to watch her under such circumstances: she was not interesting. But the moment Graham's knock sounded of an evening, a change occurred; she was instantly at the head of the staircase. Usually her welcome was a reprimand or a threat.

'You have not wiped your shoes properly on the mat. I shall tell your mama.'

'Little busybody! Are you there?'

'Yes – and you can't reach me: I am higher up than you' (peeping between the rails of the bannister; she could not look over them).

'Polly!'

'My dear boy!' (such was one of her terms for him, adopted in imitation of his mother).

'I am fit to faint with fatigue,' declared Graham, leaning against the passage-wall in seeming exhaustion. 'Dr Digby' (the headmaster) 'has quite knocked me up with over-work. Just come down and help me to carry up my book.'

'Ah! you're cunning!'

'Not at all, Polly – it is positive fact. I'm as weak as a rush. Come down.'

'Your eyes are quiet like the cat's, but you'll spring.'

'Spring? Nothing of the kind: it isn't in me. Come down.'

'Perhaps I may – if you'll promise not to touch – not to snatch me up, and not to whirl me round.'

'I? I couldn't do it!' (sinking into a chair).

'Then put the books down on the first step, and go three yards off.'

This being done, she descended warily, and not taking her eyes from the feeble Graham. Of course her approach always galvanised him to new and spasmodic life: the game of romps was sure to be exacted. Sometimes she would be angry; sometimes the matter was allowed to pass smoothly, and we could hear her say as she led him upstairs: 'Now, my dear boy, come and take your tea – I am sure you must want something.'

It was sufficiently comical to observe her as she sat beside Graham, while he took that meal. In his absence she was a still personage, but with him the most officious, fidgetty little body possible. I often wished she would mind herself and be tranquil; but no – herself was forgotten in him: he could not be sufficiently well waited on, nor carefully enough looked after; he was more than the Grand Turk in her estimation. She would gradually assemble the various plates before him, and, when one would suppose all he could possibly desire was within his reach, she would find out something else: 'Ma'am,' she would whisper to Mrs Bretton, 'perhaps your son would like a little cake – sweet cake, you know – there is some in there' (pointing to the sideboard cupboard). Mrs Bretton, as a rule, disapproved of sweet cake at tea, but still the request was urged, 'One little piece – only for him – as he goes to school: girls – such as me and Miss Snowe – don't need treats, but *he* would like it.'

Graham did like it very well, and almost always got it. To do him justice, he would have shared his prize with her to whom he owed it; but that was never allowed: to insist, was to ruffle her for the evening. To stand by his knee, and monopolise his talk and notice, was the reward she wanted – not a share of the cake.

With curious readiness did she adapt herself to such themes as interested him. One would have thought the child had no mind or life of her own, but must necessarily live, move, and have her being in another: now that her father was taken from her, she nestled to Graham, and seemed to feel by his feelings: to exist in his existence. She learned the names of all his schoolfellows in a trice; she got by heart their characters as given from his lips: a single description of an individual seemed to suffice. She never forgot, or confused identities: she would talk with him the whole evening about people she had never seen, and appear completely to realise their aspect, manners, and dispositions. Some she learned to mimic: an under-master, who was an aversion of young Bretton's, had, it seems, some peculiarities, which she caught up in a moment from Graham's representation, and rehearsed for his amusement; this, however, Mrs Bretton disapproved and forbade.

The pair seldom quarrelled; yet once a rupture occurred, in which her feelings received a severe shock.

One day Graham, on the occasion of his birthday, had some friends – lads of

his own age – to dine with him. Paulina took much interest in the coming of these friends; she had frequently heard of them; they were amongst those of whom Graham oftenest spoke. After dinner, the young gentlemen were left by themselves in the dining-room, where they soon became very merry and made a good deal of noise. Chancing to pass through the hall, I found Paulina sitting alone on the lowest step of the staircase, her eyes fixed on the glossy panels of the dining-room door, where the reflection of the hall-lamp was shining; her little brow knit in anxious meditation.

'What are you thinking about, Polly?'

'Nothing particular; only I wish that door was clear glass – that I might see through it. The boys seem very cheerful, and I want to go to them: I want to be with Graham, and watch his friends.'

'What hinders you from going?'

'I feel afraid: but may I try, do you think? May I knock at the door, and ask to be let in?'

I thought perhaps they might not object to have her as a playmate, and therefore encouraged the attempt.

She knocked – too faintly at first to be heard, but on a second essay the door unclosed; Graham's head appeared; he looked in high spirits but impatient.

'What do you want, you little monkey?'

'To come to you.'

'Do you indeed? As if I would be troubled with you! Away to mama and Mistress Snowe, and tell them to put you to bed.' The auburn head and bright flushed face vanished, the door shut peremptorily. She was stunned.

'Why does he speak so? He never spoke so before,' she said in consternation. 'What have I done?'

'Nothing, Polly; but Graham is busy with his school friends.'

'And he likes them better than me! He turns me away now they are here!'

I had some thoughts of consoling her, and of improving the occasion by inculcating some of those maxims of philosophy whereof I had ever a tolerable stock ready for application. She stopped me, however, by putting her fingers in her ears at the first words I uttered, and then lying down on the mat with her face against the flags; nor could either Warren or the cook root her from that position: she was allowed to lie, therefore, till she chose to rise of her own accord.

Graham forgot his impatience the same evening, and would have accosted her as usual when his friends were gone, but she wrenched herself from his hand; her eye quite flashed; she would not bid him good-night; she would not look in his face. The next day he treated her with indifference, and she grew like a bit of marble. The day after, he teased her to know what was the matter; her lips would not unclose. Of course he could not feel real anger on his side: the match was too unequal in every way; he tried soothing and coaxing. 'Why was she angry? What had he done?' By and by tears answered him; he petted her and they were friends. But she was one on whom such incidents were not lost: I remarked that never after this rebuff did she seek him, or follow him, or in any

way solicit his notice. I told her once to carry a book or some other article to Graham when he was shut up in his study.

'I shall wait till he comes out,' said she, proudly; 'I don't choose to give him the trouble of rising to open the door.'

Young Bretton had a favourite pony on which he often rode out; from the window she always watched his departure and return. It was her ambition to be permitted to have a ride round the courtyard on this pony; but far be it from her to ask such a favour. One day she descended to the yard to watch him dismount; as she leaned against the gate, the longing wish for the indulgence of a ride glittered in her eye.

'Come, Polly, will you have a canter?' asked Graham, half carelessly. I suppose she thought he was *too* careless.

'No thank you,' said she, turning away with the utmost coolness.

'You'd better;' pursued he. 'You will like it, I am sure.'

'Don't think I should care a fig about it,' was the response.

'That is not true. You told Lucy Snowe you longed to have a ride.'

'Lucy Snowe is a tatter-box,' I heard her say: (her imperfect articulation was the least precocious thing she had about her), and with this, she walked into the house. Graham coming in soon after, observed to his mother – 'Mama, I believe that creature is a changeling: she is a perfect cabinet of oddities; but I should be dull without her: she amuses me a great deal more than you or Lucy Snowe.'

'Miss Snowe,' said Paulina to me once (she had now got into the habit of occasionally chatting with me when we were alone in our room at night), 'do you know on what day in the week I like Graham best?'

'How can I possibly know anything so strange? Is there one day out of the seven when he is otherwise than on the other six?'

'To be sure! Can't you see? Don't you know? I find him the most excellent on a Sunday; then we have him the whole day, and he is quiet, and, in the evening, *so* kind.'

This observation was not altogether groundless: going to church, etc., kept Graham quiet on the Sunday, and the evening he generally dedicated to a serene, though rather indolent sort of enjoyment by the parlour fireside. He would take possession of the couch, and then he would call Polly.

Graham was a boy not quite as other boys are; all his delight did not lie in action: he was capable of some intervals of contemplation; he could take a pleasure too in reading, nor was his selection of books wholly indiscriminate: there were glimmerings of characteristic preference and even of instinctive taste in the choice. He rarely, it is true, remarked on what he read, but I have seen him sit and think of it.

Polly being near him, kneeling on a little cushion or the carpet, a conversation would begin in murmurs, not inaudible, though subdued. I caught a snatch of their tenor now and then; and, in truth, some influence better and finer than that of everyday, seemed to soothe Graham at such times into no ungentle mood.

'Have you learned any hymns this week, Polly?'

'I have learned a very pretty one, four verses long. Shall I say it?'

'Speak nicely, then: don't be in a hurry.'

The hymn being rehearsed, or rather half-chanted, in a little singing voice, Graham would take exceptions at the manner, and proceed to give a lesson in recitation. She was quick in learning, apt in imitating; and, besides, her pleasure was to please Graham: she proved a ready scholar. To the hymn would succeed some reading – perhaps a chapter in the Bible; correction was seldom required here, for the child could read any simple narrative chapter very well; and, when the subject was such as she could understand and take an interest in, her expression and emphasis were something remarkable. Joseph cast into the pit; the calling of Samuel; Daniel in the lion's den; these were favourite passages: of the first especially she seemed perfectly to feel the pathos.

'Poor Jacob!' she would sometimes say, with quivering lips. 'How he loved his son Joseph! As much,' she once added – 'as much, Graham, as I love you: if you were to die' (and she re-opened the book, sought the verse, and read), 'I should "refuse to be comforted, and go down into the grave to your mourning."'

With these words she gathered Graham in her little arms, drawing his long-tressed head towards her. The action, I remember, struck me as strangely rash; exciting the feeling one might experience on seeing an animal dangerous by nature, and but half-tamed by art, too heedlessly fondled. Not that I feared Graham would hurt, or very roughly check her; but I thought she ran risk of incurring such a careless, impatient repulse, as would be worse almost to her than a blow. On the whole, however, these demonstrations were borne passively: sometimes even a sort of complacent wonder at her earnest partiality would smile not unkindly in his eyes. Once he said: 'You like me almost as well as if you were my little sister, Polly.'

'Oh! I *do* like you,' said she; 'I *do* like you very much.'

I was not long allowed the amusement of this study of character. She had scarcely been at Bretton two months, when a letter came from Mr Home, signifying that he was now settled amongst his maternal kinsfolk on the Continent, that, as England was become wholly distasteful to him, he had no thoughts of returning thither, perhaps, for years; and that he wished his little girl to join him immediately.

'I wonder how she will take this news?' said Mrs Bretton, when she had read the letter. *I* wondered, too, and I took upon myself to communicate it.

Repairing to the drawing-room – in which calm and decorated apartment she was fond of being alone, and where she could be implicitly trusted, for she fingered nothing, or rather soiled nothing she fingered – I found her seated, like a little Odalisque, on a couch, half shaded by the drooping draperies of the window near. She seemed happy; all her appliances for occupation were about her; the white wood workbox, a shred or two of muslin, an end or two of ribbon, collected for conversion into doll-millinery. The doll, duly night-capped and night-gowned, lay in its cradle; she was rocking it to sleep, with an air of the most perfect faith in its possession of sentient and somnolent faculties; her eyes,

at the same time, being engaged with a picture-book, which lay open on her lap.

'Miss Snowe,' said she in a whisper, 'this is a wonderful book. Candace' (the doll, christened by Graham; for, indeed, its begrimed complexion gave it much of an Ethiopian aspect) – 'Candace is asleep now, and I may tell you about it; only we must both speak low, lest she should waken. This book was given me by Graham; it tells about distant countries, a long, long way from England, which no traveller can reach without sailing thousands of miles over the sea. Wild men live in these countries, Miss Snowe, who wear clothes different from ours: indeed, some of them wear scarcely any clothes, for the sake of being cool, you know; for they have very hot weather. Here is a picture of thousands gathered in a desolate place – a plain, spread with sand – round a man in black, a good, *good* Englishman, a missionary, who is preaching to them under a palm-tree.' (She showed a little coloured cut to that effect.) 'And here are pictures' (she went on) 'more stranger' (grammar was occasionally forgotten) 'than that. There is the wonderful Great Wall of China; here is a Chinese lady, with a foot littler than mine. There is a wild horse of Tartary; and here – most strange of all – is a land of ice and snow, without green fields, woods, or gardens. In this land, they found some mammoth bones: there are no mammoths now. You don't know what it was; but I can tell you, because Graham told me. A mighty, goblin creature, as high as this room, and as long as the hall; but not a fierce, flesh-eating thing, Graham thinks. He believes, if I met one in a forest, it would not kill me, unless I came quite in its way; when it would trample me down amongst the bushes, as I might tread on a grasshopper in a hayfield without knowing it.'

Thus she rambled on.

'Polly,' I interrupted, 'should you like to travel?'

'Not just yet,' was the prudent answer; 'but perhaps in twenty years, when I am grown a woman, as tall as Mrs Bretton, I may travel with Graham. We intend going to Switzerland, and climbing Mount Blanck; and someday we shall sail over to South America, and walk to the top of Kim – kim – borazo.'

'But how would you like to travel now, if your papa was with you?'

Her reply – not given till after a pause – evinced one of those unexpected turns of temper peculiar to her: 'Where is the good of talking in that silly way?' said she. 'Why do you mention papa? What is papa to you? I was just beginning to be happy, and not think about him so much; and there it will be all to do over again!'

Her lip trembled. I hastened to disclose the fact of a letter having been received, and to mention the directions given that she and Harriet should immediately rejoin this dear papa. 'Now, Polly, are you not glad?' I added.

She made no answer. She dropped her book, and ceased to rock her doll; she gazed at me with gravity and earnestness.

'Shall you not like to go to papa?'

'Of course,' she said at last in that trenchant manner she usually employed in speaking to me; and which was quite different from that she used with Mrs Bretton, and different again from the one dedicated to Graham. I wished to ascertain more of what she thought; but no: she would converse no more.

Hastening to Mrs Bretton, she questioned her, and received the confirmation of my news. The weight and importance of these tidings kept her perfectly serious the whole day. In the evening, at the moment Graham's entrance was heard below, I found her at my side. She began to arrange a locket-ribbon about my neck, she displaced and replaced the comb in my hair; while thus busied, Graham entered.

'Tell him by and by,' she whispered; 'tell him I am going.'

In the course of tea-time I made the desired communication. Graham, it chanced, was at that time greatly preoccupied about some school-prize, for which he was competing. The news had to be told twice before it took proper hold of his attention; and even then he dwelt on it but momently.

'Polly going? What a pity! Dear little Mousie, I shall be sorry to lose her: she must come to us again, mama.'

And hastily swallowing his tea, he took a candle and a small table to himself and his books, and was soon buried in study.

'Little Mousie' crept to his side, and lay down on the carpet at his feet, her face to the floor; mute and motionless she kept that post and position till bedtime. Once I saw Graham – wholly unconscious of her proximity – push her with his restless foot. She receded an inch or two. A minute after one little hand stole out from beneath her face, to which it had been pressed, and softly caressed the heedless foot. When summoned by her nurse she rose and departed very obediently, having bid us all a subdued good-night.

I will not say that I dreaded going to bed, an hour later; yet I certainly went with an unquiet anticipation that I should find that child in no peaceful sleep. The forewarning of my instinct was but fulfilled, when I discovered her, all cold and vigilant, perched like a white bird on the outside of the bed. I scarcely knew how to accost her; she was not to be managed like another child. She, however, accosted me. As I closed the door, and put the light on the dressing-table, she turned to me with these words: 'I cannot – *cannot* sleep; and in this way I cannot – *cannot* live!'

I asked what ailed her.

'Dedful miz-er-y!' said she, with her piteous lisp.

'Shall I call Mrs Bretton?'

'That is downright silly,' was her impatient reply; and, indeed, I well knew that if she had heard Mrs Bretton's foot approach, she would have nestled quiet as a mouse under the bedclothes. While lavishing her eccentricities regardlessly before me – for whom she professed scarcely the semblance of affection – she never showed my godmother one glimpse of her inner self: for her, she was nothing but a docile, somewhat quaint little maiden. I examined her; her cheek was crimson; her dilated eye was both troubled and glowing, and painfully restless: in this state it was obvious she must not be left till morning. I guessed how the case stood.

'Would you like to bid Graham good-night again?' I asked. 'He is not gone to his room yet.'

She at once stretched out her little arms to be lifted. Folding a shawl round her, I carried her back to the drawing-room. Graham was just coming out.

'She cannot sleep without seeing and speaking to you once more,' I said. 'She does not like the thought of leaving you.'

'I've spoilt her,' said he, taking her from me with good humour, and kissing her little hot face and burning lips. 'Polly, you care for me more than for papa, now –'

'I *do* care for you, but you care nothing for me,' was her whisper.

She was assured to the contrary, again kissed, restored to me, and I carried her away; but, alas! not soothed.

When I thought she could listen to me I said –

'Paulina, you should not grieve that Graham does not care for you so much as you care for him. It must be so.'

Her lifted and questioning eyes asked why.

'Because he is a boy and you are a girl; he is sixteen and you are only six; his nature is strong and gay, and yours is otherwise.'

'But I love him so much; he *should* love me a little.'

'He does. He is fond of you. You are his favourite.'

'Am I Graham's favourite?'

'Yes, more than any little child I know.'

The assurance soothed her; she smiled in her anguish.

'But,' I continued, 'don't fret, and don't expect too much of him, or else he will feel you to be troublesome, and then it is all over.'

'All over!' she echoed softly, 'then I'll be good. I'll try to be good, Lucy Snowe.'

I put her to bed.

'Will he forgive me this one time?' she asked, as I undressed myself. I assured her that he would; that as yet he was by no means alienated; that she had only to be careful for the future.

'There is no future,' said she: 'I am going. Shall I ever – ever – see him again, after I leave England?'

I returned an encouraging response. The candle being extinguished, a still half-hour elapsed. I thought her asleep, when the little white shape once more lifted itself in the crib, and the small voice asked, –' Do you like Graham, Miss Snowe?'

'Like him! Yes, a little.'

'Only a little! Do you like him as I do?'

'I think not. No. Not as you do.'

'Do you like him much?'

'I told you I liked him a little. Where is the use of caring for him so very much? He is full of faults.'

'Is he?'

'All boys are.'

'More than girls?'

'Very likely. Wise people say it is folly to think anybody perfect; and as to likes and dislikes, we should be friendly to all, and worship none.'

'Are you a wise person?'

'I mean to try to be so. Go to sleep.'

'I *cannot* go to sleep. Have you no pain just here' (laying her elfish hand on her elfish breast), 'when you think *you* shall have to leave Graham; for *your* home is not here?'

'Surely, Polly,' said I, 'you should not feel so much pain when you are very soon going to rejoin your father. Have you forgotten him? Do you no longer wish to be his little companion?'

Dead silence succeeded this question.

'Child, lie down and sleep,' I urged.

'My bed is cold,' said she. 'I can't warm it.'

I saw the little thing shiver. 'Come to me,' I said, wishing, yet scarcely hoping, that she would comply: for she was a most strange, capricious, little creature, and especially whimsical with me. She came, however, instantly, like a small ghost gliding over the carpet. I took her in. She was chill; I warmed her in my arms. She trembled nervously; I soothed her. Thus tranquillised and cherished she at last slumbered.

'A very unique child,' thought I, as I viewed her sleeping countenance by the fitful moonlight, and cautiously and softly wiped her glittering eyelids and her wet cheeks with my handkerchief. 'How will she get through this world, or battle with this life? How will she bear the shocks and repulses, the humiliations and desolations, which books, and my own reason tell me are prepared for all flesh?'

She departed the next day; trembling like a leaf when she took leave, but exercising self-command.

## CHAPTER 4

### *Miss Marchmont*

On quitting Bretton, which I did a few weeks after Paulina's departure – little thinking then I was never again to visit it: never more to tread its calm old streets – I betook myself home, having been absent six months. It will be conjectured that I was of course glad to return to the bosom of my kindred. Well! the amiable conjecture does no harm, and may therefore be safely left uncontradicted. Far from saying nay, indeed, I will permit the reader to picture me, for the next eight years, as a bark slumbering through halcyon weather, in a harbour still as glass – the steersman stretched on the little deck, his face up to heaven, his eyes closed: buried, if you will, in a long prayer. A great many women and girls are supposed to pass their lives something in that fashion; why not I with the rest?

Picture me then idle, basking, plump, and happy, stretched on a cushioned deck, warmed with constant sunshine, rocked by breezes indolently soft. However, it cannot be concealed that, in that case, I must somehow have fallen overboard, or that there must have been wreck at last. I too well remember a

time – a long time, of cold, of danger, of contention. To this hour, when I have the nightmare, it repeats the rush and saltness of briny waves in my throat, and their icy pressure on my lungs. I even know there was a storm, and that not of one hour nor one day. For many days and nights neither sun nor stars appeared; we cast with our own hands the tackling out of the ship; a heavy tempest lay on us; all hope that we should be saved was taken away. In fine, the ship was lost, the crew perished.

As far as I recollect, I complained to no one about these troubles. Indeed, to whom could I complain? Of Mrs Bretton I had long lost sight. Impediments, raised by others, had, years ago, come in the way of our intercourse, and cut it off. Besides, time had brought changes for her too: the handsome property of which she was left guardian for her son, and which had been chiefly invested in some joint-stock undertaking, had melted, it was said, to a fraction of its original amount. Graham, I learned from incidental rumours, had adopted a profession; both he and his mother were gone from Bretton, and were understood to be now in London. Thus, there remained no possibility of dependence on others; to myself alone could I look. I know not that I was of a self-reliant or active nature; but self-reliance and exertion were forced upon me by circumstances, as they are upon thousands besides; and when Miss Marchmont, a maiden lady of our neighbourhood, sent for me, I obeyed her behest, in the hope that she might assign me some task I could undertake.

Miss Marchmont was a woman of fortune, and lived in a handsome residence; but she was a rheumatic cripple, impotent, foot and hand, and had been so for twenty years. She always sat upstairs: her drawing-room adjoined her bedroom. I had often heard of Miss Marchmont, and of her peculiarities (she had the character of being very eccentric), but till now had never seen her. I found her a furrowed, gray-haired woman, grave with solitude, stern with long affliction, irritable also, and perhaps exacting. It seemed that a maid, or rather companion, who had waited on her for some years, was about to be married; and she, hearing of my bereaved lot, had sent for me, with the idea that I might supply this person's place. She made the proposal to me after tea, as she and I sat alone by her fireside.

'It will not be an easy life,' said she candidly, 'for I require a good deal of attention, and you will be much confined; yet, perhaps, contrasted with the existence you have lately led, it may appear tolerable.'

I reflected. Of course it ought to appear tolerable, I argued inwardly; but somehow, by some strange fatality, it would not. To live here, in this close room, the watcher of suffering, sometimes, perhaps, the butt of temper, through all that was to come of my youth; while all that was gone had passed, to say the least, not blissfully – my heart sunk one moment, then it revived; for though I forced myself to *realise* evils, I think I was too prosaic to *idealise*, and consequently to exaggerate them.

'My doubt is whether I should have strength for the undertaking,' I observed.

'That is my own scruple,' said she; 'for you look a worn-out creature.'

So I did. I saw myself in the glass, in my mourning-dress, a faded, hollow-eyed

vision. Yet I thought little of the wan spectacle. The blight, I believed, was chiefly external: I still felt life at life's sources.

'What else have you in view – anything?'

'Nothing clear as yet: but I may find something.'

'So you imagine: perhaps you are right. Try your own method, then; and if it does not succeed, test mine. The chance I have offered shall be left open to you for three months.'

This was kind. I told her so, and expressed my gratitude. While I was speaking, a paroxysm of pain came on. I ministered to her; made the necessary applications, according to her directions, and, by the time she was relieved, a sort of intimacy was already formed between us. I, for my part, had learned from the manner in which she bore this attack, that she was a firm, patient woman (patient under physical pain, though sometimes perhaps excitable under long mental canker); and she, from the goodwill with which I succoured her, discovered that she could influence my sympathies (such as they were). She sent for me the next day; for five or six successive days she claimed my company. Closer acquaintance, while it developed both faults and eccentricities, opened, at the same time, a view of a character I could respect. Stern and even morose as she sometimes was, I could wait on her and sit beside her with that calm which always blesses us when we are sensible that our manners, presence, contact, please and soothe the persons we serve. Even when she scolded me – which she did, now and then, very tartly – it was in such a way as did not humiliate, and left no sting; it was rather like an irascible mother rating her daughter, than a harsh mistress lecturing a dependent: lecture, indeed, she could not, though she could occasionally storm. Moreover, a vein of reason ever ran through her passion: she was logical even when fierce. Ere long a growing sense of attachment began to present the thought of staying with her as companion in quite a new light; in another week I had agreed to remain.

Two hot, close rooms thus became my world; and a crippled old woman, my mistress, my friend, my all. Her service was my duty – her pain, my suffering – her relief, my hope – her anger, my punishment – her regard, my reward. I forgot that there were fields, woods, rivers, seas, an everchanging sky outside the steam-dimmed lattice of this sick-chamber; I was almost content to forget it. All within me became narrowed to my lot. Tame and still by habit, disciplined by destiny, I demanded no walks in the fresh air; my appetite needed no more than the tiny messes served for the invalid. In addition she gave me the originality of her character to study: the steadiness of her virtues, I will add, the power of her passions, to admire, the truth of her feelings to trust. All these things she had, and for these things I clung to her.

For these things I would have crawled on with her for twenty years, if for twenty years longer her life of endurance had been protracted. But another decree was written. It seemed I must be stimulated into action. I must be goaded, driven, stung, forced to energy. My little morsel of human affection, which I prized as if it were a solid pearl, must melt in my fingers and slip thence like a dissolving hailstone. My small adopted duty must be snatched from my

easily contented conscience. I had wanted to compromise with Fate: to escape occasional great agonies by submitting to a whole life of privation and small pains. Fate would not so be pacified; nor would Providence sanction this shrinking sloth and cowardly indolence.

One February night – I remember it well – there came a voice near Miss Marchmont's house, heard by every inmate, but translated, perhaps, only by one. After a calm winter, storms were ushering in the spring. I had put Miss Marchmont to bed; I sat at the fireside sewing. The wind was wailing at the windows: it had wailed all day; but, as night deepened, it took a new tone – an accent keen, piercing, almost articulate to the ear; a plaint, piteous and disconsolate to the nerves, trilled in every gust.

'Oh, hush! hush!' I said in my disturbed mind, dropping my work, and making a vain effort to stop my ears against that subtle, searching cry. I had heard that very voice ere this, and compulsory observation had forced on me a theory as to what it boded. Three times in the course of my life, events had taught me that these strange accents in the storm – this restless, hopeless cry – denote a coming state of the atmosphere unpropitious to life. Epidemic diseases, I believed, were often heralded by a gasping, sobbing, tormented, long-lamenting east wind. Hence, I inferred, arose the legend of the Banshee. I fancied, too, I had noticed – but was not philosopher enough to know whether there was any connection between the circumstances – that we often at the same time hear of disturbed volcanic action in distant parts of the world; of rivers suddenly rushing above their banks; and of strange high tides flowing furiously in on low sea-coasts. 'Our globe,' I had said to myself, 'seems at such periods torn and disordered; the feeble amongst us wither in her distempered breath, rushing hot from steaming volcanoes.'

I listened, and trembled; Miss Marchmont slept.

About midnight, the storm in one half hour fell to a dead calm. The fire, which had been burning dead, glowed up vividly. I felt the air change, and become keen. Raising blind and curtain, I looked out, and saw in the stars the keen sparkle of a sharp frost.

Turning away, the object that met my eyes was Miss Marchmont awake, lifting her head from the pillow, and regarding me with unusual earnestness.

'Is it a fine night?' she asked.

I replied in the affirmative.

'I thought so,' she said; 'for I feel so strong, so well. Raise me. I feel young tonight,' she continued; 'young, light-hearted, and happy. What if my complaint be about to take a turn, and I am yet destined to enjoy health? It would be a miracle!'

'And these are not the days of miracles,' I thought to myself, and wondered to hear her talk so. She went on directing her conversation to the past, and seeming to recall its incidents, scenes, and personages with singular vividness.

'I love Memory tonight,' she said: 'I prize her as my best friend. She is just now giving me a deep delight; she is bringing back to my heart, in warm and beautiful life, realities – not mere empty ideas – but what were once realities,

and that I long have thought decayed, dissolved, mixed in with grave-mould. I possess just now the hours, the thoughts, the hopes of my youth. I renew the love of my life – its only love – almost its only affection; for I am not a particularly good woman: I am not amiable. Yet I have had my feelings, strong and concentrated; and these feelings had their object; which, in its single self, was dear to me, as, to the majority of men and women, are all the unnumbered points on which they dissipate their regard. While I loved, and while I was loved, what an existence I enjoyed! What a glorious year I can recall – how bright it comes back to me! What a living spring – what a warm, glad summer – what soft moonlight, silvering the autumn evenings – what strength of hope under the ice-bound waters and frost-hoar fields of that year's winter! Through that year my heart lived with Frank's heart. O my noble Frank – my faithful Frank – my *good* Frank! so much better than myself – his standard in all things so much higher! This I can now see and say – if few women have suffered as I did in his loss, few have enjoyed what I did in his love. It was a far better kind of love than common; I had no doubts about it or him: it was such a love as honoured, protected, and elevated, no less than it gladdened her to whom it was given. Let me now ask, just at this moment, when my mind is so strangely clear, let me reflect why it was taken from me? For what crime was I condemned, after twelve months of bliss, to undergo thirty years of sorrow?'

'I do not know,' she continued, after a pause: 'I cannot *cannot* see the reason; yet at this hour I can say with sincerity, what I never tried to say before – Inscrutable God, Thy will be done! And at this moment I can believe that death will restore me to Frank. I never believed it till now.'

'He is dead, then?' I enquired in a low voice.

'My dear girl,' she said, 'one happy Christmas Eve I dressed and decorated myself, expecting my lover, very soon to be my husband, would come that night to visit me. I sat down to wait. Once more I see that moment – I see the snow-twilight stealing through the window over which the curtain was not dropped, for I designed to watch him ride up the white walk; I see and feel the soft firelight warming me, playing on my silk dress, and fitfully showing me my own young figure in a glass. I see the moon of a calm winter night float full, clear and cold, over the inky mass of shrubbery, and the silvered turf of my grounds. I wait, with some impatience in my pulse, but no doubt in my breast. The flames had died in the fire, but it was a bright mass yet; the moon was mounting high, but she was still visible from the lattice; the clock neared ten; he rarely tarried later than this, but once or twice he had been delayed so long.

'Would he for once fail me? No – not even for once; and now he was coming – and coming fast – to atone for lost time. "Frank! you furious rider," I said inwardly, listening gladly, yet anxiously, to his approaching gallop, "you shall be rebuked for this: I will tell you it is *my* neck you are putting in peril; for whatever is yours is, in a dearer and tenderer sense, mine." There he was: I saw him; but I think tears were in my eyes; my sight was so confused. I saw the horse; I heard it stamp – I saw at least a mass; I heard a clamour. *Was* it a horse? or what heavy, dragging thing was it, crossing, strangely dark, the lawn? How

could I name that thing in the moonlight before me? or how could I utter the feeling which rose in my soul?

'I could only run out. A great animal – truly, Frank's black horse – stood trembling, panting, snorting before the door; a man held it: Frank, as I thought.

' "What is the matter?" I demanded. Thomas, my own servant, answered by saying sharply, "Go into the house, madam." And then calling to another servant, who came hurrying from the kitchen as if summoned by some instinct, "Ruth, take missis into the house directly." But I was kneeling down in the snow, beside something that lay there – something that I had seen dragged along the ground – something that sighed, that groaned on my breast, as I lifted and drew it to me. He was not dead; he was not quite unconscious. I had him carried in; I refused to be ordered about and thrust from him. I was quite collected enough, not only to be my own mistress, but the mistress of others. They had begun by trying to treat me like a child, as they always do with people struck by God's hand; but I gave place to none except the surgeon; and when he had done what he could, I took my dying Frank to myself. He had strength to fold me in his arms; he had power to speak my name; he heard me as I prayed over him very softly; he felt me as I tenderly and fondly comforted him.

' "Maria," he said, "I am dying in Paradise." He spent his last breath in faithful words for me. When the dawn of Christmas morning broke, my Frank was with God.

'And that,' she went on, 'happened thirty years ago. I have suffered since. I doubt if I have made the best use of all my calamities. Soft, amiable natures they would have refined to saintliness; of strong, evil spirits they would have made demons; as for me, I have only been a woe-struck and selfish woman.'

'You have done much good,' I said; for she was noted for her liberal almsgiving.

'I have not withheld money, you mean, where it could assuage affliction. What of that? It cost me no effort or pang to give. But I think from this day I am about to enter a better frame of mind, to prepare myself for reunion with Frank. You see I still think of Frank more than of God; and unless it be counted that in thus loving the creature so much, so long, and so exclusively, I have not at least blasphemed the Creator, small is my chance of salvation. What do you think, Lucy, of these things? Be my chaplain and tell me.'

This question I could not answer: I had no words. It seemed as if she thought I *had* answered it.

'Very right, my child. We should acknowledge God merciful, but not always for us comprehensible. We should accept our own lot whatever it be, and try to render happy that of others. Should we not? Well, tomorrow I will begin by trying to make you happy. I will endeavour to do something for you, Lucy: something that will benefit you when I am dead. My head aches now with talking too much; still I am happy. Go to bed. The clock strikes two. How late you sit up; or rather how late I, in my selfishness, keep you up. But go now; have no more anxiety for me: I feel I shall rest well.'

She composed herself as if to slumber. I, too, retired to my crib in a closet

within her room. The night passed in quietness; quietly her doom must at last have come: peacefully and painlessly: in the morning she was found without life, nearly cold, but all calm and undisturbed. Her previous excitement of spirits and change of mood had been the prelude of a fit; one stroke sufficed to sever the thread of an existence so long fretted by affliction.

## CHAPTER 5

### Turning a New Leaf

My mistress being dead, and I once more alone, I had to look out for a new place. About this time I might be a little – a very little, shaken in nerves. I grant I was not looking well, but on the contrary, thin, haggard, and hollow-eyed; like a sitter-up at night, like an overwrought servant, or a placeless person in debt. In debt, however, I was not; nor quite poor; for though Miss Marchmont had not had time to benefit me, as, on that last night, she said she intended, yet after the funeral, my wages were duly paid by her second cousin, the heir, an avaricious-looking man, with pinched nose and narrow temples, who, indeed, I heard long afterwards, turned out a thorough miser: a direct contrast to his generous kinswoman, and a foil to her memory, blessed to this day by the poor and needy. The possessor, then, of fifteen pounds; of health though worn not broken, and of a spirit in similar condition; I might still, in comparison with many people, be regarded as occupying an enviable position. An embarrassing one it was, however, at the same time; as I felt with some acuteness on a certain day, of which the corresponding one in the next week was to see my departure from my present abode, while with another I was not provided.

In this dilemma I went, as a last and sole resource, to see and consult an old servant of our family; once my nurse, now housekeeper at a grand mansion not far from Miss Marchmont's. I spent some hours with her; she comforted, but knew not how to advise me. Still all inward darkness, I left her about twilight; a walk of two miles lay before me; it was a clear, frosty night. In spite of my solitude, my poverty, and my perplexity, my heart, nourished and nerved with the vigour of a youth that had not yet counted twenty-three summers, beat light and not feebly. Not feebly, I am sure, or I should have trembled in that lonely walk, which lay through still fields, and passed neither village nor farmhouse, nor cottage; I should have quailed in the absence of moonlight, for it was by the leading of stars only I traced the dim path; I should have quailed still more in the unwonted presence of that which tonight shone in the north, a moving mystery – the Aurora Borealis. But this solemn stranger influenced me otherwise than through my fears. Some new power it seemed to bring. I drew in energy with the keen, low breeze that blew on its path. A bold thought was sent to my mind; my mind was made strong to receive it.

'Leave this wilderness,' it was said to me, 'and go out hence.'

'Where?' was the query.

I had not very far to look: gazing from this country parish in the flat, rich middle of England – I mentally saw within reach what I had never yet beheld with my bodily eyes; I saw London.

The next day I returned to the hall, and asking once more to see the housekeeper, I communicated to her my plan.

Mrs Barrett was a grave, judicious woman, though she knew little more of the world than myself; but grave and judicious as she was, she did not charge me with being out of my senses: and, indeed, I had a staid manner of my own which ere now had been as good to me as cloak and hood of hodden gray; since under its favour I had been enabled to achieve with impunity, and even approbation, deeds that if attempted with an excited and unsettled air, would in some minds have stamped me as a dreamer and zealot.

The housekeeper was slowly propounding some difficulties, while she prepared orange-rind for marmalade, when a child ran past the window and came bounding into the room. It was a pretty child, and as it danced, laughing, up to me – for we were not strangers (nor, indeed, was its mother – a young married daughter of the house – a stranger) – I took it on my knee. Different as were our social positions now, this child's mother and I had been schoolfellows, when I was a girl of ten and she a young lady of sixteen; and I remembered her – good-looking, but dull – in a lower class than mine.

I was admiring the boy's handsome dark eyes, when the mother, young Mrs Leigh, entered. What a beautiful and kind-looking woman was the good-natured and comely, but unintellectual girl become! Wifehood and maternity had changed her thus, as I have since seen them change others even less promising than she. Me she had forgotten. I was changed too; though not, I fear, for the better. I made no attempt to recall myself to her memory: why should I? She came for her son to accompany her in a walk, and behind her followed a nurse carrying an infant. I only mention the incident because, in addressing the nurse, Mrs Leigh spoke French (very bad French, by the way, and with an incorrigibly bad accent, again forcibly reminding me of our school-days); and I found the woman was a foreigner. The little boy chattered volubly in French too. When the whole party were withdrawn, Mrs Barrett remarked that her young lady had brought that foreign nurse home with her two years ago, on her return from a Continental excursion; that she was treated almost as well as a governess, and had nothing to do but walk out with the baby and chatter French with Master Charles; 'and,' added Mrs Barrett, 'she says there are many English-women in foreign families as well placed as she.'

I stored up this piece of casual information, as careful housewives store seemingly worthless shreds and fragments for which their prescient minds anticipate a possible use someday. Before I left my old friend, she gave me the address of a respectable old-fashioned inn in the city, which, she said, my uncles used to frequent in former days.

In going to London, I ran less risk and evinced less enterprise than the reader may think. In fact, the distance was only fifty miles. My means would suffice

both to take me there, to keep me a few days, and also to bring me back if I found no inducement to stay. I regarded it as a brief holiday, permitted for once to work-weary faculties, rather than as an adventure of life and death. There is nothing like taking all you do at a moderate estimate: it keeps mind and body tranquil; whereas grandiloquent notions are apt to hurry both into fever.

Fifty miles were then a day's journey, (for I speak of a time gone by: my hair which till a late period withstood the frosts of time, lies now at last, white under a white cap, like snow beneath snow.) About nine o'clock of a wet February night I reached London.

My reader, I know, is one who would not thank me for an elaborate reproduction of poetic first impressions; and it is well, inasmuch as I had neither time nor mood to cherish such; arriving as I did late, on a dark, raw, and rainy evening, in a Babylon and a wilderness of which the vastness and the strangeness tried to the utmost any powers of clear thought and steady self-possession with which, in the absence of more brilliant faculties, Nature might have gifted me.

When I left the coach, the strange speech of the cabmen and others waiting round, seemed to me odd as a foreign tongue. I had never before heard the English language chopped up in that way. However, I managed to understand and to be understood, so far as to get myself and trunk safely conveyed to the old inn whereof I had the address. How difficult, how oppressive, how puzzling seemed my flight! In London for the first time; at an inn for the first time; tired with travelling; confused with darkness; palsied with cold; unfurnished with either experience or advice to tell me how to act, and yet – to act obliged.

Into the hands of Common-sense I confided the matter. Common-sense, however, was as chilled and bewildered as all my other faculties, and it was only under the spur of an inexorable necessity that she spasmodically executed her trust. Thus urged, she paid the porter: considering the crisis, I did not blame her too much that she was hugely cheated; she asked the waiter for a room; she timorously called for the chambermaid; what is far more, she bore, without being wholly overcome, a highly supercilious style of demeanour from that young lady, when she appeared.

I recollect this same chambermaid was a pattern of town prettiness and smartness. So trim her waist, her cap, her dress – I wondered how they had all been manufactured. Her speech had an accent which in its mincing glibness seemed to rebuke mine as by authority; her spruce attire flaunted an easy scorn at my plain country garb.

'Well, it can't be helped,' I thought, 'and then the scene is new, and the circumstances; I shall gain good.'

Maintaining a very quiet manner towards this arrogant little maid, and subsequently observing the same towards the parsonic-looking, black-coated, white-neckclothed waiter, I got civility from them ere long. I believe at first they thought I was a servant; but in a little while they changed their minds, and hovered in a doubtful state between patronage and politeness.

I kept up well till I had partaken of some refreshment, warmed myself by a

fire, and was fairly shut into my room; but, as I sat down by the bed and rested
my head and arms on the pillow, a terrible oppression overcame me. All at once
my position rose on me like a ghost. Anomalous; desolate, almost blank of hope,
it stood. What was I doing here alone in great London? What should I do on
the morrow? What prospects had I in life? What friends had I on earth?
Whence did I come? Whither should I go? What should I do?

I wet the pillow, my arms, and my hair, with rushing tears. A dark interval of
most bitter thought followed this burst; but I did not regret the step taken, nor
wish to retract it. A strong, vague persuasion, that it was better to go forward
than backward, and that I *could go* forward – that a way, however narrow and
difficult, would in time open – predominated over other feelings: its influence
hushed them so far, that at last I became sufficiently tranquil to be able to say my
prayers and seek my couch. I had just extinguished my candle and lain down,
when a deep, low, mighty tone swung through the night. At first I knew it not;
but it was uttered twelve times, and at the twelfth colossal hum and trembling
knell, I said: 'I lie in the shadow of St Paul's.'

## CHAPTER 6

## *London*

The next day was the first of March, and when I awoke, rose, and opened my
curtain, I saw the risen sun struggling through fog. Above my head, above the
house-tops, co-elevate almost with the clouds, I saw a solemn, orbed mass,
dark-blue and dim – THE DOME. While I looked, my inner self moved; my spirit
shook its always-fettering wings half loose; I had a sudden feeling as if I, who
had never yet truly lived, were at last about to taste life: in that morning my soul
grew as fast as Jonah's gourd.

'I did well to come,' I said, proceeding to dress with speed and care. 'I like the
spirit of this great London which I feel around me. Who but a coward would
pass his whole life in hamlets, and for ever abandon his faculties to the eating
rust of obscurity?'

Being dressed, I went down, not travel-worn and exhausted, but tidy and
refreshed. When the waiter came in with my breakfast, I managed to accost him
sedately, yet cheerfully; we had ten minutes' discourse, in the course of which
we became usefully known to each other.

He was a gray-haired, elderly man; and, it seemed, had lived in his present
place twenty years. Having ascertained this, I was sure he must remember my
two uncles, Charles and Wilmot, who, fifteen years ago, were frequent visitors
here. I mentioned their names; he recalled them perfectly, and with respect.
Having intimated my connection, my position in his eyes was henceforth clear,
and on a right footing. He said I was like my uncle Charles: I suppose he spoke
truth, because Mrs Barrett was accustomed to say the same thing. A ready and

obliging courtesy now replaced his former uncomfortably doubtful manner: henceforth I need no longer be at a loss for a civil answer to a sensible question.

The street on which my little sitting-room window looked was narrow, perfectly quiet, and not dirty: the few passengers were just such as one sees in provincial towns: here was nothing formidable; I felt sure I might venture out alone.

Having breakfasted, out I went. Elation and pleasure were in my heart: to walk alone in London seemed of itself an adventure. Presently I found myself in Paternoster-row – classic ground this. I entered a bookseller's shop, kept by one Jones; I bought a little book – a piece of extravagance I could ill afford; but I thought I would one day give or send it to Mrs Barrett. Mr Jones, a dried-in man of business, stood behind his desk; he seemed one of the greatest, and I one of the happiest, of beings.

Prodigious was the amount of life I lived that morning. Finding myself before St Paul's, I went in; I mounted to the dome: I saw thence London, with its river, and its bridges, and its churches; I saw antique Westminster, and the green Temple Gardens, with sun upon them, and a glad, blue sky of early spring above; and, between them and it, not too dense a cloud of haze.

Descending, I went wandering whither chance might lead, in a still ecstasy of freedom and enjoyment; and I got – I knew not how – I got into the heart of city life. I saw and felt London at last: I got into the Strand; I went up Cornhill; I mixed with the life passing along; I dared the perils of crossings. To do this, and to do it utterly alone, gave me, perhaps an irrational, but a real pleasure. Since those days, I have seen the West-end, the parks, the fine squares; but I love the city far better. The city seems so much more in earnest: its business, its rush, its roar, are such serious things, sights, and sounds. The city is getting its living – the West-end but enjoying its pleasure. At the West-end you may be amused, but in the city you are deeply excited.

Faint, at last, and hungry (it was years since I had felt such healthy hunger), I returned, about two o'clock, to my dark, old, and quiet inn. I dined on two dishes – a plain joint, and vegetables; both seemed excellent (how much better than the small, dainty messes Miss Marchmont's cook used to send up to my kind, dead mistress and me, and to the discussion of which we could not bring half an appetite between us). Delightfully tired, I lay down on three chairs for an hour (the room did not boast a sofa). I slept, then I woke and thought for two hours.

My state of mind, and all accompanying circumstances, were just now such as most to favour the adoption of a new, resolute, and daring – perhaps desperate – line of action. I had nothing to lose. Unutterable loathing of a desolate existence past forbade return. If I failed in what I now designed to undertake, who, save myself, would suffer? If I died far away from – home, I was going to say, but I had no home – from England, then, who would weep?

I might suffer; I was inured to suffering: death itself had not, I thought, those terrors for me which it has for the softly reared. I had, ere this, looked on the thought of death with a quiet eye. Prepared, then, for any consequences, I formed a project.

That same evening I obtained from my friend, the waiter, information respecting the sailing of vessels for a certain continental port, Boue-Marine. No time, I found, was to be lost: that very night I must take my berth. I might, indeed, have waited till the morning before going on board, but would not run the risk of being too late.

'Better take your berth at once ma'am,' counselled the waiter. I agreed with him, and having discharged my bill, and acknowledged my friend's services at a rate which I now know was princely, and which in his eyes must have seemed absurd – and indeed, while pocketing the cash, he smiled a faint smile which intimated his opinion of the donor's *savoir-faire* – he proceeded to call a coach. To the driver he also recommended me, giving at the same time an injunction about taking me, I think, to the wharf, and not leaving me to the watermen; which that functionary promised to observe, but failed in keeping his promise. On the contrary, he offered me up as an oblation, served me as a dripping roast, making me alight in the midst of a throng of watermen.

This was an uncomfortable crisis. It was a dark night. The coachman instantly drove off as soon as he had got his fare; the watermen commenced a struggle for me and my trunk. Their oaths I hear at this moment: they shook my philosophy more than did the night, or the isolation, or the strangeness of the scene. One laid hands on my trunk. I looked on and waited quietly; but when another laid hands on me, I spoke up, shook off his touch, stepped at once into a boat, desired austerely that the trunk should be placed beside me – 'Just there,' – which was instantly done; for the owner of the boat I had chosen became now an ally: I was rowed off.

Black was the river as a torrent of ink: lights glanced on it from the piles of building round, ships rocked on its bosom. They rowed me up to several vessels; I read by lantern-light their names painted in great white letters on a dark ground. *The Ocean, The Phoenix, The Consort, The Dolphin,* were passed in turns; but *The Vivid* was my ship, and it seemed she lay further down.

Down the sable flood we glided; I thought of the Styx, and of Charon rowing some solitary soul to the Land of Shades. Amidst the strange scene, with a chilly wind blowing in my face, and midnight-clouds dropping rain above my head; with two rude rowers for companions, whose insane oaths still tortured my ear, I asked myself if I was wretched or terrified. I was neither. Often in my life have I been far more so under comparatively safe circumstances. 'How is this?' said I. 'Methinks I am animated and alert, instead of being depressed and apprehensive?' I could not tell how it was.

*The Vivid* started out, white and glaring, from the black night at last. 'Here you are!' said the waterman, and instantly demanded six shillings.

'You ask too much,' I said. He drew off from the vessel and swore he would not embark me till I paid it. A young man, the steward as I found afterwards, was looking over the ship's side; he grinned a smile in anticipation of the coming contest; to disappoint him, I paid the money. Three times that afternoon I had given crowns where I should have given shillings; but I consoled myself with the reflection, 'It is the price of experience.'

'They've cheated you!' said the steward exultantly when I got on board. I answered phlegmatically that 'I knew it,' and went below.

A stout, handsome, and showy woman was in the ladies' cabin; I asked to be shown my berth; she looked hard at me, muttered something about its being unusual for passengers to come on board at that hour, and seemed disposed to be less than civil. What a face she had – so comely – so insolent and so selfish!

'Now that I am on board, I shall certainly stay here,' was my answer. 'I will trouble you to show me my berth.'

She complied, but sullenly. I took off my bonnet, arranged my things, and lay down. Some difficulties had been passed through; a sort of victory was won: my homeless, anchorless, unsupported mind had again leisure for a brief repose: till the 'Vivid' arrived in harbour, no further action would be required of me, but then... Oh! I could not look forward. Harassed, exhausted, I lay in a half-trance.

The stewardess talked all night; not to me, but to the young steward, her son and her very picture. He passed in and out of the cabin continually: they disputed, they quarrelled, they made it up again twenty times in the course of the night. She professed to be writing a letter home, she said – to her father; she read passages of it aloud, heeding me no more than a stock – perhaps she believed me asleep: several of these passages appeared to comprise family secrets, and bore special reference to one 'Charlotte,' a younger sister who, from the bearing of the epistle, seemed to be on the brink of perpetrating a romantic and imprudent match; loud was the protest of this elder lady against the distasteful union. The dutiful son laughed his mother's correspondence to scorn. She defended it, and raved at him. They were a strange pair. She might be thirty-nine or forty, and was buxom and blooming as a girl of twenty. Hard, loud, vain and vulgar, her mind and body alike seemed brazen and imperishable. I should think, from her childhood, she must have lived in public stations; and in her youth might very likely have been a barmaid.

Towards morning her discourse ran on a new theme: 'the Watsons', a certain expected family-party of passengers, known to her, it appeared, and by her much esteemed on account of the handsome profit realised in their fees. She said, 'it was as good as a little fortune to her whenever this family crossed.'

At dawn all were astir, and by sunrise the passengers came on board. Boisterous was the welcome given by the stewardess to the 'Watsons', and great was the bustle made in their honour. They were four in number, two males and two females. Besides them, there was but one other passenger – a young lady, whom a gentlemanly, though languid-looking man escorted. The two groups offered a marked contrast. The Watsons were doubtless rich people, for they had the confidence of conscious wealth in their bearing; the women – youthful both of them, and one perfectly handsome, as far as physical beauty went – were dressed richly, gaily, and absurdly out of character for the circumstances. Their bonnets with bright flowers, their velvet cloaks and silk dresses seemed better suited for park or promenade than for a damp packet-deck. The men were of low stature, plain, fat, and vulgar; the oldest, plainest, greasiest, broadest, I soon found was the husband – the bridegroom I suppose, for she was very young – of the

beautiful girl. Deep was my amazement at this discovery; and deeper still when I perceived that, instead of being desperately wretched in such a union, she was gay even to giddiness. 'Her laughter,' I reflected, 'must be the mere frenzy of despair.' And even while this thought was crossing my mind, as I stood leaning quiet and solitary against the ship's side, she came tripping up to me, an utter stranger, with a camp stool in her hand, and smiling a smile of which the levity puzzled and startled me, though it showed a perfect set of perfect teeth, she offered me the accommodation of this piece of furniture. I declined it, of course with all the courtesy I could put into my manner; she danced off heedless and lightsome. She must have been good-natured; but what had made her marry that individual, who was at least as much like an oil-barrel as a man?

The other lady-passenger, with the gentleman-companion, was quite a girl, pretty and fair; her simple print dress, untrimmed straw-bonnet, and large shawl, gracefully worn, formed a costume plain to quakerism: yet, for her, becoming enough. Before the gentleman quitted her, I observed him throwing a glance of scrutiny over all the passengers, as if to ascertain in what company his charge would be left. With a most dissatisfied air did his eye turn from the ladies with the gay flowers: he looked at me, and then he spoke to his daughter, niece, or whatever she was; she also glanced in my direction, and slightly curled her short, pretty lip. It might be myself, or it might be my homely mourning-habit that elicited this mark of contempt; more likely both. A bell rang; her father (I afterwards knew that it was her father) kissed her and returned to land. The packet sailed.

Foreigners say that it is only English girls who can thus be trusted to travel alone, and deep is their wonder at the daring confidence of English parents and guardians. As for the 'jeunes Miss', by some their intrepidity is pronounced masculine and 'inconvenant', others regard them as the passive victims of an educational and theological system which wantonly dispenses with proper 'surveillance'. Whether this particular young lady was of the sort that can the most safely be left unwatched, I do not know: or rather did not *then* know; but it soon appeared that the dignity of solitude was not to her taste. She paced the deck once or twice backwards and forwards; she looked with a little sour air of disdain at the flaunting silks and velvets, and the bears which thereon danced attendance, and eventually she approached me and spoke.

'Are you fond of a sea-voyage?' was her question.

I explained that my *fondness* for a sea-voyage had yet to undergo the test of experience: I had never made one.

'Oh how charming!' cried she. 'I quite envy you the novelty: first impressions, you know, are so pleasant. Now I have made so many, I quite forget the first: I am quite *blasée* about the sea and all that.'

I could not help smiling.

'Why do you laugh at me?' she enquired, with a frank testiness that pleased me better than her other talk.

'Because you are so young to be *blasée* about anything.'

'I am seventeen' (a little piqued).

'You hardly look sixteen. Do you like travelling alone?'

'Bah! I care nothing about it. I have crossed the Channel ten times, alone; but then I take care never to be long alone: I always make friends.'

'You will scarcely make many friends this voyage, I think' (glancing at the Watson-group, who were now laughing and making a great deal of noise on deck).

'Not of those odious men and women,' said she: 'such people should be steerage passengers. Are you going to school?'

'No.'

'Where are you going?'

'I have not the least idea – beyond, at least, the Port of Boue-marine.'

She stared, then carelessly ran on: 'I am going to school. Oh the number of foreign schools I have been at in my life! And yet I am quite an ignoramus. I know nothing – nothing in the world – I assure you; except that I play and dance beautifully, and French and German of course I know, to speak; but I can't read or write them very well. Do you know they wanted me to translate a page of an easy German book into English the other day, and I couldn't do it. Papa was so mortified: he says it looks as if M. de Bassompierre – my god-papa, who pays all my school-bills – had thrown away all his money. And then, in matters of information – in history, geography, arithmetic, and so on, I am quite a baby; and I write English so badly – such spelling and grammar, they tell me. Into the bargain I have quite forgotten my religion; they call me a Protestant, you know, but really I am not sure whether I am one or not: I don't well know the difference between Romanism and Protestantism. However, I don't in the least care for that. I was a Lutheran once at Bonn – dear Bonn! – charming Bonn! – where there were so many handsome students. Every nice girl in our school had an admirer; they knew our hours for walking out, and almost always passed us on the promenade: "Schönes Mädchen", we used to hear them say. I was excessively happy at Bonn!'

'And where are you now?' I enquired.

'Oh! at – *chose*,' said she.

Now Miss Ginevra Fanshawe (such was this young person's name) only substituted this word '*chose*' in temporary oblivion of the real name. It was a habit she had: '*chose*' came in at every turn in her conversation – the convenient substitute for any missing word in any language she might chance at the time to be speaking. French girls often do the like; from them she had caught the custom. '*Chose*', however, I found, in this instance, stood for Villette – the great capital of the great kingdom of Labassecour.

'Do you like Villette?' I asked.

'Pretty well. The natives, you know, are intensely stupid and vulgar; but there are some nice English families.'

'Are you in a school?'

'Yes.'

'A good one?'

'Oh no! horrid: but I go out every Sunday, and care nothing about the

*maîtresses* or the *professeurs*, or the *élèves*, and send lessons *au diable* (one daren't say that in English, you know, but it sounds quite right in French); and thus I get on charmingly . . . You are laughing at me again?'

'No – I am only smiling at my own thoughts.'

'What are they?' (without waiting for an answer) – 'Now *do* tell me where you are going.'

'Where Fate may lead me. My business is to earn a living where I can find it.'

'To earn!' (in consternation) 'are you poor then?'

'As poor as Job.'

(After a pause) 'Bah! how unpleasant! But *I* know what it is to be poor: they are poor enough at home – papa and mama, and all of them. Papa is called Captain Fanshawe; he is an officer on half-pay, but well-descended, and some of our connections are great enough; but my uncle and god-papa de Bassompierre, who lives in France, is the only one that helps us: he educates us girls. I have five sisters and three brothers. By and by we are to marry – rather elderly gentlemen, I suppose, with cash: papa and mama manage that. My sister Augusta is married now to a man much older-looking than papa. Augusta is very beautiful – not in my style – but dark; her husband, Mr Davies, had the yellow fever in India, and he is still the colour of a guinea; but then he is rich, and Augusta has her carriage and establishment, and we all think she has done perfectly well. Now this is better than "earning a living", as you say. By the way, are you clever?'

'No – not at all.'

'You can play, sing, speak three or four languages?'

'By no means.'

'Still I think you are clever' (a pause and a yawn). 'Shall you be seasick?'

'Shall you?'

'Oh, immensely! as soon as ever we get in sight of the sea: I begin, indeed, to feel it already. I shall go below; and won't I order about that fat, odious stewardess? Heureusement je sais faire aller mon monde.' Down she went.

It was not long before the other passengers followed her: throughout the afternoon I remained on deck alone. When I recall the tranquil, and even happy mood in which I passed those hours, and remember, at the same time, the position in which I was placed: its hazardous – some would have said its hopeless – character; I feel that, as –

> Stone walls do not a prison make,
> Nor iron bars – a cage.

so peril, loneliness, an uncertain future, are not oppressive evils, so long as the frame is healthy and the faculties are employed; so long, especially, as Liberty lends us her wings, and Hope guides us by her star.

I was not sick till long after we passed Margate, and deep was the pleasure I drank in with the sea-breeze; divine the delight I drew from the heaving channel-waves, from the sea-birds on their ridges, from the white sails on their dark distance, from the quiet, yet beclouded sky, overhanging all. In my reverie, methought I saw the continent of Europe, like a wide dream-land, far away.

Sunshine lay on it, making the long coast one line of gold; tiniest tracery of clustered town and snow-gleaming tower, of woods deep-massed, of heights serrated, of smooth pasturage and veiny stream, embossed the metal-bright prospect. For background, spread a sky, solemn and dark-blue, and – grand with imperial promise, soft with tints of enchantment – strode from north to south a God-bent bow, an arch of hope.

Cancel the whole of that, if you please, reader – or rather let it stand, and draw thence a moral – an alternative, text-hand copy –

Day-dreams are delusions of the demon.

Becoming excessively sick, I faltered down into the cabin.

Miss Fanshawe's berth chanced to be next mine; and, I am sorry to say, she tormented me with an unsparing selfishness during the whole time of our mutual distress. Nothing could exceed her impatience and fretfulness. The Watsons, who were very sick too, and on whom the stewardess attended with shameless partiality, were stoics compared with her. Many a time since have I noticed, in persons of Ginevra Fanshawe's light, careless temperament, and fair, fragile style of beauty, an entire incapacity to endure: they seem to sour in adversity, like small-beer in thunder: the man who takes such a woman for his wife, ought to be prepared to guarantee her an existence all sunshine. Indignant at last with her teasing peevishness, I curtly requested her 'to hold her tongue.' The rebuff did her good, and it was observable that she liked me no worse for it.

As dark night drew on, the sea roughened: larger waves swayed strong against the vessel's side. It was strange to reflect that blackness and water were round us, and to feel the ship ploughing straight on her pathless way, despite noise, billow, and rising gale. Articles of furniture began to fall about, and it became needful to lash them to their places; the passengers grew sicker than ever; Miss Fanshawe declared, with groans, that she must die.

'Not just yet, honey,' said the stewardess. 'We're just in port.' Accordingly, in another quarter of an hour, a calm fell upon us all; and about midnight the voyage ended.

I was sorry: yes, I was sorry. My resting-time was past; my difficulties – my stringent difficulties – recommenced. When I went on deck, the cold air and black scowl of the night seemed to rebuke me for my presumption in being where I was: the lights of the foreign sea-port town, glimmering round the foreign harbour, met me like unnumbered threatening eyes. Friends came on board to welcome the Watsons; a whole family of friends surrounded and bore away Miss Fanshawe; I – but I dared not for one moment dwell on a comparison of positions.

Yet where should I go? I must go somewhere. Necessity dare not be nice. As I gave the stewardess her fee – and she seemed surprised at receiving a coin of more value than, from such a quarter, her coarse calculations had probably reckoned on – I said: 'Be kind enough to direct me to some quiet, respectable inn, where I can go for the night.'

She not only gave me the required direction, but called a commissionaire,

and bid him take charge of me, and – *not* my trunk, for that was gone to the custom-house.

I followed this man along a rudely-paved street, lit now by a fitful gleam of moonlight; he brought me to the inn. I offered him sixpence, which he refused to take; supposing it not enough, I changed it for a shilling; but this also he declined, speaking rather sharply, in a language to me unknown. A waiter, coming forward into the lamp-lit inn-passage, reminded me, in broken English, that my money was foreign money, not current here. I gave him a sovereign to change. This little matter settled, I asked for a bedroom; supper I could not take: I was still seasick and unnerved, and trembling all over. How deeply glad I was when the door of a very small chamber at length closed on me and my exhaustion. Again I might rest: though the cloud of doubt would be as thick tomorrow as ever; the necessity for exertion more urgent, the peril (or destitution) nearer, the conflict (for existence) more severe.

## CHAPTER 7

### *Villette*

I awoke next morning with courage revived and spirits refreshed: physical debility no longer enervated my judgement; my mind felt prompt and clear.

Just as I finished dressing, a tap came to the door; I said, 'Come in,' expecting the chambermaid, whereas a rough man walked in and said – 'Gif me your keys, Meess.'

'Why?' I asked.

'Gif!' said he impatiently; and as he half-snatched them from my hand, he added, 'All right! haf your tronc soon.'

Fortunately it did turn out all right: he was from the custom-house. Where to go to get some breakfast I could not tell; but I proceeded, not without hesitation, to descend.

I now observed what I had not noticed in my extreme weariness last night, viz., that this inn was, in fact, a large hotel; and as I slowly descended the broad staircase, halting on each step (for I was in wonderfully little haste to get down), I gazed at the high ceiling above me, at the painted walls around, at the wide windows which filled the house with light, at the veined marble I trode (for the steps were all of marble, though uncarpeted and not very clean), and contrasting all this with the dimensions of the closet assigned to me as a chamber, with the extreme modesty of its appointments, I fell into a philosophising mood.

Much I marvelled at the sagacity evinced by waiters and chambermaids in proportioning the accommodation to the guest. How could inn-servants and ship-stewardesses everywhere tell at a glance that I, for instance, was an individual of no social significance and little burdened by cash? They *did* know it, evidently: I saw quite well that they all, in a moment's calculation, estimated me

at about the same fractional value. The fact seemed to me curious and pregnant: I would not disguise from myself what it indicated, yet managed to keep up my spirits pretty well under its pressure.

Having at last landed in a great hall, full of skylight glare, I made my way somehow to what proved to be the coffee-room. It cannot be denied that on entering this room I trembled somewhat; felt uncertain, solitary, wretched; wished to Heaven I knew whether I was doing right or wrong; felt convinced it was the last, but could not help myself. Acting in the spirit and with the calm of a fatalist, I sat down at a small table, to which a waiter presently brought me some breakfast; and I partook of that meal in a frame of mind not greatly calculated to favour digestion. There were many other people breakfasting at other tables in the room; I should have felt rather more happy if amongst them all I could have seen any women; however, there was not one – all present were men. But nobody seemed to think I was doing anything strange; one or two gentlemen glanced at me occasionally, but none stared obtrusively: I suppose if there was anything eccentric in the business, they accounted for it by this word 'Anglaise!'

Breakfast over, I must again move – in what direction? 'Go to Villette,' said an inward voice; prompted doubtless by the recollection of this slight sentence uttered carelessly and at random by Miss Fanshawe, as she bid me goodbye: 'I wish you would come to Mme Beck's; she has some marmots whom you might look after: she wants an English gouvernante, or was wanting one two months ago.'

Who Mme Beck was, where she lived, I knew not; I had asked, but the question passed unheard: Miss Fanshawe, hurried away by her friends, left it unanswered. I presumed Villette to be her residence – to Villette I would go. The distance was forty miles. I knew I was catching at straws; but in the wide and weltering deep where I found myself, I would have caught at cobwebs. Having enquired about the means of travelling to Villette, and secured a seat in the Diligence, I departed on the strength of this outline – this shadow of a project. Before you pronounce on the rashness of the proceeding, reader, look back to the point whence I started; consider the desert I had left, note how little I perilled: mine was the game where the player cannot lose and may win.

Of an artistic temperament, I deny that I am; yet I must possess something of the artist's faculty of making the most of present pleasure: that is to say, when it is of the kind to my taste; I enjoyed that day, though we travelled slowly, though it was cold, though it rained. Somewhat bare, flat, and treeless was the route along which our journey lay; and slimy canals crept, like half-torpid green snakes, beside the road; and formal pollard willows edged level fields, tilled like kitchen-garden beds. The sky too was monotonously gray; the atmosphere was stagnant and humid; yet amidst all these deadening influences, my fancy budded fresh and my heart basked in sunshine. These feelings, however, were well kept in check by the secret but ceaseless consciousness of anxiety lying in wait on enjoyment, like a tiger crouched in a jungle. The breathing of that beast of prey was in my ear always; his fierce heart panted close against mine; he never stirred in his lair but I felt him: I knew he waited only for sun-down to bound ravenous from his ambush.

I had hoped we might reach Villette ere night set in, and that thus I might escape the deeper embarrassment which obscurity seems to throw round a first arrival at an unknown bourne; but, what with our slow progress and long stoppages – what with a thick fog and small, dense rain – darkness that might almost be felt, had settled on the city by the time we gained its suburbs.

I know we passed through a gate where soldiers were stationed – so much I could see by lamplight; then, having left behind us the miry Chaussée, we rattled over a pavement of strangely rough and flinty surface. At a bureau, the diligence stopped, and the passengers alighted. My first business was to get my trunk: a small matter enough, but important to me. Understanding that it was best not to be importunate or over-eager about luggage, but to wait and watch quietly the delivery of other boxes till I saw my own, and then promptly claim and secure it, I stood apart; my eye fixed on that part of the vehicle in which I had seen my little portmanteau safely stowed, and upon which, piles of additional bags and boxes were now heaped. One by one, I saw these removed, lowered, and seized on. I was sure mine ought to be by this time visible: it was not. I had tied on the direction card with a piece of green ribbon, that I might know it at a glance: not a fringe or fragment of green was perceptible. Every package was removed; every tin-case and brown paper parcel; the oil-cloth cover was lifted; I saw with distinct vision that not an umbrella, cloak, cane, hat-box or band-box remained.

And my portmanteau, with my few clothes and the little pocket-book enclasping the remnant of my fifteen pounds, where were they?

I ask this question now, but I could not ask it then. I could say nothing whatever; not possessing a phrase of *speaking* French: and it was French, and French only, the whole world seemed now gabbling round me. *What* should I do? Approaching the conductor, I just laid my hand on his arm, pointed to a trunk, then to the diligence-roof, and tried to express a question with my eyes. He misunderstood me, seized the trunk indicated, and was about to hoist it on the vehicle.

'Let that alone – will you?' said a voice in good English; then, in correction, 'Qu'est ce que vous faîtes donc? Cette malle est à moi.'

But I had heard the Fatherland accents; they rejoiced my heart; I turned: 'Sir,' said I, appealing to the stranger, without in my distress noticing what he was like, 'I cannot speak French. May I entreat you to ask this man what he has done with my trunk?'

Without discriminating, for the moment, what sort of face it was to which my eyes were raised and on which they were fixed, I felt in its expression half-surprise at my appeal and half-doubt of the wisdom of interference.

'*Do* ask him; I would do as much for you,' said I.

I don't know whether he smiled, but he said in a gentlemanly tone; that is to say, a tone not hard nor terrifying, –

'What sort of trunk was yours?'

I described it, including in my description the green ribbon. And forthwith he took the conductor under hand, and I felt, through all the storm of French which followed, that he raked him fore and aft. Presently he returned to me.

'The fellow avers he was overloaded, and confesses that he removed your trunk after you saw it put on, and has left it behind at Boue-Marine with other parcels; he has promised, however, to forward it tomorrow; the day after, therefore, you will find it safe at this bureau.'

'Thank you,' said I: but my heart sank.

Meantime what should I do? Perhaps this English gentleman saw the failure of courage in my face; he enquired kindly,

'Have you any friends in this city?'

'No, and I don't know where to go.'

There was a little pause, in the course of which, as he turned more fully to the light of a lamp above him, I saw that he was a young, distinguished, and handsome man; he might be a lord, for anything I knew: nature had made him good enough for a prince, I thought. His face was very pleasant; he looked high but not arrogant, manly but not overbearing. I was turning away, in the deep consciousness of all absence of claim to look for further help from such a one as he.

'Was all your money in your trunk?' he asked, stopping me.

How thankful was I to be able to answer with truth – 'No. I have enough in my purse' (for I had near twenty francs) 'to keep me at a quiet inn till the day after tomorrow; but I am quite a stranger in Villette, and don't know the streets and the inns.'

'I can give you the address of such an inn as you want,' said he; 'and it is not far off: with my direction you will easily find it.'

He tore a leaf from his pocket-book, wrote a few words and gave it to me. I *did* think him kind; and as to distrusting him, or his advice, or his address, I should almost as soon have thought of distrusting the Bible. There was goodness in his countenance, and honour in his bright eyes.

'Your shortest way will be to follow the boulevard, and cross the park,' he continued; 'but it is too late and too dark for a woman to go through the park alone; I will step with you thus far.'

He moved on, and I followed him, through the darkness and the small soaking rain. The Boulevard was all deserted, its path miry, the water dripping from its trees; the park was black as midnight. In the double gloom of trees and fog, I could not see my guide; I could only follow his tread. Not the least fear had I: I believe I would have followed that frank tread, through continual night, to the world's end.

'Now,' said he, when the park was traversed, 'you will go along this broad street till you come to steps; two lamps will show you where they are: these steps you will descend: a narrower street lies below; following that, at the bottom you will find your inn. They speak English there, so your difficulties are now pretty well over. Good-night.'

'Good-night, sir,' said I: 'accept my sincerest thanks.' And we parted.

The remembrance of his countenance, which I am sure wore a light not unbenignant to the friendless – the sound in my ear of his voice, which spoke a nature chivalric to the needy and feeble, as well as the youthful and fair – were a sort of cordial to me long after. He was a true young English gentleman.

On I went, hurrying fast through a magnificent street and square, with the grandest houses round, and amidst them the huge outline of more than one overbearing pile; which might be palace, or church – I could not tell. Just as I passed a portico, two moustachioed men came suddenly from behind the pillars; they were smoking cigars, their dress implied pretensions to the rank of gentlemen, but, poor things! they were very plebeian in soul. They spoke with insolence, and, fast as I walked, they kept pace with me a long way. At last I met a sort of patrol, and my dreaded hunters were turned from the pursuit; but they had driven me beyond my reckoning: when I could collect my faculties, I no longer knew where I was; the staircase I must long since have passed; puzzled, out of breath, all my pulses throbbing in inevitable agitation, I knew not where to turn. It was terrible to think of again encountering those bearded, sneering simpletons; yet the ground must be retraced, and the steps sought out.

I came at last to an old and worn flight, and, taking it for granted that this must be the one indicated, I descended them. The street into which they led was indeed narrow, but it contained no inn. On I wandered. In a very quiet and comparatively clean and well-paved street, I saw a light burning over the door of a rather large house, loftier by a storey than those round it. *This* might be the inn at last. I hastened on: my knees now trembled under me: I was getting quite exhausted.

No inn was this. A brass-plate embellished the great Porte-cochère: 'Pensionnat de Demoiselles' was the inscription; and beneath, a name, 'Mme Beck.'

I started. About a hundred thoughts volleyed through my mind in a moment. Yet I planned nothing, and considered nothing: I had not time. Providence said, 'Stop here; this is *your* inn.' Fate took me in her strong hand; mastered my will; directed my actions: I rung the doorbell.

While I waited, I would not reflect. I fixedly looked at the street-stones, where the door-lamp shone, and counted them, and noted their shapes, and the glitter of wet on their angles. I rang again. They opened at last. A bonne in a smart cap stood before me.

'May I see Mme Beck?' I enquired.

I believe if I had spoken French she would not have admitted me; but, as I spoke English, she concluded I was a foreign teacher come on business connected with the Pensionnat, and, even at that late hour, she let me in, without a word of reluctance or a moment of hesitation.

The next moment I sat in a cold, glittering salon, with porcelain stove unlit, and gilded ornaments, and polished floor. A pendule on the mantelpiece struck nine o'clock.

A quarter of an hour passed. How fast beat every pulse in my frame! How I turned cold and hot by turns! I sat with my eyes fixed on the door – a great white folding-door, with gilt mouldings: I watched to see a leaf move and open. All had been quiet: not a mouse had stirred; the white doors were closed and motionless.

'You ayre Engliss?' said a voice at my elbow. I almost bounded, so unexpected was the sound; so certain had I been of solitude.

No ghost stood beside me, nor anything of spectral aspect; merely a motherly, dumpy little woman, in a large shawl, a wrapping-gown, and a clean, trim night-cap.

I said I was English, and immediately, without further prelude, we fell to a most remarkable conversation. Mme Beck (for Mme Beck it was – she had entered by a little door behind me, and, being shod with the shoes of silence, I had heard neither her entrance nor approach) – Mme Beck had exhausted her command of insular speech when she said 'You ayre Engliss,' and she now proceeded to work away volubly in her own tongue. I answered in mine. She partly understood me, but as I did not at all understand her – though we made together an awful clamour (anything like madame's gift of utterance I had not hitherto heard or imagined) – we achieved little progress. She rang, ere long, for aid; which arrived in the shape of a 'maîtresse', who had been partly educated in an Irish convent, and was esteemed a perfect adept in the English language. A bluff little personage this maîtresse was – Labassecourienne from top to toe: and how she did slaughter the speech of Albion! However, I told her a plain tale, which she translated. I told her how I had left my own country, intent on extending my knowledge, and gaining my bread; how I was ready to turn my hand to any useful thing, provided it was not wrong or degrading: how I would be a child's-nurse or a lady's-maid, and would not refuse even housework adapted to my strength. Madame heard this; and, questioning her countenance, I almost thought the tale won her ear: 'Il n'y a que les Anglaises pour ces sortes d'entreprises,' said she: 'sont-elles donc intrépides ces femmes là!'

She asked my name, my age; she sat and looked at me – not pityingly, not with interest: never a gleam of sympathy, or a shade of compassion, crossed her countenance during the interview. I felt she was not one to be led an inch by her feelings: grave and considerate, she gazed, consulting her judgement and studying my narrative. A bell rang.

'Voilà pour la prière du soir!' said she, and rose. Through her interpreter, she desired me to depart now, and come back on the morrow; but this did not suit me: I could not bear to return to the perils of darkness and the street. With energy, yet with a collected and controlled manner, I said, addressing herself personally, and not the maîtresse: 'Be assured, madame, that by instantly securing my services, your interests will be served and not injured: you will find me one who will wish to give, in her labour, a full equivalent for her wages; and if you hire me, it will be better that I should stay here this night: having no acquaintance in Villette, and not possessing the language of the country, how can I secure a lodging?'

'It is true;' said she, 'but at least you can give a reference?'

'None.'

She enquired after my luggage: I told her when it would arrive. She mused. At that moment a man's step was heard in the vestibule, hastily proceeding to the outer door. (I shall go on with this part of my tale as if I had understood all that passed; for though it was then scarce intelligible to me, I heard it translated afterwards).

'Who goes out now?' demanded Mme Beck, listening to the tread.

'M. Paul,' replied the teacher. 'He came this evening to give a reading to the first class.'

'The very man I should at this moment most wish to see. Call him.'

The teacher ran to the salon door. M. Paul was summoned. He entered: a small, dark and spare man, in spectacles.

'Mon cousin,' began madame, 'I want your opinion. We know your skill in physiognomy; use it now. Read that countenance.'

The little man fixed on me his spectacles. A resolute compression of the lips, and gathering of the brow, seemed to say that he meant to see through me, and that a veil would be no veil for him.

'I read it,' he pronounced.

'Et qu'en dites-vous?'

'Mais – bien des choses,' was the oracular answer.

'Bad or good?'

'Of each kind, without doubt,' pursued the diviner.

'May one trust her word?'

'Are you negotiating a matter of importance?'

'She wishes me to engage her as bonne or gouvernante; tells a tale full of integrity, but gives no reference.'

'She is a stranger?'

'An Englishwoman, as one may see.'

'She speaks French?'

'Not a word.'

'She understands it?'

'No.'

'One may then speak plainly in her presence?'

'Doubtless.'

He gazed steadily. 'Do you need her services?'

'I could do with them. You know I am disgusted with Mme Svini.'

Still he scrutinised. The judgement, when it at last came, was as indefinite as what had gone before it.

'Engage her. If good predominates in that nature, the action will bring its own reward; if evil – eh bien! ma cousine, ce sera toujours une bonne oeuvre.' And with a bow and a 'bon soir,' this vague arbiter of my destiny vanished. And madame did engage me that very night – by God's blessing I was spared the necessity of passing forth again into the lonesome, dreary, hostile street.

## CHAPTER 8

## *Mme Beck*

Being delivered into the charge of the maîtresse, I was led through a long, narrow passage into a foreign kitchen, very clean but very strange. It seemed to contain no means of cooking – neither fireplace nor oven; I did not understand that the great black furnace which filled one corner, was an efficient substitute for these. Surely pride was not already beginning its whispers in my heart; yet I felt a sense of relief when, instead of being left in the kitchen, as I half-anticipated, I was led forward to a small inner room termed a 'cabinet.' A cook in a jacket, a short petticoat and sabots, brought my supper: to wit, some meat, nature unknown, served in an odd and acid, but pleasant sauce; some chopped potatoes, made savoury with, I know not what: vinegar and sugar, I think; a tartine, or slice of bread and butter, and a baked pear. Being hungry, I ate and was grateful.

After the 'Prière du Soir', madame herself came to have another look at me. She desired me to follow her upstairs. Through a series of the queerest little dormitories – which, I heard afterwards, had once been nuns' cells: for the premises were in part of ancient date – and through the oratory – a long, low, gloomy room, where a crucifix hung, pale, against the wall, and two tapers kept dim vigils – she conducted me to an apartment where three children were asleep in three tiny beds. A heated stove made the air of this room oppressive; and, to mend matters, it was scented with an odour rather strong than delicate: a perfume, indeed, altogether surprising and unexpected under the circumstances, being like the combination of smoke with some spirituous essence – a smell, in short, of whiskey.

Beside a table, on which flared the remnant of a candle guttering to waste in the socket, a coarse woman, heterogeneously clad in a broad-striped showy silk dress and a stuff apron, sat in a chair fast asleep. To complete the picture, and leave no doubt as to the state of matters, a bottle and an empty glass stood at the sleeping beauty's elbow.

Madame contemplated this remarkable tableau with great calm; she neither smiled nor scowled: no impress of anger, disgust, or surprise, ruffled the equality of her grave aspect; she did not even wake the woman. Serenely pointing to a fourth bed, she intimated that it was to be mine; then, having extinguished the candle and substituted for it a night-lamp, she glided through an inner door, which she left ajar: the entrance to her own chamber, a large, well-furnished apartment; as was discernible through the aperture.

My devotions that night were all thanksgiving: strangely had I been led since morning – unexpectedly had I been provided for. Scarcely could I believe that not forty-eight hours had elapsed since I left London, under no other guardianship

than that which protects the passenger-bird – with no prospect but the dubious cloud-tracery of hope.

I was a light sleeper; in the dead of night I suddenly awoke. All was hushed, but a white figure stood in the room – Madame in her night-dress. Moving without perceptible sound, she visited the three children in the three beds; she approached me: I feigned sleep, and she studied me long. A small pantomime ensued, curious enough. I dare say she sat a quarter of an hour on the edge of my bed, gazing at my face. She then drew nearer, bent close over me; slightly raised my cap, and turned back the border so as to expose my hair; she looked at my hand lying on the bedclothes. This done, she turned to the chair where my clothes lay: it was at the foot of the bed. Hearing her touch and lift them, I opened my eyes with precaution, for I own I felt curious to see how far her taste for research would lead her. It led her a good way: every article did she inspect. I divined her motive for this proceeding, viz., the wish to form from the garments a judgement respecting the wearer, her station, means, neatness, etc. The end was not bad, but the means were hardly fair or justifiable. In my dress was a pocket; she fairly turned it inside out: she counted the money in my purse; she opened a little memorandum-book, coolly perused its contents, and took from between the leaves a small plaited lock of Miss Marchmont's grey hair. To a bunch of three keys, being those of my trunk, desk, and workbox, she accorded special attention: with these, indeed, she withdrew a moment to her own room. I softly rose in my bed and followed her with my eye: these keys, reader, were not brought back till they had left on the toilet of the adjoining room the impress of their wards in wax. All being thus done decently and in order, my property was returned to its place, my clothes were carefully refolded. Of what nature were the conclusions deduced from this scrutiny? Were they favourable or otherwise? Vain question. Madame's face of stone (for of stone in its present night-aspect it looked: it had been human and, as I said before, motherly, in the salon) betrayed no response.

Her duty done – I felt that in her eyes this business was a duty – she rose, noiseless as a shadow: she moved towards her own chamber; at the door she turned, fixing her eye on the heroine of the bottle, who still slept and loudly snored. Mrs Svini (I presumed this was Mrs Svini, Anglicé or Hibernice, Sweeny) – Mrs Sweeny's doom was in Mme Beck's eye – an immutable purpose that eye spoke: madame's visitations for shortcomings might be slow, but they were sure. All this was very un-English: truly I was in a foreign land.

The morrow made me further acquainted with Mrs Sweeny. It seems she had introduced herself to her present employer as an English lady in reduced circumstances: a native, indeed, of Middlesex, professing to speak the English tongue with the purest metropolitan accent. Madame – reliant on her own infallible expedients for finding out the truth in time – had a singular intrepidity in hiring service offhand (as indeed seemed abundantly proved in my own case). She received Mrs Sweeny as nursery-governess to her three children. I need hardly explain to the reader that this lady was in effect a native of Ireland; her station I do not pretend to fix: she boldly declared that she had 'had the

bringing-up of the son and daughter of a marquis'. I think, myself, she might possibly have been hanger-on – nurse, fosterer, or washerwoman, in some Irish family: she spoke a smothered brogue, curiously overlaid with mincing cockney inflections. By some means or other she had acquired, and now held in possession, a wardrobe of rather suspicious splendour – gowns of stiff and costly silk, fitting her indifferently and apparently made for other proportions than those they now adorned; caps with real lace borders, and – the chief item in the inventory, the spell by which she struck a certain awe through the household, quelling the otherwise scornfully disposed teachers and servants, and, so long as her broad shoulders *wore* the folds of that majestic drapery, even influencing madame herself – a *real Indian shawl* – 'un véritable Cachmire', as Mme Beck said, with mixed reverence and amaze. I feel quite sure that without this 'Cachmire' she would not have kept her footing in the pensionnat for two days: by virtue of it, and it only, she maintained the same a month.

But when Mrs Sweeny knew that I was come to fill her shoes, then it was that she declared herself – then did she rise on Mme Beck in her full power – then come down on me with her concentrated weight. Madame bore this revelation and visitation so well, so stoically, that I for very shame could not support it otherwise than with composure. For one little moment Mme Beck absented herself from the room; ten minutes after, an agent of the police stood in the midst of us. Mrs Sweeny and her effects were removed. Madame's brow had not been ruffled during the scene – her lips had not dropped one sharply accented word.

This brisk little affair of the dismissal was all settled before breakfast: order to march given, policeman called, mutineer expelled, 'chambre d'enfants' fumigated and cleansed, windows thrown open, and every trace of the accomplished Mrs Sweeny – even to the fine essence and spiritual fragrance which gave token so subtle and so fatal of the head and front of her offending – was annihilated from the Rue Fossette: all this, I say, was done between the moment of Mme Beck's issuing like Aurora from her chamber, and that in which she coolly sat down to pour out her first cup of coffee.

About noon, I was summoned to dress madame. (It appeared my place was to be a hybrid between gouvernante and lady's-maid.) Till noon, she haunted the house in her wrapping-gown, shawl, and soundless slippers. How would the lady-chief of an English school approve this custom?

The dressing of her hair puzzled me; she had plenty of it; auburn, unmixed with grey: though she was forty years old. Seeing my embarrassment, she said, 'You have not been a femme de chambre in your own country?' And taking the brush from my hand and setting me aside, not ungently or disrespectfully, she arranged it herself. In performing other offices of the toilet, she half-directed, half-aided me, without the least display of temper or impatience. N.B. that was the first and last time I was required to dress her. Henceforth, on Rosine, the portress, devolved that duty.

When attired, Mme Beck appeared a personage of a figure rather short and stout, yet still graceful in its own peculiar way: that is, with the grace resulting from proportion of parts. Her complexion was fresh and sanguine, not too

rubicund; her eye, blue and serene; her dark silk dress fitted her as a French sempstress alone can make a dress fit; she looked well, though a little bourgeoise: as bourgeoise, indeed, she was. I know not what of harmony pervaded her whole person; and yet her face offered contrast, too; its features were by no means such as are usually seen in conjunction with a complexion of such blended freshness and repose: their outline was stern; her forehead was high but narrow; it expressed capacity and some benevolence, but no expanse; nor did her peaceful yet watchful eye ever know the fire which is kindled in the heart or the softness which flows thence. Her mouth was hard: it could be a little grim; her lips were thin. For sensibility and genius, with all their tenderness and temerity, I felt somehow that madame would be the right sort of Minos in petticoats.

In the long run, I found that she was something else in petticoats too. Her name was Modeste Maria Beck, née Kint: it ought to have been Ignacia. She was a charitable woman, and did a great deal of good. There never was a mistress whose rule was milder. I was told that she never once remonstrated with the intolerable Mrs Sweeny, despite her tipsiness, disorder, and general neglect; yet Mrs Sweeny had to go, the moment her departure became convenient. I was told, too, that neither masters nor teachers were found fault with in that establishment; yet both masters and teachers were often changed: they vanished and others filled their places, none could well explain how.

The establishment was both a pensionnat and an externat: the externes or day-pupils exceeded one hundred in number; the boarders were about a score. Madame must have possessed high administrative powers: she ruled all these, together with four teachers, eight masters, six servants, and three children, managing at the same time to perfection the pupils' parents and friends; and that without apparent effort; without bustle, fatigue, fever, or any symptom of undue excitement: occupied she always was – busy, rarely. It is true that madame had her own system for managing and regulating this mass of machinery; and a very pretty system it was: the reader has seen a specimen of it, in that small affair of turning my pocket inside out, and reading my private memoranda. 'Surveillance', 'espionage,' – these were her watchwords.

Still, madame knew what honesty was, and liked it – that is, when it did not obtrude its clumsy scruples in the way of her will and interest. She had a respect for 'Angleterre'; and as to 'les Anglaises', she would have the women of no other country about her own children, if she could help it.

Often in the evening, after she had been plotting and counter-plotting, spying and receiving the reports of spies all day, she would come up to my room – a trace of real weariness on her brow – and she would sit down and listen while the children said their little prayers to me in English: the Lord's Prayer, and the hymn beginning 'Gentle Jesus,' these little Catholics were permitted to repeat at my knee; and, when I had put them to bed, she would talk to me (I soon gained enough French to be able to understand, and even answer her) about England and Englishwomen, and the reasons for what she was pleased to term their superior intelligence, and more real and reliable probity. Very good sense she often showed; very sound opinions she often

broached: she seemed to know that keeping girls in distrustful restraint, in blind ignorance, and under a surveillance that left them no moment and no corner for retirement, was not the best way to make them grow up honest and modest women; but she averred that ruinous consequences would ensue if any other method were tried with continental children – they were so accustomed to constraint, that relaxation, however guarded, would be misunderstood and fatally presumed on: she was sick, she would declare, of the means she had to use, but use them she must; and after discoursing, often with dignity and delicacy, to me, she would move away on her 'souliers de silence,' and glide ghost-like through the house, watching and spying everywhere, peering through every keyhole, listening behind every door.

After all, madame's system was not bad – let me do her justice. Nothing could be better than all her arrangements for the physical well-being of her scholars. No minds were overtasked; the lessons were well distributed and made incomparably easy to the learner; there was a liberty of amusement, and a provision for exercise which kept the girls healthy; the food was abundant and good: neither pale nor puny faces were anywhere to be seen in the Rue Fossette. She never grudged a holiday; she allowed plenty of time for sleeping, dressing, washing, eating; her method in all these matters was easy, liberal, salutary, and rational: many an austere English schoolmistress would do vastly well to imitate it – and I believe many would be glad to do so, if exacting English parents would let them.

As Mme Beck ruled by espionage, she of course had her staff of spies: she perfectly knew the quality of the tools she used, and while she would not scruple to handle the dirtiest for a dirty occasion – flinging this sort from her like refuse rind, after the orange has been duly squeezed – I have known her fastidious in seeking pure metal for clean uses; and when once a bloodless and rustless instrument was found, she was careful of the prize, keeping it in silk and cotton-wool. Yet, woe be to that man or woman who relied on her one inch beyond the point where it was her interest to be trustworthy: interest was the master-key of madame's nature – the mainspring of her motives – the alpha and omega of her life. I have seen her *feelings* appealed to, and I have smiled in half-pity, half-scorn at the appellants. None ever gained her ear through that channel, or swayed her purpose by that means. On the contrary, to attempt to touch her heart was the surest way to rouse her antipathy, and to make of her a secret foe. It proved to her that she had no heart to be touched: it reminded her where she was impotent and dead. Never was the distinction between charity and mercy better exemplified than in her. While devoid of sympathy, she had a sufficiency of rational benevolence: she would give in the readiest manner to people she had never seen – rather, however, to classes than to individuals. 'Pour les pauvres,' she opened her purse freely – against *the poor man*, as a rule, she kept it closed. In philanthropic schemes, for the benefit of society at large, she took a cheerful part; no private sorrow touched her: no force or mass of suffering concentrated in one heart had power to pierce hers. Not the agony in Gethsemane, not the death on Calvary, could have wrung from her eyes one tear.

I say again, madame was a very great and a very capable woman. That school offered for her powers too limited a sphere; she ought to have swayed a nation: she should have been the leader of a turbulent legislative assembly. Nobody could have browbeaten her, none irritated her nerves, exhausted her patience, or overreached her astuteness. In her own single person, she could have comprised the duties of a first minister and a superintendent of police. Wise, firm, faithless; secret, crafty, passionless; watchful and inscrutable; acute and insensate – withal perfectly decorous – what more could be desired?

The sensible reader will not suppose that I gained all the knowledge here condensed for his benefit in one month, or in one half-year. No! what I saw at first was the thriving outside of a large and flourishing educational establishment. Here was a great houseful of healthy, lively girls, all well-dressed and many of them handsome, gaining knowledge by a marvellously easy method, without painful exertion or useless waste of spirits; not, perhaps, making very rapid progress in anything; taking it easy, but still always employed, and never op-pressed. Here was a corps of teachers and masters more stringently tasked, as all the real head-labour was to be done by them, in order to save the pupils, yet having their duties so arranged that they relieved each other in quick succession whenever the work was severe; here, in short, was a foreign school; of which the life, movement, and variety made it a complete and most charming contrast to many English institutions of the same kind.

Behind the house was a large garden, and, in summer, the pupils almost lived out of doors amongst the rose bushes and the fruit trees. Under the vast and vine-draped berceau, madame would take her seat on summer afternoons, and send for the classes, in turns, to sit round her and sew and read. Meantime, masters came and went, delivering short and lively lectures, rather than lessons, and the pupils made notes of their instructions, or did *not* make them – just as inclination prompted; secure that, in case of neglect, they could copy the notes of their companions. Besides the regular monthly *jours de sortie*, the Catholic fête-days brought a succession of holidays all the year round; and sometimes on a bright summer morning, or soft summer evening, the boarders were taken out for a long walk into the country, regaled with *gaufres* and *vin blanc*, or new milk and *pain bis*, or *pistolets au beurre* (rolls) and coffee. All this seemed very pleasant, and madame appeared goodness itself; and the teachers not so bad, but they might be worse; and the pupils, perhaps, a little noisy and rough, but types of health and glee.

Thus did the view appear, seen through the enchantment of distance; but there came a time when distance was to melt for me, when I was to be called down from my watch-tower of the nursery, whence I had hitherto made my observations, and was to be compelled into closer intercourse with this little world of the Rue Fossette.

I was one day sitting upstairs, as usual, hearing the children their English lessons, and at the same time turning a silk dress for madame, when she came sauntering into the room with that absorbed air, and brow of hard thought she sometimes wore, and which made her look so little genial. Dropping into a seat

opposite mine, she remained some minutes silent. Désirée, the eldest girl, was reading to me some little essay of Mrs Barbauld's, and I was making her translate currently from English to French as she proceeded, by way of ascertaining that she comprehended what she read: madame listened.

Presently, without preface or prelude, she said, almost in the tone of one making an accusation, 'Meess, in England you were a governess.'

'No, madame,' said I smiling, 'you are mistaken.'

'Is this your first essay at teaching – this attempt with my children?'

I assured her it was. Again she became silent; but looking up, as I took a pin from the cushion, I found myself an object of study: she held me under her eye; she seemed turning me round in her thoughts – measuring my fitness for a purpose, weighing my value in a plan. Madame had, ere this, scrutinised all I had, and I believe she esteemed herself cognisant of much that I was; but from that day, for the space of about a fortnight, she tried me by new tests. She listened at the nursery door when I was shut in with the children; she followed me at a cautious distance when I walked out with them, stealing within earshot whenever the trees of park or boulevard afforded a sufficient screen: a strict preliminary process having thus been observed, she made a move forward.

One morning, coming on me abruptly, and with the semblance of hurry, she said she found herself placed in a little dilemma. Mr Wilson, the English master, had failed to come at his hour, she feared he was ill; the pupils were waiting in *classe*; there was no one to give a lesson; should I, for once, object to giving a short dictation exercise, just that the pupils might not have it to say they had missed their English lesson?

'In classe, madame?' I asked.

'Yes, in classe: in the second division.'

'Where there are sixty pupils,' said I; for I knew the number, and with my usual base habit of cowardice, I shrunk into my sloth, like a snail into its shell, and alleged incapacity and impracticability as a pretext to escape action. If let to myself, I should infallibly have let this chance slip. Inadventurous, unstirred by impulses of practical ambition, I was capable of sitting twenty years teaching infants the hornbook, turning silk dresses, and making children's frocks. Not that true contentment dignified this infatuated resignation: my work had neither charm for my taste, nor hold on my interest; but it seemed to me a great thing to be without heavy anxiety, and relieved from intimate trial; the negation of severe suffering was the nearest approach to happiness I expected to know. Besides, I seemed to hold two lives – the life of thought, and that of reality; and, provided the former was nourished with a sufficiency of the strange necromantic joys of fancy, the privileges of the latter might remain limited to daily bread, hourly work, and a roof of shelter.

'Come,' said madame, as I stooped more busily than ever over the cutting out of a child's pinafore, 'leave that work.'

'But Fifine wants it, madame.'

'Fifine must want it, then, for *I* want *you*.'

And as Mme Beck did really want and was resolved to have me – as she had

long been dissatisfied with the English master, with his shortcomings in punctuality, and his careless method of tuition – as, too, *she* did not lack resolution and practical activity, whether *I* lacked them or not – she, without more ado, made me relinquish thimble and needle; my hand was taken into hers, and I was conducted down stairs. When we reached the carré, a large square hall between the dwelling-house and the pensionnat, she paused, dropped my hand, faced, and scrutinised me. I was flushed, and tremulous from head to foot; tell it not in Gath, I believe I was crying. In fact, the difficulties before me were far from being wholly imaginary; some of them were real enough; and not the least substantial lay in my want of mastery over the medium through which I should be obliged to teach. I had, indeed, studied French closely since my arrival in Villette; learning its practice by day, and its theory in every leisure moment at night, to as late an hour as the rule of the house would allow candle-light, but I was far from yet being able to trust my powers of correct oral expression.

'Dîtes donc,' said madame sternly, 'vous sentez-vous réellement trop faible?'

I might have said 'Yes,' and gone back to nursery obscurity, and there, perhaps, mouldered for the rest of my life; but, looking up at madame, I saw in her countenance a something that made me think twice ere I decided. At that instant, she did not wear a woman's aspect, but rather a man's. Power of a particular kind strongly limned itself in all her traits, and that power was not *my* kind of power: neither sympathy, nor congeniality, nor submission, were the emotions it awakened. I stood – not soothed, nor won, nor overwhelmed. It seemed as if a challenge of strength between opposing gifts was given, and I suddenly felt all the dishonour of my diffidence – all the pusillanimity of my slackness to aspire.

'Will you,' said she, 'go backward or forward?' indicating with her hand, first, the small door of communication with the dwelling-house, and then the great double portals of the classes or school-rooms.

'En avant,' I said.

'But,' pursued she, cooling as I warmed, and continuing the hard look, from very antipathy to which I drew strength and determination, 'can you face the classes, or are you over-excited?'

She sneered slightly in saying this – nervous excitability was not much to madame's taste.

'I am no more excited than this stone,' I said, tapping the flag with my toe: 'or than you,' I added, returning her look.

'Bon! But let me tell you these are not quiet, decorous English girls you are going to encounter. Ce sont des Labassecouriennes, rondes, franches, brusques, et tant soit peu rebelles.'

I said: 'I know; and I know, too, that though I have studied French hard since I came here, yet I still speak it with far too much hesitation – too little accuracy to be able to command their respect: I shall make blunders that will lay me open to the scorn of the most ignorant. Still I mean to give the lesson.'

'They always throw over timid teachers,' said she.

'I know that, too, madame; I have heard how they rebelled against and persecuted Miss Turner' – a poor, friendless English teacher, whom madame had employed, and lightly discarded; and to whose piteous history I was no stranger.

'C'est vrai,' said she, coolly. 'Miss Turner had no more command over them than a servant from the kitchen would have had. She was weak and wavering; she had neither tact nor intelligence, decision nor dignity. Miss Turner would not do for these girls at all.'

I made no reply, but advanced to the closed schoolroom door.

'You will not expect aid from me, or from anyone,' said madame. 'That would at once set you down as incompetent for your office.'

I opened the door, let her pass with courtesy, and followed her. There were three school-rooms, all large. That dedicated to the second division, where I was to figure, was considerably the largest, and accommodated an assemblage more numerous, more turbulent, and infinitely more unmanageable than the other two. In after days, when I knew the ground better, I used to think sometimes (if such a comparison may be permitted), that the quiet, polished, tame first division, was to the robust, riotous, demonstrative second division, what the English House of Lords is to the House of Commons.

The first glance informed me that many of the pupils were more than girls – quite young women; I knew that some of them were of noble family (as nobility goes in Labassecour), and I was well convinced that not one amongst them was ignorant of my position in madame's household. As I mounted the estrade (a low platform, raised a step above the flooring), where stood the teacher's chair and desk, I beheld opposite to me a row of eyes and brows that threatened stormy weather – eyes full of an insolent light, and brows hard and unblushing as marble. The continental 'female' is quite a different being to the insular 'female' of the same age and class: I never saw such eyes and brows in England. Mme Beck introduced me in one cool phrase, sailed from the room, and left me alone in my glory.

I shall never forget that first lesson, nor all the undercurrent of life and character it opened up to me. Then first did I begin rightly to see the wide difference that lies between the novelist's and poet's ideal 'jeune fille', and the said 'jeune fille' as she really is.

It seemed that three titled belles in the first row had sat down predetermined that a *bonne d'enfants* should not give them lessons in English. They knew they had succeeded in expelling obnoxious teachers before now; they knew that madame would at any time throw overboard a professeur or maîtresse who became unpopular with the school – that she never assisted a weak official to retain his place – that if he had not strength to fight, or tact to win his way – down he went: looking at 'Miss Snowe' they promised themselves an easy victory.

Mesdemoiselles Blanche, Virginie, and Angélique opened the campaign by a series of titterings and whisperings; these soon swelled into murmurs and short laughs, which the remoter benches caught up and echoed more loudly. This growing revolt of sixty against one, soon became oppressive enough; my

command of French being so limited, and exercised under such cruel constraint.

Could I but have spoken in my own tongue, I felt as if I might have gained a hearing; for, in the first place, though I knew I looked a poor creature, and in many respects actually was so, yet nature had given me a voice that could make itself heard, if lifted in excitement or deepened by emotion. In the second place, while I had no flow, only a hesitating trickle of language, in ordinary circumstances, yet – under stimulus such as was now rife through the mutinous mass – I could, in English, have rolled out readily phrases stigmatising their proceedings as such proceedings deserved to be stigmatised; and then with some sarcasm, flavoured with contemptuous bitterness, for the ringleaders, and relieved with easy banter for the weaker, but less knavish followers, it seemed to me that one might possibly get command over this wild herd and bring them into training, at least. All I could now do was to walk up to Blanche – Mlle de Melcy, a young baronne – the eldest, tallest, handsomest, and most vicious – stand before her desk, take from under her hand her exercise-book, remount the estrade, deliberately read the composition, which I found very stupid, and as deliberately, and in the face of the whole school, tear the blotted page in two.

This action availed to draw attention and check noise. One girl alone, quite in the background, persevered in the riot with undiminished energy. I looked at her attentively. She had a pale face, hair like night, broad strong eyebrows, decided features, and a dark, mutinous, sinister eye: I noted that she sat close by a little door, which door, I was well aware, opened into a small closet where books were kept. She was standing up for the purpose of conducting her clamour with freer energies. I measured her stature and calculated her strength. She seemed both tall and wiry; but, so the conflict were brief and the attack unexpected, I thought I might manage her.

Advancing up the room, looking as cool and careless as I possibly could, in short, *ayant l'air de rien*; I slightly pushed the door and found it was ajar. In an instant, and with sharpness, I had turned on her. In another instant she occupied the closet, the door was shut, and the key in my pocket.

It so happened that this girl, Dolores by name and a Catalonian by race, was the sort of character at once dreaded and hated by all her associates; the act of summary justice above noted, proved popular: there was not one present but, in her heart, liked to see it done. They were stilled for a moment; then a smile – not a laugh – passed from desk to desk: then – when I had gravely and tranquilly returned to the estrade, courteously requested silence, and commenced a dictation as if nothing at all had happened – the pens travelled peacefully over the pages, and the remainder of the lesson passed in order and industry.

'C'est bien,' said Mme Beck, when I came out of class, hot and a little exhausted, 'Ça ira.'

She had been listening and peeping through a spy-hole the whole time.

From that day I ceased to be nursery-governess, and became English teacher. Madame raised my salary; but she got thrice the work out of me she had extracted from Mr Wilson, at half the expense.

## Isidore

My time was now well and profitably filled up. What with teaching others and studying closely myself, I had hardly a spare moment. It was pleasant. I felt I was getting on; not lying the stagnant prey of mould and rust, but polishing my faculties and whetting them to a keen edge with constant use. Experience of a certain kind lay before me, on no narrow scale. Villette is a cosmopolitan city, and in this school were girls of almost every European nation, and likewise of very varied rank in life. Equality is much practised in Labassecour; though not republican in form, it is nearly so in substance, and at the desks of Mme Beck's establishment the young countess and the young bourgeoise sat side by side: nor could you always by outward indications decide which was noble and which plebeian; except that, indeed, the latter had often franker and more courteous manners, while the former bore away the bell for a delicately balanced combination of insolence and deceit. In the former there was often quick French blood mixed with their marsh-phlegm: I regret to say that the effect of this vivacious fluid chiefly appeared in the oilier glibness with which flattery and fiction ran from the tongue, and in a manner lighter and livelier, but quite heartless and insincere.

To do all parties justice, the honest aboriginal Labassecouriennes had an hypocrisy of their own too; but it was of a coarse order, such as could deceive few. Whenever a lie was necessary for their occasions, they brought it out with a careless ease and breadth altogether untroubled by the rebuke of conscience. Not a soul in Mme Beck's house, from the scullion to the directress herself, but was above being ashamed of a lie; they thought nothing of it: to invent might not be precisely a virtue, but it was the most venial of faults. 'J'ai menti plusieurs fois' formed an item of every girl's and woman's monthly confession: the priest heard unshocked, and absolved unreluctant. If they had missed going to mass, or read a chapter of a novel, that was another thing: these were crimes whereof rebuke and penance were the unfailing meed.

While yet but half-conscious of this state of things, and unlearned in its results, I got on in my new sphere very well. After the first few difficult lessons, given amidst peril and on the edge of a moral volcano, that rumbled under my feet and sent sparks and hot fumes into my eyes, the eruptive spirit seemed to subside, as far as I was concerned. My mind was a good deal bent on success: I could not bear the thought of being baffled by mere undisciplined disaffection and wanton indocility, in the first attempt to get on in life. Many hours of the night I used to lie awake thinking what plan I had best adopt to get a reliable hold on these mutineers, to bring this stiff-necked tribe under permanent influence. In the first place, I saw plainly that aid in no shape was to be expected

from Madame: her righteous plan was to maintain an unbroken popularity with the pupils, at any and every cost of justice or comfort to the teachers. For a teacher to seek her alliance in any crisis of insubordination was equivalent to securing her own expulsion. In intercourse with her pupils, Madame only took to herself what was pleasant, amiable, and recommendatory; rigidly requiring of her lieutenants sufficiency for every annoying crisis, where to act with adequate promptitude was to be unpopular. Thus, I must look only to myself.

Imprimis – it was clear as the day that this swinish multitude were not to be driven by force. They were to be humoured, borne with very patiently: a courteous though sedate manner impressed them; a very rare flash of raillery did good. Severe or continuous mental application they could not, or would not, bear: heavy demand on the memory, the reason, the attention, they rejected point-blank. Where an English girl of not more than average capacity and docility, would quietly take a theme and bind herself to the task of comprehension and mastery, a Labassecourienne would laugh in your face, and throw it back to you with the phrase, 'Dieu que c'est difficile! Je n'en veux pas. Cela m'ennuie trop.'

A teacher who understood her business would take it back at once, without hesitation, contest, or expostulation – proceed with even exaggerated care to smooth every difficulty, to reduce it to the level of their understandings, return it to them thus modified, and lay on the lash of sarcasm with unsparing hand. They would feel the sting, perhaps wince a little under it, but they bore no malice against this sort of attack, provided the sneer was not *sour* but *hearty*, and that it held well up to them, in a clear light and bold type, so that she who ran might read, their incapacity, ignorance, and sloth. They would riot for three additional lines to a lesson; but I never knew them rebel against a wound given to their self-respect: the little they had of that quality was trained to be crushed, and it rather liked the pressure of a firm heel, than otherwise.

By degrees, as I acquired fluency and freedom in their language, and could make such application of its more nervous idioms as suited their case, the elder and more intelligent girls began rather to like me, in their way: I noticed that whenever a pupil had been roused to feel in her soul the stirring of worthy emulation, or the quickening of honest shame, from that date she was won. If I could but once make their (usually large) ears burn under their thick, glossy hair, all was comparatively well. By and by bouquets began to be laid on my desk in the morning: by way of acknowledgement for this little foreign attention, I used sometimes to walk with a select few during recreation. In the course of conversation it befell once or twice that I made an unpremeditated attempt to rectify some of their singularly distorted notions of principle, especially I expressed my ideas of the evil and baseness of a lie. In an unguarded moment, I chanced to say that, of the two errors, I considered falsehood worse than an occasional lapse in church-attendance. The poor girls were tutored to report in Catholic ears whatever the Protestant teacher said. An edifying consequence ensued. Something – an unseen, an indefinite, a nameless something – stole between myself and these my best pupils: the bouquets continued to be offered,

but conversation thenceforth became impracticable. As I paced the alleys or sat in the berceau, a girl never came to my right hand but a teacher, as if by magic, appeared at my left. Also, wonderful to relate, Madame's shoes of silence brought her continually to my back, as quick, noiseless, and unexpected, as some wandering zephyr.

The opinion of my Catholic acquaintance concerning my spiritual prospects was somewhat naively expressed to me on one occasion. A pensionnaire, to whom I had rendered some little service, exclaimed one day as she sat beside me: 'Mademoiselle, what a pity you are a Protestant!'

'Why, Isabelle?'

'Parceque, quand vous serez morte – vous brûlerez tout de suite dans l'Enfer.'

'Croyez-vous?'

'Certainement que j'y crois: tout le monde le sait; et d'ailleurs le prêtre me l'a dit.'

Isabelle was an odd, blunt little creature. She added, *sotto voce*: 'Pour assurer votre salut là-haut, on ferait bien de vous brûler toute vive ici-bas.'

I laughed, as, indeed, it was impossible to do otherwise.

Has the reader forgotten Miss Ginevra Fanshawe? If so, I must be allowed to re-introduce that young lady as a thriving pupil of Mme Beck's, for such she was. On her arrival in the Rue Fossette, two or three days after my sudden settlement there, she encountered me with very little surprise. She must have had good blood in her veins, for never was any duchess more perfectly, radically, unaffectedly *nonchalante* than she: a weak, transient amaze was all she knew of the sensation of wonder. Most of her other faculties seemed to be in the same flimsy condition: her liking and disliking, her love and hate, were mere cobweb and gossamer; but she had one thing about her that seemed strong and durable enough, and that was – her selfishness.

She was not proud; and – *bonne d'enfants* as I was – she would forthwith have made of me a sort of friend and confidant. She teased me with a thousand vapid complaints about school-quarrels and household economy: the cookery was not to her taste – the people about her, teachers and pupils, she held to be despicable, because they were foreigners. I bore with her abuse of the Friday's salt-fish and hard eggs – with her invective against the soup, the bread, the coffee – with some patience for a time; but at last, wearied by iteration, I turned crusty and put her to rights – a thing I ought to have done in the very beginning, for a salutary setting down always agreed with her.

Much longer had I to endure her demands on me in the way of work. Her wardrobe, so far as concerned articles of external wear, was well and elegantly supplied; but there were other habiliments not so carefully provided: what she had, needed frequent repair. She hated needle-drudgery herself, and she would bring her hose, etc., to me in heaps, to be mended. A compliance of some weeks threatening to result in the establishment of an intolerable bore – I at last distinctly told her she must make up her mind to mend her own garments. She cried on receiving this information, and accused me of having ceased to be

her friend; but I held by my decision, and let the hysterics pass as they could.

Notwithstanding these foibles, and various others needless to mention – but by no means of a refined or elevating character – how pretty she was! How charming she looked, when she came down on a sunny Sunday morning, well-dressed and well-humoured, robed in pale lilac silk, and with her fair long curls reposing on her white shoulders. Sunday was a holiday which she always passed with friends resident in town; and amongst these friends she speedily gave me to understand was one who would fain become something more. By glimpses and hints it was shown me, and by the general buoyancy of her look and manner it was ere long proved that ardent admiration – perhaps genuine love – was at her command. She called her suitor 'Isidore': this, however, she intimated was not his real name, but one by which it pleased her to baptise him – his own, she hinted, not being 'very pretty.' Once, when she had been bragging about the vehemence of 'Isidore's' attachment, I asked if she loved him in return.

'Comme cela,' said she: 'he is handsome, and he loves me to distraction, so that I am well amused. Ça suffit.'

Finding that she carried the thing on longer than, from her very fickle tastes, I had anticipated, I one day took it upon me to make serious enquiries as to whether the gentleman was such as her parents, and especially her uncle – on whom, it appeared, she was dependent – would be likely to approve. She allowed that this was very doubtful, as she did not believe 'Isidore' had much money.

'Do you encourage him?' I asked.

'Furieusement, sometimes,' said she.

'Without being certain that you will be permitted to marry him?'

'Oh how dowdyish you are! I don't want to be married. I am too young.'

'But if he loves you as much as you say, and yet it comes to nothing in the end, he will be made miserable.'

'Of course he will break his heart. I should be shocked and disappointed if he didn't.'

'I wonder whether this M. Isidore is a fool?' said I.

'He is, about me; but he is wise in other things, à ce qu'on dit. Mrs Cholmondeley considers him extremely clever: she says he will push his way by his talents; all I know is, that he does little more than sigh in my presence, and that I can wind him round my little finger.'

Wishing to get a more definite idea of this love-stricken M. Isidore, whose position seemed to me of the least secure, I requested her to favour me with a personal description; but she could not describe: she had neither words, nor the power of putting them together so as to make graphic phrases. She even seemed not properly to have noticed him: nothing of his looks, of the changes in his countenance, had touched her heart or dwelt in her memory – that he was 'beau, mais plutôt bel homme, que joli garçon,' was all she could assert. My patience would often have failed, and my interest flagged, in listening to her, but for one thing. All the hints she dropped, all the details she gave, went unconsciously to prove, to my thinking, that M. Isidore's homage was offered with great delicacy and respect. I informed her very plainly that I believed him much too good for

her, and intimated with equal plainness my impression that she was but a vain coquette. She laughed, shook her curls from her eyes, and danced away as if I had paid her a compliment.

Miss Ginevra's school-studies were little better than nominal; there were but three things she practised in earnest, viz., music, singing, and dancing; also embroidering the fine cambric handkerchiefs which she could not afford to buy ready-worked: such mere trifles as lessons in history, geography, grammar, and arithmetic, she left undone, or got others to do for her. Very much of her time was spent in visiting. Madame, aware that her stay at school was now limited to a certain period which would not be extended whether she made progress or not, allowed her great license in this particular. Mrs Cholmondeley – her *chaperon* – a gay fashionable lady, invited her whenever she had company at her own house, and sometimes took her to evening parties at the houses of her acquaintance. Ginevra perfectly approved this mode of procedure – it had but one inconvenience; she was obliged to be well dressed, and she had not money to buy variety of dresses. All her thoughts turned on this difficulty; her whole soul was occupied with expedients for effecting its solution. It was wonderful to witness the activity of her otherwise indolent mind on this point, and to see the much-daring intrepidity to which she was spurred by a sense of necessity, and the wish to shine.

She begged boldly of Mrs Cholmondeley – boldly, I say: not with an air of reluctant shame, but in this strain: 'My darling Mrs C., I have nothing in the world fit to wear for your party next week; you *must* give me a book-muslin dress, and then a *ceinture bleu celeste: do* – there's an angel! will you?'

The 'darling Mrs C.' yielded at first; but finding that applications increased as they were complied with, she was soon obliged, like all Miss Fanshawe's friends, to oppose resistance to encroachment. After a while I heard no more of Mrs Cholmondeley's presents; but still, visiting went on, and the absolutely necessary dresses continued to be supplied: also many little expensive *etceterae* – gloves, bouquets, even trinkets. These things, contrary to her custom, and even nature – for she was not secretive – were most sedulously kept out of sight for a time; but one evening when she was going to a large party, for which particular care and elegance of costume were demanded, she could not resist coming to my chamber to show herself in all her splendour.

Beautiful she looked: so young, so fresh, and with a delicacy of skin and flexibility of shape altogether English, and not found in the list of continental female charms. Her dress was new, costly, and perfect. I saw at a glance that it lacked none of those finishing details which cost so much, and give to the general effect such an air of tasteful completeness.

I viewed her from top to toe. She turned airily round that I might survey her on all sides. Conscious of her charms, she was in her best humour: her rather small blue eyes sparkled gleefully; she was going to bestow on me a kiss, in her school girl fashion of showing her delight: but I said, 'Steady! Let us be steady, and know what we are about, and find the meaning of our magnificence' – and so put her off at arm's length, to undergo cooler inspection.

'Shall I do?' was her question.

'Do?' said I. 'There are different ways of doing; and, by my word, I don't understand yours.'

'But how do I look?'

'You look well dressed.'

She thought the praise not warm enough, and proceeded to direct attention to the various decorative points of her attire. 'Look at this *parure*,' said she. 'The brooch, the ear-rings, the bracelets: no one in the school has such a set – not madame herself.'

'I see them all.' (Pause.) 'Did M. de Bassompierre give you those jewels?'

'My uncle knows nothing about them.'

'Were they presents from Mrs Cholmondeley?'

'Not they, indeed. Mrs Cholmondeley is a mean, stingy creature; she never gives me anything now.'

I did not choose to ask any further questions, but turned abruptly away.

'Now, old Crusty – old Diogenes' (these were her familiar terms for me when we disagreed), 'what is the matter now?'

'Take yourself away. I have no pleasure in looking at you or your *parure*.'

For an instant, she seemed taken by surprise.

'What now, Mother Wisdom? I have not got into debt for it – that is, not for the jewels, nor the gloves, nor the bouquet. My dress is certainly not paid for, but uncle de Bassompierre will pay it in the bill: he never notices items, but just looks at the total; and he is so rich, one need not care about a few guineas more or less.'

'Will you go? I want to shut the door . . . Ginevra, people may tell you you are very handsome in that ball-attire; but, in *my* eyes, you will never look so pretty as you did in the gingham gown and plain straw bonnet you wore when I first saw you.'

'Other people have not your puritanical tastes:' was her angry reply. 'And, besides, I see no right you have to sermonise me.'

'Certainly! I have little right; and you, perhaps, have still less to come flourishing and fluttering into my chamber – a mere jay in borrowed plumes. I have not the least respect for your feathers, Miss Fanshawe; and especially the peacock's eyes, you call a *parure*: very pretty things, if you had bought them with money which was your own, and which you could well spare, but not at all pretty under present circumstances.'

'On est là pour Mlle Fanshawe!' was announced by the portress, and away she tripped.

This semi-mystery of the *parure* was not solved till two or three days afterwards, when she came to make a voluntary confession.

'You need not be sulky with me,' she began, 'in the idea that I am running somebody, papa or M. de Bassompierre, deeply into debt. I assure you nothing remains unpaid for, but the few dresses I have lately had: all the rest is settled.'

'There,' I thought, 'lies the mystery, considering that they were not given you by Mrs Cholmondeley, and that your own means are limited to a few shillings, of which I know you to be excessively careful.'

'Ecoutez!' she went on, drawing near and speaking in her most confidential and coaxing tone; for my 'sulkiness' was inconvenient to her: she liked me to be in a talking and listening mood, even if I only talked to chide, and listened to rail. 'Ecoutez, chère grogneuse! I will tell you all how and about it; and you will then see, not only how right the whole thing is, but how cleverly managed. In the first place, *I must* go out. Papa himself said that he wished me to see something of the world: he particularly remarked to Mrs Cholmondeley, that, though I was a sweet creature enough, I had rather a bread-and-butter-eating, schoolgirl air; of which it was his special desire that I should get rid, by an introduction to society here, before I make my regular *début* in England. Well, then, if I go out, *I must* dress. Mrs Cholmondeley is turned shabby, and will give nothing more; it would be too hard upon uncle to make him pay for *all* the things I need: *that* you can't deny – *that* agrees with your own preachments. Well, but *somebody* who heard me (quite by chance, I assure you) complaining to Mrs Cholmondeley of my distressed circumstances, and what straits I was put to for an ornament or two: *somebody*, far from grudging one a present, was quite delighted at the idea of being permitted to offer some trifle. You should have seen what a *blanc-bec* he looked when he first spoke of it: how he hesitated and blushed, and positively trembled from fear of a repulse.'

'That will do, Miss Fanshawe. I suppose I am to understand that M. Isidore is the benefactor: that it is from him you have accepted that costly *parure;* that he supplies your bouquets and your gloves?'

'You express yourself so disagreeably,' said she, 'one hardly knows how to answer; what I mean to say is, that I occasionally allow Isidore the pleasure and honour of expressing his homage, by the offer of a trifle.'

'It comes to the same thing . . . Now, Ginevra, to speak the plain truth, I don't very well understand these matters; but I believe you are doing very wrong – seriously wrong. Perhaps, however, you now feel certain that you will be able to marry M. Isidore – your parents and uncle have given their consent – and, for your part, you love him entirely?'

'Mais pas du tout!' (she always had recourse to French, when about to say something specially heartless and perverse). 'Je suis sa reine, mais il n'est pas mon roi.'

'Excuse me, I must believe this language is mere nonsense and coquetry. There is nothing great about you, yet you are above profiting by the good nature and the purse of a man to whom you feel absolute indifference. You love M. Isidore far more than you think, or will avow.'

'No. I danced with a young officer the other night, whom I love a thousand times more than he. I often wonder why I feel so very cold to Isidore, for everybody says he is handsome, and other ladies admire him; but, somehow, he bores me: let me see now how it is . . . '

And she seemed to make an effort to reflect. In this I encouraged her. 'Yes!' I said, 'try to get a clear idea of the state of your mind. To me, it seems in a great mess – chaotic as a rag-bag.'

'It is something in this fashion,' she cried out ere long: 'the man is too romantic and devoted, and he expects something more of me than I find it convenient to be.

He thinks I am perfect: furnished with all sorts of sterling qualities and solid virtues, such as I never had, nor intend to have. Now, one can't help, in his presence, rather trying to justify his good opinion; and it does so tire one to be goody, and to talk sense, for he really thinks I am sensible. I am far more at my ease with you, old lady – you, you dear crosspatch – who take me at my lowest, and know me to be coquettish, and ignorant, and flirting, and fickle, and silly, and selfish, and all the other sweet things you and I have agreed to be a part of my character.'

'This is all very well,' I said, making a strenuous effort to preserve that gravity and severity which ran risk of being shaken by this whimsical candour, 'but it does not alter that wretched business of the presents. Pack them up, Ginevra, like a good, honest girl, and send them back.'

'Indeed, I won't,' said she stoutly.

'Then you are deceiving M. Isidore. It stands to reason that by accepting his presents you give him to understand he will one day receive an equivalent, in your regard . . . '

'But he won't,' she interrupted: 'he has his equivalent now, in the pleasure of seeing me wear them – quite enough for him: he is only bourgeois.'

This phrase, in its senseless arrogance, quite cured me of the temporary weakness which had made me relax my tone and aspect. She rattled on: 'My present business is to enjoy youth, and not to think of fettering myself, by promise or vow, to this man or that. When first I saw Isidore, I believed he would help me to enjoy it. I believed he would be content with my being a pretty girl; and that we should meet and part and flutter about like two butterflies, and be happy. Lo, and behold! I find him at times as grave as a judge, and deep-feeling and thoughtful. Bah! Les penseurs, les hommes profonds et passionés, ne sont pas à mon gout. Le Colonel Alfred de Hamal suits me far better. Va pour les beaux fats et les jolis fripons! Vive les joies et les plaisirs! A bas les grandes passions et les sévères vertus!'

She looked for an answer to this tirade. I gave none.

'J'aime mon beau colonel,' she went on: 'Je n'aimerai jamais son rival. Je ne serai jamais femme de bourgeois, moi!'

I now signified that it was imperatively necessary my apartment should be relieved of the honour of her presence: she went away laughing.

CHAPTER 10

## Dr John

Mme Beck was a most consistent character; forbearing with all the world, and tender to no part of it. Her own children drew her into no deviation from the even tenor of her stoic calm. She was solicitous about her family, vigilant for their interests, and physical well-being; but she never seemed to know the wish to take her little children upon her lap, to press their rosy lips with her own, to

gather them in a genial embrace, to shower on them softly the benignant caress, the loving word.

I have watched her sometimes sitting in the garden, viewing the little ones afar off, as they walked in a distant alley with Trinette, their *bonne;* in her mien spoke care and prudence: I knew she often pondered anxiously what she called 'leur avenir;' but if the youngest, a puny and delicate, but engaging child, chancing to spy her, broke from its nurse, and toddling down the walk, came all eager and laughing and panting to clasp her knee, madame would just calmly put out one hand, so as to prevent inconvenient concussion from the child's sudden onset: 'Prends garde, mon enfant!' she would say unmoved, patiently permit it to stand near her a few moments, and then, without smile or kiss, or endearing syllable, rise and lead it back to Trinette.

Her demeanour to the eldest girl was equally characteristic in another way. This was a vicious child. 'Quelle peste que cette Désirée! Quel poison que cet enfant là!' were the expressions dedicated to her, alike in kitchen and in schoolroom. Amongst her other endowments she boasted an exquisite skill in the art of provocation, sometimes driving her *bonne* and the servants almost wild. She would steal to their attics, open their drawers and boxes, wantonly tear their best caps and soil their best shawls; she would watch her opportunity to get at the beaufet of the salle à manger, where she would smash articles of porcelain or glass – or to the cupboard of the store-room, where she would plunder the preserves, drink the sweet wine, break jars and bottles, and so contrive as to throw the onus of suspicion on the cook and the kitchen-maid. All this when madame saw, and of which when she received report, her sole observation, uttered with matchless serenity, was: 'Désirée a besoin d'une surveillance toute particulière.' Accordingly she kept this promising olive-branch a good deal at her side. Never once, I believe, did she tell her faithfully of her faults, explain the evil of such habits, and show the results which must thence ensue. Surveillance must work the whole cure. It failed of course. Désirée was kept in some measure from the servants, but she teased and pillaged her mama instead. Whatever, belonging to madame's work-table or toilet, she could lay her hands on, she stole and hid. Madame saw all this, but she still pretended not to see: she had not rectitude of soul to confront the child with her vices. When an article disappeared whose value rendered restitution necessary, she would profess to think that Désirée had taken it away in play, and beg her to restore it. Désirée was not to be so cheated: she had learned to bring falsehood to the aid of theft, and would deny having touched the brooch, ring, or scissors. Carrying on the hollow system, the mother would calmly assume an air of belief, and afterwards ceaselessly watch and dog the child till she tracked her to her hiding-places – some hole in the garden-wall – some chink or cranny in garret or out-house. This done, madame would send Désirée out for a walk with her *bonne*, and profit by her absence to rob the robber. Désirée proved herself the true daughter of her astute parent, by never suffering either her countenance or manner to betray the least sign of mortification on discovering the loss.

The second child Fifine, was said to be like its dead father. Certainly, though

the mother had given it her healthy frame, her blue eye and ruddy cheek, not from her was derived its moral being. It was an honest, gleeful little soul: a passionate, warm-tempered, bustling creature it was too, and of the sort likely to blunder often into perils and difficulties. One day it bethought itself to fall from top to bottom of a steep flight of stone steps; and when madame, hearing the noise (she always heard every noise), issued from the salle à manger and picked it up, she said quietly – 'Cet enfant a un os de cassé.'

At first we hoped this was not the case. It was, however, but too true: one little plump arm hung powerless.

'Let meess' (meaning me) 'take her,' said madame; 'et qu'on aille tout de suite chercher un fiacre.'

In a *fiacre* she promptly, but with admirable coolness and self-possession, departed to fetch a surgeon.

It appeared she did not find the family-surgeon at home; but that mattered not: she sought until she laid her hand on a substitute to her mind, and brought him back with her. Meantime I had cut the child's sleeve from its arm, undressed and put it to bed.

We none of us, I suppose (by *we* I mean the bonne, the cook, the portress, and myself, all which personages were now gathered in the small and heated chamber), looked very scrutinisingly at the new doctor when he came into the room. I, at least, was taken up with endeavouring to soothe Fifine; whose cries (for she had good lungs) were appalling to hear. These cries redoubled in intensity as the stranger approached her bed; when he took her up, 'Let alone!' she cried passionately, in her broken English (for she spoke English as did the other children). 'I will not you: I will Dr Pillule!'

'And Dr Pillule is my very good friend,' was the answer, in perfect English; 'but he is busy at a place three leagues off, and I am come in his stead. So now, when we get a little calmer, we must commence business; and we will soon have that unlucky little arm bandaged and in right order.'

Hereupon he called for a glass of *eau sucrée*, fed her with some teaspoonsful of the sweet liquid (Fifine was a frank gourmande; anybody could win her heart through her palate), promised her more when the operation should be over, and promptly went to work. Some assistance being needed, he demanded it of the cook, a robust, strong-armed woman, but she, the portress, and the nurse instantly fled. I did not like to touch that small, tortured limb, but, thinking there was no alternative, my hand was already extended to do what was requisite. I was anticipated: Mme Beck had put out her own hand – hers was steady while mine trembled.

'Ça vaudra mieux,' said the doctor, turning from me to her.

He showed wisdom in his choice. Mine would have been feigned stoicism, forced fortitude. Hers was neither forced nor feigned.

'Merci Madame: très bien, fort bien!' said the operator when he had finished. 'Voilà un sang-froid bien opportun, et qui vaut mille élans de sensibilité déplacée.'

He was pleased with her firmness, she with his compliment. It is likely too that

his whole general appearance, his voice, mien, and manner wrought impressions in his favour. Indeed, when you looked well at him, and when a lamp was brought in – for it was evening and now waxing dusk – you saw that, unless Mme Beck had been less than woman, it could not well be otherwise. This young doctor (he *was* young) had no common aspect. His stature looked imposingly tall in that little chamber, and amidst that group of Dutch-made women; his profile was clear, fine, and expressive: perhaps his eye glanced from face to face rather too vividly, too quickly, and too often, but it had a most pleasant character, and so had his mouth; his chin was full, cleft, Grecian, and perfect. As to his smile, one could not in a hurry make up one's mind as to the descriptive epithet it merited; there was something in it that pleased, but something too that brought surging up into the mind all one's foibles and weak points: all that could lay one open to a laugh; yet Fifine liked this doubtful smile, and thought the owner genial: much as he had hurt her, she held out her hand to bid him a friendly good-night. He patted the little hand kindly, and then he and madame went down stairs together; she talking in her highest tide of spirits and volubility; he listening with an air of good-natured amenity, dashed with that unconscious roguish archness I find it difficult to describe.

I noticed that though he spoke French well, he spoke English better; he had, too, an English complexion, eyes, and form. I noticed more. As he passed me in leaving the room, turning his face in my direction one moment – not to address me, but to speak to madame, yet so standing, that I almost necessarily looked up at him – a recollection which had been struggling to form in my memory, since the first moment I heard his voice, started up perfected. This was the very gentleman to whom I had spoken at the bureau; who had helped me in the matter of the trunk; who had been my guide through the dark, wet park. Listening, as he passed down the long vestibule out into the street, I recognised his very tread: it was the same firm and equal stride I had followed under the dripping trees.

It was to be concluded that this young surgeon-physician's first visit to the Rue Fossette would be his last. The respectable Dr Pillule being expected home the next day, there appeared no reason why his temporary substitute should again represent him; but the Fates had written their decree to the contrary.

Dr Pillule had been summoned to see a rich old hypochondriac at the antique university town of Bouquin-Moisi, and upon his prescribing change of air and travel as remedies, he was retained to accompany the timid patient on a tour of some weeks; it but remained, therefore, for the new doctor to continue his attendance at the Rue Fossette.

I often saw him when he came, for madame would not trust the little invalid to Trinette, but required me to spend much of my time in the nursery. I think he was skilful. Fifine recovered rapidly under his care, yet even her convalescence did not hasten his dismissal. Destiny and Mme Beck seemed in league, and both had ruled that he should make deliberate acquaintance with the vestibule, the private staircase, and upper chambers of the Rue Fossette.

No sooner did Fifine emerge from his hands than Désirée declared herself ill. That possessed child had a genius for simulation, and captivated by the attentions and indulgences of a sick-room, she came to the conclusion that an illness would perfectly accommodate her tastes, and took her bed accordingly. She acted well, and her mother still better; for while the whole case was transparent to Mme Beck as the day, she treated it with an astonishingly well-assured air of gravity and good faith.

What surprised me was that Dr John (so the young Englishman had taught Fifine to call him, and we all took from her the habit of addressing him by this name, till it became an established custom, and he was known by no other in the Rue Fossette) – that Dr John consented tacitly to adopt madame's tactics, and to fall in with her manoeuvres. He betrayed, indeed, a period of comic doubt, cast one or two rapid glances from the child to the mother, indulged in an interval of self-consultation, but finally resigned himself with a good grace to play his part in the farce. Désirée ate like a raven, gambolled day and night in her bed, pitched tents with the sheets and blankets, lounged like a Turk amidst pillows and bolsters, diverted herself with throwing her shoes at her bonne and grimacing at her sisters – overflowed, in short, with unmerited health and evil spirits – only languishing when her mama and the physician paid their diurnal visit. Mme Beck, I knew, was glad, at any price, to have her daughter in bed out of the way of mischief; but I wondered that Dr John did not tire of the business.

Every day, on this mere pretext of a motive, he gave punctual attendance; madame always received him with the same empressement, the same sunshine for himself, the same admirably counterfeited air of concern for her child. Dr John wrote harmless prescriptions for the patient, and viewed her mother with a shrewdly sparkling eye. Madame caught his rallying looks without resenting them – she had too much good sense for that. Supple as the young doctor seemed, one could not despise him – this pliant part was evidently not adopted in the design to curry favour with his employer: while he liked his office at the Pensionnat, and lingered strangely about the Rue Fossette, he was independent, almost careless in his carriage there; and yet, too, he was often thoughtful and preoccupied.

It was not perhaps my business to observe the mystery of his bearing, or search out its origin or aim; but, placed as I was, I could hardly help it. He laid himself open to my observation, according to my presence in the room just that degree of notice and consequence a person of my exterior habitually expects: that is to say, about what is given to unobtrusive articles of furniture, chairs of ordinary joiner's work, and carpets of no striking pattern. Often, while waiting for madame, he would muse, smile, watch, or listen like a man who thinks himself alone. I, meantime, was free to puzzle over his countenance and movements, and wonder what could be the meaning of that peculiar interest and attachment – all mixed up with doubt and strangeness, and inexplicably ruled by some presiding spell – which wedded him to this demi-convent, secluded in the built-up core of a capital. He, I believe, never remembered that I had eyes in my head; much less a brain behind them.

Nor would he ever have found this out, but that one day, while he sat in the sunshine, and I was observing the colouring of his hair, whiskers, and complexion – the whole being of such a tone as a strong light brings out with somewhat perilous force (indeed I recollect I was driven to compare his beamy head in my thoughts to that of the 'golden image' which Nebuchadnezzar the king had set up), an idea new, sudden, and startling, riveted my attention with an overmastering strength and power of attraction. I know not to this day how I looked at him – the force of surprise, and also of conviction, made me forget myself – and I only recovered wonted consciousness when I saw that his notice was arrested, and that it had caught my movement in a clear little oval mirror fixed in the side of the window recess – by the aid of which reflector madame often secretly spied persons walking in the garden below. Though of so gay and sanguine a temperament, he was not without a certain nervous sensitiveness which made him ill at ease under a direct, enquiring gaze. On surprising me thus, he turned and said in a tone which, though courteous, had just so much dryness in it as to mark a shade of annoyance, as well as to give to what was said the character of rebuke: 'Mademoiselle does not spare me: I am not vain enough to fancy that it is my merits which attract her attention; it must then be some defect. Dare I ask – what?'

I was confounded, as the reader may suppose, yet not with an irrecoverable confusion, being conscious that it was from no emotion of incautious admiration, nor yet in a spirit of unjustifiable inquisitiveness, that I had incurred this reproof. I might have cleared myself on the spot, but would not. I did not speak. I was not in the habit of speaking to him. Suffering him, then, to think what he chose, and accuse me of what he would, I resumed some work I had dropped, and kept my head bent over it during the remainder of his stay. There is a perverse mood of the mind which is rather soothed than irritated by misconstruction; and in quarters where we can never be rightly known, we take pleasure, I think, in being consummately ignored. What honest man on being casually taken for a housebreaker, does not feel rather tickled than vexed at the mistake?

## CHAPTER II

### The Portresse's Cabinet

It was summer and very hot. Georgette, the youngest of Mme Beck's children, took a fever. Désirée, suddenly cured of her ailments, was, together with Fifine, packed off to Bonne-Maman in the country, by way of precaution against infection. Medical aid was now really needed, and Madame, choosing to ignore the return of Dr Pillule, who had been at home a week, conjured his English rival to continue his visits. One or two of the *pensionnaires* complained of headache, and in other respects seemed slightly to participate Georgette's ailment. 'Now, at

last,' I thought, 'Dr Pillule must be recalled: the prudent directress will never venture to permit the attendance of so young a man on the pupils.'

The directress was very prudent, but she could also be intrepidly venturous. She actually introduced Dr John to the school-division of the premises, and established him in attendance on the proud and handsome Blanche de Melcy, and the vain, flirting Angélique, her friend. Dr John, I thought, testified a certain gratification at this mark of confidence; and if discretion of bearing could have justified the step, it would by him have been amply justified. Here, however, in this land of convents and confessionals, such a presence as his was not to be suffered with impunity in a 'Pensionnat de demoiselles.' The school gossiped, the kitchen whispered, the town caught the rumour, parents wrote letters and paid visits of remonstrance. Madame, had she been weak, would now have been lost: a dozen rival educational houses were ready to improve this false step – if false step it were – to her ruin; but Madame was not weak, and little Jesuit though she might be, yet I clapped the hands of my heart, and with its voice cried 'brava!' as I watched her able bearing, her skilled management, her temper and her firmness on this occasion.

She met the alarmed parents with a good-humoured, easy grace: for nobody matched her in, I know not whether to say the possession or the assumption of a certain 'rondeur et franchise de bonne femme', which on various occasions gained the point aimed at with instant and complete success, where severe gravity and serious reasoning would probably have failed.

'Ce pauvre Docteur Jean!' she would say, chuckling and rubbing joyously her fat, little, white hands; 'ce cher jeune homme! le meilleur créature du monde!' and go on to explain how she happened to be employing him for her own children, who were so fond of him they would scream themselves into fits at the thought of another doctor; how where she had confidence for her own, she thought it natural to repose trust for others, and au reste it was only the most temporary expedient in the world: Blanche and Angélique had the migraine; Dr John had written a prescription; voilà tout!

The parents' mouths were closed. Blanche and Angelique saved her all remaining trouble by chanting loud duets in their physician's praise; the other pupils echoed them, unanimously declaring that when they were ill they would have Dr John and nobody else; and madame laughed, and the parents laughed too. The Labassecouriens must have a large organ of philoprogenitiveness: at least the indulgence of offspring is carried by them to excessive lengths; the law of most households being the children's will. Madame now got credit for having acted on this occasion in a spirit of motherly partiality: she came off with flying colours; people liked her as a directress better than ever.

To this day I never fully understood why she thus risked her interest for the sake of Dr John. What people said, of course I know well: the whole house – pupils, teachers, servants included – affirmed that she was going to marry him. So they had settled it: difference of age seemed to make no obstacle in their eyes; it was to be so.

It must be admitted that appearances did not wholly discountenance this

idea; madame seemed so bent on retaining his services, so oblivious of her former protégé, Pillule. She made, too, such a point of personally receiving his visits, and was so unfailingly cheerful, blithe, and benignant in her manner to him. Moreover, she paid, about this time, marked attention to dress: the morning deshabille, the night-cap and shawl, were discarded; Dr John's early visits always found her with auburn braids all nicely arranged, silk dress trimly fitted on, neat laced brodequins in lieu of slippers: in short the whole toilette complete as a model, and fresh as a flower. I scarcely think, however, that her intention in this went further than just to show a very handsome man that she was not quite a plain woman: and plain she was not. Without beauty of feature or elegance of form, she pleased. Without youth and its gay graces, she cheered. One never tired of seeing her: she was never monotonous, or insipid, or colourless, or flat. Her unfaded hair, her eye with its temperate blue light, her cheek with its wholesome fruit-like bloom – these things pleased in moderation, but with constancy.

Had she, indeed, floating visions of adopting Dr John as a husband, taking him to her well-furnished home, endowing him with her savings, which were said to amount to a moderate competency, and making him comfortable for the rest of his life? Did Dr John suspect her of such visions? I have met him coming out of her presence with a mischievous half-smile about his lips, and in his eyes a look as of masculine vanity elate and tickled. With all his good looks and good-nature, he was not perfect; he must have been very imperfect if he roguishly encouraged aims he never intended to be successful. But did he not intend them to be successful? People said he had no money, that he was wholly dependent upon his profession. Madame – though perhaps some fourteen years his senior – was yet the sort of woman never to grow old, never to wither, never to break down. They certainly were on good terms. *He* perhaps was not in love; but how many people ever *do* love, or at least marry for love in this world? We waited the end.

For what *he* waited I do not know, nor for what he watched; but the peculiarity of his manner, his expectant, vigilant, absorbed, eager look, never wore off: it rather intensified. He had never been quite within the compass of my penetration, and I think he ranged farther and farther beyond it.

One morning little Georgette had been more feverish and consequently more peevish; she was crying and would not be pacified. I thought a particular draught ordered, disagreed with her, and I doubted whether it ought to be continued; I waited impatiently for the doctor's coming in order to consult him.

The doorbell rung, he was admitted; I felt sure of this, for I heard his voice addressing the portresse. It was his custom to mount straight to the nursery, taking about three degrees of the staircase at once, and coming upon us like a cheerful surprise. Five minutes elapsed – ten – and I saw and heard nothing of him. What could he be doing? Possibly waiting in the corridor below. Little Georgette still piped her plaintive wail, appealing to me by her familiar term, 'Minnie, Minnie, me very poorly!' till my heart ached. I descended to ascertain why he did not come. The corridor was empty. Whither was he vanished? Was he with madame in the salle à manger? Impossible: I had left her but a short time

since, dressing in her own chamber. I listened. Three pupils were just then hard
at work practising in three proximate rooms – the dining-room and the greater
and lesser drawing-rooms, between which and the corridor there was but the
portresse's cabinet communicating with the salons, and intended originally for a
boudoir. Farther off, at a fourth instrument in the oratory, a whole class of a
dozen or more were taking a singing lesson, and just then joining in a 'barcarole'
(I think they called it), whereof I yet remember these words 'fraîchë brisë' and
'Venisë'. Under these circumstances what could I hear? A great deal, certainly;
had it only been to the purpose.

Yes; I heard a giddy treble laugh in the above-mentioned little cabinet, close
by the door of which I stood – that door half-unclosed; a man's voice in a soft,
deep, pleading tone, uttered some words, whereof I only caught the adjuration,
'For God's sake!' Then, after a second's pause, forth issued Dr John, his eye
full-shining, but not with either joy or triumph; his fair English cheek high-
coloured; a baffled, tortured, anxious, and yet a tender meaning on his brow.

The open door served me as a screen; but had I been full in his way I believe he
would have passed without seeing me. Some mortification, some strong vexation
had hold of his soul: or rather, to write my impressions now as I received them at
the time, I should say some sorrow, some sense of injustice. I did not so much
think his pride was hurt, as that his affections had been wounded – cruelly
wounded it seemed to me. But who was the torturer? What being in that house
had him so much in her power? Madame I believed to be in her chamber; the
room whence he had stepped was dedicated to the portresse's sole use; and she,
Rosine Matou, an unprincipled though pretty little French grisette, airy, fickle,
dressy, vain, and mercenary – it was not, surely, to *her* hand he owed the ordeal
through which he seemed to have passed?

But while I pondered, her voice, clear though somewhat sharp, broke out in a
lightsome French song, trilling through the door still ajar: I glanced in, doubting
my senses. There at the table she sat in a smart dress of 'jaconas rose', trimming a
tiny blond cap: not a living thing save herself was in the room, except indeed
some goldfish in a glass globe, some flowers in pots, and a broad July sunbeam.

Here was a problem: but I must go upstairs to ask about the medicine.

Dr John sat in a chair at Georgette's bedside; madame stood before him; the
little patient had been examined and soothed, and now lay composed in her crib.
Mme Beck, as I entered, was discussing the physician's own health, remarking
on some real or fancied change in his looks, charging him with over-work, and
recommending rest and change of air. He listened good-naturedly, but with
laughing indifference, telling her that she was 'trop bonne', and that he felt
perfectly well. Madame appealed to me – Dr John following her movement with
a slow glance which seemed to express languid surprise at reference being made
to a quarter so insignificant.

'What do you think, Mees Lucie?' asked madame. 'Is he not paler and
thinner?'

It was very seldom that I uttered more than monosyllables in Dr John's
presence; he was the kind of person with whom I was likely ever to remain the

neutral, passive thing he thought me. Now, however, I took license to answer in a phrase: and a phrase I purposely made quite significant.

'He looks ill at this moment; but perhaps it is owing to some temporary cause: Dr John may have been vexed or harassed.' I cannot tell how he took this speech, as I never sought his face for information. Georgette here began to ask me in her broken English if she might have a glass of *eau sucrée*. I answered her in English. For the first time, I fancy, he noticed that I spoke his language; hitherto he had always taken me for a foreigner, addressing me as 'mademoiselle', and giving in French the requisite directions about the children's treatment. He seemed on the point of making a remark, but thinking better of it, held his tongue.

Madame recommenced advising him; he shook his head laughing, rose and bid her good-morning, with courtesy, but still with the regardless air of one whom too much unsolicited attention was surfeiting and spoiling.

When he was gone, madame dropped into the chair he had just left; she rested her chin in her hand; all that was animated and amiable vanished from her face: she looked stony and stern, almost mortified and morose. She sighed; a single, but a deep sigh. A loud bell rang for morning school. She got up; as she passed a dressing-table with a glass upon it, she looked at her reflected image. One single white hair streaked her nut-brown tresses; she plucked it out with a shudder. In the full summer daylight, her face, though it still had the colour, could plainly be seen to have lost the texture of youth; and then, where were youth's contours? Ah, madame! wise as you were, even *you* knew weakness. Never had I pitied madame before, but my heart softened towards her, when she turned darkly from the glass. A calamity had come upon her. That hag Disappointment was greeting her with a grisly 'all-hail!' and her soul rejected the intimacy.

But Rosine! My bewilderment there surpasses description. I embraced five opportunities of passing her cabinet that day, with a view to contemplating her charms, and finding out the secret of their influence. She was pretty, young, and wore a well-made dress. All very good points, and, I suppose, amply sufficient to account, in any philosophic mind, for any amount of agony and distraction in a young man like Dr John. Still, I could not help forming half a wish that the said doctor were my brother; or at least that he had a sister or a mother who would kindly sermonise him. I say *half* a wish; I broke it and flung it away before it became a whole one, discovering in good time its exquisite folly. 'Somebody,' I argued, 'might as well sermonise madame about her young physician: and what good would that do?'

I believe madame sermonised herself. She did not behave weakly, or make herself in any shape ridiculous. It is true she had neither strong feelings to overcome, nor tender feelings by which to be miserably pained. It is true likewise that she had an important avocation, a real business to fill her time, divert her thoughts, and divide her interest. It is especially true that she possessed a genuine good sense which is not given to all women or to all men; and by dint of these combined advantages she behaved wisely, she behaved well. Brava! once more, Mme Beck. I saw you matched against an Apollyon of a predilection; you fought a good fight, and you overcame!

## CHAPTER 12

## *The Casket*

Behind the house at the Rue Fossette there was a garden – large, considering that it lay in the heart of a city, and to my recollection at this day it seems pleasant: but time, like distance, lends to certain scenes an influence so softening; and where all is stone around, blank wall and hot pavement, how precious seems one shrub, how lovely an enclosed and planted spot of ground!

There went a tradition that Mme Beck's house had in old days been a convent. That in years gone by – how long gone by I cannot tell, but I think some centuries – before the city had overspread this quarter, and when it was tilled ground and avenue, and such deep and leafy seclusion as ought to embosom a religious house – that something had happened on this site which, rousing fear and inflicting horror, had left to the place the inheritance of a ghost story. A vague tale went of a black and white nun, sometimes, on some night or nights of the year, seen in some part of this vicinage. The ghost must have been built out ages ago, for there were houses all round now; but certain convent-relics, in the shape of old and huge fruit trees, yet consecrated the spot; and, at the foot of one – a Methuselah of a pear-tree, dead, all but a few boughs which still faithfully renewed their perfumed snow in spring, and their honey-sweet pendants in autumn – you saw, in scraping away the mossy earth between the half-bared roots, a glimpse of slab, smooth, hard, and black. The legend went, unconfirmed and unaccredited, but still propagated, that this was the portal of a vault, imprisoning deep beneath that ground, on whose surface grass grew and flowers bloomed, the bones of a girl whom a monkish conclave of the drear middle ages had here buried alive, for some sin against her vow. Her shadow it was that tremblers had feared, through long generations after her poor frame was dust; her black robe and white veil that, for timid eyes, moonlight and shade had mocked, as they fluctuated in the night-wind through the garden-thicket.

Independently of romantic rubbish, however, that old garden had its charms. On summer mornings I used to rise early, to enjoy them alone; on summer evenings, to linger solitary, to keep tryst with the rising moon, or taste one kiss of the evening breeze, or fancy rather than feel the freshness of dew descending. The turf was verdant, the gravelled walks were white; sun-bright nasturtiums clustered beautiful about the roots of the doddered orchard giants. There was a large berceau, above which spread the shade of an acacia; there was a smaller, more sequestered bower, nestled in the vines which ran all along a high and gray wall, and gathered their tendrils in a knot of beauty, and hung their clusters in loving profusion about the favoured spot where jasmine and ivy met and married them.

Doubtless at high noon, in the broad, vulgar middle of the day, when Mme Beck's large school turned out rampant, and externes and pensionnaires were spread abroad, vying with the denizens of the boys' college close at hand, in the brazen exercise of their lungs and limbs – doubtless *then* the garden was a trite, trodden-down place enough. But at sunset or the hour of *salut*, when the externes were gone home, and the boarders quiet at their studies; pleasant was it then to stray down the peaceful alleys, and hear the bells of St Jean Baptiste peal out with their sweet, soft, exalted sound.

I was walking thus one evening, and had been detained, farther within the verge of twilight than usual, by the still deepening calm, the mellow coolness, the fragrant breathing with which flowers no sunshine could win now answered the persuasion of the dew. I saw by a light in the oratory window that the Catholic household were then gathered to evening prayer – a rite, from attendance on which, I now and then, as a Protestant, exempted myself.

'One moment longer,' whispered solitude and the summer moon, 'stay with us: all is truly quiet now; for another quarter of an hour your presence will not be missed: the day's heat and bustle have tired you; enjoy these precious minutes.'

The windowless backs of houses built in this garden, and in particular the whole of one side was skirted by the rear of a long line of premises – being the boarding-houses of the neighbouring college. This rear, however, was all blank stone, with the exception of certain attic loopholes high up, opening from the sleeping-rooms of the women-servants, and also one casement in a lower story said to mark the chamber or study of a master. But, though thus secure, an alley, which ran parallel with the very high wall on that side of the garden, was forbidden to be entered by the pupils. It was called indeed 'l'allée défendue', and any girl setting foot there would have rendered herself liable to as severe a penalty as the mild rules of Mme Beck's establishment permitted. Teachers might indeed go there with impunity; but as the walk was narrow, and the neglected shrubs were grown very thick and close on each side, weaving overhead a roof of branch and leaf which the sun's rays penetrated but in rare chequers, this alley was seldom entered even during day, and after dusk was carefully shunned.

From the first I was tempted to make an exception to this rule of avoidance: the seclusion, the very gloom of the walk attracted me. For a long time the fear of seeming singular scared me away; but by degrees, as people became accustomed to me and my habits, and to such shades of peculiarity as were engrained in my nature – shades, certainly not striking enough to interest, and perhaps not prominent enough to offend, but born in and with me, and no more to be parted with than my identity – by slow degrees I became a frequenter of this strait and narrow path. I made myself gardener of some tintless flowers that grew between its closely-ranked shrubs; I cleared away the relics of past autumns, choking up a rustic seat at the far end. Borrowing of Goton, the cuisinière, a pail of water and a scrubbing-brush, I made this seat clean. Madame saw me at work and smiled approbation: whether sincerely or not I don't know; but she *seemed* sincere.

'Voyez-vous,' cried she, 'comme elle est propre cette demoiselle Lucie? Vous aimez donc cette allée, meess?'

'Yes,' I said, 'it is quiet and shady.'

'C'est juste,' cried she with her air of bonté; and she kindly recommended me to confine myself to it as much as I chose, saying, that as I was not charged with the surveillance, I need not trouble myself to walk with the pupils: only I might permit her children to come there, to talk English with me.

On the night in question, I was sitting on the hidden seat reclaimed from fungi and mould, listening to what seemed the far-off sounds of the city. Far-off, in truth, they were not: this school was in the city's centre; hence, it was but five minutes' walk to the park, scarce ten – to buildings of palatial splendour. Quite near were wide streets brightly lit, teeming at this moment with life: carriages were rolling through them, to balls or to the opera. The same hour which tolled curfew for our convent, which extinguished each lamp, and dropped the curtain round each couch, rung for the gay city about us the summons to festal enjoyment. Of this contrast I thought not, however: gay instincts my nature had few; ball or opera I had never seen; and though often I had heard them described, and even wished to see them, it was not the wish of one who hopes to partake a pleasure if she could only reach it – who feels fitted to shine in some bright distant sphere, could she but thither win her way; it was no yearning to attain, no hunger to taste; only the calm desire to look on a new thing.

A moon was in the sky, not a full moon but a young crescent. I saw her through a space in the boughs overhead. She and the stars, visible beside her, were no strangers where all else was strange: my childhood knew them. I had seen that golden sign with the dark globe in its curve leaning back on azure, beside an old thorn at the top of an old field, in Old England, in long past days, just as it now leaned back beside a stately spire in this continental capital.

Oh, my childhood! I had feelings: passive as I lived, little as I spoke, cold as I looked, when I thought of past days, I *could* feel. About the present, it was better to be stoical; about the future – such a future as mine – to be dead. And in catalepsy and a dead trance, I studiously held the quick of my nature.

At that time, I well remember whatever could excite – certain accidents of the weather, for instance, were almost dreaded by me, because they woke the being I was always lulling, and stirred up a craving cry I could not satisfy. One night a thunderstorm broke; a sort of hurricane shook us in our beds: the Catholics rose in panic and prayed to their saints. As for me, the tempest took hold of me with tyranny: I was roughly roused and obliged to live. I got up and dressed myself, and creeping outside the casement close by my bed, sat on its ledge, with my feet on the roof of a lower adjoining building. It was wet, it was wild, it was pitch-dark. Within the dormitory they gathered round the night-lamp in consternation, praying loud. I could not go in: too resistless was the delight of staying with the wild hour, black and full of thunder, pealing out such an ode as language never delivered to man – too terribly glorious, the spectacle of clouds, split and pierced by white and blinding bolts.

I did long, achingly, then and for four-and-twenty hours afterwards, for something to fetch me out of my present existence, and lead me upwards and onwards. This longing, and all of a similar kind, it was necessary to knock on the

head; which I did, figuratively, after the manner of Jael to Sisera, driving a nail through their temples. Unlike Sisera, they did not die: they were but transiently stunned, and at intervals would turn on the nail with a rebellious wrench; then did the temples bleed, and the brain thrill to its core.

Tonight, I was not so mutinous, nor so miserable. My Sisera lay quiet in the tent, slumbering; and if his pain ached through his slumbers, something like an angel – the Ideal – knelt near, dropping balm on the soothed temples, holding before the sealed eyes a magic glass, of which the sweet, solemn visions were repeated in dreams, and shedding a reflex from her moonlight wings and robe over the transfixed sleeper, over the tent threshold, over all the landscape lying without. Jael, the stern woman, sat apart, relenting somewhat over her captive; but more prone to dwell on the faithful expectation of Heber coming home. By which words I mean that the cool peace and dewy sweetness of the night filled me with a mood of hope: not hope on any definite point, but a general sense of encouragement and heart-ease.

Should not such a mood, so sweet, so tranquil, so unwonted, have been the harbinger of good? Alas, no good came of it! Presently the rude Real burst coarsely in – all evil, grovelling, and repellent as she too often is.

Amid the intense stillness of that pile of stone overlooking the walk, the trees, the high wall, I heard a sound; a casement [all the windows here are casements, opening on hinges] creaked. Ere I had time to look up and mark where, in which story, or by whom unclosed, a tree overhead shook, as if struck by a missile; some object dropped prone at my feet.

Nine was striking by St Jean Baptiste's clock; day was fading, but it was not dark: the crescent-moon aided little, but the deep gilding of that point in heaven where the sun burned last, and the crystalline clearness of a wide space above, sustained the summer twilight; even in my dark walk I could, by approaching an opening, have managed to read print of a small type. Easy was it to see then that the missile was a box, a small box of white and coloured ivory: its loose lid opened in my hand; violets lay within, violets smothering a closely-folded bit of pink paper, a note, superscribed, 'Pour la robe grise.' I wore indeed a dress of French gray.

Good. Was this a billet-doux? A thing I had heard of, but hitherto had not had the honour of seeing or handling. Was it this sort of commodity I held between my finger and thumb at this moment?

Scarcely: I did not dream it for a moment. Suitor or admirer my very thoughts had not conceived. All the teachers had dreams of some lover; one (but she was naturally of a credulous turn) believed in a future husband. All the pupils above fourteen knew of some prospective bridegroom; two or three were already affianced by their parents, and had been so from childhood: but into the realm of feelings and hopes which such prospects open, my speculations, far less my presumptions, had never once had warrant to intrude. If the other teachers went into town, or took a walk on the boulevards, or only attended mass, they were very certain (according to the accounts brought back) to meet with some individual of the 'opposite sex,' whose rapt, earnest gaze assured them of their

power to strike and to attract. I can't say that my experience tallied with theirs, in this respect. I went to church and I took walks, and am very well convinced that nobody minded me. There was not a girl or woman in the Rue Fossette who could not, and did not testify to having received an admiring beam from our young doctor's blue eyes, at one time or other. I am obliged, however humbling it may sound, to except myself: as far as I was concerned, those blue eyes were guiltless and calm as the sky, to whose tint theirs seemed akin. So it came to pass that I heard the others talk, wondered often at their gaiety, security and self-satisfaction, but did not trouble myself to look up and gaze along the path they seemed so certain of treading. This then was no billet-doux; and it was in settled conviction to the contrary that I quietly opened it. Thus it ran – I translate: 'Angel of my dreams! A thousand, thousand thanks for the promise kept: scarcely did I venture to hope its fulfilment. I believed you, indeed, to be half in jest; and then you seemed to think the enterprise beset with such danger – the hour so untimely, the alley so strictly secluded – often, you said, haunted by that dragon, the English teacher – une véritable bégueule Britannique à ce que vous dites – espèce de monstre, brusque et rude comme un vieux caporal de grenadiers, et revêche comme une religieuse' (the reader will excuse my modesty in allowing this flattering sketch of my amiable self to retain the slight veil of the original tongue). 'You are aware,' went on this precious effusion, 'that little Gustave, on account of his illness, has been removed to a master's chamber – that favoured chamber, whose lattice overlooks your prison-ground. There, I, the best uncle in the world, am admitted to visit him. How tremblingly I approached the window and glanced into your Eden – an Eden for me, though a desert for you! – how I feared to behold vacancy, or the dragon aforesaid! How my heart palpitated with delight when, through apertures in the envious boughs, I at once caught the gleam of your graceful straw-hat, and the waving of your gray dress – dress that I should recognise amongst a thousand. But why, my angel, will you not look up? Cruel, to deny me one ray of those adorable eyes! – how a single glance would have revived me! I write this in fiery haste; while the physician examines Gustave, I snatch an opportunity to enclose it in a small casket, together with a bouquet of flowers, the sweetest that blow – yet less sweet than thee, my Peri – my all-charming! Ever thine – thou well knowest whom!'

'I wish I did know whom,' was my comment; and the wish bore even closer reference to the person addressed in this choice document, than to the writer thereof. Perhaps it was from the fiancé of one of the engaged pupils; and, in that case, there was no great harm done or intended – only a small irregularity. Several of the girls, the majority indeed, had brothers or cousins at the neighbouring college. But, 'la robe grise, le chapeau de paille', here surely was a clue – a very confusing one. The straw-hat was an ordinary garden head-screen, common to a score besides myself. The gray dress hardly gave more definite indication. Mme Beck herself ordinarily wore a gray dress just now; another teacher, and three of the pensionnaires, had had gray dresses purchased of the same shade and fabric as mine: it was a sort of everyday wear which happened at that time to be in vogue.

Meanwhile, as I pondered, I knew I must go in. Lights, moving in the

dormitory, announced that prayers were over, and the pupils going to bed. Another half hour and all doors would be locked – all lights extinguished. The front door yet stood open, to admit into the heated house the coolness of the summer night; from the portresse's cabinet close by shone a lamp, showing the long vestibule with the two-leaved drawing-room doors on one side, the great street-door closing the vista.

All at once, quick rang the bell – quick, but not loud – a cautious tinkle – a sort of warning, metal whisper. Rosine darted from her cabinet and ran to open. The person she admitted stood with her two minutes in parley: there seemed a demur, a delay. Rosine came to the garden door, lamp in hand; she stood on the steps, lifting her lamp, looking round vaguely.

'Quel conte!' she cried with a coquettish laugh. 'Personne n'y a été.'

'Let me pass,' pleaded a voice I knew: 'I ask but five minutes;' and a familiar shape, tall and grand (as we of the Rue Fossette all thought it), issued from the house, and strode down amongst the beds and walks. It was sacrilege – the intrusion of a man into that spot, at that hour; but he knew himself privileged, and perhaps he trusted to the friendly night. He wandered down the alleys, looking on this side and on that – he was lost in the shrubs, trampling flowers and breaking branches in his search – he penetrated at last the 'forbidden walk.' There I met him, like some ghost, I suppose.

'Dr John! it is found.'

He did not ask by whom, for with his quick eye he perceived that I held it in my hand.

'Do not betray her,' he said, looking at me as if I were indeed a dragon.

'Were I ever so disposed to treachery, I cannot betray what I do not know,' was my answer. 'Read the note, and you will see how little it reveals.'

'Perhaps you have read it,' I thought to myself; and yet I could not believe he wrote it: that could hardly be his style: besides, I was fool enough to think there would be a degree of hardship in his calling me such names. His own look vindicated him; he grew hot, and coloured as he read.

'This is indeed too much: this is cruel, this is humiliating,' were the words that fell from him. I thought it *was* cruel, when I saw his countenance so moved. No matter whether he was to blame or not; somebody, it seemed to me, must be more to blame.

'What shall you do about it?' he enquired of me. 'Shall you tell Mme Beck what you have found, and cause a stir – an esclandre?'

I thought I ought to tell, and said so; adding that I did not believe there would be either stir or esclandre: madame was much too prudent to make a noise about an affair of that sort connected with her establishment.

He stood looking down and meditating. He was both too proud and too honourable to entreat my secrecy on a point which duty evidently commanded me to communicate. I wished to do right, yet loathed to grieve or injure him. Just then Rosine glanced out through the open door; she could not see us, though between the trees I could plainly see her: her dress was gray, like mine. This circumstance, taken in connection with prior transactions, suggested to me

that perhaps the case, however deplorable, was one in which I was under no obligation whatever to concern myself. Accordingly, I said – 'If you can assure me that none of Mme Beck's pupils are implicated in this business, I shall be very happy to stand aloof from all interference. Take the casket, the bouquet, and the billet; for my part, I gladly forget the whole affair.'

'Look there!' he whispered suddenly, as his hand closed on what I offered, and at the same time he pointed through the boughs.

I looked. Behold madame, in shawl, wrapping-gown, and slippers, softly descending the steps, and stealing like a cat round the garden: in two minutes she would have been upon Dr John. If *she* were like a cat, however, *he*, quite as much, resembled a leopard: nothing could be lighter than his tread when he chose. He watched, and as she turned a corner, he took the garden at two noiseless bounds. She reappeared, and he was gone. Rosine helped him, instantly interposing the door between him and his huntress. I too might have got away, but I preferred to meet madame openly.

Though it was my frequent and well-known custom to spend twilight in the garden, yet, never till now, had I remained so late. Full sure was I that madame had missed – was come in search of me, and designed now to pounce on the defaulter unawares. I expected a reprimand. No. Madame was all goodness. She tendered not even a remonstrance; she testified no shade of surprise. With that consummate tact of hers, in which I believe she was never surpassed by living thing, she even professed merely to have issued forth to taste 'la brise du soir.'

'Quelle belle nuit!' cried she, looking up at the stars – the moon was now gone down behind the broad tower of Jean Baptiste. 'Qu'il fait bon! que l'air est frais!'

And, instead of sending me in, she detained me to take a few turns with her down the principal alley. When at last we both re-entered, she leaned affably on my shoulder by way of support in mounting the front-door steps; at parting, her cheek was presented to my lips, and 'Bon soir, ma bonne amie; dormez bien!' was her kindly adieu for the night.

I caught myself smiling as I lay awake and thoughtful on my couch – smiling at madame. The unction, the suavity of her behaviour offered, for one who knew her, a sure token that suspicion of some kind was busy in her brain. From some aperture or summit of observation, through parted bough or open window, she had doubtless caught a glimpse, remote or near, deceptive or instructive, of that night's transactions. Finely accomplished as she was in the art of surveillance, it was next to impossible that a casket could be thrown into her garden, or an interloper could cross her walks to seek it, without that she, in shaken branch, passing shade, unwonted footfall, or stilly murmur (and though Dr John had spoken very low in the few words he dropped to me, yet the hum of his man's voice pervaded, I thought, the whole conventual ground) without, I say, that she should have caught intimation of things extraordinary transpiring on her premises. *What* things, she might by no means see, or at that time be able to discover; but a delicious little ravelled plot lay tempting her to disentanglement; and in the midst, folded round and round in cobwebs, had she not secured 'Meess Lucie', clumsily involved, like the foolish fly she was?

## *A Sneeze out of Season*

I had occasion to smile – nay, to laugh, at madame again, within the space of four and twenty hours after the little scene treated of in the last chapter.

Villette owns a climate as variable, though not so humid, as that of any English town. A night of high wind followed upon that soft sunset, and all the next day was one of dry storm – dark, be-clouded, yet rainless, the streets were dim with sand and dust, whirled from the boulevards. I know not that even lovely weather would have tempted me to spend the evening-time of study and recreation, where I had spent it yesterday. My alley, and, indeed, all the walks and shrubs in the garden, had acquired a new, but not a pleasant interest; their seclusion was now become precarious; their calm – insecure. That casement which rained billets, had vulgarised the once dear nook it overlooked; and elsewhere, the eyes of the flowers had gained vision, and the knots in the tree-boles listened like secret ears. Some plants there were, indeed, trodden down by Dr John in his search, and his hasty and heedless progress, which I wished to prop up, water, and revive; some footmarks, too, he had left on the beds: but these, in spite of the strong wind, I found a moment's leisure to efface very early in the morning, ere common eyes had discovered them. With a pensive sort of content, I sat down to my desk and my German, while the pupils settled to their evening lessons, and the other teachers took up their needlework.

The scene of the 'Etude du soir' was always the refectory, a much smaller apartment than any of the three classes or schoolrooms; for here none, save the boarders, were ever admitted, and these numbered only a score. Two lamps hung from the ceiling over the two tables; these were lit at dusk, and their kindling was the signal for school-books being set aside, a grave demeanour assumed, general silence enforced, and then commenced 'la lecture pieuse'. This said 'lecture pieuse' was, I soon found, mainly designed as a wholesome mortification of the Intellect, a useful humiliation of the Reason; and such a dose for Common Sense as she might digest at her leisure, and thrive on as she best could.

The book brought out (it was never changed, but when finished, recommenced) was a venerable volume, old as the hills – gray as the Hôtel de Ville.

I would have given two francs for the chance of getting that book once into my hands, turning over the sacred yellow leaves, ascertaining the title, and perusing with my own eyes the enormous figments which, as an unworthy heretic, it was only permitted me to drink in with my bewildered ears. This book contained legends of the saints. Good God! (I speak the words reverently) what legends they were. What gasconading rascals those saints must have been, if they first boasted these exploits or invented these miracles! These legends,

however, were no more than monkish extravagances, over which one laughed inwardly; there were, besides, priestly matters, and the priestcraft of the book was far worse than its monkery. The ears burned on each side of my head as I listened, perforce, to tales of moral martyrdom inflicted by Rome; the dread boasts of confessors, who had wickedly abused their office, trampling to deep degradation high-born ladies, making of countesses and princesses the most tormented slaves under the sun. Stories like that of Conrad and Elizabeth of Hungary, recurred again and again, with all its dreadful viciousness, sickening tyranny and black impiety: tales that were nightmares of oppression, privation, and agony.

I sat out this 'lecture pieuse' for some nights as well as I could, and as quietly too; only once breaking off the points of my scissors by involuntarily sticking them somewhat deep in the worm-eaten board of the table before me. But, at last, it made me so burning hot, and my temples and my heart and my wrist throbbed so fast, and my sleep afterwards was so broken with excitement, that I could sit no longer. Prudence recommended henceforward a swift clearance of my person from the place, the moment that guilty old book was brought out. No Mause Headrigg ever felt a stronger call to take up her testimony against Sergeant Bothwell, than I – to speak my mind in this matter of the popish 'lecture pieuse'. However, I did manage somehow to curb and rein in; and though always, as soon as Rosine came to light the lamps, I shot from the room quickly, yet also I did it quietly; seizing that vantage moment given by the little bustle before the dead silence, and vanishing whilst the boarders put their books away.

When I vanished – it was into darkness; candles were not allowed to be carried about, and the teacher who forsook the refectory, had only the unlit hall, schoolroom, or bedroom, as a refuge. In winter I sought the long classes, and paced them fast to keep myself warm – fortunate if the moon shone, and if there were only stars, soon reconciled to their dim gleam, or even to the total eclipse of their absence. In summer it was never quite dark, and then I went upstairs to my own quarter of the long dormitory, opened my own casement (that chamber was lit by five casements large as great doors), and leaning out, looked forth upon the city beyond the garden, and listened to band-music from the park or the palace-square, thinking meantime my own thoughts, living my own life in my own still, shadow-world.

This evening, fugitive as usual before the Pope and his works, I mounted the staircase, approached the dormitory, and quietly opened the door which was always kept carefully shut, and which, like every other door in this house, revolved noiselessly on well-oiled hinges. Before I *saw*, I *felt* that life was in the great room, usually void: not that there was either stir or breath, or rustle of sound, but Vacuum lacked, Solitude was not at home. All the white beds – the 'lits d'ange', as they were poetically termed – lay visible at a glance; all were empty: no sleeper reposed therein. The sound of a drawer cautiously slid out struck my ear; stepping a little to one side, my vision took a free range, unimpeded by falling curtains. I now commanded my own bed and my own toilet, with a locked workbox upon it, and locked drawers underneath.

Very good. A dumpy, motherly, little body, in decent shawl and the cleanest of possible night-caps, stood before this toilet, hard at work, apparently doing me the kindness of 'tidying out' the 'meuble'. Open stood the lid of the workbox, open the top drawer; duly and impartially was each succeeding drawer opened in turn: not an article of their contents but was lifted and unfolded, not a paper but was glanced over, not a little box but was unlidded; and beautiful was the adroitness, exemplary the care with which the search was accomplished. Madame wrought at it like a true star, 'unhasting yet unresting'. I will not deny that it was with a secret glee I watched her. Had I been a gentleman, I believe madame would have found favour in my eyes, she was so handy, neat, thorough in all she did: some people's movements provoke the soul by their loose awkwardness, hers – satisfied by their trim compactness. I stood, in short, fascinated; but it was necessary to make an effort to break this spell: a retreat must be beaten. The searcher might have turned and caught me; there would have been nothing for it then but a scene, and she and I would have had to come all at once, with a sudden clash, to a thorough knowledge of each other: down would have gone conventionalities, away swept disguises, and *I* should have looked into her eyes, and *she* into mine – we should have known that we could work together no more, and parted in this life for ever.

Where was the use of tempting such a catastrophe? I was not angry, and had no wish in the world to leave her. I could hardly get another employer whose yoke would be so light and so easy of carriage; and truly, I liked madame for her capital sense, whatever I might think of her principles: as to her system, it did me no harm; she might work me with it to her heart's content: nothing would come of the operation. Loverless and inexpectant of love, I was as safe from spies in my heart-poverty, as the beggar from thieves in his destitution of purse. I turned, then, and fled; descending the stairs with progress as swift and soundless as that of the spider, which at the same instant ran down the bannister.

How I laughed when I reached the schoolroom. I knew now she had certainly seen Dr John in the garden; I knew what her thoughts were. The spectacle of a suspicious nature so far misled by its own inventions, tickled me much. Yet as the laugh died, a kind of wrath smote me, and then bitterness followed: it was the rock struck, and Meribah's waters gushing out. I never had felt so strange and contradictory an inward tumult as I felt for an hour that evening: soreness and laughter, and fire, and grief, shared my heart between them. I cried hot tears; not because madame mistrusted me – I did not care twopence for her mistrust – but for other reasons. Complicated, disquieting thoughts broke up the whole repose of my nature. However, that turmoil subsided: next day I was again Lucy Snowe.

On revisiting my drawers, I found them all securely locked; the closest subsequent examination could not discover change or apparent disturbance in the position of one object. My few dresses were folded as I had left them; a certain little bunch of white violets that had once been silently presented to me by a stranger (a stranger to me, for we had never exchanged words), and which I had dried and kept for its sweet perfume between the folds of my best dress, lay

there unstirred; my black silk scarf, my lace chemisettes and collars were unrumpled. Had she creased one solitary article, I own I should have felt much greater difficulty in forgiving her; but finding all straight and orderly, I said, 'Let bygones be bygones. I am unharmed: why should I bear malice?'

A thing there was which puzzled myself, and I sought in my brain a key to that riddle almost as sedulously as madame had sought a guide to useful knowledge in my toilet drawers. How was it that Dr John, if he had not been accessory to the dropping of that casket into the garden, should have known that it *was* dropped, and appeared so promptly on the spot to seek it? So strong was the wish to clear up this point that I began to entertain this daring suggestion: 'Why may I not, in case I should ever have the opportunity, ask Dr John himself to explain this coincidence?'

And so long as Dr John was absent, I really believed I had courage to test him with such a question.

Little Georgette was now convalescent; and her physician accordingly made his visits very rare: indeed, he would have ceased them altogether, had not madame insisted on his giving an occasional call till the child should be quite well.

She came into the nursery one evening just after I had listened to Georgette's lisped and broken prayer, and had put her to bed. Taking the little one's hand, she said: 'Cette enfant a toujours un peu de fièvre.' And presently afterwards, looking at me with a quicker glance than was habitual to her quiet eye, 'Le Docteur John l'a-t-il vue dernièrement? Non, n'est-ce pas?'

Of course, she knew this better than any other person in the house. 'Well,' she continued, 'I am going out, pour faire quelques courses en fiacre. I shall call on Dr John, and send him to the child. I will that he sees her this very evening; her cheeks are flushed, her pulse is quick: *you* will receive him – for my part, I shall be from home.'

Now the child was well enough, only warm with the warmth of July; it was scarcely less needful to send for a priest to administer extreme unction, than for a doctor to prescribe a dose; also madame rarely made 'courses' as she called them, in the evening: moreover, this was the first time she had chosen to absent herself on the occasion of a visit from Dr John. The whole arrangement indicated some plan; this I saw, but without the least anxiety. 'Ha! ha! madame,' laughed Light-heart the Beggar, 'your crafty wits are on the wrong tack.'

She departed, attired very smartly in a shawl of price, and a certain *chapeau vert tendre* – hazardous, as to its tint, for any complexion less fresh than her own, but, to her, not unbecoming. I wondered what she intended: whether she really would send Dr John or not; or whether indeed he would come: he might be engaged.

Madame had charged me not to let Georgette sleep till the doctor came; I had therefore sufficient occupation in telling her nursery tales and palavering the little language for her benefit. I affected Georgette; she was a sensitive and a loving child: to hold her in my lap, or carry her in my arms was to me a treat. Tonight she would have me lay my head on the pillow of her crib; she even put

her little arms round my neck. Her clasp and the nestling action with which she pressed her cheek to mine, made me almost cry with a tender pain. Feeling of no kind abounded in that house; this pure little drop from a pure little source was too sweet: it penetrated deep, and subdued the heart, and sent a gush to the eyes.

Half an hour or an hour passed; Georgette murmured in her soft lisp that she was growing sleepy. 'And you *shall* sleep,' thought I, 'malgré maman and médecin, if they are not here in ten minutes.'

Hark! There was the ring, and there the tread, astonishing the staircase by the fleetness with which it left the steps behind. Rosine introduced Dr John, and, with a freedom of manner not altogether peculiar to herself, but characteristic of the domestics of Villette generally, she stayed to hear what he had to say. Madame's presence would have awed her back to her own realm of the vestibule and the cabinet – for mine, or that of any other teacher or pupil, she cared not a jot. Smart, trim and pert, she stood, a hand in each pocket of her gay grisette apron, eyeing Dr John with no more fear or shyness than if he had been a picture instead of a living gentleman.

'Le marmot n'a rien n'est ce pas?' said she, indicating Georgette with a jerk of her chin.

'Pas beaucoup,' was the answer, as the doctor hastily scribbled with his pencil some harmless prescription.

'Eh bien!' pursued Rosine, approaching him quite near, while he put up his pencil. 'And the box – did you get it? Monsieur went off like a coup de vent the other night; I had not time to ask him.'

'I found it: yes.'

'And who threw it then?' continued Rosine, speaking quite freely the very words I should so much have wished to say, but had no address or courage to bring out: how short some people make the road to a point which, for others, seems unattainable!

'That may be my secret,' rejoined Dr John briefly, but with no sort of hauteur: he seemed quite to understand the Rosine or grisette character.

'Mais enfin,' continued she, nothing abashed, 'monsieur knew it was thrown, since he came to seek it – how did he know?'

'I was attending a little patient in the college near,' said he, 'and saw it dropped out of his chamber window, and so came to pick it up.'

How simple the whole explanation! The note had alluded to a physician as then examining 'Gustave'.

'Ah ça!' pursued Rosine, 'Il n'y a donc rien là-dessous: pas de mystère, pas d'amourette, par exemple?'

'Pas plus que sur ma main,' responded the doctor, showing his palm.

'Quel dommage!' responded the grisette: 'et moi – à qui tout cela commençait à donner des idées.'

'Vraiment! vous en êtes pour vos frais,' was the doctor's cool rejoinder.

She pouted. The doctor could not help laughing at the sort of 'moue' she made: when he laughed, he had something peculiarly good-natured and genial in his look. I saw his hand incline to his pocket.

'How many times have you opened the door for me within this last month?' he asked.

'Monsieur ought to have kept count of that,' said Rosine, quite readily.

'As if I had not something better to do!' rejoined he; but I saw him give her a piece of gold, which she took unscrupulously, and then danced off to answer the doorbell, ringing just now every five minutes, as the various servants came to fetch the half-boarders.

The reader must not think too hardly of Rosine; on the whole, she was not a bad sort of person, and had no idea there could be any disgrace in grasping at whatever she could get, or any effrontery in chattering like a pie to the best gentleman in Christendom.

I had learnt something from the above scene besides what concerned the ivory box: viz., that not on the robe de jaconas, pink or gray, nor yet on the frilled and pocketted apron, lay the blame of breaking Dr John's heart: these items of array were obviously guiltless as Georgette's little blue tunic. So much the better. But who then was the culprit? What was the ground – what the origin – what the perfect explanation of the whole business? Some points had been cleared, but how many yet remained obscure as night?

'However,' I said to myself, 'it is no affair of yours;' and turning from the face on which I had been unconsciously dwelling with a questioning gaze, I looked through the window which commanded the garden below. Dr John, meantime, standing by the bedside, was slowly drawing on his gloves and watching his little patient, as her eyes closed and her rosy lips parted in coming sleep. I waited till he should depart as usual, with a quick bow and scarce articulate 'good-night.' Just as he took his hat, my eyes, fixed on the tall houses bounding the garden, saw the one lattice, already commemorated, cautiously open; forth from the aperture projected a hand and a white handkerchief; both waved. I know not whether the signal was answered from some viewless quarter of our own dwelling; but immediately after there fluttered from the lattice a falling object, white and light – billet the second, of course.

'There!' I ejaculated involuntarily.

'Where?' asked Dr John with energy, making direct for the window. 'What is it?'

'They have gone and done it again,' was my reply. 'A handkerchief waved and something fell:' and I pointed to the lattice, now closed and looking hypocritically blank.

'Go at once; pick it up and bring it here,' was his prompt direction; adding, 'nobody will take notice of *you*: *I* should be seen.'

Straight I went. After some little search, I found a folded paper, lodged on the lower branch of a shrub; I seized and brought it direct to Dr John. This time, I believe not even Rosine saw me.

He instantly tore the billet into small pieces, without reading it.

'It is not in the least *her* fault, you must remember,' he said, looking at me.

'*Whose* fault?' I asked. '*Who is* it?'

'You don't yet know, then?'

'Not in the least.'

'Have you no guess?'

'None.'

'If I knew you better, I might be tempted to risk some confidence, and thus secure you as guardian over a most innocent and excellent, but somewhat inexperienced being.'

'As a duenna?' I asked.

'Yes,' said he abstractedly. 'What snares are round her!' he added musingly: and now, certainly for the first time, he examined my face, anxious, doubtless, to see if any kindly expression there, would warrant him in recommending to my care and indulgence some ethereal creature, against whom powers of darkness were plotting. I felt no particular vocation to undertake the surveillance of ethereal creatures; but recalling the scene at the bureau, it seemed to me that I owed *him* a good turn: if I *could* help him then I would, and it lay not with me to decide how. With as little reluctance as might be, I intimated that 'I was willing to do what I could towards taking care of any person in whom he might be interested.'

'I am no farther interested than as a spectator,' said he, with a modesty, admirable, as I thought, to witness. 'I happen to be acquainted with the rather worthless character of the person who, from the house opposite, has now twice invaded the sanctity of this place; I have also met in society the object at whom these vulgar attempts are aimed. Her exquisite superiority and innate refinement ought, one would think, to scare impertinence from her very idea. It is not so, however; and innocent, unsuspicious as she is, I would guard her from evil if I could. In person, however, I can do nothing: I cannot come near her' – he paused.

'Well, I am willing to help you,' said I, 'only tell me how.' And busily, in my own mind, I ran over the list of our inmates, seeking this paragon, this pearl of great price, this gem without flaw. 'It must be madame,' I concluded. '*She* only, amongst us all, has the art even to *seem* superior: but as to being unsuspicious, inexperienced, etc., Dr John need not distract himself about that. However, this is just his whim, and I will not contradict him; he shall be humoured: his angel shall be an angel.'

'Just notify the quarter to which my care is to be directed,' I continued gravely: chuckling, however, to myself over the thought of being set to chaperon Mme Beck or any of her pupils.

Now Dr John had a fine set of nerves, and he at once felt by instinct, what no more coarsely constituted mind would have detected; namely, that I was a little amused at him. The colour rose to his cheek; with half a smile he turned and took his hat – he was going. My heart smote me.

'I will – I will help you,' said I eagerly. 'I will do what you wish. I will watch over your angel; I will take care of her, only tell me who she is.'

'But you *must* know,' said he, then with earnestness, yet speaking very low, 'So spotless, so good, so unspeakably beautiful! impossible that one house should contain two like her. I allude, of course –'

Here the latch of Mme Beck's chamber-door (opening into the nursery) gave

a sudden click, as if the hand holding it had been slightly convulsed; there was the suppressed explosion of an irrepressible sneeze. These little accidents will happen to the best of us. Madame – excellent woman! – was there on duty. She had come home quietly, stolen upstairs on tiptoe; she was in her chamber. If she had not sneezed, she would have heard all, and so should I; but that unlucky sternutation routed Dr John. While he stood aghast, she came forward alert, composed, in the best yet most tranquil spirits: no novice to her habits but would have thought she was just come in, and scouted the idea of her ear having been glued to the keyhole for at least ten minutes. She affected to sneeze again, declared she was 'enrhumée', and then proceeded volubly to recount her 'courses en fiacre'. The prayer-bell rang, and I left her with the doctor.

## CHAPTER 14

### *The Fête*

As soon as Georgette was well, madame sent her away into the country. I was sorry; I loved the child, and her loss made me poorer than before. But I must not complain. I lived in a house full of robust life; I might have had companions, and I chose solitude. Each of the teachers in turn made me overtures of special intimacy; I tried them all. One I found to be an honest woman, but a narrow thinker, a coarse feeler, and an egotist. The second was a Parisienne, externally refined – at heart, corrupt – without a creed, without a principle, without an affection: having penetrated the outward crust of decorum in this character, you found a slough beneath. She had a wonderful passion for presents; and, in this point, the third teacher – a person otherwise characterless and insignificant – closely resembled her. This last-named had also one other distinctive property – that of avarice. In her reigned the love of money for its own sake. The sight of a piece of gold would bring into her eyes a green glisten, singular to witness. She once, as a mark of high favour, took me upstairs, and, opening a secret drawer, showed me a hoard – a mass of coarse, large coin – about fifteen guineas, in five-franc pieces. She loved this hoard as a bird loves its eggs. These were her savings. She would come and talk to me about them with an infatuated and persevering dotage, strange to behold in a person not yet twenty- five.

The Parisienne, on the other hand, was prodigal and profligate (in disposition, that is: as to action, I do not know). That latter quality showed its snake-head to me but once, peering out very cautiously. A curious kind of reptile it seemed, judging from the glimpse I got; its novelty whetted my curiosity: if it would have come out boldly, perhaps I might philosophically have stood my ground, and coolly surveyed the long thing from forked tongue to scaly tail-tip; but it merely rustled in the leaves of a bad novel; and, on encountering a hasty and ill-advised demonstration of wrath, recoiled and vanished, hissing. She hated me from that day.

This Parisienne was always in debt; her salary being anticipated, not only in dress, but in perfumes, cosmetics, confectionery, and condiments. What a cold, callous epicure she was in all things! I see her now. Thin in face and figure, sallow in complexion, regular in features, with perfect teeth, lips like a thread, a large, prominent chin, a well-opened, but frozen eye, of light at once craving and ingrate. She mortally hated work, and loved what she called pleasure; being an insipid, heartless, brainless dissipation of time.

Mme Beck knew this woman's character perfectly well. She once talked to me about her, with an odd mixture of discrimination, indifference, and antipathy. I asked why she kept her in the establishment. She answered plainly, 'because it suited her interest to do so;' and pointed out a fact I had already noticed, namely, that Mlle St Pierre possessed, in an almost unique degree, the power of keeping order amongst her undisciplined ranks of scholars. A certain petrifying influence accompanied and surrounded her: without passion, noise, or violence, she held them in check as a breezeless frost-air might still a brawling stream. She was of little use as far as communication of knowledge went, but for strict surveillance and maintenance of rules she was invaluable. 'Je sais bien qu'elle n'a pas de principes, ni, peut-être, de moeurs,' admitted madame frankly; but added, with philosophy, 'son maintien en classe est toujours convenable et rempli même d'une certaine dignité: c'est tout ce qu'il faut. Ni les élèves, ni les parents ne regardent plus loin; ni, par conséquent, moi non plus.'

A strange, frolicsome, noisy little world was this school: great pains were taken to hide chains with flowers: a subtle essence of Romanism pervaded every arrangement: large sensual indulgence (so to speak) was permitted by way of counterpoise to jealous spiritual restraint. Each mind was being reared in slavery; but, to prevent reflection from dwelling on this fact, every pretext for physical recreation was seized and made the most of. There, as elsewhere, the *church* strove to bring up her children robust in body, feeble in soul, fat, ruddy, hale, joyous, ignorant, unthinking, unquestioning. 'Eat, drink, and live!' she says. 'Look after your bodies; leave your souls to me. I hold their cure – guide their course: I guarantee their final fate.' A bargain, in which every true Catholic deems himself a gainer. Lucifer just offers the same terms: 'All this power will I give thee, and the glory of it; for that is delivered unto me, and to whomsoever I will I give it. If thou, therefore, wilt worship me, all shall be thine!'

About this time – in the ripest glow of summer – Mme Beck's house became as merry a place as a school could well be. All day long the broad folding-doors and the two-leaved casements stood wide open: settled sunshine seemed naturalised in the atmosphere; clouds were far off, sailing away beyond sea, resting, no doubt, round islands such as England – that dear land of mists – but withdrawn wholly from the drier continent. We lived far more in the garden than under a roof: classes were held, and meals partaken of, in the 'grand berceau.' Moreover, there was a note of holiday preparation, which almost turned freedom into license. The autumnal long vacation was but two months distant; but before that, a great

day – an important ceremony – none other than the fête of madame – awaited celebration.

The conduct of this fête devolved chiefly on Mlle St Pierre; madame herself being supposed to stand aloof, disinterestedly unconscious of what might be going forward in her honour. Especially, she never knew, never in the least suspected that a subscription was annually levied on the whole school for the purchase of a handsome present. The polite tact of the reader will please to leave out of the account a brief, secret consultation on this point in madame's own chamber.

'What will you have this year?' was asked by her Parisian lieutenant.

'Oh, no matter! Let it alone. Let the poor children keep their francs.' And madame looked benign and modest.

The St Pierre would here protrude her chin; she knew madame by heart; she always called her airs of 'bonté' – 'des grimaces.' She never even professed to respect them one instant.

'Vite!' she would say coldly. 'Name the article. Shall it be jewellery or porcelain, haberdashery or silver?'

'Eh bien! Deux ou trois cuillers et autant de fourchettes en argent.'

And the result was a handsome case, containing 300 francs worth of plate.

The programme of the fête-day's proceedings comprised: Presentation of plate, collation in the garden, dramatic performance (with pupils and teachers for actors), a dance and supper. Very gorgeous seemed the effect of the whole to me, as I well remember. Zélie St Pierre understood these things and managed them ably.

The Play was the main point; a month's previous drilling being there required. The choice too of the actors required knowledge and care; then came lessons in elocution, in attitude, and then the fatigue of countless rehearsals. For all this, as may well be supposed, St Pierre did not suffice: other management, other accomplishments than hers were requisite here. They were supplied in the person of a master – M. Paul Emanuel, professor of literature. It was never my lot to be present at the histrionic lessons of M. Paul, but I often saw him as he crossed the *carré* (a square hall between the dwelling-house and school-house). I heard him too in the warm evenings, lecturing with open doors, and his name, with anecdotes of him, resounded in one's ears from all sides. Especially our former acquaintance, Miss Ginevra Fanshawe, who had been selected to take a prominent part in the play – used, in bestowing upon me a large portion of her leisure, to lard her discourse with frequent allusions to his sayings and doings. She esteemed him hideously plain, and used to profess herself frightened almost into hysterics at the sound of his step or voice. A dark little man he certainly was; pungent and austere. Even to me he seemed a harsh apparition, with his close-shorn, black head, his broad, sallow brow, his thin cheek, his wide and quivering nostril, his thorough glance and hurried bearing. Irritable he was; one heard that, as he apostrophised with vehemence the awkward squad under his orders. Sometimes he would break out on these raw amateur actresses with a passion of impatience at their falseness of conception, their coldness of emotion,

their feebleness of delivery. 'Ecoutez!' he would cry; and then his voice rang through the premises like a trumpet; and when, mimicking it, came the small pipe of a Ginevra, a Mathilde, or a Blanche, one understood why a hollow groan of scorn, or a fierce hiss of rage rewarded the tame echo.

'Vous n'êtes donc que des poupées?' I heard him thunder. 'Vous n'avez pas de passions – vous autres? Vous ne sentez donc rien? Votre chair est de neige, votre sang de glace? Moi, je veux que tout cela s'allume, qu'il ait une vie, une âme!'

Vain resolve! And when he at last found it *was* vain, he suddenly broke the whole business down. Hitherto he had been teaching them a grand tragedy; he tore the tragedy in morsels, and came next day with a compact little comic trifle. To this they took more kindly; he presently knocked it all into their smooth round pates.

Mlle St Pierre always presided at M. Emanuel's lessons, and I was told that the polish of her manner, her seeming attention, her tact and grace, impressed that gentleman very favourably. She had, indeed, the art of pleasing, for a given time, whom she would; but the feeling would not last: in an hour it was dried like dew, vanished like gossamer.

The day preceding madame's fête was as much a holiday as the fête itself. It was devoted to clearing out, cleaning, arranging and decorating the three schoolrooms. All within doors was the gayest bustle; neither upstairs nor down could a quiet isolated person find rest for the sole of her foot; accordingly, for my part, I took refuge in the garden. The whole day did I wander or sit there alone, finding warmth in the sun, shelter among the trees, and a sort of companionship in my own thoughts. I well remember that I exchanged but two sentences that day with any living being: not that I felt solitary; I was glad to be quiet. For a looker-on, it sufficed to pass through the rooms once or twice, observe what changes were being wrought, how a green-room and a dressing-room were being contrived, a little stage with scenery erected, how M. Paul Emanuel, in conjunction with Mlle St Pierre, was directing all, and how an eager band of pupils, amongst them Ginevra Fanshawe, were working gaily under his control.

The great day arrived. The sun rose hot and unclouded, and hot and unclouded it burned on till evening. All the doors and all the windows were set open, which gave a pleasant sense of summer freedom – and freedom the most complete seemed indeed the order of the day. Teachers and pupils descended to breakfast in dressing-gowns and curl-papers: anticipating 'avec délices' the toilette of the evening, they seemed to take a pleasure in indulging that forenoon a luxury of slovenliness; like aldermen, fasting in preparation for a feast. About nine o'clock, a.m., an important functionary, the 'coiffeur,' arrived. Sacrilegious to state, he fixed his headquarters in the oratory, and there, in presence of *bénitier*, candle, and crucifix, solemnised the mysteries of his art. Each girl was summoned in turn to pass through his hands; emerging from them with head as smooth as a shell, intersected by faultless white lines, and wreathed about with Grecian plaits that shone as if lacquered. I took my turn with the rest, and could hardly believe what the glass said when I applied to it for information afterwards;

the lavish garlandry of woven brown hair amazed me – feared it was not all my own, and it required several convincing pulls to give assurance to the contrary. I then acknowledged in the coiffeur a first-rate artist – one who certainly made the most of indifferent materials.

The oratory closed, the dormitory became the scene of ablutions, arrayings and bedizenings curiously elaborate. To me it was, and ever must be an enigma, how they contrived to spend so much time in doing so little. The operation seemed close, intricate, prolonged: the result simple. A clear white muslin dress, a blue sash (the Virgin's colours), a pair of white, or straw-colour kid gloves – such was the gala uniform, to the assumption whereof that houseful of teachers and pupils devoted three mortal hours. But though simple, it must be allowed the array was perfect – perfect in fashion, fit, and freshness; every head being also dressed with exquisite nicety, and a certain compact taste – suiting the full, firm comeliness of Labassecourien contours, though too stiff for any more flowing and flexible style of beauty – the general effect was, on the whole, commendable.

In beholding this diaphanous and snowy mass, I well remember feeling myself to be a mere shadowy spot on a field of light; the courage was not in me to put on a transparent white dress: something thin I must wear – the weather and rooms being too hot to give substantial fabrics sufferance, so I had sought through a dozen shops till I lit upon a crape-like material of purple-gray – the colour, in short, of dun mist, lying on a moor in bloom. My *tailleuse* had kindly made it as well as she could: because, as she judiciously observed, it was 'si triste – si peu voyant,' care in the fashion was the more imperative: it was well she took this view of the matter, for I had no flower, no jewel to relieve it; and, what was more, I had no natural rose of complexion.

We become oblivious of these deficiencies in the uniform routine of daily drudgery, but they *will* force upon us their unwelcome blank on those bright occasions when beauty should shine.

However, in this same gown of shadow, I felt at home and at ease; an advantage I should not have enjoyed in anything more brilliant or striking. Mme Beck, too, kept me in countenance; her dress was almost as quiet as mine, except that she wore a bracelet, and a large brooch bright with gold and fine stones. We chanced to meet on the stairs, and she gave me a nod and smile of approbation. Not that she thought I was looking well – a point unlikely to engage her interest – but she considered me dressed 'convenablement', 'décemment', and la Convenance et la Décence were the two calm deities of madame's worship. She even paused, laid on my shoulder her gloved hand, holding an embroidered and perfumed handkerchief, and confided to my ear a sarcasm on the other teachers (whom she had just been complimenting to their faces). 'Nothing so absurd,' she said, 'as for des femmes mûres "to dress themselves like girls of fifteen" – quant à la St Pierre, elle a l'air d'une vieille coquette qui fait l'ingénue.'

Being dressed at least a couple of hours before anybody else, I felt a pleasure in betaking myself – not to the garden, where servants were busy propping up long tables, placing seats, and spreading cloths in readiness for the collation – but to

the schoolrooms, now empty, quiet, cool, and clean; their walls fresh stained, their planked floors fresh scoured and scarce dry; flowers fresh gathered adorning the recesses in pots, and draperies, fresh hung, beautifying the great windows.

Withdrawing to the first classe, a smaller and neater room than the others, and taking from the glazed bookcase, of which I kept the key, a volume whose title promised some interest, I sat down to read. The glass-door of this *classe*, or schoolroom, opened into the large berceau; acacia-boughs caressed its panes, as they stretched across to meet a rose bush blooming by the opposite lintel: in this rose bush, bees murmured busy and happy. I commenced reading. Just as the stilly hum, the embowering shade, the warm, lonely calm of my retreat were beginning to steal meaning from the page, vision from my eyes, and to lure me along the track of reverie, down into some deep dell of dream-land – just then, the sharpest ring of the street-door bell to which that much-tried instrument had ever thrilled, snatched me back to consciousness.

Now, the bell had been ringing all the morning, as workmen, or servants, or *coiffeurs*, or *tailleuses*, went and came on their several errands. Moreover, there was good reason to expect it would ring all the afternoon, since about one hundred externes were yet to arrive in carriages or fiacres: nor could it be expected to rest during the evening, when parents and friends would gather thronging to the play. Under these circumstances, a ring – even a sharp ring – was a matter of course: yet this particular peal had an accent of its own, which chased my dream, and startled my book from my knee.

I was stooping to pick up this last, when – firm, fast, straight – right on through vestibule, along corridor, across carré, through first division, second division, grande salle – strode a step, quick, regular, intent. The closed door of the first classe – my sanctuary – offered no obstacle; it burst open, and a paletôt and a bonnet grec filled the void; also two eyes first vaguely struck upon, and then hungrily dived into me.

'C'est cela!' said a voice. 'Je la connais: c'est l'Anglaise. Tant pis. Toute Anglaise, et par conséquent, toute bégueule qu'elle soit – elle fera mon affaire, ou je saurai pourquoi.'

Then, with a certain stern politeness (I suppose he thought I had not caught the drift of his previous uncivil mutterings), and in a jargon the most execrable that ever was heard, 'Meess – play you must: I am planted there.'

'What can I do for you, M. Paul Emanuel?' I enquired: for M. Paul Emanuel it was, and in a state of no little excitement.

'Play you must. I will not have you shrink, or frown, or make the prude. I read your skull, that night you came; I see your moyens: play you can; play you must.'

'But how, M. Paul? What do you mean?'

'There is no time to be lost,' he went on now speaking in French; 'and let us thrust to the wall all reluctance, all excuses, all minauderies. You must take a part.'

'In the vaudeville?'

'In the vaudeville. You have said it.'

I gasped, horror-struck. *What* did the little man mean?

'Listen!' he said. 'The case shall be stated, and you shall then answer me Yes, or No; and according to your answer shall I ever after estimate you.'

The scarce-suppressed impetus of a most irritable nature glowed in his cheek, fed with sharp shafts his glances, a nature – the injudicious, the mawkish, the hesitating, the sullen, the affected, above all, the unyielding, might quickly render violent and implacable. Silence and attention was the best balm to apply: I listened.

'The whole matter is going to fail,' he began. 'Louise Vanderkelkov has fallen ill – at least so her ridiculous mother asserts; for my part, I feel sure she might play if she would: it is only goodwill that lacks. She was charged with a *rôle*, as you know, or do *not* know – it is equal: without that *rôle* the play is stopped. There are now but a few hours in which to learn it: not a girl in this school would hear reason, and accept the task. Forsooth, it is not an interesting, not an amiable, part; their vile *amour-propre* – that base quality of which women have so much – would revolt from it. Englishwomen are either the best or the worst of their sex. Dieu sait que je les déteste comme la peste, ordinairement' (this between his recreant teeth). 'I apply to an Englishwoman to rescue me. What is her answer – Yes, or No?'

A thousand objections rushed into my mind. The foreign language, the limited time, the public display. Inclination recoiled, Ability faltered, Self-respect (that 'vile quality') trembled. 'Non, non, non!' said all these; but looking up at M. Paul, and seeing in his vexed, fiery, and searching eye, a sort of appeal behind all its menace – my lips dropped the word 'oui.' For a moment, his rigid countenance relaxed with a quiver of content: quickly bent up again, however, he went on – 'Vite a l'ouvrage! Here is the book; here is your *rôle*: read.' And I read. He did not commend; at some passages he scowled and stamped. He gave me a lesson: I diligently imitated. It was a disagreeable part, a man's – an empty-headed fop's. One could put into it neither heart nor soul: I hated it. The play – a mere trifle – ran chiefly on the efforts of a brace of rivals to gain the hand of a fair coquette. One lover was called the 'Ours,' a good and gallant but unpolished man, a sort of diamond in the rough; the other was a butterfly, a talker, and a traitor: and I was to be the butterfly, talker, and traitor.

I did my best – which was bad, I know: it provoked M. Paul; he fumed. Putting both hands to the work, I endeavoured to do better than my best; I presume he gave me credit for good intentions; he professed to be partially content. 'Ça ira!' he cried; and as voices began sounding from the garden, and white dresses fluttering among the trees, he added: 'You must withdraw: you must be alone to learn this. Come with me.'

Without being allowed time or power to deliberate, I found myself in the same breath convoyed along as in a species of whirlwind, up stairs, up two pair of stairs, nay, actually up three (for this fiery little man seemed as by instinct to know his way everywhere); to the solitary and lofty attic was I borne, put in and locked in, the key being on the door, and that key he took with him, and vanished.

The attic was no pleasant place: I believe he did not know how unpleasant it was, or he never would have locked me in with so little ceremony. In this

summer weather, it was hot as Africa; as in winter, it was always cold as Greenland. Boxes and lumber filled it; old dresses draped its unstained wall – cobwebs its unswept ceiling. Well was it known to be tenanted by rats, by black beetles, and by cockroaches – nay, rumour affirmed that the ghostly Nun of the garden had once been seen here. A partial darkness obscured one end, across which, as for deeper mystery, an old russet curtain was drawn, by way of screen to a sombre band of winter cloaks, pendant each from its pin like a malefactor from his gibbet. From amongst these cloaks, and behind that curtain, the Nun was said to issue. I did not believe this, nor was I troubled by apprehension thereof; but I saw a very dark and large rat, with a long tail, come gliding out from that squalid alcove; and, moreover, my eye fell on many a black beetle, dotting the floor. These objects discomposed me more, perhaps, than it would be wise to say, as also did the dust, lumber, and stifling heat of the place. The last inconvenience would soon have become intolerable, had I not found means to open and prop up the sky-light, thus admitting some freshness. Underneath this aperture I pushed a large empty chest, and having mounted upon it a smaller box, and wiped from both the dust, I gathered my dress (my best, the reader must remember, and therefore a legitimate object of care) fastidiously round me, ascended this species of extempore throne, and being seated, commenced the acquisition of my task; while I learned, not forgetting to keep a sharp look-out on the black beetles and cockroaches, of which, more even, I believe, than of the rats, I sat in mortal dread.

My impression at first was that I had undertaken what it really was impossible to perform, and I simply resolved to do my best and be resigned to fail. I soon found, however, that one part in so short a piece was not more than memory could master at a few hours' notice. I learned and learned on, first in a whisper, and then aloud. Perfectly secure from human audience, I acted my part before the garret-vermin. Entering into its emptiness, frivolity, and falsehood, with a spirit inspired by scorn and impatience, I took my revenge on this 'fat,' by making him as fatuitous as I possibly could.

In this exercise the afternoon passed: day began to glide into evening; and I, who had eaten nothing since breakfast, grew excessively hungry. Now I thought of the collation, which doubtless they were just then devouring in the garden far below. (I had seen in the vestibule a basketful of small *pâtés à la crême*, than which nothing in the whole range of cookery seemed to me better). A *pâté*, or a square of cake, it seemed to me would come very *apropos*; and as my relish for these dainties increased, it began to appear somewhat hard that I should pass my holiday, fasting and in prison. Remote as was the attic from the street-door and vestibule, yet the ever-tinkling bell was faintly audible here; and also the ceaseless roll of wheels on the tormented pavement. I knew that the house and garden were thronged, and that all was gay and glad below; here it began to grow dusk: the beetles were fading from my sight; I trembled lest they should steal on me a march, mount my throne unseen, and, unsuspected, invade my skirts. Impatient and apprehensive, I recommenced the rehearsal of my part merely to kill time. Just as I was concluding, the long-delayed rattle of the key in the lock came to my

ear – no unwelcome sound. M. Paul (I could just see through the dusk that it *was* M. Paul, for light enough still lingered to show the velvet blackness of his close-shorn head, and the sallow ivory of his brow) looked in.

'Brava!' cried he, holding the door open, and remaining at the threshold. 'J'ai tout entendu. C'est assez bien. Encore!'

A moment I hesitated.

'Encore!' said he sternly. 'Et point de grimaces! A bas la timidité!'

Again I went through the part, but not half so well as I had spoken it alone.

'Enfin, elle le sait,' said he, half dissatisfied, 'and one cannot be fastidious or exacting under the circumstances.' Then he added, 'You may yet have twenty minutes for preparation: au revoir!' And he was going.

'Monsieur,' I called out, taking courage.

'Eh bien. Qu'est ce que c'est, mademoiselle?'

'J'ai bien faim.'

'Comment, vous avez faim! Et la collation?'

'I know nothing about it. I have not seen it, shut up here.'

'Ah! C'est vrai,' cried he.

In a moment my throne was abdicated, the attic evacuated; an inverse repetition of the impetus which had brought me up into the attic, instantly took me down – down – down to the very kitchen. I thought I should have gone to the cellar. The cook was imperatively ordered to produce food, and I, as imperatively, was commanded to eat. To my great joy this food was limited to coffee and cake: I had feared wine and sweets, which I did not like. How he guessed that I should like a *petit pâté à la crême* I cannot tell; but he went out and procured me one from some quarter. With considerable willingness I ate and drank, keeping the *petit pâté* till the last, as a *bonne bouche*. M. Paul superintended my repast, and almost forced upon me more than I could swallow.

'A la bonne heure,' he cried, when I signified that I really could take no more, and, with uplifted hands, implored to be spared the additional roll on which he had just spread butter. 'You will set me down as a species of tyrant and Bluebeard, starving women in a garret; whereas, after all, I am no such thing. Now, mademoiselle, do you feel courage and strength to appear?'

I said, I thought I did; though, in truth, I was perfectly confused, and could hardly tell how I felt: but this little man was of the order of beings who must not be opposed, unless you possessed an all-dominant force sufficient to crush him at once.

'Come then,' said he, offering his hand.

I gave him mine, and he set off with a rapid walk, which obliged me to run at his side in order to keep pace. In the carré he stopped a moment; it was lit with large lamps; the wide doors of the classes were open, and so were the equally wide garden-doors; orange trees in tubs, and tall flowers in pots, ornamented these portals on each side; groups of ladies and gentlemen in evening-dress stood and walked amongst the flowers. Within, the long vista of the school-rooms presented a thronging, undulating, murmuring, waving, streaming multitude, all

rose, and blue, and half translucent white. There were lustres burning overhead; far off there was a stage, a solemn green curtain, a row of footlights.

'N'est-ce pas que c'est beau?' demanded my companion.

I should have said it was, but my heart got up into my throat. M. Paul discovered this, and gave me a side-scowl and a little shake for my pains.

'I will do my best, but I wish it was over,' said I; then I asked: 'Are we to walk through that crowd?'

'By no means: I manage matters better: we pass through the garden – here.'

In an instant we were out of doors; the cool, calm night revived me somewhat. It was moonless, but the reflex from the many glowing windows lit the court brightly, and even the alleys – dimly. Heaven was cloudless, and grand with the quiver of its living fires. How soft are the nights of the continent! How bland, balmy, safe! No sea-fog; no chilling damp: mistless as noon, and fresh as morning.

Having crossed court and garden, we reached the glass door of the first classe. It stood open, like all other doors that night; we passed, and then I was ushered into a small cabinet, dividing the first classe from the grande salle. This cabinet dazzled me, it was so full of light: it deafened me, it was so clamorous with voices: it stifled me, it was so hot, choking, thronged.

'De l'ordre! Du silence!' cried M. Paul. 'Is this chaos?' he demanded; and there was a hush. With a dozen words, and as many gestures, he turned out half the persons present, and obliged the remnant to fall into rank. Those left were all in costume: they were the performers, and this was the green-room. M. Paul introduced me. All stared and some tittered. It was a surprise: they had not expected the Englishwoman would play in a *vaudeville*. Ginevra Fanshawe, beautifully dressed for her part, and looking fascinatingly pretty, turned on me a pair of eyes as round as beads. In the highest spirit, unperturbed by fear or bashfulness, delighted indeed at the thought of shining off before hundreds – my entrance seemed to transfix her with amazement in the midst of her joy. She would have exclaimed, but M. Paul held her and all the rest in check.

Having surveyed and criticised the whole troop, he turned to me.

'You, too, must be dressed for your part.'

'Dressed – dressed like a man!' exclaimed Zélie St Pierre, darting forwards; adding with officiousness, 'I will dress her myself.'

To be dressed like a man did not please, and would not suit me. I had consented to take a man's name and part; as to his dress – *halte là*! No. I would keep my own dress; come what might. M. Paul might storm, might rage: I would keep my own dress. I said so, with a voice as resolute in intent, as it was low, and perhaps unsteady, in utterance.

He did not immediately storm or rage, as I fully thought he would: he stood silent. But Zélie again interposed.

'She will make a capital *petit-maître*. Here are the garments, all – all complete: somewhat too large, but I will arrange all that. Come chère amie – belle Anglaise!'

And she sneered, for I was not 'belle.' She seized my hand, she was drawing me away. M. Paul stood impassible – neutral.

'You must not resist,' pursued St Pierre – for resist I did. 'You will spoil all, destroy the mirth of the piece, the enjoyment of the company, sacrifice everything to your *amour-propre*. This would be too bad – monsieur will never permit this?'

She sought his eye. I watched, likewise, for a glance. He gave her one, and then he gave me one. 'Stop!' he said slowly, arresting St Pierre, who continued her efforts to drag me after her. Everybody awaited the decision. He was not angry, not irritated; I perceived that and took heart.

'You do not like these clothes?' he asked, pointing to the masculine vestments. 'I don't object to some of them, but I won't have them all.'

'How must it be, then? How, accept a man's part, and go on the stage dressed as a woman? This is an amateur affair, it is true – a *vaudeville de pensionnat*; certain modifications I might sanction, yet something you must have to announce you as of the nobler sex.'

'And I will, monsieur; but it must be arranged in my own way: nobody must meddle; the things must not be forced upon me. Just let me dress myself.'

Monsieur, without another word, took the costume from St Pierre, gave it to me, and permitted me to pass into the dressing-room. Once alone, I grew calm, and collectedly went to work. Retaining my woman's garb without the slightest retrenchment, I merely assumed in addition, a little vest, a collar, and cravat, and a paletôt of small dimensions; the whole being the costume of a brother of one of the pupils. Having loosened my hair out of its braids, made up the long back hair close, and brushed the front hair to one side, I took my hat and gloves in my hand and came out. M. Paul was waiting and so were the others. He looked at me. 'That may pass in a Pensionnat,' he pronounced. Then added, not unkindly, 'Courage, mon ami! Un peu de sang froid – un peu d'aplomb, M. Lucien, et tout ira bien.'

St Pierre sneered again, in her cold, snaky manner.

I was irritable, because excited, and I could not help turning upon her and saying, that if she were not a lady and I a gentleman, I should feel disposed to call her out.

'After the play, after the play,' said M. Paul. 'I will then divide my pair of pistols between you, and we will settle the dispute according to form: it will only be the old quarrel of France and England.'

But now the moment approached for the performance to commence. M. Paul setting us before him, harangued us briefly, like a general addressing soldiers about to charge. I don't know what he said, except that he recommended each to penetrate herself well with a sense of her personal significance. God knows, I thought this advice superfluous for some of us. A bell tinkled. I and two more were ushered on to the stage. The bell tinkled again. I had to speak the very first words.

'Do not look at the crowd, nor think of it,' whispered M. Paul in my ear. 'Imagine yourself in the garret, acting to the rats.'

He vanished. The curtain drew up – shrivelled to the ceiling; the bright lights, the long room, the gay throng burst upon us. I thought of the black beetles, the old boxes, the worm-eaten bureaux. I said my say badly; but I said it.

That first speech was the difficulty; it revealed to me this fact, that it was not the crowd I feared, so much as my own voice. Foreigners and strangers, the crowd were nothing to me. Nor did I think of them. When my tongue once got free, and my voice took its true pitch, and found its natural tone, I thought of nothing but the personage I represented – and of M. Paul, who was listening, watching, prompting in the side-scenes.

By and by, feeling the right power come – the spring demanded gush and rise inwardly – I became sufficiently composed to notice my fellow-actors. Some of them played very well; especially Ginevra Fanshawe, who had to coquette between two suitors, and managed admirably: in fact she was in her element. I observed that she once or twice threw a certain marked fondness, and pointed partiality into her manner towards me – the fop. With such emphasis and animation did she favour me, such glances did she dart out into the listening and applauding crowd, that to me – who knew her – it presently became evident she was acting *at* someone; and I followed her eye, her smile, her gesture, and ere long discovered that she had at least singled out a handsome and distinguished aim for her shafts; full in the path of those arrows – taller than other spectators, and therefore more sure to receive them – stood, in attitude quiet but intent, a well-known form – that of Dr John.

The spectacle seemed somehow suggestive. There was language in Dr John's look, though I cannot tell what he said; it animated me: I drew out of it a history; I put my idea into the part I performed; I threw it into my wooing of Ginevra. In the 'Ours', or sincere lover, I saw Dr John. Did I pity him, as erst? No, I hardened my heart, rivalled and out-rivalled him. I knew myself but a fop, but where *he* was outcast *I* could please. Now I know I acted as if wishful and resolute to win and conquer. Ginevra seconded me; between us we half-changed the nature of the *rôle*, gilding it from top to toe. Between the acts M. Paul told us he knew not what possessed us, and half expostulated, 'C'est peut-être plus beau que votre modèle,' said he, 'mais ce n'est pas juste.' I know not what possessed me either; but somehow, my longing was to eclipse the 'Ours:' i.e., Dr John. Ginevra was tender; how could I be otherwise than chivalric? Retaining the letter, I recklessly altered the spirit of the *rôle*. Without heart, without interest, I could not play it at all. It must be played – in went the yearned-for seasoning – thus flavoured, I played it with relish.

What I felt that night, and what I did, I no more expected to feel and do, than to be lifted in a trance to the seventh heaven. Cold, reluctant, apprehensive, I had accepted a part to please another: ere long, warming, becoming interested, taking courage, I acted to please myself. Yet the next day, when I thought it over, I quite disapproved of these amateur performances; and though glad that I had obliged M. Paul, and tried my own strength for once, I took a firm resolution never to be drawn into a similar affair. A keen relish for dramatic expression had revealed itself as part of my nature; to cherish and exercise this new-found faculty might gift me with a world of delight, but it would not do for a mere looker-on at life: the strength and longing must be put by; and I put them by, and fastened them in with the lock of a resolution which neither Time nor Temptation has since picked.

No sooner was the play over and *well* over, than the choleric and arbitrary M. Paul underwent a metamorphosis. His hour of managerial responsibility past, he at once laid aside his magisterial austerity; in a moment he stood amongst us, vivacious, kind, and social, shook hands with us all round, thanked us separately, and announced his determination that each of us should in turn be his partner in the coming ball. On his claiming my promise, I told him I did not dance. 'For once I must,' was the answer; and if I had not slipped aside and kept out of his way, he would have compelled me to this second performance. But I had acted enough for one evening; it was time I retired into myself and my ordinary life. My dun-coloured dress did well enough under a paletôt on the stage, but would not suit a waltz or a quadrille. Withdrawing to a quiet nook, whence unobserved I could observe – the ball, its splendours and its pleasures passed before me as a spectacle.

Again Ginevra Fanshawe was the belle, the fairest and the gayest present; she was selected to open the ball: very lovely she looked, very gracefully she danced, very joyously she smiled. Such scenes were her triumphs – she was the child of pleasure. Work or suffering found her listless and dejected, powerless and repining; but gaiety expanded her butterfly's wings, lit up their gold-dust and bright spots, made her flash like a gem, and flush like a flower. At all ordinary diet and plain beverage she would pout; but she fed on creams and ices like a humming-bird on honeypaste: sweet wine was her element and sweet cake her daily bread. Ginevra lived her full life in a ballroom; elsewhere she drooped dispirited.

Think not, reader, that she thus bloomed and sparkled for the mere sake of M. Paul her partner, or that she lavished her best graces that night for the edification of her companions only, or for that of the parents and grandparents, who filled the carré and lined the ballroom; under circumstances so insipid and limited, with motives so chilly and vapid, Ginevra would scarce have deigned to walk one quadrille, and weariness and fretfulness would have replaced animation and good-humour, but she knew of a leaven in the otherwise heavy festal mass which lightened the whole; she tasted a condiment which gave it zest; she perceived reasons justifying the display of her choicest attractions.

In the ballroom, indeed, not a single male spectator was to be seen who was not married and a father – M. Paul excepted – that gentleman, too, being the sole creature of his sex permitted to lead out a pupil to the dance; and this exceptional part was allowed him, partly as a matter of old-established custom (for he was a kinsman of Mme Beck's, and high in her confidence), partly because he would always have his own way and do as he pleased, and partly because – wilful, passionate, partial, as he might be – he was the soul of honour, and might be trusted with a regiment of the fairest and purest, in perfect security that under his leadership they would come to no harm. Many of the girls – it may be noted in parenthesis – were not pure-minded at all, very much otherwise; but they no more dare betray their natural coarseness in M. Paul's presence, than they dare tread purposely on his corns, laugh in his face during a stormy apostrophe, or speak above their breath while some crisis of irritability was covering his human

visage with the mask of an intelligent tiger. M. Paul, then, might dance with whom he would – and woe be to the interference which put him out of step.

Others there were admitted as spectators – with (seeming) reluctance, through prayers, by influence, under restriction, by special and difficult exercise of Mme Beck's gracious good-nature, and whom she all the evening – with her own personal surveillance – kept far aloof at the remotest, drearest, coldest, darkest side of the carré – a small, forlorn, band of 'jeunes gens'; these being all of the best families, grown-up sons of mothers present, and whose sisters were pupils in the school. That whole evening was madame on duty beside these 'jeunes gens' – attentive to them as a mother, but strict with them as a dragon. There was a sort of cordon sketched before them, which they wearied her with prayers to be permitted to pass, and just to revive themselves by one dance with that 'belle blonde,' or that 'jolie brune', or 'cette jeune fille magnifique aux cheveux noirs comme le jais.'

'Taisez-vous!' madame would reply, heroically and inexorably. 'Vous ne passerez pas à moins que ce ne soit sur mon cadavre, et vous ne danserez qu'avec la nonnette du jardin' (alluding to the legend). And she majestically walked to and fro along their disconsolate and impatient line, like a little Bonaparte in a mouse-coloured silk gown.

Madame knew something of the world; madame knew much of human nature. I don't think that another directress in Villette would have dared to admit a 'jeune homme' within her walls; but madame knew that by granting such admission, on an occasion like the present, a bold stroke might be struck, and a great point gained.

In the first place, the parents were made accomplices to the deed, for it was only through their mediation it was brought about. Secondly: the admission of these rattlesnakes, so fascinating and so dangerous, served to draw out madame precisely in her strongest character – that of a first-rate *surveillante*. Thirdly: their presence furnished a most piquant ingredient to the entertainment: the pupils knew it, and saw it, and the view of such golden apples shining afar off, animated them with a spirit no other circumstance could have kindled. The children's pleasure spread to the parents; life and mirth circulated quickly round the ballroom; the 'jeunes gens' themselves, though restrained, were amused: for madame never permitted them to feel dull – and thus Mme Beck's fête annually ensured a success unknown to the fête of any other directress in the land.

I observed that Dr John was at first permitted to walk at large through the classes: there was about him a manly, responsible look, that redeemed his youth, and half-expiated his beauty; but as soon as the ball began, madame ran up to him.

'Come, Wolf; come,' said she, laughing: 'You wear sheep's clothing, but you must quit the fold notwithstanding. Come; I have a fine menagerie of twenty here in the carré: let me place you amongst my collection.'

'But first suffer me to have one dance with one pupil of my choice.'

'Have you the face to ask such a thing? It is madness: it is impiety. Sortez, sortez, et au plus vite.'

She drove him before her, and soon had him enclosed within the cordon.

Ginevra being, I suppose, tired with dancing, sought me out in my retreat. She threw herself on the bench beside me, and (a demonstration I could very well have dispensed with) cast her arms round my neck.

'Lucy Snowe! Lucy Snowe!' she cried in a somewhat sobbing voice, half hysterical.

'What in the world is the matter?' I drily said.

'How do I look – how do I look tonight?' she demanded.

'As usual,' said I; 'preposterously vain.'

'Caustic creature! You never have a kind word for me; but in spite of you, and all other envious detractors, I know I am beautiful: I feel it, I see it – for there is a great looking-glass in the dressing-room, where I can view my shape from head to foot. Will you go with me now, and let us two stand before it?'

'I will, Miss Fanshawe: you shall be humoured even to the top of your bent.'

The dressing-room was very near, and we stepped in. Putting her arm through mine, she drew me to the mirror. Without resistance, remonstrance, or remark, I stood and let her self-love have its feast and triumph: curious to see how much it could swallow – whether it was possible it could feed to satiety – whether any whisper of consideration for others could penetrate her heart, and moderate its vainglorious exultation.

Not at all. She turned me and herself round; she viewed us both on all sides; she smiled, she waved her curls, she retouched her sash, she spread her dress, and finally, letting go my arm, and curtseying with mock respect, she said: 'I would not be you for a kingdom.'

The remark was too *naïve* to rouse anger; I merely said: 'Very good.'

'And what would *you* give to be ME?' she enquired.

'Not a bad sixpence – strange as it may sound,' I replied. 'You are but a poor creature.'

'You don't think so in your heart.'

'No; for in my heart you have not the outline of a place: I only occasionally turn you over in my brain.'

'Well, but,' said she, in an expostulatory tone, 'just listen to the difference of our positions, and then see how happy am I, and how miserable are you.'

'Go on; I listen.'

'In the first place: I am the daughter of a gentleman of family, and though my father is not rich, I have expectations from an uncle. Then, I am just eighteen, the finest age possible. I have had a continental education, and though I can't spell, I have abundant accomplishments. I *am* pretty; *you* can't deny that; I may have as many admirers as I choose. This very night I have been breaking the hearts of two gentlemen, and it is the dying look I had from one of them just now, which puts me in such spirits. I do so like to watch them turn red and pale, and scowl and dart fiery glances at each other, and languishing ones at me. There is *me* – happy ME; now for *you*, poor soul!

'I suppose you are nobody's daughter, since you took care of little children when you first came to Villette: you have no relations; you can't call yourself young at twenty-three; you have no attractive accomplishments – no beauty.

As to admirers, you hardly know what they are; you can't even talk on the subject: you sit dumb when the other teachers quote their conquests. I believe you never were in love, and never will be; you don't know the feeling: and so much the better, for though you might have your own heart broken, no living heart will you ever break. Isn't it all true?'

'A good deal of it is true as gospel, and shrewd besides. There must be good in you, Ginevra, to speak so honestly; that snake, Zélie St Pierre, could not utter what you have uttered. Still, Miss Fanshawe, hapless as I am, according to your showing, sixpence I would not give to purchase you, body and soul.'

'Just because I am not clever, and that is all *you* think of. Nobody in the world but you cares for cleverness.'

'On the contrary, I consider you *are* clever, in your way – very smart indeed. But you were talking of breaking hearts – that edifying amusement into the merits of which I don't quite enter; pray on whom does your vanity lead you to think you have done execution tonight?'

She approached her lips to my ear – 'Isidore and Alfred de Hamal are both here,' she whispered.

'Oh! they are? I should like to see them.'

'There's a dear creature! your curiosity is roused at last. Follow me, I will point them out.'

She proudly led the way – 'But you cannot see them well from the classes,' said she, turning, 'Madame keeps them too far off. Let us cross the garden, enter by the corridor, and get close to them behind: we shall be scolded if we are seen, but never mind.'

For once, I did not mind. Through the garden we went – penetrated into the corridor by a quiet private entrance, and approaching the carré, yet keeping in the corridor shade, commanded a near view of the band of 'jeunes gens'.

I believe I could have picked out the conquering de Hamal even undirected. He was a straight-nosed, very correct-featured, little dandy. I say *little* dandy, though he was not beneath the middle standard in stature; but his lineaments were small, and so were his hands and feet; and he was pretty and smooth, and as trim as a doll: so nicely dressed, so nicely curled, so booted and gloved and cravated – he was charming indeed. I said so: 'What a dear personage!' cried I, and commended Ginevra's taste warmly; and asked her what she thought de Hamal might have done with the precious fragments of that heart she had broken – whether he kept them in a scent-vial, and conserved them in otto of roses? I observed, too, with a deep rapture of approbation, that the colonel's hands were scarce larger than Miss Fanshawe's own, and suggested that this circumstance might be convenient, as he could wear her gloves at a pinch. On his dear curls, I told her I doted; and as to his low, Grecian brow, and exquisite classic head-piece, I confessed I had no language to do such perfections justice.

'And if he were your lover?' suggested the cruelly exultant Ginevra.

'Oh! heavens, what bliss!' said I; 'but do not be inhuman, Miss Fanshawe: to put such thoughts into my head is like showing poor outcast Cain a far glimpse of Paradise.'

'You like him then?'

'As I like sweets, and jams, and comfits, and conservatory flowers.'

Ginevra admired my taste, for all these things were her adoration; she could then readily credit that they were mine too.

'Now for Isidore,' I went on. I own I felt still more curious to see him than his rival; but Ginevra was absorbed in the latter.

'Alfred was admitted here tonight,' said she, 'through the influence of his aunt, Mme la Baronne de Dorlodot; and now, having seen him, can you not understand why I have been in such spirits all the evening, and acted so well and danced with such life, and why I am now happy as a queen? Dieu! Dieu! It was such good fun to glance first at him and then at the other, and madden them both.'

'But that other – where is he? Show me Isidore.'

'I don't like.'

'Why not?'

'I am ashamed of him.'

'For what reason?'

'Because – because' (in a whisper) 'he has such – such whiskers, orange – red – there now!'

'The murder is out,' I subjoined. 'Never mind, show him, all the same; I engage not to faint.'

She looked round. Just then an English voice spoke behind her and me.

'You are both standing in a draught; you must leave this corridor.'

'There is no draught, Dr John,' said I turning.

'She takes cold so easily,' he pursued, looking at Ginevra with extreme kindness. 'She is delicate; she must be cared for: fetch her a shawl.'

'Permit me to judge for myself,' said Miss Fanshawe, with hauteur. 'I want no shawl.'

'Your dress is thin, you have been dancing, you are heated.'

'Always preaching,' retorted she; 'always coddling and admonishing.'

The answer Dr John would have given, did not come; that his heart was hurt became evident in his eye; darkened, and saddened, and pained, he turned a little aside, but was patient. I knew where there were plenty of shawls near at hand; I ran and fetched one.

'She shall wear this if I have strength to make her,' said I, folding it well round her muslin dress, covering carefully her neck and her arms. 'Is that Isidore?' I asked, in a somewhat fierce whisper.

She pushed up her lip, smiled, and nodded.

'*Is that* Isidore?' I repeated, giving her a shake: I could have given her a dozen.

'C'est lui-même,' said she. 'How coarse he is, compared with the Colonel-Count! And then – oh, ciel! – the whiskers!'

Dr John now passed on.

'The Colonel-Count!' I echoed. 'The doll – the puppet – the manikin – the poor inferior creature! A mere lackey for Dr John: his valet, his foot-boy! Is it possible that fine generous gentleman – handsome as a vision – offers you his

honourable hand and gallant heart, and promises to protect your flimsy person and wretchless mind through the storms and struggles of life – and you hang back – you scorn, you sting, you torture him! Have you power to do this? Who gave you that power? Where is it? Does it lie all in your beauty – your pink and white complexion and your yellow hair? Does this bind his soul at your feet, and bend his neck under your yoke? Does this purchase for you his affection, his tenderness, his thoughts, his hopes, his interest, his noble, cordial love – and will you not have it? Do you scorn it? You are only dissembling: you are not in earnest; you love him; you long for him; but you trifle with his heart to make him more surely yours?'

'Bah! How you run on! I don't understand half you have said.'

I had got her out into the garden ere this. I now set her down on a seat and told her she should not stir till she had avowed which she meant in the end to accept – the man or the monkey.

'Him you call the man,' said she, 'is bourgeois, sandy-haired, and answers to the name of John! – cela suffit: je n'en veux pas. Colonel de Hamal is a gentleman of excellent connections, perfect manners, sweet appearance, with pale interesting face, and hair and eyes like an Italian. Then too he is the most delightful company possible – a man quite in my way; not sensible and serious like the other, but one with whom I can talk on equal terms – who does not plague, and bore, and harass me with depths, and heights, and passions, and talents for which I have no taste. There now. Don't hold me so fast.'

I slackened my grasp, and she darted off. I did not care to pursue her.

Somehow I could not avoid returning once more in the direction of the corridor to get another glimpse of Dr John; but I met him on the garden-steps, standing where the light from a window fell broad. His well-proportioned figure was not to be mistaken, for I doubt whether there was another in that assemblage his equal. He carried his hat in his hand; his uncovered head, his face and fine brow were most handsome and manly. *His* features were not delicate, not slight like those of a woman, nor were they cold, frivolous, and feeble; though well cut, they were not so chiselled, so frittered away, as to lose in power and significance what they gained in unmeaning symmetry. Much feeling spoke in them at times, and more sat silent in his eye. Such at least were my thoughts of him: to me he seemed all this. An inexpressible sense of wonder occupied me as I looked at this man, and reflected that *he* could be slighted.

It was not my intention to approach or address him in the garden, our terms of acquaintance not warranting such a step; I had only meant to view him in the crowd – myself unseen: coming upon him thus alone, I withdrew. But he was looking out for me, or rather for her who had been with me; therefore he descended the steps, and followed me down the alley.

'You know Miss Fanshawe? I have often wished to ask whether you knew her,' said he.

'Yes: I know her.'

'Intimately?'

'Quite as intimately as I wish.'

'What have you done with her now?'

'Am I her keeper?' I felt inclined to ask; but I simply answered, 'I have shaken her well, and would have shaken her better, but she escaped out of my hands and ran away.'

'Would you favour me,' he asked, 'by watching over her this one evening, and observing that she does nothing imprudent – does not, for instance, run out into the night-air immediately after dancing?'

'I may, perhaps, look after her a little, since you wish it; but she likes her own way too well to submit readily to control.'

'She is so young, so thoroughly artless,' said he.

'To me she is an enigma,' I responded.

'Is she?' he asked – much interested. 'How?'

'It would be difficult to say how – difficult, at least, to tell *you* how.'

'And why me?'

'I wonder she is not better pleased that you are so much her friend.'

'But she has not the slightest idea how much I *am* her friend. That is precisely the point I cannot teach her. May I enquire did she ever speak of me to you?'

'Under the name of "Isidore" she has talked about you often; but I must add that it is only within the last ten minutes I have discovered that you and "Isidore" are identical. It is only, Dr John, within that brief space of time I have learned that Ginevra Fanshawe is the person, under this roof, in whom you have long been interested – that she is the magnet which attracts you to the Rue Fossette, that for her sake you venture into this garden, and seek out caskets dropped by rivals.'

'You know all?'

'I know so much.'

'For more than a year I have been accustomed to meet her in society. Mrs Cholmondeley, her friend, is an acquaintance of mine; thus I see her every Sunday. But you observed that under the name of "Isidore" she often spoke of me: may I – without inviting you to a breach of confidence – enquire what was the tone, what the feeling of her remarks? I feel somewhat anxious to know, being a little tormented with uncertainty as to how I stand with her.'

'Oh, she varies: she shifts and changes like the wind.'

'Still, you can gather some general idea – ?'

'I can,' thought I, 'but it would not do to communicate that general idea to you. Besides, if I said she did not love you, I know you would not believe me.'

'You are silent,' he pursued. 'I suppose you have no good news to impart. No matter. If she feels for me positive coldness and aversion, it is a sign I do not deserve her.'

'Do you doubt yourself? Do you consider yourself the inferior of Colonel de Hamal?'

'I love Miss Fanshawe far more than de Hamal loves any human being, and would care for and guard her better than he. Respecting de Hamal, I fear she is under an illusion; the man's character is known to me, all his antecedents, all his scrapes. He is not worthy of your beautiful young friend.'

'My "beautiful young friend" ought to know that, and to know or feel who is worthy of her,' said I. 'If her beauty or her brains will not serve her so far, she merits the sharp lesson of experience.'

'Are you not a little severe?'

'I am excessively severe – more severe than I choose to show you. You should hear the strictures with which I favour my "beautiful young friend", only that you would be unutterably shocked at my want of tender considerateness for her delicate nature.'

'She is so lovely, one cannot but be loving towards her. You – every woman older than herself, must feel for such a simple, innocent, girlish fairy, a sort of motherly or elder sisterly fondness. Graceful angel! Does not your heart yearn towards her when she pours into your ear her pure, childlike confidences? How you are privileged!' And he sighed.

'I cut short these confidences somewhat abruptly now and then,' said I. 'But excuse me, Dr John, may I change the theme for one instant? What a god-like person is that de Hamal! What a nose on his face – perfect! Model one in putty or clay, you could not make a better, or straighter, or neater; and then, such classic lips and chin – and his bearing – sublime!'

'De Hamal is an unutterable puppy, besides being a very white-livered hero.'

'You, Dr John, and every man of a less refined mould than he, must feel for him a sort of admiring affection, such as Mars and the coarser deities may be supposed to have borne the young, graceful Apollo.'

'An unprincipled, gambling, little jackanapes!' said Dr John curtly, 'whom, with one hand, I could lift up by the waistband any day, and lay low in the kennel, if I liked.'

'The sweet seraph!' said I. 'What a cruel idea! Are you not a little severe, Dr John?'

And now I paused. For the second time that night I was going beyond myself – venturing out of what I looked on as my natural habits – speaking in an unpremeditated, impulsive strain, which startled me strangely when I halted to reflect. On rising that morning, had I anticipated that before night I should have acted the part of a gay lover in a vaudeville; and an hour after, frankly discussed with Dr John the question of his hapless suit, and rallied him on his illusions? I had no more presaged such feats than I had looked forward to an ascent in a balloon, or a voyage to Cape Horn.

The Doctor and I, having paced down the walk, were now returning; the reflex from the window again lit his face: he smiled, but his eye was melancholy. How I wished that he could feel heart's-ease! How I grieved that he brooded over pain, and pain from such a cause! He, with his great advantages, *he* to love in vain! I did not then know that the pensiveness of reverse is the best phase for some minds; nor did I reflect that some herbs, 'though scentless when entire, yield fragrance when they're bruised.'

'Do not be sorrowful, do not grieve,' I broke out. 'If there is in Ginevra one spark of worthiness of your affection, she will – she *must* feel devotion in return. Be cheerful, be hopeful, Dr John. Who should hope, if not you?'

In return for this speech I got – what, it must be supposed, I deserved – a look of some surprise: I thought also of some disapprobation. We parted, and I went into the house very chill. The clocks struck and the bells tolled midnight; people were leaving fast: the fête was over; the lamps were fading. In another hour all the dwelling-house, and all the Pensionnat, were dark and hushed. I too was in bed, but not asleep. To me it was not easy to sleep after a day of such excitement.

## CHAPTER 15

### *The Long Vacation*

Following Mme Beck's fête, with its three preceding weeks of relaxation, its brief twelve hours' burst of hilarity and dissipation, and its one subsequent day of utter languor, came a period of reaction; two months of real application, of close, hard study. These two months, being the last of the 'année scolaire', were indeed the only genuine working months in the year. To them was procrastinated – into them concentrated, alike by professors, mistresses, and pupils – the main burden of preparation for the examinations preceding the distribution of prizes. Candidates for rewards had then to work in good earnest; masters and teachers had to set their shoulders to the wheel, to urge on the backward, and diligently aid and train the more promising. A showy demonstration – a telling exhibition – must be got up for public view, and all means were fair to this end.

I scarcely noted how the other teachers went to work; I had my own business to mind: and my task was not the least onerous, being to imbue some ninety sets of brains with a due tincture of what they considered a most complicated and difficult science, that of the English language; and to drill ninety tongues in what, for them, was an almost impossible pronunciation – the lisping and hissing dentals of the Isles.

The examination-day arrived. Awful day! Prepared for with anxious care, dressed for with silent despatch – nothing vaporous or fluttering now – no white gauze or azure streamers; the grave, close, compact was the order of the toilette. It seemed to me that I was this day especially doomed – the main burden and trial falling on me alone of all the female teachers. The others were not expected to examine in the studies they taught; the professor of literature, M. Paul, taking upon himself this duty. He, this school-autocrat, gathered all and sundry reins into the hollow of his one hand; he irefully rejected any colleague; he would not have help. Madame herself, who evidently rather wished to undertake the examination in geography – her favourite study, which she taught well – was forced to succumb, and be subordinate to her despotic kinsman's direction. The whole staff of instructors, male and female, he set aside, and stood on the examiner's estrade alone. It irked him that he was forced to make one exception to this rule. He could not manage English: he was obliged to leave that branch of education in the English teacher's hands; which he did, not without a flash of naïve jealousy.

A constant crusade against the 'amour-propre' of every human-being, but himself, was the crotchet of this able, but fiery and grasping little man. He had a strong relish for public representation in his own person, but an extreme abhorrence of the like display in any other. He quelled, he kept down where he could; and where he could not, he fumed like a bottled storm.

On the evening preceding the examination-day, I was walking in the garden, as were the other teachers and all the boarders. M. Emanuel joined me in the 'allée défendue'; his cigar was at his lips; his paletôt – a most characteristic garment of no particular shape – hung dark and menacing; the tassel of his bonnet grec sternly shadowed his left temple; his black whiskers curled like those of a wrathful cat; his blue eye had a cloud in its glitter.

'Ainsi,' he began, abruptly fronting and arresting me, 'vous allez trôner comme une reine; demain – trôner à mes côtés? Sans doute vous savourez d'avance les délices de l'autorité. Je crois voir en vous je ne sais quoi de rayonnante, petite ambitieuse!'

Now the fact was, he happened to be entirely mistaken. I did not – could not – estimate the admiration or the good opinion of tomorrow's audience at the same rate he did. Had that audience numbered as many personal friends and acquaintance for me, as for him, I know not how it might have been: I speak of the case as it stood. On me school-triumphs shed but a cold lustre. I had wondered – and I wondered now – how it was that for him they seemed to shine as with hearth-warmth and hearth-glow. *He* cared for them perhaps too much; *I*, probably, too little. However, I had my own fancies as well as he. I liked, for instance, to see M. Emanuel jealous; it lit up his nature, and woke his spirit; it threw all sorts of queer lights and shadows over his dun face, and into his violet-azure eyes (he used to say that his black hair and blue eyes were 'une de ses beautés'). There was a relish in his anger; it was artless, earnest, quite unreasonable, but never hypocritical. I uttered no disclaimer then of the complacency he attributed to me; I merely asked where the English examination was to come in – whether at the commencement or close of the day?

'I hesitate,' said he, 'whether at the very beginning, before many persons are come, and when your aspiring nature will not be gratified by a large audience, or quite at the close, when everybody is tired, and only a jaded and worn-out attention will be at your service.'

'Que vous êtes dur, monsieur!' I said, affecting dejection.

'One ought to be "dur" with you. You are one of those beings who must be *kept down*. I know you! I know you! Other people in this house see you pass, and think that a colourless shadow has gone by. As for me, I scrutinised your face once, and it sufficed.'

'You are satisfied that you understand me?'

Without answering directly, he went on, 'Were you not gratified when you succeeded in that *vaudeville*? *I* watched you, and saw a passionate ardour for triumph in your physiognomy. What fire shot into the glance! Not mere light, but flame: je me tins pour averti.'

'What feeling I had on that occasion, monsieur – and pardon me, if I say, you

immensely exaggerate both its quality and quantity – was quite abstract. I did not care for the vaudeville. I hated the part you assigned me. I had not the slightest sympathy with the audience below the stage. They are good people, doubtless, but do I know them? Are they anything to me? Can I care for being brought before their view again tomorrow? Will the examination be anything but a task to me – a task I wish well over?'

'Shall I take it out of your hands?'

'With all my heart; if you do not fear failure.'

'But I should fail. I only know three phrases of English, and a few words: par exemple, de sonn, de mone, de stare – est-ce bien dit? My opinion is that it would be better to give up the thing altogether: to have no English examination, eh?'

'If madame consents; I consent.'

'Heartily?'

'Very heartily.'

He smoked his cigar in silence. He turned suddenly.

'Donnez-moi la main,' said he, and the spite and jealousy melted out of his face, and a generous kindliness shone there instead.

'Come, we will not be rivals, we will be friends;' he pursued. 'The examination shall take place, and I will choose a good moment; and instead of vexing and hindering, as I felt half inclined ten minutes ago – for I have my malevolent moods: I always had, from childhood – I will aid you sincerely. After all, you are solitary and a stranger, and have your way to make and your bread to earn; it may be well that you should become known. We will be friends: do you agree?'

'Out of my heart, monsieur. I am glad of a friend. I like that better than a triumph.'

'Pauvrette!' said he, and turned away and left the alley.

The examination passed over well; M. Paul was as good as his word, and did his best to make my part easy. The next day came the distribution of prizes; that also passed; the school broke up; the pupils went home, and now began the long vacation.

That vacation! Shall I ever forget it? I think not. Mme Beck went, the first day of the holidays, to join her children at the sea-side; all the three teachers had parents or friends with whom they took refuge; every professor quitted the city; some went to Paris, some to Boue-Marine; M. Paul set forth on a pilgrimage to Rome; the house was left quite empty, but for me, a servant, and a poor deformed and imbecile pupil, a sort of crétin whom her stepmother in a distant province would not allow to return home.

My heart almost died within me; miserable longings strained its chords. How long were the September days! How silent, how lifeless! How vast and void seemed the desolate premises! How gloomy the forsaken garden – gray now with the dust of a town-summer departed. Looking forward at the commencement of those eight weeks, I hardly knew how I was to live to the end. My spirits had long been gradually sinking; now that the prop of employment was withdrawn, they went down fast. Even to look forward was not to hope: the dumb future spoke no comfort, offered no promise, gave no inducement to bear present evil in reliance

on future good. A sorrowful indifference to existence often pressed on me – a despairing resignation to reach betimes the end of all things earthly. Alas! When I had full leisure to look on life as life must be looked on by such as me, I found it but a hopeless desert: tawny sands, with no green field, no palm-tree, no well in view. The hopes which are dear to youth, which bear it up and lead it on, I knew not and dared not know. If they knocked at my heart sometimes, an inhospitable bar to admission must be inwardly drawn. When they turned away thus rejected, tears sad enough sometimes flowed; but it could not be helped: I dared not give such guests lodging. So mortally did I fear the sin and weakness of presumption.

Religious reader, you will preach to me a long sermon about what I have just written, and so will you, moralist; and you, stern sage: you, stoic, will frown; you, cynic, sneer; you, epicure, laugh. Well, each and all, take it your own way. I accept the sermon, frown, sneer and laugh; perhaps you are all right: and perhaps, circumstanced like me, you would have been, like me, wrong. The first month was, indeed, a long, black, heavy month to me.

The crétin did not seem unhappy. I did my best to feed her well and keep her warm, and she only asked food and sunshine, or when that lacked, fire. Her weak faculties approved of inertion: her brain, her eyes, her ears, her heart slept content; they could not wake to work, so lethargy was their Paradise.

Three weeks of that vacation were hot, fair, and dry, but the fourth and fifth were tempestuous and wet. I do not know why that change in the atmosphere made a cruel impression on me, why the raging storm and beating rain crushed me with a deadlier paralysis than I had experienced while the air remained serene: but so it was, and my nervous system could hardly support what it had for many days and nights to undergo in that huge, empty house. How I used to pray to Heaven for consolation and support! With what dread force the conviction would grasp me that Fate was my permanent foe, never to be conciliated. I did not, in my heart, arraign the mercy or justice of God for this; I concluded it to be a part of his great plan that some must deeply suffer while they live, and I thrilled in the certainty that of this number, I was one.

It was some relief when an aunt of the crétin, a kind old woman, came one day, and took away my strange, deformed companion. The hapless creature had been at times a heavy charge; I could not take her out beyond the garden, and I could not leave her a minute alone; for her poor mind, like her body, was warped: its propensity was to evil. A vague bent to mischief, an aimless malevolence made constant vigilance indispensable. As she very rarely spoke, and would sit for hours together moping and mowing and distorting her features with indescribable grimaces, it was more like being prisoned with some strange tameless animal, than associating with a human being. Then there were personal attentions to be rendered which required the nerve of a hospital nurse; my resolution was so tried, it sometimes fell dead-sick. These duties should not have fallen on me; a servant, now absent, had rendered them hitherto, and in the hurry of holiday departure, no substitute to fill this office had been provided. This tax and trial were by no means the least I have known in life. Still, menial and distasteful as they were, my mental pain was far more wasting and wearing. Attendance on the crétin deprived

me often of the power and inclination to swallow a meal, and sent me faint to the fresh air, and the well or fountain in the court; but this duty never wrung my heart, or brimmed my eyes, or scalded my cheek with tears hot as molten metal.

The crétin being gone, I was free to walk out. At first I lacked courage to venture very far from the Rue Fossette, but by degrees I sought the city-gates, and passed them, and then went wandering away far along chaussées, through fields, beyond cemeteries, Catholic and Protestant, beyond farmsteads, to lanes and little woods, and I know not where. A goad thrust me on, a fever forbade me to rest; a want of companionship maintained in my soul the cravings of a most deadly famine. I often walked all day, through the burning noon and the arid afternoon, and the dusk evening, and came back with moonrise.

While wandering in solitude, I would sometimes picture the present probable position of others, my acquaintance. There was Mme Beck at a cheerful watering-place with her children, her mother, and a whole troop of friends who had sought the same scene of relaxation. Zélie St Pierre was at Paris, with her relatives; the other teachers were at their homes. There was Ginevra Fanshawe whom certain of her connections had carried on a pleasant tour southward. Ginevra seemed to me the happiest. She was on the route of beautiful scenery; these September suns shone for her on fertile plains, where harvest and vintage matured under their mellow beam. These gold and crystal moons rose on her vision over blue horizons waved in mountain lines.

But all this was nothing; I too felt those autumn suns and saw those harvest moons, and I almost wished to be covered in with earth and turf, deep out of their influence; for I could not live on their light, nor make them comrades, nor yield them affection. But Ginevra had a kind of spirit with her, empowered to give constant strength and comfort, to gladden daylight and embalm darkness; the best of the good genii that guard humanity curtained her with his wings, and canopied her head with his bending form. By True Love was Ginevra followed: never could she be alone. Was she insensible to this presence? It seemed to me impossible: I could not realise such deadness. I imagined her grateful in secret, loving now with reserve; but purposing one day to show how much she loved: pictured her faithful hero half conscious of her coy fondness, and comforted by that consciousness: I conceived an electric chord of sympathy between them, a fine chain of mutual understanding, sustaining union through a separation of a hundred leagues – carrying, across mound and hollow, communication by prayer and wish. Ginevra gradually became with me a sort of heroine. One day, perceiving this growing illusion, I said, 'I really believe my nerves are getting overstretched: my mind has suffered somewhat too much; a malady is growing upon it – what shall I do? How shall I keep well?'

Indeed there was no way to keep well under the circumstances. At last a day and night of peculiarly agonising depression were succeeded by physical illness; I took perforce to my bed. About this time the Indian summer closed and the equinoctial storms began; and for nine dark and wet days, of which the Hours rushed on all turbulent, deaf, dishevelled – bewildered with sounding hurricane – I lay in a strange fever of the nerves and blood. Sleep went quite away. I used to

rise in the night, look round for her, beseech her earnestly to return. A rattle of the window, a cry of the blast only replied – Sleep never came!

I err. She came once, but in anger. Impatient of my importunity she brought with her an avenging dream. By the clock of St Jean Baptiste, that dream remained scarce fifteen minutes – a brief space, but sufficing to wring my whole frame with unknown anguish; to confer a nameless experience that had the hue, the mien, the terror, the very tone of a visitation from eternity. Between twelve and one that night a cup was forced to my lips, black, strong, strange, drawn from no well, but filled up seething from a bottomless and boundless sea. Suffering, brewed in temporal or calculable measure, and mixed for mortal lips, tastes not as this suffering tasted. Having drank and woke, I thought all was over: the end come and past by. Trembling fearfully – as consciousness returned – ready to cry out on some fellow-creature to help me, only that I knew no fellow-creature was near enough to catch the wild summons – Goton in her far distant attic could not hear – I rose on my knees in bed. Some fearful hours went over me: indescribably was I torn, racked and oppressed in mind. Amidst the horrors of that dream I think the worst lay here. Methought the well-loved dead, who had loved *me* well in life, met me elsewhere, alienated: galled was my inmost spirit with an unutterable sense of despair about the future. Motive there was none why I should try to recover or wish to live; and yet quite unendurable was the pitiless and haughty voice in which Death challenged me to engage his unknown terrors. When I tried to pray I could only utter these words: 'From my youth up Thy terrors have I suffered with a troubled mind.'

Most true was it.

On bringing me my tea next morning Goton urged me to call in a doctor. I would not: I thought no doctor could cure me.

One evening – and I was not delirious: I was in my sane mind, I got up – I dressed myself, weak and shaking. The solitude and the stillness of the long dormitory could not be borne any longer; the ghastly white beds were turning into spectres – the coronal of each became a death's head, huge and sun-bleached – dead dreams of an elder world and mightier race lay frozen in their wide gaping eyeholes. That evening more firmly than ever fastened into my soul the conviction that Fate was of stone, and Hope a false idol – blind, bloodless, and of granite core. I felt, too, that the trial God had appointed me was gaining its climax, and must now be turned by my own hands, hot, feeble, trembling as they were. It rained still, and blew; but with more clemency, I thought, than it had poured and raged all day. Twilight was falling, and I deemed its influence pitiful; from the lattice I saw coming night-clouds trailing low like banners drooping. It seemed to me that at this hour there was affection and sorrow in Heaven above for all pain suffered on earth beneath; the weight of my dreadful dream became alleviated – that insufferable thought of being no more loved, no more owned, half-yielded to hope of the contrary – I was sure this hope would shine clearer if I got out from under this house-roof, which was crushing as the slab of a tomb, and went outside the city to a certain quiet hill, a long way distant in the fields. Covered with a cloak (I could not be delirious, for I had sense and

recollection to put on warm clothing), forth I set. The bells of a church arrested me in passing; they seemed to call me in to the *salut*, and I went in. Any solemn rite, any spectacle of sincere worship, any opening for appeal to God was as welcome to me then as bread to one in extremity of want. I knelt down with others on the stone pavement. It was an old solemn church, its pervading gloom not gilded but purpled by light shed through stained glass.

Few worshippers were assembled, and, the *salut* over, half of them departed. I discovered soon that those left, remained to confess. I did not stir. Carefully every door of the church was shut; a holy quiet sank upon, and a solemn shade gathered about us. After a space, breathless and spent in prayer, a penitent approached the confessional. I watched. She whispered her avowal; her shrift was whispered back; she returned consoled. Another went, and another. A pale lady, kneeling near me, said in a low, kind voice: 'Go you, now; I am not quite prepared.'

Mechanically obedient, I rose and went. I knew what I was about; my mind had run over the intent with lightning-speed. To take this step could not make me more wretched than I was; it might soothe me.

The priest within the confessional never turned his eyes to regard me; he only quietly inclined his ear to my lips. He might be a good man, but this duty had become to him a sort of form: he went through it with the phlegm of custom. I hesitated; of the formula of confession, I was ignorant: instead of commencing with the prelude usual, I said: 'Mon père, je suis Protestante.'

He directly turned. He was not a native priest; of that class, the cast of physiognomy is, almost invariably, grovelling: I saw by his profile and brow he was a Frenchman; though gray and advanced in years, he did not, I think, lack either feeling or intelligence. He enquired, not unkindly, why, being a Protestant, I came to him?

I said, I was perishing for a word of advice or an accent of comfort. I had been living for some weeks quite alone; I had been ill; I had a pressure of affliction on my mind of which it would hardly any longer endure the weight.

'Was it a sin, a crime?' he enquired, somewhat startled.

I reassured him on this point, and, as well as I could, I showed him the mere outline of my experience.

He looked thoughtful, surprised, puzzled. 'You take me unawares,' said he. 'I have not had such a case as yours before: ordinarily we know our routine and are prepared, but this makes a great break in the common course of confession. I am hardly furnished with counsel fitting the circumstances.'

Of course, I had not expected he would be; but the mere relief of communication in an ear which was human and sentient, yet consecrated – the mere pouring out of some portion of long accumulating, long pent-up pain into a vessel whence it could not be again diffused – had done me good. I was already solaced.

'Must I go, father?' I asked of him, as he sat silent.

'My daughter,' he said kindly – and I am sure he was a kind man: he had a compassionate eye – 'for the present you had better go; but I assure you your words have struck me. Confession, like other things, is apt to become formal

and trivial with habit. You have come and poured your heart out; a thing seldom done. I would fain think your case over, and take it with me to my oratory. Were you of our faith I should know what to say – a mind so tossed can find repose but in the bosom of retreat, and the punctual practice of piety. The world, it is well known, has no satisfaction for that class of natures. Holy men have bidden penitents like you to hasten their path upward by penance, self-denial, and difficult good works. Tears are given them here for meat and drink – bread of affliction and waters of affliction – their recompense comes hereafter. It is my own conviction that these impressions under which you are smarting are messengers from God to bring you back to the true church. You were made for our faith: depend upon it our faith alone could heal and help you – Protestantism is altogether too dry, cold, prosaic for you. The further I look into this matter, the more plainly I see it is entirely out of the common order of things. On no account would I lose sight of you. Go, my daughter, for the present; but return to me again.'

I rose and thanked him. I was withdrawing when he signed me to return. 'You must not come to this church,' said he: 'I see you are ill, and this church is too cold; you must come to my house: I live –' (and he gave me his address). 'Be there tomorrow morning at ten.'

In reply to this appointment, I only bowed; and pulling down my veil, and gathering round me my cloak, I glided away.

Did I, do you suppose, reader, contemplate venturing again within that worthy priest's reach? As soon should I have thought of walking into a Babylonish furnace. That priest had arms which could influence me; he was naturally kind, with a sentimental French kindness, to whose softness I knew myself not wholly impervious. Without respecting some sorts of affection, there was hardly any sort, having a fibre of root in reality, which I could rely on my force wholly to withstand. Had I gone to him, he would have shown me all that was tender, and comforting, and gentle, in the honest popish superstition. Then he would have tried to kindle, blow and stir up in me the zeal of good works. I know not how it would all have ended. We all think ourselves strong in some points; we all know ourselves weak in many; the probabilities are that had I visited Numéro 10, Rue des Mages, at the hour and day appointed, I might just now, instead of writing this heretic narrative, be counting my beads in the cell of a certain Carmelite convent on the Boulevard of Crécy in Villette. There was something of Fénelon about that benign old priest; and whatever most of his brethren may be, and whatever I may think of his Church and creed (and I like neither), of himself I must ever retain a grateful recollection. He was kind when I needed kindness; he did me good. May Heaven bless him!

Twilight had passed into night, and the lamps were lit in the streets, ere I issued from that sombre church. To turn back was now become possible to me; the wild longing to breathe this October wind on the little hill far without the city-walls had ceased to be an imperative impulse, and was softened into a wish with which Reason could cope: she put it down, and I turned, as I thought, to the Rue Fossette. But I had become involved in a part of the city with which I

was not familiar; it was the old part, and full of narrow streets of picturesque, ancient, and mouldering houses. I was much too weak to be very collected, and I was still too careless of my own welfare and safety, to be cautious. I grew embarrassed; I got immeshed in a network of turns unknown. I was lost, and had no resolution to ask guidance of any passenger.

If the storm had lulled a little at sunset, it made up now for lost time. Strong and horizontal thundered the current of the wind from north-west to south-east; it brought rain like spray, and sometimes, a sharp hail like shot; it was cold and pierced me to the vitals. I bent my head to meet it, but it beat me back. My heart did not fail at all in this conflict; I only wished that I had wings and could ascend the gale, spread and repose my pinions on its strength, career in its course, sweep where it swept. While wishing this, I suddenly felt colder where before I was cold, and more powerless where before I was weak. I tried to reach the porch of a great building near, but the mass of frontage and the giant spire turned black and vanished from my eyes. Instead of sinking on the steps as I intended, I seemed to pitch headlong down an abyss. I remember no more.

## END OF VOLUME ONE

# VOLUME TWO

## CHAPTER 16

### Auld Lang Syne

Where my soul went during that swoon I cannot tell. Whatever she saw, or wherever she travelled in her trance on that strange night, she kept her own secret; never whispering a word to Memory, and baffling Imagination by an indissoluble silence. She may have gone upward, and come in sight of her eternal home, hoping for leave to rest now, and deeming that her painful union with matter was at last dissolved. While she so deemed, an angel may have warned her away from heaven's threshold, and, guiding her weeping down, have bound her, once more, all shuddering and unwilling, to that poor frame, cold and wasted, of whose companionship she was grown more than weary.

I know she re-entered her prison with pain, with reluctance, with a moan and a long shiver. The divorced mates, Spirit and Substance, were hard to reunite: they greeted each other, not in an embrace, but a racking sort of struggle. The returning sense of sight came upon me, red, as if it swam in blood; suspended hearing rushed back loud, like thunder; consciousness revived in fear: I sat up appalled, wondering into what region, amongst what strange beings I was waking. At first I knew nothing I looked on: a wall was not a wall – a lamp not a lamp. I should have understood what we call a ghost, as well as I did the commonest object; which is another way of intimating that all my eye rested on struck it as spectral. But the faculties soon settled each in its place; the life-machine presently resumed its wonted and regular working.

Still, I knew not where I was; only in time I saw I had been removed from the spot where I fell: I lay on no portico-step; night and tempest were excluded by walls, windows, and ceiling. Into some house I had been carried, but what house?

I could only think of the pensionnat in the Rue Fossette. Still half-dreaming, I tried hard to discover in what room they had put me; whether the great dormitory, or one of the little dormitories. I was puzzled, because I could not make the glimpses of furniture I saw, accord with my knowledge of any of these apartments. The empty white beds were wanting, and the long line of large windows. 'Surely,' thought I, 'it is not to Mme Beck's own chamber they have carried me!' And here my eye fell on an easy chair covered with blue damask. Other seats, cushioned to match, dawned on me by degrees; and at last I took in

the complete fact of a pleasant parlour, with a wood-fire on a clear-shining hearth, a carpet where arabesques of bright blue relieved a ground of shaded fawn; pale walls over which a slight but endless garland of azure forget-me-nots ran mazed and bewildered amongst myriad gold leaves and tendrils. A gilded mirror filled up the space between two windows, curtained amply with blue damask. In this mirror I saw myself laid, not in bed, but on a sofa. I looked spectral; my eyes larger and more hollow, my hair darker than was natural, by contrast with my thin and ashen face. It was obvious, not only from the furniture, but from the position of windows, doors, and fireplace, that this was an unknown room in an unknown house.

Hardly less plain was it that my brain was not yet settled; for, as I gazed at the blue armchair, it appeared to grow familiar; so did a certain scroll-couch, and not less so the round centre-table, with a blue covering, bordered with autumn-tinted foliage; and, above all, two little footstools with worked covers, and a small ebony-framed chair, of which the seat and back were also worked with groups of brilliant flowers on a dark ground.

Struck with these things, I explored further. Strange to say, old acquaintance were all about me, and 'auld lang syne' smiled out of every nook. There were two oval miniatures over the mantelpiece, of which I knew by heart the pearls about the high and powdered 'heads;' the velvets circling the white throats; the swell of the full muslin kerchiefs; the pattern of the lace sleeve-ruffles. Upon the mantel-shelf there were two china vases, some relics of a diminutive tea-service, as smooth as enamel and as thin as eggshell, and a white centre-ornament, a classic group in alabaster, preserved under glass. Of all these things I could have told the peculiarities, numbered the flaws or cracks, like any *clairvoyante*. Above all, there was a pair of handscreens, with elaborate pencil-drawings finished like line-engravings; these, my very eyes ached at beholding again, recalling hours when they had followed, stroke by stroke and touch by touch, a tedious, feeble, finical, schoolgirl pencil held in these fingers, now so skeleton-like.

Where was I? Not only in what spot of the world, but in what year of our Lord? For all these objects were of past days, and of a distant country. Ten years ago I bade them goodbye; since my fourteenth year they and I had never met. I gasped audibly, 'Where am I?'

A shape hitherto unnoticed, stirred, rose, came forward; a shape inharmonious with the environment, serving only to complicate the riddle further. This was no more than a sort of native bonne, in a commonplace bonne's cap and print-dress. She spoke neither French nor English, and I could get no intelligence from her, not understanding her phrases of dialect. But she bathed my temples and forehead with some cool and perfumed water, and then she heightened the cushion on which I reclined, made signs that I was not to speak, and resumed her post at the foot of the sofa.

She was busy knitting; her eyes thus drawn from me, I could gaze on her without interruption. I did mightily wonder how she came there, or what she could have to do among the scenes, or with the days of my girlhood. Still more I marvelled what those scenes and days could now have to do with me.

Too weak to scrutinise thoroughly the mystery, I tried to settle it by saying it was a mistake, a dream, a fever-fit; and yet I knew there could be no mistake, and that I was not sleeping, and I believed I was sane. I wished the room had not been so well lighted, that I might not so clearly have seen the little pictures, the ornaments, the screens, the worked chair. All these objects, as well as the blue-damask furniture, were, in fact, precisely the same, in every minutest detail, with those I so well remembered, and with which I had been so thoroughly intimate, in the drawing-room of my godmother's house at Bretton. Methought the apartment only was changed, being of different proportions and dimensions.

I thought of Bedreddin Hassan, transported in his sleep from Cairo to the gates of Damascus. Had a Genius stooped his dark wing down the storm to whose stress I had succumbed, and gathering me from the church-steps, and 'rising high into the air', as the eastern tale said, had he borne me over land and ocean, and laid me quietly down beside a hearth of Old England? But no; I knew the fire of that hearth burned before its Lares no more – it went out long ago, and the household gods had been carried elsewhere.

The bonne turned again to survey me, and seeing my eyes wide open, and, I suppose, deeming their expression perturbed and excited, she put down her knitting. I saw her busied for a moment at a little stand; she poured out water, and measured drops from a phial: glass in hand, she approached me. What dark-tinged draught might she now be offering? what Genii-elixir or Magi-distillation?

It was too late to enquire – I had swallowed it passively, and at once. A tide of quiet thought now came gently caressing my brain; softer and softer rose the flow, with tepid undulations smoother than balm. The pain of weakness left my limbs, my muscles slept. I lost power to move; but, losing at the same time wish, it was no privation. That kind bonne placed a screen between me and the lamp; I saw her rise to do this, but do not remember seeing her resume her place: in the interval between the two acts, I 'fell on sleep'.

At waking, lo! all was again changed. The light of high day surrounded me; not, indeed, a warm, summer light, but the leaden gloom of raw and blustering autumn. I felt sure now that I was in the pensionnat – sure by the beating rain on the casement; sure by the 'wuther' of wind amongst trees, denoting a garden outside; sure by the chill, the whiteness, the solitude, amidst which I lay. I say *whiteness* – for the dimity curtains, dropped before a French bed, bounded my view.

I lifted them; I looked out. My eye, prepared to take in the range of a long, large, and whitewashed chamber, blinked baffled, on encountering the limited area of a small cabinet – a cabinet with sea-green walls; also, instead of five wide and naked windows, there was one high lattice, shaded with muslin festoons: instead of two dozen little stands of painted wood, each holding a basin and an ewer, there was a toilette table dressed, like a lady for a ball, in a white robe over a pink skirt; a polished and large glass crowned, and a pretty pincushion frilled with lace adorned it. This toilette, together with a small, low, green and white chintz armchair, a washstand topped with a marble slab, and supplied with utensils of pale-green ware, sufficiently furnished the tiny chamber.

Reader, I felt alarmed! Why? you will ask. What was there in this simple and somewhat pretty sleeping-closet to startle the most timid? Merely this – These articles of furniture could not be real, solid armchairs, looking-glasses, and washstands – they must be the ghosts of such articles; or, if this were denied as too wild an hypothesis – and, confounded as I was, I *did* deny it – there remained but to conclude that I had myself passed into an abnormal state of mind; in short, that I was very ill and delirious: and even then, mine was the strangest figment with which delirium had ever harassed a victim.

I knew – I was obliged to know – the green chintz of that little chair; the little snug chair itself, the carved, shining-black, foliated frame of that glass; the smooth, milky-green of the china vessels on the stand; the very stand too, with its top of gray marble, splintered at one corner; all these I was compelled to recognise and to hail, as last night I had, perforce, recognised and hailed the rosewood, the drapery, the porcelain, of the drawing-room.

Bretton! Bretton! and ten years ago shone reflected in that mirror. And why did Bretton and my fourteenth year haunt me thus? Why, if they came at all, did they not return complete? Why hovered before my distempered vision the mere furniture, while the rooms and the locality were gone? As to that pincushion made of crimson satin, ornamented with gold beads and frilled with thread-lace, I had the same right to know it as to know the screens – I had made it myself. Rising with a start from the bed, I took the cushion in my hand and examined it. There was the cipher 'L. L. B.' formed in gold beads, and surrounded with an oval wreath embroidered in white silk. These were the initials of my godmother's name – Louisa Lucy Bretton.

Am I in England? Am I at Bretton? I muttered; and hastily pulling up the blind with which the lattice was shrouded, I looked out to try and discover *where* I was; half-prepared to meet the calm, old, handsome buildings and clean gray pavement of St Ann's Street, and to see at the end, the towers of the minster: or, if otherwise, fully expectant of a town view somewhere, a rue in Villette, if not a street in a pleasant and ancient English city.

I looked, on the contrary, through a frame of leafage, clustering round the high lattice, and forth thence to a grassy mead-like level, a lawn-terrace with trees rising from the lower ground beyond – high forest trees, such as I had not seen for many a day. They were now groaning under the gale of October, and between their trunks I traced the line of an avenue, where yellow leaves lay in heaps and drifts, or were whirled singly before the sweeping west wind. Whatever landscape might lie further must have been flat, and these tall beeches shut it out. The place seemed secluded, and was to me quite strange: I did not know it at all.

Once more I lay down. My bed stood in a little alcove; on turning my face to the wall, the room with its bewildering accompaniments became excluded. Excluded? No! For as I arranged my position in this hope, behold, on the green space between the divided and looped-up curtains, hung a broad, gilded picture-frame enclosing a portrait. It was drawn – well drawn, though but a sketch – in water-colours; a head, a boy's head, fresh, lifelike, speaking, and animated. It seemed a youth of sixteen, fair-complexioned, with sanguine

health in his cheek; hair long, not dark, and with a sunny sheen; penetrating eyes, an arch mouth, and a gay smile. On the whole a most pleasant face to look at, especially for those claiming a right to that youth's affection – parents, for instance, or sisters. Any romantic little schoolgirl might almost have loved it in its frame. Those eyes looked as if when somewhat older, they would flash a lightning response to love: I cannot tell whether they kept in store the steady-beaming shine of faith. For whatever sentiment met him in form too facile, his lips menaced, beautifully but surely, caprice and light esteem.

Striving to take each new discovery as quietly as I could, I whispered to myself – 'Ah! that portrait used to hang in the breakfast-room, over the mantel-place: somewhat too high, as I thought. I well remember how I used to mount a music-stool for the purpose of unhooking it, holding it in my hand, and searching into those bonny wells of eyes, whose glance under their hazel lashes seemed like a pencilled laugh; and well I liked to note the colouring of the cheek, and the expression of the mouth.' I hardly believed fancy could improve on the curve of that mouth, or of the chin; even my ignorance knew that both were beautiful, and pondered, perplexed over this doubt: 'How it was that what charmed so much, could at the same time so keenly pain?' Once, by way of test, I took little Missy Home, and, lifting her in my arms, told her to look at the picture.

'Do you like it, Polly?' I asked. She never answered, but gazed long, and at last a darkness went trembling through her sensitive eye, as she said, 'Put me down.' So I put her down, saying to myself: 'The child feels it too.'

All these things did I now think over, adding, 'He had his faults, yet scarce ever was a finer nature; liberal, suave, impressible.' My reflections closed in an audibly pronounced word, 'Graham!'

'Graham!' echoed a sudden voice at the bedside. 'Do you want Graham?'

I looked. The plot was but thickening; the wonder but culminating. If it was strange to see that well-remembered pictured form on the wall, still stranger was it to turn and behold the equally well-remembered living form opposite – a woman, a lady, most real and substantial, tall, well-attired, wearing widow's silk, and such a cap as best became her matron and motherly braids of hair. Hers, too, was a good face; too marked, perhaps, now for beauty, but not for sense or character. She was little changed; something sterner, something more robust – but she was my godmother still: the distinct vision of Mrs Bretton.

I kept quiet, yet internally I was much agitated: my pulse fluttered, and the blood left my cheek, which turned cold.

'Madam, where am I?' I enquired.

'In a very safe asylum; well protected for the present: make your mind quite easy till you get a little better; you look ill this morning.'

'I am so entirely bewildered, I do not know whether I can trust my senses at all, or whether they are misleading me in every particular: but you speak English, do you not, madam?'

'I should think you might hear that: it would puzzle me to hold a long discourse in French.'

'You do not come from England?'

'I am lately arrived thence. Have you been long in this country? You seem to know my son?'

'Do I, madam? Perhaps I do. Your son – the picture there?'

'That is his portrait as a youth. While looking at it, you pronounced his name.'

'Graham Bretton?'

She nodded.

'I speak to Mrs Bretton, formerly of Bretton, —shire?'

'Quite right; and you, I am told, are an English teacher in a foreign school here: my son recognised you as such.'

'How was I found, madam, and by whom?'

'My son shall tell you that by and by,' said she; 'but at present you are too confused and weak for conversation: try to eat some breakfast, and then sleep.'

Notwithstanding all I had undergone – the bodily fatigue, the perturbation of spirits, the exposure to weather – it seemed that I was better: the fever, the real malady which had oppressed my frame, was abating; for, whereas during the last nine days I had taken no solid food, and suffered from continual thirst, this morning, on breakfast being offered, I experienced a craving for nourishment: an inward faintness which caused me eagerly to taste the tea this lady offered, and to eat the morsel of dry toast she allowed in accompaniment. It was only a morsel, but it sufficed; keeping up my strength till some two or three hours afterwards, when the bonne brought me a little cup of broth and a biscuit.

As evening began to darken, and the ceaseless blast still blew wild and cold, and the rain streamed on, deluge-like, I grew weary – very weary of my bed. The room, though pretty, was small: I felt it confining; I longed for a change. The increasing chill and gathering gloom, too, depressed me; I wanted to see – to feel firelight. Besides, I kept thinking of the son of that tall matron: when should I see him? Certainly not till I left my room.

At last the bonne came to make my bed for the night. She prepared to wrap me in a blanket and place me in the little chintz chair; but, declining these attentions, I proceeded to dress myself. The business was just achieved, and I was sitting down to take breath, when Mrs Bretton once more appeared.

'Dressed!' she exclaimed, smiling with that smile I so well knew – a pleasant smile, though not soft; 'You are quite better then? Quite strong – eh?'

She spoke to me so much as of old she used to speak that I almost fancied she was beginning to know me. There was the same sort of patronage in her voice and manner that, as a girl, I had always experienced from her – a patronage I yielded to and even liked; it was not founded on conventional grounds of superior wealth or station (in the last particular there had never been any inequality; her degree was mine) but on natural reasons of physical advantage: it was the shelter the tree gives the herb. I put a request without further ceremony.

'Do let me go down stairs, madam; I am so cold and dull here.'

'I desire nothing better, if you are strong enough to bear the change,' was her reply. 'Come then; here is an arm.' And she offered me hers: I took it, and we

descended one flight of carpeted steps to a landing where a tall door, standing open, gave admission into the blue damask room. How pleasant it was in its air of perfect domestic comfort! How warm in its amber lamplight and vermilion fire-flush! To render the picture perfect, tea stood ready on the table – an English tea, whereof the whole shining service glanced at me familiarly; from the solid silver urn, of antique pattern, and the massive pot of the same metal, to the thin porcelain cups, dark with purple and gilding. I knew the very seed-cake of peculiar form, baked in a peculiar mould, which always had a place on the tea-table at Bretton. Graham liked it, and there it was as of yore – set before Graham's plate with the silver knife and fork beside it. Graham was then expected to tea: Graham was now, perhaps, in the house; ere many minutes I might see him.

'Sit down – sit down,' said my conductress, as my step faltered a little in passing to the hearth. She seated me on the sofa, but I soon passed behind it, saying the fire was too hot; in its shade I found another seat which suited me better. Mrs Bretton was never wont to make a fuss about any person or anything; without remonstrance she suffered me to have my own way. She made the tea, and she took up the newspaper. I liked to watch every action of my godmother; all her movements were so young: she must have been now above fifty, yet neither her sinews nor her spirit seemed yet touched by the rust of age. Though portly, she was alert, and though serene, she was at times impetuous – good health and an excellent temperament kept her green as in her spring.

While she read, I perceived she listened – listened for her son. She was not the woman ever to confess herself uneasy, but there was yet no lull in the weather, and if Graham were out in that hoarse wind – roaring still unsatisfied – I well knew his mother's heart would be out with him.

'Ten minutes behind his time,' said she, looking at her watch; then, in another minute, a lifting of her eyes from the page, and a slight inclination of her head towards the door, denoted that she heard some sound. Presently her brow cleared; and then even my ear, less practised, caught the iron clash of a gate swung to, steps on gravel, lastly the doorbell. He was come. His mother filled the teapot from the urn, she drew nearer the hearth the stuffed and cushioned blue chair – her own chair by right, but I saw there was one who might with impunity usurp it. And when that *one* came up the stairs – which he soon did, after, I suppose, some such attention to the toilet as the wild and wet night rendered necessary, and strode straight in – 'Is it you, Graham?' said his mother, hiding a glad smile and speaking curtly.

'Who else should it be, mama?' demanded the Unpunctual, possessing himself irreverently of the abdicated throne.

'Don't you deserve cold tea, for being late?'

'I shall not get my deserts, for the urn sings cheerily.'

'Wheel yourself to table, lazy boy: no seat will serve you but mine; if you had one spark of a sense of propriety, you would always leave that chair for the Old Lady.'

'So I should; only the dear Old Lady persists in leaving it for me. How is your patient, mama?'

'Will she come forward and speak for herself?' said Mrs Bretton, turning to my corner; and at this invitation, forward I came. Graham courteously rose up to greet me. He stood tall on the hearth, a figure justifying his mother's unconcealed pride.

'So you are come down,' said he; 'you must be better then – much better. I scarcely expected we should meet thus, or here. I was alarmed last night, and if I had not been forced to hurry away to a dying patient, I certainly would not have left you; but my mother herself is something of a doctoress, and Martha an excellent nurse. I saw the case was a fainting-fit, not necessarily dangerous. What brought it on, I have yet to learn, and all particulars; meantime, I trust you really do feel better.'

'Much better,' I said calmly. 'Much better, I thank you, Dr John.'

For, reader, this tall young man – this darling son – this host of mine – this Graham Bretton, *was* Dr John: he, and no other; and, what is more, I ascertained this identity scarcely with surprise. What is more, when I heard Graham's step on the stairs, I knew what manner of figure would enter, and for whose aspect to prepare my eyes. The discovery was not of today, its dawn had penetrated my perceptions long since. Of course I remembered young Bretton well; and though ten years (from sixteen to twenty-six) may greatly change the boy as they mature him to the man, yet they could bring no such utter difference as would suffice wholly to blind my eyes, or baffle my memory. Dr John Graham Bretton retained still an affinity to the youth of sixteen: he had his eyes; he had some of his features; to wit, all the excellently-moulded lower half of the face; I found him out soon. I first recognised him on that occasion, noted several chapters back, when my unguardedly-fixed attention had drawn on me the mortification of an implied rebuke. Subsequent observation confirmed, in every point, that early surmise. I traced in the gesture, the port, and the habits of his manhood, all his boy's promise. I heard in his now deep tones the accent of former days. Certain turns of phrase, peculiar to him of old, were peculiar to him still; and so was many a trick of eye and lip, many a smile, many a sudden ray levelled from the irid under his well-charactered brow.

To *say* anything on the subject, to *hint* at my discovery, had not suited my habits of thought, or assimilated with my system of feeling. On the contrary, I had preferred to keep the matter to myself. I liked entering his presence covered with a cloud he had not seen through, while he stood before me under a ray of special illumination, which shone all partial over his head, trembled about his feet, and cast light no farther.

Well I knew that to him it could make little difference, were I to come forward and announce 'This is Lucy Snowe!' So I kept back in my teacher's place; and as he never asked my name, so I never gave it. He heard me called 'Miss', and 'Miss Lucy'; he never heard the surname, 'Snowe'. As to spontaneous recognition – though I, perhaps, was still less changed than he – the idea never approached his mind, and why should I suggest it?

During tea, Dr John was kind, as it was his nature to be; that meal over, and the tray carried out, he made a cosy arrangement of the cushions in a corner of

the sofa, and obliged me to settle amongst them. He and his mother also drew to the fire, and ere we had sat ten minutes, I caught the eye of the latter fastened steadily upon me. Women are certainly quicker in some things than men.

'Well,' she exclaimed, presently; 'I have seldom seen a stronger likeness! Graham, have you observed it?'

'Observed what? What ails the Old Lady now? How you stare, mama! One would think you had an attack of second-sight.'

'Tell me, Graham, of whom does that young lady remind you?' pointing to me.

'Mama, you put her out of countenance. I often tell you abruptness is your fault; remember, too, that to you she is a stranger, and does not know your ways.'

'Now, when she looks down; now, when she turns sideways, who is she like, Graham?'

'Indeed, mama, since you propound the riddle, I think you ought to solve it!'

'And you have known her some time, you say – ever since you first began to attend the school in the Rue Fossette; yet you never mentioned to me that singular resemblance!'

'I could not mention a thing of which I never thought, and which I do not now acknowledge. What *can* you mean?'

'Stupid boy! look at her.'

Graham did look: but this was not to be endured; I saw how it must end, so I thought it best to anticipate.

'Dr John,' I said, 'has had so much to do and think of, since he and I shook hands at our last parting in St Ann's Street, that, while I readily found out Mr Graham Bretton, some months ago, it never occurred to me as possible that he should recognise Lucy Snowe.'

'Lucy Snowe! I thought so! I knew it!' cried Mrs Bretton. And she at once stepped across the hearth and kissed me. Some ladies would, perhaps, have made a great bustle upon such a discovery without being particularly glad of it; but it was not my godmother's habit to make a bustle, and she preferred all sentimental demonstration in bas-relief. So she and I got over the surprise with few words and a single salute; yet I dare say she was pleased, and I know I was. While we renewed old acquaintance, Graham, sitting opposite, silently disposed of his paroxysm of astonishment.

'Mama calls me a stupid boy, and I think I am so;' at length he said, 'for, upon my honour, often as I have seen you, I never once suspected this fact: and yet I perceive it all now. Lucy Snowe! To be sure! I recollect her perfectly, and there she sits; not a doubt of it. But,' he added, 'you surely have not known me as an old acquaintance all this time, and never mentioned it?'

'That I have,' was my answer.

Dr John commented not. I suppose he regarded my silence as eccentric, but he was indulgent in refraining from censure. I dare say, too, he would have deemed it impertinent to have interrogated me very closely, to have asked me the why and wherefore of my reserve; and, though he might feel a little curious,

the importance of the case was by no means such as to tempt curiosity to infringe on discretion.

For my part, I just ventured to enquire whether he remembered the circumstance of my once looking at him very fixedly; for the slight annoyance he had betrayed on that occasion, still lingered sore in my mind.

'I think I do!' said he: 'I think I was even cross with you.'

'You considered me a little bold, perhaps?' I enquired.

'Not at all. Only, shy and retiring as your general manner was, I wondered what personal or facial enormity in me proved so magnetic to your usually averted eyes.'

'You see how it was, now?'

'Perfectly.'

And here Mrs Bretton broke in with many, many questions about past times; and for her satisfaction I had to recur to gone-by troubles, to explain causes of seeming estrangement, to touch on single-handed conflict with Life, with Death, with Grief, with Fate. Dr John listened, saying little. He and she then told me of changes they had known: even with them, all had not gone smoothly, and fortune had retrenched her once abundant gifts. But so courageous a mother, with such a champion in her son, was well fitted to fight a good fight with the world, and to prevail ultimately. Dr John himself was one of those on whose birth benign planets have certainly smiled. Adversity might set against him her most sullen front: he was the man to beat her down with smiles. Strong and cheerful, and firm and courteous; not rash, yet valiant; he was the aspirant to woo Destiny herself, and to win from her stone eyeballs a beam almost loving.

In the profession he had adopted, his success was now quite decided. Within the last three months, he had taken this house (a small chateau, they told me, about half a league without the Porte de Crécy); this country site being chosen for the sake of his mother's health, with which town air did not now agree. Hither he had invited Mrs Bretton, and she, on leaving England, had brought with her such residue furniture of the former St Ann's Street mansion, as she had thought fit to keep unsold. Hence my bewilderment at the phantoms of chairs, and the wraiths of looking glasses, tea urns, and tea cups.

As the clock struck eleven, Dr John stopped his mother.

'Miss Snowe must retire now,' he said; 'she is beginning to look very pale. Tomorrow I will venture to put some questions respecting the cause of her loss of health. She is much changed indeed, since last July, when I saw her enact with no little spirit, the part of a very killing fine gentleman. As to last night's catastrophe, I am sure thereby hangs a tale, but we will enquire no further this evening. Good-night, Miss Lucy.'

And so, he kindly led me to the door, and holding a wax candle, lighted me up the one flight of steps.

When I had said my prayers, and when I was undressed and laid down, I felt that I still had friends. Friends, not professing vehement attachment, not offering the tender solace of well-matched and congenial relationship; on whom, therefore, but moderate demand of affection was to be made, of whom

but moderate expectation formed; but towards whom, my heart softened instinctively and yearned with an importunate gratitude, which I entreated Reason betimes to check.

'Do not let me think of them too often, too much, too fondly,' I implored; 'let me be content with a temperate draught of this living stream: let me not run athirst, and apply passionately to its welcome waters: let me not imagine in them a sweeter taste than earth's fountains know. Oh! would to God! I may be enabled to feel enough sustained by an occasional, amicable intercourse, rare, brief, unengrossing and tranquil: quite tranquil!'

Still repeating this word, I turned to my pillow; and, *still* repeating it, I steeped that pillow with tears.

## CHAPTER 17

## *La Terrasse*

These struggles with the natural character, the strong native bent of the heart, may seem futile and fruitless, but in the end they do good. They tend, however slightly, to give the actions, the conduct, that turn which Reason approves, and which Feeling, perhaps, too often opposes: they certainly make a difference in the general tenor of a life, and enable it to be better regulated, more equable, quieter on the surface; and it is on the surface only the common gaze will fall. As to what lies below, leave that with God. Man, your equal, weak as you, and not fit to be your judge, may be shut out thence: take it to your Maker – show Him the secrets of the spirit He gave – ask Him how you are to bear the pains He has appointed – kneel in His presence, and pray with faith for light in darkness, for strength in piteous weakness, for patience in extreme need. Certainly, at some hour, though perhaps not *your* hour, the waiting waters will stir; in *some* shape, though perhaps not the shape you dreamed, which your heart loved, and for which it bled, the healing herald will descend. The cripple and the blind, and the dumb, and the possessed, will be led to bathe. Herald, come quickly! Thousands lie round the pool, weeping and despairing, to see it, through slow years, stagnant. Long are the 'times' of Heaven: the orbits of angel messengers seem wide to mortal vision; they may en-ring ages: the cycle of one departure and return may clasp unnumbered generations; and dust, kindling to brief suffering life, and, through pain, passing back to dust, may meanwhile perish out of memory again, and yet again. To how many maimed and mourning millions is the first and sole angel visitant, him easterns call Azrael.

I tried to get up next morning, but while I was dressing, and at intervals drinking cold water from the *carafe* on my washstand, with design to brace up that trembling weakness which made dressing so difficult, in came Mrs Bretton.

'Here is an absurdity!' was her morning accost. 'Not so,' she added, and

dealing with me at once in her own brusque, energetic fashion – that fashion which I used formerly to enjoy seeing applied to her son, and by him vigorously resisted – in two minutes she consigned me captive to the French bed.

'There you lie till afternoon,' said she. 'My boy left orders before he went out that such should be the case, and I can assure you my son is master and must be obeyed. Presently you shall have breakfast.'

Presently she brought that meal – brought it with her own active hands – not leaving me to servants. She seated herself on the bed while I ate. Now it is not everybody, even amongst our respected friends and esteemed acquaintance, whom we like to have near us, whom we like to watch us, to wait on us, to approach us with the proximity of a nurse to a patient. It is not every friend whose eye is a light in a sick room, whose presence is there a solace: but all this was Mrs Bretton to me; all this she had ever been. Food or drink never pleased me so well as when it came through her hands. I do not remember the occasion when her entrance into a room had not made that room cheerier. Our natures own predilections and antipathies alike strange. There are people from whom we secretly shrink, whom we would personally avoid, though reason confesses that they are good people: there are others with faults of temper, etc., evident enough, beside whom we live content, as if the air about them did us good. My godmother's lively black eye and clear brunette cheek, her warm, prompt hand, her self-reliant mood, her decided bearing, were all beneficial to me as the atmosphere of some salubrious climate. Her son used to call her 'the old lady;' it filled me with pleasant wonder to note how the alacrity and power of five-and-twenty still breathed from her and around her.

'I would bring my work here,' she said, as she took from me the emptied teacup, 'and sit with you the whole day, if that overbearing John Graham had not put his veto upon such a proceeding. "Now, mama," said he, when he went out, "take notice, you are not to knock up your god-daughter with gossip," and he particularly desired me to keep close to my own quarters, and spare you my fine company. He says, Lucy, he thinks you have had a nervous fever, judging from your look, is that so?'

I replied that I did not quite know what my ailment had been, but that I had certainly suffered a good deal, especially in mind. Further, on this subject, I did not consider it advisable to dwell, for the details of what I had undergone belonged to a portion of my existence in which I never expected my godmother to take a share. Into what a new region would such a confidence have led that hale, serene nature! The difference between her and me might be figured by that between the stately ship, cruising safe on smooth seas, with its full complement of crew, a captain gay and brave, and venturous and provident; and the lifeboat, which most days of the year lies dry and solitary in an old, dark boat-house, only putting to sea when the billows run high in rough weather, when cloud encounters water, when danger and death divide between them the rule of the great deep. No, the 'Louisa Bretton' never was out of harbour on such a night, and in such a scene: her crew could not conceive it; so the half-drowned lifeboat man keeps his own counsel, and spins no yarns.

She left me, and I lay in bed content: it was good of Graham to remember me before he went out.

My day was lonely, but the prospect of coming evening abridged and cheered it. Then, too, I felt weak, and rest seemed welcome; and after the morning hours were gone by – those hours which always bring, even to the necessarily unoccupied, a sense of business to be done, of tasks waiting fulfilment, a vague impression of obligation to be employed – when this stirring time was past, and the silent descent of afternoon hushed housemaid steps on the stairs and in the chambers, I then passed into a dreamy mood, not unpleasant.

My calm little room seemed somehow like a cave in the sea. There was no colour about it, except that white and pale green, suggestive of foam and deep water; the blanched cornice was adorned with shell-shaped ornaments, and there were white mouldings like dolphins in the ceiling-angles. Even that one touch of colour visible in the red satin pincushion bore affinity to coral; even that dark, shining glass might have mirrored a mermaid. When I closed my eyes, I heard a gale, subsiding at last, bearing upon the house-front like a settling swell upon a rock-base. I heard it drawn and withdrawn far, far off, like a tide retiring from a shore of the upper world – a world so high above, that the rush of its largest waves, the dash of its fiercest breakers could sound down in this submarine home, only like murmurs and a lullaby.

Amidst these dreams came evening, and then Martha brought a light; with her aid I was quickly dressed, and, stronger now than in the morning, I made my way down to the blue saloon unassisted.

Dr John, it appears, had concluded his round of professional calls earlier than usual; his form was the first object that met my eyes as I entered the parlour; he stood in that window-recess opposite the door, reading the close type of a newspaper by such dull light as closing day yet gave. The fire shone clear, but the lamp stood on the table unlit, and tea was not yet brought up.

As to Mrs Bretton, my active godmother – who, I afterwards found, had been out in the open air all day – lay half-reclined in her deep-cushioned chair, actually lost in a nap. Her son seeing me, came forward. I noticed that he trod carefully, not to wake the sleeper; he also spoke low: his mellow voice never had any sharpness in it; modulated as at present, it was calculated rather to soothe than startle slumber.

'This is a quiet little chateau,' he observed, after inviting me to sit near the casement, 'I don't know whether you may have noticed it in your walks: though, indeed, from the chaussée it is not visible; just a mile beyond the Porte de Crécy, you turn down a lane which soon becomes an avenue, and that leads you on, through meadow and shade, to the very door of this house. It is not a modern place, but built somewhat in the old style of the Basse-Ville. It is rather a manoir than a chateau; they call it "La Terrasse", because its front rises from a broad turfed walk, whence steps lead down a grassy slope to the avenue. See yonder! The moon rises: she looks well through the tree boles.'

Where, indeed, does the moon not look well? What is the scene, confined or expansive, which her orb does not hallow? Rosy or fiery, she mounted now above

a not distant bank; even while we watched her flushed ascent, she cleared to gold, and in very brief space, floated up stainless into a now calm sky. Did moonlight soften or sadden Dr Bretton? Did it touch him with romance? I think it did. Albeit of no sighing mood, he sighed in watching it: sighed to himself quietly. No need to ponder the cause or the course of that sigh; I knew it was wakened by beauty: I knew it pursued Ginevra. Knowing this, the idea pressed upon me that it was in some sort my duty to speak the name he meditated. Of course he was ready for the subject: I saw in his countenance a teeming plenitude of comment, question and interest; a pressure of language and sentiment, only checked, I thought, by sense of embarrassment how to begin. To spare him this embarrassment was my best, indeed my sole use. I had but to utter the idol's name, and love's tender litany would flow out. I had just found a fitting phrase: 'You know that Miss Fanshawe is gone on a tour with the Cholmondeleys,' and was opening my lips to speak it, when he scattered my plans by introducing another theme.

'The first thing this morning,' said he, putting his sentiment in his pocket, turning from the moon, and sitting down, 'I went to the Rue Fossette, and told the cuisinière that you were safe and in good hands. Do you know I actually found that she had not yet discovered your absence from the house: she thought you safe in the great dormitory. With what care must you have been waited on!'

'Oh! all that is very conceivable,' said I. 'Goton could do nothing for me but bring me a little tisane and a crust of bread, and I had rejected both so often during the past week, that the good woman got tired of useless journeys from the dwelling-house kitchen to the school-dormitory, and only came once a day at noon, to make my bed. Believe, however, that she is a good-natured creature, and would have been delighted to cook me cotelettes de mouton, if I could have eaten them.'

'What did Mme Beck mean by leaving you alone?'

'Mme Beck could not foresee that I should fall ill.'

'Your nervous system bore a good share of the suffering?'

'I am not quite sure what my nervous system is, but I was dreadfully low-spirited.'

'Which disables me from helping you by pill or potion. Medicine can give nobody good spirits. My art halts at the threshold of Hypochondria: she just looks in and sees a chamber of torture, but can neither say nor do much. Cheerful society would be of use; you should be as little alone as possible; you should take plenty of exercise.'

Acquiescence and a pause followed these remarks. They sounded all right, I thought, and bore the safe sanction of custom, and the well-worn stamp of use.

'Miss Snowe,' recommended Dr John – my health, nervous system included, being now somewhat to my relief, discussed and done with – 'is it permitted me to ask what your religion now is? Are you a Catholic?'

I looked up in some surprise – 'A Catholic? No! Why suggest such an idea?'

'The manner in which you were consigned to me last night, made me doubt.'

'I consigned to you? But, indeed, I forget. It remains yet for me to learn how I fell into your hands.'

'Why, under circumstances that puzzled me. I had been in attendance all day yesterday on a case of singularly interesting and critical character; the disease being rare, and its treatment doubtful: I saw a similar and still finer case in a hospital at Paris; but that will not interest you. At last a mitigation of the patient's most urgent symptoms (acute pain is one of its accompaniments) liberated me, and I set out homeward. My shortest way lay through the Basse Ville, and as the night was excessively dark, wild and wet, I took it. In riding past an old church belonging to a community of Béguines, I saw by a lamp burning over the porch or deep arch of the entrance, a priest lifting some object in his arms. The lamp was bright enough to reveal the priest's features clearly, and I recognised him; he was a man I have often met by the sick beds of both rich and poor: and, chiefly, the latter. He is, I think, a good old man, far better than most of his class in this country; superior, indeed, in every way: better informed, as well as more devoted to duty. Our eyes met, he called on me to stop; what he supported was a woman, fainting or dying. I alighted.

' "This person is one of your countrywomen," he said: "save her, if she is not dead."

'My countrywoman, on examination, turned out to be the English teacher at Mme Beck's pensionnat. She was perfectly unconscious, perfectly bloodless, and nearly cold.

' "What does it all mean?" was my enquiry.

'He communicated a curious account: that you had been to him that evening at confessional; that your exhausted and suffering appearance, coupled with some things you had said –'

'Things I had said? I wonder what things!'

'Awful crimes, no doubt; but he did not tell me what: there, you know, the seal of the confessional checked his garrulity and my curiosity. Your confidences, however, had not made an enemy of the good father; it seems he was so struck, and felt so sorry that you should be out on such a night alone, he had esteemed it a Christian duty to watch when you quitted the church, and so to manage as not to lose sight of you, till you should have reached home. Perhaps the worthy man might, half unconsciously, have blent in this proceeding, some little of the subtlety of his class: it might have been his resolve to learn the locality of your home – did you impart that in your confession?'

'I did not: on the contrary, I carefully avoided the shadow of an indication; and as to my confession, Dr John, I suppose you will think me mad for taking such a step, but I could not help it: I suppose it was all the fault of what you call my "nervous system". I cannot put the case into words, but, my days and nights were grown intolerable; a cruel sense of desolation pained my mind: a feeling that would make its way, rush out, or kill me – like (and this you will understand, Dr John) the current which passes through the heart, and which, if aneurism or any other morbid cause obstructs its natural channels, seeks abnormal outlet. I wanted companionship, I wanted friendship, I wanted counsel. I could find none of these in closet, or chamber, so I went and sought them in church and confessional. As to what I said, it was no confidence, no narrative. I have done

nothing wrong: my life has not been active enough for any dark deed, either of romance or reality: all I poured out was a dreary, desperate complaint.'

'Lucy, you ought to travel for about six months: why, your calm nature is growing quite excitable! Confound Mme Beck! Has the little buxom widow no bowels, to condemn her best teacher to solitary confinement?'

'It was not Mme Beck's fault,' said I; 'it is no living being's fault, and I won't hear anyone blamed.'

'Who is in the wrong then, Lucy?'

'Me – Dr John – me; and a great abstraction on whose wide shoulders I like to lay the mountains of blame they were sculptured to bear: me and Fate.'

' "Me" must take better care in future,' said Dr John – smiling, I suppose, at my bad grammar.

'Change of air – change of scene; those are my prescriptions,' pursued the practical young doctor. 'But to return to our muttons, Lucy. As yet, Père Silas, with all his tact (they say he is a Jesuit), is no wiser than you choose him to be; for, instead of returning to the Rue Fossette, your fevered wanderings – there must have been high fever –'

'No, Dr John: the fever took its turn that night – now, don't make out that I was delirious, for I know differently.'

'Good! you were as collected as myself at this moment, no doubt! Your wanderings had taken an opposite direction to the Pensionnat. Near the Béguinage, amidst the stress of flood and gust, and in the perplexity of darkness, you had swooned and fallen. The priest came to your succour, and the physician, as we have seen, supervened. Between us we procured a fiacre and brought you here. Père Silas, old as he is, would carry you up stairs, and lay you on that couch himself. He would certainly have remained with you till suspended animation had been restored; and so should I, but, at that juncture, a hurried messenger arrived from the dying patient I had scarcely left – the last duties were called for – the physician's last visit and the priest's last rite; extreme unction could not be deferred. Père Silas and myself departed together, my mother was spending the evening abroad; we gave you in charge to Martha, leaving directions, which it seems she followed successfully. Now, are you a Catholic?'

'Not yet,' said I, with a smile. 'And never let Père Silas know where I live, or he will try to convert me; but give him my best and truest thanks when you see him, and if ever I get rich I will send him money for his charities. See, Dr John, your mother wakes; you ought to ring for tea.'

Which he did; and, as Mrs Bretton sat up – astonished and indignant at herself for the indulgence to which she had succumbed, and fully prepared to deny that she had slept at all – her son came gaily to the attack: 'Hushaby, mama! Sleep again. You look the picture of innocence in your slumbers.'

'My slumbers, John Graham! What are you talking about? You know I never *do* sleep by day: it was the slightest doze possible.'

'Exactly! a seraph's gentle lapse – a fairy's dream. Mama, under such circumstances, you always remind me of Titania.'

'That is because you, yourself, are so like Bottom.'

'Miss Snowe – did you ever hear anything like mama's wit? She is a most sprightly woman of her size and age.'

'Keep your compliments to yourself, sir, and do not neglect your own size: which seems to me a good deal on the increase. Lucy, has he not rather the air of an incipient John Bull? He used to be slender as an eel, and now I fancy in him a sort of heavy-dragoon bent – a beefeater tendency. Graham, take notice! If you grow fat I disown you.'

'As if you could not sooner disown your own personality! I am indispensable to the old lady's happiness, Lucy. She would pine away in green and yellow melancholy if she had not my six feet of iniquity to scold. It keeps her lively – it maintains the wholesome ferment of her spirits.'

The two were now standing opposite to each other, one on each side the fireplace; their words were not very fond, but their mutual looks atoned for verbal deficiencies. At least, the best treasure of Mrs Bretton's life was certainly casketed in her son's bosom; her dearest pulse throbbed in his heart. As to him, of course another love shared his feelings with filial love; and, no doubt, as the new passion was the latest born, so he assigned it in his emotions Benjamin's portion. Ginevra! Ginevra! Did Mrs Bretton yet know at whose feet her own young idol had laid his homage? Would she approve that choice? I could not tell; but I could well guess that if she knew Miss Fanshawe's conduct towards Graham: her alternations between coldness and coaxing, and repulse and allurement; if she could at all suspect the pain with which she had tried him; if she could have seen, as I had seen, his fine spirits subdued and harassed, his inferior preferred before him, his subordinate made the instrument of his humiliation – *then* Mrs Bretton would have pronounced Ginevra imbecile, or perverted, or both. Well – I thought so too.

That second evening passed as sweetly as the first – *more* sweetly indeed: we enjoyed a smoother interchange of thought; old troubles were not reverted to, acquaintance was better cemented; I felt happier, easier, more at home. That night – instead of crying myself asleep – I went down to dreamland by a pathway bordered with pleasant thoughts.

## CHAPTER 18

## *We Quarrel*

During the first days of my stay at the Terrace, Graham never took a seat near me, or in his frequent pacing of the room approached the quarter where I sat, or looked preoccupied, or more grave than usual, but I thought of Miss Fanshawe and expected her name to leap from his lips. I kept my ear and mind in perpetual readiness for the tender theme; my patience was ordered to be permanently under arms, and my sympathy desired to keep its cornucopia replenished and ready for outpouring. At last, and after a little inward struggle which I saw and respected, he

one day launched into the topic. It was introduced delicately; anonymously as it were.

'Your friend is spending her vacation in travelling, I hear?' 'Friend, forsooth!' thought I to myself: but it would not do to contradict; he must have his own way; I must own the soft impeachment: friend let it be. Still, by way of experiment, I could not help asking whom he meant?

He had taken a seat at my work-table; he now laid hands on a reel of thread which he proceeded recklessly to unwind.

'Ginevra – Miss Fanshawe, has accompanied the Cholmondeleys on a tour through the south of France?'

'She has.'

'Do you and she correspond?'

'It will astonish you to hear that I never once thought of making application for that privilege.'

'You have seen letters of her writing?'

'Yes; several to her uncle.'

'They will not be deficient in wit and naîveté; there is so much sparkle, and so little art in her soul?'

'She writes comprehensibly enough when she writes to M. de Bassompierre: he who runs may read.' (In fact, Ginevra's epistles to her wealthy kinsman were commonly business documents, unequivocal applications for cash.)

'And her handwriting? It must be pretty, light, ladylike, I should think?'

It was, and I said so.

'I verily believe that all she does is well done,' said Dr John; and as I seemed in no hurry to chime in with this remark, he added: 'You, who know her, could you name a point in which she is deficient?'

'She does several things very well.' ('Flirtation amongst the rest,' subjoined I, in thought.)

'When do you suppose she will return to town?' he soon enquired.

'Pardon me, Dr John, I must explain. You honour me too much in ascribing to me a degree of intimacy with Miss Fanshawe I have not the felicity to enjoy. I have never been the depository of her plans and secrets. You will find her particular friends in another sphere than mine: amongst the Cholmondeleys, for instance.'

He actually thought I was stung with a kind of jealous pain similar to his own! 'Excuse her;' he said, 'judge her indulgently; the glitter of fashion misleads her, but she will soon find out that these people are hollow, and will return to you with augmented attachment and confirmed trust. I know something of the Cholmondeleys; superficial, showy, selfish people: depend on it, at heart Ginevra values you beyond a score of such.'

'You are very kind,' I said briefly. A disclaimer of the sentiments attributed to me burned on my lips, but I extinguished the flame. I submitted to be looked upon as the humiliated, cast-off, and now pining confidante of the distinguished Miss Fanshawe: but, reader, it was a hard submission.

'Yet, you see,' continued Graham, 'while I comfort *you*, I cannot take the

same consolation to myself; I cannot hope she will do me justice. De Hamal is most worthless, yet I fear he pleases her: wretched delusion!'

My patience really gave way, and without notice: all at once. I suppose illness and weakness had worn it and made it brittle.

'Dr Bretton,' I broke out, 'there is no delusion like your own. On all points but one you are a man, frank, healthful, right-thinking, clear-sighted: on this exceptional point you are but a slave. I declare, where Miss Fanshawe is concerned, you merit no respect; nor have you mine.'

I got up, and left the room very much excited.

This little scene took place in the morning; I had to meet him again in the evening, and then I saw I had done mischief. He was not made of common clay, not put together out of vulgar materials; while the outlines of his nature had been shaped with breadth and vigour, the details embraced workmanship of almost feminine delicacy: finer, much finer, than you could be prepared to meet with; than you could believe inherent in him, even after years of acquaintance. Indeed, till some over-sharp contact with his nerves had betrayed, by its effects, their acute sensibility, this elaborate construction must be ignored; and the more especially because the sympathetic faculty was not prominent in him: to feel, and to seize quickly another's feelings, are separate properties; a few constructions possess both, some neither. Dr John had the one gift in exquisite perfection; and because I have admitted that he was not endowed with the other in equal degree, the reader will considerately refrain from passing to an extreme, and pronouncing him *un*sympathising, unfeeling: on the contrary, he was a kind, generous man. Make your need known, his hand was open. Put your grief into words, he turned no deaf ear. Expect refinements of perception, miracles of intuition, and realise disappointment. This night, when Dr John entered the room, and met the evening lamp, I saw well and at one glance his whole mechanism.

To one who had named him 'slave', and, on any point, banned him from respect, he must now have peculiar feelings. That the epithet was well applied, and the ban just, might be; he put forth no denial that it was so: his mind even candidly revolved that unmanning possibility. He sought in this accusation the cause of that ill-success which had got so galling a hold of his mental peace. Amid the worry of a self-condemnatory soliloquy, his demeanour seemed grave, perhaps cold, both to me and his mother. And yet there was no bad feeling, no malice, no rancour, no littleness in his countenance, beautiful with a man's best beauty, even in its depression. When I placed his chair at the table, which I hastened to do, anticipating the servant, and when I handed him his tea, which I did with trembling care, he said –

'Thank you, Lucy,' in as kindly a tone of his full pleasant voice as ever my ear welcomed.

For my part, there was only one plan to be pursued; I must expiate my culpable vehemence, or I must not sleep that night. This would not do at all; I could not stand it: I made no pretence of capacity to wage war on this footing. School solitude, conventual silence and stagnation, anything seemed preferable

to living embroiled with Dr John. As to Ginevra, she might take the silver wings of a dove, or any other fowl that flies, and mount straight up to the highest place, among the highest stars, where her lover's highest flight of fancy chose to fix the constellation of her charms: never more be it mine to dispute the arrangement. Long I tried to catch his eye. Again and again that eye just met mine; but, having nothing to say, it withdrew, and I was baffled. After tea, he sat, sad and quiet, reading a book. I wished I could have dared to go and sit near him, but it seemed that if I ventured to take that step, he would infallibly evince hostility and indignation. I longed to speak out, and I dared not whisper. His mother left the room; then, moved by insupportable regret, I just murmured the words 'Dr Bretton'.

He looked up from his book; his eyes were not cold or malevolent, his mouth was not cynical; he was ready and willing to hear what I might have to say: his spirit was of vintage too mellow and generous to sour in one thunderclap.

'Dr Bretton, forgive my hasty words: *do, do* forgive them.'

He smiled that moment I spoke. 'Perhaps I deserved them, Lucy. If you don't respect me, I am sure it is because I am not respectable. I fear I am an awkward fool: I must manage badly in some way, for where I wish to please, it seems I don't please.'

'Of that you cannot be sure; and even if such be the case, is it the fault of your character, or of another's perceptions? But now, let me unsay what I said in anger. In one thing, and in all things, I deeply respect you. If you think scarcely enough of yourself, and too much of others, what is that but an excellence?'

'Can I think too much of Ginevra?'

'*I* believe you may; *you* believe you can't. Let us agree to differ. Let me be pardoned; that is what I ask.'

'Do you think I cherish ill-will for one warm word?'

'I see you do not and cannot; but just say, "Lucy, I forgive you!" Say that, to ease me of the heartache.'

'Put away your heartache, as I will put away mine: for you wounded me a little, Lucy. Now, when the pain is gone, I more than forgive: I feel grateful, as to a sincere well-wisher.'

'I *am* your sincere well-wisher: you are right.'

Thus our quarrel ended.

Reader, if in the course of this work, you find that my opinion of Dr John undergoes modification, excuse the seeming inconsistency. I give the feeling as at the time I felt it; I describe the view of character as it appeared when discovered.

He showed the fineness of his nature by being kinder to me after that misunderstanding than before. Nay, the very incident which, by my theory, must in some degree estrange me and him, changed, indeed, somewhat our relations; but not in the sense I painfully anticipated. An invisible, but a cold something, very slight, very transparent, but very chill: a sort of screen of ice had hitherto, all through our two lives, glazed the medium through which we exchanged intercourse. Those few warm words, though only warm with anger, breathed on that frail frost-work of reserve; about this time, it gave note of

dissolution. I think from that day, so long as we continued friends, he never in discourse stood on topics of ceremony with me. He seemed to know that if he would but talk about himself, and about that in which he was most interested, my expectation would always be answered, my wish always satisfied. It follows, as a matter of course, that I continued to hear much of 'Ginevra.'

'Ginevra!' He thought her so fair, so good; he spoke so lovingly of her charms, her sweetness, her innocence, that, in spite of my plain prose knowledge of the reality, a kind of reflected glow began to settle on her idea, even for me. Still, reader, I am free to confess, that he often talked nonsense; but I strove to be unfailingly patient with him. I had had my lesson: I had learned how severe for me was the pain of crossing, or grieving, or disappointing him. In a strange and new sense, I grew most selfish, and quite powerless to deny myself the delight of indulging his mood, and being pliant to his will. He still seemed to me most absurd when he obstinately doubted, and desponded about his power to win in the end Miss Fanshawe's preference. The fancy became rooted in my own mind more stubbornly than ever, that she was only coquetting to goad him, and that, at heart, she coveted every one of his words and looks. Sometimes he harassed me, in spite of my resolution to bear and hear; in the midst of the indescribable gall-honey pleasure of thus bearing and hearing, he struck so on the flint of what firmness I owned, that it emitted fire once and again. I chanced to assert one day, with a view to stilling his impatience, that in my own mind, I felt positive Miss Fanshawe *must* intend eventually to accept him.

'Positive! It was easy to say so, but had I any grounds for such assurance?'

'The best grounds.'

'Now, Lucy, *do* tell me what!'

'You know them as well as I; and, knowing them, Dr John, it really amazes me that you should not repose the frankest confidence in her fidelity. To doubt, under the circumstances, is almost to insult.'

'Now you are beginning to speak fast and to breathe short; but speak a little faster and breathe a little shorter, till you have given an explanation – a full explanation: I must have it.'

'You shall, Dr John. In some cases, you are a lavish, generous man: you are a worshipper ever ready with the votive offering; should Père Silas ever convert *you*, you will give him abundance of alms for his poor, you will supply his altar with tapers, and the shrine of your favourite saint you will do your best to enrich: Ginevra, Dr John –'

'Hush!' said he, 'don't go on.'

'Hush, I will *not*: and go on I *will*: Ginevra has had her hands filled from your hands more times than I can count. You have sought for her the costliest flowers; you have busied your brain in devising gifts, the most delicate: such, one would have thought, as only a woman could have imagined; and in addition, Miss Fanshawe owns a set of ornaments, to purchase which your generosity must have verged on extravagance.'

The modesty Ginevra herself had never evinced in this matter, now flushed all over the face of her admirer.

'Nonsense!' he said, destructively snipping a skein of silk with my scissors. 'I offered them to please myself: I felt she did me a favour in accepting them.'

'She did more than a favour, Dr John: she pledged her very honour that she would make you some return; and if she cannot pay you in affection, she ought to hand out a businesslike equivalent, in the shape of some rouleaux of gold pieces.'

'But you don't understand her; she is far too disinterested to care for my gifts, and too simple-minded to know their value.'

I laughed out: I had heard her adjudge to every jewel its price; and well I knew money-embarrassment, money-schemes, money's worth, and endeavours to realise supplies, had, young as she was, furnished the most frequent, and the favourite stimulus of her thoughts for years.

He pursued. 'You should have seen her whenever I have laid on her lap some trifle; so cool, so unmoved: no eagerness to take, not even pleasure in contemplating. Just from amiable reluctance to grieve me, she would permit the bouquet to lie beside her, and perhaps consent to bear it away. Or, if I achieved the fastening of a bracelet on her ivory arm, however pretty the trinket might be (and I always carefully chose what seemed to *me* pretty, and what of course was not valueless), the glitter never dazzled her bright eyes: she would hardly cast one look on my gift.'

'Then, of course, not valuing it, she would unloose, and return it to you?'

'No; for such a repulse she was too good-natured. She would consent to seem to forget what I had done, and retain the offering with lady-like quiet and easy oblivion. Under such circumstances, how can a man build on acceptance of his presents as a favourable symptom? For my part, were I to offer her all I have, and she to take it, such is her incapacity to be swayed by sordid considerations, I should not venture to believe the transaction advanced me one step.'

'Dr John,' I began, 'Love is blind;' but just then a blue, subtle ray sped sideways from Dr John's eye: it reminded me of old days, it reminded me of his picture: it half led me to think that part, at least, of his professed persuasion of Miss Fanshawe's *naïveté* was assumed; it led me dubiously to conjecture that perhaps, in spite of his passion for her beauty, his appreciation of her foibles might possibly be less mistaken, more clear-sighted, than from his general language was presumable. After all it might be only a chance look, or at best, the token of a merely momentary impression. Chance or intentional, real or imaginary, it closed the conversation.

## CHAPTER 19

# The Cleopatra

My stay at La Terrasse was prolonged a fortnight beyond the close of the vacation. Mrs Bretton's kind management procured me this respite. Her son having one day delivered the dictum that 'Lucy was not yet strong enough to go back to that den of a Pensionnat,' she at once drove over to the Rue Fossette, had an interview with the directress, and procured the indulgence, on the plea of prolonged rest and change being necessary to perfect recovery. Hereupon, however, followed an attention I could very well have dispensed with, viz. a polite call from Mme Beck.

That lady – one fine day – actually came out in a fiacre as far as the chateau. I suppose she had resolved within herself to see what manner of place Dr John inhabited. Apparently, the pleasant site and neat interior surpassed her expectations; she eulogised all she saw, pronounced the blue salon 'une pièce magnifique', profusely congratulated me on the acquisition of friends, 'tellement dignes, aimables, et respectables', turned also a neat compliment in my favour, and, upon Dr John coming in, ran up to him with the utmost buoyancy, opening at the same time such a fire of rapid language, all sparkling with felicitations and protestations about his 'chateau', – 'madame sa mère, la digne châtelaine': also his looks; which indeed were very flourishing, and at the moment additionally embellished by the good-natured but amused smile with which he always listened to madame's fluent and florid French. In short, Madame shone in her very best phase that day, and came in and went out quite a living catherine-wheel of compliments, delight, and affability. Half-purposely, and half to ask some question about school-business, I followed her to the carriage, and looked in after she was seated and the door closed. In that brief fraction of time what a change had been wrought! An instant ago, all sparkles and jests, she now sat sterner than a judge and graver than a sage. Strange little woman!

I went back and teased Dr John about Madame's devotion to him. How he laughed! What fun shone in his eyes as he recalled some of her fine speeches, and repeated them, imitating her voluble delivery! He had an acute sense of humour, and was the finest company in the world – when he could forget Miss Fanshawe.

To 'sit in sunshine calm and sweet' is said to be excellent for weak people; it gives them vital force. When little Georgette Beck was recovering from her illness, I used to take her in my arms and walk with her in the garden by the hour together, beneath a certain wall hung with grapes which the Southern sun was ripening: that sun cherished her little pale frame quite as effectually as it mellowed and swelled the clustering fruit.

There are human tempers, bland, glowing, and genial, within whose influence it is as good for the poor in spirit to live, as it is for the feeble in frame to bask in the glow of noon. Of the number of these choice natures were certainly both Dr Bretton's and his mother's. They liked to communicate happiness, as some like to occasion misery: they did it instinctively; without fuss, and apparently, with little consciousness: the means to give pleasure rose spontaneously in their minds. Every day while I stayed with them, some little plan was proposed which resulted in beneficial enjoyment. Fully occupied as was Dr John's time, he still made it in his way to accompany us in each brief excursion. I can hardly tell how he managed his engagements; they were numerous, yet by dint of system, he classed them in an order which left him a daily period of liberty. I often saw him hard-worked, yet seldom over-driven; and never irritated, confused, or oppressed. What he did was accomplished with the ease and grace of all-sufficing strength; with the bountiful cheerfulness of high and unbroken energies. Under his guidance I saw, in that one happy fortnight, more of Villette, its environs, and its inhabitants, than I had seen in the whole eight months of my previous residence. He took me to places of interest in the town, of whose names I had not before so much as heard; with willingness and spirit he communicated much noteworthy information. He never seemed to think it a trouble to talk to me, and, I am sure, it was never a task to me to listen. It was not his way to treat subjects coldly and vaguely; he rarely generalised, never prosed. He seemed to like nice details almost as much as I liked them myself; he seemed observant of character: and not superficially observant, either. These points gave the quality of interest to his discourse; and the fact of his speaking direct from his own resources, and not borrowing or stealing from books – here a dry fact, and there a trite phrase, and elsewhere a hackneyed opinion – ensured a freshness, as welcome as it was rare. Before my eyes, too, his disposition seemed to unfold another phase; to pass to a fresh day: to rise in new and nobler dawn.

His mother possessed a good development of benevolence, but he owned a better and larger. I found, on accompanying him to the Basse-Ville – the poor and crowded quarter of the city – that his errands there were as much those of the philanthropist as the physician. I understood presently that – cheerfully, habitually, and in single-minded unconsciousness of any special merit distinguishing his deeds – he was achieving, amongst a very wretched population, a world of active good. The lower orders liked him well; his poor patients in the hospitals welcomed him with a sort of enthusiasm.

But stop – I must not, from the faithful narrator, degenerate into the partial eulogist. Well, full well, do I know that Dr John was not perfect, any more than I am perfect. Human fallibility leavened him throughout: there was no hour, and scarcely a moment of the times I spent with him, that in act, or speech, or look, he did not betray something that was not a god. A god could not have the cruel vanity of Dr John, nor his sometime levity. No immortal could have resembled him in his occasional temporary oblivion of all but the present – in his passing passion for that present; shown not coarsely, by devoting it to material indulgence, but selfishly, by extracting from it whatever it could yield

of nutriment to his masculine self-love: his delight was to feed that ravenous sentiment, without thought of the price of provender, or care for the cost of keeping it sleek and high-pampered.

The reader is requested to note a seeming contradiction in the two views which have been given of Graham Bretton – the public and private – the outdoor and the indoor view. In the first, the public, he is shown oblivious of self; as modest in the display of his energies, as earnest in their exercise. In the second, the fireside picture, there is expressed consciousness of what he has and what he is; pleasure in homage, some recklessness in exciting, some vanity in receiving the same. Both portraits are correct.

It was hardly possible to oblige Dr John quietly and in secret. When you thought that the fabrication of some trifle dedicated to his use had been achieved unnoticed, and that, like other men, he would use it when placed ready for his use, and never ask whence it came, he amazed you by a smilingly-uttered observation or two proving that his eye had been on the work from commencement to close: that he had noted the design, traced its progress, and marked its completion. It pleased him to be thus served, and he let his pleasure beam in his eye and play about his mouth.

This would have been all very well, if he had not added to such kindly and unobtrusive evidence a certain wilfulness in discharging what he called debts. When his mother worked for him, he paid her by showering about her his bright animal spirits, with even more affluence than his gay, taunting, teasing, loving wont. If Lucy Snowe were discovered to have put her hand to such work, he planned, in recompense, some pleasant recreation.

I often felt amazed at his perfect knowledge of Villette; a knowledge not merely confined to its open streets, but penetrating to all its galleries, salles, and cabinets: of every door which shut in an object worth seeing, of every museum, of every hall, sacred to art or science, he seemed to possess the 'Open! Sesame.' I never had a head for science, but an ignorant, blind, fond instinct inclined me to art. I liked to visit the picture-galleries, and I dearly liked to be left there alone. In company, a wretched idiosyncrasy forbade me to see much or to feel anything. In unfamiliar company, where it was necessary to maintain a flow of talk on the subjects in presence, half an hour would knock me up, with a combined pressure of physical lassitude and entire mental incapacity. I never yet saw the well-reared child, much less the educated adult, who could not put me to shame, by the sustained intelligence of its demeanour under the ordeal of a conversable sociable visitation of pictures, historical sites or buildings, or any lions of public interest. Dr Bretton was a cicerone after my own heart; he would take me betimes, ere the galleries were filled, leave me there for two or three hours, and call for me when his own engagements were discharged. Meantime, I was happy; happy, not always in admiring, but in examining, questioning, and forming conclusions. In the commencement of these visits, there was some misunderstanding and consequent struggle between Will and Power. The former faculty exacted approbation of that which it was considered orthodox to admire; the latter groaned forth its utter inability to pay the tax; it was then self-sneered at,

spurred up, goaded on to refine its taste, and whet its zest. The more it was chidden, however, the more it wouldn't praise. Discovering gradually that a wonderful sense of fatigue resulted from these conscientious efforts, I began to reflect whether I might not dispense with that great labour, and concluded eventually that I might, and so sank supine into a luxury of calm before ninety-nine out of a hundred of the exhibited frames.

It seemed to me that an original and good picture was just as scarce as an original and good book; nor did I, in the end, tremble to say to myself, standing before certain *chef d'oeuvres* bearing great names, 'These are not a whit like nature. Nature's daylight never had that colour; never was made so turbid, either by storm or cloud, as it is laid out there, under a sky of indigo: and that indigo is not ether; and those dark weeds plastered upon it are not trees.' Several very well executed and complacent-looking fat women struck me as by no means the goddesses they appeared to consider themselves. Many scores of marvellously-finished little Flemish pictures, and also of sketches, excellent for fashion-books, displaying varied costumes in the handsomest materials, gave evidence of laudable industry whimsically applied. And yet there were fragments of truth here and there which satisfied the conscience, and gleams of light that cheered the vision. Nature's power here broke through in a mountain snowstorm; and there her glory in a sunny southern day. An expression in this portrait proved clear insight into character; a face in this historical painting, by its vivid filial likeness, startlingly reminded you that genius gave it birth. These exceptions I loved: they grew dear as friends.

One day, at a quiet early hour, I found myself nearly alone in a certain gallery, wherein one particular picture of pretentious size, set up in the best light, having a cordon of protection stretched before it, and a cushioned bench duly set in front for the accommodation of worshipping connoisseurs, who, having gazed themselves off their feet, might be fain to complete the business sitting: this picture, I say, seemed to consider itself the queen of the collection.

It represented a woman, considerably larger, I thought, than the life. I calculated that this lady, put into a scale of magnitude suitable for the reception of a commodity of bulk, would infallibly turn from fourteen to sixteen stone. She was, indeed, extremely well fed: very much butcher's meat – to say nothing of bread, vegetables, and liquids – must she have consumed to attain that breadth and height, that wealth of muscle, that affluence of flesh. She lay half-reclined on a couch: why, it would be difficult to say; broad daylight blazed round her; she appeared in hearty health, strong enough to do the work of two plain cooks; she could not plead a weak spine; she ought to have been standing, or at least sitting bolt upright. She had no business to lounge away the noon on a sofa. She ought likewise to have worn decent garments; a gown covering her properly, which was not the case: out of abundance of material – seven-and-twenty yards, I should say, of drapery – she managed to make inefficient raiment. Then, for the wretched untidiness surrounding her, there could be no excuse. Pots and pans – perhaps I ought to say vases and goblets – were rolled here and there on the foreground; a perfect rubbish of flowers was mixed amongst them, and an absurd

and disorderly mass of curtain upholstery smothered the couch and cumbered the floor. On referring to the catalogue, I found that this notable production bore name 'Cleopatra'.

Well, I was sitting wondering at it (as the bench was there, I thought I might as well take advantage of its accommodation), and thinking that while some of the details – as roses, gold cups, jewels, etc. were very prettily painted, it was on the whole an enormous piece of claptrap; the room, almost vacant when I entered, began to fill. Scarcely noticing this circumstance (as, indeed, it did not matter to me) I retained my seat; rather to rest myself than with a view to studying this huge, dark-complexioned gypsy-queen; of whom, indeed, I soon tired, and betook myself for refreshment to the contemplation of some exquisite little pictures of still life: wild-flowers, wild-fruit, mossy wood-nests, casketing eggs that looked like pearls seen through clear green sea-water; all hung modestly beneath that coarse and preposterous canvas.

Suddenly a light tap visited my shoulder. Starting, turning, I met a face bent to encounter mine; a frowning, almost a shocked face it was.

'Que faites-vous ici?' said a voice.

'Mais, monsieur, je m'amuse.'

'Vous vous amusez! et à quoi, s'il vous plaît? Mais d'abord, faites-moi le plaisir de vous lever: prenez mon bras, et allons de l'autre côté.'

I did precisely as I was bid. M. Paul Emanuel (it was he) returned from Rome, and now a travelled man, was not likely to be less tolerant of insubordination now, than before this added distinction laurelled his temples.

'Permit me to conduct you to your party,' said he, as we crossed the room.

'I have no party.'

'You are not alone?'

'Yes, monsieur.'

'Did you come here unaccompanied?'

'No, monsieur. Dr Bretton brought me here.'

'Dr Bretton and Madame his mother, of course?'

'No; only Dr Bretton.'

'And he told you to look at *that* picture?'

'By no means: I found it out for myself.'

M. Paul's hair was shorn close as raven down, or I think it would have bristled on his head. Beginning now to perceive his drift, I had a certain pleasure in keeping cool, and working him up.

'Astounding insular audacity!' cried the Professor. 'Singulières femmes que ces Anglaises!'

'What is the matter, monsieur?'

'Matter! How dare you, a young person, sit coolly down, with the self-possession of a garçon, and look at *that* picture?'

'It is a very ugly picture, but I cannot at all see why I should not look at it.'

'Bon! bon! Speak no more of it. But you ought not to be here alone.'

'If, however, I have no society – no *party*, as you say? And then, what does it signify whether I am alone, or accompanied? nobody meddles with me.'

'Taisez-vous, et asseyez-vous là – là!' setting down a chair with emphasis in a particularly dull corner, before a series of most specially dreary 'cadres'.

'Mais, monsieur.'

'Mais, mademoiselle, asseyez-vous, et ne bougez pas – entendez-vous? jusqu'à ce qu'on vienne vous chercher, ou que je vous donne la permission.'

'Quel triste coin!' cried I, 'et quels laids tableaux!'

And 'laids', indeed, they were; being a set of four, denominated in the catalogue 'La vie d'une femme'. They were painted rather in a remarkable style – flat, dead, pale and formal. The first represented a 'Jeune Fille', coming out of a church-door, a missal in her hand, her dress very prim, her eyes cast down, her mouth pursed up – the image of a most villainous little precocious she-hypocrite. The second, a 'Mariée' with a long white veil, kneeling at a prie-dieu in her chamber, holding her hands plastered together, finger to finger, and showing the whites of her eyes in a most exasperating manner. The third, a 'Jeune Mère', hanging disconsolate over a clayey and puffy baby with a face like an unwholesome full moon. The fourth, a 'Veuve', being a black woman, holding by the hand a black little girl, and the twain studiously surveying an elegant French monument, set up in a corner of some Père la Chaise. All these four 'Anges' were grim and gray as burglars, and cold and vapid as ghosts. What women to live with! insincere, ill-humoured, bloodless, brainless nonentities! As bad in their way as the indolent gypsy-giantess, the Cleopatra, in hers.

It was impossible to keep one's attention long confined to these masterpieces, and so, by degrees, I veered round, and surveyed the gallery.

A perfect crowd of spectators was by this time gathered round the Lioness, from whose vicinage I had been banished; nearly half this crowd were ladies, but M. Paul afterwards told me, these were 'des dames', and it was quite proper for them to contemplate what no 'demoiselle' ought to glance at. I assured him plainly I could not agree in this doctrine, and did not see the sense of it; whereupon, with his usual absolutism, he merely requested my silence, and also, in the same breath, denounced my mingled rashness and ignorance. A more despotic little man than M. Paul never filled a professor's chair. I noticed, by the way, that he looked at the picture himself quite at his ease, and for a very long while: he did not, however, neglect to glance from time to time my way, in order, I suppose, to make sure that I was obeying orders, and not breaking bounds. By and by, he again accosted me.

'Had I not been ill?' he wished to know: 'he understood I had.'

'Yes, but I was now quite well.'

'Where had I spent the vacation?'

'Chiefly in the Rue Fossette; partly with Mme Bretton.'

'He had heard that I was left alone in the Rue Fossette; was that so?'

'Not quite alone: Marie Broc' (the crétin) 'was with me.'

He shrugged his shoulders; varied and contradictory expressions played rapidly over his countenance. Marie Broc was well known to M. Paul; he never gave a lesson in the third division (containing the least advanced pupils), that

she did not occasion in him a sharp conflict between antagonistic impressions. Her personal appearance, her repulsive manners, her often unmanageable disposition, irritated his temper, and inspired him with strong antipathy; a feeling he was too apt to conceive where his taste was offended or his will thwarted. On the other hand, her misfortunes constituted a strong claim on his forbearance and compassion – such a claim as it was not in his nature to deny; hence resulted almost daily drawn battles between impatience and disgust on the one hand, pity and a sense of justice on the other; in which, to his credit be it said, it was very seldom that the former feelings prevailed: when they did, however, M. Paul showed a phase of character which had its terrors. His passions were strong, his aversions and attachments alike vivid; the force he exerted in holding both in check, by no means mitigated an observer's sense of their vehemence. With such tendencies, it may well be supposed he often excited in ordinary minds fear and dislike; yet it was an error to fear him: nothing drove him so nearly frantic as the tremor of an apprehensive and distrustful spirit; nothing soothed him like confidence tempered with gentleness. To evince these sentiments, however, required a thorough comprehension of his nature; and his nature was of an order rarely comprehended.

'How did you get on with Marie Broc?' he asked, after some minutes' silence.

'Monsieur, I did my best; but it was terrible to be alone with her!'

'You have, then, a weak heart! You lack courage; and, perhaps, charity. Yours are not the qualities which might constitute a Sister of Mercy.'

[He was a religious little man, in his way: the self-denying and self-sacrificing part of the Catholic religion commanded the homage of his soul.]

'I don't know, indeed: I took as good care of her as I could; but when her aunt came to fetch her away, it was a great relief.'

'Ah! you are an egotist. There are women who have nursed hospitals-full of similar unfortunates. You could not do that?'

'Could Monsieur do it himself?'

'Women who are worthy the name ought infinitely to surpass our coarse, fallible, self-indulgent sex, in the power to perform such duties.'

'I washed her, I kept her clean, I fed her, I tried to amuse her; but she made mouths at me instead of speaking.'

'You think you did great things?'

'No; but as great as I *could* do.'

'Then limited are your powers, for in tending one idiot, you fell sick.'

'Not with that, monsieur; I had a nervous fever: my mind was ill.'

'Vraiment! Vous valez peu de chose. You are not cast in an heroic mould; your courage will not avail to sustain you in solitude; it merely gives you the temerity to gaze with sang-froid at pictures of Cleopatra.'

It would have been easy to show anger at the teasing, hostile tone of the little man. I had never been angry with him yet, however, and had no present disposition to begin.

'Cleopatra!' I repeated, quietly. 'Monsieur, too, has been looking at Cleopatra; what does he think of her?'

'Cela ne vaut rien,' he responded. 'Une femme superbe – une taille d'imperatrice, des formes de Junon, mais une personne dont je ne voudrais ni pour femme, ni pour fille, ni pour soeur. Aussi vous ne jeterez plus un seul coup d'oeil de sa côté.'

'But I have looked at her a great many times while Monsieur has been talking: I can see her quite well from this corner.'

'Turn to the wall and study your four pictures of a woman's life.'

'Excuse me, M. Paul; they are too hideous: but if you admire them, allow me to vacate my seat and leave you to their contemplation.'

'Mademoiselle,' he said, grimacing a half-smile, or what he intended for a smile, though it was but a grim and hurried manifestation. 'You nurslings of Protestantism astonish me. You unguarded Englishwomen walk calmly amidst red-hot ploughshares and escape burning. I believe, if some of you were thrown into Nebuchadnezzar's hottest furnace, you would issue forth untraversed by the smell of fire.'

'Will Monsieur have the goodness to move an inch to one side?'

'How! At what are you gazing now? You are not recognising an acquaintance amongst that group of jeunes gens?'

'I think so. Yes, I see there a person I know.'

In fact, I had caught a glimpse of a head too pretty to belong to any other than the redoubted Colonel de Hamal. What a very finished, highly-polished little pate it was! What a figure, so trim and natty! What womanish feet and hands! How daintily he held a glass to one of his optics! with what admiration he gazed upon the Cleopatra! and then, how engagingly he tittered and whispered a friend at his elbow! Oh, the man of sense! Oh, the refined gentleman of superior taste and tact! I observed him for about ten minutes, and perceived that he was exceedingly taken with this dusk and portly Venus of the Nile. So much was I interested in his bearing, so absorbed in divining his character by his looks and movements, I temporarily forgot M. Paul; in the interim a group came between that gentleman and me; or possibly his scruples might have received another and worse shock from my present abstraction, causing him to withdraw voluntarily: at any rate, when I again looked round, he was gone.

My eye, pursuant of the search, met not him, but another and dissimilar figure, well seen amidst the crowd, for the height as well as the port lent each its distinction. This way came Dr John, in visage, in shape, in hue, as unlike the dark, acerb, and caustic little professor, as the fruit of the Hesperides might be unlike the sloe in the wild thicket; as the high-couraged but tractable Arabian is unlike the rude and stubborn 'sheltie'. He was looking for me, but had not yet explored the corner where the schoolmaster had just put me. I remained quiet; yet another minute I would watch.

He approached de Hamal; he paused near him; I thought he had a pleasure in looking over his head; Dr Bretton, too, gazed on the Cleopatra. I doubt if it were to his taste: he did not simper like the little Count; his mouth looked fastidious, his eye cool; without demonstration he stepped aside, leaving room for others to approach. I saw now that he was waiting, and, rising, I joined him.

We took one turn round the gallery; with Graham it was very pleasant to take such a turn. I always liked dearly to hear what he had to say about either pictures or books; because, without pretending to be a connoisseur, he always spoke his thought, and that was sure to be fresh: very often it was also just and pithy. It was pleasant also to tell him some things he did not know – he listened so kindly, so teachably; unformalised by scruples lest so to bend his bright handsome head, to gather a woman's rather obscure and stammering explanation, should imperil the dignity of his manhood. And when he communicated information in return, it was with a lucid intelligence that left all his words clear graven on the memory: no explanation of his giving, no fact of his narrating, did I ever forget.

As we left the gallery, I asked him what he thought of the Cleopatra (after making him laugh by telling him how Professor Emanuel had sent me to the right-about, and taking him to see the sweet series of pictures recommended to my attention).

'Pooh!' said he, 'my mother is a better-looking woman. I heard some French fops, yonder, designating her as "le type du voluptueux"; if so, I can only say, "le voluptueux" is little to my liking. Compare that mulatto with Ginevra!'

<div align="center">

CHAPTER 20

## *The Concert*

</div>

One morning, Mrs Bretton, coming promptly into my room, desired me to open my drawers and show her my dresses; which I did, without a word.

'That will do,' said she, when she had turned them over. 'You must have a new one.'

She went out. She returned presently with a dressmaker. She had me measured. 'I mean,' said she, 'to follow my own taste, and to have my own way in this little matter.'

Two days after came home – a pink dress!

'That is not for me,' I said, hurriedly, feeling that I would almost as soon clothe myself in the costume of a Chinese lady of rank.

'We shall see whether it is for you or not,' rejoined my godmother, adding with her resistless decision: 'Mark my words. You will wear it this very evening.'

I thought I should not: I thought no human force should avail to put me into it. A pink dress! I knew it not. It knew not me. I had not proved it.

My godmother went on to decree that I was to go with her and Graham to a concert that same night: which concert, she explained, was a grand affair to be held in the large salle, or hall of the principal musical society. The most advanced of the pupils of the Conservatoire were to perform: it was to be followed by a lottery 'au bénéfice des pauvres'; and to crown all, the King, Queen, and Prince of Labassecour were to be present. Graham, in sending

tickets, had enjoined attention to costume as a compliment due to royalty: he also recommended punctual readiness by seven o'clock.

About six, I was ushered upstairs. Without any force at all, I found myself led and influenced by another's will, unconsulted, unpersuaded, quietly overruled. In short the pink dress went on, softened by some drapery of black lace. I was pronounced to be en grande tenue, and requested to look in the glass. I did so with some fear and trembling; with more fear and trembling, I turned away. Seven o'clock struck; Dr Bretton was come; my godmother and I went down. *She* was clad in brown velvet; as I walked in her shadow, how I envied her those folds of grave, dark majesty! Graham stood in the drawing-room doorway.

'*I do* hope he will not think I have been decking myself out to draw attention,' was my uneasy aspiration.

'Here, Lucy, are some flowers,' said he, giving me a bouquet. He took no further notice of my dress than was conveyed in a kind smile and satisfied nod, which calmed at once my sense of shame and fear of ridicule. For the rest, the dress was made with extreme simplicity, guiltless of flounce or furbelow; it was but the light fabric and bright tint which scared me, and since Graham found in it nothing absurd, my own eye consented soon to become reconciled.

I suppose people who go every night to places of public amusement, can hardly enter into the fresh gala feeling with which an opera or a concert is enjoyed by those for whom it is a rarity. I am not sure that I expected great pleasure from the concert, having but a very vague notion of its nature, but I liked the drive there well. The snug comfort of the close carriage on a cold though fine night, the pleasure of setting out with companions so cheerful and friendly, the sight of the stars glinting fitfully through the trees as we rolled along the avenue; then the freer burst of the night-sky when we issued forth to the open chaussée, the passage through the city gates, the lights there burning, the guards there posted, the pretence of inspection to which we there submitted, and which amused us so much – all these small matters had for me, in their novelty, a peculiar exhilarating charm. How much of it lay in the atmosphere of friendship diffused about me, I know not: Dr John and his mother were both in their finest mood, contending animatedly with each other the whole way, and as frankly kind to me as if I had been of their kin.

Our way lay through some of the best streets of Villette, streets brightly lit, and far more lively now than at high noon. How brilliant seemed the shops! How glad, gay, and abundant flowed the tide of life along the broad pavement! While I looked, the thought of the Rue Fossette came across me – of the walled-in garden and school-house, and of the dark, vast 'classes', where, as at this very hour, it was my wont to wander all solitary, gazing at the stars through the high, blindless windows, and listening to the distant voice of the reader in the refectory, monotonously exercised upon the 'lecture pieuse'. Thus must I soon again listen and wander; and this shadow of the future stole with timely sobriety across the radiant present.

By this time we had got into a current of carriages all tending in one direction, and soon the front of a great illuminated building blazed before us. Of

what I should see within this building, I had, as before intimated, but an imperfect idea; for no place of public entertainment had it ever been my lot to enter yet.

We alighted under a portico where there was a great bustle and a great crowd, but I do not distinctly remember further details, until I found myself mounting a majestic staircase wide and easy of ascent, deeply and softly carpeted with crimson, leading up to great doors closed solemnly, and whose panels were also crimson-clothed.

I hardly noticed by what magic these doors were made to roll back – Dr John managed these points; roll back they did, however, and within was disclosed a hall – grand, wide, and high, whose sweeping circular walls, and domed hollow ceiling, seemed to me all dead gold (thus with nice art was it stained), relieved by cornicing, fluting and garlandry, either bright, like gold burnished, or snow-white, like alabaster, or white and gold mingled in wreaths of gilded leaves and spotless lilies: wherever drapery hung, wherever carpets were spread, or cushions placed, the sole colour employed was deep crimson. Pendant from the dome, flamed a mass that dazzled me – a mass, I thought, of rock-crystal, sparkling with facets, streaming with drops, ablaze with stars, and gorgeously tinged with dews of gems dissolved, or fragments of rainbows shivered. It was only the chandelier, reader, but for me it seemed the work of eastern genii: I almost looked to see if a huge, dark cloudy hand – that of the Slave of the Lamp – were not hovering in the lustrous and perfumed atmosphere of the cupola, guarding its wondrous treasure.

We moved on – I was not at all conscious whither – but at some turn we suddenly encountered another party approaching from the opposite direction. I just now see that group, as it flashed upon me for one moment. A handsome middle-aged lady in dark velvet; a gentleman who might be her son – the best face, the finest figure, I thought, I had ever seen; a third person in a pink dress and black lace mantle.

I noted them all – the third person as well as the other two – and for the fraction of a moment, believed them all strangers, thus receiving an impartial impression of their appearance. But the impression was hardly felt and not fixed, before the consciousness that I faced a great mirror, filling a compartment between two pillars, dispelled it: the party was our own party. Thus for the first, and perhaps only time in my life, I enjoyed the 'giftie' of seeing myself as others see me. No need to dwell on the result. It brought a jar of discord, a pang of regret; it was not flattering, yet, after all, I ought to be thankful: it might have been worse.

At last, we were seated in places commanding a good general view of that vast and dazzling, but warm and cheerful hall. Already it was filled, and filled with a splendid assemblage. I do not know that the women were very beautiful, but their dresses were so perfect; and foreigners, even such as are ungraceful in domestic privacy, seem to possess the art of appearing graceful in public: however blunt and boisterous those everyday and home movements connected with peignoir and papillotes, there is a slide, a bend, a carriage of the head and

arms, a mien of the mouth and eyes, kept nicely in reserve for gala use – always brought out with the grande toilette, and duly put on with the 'parure'.

Some fine forms there were here and there, models of a peculiar style of beauty; a style, I think, never seen in England: a solid, firm-set, sculptural style. These shapes have no angles: a caryatid in marble is almost as flexible; a Phidian goddess is not more perfect in a certain still and stately sort. They have such features as the Dutch painters give to their madonnas: low-country classic features, regular but round, straight but stolid; and for their depth of expression-less calm, of passionless peace, a polar snow-field could alone offer a type. Women of this order need no ornament, and they seldom wear any; the smooth hair, closely braided, supplies a sufficient contrast to the smoother cheek and brow; the dress cannot be too simple; the rounded arm and perfect neck require neither bracelet nor chain.

With one of these beauties I once had the honour and rapture to be perfectly acquainted: the inert force of the deep, settled love she bore herself, was wonderful; it could only be surpassed by her proud impotency to care for any other living thing. Of blood, her cool veins conducted no flow; placid lymph filled and almost obstructed her arteries.

Such a Juno as I have described, sat full in our view – a sort of mark for all eyes, and quite conscious that so she was, but proof to the magnetic influence of gaze or glance: cold, rounded, blonde, and beauteous, as the white column, capitalled with gilding, which rose at her side.

Observing that Dr John's attention was much drawn towards her, I entreated him in a low voice 'for the love of heaven to shield well his heart. You need not fall in love with *that* lady,' I said, 'because, I tell you beforehand, you might die at her feet, and she would not love you again.'

'Very well,' said he, 'and how do you know that the spectacle of her grand insensibility might not with me be the strongest stimulus to homage? The sting of desperation is, I think, a wonderful irritant to my emotions: but' (shrugging his shoulders) 'you know nothing about these things; I'll address myself to my mother. Mama, I'm in a dangerous way. '

'As if that interested me!' said Mrs Bretton.

'Alas! the cruelty of my lot!' responded her son. 'Never man had a more unsentimental mother than mine: she never seems to think that such a calamity can befall her as a daughter-in-law.'

'If I don't, it is not for want of having that same calamity held over my head: you have threatened me with it for the last ten years. "Mama, I am going to be married soon!" was the cry before you were well out of jackets.'

'But, mother, one of these days it will be realised. All of a sudden, when you think you are most secure, I shall go forth like Jacob or Esau, or any other patriarch, and take me a wife: perhaps of these which are of the daughters of the land.'

'At your peril, John Graham! that is all.'

'This mother of mine means me to be an old bachelor. What a jealous old lady it is! But now just look at that splendid creature in the pale blue satin dress,

and hair of paler brown, with "reflets satinés" as those of her robe. Would you not feel proud, mama, if I were to bring that goddess home someday, and introduce her to you as Mrs Bretton, junior?'

'You will bring no goddess to La Terrasse: that little chateau will not contain two mistresses; especially if the second be of the height, bulk, and circumference of that mighty doll in wood and wax, and kid and satin.'

'Mama, she would fill your blue chair so admirably!'

'Fill my chair? I defy the foreign usurper! a rueful chair should it be for her: but hush, John Graham! Hold your tongue, and use your eyes.'

During the above skirmish, the hall which, I had thought, seemed full at our entrance, continued to admit party after party, until the semicircle before the stage presented one dense mass of heads, sloping from floor to ceiling. The stage, too, or rather the wide temporary platform, larger than any stage, desert half an hour since, was now overflowing with life; round two grand pianos, placed about the centre, a white flock of young girls, the pupils of the Conservatoire, had noiselessly poured. I had noticed their gathering, while Graham and his mother were engaged in discussing the belle in blue satin, and had watched with interest the process of arraying and marshalling them. Two gentlemen, in each of whom I recognised an acquaintance, officered this virgin troop. One, an artistic looking man, bearded, and with long hair, was a noted pianist, and also the first music teacher in Villette; he attended twice a week at Mme Beck's pensionnat, to give lessons to the few pupils whose parents were rich enough to allow their daughters the privilege of his instructions; his name was M. Josef Emanuel, and he was half-brother to M. Paul: which potent personage was now visible in the person of the second gentleman.

M. Paul amused me; I smiled to myself as I watched him, he seemed so thoroughly in his element – standing conspicuous in presence of a wide and grand assemblage, arranging, restraining, over-aweing about one hundred young ladies. He was, too, so perfectly in earnest – so energetic, so intent, and, above all, so absolute: and yet what business had he there? What had he to do with music or the Conservatoire – he who could hardly distinguish one note from another? I knew that it was his love of display and authority which had brought him there – a love not offensive, only because so naïve. It presently became obvious that his brother, M. Josef, was as much under his control as were the girls themselves. Never was such a little hawk of a man as that M. Paul! Ere long, some noted singers and musicians dawned upon the platform: as these stars rose, the comet-like professor set. Insufferable to him were all notorieties and celebrities: where he could not outshine, he fled.

And now all was prepared: but one compartment of the hall waited to be filled – a compartment covered with crimson, like the grand staircase and doors, furnished with stuffed and cushioned benches, ranged on each side of two red regal chairs, placed solemnly under a canopy.

A signal was given, the doors rolled back, the assembly stood up, the orchestra burst out, and, to the welcome of a choral burst, enter the King, the Queen, the Court of Labassecour.

Till then, I had never set eyes on living king or queen; it may consequently be conjectured how I strained my powers of vision to take in these specimens of European royalty. By whomsoever majesty is beheld for the first time, there will always be experienced a vague surprise bordering on disappointment, that the same does not appear seated, en permanence, on a throne, bonneted with a crown, and furnished, as to the hand, with a sceptre. Looking out for a king and queen, and seeing only a middle-aged soldier and a rather young lady, I felt half cheated, half pleased.

Well do I recall that King – a man of fifty, a little bowed, a little gray: there was no face in all that assembly which resembled his. I had never read, never been told anything of his nature or his habits; and at first the strong hieroglyphics graven as with iron stylet on his brow, round his eyes, beside his mouth, puzzled and baffled instinct. Ere long, however, if I did not *know*, at least *I felt*, the meaning of those characters written without hand. There sat a silent sufferer – a nervous, melancholy man. Those eyes had looked on the visits of a certain ghost – had long waited the comings and goings of that strangest spectre, Hypochondria. Perhaps he saw her now on that stage, over against him, amidst all that brilliant throng. Hypochondria has that wont, to rise in the midst of thousands – dark as Doom, pale as Malady, and well nigh strong as Death. Her comrade and victim thinks to be happy one moment – 'Not so,' says she; 'I come.' And she freezes the blood in his heart, and beclouds the light in his eye.

Some might say it was the foreign crown pressing the King's brows which bent them to that peculiar and painful fold; some might quote the effects of early bereavement. Something there might be of both these; but these as embittered by that darkest foe of humanity – constitutional melancholy. The Queen, his wife, knew this: it seemed to me, the reflection of her husband's grief lay, a subduing shadow, on her own benignant face. A mild, thoughtful, graceful woman that princess seemed; not beautiful, not at all like the women of solid charms and marble feelings described a page or two since. Hers was a somewhat slender shape; her features, though distinguished enough, were too suggestive of reigning dynasties and royal lines to give unqualified pleasure. The expression clothing that profile was agreeable in the present instance; but you could not avoid connecting it with remembered effigies, where similar lines appeared, under phase ignoble; feeble, or sensual, or cunning, as the case might be. The Queen's eye, however, was her own; and pity, goodness, sweet sympathy, blessed it with divinest light. She moved no sovereign, but a lady – kind, loving, elegant. Her little son, the Prince of Labassecour, and young Duc de Dindonneau, accompanied her: he leaned on his mother's knee; and, ever and anon, in the course of that evening, I saw her observant of the monarch at her side, conscious of his beclouded abstraction, and desirous to rouse him from it by drawing his attention to their son. She often bent her head to listen to the boy's remarks, and would then smilingly repeat them to his sire. The moody King started, listened, smiled, but invariably relapsed as soon as his good angel ceased speaking. Full mournful and significant was that spectacle! Not the less so because, both for the aristocracy and the honest bourgeoisie of Labassecour,

its peculiarity seemed to be wholly invisible: I could not discover that one soul present was either struck or touched.

With the King and Queen had entered their court, comprising two or three foreign ambassadors; and with them came the élite of the foreigners then resident in Villette. These took possession of the crimson benches; the ladies were seated; most of the men remained standing: their sable rank, lining the background, looked like a dark foil to the splendour displayed in front. Nor was this splendour without varying light and shade and gradation: the middle distance was filled with matrons in velvets and satins, in plumes and gems; the benches in the foreground, to the Queen's right hand, seemed devoted exclusively to young girls, the flower – perhaps, I should rather say, the bud – of Villette aristocracy. Here were no jewels, no head-dresses, no velvet pile or silken sheen: purity, simplicity, and aërial grace reigned in that virgin band. Young heads simply braided, and fair forms (I was going to write *sylph* forms, but that would have been quite untrue: several of these 'jeunes filles', who had not numbered more than sixteen or seventeen years, boasted contours as robust and solid as those of a stout Englishwoman of five-and-twenty) – fair forms robed in white, or pale rose, or placid blue, suggested thoughts of heaven and angels. I knew a couple, at least, of these 'rose et blanches' specimens of humanity. Here was a pair of Mme Beck's late pupils – Mesdemoiselles Mathilde and Angélique: pupils, who, during their last year at school, ought to have been in the first class, but whose brains had never got them beyond the second division. In English, they had been under my own charge, and hard work it was to get them to translate rationally a page of *The Vicar of Wakefield*. Also during three months I had one of them for my vis-à-vis at table, and the quantity of household bread, butter, and stewed fruit, she would habitually consume at 'second déjeuner' was a real world's wonder – to be exceeded only by the fact of her actually pocketing slices she could not eat. Here be truths – wholesome truths, too.

I knew another of these seraphs – the prettiest, or, at any rate, the least demure and hypocritical-looking of the lot: she was seated by the daughter of an English peer, also an honest, though haughty-looking girl; both had entered in the suite of the British embassy. She (i.e. my acquaintance) had a slight pliant figure, not at all like the forms of the foreign damsels; her hair, too, was not close-braided, like a shell or a skull-cap of satin; it looked *like* hair, and waved from her head, long, curled, and flowing. She chatted away volubly, and seemed full of a light-headed sort of satisfaction with herself and her position. I did not look at Dr Bretton; but I knew that he, too, saw Ginevra Fanshawe: he had become so quiet, he answered so briefly his mother's remarks, he so often suppressed a sigh. Why should he sigh? He had confessed a taste for the pursuit of love under difficulties; here was full gratification for that taste. His lady-love beamed upon him from a sphere above his own: he could not come near her; he was not certain that he could win from her a look. I watched to see if she would so far favour him. Our seat was not far from the crimson benches; we must inevitably be seen thence, by eyes so quick and roving as Miss Fanshawe's, and

very soon those optics of hers were upon us: at least, upon Dr and Mrs Bretton. I kept rather in the shade and out of sight, not wishing to be immediately recognised: she looked quite steadily at Dr John, and then she raised a glass to examine his mother; a minute or two afterwards she laughingly whispered her neighbour; upon the performance commencing, her rambling attention was attracted to the platform.

On the concert I need not dwell; the reader would not care to have my impressions thereanent: and, indeed, it would not be worth while to record them, as they were the impressions of an ignorance crasse. The young ladies of the Conservatoire, being very much frightened, made rather a tremulous exhibition on the two grand pianos. M. Josef Emanuel stood by them while they played; but he had not the tact or influence of his kinsman, who, under similar circumstances, would certainly have *compelled* pupils of his to demean themselves with heroism and self-possession. M. Paul would have placed the hysteric debutantes between two fires – terror of the audience, and terror of himself – and would have inspired them with the courage of desperation, by making the latter terror incomparably the greater: M. Josef could not do this.

Following the white muslin pianists came a fine, full-grown, sulky lady in white satin. She sang. Her singing just affected me like the tricks of a conjuror: I wondered how she did it – how she made her voice run up and down, and cut such marvellous capers; but a simple Scotch melody, played by a rude street minstrel, has often moved me more deeply.

Afterwards stepped forth a gentleman, who, bending his body a good deal in the direction of the King and Queen, and frequently approaching his white-gloved hand to the region of his heart, vented a bitter outcry against a certain 'fausse Isabelle'. I thought he seemed especially to solicit the Queen's sympathy; but, unless I am egregiously mistaken, her Majesty lent her attention rather with the calm of courtesy than the earnestness of interest. This gentleman's state of mind was very harrowing, and I was glad when he wound up his musical exposition of the same.

Some rousing choruses struck me as the best part of the evening's entertainment. There were present deputies from all the best provincial choral societies; genuine, barrel-shaped, native Labassecouriens. These worthies gave voice without mincing the matter: their hearty exertions had at least this good result – the ear drank thence a satisfying sense of power.

Through the whole performance – timid instrumental duets, conceited vocal solos, sonorous, brass-lunged choruses – my attention gave but one eye and one ear to the stage, the other being permanently retained in the service of Dr Bretton: I could not forget him, nor cease to question how he was feeling, what he was thinking, whether he was amused or the contrary. At last he spoke.

'And how do you like it all, Lucy? You are very quiet,' he said, in his own cheerful tone.

'I am quiet,' I said, 'because I am so very, *very* much interested: not merely with the music, but with everything about me.'

He then proceeded to make some further remarks, with so much equanimity

and composure that I began to think he had really not seen what I had seen, and I whispered – 'Miss Fanshawe is here: have you noticed her?'

'Oh, yes! and I observed that you noticed her too.'

'Is she come with Mrs Cholmondeley, do you think?'

'Mrs Cholmondeley is there with a very grand party. Yes: Ginevra was in *her* train; and Mrs Cholmondeley was in Lady —'s train, who was in the Queen's train. If this were not one of the compact little minor European courts, whose very formalities are little more imposing than familiarities, and whose gala grandeur is but homeliness in Sunday array, it would sound all very fine.'

'Ginevra saw you, I think?'

'So do I think so. I have had my eye on her several times since you withdrew yours; and I have had the honour of witnessing a little spectacle which you were spared.'

I did not ask what: I waited voluntary information; which was presently given.

'Miss Fanshawe,' he said, 'has a companion with her – a lady of rank. I happen to know Lady Sara by sight; her noble mother has called me in professionally. She is a proud girl, but not in the least insolent, and I doubt whether Ginevra will have gained ground in her estimation by making a butt of her neighbours.'

'What neighbours?'

'Merely myself and my mother. As to me it is all very natural: nothing, I suppose, can be fairer game than the young bourgeois doctor; but my mother? I never saw her ridiculed before. Do you know, the curling lip, and sarcastically levelled glass thus directed, gave me a most curious sensation?'

'Think nothing of it, Dr John: it is not worth while. If Ginevra were in a giddy mood, as she is eminently tonight, she would make no scruple of laughing at that mild, pensive Queen, or that melancholy King. She is not actuated by malevolence, but sheer, heedless folly. To a feather-brained schoolgirl nothing is sacred.'

'But you forget: I have not been accustomed to look on Miss Fanshawe in the light of a feather-brained schoolgirl. Was she not my divinity – the angel of my career?'

'Hem! There was your mistake.'

'To speak the honest truth, without any false rant or assumed romance, there actually was a moment, six months ago, when I thought her divine. Do you remember our conversation about the presents? I was not quite open with you in discussing that subject: the warmth with which you took it up amused me. By way of having the full benefit of your lights, I allowed you to think me more in the dark than I really was. It was that test of the presents which first proved Ginevra mortal. Still her beauty retained its fascination: three days – three hours ago, I was very much her slave. As she passed me tonight, triumphant in beauty, my emotions did her homage; but for one luckless sneer, I should yet be the humblest of her servants. She might have scoffed at me, and, while wounding, she would not soon have alienated me: through myself, she could not in ten years have done what, in a moment, she has done through my mother.'

He held his peace awhile. Never before had I seen so much fire and so little sunshine in Dr John's blue eye, as just now.

'Lucy,' he recommenced, 'look well at my mother, and say, without fear or favour, in what light she now appears to you.'

'As she always does – an English middle-class gentlewoman; well, though gravely dressed, habitually independent of pretence, constitutionally composed and cheerful.'

'So she seems to me – bless her! The merry may laugh *with* mama, but the weak only will laugh *at* her. She shall not be ridiculed, with my consent at least; nor without my – my scorn – my antipathy – my –'

He stopped: and it was time – for he was getting excited – more it seemed than the occasion warranted. I did not then know that he had witnessed double cause for dissatisfaction with Miss Fanshawe. The glow of his complexion, the expansion of his nostril, the bold curve which disdain gave his well-cut under lip, showed him in a new and striking phase. Yet the rare passion of the constitutionally suave and serene is not a pleasant spectacle; nor did I like the sort of vindictive thrill which passed through his strong young frame.

'Do I frighten you, Lucy?' he asked.

'I cannot tell why you are so very angry.'

'For this reason,' he muttered in my ear: 'Ginevra is neither a pure angel nor a pure-minded woman.'

'Nonsense! you exaggerate: she has no great harm in her.'

'Too much for me. *I* can see where *you* are blind. Now, dismiss the subject. Let me amuse myself by teasing mama: I will assert that she is flagging. Mama, pray rouse yourself.'

'John, I will certainly rouse you, if you are not better conducted. Will you and Lucy be silent, that I may hear the singing?'

They were then thundering in a chorus, under cover of which all the previous dialogue had taken place.

'*You* hear the singing, mama! Now, I will wager my studs – which are genuine – against your paste brooch –'

'My paste brooch, Graham? Profane boy! you know that it is a stone of value.'

'Oh! that is one of your superstitions: you were cheated in the business.'

'I am cheated in fewer things than you imagine. How do you happen to be acquainted with young ladies of the court, John? I have observed two of them pay you no small attention during the last half hour.'

'I wish you would not observe them.'

'Why not? Because one of them satirically levels her eyeglass at me? She is a pretty, silly girl: but are you apprehensive that her titter will discomfit the old lady?'

'The sensible, admirable old lady! Mother, you are better to me than ten wives yet.'

'Don't be demonstrative, John, or I shall faint, and you will have to carry me out; and if that burden were laid upon you, you would reverse your last speech, and exclaim, "Mother, ten wives could hardly be worse to me than you are!"'

The concert over, the Lottery 'au bénéfice des Pauvres' came next: the interval between was one of general relaxation, and the pleasantest imaginable stir and commotion. The white flock was cleared from the platform; a busy throng of gentlemen crowded it instead, making arrangements for the drawing; and amongst these – the busiest of all – reappeared that certain well-known form, not tall but active, alive with the energy and movement of three tall men. How M. Paul did work! How he issued directions, and at the same time, set his own shoulder to the wheel! Half a dozen assistants were at his beck to remove the pianos, etc.; no matter, he must add to their strength his own. The redundancy of his alertness was half-vexing, half-ludicrous: in my mind I both disapproved and derided most of this fuss. Yet, in the midst of prejudice and annoyance, I could not, while watching, avoid perceiving a certain not disagreeable naïveté in all he did and said; nor could I be blind to certain vigorous characteristics of his physiognomy, rendered conspicuous now by the contrast with a throng of tamer faces: the deep, intent keenness of his eye, the power of his forehead – pale, broad, and full – the mobility of his most flexible mouth. He lacked the calm of force, but its movement and its fire he signally possessed.

Meantime the whole hall was astir; most people rose and remained standing, for a change; some walked about, all talked and laughed. The crimson compartment presented a peculiarly animated scene. The long cloud of gentlemen, breaking into fragments, mixed with the rainbow line of ladies; two or three officer-like men approached the King and conversed with him. The Queen, leaving her chair, glided along the rank of young ladies, who all stood up as she passed; and to each in turn I saw her vouchsafe some token of kindness – a gracious word, look or smile. To the two pretty English girls, Lady Sara and Ginevra Fanshawe, she addressed several sentences; as she left them, both, and especially the latter, seemed to glow all over with gratification. They were afterwards accosted by several ladies, and a little circle of gentlemen gathered round them; amongst these – the nearest to Ginevra – stood the Count de Hamal.

'This room is stiflingly hot;' said Dr Bretton, rising with sudden impatience. 'Lucy – mother – will you come a moment to the fresh air?'

'Go with him Lucy;' said Mrs Bretton. 'I would rather keep my seat.'

Willingly would I have kept mine also, but Graham's desire must take precedence of my own; I accompanied him.

We found the night-air keen; or at least, I did: he did not seem to feel it; but it was very still, and the star-sown sky spread cloudless. I was wrapped in a fur shawl. We took some turns on the pavement; in passing under a lamp, Graham encountered my eye.

'You look pensive, Lucy: is it on my account?'

'I was only fearing that you were grieved.'

'Not at all: so be of good cheer – as I am. Whenever I die, Lucy, my persuasion is that it will not be of heart complaint. I may be stung, I may seem to droop for a time, but no pain or malady of sentiment has yet gone through my whole system. You have always seen me cheerful at home?'

'Generally.'

'I am glad she laughed at my mother. I would not give the old lady for a dozen beauties. That sneer did me all the good in the world. Thank you, Miss Fanshawe!' And he lifted his hat from his waved locks, and made a mock reverence.

'Yes,' he said, 'I thank her. She has made me feel that nine parts in ten of my heart have always been sound as a bell, and the tenth bled from a mere puncture: a lancet-prick that will heal in a trice.'

'You are angry just now, heated and indignant; you will think and feel differently tomorrow.'

'*I* heated and indignant! You don't know me. On the contrary, the heat is gone: I am cool as the night – which, by the way, may be too cool for you. We will go back.'

'Dr John – this is a sudden change.'

'Not it: or if it be, there are good reasons for it – two good reasons: I have told you one. But now let us re-enter.'

We did not easily regain our seats; the lottery was begun, and all was excited confusion; crowds blocked the sort of corridor along which we had to pass: it was necessary to pause for a time. Happening to glance round – indeed I half fancied I heard my name pronounced – I saw quite near, the ubiquitous, the inevitable M. Paul. He was looking at me gravely and intently: at me, or rather, at my pink dress – sardonic comment on which gleamed in his eye. Now it was his habit to indulge in strictures on the dress, both of the teachers and pupils, at Mme Beck's – a habit which the former, at least, held to be an offensive impertinence: as yet I had not suffered from it – my sombre daily attire not being calculated to attract notice. I was in no mood to permit any new encroachment tonight: rather than accept his banter, I would ignore his presence, and accordingly steadily turned my face to the sleeve of Dr John's coat: finding in that same black sleeve a prospect more redolent of pleasure and comfort, more genial, more friendly, I thought, than was offered by the dark little Professor's unlovely visage. Dr John seemed unconsciously to sanction the preference by looking down and saying in his kind voice, 'Ay, keep close to my side, Lucy: these crowding burghers are no respecters of persons.'

I could not, however, be true to myself. Yielding to some influence, mesmeric or otherwise – an influence unwelcome, displeasing, but effective – I again glanced round to see if M. Paul was gone. No, there he stood on the same spot, looking still, but with a changed eye; he had penetrated my thought and read my wish to shun him. The mocking but not ill-humoured gaze was turned to a swarthy frown, and when I bowed, with a view to conciliation, I got only the stiffest and sternest of nods in return.

'Whom have you made angry, Lucy?' whispered Dr Bretton, smiling. 'Who is that savage-looking friend of yours?'

'One of the professors at Mme Beck's: a very cross little man.'

'He looks mighty cross just now: what have you done to him? What is it all about? Ah, Lucy, Lucy! tell me the meaning of this.'

'No mystery, I assure you. M. Emanuel is very exigent, and because I looked

at your coat sleeve, instead of curtseying and dipping to him, he thinks I have failed in respect.'

'The little –' began Dr John: I know not what more he would have added, for at that moment I was nearly thrown down amongst the feet of the crowd. M. Paul had rudely pushed past, and was elbowing his way with such utter disregard to the convenience and security of all round him, that a very uncomfortable pressure was the consequence.

'I think he is what he himself would call "méchant',' said Dr Bretton. I thought so, too.

Slowly and with difficulty we made our way along the passage, and at last regained our seats. The drawing of the lottery lasted nearly an hour; it was an animating and amusing scene; and as we each held tickets, we shared in the alternations of hope and fear raised by each turn of the wheel. Two little girls, of five and six years old, drew the numbers; and the prizes were duly proclaimed from the platform. These prizes were numerous, though of small value. It so fell out, that Dr John and I each gained one: mine was a cigar-case, his a lady's head-dress – a most airy sort of blue and silver turban, with a streamer of plumage on one side, like a light snowy cloud. He was excessively anxious to make an exchange; but I could not be brought to hear reason, and to this day I keep my cigar-case: it serves, when I look at it, to remind me of old times, and one happy evening.

Dr John, for his part, held his turban at arm's length between his finger and thumb, and looked at it with a mixture of reverence and embarrassment highly provocative of laughter. The contemplation over, he was about coolly to deposit the delicate fabric on the ground between his feet; he seemed to have no shadow of an idea of the treatment or stowage it ought to receive: if his mother had not come to the rescue, I think he would finally have crushed it under his arm like an opera-hat; she restored it to the band-box whence it had issued.

Graham was quite cheerful all the evening, and his cheerfulness seemed natural and unforced. His demeanour, his look, is not easily described; there was something in it peculiar, and, in its way, original. I read in it no common mastery of the passions, and a fund of deep and healthy strength which, without any exhausting effort, bore down Disappointment and extracted her fang. His manner now, reminded me of qualities I had noticed in him when professionally engaged amongst the poor, the guilty, and the suffering, in the Basse-Ville: he looked at once determined, enduring, and sweet-tempered. Who could help liking him? *He* betrayed no weakness which harassed all your feelings with considerations as to how its faltering must be propped; from him broke no irritability which startled calm and quenched mirth; *his* lips let fall no caustic that burned to the bone; *his* eye shot no morose shafts that went cold and rusty and venomed through your heart: beside him was rest and refuge – around him, fostering sunshine.

And yet he had neither forgiven nor forgotten Miss Fanshawe. Once angered, I doubt if Dr Bretton were to be soon propitiated – once alienated, whether he were ever to be reclaimed. He looked at her more than once; not stealthily or

humbly, but with a movement of hardy, open observation. De Hamal was now a fixture beside her; Mrs Cholmondeley sat near, and they and she were wholly absorbed in the discourse, mirth, and excitement, with which the crimson seats were as much astir as any plebeian part of the hall. In the course of some apparently animated discussion, Ginevra once or twice lifted her hand and arm; a handsome bracelet gleamed upon the latter. I saw that its gleam flickered in Dr John's eye – quickening therein a derisive, ireful sparkle; he laughed: 'I think,' he said, 'I will lay my turban on my wonted altar of offerings; there, at any rate, it would be certain to find favour: no grisette has a more facile faculty of acceptance. Strange! for after all, I know she is a girl of family.'

'But you don't know her education, Dr John,' said I. 'Tossed about all her life from one foreign school to another, she may justly proffer the plea of ignorance in extenuation of most of her faults. And then, from what she says, I believe her father and mother were brought up much as she has been brought up.'

'I always understood she had no fortune; and once I had pleasure in the thought,' said he.

'She tells me,' I answered, 'that they are poor at home; she always speaks quite candidly on such points: you never find her lying, as these foreigners will often lie. Her parents have a large family: they occupy such a station and possess such connections as, in their opinion, demand display; stringent necessity of circumstances and inherent thoughtlessness of disposition combined, have engendered reckless unscrupulousness as to how they obtain the means of sustaining a good appearance. This is the state of things, and the only state of things she has seen from childhood upwards.'

'I believe it – and I thought to mould her to something better: but, Lucy, to speak the plain truth, I have felt a new thing tonight, in looking at her and de Hamal. I felt it before noticing the impertinence directed at my mother. I saw a look interchanged between them immediately after their entrance, which threw a most unwelcome light on my mind.'

'How do you mean? You have long been aware of the flirtation they keep up?'

'Ay, flirtation! That might be an innocent girlish wile to lure on the true lover; but what I refer to was not flirtation: it was a look marking mutual and secret understanding – it was neither girlish nor innocent. No woman, were she as beautiful as Aphrodite, who could give or receive such a glance, shall ever be sought in marriage by me: I would rather wed a paysanne in a short petticoat and high cap – and be sure that she was honest.'

I could not help smiling. I felt sure he now exaggerated the case: Ginevra, I was certain, was honest enough, with all her giddiness. I told him so. He shook his head, and said he would not be the man to trust her with his honour.

'The only thing,' said I, 'with which you may safely trust her. She would unscrupulously damage a husband's purse and property, recklessly try his patience and temper: I don't think she would breathe, or let another breathe, on his honour.'

'You are becoming her advocate,' said he. 'Do you wish me to resume my old chains?'

'No: I am glad to see you free, and trust that free you will long remain. Yet be, at the same time, just.'

'I am so: just as Rhadamanthus, Lucy. When once I am thoroughly estranged, I cannot help being severe. But look! the King and Queen are rising. I like that Queen: she has a sweet countenance. Mama, too, is excessively tired; we shall never get the old lady home if we stay longer.'

'I tired, John?' cried Mrs Bretton, looking at least as animated and as wide-awake as her son, 'I would undertake to sit you out yet: leave us both here till morning, and we should see which would look the most jaded by sunrise.'

'I should not like to try the experiment; for, in truth, mama, you are the most unfading of evergreens, and the freshest of matrons. It must then be on the plea of your son's delicate nerves and fragile constitution that I found a petition for our speedy adjournment.'

'Indolent young man! You wish you were in bed, no doubt; and I suppose you must be humoured. There is Lucy, too, looking quite done up. For shame, Lucy! At your age, a week of evenings-out would not have made me a shade paler. Come away, both of you; and you may laugh at the old lady as much as you please, but, for my part, I shall take charge of the band-box and turban.'

Which she did accordingly. I offered to relieve her, but was shaken off with kindly contempt: my godmother opined that I had enough to do to take care of myself. Not standing on ceremony now, in the midst of the gay 'confusion worse confounded' succeeding to the King and Queen's departure, Mrs Bretton preceded us, and promptly made us a lane through the crowd. Graham followed, apostrophising his mother as the most flourishing grisette it had ever been his good fortune to see charged with carriage of a band-box; he also desired me to mark her affection for the sky-blue turban, and announced his conviction that she intended one day to wear it.

The night was now very cold and very dark, but with little delay we found the carriage. Soon we were packed in it, as warm and as snug as at a fireside; and the drive home was, I think, still pleasanter than the drive to the concert. Pleasant it was, even though the coachman – having spent in the shop of a 'marchand de vin' a portion of the time we passed at the concert – drove us along the dark and solitary chaussée far past the turn leading down to La Terrasse; we, who were occupied in talking and laughing, not noticing the aberration – till at last, Mrs Bretton intimated that though she had always thought the chateau a retired spot, she did not know it was situated at the world's end, as she declared seemed now to be the case, for she believed we had been an hour and a half en route, and had not yet taken the turn down the avenue.

Then Graham looked out, and perceiving only dim-spread fields, with unfamiliar rows of pollards and limes ranged along their else invisible sunk-fences, began to conjecture how matters were, and calling a halt and descending, he mounted the box and took the reins himself. Thanks to him, we arrived safe at home about an hour and a half beyond our time.

Martha had not forgotten us; a cheerful fire was burning, and a neat supper spread in the dining-room: we were glad of both. The winter dawn was actually

breaking before we gained our chambers. I took off my pink dress and lace mantle with happier feelings than I had experienced in putting them on. Not all, perhaps, who had shone brightly arrayed at that concert could say the same; for not all had been satisfied with friendship – with its calm comfort and modest hope.

<div style="text-align:center">

CHAPTER 21

*Reaction*

</div>

Yet three days, and then I must go back to the Pensionnat. I almost numbered the moments of these days upon the clock; fain would I have retarded their flight; but they glided by while I watched them: they were already gone while I yet feared their departure.

'Lucy will not leave us today,' said Mrs Bretton, coaxingly, at breakfast; 'she knows we can procure a second respite.'

'I would not ask for one if I might have it for a word,' said I. 'I long to get the goodbye over, and to be settled in the Rue Fossette again. I must go this morning: I must go directly; my trunk is packed and corded.'

It appeared, however, that my going depended upon Graham; he had said he would accompany me, and it so fell out that he was engaged all day, and only returned home at dusk. Then ensued a little combat of words. Mrs Bretton and her son pressed me to remain one night more. I could have cried, so irritated and eager was I to be gone. I longed to leave them as the criminal on the scaffold longs for the axe to descend: that is, I wished the pang over. How much I wished it, they could not tell. On these points, mine was a state of mind out of their experience.

It was dark when Dr John handed me from the carriage at Mme Beck's door. The lamp above was lit; it rained a November drizzle, as it had rained all day: the lamplight gleamed on the wet pavement. Just such a night was it as that on which, not a year ago, I had first stopped at this very threshold; just similar was the scene. I remembered the very shapes of the paving-stones which I had noted with idle eye, while, with a thick-beating heart, I waited the unclosing of that door at which I stood – a solitary and a suppliant. On that night, too, I had briefly met him who now stood with me. Had I ever reminded him of that rencontre, or explained it? I had not, nor ever felt the inclination to do so: it was a pleasant thought, laid by in my own mind, and best kept there.

Graham rang the bell. The door was instantly opened, for it was just that period of the evening when the half-boarders took their departure – consequently, Rosine was on the alert.

'Don't come in,' said I to him; but he stepped a moment into the well-lighted vestibule. I had not wished him to see that 'the water stood in my eyes', for his was too kind a nature ever to be needlessly shown such signs of sorrow. He always wished to heal – to relieve – when, physician as he was, neither cure nor alleviation were, perhaps, in his power.

'Keep up your courage, Lucy. Think of my mother and myself as true friends. We will not forget you.'

'Nor will I forget you, Dr John.'

My trunk was now brought in. We had shaken hands; he had turned to go, but he was not satisfied: he had not done or said enough to content his generous impulses.

'Lucy,' – stepping after me – 'shall you feel very solitary here?'

'At first I shall.'

'Well, my mother will soon call to see you; and, meantime, I'll tell you what I'll do. I'll write – just any cheerful nonsense that comes into my head – shall I?'

'Good, gallant heart!' thought I to myself; but I shook my head, smiling, and said, 'Never think of it: impose on yourself no such task. *You* write to *me*! – you'll not have time.'

'Oh! I will find or make time. Goodbye!'

He was gone. The heavy door crashed to: the axe had fallen – the pang was experienced.

Allowing myself no time to think or feel – swallowing tears as if they had been wine – I passed to madame's sitting-room to pay the necessary visit of ceremony and respect. She received me with perfectly well-acted cordiality – was even demonstrative, though brief, in her welcome. In ten minutes I was dismissed. From the salle à manger I proceeded to the refectory, where pupils and teachers were now assembled for evening study: again I had a welcome, and one not, I think, quite hollow. That over, I was free to repair to the dormitory.

'And will Graham really write?' I questioned, as I sank tired on the edge of the bed.

Reason, coming stealthily up to me through the twilight of that long, dim chamber, whispered sedately, –

'He may write once. So kind is his nature, it may stimulate him for once to make the effort. But it *cannot* be continued – it *may* not be repeated. Great were that folly which should build on such a promise – insane that credulity which should mistake the transitory rain-pool, holding in its hollow one draught, for the perennial spring yielding the supply of seasons.'

I bent my head: I sat thinking an hour longer. Reason still whispered me, laying on my shoulder a withered hand, and frostily touching my ear with the chill blue lips of eld.

'If,' muttered she, 'if he *should* write, what then? Do you meditate pleasure in replying? Ah, fool! I warn you! Brief be your answer. Hope no delight of heart – no indulgence to intellect: grant no expansion to feeling – give holiday *to* no single faculty: dally with no friendly exchange: foster no genial intercommunion . . .'

'But I have talked to Graham and you did not chide,' I pleaded.

'No,' said she, 'I needed not. Talk for you is good discipline. You converse imperfectly. While you speak, there can be no oblivion of inferiority – no encouragement to delusion: pain, privation, penury stamp your language . . .'

'But,' I again broke in, 'where the bodily presence is weak and the speech

contemptible, surely there cannot be error in making written language the medium of better utterance than faltering lips can achieve?'

Reason only answered, 'At your peril you cherish that idea, or suffer its influence to animate any writing of yours!'

'But if I feel, may I *never* express?'

'*Never!*' declared Reason.

I groaned under her bitter sternness. Never – never – oh, hard word! This hag, this Reason, would not let me look up, or smile, or hope: she could not rest unless I were altogether crushed, cowed, broken-in, and broken-down. According to her, I was born only to work for a piece of bread, to await the pains of death, and steadily through all life to despond. Reason might be right; yet no wonder we are glad at times to defy her, to rush from under her rod and give a truant hour to Imagination – *her* soft, bright foe, *our* sweet Help, our divine Hope. We shall and must break bounds at intervals, despite the terrible revenge that awaits our return. Reason is vindictive as a devil: for me, she was always envenomed as a stepmother. If I have obeyed her it has chiefly been with the obedience of fear, not of love. Long ago I should have died of her ill-usage: her stint, her chill, her barren board, her icy bed, her savage, ceaseless blows; but for that kinder Power who holds my secret and sworn allegiance. Often has Reason turned me out by night, in midwinter, on cold snow, flinging for sustenance the gnawed bone dogs had forsaken: sternly has she vowed her stores held nothing more for me – harshly denied my right to ask better things. . . Then, looking up, have I seen in the sky a head amidst circling stars, of which the midmost and the brightest lent a ray sympathetic and attent. A spirit, softer and better than Human Reason, has descended with quiet flight to the waste – bringing all round her a sphere of air borrowed of eternal summer; bringing perfume of flowers which cannot fade – fragrance of trees whose fruit is life; bringing breezes pure from a world whose day needs no sun to lighten it. My hunger has this good angel appeased with food, sweet and strange, gathered amongst gleaning angels, garnering their dew-white harvest in the first fresh hour of a heavenly day; tenderly has she assuaged the insufferable tears which weep away life itself – kindly given rest to deadly weariness – generously lent hope and impulse to paralysed despair. Divine, compassionate, succourable influence! When I bend the knee to other than God, it shall be at thy white and winged feet, beautiful on mountain or on plain. Temples have been reared to the Sun – altars dedicated to the Moon. Oh, greater glory! To thee neither hands build, nor lips consecrate; but hearts, through ages, are faithful to thy worship. A dwelling thou hast, too wide for walls, too high for dome – a temple whose floors are space – rites whose mysteries transpire in presence, to the kindling, the harmony of worlds!

Sovereign complete! thou hadst, for endurance, thy great army of martyrs; for achievement, thy chosen band of worthies. Deity unquestioned, thine essence foils decay!

This daughter of Heaven remembered me tonight; she saw me weep and she came with comfort: 'Sleep,' she said. 'Sleep, sweetly – I gild thy dreams!'

She kept her word, and watched me through a night's rest; but at dawn

Reason relieved the guard. I awoke with a sort of start; the rain was dashing against the panes, and the wind uttering a peevish cry at intervals; the night-lamp was dying on the black circular stand in the middle of the dormitory: day had already broken. How I pity those whom mental pain stuns instead of rousing! This morning the pang of waking snatched me out of bed like a hand with a giant's gripe. How quickly I dressed in the cold of the raw dawn! How deeply I drank of the ice-cold water in my carafe! This was always my cordial, to which, like other dramdrinkers, I had eager recourse when unsettled by chagrin.

Ere long the bell rang its *réveillée* to the whole school. Being dressed, I descended alone to the refectory, where the stove was lit and the air was warm; through the rest of the house it was cold, with the nipping severity of a continental winter: though now but the beginning of November, a north wind had thus early brought a wintry blight over Europe. I remember the black stoves pleased me little when I first came; but now I began to associate with them a sense of comfort, and liked them, as in England, we like a fireside.

Sitting down before this dark comforter, I presently fell into a deep argument with myself on life and its chances, on destiny and her decrees. My mind, calmer and stronger now than last night, made for itself some imperious rules, prohibiting under deadly penalties all weak retrospect of happiness past; commanding a patient journeying through the wilderness of the present, enjoining a reliance on faith – a watching of the cloud and pillar which subdue while they guide, and awe while they illumine – hushing the impulse of fond idolatry, checking the longing out-look for a far-off promised land whose rivers are, perhaps, never to be reached save in dying dreams, whose sweet pastures are to be viewed but from the desolate and sepulchral summit of a Nebo.

By degrees, a composite feeling of blended strength and pain wound itself wirily round my heart, sustained, or at least restrained, its throbbings, and made me fit for the day's work. I lifted my head.

As I said before, I was sitting near the stove, let into the wall beneath the refectory and the carré, and thus sufficing to heat both apartments. Piercing the same wall, and close beside the stove, was a window, looking also into the carré; as I looked up a cap-tassel, a brow, two eyes filled a pane of that window; the fixed gaze of those two eyes hit right against my own glance: they were watching me. I had not till that moment known that tears were on my cheek, but I felt them now.

This was a strange house, where no corner was sacred from intrusion, where not a tear could be shed, nor a thought pondered, but a spy was at hand to note and to divine. And this new, this outdoor, this male spy, what business had brought him to the premises at this unwonted hour? What possible right had he to intrude on me thus? No other professor would have dared to cross the carré before the class-bell rang. M. Emanuel took no account of hours nor of claims: there was some book of reference in the first-classe library which he had occasion to consult; he had come to seek it: on his way he passed the refectory. It was very much his habit to wear eyes before, behind, and on each side of him: he had seen me through the little window – he now opened the refectory door, and there he stood.

'Mademoiselle, vous êtes triste.'

'Monsieur, j'en ai bien le droit.'

'Vous êtes malade de coeur et d'humeur,' he pursued. 'You are at once mournful and mutinous. I see on your cheek two tears which I know are hot as two sparks, and salt as two crystals of the sea. While I speak you eye me strangely. Shall I tell you of what I am reminded while watching you?'

'Monsieur, I shall be called away to prayers shortly; my time for conversation is very scant and brief at this hour – excuse –'

'I excuse everything,' he interrupted; 'my mood is so meek, neither rebuff nor, perhaps insult could ruffle it. You remind me, then, of a young she wild creature, new caught, untamed, viewing with a mixture of fire and fear the first entrance of the breaker-in.'

Unwarrantable accost! – rash and rude if addressed to a pupil; to a teacher inadmissible. He thought to provoke a warm reply; I had seen him vex the passionate to explosion before now. In me his malice should find no gratification; I sat silent.

'You look,' said he, 'like one who would snatch at a draught of sweet poison, and spurn wholesome bitters with disgust.'

'Indeed, I never liked bitters; nor do I believe them wholesome. And to whatever is sweet, be it poison or food, you cannot, at least, deny its own delicious quality – sweetness. Better, perhaps, to die quickly a pleasant death, than drag on long a charmless life.'

'Yet,' said he, 'you should take your bitter dose duly and daily, if I had the power to administer it; and, as to the well-beloved poison, I would, perhaps, break the very cup which held it.'

I sharply turned my head away, partly because his presence utterly displeased me, and partly because I wished to shun questions: lest, in my present mood, the effort of answering should overmaster self-command.

'Come,' said he, more softly, 'tell me the truth – you grieve at being parted from friends – is it not so?'

The insinuating softness was not more acceptable than the inquisitorial curiosity. I was silent. He came into the room, sat down on the bench about two yards from me, and persevered long, and, for him, patiently, in attempts to draw me into conversation – attempts necessarily unavailing, because I *could* not talk. At last I entreated to be let alone. In uttering the request, my voice faltered, my head sank on my arms and the table. I wept bitterly, though quietly. He sat a while longer. I did not look up nor speak, till the closing door and his retreating steps told me that he was gone. These tears proved a relief.

I had time to bathe my eyes before breakfast, and I suppose I appeared at that meal as serene as any other person: not, however, quite as jocund-looking as the young lady who placed herself in the seat opposite mine, fixed on me a pair of somewhat small eyes twinkling gleefully, and frankly stretched across the table a white hand to be shaken. Miss Fanshawe's travels, gaieties, and flirtations agreed with her mightily; she had become quite plump, her cheeks looked as round as apples. I had seen her last in elegant evening attire. I don't know that she looked

much less charming now in her school-dress, a kind of careless peignoir of a dark-blue material, dimly and dingily plaided with black. I even think this dusky wrapper gave her charms a triumph; enhancing by contrast the fairness of her skin, the freshness of her bloom, the golden beauty of her tresses.

'I am glad you are come back, Timon,' said she. Timon was one of her dozen names for me. 'You don't know how often I have wanted you in this dismal hole.'

'Oh! have you? Then, of course, if you wanted me, you have something for me to do: stockings to mend, perhaps?' I never gave Ginevra a minute's or a farthing's credit for disinterestedness.

'Crabbed and crusty as ever!' said she. 'I expected as much: it would not be you if you did not snub one. But now, come, grandmother, I hope you like coffee as much, and pistolets as little as ever: are you disposed to barter?'

'Take your own way.'

This way consisted in a habit she had of making me convenient. She did not like the morning cup of coffee; its school brewage not being strong or sweet enough to suit her palate; and she had an excellent appetite, like any other healthy schoolgirl, for the morning pistolets or rolls, which were new-baked and very good, and of which a certain allowance was served to each. This allowance being more than I needed, I gave half to Ginevra; never varying in my preference, though many others used to covet the superfluity; and she in return would sometimes give me a portion of her coffee. This morning I was glad of the draught; hunger I had none, and with thirst I was parched. I don't know why I chose to give my bread rather to Ginevra than to another; nor why, if two had to share the convenience of one drinking-vessel, as sometimes happened – for instance, when we took a long walk into the country, and halted for refreshment at a farm I always contrived that she should be my convive, and rather liked to let her take the lion's share, whether of the white beer, the sweet wine, or the new milk: so it was, however, and she knew it; and, therefore, while we wrangled daily, we were never alienated.

After breakfast my custom was to withdraw to the first classe, and sit and read, or think (oftenest the latter) there alone, till the nine o'clock bell threw open all doors, admitted the gathered rush of externes and demi-pensionnaires, and gave the signal for entrance on that bustle and business to which, till five p.m., there was no relax.

I was just seated this morning, when a tap came to the door.

'Pardon, mademoiselle,' said a pensionnaire, entering gently; and having taken from her desk some necessary book or paper, she withdrew on tiptoe, murmuring, as she passed me, 'Que mademoiselle est appliquée!'

Appliquée, indeed! The means of application were spread before me, but I was doing nothing; and had done nothing, and meant to do nothing. Thus does the world give us credit for merits we have not. Mme Beck herself deemed me a regular bas-bleu, and often and solemnly used to warn me not to study too much, lest 'the blood should all go to my head.' Indeed, everybody in the Rue Fossette held a superstition that 'Meess Lucie' was learned; with the

notable exception of M. Emanuel: who, by means peculiar to himself, and quite inscrutable to me, had obtained a not inaccurate inkling of my real qualifications, and used to take quiet opportunities of chuckling in my ear his malign glee over their scant measure. For my part, I never troubled myself about this penury. I dearly liked to think my own thoughts; I had great pleasure in reading a few books, but not many: preferring always those in whose style or sentiment the writer's individual nature was plainly stamped; flagging inevitably over characterless books, however clever and meritorious; perceiving well that, as far as my own mind was concerned, God had limited its powers and its action – thankful, I trust, for the gift bestowed, but unambitious of higher endowments, not restlessly eager after higher culture.

The polite pupil was scarcely gone, when, unceremoniously, without tap, in burst a second intruder. Had I been blind I should have known who this was. A constitutional reserve of manner had by this time told with wholesome and, for me, commodious effect, on the manners of my co-inmates; rarely did I now suffer from rude or intrusive treatment. When I first came, it would happen once and again that a blunt German would clap me on the shoulder, and ask me to run a race; or a riotous Labassecourienne seize me by the arm and drag me towards the playground: urgent proposals to take a swing at the 'Pas de Géant', or to join in a certain romping hide-and-seek game called 'Un, deux, trois', were formerly also of hourly occurrence; but all these little attentions had ceased some time ago – ceased, too, without my finding it necessary to be at the trouble of point-blank cutting them short. I had now no familiar demonstration to dread or endure, save from one quarter; and as that was English I could bear it. Ginevra Fanshawe made no scruple of – at times – catching me as I was crossing the carré, whirling me round in a compulsory waltz, and heartily enjoying the mental and physical discomfiture her proceeding induced. Ginevra Fanshawe it was who now broke in upon my 'learned leisure.' She carried a huge music-book under her arm.

'Go to your practising,' said I to her at once: 'away with you to the little salon!'

'Not till I have had a talk with you, chère amie. I know where you have been spending your vacation, and how you have commenced sacrificing to the graces, and enjoying life like any other belle. I saw you at the concert the other night, dressed, actually, like anybody else. Who is your tailleuse?'

'Tittle-tattle: how prettily it begins! My tailleuse! – a fiddlestick! Come, sheer off, Ginevra. I really don't want your company.'

'But when I want yours so much, ange farouche, what does a little reluctance on your part signify? Dieu merci! we know how to manoeuvre with our gifted compatriote – the learned "ourse Britannique". And so, Ourson, you know Isidore?'

'I know John Bretton.'

'Oh, hush!' (putting her fingers in her ears) 'you crack my tympanums with your rude Anglicisms. But, how is our well-beloved John? Do tell me about him. The poor man must be in a sad way. What did he say to my behaviour the other night? Wasn't I cruel?'

'Do you think I noticed you?'

'It was a delightful evening. Oh, that divine de Hamal! And then to watch the other sulking and dying in the distance; and the old lady – my future mama-in-law! But I am afraid I and Lady Sara were a little rude in quizzing her.'

'Lady Sara never quizzed her at all; and for what *you* did, don't make yourself in the least uneasy: Mrs Bretton will survive *your* sneer.'

'She may: old ladies are tough; but that poor son of hers! Do tell me what he said: I saw he was terribly cut up.'

'He said you looked as if, at heart, you were already Mme de Hamal.'

'Did he?' she cried, with delight. 'He noticed that? How charming! I thought he would be mad with jealousy.'

'Ginevra, have you seriously done with Dr Bretton? Do you want him to give you up?'

'Oh! you know he *can't* do that: but wasn't he mad?'

'Quite mad,' I assented; 'as mad as a March hare.'

'Well, and how *ever* did you get him home?'

'How *ever*, indeed! Have you no pity on his poor mother and me? Fancy us holding him tight down in the carriage, and he raving between us, fit to drive everybody delirious. The very coachman went wrong, somehow, and we lost our way.'

'You don't say so? You are laughing at me. Now, Lucy Snowe –'

'I assure you it is fact – and fact, also, that Dr Bretton would *not* stay in the carriage: he broke from us, and *would* ride outside.'

'And afterwards?'

'Afterwards – when we *did* reach home – the scene transcends description.'

'Oh, but describe it – you know it is such fun!'

'Fun for you, Miss Fanshawe; but' (with stern gravity) 'you know the proverb – "What is sport to one may be death to another."'

'Go on, there's a darling Timon.'

'Conscientiously, I cannot, unless you assure me you have some heart.'

'I have – such an immensity, you don't know!'

'Good! In that case, you will be able to conceive Dr Graham Bretton rejecting his supper in the first instance – the chicken, the sweet-bread prepared for his refreshment, left on the table untouched. Then but it is of no use dwelling at length on harrowing details. Suffice it to say, that never, in the most stormy fits and moments of his infancy, had his mother such work to tuck the sheets about him as she had that night.'

'He wouldn't lie still?'

'He wouldn't lie still: there it was. The sheets might be tucked in, but the thing was to keep them tucked in.'

'And what did he say?'

'Say! Can't you imagine him demanding his divine Ginevra, anathematising that demon, de Hamal – raving about golden locks, blue eyes, white arms, glittering bracelets?'

'No, did he? He saw the bracelet?'

'Saw the bracelet? Yes, as plain as I saw it: and, perhaps, for the first time, he saw also the brand-mark with which its pressure has circled your arm. Ginevra,' (rising, and changing my tone) 'come, we will have an end of this. Go away to your practising.' And I opened the door.

'But you've not told me all.'

'You had better not wait until I *do* tell you all. Such extra communicativeness could give you no pleasure. March!'

'Cross thing!' said she; but she obeyed: and, indeed, the first classe was my territory, and she could not there legally resist a notice of quittance from me.

Yet, to speak the truth, never had I been less dissatisfied with her than I was then. There was pleasure in thinking of the contrast between the reality and my description – to remember Dr John enjoying the drive home, eating his supper with relish, and retiring to rest with Christian composure. It was only when I saw him really unhappy that I felt really vexed with the fair, frail cause of his suffering.

A fortnight passed; I was getting once more inured to the harness of school, and lapsing from the passionate pain of change to the palsy of custom. One afternoon in crossing the carré, on my way to the first classe, where I was expected to assist at a lesson of 'style and literature', I saw, standing by one of the long and large windows, Rosine, the portress. Her attitude, as usual, was quite nonchalante. She always 'stood at ease'; one of her hands rested in her apron-pocket, the other, at this moment, held to her eyes a letter, whereof Mademoiselle coolly perused the address, and deliberately studied the seal.

A letter! The shape of a letter similar to that had haunted my brain in its very core for seven days past. I had dreamed of a letter last night. Strong magnetism drew me to that letter now; yet, whether I should have ventured to demand of Rosine so much as a glance at that white envelope, with the spot of red wax in the middle, I know not. No; I think I should have sneaked past in terror of a rebuff from Disappointment: my heart throbbed now as if I already heard the tramp of her approach. Nervous mistake! It was the rapid step of the Professor of Literature measuring the corridor. I fled before him. Could I but be seated quietly at my desk before his arrival, with the class under my orders all in disciplined readiness, he would, perhaps, exempt me from notice; but, if caught lingering in the carré, I should be sure to come in for a special harangue. I had time to get seated, to enforce perfect silence, to take out my work, and to commence it amidst the profoundest and best trained hush, ere M. Emanuel entered with his vehement burst of latch and panel, and his deep, redundant bow, prophetic of choler.

As usual he broke upon us like a clap of thunder; but instead of flashing lightning-wise from the door to the estrade, his career halted midway at my desk. Setting his face towards me and the window, his back to the pupils and the room, he gave me a look – such a look as might have licensed me to stand straight up and demand what he meant – a look of scowling distrust.

'Voilà! pour vous,' said he, drawing his hand from his waistcoat, and placing on my desk a letter – the very letter I had seen in Rosine's hand – the letter whose

face of enamelled white and single Cyclops-eye of vermilion-red had printed themselves so clear and perfect on the retina of an inward vision. I knew it, I felt it to be the letter of my hope, the fruition of my wish, the release from my doubt, the ransom from my terror. This letter M. Paul, with his unwarrantably interfering habits, had taken from the portress, and now delivered it himself.

I might have been angry, but had not a second for the sensation. Yes: I held in my hand not a slight note, but an envelope, which must, at least, contain a sheet: it felt, not flimsy, but firm, substantial, satisfying. And here was the direction, 'Miss Lucy Snowe,' in a clean, clear, equal, decided hand; and there was the seal, round, full, deftly dropped by untremulous fingers, stamped with the well-cut impress of initials, 'J. G. B.' I experienced a happy feeling – a glad emotion which went warm to my heart, and ran lively through all my veins. For once a hope was realised. I held in my hand a morsel of real solid joy: not a dream, not an image of the brain, not one of those shadowy chances imagination pictures, and on which humanity starves but cannot live; not a mess of that manna I drearily eulogised awhile ago – which, indeed, at first melts on the lips with an unspeakable and preternatural sweetness, but which, in the end, our souls full surely loathe; longing deliriously for natural and earth-grown food, wildly praying Heaven's Spirits to reclaim their own spirit-dew and essence – an aliment divine, but for mortals deadly. It was neither sweet hail, nor small coriander-seed – neither slight wafer, nor luscious honey, I had lighted on; it was the wild savoury mess of the hunter, nourishing and salubrious meat, forest-fed or desert-reared, fresh, healthful, and life-sustaining. It was what the old dying patriarch demanded of his son Esau, promising him in requital the blessing of his last breath. It was a godsend; and I inwardly thanked the God who had vouchsafed it. Outwardly I only thanked man, crying, 'Thank you, thank you, Monsieur!'

Monsieur curled his lip, gave me a vicious glance of the eye, and strode to his estrade. M. Paul was not at all a good little man, though he had good points.

Did I read my letter there and then? Did I consume the venison at once and with haste, as if Esau's shaft flew every day?

I knew better. The cover with its address; the seal, with its three clear letters, was bounty and abundance for the present. I stole from the room, I procured the key of the great dormitory which was kept locked by day. I went to my bureau; with a sort of haste and trembling lest Madame should creep upstairs and spy me, I opened a drawer, unlocked a box, and took out a case, and – having feasted my eyes with one more look, and approached the seal, with a mixture of awe and shame and delight, to my lips – I folded the untasted treasure, yet all fair and inviolate, in silver paper, committed it to the case, shut up box and drawer, reclosed, relocked the dormitory, and returned to class, feeling as if fairy tales were true and fairy gifts no dream. Strange, sweet insanity! And this letter, the source of my joy, I had not yet read: did not yet know the number of its lines.

When I re-entered the schoolroom, behold M. Paul raging like a pestilence! Some pupil had not spoken audibly or distinctly enough to suit his ear and taste, and now she and others were weeping, and he was raving from his estrade almost livid. Curious to mention, as I appeared, he fell on me.

'Was I the mistress of these girls? Did I profess to teach them the conduct befitting ladies? – and did I permit and, he doubted not, encourage them to strangle their mother-tongue in their throats, to mince and mash it between their teeth, as if they had some base cause to be ashamed of the words they uttered? Was this modesty? He knew better. It was a vile pseudo sentiment – the offspring or the forerunner of evil. Rather than submit to this mopping and mowing, this mincing and grimacing, this grinding of a noble tongue, this general affectation and sickening stubbornness of the pupils of the first class, he would throw them up for a set of insupportable petites-maîtresses, and confine himself to teaching the A B C to the babies of the third division.'

What could I say to all this? Really nothing; and I hoped he would allow me to be silent. The storm recommenced.

'Every answer to his queries was then refused? It seemed to be considered in *that* place – that conceited boudoir of a first classe, with its pretentious book-cases, its green-baized desks, its rubbish of flower-stands, its trash of framed pictures and maps, and its foreign surveillante, forsooth! – it seemed to be the fashion to think *there* that the Professor of Literature was not worthy of a reply! These were new ideas; imported, he did not doubt, straight from "la Grande Bretagne': they savoured of island insolence and arrogance.'

Lull the second – the girls, not one of whom was ever known to weep a tear for the rebukes of any other master, now all melting like snow-statues before the intemperate heat of M. Emanuel: I, not yet much shaken, sitting down, and venturing to resume my work.

Something – either in my continued silence or in the movement of my hand, stitching – transported M. Emanuel beyond the last boundary of patience; he actually sprung from his estrade. The stove stood near my desk, and he attacked it; the little iron door was nearly dashed from its hinges, the fuel was made to fly.

'Est-ce que vous avez l'intention de m'insulter?' said he to me, in a low, furious voice, as he thus outraged, under pretence of arranging, the fire.

It was time to soothe him a little if possible.

'Mais, monsieur,' said I, 'I would not insult you for the world. I remember too well that you once said we should be friends.'

I did not intend my voice to falter, but it did: more, I think, through the agitation of late delight than in any spasm of present fear. Still there certainly was something in M. Paul's anger – a kind of passion of emotion – that specially tended to draw tears. I was not unhappy, nor much afraid, yet I wept.

'Allons, allons!' said he presently, looking round and seeing the deluge universal. 'Decidedly I am a monster and a ruffian. I have only one pocket-handkerchief,' he added, 'but if I had twenty, I would offer you each one. Your teacher shall be your representative. Here, Miss Lucy.'

And he took forth and held out to me a clean silk handkerchief. Now a person who did not know M. Paul, who was unused to him and his impulses, would naturally have bungled at this offer – declined accepting the same – etcetera. But I too plainly felt this would never do: the slightest hesitation would have been fatal to the incipient treaty of peace. I rose and met the handkerchief halfway,

received it with decorum, wiped therewith my eyes, and, resuming my seat, and retaining the flag of truce in my hand and on my lap, took especial care during the remainder of the lesson to touch neither needle nor thimble, scissors nor muslin. Many a jealous glance did M. Paul cast at these implements; he hated them mortally, considering sewing a source of distraction from the attention due to himself. A very eloquent lesson he gave, and very kind and friendly was he to the close. Ere he had done, the clouds were dispersed and the sun shining out – tears were exchanged for smiles.

In quitting the room he paused once more at my desk.

'And your letter?' said he, this time not quite fiercely.

'I have not yet read it, monsieur.'

'Ah! it is too good to read at once: you save it, as, when I was a boy, I used to save a peach whose bloom was very ripe?'

The guess came so near the truth, I could not prevent a suddenly-rising warmth in my face from revealing as much.

'You promise yourself a pleasant moment,' said he, 'in reading that letter; you will open it when alone – n'est-ce pas? Ah! a smile answers. Well, well! one should not be too harsh; "la jeunesse n'a qu'un temps." '

'Monsieur, monsieur!' I cried or rather whispered after him, as he turned to go, 'do not leave me under a mistake. This is merely a friend's letter. Without reading it, I can vouch for that.'

'Je conçois, je conçois: on sait ce que c'est qu'un ami. Bonjour, mademoiselle!'

'But, monsieur, here is your handkerchief.'

'Keep it, keep it, till the letter is read, then bring it me; I shall read the billet's tenor in your eyes.'

When he was gone, the pupils having already poured out of the schoolroom into the berceau, and thence into the garden and court to take their customary recreation before the five o'clock dinner, I stood a moment thinking, and absently twisting the handkerchief round my arm. For some reason – gladdened, I think, by a sudden return of the golden glimmer of childhood, roused by an unwonted renewal of its buoyancy, made merry by the liberty of the closing hour, and, above all, solaced at heart by the joyous consciousness of that treasure in the case, box, drawer upstairs, I fell to playing with the handkerchief as if it were a ball, casting it into the air and catching it as it fell. The game was stopped by another hand than mine – a hand emerging from a paletôt-sleeve and stretched over my shoulder; it caught the extemporised plaything and bore it away with these sullen words: 'Je vois bien que vous vous moquez de moi et de mes effets.'

Really that little man was dreadful: a mere sprite of caprice and ubiquity: one never knew either his whim or his whereabout.

## CHAPTER 22

### *The Letter*

When all was still in the house; when dinner was over and the noisy recreation-hour past; when darkness had set in, and the quiet lamp of study was lit in the refectory; when the externes were gone home, the clashing door and clamorous bell hushed for the evening; when Madame was safely settled in the salle à manger in company with her mother and some friends; I then glided to the kitchen, begged a bougie for one half hour for a particular occasion, found acceptance of my petition at the hands of my friend Goton, who answered 'Mais certainement, chou-chou, vous en aurez deux, si vous voulez.' And, light in hand, I mounted noiseless to the dormitory.

Great was my chagrin to find in that apartment a pupil gone to bed indisposed, greater when I recognised amid the muslin night-cap borders, the 'figure chiffonnée' of Mistress Ginevra Fanshawe; supine at this moment, it is true – but certain to wake and overwhelm me with chatter when the interruption would be least acceptable: indeed, as I watched her, a slight twinkling of the eyelids warned me that the present appearance of repose might be but a ruse, assumed to cover sly vigilance over 'Timon's' movements: she was not to be trusted. And I had so wished to be alone, just to read my precious letter in peace.

Well, I must go to the classes. Having sought and found my prize in its casket, I descended. Ill-luck pursued me. The classes were undergoing sweeping and purification by candle-light, according to hebdomadal custom: benches were piled on desks, the air was dim with dust, damp coffee-grounds (used by Labassecourien housemaids instead of tea-leaves) darkened the floor; all was hopeless confusion. Baffled, but not beaten, I withdrew, bent as resolutely as ever on finding solitude *somewhere*.

Taking a key whereof I knew the repository, I mounted three staircases in succession, reached a dark, narrow, silent landing, opened a worm-eaten door, and dived into the deep, black, cold garret. Here none would follow me – none interrupt – not Madame herself. I shut the garret-door; I placed my light on a doddered and mouldy chest of drawers; I put on a shawl, for the air was ice-cold; I took my letter, trembling with sweet impatience; I broke its seal.

'Will it be long – will it be short?' thought I, passing my hand across my eyes to dissipate the silvery dimness of a suave, south wind shower.

It was long.

'Will it be cool? – will it be kind?'

It was kind.

To my checked, bridled, disciplined expectation, it seemed very kind; to my longing and famished thought it seemed, perhaps, kinder than it was.

So little had I hoped, so much had I feared; there was a fullness of delight in

this taste of fruition – such, perhaps, as many a human being passes through life without ever knowing. The poor English teacher in the frosty garret, reading by a dim candle guttering in the wintry air, a letter simply good-natured – nothing more: though that good-nature then seemed to me god-like – was happier than most queens in palaces.

Of course, happiness of such shallow origin could but be brief; yet, while it lasted, it was genuine and exquisite: a bubble – but a sweet bubble – of real honey-dew. Dr John had written to me at length; he had written to me with pleasure; he had written in benignant mood, dwelling with sunny satisfaction on scenes that had passed before his eyes and mine – on places we had visited together – on conversations we had held – on all the little subject-matter, in short, of the last few halcyon weeks. But the cordial core of the delight was, a conviction the blithe, genial language generously imparted, that it had been poured out – not merely to content *me* – but to gratify *himself.* A gratification he might never more desire, never more seek – an hypothesis in every point of view approaching the certain; but *that* concerned the future. This present moment had no pain, no blot, no want; full, pure, perfect, it deeply blessed me. A passing seraph seemed to have rested beside me, leaned towards my heart, and reposed on its throb a softening, cooling, healing, hallowing wing. Dr John, you pained me afterwards: forgiven be every ill – freely forgiven – for the sake of that one dear remembered good!

Are there wicked things, not human, which envy human bliss? Are there evil influences haunting the air, and poisoning it for man? What was near me? . . .

Something in that vast solitary garret sounded strangely. Most surely and certainly I heard, as it seemed, a stealthy foot on that floor: a sort of gliding out from the direction of the black recess haunted by the malefactor cloaks. I turned: my light was dim; the room was long – but, as I live! I saw in the middle of that ghostly chamber a figure all black or white; the skirts straight, narrow, black; the head bandaged, veiled, white.

Say what you will, reader – tell me I was nervous, or mad; affirm that I was unsettled by the excitement of that letter; declare that I dreamed: this I vow – I saw there – in that room – on that night – an image like – a *nun.*

I cried out; I sickened. Had the shape approached me I might have swooned. It receded: I made for the door. How I descended all the stairs I know not. By instinct I shunned the refectory, and shaped my course to Madame's sitting-room: I burst in. I said –

'There is something in the grenier: I have been there: I saw something. Go and look at it, all of you!'

I said, 'All of you;' for the room seemed to me full of people, though, in truth, there were but four present: Mme Beck; her mother, Mme Kint, who was out of health, and now staying with her on a visit; her brother M. Victor Kint, and another gentleman: who, when I entered the room, was conversing with the old lady, and had his back towards the door.

My mortal fear and faintness must have made me deadly pale. I felt cold and shaking. They all rose in consternation; they surrounded me. I urged them to go

to the grenier; the sight of the gentlemen did me good and gave me courage: it seemed as if there was some help and hope, with men at hand. I turned to the door, beckoning them to follow. They wanted to stop me; but I said they must come this way: they must see what I had seen – something strange, standing in the middle of the garret. And, now, I remembered my letter, left on the drawers with the light. This precious letter! Flesh or spirit must be defied for its sake. I flew upstairs, hastening the faster as I knew I was followed: they were obliged to come.

Lo! When I reached the garret-door, all within was dark as a pit: the light was out. Happily, someone – Madame, I think, with her usual calm sense – had brought a lamp from the room; speedily, therefore, as they came up, a ray pierced the opaque blackness. There stood the bougie quenched on the drawers; but where was the letter? And I looked for *that* now, and not for the nun.

'My letter! my letter!' I panted and plained, almost beside myself. I groped on the floor, wringing my hands wildly. Cruel, cruel doom! To have my bit of comfort preternaturally snatched from me, ere I had well tasted its virtue!

I don't know what the others were doing; I could not watch them: they asked me questions I did not answer; they ransacked all corners; they prattled about this and that, disarrangement of cloaks, a breach or crack in the sky-light – I know not what. 'Something or somebody has been here,' was sagely averred.

'Oh! they have taken my letter!' cried the grovelling, groping, monomaniac.

'What letter, Lucy? My dear girl, what letter?' asked a known voice in my ear. Could I believe that ear? No: and I looked up. Could I trust my eyes? Had I recognised the tone? Did I now look on the face of the writer of that very letter? Was this gentleman near me in this dim garret, John Graham – Dr Bretton himself?

Yes: it was. He had been called in that very evening to prescribe for some access of illness in old Mme Kint; he was the second gentleman present in the salle à manger when I entered.

'Was it *my* letter, Lucy?'

'Your own: yours – the letter you wrote to me. I had come here to read it quietly. I could not find another spot where it was possible to have it to myself. I had saved it all day – never opened it till this evening: it was scarcely glanced over: I *cannot bear* to lose it. Oh, my letter!'

'Hush! don't cry and distress yourself so cruelly. What is it worth? Hush! Come out of this cold room; they are going to send for the police now to examine further: we need not stay here – come, we will go down.'

A warm hand, taking my cold fingers, led me down to a room where there was a fire. Dr John and I sat before the stove. He talked to me and soothed me with unutterable goodness, promising me twenty letters for the one lost. If there are words and wrongs like knives, whose deep-inflicted lacerations never heal – cutting injuries and insults of serrated and poison-dripping edge – so, too, there are consolations of tone too fine for the ear not fondly and for ever to retain their echo: caressing kindnesses – loved, lingered over through a whole life, recalled with unfaded tenderness, and answering the call with undimmed shine, out of that raven cloud foreshadowing Death himself. I have been told since,

that Dr Bretton was not so nearly perfect as I thought him: that his actual character lacked the depth, height, compass, and endurance it possessed in my creed. I don't know: he was as good to me as the well is to the parched wayfarer – as the sun to the shivering gaolbird. I remember him heroic. Heroic at this moment will I hold him to be.

He asked me, smiling, why I cared for his letter so very much. I thought, but did not say, that I prized it like the blood in my veins. I only answered that I had so few letters to care for.

'I am sure you did not read it,' said he; 'or you would think nothing of it!'

'I read it, but only once. I want to read it again. I am sorry it is lost.' And I could not help weeping afresh.

'Lucy, Lucy, my poor little god-sister (if there be such a relationship), here – *here* is your letter. Why is it not better worth such tears, and such tenderly exaggerating faith?'

Curious, characteristic manœuvre! His quick eye had seen the letter on the floor where I sought it; his hand, as quick, had snatched it up. He had hidden it in his waistcoat pocket. If my trouble had wrought with a whit less stress and reality, I doubt whether he would ever have acknowledged or restored it. Tears of temperature one degree cooler than those I shed would only have amused Dr John.

Pleasure at regaining made me forget merited reproach for the teasing torment; my joy was great; it could not be concealed: yet I think it broke out more in countenance than language. I said little.

'Are you satisfied now?' asked Dr John

I replied that I was – satisfied and happy.

'Well then,' he proceeded, 'how do you feel physically? Are you growing calmer? Not much; for you tremble like a leaf still.'

It seemed to me, however, that I was sufficiently calm: at least I felt no longer terrified. I expressed myself composed.

'You are able, consequently, to tell me what you saw? Your account was quite vague, do you know? You looked white as the wall; but you only spoke of "something," not defining *what*. Was it a man? Was it an animal? *What* was it?'

'I never will tell exactly what I saw,' said I, 'unless someone else sees it too, and then I will give corroborative testimony; but otherwise, I shall be discredited and accused of dreaming.'

'Tell me,' said Dr Bretton; 'I will hear it in my professional character: I look on you now from a professional point of view, and I read, perhaps, all you would conceal – in your eye, which is curiously vivid and restless; in your cheek, which the blood has forsaken; in your hand, which you cannot steady. Come, Lucy, speak and tell me.'

'You would laugh – ?'

'If you don't tell me you shall have no more letters.'

'You are laughing now.'

'I will again take away that single epistle: being mine, I think I have a right to reclaim it.'

I felt raillery in his words: it made me grave and quiet; but I folded up the letter and covered it from sight.

'You may hide it, but I can possess it any moment I choose. You don't know my skill in sleight of hand: I might practise as a conjuror if I liked. Mama says sometimes, too, that I have a harmonising property of tongue and eye; but you never saw that in me – did you Lucy?'

'Indeed – indeed – when you were a mere boy I used to see both: far more then than now – for now you are strong, and strength dispenses with subtlety. But still, Dr John, you have what they call in this country "un air fin," that nobody can mistake. Mme Beck saw it, and –'

'And liked it,' said he, laughing, 'because she has it herself. But, Lucy, give me that letter – you don't really care for it.'

To this provocative speech I made no answer. Graham in mirthful mood must not be humoured too far. Just now there was a new sort of smile playing about his lips – very sweet, but it grieved me somehow – a new sort of light sparkling in his eyes: not hostile, but not reassuring. I rose to go – I bid him good- night a little sadly.

His sensitiveness – that peculiar, apprehensive, detective faculty of his – felt in a moment the unspoken complaint – the scarce-thought reproach. He asked quietly if I was offended. I shook my head as implying a negative.

'Permit me, then, to speak a little seriously to you before you go. You are in a highly nervous state. I feel sure from what is apparent in your look and manner, however well-controlled, that whilst alone this evening in that dismal, perishing sepulchral garret – that dungeon under the leads, smelling of damp and mould, rank with phthisis and catarrh: a place you never ought to enter – that you saw, or *thought* you saw, some appearance peculiarly calculated to impress the imagination. I know you *are* not, nor ever were, subject to material terrors, fears of robbers, etc. – I am not so sure that a visitation bearing a spectral character would not shake your very mind. Be calm now. This is all a matter of the nerves, I see: but just specify the vision.'

'You will tell nobody?'

'Nobody – most certainly. You may trust me as implicitly as you did Père Silas. Indeed, the doctor is perhaps the safer confessor of the two, though he has not gray hair.'

'You will not laugh?'

'Perhaps I may, to do you good; but not in scorn. Lucy, I feel as a friend towards you, though your timid nature is slow to trust.'

He now looked like a friend: that indescribable smile and sparkle were gone; those formidable arched curves of lip, nostril, eyebrow, were depressed; repose marked his attitude – attention sobered his aspect. Won to confidence, I told him exactly what I had seen: ere now I had narrated to him the legend of the house – whiling away with that narrative an hour of a certain mild October afternoon, when he and I rode through Bois l'Etang.

He sat and thought, and while he thought, we heard them all coming down stairs.

'Are they going to interrupt?' said he, glancing at the door with an annoyed expression.

'They will not come here,' I answered; for we were in the little salon where Madame never sat in the evening, and where it was by mere chance that heat was still lingering in the stove. They passed the door and went on to the salle à manger.

'Now,' he pursued, 'they will talk about thieves, burglars, and so on: let them do so – mind you say nothing, and keep your resolution of describing your nun to nobody. She may appear to you again: don't start.'

'You think then,' I said, with secret horror, 'she came out of my brain, and is now gone in there, and may glide out again at an hour and a day when I look not for her?'

'I think it a case of spectral illusion: I fear, following on and resulting from long-continued mental conflict.'

'Oh, Doctor John – I shudder at the thought of being liable to such an illusion! It seemed so real. Is there no cure? – no preventive?'

'Happiness is the cure – a cheerful mind the preventive: cultivate both.'

No mockery in this world ever sounds to me so hollow as that of being told to *cultivate* happiness. What does such advice mean? Happiness is not a potato, to be planted in mould, and tilled with manure. Happiness is a glory shining far down upon us out of Heaven. She is a divine dew which the soul, on certain of its summer mornings, feels dropping upon it from the amaranth bloom and golden fruitage of Paradise.

'Cultivate happiness!' I said briefly to the doctor: 'do *you* cultivate happiness? How do you manage?'

'I am a cheerful fellow by nature: and then ill-luck has never dogged me. Adversity gave me and my mother one passing scowl and brush, but we defied her, or rather laughed at her, and she went by.'

'There is no cultivation in all this.'

'I do not give way to melancholy.'

'Yes: I have seen you subdued by that feeling.'

'About Ginevra Fanshawe – eh?'

'Did she not sometimes make you miserable?'

'Pooh! stuff! nonsense! You see I am better now.'

If a laughing eye with a lively light, and a face bright with beaming and healthy energy, could attest that he was better, better he certainly was.

'You do not look much amiss, or greatly out of condition,' I allowed.

'And why, Lucy, can't you look and feel as I do – buoyant, courageous, and fit to defy all the nuns and flirts in Christendom? I would give gold on the spot just to see you snap your fingers. Try the manœuvre.'

'If I were to bring Miss Fanshawe into your presence just now?'

'I vow, Lucy, she should not move me: or, she should move me but by one thing – true, yes, and passionate love. I would accord forgiveness at no less a price.'

'Indeed! a smile of hers would have been a fortune to you a while since.'

'Transformed, Lucy: transformed! Remember, you once called me a slave! but I am a free man now!'

He stood up: in the port of his head, the carriage of his figure, in his beaming eye and mien, there revealed itself a liberty which was more than ease – a mood which was disdain of his past bondage.

'Miss Fanshawe,' he pursued, 'has led me through a phase of feeling which is over: I have entered another condition, and am now much disposed to exact love for love – passion for passion – and good measure of it too.'

'Ah, Doctor! Doctor! you said it was your nature to pursue Love under difficulties – to be charmed by a proud insensibility!'

He laughed, and answered, 'My nature varies: the mood of one hour is sometimes the mockery of the next. Well, Lucy' (drawing on his gloves), 'will the Nun come again tonight, think you?'

'I don't think she will.'

'Give her my compliments, if she does – Dr John's compliments – and entreat her to have the goodness to wait a visit from him. Lucy, was she a pretty nun? Had she a pretty face? You have not told me that yet; and *that is* the really important point.'

'She had a white cloth over her face,' said I, 'but her eyes glittered.'

'Confusion to her goblin trappings!' cried he, irreverently: 'but at least she had handsome eyes – bright and soft.'

'Cold and fixed,' was my reply.

'No, no, we'll none of her: she shall not haunt you, Lucy. Give her that shake of the hand, if she comes again. Will she stand *that*, do you think?'

I thought it too kind and cordial for a ghost to stand; and so was the smile which matched it, and accompanied his 'Good-night.'

And had there been anything in the garret? What did they discover? I believe, on the closest examination, their discoveries amounted to very little. They talked, at first, of the cloaks being disturbed; but Mme Beck told me afterwards she thought they hung much as usual: and as for the broken pane in the skylight, she affirmed that aperture was rarely without one or more panes broken or cracked: and besides, a heavy hailstorm had fallen a few days ago. Madame questioned me very closely as to what I had seen, but I only described an obscure figure clothed in black: I took care not to breathe the word 'nun,' certain that this word would at once suggest to her mind an idea of romance and unreality. She charged me to say nothing on the subject to any servant, pupil, or teacher, and highly commended my discretion in coming to her private salle à manger, instead of carrying the tale of horror to the school refectory. Thus the subject dropped. I was left secretly and sadly to wonder, in my own mind, whether that strange thing was of this world, or of a realm beyond the grave; or whether indeed it was only the child of malady, and I of that malady the prey.

# *Vashti*

To wonder sadly, did I say? No: a new influence began to act upon my life, and sadness, for a certain space, was held at bay. Conceive a dell, deep-hollowed in forest secrecy; it lies in dimness and mist: its turf is dank, its herbage pale and humid. A storm or an axe makes a wide gap amongst the oak trees; the breeze sweeps in; the sun looks down; the sad, cold dell becomes a deep cup of lustre; high summer pours her blue glory and her golden light out of that beauteous sky, which till now the starved hollow never saw.

A new creed became mine – a belief in happiness.

It was three weeks since the adventure of the garret, and I possessed in that case, box, drawer upstairs, casketed with that first letter, four companions like to it, traced by the same firm pen, sealed with the same clear seal, full of the same vital comfort. Vital comfort it seemed to me then: I read them in after years; they were kind letters enough – pleasing letters, because composed by one well-pleased; in the two last there were three or four closing lines half-gay, half-tender, 'by *feeling* touched, but not subdued'. Time, dear reader, mellowed them to a beverage of this mild quality; but when I first tasted their elixir, fresh from the fount so honoured, it seemed juice of a divine vintage: a draught which Hebe might fill, and the very gods approve.

Does the reader, remembering what was said some pages back, care to ask how I answered these letters: whether under the dry, stinting check of Reason, or according to the full, liberal impulse of Feeling?

To speak truth, I compromised matters; I served two masters: I bowed down in the house of Rimmon, and lifted the heart at another shrine. I wrote to these letters two answers – one for my own relief, the other for Graham's perusal .

To begin with: Feeling and I turned Reason out of doors, drew against her bar and bolt, then we sat down, spread our paper, dipped in the ink an eager pen, and, with deep enjoyment, poured out our sincere heart. When we had done – when two sheets were covered with the language of a strongly-adherent affection, a rooted and active gratitude – (once, for all, in this parenthesis, I disclaim, with the utmost scorn, every sneaking suspicion of what are called 'warmer feelings': women do not entertain these 'warmer feelings' where, from the commencement, through the whole progress of an acquaintance, they have never once been cheated of the conviction that to do so would be to commit a mortal absurdity: nobody ever launches into Love unless he has seen or dreamed the rising of Hope's star over Love's troubled waters) – when, then, I had given expression to a closely-clinging and deeply-honouring attachment – an attachment that wanted to attract to itself and take into its own lot all that was painful in the destiny of its object; that would, if it could, have absorbed and conducted away all storms and

lightnings from an existence viewed with a passion of solicitude – then, just at that moment, the doors of my heart would shake, bolt and bar would yield, Reason would leap in, vigorous and revengeful, snatch the full sheets, read, sneer, erase, tear up, rewrite, fold, seal, direct, and send a terse, curt missive of a page. She did right.

I did not live on letters only: I was visited, I was looked after; once a week I was taken out to La Terrasse; always I was made much of. Dr Bretton failed not to tell me *why* he was so kind: 'To keep away the nun,' he said; 'he was determined to dispute with her her prey. He had taken,' he declared, 'a thorough dislike to her, chiefly on account of that white face-cloth, and those cold gray eyes: the moment he heard of those odious particulars,' he affirmed, 'consummate disgust had incited him to oppose her; he was determined to try whether he or she was the cleverest, and he only wished she would once more look in upon me when he was present:' but *that* she never did. In short, he regarded me scientifically in the light of a patient, and at once exercised his professional skill, and gratified his natural benevolence, by a course of cordial and attentive treatment.

One evening, the first in December, I was walking by myself in the carré; it was six o'clock; the classe-doors were closed; but within, the pupils, rampant in the license of evening recreation, were counterfeiting a miniature chaos. The carré was quite dark, except a red light shining under and about the stove; the wide glass-doors and the long windows were frosted over; a crystal sparkle of starlight, here and there spangling this blanched winter veil, and breaking with scattered brilliants the paleness of its embroidery, proved it a clear night, though moonless. That I should dare to remain thus alone in darkness, showed that my nerves were regaining a healthy tone: I thought of the nun, but hardly feared her; though the staircase was behind me, leading up, through blind, black night, from landing to landing, to the haunted grenier. Yet I own my heart quaked, my pulse leaped, when I suddenly heard breathing and rustling, and turning, saw in the deep shadow of the steps a deeper shadow still – a shape that moved and descended. It paused a while at the classe door, and then it glided before me. Simultaneously came a clangor of the distant doorbell. Lifelike sounds bring lifelike feelings: this shape was too round and low for my gaunt nun: it was only Mme Beck on duty.

'Mlle Lucy!' cried Rosine, bursting in, lamp in hand, from the corridor, 'On est là pour vous au salon.'

Madame saw me, I saw Madame, Rosine saw us both: there was no mutual recognition. I made straight for the salon. There I found what I own I anticipated I should find – Dr Bretton; but he was in evening-dress.

'The carriage is at the door,' said he; 'my mother has sent it to take you to the theatre; she was going herself but an arrival has prevented her: she immediately said, "Take Lucy in my place." Will you go?'

'Just now? I am not dressed,' cried I, glancing despairingly at my dark merino.

'You have half an hour to dress. I should have given you notice, but I only determined on going since five o'clock, when I heard there was to be a genuine regale in the presence of a great actress.'

And he mentioned a name that thrilled me – a name that, in those days, could thrill Europe. It is hushed now: its once restless echoes are all still; she who bore it went years ago to her rest: night and oblivion long since closed above her; but *then* her day – a day of Sirius – stood at its full height, light and fervour.

'I'll go; I will be ready in ten minutes,' I vowed. And away I flew, never once checked, reader, by the thought which perhaps at this moment checks you: namely that to go anywhere with Graham and without Mrs Bretton could be objectionable. I could not have conceived, much less have expressed, to Graham such thought – such scruple – without risk of exciting a tyrannous self-contempt; of kindling an inward fire of shame so quenchless, and so devouring, that I think it would soon have licked up the very life in my veins. Besides, my godmother, knowing her son, and knowing me, would as soon have thought of chaperoning a sister with a brother, as of keeping anxious guard over our incomings and outgoings.

The present was no occasion for showy array; my dunmist crape would suffice, and I sought the same in the great oak-wardrobe in the dormitory, where hung no less than forty dresses. But there had been changes and reforms, and some innovating hand had pruned this same crowded wardrobe, and carried divers garments to the grenier – my crape amongst the rest. I must fetch it. I got the key, and went aloft fearless, almost thoughtless. I unlocked the door, I plunged in. The reader may believe it or not, but when I thus suddenly entered, that garret was not wholly dark as it should have been: from one point there shone a solemn light, like a star, but broader. So plainly it shone, that it revealed the deep alcove with a portion of the tarnished scarlet curtain drawn over it. Instantly, silently, before my eyes, it vanished; so did the curtain and alcove: all that end of the garret became black as night. I ventured no research; I had not time nor will; snatching my dress, which hung on the wall, happily near the door, I rushed out, relocked the door with convulsed haste, and darted downwards to the dormitory.

But I trembled too much to dress myself: impossible to arrange hair or fasten hooks-and-eyes with such fingers, so I called Rosine and bribed her to help me. Rosine liked a bribe, so she did her best, smoothed and plaited my hair as well as a coiffeur would have done, placed the lace collar mathematically straight, tied the neck-ribbon accurately – in short, did her work like the neat-handed Phillis she could be when she chose. Having given me my handkerchief and gloves, she took the candle and lighted me down stairs. After all, I had forgotten my shawl; she ran back to fetch it; and I stood with Dr John in the vestibule, waiting.

'What is this, Lucy?' said he, looking down at me narrowly. 'Here is the old excitement. Ho! the nun again?'

But I utterly denied the charge: I was vexed to be suspected of a second illusion. He was sceptical.

'She has been, as sure as I live,' said he; 'her figure crossing your eyes leaves on them a peculiar gleam and expression not to be mistaken.'

'She has *not* been,' I persisted: for, indeed, I could deny her apparition with truth.

'The old symptoms are there,' he affirmed; 'a particular pale, and what the Scotch call a "raised" look.'

He was so obstinate, I thought it better to tell him what I really *had* seen. Of course with him, it was held to be another effect of the same cause: it was all optical illusion – nervous malady, and so on. Not one bit did I believe him; but I dared not contradict: doctors are so self-opinionated, so immovable in their dry, materialist views.

Rosine brought the shawl, and I was bundled into the carriage.

The theatre was full – crammed to its roof: royal and noble were there; palace and hotel had emptied their inmates into those tiers so thronged and so hushed. Deeply did I feel myself privileged in having a place before that stage; I longed to see a being of whose powers I had heard reports which made me conceive peculiar anticipations. I wondered if she would justify her renown: with strange curiosity, with feelings severe and austere, yet of riveted interest, I waited. She was a study of such nature as had not encountered my eyes yet: a great and new planet she was: but in what state? I waited her rising.

She rose at nine that December night: above the horizon I saw her come. She could shine yet with pale grandeur and steady might; but that star verged already on its judgement day. Seen near, it was a chaos – hollow, half-consumed: an orb perished or perishing – half lava, half glow.

I had heard this woman termed 'plain,' and I expected bony harshness and grimness – something large, angular, sallow. What I saw was the shadow of a royal Vashti: a queen, fair as the day once, turned pale now like twilight, and wasted like wax in flame.

For awhile – a long while – I thought it was only a woman, though an unique woman, who moved in might and grace before this multitude. By and by I recognised my mistake. Behold! I found upon her something neither of woman nor of man: in each of her eyes sat a devil. These evil forces bore her through the tragedy, kept up her feeble strength – for she was but a frail creature; and as the action rose and the stir deepened, how wildly they shook her with their passions of the pit! They wrote HELL on her straight, haughty brow. They tuned her voice to the note of torment. They writhed her regal face to a demoniac mask. Hate and Murder and Madness incarnate, she stood.

It was a marvellous sight: a mighty revelation.

It was a spectacle low, horrible, immoral.

Swordsmen thrust through, and dying in their blood on the arena sand; bulls goring horses disembowelled, make a meeker vision for the public eye – a milder condiment for a people's palate – than Vashti torn by seven devils: devils which cried sore and rent the tenement they haunted, but still refused to be exorcised.

Suffering had struck that stage empress; and she stood before her audience neither yielding to, nor enduring, nor in finite measure, resenting it: she stood locked in struggle, rigid in resistance. She stood, not dressed, but draped in pale antique folds, long and regular like sculpture. A background and entourage and

flooring of deepest crimson threw her out, white like alabaster – like silver: rather be it said, like Death.

Where was the artist of the Cleopatra? Let him come and sit down and study this different vision. Let him seek here the mighty brawn, the muscle, the abounding blood, the full-fed flesh he worshipped: let all materialists draw nigh and look on.

I have said that she does not *resent* her grief. No; the weakness of that word would make it a lie. To her, what hurts becomes immediately embodied: she looks on it as a thing that can be attacked, worried down, torn in shreds. Scarcely a substance herself, she grapples to conflict with abstractions. Before calamity she is a tigress; she rends her woes, shivers them in convulsed abhorrence. Pain, for her, has no result in good; tears water no harvest of wisdom: on sickness, on death itself, she looks with the eye of a rebel. Wicked, perhaps, she is, but also she is strong; and her strength has conquered Beauty, has overcome Grace, and bound both at her side, captives peerlessly fair, and docile as fair. Even in the uttermost frenzy of energy is each maenad movement royally, imperially, incedingly upborne. Her hair, flying loose in revel or war, is still an angel's hair, and glorious under a halo. Fallen, insurgent, banished, she remembers the heaven where she rebelled. Heaven's light, following her exile, pierces its confines, and discloses their forlorn remoteness.

Place now the Cleopatra, or any other slug, before her as an obstacle, and see her cut through the pulpy mass as the scimitar of Saladin clove the down cushion. Let Paul Peter Rubens wake from the dead, let him rise out of his cerements, and bring into this presence all the army of his fat women; the magian power or prophet-virtue gifting that slight rod of Moses, could, at one waft, release and re-mingle a sea spell-parted, whelming the heavy host with the down-rush of overthrown sea-ramparts.

Vashti was not good, I was told; and I have said she did not look good: though a spirit, she was a spirit out of Tophet. Well, if so much of unholy force can arise from below, may not an equal efflux of sacred essence descend one day from above?

What thought Dr Graham of this being?

For long intervals I forgot to look how he demeaned himself, or to question what he thought. The strong magnetism of genius drew my heart out of its wonted orbit; the sunflower turned from the south to a fierce light, not solar – a rushing, red, cometary light – hot on vision and to sensation. I had seen acting before, but never anything like this: never anything which astonished Hope and hushed Desire; which outstripped Impulse and paled Conception; which, instead of merely irritating imagination with the thought of what *might* be done, at the same time fevering the nerves because it was *not* done, disclosed power like a deep, swollen, winter river, thundering in cataract, and bearing the soul, like a leaf, on the steep and steely sweep of its descent.

Miss Fanshawe, with her usual ripeness of judgement, pronounced Dr Bretton a serious, impassioned man, too grave and too impressible. Not in such light did I ever see him: no such faults could I lay to his charge. His natural

attitude was not the meditative, nor his natural mood the sentimental; *impressionable* he was as dimpling water, but, almost as water, *unimpressible:* the breeze, the sun, moved him – metal could not grave, nor fire brand.

Dr John *could* think, and think well, but he was rather a man of action than of thought; he *could* feel, and feel vividly in his way, but his heart had no chord for enthusiasm: to bright, soft, sweet influences his eyes and lips gave bright, soft, sweet welcome, beautiful to see as dyes of rose and silver, pearl and purple, imbuing summer clouds; for what belonged to storm, what was wild and intense, dangerous, sudden, and flaming, he had no sympathy, and held with it no communion. When I took time and regained inclination to glance at him, it amused and enlightened me to discover that he was watching that sinister and sovereign Vashti, not with wonder, nor worship, nor yet dismay, but simply with intense curiosity. Her agony did not pain him, her wild moan – worse than a shriek – did not much move him; her fury revolted him somewhat, but not to the point of horror. Cool young Briton! The pale cliffs of his own England do not look down on the tides of the channel more calmly than he watched the Pythian inspiration of that night.

Looking at his face, I longed to know his exact opinions, and at last I put a question tending to elicit them. At the sound of my voice he awoke as if out of a dream; for he had been thinking, and very intently thinking, his own thoughts, after his own manner. 'How did he like Vashti?' I wished to know.

'Hm-m-m,' was the first scarce articulate but expressive answer; and then such a strange smile went wandering round his lips, a smile so critical, so almost callous! I suppose that for natures of that order his sympathies *were* callous. In a few terse phrases he told me his opinion of, and feeling towards, the actress: he judged her as a woman, not an artist: it was a branding judgement.

That night was already marked in my book of life, not with white, but with a deep-red cross. But I had not done with it yet; and other memoranda were destined to be set down in characters of tint indelible.

Towards midnight, when the deepening tragedy blackened to the death scene, and all held their breath, and even Graham bit in his under lip, and knit his brow, and sat still and struck – when the whole theatre was hushed, when the vision of all eyes centred in one point, when all ears listened towards one quarter – nothing being seen but the white form sunk on a seat, quivering in conflict with her last, her worst-hated, her visibly-conquering foe – nothing heard but her throes, her graspings, breathing yet of mutiny, panting still defiance: when, as it seemed, an inordinate will, convulsing a perishing mortal frame, bent it to battle with doom and death, fought every inch of ground, sold dear every drop of blood, resisted to the latest the rape of every faculty, *would* see, *would* hear, *would* breathe, *would* live, up to, within, well nigh *beyond* the moment when death says to all sense and all being – 'Thus far and no farther!'

Just then a stir, pregnant with omen, rustled behind the scenes – feet ran, voices spoke. What was it? demanded the whole house. A flame, a smell of smoke replied.

'Fire!' rang through the gallery. 'Fire!' was repeated, re-echoed, yelled forth:

and then, and faster than pen can set it down, came panic, rushing, crushing – a blind, selfish, cruel chaos.

And Dr John? Reader, I see him yet, with his look of comely courage and cordial calm.

'Lucy will sit still, I know,' said he, glancing down at me with the same serene goodness, the same repose of firmness that I have seen in him when sitting at his side amid the secure peace of his mother's hearth. Yes, thus adjured, I think I would have sat still under a rocking crag: but, indeed, to sit still in actual circumstances was my instinct; and at the price of my very life, I would not have moved to give him trouble, thwart his will, or make demands on his attention. We were in the stalls, and for a few minutes there was a most terrible, ruthless pressure about us.

'How terrified are the women!' said he; 'but if the men were not almost equally so, order might be maintained. This is a sorry scene: I see fifty selfish brutes at this moment, each of whom, if I were near, I could conscientiously knock down. I see some women braver than some men. There is one yonder – Good God!'

While Graham was speaking, a young girl who had been very quietly and steadily clinging to a gentleman standing before us, was suddenly struck from her protector's arms by a big, butcherly intruder, and hurled under the feet of the crowd. Scarce two seconds lasted her disappearance. Graham rushed forwards; he and the gentleman, a powerful man though gray-haired, united their strength to thrust back the throng; her head and long hair fell back over his shoulder: she seemed unconscious.

'Trust her with me; I am a medical man,' said Dr John.

'If you have no lady with you, be it so,' was the answer. 'Hold her, and I will force a passage: we must get her to the air.'

'I have a lady,' said Graham, 'but she will be neither hindrance nor incumbrance.'

He summoned me with his eye: we were separated. Resolute, however, to rejoin him, I penetrated the living barrier, creeping under, where I could not get between or over.

'Fasten on me, and don't leave go,' he said; and I obeyed him.

Our pioneer proved strong and adroit; he opened the dense mass like a wedge; with patience and toil he at last bored through the flesh-and-blood rock – so solid, hot, and suffocating – and brought us to the fresh, freezing night.

'You are an Englishman?' said he, turning shortly on Dr Bretton, when we got into the street.

'An Englishman. And I speak to a countryman?' was the reply.

'Right. Be good enough to stand here two minutes, whilst I find my carriage.'

'Papa, I am not hurt,' said a girlish voice; 'am I with papa?'

'You are with a friend, and your father is close at hand.'

'Tell him I am not hurt, except just in my shoulder. Oh, my shoulder! They trode just here.'

'Dislocation, perhaps!' muttered the Doctor: 'let us hope there is no worse injury done. Lucy, lend a hand one instant.'

And I assisted while he made some arrangement of drapery and position for the ease of his suffering burden. She suppressed a moan, and lay in his arms quietly and patiently.

'She is very light,' said Graham, 'like a child!' and he asked in my ear, 'Is she a child, Lucy? Did you notice her age?'

'I am not a child – I am a person of seventeen,' responded the patient demurely and with dignity. Then, directly after: 'Tell papa to come; I get anxious.'

The carriage drove up; her father relieved Graham; but in the exchange from one bearer to another she was hurt, and moaned again.

'My darling!' said the father tenderly; then turning to Graham, 'You said, sir, you are a medical man?'

'I am: Dr Bretton, of La Terrasse.'

'Good. Will you step into my carriage?'

'My own carriage is here: I will seek it, and accompany you.'

'Be pleased, then, to follow us.' And he named his address: 'The Hôtel Crécy, in the Rue Crécy.'

We followed; the carriage drove fast; myself and Graham were silent. This seemed like an adventure.

Some little time being lost in seeking our own equipage, we reached the hotel, perhaps, about ten minutes after these strangers. It was an hotel in the foreign sense: a collection of dwelling-houses, not an inn – a vast, lofty pile, with a huge arch to its street-door, leading through a vaulted covered way, into a square all built round.

We alighted, passed up a wide, handsome public staircase, and stopped at Numéro 2 on the second landing; the first floor comprising the abode of I know not what 'prince Russe', as Graham informed me. On ringing the bell at a second great door, we were admitted to a suite of very handsome apartments. Announced by a servant in livery, we entered a drawing-room whose hearth glowed with an English fire, and whose walls gleamed with foreign mirrors. Near the hearth appeared a little group; a slight form sunk in a deep armchair, one or two women busy about it, the iron-gray gentleman anxiously looking on.

'Where is Harriet? I wish Harriet would come to me,' said the girlish voice, faintly.

'Where is Mrs Hurst?' demanded the gentleman impatiently and somewhat sternly of the manservant who had admitted us.

'I am sorry to say she is gone out of town, sir; my young lady gave her leave till tomorrow.'

'Yes – I did – I did. She is gone to see her sister; I said she might go: I remember now,' interposed the young lady; 'but I am so sorry, for Manon and Louison cannot understand a word I say, and they hurt me without meaning to do so.'

Dr John and the gentleman now interchanged greetings; and while they

passed a few minutes in consultation, I approached the easy-chair, and seeing what the faint and sinking girl wished to have done, I did it for her.

I was still occupied in the arrangement, when Graham drew near; he was no less skilled in surgery than medicine, and, on examination, found that no further advice than his own was necessary to the treatment of the present case. He ordered her to be carried to her chamber, and whispered to me: 'Go with the women, Lucy; they seem but dull; you can at least direct their movements, and thus spare her some pain. She must be touched very tenderly.'

The chamber was a room shadowy with pale-blue hangings, vaporous with curtainings and veilings of muslin; the bed seemed to me like snow-drift and mist – spotless, soft, and gauzy. Making the women stand apart, I undressed their mistress, without their well-meaning but clumsy aid. I was not in a sufficiently collected mood to note with separate distinctness every detail of the attire I removed, but I received a general impression of refinement, delicacy, and perfect personal cultivation; which, in a period of afterthought, offered in my reflections a singular contrast to notes retained of Miss Ginevra Fanshawe's appointments.

This girl was herself a small, delicate creature, but made like a model. As I folded back her plentiful yet fine hair, so shining and soft, and so exquisitely tended, I had under my observation a young, pale, weary, but high-bred face. The brow was smooth and clear; the eyebrows were distinct, but soft, and melting to a mere trace at the temples; the eyes were a rich gift of nature – fine and full, large, deep, seeming to hold dominion over the slighter subordinate features – capable, probably, of much significance at another hour and under other circumstances than the present, but now languid and suffering. Her skin was perfectly fair, the neck and hands veined finely like the petals of a flower; a thin glazing of the ice of pride, polished this delicate exterior, and her lip wore a curl – I doubt not inherent and unconscious, but which, if I had seen it first with the accompaniments of health and state, would have struck me as unwarranted, and proving in the little lady a quite mistaken view of life and her own consequence.

Her demeanour under the Doctor's hands at first excited a smile: it was not puerile – rather, on the whole, patient and firm – but yet, once or twice she addressed him with suddenness and sharpness, saying that he hurt her, and must contrive to give her less pain; I saw her large eyes, too, settle on his face like the solemn eyes of some pretty, wondering child. I know not whether Graham felt this examination: if he did, he was cautious not to check or discomfit it by any retaliatory look. I think he performed his work with extreme care and gentleness, sparing her what pain he could; and she acknowledged as much, when he had done, by the words: 'Thank you, Doctor, and good-night,' very gratefully pronounced: as she uttered them, however, it was with a repetition of the serious, direct gaze, I thought, peculiar in its gravity and intentness.

Her injuries, it seemed, were not dangerous: an assurance which her father received with a smile that almost made one his friend – it was so glad and gratified. He now expressed his obligations to Graham with as much earnestness as was befitting an Englishman addressing one who has served him, but is yet a stranger; he also begged him to call the next day.

'Papa,' said a voice from the veiled couch, 'thank the lady, too: is she there?'

I opened the curtain with a smile, and looked in at her. She lay now at comparative ease; she looked pretty, though pale; her face was delicately designed, and if at first sight it appeared proud, I believe custom might prove it to be soft.

'I thank the lady very sincerely,' said her father: 'I fancy she has been very good to my child. I think we scarcely dare tell Mrs Hurst who has been her substitute and done her work; she will feel at once ashamed and jealous.'

And thus, in the most friendly spirit, parting greetings were interchanged; and refreshment having been hospitably offered, but by us, as it was late, refused, we withdrew from the Hôtel Crécy.

On our way back we repassed the theatre. All was silence and darkness: the roaring, rushing crowd all vanished and gone – the lamps, as well as the incipient fire, extinct and forgotten. Next morning's papers explained that it was but some loose drapery on which a spark had fallen, and which had blazed up and been quenched in a moment.

## CHAPTER 24

### M. de Bassompierre

Those who live in retirement, whose lives have fallen amid the seclusion of schools or of other walled-in and guarded dwellings, are liable to be suddenly and for a long while dropped out of the memory of their friends, the denizens of a freer world. Unaccountably, perhaps, and close upon some space of unusually frequent intercourse – some congeries of rather exciting little circumstances, whose natural sequel would rather seem to be the quickening than the suspension of communication – there falls a stilly pause, a wordless silence, a long blank of oblivion. Unbroken always is this blank; alike entire and unexplained. The letter, the message once frequent, are cut off; the visit, formerly periodical, ceases to occur; the book, paper, or other token that indicated remembrance, comes no more.

Always there are excellent reasons for these lapses, if the hermit but knew them. Though he is stagnant in his cell, his connections without are whirling in the very vortex of life. That void interval which passes for him so slowly that the very clocks seem at a stand, and the wingless hours plod by in the likeness of tired tramps prone to rest at milestones – that same interval, perhaps, teems with events, and pants with hurry for his friends.

The hermit – if he be a sensible hermit – will swallow his own thoughts, and lock up his own emotions during these weeks of inward winter. He will know that Destiny designed him to imitate, on occasion, the dormouse, and he will be conformable: make a tidy ball of himself, creep into a hole of life's wall, and submit decently to the drift which blows in and soon blocks him up, preserving him in ice for the season.

Let him say, 'It is quite right: it ought to be so, since so it is.' And, perhaps, one day his snow-sepulchre will open, spring's softness will return, the sun and south-wind will reach him; the budding of hedges, and carolling of birds and singing of liberated streams will call him to kindly resurrection. *Perhaps* this may be the case, perhaps not: the frost may get into his heart and never thaw more; when spring comes, a crow or a pie may pick out of the wall only his dormouse-bones. Well, even in that case, all will be right: it is to be supposed he knew from the first he was mortal, and must one day go the way of all flesh, 'As well soon as syne.'

Following that eventful evening at the theatre, came for me seven weeks as bare as seven sheets of blank paper: no word was written on one of them; not a visit, not a token.

About the middle of that time I entertained fancies that something had happened to my friends at La Terrasse. The mid-blank is always a beclouded point for the solitary: his nerves ache with the strain of long expectancy; the doubts hitherto repelled gather now to a mass and – strong in accumulation – roll back upon him with a force which savours of vindictiveness. Night, too, becomes an unkindly time, and sleep and his nature cannot agree: strange starts and struggles harass his couch; the sinister band of bad dreams, with horror of calamity, and sick dread of entire desertion at their head, join the league against him. Poor wretch! He does his best to bear up, but he is a poor, pallid, wasting wretch, despite that best.

Towards the last of those long seven weeks I admitted, what through the other six I had jealously excluded – the conviction that these blanks were inevitable: the result of circumstances, the fiat of fate, a part of my life's lot, and – above all – a matter about whose origin no question must ever be asked, for whose painful sequence no murmur ever uttered. Of course I did not blame myself for suffering: I thank God I had a truer sense of justice than to fall into any imbecile extravagances of self-accusation; and as to blaming others for silence, in my reason I well knew them blameless, and in my heart acknowledged them so: but it was a rough and heavy road to travel, and I longed for better days.

I tried different expedients to sustain and fill existence: I commenced an elaborate piece of lace-work, I studied German pretty hard, I undertook a course of regular reading of the driest and thickest books in the library; in all my efforts I was as orthodox as I knew how to be. Was there error somewhere? Very likely. I only know the result was as if I had gnawed a file to satisfy hunger, or drunk brine to quench thirst.

My hour of torment was the post-hour. Unfortunately I knew it too well, and tried as vainly as assiduously to cheat myself of that knowledge; dreading the rack of expectation, and the sick collapse of disappointment which daily preceded and followed upon that well-recognised ring.

I suppose animals kept in cages, and so scantily fed as to be always upon the verge of famine, await their food as I awaited a letter. Oh! – to speak truth, and drop that tone of a false calm which long to sustain, outwears nature's endurance – I underwent in those seven weeks bitter fears and pains, strange inward trials,

miserable defections of hope, intolerable encroachments of despair. This last came so near me sometimes that her breath went right through me. I used to feel it, like a baleful air or sigh, penetrate deep, and make motion pause at my heart, or proceed only under unspeakable oppression. The letter – the well-beloved letter – would not come; and it was all of sweetness in life I had to look for.

In the very extremity of want, I had recourse again, and yet again, to the little packet in the case – the five letters. How splendid that month seemed whose skies had beheld the rising of these five stars! It was always at night I visited them, and not daring to ask every evening for a candle in the kitchen, I bought a wax-taper and matches to light it, and at the study-hour stole up to the dormitory, and feasted on my crust from the Barmecide's loaf. It did not nourish me: I pined on it, and got as thin as a shadow: otherwise I was not ill.

Reading there somewhat late one evening, and feeling that the power to read was leaving me – for the letters from incessant perusal were losing all sap and significance: my gold was withering to leaves before my eyes, and I was sorrowing over the disillusion – suddenly a quick tripping foot ran up the stairs. I knew Ginevra Fanshawe's step: she had dined in town that afternoon; she was now returned, and would come here to replace her shawl, etc., in the wardrobe.

Yes: in she came, dressed in bright silk, with her shawl falling from her shoulders, and her curls, half-uncurled in the damp of night, drooping careless and heavy upon her neck. I had hardly time to recasket my treasures and lock them up when she was at my side: her humour seemed none of the best.

'It has been a stupid evening: they are stupid people,' she began.

'Who? Mrs Cholmondeley? I thought you always found her house charming.'

'I have not been to Mrs Cholmondeley's.'

'Indeed! Have you made new acquaintance?'

'My uncle de Bassompierre is come.'

'Your uncle de Bassompierre! Are you not glad? – I thought he was a favourite.'

'You thought wrong: the man is odious; I hate him.'

'Because he is a foreigner? or for what other reason of equal weight?'

'He is not a foreigner. The man is English enough, goodness knows; and had an English name till three or four years ago; but his mother was a foreigner, a de Bassompierre, and some of her family are dead and have left him estates, a title, and this name: he is quite a great man now.'

'Do you hate him for that reason?'

'Don't I know what mama says about him? He is not my own uncle, but married mama's sister. Mama detests him; she says he killed Aunt Ginevra with unkindness: he looks like a bear. Such a dismal evening!' she went on. 'I'll go no more to his big hotel. Fancy me walking into a room alone, and a great man fifty years old coming forwards, and after a few minutes' conversation actually turning his back upon me, and then abruptly going out of the room. Such odd ways! I dare say his conscience smote him, for they all say at home I am the picture of Aunt Ginevra. Mama often declares the likeness is quite ridiculous.'

'Were you the only visitor?'

'The only visitor? Yes: then there was missy, my cousin: little spoiled, pampered thing.'

'M. de Bassompierre has a daughter?'

'Yes, yes: don't tease one with questions. Oh dear! I am so tired.'

She yawned. Throwing herself without ceremony on my bed, she added, 'It seems Mademoiselle was nearly crushed to a jelly in a hubbub at the theatre some weeks ago.'

'Ah! indeed. And they live at a large hotel in the Rue Crécy?'

'Justement. How do *you* know?'

'I have been there.'

'Oh you have? Really! You go everywhere in these days. I suppose Mother Bretton took you? She and Esculapius have the *entrée* of the de Bassompierre apartments: it seems "my son John" attended missy on the occasion of her accident – accident? Bah! All affectation! I don't think she was squeezed more than she richly deserves for her airs. And now there is quite an intimacy struck up: I heard something about "Auld lang syne," and what not? Oh, how stupid they all were!'

'*All*! You said you were the only visitor?'

'Did I? You see one forgets to particularise an old woman and her boy.'

'Dr and Mrs Bretton were at M. de Bassompierre's this evening?'

'Ay, ay! as large as life; and missy played the hostess. What a conceited doll it is!'

Soured and listless, Miss Fanshawe was beginning to disclose the causes of her prostrate condition. There had been a retrenchment of incense, a diversion or a total withholding of homage and attention: coquetry had failed of effect, vanity had undergone mortification. She lay fuming in the vapours.

'Is Miss de Bassompierre quite well now?' I asked.

'As well as you or I, no doubt; but she is an affected little thing, and gave herself invalid airs to attract medical notice. And to see the old dowager making her recline on a couch, and "my son John" prohibiting excitement, etcetera – faugh! the scene was quite sickening.'

'It would not have been so if the object of attention had been changed: if you had taken Miss de Bassompierre's place.'

'Indeed! I hate "my son John!" '

' "My son John!" – whom do you indicate by that name? Dr Bretton's mother never calls him so.'

'Then she ought. A clownish, bearish John he is.'

'You violate the truth in saying so; and as the whole of my patience is now spun off the distaff, I peremptorily desire you to rise from that bed, and vacate this room.'

'Passionate thing! Your face is the colour of a coquelicot. I wonder what always makes you so mighty testy à l'endroit du gros Jean? "John Anderson, my joe, John!" Oh! the distinguished name!'

Thrilling with exasperation, to which it would have been sheer folly to have given vent – for there was no contending with that unsubstantial feather, that

mealy-winged moth – I extinguished my taper, locked my bureau, and left her, since she would not leave me. Small-beer as she was, she had turned insufferably acid.

The morrow was Thursday and a half-holiday. Breakfast was over; I had withdrawn to the first classe. The dreaded hour, the post-hour, was nearing, and I sat waiting it, much as a ghost-seer might wait his spectre. Less than ever was a letter probable; still, strive as I would, I could not forget that it was possible. As the moments lessened, a restlessness and fear almost beyond the average assailed me. It was a day of winter east wind, and I had now for some time entered into that dreary fellowship with the winds and their changes, so little known, so incomprehensible to the healthy. The north and east owned a terrible influence, making all pain more poignant, all sorrow sadder. The south could calm, the west sometimes cheer: unless, indeed, they brought on their wings the burden of thunder-clouds, under the weight and warmth of which all energy died.

Bitter and dark as was this January day, I remember leaving the classe, and running down without bonnet to the bottom of the long garden, and there lingering amongst the stripped shrubs; in the forlorn hope that the postman's ring might occur while I was out of hearing, and I might thus be spared the thrill which some particular nerve or nerves, almost gnawed through with the unremitting tooth of a fixed idea, were becoming wholly unfit to support. I lingered as long as I dared without fear of attracting attention by my absence. I muffled my head in my apron, and stopped my ears in terror of the torturing clang, sure to be followed by such blank silence, such barren vacuum for me. At last I ventured to re-enter the first-classe, where, as it was not yet nine o'clock, no pupils had been admitted. The first thing seen was a white object on my black desk, a white, flat object. The post had, indeed, arrived; by me unheard. Rosine had visited my cell, and, like some angel, had left behind her a bright token of her presence. That shining thing on the desk was indeed a letter, a real letter; I saw so much at the distance of three yards, and as I had but one correspondent on earth, from that one it must come. He remembered me yet. How deep a pulse of gratitude sent new life through my heart.

Drawing near, bending and looking on the letter, in trembling but almost certain hope of seeing a known hand, it was my lot to find, on the contrary, an autograph for the moment deemed unknown – a pale female scrawl, instead of a firm masculine character. I then thought fate was *too* hard upon me, and I said, audibly, 'This is cruel.'

But I got over that pain also. Life is still life, whatever its pangs: our eyes and ears and their use remain with us, though the prospect of what pleases be wholly withdrawn, and the sound of what consoles be quite silenced.

I opened the billet: by this time I had recognised its handwriting as perfectly familiar. It was dated 'La Terrasse', and it ran thus:

DEAR LUCY, It occurs to me to enquire what you have been doing with yourself for the last month or two? Not that I suspect you would have the least difficulty in giving an account of your proceedings. I dare say you have

been just as busy and happy as ourselves at La Terrasse. As to Graham, his professional connection extends daily: he is so much sought after, so much engaged, that I tell him he will grow quite conceited. Like a right good mother, as I am, I do my best to keep him down: no flattery does he get from me, as you know. And yet, Lucy, he is a fine fellow; his mother's heart dances at the sight of him. After being hurried here and there the whole day, and passing the ordeal of fifty sorts of tempers, and combating a hundred caprices, and sometimes witnessing cruel sufferings – perhaps, occasionally, as I tell him, inflicting them – at night he still comes home to me in such kindly, pleasant mood, that, really, I seem to live in a sort of moral antipodes, and on these January evenings my day rises when other people's night sets in.

Still he needs keeping in order, and correcting, and repressing, and I do him that good service; but the boy is so elastic there is no such thing as vexing him thoroughly. When I think I have at last driven him to the sullens, he turns on me with jokes for retaliation: but you know him and all his iniquities, and I am but an elderly simpleton to make him the subject of this epistle.

As for me, I have had my old Bretton agent here on a visit, and have been plunged over head and ears in business matters. I do so wish to regain for Graham at least some part of what his father left him. He laughs to scorn my anxiety on this point, bidding me look and see how he can provide for himself and me too, and asking what the old lady can possibly want that she has not; hinting about sky-blue turbans; accusing me of an ambition to wear diamonds, keep livery servants, have an hotel, and lead the fashion amongst the English clan in Villette.

Talking of sky-blue turbans, I wished you had been with us the other evening. He had come in really tired; and after I had given him his tea, he threw himself into my chair with his customary presumption. To my great delight, he dropped asleep. (You know how he teases me about being drowsy; I, who never, by any chance, close an eye by daylight). While he slept, I thought he looked very bonny, Lucy: fool as I am to be so proud of him: but who can help it? Show me his peer. Look where I will I see nothing like him in Villette. Well, I took it into my head to play him a trick: so I brought out the sky-blue turban, and handling it and him with gingerly precaution, I managed to invest his brows with this grand adornment. I assure you it did not at all misbecome him; he looked quite Eastern, except that he is so fair. Nobody, however, can accuse him of having red hair *now* – it is genuine chestnut – a dark, glossy chestnut; and when I put my large Cashmere about him, there was as fine a young bey, dey, or pacha improvised as you would wish to see.

It was good entertainment; but only half-enjoyed, since I was alone: *you* should have been there.

In due time my lord awoke: the looking-glass above the fireplace soon intimated to him his plight: as you may imagine, I now live under threat and dread of vengeance.

But to come to the gist of my letter. I know Thursday is a half-holiday in

the Rue Fossette: be ready, then, by five in the afternoon, at which hour I will send the carriage to take you out to La Terrasse. Be sure to come: you may meet some old acquaintance. Goodbye, my wise, dear, grave little god-daughter.

<div align="right">Very truly yours,<br>LOUISA BRETTON</div>

Now, a letter like that sets one to rights! I might still be sad after reading that letter, but I was more composed; not exactly cheered, perhaps, but relieved. My friends, at least, were well and happy: no accident had occurred to Graham; no illness had seized his mother – calamities that had so long been my dream and thought. Their feelings for me too were – as they had been. Yet, how strange it was to look on Mrs Bretton's seven weeks and contrast them with my seven weeks! Also, how very wise it is in people placed in an exceptional position to hold their tongues and not rashly declare how such position galls them! The world can understand well enough the process of perishing for want of food: perhaps few persons can enter into or follow out that of going mad from solitary confinement. They see the long-buried prisoner disinterred, a maniac or an idiot! – how his senses left him – how his nerves first inflamed, underwent nameless agony, and then sunk to palsy – is a subject too intricate for examination, too abstract for popular comprehension. Speak of it! you might almost as well stand up in an European market-place, and propound dark sayings in that language and mood wherein Nebuchadnezzar, the imperial hypochondriac, communed with his baffled Chaldeans. And long, long may the minds to whom such themes are no mystery – by whom their bearings are sympathetically seized – be few in number, and rare of rencounter. Long may it be generally thought that physical privations alone merit compassion, and that the rest is a figment. When the world was younger and haler than now, moral trials were a deeper mystery still: perhaps in all the land of Israel there was but one Saul – certainly but one David to soothe or comprehend him.

The keen, still cold of the morning was succeeded, later in the day, by a sharp breathing from Russian wastes: the cold zone sighed over the temperate zone, and froze it fast. A heavy firmament, dull, and thick with snow, sailed up from the north, and settled over expectant Europe. Towards afternoon began the descent. I feared no carriage would come – the white tempest raged so dense and wild. But trust my godmother! Once having asked, she would have her guest. About six o'clock I was lifted from the carriage over the already blocked-up front steps of the chateau, and put in at the door of La Terrasse.

Running through the vestibule, and upstairs to the drawing-room, there I found Mrs Bretton – a summer-day in her own person. Had I been twice as cold as I was, her kind kiss and cordial clasp would have warmed me. Inured now for so long a time to rooms with bare boards, black benches, desks, and stoves, the blue saloon seemed to me gorgeous. In its Christmas-like fire alone there was a clear and crimson splendour which quite dazzled me.

When my godmother had held my hand for a little while, and chatted with me, and scolded me for having become thinner than when she last saw me, she professed to discover that the snow-wind had disordered my hair, and sent me upstairs to make it neat, and remove my shawl.

Repairing to my own little sea-green room, there also I found a bright fire, and candles too were lit: a tall waxlight stood on each side the great looking-glass; but between the candles, and before the glass, appeared something dressing itself – an airy, fairy thing – small, slight, white – a winter spirit.

I declare, for one moment I thought of Graham and his spectral illusions. With distrustful eye I noted the details of this new vision. It wore white, sprinkled slightly with drops of scarlet; its girdle was red; it had something in its hair leafy, yet shining – a little wreath with an evergreen gloss. Spectral or not, here truly was nothing frightful, and I advanced.

Turning quick upon me, a large eye, under long lashes, flashed over me, the intruder: the lashes were as dark as long, and they softened with their pencilling the orb they guarded.

'Ah! you are come!' she breathed out, in a soft, quiet voice, and she smiled slowly, and gazed intently.

I knew her now. Having only once seen that sort of face, with that cast of fine and delicate featuring, I could not but know her.

'Miss de Bassompierre,' I pronounced.

'No,' was the reply, 'not Miss de Bassompierre for *you*.' I did not enquire who then she might be, but waited voluntary information.

'You are changed, but still you are yourself,' she said, approaching nearer. 'I remember you well – your countenance, the colour of your hair, the outline of your face. . .'

I had moved to the fire, and she stood opposite, and gazed into me; and as she gazed, her face became gradually more and more expressive of thought and feeling, till at last a dimness quenched her clear vision.

'It makes me almost cry to look so far back,' said she; 'but as to being sorry, or sentimental, don't think it: on the contrary, I am quite pleased and glad.'

Interested, yet altogether at fault, I knew not what to say. At last I stammered, 'I think I never met you till that night, some weeks ago, when you were hurt . . . ?'

She smiled. 'You have forgotten then that I have sat on your knee, been lifted in your arms, even shared your pillow? You no longer remember the night when I came crying, like a naughty little child as I was, to your bedside, and you took me in? You have no memory for the comfort and protection by which you soothed an acute distress? Go back to Bretton. Remember Mr Home.'

At last I saw it all. 'And you are little Polly?'

'I am Paulina Mary Home de Bassompierre.'

How time can change! Little Polly wore in her pale, small features, her fairy symmetry, her varying expression, a certain promise of interest and grace; but Paulina Mary was become beautiful – not with the beauty that strikes the eye like a rose – orbed, ruddy, and replete; not with the plump, and pink, and flaxen attributes of her blond cousin Ginevra; but her seventeen years had brought her

a refined and tender charm which did not lie in complexion, though hers was fair and clear; nor in outline, though her features were sweet, and her limbs perfectly turned; but, I think, rather in a subdued glow from the soul outward. This was not an opaque vase, of material however costly, but a lamp chastely lucent, guarding from extinction, yet not hiding from worship, a flame vital and vestal. In speaking of her attractions, I would not exaggerate language; but, indeed, they seemed to me very real and engaging. What though all was on a small scale? It was the perfume which gave this white violet distinction, and made it superior to the broadest camellia – the fullest dahlia that ever bloomed.

'Ah! and you remember the old time at Bretton?'

'Better,' said she, 'better, perhaps, than you. I remember it with minute distinctness: not only the time, but the days of the time, and the hours of the days.'

'You must have forgotten some things?'

'Very little, I imagine.'

'You were then a little creature of quick feelings: you must, long ere this, have outgrown the impressions with which joy and grief, affection and bereavement, stamped your mind ten years ago?'

'You think I have forgotten whom I liked, and in what degree I liked them when a child?'

'The sharpness must be gone – the point, the poignancy – the deep imprint must be softened away and effaced?'

'I have a good memory for those days.'

She looked as if she had. Her eyes were the eyes of one who can remember; one whose childhood does not fade like a dream, nor whose youth vanish like a sunbeam. She would not take life, loosely and incoherently, in parts, and let one season slip as she entered on another: she would retain and add; often review from the commencement, and so grow in harmony and consistency as she grew in years. Still I could not quite admit the conviction that *all* the pictures which now crowded upon me were vivid and visible to her. Her fond attachments, her sports and contests with a well-loved playmate, the patient, true devotion of her child's heart, her fears, her delicate reserves, her little trials, the last piercing pain of separation, . . . I retraced these things, and shook my head incredulous. She persisted. 'The child of seven years lives yet in the girl of seventeen,' said she.

'You used to be excessively fond of Mrs Bretton,' I remarked, intending to test her. She set me right at once.

'Not *excessively* fond,' said she; 'I liked her: I respected her, as I should now: she seems to me very little altered.'

'She is not much changed,' I assented.

We were silent a few minutes. Glancing round the room, she said – 'There are several things here that used to be at Bretton. I remember that pincushion and that looking-glass.'

Evidently she was not deceived in her estimate of her own memory; not, at least, so far.

'You think, then, you would have known Mrs Bretton?' I went on.

'I perfectly remembered her; the turn of her features, her olive complexion, and black hair, her height, her walk, her voice.'

'Dr Bretton, of course,' I pursued, 'would be out of the question: and, indeed, as I saw your first interview with him, I am aware that he appeared to you as a stranger.'

'That first night I was puzzled,' she answered.

'How did the recognition between him and your father come about?'

'They exchanged cards. The names Graham Bretton and Home de Bassompierre gave rise to questions and explanations. That was on the second day; but before then I was beginning to know something.'

'How – know something?'

'Why,' she said, 'how strange it is that most people seem so slow to feel the truth – not to see, but *feel*! When Dr Bretton had visited me a few times, and sat near and talked to me; when I had observed the look in his eyes, the expression about his mouth, the form of his chin, the carriage of his head, and all that we *do* observe in persons who approach us – how could I avoid being led by association to think of Graham Bretton? Graham was slighter than he, and not grown so tall, and had a smoother face, and longer and lighter hair, and spoke – not so deeply – more like a girl; but yet he *is* Graham, just as *I* am little Polly, or you are Lucy Snowe.'

I thought the same, but I wondered to find my thoughts hers: there are certain things in which we so rarely meet with our double that it seems a miracle when that chance befalls.

'You and Graham were once playmates.'

'And do you remember that?' she questioned in her turn.

'No doubt he will remember it also,' said I.

'I have not asked him: few things would surprise me so much as to find that he did. I suppose his disposition is still gay and careless?'

'Was it so formerly? Did it so strike you? Do you thus remember him?'

'I scarcely remember him in any other light. Sometimes he was studious; sometimes he was merry: but whether busy with his books or disposed for play, it was chiefly the books or game he thought of; not much heeding those with whom he read or amused himself.'

'Yet to you he was partial.'

'Partial to me? Oh, no! he had other playmates – his schoolfellows; I was of little consequence to him, except on Sundays: yes, he was kind on Sundays. I remember walking with him hand in hand to St Mary's, and his finding the places in my prayer-book; and how good and still he was on Sunday evenings! So mild for such a proud, lively boy; so patient with all my blunders in reading; and so wonderfully to be depended on, for he never spent those evenings from home: I had a constant fear that he would accept some invitation and forsake us; but he never did, nor seemed ever to wish to do it. Thus, of course, it can be no more. I suppose Sunday will now be Dr Bretton's dining-out day. . .'

'Children, come down!' here called Mrs Bretton from below. Paulina would still have lingered, but I inclined to descend: we went down.

# *The Little Countess*

Cheerful as my godmother naturally was, and entertaining as, for our sakes, she made a point of being, there was no true enjoyment that evening at La Terrasse, till, through the wild howl of the winter-night, were heard the signal sounds of arrival. How often, while women and girls sit warm at snug firesides, their hearts and imaginations are doomed to divorce from the comfort surrounding their persons, forced out by night to wander through dark ways, to dare stress of weather, to contend with the snow-blast, to wait at lonely gates and stiles in wildest storms, watching and listening to see and hear the father, the son, the husband coming home.

Father and son came at last to the chateau: for the Count de Bassompierre that night accompanied Dr Bretton. I know not which of our trio heard the horses first; the asperity, the violence of the weather warranted our running down into the hall to meet and greet the two riders as they came in; but they warned us to keep our distance: both were white – two mountains of snow; and indeed Mrs Bretton, seeing their condition, ordered them instantly to the kitchen; prohibiting them, at their peril, from setting foot on her carpeted staircase till they had severally put off that mask of Old Christmas they now affected. Into the kitchen, however, we could not help following them: it was a large old Dutch kitchen, picturesque and pleasant. The little white Countess danced in a circle about her equally white sire, clapping her hands and crying – 'Papa, papa, you look like an enormous Polar bear.'

The bear shook himself, and the little sprite fled far from the frozen shower. Back she came, however, laughing, and eager to aid in removing the arctic disguise. The Count, at last issuing from his dreadnought, threatened to overwhelm her with it as with an avalanche.

'Come, then,' said she, bending to invite the fall, and when it was playfully advanced above her head, bounding out of reach like some little chamois.

Her movements had the supple softness, the velvet grace of a kitten; her laugh was clearer than the ring of silver and crystal: as she took her sire's cold hands and rubbed them, and stood on tiptoe to reach his lips for a kiss, there seemed to shine round her a halo of loving delight. The grave and reverend signior looked down on her as men *do* look on what is the apple of their eye.

'Mrs Bretton,' said he; 'what am I to do with this daughter or daughterling of mine? She neither grows in wisdom nor in stature. Don't you find her pretty nearly as much the child as she was ten years ago?'

'She cannot be more the child than this great boy of mine,' said Mrs Bretton, who was in conflict with her son about some change of dress she

deemed advisable, and which he resisted. He stood leaning against the Dutch dresser, laughing and keeping her at arm's length.

'Come, mama,' said he, 'by way of compromise, and to secure for us inward as well as outward warmth, let us have a Christmas wassail-cup, and toast Old England here, on the hearth.'

So, while the Count stood by the fire, and Paulina Mary still danced to and fro – happy in the liberty of the wide hall-like kitchen – Mrs Bretton herself instructed Martha to spice and heat the wassail-bowl, and, pouring the draught into a Bretton flagon, it was served round, reaming hot, by means of a small silver vessel, which I recognised as Graham's christening-cup.

'Here's to Auld Lang Syne!' said the Count; holding the glancing cup on high. Then, looking at Mrs Bretton:

> 'We twa ha' paidlet i' the burn
> Fra morning-sun till dine,
> But seas between us braid ha' roared
> Sin' auld lang syne.
> And surely ye'll be your pint-stoup,
> As surely I'll be mine;
> And we'll taste a cup o' kindness yet
> For auld lang syne.'

'Scotch! Scotch!' cried Paulina; 'papa is talking Scotch: and Scotch he is, partly. We are Home and De Bassompierre, Caledonian and Gallic.'

'And is that a Scotch reel you are dancing, you Highland fairy?' asked her father. 'Mrs Bretton, there will be a green ring growing up in the middle of your kitchen shortly. I would not answer for her being quite cannie: she is a strange little mortal.'

'Tell Lucy to dance with me, papa: there is Lucy Snowe.'

Mr Home (there was still quite as much about him of plain Mr Home as of proud Count de Bassompierre) held his hand out to me, saying kindly, 'he remembered me well; and, even had his own memory been less trustworthy, my name was so often on his daughter's lips, and he had listened to so many long tales about me, I should seem like an old acquaintance.'

Everyone now had tasted the wassail-cup except Paulina, whose pas de fée, ou de fantaisie, nobody thought of interrupting to offer so profanatory a draught; but she was not to be overlooked, nor baulked of her mortal privileges.

'Let me taste,' said she to Graham, as he was putting the cup on the shelf of the dresser out of her reach.

Mrs Bretton and Mr Home were now engaged in conversation. Dr John had not been unobservant of the fairy's dance; he had watched it, and he had liked it. To say nothing of the softness and beauty of the movements, eminently grateful to his grace-loving eye, that ease in his mother's house charmed him, for it set *him* at ease: again she seemed a child for him – again, almost his playmate. I wondered how he would speak to her; I had not yet seen him address her; his first words proved that the old days of 'little Polly' had been recalled to his mind by this evening's childlike light-heartedness.

'Your ladyship wishes for the tankard?'

'I think I said so. I think I intimated as much.'

'Couldn't consent to a step of the kind on any account. Sorry for it, but couldn't do it.'

'Why? I am quite well now: it can't break my collar-bone again, or dislocate my shoulder. Is it wine?'

'No; nor dew.'

'I don't want dew; I don't like dew: but what is it?'

'Ale – strong ale – old October; brewed, perhaps, when I was born.'

'It must be curious: is it good?'

'Excessively good.'

And he took it down, administered to himself a second dose of this mighty elixir, expressed in his mischievous eyes extreme contentment with the same, and solemnly replaced the cup on the shelf.

'I should like a little,' said Paulina, looking up; 'I never had any "old October:" is it sweet?'

'Perilously sweet,' said Graham.

She continued to look up exactly with the countenance of a child that longs for some prohibited dainty. At last the Doctor relented, took it down, and indulged himself in the gratification of letting her taste from his hand; his eyes, always expressive in the revelation of pleasurable feelings, luminously and smilingly avowed that it *was* a gratification; and he prolonged it by so regulating the position of the cup that only a drop at a time could reach the rosy, sipping lips by which its brim was courted.

'A little more – a little more,' said she, petulantly touching his hand with her forefinger, to make him incline the cup more generously and yieldingly. 'It smells of spice and sugar, but I can't taste it; your wrist is so stiff, and you are so stingy.'

He indulged her, whispering, however, with gravity: 'Don't tell my mother or Lucy; they wouldn't approve.'

'Nor do I,' said she, passing into another tone and manner as soon as she had fairly assayed the beverage, just as if it had acted upon her like some disenchanting draught, undoing the work of a wizard: 'I find it anything but sweet; it is bitter and hot, and takes away my breath. Your old October was only desirable while forbidden. Thank you, no more.'

And, with a slight bend – careless, but as graceful as her dance – she glided from him and rejoined her father.

I think she had spoken truth: the child of seven was in the girl of seventeen.

Graham looked after her a little baffled, a little puzzled; his eye was on her a good deal during the rest of the evening, but she did not seem to notice him.

As we ascended to the drawing-room for tea, she took her father's arm: her natural place seemed to be at his side; her eyes and her ears were dedicated to him. He and Mrs Bretton were the chief talkers of our little party, and Paulina was their best listener, attending closely to all that was said, prompting the repetition of this or that trait or adventure.

'And where were you at such a time, papa? And what did you say then? And tell Mrs Bretton what happened on that occasion.' Thus she drew him out.

She did not again yield to any effervescence of glee; the infantine sparkle was exhaled for the night: she was soft, thoughtful, and docile. It was pretty to see her bid good-night; her manner to Graham was touched with dignity: in her very slight smile and quiet bow spoke the Countess, and Graham could not but look grave, and bend responsive. I saw he hardly knew how to blend together in his ideas the dancing fairy and delicate dame.

Next day, when we were all assembled round the breakfast table, shivering and fresh from the morning's chill ablutions, Mrs Bretton pronounced a decree that nobody, who was not forced by dire necessity, should quit her house that day.

Indeed, egress seemed next to impossible; the drift darkened the lower panes of the casement, and, on looking out, one saw the sky and air vexed and dim, the wind and snow in angry conflict. There was no fall now, but what had already descended was torn up from the earth, whirled round by brief shrieking gusts, and cast into a hundred fantastic forms.

The Countess seconded Mrs Bretton.

'Papa shall not go out,' said she, placing a seat for herself beside her father's armchair. 'I will look after him. You won't go into town, will you, papa?'

'Aye, and No,' was the answer. 'If you and Mrs Bretton are *very* good to me, Polly – kind, you know, and attentive; if you pet me in a very nice manner, and make much of me, I may possibly be induced to wait an hour after breakfast and see whether this razor-edged wind settles. But, you see, you give me no breakfast; you offer me nothing: you let me starve.'

'Quick! please, Mrs Bretton, and pour out the coffee,' entreated Paulina, 'whilst I take care of the Count de Bassompierre in other respects: since he grew into a Count, he has needed *so* much attention.'

She separated and prepared a roll.

'There, papa, are your "pistolets" charged,' said she. 'And there is some marmalade, just the same sort of marmalade we used to have at Bretton, and which you said was as good as if it had been conserved in Scotland –'

'And which your little ladyship used to beg for my boy – do you remember that?' interposed Mrs Bretton. 'Have you forgotten how you would come to my elbow and touch my sleeve with the whisper, "please, ma'am, something good for Graham – a little marmalade, or honey, or jam?"'

'No, mama,' broke in Dr John, laughing, yet reddening; 'it surely was not so: I could not have cared for these things.'

'Did he or did he not, Paulina?'

'He liked them,' asserted Paulina.

'Never blush for it, John,' said Mr Home, encouragingly. 'I like them myself yet, and always did. And Polly showed her sense in catering for a friend's material comforts: it was I who put her into the way of such good manners – nor do I let her forget them. Polly, offer me a small slice of that tongue.'

'There, papa: but remember you are only waited upon with this assiduity, on condition of being persuadable, and reconciling yourself to La Terrasse for the day.'

'Mrs Bretton,' said the Count, 'I want to get rid of my daughter, to send her to school. Do you know of any good school?'

'There is Lucy's place – Mme Beck's.'

'Miss Snowe is in a school?'

'I am a teacher,' I said, and was rather glad of the opportunity of saying this. For a little while I had been feeling as if placed in a false position. Mrs Bretton and her son knew my circumstances; but the Count and his daughter did not. They might choose to vary by some shades their hitherto cordial manner towards me, when aware of my grade in society. I spoke then readily: but a swarm of thoughts I had not anticipated nor invoked, rose dim at the words, making me sigh involuntarily. Mr Home did not lift his eyes from his breakfast-plate for about two minutes, nor did he speak; perhaps he had not caught the words – perhaps he thought that on a confession of that nature, politeness would interdict comment: the Scotch are proverbially proud; and homely as was Mr Home in look, simple in habits and tastes, I have all along intimated that he was not without his share of the national quality. Was his a pseudo pride? was it real dignity? I leave the question undecided in its wide sense. Where it concerned me individually I can only answer: then, and always, he showed himself a true-hearted gentleman.

By nature he was a feeler and a thinker; over his emotions and his reflections spread a mellowing of melancholy; more than a mellowing: in trouble and bereavement it became a cloud. He did not know much about Lucy Snowe; what he knew, he did not very accurately comprehend: indeed his misconceptions of my character often made me smile; but he saw my walk in life lay rather on the shady side of the hill; he gave me credit for doing my endeavour to keep the course honestly straight; he would have helped me if he could: having no opportunity of helping, he still wished me well. When he did look at me, his eye was kind; when he did speak, his voice was benevolent.

'Yours,' said he, 'is an arduous calling. I wish you health and strength to win in it – success.'

His fair little daughter did not take the information quite so composedly: she fixed on me a pair of eyes wide with wonder – almost with dismay.

'Are you a teacher?' cried she. Then, having paused on the unpalatable idea, 'Well, I never knew what you were, nor ever thought of asking: for me, you were always Lucy Snowe.'

'And what am I now?' I could not forbear enquiring.

'Yourself, of course. But do you really teach here, in Villette?'

'I really do.'

'And do you like it?'

'Not always.'

'And why do you go on with it?'

Her father looked at, and, I feared, was going to check her; but he only said, 'Proceed, Polly, proceed with that catechism – prove yourself the little wiseacre you are. If Miss Snowe were to blush and look confused, I should have to bid you hold your tongue; and you and I would sit out the present meal in some

disgrace; but she only smiles, so push her hard, multiply the cross-questions. Well, Miss Snowe, why do you go on with it?'

'Chiefly, I fear, for the sake of the money I get.'

'Not then from motives of pure philanthropy? Polly and I were clinging to that hypothesis, as the most lenient way of accounting for your eccentricity.'

'No – no, sir. Rather for the roof of shelter I am thus enabled to keep over my head; and for the comfort of mind it gives me to think that while I can work for myself, I am spared the pain of being a burden to anybody.'

'Papa, say what you will, I pity Lucy.'

'Take up that pity, Miss de Bassompierre: take it up in both hands, as you might a little callow gosling squattering out of bounds without leave; put it back in the warm nest of a heart whence it issued, and receive in your ear this whisper. If my Polly ever came to know by experience the uncertain nature of this world's goods, I should like her to act as Lucy acts: to work for herself, that she might burden neither kith nor kin.'

'Yes, papa,' said she, pensively and tractably. 'But poor Lucy! I thought she was a rich lady, and had rich friends.'

'You thought like a little simpleton: *I* never thought so. When I had time to consider Lucy's manner and aspect, which was not often, I saw she was one who had to guard and not be guarded; to act and not be served: and this lot has, I imagine, helped her to an experience for which, if she live long enough to realise its full benefit, she may yet bless Providence. But this school,' he pursued, changing his tone from grave to gay: 'Would Mme Beck admit my Polly, do you think, Miss Lucy?'

I said, there needed but to try madame; it would soon be seen: she was fond of English pupils. 'If you, sir,' I added, 'will but take Miss de Bassompierre in your carriage this very afternoon, I think I can answer for it that Rosine, the portress, will not be very slow in answering your ring; and madame, I am sure, will put on her best pair of gloves to come into the salon to receive you.'

'In that case,' responded Mr Home, 'I see no sort of necessity there is for delay. Mrs Hurst can send, what she calls, her young lady's "things" after her; Polly can settle down to her horn-book before night; and you, Miss Lucy, I trust, will not disdain to cast an occasional eye upon her, and let me know, from time to time, how she gets on. I hope you approve of the arrangement, Countess de Bassompierre?'

The Countess hemmed and hesitated. 'I thought,' said she, 'I thought I had finished my education –'

'That only proves how much we may be mistaken in our thoughts: I hold a far different opinion, as most of those will who have been auditors of your profound knowledge of life this morning. Ah, my little girl, thou hast much to learn; and papa ought to have taught thee more than he has done! Come, there is nothing for it but to try Mme Beck; and the weather seems settling, and I have finished my breakfast.'

'But, papa!'

'Well?'

'I see an obstacle.'

'I don't at all.'

'It is enormous, papa, it can never be got over; it is as large as you in your great coat, and the snowdrift on the top.'

'And, like that snowdrift, capable of melting?'

'No! it is of too – too solid flesh: it is just your own self. Miss Lucy, warn Mme Beck not to listen to any overtures about taking me, because, in the end, it would turn out that she would have to take papa too: as he is so teasing, I will just tell tales about him. Mrs Bretton and all of you listen! About five years ago, when I was twelve years old, he took it into his head that he was spoiling me; that I was growing unfitted for the world, and I don't know what, and nothing would serve or satisfy him, but I must go to school. I cried, and so on; but M. de Bassompierre proved hard-hearted, quite firm and flinty, and to school I went. What was the result? In the most admirable manner, papa came to school likewise: every other day he called to see me. Mme Aigredoux grumbled, but it was of no use; and so, at last, papa and I were both, in a manner, expelled. Lucy can just tell Mme Beck this little trait: it is only fair to let her know what she has to expect.'

Mrs Bretton asked Mr Home what he had to say in answer to this statement. As he made no defence, judgement was given against him, and Paulina triumphed.

But she had other moods besides the arch and naïve. After breakfast, when the two elders withdrew – I suppose to talk over certain of Mrs Bretton's business matters – and the Countess, Dr Bretton, and I were, for a short time, alone together – all the child left her; with us, more nearly her companions in age, she rose at once to the little lady: her very face seemed to alter; that play of feature, and candour of look, which, when she spoke to her father, made it quite dimpled and round, yielded to an aspect more thoughtful, and lines distincter and less *mobile*.

No doubt, Graham noted the change as well as I. He stood for some minutes near the window, looking out at the snow; presently he approached the hearth, and entered into conversation, but not quite with his usual ease: fit topics did not seem to rise to his lips; he chose them fastidiously, hesitatingly, and consequently infelicitously: he spoke vaguely of Villette – its inhabitants, its notable sights and buildings. He was answered by Miss de Bassompierre in quite womanly sort; with intelligence, with a manner not indeed wholly disindividualised: a tone, a glance, a gesture, here and there, rather animated and quick than measured and stately, still recalled little Polly; but yet there was so fine and even a polish, so calm and courteous a grace, gilding and sustaining these peculiarities, that a less sensitive man than Graham would not have ventured to seize upon them as vantage points, leading to franker intimacy.

Yet while Dr Bretton continued subdued, and, for him, sedate, he was still observant. Not one of those pretty impulses and natural breaks escaped him. He did not miss one characteristic movement, one hesitation in language, or one lisp in utterance. At times, in speaking fast, she still lisped; but coloured whenever such lapse occurred, and in a painstaking, conscientious manner, quite as amusing as the slight error, repeated the word more distinctly.

Whenever she did this, Dr Bretton smiled. Gradually, as they conversed, the restraint on each side slackened: might the conference have but been prolonged, I believe it would soon have become genial: already to Paulina's lip and cheek returned the wreathing, dimpling smile; she lisped once, and forgot to correct herself. And Dr John, I know not how *he* changed, but change he did. He did not grow gayer – no raillery, no levity sparkled across his aspect – but his position seemed to become one of more pleasure to himself, and he spoke his augmented comfort in readier language, in tones more suave. Ten years ago, this pair had always found abundance to say to each other; the intervening decade had not narrowed the experience or impoverished the intelligence of either: besides, there are certain natures of which the mutual influence is such, that the more they say, the more they have to say. For these, out of association grows adhesion, and out of adhesion, amalgamation.

Graham, however, must go: his was a profession, whose claims are neither to be ignored, nor deferred. He left the room; but before he could leave the house there was a return. I am sure he came back – not for the paper, or card in his desk, which formed his ostensible errand – but to assure himself, by one more glance, that Paulina's aspect was really such as memory was bearing away: that he had not been viewing her somehow by a partial, artificial light, and making a fond mistake. No! he found the impression true – rather, indeed, he gained, than lost, by this return: he took away with him a parting look – shy, but very soft – as beautiful, as innocent, as any little fawn could lift out of its cover of fern, or any lamb from its meadow-bed.

Being left alone, Paulina and I kept silence for some time; we both took out some work, and plied a mute and diligent task. The white-wood workbox of old days, was now replaced by one inlaid with precious mosaic, and furnished with implements of gold; the tiny and trembling fingers that could scarce guide the needle, though tiny still, were now swift and skilful: but there was the same busy knitting of the brow, the same little dainty mannerisms, the same quick turns and movements – now to replace a stray tress; and anon to shake from the silken skirt some imaginary atom of dust – some clinging fibre of thread.

That morning I was disposed for silence: the austere fury of the winter-day had on me an awing, hushing influence. That passion of January, so white and so bloodless, was not yet spent: the storm had raved itself hoarse, but seemed no nearer exhaustion. Had Ginevra Fanshawe been my companion in that morning-room, she would not have suffered me to muse and listen undisturbed. The presence just gone from us would have been her theme; and how she would have rung the changes on one topic! how she would have pursued and pestered me with questions and surmises – worried and oppressed me with comments and confidences I did not want, and longed to avoid.

Paulina Mary cast once or twice towards me a quiet, but penetrating glance of her dark, full eye; her lips half opened, as if to the impulse of coming utterance: but she saw and delicately respected my inclination for silence.

'This will not hold long,' I thought to myself; for I was not accustomed to find in women or girls any power of self-control, or strength of self-denial. As

far as I knew them, the chance of a gossip about their usually trivial secrets, their often very washy and paltry feelings, was a treat not to be readily foregone.

The little Countess promised an exception: she sewed, till she was tired of sewing, and then she took a book.

As chance would have it, she had sought it in Dr Bretton's own compartment of the bookcase; and it proved to be an old Bretton book – some illustrated work of natural history. Often had I seen her standing at Graham's side, resting that volume on his knee, and reading to his tuition; and, when the lesson was over, begging, as a treat, that he would tell her all about the pictures. I watched her keenly: here was a true test of that memory she had boasted: would her recollections now be faithful?

Faithful? It could not be doubted. As she turned the leaves, over her face passed gleam after gleam of expression, the least intelligent of which was a full greeting to the Past. And then she turned to the title-page, and looked at the name written in the schoolboy hand. She looked at it long; nor was she satisfied with merely looking: she gently passed over the characters the tips of her fingers, accompanying the action with an unconscious but tender smile, which converted the touch into a caress. Paulina loved the Past; but the peculiarity of this little scene was, that she *said* nothing: she could feel, without pouring out her feelings in a flux of words.

She now occupied herself at the bookcase for nearly an hour; taking down volume after volume, and renewing her acquaintance with each. This done, she seated herself on a low stool, rested her cheek on her hand, and thought, and still was mute.

The sound of the front door opened below, a rush of cold wind, and her father's voice speaking to Mrs Bretton in the hall, startled her at last. She sprang up: she was downstairs in one second.

'Papa! papa! you are not going out?'

'My pet; I must go into town.'

'But it is too – *too* cold, papa.'

And then I heard M. de Bassompierre showing to her how he was well provided against the weather; and how he was going to have the carriage, and to be quite snugly sheltered; and, in short, proving that she need not fear for his comfort.

'But you will promise to come back here this evening, before it is quite dark; you and Dr Bretton, both, in the carriage? It is not fit to ride.'

'Well, if I see the Doctor, I will tell him a lady has laid on him her commands to take care of his precious health, and come home early under my escort.'

'Yes, you must say "a lady"; and he will think it is his mother, and be obedient. And, papa, mind to come soon, for I *shall* watch and listen.'

The door closed, and the carriage rolled softly through the snow; and back returned the Countess, pensive and anxious.

She *did* listen, and watch, when evening closed; but it was in stillest sort: walking the drawing-room with quite noiseless step. She checked at intervals her velvet march; inclined her ear, and consulted the night sounds: I should

rather say, the night silence; for now, at last, the wind was fallen. The sky, relieved of its avalanche, lay naked and pale: through the barren boughs of the avenue we could see it well, and note also the polar splendour of the new-year moon – an orb, white as a world of ice. Nor was it late when we saw also the return of the carriage.

Paulina had no dance of welcome for this evening. It was with a sort of gravity that she took immediate possession of her father, as he entered the room; but she at once made him her entire property, led him to the seat of her choice, and, while softly showering round him honeyed words of commendation for being so good and coming home so soon, you would have thought it was entirely by the power of her little hands he was put into his chair, and settled and arranged; for the strong man seemed to take pleasure in wholly yielding himself to this dominion – potent only by love.

Graham did not appear till some minutes after the Count. Paulina half turned when his step was heard: they spoke, but only a word or two; their fingers met a moment, but obviously with slight contact. Paulina remained beside her father; Graham threw himself into a seat on the other side of the room.

It was well that Mrs Bretton and Mr Home had a great deal to say to each other – almost an inexhaustible fund of discourse in old recollections; otherwise, I think, our party would have been but a still one that evening.

After tea, Paulina's quick needle and pretty golden thimble were busily plied by the lamplight, but her tongue rested, and her eyes seemed reluctant to raise often their lids so smooth and so full-fringed. Graham too must have been tired with his day's work: he listened dutifully to his elders and betters, said very little himself, and followed with his eye the gilded glance of Paulina's thimble, as if it had been some bright moth on the wing, or the golden head of some darting little yellow serpent.

## CHAPTER 26

### A Burial

From this date my life did not want variety; I went out a good deal, with the entire consent of Mme Beck, who perfectly approved the grade of my acquaintance. That worthy directress had never from the first treated me otherwise than with respect; and when she found that I was liable to frequent invitations from a chateau and a great hotel, respect improved into distinction.

Not that she was fulsome about it: madame, in all things worldly, was in nothing weak; there was measure and sense in her hottest pursuit of self-interest, calm and considerateness in her closest clutch of gain; without, then, laying herself open to my contempt as a time-server and a toadie, she marked with tact that she was pleased people connected with her establishment should frequent such associates as must cultivate and elevate, rather than those who might

568 SELECTED WORKS OF THE BRONTË SISTERS

deteriorate and depress. She never praised either me or my friends; only once when she was sitting in the sun in the garden, a cup of coffee at her elbow and the Gazette in her hand, looking very comfortable, and I came up and asked leave of absence for the evening, she delivered herself in this gracious sort: 'Oui, oui, ma bonne amie: je vous donne la permission de cœur et de gré. Votre travail dans ma maison a toujours été admirable, rempli de zèle et de discrétion: vous avez bien le droit de vous amuser. Sortez donc tant que vous voudrez. Quant à votre choix de connaissances, j'en suis contente; c'est sage, digne, louable.'

She closed her lips and resumed the Gazette.

The reader will not too gravely regard the little circumstance that about this time the triply-enclosed packet of five letters temporarily disappeared from my bureau. Blank dismay was naturally my first sensation on making the discovery; but in a moment I took heart of grace.

'Patience!' whispered I to myself. 'Let me say nothing, but wait peaceably; they will come back again.'

And they did come back: they had only been on a short visit to madame's chamber; having passed their examination, they came back duly and truly: I found them all right the next day.

I wonder what she thought of my correspondence. What estimate did she form of Dr John Bretton's epistolary powers? In what light did the often very pithy thoughts, the generally sound, and sometimes original opinions, set, without pretension, in an easily-flowing, spirited style, appear to her? How did she like that genial, half-humorous vein, which to me gave such delight? What did she think of the few kind words scattered here and there – not thickly, as the diamonds were scattered in the valley of Sinbad, but sparely, as those gems lie in unfabled beds? Oh, Mme Beck! how seemed these things to you?

I think in Mme Beck's eyes the five letters found a certain favour. One day after she had *borrowed* them (in speaking of so suave a little woman, one ought to use suave terms), I caught her examining me with a steady contemplative gaze, a little puzzled, but not at all malevolent. It was during that brief space between lessons, when the pupils turned out into the court for a quarter of an hour's recreation; she and I remained in the first classe alone: when I met her eye, her thoughts forced themselves partially through her lips.

'Il y a,' said she, 'quelquechose de bien remarquable dans le caractère Anglais.'

'How, Madame?'

She gave a little laugh, repeating the word 'how' in English.

'Je ne saurais vous dire "how"; mais, enfin, les Anglais ont des idées à eux, en amitie, en amour, en tout. Mais au moins il n'est pas besoin de les surveiller,' she added, getting up and trotting away like the compact little pony she was.

'Then I hope,' murmured I to myself, 'you will graciously let alone my letters for the future.'

Alas! something came rushing into my eyes, dimming utterly their vision, blotting from sight the schoolroom, the garden, the bright winter sun, as I remembered that never more would letters, such as she had read, come to me.

I had seen the last of them. That goodly river on whose banks I had sojourned, of whose waves a few reviving drops had trickled to my lips, was bending to another course: it was leaving my little hut and field forlorn and sand-dry, pouring its wealth of waters far away. The change was right, just, natural; not a word could be said: but I loved my Rhine, my Nile; I had almost worshipped my Ganges, and I grieved that the grand tide should roll estranged, should vanish like a false mirage. Though stoical, I was not quite a stoic; drops streamed fast on my hands, on my desk: I wept one sultry shower, heavy and brief.

But soon I said to myself, 'The Hope I am bemoaning suffered and made me suffer much: it did not die till it was full time: following an agony so lingering, death ought to be welcome.'

Welcome I endeavoured to make it. Indeed, long pain had made patience a habit. In the end I closed the eyes of my dead, covered its face, and composed its limbs with great calm.

The letters, however, must be put away, out of sight: people who have undergone bereavement always jealously gather together and lock away mementos: it is not supportable to be stabbed to the heart each moment by sharp revival of regret.

One vacant holiday afternoon (the Thursday) going to my treasure, with intent to consider its final disposal, I perceived – and this time with a strong impulse of displeasure – that it had been again tampered with: the packet was there, indeed, but the ribbon which secured it had been untied and retied; and by other symptoms I knew that my drawer had been visited.

This was a little too much. Mme Beck herself was the soul of discretion, besides having as strong a brain and sound a judgement as ever furnished a human head; that she should know the contents of my casket, was not pleasant, but might be borne. Little Jesuit inquisitress as she was, she could see things in a true light, and understand them in an unperverted sense; but the idea that she had ventured to communicate information, thus gained, to others; that she had, perhaps, amused herself with a companion over documents, in my eyes most sacred, shocked me cruelly. Yet, that such was the case I now saw reason to fear: I even guessed her confidant. Her kinsman, M. Paul Emanuel, had spent yesterday evening with her: she was much in the habit of consulting him, and of discussing with him matters she broached to no one else. This very morning, in class, that gentleman had favoured me with a glance which he seemed to have borrowed from Vashti, the actress; I had not at the moment comprehended that blue, yet lurid flash out of his angry eye, but I read its meaning now. *He*, I believed, was not apt to regard what concerned me from a fair point of view, nor to judge me with tolerance and candour: I had always found him severe and suspicious: the thought that these letters, mere friendly letters as they were, had fallen once, and might fall again, into his hands, jarred my very soul.

What should I do to prevent this? In what corner of this strange house was it possible to find security or secrecy? Where could a key be a safeguard, or a padlock a barrier?

In the grenier? No, I did not like the grenier. Besides, most of the boxes and

drawers there were mouldering, and did not lock. Rats, too, gnawed their way through the decayed wood; and mice made nests amongst the litter of their contents: my dear letters (most dear still, though Ichabod was written on their covers) might be consumed by vermin; certainly the writing would soon become obliterated by damp. No; the grenier would not do – but where then?

While pondering this problem, I sat in the dormitory window-seat. It was a fine frosty afternoon; the winter sun, already setting, gleamed pale on the tops of the garden-shrubs: in the 'allée défendue' one great old pear-tree – the nun's pear-tree – stood up a tall dryad skeleton, gray, gaunt, and stripped. A thought struck me – one of those queer fantastic thoughts that will sometimes strike solitary people. I put on my bonnet, cloak and furs, and went out into the city.

Bending my steps to the old historical quarter of the town, whose hoar and overshadowed precincts I always sought by instinct in melancholy moods, I wandered on from street to street, till, having crossed a half-deserted 'place' or square, I found myself before a sort of broker's shop; an ancient place, full of ancient things.

What I wanted was a metal box which might be soldered, or a thick glass jar or bottle which might be stoppered and sealed hermetically. Amongst miscellaneous heaps, I found and purchased the latter article.

I then made a little roll of my letters, wrapped them in oiled silk, bound them with twine, and, having put them in the bottle, got the old Jew broker to stopper, seal, and make it airtight. While obeying my directions, he glanced at me now and then, suspiciously, from under his frost-white eyelashes. I believe he thought there was some evil deed on hand. In all this I had a dreary something – not pleasure – but a sad, lonely satisfaction. The impulse under which I acted, the mood controlling me, were similar to the impulse and the mood which had induced me to visit the confessional. With quick walking I regained the pensionnat just at dark, and in time for dinner.

At seven o'clock the moon rose. At half-past seven, when the pupils and teachers were at study, and Mme Beck was with her mother and children in the salle à manger, when the half-boarders were all gone home, and Rosine had left the vestibule, and all was still – I shawled myself, and, taking the sealed jar, stole out through the first-classe door, into the berceau and thence into the 'allée défendue'.

Methusaleh, the pear-tree, stood at the further end of this walk, near my seat: he rose up, dim and gray, above the lower shrubs round him. Now Methusaleh, though so very old, was of sound timber still; only there was a hole, or rather a deep hollow, near his root. I knew there was such a hollow, hidden partly by ivy and creepers growing thick round; and there I meditated hiding my treasure. But I was not only going to hide a treasure – I meant also to bury a grief. That grief over which I had lately been weeping as I wrapped it in its winding-sheet, must be interred.

Well, I cleared away the ivy, and found the hole; it was large enough to receive the jar, and I thrust it deep in. In a tool-shed at the bottom of the garden, lay the relics of building-materials, left by masons lately employed to repair a

part of the premises. I fetched thence a slate and some mortar, put the slate on the hollow, secured it with cement, covered the whole with black mould, and, finally, replaced the ivy. This done, I rested, leaning against the tree; lingering, like any other mourner, beside a newly-sodded grave.

The air of the night was very still, but dim with a peculiar mist, which changed the moonlight into a luminous haze. In this air, or this mist, there was some quality – electrical, perhaps – which acted in strange sort upon me. I felt then as I had felt a year ago in England – on a night when the aurora borealis was streaming and sweeping round heaven, when, belated in lonely fields, I had paused to watch that mustering of an army with banners – that quivering of serried lances – that swift ascent of messengers from below the north star to the dark, high keystone of heaven's arch. I felt, not happy, far otherwise, but strong with reinforced strength.

If life be a war, it seemed my destiny to conduct it single-handed. I pondered now how to break up my winter-quarters – to leave an encampment where food and forage failed. Perhaps, to effect this change, another pitched battle must be fought with fortune; if so, I had a mind to the encounter: too poor to lose, God might destine me to gain. But what road was open? – what plan available?

On this question I was still pausing, when the moon, so dim hitherto, seemed to shine out somewhat brighter: a ray even gleamed white before me, and a shadow became distinct and marked. I looked more narrowly, to make out the cause of this well-defined contrast appearing a little suddenly in the obscure alley: whiter and blacker it grew on my eye: it took shape with instantaneous transformation. I stood about three yards from a tall, sable-robed, snowy-veiled woman.

Five minutes passed. I neither fled nor shrieked. She was there still. I spoke. 'Who are you? and why do you come to me?'

She stood mute. She had no face – no features: all below her brow was masked with a white cloth; but she had eyes, and they viewed me.

I felt, if not brave, yet a little desperate; and desperation will often suffice to fill the post and do the work of courage. I advanced one step. I stretched out my hand, for I meant to touch her. She seemed to recede. I drew nearer: her recession, still silent, became swift. A mass of shrubs, full-leaved evergreens – laurel and dense yew – intervened between me and what I followed. Having passed that obstacle, I looked and saw nothing. I waited. I said, 'If you have any errand to me, come back and deliver it.' Nothing spoke or reappeared.

This time there was no Dr John to whom to have recourse: there was no one to whom I dared whisper the words, 'I have again seen the nun.'

Paulina Mary sought my frequent presence in the Rue Crécy. In the old Bretton days, though she had never professed herself fond of me, my society had soon become to her a sort of unconscious necessary. I used to notice that if I withdrew to my room, she would speedily come trotting after me, and opening the door and peeping in, say, with her little peremptory accent – 'Come down. Why do you sit here by yourself? You must come into the parlour.'

In the same spirit she urged me now – 'Leave the Rue Fossette,' she said, 'and come and live with us. Papa would give you far more than Mme Beck gives you.'

Mr Home himself offered me a handsome sum – thrice my present salary – if I would accept the office of companion to his daughter. I declined. I think I should have declined had I been poorer than I was, and with scantier fund of resource, more stinted narrowness of future prospect. I had not that vocation. I could teach; I could give lessons; but to be either a private governess or a companion was unnatural to me. Rather than fill the former post in any great house, I would deliberately have taken a housemaid's place, bought a strong pair of gloves, swept bedrooms and staircases, and cleaned stoves and locks, in peace and independence. Rather than be a companion, I would have made shirts, and starved.

I was no bright lady's shadow – not Miss de Bassompierre's. Overcast enough it was my nature often to be; of a subdued habit I was: but the dimness and depression must both be voluntary – such as kept me docile at my desk, in the midst of my now well-accustomed pupils in Mme Beck's first classe; or alone, at my own bedside, in her dormitory, or in the alley and seat which were called mine, in her garden: my qualifications were not convertible, not adaptable; they could not be made the foil of any gem, the adjunct of any beauty, the appendage of any greatness in Christendom. Mme Beck and I, without assimilating, understood each other well. I was not *her* companion, nor her children's governess; she left me free: she tied me to nothing – not to herself – not even to her interests: once, when she had for a fortnight been called from home by a near relation's illness, and on her return, all anxious and full of care about her establishment, lest something in her absence should have gone wrong – finding that matters had proceeded much as usual, and that there was no evidence of glaring neglect – she made each of the teachers a present, in acknowledgement of steadiness. To my bedside she came at twelve o'clock at night, and told me she had no present for me. 'I must make fidelity advantageous to the St Pierre,' said she; 'if I attempt to make it advantageous to you, there will arise misunderstanding between us – perhaps separation. One thing, however, I *can* do to please you – leave you alone with your liberty: c'est ce que je ferai.'

She kept her word. Every slight shackle she had ever laid on me, she, from that time, with quiet hand removed. Thus I had pleasure in voluntarily respecting her rules; gratification in devoting double time, in taking double pains with the pupils she committed to my charge.

As to Mary de Bassompierre, I visited her with pleasure, though I would not live with her. My visits soon taught me that it was unlikely even my occasional and voluntary society would long be indispensable to her. M. de Bassompierre, for his part, seemed impervious to this conjecture, blind to this possibility; unconscious as any child to the signs, the likelihoods, the fitful beginnings of what, when it drew to an end, he might not approve.

Whether or not he would cordially approve, I used to speculate. Difficult to say. He was much taken up with scientific interests; keen, intent, and somewhat oppugnant in what concerned his favourite pursuits, but unsuspicious and trustful in the ordinary affairs of life. From all I could gather, he seemed to regard his

'daughterling' as still but a child, and probably had not yet admitted the notion that others might look on her in a different light: he would speak of what should be done when 'Polly' was a woman, when she should be grown up; and 'Polly,' standing beside his chair, would sometimes smile and take his honoured head between her little hands, and kiss his iron-gray locks; and, at other times, she would pout and toss her curls: but she never said, 'Papa, I *am* grown up.'

She had different moods for different people. With her father she really was still a child, or childlike, affectionate, merry, and playful. With me she was serious, and as womanly as thought and feeling could make her. With Mrs Bretton she was docile and reliant, but not expansive. With Graham she was shy, at present very shy; at moments she tried to be cold; on occasion she endeavoured to shun him. His step made her start; his entrance hushed her; when he spoke, her answers failed of fluency; when he took leave, she remained self-vexed and disconcerted. Even her father noticed this demeanour in her.

'My little Polly,' he said once, 'you live too retired a life; if you grow to be a woman with these shy manners, you will hardly be fitted for society. You really make quite a stranger of Dr Bretton: how is this? Don't you remember that, as a little girl, you used to be rather partial to him?'

'*Rather*, papa,' echoed she, with her slightly dry, yet gentle and simple tone.

'And you don't like him now? What has he done?'

'Nothing. Y-e-s, I like him a little; but we are grown strange to each other.'

'Then rub it off, Polly: rub the rust and the strangeness off. Talk away when he is here, and have no fear of him!'

'*He* does not talk much. Is he afraid of me, do you think, papa?'

'Oh, to be sure! What man would not be afraid of such a little silent lady?'

'Then tell him someday not to mind my being silent. Say that it is my way, and that I have no unfriendly intention.'

'Your way, you little chatter-box? So far from being your way, it is only your whim!'

'Well, I'll improve, papa.'

And very pretty was the grace with which, the next day, she tried to keep her word. I saw her make the effort to converse affably with Dr John on general topics. The attention called into her guest's face a pleasurable glow; he met her with caution, and replied to her in his softest tones, as if there was a kind of gossamer happiness hanging in the air which he feared to disturb by drawing too deep a breath. Certainly, in her timid yet earnest advance to friendship, it could not be denied that there was a most exquisite and fairy charm.

When the Doctor was gone, she approached her father's chair.

'Did I keep my word, papa? Did I behave better?'

'My Polly behaved like a queen. I shall become quite proud of her if this improvement continues. By and by we shall see her receiving my guests with quite a calm, grand manner. Miss Lucy and I will have to look about us, and polish up all our best airs and graces lest we should be thrown into the shade. Still, Polly, there is a little flutter, a little tendency to stammer now and then, and even to lisp as you lisped when you were six years old.'

'No, papa,' interrupted she, indignantly, 'that can't be true.'

'I appeal to Miss Lucy. Did she not, in answering Dr Bretton's question as to whether she had ever seen the palace of the Prince of Bois l'Etang, say "yeth", she had been there "theveral" times?'

'Papa, you are satirical, you are méchant! I can pronounce all the letters of the alphabet as clearly as you can. But tell me this: you are very particular in making me be civil to Dr Bretton, do you like him yourself?'

'To be sure: for old acquaintance sake I like him: then he is a very good son to his mother; besides being a kind-hearted fellow and clever in his profession: yes, the callant is well enough.'

'*Callant*! Ah, Scotchman! Papa, is it the Edinburgh or the Aberdeen accent you have?'

'Both, my pet, both; and doubtless the Glaswegian into the bargain: it is that which enables me to speak French so well: a gude Scots tongue always succeeds well at the French.'

'*The* French! Scotch again: incorrigible papa! You, too, need schooling.'

'Well, Polly, you must persuade Miss Snowe to undertake both you and me; to make you steady and womanly, and me refined and classical.'

The light in which M. de Bassompierre evidently regarded 'Miss Snowe,' used to occasion me much inward edification. What contradictory attributes of character we sometimes find ascribed to us, according to the eye with which we are viewed! Mme Beck esteemed me learned and blue; Miss Fanshawe, caustic, ironic, and cynical; Mr Home, a model teacher, the essence of the sedate and discreet: somewhat conventional perhaps, too strict, limited and scrupulous, but still the pink and pattern of governess-correctness; whilst another person, Professor Paul Emanuel, to wit, never lost an opportunity of intimating his opinion that mine was rather a fiery and rash nature – adventurous, indocile, and audacious. I smiled at them all. If anyone knew me it was little Paulina Mary.

As I would not be Paulina's nominal and paid companion, genial and harmonious as I began to find her intercourse, she persuaded me to join her in some study, as a regular and settled means of sustaining communication: she proposed the German language, which, like myself, she found difficult of mastery. We agreed to take our lessons in the Rue Crécy of the same mistress; this arrangement threw us together for some hours of every week. M. de Bassompierre seemed quite pleased: it perfectly met his approbation that Mme Minerva Gravity should associate a portion of her leisure with that of his fair and dear child.

That other self-elected judge of mine, the professor in the Rue Fossette, discovering by some surreptitious, spying means, that I was no longer so stationary as hitherto, but went out regularly at certain hours of certain days, took it upon himself to place me under surveillance. People said M. Emanuel had been brought up amongst Jesuits. I should more readily have accredited this report had his manœuvres been better masked. As it was I doubted it. Never was a more undisguised schemer, a franker, looser intriguer. He would analyse his own machinations: elaborately contrive plots, and forthwith indulge

in explanatory boasts of their skill. I know not whether I was more amused or provoked, by his stepping up to me one morning and whispering solemnly that he 'had his eye on me: *he* at least would discharge the duty of a friend and not leave me entirely to my own devices. My proceedings seemed at present very unsettled: he did not know what to make of them: he thought his cousin Beck very much to blame in suffering this sort of fluttering inconsistency in a teacher attached to her house. What had a person devoted to a serious calling, that of education, to do with Counts and Countesses, hotels and chateaux? To him, I seemed altogether "en l'air". On his faith, he believed I went out six days in the seven.'

I said, 'Monsieur exaggerated. I certainly had enjoyed the advantage of a little change lately, but not before it had become necessary; and the privilege was by no means exercised in excess.'

'Necessary! How was it necessary? I was well enough, he supposed? Change necessary! He would recommend me to look at the Catholic 'religieuses,' and study *their* lives. *They* asked no change.'

I am no judge of what expression crossed my face when he thus spoke, but it was one which provoked him: he accused me of being reckless, worldly, and epicurean; ambitious of greatness and feverishly athirst for the pomps and vanities of life. It seems I had no 'dévouement', no 'recueillement' in my character; no spirit of grace, faith, sacrifice, or self-abasement. Feeling the inutility of answering these charges, I mutely continued the correction of a pile of English exercises.

'He could see in me nothing Christian: like many other Protestants, I revelled in the pride and self-will of paganism.'

I slightly turned from him, nestling still closer under the wing of silence.

A vague sound grumbled between his teeth; it could not surely be a 'juron': he was too religious for that; but I am certain I heard the word *sacré*. Grievous to relate, the same word was repeated, with the unequivocal addition of *mille* something, when I passed him about two hours afterwards in the corridor, prepared to go and take my German lesson in the Rue Crécy. Never was a better little man, in some points, than M. Paul: never, in others, a more waspish little despot.

Our German mistress, Fräulein Anna Braun, was a worthy, hearty woman, of about forty-five; she ought, perhaps, to have lived in the days of Queen Elizabeth, as she habitually consumed, for her first and second breakfast, beer and beef: also, her direct and downright Deutsch nature seemed to suffer a sensation of cruel restraint from what she called our English reserve; though we thought we were very cordial with her: but we did not slap her on the shoulder, and if we consented to kiss her cheek, it was done quietly, and without any explosive smack. These omissions oppressed and depressed her considerably; still, on the whole, we got on very well. Accustomed to instruct foreign girls, who hardly ever will think and study for themselves – who have no idea of grappling with a difficulty, and overcoming it by dint of reflection or application – our progress, which, in truth, was very leisurely, seemed to astound her. In her eyes, we were a pair of glacial prodigies, cold, proud, and preternatural.

The young Countess *was* a little proud, a little fastidious: and perhaps, with her native delicacy and beauty, she had a right to these feelings; but I think it was a total mistake to ascribe them to me. I never evaded the morning salute, which Paulina would slip when she could; nor was a certain little manner of still disdain a weapon known in my armoury of defence; whereas, Paulina always kept it clear, fine and bright, and any rough German sally called forth at once its steely glisten.

Honest Anna Braun, in some measure, felt this difference; and while she half-feared, half-worshipped Paulina, as a sort of dainty nymph – an Undine – she took refuge with me, as a being all mortal, and of easier mood.

A book we liked well to read and translate was Schiller's Ballads; Paulina soon learned to read them beautifully: the Fräulein would listen to her with a broad smile of pleasure, and say her voice sounded like music. She translated them too with a facile flow of language, and in a strain of kindred and poetic fervour: her cheek would flush, her lips tremblingly smile, her beauteous eyes kindle or melt as she went on. She learnt the best by heart, and would often recite them when we were alone together. One she liked well was 'Des Mädchens Klage': that is, she liked well to repeat the words, she found plaintive melody in the sound; the sense she would criticise. She murmured, as we sat over the fire one evening:

> 'Du Heilige, rufe dein Kind zurück,
> Ich habe genossen das irdische Glück,
> Ich habe gelebt und geliebet!'

'Lived and loved!' said she, 'is that the summit of earthly happiness, the end of life – to love? I don't think it is. It may be the extreme of mortal misery, it may be sheer waste of time, and fruitless torture of feeling. If Schiller had said to *be* loved – he might have come nearer the truth. Is not that another thing, Lucy, to be loved?'

'I suppose it may be: but why consider the subject? What is love to you? What do you know about it?'

She crimsoned, half in irritation, half in shame.

'Now, Lucy,' she said, 'I won't take that from you. It may be well for papa to look on me as a baby: I rather prefer that he should thus view me; but *you* know and shall learn to acknowledge that I am verging on my nineteenth year.'

'No matter if it were your twenty-ninth; we will anticipate no feelings by discussion and conversation: we will not talk about love.'

'Indeed, indeed!' said she – all in hurry and heat – 'you may think to check and hold me in, as much as you please; but I *have* talked about it, and heard about it too; and a great deal and lately, and disagreeably and detrimentally: and in a way you wouldn't approve.'

And the vexed, triumphant, pretty, naughty being laughed. I could not discern what she meant, and I would not ask her: I was nonplussed. Seeing, however, the utmost innocence in her countenance – combined with some transient perverseness and petulance – I said at last, 'Who talks to you disagreeably and detrimentally on such matters? Who that has near access to you would dare to do it?'

'Lucy,' replied she more softly, 'it is a person who makes me miserable sometimes; and I wish she would keep away – I don't want her.'

'But who, Paulina, can it be? You puzzle me much.'

'It is – it is my cousin Ginevra. Every time she has leave to visit Mrs Cholmondeley she calls here, and whenever she finds me alone she begins to talk about her admirers. Love, indeed! You should hear all she has to say about love.'

'Oh, I have heard it,' said I, quite coolly; 'and on the whole, perhaps, it is as well you should have heard it too: it is not to be regretted, it is all right. Yet surely, Ginevra's mind cannot influence yours? You can look over both her head and her heart.'

'She does influence me very much. She has the art of disturbing my happiness and unsettling my opinions. She hurts me through the feelings and people dearest to me.'

'What does she say, Paulina? Give me some idea. There may be counteraction of the damage done.'

'The people I have longest and most esteemed are degraded by her. She does not spare Mrs Bretton – she does not spare. . . Graham –'

'No, I dare say: and how does she mix up these with her sentiment and her. . . love? She does mix them, I suppose?'

'Lucy, she is insolent; and I believe, false. You know Dr Bretton. We both know him. He may be careless and proud; but when was he ever mean or slavish? Day after day she shows him to me kneeling at her feet, pursuing her like her shadow. She – repulsing him with insult, and he imploring her with infatuation. Lucy, is it true? Is any of it true?'

'It may be true that he once thought her handsome: does she give him out as still her suitor?'

'She says she might marry him any day: he only waits her consent.'

'It is these tales which have caused that reserve in your manner towards Graham which your father noticed.'

'They have certainly made me all doubtful about his character. As Ginevra speaks, they do not carry with them the sound of unmixed truth: I believe she exaggerates – perhaps invents – but I want to know how far.'

'Suppose we bring Miss Fanshawe to some proof. Give her an opportunity of displaying the power she boasts.'

'I could do that tomorrow. Papa has asked some gentlemen to dinner, all savants. Graham who, papa is beginning to discover, is a savant, too – skilled, they say, in more than one branch of science – is among the number. Now I should be miserable to sit at table unsupported, amidst such a party. I could not talk to Messieurs A – and Z –, the Parisian academicians: all my new credit for manner would be put in peril. You and Mrs Bretton must come for my sake; Ginevra, at a word, will join you.'

'Yes; then I will carry a message of invitation, and she shall have the chance of justifying her character for veracity.'

## *The Hôtel Crécy*

The morrow turned out a more lively and busy day than we – or than I, at least – had anticipated. It seems it was the birthday of one of the young princes of Labassecour – the eldest, I think, the Duc de Dindonneau – and a general holiday was given in his honour at the schools, and especially at the principal 'Athénée', or college. The youth of that institution had also concocted, and were to present a loyal address; for which purpose they were to be assembled in the public building where the yearly examinations were conducted, and the prizes distributed. After the ceremony of presentation, an oration, or 'discours' was to follow from one of the professors.

Several of M. de Bassompierre's friends – the savants – being more or less connected with the Athénée, were expected to attend on this occasion; together with the worshipful municipality of Villette, M. le Chevalier Staas, the burgomaster, and the parents and kinsfolk of the Athenians in general. M. de Bassompierre was engaged by his friends to accompany them; his fair daughter would, of course, be of the party, and she wrote a little note to Ginevra and myself, bidding us come early that we might join her.

As Miss Fanshawe and I were dressing in the dormitory of the Rue Fossette, she (Miss F.) suddenly burst into a laugh.

'What now?' I asked; for she had suspended the operation of arranging her attire, and was gazing at me.

'It seems so odd,' she replied, with her usual half-honest, half-insolent unreserve, 'that you and I should now be so much on a level, visiting in the same sphere; having the same connections.'

'Why yes,' said I; 'I had not much respect for the connections you chiefly frequented awhile ago: Mrs Cholmondeley and Co. would never have suited me at all.'

'Who *are* you, Miss Snowe?' she enquired, in a tone of such undisguised and unsophisticated curiosity, as made me laugh in my turn.

'You used to call yourself a nursery-governess; when you first came here you really had the care of the children in this house: I have seen you carry little Georgette in your arms, like a bonne – few governesses would have condescended so far – and now Mme Beck treats you with more courtesy than she treats the Parisienne, St Pierre; and that proud chit, my cousin, makes you her bosom friend!'

'Wonderful!' I agreed, much amused at her mystification. 'Who am I indeed? Perhaps a personage in disguise. Pity I don't look the character.'

'I wonder you are not more flattered by all this,' she went on: 'you take it with strange composure. If you really are the nobody I once thought you, you must be a cool hand.'

'The nobody you once thought me!' I repeated, and my face grew a little hot; but I would not be angry: of what importance was a schoolgirl's crude use of the terms nobody and somebody? I confined myself, therefore, to the remark that I had merely met with civility; and asked 'what she saw in civility to throw the recipient into a fever of confusion?'

'One can't help wondering at some things,' she persisted.

'Wondering at marvels of your own manufacture. Are you ready at last?'

'Yes; let me take your arm.'

'I would rather not: we will walk side by side.'

When she took my arm, she always leaned upon me her whole weight; and, as I was not a gentleman, or her lover, I did not like it.

'There, again!' she cried. 'I thought, by offering to take your arm, to intimate approbation of your dress and general appearance: I meant it as a compliment.'

'You did? You meant, in short, to express that you are not ashamed to be seen in the street with me? That if Mrs Cholmondeley should be fondling her lap-dog at some window, or Colonel de Hamal picking his teeth in a balcony, and should catch a glimpse of us, you would not quite blush for your companion?'

'Yes,' said she, with that directness which was her best point – which gave an honest plainness to her very fibs when she told them – which was, in short, the salt, the sole preservative ingredient of a character otherwise not formed to keep.

I delegated the trouble of commenting on this 'yes' to my countenance; or rather, my under-lip voluntarily anticipated my tongue: of course, reverence and solemnity were not the feelings expressed in the look I gave her.

'Scornful, sneering creature!' she went on, as we crossed a great square, and entered the quiet, pleasant park, our nearest way to the Rue Crécy. 'Nobody in this world was ever such a Turk to me as you are!'

'You bring it on yourself: let me alone: have the sense to be quiet: I will let you alone.'

'As if one *could* let you alone, when you are so peculiar and so mysterious!'

'The mystery and peculiarity being entirely the conception of your own brain – maggots – neither more nor less, be so good as to keep them out of my sight.'

'But *are* you anybody?' persevered she, pushing her hand, in spite of me, under my arm; and that arm pressed itself with inhospitable closeness against my side, by way of keeping out the intruder.

'Yes,' I said, 'I am a rising character: once an old lady's companion, then a nursery-governess, now a schoolteacher.'

'Do – *do* tell me who you are? I'll not repeat it,' she urged, adhering with ludicrous tenacity to the wise notion of an incognito she had got hold of; and she squeezed the arm of which she had now obtained full possession, and coaxed and conjured till I was obliged to pause in the park to laugh. Throughout our walk she rang the most fanciful changes on this theme; proving, by her obstinate credulity, or incredulity, her incapacity to conceive how any person not bolstered up by birth or wealth, not supported by some consciousness of name or connection, could maintain an attitude of reasonable integrity. As for me, it quite sufficed to

my mental tranquillity that I was known where it imported that known I should be; the rest sat on me easily: pedigree, social position, and recondite intellectual acquisition, occupied about the same space and place in my interests and thoughts; they were my third-class lodgers – to whom could be assigned only the small sitting-room and the little back bedroom: even if the dining and drawing-rooms stood empty, I never confessed it to them, as thinking minor accommodations better suited to their circumstances. The world, I soon learned, held a different estimate: and I make no doubt, the world is very right in its view, yet believe also that I am not quite wrong in mine.

There are people whom a lowered position degrades morally, to whom loss of connection costs loss of self-respect: are not these justified in placing the highest value on that station and association which is their safeguard from debasement? If a man feels that he would become contemptible in his own eyes were it generally known that his ancestry were simple and not gentle, poor and not rich, workers and not capitalists, would it be right severely to blame him for keeping these fatal facts out of sight – for starting, trembling, quailing at the chance which threatens exposure? The longer we live, the more our experience widens; the less prone are we to judge our neighbour's conduct, to question the world's wisdom: wherever an accumulation of small defences is found, whether surrounding the prude's virtue or the man of the world's respectability, there, be sure, it is needed.

We reached the Hôtel Crécy; Paulina was ready; Mrs Bretton was with her; and, under her escort and that of M. de Bassompierre, we were soon conducted to the place of assembly, and seated in good seats, at a convenient distance from the Tribune. The youth of the Athénée were marshalled before us, the municipality and their bourgmestre were in places of honour, the young princes, with their tutors, occupied a conspicuous position, and the body of the building was crowded with the aristocracy and first burghers of the town.

Concerning the identity of the professor by whom the 'discours' was to be delivered, I had as yet entertained neither care nor question. Some vague expectation I had that a savant would stand up and deliver a formal speech, half dogmatism to the Athenians, half flattery to the princes.

The Tribune was yet empty when we entered, but in ten minutes after it was filled; suddenly, in a second of time, a head, chest and arms, grew above the crimson desk. This head I knew: its colour, shape, port, expression, were familiar both to me and Miss Fanshawe; the blackness and closeness of cranium, the amplitude and paleness of brow, the blueness and fire of glance, were details so domesticated in the memory, and so knit with many a whimsical association, as almost by this their sudden apparition, to tickle fancy to a laugh. Indeed, I confess, for my part, I did laugh till I was warm; but then I bent my head, and made my handkerchief and a lowered veil the sole confidants of my mirth.

I think I was glad to see M. Paul; I think it was rather pleasant than otherwise, to behold him set up there, fierce and frank, dark and candid, testy and fearless, as when regnant on his estrade in class. His presence was such a surprise: I had not once thought of expecting him, though I knew he filled the chair of Belles

Lettres in the college. With *him* in that Tribune, I felt sure that neither formalism nor flattery would be our doom; but for what was vouchsafed us, for what was poured suddenly, rapidly, continuously, on our heads – I own I was not prepared.

He spoke to the princes, the nobles, the magistrates and the burghers, with just the same ease, with almost the same pointed, choleric earnestness, with which he was wont to harangue the three divisions of the Rue Fossette. The collegians he addressed, not as schoolboys, but as future citizens and embryo patriots. The times which have since come on Europe had not been foretold yet, and M. Emanuel's spirit seemed new to me. Who would have thought the flat and fat soil of Labassecour could yield political convictions and national feelings, such as were now strongly expressed? Of the bearing of his opinions I need here give no special indication; yet it may be permitted me to say that I believed the little man not more earnest than right in what he said: with all his fire he was severe and sensible, he trampled Utopian theories under his heel; he rejected wild dreams with scorn; but, when he looked in the face of tyranny – oh, then there opened a light in his eye worth seeing; and when he spoke of injustice, his voice gave no uncertain sound, but reminded me rather of the band-trumpet, ringing at twilight from the park.

I do not think his audience were generally susceptible of sharing his flame in its purity; but some of the college youth caught fire as he eloquently told them what should be their path and endeavour in their country's and in Europe's future. They gave him a long, loud, ringing cheer, as he concluded: with all his fierceness, he was their favourite professor.

As our party left the Hall, he stood at the entrance; he saw and knew me, and lifted his hat; he offered his hand in passing, and uttered the words 'Qu'en dîtes-vous?' – question eminently characteristic, and reminding me, even in this his moment of triumph, of that inquisitive restlessness, that absence of what I considered desirable self-control, which were amongst his faults. He should not have cared just then to ask what I thought, or what anybody thought; but he *did* care, and he was too natural to conceal, too impulsive to repress his wish. Well! if I blamed his over-eagerness, I liked his *naïveté*. I would have praised him: I had plenty of praise in my heart; but, alas! no words on my lips. Who *has* words at the right moment? I stammered some lame expressions; but was truly glad when other people, coming up with profuse congratulations, covered my deficiency by their redundancy.

A gentleman introduced him to M. de Bassompierre; and the Count, who had likewise been highly gratified, asked him to join his friends (for the most part M. Emanuel's likewise), and to dine with them at the Hôtel Crécy. He declined dinner, for he was a man always somewhat shy in meeting the advances of the wealthy: there was a strength of sturdy independence in the stringing of his sinews – not obtrusive, but pleasant enough to discover as one advanced in knowledge of his character; he promised, however, to step in with his friend, M. A—, a French Academician, in the course of the evening.

At dinner that day, Ginevra and Paulina each looked, in her own way, very

beautiful; the former, perhaps, boasted the advantage in material charms, but the latter shone pre-eminent for attractions more subtle and spiritual: for light and eloquence of eye, for grace of mien, for winning variety of expression. Ginevra's dress of deep crimson relieved well her light curls, and harmonised with her rose-like bloom. Paulina's attire – in fashion close, though faultlessly neat, but in texture clear and white – made the eye grateful for the delicate life of her complexion, for the soft animation of her countenance, for the tender depth of her eyes, for the brown shadow and bounteous flow of her hair – darker than that of her Saxon cousin, as were also her eyebrows, her eyelashes, her full irids, and large mobile pupils – Nature having traced all these details slightly, and with a careless hand, in Miss Fanshawe's case; and in Miss de Bassompierre's, wrought them to a high and delicate finish.

Paulina was awed by the savants, but not quite to mutism: she conversed modestly, diffidently; not without effort, but with so true a sweetness, so fine and penetrating a sense, that her father more than once suspended his own discourse to listen, and fixed on her an eye of proud delight. It was a polite Frenchman, M. Z—, a very learned, but quite a courtly man, who had drawn her into discourse. I was charmed with her French; it was faultless – the structure correct, the idiom true, the accent pure; Ginevra, who had lived half her life on the Continent, could do nothing like it: not that words ever failed Miss Fanshawe, but real accuracy and purity she neither possessed, nor in any number of years would acquire. Here, too, M. de Bassompierre was gratified; for, on the point of language, he was critical.

Another listener and observer there was; one who, detained by some exigency of his profession, had come in late to dinner. Both ladies were quietly scanned by Dr Bretton, at the moment of taking his seat at the table; and that guarded survey was more than once renewed. His arrival roused Miss Fanshawe, who had hitherto appeared listless: she now became smiling and complacent, talked – though what she said was rarely to the purpose – or rather, was of a purpose somewhat mortifyingly below the standard of the occasion. Her light, disconnected prattle might have gratified Graham once; perhaps it pleased him still: perhaps it was only fancy which suggested the thought that, while his eye was filled and his ear fed, his taste, his keen zest, his lively intelligence, were not equally consulted and regaled. It is certain that, restless and exacting as seemed the demand on his attention, he yielded courteously all that was required: his manner showed neither pique nor coolness: Ginevra was his neighbour, and to her, during dinner, he almost exclusively confined his notice. She appeared satisfied, and passed to the drawing-room in very good spirits.

Yet, no sooner had we reached that place of refuge, than she again became flat and listless: throwing herself on a couch, she denounced both the 'discours' and the dinner as stupid affairs, and enquired of her cousin how she could hear such a set of prosaic 'gros-bonnets' as her father gathered about him. The moment the gentlemen were heard to move, her railings ceased: she started up, flew to the piano, and dashed at it with spirit. Dr Bretton entering, one of the first, took up his station beside her. I thought he would not long maintain that

post: there was a position near the hearth to which I expected to see him attracted: this position he only scanned with his eye; while *he* looked, others drew in. The grace and mind of Paulina charmed these thoughtful Frenchmen: the fineness of her beauty, the soft courtesy of her manner, her immature, but real and inbred tact, pleased their national taste; they clustered about her, not indeed to talk science, which would have rendered her dumb, but to touch on many subjects in letters, in arts, in actual life, on which it soon appeared that she had both read and reflected. I listened. I am sure that though Graham stood aloof, he listened too: his hearing as well as his vision was very fine, quick, discriminating. I knew he gathered the conversation; I felt that the mode in which it was sustained suited him exquisitely – pleased him almost to pain.

In Paulina there was more force, both of feeling and character, than most people thought – than Graham himself imagined – than she would ever show to those who did not wish to see it. To speak truth, reader, there is no excellent beauty, no accomplished grace, no reliable refinement, without strength as excellent, as complete, as trustworthy. As well might you look for good fruit and blossom on a rootless and sapless tree, as for charms that will endure in a feeble and relaxed nature. For a little while, the blooming semblance of beauty may flourish round weakness; but it cannot bear a blast: it soon fades, even in serenest sunshine. Graham would have started had any suggestive spirit whispered of the sinew and the stamina sustaining that delicate nature; but I, who had known her as a child, knew, or guessed, by what a good and strong root her graces held to the firm soil of reality.

While Dr Bretton listened, and waited an opening in the magic circle, his glance, restlessly sweeping the room at intervals, lighted by chance on me; where I sat in a quiet nook not far from my godmother and M. de Bassompierre, who, as usual, were engaged in what Mr Home called 'a two-handed crack': what the Count would have interpreted as a tête-à-tête. Graham smiled recognition, crossed the room, asked me how I was, told me I looked pale. I also had my own smile at my own thought: it was now about three months since Dr John had spoken to me – a lapse of which he was not even conscious. He sat down, and became silent. His wish was rather to look than converse. Ginevra and Paulina were now opposite to him: he could gaze his fill: he surveyed both forms – studied both faces.

Several new guests, ladies as well as gentlemen, had entered the room since dinner, dropping in for the evening conversation; and amongst the gentlemen, I may incidentally observe, I had already noticed by glimpses, a severe, dark professorial outline, hovering aloof in an inner saloon, seen only in vista. M. Emanuel knew many of the gentlemen present, but I think was a stranger to most of the ladies, excepting myself; in looking towards the hearth, he could not but see me, and naturally made a movement to approach; seeing, however, Dr Bretton also, he changed his mind and held back. If that had been all, there would have been no cause for quarrel; but not satisfied with holding back, he puckered his eyebrows, protruded his lip, and looked so ugly that I averted my eyes from the displeasing spectacle. M. Josef Emanuel had arrived, as well as his

austere brother, and at this very moment was relieving Ginevra at the piano. What a master-touch succeeded her schoolgirl jingle! In what grand, grateful tones the instrument acknowledged the hand of the true artist!

'Lucy,' began Dr Bretton, breaking silence and smiling, as Ginevra glided before him, casting a glance as she passed by, 'Miss Fanshawe is certainly a fine girl.'

Of course I assented.

'Is there,' he pursued, 'another in the room as lovely?'

'I think there is not another as handsome.'

'I agree with you, Lucy: you and I do often agree in opinion, in taste, I think; or at least in judgement.'

'Do we?' I said, somewhat doubtfully.

'I believe if you had been a boy, Lucy, instead of a girl – my mother's god-son instead of her god-daughter – we should have been good friends: our opinions would have melted into each other.'

He had assumed a bantering air: a light, half-caressing, half-ironic, shone aslant in his eye. Ah, Graham! I have given more than one solitary moment to thoughts and calculations of your estimate of Lucy Snowe: was it always kind or just? Had Lucy been intrinsically the same, but possessing the additional advantages of wealth and station, would your manner to her, your value for her have been quite what they actually were? And yet by these questions I would not seriously infer blame. No; you might sadden and trouble me sometimes; but then mine was a soon-depressed, an easily-deranged temperament – it fell if a cloud crossed the sun. Perhaps before the eye of severe equity, I should stand more at fault than you.

Trying then to keep down the unreasonable pain which thrilled my heart, on thus being made to feel that while Graham could devote to others the most grave and earnest, the manliest interest, he had no more than light raillery for Lucy, the friend of lang syne, I enquired calmly – 'On what points are we so closely in accordance?'

'We each have an observant faculty. You, perhaps, don't give me credit for the possession; yet I have it.'

'But you were speaking of tastes: we may see the same objects, yet estimate them differently?'

'Let us bring it to the test. Of course, you cannot but render homage to the merits of Miss Fanshawe: now, what do you think of others in the room? – my mother, for instance; or the lions, yonder, Messieurs A— and Z— ; or, let us say, that pale little lady, Miss de Bassompierre?'

'You know what I think of your mother. I have not thought of Messieurs A— and Z—.'

'And the other?'

'I think she is, as you say, a pale little lady – pale, certainly, just now, when she is fatigued with over-excitement.'

'You don't remember her as a child?'

'I wonder, sometimes, whether you do?'

'I had forgotten her; but it is noticeable, that circumstances, persons, even words and looks, that had slipped your memory, may, under certain conditions, certain aspects of your own or another's mind, revive.'

'That is possible enough.'

'Yet,' he continued, 'the revival is imperfect – needs confirmation, partakes so much of the dim character of a dream, or of the airy one of a fancy, that the testimony of a witness becomes necessary for corroboration. Were you not a guest at Bretton ten years ago, when Mr Home brought his little girl, whom we then called "little Polly", to stay with mama?'

'I was there the night she came, and also the morning she went away.'

'Rather a peculiar child; was she not? I wonder how I treated her. Was I fond of children in those days? Was there anything gracious or kindly about me – great, reckless, schoolboy as I was? But you don't recollect me, of course?'

'You have seen your own picture at La Terrasse. It is like you personally. In manner, you were almost the same yesterday as today.'

'But, Lucy, how is that? Such an oracle really whets my curiosity. What am I today? What was I the yesterday of ten years back?'

'Gracious to whatever pleased you – unkindly or cruel to nothing.'

'There you are wrong; I think I was almost a brute to you, for instance.'

'A brute! No, Graham: I should never have patiently endured brutality.'

'*This*, however, I *do* remember: quiet Lucy Snowe tasted nothing of my grace.'

'As little of your cruelty.'

'Why, had I been Nero himself, I could not have tormented a being inoffensive as a shadow.'

I smiled; but I also hushed a groan. Oh! – I wished he would just let me alone – cease allusion to me. These epithets – these attributes I put from me. His 'quiet Lucy Snowe', his 'inoffensive shadow', I gave him back; not with scorn, but with extreme weariness: theirs was the coldness and the pressure of lead; let him whelm me with no such weight. Happily, he was soon on another theme.

'On what terms were "little Polly" and I? Unless my recollections deceive me, we were not foes –'

'You speak very vaguely. Do you think little Polly's memory not more definite?'

'Oh! we don't talk of "little Polly" *now*. Pray say, Miss de Bassompierre; and, of course, such a stately personage remembers nothing of Bretton. Look at her large eyes, Lucy; can they read a word in the page of memory? Are they the same which I used to direct to a horn-book? She does not know that I partly taught her to read.'

'In the Bible on Sunday nights?'

'She has a calm, delicate, rather fine profile now: once what a little restless, anxious countenance was hers! What a thing is a child's preference – what a bubble! Would you believe it? that lady was fond of me!'

'I think she was in some measure fond of you,' said I, moderately.

'You don't remember then? I had forgotten; but I remember *now*. She liked me the best of whatever there was at Bretton.'

'You thought so.'

'I quite well recall it. I wish I could tell her all I recall; or rather, I wish someone, *you* for instance, would go behind and whisper it all in her ear, and I could have the delight – here, as I sit – of watching her look under the intelligence. Could you manage that, think you, Lucy, and make me ever grateful?'

'Could I manage to make you ever grateful?' said I. 'No, *I could not*.' And I felt my fingers work and my hands interlock: I felt, too, an inward courage, warm and resistant. In this matter I was not disposed to gratify Dr John: not at all. With a now welcome force, I realised his entire misapprehension of my character and nature. He wanted always to give me a rôle not mine. Nature and I opposed him. He did not at all guess what I felt: he did not read my eyes, or face, or gestures; though, I doubt not, all spoke. Leaning towards me coaxingly, he said, softly, '*Do* content me, Lucy.'

And I would have contented, or, at least, I would clearly have enlightened him, and taught him well never again to expect of me the part of officious soubrette in a love drama; when, following his soft, eager murmur, meeting almost his pleading, mellow – '*Do* content me, Lucy!' – a sharp hiss pierced my ear on the other side.

'Petite chatte, doucerette, coquette!' sibillated the sudden boa-constrictor; 'vous avez l'air bien triste, soumise, rêveuse, mais vous ne l'êtes pas; c'est moi qui vous le dis: Sauvage! la flamme à l'âme, l'éclair aux yeux!'

'Oui; j'ai la flamme à l'âme, et je dois l'avoir!' retorted I, turning in just wrath; but Professor Emanuel had hissed his insult and was gone.

The worst of the matter was, that Dr Bretton, whose ears, as I have said, were quick and fine, caught every word of this apostrophe; he put his handkerchief to his face and laughed till he shook.

'Well done, Lucy,' cried he; 'capital! petite chatte, petite coquette! Oh, I must tell my mother! Is it true, Lucy, or half-true? I believe it is: you redden to the colour of Miss Fanshawe's gown. And really, by my word, now I examine him, that is the same little man who was so savage with you at the concert: the very same, and in his soul he is frantic at this moment because he sees me laughing. Oh! I must tease him.'

And Graham, yielding to his bent for mischief, laughed, jested, and whispered on till I could bear no more, and my eyes filled.

Suddenly he was sobered: a vacant space appeared near Miss de Bassompierre; the circle surrounding her seemed about to dissolve. This movement was instantly caught by Graham's eye – ever-vigilant, even while laughing; he rose, took his courage in both hands, crossed the room, and made the advantage his own. Dr John, throughout his whole life, was a man of luck – a man of success. And why? Because he had the eye to see his opportunity, the heart to prompt to well-timed action, the nerve to consummate a perfect work. And no tyrant-passion dragged him back; no enthusiasms, no foibles encumbered his way.

How well he looked at this very moment! When Paulina looked up as he reached her side, her glance mingled at once with an encountering glance, animated, yet modest; his colour, as he spoke to her, became half a blush, half a glow. He stood in her presence brave and bashful: subdued and unobtrusive, yet decided in his purpose and devoted in his ardour. I gathered all this by one view. I did not prolong my observation – time failed me, had inclination served: the night wore late; Ginevra and I ought already to have been in the Rue Fossette. I rose, and bade good-night to my godmother and M. de Bassompierre.

I know not whether Professor Emanuel had noticed my reluctant acceptance of Dr Bretton's badinage, or whether he perceived that I was pained, and that, on the whole, the evening had not been one flow of exultant enjoyment for the volatile, pleasure-loving, Mlle Lucie; but, as I was leaving the room, he stepped up and enquired whether I had anyone to attend me to the Rue Fossette. The professor *now* spoke politely, and even deferentially, and he looked apologetic and repentant; but I could not recognise his civility at a word, nor meet his contrition with crude, premature oblivion. Never hitherto had I felt seriously disposed to resent his brusqueries, or freeze before his fierceness; what he had said tonight, however, I considered unwarranted: my extreme disapprobation of the proceeding must be marked, however slightly. I merely said: 'I am provided with attendance.'

Which was true, as Ginevra and I were to be sent home in the carriage; and I passed him with the sliding obeisance with which he was wont to be saluted in classe by pupils crossing his estrade.

Having sought my shawl I returned to the vestibule. M. Emanuel stood there as if waiting. He observed that the night was fine.

'Is it?' I said, with a tone and manner whose consummate chariness and frostiness I could not but applaud. It was so seldom I could properly act out my own resolution to be reserved and cool where I had been grieved or hurt, that I felt almost proud of this one successful effort. That 'Is it?' sounded just like the manner of other people. I had heard hundreds of such little minced, docked, dry phrases, from the pursed-up coral lips of a score of self-possessed, self-sufficing misses and mesdemoiselles. That M. Paul would not stand any prolonged experience of this sort of dialogue I knew; but he certainly merited a sample of the curt and arid. I believe he thought so himself, for he took the dose quietly. He looked at my shawl and objected to its lightness. I decidedly told him it was as heavy as I wished. Receding aloof, and standing apart, I leaned on the banister of the stairs, folded my shawl about me, and fixed my eyes on a dreary religious painting darkening the wall.

Ginevra was long in coming: tedious seemed her loitering. M. Paul was still there, my ear expected from his lips an angry tone. He came nearer. 'Now for another hiss!' thought I: had not the action been too uncivil I could have stopped my ears with my fingers in terror of the thrill. Nothing happens as we expect: listen for a coo or a murmur; it is then you will hear a cry of prey or pain. Await a piercing shriek, an angry threat, and welcome an amicable greeting, a low kind whisper. M. Paul spoke gently: 'Friends,' said he, 'do not

quarrel for a word. Tell me, was it I or ce grand fat d'Anglais' (so he profanely denominated Dr Bretton), 'who made your eyes so humid, and your cheeks so hot as they are even now?'

'I am not conscious of you, monsieur, or of any other having excited such emotion as you indicate,' was my answer; and in giving it, I again surpassed my usual self, and achieved a neat, frosty falsehood.

'But what did I say?' he pursued, 'tell me: I was angry: I have forgotten my words; what were they?'

'Such as it is best to forget!' said I, still quite calm and chill.

'Then it was *my* words which wounded you? Consider them unsaid: permit my retractation; accord my pardon.'

'I am not angry, monsieur.'

'Then you are worse than angry – grieved. Forgive me, Miss Lucy.'

'M. Emanuel, I *do* forgive you.'

'Let me hear you say, in the voice natural to you, and not in that alien tone, "Mon ami, je vous pardonne." '

He made me smile. Who could help smiling at his wistfulness, his simplicity, his earnestness?

'Bon!' he cried; 'Voilà que le jour va poindre! Dîtes donc, mon ami.'

'M. Paul, je vous pardonne.'

'I will have no monsieur: speak the other word, or I shall not believe you sincere: another effort – *mon ami*, or else in English, my friend!'

Now, 'my friend' had rather another sound and significancy than '*mon ami*', it did not breathe the same sense of domestic and intimate affection: '*mon ami*' I could *not* say to M. Paul; 'my friend,' I could, and did say without difficulty. This distinction existed not for him, however, and he was quite satisfied with the English phrase. He smiled. You should have seen him smile, reader; and you should have marked the difference between his countenance now, and that he wore half an hour ago. I cannot affirm that I had ever witnessed the smile of pleasure, or content, or kindness round M. Paul's lips, or in his eyes before. The ironic, the sarcastic, the disdainful, the passionately exultant, I had hundreds of times seen him express by what he called a smile, but any illuminated sign of milder or warmer feeling struck me as wholly new in his visage. It changed it as from a mask to a face: the deep lines left his features; the very complexion seemed clearer and fresher; that swart, sallow, southern darkness which spoke his Spanish blood, became displaced by a lighter hue. I know not that I have ever seen in any other human face an equal metamorphosis from a similar cause. He now took me to the carriage; at the same moment M. de Bassompierre came out with his niece.

In a pretty humour was Mistress Fanshawe; she had found the evening a grand failure: completely upset as to temper, she gave way to the most uncontrolled moroseness as soon as we were seated, and the carriage-door closed. Her invectives against Dr Bretton had something venomous in them. Having found herself impotent either to charm or sting him, hatred was her only resource; and this hatred she expressed in terms so unmeasured and proportion so monstrous,

that, after listening for a while with assumed stoicism, my outraged sense of justice at last and suddenly caught fire. An explosion ensued: for I could be passionate, too; especially with my present fair but faulty associate, who never failed to stir the worst dregs of me. It was well that the carriage-wheels made a tremendous rattle over the flinty Choseville pavement, for I can assure the reader there was neither dead silence nor calm discussion within the vehicle. Half in earnest, half in seeming, I made it my business to storm down Ginevra. She had set out rampant from the Rue Crécy; it was necessary to tame her before we reached the Rue Fossette: to this end it was indispensable to show up her sterling value and high deserts; and this must be done in language of which the fidelity and homeliness might challenge comparison with the compliments of a John Knox to a Mary Stuart. This was the right discipline for Ginevra; it suited her. I am quite sure she went to bed that night all the better and more settled in mind and mood, and slept all the more sweetly for having undergone a sound moral drubbing.

### END OF VOLUME TWO

# VOLUME THREE

## CHAPTER 28

### *The Watchguard*

M. Paul Emanuel owned an acute sensitiveness to the annoyance of interruption, from whatsoever cause, occurring during his lessons: to pass through the classe under such circumstances was considered by the teachers and pupils of the school, individually and collectively, to be as much as a woman's or girl's life was worth.

Mme Beck herself, if forced to the enterprise, would 'skurry' through, retrenching her skirts, and carefully coasting the formidable estrade, like a ship dreading breakers. As to Rosine, the portress – on whom, every half-hour, devolved the fearful duty of fetching pupils out of the very heart of one or other of the divisions, to take their music-lessons in the oratory, the great or little salon, the salle à manger, or some other piano-station – she would, upon her second or third attempt, frequently become almost tongue-tied from excess of consternation – a sentiment inspired by the unspeakable looks levelled at her through a pair of dart-dealing spectacles.

One morning I was sitting in the carré, at work upon a piece of embroidery which one of the pupils had commenced but delayed to finish, and while my fingers wrought at the frame, my ears regaled themselves with listening to the crescendos and cadences of a voice haranguing in the neighbouring classe, in tones that waxed momently more unquiet, more ominously varied. There was a good strong partition-wall between me and the gathering storm, as well as a facile means of flight through the glass-door to the court, in case it swept this way; so I am afraid I derived more amusement than alarm from these thickening symptoms. Poor Rosine was not so safe: four times that blessed morning had she made the passage of peril; and now, for the fifth time it became her dangerous duty to snatch, as it were, a brand from the burning – a pupil from under M. Paul's nose.

'Mon Dieu! mon Dieu!' cried she. 'Que vais-je devenir? Monsieur va me tuer, je suis sûre; car il est d'une colère!'

Nerved by the courage of desperation, she opened the door.

'Mlle La Malle au piano!' was her cry. Ere she could make good her retreat, or quite close the door, this voice uttered itself: 'Dès ce moment! – la classe est

défendue. La première qui ouvrira cette porte, ou passera par cette division, sera pendue – fut-ce Mme Beck elle-même!'

Ten minutes had not succeeded the promulgation of this decree, when Rosine's French pantoufles were again heard shuffling along the corridor.

'Mademoiselle,' said she, 'I would not for a five-franc piece go into that classe again just now: Monsieur's lunettes are really terrible; and here is a commission-aire come with a message from the Athénée. I have told Mme Beck I dare not deliver it, and she says I am to charge you with it.'

'Me? No, that is rather too bad! It is not in my line of duty. Come, come, Rosine! bear your own burden. Be brave – charge once more!'

'I, Mademoiselle? – impossible! Five times I have crossed him this day. Madame must really hire a gendarme for this service. Ouf! Je n'en puis plus!'

'Bah! you are only a coward. What is the message?'

'Precisely of the kind with which Monsieur least likes to be pestered: an urgent summons to go directly to the Athénée, as there is an official visitor – inspector – I know not what – arrived, and Monsieur *must* meet him: you know how he hates a *must*.'

Yes, I knew well enough. The restive little man detested spur or curb: against whatever was urgent or obligatory, he was sure to revolt. However, I accepted the responsibility – not, certainly, without fear, but fear blent with other sentiments, curiosity amongst them. I opened the door, I entered, I closed it behind me as quickly and quietly as a rather unsteady hand would permit; for to be slow or bustling, to rattle a latch, or leave a door gaping wide, were aggravations of crime, often more disastrous in result than the main crime itself. There I stood then, and there he sat; his humour was visibly bad – almost at its worst; he had been giving a lesson in arithmetic – for he gave lessons on any and every subject that struck his fancy – and arithmetic being a dry subject, invariably disagreed with him: not a pupil but trembled when he spoke of figures. He sat, bent above his desk: to look up at the sound of an entrance, at the occurrence of a direct breach of his will and law, was an effort he could not for the moment bring himself to make. It was quite as well: I thus gained time to walk up the long classe; and it suited my idiosyncrasy far better to encounter the near burst of anger like his, than to bear its menace at a distance.

At his estrade I paused, just in front; of course I was not worthy of immediate attention: he proceeded with his lesson. Disdain would not do: he must hear and he must answer my message.

Not being quite tall enough to lift my head over his desk, elevated upon the estrade, and thus suffering eclipse in my present position, I ventured to peep round, with the design, at first, of merely getting a better view of his face, which had struck me when I entered as bearing a close and picturesque resemblance to that of a black and sallow tiger. Twice did I enjoy this side-view with impunity, advancing and receding unseen; the third time my eye had scarce dawned beyond the obscuration of the desk, when it was caught and transfixed through its very pupil – transfixed by the 'lunettes'. Rosine was right; these utensils had in them a blank and immutable terror, beyond the mobile wrath of the wearer's own unglazed eyes.

I now found the advantage of proximity: these shortsighted 'lunettes' were useless for the inspection of a criminal under Monsieur's nose; accordingly, he doffed them, and he and I stood on more equal terms.

I was glad I was not really much afraid of him – that, indeed, close in his presence, I felt no terror at all; for upon his demanding cord and gibbet to execute the sentence recently pronounced, I was able to furnish him with a needleful of embroidering thread with such accommodating civility as could not but allay some portion at least of his surplus irritation. Of course I did not parade this courtesy before public view: I merely handed the thread round the angle of the desk, and attached it, ready noosed, to the barred back of the Professor's chair.

'Que me voulez-vous?' said he, in a growl of which the music was wholly confined to his chest and throat, for he kept his teeth clenched, and seemed registering to himself an inward vow, that nothing earthly should wring from him a smile. My answer commenced uncompromisingly: 'Monsieur,' I said, 'je veux l'impossible, des choses inouïes;' and thinking it best not to mince matters, but to administer the 'douche' with decision, in a low but quick voice, I delivered the Athenian message, floridly exaggerating its urgency.

Of course, he would not hear a word of it. 'He would not go; he would not leave his present class, let all the officials in Villette send for him. He would not put himself an inch out of his way at the bidding of king, cabinet, and chambers together.'

I knew, however, that he *must* go; that, talk as he would, both his duty and interest commanded an immediate and literal compliance with the summons: I stood, therefore, waiting in silence, as if he had not yet spoken. He asked what more I wanted.

'Only Monsieur's answer to deliver to the commissionaire.'

He waved an impatient negative.

I ventured to stretch my hand to the bonnet-grec which lay in grim repose on the window-sill. He followed this daring movement with his eye, no doubt in mixed pity and amazement at its presumption.

'Ah!' he muttered, 'if it came to that – if Miss Lucy meddled with his bonnet-grec – she might just put it on herself, turn garçon for the occasion, and benevolently go to the Athénée in his stead.'

With great respect, I laid the bonnet on the desk, where its tassel seemed to give me an awful nod.

'I'll write a note of apology – that will do?' said he, still bent on evasion.

Knowing well it would *not* do, I gently pushed the bonnet towards his hand. Thus impelled, it slid down the polished slope of the varnished and unbaized desk, carried before it the light steel-framed 'lunettes,' and, fearful to relate, they fell to the estrade. A score of times ere now had I seen them fall and receive no damage – this time, as Lucy Snowe's hapless luck would have it, they so fell that each clear pebble became a shivered and shapeless star.

Now, indeed, dismay seized me – dismay and regret. I knew the value of those 'lunettes': M. Paul's sight was peculiar, not easily fitted, and these glasses

suited him. I had heard him call them his treasures: as I picked them up, cracked and worthless, my hand trembled. Frightened through all my nerves I was to see the mischief I had done, but I think I was even more sorry than afraid. For some seconds I dared not look the bereaved Professor in the face; he was the first to speak.

'Là!' said he; 'me voilà veuf de mes lunettes! I think Mlle Lucy will now confess that the cord and gallows are amply earned; she trembles in anticipation of her doom. Ah, traitress! traitress! You are resolved to have me quite blind and helpless in your hands!'

I lifted my eyes: his face, instead of being irate, lowering, and furrowed, was overflowing with the smile, coloured with the bloom I had seen brightening it that evening at the Hôtel Crécy. He was not angry – not even grieved. For the real injury he showed himself full of clemency; under the real provocation, patient as a saint. This event, which seemed so untoward – which I thought had ruined at once my chance of successful persuasion – proved my best help. Difficult of management so long as I had done him no harm, he became graciously pliant as soon as I stood in his presence, a conscious and contrite offender.

Still gently railing at me as 'une forte femme – une Anglaise terrible – une petite casse-tout' – he declared that he dared not but obey one who had given such an instance of her dangerous prowess; it was absolutely like the 'grand Empereur, smashing the vase to inspire dismay'. So, at last, crowning himself with his bonnet-grec, and taking his ruined 'lunettes' from my hand with a clasp of kind pardon and encouragement, he made his bow, and went off to the Athénée in first-rate humour and spirits.

After all this amiability, the reader will be sorry for my sake to hear that I was quarrelling with M. Paul again before night; yet so it was, and I could not help it.

It was his occasional custom – and a very laudable, acceptable custom, too – to arrive of an evening, always à l'improviste, unannounced, burst in on the silent hour of study, establish a sudden despotism over us and our occupations, cause books to be put away, work-bags to be brought out, and, drawing forth a single thick volume, or a handful of pamphlets, substitute for the besotted 'lecture pieuse', drawled by a sleepy pupil, some tragedy made grand by grand reading, ardent by fiery action – some drama, whereof, for my part, I rarely studied the intrinsic merit; for M. Emanuel made it a vessel for an outpouring, and filled it with his native verve and passion like a cup with a vital brewage. Or else he would flash through our conventual darkness a reflex of a brighter world, show us a glimpse of the current literature of the day, read us passages from some enchanting tale, or the last witty feuilleton which had awakened laughter in the saloons of Paris; taking care always to expunge, with the severest hand, whether from tragedy, melodrama, tale, or essay, whatever passage, phrase, or word, could be deemed unsuited to an audience of 'jeunes filles'. I noticed more than once, that where retrenchment without substitute would have left unmeaning vacancy, or introduced weakness, he could, and did, improvise

whole paragraphs, no less vigorous than irreproachable: the dialogue – the description – he engrafted was often far better than that he pruned away.

Well, on the evening in question, we were sitting silent as nuns in a 'retreat,' the pupils studying, the teachers working. I remember my work; it was a slight matter of fancy, and it rather interested me; it had a purpose; I was not doing it merely to kill time; I meant it when finished as a gift; and the occasion of presentation being near, haste was requisite, and my fingers were busy.

We heard the sharp bell-peal which we all knew; then the rapid step familiar to each ear: the words 'Voilà Monsieur!' had scarcely broken simultaneously from every lip, when the two-leaved door split (as split it always did for his admission – such a slow word as 'open' is inefficient to describe his movements), and he stood in the midst of us.

There were two study-tables, both long and flanked with benches; over the centre of each hung a lamp; beneath this lamp, on either side the table, sat a teacher; the girls were arranged to the right hand and the left; the eldest and most studious nearest the lamps or tropics; the idlers and little ones towards the north and south poles. Monsieur's habit was politely to hand a chair to some teacher, generally Zélie St Pierre, the senior mistress; then to take her vacated seat; and thus avail himself of the full beam of Cancer or Capricorn, which, owing to his near sight, he needed.

As usual, Zélie rose with alacrity, smiling to the whole extent of her mouth, and the full display of her upper and under rows of teeth – that strange smile which passes from ear to ear, and is marked only by a sharp thin curve, which fails to spread over the countenance, and neither dimples the cheek nor lights the eye. I suppose Monsieur did not see her, or he had taken a whim that he would not notice her, for he was as capricious as women are said to be; then his 'lunettes' (he had got another pair) served him as an excuse for all sorts of little oversights and shortcomings. Whatever might be his reason, he passed by Zélie, came to the other side of the table, and before I could start up to clear the way, whispered, 'Ne bougez pas,' and established himself between me and Miss Fanshawe, who always would be my neighbour, and have her elbow in my side, however often I declared to her – 'Ginevra, I wish you were at Jericho.'

It was easy to say, 'Ne bougez pas;' but how could I help it? I must make him room, and I must request the pupils to recede that *I* might recede. It was very well for Ginevra to be gummed to me, 'keeping herself warm,' as she said, on the winter evenings, and harassing my very heart with her fidgetings and pokings, obliging me, indeed, sometimes to put an artful pin in my girdle by way of protection against her elbow; but I suppose M. Emanuel was not to be subjected to the same kind of treatment, so I swept away my working materials, to clear space for his book, and withdrew myself, to make room for his person; not, however, leaving more than a yard of interval, just what any reasonable man would have regarded as a convenient, respectful allowance of bench. But M. Emanuel never *was* reasonable; flint and tinder that he was! he struck and took fire directly.

'Vous ne voulez pas de moi pour voisin,' he growled: 'vous vous donnez des

airs de caste; vous me traitez en paria;' he scowled. 'Soit! je vais arranger la chose!' And he set to work.

'Levez vous toutes, mesdemoiselles!' cried he.

The girls rose. He made them all file off to the other table. He then placed me at one extremity of the long bench, and having duly and carefully brought me my work-basket, silk, scissors, all my implements, he fixed himself quite at the other end.

At this arrangement, highly absurd as it was, not a soul in the room dared to laugh; luckless for the giggler would have been the giggle. As for me, I took it with entire coolness. There I sat, isolated and cut off from human intercourse; I sat and minded my work, and was quiet, and not at all unhappy.

'Est-ce assez de distance?' he demanded.

'Monsieur en est l'arbitre,' said I.

'Vous savez bien que non. C'est vous qui avez créé ce vide immense: moi je n'y ai pas mis la main.'

And with this assertion he commenced the reading.

For his misfortune he had chosen a French translation of what he called 'un drame de Williams Shackspire; le faux dieu,' he further announced, 'de ces sots païens, les Anglais.' How far otherwise he would have characterised him had his temper not been upset, I scarcely need intimate.

Of course, the translation being French, was very inefficient; nor did I make any particular effort to conceal the contempt which some of its forlorn lapses were calculated to excite. Not that it behoved or beseemed me to *say* anything; but one can occasionally *look* the opinion it is forbidden to embody in words. Monsieur's lunettes being on the alert, he gleamed up every stray look; I don't think he lost one: the consequence was, his eyes soon discarded a screen, that their blaze might sparkle free, and he waxed hotter at the north pole to which he had voluntarily exiled himself, than, considering the general temperature of the room, it would have been reasonable to become under the vertical ray of Cancer itself.

The reading over, it appeared problematic whether he would depart with his anger unexpressed, or whether he would give it vent. Suppression was not much in his habits; but still, was what had been done to him definite enough to afford matter for overt reproof? I had not uttered a sound, and could not justly be deemed amenable to reprimand or penalty for having permitted a slightly freer action than usual to the muscles about my eyes and mouth.

The supper, consisting of bread, and milk diluted with tepid water, was brought in. In respectful consideration of the professor's presence, the rolls and glasses were allowed to stand instead of being immediately handed round.

'Take your supper, ladies,' said he, seeming to be occupied in making marginal notes to his 'Williams Shackspire'. They took it. I also accepted a roll and glass, but being now more than ever interested in my work, I kept my seat of punishment, and wrought while I munched my bread and sipped my beverage, the whole with easy *sang froid*; with a certain snugness of composure, indeed, scarcely in my habits, and pleasantly novel to my feelings. It seemed as if the presence of a nature so restless, chafing, thorny as that of M. Paul,

absorbed all feverish and unsettling influences like a magnet, and left me none but such as were placid and harmonious.

He rose. 'Will he go away without saying another word?' Yes; he turned to the door.

No: he re-turned on his steps; but only, perhaps, to take his pencil-case, which had been left on the table.

He took it – shut the pencil in and out, broke its point against the wood, re-cut and pocketed it, and . . . walked promptly up to me.

The girls and teachers, gathered round the other table, were talking pretty freely: they always talked at meals; and, from the constant habit of speaking fast and loud at such times, did not now subdue their voices much.

M. Paul came and stood behind me. He asked at what I was working; and I said I was making a watchguard.

He asked, 'For whom?' And I answered, 'For a gentleman – one of my friends.'

M. Paul stooped down and proceeded – as novel-writers say, and as was literally true in his case – to 'hiss' into my ear some poignant words.

He said that, of all the women he knew, I was the one who could make herself the most consummately unpleasant: I was she with whom it was least possible to live on friendly terms. I had a 'caractère intraitable' and perverse to a miracle. How I managed it, or what possessed me, he, for his part, did not know; but with whatever pacific and amicable intentions a person accosted me – crac! I turned concord to discord, goodwill to enmity. He was sure, he – M. Paul – wished me well enough; he had never done me any harm that he knew of; he might, at least, he supposed, claim a right to be regarded as a neutral acquaintance, guiltless of hostile sentiments: yet, how I behaved to him! With what pungent vivacities – what an impetus of mutiny – what a 'fougue' of injustice!

Here I could not avoid opening my eyes somewhat wide, and even slipping in a slight interjectional observation: 'Vivacities? Impetus? Fougue? I didn't know . . .'

'Chut! à l'instant! There! there I went – vive comme la poudre!' He was sorry – he was very sorry: for my sake he grieved over the hapless peculiarity. This 'emportement', this 'chaleur' – generous, perhaps, but excessive – would yet, he feared, do me a mischief. It was a pity: I was not – he believed, in his soul – wholly without good qualities; and would I but hear reason, and be more sedate, more sober, less 'en l'air', less 'coquette', less taken by show, less prone to set an undue value on outside excellence – to make much of the attentions of people remarkable chiefly for so many feet of stature, 'des couleurs de poupée', 'un nez plus ou moins bien fait', and an enormous amount of fatuity – I might yet prove an useful, perhaps an exemplary, character. But, as it was – And here, the little man's voice was for a minute choked.

I would have looked up at him, or held out my hand, or said a soothing word; but I was afraid, if I stirred, I should either laugh or cry; so odd, in all this, was the mixture of the touching and the absurd.

I thought he had nearly done: but no; he sat down that he might go on at his ease.

'While he, M. Paul, was on these painful topics, he would dare my anger for the sake of my good, and would venture to refer to a change he had noticed in my dress. He was free to confess that when he first knew me – or, rather, was in the habit of catching a passing glimpse of me from time to time – I satisfied him on this point: the gravity, the austere simplicity, obvious in this particular, were such as to inspire the highest hopes for my best interests. What fatal influence had impelled me lately to introduce flowers under the brim of my bonnet, to wear "des cols brodés", and even to appear on one occasion in a *scarlet gown* – he might indeed conjecture, but, for the present, would not openly declare.'

Again I interrupted, and this time not without an accent at once indignant and horror-struck.

'Scarlet, M. Paul? It was not scarlet! It was pink, and pale pink, too; and further subdued by black lace.'

'Pink or scarlet, yellow or crimson, pea-green or sky-blue; it was all one: these were all flaunting, giddy colours; and as to the lace I talked of, *that* was but a "colifichet de plus'.' And he sighed over my degeneracy. 'He could not, he was sorry to say, be so particular on this theme as he could wish: not possessing the exact names of these "babioles", he might run into small verbal errors which would not fail to lay him open to my sarcasm, and excite my unhappily sudden and passionate disposition. He would merely say, in general terms – and in these general terms he knew he was correct – that my costume had of late assumed "des façons mondaines", which it wounded him to see.'

What 'façons mondaines' he discovered in my present winter merino and plain white collar, I own it puzzled me to guess: and when I asked him, he said it was all made with too much attention to effect – and besides, 'had I not a bow or ribbon at my neck?'

'And if you condemn a bow of ribbon for a lady, monsieur, you would necessarily disapprove of a thing like this for a gentleman?' – holding up my bright little chainlet of silk and gold. His sole reply was a groan – I suppose over my levity.

After sitting some minutes in silence, and watching the progress of the chain, at which I now wrought more assiduously than ever, he enquired: 'Whether what he had just said would have the effect of making me entirely detest him?'

I hardly remember what answer I made, or how it came about; I don't think I spoke at all, but I know we managed to bid good-night on friendly terms: and, even after M. Paul had reached the door, he turned back just to explain, 'that he would not be understood to speak in entire condemnation of the scarlet dress' ('Pink! pink!' I threw in) 'that he had no intention to deny it the merit of *looking* rather well' (the fact was, M. Emanuel's taste in colours decidedly leaned to the brilliant); 'only he wished to counsel me, whenever I wore it, to do so in the same spirit as if its material were "bure", and its hue "gris de poussière".' 'And the flowers under my bonnet, monsieur?' I asked. 'They are very little ones – ?'

'Keep them little, then,' said he. 'Permit them not to become full-blown.'

'And the bow, monsieur – the bit of ribbon?'

'Va pour le ruban!' was the propitious answer. And so we settled it.

'Well done, Lucy Snowe!' cried I to myself; 'you have come in for a pretty lecture – brought on yourself a "rude savon", and all through your wicked fondness for worldly vanities! Who would have thought it? You deemed yourself a melancholy sober-sides enough! Miss Fanshawe there regards you as a second Diogenes. M. de Bassompierre, the other day, politely turned the conversation when it ran on the wild gifts of the actress Vashti, because, as he kindly said, "Miss Snowe looked uncomfortable." Dr John Bretton knows you only as "quiet Lucy" – "a creature inoffensive as a shadow"; he has said, and you have heard him say it: "Lucy's disadvantages spring from over-gravity in tastes and manner – want of colour in character and costume." Such are your own and your friends' impressions; and behold! there starts up a little man, differing diametrically from all these, roundly charging you with being too airy and cheery – too volatile and versatile – too flowery and coloury. This harsh little man – this pitiless censor – gathers up all your poor scattered sins of vanity, your luckless chiffon of rose-colour, your small fringe of a wreath, your scrap of ribbon, your silly bit of lace, and calls you to account for the lot, and for each item. You are well habituated to be passed by as a shadow in Life's sunshine: it is a new thing to see one testily lifting his hand to screen his eyes, because you tease him with an obtrusive ray.'

## CHAPTER 29

### Monsieur's Fête

I was up the next morning an hour before daybreak, and finished my guard, kneeling on the dormitory floor beside the centre stand, for the benefit of such expiring glimmer as the night-lamp afforded in its last watch.

All my materials – my whole stock of beads and silk – were used up before the chain assumed the length and richness I wished; I had wrought it double, as I knew, by the rule of contraries, that to suit the particular taste whose gratification was in view, an effective appearance was quite indispensable. As a finish to the ornament, a little gold clasp was needed; fortunately I possessed it in the fastening of my sole necklace; I duly detached and re-attached it, then coiled compactly the completed guard, and enclosed it in a small box I had bought for its brilliancy, made of some tropic shell of the colour called 'nacarat', and decked with a little coronal of sparkling blue stones. Within the lid of the box, I carefully graved with my scissors' point certain initials.

The reader will, perhaps, remember the description of Mme Beck's fête; nor will he have forgotten that at each anniversary, a handsome present was subscribed for and offered by the school. The observance of this day was a distinction accorded to none but Madame, and, in a modified form, to her kinsman and counsellor, M. Emanuel. In the latter case it was an honour

spontaneously awarded, not plotted and contrived beforehand, and offered an additional proof, amongst many others, of the estimation in which – despite his partialities, prejudices, and irritabilities – the professor of literature was held by his pupils. No article of value was offered to him: he distinctly gave it to be understood, that he would accept neither plate nor jewellery. Yet he liked a slight tribute; the cost, the money-value, did not touch him: a diamond ring, a gold snuff-box, presented with pomp, would have pleased him less than a flower, or a drawing, offered simply and with sincere feelings. Such was his nature. He was a man, not wise in his generation, yet could he claim a filial sympathy with 'the dayspring on high'.

M. Paul's fête fell on the first of March and a Thursday. It proved a fine sunny day, and being likewise the morning on which it was customary to attend mass; being also otherwise distinguished by the half holiday which permitted the privilege of walking out, shopping, or paying visits in the afternoon: these combined considerations induced a general smartness and freshness of dress. Clean collars were in vogue; the ordinary dingy woollen classe-dress was exchanged for something lighter and clearer. Mlle Zélie St Pierre, on this particular Thursday, even assumed a 'robe de soie', deemed in economical Labassecour an article of hazardous splendour and luxury; nay, it was remarked that she sent for a 'coiffeur' to dress her hair that morning; there were pupils acute enough to discover that she had bedewed her handkerchief and her hands with a new and fashionable perfume. Poor Zélie! It was much her wont to declare about this time, that she was tired to death of a life of seclusion and labour; that she longed to have the means and leisure for relaxation; to have someone to work for her – a husband who would pay her debts (she was wofully encumbered with debt), supply her wardrobe, and leave her at liberty, as she said, to 'goûter un peu les plaisirs'. It had long been rumoured, that her eye was upon M. Emanuel. M. Emanuel's eye was certainly often upon her. He would sit and watch her perseveringly for minutes together. I have seen him give her a quarter of an hour's gaze, while the class was silently composing, and he sat throned on his estrade, unoccupied. Conscious always of this basilisk attention, she would writhe under it, half-flattered, half-puzzled, and Monsieur would follow her sensations, sometimes looking appallingly acute; for in some cases, he had the terrible unerring penetration of instinct, and pierced in its hiding-place the last lurking thought of the heart, and discerned under florid veilings the bare, barren places of the spirit: yes, and its perverted tendencies, and its hidden false curves – all that men and women would not have known – the twisted spine, the malformed limb that was born with them, and far worse, the stain or disfigurement they have perhaps brought on themselves. No calamity so accursed but M. Emanuel could pity and forgive, if it were acknowledged candidly; but where his questioning eyes met dishonest denial – where his ruthless researches found deceitful concealment – oh, then, he could be cruel, and I thought wicked! he could exultantly snatch the screen from poor shrinking wretches, passionately hurry them to the summit of the mount of exposure, and there show them all naked, all false – poor living lies – the spawn of that horrid

Truth which cannot be looked on unveiled. He thought he did justice; for my part I doubt whether man has a right to do such justice on man: more than once in these his visitations, I have felt compelled to give tears to his victims, and not spared ire and keen reproach on himself. He deserved it; but it was difficult to shake him in his firm conviction that the work was righteous and needed.

Breakfast being over and mass attended, the school-bell rung and the rooms filled: a very pretty spectacle was presented in classe. Pupils and teachers sat neatly-arrayed, orderly, and expectant, each bearing in her hand the bouquet of felicitation – the prettiest spring-flowers – all fresh, and filling the air with their fragrance: I only had no bouquet. I like to see flowers growing, but when they are gathered, they cease to please. I look on them as things rootless and perishable; their likeness to life makes me sad. I never offer flowers to those I love; I never wish to receive them from hands dear to me. Mlle St Pierre marked my empty hands – she could not believe I had been so remiss; with avidity her eye roved over and round me: surely I must have some solitary symbolic flower somewhere: some small knot of violets, something to win to myself praise for taste, commendation for ingenuity. The unimaginative 'Anglaise' proved better than the Parisienne's fears: she sat literally unprovided, as bare of bloom or leaf as the winter tree. This ascertained, Zélie smiled well pleased.

'How wisely you have acted to keep your money, Meess Lucie,' she said: 'silly I have gone and thrown away two francs on a bouquet of hothouse flowers!'

And she showed with pride her splendid nosegay.

But hush! a step: *the* step. It came prompt, as usual, but with a promptitude, we felt disposed to flatter ourselves, inspired by other feelings than mere excitability of nerve, and vehemence of intent. We thought our professor's 'footfall' (to speak romantically) had in it a friendly promise this morning; and so it had.

He entered in a mood which made him as good as a new sunbeam to the already well-lit first-classe. The morning light, playing amongst our plants and laughing on our walls, caught an added lustre from M. Paul's all-benignant salute. Like a true Frenchman (though I don't know why I should say so, for he was of strain neither French nor Labassecourien), he had dressed for the 'situation' and the occasion. Not by the vague folds, sinister and conspirator-like, of his soot-dark paletôt were the outlines of his person obscured; on the contrary, his figure (such as it was, I don't boast of it) was well set off by a civilised coat and a silken vest quite pretty to behold. The defiant and pagan bonnet-grec had vanished: bareheaded he came upon us, carrying a Christian hat in his gloved hand. The little man looked well, very well; there was a clearness of amity in his blue eye, and a glow of good feeling on his dark complexion, which passed perfectly in the place of beauty: one really did not care to observe that his nose, though far from small, was of no particular shape, his cheek thin, his brow marked and square, his mouth no rosebud: one accepted him as he was, and felt his presence the reverse of damping or insignificant.

He passed to his desk; he placed on the same his hat and gloves. 'Bon jour, mes amies,' said he, in a tone that somehow made amends to some amongst us for many a sharp snap and savage snarl: not a jocund, good-fellow tone, still less

an unctuous priestly accent, but a voice he had belonging to himself – a voice used when his heart passed the word to his lips. That same heart *did* speak sometimes; though an irritable, it was not an ossified organ: in its core was a place, tender beyond a man's tenderness; a place that humbled him to little children, that bound him to girls and women: to whom, rebel as he would, he could not disown his affinity, nor quite deny that, on the whole, he was better with them than with his own sex.

'We all wish Monsieur a good-day, and present to him our congratulations on the anniversary of his fête,' said Mlle Zélie, constituting herself spokeswoman of the assembly; and advancing, with no more twists of affectation than with her were indispensable to the achievement of motion, she laid her costly bouquet before him. He bowed over it.

The long train of offerings followed: all the pupils, sweeping past with the gliding step foreigners practise, left their tributes as they went by. Each girl so dexterously adjusted her separate gift that, when the last bouquet was laid on the desk, it formed the apex to a blooming pyramid – a pyramid blooming, spreading, and towering with such exuberance as, in the end, to eclipse the hero behind it. This ceremony over, seats were resumed, and we sat in dead silence, expectant of a speech.

I suppose five minutes might have elapsed, and the hush remained unbroken; ten – and there was no sound.

Many present began, doubtless, to wonder for what Monsieur waited: as well they might. Voiceless and viewless, stirless and wordless, he kept his station behind the pile of flowers.

At last there issued forth a voice, rather deep, as if it spoke out of a hollow: 'Est-ce là tout?'

Mlle Zélie looked round.

'You have all presented your bouquets?' enquired she of the pupils.

Yes; they had all given their nosegays from the eldest to the youngest, from the tallest to the most diminutive. The senior mistress signified as much.

'Est-ce là tout?' was reiterated in an intonation which, deep before, had now descended some notes lower.

'Monsieur,' said Mlle St Pierre, rising, and this time speaking with her own sweet smile, 'I have the honour to tell you that, with a single exception, every person in classe has offered her bouquet. For Meess Lucie, Monsieur will kindly make allowance; as a foreigner, she probably did not know our customs, or did not appreciate their significance. Meess Lucie has regarded this ceremony as too frivolous to be honoured by her observance.'

'Famous!' I muttered between my teeth; 'you are no bad speaker, Zélie, when you begin.'

The answer vouchsafed to Mlle St Pierre from the estrade, was given in the gesticulation of a hand from behind the pyramid. This manual action seemed to deprecate words, to enjoin silence.

A form, ere long, followed the hand. Monsieur emerged from his eclipse; and producing himself upon the front of his estrade, and gazing straight and fixedly

before him at a vast 'mappe-monde' covering the wall opposite, he demanded a third time, and now in really tragic tones – 'Est-ce là tout?'

I might yet have made all right, by stepping forwards and slipping into his hand the ruddy little shell-box I, at that moment, held tight in my own. It was what I had fully purposed to do; but, first, the comic side of Monsieur's behaviour had tempted me to delay, and now, Mlle St Pierre's affected interference provoked contumacity. The reader not having hitherto had any cause to ascribe to Miss Snowe's character the most distant pretension to perfection, will be scarcely surprised to learn that she felt too perverse to defend herself from any imputation the Parisienne might choose to insinuate: and besides, M. Paul was so tragic, and took my defection so seriously, he deserved to be vexed. I kept, then, both my box and my countenance, and sat insensate as any stone.

'It is well!' dropped at length from the lips of M. Paul; and having uttered this phrase, the shadow of some great paroxysm – the swell of wrath, scorn, resolve – passed over his brow, rippled his lips, and lined his cheeks. Gulping down all further comment, he launched into his customary 'discours'.

I can't at all remember what this 'discours' was; I did not listen to it: the gulping-down process, the abrupt dismissal of his mortification or vexation, had given me a sensation which half-counteracted the ludicrous effect of the reiterated 'Est-ce là tout?'

Towards the close of the speech there came a pleasing diversion; my attention was again amusingly arrested.

Owing to some little accidental movement – I think I dropped my thimble on the floor, and in stooping to regain it, hit the crown of my head against the sharp corner of my desk; which casualties (exasperating to me, by rights, if to anybody) naturally made a slight bustle – M. Paul became irritated, and dismissing his forced equanimity, and casting to the winds that dignity and self-control with which he never cared long to encumber himself, he broke forth into the strain best calculated to give him ease.

I don't know how, in the progress of his 'discours', he had contrived to cross the channel, and land on British ground but there I found him when I began to listen.

Casting a quick, cynical glance round the room – a glance which scathed, or was intended to scathe, as it crossed me – he fell with fury upon 'les Anglaises'.

Never have I heard English women handled as M. Paul that morning handled them: he spared nothing – neither their minds, morals, manners, nor personal appearance. I specially remember his abuse of their tall stature, their long necks, their thin arms, their slovenly dress, their pedantic education, their impious scepticism (!), their insufferable pride, their pretentious virtue: over which he ground his teeth malignantly, and looked as if, had he dared, he would have said singular things. Oh! he was spiteful, acrid, savage; and, as a natural consequence, detestably ugly.

'Little wicked venomous man!' thought I; 'am I going to harass myself with fears of displeasing *you*, or hurting *your* feelings? No, indeed; you shall be indifferent to me, as the shabbiest bouquet in your pyramid.'

I grieve to say I could not quite carry out this resolution. For some time the abuse of England and the English found and left me stolid: I bore it some fifteen minutes stoically enough; but this hissing cockatrice was determined to sting, and he said such things at last – fastening not only upon our women, but upon our greatest names and best men; sullying the shield of Britannia, and dabbling the union jack in mud – that I *was* stung. With vicious relish he brought up the most spicy current continental historical falsehoods – than which nothing can be conceived more offensive. Zélie, and the whole class, became one grin of vindictive delight; for it is curious to discover how these clowns of Labassecour secretly hate England. At last, I struck a sharp stroke on my desk, opened my lips, and let loose this cry: 'Vive l'Angleterre, l'Histoire et les Héros! A bas la France, la Fiction et les Faquins!'

The class was struck of a heap. I suppose they thought me mad. The professor put up his handkerchief, and fiendishly smiled into its folds. Little monster of malice! He now thought he had got the victory, since he had made me angry. In a second he became good-humoured. With great blandness he resumed the subject of his flowers; talked poetically and symbolically of their sweetness, perfume, purity, etcetera; made Frenchified comparisons between the 'jeunes filles' and the sweet blossoms before him; paid Mlle St Pierre a very full-blown compliment on the superiority of her bouquet; and ended by announcing that the first really fine, mild, and balmy morning in spring, he intended to take the whole class out to breakfast in the country. 'Such of the class, at least,' he added, with emphasis, 'as he could count amongst the number of his friends.'

'Donc je n'y serai pas,' declared I, involuntarily.

'Soit!' was his response, and, gathering his flowers in his arms, he flashed out of classe; while I, consigning my work, scissors, thimble, and the neglected little box, to my desk, swept upstairs. I don't know whether *he* felt hot and angry, but I am free to confess that *I* did.

Yet with a strange evanescent anger, I had not sat an hour on the edge of my bed, picturing and repicturing his look, manner, words, ere I smiled at the whole scene. A little pang of regret I underwent that the box had not been offered. I had meant to gratify him. Fate would not have it so.

In the course of the afternoon, remembering that desks in classe were by no means inviolate repositories, and thinking that it was as well to secure the box, on account of the initials in the lid, P. C. D. E., for Paul Carl (or Carlos) David Emanuel – such was his full name – these foreigners must always have a string of baptismals – I descended to the schoolroom.

It slept in holiday repose. The day-pupils were all gone home, the boarders were out walking, the teachers, except the surveillante of the week, were in town, visiting or shopping; the suite of divisions was vacant; so was the grande salle, with its huge solemn globe hanging in the midst, its pair of many-branched chandeliers, and its horizontal grand piano closed, silent, enjoying its mid-week Sabbath. I rather wondered to find the first classe door ajar; this room being usually locked when empty, and being then inaccessible to any save Mme Beck

and myself, who possessed a duplicate key. I wondered still more, on approaching, to hear a vague movement as of life – a step, a chair stirred, a sound like the opening of a desk.

'It is only Mme Beck doing inspection duty,' was the conclusion following a moment's reflection. The partially-opened door gave opportunity for assurance on this point. I looked. Behold! not the inspecting garb of Mme Beck – the shawl and the clean cap – but the coat, and the close-shorn, dark head of a man. This person occupied my chair; his olive hand held my desk open, his nose was lost to view amongst my papers. His back was towards me, but there could not be a moment's question about identity. Already was the attire of ceremony discarded: the cherished and ink-stained paletôt was resumed; the perverse bonnet-grec lay on the floor, as if just dropped from the hand, culpably busy.

Now I knew, and had long known, that that hand of M. Emanuel's was on intimate terms with my desk; that it raised and lowered the lid, ransacked and arranged the contents, almost as familiarly as my own. The fact was not dubious, nor did he wish it to be so: he left signs of each visit palpable and unmistakeable; hitherto, however, I had never caught him in the act: watch as I would, I could not detect the hours and moments of his coming. I saw the brownie's work, in exercises left overnight full of faults, and found next morning carefully corrected: I profited by his capricious goodwill in loans full welcome and refreshing. Between a sallow dictionary and worn-out grammar would magically grow a fresh interesting new work, or a classic, mellow and sweet in its ripe age. Out of my work-basket would laughingly peep a romance, under it would lurk the pamphlet, the magazine, whence last evening's reading had been extracted. Impossible to doubt the source whence these treasures flowed: had there been no other indication, one condemning and traitor peculiarity common to them all, settled the question – *they smelt of cigars.* This was very shocking, of course: *I* thought so at first, and used to open the window with some bustle, to air my desk, and with fastidious finger and thumb, to hold the peccant brochures forth to the purifying breeze. I was cured of that formality suddenly. Monsieur caught me at it one day, understood the inference, instantly relieved my hand of its burden, and, in another moment, would have thrust the same into the glowing stove. It chanced to be a book on the perusal of which I was bent; so for once I proved as decided and quicker than himself, recaptured the spoil, and – having saved this volume – never hazarded a second. With all this, I had never yet been able to arrest in his visits the freakish, friendly, cigar-loving phantom.

But now at last I had him: there he was – the very brownie himself; and there, curling from his lips, was the pale blue breath of his Indian darling: he was smoking into my desk: it might well betray him. Provoked at this particular, and yet pleased to surprise him – pleased, that is, with the mixed feeling of the housewife who discovers at last her strange elfin ally busy in the dairy at the untimely churn – I softly stole forward, stood behind him, bent with precaution over his shoulder.

My heart smote me to see that – after this morning's hostility, after my seeming remissness, after the puncture experienced by his feelings, and the

ruffling undergone by his temper – he, all willing to forget and forgive, had brought me a couple of handsome volumes, of which the title and authorship were guarantees for interest. Now, as he sat bending above the desk, he was stirring up its contents; but with gentle and careful hand: disarranging indeed, but not harming. My heart smote me: as I bent over him, as he sat unconscious, doing me what good he could, and I dare say not feeling towards me unkindly, my morning's anger quite melted: I did not dislike Professor Emanuel.

I think he heard me breathe. He turned suddenly: his temperament was nervous, yet he never started, and seldom changed colour; there was something hardy about him.

'I thought you were gone into town with the other teachers,' said he, taking a grim gripe of his self-possession, which half escaped him – 'It is as well you are not. Do you think I care for being caught? Not I. I often visit your desk.'

'Monsieur, I know it.'

'You find a brochure or a tome now and then; but you don't read them, because they have passed under this?' – touching his cigar.

'They have, and are no better for the process, but I read them.'

'Without pleasure?'

'Monsieur must not be contradicted.'

'Do you like them, or any of them? – are they acceptable?'

'Monsieur has seen me reading them a hundred times, and knows I have not so many recreations as to undervalue those he provides.'

'I mean well; and, if you see that I mean well, and derive some little amusement from my efforts, why can we not be friends?'

'A fatalist would say – because we cannot.'

'This morning,' he continued, 'I awoke in a bright mood, and came into classe happy; you spoiled my day.'

'No, Monsieur, only an hour or two of it, and that unintentionally.'

'Unintentionally! No. It was my fête-day; everybody wished me happiness but you. The little children of the third division gave each her knot of violets, lisped each her congratulation: you – nothing. Not a bud, leaf, whisper – not a glance. Was this unintentional?'

'I meant no harm.'

'Then you really did not know our custom? You were unprepared? You would willingly have laid out a few centimes on a flower to give me pleasure, had you been aware that it was expected? Say so, and all is forgotten, and the pain soothed.'

'I *did* know that it was expected: I *was* prepared; yet I laid out no centimes on flowers.'

'It is well – you do right to be honest. I should almost have hated you, had you flattered and lied. Better declare at once – "Paul Carl Emanuel – je te déteste, mon garçon!" – than smile an interest, look an affection, and be false and cold at heart. False and cold, I don't think you are; but you have made a great mistake in life, that I believe: I think your judgement is warped – that you are indifferent where you ought to be grateful – and perhaps devoted and infatuated, where you

ought to be cool as your name. Don't suppose that I wish you to have a passion for me, Mademoiselle; Dieu vous en garde! What do you start for? Because I said passion? Well, I say it again. There is such a word, and there is such a thing – though not within these walls, thank Heaven! You are no child that one should not speak of what exists; but I only uttered the word – the thing, I assure you, is alien to my whole life and views. It died in the past – in the present it lies buried – its grave is deep-dug, well-heaped, and many winters old: in the future there will be a resurrection, as I believe to my soul's consolation; but all will then be changed – form and feeling: the mortal will have put on immortality – it will rise, not for earth, but heaven. All I say to *you*, Miss Lucy Snowe, is – that you ought to treat Professor Paul Emanuel decently.'

I could not, and did not, contradict such a sentiment.

'Tell me,' he pursued, 'when it is *your* fête-day, and I will not grudge a few centimes for a small offering.'

'You will be like me, monsieur: this cost more than a few centimes, and I did not grudge its price.'

And taking from the open desk the little box, I put it into his hand.

'It lay ready in my lap this morning,' I continued; 'and if Monsieur had been rather more patient, and Mlle St Pierre less interfering – perhaps I should say, too, if *I* had been calmer and wiser – I should have given it then.'

He looked at the box: I saw its clear warm tint and bright azure circlet pleased his eye. I told him to open it.

'My initials!' said he, indicating the letters in the lid. 'Who told you I was called Carl David?'

'A little bird, monsieur.'

'Does it fly from me to you? Then one can tie a message under its wing when needful?'

He took out the chain – a trifle indeed as to value, but glossy with silk and sparkling with beads. He liked that too – admired it artlessly, like a child.

'For me?'

'Yes, for you.'

'This is the thing you were working at last night?'

'The same.'

'You finished it this morning?'

'I did.'

'You commenced it with the intention that it should be mine?'

'Undoubtedly.'

'And offered on my fête-day?'

'Yes.'

'This purpose continued as you wove it?'

Again I assented.

'Then it is not necessary that I should cut out any portion – saying, this part is not mine; it was plaited under the idea and for the adornment of another?'

'By no means. It is neither necessary, nor would it be just.'

'This object is *all* mine?'

'That object is yours entirely.'

Straightway Monsieur opened his paletôt, arranged the guard splendidly across his chest, displaying as much and suppressing as little as he could: for he had no notion of concealing what he admired and thought decorative. As to the box, he pronounced it a superb bonbonnière – he was fond of bon-bons, by the way – and as he always liked to share with others what pleased himself, he would give his 'dragées' as freely as he lent his books. Amongst the kind brownie's gifts left in my desk, I forgot to enumerate many a paper of chocolate comfits. His tastes in these matters were southern, and what we think infantine. His simple lunch consisted frequently of a 'brioche', which as often as not, he shared with some child of the third division.

'A présent c'est un fait accompli,' said he, readjusting his paletôt; and we had no more words on the subject. After looking over the two volumes he had brought, and cutting away some pages with his penknife (he generally pruned before lending his books, especially if they were novels, and sometimes I was a little provoked at the severity of his censorship, the retrenchments interrupting the narrative), he rose, politely touched his bonnet-grec, and bade me a civil good-day.

'We are friends now,' thought I, 'till the next time we quarrel.'

We *might* have quarrelled again that very same evening, but, wonderful to relate! failed, for once, to make the most of our opportunity.

Contrary to all expectation, M. Paul arrived at the study-hour. Having seen so much of him in the morning, we did not look for his presence at night. No sooner were we seated at lessons, however, than he appeared. I own I was glad to see him, so glad that I could not help greeting his arrival with a smile; and when he made his way to the same seat about which so serious a misunderstanding had formerly arisen, I took good care not to make too much room for him; he watched with a jealous, sidelong look, to see whether I shrank away, but I did not, though the bench was a little crowded. I was losing the early impulse to recoil from M. Paul. Habituated to the paletôt and bonnet-grec, the neighbourhood of these garments seemed no longer uncomfortable or very formidable. I did not now sit restrained, 'asphyxiée' (as he used to say) at his side; I stirred when I wished to stir, coughed when it was necessary, even yawned when I was tired – did, in short, what I pleased, blindly reliant upon his indulgence. Nor did my temerity, this evening at least, meet the punishment it perhaps merited; he was both indulgent and good-natured; not a cross glance shot from his eyes, not a hasty word left his lips. Till the very close of the evening, he did not indeed address me at all, yet I felt, somehow, that he was full of friendliness. Silence is of different kinds, and breathes different meanings; no words could inspire a pleasanter content than did M. Paul's wordless presence. When the tray came in, and the bustle of supper commenced, he just said, as he retired, that he wished me a good-night and sweet dreams; and a good-night and sweet dreams I had.

## CHAPTER 30

## *M. Paul*

Yet the reader is advised not to be in any hurry with his kindly conclusions, or to suppose, with an over-hasty charity, that from that day M. Paul became a changed character – easy to live with, and no longer apt to flash danger and discomfort round him.

No; he was naturally a little man of unreasonable moods. When overwrought, which he often was, he became acutely irritable; and, besides, his veins were dark with a livid belladonna tincture, the essence of jealousy. I do not mean merely the tender jealousy of the heart, but that sterner, narrower sentiment whose seat is in the head.

I used to think, as I sat looking at M. Paul, while he was knitting his brow or protruding his lip over some exercise of mine, which had not as many faults as he wished (for he liked me to commit faults: a knot of blunders was sweet to him as a cluster of nuts), that he had points of resemblance to Napoleon Bonaparte. I think so still.

In a shameless disregard of magnanimity, he resembled the great Emperor. M. Paul would have quarrelled with twenty learned women, would have unblushingly carried on a system of petty bickering and recrimination with a whole capital of coteries, never troubling himself about loss or lack of dignity. He would have exiled fifty Mme de Staels, if they had annoyed, offended, outrivalled, or opposed him.

I well remember a hot episode of his with a certain Mme Panache – a lady temporarily employed by Mme Beck to give lessons in history. She was clever – that is, she knew a good deal; and, besides, thoroughly possessed the art of making the most of what she knew; of words and confidence she held unlimited command. Her personal appearance was far from destitute of advantages; I believe many people would have pronounced her 'a fine woman;' and yet there were points in her robust and ample attractions, as well as in her bustling and demonstrative presence, which, it appeared, the nice and capricious tastes of M. Paul could not away with. The sound of her voice, echoing through the carré, would put him into a strange taking; her long, free step – almost stride – along the corridor, would often make him snatch up his papers and decamp on the instant.

With malicious intent he bethought himself, one day, to intrude on her class; as quick as lightning he gathered her method of instruction; it differed from a pet plan of his own. With little ceremony, and less courtesy, he pointed out what he termed her errors. Whether he expected submission and attention, I know not; he met an acrid opposition, accompanied by a round reprimand for his certainly unjustifiable interference.

Instead of withdrawing with dignity, as he might still have done, he threw down the gauntlet of defiance. Mme Panache, bellicose as a Penthesilea, picked it up in a minute. She snapped her fingers in the intermeddler's face; she rushed upon him with a storm of words. M. Emanuel was eloquent; but Mme Panache was voluble. A system of fierce antagonism ensued. Instead of laughing in his sleeve at his fair foe, with all her sore amour propre and loud self-assertion, M. Paul detested her with intense seriousness; he honoured her with his earnest fury; he pursued her vindictively and implacably, refusing to rest peaceably in his bed, to derive due benefit from his meals, or even serenely to relish his cigar, till she was fairly rooted out of the establishment. The professor conquered, but I cannot say that the laurels of this victory shadowed gracefully his temples. Once I ventured to hint as much. To my great surprise he allowed that I might be right, but averred that when brought into contact with either men or women of the coarse, self-complacent quality, whereof Mme Panache was a specimen, he had no control over his own passions; an unspeakable and active aversion impelled him to a war of extermination.

Three months afterwards, hearing that his vanquished foe had met with reverses, and was likely to be really distressed for want of employment, he forgot his hatred, and, alike active in good and evil, he moved heaven and earth till he found her a place. Upon her coming to make up former differences, and thank him for his recent kindness, the old voice – a little loud – the old manner – a little forward – so acted upon him that in ten minutes he started up and bowed her, or rather himself, out of the room, in a transport of nervous irritation.

To pursue a somewhat audacious parallel, in a love of power, in an eager grasp after supremacy, M. Emanuel was like Bonaparte. He was a man not always to be submitted to. Sometimes it was needful to resist; it was right to stand still, to look up into his eyes and tell him that his requirements went beyond reason – that his absolutism verged on tyranny.

The dawnings, the first developments of peculiar talent appearing within his range, and under his rule, curiously excited, even disturbed him. He watched its struggle into life with a scowl; he held back his hand – perhaps said, 'Come on if you have strength,' but would not aid the birth.

When the pang and peril of the first conflict were over, when the breath of life was drawn, when he saw the lungs expand and contract, when he felt the heart beat and discovered life in the eye, he did not yet offer to foster.

'Prove yourself true ere I cherish you,' was his ordinance; and how difficult he made that proof! What thorns and briars, what flints, he strewed in the path of feet not inured to rough travel! He watched tearlessly – ordeals that he exacted should be passed through – fearlessly. He followed footprints that, as they approached the bourne, were sometimes marked in blood – followed them grimly, holding the austerest police-watch over the pain-pressed pilgrim. And when at last he allowed a rest, before slumber might close the eyelids, he opened those same lids wide, with pitiless finger and thumb, and gazed deep through the pupil and the irids into the brain, into the heart, to search if Vanity, or Pride, or Falsehood, in any of its subtlest forms, was discoverable in the furthest recess of

existence. If, at last, he let the neophyte sleep, it was but a moment; he woke him suddenly up to apply new tests; he sent him on irksome errands when he was staggering with weariness; he tried the temper, the sense, and the health; and it was only when every severest test had been applied and endured, when the most corrosive aquafortis had been used, and failed to tarnish the ore, that he admitted it genuine and, still in clouded silence, stamped it with his deep brand of approval.

I speak not ignorant of these evils.

Till the date at which the last chapter closes, M. Paul had not been my professor – he had not given me lessons, but about that time, accidentally hearing me one day acknowledge an ignorance of some branch of education (I think it was arithmetic) which would have disgraced a charity-schoolboy, as he very truly remarked, he took me in hand, examined me first, found me, I need not say, abundantly deficient, gave me some books and appointed me some tasks.

He did this at first with pleasure, indeed with unconcealed exultation, condescending to say that he believed I was 'bonne et pas trop faible' (i.e. well enough disposed, and not wholly destitute of parts) but, owing he supposed to adverse circumstances, 'as yet in a state of wretchedly imperfect mental development.'

The beginning of all efforts has indeed with me been marked by a preternatural imbecility. I never could, even in forming a common acquaintance, assert or prove a claim to average quickness. A depressing and difficult passage has prefaced every new page I have turned in life.

So long as this passage lasted, M. Paul was very kind, very good, very forbearing; he saw the sharp pain inflicted, and felt the weighty humiliation imposed by my own sense of incapacity; and words can hardly do justice to his tenderness and helpfulness. His own eyes would moisten, when tears of shame and effort clouded mine; burdened as he was with work, he would steal half his brief space of recreation to give to me.

But, strange grief! when that heavy and overcast dawn began at last to yield to day; when my faculties began to struggle themselves free, and my time of energy and fulfilment came; when I voluntarily doubled, trebled, quadrupled the tasks he set, to please him as I thought, his kindness became sternness; the light changed in his eyes from a beam to a spark; he fretted, he opposed, he curbed me imperiously; the more I did, the harder I worked, the less he seemed content. Sarcasms of which the severity amazed and puzzled me, harassed my ears; there flowed out the bitterest innuendoes against the 'pride of intellect.' I was vaguely threatened with, I know not what doom, if I ever trespassed the limits proper to my sex, and conceived a contraband appetite for unfeminine knowledge. Alas! I had no such appetite. What I loved, it joyed me by any effort to content; but the noble hunger for science in the abstract – the godlike thirst after discovery – these feelings were known to me but by briefest flashes.

Yet, when M. Paul sneered at me, I wanted to possess them more fully; his injustice stirred in me ambitious wishes – it imparted a strong stimulus – it gave wings to aspiration.

In the beginning, before I had penetrated to motives, that uncomprehended sneer of his made my heart ache, but by and by it only warmed the blood in my

veins, and sent added action to my pulses. Whatever my powers – feminine or the contrary – God had given them, and I felt resolute to be ashamed of no faculty of His bestowal.

The combat was very sharp for a time. I seemed to have lost M. Paul's affection; he treated me strangely. In his most unjust moments he would insinuate that I had deceived him when I appeared, what he called 'faible' – that is, incompetent; he said I had feigned a false incapacity. Again, he would turn suddenly round and accuse me of the most far-fetched imitations and impossible plagiarisms, asserting that I had extracted the pith out of books I had not so much as heard of – and over the perusal of which I should infallibly have fallen down in a sleep as deep as that of Eutychus.

Once, upon his preferring such an accusation, I turned upon him – I rose against him. Gathering an armful of his books out of my desk, I filled my apron and poured them in a heap upon his estrade, at his feet.

'Take them away, M. Paul,' I said, 'and teach me no more. I never asked to be made learned, and you compel me to feel very profoundly that learning is not happiness.'

And returning to my desk, I laid my head on my arms, nor would I speak to him for two days afterwards. He pained and chagrined me. His affection had been very sweet and dear – a pleasure new and incomparable: now that this seemed withdrawn, I cared not for his lessons.

The books, however, were not taken away; they were all restored with careful hand to their places, and he came as usual to teach me. He made his peace somehow – too readily, perhaps; I ought to have stood out longer, but when he looked kind and good, and held out his hand with amity, memory refused to reproduce with due force his oppressive moments. And then, reconcilement is always sweet!

On a certain morning a message came from my godmother, inviting me to attend some notable lecture to be delivered in the same public rooms before described. Dr John had brought the message himself, and delivered it verbally to Rosine, who had not scrupled to follow the steps of M. Emanuel, then passing to the first classe, and, in his presence, stand 'carrément' before my desk, hand in apron-pocket, and rehearse the same, saucily and aloud, concluding with the words – 'Qu'il est vraiment beau, mademoiselle, ce jeune docteur! Quels yeux – quel regard! Tenez! J'en ai le coeur tout ému!'

When she was gone, my professor demanded of me why I suffered 'cette fille effrontée, cette creature sans pudeur,' to address me in such terms.

I had no pacifying answer to give. The terms were precisely such as Rosine – a young lady in whose skull the organs of reverence and reserve were not largely developed – was in the constant habit of using. Besides, what she said about the young doctor was true enough. Graham *was* handsome; he *had* fine eyes and a thrilling glance. An observation to that effect actually formed itself into sound on my lips.

'Elle ne dit que la vérité,' I said.

'Ah! vous trouvez?'

'Mais, sans doute.'

The lesson to which we had that day to submit was such as to make us very glad when it terminated. At its close, the released pupils rushed out, half-trembling, half-exultant. I, too, was going. A mandate to remain arrested me. I muttered that I wanted some fresh air sadly – the stove was in a glow, the classe over-heated. An inexorable voice merely recommended silence; and this sala-mander – for whom no room ever seemed too hot – sitting down between my desk and the stove – a situation in which he ought to have felt broiled, but did not – proceeded to confront me with – a Greek quotation!

In M. Emanuel's soul rankled a chronic suspicion that I knew both Greek and Latin. As monkeys are said to have the power of speech if they would but use it, and are reported to conceal this faculty in fear of its being turned to their detriment, so to me was ascribed a fund of knowledge which I was supposed criminally and craftily to conceal. The privileges of a 'classical education,' it was insinuated, had been mine; on flowers of Hymettus I had revelled; a golden store, hived in memory, now silently sustained my efforts, and privily nurtured my wits.

A hundred expedients did M. Paul employ to surprise my secret – to wheedle, to threaten, to startle it out of me. Sometimes he placed Greek and Latin books in my way, and then watched me, as Joan of Arc's jailors tempted her with the warrior's accoutrements, and lay in wait for the issue. Again he quoted I know not what authors and passages, and while rolling out their sweet and sounding lines (the classic tones fell very musically from his lips – for he had a good voice – remarkable for compass, modulation, and matchless expression), he would fix on me a vigilant, piercing, and often malicious eye. It was evident he sometimes expected great demonstrations; they never occurred, however; not comprehending, of course I could neither be charmed nor annoyed.

Baffled – almost angry – he still clung to his fixed idea; my susceptibilities were pronounced marble – my face a mask. It appeared as if he could not be brought to accept the homely truth, and take me for what I was: men, and women too, must have delusion of some sort; if not made ready to their hand, they will invent exaggeration for themselves.

At moments I *did* wish that his suspicions had been better founded. There were times when I would have given my right hand to possess the treasures he ascribed to me. He deserved condign punishment for his testy crotchets. I could have gloried in bringing home to him his worst apprehensions astoundingly realised. I could have exulted to burst on his vision, confront and confound his 'lunettes,' one blaze of acquirements. Oh! why did nobody undertake to make me clever while I was young enough to learn, that I might, by one grand, sudden, inhuman revelation – one cold, cruel, overwhelming triumph – have for ever crushed the mocking spirit out of Paul Carl David Emanuel!

Alas! no such feat was in my power. Today, as usual, his quotations fell ineffectual: he soon shifted his ground.

'Women of intellect' was his next theme: here he was at home. A 'woman of intellect,' it appeared, was a sort of 'lusus naturae', a luckless accident, a thing for which there was neither place nor use in creation, wanted neither as wife nor

worker. Beauty anticipated her in the first office. He believed in his soul that lovely, placid, and passive feminine mediocrity was the only pillow on which manly thought and sense could find rest for its aching temples; and as to work, male mind alone could work to any good practical result – hein?

This 'hein?' was a note of interrogation intended to draw from me contradiction or objection. However, I only said – 'Cela ne me regarde pas: je ne m'en soucie pas;' and presently added – 'May I go, monsieur? They have rung the bell for the second déjeuner' (i.e., luncheon).

'What of that? You are not hungry?'

'Indeed I was,' I said; 'I had had nothing since breakfast, at seven, and should have nothing till dinner, at five, if I missed this bell.'

'Well, he was in the same plight, but I might share with him.'

And he broke in two the 'brioche', intended for his own refreshment, and gave me half. Truly his bark was worse than his bite; but the really formidable attack was yet to come. While eating his cake, I could not forbear expressing my secret wish that I really knew all of which he accused me.

'Did I sincerely feel myself to be an ignoramus?' he asked, in a softened tone.

If I had replied meekly by an unqualified affirmative, I believe he would have stretched out his hand, and we should have been friends on the spot, but I answered: 'Not exactly. I am ignorant, monsieur, in the knowledge you ascribe to me, but I *sometimes*, not *always*, feel a knowledge of my own.'

'What did I mean?' he enquired, sharply.

Unable to answer this question in a breath, I evaded it by change of subject. He had now finished his half of the brioche: feeling sure that on so trifling a fragment he could not have satisfied his appetite, as indeed I had not appeased mine, and inhaling the fragrance of baked apples afar from the refectory, I ventured to enquire whether he did not also perceive that agreeable odour. He confessed that he did. I said if he would let me out by the garden-door, and permit me just to run across the court, I would fetch him a plateful; and added that I believed they were excellent, as Goton had a very good method of baking, or rather stewing fruit, putting in a little spice, sugar, and a glass or two of vin blanc – might I go?

'Petite gourmande!' said he, smiling. 'I have not forgotten how pleased you were with the pâté à la crême I once gave you, and you know very well, at this moment, that to fetch the apples for me will be the same as getting them for yourself. Go, then, but come back quickly.'

And at last he liberated me on parole. My own plan was to go and return with speed and good faith, to put the plate in at the door, and then to vanish incontinent, leaving all consequences for future settlement.

That intolerably keen instinct of his seemed to have anticipated my scheme; he met me at the threshold, hurried me into the room, and fixed me in a minute in my former seat. Taking the plate of fruit from my hand, he divided the portion intended only for himself, and ordered me to eat my share. I complied with no good grace, and vexed, I suppose, by my reluctance, he opened a masked and dangerous battery. All he had yet said, I could count as mere sound and fury, signifying nothing; not so of the present attack.

It consisted in an unreasonable proposition with which he had before afflicted me: namely, that on the next public examination-day I should engage – foreigner as I was – to take my place on the first form of first-class pupils, and with them improvise a composition in French, on any subject any spectator might dictate, without benefit of grammar or lexicon.

I knew what the result of such an experiment would be. I, to whom nature had denied the impromptu faculty; who, in public, was by nature a cypher; whose time of mental activity, even when alone, was not under the meridian sun; who needed the fresh silence of morning, or the recluse peace of evening, to win from the Creative Impulse one evidence of his presence, one proof of his force; I, with whom that Impulse was the most intractable, the most capricious, the most maddening of masters (him before me always excepted) – a deity, which sometimes, under circumstances apparently propitious, would not speak when questioned, would not hear when appealed to, would not, when sought, be found; but would stand, all cold, all indurated, all granite, a dark Baal with carven lips and blank eyeballs, and breast like the stone face of a tomb; and again, suddenly, at some turn, some sound, some long-trembling sob of the wind, at some rushing past of an unseen stream of electricity, the irrational demon would wake unsolicited, would stir strangely alive, would rush from its pedestal like a perturbed Dagon, calling to its votary for a sacrifice, whatever the hour – to its victim for some blood or some breath, whatever the circumstance or scene – rousing its priest, treacherously promising vaticination, perhaps filling its temple with a strange hum of oracles, but sure to give half the significance to fateful winds, and grudging to the desperate listener even a miserable remnant – yielding it sordidly, as though each word had been a drop of the deathless ichor of its own dark veins. And this tyrant I was to compel into bondage, and make it improvise a theme, on a school estrade, between a Mathilde and a Coralie, under the eye of a Mme Beck, for the pleasure and to the inspiration of a bourgeois of Labassecour!

Upon this argument M. Paul and I did battle more than once – strong battle, with confused noise of demand and rejection, exaction and repulse.

On this particular day I was soundly rated. 'The obstinacy of my whole sex,' it seems, was concentrated in me; I had an 'orgueil de diable'. I feared to fail, forsooth! What did it matter whether I failed or not? Who was I that I should not fail like my betters? It would do me good to fail. He wanted to see me worsted (I knew he did), and one minute he paused to take breath.

'Would I speak now and be tractable?'

'Never would I be tractable in this matter. Law itself should not compel me. I would pay a fine, or undergo an imprisonment, rather than write for a show and to order, perched up on a platform.'

'Could softer motives influence me? Would I yield for friendship's sake?'

'Not a whit, not a hair-breadth. No form of friendship under the sun had a right to exact such a concession. No true friendship would harass me thus.'

He supposed then (with a sneer – M. Paul could sneer supremely, curling his lip, opening his nostrils, contracting his eyelids) – he supposed there was but one

form of appeal to which I would listen, and of that form it was not for him to make use.

'Under certain persuasions, from certain quarters, je vous vois d'ici,' said he, 'eagerly subscribing to the sacrifice, passionately arming for the effort.'

'Making a simpleton, a warning, and an example of myself, before a hundred and fifty of the "papas" and "mamans" of Villette.'

And here, losing patience, I broke out afresh with a cry that I wanted to be liberated, to get out to the air – I was almost in a fever.

'Chut!' said the inexorable, 'this was a mere pretext to run away: he was not hot, with the stove close at his back; how could I suffer, thoroughly screened by his person?'

'I did not understand his constitution. I knew nothing of the natural history of salamanders. For my own part, I was a phlegmatic islander, and sitting in an oven did not agree with me; at least, might I step to the well, and get a glass of water – the sweet apples had made me thirsty?'

'If that was all, he would do my errand.'

He went to fetch the water. Of course, with a door only on the latch behind me, I lost not my opportunity. Ere his return, his half-worried prey had escaped.

## CHAPTER 31

### *The Dryad*

The spring was advancing, and the weather had turned suddenly warm. This change of temperature brought with it for me, as probably for many others, temporary decrease of strength. Slight exertion at this time left me overcome with fatigue – sleepless nights entailed languid days.

One Sunday afternoon, having walked the distance of half a league to the Protestant church, I came back weary and exhausted; and taking refuge in my solitary sanctuary, the first classe, I was glad to sit down, and to make of my desk a pillow for my arms and head.

Awhile I listened to the lullaby of bees humming in the berceau, and watched, through the glass door, and the tender, lightly-strewn spring foliage, Mme Beck and a gay party of friends, whom she had entertained that day at dinner after morning-mass, walking in the centre-alley under orchard boughs dressed at this season in blossom, and wearing a colouring as pure and warm as mountain-snow at sunrise.

My principal attraction towards this group of guests lay, I remember, in one figure – that of a handsome young girl whom I had seen before as a visitor at Mme Beck's, and of whom I had been vaguely told that she was a 'filleule', or god-daughter, of M. Emanuel's, and that between her mother, or aunt, or some other female relation of hers, and the professor – had existed of old a special friendship. M. Paul was not of the holiday band today, but I had seen this young

girl with him ere now, and as far as distant observation could enable me to judge, she seemed to enjoy with him the frank ease of a ward with an indulgent guardian. I had seen her run up to him, put her arm through his and hang upon him. Once, when she did so, a curious sensation had struck through me – a disagreeable anticipatory sensation – one of the family of presentiments, I suppose – but I refused to analyse or dwell upon it. While watching this girl, Mlle Sauveur by name, and following the gleam of her bright silk robe (she was always richly dressed, for she was said to be wealthy) through the flowers and the glancing leaves of tender emerald, my eyes became dazzled – they closed; my lassitude, the warmth of the day, the hum of bees and birds, all lulled me, and at last I slept.

Two hours stole over me. Ere I woke, the sun had declined out of sight behind the towering houses, the garden and the room were gray, bees had gone homeward, and the flowers were closing; the party of guests, too, had vanished; each alley was void.

On waking, I felt much at ease – not chill, as I ought to have been after sitting so still for at least two hours; my cheek and arms were not benumbed by pressure against the hard desk. No wonder. Instead of the bare wood on which I had laid them, I found a thick shawl, carefully folded, substituted for support, and another shawl (both taken from the corridor where such things hung) wrapped warmly round me.

Who had done this? Who was my friend? Which of the teachers? Which of the pupils? None, except St Pierre, was inimical to me; but which of them had the art, the thought, the habit, of benefiting thus tenderly? Which of them had a step so quiet, a hand so gentle, but I should have heard or felt her, if she had approached or touched me in a day-sleep?

As to Ginevra Fanshawe, that bright young creature was not gentle at all, and would certainly have pulled me out of my chair, if she had meddled in the matter. I said at last: 'It is Mme Beck's doing; she has come in, seen me asleep, and thought I might take cold. She considers me a useful machine, answering well the purpose for which it was hired; so would not have me needlessly injured. And now,' methought, 'I'll take a walk; the evening is fresh, and not very chill.'

So I opened the glass door and stepped into the berceau.

I went to my own alley: had it been dark, or even dusk, I should hardly have ventured there, for I had not yet forgotten the curious illusion of vision (if illusion it were) experienced in that place some months ago. But a ray of the setting sun burnished still the gray crown of Jean Baptiste; nor had all the birds of the garden yet vanished into their nests amongst the tufted shrubs and thick wall-ivy. I paced up and down, thinking almost the same thoughts I had pondered that night when I buried my glass jar – how I should make some advance in life, take another step towards an independent position; for this train of reflection, though not lately pursued, had never by me been wholly abandoned; and whenever a certain eye was averted from me, and a certain countenance grew dark with unkindness and injustice, into that track of speculation did I at once strike; so that, little by little, I had laid half a plan.

'Living costs little,' said I to myself, 'in this economical town of Villette, where people are more sensible than I understand they are in dear old England – infinitely less worried about appearance, and less emulous of display – where nobody is in the least ashamed to be quite as homely and saving as he finds convenient. House-rent, in a prudently chosen situation, need not be high. When I shall have saved one thousand francs, I will take a tenement with one large room, and two or three smaller ones, furnish the first with a few benches and desks, a black tableau, an estrade for myself; upon it a chair and table, with a sponge and some white chalks; begin with taking day-pupils, and so work my way upwards. Mme Beck's commencement was – as I have often heard her say – from no higher starting-point, and where is she now? All these premises and this garden are hers, bought with her money; she has a competency already secured for old age, and a flourishing establishment under her direction, which will furnish a career for her children.

Courage, Lucy Snowe! With self-denial and economy now, and steady exertion by and by, an object in life need not fail you. Venture not to complain that such an object is too selfish, too limited, and lacks interest; be content to labour for independence until you have proved, by winning that prize, your right to look higher. But afterwards, is there nothing more for me in life – no true home – nothing to be dearer to me than myself, and by its paramount preciousness, to draw from me better things than I care to culture for myself only? Nothing, at whose feet I can willingly lay down the whole burden of human egotism, and gloriously take up the nobler charge of labouring and living for others?' I suppose, Lucy Snowe, the orb of your life is not to be so rounded; for you the crescent-phase must suffice. Very good. I see a huge mass of my fellow-creatures in no better circumstances. I see that a great many men, and more women, hold their span of life on conditions of denial and privation. I find no reason why I should be of the few favoured. I believe in some blending of hope and sunshine sweetening the worst lots. I believe that this life is not all; neither the beginning nor the end. I believe while I tremble; I trust while I weep.

So this subject is done with. It is right to look our life-accounts bravely in the face now and then, and settle them honestly. And he is a poor self-swindler who lies to himself while he reckons the items, and sets down under the head happiness that which is misery. Call anguish – anguish, and despair – despair; write both down in strong characters with a resolute pen: you will the better pay your debt to Doom. Falsify; insert 'privilege' where you should have written 'pain;' and see if your mighty creditor will allow the fraud to pass, or accept the coin with which you would cheat him. Offer to the strongest – if the darkest angel of God's host – water, when he has asked blood – will he take it? Not a whole pale sea for one red drop. I settled another account.

Pausing before Methusaleh – the giant and patriarch of the garden – and leaning my brow against his knotty trunk, my foot rested on the stone sealing the small sepulchre at his root; and I recalled the passage of feeling therein buried. I recalled Dr John; my warm affection for him; my faith in his excellence; my delight in his grace. What was become of that curious one-sided friendship

which was half marble and half life; only on one hand truth, and on the other perhaps a jest?

Was this feeling dead? I do not know, but it was buried. Sometimes I thought the tomb unquiet, and dreamed strangely of disturbed earth, and of hair, still golden and living, obtruded through coffin-chinks.

Had I been too hasty? I used to ask myself; and this question would occur with a cruel sharpness after some brief chance interview with Dr John. He had still such kind looks, such a warm hand; his voice still kept so pleasant a tone for my name; I never liked 'Lucy' so well as when he uttered it. But I learned in time that this benignity, this cordiality, this music, belonged in no shape to me: it was a part of himself; it was the honey of his temper; it was the balm of his mellow mood; he imparted it, as the ripe fruit rewards with sweetness the rifling bee; he diffused it about him, as sweet plants shed their perfume. Does the nectarine love either the bee or bird it feeds? Is the sweet-briar enamoured of the air?

'Good-night, Dr John; you are good, you are beautiful; but you are not mine. Good-night, and God bless you!'

Thus I closed my musings. 'Good-night' left my lips in sound; I heard the two words spoken, and then I heard an echo – quite close.

'Good-night, mademoiselle; or, rather, good-evening – the sun is scarce set; I hope you slept well?'

I started, but was only discomposed a moment; I knew the voice and speaker.

'Slept, monsieur! When? where?'

'You may well enquire when – where. It seems you turn day into night, and choose a desk for a pillow; rather hard lodging – ?'

'It was softened for me, monsieur, while I slept. That unseen, gift-bringing thing which haunts my desk, remembered me. No matter how I fell asleep; I awoke pillowed and covered.'

'Did the shawls keep you warm?'

'Very warm. Do you ask thanks for them?'

'No. You looked pale in your slumbers; are you homesick?'

'To be homesick, one must have a home; which I have not.'

'Then you have more need of a careful friend. I scarcely know anyone, Miss Lucy, who needs a friend more absolutely than you; your very faults imperatively require it. You want so much checking, regulating, and keeping down.'

This idea of 'keeping down' never left M. Paul's head; the most habitual subjugation would, in my case, have failed to relieve him of it. No matter; what did it signify? I listened to him, and did not trouble myself to be too submissive; his occupation would have been gone, had I left him nothing to 'keep down.'

'You need watching, and watching over,' he pursued; 'and it is well for you that I see this, and do my best to discharge both duties. I watch you and others pretty closely, pretty constantly, nearer and oftener than you or they think. Do you see that window with a light in it?'

He pointed to a lattice in one of the college boarding-houses.

'That,' said he, 'is a room I have hired, nominally for a study – virtually for a post of observation. There I sit and read for hours together: it is my way – my

taste. My book is this garden; its contents are human nature – female human nature. I know you all by heart. Ah! I know you well – St Pierre the Parisienne – cette maîtresse-femme, my cousin Beck herself.'

'It is not right, monsieur.'

'Comment – it is not right? By whose creed? Does some dogma of Calvin or Luther condemn it? What is that to me? I am no Protestant. My rich father (for, though I have known poverty, and once starved for a year in a garret in Rome – starved wretchedly, often on a meal a day, and sometimes not that – yet I was born to wealth) – my rich father was a good Catholic; and he gave me a priest and a Jesuit for a tutor. I retain his lessons; and to what discoveries, grand Dieu! have they not aided me!'

'Discoveries made by stealth seem to me dishonourable discoveries.'

'Puritaine! I doubt it not. Yet see how my Jesuit's system works. You know the St Pierre?'

'Partially.'

He laughed. 'You say right – "*partially*"; whereas, *I* know her *thoroughly*; there is the difference. She played before me the amiable; offered me patte de velours; caressed, flattered, fawned on me. Now, I am accessible to a woman's flattery – accessible against my reason. Though never pretty, she was – when I first knew her – young, or knew how to look young. Like all her countrywomen, she had the art of dressing – she had a certain, cool, easy, social assurance, which spared me the pain of embarrassment –'

'Monsieur, that must have been unnecessary. I never saw you embarrassed in my life.'

'Mademoiselle, you know little of me; I can be embarrassed as a petite pensionnaire; there is a fund of modesty and diffidence in my nature –'

'Monsieur, I never saw it.'

'Mademoiselle, it is there. You ought to have seen it.'

'Monsieur, I have observed you in public – on platforms, in tribunes, before titles and crowned heads – and you were as easy as you are in the third division.'

'Mademoiselle, neither titles nor crowned heads excite my modesty; and publicity is very much my element. I like it well, and breathe in it quite freely; but – but – in short, here is the sentiment brought into action, at this very moment; however, I disdain to be worsted by it. If, mademoiselle, I were a marrying man (which I am not; and you may spare yourself the trouble of any sneer you may be contemplating at the thought), and found it necessary to ask a lady whether she could look upon me in the light of a future husband, then would it be proved that I am as I say – modest.'

I quite believed him now; and, in believing, I honoured him with a sincerity of esteem which made my heart ache.

'As to the St Pierre,' he went on, recovering himself, for his voice had altered a little, 'she once intended to be Mme Emanuel; and I don't know whither I might have been led, but for yonder little lattice with the light. Ah, magic lattice! what miracles of discovery hast thou wrought! Yes,' he pursued, 'I have seen her rancours, her vanities, her levities – not only here, but elsewhere: I

have witnessed what bucklers me against all her arts: I am safe from poor Zélie.'

'And my pupils,' he presently recommenced, 'those blondes jeunes filles – so mild and meek – I have seen the most reserved – romp like boys, the demurest – snatch grapes from the walls, shake pears from the trees. When the English teacher came, I saw her, marked her early preference for this alley, noted her taste for seclusion, watched her well, long before she and I came to speaking terms; do you recollect my once coming silently and offering you a little knot of white violets when we were strangers?'

'I recollect it. I dried the violets, kept them, and have them still.'

'It pleased me when you took them peacefully and promptly, without prudery – that sentiment which I ever dread to excite, and which, when it is revealed in eye or gesture, I vindictively detest. To return. Not only did I watch you, but often – especially at eventide – another guardian angel was noiselessly hovering near: night after night my cousin Beck has stolen down yonder steps, and glidingly pursued your movements when you did not see her.'

'But, Monsieur, you could not from the distance of that window see what passed in this garden at night?'

'By moonlight I possibly might with a glass – I use a glass – but the garden itself is open to me. In the shed, at the bottom, there is a door leading into a court, which communicates with the college; of that door I possess the key, and thus come and go at pleasure. This afternoon I came through it, and found you asleep in class; again this evening, I have availed myself of the same entrance.'

I could not help saying, 'If you were a wicked, designing man, how terrible would all this be!'

His attention seemed incapable of being arrested by this view of the subject: he lit his cigar, and while he puffed it, leaning against a tree, and looking at me in a cool, amused way he had when his humour was tranquil, I thought proper to go on sermonising him: he often lectured me by the hour together – I did not see why I should not speak my mind for once. So I told him my impressions concerning his Jesuit-system.

'The knowledge it brings you is bought too dear, monsieur; this coming and going by stealth degrades your own dignity.'

'My dignity!' he cried, laughing; 'when did you ever see me trouble my head about my dignity? It is you, Miss Lucy, who are "digne". How often, in your high insular presence, have I taken a pleasure in trampling upon, what you are pleased to call, my dignity; tearing it, scattering it to the winds, in those mad transports you witness with such hauteur, and which I know you think very like the ravings of a third-rate London actor.'

'Monsieur, I tell you every glance you cast from that lattice is a wrong done to the best part of your own nature. To study the human heart thus, is to banquet secretly and sacrilegiously on Eve's apples. I wish you were a Protestant.'

Indifferent to the wish, he smoked on. After a space of smiling yet thoughtful silence, he said, rather suddenly – 'I have seen other things.'

'What other things?'

Taking the weed from his lips, he threw the remnant amongst the shrubs, where, for a moment, it lay glowing in the gloom.

'Look at it,' said he: 'is not that spark like an eye watching you and me?'

He took a turn down the walk; presently returning, he went on: 'I have seen, Miss Lucy, things to me unaccountable, that have made me watch all night for a solution, and I have not yet found it.'

His tone was peculiar; my veins thrilled; he saw me shiver.

'Are you afraid? Whether is it of my words or of that red jealous eye just winking itself out?'

'I am cold; the night grows dark and late, and the air is changed; it is time to go in.'

'It is little past eight, but you shall go in soon. Answer me only this question.'

Yet he paused ere he put it. The garden was truly growing dark; dusk had come on with clouds, and drops of rain began to patter through the trees. I hoped he would feel this, but, for the moment, he seemed too much absorbed to be sensible of the change.

'Mademoiselle, do you Protestants believe in the supernatural?'

'There is a difference of theory and belief on this point amongst Protestants, as amongst other sects,' I answered. 'Why, monsieur, do you ask such a question?'

'Why do you shrink and speak so faintly? Are you superstitious?'

'I am constitutionally nervous. I dislike the discussion of such subjects. I dislike it the more because –'

'You believe?'

'No: but it has happened to me to experience impressions –'

'Since you came here?'

'Yes: not many months ago.'

'Here? – in this house?'

'Yes.'

'Bon! I am glad of it. I knew it somehow before you told me. I was conscious of rapport between you and myself. You are patient, and I am choleric; you are quiet and pale, and I am tanned and fiery; you are a strict Protestant, and I am a sort of lay Jesuit: but we are alike – there is affinity. Do you see it, mademoiselle, when you look in the glass? Do you observe that your forehead is shaped like mine – that your eyes are cut like mine? Do you hear that you have some of my tones of voice? Do you know that you have many of my looks? I perceive all this, and believe that you were born under my star. Yes, you were born under my star! Tremble! for where that is the case with mortals, the threads of their destinies are difficult to disentangle; knottings and catchings occur – sudden breaks leave damage in the web. But these "impressions", as you say, with English caution. I, too, have had my "impressions".'

'Monsieur, tell me them.'

'I desire no better, and intend no less. You know the legend of this house and garden?'

'I know it. Yes. They say that hundreds of years ago a nun was buried here alive at the foot of this very tree, beneath the ground which now bears us.'

'And that in former days a nun's ghost used to come and go here.'

'Monsieur, what if it comes and goes here still?'

'Something comes and goes here: there is a shape frequenting this house by night, different to any forms that show themselves by day. I have indisputably seen a something, more than once; and to me its conventual weeds were a strange sight, saying more than they can do to any other living being. A nun!'

'Monsieur, I, too, have seen it.'

'I anticipated that. Whether this nun be flesh and blood, or something that remains when blood is dried and flesh wasted, her business is as much with you as with me, probably. Well, I mean to make it out: it has baffled me so far, but I mean to follow up the mystery. I mean –'

Instead of telling what he meant, he raised his head suddenly; I made the same movement in the same instant; we both looked to one point – the high tree shadowing the great berceau, and resting some of its boughs on the roof of the first classe. There had been a strange and inexplicable sound from that quarter, as if the arms of that tree had swayed of their own motion, and its weight of foliage had rushed and crushed against the massive trunk. Yes; there scarce stirred a breeze, and that heavy tree was convulsed, whilst the feathery shrubs stood still. For some minutes amongst the wood and leafage a rending and heaving went on. Dark as it was, it seemed to me that something more solid than either night-shadow, or branch-shadow, blackened out of the boles. At last the struggle ceased. What birth succeeded this travail? What Dryad was born of these throes? We watched fixedly. A sudden bell rang in the house – the prayer-bell. Instantly into our alley there came, out of the bureau, an apparition, all black and white. With a sort of angry rush – close, close past our faces – swept swiftly the very *nun* herself! Never had I seen her so clearly. She looked tall of stature, and fierce of gesture. As she went, the wind rose sobbing; the rain poured wild and cold; the whole night seemed to feel her.

CHAPTER 32

*The First Letter*

Where, it becomes time to enquire, was Paulina Mary? How fared my intercourse with the sumptuous Hôtel Crécy? That intercourse had, for an interval, been suspended by absence; M. and Miss de Bassompierre had been travelling, dividing some weeks between the provinces and the capital of France. Chance apprised me of their return very shortly after it took place.

I was walking one mild afternoon on a quiet boulevard, wandering slowly on, enjoying the benign April sun, and some thoughts not unpleasing, when I saw before me a group of riders, stopping as if they had just encountered, and exchanging greetings in the midst of the broad, smooth, linden-bordered path; on one side a middle-aged gentleman and young lady, on the other – a young and

handsome man. Very graceful was the lady's mien, choice her appointments, delicate and stately her whole aspect. Still, as I looked, I felt they were known to me, and, drawing a little nearer, I fully recognised them all; the Count Home de Bassompierre, his daughter, and Dr Graham Bretton.

How animated was Graham's face! How true, how warm, yet how retiring the joy it expressed! This was the state of things, this the combination of circumstances, at once to attract and enchain, to subdue and excite Dr John. The pearl he admired was in itself of great price and truest purity, but he was not the man who, in appreciating the gem, could forget its setting. Had he seen Paulina with the same youth, beauty, and grace, but on foot, alone, unguarded, and in simple attire, a dependent worker, a demi-grisette, he would have thought her a pretty little creature, and would have loved with his eye her movements and her mien, but it required other than this to conquer him as he was now vanquished, to bring him safe under dominion as now, without loss, and even with gain to his manly honour – one saw that he was reduced; there was about Dr John all the man of the world; to satisfy himself did not suffice; society must approve – the world must admire what he did, or he counted his measures false and futile. In his victrix he required all that was here visible – the imprint of high cultivation, the consecration of a careful and authoritative protection, the adjuncts that Fashion decrees, Wealth purchases, and Taste adjusts; for these conditions his spirit stipulated ere it surrendered: they were here to the utmost fulfilled; and now, proud, impassioned, yet fearing, he did homage to Paulina as his sovereign. As for her, the smile of feeling, rather than of conscious power, slept soft in her eyes.

They parted. He passed me at speed, hardly feeling the earth he skimmed, and seeing nothing on either hand. He looked very handsome; mettle and purpose were roused in him fully.

'Papa, there is Lucy!' cried a musical, friendly voice, 'Lucy, dear Lucy – *do* come here!'

I hastened to her. She threw back her veil, and stooped from her saddle to kiss me.

'I was coming to see you tomorrow,' said she; 'but now, tomorrow you will come and see me.'

She named the hour, and I promised compliance.

The morrow's evening found me with her – she and I shut into her own room. I had not seen her since that occasion when her claims were brought into comparison with those of Ginevra Fanshawe, and had so signally prevailed; she had much to tell me of her travels in the interval. A most animated, rapid speaker was she in such tête-à-tête, a most lively describer; yet with her artless diction and clear, soft voice, she never seemed to speak too fast or say too much. My own attention I think would not soon have flagged, but by and by, she herself seemed to need some change of subject; she hastened to wind up her narrative briefly. Yet why she terminated with so concise an abridgement did not immediately appear; silence followed – a restless silence, not without symptoms of abstraction. Then, turning to me, in a diffident, half-appealing voice – 'Lucy –'

'Well, I am at your side.'

'Is my cousin Ginevra still at Mme Beck's?'

'Your cousin is still there; you must be longing to see her.'

'No – not much.'

'You want to invite her to spend another evening?'

'No. . . I suppose she still talks about being married?'

'Not to anyone you care for.'

'But of course she still thinks of Dr Bretton? She cannot have changed her mind on that point, because it was so fixed two months ago?'

'Why, you know, it does not matter. You saw the terms on which they stood.'

'There was a little misunderstanding that evening, certainly; does she seem unhappy?'

'Not she. To change the subject. Have you heard or seen nothing of, or from Graham during your absence?'

'Papa had letters from him once or twice, about business I think. He undertook the management of some affair which required attention, while we were away. Dr Bretton seems to respect papa, and to have pleasure in obliging him.'

'Yes: you met him yesterday on the boulevard; you would be able to judge from his aspect that his friends need not be painfully anxious about his health?'

'Papa seems to have thought with you. I could not help smiling. He is not particularly observant, you know, because he is often thinking of other things than what pass before his eyes; but he said, as Dr Bretton rode away, "Really it does a man good to see the spirit and energy of that boy." He called Dr Bretton a boy; I believe he almost thinks him so, just as he thinks me a little girl; he was not speaking to me, but dropped that remark to himself. Lucy . . .'

Again fell the appealing accent, and at the same instant she left her chair, and came and sat on the stool at my feet.

I liked her. It is not a declaration I have often made concerning my acquaintance, in the course of this book; the reader will bear with it for once. Intimate intercourse, close inspection, disclosed in Paulina only what was delicate, intelligent, and sincere; therefore my regard for her lay deep. An admiration more superficial might have been more demonstrative; mine, however, was quiet.

'What have you to ask of Lucy?' said I; 'be brave, and speak out.'

But there was no courage in her eye; as it met mine, it fell; and there was no coolness on her cheek – not a transient surface-blush, but a gathering inward excitement raised its tint and its temperature.

'Lucy, I *do* wish to know your thoughts of Dr Bretton. Do, *do* give me your real opinion of his character – his disposition.'

'His character stands high, and deservedly high.'

'And his disposition? Tell me about his disposition,' she urged; 'you know him well.'

'I know him pretty well.'

'You know his home-side. You have seen him with his mother; speak of him as a son.'

'He is a fine-hearted son; his mother's comfort and hope, her pride and pleasure.'

She held my hand between hers, and at each favourable word gave it a little caressing stroke.

'In what other way is he good, dear Lucy?'

'Dr Bretton is benevolent – humanely disposed towards all his race. Dr Bretton would have benignity for the lowest savage, or the worst criminal.'

'I heard some gentlemen, some of papa's friends, who were talking about him, say the same. They say many of the poor patients at the hospitals, who tremble before some pitiless and selfish surgeons, welcome him.'

'They are right; I have witnessed as much. He once took me over a hospital; I saw how he was received: your father's friends are right.'

The softest gratitude animated her eye as she lifted it a moment. She had yet more to say, but seemed hesitating about time and place. Dusk was beginning to reign; her parlour fire already glowed with twilight ruddiness; but I thought she wished the room dimmer, the hour later.

'How quiet and secluded we feel here!' I remarked, to reassure her.

'Do we? Yes; it is a still evening, and I shall not be called down to tea; papa is dining out.'

Still holding my hand, she played with the fingers unconsciously, dressed them, now in her own rings, and now circled them with a twine of her beautiful hair; she patted the palm against her hot cheek, and at last, having cleared a voice that was naturally liquid as a lark's, she said: 'You must think it rather strange that I should talk so much about Dr Bretton, ask so many questions, take such an interest, but –'

'Not at all strange; perfectly natural; you like him.'

'And if I did,' said she, with slight quickness, 'is that a reason why I should talk? I suppose you think me weak, like my cousin Ginevra?'

'If I thought you one whit like Mme Ginevra, I would not sit here waiting for your communications. I would get up, walk at my ease about the room, and anticipate all you had to say by a round lecture. Go on.'

'I mean to go on,' retorted she; 'what else do you suppose I mean to do?' And she looked and spoke – the little Polly of Bretton – petulant, sensitive. 'If,' said she emphatically, 'if I liked Dr John till I was fit to die for liking him, that alone could not license me to be otherwise than dumb – dumb as the grave – dumb as you, Lucy Snowe – you know it – and you know you would despise me if I failed in self-control, and whined about some ricketty liking that was all on my side.'

'It is true I little respect women or girls who are loquacious either in boasting the triumphs, or bemoaning the mortifications, of feeling. But as to *you*, Paulina, speak, for I earnestly wish to hear you. Tell me all it will give you pleasure or relief to tell; I ask no more.'

'Do you care for me, Lucy?'

'Yes, I do, Paulina.'

'And I love you. I had an odd content in being with you even when I was a little, troublesome, disobedient girl; it was charming to me then to lavish on you my naughtinesses and whims. Now you are acceptable to me, and I like to talk with and trust you. So listen, Lucy.'

And she settled herself, resting against my arm – resting gently, not with honest Mistress Fanshawe's fatiguing and selfish weight.

'A few minutes since you asked whether we had not heard from Graham during our absence, and I said there were two letters for papa on business; this was true, but I did not tell you all.'

'You evaded?'

'I shuffled and equivocated, you know. However, I am going to speak the truth now; it is getting darker; one can talk at one's ease. Papa often lets me open the letter-bag and give him out the contents. One morning, about three weeks ago, you don't know how surprised I was to find, amongst a dozen letters for M. de Bassompierre, a note addressed to Miss de Bassompierre. I spied it at once, amidst all the rest; the handwriting was not strange; it attracted me directly. I was going to say, "Papa, here is another letter from Dr Bretton"; but the "Miss" struck me mute. I actually never received a letter from a gentleman before. Ought I to have shown it to papa, and let him open it and read it first? I could not for my life, Lucy. I know so well papa's ideas about me: he forgets my age; he thinks I am a mere schoolgirl; he is not aware that other people see I am grown up as tall as I shall be; so, with a curious mixture of feelings, some of them self-reproachful, and some so fluttering and strong, I cannot describe them, I gave papa his twelve letters – his herd of possessions – and kept back my one, my ewe-lamb. It lay in my lap during breakfast, looking up at me with an inexplicable meaning, making me feel myself a thing double-existent – a child to that dear papa, but no more a child to myself. After breakfast I carried my letter upstairs, and having secured myself by turning the key in the door, I began to study the outside of my treasure: it was some minutes before I could get over the direction and penetrate the seal; one does not take a strong place of this kind by instant storm – one sits down awhile before it, as beleaguers say. Graham's hand is like himself, Lucy, and so is his seal – all clear, firm, and rounded – no slovenly splash of wax – a full, solid, steady drop – a distinct impress: no pointed turns harshly pricking the optic nerve, but a clean, mellow, pleasant manuscript, that soothes you as you read. It is like his face – just like the chiselling of his features: do you know his autograph?'

'I have seen it: go on.'

'The seal was too beautiful to be broken, so I cut it round with my scissors. On the point of reading the letter at last, I once more drew back voluntarily; it was too soon yet to drink that draught – the sparkle in the cup was so beautiful – I would watch it yet a minute. Then I remembered all at once that I had not said my prayers that morning. Having heard papa go down to breakfast a little earlier than usual, I had been afraid of keeping him waiting, and had hastened to join him as soon as dressed, thinking no harm to put off prayers till afterwards. Some people would say I ought to have served God first and then man; but I don't think Heaven could be jealous of anything I might do for papa. I believe I am superstitious. A voice seemed now to say that another feeling than filial affection was in question – to urge me to pray before I dared to read what I so longed to read – to deny myself yet a moment, and remember first a great duty. I have had

these impulses ever since I can remember. I put the letter down and said my prayers, adding, at the end, a strong entreaty that whatever happened, I might not be tempted or led to cause papa any sorrow, and might never, in caring for others, neglect him. The very thought of such a possibility so pierced my heart that it made me cry. But still, Lucy, I felt that in time papa would have to be taught the truth, managed, and induced to hear reason.

'I read the letter. Lucy, life is said to be all disappointment. *I* was not disappointed. Ere I read, and while I read, my heart did more than throb – it trembled fast – every quiver seemed like the pant of an animal athirst, laid down at a well and drinking; and the well proved quite full, gloriously clear; it rose up munificently of its own impulse; I saw the sun through its gush, and not a mote, Lucy, no moss, no insect, no atom in the thrice-refined golden gurgle.

'Life,' she went on, 'is said to be full of pain to some. I have read biographies where the wayfarer seemed to journey on from suffering to suffering; where Hope flew before him fast, never alighting so near, or lingering so long, as to give his hand a chance of one realising grasp. I have read of those who sowed in tears, and whose harvest, so far from being reaped in joy, perished by untimely blight, or was borne off by sudden whirlwind; and, alas! some of these met the winter with empty garners, and died of utter want in the darkest and coldest of the year.'

'Was it their fault, Paulina, that they of whom you speak thus died?'

'Not always their fault. Some of them were good, endeavouring people. I am not endeavouring, nor actively good, yet God has caused me to grow in sun, due moisture, and safe protection, sheltered, fostered, taught, by my dear father; and now – now – another comes. Graham loves me.'

For some minutes we both paused on this climax.

'Does your father know?' I enquired, in a low voice.

'Graham spoke with deep respect of papa, but implied that he dared not approach that quarter as yet; he must first prove his worth: he added that he must have some light respecting myself and my own feelings ere he ventured to risk a step in the matter elsewhere.'

'How did you reply?'

'I replied briefly, but I did not repulse him. Yet I almost trembled for fear of making the answer too cordial: Graham's tastes are so fastidious. I wrote it three times – chastening and subduing the phrases at every rescript; at last, having confected it till it seemed to me to resemble a morsel of ice flavoured with ever so slight a zest of fruit or sugar, I ventured to seal and despatch it.'

'Excellent, Paulina! Your instinct is fine; you understand Dr Bretton.'

'But how must I manage about papa? There I am still in pain.'

'Do not manage at all. Wait now. Only maintain no further correspondence till your father knows all, and gives his sanction.'

'Will he ever give it?'

'Time will show. Wait.'

'Dr Bretton wrote one other letter, deeply grateful for my calm, brief note; but I anticipated your advice, by saying, that while my sentiments continued the same, I could not without my father's knowledge write again.'

'You acted as you ought to have done; so Dr Bretton will feel: it will increase his pride in you, his love for you, if either be capable of increase. Paulina, that gentle hoar-frost of yours, surrounding so much pure, fine flame, is a priceless privilege of nature.'

'You see I feel Graham's disposition,' said she. 'I feel that no delicacy can be too exquisite for his treatment.'

'It is perfectly proved that you comprehend him, and then – whatever Dr Bretton's disposition, were he one who expected to be more nearly met – you would still act truthfully, openly, tenderly, with your father.'

'Lucy, I trust I shall thus act always. Oh, it will be pain to wake papa from his dream, and tell him I am no more a little girl!'

'Be in no hurry to do so, Paulina. Leave the revelation to Time and your kind Fate. I also have noticed the gentleness of her cares for you: doubt not she will benignantly order the circumstances, and fitly appoint the hour. Yes; I have thought over your life just as you have yourself thought it over; I have made comparisons like those to which you adverted. We know not the future, but the past has been propitious.

'As a child I feared for you; nothing that has life was ever more susceptible than your nature in infancy: under harshness, or neglect, neither your outward nor your inward self would have ripened to what they now are. Much pain, much fear, much struggle would have troubled the very lines of your features, broken their regularity, would have harassed your nerves into the fever of habitual irritation: you would have lost in health and cheerfulness, in grace and sweetness. Providence has protected and cultured you, not only for your own sake, but I believe for Graham's. His star, too, was fortunate: to develop fully the best of his nature, a companion like you was needed; there you are, ready. You must be united. I knew it the first day I saw you together at La Terrasse. In all that mutually concerns you and Graham there seems to me promise, plan, harmony. I do not think the sunny youth of either will prove the forerunner of stormy age. I think it is deemed good that you two should live in peace and be happy – not as angels, but as few are happy amongst mortals. Some lives *are* thus blessed: it is God's will: it is the attesting trace and lingering evidence of Eden. Other lives run from the first another course. Other travellers encounter weather fitful and gusty, wild and variable – breast adverse winds, are belated and overtaken by the early closing winter night. Neither can this happen without the sanction of God; and I know that, amidst His boundless works, is somewhere stored the secret of this last fate's justice: I know that His treasures contain the proof as the promise of its mercy.'

## *M. Paul Keeps His Promise*

On the first of may, we had all – i.e. the twenty boarders and the four teachers – notice to rise at five o'clock of the morning, to be dressed and ready by six, to put ourselves under the command of M. le Professeur Emanuel, who was to head our march forth from Villette, for it was on this day he proposed to fulfil his promise of taking us to breakfast in the country. I, indeed, as the reader may perhaps remember, had not had the honour of an invitation when this excursion was first projected – rather the contrary; but on my now making allusion to this fact, and wishing to know how it was to be, my ear received a pull, of which I did not venture to challenge the repetition by raising further difficulties.

'Je vous conseille de vous faire prier,' said M. Emanuel, imperially menacing the other ear. One Napoleonic compliment, however, was enough, so I made up my mind to be of the party.

The morning broke calm as summer, with singing of birds in the garden, and a light dew-mist that promised heat. We all said it would be warm, and we all felt pleasure in folding away heavy garments, and in assuming the attire suiting a sunny season. The clean fresh print dress, and the light straw bonnet, each made and trimmed as the French workwoman alone can make and trim, so as to unite the utterly unpretending with the perfectly becoming, was the rule of costume. Nobody flaunted in faded silk; nobody wore a second-hand best article.

At six the bell rang merrily, and we poured down the staircase, through the carré, along the corridor, into the vestibule. There stood our Professor, wearing, not his savage-looking paletôt and severe bonnet-grec, but a young-looking belted blouse and cheerful straw hat. He had for us all the kindest good-morrow, and most of us for him had a thanksgiving smile. We were marshalled in order and soon started.

The streets were yet quiet, and the boulevards were fresh and peaceful as fields. I believe we were very happy as we walked along. This chief of ours had the secret of giving a certain impetus to happiness when he would; just as, in an opposite mood, he could give a thrill to fear.

He did not lead nor follow us, but walked along the line, giving a word to everyone, talking much to his favourites, and not wholly neglecting even those he disliked. It was rather my wish, for a reason I had, to keep slightly aloof from notice, and being paired with Ginevra Fanshawe, bearing on my arm the dear pressure of that angel's not unsubstantial limb – (she continued in excellent case, and I can assure the reader it was no trifling business to bear the burden of her loveliness; many a time in the course of that warm day I wished to goodness there had been less of the charming commodity) – however, having her, as I said, I tried to make her useful by interposing her always between myself and

M. Paul, shifting my place, according as I heard him coming up to the right hand or to the left. My private motive for this manoeuvre might be traced to the circumstance of the new print dress I wore, being pink in colour – a fact which, under our present convoy, made me feel something as I have felt, when, clad in a shawl with a red border, necessitated to traverse a meadow where pastured a bull.

For awhile, the shifting system, together with some modifications in the arrangement of a black silk scarf, answered my purpose; but, by and by, he found out, that whether he came to this side or to that, Miss Fanshawe was still his neighbour. The course of acquaintance between Ginevra and him had never run so smooth that his temper did not undergo a certain crisping process whenever he heard her English accent: nothing in their dispositions fitted; they jarred if they came in contact; he held her empty and affected; she deemed him bearish, meddling, repellent.

At last, when he had changed his place for about the sixth time, finding still the same untoward result to the experiment – he thrust his head forward, settled his eyes on mine, and demanded with impatience – 'Qu'est-ce que c'est? Vous me jouez des tours?'

The words were hardly out of his mouth, however, ere, with his customary quickness, he seized the root of this proceeding: in vain I shook out the long fringe, and spread forth the broad end of my scarf. 'A – h – h! c'est la robe rose!' broke from his lips, affecting me very much like the sudden and irate low of some lord of the meadow.

'It is only cotton,' I alleged, hurriedly; 'and cheaper, and washes better than any other colour.'

'Et Mlle Lucie est coquette comme dix Parisiennes,' he answered. 'A-t-on jamais vu une Anglaise pareille? Regardez plutot son chapeau, et ses gants, et ses brodequins!' These articles of dress were just like what my companions wore; certainly not one whit smarter – perhaps rather plainer than most – but monsieur had now got hold of his text, and I began to chafe under the expected sermon. It went off, however, as mildly as the menace of a storm sometimes passes on a summer day. I got but one flash of sheet lightning in the shape of a single bantering smile from his eyes; and then he said: 'Courage! – à vrai dire je ne suis pas fâché, peut-être même suis-je content qu'on s'est fait si belle pour ma petite fête.'

'Mais ma robe n'est pas belle, monsieur – elle n'est que propre.'

'J'aime la propreté,' said he. In short, he was not to be dissatisfied; the sun of good humour was to triumph on this auspicious morning; it consumed scudding clouds ere they sullied its disk.

And now we were in the country, amongst what they called 'les bois et les petits sentiers'. These woods and lanes a month later, would offer but a dusty and doubtful seclusion: now, however, in their May greenness and morning repose, they looked very pleasant.

We reached a certain well, planted round, in the taste of Labassecour, with an orderly circle of lime trees: here a halt was called; on the green swell of ground surrounding this well, we were ordered to be seated, monsieur taking his place

in our midst, and suffering us to gather in a knot round him. Those who liked him more than they feared, came close, and these were chiefly little ones; those who feared more than they liked, kept somewhat aloof; those in whom much affection had given, even to what remained of fear, a pleasurable zest, observed the greatest distance.

He began to tell us a story. Well could he narrate: in such a diction as children love, and learned men emulate; a diction simple in its strength, and strong in its simplicity. There were beautiful touches in that little tale; sweet glimpses of feeling and hues of description that, while I listened, sunk into my mind, and since have never faded. He tinted a twilight scene – I hold it in memory still – such a picture I have never looked on from artists' pencil.

I have said that, for myself, I had no impromptu faculty; and perhaps that very deficiency made me marvel the more at one who possessed it in perfection. M. Emanuel was not a man to write books; but I have heard him lavish, with careless, unconscious prodigality, such mental wealth as books seldom boast; his mind was indeed my library, and whenever it was opened to me, I entered bliss. Intellectually imperfect as I was, I could read little; there were few bound and printed volumes that did not weary me – whose perusal did not fag and blind – but his tomes of thought were collyrium to the spirit's eyes; over their contents, inward sight grew clear and strong. I used to think what a delight it would be for one who loved him better than he loved himself, to gather and store up those handfuls of gold-dust, so recklessly flung to heaven's reckless winds.

His story done, he approached the little knoll where I and Ginevra sat apart. In his usual mode of demanding an opinion (he had not reticence to wait till it was voluntarily offered) he asked: 'Were you interested?'

According to my wonted undemonstrative fashion, I simply answered – 'Yes.'

'Was it good?'

'Very good.'

'Yet I could not write that down,' said he.

'Why not, monsieur?'

'I hate the mechanical labour; I hate to stoop and sit still. I could dictate it, though, with pleasure to an amanuensis who suited me. Would Mlle Lucy write for me if I asked her?'

'Monsieur would be too quick; he would urge me, and be angry, if my pen did not keep pace with his lips.'

'Try someday; let us see the monster I can make of myself under the circumstances. But just now, there is no question of dictation; I mean to make you useful in another office. Do you see yonder farmhouse?'

'Surrounded with trees? Yes.'

'There we are to breakfast; and while the good fermière makes the café au lait in a caldron, you and five others, whom I shall select, will spread with butter half a hundred rolls.'

Having formed his troop into line once more, he marched us straight on the farm, which, on seeing our force, surrendered without capitulation.

Clean knives and plates, and fresh butter being provided, half a dozen of us,

chosen by our professor, set to work under his directions, to prepare for breakfast a huge basket of rolls, with which the baker had been ordered to provision the farm, in anticipation of our coming. Coffee and chocolate were already made hot; cream and new-laid eggs were added to the treat, and M. Emanuel, always generous, would have given a large order for 'jambon' and 'confitures' in addition, but that some of us, who presumed perhaps upon our influence, insisted that it would be a most reckless waste of victual. He railed at us for our pains, terming us 'des ménagères avares'; but we let him talk, and managed the economy of the repast our own way.

With what a pleasant countenance he stood on the farm-kitchen hearth looking on! He was a man whom it made happy to see others happy; he liked to have movement, animation, abundance and enjoyment round him. We asked where he would sit. He told us, we knew well he was our slave, and we his tyrants, and that he dared not so much as choose a chair without our leave; so we set him the farmer's great chair at the head of the long table, and put him into it.

Well might we like him, with all his passions and hurricanes, when he could be so benignant and docile at times, as he was just now. Indeed, at the worst, it was only his nerves that were irritable, not his temper that was radically bad; soothe, comprehend, comfort him, and he was a lamb; he would not harm a fly. Only to the very stupid, perverse, or unsympathising, was he in the slightest degree dangerous.

Mindful always of his religion, he made the youngest of the party say a little prayer before we begun breakfast, crossing himself as devoutly as a woman. I had never seen him pray before, or make that pious sign; he did it so simply, with such childlike faith, I could not help smiling pleasurably as I watched; his eyes met my smile; he just stretched out his kind hand, saying,

'Donnez-moi la main! I see we worship the same God, in the same spirit, though by different rites.'

Most of M. Emanuel's brother professors were emancipated free-thinkers, infidels, atheists; and many of them men whose lives would not bear scrutiny: he was more like a knight of old, religious in his way, and of spotless fame. Innocent childhood, beautiful youth were safe at his side. He had vivid passions, keen feelings, but his pure honour and his artless piety were the strong charm that kept the lions couchant.

That breakfast was a merry meal, and the merriment was not mere vacant clatter: M. Paul originated, led, controlled and heightened it; his social, lively temper played unfettered and unclouded; surrounded only by women and children there was nothing to cross and thwart him; he had his own way, and a pleasant way it was.

The meal over, the party were free to run and play in the meadows; a few stayed to help the farmer's wife to put away her earthenware. M. Paul called me from among these to come out and sit near him under a tree – whence he could view the troop gambolling over a wide pasture – and read to him whilst he took his cigar. He sat on a rustic bench, and I at the tree-root. While I read (a pocket-classic – a Corneille – I did not like it, but he did, finding therein

beauties I never could be brought to perceive), he listened with a sweetness of calm the more impressive from the impetuosity of his general nature; the deepest happiness filled his blue eye and smoothed his broad forehead. I too was happy – happy with the bright day, happier with his presence, happiest with his kindness.

He asked, by and by, if I would not rather run to my companions than sit there? I said, no; I felt content to be where he was. He asked whether, if I were his sister, I should always be content to stay with a brother such as he. I said, I believed I should; and I felt it. Again, he enquired whether, if he were to leave Villette, and go far away, I should be sorry; and I dropped Corneille, and made no reply.

'Petite soeur,' said he; 'how long could you remember me if we were separated?'

'That, monsieur, I can never tell, because I do not know how long it will be before I shall cease to remember everything earthly.'

'If I were to go beyond seas for two – three – five years, should you welcome me on my return?'

'Monsieur, how could I live in the interval?'

'Pourtant j'ai été pour vous bien dur, bien exigeant.'

I hid my face with the book, for it was covered with tears. I asked him why he talked so; and he said he would talk so no more, and cheered me again with the kindest encouragement. Still, the gentleness with which he treated me during the rest of the day, went somehow to my heart. It was too tender. It was mournful. I would rather he had been abrupt, whimsical, and irate as was his wont.

When hot noon arrived – for the day turned out as we had anticipated; glowing as June – our shepherd collected his sheep from the pasture, and proceeded to lead us all softly home. But we had a whole league to walk – thus far from Villette was the farm where we had breakfasted; the children, especially, were tired with their play; the spirits of most flagged at the prospect of this midday walk over chaussées flinty, glaring and dusty. This state of things had been foreseen and provided for. Just beyond the boundary of the farm we met two spacious vehicles coming to fetch us – such conveyances as are hired out purposely for the accommodation of school-parties; here, with good management, room was found for all, and in another hour M. Paul made safe consignment of his charge at the Rue Fossette. It had been a pleasant day: it would have been perfect, but for the breathing of melancholy which had dimmed its sunshine a moment.

That tarnish was renewed the same evening.

Just about sunset, I saw M. Emanuel come out of the front-door, accompanied by Mme Beck. They paced the centre-alley for nearly an hour, talking earnestly: he – looking grave, yet restless; she – wearing an amazed, expostulatory, dissuasive air.

I wondered what was under discussion; and when Mme Beck re-entered the house as it darkened, leaving her kinsman Paul yet lingering in the garden, I said to myself – 'He called me "petite soeur" this morning. If he were really my

brother, how I should like to go to him just now, and ask what it is that presses on his mind. See how he leans against that tree, with his arms crossed and his brow bent. He wants consolation, I know: Madame does not console; she only remonstrates. What now – ?'

Starting from quiescence to action, M. Paul came striding erect and quick down the garden. The carré doors were yet open: I thought he was probably going to water the orange trees in the tubs, after his occasional custom; on reaching the court, however, he took an abrupt turn and made for the berceau and the first classe glass-door. There, in that first classe I was, thence I had been watching him; but there I could not find courage to await his approach. He had turned so suddenly, he strode so fast, he looked so strange; the coward within me grew pale, shrunk and – not waiting to listen to reason, and hearing the shrubs crush and the gravel crunch to his advance – she was gone on the wings of panic.

Nor did I pause till I had taken sanctuary in the oratory, now empty. Listening there with beating pulses, and an unaccountable, undefined apprehension, I heard him pass through all the schoolrooms, clashing the doors impatiently as he went; I heard him invade the refectory which the 'lecture pieuse' was now holding under hallowed constraint; I heard him pronounce these words – 'Où est Mlle Lucie?'

And just as, summoning my courage, I was preparing to go down and do what, after all, I most wished to do in the world – viz., meet him – the wiry voice of St Pierre replied glibly and falsely, 'Elle est au lit.' And he passed, with the stamp of vexation, into the corridor. There Mme Beck met, captured, chid, convoyed to the street-door, and finally dismissed him.

As that street-door closed, a sudden amazement at my own perverse proceeding struck like a blow upon me. I felt from the first it was me he wanted – me he was seeking – and had not I wanted him too? What, then, had carried me away? What had rapt me beyond his reach? He had something to tell: he was going to tell me that something: my ear strained its nerve to hear it, and I had made the confidence impossible. Yearning to listen and console, while I thought audience and solace beyond hope's reach – no sooner did opportunity suddenly and fully arrive, than I evaded it, as I would have evaded the levelled shaft of mortality.

Well, my insane inconsistency had its reward. Instead of the comfort, the certain satisfaction, I might have won – could I but have put choking panic down, and stood firm two minutes – here was dead blank, dark doubt, and drear suspense.

I took my wages to my pillow, and passed the night counting them.

## *Malevola*

Mme Beck called me on Thursday afternoon, and asked whether I had any occupation to hinder me from going into town and executing some little commissions for her at the shops.

Being disengaged, and placing myself at her service, I was presently furnished with a list of the wools, silks, embroidering thread, etcetera, wanted in the pupils' work, and having equipped myself in a manner suiting the threatening aspect of a clouded and sultry day, I was just drawing the spring-bolt of the street-door, in act to issue forth, when Madame's voice again summoned me to the salle à manger.

'Pardon, Meess Lucie!' cried she, in the seeming haste of an impromptu thought, 'I have just recollected one more errand for you, if your good nature will not deem itself overburdened?'

Of course I 'confounded myself' in asseverations to the contrary; and Madame, running into the little salon, brought thence a pretty basket, filled with fine hothouse fruit, rosy, perfect, and tempting, reposing amongst the dark green, wax-like leaves, and pale yellow stars of, I know not what, exotic plant.

'There,' she said, 'it is not heavy, and will not shame your neat toilette, as if it were a household, servant-like detail. Do me the favour to leave this little basket at the house of Mme Walravens, with my felicitations on her fête. She lives down in the old town, Numéro 3, Rue des Mages. I fear you will find the walk rather long, but you have the whole afternoon before you, and do not hurry; if you are not back in time for dinner, I will order a portion to be saved, or Goton, with whom you are a favourite, will have pleasure in tossing up some trifle, for your especial benefit. You shall not be forgotten, ma bonne meess. And oh! please!' (calling me back once more) 'be sure to insist on seeing Mme Walravens herself, and giving the basket into her own hands, in order that there may be no mistake, for she is rather a punctilious personage. Adieu! Au revoir!'

And at last I got away. The shop-commissions took some time to execute, that choosing and matching of silks and wools being always a tedious business, but at last I got through my list. The patterns for the slippers, the bell-ropes, the cabas were selected – the slides and tassels for the purses chosen – the whole 'tripotage', in short, was off my mind; nothing but the fruit and the felicitations remained to be attended to.

I rather liked the prospect of a long walk, deep into the old and grim Basse-Ville; and I liked it no worse because the evening sky, over the city, was settling into a mass of black-blue metal, heated at the rim, and inflaming slowly to a heavy red.

I fear a high wind, because storm demands that exertion of strength and use of

action I always yield with pain; but the sullen downfall, the thick snow-descent, or dark rush of rain, asks only resignation – the quiet abandonment of garments and person to be drenched. In return, it sweeps a great capital clean before you; it makes you a quiet path through broad, grand streets; it petrifies a living city, as if by eastern enchantment; it transforms a Villette into a Tadmor. Let, then, the rains fall, and the floods descend – only I must first get rid of this basket of fruit.

An unknown clock from an unknown tower (Jean Baptiste's voice was now too distant to be audible) was tolling the third quarter past five, when I reached that street and house whereof Mme Beck had given me the address. It was no street at all; it seemed rather to be part of a square; it was quiet, grass grew between the broad gray flags, the houses were large and looked very old – behind them rose the appearance of trees, indicating gardens at the back. Antiquity brooded above this region, business was banished thence. Rich men had once possessed this quarter, and once grandeur had made her seat here. That church whose dark, half-ruinous turrets overlooked the square, was the venerable and formerly opulent shrine of the Magi. But wealth and greatness had long since stretched their gilded pinions and fled hence, leaving these their ancient nests, perhaps to house Penury for a time, or perhaps to stand cold and empty, mouldering untenanted in the course of winters.

As I crossed this deserted 'place,' on whose pavement drops almost as large as a five-franc piece were now slowly darkening, I saw, in its whole expanse, no symptom or evidence of life, except what was given in the figure of an infirm old priest, who went past, bending and propped on a staff – the type of eld and decay.

He had issued from the very house to which I was directed; and when I paused before the door just closed after him, and rang the bell, he turned to look at me. Nor did he soon avert his gaze; perhaps he thought me, with my basket of summer fruit, and my lack of the dignity age confers, an incongruous figure in such a scene. I know, had a young ruddy-faced bonne opened the door to admit me, I should have thought such a one little in harmony with her dwelling; but when I found myself confronted by a very old woman, wearing a very antique peasant costume, a cap alike hideous and costly, with long flaps of native lace, a petticoat and jacket of cloth, and sabots more like little boats than shoes, it seemed all right, and soothingly in character.

The expression of her face was not quite so soothing as the cut of her costume; anything more cantankerous I have seldom seen; she would scarcely reply to my enquiry after Mme Walravens; I believe she would have snatched the basket of fruit from my hand, had not the old priest, hobbling up, checked her, and himself lent an ear to the message with which I was charged.

His apparent deafness rendered it a little difficult to make him fully understand that I must see Mme Walravens, and consign the fruit into her own hands. At last, however, he comprehended the fact that such were my orders, and that duty enjoined their literal fulfilment. Addressing the aged bonne, not in French, but in the aboriginal tongue of Labassecour, he persuaded her, at last, to let me cross the inhospitable threshold, and himself escorting me upstairs, I was ushered into a sort of salon, and there left.

The room was large, and had a fine old ceiling, and almost church-like windows of coloured glass; but it was desolate, and in the shadow of the coming storm, looked strangely lowering. Within – opened a smaller room; there, however, the blind of the single casement was closed; through the deep gloom few details of furniture were apparent. These few I amused myself by puzzling to make out; and, in particular, I was attracted by the outline of a picture on the wall.

By and by the picture seemed to give way: to my bewilderment, it shook, it sunk, it rolled back into nothing; its vanishing left an opening – arched, leading into an arched passage, with a mystic winding stair; both passage and stair were of cold stone, uncarpeted and unpainted. Down this donjon stair descended a tap, tap, like a stick; soon, there fell on the steps a shadow, and last of all, I was aware of a substance.

Yet, was it actual substance, this appearance approaching me? this obstruction, partially darkening the arch?

It drew near, and I saw it well. I began to comprehend where I was. Well might this old square be named quarter of the Magi – well might the three towers, overlooking it, own for godfathers three mystic sages of a dead and dark art. Hoar enchantment here prevailed; a spell had opened for me elf-land – that cell-like room, that vanishing picture, that arch and passage, and stair of stone, were all parts of a fairy tale. Distincter even than these scenic details stood the chief figure – Cunegonde, the sorceress! Malevola, the evil fairy. How was she?

She might be three feet high, but she had no shape; her skinny hands rested upon each other, and pressed the gold knob of a wand-like ivory staff. Her face was large, set, not upon her shoulders, but before her breast; she seemed to have no neck; I should have said there were a hundred years in her features, and more perhaps in her eyes – her malign, unfriendly eyes, with thick gray brows above, and livid lids all round. How severely they viewed me, with a sort of dull displeasure!

This being wore a gown of brocade, dyed bright blue, full-tinted as the gentianella flower, and covered with satin foliage in a large pattern; over the gown a costly shawl, gorgeously bordered, and so large for her, that its many-coloured fringe swept the floor. But her chief points were her jewels: she had long, clear ear-rings, blazing with a lustre which could not be borrowed or false; she had rings on her skeleton hands, with thick gold hoops, and stones – purple, green, and blood-red. Hunchbacked, dwarfish, and doting, she was adorned like a barbarian queen.

'Que me voulez-vous?' said she hoarsely, with the voice rather of male than of female old age; and, indeed, a silver beard bristled her chin.

I delivered my basket and my message.

'Is that all?' she demanded.

'It is all,' said I.

'Truly, it was well worth while,' she answered. 'Return to Mme Beck, and tell her I can buy fruit when I want it, et quant à ses félicitations, je m'en moque!' And this courteous dame turned her back.

Just as she turned, a peal of thunder broke, and a flash of lightning blazed broad over salon and boudoir. The tale of magic seemed to proceed with due accompaniment of the elements. The wanderer, decoyed into the enchanted castle, heard rising, outside, the spell-wakened tempest.

What, in all this, was I to think of Mme Beck? She owned strange acquaintance; she offered messages and gifts at an unique shrine, and inauspicious seemed the bearing of the uncouth thing she worshipped. There went that sullen Sidonia, tottering and trembling like palsy incarnate, tapping her ivory staff on the mosaic parquet, and muttering venomously as she vanished.

Down washed the rain, deep lowered the welkin; the clouds, ruddy a while ago, had now, through all their blackness, turned deadly pale, as if in terror. Notwithstanding my late boast about not fearing a shower, I hardly liked to go out under this water-spout. Then, the gleams of lightning were very fierce, the thunder crashed very near; this storm had gathered immediately above Villette; it seemed to have burst at the zenith; it rushed down prone; the forked, slant bolts pierced athwart vertical torrents; red zigzags interlaced a descent blanched as white metal: and all broke from a sky heavily black in its swollen abundance.

Leaving Mme Walravens' inhospitable salon, I betook myself to her cold staircase; there was a seat on the landing – there I waited. Somebody came gliding along the gallery just above; it was the old priest.

'Indeed Mademoiselle shall not sit there,' said he. 'It would displease our benefactor if he knew a stranger was so treated in this house.'

And he begged me so earnestly to return to the salon, that, without discourtesy, I could not but comply. The smaller room was better furnished and more habitable than the larger; thither he introduced me. Partially withdrawing the blind, he disclosed what seemed more like an oratory than a boudoir, a very solemn little chamber, looking as if it were a place rather dedicated to relics and remembrance, than designed for present use and comfort.

The good father sat down, as if to keep me company; but instead of conversing, he took out a book, fastened on the page his eyes, and employed his lips in whispering – what sounded like a prayer or litany. A yellow electric light from the sky gilded his bald head; his figure remained in shade – deep and purple; he sat still as sculpture; he seemed to forget me for his prayers; he only looked up when a fiercer bolt, or a harsher, closer rattle told of nearing danger; even then, it was not in fear, but in seeming awe, he raised his eyes. I too was awestruck; being, however, under no pressure of slavish terror, my thoughts and observations were free.

To speak truth, I was beginning to fancy that the old priest resembled that Père Silas, before whom I had kneeled in the church of the Béguinage. The idea was vague, for I had seen my confessor only in dusk and in profile, yet still I seemed to trace a likeness: I thought also I recognised the voice. While I watched him, he betrayed, by one lifted look, that he felt my scrutiny; I turned to note the room; that too had its half-mystic interest.

Beside a cross of curiously carved old ivory, yellow with time, and sloped above a dark-red *prie-dieu*, furnished duly with rich missal and ebon rosary – hung the

picture whose dim outline had drawn my eyes before – the picture which moved, fell away with the wall and let in phantoms. Imperfectly seen, I had taken it for a Madonna; revealed by clearer light, it proved to be a woman's portrait in a nun's dress. The face, though not beautiful, was pleasing; pale, young, and shaded with the dejection of grief or ill health. I say again it was not beautiful; it was not even intellectual; its very amiability was the amiability of a weak frame, inactive passions, acquiescent habits; yet I looked long at that picture, and could not choose but look.

The old priest, who at first had seemed to me so deaf and infirm, must yet have retained his faculties in tolerable preservation; absorbed in his book as he appeared, without once lifting his head, or, as far as I knew, turning his eyes, he perceived the point towards which my attention was drawn, and, in a slow, distinct voice, dropped concerning it, these four observations.

'She was much beloved.

'She gave herself to God.

'She died young.

'She is still remembered, still wept.'

'By that aged lady, Mme Walravens?' I enquired, fancying that I had discovered in the incurable grief of bereavement, a key to that same aged lady's desperate ill-humour.

The father shook his head with half a smile.

'No, no;' said he, 'a grand-dame's affection for her children's children may be great, and her sorrow for their loss, lively; but it is only the affianced lover, to whom Fate, Faith, and Death, have trebly denied the bliss of union, who mourns what he has lost, as Justine Marie is still mourned.'

I thought the father rather wished to be questioned, and therefore I enquired who had lost and who still mourned 'Justine Marie.' I got, in reply, quite a little romantic narrative, told not unimpressively, with the accompaniment of the now subsiding storm. I am bound to say it might have been made much more truly impressive, if there had been less French, Rousseau-like sentimentalising and wire-drawing; and rather more healthful carelessness of effect. But the worthy father was obviously a Frenchman born and bred (I became more and more persuaded of his resemblance to my confessor) – he was a true son of Rome; when he did lift his eyes, he looked at me out of their corners, with more and sharper subtlety than, one would have thought, could survive the wear and tear of seventy years. Yet, I believe, he was a good old man.

The hero of his tale was some former pupil of his, whom he now called his benefactor, and who, it appears, had loved this pale Justine Marie, the daughter of rich parents, at a time when his own worldly prospects were such as to justify his aspiring to a well-dowered hand. The pupil's father – once a rich banker – had failed, died, and left behind him only debts and destitution. The son was then forbidden to think of Marie – especially that old witch of a grand-dame I had seen, Mme Walravens, opposed the match with all the violence of a temper which deformity made sometimes demoniac. The mild Marie had neither the treachery to be false, nor the force to be quite staunch to her lover; she gave up

her first suitor, but, refusing to accept a second with a heavier purse, withdrew to a convent, and there died in her noviciate.

Lasting anguish, it seems, had taken possession of the faithful heart which worshipped her, and the truth of that love and grief had been shown in a manner which touched even me, as I listened.

Some years after Justine Marie's death, ruin had come on her house too; her father, by nominal calling a jeweller, but who also dealt a good deal on the Bourse, had been concerned in some financial transactions which entailed exposure and ruinous fines. He died of grief for the loss, and shame for the infamy. His old hunchbacked mother and his bereaved wife were left penniless, and might have died too, of want; but their lost daughter's once despised, yet most true-hearted suitor, hearing of the condition of these ladies, came with singular devotedness to the rescue. He took on their insolent pride the revenge of the purest charity – housing, caring for, befriending them, so as no son could have done it more tenderly and efficiently. The mother – on the whole a good woman – died blessing him; the strange, godless, loveless, misanthrope grand-mother lived still, entirely supported by this self-sacrificing man. She, who had been the bane of his life, blighting his hope, and awarding him, for love and domestic happiness, long mourning and cheerless solitude, he treated with the respect a good son might offer a kind mother. He had brought her to this house, 'and,' continued the priest, while genuine tears rose to his eyes, 'here, too, he shelters me, his old tutor, and Agnes, a superannuated servant of his father's family. To our sustenance, and to other charities, I know he devotes three parts of his income, keeping only the fourth to provide himself with bread and the most modest accommodations. By this arrangement he has rendered it impossible to himself ever to marry: he has given himself to God and to his angel-bride as much as if he were a priest, like me.'

The father had wiped away his tears before he uttered these last words, and in pronouncing them, he for one instant raised his eyes to mine. I caught that glance, despite its veiled character; the momentary gleam shot a meaning which struck me.

These Romanists are strange beings. Such a one among them – whom you know no more than the last Inca of Peru, or the first Emperor of China – knows you and all your concerns; and has his reasons for saying to you so and so, when you simply thought the communication sprang impromptu from the instant's impulse: his plan in bringing it about that you shall come on such a day, to such a place, under such and such circumstances, when the whole arrangement seems to your crude apprehension the ordinance of chance, or the sequel of exigency. Mme Beck's suddenly recollected message and present, my artless embassy to the Place of the Magi, the old priest, accidentally descending the steps and crossing the square, his interposition on my behalf with the bonne who would have sent me away, his reappearance on the staircase, my introduction to this room, the portrait, the narrative so affably volunteered – all these little incidents, taken as they fell out, seemed each independent of its successor; a handful of loose beads; but threaded through by

that quick-shot and crafty glance of a Jesuit-eye, they dropped pendant in a long string, like that rosary on the prie-dieu. Where lay the link of junction, where the little clasp of this monastic necklace? I saw or felt union, but could not yet find the spot, or detect the means of connection.

Perhaps the musing-fit into which I had by this time fallen, appeared somewhat suspicious in its abstraction; he gently interrupted: 'Mademoiselle,' said he, 'I trust you have not far to go through these inundated streets?'

'More than half a league.'

'You live – ?'

'In the Rue Fossette.'

'Not' (with animation), 'not at the pensionnat of Mme Beck?'

'The same.'

'Donc' (clapping his hands), 'donc, vous devez connaître mon noble élève, mon Paul?'

'M. Paul Emanuel, Professor of Literature?'

'He, and none other.'

A brief silence fell. The spring of junction seemed suddenly to have become palpable; I felt it yield to pressure.

'Was it of M. Paul you have been speaking?' I presently enquired. 'Was he your pupil and the benefactor of Mme Walravens?'

'Yes, and of Agnes, the old servant; and moreover' (with a certain emphasis), 'he was and *is* the lover, true, constant and eternal, of that saint in Heaven – Justine Marie.'

'And who, father, are *you*?' I continued; and though I accentuated the question, its utterance was well-nigh superfluous; I was ere this quite prepared for the answer which actually came.

'I, daughter, am Père Silas; that unworthy son of Holy Church whom you once honoured with a noble and touching confidence, showing me the core of a heart, and the inner shrine of a mind whereof, in solemn truth, I coveted the direction, in behalf of the only true faith. Nor have I for a day lost sight of you, nor for an hour failed to take in you a rooted interest. Passed under the discipline of Rome, moulded by her high training, inoculated with her salutary doctrines, inspired by the zeal she alone gives – I realise what then might be your spiritual rank, your practical value; and I envy Heresy her prey.'

This struck me as a special state of things – I half-realised myself in that condition also; passed under discipline, moulded, trained, inoculated, and so on. 'Not so,' thought I, but I restrained deprecation and sat quietly enough.

'I suppose M. Paul does not live here?' I resumed, pursuing a theme which I thought more to the purpose than any wild renegade dreams.

'No; he only comes occasionally to worship his beloved saint, to make his confession to me, and to pay his respects to her he calls his mother. His own lodging consists but of two rooms; he has no servant, and yet he will not suffer Mme Walravens to dispose of those splendid jewels with which you see her adorned, and in which she takes a puerile pride as the ornaments of her youth, and the last relics of her son, the jeweller's wealth.'

'How often,' murmured I to myself, 'has this man, this M. Emanuel, seemed to me to lack magnanimity in trifles, yet how great he is in great things!'

I own I did not reckon amongst the proofs of his greatness, either the act of confession, or the saint-worship.

'How long is it since that lady died?' I enquired, looking at Justine Marie.

'Twenty years. She was somewhat older than M. Emanuel; he was then very young, for he is not now much beyond forty.'

'Does he yet weep her?'

'His heart will weep her always: the essence of Emanuel's nature is – constancy.'

This was said with marked emphasis.

And now the sun broke out pallid and waterish; the rain yet fell, but there was no more tempest; that hot firmament had cloven and poured out its lightnings. A longer delay would scarce leave daylight for my return, so I rose, thanked the father for his hospitality and his tale, was benignantly answered by a 'pax vobiscum', which I made kindly welcome, because it seemed uttered with a true benevolence; but I liked less the mystic phrase accompanying it: 'Daughter, you *shall* be what you *shall* be!' an oracle that made me shrug my shoulders as soon as I had got outside the door. Few of us know what we are to come to certainly, but for all that had happened yet, I had good hopes of living and dying a sober-minded protestant: there was a hollowness within, and a flourish around 'Holy Church' which tempted me but moderately. I went on my way pondering many things. Whatever Romanism may be, there are good Romanists: this man, Emanuel, seemed of the best; touched with superstition, influenced by priestcraft, yet wondrous for fond faith, for pious devotion, for sacrifice of self, for charity unbounded. It remained to see how Rome, by her agents, handled such qualities; whether she cherished them for their own sake and for God's, or put them out to usury and made booty of the interest.

By the time I reached home, it was sundown. Goton had kindly saved me a portion of dinner, which indeed I needed. She called me into the little cabinet to partake of it, and there Mme Beck soon made her appearance, bringing me a glass of wine.

'Well,' began she, chuckling, 'and what sort of a reception did Mme Walravens give you? Elle est drôle, n'est ce pas?'

I told her what had passed, delivering verbatim the courteous message with which I had been charged.

'Oh la singulière petite bossue!' laughed she: 'Et figurez-vous qu'elle me déteste, parcequ'elle me croit amoureuse de mon cousin Paul; ce petit devot qui n'ose pas bouger, à moins que son confesseur ne lui donne la permission! Au reste' (she went on), 'if he wanted to marry ever so much – soit moi, soit une autre – he could not do it; he has too large a family already on his hands; Mère Walravens, Père Silas, Dame Agnes, and a whole troop of nameless paupers. There never was a man like him for laying on himself burdens greater than he can bear, voluntarily incurring needless responsibilities. Besides, he harbours a romantic idea about some pale-faced Marie Justine – personnage assez niaise à

ce que je pense' (such was Madame's irreverent remark), 'who has been an angel in Heaven, or elsewhere, this score of years, and to whom he means to go, free from all earthly ties, pure comme un lis, à ce qu'il dit. Oh, you would laugh could you but know half M. Emanuel's crotchets and eccentricities! But I hinder you from taking refreshment, ma bonne meess, which you must need; eat your supper, drink your wine, oubliez les anges, les bossues, et surtout, les Professeurs – et bon soir!'

CHAPTER 35

*Fraternity*

'Oubliez les professeurs.' So said Mme Beck. Mme Beck was a wise woman, but she should not have uttered those words. To do so was a mistake. That night she should have left me calm – not excited, indifferent – not interested, isolated in my own estimation and that of others – not connected, even in idea, with this second person whom I was to forget.

Forget him? Ah! they took a sage plan to make me forget him – the wiseheads! They showed me how good he was; they made of my dear little man a stainless little hero. And then they had prated about his manner of loving. What means had I, before this day, of being certain whether he could love at all or not?

I had known him jealous, suspicious; I had seen about him certain tendernesses, fitfulnesses – a softness which came like a warm air, and a ruth which passed like early dew, dried in the heat of his irritabilities: *this* was all I had seen. And they, Père Silas and Modeste Maria Beck (that these two wrought in concert I could not doubt) opened up the adytum of his heart – showed me one grand love, the child of this southern nature's youth, born so strong and perfect, that it had laughed at Death himself, despised his mean rape of matter, clung to immortal spirit, and, in victory and faith, had watched beside a tomb twenty years.

This had been done – not idly: this was not a mere hollow indulgence of sentiment; he had proven his fidelity by the consecration of his best energies to an unselfish purpose, and attested it by limitless personal sacrifices: for those once dear to her he prized – he had laid down vengeance, and taken up a cross.

Now, as for Justine Marie, I knew what she was as well as if I had seen her. I knew she was well enough; there were girls like her in Mme Beck's school – phlegmatics – pale, slow, inert, but kind-natured, neutral of evil, undistinguished for good.

If she wore angel's wings, I knew whose poet-fancy conferred them. If her forehead shone luminous with the reflex of a halo, I knew in the fire of whose irids that circlet of holy flame had generation.

Was I, then, to be frightened by Justine Marie? Was the picture of a pale

dead nun to rise, an eternal barrier? And what of the charities which absorbed his worldly goods? What of his heart, sworn to virginity?

Mme Beck – Père Silas – you should not have suggested these questions. They were at once the deepest puzzle, the strongest obstruction, and the keenest stimulus, I had ever felt. For a week of nights and days I fell asleep – I dreamt, and I woke upon these two questions. In the whole world there was no answer to them, except where one dark little man stood, sat, walked, lectured, under the head-piece of a bandit bonnet-grec, and within the girth of a sorry paletôt, much be-inked, and no little adust.

After that visit to the Rue des Mages, I *did* want to see him again. I felt as if – knowing what I now knew – his countenance would offer a page more lucid, more interesting than ever; I felt a longing to trace in it the imprint of that primitive devotedness, the signs of that half-knightly, half-saintly chivalry which the priest's narrative imputed to his nature. He had become my Christian hero: under that character I wanted to view him.

Nor was opportunity slow to favour: my new impressions underwent her test the next day. Yes: I was granted an interview with my 'Christian hero' – an interview not very heroic, or sentimental, or biblical, but lively enough in its way.

About three o'clock of the afternoon, the peace of the first classe – safely established, as it seemed, under the serene sway of Mme Beck, who, in *propria persona*, was giving one of her orderly and useful lessons – this peace, I say, suffered a sudden fracture by the wild inburst of a paletôt.

Nobody at the moment was quieter than myself. Eased of responsibility by Mme Beck's presence, soothed by her uniform tones, pleased and edified with her clear exposition of the subject in hand (for she taught well), I sat bent over my desk, drawing – that is, copying an elaborate line engraving, tediously working up my copy to the finish of the original, for that was my practical notion of art; and, strange to say, I took extreme pleasure in the labour, and could even produce curiously finical Chinese facsimiles of steel or mezzotint plates – things about as valuable as so many achievements in worsted-work, but I thought pretty well of them in those days.

What was the matter? My drawing, my pencils, my precious copy, gathered into one crushed-up handful, perished from before my sight; I myself appeared to be shaken or emptied out of my chair, as a solitary and withered nutmeg might be emptied out of a spice-box by an excited cook. That chair, and my desk, seized by the wild paletôt, one under each sleeve, were borne afar; in a second, I followed the furniture: in two minutes they and I were fixed in the centre of the grande salle – a vast adjoining room, seldom used save for dancing and choral singing-lessons – fixed with an emphasis which seemed to prohibit the remotest hope of our ever being permitted to stir thence again.

Having partially collected my scared wits, I found myself in the presence of two men – gentlemen, I suppose I should say – one dark, the other light – one having a stiff, half-military air, and wearing a braided surtout; the other partaking, in garb and bearing, more of the careless aspect of the student or artist class: both flourishing in full magnificence of moustaches, whiskers, and

imperial. M. Emanuel stood a little apart from these; his countenance and eyes expressed strong choler; he held forth his hand with his tribune gesture.

'Mademoiselle,' said he, 'your business is to prove to these gentlemen that I am no liar. You will answer, to the best of your ability, such questions as they shall put. You will also write on such theme as they shall select. In their eyes, it appears I hold the position of an unprincipled impostor. I write essays; and, with deliberate forgery, sign to them my pupils' names, and boast of them as their work. You will disprove this charge.'

Grand Ciel! Here was the show-trial, so long evaded, come on me like a thunderclap. These two fine, braided, moustachioed, sneering personages, were none other than dandy professors of the college – Messieurs Boissec and Rochemorte – a pair of cold-blooded fops and pedants, sceptics, and scoffers. It seems that M. Paul had been rashly exhibiting something I had written – something he had never once praised, or even mentioned, in my hearing, and which I deemed forgotten. The essay was not remarkable at all; it only *seemed* remarkable, compared with the average productions of foreign schoolgirls; in an English establishment it would have passed scarce noticed. Messrs Boissec and Rochemorte had thought proper to question its genuineness, and insinuate a cheat; I was now to bear my testimony to the truth, and to be put to the torture of their examination.

A memorable scene ensued.

They began with classics. A dead blank. They went on to French history. I hardly knew Mérovée from Pharamond. They tried me in various 'ologies, and still only got a shake of the head, and an unchanging 'Je n'en sais rien.'

After an expressive pause, they proceeded to matters of general information, broaching one or two subjects which I knew pretty well, and on which I had often reflected. M. Emanuel, who had hitherto stood looking on, dark as the winter-solstice, brightened up somewhat; he thought I should now show myself at least no fool.

He learned his error. Though answers to the questions surged up fast, my mind filling like a rising well, ideas were there, but not words. I either *could* not, or *would* not speak – I am not sure which: partly, I think my nerves had got wrong, and partly my humour was crossed.

I heard one of my examiners – he of the braided surtout – whisper to his co-professor: 'Est-elle donc idiote?'

'Yes,' I thought, 'an idiot she is, and always will be, for such as you.'

But I suffered – suffered cruelly; I saw the damps gather on M. Paul's brow, and his eye spoke a passionate yet sad reproach. He would not believe in my total lack of popular cleverness; he thought I *could* be prompt if I *would*.

At last, to relieve him, the professors, and myself, I stammered out: 'Gentlemen, you had better let me go; you will get no good of me; as you say, I am an idiot.'

I wish I could have spoken with calm and dignity, or I wish my sense had sufficed to make me hold my tongue; that traitor tongue tripped, faltered. Beholding the judges cast on M. Emanuel a hard look of triumph, and hearing

the distressed tremor of my own voice, out I burst in a fit of choking tears. The emotion was far more of anger than grief; had I been a man and strong, I could have challenged that pair on the spot – but it *was* emotion, and I would rather have been scourged, than betrayed it.

The incapables! Could they not see at once the crude hand of a novice in that composition they called a forgery? The subject was classical. When M. Paul dictated the trait on which the essay was to turn, I heard it for the first time; the matter was new to me, and I had no material for its treatment. But I got books, read up the facts, laboriously constructed a skeleton out of the dry bones of the real, and then clothed them, and tried to breathe into them life, and in this last aim I had pleasure. With me it was a difficult and anxious time till my facts were found, selected, and properly pointed; nor could I rest from research and effort till I was satisfied of correct anatomy; the strength of my inward repugnance to the idea of flaw or falsity sometimes enabled me to shun egregious blunders; but the knowledge was not there in my head, ready and mellow; it had not been sown in Spring, grown in Summer, harvested in Autumn, and garnered through Winter; whatever I wanted I must go out and gather fresh; glean of wild herbs my lap full, and shred them green into the pot. Messieurs Boissec and Rochemorte did not perceive this. They mistook my work for the work of a ripe scholar.

They would not yet let me go: I must sit down and write before them. As I dipped my pen in the ink with a shaking hand, and surveyed the white paper with eyes half-blinded and overflowing, one of my judges began mincingly to apologise for the pain he caused.

'Nous agissons dans l'intêret de la verité. Nous ne voulons pas vous blesser,' said he.

Scorn gave me nerve. I only answered – 'Dictate, Monsieur.'

Rochemorte named this theme: 'Human Justice.'

Human Justice! What was I to make of it? Blank, cold abstraction, unsuggestive to me of one inspiring idea; and there stood M. Emanuel, sad as Saul, and stern as Joab, and there triumphed his accusers.

At these two I looked. I was gathering my courage to tell them that I would neither write nor speak another word for their satisfaction, that their theme did not suit, nor their presence inspire me, and that, notwithstanding, whoever threw the shadow of a doubt on M. Emanuel's honour, outraged that truth of which they had announced themselves the champions: I *meant* to utter all this, I say, when, suddenly, a light darted on memory.

Those two faces looking out of the forest of long hair, moustache, and whisker – those two cold yet bold, trustless yet presumptuous visages – were the same faces, the very same that, projected in full gas-light from behind the pillars of a portico, had half frightened me to death on the night of my desolate arrival in Villette. These, I felt morally certain, were the very heroes who had driven a friendless foreigner beyond her reckoning and her strength, chased her breathless over a whole quarter of the town.

'Pious mentors!' thought I. 'Pure guides for youth! If "Human Justice" were

what she ought to be, you two would scarce hold your present post, or enjoy your present credit.'

An idea once seized, I fell to work. 'Human Justice' rushed before me in novel guise, a red, random beldame with arms akimbo. I saw her in her house, the den of confusion: servants called to her for orders or help which she did not give; beggars stood at her door waiting and starving unnoticed; a swarm of children, sick and quarrelsome, crawled round her feet and yelled in her ears appeals for notice, sympathy, cure, redress. The honest woman cared for none of these things. She had a warm seat of her own by the fire, she had her own solace in a short black pipe, and a bottle of Mrs Sweeny's soothing syrup; she smoked and she sipped and she enjoyed her paradise, and whenever a cry of the suffering souls about her pierced her ears too keenly – my jolly dame seized the poker or the hearth-brush: if the offender was weak, wronged, and sickly, she effectually settled him; if he was strong, lively, and violent, she only menaced, then plunged her hand in her deep pouch, and flung a liberal shower of sugar-plums.

Such was the sketch of 'Human Justice', scratched hurriedly on paper, and placed at the service of Messrs Boissec and Rochemorte. M. Emanuel read it over my shoulder. Waiting no comment, I curtsied to the trio, and withdrew.

After school that day, M. Paul and I again met. Of course the meeting did not at first run smooth; there was a crow to pluck with him: that forced examination could not be immediately digested. A crabbed dialogue terminated in my being called, 'une petite moqueuse et sans-cœur', and in Monsieur's temporary departure.

Not wishing him to go quite away, only desiring he should feel that such a transport as he had that day given way to, could not be indulged with perfect impunity, I was not sorry to see him, soon after, gardening in the berceau. He approached the glass door; I drew near also. We spoke of some flowers growing round it. By and by Monsieur laid down his spade; by and by he recommended conversation, passed to other subjects, and at last touched a point of interest.

Conscious that his proceeding of that day was specially open to a charge of extravagance, M. Paul half apologised; he half regretted too the fitfulness of his moods at all times, yet he hinted that some allowance ought to be made for him. 'But,' said he, 'I can hardly expect it at your hands, Miss Lucy; you know neither me, nor my position, nor my history.'

His history. I took up the word at once; I pursued the idea.

'No, monsieur,' I rejoined. 'Of course, as you say, I know neither your history, nor your position, nor your sacrifices, nor any of your sorrows, or trials, or affections, or fidelities. Oh, no! I know nothing about you; you are for me altogether a stranger.'

'Hein?' he murmured, arching his brows in surprise.

'You know, monsieur, I only see you in classe – stern, dogmatic, hasty, imperious. I only hear of you in town as active and wilful, quick to originate, hasty to lead, but slow to persuade, and hard to bend. A man like you, without ties, can have no attachments; without dependents, no duties. All we, with whom you come in contact, are machines, which you thrust here and there,

inconsiderate of their feelings. You seek your recreations in public, by the light of the evening chandelier: this school and yonder college are your workshops, where you fabricate the ware called pupils. I don't so much as know where you live; it is natural to take it for granted that you have no home, and need none.'

'I am judged,' said he. 'Your opinion of me is just what I thought it was. For you – I am neither a man nor a Christian. You see me void of affection and religion, unattached by friend or family, unpiloted by principle or faith. It is well, mademoiselle; such is our reward in this life.'

'You are a philosopher, monsieur; a cynic philosopher' (and I looked at his paletôt, of which he straightway brushed the dim sleeve with his hand), 'despising the foibles of humanity – above its luxuries – independent of its comforts.'

'Et vous, mademoiselle; vous êtes proprette et douillette, et affreusement insensible, par-dessus le marché.'

'But, in short, monsieur, now I think of it, you *must* live somewhere? Do tell me where; and what establishment of servants do you keep?'

With a fearful projection of the under lip, implying an impetus of scorn the most decided, he broke out – 'Je vis dans un trou! I inhabit a den, miss – a cavern, where you would not put your dainty nose. Once, with base shame of speaking the whole truth, I talked about my "study" in that college: know now that this "study" is my whole abode; my chamber is there and my drawing-room. As for my "establishment of servants"' (mimicking my voice) 'they number ten: les voilà!'

And he grimly spread, close under my eyes, his ten fingers.

'I black my boots,' pursued he, savagely. 'I brush my paletôt –'

'No, monsieur, it is too plain; you never do that,' was my parenthesis.

'Je fais mon lit et mon ménage; I seek my dinner in a restaurant; my supper takes care of itself; I pass days laborious and loveless; nights long and lonely; I am ferocious, and bearded, and monkish; and nothing now living in this world loves me, except some old hearts worn like my own, and some few beings, impoverished, suffering, poor in purse and in spirit, whom the kingdoms of this world own not, but to whom a will and testament not to be disputed, has bequeathed the kingdom of heaven.'

'Ah, monsieur; but I know!'

'What do you know? many things, I verily believe; yet not me, Lucy!'

'I know that you have a pleasant old house in a pleasant old square of the Basse-Ville – why don't you go and live there?'

'Hein?' muttered he again.

'I liked it much, monsieur; with the steps ascending to the door, the gray flags in front, the nodding trees behind – real trees, not shrubs – trees dark, high, and of old growth. And the boudoir-oratoire – you should make that room your study; it is so quiet and solemn.'

He eyed me closely; he half-smiled, half-coloured. 'Where did you pick up all that? Who told you?' he asked.

'Nobody told me. Did I dream it, monsieur, do you think?'

'Can I enter into your visions? Can I guess a woman's waking thoughts, much less her sleeping fantasies?'

'If I dreamt it, I saw in my dream human beings as well as a house. I saw a priest, old, bent, and gray, and a domestic – old, too, and picturesque; and a lady, splendid but strange; her head would scarce reach to my elbow – her magnificence might ransom a duke. She wore a gown bright as lapis-lazuli – a shawl worth a thousand francs: she was decked with ornaments so brilliant, I never saw any with such a beautiful sparkle; but her figure looked as if it had been broken in two and bent double; she seemed also to have outlived the common years of humanity, and to have attained those which are only labour and sorrow. She was become morose – almost malevolent; yet *somebody*, it appears, cared for her in her infirmities – somebody forgave her trespasses, hoping to have his trespasses forgiven. They lived together, these three people – the mistress, the chaplain, the servant – all old, all feeble, all sheltered under one kind wing.'

He covered with his hand the upper part of his face, but did not conceal his mouth, where I saw hovering an expression I liked.

'I see you have entered into my secrets,' said he, 'but how was it done?'

So I told him how – the commission on which I had been sent, the storm which had detained me, the abruptness of the lady, the kindness of the priest. 'As I sat waiting for the rain to cease, Père Silas whiled away the time with a story,' I said.

'A story! What story? Père Silas is no romancist.'

'Shall I tell monsieur the tale?'

'Yes: begin at the beginning. Let me hear some of Miss Lucy's French – her best or her worst – I don't much care which: let us have a good poignée of barbarisms, and a bounteous dose of the insular accent.'

'Monsieur is not going to be gratified by a tale of ambitious proportions, and the spectacle of the narrator sticking fast in the midst. But I will tell him the title – "The Priest's Pupil".'

'Bah!' said he, the swarthy flush again dyeing his dark cheek. 'The good old father could not have chosen a worse subject: it is his weak point. But what of "The Priest's Pupil"?'

'Oh! many things.'

'You may as well at once define *what* things. I mean to know.'

'There was the pupil's youth, the pupil's manhood – his avarice, his ingratitude, his implacability, his inconstancy. Such a bad pupil, monsieur! – so thankless, cold-hearted, unchivalrous, unforgiving!'

'Et puis?' said he, taking a cigar.

'Et puis,' I pursued, 'he underwent calamities which one did not pity – bore them in a spirit one did not admire – endured wrongs for which one felt no sympathy; finally, took the unchristian revenge of heaping coals of fire on his adversary's head.'

'You have not told me all,' said he.

'Nearly all, I think: I have indicated the heads of Père Silas's chapters.'

'You have forgotten one – that which touched on the pupil's lack of affection – on his hard, cold, monkish heart.'

'True; I remember now. Père Silas *did* say that his vocation was almost that of a priest – that his life was considered consecrated.'

'By what bonds or duties?'

'By the ties of the past and the charities of the present.'

'You have, then, the whole situation?'

'I have now told monsieur all that was told me.' Some meditative minutes passed.

'Now, Mlle Lucy, look at me, and with that truth which I believe you never knowingly violate, answer me one question. Raise your eyes; rest them on mine; have no hesitation; fear not to trust me – I am a man to be trusted.'

I raised my eyes.

'Knowing me thoroughly now – all my antecedents, all my responsibilities – having long known my faults, can you and I still be friends?'

'If monsieur wants a friend in me, I shall be glad to have a friend in him.'

'But a close friend I mean – intimate and real – kindred in all but blood? Will Miss Lucy be the sister of a very poor, fettered, burdened, encumbered man?'

I could not answer him in words, yet I suppose I *did* answer him; he took my hand, which found comfort in the shelter of his. *His* friendship was not a doubtful, wavering benefit – a cold, distant hope – a sentiment so brittle as not to bear the weight of a finger: I at once felt (or *thought* I felt) its support like that of some rock.

'When I talk of friendship, I mean *true* friendship,' he repeated emphatically; and I could hardly believe that words so earnest had blessed my ear; I hardly could credit the reality of that kind, anxious look he gave. If he *really* wished for my confidence and regard, and *really* would give me his – why, it seemed to me that life could offer nothing more or better. In that case, I was become strong and rich: in a moment I was made substantially happy. To ascertain the fact, to fix and seal it, I asked – 'Is monsieur quite serious? Does he really think he needs me, and can take an interest in me as a sister?'

'Surely, surely,' said he; 'a lonely man like me, who has no sister, must be but too glad to find in some woman's heart a sister's pure affection.'

'And dare I rely on monsieur's regard? Dare I speak to him when I am so inclined?'

'My little sister must make her own experiments,' said he; 'I will give no promises. She must tease and try her wayward brother till she has drilled him into what she wishes. After all, he is no inductile material in some hands.'

While he spoke, the tone of his voice, the light of his now affectionate eye, gave me such a pleasure as, certainly, I had never felt. I envied no girl her lover, no bride her bridegroom, no wife her husband; I was content with this my voluntary, self-offering friend. If he would but prove reliable, and he *looked* reliable, what, beyond his friendship, could I ever covet? But, if all melted like a dream, as once before had happened – ?

'Qu'est-ce donc? What is it?' said he, as this thought threw its weight on my heart, its shadow on my countenance. I told him; and after a moment's pause, and a thoughtful smile, he showed me how an equal fear – lest I should weary of him, a man of moods so difficult and fitful – had haunted his mind for more than one day, or one month.

On hearing this, a quiet courage cheered me. I ventured a word of reassurance. That word was not only tolerated; its repetition was courted. I grew quite happy – strangely happy – in making him secure, content, tranquil. Yesterday, I could not have believed that earth held, or life afforded, moments like the few I was now passing. Countless times it had been my lot to watch apprehended sorrow close darkly in; but to see unhoped-for happiness take form, find place, and grow more real as the seconds sped, was indeed a new experience.

'Lucy,' said M. Paul, speaking low and still holding my hand, 'did you see a picture in the boudoir of the old house?'

'I did; a picture painted on a panel.'

'The portrait of a nun?'

'Yes.'

'You heard her history?'

'Yes.'

'You remember what we saw that night in the berceau?'

'I shall never forget it.'

'You did not connect the two ideas; that would be folly?'

'I thought of the apparition when I saw the portrait,' said I; which was true enough.

'You did not, nor will you fancy,' pursued he, 'that a saint in Heaven perturbs herself with rivalries of earth? Protestants are rarely superstitious; these morbid fancies will not beset you?'

'I know not what to think of this matter; but I believe a perfectly natural solution of this seeming mystery will one day be arrived at.'

'Doubtless, doubtless. Besides, no good living woman – much less a pure, happy spirit – would trouble amity like ours – n'est-il pas vrai?'

Ere I could answer, Fifine Beck burst in, rosy and abrupt, calling out that I was wanted. Her mother was going into town to call on some English family, who had applied for a prospectus: my services were needed as interpreter. The interruption was not unseasonable: sufficient for the day is always the evil; for this hour, its good sufficed. Yet I should have liked to ask M. Paul whether the 'morbid fancies,' against which he warned me, wrought in his own brain.

## CHAPTER 36

### The Apple of Discord

Besides Fifine Beck's mother, another power had a word to say to M. Paul and me, before that covenant of friendship could be ratified. We were under the surveillance of a sleepless eye: Rome watched jealously her son through that mystic lattice at which I had knelt once, and to which M. Emanuel drew nigh month by month – the sliding panel of the confessional.

'Why were you so glad to be friends with M. Paul?' asks the reader. 'Had he

not long been a friend to you? Had he not given proof on proof of a certain partiality in his feelings?'

Yes, he had; but still I liked to hear him say so earnestly – that he was my close, true friend; I liked his modest doubts, his tender deference – that trust which longed to rest, and was grateful when taught how. He had called me 'sister.' It was well. Yes; he might call me what he pleased, so long as he confided in me. I was willing to be his sister, on condition that he did not invite me to fill that relation to some future wife of his; and tacitly vowed as he was to celibacy, of this dilemma there seemed little danger.

Through most of the succeeding night, I pondered that evening's interview. I wanted much the morning to break, and then listened for the bell to ring; and, after rising and dressing, I deemed prayers and breakfast slow, and all the hours lingering, till that arrived at last which brought the lesson of literature. My wish was to get a more thorough comprehension of this fraternal alliance: to note with how much of the brother he would demean himself when we met again; to prove how much of the sister was in my own feelings; to discover whether I could summon a sister's courage, and he a brother's frankness.

He came. Life is so constructed, that the event does not, cannot, will not, match the expectation. That whole day he never accosted me. His lesson was given rather more quietly than usual, more mildly, and also more gravely. He was fatherly to his pupils, but he was not brotherly to me. Ere he left the classe, I expected a smile, if not a word; I got neither: to my portion fell one nod – hurried, shy.

This distance, I argued, is accidental – it is involuntary; patience, and it will vanish. It vanished not; it continued for days; it increased. I suppressed my surprise, and swallowed whatever other feelings began to surge.

Well might I ask when he offered fraternity – 'Dare I rely on you?' Well might he, doubtless knowing himself, withhold all pledge. True, he had bid me make my own experiments – tease and try him. Vain injunction! Privilege nominal and unavailable! Some women might use it! Nothing in my powers or instinct placed me amongst this brave band. Left alone, I was passive; repulsed, I withdrew; forgotten – my lips would not utter, nor my eyes dart a reminder. It seemed there had been an error somewhere in my calculations, and I waited for time to disclose it.

But the day came when, as usual, he was to give me a lesson. One evening in seven he had long generously bestowed on me, devoting it to the examination of what had been done in various studies during the past week, and to the preparation of work for the week in prospect. On these occasions my schoolroom was anywhere, wherever the pupils and the other teachers happened to be, or in their close vicinage, very often in the large second division, where it was easy to choose a quiet nook when the crowding day-pupils were absent, and the few boarders gathered in a knot about the surveillante's estrade.

On the customary evening, hearing the customary hour strike, I collected my books and papers, my pen and ink, and sought the large division.

In classe there was no one, and it lay all in cool deep shadow; but through the

open double doors was seen the carré, filled with pupils and with light; over hall and figures blushed the westering sun. It blushed so ruddily and vividly, that the hues of the walls and the variegated tints of the dresses seemed all fused in one warm glow. The girls were seated, working or studying; in the midst of their circle stood M. Emanuel, speaking good-humouredly to a teacher. His dark paletôt, his jetty hair, were tinged with many a reflex of crimson; his Spanish face, when he turned it momentarily, answered the sun's animated kiss with an animated smile. I took my place at a desk.

The orange trees, and several plants, full and bright with bloom, basked also in the sun's laughing bounty; they had partaken it the whole day, and now asked water. M. Emanuel had a taste for gardening; he liked to tend and foster plants. I used to think that working amongst shrubs with a spade or a watering-pot soothed his nerves; it was a recreation to which he often had recourse; and now he looked to the orange trees, the geraniums, the gorgeous cactuses, and revived them all with the refreshment their drought needed. His lips meantime sustained his precious cigar, that (for him) first necessary and prime luxury of life; its blue wreaths curled prettily enough amongst the flowers, and in the evening light. He spoke no more to the pupils, nor to the mistresses, but gave many an endearing word to a small spanieless (if one may coin a word), that nominally belonged to the house, but virtually owned him as master, being fonder of him than of any inmate. A delicate, silky, loving, and loveable little doggie she was, trotting at his side, looking with expressive, attached eyes into his face; and whenever he dropped his bonnet-grec or his handkerchief, which he occasionally did in play, crouching beside it with the air of a miniature lion guarding a kingdom's flag.

There were many plants, and as the amateur gardener fetched all the water from the well in the court, with his own active hands, his work spun out to some length. The great school-clock ticked on. Another hour struck. The carré and the youthful group lost the illusion of sunset. Day was drooping. My lesson, I perceived, must tonight be very short; but the orange trees, the cacti, the camelias were all served now. Was it my turn?

Alas! in the garden were more plants to be looked after, favourite rose bushes, certain choice flowers; little Sylvie's glad bark and whine followed the receding paletôt down the alleys. I put up some of my books; I should not want them all; I sat and thought, and waited, involuntarily deprecating the creeping invasion of twilight.

Sylvie, gaily frisking, emerged into view once more, heralding the returning paletôt; the watering-pot was deposited beside the well; it had fulfilled its office; how glad I was! Monsieur washed his hands in a little stone bowl. There was no longer time for a lesson now; ere long the prayer-bell must ring; but still we should meet; he would speak; a chance would be offered of reading in his eyes the riddle of his shyness. His ablutions over, he stood, slowly rearranging his cuffs, looking at the horn of a young moon, set pale in the opal sky, and glimmering faint on the oriel of Jean Baptiste. Sylvie watched the mood contemplative; its stillness irked her; she whined and jumped to break it. He looked down.

'Petite exigeante!' said he; 'you must not be forgotten one moment, it seems.'

He stooped, lifted her in his arms, sauntered across the court, within a yard of the line of windows near one of which I sat: he sauntered lingeringly, fondling the spaniel in his bosom, calling her tender names in a tender voice. On the front-door steps he turned; once again he looked at the moon, at the gray cathedral, over the remoter spires and house-roofs fading into a blue sea of night-mist; he tasted the sweet breath of dusk, and noted the folded bloom of the garden; he suddenly looked round; a keen beam out of his eye rased the white façade of the classes, swept the long line of croisées. I think he bowed; if he did, I had no time to return the courtesy. In a moment he was gone; the moonlit threshold lay pale and shadowless before the closed front-door.

Gathering in my arms all that was spread on the desk before me, I carried back the unused heap to its place in the third classe. The prayer-bell rang; I obeyed its summons.

The morrow would not restore him to the Rue Fossette, that day being devoted entirely to his college. I got through my teaching; I got over the intermediate hours; I saw evening approaching, and armed myself for its heavy ennuis. Whether it was worse to stay with my co-inmates, or to sit alone, I had not considered; I naturally took up the latter alternative; if there was a hope of comfort for any moment, the heart or head of no human being in this house could yield it; only under the lid of my desk could it harbour, nestling between the leaves of some book, gilding a pencil-point, the nib of a pen, or tinging the black fluid in that ink-glass. With a heavy heart I opened my desk-lid; with a weary hand I turned up its contents.

One by one, well-accustomed books, volumes sewn in familiar covers, were taken out and put back hopeless; they had no charm; they could not comfort. Is this something new, this pamphlet in lilac? I have not seen it before, and I rearranged my desk this very day – this very afternoon; the tract must have been introduced within the last hour, while we were at dinner.

I opened it. What was it? What would it say to me?

It was neither tale nor poem, neither essay nor history; it neither sung, nor related, nor discussed. It was a theological work; it preached and it persuaded.

I lent to it my ear very willingly, for, small as it was, it possessed its own spell, and bound my attention at once. It preached Romanism; it persuaded to conversion. The voice of that sly little book was a honied voice; its accents were all unction and balm. Here roared no utterance of Rome's thunders, no blasting of the breath of her displeasure. The Protestant was to turn Papist, not so much in fear of the heretic's hell, as on account of the comfort, the indulgence, the tenderness Holy Church offered: far be it from her to threaten or to coerce; her wish was to guide and win. *She* persecute? Oh dear no! not on any account!

This meek volume was not addressed to the hardened and worldly; it was not even strong meat for the strong: it was milk for babes; the mild effluence of a mother's love towards her tenderest and her youngest; intended wholly and solely for those whose head is to be reached through the heart. Its appeal was

not to intellect; it sought to win the affectionate through their affections, the sympathising through their sympathies: St Vincent de Paul, gathering his orphans about him, never spoke more sweetly.

I remember one capital inducement to apostasy was held out in the fact that a Catholic who had lost dear friends by death could enjoy the unspeakable solace of praying them out of purgatory. The writer did not touch on the firmer peace of those whose belief dispenses with purgatory altogether; but I thought of this, and, on the whole, preferred the latter doctrine as the most consolatory.

The little book amused, and did not painfully displease me. It was a canting, sentimental, shallow little book, yet something about it cheered my gloom and made me smile; I was amused with the gambols of this unlicked wolf-cub muffled in the fleece, and mimicking the bleat of a guileless lamb. Portions of it reminded me of certain Wesleyan Methodist tracts I had once read when a child; they were flavoured with about the same seasoning of excitation to fanaticism. He that had written it was no bad man, and while perpetually betraying the trained cunning – the cloven hoof of his system – I should pause before accusing himself of insincerity. His judgement, however, wanted surgical props; it was ricketty.

I smiled then over this dose of maternal tenderness, coming from the ruddy old lady of the Seven Hills; smiled, too, at my own disinclination, not to say disability, to meet these melting favours. Glancing at the title-page, I found the name of 'Père Silas.' A fly-leaf bore in small, but clear and well-known pencil characters: 'From P. C. D. E. to L—y.' And when I saw this I laughed; but not in my former spirit. I was revived.

A mortal bewilderment cleared suddenly from my head and vision; the solution of the Sphynx-riddle was won; the conjunction of those two names, Père Silas and Paul Emanuel, gave the key to all. The penitent had been with his director; permitted to withhold nothing; suffered to keep no corner of his heart sacred to God and to himself; the whole narrative of our late interview had been drawn from him; he had avowed the covenant of fraternity, and spoken of his adopted sister. How could such covenant, such adoption, be sanctioned by the Church? Fraternal communion with a heretic! I seemed to hear Père Silas annulling the unholy pact; warning his penitent of its perils; entreating, enjoining reserve, nay, by the authority of his office, and in the name, and by the memory of all M. Emanuel held most dear and sacred, commanding the enforcement of that new system whose frost had pierced to the marrow of my bones.

These may not seem pleasant hypotheses; yet, by comparison, they were welcome. The vision of a ghostly troubler hovering in the background, was as nothing, matched with the fear of spontaneous change arising in M. Paul himself.

At this distance of time, I cannot be sure how far the above conjectures were self-suggested: or in what measure they owed their origin and confirmation to another quarter. Help was not wanting.

This evening there was no bright sunset; west and east were one cloud; no

summer night-mist, blue, yet rose-tinged, softened the distance; a clammy fog from the marshes crept gray round Villette. Tonight the watering-pot might rest in its niche by the well; a small rain had been drizzling all the afternoon, and still it fell fast and quietly. This was no weather for rambling in the wet alleys, under the dripping trees; and I started to hear Sylvie's sudden bark in the garden – her bark of welcome. Surely she was not accompanied; and yet this glad, quick bark was never uttered, save in homage to one presence.

Through the glass-door and the arching berceau, I commanded the deep vista of the allée défendue: thither rushed Sylvie, glistening through its gloom like a white guelder-rose. She ran to and fro, whining, springing, harassing little birds amongst the bushes. I watched five minutes; no fulfilment followed the omen. I returned to my books: Sylvie's sharp bark suddenly ceased. Again I looked up. She was standing not many yards distant, wagging her white, feathery tail as fast as the muscle would work, and intently watching the operations of a spade, plied fast by an indefatigable hand. There was M. Emanuel, bent over the soil, digging in the wet mould amongst the rain-laden and streaming shrubs, working as hard as if his day's pittance were yet to earn by the literal sweat of his brow.

In this sign I read a ruffled mood. He would dig thus in frozen snow on the coldest winter day, when urged inwardly by painful emotion, whether of nervous excitation, or sad thoughts, or self-reproach. He would dig, by the hour, with knit brow and set teeth, nor once lift his head, or open his lips.

Sylvie watched till she was tired. Again scampering devious, bounding here, rushing there, snuffing and sniffing everywhere, she at last discovered me in classe. Instantly she flew barking at the panes, as if to urge me forth to share her pleasure or her master's toil; she had seen me occasionally walking in that alley with M. Paul; and I doubt not, considered it my duty to join him now, wet as it was.

She made such a bustle that M. Paul at last looked up, and of course perceived why, and at whom she barked. He whistled to call her off; she only barked the louder. She seemed quite bent upon having the glass-door opened. Tired, I suppose, with her importunity, he threw down his spade, approached, and pushed the door ajar. Sylvie burst in all impetuous, sprang to my lap, and with her paws at my neck, and her little nose and tongue somewhat overpoweringly busy about my face, mouth, and eyes, flourished her bushy tail over the desk, and scattered books and papers far and wide.

M. Emanuel advanced to still the clamour and repair the disarrangement. Having gathered up the books, he captured Sylvie, and stowed her away under his paletôt, where she nestled as quiet as a mouse, her head just peeping forth. She was very tiny, and had the prettiest little innocent face, the silkiest long ears, the finest dark eyes in the world. I never saw her, but I thought of Paulina de Bassompierre: forgive the association, reader, it *would* occur.

M. Paul petted and patted her; the endearments she received were not to be wondered at; she invited affection by her beauty and her vivacious life.

While caressing the spaniel, his eye roved over the papers and books just replaced; it settled on the religious tract. His lips moved; he half-checked the

impulse to speak. What! had he promised never to address me more? If so, his better nature pronounced the vow 'more honoured in the breach than in the observance,' for with a second effort, he spoke: 'You have not yet read the brochure, I presume? It is not sufficiently inviting?'

I replied that I had read it.

He waited, as if wishing me to give an opinion upon it unasked. Unasked, however, I was in no mood to do or say anything. If any concessions were to be made – if any advances were demanded – that was the affair of the very docile pupil of Père Silas, not mine. His eye settled upon me gently; there was mildness at the moment in its blue ray – there was solicitude – a shade of pathos; there were meanings composite and contrasted – reproach melting into remorse. At the moment, probably, he would have been glad to see something emotional in me. I could not show it. In another minute, however, I should have betrayed confusion, had I not bethought myself to take some quill-pens from my desk, and begin soberly to mend them.

I knew that action would give a turn to his mood. He never liked to see me mend pens; my knife was always dull-edged – my hand, too, was unskilful; I hacked and chipped. On this occasion I cut my own finger – half on purpose. I wanted to restore him to his natural state, to set him at his ease, to get him to chide.

'Maladroite!' he cried at last, 'she will make mincemeat of her hands.'

He put Sylvie down, making her lie quiet beside his bonnet-grec, and, depriving me of the pens and penknife, he proceeded to slice, nib, and point with the accuracy and celerity of a machine.

'Did I like the little book?' he now enquired.

Suppressing a yawn, I said I hardly knew.

'Had it moved me?'

'I thought it had made me a little sleepy.'

(After a pause) 'Allons donc! It was of no use taking that tone with him. Bad as I was – and he should be sorry to have to name all my faults at a breath – God and nature had given me "trop de sensibilité et de sympathie" not to be profoundly affected by an appeal so touching.'

'Indeed!' I responded, rousing myself quickly, 'I was not affected at all – not a whit.'

And in proof, I drew from my pocket a perfectly dry handkerchief, still clean and in its folds.

Hereupon I was made the object of a string of strictures rather piquant than polite. I listened with zest. After those two days of unnatural silence, it was better than music to hear M. Paul haranguing again just in his old fashion. I listened, and meantime solaced myself and Sylvie with the contents of a bonbonnière, which M. Emanuel's gifts kept well supplied with chocolate comfits. It pleased him to see even a small matter from his hand duly appreciated. He looked at me and the spaniel while we shared the spoil; he put up his penknife. Touching my hand with the bundle of new-cut quills, he said: 'Dites-donc, petite soeur – speak frankly – what have you thought of me during the last two days?'

But of this question I would take no manner of notice; its purport made my eyes fill. I caressed Sylvie assiduously. M. Paul, leaning over the desk, bent towards us: 'I called myself your brother,' he said; 'I hardly know what I am – brother – friend – I cannot tell. I know I think of you – I feel I wish you well – but I must check myself; you are to be feared. My best friends point out danger, and whisper caution.'

'You do right to listen to your friends. By all means be cautious.'

'It is your religion – your strange, self-reliant, invulnerable creed, whose influence seems to clothe you in, I know not what unblessed panoply. You are good – Père Silas calls you good, and loves you – but your terrible, proud, earnest Protestantism, there is the danger. It expresses itself by your eye at times; and again, it gives you certain tones and certain gestures that make my flesh creep. You are not demonstrative, and yet, just now – when you handled that tract – my God! I thought Lucifer smiled.'

'Certainly I don't respect that tract – what then?'

'Not respect that tract? But it is the pure essence of faith, love, charity! I thought it would touch you: in its gentleness, I trusted that it could not fail. I laid it in your desk with a prayer. I must indeed be a sinner: Heaven will not hear the petitions that come warmest from my heart. You scorn my little offering. Oh, cela me fait mal!'

'Monsieur, I don't scorn it – at least, not as your gift. Monsieur, sit down; listen to me. I am not a heathen, I am not hard-hearted, I am not unchristian, I am not dangerous, as they tell you; I would not trouble your faith; you believe in God and Christ and the Bible, and so do I.'

'But do you believe in the Bible? Do you receive Revelation? What limits are there to the wild, careless daring of your country and sect? Père Silas dropped dark hints.'

By dint of persuasion, I made him half-define these hints; they amounted to crafty Jesuit-slanders. That night M. Paul and I talked seriously and closely. He pleaded, he argued. I could not argue – a fortunate incapacity; it needed but triumphant, logical opposition to effect all the director wished to be effected; but I could talk in my own way – the way M. Paul was used to – and of which he could follow the meanderings and fill the hiatus, and pardon the strange stammerings, strange to him no longer. At ease with him, I could defend my creed and faith in my own fashion; in some degree I could lull his prejudices. He was not satisfied when he went away, hardly was he appeased; but he was made thoroughly to feel that Protestants were not necessarily the irreverent Pagans his director had insinuated; he was made to comprehend something of their mode of honouring the Light, the Life, the Word; he was enabled partly to perceive that, while their veneration for things venerable was not quite like that cultivated in his Church, it had its own, perhaps, deeper power – its own more solemn awe.

I found that Père Silas (himself, I must repeat, not a bad man, though the advocate of a bad cause) had darkly stigmatised Protestants in general, and myself by inference, with strange names, had ascribed to us strange 'isms'; M. Emanuel

revealed all this in his frank fashion, which knew not secretiveness, looking at me as he spoke with a kind, earnest fear, almost trembling lest there should be truth in the charges. Père Silas, it seems, had closely watched me, had ascertained that I went by turns, and indiscriminately, to the three Protestant Chapels of Villette – the French, German, and English – *id est*, the Presbyterian, Lutheran, Episcopalian. Such liberality argued in the Father's eyes profound indifference – who tolerates all, he reasoned, can be attached to none. Now, it happened that I had often secretly wondered at the minute and unimportant character of the differences between these three sects – at the unity and identity of their vital doctrines: I saw nothing to hinder them from being one day fused into one grand Holy Alliance, and I respected them all, though I thought that in each there were faults of form; incumbrances, and trivialities. Just what I thought, that did I tell M. Emanuel, and explained to him that my own last appeal, the guide to which I looked, and the teacher which I owned, must always be the Bible itself, rather than any sect, of whatever name or nation.

He left me soothed, yet full of solicitude, breathing a wish, as strong as a prayer, that if I were wrong, Heaven would lead me right. I heard, poured forth on the threshold, some fervid murmurings to 'Marie, Reine du Ciel,' some deep aspiration that *his* hope might yet be *mine*.

Strange! I had no such feverish wish to turn him from the faith of his fathers. I thought Romanism wrong, a great mixed image of gold and clay; but it seemed to me that *this* Romanist held the purer elements of his creed with an innocency of heart which God must love.

The preceding conversation passed between eight and nine o'clock of the evening, in a schoolroom of the quiet Rue Fossette, opening on a sequestered garden. Probably about the same, or a somewhat later hour of the succeeding evening, its echoes, collected by holy obedience, were breathed verbatim in an attent ear, at the panel of a confessional, in the hoary church of the Magi. It ensued that Père Silas paid a visit to Mme Beck, and stirred by I know not what mixture of motives, persuaded her to let him undertake for a time the heretic Englishwoman's spiritual direction.

Hereupon I was put through a course of reading – that is, I just glanced at the books lent me; they were too little in my way to be thoroughly read, marked, learned, or inwardly digested. And besides, I had a book upstairs, under my pillow, whereof certain chapters satisfied my needs in the article of spiritual lore, furnishing such precept and example as, to my heart's core, I was convinced could not be improved on.

Then Père Silas showed me the fair side of Rome, her good works, and bade me judge the tree by its fruits.

In answer, I felt and I avowed that these works were *not* the fruits of Rome; they were but her abundant blossoming, but the fair promise she showed the world. That bloom, when set, savoured not of charity; the apple full-formed was ignorance, abasement, and bigotry. Out of men's afflictions and affections were forged the rivets of their servitude. Poverty was fed and clothed, and sheltered, to bind it by obligation to 'the Church'; orphanage was reared and educated that

it might grow up in the fold of 'the Church'; sickness was tended that it might die after the formula and in the ordinance of 'the Church;' and men were overwrought, and women most murderously sacrificed, and all laid down a world God made pleasant for his creatures' good, and took up a cross, monstrous in its galling weight, that they might serve Rome, prove her sanctity, confirm her power, and spread the reign of her tyrant 'Church.'

For man's good was little done; for God's glory less. A thousand ways were opened with pain, with blood-sweats, with lavishing of life; mountains were cloven through their breasts, and rocks were split to their base; and all for what? That a Priesthood might march straight on and straight upward to an all-dominating eminence, whence they might at last stretch the sceptre of their Moloch 'Church'.

It will not be. God is not with Rome, and, were human sorrows still for the Son of God, would he not mourn over her cruelties and ambitions, as once he mourned over the crimes and woes of doomed Jerusalem!

Oh, lovers of power! Oh, mitred aspirants for this world's kingdoms! an hour will come, even to you, when it will be well for your hearts – pausing faint at each broken beat – that there is a Mercy beyond human compassions, a Love stronger than this strong death which even you must face, and before it, fall; a Charity more potent than any sin, even yours; a Pity which redeems worlds – nay, absolves Priests.

My third temptation was held out in the pomp of Rome, the glory of her kingdom. I was taken to the churches on solemn occasions – days of fête and state; I was shown the Papal ritual and ceremonial. I looked at it.

Many people – men and women – no doubt far my superiors in a thousand ways, have felt this display impressive, have declared that though their Reason protested, their Imagination was subjugated. I cannot say the same. Neither full procession, nor high mass, nor swarming tapers, nor swinging censers, nor ecclesiastical millinery, nor celestial jewellery, touched my imagination a whit. What I saw struck me as tawdry, not grand; as grossly material, not poetically spiritual.

This I did not tell Père Silas; he was old, he looked venerable, through every abortive experiment, under every repeated disappointment, he remained personally kind to me, and I felt tender of hurting his feelings. But on the evening of a certain day when, from the balcony of a great house, I had been made to witness a huge mingled procession of the church and the army – priests with relics, and soldiers with weapons, an obese and aged archbishop, habited in cambric and lace, looking strangely like a gray daw in bird-of-paradise plumage, and a band of young girls fantastically robed and garlanded – then I spoke my mind to M. Paul.

'I did not like it,' I told him, 'I did not respect such ceremonies; I wished to see no more.'

And having relieved my conscience by this declaration, I was able to go on, and, speaking more currently and clearly than my wont, to show him that I had a mind to keep to my reformed creed; that the more I saw of Popery the closer I

clung to Protestantism; doubtless there were errors in every Church, but I now perceived by contrast how severely pure was my own, compared with her whose painted and meretricious face had been unveiled for my admiration. I told him how we kept fewer forms between us and God; retaining, indeed, no more than, perhaps, the nature of mankind in the mass rendered necessary for due observance. I told him I could not look on flowers and tinsel, on wax-lights and embroidery, at such times and under such circumstances as should be devoted to lifting the secret vision to Him whose home is Infinity, and his being – Eternity. That when I thought of sin and sorrow, of earthly corruption, mortal depravity, weighty temporal woe – I could not care for chanting priests or murmuring officials; that when the pains of existence and the terrors of dissolution pressed before me – when the mighty hope and measureless doubt of the future arose in view – *then*, even the scientific strain, or the prayer in a language learned and dead, harassed with hindrance a heart which only longed to cry – 'God be merciful to me, a sinner!'

When I had so spoken, so declared my faith, and so widely severed myself from him I addressed – then, at last, came a tone accordant, an echo responsive, one sweet chord of harmony in two conflicting spirits.

'Whatever say priests or controversialists,' murmured M. Emanuel, 'God is good, and loves all the sincere. Believe, then, what you can; believe it as you can; one prayer, at least, we have in common; I also cry – "O Dieu, sois appaisé envers moi qui suis pécheur!" '

He leaned on the back of my chair. After some thought he again spoke: 'How seem in the eyes of that God who made all firmaments, from whose nostrils issued whatever of life is here, or in the stars shining yonder – how seem the differences of man? But as Time is not for God, nor Space, so neither is Measure, nor Comparison. We abase ourselves in our littleness, and we do right; yet it may be that the constancy of one heart, the truth and faith of one mind according to the light He has appointed, import as much to Him as the just motion of satellites about their planets, of planets about their suns, of suns around that mighty unseen centre incomprehensible, irrealisable, with strange mental effort only divined.

'God guide us all! God bless you, Lucy!'

## CHAPTER 37

### Sunshine

It was very well for Paulina to decline further correspondence with Graham till her father had sanctioned the intercourse, but Dr Bretton could not live within a league of the Hôtel Crécy, and not contrive to visit there often. Both lovers meant at first, I believe, to be distant; they kept their intention so far as demonstrative courtship went, but in feeling they soon drew very near.

All that was best in Graham sought Paulina; whatever in him was noble,

awoke, and grew in her presence. With his past admiration of Miss Fanshawe, I suppose his intellect had little to do, but his whole intellect, and his highest tastes, came in question now. These, like all his faculties, were active, eager for nutriment, and alive to gratification when it came.

I cannot say that Paulina designedly led him to talk of books, or formally proposed to herself for a moment the task of winning him to reflection, or planned the improvement of his mind, or so much as fancied his mind could in any one respect be improved. She thought him very perfect; it was Graham himself, who, at first by the merest chance, mentioned some book he had been reading, and when in her response, sounded a welcome harmony of sympathies, something pleasant to his soul, he talked on, more and better perhaps than he had ever talked before on such subjects. She listened with delight, and answered with animation. In each successive answer, Graham heard a music waxing finer and finer to his sense; in each he found a suggestive, persuasive, magic accent that opened a scarce known treasure-house within, showed him unsuspected power in his own mind, and what was better, latent goodness in his heart. Each liked the way in which the other talked; the voice, the diction, the expression pleased; each keenly relished the flavour of the other's wit; they met each other's meaning with strange quickness, their thoughts often matched like carefully-chosen pearls. Graham had a wealth of mirth by nature; Paulina possessed no such inherent flow of animal spirits – unstimulated, she inclined to be thoughtful and pensive – but now she seemed merry as a lark; in her lover's genial presence, she glanced like some soft glad light. How beautiful she grew in her happiness, I can hardly express, but I wondered to see her. As to that gentle ice of hers – that reserve on which she had depended; where was it now? Ah! Graham would not long bear it; he brought with him a generous influence that soon thawed the timid, self-imposed restriction.

Now were the old Bretton days talked over; perhaps brokenly at first, with a sort of smiling diffidence, then with opening candour and still growing confidence. Graham had made for himself a better opportunity than that he had wished me to give; he had earned independence of the collateral help that disobliging Lucy had refused; all his reminiscences of 'little Polly' found their proper expression in his own pleasant tones, by his own kind and handsome lips – how much better than if suggested by me.

More than once when we were alone, Paulina would tell me how wonderful and curious it was to discover the richness and accuracy of his memory in this matter. How, while he was looking at her, recollections would seem to be suddenly quickened in his mind. He reminded her that she had once gathered his head in her arms, caressed his leonine graces, and cried out, 'Graham, I *do* like you!' He told her how she would set a footstool beside him, and climb by its aid to his knee. At this day he said he could recall the sensation of her little hands smoothing his cheek, or burying themselves in his thick mane. He remembered the touch of her small forefinger, placed half tremblingly, half curiously, in the cleft in his chin, the lisp, the look with which she would name it 'a pretty dimple', then seek his eyes and question why they pierced so, telling him he had

a 'nice, strange face; far nicer, far stranger, than either his mama or Lucy Snowe'.

'Child as I was,' remarked Paulina, 'I wonder how I dared be so venturous. To me he seems now all sacred, his locks are inaccessible, and, Lucy, I feel a sort of fear when I look at his firm, marble chin, at his straight Greek features. Women are called beautiful, Lucy; he is not like a woman, therefore I suppose he is not beautiful, but what is he then? Do other people see him with my eyes? Do *you* admire him?'

'I'll tell you what I do, Paulina,' was once my answer to her many questions. '*I never see him.* I looked at him twice or thrice about a year ago, before he recognised me, and then I shut my eyes; and if he were to cross their balls twelve times between each day's sunset and sunrise, except from memory, I should hardly know what shape had gone by.'

'Lucy, what do you mean?' said she, under her breath.

'I mean that I value vision, and dread being struck stone blind.' It was best to answer her strongly at once, and to silence for ever the tender, passionate confidences which left her lips, sweet honey, and sometimes dropped in my ear – molten lead. To me, she commented no more on her lover's beauty.

Yet speak of him she would; sometimes shyly in quiet, brief phrases; sometimes with a tenderness of cadence, and music of voice exquisite in itself, but which chafed me at times miserably; and then, I know, I gave her stern looks and words; but cloudless happiness had dazzled her native clear sight, and she only thought Lucy – fitful.

'Spartan girl! Proud Lucy!' she would say, smiling at me. 'Graham says you are the most peculiar, capricious little woman he knows; but yet you are excellent; we both think so.'

'You both think you know not what,' said I. 'Have the goodness to make me as little the subject of your mutual talk and thoughts as possible. I have my sort of life apart from yours.'

'But ours, Lucy, is a beautiful life, or it will be; and you shall share it.'

'I shall share no man's or woman's life in this world, as you understand sharing. I think I have one friend of my own, but am not sure; and till I *am* sure, I live solitary.'

'But solitude is sadness.'

'Yes; it is sadness. Life, however, has worse than that. Deeper than melancholy, lies heartbreak.'

'Lucy, I wonder if anybody will ever comprehend you altogether.'

There is, in lovers, a certain infatuation of egotism; they will have a witness of their happiness, cost that witness what it may. Paulina had forbidden letters, yet Dr Bretton wrote; she had resolved against correspondence, yet she answered, were it only to chide. She showed me these letters; with something of the spoiled child's wilfulness, and of the heiress's imperiousness, she *made* me read them. As I read Graham's, I scarce wondered at her exaction, and understood her pride: they were fine letters – manly and fond – modest and gallant. Hers must have appeared to him beautiful. They had not been written to show her talents; still

less, I think, to express her love. On the contrary, it appeared that she had proposed to herself the task of hiding that feeling, and bridling her lover's ardour. But how could such letters serve such a purpose? Graham was become dear as her life; he drew her like a powerful magnet. For her there was influence unspeakable in all he uttered, wrote, thought, or looked. With this unconfessèd confession, her letters glowed; it kindled them, from greeting to adieu.

'I wish papa knew; I *do* wish papa knew!' began now to be her anxious murmur. 'I wish, and yet I fear. I can hardly keep Graham back from telling him. There is nothing I long for more than to have this affair settled – to speak out candidly; and yet I dread the crisis. I know, I am certain, papa will be angry at the first; I fear he will dislike me almost; it will seem to him an untoward business; it will be a surprise, a shock; I can hardly foresee its whole effect on him.'

The fact was – her father, long calm, was beginning to be a little stirred: long blind on one point, an importunate light was beginning to trespass on his eye.

To *her*, he said nothing; but when she was not looking at, or perhaps thinking of him, I saw him gaze and meditate on her.

One evening – Paulina was in her dressing-room, writing, I believe, to Graham; she had left me in the library, reading – M. de Bassompierre came in; he sat down: I was about to withdraw; he requested me to remain – gently, yet in a manner which showed he wished compliance. He had taken his seat near the window, at a distance from me; he opened a desk; he took from it what looked like a memorandum-book; of this book he studied a certain entry for several minutes.

'Miss Snowe,' said he, laying it down, 'do you know my little girl's age?'

'About eighteen, is it not, sir?'

'It seems so. This old pocket-book tells me she was born on the 5th of May, in the year 18—, eighteen years ago. It is strange; I had lost the just reckoning of her age. I thought of her as twelve – fourteen – an indefinite date; but she seemed a child.'

'She is about eighteen,' I repeated. 'She is grown up; she will be no taller.'

'My little jewel!' said M. de Bassompierre, in a tone which penetrated like some of his daughter's accents.

He sat very thoughtful.

'Sir, don't grieve,' I said; for I knew his feelings, utterly unspoken as they were.

'She is the only pearl I have,' he said; 'and now others will find out that she is pure and of price; they will covet her.'

I made no answer. Graham Bretton had dined with us that day; he had shone both in converse and looks: I know not what pride of bloom embellished his aspect and mellowed his intercourse. Under the stimulus of a high hope, something had unfolded in his whole manner which compelled attention. I think he had purposed on that day to indicate the origin of his endeavours, and the aim of his ambition. M. de Bassompierre had found himself forced, in a manner, to descry the direction and catch the character of his homage. Slow in remarking, he was logical in reasoning; having once seized the thread, it had guided him through a long labyrinth.

'Where is she?' he asked.

'She is upstairs.'

'What is she doing?'

'She is writing.'

'She writes, does she? Does she receive letters?'

'None but such as she can show me. And – sir – she – *they* have long wanted to consult you.'

'Pshaw! They don't think of me – an old father! I am in the way.'

'Ah, M. de Bassompierre – not so – that can't be! But Paulina must speak for herself; and Dr Bretton, too, must be his own advocate.'

'It is a little late. Matters are advanced, it seems.'

'Sir, till you approve, nothing is done – only they love each other.'

'Only!' he echoed.

Invested by fate with the part of confidante and mediator, I was obliged to go on: 'Hundreds of times has Dr Bretton been on the point of appealing to you, sir; but, with all his high courage, he fears you mortally.'

'He may well – he may well fear me. He has touched the best thing I have. Had he but let her alone, she would have remained a child for years yet. So. Are they engaged?'

'They could not become engaged without your permission.'

'It is well for you, Miss Snowe, to talk and think with that propriety which always characterises you; but this matter is a grief to me; my little girl was all I had; I have no more daughters and no son; Bretton might as well have looked elsewhere; there are scores of rich and pretty women who would not, I dare say, dislike him; he has looks, and conduct, and connection. Would nothing serve him but my Polly?'

'If he had never seen your "Polly", others might and would have pleased him – your niece, Miss Fanshawe, for instance.'

'Ah! I would have given him Ginevra with all my heart; but Polly! – I can't let him have her. No – I can't. He is not her equal,' he affirmed, rather gruffly. 'In what particular is he her match? They talk of fortune! I am not an avaricious or interested man, but the world thinks of these things – and Polly will be rich.'

'Yes, that is known,' said I: 'all Villette knows her as an heiress.'

'Do they talk of my little girl in that light?'

'They do, sir.'

He fell into deep thought. I ventured to say: 'Would you, sir, think anyone Paulina's match? Would you prefer any other to Dr Bretton? Do you think higher rank or more wealth would make much difference in your feelings towards a future son-in-law?'

'You touch me there,' said he.

'Look at the aristocracy of Villette – you would not like them, sir?'

'I should not – never a duc, baron, or vicomte of the lot.'

'I am told many of these persons think about her, sir,' I went on, gaining courage on finding that I met attention rather than repulse. 'Other suitors will come, therefore, if Dr Bretton is refused. Wherever you go, I suppose, aspirants

will not be wanting. Independent of heiress-ship, it appears to me that Paulina charms most of those who see her.'

'Does she? How? My little girl is not thought a beauty.'

'Sir, Miss de Bassompierre is very beautiful.'

'Nonsense! – begging your pardon, Miss Snowe, but I think you are too partial. *I* like Polly: I like all her ways and all her looks – but then I am her father; and even *I* never thought about beauty. She is amusing, fairy-like, interesting to me; you must be mistaken in supposing her handsome?'

'She attracts, sir: she would attract without the advantages of your wealth and position.'

'My wealth and position! Are these any bait to Graham? If I thought so – '

'Dr Bretton knows these points perfectly, as you may be sure, M. de Bassompierre, and values them as any gentleman would – as *you* would yourself, under the same circumstances – but they are not his baits. He loves your daughter very much; he feels her finest qualities, and they influence him worthily.'

'What! has my little pet "fine qualities?"'

'Ah, sir! did you observe her that evening when so many men of eminence and learning dined here?'

'I certainly was rather struck and surprised with her manner that day; its womanliness made me smile.'

'And did you see those accomplished Frenchmen gather round her in the drawing-room?'

'I did; but I thought it was by way of relaxation – as one might amuse oneself with a pretty infant.'

'Sir, she demeaned herself with distinction; and I heard the French gentlemen say she was "pétrie d'esprit et de graces". Dr Bretton thought the same.'

'She is a good, dear child, that is certain; and I *do* believe she has some character. When I think of it, I was once ill; Polly nursed me; they thought I should die; she, I recollect, grew at once stronger and tenderer as I grew worse in health. And as I recovered, what a sunbeam she was in my sick-room! Yes; she played about my chair as noiseless and as cheerful as light. And now she is sought in marriage! I don't want to part with her,' said he, and he groaned.

'You have known Dr and Mrs Bretton so long,' I suggested, 'it would be less like separation to give her to him than to another.'

He reflected rather gloomily.

'True. I have long known Louisa Bretton,' he murmured. 'She and I are indeed old, old friends: a sweet, kind girl she was when she was young. You talk of beauty, Miss Snowe! *she* was handsome, if you will – tall, straight, and blooming – not the mere child or elf my Polly seems to me: at eighteen, Louisa had a carriage and stature fit for a princess. She is a comely and a good woman now. The lad is like her; I have always thought so, and favoured and wished him well. Now he repays me by this robbery! My little treasure used to love her old father dearly and truly. It is all over now, doubtless – I am an encumbrance.'

The door opened – his 'little treasure' came in. She was dressed, so to speak,

in evening beauty; that animation which sometimes comes with the close of day, warmed her eye and cheek; a tinge of summer crimson heightened her complexion; her curls fell full and long on her lily neck; her white dress suited the heat of June. Thinking me alone, she had brought in her hand the letter just written – brought it folded but unsealed. I was to read it. When she saw her father, her tripping step faltered a little, paused a moment – the colour in her cheek flowed rosy over her whole face.

'Polly,' said M. de Bassompierre, in a low voice, with a grave smile, 'do you blush at seeing papa? That is something new.'

'I don't blush – I never *do* blush,' affirmed she, while another eddy from the heart sent up its scarlet. 'But I thought you were in the dining-room, and I wanted Lucy.'

'You thought I was with John Graham Bretton, I suppose? But he has just been called out: he will be back soon, Polly. He can post your letter for you; it will save Matthieu a "course", as he calls it.'

'I don't post letters,' said she, rather pettishly.

'What do you do with them, then? – come here and tell me.'

Both her mind and gesture seemed to hesitate a second – to say 'Shall I come?' – but she approached.

'How long is it since you became a letter-writer, Polly? It only seems yesterday when you were at your pot-hooks, labouring away absolutely with both hands at the pen.'

'Papa, they are not letters to send to the post in your letter-bag; they are only notes, which I give now and then into the person's hand, just to satisfy.'

'The person! That means Miss Snowe, I suppose?'

'No, papa – not Lucy.'

'Who then? Perhaps Mrs Bretton?'

'No, papa – not Mrs Bretton.'

'Who then, my little daughter? Tell papa the truth.'

'Oh, papa!' she cried with earnestness, 'I will – I *will* tell you the truth – all the truth; I am glad to tell you – glad, though I tremble.'

She *did* tremble: growing excitement, kindling feeling, and also gathering courage, shook her.

'I hate to hide my actions from you, papa. I fear you and love you above everything but God. Read the letter; look at the address.'

She laid it on his knee. He took it up and read it through; his hand shaking, his eyes glistening meantime.

He re-folded it, and viewed the writer with a strange, tender, mournful amaze.

'Can *she* write so – the little thing that stood at my knee but yesterday? Can she feel so?'

'Papa, is it wrong? Does it pain you?'

'There is nothing wrong in it, my innocent little Mary; but it pains me.'

'But, papa, listen! You shall not be pained by me. I would give up everything – almost' (correcting herself): 'I would die rather than make you unhappy; that would be too wicked!'

She shuddered.

'Does the letter not please you? Must it not go? Must it be torn? It shall, for your sake, if you order it.'

'I order nothing.'

'Order something, papa; express your wish; only don't hurt, don't grieve Graham. I cannot, *cannot* bear that. I love you, papa; but I love Graham too, because – because – it is impossible to help it.'

'This splendid Graham is a young scamp, Polly – that is my present notion of him: it will surprise you to hear that, for my part, I do not love him one whit. Ah! years ago I saw something in that lad's eye I never quite fathomed – something his mother had not – a depth which warned a man not to wade into that stream too far; now, suddenly, I find myself taken over the crown of the head.'

'Papa, you don't – you have not fallen in; you are safe on the bank; you can do as you please; your power is despotic; you can shut me up in a convent, and break Graham's heart tomorrow, if you choose to be so cruel. Now autocrat, now czar, will you do this?'

'Off with him to Siberia, red whiskers and all; I say, I don't like him, Polly, and I wonder that you should.'

'Papa,' said she, 'do you know you are very naughty? I never saw you look so disagreeable, so unjust, so almost vindictive before. There is an expression in your face which does not belong to you.'

'Off with him!' pursued Mr Home, who certainly did look sorely crossed and annoyed – even a little bitter; 'but, I suppose, if he went, Polly would pack a bundle and run after him; her heart is fairly won – won, and weaned from her old father.'

'Papa, I say it is naughty, it is decidedly wrong, to talk in that way. I am *not* weaned from you, and no human being and no mortal influence *can* wean me.'

'Be married, Polly! Espouse the red whiskers. Cease to be a daughter; go and be a wife!'

'Red whiskers! I wonder what you mean, papa. You should take care of prejudice. You sometimes say to me that all the Scotch, your countrymen, are the victims of prejudice. It is proved now, I think, when no distinction is to be made between red and deep nut-brown.'

'Leave the prejudiced old Scotchman; go away.'

She stood looking at him a minute. She wanted to show firmness, superiority to taunts; knowing her father's character, guessing his few foibles, she had expected the sort of scene which was now transpiring; it did not take her by surprise, and she desired to let it pass with dignity, reliant upon reaction. Her dignity stood her in no stead. Suddenly her soul melted in her eyes; she fell on his neck: 'I won't leave you, papa; I'll never leave you. I won't pain you; I'll never pain you!' was her cry.

'My lamb! my treasure!' murmured the loving though rugged sire. He said no more for the moment; indeed, those two words were hoarse.

The room was now darkening; I heard a movement, a step without. Thinking it might be a servant coming with candles, I gently opened, to prevent intrusion.

In the ante-room stood no servant; a tall gentleman was placing his hat on the table, drawing off his gloves slowly – lingering, waiting, it seemed to me. He called me neither by sign nor word; yet his eye said: 'Lucy, come here.' And I went.

Over his face a smile flowed, while he looked down on me: no temper, save his own, would have expressed by a smile the sort of agitation which now fevered him.

'Mr de Bassompierre is there – is he not?' he enquired, pointing to the library.

'Yes.'

'He noticed me at dinner? He understood me?'

'Yes, Graham.'

'I am brought up for judgement, then, and so is *she*?'

'Mr Home' (we now and always continued to term him Mr Home at times) 'is talking to his daughter.'

'Ha! These are sharp moments, Lucy!'

He was quite stirred up; his young hand trembled; a vital (I was going to write *mortal*, but such words ill apply to one all living like him) – a vital suspense now held, now hurried, his breath: in all this trouble his smile never faded.

'Is he *very* angry, Lucy?'

'*She* is very faithful, Graham.'

'What will be done unto me?'

'Graham, your star must be fortunate.'

'Must it? Kind prophet! So cheered, I should be a faint heart indeed to quail. I think I find all women faithful, Lucy. I ought to love them, and I do. My mother is good; *she* is divine; and *you* are true as steel. Are you not?'

'Yes, Graham.'

'Then give me thy hand, my little god-sister; it is a friendly little hand to me, and always has been. And now for the great venture. God be with the right! Lucy, say, Amen!'

He turned, and waited till I said 'Amen!' – which I did to please him: the old charm, in doing as he bid me, came back. I wished him success; and successful I knew he would be. He was born victor, as some are born vanquished.

'Follow me!' he said; and I followed him into Mr Home's presence.

'Sir,' he asked, 'what is my sentence?'

The father looked at him; the daughter kept her face hid.

'Well, Bretton,' said Mr Home, 'you have given me the usual reward of hospitality. I entertained you; you have taken my best. I was always glad to see you; you were glad to see the one precious thing I had. You spoke me fair; and, meantime, I will not say you *robbed* me, but I am bereaved, and what I have lost, *you*, it seems, have won.'

'Sir, I cannot repent.'

'Repent! Not you! You triumph, no doubt: John Graham, you descended partly from a Highlander and a chief, and there is a trace of the Celt in all you look, speak, and think. You have his cunning and his charm. The red – (well,

then, Polly, the *fair)* hair, the tongue of guile, and brain of wile, are all come down by inheritance.'

'Sir, I *feel* honest enough,' said Graham; and a genuine English blush covered his face with its warm witness of sincerity. 'And yet,' he added, 'I won't deny that in some respects you accuse me justly. In your presence I have always had a thought which I dared not show you. I did truly regard you as the possessor of the most valuable thing the world owns for me. I wished for it; I tried for it. Sir, I ask for it now.'

'John, you ask much.'

'Very much, sir. It must come from your generosity, as a gift; from your justice, as a reward. I can never earn it.'

'Ay! Listen to the Highland tongue!' said Mr Home. 'Look up, Polly! Answer this "braw wooer"; send him away!'

She looked up. She shyly glanced at her eager, handsome suitor. She gazed tenderly on her furrowed sire.

'Papa, I love you both,' said she; 'I can take care of you both. I need not send Graham away – he can live here; he will be no inconvenience,' she alleged with that simplicity of phraseology which at times was wont to make both her father and Graham smile. They smiled now.

'He will be a prodigious inconvenience to me,' still persisted Mr Home. 'I don't want him, Polly; he is too tall; he is in my way. Tell him to march.'

'You will get used to him, papa. He seemed exceedingly tall to me at first – like a tower when I looked up at him; but, on the whole, I would rather not have him otherwise.'

'I object to him altogether, Polly; I can do without a son-in-law. I should never have requested the best man in the land to stand to me in that relation. Dismiss this gentleman.'

'But he has known you so long, papa, and suits you so well.'

'Suits *me*, forsooth! Yes; he has pretended to make my opinions and tastes his own. He has humoured me for good reasons. I think, Polly, you and I will bid him goodbye.'

'Till tomorrow only. Shake hands with Graham, papa.'

'No: I think not: I am not friends with him. Don't think to coax me between you.'

'Indeed, indeed, you *are* friends. Graham, stretch out your right hand. Papa, put out yours. Now, let them touch. Papa, don't be stiff; close your fingers; be pliant – there! But that is not a clasp – it is a grasp! Papa, you gripe like a vice. You crush Graham's hand to the bone; you hurt him!'

He must have hurt him; for he wore a massive ring, set round with brilliants, of which the sharp facets cut into Graham's flesh and drew blood: but pain only made Dr John laugh, as anxiety had made him smile.

'Come with me into my study,' at last said Mr Home to the doctor. They went. Their interview was not long, but I suppose it was conclusive. The suitor had to undergo an interrogatory and a scrutiny on many things. Whether Dr Bretton was at times guileful in look and language or not, there was a sound

foundation below. His answers, I understood afterwards, evinced both wisdom and integrity. He had managed his affairs well. He had struggled through entanglements; his fortunes were in the way of retrieval; he proved himself in a position to marry.

Once more the father and lover appeared in the library. M. de Bassompierre shut the door; he pointed to his daughter.

'Take her,' he said. 'Take her, John Bretton; and may God deal with you as you deal with her!'

Not long after, perhaps a fortnight, I saw three persons, Count de Bassompierre, his daughter, and Dr Graham Bretton, sitting on one seat, under a low-spreading and umbrageous tree, in the grounds of the palace at Bois l'Etang. They had come thither to enjoy a summer evening: outside the magnificent gates their carriage waited to take them home; the green sweeps of turf spread round them quiet and dim; the palace rose at a distance, white as a crag on Pentelicus; the evening star shone above it; a forest of flowering shrubs embalmed the climate of this spot; the hour was still and sweet; the scene, but for this group, was solitary.

Paulina sat between the two gentlemen; while they conversed, her little hands were busy at some work; I thought at first she was binding a nosegay. No; with the tiny pair of scissors, glittering in her lap, she had severed spoils from each manly head beside her, and was now occupied in plaiting together the gray lock and the golden wave. The plait woven – no silk-thread being at hand to bind it – a tress of her own hair was made to serve that purpose; she tied it like a knot, prisoned it in a locket, and laid it on her heart.

'Now,' said she, 'there is an amulet made, which has virtue to keep you two always friends. You can never quarrel so long as I wear this.'

An amulet was indeed made, a spell framed which rendered enmity impossible. She was become a bond to both, an influence over each, a mutual concord. From them she drew her happiness, and what she borrowed, she, with interest, gave back.

Is there, indeed, such happiness on earth? I asked, as I watched the father, the daughter, the future husband, now united – all blessed and blessing.

Yes; it is so. Without any colouring of romance, or any exaggeration of fancy, it is so. Some real lives do – for some certain days or years – actually anticipate the happiness of Heaven; and, I believe, if such perfect happiness is once felt by good people (to the wicked it never comes), its sweet effect is never wholly lost. Whatever trials follow, whatever pains of sickness or shades of death, the glory precedent still shines through, cheering the keen anguish, and tinging the deep cloud.

I will go farther. I *do* believe there are some human beings so born, so reared, so guided from a soft cradle to a calm and late grave, that no excessive suffering penetrates their lot, and no tempestuous blackness overcasts their journey. And often, these are not pampered, selfish beings, but natures elect, harmonious and benign; men and women mild with charity, kind agents of God's kind attributes.

Let me not delay the happy truth. Graham Bretton and Paulina de

Bassompierre were married, and such an agent did Dr Bretton prove. He did not with time degenerate; his faults decayed, his virtues ripened; he rose in intellectual refinement, he won in moral profit: all dregs filtered away, the clear wine settled bright and tranquil. Bright, too, was the destiny of his sweet wife. She kept her husband's love, she aided in his progress – of his happiness she was the corner stone.

This pair was blessed indeed, for years brought them, with great prosperity, great goodness; they imparted with open hand, yet wisely. Doubtless they knew crosses, disappointments, difficulties; but these were well borne. More than once, too, they had to look on Him whose face flesh scarce can see and live: they had to pay their tribute to the King of Terrors. In the fullness of years, M. de Bassompierre was taken; in ripe old age departed Louisa Bretton. Once even there rose a cry in their halls, of Rachel weeping for her children; but others sprang healthy and blooming to replace the lost: Dr Bretton saw himself live again in a son who inherited his looks and his disposition; he had stately daughters, too, like himself; these children he reared with a suave, yet a firm hand; they grew up according to inheritance and nurture.

In short, I do but speak the truth when I say that these two lives of Graham and Paulina were blessed, like that of Jacob's favoured son, with 'blessings of Heaven above, blessings of the deep that lies under.' It was so, for God saw that it was good.

## CHAPTER 38

## *Cloud*

But it is not so for all. What then? His will be done, as done it surely will be, whether we humble ourselves to resignation or not. The impulse of creation forwards it; the strength of powers, seen and unseen, has its fulfilment in charge. Proof of a life to come must be given. In fire and in blood, if needful, must that proof be written. In fire and in blood do we trace the record throughout nature. In fire and in blood does it cross our own experience. Sufferer, faint not through terror of this burning evidence. Tired wayfarer, gird up thy loins, look upward, march onward. Pilgrims and brother mourners, join in friendly company. Dark through the wilderness of this world stretches the way for most of us: equal and steady be our tread; be our cross our banner. For staff we have His promise, whose 'word is tried, whose way perfect:' for present hope His providence, 'who gives the shield of salvation, whose gentleness makes great;' for final home His bosom, who 'dwells in the height of Heaven;' for crowning prize a glory, exceeding and eternal. Let us so run that we may obtain; let us endure hardness as good soldiers; let us finish our course, and keep the faith, reliant in the issue to come off more than conquerors: 'Art thou not from everlasting mine Holy One? WE SHALL NOT DIE!'

On a Thursday morning we were all assembled in classe, waiting for the lesson of literature. The hour was come; we expected the master.

The pupils of the first classe sat very still; the cleanly-written compositions prepared since the last lesson lay ready before them, neatly tied with ribbon, waiting to be gathered by the hand of the professor as he made his rapid round of the desks. The month was July, the morning fine, the glass-door stood ajar, through it played a fresh breeze, and plants, growing at the lintel, waved, bent, looked in, seeming to whisper tidings.

M. Emanuel was not always quite punctual; we scarcely wondered at his being a little late, but we wondered when the door at last opened and, instead of him with his swiftness and his fire, there came quietly upon us, the cautious Mme Beck.

She approached M. Paul's desk; she stood before it; she drew round her the light shawl covering her shoulders; beginning to speak in low, yet firm tones, and with a fixed gaze, she said –

'This morning there will be no lesson of literature.'

The second paragraph of her address followed, after about two minutes' pause.

'It is probable the lessons will be suspended for a week. I shall require at least that space of time to find an efficient substitute for M. Emanuel. Meanwhile, it shall be our study to fill the blanks usefully.

'Your professor, ladies,' she went on, 'intends, if possible, duly to take leave of you. At the present moment he has not leisure for that ceremony. He is preparing for a long voyage. A very sudden and urgent summons of duty calls him to a great distance. He has decided to leave Europe for an indefinite time. Perhaps he may tell you more himself. Ladies, instead of the usual lesson with M. Emanuel, you will, this morning, read English with Mlle Lucy.'

She bent her head courteously, drew closer the folds of her shawl, and passed from the classe.

A great silence fell: then a murmur went round the room: I believe some pupils wept.

Some time elapsed. The noise, the whispering, the occasional sobbing increased. I became conscious of a relaxation of discipline, a sort of growing disorder, as if my girls felt that vigilance was withdrawn, and that surveillance had virtually left the classe. Habit and the sense of duty enabled me to rally quickly, to rise in my usual way, to speak in my usual tone, to enjoin, and finally to establish quiet. I made the English reading long and close. I kept them at it the whole morning. I remember feeling a sentiment of impatience towards the pupils who sobbed. Indeed, their emotion was not of much value; it was only an hysteric agitation. I told them so unsparingly. I half ridiculed them. I was severe. The truth was, I could not do with their tears, or that gasping sound; I could not bear it. A rather weak-minded, low-spirited pupil kept it up when the others had done; relentless necessity obliged and assisted me so to accost her, that she dared not carry on the demonstration, that she was forced to conquer the convulsion.

That girl would have had a right to hate me, except that, when school was over and her companions departing, I ordered her to stay, and when they were gone, I did what I had never done to one among them before – pressed her to my heart and kissed her cheek. But, this impulse yielded to, I speedily put her out of the classe, for, upon that poignant strain, she wept more bitterly than ever.

I filled with occupation every minute of that day, and should have liked to sit up all night if I might have kept a candle burning; the night, however, proved a bad time, and left bad effects, preparing me ill for the next day's ordeal of insufferable gossip. Of course this news fell under general discussion. Some little reserve had accompanied the first surprise: that soon wore off; every mouth opened; every tongue wagged; teachers, pupils, the very servants, mouthed the name of 'Emanuel'. He, whose connection with the school was contemporary with its commencement, thus suddenly to withdraw! All felt it strange.

They talked so much, so long, so often, that, out of the very multitude of their words and rumours, grew at last some intelligence. About the third day I heard it said that he was to sail in a week; then – that he was bound for the West Indies. I looked at Mme Beck's face, and into her eyes, for disproof or confirmation of this report; I perused her all over for information, but no part of her disclosed more than what was unperturbed and commonplace.

'This secession was an immense loss to her,' she alleged. 'She did not know how she should fill up the vacancy. She was so used to her kinsman, he had become her right hand; what should she do without him? She had opposed the step, but M. Paul had convinced her it was his duty.'

She said all this in public, in classe, at the dinner-table, speaking audibly to Zélie St Pierre.

'Why was it his duty?' I could have asked her that. I had impulses to take hold of her suddenly, as she calmly passed me in classe, to stretch out my hand and grasp her fast, and say, 'Stop. Let us hear the conclusion of the whole matter. *Why* is it his duty to go into banishment?' But Madame always addressed some other teacher, and never looked at me, never seemed conscious I could have a care in the question.

The week wore on. Nothing more was said about M. Emanuel coming to bid us goodbye; none seemed anxious for his coming; none questioned whether or not he would come; none betrayed torment lest he should depart silent and unseen; incessantly did they talk, and never, in all their talk, touched on this vital point. As to Madame, she of course could see him, and say to him as much as she pleased. What should *she* care whether or not he appeared in the schoolroom?

The week consumed. We were told that he was going on such a day, that his destination was 'Basseterre in Guadaloupe:' the business which called him abroad related to a friend's interests, not his own: I thought as much.

'Basseterre in Guadaloupe.' I had little sleep about this time, but whenever I *did* slumber, it followed infallibly that I was quickly roused with a start, while the words 'Basseterre', 'Guadaloupe', seemed pronounced over my pillow, or ran athwart the darkness around and before me, in zigzag characters of red or violet light.

For what I felt there was no help, and how could I help feeling? M. Emanuel had been very kind to me of late days; he had been growing hourly better and kinder. It was now a month since we had settled the theological difference, and in all that time there had been no quarrel. Nor had our peace been the cold daughter of divorce; we had not lived aloof; he had come oftener, he had talked with me more than before; he had spent hours with me, with temper soothed, with eye content, with manner home-like and mild. Kind subjects of conversation had grown between us; he had enquired into my plans of life, and I had communicated them; the school-project pleased him; he made me repeat it more than once, though he called it an Alnaschar dream. The jar was over; the mutual understanding was settling and fixing; feelings of union and hope made themselves profoundly felt in the heart; affection and deep esteem and dawning trust had each fastened its bond.

What quiet lessons I had about this time! No more taunts on my 'intellect,' no more menaces of grating public shows! How sweetly, for the jealous gibe, and the more jealous, half-passionate eulogy, were substituted a mute, indulgent help, a fond guidance, and a tender forbearance which forgave but never praised. There were times when he would sit for many minutes and not speak at all; and when dusk or duty brought separation, he would leave with words like these: 'Il est doux, le repos! Il est précieux, le calme bonheur!'

One evening, not ten short days since, he joined me whilst walking in my alley. He took my hand. I looked up in his face; I thought he meant to arrest my attention.

'Bonne petite amie!' said he, softly; 'douce consolatrice!' But through his touch, and with his words, a new feeling and a strange thought found a course. Could it be that he was becoming more than friend or brother? Did his look speak a kindness beyond fraternity or amity?

His eloquent look had more to say, his hand drew me forward, his interpreting lips stirred. No. Not now. Here into the twilight alley broke an interruption: it came dual and ominous: we faced two bodeful forms – a woman's and a priest's – Mme Beck and Père Silas.

The aspect of the latter I shall never forget. On the first impulse, it expressed a Jean-Jacques sensibility, stirred by the signs of affection just surprised; then, immediately, darkened over it the jaundice of ecclesiastical jealousy. He spoke to *me* with unction. He looked on his pupil with sternness. As to Mme Beck, she, of course, saw nothing – nothing; though her kinsman retained in her presence the hand of the heretic foreigner, not suffering withdrawal, but clasping it close and fast.

Following these incidents, that sudden announcement of departure had struck me at first as incredible. Indeed, it was only frequent repetition, and the credence of the hundred and fifty minds round me, which forced on me its full acceptance. As to that week of suspense, with its blank yet burning days, which brought from him no word of explanation – I remember, but I cannot describe its passage.

The last day broke. Now would he visit us. Now he would come and speak his farewell, or he would vanish mute, and be seen by us nevermore.

This alternative seemed to be present in the mind of not a living creature in that school. All rose at the usual hour; all breakfasted as usual; all, without reference to, or apparent thought of their late professor, betook themselves with wonted phlegm to their ordinary duties.

So oblivious was the house, so tame, so trained its proceedings, so inexpectant its aspect – I scarce knew how to breathe in an atmosphere thus stagnant, thus smothering. Would no one lend me a voice? Had no one a wish, no one a word, no one a prayer to which I could say – Amen?

I had seen them unanimous in demand for the merest trifle – a treat, a holiday, a lesson's remission; they could not, they *would* not now band to besiege Mme Beck, and insist on a last interview with a Master who had certainly been loved, at least by some – loved as *they* could love – but, oh! what is the love of the multitude?

I knew where he lived: I knew where he was to be heard of, or communicated with; the distance was scarce a stone's-throw; had it been in the next room – unsummoned, I could make no use of my knowledge. To follow, to seek out, to remind, to recall – for these things I had no faculty.

M. Emanuel might have passed within reach of my arm: had he passed silent and unnoticing – silent and stirless, should I have suffered him to go by.

Morning wasted. Afternoon came, and I thought all was over. My heart trembled in its place. My blood was troubled in its current. I was quite sick, and hardly knew how to keep at my post or do my work. Yet the little world round me plodded on indifferent; all seemed jocund, free of care, or fear, or thought: the very pupils who, seven days since, had wept hysterically at a startling piece of news, appeared quite to have forgotten the news, its import, and their emotion.

A little before five o'clock, the hour of dismissal, Mme Beck sent for me to her chamber, to read over and translate some English letter she had received, and to write for her the answer. Before settling to this work, I observed that she softly closed the two doors of her chamber; she even shut and fastened the casement, though it was a hot day, and free circulation of air was usually regarded by her as indispensable. Why this precaution? A keen suspicion, an almost fierce distrust, suggested such question. Did she want to exclude sound? what sound?

I listened as I had never listened before; I listened like the evening and winter-wolf, snuffing the snow, scenting prey, and hearing far off the traveller's tramp. Yet I could both listen and write. About the middle of the letter I heard – what checked my pen – a tread in the vestibule. No doorbell had rung; Rosine – acting doubtless by orders – had anticipated such reveillée. Madame saw me halt. She coughed, made a bustle, spoke louder. The tread had passed on to the classes.

'Proceed,' said Madame; but my hand was fettered, my ear enchained, my thoughts were carried off captive.

The classes formed another building; the hall parted them from the dwelling-house: despite distance and partition, I heard the sudden stir of numbers, a whole division rising at once.

'They are putting away work,' said Madame.

It was indeed the hour to put away work, but why that sudden hush – that instant quell of the tumult?

'Wait, madame – I will see what it is.'

And I put down my pen and left her. Left her? No: she would not be left: powerless to detain me, she rose and followed, close as my shadow. I turned on the last step of the stairs: 'Are you coming too?' I asked.

'Yes,' said she; meeting my glance with a peculiar aspect – a look, clouded, yet resolute. We proceeded then, not together, but she walked in my steps.

He was come. Entering the first classe, I saw him. There, once more appeared the form most familiar. I doubt not they had tried to keep him away, but he was come.

The girls stood in a semicircle; he was passing round, giving his farewells, pressing each hand, touching with his lips each cheek. This last ceremony, foreign custom permitted at such a parting – so solemn, to last so long.

I felt it hard that Mme Beck should dog me thus; following and watching me close, my neck and shoulder shrunk in fever under her breath; I became terribly goaded.

He was approaching; the semicircle was almost travelled round; he came to the last pupil; he turned. But Madame was before me; she had stepped out suddenly; she seemed to magnify her proportions and amplify her drapery; she eclipsed me; I was hid. She knew my weakness and deficiency; she could calculate the degree of moral paralysis – the total default of self-assertion – with which, in a crisis, I could be struck. She hastened to her kinsman, she broke upon him volubly, she mastered his attention, she hurried him to the door – the glass-door opening on the garden. I think he looked round; could I but have caught his eye, courage, I think, would have rushed in to aid feeling, and there would have been a charge, and, perhaps a rescue; but already the room was all confusion, the semicircle broken into groups, my figure was lost among thirty more conspicuous. Madame had her will; yes, she got him away, and he had not seen me; he thought me absent. Five o'clock struck, the loud dismissal bell rung, the school separated, the room emptied.

There seems, to my memory, an entire darkness and distraction in some certain minutes I then passed alone – a grief inexpressible over a loss unendurable. *What* should I do; oh! *what* should I do; when all my life's hope was thus torn by the roots out of my riven, outraged heart?

What I *should* have done, I know not, when a little child – the least child in the school – broke with its simplicity and its unconsciousness into the raging yet silent centre of that inward conflict.

'Mademoiselle,' lisped the treble voice, 'I am to give you that. M. Paul said I was to seek you all over the house, from the grenier to the cellar, and when I found you, to give you that.'

And the child delivered a note; the little dove dropped on my knee its olive-leaf plucked off. I found neither address nor name, only these words:

It was not my intention to take leave of you when I said goodbye to the rest, but I hoped to see you in classe. I was disappointed. The interview is deferred. Be ready for me. Ere I sail, I must see you at leisure, and speak with you at length. Be ready; my moments are numbered, and, just now, monopolised; besides I have a private business on hand which I will not share with any, nor communicate – even to you.

PAUL

'Be ready?' Then it must be this evening; was he not to go on the morrow? Yes; of that point I was certain. I had seen the date of his vessel's departure advertised. Oh! *I* would be ready, but could that longed-for meeting really be achieved? the time was so short, the schemers seemed so watchful, so active, so hostile; the way of access appeared strait as a gully, deep as a chasm – Apollyon straddled across it, breathing flames. Could my Greatheart overcome? Could my guide reach me?

Who might tell? Yet I began to take some courage, some comfort; it seemed to me that I felt a pulse of his heart beating yet true to the whole throb of mine.

I waited my champion. Apollyon came trailing his Hell behind him. I think if Eternity held torment, its form would not be fiery rack, nor its nature, despair. I think that on a certain day amongst those days which never dawned, and will not set, an angel entered Hades – stood, shone, smiled, delivered a prophecy of conditional pardon, kindled a doubtful hope of bliss to come, not now, but at a day and hour unlooked for, revealed in his own glory and grandeur the height and compass of his promise; spoke thus – then towering, became a star, and vanished into his own Heaven. His legacy was suspense – a worse boon than despair.

All that evening I waited, trusting in the dove-sent olive-leaf, yet in the midst of my trust, terribly fearing. My fear pressed heavy. Cold and peculiar, I knew it for the partner of a rarely-belied presentiment. The first hours seemed long and slow; in spirit I clung to the flying skirts of the last. They passed like drift cloud – like the rack scudding before a storm.

They passed. All the long, hot summer day burned away like a Yule-log; the crimson of its close perished; I was left bent among the cool blue shades, over the pale and ashen gleams of its night.

Prayers were over; it was bedtime; my co-inmates were all retired. I still remained in the gloomy first-classe, forgetting, or at least disregarding, rules I had never forgotten or disregarded before.

How long I paced that classe I cannot tell; I must have been afoot many hours; mechanically had I moved aside benches and desks, and had made for myself a path down its length. There I walked, and there, when certain that the whole household were abed, and quite out of hearing – there, I at last wept. Reliant on Night, confiding in Solitude, I kept my tears sealed, my sobs chained, no longer; they heaved my heart; they tore their way. In this house, what grief could be sacred?

Soon after eleven o'clock – a very late hour for the Rue Fossette – the door

unclosed, quietly but not stealthily; a lamp's flame invaded the moonlight; Mme Beck entered, with the same composed air, as if coming on an ordinary occasion, at an ordinary season. Instead of at once addressing me, she went to her desk, took her keys, and seemed to seek something; she loitered over this feigned search long, too long. She was calm, too calm; my mood scarce endured the pretence; driven beyond common range, two hours since I had left behind me wonted respects and fears. Led by a touch, and ruled by a word, under usual circumstances, no yoke could now be borne – no curb obeyed.

'It is more than time for retirement,' said Madame; 'the rule of the house has already been transgressed too long.'

Madame met no answer: I did not check my walk; when she came in my way, I put her out of it.

'Let me persuade you to calm, meess; let me lead you to your chamber,' said she, trying to speak softly.

'No!' I said; 'neither you nor another shall persuade or lead me.'

'Your bed shall be warmed. Goton is sitting up still. She shall make you comfortable: she shall give you a sedative.'

'Madame,' I broke out, 'you are a sensualist. Under all your serenity, your peace, and your decorum, you are an undenied sensualist. Make your own bed warm and soft; take sedatives, and meats and drinks spiced and sweet, as much as you will. If you have any sorrow or disappointment – and, perhaps, you have – nay, I *know* you have – seek your own palliatives, in your own chosen resources. Leave me, however. *Leave me*, I say!'

'I must send another to watch you, meess; I must send Goton.'

'I forbid it. Let me alone. Keep your hand off me, and my life, and my troubles. Oh, Madame! in *your* hand there is both chill and poison. You en-venom and you paralyse.'

'What have I done, meess? You must not marry Paul. He cannot marry.'

'Dog in the manger!' I said; for I knew she secretly wanted him, and had always wanted him. She called him 'insupportable;' she railed at him for a 'dévot'; she did not love, but she wanted to marry, that she might bind him to her interest. Deep into some of Madame's secrets I had entered – I know not how; by an intuition or an inspiration which came to me – I know not whence. In the course of living with her, too, I had slowly learned, that, unless with an inferior, she must ever be a rival. She was *my* rival, heart and soul, though secretly, under the smoothest bearing, and utterly unknown to all save her and myself.

Two minutes I stood over Madame, feeling that the whole woman was in my power, because in some moods, such as the present – in some stimulated states of perception, like that of this instant – her habitual disguise, her mask and her domino, were to me a mere network reticulated with holes; and I saw underneath a being heartless, self-indulgent, and ignoble. She quietly retreated from me; meek and self-possessed, though very uneasy, she said, 'If I would not be persuaded to take rest, she must reluctantly leave me.' Which she did incontinent, perhaps even more glad to get away, than I was to see her vanish.

This was the sole flash-eliciting, truth-extorting, rencontre which ever occurred between me and Mme Beck; this short night-scene was never repeated. It did not one whit change her manner to me. I do not know that she revenged it. I do not know that she hated me the worse for my fell candour. I think she bucklered herself with the secret philosophy of her strong mind, and resolved to forget what it irked her to remember. I know that to the end of our mutual lives there occurred no repetition of, no allusion to, that fiery passage.

That night passed: all nights – even the starless night before dissolution – must wear away. About six o'clock, the hour which called up the household, I went out to the court, and washed my face in its cold, fresh, well-water. Entering by the carré, a piece of mirror-glass, set in an oaken cabinet, repeated my image. It said I was changed; my cheeks and lips were sodden-white, my eyes were glassy, and my eyelids swollen and purple.

On rejoining my companions, I knew they all looked at me – my heart seemed discovered to them; I believed myself self-betrayed. Hideously certain did it seem that the very youngest of the school must guess why and for whom I despaired.

Isabelle, the child whom I had once nursed in sickness, approached me. Would she, too, mock me?

'Que vous êtes pâle! Vous êtes donc bien malade, mademoiselle!' said she, putting her finger in her mouth, and staring with a wistful stupidity which at the moment seemed to me more beautiful than the keenest intelligence.

Isabelle did not long stand alone in the recommendation of ignorance; before the day was over, I gathered cause of gratitude towards the whole blind household. The multitude have something else to do than to read hearts and interpret dark sayings. Who wills, may keep his own counsel – be his own secret's sovereign. In the course of that day, proof met me on proof, not only that the cause of my present sorrow was unguessed, but that my whole inner life for the last six months, was still mine only. It was not known – it had not been noted – that I held in peculiar value one life among all lives. Gossip had passed me by; curiosity had looked me over: both subtle influences, hovering always round, had never become centred upon me. A given organisation may live in a full fever-hospital, and escape typhus. M. Emanuel had come and gone; I had been taught and sought; in season and out of season he had called me, and I had obeyed him: 'M. Paul' – such had been the perpetual bulletin; and nobody commented, far less condemned. Nobody hinted, nobody jested. Mme Beck read the riddle; none else resolved it. What I now suffered was called illness – a headache: I accepted the baptism.

But what bodily illness was ever like this pain? This certainty that he was gone without a farewell – this cruel conviction that fate and pursuing furies – a woman's envy and a priest's bigotry – would suffer me to see him no more? What wonder that the second evening found me like the first – untamed, tortured, again pacing a solitary room in an unalterable passion of silent desolation?

Mme Beck did not herself summon me to bed that night – she did not come

near me; she sent Ginevra Fanshawe – a more efficient agent for the purpose she could not have employed. Ginevra's first words – 'Is your headache very bad tonight?' (for Ginevra, like the rest, thought I had a headache – an intolerable headache which made me frightfully white in the face, and insanely restless in the foot) – her first words, I say, inspired the impulse to flee anywhere, so that it were only out of reach. And soon, what followed – plaints about her own headaches – completed the business.

I went upstairs. Presently I was in my bed – my miserable bed – haunted with quick scorpions. I had not been laid down five minutes, when another emissary arrived: Goton came, bringing me something to drink. I was consumed with thirst – I drank eagerly; the beverage was sweet, but I tasted a drug.

'Madame says it will make you sleep, chou-chou,' said Goton, as she received back the emptied cup.

Ah! the sedative had been administered. In fact, they had given me a strong opiate. I was to be held quiet for one night.

The household came to bed, the night-light was lit, the dormitory hushed. Sleep soon reigned: over those pillows, sleep won an easy supremacy; contented sovereign over heads and hearts which did not ache – he passed by the unquiet.

The drug wrought. I know not whether Madame had over-charged or under-charged the dose; its result was not that she intended. Instead of stupor, came excitement. I became alive to new thought – to reverie peculiar in colouring. A gathering call ran among the faculties, their bugles sang, their trumpets rang an untimely summons. Imagination was roused from her rest, and she came forth impetuous and venturous. With scorn she looked on Matter, her mate –

'Rise!' she said. 'Sluggard! this night I will have *my* will; nor shalt thou prevail.'

'Look forth and view the night!' was her cry; and when I lifted the heavy blind from the casement close at hand – with her own royal gesture, she showed me a moon supreme, in an element deep and splendid.

To my gasping senses she made the glimmering gloom, the narrow limits, the oppressive heat of the dormitory, intolerable. She lured me to leave this den and follow her forth into dew, coolness, and glory.

She brought upon me a strange vision of Villette at midnight. Especially she showed the park, the summer-park, with its long alleys all silent, lone and safe; among these lay a huge stone basin – that basin I knew, and beside which I had often stood – deep-set in the tree-shadows, brimming with cool water, clear, with a green, leafy, rushy bed. What of all this? The park gates were shut up, locked, sentinelled; the place could not be entered.

Could it not? A point worth considering; and while revolving it, I mechanically dressed. Utterly incapable of sleeping or lying still – excited from head to foot – what could I do better than dress?

The gates were locked, soldiers set before them; was there, then, no admission to the park?

The other day, in walking past, I had seen, without then attending to the circumstance, a gap in the paling – one stake broken down: I now saw this gap

again in recollection – saw it very plainly – the narrow, irregular aperture visible between the stems of the lindens, planted orderly as a colonnade. A man could not have made his way through that aperture, nor could a stout woman, perhaps not Mme Beck; but I thought I might: I fancied I should like to try, and once within, at this hour the whole park would be mine – the moonlight, midnight park!

How soundly the dormitory slept! What deep slumbers! What quiet breathing! How very still the whole large house! What was the time? I felt restless to know. There stood a clock in the classe below; what hindered me from venturing down to consult it? By such a moon, its large white face and jet black figures must be vividly distinct.

As for hindrance to this step, there offered not so much as a creaking hinge or a clicking latch. On these hot July nights, close air could not be tolerated, and the chamber-door stood wide open. Will the dormitory-planks sustain my tread untraitorous? Yes. I know wherever a board is loose, and will avoid it. The oak staircase creaks somewhat as I descend, but not much: I am in the carré.

The great classe-doors are close shut; they are bolted. On the other hand, the entrance to the corridor stands open. The classes seem to my thought, great dreary jails, buried far back beyond thoroughfares, and for me, filled with spectral and intolerable memories, laid miserable amongst their straw and their manacles. The corridor offers a cheerful vista, leading to the high vestibule which opens direct upon the street.

Hush! – the clock strikes. Ghostly deep as is the stillness of this convent, it is only eleven. While my ear follows to silence the hum of the last stroke, I catch faintly from the built-out capital, a sound like bells or like a band – a sound where sweetness, where victory, where mourning blend. Oh, to approach this music nearer, to listen to it alone by the rushy basin! Let me go – oh, let me go! What hinders, what does not aid freedom?

There, in the corridor, hangs my garden-costume, my large hat, my shawl. There is no lock on the huge, heavy, porte-cochère; there is no key to seek; it fastens with a sort of spring-bolt, not to be opened from the outside, but which, from within, may be noiselessly withdrawn. Can I manage it? It yields to my hand, yields with propitious facility. I wonder as that great portal seems almost spontaneously to unclose; I wonder as I cross the threshold and step on the paved street, wonder at the strange ease with which this prison has been forced. It seems as if I had been pioneered invisibly, as if some dissolving force had gone before me; for myself, I have scarce made an effort.

Quiet Rue Fossette! I find on this pavement that wanderer-wooing summer night of which I mused; I see its moon over me; I feel its dew in the air. But here I cannot stay; I am still too near old haunts; so close under the dungeon, I can hear the prisoners moan. This solemn peace is not what I seek, it is not what I can bear; to me the face of that sky bears the aspect of a world's death. The park also will be calm – I know, a mortal serenity prevails everywhere – yet let me seek the park.

I took a route well-known, and went up towards the palatial and royal

Haute-Ville; thence the music I had heard, certainly floated; it was hushed now, but it might re-waken. I went on; neither band nor bell-music came to meet me; another sound replaced it, a sound like a strong tide, a great flow, deepening as I proceeded. Light broke, movement gathered, chimes pealed – to what was I coming? Entering on the level of a Grande Place, I found myself, with the suddenness of magic, plunged amidst a gay, living, joyous crowd.

Villette is one blaze, one broad illumination; the whole world seems abroad; moonlight and heaven are banished: the town, by her own flambeaux, beholds her own splendour – gay dresses, grand equipages, fine horses and gallant riders throng the bright streets. I see even scores of masks. It is a strange scene, stranger than dreams. But where is the park? – I ought to be near it. In the midst of this glare the park must be shadowy and calm – *there*, at least, are neither torches, lamps, nor crowd?

I was asking this question, when an open carriage passed me filled with known faces. Through the deep throng it could pass but slowly; the spirited horses fretted in their curbed ardour. I saw the occupants of that carriage well; me they could not see, or, at least, not know, folded close in my large shawl, screened with my straw hat (in that motley crowd no dress was noticeably strange). I saw the Count de Bassompierre; I saw my godmother, handsomely apparelled, comely and cheerful; I saw, too, Paulina Mary, compassed with the triple halo of her beauty, her youth, and her happiness. In looking on her countenance of joy, and eyes of festal light, one scarce remembered to note the gala elegance of what she wore; I know only that the drapery floating about her was all white and light and bridal: seated opposite to her I saw Graham Bretton; it was in looking up at him her aspect had caught its lustre – the light repeated in *her* eyes beamed first out of his.

It gave me strange pleasure to follow these friends viewlessly, and I *did* follow them, as I thought, to the park. I watched them alight (carriages were inadmissible) amidst new and unanticipated splendours. Lo! the iron gateway, between the stone columns, was spanned by a flaming arch built of massed stars; and, following them cautiously beneath that arch, where were they, and where was I?

In a land of enchantment, a garden most gorgeous, a plain sprinkled with coloured meteors, a forest with sparks of purple and ruby and golden fire gemming the foliage; a region, not of trees and shadow, but of strangest architectural wealth – of altar and of temple, of pyramid, obelisk, and sphynx; incredible to say, the wonders and the symbols of Egypt teemed throughout the park of Villette.

No matter that in five minutes the secret was mine – the key of the mystery picked up, and its illusion unveiled – no matter that I quickly recognised the material of these solemn fragments – the timber, the paint, and the pasteboard – these inevitable discoveries failed to quite destroy the charm, or undermine the marvel of that night. No matter that I now seized the explanation of the whole great fête – a fête of which the conventual Rue Fossette had not tasted, though it had opened at dawn that morning, and was still in full vigour near midnight.

In past days there had been, said history, an awful crisis in the fate of Labassecour, involving I know not what peril to the rights and liberties of her gallant citizens. Rumours of wars, there had been, if not wars themselves; a kind of struggling in the streets – a bustle – a running to and fro, some rearing of barricades, some burgher-rioting, some calling out of troops, much interchange of brick-bats, and even a little of shot. Tradition held that patriots had fallen: in the old Basse-Ville was shown an enclosure, solemnly built in and set apart, holding, it was said, the sacred bones of martyrs. Be this as it may, a certain day in the year was still kept as a festival in honour of the said patriots and martyrs of somewhat apocryphal memory – the morning being given to a solemn *Te Deum* in St Jean Baptiste, the evening devoted to spectacles, decorations, and illuminations, such as these I now saw.

While looking up at the image of a white ibis, fixed on a column – while fathoming the deep, torch-lit perspective of an avenue, at the close of which was couched a sphinx – I lost sight of the party which, from the middle of the great square, I had followed – or, rather, they vanished like a group of apparitions. On this whole scene was impressed a dream-like character; every shape was wavering, every movement floating, every voice echo-like – half-mocking, half-uncertain. Paulina and her friends being gone, I scarce could avouch that I had really seen them; nor did I miss them as guides through the chaos, far less regret them as protectors amidst the night.

That festal night would have been safe for a very child. Half the peasantry had come in from the outlying environs of Villette, and the decent burghers were all abroad and around, dressed in their best. My straw-hat passed amidst cap and jacket, short petticoat, and long calico mantle, without, perhaps, attracting a glance; I only took the precaution to bind down the broad leaf gypsy-wise, with a supplementary ribbon; and then I felt safe as if masked.

Safe I passed down the avenues – safe I mixed with the crowd where it was deepest. To be still was not in my power, nor quietly to observe. I took a revel of the scene; I drank the elastic night-air – the swell of sound, the dubious light, now flashing, now fading. As to Happiness or Hope, they and I had shaken hands, but just now – I scorned Despair.

My vague aim, as I went, was to find the stone basin, with its clear depth and green lining: of that coolness and verdure I thought, with the passionate thirst of unconscious fever. Amidst the glare, and hurry, and throng, and noise, I still secretly and chiefly longed to come on that circular mirror of crystal, and surprise the moon glassing therein her pearly front.

I knew my route, yet it seemed as if I was hindered from pursuing it direct: now a sight, and now a sound, called me aside, luring me down this alley and down that. Already I saw the thick-planted trees which framed this tremulous and rippled glass, when, choiring out of a glade to the right, broke such a sound as I thought might be heard if Heaven were to open – such a sound, perhaps, as *was* heard above the plain of Bethlehem, on the night of glad tidings.

The song, the sweet music, rose afar, but rushing swiftly on fast-strengthening pinions – there swept through these shades so full a storm of harmonies that, had

no tree been near against which to lean, I think I must have dropped. Voices were there, it seemed to me, unnumbered; instruments varied and countless – bugle, horn, and trumpet I knew. The effect was as a sea breaking into song with all its waves.

The swaying tide swept this way, and then it fell back, and I followed its retreat. It led me towards a Byzantine building – a sort of kiosk near the park's centre. Round about stood crowded thousands, gathered to a grand concert in the open air. What I had heard was, I think, a wild Jager chorus; the night, the space, the scene, and my own mood, had but enhanced the sounds and their impression.

Here were assembled ladies, looking by this light most beautiful; some of their dresses were gauzy, and some had the sheen of satin; the flowers and the blond trembled, and the veils waved about their decorated bonnets, as that host-like chorus, with its greatly-gathering sound, sundered the air above them. Most of these ladies occupied the little light park-chairs, and behind and beside them stood guardian gentlemen. The outer ranks of the crowd were made up of citizens, plebeians and police.

In this outer rank I took my place. I rather liked to find myself the silent, unknown, consequently unaccosted neighbour of the short petticoat and the sabot; and only the distant gazer at the silk robe, the velvet mantle, and the plumed chapeau. Amidst so much life and joy, too, it suited me to be alone – quite alone. Having neither wish nor power to force my way through a mass so close-packed, my station was on the farthest confines, where, indeed, I might hear, but could see little.

'Mademoiselle is not well placed,' said a voice at my elbow. Who dared accost *me*, a being in a mood so little social? I turned, rather to repel than to reply. I saw a man – a burgher – an entire stranger, as I deemed him for one moment, but the next, recognised in him a certain tradesman – a bookseller, whose shop furnished the Rue Fossette with its books and stationery; a man notorious in our pensionnat for the excessive brittleness of his temper, and frequent snappishness of his manner, even to us, his principal customers; but whom, for my solitary self, I had ever been disposed to like, and had always found civil, sometimes kind; once, in aiding me about some troublesome little exchange of foreign money, he had done me a service. He was an intelligent man; under his asperity, he was a good-hearted man; the thought had sometimes crossed me, that a part of his nature bore affinity to a part of M. Emanuel's, (whom he knew well, and whom I had often seen sitting on Miret's counter, turning over the current month's publications); and it was in this affinity I read the explanation of that conciliatory feeling with which I instinctively regarded him.

Strange to say, this man knew me under my straw-hat and closely-folded shawl; and, though I deprecated the effort, he insisted on making a way for me through the crowd, and finding me a better situation. He carried his disinterested civility further, and, from some quarter, procured me a chair. Once and again, I have found that the most cross-grained are by no means the worst of mankind; nor the humblest in station, the least polished in feeling. This man, in his

courtesy, seemed to find nothing strange in my being here alone; only a reason for extending to me, as far as he could, a retiring, yet efficient attention. Having secured me a place and a seat, he withdrew without asking a question, without obtruding a remark, without adding a superfluous word. No wonder that Professor Emanuel liked to take his cigar and his lounge, and to read his feuilleton in M. Miret's shop; the two must have suited.

I had not been seated five minutes, ere I became aware that chance and my worthy burgher friend had brought me once more within view of a familiar and domestic group. Right before me sat the Brettons and De Bassompierres. Within reach of my hand – had I chosen to extend it – sat a figure like a fairy-queen, whose array, lilies and their leaves seemed to have suggested; whatever was not spotless white, being forest-green. My godmother, too, sat so near, that, had I leaned forward, my breath might have stirred the ribbon of her bonnet. They were too near; having been just recognised by a comparative stranger, I felt uneasy at this close vicinage of intimate acquaintance.

It made me quite start when Mrs Bretton, turning to Mr Home, and speaking out of a kind impulse of memory, said – 'I wonder what my steady little Lucy would say to all this if she were here? I wish we had brought her, she would have enjoyed it much.'

'So she would, so she would, in her grave sensible fashion; it is a pity but we had asked her,' rejoined the kind gentleman; and added, 'I like to see her so quietly pleased; so little moved, yet so content.'

Dear were they both to me, dear are they to this day in their remembered benevolence. Little knew they the rack of pain which had driven Lucy almost into fever, and brought her out, guideless and reckless, urged and drugged to the brink of frenzy. I had half a mind to bend over the elders' shoulders, and answer their goodness with the thanks of my eyes. M. de Bassompierre did not well know *me*, but I knew *him*, and honoured and admired his nature, with all its plain sincerity, its warm affection, and unconscious enthusiasm. Possibly I might have spoken, but just then Graham turned, he turned with one of his stately firm movements, so different from those of a sharp-tempered undersized man; there was behind him a throng, a hundred ranks deep; there were thousands to meet his eye and divide its scrutiny – why then did he concentrate all on me – oppressing me with the whole force of that full, blue, steadfast orb? Why, if he *would* look, did not one glance satisfy him? why did he turn on his chair, rest his elbow on its back, and study me leisurely? He could not see my face, I held it down; surely, he *could* not recognise me; I stooped, I turned, I *would* not be known. He rose, by some means he contrived to approach, in two minutes he would have had my secret; my identity would have been grasped between his never tyrannous, but always powerful hands. There was but one way to evade or to check him. I implied, by a sort of supplicatory gesture, that it was my prayer to be let alone; after that, had he persisted, he would perhaps have seen the spectacle of Lucy incensed: not all that was grand, or good, or kind in him (and Lucy felt the full amount) should have kept her quite tame, or absolutely inoffensive and shadowlike. He looked, but he desisted. He shook his handsome head, but he was mute. He resumed his seat, nor

did he again turn or disturb me by a glance, except indeed for one single instant, when a look, rather solicitous than curious, stole my way – speaking what somehow stilled my heart like 'the south-wind quieting the earth.' Graham's thoughts of me were not entirely those of a frozen indifference, after all. I believe in that goodly mansion, his heart, he kept one little place under the skylights where Lucy might have entertainment, if she chose to call. It was not so handsome as the chambers where he lodged his male friends; it was not like the hall where he accommodated his philanthropy, or the library where he treasured his science, still less did it resemble the pavilion where his marriage feast was splendidly spread; yet, gradually, by long and equal kindness, he proved to me that he kept one little closet, over the door of which was written 'Lucy's Room'. I kept a place for him, too – a place of which I never took the measure, either by rule or compass: I think it was like the tent of Peri-Banou. All my life long I carried it folded in the hollow of my hand – yet, released from that hold and constriction, I know not but its innate capacity for expanse might have magnified it into a tabernacle for a host.

Forbearing as he was tonight, I could not stay in this proximity; this dangerous place and seat must be given up; I watched my opportunity, rose, and stole away. He might think, he might even believe that Lucy was contained within that shawl, and sheltered under that hat; he could never be certain, for he did not see my face.

Surely the spirit of restlessness was by this time appeased? Had I not had enough of adventure? Did I not begin to flag, quail, and wish for safety under a roof? Not so. I still loathed my bed in the school-dormitory more than words can express; I clung to whatever could distract thought. Somehow I felt, too, that the night's drama was but begun, that the prologue was scarce spoken: throughout this woody and turfy theatre reigned a shadow of mystery; actors and incidents unlooked-for, waited behind the scenes: I thought so: foreboding told me as much.

Straying at random, obeying the push of every chance elbow, I was brought to a quarter where trees planted in clusters, or towering singly, broke up somewhat the dense packing of the crowd, and gave it a more scattered character. These confines were far from the music, and somewhat aloof even from the lamps, but there was sound enough to soothe, and with that full, high moon, lamps were scarce needed. Here had chiefly settled family-groups, burgher-parents; some of them, late as was the hour, actually surrounded by their children, with whom it had not been thought advisable to venture into the closer throng.

Three fine tall trees growing close, almost twined stem within stem, lifted a thick canopy of shade above a green knoll, crowned with a seat – a seat which might have held several, yet it seemed abandoned to one, the remaining members of the fortunate party in possession of this site standing dutifully round; yet, amongst this reverent circle was a lady, holding by the hand a little girl.

When I caught sight of this little girl, she was twisting herself round on her heel, swinging from her conductress's hand, flinging herself from side to side

with wanton and fantastic gyrations. These perverse movements arrested my attention, they struck me as of a character fearfully familiar. On close inspection, no less so appeared the child's equipment; the lilac silk pelisse, the small swansdown boa, the white bonnet – the whole holiday toilette, in short, was the gala garb of a cherub but too-well known, of that tadpole, Désirée Beck – and Désirée Beck it was – she, or an imp in her likeness.

I might have taken this discovery as a thunderclap, but such hyperbole would have been premature; discovery was destined to rise more than one degree, ere it reached its climax.

On whose hand could the amiable Désirée swing thus selfishly, whose glove could she tear thus recklessly, whose arm thus strain with impunity, or on the borders of whose dress thus turn and trample insolently, if not the hand, glove, arm, and robe of her lady-mother? And there, in an Indian shawl and a pale-green crape bonnet – there, fresh, portly, blithe, and pleasant – there stood Mme Beck.

Curious! I had certainly deemed Madame in her bed, and Désirée in her crib, at this blessed minute, sleeping, both of them, the sleep of the just, within the sacred walls, amidst the profound seclusion of the Rue Fossette. Most certainly also they did not picture 'Meess Lucie' otherwise engaged; and here we all three were taking our 'ébats' in the fête-blazing park at midnight!

The fact was, Madame was only acting according to her quite justifiable wont. I remembered now I had heard it said among the teachers – though without at the time particularly noticing the gossip – that often, when we thought Madame in her chamber, sleeping, she was gone, full-dressed, to take her pleasure at operas, or plays, or balls. Madame had no sort of taste for a monastic life, and took care – largely, though discreetly – to season her existence with a relish of the world.

Half a dozen gentlemen of her friends stood about her. Amongst these, I was not slow to recognise two or three. There was her brother, M. Victor Kint; there was another person, moustached and with long hair – a calm, taciturn man, but whose traits bore a stamp and a semblance I could not mark unmoved. Amidst reserve and phlegm, amidst contrasts of character and of countenance, something there still was which recalled a face – mobile, fervent, feeling – a face changeable, now clouded, and now alight – a face from my world taken away, for my eyes lost, but where my best spring-hours of life had alternated in shadow and in glow – that face, where I had often seen movements, so near the signs of genius – that why there did not shine fully out, the undoubted fire, the thing, the spirit, and the secret itself – I could never tell. Yes – this Josef Emanuel – this man of peace – reminded me of his ardent brother.

Besides Messieurs Victor and Josef, I knew another of this party. This third person stood behind and in the shade, his attitude too was stooping, yet his dress and bald white head made him the most conspicuous figure of the group. He was an ecclesiastic: he was Père Silas. Do not fancy, reader, that there was any inconsistency in the priest's presence at this fête. This was not considered a show of Vanity Fair, but a commemoration of patriotic sacrifice. The Church patronised it, even with ostentation. There were troops of priests in the park that night.

Père Silas stooped over the seat with its single occupant, the rustic bench and that which sat upon it: a strange mass it was – bearing no shape, yet magnificent. You saw, indeed, the outline of a face and features, but these were so cadaverous and so strangely placed, you could almost have fancied a head severed from its trunk, and flung at random on a pile of rich merchandise. The distant lamp-rays glanced on clear pendants, on broad rings; neither the chasteness of moonlight, nor the distance of the torches, could quite subdue the gorgeous dyes of the drapery. Hail, Mme Walravens! I think you looked more witch-like than ever. And presently the good lady proved that she was indeed no corpse or ghost, but a harsh and hardy old woman; for, upon some aggravation in the clamorous petition of Désirée Beck to her mother, to go to the kiosk and take sweetmeats, the hunchback suddenly fetched her a resounding rap with her gold-knobbed cane.

There, then, were Mme Walravens, Mme Beck, Père Silas – the whole conjuration, the secret junta. The sight of them thus assembled did me good. I cannot say that I felt weak before them, or abashed, or dismayed. They outnumbered me, and I was worsted and under their feet; but, as yet, I was not dead.

CHAPTER 39

## Old and New Acquaintance

Fascinated as by a basilisk with three heads, I could not leave this clique; the ground near them seemed to hold my feet. The canopy of entwined trees held out shadow, the night whispered a pledge of protection, and an officious lamp flashed just one beam to show me an obscure, safe seat, and then vanished. Let me now briefly tell the reader all that, during the past dark fortnight, I have been silently gathering from Rumour, respecting the origin and the object of M. Emanuel's departure. The tale is short, and not new: its alpha is Mammon, and its omega, Interest.

If Mme Walravens was hideous as a Hindu idol, she seemed also to possess, in the estimation of these her votaries, an idol's consequence. The fact was, she had been rich – very rich; and though for the present, without the command of money, she was likely one day to be rich again. At Basseterre, in Guadaloupe, she possessed a large estate, received in dowry on her marriage sixty years ago, sequestered since her husband's failure; but now, it was supposed, cleared of claim, and, if duly looked after by a competent agent of integrity, considered capable of being made, in a few years, largely productive.

Père Silas took an interest in this prospective improvement for the sake of religion and the church, whereof Magloire Walravens was a devout daughter. Mme Beck, distantly related to the hunchback, and knowing her to be without family of her own, had long brooded over contingencies with a mother's calculating forethought, and, harshly treated as she was by Mme Walravens, never ceased to court her for interest's sake. Mme Beck and the priest were thus, for

money reasons, equally and sincerely interested in the nursing of the West-Indian estate.

But the distance was great, and the climate hazardous. The competent and upright agent wanted, must be a devoted man. Just such a man had Mme Walravens retained for twenty years in her service, blighting his life, and then living on him, like an old fungus; such a man had Père Silas trained, taught, and bound to him by the ties of gratitude, habit, and belief. Such a man Mme Beck knew, and could in some measure influence. 'My pupil,' said Père Silas, 'if he remains in Europe, runs risk of apostasy, for he has become entangled with a heretic.' Mme Beck made also her private comment, and preferred in her own heart her secret reason for desiring expatriation. The thing she could not obtain, she desired not another to win; rather would she destroy it. As to Mme Walravens, she wanted her money and her land, and knew Paul, if he liked, could make the best and faithfullest steward: so the three self-seekers banded and beset the one unselfish. They reasoned, they appealed, they implored; on his mercy they cast themselves, into his hands they confidingly thrust their interests. They asked but two or three years of devotion – after that, he should live for himself: one of the number, perhaps, wished that in the mean time he might die.

No living being ever humbly laid his advantage at M. Emanuel's feet, or confidingly put it into his hands, that he spurned the trust, or repulsed the repository. What might be his private pain or inward reluctance to leave Europe – what his calculations for his own future – none asked, or knew, or reported. All this was a blank to me. His conferences with his confessor I might guess; the part duty and religion were made to play in the persuasions used, I might conjecture. He was gone, and had made no sign. There my knowledge closed.

With my head bent, and my forehead resting on my hands, I sat amidst grouped tree-stems and branching brushwood. Whatever talk passed amongst my neighbours, I might hear, if I would; I was near enough; but, for some time, there was scarce motive to attend. They gossiped about the dresses, the music, the illuminations, the fine night. I listened to hear them say, 'It is calm weather for *his* voyage; the "Antigua" (his ship) 'will sail prosperously.' No such remark fell: neither the 'Antigua,' nor her course, nor her passenger, were named.

Perhaps the light chat scarcely interested old Mme Walravens more than it did me; she appeared restless, turning her head now to this side, now that, looking through the trees, and among the crowd, as if expectant of an arrival and impatient of a delay. 'Où sont-ils? Pourquoi ne viennent-ils?' I heard her mutter more than once; and at last, as if determined to have an answer to her questions – which hitherto none seemed to mind, she spoke aloud this phrase – a phrase brief enough, simple enough, but it sent a shock through me – 'Messieurs et mesdames,' said she, 'où donc est Justine Marie?'

'Justine Marie!' What name was this? Justine Marie – the dead nun – where was she? Why in her grave, Mme Walravens – what can you want with her? You shall go to her, but she shall not come to you.

Thus *I* should have answered, had the response lain with me, but nobody seemed to be of my mind; nobody seemed surprised, startled, or at a loss. The quietest commonplace answer met the strange, the dead-disturbing, the Witch-of-Endor query of the hunchback.

'Justine Marie,' said one, 'is coming; she is in the kiosk; she will be here presently.'

Out of this question and reply sprang a change in the chat – chat it still remained – easy, desultory, familiar gossip. Hint, allusion, comment, went round the circle, but all so broken, so dependent on references to persons not named, or circumstances not defined, that, listen intently as I would – and I *did* listen *now* with a fated interest – I could make out no more than that some scheme was on foot, in which this ghostly Justine Marie – dead or alive – was concerned. This family-junta seemed grasping at her somehow, for some reason; there seemed question of a marriage, of a fortune, for whom I could not quite make out – perhaps for Victor Kint, perhaps for Josef Emanuel – both were bachelors. Once I thought the hints and jests rained upon a young fair-haired foreigner of the party, whom they called Heinrich Mühler. Amidst all the badinage, Mme Walravens still obtruded, from time to time, hoarse, cross-grained speeches; her impatience being diverted only by an implacable surveillance of Désirée, who could not stir but the old woman menaced her with her staff.

'Là voilà!' suddenly cried one of the gentlemen, 'voilà Justine Marie qui arrive!'

This moment was for me peculiar. I called up to memory the pictured nun on the panel; present to my mind was the sad love-story; I saw in thought the vision of the garret, the apparition of the alley, the strange birth of the berceau: I underwent a presentiment of discovery, a strong conviction of coming disclosure. Ah! when imagination once runs riot where do we stop? What winter tree so bare and branchless – what wayside, hedge-munching animal so humble, that Fancy, a passing cloud, and a struggling moonbeam, will not clothe it in spirituality, and make of it a phantom?

With solemn force pressed on my heart the expectation of mystery breaking up: hitherto I had seen this spectre only through a glass darkly; now was I to behold it face to face. I leaned forward: I looked.

'She comes!' cried Josef Emanuel.

The circle moved as if opening to admit a new and welcome member. At this instant a torch chanced to be carried past; its blaze aided the pale moon in doing justice to the crisis, in lighting to perfection the dénouement pressing on. Surely those near me must have felt some little of the anxiety I felt, in degree so unmeted. Of that group, the coolest must have 'held his breath for a time!' As for me, my life stood still.

It is over. The moment and the nun are come. The crisis and the revelation are passed by.

The flambeau glares still within a yard, held up in a parkkeeper's hand; its long eager tongue of flame almost licks the figure of the Expected – there – where she stands full in my sight. What is she like? What does she wear? How does she look? Who is she?

There are many masks in the Park tonight, and as the hour wears late, so strange a feeling of revelry and mystery begins to spread abroad, that scarce would you discredit me, reader, were I to say that she is like the nun of the attic, that she wears black skirts and white head-clothes, that she looks the resurrection of the flesh, and that she is a risen ghost.

All falsities – all figments! We will not deal in this gear. Let us be honest, and cut, as heretofore, from the homely web of truth.

*Homely*, though, is an ill-chosen word. What I see is not precisely homely. A girl of Villette stands there – a girl fresh from her pensionnat. She is very comely, with the beauty indigenous to this country; she looks well-nourished, fair, and fat of flesh. Her cheeks are round, her eyes good; her hair is abundant. She is handsomely dressed. She is not alone; her escort consists of three persons – two being elderly; these she addresses as 'Mon Oncle' and 'Ma Tante'. She laughs, she chats: good-humoured, buxom, and blooming, she looks, at all points, the bourgeoise belle.

So much for 'Justine Marie'; so much for ghosts and mystery: not that this last was solved – this girl certainly is not my nun; what I saw in the garret and garden must have been taller by a span.

We have looked at the city belle; we have cursorily glanced at the respectable old uncle and aunt. Have we a stray glance to give to the third member of this company? Can we spare him a moment's notice? We ought to distinguish him so far, reader; he has claims on us; we do not now meet him for the first time. I clasped my hands very hard, and I drew my breath very deep; I held in the cry, I devoured the ejaculation, I forbade the start, I spoke and I stirred no more than a stone; but I knew what I looked on; through the dimness left in my eyes by many nights' weeping, I knew him. They said he was to sail by the 'Antigua.' Mme Beck said so. She lied, or she had uttered what was once truth, and failed to contradict it, when it became false. The 'Antigua' was gone, and there stood Paul Emanuel .

Was I glad? A huge load left me. Was it a fact to warrant joy? I know not. Ask first what were the circumstances attendant on this respite? How far did this delay concern *me*? Were there not those whom it might touch more nearly?

After all, who may this young girl, this Justine Marie be? Not a stranger, reader; she is known to me by sight; she visits at the Rue Fossette; she is often of Mme Beck's Sunday parties. She is a relation of both the Becks and Walravens; she derives her baptismal name from the sainted nun who would have been her aunt had she lived; her patronymic is Sauveur; she is an heiress and an orphan, and M. Emanuel is her guardian; some say her godfather. The family junta wish this heiress to be married to one of their band – which is it? Vital question – which is it?

I felt very glad now, that the drug administered in the sweet draught had filled me with a possession which made bed and chamber intolerable. I always, through my whole life, liked to penetrate to the real truth; I like seeking the goddess in her temple, and handling the veil, and daring the dread glance. O Titaness amongst deities! The covered outline of thine aspect sickens often

through its uncertainty, but define to us one trait, show us one lineament, clear in awful sincerity; we may gasp in untold terror, but with that gasp we drink in a breath of thy divinity; our heart shakes, and its currents sway like rivers lifted by earthquake, but we have swallowed strength. To see and know the worst is to take from Fear her main advantage.

The Walravens' party, augmented in numbers, now became very gay. The gentlemen fetched refreshments from the kiosk, all sat down on the turf under the trees; they drank healths and sentiments; they laughed, they jested. M. Emanuel underwent some raillery, half good-humoured, half, I thought, malicious, especially on Mme Beck's part. I soon gathered that his voyage had been temporarily deferred of his own will, without the concurrence, even against the advice of his friends; he had let the 'Antigua' go, and had taken his berth in the 'Paul et Virginie', appointed to sail a fortnight later. It was his reason for this resolve which they teased him to assign, and which he would only vaguely indicate as 'the settlement of a little piece of business which he had set his heart upon.' What *was* this business? Nobody knew. Yes, there was one who seemed partly, at least, in his confidence; a meaning look passed between him and Justine Marie. 'La petite va m'aider – n'est-ce pas?' said he. The answer was prompt enough, God knows!

'Mais oui, je vous aiderai de tout mon cœur. Vous ferez de moi tout ce que vous voudrez, mon parrain.'

And this dear 'parrain' took her hand and lifted it to his grateful lips. Upon which demonstration, I saw the light-complexioned young Teuton, Heinrich Mühler, grow restless, as if he did not like it. He even grumbled a few words, whereat M. Emanuel actually laughed in his face, and with the ruthless triumph of the assured conqueror, he drew his ward nearer to him.

M. Emanuel was indeed very joyous that night. He seemed not one whit subdued by the change of scene and action impending. He was the true life of the party; a little despotic perhaps, determined to be chief in mirth, as well as in labour, yet from moment to moment proving indisputably his right of leadership. His was the wittiest word, the pleasantest anecdote, the frankest laugh. Restlessly active, after his manner, he multiplied himself to wait on all; but oh! I saw which was his favourite. I saw at whose feet he lay on the turf, I saw whom he folded carefully from the night air, whom he tended, watched, and cherished as the apple of his eye.

Still, hint and raillery flew thick, and still I gathered that while M. Paul should be absent, working for others, these others, not quite ungrateful, would guard for him the treasure he left in Europe. Let him bring them an Indian fortune; they would give him in return a young bride and a rich inheritance. As for the saintly consecration, the vow of constancy, that was forgotten: the blooming and charming Present prevailed over the Past; and at length his nun was indeed buried.

Thus it must be. The revelation was indeed come. Presentiment had not been mistaken in her impulse; there is a kind of presentiment which never *is* mistaken; it was I who had for a moment miscalculated; not seeing the true

bearing of the oracle, I had thought she muttered of vision when, in truth, her prediction touched reality.

I might have paused longer upon what I saw; I might have deliberated ere I drew inferences. Some perhaps would have held the premises doubtful, the proofs insufficient; some slow sceptics would have incredulously examined, ere they conclusively accepted the project of a marriage between a poor and unselfish man of forty, and his wealthy ward of eighteen; but far from me such shifts and palliatives, far from me such temporary evasion of the actual, such coward fleeing from the dread, the swift-footed, the all-overtaking Fact, such feeble suspense of submission to her the sole sovereign, such paltering and faltering resistance to the Power whose errand is to march conquering and to conquer, such traitor defection from the TRUTH.

No. I hastened to accept the whole plan. I extended my grasp and took it all in. I gathered it to me with a sort of rage of haste, and folded it round me, as the soldier struck on the field folds his colours about his breast. I invoked Conviction to nail upon me the certainty, abhorred while embraced, to fix it with the strongest spikes her strongest strokes could drive; and when the iron had entered well my soul, I stood up, as I thought renovated.

In my infatuation, I said, 'Truth, you are a good mistress to your faithful servants! While a Lie pressed me, how I suffered! Even when the Falsehood was still sweet, still flattering to the fancy, and warm to the feelings, it wasted me with hourly torment. The persuasion that affection was won could not be divorced from the dread that, by another turn of the wheel, it might be lost. Truth stripped away Falsehood, and Flattery, and Expectancy, and here I stand – free!'

Nothing remained now but to take my freedom to my chamber, to carry it with me to my bed and see what I could make of it. The play was not yet indeed quite played out, I might have waited and watched longer that love scene under the trees, that sylvan courtship. Had there been nothing of love in the demonstration, my Fancy in this hour was so generous, so creative, she could have modelled for it the most salient lineaments, and given it the deepest life and highest colour of passion. But I *would* not look; I had fixed my resolve, but I would not violate my nature. And then – something tore me so cruelly under my shawl, something so dug into my side, a vulture so strong in beak and talon, I must be alone to grapple with it. I think I never felt jealousy till now. This was not like enduring the endearments of Dr John and Paulina, against which while I sealed my eyes and my ears, while I withdrew thence my thoughts, my sense of harmony still acknowledged in it a charm. This was an outrage. The love born of beauty was not mine; I had nothing in common with it: I could not dare to meddle with it, but another love, venturing diffidently into life after long acquaintance, furnace-tried by pain, stamped by constancy, consolidated by affection's pure and durable alloy, submitted by intellect to intellect's own tests, and finally wrought up, by his own process, to his own unflawed completeness, this Love that laughed at Passion, his fast frenzies and his hot and hurried extinction, in *this* Love I had a vested interest; and whatever tended either to its culture or its destruction, I could not view impassibly.

I turned from the group of trees and the 'merrie companie' in its shade. Midnight was long past; the concert was over, the crowds were thinning. I followed the ebb. Leaving the radiant park and well-lit Haute-Ville (still well-lit, for this it seems was to be a 'nuit blanche' in Villette), I sought the dim lower quarter.

Dim I should not say, for the beauty of moonlight – forgotten in the park – here once more flowed in upon perception. High she rode, and calm and stainlessly she shone. The music and the mirth of the fête, the fire and bright hues of those lamps had out-done and out-shone her for an hour, but now, again, her glory and her silence triumphed. The rival lamps were dying: she held her course like a white fate. Drum, trumpet, bugle, had uttered their clangour and were forgotten: with pencil-ray she wrote on heaven and on earth records for archives everlasting. She and those stars seemed to me at once the types and witnesses of truth all regnant. The night-sky lit her reign: like its slow-wheeling progress, advanced her victory – that onward movement which has been, and is, and will be from eternity to eternity.

These oil-twinkling streets are very still: I like them for their lowliness and peace. Homeward-bound burghers pass me now and then, but these companies are pedestrian, make little noise, and are soon gone. So well do I love Villette under her present aspect, not willingly would I re-enter under a roof, but that I am bent on pursuing my strange adventure to a successful close, and quietly regaining my bed in the great dormitory, before Mme Beck comes home.

Only one street lies between me and the Rue Fossette; as I enter it, for the first time, the sound of a carriage tears up the deep peace of this quarter. It comes this way – comes very fast. How loud sounds its rattle on the paved path! The street is narrow and I keep carefully to the causeway. The carriage thunders past, but what do I see, or fancy I see, as it rushes by? Surely something white fluttered from that window – surely a hand waved a handkerchief. Was that signal meant for me? Am I known? Who could recognise me? That is not M. de Bassompierre's carriage, nor Mrs Bretton's; and besides, neither the Hôtel Crécy nor the chateau of La Terrasse lies in that direction. Well, I have no time for conjecture: I must hurry home.

Gaining the Rue Fossette, reaching the Pensionnat, all there was still; no fiacre had yet arrived with Madame and Désirée. I had left the great door ajar; should I find it thus? Perhaps the wind or some other accident may have thrown it to with sufficient force to start the spring-bolt? In that case, hopeless became admission; my adventure must issue in catastrophe. I lightly pushed the heavy leaf: would it yield?

Yes. As soundless, as unresisting, as if some propitious genius had waited on a sesame-charm, in the vestibule within. Entering with bated breath, quietly making all fast, shoelessly mounting the staircase, I sought the dormitory, and reached my couch.

Aye! I reached it, and once more drew a free inspiration. The next moment, I almost shrieked – almost, but not quite, thank Heaven!

Throughout the dormitory, throughout the house, there reigned at this hour the stillness of death. All slept, and in such hush, it seemed that none dreamed. Stretched on the nineteen beds lay nineteen forms, at full-length and motionless. On mine – the twentieth couch – nothing *ought* to have lain: I had left it void, and void should have found it. What, then, do I see between the half-drawn curtains? What dark, usurping shape, supine, long, and strange? Is it a robber who has made his way through the open street-door, and lies there in wait? It looks very black, I think it looks – not human. Can it be a wandering dog that has come in from the street and crept and nestled hither? Will it spring, will it leap out if I approach? Approach I must. Courage! One step! –

My head reeled, for by the faint night-lamp, I saw stretched on my bed the old phantom – the NUN.

A cry at this moment might have ruined me. Be the spectacle what it might, I could afford neither consternation, scream, nor swoon. Besides, I was not overcome. Tempered by late incidents, my nerves disdained hysteria. Warm from illuminations, and music, and thronging thousands, thoroughly lashed up by a new scourge, I defied spectra. In a moment, without exclamation, I had rushed on the haunted couch; nothing leaped out, or sprung, or stirred; all the movement was mine, so was all the life, the reality, the substance, the force; as my instinct felt. I tore her up – the incubus! I held her on high – the goblin! I shook her loose – the mystery! And down she fell – down all round me – down in shreds and fragments – and I trode upon her.

Here again – behold the branchless tree, the unstabled Rosinante; the film of cloud, the flicker of moonshine. The long nun proved a long bolster dressed in a long black stole, and artfully invested with a white veil. The garments in very truth – strange as it may seem – were genuine nun's garments, and by some hand they had been disposed with a view to illusion. Whence came these vestments? Who contrived this artifice? These questions still remained. To the head-bandage was pinned a slip of paper: it bore in pencil these mocking words: 'The nun of the attic bequeaths to Lucy Snowe her wardrobe. She will be seen in the Rue Fossette no more.'

And what and who was she that had haunted me? She, I had actually seen three times? Not a woman of my acquaintance had the stature of that ghost. She was not of female height. Not to any man I knew could the machination, for a moment, be attributed.

Still mystified beyond expression, but as thoroughly, as suddenly, relieved from all sense of the spectral and unearthly; scorning also to wear out my brain with the fret of a trivial though insoluble riddle – I just bundled together stole, veil, and bandages, thrust them beneath my pillow, lay down, listened till I heard the wheels of Madame's home-returning fiacre, then turned, and worn out by many nights' vigils, conquered, too, perhaps, by the now reacting narcotic, I deeply slept.

CHAPTER 40

## The Happy Pair

The day succeeding this remarkable Midsummer night, proved no common day. I do not mean that it brought signs in heaven above, or portents on the earth beneath; nor do I allude to meteorological phenomena, to storm, flood, or whirlwind. On the contrary: the sun rose jocund, with a July face. Morning decked her beauty with rubies, and so filled her lap with roses, that they fell from her in showers, making her path blush: the Hours woke fresh as nymphs, and emptying on the early hills their dew-vials, they stepped out dismantled of vapour: shadowless, azure, and glorious, they led the sun's steeds on a burning and unclouded course.

In short, it was as fine a day as the finest summer could boast: but I doubt whether I was not the sole inhabitant of the Rue Fossette, who cared or remembered to note this pleasant fact. Another thought busied all other heads; a thought, indeed, which had its share in my meditations; but this master consideration, not possessing for me so entire a novelty, so overwhelming a suddenness, especially so dense a mystery, as it offered to the majority of my co-speculators thereon, left me somewhat more open than the rest, to any collateral observation or impression.

Still, while walking in the garden, feeling the sunshine, and marking the blooming and growing plants, I pondered the same subject the whole house discussed.

What subject?

Merely this. When matins came to be said, there was a place vacant in the first rank of boarders. When breakfast was served, there remained a coffee-cup unclaimed. When the housemaid made the beds, she found in one, a bolster laid lengthwise, clad in a cap and nightgown; and when Ginevra Fanshawe's music-mistress came early, as usual, to give the morning lesson, that accomplished and promising young person, her pupil, failed utterly to be forthcoming.

High and low was Miss Fanshawe sought; through length and breadth was the house ransacked; vainly; not a trace, not an indication, not so much as a scrap of a billet rewarded the search; the nymph was vanished, engulfed in the past night, like a shooting star swallowed up by darkness.

Deep was the dismay of surveillante teachers, deeper the horror of the defaulting directress. Never had I seen Mme Beck so pale or so appalled. Here was a blow struck at her tender part, her weak side; here was damage done to her interest. How, too, had the untoward event happened? By what outlet had the fugitive taken wing? Not a casement was found unfastened, not a pane of glass broken; all the doors were bolted secure. Never to this day has Mme Beck obtained satisfaction on this point, nor indeed has anybody else concerned, save

and excepting one, Lucy Snowe, who could not forget how, to facilitate a certain enterprise, a certain great door had been drawn softly to its lintel, closed, indeed, but neither bolted nor secure. The thundering carriage-and-pair encountered were now likewise recalled, as well as that puzzling signal, the waved handkerchief.

From these premises, and one or two others, inaccessible to any but myself, I could draw but one inference. It was a case of elopement. Morally certain on this head, and seeing Mme Beck's profound embarrassment, I at last communicated my conviction. Having alluded to M. de Hamal's suit, I found, as I expected, that Mme Beck was perfectly au fait to that affair. She had long since discussed it with Mrs Cholmondeley, and laid her own responsibility, in the business, on that lady's shoulders. To Mrs Cholmondeley and M. de Bassompierre she now had recourse.

We found that the Hôtel Crécy was already alive to what had happened. Ginevra had written to her cousin Paulina, vaguely signifying hymeneal intentions; communications had been received from the family of de Hamal; M. de Bassompierre was on the track of the fugitives. He overtook them too late.

In the course of the week, the post brought me a note. I may as well transcribe it; it contains explanation on more than one point:

DEAR OLD TIM [short for Timon] – I am off you see – gone like a shot. Alfred and I intended to be married in this way almost from the first; we never meant to be spliced in the humdrum way of other people; Alfred has too much spirit for that, and so have I – Dieu merci! Do you know, Alfred, who used to call you 'the dragon', has seen so much of you during the last few months, that he begins to feel quite friendly towards you. He hopes you won't miss him now that he is gone; he begs to apologise for any little trouble he may have given you. He is afraid he rather inconvenienced you once when he came upon you in the grenier, just as you were reading a letter seemingly of the most special interest; but he could not resist the temptation to give you a start, you appeared so wonderfully taken up with your correspondent. En revanche, he says you once frightened him by rushing in for a dress or a shawl, or some other chiffon, at the moment when he had struck a light, and was going to take a quiet whiff of his cigar, while waiting for me.

Do you begin to comprehend by this time that M. le Comte de Hamal was the nun of the attic, and that he came to see your humble servant? I will tell you how he managed it. You know he has the entrée of the Athénée, where two or three of his nephews, the sons of his eldest sister, Mme de Melcy, are students. You know the court of the Athénée is on the other side of the high wall bounding your walk, the allée défendue. Alfred can climb as well as he can dance or fence; his amusement was to make the escalade of our pensionnat by mounting, first the wall; then – by the aid of that high tree overspreading the grand berceau, and resting some of its boughs on the roof of the lower buildings of our premises – he managed to scale the first classe and the grande salle. One night, by the way, he fell out of this tree, tore down

some of the branches, nearly broke his own neck, and after all, in running away, got a terrible fright, and was nearly caught by two people, Mme Beck and M. Emanuel, he thinks, walking in the alley. From the grande salle the ascent is not difficult to the highest block of building, finishing in the great garret. The skylight, you know, is day and night left half-open for air; by the skylight he entered. Nearly a year ago, I chanced to tell him our legend of the nun, that suggested his romantic idea of the spectral disguise, which I think you must allow he has very cleverly carried out.

But for the nun's black gown and white veil, he would have been caught again and again both by you and that tiger-Jesuit, M. Paul. He thinks you both capital ghost-seers, and very brave. What I wonder at is, rather your secretiveness than your courage. How could you endure the visitations of that long spectre, time after time, without crying out, telling everybody, and rousing the whole house and neighbourhood?

Oh, and how did you like the nun as a bedfellow? I dressed her up – didn't I do it well? Did you shriek when you saw her? *I* should have gone mad; but then you have such nerves! – real iron and bend leather! I believe you feel nothing. You haven't the same sensitiveness that a person of my constitution has. You seem to me insensible both to pain and fear and grief. You are a real old Diogenes.

Well, dear grandmother! and are you not mightily angry at my moonlight flitting and run-away match? I assure you it is excellent fun, and I did it partly to spite that minx, Paulina, and that bear, Dr John – to show them that, with all their airs, I could get married as well as they. M. de Bassompierre was at first in a strange fume with Alfred; he threatened a prosecution for 'détournement de mineur', and I know not what; he was so abominably in earnest, that I found myself forced to do a little bit of the melodramatic – go down on my knees, sob, cry, drench three pocket-handkerchiefs. Of course, 'mon oncle' soon gave in; indeed, where was the use of making a fuss? I am married, and that's all about it. He still says our marriage is not legal, because I am not of age, forsooth! As if that made any difference! I am just as much married as if I were a hundred. However, we are to be married again, and I am to have a trousseau, and Mrs Cholmondeley is going to superintend it; and there are some hopes that M. de Bassompierre will give me a decent portion, which will be very convenient, as dear Alfred has nothing but his nobility, native and hereditary, and his pay. I only wish uncle would do things unconditionally, in a generous, gentleman-like fashion; he is so disagreeable as to make the dowry depend on Alfred's giving his written promise that he will never touch cards or dice from the day it is paid down. They accuse my angel of a tendency to play: I don't know anything about that, but I *do* know he is a dear, adorable creature.

I cannot sufficiently extol the genius with which De Hamal managed our flight. How clever in him to select the night of the fête, when Mme (for he knows her habits), as he said, would infallibly be absent at the concert in the park. I suppose *you* must have gone with her. I watched you rise and leave the

dormitory about eleven o'clock. How you returned alone, and on foot, I cannot conjecture. That surely was *you* we met in the narrow old Rue St Jean? Did you see me wave my handkerchief from the carriage window?

Adieu! Rejoice in my good luck: congratulate me on my supreme happiness, and believe me, dear cynic and misanthrope, yours, in the best of health and spirits,

<div align="right">Ginevra Laura de Hamal, née Fanshawe</div>

P.S. Remember, I am a countess now. Papa, mama, and the girls at home, will be delighted to hear that. 'My daughter, the Countess! My sister, the Countess.' Bravo! Sounds rather better than Mrs John Bretton, hein?

In winding up Mistress Fanshawe's memoirs, the reader will no doubt expect to hear that she came finally to bitter expiation of her youthful levities. Of course, a large share of suffering lies in reserve for her future.

A few words will embody my farther knowledge respecting her.

I saw her towards the close of her honeymoon. She called on Mme Beck, and sent for me into the salon. She rushed into my arms laughing. She looked very blooming and beautiful: her curls were longer, her cheeks rosier than ever: her white bonnet and her Flanders veil, her orange flowers and her bride's dress, became her mightily.

'I have got my portion!' she cried at once (Ginevra ever stuck to the substantial; I always thought there was a good trading element in her composition, much as she scorned the 'bourgeoisie'); 'and uncle de Bassompierre is quite reconciled. I don't mind his calling Alfred a "nincompoop" – that's only his coarse Scotch breeding; and I believe Paulina envies me, and Dr John is wild with jealousy – fit to blow his brains out – and I'm so happy! I really think I've hardly anything left to wish for – unless it be a carriage and a hotel, and – oh! I must introduce you to "mon mari". Alfred, come here!'

And Alfred appeared from the inner salon, where he was talking to Mme Beck, receiving the blended felicitations and reprimands of that lady. I was presented under my various names: the Dragon, Diogenes, and Timon. The young Colonel was very polite. He made me a prettily-turned, neatly-worded apology, about the ghost-visits, etc., concluding with saying that 'the best excuse for all his iniquities stood there!' pointing to his bride.

And then the bride sent him back to Mme Beck, and she took me to herself, and proceeded literally to suffocate me with her unrestrained spirits, her girlish, giddy, wild nonsense. She showed her ring exultingly; she called herself Mme la Comtesse de Hamal, and asked how it sounded, a score of times. I said very little. I gave her only the crust of my nature. No matter: she expected of me nothing better – she knew me too well to look for compliments – my dry gibes pleased her well enough, and the more impassible and prosaic my mien, the more merrily she laughed.

Soon after his marriage, M. de Hamal was persuaded to leave the army as the surest way of weaning him from certain unprofitable associates and habits; a

post of attaché was procured for him, and he and his young wife went abroad. I thought she would forget me now, but she did not. For many years, she kept up a capricious, fitful sort of correspondence. During the first year or two, it was only of herself and Alfred she wrote; then, Alfred faded in the background; herself and a certain newcomer prevailed; one Alfred Fanshawe de Bassompierre de Hamal began to reign in his father's stead. There were great boastings about this personage, extravagant amplifications upon miracles of precocity, mixed with vehement objurgations against the phlegmatic incredulity with which I received them. I didn't know 'what it was to be a mother:' 'unfeeling thing that I was, the sensibilities of the maternal heart were Greek and Hebrew to me,' and so on. In due course of nature this young gentleman took his degrees in teething, measles, whooping-cough: that was a terrible time for me – the mama's letters became a perfect shout of affliction – never woman was so put upon by calamity: never human being stood in such need of sympathy. I was frightened at first, and wrote back pathetically; but I soon found out there was more cry than wool in the business, and relapsed into my natural cruel insensibility. As to the youthful sufferer, he weathered each storm like a hero. Five times was that youth 'in articulo mortis', and five times did he miraculously revive.

In the course of years there arose ominous murmurings against Alfred the First; M. de Bassompierre had to be appealed to, debts had to be paid, some of them of that dismal and dingy order called 'debts of honour;' ignoble plaints and difficulties became frequent. Under every cloud, no matter what its nature, Ginevra, as of old, called out lustily for sympathy and aid. She had no notion of meeting any distress single-handed. In some shape, from some quarter or other, she was pretty sure to obtain her will, and so she got on – fighting the battle of life by proxy, and, on the whole, suffering as little as any human being I have ever known.

CHAPTER 41

*Faubourg Clotilde*

Must I, ere I close, render some account of that Freedom and Renovation which I won on the fête-night? Must I tell how I and the two stalwart companions I brought home from the illuminated park bore the test of intimate acquaintance?

I tried them the very next day. They had boasted their strength loudly when they reclaimed me from love and its bondage, but upon my demanding deeds, not words, some evidence of better comfort, some experience of a relieved life – Freedom excused himself, as for the present, impoverished and disabled to assist; and Renovation never spoke; he had died in the night suddenly.

I had nothing left for it then but to trust secretly that conjecture might have hurried me too fast and too far, to sustain the oppressive hour by reminders of

the distorting and discolouring magic of jealousy. After a short and vain struggle, I found myself brought back captive to the old rack of suspense, tied down and strained anew.

Shall I yet see him before he goes? Will he bear me in mind? Does he purpose to come? Will this day – will the next hour bring him? or must I again assay that corroding pain of long attent – that rude agony of rupture at the close, that mute, mortal wrench, which, in at once uprooting hope and doubt, shakes life; while the hand that does the violence cannot be caressed to pity, because absence interposes her barrier!

It was the Feast of the Assumption; no school was held. The boarders and teachers, after attending mass in the morning, were gone on a long walk into the country to take their goûter, or afternoon meal at some farmhouse. I did not go with them, for now but two days remained ere the 'Paul et Virginie' must sail, and I was clinging to my last chance, as the living waif of a wreck clings to his last raft or cable.

There was some joiners' work to do in the first classe, some bench or desk to repair; holidays were often turned to account for the performance of these operations, which could not be executed when the rooms were filled with pupils. As I sat solitary, purposing to adjourn to the garden and leave the coast clear, but too listless to fulfil my own intent, I heard the workman coming.

Foreign artisans and servants do everything by couples: I believe it would take two Labassecourien carpenters to drive a nail. While tying on my bonnet, which had hitherto hung by its ribbons from my idle hand, I vaguely and momentarily wondered to hear the step of but one 'ouvrier'. I noted, too – as captives in dungeons find sometimes dreary leisure to note the merest trifles – that this man wore shoes, and not sabots: I concluded that it must be the master-carpenter, coming to inspect, before he sent his journeymen. I threw round me my scarf. He advanced; he opened the door; my back was towards it; I felt a little thrill – a curious sensation, too quick and transient to be analysed. I turned, I stood in the supposed master-artisan's presence: looking towards the doorway, I saw it filled with a figure, and my eyes printed upon my brain the picture of M. Paul.

Hundreds of the prayers with which we weary Heaven, bring to the suppliant no fulfilment. Once haply in life, one golden gift falls prone in the lap – one boon full and bright, perfect from Fruition's mint.

M. Emanuel wore the dress in which he probably purposed to travel – a surtout, guarded with velvet; I thought him prepared for instant departure, and yet I had understood that two days were yet to run before the ship sailed. He looked well, and cheerful. He looked kind and benign: he came in with eagerness; he was close to me in one second; he was all amity. It might be his bridegroom-mood which thus brightened him. Whatever the cause, I could not meet his sunshine with cloud. If this were my last moment with him, I would not waste it in forced, unnatural distance. I loved him well – too well not to smite out of my path even Jealousy herself, when she would have obstructed a kind farewell. A cordial word from his lips, or a gentle look from his eyes, would do

me good, for all the span of life that remained to me; it would be comfort in the last strait of loneliness; I would take it – I would taste the elixir, and pride should not spill the cup.

The interview would be short, of course: he would say to me just what he had said to each of the assembled pupils; he would take and hold my hand two minutes; he would touch my cheek with his lips for the first, last, only time – and then – no more. Then, indeed, the final parting, then the wide separation, the great gulf I could not pass to go to him – across which, haply, he would not glance, to remember me.

He took my hand in one of his, with the other he put back my bonnet; he looked into my face, his luminous smile went out, his lips expressed something almost like the wordless language of a mother who finds a child greatly and unexpectedly changed, broken with illness, or worn-out by want. A check supervened.

'Paul, Paul!' said a woman's hurried voice behind, 'Paul, come into the salon; I have yet a great many things to say to you – conversation for the whole day – and so has Victor; and Josef is here. Come, Paul, come to your friends.'

Mme Beck, brought to the spot by vigilance or an inscrutable instinct, pressed so near, she almost thrust herself between me and M. Emanuel. 'Come, Paul!' she reiterated, her eye grazing me with its hard ray like a steel stylet. She pushed against her kinsman. I thought he receded; I thought he would go. Pierced deeper than I could endure, made now to feel what defied suppression, I cried – 'My heart will break!'

What I felt seemed literal heart-break; but the seal of another fountain yielded under the strain: one breath from M. Paul, the whisper, 'Trust me!' lifted a load, opened an outlet. With many a deep sob, with thrilling, with icy shiver, with strong trembling, and yet with relief – I wept.

'Leave her to me; it is a crisis; I will give her a cordial, and it will pass,' said the calm Mme Beck.

To be left to her and her cordial, seemed to me something like being left to the poisoner and her bowl. When M. Paul answered deeply, harshly, and briefly – 'Laissez-moi!' in the grim sound I felt a music strange, strong, but life-giving.

'Laissez-moi!' he repeated, his nostrils opening, and his facial muscles all quivering as he spoke.

'But this will never do,' said Madame, with sternness. More sternly rejoined her kinsman – 'Sortez d'ici!'

'I will send for Père Silas; on the spot I will send for him,' she threatened pertinaciously.

'Femme!' cried the professor, not now in his deep tones, but in his highest and most excited key, 'Femme! sortez à l'instant!'

He was roused, and I loved him in his wrath with a passion beyond what I had yet felt.

'What you do is wrong,' pursued Madame; 'it is an act characteristic of men of your unreliable, imaginative temperament; a step impulsive, injudicious,

inconsistent – a proceeding vexatious, and not estimable in the view of persons of steadier and more resolute character.'

'You know not what I have of steady and resolute in me,' said he, 'but you shall see; the event shall teach you. Modeste,' he continued less fiercely, 'be gentle, be pitying, be a woman; look at this poor face, and relent. You know I am your friend, and the friend of your friends; in spite of your taunts, you well and deeply know I may be trusted. Of sacrificing myself I made no difficulty, but my heart is pained by what I see; it *must* have and give solace. *Leave me!*'

This time, in the *'leave me'*, there was an intonation so bitter and so imperative, I wondered that even Mme Beck herself could for one moment delay obedience; but she stood firm; she gazed upon him dauntless; she met his eye, forbidding and fixed as stone. She was opening her lips to retort; I saw over all M. Paul's face a quick-rising light and fire: I can hardly tell how he managed the movement; it did not seem violent; it kept the form of courtesy; he gave his hand; it scarce touched her, I thought; she ran, she whirled from the room; she was gone and the door shut in one second.

This flash of passion was all over very soon. He smiled as he told me to wipe my eyes; he waited quietly till I was calm, dropping from time to time a stilling, solacing word. Ere long I sat beside him once more myself – reassured – not desperate, nor yet desolate; not friendless, not hopeless, not sick of life, and seeking death.

'It made you very sad then to lose your friend?' said he.

'It kills me to be forgotten, monsieur,' I said. 'All these weary days I have not heard from you one word, and I was crushed with the possibility, growing to certainty, that you would depart without saying farewell!'

'Must I tell you what I told Modeste Beck – that you do not know me? Must I show and teach you my character? You *will* have proof that I can be a firm friend? Without clear proof this hand will not lie still in mine, it will not trust my shoulder as a safe stay? Good. The proof is ready. I come to justify myself.'

'Say anything, teach anything, prove anything, monsieur: I can listen now.'

'Then, in the first place, you must go out with me a good distance into the town. I came on purpose to fetch you.'

Without questioning his meaning, or sounding his plan, or offering the semblance of an objection, I retied my bonnet: I was ready.

The route he took was by the boulevards: he several times made me sit down on the seats stationed under the lime trees; he did not ask if I was tired, but looked, and drew his own conclusions.

'All these weary days,' said he, repeating my words, with a gentle, kindly mimicry of my voice and foreign accent, not new from his lips, and of which the playful banter never wounded, not even when coupled as it often was, with the assertion, that however I might *write* his language, I *spoke* and always should speak it imperfectly and hesitatingly. ' "All these weary days," I have not for one hour forgotten you. Faithful women err in this, that they think themselves the sole faithful of God's creatures. On a very fervent and living truth to myself, I, too, till lately scarce dared count, from any quarter; but – look at me.'

I lifted my happy eyes: they *were* happy now, or they would have been no interpreters of my heart.

'Well,' said he, after some seconds' scrutiny, 'there is no denying that signature: Constancy wrote it; her pen is of iron. Was the record painful?'

'Severely painful,' I said, with truth. 'Withdraw her hand, monsieur; I can bear its inscribing force no more.'

'Elle est toute pâle,' said he, speaking to himself; 'cette figure là me fait mal.'

'Ah! I am not pleasant to look at – ?'

I could not help saying this; the words came unbidden: I never remember the time when I had not a haunting dread of what might be the degree of my outward deficiency; this dread pressed me at the moment with special force.

A great softness passed upon his countenance; his violet eyes grew suffused and glistening under their deep Spanish lashes: he started up; 'Let us walk on.'

'Do I displease your eyes *much*?' I took courage to urge: the point had its vital import for me.

He stopped, and gave me a short, strong answer – an answer which silenced, subdued, yet profoundly satisfied. Ever after that, I knew what I was for *him*; and what I might be for the rest of the world, I ceased painfully to care. Was it weak to lay so much stress on an opinion about appearance? I fear it might be – I fear it was; but in that case I must avow no light share of weakness. I must own a great fear of displeasing – a strong wish moderately to please M. Paul.

Whither we rambled, I scarce knew. Our walk was long, yet seemed short; the path was pleasant, the day lovely. M. Emanuel talked of his voyage – he thought of staying away three years. On his return from Guadaloupe, he looked forward to release from liabilities and a clear course; and what did I purpose doing in the interval of his absence? he asked. I had talked once, he reminded me, of trying to be independent and keeping a little school of my own: had I dropped the idea?

'Indeed, I had not: I was doing my best to save what would enable me to put it in practice.'

'He did not like leaving me in the Rue Fossette; he feared I should miss him there too much – I should feel desolate – I should grow sad – ?'

This was certain; but I promised to do my best to endure.

'Still,' said he, speaking low, 'there is another objection to your present residence. I should wish to write to you sometimes: it would not be well to have any uncertainty about the safe transmission of letters; and in the Rue Fossette – in short, our Catholic discipline in certain matters – though justifiable and expedient – might possibly, under peculiar circumstances, become liable to misapplication – perhaps abuse.'

'But if you write,' said I, 'I *must* have your letters; and I *will* have them: ten directors, twenty directresses, shall not keep them from me. I am a Protestant: I will not bear that kind of discipline: monsieur, I *will not*.'

'Doucement – doucement,' rejoined he; 'we will contrive a plan; we have our resources: soyez tranquille.'

So speaking, he paused.

We were now returning from the long walk. We had reached the middle of a clean Faubourg, where the houses were small, but looked pleasant. It was before the white doorstep of a very neat abode that M. Paul had halted.

'I call here,' said he.

He did not knock, but taking from his pocket a key, he opened and entered at once. Ushering me in, he shut the door behind us. No servant appeared. The vestibule was small, like the house, but freshly and tastefully painted; its vista closed in a French window with vines trained about the panes, tendrils and green leaves kissing the glass. Silence reigned in this dwelling.

Opening an inner door, M. Paul disclosed a parlour, or salon – very tiny, but I thought, very pretty. Its delicate walls were tinged like a blush; its floor was waxed; a square of brilliant carpet covered its centre; its small round table shone like the mirror over its hearth; there was a little couch, a little chiffonnière – the half-open, crimson-silk door of which, showed porcelain on the shelves; there was a French clock, a lamp; there were ornaments in biscuit china; the recess of the single ample window was filled with a green stand, bearing three green flower-pots, each filled with a fine plant glowing in bloom; in one corner appeared a guéridon with a marble top, and upon it a workbox, and a glass filled with violets in water. The lattice of this room was open; the outer air breathing through, gave freshness, the sweet violets lent fragrance.

'Pretty, pretty place!' said I. M. Paul smiled to see me so pleased.

'Must we sit down here and wait?' I asked in a whisper, half-awed by the deep-pervading hush.

'We will first peep into one or two other nooks of this nut-shell,' he replied.

'Dare you take the freedom of going all over the house?' I enquired.

'Yes, I dare,' said he, quietly.

He led the way. I was shown a little kitchen with a little stove and oven, with few but bright brasses, two chairs and a table. A small cupboard held a diminutive but commodious set of earthenware.

'There is a coffee service of china in the salon,' said M. Paul, as I looked at the six green and white dinner-plates; the four dishes, the cups and jugs to match.

Conducted up the narrow but clean staircase, I was permitted a glimpse of two pretty cabinets of sleeping-rooms; finally, I was once more led below, and we halted with a certain ceremony before a larger door than had yet been opened.

Producing a second key, M. Emanuel adjusted it to the lock of this door. He opened, put me in before him.

'Voici!' he cried.

I found myself in a good-sized apartment, scrupulously clean, though bare, compared with those I had hitherto seen. The well-scoured boards were carpetless; it contained two rows of green benches and desks, with an alley down the centre, terminating in an estrade, a teacher's chair and table; behind them a tableau. On the walls hung two maps; in the windows flowered a few hardy plants; in short, here was a miniature classe – complete, neat, pleasant.

'It is a school then?' said I. 'Who keeps it? I never heard of an establishment in this faubourg.'

'Will you have the goodness to accept of a few prospectuses for distribution in behalf of a friend of mine?' asked he, taking from his surtout-pocket some quires of these documents, and putting them into my hand. I looked, I read – printed in fair characters: 'Externat de demoiselles. Numéro 7, Faubourg Clotilde. Directrice, Mlle Lucy Snowe.'

And what did I say to M. Paul Emanuel?

Certain junctures of our lives must always be difficult of recall to memory. Certain points, crises, certain feelings, joys, griefs, and amazements, when reviewed, must strike us as things wildered and whirling, dim as a wheel fast spun.

I can no more remember the thoughts or the words of the ten minutes succeeding this disclosure, than I can retrace the experience of my earliest year of life: and yet the first thing distinct to me is the consciousness that I was speaking very fast, repeating over and over again: 'Did you do this, M. Paul? Is this your house? Did you furnish it? Did you get these papers printed? Do you mean me? Am I the directress? Is there another Lucy Snowe? Tell me: say something.'

But he would not speak. His pleased silence, his laughing down-look, his attitude, are visible to me now.

'How is it? I must know all – *all*,' I cried.

The packet of papers fell on the floor. He had extended his hand, and I had fastened thereon, oblivious of all else.

'Ah! you said I had forgotten you all these weary days,' said he. 'Poor old Emanuel! These are the thanks he gets for trudging about three mortal weeks – from house-painter to upholsterer, from cabinet-maker to charwoman – Lucy and Lucy's cot, the sole thoughts in his head!'

I hardly knew what to do. I first caressed the soft velvet on his cuff, and then I stroked the hand it surrounded. It was his foresight, his goodness, his silent, strong, effective goodness, that overpowered me by their proved reality. It was the assurance of his sleepless interest which broke on me like a light from heaven; it was his (I will dare to say it) his fond, tender look, which now shook me indescribably. In the midst of all, I forced myself to look at the practical.

'The trouble!' I cried, 'and the cost! Had you money, M. Paul?'

'Plenty of money!' said he heartily. 'The disposal of my large teaching-connection put me in possession of a handsome sum: with part of it I determined to give myself the richest treat that I *have* known or *shall* know. I like this. I have reckoned on this hour day and night lately. I would not come near you, because I would not forestall it. Reserve is neither my virtue nor my vice. If I had put myself into your power, and you had begun with your questions of look and lip – Where have you been, M. Paul? What have you been doing? What is your mystery? – my solitary first and last secret would presently have unravelled itself in your lap. Now,' he pursued, 'you shall live here and have a school; you shall employ yourself while I am away; you shall think of me sometimes; you shall mind your health and happiness for my sake, and when I come back –'

Here he left a blank.

I promised to do all he told me. I promised to work hard and willingly. 'I will be your faithful steward,' I said; 'I trust at your coming the account will be ready. Monsieur, monsieur, you are *too* good!'

In such inadequate language my feelings struggled for expression: they could not get it; speech, brittle and unmalleable, and cold as ice, dissolved or shivered in the effort. He watched me still: he gently raised his hand to stroke my hair; it touched my lips in passing; I pressed it close, I paid it tribute. He was my king; royal for me had been that hand's bounty; to offer homage was both a joy and a duty.

The afternoon hours were over, and the stiller time of evening shaded the quiet faubourg. M. Paul claimed my hospitality; occupied and afoot since morning, he needed refreshment; he said I should offer him chocolate in my pretty gold and white china service. He went out and ordered what was needful from the restaurant; he placed the small guéridon and two chairs in the balcony outside the French window under the screening vines. With what shy joy I accepted my part as hostess, arranged the salver, served the benefactor-guest.

This balcony was in the rear of the house, the gardens of the faubourg were round us, fields extended beyond. The air was still, mild, and fresh. Above the poplars, the laurels, the cypresses, and the roses, looked up a moon so lovely and so halcyon, the heart trembled under her smile; a star shone subject beside her, with the unemulous ray of pure love. In a large garden near us, a jet rose from a well, and a pale statue leaned over the play of waters.

M. Paul talked to me. His voice was so modulated that it mixed harmonious with the silver whisper, the gush, the musical sigh, in which light breeze, fountain, and foliage intoned their lulling vesper.

Happy hour – stay one moment! droop those plumes, rest those wings; incline to mine that brow of Heaven! White Angel! let thy light linger; leave its reflection on succeeding clouds; bequeath its cheer to that time which needs a ray in retrospect!

Our meal was simple: the chocolate, the rolls, the plate of fresh summer fruit, cherries and strawberries bedded in green leaves, formed the whole; but it was what we both liked better than a feast, and I took a delight inexpressible in tending M. Paul. I asked him whether his friends, Père Silas and Mme Beck knew what he had done – whether they had seen my house?

'Mon amie,' said he, 'none knows what I have done save you and myself: the pleasure is consecrated to us two, unshared and unprofaned. To speak truth, there has been to me in this matter a refinement of enjoyment I would not make vulgar by communication. Besides' (smiling), 'I wanted to prove to Miss Lucy that I *could* keep a secret. How often has she taunted me with lack of dignified reserve and needful caution! How many times has she saucily insinuated that all my affairs are the secret of Polichinelle!'

This was true enough: I had not spared him on this point, nor perhaps on any other that was assailable. Magnificent minded, grand-hearted, dear, faulty little man! You deserved candour, and from me always had it.

Continuing my queries, I asked to whom the house belonged, who was my landlord, the amount of my rent. He instantly gave me these particulars in writing; he had foreseen and prepared all things.

The house was not M. Paul's – that I guessed; he was hardly the man to become a proprietor; I more than suspected in him a lamentable absence of the saving faculty; he could get, but not keep; he needed a treasurer. The tenement, then, belonged to a citizen in the Basse-Ville – a man of substance, M. Paul said; he startled me by adding: 'a friend of yours, Miss Lucy, a person who has a most respectful regard for you.' And, to my pleasant surprise, I found the landlord was none other than M. Miret, the short-tempered and kind-hearted bookseller, who had so kindly found me a seat that eventful night in the Park. It seems M. Miret was in his station, rich, as well as much respected, and possessed several houses in this faubourg; the rent was moderate, scarce half of what it would have been, for a house of equal size, nearer the centre of Villette.

'And then,' observed M. Paul, 'should fortune not favour you, though I think she will, I have the satisfaction to think you are in good hands; M. Miret will not be extortionate: the first year's rent you already have in your savings; afterwards Miss Lucy must trust God, and herself. But now, what will you do for pupils?'

'I must distribute my prospectuses.'

'Right! By way of losing no time, I gave one to M. Miret yesterday. Should you object to beginning with three petites bourgeoises – the Demoiselles Miret? They are at your service.'

'Monsieur, you forget nothing; you are wonderful. Object? It would become me indeed to object! I suppose I hardly expect at the outset to number aristocrats in my little day-school; I care not if they never come. I shall be proud to receive M. Miret's daughters.'

'Besides these,' pursued he, 'another pupil offers, who will come daily to take lessons in English; and, as she is rich, she will pay handsomely. I mean my god-daughter and ward, Justine Marie Sauveur.'

What is in a name? – what in three words? Till this moment I had listened with living joy – I had answered with gleeful quickness; a name froze me; three words struck me mute. The effect could not be hidden, and indeed I scarce tried to hide it.

'What now?' said M. Paul.

'Nothing.'

'Nothing! Your countenance changes; your colour and your very eyes fade. Nothing! You must be ill; you have some suffering; tell me what?'

I had nothing to tell.

He drew his chair nearer. He did not grow vexed, though I continued silent and icy. He tried to win a word; he entreated with perseverance, he waited with patience.

'Justine Marie is a good girl,' said he; 'docile and amiable; not quick – but you will like her.'

'I think not. I think she must not come here.' Such was my speech.

'Do you wish to puzzle me? Do you know her? But, in truth, there *is*

something. Again you are pale as that statue. Rely on Paul Carlos: tell him the grief.'

His chair touched mine; his hand, quietly advanced, turned me towards him. 'Do you know Marie Justine?' said he again.

The name re-pronounced by his lips overcame me unaccountably. It did not prostrate – no, it stirred me up, running with haste and heat through my veins – recalling an hour of quick pain, many days and nights of heart-sickness. Near me as he now sat, strongly and closely as he had long twined his life in mine – far as had progressed, and near as was achieved our minds' and affections' assimilation – the very suggestion of interference, of heart-separation, could be heard only with a fermenting excitement, an impetuous throe, a disdainful resolve, an ire, a resistance of which no human eye or cheek could hide the flame, nor any truth-accustomed human tongue curb the cry.

'I want to tell you something,' I said; 'I want to tell you all.'

'Speak, Lucy; come near; speak. Who prizes you if I do not? Who is your friend, if not Emanuel? Speak!'

I spoke. All leaped from my lips. I lacked not words now; fast I narrated; fluent I told my tale; it streamed on my tongue. I went back to the night in the park; I mentioned the medicated draught – why it was given – its goading effect – how it had torn rest from under my head, shaken me from my couch, carried me abroad with the lure of a vivid yet solemn fancy – a summer-night solitude on turf, under trees, near a deep, cool lakelet. I told the scene realised; the crowd, the masques, the music, the lamps, the splendours, the guns booming afar, the bells sounding on high. All I had encountered I detailed, all I had recognised, heard, and seen; how I had beheld and watched himself; how I listened, how much heard, what conjectured; the whole history, in brief, summoned to his confidence, rushed thither truthful, literal, ardent, bitter.

Still as I narrated, instead of checking, he incited me to proceed; he spurred me by the gesture, the smile, the half-word. Before I had half done, he held both my hands, he consulted my eyes with a most piercing glance: there was something in his face which tended neither to calm nor to put me down; he forgot his own doctrine, he forsook his own system of repression when I most challenged its exercise. I think I deserved strong reproof; but when have we our deserts? I merited severity; he looked indulgence. To my very self I seemed imperious and unreasonable; for I forbade Justine Marie my door and roof; he smiled, betraying delight. Warm, jealous, and haughty, I knew not till now that my nature had such a mood; he gathered me near his heart. I was full of faults; he took them and me all home. For the moment of utmost mutiny, he reserved the one deep spell of peace. These words caressed my ear: 'Lucy, take my love. One day share my life. Be my dearest, first on earth.'

We walked back to the Rue Fossette by moonlight – such moonlight as fell on Eden – shining through the shades of the Great Garden, and haply gilding a path glorious, for a step divine – a Presence nameless. Once in their lives some men and women go back to these first fresh days of our great Sire and Mother – taste that grand morning's dew – bathe in its sunrise.

In the course of the walk I was told how Justine Marie Sauveur had always been regarded with the affection proper to a daughter – how, with M. Paul's consent, she had been affianced for months to one Heinrich Mühler, a wealthy young German merchant, and was to be married in the course of a year. Some of M. Emanuel's relations and connections would, indeed, it seems, have liked him to marry her, with a view to securing her fortune in the family; but to himself the scheme was repugnant, and the idea totally inadmissible.

We reached Mme Beck's door. Jean Baptiste's clock tolled nine. At this hour, in this house, eighteen months since, had this man at my side, bent before me, looked into my face and eyes, and arbitered my destiny. This very evening he had again stooped, gazed and decreed. How different the look – how far otherwise the fate!

He deemed me born under his star: he seemed to have spread over me its beam like a banner. Once – unknown, and unloved, I held him harsh and strange; the low stature, the wiry make, the angles, the darkness, the manner, displeased me. Now, penetrated with his influence, and living by his affection, having his worth by intellect, and his goodness by heart – I preferred him before all humanity.

We parted: he gave me his pledge, and then his farewell. We parted: the next day – he sailed.

## CHAPTER 42

## *Finis*

Man cannot prophesy. Love is no oracle. Fear sometimes imagines a vain thing. Those years of absence! How had I sickened over their anticipation! The woe they must bring seemed certain as death. I knew the nature of their course: I never had doubt how it would harrow as it went. The Juggernaut on his car towered there a grim load. Seeing him draw nigh, burying his broad wheels in the oppressed soil – I, the prostrate votary – felt beforehand the annihilating craunch.

Strange to say – strange, yet true, and owning many parallels in life's experience – that anticipatory craunch proved all – yes – nearly *all* the torture. The great Juggernaut, in his great chariot, drew on lofty, loud, and sullen. He passed quietly, like a shadow sweeping the sky at noon. Nothing but a chilling dimness was seen or felt. I looked up. Chariot and demon charioteer were gone by; the votary still lived.

M. Emanuel was away three years. Reader, they were the three happiest years of my life. Do you scout the paradox? Listen.

I commenced my school; I worked – I worked hard. I deemed myself the steward of his property, and determined, God willing, to render a good account. Pupils came – burghers at first – a higher class ere long. About the middle of the

second year an unexpected chance threw into my hands an additional hundred pounds: one day I received from England a letter containing that sum. It came from Mr Marchmont, the cousin and heir of my dear and dead mistress. He was just recovering from a dangerous illness; the money was a peace-offering to his conscience, reproaching him in the matter of, I know not what, papers or memoranda found after his kinswoman's death – naming or recommending Lucy Snowe. Mrs Barrett had given him my address. How far his conscience had been sinned against, I never enquired. I asked no questions, but took the cash and made it useful.

With this hundred pounds I ventured to take the house adjoining mine. I would not leave that which M. Paul had chosen, in which he had left, and where he expected again to find me. My externat became a pensionnat; that also prospered.

The secret of my success did not lie so much in myself, in any endowment, any power of mine, as in a new state of circumstances, a wonderfully changed life, a relieved heart. The spring which moved my energies lay far away beyond seas, in an Indian isle. At parting, I had been left a legacy; such a thought for the present, such a hope for the future, such a motive for a persevering, a laborious, an enterprising, a patient and a brave course – I *could* not flag. Few things shook me now; few things had importance to vex, intimidate, or depress me: most things pleased – mere trifles had a charm.

Do not think that this genial flame sustained itself, or lived wholly on a bequeathed hope or a parting promise. A generous provider supplied bounteous fuel. I was spared all chill, all stint; I was not suffered to fear penury; I was not tried with suspense. By every vessel he wrote; he wrote as he gave and as he loved, in full-handed, full-hearted plenitude. He wrote because he liked to write; he did not abridge, because he cared not to abridge. He sat down, he took pen and paper, because he loved Lucy and had much to say to her; because he was faithful and thoughtful, because he was tender and true. There was no sham and no cheat, and no hollow unreal in him. Apology never dropped her slippery oil on his lips – never proffered, by his pen, her coward feints and paltry nullities: he would give neither a stone, nor an excuse – neither a scorpion, nor a disappointment; his letters were real food that nourished, living water that refreshed.

And was I grateful? God knows! I believe that scarce a living being so remembered, so sustained, dealt with in kind so constant, honourable and noble, could be otherwise than grateful to the death.

Adherent to his own religion (in him was not the stuff of which is made the facile apostate), he freely left me my pure faith. He did not tease nor tempt. He said: 'Remain a Protestant. My little English Puritan, I love Protestantism in you. I own its severe charm. There is something in its ritual I cannot receive myself, but it is the sole creed for "Lucy".'

All Rome could not put into him bigotry, nor the Propaganda itself make him a real Jesuit. He was born honest, and not false – artless, and not cunning – a freeman, and not a slave. His tenderness had rendered him ductile in a priest's

hands, his affection, his devotedness, his sincere pious enthusiasm blinded his kind eyes sometimes, made him abandon justice to himself to do the work of craft, and serve the ends of selfishness; but these are faults so rare to find, so costly to their owner to indulge, we scarce know whether they will not one day be reckoned amongst the jewels.

And now the three years are past: M. Emanuel's return is fixed. It is Autumn; he is to be with me ere the mists of November come. My school flourishes, my house is ready: I have made him a little library, filled its shelves with the books he left in my care: I have cultivated out of love for him (I was naturally no florist) the plants he preferred, and some of them are yet in bloom. I thought I loved him when he went away; I love him now in another degree; he is more my own.

The sun passes the equinox; the days shorten, the leaves grow sere; but – he is coming.

Frosts appear at night; November has sent his fogs in advance; the wind takes its autumn moan; but – he is coming.

The skies hang full and dark – a rack sails from the west; the clouds cast themselves into strange forms – arches and broad radiations; there rise resplendent mornings – glorious, royal, purple as monarch in his state; the heavens are one flame; so wild are they, they rival battle at its thickest – so bloody, they shame Victory in her pride. I know some signs of the sky; I have noted them ever since childhood. God, watch that sail! Oh! guard it!

The wind shifts to the west. Peace, peace, Banshee – 'keening' at every window! It will rise – it will swell – it shrieks out long: wander as I may through the house this night, I cannot lull the blast. The advancing hours make it strong: by midnight, all sleepless watchers hear and fear a wild south-west storm.

That storm roared frenzied for seven days. It did not cease till the Atlantic was strewn with wrecks: it did not lull till the deeps had gorged their full of sustenance. Not till the destroying angel of tempest had achieved his perfect work, would he fold the wings whose waft was thunder – the tremor of whose plumes was storm.

Peace, be still! Oh! a thousand weepers, praying in agony on waiting shores, listened for that voice, but it was not uttered – not uttered till, when the hush came, some could not feel it: till, when the sun returned, his light was night to some!

Here pause: pause at once. There is enough said. Trouble no quiet, kind heart; leave sunny imaginations hope. Let it be theirs to conceive the delight of joy born again fresh out of great terror, the rapture of rescue from peril, the wondrous reprieve from dread, the fruition of return. Let them picture union and a happy succeeding life.

Mme Beck prospered all the days of her life; so did Père Silas; Mme Walravens fulfilled her ninetieth year before she died. Farewell.

# WUTHERING HEIGHTS

# Wuthering Heights

EMILY BRONTË

## Editor's Preface to the 1850 Edition

I have just read over *Wuthering Heights*, and, for the first time, have obtained a clear glimpse of what are termed (and, perhaps, really are) its faults; have gained a definite notion of how it appears to other people – to strangers who knew nothing of the author; who are unacquainted with the locality where the scenes of the story are laid; to whom the inhabitants, the customs, the natural characteristics of the outlying hills and hamlets in the West-Riding of Yorkshire are things alien and unfamiliar.

To all such *Wuthering Heights* must appear a rude and strange production. The wild moors of the north of England can for them have no interest; the language, the manners, the very dwellings and household customs of the scattered inhabitants of those districts, must be to such readers in a great measure unintelligible, and – where intelligible – repulsive. Men and women who, perhaps, naturally very calm, and with feelings moderate in degree, and little marked in kind, have been trained from their cradle to observe the utmost evenness of manner and guardedness of language, will hardly know what to make of the rough, strong utterance, the harshly manifested passions, the unbridled aversions, and headlong partialities of unlettered moorland hinds and rugged moorland squires, who have grown up untaught and unchecked, except by mentors as harsh as themselves. A large class of readers, likewise, will suffer greatly from the introduction into the pages of this work of words printed with all their letters, which it has become the custom to represent by the initial and final letter only – a blank line filling the interval. I may as well say at once that, for this circumstance, it is out of my power to apologise; deeming it, myself, a rational plan to write words at full length. The practice of hinting by single letters those expletives with which profane and violent people are wont to garnish their discourse, strikes me as a proceeding which, however well meant, is weak and futile. I cannot tell what good it does – what feeling it spares – what horror it conceals.

With regard to the rusticity of *Wuthering Heights*, I admit the charge, for I feel the quality. It is rustic all through. It is moorish, and wild, and knotty as the root of heath. Nor was it natural that it should be otherwise; the author being herself a native and nursling of the moors. Doubtless, had her lot been cast in a town, her writings, if she had written at all, would have possessed another character. Even had chance or taste led her to choose a similar subject, she would have treated it otherwise. Had Ellis Bell been a lady or a gentleman accustomed to what is called 'the world', her view of a remote and unreclaimed region, as well as of the dwellers therein, would have differed greatly from that actually taken by the homebred country girl. Doubtless it would have been wider – more comprehensive: whether it would have been more original or

more truthful is not so certain. As far as the scenery and locality are concerned, it could scarcely have been so sympathetic: Ellis Bell did not describe as one whose eye and taste alone found pleasure in the prospect; her native hills were far more to her than a spectacle; they were what she lived in, and by, as much as the wild birds, their tenants, or as the heather, their produce. Her descriptions, then, of natural scenery, are what they should be, and all they should be.

Where delineation of human character is concerned, the case is different. I am bound to avow that she had scarcely more practical knowledge of the peasantry amongst whom she lived, than a nun has of the country people who sometimes pass her convent gates. My sister's disposition was not naturally gregarious; circumstances favoured and fostered her tendency to seclusion; except to go to church or take a walk on the hills, she rarely crossed the threshold of home. Though her feeling for the people round was benevolent, intercourse with them she never sought; nor, with very few exceptions, ever experienced. And yet she knew them: knew their ways, their language, their family histories; she could hear of them with interest, and talk of them with detail, minute, graphic, and accurate; but *with* them she rarely exchanged a word. Hence it ensued that what her mind had gathered of the real concerning them, was too exclusively confined to those tragic and terrible traits of which, in listening to the secret annals of every rude vicinage, the memory is sometimes compelled to receive the impress. Her imagination, which was a spirit more sombre than sunny, more powerful than sportive, found in such traits material whence it wrought creations like Heathcliff, like Earnshaw, like Catherine. Having formed these beings, she did not know what she had done. If the auditor of her work, when read in manuscript, shuddered under the grinding influence of natures so relentless and implacable, of spirits so lost and fallen; if it was complained that the mere hearing of certain vivid and fearful scenes banished sleep by night, and disturbed mental peace by day, Ellis Bell would wonder what was meant, and suspect the complainant of affectation. Had she but lived, her mind would of itself have grown like a strong tree, loftier, straighter, wider-spreading, and its matured fruits would have attained a mellower ripeness and sunnier bloom; but on that mind time and experience alone could work: to the influence of other intellects, it was not amenable.

Having avowed that over much of *Wuthering Heights* there broods 'a horror of great darkness'; that, in its storm-heated and electrical atmosphere, we seem at times to breathe lightning, let me point to those spots where clouded daylight and the eclipsed sun still attest their existence. For a specimen of true benevolence and homely fidelity, look at the character of Nelly Dean; for an example of constancy and tenderness, remark that of Edgar Linton. (Some people will think these qualities do not shine so well incarnate in a man as they would do in a woman, but Ellis Bell could never be brought to comprehend this notion: nothing moved her more than any insinuation that the faithfulness and clemency, the long-suffering and loving-kindness which are esteemed virtues in the daughters of Eve, become foibles in the sons of Adam. She held that mercy and forgiveness are the divinest attributes of the Great Being who made

both man and woman, and that what clothes the Godhead in glory, can disgrace no form of feeble humanity.) There is a dry saturnine humour in the delineation of old Joseph, and some glimpses of grace and gaiety animate the younger Catherine. Nor is even the first heroine of the name destitute of a certain strange beauty in her fierceness, or of honesty in the midst of perverted passion and passionate perversity.

Heathcliff, indeed, stands unredeemed; never once swerving in his arrow-straight course to perdition, from the time when 'the little black-haired, swarthy thing, as dark as if it came from the Devil', was first unrolled out of the bundle and set on its feet in the farmhouse kitchen, to the hour when Nelly Dean found the grim, stalwart corpse laid on its back in the panel-enclosed bed, with wide-gazing eyes that seemed 'to sneer at her attempt to close them, and parted lips and sharp white teeth that sneered too'.

Heathcliff betrays one solitary human feeling, and that is *not* his love for Catherine; which is a sentiment fierce and inhuman: a passion such as might boil and glow in the bad essence of some evil genius; a fire that might form the tormented centre – the ever-suffering soul of a magnate of the infernal world: and by its quenchless and ceaseless ravage effect the execution of the decree which dooms him to carry Hell with him wherever he wanders. No; the single link that connects Heathcliff with humanity is his rudely confessed regard for Hareton Earnshaw – the young man whom he has ruined; and then his half-implied esteem for Nelly Dean. These solitary traits omitted, we should say he was child neither of Lascar nor gypsy, but a man's shape animated by demon life – a Ghoul – an Afreet.

Whether it is right or advisable to create beings like Heathcliff, I do not know: I scarcely think it is. But this I know; the writer who possesses the creative gift owns something of which he is not always master – something that at times strangely wills and works for itself. He may lay down rules and devise principles, and to rules and principles it will perhaps for years lie in subjection; and then, haply without any warning of revolt, there comes a time when it will no longer consent to 'harrow the valleys, or be bound with a band in the furrow' – when it 'laughs at the multitude of the city, and regards not the crying of the driver' – when, refusing absolutely to make ropes out of sea-sand any longer, it sets to work on statue-hewing, and you have a Pluto or a Jove, a Tisiphone or a Psyche, a Mermaid or a Madonna, as Fate or Inspiration direct. Be the work grim or glorious, dread or divine, you have little choice left but quiescent adoption. As for you – the nominal artist – your share in it has been to work passively under dictates you neither delivered nor could question – that would not be uttered at your prayer, nor suppressed nor changed at your caprice. If the result be attractive, the World will praise you, who little deserve praise; if it be repulsive, the same World will blame you, who almost as little deserve blame.

*Wuthering Heights* was hewn in a wild workshop, with simple tools, out of homely materials. The statuary found a granite block on a solitary moor: gazing thereon, he saw how from the crag might be elicited a head, savage, swart, sinister; a form moulded with at least one element of grandeur – power. He

wrought with a rude chisel, and from no model but the vision of his meditations. With time and labour, the crag took human shape; and there it stands colossal, dark, and frowning, half statue, half rock: in the former sense, terrible and goblin-like; in the latter, almost beautiful, for its colouring is of mellow grey, and moorland moss clothes it; and heath, with its blooming bells and balmy fragrance, grows faithfully close to the giant's foot.

CURRER BELL
1850

## *Chapter 1*

1801 – I have just returned from a visit to my landlord – the solitary neighbour that I shall be troubled with. This is certainly a beautiful country! In all England, I do not believe that I could have fixed on a situation so completely removed from the stir of society. A perfect misanthropist's Heaven: and Mr Heathcliff and I are such a suitable pair to divide the desolation between us. A capital fellow! He little imagined how my heart warmed towards him when I beheld his black eyes withdraw so suspiciously under their brows, as I rode up, and when his fingers sheltered themselves, with a jealous resolution, still further in his waistcoat, as I announced my name.

'Mr Heathcliff?' I said.

A nod was the answer.

'Mr Lockwood your new tenant, sir. I do myself the honour of calling as soon as possible after my arrival, to express the hope that I have not inconvenienced you by my perseverance in soliciting the occupation of Thrushcross Grange: I heard yesterday you had had some thoughts – '

'Thrushcross Grange is my own, sir,' he interrupted, wincing. 'I should not allow anyone to inconvenience me, if I could hinder it – walk in!'

The 'walk in' was uttered with closed teeth, and expressed the sentiment, 'Go to the Deuce': even the gate over which he leant manifested no sympathising movement to the words; and I think that circumstance determined me to accept the invitation: I felt interested in a man who seemed more exaggeratedly reserved than myself.

When he saw my horse's breast fairly pushing the barrier, he did pull out his hand to unchain it, and then sullenly preceded me up the causeway, calling, as we entered the court – 'Joseph, take Mr Lockwood's horse; and bring up some wine.'

'Here we have the whole establishment of domestics, I suppose,' was the reflection, suggested by this compound order. 'No wonder the grass grows up between the flags, and cattle are the only hedge-cutters.'

Joseph was an elderly, nay, an old man: very old, perhaps, though hale and sinewy. 'The Lord help us!' he soliloquised in an undertone of peevish displeasure, while relieving me of my horse: looking, meantime, in my face so sourly that I charitably conjectured he must have need of divine aid to digest his dinner, and his pious ejaculation had no reference to my unexpected advent.

Wuthering Heights is the name of Mr Heathcliff's dwelling. 'Wuthering' being a significant provincial adjective, descriptive of the atmospheric tumult to which its station is exposed in stormy weather. Pure, bracing ventilation they must have up there at all times, indeed: one may guess the power of the north wind blowing over the edge, by the excessive slant of a few stunted firs at the end

of the house; and by a range of gaunt thorns all stretching their limbs one way, as if craving alms of the sun. Happily, the architect had foresight to build it strong: the narrow windows are deeply set in the wall, and the corners defended with large jutting stones.

Before passing the threshold, I paused to admire a quantity of grotesque carving lavished over the front, and especially about the principal door; above which, among a wilderness of crumbling griffins and shameless little boys, I detected the date '1500', and the name 'Hareton Earnshaw'. I would have made a few comments, and requested a short history of the place from the surly owner; but his attitude at the door appeared to demand my speedy entrance, or complete departure, and I had no desire to aggravate his impatience previous to inspecting the penetralium.

One step brought us into the family sitting-room, without any introductory lobby or passage: they call it here 'the house' pre-eminently. It includes kitchen and parlour, generally; but I believe at Wuthering Heights the kitchen is forced to retreat altogether into another quarter: at least I distinguished a chatter of tongues, and a clatter of culinary utensils, deep within; and I observed no signs of roasting, boiling, or baking, about the huge fireplace; nor any glitter of copper saucepans and tin colanders on the walls. One end, indeed, reflected splendidly both light and heat from ranks of immense pewter dishes, interspersed with silver jugs and tankards, towering row after row, on a vast oak dresser, to the very roof. The latter had never been underdrawn: its entire anatomy lay bare to an enquiring eye, except where a frame of wood laden with oatcakes and clusters of legs of beef, mutton, and ham, concealed it. Above the chimney were sundry villainous old guns, and a couple of horse-pistols: and, by way of ornament, three gaudily painted canisters disposed along its ledge. The floor was of smooth, white stone; the chairs, high-backed, primitive structures, painted green: one or two heavy black ones lurking in the shade. In an arch under the dresser, reposed a huge, liver-coloured bitch pointer, surrounded by a swarm of squealing puppies; and other dogs haunted other recesses.

The apartment and furniture would have been nothing extraordinary as belonging to a homely, northern farmer, with a stubborn countenance, and stalwart limbs set out to advantage in knee-breeches and gaiters. Such an individual seated in his armchair, his mug of ale frothing on the round table before him, is to be seen in any circuit of five or six miles among these hills, if you go at the right time after dinner. But Mr Heathcliff forms a singular contrast to his abode and style of living. He is a dark-skinned gypsy in aspect, in dress and manners a gentleman: that is, as much a gentleman as many a country squire: rather slovenly, perhaps, yet not looking amiss with his negligence, because he has an erect and handsome figure; and rather morose. Possibly, some people might suspect him of a degree of underbred pride; I have a sympathetic chord within that tells me it is nothing of the sort: I know, by instinct, his reserve springs from an aversion to showy displays of feeling – to manifestations of mutual kindliness. He'll love and hate equally under cover, and esteem it a species of impertinence to be loved or hated again. No, I'm running on too fast:

I bestow my own attributes over liberally on him. Mr Heathcliff may have entirely dissimilar reasons for keeping his hand out of the way when he meets a would-be acquaintance, to those which actuate me. Let me hope my constitution is almost peculiar: my dear mother used to say I should never have a comfortable home; and only last summer I proved myself perfectly unworthy of one.

While enjoying a month of fine weather at the seacoast, I was thrown into the company of a most fascinating creature: a real goddess in my eyes, as long as she took no notice of me. I 'never told my love' vocally; still, if looks have language, the merest idiot might have guessed I was over head and ears: she understood me at last, and looked a return – the sweetest of all imaginable looks. And what did I do? I confess it with shame – shrunk icily into myself, like a snail; at every glance retired colder and farther; till finally the poor innocent was led to doubt her own senses, and, overwhelmed with confusion at her supposed mistake, persuaded her mamma to decamp. By this curious turn of disposition I have gained the reputation of deliberate heartlessness; how undeserved, I alone can appreciate.

I took a seat at the end of the hearthstone opposite that towards which my landlord advanced, and filled up an interval of silence by attempting to caress the canine mother, who had left her nursery, and was sneaking wolfishly to the back of my legs, her lip curled up, and her white teeth watering for a snatch. My caress provoked a long, guttural gnarl.

'You'd better let the dog alone,' growled Mr Heathcliff in unison, checking fiercer demonstrations with a punch of his foot. 'She's not accustomed to be spoiled – not kept for a pet.' Then, striding to a side door, he shouted again, 'Joseph!'

Joseph mumbled indistinctly in the depths of the cellar, but gave no intimation of ascending; so his master dived down to him, leaving me *vis-à-vis* the ruffianly bitch and a pair of grim shaggy sheepdogs, who shared with her a jealous guardianship over all my movements. Not anxious to come in contact with their fangs, I sat still; but, imagining they would scarcely understand tacit insults, I unfortunately indulged in winking and making faces at the trio, and some turn of my physiognomy so irritated madam, that she suddenly broke into a fury, and leapt on my knees. I flung her back, and hastened to interpose the table between us. This proceeding roused the whole hive. Half a dozen four-footed fiends, of various sizes and ages, issued from hidden dens to the common centre. I felt my heels and coat-laps peculiar subjects of assault; and, parrying off the larger combatants as effectually as I could with the poker, I was constrained to demand, aloud, assistance from some of the household in re-establishing peace.

Mr Heathcliff and his man climbed the cellar steps with vexatious phlegm: I don't think they moved one second faster than usual, though the hearth was an absolute tempest of worrying and yelping. Happily, an inhabitant of the kitchen made more dispatch: a lusty dame, with tucked-up gown, bare arms, and fire-flushed cheeks, rushed into the midst of us flourishing a frying-pan: and used that weapon, and her tongue, to such purpose, that the storm subsided magically, and she only remained, heaving like a sea after a high wind, when her master entered on the scene.

'What the devil is the matter?' he asked, eyeing me in a manner I could ill endure after this inhospitable treatment.

'What the devil, indeed!' I muttered. 'The herd of possessed swine could have had no worse spirits in them than those animals of yours, sir. You might as well leave a stranger with a brood of tigers!'

'They won't meddle with persons who touch nothing,' he remarked, putting the bottle before me, and restoring the displaced table. 'The dogs do right to be vigilant. Take a glass of wine?'

'No thank you.'

'Not bitten, are you?'

'If I had been, I would have set my signet on the biter.'

Heathcliff's countenance relaxed into a grin.

'Come, come,' he said, 'you are flurried, Mr Lockwood. Here, take a little wine. Guests are so exceedingly rare in this house that I and my dogs, I am willing to own, hardly know how to receive them. Your health, sir!'

I bowed and returned the pledge; beginning to perceive that it would be foolish to sit sulking for the misbehaviour of a pack of curs: besides, I felt loath to yield the fellow further amusement at my expense; since his humour took that turn. He – probably swayed by prudential considerations of the folly of offending a good tenant – relaxed a little in the laconic style of chipping off his pronouns and auxiliary verbs, and introduced what he supposed would be a subject of interest to me – a discourse on the advantages and disadvantages of my present place of retirement. I found him very intelligent on the topics we touched; and before I went home, I was encouraged so far as to volunteer another visit tomorrow. He evidently wished no repetition of my intrusion. I shall go, notwithstanding. It is astonishing how sociable I feel myself compared with him.

## Chapter 2

Yesterday afternoon set in misty and cold. I had half a mind to spend it by my study fire, instead of wading through heath and mud to Wuthering Heights. On coming up from dinner, however (N.B. – I dine between twelve and one o'clock; the housekeeper, a matronly lady, taken as a fixture along with the house, could not, or would not, comprehend my request that I might be served at five), on mounting the stairs with this lazy intention, and stepping into the room, I saw a servant-girl on her knees, surrounded by brushes, and coal-scuttles; and raising an infernal dust as she extinguished the flames with heaps of cinders. This spectacle drove me back immediately; I took my hat, and, after a four miles' walk, arrived at Heathcliff's garden gate just in time to escape the first feathery flakes of a snow-shower.

On that bleak hilltop the earth was hard with a black frost, and the air made me shiver through every limb. Being unable to remove the chain, I jumped over, and,

running up the flagged causeway bordered with straggling gooseberry bushes, knocked vainly for admittance, till my knuckles tingled, and the dogs howled.

'Wretched inmates!' I ejaculated, mentally, 'you deserve perpetual isolation from your species for your churlish inhospitality. At least, I would not keep my doors barred in the daytime. I don't care – I will get in!' So resolved, I grasped the latch and shook it vehemently. Vinegar-faced Joseph projected his head from a round window of the barn.

'Whet are ye for?' he shouted. 'T' maister's dahn i' t' fowld. Goa rahnd by th' end ut' laith, if yah went tuh spake tull him.'

'Is there nobody inside to open the door?' I hallooed, responsively.

'They's nobbut t' missis; and shoo'll nut oppen 't an ye mak yer flaysome dins till neeght.'

'Why? cannot you tell her who I am, eh, Joseph?'

'Nor-ne me! Aw'll hae noa hend wi't,' muttered the head vanishing.

The snow began to drive thickly. I seized the handle to essay another trial; when a young man without coat, and shouldering a pitchfork, appeared in the yard behind. He hailed me to follow him, and, after marching through a wash-house, and a paved area containing a coal-shed, pump, and pigeon-cote, we at length arrived in the huge, warm, cheerful apartment, where I was formerly received. It glowed delightfully in the radiance of an immense fire, compounded of coal, peat, and wood; and near the table, laid for a plentiful evening meal, I was pleased to observe the 'missis,' an individual whose existence I had never previously suspected. I bowed and waited, thinking she would bid me take a seat. She looked at me, leaning back in her chair, and remained motionless and mute.

'Rough weather!' I remarked. 'I'm afraid, Mrs Heathcliff, the door must bear the consequence of your servants' leisure attendance: I had hard work to make them hear me!'

She never opened her mouth. I stared – she stared also. At any rate, she kept her eyes on me in a cool, regardless manner, exceedingly embarrassing and disagreeable.

'Sit down,' said the young man, gruffly. 'He'll be in soon.'

I obeyed; and hemmed, and called the villain Juno, who deigned, at this second interview, to move the extreme tip of her tail, in token of owning my acquaintance.

'A beautiful animal!' I commenced again. 'Do you intend parting with the little ones, madam?'

'They are not mine,' said the amiable hostess, more repellingly than Heathcliff himself could have replied.

'Ah, your favourites are among these!' I continued, turning to an obscure cushion full of something like cats.

'A strange choice of favourites!' she observed scornfully.

Unluckily, it was a heap of dead rabbits. I hemmed once more, and drew closer to the hearth, repeating my comment on the wildness of the evening.

'You should not have come out,' she said, rising and reaching from the chimney-piece two of the painted canisters.

Her position before was sheltered from the light; now, I had a distinct view of her whole figure and countenance. She was slender, and apparently scarcely past girlhood: an admirable form, and the most exquisite little face that I have ever had the pleasure of beholding: small features, very fair; flaxen ringlets, or rather golden, hanging loose on her delicate neck; and eyes, had they been agreeable in expression, they would have been irresistible: fortunately for my susceptible heart, the only sentiment they evinced hovered between scorn and a kind of desperation, singularly unnatural to be detected there.

The canisters were almost out of her reach; I made a motion to aid her; she turned upon me as a miser might turn if anyone attempted to assist him in counting his gold.

'I don't want your help,' she snapped; 'I can get them for myself.'

'I beg your pardon,' I hastened to reply.

'Were you asked to tea?' she demanded, tying an apron over her neat black frock, and standing with a spoonful of the leaf poised over the pot.

'I shall be glad to have a cup,' I answered.

'Were you asked?' she repeated.

'No,' I said, half smiling. 'You are the proper person to ask me.'

She flung the tea back, spoon and all; and resumed her chair in a pet, her forehead corrugated, and her red under-lip pushed out, like a child's, ready to cry.

Meanwhile, the young man had slung on to his person a decidedly shabby upper garment, and, erecting himself before the blaze, looked down on me, from the corner of his eyes, for all the world as if there were some mortal feud unavenged between us. I began to doubt whether he were a servant or not: his dress and speech were both rude, entirely devoid of the superiority observable in Mr and Mrs Heathcliff; his thick, brown curls were rough and uncultivated, his whiskers encroached bearishly over his cheeks, and his hands were embrowned like those of the common labourer: still his bearing was free, almost haughty, and he showed none of a domestic's assiduity in attending on the lady of the house. In the absence of clear proofs of his condition, I deemed it best to abstain from noticing his curious conduct; and, five minutes afterwards, the entrance of Heathcliff relieved me, in some measure, from my uncomfortable state.

'You see, sir, I am come, according to promise!' I exclaimed, assuming the cheerful; 'and I fear I shall be weather-bound for half an hour, if you can afford me shelter during that space.'

'Half an hour?' he said, shaking the white flakes from his clothes; 'I wonder you should select the thick of a snowstorm to ramble about in. Do you know that you run a risk of being lost in the marshes? People familiar with these moors often miss their road on such evenings; and, I can tell you, there is no chance of a change at present.'

'Perhaps I can get a guide among your lads, and he might stay at the Grange till morning – could you spare me one?'

'No, I could not.'

'Oh, indeed! Well, then, I must trust to my own sagacity.'

'Umph!'

'Are you going to mak' th' tea?' demanded he of the shabby coat, shifting his ferocious gaze from me to the young lady.

'Is *he* to have any?' she asked, appealing to Heathcliff.

'Get it ready, will you?' was the answer uttered so savagely that I started. The tone in which the words were said, revealed a genuine bad nature. I no longer felt inclined to call Heathcliff a capital fellow. When the preparations were finished, he invited me with – 'Now, sir, bring forward your chair.' And we all, including the rustic youth, drew round the table: an austere silence prevailing while we discussed our meal.

I thought, if I had caused the cloud, it was my duty to make an effort to dispel it. They could not every day sit so grim and taciturn; and it was impossible, however ill-tempered they might be, that the universal scowl they wore was their everyday countenance.

'It is strange,' I began, in the interval of swallowing one cup of tea and receiving another – 'it is strange how custom can mould our tastes and ideas: many could not imagine the existence of happiness in a life of such complete exile from the world as you spend, Mr Heathcliff; yet, I'll venture to say, that, surrounded by your family, and with your amiable lady as the presiding genius over your home and heart – '

'My amiable lady!' he interrupted, with an almost diabolical sneer on his face. 'Where is she – my amiable lady?'

'Mrs Heathcliff, your wife, I mean.'

'Well, yes – Oh! you would intimate that her spirit has taken the post of ministering angel, and guards the fortunes of Wuthering Heights, even when her body is gone. Is that it?'

Perceiving myself in a blunder, I attempted to correct it. I might have seen that there was too great a disparity between the ages of the parties to make it likely that they were man and wife. One was about forty; a period of mental vigour at which men seldom cherish the delusion of being married for love, by girls: that dream is reserved for the solace of our declining years. The other did not look seventeen.

Then it flashed upon me – 'The clown at my elbow, who is drinking his tea out of a basin and eating his bread with unwashed hands, may be her husband. Heathcliff, junior, of course. Here is the consequence of being buried alive: she has thrown herself away upon that boor, from sheer ignorance that better individuals existed! A sad pity – I must beware how I cause her to regret her choice.' The last reflection may seem conceited; it was not. My neighbour struck me as bordering on repulsive; I knew, through experience, that I was tolerably attractive.

'Mrs Heathcliff is my daughter-in-law,' said Heathcliff, corroborating my surmise. He turned, as he spoke, a peculiar look in her direction, a look of hatred unless he has a most perverse set of facial muscles that will not, like those of other people, interpret the language of his soul.

'Ah, certainly – I see now: you are the favoured possessor of the beneficent fairy,' I remarked, turning to my neighbour.

This was worse than before: the youth grew crimson, and clenched his fist, with every appearance of a meditated assault. But he seemed to recollect himself, presently; and smothered the storm in a brutal curse, muttered on my behalf: which, however, I took care not to notice.

'Unhappy in your conjectures, sir!' observed my host: 'we neither of us have the privilege of owning your good fairy; her mate is dead. I said she was my daughter-in-law, therefore, she must have married my son.'

'And this young man is –'

'Not my son, assuredly!'

Heathcliff smiled again, as if it were rather too bold a jest to attribute the paternity of that bear to him.

'My name is Hareton Earnshaw,' growled the other; 'and I'd counsel you to respect it!'

'I've shown no disrespect,' was my reply, laughing internally at the dignity with which he announced himself.

He fixed his eye on me longer than I cared to return the stare, for fear I might be tempted either to box his ears, or render my hilarity audible. I began to feel unmistakably out of place in that pleasant family circle. The dismal spiritual atmosphere overcame, and more than neutralised the glowing physical comforts round me; and I resolved to be cautious how I ventured under those rafters a third time.

The business of eating being concluded, and no one uttering a word of sociable conversation, I approached a window to examine the weather. A sorrowful sight I saw: dark night coming down prematurely, and sky and hills mingled in one bitter whirl of wind and suffocating snow.

'I don't think it possible for me to get home now, without a guide,' I could not help exclaiming. 'The roads will be buried already; and, if they were bare, I could scarcely distinguish a foot in advance.'

'Hareton, drive those dozen sheep into the barn porch. They'll be covered if left in the fold all night: and put a plank before them,' said Heathcliff.

'How must I do?' I continued, with rising irritation.

There was no reply to my question; and on looking round I saw only Joseph bringing in a pail of porridge for the dogs, and Mrs Heathcliff leaning over the fire, diverting herself with burning a bundle of matches which had fallen from the chimney-piece as she restored the tea-canister to its place.

The former, when he had deposited his burden, took a critical survey of the room; and, in cracked tones, grated out – 'Aw woonder hagh yah can faishion tuh stand thear i' idleness un war, when all on 'em's goan aght! Bud yah 're a nowt, and it's noa use talking – yah'll niver mend uh yer ill ways; bud, goa raight tuh t' divil, like yer mother afore ye!'

I imagined, for a moment, that this piece of eloquence was addressed to me; and, sufficiently enraged, stepped towards the aged rascal with an intention of kicking him out of the door. Mrs Heathcliff, however, checked me by her answer.

'You scandalous old hypocrite!' she replied. 'Are you not afraid of being carried away bodily, whenever you mention the devil's name? I warn you to

refrain from provoking me, or I'll ask your adduction as a special favour. Stop, look here, Joseph,' she continued, taking a long, dark book from a shelf. 'I'll show you how far I've progressed in the Black Art: I shall soon be competent to make a clear house of it. The red cow didn't die by chance; and your rheumatism can hardly be reckoned among providential visitations!'

'Oh, wicked, wicked!' gasped the elder; 'may the Lord deliver us from evil!'

'No, reprobate! you are a castaway – be off, or I'll hurt you seriously! I'll have you all modelled in wax and clay; and the first who passes the limits I fix, shall – I'll not say what he shall be done to – but, you'll see! Go, I'm looking at you!'

The little witch put a mock malignity into her beautiful eyes, and Joseph, trembling with sincere horror, hurried out praying and ejaculating 'wicked' as he went. I thought her conduct must be prompted by a species of dreary fun; and, now that we were alone, I endeavoured to interest her in my distress.

'Mrs Heathcliff,' I said, earnestly, 'you must excuse me for troubling you – I presume, because, with that face, I'm sure you cannot help being good-hearted. Do point out some landmarks by which I may know my way home: I have no more idea how to get there than you would have how to get to London!'

'Take the road you came,' she answered, ensconcing herself in a chair, with a candle, and the long book open before her. 'It is brief advice, but as sound as I can give.'

'Then, if you hear of me being discovered dead in a bog or a pit full of snow, your conscience won't whisper that it is partly your fault?'

'How so? I cannot escort you. They wouldn't let me go to the end of the garden-wall.'

'*You!* I should be very sorry to ask you to cross the threshold, for my convenience, on such a night,' I cried. 'I want you to *tell* me my way, not to *show* it; or else to persuade Mr Heathcliff to give me a guide.'

'Who? There is himself, Earnshaw, Zillah, Joseph, and I. Which would you have?'

'Are there no boys at the farm?'

'No, those are all.'

'Then, it follows that I am compelled to stay.'

'That you may settle with your host. I have nothing to do with it.'

'I hope it will be a lesson to you, to make no more rash journeys on these hills,' cried Heathcliff's stern voice from the kitchen entrance. 'As to staying here, I don't keep accommodations for visitors: you must share a bed with Hareton, or Joseph, if you do.'

'I can sleep on a chair in this room,' I replied.

'No, no! A stranger is a stranger, be he rich or poor: it will not suit me to permit anyone the range of the place while I am off guard!' said the unmannerly wretch.

With this insult, my patience was at an end. I uttered an expression of disgust, and pushed past him into the yard, running against Earnshaw in my haste. It was so dark that I could not see the means of exit; and, as I wandered round, I heard another specimen of their civil behaviour amongst each other. At first, the young man appeared about to befriend me.

'I'll go with him as far as the park,' he said.

'You'll go with him to hell!' exclaimed his master, or whatever relation he bore. 'And who is to look after the horses, eh?'

'A man's life is of more consequence than one evening's neglect of the horses: somebody must go,' murmured Mrs Heathcliff, more kindly than I expected.

'Not at your command!' retorted Hareton. 'If you set store on him, you'd better be quiet.'

'Then I hope his ghost will haunt you; and I hope Mr Heathcliff will never get another tenant, till the Grange is a ruin!' she answered sharply.

'Hearken, hearken, shoo's cursing on em!' muttered Joseph, towards whom I had been steering.

He sat within earshot, milking the cows by the light of a lantern, which I seized unceremoniously, and, calling out that I would send it back on the morrow, rushed to the nearest postern.

'Maister, maister, he's staling t' lantern!' shouted the ancient, pursuing my retreat. 'Hey, Gnasher! Hey, dog! Hey, Wolf, holld him, holld him!'

On opening the little door, two hairy monsters flew at my throat, bearing me down and extinguishing the light; while a mingled guffaw, from Heathcliff and Hareton, put the copestone on my rage and humiliation. Fortunately, the beasts seemed more bent on stretching their paws, and yawning, and flourishing their tails, than devouring me alive; but they would suffer no resurrection, and I was forced to lie till their malignant masters pleased to deliver me: then hatless, and trembling with wrath, I ordered the miscreants to let me out – on their peril to keep me one minute longer – with several incoherent threats of retaliation that, in their indefinite depth of virulency, smacked of King Lear.

The vehemence of my agitation brought on a copious bleeding at the nose, and still Heathcliff laughed, and still I scolded. I don't know what would have concluded the scene, had there not been one person at hand rather more rational than myself, and more benevolent than my entertainer. This was Zillah, the stout housewife; who at length issued forth to enquire into the nature of the uproar. She thought that some of them had been laying violent hands on me; and, not daring to attack her master, she turned her vocal artillery against the younger scoundrel.

'Well, Mr Earnshaw,' she cried, 'I wonder what you'll have agait next! Are we going to murder folk on our very door-stones? I see this house will never do for me – look at t' poor lad, he's fair choking! Wisht, wisht! you mun'n't go on so. Come in, and I'll cure that. There now, hold ye still.'

With these words she suddenly splashed a pint of icy water down my neck, and pulled me into the kitchen. Mr Heathcliff followed, his accidental merriment expiring quickly in his habitual moroseness.

I was sick exceedingly, and dizzy and faint; and thus compelled, perforce, to accept lodgings under his roof. He told Zillah to give me a glass of brandy, and then passed on to the inner room; while she condoled with me on my sorry predicament, and having obeyed his orders, whereby I was somewhat revived, ushered me to bed.

While leading the way upstairs, she recommended that I should hide the candle, and not make a noise; for her master had an odd notion about the chamber she would put me in, and never let anybody lodge there willingly. I asked the reason. She did not know, she answered: she had only lived there a year or two; and they had so many queer goings on, she could not begin to be curious.

Too stupified to be curious myself, I fastened my door and glanced round for the bed. The whole furniture consisted of a chair, a clothes-press, and a large oak case, with squares cut out near the top, resembling coach windows. Having approached this structure, I looked inside, and perceived it to be a singular sort of old-fashioned couch, very conveniently designed to obviate the necessity for every member of the family having a room to himself. In fact, it formed a little closet, and the ledge of a window, which it enclosed, served as a table. I slid back the panelled sides, got in with my light, pulled them together again, and felt secure against the vigilance of Heathcliff, and everyone else.

The ledge, where I placed my candle, had a few mildewed books piled up in one corner; and it was covered with writing scratched on the paint. This writing, however, was nothing but a name repeated in all kinds of characters, large and small – *Catherine Earnshaw*, here and there varied to *Catherine Heathcliff*, and then again to *Catherine Linton*.

In vapid listlessness I leant my head against the window, and continued spelling over Catherine Earnshaw – Heathcliff – Linton, till my eyes closed; but they had not rested five minutes when a glare of white letters started from the dark, as vivid as spectres – the air swarmed with Catherines; and rousing myself to dispel the obtrusive name, I discovered my candle wick reclining on one of the antique volumes, and perfuming the place with an odour of roasted calfskin. I snuffed it off, and, very ill at ease under the influence of cold and lingering nausea, sat up and spread open the injured tome on my knee. It was a Testament, in lean type, and smelling dreadfully musty: a flyleaf bore the inscription – ' Catherine Earnshaw, her book,' and a date some quarter of a century back. I shut it, and took up another, and another, till I had examined all. Catherine's library was select, and its state of dilapidation proved it to have been well used; though not altogether for a legitimate purpose: scarcely one chapter had escaped a pen-and-ink commentary – at least, the appearance of one – covering every morsel of blank that the printer had left. Some were detached sentences; other parts took the form of a regular diary, scrawled in an unformed, childish hand. At the top of an extra page (quite a treasure, probably, when first lighted on) I was greatly amused to behold an excellent caricature of my friend Joseph – rudely yet powerfully sketched. An immediate interest kindled within me for the unknown Catherine, and I began, forthwith, to decipher her faded hieroglyphics.

'An awful Sunday!' commenced the paragraph beneath. 'I wish my father

were back again. Hindley is a detestable substitute – his conduct to Heathcliff is atrocious – H. and I are going to rebel – we took our initiatory step this evening.

'All day had been flooding with rain; we could not go to church, so Joseph must needs get up a congregation in the garret; and, while Hindley and his wife basked downstairs before a comfortable fire – doing anything but reading their Bibles, I'll answer for it – Heathcliff, myself, and the unhappy ploughboy were commanded to take our prayer-books, and mount: we were ranged in a row, on a sack of corn, groaning and shivering, and hoping that Joseph would shiver too, so that he might give us a short homily for his own sake. A vain idea! The service lasted precisely three hours; and yet my brother had the face to exclaim, when he saw us descending, "What, done already?" On Sunday evenings we used to be permitted to play, if we did not make much noise; now a mere titter is sufficient to send us into corners!

' "You forget you have a master here," says the tyrant. "I'll demolish the first who puts me out of temper! I insist on perfect sobriety and silence. Oh, boy! was that you? Frances, darling, pull his hair as you go by: I heard him snap his fingers." Frances pulled his hair heartily, and then went and seated herself on her husband's knee; and there they were, like two babies, kissing and talking nonsense by the hour – foolish palaver that we should be ashamed of. We made ourselves as snug as our means allowed in the arch of the dresser. I had just fastened our pinafores together, and hung them up for a curtain, when in comes Joseph, on an errand from the stables.

'He tears down my handiwork, boxes my ears, and croaks – "T' maister nobbut just buried, and Sabbath nut oe'red, und t' sahnd uh't gospel still i' yer lugs, and yah darr be laiking! shame on ye! sit ye dahn, ill childer! they's good books eneugh if ye'll read 'em: sit ye dahn, and think uh yer sowls!"

'Saying this, he compelled us so to square our positions that we might receive from the far-off fire a dull ray to show us the text of the lumber he thrust upon us. I could not bear the employment. I took my dingy volume by the scroop, and hurled it into the dog-kennel, vowing I hated a good book. Heathcliff kicked his to the same place. Then there was a hubbub!

' "Maister Hindley!" shouted our chaplain. "Maister, coom hither! Miss Cathy's riven th' back off *Th' Helmet uh Salvation*, un' Heathcliff's pawsed his fit intuh t' first part uh *T' Brooad Way to Destruction*! It's fair flaysome ut yah let 'em goa on this gait. Ech! th' owd man ud uh laced 'em properly – bud he's goan!"

'Hindley hurried up from his paradise on the hearth, and seizing one of us by the collar, and the other by the arm, hurled both into the back-kitchen; where, Joseph asseverated, "owd Nick" would fetch us as sure as we were living: and, so comforted, we each sought a separate nook to await his advent. I reached this book, and a pot of ink from the shelf, and pushed the house-door ajar to give me light, and I have got the time on with writing for twenty minutes; but my companion is impatient, and proposes that we should appropriate the dairy woman's cloak, and have a scamper on the moors, under its shelter. A pleasant suggestion – and then, if the surly old man come in, he may

believe his prophecy verified – we cannot be damper, or colder, in the rain than we are here.'

I suppose Catherine fulfilled her project, for the next sentence took up another subject: she waxed lachrymose.

'How little did I dream that Hindley would ever make me cry so!' she wrote. 'My head aches, till I cannot keep it on the pillow; and still I can't give over. Poor Heathcliff! Hindley calls him a vagabond, and won't let him sit with us, nor eat with us any more; and, he says, he and I must not play together, and threatens to turn him out of the house if we break his orders. He has been blaming our father (how dared he?) for treating H. too liberally; and swears he will reduce him to his right place – '

I began to nod drowsily over the dim page: my eye wandered from manuscript to print. I saw a red ornamented title – 'Seventy Times Seven, and the First of the Seventy-First. A Pious Discourse delivered by the Reverend Jabes Branderham, in the Chapel of Gimmerden Sough'. And while I was, half consciously, worrying my brain to guess what Jabes Branderham would make of his subject, I sank back in bed, and fell asleep. Alas, for the effects of bad tea and bad temper! What else could it be that made me pass such a terrible night? I don't remember another that I can at all compare with it since I was capable of suffering.

I began to dream, almost before I ceased to be sensible of my locality. I thought it was morning; and I had set out on my way home, with Joseph for a guide. The snow lay yards deep in our road; and, as we floundered on, my companion wearied me with constant reproaches that I had not brought a pilgrim's staff: telling me that I could never get into the house without one, and boastfully flourishing a heavy-headed cudgel, which I understood to be so denominated. For a moment I considered it absurd that I should need such a weapon to gain admittance into my own residence. Then a new idea flashed across me. I was not going there: we were journeying to hear the famous Jabes Branderham preach from the text – 'Seventy Times Seven'; and either Joseph, the preacher, or I had committed the 'First of the Seventy-First', and were to be publicly exposed and excommunicated.

We came to the chapel. I have passed it really in my walks, twice or thrice; it lies in a hollow, between two hills: an elevated hollow, near a swamp, whose peaty moisture is said to answer all the purposes of embalming on the few corpses deposited there. The roof has been kept whole hitherto; but as the clergyman's stipend is only twenty pounds per annum, and a house with two rooms, threatening speedily to determine into one, no clergyman will undertake the duties of pastor: especially as it is currently reported that his flock would rather let him starve than increase the living by one penny from their own pockets. However, in my dream, Jabes had a full and attentive congregation; and he preached – good God! what a sermon: divided into *four hundred and ninety* parts, each fully equal to an ordinary address from the pulpit, and each discussing

a separate sin! Where he searched for them, I cannot tell. He had his private manner of interpreting the phrase, and it seemed necessary the brother should sin different sins on every occasion. They were of the most curious character: odd transgressions that I never imagined previously.

Oh, how weary I grew. How I writhed, and yawned, and nodded, and revived! How I pinched and pricked myself, and rubbed my eyes, and stood up, and sat down again, and nudged Joseph to inform me if he would *ever* have done. I was condemned to hear all out: finally, he reached the '*First of the Seventy-First*'. At that crisis, a sudden inspiration descended on me; I was moved to rise and denounce Jabes Branderham as the sinner of the sin that no Christian need pardon.

'Sir,' I exclaimed, 'sitting here within these four walls, at one stretch, I have endured and forgiven the four hundred and ninety heads of your discourse. Seventy times seven times have I plucked up my hat and been about to depart – Seventy times seven times have you preposterously forced me to resume my seat. The four hundred and ninety first is too much. Fellow-martyrs, have at him! Drag him down, and crush him to atoms, that the place which knows him may know him no more!'

'*Thou art the Man!*' cried Jabes, after a solemn pause, leaning over his cushion. 'Seventy times seven times didst thou gapingly contort thy visage – seventy times seven did I take counsel with my soul – Lo, this is human weakness: this also may be absolved! The First of the Seventy-First is come. Brethren, execute upon him the judgement written. Such honour have all His saints!'

With that concluding word the whole assembly, exalting their pilgrim's staves, rushed round me in a body; and I, having no weapon to raise in self-defence, commenced grappling with Joseph, my nearest and most ferocious assailant, for his. In the confluence of the multitude, several clubs crossed; blows, aimed at me, fell on other sconces. Presently the whole chapel resounded with rappings and counter-rappings: every man's hand was against his neighbour; and Branderham, unwilling to remain idle, poured forth his zeal in a shower of loud taps on the boards of the pulpit, which responded so smartly that, at last, to my unspeakable relief, they woke me. And what was it that had suggested the tremendous tumult? What had played Jabes's part in the row? Merely the branch of a fir tree that touched my lattice, as the blast wailed by, and rattled its dry cones against the panes! I listened doubtingly an instant; detected the disturber, then turned and dosed, and dreamt again: if possible, still more disagreeably than before.

This time, I remembered I was lying in the oak closet, and I heard distinctly the gusty wind, and the driving of the snow; I heard, also, the fir bough repeat its teasing sound, and ascribed it to the right cause: but it annoyed me so much, that I resolved to silence it, if possible; and, I thought, I rose and endeavoured to unhasp the casement. The hook was soldered into the staple: a circumstance observed by me when awake, but forgotten. 'I must stop it, nevertheless!' I muttered, knocking my knuckles through the glass, and stretching an arm out to seize the importunate branch; instead of which, my fingers closed on the fingers

of a little, ice-cold hand! The intense horror of nightmare came over me: I tried
to draw back my arm, but the hand clung to it, and a most melancholy voice
sobbed, 'Let me in – let me in!' 'Who are you?' I asked, struggling, meanwhile,
to disengage myself. 'Catherine Linton,' it replied shiveringly (why did I think
of *Linton*? I had read *Earnshaw* twenty times for Linton). 'I'm come home: I'd
lost my way on the moor!' As it spoke, I discerned, obscurely, a child's face
looking through the window. Terror made me cruel; and, finding it useless to
attempt shaking the creature off, I pulled its wrist on to the broken pane, and
rubbed it to and fro till the blood ran down and soaked the bedclothes: still it
wailed, 'Let me in!' and maintained its tenacious gripe, almost maddening me
with fear. 'How can I!' I said at length. 'Let *me* go, if you want me to let you in!'
The fingers relaxed, I snatched mine through the hole, hurriedly piled the
books up in a pyramid against it, and stopped my ears to exclude the lamentable
prayer. I seemed to keep them closed above a quarter of an hour; yet, the instant
I listened again, there was the doleful cry moaning on! 'Begone!' I shouted, 'I'll
never let you in, not if you beg for twenty years.' 'It is twenty years,' mourned
the voice: 'twenty years. I've been a waif for twenty years!' Thereat began a
feeble scratching outside, and the pile of books moved as if thrust forward. I
tried to jump up; but could not stir a limb; and so yelled aloud, in a frenzy of
fright. To my confusion, I discovered the yell was not ideal: hasty footsteps
approached my chamber door; somebody pushed it open, with a vigorous hand,
and a light glimmered through the squares at the top of the bed. I sat shuddering
yet, and wiping the perspiration from my forehead: the intruder appeared to
hesitate, and muttered to himself. At last, he said in a half-whisper, plainly not
expecting an answer, 'Is anyone here?' I considered it best to confess my
presence; for I knew Heathcliff's accents, and feared he might search further, if I
kept quiet. With this intention, I turned and opened the panels. I shall not soon
forget the effect my action produced.

Heathcliff stood near the entrance, in his shirt and trousers; with a candle
dripping over his fingers, and his face as white as the wall behind him. The first
creak of the oak startled him like an electric shock: the light leaped from his hold
to a distance of some feet, and his agitation was so extreme, that he could hardly
pick it up.

'It is only your guest, sir,' I called out, desirous to spare him the humiliation
of exposing his cowardice further. 'I had the misfortune to scream in my sleep,
owing to a frightful nightmare. I'm sorry I disturbed you.'

'Oh, God confound you, Mr Lockwood! I wish you were at the —' commenced
my host, setting the candle on a chair, because he found it impossible to hold it
steady. 'And who showed you up to this room?' he continued, crushing his nails
into his palms, and grinding his teeth to subdue the maxillary convulsions. 'Who
was it? I've a good mind to turn them out of the house this moment!'

'It was your servant, Zillah,' I replied, flinging myself on to the floor, and
rapidly resuming my garments. 'I should not care if you did, Mr Heathcliff; she
richly deserves it. I suppose that she wanted to get another proof that the place
was haunted, at my expense. Well, it is – swarming with ghosts and goblins! You

have reason in shutting it up, I assure you. No one will thank you for a dose in such a den!"

'What do you mean?' asked Heathcliff, 'and what are you doing? Lie down and finish out the night, since you *are* here; but, for Heaven's sake! Don't repeat that horrid noise: nothing could excuse it, unless you were having your throat cut!'

'If the little fiend had got in at the window, she probably would have strangled me!' I returned. 'I'm not going to endure the persecutions of your hospitable ancestors again. Was not the Reverend Jabes Branderham akin to you on the mother's side? And that minx, Catherine Linton, or Earnshaw, or however she was called – she must have been a changeling – wicked little soul! She told me she had been walking the earth these twenty years; a just punishment for her mortal transgressions, I've no doubt!'

Scarcely were these words uttered, when I recollected the association of Heathcliff's with Catherine's name in the book, which had completely slipped from my memory, till thus awakened. I blushed at my inconsideration; but, without showing further consciousness of the offence, I hastened to add – 'The truth is, sir, I passed the first part of the night in' – here I stopped afresh – I was about to say 'perusing those old volumes', then it would have revealed my knowledge of their written, as well as their printed, contents; so, correcting myself, I went on – 'in spelling over the name scratched on that window-ledge. A monotonous occupation, calculated to set me asleep, like counting, or –'

'What *can* you mean by talking in this way to *me*?' thundered Heathcliff with savage vehemence. 'How – how *dare* you, under my roof? – God! he's mad to speak so!' And he struck his forehead with rage.

I did not know whether to resent this language or pursue my explanation; but he seemed so powerfully affected that I took pity and proceeded with my dreams; affirming I had never heard the appellation of 'Catherine Linton' before, but reading it often over produced an impression which personified itself when I had no longer my imagination under control. Heathcliff gradually fell back into the shelter of the bed, as I spoke; finally sitting down almost concealed behind it. I guessed, however, by his irregular and intercepted breathing, that he struggled to vanquish an excess of violent emotion. Not liking to show him that I heard the conflict, I continued my toilette rather noisily, looked at my watch, and soliloquised on the length of the night: 'Not three o'clock yet! I could have taken oath it had been six. Time stagnates here: we must surely have retired to rest at eight!'

'Always at nine in winter, and always rise at four,' said my host, suppressing a groan: and, as I fancied, by the motion of his shadow's arm, dashing a tear from his eyes. 'Mr Lockwood,' he added, 'you may go into my room: you'll only be in the way, coming downstairs so early; and your childish outcry has sent sleep to the devil for me.'

'And for me, too,' I replied. 'I'll walk in the yard till daylight, and then I'll be off; and you need not dread a repetition of my intrusion. I am now quite cured of seeking pleasure in society, be it country or town. A sensible man ought to find sufficient company in himself.'

'Delightful company!' muttered Heathcliff. 'Take the candle, and go where you please. I shall join you directly. Keep out of the yard, though, the dogs are unchained; and the house – Juno mounts sentinel there, and – nay, you can only ramble about the steps and passages. But, away with you! I'll come in two minutes!'

I obeyed, so far as to quit the chamber; when, ignorant where the narrow lobbies led, I stood still, and was witness, involuntarily, to a piece of superstition on the part of my landlord, which belied, oddly, his apparent sense. He got on to the bed, and wrenched open the lattice, bursting, as he pulled at it, into an uncontrollable passion of tears. 'Come in! come in!' he sobbed. 'Cathy, do come. Oh do – *once* more! Oh! My heart's darling! hear me *this* time, Catherine, at last!' The spectre showed a spectre's ordinary caprice; it gave no sign of being; but the snow and wind whirled wildly through, even reaching my station, and blowing out the light.

There was such anguish in the gush of grief that accompanied this raving, that my compassion made me overlook its folly, and I drew off, half angry to have listened at all, and vexed at having related my ridiculous nightmare, since it produced that agony; though *why*, was beyond my comprehension. I descended cautiously to the lower regions, and landed in the back-kitchen, where a gleam of fire, raked compactly together, enabled me to rekindle my candle. Nothing was stirring except a brindled, grey cat, which crept from the ashes, and saluted me with a querulous mew.

Two benches, shaped in sections of a circle, nearly enclosed the hearth; on one of these I stretched myself, and Grimalkin mounted the other. We were both of us nodding, ere anyone invaded our retreat, and then it was Joseph, shuffling down a wooden ladder that vanished in the roof, through a trap: the ascent to his garret, I suppose. He cast a sinister look at the little flame which I had enticed to play between the ribs, swept the cat from its elevation, and bestowing himself in the vacancy, commenced the operation of stuffing a three-inch pipe with tobacco. My presence in his sanctum was evidently esteemed a piece of impudence too shameful for remark: he silently applied the tube to his lips, folded his arms, and puffed away. I let him enjoy the luxury unannoyed; and after sucking out the last wreath, and heaving a profound sigh, he got up, and departed as solemnly as he came.

A more elastic footstep entered next; and now I opened my mouth for a 'good-morning', but closed it again, the salutation unachieved; for Hareton Earnshaw was performing his orisons *sotto voce*, in a series of curses directed against every object he touched, while he rummaged a corner for a spade or shovel to dig through the drifts. He glanced over the back of the bench, dilating his nostrils, and thought as little of exchanging civilities with me as with my companion the cat. I guessed, by his preparations, that egress was allowed, and, leaving my hard couch, made a movement to follow him. He noticed this, and thrust at an inner door with the end of his spade, intimating by an inarticulate sound that there was the place where I must go, if I changed my locality.

It opened into the house, where the females were already astir. Zillah urging flakes of flame up the chimney with a colossal bellows; and Mrs Heathcliff, kneeling on the hearth, reading a book by the aid of the blaze. She held her hand interposed between the furnace-heat and her eyes, and seemed absorbed in her occupation; desisting from it only to chide the servant for covering her with sparks, or to push away a dog, now and then, that snoozled its nose over-forwardly into her face. I was surprised to see Heathcliff there also. He stood by the fire, his back towards me, just finishing a stormy scene to poor Zillah; who ever and anon interrupted her labour to pluck up the corner of her apron, and heave an indignant groan.

'And you, you worthless —,' he broke out as I entered, turning to his daughter-in-law, and employing an epithet as harmless as duck, or sheep, but generally represented by a dash. 'There you are, at your idle tricks again? The rest of them do earn their bread – you live on my charity! Put your trash away, and find something to do. You shall pay me for the plague of having you eternally in my sight – do you hear, damnable jade?'

'I'll put my trash away, because you can make me, if I refuse,' answered the young lady, closing her book, and throwing it on a chair. 'But I'll not do anything, though you should swear your tongue out, except what I please!'

Heathcliff lifted his hand, and the speaker sprang to a safer distance, obviously acquainted with its weight. Having no desire to be entertained by a cat-and-dog combat, I stepped forward briskly, as if eager to partake the warmth of the hearth, and innocent of any knowledge of the interrupted dispute. Each had enough decorum to suspend further hostilities: Heathcliff placed his fists, out of temptation, in his pockets; Mrs Heathcliff curled her lip, and walked to a seat far off, where she kept her word by playing the part of a statue during the remainder of my stay. That was not long. I declined joining their breakfast, and, at the first gleam of dawn, took an opportunity of escaping into the free air, now clear and still, and cold as impalpable ice.

My landlord hallooed for me to stop, ere I reached the bottom of the garden, and offered to accompany me across the moor. It was well he did, for the whole hill-back was one billowy, white ocean; the swells and falls not indicating corresponding rises and depressions in the ground: many pits, at least, were filled to a level; and entire ranges of mounds, the refuse of the quarries, blotted out from the chart which my yesterday's walk left pictured in my mind. I had remarked on one side of the road, at intervals of six or seven yards, a line of upright stones, continued through the whole length of the barren: these were erected, and daubed with lime on purpose to serve as guides in the dark; and also when a fall, like the present, confounded the deep swamps on either hand with the firmer path: but, excepting a dirty dot pointing up here and there, all traces of their existence had vanished: and my companion found it necessary to warn me frequently to steer to the right or left, when I imagined I was following, correctly, the windings of the road.

We exchanged little conversation, and he halted at the entrance of Thrushcross park, saying I could make no error there. Our adieux were limited to

a hasty bow, and then I pushed forward, trusting to my own resources; for the porter's lodge is untenanted as yet. The distance from the gate to the Grange is two miles: I believe I managed to make it four; what with losing myself among the trees, and sinking up to the neck in snow: a predicament which only those who have experienced it can appreciate. At any rate, whatever were my wanderings, the clock chimed twelve as I entered the house; and that gave exactly an hour for every mile of the usual way from Wuthering Heights.

My human fixture and her satellites rushed to welcome me; exclaiming, tumultuously, they had completely given me up: everybody conjectured that I perished last night; and they were wondering how they must set about the search for my remains. I bid them be quiet, now that they saw me returned, and, benumbed to my very heart, I dragged upstairs; whence, after putting on dry clothes, and pacing to and fro thirty or forty minutes, to restore the animal heat, I am adjourned to my study, feeble as a kitten: almost too much so to enjoy the cheerful fire and smoking coffee which the servant has prepared for my refreshment.

## Chapter 4

What vain weathercocks we are! I, who had determined to hold myself independent of all social intercourse, and thanked my stars that, at length, I had lighted on a spot where it was next to impracticable – I, weak wretch, after maintaining till dusk a struggle with low spirits and solitude, was finally compelled to strike my colours: and, under pretence of gaining information concerning the necessities of my establishment, I desired Mrs Dean, when she brought in supper, to sit down while I ate it; hoping sincerely she would prove a regular gossip, and either rouse me to animation or lull me to sleep by her talk.

'You have lived here a considerable time,' I commenced; 'did you not say sixteen years?'

'Eighteen, sir: I came, when the mistress was married, to wait on her; after she died, the master retained me for his housekeeper.'

'Indeed.'

There ensued a pause. She was not a gossip, I feared; unless about her own affairs, and those could hardly interest me. However, having studied for an interval, with a fist on either knee, and a cloud of meditation over her ruddy countenance, she ejaculated – 'Ah, times are greatly changed since then!'

'Yes,' I remarked, 'you've seen a good many alterations, I suppose?'

'I have: and troubles too,' she said.

'Oh, I'll turn the talk on my landlord's family!' I thought to myself. 'A good subject to start – and that pretty girl-widow, I should like to know her history: whether she be a native of the country, or, as is more probable, an exotic that the surly *indigenae* will not recognise for kin.' With this intention I asked Mrs Dean

why Heathcliff let Thrushcross Grange, and preferred living in a situation and residence so much inferior. 'Is he not rich enough to keep the estate in good order?' I enquired.

'Rich, sir!' she returned. 'He has nobody knows what money, and every year it increases. Yes, yes, he's rich enough to live in a finer house than this: but he's very near – close-handed; and, if he had meant to flit to Thrushcross Grange, as soon as he heard of a good tenant he could not have borne to miss the chance of getting a few hundreds more. It is strange people should be so greedy, when they are alone in the world!'

'He had a son, it seems?'

'Yes, he had one – he is dead.'

'And that young lady, Mrs Heathcliff, is his widow?'

'Yes.'

'Where did she come from originally?'

'Why, sir, she is my late master's daughter: Catherine Linton was her maiden name. I nursed her, poor thing! I did wish Mr Heathcliff would remove here, and then we might have been together again.'

'What! Catherine Linton?' I exclaimed, astonished. But a minute's reflection convinced me it was not my ghostly Catherine. 'Then,' I continued, 'my predecessor's name was Linton?'

'It was.'

'And who is that Earnshaw, Hareton Earnshaw, who lives with Mr Heathcliff? Are they relations?'

'No; he is the late Mrs Linton's nephew.'

'The young lady's cousin, then?'

'Yes; and her husband was her cousin also: one on the mother's, the other on the father's side: Heathcliff married Mr Linton's sister.'

'I see the house at Wuthering Heights has "Earnshaw" carved over the front door. Are they an old family?'

'Very old, sir; and Hareton is the last of them, as our Miss Cathy is of us – I mean, of the Lintons. Have you been to Wuthering Heights? I beg pardon for asking; but I should like to hear how she is.'

'Mrs Heathcliff? she looked very well, and very handsome; yet, I think, not very happy.'

'Oh dear, I don't wonder! And how did you like the master?'

'A rough fellow, rather, Mrs Dean. Is not that his character?'

'Rough as a saw-edge, and hard as whinstone! The less you meddle with him the better.'

'He must have had some ups and downs in life to make him such a churl. Do you know anything of his history?'

'It's a cuckoo's, sir – I know all about it: except where he was born, and who were his parents, and how he got his money, at first. And Hareton has been cast out like an unfledged dunnock! The unfortunate lad is the only one in all this parish that does not guess how he has been cheated.'

'Well, Mrs Dean, it will be a charitable deed to tell me something of my

neighbours: I feel I shall not rest, if I go to bed; so be good enough to sit and chat an hour.'

'Oh, certainly, sir! I'll just fetch a little sewing, and then I'll sit as long as you please. But you've caught cold: I saw you shivering, and you must have some gruel to drive it out.'

The worthy woman bustled off, and I crouched nearer the fire; my head felt hot, and the rest of me chill: moreover I was excited, almost to a pitch of foolishness, through my nerves and brain. This caused me to feel, not uncomfortable, but rather fearful (as I am still) of serious effects from the incidents of today and yesterday. She returned presently, bringing a smoking basin and a basket of work; and, having placed the former on the hob, drew in her seat, evidently pleased to find me so companionable.

Before I came to live here, she commenced – waiting no further invitation to her story – I was almost always at Wuthering Heights; because my mother had nursed Mr Hindley Earnshaw, that was Hareton's father, and I got used to playing with the children: I ran errands too, and helped to make hay, and hung about the farm ready for anything that anybody would set me to. One fine summer morning – it was the beginning of harvest, I remember – Mr Earnshaw, the old master, came downstairs, dressed for a journey; and after he had told Joseph what was to be done during the day, he turned to Hindley, and Cathy, and me – for I sat eating my porridge with them – and he said, speaking to his son, 'Now, my bonny man, I'm going to Liverpool today, what shall I bring you? You may choose what you like: only let it be little, for I shall walk there and back: sixty miles each way, that is a long spell!' Hindley named a fiddle, and then he asked Miss Cathy; she was hardly six years old, but she could ride any horse in the stable, and she chose a whip. He did not forget me; for he had a kind heart, though he was rather severe sometimes. He promised to bring me a pocketful of apples and pears, and then he kissed his children, goodbye, and set off.

It seemed a long while to us all – the three days of his absence – and often did little Cathy ask when he would be home. Mrs Earnshaw expected him by supper-time, on the third evening, and she put the meal off hour after hour; there were no signs of his coming, however, and at last the children got tired of running down to the gate to look. Then it grew dark; she would have had them to bed, but they begged sadly to be allowed to stay up; and, just about eleven o'clock, the door-latch was raised quietly, and in stepped the master. He threw himself into a chair, laughing and groaning, and bid them all stand off, for he was nearly killed – he would not have such another walk for the three kingdoms.

'And at the end of it, to be flighted to death!' he said, opening his greatcoat, which he held bundled up in his arms. 'See here, wife! I was never so beaten with anything in my life: but you must e'en take it as a gift of God; though it's as dark almost as if it came from the devil.'

We crowded round, and over Miss Cathy's head I had a peep at a dirty, ragged, black-haired child; big enough both to walk and talk: indeed, its face looked older than Catherine's; yet, when it was set on its feet, it only stared

round, and repeated over and over again some gibberish, that nobody could understand. I was frightened, and Mrs Earnshaw was ready to fling it out of doors: she did fly up, asking how he could fashion to bring that gypsy brat into the house, when they had their own bairns to feed and fend for? What he meant to do with it, and whether he were mad? The master tried to explain the matter; but he was really half dead with fatigue, and all that I could make out, amongst her scolding, was a tale of his seeing it starving, and houseless, and as good as dumb, in the streets of Liverpool; where he picked it up and enquired for its owner. Not a soul knew to whom it belonged, he said; and his money and time being both limited, he thought it better to take it home with him at once, than run into vain expenses there: because he was determined he would not leave it as he found it. Well, the conclusion was that my mistress grumbled herself calm; and Mr Earnshaw told me to wash it, and give it clean things, and let it sleep with the children.

Hindley and Cathy contented themselves with looking and listening till peace was restored: then, both began searching their father's pockets for the presents he had promised them. The former was a boy of fourteen, but when he drew out what had been a fiddle, crushed to morsels in the greatcoat, he blubbered aloud; and Cathy, when she learnt the master had lost her whip in attending on the stranger, showed her humour by grinning and spitting at the stupid little thing; earning for her pains a sound blow from her father to teach her cleaner manners. They entirely refused to have it in bed with them, or even in their room; and I had no more sense, so I put it on the landing of the stairs, hoping it might be gone on the morrow. By chance, or else attracted by hearing his voice, it crept to Mr Earnshaw's door, and there he found it on quitting his chamber. Enquiries were made as to how it got there; I was obliged to confess, and in recompense for my cowardice and inhumanity was sent out of the house.

This was Heathcliff's first introduction to the family. On coming back a few days afterwards (for I did not consider my banishment perpetual) I found they had christened him 'Heathcliff': it was the name of a son who died in childhood, and it has served him ever since, both for Christian and surname. Miss Cathy and he were now very thick; but Hindley hated him: and to say the truth I did the same; and we plagued and went on with him shamefully: for I wasn't reasonable enough to feel my injustice, and the mistress never put in a word on his behalf when she saw him wronged.

He seemed a sullen, patient child; hardened, perhaps, to ill-treatment: he would stand Hindley's blows without winking or shedding a tear, and my pinches moved him only to draw in a breath and open his eyes, as if he had hurt himself by accident and nobody was to blame. This endurance made old Earnshaw furious, when he discovered his son persecuting the poor, fatherless child, as he called him. He took to Heathcliff strangely, believing all he said (for that matter, he said precious little, and generally the truth), and petting him up far above Cathy, who was too mischievous and wayward for a favourite.

So, from the very beginning, he bred bad feeling in the house; and at Mrs Earnshaw's death, which happened in less than two years after, the young

master had learnt to regard his father as an oppressor rather than a friend, and Heathcliff as a usurper of his father's affections and his privileges, and he grew bitter with brooding over these injuries. I sympathised awhile; but when the children fell ill of the measles, and I had to tend them, and take on me the cares of a woman at once, I changed my ideas. Heathcliff was dangerously sick; and while he lay at the worst he would have me constantly by his pillow: I suppose he felt I did a good deal for him, and he hadn't the wit to guess that I was compelled to do it. However, I will say this, he was the quietest child that ever nurse watched over. The difference between him and the others forced me to be less partial. Cathy and her brother harassed me terribly; *he* was as uncomplaining as a lamb; though hardness, not gentleness, made him give little trouble.

He got through, and the doctor affirmed it was in a great measure owing to me, and praised me for my care. I was vain of his commendations, and softened towards the being by whose means I earned them, and thus Hindley lost his last ally: still I couldn't dote on Heathcliff, and I wondered often what my master saw to admire so much in the sullen boy, who never, to my recollection, repaid his indulgence by any sign of gratitude. He was not insolent to his benefactor, he was simply insensible; though knowing perfectly the hold he had on his heart, and conscious he had only to speak and all the house would be obliged to bend to his wishes.

As an instance, I remember Mr Earnshaw once bought a couple of colts at the parish fair, and gave the lads each one. Heathcliff took the handsomest, but it soon fell lame, and when he discovered it, he said to Hindley – 'You must exchange horses with me: I don't like mine; and if you won't I shall tell your father of the three thrashings you've given me this week, and show him my arm, which is black to the shoulder.' Hindley put out his tongue, and cuffed him over the ears. 'You'd better do it at once,' he persisted, escaping to the porch (they were in the stable): 'you will have to; and if I speak of these blows, you'll get them again with interest.' 'Off, dog!' cried Hindley, threatening him with an iron weight used for weighing potatoes and hay. 'Throw it,' he replied, standing still, 'and then I'll tell how you boasted that you would turn me out of doors as soon as he died, and see whether he will not turn you out directly.' Hindley threw it, hitting him on the breast, and down he fell, but staggered up immediately, breathless and white; and, had not I prevented it, he would have gone just so to the master, and got full revenge by letting his condition plead for him, intimating who had caused it. 'Take my colt, gypsy, then!' said young Earnshaw. 'And I pray that he may break your neck: take him, and be damned, you beggarly interloper! and wheedle my father out of all he has: only afterwards show him what you are, imp of Satan – And take that, I hope he'll kick out your brains!'

Heathcliff had gone to loose the beast, and shift it to his own stall; he was passing behind it, when Hindley finished his speech by knocking him under its feet, and without stopping to examine whether his hopes were fulfilled, ran away as fast as he could. I was surprised to witness how coolly the child gathered himself up, and went on with his intention; exchanging saddles and all, and then

sitting down on a bundle of hay to overcome the qualm which the violent blow occasioned, before he entered the house. I persuaded him easily to let me lay the blame of his bruises on the horse: he minded little what tale was told since he had what he wanted. He complained so seldom, indeed, of such stirs as these, that I really thought him not vindictive: I was deceived completely, as you will hear.

## *Chapter 5*

In the course of time, Mr Earnshaw began to fail. He had been active and healthy, yet his strength left him suddenly; and when he was confined to the chimney-corner he grew grievously irritable. A nothing vexed him; and suspected slights of his authority nearly threw him into fits. This was especially to be remarked if anyone attempted to impose upon, or domineer over, his favourite: he was painfully jealous lest a word should be spoken amiss to him; seeming to have got into his head the notion that, because he liked Heathcliff, all hated, and longed to do him an ill-turn. It was a disadvantage to the lad; for the kinder among us did not wish to fret the master, so we humoured his partiality; and that humouring was rich nourishment to the child's pride and black tempers. Still it became in a manner necessary; twice, or thrice, Hindley's manifestations of scorn, while his father was near, roused the old man to a fury: he seized his stick to strike him, and shook with rage that he could not do it.

At last, our curate, (we had a curate then who made the living answer by teaching the little Lintons and Earnshaws, and farming his bit of land himself), he advised that the young man should be sent to college; and Mr Earnshaw agreed, though with a heavy spirit, for he said – 'Hindley was naught, and would never thrive as where he wandered.'

I hoped heartily we should have peace now. It hurt me to think the master should be made uncomfortable by his own good deed. I fancied the discontent of age and disease arose from his family disagreements; as he would have it that it did: really, you know, sir, it was in his sinking frame. We might have got on tolerably, notwithstanding, but for two people, Miss Cathy and Joseph, the servant: you saw him, I dare say, up yonder. He was, and is yet, most likely, the wearisomest, self-righteous pharisee that ever ransacked a Bible to rake the promises to himself and fling the curses on his neighbours. By his knack of sermonising and pious discoursing, he contrived to make a great impression on Mr Earnshaw; and the more feeble the master became, the more influence he gained. He was relentless in worrying him about his soul's concerns, and about ruling his children rigidly. He encouraged him to regard Hindley as a reprobate; and, night after night, he regularly grumbled out a long string of tales against Heathcliff and Catherine: always minding to flatter Earnshaw's weakness by heaping the heaviest blame on the last.

Certainly, she had ways with her such as I never saw a child take up before;

and she put all of us past our patience fifty times and oftener in a day: from the hour she came downstairs till the hour she went to bed, we had not a minute's security that she wouldn't be in mischief. Her spirits were always at high-watermark, her tongue always going – singing, laughing, and plaguing everybody who would not do the same. A wild, wicked slip she was – but she had the bonniest eye, and sweetest smile, and lightest foot in the parish: and, after all, I believe she meant no harm; for when once she made you cry in good earnest, it seldom happened that she would not keep you company, and oblige you to be quiet that you might comfort her. She was much too fond of Heathcliff. The greatest punishment we could invent for her was to keep her separate from him; yet she got chided more than any of us on his account. In play, she liked exceedingly to act the little mistress; using her hands freely, and commanding her companions: she did so to me, but I would not bear slapping and ordering: and so I let her know.

Now, Mr Earnshaw did not understand jokes from his children: he had always been strict and grave with them; and Catherine, on her part, had no idea why her father should be crosser and less patient in his ailing condition, than he was in his prime. His peevish reproofs wakened in her a naughty delight to provoke him: she was never so happy as when we were all scolding her at once, and she defying us with her bold, saucy look, and her ready words; turning Joseph's religious curses into ridicule, baiting me, and doing just what her father hated most, showing how her pretended insolence, which he thought real, had more power over Heathcliff than his kindness: how the boy would do *her* bidding in anything, and *his* only when it suited his own inclination. After behaving as badly as possible all day, she sometimes came fondling to make it up at night. 'Nay, Cathy,' the old man would say, 'I cannot love thee; thou'rt worse than thy brother. Go, say thy prayers, child, and ask God's pardon. I doubt thy mother and I must rue that we ever reared thee!' That made her cry, at first; and then, being repulsed continually hardened her, and she laughed if I told her to say she was sorry for her faults, and beg to be forgiven.

But the hour came, at last, that ended Mr Earnshaw's troubles on earth. He died quietly in his chair one October evening, seated by the fireside. A high wind blustered round the house, and roared in the chimney: it sounded wild and stormy, yet it was not cold, and we were all together – I, a little removed from the hearth, busy at my knitting, and Joseph reading his Bible near the table (for the servants generally sat in the house then, after their work was done). Miss Cathy had been sick, and that made her still; she leant against her father's knee, and Heathcliff was lying on the floor with his head in her lap. I remember the master, before he fell into a doze, stroking her bonny hair – it pleased him rarely to see her gentle – and saying – 'Why canst thou not always be a good lass, Cathy?' And she turned her face up to his, and laughed, and answered, 'Why cannot you always be a good man, father?' But as soon as she saw him vexed again, she kissed his hand, and said she would sing him to sleep. She began singing very low, till his fingers dropped from hers, and his head sank on his breast. Then I told her to hush, and not stir, for fear she should wake him. We

all kept as mute as mice a full half-hour, and should have done longer, only Joseph, having finished his chapter, got up and said that he must rouse the master for prayers and bed. He stepped forward, and called him by name, and touched his shoulder; but he would not move, so he took the candle and looked at him. I thought there was something wrong as he set down the light, and seizing the children each by an arm, whispered them to 'frame upstairs, and make little din – they might pray alone that evening – he had summut to do'.

'I shall bid father good-night first,' said Catherine, putting her arms round his neck before we could hinder her. The poor thing discovered her loss directly – she screamed out – 'Oh, he's dead, Heathcliff! he's dead!' And they both set up a heartbreaking cry.

I joined my wail to theirs, loud and bitter; but Joseph asked what we could be thinking of to roar in that way over a saint in heaven. He told me to put on my cloak and run to Gimmerton for the doctor and the parson. I could not guess the use that either would be of, then. However, I went, through wind and rain, and brought one, the doctor, back with me; the other said he would come in the morning. Leaving Joseph to explain matters, I ran to the children's room: their door was ajar, I saw they had never laid down, though it was past midnight; but they were calmer, and did not need me to console them. The little souls were comforting each other with better thoughts than I could have hit on: no parson in the world ever pictured heaven so beautifully as they did, in their innocent talk; and, while I sobbed, and listened, I could not help wishing we were all there safe together.

## *Chapter 6*

Mr Hindley came home to the funeral; and – a thing that amazed us, and set the neighbours gossiping right and left – he brought a wife with him. What she was, and where she was born, he never informed us: probably, she had neither money nor name to recommend her, or he would scarcely have kept the union from his father.

She was not one that would have disturbed the house much on her own account. Every object she saw, the moment she crossed the threshold, appeared to delight her; and every circumstance that took place about her: except the preparing for the burial, and the presence of the mourners. I thought she was half silly, from her behaviour while that went on: she ran into her chamber, and made me come with her, though I should have been dressing the children; and there she sat shivering and clasping her hands, and asking repeatedly – 'Are they gone yet?' Then she began describing with hysterical emotion the effect it produced on her to see black; and started, and trembled, and, at last, fell a-weeping – and when I asked what was the matter? answered, she didn't know; but she felt so afraid of dying! I imagined her as little likely to die as myself. She was rather thin, but young, and fresh complexioned, and her eyes sparkled as bright as diamonds.

I did remark, to be sure, that mounting the stairs made her breathe very quick; that the least sudden noise set her all in a quiver, and that she coughed troublesomely sometimes: but I knew nothing of what these symptoms portended, and had no impulse to sympathise with her. We don't in general take to foreigners, here, Mr Lockwood, unless they take to us first.

Young Earnshaw was altered considerably in the three years of his absence. He had grown sparer, and lost his colour, and spoke and dressed quite differently; and, on the very day of his return, he told Joseph and me we must thenceforth quarter ourselves in the back-kitchen, and leave the house for him. Indeed, he would have carpeted and papered a small spare room for a parlour; but his wife expressed such pleasure at the white floor and huge glowing fireplace, at the pewter dishes and delf-case, and dog-kennel, and the wide space there was to move about in where they usually sat, that he thought it unnecessary to her comfort, and so dropped the intention.

She expressed pleasure, too, at finding a sister among her new acquaintance; and she prattled to Catherine, and kissed her, and ran about with her, and gave her quantities of presents, at the beginning. Her affection tired very soon, however, and when she grew peevish, Hindley became tyrannical. A few words from her, evincing a dislike to Heathcliff, were enough to rouse in him all his old hatred of the boy. He drove him from their company to the servants, deprived him of the instructions of the curate, and insisted that he should labour out of doors instead; compelling him to do so as hard as any other lad on the farm.

He bore his degradation pretty well at first, because Cathy taught him what she learnt, and worked or played with him in the fields. They both promised fair to grow up as rude as savages; the young master being entirely negligent how they behaved, and what they did, so they kept clear of him. He would not even have seen after their going to church on Sundays, only Joseph and the curate reprimanded his carelessness when they absented themselves; and that reminded him to order Heathcliff a flogging, and Catherine a fast from dinner or supper. But it was one of their chief amusements to run away to the moors in the morning and remain there all day, and the after punishment grew a mere thing to laugh at. The curate might set as many chapters as he pleased for Catherine to get by heart, and Joseph might thrash Heathcliff till his arm ached; they forgot everything the minute they were together again: at least the minute they had contrived some naughty plan of revenge; and many a time I've cried to myself to watch them growing more reckless daily, and I not daring to speak a syllable, for fear of losing the small power I still retained over the unfriended creatures. One Sunday evening, it chanced that they were banished from the sitting-room, for making a noise, or a light offence of the kind; and when I went to call them to supper, I could discover them nowhere. We searched the house, above and below, and the yard and stables; they were invisible: and, at last, Hindley in a passion told us to bolt the doors, and swore nobody should let them in that night. The household went to bed; and I, too anxious to lie down, opened my lattice and put my head out to hearken, though it rained: determined to admit them in spite of the prohibition, should they return. In a while, I

distinguished steps coming up the road, and the light of a lantern glimmered through the gate. I threw a shawl over my head and ran to prevent them from waking Mr Earnshaw by knocking. There was Heathcliff, by himself: it gave me a start to see him alone.

'Where is Miss Catherine?' I cried hurriedly. 'No accident, I hope?' 'At Thrushcross Grange,' he answered; 'and I would have been there too, but they had not the manners to ask me to stay.' 'Well, you will catch it!' I said: 'you'll never be content till you're sent about your business. What in the world led you wandering to Thrushcross Grange?' 'Let me get off my wet clothes, and I'll tell you all about it, Nelly,' he replied. I bid him beware of rousing the master, and while he undressed and I waited to put out the candle, he continued – 'Cathy and I escaped from the wash-house to have a ramble at liberty, and getting a glimpse of the Grange lights, we thought we would just go and see whether the Lintons passed their Sunday evenings standing shivering in corners, while their father and mother sat eating and drinking, and singing and laughing, and burning their eyes out before the fire. Do you think they do? Or reading sermons, and being catechised by their manservant, and set to learn a column of Scripture names, if they don't answer properly?' 'Probably not,' I responded. 'They are good children, no doubt, and don't deserve the treatment you receive, for your bad conduct.' 'Don't you cant, Nelly,' he said: 'nonsense! We ran from the top of the Heights to the park, without stopping – Catherine completely beaten in the race, because she was barefoot. You'll have to seek for her shoes in the bog tomorrow. We crept through a broken hedge, groped our way up the path, and planted ourselves on a flower-plot under the drawing-room window. The light came from thence; they had not put up the shutters, and the curtains were only half closed. Both of us were able to look in by standing on the basement, and clinging to the ledge, and we saw – ah! it was beautiful – a splendid place carpeted with crimson, and crimson-covered chairs and tables, and a pure white ceiling bordered by gold, a shower of glass-drops hanging in silver chains from the centre, and shimmering with little soft tapers. Old Mr and Mrs Linton were not there; Edgar and his sister had it entirely to themselves. Shouldn't they have been happy? We should have thought ourselves in heaven! And now, guess what your good children were doing? Isabella – I believe she is eleven, a year younger than Cathy – lay screaming at the farther end of the room, shrieking as if witches were running red-hot needles into her. Edgar stood on the hearth weeping silently, and in the middle of the table sat a little dog, shaking its paw and yelping; which, from their mutual accusations, we understood they had nearly pulled in two between them. The idiots! That was their pleasure! to quarrel who should hold a heap of warm hair, and each begin to cry because both, after struggling to get it, refused to take it. We laughed outright at the petted things; we did despise them! When would you catch me wishing to have what Catherine wanted? Or find us by ourselves, seeking entertainment in yelling, and sobbing, and rolling on the ground, divided by the whole room? I'd not exchange, for a thousand lives, my condition here, for Edgar Linton's at Thrushcross Grange – not if I might have the privilege of

flinging Joseph off the highest gable, and painting the house-front with Hindley's blood!'

'Hush, hush!' I interrupted. 'Still you have not told me, Heathcliff, how Catherine is left behind?'

'I told you we laughed,' he answered. 'The Lintons heard us, and with one accord, they shot like arrows to the door; there was silence, and then a cry, "Oh, mamma, mamma! Oh, papa! Oh, mamma, come here. Oh, papa, oh!" They really did howl out something in that way. We made frightful noises to terrify them still more, and then we dropped off the ledge, because somebody was drawing the bars, and we felt we had better flee. I had Cathy by the hand, and was urging her on, when all at once she fell down. "Run, Heathcliff, run!" she whispered. "They have let the bulldog loose, and he holds me!" The devil had seized her ankle, Nelly: I heard his abominable snorting. She did not yell out – no! She would have scorned to do it, if she had been spitted on the horns of a mad cow. I did, though: I vociferated curses enough to annihilate any fiend in Christendom; and I got a stone and thrust it between his jaws, and tried with all my might to cram it down his throat. A beast of a servant came up with a lantern, at last, shouting – "Keep fast, Skulker, keep fast!" He changed his note, however, when he saw Skulker's game. The dog was throttled off; his huge, purple tongue hanging half a foot out of his mouth, and his pendant lips streaming with bloody slaver. The man took Cathy up; she was sick, not from fear, I'm certain, but from pain. He carried her in; I followed, grumbling execrations and vengeance. "What prey, Robert?" hallooed Linton from the entrance. "Skulker has caught a little girl, sir," he replied; "and there's a lad here," he added, making a clutch at me, "who looks an out-and-outer! Very like, the robbers were for putting them through the window to open the doors to the gang after all were asleep, that they might murder us at their ease. Hold your tongue, you foul-mouthed thief, you! You shall go to the gallows for this. Mr Linton, sir, don't lay by your gun." "No, no, Robert," said the old fool. "The rascals knew that yesterday was my rent-day: they thought to have me cleverly. Come in; I'll furnish them a reception. There, John, fasten the chain. Give Skulker some water, Jenny. To beard a magistrate in his stronghold, and on the Sabbath, too! Where will their insolence stop? Oh, my dear Mary, look here! Don't be afraid, it is but a boy – yet the villain scowls so plainly in his face; would it not be a kindness to the country to hang him at once, before he shows his nature in acts as well as features?" He pulled me under the chandelier, and Mrs Linton placed her spectacles on her nose and raised her hands in horror. The cowardly children crept nearer, also, Isabella lisping – "Frightful thing! Put him in the cellar, papa. He's exactly like the son of the fortune-teller, that stole my tame pheasant. Isn't he, Edgar?"

'While they examined me, Cathy came round; she heard the last speech, and laughed. Edgar Linton, after an inquisitive stare, collected sufficient wit to recognise her. They see us at church, you know, though we seldom meet them elsewhere. "That's Miss Earnshaw!" he whispered to his mother, "and look how Skulker has bitten her – how her foot bleeds!"

' "Miss Earnshaw? Nonsense!" cried the dame; "Miss Earnshaw scouring the country with a gypsy! And yet, my dear, the child is in mourning – surely it is – and she may be lamed for life!"

' "What culpable carelessness in her brother!" exclaimed Mr Linton, turning from me to Catherine. "I've understood from Shielders" ' (that was the curate, sir) ' "that he lets her grow up in absolute heathenism. But who is this? Where did she pick up this companion? Oho! I declare he is that strange acquisition my late neighbour made, in his journey to Liverpool – a little Lascar, or an American or Spanish castaway."

' "A wicked boy, at all events," remarked the old lady, "and quite unfit for a decent house! Did you notice his language, Linton? I'm shocked that my children should have heard it."

'I recommenced cursing – don't be angry, Nelly – and so Robert was ordered to take me off. I refused to go without Cathy; he dragged me into the garden, pushed the lantern into my hand, assured me that Mr Earnshaw should be informed of my behaviour, and, bidding me march directly, secured the door again. The curtains were still looped up at one corner, and I resumed my station as spy; because, if Catherine had wished to return, I intended shattering their great glass panes to a million of fragments, unless they let her out. She sat on the sofa quietly. Mrs Linton took off the grey cloak of the dairy maid which we had borrowed for our excursion, shaking her head and expostulating with her, I suppose: she was a young lady, and they made a distinction between her treatment and mine. Then the woman-servant brought a basin of warm water, and washed her feet; and Mr Linton mixed a tumbler of negus, and Isabella emptied a plateful of cakes into her lap, and Edgar stood gaping at a distance. Afterwards, they dried and combed her beautiful hair, and gave her a pair of enormous slippers, and wheeled her to the fire; and I left her, as merry as she could be, dividing her food between the little dog and Skulker, whose nose she pinched as she ate; and kindling a spark of spirit in the vacant blue eyes of the Lintons – a dim reflection from her own enchanting face. I saw they were full of stupid admiration; she is so immeasurably superior to them – to everybody on earth, is she not, Nelly?'

'There will more come of this business than you reckon on,' I answered, covering him up and extinguishing the light. 'You are incurable, Heathcliff; and Mr Hindley will have to proceed to extremities, see if he won't.' My words came truer than I desired. The luckless adventure made Earnshaw furious. And then Mr Linton, to mend matters, paid us a visit himself on the morrow; and read the young master such a lecture on the road he guided his family, that he was stirred to look about him, in earnest. Heathcliff received no flogging, but he was told that the first word he spoke to Miss Catherine should ensure a dismissal; and Miss Earnshaw undertook to keep her sister-in-law in due restraint when she returned home; employing art, not force: with force she would have found it impossible.

Cathy stayed at Thrushcross Grange five weeks: till Christmas. By that time her ankle was thoroughly cured, and her manners much improved. The mistress visited her often in the interval, and commenced her plan of reform by trying to raise her self-respect with fine clothes and flattery, which she took readily; so that, instead of a wild, hatless little savage jumping into the house, and rushing to squeeze us all breathless, there lighted from a handsome black pony a very dignified person, with brown ringlets falling from the cover of a feathered beaver, and a long cloth habit, which she was obliged to hold up with both hands that she might sail in. Hindley lifted her from her horse, exclaiming delightedly, 'Why, Cathy, you are quite a beauty! I should scarcely have known you: you look like a lady now. Isabella Linton is not to be compared with her, is she, Frances?' 'Isabella has not her natural advantages,' replied his wife: 'but she must mind and not grow wild again here. Ellen, help Miss Catherine off with her things – Stay, dear, you will disarrange your curls – let me untie your hat.'

I removed the habit, and there shone forth, beneath a grand plaid silk frock, white trousers, and burnished shoes; and, while her eyes sparkled joyfully when the dogs came bounding up to welcome her, she dare hardly touch them lest they should fawn upon her splendid garments. She kissed me gently: I was all flour making the Christmas cake, and it would not have done to give me a hug; and, then, she looked round for Heathcliff. Mr and Mrs Earnshaw watched anxiously their meeting; thinking it would enable them to judge, in some measure, what grounds they had for hoping to succeed in separating the two friends.

Heathcliff was hard to discover, at first. If he were careless, and uncared for, before Catherine's absence, he had been ten times more so since. Nobody but I even did him the kindness to call him a dirty boy, and bid him wash himself, once a week; and children of his age seldom have a natural pleasure in soap and water. Therefore, not to mention his clothes, which had seen three months' service in mire and dust, and his thick uncombed hair, the surface of his face and hands was dismally beclouded. He might well skulk behind the settle, on beholding such a bright, graceful damsel enter the house, instead of a rough-headed counterpart of himself, as he expected. 'Is Heathcliff not here?' she demanded, pulling off her gloves, and displaying fingers wonderfully whitened with doing nothing and staying in doors.

'Heathcliff, you may come forward,' cried Mr Hindley, enjoying his discomfiture, and gratified to see what a forbidding young blackguard he would be compelled to present himself. 'You may come and wish Miss Catherine welcome, like the other servants.'

Cathy, catching a glimpse of her friend in his concealment, flew to embrace him; she bestowed seven or eight kisses on his cheek within the second, and then

stopped, and drawing back, burst into a laugh, exclaiming, 'Why, how very black and cross you look! and how – how funny and grim! But that's because I'm used to Edgar and Isabella Linton. Well, Heathcliff, have you forgotten me?'

She had some reason to put the question, for shame and pride threw double gloom over his countenance, and kept him immoveable.

'Shake hands, Heathcliff,' said Mr Earnshaw, condescendingly; 'once in a way, that is permitted.'

'I shall not,' replied the boy, finding his tongue at last; 'I shall not stand to be laughed at. I shall not bear it!'

And he would have broken from the circle, but Miss Cathy seized him again.

'I did not mean to laugh at you,' she said; 'I could not hinder myself: Heathcliff, shake hands, at least! What are you sulky for? It was only that you looked odd. If you wash your face, and brush your hair, it will be all right: but you are so dirty!'

She gazed concernedly at the dusky fingers she held in her own, and also at her dress; which she feared had gained no embellishment from its contact with his.

'You needn't have touched me!' he answered, following her eye and snatching away his hand. 'I shall be as dirty as I please: and I like to be dirty, and I will be dirty.'

With that he dashed head foremost out of the room, amid the merriment of the master and mistress, and to the serious disturbance of Catherine; who could not comprehend how her remarks should have produced such an exhibition of bad temper.

After playing lady's maid to the new comer, and putting my cakes in the oven, and making the house and kitchen cheerful with great fires, befitting Christmas Eve, I prepared to sit down and amuse myself by singing carols, all alone; regardless of Joseph's affirmations that he considered the merry tunes I chose as next door to songs. He had retired to private prayer in his chamber, and Mr and Mrs Earnshaw were engaging missy's attention by sundry gay trifles bought for her to present to the little Lintons, as an acknowledgment of their kindness. They had invited them to spend the morrow at Wuthering Heights, and the invitation had been accepted, on one condition: Mrs Linton begged that her darlings might be kept carefully apart from that 'naughty swearing boy'.

Under these circumstances I remained solitary. I smelt the rich scent of the heating spices: and admired the shining kitchen utensils, the polished clock, decked in holly, the silver mugs ranged on a tray ready to be filled with mulled ale for supper; and above all, the speckless purity of my particular care – the scoured and well-swept floor. I gave due inward applause to every object, and then I remembered how old Earnshaw used to come in when all was tidied, and call me a cant lass, and slip a shilling into my hand as a Christmas box; and from that I went on to think of his fondness for Heathcliff, and his dread lest he should suffer neglect after death had removed him; and that naturally led me to consider the poor lad's situation now, and from singing I changed my mind to crying. It struck me soon, however, there would be more sense in

endeavouring to repair some of his wrongs than shedding tears over them: I got up and walked into the court to seek him. He was not far; I found him smoothing the glossy coat of the new pony in the stable, and feeding the other beasts, according to custom.

'Make haste, Heathcliff!' I said, 'the kitchen is so comfortable; and Joseph is upstairs: make haste, and let me dress you smart before Miss Cathy comes out, and then you can sit together, with the whole hearth to yourselves, and have a long chatter till bedtime.'

He proceeded with his task and never turned his head towards me.

'Come – are you coming?' I continued. 'There's a little cake for each of you, nearly enough; and you'll need half-an-hour's donning.'

I waited five minutes, but getting no answer left him . . . Catherine supped with her brother and sister-in-law: Joseph and I joined at an unsociable meal, seasoned with reproofs on one side and sauciness on the other. His cake and cheese remained on the table all night for the fairies. He managed to continue work till nine o'clock, and then marched dumb and dour to his chamber.

Cathy sat up late, having a world of things to order for the reception of her new friends: she came into the kitchen once to speak to her old one; but he was gone, and she only stayed to ask what was the matter with him, and then went back. In the morning he rose early; and as it was a holiday, carried his ill-humour on to the moors; not reappearing till the family were departed for church. Fasting and reflection seemed to have brought him to a better spirit.

He hung about me for a while, and having screwed up his courage, exclaimed abruptly – 'Nelly, make me decent, I'm going to be good.'

'High time, Heathcliff,' I said; 'you *have* grieved Catherine: she's sorry she ever came home, I dare say! It looks as if you envied her, because she is more thought of than you.'

The notion of *envying* Catherine was incomprehensible to him, but the notion of grieving her he understood clearly enough.

'Did she say she was grieved?' he enquired, looking very serious.

'She cried when I told her you were off again this morning.'

'Well, *I* cried last night,' he returned, 'and I had more reason to cry than she.'

'Yes; you had the reason of going to bed with a proud heart and an empty stomach,' said I. 'Proud people breed sad sorrows for themselves. But, if you be ashamed of your touchiness, you must ask pardon, mind, when she comes in. You must go up and offer to kiss her, and say – you know best what to say; only do it heartily, and not as if you thought her converted into a stranger by her grand dress. And now, though I have dinner to get ready, I'll steal time to arrange you so that Edgar Linton shall look quite a doll beside you: and that he does. You are younger, and yet, I'll be bound, you are taller and twice as broad across the shoulders: you could knock him down in a twinkling; don't you feel that you could?'

Heathcliff's face brightened a moment; then it was overcast afresh, and he sighed.

'But, Nelly, if I knocked him down twenty times, that wouldn't make him less

handsome or me more so. I wish I had light hair and a fair skin, and was dressed and behaved as well, and had a chance of being as rich as he will be!'

'And cried for mama, at every turn,' I added, 'and trembled if a country lad heaved his fist against you, and sat at home all day for a shower of rain. Oh, Heathcliff, you are showing a poor spirit! Come to the glass, and I'll let you see what you should wish. Do you mark those two lines between your eyes; and those thick brows, that instead of rising arched, sink in the middle; and that couple of black fiends, so deeply buried, who never open their windows boldly, but lurk glinting under them, like devil's spies? Wish and learn to smooth away the surly wrinkles, to raise your lids frankly, and change the fiends to confident, innocent angels, suspecting and doubting nothing, and always seeing friends where they are not sure of foes. Don't get the expression of a vicious cur that appears to know the kicks it gets are its desert, and yet hates all the world, as well as the kicker, for what it suffers.'

'In other words, I must wish for Edgar Linton's great blue eyes and even forehead,' he replied. 'I do – and that won't help me to them.'

'A good heart will help you to a bonny face, my lad,' I continued, 'if you were a regular black; and a bad one will turn the bonniest into something worse than ugly. And now that we've done washing, and combing, and sulking – tell me whether you don't think yourself rather handsome? I'll tell you, I do. You're fit for a prince in disguise. Who knows but your father was Emperor of China, and your mother an Indian queen, each of them able to buy up, with one week's income, Wuthering Heights and Thrushcross Grange together? And you were kidnapped by wicked sailors and brought to England. Were I in your place, I would frame high notions of my birth; and the thoughts of what I was should give me courage and dignity to support the oppressions of a little farmer!'

So I chattered on; and Heathcliff gradually lost his frown and began to look quite pleasant, when all at once our conversation was interrupted by a rumbling sound moving up the road and entering the court. He ran to the window and I to the door, just in time to behold the two Lintons descend from the family carriage, smothered in cloaks and furs, and the Earnshaws dismount from their horses: they often rode to church in winter. Catherine took a hand of each of the children, and brought them into the house and set them before the fire, which quickly put colour into their white faces.

I urged my companion to hasten now and show his amiable humour, and he willingly obeyed; but ill-luck would have it that, as he opened the door leading from the kitchen on one side, Hindley opened it on the other. They met, and the master, irritated at seeing him clean and cheerful; or, perhaps, eager to keep his promise to Mrs Linton, shoved him back with a sudden thrust, and angrily bade Joseph 'keep the fellow out of the room – send him into the garret till dinner is over. He'll be cramming his fingers in the tarts and stealing the fruit, if left alone with them a minute.'

'Nay, sir,' I could not avoid answering, 'he'll touch nothing, not he: and I suppose he must have his share of the dainties as well as we.'

'He shall have his share of my hand, if I catch him downstairs again till dark,'

cried Hindley. Begone, you vagabond! What! you are attempting the coxcomb, are you? Wait till I get hold of those elegant locks – see if I won't pull them a bit longer!'

'They are long enough already,' observed Master Linton, peeping from the doorway; 'I wonder they don't make his head ache. It's like a colt's mane over his eyes!'

He ventured this remark without any intention to insult; but Heathcliff's violent nature was not prepared to endure the appearance of impertinence from one whom he seemed to hate, even then, as a rival. He seized a tureen of hot apple sauce, the first thing that came under his gripe, and dashed it full against the speaker's face and neck; who instantly commenced a lament that brought Isabella and Catherine hurrying to the place. Mr Earnshaw snatched up the culprit directly and conveyed him to his chamber; where, doubtless, he administered a rough remedy to cool the fit of passion, for he reappeared red and breathless. I got the dishcloth, and, rather spitefully, scrubbed Edgar's nose and mouth, affirming it served him right for meddling. His sister began weeping to go home, and Cathy stood by, confounded, blushing for all.

'You should not have spoken to him!' she expostulated with Master Linton. 'He was in a bad temper, and now you've spoilt your visit; and he'll be flogged: I hate him to be flogged! I can't eat my dinner. Why did you speak to him, Edgar?'

'I didn't,' sobbed the youth, escaping from my hands, and finishing the remainder of the purification with his cambric pocket-handkerchief. 'I promised mamma that I wouldn't say one word to him, and I didn't.'

'Well, don't cry,' replied Catherine, contemptuously; 'you're not killed. Don't make more mischief; my brother is coming: be quiet! Give over, Isabella! Has anybody hurt *you*?'

'There, there, children – to your seats!' cried Hindley, bustling in. 'That brute of a lad has warmed me nicely. Next time, Master Edgar, take the law into your own fists – it will give you an appetite!'

The little party recovered its equanimity at sight of the fragrant feast. They were hungry after their ride, and easily consoled, since no real harm had befallen them. Mr Earnshaw carved bountiful platefuls, and the mistress made them merry with lively talk. I waited behind her chair, and was pained to behold Catherine, with dry eyes and an indifferent air, commence cutting up the wing of a goose before her. 'An unfeeling child,' I thought to myself; 'how lightly she dismisses her old playmate's troubles. I could not have imagined her to be so selfish.' She lifted a mouthful to her lips; then she set it down again: her cheeks flushed, and the tears gushed over them. She slipped her fork to the floor, and hastily dived under the cloth to conceal her emotion. I did not call her unfeeling long; for I perceived she was in purgatory throughout the day, and wearying to find an opportunity of getting by herself, or paying a visit to Heathcliff, who had been locked up by the master: as I discovered, on endeavouring to introduce to him a private mess of victuals.

In the evening we had a dance. Cathy begged that he might be liberated then,

as Isabella Linton had no partner; her entreaties were vain, and I was appointed to supply the deficiency. We got rid of all gloom in the excitement of the exercise, and our pleasure was increased by the arrival of the Gimmerton band, mustering fifteen strong: a trumpet, a trombone, clarionets, bassoons, French horns, and a bass viol, besides singers. They go the rounds of all the respectable houses, and receive contributions every Christmas, and we esteemed it a first-rate treat to hear them. After the usual carols had been sung, we set them to songs and glees. Mrs Earnshaw loved the music, and so they gave us plenty.

Catherine loved it too; but she said it sounded sweetest at the top of the steps, and she went up in the dark: I followed. They shut the house door below, never noting our absence, it was so full of people. She made no stay at the stairs' head, but mounted farther, to the garret where Heathcliff was confined, and called him. He stubbornly declined answering for a while; she persevered, and finally persuaded him to hold communion with her through the boards. I let the poor things converse unmolested, till I supposed the songs were going to cease, and the singers to get some refreshment; then, I clambered up the ladder to warn her. Instead of finding her outside, I heard her voice within. The little monkey had crept by the skylight of one garret along the roof, into the skylight of the other, and it was with the utmost difficulty I could coax her out again. When she did come, Heathcliff came with her, and she insisted that I should take him into the kitchen, as my fellow-servant had gone to a neighbour's to be removed from the sound of our 'devil's psalmody', as it pleased him to call it. I told them I intended by no means to encourage their tricks; but as the prisoner had never broken his fast since yesterday's dinner, I would wink at his cheating Mr Hindley that once. He went down; I set him a stool by the fire, and offered him a quantity of good things; but he was sick and could eat little, and my attempts to entertain him were thrown away. He leant his two elbows on his knees, and his chin on his hands, and remained wrapped in dumb meditation.

On my enquiring the subject of his thoughts, he answered gravely – 'I'm trying to settle how I shall pay Hindley back. I don't care how long I wait, if I can only do it at last. I hope he will not die before I do!'

'For shame, Heathcliff!' said I. 'It is for God to punish wicked people; we should learn to forgive.'

'No, God won't have the satisfaction that I shall,' he returned. 'I only wish I knew the best way! Let me alone, and I'll plan it out: while I'm thinking of that I don't feel pain.'

But, Mr Lockwood, I forget these tales cannot divert you. I'm annoyed how I should dream of chattering on at such a rate: and your gruel cold, and you nodding for bed! I could have told Heathcliff's history, all that you need hear, in half a dozen words.

Thus interrupting herself, the housekeeper rose, and proceeded to lay aside her sewing; but I felt incapable of moving from the hearth, and I was very far from nodding. 'Sit still, Mrs Dean,' I cried, 'do sit still, another half-hour! You've done just right to tell the story leisurely. That is the method I like; and you must

finish in the same style. I am interested in every character you have mentioned, more or less.'

'The clock is on the stroke of eleven, sir.'

'No matter – I'm not accustomed to go to bed in the long hours. One or two is early enough for a person who lies till ten.'

'You shouldn't lie till ten. There's the very prime of the morning gone long before that time. A person who has not done one half his day's work by ten o'clock, runs a chance of leaving the other half undone.'

'Nevertheless, Mrs Dean, resume your chair; because tomorrow I intend lengthening the night till afternoon. I prognosticate for myself an obstinate cold, at least.'

'I hope not, sir. Well, you must allow me to leap over some three years; during that space Mrs Earnshaw – '

'No, no, I'll allow nothing of the sort! Are you acquainted with the mood of mind in which, if you were seated alone, and the cat licking its kitten on the rug before you, you would watch the operation so intently that puss's neglect of one ear would put you seriously out of temper?'

'A terribly lazy mood, I should say.'

'On the contrary, a tiresomely active one. It is mine, at present: and, therefore, continue minutely. I perceive that people in these regions acquire over people in towns the value that a spider in a dungeon does over a spider in a cottage, to their various occupants; and yet the deepened attraction is not entirely owing to the situation of the looker-on. They *do* live more in earnest, more in themselves, and less in surface change, and frivolous external things. I could fancy a love for life here almost possible; and I was a fixed unbeliever in any love of a year's standing. One state resembles setting a hungry man down to a single dish, on which he may concentrate his entire appetite and do it justice; the other, introducing him to a table laid out by French cooks: he can perhaps extract as much enjoyment from the whole; but each part is a mere atom in his regard and remembrance.'

'Oh! here we are the same as anywhere else, when you get to know us,' observed Mrs Dean, somewhat puzzled at my speech.

'Excuse me,' I responded; 'you, my good friend, are a striking evidence against that assertion. Excepting a few provincialisms of slight consequence, you have no marks of the manners which I am habituated to consider peculiar to your class. I am sure you have thought a great deal more than the generality of servants think. You have been compelled to cultivate your reflective faculties for want of occasions for frittering your life away in silly trifles.'

Mrs Dean laughed.

'I certainly esteem myself a steady, reasonable kind of body,' she said; 'not exactly from living among the hills and seeing one set of faces, and one series of actions, from year's end to year's end; but I have undergone sharp discipline, which has taught me wisdom: and then, I have read more than you would fancy, Mr Lockwood. You could not open a book in this library that I have not looked into, and got something out of also: unless it be that range of Greek and Latin,

and that of French; and those I know one from another: it is as much as you can expect of a poor man's daughter. However, if I am to follow my story in true gossip's fashion, I had better go on; and instead of leaping three years, I will be content to pass to the next summer – the summer of 1778, that is nearly twenty-three years ago.'

## *Chapter 8*

On the morning of a fine June day, my first bonny little nursling, and the last of the ancient Earnshaw stock, was born. We were busy with the hay in a far away field, when the girl that usually brought our breakfasts came running an hour too soon, across the meadow and up the lane, calling me as she ran.

'Oh, such a grand bairn!' she panted out. 'The finest lad that ever breathed! But the doctor says missis must go: he says she's been in a consumption these many months. I heard him tell Mr Hindley: and now she has nothing to keep her, and she'll be dead before winter. You must come home directly. You're to nurse it, Nelly: to feed it with sugar and milk, and take care of it day and night. I wish I were you, because it will be all yours when there is no missis!'

'But is she very ill?' I asked, flinging down my rake, and tying my bonnet.

'I guess she is; yet she looks bravely,' replied the girl, 'and she talks as if she thought of living to see it grow a man. She's out of her head for joy, it's such a beauty! If I were her, I'm certain I should not die: I should get better at the bare sight of it, in spite of Kenneth. I was fairly mad at him. Dame Archer brought the cherub down to master, in the house, and his face just began to light up, then the old croaker steps forward, and says he – "Earnshaw, it's a blessing your wife has been spared to leave you this son. When she came, I felt convinced we shouldn't keep her long; and now, I must tell you, the winter will probably finish her. Don't take on, and fret about it too much: it can't be helped. And besides, you should have known better than to choose such a rush of a lass!"'

'And what did the master answer?' I enquired.

'I think he swore: but I didn't mind him, I was straining to see the bairn,' and she began again to describe it rapturously. I, as zealous as herself, hurried eagerly home to admire, on my part; though I was very sad for Hindley's sake. He had room in his heart only for two idols – his wife and himself: he doted on both, and adored one, and I couldn't conceive how he would bear the loss.

When we got to Wuthering Heights, there he stood at the front door; and, as I passed in, I asked, 'how was the baby?'

'Nearly ready to run about, Nell!' he replied, putting on a cheerful smile.

'And the mistress?' I ventured to enquire; 'the doctor says she's –'

'Damn the doctor!' he interrupted, reddening. 'Frances is quite right: she'll be perfectly well by this time next week. Are you going upstairs? will you tell her that I'll come, if she'll promise not to talk. I left her because she would not hold her tongue; and she must – tell her Mr Kenneth says she must be quiet.'

I delivered this message to Mrs Earnshaw: she seemed in flighty spirits, and replied merrily – 'I hardly spoke a word, Ellen, and there he has gone out twice, crying. Well, say I promise I won't speak: but that does not bind me not to laugh at him!'

Poor soul! Till within a week of her death that gay heart never failed her; and her husband persisted doggedly, nay, furiously, in affirming her health improved every day.

When Kenneth warned him that his medicines were useless at that stage of the malady, and he needn't put him to further expense by attending her, he retorted – 'I know you need not – she 's well – she does not want any more attendance from you! She never was in a consumption. It was a fever; and it is gone: her pulse is as slow as mine now, and her cheek as cool.'

He told his wife the same story, and she seemed to believe him: but one night, while leaning on his shoulder in the act of saying she thought she should be able to get up tomorrow, a fit of coughing took her – a very slight one – he raised her in his arms; she put her two hands about his neck, her face changed, and she was dead.

As the girl had anticipated, the child Hareton fell wholly into my hands. Mr Earnshaw, provided he saw him healthy and never heard him cry, was contented, as far as regarded him. For himself, he grew desperate: his sorrow was of that kind that will not lament. He neither wept nor prayed; he cursed and defied: execrated God and man, and gave himself up to reckless dissipation. The servants could not bear his tyrannical and evil conduct long: Joseph and I were the only two that would stay. I had not the heart to leave my charge; and besides, you know, I had been his foster-sister, and excused his behaviour more readily than a stranger would. Joseph remained to hector over tenants and labourers; and because it was his vocation to be where he had plenty of wickedness to reprove.

The master's bad ways and bad companions formed a pretty example for Catherine and Heathcliff. His treatment of the latter was enough to make a fiend of a saint. And, truly, it appeared as if the lad *were* possessed of something diabolical at that period. He delighted to witness Hindley degrading himself past redemption; and became daily more notable for savage sullenness and ferocity. I could not half tell what an infernal house we had. The curate dropped calling, and nobody decent came near us, at last; unless Edgar Linton's visits to Miss Cathy might be an exception. At fifteen she was the queen of the country-side; she had no peer; and she did turn out a haughty, headstrong creature! I own I did not like her, after her infancy was past; and I vexed her frequently by trying to bring down her arrogance: she never took an aversion to me, though. She had a wondrous constancy to old attachments: even Heathcliff kept his hold on her affections unalterably; and young Linton, with all his superiority, found it difficult to make an equally deep impression. He was my late master: that is his portrait over the fireplace. It used to hang on one side, and his wife's on the other; but hers has been removed, or else you might see something of what she was. Can you make that out?

Mrs Dean raised the candle, and I discerned a soft-featured face, exceedingly resembling the young lady at the Heights, but more pensive and amiable in expression. It formed a sweet picture. The long light hair curled slightly on the temples; the eyes were large and serious; the figure almost too graceful. I did not marvel how Catherine Earnshaw could forget her first friend for such an individual. I marvelled much how he, with a mind to correspond with his person, could fancy my idea of Catherine Earnshaw.

'A very agreeable portrait, I observed to the housekeeper. 'Is it like?'

'Yes,' she answered; 'but he looked better when he was animated; that is his everyday countenance: he wanted spirit in general.'

Catherine had kept up her acquaintance with the Lintons since her five weeks' residence among them; and as she had no temptation to show her rough side in their company, and had the sense to be ashamed of being rude where she experienced such invariable courtesy, she imposed unwittingly on the old lady and gentleman, by her ingenious cordiality; gained the admiration of Isabella, and the heart and soul of her brother: acquisitions that flattered her from the first, for she was full of ambition, and led her to adopt a double character without exactly intending to deceive anyone. In the place where she had heard Heathcliff termed a 'vulgar young ruffian,' and 'worse than a brute,' she took care not to act like him; but at home she had small inclination to practise politeness that would only be laughed at, and restrain an unruly nature when it would bring her neither credit nor praise.

Mr Edgar seldom mustered courage to visit Wuthering Heights openly. He had a terror of Earnshaw's reputation, and shrunk from encountering him; and yet he was always received with our best attempts at civility: the master himself avoided offending him, knowing why he came; and if he could not be gracious, kept out of the way. I rather think his appearance there was distasteful to Catherine: she was not artful, never played the coquette, and had evidently an objection to her two friends meeting at all; for when Heathcliff expressed contempt of Linton in his presence, she could not half coincide, as she did in his absence; and when Linton evinced disgust and antipathy to Heathcliff, she dare not treat his sentiments with indifference, as if depreciation of her playmate were of scarcely any consequence to her. I've had many a laugh at her perplexities and untold troubles, which she vainly strove to hide from my mockery. That sounds ill-natured: but she was so proud, it became really impossible to pity her distresses, till she should be chastened into more humility. She did bring herself, finally, to confess, and confide in me: there was not a soul else that she might fashion into an adviser.

Mr Hindley had gone from home, one afternoon, and Heathcliff presumed to give himself a holiday on the strength of it. He had reached the age of sixteen then, I think, and without having bad features, or being deficient in intellect, he contrived to convey an impression of inward and outward repulsiveness that his present aspect retains no traces of. In the first place, he had by that time lost the benefit of his early education: continual hard work, begun soon and concluded late, had extinguished any curiosity he once possessed in

pursuit of knowledge, and any love for books or learning. His childhood's sense of superiority, instilled into him by the favours of old Mr Earnshaw, was faded away. He struggled long to keep up an equality with Catherine in her studies, and yielded with poignant though silent regret: but he yielded completely; and there was no prevailing on him to take a step in the way of moving upward, when he found he must, necessarily, sink beneath his former level. Then personal appearance sympathised with mental deterioration: he acquired a slouching gait, and ignoble look; his naturally reserved disposition was exaggerated into an almost idiotic excess of unsociable moroseness; and he took a grim pleasure, apparently, in exciting the aversion rather than the esteem of his few acquaintance.

Catherine and he were constant companions still at his seasons of respite from labour; but he had ceased to express his fondness for her in words, and recoiled with angry suspicion from her girlish caresses, as if conscious there could be no gratification in lavishing such marks of affection on him. On the before-named occasion he came into the house to announce his intention of doing nothing, while I was assisting Miss Cathy to arrange her dress: she had not reckoned on his taking it into his head to be idle: and imagining she would have the whole place to herself, she managed, by some means, to inform Mr Edgar of her brother's absence, and was then preparing to receive him.

'Cathy, are you busy this afternoon?' asked Heathcliff. 'Are you going anywhere?'

'No, it is raining,' she answered.

'Why have you that silk frock on, then?' he said. 'Nobody coming here, I hope?'

'Not that I know of,' stammered miss: 'but you should be in the field now, Heathcliff. It is an hour past dinner time: I thought you were gone.'

'Hindley does not often free us from his accursed presence,' observed the boy. 'I'll not work any more today: I'll stay with you.'

'Oh, but Joseph will tell,' she suggested: 'you'd better go!'

'Joseph is loading lime on the farther side of Pennistow Crag; it will take him till dark, and he'll never know.'

So saying, he lounged to the fire, and sat down. Catherine reflected an instant, with knitted brows – she found it needful to smooth the way for an intrusion. 'Isabella and Edgar Linton talked of calling this afternoon,' she said, at the conclusion of a minute's silence. 'As it rains, I hardly expect them; but they may come, and if they do, you run the risk of being scolded for no good.'

'Order Ellen to say you are engaged, Cathy,' he persisted; 'don't turn me out for those pitiful, silly friends of yours! I'm on the point, sometimes, of complaining that they – but I'll not – '

'That they what?' cried Catherine, gazing at him with a troubled countenance. 'Oh, Nelly!' she added petulantly, jerking her head away from my hands, 'you've combed my hair quite out of curl! That's enough; let me alone. What are you on the point of complaining about, Heathcliff?'

'Nothing – only look at the almanac on that wall,' he pointed to a framed

sheet hanging near the window, and continued – 'The crosses are for the evenings you have spent with the Lintons, the dots for those spent with me. Do you see? I've marked every day.'

'Yes – very foolish: as if I took notice!' replied Catherine in a peevish tone. 'And where is the sense of that?'

'To show that I *do* take notice,' said Heathcliff.

'And should I always be sitting with you?' she demanded, growing more irritated. 'What good do I get? What do you talk about? You might be dumb, or a baby, for anything you say to amuse me, or for anything you do, either!'

'You never told me before that I talked too little, or that you disliked my company, Cathy!' exclaimed Heathcliff in much agitation.

'It's no company at all, when people know nothing and say nothing,' she muttered.

Her companion rose up, but he hadn't time to express his feelings further, for a horse's feet were heard on the flags, and having knocked gently, young Linton entered, his face brilliant with delight at the unexpected summons he had received. Doubtless Catherine marked the difference between her friends, as one came in and the other went out. The contrast resembled what you see in exchanging a bleak, hilly, coal country for a beautiful fertile valley; and his voice and greeting were as opposite as his aspect. He had a sweet, low manner of speaking, and pronounced his words as you do: that's less gruff than we talk here, and softer.

'I'm not come too soon, am I?' he said, casting a look at me: I had begun to wipe the plate, and tidy some drawers at the far end in the dresser.

'No,' answered Catherine. 'What are you doing there, Nelly?'

'My work, miss,' I replied. (Mr Hindley had given me directions to make a third party in any private visits Linton chose to pay.)

She stepped behind me and whispered crossly, 'Take yourself and your dusters off; when company are in the house, servants don't commence scouring and cleaning in the room where they are!'

'It's a good opportunity, now that master is away,' I answered aloud: 'he hates me to be fidgeting over these things in his presence. I'm sure Mr Edgar will excuse me.'

'I hate you to be fidgeting in *my* presence,' exclaimed the young lady imperiously, not allowing her guest time to speak: she had failed to recover her equanimity since the little dispute with Heathcliff.

'I'm sorry for it, Miss Catherine,' was my response; and I proceeded assiduously with my occupation.

She, supposing Edgar could not see her, snatched the cloth from my hand, and pinched me, with a prolonged wrench, very spitefully on the arm. I've said I did not love her, and rather relished mortifying her vanity now and then: besides, she hurt me extremely; so I started up from my knees, and screamed out, 'Oh, miss, that's a nasty trick! You have no right to nip me, and I'm not going to bear it.'

'I didn't touch you, you lying creature!' cried she, her fingers tingling to

repeat the act, and her ears red with rage. She never had power to conceal her passion, it always set her whole complexion in a blaze.

'What's that, then?' I retorted, showing a decided purple witness to refute her.

She stamped her foot, wavered a moment, and then, irresistibly impelled by the naughty spirit within her, slapped me on the cheek a stinging blow that filled both eyes with water.

'Catherine, love! Catherine!' interposed Linton, greatly shocked at the double fault of falsehood and violence which his idol had committed.

'Leave the room, Ellen!' she repeated, trembling all over.

Little Hareton, who followed me everywhere, and was sitting near me on the floor, at seeing my tears commenced crying himself, and sobbed out complaints against 'wicked aunt Cathy,' which drew her fury on to his unlucky head: she seized his shoulders, and shook him till the poor child waxed livid, and Edgar thoughtlessly laid hold of her hands to deliver him. In an instant one was wrung free, and the astonished young man felt it applied over his own ear in a way that could not be mistaken for jest. He drew back in consternation. I lifted Hareton in my arms, and walked off to the kitchen with him, leaving the door of communication open, for I was curious to watch how they would settle their disagreement. The insulted visitor moved to the spot where he had laid his hat, pale and with a quivering lip.

'That's right!' I said to myself. 'Take warning and begone! It's a kindness to let you have a glimpse of her genuine disposition.'

'Where are you going?' demanded Catherine, advancing to the door.

He swerved aside, and attempted to pass.

'You must not go!' she exclaimed energetically.

'I must and shall!' he replied in a subdued voice.

'No,' she persisted, grasping the handle; 'not yet, Edgar Linton: sit down; you shall not leave me in that temper. I should be miserable all night, and I won't be miserable for you!'

'Can I stay after you have struck me?' asked Linton.

Catherine was mute.

'You've made me afraid and ashamed of you,' he continued; 'I'll not come here again!'

Her eyes began to glisten, and her lids to twinkle.

'And you told a deliberate untruth!' he said.

'I didn't!' she cried, recovering her speech; 'I did nothing deliberately. Well, go, if you please – get away! And now I'll cry – I'll cry myself sick!'

She dropped down on her knees by a chair, and set to weeping in serious earnest. Edgar persevered in his resolution as far as the court; there he lingered. I resolved to encourage him.

'Miss is dreadfully wayward, sir,' I called out. 'As bad as any marred child: you'd better be riding home, or else she will be sick, only to grieve us.'

The soft thing looked askance through the window: he possessed the power to depart, as much as a cat possesses the power to leave a mouse half killed, or

a bird half eaten. Ah, I thought, there will be no saving him – He's doomed, and flies to his fate! And so it was: he turned abruptly, hastened into the house again, shut the door behind him; and when I went in a while after to inform them that Earnshaw had come home rabid drunk, ready to pull the old place about our ears (his ordinary frame of mind in that condition), I saw the quarrel had merely effected a closer intimacy – had broken the outworks of youthful timidity, and enabled them to forsake the disguise of friendship, and confess themselves lovers.

Intelligence of Mr Hindley's arrival drove Linton speedily to his horse, and Catherine to her chamber. I went to hide little Hareton, and to take the shot out of the master's fowling-piece, which he was fond of playing with in his insane excitement, to the hazard of the lives of any who provoked, or even attracted his notice too much; and I had hit upon the plan of removing it, that he might do less mischief if he did go the length of firing the gun.

## *Chapter 9*

He entered, vociferating oaths dreadful to hear; and caught me in the act of stowing his son away in the kitchen cupboard. Hareton was impressed with a wholesome terror of encountering either his wild-beast's fondness or his madman's rage; for in one he ran a chance of being squeezed and kissed to death, and in the other of being flung into the fire, or dashed against the wall; and the poor thing remained perfectly quiet wherever I chose to put him.

'There, I've found it out at last!' cried Hindley, pulling me back by the skin of my neck, like a dog. 'By heaven and hell, you've sworn between you to murder that child! I know how it is, now, that he is always out of my way. But, with the help of Satan, I shall make you swallow the carving-knife, Nelly! You needn't laugh; for I've just crammed Kenneth, head-downmost, in the Blackhorse marsh; and two is the same as one – and I want to kill some of you: I shall have no rest till I do!'

'But I don't like the carving-knife, Mr Hindley,' I answered; 'it has been cutting red herrings. I'd rather be shot, if you please.'

'You'd rather be damned!' he said; 'and so you shall. No law in England can hinder a man from keeping his house decent, and mine's abominable! open your mouth.'

He held the knife in his hand, and pushed its point between my teeth: but, for my part, I was never much afraid of his vagaries. I spat out, and affirmed it tasted detestably – I would not take it on any account.

'Oh!' said he, releasing me, 'I see that hideous little villain is not Hareton: I beg your pardon, Nell. If it be, he deserves flaying alive for not running to welcome me, and for screaming as if I were a goblin. Unnatural cub, come hither! I'll teach thee to impose on a good-hearted, deluded father. Now, don't you think the lad would be handsomer cropped? It makes a dog fiercer, and I

love something fierce – get me a scissors – something fierce and trim! Besides, it's infernal affectation – devilish conceit it is, to cherish our ears – we're asses enough without them. Hush, child, hush! Well then, it is my darling! wisht, dry thy eyes – there's a joy; kiss me. What! it won't? Kiss me, Hareton! Damn thee, kiss me! By God, as if I would rear such a monster! As sure as I'm living, I'll break the brat's neck.'

Poor Hareton was squalling and kicking in his father's arms with all his might, and redoubled his yells when he carried him upstairs and lifted him over the bannister. I cried out that he would frighten the child into fits, and ran to rescue him. As I reached them, Hindley leant forward on the rails to listen to a noise below; almost forgetting what he had in his hands. 'Who is that?' he asked, hearing someone approaching the stair's foot. I leant forward also, for the purpose of signing to Heathcliff, whose step I recognised, not to come further; and, at the instant when my eye quitted Hareton, he gave a sudden spring, delivered himself from the careless grasp that held him, and fell.

There was scarcely time to experience a thrill of horror before we saw that the little wretch was safe. Heathcliff arrived underneath just at the critical moment; by a natural impulse, he arrested his descent, and setting him on his feet, looked up to discover the author of the accident. A miser who has parted with a lucky lottery ticket for five shillings, and finds next day he has lost in the bargain five thousand pounds, could not show a blanker countenance than he did on beholding the figure of Mr Earnshaw above. It expressed, plainer than words could do, the intensest anguish at having made himself the instrument of thwarting his own revenge. Had it been dark, I dare say, he would have tried to remedy the mistake by smashing Hareton's skull on the steps; but, we witnessed his salvation; and I was presently below with my precious charge pressed to my heart. Hindley descended more leisurely, sobered and abashed.

'It is your fault, Ellen,' he said; 'you should have kept him out of sight: you should have taken him from me! Is he injured anywhere?'

'Injured!' I cried angrily. 'If he's not killed, he'll be an idiot! Oh! I wonder his mother does not rise from her grave to see how you use him. You're worse than a heathen – treating your own flesh and blood in that manner!'

He attempted to touch the child, who, on finding himself with me, sobbed off his terror directly. At the first finger his father laid on him, however, he shrieked again louder than before, and struggled as if he would go into convulsions.

'You shall not meddle with him!' I continued. 'He hates you – they all hate you – that's the truth! A happy family you have; and a pretty state you're come to!'

'I shall come to a prettier, yet, Nelly,' laughed the misguided man, recovering his hardness. 'At present, convey yourself and him away. And, hark you, Heathcliff! clear you too, quite from my reach and hearing . . . I wouldn't murder you tonight, unless, perhaps, I set the house on fire: but that's as my fancy goes.'

While saying this he took a pint bottle of brandy from the dresser, and poured some into a tumbler.

'Nay, don't!' I entreated. 'Mr Hindley, do take warning. Have mercy on this unfortunate boy, if you care nothing for yourself!'

'Anyone will do better for him than I shall,' he answered.

'Have mercy on your own soul!' I said, endeavouring to snatch the glass from his hand.

'Not I! On the contrary, I shall have great pleasure in sending it to perdition to punish its Maker,' exclaimed the blasphemer. 'Here's to its hearty damnation!'

He drank the spirits and impatiently bade us go; terminating his command with a sequel of horrid imprecations, too bad to repeat or remember.

'It's a pity he cannot kill himself with drink,' observed Heathcliff, muttering an echo of curses back when the door was shut. 'He's doing his very utmost; but his constitution defies him. Mr Kenneth says he would wager his mare, that he'll outlive any man on this side Gimmerton, and go to the grave a hoary sinner; unless some happy chance out of the common course befall him.'

I went into the kitchen, and sat down to lull my little lamb to sleep. Heathcliff, as I thought, walked through to the barn. It turned out afterwards that he only got as far as the other side the settle, when he flung himself on a bench by the wall, removed from the fire, and remained silent.

I was rocking Hareton on my knee, and humming a song that began –

> 'It was far in the night, and the bairnies grat,
> The mither beneath the mools heard that,'

when Miss Cathy, who had listened to the hubbub from her room, put her head in and whispered – 'Are you alone, Nelly?'

'Yes, miss,' I replied.

She entered and approached the hearth. I, supposing she was going to say something, looked up. The expression of her face seemed disturbed and anxious. Her lips were half asunder, as if she meant to speak, and she drew a breath; but it escaped in a sigh instead of a sentence. I resumed my song; not having forgotten her recent behaviour.

'Where's Heathcliff?' she said, interrupting me.

'About his work in the stable,' was my answer.

He did not contradict me; perhaps he had fallen into a dose. There followed another long pause, during which I perceived a drop or two trickle from Catherine's cheek to the flags. Is she sorry for her shameful conduct? I asked myself. That will be a novelty: but she may come to the point as she will – I shan't help her! No, she felt small trouble regarding any subject, save her own concerns.

'Oh, dear!' she cried at last. 'I'm very unhappy!'

'A pity,' observed I. 'You're hard to please: so many friends and so few cares, and can't make yourself content!'

'Nelly, will you keep a secret for me?' she pursued, kneeling down by me, and lifting her winsome eyes to my face with that sort of look which turns off bad temper, even when one has all the right in the world to indulge it.

'Is it worth keeping?' I enquired, less sulkily.

'Yes, and it worries me, and I must let it out! I want to know what I should do.

Today, Edgar Linton has asked me to marry him, and I've given him an answer. Now, before I tell you whether it was a consent or denial, you tell me which it ought to have been.'

'Really, Miss Catherine, how can I know?' I replied. 'To be sure, considering the exhibition you performed in his presence this afternoon, I might say it would be wise to refuse him: since he asked you after that, he must be either hopelessly stupid or a venturesome fool.'

'If you talk so, I won't tell you any more,' she returned, peevishly, rising to her feet. 'I accepted him, Nelly. Be quick, and say whether I was wrong!'

'You accepted him! then what good is it discussing the matter? You have pledged your word, and cannot retract.'

'But, say whether I should have done so – do!' she exclaimed in an irritated tone; chafing her hands together, and frowning.

'There are many things to be considered before that question can be answered properly,' I said sententiously. 'First and foremost, do you love Mr Edgar?'

'Who can help it? Of course I do,' she answered.

Then I put her through the following catechism: for a girl of twenty-two, it was not injudicious.

'Why do you love him, Miss Cathy?'

'Nonsense, I do – that's sufficient.'

'By no means; you must say why?'

'Well, because he is handsome, and pleasant to be with.'

'Bad!' was my commentary.

'And because he is young and cheerful.'

'Bad, still.'

'And because he loves me.'

'Indifferent, coming there.'

'And he will be rich, and I shall like to be the greatest woman of the neighbourhood, and I shall be proud of having such a husband.'

'Worst of all. And now say how you love him?'

'As everybody loves – You're silly, Nelly.'

'Not at all – Answer.'

'I love the ground under his feet, and the air over his head, and everything he touches, and every word he says. I love all his looks, and all his actions, and him entirely and altogether. There now!'

'And why?'

'Nay, you are making a jest of it: it is exceedingly ill-natured! It's no jest to me!' said the young lady, scowling, and turning her face to the fire.

'I'm very far from jesting, Miss Catherine,' I replied. 'You love Mr Edgar, because he is handsome, and young, and cheerful, and rich, and loves you. The last, however, goes for nothing: you would love him without that, probably; and with it you wouldn't, unless he possessed the four former attractions.'

'No, to be sure not: I should only pity him – hate him, perhaps, if he were ugly, and a clown.'

'But there are several other handsome, rich young men in the world:

handsomer, possibly, and richer than he is. What should hinder you from loving them?'

'If there be any, they are out of my way: I've seen none like Edgar.'

'You may see some; and he won't always be handsome, and young, and may not always be rich.'

'He is now; and I have only to do with the present. I wish you would speak rationally.'

'Well, that settles it: if you have only to do with the present, marry Mr Linton.'

'I don't want your permission for that – I *shall* marry him: and yet you have not told me whether I'm right.'

'Perfectly right; if people be right to marry only for the present. And now, let us hear what you are unhappy about. Your brother will be pleased . . . The old lady and gentleman will not object, I think; you will escape from a disorderly comfortless home into a wealthy, respectable one; and you love Edgar, and Edgar loves you. All seems smooth and easy: where is the obstacle?'

'*Here!* and *here!*' replied Catherine, striking one hand on her forehead, and the other on her breast 'in whichever place the soul lives. In my soul and in my heart, I'm convinced I'm wrong!'

'That's very strange! I cannot make it out.'

'It's my secret. But if you will not mock at me, I'll explain it: I can't do it distinctly; but I'll give you a feeling of how I feel.'

She seated herself by me again: her countenance grew sadder and graver, and her clasped hands trembled.

'Nelly, do you never dream queer dreams?' she said, suddenly, after some minutes' reflection.

'Yes, now and then,' I answered.

'And so do I. I've dreamt in my life dreams that have stayed with me ever after, and changed my ideas: they've gone through and through me, like wine through water, and altered the colour of my mind. And this is one: I'm going to tell it – but take care not to smile at any part of it.'

'Oh! don't, Miss Catherine!' I cried. 'We're dismal enough without conjuring up ghosts and visions to perplex us. Come, come, be merry and like yourself! Look at little Hareton! *He's* dreaming nothing dreary. How sweetly he smiles in his sleep!'

'Yes; and how sweetly his father curses in his solitude! You remember him, I dare say, when he was just such another as that chubby thing: nearly as young and innocent. However, Nelly, I shall oblige you to listen: it's not long: and I've no power to be merry tonight.'

'I won't hear it, I won't hear it!' I repeated, hastily.

I was superstitious about dreams then, and am still; and Catherine had an unusual gloom in her aspect, that made me dread something from which I might shape a prophecy, and foresee a fearful catastrophe. She was vexed, but she did not proceed. Apparently taking up another subject, she recommenced in a short time.

'If I were in heaven, Nelly, I should be extremely miserable.'

'Because you are not fit to go there,' I answered. 'All sinners would be miserable in heaven.'

'But it is not for that. I dreamt once that I was there.'

'I tell you I won't harken to your dreams, Miss Catherine! I'll go to bed,' I interrupted again.

She laughed, and held me down; for I made a motion to leave my chair.

'This is nothing,' cried she: 'I was only going to say that heaven did not seem to be my home; and I broke my heart with weeping to come back to earth; and the angels were so angry that they flung me out into the middle of the heath on the top of Wuthering Heights; where I woke sobbing for joy. That will do to explain my secret, as well as the other. I've no more business to marry Edgar Linton than I have to be in heaven; and if the wicked man in there had not brought Heathcliff so low, I shouldn't have thought of it. It would degrade me to marry Heathcliff now; so he shall never know how I love him: and that, not because he's handsome, Nelly, but because he's more myself than I am. Whatever our souls are made of, his and mine are the same; and Linton's is as different as a moonbeam from lightning, or frost from fire.'

Ere this speech ended, I became sensible of Heathcliff's presence. Having noticed a slight movement, I turned my head, and saw him rise from the bench, and steal out noiselessly. He had listened till he heard Catherine say it would degrade her to marry him, and then he staid, to hear no farther. My companion, sitting on the ground, was prevented by the back of the settle from remarking his presence or departure; but I started, and bade her hush!

'Why?' she asked, gazing nervously round.

'Joseph is here,' I answered, catching opportunely the roll of his cartwheels up the road; 'and Heathcliff will come in with him. I'm not sure whether he were not at the door this moment.'

'Oh, he couldn't overhear me at the door!' said she. 'Give me Hareton, while you get the supper, and when it is ready ask me to sup with you. I want to cheat my uncomfortable conscience, and be convinced that Heathcliff has no notion of these things. He has not, has he? He does not know what being in love is?'

'I see no reason that he should not know, as well as you,' I returned; 'and if *you* are his choice, he'll be the most unfortunate creature that ever was born! As soon as you become Mrs Linton, he loses friend, and love, and all! Have you considered how you'll bear the separation, and how he'll bear to be quite deserted in the world? Because, Miss Catherine – '

'He quite deserted! We separated!' she exclaimed, with an accent of indignation. 'Who is to separate us, pray? They'll meet the fate of Milo! Not as long as I live, Ellen: for no mortal creature. Every Linton on the face of the earth might melt into nothing, before I could consent to forsake Heathcliff. Oh, that's not what I intend – that's not what I mean! I shouldn't be Mrs Linton were such a price demanded! He'll be as much to me as he has been all his lifetime. Edgar must shake off his antipathy, and tolerate him, at least. He will, when he learns my true feelings towards him. Nelly, I see now, you think me a

selfish wretch; but did it never strike you that if Heathcliff and I married, we should be beggars? Whereas, if I marry Linton, I can aid Heathcliff to rise, and place him out of my brother's power.'

'With your husband's money, Miss Catherine?' I asked. 'You'll find him not so pliable as you calculate upon: and though I'm hardly a judge, I think that's the worst motive you've given yet for being the wife of young Linton.'

'It is not,' retorted she; 'it is the best! The others were the satisfaction of my whims: and for Edgar's sake, too, to satisfy him. This is for the sake of one who comprehends in his person my feelings to Edgar and myself. I cannot express it; but surely you and everybody have a notion that there is or should be an existence of yours beyond you. What were the use of my creation, if I were entirely contained here? My great miseries in this world have been Heathcliff's miseries, and I watched and felt each from the beginning: my great thought in living is himself. If all else perished, and *he* remained, I should still continue to be; and if all else remained, and he were annihilated, the universe would turn to a mighty stranger: I should not seem a part of it. My love for Linton is like the foliage in the woods: time will change it, I'm well aware, as winter changes the trees. My love for Heathcliff resembles the eternal rocks beneath: a source of little visible delight, but necessary. Nelly, I *am* Heathcliff! He's always, always in my mind: not as a pleasure, any more than I am always a pleasure to myself, but as my own being. So don't talk of our separation again: it is impracticable; and – '

She paused, and hid her face in the folds of my gown; but I jerked it forcibly away. I was out of patience with her folly!

'If I can make any sense of your nonsense, miss,' I said, 'it only goes to convince me that you are ignorant of the duties you undertake in marrying; or else that you are a wicked, unprincipled girl. But trouble me with no more secrets: I'll not promise to keep them.'

'You'll keep that?' she asked, eagerly.

'No, I'll not promise,' I repeated.

She was about to insist, when the entrance of Joseph finished our conversation; and Catherine removed her seat to a corner, and nursed Hareton, while I made the supper. After it was cooked, my fellow-servant and I began to quarrel who should carry some to Mr Hindley; and we didn't settle it till all was nearly cold. Then we came to the agreement that we would let him ask, if he wanted any; for we feared particularly to go into his presence when he had been some time alone.

'Und hah isn't that nowt comed in frough th' field, be this time? What is he abaht? girt eedle seeght!' demanded the old man, looking round for Heathcliff.

'I'll call him,' I replied. 'He's in the barn, I've no doubt.'

I went and called, but got no answer. On returning, I whispered to Catherine that he had heard a good part of what she said, I was sure; and told how I saw him quit the kitchen just as she complained of her brother's conduct regarding him. She jumped up in a fine fright, flung Hareton on to the settle, and ran to seek for her friend herself; not taking leisure to consider why she

was so flurried, or how her talk would have affected him. She was absent such a while that Joseph proposed we should wait no longer. He cunningly conjectured they were staying away in order to avoid hearing his protracted blessing. They were 'ill eneugh for ony fahl manners,' he affirmed. And on their behalf he added that night a special prayer to the usual quarter of an hour's supplication before meat, and would have tacked another to the end of the grace, had not his young mistress broken in upon him with a hurried command that he must run down the road, and, wherever Heathcliff had rambled, find and make him re-enter directly!

'I want to speak to him, and I *must*, before I go upstairs,' she said. 'And the gate is open: he is somewhere out of hearing; for he would not reply, though I shouted at the top of the fold as loud as I could.'

Joseph objected at first; she was too much in earnest, however, to suffer contradiction; and at last he placed his hat on his head, and walked grumbling forth.

Meantime, Catherine paced up and down the floor, exclaiming – 'I wonder where he is – I wonder where he *can* be! What did I say, Nelly? I've forgotten. Was he vexed at my bad humour this afternoon? Dear! tell me what I've said to grieve him? I do wish he'd come. I do wish he would!'

'What a noise for nothing!' I cried, though rather uneasy myself. 'What a trifle scares you! It's surely no great cause of alarm that Heathcliff should take a moonlight saunter on the moors, or even lie too sulky to speak to us in the hayloft. I'll engage he's lurking there. See if I don't ferret him out!'

I departed to renew my search; its result was disappointment, and Joseph's quest ended in the same.

'You lad gets war un war!' observed he on re-entering. 'He's left th' yate ut t'full swing, and miss's pony has trodden dahn two rigs uh corn, un plottered through, raight o'er intuh t'meadow! Hahsomdiver, t' maister 'ull play t' devil to morn, and he'll do weel. He's patience itsseln wi'sich careless, offald craters – patience itsseln he is! Bud he'll nut be soa allus – yah's see, all on ye! Yah mum'n't drive him aht uf his heead fur nowt!'

'Have you found Heathcliff, you ass?' interrupted Catherine. 'Have you been looking for him, as I ordered?'

'Aw sud more likker look for th' horse,' he replied. 'It 'ud be tuh more sense. Bud, aw can look for norther horse, nur man uf a neeght loike this – as black as t' chimbley! Und Hathecliff's noan t' chap tuh coom ut *maw* whistle – happen he'll be less hard uh hearing wi' *ye*!'

It *was* a very dark evening for summer: the clouds appeared inclined to thunder, and I said we had better all sit down: the approaching rain would be certain to bring him home without further trouble. However, Catherine would not be persuaded into tranquillity. She kept wandering to and fro, from the gate to the door, in a state of agitation which permitted no repose; and at length took up a permanent position on one side of the wall, near the road: where, heedless of my expostulations and the growling thunder, and the great drops

that began to plash around her, she remained, calling at intervals, and then listening, and then crying outright. She beat Hareton, or any child, at a good passionate fit of crying.

About midnight, while we still sat up, the storm came rattling over the Heights in full fury. There was a violent wind, as well as thunder, and either one or the other split a tree off at the corner of the building: a huge bough fell across the roof, and knocked down a portion of the east chimney-stack, sending a clatter of stones and soot into the kitchen fire. We thought a bolt had fallen in the middle of us; and Joseph swung on to his knees, beseeching the Lord to remember the patriarchs Noah and Lot, and, as in former times, spare the righteous, though he smote the ungodly. I felt some sentiment that it must be a judgement on us also. The Jonah, in my mind, was Mr Earnshaw; and I shook the handle of his den that I might ascertain if he were yet living. He replied audibly enough, in a fashion which made my companion vociferate, more clamorously than before, that a wide distinction might be drawn between saints like himself and sinners like his master. But the uproar passed away in twenty minutes, leaving us all unharmed; excepting Cathy, who got thoroughly drenched for her obstinacy in refusing to take shelter, and standing bonnetless and shawlless to catch as much water as she could with her hair and clothes. She came in and lay down on the settle, all soaked as she was, turning her face to the back, and putting her hands before it.

'Well, miss!' I exclaimed, touching her shoulder; 'you are not bent on getting your death, are you? Do you know what o'clock it is? Half-past twelve. Come, come to bed! there's no use waiting longer on that foolish boy: he'll be gone to Gimmerton, and he'll stay there now. He guesses we shouldn't wake for him till this late hour: at least, he guesses that only Mr Hindley would be up; and he'd rather avoid having the door opened by the master.'

'Nay, nay, he's noan at Gimmerton!' said Joseph. 'Aw'sniver wonder, bud he's at t' bothom ufa bug-hoile. This visitation worn't for nowt, und aw wod hev ye tuh look aht, miss – yah muh be t' next. Thank Hivin for all! All warks togither for gooid tuh them as is chozzen, and piked aht froo' th' rubbidge! Yah knaw whet t' Scripture ses – ' And he began quoting several texts, referring us to the chapters and verses, where we might find them.

I, having vainly begged the wilful girl to rise and remove her wet things, left him preaching and her shivering, and betook myself to bed with little Hareton, who slept as fast as if everyone had been sleeping round him. I heard Joseph read on a while afterwards; then I distinguished his slow step on the ladder, and then I dropped asleep.

Coming down somewhat later than usual, I saw, by the sunbeams piercing the chinks of the shutters, Miss Catherine still seated near the fireplace. The house door was ajar, too; light entered from its unclosed windows; Hindley had come out, and stood on the kitchen hearth, haggard and drowsy.

'What ails you, Cathy?' he was saying when I entered: 'you look as dismal as a drowned whelp. Why are you so damp and pale, child?'

'I've been wet,' she answered reluctantly, 'and I'm cold, that's all.'

'Oh, she is naughty!' I cried, perceiving the master to be tolerably sober. 'She got steeped in the shower of yesterday evening, and there she has sat the night through, and I couldn't prevail on her to stir.'

Mr Earnshaw stared at us in surprise. 'The night through,' he repeated. 'What kept her up? Not fear of the thunder, surely? That was over hours since.'

Neither of us wished to mention Heathcliff's absence, as long as we could conceal it; so I replied, I didn't know how she took it into her head to sit up; and she said nothing. The morning was fresh and cool; I threw back the lattice, and presently the room filled with sweet scents from the garden; but Catherine called peevishly to me, 'Ellen, shut the window. I'm starving!' And her teeth chattered as she shrunk closer to the almost extinguished embers.

'She's ill,' said Hindley, taking her wrist; 'I suppose that's the reason she would not go to bed. Damn it! I don't want to be troubled with more sickness here. What took you into the rain?'

'Running after t' lads, as usuald!' croaked Joseph, catching an opportunity, from our hesitation, to thrust in his evil tongue. 'If Aw wur yah, maister, Aw'd just slam t' boards i' their faces all on 'em, gentle and simple! Never a day ut yah're off, but yon cat uh Linton comes sneaking hither; and Miss Nelly shoo's a fine lass! shoo sits watching for ye i' t' kitchen; and as yah're in at one door, he's aht at t' other; und, then, wer grand lady goes a coorting uf hor side! It's bonny behaviour, lurking amang t' fields, after twelve ut' night, wi' that fahl, flaysome divil uf a gipsy, Heathcliff! They think *Aw*'m blind; but Aw'm noan, nowt ut t'soart! Aw seed young Linton, boath coming and going, and Aw seed *yah*' (directing his discourse to me). 'Yah gooid fur nowt, slattenly witch! nip up und bolt intuh th' hahs, t' minute yah heard t' maister's horse fit clatter up t' road.'

'Silence, eavesdropper!' cried Catherine; 'None of your insolence, before me! Edgar Linton came yesterday, by chance, Hindley; and it was *I* who told him to be off: because, I knew you would not like to have met him as you were.'

'You lie, Cathy, no doubt,' answered her brother, 'and you are a confounded simpleton! But never mind Linton at present: tell me, were you not with Heathcliff last night? Speak the truth, now. You need not be afraid of harming him: though I hate him as much as ever, he did me a good turn a short time since, that will make my conscience tender of breaking his neck. To prevent it, I shall send him about his business, this very morning; and after he's gone, I'd advise you all to look sharp: I shall only have the more humour for you.'

'I never saw Heathcliff last night,' answered Catherine, beginning to sob bitterly: 'and if you do turn him out of doors, I'll go with him. But, perhaps, you'll never have an opportunity: perhaps he's gone.' Here she burst into uncontrollable grief, and the remainder of her words were inarticulate.

Hindley lavished on her a torrent of scornful abuse, and bade her get to her room immediately, or she shouldn't cry for nothing! I obliged her to obey; and I shall never forget what a scene she acted when we reached her chamber: it terrified me. I thought she was going mad, and I begged Joseph to run for the doctor. It proved the commencement of delirium: Mr Kenneth, as soon as he

saw her, pronounced her dangerously ill; she had a fever. He bled her, and he told me to let her live on whey, and water gruel; and take care she did not throw herself downstairs or out of the window; and then he left: for he had enough to do in the parish, where two or three miles was the ordinary distance between cottage and cottage.

Though I cannot say I made a gentle nurse, and Joseph and the master were no better; and though our patient was as wearisome and headstrong as a patient could be, she weathered it through. Old Mrs Linton paid us several visits, to be sure, and set things to rights, and scolded and ordered us all; and when Catherine was convalescent, she insisted on conveying her to Thrushcross Grange: for which deliverance we were very grateful. But the poor dame had reason to repent of her kindness: she and her husband both took the fever, and died within a few days of each other.

Our young lady returned to us, saucier and more passionate, and haughtier than ever. Heathcliff had never been heard of since the evening of the thunderstorm; and, one day, I had the misfortune, when she provoked me exceedingly, to lay the blame of his disappearance on her: where indeed it belonged, as she well knew. From that period, for several months, she ceased to hold any communication with me, save in the relation of a mere servant. Joseph fell under a ban also: he *would* speak his mind, and lecture her all the same as if she were a little girl; and she esteemed herself a woman, and our mistress, and thought that her recent illness gave her a claim to be treated with consideration. Then the doctor had said that she would not bear crossing much; she ought to have her own way; and it was nothing less than murder in her eyes for anyone to presume to stand up and contradict her. From Mr Earnshaw and his companions she kept aloof; and tutored by Kenneth, and serious threats of a fit that often attended her rages, her brother allowed her whatever she pleased to demand, and generally avoided aggravating her fiery temper. He was rather *too* indulgent in humouring her caprices; not from affection, but from pride: he wished earnestly to see her bring honour to the family by an alliance with the Lintons, and as long as she let him alone she might trample us like slaves, for aught he cared! Edgar Linton, as multitudes have been before and will be after him, was infatuated; and believed himself the happiest man alive on the day he led her to Gimmerton chapel, three years subsequent to his father's death.

Much against my inclination, I was persuaded to leave Wuthering Heights and accompany her here. Little Hareton was nearly five years old, and I had just begun to teach him his letters. We made a sad parting; but Catherine's tears were more powerful than ours. When I refused to go, and when she found her entreaties did not move me, she went lamenting to her husband and brother. The former offered me munificent wages; the latter ordered me to pack up: he wanted no women in the house, he said, now that there was no mistress; and as to Hareton, the curate should take him in hand, by and by. And so I had but one choice left: to do as I was ordered. I told the master he got rid of all decent people only to run to ruin a little faster; I kissed Hareton goodbye; and since then he has been a stranger: and it's very queer to think it, but I've no doubt he

has completely forgotten all about Ellen Dean, and that he was ever more than all the world to her, and she to him!

At this point of the housekeeper's story, she chanced to glance towards the timepiece over the chimney; and was in amazement on seeing the minute-hand measure half-past one. She would not hear of staying a second longer: in truth, I felt rather disposed to defer the sequel of her narrative myself. And now that she is vanished to her rest, and I have meditated for another hour or two, I shall summon courage to go, also, in spite of aching laziness of head and limbs.

## *Chapter 10*

A charming introduction to a hermit's life! Four weeks' torture, tossing and sickness! Oh, these bleak winds and bitter northern skies, and impassable roads, and dilatory country surgeons!

And, oh, this dearth of the human physiognomy! and, worse than all, the terrible intimation of Kenneth that I need not expect to be out of doors till spring!

Mr Heathcliff has just honoured me with a call. About seven days ago he sent me a brace of grouse – the last of the season. Scoundrel! He is not altogether guiltless in this illness of mine; and that I had a great mind to tell him. But, alas! how could I offend a man who was charitable enough to sit at my bedside a good hour, and talk on some other subject than pills, and draughts, blisters, and leeches? This is quite an easy interval. I am too weak to read; yet I feel as if I could enjoy something interesting. Why not have up Mrs Dean to finish her tale? I can recollect its chief incidents, as far as she had gone. Yes: I remember her hero had run off, and never been heard of for three years; and the heroine was married. I'll ring: she'll be delighted to find me capable of talking cheerfully. Mrs Dean came.

'It wants twenty minutes, sir, to taking the medicine,' she commenced.

'Away, away with it!' I replied; 'I desire to have —'

'The doctor says you must drop the powders.'

'With all my heart! Don't interrupt me. Come and take your seat here. Keep your fingers from that bitter phalanx of vials. Draw your knitting out of your pocket – that will do – now continue the history of Mr Heathcliff, from where you left off, to the present day. Did he finish his education on the Continent, and come back a gentleman? Or did he get a sizar's place at college, or escape to America, and earn honours by drawing blood from his foster country? Or make a fortune more promptly, on the English highways?'

'He may have done a little in all these vocations, Mr Lockwood; but I couldn't give my word for any. I stated before that I didn't know how he gained his money; neither am I aware of the means he took to raise his mind from the savage ignorance into which it was sunk: but, with your leave, I'll proceed in my

own fashion, if you think it will amuse and not weary you. Are you feeling better this morning?'

'Much.'

'That's good news.'

I got Miss Catherine and myself to Thrushcross Grange; and, to my agreeable disappointment, she behaved infinitely better than I dared to expect. She seemed almost over fond of Mr Linton; and even to his sister, she showed plenty of affection. They were both very attentive to her comfort, certainly. It was not the thorn bending to the honeysuckles, but the honeysuckles embracing the thorn. There were no mutual concessions: one stood erect, and the others yielded: and who *can* be ill-natured and bad-tempered when they encounter neither opposition nor indifference? I observed that Mr Edgar had a deep-rooted fear of ruffling her humour. He concealed it from her; but if ever he heard me answer sharply, or saw any other servant grow cloudy at some imperious order of hers, he would show his trouble by a frown of displeasure that never darkened on his own account. He many a time spoke sternly to me about my pertness; and averred that the stab of a knife could not inflict a worse pang than he suffered at seeing his lady vexed. Not to grieve a kind master, I learned to be less touchy; and, for the space of half a year, the gunpowder lay as harmless as sand, because no fire came near to explode it. Catherine had seasons of gloom and silence, now and then: they were respected with sympathising silence by her husband, who ascribed them to an alteration in her constitution, produced by her perilous illness; as she was never subject to depression of spirits before. The return of sunshine was welcomed by answering sunshine from him. I believe I may assert that they were really in possession of deep and growing happiness.

It ended. Well, we *must* be for ourselves in the long run; the mild and generous are only more justly selfish than the domineering; and it ended when circumstances caused each to feel that the one's interest was not the chief consideration in the other's thoughts. On a mellow evening in September, I was coming from the garden with a heavy basket of apples which I had been gathering. It had got dusk, and the moon looked over the high wall of the court, causing undefined shadows to lurk in the corners of the numerous projecting portions of the building. I set my burden on the house steps by the kitchen door, and lingered to rest, and drew in a few more breaths of the soft, sweet air; my eyes were on the moon, and my back to the entrance, when I heard a voice behind me say – 'Nelly, is that you?'

It was a deep voice, and foreign in tone; yet there was something in the manner of pronouncing my name which made it sound familiar. I turned about to discover who spoke, fearfully; for the doors were shut, and I had seen nobody on approaching the steps. Something stirred in the porch; and, moving nearer, I distinguished a tall man dressed in dark clothes, with dark face and hair. He leant against the side, and held his fingers on the latch as if intending to open for himself. 'Who can it be?' I thought. 'Mr Earnshaw? Oh, no! The voice has no resemblance to his.'

'I have waited here an hour,' he resumed, while I continued staring; 'and the whole of that time all round has been as still as death. I dared not enter. You do not know me? Look, I'm not a stranger!'

A ray fell on his features; the cheeks were sallow, and half covered with black whiskers; the brows lowering, the eyes deep set and singular. I remembered the eyes.

'What!' I cried, uncertain whether to regard him as a worldly visitor, and I raised my hands in amazement. 'What! you come back? Is it really you? Is it?'

'Yes, Heathcliff,' he replied, glancing from me up to the windows, which reflected a score of glittering moons, but showed no lights from within. 'Are they at home? Where is she? Nelly, you are not glad! You needn't be so disturbed. Is she here? Speak! I want to have one word with her – your mistress. Go, and say some person from Gimmerton desires to see her.'

'How will she take it?' I exclaimed. 'What will she do? The surprise bewilders me – it will put her out of her head! And you *are* Heathcliff? But altered! Nay, there's no comprehending it. Have you been for a soldier?'

'Go and carry my message,' he interrupted impatiently. 'I'm in hell till you do!'

He lifted the latch, and I entered; but when I got to the parlour where Mr and Mrs Linton were, I could not persuade myself to proceed. At length, I resolved on making an excuse to ask if they would have the candles lighted, and I opened the door.

They sat together in a window whose lattice lay back against the wall, and displayed, beyond the garden trees and the wild green park, the valley of Gimmerton, with a long line of mist winding nearly to its top (for very soon after you pass the chapel, as you may have noticed, the sough that runs from the marshes joins a beck which follows the bend of the glen). Wuthering Heights rose above this silvery vapour; but our old house was invisible; it rather dips down on the other side. Both the room and its occupants, and the scene they gazed on, looked wondrously peaceful. I shrank reluctantly from performing my errand; and was actually going away leaving it unsaid, after having put my question about the candles, when a sense of my folly compelled me to return, and mutter, 'A person from Gimmerton wishes to see you, ma'am.'

'What does he want?' asked Mrs Linton.

'I did not question him,' I answered.

'Well, close the curtains, Nelly,' she said; 'and bring up tea. I'll be back again directly.'

She quitted the apartment; Mr Edgar enquired, carelessly, who it was.

'Someone mistress does not expect,' I replied. 'That Heathcliff – you recollect him, sir – who used to live at Mr Earnshaw's.'

'What, the gipsy – the plough-boy?' he cried. 'Why did you not say so to Catherine?'

'Hush! you must not call him by those names, master,' I said. 'She'd be sadly grieved to hear you. She was nearly heartbroken when he ran off. I guess his return will make a jubilee to her.'

Mr Linton walked to a window on the other side of the room that overlooked

the court. He unfastened it, and leant out. I suppose they were below, for he exclaimed quickly, 'Don't stand there, love! Bring the person in, if it be anyone particular.' Ere long, I heard the click of the latch, and Catherine flew upstairs, breathless and wild; too excited to show gladness: indeed, by her face, you would rather have surmised an awful calamity.

'Oh, Edgar, Edgar!' she panted, flinging her arms round his neck. 'Oh, Edgar, darling! Heathcliff's come back – he is!' And she tightened her embrace to a squeeze.

'Well, well,' cried her husband, crossly, 'don't strangle me for that! He never struck me as such a marvellous treasure. There is no need to be frantic!'

'I know you didn't like him,' she answered, repressing a little the intensity of her delight. 'Yet, for my sake, you must be friends now. Shall I tell him to come up now?'

'Here?' he said, 'into the parlour?'

'Where else?' she asked.

He looked vexed, and suggested the kitchen as a more suitable place for him. Mrs Linton eyed him with a droll expression – half angry, half laughing at his fastidiousness.

'No,' she added, after a while; 'I cannot sit in the kitchen. Set two tables here, Ellen: one for your master and Miss Isabella, being gentry; the other for Heathcliff and myself, being of the lower orders. Will that please you, dear? Or must I have a fire lighted elsewhere? If so, give directions. I'll run down and secure my guest. I'm afraid the joy is too great to be real!'

She was about to dart off again; but Edgar arrested her.

'*You* bid him step up,' he said, addressing me; 'and, Catherine, try to be glad, without being absurd! The whole household need not witness the sight of your welcoming a runaway servant as a brother.'

I descended, and found Heathcliff waiting under the porch, evidently anticipating an invitation to enter. He followed my guidance with out waste of words, and I ushered him into the presence of the master and mistress, whose flushed cheeks betrayed signs of warm talking. But the lady's glowed with another feeling when her friend appeared at the door: she sprang forward, took both his hands, and led him to Linton; and then she *seized* Linton's reluctant fingers and crushed them into his. Now fully revealed by the fire and candlelight, I was amazed, more than ever, to behold the transformation of Heathcliff. He had grown a tall, athletic, well-formed man; beside whom, my master seemed quite slender and youth-like. His upright carriage suggested the idea of his having been in the army. His countenance was much older in expression and decision of feature than Mr Linton's; it looked intelligent, and retained no marks of former degradation. A half-civilised ferocity lurked yet in the depressed brows and eyes full of black fire, but it was subdued; and his manner was even dignified: quite divested of roughness, though too stern for grace. My master's surprise equalled or exceeded mine: he remained for a minute at a loss how to address the ploughboy, as he had called him. Heathcliff dropped his slight hand, and stood looking at him coolly till he chose to speak.

'Sit down, sir,' he said, at length. 'Mrs Linton, recalling old times, would have me give you a cordial reception; and, of course, I am gratified when anything occurs to please her.'

'And I also,' answered Heathcliff, 'especially if it be anything in which I have a part. I shall stay an hour or two willingly.'

He took a seat opposite Catherine, who kept her gaze fixed on him as if she feared he would vanish were she to remove it. He did not raise his to her often: a quick glance now and then sufficed; but it flashed back, each time more confidently, the undisguised delight he drank from hers. They were too much absorbed in their mutual joy to suffer embarrassment. Not so Mr Edgar: he grew pale with pure annoyance: a feeling that reached its climax when his lady rose, and stepping across the rug, seized Heathcliff's hands again, and laughed like one beside herself.

'I shall think it a dream tomorrow!' she cried. 'I shall not be able to believe that I have seen, and touched, and spoken to you once more. And yet, cruel Heathcliff! you don't deserve this welcome. To be absent and silent for three years, and never to think of me!'

'A little more than you have thought of me,' he murmured. 'I heard of your marriage, Cathy, not long since; and, while waiting in the yard below, I meditated this plan – just to have one glimpse of your face: a stare of surprise, perhaps, and pretended pleasure; afterwards settle my score with Hindley; and then prevent the law by doing execution on myself. Your welcome has put these ideas out of my mind; but beware of meeting me with another aspect next time! Nay, you'll not drive me off again. You were really sorry for me, were you? Well, there was cause. I've fought through a bitter life since I last heard your voice; and you must forgive me, for I struggled only for you!'

'Catherine, unless we are to have cold tea, please to come to the table,' interrupted Linton, striving to preserve his ordinary tone, and a due measure of politeness. 'Mr Heathcliff will have a long walk, wherever he may lodge tonight; and I'm thirsty.'

She took her post before the urn; and Miss Isabella came, summoned by the bell; then, having handed their chairs forward, I left the room. The meal hardly endured ten minutes. Catherine's cup was never filled: she could neither eat nor drink. Edgar had made a slop in his saucer, and scarcely swallowed a mouthful. Their guest did not protract his stay that evening above an hour longer. I asked, as he departed, if he went to Gimmerton?

'No, to Wuthering Heights,' he answered: 'Mr Earnshaw invited me, when I called this morning.'

Mr Earnshaw invited *him*! and *he* called on Mr Earnshaw! I pondered this sentence painfully after he was gone. Is he turning out a bit of a hypocrite and coming into the country to work mischief under a cloak? I mused: I had a presentiment, in the bottom of my heart, that he had better have remained away.

About the middle of the night, I was wakened from my first nap by Mrs Linton gliding into my chamber, taking a seat on my bedside, and pulling me by the hair to rouse me.

'I cannot rest, Ellen,' she said, by way of apology. 'And I want some living creature to keep me company in my happiness! Edgar is sulky, because I'm glad of a thing that does not interest him: he refuses to open his mouth, except to utter pettish, silly speeches; and he affirmed I was cruel and selfish for wishing to talk when he was so sick and sleepy. He always contrives to be sick at the least cross! I gave a few sentences of commendation to Heathcliff, and he, either for a headache or a pang of envy, began to cry: so I got up and left him.'

'What use is it praising Heathcliff to him?' I answered. 'As lads they had an aversion to each other, and Heathcliff would hate just as much to hear him praised: it's human nature. Let Mr Linton alone about him, unless you would like an open quarrel between them.'

'But does it not show great weakness?' pursued she. 'I'm not envious; I never feel hurt at the brightness of Isabella's yellow hair and the whiteness of her skin, at her dainty elegance, and the fondness all the family exhibit for her. Even you, Nelly, if we have a dispute sometimes, you back Isabella at once; and I yield like a foolish mother: I call her a darling, and flatter her into a good temper. It pleases her brother to see us cordial, and that pleases me. But they are very much alike: they are spoiled children, and fancy the world was made for their accommodation; and though I humour both, I think a smart chastisement might improve them, all the same.'

'You're mistaken, Mrs Linton,' said I. 'They humour you: I know what there would be to do if they did not. You can well afford to indulge their passing whims as long as their business is to anticipate all your desires. You may, however, fall out, at last, over something of equal consequence to both sides; and then those you term weak are very capable of being as obstinate as you.'

'And then we shall fight to the death, shan't we, Nelly?' she returned, laughing. 'No! I tell you, I have such faith in Linton's love, that I believe I might kill him, and he wouldn't wish to retaliate.'

I advised her to value him the more for his affection.

'I do,' she answered, 'but he needn't resort to whining for trifles. It is childish; and, instead of melting into tears because I said that Heathcliff was now worthy of anyone's regard, and it would honour the first gentleman in the country to be his friend, he ought to have said it for me, and been delighted from sympathy. He must get accustomed to him, and he may as well like him: considering how Heathcliff has reason to object to him, I'm sure he behaved excellently!'

'What do you think of his going to Wuthering Heights?' I enquired. 'He is reformed in every respect, apparently: quite a Christian: offering the right hand of fellowship to his enemies all around!'

'He explained it,' she replied. 'I wondered as much as you. He said he called to gather information concerning me from you, supposing you resided there still, and Joseph told Hindley, who came out and fell to questioning him of what he had been doing, and how he had been living; and finally, desired him to walk in. There were some persons sitting at cards; Heathcliff joined them; my brother lost some money to him, and, finding him plentifully supplied, he requested that he would come again in the evening: to which he consented.

Hindley is too reckless to select his acquaintance prudently: he doesn't trouble himself to reflect on the causes he might have for mistrusting one whom he has basely injured. But, Heathcliff affirms his principal reason for resuming a connection with his ancient persecutor is a wish to install himself in quarters at walking distance from the Grange, and an attachment to the house where we lived together; and likewise a hope that I shall have more opportunities of seeing him there than I could have if he settled in Gimmerton. He means to offer liberal payment for permission to lodge at the Heights; and doubtless my brother's covetousness will prompt him to accept the terms: he was always greedy; though what he grasps with one hand he flings away with the other.'

'It's a nice place for a young man to fix his dwelling in!' said I. 'Have you no fear of the consequences, Mrs Linton?'

'None for my friend,' she replied: 'his strong head will keep him from danger; a little for Hindley: but he can't be made morally worse than he is; and I stand between him and bodily harm. The event of this evening has reconciled me to God and humanity! I had risen in angry rebellion against Providence. Oh, I've endured very, very bitter misery, Nelly! If that creature knew how bitter, he'd be ashamed to cloud its removal with idle petulance. It was kindness for him which induced me to bear it alone: had I expressed the agony I frequently felt, he would have been taught to long for its alleviation as ardently as I. However, it's over, and I'll take no revenge on his folly; I can afford to suffer anything hereafter! Should the meanest thing alive slap me on the cheek, I'd not only turn the other, but I'd ask pardon for provoking it; and, as a proof, I'll go make my peace with Edgar instantly. Good-night! I'm an angel!'

In this self-complacent conviction she departed; and the success of her fulfilled resolution was obvious on the morrow: Mr Linton had not only abjured his peevishness (though his spirits seemed still subdued by Catherine's exuberance of vivacity), but he ventured no objection to her taking Isabella with her to Wuthering Heights in the afternoon; and she rewarded him with such a summer of sweetness and affection in return, as made the house a paradise for several days; both master and servants profiting from the perpetual sunshine.

Heathcliff – Mr Heathcliff I should say in future – used the liberty of visiting at Thrushcross Grange cautiously, at first: he seemed estimating how far its owner would bear his intrusion. Catherine, also, deemed it judicious to moderate her expressions of pleasure in receiving him; and he gradually established his right to be expected. He retained a great deal of the reserve for which his boyhood was remarkable; and that served to repress all startling demonstrations of feeling. My master's uneasiness experienced a lull, and further circumstances diverted it into another channel for a space.

His new source of trouble sprang from the not anticipated misfortune of Isabella Linton evincing a sudden and irresistible attraction towards the tolerated guest. She was at that time a charming young lady of eighteen; infantile in manners, though possessed of keen wit, keen feelings, and a keen temper, too, if irritated. Her brother, who loved her tenderly, was appalled at this fantastic preference. Leaving aside the degradation of an alliance with a nameless man,

and the possible fact that his property, in default of heirs male, might pass into such a one's power, he had sense to comprehend Heathcliff's disposition: to know that, though his exterior was altered, his mind was unchangeable, and unchanged. And he dreaded that mind: it revolted him: he shrank forebodingly from the idea of committing Isabella to its keeping. He would have recoiled still more had he been aware that her attachment rose unsolicited, and was bestowed where it awakened no reciprocation of sentiment; for the minute he discovered its existence, he laid the blame on Heathcliff's deliberate designing.

We had all remarked, during some time, that Miss Linton fretted and pined over something. She grew cross and wearisome; snapping at and teasing Catherine continually, at the imminent risk of exhausting her limited patience. We excused her to a certain extent, on the plea of ill-health: she was dwindling and fading before our eyes. But one day, when she had been particularly wayward, rejecting her breakfast, complaining that the servants did not do what she told them; that the mistress would allow her to be nothing in the house, and Edgar neglected her; that she had caught a cold with the doors being left open, and we let the parlour fire go out on purpose to vex her, with a hundred yet more frivolous accusations, Mrs Linton peremptorily insisted that she should get to bed; and, having scolded her heartily, threatened to send for the doctor. Mention of Kenneth caused her to exclaim, instantly, that her health was perfect, and it was only Catherine's harshness which made her unhappy.

'How can you say I am harsh, you naughty fondling?' cried the mistress, amazed at the unreasonable assertion. 'You are surely losing your reason. When have I been harsh, tell me?'

'Yesterday,' sobbed Isabella, 'and now!'

'Yesterday!' said her sister-in-law. 'On what occasion?'

'In our walk along the moor: you told me to ramble where I pleased, while you sauntered on with Mr Heathcliff!'

'And that's your notion of harshness?' said Catherine, laughing. 'It was no hint that your company was superfluous: we didn't care whether you kept with us or not; I merely thought Heathcliff's talk would have nothing entertaining for your ears.'

'Oh no,' wept the young lady; 'you wished me away, because you know I liked to be there!'

'Is she sane?' asked Mrs Linton, appealing to me. 'I'll repeat our conversation, word for word, Isabella; and you point out any charm it could have had for you.'

'I don't mind the conversation,' she answered. 'I wanted to be with – '

'Well!' said Catherine, perceiving her hesitate to complete the sentence.

'With him: and I won't be always sent off!' she continued, kindling up. 'You are a dog in the manger, Cathy, and desire no one to be loved but yourself!'

'You are an impertinent little monkey!' exclaimed Mrs Linton, in surprise. 'But I'll not believe this idiocy! It is impossible that you can covet the admiration of Heathcliff – that you can consider him an agreeable person! I hope I have misunderstood you, Isabella?

'No, you have not,' said the infatuated girl. 'I love him more than ever you loved Edgar; and he might love me, if you would let him!'

'I wouldn't be you for a kingdom, then!' Catherine declared, emphatically: and she seemed to speak sincerely. 'Nelly, help me to convince her of her madness. Tell her what Heathcliff is: an unreclaimed creature, without refinement, without cultivation: an arid wilderness of furze and whinstone. I'd as soon put that little canary into the park on a winter's day, as recommend you to bestow your heart on him! It is deplorable ignorance of his character, child, and nothing else, which makes that dream enter your head. Pray, don't imagine that he conceals depths of benevolence and affection beneath a stern exterior! He's not a rough diamond – a pearl-containing oyster of a rustic: he's a fierce, pitiless, wolfish man. I never say to him, "Let this or that enemy alone, because it would be ungenerous or cruel to harm them"; I say, "Let them alone, because *I* should hate them to be wronged": and he'd crush you like a sparrow's egg, Isabella, if he found you a troublesome charge. I know he couldn't love a Linton; and yet he'd be quite capable of marrying your fortune and expectations: avarice is growing with him a besetting sin. There's my picture: and I'm his friend – so much so, that had he thought seriously to catch you, I should, perhaps, have held my tongue, and let you fall into his trap.'

Miss Linton regarded her sister-in-law with indignation. 'For shame! for shame!' she repeated, angrily. 'You are worse than twenty foes, you poisonous friend!'

'Ah! you won't believe me, then?' said Catherine. 'You think I speak from wicked selfishness?'

'I'm certain you do,' retorted Isabella; 'and I shudder at you!'

'Good!' cried the other. 'Try for yourself, if that be your spirit: I have done, and yield the argument to your saucy insolence.'

'And I must suffer for her egotism!' she sobbed, as Mrs Linton left the room. 'All, all is against me: she has blighted my single consolation. But she uttered falsehoods, didn't she? Mr Heathcliff is not a fiend: he has an honourable soul, and a true one, or how could he remember her?'

'Banish him from your thoughts, miss,' I said. 'He's a bird of bad omen: no mate for you. Mrs Linton spoke strongly, and yet I can't contradict her. She is better acquainted with his heart than I, or anyone besides; and she never would represent him as worse than he is. Honest people don't hide their deeds. How has he been living? How has he got rich? Why is he staying at Wuthering Heights, the house of a man whom he abhors? They say Mr Earnshaw is worse and worse since he came. They sit up all night together continually, and Hindley has been borrowing money on his land, and does nothing but play and drink: I heard only a week ago – it was Joseph who told me – I met him at Gimmerton: "Nelly," he said, "we's hae a Crahnr's 'quest enah, at ahr folks. One on 'em's a'most getten his finger cut off wi' hauding t' other froo'sticking hisseln loike a cawlf. That's maister, yah knaw, ut's soa up uh going tuh t' grand 'sizes. He 's noan feard uh t' Bench uh judges, norther Paul, nur Peter, nur John, nor Mathew, nor noan on 'em, nut he! He fair like's he langs tuh set his brazened face agean 'em! And yon

bonny lad Heathcliff, yah mind, he's a rare un! He can girn a laugh, as weel's onybody at a raight divil's jest. Does he niver say nowt of his fine living amang us, when he goas tuh t' Grange? This is t' way on 't – up at sun-dahn; dice, brandy, cloised shutters, und can'le lught till next day, at nooin: then, t'fooil gangs banning un raving tuh his cham'er, makking dacent fowks dig thur fingers i' thur lugs fur varry shaume; un' the knave, wah, he earn cahnt his brass, un' ate, un' sleep, un' off tuh his neighbour's tuh gossip wi' t' wife. I' course, he tells Dame Catherine hah hor father's goold runs intuh his pocket, and her fathur's son gallops dahn t' Broad road, while he flees afore tuh oppen t' pikes?" Now, Miss Linton, Joseph is an old rascal, but no liar; and, if his account of Heathcliff's conduct be true, you would never think of desiring such a husband, would you?'

'You are leagued with the rest, Ellen!' she replied. 'I'll not listen to your slanders. What malevolence you must have to wish to convince me that there is no happiness in the world!'

Whether she would have got over this fancy if left to herself, or persevered in nursing it perpetually, I cannot say: she had little time to reflect. The day after, there was a justice-meeting at the next town; my master was obliged to attend; and Mr Heathcliff, aware of his absence, called rather earlier than usual. Catherine and Isabella were sitting in the library, on hostile terms, but silent. The latter alarmed at her recent indiscretion, and the disclosure she had made of her secret feelings in a transient fit of passion; the former, on mature consideration, really offended with her companion; and, if she laughed again at her pertness, inclined to make it no laughing matter to *her*. She did laugh as she saw Heathcliff pass the window. I was sweeping the hearth, and I noticed a mischievous smile on her lips. Isabella, absorbed in her meditations, or a book, remained till the door opened; and it was too late to attempt an escape, which she would gladly have done had it been practicable.

'Come in, that's right!' exclaimed the mistress, gaily, pulling a chair to the fire. 'Here are two people sadly in need of a third to thaw the ice between them; and you are the very one we should both of us choose. Heathcliff, I'm proud to show you, at last, somebody that dotes on you more than myself. I expect you to feel flattered. Nay, it's not Nelly; don't look at her! My poor little sister-in-law is breaking her heart by mere contemplation of your physical and moral beauty. It lies in your own power to be Edgar's brother! No, no, Isabella, you sha'n't run off,' she continued, arresting, with feigned playfulness, the confounded girl, who had risen indignantly. 'We were quarrelling like cats about you, Heathcliff, and I was fairly beaten in protestations of devotion and admiration: and, moreover, I was informed that if I would but have the manners to stand aside, my rival, as she will have herself to be, would shoot a shaft into your soul that would fix you for ever, and send my image into eternal oblivion!'

'Catherine!' said Isabella, calling up her dignity, and disdaining to struggle from the tight grasp that held her. 'I'd thank you to adhere to the truth and not slander me, even in joke! Mr Heathcliff, be kind enough to bid this friend of yours release me: she forgets that you and I are not intimate acquaintances; and what amuses her is painful to me beyond expression.'

As the guest answered nothing, but took his seat, and looked thoroughly indifferent what sentiments she cherished concerning him, she turned and whispered an earnest appeal for liberty to her tormentor.

'By no means!' cried Mrs Linton in answer.

'I won't be named a dog in the manger again. You *shall* stay: now then! Heathcliff, why don't you evince satisfaction at my pleasant news? Isabella swears that the love Edgar has for me is nothing to that she entertains for you. I'm sure she made some speech of the kind; did she not, Ellen? And she has fasted ever since the day before yesterday's walk, from sorrow and rage that I despatched her out of your society under the idea of its being unacceptable.'

'I think you belie her,' said Heathcliff, twisting his chair to face them. 'She wishes to be out of my society now, at any rate!'

And he stared hard at the object of discourse, as one might do at a strange repulsive animal: a centipede from the Indies, for instance, which curiosity leads one to examine in spite of the aversion it raises. The poor thing couldn't bear that: she grew white and red in rapid succession, and, while tears beaded her lashes, bent the strength of her small fingers to loosen the firm clutch of Catherine; and perceiving that as fast as she raised one finger off her arm another closed down, and she could not remove the whole together, she began to make use of her nails; and their sharpness presently ornamented the detainer's with crescents of red.

'There's a tigress!' exclaimed Mrs Linton, setting her free, and shaking her hand with pain. 'Begone, for God's sake, and hide your vixen face! How foolish to reveal those talons to *him*. Can't you fancy the conclusions he'll draw? Look, Heathcliff! they are instruments that will do execution – you must beware of your eyes.'

'I'd wrench them off her fingers, if they ever menaced me,' he answered, brutally, when the door had closed after her. 'But what did you mean by teasing the creature in that manner, Cathy? You were not speaking the truth, were you?'

'I assure you I was,' she returned. 'She has been pining for your sake several weeks; and raving about you this morning, and pouring forth a deluge of abuse, because I represented your failings in a plain light, for the purpose of mitigating her adoration. But don't notice it further: I wished to punish her sauciness, that's all. I like her too well, my dear Heathcliff, to let you absolutely seize and devour her up.'

'And I like her too ill to attempt it,' said he, 'except in a very ghoulish fashion. You'd hear of odd things if I lived alone with that mawkish, waxen face: the most ordinary would be painting on its white the colours of the rainbow, and turning the blue eyes black, every day or two: they detestably resemble Linton's.'

'Delectably!' observed Catherine. 'They are dove's eyes – angel's!'

'She's her brother's heir, is she not?' he asked, after a brief silence.

'I should be sorry to think so,' returned his companion. 'Half a dozen nephews shall erase her title, please Heaven. Abstract your mind from the subject at present: you are too prone to covet your neighbour's goods; remember *this* neighbour's goods are mine.'

'If they were *mine*, they would be none the less that,' said Heathcliff; 'but though Isabella Linton may be silly, she is scarcely mad; and, in short, we'll dismiss the matter, as you advise.'

From their tongues, they did dismiss it; and Catherine, probably, from her thoughts. The other, I felt certain, recalled it often in the course of the evening. I saw him smile to himself – grin rather – and lapse into ominous musing whenever Mrs Linton had occasion to be absent from the apartment.

I determined to watch his movements. My heart invariably cleaved to the master's, in preference to Catherine's side: with reason I imagined, for he was kind, and trustful, and honourable; and she – she could not be called the *opposite*, yet she seemed to allow herself such wide latitude, that I had little faith in her principles, and still less sympathy for her feelings. I wanted something to happen which might have the effect of freeing both Wuthering Heights and the Grange of Mr Heathcliff, quietly; leaving us as we had been prior to his advent. His visits were a continual nightmare to me; and, I suspected, to my master also. His abode at the Heights was an oppression past explaining. I felt that God had forsaken the stray sheep there to its own wicked wanderings, and an evil beast prowled between it and the fold, waiting his time to spring and destroy.

## *Chapter 11*

Sometimes, while meditating on these things in solitude, I've got up in a sudden terror, and put on my bonnet to go and see how all was at the farm. I've persuaded my conscience that it was a duty to warn him how people talked regarding his ways; and then I've recollected his confirmed bad habits, and, hopeless of benefiting him, have flinched from re-entering the dismal house, doubting if I could bear to be taken at my word.

One time I passed the old gate, going out of my way, on a journey to Gimmerton. It was about the period that my narrative has reached: a bright frosty afternoon; the ground bare, and the road hard and dry. I came to a stone where the highway branches off on to the moor at your left hand; a rough sand-pillar, with the letters W. H. cut on its north side, on the east, G., and on the southwest, T. G. It serves as guidepost to the Grange, and Heights, and village. The sun shone yellow on its grey head, reminding me of summer; and I cannot say why, but all at once, a gush of child's sensations flowed into my heart. Hindley and I held it a favourite spot twenty years before I gazed long at the weather-worn block; and, stooping down, perceived a hole near the bottom still full of snail-shells and pebbles, which we were very fond of storing there with more perishable things; and, as fresh as reality, it appeared that I beheld my early playmate seated on the withered turf: his dark, square head bent forward, and his little hand scooping out the earth with a piece of slate. 'Poor Hindley!' I exclaimed, involuntarily. I started: my bodily eye was cheated into a momentary belief that the child lifted its face and stared straight into mine! It vanished in a

twinkling; but immediately I felt an irresistible yearning to be at the Heights. Superstition urged me to comply with this impulse: supposing he should be dead! I thought – or should die soon! – supposing it were a sign of death! The nearer I got to the house the more agitated I grew; and on catching sight of it I trembled every limb. The apparition had outstripped me: it stood looking through the gate. That was my first idea on observing an elf-locked, brown-eyed boy setting his ruddy countenance against the bars. Further reflection suggested this must be Hareton, *my* Hareton, not altered greatly since I left him, ten months since.

'God bless thee, darling!' I cried, forgetting instantaneously my foolish fears. 'Hareton, it's Nelly! Nelly, thy nurse.'

He retreated out of arm's length, and picked up a large flint.

'I am come to see thy father, Hareton,' I added, guessing from the action that Nelly, if she lived in his memory at all, was not recognised as one with me.

He raised his missile to hurl it; I commenced a soothing speech, but could not stay his hand: the stone struck my bonnet; and then ensued, from the stammering lips of the little fellow, a string of curses, which, whether he comprehended them or not, were delivered with practised emphasis, and distorted his baby features into a shocking expression of malignity. You may be certain this grieved more than angered me. Fit to cry, I took an orange from my pocket, and offered it to propitiate him. He hesitated, and then snatched it from my hold; as if he fancied I only intended to tempt and disappoint him. I showed another, keeping it out of his reach.

'Who has taught you those fine words, my bairn?' I enquired. 'The curate?'

'Damn the curate, and thee! Gie me that,' he replied.

'Tell us where you got your lessons, and you shall have it,' said I. 'Who's your master?'

'Devil daddy,' was his answer.

'And what do you learn from daddy?' I continued.

He jumped at the fruit; I raised it higher. 'What does he teach you?' I asked.

'Naught,' said he, 'but to keep out of his gait. Daddy cannot bide me, because I swear at him.'

'Ah! and the devil teaches you to swear at daddy?' I observed.

'Ay – nay,' he drawled.

'Who, then?'

'Heathcliff.'

I asked if he liked Mr Heathcliff.

'Ay!' he answered again.

Desiring to have his reasons for liking him, I could only gather the sentences – 'I known't: he pays dad back what he gies to me – he curses daddy for cursing me. He says I mun do as I will.'

'And the curate does not teach you to read and write, then?' I pursued.

'No, I was told the curate should have his — teeth dashed down his — throat, if he stepped over the threshold – Heathcliff had promised that!'

I put the orange in his hand, and bade him tell his father that a woman called

Nelly Dean was waiting to speak with him, by the garden gate. He went up the walk, and entered the house; but, instead of Hindley, Heathcliff appeared on the door stones; and I turned directly and ran down the road as hard as ever I could race, making no halt till I gained the guide post, and feeling as scared as if I had raised a goblin. This is not much connected with Miss Isabella's affair; except that it urged me to resolve further on mounting vigilant guard, and doing my utmost to check the spread of such bad influence at the Grange: even though I should wake a domestic storm, by thwarting Mrs Linton's pleasure.

The next time Heathcliff came, my young lady chanced to be feeding some pigeons in the court. She had never spoken a word to her sister-in-law for three days; but she had likewise dropped her fretful complaining, and we found it a great comfort. Heathcliff had not the habit of bestowing a single unnecessary civility on Miss Linton, I knew. Now, as soon as he beheld her, his first precaution was to take a sweeping survey of the house-front. I was standing by the kitchen window, but I drew out of sight. He then stepped across the pavement to her, and said something: she seemed embarrassed, and desirous of getting away; to prevent it, he laid his hand on her arm. She averted her face: he apparently put some question which she had no mind to answer. There was another rapid glance at the house, and supposing himself unseen, the scoundrel had the impudence to embrace her.

'Judas! Traitor!' I ejaculated. 'You are a hypocrite, too, are you? A deliberate deceiver.'

'Who is, Nelly?' said Catherine's voice at my elbow: I had been over-intent on watching the pair outside to mark her entrance.

'Your worthless friend!' I answered warmly: 'the sneaking rascal yonder. Ah, he has caught a glimpse of us – he is coming in! I wonder will he have the art to find a plausible excuse for making love to miss, when he told you he hated her?'

Mrs Linton saw Isabella tear herself free, and run into the garden; and a minute after, Heathcliff opened the door. I couldn't withhold giving some loose to my indignation; but Catherine angrily insisted on silence, and threatened to order me out of the kitchen, if I dared to be so presumptuous as to put in my insolent tongue.

'To hear you, people might think you were the mistress!' she cried. 'You want setting down in your right place! Heathcliff, what are you about, raising this stir? I said you must let Isabella alone! I beg you will, unless you are tired of being received here, and wish Linton to draw the bolts against you!'

'God forbid that he should try!' answered the black villain. I detested him just then. 'God keep him meek and patient! Every day I grow madder after sending him to heaven!'

'Hush!' said Catherine, shutting the inner door. 'Don't vex me. Why have you disregarded my request? Did she come across you on purpose?'

'What is it to you?' he growled. 'I have a right to kiss her, if she chooses; and you have no right to object. I'm not *your* husband: *you* needn't be jealous of me!'

'I'm not jealous of you,' replied the mistress; 'I'm jealous for you. Clear your face: you shan't scowl at me! If you like Isabella, you shall marry her. But do

you like her? Tell the truth, Heathcliff! There, you won't answer. I'm certain you don't!'

'And would Mr Linton approve of his sister marrying that man?' I enquired.

'Mr Linton should approve,' returned my lady decisively.

'He might spare himself the trouble,' said Heathcliff: 'I could do as well without his approbation. And as to you, Catherine, I have a mind to speak a few words now, while we are at it. I want you to be aware that I *know* you have treated me infernally – infernally! Do you hear? And if you flatter yourself that I don't perceive it, you are a fool; and if you think I can be consoled by sweet words, you are an idiot; and if you fancy I'll suffer unrevenged, I'll convince you of the contrary, in a very little while! Meantime, thank you for telling me your sister-in-law's secret: I swear I'll make the most of it. And stand you aside!'

'What new phase of his character is this?' exclaimed Mrs Linton, in amazement. 'I've treated you infernally – and you'll take revenge! How will you take it, ungrateful brute? How have I treated you infernally?'

'I seek no revenge on you,' replied Heathcliff less vehemently. 'That's not the plan. The tyrant grinds down his slaves and they don't turn against him; they crush those beneath them. You are welcome to torture me to death for your amusement, only allow me to amuse myself a little in the same style, and refrain from insult as much as you are able. Having levelled my palace, don't erect a hovel and complacently admire your own charity in giving me that for a home. If I imagined you really wished me to marry Isabella, I'd cut my throat!'

'Oh, the evil is that I am *not* jealous, is it?' cried Catherine. 'Well, I won't repeat my offer of a wife: it is as bad as offering Satan a lost soul. Your bliss lies, like his, in inflicting misery. You prove it. Edgar is restored from the ill-temper he gave way to at your coming; I begin to be secure and tranquil; and you, restless to know us at peace, appear resolved on exciting a quarrel. Quarrel with Edgar, if you please, Heathcliff, and deceive his sister: you'll hit on exactly the most efficient method of revenging yourself on me.'

The conversation ceased. Mrs Linton sat down by the fire, flushed and gloomy. The spirit which served her was growing intractable: she could neither lay nor control it. He stood on the hearth with folded arms, brooding on his evil thoughts; and in this position I left them to seek the master, who was wondering what kept Catherine below so long.

'Ellen,' said he, when I entered, 'have you seen your mistress?'

'Yes; she's in the kitchen, sir,' I answered. 'She's sadly put out by Mr Heathcliff's behaviour: and, indeed, I do think it's time to arrange his visits on another footing. There's harm in being too soft, and now it's come to this – ' And I related the scene in the court, and, as near as I dared, the whole subsequent dispute. I fancied it could not be very prejudicial to Mrs Linton; unless she made it so afterwards, by assuming the defensive for her guest. Edgar Linton had difficulty in hearing me to the close. His first words revealed that he did not clear his wife of blame.

'This is insufferable!' he exclaimed. 'It is disgraceful that she should own him for a friend, and force his company on me! Call me two men out of the hall, Ellen. Catherine shall linger no longer to argue with the low ruffian – I have humoured her enough.'

He descended, and bidding the servants wait in the passage, went, followed by me, to the kitchen. Its occupants had recommenced their angry discussion: Mrs Linton, at least, was scolding with renewed vigour; Heathcliff had moved to the window, and hung his head, somewhat cowed by her violent rating apparently. He saw the master first, and made a hasty motion that she should be silent; which she obeyed, abruptly, on discovering the reason of his intimation. 'How is this?' said Linton, addressing her; 'what notion of propriety must you have to remain here, after the language which has been held to you by that blackguard? I suppose, because it is his ordinary talk, you think nothing of it: you are habituated to his baseness, and, perhaps, imagine I can get used to it too!'

'Have you been listening at the door, Edgar?' asked the mistress, in a tone particularly calculated to provoke her husband, implying both carelessness and contempt of his irritation. Heathcliff, who had raised his eyes at the former speech, gave a sneering laugh at the latter; on purpose, it seemed, to draw Mr Linton's attention to him. He succeeded; but Edgar did not mean to entertain him with any high flights of passion.

'I have been so far forbearing with you, sir,' he said, quietly; 'not that I was ignorant of your miserable, degraded character, but I felt you were only partly responsible for that; and Catherine wishing to keep up your acquaintance, I acquiesced – foolishly. Your presence is a moral poison that would contaminate the most virtuous: for that cause, and to prevent worse consequences, I shall deny you hereafter admission into this house, and give notice now that I require your instant departure. Three minutes' delay will render it involuntary and ignominious.'

Heathcliff measured the height and breadth of the speaker with an eye full of derision.

'Cathy, this lamb of yours threatens like a bull!' he said. 'It is in danger of splitting its skull against my knuckles. By God! Mr Linton, I'm mortally sorry that you are not worth knocking down!'

My master glanced towards the passage, and signed me to fetch the men: he had no intention of hazarding a personal encounter. I obeyed the hint; but Mrs Linton, suspecting something, followed; and when I attempted to call them, she pulled me back, slammed the door to, and locked it.

'Fair means!' she said, in answer to her husband's look of angry surprise. 'If you have not the courage to attack him, make an apology, or allow yourself to be beaten. It will correct you of feigning more valour than you possess. No, I'll swallow the key before you shall get it! I'm delightfully rewarded for my kindness to each! After constant indulgence of one's weak nature, and the other's bad one, I earn, for thanks, two samples of blind ingratitude, stupid to absurdity! Edgar, I was defending you and yours; and I wish Heathcliff may flog you sick, for daring to think an evil thought of me!'

It did not need the medium of a flogging to produce that effect on the master. He tried to wrest the key from Catherine's grasp, and for safety she flung it into the hottest part of the fire; whereupon Mr Edgar was taken with a nervous trembling, and his countenance grew deadly pale. For his life he could not avert that access of emotion: mingled anguish and humiliation overcame him completely. He leant on the back of a chair, and covered his face.

'Oh! Heavens! In old days this would win you knight- hood!' exclaimed Mrs Linton. 'We are vanquished! we are vanquished! Heathcliff would as soon lift a finger at you as the king would march his army against a colony of mice. Cheer up! you sha'n't be hurt! Your type is not a lamb, it's a sucking leveret.'

'I wish you joy of the milk-blooded coward, Cathy!' said her friend. 'I compliment you on your taste. And that is the slavering, shivering thing you preferred to me! I would not strike him with my fist, but I'd kick him with my foot, and experience considerable satisfaction. Is he weeping, or is he going to faint for fear?'

The fellow approached and gave the chair on which Linton rested a push. He'd better have kept his distance: my master quickly sprang erect, and struck him full on the throat a blow that would have levelled a slighter man. It took his breath for a minute; and, while he choked, Mr Linton walked out by the back door into the yard, and from thence, to the front entrance.

'There! you've done with coming here,' cried Catherine. 'Get away, now; he'll return with a brace of pistols, and half a dozen assistants. If he did overhear us, of course, he'd never forgive you. You've played me an ill turn, Heathcliff! But, go – make haste! I'd rather see Edgar at bay than you.'

'Do you suppose I'm going with that blow burning in my gullet?' he thundered. 'By hell, no! I'll crush his ribs in like a rotten hazelnut, before I cross the threshold! If I don't floor him now, I shall murder him some time; so, as you value his existence, let me get at him!'

'He is not coming,' I interposed, framing a bit of a lie. 'There's the coach-man, and the two gardeners; you'll surely not wait to be thrust into the road by them! Each has a bludgeon; and master will, very likely, be watching from the parlour windows to see that they fulfil his orders.'

The gardeners and coachman *were* there; but Linton was with them. They had already entered the court. Heathcliff, on second thoughts, resolved to avoid a struggle against three underlings: he seized the poker, smashed the lock from the inner door, and made his escape as they tramped in.

Mrs Linton, who was very much excited, bade me accompany her upstairs. She did not know my share in contributing to the disturbance, and I was anxious to keep her in ignorance.

'I'm nearly distracted, Nelly!' she exclaimed, throwing herself on the sofa. 'A thousand smiths' hammers are beating in my head! Tell Isabella to shun me; this uproar is owing to her; and should she or anyone else aggravate my anger at present, I shall get wild. And, Nelly, say to Edgar, if you see him again tonight, that I'm in danger of being seriously ill. I wish it may prove true. He has startled and distressed me shockingly! I want to frighten him. Besides, he might come

and begin a string of abuse or complainings; I'm certain I should recriminate, and God knows where we should end! Will you do so, my good Nelly? You are aware that I am no way blameable in this matter. What possessed him to turn listener? Heathcliff's talk was outrageous, after you left us; but I could soon have diverted him from Isabella, and the rest meant nothing. Now, all is dashed wrong by the fool's-craving to hear evil of self that haunts some people like a demon! Had Edgar never gathered our conversation, he would never have been the worse for it. Really, when he opened on me in that unreasonable tone of displeasure, after I had scolded Heathcliff till I was hoarse for *him*, I did not care, hardly, what they did to each other; especially as I felt that, however the scene closed, we should all be driven asunder for nobody knows how long! Well, if I cannot keep Heathcliff for my friend – if Edgar will be mean and jealous, I'll try to break their hearts by breaking my own. That will be a prompt way of finishing all, when I am pushed to extremity! But it's a deed to be reserved for a forlorn hope; I'd not take Linton by surprise with it. To this point he has been discreet in dreading to provoke me; you must represent the peril of quitting that policy, and remind him of my passionate temper, verging, when kindled, on frenzy. I wish you could dismiss that apathy out of your countenance, and look rather more anxious about me!'

The stolidity with which I received these instructions was, no doubt, rather exasperating: for they were delivered in perfect sincerity; but I believed a person who could plan the turning of her fits of passion to account, beforehand, might, by exerting her will, manage to control herself tolerably, even while under their influence; and I did not wish to 'frighten' her husband, as she said, and multiply his annoyances for the purpose of serving her selfishness. Therefore I said nothing when I met the master coming towards the parlour; but I took the liberty of turning back to listen whether they would resume their quarrel together. He began to speak first.

'Remain where you are, Catherine,' he said; without any anger in his voice, but with much sorrowful despondency. 'I shall not stay. I am neither come to wrangle nor be reconciled; but I wish just to learn whether, after this evening's events, you intend to continue your intimacy with – '

'Oh, for mercy's sake,' interrupted the mistress, stamping her foot, 'for mercy's sake, let us hear no more of it now! Your cold blood cannot be worked into a fever: your veins are full of ice-water; but mine are boiling, and the sight of such chillness makes them dance.'

'To get rid of me, answer my question,' persevered Mr Linton. 'You *must* answer it; and that violence does not alarm me. I have found that you can be as stoical as anyone, when you please. Will you give up Heathcliff hereafter, or will you give up me? It is impossible for you to be *my* friend and *his* at the same time; and I absolutely *require* to know which you choose.'

'I require to be let alone!' exclaimed Catherine, furiously. 'I demand it! Don't you see I can scarcely stand? Edgar, you – you leave me!'

She rung the bell till it broke with a twang; I entered leisurely. It was enough to try the temper of a saint, such senseless, wicked rages! There she lay dashing

her head against the arm of the sofa, and grinding her teeth, so that you might fancy she would crash them to splinters! Mr Linton stood looking at her in sudden compunction and fear. He told me to fetch some water. She had no breath for speaking. I brought a glass full; and, as she would not drink, I sprinkled it on her face. In few seconds she stretched herself out stiff, and turned up her eyes, while her cheeks, at once blanched and livid, assumed the aspect of death. Linton looked terrified.

'There is nothing in the world the matter,' I whispered. I did not want him to yield, though I could not help being afraid in my heart.

'She has blood on her lips!' he said, shuddering.

'Never mind!' I answered, tartly. And I told him how she had resolved, previous to his coming, on exhibiting a fit of frenzy. I incautiously gave the account aloud, and she heard me; for she started up – her hair flying over her shoulders, her eyes flashing, the muscles of her neck and arms standing out preternaturally. I made up my mind for broken bones, at least; but she only glared about her for an instant, and then rushed from the room. The master directed me to follow; I did, to her chamber door: she hindered me from going farther by securing it against me.

As she never offered to descend to breakfast next morning, I went to ask whether she would have some carried up. 'No!' she replied, peremptorily. The same question was repeated at dinner and tea; and again on the morrow after, and received the same answer. Mr Linton, on his part, spent his time in the library, and did not enquire concerning his wife's occupations. Isabella and he had had an hour's interview, during which he tried to elicit from her some sentiment of proper horror for Heathcliff's advances: but he could make nothing of her evasive replies, and was obliged to close the examination unsatisfactorily; adding, however, a solemn warning, that if she were so insane as to encourage that worthless suitor, it would dissolve all bonds of relationship between herself and him.

## Chapter 12

While Miss Linton moped about the park and garden, always silent, and almost always in tears; and her brother shut himself up among books that he never opened – wearying, I guessed, with a continual vague expectation that Catherine, repenting her conduct, would come of her own accord to ask pardon, and seek a reconciliation – and *she* fasted pertinaciously, under the idea, probably, that at every meal, Edgar was ready to choke for her absence, and pride alone held him from running to cast himself at her feet; I went about my household duties, convinced that the Grange had but one sensible soul in its walls, and that lodged in my body. I wasted no condolences on miss, nor any expostulations on my mistress; nor did I pay attention to the sighs of my master, who yearned to hear his lady's name, since he might not hear her voice.

I determined they should come about as they pleased for me; and though it was a tiresomely slow process, I began to rejoice at length in a faint dawn of its progress: as I thought at first.

Mrs Linton on the third day unbarred her door, and having finished the water in her pitcher and decanter, desired a renewed supply, and a basin of gruel, for she believed she was dying. That I set down as a speech meant for Edgar's ears; I believed no such thing, so I kept it to myself, and brought her some tea and dry toast. She eat and drank eagerly; and sank back on her pillow again, clenching her hands and groaning. 'Oh, I will die,' she exclaimed, 'since no one cares anything about me. I wish I had not taken that.' Then a good while after I heard her murmur, 'No, I'll not die – he'd be glad – he does not love me at all – he would never miss me!'

'Did you want anything, ma'am?' I enquired, still preserving my external composure, in spite of her ghastly countenance and strange exaggerated manner.

'What is that apathetic being doing?' she demanded, pushing the thick entangled locks from her wasted face. 'Has he fallen into a lethargy, or is he dead?'

'Neither,' replied I; 'if you mean Mr Linton. He's tolerably well, I think, though his studies occupy him rather more than they ought: he is continually among his books, since he has no other society.'

I should not have spoken so if I had known her true condition, but I could not get rid of the notion that she acted a part of her disorder.

'Among his books!' she cried, confounded. 'And I dying! I on the brink of the grave! My God! does he know how I'm altered?' continued she, staring at her reflection in a mirror hanging against the opposite wall. 'Is that Catherine Linton? He imagines me in a pet – in play, perhaps. Cannot you inform him that it is frightful earnest? Nelly, if it be not too late, as soon as I learn how he feels, I'll choose between these two; either to starve at once – that would be no punishment unless he had a heart – or to recover, and leave the country. Are you speaking the truth about him now? Take care. Is he actually so utterly indifferent for my life?

'Why, ma'am,' I answered, 'the master has no idea of your being deranged; and of course he does not fear that you will let yourself die of hunger.'

'You think not? Cannot you tell him I will?' she returned. 'Persuade him! speak of your own mind: say you are certain I will!'

'No, you forget, Mrs Linton,' I suggested, 'that you have eaten some food with a relish this evening, and tomorrow you will perceive its good effects.'

'If I were only sure it would kill him,' she interrupted, 'I'd kill myself directly! These three awful nights, I've never closed my lids – and oh, I've been tormented! I've been haunted, Nelly! But I begin to fancy you don't like me. How strange! I thought, though everybody hated and despised each other, they could not avoid loving me. And they have all turned to enemies in a few hours: *they* have, I'm positive; the people *here*. How dreary to meet death, surrounded by their cold faces! Isabella, terrified and repelled, afraid to enter the room, it would be so terrible to watch Catherine go. And Edgar standing solemnly by to see it over;

then offering prayers of thanks to God for restoring peace to his house, and going back to his *books*! What in the name of all that feels has he to do with *books* when I am dying?'

She could not bear the notion which I had put into her head of Mr Linton's philosophical resignation. Tossing about, she increased her feverish bewilderment to madness, and tore the pillow with her teeth; then raising herself up all burning, desired that I would open the window. We were in the middle of winter, the wind blew strong from the north-east, and I objected. Both the expressions flitting over her face, and the changes of her moods, began to alarm me terribly; and brought to my recollection her former illness, and the doctor's injunction that she should not be crossed. A minute previously she was violent; now, supported on one arm, and not noticing my refusal to obey her, she seemed to find childish diversion in pulling the feathers from the rents she had just made, and ranging them on the sheet according to their different species: her mind had strayed to other associations.

'That's a turkey's,' she murmured to herself; 'and this is a wild duck's; and this is a pigeon's. Ah, they put pigeons' feathers in the pillows – no wonder I couldn't die! Let me take care to throw it on the floor when I lie down. And here is a moorcock's; and this – I should know it among a thousand – it's a lapwing's. Bonny bird; wheeling over our heads in the middle of the moor. It wanted to get to its nest, for the clouds had touched the swells, and it felt rain coming. This feather was picked up from the heath, the bird was not shot: we saw its nest in the winter, full of little skeletons. Heathcliff set a trap over it, and the old ones dare not come. I made him promise he'd never shoot a lapwing after that, and he didn't. Yes, here are more! Did he shoot my lapwings, Nelly? Are they red, any of them? Let me look.'

'Give over with that baby-work!' I interrupted, dragging the pillow away, and turning the holes towards the mattress, for she was removing its contents by handfuls. 'Lie down and shut your eyes: you're wandering. There's a mess! The down is flying about like snow.'

I went here and there collecting it.

'I see in you, Nelly,' she continued, dreamily, 'an aged woman: you have grey hair and bent shoulders. This bed is the fairy cave under Penistone Crag, and you are gathering elf-bolts to hurt our heifers; pretending, while I am near, that they are only locks of wool. That's what you'll come to fifty years hence: I know you are not so now. I'm not wandering: you're mistaken, or else I should believe you really *were* that withered hag, and I should think I *was* under Penistone Crag; and I'm conscious it's night, and there are two candles on the table making the black press shine like jet.'

'The black press? Where is that?' I asked. 'You are talking in your sleep!'

'It's against the wall, as it always is,' she replied. 'It *does* appear odd – I see a face in it!'

'There is no press in the room, and never was,' said I, resuming my seat, and looping up the curtain that I might watch her.

'Don't *you* see that face?' she enquired, gazing earnestly at the mirror.

And say what I could, I was incapable of making her comprehend it to be her own; so I rose and covered it with a shawl.

'It's behind there still!' she pursued, anxiously. 'And it stirred. Who is it? I hope it will not come out when you are gone! Oh! Nelly, the room is haunted! I'm afraid of being alone!'

I took her hand in mine, and bid her be composed; for a succession of shudders convulsed her frame, and she *would* keep straining her gaze towards the glass.

'There's nobody here!' I insisted. 'It was *yourself*, Mrs Linton: you knew it a while since.'

'Myself!' she gasped, 'and the clock is striking twelve! It's true, then! that's dreadful!'

Her fingers clutched the clothes, and gathered them over her eyes. I attempted to steal to the door with an intention of calling her husband; but I was summoned back by a piercing shriek – the shawl had dropped from the frame.

'Why, what *is* the matter?' cried I. 'Who is coward now? Wake up! That is the glass – the mirror, Mrs Linton; and you see yourself in it and there am I, too, by your side.'

Trembling and bewildered, she held me fast, but the horror gradually passed from her countenance; its paleness gave place to a glow of shame.

'Oh, dear! I thought I was at home,' she sighed. 'I thought I was lying in my chamber at Wuthering Heights. Because I'm weak, my brain got confused, and I screamed unconsciously. Don't say anything; but stay with me. I dread sleeping: my dreams appal me.'

'A sound sleep would do you good, ma'am,' I answered; 'and I hope this suffering will prevent your trying starving again.'

'Oh, if I were but in my own bed in the old house!' she went on bitterly, wringing her hands. 'And that wind sounding in the firs by the lattice. Do let me feel it – it comes straight down the moor – do let me have one breath!'

To pacify her, I held the casement ajar a few seconds. A cold blast rushed through; I closed it, and returned to my post. She lay still now, her face bathed in tears. Exhaustion of body had entirely subdued her spirit: our fiery Catherine was no better than a wailing child.

'How long is it since I shut myself in here?' she asked, suddenly reviving.

'It was Monday evening,' I replied, 'and this is Thurs-day night, or rather Friday morning, at present.'

'What! of the same week?' she exclaimed. 'Only that brief time?'

'Long enough to live on nothing but cold water and ill-temper,' observed I.

'Well, it seems a weary number of hours,' she muttered doubtfully: 'it must be more. I remember being in the parlour after they had quarrelled, and Edgar being cruelly provoking, and me running into this room desperate. As soon as ever I had barred the door, utter blackness overwhelmed me, and I fell on the floor. I couldn't explain to Edgar how certain I felt of having a fit, or going raging mad, if he persisted in teasing me! I had no command of tongue, or brain, and he did not guess my agony, perhaps: it barely left me sense to try to

escape from him and his voice. Before I recovered sufficiently to see and hear, it began to be dawn, and, Nelly, I'll tell you what I thought, and what has kept recurring and recurring till I feared for my reason. I thought as I lay there, with my head against that table leg, and my eyes dimly discerning the grey square of the window, that I was enclosed in the oak-panelled bed at home; and my heart ached with some great grief which, just waking, I could not recollect. I pondered, and worried myself to discover what it could be, and, most strangely, the whole last seven years of my life grew a blank! I did not recall that they had been at all. I was a child; my father was just buried, and my misery arose from the separation that Hindley had ordered between me and Heathcliff. I was laid alone, for the first time; and, rousing from a dismal dose after a night of weeping, I lifted my hand to push the panels aside: it struck the table-top! I swept it along the carpet, and then memory burst in: my late anguish was swallowed in a paroxysm of despair. I cannot say why I felt so wildly wretched: it must have been temporary derangement, for there is scarcely cause – but, supposing at twelve years old, I had been wrenched from the Heights, and every early association, and my all in all, as Heathcliff was at that time, and been converted at a stroke into Mrs Linton, the lady of Thrushcross Grange, and the wife of a stranger: an exile, and outcast, thenceforth, from what had been my world – you may fancy a glimpse of the abyss where I grovelled! Shake your head as you will, Nelly, *you* have helped to unsettle me! You should have spoken to Edgar, indeed you should, and compelled him to leave me quiet! Oh, I'm burning!

'I wish I were out of doors! I wish I were a girl again, half savage and hardy, and free . . . and laughing at injuries, not maddening under them! Why am I so changed? why does my blood rush into a hell of tumult at a few words? I'm sure I should be myself were I once among the heather on those hills. Open the window again wide: fasten it open! Quick, why don't you move?'

'Because I won't give you your death of cold,' I answered.

'You won't give me a chance of life, you mean,' she said sullenly. 'However, I'm not helpless yet; I'll open it myself.'

And sliding from the bed before I could hinder her, she crossed the room, walking very uncertainly, threw it back, and bent out, careless of the frosty air that cut about her shoulders as keen as a knife. I entreated, and finally attempted to force her to retire. But I soon found her delirious strength much surpassed mine (she *was* delirious, I became convinced by her subsequent actions and ravings). There was no moon, and everything beneath lay in misty darkness: not a light gleamed from any house, far or near – all had been extinguished long ago; and those at Wuthering Heights were never visible – still she asserted she caught their shining.

'Look!' she cried eagerly, 'that's my room with the candle in it, and the trees swaying before it . . . and the other candle is in Joseph's garret . . . Joseph sits up late, doesn't he? He's waiting till I come home that he may lock the gate . . . Well, he'll wait a while yet. It's a rough journey, and a sad heart to travel it; and we must pass by Gimmerton kirk, to go that journey! We've braved its ghosts

often together, and dared each other to stand among the graves and ask them to come . . . But Heathcliff, if I dare you now, will you venture? If you do, I'll keep you. I'll not lie there by myself: they may bury me twelve feet deep, and throw the church down over me, but I won't rest till you are with me. I never will!'

She paused, and resumed with a strange smile. 'He's considering – he'd rather I'd come to him! Find a way, then! not through that kirkyard . . . You are slow! Be content, you always followed me!'

Perceiving it vain to argue against her insanity, I was planning how I could reach something to wrap about her, without quitting my hold of herself, for I could not trust her alone by the gaping lattice; when, to my consternation, I heard the rattle of the door-handle, and Mr Linton entered. He had only then come from the library; and, in passing through the lobby, had noticed our talking and been attracted by curiosity, or fear, to examine what it signified, at that late hour.

'Oh, sir!' I cried, checking the exclamation risen to his lips at the sight which met him, and the bleak atmosphere of the chamber. 'My poor mistress is ill, and she quite masters me: I cannot manage her at all; pray, come and persuade her to go to bed. Forget your anger, for she's hard to guide any way but her own.'

'Catherine ill?' he said, hastening to us. 'Shut the window, Ellen! Catherine! why . . .'

He was silent; the haggardness of Mrs Linton's appearance smote him speechless, and he could only glance from her to me in horrified astonishment.

'She's been fretting here,' I continued, 'and eating scarcely anything, and never complaining: she would admit none of us till this evening, and so we couldn't inform you of her state, as we were not aware of it ourselves; but it is nothing.'

I felt I uttered my explanations awkwardly; the master frowned. 'It is nothing, is it, Ellen Dean?' he said sternly. 'You shall account more clearly for keeping me ignorant of this!' And he took his wife in his arms, and looked at her with anguish.

At first she gave him no glance of recognition: he was invisible to her abstracted gaze. The delirium was not fixed, however; having weaned her eyes from contemplating the outer darkness, by degrees she centred her attention on him, and discovered who it was that held her.

'Ah! You are come, are you, Edgar Linton?' she said with angry animation . . . 'You are one of those things that are ever found when least wanted, and when you are wanted, never! I suppose we shall have plenty of lamentations now . . . I see we shall . . . but they can't keep me from my narrow home out yonder: my resting-place, where I'm bound before spring is over! There it is: not among the Lintons, mind, under the chapel-roof, but in the open air, with a headstone; and you may please yourself, whether you go to them or come to me!'

'Catherine, what have you done?' commenced the master. 'Am I nothing to you any more? Do you love that wretch Heath –'

'Hush!' cried Mrs Linton. 'Hush, this moment! You mention that name and I end the matter instantly, by a spring from the window!

What you touch at present you may have; but my soul will be on that hilltop

before you lay hands on me again. I don't want you, Edgar: I'm past wanting you. Return to your books. I'm glad you possess a consolation, for all you had in me is gone.'

'Her mind wanders, sir,' I interposed. 'She has been talking nonsense the whole evening; but, let her have quiet, and proper attendance, and she'll rally . . . Hereafter, we must be cautious how we vex her.'

'I desire no further advice from you,' answered Mr Linton. 'You knew your mistress's nature, and you encouraged me to harass her. And not to give me one hint of how she has been these three days! It was heartless! Months of sickness could not cause such a change!'

I began to defend myself, thinking it too bad to be blamed for another's wicked waywardness. 'I knew Mrs Linton's nature to be headstrong and domi-neering,' cried I; 'but I didn't know that you wished to foster her fierce temper! I didn't know that, to humour her, I should wink at Mr Heathcliff. I performed the duty of a faithful servant in telling you, and I have got a faithful servant's wages! Well, it will teach me to be careful next time. Next time you may gather intelligence for yourself!'

'The next time you bring a tale to me, you shall quit my service, Ellen Dean,' he replied.

'You'd rather hear nothing about it, I suppose, then, Mr Linton?' said I. 'Heathcliff has your permission to come a-courting to miss, and to drop in at every opportunity your absence offers, on purpose to poison the mistress against you?'

Confused as Catherine was, her wits were alert at applying our conversation.

'Ah! Nelly has played traitor,' she exclaimed, passionately. 'Nelly is my hidden enemy. You witch! So you do seek elf-bolts to hurt us! Let me go, and I'll make her rue! I'll make her howl a recantation!'

A maniac's fury kindled under her brows; she struggled desperately to disengage herself from Linton's arms. I felt no inclination to tarry the event; and, resolving to seek medical aid on my own responsibility, I quitted the chamber.

In passing the garden to reach the road, at a place where a bridle hook is driven into the wall, I saw something white moved irregularly, evidently by another agent than the wind. Notwithstanding my hurry, I staid to examine it, lest ever after I should have the conviction impressed on my imagination that it was a creature of the other world. My surprise and perplexity were great to discover, by touch more than vision, Miss Isabella's springer, Fanny, suspended to a handkerchief, and nearly at its last gasp. I quickly released the animal, and lifted it into the garden. I had seen it follow its mistress upstairs, when she went to bed; and wondered much how it could have got out there, and what mischie-vous person had treated it so. While untying the knot round the hook, it seemed to me that I repeatedly caught the beat of horses' feet galloping at some distance; but there were such a number of things to occupy my reflections that I hardly gave the circumstance a thought: though it was a strange sound, in that place, at two o'clock in the morning.

Mr Kenneth was fortunately just issuing from his house to see a patient in the village as I came up the street; and my account of Catherine Linton's malady induced him to accompany me back immediately. He was a plain rough man; and he made no scruple to speak his doubts of her surviving this second attack; unless she were more submissive to his directions than she had shown herself before.

'Nelly Dean,' said he, 'I can't help fancying there's an extra cause for this. What has there been to do at the Grange? We've odd reports up here. A stout, hearty lass like Catherine does not fall ill for a trifle; and that sort of people should not either. It's hard work bringing them through fevers, and such things. How did it begin?'

'The master will inform you,' I answered; 'but you are acquainted with the Earnshaws' violent dispositions, and Mrs Linton caps them all. I may say this; it commenced in a quarrel. She was struck during a tempest of passion with a kind of fit. That's her account, at least; for she flew off in the height of it, and locked herself up. Afterwards, she refused to eat, and now she alternately raves and remains in a half-dream; knowing those about her, but having her mind filled with all sorts of strange ideas and illusions.'

'Mr Linton will be sorry?' observed Kenneth, interrogatively.

'Sorry? he'll break his heart should anything happen!' I replied. 'Don't alarm him more than necessary.'

'Well, I told him to beware,' said my companion; 'and he must bide the consequences of neglecting my warning! Hasn't he been thick with Mr Heathcliff lately?'

'Heathcliff frequently visits at the Grange,' answered I, 'though more on the strength of the mistress having known him when a boy, than because the master likes his company. At present, he's discharged from the trouble of calling; owing to some presumptuous aspirations after Miss Linton which he manifested. I hardly think he'll be taken in again.'

'And does Miss Linton turn a cold shoulder on him?' was the doctor's next question.

'I'm not in her confidence,' returned I, reluctant to continue the subject.

'No, she's a sly one,' he remarked, shaking his head. 'She keeps her own counsel! But she's a real little fool. I have it from good authority, that, last night (and a pretty night it was!) she and Heathcliff were walking in the plantation at the back of your house, above two hours; and he pressed her not to go in again, but just mount his horse and away with him! My informant said she could only put him off by pledging her word of honour to be prepared on their first meeting after that: when it was to be, he didn't hear; but you urge Mr Linton to look sharp!'

This news filled me with fresh fears; I outstripped Kenneth, and ran most of the way back. The little dog was yelping in the garden yet. I spared a minute to open the gate for it, but instead of going to the house door, it coursed up and down snuffing the grass, and would have escaped to the road, had I not seized and conveyed it in with me. On ascending to Isabella's room, my suspicions

were confirmed: it was empty. Had I been a few hours sooner, Mrs Linton's illness might have arrested her rash step.

But what could be done now? There was a bare possibility of overtaking them if I pursued instantly. *I* could not pursue them, however; and I dare not rouse the family, and fill the place with confusion; still less unfold the business to my master, absorbed as he was in his present calamity, and having no heart to spare for a second grief! I saw nothing for it but to hold my tongue, and suffer matters to take their course; and Kenneth being arrived, I went with a badly composed countenance to announce him. Catherine lay in a troubled sleep: her husband had succeeded in soothing the access of frenzy; he now hung over her pillow, watching every shade, and every change of her painfully expressive features.

The doctor, on examining the case for himself, spoke hopefully to him of its having a favourable termination, if we could only preserve around her perfect and constant tranquillity. To me, he signified the threatening danger was not so much death, as permanent alienation of intellect.

I did not close my eyes that night, nor did Mr Linton: indeed, we never went to bed; and the servants were all up long before the usual hour, moving through the house with stealthy tread, and exchanging whispers as they encountered each other in their vocations. Everyone was active, but Miss Isabella; and they began to remark how sound she slept: her brother, too, asked if she had risen, and seemed impatient for her presence, and hurt that she showed so little anxiety for her sister-in-law. I trembled lest he should send me to call her; but I was spared the pain of being the first proclaimant of her flight. One of the maids, a thoughtless girl, who had been on an early errand to Gimmerton, came panting upstairs, open-mouthed, and dashed into the chamber, crying – 'Oh, dear, dear! What mun we have next? Master, master, our young lady – '

'Hold your noise!' cried I hastily, enraged at her clamorous manner.

'Speak lower, Mary – What is the matter?' said Mr Linton. 'What ails your young lady?'

'She's gone, she's gone! Yon' Heathcliff's run off wi' her!' gasped the girl.

'That is not true!' exclaimed Linton, rising in agitation. 'It cannot be: how has the idea entered your head? Ellen Dean, go and seek her. It is incredible: it cannot be.'

As he spoke he took the servant to the door, and then repeated his demand to know her reasons for such an assertion.

'Why, I met on the road a lad that fetches milk here,' she stammered, 'and he asked whether we wern't in trouble at the Grange. I thought he meant for missis's sickness, so I answered, yes. Then says he, "they's somebody gone after 'em, I guess?" I stared. He saw I knew naught about it, and he told how a gentleman and lady had stopped to have a horse's shoe fastened at a blacksmith's shop, two miles out of Gimmerton, not very long after midnight! and how the blacksmith's lass had got up to spy who they were: she knew them both directly. And she noticed the man – Heathcliff it was, she felt certain, nob'dy could mistake him, besides – put a sovereign in her father's hand for payment. The

lady had a cloak about her face; but having desired a sup of water, while she drank, it fell back, and she saw her very plain. Heathcliff held both bridles as they rode on, and they set their faces from the village, and went as fast as the rough roads would let them. The lass said nothing to her father, but she told it all over Gimmerton this morning.'

I ran and peeped, for form's sake, into Isabella's room; confirming, when I returned, the servant's statement. Mr Linton had resumed his seat by the bed; on my re-entrance, he raised his eyes, read the meaning of my blank aspect, and dropped them without giving an order, or uttering a word.

'Are we to try any measures for overtaking and bringing her back,' I enquired. 'How should we do?'

'She went of her own accord,' answered the master; 'she had a right to go if she pleased. Trouble me no more about her. Hereafter she is only my sister in name: not because I disown her, but because she has disowned me.'

And that was all he said on the subject: he did not make a single enquiry further, nor mention her in any way, except directing me to send what property she had in the house to her fresh home, wherever it was, when I knew it.

## Chapter 13

For two months the fugitives remained absent; in those two months, Mrs Linton encountered and conquered the worst shock of what was denominated a brain fever. No mother could have nursed an only child more devotedly than Edgar tended her. Day and night he was watching, and patiently enduring all the annoyances that irritable nerves and a shaken reason could inflict; and, though Kenneth remarked that what he saved from the grave would only recompense his care by forming the source of constant future anxiety – in fact, that his health and strength were being sacrificed to preserve a mere ruin of humanity – he knew no limits in gratitude and joy when Catherine's life was declared out of danger; and hour after hour he would sit beside her, tracing the gradual return to bodily health, and flattering his too sanguine hopes with the illusion that her mind would settle back to its right balance also, and she would soon be entirely her former self.

The first time she left her chamber was at the commencement of the following March. Mr Linton had put on her pillow, in the morning, a handful of golden crocuses; her eye, long stranger to any gleam of pleasure, caught them in waking, and shone delighted as she gathered them eagerly together.

'These are the earliest flowers at the Heights,' she exclaimed. 'They remind me of soft thaw winds, and warm sunshine, and nearly melted snow. Edgar, is there not a south wind, and is not the snow almost gone?'

'The snow is quite gone down here, darling,' replied her husband; 'and I only see two white spots on the whole range of moors: the sky is blue, and the larks are singing, and the becks and brooks are all brim full. Catherine, last spring at

this time, I was longing to have you under this roof: now, I wish you were a mile or two up those hills: the air blows so sweetly, I feel that it would cure you.'

'I shall never be there, but once more,' said the invalid; 'and then you'll leave me, and I shall remain for ever. Next spring you'll long again to have me under this roof, and you'll look back and think you were happy today.'

Linton lavished on her the kindest caresses, and tried to cheer her by the fondest words; but, vaguely regarding the flowers, she let the tears collect on her lashes and stream down her cheeks unheeding. We knew she was really better, and, therefore, decided that long confinement to a single place produced much of this despondency, and it might be partially removed by a change of scene. The master told me to light a fire in the many-weeks'-deserted parlour, and to set an easy-chair in the sunshine by the window; and then he brought her down, and she sat a long while enjoying the genial heat, and, as we expected, revived by the objects round her: which, though familiar, were free from the dreary associations investing her hated sick-chamber. By evening, she seemed greatly exhausted; yet no arguments could persuade her to return to that apartment, and I had to arrange the parlour sofa for her bed, till another room could be prepared. To obviate the fatigue of mounting and descending the stairs, we fitted up this, where you lie at present: on the same floor with the parlour; and she was soon strong enough to move from one to the other, leaning on Edgar's arm. Ah, I thought myself, she might recover, so waited on as she was. And there was double cause to desire it, for on her existence depended that of another: we cherished the hope that in a little while, Mr Linton's heart would be gladdened, and his lands secured from a stranger's gripe, by the birth of an heir.

I should mention that Isabella sent to her brother, some six weeks from her departure, a short note, announcing her marriage with Heathcliff. It appeared dry and cold; but at the bottom was dotted in with pencil an obscure apology, and an entreaty for kind remembrance and reconciliation, if her proceeding had offended him: asserting that she could not help it then, and being done, she had now no power to repeal it. Linton did not reply to this, I believe; and, in a fortnight more, I got a long letter which I considered odd, coming from the pen of a bride just out of the honeymoon. I'll read it: for I keep it yet. Any relic of the dead is precious, if they were valued living.

DEAR ELLEN, it begins. I came last night to Wuthering Heights, and heard, for the first time, that Catherine has been, and is yet, very ill. I must not write to her, I suppose, and my brother is either too angry or too distressed to answer what I send him. Still, I must write to somebody, and the only choice left me is you.

Inform Edgar that I'd give the world to see his face again – that my heart returned to Thrushcross Grange in twenty-four hours after I left it, and is there at this moment, full of warm feelings for him, and Catherine! *I can't follow it though* – (those words are underlined) they need not expect me, and they may draw what conclusions they please; taking care, however, to lay nothing it the door of my weak will or deficient affection.

The remainder of the letter is for yourself alone. I want to ask you two questions; the first is – How did you contrive to preserve the common sympathies of human nature when you resided here? I cannot recognise any sentiment which those around share with me.

The second question, I have great interest in; it is this – Is Mr Heathcliff a man? If so, is he mad? And if not, is he a devil? I shan't tell my reasons for making this enquiry; but I beseech you to explain, if you can, what I have married: that is, when you call to see me; and you must call, Ellen, very soon. Don't write but come, and bring me something from Edgar.

Now, you shall hear how I have been received in my new home, as I am led to imagine the Heights will be. It is to amuse myself that I dwell on such subjects as the lack of external comforts: they never occupy my thoughts, except at the moment when I miss them. I should laugh and dance for joy, if I found their absence was the total of my miseries, and the rest was an unnatural dream!

The sun set behind the Grange, as we turned on to the moors; by that, I judged it to be six o'clock; and my companion halted half an hour, to inspect the park, and the gardens, and, probably, the place itself, as well as he could; so it was dark when we dismounted in the paved yard of the farmhouse, and your old fellow-servant, Joseph, issued out to receive us by the light of a dip candle. He did it with a courtesy that redounded to his credit. His first act was to elevate his torch to a level with my face, squint malignantly, project his under lip, and turn away.

Then he took the two horses, and led them into the stables; reappearing for the purpose of locking the outer gate, as if we lived in an ancient castle.

Heathcliff stayed to speak to him, and I entered the kitchen – a dingy, untidy hole; I dare say you would not know it, it is so changed since it was in your charge. By the fire stood a ruffianly child, strong in limb and dirty in garb, with a look of Catherine in his eyes and about his mouth.

'This is Edgar's legal nephew,' I reflected – 'mine in a manner; I must shake hands, and – yes – I must kiss him. It is right to establish a good understanding at the beginning.'

I approached, and, attempting to take his chubby fist, said – 'How do you do, my dear?'

He replied in a jargon I did not comprehend. 'Shall you and I be friends, Hareton?' was my next essay at conversation.

An oath, and a threat to set Throttler on me if I did not 'frame off', rewarded my perseverance.

'Hey, Throttler, lad!' whispered the little wretch, rousing a half-bred bulldog from its lair in a corner. 'Now, wilt tuh be ganging?' he asked authoritatively.

Love for my life urged a compliance; I stepped over the threshold to wait till the others should enter. Mr Heathcliff was nowhere visible; and Joseph, whom I followed to the stables, and requested to accompany me in, after staring and muttering to himself, screwed up his nose and replied – 'Mim! mim! mim! Did iver Christian body hear owt like it? Minching un' munching! Hah can Aw tell whet ye say?'

'I say, I wish you to come with me into the house!' I cried, thinking him deaf, yet highly disgusted at his rudeness.

'Nor nuh me! Aw getten summut else to do,' he answered, and continued his work; moving his lantern jaws meanwhile, and surveying my dress and countenance (the former a great deal too fine, but the latter, I'm sure, as sad as he could desire) with sovereign contempt.

I walked round the yard, and through a wicket, to another door, at which I took the liberty of knocking, in hopes some more civil servant might show himself. After a short suspense, it was opened by a tall, gaunt man, without neckerchief, and otherwise extremely slovenly; his features were lost in masses of shaggy hair that hung on his shoulders; and *his* eyes, too, were like a ghostly Catherine's, with all their beauty annihilated.

'What's your business here?' he demanded, grimly. 'Who are you?'

'My name *was* Isabella Linton,' I replied. 'You've seen me before, sir. I'm lately married to Mr Heathcliff, and he has brought me here – I suppose by your permission.'

'Is he come back, then?' asked the hermit, glaring like a hungry wolf.

'Yes – we came just now,' I said; 'but he left me by the kitchen door; and when I would have gone in, your little boy played sentinel over the place, and frightened me off by the help of a bulldog.'

'It's well the hellish villain has kept his word!' growled my future host, searching the darkness beyond me in expectation of discovering Heathcliff; and then he indulged in a soliloquy of execrations, and threats of what he would have done had the 'fiend' deceived him.

I repented having tried this second entrance, and was almost inclined to slip away before he finished cursing, but ere I could execute that intention, he ordered me in, and shut and re-fastened the door. There was a great fire, and that was all the light in the huge apartment, whose floor had grown a uniform grey; and the once brilliant pewter dishes, which used to attract my gaze when I was a girl, partook of a similar obscurity, created by tarnish and dust. I enquired whether I might call the maid, and be conducted to a bedroom? Mr Earnshaw vouchsafed no answer. He walked up and down, with his hands in his pockets, apparently quite forgetting my presence; and his abstraction was evidently so deep, and his whole aspect so misanthropical, that I shrank from disturbing him again.

You'll not be surprised, Ellen, at my feeling particularly cheerless, seated in worse than solitude on that inhospitable hearth, and remembering that four miles distant lay my delightful home, containing the only people I loved on earth; and there might as well be the Atlantic to part us, instead of those four miles: I could not overpass them! I questioned with myself – where must I turn for comfort? And – mind you don't tell Edgar, or Catherine – above every sorrow beside, this rose pre-eminent: despair at finding nobody who could or would be my ally against Heathcliff! I had sought shelter at Wuthering Heights, almost gladly, because I was secured by that arrangement from living alone with him; but he knew the people we were coming amongst, and he did not fear their intermeddling.

I sat and thought a doleful time; the clock struck eight, and nine, and still my companion paced to and fro, his head bent on his breast, and perfectly silent, unless a groan or a bitter ejaculation forced itself out at intervals. I listened to detect a woman's voice in the house, and filled the interim with wild regrets and dismal anticipations, which, at last, spoke audibly in irrepressible sighing and weeping. I was not aware how openly I grieved, till Earnshaw halted opposite, in his measured walk, and gave me a stare of newly-awakened surprise.

Taking advantage of his recovered attention, I exclaimed – 'I'm tired with my journey, and I want to go to bed! Where is the maidservant? Direct me to her, as she won't come to me!'

'We have none,' he answered; 'you must wait on yourself!'

'Where must I sleep, then?' I sobbed; I was beyond regarding self-respect, weighed down by fatigue and wretchedness.

'Joseph will show you Heathcliff's chamber,' said he; 'open that door – he's in there.'

I was going to obey, but he suddenly arrested me, and added in the strangest tone – 'Be so good as to turn your lock, and draw your bolt – don't omit it!'

'Well!' I said. 'But why, Mr Earnshaw?' I did not relish the notion of deliberately fastening myself in with Heathcliff.

'Look here!' he replied, pulling from his waistcoat a curiously constructed pistol, having a double-edged spring knife attached to the barrel. 'That's a great tempter to a desperate man, is it not? I cannot resist going up with this every night, and trying his door. If once I find it open, he's done for! I do it invariably, even though the minute before I have been recalling a hundred reasons that should make me refrain: it is some devil that urges me to thwart my own schemes by killing him – you fight against that devil for love as long as you may; when the time comes, not all the angels in heaven shall save him!'

I surveyed the weapon inquisitively; a hideous notion struck me: how powerful I should be possessing such an instrument! I took it from his hand, and touched the blade. He looked astonished at the expression my face assumed during a brief second: it was not horror, it was covetousness. He snatched the pistol back, jealously; shut the knife, and returned it to its concealment.

'I don't care if you tell him,' said he. 'Put him on his guard, and watch for him. You know the terms we are on, I see: his danger does not shock you.'

'What has Heathcliff done to you?' I asked. 'In what has he wronged you, to warrant this appalling hatred? Wouldn't it be wiser to bid him quit the house?'

'No!' thundered Earnshaw; 'should he offer to leave me, he's a dead man: persuade him to attempt it, and you are a murderess! Am I to lose *all*, without a chance of retrieval? Is Hareton to be a beggar? Oh, damnation! I *will* have it back: and I'll have *his* gold too: and then his blood; and hell shall have his soul! It will be ten times blacker with that guest than ever it was before!'

You've acquainted me, Ellen, with your old master's habits. He is clearly on the verge of madness: he was so last night at least. I shuddered to be near him, and thought on the servant's ill-bred moroseness as comparatively agreeable. He now recommenced his moody walk, and I raised the latch, and escaped into

the kitchen. Joseph was bending over the fire, peering into a large pan that swung above it; and a wooden bowl of oatmeal stood on the settle close by. The contents of the pan began to boil, and he turned to plunge his hand into the bowl; I conjectured that this preparation was probably for our supper, and, being hungry, I resolved it should be eatable; so, crying out sharply, 'I'll make the porridge!' I removed the vessel out of his reach, and proceeded to take off my hat and riding habit. 'Mr Earnshaw,' I continued, 'directs me to wait on myself: I will. I'm not going to act the lady among you, for fear I should starve.'

'Gooid Lord!' he muttered, sitting down, and stroking his ribbed stockings from the knee to the ankle. 'If they's tuh be fresh ortherings – just when aw getten used tuh two maisters, if aw mun hev a *mistress* set o'er my heead, it's loike time tuh be flitting. Aw niver *did* think tuh say t' day ut aw mud lave th' owld place – but aw daht it's nigh at hend!'

This lamentation drew no notice from me: I went briskly to work, sighing to remember a period when it would have been all merry fun; but compelled speedily to drive off the remembrance. It racked me to recall past happiness, and the greater peril there was of conjuring up its apparition, the quicker the thible ran round, and the faster the handfuls of meal fell into the water. Joseph beheld my style of cookery with growing indignation.

'Thear!' he ejaculated. 'Hareton, thah willut sup thy porridge tuh neeght; they'll be nowt bud lumps as big as maw nave. Thear, agean! Aw'd fling in bowl un all, if aw wer yah! Thear, pale t' guilp off, un' then yah'll hae done wi't. Bang, bang. It's a marcy t' bothom isn't deaved aht!'

It *was* rather a rough mess, I own, when poured into the basins; four had been provided, and a gallon pitcher of new milk was brought from the dairy, which Hareton seized and commenced drinking and spilling from the expansive lip. I expostulated, and desired that he should have his in a mug; affirming that I could not taste the liquid treated so dirtily. The old cynic chose to be vastly offended at this nicety; assuring me, repeatedly, that 'the barn was every bit as gooid' as I, 'and every bit as wollsome,' and wondering how I could fashion to be so conceited. Meanwhile, the infant ruffian continued sucking; and glowered up at me defyingly, as he slavered into the jug.

'I shall have my supper in another room,' I said. 'Have you no place you call a parlour?'

'*Parlour!*' he echoed, sneeringly, '*parlour!* Nay, we've noa *parlours*. If yah dunnut loike wer company, they's maister's; un' if yah dunnut loike maister, they's us.'

'Then I shall go upstairs,' I answered; 'shew me a chamber.'

I put my basin on a tray, and went myself to fetch some more milk. With great grumblings, the fellow rose, and preceded me in my ascent: we mounted to the garrets; he opening a door, now and then, to look into the apartments we passed.

'Here's a rahm,' he said, at last, flinging back a cranky board on hinges. 'It's weel eneugh tuh ate a few porridge in. They's a pack uh corn i' t' corner, thear, meeterly clane; if yah're feared uh muckying yer grand silk cloes, spread yer hankerchir ut t' top on 't.'

The 'rahm' was a kind of lumber-hole smelling strong of malt and grain; various sacks of which articles were piled around, leaving a wide, bare space in the middle.

'Why, man!' I exclaimed, facing him angrily, 'this is not a place to sleep in. I wish to see my bedroom.'

'*Bed–rume!*' he repeated, in a tone of mockery. 'Yah's see all t' *bed–rumes* thear is – yon's mine.'

He pointed into the second garret, only differing from the first in being more naked about the walls, and having a large, low, curtainless bed, with an indigo-coloured quilt, at one end.

'What do I want with yours?' I retorted. 'I suppose Mr Heathcliff does not lodge at the top of the house, does he?'

'Oh, it's Maister *Hathecliff's* yah're wenting?' cried he, as if making a new discovery. 'Couldn't ye uh said soa, at onst? Un then, aw mud uh telled ye, baht all this wark, ut that's just one yah cannut sea – he allas keeps it locked, un' nob'dy iver mells on 't but hisseln.'

'You've a nice house, Joseph,' I could not refrain from observing, 'and pleasant inmates; and I think the concentrated essence of all the madness in the world took up its abode in my brain the day I linked my fate with theirs! However, that is not to the present purpose – there are other rooms. For Heaven's sake, be quick, and let me settle somewhere!'

He made no reply to this adjuration; only plodding doggedly down the wooden steps, and halting before an apartment which, from that halt and the superior quality of its furniture, I conjectured to be the best one. There was a carpet: a good one, but the pattern was obliterated by dust; a fireplace hung with cut paper, dropping to pieces; a handsome oak-bedstead with ample crimson curtains of rather expensive material and modern make; but they had evidently experienced rough usage; the valances hung in festoons, wrenched from their rings, and the iron rod supporting them was bent in an arc, on one side, causing the drapery to trail upon the floor. The chairs were also damaged, many of them severely; and deep indentations deformed the panels of the walls. I was endeavouring to gather resolution for entering, and taking possession, when my fool of a guide announced, 'This here is t' maister's.' My supper by this time was cold, my appetite gone, and my patience exhausted. I insisted on being provided instantly with a place of refuge, and means of repose.

'Whear the divil,' began the religious elder. 'The Lord bless us! The Lord forgie us! Whear the *hell*, wold ye gang? Ye marred, wearisome nowt! Yah seen all bud Hareton's bit uf a cham'er. They's nut another hoile tuh lig dahn in i' th' hahse!'

I was so vexed, I flung my tray and its contents on the ground; and then seated myself at the stair head, hid my face in my hands, and cried.

'Ech! ech!' exclaimed Joseph. 'Weel done, Miss Cathy! Weel done, Miss Cathy! Hahsiver, t' maister sall just tum'le o'er them brocken pots; un' then we's hear summut; we's hear hah it's tuh be. Gooid-for-nowt madling! yah desarve pining froo this tuh Churstmas, flinging t' precious gifts uh God under fooit i'

yer flaysome rages! Bud, aw'm mista'en if yah shew yer sperrit lang. Will Hathecliff bide sich bonny ways, think ye? Aw nobbut wish he muh cotch ye i' that plisky. Aw nobbut wish he may.'

And so he went scolding to his den beneath, taking the candle with him; and I remained in the dark. The period of reflection succeeding this silly action, compelled me to admit the necessity of smothering my pride and choking my wrath, and bestirring myself to remove its effects. An unexpected aid presently appeared in the shape of Throttler, whom I now recognised as a son of our old Skulker: it had spent its whelphood at the Grange, and was given by my father to Mr Hindley. I fancy it knew me: it pushed its nose against mine by way of salute, and then hastened to devour the porridge; while I groped from step to step, collecting the shattered earthenware, and drying the spatters of milk from the bannister with my pocket-handkerchief. Our labours were scarcely over when I heard Earnshaw's tread in the passage; my assistant tucked in his tail, and pressed to the wall: I stole into the nearest doorway. The dog's endeavour to avoid him was unsuccessful; as I guessed by a scutter downstairs, and a pro-longed, piteous yelping. I had better luck: he passed on, entered his chamber, and shut the door.

Directly after Joseph came up with Hareton, to put him to bed. I had found shelter in Hareton's room, and the old man, on seeing me, said – 'They's rahm fur boath yah, un yer pride, nah, aw sud think i' th' hahse. It's empty; yah muh hev it all tuh yerseln, un Him as allas maks a third, i' sich ill company!'

Gladly did I take advantage of this intimation; and the minute I flung myself into a chair, by the fire, I nodded, and slept. My slumber was deep and sweet, though over far too soon. Mr Heathcliff awoke me; he had just come in, and demanded, in his loving manner, what I was doing there? I told him the cause of my staying up so late – that he had the key of our room in his pocket. The adjective *our* gave mortal offence. He swore it was not, nor ever should be mine; and he'd – but I'll not repeat his language, nor describe his habitual conduct: he is ingenious and unresting in seeking to gain my abhorrence! I sometimes wonder at him with an intensity that deadens my fear: yet, I assure you, a tiger or a venomous serpent could not rouse terror in me equal to that which he wakens. He told me of Catherine's illness, and accused my brother of causing it; promising that I should be Edgar's proxy in suffering, till he could get hold of him.

I do hate him – I am wretched – I have been a fool! Beware of uttering one breath of this to anyone at the Grange. I shall expect you every day – don't disappoint me! ISABELLA.

## Chapter 14

As soon as I had perused this epistle, I went to the master, and informed him that his sister had arrived at the Heights, and sent me a letter expressing her sorrow for Mrs Linton's situation, and her ardent desire to see him; with a wish that he would transmit to her, as early as possible, some token of forgiveness by me.

'Forgiveness!' said Linton. 'I have nothing to forgive her, Ellen. You may call at Wuthering Heights this afternoon, if you like, and say that I am not *angry*, but I'm *sorry* to have lost her; especially as I can never think she'll be happy. It is out of the question my going to see her, however: we are eternally divided; and should she really wish to oblige me, let her persuade the villain she has married to leave the country.'

'And you won't write her a little note, sir?' I asked imploringly.

'No,' he answered. 'It is needless. My communication with Heathcliff's family shall be as sparing as his with mine. It shall not exist!'

Mr Edgar's coldness depressed me exceedingly; and all the way from the Grange I puzzled my brains how to put more heart into what he said, when I repeated it; and how to soften his refusal of even a few lines to console Isabella. I dare say she had been on the watch for me since morning: I saw her looking through the lattice, as I came up the garden causeway, and I nodded to her; but she drew back, as if afraid of being observed. I entered without knocking. There never was such a dreary, dismal scene as the formerly cheerful house presented! I must confess, that if I had been in the young lady's place, I would, at least, have swept the hearth, and wiped the tables with a duster. But she already partook of the pervading spirit of neglect which encompassed her. Her pretty face was wan and listless; her hair uncurled: some locks hanging lankly down, and some carelessly twisted round her head. Probably she had not touched her dress since yester-evening. Hindley was not there. Mr Heathcliff sat at a table, turning over some papers in his pocketbook; but he rose when I appeared, asked me how I did, quite friendly, and offered me a chair. He was the only thing there that seemed decent; and I thought he never looked better. So much had circumstances altered their positions, that he would certainly have struck a stranger as a born and bred gentleman, and his wife as a thorough little slattern! She came forward eagerly to greet me; and held out one hand to take the expected letter. I shook my head. She wouldn't understand the hint, but followed me to a sideboard, where I went to lay my bonnet, and importuned me in a whisper to give her directly what I had brought.

Heathcliff guessed the meaning of her manoeuvres, and said – 'If you have got anything for Isabella (as no doubt you have, Nelly), give it to her. You needn't make a secret of it: we have no secrets between us.'

'Oh, I have nothing,' I replied, thinking it best to speak the truth at once. 'My master bid me tell his sister that she must not expect either a letter or a visit from

him at present. He sends his love, ma'am, and his wishes for your happiness, and his pardon for the grief you have occasioned; but he thinks that after this time, his household and the household here should drop intercommunication, as nothing good could come of keeping it up.'

Mrs Heathcliff's lip quivered slightly, and she returned to her seat in the window. Her husband took his stand on the hearthstone, near me, and began to put questions concerning Catherine. I told him as much as I thought proper of her illness, and he extorted from me, by cross-examination, most of the facts connected with its origin. I blamed her, as she deserved, for bringing it all on herself; and ended by hoping that he would follow Mr Linton's example, and avoid future interference with his family, for good or evil.

'Mrs Linton is now just recovering,' I said; 'she'll never be like she was, but her life is spared; and if you really have a regard for her, you'll shun crossing her way again: nay, you'll move out of this country entirely; and that you may not regret it, I'll inform you Catherine Linton is as different now from your old friend Catherine Earnshaw, as that young lady is different from me. Her appearance is changed greatly, her character much more so; and the person who is compelled, of necessity, to be her companion, will only sustain his affection hereafter by the remembrance of what she once was, by common humanity, and a sense of duty!'

'That is quite possible,' remarked Heathcliff, forcing himself to seem calm: 'quite possible that your master should have nothing but common humanity and a sense of duty to fall back upon. But do you imagine that I shall leave Catherine to his *duty* and *humanity*? and can you compare my feelings respecting Catherine to his? Before you leave this house, I must exact a promise from you, that you'll get me an interview with her: consent, or refuse, I *will* see her! What do you say?'

'I say, Mr Heathcliff,' I replied, 'you must not: you never shall, through my means. Another encounter between you and the master would kill her altogether.'

'With your aid, that may be avoided,' he continued; 'and should there be danger of such an event – should he be the cause of adding a single trouble more to her existence – why, I think, I shall be justified in going to extremes! I wish you had sincerity enough to tell me whether Catherine would suffer greatly from his loss: the fear that she would restrains me. And there you see the distinction between our feelings: had he been in my place and I in his, though I hated him with a hatred that turned my life to gall, I never would have raised a hand against him. You may look incredulous, if you please! I never would have banished him from her society as long as she desired his. The moment her regard ceased, I would have torn his heart out, and drank his blood! But, till then – if you don't believe me, you don't know me – till then, I would have died by inches before I touched a single hair of his head!'

'And yet,' I interrupted, 'you have no scruples in completely ruining all hopes of her perfect restoration, by thrusting yourself into her remembrance now, when she has nearly forgotten you, and involving her in a new tumult of discord and distress.'

'You suppose she has nearly forgotten me?' he said. 'Oh, Nelly! You know she has not! You know as well as I do, that for every thought she spends on Linton, she spends a thousand on me! At a most miserable period of my life, I had a notion of the kind: it haunted me on my return to the neighbourhood last summer; but only her own assurance could make me admit the horrible idea again. And then, Linton would be nothing, nor Hindley, nor all the dreams that ever I dreamt. Two words would comprehend my future – *death* and *hell*: existence, after losing her, would be hell. Yet I was a fool to fancy for a moment that she valued Edgar Linton's attachment more than mine. If he loved with all the powers of his puny being, he couldn't love as much in eighty years as I could in a day. And Catherine has a heart as deep as I have: the sea could be as readily contained in that horse-trough, as her whole affection be monopolised by him. Tush! He is scarcely a degree dearer to her than her dog, or her horse. It is not in him to be loved like me: how can she love in him what he has not?'

'Catherine and Edgar are as fond of each other as any two people can be,' cried Isabella, with sudden vivacity. 'No one has a right to talk in that manner, and I won't hear my brother depreciated in silence!'

'Your brother is wondrous fond of you too, isn't he?' observed Heathcliff scornfully. 'He turns you adrift on the world with surprising alacrity.'

'He is not aware of what I suffer,' she replied. 'I didn't tell him that.'

'You have been telling him something, then: you have written, have you?'

'To say that I was married, I did write – you saw the note.'

'And nothing since?'

'No.'

'My young lady is looking sadly the worse for her change of condition,' I remarked. 'Somebody's love comes short in her case, obviously: whose, I may guess; but, perhaps, I shouldn't say.'

'I should guess it was her own,' said Heathcliff. 'She degenerates into a mere slut! She is tired of trying to please me, uncommonly early. You'd hardly credit it, but the very morrow of our wedding, she was weeping to go home. However, she'll suit this house so much the better for not being over nice, and I'll take care she does not disgrace me by rambling abroad.'

'Well, sir,' returned I, 'I hope you'll consider that Mrs Heathcliff is accustomed to be looked after and waited on; and that she has been brought up like an only daughter, whom, everyone was ready to serve. You must let her have a maid to keep things tidy about her, and you must treat her kindly. Whatever be your notion of Mr Edgar, you cannot doubt that she has a capacity for strong attachments, or she wouldn't have abandoned the elegancies, and comforts, and friends of her former home, to fix contentedly, in such a wilderness as this, with you.'

'She abandoned them under a delusion,' he answered; 'picturing in me a hero of romance, and expecting unlimited indulgences from my chivalrous devotion. I can hardly regard her in the light of a rational creature, so obstinately has she persisted in forming a fabulous notion of my character, and acting on the false impressions she cherished. But, at last, I think she begins to know me: I don't

perceive the silly smiles and grimaces that provoked me at first; and the senseless incapability of discerning that I was in earnest when I gave her my opinion of her infatuation and herself. It was a marvellous effort of perspicacity to discover that I did not love her. I believed, at one time, no lessons could teach her that! And yet it is poorly learnt; for this morning she announced, as a piece of appalling intelligence, that I had actually succeeded in making her hate me! A positive labour of Hercules, I assure you! If it be achieved, I have cause to return thanks. Can I trust your assertion, Isabella? Are you sure you hate me? If I let you alone for half a day, won't you come sighing and wheedling to me again? I dare say she would rather I had seemed all tenderness before you: it wounds her vanity to have the truth exposed. But I don't care who knows that the passion was wholly on one side; and I never told her a lie about it. She cannot accuse me of showing a bit of deceitful softness. The first thing she saw me do, on coming out of the Grange, was to hang up her little dog; and when she pleaded for it, the first words I uttered were a wish that I had the hanging of every being belonging to her, except one: possibly she took that exception for herself. But no brutality disgusted her: I suppose she has an innate admiration of it, if only her precious person were secure from injury! Now, was it not the depth of absurdity – of genuine idiocy, for that pitiful, slavish, mean-minded brach to dream that I could love her? Tell your master, Nelly, that I never, in all my life, met with such an abject thing as she is. She even disgraces the name of Linton; and I've sometimes relented, from pure lack of invention, in my experiments on what she could endure, and still creep shamefully cringing back! But tell him, also, to set his fraternal and magisterial heart at ease, that I keep strictly within the limits of the law. I have avoided, up to this period, giving her the slightest right to claim a separation; and, what's more, she'd thank nobody for dividing us. If she desired to go she might: the nuisance of her presence outweighs the gratification to be derived from tormenting her!'

'Mr Heathcliff,' said I, 'this is the talk of a madman, and your wife, most likely, is convinced you are mad; and, for that reason, she has borne with you hitherto: but now that you say she may go, she'll doubtless avail herself of the permission. You are not so bewitched, ma'am, are you, as to remain with him of your own accord?'

'Take care, Ellen!' answered Isabella, her eyes sparkling irefully; there was no misdoubting by their expression, the full success of her partner's endeavours to make himself detested. 'Don't put faith in a single word he speaks. He's a lying fiend! A monster, and not a human being! I've been told I might leave him before; and I've made the attempt, but I dare not repeat it! Only, Ellen, promise you'll not mention a syllable of his infamous conversation to my brother or Catherine. Whatever he may pretend, he wishes to provoke Edgar to desperation: he says he has married me on purpose to obtain power over him; and he shan't obtain it – I'll die first! I just hope, I pray, that he may forget his diabolical prudence, and kill me! The single pleasure I can imagine, is to die, or to see him dead!'

'There – that will do for the present!' said Heathcliff. 'If you are called upon

in a court of law, you'll remember her language, Nelly! And take a good look at that countenance: she's near the point which would suit me. No; you're not fit to be your own guardian, Isabella, now; and I, being your legal protector, must retain you in my custody, however distasteful the obligation may be. Go upstairs; I have something to say to Ellen Dean in private. That's not the way: upstairs, I tell you! Why, this is the road upstairs, child!'

He seized, and thrust her from the room; and returned muttering – 'I have no pity! I have no pity! The more the worms writhe, the more I yearn to crush out their entrails! It is a moral teething; and I grind with greater energy, in proportion to the increase of pain.'

'Do you understand what the word pity means?' I said, hastening to resume my bonnet. 'Did you ever feel a touch of it in your life?'

'Put that down!' he interrupted, perceiving my intention to depart. 'You are not going yet. Come here now, Nelly: I must either persuade or compel you to aid me in fulfilling my determination to see Catherine, and that without delay. I swear that I meditate no harm: I don't desire to cause any disturbance, or to exasperate or insult Mr Linton; I only wish to hear from herself how she is, and why she has been ill; and to ask if anything that I could do would be of use to her. Last night, I was in the Grange garden six hours, and I'll return there tonight; and every night I'll haunt the place, and every day, till I find an opportunity of entering. If Edgar Linton meets me, I shall not hesitate to knock him down, and give him enough to ensure his quiescence while I stay. If his servants oppose me, I shall threaten them off with these pistols. But wouldn't it be better to prevent my coming in contact with them, or their master? And you could do it so easily. I'd warn you when I came, and then you might let me in unobserved, as soon as she was alone, and watch till I departed, your conscience quite calm: you would be hindering mischief.'

I protested against playing that treacherous part in my employer's house: and besides, I urged the cruelty and selfishness of his destroying Mrs Linton's tranquillity for his satisfaction. 'The commonest occurrence startles her painfully,' I said. 'She's all nerves, and she couldn't bear the surprise, I'm positive. Don't persist, sir! Or else, I shall be obliged to inform my master of your designs; and he'll take measures to secure his house and its inmates from any such unwarrantable intrusions!'

'In that case, I'll take measures to secure you, woman!' exclaimed Heathcliff; 'you shall not leave Wuthering Heights till tomorrow morning. It is a foolish story to assert that Catherine could not bear to see me; and as to surprising her, I don't desire it: you must prepare her – ask her if I may come. You say she never mentions my name, and that I am never mentioned to her. To whom should she mention me if I am a forbidden topic in the house? She thinks you are all spies for her husband. Oh, I've no doubt she's in hell among you! I guess by her silence, as much as anything, what she feels. You say she is often restless, and anxious looking: is that a proof of tranquillity? You talk of her mind being unsettled. How the devil could it be otherwise in her frightful isolation? And that insipid, paltry creature attending her from *duty* and *humanity*! From *pity* and

*charity*! He might as well plant an oak in a flowerpot, and expect it to thrive, as imagine he can restore her to vigour in the soil of his shallow cares! Let us settle it at once; will you stay here, and am I to fight my way to Catherine over Linton and his footmen? Or will you be my friend, as you have been hitherto, and do what I request? Decide! because there is no reason for my lingering another minute, if you persist in your stubborn ill-nature!'

Well, Mr Lockwood, I argued and complained, and flatly refused him fifty times; but in the long run he forced me to an agreement. I engaged to carry a letter from him to my mistress; and should she consent, I promised to let him have intelligence of Linton's next absence from home, when he might come, and get in as he was able: I wouldn't be there, and my fellow servants should be equally out of the way. Was it right or wrong? I fear it was wrong, though expedient. I thought I prevented another explosion by my compliance; and I thought, too, it might create a favourable crisis in Catherine's mental illness: and then I remembered Mr Edgar's stern rebuke of my carrying tales; and I tried to smooth away all disquietude on the subject, by affirming, with frequent iteration, that that betrayal of trust, if it merited so harsh an appellation, should be the last. Notwithstanding, my journey homeward was sadder than my journey thither; and many misgivings I had, ere I could prevail on myself to put the missive into Mrs Linton's hand.

But here is Kenneth; I'll go down, and tell him how much better you are. My history is *dree*, as we say, and will serve to wile away another morning.

Dree, and dreary! I reflected as the good woman descended to receive the doctor; and not exactly of a kind which I should have chosen to amuse me. But never mind! I'll extract wholesome medicines from Mrs Dean's bitter herbs; and firstly, let me beware of the fascination that lurks in Catherine Heathcliff's brilliant eyes. I should be in a curious taking if I surrendered my heart to that young person, and the daughter turned out a second edition of the mother!

## Chapter 15

Another week over – and I am so many days nearer health, and spring! I have now heard all my neighbour's history, at different sittings, as the housekeeper could spare time from more important occupations. I'll continue it in her own words, only a little condensed. She is, on the whole, a very fair narrator, and I don't think I could improve her style.

In the evening, she said, the evening of my visit to the Heights, I knew, as well as if I saw him, that Mr Heathcliff was about the place; and I shunned going out, because I still carried his letter in my pocket, and didn't want to be threatened, or teased any more. I had made up my mind not to give it till my master went somewhere, as I could not guess how its receipt would affect Catherine. The consequence was, that it did not reach her before the lapse of

three days. The fourth was Sunday, and I brought it into her room after the family were gone to church. There was a man servant left to keep the house with me, and we generally made a practice of locking the doors during the hours of service; but on that occasion the weather was so warm and pleasant that I set them wide open, and, to fulfil my engagement, as I knew who would be coming, I told my companion that the mistress wished very much for some oranges, and he must run over to the village and get a few, to be paid for on the morrow. He departed, and I went upstairs.

Mrs Linton sat in a loose, white dress, with a light shawl over her shoulders, in the recess of the open window, as usual. Her thick, long hair had been partly removed at the beginning of her illness, and now she wore it simply combed in its natural tresses over her temples and neck. Her appearance was altered, as I had told Heathcliff; but when she was calm, there seemed unearthly beauty in the change. The flash of her eyes had been succeeded by a dreamy and melancholy softness; they no longer gave the impression of looking at the objects around her: they appeared always to gaze beyond, and far beyond – you would have said out of this world. Then, the paleness of her face – its haggard aspect having vanished as she recovered flesh – and the peculiar expression arising from her mental state, though painfully suggestive of their causes, added to the touching interest which she awakened; and – invariably to me, I know, and to any person who saw her, I should think – refuted more tangible proofs of convalescence, and stamped her as one doomed to decay.

A book lay spread on the sill before her, and the scarcely perceptible wind fluttered its leaves at intervals. I believe Linton had laid it there: for she never endeavoured to divert herself with reading, or occupation of any kind, and he would spend many an hour in trying to entice her attention to some subject which had formerly been her amusement. She was conscious of his aim, and in her better moods endured his efforts placidly, only showing their uselessness by now and then suppressing a wearied sigh, and checking him at last with the saddest of smiles and kisses. At other times, she would turn petulantly away, and hide her face in her hands, or even push him off angrily; and then he took care to let her alone, for he was certain of doing no good.

Gimmerton chapel bells were still ringing; and the full, mellow flow of the beck in the valley came soothingly on the ear. It was a sweet substitute for the yet absent murmur of the summer foliage, which drowned that music about the Grange when the trees were in leaf. At Wuthering Heights it always sounded on quiet days following a great thaw or a season of steady rain. And of Wuthering Heights Catherine was thinking as she listened: that is, if she thought or listened at all; but she had the vague, distant look I mentioned before, which expressed no recognition of material things either by ear or eye.

'There's a letter for you, Mrs Linton,' I said, gently inserting it in one hand that rested on her knee. 'You must read it immediately, because it wants an answer. Shall I break the seal?' 'Yes,' she answered, without altering the direction of her eyes. I opened it – it was very short. 'Now,' I continued, 'read it.'

She drew away her, hand, and let it fall. I replaced it in her lap, and stood

waiting till it should please her to glance down; but that movement was so long delayed that at last I resumed – 'Must I read it, ma'am? It is from Mr Heathcliff.'

There was a start and a troubled gleam of recollection, and a struggle to arrange her ideas. She lifted the letter, and seemed to peruse it; and when she came to the signature she sighed: yet still I found she had not gathered its import, for, upon my desiring to hear her reply, she merely pointed to the name, and gazed at me with mournful and questioning eagerness.

'Well, he wishes to see you,' said I, guessing her need of an interpreter. 'He's in the garden by this time, and impatient to know what answer I shall bring.'

As I spoke, I observed a large dog lying on the sunny grass beneath, raise its ears as if about to bark, and then smoothing them back, announce, by a wag of the tail, that someone approached whom it did not consider a stranger. Mrs Linton bent forward, and listened breathlessly. The minute after a step traversed the hall; the open house was too tempting for Heathcliff to resist walking in: most likely he supposed that I was inclined to shirk my promise, and so resolved to trust to his own audacity. With straining eagerness Catherine gazed towards the entrance of her chamber. He did not hit the right room directly; she motioned me to admit him; but he found it out, ere I could reach the door, and in a stride or two was at her side, and had her grasped in his arms.

He neither spoke nor loosed his hold for some five minutes, during which period he bestowed more kisses than ever he gave in his life before, I dare say: but then my mistress had kissed him first, and I plainly saw that he could hardly bear, for downright agony, to look into her face! The same conviction had stricken him as me, from the instant he beheld her, that there was no prospect of ultimate recovery there – she was fated, sure to die.

'Oh, Cathy! Oh, my life! how can I bear it?' Was the first sentence he uttered, in a tone that did not seek to disguise his despair. And now he stared at her so earnestly that I thought the very intensity of his gaze would bring tears into his eyes; but they burned with anguish: they did not melt.

'What now?' said Catherine, leaning back, and returning his look with a suddenly clouded brow: her humour was a mere vane for constantly varying caprices. 'You and Edgar have broken my heart, Heathcliff! And you both come to bewail the deed to me, as if you were the people to be pitied! I shall not pity you, not I. You have killed me – and thriven on it, I think. How strong you are! How many years do you mean to live after I am gone?'

Heathcliff had knelt on one knee to embrace her; he attempted to rise, but she seized his hair, and kept him down.

'I wish I could hold you,' she continued, bitterly, 'till we were both dead! I shouldn't care what you suffered. I care nothing for your sufferings. Why shouldn't you suffer? I do! Will you forget me? Will you be happy when I am in the earth? Will you say twenty years hence, "That's the grave of Catherine Earnshaw. I loved her long ago, and was wretched to lose her; but it is past. I've loved many others since: my children are dearer to me than she was; and, at death, I shall not rejoice that I am going to her: I shall be sorry that I must leave them!" Will you say so, Heathcliff?'

'Don't torture me till I'm as mad as yourself,' cried he, wrenching his head free, and grinding his teeth.

The two, to a cool spectator, made a strange and fearful picture. Well might Catherine deem that heaven would be a land of exile to her, unless with her mortal body she cast away her mortal character also. Her present countenance had a wild vindictiveness in its white cheek, and a bloodless lip and scintillating eye; and she retained in her closed fingers a portion of the locks she had been grasping. As to her companion, while raising himself with one hand, he had taken her arm with the other; and so inadequate was his stock of gentleness to the requirements of her condition, that on his letting go I saw four distinct impressions left blue in the colourless skin.

'Are you possessed with a devil,' he pursued, savagely, 'to talk in that manner to me when you are dying? Do you reflect that all those words will be branded in my memory, and eating deeper eternally after you have left me? You know you lie to say I have killed you: and, Catherine, you know that I could as soon forget you as my existence! Is it not sufficient for your infernal selfishness, that while you are at peace I shall writhe in the torments of hell?'

'I shall not be at peace,' moaned Catherine, recalled to a sense of physical weakness by the violent, unequal throbbing of her heart, which beat visibly and audibly under this excess of agitation.

She said nothing further till the paroxysm was over; then she continued, more kindly – 'I'm not wishing you greater torment than I have, Heathcliff. I only wish us never to be parted: and should a word of mine distress you hereafter, think I feel the same distress underground, and for my own sake, forgive me! Come here and kneel down again! You never harmed me in your life. Nay, if you nurse anger, that will be worse to remember than my harsh words! Won't you come here again? Do!'

Heathcliff went to the back of her chair, and leant over, but not so far as to let her see his face, which was livid with emotion. She bent round to look at him; he would not permit it: turning abruptly, he walked to the fireplace, where he stood, silent, with his back towards us. Mrs Linton's glance followed him suspiciously: every movement woke a new sentiment in her.

After a pause, and a prolonged gaze, she resumed; addressing me in accents of indignant disappointment – 'Oh, you see, Nelly, he would not relent a moment to keep me out of the grave. *That* is how I'm loved! Well, never mind. That is not *my* Heathcliff. I shall love mine yet; and take him with me: he's in my soul. And,' added she musingly, 'the thing that irks me most is this shattered prison, after all. I'm tired, tired of being enclosed here. I'm wearying to escape into that glorious world, and to be always there: not seeing it dimly through tears, and yearning for it through the walls of an aching heart; but really with it, and in it. Nelly, you think you are better and more fortunate than I; in full health and strength: you are sorry for me – very soon that will be altered. I shall be sorry for *you*. I shall be incomparably beyond and above you all. I *wonder* he won't be near me!' She went on to herself. 'I thought he wished it. Heathcliff, dear! you should not be sullen now. Do come to me, Heathcliff.'

In her eagerness she rose and supported herself on the arm of the chair. At that earnest appeal he turned to her, looking absolutely desperate. His eyes wide, and wet at last, flashed fiercely on her; his breast heaved convulsively. An instant they held asunder, and then how they met I hardly saw, but Catherine made a spring, and he caught her, and they were locked in an embrace from which I thought my mistress would never be released alive: in fact, to my eyes, she seemed directly insensible. He flung himself into the nearest seat, and on my approaching hurriedly to ascertain if she had fainted, he gnashed at me, and foamed like a mad dog, and gathered her to him with greedy jealousy. I did not feel as if I were in the company of a creature of my own species: it appeared that he would not understand, though I spoke to him; so I stood off, and held my tongue, in great perplexity.

A movement of Catherine's relieved me a little presently: she put up her hand to clasp his neck, and bring her cheek to his as he held her; while he, in return, covering her with frantic caresses, said wildly – 'You teach me now how cruel you've been – cruel and false. *Why* did you despise me? *Why* did you betray your own heart, Cathy? I have not one word of comfort. You deserve this. You have killed yourself. Yes, you may kiss me, and cry; and wring out my kisses and tears: they'll blight you – they'll damn you. You loved me – then what *right* had you to leave me? What right – answer me – for the poor fancy you felt for Linton? Because misery, and degradation, and death, and nothing that God or satan could inflict would have parted us, *you*, of your own will, did it. I have not broken your heart – *you* have broken it; and in breaking it, you have broken mine. So much the worse for me, that I am strong. Do I want to live? What kind of living will it be when you – oh, God! Would *you* like to live with your soul in the grave?'

'Let me alone. Let me alone,' sobbed Catherine. 'If I've done wrong, I'm dying for it. It is enough! You left me too: but I won't upbraid you! I forgive you. Forgive me!'

'It is hard to forgive, and to look at those eyes, and feel those wasted hands,' he answered. 'Kiss me again; and don't let me see your eyes! I forgive what you have done to me. I love *my* murderer – but *yours*! How can I?'

They were silent – their faces hid against each other, and washed by each other's tears. At least, I suppose the weeping was on both sides; as it seemed Heathcliff *could* weep on a great occasion like this.

I grew very uncomfortable, meanwhile; for the afternoon wore fast away, the man whom I had sent off returned from his errand, and I could distinguish, by the shine of the westering sun up the valley, a concourse thickening outside Gimmerton chapel porch.

'Service is over,' I announced. 'My master will be here in half an hour.'

Heathcliff groaned a curse, and strained Catherine closer: she never moved.

Ere long I perceived a group of the servants passing up the road towards the kitchen wing. Mr Linton was not far behind; he opened the gate himself and sauntered slowly up, probably enjoying the lovely afternoon that breathed as soft as summer.

'Now he is here,' I exclaimed. 'For Heaven's sake, hurry down! You'll not

meet anyone on the front stairs. Do be quick; and stay among the trees till he is fairly in.'

'I must go, Cathy,' said Heathcliff, seeking to extricate himself from his companion's arms. 'But, if I live, I'll see you again before you are asleep. I won't stray five yards from your window.'

'You must not go!' she answered, holding him as firmly as her strength allowed. 'You shall not, I tell you.'

'For one hour,' he pleaded, earnestly.

'Not for one minute,' she replied.

'I *must* – Linton will be up immediately,' persisted the alarmed intruder.

He would have risen, and unfixed her fingers by the act – she clung fast, gasping: there was mad resolution in her face.

'No!' she shrieked. 'Oh, don't, don't go. It is the last time! Edgar will not hurt us. Heathcliff, I shall die! I shall die!'

'Damn the fool! There he is,' cried Heathcliff, sinking back into his seat. 'Hush, my darling! Hush, hush, Catherine! I'll stay. If he shot me so, I'd expire with a blessing on my lips.'

And there they were fast again. I heard my master mounting the stairs – the cold sweat ran from my forehead: I was horrified.

'Are you going to listen to her ravings?' I said, passionately. 'She does not know what she says. Will you ruin her, because she has not wit to help herself? Get up! You could be free instantly. That is the most diabolical deed that ever you did. We are all done for – master, mistress, and servant.'

I wrung my hands, and cried out; and Mr Linton hastened his step at the noise. In the midst of my agitation, I was sincerely glad to observe that Catherine's arms had fallen relaxed, and her head hung down.

'She's fainted, or dead,' I thought: 'so much the better. Far better that she should be dead, than lingering a burden and a misery-maker to all about her.'

Edgar sprang to his unbidden guest, blanched with astonishment and rage. What he meant to do, I cannot tell; however, the other stopped all demonstrations, at once, by placing the lifeless-looking form in his arms.

'Look there!' he said. 'Unless you be a fiend, help her first – then you shall speak to me!'

He walked into the parlour, and sat down. Mr Linton summoned me, and with great difficulty, and after resorting to many means, we managed to restore her to sensation; but she was all bewildered; she sighed, and moaned, and knew nobody. Edgar, in his anxiety for her, forgot her hated friend. I did not. I went, at the earliest opportunity, and besought him to depart; affirming that Catherine was better, and he should hear from me in the morning, how she passed the night.

'I shall not refuse to go out of doors,' he answered; 'but I shall stay in the garden: and, Nelly, mind you keep your word tomorrow. I shall be under those larch trees. Mind! Or I pay another visit, whether Linton be in or not.'

He sent a rapid glance through the half-open door of the chamber, and, ascertaining that what I stated was apparently true, delivered the house of his luckless presence.

## *Chapter 16*

About twelve o'clock, that night, was born the Catherine you saw at Wuthering Heights: a puny, seven months' child; and two hours after the mother died, having never recovered sufficient consciousness to miss Heathcliff, or know Edgar. The latter's distraction at his bereavement is a subject too painful to be dwelt on; its after effects showed how deep the sorrow sank. A great addition, in my eyes, was his being left without an heir. I bemoaned that, as I gazed on the feeble orphan; and I mentally abused old Linton for (what was only natural partiality) the securing his estate to his own daughter, instead of his son's. An unwelcomed infant it was, poor thing! It might have wailed out of life, and nobody cared a morsel, during those first hours of existence. We redeemed the neglect afterwards; but its beginning was as friendless as its end is likely to be.

Next morning – bright and cheerful out of doors – stole softened in through the blinds of the silent room, and suffused the couch and its occupant with a mellow, tender glow. Edgar Linton had his head laid on the pillow, and his eyes shut. His young and fair features were almost as deathlike as those of the form beside him, and almost as fixed: but *his* was the hush of exhausted anguish, and *hers* of perfect peace. Her brow smooth, her lids closed, her lips wearing the expression of a smile; no angel in heaven could be more beautiful than she appeared. And I partook of the infinite calm in which she lay: my mind was never in a holier frame than while I gazed on that untroubled image of Divine rest. I instinctively echoed the words she had uttered a few hours before: 'Incomparably beyond and above us all! Whether still on earth or now in heaven, her spirit is at home with God!'

I don't know if it be a peculiarity in me, but I am seldom otherwise than happy while watching in the chamber of death, should no frenzied or despairing mourner share the duty with me. I see a repose that neither earth nor hell can break, and I feel an assurance of the endless and shadowless hereafter – the Eternity they have entered – where life is boundless in its duration, and love in its sympathy, and joy in its fullness. I noticed on that occasion how much selfishness there is even in a love like Mr Linton's, when he so regretted Catherine's blessed release! To be sure, one might have doubted, after the wayward and impatient existence she had led, whether she merited a haven of peace at last. One might doubt in seasons of cold reflection; but not then, in the presence of her corpse. It asserted its own tranquillity, which seemed a pledge of equal quiet to its former inhabitant.

Do you believe such people *are* happy in the other world, sir? I'd give a great deal to know. I declined answering Mrs Dean's question, which struck me as something heterodox. She proceeded:

Retracing the course of Catherine Linton, I fear we have no right to think she is; but we'll leave her with her Maker.

The master looked asleep, and I ventured soon after sunrise to quit the room and steal out to the pure refreshing air. The servants thought me gone to shake off the drowsiness of my protracted watch; in reality, my chief motive was seeing Mr Heathcliff. If he had remained among the larches all night, he would have heard nothing of the stir at the Grange; unless, perhaps, he might catch the gallop of the messenger going to Gimmerton. If he had come nearer, he would probably be aware, from the lights flitting to and fro, and the opening and shutting of the outer doors, that all was not right within. I wished, yet feared, to find him. I felt the terrible news must be told, and I longed to get it over; but *how* to do it, I did not know. He was there – at least a few yards further in the park; leant against an old ash tree, his hat off, and his hair soaked with the dew that had gathered on the budded branches, and fell pattering round him. He had been standing a long time in that position, for I saw a pair of ouzels passing and repassing scarcely three feet from him, busy in building their nest, and regarding his proximity no more than that of a piece of timber. They flew off at my approach, and he raised his eyes and spoke: 'She's dead!' he said; 'I've not waited for you to learn that. Put your hand-kerchief away – don't snivel before me. Damn you all! she wants none of *your* tears!'

I was weeping as much for him as her: we do sometimes pity creatures that have none of the feeling either for themselves or others; and when I first looked into his face, I perceived that he had got intelligence of the catastrophe; and a foolish notion struck me that his heart was quelled and he prayed, because his lips moved and his gaze was bent on the ground.

'Yes, she's dead!' I answered, checking my sobs and drying my cheeks. 'Gone to heaven, I hope; where we may, everyone, join her, if we take due warning and leave our evil ways to follow good!'

'Did *she* take due warning, then?' asked Heathcliff, attempting a sneer. 'Did she die like a saint? Come, give me a true history of the event. How did –'

He endeavoured to pronounce the name, but could not manage it; and compressing his mouth he held a silent combat with his inward agony, defying, meanwhile, my sympathy with an unflinching, ferocious stare. 'How did she die?' he resumed, at last – fain, notwithstanding his hardihood, to have a support behind him; for, after the struggle, he trembled, in spite of himself, to his very finger-ends.

'Poor wretch!' I thought; 'you have a heart and nerves the same as your brother men! Why should you be anxious to conceal them? Your pride cannot blind God! You tempt him to wring them, till he forces a cry of humiliation.'

'Quietly as a lamb!' I answered, aloud. 'She drew a sigh, and stretched herself, like a child reviving, and sinking again to sleep; and five minutes after I felt one little pulse at her heart, and nothing more!'

'And – did she ever mention me?' he asked, hesitating, as if he dreaded the answer to his question would introduce details that he could not bear to hear.

'Her senses never returned: she recognised nobody from the time you left her,' I said. 'She lies with a sweet smile on her face; and her latest ideas wandered

back to pleasant early days. Her life closed in a gentle dream – may she wake as kindly in the other world!'

'May she wake in torment!' he cried, with frightful vehemence, stamping his foot, and groaning in a sudden paroxysm of ungovernable passion. 'Why, she's a liar to the end! Where is she? Not *there* – not in heaven – not perished – where? Oh! you said you cared nothing for my sufferings! And I pray one prayer – I repeat it till my tongue stiffens – Catherine Earnshaw, may you not rest as long as I am living! You said I killed you – haunt me, then! The murdered *do* haunt their murderers. I believe – I know that ghosts *have* wandered on earth. Be with me always – take any form – drive me mad! Only *do* not leave me in this abyss, where I cannot find you! Oh, God! It is unutterable! I *cannot* live without my life! I *cannot* live without my soul!'

He dashed his head against the knotted trunk; and, lifting up his eyes, howled, not like a man, but like a savage beast getting goaded to death with knives and spears. I observed several splashes of blood about the bark of the tree, and his hand and forehead were both stained; probably the scene I witnessed was a repetition of others acted during the night. It hardly moved my compassion – it appalled me: still I felt reluctant to quit him so. But the moment he recollected himself enough to notice me watching, he thundered a command for me to go, and I obeyed. He was beyond my skill to quiet or console!

Mrs Linton's funeral was appointed to take place on the Friday following her decease; and till then her coffin remained uncovered, and strewn with flowers and scented leaves, in the great drawing-room. Linton spent his days and nights there, a sleepless guardian; and – a circumstance concealed from all but me – Heathcliff spent his nights, at least, outside, equally a stranger to repose. I held no communication with him: still I was conscious of his design to enter, if he could; and on the Tuesday, a little after dark, when my master, from sheer fatigue, had been compelled to retire a couple of hours, I went and opened one of the windows, moved by his perseverance to give him a chance of bestowing on the fading image of his idol one final adieu. He did not omit to avail himself of the opportunity, cautiously and briefly: too cautiously to betray his presence by the slightest noise. Indeed, I shouldn't have discovered that he had been there, except for the disarrangement of the drapery about the corpse's face, and for observing on the floor a curl of light hair, fastened with a silver thread; which, on examination, I ascertained to have been taken from a locket hung round Catherine's neck. Heathcliff had opened the trinket and cast out its contents, replacing them by a black lock of his own. I twisted the two, and enclosed them together.

Mr Earnshaw was, of course, invited to attend the remains of his sister to the grave; and he sent no excuse, but he never came; so that, besides her husband, the mourners were wholly composed of tenants and servants. Isabella was not asked.

The place of Catherine's interment, to the surprise of the villagers, was neither in the chapel, under the carved monument of the Lintons, nor yet by the

tombs of her own relations, outside. It was dug on a green slope in a corner of the kirkyard, where the wall is so low that heath and bilberry plants have climbed over it from the moor; and peat mould almost buries it. Her husband lies in the same spot now; and they have each a simple headstone above, and a plain grey block at their feet, to mark the graves.

## *Chapter 17*

That Friday made the last of our fine days, for a month. In the evening, the weather broke; the wind shifted from south to northeast, and brought rain first, and then sleet and snow. On the morrow one could hardly imagine that there had been three weeks of summer: the primroses and crocuses were hidden under wintry drifts; the larks were silent, the young leaves of the early trees smitten and blackened. And dreary, and chill, and dismal that morrow did creep over! My master kept his room; I took possession of the lonely parlour, converting it into a nursery: and there I was sitting, with the moaning doll of a child laid on my knee; rocking it to and fro, and watching, meanwhile, the still driving flakes build up the uncurtained window, when the door opened, and some person entered, out of breath and laughing! My anger was greater than my astonishment for a minute. I supposed it one of the maids, and I cried – 'Have done! How dare you show your giddiness here? What would Mr Linton say if he heard you?'

'Excuse me!' answered a familiar voice; 'but I know Edgar is in bed, and I cannot stop myself.'

With that the speaker came forward to the fire, panting and holding her hand to her side.

'I have run the whole way from Wuthering Heights!' she continued, after a pause; 'except where I've flown. I couldn't count the number of falls I've had. Oh, I'm aching all over! Don't be alarmed! There shall be an explanation as soon as I can give it; only just have the goodness to step out and order the carriage to take me on to Gimmerton, and tell a servant to seek up a few clothes in my wardrobe.'

The intruder was Mrs Heathcliff. She certainly seemed in no laughing predicament: her hair streamed on her shoulders, dripping with snow and water; she was dressed in the girlish dress she commonly wore, befitting her age more than her position: a low frock with short sleeves, and nothing on either head or neck. The frock was of light silk, and clung to her with wet, and her feet were protected merely by thin slippers; add to this a deep cut under one ear, which only the cold prevented from bleeding profusely, a white face scratched and bruised, and a frame hardly able to support itself, through fatigue; and you may fancy my first fright was not much allayed when I had leisure to examine her.

'My dear young lady,' I exclaimed, 'I'll stir nowhere, and hear nothing, till you have removed every article of your clothes, and put on dry things; and certainly you shall not go to Gimmerton tonight, so it is needless to order the carriage.'

'Certainly, I shall,' she said; 'walking or riding: yet I've no objection to dress myself decently. And – ah, see how it flows down my neck now! The fire does make it smart.'

She insisted on my fulfilling her directions, before she would let me touch her; and not till after the coachman had been instructed to get ready, and a maid set to pack up some necessary attire, did I obtain her consent for binding the wound and helping to change her garments.

'Now, Ellen,' she said, when my task was finished, and she was seated in an easy chair on the hearth, with a cup of tea before her, 'you sit down opposite me, and put poor Catherine's baby away: I don't like to see it! You mustn't think I care little for Catherine, because I behaved so foolishly on entering: I've cried too, bitterly – yes, more than anyone else has reason to cry. We parted unreconciled, you remember, and I shan't forgive myself. But, for all that, I was not going to sympathise with him – the brute beast! O, give me the poker! This is the last thing of his I have about me:' she slipped the gold ring from her third finger, and threw it on the floor. 'I'll smash it!' she continued, striking it with childish spite, 'and then I'll burn it!' And she took and dropped the misused article among the coals. 'There! he shall buy another, if he gets me back again. He'd be capable of coming to seek me, to tease Edgar – I dare not stay, lest that notion should possess his wicked head! And besides, Edgar has not been kind, has he? And I won't come suing for his assistance; nor will I bring him into more trouble. Necessity compelled me to seek shelter here; though, if I had not learnt he was out of the way, I'd have halted at the kitchen, washed my face, warmed myself, got you to bring what I wanted, and departed again to anywhere out of the reach of my accursed – of that incarnate goblin! Ah, he was in such a fury! If he had caught me! It's a pity Earnshaw is not his match in strength: I wouldn't have run till I'd seen him all but demolished, had Hindley been able to do it!'

'Well, don't talk so fast, miss!' I interrupted, 'you'll disorder the handkerchief I have tied round your face, and make the cut bleed again. Drink your tea, and take breath, and give over laughing: laughter is sadly out of place under this roof, and in your condition!'

'An undeniable truth,' she replied. 'Listen to that child! It maintains a constant wail – send it out of my hearing for an hour; I shan't stay any longer.'

I rang the bell, and committed it to a servant's care; and then I enquired what had urged her to escape from Wuthering Heights in such an unlikely plight, and where she meant to go, as she refused remaining with us.

'I ought, and I wish to remain,' answered she, 'to cheer Edgar and take care of the baby, for two things, and because the Grange is my right home. But I tell you he wouldn't let me! Do you think he could bear to see me grow fat and merry; and could bear to think that we were tranquil, and not resolve on poisoning our comfort? Now, I have the satisfaction of being sure that he detests me to the point of its annoying him seriously to have me within earshot, or eyesight: I notice, when I enter his presence, the muscles of his countenance are involuntarily distorted into an expression of hatred; partly arising from his

knowledge of the good causes I have to feel that sentiment for him, and partly from original aversion. It is strong enough to make me feel pretty certain that he would not chase me over England, supposing I contrived a clear escape; and therefore I must get quite away. I've recovered from my first desire to be killed by him: I'd rather he'd kill himself! He has extinguished my love effectually, and so I'm at my ease. I can recollect yet how I loved him; and can dimly imagine that I could still be loving him, if – no, no! Even if he had doted on me, the devilish nature would have revealed its existence somehow. Catherine had an awfully perverted taste to esteem him so dearly, knowing him so well. Monster! would that he could be blotted out of creation, and out of my memory!'

'Hush, hush! He's a human being,' I said. 'Be more charitable: there are worse men than he is yet!'

'He's not a human being,' she retorted; 'and he has no claim on my charity. I gave him my heart, and he took and pinched it to death; and flung it back to me. People feel with their hearts, Ellen: and since he has destroyed mine, I have not power to feel for him: and I would not, though he groaned from this to his dying day, and wept tears of blood for Catherine! No, indeed, indeed, I wouldn't!' And here Isabella began to cry; but, immediately dashing the water from her lashes, she recommenced. 'You asked, what has driven me to flight at last? I was compelled to attempt it, because I had succeeded in rousing his rage a pitch above his malignity. Pulling out the nerves with red hot pincers requires more coolness than knocking on the head. He was worked up to forget the fiendish prudence he boasted of, and proceeded to murderous violence. I experienced pleasure in being able to exasperate him: the sense of pleasure woke my instinct of self-preservation, so I fairly broke free; and if ever I come into his hands again he is welcome to a signal revenge.

'Yesterday, you know, Mr Earnshaw should have been at the funeral. He kept himself sober for the purpose – tolerably sober: not going to bed mad at six o'clock and getting up drunk at twelve. Consequently, he rose, in suicidal low spirits, as fit for the church as for a dance; and instead, he sat down by the fire and swallowed gin or brandy by tumblerfuls.

'Heathcliff – I shudder to name him! has been a stranger in the house from last Sunday till today. Whether the angels have fed him, or his kin beneath, I cannot tell; but he has not eaten a meal with us for nearly a week. He has just come home at dawn, and gone upstairs to his chamber; locking himself in – as if anybody dreamt of coveting his company! There he has continued, praying like a methodist: only the deity he implored is senseless dust and ashes; and God, when addressed, was curiously confounded with his own black father! After concluding these precious orisons – and they lasted generally till he grew hoarse and his voice was strangled in his throat – he would be off again; always straight down to the Grange! I wonder Edgar did not send for a constable, and give him into custody! For me, grieved as I was about Catherine, it was impossible to avoid regarding this season of deliverance from degrading oppression as a holiday.

'I recovered spirits sufficient to hear Joseph's eternal lectures without weeping, and to move up and down the house less with the foot of a frightened thief than

formerly. You wouldn't think that I should cry at anything Joseph could say; but he and Hareton are detestable companions. I'd rather sit with Hindley, and hear his awful talk, than with "t' little maister" and his staunch supporter, that odious old man! When Heathcliff is in, I'm often obliged to seek the kitchen and their society, or starve among the damp uninhabited chambers; when he is not, as was the case this week, I establish a table and chair at one corner of the house fire, and never mind how Mr Earnshaw may occupy himself; and he does not interfere with my arrangements. He is quieter now than he used to be, if no one provokes him: more sullen and depressed, and less furious. Joseph affirms he's sure he's an altered man: that the Lord has touched his heart, and he is saved "so as by fire". I'm puzzled to detect signs of the favourable change: but it is not my business.

'Yester-evening I sat in my nook reading some old books till late on towards twelve. It seemed so dismal to go upstairs, with the wild snow blowing outside, and my thoughts continually reverting to the kirkyard and the new-made grave! I dared hardly lift my eyes from the page before me, that melancholy scene so instantly usurped its place. Hindley sat opposite, his head leant on his hand; perhaps meditating on the same subject. He had ceased drinking at a point below irrationality, and had neither stirred nor spoken during two or three hours. There was no sound through the house but the moaning wind which shook the windows every now and then, the faint crackling of the coals, and the click of my snuffers as I removed at intervals the long wick of the candle. Hareton and Joseph were probably fast asleep in bed. It was very, very sad: and while I read I sighed, for it seemed as if all joy had vanished from the world, never to be restored.

'The doleful silence was broken at length by the sound of the kitchen latch: Heathcliff had returned from his watch earlier than usual; owing, I suppose, to the sudden storm. That entrance was fastened, and we heard him coming round to get in by the other. I rose with an irrepressible expression of what I felt on my lips, which induced my companion, who had been staring towards the door, to turn and look at me.

' "I'll keep him out five minutes," he exclaimed. "You won't object?"

' "No, you may keep him out the whole night for me," I answered. "Do! put the key in the lock, and draw the bolts."

'Earnshaw accomplished this ere his guest reached the front; he then came and brought his chair to the other side of my table, leaning over it, and searching in my eyes, a sympathy with the burning hate that gleamed from his: as he both looked and felt like an assassin, he couldn't exactly find that; but he discovered enough to encourage him to speak.

' "You, and I," he said, "have each a great debt to settle with the man out yonder! If we were neither of us cowards, we might combine to discharge it. Are you as soft as your brother? Are you willing to endure to the last, and not once attempt a repayment?"

' "I'm weary of enduring now," I replied; "and I'd be glad of a retaliation that wouldn't recoil on myself; but treachery and violence are spears pointed at both ends: they wound those who resort to them, worse than their enemies."

' "Treachery and violence are a just return for treachery and violence!" cried Hindley. "Mrs Heathcliff, I'll ask you to do nothing, but sit still and be dumb. Tell me now, can you? I'm sure you would have as much pleasure as I in witnessing the conclusion of the fiend's existence; he'll be *your* death unless you overreach him; and he'll be *my* ruin. Damn the hellish villain! He knocks at the door as if he were master here already! Promise to hold your tongue, and before that clock strikes – it wants three minutes of one – you're a free woman!"

'He took the implements which I described to you in my letter from his breast, and would have turned down the candle. I snatched it away, however, and seized his arm.

' "I'll not hold my tongue!" I said; "you mustn't touch him. Let the door remain shut, and be quiet!"

' "No! I've formed my resolution, and by God, I'll execute it!" cried the desperate being. "I'll do you a kindness in spite of yourself, and Hareton justice! And you needn't trouble your head to screen me; Catherine is gone. Nobody alive would regret me, or be ashamed, though I cut my throat this minute – and it's time to make an end!"

'I might as well have struggled with a bear, or reasoned with a lunatic. The only resource left me was to run to a lattice and warn his intended victim of the fate which awaited him.

' "You'd better seek shelter somewhere else tonight!" I exclaimed in a rather triumphant tone. "Mr Earnshaw has a mind to shoot you, if you persist in endeavouring to enter."

' "You'd better open the door, you – ," he answered, addressing me by some elegant term that I don't care to repeat.

' "I shall not meddle in the matter," I retorted again. "Come in and get shot, if you please! I've done my duty."

'With that I shut the window and returned to my place by the fire; having too small a stock of hypocrisy at my command to pretend any anxiety for the danger that menaced him. Earnshaw swore passionately at me: affirming that I loved the villain yet; and calling me all sorts of names for the base spirit I evinced. And I, in my secret heart, (and conscience never reproached me) thought what a blessing it would be for *him*, should Heathcliff put him out of misery; and what a blessing for *me*, should he send Heathcliff to his right abode! As I sat nursing these reflections, the casement behind me was banged on to the floor by a blow from the latter individual, and his black countenance looked blightingly through. The stanchions stood too close to suffer his shoulders to follow, and I smiled, exulting in my fancied security. His hair and clothes were whitened with snow, and his sharp cannibal teeth, revealed by cold and wrath, gleamed through the dark.

' "Isabella, let me in, or I'll make you repent!" he "girned", as Joseph calls it.

' "I cannot commit murder," I replied. "Mr Hindley stands sentinel with a knife and loaded pistol."

' "Let me in by the kitchen door," he said.

' "Hindley will be there before me," I answered: "and that's a poor love of

yours that cannot bear a shower of snow! We were left at peace in our beds as long as the summer moon shone, but the moment a blast of winter returns, you must run for shelter! Heathcliff, if I were you, I'd go stretch myself over her grave and die like a faithful dog. The world is surely not worth living in now, is it? You had distinctly impressed on me the idea that Catherine was the whole joy of your life: I can't imagine how you think of surviving her loss."

' "He's there, is he?" exclaimed my companion, rushing to the gap. "If I can get my arm out I can hit him!"

'I'm afraid, Ellen, you'll set me down as really wicked; but you don't know all, so don't judge. I wouldn't have aided or abetted an attempt on even *his* life for anything. Wish that he were dead, I must; and therefore I was fearfully disappointed, and unnerved by terror for the consequences of my taunting speech, when he flung himself on Earnshaw's weapon and wrenched it from his grasp.

'The charge exploded, and the knife, in springing back, closed into its owner's wrist. Heathcliff pulled it away by main force, slitting up the flesh as it passed on, and thrust it dripping into his pocket. He then took a stone, struck down the division between two windows, and sprung in. His adversary had fallen senseless with excessive pain, and the flow of blood that gushed from an artery or a large vein. The ruffian kicked and trampled on him, and dashed his head repeatedly against the flags, holding me with one hand, meantime, to prevent me summoning Joseph. He exerted preter-human self-denial in abstaining from finishing him completely; but getting out of breath he finally desisted, and dragged the apparently inanimate body on to the settle. There he tore off the sleeve of Earnshaw's coat, and bound up the wound with brutal roughness; spitting and cursing during the operation as energetically as he had kicked before. Being at liberty, I lost no time in seeking the old servant; who, having gathered by degrees the purport of my hasty tale, hurried below, gasping, as he descended the steps two at once.

' "Whet is thur tuh do, nah? Whet is thur tuh do, nah?"

' "There's this to do," thundered Heathcliff, "that your master's mad; and should he last another month, I'll have him to an asylum. And how the devil did you come to fasten me out, you toothless hound? Don't stand muttering and mumbling there. Come, I'm not going to nurse him. Wash that stuff away; and mind the sparks of your candle – it is more than half brandy!"

' "Und soa, yah been murthering on him?" exclaimed Joseph, lifting his hands and eyes in horror. "If iver Aw seed a seeght loike this! May the Lord – "

'Heathcliff gave him a push on to his knees in the middle of the blood, and flung a towel to him; but instead of proceeding to dry it up, he joined his hands, and began a prayer which excited my laughter from its odd phraseology. I was in the condition of mind to be shocked at nothing: in fact, I was as reckless as some malefactors show themselves at the foot of the gallows.

' "Oh, I forgot you," said the tyrant. "You shall do that. Down with you. And you conspire with him against me, do you, viper? There, that is work fit for you!'

'He shook me till my teeth rattled, and pitched me beside Joseph, who

steadily concluded his supplications and then rose, vowing he would set off for the Grange directly. Mr Linton was a magistrate, and though he had fifty wives dead, he should enquire into this. He was so obstinate in his resolution, that Heathcliff deemed it expedient to compel from my lips a recapitulation of what had taken place; standing over me, heaving with malevolence, as I reluctantly delivered the account in answer to his questions. It required a great deal of labour to satisfy the old man that he was not the aggressor; especially with my hardly wrung replies. However, Mr Earnshaw soon convinced him that he was alive still; he hastened to administer a dose of spirits, and by their succour his master presently regained motion and consciousness. Heathcliff, aware that he was ignorant of the treatment received while insensible, called him deliriously intoxicated; and said he should not notice his atrocious conduct further, but advised him to get to bed. To my joy, he left us, after giving this judicious counsel, and Hindley stretched himself on the hearthstone. I departed to my own room, marvelling that I had escaped so easily.

'This morning, when I came down, about half an hour before noon, Mr Earnshaw was sitting by the fire, deadly sick; his evil genius, almost as gaunt and ghastly, leant against the chimney. Neither appeared inclined to dine, and, having waited till all was cold on the table, I commenced alone. Nothing hindered me from eating heartily, and I experienced a certain sense of satisfaction and superiority, as, at intervals, I cast a look towards my silent companions, and felt the comfort of a quiet conscience within me. After I had done, I ventured on the unusual liberty of drawing near the fire, going round Earnshaw's seat, and kneeling in the corner beside him.

'Heathcliff did not glance my way, and I gazed up, and contemplated his features almost as confidently as if they had been turned to stone. His forehead, that I once thought so manly, and that I now think so diabolical, was shaded with a heavy cloud; his basilisk eyes were nearly quenched by sleeplessness – and weeping, perhaps, for the lashes were wet then; his lips devoid of their ferocious sneer, and sealed in an expression of unspeakable sadness. Had it been another, I would have covered my face, in the presence of such grief. In *his* case, I was gratified; and, ignoble as it seems to insult a fallen enemy, I couldn't miss this chance of sticking in a dart: his weakness was the only time when I could taste the delight of paying wrong for wrong.'

'Fie, fie, miss!' I interrupted. 'One might suppose you had never opened a Bible in your life. If God afflict your enemies, surely that ought to suffice you. It is both mean and presumptuous to add your torture to his!'

'In general, I'll allow that it would be, Ellen,' she continued; 'but what misery laid on Heathcliff could content me, unless I have a hand in it? I'd rather he suffered *less*, if I might cause his sufferings and he might *know* that I was the cause. Oh, I owe him so much. On only one condition can I hope to forgive him. It is, if I may take an eye for an eye, a tooth for a tooth; for every wrench of agony return a wrench: reduce him to my level. As he was the first to injure, make him the first to implore pardon; and then – why then, Ellen, I might show you some generosity. But it is utterly impossible I can ever be revenged, and

therefore I cannot forgive him. Hindley wanted some water, and I handed him a glass, and asked him how he was.

' "Not as ill as I wish," he replied. "But leaving out my arm, every inch of me is as sore as if I had been fighting with a legion of imps!"

' "Yes, no wonder," was my next remark. "Catherine used to boast that she stood between you and bodily harm: she meant that certain persons would not hurt you for fear of offending her. It's well people don't *really* rise from their grave, or, last night, she might have witnessed a repulsive scene! Are not you bruised, and cut over your chest and shoulders?"

' "I can't say," he answered: "but what do you mean? Did he dare to strike me when I was down?"

' "He trampled on, and kicked you, and dashed you on the ground," I whispered. "And his mouth watered to tear you with his teeth; because, he's only half a man – not so much."

'Mr Earnshaw looked up, like me, to the countenance of our mutual foe; who, absorbed in his anguish, seemed insensible to anything around him: the longer he stood, the plainer his reflections revealed their blackness through his features.

' "Oh, if God would but give me strength to strangle him in my last agony, I'd go to hell with joy," groaned the impatient man, writhing to rise, and sinking back in despair, convinced of his inadequacy for the struggle.

' "Nay, it's enough that he has murdered one of you," I observed aloud. "At the Grange, everyone knows your sister would have been living now, had it not been for Mr Heathcliff. After all, it is preferable to be hated than loved by him. When I recollect how happy we were – how happy Catherine was before he came – I'm fit to curse the day."

'Most likely, Heathcliff noticed more the truth of what was said, than the spirit of the person who said it. His attention was roused, I saw, for his eyes rained down tears among the ashes, and he drew his breath in suffocating sighs. I stared full at him, and laughed scornfully. The clouded windows of hell flashed a moment towards me; the fiend which usually looked out, however, was so dimmed and drowned that I did not fear to hazard another sound of derision.

' "Get up, and begone out of my sight," said the mourner.

'I guessed he uttered those words, at least, though his voice was hardly intelligible.

' "I beg your pardon," I replied. "But I loved Catherine too; and her brother requires attendance which, for her sake, I shall supply. Now that she's dead, I see her in Hindley: Hindley has exactly her eyes, if you had not tried to gouge them out, and made them black and red; and her – "

' "Get up, wretched idiot, before I stamp you to death!" he cried, making a movement that caused me to make one also.

' "But then," I continued, holding myself ready to flee; "if poor Catherine had trusted you, and assumed the ridiculous, contemptible, degrading title of Mrs Heathcliff, she would soon have presented a similar picture! *She* wouldn't have borne your abominable behaviour quietly: her detestation and disgust must have found voice."

'The back of the settle and Earnshaw's person interposed between me and him; so instead of endeavouring to reach me, he snatched a dinner knife from the table and flung it at my head. It struck beneath my ear, and stopped the sentence I was uttering; but, pulling it out, I sprang to the door and delivered another which I hope went a little deeper than his missile. The last glimpse I caught of him was a furious rush on his part, checked by the embrace of his host; and both fell locked together on the hearth. In my flight through the kitchen I bid Joseph speed to his master; I knocked over Hareton, who was hanging a litter of puppies from a chair-back in the doorway; and, blest as a soul escaped from purgatory, I bounded, leaped, and flew down the steep road; then, quitting its windings, shot direct across the moor, rolling over banks, and wading through marshes: precipitating myself, in fact, towards the beacon light of the Grange. And far rather would I be condemned to a perpetual dwelling in the infernal regions, than, even for one night, abide beneath the roof of Wuthering Heights again.'

Isabella ceased speaking, and took a drink of tea; then she rose, and bidding me put on her bonnet, and a great shawl I had brought, and turning a deaf ear to my entreaties for her to remain another hour, she stepped on to a chair, kissed Edgar's and Catherine's portraits, bestowed a similar salute on me, and descended to the carriage, accompanied by Fanny, who yelped wild with joy at recovering her mistress. She was driven away, never to revisit this neighbourhood: but a regular correspondence was established between her and my master when things were more settled. I believe her new abode was in the south, near London; there she had a son born, a few months subsequent to her escape. He was christened Linton, and, from the first, she reported him to be an ailing, peevish creature.

Mr Heathcliff, meeting me one day in the village, enquired where she lived. I refused to tell. He remarked that it was not of any moment, only she must beware of coming to her brother: she should not be with him, if he had to keep her himself. Though I would give no information, he discovered, through some of the other servants, both her place of residence and the existence of the child. Still he didn't molest her: for which forbearance she might thank his aversion, I suppose.

He often asked about the infant, when he saw me; and on hearing its name, smiled grimly, and observed – 'They wish me to hate it too, do they?'

'I don't think they wish you to know anything about it,' I answered.

'But I'll have it,' he said, 'when I want it. They may reckon on that!'

Fortunately, its mother died before the time arrived, some thirteen years after the decease of Catherine, when Linton was twelve, or a little more.

On the day succeeding Isabella's unexpected visit, I had no opportunity of speaking to my master: he shunned conversation, and was fit for discussing nothing. When I could get him to listen, I saw it pleased him that his sister had left her husband; whom he abhorred with an intensity which the mildness of his nature would scarcely seem to allow. So deep and sensitive was his aversion, that he refrained from going anywhere where he was likely to see or hear of Heathcliff. Grief, and that together, transformed him into a complete hermit:

he threw up his office of magistrate, ceased even to attend church, avoided the village on all occasions, and spent a life of entire seclusion within the limits of his park and grounds; only varied by solitary rambles on the moors, and visits to the grave of his wife, mostly at evening, or early morning before other wanderers were abroad. But he was too good to be thoroughly unhappy long. *He* didn't pray for Catherine's soul to haunt him: time brought resignation, and a melancholy sweeter than common joy. He recalled her memory with ardent, tender love, and hopeful aspiring to the better world, where, he doubted not, she was gone.

And he had earthly consolation and affections, also. For a few days, I said, he seemed regardless of the puny successor to the departed: that coldness melted as fast as snow in April, and ere the tiny thing could stammer a word or totter a step, it wielded a despot's sceptre in his heart. It was named Catherine; but he never called it the name in full, as he had never called the first Catherine short: probably because Heathcliff had a habit of doing so. The little one was always Cathy: it formed to him a distinction from the mother, and yet, a connection with her; and his attachment sprang from its relation to her, far more than from its being his own.

I used to draw a comparison between him and Hindley Earnshaw, and perplex myself to explain satisfactorily why their conduct was so opposite in similar circumstances. They had both been fond husbands, and were both attached to their children; and I could not see how they shouldn't both have taken the same road, for good or evil. But, I thought in my mind, Hindley, with apparently the stronger head, has shown himself sadly the worse and the weaker man. When his ship struck, the captain abandoned his post; and the crew, instead of trying to save her, rushed into riot and confusion, leaving no hope for their luckless vessel. Linton, on the contrary, displayed the true courage of a loyal and faithful soul: he trusted God; and God comforted him. One hoped, and the other despaired: they chose their own lots, and were righteously doomed to endure them. But you'll not want to hear my moralising, Mr Lockwood; you'll judge as well as I can, all these things: at least, you'll think you will, and that's the same. The end of Earnshaw was what might have been expected; it followed fast on his sister's: there were scarcely six months between them. We, at the Grange, never got a very succinct account of his state preceding it; all that I did learn was on occasion of going to aid in the preparations for the funeral.

Mr Kenneth came to announce the event to my master.

'Well, Nelly,' said he, riding into the yard one morning, too early not to alarm me with an instant presentiment of bad news, 'It's yours and my turn to go into mourning at present. Who's given us the slip now, do you think?'

'Who?' I asked in a flurry.

'Why, guess!' he returned, dismounting, and slinging his bridle on a hook by the door. 'And nip up the corner of your apron: I'm certain you'll need it.'

'Not Mr Heathcliff, surely?' I exclaimed.

'What! would you have tears for him?' said the doctor. 'No, Heathcliff's a

tough young fellow: he looks blooming today. I've just seen him. He's rapidly regaining flesh since he lost his better half.'

'Who is it, then, Mr Kenneth?' I repeated impatiently.

'Hindley Earnshaw! Your old friend Hindley,' he replied, 'and my wicked gossip: though he's been too wild for me this long while. There! I said we should draw water. But cheer up! He died true to his character: drunk as a lord. Poor lad; I'm sorry, too. One can't help missing an old companion: though he had the worst tricks with him that ever man imagined, and has done me many a rascally turn. He's barely twenty-seven, it seems; that's your own age: who would have thought you were born in one year?'

I confess this blow was greater to me than the shock of Mrs Linton's death: ancient associations lingered round my heart; I sat down in the porch and wept as for a blood relation, desiring Kenneth to get another servant to introduce him to the master. I could not hinder myself from pondering on the question – 'Had he had fair play?' Whatever I did, that idea would bother me: it was so tiresomely pertinacious that I resolved on requesting leave to go to Wuthering Heights, and assist in the last duties to the dead. Mr Linton was extremely reluctant to consent, but I pleaded eloquently for the friendless condition in which he lay; and I said my old master and foster-brother had a claim on my services as strong as his own. Besides, I reminded him that the child Hareton was his wife's nephew, and, in the absence of nearer kin, he ought to act as its guardian; and he ought to and must enquire how the property was left, and look over the concerns of his brother-in-law. He was unfit for attending to such matters then, but he bid me speak to his lawyer; and at length permitted me to go. His lawyer had been Earnshaw's also: I called at the village, and asked him to accompany me. He shook his head, and advised that Heathcliff should be let alone; affirming, if the truth were known, Hareton would be found little else than a beggar.

'His father died in debt,' he said; 'the whole property is mortgaged, and the sole chance for the natural heir is to allow him an opportunity of creating some interest in the creditor's heart, that he may be inclined to deal leniently towards him.'

When I reached the Heights, I explained that I had come to see everything carried on decently; and Joseph, who appeared in sufficient distress, expressed satisfaction at my presence. Mr Heathcliff said he did not perceive that I was wanted; but I might stay and order the arrangements for the funeral, if I chose.

'Correctly,' he remarked, 'that fool's body should be buried at the crossroads, without ceremony of any kind. I happened to leave him ten minutes yesterday afternoon, and in that interval he fastened the two doors of the house against me, and he has spent the night in drinking himself to death deliberately! We broke in this morning, for we heard him snorting like a horse; and there he was, laid over the settle: flaying and scalping would not have wakened him. I sent for Kenneth, and he came; but not till the beast had changed into carrion; he was both dead and cold, and stark; and so you'll allow, it was useless making more stir about him!'

The old servant confirmed this statement, but muttered – 'Aw'd rayther he'd goan hisseln fur t' doctor! Aw sud uh taen tent uh t' maister better nur him – un he warn't deead when Aw left, nowt uh t' soart!'

I insisted on the funeral being respectable. Mr Heathcliff said I might have my own way there too: only, he desired me to remember that the money for the whole affair came out of his pocket. He maintained a hard, careless deportment, indicative of neither joy nor sorrow: if anything, it expressed a flinty gratification at a piece of difficult work successfully executed. I observed once, indeed, something like exultation in his aspect: it was just when the people were bearing the coffin from the house. He had the hypocrisy to represent a mourner: and previous to following with Hareton, he lifted the unfortunate child on to the table and muttered, with peculiar gusto, 'Now, my bonny lad, you are *mine*! And we'll see if one tree won't grow as crooked as another, with the same wind to twist it!' The unsuspecting thing was pleased at this speech: he played with Heathcliff's whiskers, and stroked his cheek; but I divined its meaning, and observed tartly, 'That boy must go back with me to Thrushcross Grange, sir. There is nothing in the world less yours than he is!'

'Does Linton say so?' he demanded.

'Of course – he has ordered me to take him,' I replied.

'Well,' said the scoundrel, 'we'll not argue the subject now: but I have a fancy to try my hand at rearing a young one; so intimate to your master that I must supply the place of this with my own, if he attempt to remove it. I don't engage to let Hareton go, undisputed; but I'll be pretty sure to make the other come! Remember to tell him.'

This hint was enough to bind our hands. I repeated its substance on my return; and Edgar Linton, little interested at the commencement, spoke no more of interfering. I'm not aware that he could have done it to any purpose, had he been ever so willing.

The guest was now the master of Wuthering Heights: he held firm possession, and proved to the attorney – who, in his turn, proved it to Mr Linton – that Earnshaw had mortgaged every yard of land he owned, for cash to supply his mania for gaming; and he, Heathcliff, was the mortgagee. In that manner Hareton, who should now be the first gentleman in the neighbourhood, was reduced to a state of complete dependence on his father's inveterate enemy; and lives in his own house as a servant, deprived of the advantage of wages, and quite unable to right himself, because of his friendlessness, and his ignorance that he has been wronged.

## Chapter 18

The twelve years, continued Mrs Dean, following that dismal period, were the happiest of my life: my greatest troubles in their passage rose from our little lady's trifling illnesses, which she had to experience in common with all children, rich and poor. For the rest, after the first six months, she grew like a larch, and could walk and talk too, in her own way, before the heath blossomed a second time over Mrs Linton's dust. She was the most winning thing that ever brought sunshine into a desolate house: a real beauty in face, with the Earnshaws' handsome dark eyes, but the Lintons' fair skin, and small features, and yellow curling hair. Her spirit was high, though not rough, and qualified by a heart sensitive and lively to excess in its affections. That capacity for intense attachments reminded me of her mother: still she did not resemble her; for she could be soft and mild as a dove, and she had a gentle voice and pensive expression: her anger was never furious; her love never fierce: it was deep and tender. However, it must be acknowledged, she had faults to foil her gifts. A propensity to be saucy was one; and a perverse will, that indulged children invariably acquire, whether they be good tempered or cross. If a servant chanced to vex her, it was always – 'I shall tell papa!' And if he reproved her, even by a look, you would have thought it a heartbreaking business: I don't believe he ever did speak a harsh word to her. He took her education entirely on himself, and made it an amusement. Fortunately, curiosity and a quick intellect urged her into an apt scholar: she learnt rapidly and eagerly, and did honour to his teaching.

Till she reached the age of thirteen, she had not once been beyond the range of the park by herself. Mr Linton would take her with him a mile or so outside, on rare occasions; but he trusted her to no one else. Gimmerton was an unsubstantial name in her ears; the chapel, the only building she had approached or entered, except her own home. Wuthering Heights and Mr Heathcliff did not exist for her: she was a perfect recluse; and, apparently, perfectly contented. Sometimes, indeed, while surveying the country from her nursery window, she would observe – 'Ellen, how long will it be before I can walk to the top of those hills? I wonder what lies on the other side – is it the sea?'

'No, Miss Cathy,' I would answer; 'it is hills again, just like these.'

'And what are those golden rocks like, when you stand under them?' she once asked.

The abrupt descent of Penistone Craggs particularly attracted her notice; especially when the setting sun shone on it and the topmost heights, and the whole extent of landscape besides lay in shadow. I explained that they were bare masses of stone, with hardly enough earth in their clefts to nourish a stunted tree.

'And why are they bright so long after it is evening here?' she pursued.

'Because they are a great deal higher up than we are,' replied I; 'you could not

climb them, they are too high and steep. In winter the frost is always there before it comes to us; and deep into summer I have found snow under that black hollow on the northeast side!'

'Oh, you have been on them!' she cried, gleefully. 'Then I can go, too, when I am a woman. Has papa been, Ellen?'

'Papa would tell you, miss,' I answered, hastily, 'that they are not worth the trouble of visiting. The moors, where you ramble with him, are much nicer; and Thrushcross park is the finest place in the world.'

'But I know the park, and I don't know those,' she murmured to herself. 'And I should delight to look round me from the brow of that tallest point: my little pony Minny shall take me sometime.'

One of the maids mentioning the Fairy cave, quite turned her head with a desire to fulfil this project: she teased Mr Linton about it; and he promised she should have the journey when she got older. But Miss Catherine measured her age by months, and, 'Now, am I old enough to go to Penistone Craggs?' was the constant question in her mouth. The road thither wound close by Wuthering Heights. Edgar had not the heart to pass it; so she received as constantly the answer, 'Not yet, love: not yet.'

I said Mrs Heathcliff lived above a dozen years after quitting her husband. Her family were of a delicate constitution: she and Edgar both lacked the ruddy health that you will generally meet in these parts. What her last illness was, I am not certain: I conjecture, they died of the same thing, a kind of fever, slow at its commencement, but incurable, and rapidly consuming life towards the close. She wrote to inform her brother of the probable conclusion of a four months' indisposition under which she had suffered; and entreated him to come to her, if possible; for she had much to settle, and she wished to bid him adieu, and deliver Linton safely into his hands. Her hope was, that Linton might be left with him, as he had been with her: his father, she would fain convince herself, had no desire to assume the burden of his maintenance or education. My master hesitated not a moment in complying with her request: reluctant as he was to leave home at ordinary calls, he flew to answer this; commending Catherine to my peculiar vigilance, in his absence, with reiterated orders that she must not wander out of the park, even under my escort: he did not calculate on her going unaccompanied.

He was away three weeks: the first day or two, my charge sat in a corner of the library, too sad for either reading or playing: in that quiet state she caused me little trouble; but it was succeeded by an interval of impatient, fretful weariness; and being too busy, and too old then, to run up and down amusing her, I hit on a method by which she might entertain herself. I used to send her on travels round the grounds – now on foot, and now on a pony: indulging her with a patient audience of all her real and imaginary adventures, when she returned.

The summer shone in full prime; and she took such a taste for this solitary rambling that she often contrived to remain out from breakfast till tea; and then the evenings were spent in recounting her fanciful tales. I did not fear her

breaking bounds; because the gates were generally locked, and I thought she would scarcely venture forth alone, if they had stood wide open. Unluckily, my confidence proved misplaced. Catherine came to me, one morning, at eight o'clock, and said she was that day an Arabian merchant, going to cross the desert with his caravan; and I must give her plenty of provision for herself and beasts: a horse, and three camels, personated by a large hound and a couple of pointers. I got together good store of dainties, and slung them in a basket on one side of the saddle; and she sprang up as gay as a fairy, sheltered by her wide-brimmed hat and gauze veil from the July sun, and trotted off with a merry laugh, mocking my cautious counsel to avoid galloping, and come back early. The naughty thing never made her appearance at tea. One traveller, the hound, being an old dog and fond of its ease, returned; but neither Cathy, nor the pony, nor the two pointers were visible in any direction; and I despatched emissaries down this path, and that path, and at last went wandering in search of her myself. There was a labourer working at a fence round a plantation, on the borders of the grounds. I enquired of him if he had seen our young lady.

'I saw her at morn,' he replied; 'she would have me to cut her a hazel switch, and then she leapt her galloway over the hedge yonder, where it is lowest, and galloped out of sight.'

You may guess how I felt at hearing this news. It struck me directly she must have started for Penistone Craggs. 'What will become of her?' I ejaculated, pushing through a gap which the man was repairing, and making straight to the highroad. I walked as if for a wager, mile after mile, till a turn brought me in view of the Heights; but no Catherine could I detect, far or near. The Craggs lie about a mile and a half beyond Mr Heathcliff's place, and that is four from the Grange, so I began to fear night would fall ere I could reach them. 'And what if she should have slipped in clambering among them,' I reflected, 'and been killed, or broken some of her bones?' My suspense was truly painful; and, at first, it gave me delightful relief to observe, in hurrying by the farmhouse, Charlie, the fiercest of the pointers, lying under a window, with swelled head and bleeding ear. I opened the wicket and ran to the door, knocking vehemently for admittance. A woman whom I knew, and who formerly lived at Gimmerton, answered: she had been servant there since the death of Mr Earnshaw.

'Ah,' said she, 'you are come a seeking your little mistress! Don't be frightened. She's here safe: but I'm glad it isn't the master.'

'He is not at home then, is he?' I panted, quite breathless with quick walking and alarm.

'No, no,' she replied: 'both he and Joseph are off, and I think they won't return this hour or more. Step in and rest you a bit.'

I entered, and beheld my stray lamb seated on the hearth, rocking herself in a little chair that had been her mother's when a child. Her hat was hung against the wall and she seemed perfectly at home, laughing and chattering, in the best spirits imaginable, to Hareton – now a great, strong lad of eighteen – who stared at her with considerable curiosity and astonishment: comprehending precious

little of the fluent succession of remarks and questions which her tongue never ceased pouring forth.

'Very well, miss!' I exclaimed, concealing my joy under an angry countenance. 'This is your last ride, till papa comes back. I'll not trust you over the threshold again, you naughty, naughty girl!'

'Aha, Ellen!' she cried, gaily, jumping up, and running to my side. 'I shall have a pretty story to tell tonight: and so you've found me out. Have you ever been here in your life before?'

'Put that hat on, and home at once,' said I. 'I'm dreadfully grieved at you, Miss Cathy: you've done extremely wrong! It's no use pouting and crying: that won't repay the trouble I've had, scouring the country after you. To think how Mr Linton charged me to keep you in; and you stealing off so! It shows you are a cunning little fox, and nobody will put faith in you any more.'

'What have I done?' sobbed she, instantly checked. 'Papa charged me nothing: he'll not scold me, Ellen – he's never cross, like you!'

'Come, come!' I repeated. 'I'll tie the riband. Now, let us have no petulance. Oh, for shame. You thirteen years old, and such a baby!'

This exclamation was caused by her pushing the hat from her head, and retreating to the chimney out of my reach.

'Nay,' said the servant, 'don't be hard on the bonny lass, Mrs Dean. We made her stop: she'd fain have ridden forwards, afeard you should be uneasy. But Hareton offered to go with her, and I thought he should: it's a wild road over the hills.'

Hareton, during the discussion, stood with his hands in his pockets, too awkward to speak; though he looked as if he did not relish my intrusion.

'How long am I to wait?' I continued, disregarding the woman's interference. 'It will be dark in ten minutes. Where is the pony, Miss Cathy? And where is Phoenix? I shall leave you unless you be quick; so please yourself.'

'The pony is in the yard,' she replied, 'and Phoenix is shut in there. He's bitten – and so is Charlie. I was going to tell you all about it; but you are in a bad temper, and don't deserve to hear.'

I picked up her hat, and approached to reinstate it; but perceiving that the people of the house took her part, she commenced capering round the room; and on my giving chase, ran like a mouse over and under and behind the furniture, rendering it ridiculous for me to pursue. Hareton and the woman laughed, and she joined them, and waxed more impertinent still; till I cried, in great irritation – 'Well, Miss Cathy, if you were aware whose house this is, you'd be glad enough to get out.'

'It's *your* father's, isn't it?' said she, turning to Hareton.

'Nay,' he replied, looking down, and blushing bashfully.

He could not stand a steady gaze from her eyes, though they were just his own.

'Whose, then – your master's?' she asked.

He coloured deeper, with a different feeling, muttered an oath, and turned away.

'Who is his master?' continued the tiresome girl, appealing to me. 'He talked

about "our house", and "our folk". I thought he had been the owner's son. And he never said, miss: he should have done, shouldn't he, if he's a servant?'

Hareton grew black as a thundercloud, at this childish speech. I silently shook my questioner, and at last succeeded in equipping her for departure.

'Now, get my horse,' she said, addressing her unknown kinsman as she would one of the stable-boys at the Grange. 'And you may come with me. I want to see where the goblin-hunter rises in the marsh, and to hear about the *fairishes*, as you call them: but make haste! What's the matter? Get my horse, I say.'

'I'll see thee damned before I be *thy* servant!' growled the lad.

'You'll see me *what*?' asked Catherine in surprise.

'Damned – thou saucy witch!' he replied.

'There, Miss Cathy! You see you have got into pretty company,' I interposed. 'Nice words to be used to a young lady! Pray don't begin to dispute with him. Come, let us seek for Minny ourselves, and begone.'

'But Ellen,' cried she, staring, fixed in astonishment. 'How dare he speak so to me? Mustn't he be made to do as I ask him? You wicked creature, I shall tell papa what you said – Now then!'

Hareton did not appear to feel this threat; so the tears sprung into her eyes with indignation.

'You bring the pony,' she exclaimed, turning to the woman, 'and let my dog free this moment!'

'Softly, miss,' answered the addressed: 'you'll lose nothing by being civil. Though Mr Hareton, there, be not the master's son, he's your cousin; and I was never hired to serve you.'

'*He* my cousin!' cried Cathy, with a scornful laugh.

'Yes, indeed,' responded her reprover.

'Oh, Ellen! Don't let them say such things,' she pursued in great trouble. 'Papa is gone to fetch my cousin from London: my cousin is a gentleman's son. That my – ' she stopped, and wept outright; upset at the bare notion of relationship with such a clown.

'Hush, hush!' I whispered, 'people can have many cousins and of all sorts, Miss Cathy, without being any the worse for it; only they needn't keep their company, if they be disagreeable and bad.'

'He's not – he's not my cousin, Ellen!' she went on, gathering fresh grief from reflection, and flinging herself into my arms for refuge from the idea.

I was much vexed at her and the servant for their mutual revelations; having no doubt of Linton's approaching arrival, communicated by the former, being reported to Mr Heathcliff; and feeling as confident that Catherine's first thought on her father's return would be to seek an explanation of the latter's assertion concerning her rude-bred kindred. Hareton, recovering from his disgust at being taken for a servant, seemed moved by her distress; and, having fetched the pony round to the door, he took, to propitiate her, a fine crooked-legged terrier whelp from the kennel, and putting it into her hand bid her wisht! For he meant naught. Pausing in her lamentations, she surveyed him with a glance of awe and horror, then burst forth anew.

I could scarcely refrain from smiling at this antipathy to the poor fellow; who was a well-made, athletic youth, good looking in features, and stout and healthy, but attired in garments befitting his daily occupations of working on the farm, and lounging among the moors after rabbits and game. Still, I thought I could detect in his physiognomy a mind owning better qualities than his father ever possessed. Good things lost amid a wilderness of weeds, to be sure, whose rankness far over-topped their neglected growth; yet, notwith-standing, evidence of a wealthy soil, that might yield luxuriant crops under other and favourable circumstances. Mr Heathcliff, I believe, had not treated him physically ill; thanks to his fearless nature, which offered no temptation to that course of oppression: it had none of the timid susceptibility that would have given zest to ill-treatment, in Heathcliff's judgement. He appeared to have bent his malevolence on making him a brute: he was never taught to read or write; never rebuked for any bad habit which did not annoy his keeper; never led a single step towards virtue, or guarded by a single precept against vice. And from what I heard, Joseph contributed much to his deterioration, by a narrow-minded partiality which prompted him to flatter and pet him, as a boy, because he was the head of the old family. And as he had been in the habit of accusing Catherine Earnshaw and Heathcliff, when children, of putting the master past his patience, and compelling him to seek solace in drink by what he termed their 'offalld ways', so at present he laid the whole burden of Hareton's faults on the shoulders of the usurper of his property. If the lad swore, he wouldn't correct him: nor however culpably he behaved. It gave Joseph satisfaction, apparently, to watch him go the worst lengths: he allowed that he was ruined: that his soul was abandoned to perdition; but then, he reflected that Heathcliff must answer for it. Hareton's blood would be required at his hands; and there lay immense consolation in that thought. Joseph had instilled into him a pride of name, and of his lineage; he would, had he dared, have fostered hate between him and the present owner of the Heights: but his dread of that owner amounted to superstition; and he confined his feelings regarding him to mut-tered innuendoes and private comminations. I don't pretend to be intimately acquainted with the mode of living customary in those days at Wuthering Heights: I only speak from hearsay; for I saw little. The villagers affirmed Mr Heathcliff was *near*, and a cruel hard landlord to his tenants; but the house, inside, had regained its ancient aspect of comfort under female management, and the scenes of riot common in Hindley's time were not now enacted within its walls. The master was too gloomy to seek companionship with any people, good or bad; and he is yet.

This, however, is not making progress with my story. Miss Cathy rejected the peace-offering of the terrier, and demanded her own dogs, Charlie and Phoenix. They came limping, and hanging their heads; and we set out for home, sadly out of sorts, every one of us. I could not wring from my little lady how she had spent the day; except that, as I supposed, the goal of her pilgrimage was Penistone Craggs; and she arrived without adventure to the gate of the farmhouse, when Hareton happened to issue forth, attended by some canine followers, who

attacked her train. They had a smart battle, before their owners could separate them: that formed an introduction. Catherine told Hareton who she was, and where she was going; and asked him to show her the way; finally, beguiling him to accompany her. He opened the mysteries of the fairy cave, and twenty other queer places. But, being in disgrace, I was not favoured with a description of the interesting objects she saw. I could gather, however, that her guide had been a favourite till she hurt his feelings by addressing him as a servant; and Heathcliff's housekeeper hurt hers by calling him her cousin. Then the language he had held to her rankled in her heart; she who was always 'love', and 'darling', and 'queen', and 'angel', with everybody at the Grange, to be insulted so shockingly by a stranger! She did not comprehend it; and hard work I had to obtain a promise that she would not lay the grievance before her father. I explained how he objected to the whole household at the Heights, and how sorry he would be to find she had been there; but I insisted most on the fact, that if she revealed my negligence of his orders, he would perhaps be so angry, that I should have to leave; and Cathy couldn't bear that prospect: she pledged her word, and kept it, for my sake. After all, she was a sweet little girl.

## Chapter 19

A letter, edged with black, announced the day of my master's return. Isabella was dead; and he wrote to bid me get mourning for his daughter, and arrange a room, and other accommodations, for his youthful nephew. Catherine ran wild with joy at the idea of welcoming her father back; and indulged most sanguine anticipations of the innumerable excellences of her 'real' cousin. The evening of their expected arrival came. Since early morning, she had been busy ordering her own small affairs; and now, attired in her new black frock – poor thing! Her aunt's death impressed her with no definite sorrow – she obliged me, by constant worrying, to walk with her down through the grounds to meet them.

'Linton is just six months younger than I am,' she chattered, as we strolled leisurely over the swells and hollows of mossy turf, under shadow of the trees. 'How delightful it will be to have him for a playfellow! Aunt Isabella sent papa a beautiful lock of his hair; it was lighter than mine – more flaxen, and quite as fine. I have it carefully preserved in a little glass box; and I've often thought what pleasure it would be to see its owner. Oh! I am happy – and papa, dear, dear papa! Come, Ellen, let us run! Come run!'

She ran, and returned and ran again, many times before my sober footsteps reached the gate, and then she seated herself on the grassy bank beside the path, and tried to wait patiently, but that was impossible: she couldn't be still a minute.

'How long they are!' she exclaimed. 'Ah, I see some dust on the road – they are coming! No! When will they be here? May we not go a little way – half a mile, Ellen: only just half a mile? Do say yes, to that clump of birches at the turn!'

I refused staunchly: and, at length, her suspense was ended: the travelling

carriage rolled in sight. Miss Cathy shrieked, and stretched out her arms, as soon as she caught her father's face looking from the window. He descended, nearly as eager as herself; and a considerable interval elapsed ere they had a thought to spare for any but themselves. While they exchanged caresses, I took a peep in to see after Linton. He was asleep in a corner, wrapped in a warm, fur-lined cloak, as if it had been winter. A pale, delicate, effeminate boy, who might have been taken for my master's younger brother, so strong was the resemblance: but there was a sickly peevishness in his aspect that Edgar Linton never had. The latter saw me looking; and having shaken hands, advised me to close the door, and leave him undisturbed; for the journey had fatigued him. Cathy would fain have taken one glance, but her father told her to come on, and they walked together up the park, while I hastened before to prepare the servants.

'Now, darling,' said Mr Linton, addressing his daughter, as they halted at the bottom of the front steps: 'your cousin is not so strong or so merry as you are, and he has lost his mother, remember, a very short time since; therefore, don't expect him to play and run about with you directly. And don't harass him much by talking: let him be quiet this evening, at least, will you?

'Yes, yes, papa,' answered Catherine: 'but I do want to see him; and he hasn't once looked out.'

The carriage stopped; and the sleeper, being roused, was lifted to the ground by his uncle.

'This is your cousin Cathy, Linton,' he said, putting their little hands together. 'She's fond of you already; and mind you don't grieve her by crying tonight. Try to be cheerful now; the travelling is at an end, and you have nothing to do but rest and amuse yourself as you please.'

'Let me go to bed, then,' answered the boy, shrinking from Catherine's salute; and he put his fingers to his eyes to remove incipient tears.

'Come, come, there's a good child,' I whispered, leading him in. 'You'll make her weep too – see how sorry she is for you!'

I do not know whether it were sorrow for him, but his cousin put on as sad a countenance as himself, and returned to her father. All three entered, and mounted to the library, where tea was laid ready. I proceeded to remove Linton's cap and mantle, and placed him on a chair by the table; but he was no sooner seated than he began to cry afresh. My master enquired what was the matter.

'I can't sit on a chair,' sobbed the boy.

'Go to the sofa, then, and Ellen shall bring you some tea,' answered his uncle, patiently.

He had been greatly tried during the journey, I felt convinced, by his fretful ailing charge. Linton slowly trailed himself off, and lay down. Cathy carried a footstool and her cup to his side. At first she sat silent; but that could not last: she had resolved to make a pet of her little cousin, as she would have him to be; and she commenced stroking his curls, and kissing his cheek, and offering him tea in her saucer, like a baby. This pleased him, for he was not much better: he dried his eyes, and lightened into a faint smile.

'Oh, he'll do very well,' said the master to me, after watching them a minute. 'Very well, if we can keep him, Ellen. The company of a child of his own age will instil new spirit into him soon, and by wishing for strength he'll gain it.'

'Ay, if we can keep him!' I mused to myself; and sore misgivings came over me that there was slight hope of that. And then, I thought, however will that weakling live at Wuthering Heights, between his father and Hareton? what playmates and instructors they'll be. Our doubts were presently decided – even earlier than I expected. I had just taken the children upstairs, after tea was finished, and seen Linton asleep – he would not suffer me to leave him till that was the case – I had come down, and was standing by the table in the hall, lighting a bedroom candle for Mr Edgar, when a maid stepped out of the kitchen and informed me that Mr Heathcliff's servant Joseph was at the door, and wished to speak with the master.

'I shall ask him what he wants first,' I said, in considerable trepidation. 'A very unlikely hour to be troubling people, and the instant they have returned from a long journey. I don't think the master can see him.'

Joseph had advanced through the kitchen as I uttered these words, and now presented himself in the hall. He was donned in his Sunday garments, with his most sanctimonious and sourest face, and, holding his hat in one hand and his stick in the other, he proceeded to clean his shoes on the mat.

'Good-evening, Joseph,' I said, coldly. 'What business brings you here tonight?'

'It's Maister Linton Aw mun spake tull,' he answered, waving me disdainfully aside.

'Mr Linton is going to bed; unless you have something particular to say, I'm sure he won't hear it now,' I continued. 'You had better sit down in there, and entrust your message to me.'

'Which is his rahm?' pursued the fellow, surveying the range of closed doors.

I perceived he was bent on refusing my mediation, so very reluctantly I went up to the library, and announced the unseasonable visitor, advising that he should be dismissed till next day. Mr Linton had no time to empower me to do so, for he mounted close at my heels, and, pushing into the apartment, planted himself at the far side of the table, with his two fists clapped on the head of his stick, and began in an elevated tone, as if anticipating opposition – 'Hathecliff has send me for his lad, un Aw munn't goa back 'baht him.'

Edgar Linton was silent a minute; an expression of exceeding sorrow overcast his features: he would have pitied the child on his own account; but, recalling Isabella's hopes and fears, and anxious wishes for her son, and her commendations of him to his care, he grieved bitterly at the prospect of yielding him up, and searched in his heart how it might be avoided. No plan offered itself: the very exhibition of any desire to keep him would have rendered the claimant more peremptory: there was nothing left but to resign him. However, he was not going to rouse him from his sleep.

'Tell Mr Heathcliff,' he answered, calmly, 'that his son shall come to

Wuthering Heights tomorrow. He is in bed, and too tired to go the distance now. You may also tell him that the mother of Linton desired him to remain under my guardianship; and, at present, his health is very precarious.'

'Noa!' said Joseph, giving a thud with his prop on the floor, and assuming an authoritative air. 'Noa! that manes nowt – Hathecliff maks noa 'cahnt uh t' mother, nur yah norther; Bud he'll hev his lad; und Aw mun tak him – soa nah yah knaw!'

'You shall not tonight!' answered Linton, decisively. 'Walk downstairs at once, and repeat to your master what I have said. Ellen, show him down. Go –'

And, aiding the indignant elder with a lift by the arm, he rid the room of him, and closed the door.

'Varrah weel!' shouted Joseph, as he slowly drew off. 'Tuh morn, he's come hisseln, un'thrust *him* aht, if yah darr!'

## *Chapter 20*

To obviate the danger of this threat being fulfilled, Mr Linton commissioned me to take the boy home early, on Catherine's pony; and, said he – 'As we shall now have no influence over his destiny, good or bad, you must say nothing of where he is gone to my daughter: she cannot associate with him hereafter, and it is better for her to remain in ignorance of his proximity; lest she should be restless, and anxious to visit the Heights – merely tell her, his father sent for him suddenly, and he has been obliged to leave us.'

Linton was very reluctant to be roused from his bed at five o'clock, and astonished to be informed that he must prepare for further travelling; but I softened off the matter by stating that he was going to spend some time with his father, Mr Heathcliff, who wished to see him so much, he did not like to defer the pleasure till he should recover from his late journey.

'My father!' he cried, in strange perplexity. 'Mamma never told me I had a father. Where does he live? I'd rather stay with uncle.'

'He lives a little distance from the Grange,' I replied; 'just beyond those hills: not so far, but you may walk over here when you get hearty. And you should be glad to go home, and to see him. You must try to love him, as you did your mother, and then he will love you.'

'But why have I not heard of him before?' asked Linton. 'Why didn't mamma and he live together, as other people do?'

'He had business to keep him in the north,' I answered, 'and your mother's health required her to reside in the south.'

'And why didn't mamma speak to me about him?' persevered the child. 'She often talked of uncle, and I learnt to love him long ago. How am I to love papa? I don't know him.'

'Oh, all children love their parents,' I said. 'Your mother, perhaps, thought you would want to be with him if she mentioned him often to you. Let us make

haste. An early ride on such a beautiful morning is much preferable to an hour's more sleep.'

'Is *she* to go with us,' he demanded: 'the little girl I saw yesterday?'

'Not now,' replied I.

'Is uncle?' he continued.

'No, I shall be your companion there,' I said.

Linton sank back on his pillow, and fell into a brown study.

'I won't go without uncle,' he cried at length; 'I can't tell where you mean to take me.'

I attempted to persuade him of the naughtiness of showing reluctance to meet his father; still he obstinately resisted any progress towards dressing, and I had to call for my master's assistance in coaxing him out of bed. The poor thing was finally got off with several delusive assurances that his absence should be short; that Mr Edgar and Cathy would visit him, and other promises, equally ill-founded, which I invented and reiterated at intervals throughout the way. The pure heather-scented air, and the bright sunshine, and the gentle canter of Minny, relieved his despondency, after a while. He began to put questions concerning his new home, and its inhabitants, with greater interest and liveliness.

'Is Wuthering Heights as pleasant a place as Thrushcross Grange?' he enquired, turning to take a last glance into the valley, whence a light mist mounted and formed a fleecy cloud on the skirts of the blue.

'It is not so buried in trees,' I replied, 'and it is not quite so large, but you can see the country beautifully, all round; and the air is healthier for you – fresher and dryer. You will, perhaps, think the building old and dark at first; though it is a respectable house: the next best in the neighbourhood. And you will have such nice rambles on the moors. Hareton Earnshaw – that is Miss Cathy's other cousin, and so yours in a manner – will show you all the sweetest spots; and you can bring a book in fine weather, and make a green hollow your study; and, now and then, your uncle may join you in a walk: he does, frequently, walk out on the hills.'

'And what is my father like?' he asked. 'Is he as young and handsome as uncle?'

'He's as young,' said I; 'but he has black hair and eyes, and looks sterner; and he is taller and bigger altogether. He'll not seem to you so gentle and kind at first, perhaps, because it is not his way – still, mind you be frank and cordial with him; and naturally he'll be fonder of you than any uncle, for you are his own.'

'Black hair and eyes!' mused Linton. 'I can't fancy him. Then I am not like him, am I?'

'Not much,' I answered . . . not a morsel, I thought, surveying with regret the white complexion and slim frame of my companion, and his large languid eyes . . . his mother's eyes, save that, unless a morbid touchiness kindled them a moment, they had not a vestige of her sparkling spirit.

'How strange that he should never come to see mama, and me!' he murmured. 'Has he ever seen me? If he have, I must have been a baby – I remember not a single thing about him!'

'Why, Master Linton,' said I, 'three hundred miles is a great distance; and ten

years seem very different in length to a grown-up person compared with what they do to you. It is probable Mr Heathcliff proposed going, from summer to summer, but never found a convenient opportunity; and now it is too late. Don't trouble him with questions on the subject: it will disturb him for no good.'

The boy was fully occupied with his own cogitations for the remainder of the ride, till we halted before the farmhouse garden gate. I watched to catch his impressions in his countenance. He surveyed the carved front and low-browed lattices, the straggling gooseberry bushes and crooked firs, with solemn intentness, and then shook his head: his private feelings entirely disapproved of the exterior of his new abode. But he had sense to postpone complaining: there might be compensation within. Before he dismounted, I went and opened the door. It was half-past six; the family had just finished breakfast; the servant was clearing and wiping down the table: Joseph stood by his master's chair telling some tale concerning a lame horse; and Hareton was preparing for the hayfield.

'Hallo, Nelly!' cried Mr Heathcliff, when he saw me. 'I feared I should have to come down and fetch my property myself. You've brought it, have you? Let us see what we can make of it.'

He got up and strode to the door: Hareton and Joseph followed in gaping curiosity. Poor Linton ran a frightened eye over the faces of the three.

'Sure–ly,' said Joseph after a grave inspection, 'he's swopped wi' ye, maister, an' yon's his lass!'

Heathcliff, having stared his son into an ague of confusion, uttered a scornful laugh.

'God! What a beauty! What a lovely, charming thing!' he exclaimed. 'Haven't they reared it on snails and sour milk, Nelly? Oh, damn my soul! But that's worse than I expected – and the devil knows I was not sanguine!'

I bid the trembling and bewildered child get down, and enter. He did not thoroughly comprehend the meaning of his father's speech, or whether it were intended for him: indeed, he was not yet certain that the grim, sneering stranger was his father; but he clung to me with growing trepidation; and on Mr Heathcliff's taking a seat, and bidding him 'come hither', he hid his face on my shoulder, and wept.

'Tut, tut!' said Heathcliff, stretching out a hand and dragging him roughly between his knees, and then holding up his head by the chin. 'None of that nonsense! We're not going to hurt thee, Linton – isn't that thy name? Thou art thy mother's child, entirely! Where is *my* share in thee, puling chicken?'

He took off the boy's cap and pushed back his thick flaxen curls, felt his slender arms and his small fingers; during which examination Linton ceased crying, and lifted his great blue eyes to inspect the inspector.

'Do you know me?' asked Heathcliff, having satisfied himself that the limbs were all equally frail and feeble.

'No,' said Linton, with a gaze of vacant fear.

'You've heard of me, I dare say?'

'No,' he replied again.

'No? What a shame of your mother, never to waken your filial regard for me!

You are my son, then, I'll tell you; and your mother was a wicked slut to leave you in ignorance of the sort of father you possessed. Now, don't wince, and colour up! Though it *is* something to see you have not white blood. Be a good lad; and I'll do for you. Nelly, if you be tired you may sit down; if not, get home again. I guess you'll report what you hear, and see, to the cipher at the Grange; and this thing won't be settled while you linger about it.'

'Well,' replied I, 'I hope you'll be kind to the boy, Mr Heathcliff, or you'll not keep him long; and he's all you have akin in the wide world, that you will ever know – remember.'

'I'll be *very* kind to him, you needn't fear,' he said, laughing. 'Only nobody else must be kind to him: I'm jealous of monopolising his affection. And, to begin my kindness, Joseph! Bring the lad some breakfast. Hareton, you infernal calf, begone to your work. Yes, Nell,' he added when they had departed, 'my son is prospective owner of your place, and I should not wish him to die till I was certain of being his successor. Besides, he's *mine*, and I want the triumph of seeing *my* descendant fairly lord of their estates: my child hiring their children to till their fathers' lands for wages. That is the sole consideration which can make me endure the whelp: I despise him for himself, and hate him for the memories he revives! But that consideration is sufficient: he's as safe with me, and shall be tended as carefully as your master tends his own. I have a room upstairs, furnished for him in handsome style; I've engaged a tutor, also, to come three times a week, from twenty miles distance, to teach him what he pleases to learn. I've ordered Hareton to obey him: and in fact I've arranged everything with a view to preserve the superior and the gentleman in him, above his associates. I do regret, however, that he so little deserves the trouble: if I wished any blessing in the world, it was to find him a worthy object of pride; and I'm bitterly disappointed with the wheyfaced whining wretch!'

While he was speaking, Joseph returned, bearing a basin of milk-porridge, and placed it before Linton. He stirred round the homely mess with a look of aversion, and affirmed he could not eat it. I saw the old manservant shared largely in his master's scorn of the child; though he was compelled to retain the sentiment in his heart, because Heathcliff plainly meant his underlings to hold him in honour.

'Cannot ate it?' repeated he, peering in Linton's face, and subduing his voice to a whisper, for fear of being overheard. 'But Maister Hareton nivir ate nowt else, when he wer a little un: und what wer gooid eneugh fur him's gooid eneugh fur yah, Aw's rayther think!'

'I *shan't* eat it!' answered Linton, snappishly. 'Take it away.'

Joseph snatched up the food indignantly, and brought it to us.

'Is there owt ails th' victuals?' he asked, thrusting the tray under Heathcliff's nose.

'What should ail them?' he said.

'Wah!' answered Joseph, 'yon dainty chap says he cannut ate 'em. Bud Aw guess it's raight! His mother wer just soa – we wer a'most too mucky tuh sow t' corn fur makking her breead.'

'Don't mention his mother to me,' said the master, angrily. 'Get him something that he can eat, that's all. What is his usual food, Nelly?'

I suggested boiled milk or tea; and the housekeeper received instructions to prepare some. Come, I reflected, his father's selfishness may contribute to his comfort. He perceives his delicate constitution, and the necessity of treating him tolerably. I'll console Mr Edgar by acquainting him with the turn Heathcliff's humour has taken. Having no excuse for lingering longer, I slipped out, while Linton was engaged in timidly rebuffing the advances of a friendly sheepdog. But he was too much on the alert to be cheated: as I closed the door, I heard a cry, and a frantic repetition of the words – 'Don't leave me! I'll not stay here! I'll not stay here!'

Then the latch was raised and fell: they did not suffer him to come forth. I mounted Minny, and urged her to a trot; and so my brief guardianship ended.

## Chapter 21

We had sad work with little Cathy that day: she rose in high glee, eager to join her cousin; and such passionate tears and lamentations followed the news of his departure, that Edgar himself was obliged to sooth her, by affirming he should come back soon: he added, however, 'if I can get him'; and there were no hopes of that. This promise poorly pacified her; but time was more potent; and though still at intervals she enquired of her father when Linton would return, before she did see him again his features had waxed so dim in her memory that she did not recognise him.

When I chanced to encounter the housekeeper of Wuthering Heights, in paying business-visits to Gimmerton, I used to ask how the young master got on; for he lived almost as secluded as Catherine herself, and was never to be seen. I could gather from her that he continued in weak health, and was a tiresome inmate. She said Mr Heathcliff seemed to dislike him ever longer and worse, though he took some trouble to conceal it. He had an antipathy to the sound of his voice, and could not do at all with his sitting in the same room with him many minutes together. There seldom passed much talk between them: Linton learnt his lessons and spent his evenings in a small apartment they called the parlour: or else lay in bed all day: for he was constantly getting coughs, and colds, and aches, and pains of some sort.

'And I never knew such a fainthearted creature,' added the woman; 'nor one so careful of hisseln. He *will* go on, if I leave the window open a bit late in the evening. Oh! it's killing, a breath of night air! And he must have a fire in the middle of summer; and Joseph's bacca pipe is poison; and he must always have sweets and dainties, and always milk, milk for ever – heeding naught how the rest of us are pinched in winter; and there he'll sit, wrapped in his furred cloak in his chair by the fire, and some toast and water or other slop on the hob to sip at; and if Hareton, for pity, comes to amuse him – Hareton is not bad-natured,

though he's rough – they're sure to part, one swearing and the other crying. I believe the master would relish Earnshaw's thrashing him to a mummy, if he were not his son; and I'm certain he would be fit to turn him out of doors, if he knew half the nursing he gives hisseln. But then, he won't go into danger of temptation: he never enters the parlour, and should Linton show those ways in the house where he is, he sends him upstairs directly.'

I divined, from this account, that utter lack of sympathy had rendered young Heathcliff selfish and disagreeable, if he were not so originally; and my interest in him, consequently, decayed: though still I was moved with a sense of grief at his lot, and a wish that he had been left with us.

Mr Edgar encouraged me to gain information: he thought a great deal about him, I fancy, and would have run some risk to see him; and he told me once to ask the housekeeper whether he ever came into the village? She said he had only been twice, on horseback, accompanying his father; and both times he pretended to be quite knocked up for three or four days afterwards. That housekeeper left, if I recollect rightly, two years after he came; and another, whom I did not know, was her successor: she lives there still.

Time wore on at the Grange in its former pleasant way, till Miss Cathy reached sixteen. On the anniversary of her birth we never manifested any signs of rejoicing, because it was also the anniversary of my late mistress's death. Her father invariably spent that day alone in the library; and walked, at dusk, as far as Gimmerton kirkyard, where he would frequently prolong his stay beyond midnight. Therefore Catherine was thrown on her own resources for amusement.

This twentieth of March was a beautiful spring day, and when her father had retired, my young lady came down dressed for going out, and said she had asked to have a ramble on the edge of the moors with me; and Mr Linton had given her leave, if we went only a short distance and were back within the hour.

'So make haste, Ellen!' she cried. 'I know where I wish to go; where a colony of moor-game are settled: I want to see whether they have made their nests yet.'

'That must be a good distance up,' I answered; 'they don't breed on the edge of the moor.'

'No, it's not,' she said. 'I've gone very near with papa.'

I put on my bonnet and sallied out, thinking nothing more of the matter. She bounded before me, and returned to my side, and was off again like a young greyhound; and, at first, I found plenty of entertainment in listening to the larks singing far and near, and enjoying the sweet, warm sunshine; and watching her, my pet, and my delight, with her golden ringlets flying loose behind, and her bright cheek, as soft and pure in its bloom as a wild rose, and her eyes radiant with cloudless pleasure. She was a happy creature, and an angel, in those days. It's a pity she could not be content.

'Well,' said I, 'where are your moor-game, Miss Cathy? We should be at them: the Grange park-fence is a great way off now.'

'Oh, a little farther – only a little farther, Ellen,' was her answer, continually. 'Climb to that hillock, pass that bank, and by the time you reach the other side I shall have raised the birds.'

But there were so many hillocks and banks to climb and pass, that, at length, I began to be weary, and told her we must halt, and retrace our steps. I shouted to her, as she had outstripped me, a long way; she either did not hear or did not regard, for she still sprang on, and I was compelled to follow. Finally, she dived into a hollow; and before I came in sight of her again, she was two miles nearer Wuthering Heights than her own home; and I beheld a couple of persons arrest her, one of whom I felt convinced was Mr Heathcliff himself.

Cathy had been caught in the fact of plundering, or, at least, hunting out the nests of the grouse. The Heights were Heathcliff's land, and he was reproving the poacher.

'I've neither taken any nor found any,' she said, as I toiled to them, expanding her hands in corroboration of the statement. 'I didn't mean to take them; but papa told me there were quantities up here, and I wished to see the eggs.'

Heathcliff glanced at me with an ill-meaning smile, expressing his acquaintance with the party, and, consequently, his malevolence towards it, and demanded who 'papa' was?

'Mr Linton of Thrushcross Grange,' she replied. 'I thought you did not know me, or you wouldn't have spoken in that way.'

'You suppose papa is highly esteemed and respected, then?' he said, sarcastically.

'And what are you?' enquired Catherine, gazing curiously on the speaker. 'That man I've seen before. Is he your son?'

She pointed to Hareton, the other individual, who had gained nothing but increased bulk and strength by the addition of two years to his age: he seemed as awkward and rough as ever.

'Miss Cathy,' I interrupted, 'it will be three hours instead of one that we are out, presently. We really must go back.'

'No, that man is not my son,' answered Heathcliff, pushing me aside. 'But I have one, and you have seen him before, too; and, though your nurse is in a hurry, I think both you and she would be the better for a little rest. Will you just turn this nab of heath, and walk into my house ? You'll get home earlier for the ease; and you shall receive a kind welcome.'

I whispered Catherine that she mustn't, on any account, accede to the proposal: it was entirely out of the question.

'Why?' she asked, aloud. 'I'm tired of running, and the ground is dewy: I can't sit here. Let us go, Ellen. Besides, he says I have seen his son. He's mistaken, I think; but I guess where he lives: at the farmhouse I visited in coming from Penistone Craggs. Don't you?'

'I do. Come, Nelly, hold your tongue – it will be a treat for her to look in on us. Hareton, get forwards with the lass. You shall walk with me, Nelly.'

'No, she's not going to any such place,' I cried, struggling to release my arm, which he had seized: but she was almost at the door-stones already, scampering round the brow at full speed. Her appointed companion did not pretend to escort her: he shied off by the roadside, and vanished.

'Mr Heathcliff, it's very wrong,' I continued: 'you know you mean no good.

And there she'll see Linton, and all will be told, as soon as ever we return; and I shall have the blame.'

'I want her to see Linton,' he answered; 'he's looking better these few days: it's not often he's fit to be seen. And we'll soon persuade her to keep the visit secret: where is the harm of it?'

'The harm of it is, that her father would hate me if he found I suffered her to enter your house; and I am convinced you have a bad design in encouraging her to do so,' I replied.

'My design is as honest as possible. I'll inform you of its whole scope,' he said. 'That the two cousins may fall in love, and get married. I'm acting generously to your master: his young chit has no expectations, and should she second my wishes, she'll be provided for at once as joint successor with Linton.'

'If Linton died,' I answered, 'and his life is quite uncertain, Catherine would be the heir.'

'No, she would not,' he said. 'There is no clause in the will to secure it so: his property would go to me; but, to prevent disputes, I desire their union, and am resolved to bring it about.'

'And I'm resolved she shall never approach your house with me again,' I returned, as we reached the gate, where Miss Cathy waited our coming.

Heathcliff bid me be quiet; and, preceding us up the path, hastened to open the door. My young lady gave him several looks, as if she could not exactly make up her mind what to think of him; but now he smiled when he met her eye, and softened his voice in addressing her; and I was foolish enough to imagine the memory of her mother might disarm him from desiring her injury. Linton stood on the hearth. He had been out, walking in the fields, for his cap was on, and he was calling to Joseph to bring him dry shoes. He had grown tall of his age, still wanting some months of sixteen. His features were pretty yet, and his eye and complexion brighter than I remembered them, though with merely temporary lustre borrowed from the salubrious air and genial sun.

'Now, who is that?' asked Mr Heathcliff, turning to Cathy. 'Can you tell?'

'Your son?' she said, having doubtfully surveyed, first one and then the other.

'Yes, yes,' answered he: 'but is this the only time you have beheld him? Think! Ah! you have a short memory. Linton, don't you recall your cousin, that you used to tease us so with wishing to see?'

'What, Linton!' cried Cathy, kindling into joyful surprise at the name. 'Is that little Linton? He's taller than I am! Are you, Linton?'

The youth stepped forward, and acknowledged himself: she kissed him fervently, and they gazed with wonder at the change time had wrought in the appearance of each. Catherine had reached her full height; her figure was both plump and slender, elastic as steel, and her whole aspect sparkling with health and spirits. Linton's looks and movements were very languid, and his form extremely slight; but there was a grace in his manner that mitigated these defects, and rendered him not unpleasing. After exchanging numerous marks of fondness with him, his cousin went to Mr Heathcliff, who lingered by the door, dividing his attention between the objects inside and those that lay

without: pretending, that is, to observe the latter, and really noting the former alone.

'And you are my uncle, then!' she cried, reaching up to salute him. 'I thought I liked you, though you were cross, at first. Why don't you visit at the Grange with Linton? To live all these years such close neighbours, and never see us, is odd: what have you done so for?'

'I visited it once or twice too often before you were born,' he answered. 'There – damn it! If you have any kisses to spare, give them to Linton: they are thrown away on me.'

'Naughty Ellen!' exclaimed Catherine, flying to attack me next with her lavish caresses. 'Wicked Ellen! to try to hinder me from entering. But I'll take this walk every morning in future: may I, uncle? And sometimes bring papa. Won't you be glad to see us?'

'Of course!' replied the uncle, with a hardly suppressed grimace, resulting from his deep aversion to both the proposed visitors. 'But stay,' he continued, turning towards the young lady. 'Now I think of it, I'd better tell you. Mr Linton has a prejudice against me: we quarrelled at one time of our lives, with unchristian ferocity; and, if you mention coming here to him, he'll put a veto on your visits altogether. Therefore, you must not mention it, unless you be careless of seeing your cousin hereafter: you may come, if you will, but you must not mention it.'

'Why did you quarrel?' asked Catherine, considerably crestfallen.

'He thought me too poor to wed his sister,' answered Heathcliff, 'and was grieved that I got her: his pride was hurt, and he'll never forgive it.'

'That's wrong!' said the young lady: 'some time, I'll tell him so. But Linton and I have no share in your quarrel. I'll not come here, then; he shall come to the Grange.'

'It will be too far for me,' murmured her cousin: 'to walk four miles would kill me. No, come here, Miss Catherine, now and then: not every morning, but once or twice a week.'

The father launched towards his son a glance of bitter contempt.

'I am afraid, Nelly, I shall lose my labour,' he muttered to me. 'Miss Catherine, as the ninny calls her, will discover his value, and send him to the devil. Now, if it had been Hareton! – Do you know that, twenty times a day, I covet Hareton, with all his degradation? I'd have loved the lad had he been someone else. But I think he's safe from *her* love. I'll pit him against that paltry creature, unless it bestir itself briskly. We calculate it will scarcely last till it is eighteen. Oh, confound the vapid thing! He's absorbed in drying his feet, and never looks at her – Linton!'

'Yes, father,' answered the boy.

'Have you nothing to show your cousin, anywhere about; not even a rabbit, or a weasel's nest? Take her into the garden, before you change your shoes; and into the stable to see your horse.'

'Wouldn't you rather sit here?' asked Linton, addressing Cathy in a tone which expressed reluctance to move again.

'I don't know,' she replied, casting a longing look to the door, and evidently eager to be active.

He kept his seat, and shrank closer to the fire. Heathcliff rose, and went into the kitchen, and from thence to the yard, calling out for Hareton. Hareton responded, and presently the two re-entered. The young man had been washing himself, as was visible by the glow on his cheeks, and his wetted hair.

'Oh, I'll ask *you*, uncle,' cried Miss Cathy, recollecting the housekeeper's assertion. 'That is not my cousin, is he?'

'Yes,' he replied, 'your mother's nephew. Don't you like him?'

Catherine looked queer.

'Is he not a handsome lad?' he continued.

The uncivil little thing stood on tiptoe, and whispered a sentence in Heathcliff's ear. He laughed; Hareton darkened: I perceived he was very sensitive to suspected slights, and had obviously a dim notion of his inferiority. But his master or guardian chased the frown by exclaiming – 'You'll be the favourite among us, Hareton! She says you are a – what was it? Well, something very flattering. Here! you go with her round the farm. And behave like a gentleman, mind! Don't use any bad words; and don't stare, when the young lady is not looking at you, and be ready to hide your face when she is; and, when you speak, say your words slowly, and keep your hands out of your pockets. Be off, and entertain her as nicely as you can.'

He watched the couple walking past the window. Earnshaw had his countenance completely averted from his companion. He seemed studying the familiar landscape with a stranger's and an artist's interest. Catherine took a sly look at him, expressing small admiration. She then turned her attention to seeking out objects of amusement for herself, and tripped merrily on, lilting a tune to supply the lack of conversation.

'I've tied his tongue,' observed Heathcliff. 'He'll not venture a single syllable, all the time! Nelly, you recollect me at his age – nay, some years younger. Did I ever look so stupid: so "gaumless", as Joseph calls it?'

'Worse,' I replied, 'because more sullen with it.'

'I've a pleasure in him,' he continued reflecting aloud. 'He has satisfied my expectations. If he were a born fool I should not enjoy it half so much. But he's no fool; and I can sympathise with all his feelings, having felt them myself. I know what he suffers now, for instance, exactly: it is merely a beginning of what he shall suffer, though. And he'll never be able to emerge from his bathos of coarseness and ignorance. I've got him faster than his scoundrel of a father secured me, and lower; for he takes a pride in his brutishness. I've taught him to scorn everything extra animal as silly and weak. Don't you think Hindley would be proud of his son, if he could see him? almost as proud as I am of mine. But there's this difference; one is gold put to the use of paving-stones, and the other is tin polished to ape a service of silver. *Mine* has nothing valuable about it; yet I shall have the merit of making it go as far as such poor stuff can go. *His* had first rate qualities, and they are lost: rendered worse than unavailing. I have nothing to regret; he would have more than any, but I, are aware of. And the best of it is,

Hareton is damnably fond of me! You'll own that I've out-matched Hindley there. If the dead villain could rise from his grave to abuse me for his offspring's wrongs, I should have the fun of seeing the said offspring fight him back again, indignant that he should dare to rail at the one friend he has in the world!'

Heathcliff chuckled a fiendish laugh at the idea. I made no reply, because I saw that he expected none. Meantime, our young companion, who sat too removed from us to hear what was said, began to evince symptoms of uneasiness, probably repenting that he had denied himself the treat of Catherine's society for fear of a little fatigue. His father remarked the restless glances wandering to the window, and the hand irresolutely extended towards his cap.

'Get up, you idle boy!' he exclaimed with assumed heartiness. 'Away after them! they are just at the corner, by the stand of hives.'

Linton gathered his energies, and left the hearth. The lattice was open, and, as he stepped out, I heard Cathy enquiring of her unsociable attendant, what was that inscription over the door? Hareton stared up, and scratched his head like a true clown.

'It's some damnable writing,' he answered. 'I cannot read it.'

'Can't read it?' cried Catherine; 'I can read it: it's English. But I want to know why it is there.'

Linton giggled – the first appearance of mirth he had exhibited.

'He does not know his letters,' he said to his cousin. 'Could you believe in the existence of such a colossal dunce?'

'Is he all as he should be?' asked Miss Cathy seriously; 'or is he simple: not right? I've questioned him twice now, and each time he looked so stupid I think he does not understand me. I can hardly understand *him*, I'm sure!'

Linton repeated his laugh, and glanced at Hareton tauntingly; who certainly did not seem quite clear of comprehension at that moment.

'There's nothing the matter, but laziness, is there, Earnshaw?' he said. 'My cousin fancies you are an idiot. There you experience the consequence of scorning "book-larning", as you would say. Have you noticed, Catherine, his frightful Yorkshire pronunciation?'

'Why, where the devil is the use on 't?' growled Hareton, more ready in answering his daily companion. He was about to enlarge further, but the two youngsters broke into a noisy fit of merriment; my giddy miss being delighted to discover that she might turn his strange talk to matter of amusement.

'Where is the use of the devil in that sentence?' tittered Linton. 'Papa told you not to say any bad words, and you can't open your mouth without one. Do try to behave like a gentleman, now do!'

'If thou wern't more a lass than a lad, I'd fell thee this minute, I would; pitiful lath of a crater!' retorted the angry boor, retreating, while his face burnt with mingled rage and mortification; for he was conscious of being insulted, and embarrassed how to resent it.

Mr Heathcliff having overheard the conversation, as well as I, smiled when he saw him go; but immediately afterwards cast a look of singular aversion on the flippant pair, who remained chattering in the doorway: the boy finding

animation enough while discussing Hareton's faults and deficiencies, and relating anecdotes of his goings on; and the girl relishing his pert and spiteful sayings, without considering the ill-nature they evinced: but I began to dislike, more than to compassionate, Linton, and to excuse his father, in some measure, for holding him cheap.

We stayed till afternoon: I could not tear Miss Cathy away, before; but happily my master had not quitted his apartment, and remained ignorant of our prolonged absence. As we walked home, I would fain have enlightened my charge on the characters of the people we had quitted; but she got it into her head that I was prejudiced against them.

'Aha!' she cried, 'you take papa's side, Ellen: you are partial, I know; or else you wouldn't have cheated me so many years into the notion that Linton lived a long way from here. I'm really extremely angry, only, I'm so pleased, I can't show it! But you must hold your tongue about my uncle: he's *my* uncle, remember; and I'll scold papa for quarrelling with him.'

And so she ran on, till I dropped endeavouring to convince her of her mistake. She did not mention the visit that night, because she did not see Mr Linton. Next day it all came out, sadly to my chagrin; and still I was not altogether sorry: I thought the burden of directing and warning would be more efficiently borne by him than me, but he was too timid in giving satisfactory reasons for his wish that she would shun connection with the household of the Heights, and Catherine liked good reasons for every restraint that harassed her petted will.

'Papa!' she exclaimed, after the morning's salutations, 'guess whom I saw yesterday, in my walk on the moors. Ah, papa, you started! You've not done right, have you, now? I saw – But listen, and you shall hear how I found you out, and Ellen, who is in league with you, and yet pretended to pity me so, when I kept hoping, and was always disappointed about Linton's coming back!'

She gave a faithful account of her excursion and its consequences; and my master, though he cast more than one reproachful look at me, said nothing till she had concluded. Then he drew her to him, and asked if she knew why he had concealed Linton's near neighbourhood from her? Could she think it was to deny her a pleasure that she might harmlessly enjoy?

'It was because you disliked Mr Heathcliff,' she answered.

'Then you believe I care more for my own feelings than yours, Cathy?' he said. 'No, it was not because I disliked Mr Heathcliff, but because Mr Heathcliff dislikes me; and is a most diabolical man, delighting to wrong and ruin those he hates, if they give him the slightest opportunity. I knew that you could not keep up an acquaintance with your cousin, without being brought into contact with him; and I knew he would detest you, on my account; so for your own good, and nothing else, I took precautions that you should not see Linton again. I meant to explain this some time as you grew older, and I'm sorry I delayed it.'

'But Mr Heathcliff was quite cordial, papa,' observed Catherine, not at all convinced; 'and *he* didn't object to our seeing each other: he said I might come to his house when I pleased; only I must not tell you, because you had quarrelled

with him, and would not forgive him for marrying Aunt Isabella. And you won't. *You* are the one to be blamed: he is willing to let *us* be friends, at least; Linton and I; and you are not.'

My master, perceiving that she would not take his word for her uncle-in-law's evil disposition, gave a hasty sketch of his conduct to Isabella, and the manner in which Wuthering Heights became his property. He could not bear to discourse long upon the topic; for though he spoke little of it, he still felt the same horror and detestation of his ancient enemy that had occupied his heart ever since Mrs Linton's death. 'She might have been living yet, if it had not been for him!' was his constant bitter reflection; and, in his eyes, Heathcliff seemed a murderer. Miss Cathy – conversant with no bad deeds except her own slight acts of disobedience, injustice, and passion, rising from hot temper and thoughtlessness, and repented of on the day they were committed – was amazed at the blackness of spirit that could brood on and cover revenge for years, and deliberately prosecute its plans without a visitation of remorse. She appeared so deeply impressed and shocked at this new view of human nature – excluded from all her studies and all her ideas till now – that Mr Edgar deemed it unnecessary to pursue the subject. He merely added – 'You will know hereafter, darling, why I wish you to avoid his house and family; now, return to your old employments and amusements, and think no more about them!'

Catherine kissed her father, and sat down quietly to her lessons for a couple of hours, according to custom; then she accompanied him into the grounds, and the whole day passed as usual: but in the evening, when she had retired to her room, and I went to help her to undress, I found her crying, on her knees by the bedside.

'Oh, fie, silly child!' I exclaimed. 'If you had any real griefs, you'd be ashamed to waste a tear on this little contrariety. You never had one shadow of substantial sorrow, Miss Catherine. Suppose, for a minute, that master and I were dead, and you were by yourself in the world: how would you feel then? Compare the present occasion with such an affliction as that, and be thankful for the friends you have, instead of coveting more.'

'I'm not crying for myself, Ellen,' she answered, 'it's for him. He expected to see me again tomorrow, and there, he'll be so disappointed: and he'll wait for me, and I shan't come!'

'Nonsense!' said I, 'do you imagine he has thought as much of you as you have of him? Hasn't he Hareton for a companion? Not one in a hundred would weep at losing a relation they had just seen twice, for two afternoons. Linton will conjecture how it is, and trouble himself no further about you.'

'But may I not write a note to tell him why I cannot come?' she asked, rising to her feet. 'And just send those books I promised to lend him? His books are not as nice as mine, and he wanted to have them extremely, when I told him how interesting they were. May I not, Ellen?'

'No, indeed! no, indeed!' replied I with decision. 'Then he would write to you, and there'd never be an end of it. No, Miss Catherine, the acquaintance must be dropped entirely: so papa expects, and I shall see that it is done.'

'But how can one little note – ' she recommenced, putting on an imploring countenance.

'Silence!' I interrupted. 'We'll not begin with your little notes. Get into bed.'

She threw at me a very naughty look, so naughty that I would not kiss her good-night at first: I covered her up, and shut her door, in great displeasure; but, repenting halfway, I returned softly, and lo! there was miss, standing at the table with a bit of blank paper before her and a pencil in her hand, which she guiltily slipped out of sight, on my re-entrance.

'You'll get nobody to take that, Catherine,' I said, 'if you write it; and at present I shall put out your candle.'

I set the extinguisher on the flame, receiving as I did so a slap on my hand, and a petulant 'cross thing!' I then quitted her again, and she drew the bolt in one of her worst, most peevish humours. The letter was finished and forwarded to its destination by a milk-fetcher who came from the village: but that I didn't learn till some time afterwards. Weeks passed on, and Cathy recovered her temper; though she grew wondrous fond of stealing off to corners by herself; and often, if I came near her suddenly while reading, she would start and bend over the book, evidently desirous to hide it; and I detected edges of loose paper sticking out beyond the leaves. She also got a trick of coming down early in the morning, and lingering about the kitchen, as if she were expecting the arrival of something: and she had a small drawer in a cabinet in the library, which she would trifle over for hours, and whose key she took special care to remove when she left it.

One day, as she inspected this drawer, I observed that the playthings and trinkets, which recently formed its contents, were transmuted into bits of folded paper. My curiosity and suspicions were roused; I determined to take a peep at her mysterious treasures; so, at night, as soon as she and my master were safe upstairs, I searched and readily found among my house keys one that would fit the lock. Having opened, I emptied the whole contents into my apron, and took them with me to examine at leisure in my own chamber. Though I could not but suspect, I was still surprised to discover that they were a mass of correspondence – daily, almost, it must have been – from Linton Heathcliff: answers to documents forwarded by her. The earlier dated were embarrassed and short; gradually, however, they expanded into copious love letters, foolish as the age of the writer rendered natural, yet with touches, here and there, which I thought were borrowed from a more experienced source. Some of them struck me as singularly odd compounds of ardour and flatness; commencing in strong feeling, and concluding in the affected, wordy way that a schoolboy might use to a fancied, incorporeal sweetheart. Whether they satisfied Cathy, I don't know; but they appeared very worthless trash to me. After turning over as many as I thought proper, I tied them in a handkerchief and set them aside, re-locking the vacant drawer.

Following her habit, my young lady descended early, and visited the kitchen: I watched her go to the door, on the arrival of a certain little boy; and, while the dairy maid filled his can, she tucked something into his jacket pocket, and

plucked something out. I went round by the garden, and laid wait for the messenger; who fought valorously to defend his trust, and we spilt the milk between us; but I succeeding in abstracting the epistle; and, threatening serious consequences if he did not look sharp home, I remained under the wall and perused Miss Cathy's affectionate composition. It was more simple and more eloquent than her cousin's: very pretty and very silly. I shook my head, and went meditating into the house. The day being wet, she could not divert herself with rambling about the park; so, at the conclusion of her morning studies, she resorted to the solace of the drawer. Her father sat reading at the table; and I, on purpose, had sought a bit of work in some unripped fringes of the window curtain, keeping my eye steadily fixed on her proceedings. Never did any bird flying back to a plundered nest which it had left brimfull of chirping young ones, express more complete despair in its anguished cries and flutterings, than she by her single 'Oh!' and the change that transfigured her late happy countenance. Mr Linton looked up.

'What is the matter, love? Have you hurt yourself?' he said.

His tone and look assured her *he* had not been the discoverer of the hoard.

'No, papa – ' she gasped. 'Ellen! Ellen! Come upstairs – I'm sick!'

I obeyed her summons, and accompanied her out.

'Oh, Ellen! You have got them,' she commenced immediately, dropping on her knees, when we were enclosed alone. 'O, give them to me, and I'll never never do so again! Don't tell papa. You have not told papa, Ellen, say you have not! I've been exceedingly naughty, but I won't do it any more!'

With a grave severity in my manner, I bid her stand up.

'So,' I exclaimed, 'Miss Catherine, you are tolerably far on, it seems: you may well be ashamed of them! A fine bundle of trash you study in your leisure hours, to be sure: why it's good enough to be printed! And what do you suppose the master will think, when I display it before him? I haven't shown it yet, but you needn't imagine I shall keep your ridiculous secrets. For shame! And you must have led the way in writing such absurdities: he would not have thought of beginning, I'm certain.'

'I didn't! I didn't!' sobbed Cathy, fit to break her heart. 'I didn't once think of loving him till – '

'*Loving!*' cried I, as scornfully as I could utter the word. '*Loving!* Did anybody ever hear the like! I might just as well talk of loving the miller who comes once a year to buy our corn. Pretty loving, indeed! and both times together you have seen Linton hardly four hours in your life! Now here is the babyish trash. I'm going with it to the library; and we'll see what your father says to such *loving*.'

She sprang at her precious epistles, but I held them above my head; and then she poured out further frantic entreaties that I would burn them – do anything rather than show them. And being really fully as inclined to laugh as scold – for I esteemed it all girlish vanity – I at length relented in a measure, and asked – 'If I consent to burn them, will you promise faithfully, neither to send nor receive a letter again, nor a book (for I perceive you have sent him books), nor locks of hair, nor rings, nor playthings?'

'We don't send playthings!' cried Catherine, her pride overcoming her shame.

'Nor anything at all, then, my lady!' I said. 'Unless you will, here I go.'

'I promise, Ellen!' she cried, catching my dress. 'Oh, put them in the fire, do, do!'

But when I proceeded to open a place with the poker, the sacrifice was too painful to be borne. She earnestly supplicated that I would spare her one or two.

'One or two, Ellen, to keep for Linton's sake!'

I unknotted the handkerchief, and commenced dropping them in from an angle, and the flame curled up the chimney.

'I will have one, you cruel wretch!' she screamed, darting her hand into the fire, and drawing forth some half consumed fragments, at the expense of her fingers.

'Very well – and I will have some to exhibit to papa!' I answered, shaking back the rest into the bundle, and turning anew to the door.

She emptied her blackened pieces into the flames, and motioned me to finish the immolation. It was done; I stirred up the ashes, and interred them under a shovel full of coals; and she mutely, and with a sense of intense injury, retired to her private apartment. I descended to tell my master that the young lady's qualm of sickness was almost gone, but I judged it best for her to lie down a while. She wouldn't dine; but she reappeared at tea, pale, and red about the eyes, and marvellously subdued in outward aspect.

Next morning, I answered the letter by a slip of paper, inscribed, 'Master Heathcliff is requested to send no more notes to Miss Linton, as she will not receive them.' And, thenceforth, the little boy came with vacant pockets.

## Chapter 22

Summer drew to an end, and early autumn: it was past Michaelmas, but the harvest was late that year, and a few of our fields were still uncleared. Mr Linton and his daughter would frequently walk out among the reapers; at the carrying of the last sheaves, they stayed till dusk, and the evening happening to be chill and damp, my master caught a bad cold, that settling obstinately on his lungs, confined him indoors throughout the whole of the winter, nearly without intermission.

Poor Cathy, frightened from her little romance, had been considerably sadder and duller since its abandonment; and her father insisted on her reading less, and taking more exercise. She had his companionship no longer; I esteemed it a duty to supply its lack, as much as possible, with mine: an inefficient substitute, for I could only spare two or three hours, from my numerous diurnal occupations, to follow her footsteps, and then my society was obviously less desirable than his.

On an afternoon in October, or the beginning of November – a fresh watery afternoon, when the turf and paths were rustling with moist, withered leaves,

and the cold, blue sky was half hidden by clouds – dark grey streamers, rapidly mounting from the west, and boding abundant rain – I requested my young lady to forego her ramble because I was certain of showers. She refused; and I unwillingly donned a cloak, and took my umbrella to accompany her on a stroll to the bottom of the park: a formal walk which she generally affected if low-spirited – and that she invariably was when Mr Edgar had been worse than ordinary; a thing never known from his confession, but guessed both by her and me from his increased silence, and the melancholy of his countenance. She went sadly on: there was no running or bounding now, though the chill wind might well have tempted her to a race. And often, from the side of my eye, I could detect her raising a hand, and brushing something off her cheek. I gazed round for a means of diverting her thoughts. On one side of the road rose a high, rough bank, where hazels and stunted oaks, with their roots half exposed, held uncertain tenure: the soil was too loose for the latter; and strong winds had blown some nearly horizontal. In summer, Miss Catherine delighted to climb along these trunks, and sit in the branches, swinging twenty feet above the ground; and I, pleased with her agility and her light, childish heart, still considered it proper to scold every time I caught her at such an elevation, but so that she knew there was no necessity for descending. From dinner to tea she would lie in her breeze-rocked cradle, doing nothing except singing old songs – my nursery lore – to herself, or watching the birds, joint tenants, feed and entice their young ones to fly: or nestling with closed lids, half thinking, half dreaming, happier than words can express.

'Look, miss!' I exclaimed, pointing to a nook under the roots of one twisted tree. 'Winter is not here yet. There's a little flower, up yonder, the last bud from the multitude of bluebells that clouded those turf steps in July with a lilac mist. Will you clamber up, and pluck it to show to papa?'

Cathy stared a long time at the lonely blossom trembling in its earthy shelter, and replied, at length – 'No, I'll not touch it: but it looks melancholy, does it not, Ellen?'

'Yes,' I observed, 'about as starved and sackless as you: your cheeks are bloodless; let us take hold of hands and run. You're so low, I dare say I shall keep up with you.'

'No,' she repeated, and continued sauntering on, pausing, at intervals, to muse over a bit of moss, or a tuft of blanched grass, or a fungus spreading its bright orange among the heaps of brown foliage; and, ever and anon, her hand was lifted to her averted face.

'Catherine, why are you crying, love?' I asked, approaching and putting my arm over her shoulder. 'You mustn't cry because papa has a cold; be thankful it is nothing worse.'

She now put no further restraint on her tears; her breath was stifled by sobs.

'Oh, it *will* be something worse,' she said. 'And what shall I do when papa and you leave me, and I am by myself? I can't forget your words, Ellen; they are always in my ear. How life will be changed, how dreary the world will be, when papa and you are dead.'

'None can tell, whether you won't die before us,' I replied. 'It's wrong to anticipate evil. We'll hope there are years and years to come before any of us go: master is young, and I am strong, and hardly forty-five. My mother lived till eighty, a canty dame to the last. And suppose Mr Linton were spared till he saw sixty, that would be more years than you have counted, miss. And would it not be foolish to mourn a calamity above twenty years beforehand?'

'But Aunt Isabella was younger than papa,' she remarked, gazing up with timid hope to seek further consolation.

'Aunt Isabella had not you and me to nurse her,' I replied. 'She wasn't as happy as master: she hadn't as much to live for. All you need do, is to wait well on your father, and cheer him by letting him see you cheerful; and avoid giving him anxiety on any subject: mind that, Cathy! I'll not disguise but you might kill him, if you were wild and reckless, and cherished a foolish, fanciful affection for the son of a person who would be glad to have him in his grave; and allowed him to discover that you fretted over the separation he has judged it expedient to make.'

'I fret about nothing on earth except papa's illness,' answered my companion. 'I care for nothing in comparison with papa. And I'll never – never – oh, never, while I have my senses, do an act or say a word to vex him. I love him better than myself, Ellen; and I know it by this: I pray every night that I may live after him; because I would rather be miserable than that he should be: that proves I love him better than myself.'

'Good words,' I replied. 'But deeds must prove it also; and after he is well, remember you don't forget resolutions formed in the hour of fear.'

As we talked, we neared a door that opened on the road; and my young lady, lightening into sunshine again, climbed up, and seated herself on the top of the wall, reaching over to gather some hips that bloomed scarlet on the summit branches of the wild rose trees, shadowing the highway side: the lower fruit had disappeared, but only birds could touch the upper, except from Cathy's present station. In stretching to pull them, her hat fell off; and as the door was locked, she proposed scrambling down to recover it. I bid her be cautious lest she got a fall, and she nimbly disappeared. But the return was no such easy matter: the stones were smooth and neatly cemented, and the rosebushes and blackberry stragglers could yield no assistance in re-ascending. I, like a fool, didn't recollect that, till I heard her laughing and exclaiming – 'Ellen, you'll have to fetch the key, or else I must run round to the porter's lodge. I can't scale the ramparts on this side!'

'Stay where you are,' I answered, 'I have my bundle of keys in my pocket: perhaps I may manage to open it; if not, I'll go.'

Catherine amused herself with dancing to and fro before the door, while I tried all the large keys in succession. I had applied the last, and found that none would do; so, repeating my desire that she would remain there, I was about to hurry home as fast as I could, when an approaching sound arrested me. It was the trot of a horse; Cathy's dance stopped; and in a minute the horse stopped also.

'Who is that?' I whispered.

'Ellen, I wish you could open the door,' whispered back my companion, anxiously.

'Ho, Miss Linton!' cried a deep voice (the rider's). 'I'm glad to meet you. Don't be in haste to enter, for I have an explanation to ask and obtain.'

'I shan't speak to you, Mr Heathcliff,' answered Catherine. 'Papa says you are a wicked man, and you hate both him and me; and Ellen says the same.'

'That is nothing to the purpose,' said Heathcliff. (He it was.) 'I don't hate my son, I suppose; and it is concerning him that I demand your attention. Yes! You have cause to blush. Two or three months since, were you not in the habit of writing to Linton? Making love in play, eh? You deserved, both of you, flogging for that!

You especially, the elder, and less sensitive, as it turns out. I've got your letters, and if you give me any pertness I'll send them to your father. I presume you grew weary of the amusement and dropped it, didn't you? Well, you dropped Linton with it, into a Slough of Despond. He was in earnest: in love, really. As true as I live, he's dying for you; breaking his heart at your fickleness: not figuratively, but actually. Though Hareton has made him a standing jest for six weeks, and I have used more serious measures, and attempted to frighten him out of his idiocy, he gets worse daily; and he'll be under the sod before summer, unless you restore him!'

'How can you lie so glaringly to the poor child!' I called from the inside. 'Pray ride on! How can you deliberately get up such paltry falsehoods? Miss Cathy, I'll knock the lock off with a stone: you won't believe that vile nonsense. You can feel in yourself, it is impossible that a person should die for the love of a stranger.'

'I was not aware there were eavesdroppers,' muttered the detected villain. 'Worthy Mrs Dean, I like you, but I don't like your double dealing,' he added, aloud. 'How could you lie so glaringly, as to affirm I hated the "poor child"? and invent bugbear stories to terrify her from my door-stones? Catherine Linton (the very name warms me), my bonny lass, I shall be from home all this week; go and see if I have not spoken truth: do, there's a darling! Just imagine your father in my place, and Linton in yours; then think how you would value your careless lover if he refused to stir a step to comfort you, when your father, himself, entreated him; and don't, from pure stupidity, fall into the same error. I swear, on my salvation, he's going to his grave, and none but you can save him!'

The lock gave way, and I issued out.

'I swear Linton is dying,' repeated Heathcliff, looking hard at me. 'And grief and disappointment are hastening his death. Nelly, if you won't let her go, you can walk over yourself. But I shall not return till this time next week; and I think your master himself would scarcely object to her visiting her cousin!'

'Come in,' said I, taking Cathy by the arm and half forcing her to re-enter; for she lingered, viewing with troubled eyes the features of the speaker, too stern to express his inward deceit.

He pushed his horse close, and, bending down, observed – 'Miss Catherine, I'll own to you that I have little patience with Linton; and Hareton and Joseph

have less. I'll own that he's with a harsh set. He pines for kindness, as well as love; and a kind word from you would be his best medicine. Don't mind Mrs Dean's cruel cautions; but be generous, and contrive to see him. He dreams of you day and night, and cannot be persuaded that you don't hate him, since you neither write nor call.'

I closed the door, and rolled a stone to assist the loosened lock in holding it; and spreading my umbrella, I drew my charge underneath: for the rain began to drive through the moaning branches of the trees, and warned us to avoid delay. Our hurry prevented any comment on the encounter with Heathcliff, as we stretched towards home; but I divined instinctively that Catherine's heart was clouded now in double darkness. Her features were so sad, they did not seem hers: she evidently regarded what she had heard as every syllable true.

The master had retired to rest before we came in. Cathy stole to his room to enquire how he was; he had fallen asleep. She returned, and asked me to sit with her in the library. We took our tea together; and afterwards she lay down on the rug, and told me not to talk for she was weary. I got a book, and pretended to read. As soon as she supposed me absorbed in my occupation, she recommenced her silent weeping: it appeared, at present, her favourite diversion. I suffered her to enjoy it a while; then I expostulated: deriding and ridiculing all Mr Heathcliff's assertions about his son, as if I were certain she would coincide. Alas! I hadn't the skill to counteract the effect his account had produced: it was just what he intended.

'You may be right, Ellen,' she answered; 'but I shall never feel at ease till I know. And I must tell Linton it is not my fault that I don't write; and convince him that I shall not change.'

What use were anger and protestations against her silly credulity? We parted that night – hostile; but next day beheld me on the road to Wuthering Heights, by the side of my wilful young mistress's pony. I couldn't bear to witness her sorrow: to see her pale, dejected countenance, and heavy eyes; and I yielded, in the faint hope that Linton himself might prove, by his reception of us, how little of the tale was founded on fact.

## Chapter 23

The rainy night had ushered in a misty morning – half frost, half drizzle – and temporary brooks crossed our path, gurgling from the uplands. My feet were thoroughly wetted; I was cross and low: exactly the humour suited for making the most of these disagreeable things. We entered the farmhouse by the kitchen way, to ascertain whether Mr Heathcliff were really absent; because I put slight faith in his own affirmation.

Joseph seemed sitting in a sort of elysium alone, beside a roaring fire; a quart of ale on the table near him, bristling with large pieces of toasted oat cake; and his black, short pipe in his mouth. Catherine ran to the hearth to warm herself. I

asked if the master was in? My question remained so long unanswered, that I thought the old man had grown deaf, and repeated it louder.

'Na–ay!' he snarled, or rather screamed through his nose. 'Na–ay! yah muh goa back whear yah coom frough.'

'Joseph!' cried a peevish voice, simultaneously with me, from the inner room. 'How often am I to call you? There are only a few red ashes now. Joseph! Come this moment.'

Vigorous puffs, and a resolute stare into the grate, declared he had no ear for this appeal. The housekeeper and Hareton were invisible; one gone on an errand, and the other at his work, probably. We knew Linton's tones and entered.

'Oh, I hope you'll die in a garret! Starved to death,' said the boy, mistaking our approach for that of his negligent attendant.

He stopped, on observing his error; his cousin flew to him.

'Is that you, Miss Linton?' he said, raising his head from the arm of the great chair, in which he reclined. 'No – don't kiss me. It takes my breath – dear me! Papa said you would call,' continued he, after recovering a little from Catherine's embrace; while she stood by looking very contrite. 'Will you shut the door, if you please? you left it open; and those – those *detestable* creatures won't bring coals to the fire. It's so cold!'

I stirred up the cinders, and fetched a scuttle full myself. The invalid complained of being covered with ashes; but he had a tiresome cough, and looked feverish and ill, so I did not rebuke his temper.

'Well, Linton,' murmured Catherine, when his corrugated brow relaxed. 'Are you glad to see me? Can I do you any good?'

'Why didn't you come before?' he said. 'You should have come, instead of writing. It tired me dreadfully, writing those long letters. I'd far rather have talked to you. Now, I can neither bear to talk, nor anything else. I wonder where Zillah is! Will you,' looking at me, 'step into the kitchen and see?'

I had received no thanks for my other service; and being unwilling to run to and fro at his behest, I replied – 'Nobody is out there but Joseph.'

'I want to drink,' he exclaimed, fretfully, turning away. 'Zillah is constantly gadding off to Gimmerton since papa went. It's miserable! And I'm obliged to come down here – they resolved never to hear me upstairs.'

'Is your father attentive to you, Master Heathcliff?' I asked, perceiving Catherine to be checked in her friendly advances.

'Attentive? He makes *them* a little more attentive, at least,' he cried. 'The wretches! Do you know, Miss Linton, that brute Hareton laughs at me! I hate him! indeed, I hate them all: they are odious beings.'

Cathy began searching for some water; she lighted on a pitcher in the dresser, filled a tumbler, and brought it. He bid her add a spoonful of wine from a bottle on the table; and having swallowed a small portion, appeared more tranquil, and said she was very kind.

'And are you glad to see me?' asked she, reiterating her former question, and pleased to detect the faint dawn of a smile.

'Yes, I am. It's something new to hear a voice like yours!' he replied. 'But I

*have* been vexed, because you wouldn't come. And papa swore it was owing to me: he called me a pitiful, shuffling, worthless thing; and said you despised me; and if he had been in my place, he would be more the master of the Grange than your father, by this time. But you don't despise me, do you miss – '

'I wish you would say Catherine, or Cathy,' interrupted my young lady. 'Despise you? No! Next to papa, and Ellen, I love you better than anybody living. I don't love Mr Heathcliff, though; and I dare not come when he returns: will he stay away many days?'

'Not many,' answered Linton; 'but he goes on to the moors frequently, since the shooting season commenced; and you might spend an hour or two with me, in his absence. Do! Say you will! I think I should not be peevish with you: you'd not provoke me, and you'd be always ready to help me, wouldn't you?'

'Yes,' said Catherine, stroking his long soft hair; 'if I could only get papa's consent, I'd spend half my time with you. Pretty Linton! I wish you were my brother.'

'And then you would like me as well as your father?' observed he, more cheerfully. 'But papa says you would love me better than him and all the world, if you were my wife; so I'd rather you were that.'

'No! I should never love anybody better than papa,' she returned gravely. 'And people hate their wives, sometimes; but not their sisters and brothers: and if you were the latter, you would live with us, and papa would be as fond of you as he is of me.'

Linton denied that people ever hated their wives; but Cathy affirmed they did, and, in her wisdom, instanced his own father's aversion to her aunt. I endeavoured to stop her thoughtless tongue. I couldn't succeed till everything she knew was out. Master Heathcliff, much irritated, asserted her relation was false.

'Papa told me; and papa does not tell falsehoods!' she answered pertly.

'*My* papa scorns yours!' cried Linton. 'He calls him a sneaking fool!'

'Yours is a wicked man,' retorted Catherine; 'and you are very naughty to dare to repeat what he says. He must be wicked, to have made Aunt Isabella leave him as she did!'

'She didn't leave him,' said the boy: 'you shan't contradict me!'

'She did!' cried my young lady.

'Well, I'll tell *you* something!' said Linton. 'Your mother hated your father: now then.'

'Oh!' exclaimed Catherine, too enraged to continue.

'And she loved mine!' added he.

'You little liar! I hate you now,' she panted, and her face grew red with passion.

'She did! She did!' sang Linton, sinking into the recess of his chair, and leaning back his head to enjoy the agitation of the other disputant, who stood behind.

'Hush, Master Heathcliff!' I said; 'that's your father's tale too, I suppose.'

'It isn't: you hold your tongue!' he answered. 'She did, she did, Catherine! She did, she did!'

Cathy, beside herself, gave the chair a violent push, and caused him to fall

against one arm. He was immediately seized by a suffocating cough that soon ended his triumph. It lasted so long that it frightened even me. As to his cousin, she wept with all her might; aghast at the mischief she had done: though she said nothing. I held him till the fit exhausted itself. Then he thrust me away, and leant his head down silently. Catherine quelled her lamentations also, took a seat opposite, and looked solemnly into the fire.

'How do you feel now, Master Heathcliff?' I enquired after waiting ten minutes.

'I wish *she* felt as I do,' he replied: 'spiteful, cruel thing! Hareton never touches me: he never struck me in his life. And I was better today: and there – ' his voice died in a whimper.

'*I* didn't strike you!' muttered Cathy, chewing her lip to prevent another burst of emotion.

He sighed and moaned like one under great suffering, and kept it up for a quarter of an hour; on purpose to distress his cousin, apparently, for whenever he caught a stifled sob from her he put renewed pain and pathos into the inflections of his voice.

'I'm sorry I hurt you, Linton,' she said at length, racked beyond endurance. 'But *I* couldn't have been hurt by that little push, and I had no idea that you could, either: you're not much, are you, Linton? Don't let me go home thinking I've done you harm. Answer! Speak to me.'

'I can't speak to you,' he murmured; 'you've hurt me so, that I shall lie awake all night, choking with this cough! If you had it you'd know what it was: but *you*'ll be comfortably asleep, while I'm in agony – and nobody near me! I wonder how you would like to pass those fearful nights!' And he began to wail aloud, for very pity of himself.

'Since you are in the habit of passing dreadful nights,' I said, 'it won't be miss who spoils your ease: you'd be the same had she never come. However, she shall not disturb you again; and perhaps you'll get quieter when we leave you.'

'Must I go?' asked Catherine dolefully, bending over him. 'Do you want me to go, Linton?'

'You can't alter what you've done,' he replied pettishly, shrinking from her, 'unless you alter it for the worse, by teasing me into a fever.'

'Well, then I must go?' she repeated.

'Let me alone, at least,' said he; 'I can't bear your talking!'

She lingered, and resisted my persuasions to departure, a tiresome while; but as he neither looked up nor spoke, she finally made a movement to the door and I followed. We were recalled by a scream. Linton had slid from his seat on to the hearthstone, and lay writhing in the mere perverseness of an indulged plague of a child, determined to be as grievous and harassing as it can. I thoroughly gauged his disposition from his behaviour, and saw at once it would be folly to attempt humouring him. Not so my companion: she ran back in terror, knelt down, and cried, and soothed, and entreated, till he grew quiet from lack of breath: by no means from compunction at distressing her.

'I shall lift him on the settle,' I said, 'and he may roll about as he pleases: we

can't stop to watch him. I hope you are satisfied, Miss Cathy, that *you* are not the person to benefit him, and that his condition of health is not occasioned by attachment to you. Now then, there he is! Come away: as soon as he knows there is nobody by to care for his nonsense, he'll be glad to lie still!'

She placed a cushion under his head, and offered him some water; he rejected the latter, and tossed uneasily on the former, as if it were a stone or a block of wood. She tried to put it more comfortably.

'I can't do with that,' he said; 'it's not high enough!'

Catherine brought another to lay above it.

'That's *too* high!' murmured the provoking thing.

'How must I arrange it, then?' she asked despairingly.

He twined himself up to her, as she half knelt by the settle, and converted her shoulder into a support.

'No, that won't do,' I said. 'You'll be content with the cushion, Master Heathcliff. Miss has wasted too much time on you already: we cannot remain five minutes longer.'

'Yes, yes, we can!' replied Cathy. 'He's good and patient now. He's beginning to think I shall have far greater misery than he will tonight, if I believe he is the worse for my visit; and then, I dare not come again. Tell the truth about it, Linton; for I mustn't come, if I have hurt you.'

'You must come, to cure me,' he answered. 'You ought to come because you have hurt me: you know you have, extremely! I was not as ill when you entered as I am at present – was I?'

'But you've made yourself ill by crying, and being in a passion.'

'I didn't do it all,' said his cousin. 'However, we'll be friends now. And you want me: you would wish to see me sometimes, really?'

'I told you I did,' he replied impatiently. 'Sit on the settle and let me lean on your knee. That's as mama used to do, whole afternoons together. Sit quite still, and don't talk: but you may sing a song if you can sing; or you may say a nice long interesting ballad – one of those you promised to teach me; or a story. I'd rather have a ballad, though: begin.'

Catherine repeated the longest she could remember. The employment pleased both mightily. Linton would have another, and after that another, notwithstanding my strenuous objections; and so they went on until the clock struck twelve, and we heard Hareton in the court, returning for his dinner.

'And tomorrow, Catherine, will you be here tomorrow?' asked young Heathcliff, holding her frock as she rose reluctantly.

'No!' I answered, 'nor next day neither.' She, however, gave a different response, evidently, for his forehead cleared as she stooped and whispered in his ear.

'You won't go tomorrow, recollect, miss!' I commenced, when we were out of the house. 'You are not dreaming of it, are you?'

She smiled.

'Oh, I'll take good care,' I continued: 'I'll have that lock mended, and you can escape by no way else.'

'I can get over the wall,' she said, laughing. 'The Grange is not a prison, Ellen, and you are not my jailer. And besides, I'm almost seventeen: I'm a woman. And I'm certain Linton would recover quickly if he had me to look after him. I'm older than he is, you know, and wiser: less childish, am I not? And he'll soon do as I direct him, with some slight coaxing. He's a pretty little darling when he's good. I'd make such a pet of him, if he were mine. We should never quarrel, should we, after we were used to each other? Don't you like him, Ellen?'

'Like him?' I exclaimed. 'The worst-tempered bit of a sickly slip that ever struggled into its teens! Happily, as Mr Heathcliff conjectured, he'll not win twenty! I doubt whether he'll see spring, indeed. And small loss to his family whenever he drops off. And lucky it is for us that his father took him: the kinder he was treated, the more tedious and selfish he'd be! I'm glad you have no chance of having him for a husband, Miss Catherine!'

My companion waxed serious at hearing this speech. To speak of his death so regardlessly wounded her feelings.

'He's younger than I,' she answered, after a protracted pause of meditation, 'and he ought to live the longest: he will – he must live as long as I do. He's as strong now as when he first came into the North; I'm positive of that! It's only a cold that ails him, the same as papa has. You say papa will get better, and why shouldn't he?'

'Well, well,' I cried, 'after all, we needn't trouble ourselves; for listen, miss – and mind, I'll keep my word – if you attempt going to Wuthering Heights again, with or without me, I shall inform Mr Linton, and, unless he allow it, the intimacy with your cousin must not be revived.'

'It has been revived!' muttered Cathy sulkily.

'Must not be continued, then!' I said.

'We'll see!' was her reply, and she set off at a gallop, leaving me to toil in the rear.

We both reached home before our dinner-time; my master supposed we had been wandering through the park, and therefore he demanded no explanation of our absence. As soon as I entered, I hastened to change my soaked shoes and stockings; but sitting such a while at the Heights had done the mischief. On the succeeding morning I was laid up, and during three weeks I remained incapacitated for attending to my duties: a calamity never experienced prior to that period, and never, I am thankful to say, since.

My little mistress behaved like an angel in coming to wait on me, and cheer my solitude: the confinement brought me exceedingly low. It is wearisome, to a stirring active body: but few have slighter reasons for complaint than I had. The moment Catherine left Mr Linton's room, she appeared at my bedside. Her day was divided between us; no amusement usurped a minute: she neglected her meals, her studies, and her play; and she was the fondest nurse that ever watched. She must have had a warm heart, when she loved her father so, to give so much to me!

I said her days were divided between us; but the master retired early, and I generally needed nothing after six o'clock, thus the evening was her own. Poor

thing! I never considered what she did with herself after tea. And though frequently, when she looked in to bid me good-night, I remarked a fresh colour in her cheeks and a pinkness over her slender fingers; instead of fancying the hue borrowed from a cold ride across the moors, I laid it to the charge of a hot fire in the library.

## *Chapter 24*

At the close of three weeks, I was able to quit my chamber, and move about the house. And on the first occasion of my sitting up in the evening, I asked Catherine to read to me, because my eyes were weak. We were in the library, the master having gone to bed: she consented, rather unwillingly, I fancied; and imagining my sort of books did not suit her, I bid her please herself in the choice of what she perused. She selected one of her own favourites, and got forward steadily about an hour; then came frequent questions.

'Ellen, are not you tired? Hadn't you better lie down now? You'll be sick, keeping up so long, Ellen.'

'No, no, dear, I'm not tired,' I returned, continually.

Perceiving me immovable, she essayed another method of showing her dis-relish for her occupation. It changed to yawning, and stretching, and – 'Ellen, I'm tired.'

'Give over then and talk,' I answered.

That was worse: she fretted and sighed, and looked at her watch till eight, and finally went to her room, completely overdone with sleep; judging by her peevish, heavy look, and the constant rubbing she inflicted on her eyes. The following night she seemed more impatient still; and on the third from recovering my company, she complained of a headache, and left me. I thought her conduct odd; and having remained alone a long while, I resolved on going, and enquiring whether she were better, and asking her to come and lie on the sofa, instead of upstairs in the dark. No Catherine could I discover upstairs, and none below. The servants affirmed they had not seen her. I listened at Mr Edgar's door; all was silence. I returned to her apartment, extinguished my candle, and seated myself in the window.

The moon shone bright; a sprinkling of snow covered the ground, and I reflected that she might, possibly, have taken it into her head to walk about the garden, for refreshment. I did detect a figure creeping along the inner fence of the park; but it was not my young mistress: on its emerging into the light, I recognised one of the grooms. He stood a considerable period, viewing the carriage-road through the grounds; then started off at a brisk pace, as if he had detected something, and reappeared presently, leading miss's pony; and there she was, just dismounted, and walking by its side. The man took his charge stealthily across the grass towards the stable. Cathy entered by the casement-window of the drawing-room, and glided noiselessly up to where I awaited her.

She put the door gently to, slipped off her snowy shoes, untied her hat, and was proceeding, unconscious of my espionage, to lay aside her mantle, when I suddenly rose and revealed myself. The surprise petrified her an instant: she uttered an inarticulate exclamation, and stood fixed.

'My dear Miss Catherine,' I began, too vividly impressed by her recent kindness to break into a scold, 'where have you been riding out at this hour? And why should you try to deceive me, by telling a tale? Where have you been? Speak!'

'To the bottom of the park,' she stammered. 'I didn't tell a tale.'

'And nowhere else?' I demanded.

'No,' was the muttered reply.

'Oh, Catherine!' I cried, sorrowfully. 'You know you have been doing wrong, or you wouldn't be driven to uttering an untruth to me. That does grieve me. I'd rather be three months ill, than hear you frame a deliberate lie.'

She sprang forward, and bursting into tears, threw her arms round my neck.

'Well Ellen, I'm so afraid of you being angry,' she said. 'Promise not to be angry, and you shall know the very truth. I hate to hide it.'

We sat down in the window-seat; I assured her I would not scold, whatever her secret might be, and I guessed it, of course; so she commenced – 'I've been to Wuthering Heights, Ellen, and I've never missed going a day since you fell ill; except thrice before, and twice after you left your room. I gave Michael books and pictures to prepare Minny every evening, and to put her back in the stable: you mustn't scold *him* either, mind. I was at the Heights by half-past six, and generally stayed till half-past eight, and then galloped home. It was not to amuse myself that I went: I was often wretched all the time. Now and then, I was happy: once in a week perhaps. At first, I expected there would be sad work persuading you to let me keep my word to Linton: for I had engaged to call again next day, when we quitted him; but, as you stayed upstairs on the morrow, I escaped that trouble; and while Michael was refastening the lock of the park door in the afternoon, I got possession of the key, and told him how my cousin wished me to visit him, because he was sick, and couldn't come to the Grange; and how papa would object to my going; and then I negotiated with him about the pony.

'He is fond of reading, and he thinks of leaving soon to get married; so he offered, if I would lend him books out of the library, to do what I wished: but I preferred giving him my own, and that satisfied him better.

'On my second visit, Linton seemed in lively spirits; and Zillah (that is their housekeeper) made us a clean room and a good fire, and told us that, as Joseph was out at a prayer-meeting and Hareton Earnshaw was off with his dogs – robbing our woods of pheasants, as I heard afterwards – we might do what we liked. She brought me some warm wine and gingerbread, and appeared exceedingly good-natured; and Linton sat in the armchair, and I in the little rocking chair on the hearthstone, and we laughed and talked so merrily, and found so much to say: we planned where we would go, and what we would do in summer. I needn't repeat that, because you would call it silly.

'One time, however, we were near quarrelling. He said the pleasantest

manner of spending a hot July day was lying from morning till evening on a bank of heath in the middle of the moors, with the bees humming dreamily about among the bloom, and the larks singing high up over head, and the blue sky and bright sun shining steadily and cloudlessly. That was his most perfect idea of heaven's happiness: mine was rocking in a rustling green tree, with a west wind blowing, and bright white clouds flitting rapidly above; and not only larks, but throstles, and blackbirds, and linnets, and cuckoos pouring out music on every side, and the moors seen at a distance, broken into cool dusky dells; but close by great swells of long grass undulating in waves to the breeze; and woods and sounding water, and the whole world awake and wild with joy. He wanted all to lie in an ecstacy of peace; I wanted all to sparkle, and dance in a glorious jubilee. I said his heaven would be only half alive; and he said mine would be drunk: I said I should fall asleep in his; and he said he could not breathe in mine, and began to grow very snappish. At last, we agreed to try both, as soon as the right weather came; and then we kissed each other and were friends.

'After sitting still an hour, I looked at the great room with its smooth uncarpeted floor, and thought how nice it would be to play in, if we removed the table; and I asked Linton to call Zillah in to help us, and we'd have a game at blind-man's buff; she should try to catch us; you used to, you know, Ellen. He wouldn't: there was no pleasure in it, he said; but he consented to play at ball with me. We found two in a cupboard, among a heap of old toys: tops, and hoops, battledores, and shuttlecocks. One was marked C., and the other H.; I wished to have the C., because that stood for Catherine, and the H. might be for Heathcliff, his name; but the bran came out of H., and Linton didn't like it. I beat him constantly: and he got cross again, and coughed, and returned to his chair. That night, though, he easily recovered his good humour: he was charmed with two or three pretty songs – *your* songs, Ellen; and when I was obliged to go, he begged and entreated me to come the following evening; and I promised. Minny and I went flying home as light as air; and I dreamt of Wuthering Heights and my sweet, darling cousin, till morning.

'On the morrow, I was sad; partly because you were poorly, and partly that I wished my father knew, and approved of my excursions: but it was beautiful moonlight after tea; and, as I rode on, the gloom cleared. I shall have another happy evening, I thought to myself; and what delights me more, my pretty Linton will. I trotted up their garden, and was turning round to the back, when that fellow Earnshaw met me, took my bridle, and bid me go in by the front entrance. He patted Minny's neck, and said she was a bonny beast, and appeared as if he wanted me to speak to him. I only told him to leave my horse alone, or else it would kick him. He answered in his vulgar accent, "It wouldn't do mitch hurt if it did"; and surveyed its legs with a smile. I was half inclined to make it try; however, he moved off to open the door, and, as he raised the latch, he looked up to the inscription above, and said, with a stupid mixture of awkwardness and elation – ' "Miss Catherine! I can read yon, nah."

' "Wonderful," I exclaimed. "Pray let us hear you – you *are* grown clever!"

'He spelt, and drawled over by syllables, the name – "Hareton Earnshaw."

' "And the figures?" I cried, encouragingly, perceiving that he came to a dead halt.

' "I cannot tell them yet," he answered.

' "Oh, you dunce!" I said, laughing heartily at his failure.

'The fool stared, with a grin hovering about his lips, and a scowl gathering over his eyes, as if uncertain whether he might not join in my mirth: whether it were not pleasant familiarity, or what it really was, contempt. I settled his doubts, by suddenly retrieving my gravity and desiring him to walk away, for I came to see Linton not him. He reddened – I saw that by the moonlight – dropped his hand from the latch, and skulked off, a picture of mortified vanity. He imagined himself to be as accomplished as Linton, I suppose, because he could spell his own name; and was marvellously discomfited that I didn't think the same.'

'Stop, Miss Catherine, dear!' I interrupted. 'I shall not scold, but I don't like your conduct there. If you had remembered that Hareton was your cousin as much as Master Heathcliff, you would have felt how improper it was to behave in that way. At least, it was praiseworthy ambition for him to desire to be as accomplished as Linton; and probably he did not learn merely to show off: you had made him ashamed of his ignorance before, I have no doubt; and he wished to remedy it and please you. To sneer at his imperfect attempt was very bad breeding. Had *you* been brought up in his circumstances, would you be less rude? He was as quick and as intelligent a child as ever you were; and I'm hurt that he should be despised now, because that base Heathcliff has treated him so unjustly.'

'Well, Ellen, you won't cry about it, will you?' she exclaimed, surprised at my earnestness. 'But wait, and you shall hear if he conned his A B C to please me; and if it were worth while being civil to the brute. I entered; Linton was lying on the settle, and half got up to welcome me.

' "I'm ill tonight, Catherine, love," he said; "and you must have all the talk, and let me listen. Come, and sit by me. I was sure you wouldn't break your word, and I'll make you promise again, before you go."

'I knew now that I mustn't tease him, as he was ill; and I spoke softly and put no questions, and avoided irritating him in any way. I had brought some of my nicest books for him; he asked me to read a little of one, and I was about to comply, when Earnshaw burst the door open: having gathered venom with reflection. He advanced direct to us, seized Linton by the arm, and swung him off the seat.

' "Get to thy own room!" he said in a voice almost inarticulate with passion; and his face looked swelled and furious. "Take her there if she comes to see thee: thou shalln't keep me out of this. Begone, wi' ye both!"

'He swore at us, and left Linton no time to answer, nearly throwing him into the kitchen; and he clenched his fist as I followed, seemingly longing to knock me down. I was afraid for a moment, and I let one volume fall; he kicked it after me, and shut us out. I heard a malignant, crackly laugh by the fire, and turning, beheld that odious Joseph standing rubbing his bony hands, and quivering.

' "Aw wer sure he'd sarve ye eht! He's a grand lad! He's getten t' raight sperrit in him! *He* knaws – aye, he knaws, as weel as Aw do, who sud be t' maister yonder – ech, ech, ech! He mad ye skift properly! Ech, ech, ech!"

' "Where must we go?" I said to my cousin, disregarding the old wretch's mockery.

'Linton was white and trembling. He was not pretty then, Ellen: Oh no! He looked frightful! For his thin face and large eyes were wrought into an expression of frantic, powerless fury. He grasped the handle of the door, and shook it: it was fastened inside.

' "If you don't let me in I'll kill you! – if you don't let me in I'll kill you!" he rather shrieked than said. "Devil! devil! – I'll kill you – I'll kill you!"

'Joseph uttered his croaking laugh again.

' "Thear that's t' father!" he cried. "That's father! We've allas summut uh orther side in us. Niver heed Hareton, lad – dunnut be 'feard – he cannot get at thee!"

'I took hold of Linton's hands, and tried to pull him away; but he shrieked so shockingly that I dared not proceed. At last, his cries were choked by a dreadful fit of coughing; blood gushed from his mouth, and he fell on the ground. I ran into the yard, sick with terror; and called for Zillah, as loud as I could. She soon heard me: she was milking the cows in a shed behind the barn, and hurrying from her work, she enquired what there was to do? I hadn't breath to explain; dragging her in, I looked about for Linton. Earnshaw had come out to examine the mischief he had caused, and he was then conveying the poor thing upstairs. Zillah and I ascended after him; but he stopped me at the top of the steps, and said I shouldn't go in: I must go home. I exclaimed that he had killed Linton, and I *would* enter. Joseph locked the door, and declared I should do "no sich stuff", and asked me whether I were "bahn to be as mad as him". I stood crying, till the housekeeper reappeared. She affirmed that he would be better in a bit, but he couldn't do with that shrieking and din; and she took me, and nearly carried me into the house.

'Ellen, I was ready to tear my hair off my head! I sobbed and wept so that my eyes were almost blind; and the ruffian you have such sympathy with stood opposite: presuming every now and then to bid me "wisht", and denying that it was his fault; and finally, frightened by my assertions that I would tell papa, and that he should be put in prison and hanged, he commenced blubbering himself, and hurried out to hide his cowardly agitation. Still, I was not rid of him: when at length they compelled me to depart, and I had got some hundred yards off the premises, he suddenly issued from the shadow of the roadside, and checked Minny and took hold of me.

' "Miss Catherine, I'm ill grieved," he began, "but it's rayther too bad – "

'I gave him a cut with my whip, thinking perhaps he would murder me. He let go, thundering one of his horrid curses, and I galloped home more than half out of my senses.

'I didn't bid you good-night, that evening, and I didn't go to Wuthering Heights, the next: I wished to, exceedingly; but I was strangely excited, and

dreaded to hear that Linton was dead, sometimes; and sometimes shuddered at the thought of encountering Hareton. On the third day I took courage: at least, I couldn't bear longer suspense, and stole off once more. I went at five o'clock, and walked; fancying I might manage to creep into the house, and up to Linton's room, unobserved. However, the dogs gave notice of my approach. Zillah received me, and saying "the lad was mending nicely", showed me into a small, tidy, carpeted apartment, where, to my inexpressible joy, I beheld Linton laid on a little sofa, reading one of my books. But he would neither speak to me nor look at me, through a whole hour, Ellen: he has such an unhappy temper. And what quite confounded me, when he did open his mouth it was to utter the falsehood that I had occasioned the uproar, and Hareton was not to blame! Unable to reply, except passionately, I got up and walked from the room. He sent after me a faint "Catherine!" He did not reckon on being answered so: but I wouldn't turn back; and the morrow was the second day on which I stayed at home, nearly determined to visit him no more. But it was so miserable going to bed, and getting up, and never hearing anything about him, that my resolution melted into air before it was properly formed. It *had* appeared wrong to take the journey once; now it seemed wrong to refrain. Michael came to ask if he must saddle Minny; I said "Yes," and considered myself doing a duty as she bore me over the hills. I was forced to pass the front windows to get to the court: it was no use trying to conceal my presence.

' "Young master is in the house," said Zillah, as she saw me making for the parlour. I went in; Earnshaw was there also, but he quitted the room directly. Linton sat in the great arm chair half asleep; walking up to the fire, I began in a serious tone, partly meaning it to be true – ' "As you don't like me, Linton, and as you think I come on purpose to hurt you, and pretend that I do so every time, this is our last meeting: let us say goodbye; and tell Mr Heathcliff that you have no wish to see me, and that he mustn't invent any more falsehoods on the subject.'

' "Sit down and take your hat off, Catherine," he answered. "You are so much happier than I am, you ought to be better. Papa talks enough of my defects, and shows enough scorn of me, to make it natural I should doubt myself. I doubt whether I am not altogether as worthless as he calls me, frequently; and then I feel so cross and bitter, I hate everybody! I *am* worthless, and bad in temper, and bad in spirit, almost always; and if you choose, you *may* say goodbye: you'll get rid of an annoyance. Only, Catherine, do me this justice: believe that if I might be as sweet, and as kind, and as good as you are, I would be; as willingly, and more so, than as happy and as healthy. And believe that your kindness has made me love you deeper than if I deserved your love: and though I couldn't, and cannot help showing my nature to you, I regret it and repent it; and shall regret and repent it till I die!"

'I felt he spoke the truth; and I felt I must forgive him: and, though he should quarrel the next moment, I must forgive him again. We were reconciled; but we cried, both of us, the whole time I stayed: not entirely for sorrow; yet I *was* sorry Linton had that distorted nature. He'll never let his friends be at ease, and he'll

never be at ease himself! I have always gone to his little parlour, since that night; because his father returned the day after.

'About three times, I think, we have been merry and hopeful, as we were the first evening; the rest of my visits were dreary and troubled: now with his selfishness and spite, and now with his sufferings: but I've learnt to endure the former with nearly as little resentment as the latter. Mr Heathcliff purposely avoids me; I have hardly seen him at all. Last Sunday, indeed, coming earlier than usual, I heard him abusing poor Linton, cruelly, for his conduct of the night before. I can't tell how he knew of it, unless he listened. Linton had certainly behaved provokingly: however, it was the business of nobody but me, and I interrupted Mr Heathcliff's lecture by entering and telling him so. He burst into a laugh, and went away, saying he was glad I took that view of the matter. Since then, I've told Linton he must whisper his bitter things. Now, Ellen, you have heard all; and I can't be prevented from going to Wuthering Heights, except by inflicting misery on two people; whereas, if you'll only not tell papa, my going need disturb the tranquillity of none. You'll not tell, will you? It will be very heartless if you do.'

'I'll make up my mind on that point by tomorrow, Miss Catherine,' I replied. 'It requires some study; and so I'll leave you to your rest, and go think it over.'

I thought it over aloud, in my master's presence; walking straight from her room to his, and relating the whole story: with the exception of her conversations with her cousin, and any mention of Hareton. Mr Linton was alarmed and distressed more than he would acknowledge to me. In the morning, Catherine learnt my betrayal of her confidence, and she learnt also that her secret visits were to end. In vain she wept and writhed against the interdict, and implored her father to have pity on Linton: all she got to comfort her was a promise that he would write, and give him leave to come to the Grange when he pleased; but explaining that he must no longer expect to see Catherine at Wuthering Heights. Perhaps, had he been aware of his nephew's disposition and state of health, he would have seen fit to withhold even that slight consolation.

## Chapter 25

'These things happened last winter, sir,' said Mrs Dean; 'hardly more than a year ago. Last winter, I did not think, at another twelve months' end, I should be amusing a stranger to the family with relating them! Yet, who knows how long you'll be a stranger? You're too young to rest always contented, living by yourself; and I some way fancy, no one could see Catherine Linton, and not love her. You smile; but why do you look so lively and interested, when I talk about her? And why have you asked me to hang her picture over your fireplace? and why – '

'Stop, my good friend!' I cried. 'It may be very possible that *I* should love her; but would she love me? I doubt it too much to venture my tranquillity by

running into temptation: and then my home is not here. I'm of the busy world, and to its arms I must return. Go on. Was Catherine obedient to her father's commands?'

'She was,' continued the housekeeper. 'Her affection for him was still the chief sentiment in her heart; and he spoke without anger: he spoke in the deep tenderness of one about to leave his treasure amid perils and foes, where his remembered words would be the only aid that he could bequeath to guide her. He said to me, a few days afterwards,

' "I wish my nephew would write, Ellen, or call. Tell me, sincerely, what you think of him: is he changed for the better, or is there a prospect of improvement, as he grows a man?"

' "He's very delicate, sir," I replied; "and scarcely likely to reach manhood: but this I can say, he does not resemble his father; and if Miss Catherine had the misfortune to marry him, he would not be beyond her control: unless she were extremely and foolishly indulgent. However, master, you'll have plenty of time to get acquainted with him, and see whether he would suit her: it wants four years and more to his being of age."

Edgar sighed; and, walking to the window, looked out towards Gimmerton kirk. It was a misty afternoon, but the February sun shone dimly, and we could just distinguish the two fir trees in the yard, and the sparely scattered grave-stones.

'I've prayed often,' he half soliloquised, 'for the approach of what is coming; and now I begin to shrink, and fear it. I thought the memory of the hour I came down that glen a bridegroom would be less sweet than the anticipation that I was soon, in a few months, or, possibly, weeks, to be carried up, and laid in its lonely hollow! Ellen, I've been very happy with my little Cathy. Through winter nights and summer days she was a living hope at my side. But I've been as happy musing by myself among those stones, under that old church: lying, through the long June evenings, on the green mound of her mother's grave, and wishing, yearning for the time when I might lie beneath it. What can I do for Cathy? How must I quit her? I'd not care one moment for Linton being Heathcliff's son; nor for his taking her from me, if he could console her for my loss. I'd not care that Heathcliff gained his ends, and triumphed in robbing me of my last blessing! But should Linton be unworthy – only a feeble tool to his father – I cannot abandon her to him! And, hard though it be to crush her buoyant spirit, I must persevere in making her sad while I live, and leaving her solitary when I die. Darling! I'd rather resign her to God, and lay her in the earth before me.'

'Resign her to God, as it is, sir,' I answered, 'and if we should lose you – which may He forbid – under His providence, I'll stand her friend and counsellor to the last. Miss Catherine is a good girl: I don't fear that she will go wilfully wrong; and people who do their duty are always finally rewarded.'

Spring advanced; yet my master gathered no real strength, though he resumed his walks in the grounds with his daughter. To her inexperienced notions, this itself was a sign of convalescence; and then his cheek was often flushed, and his eyes were bright: she felt sure of his recovering.

On her seventeenth birthday, he did not visit the churchyard: it was raining, and I observed – 'You'll surely not go out tonight, sir?'

He answered – 'No, I'll defer it, this year, a little longer.'

He wrote again to Linton, expressing his great desire to see him; and, had the invalid been presentable, I've no doubt his father would have permitted him to come. As it was, being instructed, he returned an answer, intimating that Mr Heathcliff objected to his calling at the Grange; but his uncle's kind remembrance delighted him, and he hoped to meet him, sometimes, in his rambles, and personally to petition that his cousin and he might not remain long so utterly divided.

That part of his letter was simple, and probably his own. Heathcliff knew he could plead eloquently enough for Catherine's company, then – 'I do not ask,' he said, 'that she may visit here; but, am I never to see her, because my father forbids me to go to her home, and you forbid her to come to mine? Do, now and then, ride with her towards the Heights; and let us exchange a few words, in your presence! We have done nothing to deserve this separation; and you are not angry with me: you have no reason to dislike me, you allow, yourself. Dear uncle! Send me a kind note tomorrow, and leave to join you anywhere you please, except at Thrushcross Grange. I believe an interview would convince you that my father's character is not mine: he affirms I am more your nephew than his son; and though I have faults which render me unworthy of Catherine, she has excused them, and, for her sake, you should also. You enquire after my health – it is better; but while I remain cut off from all hope, and doomed to solitude, or the society of those who never did and never will like me, how can I be cheerful and well?'

Edgar, though he felt for the boy, could not consent to grant his request; because he could not accompany Catherine. He said, in summer, perhaps, they might meet: meantime, he wished him to continue writing at intervals, and engaged to give him what advice and comfort he was able by letter; being well aware of his hard position in his family. Linton complied; and had he been unrestrained, would probably have spoiled all by filling his epistles with complaints and lamentations: but his father kept a sharp watch over him; and, of course, insisted on every line that my master sent being shown; so, instead of penning his peculiar personal sufferings and distresses, the themes constantly uppermost in his thoughts, he harped on the cruel obligation of being held asunder from his friend and love; and gently intimated that Mr Linton must allow an interview soon, or he should fear he was purposely deceiving him with empty promises.

Cathy was a powerful ally at home; and, between them, they at length persuaded my master to acquiesce in their having a ride or a walk together, about once a week, under my guardianship, and on the moors nearest the Grange: for June found him still declining; and though he had set aside, yearly, a portion of his income for my young lady's fortune, he had a natural desire that she might retain – or at least return in a short time to – the house of her ancestors; and he considered her only prospect of doing that was by a union with

his heir; he had no idea that the latter was failing almost as fast as himself; nor had anyone, I believe: no doctor visited the Heights, and no one saw Master Heathcliff to make report of his condition, among us. I, for my part, began to fancy my forebodings were false, and that he must be actually rallying, when he mentioned riding and walking on the moors, and seemed so earnest in pursuing his object. I could not picture a father treating a dying child as tyrannically and wickedly as I afterwards learnt Heathcliff had treated him, to compel this apparent eagerness: his efforts redoubling the more imminently his avaricious and unfeeling plans were threatened with defeat by death.

## *Chapter 26*

Summer was already past its prime, when Edgar reluctantly yielded his assent to their entreaties, and Catherine and I set out on our first ride to join her cousin. It was a close, sultry day: devoid of sunshine, but with a sky too dappled and hazy to threaten rain; and our place of meeting had been fixed at the guide-stone, by the crossroads.

On arriving there, however, a little herd-boy, despatched as a messenger, told us that – 'Maister Linton wer just ut this side th' Heights: and he'd be mitch obleeged to us to gang on a bit further.'

'Then Master Linton has forgot the first injunction of his uncle,' I observed: 'he bid us keep on the Grange land, and here we are, off at once.'

'Well, we'll turn our horses' heads round, when we reach him,' answered my companion, 'our excursion shall lie towards home.'

But when we reached him, and that was scarcely a quarter of a mile from his own door, we found he had no horse; and we were forced to dismount, and leave ours to graze.

He lay on the heath, awaiting our approach, and did not rise till we came within a few yards. Then he walked so feebly, and looked so pale, that I immediately exclaimed – 'Why, Master Heathcliff, you are not fit for enjoying a ramble, this morning. How ill you do look!'

Catherine surveyed him with grief and astonishment; and changed the ejaculation of joy on her lips, to one of alarm; and the congratulation on their long postponed meeting to an anxious enquiry, whether he were worse than usual?

'No – better – better!' he panted, trembling, and retaining her hand as if he needed its support, while his large blue eyes wandered timidly over her; the hollowness round them transforming to haggard wildness the languid expression they once possessed.

'But you have been worse,' persisted his cousin; 'worse than when I saw you last – you are thinner, and – '

'I'm tired,' he interrupted, hurriedly. 'It is too hot for walking, let us rest here. And, in the morning, I often feel sick – papa says I grow so fast.'

Badly satisfied, Cathy sat down, and he reclined beside her.

'This is something like your paradise,' said she, making an effort at cheerfulness. 'You recollect the two days we agreed to spend in the place and way each thought pleasantest? This is nearly yours, only there are clouds; but then they are so soft and mellow, it is nicer than sunshine. Next week, if you can, we'll ride down to the Grange Park, and try mine.'

Linton did not appear to remember what she talked of; and he had evidently great difficulty in sustaining any kind of conversation. His lack of interest in the subjects she started, and his equal incapacity to contribute to her entertainment, were so obvious, that she could not conceal her disappointment. An indefinite alteration had come over his whole person and manner. The pettishness that might be caressed into fondness, had yielded to a listless apathy; there was less of the peevish temper of a child which frets and teases on purpose to be soothed, and more of the self-absorbed moroseness of a confirmed invalid, repelling consolation, and ready to regard the good-humoured mirth of others, as an insult. Catherine perceived, as well as I did, that he held it rather a punishment, than a gratification, to endure our company; and she made no scruple of proposing, presently, to depart. That proposal, unexpectedly, roused Linton from his lethargy, and threw him into a strange state of agitation. He glanced fearfully towards the Heights, begging she would remain another half-hour, at least.

'But, I think,' said Cathy, 'you'd be more comfortable at home than sitting here; and I cannot amuse you today, I see, by my tales, and songs, and chatter: you have grown wiser than I, in these six months; you have little taste for my diversions now; or else, if I could amuse you, I'd willingly stay.'

'Stay to rest yourself,' he replied. 'And, Catherine, don't think, or say that I'm *very* unwell: it is the heavy weather and heat that make me dull; and I walked about, before you came, a great deal, for me. Tell uncle, I'm in tolerable health, will you?'

'I'll tell him that *you* say so, Linton. I couldn't affirm that you are,' observed my young lady, wondering at his pertinacious assertion of what was evidently an untruth.

'And be here again next Thursday,' continued he, shunning her puzzled gaze. 'And give him my thanks for permitting you to come – my best thanks, Catherine. And – and, if you *did* meet my father, and he asked you about me, don't lead him to suppose that I've been extremely silent and stupid: don't look sad and downcast, as you *are* doing – he'll be angry.'

'I care nothing for his anger,' exclaimed Cathy, imagining she would be its object.

'But I do,' said her cousin, shuddering. '*Don't* provoke him against me, Catherine, for he is very hard.'

'Is he severe to you, Master Heathcliff?' I enquired. 'Has he grown weary of indulgence, and passed from passive, to active hatred?'

Linton looked at me, but did not answer; and, after keeping her seat by his side another ten minutes, during which his head fell drowsily on his breast, and

he uttered nothing except suppressed moans of exhaustion or pain, Cathy began to seek solace in looking for bilberries, and sharing the produce of her researches with me: she did not offer them to him, for she saw further notice would only weary and annoy.

'Is it half an hour now, Ellen!' she whispered in my ear, at last. 'I can't tell why we should stay. He's asleep, and papa will be wanting us back.'

'Well, we must not leave him asleep,' I answered; 'wait till he wakes, and be patient. You were mighty eager to set off, but your longing to see poor Linton has soon evaporated!'

'Why did *he* wish to see me?' returned Catherine. 'In his crassest humours, formerly, I liked him better than I do in his present curious mood. It's just as if it were a task he was compelled to perform – this interview – for fear his father should scold him. But I'm hardly going to come to give Mr Heathcliff pleasure; whatever reason he may have for ordering Linton to undergo this penance. And, though I'm glad he's better in health, I'm sorry he's so much less pleasant, and so much less affectionate to me.'

'You think he *is* better in health, then?' I said.

'Yes,' she answered; 'because he always made such a great deal of his sufferings, you know. He is not tolerably well, as he told me to tell papa; but he's better, very likely.'

'There you differ with me, Miss Cathy,' I remarked; 'I should conjecture him to be far worse.'

Linton here started from his slumber in bewildered terror, and asked if anyone had called his name.

'No,' said Catherine; 'unless in dreams. I cannot conceive how you manage to close, out of doors, in the morning.'

'I thought I heard my father,' he gasped, glancing up to the frowning nab above us. 'You are sure nobody spoke?'

'Quite sure,' replied his cousin. 'Only Ellen and I were disputing concerning your health. Are you truly stronger, Linton, than when we separated in winter? If you be, I'm certain one thing is not stronger – your regard for me – speak, are you?'

The tears gushed from Linton's eyes as he answered, 'Yes, yes, I am!' And, still under the spell of the imaginary voice, his gaze wandered up and down to detect its owner. Cathy rose. 'For today we must part,' she said. 'And I won't conceal that I have been sadly disappointed with our meeting, though I'll mention it to nobody but you: not that I stand in awe of Mr Heathcliff!'

'Hush,' murmured Linton; 'for God's sake, hush! He's coming.' And he clung to Catherine's arm, striving to detain her; but at that announcement she hastily disengaged herself, and whistled to Minny, who obeyed like a dog.

'I'll be here next Thursday,' she cried, springing to the saddle. 'Goodbye. Quick, Ellen!'

And so we left him, scarcely conscious of our departure, so absorbed was he in anticipating his father's approach.

Before we reached home, Catherine's displeasure softened into a perplexed

sensation of pity and regret, largely blended with vague, uneasy doubts about Linton's actual circumstances, physical and social: in which I partook, though I counselled her not to say much; for a second journey would make us better judges. My master requested an account of our on-goings: His nephew's offering of thanks was duly delivered, Miss Cathy gently touching on the rest: I also, threw little light on his enquiries, for I hardly knew what to hide, and what to reveal.

## Chapter 27

Seven days glided away, every one marking its course by the henceforth rapid alteration of Edgar Linton's state. The havoc that months had previously wrought was now emulated by the inroads of hours. Catherine, we would fain have deluded yet; but her own quick spirit refused to delude her: it divined in secret, and brooded on the dreadful probability, gradually ripening into certainty. She had not the heart to mention her ride, when Thursday came round; I mentioned it for her, and obtained permission to order her out of doors: for the library, where her father stopped a short time daily – the brief period he could bear to sit up – and his chamber, had become her whole world. She grudged each moment that did not find her bending over his pillow, or seated by his side. Her countenance grew wan with watching and sorrow, and my master gladly dismissed her to what he flattered himself would be a happy change of scene and society; drawing comfort from the hope that she would not now be left entirely alone after his death.

He had a fixed idea, I guessed by several observations he let fall, that as his nephew resembled him in person, he would resemble him in mind; for Linton's letters bore few or no indications of his defective character. And I, through pardonable weakness, refrained from correcting the error; asking myself what good there would be in disturbing his last moments with information that he had neither power nor opportunity to turn to account.

We deferred our excursion till the afternoon; a golden afternoon of August: every breath from the hills so full of life, that it seemed whoever respired it, though dying, might revive. Catherine's face was just like the landscape – shadows and sunshine flitting over it in rapid succession; but the shadows rested longer, and the sunshine was more transient; and her poor little heart reproached itself for even that passing forgetfulness of its cares.

We discerned Linton watching at the same spot he had selected before. My young mistress alighted, and told me that as she was resolved to stay a very little while, I had better hold the pony and remain on horseback; but I dissented: I wouldn't risk losing sight of the charge committed to me a minute; so we climbed the slope of heath together. Master Heathcliff received us with greater animation on this occasion: not the animation of high spirits though, nor yet of joy; it looked more like fear.

'It is late!' he said, speaking short and with difficulty. 'Is not your father very ill? I thought you wouldn't come.'

'*Why* won't you be candid?' cried Catherine, swallowing her greeting. 'Why cannot you say at once, you don't want me? It is strange Linton, that for the second time, you have brought me here on purpose, apparently, to distress us both, and for no reason besides!'

Linton shivered, and glanced at her, half supplicating, half ashamed; but his cousin's patience was not sufficient to endure this enigmatical behaviour.

'My father *is* very ill,' she said; 'and why am I called from his bedside – why didn't you send to absolve me from my promise, when you wished I wouldn't keep it? Come! I desire an explanation: playing and trifling are completely banished out of my mind; and I can't dance attendance on your affectations, now!'

'My affectations!' he murmured; 'what are they? For Heaven's sake Catherine, don't look so angry! Despise me as much as you please; I am a worthless, cowardly wretch: I can't be scorned enough! but I'm too mean for your anger – hate my father, and spare me, for contempt.'

'Nonsense!' cried Catherine, in a passion. 'Foolish, silly boy! And there! He trembles, as if I were really going to touch him! You needn't bespeak contempt, Linton: anybody will have it spontaneously, at your service. Get off! I shall return home: it is folly dragging you from the hearthstone, and pretending – what do we pretend? Let go my frock! If I pitied you for crying and looking so very frightened, you should spurn such pity. Ellen, tell him how disgraceful this conduct is. Rise, and don't degrade yourself into an abject reptile – *don't*.'

With streaming face and an expression of agony, Linton had thrown his nerveless frame along the ground: he seemed convulsed with exquisite terror.

'Oh!' he sobbed, 'I cannot bear it! Catherine, Catherine, I'm a traitor too, and I dare not tell you! But leave me and I shall be killed! *Dear* Catherine, my life is in your hands: and you have said you loved me – and if you did, it wouldn't harm you. You'll not go, then? kind, sweet, good Catherine! And perhaps you *will* consent – and he'll let me die with you!'

My young lady, on witnessing his intense anguish, stooped to raise him. The old feeling of indulgent tenderness overcame her vexation, and she grew thoroughly moved and alarmed.

'Consent to what?' she asked. 'To stay? Tell me the meaning of this strange talk, and I will. You contradict your own words, and distract me! Be calm and frank, and confess at once all that weighs on your heart. You wouldn't injure me, Linton, would you? You wouldn't let any enemy hurt me, if you could prevent it? I'll believe you are a coward, for yourself, but not a cowardly betrayer of your best friend.'

'But my father threatened me,' gasped the boy, clasping his attenuated fingers, 'and I dread him – I dread him! I *dare* not tell!'

'Oh well!' said Catherine, with scornful compassion, 'keep your secret, *I'm* no coward – save yourself: I'm not afraid!'

Her magnanimity provoked his tears: he wept wildly, kissing her supporting hands, and yet could not summon courage to speak out. I was cogitating what

the mystery might be, and determined Catherine should never suffer to benefit him or anyone else, by my good will; when hearing a rustle among the ling, I looked up, and saw Mr Heathcliff almost close upon us, descending the Heights. He didn't cast a glance towards my companions, though they were sufficiently near for Linton's sobs to be audible; but hailing me in the almost hearty tone he assumed to none besides, and the sincerity of which, I couldn't avoid doubting, he said – 'It is something to see you so near to my house, Nelly! How are you at the Grange? Let us hear! The rumour goes,' he added in a lower tone, 'that Edgar Linton is on his deathbed: perhaps they exaggerate his illness?'

'No; my master is dying,' I replied: 'it is true enough. A sad thing it will be for us all, but a blessing for him!'

'How long will he last, do you think?' he asked.

'I don't know,' I said.

'Because,' he continued, looking at the two young people, who were fixed under his eye – Linton appeared as if he could not venture to stir, or raise his head, and Catherine could not move, on his account – 'Because that lad yonder, seems determined to beat me; and I'd thank his uncle to be quick, and go before him – Hallo! Has the whelp been playing that game long? I *did* give him some lessons about snivelling. Is he pretty lively with Miss Linton generally?'

'Lively? no – he has shown the greatest distress,' I answered. 'To see him, I should say, that instead of rambling with his sweetheart on the hills, he ought to be in bed, under the hands of a doctor.'

'He shall be, in a day or two,' muttered Heathcliff. 'But first – get up, Linton! Get up!' he shouted. 'Don't grovel on the ground, there – up this moment!'

Linton had sunk prostrate again in another paroxysm of helpless fear, caused by his father's glance towards him, I suppose: there was nothing else to produce such humiliation. He made several efforts to obey, but his little strength was annihilated for the time, and he fell back again with a moan. Mr Heathcliff advanced, and lifted him to lean against a ridge of turf.

'Now,' said he, with curbed ferocity, 'I'm getting angry; and if you don't command that paltry spirit of yours – *Damn* you! Get up, directly!'

'I will, father!' he panted. 'Only, let me alone, or I shall faint! I've done as you wished, I'm sure. Catherine will tell you that I – that I – have been cheerful. Ah! keep by me Catherine; give me your hand.'

'Take mine,' said his father; 'stand on your feet. There now – she'll lend you her arm: that's right, look at *her*. You would imagine I was the devil himself, Miss Linton, to excite such horror. Be so kind as to walk home with him, will you? He shudders, if I touch him.'

'Linton, dear!' whispered Catherine, 'I can't go to Wuthering Heights . . . papa has forbidden me . . . He'll not harm you: why are you so afraid?'

'I can never re-enter that house,' he answered. 'I'm *not* to re-enter it without you!'

'Stop . . .' cried his father. 'We'll respect Catherine's filial scruples. Nelly, take him in, and I'll follow your advice concerning the doctor, without delay.'

'You'll do well,' replied I, 'but I must remain with my mistress. To mind your son is not my business.'

'You are very stiff,' said Heathcliff, 'I know that: but you'll force me to pinch the baby, and make it scream, before it moves your charity. Come then, my hero. Are you willing to return, escorted by me?'

He approached once more, and made as if he would seize the fragile being; but shrinking back, Linton clung to his cousin, and implored her to accompany him, with a frantic importunity that admitted no denial. However I disapproved, I couldn't hinder her: indeed how could she have refused him herself? What was filling him with dread we had no means of discerning; but there he was, powerless under its gripe, and any addition seemed capable of shocking him into idiocy.

We reached the threshold; Catherine walked in; and I stood waiting till she had conducted the invalid to a chair, expecting her out immediately; when Mr Heathcliff, pushing me forward, exclaimed – 'My house is not stricken with the plague, Nelly; and I have a mind to be hospitable today: sit down, and allow me to shut the door.'

He shut and locked it also. I started.

'You shall have tea, before you go home,' he added. 'I am by myself. Hareton is gone with some cattle to the lees – and Zillah and Joseph are off on a journey of pleasure. And, though I'm used to being alone, I'd rather have some interesting company, if I can get it. Miss Linton, take your seat by *him*. I give you what I have: the present is hardly worth accepting; but, I have nothing else to offer. It is Linton, I mean. How she does stare! It's odd what a savage feeling I have to anything that seems afraid of me! Had I been born where laws are less strict, and tastes less dainty, I should treat myself to a slow vivisection of those two, as an evening's amusement.'

He drew in his breath, struck the table, and swore to himself, 'By hell! I hate them.'

'I'm not afraid of you!' exclaimed Catherine, who could not hear the latter part of his speech. She stepped close up; her black eyes flashing with passion and resolution. 'Give me that key: I will have it!' she said. 'I wouldn't eat or drink here, if I were starving.'

Heathcliff had the key in his hand that remained on the table. He looked up, seized with a sort of surprise at her boldness; or, possibly, reminded by her voice and glance, of the person from whom she inherited it. She snatched at the instrument, and half succeeded in getting it out of his loosened fingers: but her action recalled him to the present; he recovered it speedily.

'Now, Catherine Linton,' he said, 'stand off, or I shall knock you down; and that will make Mrs Dean mad.'

Regardless of this warning, she captured his closed hand and its contents again. 'We *will* go!' she repeated, exerting her utmost efforts to cause the iron muscles to relax; and finding that her nails made no impression, she applied her teeth pretty sharply. Heathcliff glanced at me a glance that kept me from interfering a moment. Catherine was too intent on his fingers to notice his face. He opened them suddenly, and resigned the object of dispute; but, ere she had

well secured it, he seized her with the liberated hand, and, pulling her on his knee, administered with the other a shower of terrific slaps on both sides of the head, each sufficient to have fulfilled his threat, had she been able to fall.

At this diabolical violence, I rushed on him furiously. 'You villain!' I began to cry, 'you villain!' A touch on the chest silenced me: I am stout, and soon put out of breath; and, what with that and the rage, I staggered dizzily back, and felt ready to suffocate, or to burst a blood-vessel.

The scene was over in two minutes; Catherine, released, put her two hands to her temples, and looked just as if she were not sure whether her ears were off or on. She trembled like a reed, poor thing, and leant against the table perfectly bewildered.

'I know how to chastise children, you see,' said the scoundrel, grimly, as he stooped to repossess himself of the key, which had dropped to the floor. 'Go to Linton now, as I told you; and cry at your ease! I shall be your father, tomorrow – all the father you'll have in a few days – and you shall have plenty of that – you can bear plenty – you're no weakling – you shall have a daily taste, if I catch such a devil of a temper in your eyes again!'

Cathy ran to me instead of Linton, and knelt down, and put her burning cheek on my lap, weeping aloud. Her cousin had shrunk into a corner of the settle, as quiet as a mouse, congratulating himself, I dare say, that the correction had lighted on another than him. Mr Heathcliff, perceiving us all confounded, rose, and expeditiously made the tea himself. The cups and saucers were laid ready. He poured it out, and handed me a cup.

'Wash away your spleen,' he said. 'And help your own naughty pet and mine. It is not poisoned, though I prepared it. I'm going out to seek your horses.'

Our first thought, on his departure, was to force an exit somewhere. We tried the kitchen door, but that was fastened outside: we looked at the windows – they were too narrow for even Cathy's little figure.

'Master Linton,' I cried, seeing we were regularly imprisoned; 'you know what your diabolical father is after, and you shall tell us, or I'll box your ears, as he has done your cousin's.'

'Yes, Linton; you must tell,' said Catherine. 'It was for your sake I came; and it will be wickedly ungrateful if you refuse.'

'Give me some tea, I'm thirsty, and then I'll tell you,' he answered. 'Mrs Dean, go away. I don't like you standing over me. Now, Catherine, you are letting your tears fall into my cup! I won't drink that. Give me another.'

Catherine pushed another to him, and wiped her face. I felt disgusted at the little wretch's composure, since he was no longer in terror for himself. The anguish he had exhibited on the moor subsided as soon as ever he entered Wuthering Heights; so I guessed he had been menaced with an awful visitation of wrath if he failed in decoying us there; and, that accomplished, he had no further immediate fears.

'Papa wants us to be married,' he continued, after sipping some of the liquid. 'And he knows your papa wouldn't let us marry now; and he's afraid of my dying, if we wait; so we are to be married in the morning, and you are to stay

here all night; and, if you do as he wishes, you shall return home next day, and take me with you.'

'Take you with her, pitiful changeling?' I exclaimed. '*You* marry? Why, the man is mad! Or he thinks us fools, everyone. And do you imagine that beautiful young lady, that healthy, hearty girl, will tie herself to a little perishing monkey like you? Are you cherishing the notion that *anybody*, let alone Miss Catherine Linton, would have you for a husband? You want whipping for bringing us in here at all, with your dastardly, puling tricks; and – don't look so silly now! I've a very good mind to shake you severely, for your contemptible treachery, and your imbecile conceit.'

I did give him a slight shaking; but it brought on the cough, and he took to his ordinary resource of moaning and weeping, and Catherine rebuked me.

'Stay all night? No!' she said, looking slowly round. 'Ellen, I'll burn that door down, but I'll get out.'

And she would have commenced the execution of her threat directly, but Linton was up in alarm, for his dear self, again.

He clasped her in his two feeble arms, sobbing – 'Won't you have me, and save me – not let me come to the Grange? Oh! darling Catherine! you mustn't go, and leave me, after all. You *must* obey my father, you *must*!'

'I must obey my own,' she replied, 'and relieve him from this cruel suspense. The whole night! What would he think? he'll be distressed already. I'll either break or burn a way out of the house. Be quiet! You're in no danger – but, if you hinder me – Linton, I love papa better than you!'

The mortal terror he felt of Mr Heathcliff's anger, restored to the boy his coward's eloquence. Catherine was near distraught: still, she persisted that she must go home, and tried entreaty, in her turn, persuading him to subdue his selfish agony.

While they were thus occupied, our jailer re-entered.

'Your beasts have trotted off;' he said, 'and – Now, Linton! Snivelling again? What has she been doing to you? Come, come – have done, and get to bed. In a month or two, my lad, you'll be able to pay her back her present tyrannies, with a vigorous hand. You're pining for pure love, are you not? Nothing else in the world: and she shall have you! There, to bed! Zillah won't be here tonight; you must undress yourself. Hush! Hold your noise! Once in your own room, I'll not come near you, you needn't fear. By chance, you've managed tolerably. I'll look to the rest.'

He spoke these words, holding the door open for his son to pass; and the latter achieved his exit exactly as a spaniel might, which suspected the person who attended on it of designing a spiteful squeeze. The lock was re-secured. Heathcliff approached the fire, where my mistress and I stood silent.

Catherine looked up, and instinctively raised her hand to her cheek: his neighbourhood revived a painful sensation. Anybody else would have been incapable of regarding the childish act with sternness, but he scowled on her, and muttered – 'Oh, you are not afraid of me? Your courage is well disguised: you *seem* damnably afraid!'

'I *am* afraid now,' she replied; 'because if I stay, papa will be miserable; and how can I endure making him miserable – when he – when he – Mr Heathcliff, *let* me go home! I promise to marry Linton: papa would like me to, and I love him – and why should you wish to force me to do what I'll willingly do of myself?'

'Let him dare to force you!' I cried. 'There's law in the land, thank God, there is! Though we *be* in an out-of-the-way place. I'd inform, if he were my own son, and it's felony without benefit of clergy!'

'Silence!' said the ruffian. 'To the devil with your clamour! I don't want *you* to speak. Miss Linton, I shall enjoy myself remarkably in thinking your father will be miserable: I shall not sleep for satisfaction. You could have hit on no surer way of fixing your residence under my roof, for the next twenty-four hours, than informing me that such an event would follow. As to your promise to marry Linton, I'll take care you shall keep it; for you shall not quit this place till it is fulfilled.'

'Send Ellen then, to let papa know I'm safe!' exclaimed Catherine, weeping bitterly. 'Or marry me now. Poor papa! Ellen, he'll think we're lost. What shall we do?'

'Not he! He'll think you are tired of waiting on him, and run off, for a little amusement,' answered Heathcliff. 'You cannot deny that you entered my house of your own accord, in contempt of his injunctions to the contrary. And it is quite natural that you should desire amusement at your age; and that you should weary of nursing a sick man, and that man *only* your father. Catherine, his happiest days were over when your days began. He cursed you, I dare say, for coming into the world (I did, at least). And it would just do if he cursed you as *he* went out of it. I'd join him. I don't love you! How should I? Weep away. As far as I can see, it will be your chief diversion hereafter; unless Linton make amends for other losses: and your provident parent appears to fancy he may. His letters of advice and consolation entertained me vastly. In his last, he recommended my jewel to be careful of his; and kind to her when he got her. Careful and kind – that's paternal. But Linton requires his whole stock of care and kindness for himself. Linton can play the little tyrant well. He'll undertake to torture any number of cats if their teeth be drawn, and their claws pared. You'll be able to tell his uncle fine tales of his *kindness*, when you get home again, I assure you.'

'You're right there!' I said; 'explain your son's character. Show his resemblance to yourself; and then, I hope, Miss Cathy will think twice before she takes the cockatrice!'

'I don't much mind speaking of his amiable qualities now,' he answered; 'because she must either accept him or remain a prisoner, and you along with her, till your master dies. I can detain you both, quite concealed, here. If you doubt, encourage her to retract her word, and you'll have an opportunity of judging!'

'I'll not retract my word,' said Catherine. 'I'll marry him, within this hour, if I may go to Thrushcross Grange afterwards. Mr Heathcliff, you're a cruel man, but you're not a fiend; and you won't, from *mere* malice, destroy, irrevocably, all my happiness. If papa thought I had left him, on purpose, and if he died before I

returned, could I bear to live? I've given over crying: but I'm going to kneel here, at your knee; and I'll not get up, and I'll not take my eyes from your face, till you look back at me! No, don't turn away! *Do* look! You'll see nothing to provoke you. I don't hate you. I'm not angry that you struck me. Have you never loved *anybody*, in all your life, uncle? *Never?* Ah! you must look once – I'm so wretched – you can't help being sorry and pitying me.'

'Keep your eft's fingers off; and move, or I'll kick you!' cried Heathcliff, brutally repulsing her. 'I'd rather be hugged by a snake. How the devil can you dream of fawning on me? I *detest* you!'

He shrugged his shoulders: shook himself, indeed, as if his flesh crept with aversion; and thrust back his chair; while I got up, and opened my mouth, to commence a downright torrent of abuse; but I was rendered dumb in the middle of the first sentence, by a threat that I should be shown into a room by myself, the very next syllable I uttered. It was growing dark – we heard a sound of voices at the garden gate. Our host hurried out instantly: *he* had his wits about him; *we* had not. There was a talk of two or three minutes, and he returned alone.

'I thought it had been your cousin Hareton,' I observed to Catherine. 'I wish he would arrive! Who knows but he might take our part?'

'It was three servants sent to seek you from the Grange,' said Heathcliff, overhearing me. 'You should have opened a lattice and called out: but I could swear that chit is glad you didn't. She's glad to be obliged to stay, I'm certain.'

At learning the chance we had missed, we both gave vent to our grief without control; and he allowed us to wail on till nine o'clock. Then he bade us go upstairs, through the kitchen, to Zillah's chamber; and I whispered my companion to obey: perhaps we might contrive to get through the window there, or into a garret, and out by its skylight. The window, however, was narrow, like those below, and the garret trap was safe from our attempts; for we were fastened in as before. We neither of us lay down: Catherine took her station by the lattice, and watched anxiously for morning; a deep sigh being the only answer I could obtain to my frequent entreaties that she would try to rest. I seated myself in a chair, and rocked, to and fro, passing harsh judgement on my many derelictions of duty; from which, it struck me then, all the misfortunes of all my employers sprang. It was not the case, in reality, I am aware; but it was, in my imagination, that dismal night; and I thought Heathcliff himself less guilty than I.

At seven o'clock he came, and enquired if Miss Linton had risen. She ran to the door immediately, and answered, 'Yes.'

'Here, then,' he said, opening it, and pulling her out. I rose to follow, but he turned the lock again. I demanded my release.

'Be patient,' he replied; 'I'll send up your breakfast in a while.'

I thumped on the panels, and rattled the latch angrily; and Catherine asked why I was still shut up? He answered, I must try to endure it another hour, and they went away. I endured it two or three hours; at length, I heard a footstep, not Heathcliff's.

'I've brought you something to eat,' said a voice; 'oppen t' door!'

Complying eagerly, I beheld Hareton, laden with food enough to last me all day.

'Tak it,' he added, thrusting the tray into my hand.

'Stay one minute,' I began.

'Nay!' cried he, and retired, regardless of any prayers I could pour forth to detain him.

And there I remained enclosed, the whole day, and the whole of the next night; and another, and another. Five nights and four days I remained, altogether, seeing nobody but Hareton, once every morning; and he was a model of a jailer: surly, and dumb, and deaf to every attempt at moving his sense of justice or compassion.

## Chapter 28

On the fifth morning, or rather afternoon, a different step approached – lighter and shorter; and, this time, the person entered the room. It was Zillah; donned in her scarlet shawl, with a black silk bonnet on her head, and a willow basket swung to her arm.

'Eh, dear! Mrs Dean,' she exclaimed. 'Well! There is a talk about you at Gimmerton. I never thought but you were sunk in the Blackhorse marsh, and missy with you, till master told me you'd been found, and he'd lodged you here! What, and you must have got on an island, sure? And how long were you in the hole? Did master save you, Mrs Dean? But you're not so thin – you've not been so poorly, have you?'

'Your master is a true scoundrel!' I replied. 'But he shall answer for it. He needn't have raised that tale: it shall all be laid bare!'

'What do you mean?' asked Zillah. 'It's not his tale: they tell that in the village – about your being lost in the marsh; and I calls to Earnshaw, when I come in – "Eh, they's queer things, Mr Hareton, happened since I went off. It's a sad pity of that likely young lass, and cant Nelly Dean." He stared. I thought he had not heard aught, so I told him the rumour. The master listened, and he just smiled to himself, and said, "If they have been in the marsh, they are out now, Zillah. Nelly Dean is lodged, at this minute, in your room. You can tell her to flit, when you go up; here is the key. The bog-water got into her head, and she would have run home, quite flighty, but I fixed her, till she came round to her senses. You can bid her go to the Grange, at once, if she be able, and carry a message from me, that her young lady will follow in time to attend the squire's funeral." '

'Mr Edgar is not dead?' I gasped. 'Oh! Zillah, Zillah!'

'No, no; sit you down, my good mistress,' she replied; 'your right sickly yet. He's not dead; Doctor Kenneth thinks he may last another day. I met him on the road and asked.'

Instead of sitting down, I snatched my outdoor things, and hastened below, for the way was free. On entering the house, I looked about for someone to give

information of Catherine. The place was filled with sunshine, and the door stood wide open; but nobody seemed at hand. As I hesitated whether to go off at once, or return and seek my mistress, a slight cough drew my attention to the hearth. Linton lay on the settle, sole tenant, sucking a stick of sugar-candy, and pursuing my movements with apathetic eyes. 'Where is Miss Catherine?' I demanded, sternly, supposing I could frighten him into giving intelligence, by catching him thus, alone. He sucked on like an innocent.

'Is she gone?' I said.

'No,' he replied; she's upstairs: she's not to go; we won't let her.'

'You won't let her, little idiot!' I exclaimed. 'Direct me to her room immediately, or I'll make you sing out sharply.'

'Papa would make you sing out, if you attempted to get there,' he answered. 'He says I'm not to be soft with Catherine: she's my wife, and it's shameful that she should wish to leave me! He says, she hates me, and wants me to die, that she may have my money; but she shan't have it: and she shan't go home! She never shall! – She may cry, and be sick as much as she pleases!'

He resumed his former occupation, closing his lids, as if he meant to drop asleep.

'Master Heathcliff,' I resumed, 'have you forgotten all Catherine's kindness to you, last winter, when you affirmed you loved her, and when she brought you books, and sung you songs, and came many a time through wind and snow to see you? She wept to miss one evening, because you would be disappointed; and you felt then, that she was a hundred times too good to you: and now you believe the lies your father tells, though you know he detests you both! And you join him against her. That's fine gratitude, is it not?'

The corner of Linton's mouth fell, and he took the sugar-candy from his lips.

'Did she come to Wuthering Heights, because she hated you?' I continued. 'Think for yourself!

As to your money, she does not even know that you will have any. And you say she's sick; and yet, you leave her alone, up there in a strange house! *You*, who have felt what it is to be so neglected! You could pity your own sufferings, and she pitied them, too, but you won't pity hers! I shed tears Master Heathcliff, you see – an elderly woman, and a servant merely – and you, after pretending such affection, and having reason to worship her, almost, store up every tear you have for yourself, and lie there quite at ease. Ah! You're a heartless, selfish boy!'

'I can't stay with her,' he answered crossly. 'I can't stay, by myself. She cries so I can't bear it. And she won't give over, though I say I'll call my father. I did call him once; and he threatened to strangle her, if she was not quiet; but she began again, the instant he left the room; moaning and grieving all night long, though I screamed for vexation that I couldn't sleep.'

'Is Mr Heathcliff out?' I enquired, perceiving that the wretched creature had no power to sympathise with his cousin's mental tortures.

'He's in the court,' he replied, 'talking to Doctor Kenneth who says uncle is dying, truly, at last. I'm glad, for I shall be master of the Grange after him – and Catherine always spoke of it as her house. It isn't hers! It's mine: papa says

everything she has is mine. All her nice books are mine; she offered to give me them, and her pretty birds, and her pony Minny, if I would get the key of our room, and let her but; but I told her she had nothing to give, they were all, all mine. And then she cried, and took a little picture from her neck, and said I should have that two pictures in a gold case – on one side her mother, and on the other, uncle, when they were young. That was yesterday – I said *they* were mine, too; and tried to get them from her. The spiteful thing wouldn't let me: she pushed me off, and hurt me. I shrieked out – that frightens her – she heard papa coming, and she broke the hinges, and divided the case and gave me her mother's portrait; the other she attempted to hide: but papa asked what was the matter and I explained it. He took the one I had away; and ordered her to resign hers to me; she refused, and he – he struck her down, and wrenched it off the chain, and crushed it with his foot.'

'And were you pleased to see her struck?' I asked: having my designs in encouraging his talk.

'I winked,' he answered. 'I wink to see my father strike a dog, or a horse, he does it so hard. Yet I was glad at first – she deserved punishing for pushing me: but when papa was gone, she made me come to the window and showed me her cheek cut on the inside, against her teeth, and her mouth filling with blood; and then she gathered up the bits of the picture, and went and sat down with her face to the wall, and she has never spoken to me since: and I sometimes think she can't speak for pain. I don't like to think so! But she's a naughty thing for crying continually; and she looks so pale and wild, I'm afraid of her!'

'And you can get the key if you choose?' I said.

'Yes, when I am upstairs,' he answered; 'but I can't walk upstairs now.'

'In what apartment is it?' I asked.

'Oh,' he cried, 'I shan't tell *you* where it is! It is our secret. Nobody, neither Hareton, nor Zillah are to know. There! You've tired me – go away, go away!' And he turned his face on to his arm, and shut his eyes, again.

I considered it best to depart without seeing Mr Heathcliff; and bring a rescue for my young lady, from the Grange. On reaching it, the astonishment of my fellow servants to see me, and their joy also, was intense; and when they heard that their little mistress was safe, two or three were about to hurry up, and shout the news at Mr Edgar's door: but I bespoke the announcement of it, myself. How changed I found him, even in those few days! He lay an image of sadness, and resignation, waiting his death. Very young he looked: though his actual age was thirty-nine; one would have called him ten years younger, at least. He thought of Catherine for he murmured her name. I touched his hand, and spoke.

'Catherine is coming, dear master!' I whispered; 'she is alive, and well; and will be here I hope tonight.'

I trembled at the first effects of this intelligence: he half rose up, looked eagerly round the apartment, and then sunk back in a swoon. As soon as he recovered, I related our compulsory visit, and detention at the Heights. I said Heathcliff forced me to go in: which was not quite true. I uttered as little as possible against

Linton; nor did I describe all his father's brutal conduct – my intentions being to add no bitterness, if I could help it, to his already overflowing cup.

He divined that one of his enemy's purposes was to secure the personal property, as well as the estate, to his son, or rather himself; yet why he did not wait till his decease, was a puzzle to my master, because ignorant how nearly he and his nephew would quit the world together. However, he felt that his will had better be altered: instead of leaving Catherine's fortune at her own disposal, he determined to put it in the hands of trustees, for her use during life; and for her children, if she had any, after her. By that means, it could not fall to Mr Heathcliff should Linton die.

Having received his orders, I despatched a man to fetch the attorney, and four more, provided with serviceable weapons, to demand my young lady of her jailer. Both parties were delayed very late. The single servant returned first. He said Mr Green, the lawyer, was out when he arrived at his house, and he had to wait two hours for his re-entrance; and then Mr Green told him he had a little business in the village that must be done; but he would be at Thrushcross Grange before morning. The four men came back unaccompanied, also. They brought word that Catherine was ill: too ill to quit her room; and Heathcliff would not suffer them to see her. I scolded the stupid fellows well, for listening to that tale, which I would not carry to my master; resolving to take a whole bevy up to the Heights, at daylight, and storm it, literally, unless the prisoner were quietly surrendered to us. Her father *shall* see her, I vowed, and vowed again, if that devil be killed on his own door-stones in trying to prevent it!

Happily, I was spared the journey, and the trouble. I had gone downstairs at three o'clock to fetch a jug of water; and was passing through the hall with it in my hand, when a sharp knock at the front door made me jump. 'Oh! It is Green,' I said, recollecting myself – 'only Green,' and I went on, intending to send somebody else to open it; but the knock was repeated: not loud, and still importunately. I put the jug on the bannister, and hastened to admit him myself. The harvest moon shone clear outside. It was not the attorney. My own sweet little mistress sprung on my neck, sobbing – 'Ellen! Ellen! Is papa alive?'

'Yes!' I cried: 'yes, my angel, he is. God be thanked, you are safe with us again!'

She wanted to run, breathless as she was, upstairs to Mr Linton's room; but I compelled her to sit down on a chair, and made her drink, and washed her pale face, chafing it into a faint colour with my apron. Then I said I must go first and tell of her arrival, imploring her to say she should be happy with young Heathcliff. She stared, but soon comprehending why I counselled her to utter the falsehood, she assured me she would not complain.

I couldn't abide to be present at their meeting. I stood outside the chamber-door a quarter of an hour, and hardly ventured near the bed, then. All was composed, however: Catherine's despair was as silent as her father's joy. She supported him calmly, in appearance; and he fixed on her features his raised eyes, that seemed dilating with ecstacy.

He died blissfully, Mr Lockwood: he died so. Kissing her cheek, he murmured,

'I am going to her; and you darling child shall come to us;' and never stirred or spoke again; but continued that rapt, radiant gaze, till his pulse imperceptibly stopped, and his soul departed. None could have noticed the exact minute of his death, it was so entirely without a struggle.

Whether Catherine had spent her tears, or whether the grief were too weighty to let them flow, she sat there dry-eyed till the sun rose: she sat till noon, and would still have remained, brooding over that deathbed, but I insisted on her coming away, and taking some repose. It was well I succeeded in removing her, for at dinner-time appeared the lawyer, having called at Wuthering Heights to get his instructions how to behave. He had sold himself to Mr Heathcliff, and that was the cause of his delay in obeying my master's summons. Fortunately, no thought of worldly affairs crossed the latter's mind, to disturb him, after his daughter's arrival.

Mr Green took upon himself to order everything and everybody about the place. He gave all the servants but me, notice to quit. He would have carried his delegated authority to the point of insisting that Edgar Linton should not be buried beside his wife, but in the chapel, with his family. There was the will however, to hinder that, and my loud protestations against any infringement of its directions. The funeral was hurried over; Catherine, Mrs Linton Heathcliff now, was suffered to stay at the Grange till her father's corpse had quitted it.

She told me that her anguish had at last spurred Linton to incur the risk of liberating her. She heard the men I sent, disputing at the door, and she gathered the sense of Heathcliff's answer. It drove her desperate. Linton, who had been conveyed up to the little parlour soon after I left, was terrified into fetching the key before his father re-ascended. He had the cunning to unlock, and re-lock the door, without shutting it; and when he should have gone to bed, he begged to sleep with Hareton, and his petition was granted, for once. Catherine stole out before break of day. She dare not try the doors, lest the dogs should raise an alarm; she visited the empty chambers, and examined their windows; and, luckily, lighting on her mother's, she got easily out of its lattice, and on to the ground, by means of the fir tree, close by. Her accomplice suffered for his share in the escape, notwithstanding his timid contrivances.

## Chapter 29

The evening after the funeral, my young lady and I were seated in the library; now musing mournfully – one of us despairingly – on our loss, now venturing conjectures as to the gloomy future.

We had just agreed the best destiny which could await Catherine, would be a permission to continue resident at the Grange; at least during Linton's life: he being allowed to join her there, and I to remain as housekeeper. That seemed rather too favourable an arrangement to be hoped for; and yet I did hope, and began to cheer up under the prospect of retaining my home, and my

employment, and, above all, my beloved young mistress, when a servant –
one of the discarded ones, not yet departed – rushed hastily in, and said, 'that
devil Heathcliff' was coming through the court: should he fasten the door
in his face?

If we had been mad enough to order that proceeding, we had not time. He
made no ceremony of knocking, or announcing his name: he was master, and
availed himself of the master's privilege to walk straight in, without saying a
word. The sound of our informant's voice directed him to the library; he
entered, and motioning him out, shut the door.

It was the same room into which he had been ushered, as a guest, eighteen
years before: the same moon shone through the window; and the same autumn
landscape lay outside. We had not yet lighted a candle, but all the apartment
was visible, even to the portraits on the wall – the splendid head of Mrs Linton,
and the graceful one of her husband. Heathcliff advanced to the hearth. Time
had little altered his person either. There was the same man: his dark face
rather sallower, and more composed, his frame a stone or two heavier, perhaps,
and no other difference. Catherine had risen, with an impulse to dash out,
when she saw him.

'Stop!' he said, arresting her by the arm. 'No more runnings away! Where
would you go? I'm come to fetch you home; and I hope you'll be a dutiful
daughter, and not encourage my son to further disobedience. I was embarrassed
how to punish him, when I discovered his part in the business: he's such a
cobweb, a pinch would annihilate him; but you'll see by his look that he has
received his due! I brought him down one evening, the day before yesterday,
and just set him in a chair, and never touched him afterwards. I sent Hareton
out, and we had the room to ourselves. In two hours, I called Joseph to carry
him up again; and, since then, my presence is as potent on his nerves as a ghost;
and I fancy he sees me often, though I am not near. Hareton says he wakes and
shrieks in the night by the hour together; and calls you to protect him from me;
and, whether you like your precious mate or not, you must come: he's your
concern now; I yield all my interest in him to you.'

'Why not let Catherine continue here?' I pleaded, 'and send Master Linton
to her. As you hate them both, you'd not miss them: they *can* only be a daily
plague to your unnatural heart.'

'I'm seeking a tenant for the Grange,' he answered; 'and I want my children
about me, to be sure – besides, that lass owes me her services for her bread; I'm
not going to nurture her in luxury and idleness after Linton is gone. Make haste
and get ready now. And don't oblige me to compel you.'

'I shall,' said Catherine. 'Linton is all I have to love in the world, and, though
you have done what you could to make him hateful to me, and me to him, you
*cannot* make us hate each other! And I defy you to hurt him when I am by, and I
defy you to frighten me.'

'You are a boastful champion,' replied Heathcliff; 'but I don't like you well
enough to hurt him: you shall get the full benefit of the torment, as long as it
lasts. It is not I who will make him hateful to you – it is his own sweet spirit. He's

as bitter as gall at your desertion, and its consequences; don't expect thanks for this noble devotion. I heard him draw a pleasant picture to Zillah of what he would do, if he were as strong as I: the inclination is there, and his very weakness will sharpen his wits to find a substitute for strength.'

'I know he has a bad nature,' said Catherine: 'he's your son. But I'm glad I've a better, to forgive it; and I know he loves me, and for that reason I love him. Mr Heathcliff, *you* have *nobody* to love you; and, however miserable you make us, we shall still have the revenge of thinking that your cruelty arises from your greater misery! You *are* miserable, are you not? Lonely, like the devil, and envious like him? *Nobody* loves you – *nobody* will cry for you when you die! I wouldn't be you!'

Catherine spoke with a kind of dreary triumph: she seemed to have made up her mind to enter into the spirit of her future family, and draw pleasure from the griefs of her enemies.

'You shall be sorry to be yourself presently,' said her father-in-law, 'if you stand there another minute. Begone, witch, and get your things.'

She scornfully withdrew. In her absence, I began to beg for Zillah's place at the Heights, offering to resign mine to her; but he would suffer it on no account.

He bid me be silent; and then, for the first time, allowed himself a glance round the room, and a look at the pictures. Having studied Mrs Linton, he said – 'I shall have that home. Not because I need it, but – ' He turned abruptly to the fire, and continued, with what, for lack of a better word, I must call a smile – 'I'll tell you what I did yesterday! I got the sexton, who was digging Linton's grave, to remove the earth off her coffin-lid, and I opened it. I thought, once, I would have stayed there, when I saw her face again – it is hers yet – he had hard work to stir me; but he said it would change, if the air blew on it, and so I struck one side of the coffin loose, and covered it up: not Linton's side, damn him! I wish he'd been soldered in lead – and I bribed the sexton to pull it away, when I'm laid there, and slide mine out too. I'll have it made so, and then, by the time Linton gets to us, he'll not know which is which!'

'You were very wicked, Mr Heathcliff!' I exclaimed; 'were you not ashamed to disturb the dead?'

'I disturbed nobody, Nelly,' he replied; 'and I gave some ease to myself. I shall be a great deal more comfortable now; and you'll have a better chance of keeping me underground, when I get there. Disturbed her? No! She has disturbed me, night and day, through eighteen years – incessantly – remorselessly – till yesternight; and yesternight I was tranquil. I dreamt I was sleeping the last sleep by that sleeper, with my heart stopped and my cheek frozen against hers.'

'And if she had been dissolved into earth, or worse, what would you have dreamt of then?' I said.

'Of dissolving with her, and being more happy still!' he answered. 'Do you suppose I dread any change of that sort? I expected such a transformation on raising the lid, but I'm better pleased that it should not commence till I share it. Besides, unless I had received a distinct impression of her passionless features, that strange feeling would hardly have been removed. It began oddly. You know, I was wild after she died; and eternally, from dawn to dawn, praying her

to return to me – her spirit – I have a strong faith in ghosts: I have a conviction that they can, and do exist, among us! The day she was buried, there came a fall of snow. In the evening I went to the churchyard. It blew bleak as winter – all round was solitary: I didn't fear that her fool of a husband would wander up the den so late; and no one else had business to bring them there. Being alone, and conscious two yards of loose earth was the sole barrier between us, I said to myself – "I'll have her in my arms again! If she be cold, I'll think it is this north wind that chills *me*; and if she be motionless, it is sleep." I got a spade from the toolhouse, and began to delve with all my might – it scraped the coffin; I fell to work with my hands; the wood commenced cracking about the screws, I was on the point of attaining my object, when it seemed that I heard a sigh from someone above, close at the edge of the grave, and bending down. "If I can only get this off," I muttered, "I wish they may shovel in the earth over us both!" and I wrenched more desperately still. There was another sigh, close at my ear. I appeared to feel the warm breath of it displacing the sleet-laden wind. I knew no living thing in flesh and blood was by; but as certainly as you perceive the approach to some substantial body in the dark, though it cannot be discerned, so certainly I felt that Cathy was there: not under me, but on the earth. A sudden sense of relief flowed, from my heart, through every limb. I relinquished my labour of agony, and turned consoled at once: unspeakably consoled. Her presence was with me: it remained while I refilled the grave, and led me home. You may laugh, if you will; but I was sure I should see her there. I was sure she was with me, and I could not help talking to her. Having reached the Heights, I rushed eagerly to the door. It was fastened; and, I remember, that accursed Earnshaw and my wife opposed my entrance. I remember stopping to kick the breath out of him, and then hurrying upstairs, to my room, and hers. I looked round impatiently – I felt her by me – I could *almost* see her, and yet I *could not*! I ought to have sweat blood then, from the anguish of my yearning – from the fervour of my supplications to have but one glimpse! I had not one. She showed herself, as she often was in life, a devil to me! And, since then, sometimes more and sometimes less, I've been the sport of that intolerable torture! Infernal – keeping my nerves at such a stretch, that, if they had not resembled catgut, they would, long ago, have relaxed to the feebleness of Linton's. When I sat in the house with Hareton, it seemed that on going out, I should meet her; when I walked on the moors I should meet her coming in. When I went from home, I hastened to return: she *must* be somewhere at the Heights, I was certain! And when I slept in her chamber – I was beaten out of that – I couldn't lie there; for the moment I closed my eyes, she was either outside the window, or sliding back the panels, or entering the room, or even resting her darling head on the same pillow as she did when a child. And I must open my lids to see. And so I opened and closed them a hundred times a night – to be always disappointed! It racked me! I've often groaned aloud, till that old rascal Joseph no doubt believed that my conscience was playing the fiend inside of me. Now, since I've seen her, I'm pacified – a little. It was a strange way of killing, not by inches, but by fractions of hairbreadths, to beguile me with the spectre of a hope, through eighteen years!'

Mr Heathcliff paused and wiped his forehead; his hair clung to it, wet with perspiration; his eyes were fixed on the red embers of the fire; the brows not contracted, but raised next the temples; diminishing the grim aspect of his countenance, but imparting a peculiar look of trouble, and a painful appearance of mental tension towards one absorbing subject. He only half addressed me, and I maintained silence – I didn't like to hear him talk! After a short period, he resumed his meditation on the picture, took it down and leant it against the sofa to contemplate it at better advantage; and while so occupied Catherine entered, announcing that she was ready, when her pony should be saddled.

'Send that over tomorrow,' said Heathcliff to me, then turning to her he added, 'You may do without your pony: it is a fine evening, and you'll need no ponies at Wuthering Heights; for what journeys you take, your own feet will serve you – come along.'

'Goodbye, Ellen!' whispered my dear little mistress. As she kissed me, her lips felt like ice. 'Come and see me Ellen, don't forget.'

'Take care you do no such thing, Mrs Dean!' said her new father. 'When I wish to speak to you I'll come here. I want none of your prying at my house!'

He signed her to precede him; and casting back a look that cut my heart, she obeyed. I watched them from the window, walk down the garden. Heathcliff fixed Catherine's arm under his: though she disputed the act, at first, evidently; and with rapid strides, he hurried her into the alley, whose trees concealed them.

## Chapter 30

I have paid a visit to the Heights, but I have not seen her since she left: Joseph held the door in his hand, when I called to ask after her, and wouldn't let me pass. He said Mrs Linton was 'thrang', and the master was not in. Zillah has told me something of the way they go on, otherwise I should hardly know who was dead and who living. She thinks Catherine haughty, and does not like her, I can guess by her talk. My young lady asked some aid of her when she first came; but Mr Heathcliff told her to follow her own business, and let his daughter-in-law look after herself; and Zillah willingly acquiesced, being a narrow-minded selfish woman. Catherine evinced a child's annoyance at this neglect; repaid it with contempt, and thus enlisted my informant among her enemies, as securely as if she had done her some great wrong. I had a long talk with Zillah, about six weeks ago, a little before you came, one day, when we foregathered on the moor; and this is what she told me.

'The first thing Mrs Linton did,' she said, 'on her arrival at the Heights, was to run upstairs without even wishing good-evening to me and Joseph; she shut herself into Linton's room, and remained till morning. Then, while the master and Earnshaw were at breakfast, she entered the house, and asked all in a quiver if the doctor might be sent for? Her cousin was very ill.

' "We know that!" answered Heathcliff; "but his life is not worth a farthing, and I won't spend a farthing on him."

' "But I cannot tell how to do," she said; "and if nobody will help me, he'll die!"

' "Walk out of the room," cried the master, "and let me never hear a word more about him! None here care what becomes of him; if you do, act the nurse; if you do not, lock him up and leave him."

'Then she began to bother me, and I said I'd had enough plague with the tiresome thing; we each had our tasks, and hers was to wait on Linton, Mr Heathcliff bid me leave that labour to her.

'How they managed together, I can't tell. I fancy he fretted a great deal, and moaned hisseln, night and day; and she had precious little rest, one could guess by her white face, and heavy eyes – she sometimes came into the kitchen all wildered like, and looked as if she would fain beg assistance; but I was not going to disobey the master: I never dare disobey him, Mrs Dean, and though I thought it wrong that Kenneth should not be sent for, it was no concern of mine, either to advise or complain; and I always refused to meddle. Once or twice, after we had gone to bed, I've happened to open my door again, and seen her sitting crying, on the stairs' top; and then I've shut myself in, quick, for fear of being moved to interfere. I did pity her then, I'm sure: still I didn't want to lose my place, you know!

'At last, one night she came boldly into my chamber, and frightened me out of my wits, by saying – ' "Tell Mr Heathcliff that his son is dying – I'm sure he is, this time. Get up, instantly, and tell him!"

'Having uttered this speech, she vanished again. I lay a quarter of an hour listening and trembling. Nothing stirred – the house was quiet.

' "She's mistaken," I said to myself. "He's got over it. I needn't disturb them." And I began to dose. But my sleep was marred a second time, by a sharp ringing of the bell – the only bell we have, put up on purpose for Linton; and the master called to me to see what was the matter, and inform them that he wouldn't have that noise repeated.

'I delivered Catherine's message. He cursed to himself, and in a few minutes came out with a lighted candle, and proceeded to their room. I followed. Mrs Heathcliff was seated by the bedside, with her hands folded on her knees. Her father-in-law went up, held the light to Linton's face, looked at him, and touched him; afterwards he turned to her.

' "Now – Catherine," he said, "how do you feel?"

'She was dumb.

' "How do you feel, Catherine?" he repeated.

' "He's safe, and I'm free," she answered: "I should feel well – but," she continued with a bitterness she couldn't conceal, "you have left me so long to struggle against death, alone, that I feel and see only death! I feel like death!"

'And she looked like it, too! I gave her a little wine. Hareton and Joseph, who had been wakened by the ringing, and the sound of feet, and heard our talk from outside, now entered. Joseph was fain, I believe, of the lad's removal; Hareton seemed a thought bothered: though he was more taken up with staring at

Catherine than thinking of Linton. But the master bid him get off to bed again: we didn't want his help. He afterwards made Joseph remove the body to his chamber, and told me to return to mine, and Mrs Heathcliff remained by herself.

'In the morning, he sent me to tell her she must come down to breakfast: she had undressed, and appeared going to sleep; and said she was ill; at which I hardly wondered. I informed Mr Heathcliff, and he replied – "Well, let her be till after the funeral; and go up now and then to get her what is needful; and as soon as she seems better, tell me." '

Cathy stayed upstairs a fortnight, according to Zillah, who visited her twice a day, and would have been rather more friendly, but her attempts at increasing kindness were proudly and promptly repelled.

Heathcliff went up at once, to show her Linton's will. He had bequeathed the whole of his, and what had been her moveable property to his father. The poor creature was threatened, or coaxed, into that act during her week's absence, when his uncle died. The lands, being a minor, he could not meddle with. However, Mr Heathcliff has claimed and kept them in his wife's right, and his also: I suppose legally, at any rate Catherine, destitute of cash and friends, cannot disturb his possession.

'Nobody,' said Zillah, 'ever approached her door, except that once, but I . . . and nobody asked anything about her. The first occasion of her coming down into the house, was on a Sunday afternoon. She had cried out, when I carried up her dinner, that she couldn't bear any longer being in the cold; and I told her the master was going to Thrushcross Grange; and Earnshaw and I needn't hinder her from descending; so, as soon as she heard Heathcliff's horse trot off, she made her appearance, donned in black, and her yellow curls combed back behind her ears, as plain as a quaker: she couldn't comb them out.

'Joseph and I generally go to chapel on Sundays. (The kirk, you know, has no minister now,' explained Mrs Dean; 'and they call the Methodists' or Baptists' place, I can't say which it is, at Gimmerton, a chapel.) Joseph had gone,' she continued, 'but I thought proper to bide at home. Young folks are always the better for an elder's overlooking; and Hareton, with all his bashfulness, isn't a model of nice behaviour. I let him know that his cousin would very likely sit with us, and she had been always used to see the Sabbath respected; so he had as good leave his guns, and bits of indoor work alone, while she stayed. He coloured up at the news, and cast his eyes over his hands and clothes. The train-oil and gunpowder were shoved out of sight in a minute. I saw he meant to give her his company; and I guessed, by his way, he wanted to be presentable; so, laughing, as I durst not laugh when the master is by, I offered to help him, if he would, and joked at his confusion. He grew sullen, and began to swear.

'Now, Mrs Dean,' she went on, seeing me not pleased by her manner, 'you happen think your young lady too fine for Mr Hareton; and happen you're right: but, I own, I should love well to bring her pride a peg lower. And what will all her learning and her daintiness do for her, now? She's as poor as you or I: poorer, I'll be bound: you're saving, and I'm doing my little all, that road.'

Hareton allowed Zillah to give him her aid; and she flattered him into a good

humour; so, when Catherine came, half forgetting her former insults, he tried to make himself agreeable, by the housekeeper's account.

'Missis walked in,' she said, 'as chill as an icicle, and as high as a princess. I got up and offered her my seat in the armchair. No, she turned up her nose at my civility. Earnshaw rose too, and bid her come to the settle, and sit close by the fire: he was sure she was starved.

' "I've been starved a month and more," she answered, resting on the word, as scornful as she could.

'And she got a chair for herself, and placed it at a distance from both of us. Having sat till she was warm, she began to look round, and discovered a number of books in the dresser; she was instantly upon her feet again, stretching to reach them: but they were too high up. Her cousin, after watching her endeavours a while, at last summoned courage to help her; she held her frock, and he filled it with the first that came to hand.

'That was a great advance for the lad. She didn't thank him: still, he felt gratified that she had accepted his assistance, and ventured to stand behind as she examined them, and even to stoop and point out what struck his fancy in certain old pictures which they contained; nor was he daunted by the saucy style in which she jerked the page from his finger: he contented himself with going a bit farther back, and looking at her instead of the book. She continued reading, or seeking for something to read. His attention became, by degrees, quite centred in the study of her thick, silky curls: her face he couldn't see, and she couldn't see him. And, perhaps, not quite awake to what he did, but attracted like a child to a candle, at last he proceeded from staring to touching; he put out his hand and stroked one curl, as gently as if it were a bird. He might have stuck a knife into her neck, she started round in such a taking.

' "Get away, this moment! How dare you touch me? Why are you stopping there?" she cried, in a tone of disgust. "I can't endure you! I'll go upstairs again, if you come near me."

'Mr Hareton recoiled, looking as foolish as he could do: he sat down in the settle, very quiet, and she continued turning over her volumes, another half-hour; finally, Earnshaw crossed over, and whispered to me.

' "Will you ask her to read to us, Zillah? I'm stalled of doing naught; and I do like – I could like to hear her! Dunnot say I wanted it, but ask of yourseln."

' "Mr Hareton wishes you would read to us, ma'am," I said, immediately. "He'd take it very kind – he'd be much obliged."

'She frowned; and, looking up, answered – "Mr Hareton, and the whole set of you, will be good enough to understand that I reject any pretence at kindness you have the hypocrisy to offer! I despise you, and will have nothing to say to any of you! When I would have given my life for one kind word, even to see one of your faces, you all kept off. But I won't complain to you! I'm driven down here by the cold, not either to amuse you, or enjoy your society."

' "What could I ha' done?" began Earnshaw. "How was I to blame?"

' "Oh! you are an exception," answered Mrs Heathcliff. "I never missed such a concern as you."

' "But, I offered more than once, and asked," he said, kindling up at her pertness, "I asked Mr Heathcliff to let me wake for you – "

' "Be silent! I'll go out of doors, or anywhere, rather than have your disagreeable voice in my ear!" said my lady.

'Hareton muttered, she might go to hell, for him! and unslinging his gun, restrained himself from his Sunday occupations no longer. He talked now, freely enough; and she presently saw fit to retreat to her solitude: but the frost had set in, and, in spite of her pride, she was forced to condescend to our company, more and more. However, I took care there should be no further scorning at my good nature: ever since, I've been as stiff as herself; and she has no lover or liker among us: and she does not deserve one; for, let them say the least word to her, and she'll curl back without respect of anyone! She'll snap at the master himself, and as good as dares him to thrash her; and the more hurt she gets, the more venomous she grows.'

At first, on hearing this account from Zillah, I determined to leave my situation, take a cottage, and get Catherine to come and live with me: but Mr Heathcliff would as soon permit that, as he would set up Hareton in an independent house; and I can see no remedy, at present, unless she could marry again: and that scheme it does not come within my province to arrange.

Thus ended Mrs Dean's story. Notwithstanding the doctor's prophecy, I am rapidly recovering strength; and, though it be only the second week in January, I propose getting out on horseback in a day or two, and riding over to Wuthering Heights, to inform my landlord that I shall spend the next six months in London; and, if he likes, he may look out for another tenant to take the place, after October – I would not pass another winter here for much.

## Chapter 31

Yesterday was bright, calm, and frosty. I went to the Heights as I proposed: my housekeeper entreated me to bear a little note from her to her young lady, and I did not refuse, for the worthy woman was not conscious of anything odd in her request. The front door stood open, but the jealous gate was fastened, as at my last visit; I knocked, and invoked Earnshaw from among the garden beds; he unchained it, and I entered. The fellow is as handsome a rustic as need be seen. I took particular notice of him this time; but then he does his best, apparently, to make the least of his advantages.

I asked if Mr Heathcliff were at home? He answered, no; but he would be in at dinner time. It was eleven o'clock, and I announced my intention of going in, and waiting for him, at which he immediately flung down his tools and accompanied me, in the office of watchdog, not as a substitute for the host.

We entered together; Catherine was there, making herself useful in preparing some vegetables for the approaching meal; she looked more sulky, and less

spirited than when I had seen her first. She hardly raised her eyes to notice me, and continued her employment with the same disregard to common forms of politeness, as before; never returning my bow and good-morning by the slightest acknowledgment.

'She does not seem so amiable,' I thought, 'as Mrs Dean would persuade me to believe. She's a beauty, it is true; but not an angel.'

Earnshaw surlily bid her remove her things to the kitchen. 'Remove them yourself,' she said, pushing them from her as soon as she had done; and retiring to a stool by the window, where she began to carve figures of birds and beasts out of the turnip parings in her lap. I approached her, pretending to desire a view of the garden; and, as I fancied, adroitly dropped Mrs Dean's note on to her knee, unnoticed by Hareton – but she asked aloud, 'What is that?' and chucked it off.

'A letter from your old acquaintance, the housekeeper at the Grange,' I answered, annoyed at her exposing my kind deed, and fearful lest it should be imagined a missive of my own. She would gladly have gathered it up at this information, but Hareton beat her; he seized, and put it in his waistcoat, saying Mr Heathcliff should look at it first. Thereat, Catherine silently turned her face from us, and, very stealthily, drew out her pocket-handkerchief and applied it to her eyes; and her cousin, after struggling a while to keep down his softer feelings, pulled out the letter and flung it on the floor beside her, as ungraciously as he could.

Catherine caught and perused it eagerly; then she put a few questions to me concerning the inmates, rational and irrational, of her former home; and gazing towards the hills, murmured in soliloquy – 'I should like to be riding Minny down there! I should like to be climbing up there – Oh! I'm tired – I'm *stalled*, Hareton!' And she leant her pretty head back against the sill, with half a yawn and half a sigh, and lapsed into an aspect of abstracted sadness: neither caring nor knowing whether we remarked her.

'Mrs Heathcliff,' I said, after sitting some time mute, 'are you not aware that I am an acquaintance of yours? So intimate, that I think it strange you won't come and speak to me. My housekeeper never wearies of talking about and praising you; and she'll be greatly disappointed if I return with no news of, or from you, except that you received her letter and said nothing!'

She appeared to wonder at this speech and asked – 'Does Ellen like you?'

'Yes, very well,' I replied unhesitatingly.

'You must tell her,' she continued, 'that I would answer her letter, but I have no materials for writing: not even a book from which I might tear a leaf.'

'No books!' I exclaimed. 'How do you contrive to live here without them? If I may take the liberty to enquire. Though provided with a large library, I'm frequently very dull at the Grange; take my books away, and I should be desperate!'

'I was always reading, when I had them,' said Catherine: 'and Mr Heathcliff never reads; so he took it into his head to destroy my books. I have not had a glimpse of one, for weeks. Only once, I searched through Joseph's store of

theology, to his great irritation; and once, Hareton, I came upon a secret stock in your room . . . some Latin and Greek, and some tales and poetry: all old friends – I brought the last here – and you gathered them, as a magpie gathers silver spoons, for the mere love of stealing! They are of no use to you; or else you concealed them in the bad spirit, that as you cannot enjoy them, nobody else shall. Perhaps *your* envy counselled Mr Heathcliff to rob me of my treasures? But I've most of them written on my brain and printed in my heart, and you cannot deprive me of those!'

Earnshaw blushed crimson when his cousin made this revelation of his private literary accumulations, and stammered an indignant denial of her accusations.

'Mr Hareton is desirous of increasing his amount of knowledge,' I said, coming to his rescue. 'He is not *envious* but *emulous* of your attainments – He'll be a clever scholar in a few years!'

'And he wants *me* to sink into a dunce, meantime,' answered Catherine. 'Yes, I hear him trying to spell and read to himself, and pretty blunders he makes! I wish you would repeat Chevy Chase as you did yesterday: it was extremely funny! I heard you . . . and I heard you turning over the dictionary, to seek out the hard words, and then cursing, because you couldn't read their explanations!'

The young man evidently thought it too bad that he should be laughed at for his ignorance, and then laughed at for trying to remove it. I had a similar notion, and, remembering Mrs Dean's anecdote of his first attempt at enlightening the darkness in which he had been reared, I observed – 'But, Mrs Heathcliff, we have each had a commencement, and each stumbled and tottered on the threshold, and had our teachers scorned, instead of aiding us, we should stumble and totter yet.'

'Oh!' she replied, 'I don't wish to limit his acquirements . . . still, he has no right to appropriate what is mine, and make it ridiculous to me with his vile mistakes and mispronunciations! Those books, both prose and verse, were consecrated to me by other associations, and I hate to have them debased and profaned in his mouth! Besides, of all, he has selected my favourite pieces that I love the most to repeat, as if out of deliberate malice!'

Hareton's chest heaved in silence a minute: he laboured under a severe sense of mortification and wrath, which it was no easy task to suppress.

I rose and, from a gentlemanly idea of relieving his embarrassment, took up my station in the doorway, surveying the external prospect as I stood. He followed my example, and left the room; but presently reappeared, bearing half a dozen volumes in his hands, which he threw into Catherine's lap, exclaiming – 'Take them! I never want to hear, or read, or think of them again!'

'I won't have them, now,' she answered. 'I shall connect them with you, and hate them.'

She opened one that had obviously been often turned over, and read a portion in the drawling tone of a beginner; then laughed, and threw it from her. 'And listen,' she continued provokingly, commencing a verse of an old ballad in the same fashion.

But his self-love would endure no further torment: I heard, and not altogether

disapprovingly, a manual check given to her saucy tongue – The little wretch had done her utmost to hurt her cousin's sensitive though uncultivated feelings, and a physical argument was the only mode he had of balancing the account and repaying its effects on the inflicter. He afterwards gathered the books and hurled them on the fire. I read in his countenance what anguish it was to offer that sacrifice to spleen – I fancied that as they consumed, he recalled the pleasure they had already imparted, and the triumph and ever-increasing pleasure he had anticipated from them; and I fancied, I guessed the incitement to his secret studies, also. He had been content with daily labour and rough animal enjoyments, till Catherine crossed his path. Shame at her scorn, and hope of her approval, were his first prompters to higher pursuits; and instead of guarding him from one, and winning him the other, his endeavours to raise himself had produced just the contrary result.

'Yes; that's all the good that such a brute as you can get from them!' cried Catherine, sucking her damaged lip, and watching the conflagration with indignant eyes.

'You'd *better* hold your tongue, now!' he answered fiercely.

And his agitation precluding further speech, he advanced hastily to the entrance, where I made way for him to pass. But, ere he had crossed the door-stones, Mr Heathcliff, coming up the causeway, encountered him, and laying hold of his shoulder, asked – 'What's to do now, my lad?'

'Naught, naught!' he said, and broke away, to enjoy his grief and anger in solitude.

Heathcliff gazed after him, and sighed.

'It will be odd, if I thwart myself!' he muttered, unconscious that I was behind him. 'But, when I look for his father in his face, I find *her* every day more! How the devil is he so like? I can hardly bear to see him.'

He bent his eyes to the ground, and walked moodily in. There was a restless, anxious expression in his countenance I had never remarked there before; and he looked sparer in person. His daughter-in-law, on perceiving him through the window, immediately escaped to the kitchen, so that I remained alone.

'I'm glad to see you out of doors again, Mr Lockwood.' he said in reply to my greeting, 'from selfish motives partly: I don't think I could readily supply your loss in this desolation. I've wondered, more than once, what brought you here.'

'An idle whim, I fear, sir,' was my answer; 'or else an idle whim is going to spirit me away. I shall set out for London, next week; and I must give you warning, that I feel no disposition to retain Thrushcross Grange beyond the twelve-months I agreed to rent it. I believe I shall not live there any more.'

'Oh, indeed! You're tired of being banished from the world, are you?' he said. 'But, if you be coming to plead off paying for a place you won't occupy, your journey is useless: I never relent in exacting my due, from anyone.'

'I'm coming to plead off nothing about it!' I exclaimed, considerably irritated. 'Should you wish it, I'll settle with you now,' and I drew my notebook from my pocket.

'No, no,' he replied coolly; 'you'll leave sufficient behind to cover your debts,

if you fail to return: I'm not in such a hurry – sit down and take your dinner with us; a guest that is safe from repeating his visit can generally be made welcome. Catherine! Bring the things in: where are you?'

Catherine reappeared, bearing a tray of knives and forks.

'You may get your dinner with Joseph,' muttered Heathcliff aside, 'and remain in the kitchen till he is gone.'

She obeyed his directions very punctually: perhaps she had no temptation to transgress. Living among clowns and misanthropists, she probably cannot appreciate a better class of people, when she meets them.

With Mr Heathcliff, grim and saturnine, on one hand, and Hareton, absolutely dumb, on the other, I made a somewhat cheerless meal, and bid adieu early. I would have departed by the back way, to get a last glimpse of Catherine, and annoy old Joseph; but Hareton received orders to lead up my horse, and my host himself escorted me to the door, so I could not fulfil my wish.

'How dreary life gets over in that house!' I reflected, while riding down the road. 'What a realisation of something more romantic than a fairy tale it would have been for Mrs Linton Heathcliff, had she and I struck up an attachment, as her good nurse desired, and migrated together into the stirring atmosphere of the town!'

## *Chapter 32*

1802 – This September, I was invited to devastate the moors of a friend, in the North; and, on my journey to his abode, I unexpectedly came within fifteen miles of Gimmerton.

The ostler at a roadside public-house was holding a pail of water to refresh my horses, when a cart of very green oats, newly reaped, passed by, and he remarked – 'Yon's frough Gimmerton, nah! They're alias three wick' after other folk wi' ther harvest.'

'Gimmerton?' I repeated – my residence in that locality had already grown dim and dreamy. 'Ah! I know! How far is it from this?'

'Happen fourteen mile' o'er th' hills, and a rough road,' he answered.

A sudden impulse seized me to visit Thrushcross Grange. It was scarcely noon, and I conceived that I might as well pass the night under my own roof, as in an inn. Besides, I could spare a day easily, to arrange matters with my landlord, and thus save myself the trouble of invading the neighbourhood again. Having rested a while, I directed my servant to enquire the way to the village; and, with great fatigue to our beasts, we managed the distance in some three hours.

I left him there, and proceeded down the valley alone. The grey church looked greyer, and the lonely churchyard lonelier. I distinguished a moor sheep cropping the short turf on the graves. It was sweet, warm weather – too warm for travelling; but the heat did not hinder me from enjoying the delightful scenery above and below: had I seen it nearer August, I'm sure it would have

tempted me to waste a month among its solitudes. In winter nothing more dreary, in summer nothing more divine, than those glens shut in by hills, and those bluff, bold swells of heath.

I reached the Grange before sunset, and knocked for admittance; but the family had retreated into the back premises, I judged by one thin, blue wreath curling from the kitchen chimney, and they did not hear. I rode into the court. Under the porch, a girl of nine or ten sat knitting, and an old woman reclined on the horse-steps, smoking a meditative pipe.

'Is Mrs Dean within?' I demanded of the dame.

'Mistress Dean? Nay!' she answered, 'shoo doesn't bide here; shoo's up at th' Heights.'

'Are you the housekeeper, then?' I continued.

'Eea, Aw keep th' hause,' she replied.

'Well, I'm Mr Lockwood, the master. Are there any rooms to lodge me in, I wonder? I wish to stay here all night.'

'T' maister!' she cried in astonishment. 'Whet, whoiver knew yah wur coming? Yah sud ha' send word! They's nowt norther dry – nor mensful abaht t' place: nowt there is n't!'

She threw down her pipe and bustled in, the girl followed, and I entered too; soon perceiving that her report was true, and, moreover, that I had almost upset her wits by my unwelcome apparition. I bid her be composed – I would go out for a walk; and, meantime, she must try to prepare a corner of a sitting-room for me to sup in, and a bedroom to sleep in. No sweeping and dusting, only good fires and dry sheets were necessary. She seemed willing to do her best; though she thrust the hearth-brush into the grates in mistake for the poker, and malappropriated several other articles of her craft: but I retired, confiding in her energy for a resting-place against my return. Wuthering Heights was the goal of my proposed excursion. An afterthought brought me back, when I had quitted the court.

'All well at the Heights?' I enquired of the woman.

'Eea, fr owt Ee knaw!' she answered, skurrying away with a pan of hot cinders.

I would have asked why Mrs Dean had deserted the Grange, but it was impossible to delay her at such a crisis, so I turned away and made my exit, rambling leisurely along, with the glow of a sinking sun behind, and the mild glory of a rising moon in front – one fading, and the other brightening, as I quitted the park, and climbed the stony by-road branching off to Mr Heathcliff's dwelling. Before I arrived in sight of it, all that remained of day was a beamless, amber light along the west: but I could see every pebble on the path, and every blade of grass, by that splendid moon. I had neither to climb the gate, nor to knock – it yielded to my hand. That is an improvement! I thought. And I noticed another, by the aid of my nostrils; a fragrance of stocks and wall flowers, wafted on the air, from amongst the homely fruit trees.

Both doors and lattices were open; and yet, as is usually the case in a coal district, a fine, red fire illumined the chimney: the comfort which the eye derives from it, renders the extra heat endurable. But the house of Wuthering Heights

is so large, that the inmates have plenty of space for withdrawing out of its influence; and, accordingly, what inmates there were had stationed themselves not far from one of the windows. I could both see them and hear them talk before I entered, and looked and listened in consequence; being moved thereto by a mingled sense of curiosity, and envy that grew as I lingered.

'Con–*trary*!' said a voice, as sweet as a silver bell – 'That for the third time, you dunce! I'm not going to tell you, again – Recollect, or I pull your hair!'

'Contrary, then,' answered another, in deep but softened tones. 'And now, kiss me, for minding so well.'

'No, read it over first correctly, without a single mistake.'

The male speaker began to read: he was a young man, respectably dressed, and seated at a table, having a book before him. His handsome features glowed with pleasure, and his eyes kept impatiently wandering from the page to a small white hand over his shoulder, which recalled him by a smart slap on the cheek, whenever its owner detected such signs of inattention. Its owner stood behind; her light shining ringlets blending, at intervals, with his brown locks, as she bent to superintend his studies; and her face – it was lucky he could not see her face, or he would never have been so steady – I could, and I bit my lip, in spite, at having thrown away the chance I might have had, of doing something besides staring at its smiting beauty.

The task was done, not free from further blunders; but the pupil claimed a reward, and received at least five kisses: which, however, he generously returned. Then, they came to the door, and from their conversation, I judged they were about to issue out and have a walk on the moors. I supposed I should be condemned in Hareton Earnshaw's heart, if not by his mouth, to the lowest pit in the infernal regions, if I showed my unfortunate person in his neighbourhood then; and feeling very mean and malignant, I skulked round to seek refuge in the kitchen.

There was unobstructed admittance on that side also; and, at the door, sat my old friend, Nelly Dean, sewing and singing a song, which was often interrupted from within, by harsh words of scorn and intolerance, uttered in far from musical accents.

'Aw'd rayther, by th' haulf, hev 'em swearing i' my lugs frough morn tuh neeght, nur hearken yah, hahsiver!' said the tenant of the kitchen, in answer to an unheard speech of Nelly's. 'It's a blazing shaime, ut Aw cannut oppen t' Blessed Book, bud yah set up them glories tuh sattan, un' all t' flay-some wickednesses ut iver wer born intuh t' warld! Oh! yah're a raight nowt; un' shoo's another; un' that poor lad 'ull be lost, atween ye. Poor lad!' he added, with a groan; 'he's witched, Aw'm sartin on 't! O, Lord, judge 'em, fur they's norther law nur justice amang wer rullers!'

'No! or we should be sitting in flaming faggots, I suppose,' retorted the singer. 'But wisht, old man, and read your Bible, like a Christian, and never mind me. This is "Fairy Annie's Wedding" – a bonny tune – it goes to a dance.'

Mrs Dean was about to recommence, when I advanced; and recognising me directly, she jumped to her feet, crying – 'Why, bless you, Mr Lockwood! How

could you think of returning in this way? All's shut up at Thrushcross Grange. You should have given us notice!'

'I've arranged to be accommodated there, for as long as I shall stay,' I answered. 'I depart again tomorrow. And how are you transplanted here, Mrs Dean? tell me that.'

'Zillah left, and Mr Heathcliff wished me to come, soon after you went to London, and stay till you returned. But, step in, pray! Have you walked from Gimmerton this evening?'

'From the Grange,' I replied; 'and, while they make me lodging room there, I want to finish my business with your master; because I don't think of having another opportunity in a hurry.'

'What business, sir?' said Nelly, conducting me into the house. 'He's gone out at present, and won't return soon.'

'About the rent,' I answered.

'Oh! Then it is with Mrs Heathcliff you must settle,' she observed; 'or rather with me. She has not learnt to manage her affairs yet, and I act for her: there's nobody else.'

I looked surprised.

'Ah! You have not heard of Heathcliff's death, I see!' she continued.

'Heathcliff dead?' I exclaimed, astonished. 'How long ago?'

'Three months since: but, sit down, and let me take your hat, and I'll tell you all about it. Stop, you have had nothing to eat, have you?'

'I want nothing. I have ordered supper at home. You sit down too. I never dreamt of his dying! Let me hear how it came to pass. You say you don't expect them back for some time – the young people?'

'No – I have to scold them every evening, for their late rambles: but they don't care for me. At least, have a drink of our old ale; it will do you good: you seem weary.'

She hastened to fetch it, before I could refuse, and I heard Joseph asking whether 'it warn't a crying scandal that she should have fellies at her time of life? And then, to get them jocks out uh' t' Maister's cellar! He fair shaamed to 'bide still and see it.'

She did not stay to retaliate, but re-entered, in a minute, bearing a reaming silver pint, whose contents I lauded with becoming earnestness. And afterwards she furnished me with the sequel of Heathcliff's history. He had a 'queer' end, as she expressed it.

I was summoned to Wuthering Heights, within a fortnight of your leaving us, she said; and I obeyed joyfully, for Catherine's sake. My first interview with her grieved and shocked me! She had altered so much since our separation. Mr Heathcliff did not explain his reasons for taking a new mind about my coming here; he only told me he wanted me, and he was tired of seeing Catherine: I must make the little parlour my sitting-room, and keep her with me. It was enough if he were obliged to see her once or twice a day. She seemed pleased at this arrangement; and, by degrees, I smuggled over a great number of books, and other articles, that had formed her amusement at the Grange; and flattered

myself we should get on in tolerable comfort. The delusion did not last long. Catherine, contented at first, in a brief space grew irritable and restless. For one thing, she was forbidden to move out of the garden, and it fretted her sadly to be confined to its narrow bounds, as Spring drew on; for another, in following the house, I was forced to quit her frequently, and she complained of loneliness: she preferred quarrelling with Joseph in the kitchen, to sitting at peace in her solitude. I did not mind their skirmishes: but Hareton was often obliged to seek the kitchen also, when the master wanted to have the house to himself; and though, in the beginning, she either left it at his approach, or quietly joined in my occupations, and shunned remarking or addressing him – and though he was always as sullen and silent as possible – after a while, she changed her behaviour, and became incapable of letting him alone: talking at him; commenting on his stupidity and idleness; expressing her wonder how he could endure the life he lived – how he could sit a whole evening staring into the fire, and dozing.

'He's just like a dog, is he not, Ellen?' she once observed, 'or a carthorse? He does his work, eats his food, and sleeps, eternally! What a blank, dreary mind he must have! Do you ever dream, Hareton? And, if you do, what is it about? But you can't speak to me!'

Then she looked at him; but he would neither open his mouth nor look again.

'He's perhaps dreaming now,' she continued. 'He twitched his shoulder as Juno twitches hers. Ask him, Ellen.'

'Mr Hareton will ask the master to send you upstairs, if you don't behave!' I said. He had not only twitched his shoulder but clenched his fist, as if tempted to use it.

'I know why Hareton never speaks, when I am in the kitchen,' she exclaimed, on another occasion. 'He is afraid I shall laugh at him. Ellen, what do you think? He began to teach himself to read once; and, because I laughed, he burned his books, and dropped it: was he not a fool?'

'Were not you naughty?' I said; 'answer me that.'

'Perhaps I was,' she went on; 'but I did not expect him to be so silly. Hareton, if I gave you a book, would you take it now? I'll try!'

She placed one she had been perusing on his hand; he flung it off, and muttered, if she did not give over, he would break her neck.

'Well, I shall put it here,' she said, 'in the table drawer; and I'm going to bed.'

Then she whispered me to watch whether he touched it, and departed. But he would not come near it; and so I informed her in the morning, to her great disappointment. I saw she was sorry for his persevering sulkiness and indolence: her conscience reproved her for frightening him off improving himself: she had done it effectually.

But her ingenuity was at work to remedy the injury: while I ironed, or pursued other stationary employments I could not well do in the parlour, she would bring some pleasant volume and read it aloud to me. When Hareton was there, she generally paused in an interesting part, and left the book lying about: that she did repeatedly; but he was as obstinate as a mule, and, instead of snatching at her bait, in wet weather he took to smoking with Joseph, and they

sat like automatons, one on each side of the fire, the elder happily too deaf to understand her wicked nonsense, as he would have called it, the younger doing his best to seem to disregard it. On fine evenings the latter followed his shooting expeditions, and Catherine yawned and sighed, and teased me to talk to her, and ran off into the court or garden, the moment I began; and, as a last resource, cried and said, she was tired of living: her life was useless.

Mr Heathcliff, who grew more and more disinclined to society, had almost banished Earnshaw out of his apartment. Owing to an accident, at the commencement of March, he became for some days a fixture in the kitchen. His gun burst while out on the hills by himself; a splinter cut his arm, and he lost a good deal of blood before he could reach home. The consequence was, that, perforce, he was condemned to the fireside and tranquillity, till he made it up again. It suited Catherine to have him there: at any rate, it made her hate her room upstairs more than ever: and she would compel me to find out business below, that she might accompany me.

On Easter Monday, Joseph went to Gimmerton fair with some cattle; and, in the afternoon, I was busy getting up linen in the kitchen. Earnshaw sat, morose as usual, at the chimney corner, and my little mistress was beguiling an idle hour with drawing pictures on the window panes, varying her amusement by smothered bursts of songs, and whispered ejaculations, and quick glances of annoyance and impatience in the direction of her cousin, who steadfastly smoked, and looked into the grate.

At a notice that I could do with her no longer, intercepting my light, she removed to the hearthstone. I bestowed little attention on her proceedings, but, presently, I heard her begin – 'I've found out, Hareton, that I want – that I'm glad – that I should like you to be my cousin, now, if you had not grown so cross to me, and so rough.'

Hareton returned no answer.

'Hareton, Hareton, Hareton! do you hear?' she continued.

'Get off wi' ye!' he growled, with uncompromising gruffness.

'Let me take that pipe,' she said, cautiously advancing her hand, and abstracting it from his mouth.

Before he could attempt to recover it, it was broken, and behind the fire. He swore at her and seized another.

'Stop,' she cried, 'you must listen to me, first; and I can't speak while those clouds are floating in my face.'

'Will you go to the devil!' he exclaimed, ferociously, 'and let me be!'

'No,' she persisted, 'I won't: I can't tell what to do to make you talk to me; and you are determined not to understand. When I call you stupid, I don't mean anything: I don't mean that I despise you. Come, you shall take notice of me, Hareton: you are my cousin, and you shall own me.'

'I shall have naught to do wi' you, and your mucky pride, and your damned, mocking tricks!' he answered. 'I'll go to hell, body and soul, before I look sideways after you again! Side out of t' gait, now; this minute!'

Catherine frowned, and retreated to the window-seat, chewing her lip, and

endeavouring, by humming an eccentric tune, to conceal a growing tendency to sob.

'You should be friends with your cousin, Mr Hareton,' I interrupted, 'since she repents of her sauciness! It would do you a great deal of good: it would make you another man, to have her for a companion.'

'A companion?' he cried; 'when she hates me, and does not think me fit to wipe her shoon! Nay, if it made me a king, I'd not be scorned for seeking her good will any more.'

'It is not I who hate you, it is you who hate me!' wept Cathy, no longer disguising her trouble. 'You hate me as much as Mr Heathcliff does, and more.'

'You're a damned liar,' began Earnshaw: 'why have I made him angry, by taking your part then, a hundred times? And that, when you sneered at, and despised me, and – Go on plaguing me, and I'll step in yonder, and say you worried me out of the kitchen!'

'I didn't know you took my part,' she answered, drying her eyes; 'and I was miserable and bitter at everybody; but, now I thank you, and beg you to forgive me, what can I do besides?'

She returned to the hearth, and frankly extended her hand. He blackened, and scowled like a thundercloud, and kept his fists resolutely clenched, and his gaze fixed on the ground.

Catherine, by instinct, must have divined it was obdurate perversity, and not dislike, that prompted this dogged conduct; for, after remaining an instant undecided, she stooped, and impressed on his cheek a gentle kiss. The little rogue thought I had not seen her, and, drawing back, she took her former station by the window, quite demurely. I shook my head reprovingly; and then she blushed, and whispered – 'Well! what should I have done, Ellen? He wouldn't shake hands, and he wouldn't look: I must show him some way that I like him – that I want to be friends.'

Whether the kiss convinced Hareton, I cannot tell: he was very careful, for some minutes, that his face should not be seen; and when he did raise it, he was sadly puzzled where to turn his eyes.

Catherine employed herself in wrapping a handsome book neatly in white paper; and having tied it with a bit of ribband, and addressed it to 'Mr Hareton Earnshaw,' she desired me to be her ambassadress, and convey the present to its destined recipient.

'And tell him, if he'll take it, I'll come and teach him to read it right,' she said; 'and, if he refuse it, I'll go upstairs, and never tease him again.'

I carried it, and repeated the message, anxiously watched by my employer. Hareton would not open his fingers, so I laid it on his knee. He did not strike it off, either. I returned to my work: Catherine leaned her head and arms on the table, till she heard the slight rustle of the covering being removed; then she stole away, and quietly seated herself beside her cousin. He trembled, and his face glowed: all his rudeness and all his surly harshness had deserted him: he could not summon courage, at first, to utter a syllable, in reply to her questioning look, and her murmured petition.

'Say you forgive me, Hareton, do! You can make me so happy, by speaking that little word.'

He muttered something inaudible.

'And you'll be my friend?' added Catherine, interrogatively.

'Nay! you'll be ashamed of me every day of your life,' he answered. 'And the more, the more you know me, and I cannot bide it.'

'So, you won't be my friend?' she said, smiling as sweet as honey, and creeping close up.

I overheard no further distinguishable talk, but on looking round again, I perceived two such radiant countenances bent over the page of the accepted book, that I did not doubt the treaty had been ratified, on both sides, and the enemies were, thenceforth, sworn allies.

The work they studied was full of costly pictures; and those, and their position, had charm enough to keep them unmoved, till Joseph came home. He, poor man, was perfectly aghast at the spectacle of Catherine seated on the same bench with Hareton Earnshaw, leaning her hand on his shoulder; and confounded at his favourite's endurance of her proximity. It affected him too deeply to allow an observation on the subject that night. His emotion was only revealed by the immense sighs he drew, as he solemnly spread his large Bible on the table, and overlaid it with dirty banknotes from his pocketbook, the produce of the day's transactions. At length, he summoned Hareton from his seat.

'Tak' these in tuh t' maister, lad,' he said, 'un' bide theare; Aw's gang up tuh my awn rahm. This hoile's norther mensful, nor seemly fur us – we mun side aht, and seearch another!'

'Come, Catherine,' I said, 'we must "side out" too: I've done my ironing, are you ready to go?'

'It is not eight o'clock!' she answered, rising unwillingly. 'Hareton, I'll leave this book upon the chimney-piece, and I'll bring some more tomorrow.'

'Ony books ut yah leave, Aw suall tak' intuh th' hahse,' said Joseph, 'un' it'ull be mitch if yah find 'em agean; soa, yah muh plase yourseln!'

Cathy threatened that his library should pay for hers; and, smiling as she passed Hareton, went singing upstairs: lighter of heart, I venture to say, than ever she had been under that roof before; except, perhaps, during her earliest visits to Linton.

The intimacy thus commenced, grew rapidly: though it encountered temporary interruptions. Earnshaw was not to be civilised with a wish; and my young lady was no philosopher, and no paragon of patience; but both their minds tending to the same point – one loving and desiring to esteem, and the other loving and desiring to be esteemed – they contrived in the end to reach it.

You see, Mr Lockwood, it was easy enough to win Mrs Heathcliff's heart. But now, I'm glad you did not try. The crown of all my wishes will be the union of those two. I shall envy no one on their wedding-day: there won't be a happier woman than myself in England!

On the morrow of that Monday, Earnshaw being still unable to follow his ordinary employments, and therefore remaining about the house, I speedily found it would be impracticable to retain my charge beside me, as heretofore. She got downstairs before me, and out into the garden, where she had seen her cousin performing some easy work; and when I went to bid them come to breakfast, I saw she had persuaded him to clear a large space of ground from currant and gooseberry bushes, and they were busy planning together an importation of plants from the Grange.

I was terrified at the devastation which had been accomplished in a brief half-hour; the black currant trees were the apple of Joseph's eye, and she had just fixed her choice of a flower bed in the midst of them!

'There! That will be all shewn to the master,' I exclaimed, 'the minute it is discovered. And what excuse have you to offer for taking such liberties with the garden? We shall have a fine explosion on the head of it: see if we don't! Mr Hareton, I wonder you should have no more wit, than to go and make that mess at her bidding!'

'I'd forgotten they were Joseph's,' answered Earnshaw, rather puzzled; 'but I'll tell him I did it.'

We always ate our meals with Mr Heathcliff. I held the mistress's post in making tea and carving; so I was indispensable at table. Catherine usually sat by me; but today, she stole nearer to Hareton, and I presently saw she would have no more discretion in her friendship, than she had in her hostility.

'Now, mind you don't talk with and notice your cousin too much,' were my whispered instructions as we entered the room. 'It will certainly annoy Mr Heathcliff, and he'll be mad at you both.'

'I'm not going to,' she answered.

The minute after, she had sidled to him, and was sticking primroses in his plate of porridge.

He dared not speak to her, there: he dared hardly look; and yet she went on teasing, till he was twice on the point of being provoked to laugh; and I frowned, and then, she glanced towards the master, whose mind was occupied on other subjects than his company, as his countenance evinced, and she grew serious for an instant, scrutinising him with deep gravity. Afterwards she turned, and recommenced her nonsense; at last, Hareton uttered a smothered laugh. Mr Heathcliff started; his eye rapidly surveyed our faces. Catherine met it with her accustomed look of nervousness, and yet defiance, which he abhorred.

'It is well you are out of my reach,' he exclaimed. 'What fiend possesses you to stare back at me, continually, with those infernal eyes? Down with them! And don't remind me of your existence again. I thought I had cured you of laughing!'

'It was me,' muttered Hareton.

'What do you say?' demanded the master.

Hareton looked at his plate, and did not repeat the confession. Mr Heathcliff looked at him a bit, and then silently resumed his breakfast, and his interrupted musing. We had nearly finished, and the two young people prudently shifted wider asunder, so I anticipated no further disturbance during that sitting; when Joseph appeared at the door, revealing by his quivering lip and furious eyes, that the outrage committed on his precious shrubs was detected.

He must have seen Cathy and her cousin about the spot before he examined it, for while his jaws worked like those of a cow chewing its cud, and rendered his speech difficult to understand, he began – 'Aw mun hev my wage, and Aw mun goa! Aw *hed* aimed tuh dee, wheare Aw'd sarved fur sixty year; un' Aw thowt Aw'd lug my books up intuht' garret, 'un all my bits uh stuff, un' they sud hev t' kitchen tuh theirseln; fur t' sake uh quietness. It wur hard tuh gie up my awn hearthstun, bud Aw thowt Aw *could* do that! Bud, nah, shoo's taan my garden frough me, un' by th' heart! Maister, Aw cannot stand it! Yah muh bend tuh th' yoak, an ye will – *Aw'* noan used to 't and an ow'd man doesn't sooin get used tuh new barthens – Aw'd rayther arn my bite, an' my sup, wi' a hammer in th' road!'

'Now, now, idiot!' interrupted Heathcliff, 'cut it short! What's your grievance? I'll interfere in no quarrels between you and Nelly – She may thrust you into the coal-hole for anything I care.'

'It's noan Nelly!' answered Joseph. 'Aw sudn't shift fur Nelly – Nasty, ill nowt as shoo is, Thank God! *Shoo* cannot stale t' sowl uh nob'dy! Shoo wer niver soa handsome, bud whet a body mud look at her 'baht winking. It's yon flaysome, graceless quean, ut's witched ahr lad, wi' her bold een, un' her forrard ways – till – Nay! It fair brusts my heart! He's forgetten all E done for him, un made on him, un' goan un' riven up a whole row ut t' grandest currant trees, i' t' garden!' and here he lamented outright, unmanned by a sense of his bitter injuries, and Earnshaw's ingratitude and dangerous condition.

'Is the fool drunk?' asked Mr Heathcliff. 'Hareton, is it you he's finding fault with?'

'I've pulled up two or three bushes,' replied the young man; 'but I'm going to set 'em again.'

'And why have you pulled them up?' said the master.

Catherine wisely put in her tongue.

'We wanted to plant some flowers there,' she cried. 'I'm the only person to blame, for I wished him to do it.'

'And who the devil gave *you* leave to touch a stick about the place?' demanded her father-in-law, much surprised. 'And who ordered *you* to obey her?' he added, turning to Hareton.

The latter was speechless; his cousin replied – 'You shouldn't grudge a few yards of earth, for me to ornament, when you have taken all my land!'

'Your land, insolent slut? You never had any!' said Heathcliff.

'And my money,' she continued, returning his angry glare, and meantime, biting a piece of crust, the remnant of her breakfast.

'Silence!' he exclaimed. 'Get done, and begone!'

'And Hareton's land, and his money,' pursued the reckless thing. 'Hareton and I are friends now; and I shall tell him all about you!'

The master seemed confounded a moment: he grew pale, and rose up, eyeing her all the while, with an expression of mortal hate.

'If you strike me, Hareton will strike you!' she said; 'so you may as well sit down.'

'If Hareton does not turn you out of the room, I'll strike him to Hell,' thundered Heathcliff. 'Damnable witch! Dare you pretend to rouse him against me? Off with her! Do you hear? Fling her into the kitchen! I'll kill her, Ellen Dean, if you let her come into my sight again!'

Hareton tried under his breath to persuade her to go.

'Drag her away!' he cried savagely. 'Are you staying to talk?' And he approached to execute his own command.

'He'll not obey you, wicked man, any more!' said Catherine; 'and he'll soon detest you, as much as I do!'

'Wisht! wisht!' muttered the young man reproachfully. 'I will not hear you speak so to him – Have done.'

'But you won't let him strike me?' she cried.

'Come then!' he whispered earnestly.

It was too late: Heathcliff had caught hold of her.

'Now *you* go!' he said to Earnshaw. 'Accursed witch! this time she has provoked me, when I could not bear it; and I'll make her repent it for ever!'

He had his hand in her hair; Hareton attempted to release the locks, entreating him not to hurt her that once. His black eyes flashed; he seemed ready to tear Catherine in pieces, and I was just worked up to risk coming to the rescue, when of a sudden, his fingers relaxed, he shifted his grasp from her head, to her arm, and gazed intently in her face – Then, he drew his hand over his eyes, stood a moment to collect himself apparently, and turning anew to Catherine, said with assumed calmness, 'You must learn to avoid putting me in a passion, or I shall really murder you, some time! Go with Mrs Dean, and keep with her, and confine your insolence to her ears. As to Hareton Earnshaw, if I see him listen to you, I'll send him seeking his bread where he can get it! Your love will make him an outcast, and a beggar. Nelly, take her, and leave me, all of you! Leave me!'

I led my young lady out: she was too glad of her escape, to resist; the other followed, and Mr Heathcliff had the room to himself, till dinner. I had counselled Catherine to get hers upstairs; but, as soon as he perceived her vacant seat, he sent me to call her. He spoke to none of us, eat very little, and went out directly afterwards, intimating that he should not return before evening.

'The two new friends established themselves in the house, during his absence, where I heard Hareton sternly check his cousin, on her offering a revelation of her father-in-law's conduct to his father. He said he wouldn't suffer a word to be uttered to him, in his disparagement: if he were the devil, it didn't signify; he would stand by him; and he'd rather she would abuse himself, as she used to, than begin on Mr Heathcliff. Catherine was waxing cross at this;

but he found means to make her hold her tongue, by asking, how she would like *him* to speak ill of her father? And then she comprehended that Earnshaw took the master's reputation home to himself; and was attached by ties stronger than reason could break – chains, forged by habit, which it would be cruel to attempt to loosen. She showed a good heart, thenceforth, in avoiding both complaints and expressions of antipathy concerning Heathcliff; and confessed to me her sorrow that she had endeavoured to raise a bad spirit between him and Hareton: indeed, I don't believe she has ever breathed a syllable, in the latter's hearing, against her oppressor, since.

When this slight disagreement was over, they were thick again, and as busy as possible, in their several occupations, of pupil, and teacher. I came in to sit with them, after I had done my work; and I felt so soothed and comforted to watch them, that I did not notice how time got on. You know, they both appeared in a measure my children: I had long been proud of one; and now, I was sure, the other would be a source of equal satisfaction. His honest, warm, and intelligent nature shook off rapidly the clouds of ignorance and degradation in which it had been bred; and Catherine's sincere commendations acted as a spur to his industry. His brightening mind brightened his features, and added spirit and nobility to their aspect: I could hardly fancy it the same individual I had beheld on the day I discovered my little lady at Wuthering Heights, after her expedition to the crags. While I admired, and they laboured, dusk drew on, and with it returned the master. He came upon us quite unexpectedly, entering by the front way, and had a full view of the whole three, ere we could raise our heads to glance at him. Well, I reflected, there was never a pleasanter, or more harmless sight; and it will be a burning shame to scold them. The red firelight glowed on their two bonny heads, and revealed their faces, animated with the eager interest of children; for, though he was twenty-three, and she eighteen, each had so much of novelty to feel and learn, that neither experienced nor evinced the sentiments of sober disenchanted maturity.

They lifted their eyes together, to encounter Mr Heathcliff: perhaps you have never remarked that their eyes are precisely similar, and they are those of Catherine Earnshaw. The present Catherine has no other likeness to her, except a breadth of forehead, and a certain arch of the nostril that makes her appear rather haughty, whether she will or not. With Hareton the resemblance is carried farther: it is singular, at all times – then it was particularly striking: because his senses were alert, and his mental faculties wakened to unwonted activity. I suppose this resemblance disarmed Mr Heathcliff: he walked to the hearth in evident agitation; but it quickly subsided, as he looked at the young man: or, I should say, altered its character; for it was there yet. He took the book from his hand, and glanced at the open page, then returned it without any observation; merely signing Catherine away: her companion lingered very little behind her, and I was about to depart also, but he bid me sit still.

'It is a poor conclusion, is it not,' he observed, having brooded a while on the scene he had just witnessed. 'An absurd termination to my violent exertions? I get levers and mattocks to demolish the two houses, and train myself to be

capable of working like Hercules, and when everything is ready, and in my power, I find the will to lift a slate off either roof has vanished! My old enemies have not beaten me; now would be the precise time to revenge myself on their representatives: I could do it; and none could hinder me. But where is the use? I don't care for striking: I can't take the trouble to raise my hand! That sounds as if I had been labouring the whole time, only to exhibit a fine trait of magnanimity. It is far from being the case – I have lost the faculty of enjoying their destruction, and I am too idle to destroy for nothing.

'Nelly, there is a strange change approaching: I'm in its shadow at present. I take so little interest in my daily life, that I hardly remember to eat and drink. Those two, who have left the room are the only objects which retain a distinct material appearance to me; and, that appearance causes me pain, amounting to agony. About *her* I won't speak; and I don't desire to think; but I earnestly wish she were invisible: her presence invokes only maddening sensations. *He* moves me differently: and yet if I could do it without seeming insane, I'd never see him again! You'll perhaps think me rather inclined to become so,' he added, making an effort to smile, 'if I try to describe the thousand forms of past associations, and ideas he awakens, or embodies – But you'll not talk of what I tell you; and my mind is so eternally secluded in itself, it is tempting, at last, to turn it out to another.

'Five minutes ago, Hareton seemed a personification of my youth, not a human being: I felt to him in such a variety of ways, that it would have been impossible to have accosted him rationally.

'In the first place, his startling likeness to Catherine connected him fearfully with her. That however which you may suppose the most potent to arrest my imagination, is actually the least: for what is not connected with her to me? And what does not recall her? I cannot look down to this floor, but her features are shaped on the flags! In every cloud, in every tree – filling the air at night, and caught by glimpses in every object, by day I am surrounded with her image! The most ordinary faces of men, and women – my own features mock me with a resemblance. The entire world is a dreadful collection of memoranda that she did exist, and that I have lost her!

'Well, Hareton's aspect was the ghost of my immortal love, of my wild endeavours to hold my right, my degradation, my pride, my happiness, and my anguish –

'But it is frenzy to repeat these thoughts to you: only it will let you know, why, with a reluctance to be always alone, his society is no benefit, rather an aggravation of the constant torment I suffer: and it partly contributes to render me regardless how he and his cousin go on together. I can give them no attention, any more.'

'But what do you mean by a *change*, Mr Heathcliff?' I said, alarmed at his manner, though he was neither in danger of losing his senses, nor dying; according to my judgement he was quite strong and healthy; and, as to his reason, from childhood he had a delight in dwelling on dark things, and entertaining odd fancies. He might have had a monomania on the subject of his departed idol; but on every other point his wits were as sound as mine.

'I shall not know that, till it comes,' he said; 'I'm only half conscious of it now.'

'You have no feeling of illness, have you?' I asked.

'No, Nelly, I have not,' he answered.

'Then, you are not afraid of death?' I pursued.

'Afraid? No!' he replied. 'I have neither a fear, nor a presentiment, nor a hope of death. Why should I? With my hard constitution and temperate mode of living, and unperilous occupations, I ought to, and probably *shall* remain above ground, till there is scarcely a black hair on my head – And yet I cannot continue in this condition! I have to remind myself to breathe – almost to remind my heart to beat! And it is like bending back a stiff spring: it is by compulsion that I do the slightest act not prompted by one thought, and by compulsion, that I notice anything alive or dead, which is not associated with one universal idea. I have a single wish, and my whole being and faculties are yearning to attain it. They have yearned towards it so long, and so unwaveringly, that I'm convinced it *will* be reached – and *soon* – because it has devoured my existence: I am swallowed in the anticipation of its fulfilment. My confessions have not relieved me; but they may account for some otherwise unaccountable phases of humour which I show. O, God! It is a long fight, I wish it were over!'

He began to pace the room, muttering terrible things to himself, till I was inclined to believe, as he said Joseph did, that conscience had turned his heart to an earthly hell. I wondered greatly how it would end. Though he seldom before had revealed this state of mind, even by looks, it was his habitual mood, I had no doubt: he asserted it himself; but not a soul, from his general bearing, would have conjectured the fact. You did not, when you saw him, Mr Lockwood: and at the period of which I speak, he was just the same as then, only fonder of continued solitude, and perhaps still more laconic in company.

## Chapter 34

For some days after that evening, Mr Heathcliff shunned meeting us at meals; yet he would not consent, formally, to exclude Hareton and Cathy. He had an aversion to yielding so completely to his feelings, choosing rather to absent himself; and eating once in twenty-four hours seemed sufficient sustenance for him.

One night, after the family were in bed, I heard him go downstairs, and out at the front door. I did not hear him re-enter, and in the morning I found he was still away. We were in April then: the weather was sweet and warm, the grass as green as showers and sun could make it, and the two dwarf apple trees, near the southern wall, in full bloom. After breakfast, Catherine insisted on my bringing a chair, and sitting with my work under the fir trees at the end of the house; and she beguiled Hareton, who had perfectly recovered from his accident, to dig and arrange her little garden, which was shifted to that corner by the influence of

Joseph's complaints. I was comfortably revelling in the spring fragrance around, and the beautiful soft blue overhead, when my young lady, who had run down near the gate to procure some primrose roots for a border, returned only half laden, and informed us that Mr Heathcliff was coming in. 'And he spoke to me,' she added, with a perplexed countenance.

'What did he say?' asked Hareton.

'He told me to begone as fast as I could,' she answered. 'But he looked so different from his usual look that I stopped a moment to stare at him.'

'How?' he enquired.

'Why, almost bright and cheerful – No, almost nothing – *very much* excited, and wild and glad!' she replied.

'Night-walking amuses him, then,' I remarked, affecting a careless manner: in reality, as surprised as she was; and, anxious to ascertain the truth of her statement, for to see the master looking glad would not be an everyday spectacle, I framed an excuse to go in. Heathcliff stood at the open door; he was pale, and he trembled: yet, certainly, he had a strange joyful glitter in his eyes that altered the aspect of his whole face.

'Will you have some breakfast?' I said. 'You must be hungry, rambling about all night!' I wanted to discover where he had been, but I did not like to ask directly.

'No, I'm not hungry,' he answered, averting his head, and speaking rather contemptuously, as if he guessed I was trying to divine the occasion of his good humour.

I felt perplexed: I didn't know whether it were not a proper opportunity to offer a bit of admonition.

'I don't think it right to wander out of doors,' I observed, 'instead of being in bed: it is not wise, at any rate, this moist season. I dare say you'll catch a bad cold, or a fever: you have something the matter with you now!'

'Nothing but what I can bear,' he replied; 'and with the greatest pleasure, provided you'll leave me alone: get in, and don't annoy me.'

I obeyed; and, in passing, I noticed he breathed as fast as a cat.

'Yes!' I reflected to myself, 'we shall have a fit of illness. I cannot conceive what he has been doing!'

That noon, he sat down to dinner with us, and received a heaped-up plate from my hands, as if he intended to make amends for previous fasting.

'I've neither cold nor fever, Nelly,' he remarked, in allusion to my morning's speech; 'and I'm ready to do justice to the food you give me.'

He took his knife and fork, and was going to commence eating, when the inclination appeared to become suddenly extinct. He laid them on the table, looked eagerly towards the window, then rose and went out. We saw him walking to and fro in the garden while we concluded our meal, and Earnshaw said he'd go and ask why he would not dine: he thought we had grieved him some way.

'Well, is he coming?' cried Catherine, when her cousin returned.

'Nay,' he answered; 'but he's not angry: he seemed rare and pleased indeed;

only, I made him impatient by speaking to him twice; and then he bid me be off to you: he wondered how I could want the company of anybody else.'

I set his plate to keep warm on the fender: and after an hour or two he re-entered, when the room was clear, in no degree calmer: the same unnatural – it was unnatural – appearance of joy under his black brows; the same bloodless hue, and his teeth visible, now and then, in a kind of smile; his frame shivering, not as one shivers with chill or weakness, but as a tight-stretched cord vibrates – a strong thrilling, rather than trembling.

I will ask what is the matter, I thought, or who should? And I exclaimed – 'Have you heard any good news, Mr Heathcliff? You look uncommonly animated.'

'Where should good news come from, to me?' he said. 'I'm animated with hunger; and, seemingly, I must not eat.'

'Your dinner is here', I returned; 'why won't you get it?'

'I don't want it now,' he muttered, hastily: 'I'll wait till supper. And, Nelly, once for all, let me beg you to warn Hareton and the other away from me. I wish to be troubled by nobody: I wish to have this place to myself.'

'Is there some new reason for this banishment?' I enquired. 'Tell me why you are so queer, Mr Heathcliff? Where were you last night? I'm not putting the question through idle curiosity, but – '

'You are putting the question through very idle curiosity,' he interrupted, with a laugh. 'Yet, I'll answer it. Last night, I was on the threshold of hell. Today, I am within sight of my heaven. I have my eyes on it: hardly three feet to sever me! And now you'd better go – You'll neither see nor hear anything to frighten you, if you refrain from prying.'

Having swept the hearth and wiped the table, I departed more perplexed than ever.

He did not quit the house again that afternoon, and no one intruded on his solitude, till, at eight o'clock, I deemed it proper, though unsummoned, to carry a candle and his supper to him.

He was leaning against the ledge of an open lattice, but not looking out: his face was turned to the interior gloom. The fire had smouldered to ashes; the room was filled with the damp, mild air of the cloudy evening; and so still, that not only the murmur of the beck down Gimmerton was distinguishable, but its ripples and its gurgling over the pebbles, or through the large stones which it could not cover. I uttered an ejaculation of discontent at seeing the dismal grate, and commenced shutting the casements, one after another, till I came to his.

'Must I close this?' I asked, in order to rouse him; for he would not stir.

The light flashed on his features as I spoke. Oh, Mr Lockwood, I cannot express what a terrible start I got, by the momentary view! Those deep black eyes! That smile, and ghastly paleness! It appeared to me, not Mr Heathcliff, but a goblin; and, in my terror, I let the candle bend towards the wall, and it left me in darkness.

'Yes, close it,' he replied, in his familiar voice. 'There, that is pure awkward-ness! Why did you hold the candle horizontally? Be quick, and bring another.'

I hurried out in a foolish state of dread, and said to Joseph – 'The master wishes you to take him a light and rekindle the fire.' For I dare not go in myself again just then.

Joseph rattled some fire into the shovel, and went: but he brought it back immediately, with the supper tray in his other hand, explaining that Mr Heathcliff was going to bed, and he wanted nothing to eat till morning. We heard him mount the stairs directly; he did not proceed to his ordinary chamber, but turned into that with the panelled bed: its window, as I mentioned before, is wide enough for anybody to get through; and it struck me that he plotted another midnight excursion, which he had rather we had no suspicion of.

'Is he a ghoul, or a vampire?' I mused. I had read of such hideous, incarnate demons. And then I set myself to reflect how I had tended him in infancy; and watched him grow to youth; and followed him almost through his whole course; and what absurd nonsense it was to yield to that sense of horror. 'But where did he come from, the little dark thing, harboured by a good man to his bane?' muttered superstition, as I dozed into unconsciousness. And I began, half dreaming, to weary myself with imaging some fit parentage for him; and repeating my waking meditations, I tracked his existence over again, with grim variations; at last, picturing his death and funeral: of which, all I can remember is, being exceedingly vexed at having the task of dictating an inscription for his monument, and consulting the sexton about it; and, as he had no surname, and we could not tell his age, we were obliged to content ourselves with the single word, 'Heathcliff'. That came true: we were. If you enter the kirkyard, you'll read on his headstone, only that, and the date of his death.

Dawn restored me to common sense. I rose, and went into the garden, as soon as I could see, to ascertain if there were any footmarks under his window. There were none. 'He has stayed at home,' I thought, 'and he'll be all right today!'

I prepared breakfast for the household, as was my usual custom, but told Hareton and Catherine to get theirs ere the master came down, for he lay late. They preferred taking it out of doors, under the trees, and I set a little table to accommodate them.

On my re-entrance, I found Mr Heathcliff below. He and Joseph were conversing about some farming business; he gave clear, minute directions concerning the matter discussed, but he spoke rapidly, and turned his head continually aside, and had the same excited expression, even more exaggerated. When Joseph quitted the room, he took his seat in the place he generally chose, and I put a basin of coffee before him. He drew it nearer, and then rested his arms on the table, and looked at the opposite wall, as I supposed, surveying one particular portion, up and down, with glittering, restless eyes, and with such eager interest that he stopped breathing, during half a minute together.

'Come now,' I exclaimed, pushing some bread against his hand. 'Eat and drink that, while it is hot: it has been waiting near an hour.'

He didn't notice me, and yet he smiled. I'd rather have seen him gnash his teeth than smile so.

'Mr Heathcliff! Master!' I cried. 'Don't for God's sake, stare as if you saw an unearthly vision.'

'Don't, for God's sake, shout so loud,' he replied. 'Turn round, and tell me, are we by ourselves?'

'Of course,' was my answer; 'of course we are!'

Still. I involuntarily obeyed him, as if I were not quite sure. With a sweep of his hand he cleared a vacant space in front among the breakfast things, and leant forward to gaze more at his ease.

Now, I perceived he was not looking at the wall; for when I regarded him alone, it seemed exactly that he gazed at something within two yards distance. And whatever it was, it communicated, apparently, both pleasure and pain, in exquisite extremes: at least, the anguished, yet raptured expression of his countenance suggested that idea. The fancied object was not fixed, either; his eyes pursued it with unwearied vigilance, and, even in speaking to me, were never weaned away. I vainly reminded him of his protracted abstinence from food: if he stirred to touch anything in compliance with my entreaties, if he stretched his hand out to get a piece of bread, his fingers clenched before they reached it, and remained on the table, forgetful of their aim.

I sat, a model of patience, trying to attract his absorbed attention from its engrossing speculation; till he grew irritable, and got up, asking why I would not allow him to have his own time in taking his meals? and saying that, on the next occasion, I needn't wait: I might set the things down and go. Having uttered these words he left the house, slowly sauntered down the garden path, and disappeared through the gate.

The hours crept anxiously by: another evening came. I did not retire to rest till late, and when I did, I could not sleep. He returned after midnight, and, instead of going to bed, shut himself into the room beneath. I listened, and tossed about; and, finally, dressed, and descended. It was too irksome to lie up there, harassing my brain with a hundred idle misgivings.

I distinguished Mr Heathcliff's step, restlessly measuring the floor; and he frequently broke the silence by a deep inspiration, resembling a groan. He muttered detached words also; the only one I could catch was the name of Catherine, coupled with some wild term of endearment or suffering; and spoken as one would speak to a person present: low and earnest, and wrung from the depth of his soul. I had not courage to walk straight into the apartment; but I desired to divert him from his reverie, and therefore fell foul of the kitchen fire, stirred it, and began to scrape the cinders. It drew him forth sooner than I expected. He opened the door immediately, and said – 'Nelly, come here – is it morning? Come in with your light.'

'It is striking four,' I answered. 'You want a candle to take upstairs: you might have lit one at this fire.'

'No, I don't wish to go upstairs,' he said. 'Come in, and kindle *me* a fire, and do anything there is to do about the room.'

'I must blow the coals red first, before I can carry any,' I replied, getting a chair and the bellows.

He roamed to and fro, meantime, in a state approaching distraction; his heavy sighs succeeding each other so thick as to leave no space for common breathing between.

'When day breaks I'll send for Green,' he said; 'I wish to make some legal enquiries of him while I can bestow a thought on those matters, and while I can act calmly. I have not written my will yet; and how to leave my property I cannot determine! I wish I could annihilate it from the face of the earth.'

'I would not talk so, Mr Heathcliff,' I interposed. 'Let your will be, a while: you'll be spared to repent of your many injustices, yet! I never expected that your nerves would be disordered: they are, at present, marvellously so, however; and almost entirely through your own fault. The way you've passed these three last days might knock up a Titan. Do take some food, and some repose. You need only look at yourself in a glass to see how you require both. Your cheeks are hollow, and your eyes bloodshot, like a person starving with hunger, and going blind with loss of sleep.'

'It is not my fault that I cannot eat or rest,' he replied. 'I assure you it is through no settled designs. I'll do both, as soon as I possibly can. But you might as well bid a man struggling in the water, rest within arm's length of the shore! I must reach it first, and then I'll rest. Well, never mind Mr Green: as to repenting of my injustices, I've done no injustice, and I repent of nothing – I'm too happy, and yet I'm not happy enough. My soul's bliss kills my body, but does not satisfy itself.'

'Happy, master?' I cried. 'Strange happiness! If you would hear me without being angry, I might offer some advice that would make you happier.'

'What is that?' he asked. 'Give it.'

'You are aware, Mr Heathcliff,' I said, 'that from the time you were thirteen years old, you have lived a selfish, unchristian life; and probably hardly had a Bible in your hands during all that period. You must have forgotten the contents of the book, and you may not have space to search it now. Could it be hurtful to send for someone – some minister of any denomination, it does not matter which, to explain it, and show you how very far you have erred from its precepts, and how unfit you will be for its heaven, unless a change takes place before you die?'

'I'm rather obliged than angry, Nelly,' he said, 'for you remind me of the manner that I desire to be buried in – It is to be carried to the churchyard, in the evening. You and Hareton may, if you please, accompany me: and mind, particularly, to notice that the sexton obeys my directions concerning the two coffins! No minister need come; nor need anything be said over me – I tell you, I have nearly attained *my* heaven; and that of others is altogether unvalued and uncoveted by me!'

'And supposing you persevered in your obstinate fast, and died by that means, and they refused to bury you in the precincts of the kirk?' I said, shocked at his godless indifference. 'How would you like it?'

'They won't do that,' he replied: 'if they did, you must have me removed secretly; and if you neglect it, you shall prove, practically, that the dead are not annihilated!'

As soon as he heard the other members of the family stirring he retired to his den, and I breathed freer. But in the afternoon, while Joseph and Hareton were at their work, he came into the kitchen again, and with a wild look, bid me come, and sit in the house: he wanted somebody with him. I declined; telling him plainly that his strange talk and manner frightened me, and I had neither the nerve nor the will to be his companion, alone.

'I believe you think me a fiend!' he said, with his dismal laugh: 'something too horrible to live under a decent roof!' Then turning to Catherine, who was there, and who drew behind me at his approach, he added, half sneeringly – 'Will *you* come, chuck? I'll not hurt you. No! To you, I've made myself worse than the devil. Well, there is *one* who won't shrink from my company! By God! She's relentless. Oh, damn it! It's unutterably too much for flesh and blood to bear – even mine.'

He solicited the society of no one more. At dusk, he went into his chamber. Through the whole night, and far into the morning, we heard him groaning, and murmuring to himself. Hareton was anxious to enter; but I bid him fetch Mr Kenneth, and he should go in and see him.

When he came, and I requested admittance and tried to open the door, I found it locked; and Heathcliff bid us be damned. He was better, and would be left alone; so the doctor went away.

The following evening was very wet: indeed it poured down, till day-dawn; and, as I took my morning walk round the house, I observed the master's window swinging open, and the rain driving straight in. He cannot be in bed, I thought: those showers would drench him through! He must either be up or out. But I'll make no more ado, I'll go boldly and look!

Having succeeded in obtaining entrance with another key, I ran to unclose the panels, for the chamber was vacant; quickly pushing them aside, I peeped in. Mr Heathcliff was there – laid on his back. His eyes met mine so keen and fierce, I started; and then he seemed to smile.

I could not think him dead: but his face and throat were washed with rain; the bedclothes dripped, and he was perfectly still. The lattice, flapping to and fro, had grazed one hand that rested on the sill; no blood trickled from the broken skin, and when I put my fingers to it, I could doubt no more: he was dead and stark!

I hasped the window; I combed his black long hair from his forehead; I tried to close his eyes: to extinguish, if possible, that frightful, lifelike gaze of exultation, before anyone else beheld it. They would not shut: they seemed to sneer at my attempts; and his parted lips and sharp white teeth sneered too! Taken with another fit of cowardice, I cried out for Joseph. Joseph shuffled up and made a noise, but resolutely refused to meddle with him.

'Th' divil's harried off his soul,' he cried, 'and he muh hev his carcass intuh t' bargin, for ow't Aw care! Ech! what a wicked un he looks girnning at death!' and the old sinner grinned in mockery.

I thought he intended to cut a caper round the bed; but suddenly composing himself, he fell on his knees, and raised his hands, and returned thanks that the lawful master and the ancient stock were restored to their rights.

I felt stunned by the awful event; and my memory unavoidably recurred to former times with a sort of oppressive sadness. But poor Hareton, the most wronged, was the only one that really suffered much. He sat by the corpse all night, weeping in bitter earnest. He pressed its hand, and kissed the sarcastic, savage face that everyone else shrank from contemplating; and bemoaned him with that strong grief which springs naturally from a generous heart, though it be tough as tempered steel.

Kenneth was perplexed to pronounce of what disorder the master died. I concealed the fact of his having swallowed nothing for four days, fearing it might lead to trouble, and then, I am persuaded he did not abstain on purpose: it was the consequence of his strange illness, not the cause.

We buried him, to the scandal of the whole neighbourhood, as he had wished. Earnshaw, and I, the sexton and six men to carry the coffin, comprehended the whole attendance. The six men departed when they had let it down into the grave: we stayed to see it covered. Hareton, with a streaming face, dug green sods, and laid them over the brown mould himself: at present it is as smooth and verdant as its companion mounds – and I hope its tenant sleeps as soundly. But the country folks, if you asked them, would swear on their Bible that he *walks*. There are those who speak to having met him near the church, and on the moor, and even within this house. Idle tales, you'll say, and so say I. Yet that old man by the kitchen fire affirms he has seen two on 'em looking out of his chamber window, on every rainy night since his death – and an odd thing happened to me about a month ago. I was going to the Grange one evening – a dark evening threatening thunder – and, just at the turn of the Heights, I encountered a little boy with a sheep and two lambs before him; he was crying terribly, and I supposed the lambs were skittish, and would not be guided.

'What is the matter, my little man?' I asked.

'They's Heathcliff, and a woman, yonder, under t' Nab,' he blubbered, 'un' Aw darnut pass 'em.'

I saw nothing; but neither the sheep nor he would go on; so I bid him take the road lower down. He probably raised the phantoms from thinking, as he traversed the moors alone, on the nonsense he had heard his parents and companions repeat – yet still, I don't like being out in the dark, now; and I don't like being left by myself in this grim house: I cannot help it; I shall be glad when they leave it, and shift to the Grange!

'They are going to the Grange then?' I said.

'Yes,' answered Mrs Dean, 'as soon as they are married; and that will be on New Year's Day.'

'And who will live here then?'

'Why, Joseph will take care of the house, and, perhaps, a lad to keep him company. They will live in the kitchen, and the rest will be shut up.'

'For the use of such ghosts as choose to inhabit it,' I observed.

'No, Mr Lockwood,' said Nelly, shaking her head. 'I believe the dead are at peace, but it is not right to speak of them with levity.'

At that moment the garden gate swung to; the ramblers were returning.

'*They* are afraid of nothing,' I grumbled, watching their approach through the window.

'Together, they would brave satan and all his legions.'

As they stepped on to the door-stones, and halted to take a last look at the moon – or, more correctly, at each other, by her light – I felt irresistibly impelled to escape them again; and, pressing a remembrance into the hand of Mrs Dean, and disregarding her expostulations at my rudeness, I vanished through the kitchen as they opened the house door: and so should have confirmed Joseph in his opinion of his fellow-servant's gay indiscretions, had he not fortunately recognised me for a respectable character by the sweet ring of a sovereign at his feet.

My walk home was lengthened by a diversion in the direction of the kirk. When beneath its walls, I perceived decay had made progress, even in seven months: many a window showed black gaps deprived of glass; and slates jutted off, here and there, beyond the right line of the roof, to be gradually worked off in coming autumn storms.

I sought, and soon discovered, the three headstones on the slope next the moor: the middle one grey, and half buried in heath; Edgar Linton's only harmonised by the turf, and moss creeping up its foot; Heathcliff's still bare.

I lingered round them, under that benign sky: watched the moths fluttering among the heath and harebells; listened to the soft wind breathing through the grass; and wondered how anyone could ever imagine unquiet slumbers for the sleepers in that quiet earth.

# AGNES GREY

# Agnes Grey

## ANNE BRONTË

# Contents

**CHAPTER I**

## The Parsonage

All true histories contain instruction; though, in some, the treasure may be hard to find, and when found, so trivial in quantity, that the dry, shrivelled kernel scarcely compensates for the trouble of cracking the nut. Whether this be the case with my history or not, I am hardly competent to judge. I sometimes think it might prove useful to some, and entertaining to others; but the world may judge for itself. Shielded by my own obscurity, and by the lapse of years, and a few fictitious names, I do not fear to venture; and will candidly lay before the public what I would not disclose to the most intimate friend.

My father was a clergyman of the north of England, who was deservedly respected by all who knew him; and, in his younger days, lived pretty comfortably on the joint income of a small incumbency and a snug little property of his own. My mother, who married him against the wishes of her friends, was a squire's daughter, and a woman of spirit. In vain it was represented to her, that if she became the poor parson's wife, she must relinquish her carriage and her lady's-maid, and all the luxuries and elegancies of affluence; which to her were little less than the necessaries of life. A carriage and a lady's-maid were great conveniences; but, thank Heaven, she had feet to carry her, and hands to minister to her own necessities. An elegant house and spacious grounds were not to be despised; but she would rather live in a cottage with Richard Grey than in a palace with any other man in the world.

Finding arguments of no avail, her father, at length, told the lovers they might marry if they pleased; but, in so doing, his daughter would forfeit every fraction of her fortune. He expected this would cool the ardour of both; but he was mistaken. My father knew too well my mother's superior worth not to be sensible that she was a valuable fortune in herself: and if she would but consent to embellish his humble hearth, he should be happy to take her on any terms; while she, on her part, would rather labour with her own hands than be divided from the man she loved, whose happiness it would be her joy to make, and who was already one with her in heart and soul. So her fortune went to swell the purse of a wiser sister, who had married a rich nabob; and she, to the wonder and compassionate regret of all who knew her, went to bury herself in the homely village parsonage among the hills of —. And yet, in spite of all this, and in spite of my mother's high spirit and my father's whims, I believe you might search all England through, and fail to find a happier couple.

Of six children, my sister Mary and myself were the only two that survived the perils of infancy and early childhood. I, being the younger by five or six years, was always regarded as the *child*, and the pet of the family: father, mother, and sister, all combined to spoil me – not by foolish indulgence, to render me

fractious and ungovernable, but by ceaseless kindness, to make me too helpless and dependent – too unfit for buffeting with the cares and turmoils of life.

Mary and I were brought up in the strictest seclusion. My mother, being at once highly accomplished, well-informed, and fond of employment, took the whole charge of our education on herself, with the exception of Latin – which my father undertook to teach us – so that we never even went to school; and, as there was no society in the neighbourhood, our only intercourse with the world consisted in a stately tea-party, now and then, with the principal farmers and tradespeople of the vicinity (just to avoid being stigmatised as too proud to consort with our neighbours), and an annual visit to our paternal grandfather's; where himself, our kind grandmamma, a maiden aunt, and two or three elderly ladies and gentlemen, were the only persons we ever saw. Sometimes our mother would amuse us with stories and anecdotes of her younger days, which, while they entertained us amazingly, frequently awoke – in me, at least – a secret wish to see a little more of the world.

I thought she must have been very happy: but she never seemed to regret past times. My father, however, whose temper was neither tranquil nor cheerful by nature, often unduly vexed himself with thinking of the sacrifices his dear wife had made for him; and troubled his head with revolving endless schemes for the augmentation of his little fortune, for her sake and ours. In vain my mother assured him she was quite satisfied; and if he would but lay by a little for the children, we should all have plenty, both for time present and to come: but saving was not my father's forte. He would not run in debt (at least, my mother took good care he should not), but while he had money he must spend it: he liked to see his house comfortable, and his wife and daughters well clothed, and well attended; and besides, he was charitably disposed, and liked to give to the poor, according to his means: or, as some might think, beyond them.

At length, however, a kind friend suggested to him a means of doubling his private property at one stroke; and further increasing it, hereafter, to an untold amount. This friend was a merchant, a man of enterprising spirit and un-doubted talent, who was somewhat straitened in his mercantile pursuits for want of capital; but generously proposed to give my father a fair share of his profits, if he would only entrust him with what he could spare; and he thought he might safely promise that whatever sum the latter chose to put into his hands, it should bring him in cent per cent. The small patrimony was speedily sold, and the whole of its price was deposited in the hands of the friendly merchant; who as promptly proceeded to ship his cargo, and prepare for his voyage.

My father was delighted, so were we all, with our brightening prospects. For the present, it is true, we were reduced to the narrow income of the curacy; but my father seemed to think there was no necessity for scrupulously restricting our expenditure to that; so, with a standing bill at Mr Jackson's, another at Smith's and a third at Hobson's, we got along even more comfortably than before: though my mother affirmed we had better keep within bounds, for our prospects of wealth were but precarious, after all; and if my father would only

trust everything to her management, he should never feel himself stinted: but he, for once, was incorrigible.

What happy hours Mary and I have passed, while sitting at our work by the fire, or wandering on the heath-clad hills, or idling under the weeping birch (the only considerable tree in the garden), talking of future happiness to ourselves and our parents, of what we would do, and see, and possess; with no firmer foundation for our goodly superstructure, than the riches that were expected to flow in upon us from the success of the worthy merchant's speculations. Our father was nearly as bad as ourselves; only, that he affected not to be so much in earnest: expressing his bright hopes and sanguine expectations, in jests and playful sallies, that always struck me as being exceedingly witty and pleasant. Our mother laughed with delight to see him so hopeful and happy: but still she feared he was setting his heart too much upon the matter; and once I heard her whisper as she left the room, 'God grant he be not disappointed! I know not how he would bear it.'

Disappointed he was; and bitterly, too. It came like a thunderclap on us all, that the vessel which contained our fortune had been wrecked, and gone to the bottom with all its stores, together with several of the crew, and the unfortunate merchant himself. I was grieved for him. I was grieved for the overthrow of all our air-built castles: but, with the elasticity of youth, I soon recovered the shock.

Though riches had charms, poverty had no terrors for an inexperienced girl like me. Indeed, to say the truth, there was something exhilarating in the idea of being driven to straits, and thrown upon our own resources. I only wished papa, mamma, and Mary, were all of the same mind as myself; and then, instead of lamenting past calamities, we might all cheerfully set to work to remedy them; and the greater the difficulties, the harder our present privations, the greater should be our cheerfulness to endure the latter, and our vigour to contend against the former.

Mary did not lament, but she brooded continually over the misfortune, and sank into a state of dejection from which no effort of mine could rouse her. I could not possibly bring her to regard the matter on its bright side as I did: and indeed I was so fearful of being charged with childish frivolity, or stupid insensibility, that I carefully kept most of my bright ideas and cheering notions to myself; well knowing they could not be appreciated.

My mother thought only of consoling my father, and paying our debts and retrenching our expenditure by every available means; but my father was completely overwhelmed by the calamity: health, strength, and spirits sank beneath the blow; and he never wholly recovered them. In vain my mother strove to cheer him, by appealing to his piety, to his courage, to his affection for herself and us. The very affection was his greatest torment: it was for our sakes he had so ardently longed to increase his fortune – it was our interest that had lent such brightness to his hopes, and that imparted such bitterness to his present distress. He now tormented himself with remorse at having neglected my mother's advice; which would at least have saved him from the additional burden of debt – he vainly reproached himself for having brought her from the

dignity, the ease, the luxury of her former station to toil with him through the cares and toils of poverty. It was gall and wormwood to his soul to see that splendid, highly accomplished woman, once so courted and admired, transformed into an active managing housewife, with hands and head continually occupied with household labours and household economy. The very willingness with which she performed these duties, the cheerfulness with which she bore her reverses, and the kindness which withheld her from imputing the smallest blame to him, were all perverted by this ingenious self-tormentor, into further aggravations of his sufferings. And thus the mind preyed upon the body, and disordered the system of the nerves, and they in turn increased the troubles of the mind, till by action and reaction his health was seriously impaired, and not one of us could convince him that the aspect of our affairs was not half so gloomy, so utterly hopeless, as his morbid imagination represented it to be.

The useful pony phaeton was sold, together with the stout well-fed pony – the old favourite that we had fully determined should end its days in peace, and never pass from our hands; the little coach-house and stable were let; the servant boy, and the more efficient (being the more expensive) of the two maidservants were dismissed. Our clothes were mended, turned, and darned to the utmost verge of decency; our food, always plain, was now simplified to an unprecedented degree – except my father's favourite dishes; our coals and candles were painfully economised – the pair of candles reduced to one, and that most sparingly used; the coals carefully husbanded in the half-empty grate: especially when my father was out on his parish duties, or confined to bed through illness – then we sat with our feet on the fender, scraping the perishing embers together from time to time, and occasionally adding a slight scattering of the dust and fragments of coal, just to keep them alive. As for our carpets, they in time were worn threadbare, and patched and darned even to a greater extent than our garments. To save the expense of a gardener, Mary and I undertook to keep the garden in order; and all the cooking and household work that could not easily be managed by one servant girl, was done by my mother and sister, with a little occasional help from me: only a little, because, though a woman in my own estimation, I was still a child in theirs; and my mother, like most active managing women, was not gifted with very active daughters: for this reason – that being so clever and diligent herself, she was never tempted to trust her affairs to a deputy, but on the contrary was willing to act and think for others as well as for number one; and whatever was the business in hand, she was apt to think that no one could do it so well as herself: so that whenever I offered to assist her, I received such an answer as – 'No, love, you cannot indeed – there's nothing here you can do. Go and help your sister or get her to take a walk with you – tell her she must not sit so much, and stay so constantly in the house as she does – she may well look thin and dejected.'

'Mary, mamma says I'm to help you; or get you to take a walk with me: she says you may well look thin and dejected, if you sit so constantly in the house.'

'Help me you cannot, Agnes; and I cannot go out with *you* – I have far too much to do.'

'Then let me help you.'

'You cannot, indeed, dear child. Go and practise your music, or play with the kitten.'

There was always plenty of sewing on hand; but I had not been taught to cut out a single garment, and except plain hemming and seaming, there was little I could do, even in that line; for they both asserted that it was far easier to do the work themselves than to prepare it for me: and, besides, they liked better to see me prosecuting my studies, or amusing myself – it was time enough for me to sit bending over my work, like a grave matron, when my favourite little pussy was become a steady old cat. Under such circumstances, although I was not many degrees more useful than the kitten, my idleness was not entirely without excuse.

Through all our troubles, I never but once heard my mother complain of our want of money. As summer was coming on, she observed to Mary and me, 'What a desirable thing it would be for your papa to spend a few weeks at a watering-place. I am convinced the sea air and the change of scene would be of incalculable service to him. But then, you see, there's no money,' she added, with a sigh. We both wished exceedingly that the thing might be done, and lamented greatly that it could not. 'Well well!' said she, 'it's no use complaining. Possibly something might be done to further the project after all. Mary, you are a beautiful drawer. What do you say to doing a few more pictures in your best style, and getting them framed, with the water-coloured drawings you have already done, and trying to dispose of them to some liberal picture-dealer, who has the sense to discern their merits?'

'Mamma, I should be delighted if you think they *could* be sold; and for anything worth while.'

'It's worth while trying, however, my dear; do you procure the drawings, and I'll endeavour to find a purchaser.'

'I wish I could do something,' said I.

'You, Agnes! well, who knows? You draw pretty well, too: if you choose some simple piece for your subject, I dare say you will be able to produce something we shall all be proud to exhibit.'

'But I have another scheme in my head, mamma, and have had long, only I did not like to mention it.'

'Indeed! pray tell us what it is.'

'I should like to be a governess.'

My mother uttered an exclamation of surprise, and laughed. My sister dropped her work in astonishment, exclaiming, '*You* a governess, Agnes! What can you be dreaming of?'

'Well! I don't see anything so very extraordinary in it. I do not pretend to be able to instruct great girls; but surely, I could teach little ones: and I should like it *so* much; I am so fond of children. Do let me, mamma!'

'But, my love, you have not learned to take care of *yourself* yet: and young children require more judgement and experience to manage than elder ones.'

'But, mamma, I am above eighteen, and quite able to take care of myself, and

others too. You do not know half the wisdom and prudence I possess, because I have never been tried.'

'Only think,' said Mary, 'what would you do in a house full of strangers, without me or mamma to speak and act for you – with a parcel of children, besides yourself, to attend to; and no one to look to for advice? You would not even know what clothes to put on.'

'You think, because I always do as you bid me, I have no judgement of my own: but only try me – that is all I ask – and you shall see what I can do.'

At that moment my father entered, and the subject of our discussion was explained to him.

'What, my little Agnes a governess;' cried he, and, in spite of his dejection, he laughed at the idea.

'Yes, papa, don't *you* say anything against it: I should like it *so* much; and I am sure I could manage delightfully.'

'But, my darling, we could not spare you.' And a tear glistened in his eye as he added – 'No, no! afflicted as we are, surely we are not brought to that pass yet.'

'Oh, no!' said my mother. 'There is no necessity whatever for such a step; it is merely a whim of her own. So you must hold your tongue, you naughty girl; for, though you are so ready to leave us, you know very well we cannot part with you.'

I was silenced for that day, and for many succeeding ones; but still I did not wholly relinquish my darling scheme. Mary got her drawing materials, and steadily set to work. I got mine too; but while I drew, I thought of other things. How delightful it would be to be a governess! To go out into the world; to enter upon a new life; to act for myself; to exercise my unused faculties; to try my unknown powers; to earn my own maintenance, and something to comfort and help my father, mother, and sister, besides exonerating them from the provision of my food and clothing; to show papa what his little Agnes could do; to convince mamma and Mary that I was not quite the helpless, thoughtless being they supposed. And then, how charming to be entrusted with the care and education of children! Whatever others said, I felt I was fully competent to the task: the clear remembrance of my own thoughts in early childhood would be a surer guide than the instructions of the most mature adviser. I had but to turn from my little pupils to myself at their age, and I should know, at once, how to win their confidence and affections: how to waken the contrition of the erring; how to embolden the timid, and console the afflicted; how to make Virtue practicable, Instruction desirable, and Religion lovely and comprehensible.

– Delightful task!
To teach the young idea how to shoot!

To train the tender plants, and watch their buds unfolding day by day!

Influenced by so many inducements, I determined still to persevere; though the fear of displeasing my mother, or distressing my father's feelings, prevented me from resuming the subject for several days. At length, again I mentioned it to my mother in private; and, with some difficulty, got her to

promise to assist me with her endeavours. My father's reluctant consent was next obtained, and then, though Mary still sighed her disapproval, my dear, kind mother began to look out for a situation for me. She wrote to my father's relations, and consulted the newspaper advertisements – her own relations she had long dropped all communication with: a formal interchange of occasional letters was all she had ever had since her marriage, and she would not at any time have applied to them in a case of this nature. But so long and so entire had been my parents' seclusion from the world, that many weeks elapsed before a suitable situation could be procured. At last, to my great joy, it was decreed that I should take charge of the young family of a certain Mrs Bloomfield; whom my kind, prim aunt Grey had known in her youth, and asserted to be a very nice woman. Her husband was a retired tradesman, who had realised a very comfortable fortune; but could not be prevailed upon to give a greater salary than twenty-five pounds to the instructress of his children. I, however, was glad to accept this, rather than refuse the situation – which my parents were inclined to think the better plan.

But some weeks more were yet to be devoted to preparation. How long, how tedious those weeks appeared to me! Yet they were happy ones in the main – full of bright hopes and ardent expectations. With what peculiar pleasure I assisted at the making of my new clothes, and, subsequently, the packing of my trunks! But there was a feeling of bitterness mingling with the latter occupation too; and when it was done – when all was ready for my departure on the morrow, and the last night at home approached – a sudden anguish seemed to swell my heart. My dear friends looked so sad, and spoke so very kindly, that I could scarcely keep my eyes from overflowing: but I still affected to be gay. I had taken my last ramble with Mary on the moors, my last walk in the garden, and round the house; I had fed, with her, our pet pigeons for the last time – the pretty creatures that we had tamed to peck their food from our hands: I had given a farewell stroke to all their silky backs as they crowded in my lap. I had tenderly kissed my own peculiar favourites, the pair of snow-white fantails; I had played my last tune on the old familiar piano, and sung my last song to papa: not the last, I hoped, but the last for, what appeared to me, a very long time. And, perhaps, when I did these things again, it would be with different feelings: circumstances might be changed, and this house might never be my settled home again. My dear little friend, the kitten, would certainly be changed: she was already growing a fine cat; and when I returned, even for a hasty visit at Christmas, would, most likely, have forgotten both her playmate and her merry pranks. I had romped with her for the last time; and when I stroked her soft bright fur, while she lay purring herself to sleep in my lap, it was with a feeling of sadness I could not easily disguise. Then, at bedtime, when I retired with Mary to our quiet little chamber, where already my drawers were cleared out and my share of the bookcase was empty – and where, hereafter, she would have to sleep alone, in dreary solitude, as she expressed it – my heart sank more than ever: I felt as if I had been selfish and wrong to persist in leaving her; and when I knelt once more beside our little bed, I prayed for a blessing on her and on my parents more

fervently than ever I had done before. To conceal my emotion, I buried my face in my hands, and they were presently bathed in tears. I perceived, on rising, that she had been crying too: but neither of us spoke; and in silence we betook ourselves to our repose, creeping more closely together from the consciousness that we were to part so soon.

But the morning brought a renewal of hope and spirits. I was to depart early, that the conveyance which took me (a gig, hired from Mr Smith, the draper, grocer, and tea-dealer of the village) might return the same day. I rose, washed, dressed, swallowed a hasty breakfast, received the fond embraces of my father, mother, and sister, kissed the cat – to the great scandal of Sally, the maid – shook hands with her, mounted the gig, drew my veil over my face, and then, but not till then, burst into a flood of tears. The gig rolled on; I looked back; my dear mother and sister were still standing at the door, looking after me, and waving their adieux. I returned their salute, and prayed God to bless them from my heart: we descended the hill, and I could see them no more.

'It's a coldish mornin' for you, Miss Agnes,' observed Smith; 'and a darksome un too; but we's, happen, get to yon' spot afore there come much rain to signify.'

'Yes, I hope so,' replied I, as calmly as I could.

'It's comed a good sup last night too.'

'Yes.'

'But this cold wind will, happen, keep it off.'

'Perhaps it will.'

Here ended our colloquy. We crossed the valley, and began to ascend the opposite hill. As we were toiling up, I looked back again: there was the village spire, and the old grey parsonage beyond it, basking in a slanting beam of sunshine – it was but a sickly ray, but the village and surrounding hills were all in sombre shade, and I hailed the wandering beam as a propitious omen to my home. With clasped hands, I fervently implored a blessing on its inhabitants, and hastily turned away; for I saw the sunshine was departing; and I carefully avoided another glance, lest I should see it in gloomy shadow, like the rest of the landscape.

## CHAPTER 2

## *First Lessons in the Art of Instruction*

As we drove along, my spirits revived again, and I turned, with pleasure, to the contemplation of the new life upon which I was entering. But though it was not far past the middle of September, the heavy clouds and strong north-easterly wind combined to render the day extremely cold and dreary; and the journey seemed a very long one, for, as Smith observed, the roads were 'very heavy'; and certainly, his horse was very heavy too: it crawled up the hills, and crept down

them, and only condescended to shake its sides in a trot where the road was at a dead level or a very gentle slope, which was rarely the case in those rugged regions; so that it was nearly one o'clock before we reached the place of our destination. Yet, after all, when we entered the lofty iron gateway, when we drove softly up the smooth, well-rolled carriage road, with the green lawn on each side, studded with young trees, and approached the new but stately mansion of Wellwood, rising above its mushroom poplar-groves, my heart failed me, and I wished it were a mile or two farther off. For the first time in my life, I must stand alone: there was no retreating now. I must enter that house, and introduce myself among its strange inhabitants. But how was it to be done? True, I was near nineteen; but, thanks to my retired life and the protecting care of my mother and sister, I well knew that many a girl of fifteen, or under, was gifted with a more womanly address, and greater ease and self-possession, than I was. Yet, if Mrs Bloomfield were a kind, motherly woman, I might do very well, after all; and the children, of course, I should soon be at ease with them – and Mr Bloomfield, I hoped, I should have but little to do with.

'Be calm, be calm, whatever happens,' I said within myself; and truly I kept this resolution so well, and was so fully occupied in steadying my nerves and stilling the rebellious flutter of my heart, that when I was admitted into the hall, and ushered into the presence of Mrs Bloomfield, I almost forgot to answer her polite salutation; and it afterwards struck me, that the little I did say was spoken in the tone of one half-dead or half-asleep. The lady, too, was somewhat chilly in her manner, as I discovered when I had time to reflect. She was a tall, spare, stately woman, with thick black hair, cold grey eyes and extremely sallow complexion.

With due politeness, however, she showed me my bedroom, and left me there to take a little refreshment. I was somewhat dismayed at my appearance on looking in the glass: the cold wind had swelled and reddened my hands, uncurled and entangled my hair, and dyed my face of a pale purple; add to this my collar was horridly crumpled, my frock splashed with mud, my feet clad in stout new boots, and as the trunks were not brought up, there was no remedy; so having smoothed my hair as well as I could, and repeatedly twitched my obdurate collar, I proceeded to clomp down the two flights of stairs, philos- ophising as I went; and with some difficulty found my way into the room where Mrs Bloomfield awaited me.

She led me into the dining-room, where the family luncheon had been laid out. Some beefsteaks and half-cold potatoes were set before me; and while I dined upon these, she sat opposite, watching me (as I thought) and endeavouring to sustain something like a conversation – consisting chiefly of a succession of commonplace remarks, expressed with frigid formality: but this might be more my fault than hers, for I really *could* not converse. In fact, my attention was almost wholly absorbed in my dinner: not from ravenous appetite, but from distress at the toughness of the beefsteaks, and the numbness of my hands, almost palsied by their five hours' exposure to the bitter wind. I would gladly have eaten the potatoes and let the meat alone, but having got a large piece of

the latter on to my plate, I could not be so impolite as to leave it; so, after many awkward and unsuccessful attempts to cut it with the knife, or tear it with the fork, or pull it asunder between them, sensible that the awful lady was a spectator to the whole transaction, I at last desperately grasped the knife and fork in my fists, like a child of two years old, and fell to work with all the little strength I possessed. But this needed some apology – with a feeble attempt at a laugh, I said, 'My hands are so benumbed with the cold that I can scarcely handle my knife and fork.'

'I dare say you would find it cold,' replied she with a cool, immutable gravity that did not serve to reassure me.

When the ceremony was concluded, she led me into the sitting-room again, where she rang and sent for the children.

'You will find them not very far advanced in their attainments,' said she, 'for I have had so little time to attend to their education myself, and we have thought them too young for a governess till now; but I think they are clever children, and very apt to learn, especially the little boy: he is, I think, the flower of the flock – a generous, noble-spirited boy, one to be led, but not driven, and remarkable for always speaking the truth. He seems to scorn deception' (this was good news). 'His sister Mary Ann will require watching,' continued she, 'but she is a very good girl upon the whole: though I wish her to be kept out of the nursery as much as possible, as she is now almost six years old, and might acquire bad habits from the nurses. I have ordered her crib to be placed in your room, and if you will be so kind as to overlook her washing and dressing, and take charge of her clothes, she need have nothing further to do with the nursery-maid.'

I replied I was quite willing to do so; and at that moment my young pupils entered the apartment, with their two younger sisters. Master Tom Bloomfield was a well-grown boy of seven with a somewhat wiry frame, flaxen hair, blue eyes, small turned up nose, and fair complexion. Mary Ann was a tall girl too, somewhat dark like her mother, but with a round full face and a high colour in her cheeks. The second sister was Fanny, a very pretty little girl; Mrs Bloomfield assured me she was a remarkably gentle child, and required encouragement: she had not learned anything yet; but in a few days, she would be four years old, and then she might take her first lesson in the alphabet, and be promoted to the schoolroom. The remaining one was Harriet, a little broad, fat, merry, playful thing of scarcely two, that I coveted more than all the rest – but with her I had nothing to do.

I talked to my little pupils as well as I could, and tried to render myself agreeable; but with little success, I fear, for their mother's presence kept me under an unpleasant restraint. They, however, were remarkably free from shyness. They seemed bold, lively children, and I hoped I should soon be on friendly terms with them – the little boy especially, of whom I had heard such a favourable character from his mamma. In Mary Ann there was a certain affected simper, and a craving for notice, that I was sorry to observe. But her brother claimed all my attention to himself; he stood bolt upright between me and the fire, with his hands behind his back, talking away like an orator, occasionally

interrupting his discourse with a sharp reproof to his sisters when they made too much noise.

'Oh, Tom, what a darling you are!' exclaimed his mother. 'Come and kiss dear mamma; and then won't you show Miss Grey your schoolroom, and your nice new books?'

'I won't kiss you, mamma; but I *will* show Miss Grey my schoolroom, and my new books.'

'And *my* schoolroom, and *my* new books, Tom,' said Mary Ann. 'They're mine too.'

'They're *mine*,' replied he decisively. 'Come along, Miss Grey – I'll escort you.'

When the room and books had been shown, with some bickerings between the brother and sister that I did my utmost to appease or mitigate, Mary Ann brought me her doll, and began to be very loquacious on the subject of its fine clothes, its bed, its chest of drawers, and other appurtenances; but Tom told her to hold her clamour, that Miss Grey might see his rocking-horse, which, with a most important bustle, he dragged forth from its corner into the middle of the room loudly calling on me to attend to it. Then, ordering his sister to hold the reins, he mounted, and made me stand for ten minutes, watching how manfully he used his whip and spurs. Meantime, however, I admired Mary Ann's pretty doll, and all its possessions; and then told Master Tom he was a capital rider, but I hoped he would not use his whip and spurs so much when he rode a real pony.

'Oh, yes, I will!' said he, laying on with redoubled ardour. 'I'll cut into him like smoke! Eh! my word! but he shall sweat for it.'

This was very shocking: but I hoped in time to be able to work a reformation.

'Now you must put on your bonnet and shawl,' said the little hero, 'and I'll show you my garden.'

'And *mine*,' said Mary Ann.

Tom lifted his fist with a menacing gesture; she uttered a loud, shrill scream, ran to the other side of me, and made a face at him.

'Surely, Tom, you would not strike your sister! I hope I shall *never* see you do that.'

'You will sometimes: I'm obliged to do it now and then to keep her in order.'

'But it is not your business to keep her in order, you know – that is for –'

'Well, now go and put on your bonnet.'

'I don't know – it is so very cloudy and cold, it seems likely to rain; and you know I have had a long drive.'

'No matter – you *must* come; I shall allow of no excuses,' replied the consequential little gentleman. And as it was the first day of our acquaintance, I thought I might as well indulge him. It was too cold for Mary Ann to venture, so she stayed with her mamma; to the great relief of her brother, who liked to have me all to himself.

The garden was a large one, and tastefully laid out; besides several splendid dahlias, there were some other fine flowers still in bloom: but my companion would not give me time to examine them: I must go with him across the wet

grass, to a remote sequestered corner, the most important place in the grounds, because it contained *his* garden. There were two round beds, stocked with a variety of plants. In one there was a pretty little rose tree. I paused to admire its lovely blossoms.

'Oh, never mind that!' said he, contemptuously. 'That's only *Mary Ann's* garden; look, this is mine.'

After I had observed every flower, and listened to a disquisition on every plant, I was permitted to depart; but first, with great pomp, he plucked a polyanthus and presented it to me, as one conferring a prodigious favour. I observed, on the grass about his garden, certain apparatus of sticks and cord, and asked what they were.'

'Traps for birds.'

'Why do you catch them?'

'Papa says they do harm.'

'And what do you do with them when you catch them?'

'Different things. Sometimes I give them to the cat; sometimes I cut them in pieces with my penknife; but the next, I mean to roast alive.'

'And why do you mean to do such a horrible thing?'

'For two reasons; first, to see how long it will live – and then, to see what it will taste like.'

'But don't you know it is extremely wicked to do such things. Remember, the birds can feel as well as you; and think, how would you like it yourself.'

'Oh, that's nothing! I'm not a bird, and I can't feel what I do to them.'

'But you will have to feel it sometime, Tom: you have heard where wicked people go to when they die; and if you don't leave off torturing innocent birds, remember, you will have to go there, and suffer just what you have made them suffer.'

'Oh, pooh! I shan't. Papa knows how I treat them, and he never blames me for it: he says it is just what *he* used to do when *he* was a boy. Last summer, he gave me a nest full of young sparrows, and he saw me pulling off their legs and wings and heads, and never said anything; except that they were nasty things, and I must not let them soil my trousers: and Uncle Robson was there too, and he laughed, and said I was a fine boy.'

'But what would your mamma say?'

'Oh, she doesn't care! she says it's a pity to kill the pretty singing birds, but the naughty sparrows, and mice and rats, I may do what I like with. So now, Miss Grey, you see it is *not* wicked.'

'I still think it is, Tom; and perhaps your papa and mamma would think so too, if they thought much about it. However,' I internally added, 'they may say what they please, but I am determined you shall do nothing of the kind, as long as I have power to prevent it.'

He next took me across the lawn to see his mole-traps, and then into the stack-yard to see his weasel-traps: one of which, to his great joy, contained a dead weasel; and then into the stable to see, not the fine carriage horses, but a little rough colt, which he informed me had been bred on purpose for him, and

he was to ride it as soon as it was properly trained. I tried to amuse the little fellow, and listened to all his chatter as complacently as I could; for I thought if he had any affections at all, I would endeavour to win them; and then, in time, I might be able to show him the error of his ways: but I looked in vain for that generous, noble spirit his mother talked of; though I could see he was not without a certain degree of quickness and penetration, when he chose to exert it.

When we re-entered the house it was nearly tea-time. Master Tom told me that, as papa was from home, he and I and Mary Ann were to have tea with mamma, for a treat; for, on such occasions, she always dined at luncheon time with them, instead of at six o'clock. Soon after tea, Mary Ann went to bed, but Tom favoured us with his company and conversation till eight. After he was gone, Mrs Bloomfield further enlightened me on the subject of her children's dispositions and acquirements, and on what they were to learn, and how they were to be managed, and cautioned me to mention their defects to no one but herself. My mother had warned me before to mention them as little as possible to her, for people did not like to be told of their children's faults, and so I concluded I was to keep silence on them altogether. About half-past nine, Mrs Bloomfield invited me to partake of a frugal supper of cold meat and bread. I was glad when that was over, and she took her bedroom candlestick and retired to rest; for though I wished to be pleased with her, her company was extremely irksome to me; and I could not help feeling that she was cold, grave, and forbidding – the very opposite of the kind warm-hearted matron my hopes had depicted her to be.

### CHAPTER 3

## A Few More Lessons

I rose next morning with a feeling of hopeful exhilaration, in spite of the disappointments already experienced; but I found the dressing of Mary Ann was no light matter, as her abundant hair was to be smeared with pomade, plaited in three long tails, and tied with bows of ribbon: a task my unaccustomed fingers found great difficulty in performing. She told me her nurse could do it in half the time, and, by keeping up a constant fidget of impatience, contrived to render me still longer. When all was done, we went into the schoolroom, where I met my other pupil, and chatted with the two till it was time to go down to breakfast. That meal being concluded and a few civil words having been exchanged with Mrs Bloomfield, we repaired to the schoolroom again, and commenced the business of the day. I found my pupils very backward, indeed; but Tom, though averse to every species of mental exertion, was not without abilities. Mary Ann could scarcely read a word, and was so careless and inattentive that I could hardly get on with her at all. However, by dint of great labour and patience, I managed to get something done in the course of the morning, and then accompanied my

young charges out into the garden and adjacent grounds, for a little recreation before dinner. There we got along tolerably together, except that I found they had no notion of going with *me:* I must go with *them* wherever they chose to lead me. I must run, walk, or stand, exactly as it suited their fancy. This, I thought, was reversing the order of things; and I found it doubly disagreeable, as on this as well as subsequent occasions, they seemed to prefer the dirtiest places and the most dismal occupations. But there was no remedy; either I must follow them, or keep entirely apart from them, and thus appear neglectful of my charge. Today, they manifested a particular attachment to a well at the bottom of the lawn, where they persisted in dabbling with sticks and pebbles for above half an hour. I was in constant fear that their mother would see them from the window, and blame me for allowing them thus to draggle their clothes and wet their feet and hands, instead of taking exercise; but no arguments, commands, or entreaties could draw them away. If *she* did not see them, someone else did – a gentleman on horseback had entered the gate and was proceeding up the road; at the distance of a few paces from us he paused, and calling to the children in a waspish penetrating tone, bade them 'Keep out of that water.' 'Miss Grey,' said he, '(I suppose it is Miss Grey) I am surprised that you should allow them to dirty their clothes in that manner! Don't you see how Miss Bloomfield has soiled her frock? and that Master Bloomfield's socks are quite wet? and both of them without gloves? Dear, dear! Let me *request* that in future you will keep them *decent* at least!' so saying, he turned away, and continued his ride up to the house. This was Mr Bloomfield. I was surprised that he should nominate his children Master and Miss Bloomfield; and still more so, that he should speak so uncivilly to me, their governess, and a perfect stranger to himself. Presently the bell rang to summon us in. I dined with the children at one, while he and his lady took their luncheon at the same table. His conduct there did not greatly raise him in my estimation. He was a man of ordinary stature – rather below than above – and rather thin than stout, apparently between thirty and forty years of age: he had a large mouth, pale, dingy complexion, milky blue eyes, and hair the colour of a hempen cord. There was a roast leg of mutton before him: he helped Mrs Bloomfield, the children, and me, desiring me to cut up the children's meat; then, after twisting about the mutton in various directions, and eyeing it from different points, he pronounced it not fit to be eaten and called for the cold beef.

'What is the matter with the mutton, my dear?' asked his mate.

'It is quite overdone. Don't you taste, Mrs Bloomfield, that all the goodness is roasted out of it? And can't you see that all that nice, red gravy is completely dried away?'

'Well, I think the *beef* will suit you.'

The beef was set before him, and he began to carve, but with the most rueful expressions of discontent

'What is the matter with the *beef,* Mr Bloomfield? I'm sure I thought it was very nice.'

'And so it *was* very nice. A nicer joint could not be; but it is *quite* spoiled,' replied he dolefully.

'How so?'

'How so! Why, don't you see how it is cut? Dear – dear! it is quite shocking!'

'They must have cut it wrong in the kitchen, then, for I'm sure I carved it quite properly here, yesterday.'

'*No doubt* they cut it wrong in the kitchen – the savages! Dear – dear! Did ever anyone see such a fine piece of beef so completely ruined? But remember that, in future, when a decent dish leaves this table, they shall not *touch* it in the kitchen. Remember *that* Mrs Bloomfield!'

Notwithstanding the ruinous state of the beef, the gentleman managed to cut himself some delicate slices, part of which he ate in silence. When he next spoke, it was, in a less querulous tone, to ask what there was for dinner.

'Turkey and grouse,' was the concise reply.

'And what besides?'

'Fish.'

'What kind of fish?'

'I don't know.'

'*You don't know?*' cried he, looking solemnly up from his plate and suspending his knife and fork in astonishment.

'No. I told the cook to get some fish – I did not particularise what.'

'Well, that beats everything! A lady professes to keep house, and doesn't even know what fish is for dinner! professes to order fish, and doesn't specify what!'

'Perhaps, Mr Bloomfield, you will order dinner yourself in future.'

Nothing more was said; and I was very glad to get out of the room with my pupils; for I never felt so ashamed and uncomfortable in my life for anything that was not my own fault.

In the afternoon we applied to lessons again: then went out again; then had tea in the schoolroom; then I dressed Mary Ann for dessert; and when she and her brother had gone down to the dining-room, I took the opportunity of beginning a letter to my dear friends at home: but the children came up before I had half-completed it. At seven I had to put Mary Anne to bed: then I played with Tom till eight, when he, too, went; and I finished my letter and unpacked my clothes which I had hitherto found no opportunity for doing, and, finally, went to bed myself.

But this is a very favourable specimen of a day's proceedings.

My task of instruction and surveillance, instead of becoming easier as my charges and I got better accustomed to each other, became more arduous as their characters unfolded. The name of governess, I soon found, was a mere mockery as applied to me: my pupils had no more notion of obedience than a wild, unbroken colt. The habitual fear of their father's peevish temper, and the dread of the punishments he was wont to inflict when irritated, kept them generally within bounds in his immediate presence. The girls, too, had some fear of their mother's anger; and the boy might occasionally be bribed to do as she bid him by the hope of reward: but I had no rewards to offer; and as for punishments, I was given to understand, the parents reserved that privilege to themselves; and yet they expected me to keep my pupils in order. Other

children might be guided by the fear of anger, and the desire of approbation; but neither the one nor the other had any effect upon these.

Master Tom, not content with refusing to be ruled, must needs set up as a ruler, and manifested a determination to keep, not only his sisters, but his governess in order, by violent manual and pedal applications; and as he was a tall, strong boy of his years, this occasioned no trifling inconvenience. A few sound boxes in the ear, on such occasions, might have settled the matter easily enough: but as, in that case, he might make up some story to his mother, which she would be sure to believe, as she had such unshaken faith in his veracity – though I had already discovered it to be by no means unimpeachable – I determined to refrain from striking him, even in self-defence; and, in his most violent moods, my only resource was to throw him on his back, and hold his hands and feet till the frenzy was somewhat abated. To the difficulty of preventing him from doing what he ought not, was added that of forcing him to do what he ought. Often he would positively refuse to learn, or to repeat his lessons, or even to look at his book. Here, again, a good birch rod might have been serviceable; but, as my powers were so limited, I must make the best use of what I had.

As there were no settled hours for study and play, I resolved to give my pupils a certain task, which, with moderate attention, they could perform in a short time; and till this was done, however weary I was, or however perverse they might be, nothing short of parental interference should induce me to suffer them to leave the schoolroom; even if I should sit with my chair against the door to keep them in. Patience, Firmness, and Perseverance, were my only weapons; and these I resolved to use to the utmost. I determined always strictly to fulfil the threats and promises I made, and, to that end, I must be cautious to threaten and promise nothing that I could not perform. Then, I would carefully refrain from all useless irritability and indulgence of my own ill-temper: when they behaved tolerably, I would be as kind and obliging as it was in my power to be, in order to make the widest possible distinction between good and bad conduct; I would reason with them, too, in the simplest and most effective manner. When I reproved them or refused to gratify their wishes, after a glaring fault, it should be more in sorrow than in anger: their little hymns and prayers I would make plain and clear to their understanding; when they said their prayers at night, and asked pardon for their offences, I would remind them of the sins of the past day, solemnly, but in perfect kindness, to avoid raising a spirit of opposition; penitential hymns should be said by the naughty; cheerful ones by the comparatively good; and every kind of instruction I would convey to them, as much as possible, by entertaining discourse – apparently with no other object than their present amusement in view.

By these means I hoped, in time, both to benefit the children and to gain the approbation of their parents; and also to convince my friends at home that I was not so wanting in skill and prudence as they supposed. I knew the difficulties I had to contend with were great; but I knew (at least I believed) unremitting patience and perseverance could overcome them; and night and morning I implored

Divine assistance to this end. But either the children were so incorrigible, the parents so unreasonable, or myself so mistaken in my views, or so unable to carry them out, that my best intentions and most strenuous efforts seemed productive of no better result than sport to the children, dissatisfaction to their parents, and torment to myself.

The task of instruction was as arduous for the body as the mind. I had to run after my pupils to catch them, to carry or drag them to the table, and often forcibly to hold them there till the lesson was done. Tom I frequently put into a corner, seating myself before him in a chair, with a book which contained the little task that must be said or read, before he was released, in my hand. He was not strong enough to push both me and the chair away, so he would stand twisting his body and face into the most grotesque and singular contortions – laughable, no doubt, to an unconcerned spectator, but not to me – and uttering loud yells and doleful outcries, intended to represent weeping, but wholly without the accompaniment of tears. I knew this was done solely for the purpose of annoying me; and, therefore, however I might inwardly tremble with impatience and irritation, I manfully strove to suppress all visible signs of molestation, and affected to sit with calm indifference, waiting till it should please him to cease this pastime, and prepare for a run in the garden, by casting his eye on the book and reading or repeating the few words he was required to say. Sometimes he was determined to do his writing badly; and I had to hold his hand to prevent him from purposely blotting or disfiguring the paper. Frequently I threatened that, if he did not do better he should have another line: then he would stubbornly refuse to write this line; and I, to save my word, had finally to resort to the expedient of holding his fingers upon the pen, and forcibly drawing his hand up and down, till, in spite of his resistance, the line was in some sort completed.

Yet Tom was by no means the most unmanageable of my pupils: sometimes, to my great joy, he would have the sense to see that his wisest policy was to finish his tasks, and go out and amuse himself till I and his sisters came to join him; which frequently was not at all, for Mary Ann seldom followed his example in this particular: she apparently preferred rolling on the floor to any other amusement: down she would drop like a leaden weight; and when I, with great difficulty, had succeeded in rooting her thence, I had still to hold her up with one arm, while with the other I held the book from which she was to read or spell her lesson. As the dead weight of the big girl of six became too heavy for one arm to bear, I transferred it to the other; or, if both were weary of the burden, I carried her into a corner, and told her she might come out when she should find the use of her feet, and stand up: but she generally preferred lying there like a log till dinner or tea-time, when, as I could not deprive her of her meals, she must be liberated, and would come crawling out with a grin of triumph on her round, red face. Often she would stubbornly refuse to pronounce some particular word in her lesson; and now I regret the lost labour I have had in striving to conquer her obstinacy. If I had passed it over as a matter of no consequence, it would have been better for both parties, than vainly striving to overcome it as I did; but I thought it my

absolute duty to crush this vicious tendency in the bud: and so it was if I could have done it; and, had my powers been less limited, I might have enforced obedience; but, as it was, it was a trial of strength between her and me, in which she generally came off victorious; and every victory served to encourage and strengthen her for a future contest. In vain I argued, coaxed, entreated, threatened, scolded; in vain I kept her in from play, or, if obliged to take her out, refused to play with her, or to speak kindly, or have anything to do with her; in vain I tried to set before her the advantages of doing as she was bid, and being loved, and kindly treated in consequence, and the disadvantages of persisting in her absurd perversity. Sometimes, when she would ask me to do something for her, I would answer – 'Yes, I will, Mary Ann, if you will only say that word. Come! you'd better say it at once, and have no more trouble about it.'

'No.'

'Then, of course, I can do nothing for you.'

With me, at her age, or under, neglect and disgrace were the most dreadful of punishments; but on her they made no impression. Sometimes, exasperated to the utmost pitch I would shake her violently by the shoulder, or pull her long hair, or put her in the corner; for which she punished me with loud, shrill, piercing screams, that went through my head like a knife. She knew I hated this, and when she had shrieked her utmost, would look into my face with an air of vindictive satisfaction, exclaiming – '*Now*, then! that's for you!' And then shriek again and again, till I was forced to stop my ears. Often these dreadful cries would bring Mrs Bloomfield up to enquire what was the matter.

'Mary Ann is a naughty girl, ma'am.'

'But what are these shocking screams?'

'She is screaming in a passion.'

'I never heard such a dreadful noise! You might be killing her. Why is she not out with her brother?'

'I cannot get her to finish her lessons.'

'But Mary Ann must be a *good* girl, and finish her lessons.' This was blandly spoken to the child. 'And I hope I shall never hear such terrible cries again!'

And fixing her cold, stony eyes upon me with a look that could not be mistaken, she would shut the door, and walk away. Sometimes I would try to take the little obstinate creature by surprise, and casually ask her the word while she was thinking of something else; frequently she would begin to say it, and then suddenly check herself, with a provoking look that seemed to say, 'Ah! I'm too sharp for you; you shan't trick it out of me, either.'

On another occasion, I pretended to forget the whole affair; and talked and played with her as usual, till night, when I put her to bed; then bending over her, while she lay all smiles and good humour, just before departing, I said, as cheerfully and kindly as before – 'Now, Mary Ann, just tell me that word before I kiss you good-night: you are a good girl now, and, of course, you will say it.'

'No, I won't.'

'Then I can't kiss you.'

'Well, I don't care.'

In vain I expressed my sorrow; in vain I lingered for some symptom of contrition; she really 'didn't care' and I left her alone, and in darkness, wondering most of all at this last proof of insensate stubbornness. In my childhood I could not imagine a more afflictive punishment, than for my mother to refuse to kiss me at night: the very idea was terrible. More than the idea I never felt, for, happily, I never committed a fault that was deemed worthy of such a penalty; but once I remember, for some transgression of my sister's, our mother thought proper to inflict it upon her: what she felt, I cannot tell; but my sympathetic tears and suffering for her sake, I shall not soon forget.

Another troublesome trait in Mary Ann, was her incorrigible propensity to keep running into the nursery, to play with her little sisters and the nurse. This was natural enough, but, as it was against her mother's express desire, I, of course, forbade her to do so, and did my utmost to keep her with me; but that only increased her relish for the nursery, and the more I strove to keep her out of it, the oftener she went, and the longer she stayed: to the great dissatisfaction of Mrs Bloomfield, who, I well knew, would impute all the blame of the matter to me. Another of my trials was the dressing in the morning: at one time she would not be washed; at another she would not be dressed, unless she might wear some particular frock, that I knew her mother would not like her to have; at another she would scream and run away if I attempted to touch her hair. So that, frequently, when, after much trouble and toil, I had, at length, succeeded in bringing her down, the breakfast was nearly half over; and black looks from 'mamma', and testy observations from 'papa', spoken at me, if not to me, were sure to be my meed: for few things irritated the latter so much as want of punctuality at meal times. Then, among the minor annoyances, was my inability to satisfy Mrs Bloomfield with her daughter's dress and the child's hair 'was never fit to be seen.' Sometimes, as a powerful reproach to me, she would perform the office of tire-woman herself, and then complain bitterly of the trouble it gave her.

When little Fanny came into the schoolroom, I hoped she would be mild and inoffensive, at least; but a few days, if not a few hours, sufficed to destroy the illusion: I found her a mischievous, intractable little creature, given up to false-hood and deception, young as she was, and alarmingly fond of exercising her two favourite weapons of offence and defence; that of spitting in the faces of those who incurred her displeasure, and bellowing like a bull when her unreasonable desires were not gratified. As she, generally, was pretty quiet in her parents' presence, and they were impressed with the notion of her being a remarkably gentle child, her falsehoods were readily believed, and her loud uproars led them to suspect harsh and injudicious treatment on my part; and when, at length, her bad disposition became manifest even to their prejudiced eyes, I felt that the whole was attributed to me.

'What a naughty girl Fanny is getting!' Mrs Bloomfield would say to her spouse. 'Don't you observe, my dear, how she is altered since she entered the schoolroom? She will soon be as bad as the other two; and, I am sorry to say, they have quite deteriorated of late.'

'You may say that,' was the answer. 'I've been thinking that same myself. I thought when we got them a governess they'd improve; but, instead of that, they get worse and worse: I don't know how it is with their learning; but their habits, I know, make no sort of improvement; they get rougher, and dirtier, and more unseemly, every day.'

I knew this was all pointed at me; and these, and all similar innuendoes, affected me far more deeply than any open accusations would have done; for against the latter I should have been roused to speak in my own defence: now I judged it my wisest plan to subdue every resentful impulse, suppress every sensitive shrinking, and go on perseveringly, doing my best; for, irksome as my situation was, I earnestly wished to retain it. I thought, if I could struggle on with unremitting firmness and integrity, the children would in time become more humanised: every month would contribute to make them some little wiser, and, consequently, more manageable; for a child of nine or ten as frantic and ungovernable as these at six and seven would be a maniac.

I flattered myself I was benefiting my parents and sister by my continuance here; for small as the salary was, I still was earning something, and with strict economy I could easily manage to have something to spare for them, if they would favour me by taking it. Then it was by my own will that I had got the place: I had brought all this tribulation on myself, and I was determined to bear it; nay, more than that, I did not even regret the step I had taken. I longed to show my friends that, even now, I was competent to undertake the charge, and able to acquit myself honourably to the end; and if ever I felt it degrading to submit so quietly, or intolerable to toil so constantly, I would turn towards my home and say within myself –

> They may crush, but they shall not subdue me!
> 'Tis of thee that I think, not of them.

About Christmas I was allowed to visit home; but my holiday was only of a fortnight's duration: 'For,' said Mrs Bloomfield, 'I thought, as you had seen your friends so lately, you would not care for a longer stay.' I left her to think so still: but she little knew how long, how wearisome those fourteen weeks of absence had been to me; how intensely I had longed for my holidays, how greatly I was disappointed at their curtailment. Yet she was not to blame in this. I had never told her my feelings, and she could not be expected to divine them; I had not been with her a full term, and she was justified in not allowing me a full vacation.

## CHAPTER 4

## *The Grandmamma*

I spare my readers the account of my delight on coming home, my happiness while there – enjoying a brief space of rest and liberty in that dear, familiar place, among the loving and the loved – and my sorrow on being obliged to bid them, once more, a long adieu.

I returned, however, with unabated vigour to my work – a more arduous task than anyone can imagine, who has not felt something like the misery of being charged with the care and direction of a set of mischievous turbulent rebels, whom his utmost exertions cannot bind to their duty; while, at the same time, he is responsible for their conduct to a higher power, who exacts from him what cannot be achieved without the aid of the superior's more potent authority: which, either from indolence, or the fear of becoming unpopular with the said rebellious gang, the latter refuses to give. I can conceive few situations more harassing than that wherein, however you may long for success, however you may labour to fulfil your duty, your efforts are baffled and set at naught by those beneath you, and unjustly censured and misjudged by those above.

I have not enumerated half the vexatious propensities of my pupils, or half the troubles resulting from my heavy responsibilities, for fear of trespassing too much upon the reader's patience; as, perhaps, I have already done; but my design, in writing the few last pages, was not to amuse, but to benefit those whom it might concern: he that has no interest in such matters will doubtless have skipped them over with cursory glance, and, perhaps, a malediction against the prolixity of the writer; but if a parent has therefrom gathered any useful hint, or an unfortunate governess received thereby the slightest benefit, I am well rewarded for my pains.

To avoid trouble and confusion, I have taken my pupils one by one, and discussed their various qualities; but this can give no adequate idea of being worried by the whole three together; when, as was often the case, all were determined to 'be naughty, and to tease Miss Grey, and put her in a passion'.

Sometimes, on such occasions, the thought had suddenly occurred to me – 'If *they* could see me now!' meaning, of course, my friends at home; and the idea of how they would pity me has made me pity myself – so greatly that I have had the utmost difficulty to restrain my tears: but I have restrained them, till my little tormentors were gone to dessert, or cleared off to bed (my only prospects of deliverance), and then, in all the bliss of solitude, I have given myself up to the luxury of an unrestricted burst of weeping. But this was a weakness I did not often indulge: my employments were too numerous, my leisure moments too precious, to admit of much time being given to fruitless lamentations.

I particularly remember one wild, snowy afternoon, soon after my return in

January; the children had all come up from dinner, loudly declaring that they meant 'to be naughty'; and they had well kept their resolution, though I had talked myself hoarse, and wearied every muscle in my throat, in the vain attempt to reason them out of it. I had got Tom pinned up in a corner, whence, I told him, he should not escape till he had done his appointed task. Meantime, Fanny had possessed herself of my work-bag, and was rifling its contents – and spitting into it besides. I told her to let it alone, but to no purpose, of course. 'Burn it, Fanny!' cried Tom: and *this* command she hastened to obey. I sprang to snatch it from the fire, and Tom darted to the door. 'Mary Ann, throw her desk out of the window!' cried he: and my precious desk containing my letters and papers, my small amount of cash, and all my valuables, was about to be precipitated from the three-storey window. I flew to rescue it. Meanwhile Tom had left the room, and was rushing down the stairs, followed by Fanny. Having secured my desk, I ran to catch them, and Mary Ann came scampering after. All three escaped me, and ran out of the house into the garden, where they plunged about in the snow, shouting and screaming in exultant glee.

What must I do? If I followed them, I should probably be unable to capture one, and only drive them farther away, if I did not, how was I to get them in? and what would their parents think of me, if they saw or heard the children rioting, hatless, bonnetless, gloveless, and bootless, in the deep, soft snow? While I stood in this perplexity, just without the door, trying, by grim looks and angry words, to awe them into subjection, I heard a voice behind me, in harshly piercing tones, exclaiming – 'Miss Grey! Is it possible! What, in the devil's name, can you be thinking about?'

'I can't get them in, sir,' said I, turning round, and beholding Mr Bloomfield, with his hair on end, and his pale blue eyes bolting from their sockets.

'But I INSIST upon their being got in!' cried he, approaching nearer, and looking perfectly ferocious.

'Then, sir, you must call them yourself, if you please, for they won't listen to me,' I replied, stepping back.

'Come in with you, you filthy brats; or I'll horsewhip you every one!' roared he; and the children instantly obeyed. 'There, you see! they come at the first word!'

'Yes, when *you* speak.'

'And it's very strange, that when you've the care of 'em, you've no better control over 'em than that! – Now, there they are – gone upstairs with their nasty snowy feet! Do go after 'em and see them made decent, for Heaven's sake!'

That gentleman's mother was then staying in the house; and, as I ascended the stairs and passed the drawing-room door, I had the satisfaction of hearing the old lady declaiming aloud to her daughter-in-law to this effect (for I could only distinguish the most emphatic words) – 'Gracious heavens! – never in all my life – ! – get their death as sure as – ! Do you think, my dear, she's a *proper person?* Take my word for it – '

I heard no more; but that sufficed.

The senior Mrs Bloomfield had been very attentive and civil to me; and till

now, I had thought her a nice, kind-hearted, chatty old body. She would often come to me and talk in a confidential strain; nodding and shaking her head, and gesticulating with hands and eyes as a certain class of old ladies are wont to do: though I never knew one that carried the peculiarity to so great an extent. She would even sympathise with me for the trouble I had with the children, and express at times, by half sentences, interspersed with nods and knowing winks, her sense of the injudicious conduct of their mamma in so restricting my power, and neglecting to support me with her authority. Such a mode of testifying disapprobation was not much to my taste; and I generally refused to take it in, or understand anything more than was openly spoken: at least, I never went farther than an implied acknowledgement that, if matters were otherwise ordered, my task would be a less difficult one, and I should be better able to guide and instruct my charge; but now I must be doubly cautious. Hitherto, though I saw the old lady had her defects (of which one was a proneness to proclaim her perfections), I had always been wishful to excuse them, and to give her credit for all the virtues she professed, and even imagine others yet untold. Kindness, which had been the food of my life through so many years, had lately been so entirely denied me, that I welcomed with grateful joy the slightest semblance of it. No wonder, then, that my heart warmed to the old lady, and always gladdened at her approach and regretted her departure.

But now, the few words luckily or unluckily heard in passing had wholly revolutionised my ideas respecting her: now I looked upon her as hypocritical and insincere, a flatterer, and a spy upon my words and deeds. Doubtless it would have been my interest still to meet her with the same cheerful smile and tone of respectful cordiality as before; but I could not, if I would: my manner altered with my feelings, and became so cold and shy that she could not fail to notice it. She soon did notice it, and *her* manner altered too: the familiar nod was changed to a stiff bow, the gracious smile gave place to a glare of Gorgon ferocity; her vivacious loquacity was entirely transferred from me to 'the darling boy and girls', whom she flattered and indulged more absurdly than ever their mother had done.

I confess I was somewhat troubled at this change: I feared the consequences of her displeasure, and even made some efforts to recover the ground I had lost – and with better apparent success than I could have anticipated. At one time, I, merely in common civility, asked after her cough; immediately her long visage relaxed into a smile, and she favoured me with a particular history of that and her other infirmities, followed by an account of her pious resignation, delivered in the usual emphatic, declamatory style, which no writing can portray.

'But there's one remedy for all, my dear, and that's resignation' (a toss of the head), 'resignation to the will of Heaven!' (an uplifting of the hands and eyes). 'It has always supported me through all my trials, and always will do' (a succession of nods). 'But then, it isn't everybody that can say that' (a shake of the head); 'but I'm one of the pious ones, Miss Grey!' (a very significant nod and toss). 'And thank Heaven, I always was' (another nod), 'and I glory in it!' (an emphatic clasping of the hands and shaking of the head). And with several texts of

scripture misapplied, and religious exclamations so redolent of the ludicrous in the style of delivery and manner of bringing in, if not in the expressions themselves, that I decline repeating them, she withdrew; tossing her large head in high good-humour – with herself at least – and left me hoping that, after all, she was rather weak than wicked.

At her next visit to Wellwood House, I went so far as to say I was glad to see her looking so well. The effect of this was magical: the words, intended as a mark of civility, were received as a flattering compliment; her countenance brightened up, and from that moment she became as gracious and benign as heart could wish – in outward semblance at least. From what I now saw of her, and what I heard from the children, I knew that, in order to gain her cordial friendship, I had but to utter a word of flattery at each convenient opportunity: but this was against my principles; and for lack of this, the capricious old dame soon deprived me of her favour again and I believe did me much secret injury.

She could not greatly influence her daughter-in-law against me, because, between that lady and herself, there was a mutual dislike – chiefly shown by her in secret detractions and calumniations; by the other, in an excess of frigid formality in her demeanour; and no fawning flattery of the elder could thaw away the wall of ice which the younger interposed between them. But with her son, the old lady had better success: he would listen to all she had to say, provided she could soothe his fretful temper, and refrain from irritating him by her own asperities; and I have reason to believe that she considerably strengthened his prejudice against me. She would tell him that I shamefully neglected the children, and even his wife did not attend to them as she ought; and that he must look after them himself, or they would all go to ruin.

Thus urged, he would frequently give himself the trouble of watching them from the windows during their play; at times, he would follow them through the grounds, and too often came suddenly upon them while they were dabbling in the forbidden well, talking to the coachman in the stables, or revelling in the filth of the farmyard – and I, meanwhile, wearily standing by, having previously exhausted my energy in vain attempts to get them away. Often, too, he would unexpectedly pop his head into the schoolroom while the young people were at meals, and find them spilling their milk over the table and themselves, plunging their fingers into their own or each other's mugs, or quarrelling over their victuals like a set of tiger's cubs. If I were quiet at the moment, I was conniving at their disorderly conduct; if (as was frequently the case) I happened to be exalting my voice to enforce order, I was using undue violence, and setting the girls a bad example by such ungentleness of tone and language.

I remember one afternoon in spring when, owing to the rain, they could not go out; but, by some amazing good fortune, they had all finished their lessons, and yet abstained from running down to tease their parents – a trick that annoyed me greatly, but which, on rainy days, I seldom could prevent their doing; because, below, they found novelty and amusement – especially when visitors were in the house; and their mother, though she bid me keep them in the schoolroom, would never chide them for leaving it, or trouble herself to

send them back. But this day they appeared satisfied with their present abode, and what is more wonderful still, seemed disposed to play together without depending on me for amusement, and without quarrelling with each other. Their occupation was a somewhat puzzling one: they were all squatted together on the floor by the window, over a heap of broken toys and a quantity of birds' eggs – or rather eggshells, for the contents had luckily been abstracted. These shells they had broken up and were pounding into small fragments, to what end I could not imagine; but so long as they were quiet and not in positive mischief, I did not care; and, with a feeling of unusual repose, I sat by the fire, putting the finishing stitches to a frock for Mary Ann's doll; intending, when that was done, to begin a letter to my mother. Suddenly, the door opened, and the dingy head of Mr Bloomfield looked in.

'All very quiet here! What are you doing?' said he. 'No harm *today*, at least,' thought I. But he was of a different opinion. Advancing to the window, and seeing the children's occupations, he testily exclaimed – 'What in the world are you about?'

'We're grinding eggshells, papa!' cried Tom.

'How *dare you* make such a mess, you little devils? Don't you see what confounded work you're making of the carpet?' (the carpet was a plain, brown drugget). 'Miss Grey, did you know what they were doing?'

'Yes, sir.'

'*You knew* it?'

'Yes.'

'*You knew* it! and you actually sat there and permitted them to go on, without a word of reproof!'

'I didn't think they were doing any harm.'

'Any harm! Why look there! Just look at that carpet, and see – was there ever anything like it in a Christian house before? No wonder your room is not fit for a pigsty – no wonder your pupils are worse than a litter of pigs! – no wonder – oh! I declare, it puts me quite past my patience!' and he departed, shutting the door after him with a bang, that made the children laugh.

'It puts *me* quite past my patience too!' muttered I, getting up; and, seizing the poker, I dashed it repeatedly into the cinders, and stirred them up with unwonted energy; thus easing my irritation, under pretence of mending the fire.

After this, Mr Bloomfield was continually looking in to see if the schoolroom was in order; and, as the children were continually littering the floor with fragments of toys, sticks, stones, stubble, leaves, and other rubbish, which I could not prevent their bringing, or oblige them to gather up, and which the servants refused to 'clean after them', I had to spend a considerable portion of my valuable leisure moments on my knees upon the floor, in painfully reducing things to order. Once I told them that they should not taste their supper till they had picked up everything from the carpet. Fanny might have hers when she had taken up a certain quantity, Mary Ann when she had gathered twice as many, and Tom was to clear away the rest. Wonderful to state, the girls did their part;

but Tom was in such a fury that he flew upon the table scattered the bread and milk about the floor, struck his sisters, kicked the coals out of the coal-pan, attempted to overthrow the table and chairs, and seemed inclined to make a Douglas-larder of the whole contents of the room: but I seized upon him, and, sending Mary Ann to call her mamma, held him, in spite of kicks, blows, yells, and execrations, till Mrs Bloomfield made her appearance.

'What is the matter with my boy?' said she.

And when the matter was explained to her, all she did was to send for the nursery-maid to put the room in order, and bring Master Bloomfield his supper.

'There now,' cried Tom triumphantly, looking up from his viands with his mouth almost too full for speech. 'There now, Miss Grey! you see I have got my supper in spite of you: and I haven't picked up a single thing!'

The only person in the house who had any real sympathy for me was the nurse; for she had suffered like afflictions, though in a smaller degree; as she had not the task of teaching, nor was she so responsible for the conduct of her charge.

'Oh, Miss Grey!' she would say, 'you have some trouble with them childer!'

'I have indeed, Betty; and I dare say you know what it is.'

'Ay, I do so! But I don't vex myself o'er 'em as you do. And then, you see, I hit 'em a slap sometimes: and them little uns – I gives 'em a good whipping now and then: there's nothing else will do for 'em, as what they say. Howsoever, I've lost my place for it.'

'Have you, Betty? I heard you were going to leave.'

'Eh bless you, yes! Missis gave me warning a three-wik sin'. She told me afore Christmas how it mud be, if I hit 'em again; but I couldn't hold my hand off 'em at nothing. I know not how you do, for Miss Mary Ann's worse by the half nor her sisters!'

## CHAPTER 5

## The Uncle

Besides the old lady, there was another relative of the family, whose visits were a great annoyance to me – this was 'Uncle Robson', Mrs Bloomfield's brother; a tall, self-sufficient fellow, with dark hair and sallow complexion like his sister, a nose that seemed to disdain the earth, and little grey eyes, frequently half-closed, with a mixture of real stupidity and affected contempt of all surrounding objects. He was a thickset, strongly-built man, but he had found some means of compressing his waist into a remarkably small compass; and that, together with the unnatural stiffness of his form, showed that the lofty-minded, manly Mr Robson, the scorner of the female sex, was not above the foppery of stays. He seldom deigned to notice me; and, when he did, it was with a certain supercilious insolence of tone and manner that convinced me he was no gentleman: though it was intended to have a contrary effect. But it was not for

that I disliked his coming, so much as for the harm he did the children – encouraging all their evil propensities, and undoing, in a few minutes, the little good it had taken me months of labour to achieve.

Fanny and little Harriet he seldom condescended to notice; but Mary Ann was something of a favourite. He was continually encouraging her tendency to affectation (which I had done my utmost to crush), talking about her pretty face, and filling her head with all manner of conceited notions concerning her personal appearance (which I had instructed her to regard as dust in the balance compared with the cultivation of her mind and manners); and I never saw a child so susceptible of flattery as she was. Whatever was wrong, in either her or her brother, he would encourage by laughing at, if not by actually praising: people little know the injury they do to children by laughing at their faults, and making a pleasant jest of what their true friends have endeavoured to teach them to hold in grave abhorrence.

Though not a positive drunkard, Mr Robson habitually swallowed great quantities of wine, and took with relish an occasional glass of brandy and water. He taught his nephew to imitate him in this to the utmost of his ability, and to believe that the more wine and spirits he could take, and the better he liked them, the more he manifested his bold and manly spirit, and rose superior to his sisters. Mr Bloomfield had not much to say against it, for his favourite beverage was gin and water; of which he took a considerable portion every day, by dint of constant sipping – and to that, I chiefly attributed his dingy complexion and waspish temper.

Mr Robson likewise encouraged Tom's propensity to persecute the lower creation, both by precept and example. As he frequently came to course or shoot over his brother-in-law's grounds, he would bring his favourite dogs with him; and he treated them so brutally that, poor as I was, I would have given a sovereign any day to see one of them bite him, provided the animal could have done it with impunity. Sometimes, when in a very complacent mood, he would go a bird-nesting with the children: a thing that irritated and annoyed me exceedingly; as, by frequent and persevering attempts, I flattered myself I had partly shown them the evil of this pastime, and hoped, in time, to bring them to some general sense of justice and humanity, but ten minutes' bird-nesting with uncle Robson, or even a laugh from him at some relation of their former barbarities, was sufficient at once to destroy the effect of my whole elaborate course of reasoning and persuasion. Happily, however, during that spring, they never, but once, got anything but empty nests, or eggs – being too impatient to leave them till the birds were hatched; that once, Tom, who had been with his uncle into the neighbouring plantation, came running in high glee into the garden, with a brood of little callow nestlings in his hands. Mary Ann and Fanny, whom I was just bringing out, ran to admire his spoils, and to beg each a bird for themselves. 'No, not one!' cried Tom. 'They're all mine: uncle Robson gave them to me – one, two, three, four, five – you shan't touch one of them! no, not one, for your lives!' continued he exultingly; laying the nest on the ground, and standing over it with his legs wide apart, his hands thrust into his

breeches pockets his body bent forward, and his face twisted into all manner of contortions in the ecstasy of his delight.

'But you shall see me fettle 'em off. My word, but I *will* wallop 'em! See if I don't now. By gum! but there's rare sport for me in that nest.'

'But, Tom,' said I. 'I shall not allow you to torture those birds. They must either be killed at once or carried back to the place you took them from, that the old birds may continue to feed them.'

'But you don't know where that is, madam: it's only me and uncle Robson that knows that.'

'But if you don't tell me, I shall kill them myself – much as I hate it.'

'You daren't. You daren't touch them for your life! because you know papa and mamma, and uncle Robson, would be angry. Ha, ha! I've caught you there, miss!'

'I shall do what I think right in a case of this sort without consulting anyone. If your papa and mamma don't happen to approve of it, I shall be sorry to offend them; but your uncle Robson's opinions, of course, are nothing to me.'

So saying – urged by a sense of duty – at the risk of both making myself sick and incurring the wrath of my employers – I got a large flat stone, that had been reared up for a mousetrap by the gardener, then, having once more vainly endeavoured to persuade the little tyrant to let the birds be carried back, I asked what he intended to do with them. With fiendish glee he commenced a list of torments; and while he was busied in the relation, I dropped the stone upon his intended victims and crushed them flat beneath it. Loud were the outcries, terrible the execrations, consequent upon this daring outrage; uncle Robson had been coming up the walk with his gun, and was just then pausing to kick his dog. Tom flew towards him, vowing he would make him kick me instead of Juno. Mr Robson leant upon his gun, and laughed excessively at the violence of his nephew's passion, and the bitter maledictions and opprobrious epithets he heaped upon me. 'Well, you *are* a good un!' exclaimed he, at length, taking up his weapon and proceeding towards the house. 'Damme, but the lad has some spunk in him, too. Curse me, if ever I saw a nobler little scoundrel than that. He's beyond petticoat government already: by God! he defies mother, granny, governess, and all! Ha, ha, ha! Never mind, Tom, I'll get you another brood tomorrow.'

'If you do, Mr Robson, I shall kill them too,' said I.

'Humph!' replied he, and having honoured me with a broad stare – which, contrary to his expectations, I sustained without flinching – he turned away with an air of supreme contempt, and stalked into the house. Tom next went to tell his mamma. It was not her way to say much on any subject; but, when she next saw me, her aspect and demeanour were doubly dark and chill. After some casual remark about the weather, she observed – 'I am sorry, Miss Grey you should think it necessary to interfere with Master Bloomfield's amusements; he was *very* much distressed about your destroying the birds.'

'When Master Bloomfield's amusements consist in injuring sentient creatures,' I answered, 'I think it my duty to interfere.'

'You seemed to have forgotten,' said she calmly, 'that the creatures were all created for our convenience.'

I thought that doctrine admitted some doubt, but merely replied – 'If they were, we have no right to torment them for our amusement.'

'I think,' said she, 'a child's amusement is scarcely to be weighed against the welfare of a soulless brute.'

'But, for the child's own sake, it ought not to be encouraged to have such amusements,' answered I, as meekly as I could, to make up for such unusual pertinacity. ' "Blessed are the merciful for they shall obtain mercy." '

'Oh! of course; but that refers to our conduct towards each other.'

' "The merciful man shows mercy to his beast," ' I ventured to add.

'I think you have not shown much mercy,' replied she with a short, bitter laugh: 'killing the poor birds by wholesale in that shocking manner, and putting the dear boy to such misery for a mere whim.'

I judged it prudent to say no more. This was the nearest approach to a quarrel I ever had with Mrs Bloomfield; as well as the greatest number of words I ever exchanged with her at one time, since the day of my first arrival.

But Mr Robson and old Mrs Bloomfield were not the only guests whose coming to Wellwood House annoyed me; every visitor disturbed me more or less; not so much because they neglected me (though I did feel their conduct strange and disagreeable in that respect), as because I found it impossible to keep my pupils away from them, as I was repeatedly desired to do: Tom must talk to them, and Mary Ann must be noticed by them. Neither the one nor the other knew what it was to feel any degree of shamefacedness, or even common modesty. They would indecently and clamorously interrupt the conversation of their elders, tease them with the most impertinent questions, roughly collar the gentlemen, climb their knees uninvited, hang about their shoulders or rifle their pockets, pull the ladies' gowns, disorder their hair, tumble their collars, and importunately beg for their trinkets.

Mrs Bloomfield had the sense to be shocked and annoyed at all this, but she had not sense to prevent it: she expected me to prevent it. But how could I – when the guests, with their fine clothes and new faces, continually flattered and indulged them, out of complaisance to their parents – how could I, with my homely garments, everyday face, and honest words, draw them away? I strained every nerve to do so: by striving to amuse them, I endeavoured to attract them to my side; by the exertion of such authority as I possessed, and by such severity as I dared to use, I tried to deter them from tormenting the guests; and by reproaching their unmannerly conduct, to make them ashamed to repeat it. But they knew no shame; they scorned authority which had no terrors to back it; and as for kindness and affection, either they had no hearts, or such as they had were so strongly guarded, and so well concealed, that I, with all my efforts, had not yet discovered how to reach them.

But soon my trials in this quarter came to a close – sooner than I either expected or desired; for one sweet evening towards the close of May, as I was rejoicing in the near approach of the holidays, and congratulating myself upon

having made some progress with my pupils (as far as their learning went at least, for I *had* instilled *something* into their heads, and I had at length brought them to be a little – a very little – more rational about getting their lessons done in time to leave some space for recreation, instead of tormenting themselves and me all day long to no purpose), Mrs Bloomfield sent for me, and calmly told me that after Midsummer my services would be no longer required. She assured me that my character and general conduct were unexceptionable; but the children had made so little improvement since my arrival, that Mr Bloomfield and she felt it their duty to seek some other mode of instruction. Though superior to most children of their years in abilities, they were decidedly behind them in attainments: their manners were uncultivated, and their tempers unruly. And this she attributed to a want of sufficient firmness, and diligent, persevering care on my part.

Unshaken firmness, devoted diligence, unwearied perseverance, unceasing care, were the very qualifications on which I had secretly prided myself; and by which I had hoped in time to overcome all difficulties, and obtain success at last. I wished to say something in my own justification: but in attempting to speak, I felt my voice falter; and rather than testify any emotion, or suffer the tears to overflow that were already gathering in my eyes, I chose to keep silence, and bear all like a self-convicted culprit.

Thus was I dismissed and thus I sought my home. Alas! what would they think of me? unable, after all my boasting, to keep my place, even for a single year, as governess to three small children, whose mother was asserted by my own aunt, to be a 'very nice woman'. Having been thus weighed in the balance and found wanting, I need not hope they would be willing to try me again. And this was an unwelcome thought; for vexed, harassed, disappointed as I had been, and greatly as I had learned to love and value my home, I was not yet weary of adventure, nor willing to relax my efforts. I knew that all parents were not like Mr and Mrs Bloomfield, and I was certain all children were not like theirs. The next family must be different, and any change must be for the better. I had been seasoned by adversity, and tutored by experience, and I longed to redeem my lost honour in the eyes of those whose opinion was more than that of all the world to me.

## CHAPTER 6

### The Parsonage Again

For a few months I remained peaceably at home, in the quiet enjoyment of liberty and rest, and genuine friendship, from all of which I had fasted so long; and in the earnest prosecution of my studies, to recover what I had lost during my stay at Wellwood House, and to lay in new stores for future use. My father's health was still very infirm, but not materially worse than when I last saw him; and I was glad I had it in my power to cheer him by my return, and to amuse him with singing his favourite songs.

No one triumphed over my failure, or said I had better have taken his or her advice, and quietly stayed at home. All were glad to have me back again, and lavished more kindness than ever upon me, to make up for the sufferings I had undergone; but not one would touch a shilling of what I had so cheerfully earned and so carefully saved, in the hope of sharing it with them. By dint of pinching here, and scraping there, our debts were already nearly paid. Mary had had good success with her drawings; but our father had insisted upon *her* likewise keeping all the produce of her industry to herself. All we could spare from the supply of our humble wardrobe and our little casual expenses, he directed us to put into the savings' bank; saying, we knew not how soon we might be dependent on that alone for support: for he felt he had not long to be with us, and what would become of our mother and us when he was gone, God only knew!

Dear papa! if he had troubled himself less about the afflictions that threatened us in case of his death, I am convinced that dreaded event would not have taken place so soon. My mother would never suffer him to ponder on the subject if she could help it.

'Oh, Richard!' exclaimed she, on one occasion, 'if you would but dismiss such gloomy subjects from your mind, you would live as long as any of us; at least you would live to see the girls married, and yourself a happy grandfather, with a canty old dame for your companion.'

My mother laughed, and so did my father: but his laugh soon perished in a dreary sigh.

'*They* married – poor penniless things!' said he, 'who will take them, I wonder!'

'Why nobody shall that isn't thankful for them. Wasn't I penniless when you took me? and you *pretended*, at least, to be vastly pleased with your acquisition. But it's no matter whether they get married or not: we can devise a thousand honest ways of making a livelihood. And I wonder, Richard, you can think of bothering your head about our *poverty* in case of your death; as if *that* would be anything compared with the calamity of losing you – an affliction that you well

know, would swallow up all others, and which you ought to do your utmost to preserve us from: and there is nothing like a cheerful mind for keeping the body in health.'

'I know, Alice, it is wrong to keep repining as I do, but I cannot help it: you must bear with me.'

'*I won't* bear with you, if I can alter you,' replied my mother: but the harshness of her words was undone by the earnest affection of her tone and pleasant smile, that made my father smile again, less sadly and less transiently than was his wont.

'Mamma,' said I, as soon as I could find an opportunity of speaking with her alone, 'my money is but little, and cannot last long; if I could increase it, it would lessen papa's anxiety, on one subject at least. I cannot draw like Mary, and so the best thing I could do would be to look out for another situation.'

'And so you would actually try again, Agnes?'

'Decidedly, I would.'

'Why, my dear, I should have thought you had had enough of it.'

'I know,' said I, 'everybody is not like Mr and Mrs Bloomfield – '

'Some are worse,' interrupted my mother.

'But not many, I think,' replied I, 'and I'm sure all children are not like theirs; for I and Mary were not: we always did as you bid us, didn't we?'

'Generally: but then, I did not spoil you; and you were not perfect angels after all: Mary had a fund of quiet obstinacy, and you were somewhat faulty in regard to temper; but you were very good children on the whole.'

'I know I was sulky sometimes, and I should have been glad to see these children sulky sometimes too; for then I could have understood them: but they never were, for they *could* not be offended, nor hurt, nor ashamed: they could not be unhappy in any way, except when they were in a passion.'

'Well, if they *could* not, it was not their fault: you cannot expect stone to be as pliable as clay.'

'No, but still it is very unpleasant to live with such unimpressible, incomprehensible creatures. You cannot love them; and if you could, your love would be utterly thrown away: they could neither return it, nor value, nor understand it. But, however, even if I should stumble on such a family again, which is quite unlikely, I have all this experience to begin with, and I should manage better another time; and the end and aim of this preamble is, let me try again.'

'Well, my girl, you are not easily discouraged, I see: I am glad of that. But, let me tell you, you are a good deal paler and thinner than when you first left home; and we cannot have you undermining your health to hoard up money, either for yourself or others.'

'Mary tells me I am changed too; and I don't much wonder at it, for I was in a constant state of agitation and anxiety all day long; but next time I am determined to take things coolly.'

After some further discussion, my mother promised once more to assist me, provided I would wait and be patient; and I left her to broach the matter to my father, when and how she deemed it most advisable: never doubting her ability

to obtain his consent. Meantime, I searched, with great interest the advertising columns of the newspapers, and wrote answers to every 'Wanted a Governess,' that appeared at all eligible; but all my letters, as well as the replies, when I got any, were dutifully shown to my mother; and she, to my chagrin, made me reject the situations one after another: these were low people, these were too exacting in their demands, and these too niggardly in their remuneration.

'Your talents are not such as every poor clergyman's daughter possesses, Agnes,' she would say, 'and you must not throw them away. Remember, you promised to be patient: there is no need of hurry: you have plenty of time before you, and may have many chances yet.'

At length, she advised me to put an advertisement myself in the paper, stating my qualifications, etc.

'Music, singing, drawing, French, Latin, and German,' said she, 'are no mean assemblage: many will be glad to have so much in one instructor; and this time, you shall try your fortune in a somewhat higher family – in that of some genuine, thoroughbred gentleman; for such are far more likely to treat you with proper respect and consideration than those purse-proud tradespeople and arrogant upstarts. I have known several among the higher ranks who treated their governesses quite as one of the family; though some, I allow, are as insolent and exacting as anyone else can be: for there are bad and good in all classes.'

The advertisement was quickly written and despatched. Of the two parties who answered it, but one would consent to give me fifty pounds, the sum my mother bade me name as the salary I should require; and here, I hesitated about engaging myself, as I feared the children would be too old, and their parents would require someone more showy, or more experienced, if not more accomplished than I. But my mother dissuaded me from declining it on that account: I should do vastly well, she said, if I would only throw aside my diffidence, and acquire a little more confidence in myself. I was just to give a plain, true statement of my acquirements and qualifications, and name what stipulations I chose to make, and then await the result. The only stipulation I ventured to propose, was that I might be allowed two months holidays during the year to visit my friends, at Midsummer and Christmas. The unknown lady, in her reply, made no objection to this, and stated that, as to my acquirements, she had no doubt, I should be able to give satisfaction; but in the engagement of governesses, she considered these things as but subordinate points; as, being situated in the neighbourhood of O—, she could get masters to supply any deficiencies in that respect: but, in her opinion, next to unimpeachable morality, a mild and cheerful temper and obliging disposition were the most essential requisites.

My mother did not relish this at all, and now made many objections to my accepting the situation; in which my sister warmly supported her: but, unwilling to be balked again, I overruled them all; and, having first obtained the consent of my father (who had, a short time previously, been apprised of these transactions), I wrote a most obliging epistle to my unknown correspondent, and, finally, the bargain was concluded.

It was decreed that on the last day of January, I was to enter upon my new office as governess in the family of Mr Murray, of Horton Lodge, near O—, about seventy miles from our village: a formidable distance to me, as I had never been above twenty miles from home in all the course of my twenty years' sojourn on earth; and as, moreover, every individual in that family and in the neighbourhood was utterly unknown to myself and all my acquaintances. But this rendered it only the more piquant to me. I had now, in some measure, got rid of the *mauvaise honte* that had formerly oppressed me so much; there was a pleasing excitement in the idea of entering these unknown regions, and making my way alone among its strange inhabitants. I now flattered myself I was going to see something of the world: Mr Murray's residence was near a large town, and not in a manufacturing district, where the people had nothing to do but to make money; his rank, from what I could gather, appeared to be higher than that of Mr Bloomfield; and, doubtless, he was one of those genuine thorough-bred gentry my mother spoke of, who would treat his governess with due consideration as a respectable, well-educated lady, the instructor and guide of his children, and not a mere upper servant. Then, my pupils being older, would be more rational, more teachable, and less troublesome than the last; they would be less confined to the schoolroom, and not require that constant labour and incessant watching; and, finally, bright visions mingled with my hopes, with which the care of children and the mere duties of a governess had little or nothing to do. Thus, the reader will see that I had no claim to be regarded as a martyr to filial piety, going forth to sacrifice peace and liberty for the sole purpose of laying up stores for the comfort and support of my parents: though certainly the comfort of my father, and the future support of my mother, had a large share in my calculations; and fifty pounds appeared to me no ordinary sum. I must have decent clothes becoming my station; I must, it seemed, put out my washing, and also pay for my four annual journeys between Horton Lodge and home; but with strict attention to economy, surely twenty pounds, or little more, would cover those expenses, and then there would be thirty for the bank or little less: what a valuable addition to our stock! Oh, I must struggle to keep this situation, whatever it might be! both for my own honour among my friends and for the solid services I might render them by my continuance there.

## CHAPTER 7
### *Horton Lodge*

The 31st of January was a wild, tempestuous day: there was a strong north wind, with a continual storm of snow drifting on the ground and whirling through the air. My friends would have had me delay my departure, but fearful of prejudicing my employers against me by such want of punctuality at the commencement of my undertaking, I persisted in keeping the appointment.

I will not inflict upon my readers an account of my leaving home on that dark winter morning: the fond farewells, the long, long, journey to O—, the solitary waitings in inns for coaches or trains – for there were some railways then – and, finally, the meeting at O— with Mr Murray's servant, who had been sent with the phaeton to drive me from thence to Horton Lodge. I will just state that the heavy snow had thrown such impediments in the way of both horses and steam-engines, that it was dark some hours before I reached my journey's end, and that a most bewildering storm came on at last, which made the few miles space between O— and Horton Lodge a long and formidable passage. I sat resigned, with the cold, sharp snow drifting through my veil and filling my lap, seeing nothing, and wondering how the unfortunate horse and driver could make their way even as well as they did: and indeed it was but a toilsome, creeping style of progression to say the best of it. At length we paused; and, at the call of the driver someone unlatched and rolled back upon their creaking hinges what appeared to be the park gates. Then we proceeded along a smoother road, whence, occasionally, I perceived some huge hoary mass gleaming through the darkness, which I took to be a portion of a snow-clad tree. After a considerable time we paused again, before the stately portico of a large house with long windows descending to the ground.

I rose with some difficulty from under the superincumbent snow-drift, and alighted from the carriage, expecting that a kind and hospitable reception would indemnify me for the toils and hardships of the day. A gentlemanly person in black opened the door, and admitted me into a spacious hall, lighted by an amber-coloured lamp suspended from the ceiling; he led me through this, along a passage, and, opening the door of a back room, told me that was the school-room. I entered, and found two young ladies and two young gentlemen – my future pupils, I supposed. After a formal greeting, the elder girl, who was trifling over a piece of canvas and a basket of German wools, asked if I should like to go upstairs. I replied in the affirmative, of course.

'Matilda, take a candle, and show her her room,' said she.

Miss Matilda, a strapping hoyden of about fourteen, with a short frock and trousers, shrugged her shoulders and made a slight grimace, but took a candle and proceeded before me, up the back stairs (a long, steep, double flight), and

through a long, narrow passage, to a small but tolerably comfortable room. She then asked me if I would take some tea or coffee. I was about to answer No; but remembering that I had taken nothing since seven o'clock that morning, and feeling faint in consequence, I said I would take a cup of tea. Saying she would tell 'Brown,' the young lady departed; and by the time I had divested myself of my heavy, wet cloak, shawl, bonnet, etc., a mincing damsel came to say the young ladies desired to know whether I would take my tea up there or in the schoolroom. Under the plea of fatigue, I chose to take it there. She withdrew; and, after a while, returned again with a small tea-tray, and placed it on the chest of drawers which served as a dressing table. Having civilly thanked her, I asked at what time I should be expected to rise in the morning.

'The young ladies and gentlemen breakfast at half-past eight, ma'am,' said she; 'they rise early; but, as they seldom do any lessons before breakfast, I should think it will do if you rise soon after seven.'

I desired her to be so kind as to call me at seven, and, promising to do so, she withdrew. Then, having broken my long fast on a cup of tea and a little thin bread and butter, I sat down beside the small, smouldering fire, and amused myself with a hearty fit of crying; after which I said my prayers, and then, feeling considerably relieved, began to prepare for bed. Finding that none of my luggage was brought up, I instituted a search for the bell; and failing to discover any signs of such a convenience in any corner of the room, I took my candle and ventured through the long passage, and down the steep stairs, on a voyage of discovery. Meeting a well-dressed female on the way, I told her what I wanted; but not without considerable hesitation, as I was not quite sure whether it was one of the upper servants, or Mrs Murray herself: it happened, however, to be the lady's-maid. With the air of one conferring an unusual favour, she vouchsafed to undertake the sending up of my things; and when I had re-entered my room, and waited and wondered a long time (greatly fearing that she had forgotten or neglected to perform her promise, and doubting whether to keep waiting or to go to bed, or go down again, my hopes, at length, were revived by the sound of voices and laughter, accompanied by the tramp of feet along the passage; and presently the luggage was brought in by a rough-looking maid and a man, neither of them very respectful in their demeanour to me. Having shut the door upon their retiring footsteps, and unpacked a few of my things, I betook myself to rest; gladly enough, for I was weary in body and mind.

It was with a strange feeling of desolation, mingled with a strong sense of the novelty of my situation, and a joyless kind of curiosity concerning what was yet unknown, that I awoke the next morning; feeling like one whirled away by enchantment, and suddenly dropped from the clouds into a remote and unknown land, widely and completely isolated from all he had ever seen or known before; or like a thistle-seed borne on the wind to some strange nook of uncongenial soil, where it must lie long enough before it can take root and germinate, extracting nourishment from what appears so alien to its nature: if, indeed, it ever can. But this gives no proper idea of my feelings at all; and no one that has not lived such a retired, stationary life as mine, can possible imagine what they were: hardly even if

he has known what it is to awake some morning, and find himself in Port Nelson, in New Zealand, with a world of waters between himself and all that knew him.

I shall not soon forget the peculiar feeling with which I raised my blind and looked out upon the unknown world: a wide, white wilderness was all that met my gaze; a waste of

> Deserts tossed in snows
> And heavy laden groves.

I descended to the schoolroom with no remarkable eagerness to join my pupils, though not without some feeling of curiosity respecting what a further acquaintance would reveal. One thing, among others of more obvious importance, I determined with myself – I must begin with calling them Miss and Master. It seemed to me a chilling and unnatural piece of punctilio between the children of a family and their instructor and daily companion; especially where the former were in their early childhood, as at Wellwood House; but even there, my calling the little Bloomfields by their simple names had been regarded as an offensive liberty: as their parents had taken care to show me, by carefully designating them *Master* and *Miss* Bloomfield, etc., in speaking to me. I had been very slow to take the hint, because the whole affair struck me as so very absurd; but now I determined to be wiser, and begin at once with as much form and ceremony as any member of the family would be likely to require: and indeed, the children being so much older, there would be less difficulty; though the little words Miss and Master seemed to have a surprising effect in repressing all familiar, open-hearted kindness, and extinguishing every gleam of cordiality that might arise between us.

As I cannot, like Dogberry, find it in my heart to bestow *all* my tediousness upon the reader, I will not go on to bore him with a minute detail of all the discoveries and proceedings of this and the following day. No doubt he will be amply satisfied with a slight sketch of the different members of the family, and a general view of the first year of two of my sojourn among them.

To begin with the head: Mr Murray was, by all accounts a blustering, roistering, country squire; a devoted fox-hunter, a skilful horse-jockey and farrier, an active, practical farmer, and a hearty *bon-vivant*. By all accounts, I say; for, except on Sundays when he went to church, I never saw him from month to month: unless, in crossing the hall or walking in the grounds, the figure of a tall, stout gentleman, with scarlet cheeks and crimson nose, happened to come across me; on which occasions, if he passed near enough to speak, an unceremonious nod, accompanied by a 'Morning, Miss Grey,' or some such brief salutation, was usually vouchsafed. Frequently, indeed, his loud laugh reached me from afar; and oftener still I heard him swearing and blaspheming against the footmen, groom, coachman, or some other hapless dependant.

Mrs Murray was a handsome, dashing lady of forty, who certainly required neither rouge nor padding to add to her charms; and whose chief enjoyments were, or seemed to be, in giving or frequenting parties, and in dressing at the very top of the fashion. I did not see her till eleven o'clock on the morning after

my arrival; when she honoured me with a visit, just as my mother might step into the kitchen to see a new servant girl: yet not so, either, for my mother would have seen her immediately after her arrival, and not waited till the next day; and, moreover, she would have addressed her in a more kind and friendly manner, and given her some words of comfort as well as a plain exposition of her duties; but Mrs Murray did neither the one nor the other. She just stepped into the schoolroom on her return from ordering dinner in the housekeeper's room, bade me good-morning, stood for two minutes by the fire, said a few words about the weather and the 'rather rough' journey I must have had yesterday; petted her youngest child – a boy of ten – who had just been wiping his mouth and hands on her gown, after indulging in some savoury morsel from the housekeeper's stores; told me what a sweet, good boy he was; and then sailed out, with a self-complacent smile upon her face: thinking, no doubt, that she had done quite enough for the present, and had been delightfully condescending into the bargain. Her children evidently held the same opinion, and I alone thought otherwise.

After this she looked in upon me once or twice, during the absence of my pupils, to enlighten me concerning my duties towards them. For the girls, she seemed anxious only to render them as superficially attractive and showily accomplished as they could possibly be made, without present trouble or discomfort to themselves; and I was to act accordingly – to study and strive to amuse and oblige, instruct, refine, and polish, with the least possible exertion on their part, and no exercise of authority on mine. With regard to the two boys, it was much the same; only instead of accomplishments, I was to get the greatest possible quantity of Latin grammar and Valpy's Delectus into their heads, in order to fit them for school – the greatest possible quantity at least *without* trouble to themselves. John might be a 'little high-spirited,' and Charles might be a little 'nervous and tedious – '

'But at all events, Miss Grey,' said she, 'I hope you will keep your temper, and be mild and patient throughout; especially with the dear little Charles: he is so extremely nervous and susceptible, and so utterly unaccustomed to anything but the tenderest treatment. You will excuse my naming these things to you; for the fact is, I have hitherto found all the governesses, even the very best of them, faulty in this particular. They wanted that meek and quiet spirit, which St Matthew, or some of them, says is better than the putting on of apparel – you will know the passage to which I allude, for you are a clergyman's daughter. But I have no doubt you will give satisfaction in this respect as well as the rest. And remember, on all occasions, when any of the young people do anything improper, if persuasion and gentle remonstrance will not do, let one of the others come and tell me; for I can speak to them more plainly that it would be proper for you to do. And make them as happy as you can, Miss Grey, and I dare say you will do very well.'

I observed that while Mrs Murray was so extremely solicitious for the comfort and happiness of her children, and continually talking about it, she never once mentioned mine; though they were at home surrounded by friends, and I am

alien among strangers; and I did not yet know enough of the world, not to be considerably surprised at this anomaly.

Miss Murray, otherwise Rosalie, was about sixteen when I came, and decidedly a very pretty girl; and in two years longer, as time more completely developed her form and added grace to her carriage and deportment, she became positively beautiful; and that in no common degree. She was tall and slender, yet not thin; perfectly formed, exquisitely fair, though not without a brilliant, healthy bloom; her hair, which she wore in a profusion of long ringlets, was of a very light brown inclining to yellow; her eyes were pale blue, but so clear and bright that few would wish them darker; the rest of her features were small, not quite regular, and not remarkably otherwise: but altogether you could not hesitate to pronounce her a very lovely girl. I wish I could say as much for mind and disposition as I can for her form and face.

Yet think not I have any dreadful disclosures to make: she was lively, light-hearted, and could be very agreeable, with those who did not cross her will. Towards me, when I first came, she was cold and haughty, then insolent and overbearing; but on a further acquaintance, she gradually laid aside her airs, and in time became as deeply attached to me as it was possible for *her* to be to one of my character and position: for she seldom lost sight, for above half an hour at a time, of the fact of my being a hireling and a poor curate's daughter. And yet, upon the whole, I believe she respected me more than she herself was aware of; because I was the only person in the house who steadily professed good principles, habitually spoke the truth, and generally endeavoured to make inclination bow to duty: and this I say, not, of course, in commendation of myself, but to show the unfortunate state of the family to which my services were, for the present, devoted. There was no member of it in whom I regretted this sad want of principle so much as Miss Murray herself; not only because she had taken a fancy to me, but because there was so much of what was pleasant and pre-possessing in herself, that, in spite of her failings, I really liked her – when she did not rouse my indignation, or ruffle my temper by *too* great a display of her faults. These, however, I would fain persuade myself, were rather the effect of her education than her disposition: she had never been perfectly taught the distinction between right and wrong; she had, like her brothers and sisters, been suffered, from infancy, to tyrannise over nurses, governesses, and servants; she had not been taught to moderate her desires, to control her temper, or bridle her will, or to sacrifice her own pleasure for the good of others. Her temper being naturally good, she was never violent or morose, but from constant indulgence and habitual scorn of reason, she was often testy and capricious; her mind had never been cultivated: her intellect, at best, was somewhat shallow; she possessed considerable vivacity, some quickness of perception, and some talent for music and the acquisition of languages, but till fifteen she had troubled herself to acquire nothing; then the love of display had roused her faculties, and induced her to apply herself, but only to the more showy accomplishments. And when I came it was the same: everything was neglected but French, German, music, singing; dancing, fancy-work, and a little drawing – such drawing as

might produce the greatest show with the smallest labour, and the principal parts of which were generally done by me. For music and singing, besides my occasional instructions, she had the attendance of the best master the country afforded; and in these accomplishments, as well as in dancing, she certainly attained great proficiency. To music, indeed, she devoted too much of her time: as, governess though I was, I frequently told her; but her mother thought that if she liked it, she *could* not give too much time to the acquisition of so attractive an art. Of fancy-work I knew nothing but what I gathered from my pupil and my own observation; but no sooner was I initiated, than she made me useful in twenty different ways: all the tedious parts of her work were shifted on to my shoulders; such as stretching the frames, stitching in the canvas, sorting the wools and silks, putting in the grounds, counting the stitches, rectifying mistakes, and finishing the pieces she was tired of.

At sixteen, Miss Murray was something of a romp, yet not more so than is natural and allowable for a girl of that age; but at seventeen, that propensity, like all other things, began to give way to the ruling passion, and soon was swallowed up in the all-absorbing ambition to attract and dazzle the other sex. But enough of her: now let us turn to her sister.

Miss Matilda Murray was a veritable hoyden, of whom little need be said. She was about two years and a half younger than her sister; her features were larger, her complexion much darker. She might possibly make a handsome woman; but she was far too big-boned and awkward ever to be called a pretty girl, and at present she cared little about it. Rosalie knew all her charms, and thought them even greater than they were, and valued them more highly than she ought to have done, had they been three times as great; Matilda thought she was well enough, but cared little about the matter; still less did she care about the cultivation of her mind and the acquisition of ornamental accomplishments. The manner in which she learnt her lessons and practised her music was calculated to drive any governess to despair. Short and easy as her tasks were, if done at all, they were slurred over, at any time and in any way; but generally at the least convenient times, and in the way least beneficial to herself, and least satisfactory to me: the short half-hour of practising was horribly strummed through; she meantime, unsparingly abusing me, either for interrupting her with corrections, or for not rectifying her mistakes before they were made, or something equally unreasonable. Once or twice, I ventured to remonstrate with her seriously for such irrational conduct; but on each of those occasions, I received such reprehensive expostulations from her mother, as convinced me that, if I wished to keep the situation, I must even let Miss Matilda go on in her own way,

When her lessons were over, however, her ill-humour was generally over too: while riding her spirited pony or romping with the dogs or her brothers and sister, but especially with her dear brother John, she was as happy as a lark. As an animal, Matilda was all right, full of life, vigour, and activity; as an intelligent being, she was barbarously ignorant, indocile, careless and irrational; and, consequently, very distressing to one who had the task of cultivating her understanding, reforming her manners, and aiding her to acquire those

ornamental attainments which, unlike her sister, she despised as much as the rest. Her mother was partly aware of her deficiencies, and gave me many a lecture as to how I should try to form her tastes, and endeavour to rouse and cherish her dormant vanity; and, by insinuating, skilful flattery, to win her attention to the desired objects – which I would not do; and how I could prepare and smooth the path of learning till she could glide along it without the least exertion to herself: which I could not, for nothing can be taught to any purpose without some little exertion on the part of the learner.

As a moral agent, Matilda was reckless, headstrong, violent, and unamenable to reason. One proof of the deplorable state of her mind was, that from her father's example she had learned to swear like a trooper. Her mother was greatly shocked at the 'unlady-like trick', and wondered 'how she had picked it up'. 'But you can soon break her of it Miss Grey,' said she: 'it is only a habit; and if you will just gently remind her every time she does so, I am sure she will soon lay it aside.' I not only 'gently reminded' her, I tried to impress upon her how wrong it was, and how distressing to the ears of decent people; but all in vain: I was only answered by a careless laugh, and, 'oh, Miss Grey, how shocked you are! I'm so glad!' or, 'Well! I can't help it. Papa shouldn't have taught me: I learned it all from him; and maybe a bit from the coachman.'

Her brother John, *alias* Master Murray, was about eleven when I came: a fine, stout, healthy boy, frank and good-natured in the main, and might have been a decent lad had he been properly educated: but now he was as rough as a young bear, boisterous, unruly, unprincipled, untaught, unteachable – at least, for a governess under his mother's eye. His masters at school might be able to manage him better – for to school he was sent, greatly to my relief, in the course of a year; in a state, it is true, of scandalous ignorance as to Latin, as well as the more useful though more neglected things: and this, doubtless, would all be laid to the account of his education having been entrusted to an ignorant female teacher, who had presumed to take in hand what she was wholly incompetent to perform. I was not delivered from his brother till full twelve months after, when he also was despatched in the same state of disgraceful ignorance as the former.

Master Charles was his mother's peculiar darling. He was little more than a year younger than John, but much smaller, paler, and less active and robust; a pettish, cowardly, capricious, selfish little fellow, only active in doing mischief, and only clever in inventing falsehoods: not simply to hide his faults, but, in mere malicious wantonness, to bring odium upon others. In fact, Master Charles was a very great nuisance to me: it was a trial of patience to live with him peaceably; to watch over him was worse; and to teach him, or pretend to teach him, was inconceivable. At ten years old, he could not read correctly the easiest line in the simplest book; and as, according to his mother's principle, he was to be told every word, before he had time to hesitate or examine its orthography, and never even to be informed, as a stimulant to exertion that other boys were more forward than he, it is not surprising that he made but little progress during the two years I had charge of his education. His minute portions of Latin grammar, etc., were to be repeated over to him, till he chose to say he knew

them, and then he was to be helped to say them; if he made mistakes in his little easy sums in arithmetic, they were to be shown him at once, and the sum done for him, instead of his being left to exercise his faculties in finding them out himself; so that, of course, he took no pains to avoid mistakes, but frequently set down his figures at random, without any calculation at all.

I did not invariably confine myself to these rules: it was against my conscience to do so; but I seldom could venture to deviate from them in the slightest degree, without incurring the wrath of my little pupil, and subsequently of his mamma; to whom he would relate my transgressions, maliciously exaggerated, or adorned with embellishments of his own; and often, in consequence, was I on the point of losing or resigning my situation. But, for their sakes at home, I smothered my pride and suppressed my indignation, and managed to struggle on till my little tormentor was despatched to school; his father declaring that home education was 'no go for him, it was plain: his mother spoiled him outrageously, and his governess could make no hand of him at all.'

A few more observations about Horton Lodge and its ongoings, and I have done with dry description for the present. The house was a very respectable one; superior to Mr Bloomfield's, both in age, size, and magnificence: the garden was not so tastefully laid out; but instead of the smooth-shaven lawn, the young trees guarded by palings, the grove of upstart poplars, and the plantation of firs, there was a wide park, stocked with deer, and beautified by fine old trees. The surrounding country itself was pleasant, as far as fertile fields, flourishing trees, quiet green lanes, and smiling hedges with wild flowers scattered along their banks, could make it; but it was depressingly flat to one born and nurtured among the rugged hills of —.

We were situated nearly two miles from the village church, and, consequently, the family carriage was put in requisition every Sunday morning, and sometimes oftener. Mr and Mrs Murray generally thought it sufficient to show themselves at church once in the course of the day; but frequently the children preferred going a second time to wandering about the grounds all the day with nothing to do. If some of my pupils chose to walk and take me with them, it was well for me; for otherwise, my position in the carriage was to be crushed into the corner farthest from the open window, and with my back to the horses: a position which invariably made me sick; and, if I were not actually obliged to leave the church in the middle of the service, my devotions were disturbed with a feeling of languor and sickliness, and the tormenting fear of its becoming worse; and a depressing headache was generally my companion throughout the day, which would otherwise have been one of welcome rest, and holy, calm, enjoyment.

'It's very odd, Miss Grey, that the carriage should always make you sick: it never makes me,' remarked Miss Matilda.

'Nor me either,' said her sister; 'but I dare say it would, if I sat where she does – such a nasty, horrid place, Miss Grey; I wonder how you can bear it!'

I am obliged to bear it, since no choice is left me – I might have answered; but in tenderness for their feelings I only replied – 'oh! it is but a short way, and if I am not sick in church, I don't mind it.'

If I were called upon to give a description of the usual divisions and arrangements of the day, I should find it a very difficult matter. I had all my meals in the schoolroom with my pupils, at such times as suited their fancy: sometimes they would ring for dinner before it was half-cooked; sometimes they would keep it waiting on the table for above an hour, and then be out of humour because the potatoes were cold, and the gravy covered with cakes of solid fat; sometimes they would have tea at four; frequently, they would storm at the servants because it was not in precisely at five; and when these orders were obeyed, by way of encouragement to punctuality, they would keep it on the table till seven or eight.

Their hours of study were managed in much the same way; my judgement or convenience was never once consulted. Sometimes Matilda and John would determine 'to get all the plaguey business over before breakfast', and send the maid to call me up at half-past five, without any scruple or apology; sometimes, I was told to be ready precisely at six, and, having dressed in a hurry, came down to an empty room, and after waiting a long time in suspense, discovered that they had changed their minds, and were still in bed; or, perhaps, if it were a fine summer morning, Brown would come to tell me that the young ladies and gentlemen had taken a holiday, and were gone out; and then, I was kept waiting for breakfast till I was almost ready to faint: they having fortified themselves with something before they went.

Often they would do their lessons in the open air; which I had nothing to say against: except that I frequently caught cold by sitting on the damp grass, or from exposure to the evening dew, or some insidious draught, which seemed to have no injurious effect on them. It was quite right that they should be hardy; yet, surely, they might have been taught some consideration for others who were less so. But I must not blame them for what was, perhaps, my own fault; for I never made any particular objections to sitting where they pleased; foolishly choosing to risk the consequences rather than trouble them for my convenience. Their indecorous manner of doing their lessons was quite as remarkable as the caprice displayed in their choice of time and place. While receiving my instructions, or repeating what they had learned, they would lounge upon the sofa, lie on the rug, stretch, yawn, talk to each other, or look out of the window; whereas, I could not so much as stir the fire, or pick up the handkerchief I had dropped, without being rebuked for inattention by one of my pupils, or told that 'mamma would not like me to be so careless.'

The servants, seeing in what little estimation the governess was held by both parents and children, regulated their behaviour by the same standard. I have frequently stood up for them, at the risk of some injury to myself, against the tyranny and injustice of their young masters and mistresses; and I always endeavoured to give them as little trouble as possible: but they entirely neglected my comfort, despised my requests, and slighted my directions. All servants, I am convinced, would not have done so; but domestics in general, being ignorant and little accustomed to reason and reflection, are too easily corrupted by the carelessness and bad example of those above them; and these, I think, were not of the best order to begin with.

I sometimes felt myself degraded by the life I led and ashamed of submitting to so many indignities. And sometimes I thought myself a fool for caring so much about them, and feared I must be sadly wanting in Christian humility, or that charity which 'suffereth long and is kind, seeketh not her own, is not easily provoked, beareth all things, endureth all things'. But, with time and patience, matters began to be slightly ameliorated: slowly, it is true, and almost imperceptibly; but I got rid of my male pupils (that was no trifling advantage), and the girls, as I intimated before concerning one of them, became a little less insolent, and began to show some symptoms of esteem. 'Miss Grey was a queer creature: she never flattered, and did not praise them half enough; but whenever she did speak favourably of them, or anything belonging to them, they could be quite sure her approbation was sincere. She was very obliging, quiet, and peaceable in the main, but there were some things that put her out of temper: they did not much care for that, to be sure, but still it was better to keep her in tune; as when she was in a good humour she would talk to them, and be very agreeable and amusing sometimes, in her way; which was quite different to mamma's, but still very well for a change. She had her own opinions on every subject, and kept steadily to them – very tiresome opinions they often were; as she was always thinking of what was right and what was wrong, and had a strange reverence for matters connected with religion, and an unaccountable liking to good people.'

## CHAPTER 8

### *The 'Coming Out'*

At eighteen, Miss Murray was to emerge from the quiet obscurity of the schoolroom into the full blaze of the fashionable world – as much of it, at least, as could be had out of London; for her papa could not be persuaded to leave his rural pleasures and pursuits, even for a few weeks' residence in town. She was to make her debut on the third of January, at a magnificent ball, which her mamma proposed to give to all nobility and choice gentry of O— and its neighbourhood for twenty miles round. Of course, she looked forward to it with the wildest impatience, and the most extravagant anticipations of delight.

'Miss Grey,' said she, one evening, a month before the all-important day, as I was perusing a long and extremely interesting letter of my sister's – which I had just glanced at in the morning to see that it contained no very bad news, and kept till now, unable before to find a quiet moment for reading it, 'Miss Grey, do put away that dull, stupid letter, and listen to me! I'm sure my talk must be far more amusing than that.'

She seated herself on the low stool at my feet; and I, suppressing a sigh of vexation, began to fold up the epistle.

'You should tell the good people at home not to bore you with such long letters,' said she; 'and above all, do bid them write on proper note-paper, and

not on those great vulgar sheets. You should see the charming little lady-like notes mamma writes to her friends.'

'The good people at home,' replied I, 'know very well that the longer their letters are, the better I like them. I should be very sorry to receive a charming little lady-like note from any of them; and I thought you were too much of a lady yourself, Miss Murray, to talk about the "vulgarity" of writing on a large sheet of paper.'

'Well, I only said it to tease you. But now I want to talk about the ball; and to tell you that you positively must put off your holidays till it is over.'

'Why so? – I shall not be present at the ball.'

'No, but you will see the rooms decked out before it begins, and hear the music, and, above all, see me in my splendid new dress. I shall be so charming, you'll be ready to worship me – you really must stay.'

'I should like to see you very much; but I shall have many opportunities of seeing you equally charming, on the occasion of some of the numberless balls and parties that are to be and I cannot disappoint my friends by postponing my return so long.'

'Oh, never mind your friends! Tell them we won't let you go.'

'But, to say the truth, it would be a disappointment to myself: I long to see them as much as they to see me – perhaps more.'

'Well, but it is such a short time.'

'Nearly a fortnight by my computation; and, besides, I cannot bear the thoughts of a Christmas spent from home: and, moreover, my sister is going to be married.'

'Is she – when?'

'Not till next month; but I want to be there to assist her in making preparations, and to make the best of her company while we have her.'

'Why didn't you tell me before?'

'I've only got the news in this letter, which you stigmatise as dull and stupid, and won't let me read.'

'To whom is she to be married?'

'To Mr Richardson, the vicar of a neighbouring parish.'

'Is he rich?'

'No; only comfortable.'

'Is he handsome?'

'No; only decent.'

'Young?'

'No. Only middling.'

'O mercy! what a wretch! What sort of a house is it?'

'A quiet little vicarage, with an ivy-clad porch, an old-fashioned garden, and – '

'Oh, stop! – you'll make me sick. How *can* she bear it?'

'I expect she'll not only be able to bear it, but to be very happy. You did not ask me if Mr Richardson were a good, wise, or amiable man. I could have answered Yes, to all these questions – at least so Mary thinks, and I hope she will not find herself mistaken.'

'But – miserable creature! how can she think of spending her life there, cooped up with that nasty old man; and no hope of change?'

'He is not old: he's only six or seven and thirty; and she herself is twenty-eight, and as sober as if she were fifty.'

'Oh! that's better then – they're well matched: but do they call him the "worthy vicar"?'

'I don't know; but if they do, I believe he merits the epithet.'

'Mercy, how shocking! and will she wear a white apron, and make pies and puddings?'

'I don't know about the white apron, but I dare say she will make pies and puddings now and then; but that will be no great hardship, as she has done it before.'

'And will she go about in a plain shawl, and a large straw bonnet, carrying tracts and bone soup to her husband's poor parishioners?'

'I'm not clear about that; but I dare say she will do her best to make them comfortable in body and mind, in accordance with our mother's example.'

## CHAPTER 9

## *The Ball*

'Now, Miss Grey,' exclaimed Miss Murray, immediately I entered the schoolroom, after having taken off my outdoor garments, upon returning from my four weeks' recreation, 'Now – shut the door, and sit down, and I'll tell you all about the ball.'

'No, damn it, no!' shouted Miss Matilda. 'Hold your tongue, can't ye? and let me tell her about my new mare – *such* a splendour, Miss Grey! a fine blood mare – '

'Do be quiet, Matilda; and let me tell my news first.'

'No, no, Rosalie; you'll be such a damned long time over it – she shall hear me first – I'll be hanged if she doesn't!'

'I'm sorry to hear, Miss Matilda, that you've not got rid of that shocking habit yet.'

'Well, I can't help it: but I'll never say a wicked word again, if you'll only listen to me, and tell Rosalie to hold her confounded tongue.'

Rosalie remonstrated, and I thought I should have been torn in pieces between them; but Miss Matilda having the loudest voice, her sister at length gave in, and suffered her to tell her story first: so I was doomed to hear a long account of her splendid mare, its breeding and pedigree, its paces, its action, its spirit, etc., and of her own amazing skill and courage in riding it; concluding with an assertion that she could clear a five-barred gate 'like winking', that papa said she might hunt the next time the hounds met, and mamma had ordered a bright scarlet hunting-habit for her.

'Oh, Matilda! what stories you are telling!' exclaimed her sister.

'Well,' answered she, no whit abashed, 'I know I *could* clear a five-barred gate, if I tried, and papa *will* say I may hunt, and mamma *will* order the habit when I ask it.'

'Well, now get along,' replied Miss Murray; 'and do, dear Matilda, try to be a little more lady-like. Miss Grey, I wish you *would* tell her not to use such shocking words; she *will* call her horse a mare: it is *so inconceivably* shocking! and then she uses such dreadful expressions in describing it: she *must* have learned it from the grooms. It nearly puts me into fits when she begins.'

'I learned it from papa, you ass! and his jolly friends,' said the young lady, vigorously cracking a hunting-whip, which she habitually carried in her hand. 'I'm as good a judge of horseflesh as the best of 'm.'

'Well, now get along, you shocking girl! I really shall take a fit if you go on in such a way. And now, Miss Grey, attend to me; I'm going to tell you about the ball. You must be dying to hear about it, I know. Oh, *such* a ball! You never saw or heard, or read, or dreamt of anything like it in all your life! The decorations, the entertainment, the supper, the music were indescribable! and then the guests! There were two noblemen, three baronets, and five titled ladies, and other ladies and gentlemen innumerable. The ladies, of course, were of no consequence to me, except to put me in a good humour with myself, by showing how ugly and awkward most of them were; and the best, mamma told me, the most transcendent beauties among them, were nothing to me. As for *me*, Miss Grey – I'm so *sorry* you didn't see me! I was *charming* – wasn't I, Matilda?'

'Middling.'

'No, but I really *was* – at least so mamma said – and Brown and Williamson. Brown said she was sure no gentleman could set eyes on me without falling in love that minute; and so I may be allowed to be a little vain. I know you think me a shocking, conceited, frivolous girl; but, then, you know, I don't attribute it *all* to my personal attractions: I give some praise to the hairdresser, and some to my exquisitely lovely dress – you must see it tomorrow – white gauze over pink satin – and so *sweetly* made! and a necklace and bracelet of beautiful large pearls!'

'I have no doubt you looked very charming: but should that delight you so very much?'

'Oh, no! – not that alone: but, then, I was so much admired; and I made so *many* conquests in that one night – you'd be astonished to hear – '

'But what goodwill they do you?'

'What good! Think of any woman asking that!'

'Well, I should think one conquest would be enough; and too much, unless the subjugation were mutual.'

'Oh, but you know I never agree with you on those points. Now, wait a bit, and I'll tell you my principal admirers – those who made themselves very conspicuous that night and after: for I've been to two parties since. Unfortunately the two noblemen Lord G— and Lord F—, were married, or I might have condescended to be particularly gracious to *them*; as it was, I did not: though Lord F—, who hates his wife, was evidently much struck with me. He asked me to dance with

him twice – he is a charming dancer, by the by, and so am I: you can't think how well I did – I was astonished at myself. My lord was very complimentary too – rather too much so, in fact – and I thought proper to be a little haughty and repellent; but I had the pleasure of seeing his nasty, cross wife ready to perish with spite and vexation – '

'Oh, Miss Murray! you don't mean to say that such a thing could really give you pleasure! However cross or – '

'Well, I know it's very wrong; but never mind! I mean to be good sometime – only don't preach now, there's a good creature. I haven't told you half yet. Let me see. Oh! I was going to tell you how many unmistakable admirers I had: Sir Thomas Ashby was one, Sir Hugh Meltham and Sir Broadley Wilson are old codgers, only fit companions for papa and mamma. Sir Thomas is young, rich and gay; but an ugly beast, nevertheless: however mamma says I should not mind that after a few months' acquaintance. Then, there was Henry Meltham, Sir Hugh's younger son; rather good-looking, and a pleasant fellow to flirt with: but *being* a younger son, that is all he is good for; then there was young Mr Green, rich enough, but of no family, and a great stupid fellow, a mere country booby; and then, our good rector, Mr Hatfield: an *humble* admirer he ought to consider himself, but I fear he has forgotten to number humility among his stock of Christian virtues.'

'Was Mr Hatfield at the ball?'

'Yes, to be sure. Did you think he was too good to go?'

'I thought he might consider it unclerical.'

'By no means. He did not profane his cloth by dancing: but it was with difficulty he could refrain, poor man; he looked as if he were dying to ask my hand just for *one* set; and – oh! by the by – he's got a new curate: that seedy old fellow Mr Bligh has got his long-wished-for living at last, and is gone.'

'And what is the new one like?'

'*Oh, such* a beast! Weston his name is. I can give you his description in three words – an insensate, ugly, stupid blockhead. That's four, but no matter – enough *of him* now.'

Then she returned to the ball, and gave me a further account of her deportment there, and at the several parties she had since attended; and further particulars respecting Sir Thomas Ashby and Messrs Meltham, Green, and Hatfield, and the ineffaceable impression she had wrought upon each of them.

'Well, which of the four do you like best?' said I, suppressing my third or fourth yawn.

'I detest them all!' replied she, shaking her bright ringlets in vivacious scorn.

'That means, I suppose, I like them all – but which most?'

'No, I really detest them all; but Harry Meltham is the handsomest and most amusing and Mr Hatfield the cleverest, Sir Thomas the wickedest, and Mr Green the most stupid. But the one I'm to have, I suppose, if I'm doomed to have any of them, is Sir Thomas Ashby.'

'Surely not, if he's so wicked, and if you dislike him?'

'Oh, I don't mind his being wicked: he's all the better for that; and as for

disliking him – I shouldn't greatly object to being Lady Ashby of Ashby Park if I must marry. But if I could be always young, I would be always single. I should like to enjoy myself thoroughly, and coquet with all the world, till I am on the verge of being called an old maid; and then, to escape the infamy of that, after having made ten thousand conquests, to break all their hearts save one, by marrying some high-born, rich, indulgent husband, whom, on the other hand, fifty ladies were dying to have.'

'Well, as long as you entertain these views, keep single by all means, and never marry at all: not even to escape the infamy of old-maidenhood.'

### CHAPTER 10

## *The Church*

'Well, Miss Grey, WHAT do you think of the new curate?' asked Miss Murray, on our return from church the Sunday after the recommencement of our duties.

'I can scarcely tell,' was my reply: 'I have not even heard him preach.'

'Well, but you saw him, didn't you?'

'Well, but I cannot pretend to judge of a man's character by a single, cursory glance at his face.'

'But isn't he ugly?'

'He did not strike me as being particularly so; I don't dislike that cast of countenance: but the only thing I particularly noticed about him was his style of reading; which appeared to me good – infinitely better, at least, than Mr Hatfield's. He read the Lessons as if he were bent on giving full effect to every passage: it seemed as if the most careless person could not have helped attending, nor the most ignorant have failed to understand; and the prayers he read as if he were not reading at all, but praying earnestly and sincerely from his own heart.'

'Oh, yes, that's all he is good for: he can plod through the service well enough; but he has not a single idea beyond it.'

'How do you know?'

'Oh! I know perfectly well; I am an excellent judge in such matters. Did you see how he went out of church? stumping along – never looking to the right hand or the left, and evidently thinking of nothing but just getting out of the church, and, perhaps, home to his dinner: his great stupid head could contain no other idea.'

'I suppose you would have had him cast a glance into the squire's pew,' said I, laughing at the vehemence of her hostility.

'Indeed! I should have been highly indignant if he had dared to do such a thing!' replied she, haughtily tossing her head; then, after a moment's reflection, she added – 'Well, well! I suppose he's good enough for his place: but I'm glad I'm not dependent on *him* for amusement – that's all. Did you see how Mr Hatfield hurried out to get a bow from me, and be in time to put us into the carriage?'

'Yes,' answered I; internally adding, 'and I thought it somewhat derogatory to his dignity as a clergyman to come flying from the pulpit in such eager haste to shake hands with the squire, and hand his wife and daughters into their carriage: and, moreover, I owe him a grudge for nearly shutting me out of it;' for, in fact, though I was standing before his face, close beside the carriage steps, waiting to get in, he would persist in putting them up and closing the door, till one of the family stopped him by calling out that the governess was not in yet; then, without a word of apology, he departed, wishing them good-morning, and leaving the footman to finish the business.

*Nota bene.* Mr Hatfield never spoke to me, neither did Sir Hugh or Lady Meltham, nor Mr Harry or Miss Meltham, nor Mr Green or his sisters, nor any other lady or gentleman who frequented that church: nor, in fact, anyone that visited at Horton Lodge.

Miss Murray ordered the carriage again, in the afternoon, for herself and her sister: she said it was too cold for them to enjoy themselves in the garden: and besides, she believed Harry Meltham would be at church. 'For,' said she, smiling slyly at her own fair image in the glass, 'he has been a most exemplary attendant at church these last few Sundays: you would think he was quite a good Christian. And you may go with us, Miss Grey: I want you to see him; he is so greatly improved since he returned from abroad – you can't think! And besides, then you will have an opportunity of seeing the beautiful Mr Weston again, and of hearing him preach.'

I did hear him preach, and was decidedly pleased with the evangelical truth of his doctrine, as well as the earnest simplicity of his manner, and the clearness and force of his style. It was truly refreshing to hear such a sermon, after being so long accustomed to the dry, prosy discourses of the former curate, and the still less edifying harangues of the rector. Mr Hatfield would come sailing up the aisle, or rather sweeping along like a whirlwind, with his rich silk gown flying behind him and rustling against the pew doors, mount the pulpit like a conqueror ascending his triumphal car; then, sinking on the velvet cushion in an attitude of studied grace, remain in silent prostration for a certain time; then mutter over a Collect, and gabble through the Lord's Prayer, rise, draw off one bright lavender glove, to give the congregation the benefit of his sparkling rings, lightly pass his fingers through his well-curled hair, flourish a cambric handkerchief, recite a very short passage, or perhaps, a mere phrase of Scripture, as a head-piece to his discourse, and, finally, deliver a composition which, as a composition, might be considered good, though far too studied and too artificial to be pleasing to me: the propositions were well laid down, the arguments logically conducted; and yet, it was sometimes hard to listen quietly throughout, without some slight demonstrations of disapproval or impatience.

His favourite subjects were church discipline, rites and ceremonies, apostolical succession, the duty of reverence and obedience to the clergy, the atrocious criminality of dissent, the absolute necessity of observing all the forms of godliness, the reprehensible presumption of individuals who attempted to think for themselves in matters connected with religion, or to be guided by their

own interpretations of Scripture, and, occasionally (to please his wealthy parish-ioners), the necessity of deferential obedience from the poor to the rich – supporting his maxims and exhortations throughout with quotations from the Fathers: with whom he appeared to be far better acquainted than with the Apostles and Evangelists, and whose importance he seemed to consider at least equal to theirs. But now and then he gave us a sermon of a different order – what some would call a very good one; but sunless and severe: representing the Deity as a terrible taskmaster, rather than a benevolent father. Yet, as I listened, I felt inclined to think the man was sincere in all he said: he must have changed his views, and become decidedly religious; gloomy and austere, yet still devout. But such illusions were usually dissipated, on coming out of church, by hearing his voice in jocund colloquy with some of the Melthams or Greens, or, perhaps, the Murrays themselves; probably laughing at his own sermon, and hoping that he had given the rascally people something to think about; perchance, exulting in the thought that old Betty Holmes would now lay aside the sinful indulgence of her pipe, which had been her daily solace for upwards of thirty years; that George Higgins would be frightened out of his Sabbath evening walks, and Thomas Jackson would be sorely troubled in his conscience, and shaken in his sure and certain hope of a joyful resurrection at the last day.

Thus, I could not but conclude that Mr Hatfield was one of those who 'bind heavy burdens, and grievous to be borne, and lay them upon men's shoulders, while they themselves will not move them with one of their fingers'; and who 'make the word of God of none effect by their traditions, teaching for doctrines the commandments of men.' I was well pleased to observe that the new curate resembled him, as far as I could see, in none of these particulars.

'Well, Miss Grey, what do you think of him now?' said Miss Murray, as we took our places in the carriage after service.

'No harm still,' repeated I.

'No harm!' repeated she, in amazement. 'What do you mean?'

'I mean, I think no worse of him than I did before.'

'No worse! I should think not indeed – quite the contrary! Is he not greatly improved?'

'Oh, yes; very much indeed,' replied I; for I had now discovered that it was Harry Meltham she meant, not Mr Weston. That gentleman had eagerly come forward to speak to the young ladies: a thing he would hardly have ventured to do had their mother been present; he had likewise politely handed them into the carriage. He had not attempted to shut me out, like Mr Hatfield; neither, of course, had he offered me his assistance (I should not have accepted it, if he had), but as long as the door remained open he had stood smirking and chatting with them, and then lifted his hat and departed to his own abode: but I scarcely noticed him all the time. My companions, however, had been more observant; and, as we rolled along, they discussed between them not only his looks, words, and actions, but every feature of his face, and every article of his apparel.

'You shan't have him all to yourself, Rosalie,' said Miss Matilda at the close of this discussion; 'I like him: I know he'd make a nice, jolly companion for me.'

'Well, you're quite welcome to him, Matilda,' replied her sister, in a tone of affected indifference.

'And I'm sure,' continued the other, 'he admires me quite as much as he does you; doesn't he, Miss Grey?'

'I don't know. I'm not acquainted with his sentiments.'

'Well, but he *does* though.'

'My *dear* Matilda! nobody will ever admire you till you get rid of your rough, awkward manners.'

'Oh, stuff! Harry Meltham likes such manners; and so do papa's friends.'

'Well, you *may* captivate old men, and younger sons; but nobody else, I am sure, will ever take a fancy to you.'

'I don't care: I'm not always grubbing after money, like you and mamma. If my husband is able to keep a few good horses and dogs, I shall be quite satisfied; and all the rest may go to the devil!'

'Well, if you use such shocking expressions, I'm sure no real gentleman will ever venture to come near you. Really, Miss Grey, you should not let her do so.'

'I can't possibly prevent it, Miss Murray.'

'And you're quite mistaken, Matilda, in supposing that Harry Meltham admires you: I assure you he does nothing of the kind.'

Matilda was beginning an angry reply; but, happily, our journey was now at an end; and the contention was cut short by the footman opening the carriage door, and letting down the steps for our descent.

## CHAPTER 11

### *The Cottagers*

As I had now only one regular pupil – though she contrived to give me as much trouble as three or four ordinary ones, and though her sister still took lessons in German and drawing – I had considerably more time at my own disposal than I had ever been blessed with before, since I had taken upon me the governess' yoke; which time I devoted partly to correspondence with my friends, partly to reading, study, and the practice of music, singing, etc., partly to wandering in the grounds or adjacent fields, with my pupils if they wanted me, alone if they did not.

Often, when they had no more agreeable occupation at hand, the Misses Murray would amuse themselves with visiting the poor cottagers on their father's estate, to receive their flattering homage, or to hear the old stories or gossiping news of the garrulous old women; or, perhaps to enjoy the purer pleasure of making the poor people happy with their cheering presence and their occasional gifts, so easily bestowed, so thankfully received. Sometimes, I was called upon to accompany one or both of the sisters in these visits; and sometimes I was desired to go alone, to fulfil some promise which they had been

more ready to make than to perform; to carry some small donation, or read to one who was sick or seriously disposed: and thus I made a few acquaintances among the cottagers; and, occasionally, I went to see them on my own account.

I generally had more satisfaction in going alone than with either of the young ladies; for they, chiefly owing to their defective education, comported themselves towards their inferiors in a manner that was highly disagreeable for me to witness. They never, in thought, exchanged places with them; and, consequently, had no consideration for their feelings, regarding them as an order of beings entirely different from themselves. They would watch the poor creatures at their meals, making uncivil remarks about their food, and their manner of eating; they would laugh at their simple notions and provincial expressions, till some of them scarcely durst venture to speak; they would call the grave elderly men and women old fools and silly old blockheads to their faces; and all this without meaning to offend. I could see that the people were often hurt and annoyed by such conduct, though their fear of the 'grand ladies' prevented them from testifying any resentment; but they never perceived it. They thought that, as these cottagers were poor and untaught, they must be stupid and brutish; and as long as they, their superiors, condescended to talk to them, and to give them shillings and half-crowns, or articles of clothing, they had a right to amuse themselves, even at their expense; and the people must adore them as angels of light, condescending to minister to their necessities, and enlighten their humble dwellings.

I made many and various attempts to deliver my pupils from these delusive notions without alarming their pride – which was easily offended, and not soon appeased – but with little apparent result; and I know not which was the more reprehensible of the two: Matilda was more rude and boisterous; but from Rosalie's womanly age and lady-like exterior better things were expected: yet she was as provokingly careless and inconsiderate as a giddy child of twelve.

One bright day in the last week of February, I was walking in the park, enjoying the threefold luxury of solitude, a book, and pleasant weather; for Miss Matilda had set out on her daily ride, and Miss Murray was gone in the carriage with her mamma to pay some morning calls. But it struck me that I ought to leave these selfish pleasures, and the park with its glorious canopy of bright blue sky, the west wind sounding through its yet leafless branches, the snow-wreaths still lingering in its hollows, but melting fast beneath the sun, and the graceful deer browsing on its moist herbage already assuming the freshness and verdure of spring – and go to the cottage of one Nancy Brown, a widow, whose son was at work all day in the fields, and who was afflicted with an inflammation in the eyes; which had for some time incapacitated her from reading: to her own great grief, for she was a woman of a serious, thoughtful turn of mind. I accordingly went, and found her alone, as usual, in her little, close, dark cottage, redolent of smoke and confined air, but as tidy and clean as she could make it. She was seated beside her little fire (consisting of a few red cinders and a bit of stick), busily knitting, with a small sackcloth cushion at her feet, placed for the accommodation of her gentle friend the cat; who was seated

thereon with her long tail half encircling her velvet paws, and her half-closed eyes dreamily gazing on the low, crooked fender.

'Well, Nancy, how are you today?'

'Why, middling, miss, i' myseln – my eyes is no better, but I'm a deal easier i' my mind nor I have been,' replied she, rising to welcome me with a contented smile: which I was glad to see, for Nancy had been somewhat afflicted with religious melancholy. I congratulated her upon the change. She agreed that it was a great blessing, and expressed herself 'right down thankful for it'; adding, 'If it please God to spare my sight, and make me so as I can read my Bible again, I think I shall be as happy as a queen.'

'I hope He will, Nancy,' replied I; 'and, meantime, I'll come and read to you now and then, when I have a little time to spare.'

With expressions of grateful pleasure, the poor woman moved to get me a chair; but, as I saved her the trouble, she busied herself with stirring the fire, and adding a few more sticks to the decaying embers; and then, taking her well-used Bible from the shelf, dusted it carefully, and gave it me. On my asking if there was any particular part she should like me to read, she answered – 'Well, Miss Grey, if it's all the same to you I should like to hear that chapter in the First Epistle of St John, that says, "God is love, and he that dwelleth in love dwelleth in God, and God in him."'

With a little searching, I found these words in the fourth chapter. When I came to the seventh verse she interrupted me, and, with needless apologies for such a liberty, desired me to read it very slowly, that she might take it all in, and dwell on every word; hoping I would excuse her, as she was but a 'simple body'.

"The wisest person,' I replied, 'might think over each of these verses for an hour, and be all the better for it; and I would rather read them slowly than not.'

Accordingly, I finished the chapter as slowly as need be, and at the same time as impressively as I could; my auditor listened most attentively all the while, and sincerely thanked me when I had done. I sat still about half a minute to give her time to reflect upon it; when, somewhat to my surprise, she broke the pause by asking me how I liked Mr Weston?

'I don't know,' I replied, a little startled by the suddenness of the question. 'I think he preaches very well.'

'Ay, he does so; and talks well too.'

'Does he?'

'He does. Maybe, you haven't seen him – not to talk to him much, yet?'

'No, I never see anyone to talk to – except the young ladies of the hall.'

'Ah; they're nice, kind young ladies; but they can't talk as he does.'

'Then he comes to see you, Nancy?'

'He does, miss; and I'se thankful for it. He comes to see all us poor bodies a deal ofter nor Maister Bligh, or th' Rector ever did; an' it's well he does, for he's always welcome: we can't say as much for th' Rector – there is 'at says they're fair feared on him. When he comes into a house, they say he's sure to find summut wrong, and begin a-calling 'em as soon as he crosses th' door-stuns: but maybe he thinks it his duty-like to tell 'em what's wrong. And very oft he comes

o' purpose to reprove folk for not coming to church, or not kneeling an' standing when other folk does, or going to the Methody chapel, or summut o' that sort: but I can't say 'at he ever fund much fault wi' me. He came to see me once or twice, afore Maister Weston come, when I was so ill troubled in my mind; and as I had only very poor health besides, I made bold to send for him – and he came right enough. I was sore distressed, Miss Grey – thank God, it's owered now – but when I took my Bible, I could get no comfort of it at all. That very chapter 'at you've just been reading troubled me as much as aught – "He that loveth not, knoweth not God." It seemed fearsome to me; for I felt that I loved neither God nor man as I should do, and could not, if I tried ever so. And th' chapter afore, where it says – "He that is born of God cannot commit sin." And another place where it says – "Love is the fulfilling of the Law." And many, many others, miss: I should fair weary you out, if I was to tell them all. But all seemed to condemn me, and to show me 'at I was not in the right way; and as I knew not how to get into it, I sent our Bill to beg Maister Hatfield to be as kind as look in on me someday: and when he came, I telled him all my troubles.'

'And what did he say, Nancy?'

'Why, miss, he seemed to scorn me. I might be mista'en – but he like gave a sort of a whistle, and I saw a bit of a smile on his face; and he said, "Oh, it's all stuff! You've been among the Methodists, my good woman." But I telled him I'd never been near the Methodies. And then he said – ' "Well," says he, "you must come to church, where you'll hear the Scriptures properly explained, instead of sitting poring over your Bible at home."

'But I telled him I always used coming to church when I had my health; but this very cold winter weather I hardly durst venture so far – and me so bad wi' th' rheumatis and all.

'But he says, "It'll do your rheumatis good to hobble to church: there's nothing like exercise for the rheumatis. You can walk about the house well enough; why can't you walk to church? The fact is," says he, "you're getting too fond of your ease. It's always easy to find excuses for shirking one's duty."

'But then, you know, Miss Grey, it wasn't so. However, I telled him I'd try. "But please, sir," says I, "if I do go to church, what the better shall I be? I want to have my sins blotted out, and to feel that they are remembered no more against me, and that the love of God is shed abroad in my heart; and if I can get no good by reading my Bible an' saying my prayers at home, what good shall I get by going to church?"

' "The church," says he, "is the place appointed by God for His worship. It's your duty to go there as often as you can. If you want comfort, you must seek it in the path of duty" – an' a deal more he said, but I cannot remember all his fine words. However, it all came to this, that I was to come to church as oft as ever I could, and bring my prayer-book with me, an' read up all the sponsers after the clerk, an' stand, an' kneel, an' sit, an' do all as I should, and take the Lord's supper at every opportunity, an' hearken his sermons, and Maister Bligh's, and it "ud be all right: if I went on doing my duty, I should get a blessing at last".

‘ "But if you get no comfort that way," says he, "it's all up."

‘ "Then, sir," says I, "should you think I'm a reprobate?"

‘ "Why," says he – he says, "if you do your best to get to heaven and can't manage it, you must be one of those that seek to enter in at the strait gate and shall not be able."

'An' then he asked me if I'd seen any of the ladies o' th' Hall about that mornin'; so I told him where I had seen the young missis go on th' Moss Lane; an' he kicked my poor cat right across th' floor, an' went after 'em as gay as a lark: but I was very sad. That last word o' his fair sunk into my heart, an' lay there like a lump o' lead, till I was weary to bear it.

'Howsever, I follered his advice: I thought he meant it all for th' best, though he *had* a queer way with him. But you know, miss, he's rich an' young, and suchlike cannot right understand the thoughts of a poor old woman such as me. But, however, I did my best to do all as he bade me – but maybe I'm plaguing you, miss, wi' my chatter.'

'Oh, no, Nancy! Go on, and tell me all.'

'Well, my rheumatis got better – I know not whether wi' going to church or not, but one frosty Sunday I got this cold i' my eyes. Th' inflammation didn't come on all at once like, but bit by bit – but I wasn't going to tell you about my eyes, I was talking about my trouble o' mind; and to tell the truth, Miss Grey, I don't think it was anyways eased by coming to church – naught to speak on, at least: I like got my health better; but that didn't mend my soul. I hearkened and hearkened the ministers, and read an' read at my prayer-book; but it was all like sounding brass, and a tinkling cymbal: the sermons I couldn't understand, an' th' prayer-book only served to show me how wicked I was, that I could read such good words an' never be no better for it, and oftens feel it a sore labour an' a heavy task beside, instead of a blessing and a privilege as all good Christians does. It seemed like as all were barren an' dark to me. And then, them dreadful words, "Many shall seek to enter in, and shall not be able." They like as they fair dried up my sperrit.

'But one Sunday, when Maister Hatfield gave out about the sacrament, I noticed where he said, "If there be any of you that cannot quiet his own conscience, but requireth further comfort or counsel, let him come to me, or some other discreet and learned minister of God's Word, and open his grief!" So, next Sunday morning, afore service, I just looked into the vestry, an' began a-talking to th' Rector again. I hardly could fashion to take such a liberty, but I thought when my soul was at stake I shouldn't stick at a trifle. But he said he hadn't time to attend to me then.

‘ "And, indeed," says he, "I've nothing to say to you but what I've said before. Take the sacrament, of course, and go on doing your duty; and if that won't serve you, nothing will. So don't bother me any more."

'So then, I went away. But I heard Maister Weston – Maister Weston was there, miss – this was his first Sunday at Horton, you know, an' he was i' th' vestry in his surplice, helping th' Rector on with his gown.'

'Yes. Nancy.'

'And I heard him ask Maister Hatfield who I was; an' he says, "Oh, she's a canting old fool."

'And I was very ill grieved, Miss Grey; but I went to my seat, and I tried to do my duty as aforetime: but I like got no peace. An' I even took the sacrament; but I felt as though I were eating and drinking to my own damnation all th' time. So I went home, sorely troubled.

'But next day, afore I'd gotten fettled up – for indeed, miss, I'd no heart to sweeping an' fettling, an' washing pots; so I sat me down i' th' muck – who should come in but Maister Weston! I started siding stuff then, an' sweeping an' doing; and I expected he'd begin a-calling me for my idle ways, as Maister Hatfield would a' done; but I was mista'en: he only bid me good-mornin' like, in a quiet dacent way. So I dusted him a chair, an' fettled up th' fireplace a bit; but I hadn't forgotten th' Rector's words, so says I, "I wonder, sir, you should give yourself that trouble to come so far to see a 'canting old fool', such as me."

'He seemed taken aback at that; but he would fain persuade me 'at the Rector was only in jest; and when that wouldn't do, he says, "Well, Nancy, you shouldn't think so much about it: Mr Hatfield was a little out of humour just then: you know we're none of us perfect – even Moses spoke unadvisedly with his lips. But now sit down a minute, if you can spare the time, and tell me all your doubts and fears; and I'll try to remove them."

'So I sat me down anent him. He was quite a stranger, you know, Miss Grey, and even *younger* nor Maister Hatfield, I believe; an' I had thought him not so pleasant looking as him, and rather a bit crossish, at first to look at; but he spake so civil like – and when th' cat, poor thing, jumped on to his knee, he only stroked her, and gave a bit of a smile: so I thought that was a good sign; for once when she did so to th' Rector, he knocked her off, like as it might be in scorn and anger, poor thing. But you can't expect a cat to know manners like a Christian, you know, Miss Grey.'

'No; of course not, Nancy. But what did Mr Weston say then?'

'He said naught; but he listened to me as steady an' patient as could be, an' never a bit o' scorn about him; so I went on, an' telled him all, just as I've telled you – an' more too.

' "Well," says he, "Mr Hatfield was quite right in telling you to persevere in doing your duty; but in advising you to go to church and attend to the service, and so on, he didn't mean that was the whole of a Christian's duty: he only thought you might there learn what more was to be done, and be led to take delight in those exercises, instead of finding them a task and a burden. And if you had asked him to explain those words that trouble you so much, I think he would have told you, that if many shall seek to enter in at the strait gate and shall not be able, it is their own sins that hinder them; just as a man with a large sack on his back might wish to pass through a narrow doorway, and find it impossible to do so unless he would leave his sack behind him. But you, Nancy, I dare say, have no sins that you would not gladly throw aside, if you "knew how"?

' "Indeed, sir, you speak truth," said I.

' "Well," says he, "you know the first and great commandment – and the

second, which is like unto it – on which two commandments hang all the law and the prophets? You say you cannot love God; but it strikes me that if you rightly consider who and what He is, you cannot help it. He is your Father, your best friend: every blessing, everything good, pleasant, or useful, comes from Him; and everything evil, everything you have reason to hate, to shun, or to fear, comes from Satan – *His* enemy as well as ours. And for *this* cause was God manifest in the flesh, that He might destroy the works of the devil: in one word, God is love; and the more of love we have within us, the nearer we are to Him, and the more of His spirit we possess."

' "Well, sir," I said, "if I can always think on these things, I think I might well love God: but how can I love my neighbours, when they vex me, and be so contrairy and sinful as some on 'em is?"

' "It may seem a hard matter," says he, "to love our neighbours, who have so much of what is evil about them, and whose faults so often awaken the evil that lingers within ourselves; but remember that *He* made them, and *He* loves them; and whosoever loveth Him that begat, lovest Him that is begotten also. And if God so loveth us, that He gave His only begotten Son to die for us, we ought also to love one another. But if you cannot feel positive affection for those who do not care for you, you can at least try to do to them as you would they should do unto you: you can endeavour to pity their failings and excuse their offences, and to do all the good you can to those about you. And if you accustom yourself to this, Nancy, the very effort itself will make you love them in some degree – to say nothing of the goodwill your kindness would beget in them, though they might have little else that is good about them. If we love God and wish to serve Him, let us try to be like Him, to do His work, to labour for His glory – which is the good of man – to hasten the coming of His kingdom, which is the peace and happiness of all the world: however powerless we may seem to be, in doing all the good we can through life, the humblest of us may do much towards it; and let us dwell in love, that He may dwell in us and we in Him. The more happiness we bestow, the more we shall receive, even here; and the greater will be our reward in heaven when we rest from our labours." I believe, miss, them is his very words, for I've thought 'em ower many a time. An' then he took that Bible, and read bits here and there, an' explained em' as clear as the day: and it seemed like as a new light broke in on my soul; an' I felt fair a glow about my heart, an' only wished poor Bill an' all the world could ha' been there, an' heard it all, and rejoiced wi' me.

'After he was gone, Hannah Rogers, one o' th' neighbours, came in and wanted me to help her to wash. I told her I couldn't just then, for I hadn't set on the potaties for th' dinner, nor washed up th' breakfast stuff yet. So then she began a-calling me for my nasty idle ways. I was a little bit vexed at first, but I never said nothing wrong to her: I only told her, like all in a quiet way, 'at I'd had th' new parson to see me; but I'd get done as quick as ever I could, an' then come an' help her. So then she softened down; and my heart like as it warmed towards her, an' in a bit we was very good friends. An' so it is, Miss Grey, "a soft answer turneth away wrath; but grievous words stir up anger". It isn't only in them you speak to, but in yourself.'

'Very true, Nancy, if we could always remember it.'

'Ay, if we could!'

'And did Mr Weston ever come to see you again?'

'Yes, many a time; and since my eyes has been so bad, he's sat an' read to me by the half-hour together: but you know miss, he has other folks to see, and other things to do – God bless him! An' that next Sunday he preached *such* a sermon! His text was "Come unto me all ye that labour and are heavy laden, and I will give you rest," and them two blessed verses that follows. You wasn't there, miss, you was with your friends then – but it made me *so* happy! And I *am* happy now, thank God! an' I take a pleasure now, in doing little bits o' jobs for my neighbours – such as a poor old body 'at's half blind can do; and they take it kindly of me, just as he said. You see, miss, I'm knitting a pair o' stockings now – they're for Thomas Jackson: he's a queerish old body, an' we've had many a bout at threaping, one anent t'other; an' at times we've differed sorely. So I thought I couldn't do better nor knit him a pair o' warm stockings; an' I've felt to like him a deal better, poor old man, sin' I began. It's turned out just as Maister Weston said.'

'Well, I'm very glad to see you so happy, Nancy, and so wise: but I must go now; I shall be wanted at the Hall,' said I; and bidding her goodbye, I departed, promising to come again when I had time, and feeling nearly as happy as herself.

At another time, I went to read to a poor labourer who was in the last stage of consumption. The young ladies had been to see him, and somehow a promise of reading had been extracted from them; but it was too much trouble, so they begged *me* to do it instead. I went, willingly enough; and there too I was gratified with the praises of Mr Weston, both from the sick man and his wife. The former told me that he derived great comfort and benefit from the visits of the new parson, who frequently came to see him and was 'another-guess sort of man' to Mr Hatfield; who before the other's arrival at Horton had now and then paid him a visit. On which occasions he would always insist upon having the cottage door kept open, to admit the fresh air for his own convenience without considering how it might injure the sufferer; and having opened his prayer-book and hastily read over a part of the service for the sick, would hurry away again: if he did not stay to administer some harsh rebuke to the afflicted wife, or to make some thoughtless, not to say heartless, observation, rather calculated to increase than diminish the troubles of the suffering pair.

'Whereas,' said the man, 'Maister Weston 'ull pray with me quite in a different fashion, an' talk to me as kind as owt; an' oft read to me too, an' sit beside me just like a brother.'

'Just for all the world!' exclaimed his wife; 'an about a three wik sin', when he seed how poor Jem shivered wi' cold, an' what pitiful fires we kept, he axed if wer stock of coals was nearly done. I told him it was, an' we was ill set to get more: but you know, mum, I didn't think o' him helping us; but howsever, he sent us a sack o' coals next day; an' we've had good fires ever sin: an' a great blessing it is, this winter time. But that's his way, Miss Grey: when he comes into a poor body's house a seein' sick folk, he like notices what they most stand i' need on; an' if he thinks they can't readily get it therseln, he never says nowt

about it, but just gets it for 'em. An' it isn't everybody 'at 'ud do that, 'at has as little as he has: for you know, mum, he's now't at all to live on but what he get's fra' th' rector, an' that's little enough, they say.'

I remembered then, with a species of exultation, that he had frequently been styled a vulgar brute by the amiable Miss Murray, because he wore a silver watch, and clothes not quite so bright and fresh as Mr Hatfield's.

In returning to the lodge I felt very happy, and thanked God that I had now something to think about; something to dwell on as a relief from the weary monotony, the lonely drudgery, of my present life: for I *was* lonely. Never, from month to month, from year to year, except during my brief intervals of rest at home, did I see one creature to whom I could open my heart, or freely speak my thoughts with any hope of sympathy, or even comprehension: never one, unless it were poor Nancy Brown, with whom I could enjoy a single moment of real social intercourse, or whose conversation was calculated to render me better, wiser, or happier than before; or who, as far as I could see, could be greatly benefited by mine. My only companions had been unamiable children, and ignorant, wrong-headed girls; from whose fatiguing folly, unbroken solitude was often a relief most earnestly desired and dearly prized. But to be restricted to such associates was a serious evil, both in its immediate effects and the consequences that were likely to ensue. Never a new idea or stirring thought came to me from without; and such as rose within me were, for the most part miserably crushed at once, or doomed to sicken and fade away, because they could not see the light.

Habitual associates are known to exercise a great influence over each other's minds and manners. Those whose actions are for ever before our eyes, whose words are ever in our ears, will naturally lead us, albeit against our will, slowly, gradually, imperceptibly, perhaps, to act and speak as they do. I will not presume to say how far this irresistible power of assimilation extends; but if one civilised man were doomed to pass a dozen years amid a race of intractable savages, unless he had power to improve them, I greatly question whether, at the close of that period, he would not have become, at least, a barbarian himself. And I, as I could not make my young companions better, feared exceedingly that they would make me worse – would gradually bring my feelings, habits, capacities, to the level of their own; without, however, imparting to me their light-heartedness and cheerful vivacity.

Already, I seemed to feel my intellect deteriorating, my heart petrifying, my soul contracting; and I trembled lest my very moral perceptions should become deadened, my distinctions of right and wrong confounded, and all my better faculties be sunk, at last, beneath the baneful influence of such a mode of life. The gross vapours of earth were gathering around me, and closing in upon my inward heaven; and thus it was that Mr Weston rose at length upon me, appearing like the morning-star in my horizon, to save me from the fear of utter darkness; and I rejoiced that I had now a subject for contemplation, that was above me, not beneath. I was glad to see that all the world was not made up of Bloomfields, Murrays, Hatfields, Ashbys, etc., and that human excellence was

not a mere dream of the imagination. When we hear a little good and no harm of a person, it is easy and pleasant to imagine more: in short, it is needless to analyse all my thoughts; but Sunday was now become a day of peculiar delight to me (I was now almost broken-in to the back corner in the carriage), for I liked to hear him – and I liked to see him, too; though I knew he was not handsome, or even what is called agreeable, in outward aspect: but, certainly, he was not ugly.

In stature he was a little, a very little, above the middle size, the outline of his face would be pronounced too square for beauty but to me it announced decision of character; his dark brown hair was not carefully curled, like Mr Hatfield's, but simply brushed aside over a broad white forehead; the eyebrows, I suppose, were too projecting, but from under those dark brows there gleamed an eye of singular power, brown in colour, not large, and somewhat deep-set, but strikingly brilliant, and full of expression; there was character, too, in the mouth, something that bespoke a man of firm purpose and a habitual thinker; and when he smiled – but I will not speak of that yet, for, at the time I mention, I had never seen him smile: and, indeed, his general appearance did not impress me with the idea of a man given to such a relaxation, nor of such an individual as the cottagers described him. I had early formed my opinion of him; and, in spite of Miss Murray's objurgations, was fully convinced that he was a man of strong sense, firm faith, and ardent piety, but thoughtful and stern: and when I found that, to his other good qualities, was added that of true benevolence and gentle, considerate kindness, the discovery perhaps, delighted me the more, as I had not been prepared to expect it.

## CHAPTER 12

## *The Shower*

The next visit I paid to Nancy Brown was in the second week in March: for, though I had many spare minutes during the day, I seldom could look upon an hour as entirely my own; since where everything was left to the caprices of Miss Matilda and her sister, there could be no order or regularity. Whatever occupation I chose, when not actually busied about them or their concerns, I had, as it were, to keep my loins girded, my shoes on my feet, and my staff in my hand; for not to be immediately forthcoming when called for, was regarded as a grave and inexcusable offence: not only by my pupils and their mother, but by the very servant who came in breathless haste to call me, exclaiming, 'You're to go to the schoolroom *directly*, mum – the young ladies is waiting!!' Climax of horror! actually waiting for their governess!!!

But this time I was pretty sure of an hour or two to myself; for Matilda was preparing for a long ride, and Rosalie was dressing for a dinner party at Lady Ashby's: so I took the opportunity of repairing to the widow's cottage, where I found her in some anxiety about her cat, which had been absent all day. I

comforted her with as many anecdotes of that animal's roving propensities as I could recollect. 'I'm feared o' th' gamekeepers,' said she, 'that's all t'a I think on. If th' young gentlemen had been at home, I should a' thought they'd been setting their dogs at her, 'an' worried her, poor thing, as they did *many* a poor thing's cat; but I haven't that to be feared on now.' Nancy's eyes were better, but still far from well: she had been trying to make a Sunday shirt for her son, but told me she could only bear to do a little bit at it now and then, so that it progressed but slowly, though the poor lad wanted it sadly. So I proposed to help her a little after I had read to her, for I had plenty of time that evening, and need not return till dusk. She thankfully accepted the offer. 'An' you'll be a bit o' company for me too, miss,' said she; 'I like as I feel lonesome without my cat.' But when I had finished reading, and done the half of a seam, with Nancy's capacious brass thimble fitted on to my finger by means of a roll of paper, I was disturbed by the entrance of Mr Weston, with the identical cat in his arms. I now saw that he could smile, and very pleasantly too.

'I've done you a piece of good service, Nancy,' he began: then seeing me, he acknowledged my presence by a slight bow. I should have been invisible to Hatfield, or any other gentleman of those parts. 'I've delivered your cat,' he continued, 'from the hands, or rather the gun, of Mr Murray's gamekeeper.'

'God bless you, sir!' cried the grateful old woman, ready to weep for joy as she received her favourite from his arms.

'Take care of it,' said he, 'and don't let it go near the rabbit warren, for the gamekeeper swears he'll shoot it if he sees it there again: he would have done so today, if I had not been in time to stop him. I believe it is raining, Miss Grey,' added he, more quietly, observing that I had put aside my work, and was preparing to depart. 'Don't let me disturb you – I shan't stay two minutes.'

'You'll *both* stay while this shower gets owered,' said Nancy, as she stirred the fire, and placed another chair beside it; 'what! there's room for all.'

'I can see better here, thank you, Nancy,' replied I, taking my work to the window, where she had the goodness to suffer me to remain unmolested, while she got a brush to remove the cat's hairs from Mr Weston's coat, carefully wiped the rain from his hat, and gave the cat its supper, busily talking all the time: now thanking her clerical friend for what he had done; now wondering how the cat had found out the warren; and now lamenting the probable consequences of such a discovery. He listened with a quiet, good-natured smile, and at length took a seat in compliance with her pressing invitations, but repeated that he did not mean to stay.

'I have another place to go to,' said he, 'and I see' (glancing at the book on the table) 'someone else has been reading to you.'

'Yes, sir; Miss Grey has been as kind as to read me a chapter; an' now she's helping me with a shirt for our Bill – but I'm feared she'll be cold there. Won't you come to th' fire, miss?'

'No, thank you, Nancy, I'm quite warm. I must go as soon as this shower is over.'

'Oh, miss! You said you could stop while dusk!' cried the provoking old

woman, and Mr Weston seized his hat. 'Nay, sir,' exclaimed she, 'pray don't go now, while it rains so fast.'

'But it strikes me I'm keeping your visitor away from the fire.'

'No, you're not, Mr Weston,' replied I, hoping there was no harm in a falsehood of that description.

'No, sure!' cried Nancy. 'What, there's lots o' room!'

'Miss Grey,' said he half-jestingly, as if he felt it necessary to change the present subject, whether he had anything particular to say or not, 'I wish you would make my peace with the squire, when you see him. He was by when I rescued Nancy's cat and did not quite approve of the deed. I told him I thought he might better spare all his rabbits than she her cat, for which audacious assertion he treated me to some rather ungentlemanly language; and I fear I retorted a trifle too warmly.'

'Oh, lawful sir! I hope you didn't fall out wi' th' maister for sake o' my cat! he cannot bide answering again – can th' maister.'

'Oh, it's no matter, Nancy: I don't care about it, really. I said nothing very uncivil; and I suppose Mr Murray is accustomed to use rather strong language when he's heated.'

'Ay, sir: it's a pity!'

'And now, I really must go, I have to visit a place a mile beyond this; and you would not have me to return in the dark: besides, it has nearly done raining now – so good-evening, Nancy. Good-evening, Miss Grey.'

'Good-evening, Mr Weston; but don't depend upon me for making your peace with Mr Murray, for I never see him – to speak to.'

'Don't you? it can't be helped then,' replied he, in dolorous resignation: then with a peculiar half-smile, he added, 'But never mind; I imagine the squire has more to apologise for than I.' And he left the cottage.

I went on with my sewing as long as I could see, and then bade Nancy good-evening; checking her too lively gratitude by the undeniable assurance that I had only done for her what she would have done for me, if she had been in my place and I in hers. I hastened back to Horton Lodge, where having entered the schoolroom, I found the tea-table all in confusion, the tray flooded with slops, and Miss Matilda in a most ferocious humour.

'Miss Grey, whatever have you been about? I've had tea half an hour ago, and had to make it myself, and drink it all alone! I wish you *would* come in sooner!'

'I've been to see Nancy Brown. I thought you would not be back from your ride.'

'How could I ride in the rain, I should like to know? That damned pelting shower was vexatious enough – coming on when I was just in full swing: and then to come and find nobody in to tea! – and you know I can't make the tea as I like it.'

'I didn't think of the shower,' replied I (and, indeed, the thought of its driving her home had never entered my head).

'No, of course; you were under shelter yourself, and you never thought of other people.'

I bore her coarse reproaches with astonishing equanimity, even with cheerfulness; for I was sensible that I had done more good to Nancy Brown than harm to her: and perhaps some other thoughts assisted to keep up my spirits, and impart a relish to the cup of cold, over-drawn tea, and a charm to the otherwise unsightly table; and – I had almost said – to Miss Matilda's unamiable face. But she soon betook herself to the stables, and left me to the quiet enjoyment of my solitary meal.

<div align="center">CHAPTER 13</div>

## The Primroses

Miss Murray now always went twice to church, for she so loved admiration that she could not bear to lose a single opportunity of obtaining it; and she was so sure of it wherever she showed herself, that whether Harry Meltham and Mr Green were there or not, there was certain to be somebody present who would not be insensible to her charms: besides the Rector, whose official capacity generally obliged him to attend. Usually, also, if the weather permitted, both she and her sister would walk home; Matilda, because she hated the confinement of the carriage; she, because she disliked the privacy of it, and enjoyed the company that generally enlivened the first mile of the journey in walking from the church to Mr Green's park, near which commenced the private road to Horton Lodge, which lay in the opposite direction; while the highway conducted in a straightforward course to the still more distant mansion of Sir Hugh Meltham. Thus there was always a chance of being accompanied, so far, either by Harry Meltham, with or without Miss Meltham, or Mr Green, with perhaps one or both of his sisters, and any gentlemen visitors they might have.

Whether I walked with the young ladies or rode with their parents, depended upon their own capricious will: if they chose to 'take' me, I went; if, for reasons best known to themselves they chose to go alone, I took my seat in the carriage. I liked walking better, but a sense of reluctance to obtrude my presence on anyone who did not desire it, always kept me passive on these and similar occasions; and I never enquired into the causes of their varying whims. Indeed, this was the best policy – for to submit and oblige was the governess's part, to consult their own pleasure was that of the pupils. But when I did walk, the first half of the journey was generally a great nuisance to me. As none of the beforementioned ladies and gentlemen ever noticed me, it was disagreeable to walk beside them, as if listening to what they said, or wishing to be thought one of them, while they talked over me, or across; and if their eyes, in speaking, chanced to fall on me, it seemed as if they looked on vacancy – as if they either did not see me, or were very desirous to make it appear so. It was disagreeable, too, to walk behind, and thus appear to acknowledge my own inferiority; for, in truth, I considered myself pretty nearly as good as the best of them, and wished

them to know that I did so, and not to imagine that I looked upon myself as a mere domestic, who knew her own place too well to walk beside such fine ladies and gentlemen as they were – though her young ladies might choose to have her with them, and even condescend to converse with her when no better company were at hand. Thus – I am almost ashamed to confess it – but indeed I gave myself no little trouble in my endeavours (if I did keep up with them) to appear perfectly unconscious or regardless of their presence, as if I were wholly absorbed in my own reflections, or the contemplation of surrounding objects; or, if I lingered behind, it was some bird or insect, some tree or flower, that attracted my attention, and having duly examined that, I would pursue my walk alone, at a leisurely pace, until my pupils had bidden adieu to their companions, and turned off into the quiet, private road.

One such occasion I particularly well remember: it was a lovely afternoon about the close of March; Mr Green and his sisters had sent their carriage back empty, in order to enjoy the bright sunshine and balmy air in a sociable walk home along with their visitors, Captain Somebody and Lieutenant Somebody else (a couple of military fops), and the Misses Murray, who, of course, contrived to join them. Such a party was highly agreeable to Rosalie; but not finding it equally suitable to my taste, I presently fell back, and began to botanise and entomologise along the green banks and budding hedges, till the company was considerably in advance of me, and I could hear the sweet song of the happy lark; then my spirit of misanthropy began to melt away beneath the soft, pure air and genial sunshine: but sad thoughts of early childhood, and yearnings for departed joys, or for a brighter future lot, arose instead. As my eyes wandered over the steep banks covered with young grass and green-leaved plants, and surmounted by budding hedges, I longed intensely for some familiar flower that might recall the woody dales or green hillsides of home: the brown moor-lands, of course, were out of the question. Such a discovery would make my eyes gush out with water, no doubt; but that was one of my greatest enjoyments now. At length I descried, high up between the twisted roots of an oak, three lovely primroses, peeping so sweetly from their hiding-place that the tears already started at the sight; but they grew so high above me that I tried in vain to gather one or two, to dream over and to carry with me: I could not reach them unless I climbed the bank, which I was deterred from doing by hearing a footstep at that moment behind me, and was, therefore, about to turn away, when I was startled by the words, 'Allow me to gather them for you, Miss Grey,' spoken in the grave, low tones of a well-known voice. Immediately the flowers were gathered, and in my hand. It was Mr Weston, of course – who else would trouble himself to do so much for *me*?

I thanked him; whether warmly or coldly, I cannot tell: but certain I am that I did not express half the gratitude I felt. It was foolish, perhaps, to feel any gratitude at all; but it seemed to me, at that moment, as if this were a remarkable instance of his good-nature: an act of kindness which I could not repay, but never should forget: so utterly unaccustomed was I to receive such civilities, so little prepared to expect them from anyone within fifty miles of Horton Lodge.

Yet this did not prevent me from feeling a little uncomfortable in his presence; and I proceeded to follow my pupils at a much quicker pace than before; though, perhaps, if Mr Weston had taken the hint and let me pass without another word, I might have repented it an hour after: but he did not. A somewhat rapid walk for me, was but an ordinary pace for him.

'Your young ladies have left you alone,' said he.

'Yes, they are occupied with more agreeable company.'

'Then don't trouble yourself to overtake them.'

I slackened my pace; but next moment regretted having done so: my companion did not speak; and I had nothing in the world to say, and feared he might be in the same predicament. At length, however, he broke the pause by asking, with a certain quiet abruptness peculiar to himself, if I liked flowers.

'Yes; very much,' I answered: 'wild flowers especially.'

'I like wild flowers,' said he. 'Others I don't care about, because I have no particular associations connected with them – except one or two. What are your favourite flowers?'

'Primroses, bluebells, and heath-blossoms.'

'Not violets?'

'No; because, as you say, I have no particular associations connected with them; for there are no sweet violets among the hills and valleys round my home.'

'It must be a great consolation to you to have a home, Miss Grey,' observed my companion after a short pause: 'however remote, or however seldom visited, still it is something to look to.'

'It is so much that I think I could not live without it,' replied I, with an enthusiasm of which I immediately repented; for I thought it must have sounded essentially silly.

'Oh, yes; you could,' said he, with a thoughtful smile. 'The ties that bind us to life are tougher than you imagine, or than anyone can who has not felt how roughly they may be pulled without breaking. You might be miserable without a home, but even you could live; and not *so* miserably as you suppose. The human heart is like Indian rubber: a little swells it, but a great deal will not burst it. If "little more than nothing will disturb it, little less than all things will suffice" to break it. As in the outer members of our frame, there is a vital power inherent in itself, that strengthens it against external violence. Every blow that shakes it will serve to harden it against a future stroke; as constant labour thickens the skin of the hand, and strengthens its muscles instead of wasting them away: so that a day of arduous toil that might excoriate a lady's palm, would make no sensible impression on that of a hardy ploughman.

'I speak from experience – partly my own. There was a time when I thought as you do – at least, I was fully persuaded that home and its affections were the only things that made life tolerable: that, if deprived of these, existence would become a burden hard to be endured; but now I have no home – unless you would dignify my two hired rooms at Horton by such a name – and not twelve months ago, I lost the last and dearest of my early friends; and yet, not only I live, but I am not wholly destitute of hope and comfort, even for this life: though

I must acknowledge that I can seldom enter even an humble cottage at the close of day, and see its inhabitants peaceably gathered around their cheerful hearth, without a feeling *almost* of envy at their domestic enjoyment.'

'You don't know what happiness lies before you yet,' said I; 'you are now only in the commencement of your journey.'

'The best of happiness,' replied he, 'is mine already – the power and the will to be useful.'

We now approached a stile communicating with a footpath that conducted to a farmhouse, where, I suppose, Mr Weston purposed to make himself 'useful;' for he presently took leave of me crossed the stile, and traversed the path with his usual firm, elastic tread, leaving me to ponder his words as I continued my course alone. I had heard before that he had lost his mother not many months before he came. She then was the last and dearest of his early friends; and he had *no home*. I pitied him from my heart: I almost wept for sympathy. And this, I thought, accounted for the shade of premature thoughtfulness that so frequently clouded his brow, and obtained for him the reputation of a morose and sullen disposition with the charitable Miss Murray and all her kin. 'But,' thought I, 'he is not so miserable as I should be under such a deprivation: he leads an active life; and a wide field for useful exertion lies before him. He can *make* friends; and he can make a home too, if he pleases; and, doubtless, he will please sometime. God grant the partner of that home may be worthy of his choice and make it a happy one – such a home as he deserves to have! And how delightful it would be to –' But no matter what I thought.

I began this book with the intention of concealing nothing; that those who liked might have the benefit of perusing a fellow creature's heart: but we have *some* thoughts that all the angels in heaven are welcome to behold, but not our brother-men – not even the best and kindest amongst them.

By this time the Greens had taken themselves to their own abode, and the Murrays had turned down the private road, whither I hastened to follow them. I found the two girls warm in an animated discussion on the respective merits of the two young officers; but on seeing me Rosalie broke off in the middle of a sentence to exclaim, with malicious glee – 'Oh, ho, Miss Grey! you're come at last, are you? No *wonder* you lingered so long behind; and no *wonder you* always stand up so vigorously for Mr Weston when I abuse him. Ah, ha! I see it all now!'

'Now, come, Miss Murray, don't be foolish,' said I, attempting a good-natured laugh; 'you know such nonsense can make no impression on me.'

But she still went on talking such intolerable stuff – her sister helping her with appropriate fiction coined for the occasion – that I thought it necessary to say something in my own justification.

'What folly all this is!' I exclaimed. 'If Mr Weston's road happened to be the same as mine for a few yards, and if he chose to exchange a word or two in passing, what is there so remarkable in that? I assure you, I never spoke to him before: except once.'

'Where? where? and when?' cried they eagerly.

'In Nancy's cottage.'

'Ah, ha! you've met him there, have you?' exclaimed Rosalie, with exultant laughter. 'Ah! now, Matilda, I've found out why she's so fond of going to Nancy Brown's! she goes there to flirt with Mr Weston.'

'Really, that is not worth contradicting! – I only saw him there once, I tell you – and how could I know he was coming?'

Irritated as I was at their foolish mirth and vexatious imputations, the uneasiness did not continue long: when they had had their laugh out, they returned again to the captain and lieutenant; and, while they disputed and commented upon them, my indignation rapidly cooled; the cause of it was quickly forgotten, and I turned my thoughts into a pleasanter channel. Thus we proceeded up the park, and entered the hall; and as I ascended the stairs to my own chamber, I had but one thought within me: my heart was filled to over-flowing with one single earnest wish. Having entered the room, and shut the door, I fell upon my knees and offered up a fervent but not impetuous prayer: 'Thy will be done,' I strove to say throughout; but, 'Father, all things are possible with Thee, and may it be Thy will,' was sure to follow. That wish – that prayer – both men and women would have scorned me for – 'But Father, *thou* wilt *not* despise!' I said, and felt that it was true. It seemed to me that another's welfare was at least as ardently implored for as my own; nay, even *that* was the principal object of my heart's desire. I might have been deceiving myself; but that idea gave me confidence to ask, and power to hope I did not ask in vain. As for the primroses, I kept two of them in a glass in my room until they were completely withered, and the housemaid threw them out; and the petals of the other I pressed between the leaves of my Bible – I have them still, and mean to keep them always.

## CHAPTER 14

### *The Rector*

The following day was as fine as the preceding one. Soon after breakfast Miss Matilda, having galloped and blundered through a few unprofitable lessons, and vengeably thumped the piano for an hour, in a terrible humour with both me and it because her mamma would not give her a holiday, had betaken herself to her favourite places of resort, the yards, the stables, and the dog-kennels; and Miss Murray was gone forth to enjoy a quiet ramble with a new fashionable novel for her companion, leaving me in the schoolroom hard at work upon a water-colour drawing which I had promised to do for her, and which she insisted upon my finishing that day.

At my feet lay a little rough terrier. It was the property of Miss Matilda; but she hated the animal, and intended to sell it, alleging that it was quite spoiled. It was really an excellent dog of its kind; but she affirmed it was fit for nothing, and had not even the sense to know its own mistress.

The fact was, she had purchased it when but a small puppy insisting at first

that no one should touch it but herself; but, soon becoming tired of so helpless and troublesome a nursling, she had gladly yielded to my entreaties to be allowed to take charge of it; and I, by carefully nursing the little creature from infancy to adolescence, of course, had obtained its affections: a reward I should have greatly valued, and looked upon as far outweighing all the trouble I had had with it, had not poor Snap's grateful feelings exposed him to many a harsh word and many a spiteful kick and pinch from his owner, and were he not now in danger of being 'put away,' in consequence, or transferred to some rough, stony-hearted master. But how could I help it? I could not make the dog hate me, by cruel treatment; and she would not propitiate him by kindness.

However, while I thus sat, working away with my pencil, Mrs Murray came, half-sailing, half-bustling, into the room.

'Miss Grey,' she began, 'dear! how can you sit at your drawing such a day as this?' (She thought I was doing it for my own pleasure.) 'I *wonder you* don't put on your bonnet and go out with the young ladies.'

'I think, ma'am, Miss Murray is reading; and Miss Matilda is amusing herself with her dogs.'

'If you would try to amuse Miss Matilda yourself a little more, I think she would not be *driven* to seek amusement in the companionship of dogs and horses, and grooms, so much as she is; and if you would be a little more cheerful and conversable with Miss Murray, she would not so often go wandering in the fields with a book in her hand. However, I don't want to vex you,' added she, seeing, I suppose, that my cheeks burned and my hand trembled with some unamiable emotion. 'Do, pray, try not to be so touchy – there's no speaking to you else. And tell me if you know where Rosalie is gone; and why she likes to be so much alone?'

'She says she likes to be alone when she has a new book to read.'

'But why can't she read it in the park or the garden? – why should she go into the fields and lanes? And how is it that that Mr Hatfield so often finds her out? She told me last week he'd walked his horse by her side all up Moss Lane; and now I'm sure it was he I saw from my dressing-room window, walking so briskly past the park gates, and on towards the field where she so frequently goes. I wish you would go and see if she is there; and just gently remind her that it is not proper for a young lady of her rank and prospects to be wandering about by herself in that manner, exposed to the attentions of anyone that presumes to address her; like some poor neglected girl that has no park to walk in, and no friends to take care of her; and tell her that her papa would be extremely angry if he knew of her treating Mr Hatfield in the familiar manner that I fear she does; and – oh! if you – if *any* governess had but half a mother's watchfulness – half a mother's anxious care, I should be saved this trouble; and you would see at once the necessity of keeping your eye upon her, and making your company agreeable to – Well, go – go; there's no time to be lost,' cried she, seeing that I had put away my drawing materials, and was waiting in the doorway for the conclusion of her address.

According to her prognostications, I found Miss Murray in her favourite field

just without the park; and, unfortunately, not alone; for the tall, stately figure of Mr Hatfield was slowly sauntering by her side.

Here was a poser for me. It was my duty to interrupt the tête-à-tête: but how was it to be done? Mr Hatfield could not be driven away by so insignificant a person as I; and to go and place myself on the other side of Miss Murray, and intrude my unwelcome presence upon her without noticing her companion was a piece of rudeness I could not be guilty of: neither had I the courage to cry aloud from the top of the field that she was wanted elsewhere. So I took the intermediate course of walking slowly, but steadily towards them; resolving, if my approach failed to scare away the beau, to pass by and tell Miss Murray her mamma wanted her.

She certainly looked very charming as she strolled, lingering along under the budding horse-chestnut trees that stretched their long arms over the park palings, with her closed book in one hand and in the other a graceful sprig of myrtle, which served her as a very pretty plaything; her bright ringlets escaping profusely from her little bonnet, and gently stirred by the breeze, her fair cheek flushed with gratified vanity, her smiling blue eyes, now slyly glancing towards her admirer, now gazing downward at her myrtle sprig. But Snap, running before me, interrupted her in the midst of some half-pert, half-playful repartee, by catching hold of her dress and vehemently tugging thereat; till Mr Hatfield with his cane administered a resounding thwack upon the animal's skull, and sent it yelping back to me, with a clamorous outcry that afforded the reverend gentleman great amusement: but seeing me so near he thought, I suppose, he might as well be taking his departure, and as I stooped to caress the dog, with ostentatious pity to show my disapproval of his severity, I heard him say – 'When shall I see you again, Miss Murray?'

'At church, I suppose,' replied she, 'unless your business chances to bring you here again, at the precise moment when I happen to be walking by.'

'I could always manage to have business here, if I knew precisely when and where to find you.'

'But if I would, I could not inform you, for I am so unmethodical, I never can tell today what I shall do tomorrow.'

'Then give me that, meantime, to comfort me,' said he, half-jestingly and half in earnest, extending his hand for the sprig of myrtle.

'No, indeed, I shan't.'

'Do! *prey* do! I shall be the most miserable of men if you don't. You cannot be so cruel as to deny me a favour so easily granted and yet so highly prized!' pleaded he as ardently as if his life depended on it.

By this time, I stood within a very few yards of them, impatiently waiting his departure.

'There then! take it and go,' said Rosalie.

He joyfully received the gift, murmured something that made her blush and toss her head, but with a little laugh that showed her displeasure was entirely affected; and then with a courteous salutation withdrew.

'Did you ever see such a man, Miss Grey?' said she, turning to me; 'I'm so

*glad you* came! I thought I never *should* get rid of him; and I was so terribly afraid of papa seeing him.'

'Has he been with you long?'

'No, not long, but he's so extremely impertinent: and he's always hanging about, pretending his business or his clerical duties require his attendance in these parts, and really watching for poor me, and pouncing upon me wherever he sees me.'

'Well, your mamma thinks you ought not to go beyond the park or garden without some discreet, matronly person like me to accompany you, and keep off all intruders. She descried Mr Hatfield hurrying past the park gates, and forthwith despatched me with instructions to seek you up and to take care of you, and likewise to warn – '

'Oh, mamma's so tiresome! As if I couldn't take care of myself. She bothered me before about Mr Hatfield; and I told her she might trust me: I never should forget my rank and station for the most delightful man that ever breathed. I wish he would go down on his knees tomorrow, and implore me to be his wife, that I might just show her how mistaken she is in supposing that I could ever – oh, it provokes me so! To think that I could be such a fool as to fall in *love!* It is quite beneath the dignity of a woman to do such a thing. Love! I detest the word! as applied to one of our sex, I think it a perfect insult. A preference I *might* acknowledge; but never for one like poor Mr Hatfield, who has not seven hundred a year to bless himself with. I like to talk to him, because he's so clever and amusing – I wish Sir Thomas Ashby were half as nice; besides, I must have *somebody* to flirt with, and no one else has the sense to come here; and when we go out, mamma won't let me flirt with anybody but Sir Thomas – if he's there; and if he's *not* there, I'm bound hand and foot, for fear somebody should go and make up some exaggerated story, and put it into his head that I'm engaged, or likely to be engaged, to somebody else; or, what is more probable, for fear his nasty old mother should see or hear of my ongoings, and conclude that I'm not a fit wife for her excellent son: as if the said son were not the greatest scamp in Christendom; and as if any woman of common decency were not a world too good for him.'

'Is it really so, Miss Murray? and does your mamma know it, and yet wish you to marry him?'

'To be sure, she does! She knows more against him than I do, I believe: she keeps it from me lest I should be discouraged; not knowing how little I care about such things. For it's no great matter, really: he'll be all right when he's married, as mamma says; and reformed rakes make the best husbands, *everybody* knows. I only wish he were not so ugly – *that's* all I think about: but then there's no choice here in the country; and papa *will not* let us go to London – '

'But I should think Mr Hatfield would be far better.'

'And so he would, if he were lord of Ashby Park – there's not a doubt of it: but the fact is, *I must* have Ashby Park, whoever shares it with me.'

'But Mr Hatfield thinks you like him all this time; you don't consider how bitterly he will be disappointed when he finds himself mistaken.'

'*No*, indeed! It will be a proper punishment for his presumption – for ever

*daring* to think I could like him. I should enjoy nothing so much as lifting the veil from his eyes.'

'The sooner you do it the better then.'

'No; I tell you, I like to amuse myself with him. Besides, he doesn't really think I like him. I take good care of that: you don't know how cleverly I manage. He may presume to think he can *induce* me to like him; for which I shall punish him as he deserves.'

'Well, mind you don't give too much reason for such presumption – that's all,' replied I.

But all my exhortations were in vain; they only made her somewhat more solicitous to disguise her wishes and her thoughts from me. She talked no more to me about the Rector; but I could see that her mind, if not her heart, was fixed upon him still, and that she was intent upon obtaining another interview: for though, in compliance with her mother's request, I was now constituted the companion of her rambles for a time, she still persisted in wandering in the fields and lanes that lay in the nearest proximity to the road; and, whether she talked to me or read the book she carried in her hand, she kept continually pausing to look round her, or gaze up the road to see if anyone was coming; and if a horseman trotted by, I could tell by her unqualified abuse of the poor equestrian, whoever he might be, that she hated him *because* he was not Mr Hatfield.

'Surely,' thought I, 'she is not so indifferent to him as she believes herself to be, or would have others to believe her; and her mother's anxiety is not so wholly causeless as she affirms.'

Three days passed away, and he did not make his appearance. On the afternoon of the fourth, as we were walking beside the park palings in the memorable field, each furnished with a book (for I always took care to provide myself with something to be doing when she did not require me to talk), she suddenly interrupted my studies by exclaiming –

'Oh, Miss Grey! do be so kind as to go and see Mark Wood, and take his wife half a crown from me – I should have given or sent it a week ago, but quite forgot. There!' said she, throwing me her purse, and speaking very fast – 'Never mind getting it out now, but take the purse and give them what you like; I would go with you, but I want to finish this volume. I'll come and meet you when I've done it. Be quick, will you – and – oh, wait; hadn't you better read to him a bit? Run to the house and get some sort of a good book. Anything will do.'

I did as I was desired; but, suspecting something from her hurried manner and the suddenness of the request, I just glanced back before I quitted the field, and there was Mr Hatfield about to enter at the gate below. By sending me to the house for a book, she had just prevented my meeting him on the road.

'Never mind!' thought I, 'there'll be no great harm done. Poor Mark will be glad of the half-crown, and perhaps of the good book too; and if the Rector does steal Miss Rosalie's heart, it will only humble her pride a little; and if they do get married at last, it will only save her from a worse fate; and she will be quite a good enough partner for him, and he for her.'

Mark Wood was the consumptive labourer whom I mentioned before. He

was now rapidly wearing away. Miss Murray, by her liberality, obtained literally the blessing of him that was ready to perish; for though the half-crown could be of very little service to him, he was glad of it for the sake of his wife and children, so soon to be widowed and fatherless. After I had sat a few minutes, and read a little for the comfort and edification of himself and his afflicted wife, I left them; but I had not proceeded fifty yards before I encountered Mr Weston, apparently on his way to the same abode. He greeted me in his usual quiet, unaffected way, stopped to enquire about the condition of the sick man and his family, and with a sort of unconscious, brotherly disregard to ceremony, took from my hand the book out of which I had been reading, turned over its pages, made a few brief but very sensible remarks, and restored it; then told me about some poor sufferer he had just been visiting, talked a little about Nancy Brown, made a few observations upon my little rough friend, the terrier, that was frisking at his feet, and finally upon the beauty of the weather and departed.

I have omitted to give a detail of his words, from a notion that they would not interest the reader as they did me, and not because I have forgotten them. No; I remember them well; for I thought them over and over again in the course of that day and many succeeding ones, I know not how often; and recalled every intonation of his deep, clear voice, every flash of his quick, brown eye, and every gleam of his pleasant, but too transient smile. Such a confession will look very absurd, I fear; but no matter: I have written it: and they that read it will not know the writer.

While I was walking along, happy within, and pleased with all around, Miss Murray came hastening to meet me: her buoyant step, flushed cheek, and radiant smiles showing that she, too, was happy, in her own way. Running up to me, she put her arm through mine, and without waiting to recover breath, began – 'Now, Miss Grey, think yourself highly honoured, for I'm come to tell you my news before I've breathed a word of it to anyone else.'

'Well, what is it?'

'*Oh, such* news! In the first place, you must know that Mr Hatfield came upon me just after you were gone. I was in *such* a way for fear papa or mamma should see him; but you know I couldn't call you back again, and so I – oh, dear! I can't tell you all about it now, for there's Matilda, I see, in the park, and I must go and open my budget to her. But, however, Hatfield was most uncommonly audacious, unspeakably complimentary, and unprecedentedly tender – tried to be so, at least – he didn't succeed very well in *that*, because it's not his vein. I'll tell you all he said another time.'

'But what did *you* say – I'm more interested in that?'

'I'll tell you that, too, at some future period. I happened to be in a very good humour just then; but, though I was complaisant and gracious enough, I took care not to compromise myself in any possible way. But, however, the conceited wretch chose to interpret my amiability of temper his own way, and at length presumed upon my indulgence so far – what do you think? – he actually – made me an offer!'

'And you – '

'I proudly drew myself up, and with the greatest coolness expressed my astonishment at such an occurrence, and hoped he had seen nothing in my conduct to justify his expectations. You should have *seen* how his countenance fell! He went perfectly white in the face. I assured him that I esteemed him and all that, but could not possibly accede to his proposals; and if I did, papa and mamma could never be brought to give their consent.'

' "But if they could," said he, "would yours be wanting?"

' "Certainly, Mr Hatfield," I replied, with a cool decision which quelled all hope at once. Oh, if you had seen how dreadfully mortified he was – how crushed to the earth by his disappointment! really, I almost pitied him myself.

'One more desperate attempt, however, he made. After a silence of considerable duration, during which he struggled to be calm, and I to be grave – for I felt a strong propensity to laugh – which would have ruined all – he said, with the ghost of a smile, "But tell me plainly, Miss Murray, if I had the wealth of Sir Hugh Meltham, or the prospects of his eldest son, would you still refuse me? answer me truly, upon your honour."

' "Certainly," said I. "That would make no difference whatever."

'It was a great lie, but he looked so confident in his own attractions still, that I determined not to leave him one stone upon another. He looked me full in the face; but I kept my countenance so well that he could not imagine I was saying anything more than the actual truth.

' "Then it's all over, I suppose," he said, looking as if he could have died on the spot with vexation and the intensity of his despair. But he was angry as well as disappointed. There was he, suffering so unspeakably, and there was I, the pitiless cause of it all, so utterly impenetrable to all the artillery of his looks and words, so calmly cold and proud, he could not but feel some resentment; and with singular bitterness he began, "I certainly did not expect this, Miss Murray. I might say something about your past conduct, and the hopes you have led me to foster, but I forbear, on condition – "

' "No conditions, Mr Hatfield!" said I, now truly indignant at his insolence.

' "Then let me beg it as a favour," he replied, lowering his voice at once, and taking a humbler tone: "let me entreat that you will not mention this affair to anyone whatever. If you will keep silence about it, there need be no unpleasantness on either side – nothing, I mean, beyond what is quite unavoidable: for my own feelings I will endeavour to keep to myself, if I cannot annihilate them – I will try to forgive, if I cannot forget the cause of my sufferings. I will not suppose, Miss Murray, that you know how deeply you have injured me. I would not have you aware of it; but if, in addition to the injury you have already done me – pardon me, but whether innocently or not, you *have* done it – and if you add to it by giving publicity to this unfortunate affair, or naming it *at all*, you will find that I too can speak, and though you scorned my love, you will hardly scorn my – "

'He stopped, but he bit his bloodless lip, and looked so terribly fierce that I was quite frightened. However, my pride upheld me still, and I answered disdainfully – "I do not know what motive you suppose I could have for naming

it to anyone, Mr Hatfield; but if I were disposed to do so, you would not deter me by threats; and it is scarcely the part of a gentleman to attempt it."

' "Pardon me, Miss Murray," said he, "I have loved you so intensely – I do still adore you so deeply, that I would not willingly offend you; but though I never have loved, and never *can* love any woman as I have loved you, it is equally certain that I never was so ill-treated by any. On the contrary, I have always found your sex the kindest and most tender and obliging of God's creation, till now." (Think of the conceited fellow saying that!) "And the novelty and harshness of the lesson you have taught me today, and the bitterness of being disappointed in the only quarter on which the happiness of my life depended, must excuse any appearance of asperity. If my presence is disagreeable to you, Miss Murray," he said (for I was looking about me to show how little I cared for him, so he thought I was tired of him, I suppose), "if my presence is disagreeable to you, Miss Murray, you have only to promise me the favour I named, and I will relieve you at once. There are many ladies – some even in this parish – who would be delighted to accept what you have so scornfully trampled under your feet. They would be naturally inclined to hate one whose surpassing loveliness has so completely estranged my heart from them and blinded me to their attractions; and a single hint of the truth from me to one of these would be sufficient to raise such a talk against you as would seriously injure your prospects, and diminish your chance of success with any other gentleman you or your mamma might design to entangle."

' "What do you mean, sir?" said I, ready to stamp with passion.

' "I mean that this affair from beginning to end appears to me like a case of arrant flirtation, to say the least of it – such a case as you would find it rather inconvenient to have blazoned through the world: especially with the additions and exaggerations of your female rivals, who would be too glad to publish the matter, if I only gave them a handle to it. But I promise you, on the faith of a gentleman, that no word or syllable that could tend to your prejudice shall ever escape my lips, provided you will – "

' "Well, well, I won't mention it," said I. "You may rely upon my silence, if that can afford you any consolation."

' "You promise it?"

' "Yes," I answered, for I wanted to get rid of him now.

' "Farewell, then!" said he, in a most doleful heart-sick tone; and with a look where pride vainly struggled against despair, he turned and went away: longing, no doubt, to get home, that he might shut himself up in his study and cry – if he doesn't burst into tears before he gets there.'

'But you have broken your promise already,' said I, truly horrified at her perfidy.

'Oh! it's only to you; I know you won't repeat it.'

'Certainly, I shall not: but you say you are going to tell your sister; and she will tell your brothers when they come home, and Brown immediately, if you do not tell her yourself; and Brown will blazon it, or be the means of blazoning it throughout the country.'

'No, indeed, she won't. We shall not tell her at all, unless it be under the promise of the strictest secrecy.'

'But how can you expect her to keep her promises better than her more enlightened mistress?'

'Well, well, she shan't hear it then,' said Miss Murray, somewhat snappishly.

'But you will tell your mamma, of course,' pursued I; 'and she will tell your papa.'

'Of course, I shall tell mamma, that is the very thing that pleases me so much. I shall now be able to convince her how mistaken she was in her fears about me.'

'*Oh, that's* it, is it? I was wondering what it was that delighted you so much.'

'Yes; and another thing is, that I've humbled Mr Hatfield so charmingly; and another – why, you must allow me some share of female vanity: I don't pretend to be without that most essential attribute of our sex – and if you had seen poor Hatfield's intense eagerness in making his ardent declaration, and his flattering proposal, and his agony of mind, that no effort of pride could conceal, on being refused, you would have allowed I had some cause to be gratified.'

'The greater his agony, I should think, the less your cause for gratification.'

'Oh, nonsense!' cried the young lady, shaking herself with vexation. 'You either can't understand me or you won't. If I had not confidence in your magnanimity, I should think you envied me. But you will, perhaps, comprehend this cause of pleasure – which is as great as any – namely, that I am delighted with myself for my prudence, my self-command, my heartlessness, if you please. I was not a bit taken by surprise, not a bit confused, or awkward, or foolish; I just acted and spoke as I ought to have done, and was completely my own mistress throughout. And here was a man, decidedly good-looking – Jane and Susan Green call him bewitchingly handsome – I suppose they're two of the ladies he pretends would be so glad to have him; but, however, he was certainly a very clever, witty, agreeable companion – not what you call clever, but just enough to make him entertaining; and a man one needn't be ashamed of anywhere, and would not soon grow tired of; and to confess the truth, I rather liked him – better even, of late, than Harry Meltham – and he evidently idolised me; and yet, though he came upon me all alone and unprepared, I had the wisdom, and the pride, and the strength to refuse him – and so scornfully and coolly as I did: I have good reason to be proud of that!'

'And are you equally proud of having told him that his having the wealth of Sir Hugh Meltham would make no difference to you when that was not the case; and of having promised to tell no one of his misadventure, apparently without the slightest intention of keeping your promise?'

'Of course! what else could I do? You would not have had me – but I see, Miss Grey, you're not in a good temper. Here's Matilda; I'll see what she and mamma have to say about it.'

She left me, offended at my want of sympathy, and thinking no doubt, that I envied her. I did not – at least, I firmly believed I did not. I was sorry for her; I was amazed, disgusted at her heartless vanity; I wondered why so much beauty should be given to those who made so bad a use of it, and denied to some who would make it a benefit to both themselves and others.

But, God knows best, I concluded. There are, I suppose, some men as vain, as selfish, and as heartless as she is, and, perhaps, such women may be useful to punish them.

## CHAPTER 15

# The Walk

'Oh dear! I wish Hatfield had not been so precipitate!' said Rosalie next day at four p.m., as, with a portentous yawn, she laid down her worsted-work and looked listlessly towards the window. 'There's no inducement to go out now; and nothing to look forward to. The days will be so long and dull when there are no parties to enliven them; and there are none this week, or next either, that I know of.'

'Pity you were so cross to him,' observed Matilda, to whom this lamentation was addressed. 'He'll never come again: and I suspect you liked him after all. I hoped you would have taken him for your beau, and left dear Harry to me.'

'Humph! my beau must be an Adonis indeed, Matilda, the admired of all beholders, if I am to be contented with him alone. I'm sorry to lose Hatfield, I confess; but the first decent man, or number of men, that come to supply his place, will be more than welcome. It's Sunday tomorrow – I do wonder how he'll look, and whether he'll be able to go through the service. Most likely he'll pretend he's got a cold and make Mr Weston do it all.'

'Not he!' exclaimed Matilda, somewhat contemptuously. 'Fool as he is, he's not so soft as that comes to.'

Her sister was slightly offended; but the event proved Matilda was right: the disappointed lover performed his pastoral duties as usual. Rosalie, indeed, affirmed he looked very pale and dejected: he might be a little paler; but the difference, if any, was scarcely perceptible. As for his dejection, I certainly did not hear his laugh ringing from the vestry as usual, nor his voice loud in hilarious discourse; though I did hear it uplifted in rating the sexton in a manner that made the congregation stare; and, in his transits to and from the pulpit and the communion-table there was more of solemn pomp, and less of that irreverent, self-confident, or rather self-delighted imperiousness with which he usually swept along – that air that seemed to say, 'You all reverence and adore me, I know; but if anyone does not, I defy him to the teeth!' But the most remarkable change was, that he never once suffered his eyes to wander in the direction of Mr Murray's pew, and did not leave the church till we were gone.

Mr Hatfield had doubtless received a very severe blow; but his pride impelled him to use every effort to conceal the effects of it. He had been disappointed in his certain hope of obtaining not only a beautiful, and, to him, highly attractive wife, but one whose rank and fortune might give brilliance to far inferior charms: he was likewise, no doubt, intensely mortified by his repulse, and deeply

offended at the conduct of Miss Murray throughout. It would have given him no little consolation to have known how disappointed she was to find him apparently so little moved, and to see that he was able to refrain from casting a single glance at her throughout both services; though, she declared, it showed he was thinking of her all the time, or his eyes would have fallen upon her, if it were only by chance: but if they had so chanced to fall, she would have affirmed it was because they could not resist the attraction. It might have pleased him too, in some degree, to have seen how dull and dissatisfied she was throughout that week (the greater part of it, at least), for lack of her usual source of excitement; and how often she regretted having 'used him up so soon', like a child that, having devoured its plum-cake too hastily, sits sucking its fingers, and vainly lamenting its greediness.

At length I was called upon, one fine morning, to accompany her in a walk to the village. Ostensibly she went to get some shades of Berlin wool, at a tolerably respectable shop that was chiefly supported by the ladies of the vicinity: really – I trust there is no breach of charity in supposing that she went with the idea of meeting either with the Rector himself, or some other admirer by the way; for as we went along, she kept wondering 'what Hatfield would do or say, if we met him', etc., etc.; as we passed Mr Green's park gates, she 'wondered whether he was at home – great stupid blockhead'; as Lady Meltham's carriage passed us, she 'wondered what Mr Harry was doing this fine day', and then began to abuse his elder brother for being 'such a fool as to get married and go and live in London'.

'Why,' said I, 'I thought you wanted to live in London yourself.'

'Yes, because it's so dull here; but then he makes it still duller by taking himself off; and if he were not married I might have him instead of that odious Sir Thomas.'

Then, observing the prints of a horse's feet on the somewhat miry road, she 'wondered whether it was a gentleman's horse', and finally concluded it was, for the impressions were too small to have been made by a 'great, clumsy cart-horse'; and then she 'wondered who the rider could be', and whether we should meet him coming back for she was sure he had only passed that morning; and lastly, when we entered the village and saw only a few of its humble inhabitants moving about, she 'wondered why the stupid people couldn't keep in their houses; she was sure she didn't want to see their ugly faces, and dirty, vulgar clothes – it wasn't for that she came to Horton!'

Amid all this, I confess, I wondered, too, in secret, whether we should meet, or catch a glimpse of somebody else; and as we passed his lodgings, I even went so far as to wonder whether he was at the window. On entering the shop, Miss Murray desired me to stand in the doorway while she transacted her business and tell her if anyone passed. But alas! there was no one visible besides the villagers, except Jane and Susan Green coming down the single street, apparently returning from a walk.

'Stupid things!' muttered she, as she came out after having concluded her bargain. 'Why couldn't they have their dolt of a brother with them? even *he* would be better than nothing.'

She greeted them, however, with a cheerful smile, and protestations of pleasure at the happy meeting equal to their own. They placed themselves one on each side of her, and all three walked away chatting and laughing as young ladies do when they get together, if they be but on tolerably intimate terms. But I, feeling myself to be one too many, left them to their merriment and lagged behind, as usual on such occasions: I had no relish for walking beside Miss Green or Miss Susan like one deaf and dumb, who could neither speak nor be spoken to.

But this time I was not long alone. It struck me, at first, as very odd, but just as I was thinking about Mr Weston he should come up and accost me; but afterwards, on due reflection, I thought there was nothing odd about it, unless it were the fact of his speaking to me; for on such a morning and so near his own abode, it was natural enough that he should be about; and as for my thinking of him, I had been doing that, with little intermission, ever since we set out on our journey; so there was nothing remarkable in that.

'You are alone again, Miss Grey,' said he.

'Yes.'

'What kind of people are those ladies – the Misses Green?'

'I really don't know.'

'That's strange – when you live so near and see them so often!'

'Well, I suppose they are lively, good-tempered girls; but, I imagine you must know them better than I do yourself, for I never exchanged a word with either of them.'

'Indeed! They don't strike me as being particularly reserved.'

'Very likely they are not so to people of their own class; but they consider themselves as moving in quite a different sphere from me!'

He made no reply to this; but after a short pause, he said – 'I suppose it's these things, Miss Grey, that make you think you could not live without a home?'

'Not exactly. The fact is I am too socially disposed to be able to live contentedly without a friend; and as the only friends I have, or am likely to have, are at home, if it or rather, if they were gone – I will not say I could not live – but I would rather not live in such a desolate world.'

'But why do you say the only friends you are likely to have? Are you so unsociable that you cannot make friends?'

'No, but I never made one yet; and in my present position there is no possibility of doing so, or even of forming a common acquaintance. The fault may be partly in myself, but I hope not altogether.'

'The fault is partly in society, and partly, I should think, in your immediate neighbours: and partly, too, in yourself; for many ladies, in your position, would make themselves be noticed and accounted of. But your pupils should be companions for you in some degree; they cannot be many years younger than yourself.'

'Oh, yes, they are good company sometimes; but I cannot call them friends, nor would they think of bestowing such a name on me – they have other companions better suited to their tastes.'

'Perhaps you are too wise for them. How do you amuse yourself when alone – do you read much?'

'Reading is my favourite occupation, when I have leisure for it and books to read.'

From speaking of books in general, he passed to different books in particular, and proceeded by rapid transitions from topic to topic, till several matters, both of taste and opinion, had been discussed considerably within the space of half an hour, but without the embellishment of many observations from himself; he being evidently less bent upon communicating his own thoughts and predilections, than on discovering mine. He had not the tact, or the art, to effect such a purpose by skilfully drawing out my sentiments or ideas through the real or apparent statement of his own, or leading the conversation by imperceptible gradations to such topics as he wished to advert to: but such gentle abruptness, and such single-minded straightforwardness could not possibly offend me.

'And why should he interest himself at all in my moral and intellectual capacities: what is it to him what I think or feel?' I asked myself. And my heart throbbed in answer to the question.

But Jane and Susan Green soon reached their home. As they stood parleying at the park gates, attempting to persuade Miss Murray to come in, I wished Mr Weston would go, that she might not see him with me when she turned round; but, unfortunately, his business, which was to pay one more visit to poor Mark Wood, led him to pursue the same path as we did, till nearly the close of our journey. When, however, he saw that Rosalie had taken leave of her friends and I was about to join her, he would have left me and passed on at a quicker pace; but, as he civilly lifted his hat in passing her, to my surprise, instead of returning the salute with a stiff, ungracious bow, she accosted him with one of her sweetest smiles, and, walking by his side, began to talk to him with all imaginable cheerfulness and affability; and so we proceeded all three together.

After a short pause in the conversation, Mr Weston made some remark addressed particularly to me, as referring to something we had been talking of before; but, before I could answer, Miss Murray replied to the observation and enlarged upon it: he rejoined; and, from thence to the close of the interview, she engrossed him entirely to herself. It might be partly owing to my own stupidity, my want of tact and assurance: but I felt myself wronged: I trembled with apprehension; and I listened with envy to her easy, rapid flow of utterance, and saw with anxiety the bright smile with which she looked into his face from time to time: for she was walking a little in advance, for the purpose (as I judged) of being seen as well as heard. If her conversation was light and trivial, it was amusing, and she was never at a loss for something to say, or for suitable words to express it in. There was nothing pert or flippant in her manner now, as when she walked with Mr Hatfield; there was only a gentle, playful kind of vivacity, which I thought must be peculiarly pleasing to a man of Mr Weston's disposition and temperament.

When he was gone she began to laugh, and muttered to herself, 'I thought I could do it!'

'Do what?' I asked.

'Fix that man.'

'What in the world do you mean?"

'I mean that he will go home and dream of me. I have shot him through the heart!'

'How do you know?'

'By many infallible proofs: more especially the look he gave me when he went away. It was not an impudent look – I exonerate him from that – it was a look of reverential, tender adoration. Ha, ha! he's not quite such a stupid blockhead as I thought him!'

I made no answer, for my heart was in my throat, or something like it, and I could not trust myself to speak. 'Oh, God, avert it!' I cried internally – 'for his sake, not for mine!'

Miss Murray made several trivial observations as we passed up the park, to which (in spite of my reluctance to let one glimpse of my feelings appear) I could only answer by monosyllables. Whether she intended to torment me, or merely to amuse herself, I could not tell – and did not much care; but I thought of the poor man and his one lamb, and the rich man with his thousand flocks; and I dreaded I knew not what for Mr Weston, independently of my own blighted hopes.

Right glad was I to get into the house, and find myself alone once more in my own room. My first impulse was to sink into the chair beside the bed; and laying my head on the pillow, to seek relief in a passionate burst of tears: there was an imperative craving for such an indulgence; but, alas! I must restrain and swallow back my feelings still: there was the bell – the odious bell for the schoolroom dinner; and I must go down with a calm face, and smile, and laugh, and talk nonsense – yes, and eat, too, if possible, as if all was right, and I was just returned from a pleasant walk.

## CHAPTER 16

## *The Substitution*

Next Sunday was one of the gloomiest of April days – a day of thick, dark clouds, and heavy showers. None of the Murrays were disposed to attend church in the afternoon, excepting Rosalie: she was bent upon going as usual; so she ordered the carriage, and I went with her: nothing loth, of course, for at church I might look without fear of scorn or censure upon a form and face more pleasing to me than the most beautiful of God's creations; I might listen without disturbance to a voice more charming than the sweetest music to my ears; I might seem to hold communion with that soul in which I felt so deeply interested, and imbibe its purest thoughts and holiest aspirations, with no alloy to such felicity except the secret reproaches of my conscience, which would too often whisper that I was

deceiving my own self, and mocking God with the service of a heart more bent upon the creature than the Creator.

Sometimes such thoughts would give me trouble enough; but sometimes I could quiet them with thinking – it is not the man, it is his goodness that I love. 'Whatsoever things are pure, whatsoever things are lovely, whatsoever things are honest and of good report, think on these things.' We do well to worship God in His works; and I know none of them in which so many of His attributes – so much of His own spirit shines, as in this His faithful servant; whom to know and not to appreciate, were obtuse insensibility in me, who have so little else to occupy my heart.

Almost immediately after the conclusion of the service, Miss Murray left the church. We had to stand in the porch, for it was raining, and the carriage was not yet come. I wondered at her coming forth so hastily, for neither young Meltham nor Squire Green was there; but I soon found it was to secure an interview with Mr Weston as he came out, which he presently did. Having saluted us both, he would have passed on, but she detained him; first with observations upon the disagreeable weather, and then with asking if he would be so kind as to come sometime tomorrow to see the granddaughter of the old woman who kept the porter's lodge, for the girl was ill of a fever, and wished to see him. He promised to do so.

'And at what time will you be most likely to come, Mr Weston? The old woman will like to know when to expect you – you know such people think more about having their cottages in order when decent people come to see them than we are apt to suppose.'

Here was a wonderful instance of consideration from the thoughtless Miss Murray. Mr Weston named an hour in the morning at which he would endeavour to be there. By this time the carriage was ready, and the footman was waiting, with an open umbrella, to escort Miss Murray through the churchyard. I was about to follow; but Mr Weston had an umbrella too, and offered me the benefit of its shelter, for it was raining heavily.

'No, thank you, I don't mind the rain,' I said. I always lacked common sense when taken by surprise.

'But you don't *like* it, I suppose? – an umbrella will do you no harm at any rate,' he replied, with a smile that showed he was not offended; as a man of worse temper or less penetration would have been at such a refusal of his aid. I could not deny the truth of his assertion, and so went with him to the carriage; he even offered me his hand on getting in: an unnecessary piece of civility, but I accepted that too, for fear of giving offence. One glance he gave, one little smile at parting – it was but for a moment; but therein I read, or thought I read, a meaning that kindled in my heart a brighter flame of hope than had ever yet arisen.

'I would have sent the footman back for you, Miss Grey, if you'd waited a moment – you needn't have taken Mr Weston's umbrella,' observed Rosalie, with a very unamiable cloud upon her pretty face.

'I would have come without an umbrella, but Mr Weston offered me the

benefit of his, and I could not have refused it more than I did without offending him,' replied I, smiling placidly; for my inward happiness made that amusing which would have wounded me at another time.

The carriage was now in motion. Miss Murray bent forwards and looked out of the window as we were passing Mr Weston. He was pacing homewards along the causeway, and did not turn his head.

'Stupid ass!' cried she, throwing herself back again in the seat. 'You don't know *what* you've lost by not looking this way!'

'What has he lost?'

'A bow from me, that would have raised him to the seventh heaven!'

I made no answer. I saw she was out of humour, and I derived a secret gratification from the fact, not that she was vexed, but that she thought she had reason to be so. It made me think my hopes were not entirely the offspring of my wishes and imagination.

'I mean to take up Mr Weston instead of Mr Hatfield,' said my companion, after a short pause, resuming something of her usual cheerfulness. 'The ball at Ashby Park takes places on Tuesday, you know; and mamma thinks it very likely that Sir Thomas will propose to me then: such things are often done in the privacy of the ballroom, when gentlemen are most easily ensnared, and ladies most enchanting. But if I am to be married so soon, I must make the best of the present time: I am determined Hatfield shall not be the only man who shall lay his heart at my feet, and implore me to accept the worthless gift in vain.'

'If you mean Mr Weston to be one of your victims,' said I with affected indifference, 'you will have to make such overtures yourself that you will find it difficult to draw back when he asks you to fulfil the expectations you have raised.'

'I don't suppose he will ask me to *marry* him – nor should I desire it: that would be *rather* too much presumption! but I intend him to feel my power. He has felt it already, indeed: but he shall *acknowledge* it too; and what visionary hopes he may have, he must keep to himself, and only amuse me with the result of them – for a time.'

'Oh! that some kind spirit would whisper those words in his ear!' I inwardly exclaimed. I was far too indignant to hazard a reply to her observation aloud; and nothing more was said about Mr Weston that day, by me or in my hearing. But next morning, soon after breakfast, Miss Murray came into the schoolroom, where her sister was employed at her studies, or rather her lessons, for studies they were not, and said, 'Matilda, I want you to take a walk with me about eleven o'clock.'

'Oh, I can't, Rosalie! I have to give orders about my new bridle and saddle-cloth, and speak to the rat-catcher about his dogs: Miss Grey must go with you.'

'No, I want *you*,' said Rosalie; and calling her sister to the window, she whispered an explanation in her ear; upon which the latter consented to go.

I remembered that eleven was the hour at which Mr Weston proposed to come to the porter's lodge; and remembering that I beheld the whole contrivance. Accordingly, at dinner, I was entertained with a long account of

how Mr Weston had overtaken them as they were walking along the road; and how they had had a long walk and talk with him, and really found him quite an agreeable companion; and how he must have been, and evidently was, delighted with them and their amazing condescension, etc. etc.

## CHAPTER 17

### *Confessions*

As I am in the way of confessions, I may as well acknowledge that, about this time, I paid more attention to dress than ever I had done before. This is not saying much; for hitherto I had been a little neglectful in that particular: but now, also, it was no uncommon thing to spend as much as two minutes in the contemplation of my own image in the glass; though I never could derive any consolation from such a study. I could discover no beauty in those marked features, that pale hollow cheek, and ordinary dark brown hair; there might be intellect in the forehead, there might be expression in the dark grey eyes: but what of that? – a low Grecian brow, and large black eyes devoid of sentiment would be esteemed far preferable. It is foolish to wish for beauty. Sensible people never either desire it for themselves, or care about it in others. If the mind be but well cultivated, and the heart well disposed, no one ever cares for the exterior. So said the teachers of our childhood; and so say we to the children of the present day. All very judicious and proper, no doubt; but are such assertions supported by actual experience?

We are naturally disposed to love what gives us pleasure, and what more pleasing than a beautiful face – when we know no harm of the possessor at least? A little girl loves her bird – Why? Because it lives and feels; because it is helpless and harmless? A toad, likewise, lives and feels, and is equally helpless and harmless; but though she would not hurt a toad, she cannot love it like the bird, with its graceful form, soft feathers, and bright, speaking eyes. If a woman is fair and amiable, she is praised for both qualities, but especially the former, by the bulk of mankind: if, on the other hand, she is disagreeable in person and character, her plainness is commonly inveighed against as her greatest crime, because, to common observers, it gives the greatest offence; while if she is plain and good, provided she is a person of retired manners and secluded life, no one ever knows of her goodness, except her immediate connections. Others, on the contrary, are disposed to form unfavourable opinions of her mind and disposition, if it be but to excuse themselves for their instinctive dislike of one so unfavoured by nature; and vice versa with her whose angel form conceals a vicious heart, or sheds a false, deceitful charm over defects and foibles that would not be tolerated in another. They that have beauty, let them be thankful for it, and make a good use of it, like any other talent; they that have it not, let them console themselves, and do the best they can without it: certainly, though liable to be overestimated, it is a gift of

God, and not to be despised. Many will feel this who have felt that they could love, and whose hearts tell them that they are worthy to be loved again; while yet they are debarred by the lack of this or some such seeming trifle, from giving and receiving that happiness they seem almost made to feel and to impart. As well might the humble glow-worm despise that power of giving light without which the roving fly might pass her and repass her a thousand times, and never rest beside her: she might hear her winged darling buzzing over and around her; he vainly seeking her, she longing to be found, but with no power to make her presence known, no voice to call him, no wings to follow his flight; the fly must seek another mate, the worm must live and die alone.

Such were some of my reflections about this period. I might go on prosing more and more, I might dive much deeper, and disclose other thoughts, propose questions the reader might be puzzled to answer, and deduce arguments that might startle his prejudices, or, perhaps, provoke his ridicule, because he could not comprehend them; but I forbear.

Now, therefore, let us return to Miss Murray. She accompanied her mamma to the ball on Tuesday; of course splendidly attired, and delighted with her prospects and her charms. As Ashby Park was nearly ten miles distant from Horton Lodge, they had to set out pretty early, and I intended to have spent the evening with Nancy Brown, whom I had not seen for a long time; but my kind pupil took care I should spend it neither there nor anywhere else beyond the limits of the schoolroom, by giving me a piece of music to copy, which kept me closely occupied till bedtime. About eleven next morning, as soon as she had left her room, she came to tell me her news. Sir Thomas had indeed proposed to her at the ball: an event which reflected great credit on her mamma's sagacity, if not upon her skill in contrivance. I rather incline to the belief that she had first laid her plans, and then predicted their success. The offer had been accepted, of course, and the bridegroom elect was coming that day to settle matters with Mr Murray.

Rosalie was pleased with the thoughts of becoming mistress of Ashby Park; she was elated with the prospect of the bridal ceremony and its attendant splendour and éclat, the honeymoon spent abroad, and the subsequent gaieties she expected to enjoy in London and elsewhere; she appeared pretty well pleased too, for the time being, with Sir Thomas himself, because she had so lately seen him, danced with him, and been flattered by him; but after all, she seemed to shrink from the idea of being so soon united: she wished the ceremony to be delayed some months, at least; and I wished it too. It seemed a horrible thing to hurry on the inauspicious match, and not to give the poor creature time to think and reason on the irrevocable step she was about to take. I made no pretension to 'a mother's watchful, anxious care', but I was amazed and horrified at Mrs Murray's heartlessness, or want of thought for the real good of her child; and, by my unheeded warnings and exhortations, I vainly strove to remedy the evil. Miss Murray only laughed at what I said; and I soon found that her reluctance to an immediate union arose chiefly from a desire to do what execution she could among the young gentlemen of her acquaintance, before she was incapacitated from further mischief of the kind. It was for this cause

that, before confiding to me the secret of her engagement, she had extracted a promise that I would not mention a word on the subject to anyone. And when I saw him, and when I beheld her plunge more recklessly than ever into the depths of heartless coquetry, I had no more pity for her. 'Come what will,' I thought, 'she deserves it. Sir Thomas cannot be too bad for her; and the sooner she is incapacitated from deceiving and injuring others the better.'

The wedding was fixed for the first of June. Between that and the critical ball was little more than six weeks; but, with Rosalie's accomplished skill and resolute exertion, much might be done even within that period: especially as Sir Thomas spent most of the interim in London; whither he went up, it was said, to settle affairs with his lawyer, and make other preparations for the approaching nuptials. He endeavoured to supply the want of his presence by a pretty constant fire of billets-doux; but these did not attract the neighbours' attention, and open their eyes, as personal visits would have done; and old Lady Ashby's haughty, sour spirit of reserve withheld her from spreading the news, while her indifferent health prevented her coming to visit her future daughter-in-law; so that, altogether, this affair was kept far closer than such things usually are.

Rosalie would sometimes show her lover's epistles to me, to convince me what a kind, devoted husband he would make. She showed me the letters of another individual, too, the unfortunate Mr Green, who had not the courage, or, as she expressed it, the 'spunk', to plead his cause in person, but whom one denial would not satisfy: he must write again and again. He would not have done so if he could have seen the grimaces his fair idol made over his moving appeals to her feelings, and heard her scornful laughter, and the opprobrious epithets she heaped upon him for his perseverance.

'Why don't you tell him, at once, that you are engaged?' I asked.

'Oh, I don't want him to know that,' replied she. 'If he knew it, his sisters and everybody would know it, and then there would be an end of my – ahem! And, besides, if I told him that, he would think my engagement was the only obstacle, and that I would have him if I were free; which I could not bear that any man should think, and he, of all others, at least. Besides, I don't care for his letters,' she added contemptuously; 'he may write as often as he pleases, and look as great a calf as he likes when I meet him; it only amuses me.'

Meantime, young Meltham was pretty frequent in his visits to the house or transits past it; and, judging by Matilda's execrations and reproaches, her sister paid more attention to him than civility required: in other words, she carried on as animated a flirtation as the presence of her parents would admit. She made some attempts to bring Mr Hatfield once more to her feet; but finding them unsuccessful, she repaid his haughty indifference with still loftier scorn, and spoke of him with as much disdain and detestation as she had formerly done of his curate. But, amid all this, she never for a moment lost sight of Mr Weston. She embraced every opportunity of meeting him, tried every art to fascinate him, and pursued him with as much perseverance as if she really loved him and no other, and the happiness of her life depended upon eliciting a return of affection. Such conduct was completely beyond my comprehension. Had I seen

it depicted in a novel, I should have thought it unnatural; had I heard it described by others, I should have deemed it a mistake or an exaggeration; but when I saw it with my own eyes, and suffered from it too, I could only conclude that excessive vanity, like drunkenness, hardens the heart, enslaves the faculties, and perverts the feelings; and that dogs are not the only creatures which, when gorged to the throat, will yet gloat over what they cannot devour, and grudge the smallest morsel to a starving brother.

She now became extremely beneficent to the poor cottagers. Her acquaintance among them was more widely extended, her visits to their humble dwellings were more frequent and excursive than they had ever been before. Hereby, she earned among them the reputation of a condescending and very charitable young lady; and their encomiums were sure to be repeated to Mr Weston: whom also she had thus a daily chance of meeting in one or other of their abodes, or in her transits to and fro; and often, likewise, she could gather, through their gossip, to what places he was likely to go at such and such a time, whether to baptise a child, or to visit the aged, the sick, the sad, or the dying; and most skilfully she laid her plans accordingly. In these excursions she would sometimes go with her sister – whom, by some means, she had persuaded or bribed to enter into her schemes – sometimes alone, never, now, with me; so that I was debarred the pleasure of seeing Mr Weston, or hearing his voice even in conversation with another: which would certainly have been a very great pleasure, however hurtful or however fraught with pain. I could not even see him at church: for Miss Murray, under some trivial pretext, chose to take possession of that corner in the family pew which had been mine ever since I came; and, unless I had the presumption to station myself between Mr and Mrs Murray, I must sit with my back to the pulpit, which I accordingly did.

Now, also, I never walked home with my pupils: they said their mamma thought it did not look well to see three people out of the family walking, and only two going in the carriage; and, as they greatly preferred walking in fine weather, I should be honoured by going with the seniors. 'And, besides,' said they, 'you can't walk as fast as we do; you know you're always lagging behind.' I knew these were false excuses, but I made no objections, and never contradicted such assertions, well knowing the motives which dictated them. And in the afternoons, during those six memorable weeks, I never went to church at all. If I had a cold, or any slight indisposition, they took advantage of that to make me stay at home; and often they would tell me they were not going again that day, themselves, and then pretend to change their minds, and set off without telling me: so managing their departure that I never discovered the change of purpose till too late. Upon their return home, on one of these occasions, they entertained me with an animated account of a conversation they had had with Mr Weston as they came along. 'And he asked if you were ill, Miss Grey,' said Matilda; 'but we told him you were quite well, only you didn't want to come to church – so he'll think you're turned wicked.'

All chance meetings on weekdays were likewise carefully prevented; for, lest I should go to see poor Nancy Brown or any other person, Miss Murray took

good care to provide sufficient employment for all my leisure hours. There was always some drawing to finish, some music to copy, or some work to do, sufficient to incapacitate me from indulging in anything beyond a short walk about the grounds, however she or her sister might be occupied.

One morning, having sought and waylaid Mr Weston, they returned in high glee to give me an account of their interview. 'And he asked after you again,' said Matilda, in spite of her sister's silent but imperative intimation that she should hold her tongue. 'He wondered why you were never with us, and thought you must have delicate health, as you came out so seldom.'

'He didn't, Matilda – what nonsense you're talking!'

'Oh, Rosalie, what a lie! He did, you know; and you said – Don't Rosalie – hang it! – I won't be pinched so! And, Miss Grey, Rosalie told him you were quite well, but you were always so buried in your books that you had no pleasure in anything else!'

'What an idea he must have of me!' I thought.

'And,' I asked, 'does old Nancy ever enquire about me?'

'Yes; and we tell her you are so fond of reading and drawing that you can do nothing else.'

'That is not the case though; if you had told her I was so busy I *could* not come to see her, it would have been nearer the truth.'

'I don't think it would,' replied Miss Murray, suddenly kindling up; 'I'm sure you have plenty of time to yourself now, when you have so little teaching to do.'

It was no use beginning to dispute with such indulged, unreasoning creatures: so I held my peace. I was accustomed, now, to keeping silence when things distasteful to my ear were uttered; and now, too, I was used to wearing a placid smiling countenance when my heart was bitter within me. Only those who have felt the like can imagine my feelings, as I sat with an assumption of smiling indifference, listening to the accounts of those meetings and interviews with Mr Weston, which they seemed to find such pleasure in describing to me; and hearing things asserted of him which, from the character of the man, I knew to be exaggerations and perversions of the truth, if not entirely false – things derogatory to him, and flattering to them – especially to Miss Murray – which I burned to contradict, or, at least, to show my doubts about, but dared not; lest, in expressing my disbelief, I should display my interest too. Other things I heard, which I felt or feared were indeed too true: but I must still conceal my anxiety respecting him, my indignation against them, beneath a careless aspect; others, again, mere hints of something said or done, which I longed to hear more of, but could not venture to enquire. So passed the weary time, I could not even comfort myself with saying, 'She will soon be married; and then there may be hope.'

Soon after her marriage the holidays would come; and when I returned from home, most likely, Mr Weston would be gone, for I was told that he and the Rector could not agree (the Rector's fault, of course), and he was about to remove to another place.

No – besides my hope in God, my only consolation was in thinking that, though he knew it not, I was more worthy of his love than Rosalie Murray,

charming and engaging as she was; for I could appreciate his excellence, which she could not: I would devote my life to the promotion of his happiness; she would destroy his happiness for the momentary gratification of her own vanity. 'Oh, if he could but know the difference!' I would earnestly exclaim. 'But no! I would not have him see my heart: yet, if he could but know her hollowness, her worthless, heartless frivolity, he would then be safe, and I should be – *almost* happy, though I might never see him more!'

I fear, by this time, the reader is well-nigh disgusted with the folly and weakness I have so freely laid before him. I never disclosed it then, and would not have done so had my own sister or my mother been with me in the house. I was a close and resolute dissembler – in this one case at least. My prayers, my tears, my wishes, fears, and lamentations, were witnessed by myself and Heaven alone.

When we are harassed by sorrows or anxieties, or long oppressed by any powerful feelings which we must keep to ourselves, for which we can obtain and seek no sympathy from any living creature, and which yet we cannot, or will not wholly crush, we often naturally seek relief in poetry – and often find it, too – whether in the effusions of others, which seem to harmonise with our existing case, or in our own attempts to give utterance to those thoughts and feelings in strains less musical, perchance, but more appropriate, and therefore more penetrating and sympathetic, and, for the time, more soothing, or more powerful to rouse and to unburden the oppressed and swollen heart. Before this time, at Wellwood House and here, when suffering from homesick melancholy, I had sought relief twice or thrice at this secret source of consolation; and now I fly to it again, with greater avidity than ever, because I seemed to need it more. I still preserve those relics of past sufferings and experience, like pillars of witness set up in travelling through the vale of life, to mark particular occurrences. The footsteps are obliterated now; the face of the country may be changed; but the pillar is still there, to remind me how all things were when it was reared. Lest the reader should be curious to see any of these effusions, I will favour him with one short specimen: cold and languid as the lines may seem, it was almost a passion of grief to which they owed their being.

> Oh, they have robbed me of the hope
> My spirit held so dear;
> They will not let me hear that voice
> My soul delights to hear.
>
> They will not let me see that face
> I so delight to see;
> And they have taken all thy smiles,
> And all thy love from me.
>
> Well, let them seize on all they can;
> One treasure still is mine –
> A heart that loves to think on thee,
> And feels the worth of thine.

Yes, at least, they could not deprive me of that: I could think of him day and night; and I could feel that he was worthy to be thought of. Nobody knew him as I did; nobody could appreciate him as I did; nobody could love him as I – could, if I might: but there was the evil. What business had I to think so much of one that never thought of me? Was it not foolish? was it not wrong? Yet, if I found such deep delight in thinking of him, and if I kept those thoughts to myself, and troubled no one else with them where was the harm of it? I would ask myself. And such reasoning prevented me from making any sufficient effort to shake off my fetters.

But, if those thoughts brought delight, it was a painful, troubled pleasure, too near akin to anguish; and one that did me more injury than I was aware of. It was an indulgence that a person of more wisdom or more experience would doubtless have denied herself. And yet, how dreary to turn my eyes from the contemplation of that bright object and force them to dwell on the dull, grey, desolate prospect around: the joyless, hopeless, solitary path that lay before me. It was wrong to be so joyless, so desponding; I should have made God my friend, and to do His will the pleasure and the business of my life; but faith was weak, and passion was too strong.

In this time of trouble I had two other causes of affliction, The first may seem a trifle, but it cost me many a tear: Snap, my little dumb, rough-visaged, but bright-eyed, warm-hearted companion, the only thing I had to love me, was taken away, and delivered over to the tender mercies of the village rat-catcher, a man notorious for his brutal treatment of his canine slaves. The other was serious enough: my letters from home gave intimation that my father's health was worse. No boding fears were expressed, but I was grown timid and despondent, and could not help fearing that some dreadful calamity awaited us there. I seemed to see the black clouds gathering around my native hills, and to hear the angry muttering of a storm that was about to burst, and desolate our hearth.

## CHAPTER 18

### Mirth and Mourning

The 1st of June arrived at last: and Rosalie Murray was transmuted into Lady Ashby. Most splendidly beautiful she looked in her bridal costume. Upon her return from church, after the ceremony, she came flying into the schoolroom, flushed with excitement, and laughing, half in mirth, and half in reckless desperation, as it seemed to me.

'Now, Miss Grey, I'm Lady Ashby!' she exclaimed. 'It's done, my fate is sealed: there's no drawing back now. I'm come to receive your congratulations and bid you goodbye; and then I'm off for Paris, Rome, Naples, Switzerland, London oh dear! what a deal I shall see and hear before I come back again. But

don't forget me: I shan't forget you, though I've been a naughty girl. Come, why don't you congratulate me?'

'I cannot congratulate you,' I replied, 'till I know whether this change is really for the better: but I sincerely hope it is; and I wish you true happiness and the best of blessings.'

'Well, goodbye, the carriage is waiting, and they're calling me.'

She gave me a hasty kiss, and was hurrying away; but, suddenly returning, embraced me with more affection than I thought her capable of evincing, and departed with tears in her eyes. Poor girl! I really loved her then; and forgave her from my heart all the injury she had done me – and others also: she had not half-known it, I was sure; and I prayed God to pardon her too.

During the remainder of that day of festal sadness, I was left to my own devices. Being too much unhinged for any steady occupation, I wandered about with a book in my hand for several hours, more thinking than reading, for I had many things to think about. In the evening, I made use of my liberty to go and see my old friend Nancy once again; to apologise for my long absence (which must have seemed so neglectful and unkind) by telling her how busy I had been: and to talk, or read, or work for her, whichever might be most acceptable, and also, of course, to tell her the news of this important day: and perhaps to obtain a little information from her in return, respecting Mr Weston's expected departure. But of this she seemed to know nothing, and I hoped, as she did, that it was all a false report. She was very glad to see me; but, happily, her eyes were now so nearly well that she was almost independent of my services. She was deeply interested in the wedding; but while I amused her with the details of the festive day the splendours of the bridal party and of the bride herself, she often sighed and shook her head, and wished good might come of it; she seemed, like me, to regard it rather as a theme for sorrow than rejoicing. I sat a long time talking to her about that and other things – but *no one came*.

Shall I confess that I sometimes looked towards the door with a half-expectant wish to see it open and give entrance to Mr Weston, as had happened once before? and that, returning through the lanes and fields, I often paused to look round me, and walked more slowly than was at all necessary – for, though a fine evening, it was not a hot one – and, finally, felt a sense of emptiness and disappointment at having reached the house without meeting or even catching a distant glimpse of anyone, except a few labourers returning from their work?

Sunday, however, was approaching: I should see him then; for now that Miss Murray was gone, I could have my old corner again. I should see him, and by look, speech, and manner, I might judge whether the circumstance of her marriage had very much afflicted him. Happily, I could perceive no shadow of a difference: he wore the same aspect as he had worn two months ago – voice, look, manner, all alike unchanged: there was the same keen-sighted, unclouded truthfulness in his discourse, the same forcible clearness in his style, the same earnest simplicity in all he said and did, that made itself, not marked by the eye and ear, but felt upon the hearts of his audience.

I walked home with Miss Matilda; but *he did not join us*. Matilda was now sadly

at a loss for amusement, and woefully in want of a companion: her brothers at school, her sister married and gone, she too young to be admitted into society; for which, from Rosalie's example, she was in some degree beginning to acquire a taste – a taste at least for the company of certain classes of gentlemen; at this dull time of year – no hunting going on, no shooting even – for, though she might not join in that, it was *something* to see her father or the gamekeeper go out with the dogs, and to talk with them on their return, about the different birds they had bagged. Now, also, she was denied the solace which the companionship of the coachman, grooms, horses, greyhounds, and pointers might have afforded; for her mother having, notwithstanding the disadvantages of a country life, so satisfactorily disposed of her elder daughter, the pride of her heart had begun seriously to turn her attention to the younger; and, being truly alarmed at the roughness of her manners, and thinking it high time to work a reform, had been roused at length to exert her authority, and prohibited entirely the yards, stables, kennels, and coach-house. Of course, she was not implicitly obeyed; but, indulgent as she had hitherto been, when once her spirit was roused, her temper was not so gentle as she required that of her governesses to be, and her will was not to be thwarted with impunity. After many a scene of contention between mother and daughter, many a violent outbreak which I was ashamed to witness, in which the father's authority was often called in to confirm with oaths and threats the mother's slighted prohibitions – for even *he* could see that 'Tilly, though she would have made a fine lad, was not quite what a young lady ought to be' – Matilda at length found that her easiest plan was to keep clear of the forbidden regions; unless she could now and then steal a visit without her watchful mother's knowledge.

Amid all this, let it not be imagined that I escaped without many a reprimand, and many an implied reproach, that lost none of its sting from not being openly worded; but rather wounded the more deeply because, from that very reason, it seemed to preclude self-defence. Frequently, I was told to amuse Miss Matilda with other things, and to *remind* her of her mother's precepts and prohibitions. I did so to the best of my power: but she would not be amused against her will and could not against her taste; and though I went beyond mere reminding, such gentle remonstrances as I could use were utterly ineffectual.

'*Dear* Miss Grey! it is the *strangest* thing. I suppose you can't help it, if it's not in your nature – but I *wonder* you can't win the confidence of that girl, and make your society at *least* as agreeable to her as that of Robert or Joseph!'

'They can talk the best about the things in which she is most interested,' I replied.

'Well! that is a strange confession, *however*, to come from her *governess!* Who is to form a young lady's tastes, I wonder, if the governess doesn't do it? I *have* known governesses who have so completely identified themselves with the reputation of their young ladies for elegance and propriety in mind and manners, that they would *blush* to speak a word against them; and to hear the slightest blame imputed to their pupils was worse than to be censured in their own persons – and I really think it very natural, for my part.'

'Do you, ma'am?'

'Yes, of course: the young lady's proficiency and elegance is of more con-
sequence to the governess than her own, as well as to the world. If she wishes to
prosper in her vocation she must devote all her energies to her business: all her
ideas and all her ambition will tend to the accomplishment of that one object.
When we wish to decide upon the merits of a governess, we naturally look at
the young ladies she professes to have educated, and judge accordingly. The
*judicious* governess knows this: she knows that, while she lives in obscurity
herself, her pupil's virtues and defects will be open to every eye; and that, unless
she loses sight of herself in their cultivation, she need not hope for success. You
see, Miss Grey, it is just the same as any other trade or profession: they that wish
to prosper must devote themselves body and soul to their calling; and if they
begin to yield to indolence or self-indulgence they are speedily distanced by
wiser competitors: there is little to choose between a person that ruins her pupils
by neglect, and one that corrupts them by her example. You will excuse my
dropping these little hints: you know it is all for your own good. Many ladies
would speak to you much more strongly; and many would not trouble them-
selves to speak at all, but quietly look out for a substitute. That, of course, would
be the *easiest* plan: but I know the advantage of a place like this to a person in
your situation; and I have no desire to part with you, as I am sure you would do
very well if you will only think of these things and try to exert yourself a *little*
more: then, I am convinced, you would *soon* acquire that delicate tact which
alone is wanting to give you a proper influence over the mind of your pupil.'

I was about to give the lady some idea of the fallacy of her expectations; but
she sailed away as soon as she had concluded her speech. Having said what she
wished, it was not part of her plan to await my answer: it was my business to
hear, and not to speak.

However, as I have said, Matilda at length yielded in some degree to her
mother's authority (pity it had not been exerted before); and being thus deprived
of almost every source of amusement, there was nothing for it but to take long
rides with the groom and long walks with the governess, and to visit the cottages
and farmhouses on her father's estate, to kill time in chatting with the old men
and women that inhabited them. In one of these walks it was our chance to meet
Mr Weston. This was what I had long desired; but now, for a moment, I wished
either her or I were away: I felt my heart throb so violently that I dreaded lest
some outward signs of emotion should appear; but I think he hardly glanced at
me, and I was soon calm enough. After a brief salutation to both, he asked
Matilda if she had lately heard from her sister.

'Yes,' replied she. 'She was at Paris when she wrote, and very well and very
happy.'

She spoke the last word emphatically, and with a glance impertinently sly. He
did not seem to notice it, but replied, with equal emphasis, and very seriously –
'I hope she will continue to be so.'

'Do you think it likely?' I ventured to enquire: for Matilda had started off in
pursuit of her dog, that was chasing a leveret.

'I cannot tell,' replied he. 'Sir Thomas may be a better man than I suppose; but, from all I have heard and seen, it seems a pity that one so young and gay, and – and *interesting*, to express many things by one word – whose greatest, if not her only fault, appears to be thoughtlessness – no trifling fault to be sure, since it renders the possessor liable to almost every other, and exposes him to so many temptations: but it seems a pity that she should be thrown away on such a man. It was her mother's wish, I suppose?'

'Yes; and her own too, I think, for she always laughed at my attempts to dissuade her from the step.'

'You did attempt it? Then, at least, you will have the satisfaction of knowing that it is no fault of yours, if any harm should come of it. As for Mrs Murray, I don't know how she can justify her conduct: if I had sufficient acquaintance with her, I'd ask her.'

'It seems unnatural: but some people think rank and wealth the chief good; and, if they can secure that for their children, they think they have done their duty.'

'True: but is it not strange that persons of experience, who have been married themselves, should judge so falsely?'

Matilda now came panting back, with the lacerated body of the young hare in her hand.

'Was it your intention to kill that hare, or to save it, Miss Murray?' asked Mr Weston, apparently puzzled at her gleeful countenance.

'I pretended to want to save it,' she answered honestly enough, 'as it was so glaringly out of season; but I was better pleased to see it killed. However, you can both witness that I couldn't help it: Prince was determined to have her; and he clutched her by the back, and killed her in a minute! Wasn't it a noble chase?'

'Very! for a young lady after a leveret.'

There was a quiet sarcasm in the tone of his reply which was not lost upon her; she shrugged her shoulders, and, turning away with a significant 'Humph!' asked me how I had enjoyed the fun. I replied that I saw no fun in the matter; but admitted that I had not observed the transaction very narrowly.

'Didn't you see how it doubled – just like an old hare and didn't you hear it scream?'

'I'm happy to say I did not.'

'It cried out just like a child.'

'Poor little thing! What will you do with it?'

'Come along – I shall leave it in the first house we come to. I don't want to take it home, for fear papa should scold me for letting the dog kill it.'

Mr Weston was now gone, and we too went on our way; but as we returned, after having deposited the hare in a farmhouse, and demolished some spice-cake and currant wine in exchange, we met him returning also from the execution of his mission, whatever it might be. He carried in his hand a cluster of beautiful bluebells which he offered to me; observing, with a smile, that though he had seen so little of me for the last two months, he had not forgotten that bluebells were numbered among my favourite flowers. It was done as a simple act of

goodwill, without compliment or remarkable courtesy, or any look that could be construed into 'reverential, tender adoration' (*vide* Rosalie Murray); but still it was something to find my unimportant saying so well remembered: it was something that he had noticed so accurately the time I had ceased to be visible.

'I was told,' said he, 'that you were a perfect bookworm Miss Grey: so completely absorbed in your studies that you were lost to every other pleasure.'

'Yes, and it's quite true!' cried Matilda.

'No, Mr Weston; don't believe it: it's a scandalous libel. These young ladies are too fond of making random assertions at the expense of their friends; and you ought to be careful how you listen to them.'

'I hope *this* assertion is groundless, at any rate.'

'Why? Do you particularly object to ladies studying?'

'No; but I object to anyone so devoting himself or herself to study as to lose sight of everything else. Except under peculiar circumstances, I consider very close and constant study as a waste of time, and an injury to the mind as well as the body.'

'Well, I have neither the time nor the inclination for such transgressions.'

We parted again.

Well! what is there remarkable in all this? Why have I recorded it? Because, reader, it was important enough to give me a cheerful evening, a night of pleasing dreams and a morning of felicitous hopes. Shallow-brained cheerfulness, foolish dreams, unfounded hopes, you would say; and I will not venture to deny it: suspicions to that effect arose too frequently in my own mind. But our wishes are like tinder: the flint and steel of circumstances are continually striking our sparks, which vanish immediately, unless they chance to fall upon the tinder of our wishes; then, they instantly ignite, and the flame of hope is kindled in a moment.

But alas! that very morning, my flickering flame of hope was dismally quenched by a letter from my mother, which spoke so seriously of my father's increasing illness, that I feared there was little or no chance of his recovery; and, close at hand as the holidays were, I almost trembled lest they should come too late for me to meet him in this world. Two days after, a letter from Mary told me his life was despaired of, and his end seemed fast approaching. Then, immediately, I sought permission to anticipate the vacation, and go without delay. Mrs Murray stared, and wondered at the unwonted energy and boldness with which I urged the request, and thought there was no occasion to hurry; but finally gave me leave, stating, however, that there was 'no need to be in such agitation about the matter – it might prove a false alarm after all; and if not – why, it was only in the common course of nature: we must all die sometime; and I was not to suppose myself the only afflicted person in the world;' and concluding with saying I might have the phaeton to take me to O—. 'And instead of *repining*, Miss Grey, be thankful for the privileges you enjoy. There's many a poor clergyman whose family would be plunged into ruin by the event of his death; but *you*, you see, have influential friends ready to continue their patronage, and to show you every consideration.'

I thanked her for her 'consideration', and flew to my room to make some

hurried preparations for my departure. My bonnet and shawl being on, and a few things hastily crammed into my largest trunk, I descended. But I might have done the work more leisurely, for no one else was in a hurry; and I had still a considerable time to wait for the phaeton. At length it came to the door, and I was off: but, oh, what a dreary journey was that! how utterly different from my former passages homewards! Being too late for the last coach to —, I had to hire a cab for ten miles, and then a car to take me over the rugged hills. It was half-past ten before I reached home. They were not in bed.

My mother and sister both met me in the passage – sad – silent pale! I was so much shocked and terror-stricken that I could not speak, to ask the information I so much longed yet dreaded to obtain.

'Agnes!' said my mother, struggling to repress some strong emotion.

'Oh, Agnes!' cried Mary, and burst into tears.

'How is he?' I asked, gasping for the answer.

'Dead!'

It was the reply I had anticipated: but the shock seemed none the less tremendous.

## CHAPTER 19

### *The Letter*

My father's mortal remains had been consigned to the tomb; and we, with sad faces and sombre garments, sat lingering over the frugal breakfast-table, revolving plans for our future life. My mother's strong mind had not given way beneath even this affliction: her spirit, though crushed, was not broken. Mary's wish was that I should go back to Horton Lodge, and that our mother should come and live with her and Mr Richardson at the vicarage: she affirmed that he wished it no less than herself, and that such an arrangement could not fail to benefit all parties; for my mother's society and experience would be of inestimable value to them, and they would do all they could to make her happy. But no arguments or entreaties could prevail: my mother was determined not to go. Not that she questioned, for a moment, the kind wishes and intentions of her daughter; but she affirmed that so long as God spared her health and strength, she would make use of them to earn her own livelihood, and be chargeable to no one; whether her dependence would be felt as a burden or not. If she could afford to reside as a lodger in — vicarage, she would choose that house before all others as the place of her abode; but not being so circumstanced, she would never come under its roof, except as an occasional visitor: unless sickness or calamity should render her assistance really needful, or until age or infirmity made her incapable of maintaining herself.

'No, Mary,' said she, 'if Richardson and you have anything to spare, you must lay it aside for your family; and Agnes and I must gather honey for ourselves.

Thanks to my having had daughters to educate, I have not forgotten my accomplishments. God willing, I will check this vain repining,' she said, while the tears coursed one another down her cheeks in spite of her efforts; but she wiped them away, and resolutely shaking back her head, continued, 'I will exert myself and look out for a small house, commodiously situated in some populous but healthy district where we will take a few young ladies to board and educate – if we can get them – and as many day pupils as will come, or as we can manage to instruct. Your father's relations and old friends will be able to send us some pupils, or to assist us with their recommendations, no doubt: I shall not apply to my own. What say you to it, Agnes? will you be willing to leave your present situation and try?'

'Quite willing, mamma; and the money I have saved will do to furnish the house. It shall be taken from the bank directly.'

'When it is wanted: we must get the house, and settle all preliminaries first.'

Mary offered to lend the little she possessed; but my mother declined it, saying that we must begin on an economical plan; and she hoped that the whole or part of mine, added to what we could get by the sale of the furniture, and what little our dear papa had contrived to lay aside for her since the debts were paid, would be sufficient to last us till Christmas; when, it was hoped, something would accrue from our united labours. It was finally settled that this should be our plan; and that enquiries and preparations should immediately be set on foot; and while my mother busied herself with these, I should return to Horton Lodge at the close of my four weeks' vacation, and give notice for my final departure when things were in train for the speedy commencement of our school.

We were discussing these affairs on the morning I have mentioned, about a fortnight after my father's death, when a letter was brought in for my mother, on beholding which the colour mounted to her face – lately pale enough with anxious watchings and excessive sorrow. 'From my father!' murmured she, as she hastily tore off the cover. It was many years since she had heard from any of her own relations before. Naturally wondering what the letter might contain, I watched her countenance while she read it, and was somewhat surprised to see her bite her lip and knit her brows as if in anger. When she had done, she somewhat irreverently cast it on the table, saying with a scornful smile – 'Your grandpapa has been so kind as to write to me. He says he has no doubt that I have long repented of my "unfortunate marriage", and if I will only acknowledge this, and confess I was wrong in neglecting his advice, and that I have justly suffered for it, he will make a lady of me once again – if that be possible after my long degradation – and remember my girls in his will. Get my desk, Agnes, and send these things away: I will answer the letter directly. But first, as I may be depriving you both of a legacy, it is just that I should tell you what I mean to say. I shall say that he is mistaken in supposing that I can regret the birth of my daughters (who have been the pride of my life, and are likely to be the comfort of my old age), or the thirty years I have passed in the company of my best and dearest friend; that, had our misfortunes been three times as great as they were (unless they had been

of my bringing on), I should still the more rejoice to have shared them with your father, and administered what consolation I was able; and, had his sufferings in illness been ten times what they were, I could not regret having watched over and laboured to relieve them; that, if he married a richer wife, misfortunes and trials would no doubt have come upon him still; while I am egotist enough to imagine that no other woman could have cheered him through them so well: not that I am superior to the rest, but I was made for him, and he for me; and I can no more repent the hours, days, years of happiness we have spent together, and which neither could have had without the other, than I can the privilege of having been his nurse in sickness, and his comfort in affliction.

'Will this do, children? – or shall I say we are all very sorry for what has happened during the last thirty years, and my daughters wish they had never been born; but since they have had that misfortune, they will be thankful for any trifle their grandpapa will be kind enough to bestow?'

Of course, we both applauded our mother's resolution; Mary cleared away the breakfast things; I brought the desk; the letter was quickly written and despatched; and, from that day, we heard no more of our grandfather, till we saw his death announced in the newspaper a considerable time after – all his worldly possessions, of course, being left to our wealthy, unknown cousins.

## CHAPTER 20

### *The Farewell*

A House in A—, THE fashionable watering-place, was hired for our seminary; and a promise of two or three pupils was obtained to commence with. I returned to Horton Lodge about the middle of July, leaving my mother to conclude the bargain for the house, to obtain more pupils, to sell off the furniture of our old abode, and to fit out the new one.

We often pity the poor, because they have no leisure to mourn their departed relatives, and necessity obliges them to labour through their severest afflictions: but is not active employment the best remedy for overwhelming sorrow – the surest antidote for despair? It may be a rough comforter: it may seem hard to be harassed with the cares of life when we have no relish for its enjoyments; to be goaded to labour when the heart is ready to break, and the vexed spirit implores for rest only to weep in silence: but is not labour better than the rest we covet? and are not those petty, tormenting cares less hurtful than a continual brooding over the great affliction that oppresses us? Besides, we cannot have cares, and anxieties, and toil, without hope – if it be but the hope of fulfilling our joyless task, accomplishing some needful project, or escaping some further annoyance. At any rate, I was glad my mother had so much employment for every faculty of her action-loving frame. Our kind neighbours lamented that she, once so exalted in wealth and station, should be

reduced to such extremity in her time of sorrow; but I am persuaded that she would have suffered thrice as much had she been left in affluence, with liberty to remain in that house, the scene of her early happiness and late affliction, and no stern necessity to prevent her from incessantly brooding over and lamenting her bereavement.

I will not dilate upon the feelings with which I left the old house the well-known garden, the little village church – then doubly dear to me, because my father, who, for thirty years, had taught and prayed within its walls, lay slumbering now beneath its flags – and the old bare hills, delightful in their very desolation, with the narrow vales between, smiling in green wood and sparkling water – the house where I was born, the scene of all my early associations, the place where throughout life my earthly affections had been centred; and left them to return no more! True, I was going back to Horton Lodge, where, amid many evils, one source of pleasure yet remained; but it was pleasure mingled with excessive pain; and my stay, alas! was limited to six weeks. And even of that previous time, day after day slipped by and I did not see him: except at church, I never saw him for a fortnight after my return. It seemed a long time to me: and, as I was often out with my rambling pupil, of course hopes would keep rising, and disappointments would ensue; and, then, I would say to my own heart, 'Here is a convincing proof – if you would but have the sense to see it, or the candour to acknowledge it – that he does not care for you. If he only thought *half* as much about you as you do about him, he would have contrived to meet you many times ere this: you must know that, by consulting your own feelings. Therefore, have done with this nonsense: you have no ground for hope: dismiss, at once, these hurtful thoughts and foolish wishes from your mind and turn to your own duty, and the dull blank life that lies before you. You might have *known* such happiness was not for you.'

But I saw him at last. He came suddenly upon me as I was crossing a field in returning from a visit to Nancy Brown, which I had taken the opportunity of paying while Matilda Murray was riding her matchless mare. He must have heard of the heavy loss I had sustained: he expressed no sympathy, offered no condolence: but almost the first words he uttered were, 'How is your mother?' And this was no matter-of-course question, for I never told him that I *had* a mother: he must have learned the fact from others, if he knew it at all; and, besides, there was sincere goodwill, and even deep, touching, unobtrusive sympathy in the tone and manner of the enquiry. I thanked him with due civility, and told him she was as well as could be expected. 'What will she do?' was the next question. Many would have deemed it an impertinent one, and given an evasive reply; but such an idea never entered my head, and I gave a brief but plain statement of mother's plans and prospects.

'Then you will leave this place shortly?' said he.

'Yes, in a month.'

He paused a minute, as if in thought. When he spoke again, I hoped it would be to express his concern at my departure; but it was only to say – 'I should think you will be willing enough to go?'

'Yes – for some things,' I replied.

'For *some* things only – I wonder what should make you regret it!'

*I was* annoyed at this in some degree; because it embarrassed me: I had only one reason for regretting it; and that was a profound secret, which he had no business to trouble me about.

'Why,' said I – 'why should you suppose that I dislike the place?'

'You told me so yourself,' was the decisive reply. 'You said, at least, that you could not live contentedly, without a friend; and that you had no friend here, and no possibility of making one – and besides, I know you *must* dislike it.'

'But if you remember rightly, I said, or meant to say, I could not live contentedly without a friend in the *world*: I was not so unreasonable as to require one always near me. I think I could be happy in a house full of enemies, if –' but no; that sentence must not be continued – I paused, and hastily added – 'And besides, we cannot well leave a place where we have lived for two or three years, without some feeling of regret.'

'Will you regret to part with Miss Murray, your sole remaining pupil and companion?'

'I dare say I shall in some degree: it was not without sorrow I parted with her sister.'

'I can imagine that.'

'Well, Miss Matilda is quite as good – better, in one respect.'

'What is that?'

'She's honest.'

'And the other is not?'

'I should not call her dishonest; but it must be confessed, she's a little artful.'

'*Artful* is she? – I saw she was giddy and vain – and now,' he added after a pause, 'I can well believe she was artful too; but so excessively so as to assume an aspect of extreme simplicity and unguarded openness. Yes,' continued he, musingly, 'that accounts for some little things that puzzled me a trifle before.'

After that, he turned the conversation to more general subjects. He did not leave me till we had nearly reached the park gates: he had certainly stepped a little out of his way to accompany me so far, for he now went back and disappeared down Moss Lane, the entrance of which we had passed sometime before. Assuredly I did not regret this circumstance: if sorrow had any place in my heart, it was that he was gone at last – that he was no longer walking by my side, and that that short interval of delightful intercourse was at an end. He had not breathed a word of love, or dropped one hint of tenderness or affection, and yet I had been supremely happy. To be near him, to hear him talk as he did talk; and to feel that he thought me worthy to be spoken to – capable of understanding and duly appreciating such discourse – was enough.

'Yes, Edward Weston, I could indeed be happy in a house full of enemies, if I had but one friend, who truly, deeply, and faithfully loved me; and if that friend were you – though we might be far apart – seldom to hear from each other, still more seldom to meet – though toil, and trouble, and vexation might surround me still – it would be too much happiness for me to dream of! Yet

who can tell,' said I within myself, as I proceeded up the park, 'who can tell what this one month may bring forth? I have lived nearly three-and-twenty years, and I have suffered much, and tasted little pleasure yet: is it likely my life all through will be so clouded? is it possible that God may hear my prayers, disperse these gloomy shadows, and grant me some beams of heaven's s unshine yet? Will He entirely deny to me those blessings which are so freely given to others, who neither ask them nor acknowledge them when received? May I not still hope and trust?' I did hope and trust for a while: but, alas, alas! the time ebbed away: one week followed another, and, excepting one distant glimpse and two transient meetings – during which scarcely anything was said – while I was walking with Miss Matilda, I saw nothing of him: except, of course, at church.

And now, the last Sunday was come, and the last service. I was often on the point of melting into tears during the sermon – the last I was to hear from him: the best I should hear from anyone, I was well assured. It was over – the congregation were departing; and I must follow. I had then seen him, and heard his voice, too, probably for the last time. In the churchyard, Matilda was pounced upon by the two Misses Green. They had many enquiries to make about her sister, and I know not what besides. I only wished they would have done, that we might hasten back to Horton Lodge: I longed to seek the retirement of my own room or some sequestered nook in the grounds, that I might deliver myself up to my feelings – to weep my last farewell, and lament my false hopes and vain delusions. Only this once, and then adieu to fruitless dreaming – thenceforth, only sober, solid, sad reality should occupy my mind. But while I thus resolved, a low voice close beside me said – 'I suppose you are going this week, Miss Grey?' 'Yes,' I replied. I was very much startled; and had I been at all hysterically inclined, I certainly should have committed myself in some way then. Thank God, I was not.

'Well,' said Mr Weston, 'I want to bid you goodbye – it is not likely I shall see you again before you go.'

'Goodbye, Mr Weston,' I said. Oh, how I struggled to say it calmly! I gave him my hand. He retained it a few seconds in his.

'It is possible we may meet again,' said he; 'will it be of any consequence to you whether we do or not?'

'Yes, I should be very glad to see you again.'

*I could* say no less. He kindly pressed my hand, and went. Now, I was happy again – though more inclined to burst into tears than ever. If I had been forced to speak at that moment, a succession of sobs would have inevitably ensued; and as it was, I could not keep the water out of my eyes. I walked along with Miss Murray, turning aside my face, and neglecting to notice several successive remarks, till she bawled out that I was either deaf or stupid; and then (having recovered my self-possession), as one awakened from a fit of abstraction, I suddenly looked up and asked what she had been saying.

## *The School*

I left Horton Lodge, and went to join my mother in our new abode at A—. I found her well in health, resigned in spirit, and even cheerful, though subdued and sober, in her general demeanour. We had only three boarders and half a dozen day-pupils to commence with; but by due care and diligence we hoped ere long to increase the number of both.

I set myself with befitting energy to discharge the duties of this new mode of life. I call it new, for there was, indeed, a considerable difference between working with my mother in a school of our own, and working as a hireling among strangers, despised and trampled upon by old and young; and for the first few weeks I was by no means unhappy. 'It is possible we may meet again,' and 'will it be of any consequence to you whether we do or not?' – Those words still rang in my ear and rested on my heart: they were my secret solace and support. 'I shall see him again. He will come; or he will write.' No promise, in fact, was too bright or too extravagant for Hope to whisper in my ear. I did not believe half of what she told me: I pretended to laugh at it all; but I was far more credulous than I myself supposed; otherwise why did my heart leap up when a knock was heard at the front door, and the maid, who opened it, came to tell my mother a gentleman wished to see her? and why was I out of humour for the rest of the day because it proved to be a music-master come to offer his services to our school? and what stopped my breath for a moment, when the postman having brought a couple of letters, my mother said, 'Here, Agnes, this is for you,' and threw one of them to me? and what made the hot blood rush into my face when I saw it was directed in a gentleman's hand? and why – oh! why did that cold sickening sense of disappointment fall upon me, when I had torn open the cover and found it was *only* a letter from Mary, which, for some reason or other, her husband had directed for her?

Was it then come to this – that I should be *disappointed* to receive a letter from my only sister: and because it was not written by a comparative stranger? Dear Mary! and she had written it so kindly – and thinking I should be so pleased to have it! – I was not worthy to read it! And I believe, in my indignation against myself I should have put it aside till I had schooled myself into a better frame of mind, and was become more deserving of the honour and privilege of its perusal: but there was my mother looking on, and wishful to know what news it contained; so I read it and delivered it to her, and then went into the school-room to attend to the pupils; but amidst the cares of copies and sums – in the intervals of correcting errors here, and reproving derelictions of duty there, I was inwardly taking myself to task with far sterner severity. 'What a fool you must be,' said my head to my heart, or my sterner to my softer self; 'how could

you ever dream that he would write to you? What grounds have you for such a hope – or that he will see you, or give himself any trouble about you – or even think of you again?' 'What grounds?' – and then Hope set before me that last, short interview, and repeated the words I had so faithfully treasured in my memory. 'Well, and what was there in that? – Who ever hung his hopes upon so frail a twig? What was there in those words that any common acquaintance might not say to another? Of course, it was possible you might meet again: he might have said so if you had been going to New Zealand; but that did not imply any *intention* of seeing you – and then, as to the question that followed, anyone might ask that: and how did you answer? – Merely with a stupid, commonplace reply, such as you would have given to Master Murray, or anyone else you had been on tolerably civil terms with.' 'But, then,' persisted Hope, 'the tone and manner in which he spoke.' 'Oh, that is nonsense! he always speaks impressively; and at that moment there were the Greens and Miss Matilda Murray just before, and other people passing by, and he was obliged to stand close beside you, and to speak very low, unless he wished everybody to hear what he said; which – though it was nothing at all particular – of course, he would rather not.' But then, above all, that emphatic, yet gentle pressure of the hand, which seemed to say, '*Trust me*'; and many other things besides – too delightful, almost too flattering, to be repeated even to oneself. 'Egregious folly – too absurd to require contradiction – mere inventions of the imagination, which you ought to be ashamed of. If you would but consider your own unattractive exterior, your unamiable reserve, your foolish diffidence – which must make you appear cold, dull, awkward, and perhaps ill-tempered too; if you had but rightly considered these from the beginning, you would never have harboured such presumptuous thoughts: and now that you have been so foolish, pray repent and amend, and let us have no more of it!'

I cannot say that I implicitly obeyed my own injunctions: but such reasoning as this became more and more effective as time wore on, and nothing was seen or heard of Mr Weston, until at last, I gave up hoping, for even my heart acknowledged it was all it vain. But still, I would think of him: I would cherish his image in my mind; and treasure every word, look, and gesture that my memory could retain; and brood over his excellences and peculiarities, and, in fact, all I had seen, heard, or imagined respecting him.

'Agnes, this sea air and change of scene do *you* no good, I think: I never saw you look so wretched. It must be that you sit too much, and allow the cares of the schoolroom to worry you. You must learn to take things easy, and to be more active and cheerful; you must take exercise whenever you can get it, and leave the most tiresome duties to me: they will only serve to exercise my patience, and, perhaps, try my temper a little.'

So said my mother, as we sat at work one morning during the Easter holidays, I assured her that my employments were not at all oppressive; that I was well; or, if there was anything amiss, it would be gone as soon as the trying months of spring were over: when summer came I should be as strong and hearty as she could wish to see me: but inwardly her observation startles me. I knew my strength was declining, my appetite had failed, and I was grown listless

and desponding; and if, indeed, he could never care for me, and I could never see him more – if I was forbidden to minister to his happiness – forbidden, for ever, to taste the joys of love, to bless and to be blessed – then, life must be a burden, and if my Heavenly Father would call me away, I should be glad to rest. But it would not do to die and leave my mother. Selfish, unworthy daughter, to forget her for a moment! Was not her happiness committed in a great measure to my charge? – and the welfare of our young pupils too? Should I shrink from the work that God had set before me, because it was not fitted to my taste? Did not He know best what I should do, and where I ought to labour? and should I long to quit His service before I had finished my task, and expect to enter into His rest without having laboured to earn it? 'No; by His help I will arise and address myself diligently to my appointed duty. If happiness in this world is not for me, I will endeavour to promote the welfare of those around me, and my reward shall be hereafter.' So said I in my heart; and from that hour I only permitted my thoughts to wander to Edward Weston – or at least to dwell upon him now and then – as a treat for rare occasions: and, whether it was really the approach of summer, or the effect of these good resolutions, or the lapse of time, or all together, tranquillity of mind was soon restored; and bodily health and vigour began likewise, slowly, but surely, to return.

Early in June, I received a letter from Lady Ashby, late Miss Murray. She had written to me twice or thrice before, from the different stages of her bridal tour, always in good spirits, and professing to be very happy. I wondered every time that she had not forgotten me, in the midst of so much gaiety and variety of scene. At length, however, there was a pause; and it seemed she had forgotten me, for upwards of seven months passed away and no letter. Of course, I did not break my heart about *that*, though I often wondered how she was getting on; and when this last epistle so unexpectedly arrived, I was glad enough to receive it. It was dated from Ashby Park where she was come to settle down at last, having previously divided her time between the continent and the metropolis. She made many apologies for having neglected me so long, assured me she had not forgotten me, and had often intended to write, etc., etc., but had always been prevented by something. She acknowledged that she had been leading a very dissipated life, and I should think her very wicked and very thoughtless; but, notwithstanding that, she thought a great deal, and, among other things, that she should vastly like to see me.

We have been several days here already [wrote she]. We have not a single friend with us, and are likely to be very dull. You know I never had a fancy for living with my husband like two turtles in a nest, were he the most delightful creature that ever wore a coat; so do take pity upon me and come. I suppose your Midsummer holidays commence in June, the same as other people's, therefore you cannot plead want of time; and you must and shall come – in fact, I shall die if you don't. I want you to visit me as a friend, and stay a long time. There is nobody with me, as I told you before, but Sir Thomas and old Lady Ashby: but you needn't mind them – they'll trouble us but little with

their company. And you shall have a room to yourself, whenever you like to retire to it, and plenty of books to read when my company is not sufficiently amusing. I forget whether you like babies; if you do, you may have the pleasure of seeing mine – the most charming child in the world, no doubt; and all the more so, that I am not troubled with nursing it – I was determined I wouldn't be bothered with that. Unfortunately, it is a girl, and Sir Thomas has never forgiven me: but, however, if you will only come, I promise you shall be its governess as soon as it can speak; and you shall bring it up in the way it should go, and make a better woman of it than its mamma. And you shall see my poodle, too: a splendid little charmer imported from Paris: and two fine Italian paintings of great value – I forget the artist. Doubtless you will be able to discover prodigious beauties in them, which you must point out to me, as I only admire by hearsay; and many elegant curiosities besides, which I purchased at Rome and elsewhere; and, finally, you shall see my new home – the splendid house and grounds I used to covet so greatly. Alas! how far the promise of anticipation exceeds the pleasure of possession! There's a fine sentiment! I assure you I am become quite a grave old matron: pray come, if it be only to witness the wonderful change. Write by return of post, and tell me when your vacation commences, and say that you will come the day after, and stay till the day before it closes – in mercy to,

Yours affectionately,

ROSALIE ASHBY

I showed this strange epistle to my mother, and consulted her on what I ought to do. She advised me to go; and I went – willing enough to see Lady Ashby, and her baby too, and to do anything I could to benefit her, by consolation or advice; for I imagined she must be unhappy, or she would not have applied to me thus – but feeling, as may readily be conceived, that, in accepting the invitation, I made a great sacrifice for her, and did violence to my feelings in many ways, instead of being delighted with the honourable distinction of being entreated by the baronet's lady to visit her as a friend. However, I determined my visit should be only for a few days at most; and I will not deny that I derived some consolation from the idea that, as Ashby Park was not very far from Horton, I might possible see Mr Weston, or, at least, hear something about him.

## CHAPTER 22

### The Visit

Ashby Park was certainly a very delightful residence. The mansion was stately without, commodious and elegant within; the park was spacious and beautiful, chiefly on account of its magnificent old trees, its stately herds of deer, its broad sheet of water, and the ancient woods that stretched beyond it: for there was no

broken ground to give variety to the landscape, and but very little of that undulating swell which adds so greatly to the charm of park scenery. And so, this was the place Rosalie Murray had so longed to call her own, that she must have a share of it, on whatever terms it might be offered – whatever price was to be paid for the title of mistress, and whoever was to be her partner in the honour and bliss of such a possession! Well! I am not disposed to censure her now.

She received me very kindly; and, though I was a poor clergyman's daughter, a governess, and a schoolmistress, she welcomed me with unaffected pleasure to her home; and – what surprised me rather – took some pains to make my visit agreeable. I could see, it is true, that she expected me to be greatly struck with the magnificence that surrounded her; and, I confess, I was rather annoyed at her evident efforts to reassure me, and prevent me from being overwhelmed by so much grandeur – too much awed at the idea of encountering her husband and mother-in-law, or too much ashamed of my own humble appearance. I was not ashamed of it at all; for, though plain, I had taken good care not to be shabby or mean, and should have been pretty considerably at my ease, if my condescending hostess had not taken such manifest pains to make me so; and, as for the magnificence that surrounded her, nothing that met my eyes struck me or affected me half so much as her own altered appearance. Whether from the influence of fashionable dissipation, or some other evil, a space of little more than twelve months had had the effect that might be expected from as many years, in reducing the plumpness of her form, the freshness of her complexion, the vivacity of her movements, and the exuberance of her spirits.

I wished to know if she was unhappy; but I felt it was not my province to enquire: I might endeavour to win her confidence; but if she chose to conceal her matrimonial cares from me, I would trouble her with no obtrusive questions. I, therefore, at first, confined myself to a few general enquiries about her health and welfare, and a few commendations on the beauty of the park, and of the little girl that should have been a boy: a small delicate infant of seven or eight weeks old, whom its mother seemed to regard with no remarkable degree of interest or affection, though full as much as I expected her to show.

Shortly after my arrival, she commissioned her maid to conduct me to my room and see that I had everything I wanted: it was a small, unpretending, but sufficiently comfortable apartment. When I descended thence – having divested myself of all travelling encumberances, and arranged my toilet with due consideration for the feelings of my lady hostess – she conducted me herself to the room I was to occupy when I chose to be alone, or when she was engaged with visitors, or obliged to be with her mother-in-law, or otherwise prevented, as she said, from enjoying the pleasure of my society. It was a quiet, tidy little sitting-room; and I was not sorry to be provided with such a harbour of refuge.

'And sometime,' said she, 'I will show you the library: I never examined its shelves, but, I dare say, it is full of wise books; and you may go and burrow among them whenever you please. And now you shall have some tea – it will soon be dinner-time, but, I thought as you were accustomed to dine at one, you would perhaps like better to have a cup of tea about this time, and to dine when

we lunch; and then, you know, you can have your tea in this room, and that will save you from having to dine with Lady Ashby and Sir Thomas: which would be rather awkward – at least, not awkward but rather – a – you know what I mean. I thought you mightn't like it so well – especially as we may have other ladies and gentlemen to dine with us occasionally.'

'Certainly,' said I, 'I would much rather have it as you say; and, if you have no objection, I should prefer having all my meals in this room.'

'Why so?'

'Because, I imagine, it would be more agreeable to Lady Ashby and Sir Thomas.'

'Nothing of the kind.'

'At any rate, it would be more agreeable to me.'

She made some faint objections, but soon conceded; and I could see that the proposal was a considerable relief to her.

'Now, come into the drawing-room,' said she. 'There's the dressing-bell; but I won't go yet; it's no use dressing when there's no one to see you; and I want to have a little discourse.'

The drawing-room was certainly an imposing apartment, and very elegantly furnished; but I saw its young mistress glance towards me as we entered, as if to notice how I was impressed by the spectacle, and accordingly I determined to preserve an aspect of stony indifference, as if I saw nothing at all remarkable. But this was only for a moment: immediately conscience whispered, 'Why should I disappoint her to save my pride? No – rather let me sacrifice my pride to give her a little innocent gratification.' And I honestly looked round, and told her it was a noble room, and very tastefully furnished. She said little, but I saw she was pleased.

She showed me her fat French poodle, that lay curled up on a silk cushion, and the two fine Italian paintings: which, however she would not give me time to examine, but, saying I must look at them some other day, insisted upon my admiring the little jewelled watch she had purchased in Geneva; and then she took me round the room to point out sundry articles of *vertu* she had brought from Italy: an elegant little timepiece, and several busts, small graceful figures, and vases, all beautifully carved in white marble. She spoke of these with animation, and heard my admiring comments with a smile of pleasure: that soon, however, vanished, and was followed by a melancholy sigh; as if in consideration of the insufficiency of all such baubles to the happiness of the human heart, and their woeful inability to supply its insatiate demands.

Then, stretching herself upon a couch, she motioned me to a capacious easy chair that stood opposite – not before the fire, but before a wide open window; for it was summer, be it remembered; a sweet, warm evening in the latter half of June. I sat for a moment in silence, enjoying the still, pure air, and the delightful prospect of the park that lay before me, rich in verdure and foliage, and basking in yellow sunshine, relieved by the long shadows of declining day. But I must take advantage of this pause: I had enquiries to make, and, like the substance of a lady's postcript, the most important must come last. So I

began with asking after Mr and Mrs Murray, and Miss Matilda and the young gentlemen.

I was told that papa had the gout, which made him very ferocious; and that he would not give up his choice wines, and his substantial dinners and suppers, and had quarrelled with his physician, because the latter had dared to say that no medicine could cure him while he lived so freely; that mamma and the rest were well. Matilda was still wild and reckless, but she had got a fashionable governess, and was considerably improved in her manners, and soon to be introduced to the world; and John and Charles (now at home for the holidays) were, by all accounts 'fine, bold, unruly, mischievous boys.'

'And how are the other people getting on?' said I – 'the Greens, for instance?'

'Ah! Mr Green is heart-broken, you know,' replied she, with a languid smile: 'he hasn't got over his disappointment yet, and never will, I suppose. He's doomed to be an old bachelor; and his sisters are doing their best to get married.'

'And the Melthams?'

'Oh, they're jogging on as usual, I suppose: but I know very little about any of them – except Harry,' said she, blushing slightly, and smiling again. 'I saw a great deal of him while we were in London; for, as soon as he heard we were there, he came up under pretence of visiting his brother, and either followed me, like a shadow, wherever I went, or met me, like a reflection, at every turn. You needn't look so shocked, Miss Grey; I was very discreet, I assure you: but, you know, one can't help being admired. Poor fellow! He was not my only worshipper; though he was certainly the most conspicuous, and, I think, the most devoted among them all. And that detestable – ahem – and Sir Thomas chose to take offence at him – or my profuse expenditure, or something – I don't exactly know what – and hurried me down to the country at a moment's notice; where I'm to play the hermit, I suppose, for life.'

And she bit her lip, and frowned vindictively upon the fair domain she had once so coveted to call her own.

'And Mr Hatfield,' said I, 'what is become of him?'

Again she brightened up, and answered gaily, 'Oh! he made up to an elderly spinster, and married her, not long since; weighing her heavy purse against her faded charms, and expecting to find that solace in gold which was denied him in love, ha, ha!'

'Well, and I think that's all – except Mr Weston: what is he doing?'

'I don't know, I'm sure. He's gone from Horton.'

'How long since? and where is he gone to?'

'I know nothing about him,' replied she, yawning – 'except that he went about a month ago – I never asked where' (I would have asked whether it was to a living or merely another curacy, but thought it better not); 'and the people made a great rout about his leaving,' continued she, 'much to Mr Hatfield's displeasure; for Hatfield didn't like him, because he had too much influence with the common people, and because he was not sufficiently tractable and submissive to him – and for some other unpardonable sins, I don't know what.

But now I positively must go and dress: the second bell will ring directly, and if I come to dinner in this guise, I shall never hear the end of it from Lady Ashby. It's a strange thing one can't be mistress in one's own house! Just ring the bell and I'll send for my maid, and tell them to get you some tea. Only think of that intolerable woman – '

'Who your maid?'

'No; my mother-in-law – and my unfortunate mistake! Instead of letting her take herself off to some other house, as she offered to do when I married, I was fool enough to ask her to live here still, and direct the affairs of the house for me; because, in the first place, I hoped we should spend the greater part of the year in town, and in the second place, being so young and inexperienced, I was frightened at the idea of having a houseful of servants to manage, and dinners to order, and parties to entertain, and all the rest of it, and I thought she might assist me with her experience; never dreaming she would prove a usurper, a tyrant, an incubus, a spy and everything else that's detestable. I wish she was dead!'

She then turned to give her orders to the footman, who had been standing bolt upright within the door for the last half-minute, and had heard the latter part of her animadversions; and, of course, made his own reflections upon them, notwithstanding the inflexible, wooden countenance he thought proper to preserve in the drawing-room. On my remarking afterwards that he must have heard her, she replied, 'Oh, no matter! I never care about the footmen; they're mere automatons: it's nothing to them what their superiors say or do; they won't dare to repeat it; and as to what they think – if they presume to think at all – of course, nobody cares for that. It would be a pretty thing indeed, if we were to be tongue-tied by our servants!'

So saying, she ran off to make her hasty toilet, leaving me to pilot my way back to my sitting-room, where, in due time, I was served with a cup of tea. After that, I sat musing on Lady Ashby's past and present condition; and on what little information I had obtained respecting Mr Weston, and the small chance there was of ever seeing or hearing anything more of him throughout my quiet, drab-colour life: which, henceforth, seemed to offer no alternative between positive rainy days and days of dull grey clouds without downfall. At length, however, I began to weary of my thoughts, and to wish I knew where to find the library my hostess had spoken of; and to wonder whether I was to remain there doing nothing till bedtime.

As I was not rich enough to possess a watch, I could not tell how time was passing, except by observing the slowly lengthening shadows from the window; which presented a side view, including a corner of the park, a clump of trees, whose topmost branches had been colonised by an innumerable company of noisy rooks, and a high wall with a massive wooden gate: no doubt communicating with the stable yard, as a broad carriage road swept up to it from the park. The shadow of this wall soon took possession of the whole of the ground as far as I could see, forcing the golden sunlight to retreat inch by inch, and at last take refuge in the very tops of the trees. Ere long, even they were left in shadow – the

shadow of the distant hills, or of the earth itself; and, in sympathy for the busy citizens of the rookery, I regretted to see their habitation, so lately bathed in glorious light, reduced to the sombre, workaday hue of the lower world, or of my own world within. For a moment, such birds as soared above the rest might still receive the lustre on their wings, which imparted to their sable plumage the hue and brilliance of deep red gold; at last, that too departed. Twilight came stealing on; the rooks became more quiet; I became more weary, and wished I were going home tomorrow. At length it grew dark, and I was thinking of ringing for a candle, and betaking myself to bed, when my hostess appeared, with many apologies for having neglected me so long, and laying all the blame upon that 'nasty old woman,' as she called her mother-in-law.

'If I didn't sit with her in the drawing-room while Sir Thomas is taking his wine,' said she, 'she would never forgive me; and, then, if I leave the room the instant he comes – as I have done once or twice – it is an unpardonable offence against her dear Thomas. *She* never showed such disrespect to *her* husband; and as for affection, wives never think of that nowadays, she supposes: but things were different in *her* time – as if there was any good to be done by staying in the room, when he does nothing but grumble and scold when he's in a bad humour, talk disgusting nonsense when he's in a good one, and go to sleep on the sofa when he's too stupid for either; which is most frequently the case now, when he has nothing to do but to sot over his wine.'

'But could you not try to occupy his mind with something better; and engage him to give up such habits? I'm sure you have powers of persuasion, and qualifications for amusing a gentleman, which many ladies would be glad to possess.'

'And so you think I would lay myself out for his amusement! No; that's not *my* idea of a wife. It's the husband's part to please the wife, not hers to please him; and if he isn't satisfied with her as she is – and thankful to possess her too – he isn't worthy of her, that's all. And as for persuasion, I assure you I shan't trouble myself with that: I've enough to do to bear with him as he is, without attempting to work a reform. But I'm sorry I left you so long alone, Miss Grey. How have you passed the time?'

'Chiefly in watching the rooks.'

'Mercy, how dull you must have been! I really must show you the library; and you must ring for everything you want, just as you would in an inn, and make yourself comfortable. I have selfish reasons for wishing to make you happy, because I want you to stay with me, and not fulfil your horrid threat of running away in a day or two.'

'Well, don't let me keep you out of the drawing-room any longer tonight, for at present I am tired, and wish to go to bed.'

## CHAPTER 23

# *The Park*

I came down a little before eight, next morning, as I knew by the striking of a distant clock. There was no appearance of breakfast. I waited above an hour before it came, still vainly longing for access to the library; and, after that lonely repast was concluded, I waited again about an hour and a half in great suspense and discomfort, uncertain what to do. At length, Lady Ashby came to bid me good-morning. She informed me she had only just breakfasted, and now wanted me to take an early walk with her in the park. She asked how long I had been up, and on receiving my answer expressed the deepest regret, and again promised to show me the library. I suggested she had better do so at once, and then there would be no further trouble either with remembering or forgetting. She complied, on condition that I would not think of reading, or bothering with the books now; for she wanted to show me the gardens, and take a walk in the park with me, before it became too hot for enjoyment: which, indeed, was nearly the case already. Of course, I readily assented; and we took our walk accordingly.

As we were strolling in the park, talking of what my companion had seen and heard during her travelling experience, a gentleman on horseback rode up and passed us. As he turned, in passing, and stared me full in the face, I had a good opportunity of seeing what he was like. He was tall, thin, and wasted, with a slight stoop in the shoulders, a pale face, but somewhat blotchy, and disagreeably red about the eyelids, plain features, and a general appearance of languor and flatness, relieved by a sinister expression in the mouth and the dull, soulless eyes.

'I detest that man!' whispered Lady Ashby, with bitter emphasis, as he slowly trotted by.

'Who is it?' I asked, unwilling to suppose that she should so speak of her husband.

'Sir Thomas Ashby,' she replied, with dreary composure.

'And do you *detest* him, Miss Murray?' said I, for I was too much shocked to remember her name at the moment.

'Yes, I do, Miss Grey, and despise him too; and if you knew him you would not blame me.'

'But you knew what he was before you married him.'

'No; I only thought so: I did not half know him really. I know you warned me against it, and I wish I had listened to you: but it's too late to regret that now. And besides, mamma ought to have known better than either of us, and she never said anything against it – quite the contrary. And then I thought he adored me, and would let me have my own way: he did pretend to do so at first but now he does not care a bit about me. Yet I should not care for that: he might do as he

pleased, if I might only be free to amuse myself and to stay in London, or have a few friends down here: but *he will* do as he pleases, and I must be a prisoner and a slave. The moment he saw I could enjoy myself without him, and that others knew my value better than himself, the selfish wretch began to accuse me of coquetry and extravagance; and to abuse Harry Meltham, whose shoes he was not worthy to clean. And then, he must needs have me down in the country, to lead the life of a nun lest I should dishonour him or bring him to ruin; as if he had not been ten times worse every way, with his betting book, and his gaming table, and his opera girls, and his Lady This and Mrs That – yes, and his bottles of wine, and glasses of brandy and water too! Oh, I would give ten thousand worlds to be Miss Murray again! It is *too* bad to feel life, health, and beauty wasting away unfelt and unenjoyed, for such a brute as that!' exclaimed she, fairly bursting into tears in the bitterness of her vexation.

Of course, I pitied her exceedingly; as well for her false idea of happiness and disregard of duty, as for the wretched partner with whom her fate was linked. I said what I could to comfort her, and offered such counsels as I though she most required: advising her, first, by gentle reasoning, by kindness, example, and persuasion, to try to ameliorate her husband; and then, when she had done all she could, if she still found him incorrigible, to endeavour to abstract herself from him – to wrap herself up in her own integrity and trouble herself as little about him as possible. I exhorted her to seek consolation in doing her duty to God and man, to put her trust in Heaven, and solace herself with the care and nurture of her little daughter; assuring her she would be amply rewarded by witnessing its progress in strength and wisdom, and receiving its genuine affection.

'But I can't devote myself entirely to a child,' said she: 'it may die – which is not at all improbable.'

'But, with care, many a delicate infant has become a strong man or woman.'

'But it may grow so intolerably like its father that I shall hate it.'

'That is not likely; it is a little girl, and strongly resembles its mother.'

'No matter; I should like it better if it were a boy – only that its father will leave it no inheritance that he can possibly squander away. What pleasure can I have in seeing a girl grow up to eclipse me, and enjoy those pleasures that I am for ever debarred from? But supposing I could be so generous as to take delight in this, still it is *only* a child; and I can't centre all my hopes in a child: that is only one degree better than devoting oneself to a dog. And as for all the wisdom and goodness you have been trying to instil into me – that is all very right and proper I dare say, and if I were some twenty years older, I might fructify by it: but people must enjoy themselves when they are young; and if others won't let them – why, they must hate them for it!'

'The best way to enjoy yourself is to do what is right and hate nobody. The end of Religion is not to teach us how to die, but how to live; and the earlier you become wise and good, the more of happiness you secure. And now, Lady Ashby, I have one more piece of advice to offer you, which is, that you will not make an enemy of your mother-in-law. Don't get into the way of holding her at arm's length, and regarding her with jealous distrust. I never saw her, but I have

heard good as well as evil respecting her; and I imagine that, though cold and haughty in her general demeanour, and even exacting in her requirements, she has strong affections for those who can reach them; and, though so blindly attached to her son, she is not without good principles, or incapable of hearing reason. If you would but conciliate her a little, and adopt a friendly, open manner – and even confide your grievances to her – *real* grievances, such as you have a right to complain of – it is my firm belief that she would, in time, become your faithful friend, and a comfort and support to you, instead of the incubus you describe her.'

But I fear my advice had little effect upon the unfortunate young lady; and, finding I could render myself so little serviceable, my residence at Ashby Park became doubly painful. But still, I must stay out that day and the following one, as I had promised to do so: though, resisting all entreaties and inducements to prolong my visit further, I insisted upon departing the next morning; affirming that my mother would be lonely without me, and that she impatiently expected my return. Nevertheless, it was with a heavy heart that I bade adieu to poor Lady Ashby and left her in her princely home. It was no slight additional proof of her unhappiness, that she should so cling to the consolation of my presence, and earnestly desire the company of one whose general tastes and ideas were so little congenial to her own – whom she had completely forgotten in her hours of prosperity, and whose presence would be rather a nuisance than a pleasure, if she could but have half her heart's desire.

## CHAPTER 24

### The Sands

Our school was not situated in the heart of the town: on entering A— from the north-west there is a row of respectable-looking houses, on each side of the broad, white road, with narrow slips of garden-ground before them, Venetian blinds to the windows, and a flight of steps leading to each trim, brass-handled door. In one of the largest of these habitations dwelt my mother and I, with such young ladies as our friends and the public chose to commit to our charge. Consequently, we were a considerable distance from the sea, and divided from it by a labyrinth of streets and houses. But the sea was my delight; and I would often gladly pierce the town to obtain the pleasure of a walk beside it, whether with the pupils or alone with my mother during the vacations. It was delightful to me at all times and seasons, but especially in the wild commotion of a rough sea-breeze, and in the brilliant freshness of a summer morning.

I awoke early on the third morning after my return from Ashby Park – the sun was shining through the blind, and I thought how pleasant it would be to pass through the quiet town and take a solitary ramble on the sands while half the world was in bed. I was not long in forming the resolution, nor slow to act

upon it. Of course I would not disturb my mother, so I stole noiselessly downstairs, and quietly unfastened the door. I was dressed and out, when the church clock struck a quarter to six. There was a feeling of freshness and vigour in the very streets; and when I got free of the town, when my foot was on the sands and my face towards the broad, bright bay, no language can describe the effect of the deep, clear azure of the sky and ocean, the bright morning sunshine on the semicircular barrier of craggy cliffs surmounted by green swelling hills, and on the smooth wide sands, and the low rocks out at sea – looking, with their clothing of weeds and moss, like little grass-grown islands – and above all, on the brilliant, sparkling waves. And then, the unspeakable purity and freshness of the air! there was just enough heat to enhance the value of the breeze, and just enough wind to keep the whole sea in motion, to make the waves come bounding to the shore, foaming and sparkling, as if wild with glee. Nothing else was stirring – no living creature was visible besides myself. My footsteps were the first to press the firm, unbroken sands – nothing before had trampled them since last night's flowing tide had obliterated the deepest marks of yesterday, and left it fair and even, except where the subsiding water had left behind it the traces of dimpled pools, and little running streams.

Refreshed, delighted, invigorated, I walked along, forgetting all my cares, feeling as if I had wings to my feet, and could go at least forty miles without fatigue, and experiencing a sense of exhilaration to which I had been an entire stranger since the days of early youth. About half-past six, however, the grooms began to come down to air their masters' horses – first one, and then another till there were some dozen horses and five or six riders: but that need not trouble me, for they would not come as far as the low rocks which I was now approaching. When I had reached these, and walked over the moist, slippery seaweed (at the risk of floundering into one of the numerous pools of clear, salt water that lay between them), to a little mossy promontory with the sea splashing round it, I looked back again to see who next was stirring. Still, there were only the early grooms with their horses, and one gentleman with a little dark speck of a dog running before him, and one water-cart coming out of the town to get water for the baths. In another minute or two, the distant bathing machines would begin to move, and then the elderly gentlemen of regular habits, and sober Quaker ladies would be coming to take their salutary morning walks. But however interesting such a scene might be, I could not wait to witness it, for the sun and the sea so dazzled my eyes in that direction, that I could but afford one glance; and then I turned again to delight myself with the sight and the sound of the sea dashing against my promontory – with no prodigious force, for the swell was broken by the tangled seaweed and the unseen rocks beneath; otherwise I should soon have been deluged with spray. But the tide was coming in; the water was rising; the gulfs and lakes were filling; the straits were widening, it was time to seek some safer footing; so I walked, skipped, and stumbled back to the smooth, wide sands, and resolved to proceed to a certain bold projection in the cliffs, and then return.

Presently, I heard a snuffling sound behind me, and then a dog came frisking and wriggling at my feet. It was my own Snap – the little, dark, wire-haired

terrier! When I spoke his name, he leapt up in my face and yelled for joy. Almost as much delighted as himself, I caught the little creature in my arms, and kissed him repeatedly. But how came he to be there? He could not have dropped from the sky, or come all that way alone: it must be either his master, the rat-catcher, or somebody else that had brought him; so, repressing my extravagant caresses, and endeavouring to repress his likewise, I looked round, and beheld – Mr Weston!

'Your dog remembers you well, Miss Grey,' said he, warmly grasping the hand I offered him without clearly knowing what I was about. 'You rise early.'

'Not often so early as this,' I replied, with amazing composure, considering all the circumstances of the case.

'How far do you propose to extend your walk?'

'I was thinking of returning – it must be almost time, I think.'

He consulted his watch – a gold one now – and told me it was only five minutes past seven. 'But, doubtless, you have had a long enough walk,' said he, turning towards the town, to which I now proceeded leisurely to retrace my steps; and he walked beside me.

'In what part of the town do you live?' asked he. 'I never could discover.'

Never could discover? Had he endeavoured to do so then? I told him the place of our abode. He asked how we prospered in our affairs. I told him we were doing very well – that we had had a considerable addition to our pupils after the Christmas vacation, and expected a still further increase at the close of this.

'You must be an accomplished instructor,' he observed.

'No, it is my mother,' I replied. 'she manages things so well and is so active, and clever, and kind.'

'I should like to know your mother. Will you introduce me to her sometime, if I call?'

'Yes, willingly.'

'And will you allow me the privilege of an old friend, of looking in upon you now and then – '

'Yes, if – I suppose so.'

This was a very foolish answer, but the truth was, I considered that I had no right to invite anyone to my mother's house without her knowledge; and if I had said, 'yes, if mother does not object,' it would appear as if by his question I understood more than was expected; so, *supposing* she would not, I added, 'I suppose so'; but of course I should have said something more sensible and more polite, if I had had my wits about me. We continued our walk for a minute in silence; which, however, was shortly relieved (no small relief to me), by Mr Weston commenting upon the brightness of the morning and the beauty of the bay, and then upon the advantages A— possessed over many other fashionable places of resort.

'You don't ask what brings me to A—,' said he. 'You can't suppose I'm rich enough to come for my own pleasure.'

'I heard you had left Horton.'

'You didn't hear, then, that I had got the living of F— ?'

F— was a village about two miles distant from A—.

'No,' said I; 'we live so completely out of the world even here, that news seldom reaches me through any quarter, except through the medium of the — *Gazette*. But, I hope you like your new parish; and that I may congratulate you on the acquisition?'

'I expect to like my parish better a year or two hence, when I have worked certain reforms I have set my heart upon – or, at least, progressed some steps towards such an achievement. But you may congratulate me now; for I find it very agreeable to *have* a parish all to myself, with nobody to interfere with me – to thwart my plans or cripple my exertions: and besides, I have a respectable house in a rather pleasant neighbourhood, and three hundred pounds a year; and, in fact, I have nothing but solitude to complain of, and nothing but a companion to wish for.'

He looked at me as he concluded; and the flash of his dark eyes seemed to set my face on fire; greatly to my own discomfiture, for to evince confusion at such a juncture was intolerable. I made an effort, therefore, to remedy the evil, and disclaim all personal application of the remark by a hasty, ill-expressed reply, to the effect that, if he waited till he was well known in the neighbourhood, he might have numerous opportunities for supplying his want among the residents of F— and its vicinity, or the visitors of A—, if he required so ample a choice: not considering the compliment implied by such an assertion, till his answer made me aware of it.

'I am not so presumptuous as to believe that,' said he, 'though you tell it me; but if it were so, I am rather particular in my notions of a companion for life, and perhaps I might not find one to suit me among the ladies you mention.'

'If you require perfection, you never will.'

'I do not – I have no right to require it, as being so far from perfect myself.'

Here the conversation was interrupted by a water-cart lumbering past us, for we were now come to the busy part of the sands; and, for the next eight or ten minutes, between carts and horses, and asses and men, there was little room for social intercourse, till we had turned our backs upon the sea, and began to ascend the precipitous road leading into the town. Here my companion offered me his arm, which I accepted, though not with the intention of using it as a support.

'You don't often come on to the sands, I think,' said he, 'for I have walked there many times, both morning and evening, since I came, and never seen you till now; and several times, in passing through the town, too, I have looked about for your school – but I did not think of the — Road; and once or twice I made enquiries, but without obtaining the requisite information.'

When we had surmounted the acclivity, I was about to withdraw my arm from his, but by a slight tightening of the elbow was tacitly informed that such was not his will, and accordingly desisted. Discoursing on different subjects, we entered the town, and passed through several streets. I saw that he was going out of his way to accompany me, notwithstanding the long walk that was yet before him; and, fearing that he might be inconveniencing himself from motives of politeness, I observed, 'I fear I am taking you out of your way, Mr Weston – I believe the road to F— lies quite in another direction.'

'I'll leave you at the end of the next street,' said he.

'And when will you come to see mamma?'

'Tomorrow – God willing.'

The end of the next street was nearly the conclusion of my journey. He stopped there, however, bid me good-morning, and called Snap, who seemed a little doubtful whether to follow his old mistress or his new master, but trotted away upon being summoned by the latter.

'I won't offer to restore him to you, Miss Grey,' said Mr Weston, smiling, 'because I like him.'

'Oh, I don't want him,' replied I, 'now that he has a good master; I'm quite satisfied.'

'You take it for granted that I *am* a good one, then?'

The man and the dog departed, and I returned home, full of gratitude to Heaven for so much bliss, and praying that my hopes might not again be crushed.

CHAPTER 25

## *Conclusion*

'Well, Agnes, you must not take such long walks again before breakfast,' said my mother, observing that I drank an extra cup of coffee and ate nothing – pleading the heat of the weather, and the fatigue of my long walk as an excuse. I certainly did feel feverish, and tired too.

'You always do things by extremes: now, if you had taken a *short* walk every morning, and would continue to do so, it would do you good.'

'Well, mamma, I will.'

'But this is worse than lying in bed or bending over your books: you have quite put yourself into a fever.'

'I won't do it again,' said I.

I was racking my brains with thinking how to tell her about Mr Weston, for she must know he was coming tomorrow. However, I waited till the breakfast things were removed, and I was more calm and cool; and then, having sat down to my drawing, I began, 'I met an old friend on the sands today, mamma.'

'An old friend. Who could it be?'

'Two old friends, indeed. One was a dog;' and then I reminded her of Snap, whose history I had recounted before, and related the incident of his sudden appearance and remarkable recognition; 'and the other,' continued I, 'was Mr Weston, the curate of Horton.'

'Mr Weston! I never heard of him before.'

'Yes, you have: I've mentioned him several times, I believe: but you don't remember.'

'I've heard you speak of Mr Hatfield.'

'Mr Hatfield was the rector, and Mr Weston the curate: I used to mention

him sometimes in contradistinction to Mr Hatfield, as being a more efficient clergyman. However, he was on the sands this morning with the dog – he had bought it, I suppose, from the rat-catcher; and he knew me as well as it did – probably through its means: and I had a little conversation with him, in the course of which, as he asked about our school, I was led to say something about you and your good management; and he said he should like to know you, and asked if I would introduce him to you, if he should take the liberty of calling tomorrow; so I said I would. Was I right?'

'Of course. What kind of a man is he?'

'A very *respectable* man, I think: but you will see him tomorrow. He is the new vicar of F—, and as he has only been there a few weeks, I suppose he has made no friends yet, and wants a little society.'

The morrow came. What a fever of anxiety and expectation I was in from breakfast till noon – at which time he made his appearance! Having introduced him to my mother, I took my work to the window, and sat down to await the result of the interview. They got on extremely well together; greatly to my satisfaction, for I had felt very anxious about what my mother would think of him. He did not stay long that time: but when he rose to take leave, she said she should be happy to see him, whenever he might find it convenient to call again; and when he was gone, I was gratified by hearing her say, 'Well! I think he's a very sensible man. But why did you sit back there, Agnes,' she added, 'and talk so little?'

'Because you talked so well, mamma, I thought you required no assistance from me: and, besides, he was your visitor, not mine.'

After that, he often called upon us – several times in the course of a week. He generally addressed most of his conversation to my mother: and no wonder, for she *could* converse. I almost envied the unfettered, vigorous fluency of her discourse, and the strong sense evinced by everything she said – and yet, I did not; for, though I occasionally regretted my own deficiencies for his sake, it gave me very great pleasure to sit and hear the two beings I loved and honoured above everyone else in the world, discoursing together so amicably, so wisely, and so well. I was not always silent, however; nor was I at all neglected. I was quite as much noticed as I would wish to be: there was no lack of kind words and kinder looks, no end of delicate attentions, too fine and subtle to be grasped by words, and therefore indescribable – but deeply felt at heart.

Ceremony was quickly dropped between us: Mr Weston came as an expected guest, welcome at all times, and never deranging the economy of our household affairs. He even called me 'Agnes': the name had been timidly spoken at first, but, finding it gave no offence in any quarter, he seemed greatly to prefer that appellation to 'Miss Grey'; and so did I. How tedious and gloomy were those days in which he did not come! And yet not miserable; for I had still the remembrance of the last visit and the hope of the next to cheer me. But when two or three days passed without my seeing him, I certainly felt very anxious – absurdly, unreasonably, so; for, of course, he had his own business and the affairs of his parish to attend to. And I dreaded the close of the holidays, when my business also would begin, and I should be sometimes unable to see him, and

sometimes – when my mother was in the schoolroom – obliged to be with him alone: a position I did not at all desire, in the house; though to meet him out of doors, and walk beside him, had proved by no means disagreeable.

One evening, however, in the last week of the vacation, he arrived – unexpectedly; for a heavy and protracted thundershower during the afternoon had almost destroyed my hopes of seeing him that day; but now the storm was over, and the sun was shining brightly.

'A beautiful evening, Mrs Grey!' said he, as he entered. 'Agnes, I want you to take a walk with me to – ' (he named a certain part of the coast – a bold hill on the land side, and towards the sea a steep precipice, from the summit of which a glorious view is to be had). 'The rain has laid the dust, and cooled and cleared the air, and the prospect will be magnificent. Will you come?'

'Can I go, mamma?'

'Yes; to be sure.'

I went to get ready and was down again in a few minutes; though, of course, I took a little more pains with my attire than if I had merely been going out on some shopping expedition alone. The thunder-shower had certainly had a most beneficial effect upon the weather, and the evening was most delightful. Mr Weston would have me to take his arm: he said little during our passage through the crowded streets, but walked very fast, and appeared grave and abstracted. I wondered what was the matter and felt an indefinite dread that something unpleasant was on his mind; and vague surmises, concerning what it might be, troubled me not a little, and made me grave and silent enough. But these fantasies vanished upon reaching the quiet outskirts of the town; for as soon as we came within sight of the venerable old church, and the hill, with the deep, blue sea beyond it, I found my companion was cheerful enough.

'I'm afraid I've been walking too fast for you, Agnes,' said he; 'in my impatience to be rid of the town, I forgot to consult your convenience; but now, we'll walk as slowly as you please. I see, by those light clouds in the west, there will be a brilliant sunset, and we shall be in time to witness its effect upon the sea, at the most moderate rate of progression.'

When we had got about halfway up the hill, we fell into silence which as usual, he was the first to break.

'My house is desolate yet, Miss Grey,' he smilingly observed 'and I am acquainted now with all the ladies in my parish, and several in this town too; and many others I know by sight and by report; but not one of them will suit me for a companion: in fact there is only one person in the world that will; and that is yourself and I want to know your decision?'

'Are you in earnest, Mr Weston?'

'In earnest! How could you think I should jest on such a subject?'

He laid his hand on mine that rested on his arm: he must have felt it tremble – but it was no great matter now.

'I hope I have not been too precipitate,' he said, in a serious tone. 'You must have known that it was not my way to flatter and talk soft nonsense, or even to speak the admiration that I felt; and that a single word or glance of mine meant

more than the honeyed phrases and fervent protestations of most other men.'

I said something about not liking to leave my mother, and doing nothing without her consent.

'I settled everything with Mrs Grey, while you were putting on your bonnet,' replied he. 'She said I might have her consent, if I could obtain yours; and I asked her, in case I should be so happy, to come and live with us – for I was sure you would like it better. But she refused, saying she could now afford to employ an assistant; and would continue the school till she could purchase an annuity sufficient to maintain her in comfortable lodgings; and, meantime she would spend her vacations alternately with us and your sister, and should be quite contented if you were happy. And so now I have overruled your objections on her account. Have you any other?'

'No – none.'

'You love me then?' said he, fervently pressing my hand.

'Yes.'

\*        \*        \*

Here I pause, My diary, from which I have compiled these pages, goes but little further. I could go on for years; but I will content myself with adding that I shall never forget that glorious summer evening, and always remember with delight that steep hill, and the edge of the precipice where we stood together watching the splendid sunset mirrored in the restless world of waters at our feet – with hearts filled with gratitude to Heaven, and happiness and love – almost too full for speech.

A few weeks after that, when my mother had supplied herself with an assistant, I became the wife of Edward Weston; and never have found cause to repent it, and am certain that I never shall. We have had trials, and we know that we must have them again; but we bear them well together, and endeavour to fortify ourselves and each other against the final separation – that greatest of all afflictions to the survivor. But, if we keep in mind the glorious heaven beyond, where both may meet again, and sin and sorrow are unknown, surely that too may be borne: and, meantime, we endeavour to live to the glory of Him who has scattered so many blessings in our path.

Edward, by his strenuous exertions, has worked surprising reforms in his parish, and is esteemed and loved by its inhabitants – as he deserves; for whatever his faults may be as a man (and no one is entirely without), I defy anybody to blame him as a pastor, a husband, or a father.

Our children, Edward, Agnes, and little Mary, promise well; their education, for the time being, is chiefly committed to me; and they shall want no good thing that a mother's care can give. Our modest income is amply sufficient for our requirements: and by practising the economy we learnt in harder times, and never attempting to imitate our richer neighbours, we manage not only to enjoy comfort and contentment ourselves, but to have every year something to lay by for our children, and something to give to those who need it.

And now I think I have said sufficient.

# THE TENANT OF WILDFELL HALL

# The Tenant of Wildfell Hall

ANNE BRONTË

# Contents

## Preface to the Second Edition

While I acknowledge the success of the present work to have been greater than I anticipated, and the praises it has elicited from a few kind critics to have been greater than it deserved, I must also admit that from some other quarters it has been censured with an asperity which I was as little prepared to expect, and which my judgement, as well as my feelings, assures me is more bitter than just. It is scarcely the province of an author to refute the arguments of his censors and vindicate his own productions, but I may be allowed to make here a few observations with which I would have prefaced the first edition had I foreseen the necessity of such precautions against the misapprehensions of those who would read it with a prejudiced mind or be content to judge it by a hasty glance.

My object in writing the following pages, was not simply to amuse the Reader, neither was it to gratify my own taste, nor yet to ingratiate myself with the Press and the Public: I wished to tell the truth, for truth always conveys its own moral to those who are able to receive it. But as the priceless treasure too frequently hides at the bottom of a well, it needs some courage to dive for it, especially as he that does so will be likely to incur more scorn and obloquy for the mud and water into which he has ventured to plunge than thanks for the jewel he procures; as, in like manner, she who undertakes the cleansing of a careless bachelor's apartment will be liable to more abuse for the dust she raises than commendation for the clearance she effects. Let it not be imagined, however, that I consider myself competent to reform the errors and abuses of society, but only that I would fain contribute my humble quota towards so good an aim, and if I can gain the public ear at all, I would rather whisper a few wholesome truths therein than much soft nonsense.

As the story of 'Agnes Grey' was accused of extravagant over-colouring in those very parts that were carefully copied from the life, with a most scrupulous avoidance of all exaggeration, so, in the present work, I find myself censured for depicting *con amore*, with 'a morbid love of the coarse, if not of the brutal', those scenes which, I will venture to say, have not been more painful for the most fastidious of my critics to read than they were for me to describe. I may have gone too far, in which case I shall be careful not to trouble myself or my readers in the same way again; but when we have to do with vice and vicious characters, I maintain it is better to depict them as they really are than as they would wish to appear. To represent a bad thing in its least offensive light is doubtless the most agreeable course for a writer of fiction to pursue; but is it the most honest, or the safest? Is it better to reveal the snares and pitfalls of life to the young and thoughtless traveller, or to cover them with branches and flowers? O Reader! if there were less of this delicate concealment of facts – this whispering 'Peace, peace,' when there is no peace, there would be less of sin

and misery to the young of both sexes who are left to wring their bitter knowledge from experience.

I would not be understood to suppose that the proceedings of the unhappy scapegrace with his few profligate companions I have here introduced are a specimen of the common practices of society: the case is an extreme one, as I trusted none would fail to perceive; but I know that such characters do exist, and if I have warned one rash youth from following in their steps, or prevented one thoughtless girl from falling into the very natural error of my heroine, the book has not been written in vain. But, at the same time, if any honest reader shall have derived more pain than pleasure from its perusal, and have closed the last volume with a disagreeable impression on his mind, I humbly crave his pardon, for such was far from my intention; and I will endeavour to do better another time, for I love to give innocent pleasure. Yet, be it understood, I shall not limit my ambition to this – or even to producing 'a perfect work of art': time and talents so spent, I should consider wasted and misapplied. Such humble talents as God has given me I will endeavour to put to their greatest use; if I am able to amuse I will try to benefit too; and when I feel it my duty to speak an unpalatable truth, with the help of God, I *will* speak it, though it be to the prejudice of my name and to the detriment of my reader's immediate pleasure as well as my own.

One word more, and I have done. Respecting the author's identity, I would have it to be distinctly understood that Acton Bell is neither Currer nor Ellis Bell, and therefore, let not his faults be attributed to them. As to whether the name be real or fictitious, it cannot greatly signify to those who know him only by his works. As little, I should think, can it matter whether the writer so designated is a man, or a woman as one or two of my critics profess to have discovered. I take the imputation in good part, as a compliment to the just delineation of my female characters; and though I am bound to attribute much of the severity of my censors to this suspicion, I make no effort to refute it, because, in my own mind, I am satisfied that if a book is a good one, it is so whatever the sex of the author may be. All novels are or should be written for both men and women to read, and I am at a loss to conceive how a man should permit himself to write anything that would be really disgraceful to a woman, or why a woman should be censured for writing anything that would be proper and becoming for a man.

ANNE BRONTË
July 22nd, 1848

## *To J. Halford, Esq.*

DEAR HALFORD – When we were together last, you gave me a very particular and interesting account of the most remarkable occurrences of your early life, previous to our acquaintance; and then you requested a return of confidence from me. Not being in a story-telling humour at the time, I declined, under the plea of having nothing to tell, and the like shuffling excuses, which were regarded as wholly inadmissible by you; for though you instantly turned the conversation, it was with the air of an uncomplaining, but deeply injured man, and your face was overshadowed with a cloud which darkened it to the end of our interview, and, for what I know, darkens it still; for your letters have, ever since, been distinguished by a certain dignified, semi-melancholy stiffness and reserve, that would have been very affecting, if my conscience had accused me of deserving it.

Are you not ashamed, old boy – at your age, and when we have known each other so intimately and so long, and when I have already given you so many proofs of frankness and confidence, and never resented your comparative closeness and taciturnity? But there it is, I suppose; you are not naturally communicative, and you thought you had done great things, and given an unparalleled proof of friendly confidence on that memorable occasion – which, doubtless, you have sworn shall be the last of the kind – and you deemed that the smallest return I could make for so mighty a favour, would be to follow your example without a moment's hesitation.

Well! – I did not take up my pen to reproach you, nor to defend myself, nor to apologise for past offences, but, if possible, to atone for them.

It is a soaking, rainy day, the family are absent on a visit, I am alone in my library and have been looking over certain musty old letters and papers and musing on past times; so that I am now in a very proper frame of mind for amusing you with an old-world story; and, having withdrawn my well-roasted feet from the hobs, wheeled round to the table and indited the above lines to my crusty old friend, I am about to give him a sketch – no not a sketch, a full and faithful account of certain circumstances connected with the most important event of my life – previous to my acquaintance with Jack Halford at least; and when you have read it, charge me with ingratitude and unfriendly reserve if you can.

I know you like a long story, and are as great a stickler for particularities and circumstantial details as my grandmother, so I will not spare you: my own patience and leisure shall be my only limits.

Among the letters and papers I spoke of, there is a certain faded old journal of mine, which I mention by way of assurance that I have not my memory alone – tenacious as it is – to depend upon, in order that your credulity may not be too severely taxed in following me through the minute details of my narrative. To begin then, at once, with Chapter 1 – for it shall be a tale of many chapters.

**CHAPTER I**

## A Discovery

You must go back with me to the autumn of 1827.

My father, as you know, was a sort of gentleman farmer in —shire; and I, by his express desire, succeeded him in the same quiet occupation, not very willingly, for ambition urged me to higher aims, and self-conceit assured me that, in disregarding its voice, I was burying my talent in the earth, and hiding my light under a bushel. My mother had done her utmost to persuade me that I was capable of great achievements; but my father, who thought ambition was the surest road to ruin, and change but another word for destruction, would listen to no scheme for bettering either my own condition, or that of my fellow mortals. He assured me it was all rubbish, and exhorted me, with his dying breath, to continue in the good old way, to follow his steps, and those of his father before him, and let my highest ambition be, to walk honestly through the world, looking neither to the right hand nor to the left, and to transmit the paternal acres to my children in, at least, as flourishing a condition as he left them to me.

'Well! – an honest and industrious farmer is one of the most useful members of society; and if I devote my talents to the cultivation of my farm, and the improvement of agriculture in general, I shall thereby benefit, not only my own immediate connections and dependants, but in some degree, mankind at large – hence I shall not have lived in vain.'

With such reflections as these, I was endeavouring to console myself, as I plodded home from the fields, one cold, damp, cloudy evening towards the close of October. But the gleam of a bright red fire through the parlour window, had more effect in cheering my spirits, and rebuking my thankless repinings, than all the sage reflections and good resolutions I had forced my mind to frame; for I was young then, remember – only four and twenty – and had not acquired half the rule over my own spirit, that I now possess – trifling as that may be.

However, that haven of bliss must not be entered till I had exchanged my miry boots, for a clean pair of shoes, and my rough surtout for a respectable coat, and made myself generally presentable before decent society; for my mother, with all her kindness, was vastly particular on certain points.

In ascending to my room, I was met upon the stairs by a smart, pretty girl of nineteen, with a tidy, dumpy figure, a round face, bright, blooming cheeks, glossy, clustering curls, and little merry brown eyes. I need not tell you this was my sister Rose. She is, I know, a comely matron still, and, doubtless, no less lovely – in *your* eyes – than on the happy day you first beheld her. Nothing told me then, that she, a few years hence, would be the wife of one – entirely unknown to me as yet, but destined hereafter to become a closer friend than even herself, more intimate than that unmannerly lad of seventeen, by whom I

was collared in the passage, on coming down, and wellnigh jerked off my equilibrium, and who, in correction for his impudence, received a resounding whack over the sconce, which, however, sustained no serious injury from the infliction; as besides being more than commonly thick, it was protected by a redundant shock of short, reddish curls, that my mother called auburne.

On entering the parlour, we found that honoured lady seated in her armchair at the fireside, working away at her knitting, according to her usual custom, when she had nothing else to do. She had swept the hearth, and made a bright blazing fire for our reception; the servant had just brought in the tea-tray; and Rose was producing the sugar-basin and tea-caddy, from the cupboard in the black, oak sideboard, that shone like polished ebony, in the cheerful parlour twilight.

'Well! here they both are,' cried my mother, looking round upon us without retarding the motion of her nimble fingers, and glittering needles. 'Now shut the door, and come to the fire, while Rose gets the tea ready; I'm sure you must be starved; and tell me what you've been about all day; I like to know what my children have been about.'

'I've been breaking in the grey colt – no easy business that – directing the ploughing of the last wheat stubble – for the ploughboy has not the sense to direct himself – and carrying out a plan for the extensive and efficient draining of the low meadow-lands.'

'That's my brave boy! – and Fergus – what have you been doing?'

'Badger-baiting.'

And here he proceeded to give a particular account of his sport, and the respective traits of prowess evinced by the badger and the dogs; my mother pretending to listen with deep attention, and watching his animated countenance with a degree of maternal admiration I thought highly disproportioned to its object.

'It's time you should be doing something else, Fergus,' said I, as soon as a momentary pause in his narration, allowed me to get in a word.

'What *can* I do?' replied he, 'my mother won't let me go to sea or enter the army; and I'm determined to do nothing else – except make myself such a nuisance to you all, that you will be thankful to get rid of me, on any terms.'

Our parent soothingly stroked his stiff, short curls. He growled, and tried to look sulky, and then, we all took our seats at the table, in obedience to the thrice repeated summons of Rose.

'Now take your tea,' said she; 'and I'll tell you what *I've* been doing. I've been to call on the Wilsons; and it's a *thousand* pities you didn't go with me, Gilbert, for Eliza Millward was there!'

'Well! what of her?'

'Oh nothing! – I'm not going to tell you about her; only that she's a nice, amusing little thing, when she is in a merry humour, and I shouldn't mind calling her –'

'Hush, hush, my dear! your brother has no such idea!' whispered my mother earnestly, holding up her finger.

'Well,' resumed Rose; 'I was going to tell you an important piece of news I heard there – I've been bursting with it ever since. You know it was reported a month ago, that somebody was going to take Wildfell Hall – and – what do you think? It has actually been inhabited above a week! – and we never knew!'

'Impossible!' cried my mother.

'Preposterous!!!' shrieked Fergus.

'It has indeed! – and by a single lady!'

'Good gracious, my dear! The place is in ruins!'

'She has had two or three rooms made habitable; and there she lives, all alone – except an old woman for a servant!'

'Oh dear! that spoils it – I'd hoped she was a witch,' observed Fergus, while carving his inch-thick slice of bread and butter.

'Nonsense, Fergus! But isn't it strange mamma?'

'Strange! I can hardly believe it.'

'But you may believe it; for Jane Wilson has seen her. She went with her mother, who, of course, when she heard of a stranger being in the neighbourhood, would be on pins and needles till she had seen her and got all she could out of her. She is called Mrs Graham, and she is in mourning – not widow's weeds, but slightish mourning – and she is quite young, they say – not above five or six and twenty – but *so* reserved! They tried all they could to find out who she was, and where she came from, and all about her, but neither Mrs Wilson, with her pertinacious and impertinent home thrusts, nor Miss Wilson, with her skilful manoeuvring, could manage to elicit a single satisfactory answer, or even a casual remark, or chance expression calculated to allay their curiosity, or throw the faintest ray of light upon her history, circumstances, or connections. Moreover, she was barely civil to them, and evidently better pleased to say "goodbye", than "how do you do". But Eliza Millward says her father intends to call upon her soon, to offer some pastoral advice, which he fears she needs, as though she is known to have entered the neighbourhood early last week she did not make her appearance at church on Sunday; and she – Eliza, that is – will beg to accompany him, and is sure *she* can succeed in wheedling something out of her – you know, Gilbert, *she* can do anything. And *we* should call sometime, mamma; it's only proper, you know.'

'Of course, my dear. Poor thing! how lonely she must feel!'

'And pray, be quick about it; and mind you bring me word how much sugar she puts in her tea, and what sort of caps and aprons she wears, and all about it; for I don't know how I can live till I know,' said Fergus, very gravely.

But if he intended the speech to be hailed as a master-stroke of wit, he signally failed, for nobody laughed. However, he was not much disconcerted at that; for when he had taken a mouthful of bread and butter, and was about to swallow a gulp of tea, the humour of the thing burst upon him with such irresistible force, that he was obliged to jump up from the table, and rush snorting and choking from the room; and a minute after, was heard screaming in fearful agony in the garden.

As for me, I was hungry, and contented myself with silently demolishing the

tea, ham, and toast, while my mother and sister went on talking, and continued to discuss the apparent, or nonapparent circumstances, and probable or improbable history of the mysterious lady; but I must confess that, after my brother's misadventure, I once or twice, raised the cup to my lips, and put it down again without daring to taste the contents, lest I should injure my dignity by a similar explosion.

The next day, my mother and Rose hastened to pay their compliments to the fair recluse; and came back but little wiser than they went; though my mother declared she did not regret the journey, for if she had not gained much good, she flattered herself she had imparted some, and that was better: she had given some useful advice, which, she hoped, would not be thrown away; for Mrs Graham, though she said little to any purpose, and appeared somewhat self-opinionated, seemed not incapable of reflection – though she did not know where she had been all her life, poor thing, for she betrayed a lamentable ignorance on certain points, and had not even the sense to be ashamed of it.

'On what points, mother?' asked I.

'On household matters, and all the little niceties of cookery, and such things, that every lady ought to be familiar with, whether she be required to make a practical use of her knowledge or not. I gave her some useful pieces of information, however, and several excellent receipts, the value of which, she evidently could not appreciate, for she begged I would not trouble myself, as she lived in such a plain, quiet way, that she was sure she should never make use of them. "No matter, my dear," said I; "it is what every respectable female ought to know; and besides, though you are alone now, you will not be always so; you *have* been married, and probably – I might say almost certainly – will be again." "You are mistaken there, ma'am," said she, almost haughtily; "I am certain I never shall." – But I told her *I* knew better.'

'Some romantic young widow, I suppose,' said I, 'come there to end her days in solitude, and mourn in secret for the dear departed – but it won't last long.'

'No, I think not,' observed Rose; 'for she didn't seem *very* disconsolate after all; and she's excessively pretty – handsome rather – you must see her Gilbert; you will call her a perfect beauty, though you could hardly pretend to discover a resemblance between her and Eliza Millward.'

'Well, I can imagine many faces more beautiful than Eliza's, though not more charming. I allow she has small claims to perfection; but then, I maintain that, if she were more perfect, she would be less interesting.'

'And so you prefer her faults to other people's perfections?'

'Just so – saving my mother's presence.'

'Oh, my dear Gilbert, what nonsense you talk! – I know you don't mean it; it's quite out of the question,' said my mother, getting up, and bustling out of the room, under pretence of household business, in order to escape the contradiction that was trembling on my tongue.

After that, Rose favoured me with further particulars respecting Mrs Graham. Her appearance, manners, and dress, and the very furniture of the room she inhabited, were all set before me, with rather more clearness and

precision than I cared to see them; but, as I was not a very attentive listener, I could not repeat the description if I would.

The next day was Saturday; and, on Sunday, everybody wondered whether or not the fair unknown would profit by the vicar's remonstrance, and come to church. I confess, I looked with some interest myself towards the old family pew, appertaining to Wildfell Hall, where the faded crimson cushions and lining had been unpressed and unrenewed so many years, and the grim escutcheons, with their lugubrious borders of rusty black cloth, frowned so sternly from the wall above.

And there I beheld a tall, ladylike figure, clad in black. Her face was towards me, and there was something in it, which, once seen, invited me to look again. Her hair was raven black, and disposed in long glossy ringlets, a style of coiffure, rather unusual in those days, but always graceful and becoming; her complexion was clear and pale; her eyes I could not see, for being bent upon her prayer-book they were concealed by their drooping lids and long black lashes, but the brows above were expressive and well defined, the forehead was lofty and intellectual, the nose, a perfect aquiline, and the features in general, unexceptionable – only there was a slight hollowness about the cheeks and eyes and the lips, though finely formed, were a little too thin, a little too firmly compressed, and had something about them that betokened, I thought, no very soft or amiable temper; and I said in my heart – 'I would rather admire you from this distance, fair lady, than be the partner of your home.'

Just then, she happened to raise her eyes, and they met mine; I did not choose to withdraw my gaze, and she turned again to her book, but with a momentary, indefinable expression of quiet scorn, that was inexpressibly provoking to me.

'She thinks me an impudent puppy,' thought I. 'Humph! – she shall change her mind before long, if I think it worth while.'

But then, it flashed upon me that these were very improper thoughts for a place of worship, and that my behaviour, on the present occasion, was anything but what it ought to be. Previous, however, to directing my mind to the service, I glanced round the church to see if anyone had been observing me; but no – all, who were not attending to their prayer-books, were attending to the strange lady – my good mother and sister among the rest, and Mrs Wilson and her daughter; and even Eliza Millward was slyly glancing from the corners of her eyes towards the object of general attraction. Then, she glanced at me, simpered a little, and blushed – modestly looked at her prayer-book, and endeavoured to compose her features.

Here I was transgressing again; and this time I was made sensible of it by a sudden dig in the ribs, from the elbow of my pert brother. For the present, I could only resent the insult by pressing my foot upon his toes, deferring further vengeance till we got out of church.

Now, Halford, before I close this letter, I'll tell you who Eliza Millward was: she was the vicar's younger daughter, and a very engaging little creature, for whom I felt no small degree of partiality; and she knew it, though I had never come to any direct explanation, and had no definite intention of so doing, for my

mother, who maintained there was no one good enough for me, within twenty miles round, could not bear the thoughts of my marrying that insignificant, little thing, who, in addition to her numerous other disqualifications, had not twenty pounds to call her own. Eliza's figure was at once slight and plump, her face small, and nearly as round as my sister's – complexion, something similar to hers, but more delicate and less decidedly blooming – nose, *retroussé* – features, generally irregular; and, altogether, she was rather charming than pretty. But her eyes – I must not forget those remarkable features, for therein her chief attraction lay – in outward aspect at least; they were long and narrow in shape, the irids black, or very dark brown, the expression various, and ever changing, but always either preternaturally – I had almost said *diabolically* – wicked, or irresistibly bewitching – often both. Her voice was gentle and childish, her tread light and soft as that of a cat; but her manners more frequently resembled those of a pretty, playful kitten, that is now pert and roguish, now timid and demure, according to its own sweet will.

Her sister, Mary, was several years older, several inches taller, and of a larger, coarser build – a plain, quiet, sensible girl, who had patiently nursed their mother, through her last long, tedious illness, and been the housekeeper, and family drudge, from thence to the present time. She was trusted and valued by her father, loved and courted by all dogs, cats, children, and poor people, and slighted and neglected by everybody else.

The Reverend Michael Millward, himself was a tall, ponderous, elderly gentleman, who placed a shovel hat above his large, square, massive-featured face, carried a stout walking stick in his hand, and incased his still powerful limbs in knee breeches and gaiters – or black silk stockings on state occasions. He was a man of fixed principles, strong prejudices, and regular habits – intolerant of dissent in any shape, acting under a firm conviction that *his* opinions were always right, and whoever differed from them, must be, either most deplorably ignorant, or wilfully blind.

In childhood, I had always been accustomed to regard him with a feeling of reverential awe – but lately, even now, surmounted, for, though he had a fatherly kindness for the well-behaved, he was a strict disciplinarian, and had often sternly reproved our juvenile failings and peccadillos; and moreover, in those days whenever he called upon our parents, we had to stand up before him, and say our catechism, or repeat 'How doth the little busy bee', or some other hymn, or – worse than all – be questioned about his last text and the heads of the discourse, which we never could remember. Sometimes, the worthy gentleman would reprove my mother for being over indulgent to her sons, with a reference to old Eli, or David and Absalom, which was particularly galling to her feelings; and, very highly as she respected him, and all his sayings, I once heard her exclaim, 'I wish to goodness he had a son himself! He wouldn't be so ready with his advice to other people then; he'd see what it *is* to have a couple of boys to keep in order.'

He had a laudable care for his own bodily health – kept very early hours, regularly took a walk before breakfast, was vastly particular about warm and

dry clothing, had never been known to preach a sermon without previously swallowing a raw egg – albeit he was gifted with good lungs and a powerful voice – and was, generally, extremely particular about what he eat and drank, though by no means abstemious, and having a mode of dietary peculiar to himself – being a great despiser of tea and such slops, and a patron of malt liquors, bacon and eggs, ham, hung beef, and other strong meats, which agreed well enough with his digestive organs, and therefore were maintained by him to be good and wholesome for everybody, and confidently recommended to the most delicate convalescents or dyspeptics, who, if they failed to derive the promised benefit from his prescriptions, were told it was because they had not persevered, and if they complained of inconvenient results therefrom, were assured it was all fancy.

I will just touch upon two other persons whom I have mentioned, and then bring this long letter to a close. These are Mrs Wilson and her daughter. The former was the widow of a substantial farmer, a narrow-minded, tattling old gossip, whose character is not worth describing. She had two sons, Robert, a rough countrified farmer, and Richard, a retiring, studious young man, who was studying the classics with the vicar's assistance, preparing for college, with a view to enter the church.

Their sister Jane was a young lady of some talents and more ambition. She had at her own desire, received a regular boarding-school education, superior to what any member of the family had obtained before. She had taken the polish well, acquired considerable elegance of manners, quite lost her provincial accent, and could boast of more accomplishments than the vicar's daughters. She was considered a beauty besides; but never for a moment could she number me amongst her admirers. She was about six and twenty, rather tall and very slender, her hair was neither chesnut nor auburne, but a most decided, bright, light red, her complexion was remarkably fair and brilliant, her head small, neck long, chin well turned, but very short, lips thin and red, eyes clear hazel, quick and penetrating, but entirely destitute of poetry or feeling. She had, or might have had many suitors in her own rank of life, but scornfully repulsed or rejected them all; for none but a gentleman could please her refined taste, and none but a rich one could satisfy her soaring ambition. One gentleman there was, from whom she had lately received some rather pointed attentions, and upon whose heart, name, and fortune, it was whispered, she had serious designs. This was Mr Lawrence, the young squire whose family had formerly occupied Wildfell Hall, but had deserted it, some fifteen years ago, for a more modern and commodious mansion in the neighbouring parish.

Now Halford, I bid you adieu for the present. This is the first instalment of my debt. If the coin suits you, tell me so, and I'll send you the rest at my leisure: if you would rather remain my creditor than stuff your purse with such ungainly heavy pieces – tell me still, and I'll pardon your bad taste, and willingly keep the treasure to myself.

Yours immutably,

GILBERT MARKHAM

## CHAPTER 2

## *An Interview*

I perceive, with joy, my most valued friend, that the cloud of your displeasure has past away; the light of your countenance blesses me once more, and you desire the continuation of my story: therefore, without more ado, you shall have it.

I think the day I last mentioned, was a certain Sunday, the latest in the October of 1827. On the following Tuesday I was out with my dog and gun, in pursuit of such game as I could find within the territory of Linden-car; but finding none at all, I turned my arms against the hawks and carrion crows, whose depredations, as I suspected, had deprived me of better prey. To this end, I left the more frequented regions, the wooded valleys, the cornfields, and the meadow lands, and proceeded to mount the steep acclivity of Wildfell, the wildest and the loftiest eminence in our neighbourhood, where, as you ascend, the hedges, as well as the trees, become scanty and stunted, the former, at length, giving place to rough stone fences, partly greened over with ivy and moss, the latter to larches and Scotch fir trees or isolated black thorns. The fields, being rough and stony and wholly unfit for the plough, were mostly devoted to the pasturing of sheep and cattle; the soil was thin and poor: bits of grey rock here and there peeped out from the grassy hillocks; bilberry plants and heather – relics of more savage wildness – grew under the walls; and in many of the enclosures, ragweeds and rushes usurped supremacy over the scanty herbage – but these were not *my* property.

Near the top of this hill, about two miles from Linden-car, stood Wildfell Hall, a superannuated mansion of the Elizabethan era built of dark grey stone – venerable and picturesque to look at, but, doubtless, cold and gloomy enough to inhabit, with its thick stone mullions and little latticed panes, its time-eaten air-holes, and its too lonely, too unsheltered situation – only shielded from the war of wind and weather by a group of Scotch firs, themselves half blighted with storms, and looking as stern and gloomy as the Hall itself. Behind it lay a few desolate fields, and then, the brown, heath-clad summit of the hill; before it (enclosed by stone walls, and entered by an iron gate with large balls of grey granite – similar to those which decorated the roof and gables – surmounting the gateposts), was a garden – once, stocked with such hardy plants and flowers as could best brook the soil and climate, and such trees and shrubs as could best endure the gardener's torturing shears, and most readily assume the shapes he chose to give them – now, having been left so many years, untilled and untrimmed, abandoned to the weeds and the grass, to the frost and the wind, the rain and the drought, it presented a very singular appearance indeed. The close green walls of privet, that had bordered the principal walk, were two-thirds withered away, and the rest grown beyond all reasonable bounds; the old

boxwood swan, that sat beside the scraper, had lost its neck and half its body; the castellated towers of laurel in the middle of the garden, the gigantic warrior that stood on one side of the gateway, and the lion that guarded the other, were sprouted into such fantastic shapes as resembled nothing either in heaven or earth, or in the waters under the earth; but, to my young imagination, they presented all of them a goblinish appearance, that harmonised well with the ghostly legends and dark traditions our old nurse had told us respecting the haunted hall and its departed occupants.

I had succeeded in killing a hawk and two crows when I came within sight of the mansion; and then, relinquishing further depredations, I sauntered on, to have a look at the old place, and see what changes had been wrought in it by its new inhabitant. I did not like to go quite to the front and stare in at the gate; but I paused beside the garden wall, and looked, and saw no change – except in one wing where the broken windows and dilapidated roof had evidently been repaired, and where a thin wreath of smoke was curling up from the stack of chimneys.

While I thus stood, leaning on my gun, and looking up at the dark gables, sunk in an idle reverie, weaving a tissue of wayward fancies, in which old associations and the fair young hermit, now within those walls, bore a nearly equal part, I heard a slight rustling and scrambling just within the garden; and, glancing in the direction whence the sound proceeded, I beheld a tiny hand elevated above the wall: it clung to the topmost stone, and then another little hand was raised to take a firmer hold, and then appeared a small white forehead, surmounted with wreaths of light brown hair, with a pair of deep blue eyes beneath, and the upper portion of a diminutive ivory nose.

The eyes did not notice me, but sparkled with glee on beholding Sancho, my beautiful black and white setter, that was coursing about the field with its muzzle to the ground. The little creature raised its face and called aloud to the dog. The good-natured animal paused, looked up, and wagged his tail, but made no further advances. The child (a little boy, apparently about five years old) scrambled up to the top of the wall and called again and again; but finding this of no avail, apparently made up his mind, like Muhammad, to go to the mountain since the mountain would not come to him, and attempted to get over; but a crabbed old cherry tree, that grew hard by, caught him by the frock in one of its crooked scraggy arms that stretched over the wall. In attempting to disengage himself, his foot slipped, and down he tumbled – but not to the earth – the tree still kept him suspended. There was a silent struggle, and then a piercing shriek – but, in an instant, I had dropped my gun on the grass, and caught the little fellow in my arms.

I wiped his eyes with his frock, told him he was all right, and called Sancho to pacify him. He was just putting his little hand on the dog's neck and beginning to smile through his tears, when I heard, behind me, a click of the iron gate and a rustle of female garments, and lo! Mrs Graham darted upon me – her neck uncovered, her black locks streaming in the wind.

'Give me the child!' she said in a voice scarce louder than a whisper, but with a

tone of startling vehemence, and, seizing the boy, she snatched him from me, as if some dire contamination were in my touch, and then stood with one hand firmly clasping his, the other on his shoulder, fixing upon me her large, luminous, dark eyes – pale, breathless, quivering with agitation.

'I was not harming the child, madam,' said I, scarce knowing whether to be most astonished or displeased, 'he was tumbling off the wall there; and I was so fortunate as to catch him, while he hung suspended headlong from that tree, and prevent I know not what catastrophe.'

'I beg your pardon, sir,' stammered she; suddenly calming down – the light of reason seeming to break upon her beclouded spirit and a faint blush mantling on her cheek – 'I did not know you; and I thought' – She stooped to kiss the child, and fondly clasped her arm round his neck.

'You thought I was going to kidnap your son, I suppose?'

She stroked his head with a half-embarrassed laugh, and replied – 'I did not know he had attempted to climb the wall. I have the pleasure of addressing Mr Markham, I believe?' she added somewhat abruptly.

I bowed, but ventured to ask how she knew me.

'Your sister called here, a few days ago, with Mrs Markham.'

'Is the resemblance so strong then?' I asked in some surprise, and not so greatly flattered at the idea as I ought to have been.

'There is a likeness about the eyes and complexion I think,' replied she, somewhat dubiously surveying my face; 'and I think I saw you at church on Sunday.'

I smiled. There was something either in that smile or the recollections it awakened that was particularly displeasing to her, for she suddenly assumed again that proud, chilly look that had so unspeakably roused my corruption at church – a look of repellent scorn, so easily assumed, and so entirely without the least distortion of a single feature that, while there, it seemed like the natural expression of the face, and was the more provoking to me, because I could not think it affected.

'Good-morning, Mr Markham,' said she; and without another word or glance, she withdrew with her child into the garden; and I returned home, angry and dissatisfied – I could scarcely tell you why – and therefore will not attempt it.

I only stayed to put away my gun and powder-horn, and give some requisite directions to one of the farming-men, and then repaired to the vicarage, to solace my spirit and soothe my ruffled temper with the company and conversation of Eliza Millward.

I found her, as usual, busy with some piece of soft embroidery (the mania for Berlin wools had not yet commenced), while her sister was seated at the chimney-corner, with the cat on her knee, mending a heap of stockings.

'Mary – Mary! put them away!' Eliza was hastily saying just as I entered the room.

'Not I, indeed!' was the phlegmatic reply; and my appearance prevented further discussion.

'You're *so* unfortunate, Mr Markham!' observed the younger sister, with one

of her arch, sidelong glances. 'Papa's just gone out into the parish, and not likely to be back for an hour!'

'Never mind; I can manage to spend a few minutes with his daughters, if they'll allow me,' said I, bringing a chair to the fire, and seating myself therein, without waiting to be asked.

'Well, if you'll be very good and amusing, we shan't object.'

'Let your permission be unconditional, pray; for I came not to give pleasure, but to seek it,' I answered.

However, I thought it but reasonable to make some slight exertion to render my company agreeable; and what little effort I made, was apparently pretty successful, for Miss Eliza was never in a better humour. We seemed, indeed, to be mutually pleased with each other, and managed to maintain between us a cheerful and animated, though not very profound conversation. It was little better than a tête-à-tête, for Miss Millward never opened her lips, except occasionally to correct some random assertion or exaggerated expression of her sister's, and once to ask her to pick up the ball of cotton, that had rolled under the table. I did this myself, however, as in duty bound.

'Thank you, Mr Markham,' said she, as I presented it to her. 'I would have picked it up myself; only I did not want to disturb the cat.'

'Mary, dear, *that* won't excuse you in Mr Markham's eyes,' said Eliza; 'he hates cats, I dare say, as cordially as he does old maids – like all other gentlemen – don't you Mr Markham?'

'I believe it is natural for our unamiable sex, to dislike the creatures,' replied I; 'for you ladies lavish so many caresses upon them.'

'Bless them – little darlings!' cried she, in a sudden burst of enthusiasm, turning round and overwhelming her sister's pet with a shower of kisses.

'Don't Eliza!' said Miss Millward, somewhat gruffly as she impatiently pushed her away.

But it was time for me to be going: make what haste I would, I should still be too late for tea; and my mother was the soul of order and punctuality.

My fair friend was evidently unwilling to bid me adieu. I tenderly squeezed her little hand at parting; and she repaid me with one of her softest smiles and most bewitching glances. I went home very happy, with a heart brimful of complacency for myself, and overflowing with love for Eliza.

## CHAPTER 3

### A Controversy

Two days after, Mrs Graham called at Linden-car, contrary to the expectation of Rose, who entertained an idea that the mysterious occupant of Wildfell Hall would wholly disregard the common observances of civilised life – in which opinion she was supported by the Wilsons, who testified that neither their call

nor the Millwards' had been returned as yet. Now however, the cause of that omission was explained, though not entirely to the satisfaction of Rose. Mrs Graham had brought her child with her, and on my mother's expressing surprise that he could walk so far, she replied, 'It is a long walk for him; but I must have either taken him with me, or relinquished the visit altogether: for I never leave him alone; and I think, Mrs Markham, I must beg you to make my excuses to the Millwards and Mrs Wilson, when you see them, as I fear I cannot do myself the pleasure of calling upon them till my little Arthur is able to accompany me.'

'But you have a servant,' said Rose; 'could you not leave him with her?'

'She has her own occupations to attend to; and besides, she is too old to run after a child, and he is too mercurial to be tied to an elderly woman.'

'But you left him to come to church.'

'Yes, once; but I would not have left him for any other purpose; and I think, in future, I must contrive to bring him with me, or stay at home.'

'Is he so mischievous?' asked my mother, considerably shocked.

'No,' replied the lady, sadly smiling, as she stroked the wavy locks of her son, who was seated on a low stool at her feet, 'but he is my only treasure; and I am his only friend, so we don't like to be separated.'

'But my dear, I call that doting,' said my plain-spoken parent. 'You should try to suppress such foolish fondness, as well to save your son from ruin as yourself from ridicule.'

'*Ruin*, Mrs Markham?'

'Yes; it is spoiling the child. Even at *his* age, he ought not to be always tied to his mother's apron string; he should learn to be ashamed of it.'

'Mrs Markham, I beg you will not say such things in *his* presence, at least. I trust my son will *never* be ashamed to love his mother!' said Mrs Graham, with a serious energy that startled the company.

My mother attempted to appease her by an explanation; but she seemed to think enough had been said on the subject, and abruptly turned the conversation.

'Just as I thought,' said I to myself: 'the lady's temper is none of the mildest, notwithstanding her sweet, pale face and lofty brow, where thought and suffering seem equally to have stamped their impress.'

All this time, I was seated at a table on the other side of the room, apparently immersed in the perusal of a volume of the *Farmer's Magazine*, which I happened to have been reading at the moment of our visitor's arrival; and, not choosing to be over civil, I had merely bowed as she entered, and continued my occupation as before.

In a little while, however, I was sensible that someone was approaching me, with a light, but slow and hesitating tread. It was little Arthur, irresistibly attracted by my dog Sancho, that was lying at my feet. On looking up, I beheld him standing about two yards off, with his clear blue eyes wistfully gazing on the dog, transfixed to the spot, not by fear of the animal, but by a timid disinclination to approach its master. A little encouragement, however, induced him to come forward. The child, though shy, was not sullen. In a minute he was

kneeling on the carpet, with his arms round Sancho's neck, and in a minute or two more, the little fellow was seated on my knee, surveying with eager interest the various specimens of horses, cattle, pigs, and model farms portrayed in the volume before me. I glanced at his mother now and then, to see how she relished the new-sprung intimacy; and I saw, by the unquiet aspect of her eye, that for some reason or other, she was uneasy at the child's position.

'Arthur,' said she, at length, 'come here. You are troublesome to Mr Markham: he wishes to read.'

'By no means, Mrs Graham; pray let him stay. I am as much amused as he is,' pleaded I. But still, with hand and eye, she silently called him to her side.

'No, mamma,' said the child; 'let me look at these pictures first; and then I'll come, and tell you all about them.'

'We are going to have a small party on Monday, the fifth of November,' said my mother; 'and I hope you will not refuse to make one, Mrs Graham. You can bring your little boy with you, you know – I dare say we shall be able to amuse him; and then you can make your own apologies to the Millwards and Wilsons – they will all be here I expect.'

'Thank you, I never go to parties.'

'Oh! but this will be quite a family concern – early hours, and nobody here but ourselves, and just the Millwards and Wilsons, most of whom you already know, and Mr Lawrence, your landlord, whom you ought to make acquaintance with.'

'I do know something of him – but you must excuse me this time; for the evenings, now, are dark and damp, and Arthur, I fear, is too delicate to risk exposure to their influence with impunity. We must defer the enjoyment of your hospitality, till the return of longer days and warmer nights.'

Rose, now, at a hint from my mother, produced a decanter of wine, with accompaniments of glasses and cake, from the cupboard under the oak sideboard, and the refreshment was duly presented to the guests. They both partook of the cake, but obstinately refused the wine, in spite of their hostess's hospitable attempts to force it upon them. Arthur especially shrank from the ruby nectar as if in terror and disgust, and was ready to cry when urged to take it.

'Never mind, Arthur,' said his mamma, 'Mrs Markham thinks it will do you good, as you were tired with your walk; but she will not oblige you to take it; I dare say you will do very well without. He detests the very sight of wine,' she added, 'and the smell of it almost makes him sick. I have been accustomed to make him swallow a little wine or weak spirits-and-water, by way of medicine when he was sick, and, in fact, I have done what I could to make him hate them.'

Everybody laughed, except the young widow and her son.

'Well, Mrs Graham,' said my mother, wiping the tears of merriment from her bright, blue eyes – 'well, you surprise me! I really gave you credit for having more sense – the poor child will be the veriest milksop that ever was sopped! Only think what a man you will make of him, if you persist in – '

'I think it a very excellent plan,' interrupted Mrs Graham with imperturbable gravity. 'By that means I hope to save him from one degrading vice at

least. I wish I could render the incentives to every other equally innoxious in his case.'

'But by such means,' said I, 'you will never render him virtuous. What is it that constitutes virtue, Mrs Graham? Is it the circumstance of being able and willing to resist temptation; or that of having no temptations to resist? – Is he a strong man that overcomes great obstacles and performs surprising achievements, though by dint of great muscular exertion, and at the risk of some subsequent fatigue, or he that sits in his chair all day, with nothing to do more laborious than stirring the fire, and carrying his food to his mouth? If you would have your son to walk honourably through the world, you must not attempt to clear the stones from his path, but teach him to walk firmly over them – not insist upon leading him by the hand, but let him learn to go alone.'

'I will lead him by the hand, Mr Markham, till he has strength to go alone; and I will clear as many stones from his path as I can, and teach him to avoid the *rest* – or walk firmly over them, as you say; for when I have done my utmost, in the way of clearance, there will still be plenty left to exercise all the agility, steadiness, and circumspection he will ever have. It is all very well to talk about noble resistance, and trials of virtue; but for fifty – or five hundred men that have yielded to temptation, show me one that has had virtue to resist. And why should I take it for granted that my son will be one in a thousand? – and not rather prepare for the worst, and suppose he will be like his – like the rest of mankind, unless I take care to prevent it?'

'You are very complimentary to us all,' I observed.

'I know nothing about *you* – I speak of those I do know – and when I see the whole race of mankind (with a few rare exceptions), stumbling and blundering along the path of life, sinking into every pitfall, and breaking their shins over every impediment that lies in their way, shall I not use all the means in my power to ensure for him, a smoother and a safer passage?'

'Yes, but the surest means will be, to endeavour to fortify him *against* temptation, not to remove it out of his way.'

'I will do both, Mr Markham. God knows he will have temptations enough to assail him, both from within and without, when I have done all I can to render vice as uninviting to him, as it is abominable in its own nature – I myself, have had, indeed, but few incentives to what the world calls vice, but yet, I have experienced temptations and trials of another kind, that have required, on many occasions, more watchfulness and firmness to resist, than I have hitherto been able to muster against them. And this, I believe, is what most others would acknowledge, who are accustomed to reflection, and wishful to strive against their natural corruptions.'

'Yes,' said my mother, but half apprehending her drift; 'but you would not judge of a boy by yourself – and my dear Mrs Graham, let me warn you in good time against the error – the fatal error, I may call it – of taking that boy's education upon yourself. Because you are clever, in some things, and well informed, you may fancy yourself equal to the task; but indeed you are not; and, if you persist in the attempt, believe me, you will bitterly repent it when the mischief is done.'

'I am to send him to school, I suppose, to learn to despise his mother's authority and affection!' said the lady, with a rather bitter smile.

'Oh, *no*! – But if you would have a boy to despise his mother let her keep him at home, and spend her life in petting him up, and slaving to indulge his follies and caprices.'

'I perfectly agree with you Mrs Markham; but nothing can be further from my principle and practice than such criminal weakness as that.'

'Well, but you will treat him like a girl – you'll spoil his spirit, and make a mere Miss Nancy of him – you will indeed, Mrs Graham, whatever you may think – but I'll get Mr Millward to talk to you about it – *he'll* tell you the consequences; he'll set it before you as plain as the day; and tell you what you ought to do, and all about it; and, I don't doubt, he'll be able to convince you in a minute.'

'No occasion to trouble the vicar,' said Mrs Graham, glancing at me – I suppose I was smiling at my mother's unbounded confidence in that worthy gentleman – 'Mr Markham here, thinks his powers of conviction at least equal to Mr Millward's. If I hear not him, neither should I be convinced though one rose from the dead, he would tell you. Well Mr Markham, you that maintain that a boy should not be shielded from evil, but sent out to battle against it, alone and unassisted – not taught to avoid the snares of life, but boldly to rush into them, or over them, as he may – to seek danger rather than shun it, and feed his virtue by temptation – would you –'

'I beg your pardon, Mrs Graham – but you get on too fast. I have not yet said that a boy should be taught to rush into the snares of life – or even wilfully to seek temptation for the sake of exercising his virtue by overcoming it; I only say that it is better to arm and strengthen your hero, than to disarm and enfeeble the foe; and if you were to rear an oak sapling in a hothouse, tending it carefully night and day, and shielding it from every breath of wind, you could not expect it to become a hardy tree, like that which has grown up on the mountain-side, exposed to all the action of the elements, and not even sheltered from the shock of the tempest.'

'Granted; but would you use the same argument with regard to a girl?'

'Certainly not.'

'No; you would have her to be tenderly and delicately nurtured, like a hot-house plant – taught to cling to others for direction and support, and guarded, as much as possible, from the very knowledge of evil. But will you be so good as to inform me, why you make this distinction? Is it that you think she *has* no virtue?'

'Assuredly not.'

'Well, but you affirm that virtue is only elicited by temptation; and you think that a woman cannot be too little exposed to temptation, or too little acquainted with vice, or anything connected therewith – It *must* be, either, that you think she is essentially so vicious, or so feeble-minded that she *cannot* withstand temptation – and though she may be pure and innocent as long as she is kept in ignorance and restraint, yet, being destitute of *real* virtue, to teach her how to sin, is at once to make her a sinner, and the greater her knowledge, the wider her

liberty, the deeper will be her depravity – whereas, in the nobler sex, there is a natural tendency to goodness, guarded by a superior fortitude, which, the more it is exercised by trials and dangers, is only the further developed – '

'Heaven forbid that I should think so!' I interrupted at last.

'Well then, it must be that you think they are *both* weak and prone to err, and the slightest error, the merest shadow of pollution will ruin the one, while the character of the other will be strengthened and embellished – his education properly finished by a little practical acquaintance with forbidden things. Such experience, to him (to use a trite simile), will be like the storm to the oak, which, though it may scatter the leaves, and snap the smaller branches, serves but to rivet the roots, and to harden and condense the fibres of the tree. You would have us encourage our sons to prove all things by their own experience, while our daughters must not even profit by the experience of others. Now *I* would have both so to benefit by the experience of others, and the precepts of a higher authority, that they should know beforehand to refuse the evil and choose the good, and require no experimental proofs to teach them the evil of transgression. I would not send a poor girl into the world, unarmed against her foes, and ignorant of the snares that beset her path: nor would I watch and guard her, till, deprived of self-respect and self-reliance, she lost the power, or the will to catch and guard herself; and as for my son – if I thought he would grow up to be what you call a man of the world – one that has "*seen life*", and glories in his experience, even though he should so far profit by it, as to sober down, at length, into a useful and respected member of society – I would rather that he died tomorrow! – rather a thousand times!' she earnestly repeated, pressing her darling to her side and kissing his forehead with intense affection. He had, already, left his new companion, and been standing for some time beside his mother's knee, looking up into her face, and listening in silent wonder to her incomprehensible discourse.

'Well! you ladies must always have the last word, I suppose,' said I, observing her rise, and begin to take leave of my mother.

'You may have as many words as you please – only I can't stay to hear them.'

'No; that is the way: you hear just as much of an argument as you please; and the rest may be spoken to the wind.'

'If you are anxious to say anything more on the subject,' replied she, as she shook hands with Rose, 'you must bring your sister to see me some fine day, and I'll listen, as patiently as you could wish, to whatever you please to say. I would rather be lectured by you than the vicar, because, I should have less remorse in telling you, at the end of the discourse, that I preserve my own opinion precisely the same as at the beginning – as would be the case, I am persuaded, with regard to either logician.'

'Yes, of course,' replied I, determined to be as provoking as herself; 'for, when a lady does consent to listen to an argument against her own opinions, she is always predetermined to withstand it – to listen only with her bodily ears, keeping the mental organs resolutely closed against the strongest reasoning.'

'Good-morning, Mr Markham,' said my fair antagonist with a pitying smile;

and deigning no further rejoinder, she slightly bowed, and was about to with-draw; but her son, with childish impertinence, arrested her by exclaiming,

'Mamma, you have not shaken hands with Mr Markham!'

She laughingly turned round, and held out her hand. I gave it a spiteful squeeze; for I was annoyed at the continual injustice she had done me from the very dawn of our acquaintance. Without knowing anything about my real disposition and principles, she was evidently prejudiced against me, and seemed bent upon showing me that her opinions respecting me, on every particular, fell far below those I entertained of myself. I was naturally touchy, or, it would not have vexed me so much. Perhaps, too, I was a little bit spoiled by my mother and sister, and some other ladies of my acquaintance; and yet, I was by no means a fop – of that I am fully convinced, whether *you* are or not.

## CHAPTER 4

## *The Party*

Our party, on the fifth of November, passed off very well in spite of Mrs Graham's refusal to grace it with her presence. Indeed, it is probable that, had she been there, there would have been less cordiality, freedom, and frolic amongst us than there was without her.

My mother, as usual, was cheerful and chatty, full of activity and good nature, and only faulty in being too anxious to make her guests happy, thereby forcing several of them to do what their soul abhorred, in the way of eating or drinking, sitting opposite the blazing fire, or talking when they would be silent. Nevertheless, they bore it very well, being all in their holiday humours.

Mr Millward was mighty in important dogmas and sententious jokes, pompous anecdotes and oracular discourses, dealt out for the edification of the whole assembly in general, and of the admiring Mrs Markham, the polite Mr Lawrence, the sedate Mary Millward, the quiet Richard Wilson, and the matter of fact Robert, in particular – as being the most attentive listeners.

Mrs Wilson was more brilliant than ever, with her budgets of fresh news and old scandal, strung together with trivial questions and remarks, and oft repeated observations, uttered apparently for the sole purpose of denying a moment's rest to her inexhaustible organs of speech. She had brought her knitting with her, and it seemed as if her tongue had laid a wager with her fingers, to outdo them in swift and ceaseless motion.

Her daughter Jane was, of course, as graceful and elegant, as witty and seduc-tive as she could possibly manage to be; for here were all the ladies to outshine, and all the gentlemen to charm – and Mr Lawrence, especially, to capture and subdue. Her little arts to effect his subjugation were too subtle and impalpable to attract my observation; but I thought there was a certain *refined* affectation of superiority, and an ungenial self-consciousness about her, that negatived all her

advantages, and after she was gone Rose interpreted to me her various looks, words, and actions with a mingled acuteness and asperity that made me wonder, equally, at the lady's artifice and my sister's penetration, and ask myself if she too had an eye to the squire – but never mind, Halford; she had not.

Richard Wilson, Jane's younger brother, sat in a corner, apparently good-tempered, but silent and shy, desirous to escape observation, but willing enough to listen and observe: and, although somewhat out of his element, he would have been happy enough in his own quiet way, if my mother could only have let him alone, but in her mistaken kindness, she would keep persecuting him with her attentions – pressing upon him all manner of viands, under the notion that he was too bashful to help himself, and obliging him to shout across the room his monosyllabic replies to the numerous questions and observations by which she vainly attempted to draw him into conversation.

Rose informed me that he never would have favoured us with his company, but for the importunities of his sister Jane, who was most anxious to show Mr Lawrence that she had at least one brother more gentlemanly and refined than Robert. That worthy individual she had been equally solicitous to keep away; but he affirmed that he saw no reason why he should not enjoy a crack with Markham and the old lady (my mother was not old really), and bonny Miss Rose and the parson, as well as the best; and he was in the right of it too. So he talked commonplace with my mother and Rose, and discussed parish affairs with the vicar, farming matters with me, and politics with us both.

Mary Millward was another mute – not so much tormented with cruel kindness as Dick Wilson, because she had a certain short, decided way of answering and refusing, and was supposed to be rather sullen than diffident. However that might be, she certainly did not give much pleasure to the company; nor did she appear to derive much from it. Eliza told me she had only come because her father insisted upon it, having taken it into his head that she devoted herself too exclusively to her household duties, to the neglect of such relaxations and innocent enjoyments as were proper to her age and sex. She seemed, to me, to be good-humoured enough on the whole. Once or twice she was provoked to laughter by the wit, or the merriment of some favoured individual amongst us; and then I observed she sought the eye of Richard Wilson, who sat over against her. As he studied with her father, she had some acquaintance with him, in spite of the retiring habits of both, and I suppose there was a kind of fellow-feeling established between them.

My Eliza was charming beyond description, coquettish without affectation, and evidently more desirous to engage my attention than that of all the room besides. Her delight in having me near her, seated or standing by her side, whispering in her ear, or pressing her hand in the dance, was plainly legible in her glowing face and heaving bosom, however belied by saucy words and gestures. But I had better hold my tongue: if I boast of these things now, I shall have to blush hereafter.

To proceed then, with the various individuals of our party; Rose was simple and natural as usual, and full of mirth and vivacity.

Fergus was impertinent and absurd; but his impertinence and folly served to make others laugh, if they did not raise himself in their estimation.

And finally (for I omit myself), Mr Lawrence was gentlemanly and inoffensive to all, and polite to the vicar and the ladies, especially his hostess and her daughter, and Miss Wilson – misguided man; he had not the taste to prefer Eliza Millward. Mr Lawrence and I were on tolerably intimate terms. Essentially of reserved habits, and but seldom quitting the secluded place of his birth, where he had lived in solitary state since the death of his father, he had neither the opportunity nor the inclination for forming many acquaintances; and, of all he had ever known, I (judging by the results) was the companion most agreeable to his taste. I liked the man well enough, but he was too cold, and shy, and self-contained, to obtain my cordial sympathies. A spirit of candour and frankness, when wholly unaccompanied with coarseness, he admired in others, but he could not acquire it himself. His excessive reserve upon all his own concerns was, indeed, provoking and chilly enough; but I forgave it, from a conviction that it originated, less in pride and want of confidence in his friends, than in a certain morbid feeling of delicacy, and a peculiar diffidence, that he was sensible of, but wanted energy to overcome. His heart was like a sensitive plant, that opens for a moment in the sunshine, but curls up and shrinks into itself at the slightest touch of the finger, or the lightest breath of wind. And, upon the whole, our intimacy was rather a mutual predilection than a deep and solid friendship, such as has since arisen between myself and you, Halford, whom, in spite of your occasional crustiness, I can liken to nothing so well as an old coat, unimpeachable in texture, but easy and loose – that has conformed itself to the shape of the wearer, and which he may use as he pleases, without being bothered with the fear of spoiling it; whereas Mr Lawrence was like a new garment, all very neat and trim to look at, but so tight in the elbows that you would fear to split the seams by the unrestricted motion of your arms, and so smooth and fine in surface that you scruple to expose it to a single drop of rain.

Soon after the arrival of the guests, my mother mentioned Mrs Graham, regretted she was not there to meet them, and explained to the Millwards and Wilsons, the reasons she had given for neglecting to return their calls, hoping they would excuse her, as she was sure she did not mean to be uncivil, and would be glad to see them at any time;

'But she is a very singular lady, Mr Lawrence,' added she; 'we don't know what to make of her – but I dare say you can tell us something about her; for she is your tenant, you know – and she said she knew you a little.'

All eyes were turned to Mr Lawrence. I thought he looked unnecessarily confused at being so appealed to.

'I, Mrs Markham!' said he, 'you are mistaken – I don't – that is – I have seen her certainly; but I am the last person you should apply to for information respecting Mrs Graham.'

He then immediately turned to Rose, and asked her to favour the company with a song, or a tune on the piano.

'No,' said she; 'you must ask Miss Wilson: she outshines us all in singing, and music too.'

Miss Wilson demurred.

'*She'll* sing readily enough,' said Fergus, 'if you'll undertake to stand by her, Mr Lawrence, and turn over the leaves for her.'

'I shall be most happy to do so. Miss Wilson, will you allow me?'

She bridled her long neck and smiled, and suffered him to lead her to the instrument, where she played and sang, in her very best style, one piece after another; while he stood patiently by, leaning one hand on the back of her chair, and turning over the leaves of her book with the other. Perhaps, he was as much charmed with her performance as she was. It was all very fine in its way; but I cannot say that it moved me very deeply. There was plenty of skill and execution, but precious little feeling.

But we had not done with Mrs Graham yet.

'I don't take wine, Mrs Markham,' said Mr Millward, upon the introduction of that beverage; 'I'll take a little of your home-brewed ale. I always prefer your home-brewed to anything else.'

Flattered at this compliment, my mother rang the bell, and a china jug of our best ale was presently brought, and set before the worthy gentleman who so well knew how to appreciate its excellencies.

'Now this is the thing!' cried he, pouring out a glass of the same in a long stream, skilfully directed from the jug to the tumbler, so as to produce much foam without spilling a drop; and, having surveyed it for a moment opposite the candle, he took a deep draught, and then smacked his lips, drew a long breath, and refilled his glass, my mother looking on with the greatest satisfaction.

'There's nothing like this, Mrs Markham!' said he, 'I always maintain that there's nothing to compare with your home-brewed ale.'

'I'm sure I'm glad you like it, sir. I always look after the brewing myself, as well as the cheese and the butter – I like to have things well done, while we're about it.'

'*Quite right*, Mrs Markham!'

'But then, Mr Millward, you don't think it *wrong* to take a little wine now and then – or a little spirits either?' said my mother, as she handed a smoking tumbler of gin and water to Mrs Wilson, who affirmed that wine sat heavy on her stomach, and whose son Robert was at that moment helping himself to a pretty stiff glass of the same.

'By no means!' replied the oracle with a Jove-like nod; 'these things are all blessings and mercies, if we only knew how to make use of them.'

'But Mrs Graham doesn't think so. You shall just hear now, what she told us the other day – I *told* her I'd tell you.'

And my mother favoured the company with a particular account of that lady's mistaken ideas and conduct regarding the matter in hand, concluding with, 'Now don't you think it is wrong?'

'Wrong!' repeated the vicar, with more than common solemnity – 'criminal, I should say – criminal! – Not only is it making a fool of the boy, but it is

despising the gifts of Providence, and teaching him to trample them under his feet.'

He then entered more fully into the question, and explained at large the folly and impiety of such a proceeding. My mother heard him with profoundest reverence; and even Mrs Wilson vouchsafed to rest her tongue for a moment, and listen in silence, while she complacently sipped her gin and water. Mr Lawrence sat with his elbow on the table, carelessly playing with his half-empty wineglass, and covertly smiling to himself.

'But don't you think, Mr Millward,' suggested he, when at length that gentleman paused in his discourse, 'that when a child may be naturally prone to intemperance – by the fault of its parents or ancestors, for instance – some precautions are advisable?' (Now it was generally believed that Mr Lawrence's father had shortened his days by intemperance.)

'Some precautions, it may be; but temperance, sir, is one thing, and abstinence another.'

'But I have heard that, with some persons, temperance – that is moderation – is almost impossible; and if abstinence be an evil (which some have doubted), no one will deny that excess is a greater. Some parents have entirely prohibited their children from tasting intoxicating liquors; but a parent's authority cannot last for ever: children are naturally prone to hanker after forbidden things; and a child, in such a case, would be likely to have a strong curiosity to taste, and try the effect of what has been so lauded and enjoyed by others, so strictly forbidden to himself – which curiosity would generally be gratified on the first convenient opportunity; and the restraint once broken, serious consequences might ensue. I don't pretend to be a judge of such matters, but it seems to me, that this plan of Mrs Graham's, as you describe it, Mrs Markham, extraordinary as it may be, is not without its advantages; for here you see, the child is delivered at once from temptation; he has no secret curiosity, no hankering desire; he is as well acquainted with the tempting liquors as he ever wishes to be; and is thoroughly disgusted with them without having suffered from their effects.'

'And is that right, sir? Have I not proven to you how wrong it is – how contrary to Scripture and to reason to teach a child to look with contempt and disgust upon the blessings of Providence, instead of to use them aright?'

'You may consider laudanum a blessing of Providence, sir,' replied Mr Lawrence, smiling; 'and yet, you will allow that most of us had better abstain from it, even in moderation; but,' added he, 'I would not desire you to follow out my simile too closely – in witness whereof I finish my glass.'

'And take another I hope, Mr Lawrence,' said my mother, pushing the bottle towards him.

He politely declined, and pushing his chair a little away from the table, leant back towards me – I was seated a trifle behind, on the sofa beside Eliza Millward – and carelessly asked me if I knew Mrs Graham.

'I have met her once or twice,' I replied.

'What do you think of her?'

'I cannot say that I like her much. She is handsome – or rather I should say

distinguished and interesting – in her appearance, but by no means amiable – a woman liable to take strong prejudices, I should fancy, and stick to them through thick and thin, twisting everything into conformity with her own preconceived opinions – too hard, too sharp, too bitter for my taste.'

He made no reply, but looked down and bit his lip and shortly after rose and sauntered up to Miss Wilson, as much repelled by me, I fancy, as attracted by her. I scarcely noticed it at the time, but afterwards, I was led to recall this and other trifling facts, of a similar nature, to my remembrance, when – but I must not anticipate.

We wound up the evening with dancing – our worthy pastor thinking it no scandal to be present on the occasion, though one of the village musicians was engaged to direct our evolutions with his violin. But Mary Millward obstinately refused to join us; and so did Richard Wilson, though my mother earnestly entreated him to do so, and even offered to be his partner.

We managed very well without them, however. With a single set of quadrilles, and several country dances, we carried it on to a pretty late hour; and at length, having called upon our musician to strike up a waltz, I was just about to whirl Eliza round in that delightful dance, accompanied by Lawrence and Jane Wilson and Fergus and Rose, when Mr Millward interposed with – 'No, no, I don't allow that! Come it's time to be going now.'

'Oh, no, papa!' pleaded Eliza.

'High time my girl – high time! – Moderation in all things remember! That's the plan – "Let your moderation be known unto all men!" '

But in revenge, I followed Eliza into the dimly lighted passage, where under pretence of helping her on with her shawl, I fear I must plead guilty to snatching a kiss behind her father's back, while he was enveloping his throat and chin in the folds of a mighty comforter. But alas! in turning round, there was my mother close beside me. The consequence was, that no sooner were the guests departed, than I was doomed to a very serious remonstrance, which unpleasantly checked the galloping course of my spirits, and made a disagreeable close to the evening.

'My dear Gilbert,' said she, 'I wish you wouldn't do so! You know how deeply I have your advantage at heart, how I love you and prize you above everything else in the world, and how much I long to see you well settled in life – and how bitterly it would grieve me to see you married to that girl – or any other in the neighbourhood. What you *see* in her I don't know. It isn't only the want of money that I think about – nothing of the kind – but there's neither beauty, nor cleverness, nor goodness, nor anything else that's desirable. If you knew your own value as I do, you wouldn't dream of it. Do wait awhile and see! If you bind yourself to her, you'll repent it all your lifetime when you look round you and see how many better there are. Take my word for it, you will.'

'Well, mother, do be quiet! – I hate to be lectured! – I'm not going to marry yet, I tell you; but – dear me! mayn't I enjoy myself at *all*?'

'Yes, my dear boy, but not in that way. Indeed you shouldn't do such things. You would be wronging the girl, if she were what she ought to be; but I assure you she is as artful a little hussy as anybody need wish to see; and you'll get

entangled in her snares before you know where you are. And if you *do* marry her Gilbert, you'll break my heart – so there's an end of it.'

'Well, don't cry about it, mother,' said I, for the tears were gushing from her eyes, 'there, let that kiss efface the one I gave Eliza; don't abuse her any more, and set your mind at rest; for I'll promise never to – that is, I'll promise to – to think twice before I take any important step you seriously disapprove of.'

So saying, I lighted my candle, and went to bed, considerably quenched in spirit.

## CHAPTER 5

### *The Studio*

It was about the close of the month, that, yielding at length to the urgent importunities of Rose, I accompanied her in a visit to Wildfell Hall. To our surprise, we were ushered into a room where the first object that met the eye was a painter's easel, with a table beside it covered with rolls of canvas, bottles of oil and varnish, palette, brushes, paints, etc. Leaning against the wall were several sketches in various stages of progression, and a few finished paintings – mostly of landscapes and figures.

'I must make you welcome to my studio,' said Mrs Graham; 'there is no fire in the sitting-room today, and it is rather too cold to show you into a place with an empty grate.'

And disengaging a couple of chairs from the artistical lumber that usurped them, she bid us be seated, and resumed her place beside the easel – not facing it exactly, but now and then glancing at the picture upon it while she conversed, and giving it an occasional touch with her brush, as if she found it impossible to wean her attention entirely from her occupation to fix it upon her guests. It was a view of Wildfell Hall, as seen at early morning from the field below, rising in dark relief against a sky of clear silvery blue, with a few red streaks on the horizon, faithfully drawn and coloured, and very elegantly and artistically handled.

'I see your heart is in your work, Mrs Graham,' observed I: 'I must beg you to go on with it; for if you suffer our presence to interrupt you, we shall be constrained to regard ourselves as unwelcome intruders.'

'Oh, no!' replied she, throwing her brush on to the table, as if startled into politeness. 'I am not so beset with visitors, but that I can readily spare a few minutes to the few that do favour me with their company.'

'You have almost completed your painting,' said I, approaching to observe it more closely, and surveying it with a greater degree of admiration and delight than I cared to express. 'A few more touches in the foreground will finish it I should think. But why have you called it Fernley Manor, Cumberland, instead of Wildfell Hall, —shire?' I asked, alluding to the name she had traced in small characters at the bottom of the canvas.

But immediately I was sensible of having committed an act of impertinence in so doing; for she coloured and hesitated; but after a moment's pause, with a kind of desperate frankness, she replied – 'Because I have friends – acquaintances at least – in the world, from whom I desire my present abode to be concealed; and as they might see the picture, and might possibly recognise the style in spite of the false initials I have put in the corner, I take the precaution to give a false name to the place also, in order to put them on a wrong scent, if they should attempt to trace me out by it.'

'Then you don't intend to keep the picture?' said I, anxious to say anything to change the subject.

'No; I cannot afford to paint for my own amusement.'

'Mamma sends all her pictures to London,' said Arthur; 'and somebody sells them for her there, and sends us the money.'

In looking round upon the other pieces, I remarked a pretty sketch of Lindenhope from the top of the hill; another view of the old hall, basking in the sunny haze of a quiet summer afternoon; and a simple but striking little picture of a child brooding with looks of silent, but deep and sorrowful regret, over a handful of withered flowers, with glimpses of dark low hills and autumnal fields behind it, and a dull beclouded sky above.

'You see there is a sad dearth of subjects,' observed the fair artist. 'I took the old hall once on a moonlight night, and I suppose I must take it again on a snowy winter's day, and then again on a dark cloudy evening; for I really have nothing else to paint. I have been told that you have a fine view of the sea somewhere in the neighbourhood – is it true? – and is it within walking distance?'

'Yes, if you don't object to walking four miles – or nearly so – little short of eight miles there and back – and over a somewhat rough, fatiguing road.'

'In what direction does it lie?'

I described the situation as well as I could, and was entering upon an explanation of the various roads, lanes, and fields to be traversed in order to reach it, the goings straight on, and turnings to the right, and the left, when she checked me with – 'Oh, stop! – don't tell me now: I shall forget every word of your directions before I require them. I shall not think about going till next spring; and then, perhaps, I may trouble you. At present we have the winter before us, and – '

She suddenly paused, with a suppressed exclamation started up from her seat, and saying, 'Excuse me one moment,' hurried from the room, and shut the door behind her.

Curious to see what had startled her so, I looked towards the window – for her eyes had been carelessly fixed upon it the moment before – and just beheld the skirts of a man's coat vanishing behind a large holly bush that stood between the window and the porch.

'It's mamma's friend,' said Arthur.

Rose and I looked at each other.

'I don't know what to make of her, at all,' whispered Rose.

The child looked at her in grave surprise. She straightway began to talk to him

on indifferent matters, while I amused myself with looking at the pictures. There was one in an obscure corner that I had not before observed. It was a little child, seated on the grass with its lap full of flowers. The tiny features and large, blue eyes, smiling through a shock of light brown curls, shaken over the forehead as it bent above its treasure, bore sufficient resemblance to those of the young gentleman before me, to proclaim it a portrait of Arthur Graham in his early infancy.

In taking this up to bring it to the light, I discovered another behind it, with its face to the wall. I ventured to take that up too. It was the portrait of a gentleman in the full prime of youthful manhood – handsome enough, and not badly executed; but, if done by the same hand as the others, it was evidently some years before; for there was far more careful minuteness of detail, and less of that freshness of colouring and freedom of handling, that delighted and surprised me in them. Nevertheless, I surveyed it with considerable interest. There was a certain individuality in the features and expression that stamped it, at once, a successful likeness. The bright, blue eyes regarded the spectator with a kind of lurking drollery – you almost expected to see them wink; the lips – a little too voluptuously full – seemed ready to break into a smile; the warmly tinted cheeks were embellished with a luxuriant growth of reddish whiskers; while the bright chesnut hair, clustering in abundant, wavy curls, trespassed too much upon the forehead, and seemed to intimate that the owner thereof was prouder of his beauty than his intellect – as perhaps, he had reason to be; and yet he looked no fool.

I had not had the portrait in my hands two minutes before the fair artist returned.

'Only someone come about the pictures,' said she, in apology for her abrupt departure: 'I told him to wait.'

'I fear it will be considered an act of impertinence,' said I, 'to presume to look at a picture that the artist has turned to the wall; but may I ask – '

'It *is* an act of very great impertinence, sir; and therefore, I beg you will ask nothing about it, for your curiosity will not be gratified,' replied she, attempting to cover the tartness of her rebuke with a smile; but I could see, by her flushed cheek and kindling eye, that she was seriously annoyed.

'I was only going to ask if you had painted it yourself,' said I, sulkily resigning the picture into her hands; for without a grain of ceremony, she took it from me; and quickly restoring it to the dark corner, with its face to the wall, placed the other against it as before, and then turned to me and laughed.

But I was in no humour for jesting. I carelessly turned to the window, and stood looking out upon the desolate garden, leaving her to talk to Rose for a minute or two; and then, telling my sister it was time to go, shook hands with the little gentleman, coolly bowed to the lady, and moved towards the door. But, having bid adieu to Rose, Mrs Graham presented her hand to me, saying, with a soft voice, and by no means a disagreeable smile – 'Let not the sun go down upon your wrath, Mr Markham. I'm sorry I offended you by my abruptness.'

When a lady condescends to apologise, there is no keeping one's anger of course; so we parted good friends for once; and *this* time, I squeezed her hand with a cordial, not a spiteful pressure.

## CHAPTER 6

## *Progression*

During the next four months, I did not enter Mrs Graham's house, nor she mine; but still, the ladies continued to talk about her, and still, our acquaintance continued, though slowly, to advance. As for their talk, I paid but little attention to that (when it related to the fair hermit, I mean), and the only information I derived from it, was that, one fine, frosty day, she had ventured to take her little boy as far as the vicarage, and that, unfortunately, nobody was at home but Miss Millward; nevertheless, she had sat a long time, and, by all accounts, they had found a good deal to say to each other, and parted with a mutual desire to meet again. But Mary liked children, and fond mammas like those who can duly appreciate their treasures.

But sometimes, I saw her myself – not only when she came to church, but when she was out on the hills with her son, whether taking a long, purpose-like walk, or – on specially fine days – leisurely rambling over the moor or the bleak pasture-lands, surrounding the old hall, herself with a book in her hand, her son gambolling about her; and, on any of these occasions, when I caught sight of her in my solitary walks or rides, or while following my agricultural pursuits, I generally contrived to meet or overtake her; for I rather liked to see Mrs Graham, and to talk to her, and I decidedly liked to talk to her little companion, whom, when once the ice of his shyness was fairly broken, I found to be a very amiable, intelligent, and entertaining little fellow; and we soon became excellent friends – how much to the gratification of his mamma, I cannot undertake to say. I suspected at first, that she was desirous of throwing cold water on this growing intimacy – to quench, as it were, the kindling flame of our friendship – but discovering, at length, in spite of her prejudice against me, that I was perfectly harmless, and even well intentioned, and that, between myself and my dog, her son derived a great deal of pleasure from the acquaintance, that he would not otherwise have known, she ceased to object, and even welcomed my coming with a smile.

As for Arthur, he would shout his welcome from afar, and run to meet me fifty yards from his mother's side. If I happened to be on horseback, he was sure to get a canter or a gallop; or, if there was one of the draught horses within an available distance, he was treated to a steady ride upon that, which served his turn almost as well; but his mother would always follow and trudge beside him – not so much, I believe, to ensure his safe conduct, as to see that I instilled no objectionable notions into his infant mind; for she was ever on the watch, and never would allow him to be taken out of her sight. What pleased her best of all, was to see him romping and racing with Sancho, while I walked by her side – not, I fear, for love of my company (though I sometimes deluded myself with

that idea), so much as for the delight she took in seeing her son thus happily engaged in the enjoyment of those active sports, so invigorating to his tender frame, yet so seldom exercised for want of playmates suited to his years; and, perhaps, her pleasure was sweetened, not a little, by the fact of my being with *her* instead of with *him*; and therefore – incapable of doing him any injury directly or indirectly, designedly or otherwise – small thanks to her for that same.

But sometimes, I believe, she really had some little gratification in conversing with me; and one bright February morning, during twenty minutes' stroll along the moor, she laid aside her usual asperity and reserve, and fairly entered into conversation with me discoursing with so much eloquence, and depth of thought and feeling, on a subject, happily coinciding with my own ideas, and looking so beautiful withal, that I went home enchanted; and on the way (morally) started to find myself thinking that, after all, it would, perhaps, be better to spend one's days with such a woman than with Eliza Millward; and then, I (figuratively) blushed for my inconstancy.

On entering the parlour, I found Eliza there, with Rose and no one else. The surprise was not altogether so agreeable as it ought to have been. We chatted together a long time; but I found her rather frivolous, and even a little insipid, compared with the more mature and earnest Mrs Graham – Alas, for human constancy!

'However,' thought I, 'I ought not to marry Eliza since my mother so strongly objects to it, and I ought not to delude the girl with the idea that I intended to do so. Now, if this mood continue, I shall have less difficulty in emancipating my affections from her soft, yet unrelenting sway; and, though Mrs Graham might be equally objectionable, I may be permitted, like the doctors, to cure a greater evil by a less; for I shall not fall seriously in love with the young widow, I think – nor she with me – that's certain – but if I find a little pleasure in her society, I may surely be allowed to seek it; and if the star of her divinity be bright enough to dim the lustre of Eliza's, so much the better; but I scarcely can think it.'

And thereafter, I seldom suffered a fine day to pass without paying a visit to Wildfell, about the time my new acquaintance usually left her hermitage; but so frequently was I balked in my expectations of another interview, so changeable was she in her times of coming forth, and in her places of resort, so transient were the occasional glimpses I was able to obtain, that I felt half inclined to think she took as much pains to avoid my company, as I to seek hers; but this was too disagreeable a supposition to be entertained a moment after it could, conveniently, be dismissed.

One calm, clear afternoon, however, in March, as I was superintending the rolling of the meadowland, and the repairing of a hedge in the valley, I saw Mrs Graham down by the brook, with a sketch-book in her hand, absorbed in the exercise of her favourite art, while Arthur was putting on the time with constructing dams and breakwaters in the shallow, stony stream. I was rather in want of amusement, and so rare an opportunity was not to be neglected; so, leaving both meadow and hedge, I quickly repaired to the spot – but not before

Sancho, who, immediately upon perceiving his young friend, scoured at full gallop the intervening space, and pounced upon him with an impetuous mirth that precipitated the child almost into the middle of the beck; but, happily, the stones preserved him from any serious wetting, while their smoothness prevented his being too much hurt to laugh at the untoward event.

Mrs Graham was studying the distinctive characters of the different varieties of trees in their winter nakedness, and copying, with a spirited, though delicate touch, their various ramifications. She did not talk much; but I stood and watched the progress of her pencil: it was a pleasure to behold it so dexterously guided by those fair and graceful fingers. But erelong their dexterity became impaired, they began to hesitate, to tremble slightly, and make false strokes, and, then, suddenly came to a pause, while their owner laughingly raised her face to mine, and told me that her sketch did not profit by my superintendence.

'Then,' said I, 'I'll talk to Arthur, till you've done.'

'I should like to have a ride, Mr Markham, if mamma will let me,' said the child.

'What on, my boy?'

'I think there's a horse in that field,' replied he, pointing to where the strong black mare was pulling the roller.

'No, no, Arthur; it's too far,' objected his mother.

But I promised to bring him safe back, after a turn or two up and down the meadow; and when she looked at his eager face, she smiled and let him go. It was the first time she had even allowed me to take him so much as half a field's length from her side.

Enthroned upon his monstrous steed, and solemnly proceeding up and down the wide, steep field, he looked the very incarnation of quiet, gleeful satisfaction and delight. The rolling, however, was soon completed; but when I dismounted the gallant horseman, and restored him to his mother, she seemed rather displeased at my keeping him so long. She had shut up her sketch-book, and been, probably for some minutes, impatiently waiting his return.

It was now high time to go home she said, and would have bid me good-evening; but I was not going to leave her yet: I accompanied her half way up the hill. She became more sociable; and I was beginning to be very happy; but, on coming within sight of the grim old hall, she stood still and turned towards me while she spoke, as if expecting I should go no further, that the conversation would end here, and I should now take leave and depart – as, indeed, it was time to do; for 'the clear, cold eve' was fast 'declining', the sun had set, and the gibbous moon was visibly brightening in the pale grey sky; but a feeling almost of compassion riveted me to the spot. It seemed hard to leave her to such a lonely, comfortless home. I looked up at it. Silent and grim it frowned before us. A faint, red light was gleaming from the lower windows of one wing; but all the other windows were in darkness, and many exhibited their black, cavernous gulfs, entirely destitute of glazing or frame work.

'Do you not find it a desolate place to live in?' said I, after a moment of silent contemplation.

'I do, sometimes,' replied she. 'On winter evenings, when Arthur is in bed, and I am sitting there alone, hearing the bleak wind moaning round me and howling through the ruinous old chambers, no books or occupations can repress the dismal thoughts and apprehensions that come crowding in – but it is folly to give way to such weakness I know – If Rachel is satisfied with such a life, why should not I? – Indeed I cannot be too thankful for such an asylum, while it is left me.'

The closing sentence was uttered in an undertone, as if spoken rather to herself than to me. She then bid me good-evening and withdrew.

I had not proceeded many steps on my way homewards, when I perceived Mr Lawrence, on his pretty grey pony, coming up the rugged lane that crossed over the hilltop. I went a little out of my way to speak to him; for we had not met for some time.

'Was that Mrs Graham you were speaking to just now?' said he, after the first few words of greeting had passed between us.

'Yes.'

'Humph! I thought so.' He looked contemplatively at his horse's mane, as if he had some serious cause of dissatisfaction with it, or something else.

'Well! what then?'

'Oh, nothing! replied he. 'Only, I thought you disliked her,' he quietly added, curling his classic lip with a slightly sarcastic smile.

'Suppose I did; mayn't a man change his mind on further acquaintance?'

'Yes, of course,' returned he, nicely reducing an entanglement in the pony's redundant, hoary mane. Then suddenly turning to me, and fixing his shy, hazel eyes upon me with a steady penetrating gaze, he added, 'Then you *have* changed your mind?'

'I can't say that I have exactly. No; I think I hold the same opinion respecting her as before – but slightly ameliorated.'

'Oh.' He looked round for something else to talk about; and glancing up at the moon, made some remark upon the beauty of the evening, which I did not answer, as being irrelevant to the subject.

'Lawrence,' said I, calmly looking him in the face, 'are you in love with Mrs Graham?'

Instead of his being deeply offended at this, as I more than half expected he would, the first start of surprise, at the audacious question, was followed by a tittering laugh, as if he was highly amused at the idea.

'*I* in love with her!' repeated he. 'What makes you dream of such a thing?'

'From the interest you take in the progress of my acquaintance with the lady, and the changes of my opinion concerning her, I thought you might be jealous.'

He laughed again. 'Jealous! no – but I thought you were going to marry Eliza Millward.'

'You thought wrong then; I am not going to marry either one or the other – that I know of.'

'Then I think you'd better let them alone.'

'Are you going to marry Jane Wilson?'

He coloured, and played with the mane again, but answered – 'No, I think not.'

'Then you had better let her alone.'

She won't let me alone – he might have said; but he only looked silly and said nothing for the space of half a minute, and then made another attempt to turn the conversation; and, this time, I let it pass; for he had borne enough: another word on the subject would have been like the last atom that breaks the camel's back.

I was too late for tea; but my mother had kindly kept the teapot and muffin warm upon the hobs, and, though she scolded me a little, readily admitted my excuses; and when I complained of the flavour of the overdrawn tea, she poured the remainder into the slop basin, and bade Rose put some fresh into the pot, and reboil the kettle, which offices were performed with great commotion, and certain remarkable comments.

'Well! – if it had been *me* now, I should have had no tea at all – if it had been Fergus, even, he would have had to put up with such as there was, and been told to be thankful, for it was far too good for him; but *you* – we can't do too much for you – it's always so – if there's anything particularly nice at table, mamma winks and nods at me, to abstain from it, and if I don't attend to that, she whispers, "Don't eat so much of that, Rose, Gilbert will like it for his supper" – *I'm* nothing at all – in the parlour, it's, "Come Rose, put away your things, and let's have the room nice and tidy against they come in; and keep up a good fire; Gilbert likes a cheerful fire." In the kitchen – "Make that pie a large one, Rose, I dare say the boys'll be hungry; and don't put so much pepper in, they'll not like it I'm sure" – or, "Rose, don't put so many spices in the pudding, Gilbert likes it plain," – or, "Mind you put plenty of currants in the cake, Fergus likes plenty." If I say, "Well, mamma, *I* don't," I'm told I ought not to think of myself – "You know Rose, in all household matters, we have only two things to consider, first, what's proper to be done, and secondly, what's most agreeable to the gentlemen of the house – anything will do for the ladies." '

'And very good doctrine too,' said my mother. 'Gilbert thinks so, I'm sure.'

'Very convenient doctrine, for us at all events,' said I; 'but if you would really study my pleasure, mother, you must consider your own comfort and convenience a little more than you do – as for Rose, I have no doubt she'll take care of herself; and whenever she does make a sacrifice or perform a remarkable act of devotedness, she'll take good care to let me know the extent of it. But for *you*, I might sink into the grossest condition of self-indulgence and carelessness about the wants of others, from the mere habit of being constantly cared for myself, and having all my wants anticipated or immediately supplied, while left in total ignorance of what is done for me – if Rose did not enlighten me now and then; and I should receive all your kindness as a matter of course, and never know how much I owe you.'

'Ah! and you never *will* know, Gilbert, till you're married. Then, when you've got some trifling, self-conceited girl like Eliza Millward, careless of everything but her own immediate pleasure and advantage, or some misguided, obstinate woman like Mrs Graham, ignorant of her principal duties, and clever only in what concerns her least to know – then, you'll find the difference.'

'It will do me good, mother; I was not sent into the world merely to exercise the good capacities and good feelings of others – was I? – but to exert my own towards them; and when I marry, I shall expect to find more pleasure in making my wife happy and comfortable, than in being made so by her: I would rather give than receive.'

'Oh! that's all nonsense, my dear – it's mere boy's talk that! You'll soon tire of petting and humouring your wife, be she ever so charming, and *then* comes the trial.'

'Well, then, we must bear one another's burdens.'

'Then you must fall each into your proper place. You'll do your business, and she, if she's worthy of you, will do hers; but it's your business to please yourself, and hers to please you. I'm sure your poor, dear father was as good a husband as ever lived, and after the first six months or so were over, I should as soon have expected him to fly, as to put himself out of his way to pleasure me. He always said I was a good wife, and did my duty; and he always did his – bless him! – he was steady and punctual, seldom found fault without a reason, always did justice to my good dinners and hardly ever spoiled my cookery by delay – and that's as much as any woman can expect of any man.'

Is it so Halford? Is that the extent of *your* domestic virtues; and does your happy wife exact no more?

## CHAPTER 7

### *The Excursion*

Not many days after this, on a mild sunny morning – rather soft under foot; for the last fall of snow was only just wasted away, leaving yet a thin ridge, here and there, lingering on the fresh, green grass beneath the hedges; but beside them already, the young primroses were peeping from among their moist, dark foliage, and the lark above was singing of summer, and hope, and love, and every heavenly thing – I was out on the hillside, enjoying these delights, and looking after the well-being of my young lambs and their mothers, when, on glancing round me, I beheld three persons ascending from the vale below. They were Eliza Millward, Fergus and Rose; so I crossed the field to meet them; and, being told they were going to Wildfell Hall, I declared myself willing to go with them, and offering my arm to Eliza, who readily accepted it in lieu of my brother's, told the latter he might go back, for I would accompany the ladies.

'I beg *your* pardon!' exclaimed he – 'it's the ladies that are accompanying me, not I them. You had all had a peep at this wonderful stranger, but me, and I could endure my wretched ignorance no longer – come what would, I must be satisfied; so I begged Rose to go with me to the Hall, and introduce me to her at once. She swore she would not unless Miss Eliza would go too; so I ran to the vicarage and fetched her; and we've come hooked all the way, as fond as a pair of

lovers – and now you've taken her from me; and you want to deprive me of my walk and my visit besides – go back to your fields and your cattle, you lubberly fellow; you're not fit to associate with ladies and gentlemen, like us, that have nothing to do but to run snooking about to our neighbours' houses, peeping into their private corners; and scenting out their secrets, and picking holes in their coats, when we don't find them ready made to our hands – you don't understand such refined sources of enjoyment.'

'Can't you both go?' suggested Eliza, disregarding the latter half of the speech.

'Yes, both to be sure!' cried Rose; 'the more the merrier – and I'm sure we shall want all the cheerfulness we can carry with us to that great, dark, gloomy room, with its narrow latticed windows, and its dismal old furniture – unless she shows us into her studio again.'

So we went all in a body; and the meagre old maidservant, that opened the door, ushered us into an apartment, such as Rose had described to me as the scene of her first introduction to Mrs Graham, a tolerably spacious and lofty room, but obscurely lighted by the old-fashioned windows, the ceiling, panels and chimney-piece of grim black oak – the latter elaborately, but not very tastefully carved – with tables and chairs to match, an old bookcase on one side of the fireplace, stocked with a motley assemblage of books, and an elderly cabinet piano on the other.

The lady was seated in a stiff, high-backed armchair, with a small, round table, containing a desk and a work basket, on one side of her, and her little boy on the other, who stood leaning his elbow on her knee, and reading to her, with wonderful fluency, from a small volume that lay in her lap; while she rested her hand on his shoulder, and abstractedly played with the long, wavy curls that fell on his ivory neck. They struck me as forming a pleasing contrast to all the surrounding objects; but of course their position was immediately changed on our entrance; I could only observe the picture during the few brief seconds that Rachel held the door for our admittance.

I do not think Mrs Graham was particularly delighted to see us: there was something indescribably chilly in her quiet, calm civility; but I did not talk much to her. Seating myself near the window, a little back from the circle, I called Arthur to me, and he and I and Sancho amused ourselves very pleasantly together, while the two young ladies baited his mother with small talk, and Fergus sat opposite, with his legs crossed, and his hands in his breeches pockets, leaning back in his chair, and staring now up at the ceiling, now straight forward at his hostess (in a manner that made me strongly inclined to kick him out of the room), now whistling *sotto voce* to himself a snatch of a favourite air, now interrupting the conversation, or filling up a pause (as the case might be), with some most impertinent question or remark. At one time it was – 'It amazes me, Mrs Graham, how you could choose such a dilapidated, rickety old place as this to live in. If you couldn't afford to occupy the whole house, and have it mended up, why couldn't you take a neat little cottage?'

'Perhaps, I was too proud, Mr Fergus,' replied she smiling; 'perhaps I took a particular fancy for this romantic old-fashioned place – but indeed, it has many

advantages over a cottage – in the first place, you see, the rooms are larger and more airy; in the second place, the unoccupied apartments, which I don't pay for, may serve as lumber-rooms, if I have anything to put in them; and they are very useful for my little boy to run about in on rainy days when he can't go out; and then, there is the garden for him to play in, and for me to work in. You see I have effected some little improvement already,' continued she, turning to the window. 'There is a bed of young vegetables in that corner, and here are some snowdrops and primroses already in bloom – and there, too, is a yellow crocus just opening in the sunshine.'

'But then how can you bear such a situation – your nearest neighbours two miles distant, and nobody looking in or passing by? – Rose would go stark mad in such a place. She can't put on life unless she sees half a dozen fresh gowns and bonnets a day – not to speak of the faces within, but you might sit watching at these windows all day long, and never see so much as an old woman carrying her eggs to market.'

'I am not sure the loneliness of the place was not one of its chief recommendations – I take no pleasure in watching people pass the windows; and I like to be quiet.'

'Oh! as good as to say, you wish we would all of us mind our own business, and let you alone.'

'No, I dislike an extensive acquaintance; but if I have a few friends, of course I am glad to see them occasionally. No one can be happy in eternal solitude. Therefore, Mr Fergus, if you choose to enter my house as a friend, I will make you welcome; if not, I must confess, I would rather you kept away.' She then turned and addressed some observation to Rose or Eliza.

'And, Mrs Graham,' said he again, five minutes after, 'we were disputing, as we came along, a question that you can readily decide for us, as it mainly regarded yourself – and indeed, we often hold discussions about you; for some of us have nothing better to do than to talk about our neighbours' concerns, and we, the indigenous plants of the soil, have known each other so long, and talked each other over so often, that we are quite sick of that game; so that a stranger coming amongst us makes an invaluable addition to our exhausted sources of amusement. Well, the question, or questions you are requested to solve – '

'Hold your tongue, Fergus!' cried Rose, in a fever of apprehension and wrath.

'I won't tell you. The questions you are requested to solve are these – First, concerning your birth, extraction, and previous residence. Some will have it that you are a foreigner, and some an Englishwoman; some a native of the north country, and some of the south; some say – '

'Well, Mr Fergus, I'll tell you. I'm an Englishwoman – and I don't see why anyone should doubt it – and I was born in the country neither in the extreme north nor south of our happy isle; and in the country I have chiefly passed my life, and now, I hope, you are satisfied; for I am not disposed to answer any more questions at present.'

'Except this – '

'No, not one more!' laughed she, and instantly quitting her seat, she sought

refuge at the window by which I was seated, and, in very desperation, to escape my brother's persecutions, endeavoured to draw me into conversation.

'Mr Markham,' said she, her rapid utterance and heightened colour too plainly evincing her disquietude; 'have you forgotten the fine sea view we were speaking of some time ago? I think I must trouble you, now, to tell me the nearest way to it; for if this beautiful weather continue, I shall, perhaps, be able to walk there, and take my sketch; I have exhausted every other subject for painting, and I long to see it.'

I was about to comply with her request; but Rose would not suffer me to proceed.

'Oh, don't tell her, Gilbert!' cried she; 'she shall go with us. It's — Bay you are thinking about I suppose, Mrs Graham. It is a very long walk, too far for you, and out of the question for Arthur. But we were thinking about making a picnic to see it, some fine day; and, if you will wait till the settled fine weather comes, I'm sure we shall all be delighted to have you amongst us.'

Poor Mrs Graham looked dismayed, and attempted to make excuses, but Rose, either compassionating her lonely life, or anxious to cultivate her acquaintance, was determined to have her; and every objection was overruled. She was told it would only be a small party, and all friends, and that the best view of all was from — Cliffs, full five miles distant.

'Just a nice walk for the gentlemen,' continued Rose; 'but the ladies will drive and walk by turns; for we shall have our pony-carriage, which will be plenty large enough to contain little Arthur and three ladies, together with your sketching apparatus, and our provisions.'

So the proposal was finally acceded to; and, after some further discussion respecting the time and manner of the projected excursion, we rose, and took our leave.

But this was only March: a cold, wet April, and two weeks of May passed over before we could venture forth on our expedition with the reasonable hope of obtaining that pleasure we sought in pleasant prospects, cheerful society, fresh air, good cheer, and exercise, without the alloy of bad roads, cold winds, or threatening clouds. Then, on a glorious morning, are gathered our forces and set forth. The company consisted of Mrs and Master Graham, Mary and Eliza Millward, Jane and Richard Wilson, and Rose, Fergus, and Gilbert Markham.

Mr Lawrence had been invited to join us, but, for some reason best known to himself, had refused to give us his company. I had solicited the favour myself. When I did so, he hesitated, and asked who were going. Upon my naming Miss Wilson among the rest, he seemed half inclined to go, but when I mentioned Mrs Graham, thinking it might be a further inducement, it appeared to have a contrary effect, and he declined it altogether, and, to confess the truth, the decision was not displeasing to me, though I could scarcely tell you why.

It was about midday, when we reached the place of our destination. Mrs Graham walked all the way to the cliffs; and little Arthur walked the greater part of it too; for he was now much more hardy and active, than when he first entered the neighbourhood, and he did not like being in the carriage with

strangers, while all his four friends, mamma, and Sancho, and Mr Markham, and Miss Millward, were on foot, journeying far behind, or passing through distant fields and lanes.

I have a very pleasant recollection of that walk, along the hard, white, sunny road, shaded here and there with bright green trees, and adorned with flowery banks and blossoming hedges of delicious fragrance; or through pleasant fields and lanes, all glorious in the sweet flowers, and brilliant verdure of delightful May. It was true, Eliza was not beside me; but she was with her friends in the pony-carriage, as happy, I trusted, as I was; and even when we pedestrians, having forsaken the highway for a short cut across the fields, beheld the little carriage far away, disappearing amid the green, embowering trees, I did not hate those trees for snatching the dear little bonnet and shawl from my sight, nor did I feel that all those intervening objects lay between my happiness and me; for, to confess the truth, I was too happy in the company of Mrs Graham, to regret the absence of Eliza Millward.

The former, it is true, was most provokingly unsociable at first – seemingly bent upon talking to no one but Mary Millward and Arthur. She and Mary journeyed along together, generally with the child between them; but where the road permitted, I always walked on the other side of her, Richard Wilson taking the other side of Miss Millward, and Fergus roving here and there according to his fancy; and after a while, she became more friendly, and at length, I succeeded in securing her attention, almost entirely to myself – and then I was happy indeed; for whenever she did condescend to converse, I liked to listen. Where her opinions and sentiments tallied with mine, it was her extreme good sense, her exquisite taste and feeling that delighted me; where they differed, it was still her uncompromising boldness in the avowal or defence of that difference – her earnestness and keenness that piqued my fancy: and even when she angered me by her unkind words or looks, and her uncharitable conclusions respecting me, it only made me the more dissatisfied with myself for having so unfavourably impressed her, and the more desirous to vindicate my character and disposition in her eyes, and if possible, to win her esteem.

At length our walk was ended. The increasing height and boldness of the hills had for some time intercepted the prospect; but, on gaining the summit of a steep acclivity, and looking downward, an opening lay before us – and the blue sea burst upon our sight! – deep violet blue – not deadly calm, but covered with glinting breakers – diminutive white specks twinkling on its bosom, and scarcely to be distinguished by the keenest vision, from the little sea-mews that sported above, their white wings glittering in the sunshine: only one or two vessels were visible; and those were far away.

I looked at my companion to see what she thought of this glorious scene. She said nothing: but she stood still, and fixed her eyes upon it with a gaze that assured me she was not disappointed. She had very fine eyes by the by – I don't know whether I've told you before, but they were full of soul, large, clear, and nearly black – not brown, but very dark grey. A cool, reviving breeze blew from the sea – soft, pure, salubrious: it waved her drooping ringlets, and imparted a

livelier colour to her usually too pallid lip and cheek. She felt its exhilarating influence, and so did I – I felt it tingling through my frame, but dared not give way to it while she remained so quiet. There was an aspect of subdued exhilaration in her face, that kindled into almost a smile of exalted, glad intelligence as her eye met mine. Never had she looked so lovely: never had my heart so warmly cleaved to her as now. Had we been left two minutes longer, standing there alone, I cannot answer for the consequences. Happily for my discretion, perhaps for my enjoyment during the remainder of the day, we were speedily summoned to the repast – a very respectable collation, which Rose, assisted by Miss Wilson and Eliza, who, having shared her seat in the carriage, had arrived with her a little before the rest, had set out upon an elevated platform overlooking the sea, and sheltered from the hot sun by a shelving rock and overhanging trees.

Mrs Graham seated herself at a distance from me. Eliza was my nearest neighbour. She exerted herself to be agreeable, in her gentle, unobtrusive way, and was, no doubt, as fascinating and charming as ever, if I could only have felt it. But soon, my heart began to warm towards her once again; and we were all very merry and happy together – as far as I could see – throughout the protracted, social meal.

When that was over, Rose summoned Fergus to help her to gather up the fragments, and the knives, dishes, etc. and restore them to the baskets; and Mrs Graham took her camp-stool and drawing materials; and having begged Miss Millward to take charge of her precious son, and strictly enjoined him not to wander from his new guardian's side, she left us and proceeded along the steep, stony hill, to a loftier, more precipitous eminence at some distance, whence a still finer prospect was to be had, where she preferred taking her sketch, though some of the ladies told her it was a frightful place, and advised her not to attempt it.

When she was gone, I felt as if there was to be no more fun – though it is difficult to say what she had contributed to the hilarity of the party. No jests, and little laughter had escaped her lips; but her smile had animated my mirth, a keen observation or a cheerful word from her had insensibly sharpened my wits, and thrown an interest over all that was done and said by the rest. Even my conversation with Eliza had been enlivened by her presence, though I knew it not; and now that she was gone, Eliza's playful nonsense ceased to amuse me – nay, grew wearisome to my soul, and I grew weary of amusing her: I felt myself drawn by an irresistible attraction to that distant point where the fair artist sat and plied her solitary task – and not long did I attempt to resist it: while my little neighbour was exchanging a few words with Miss Wilson, I rose and cannily slipped away. A few rapid strides, and a little active clambering, soon brought me to the place when she was seated – a narrow ledge of rock at the very verge of the cliff which descended with a steep, precipitous slant, quite down to the rocky shore.

She did not hear me coming: the falling of my shadow across her paper, gave her an electric start; and she looked hastily round – any other lady of my acquaintance would have screamed under such a sudden alarm.

'Oh! I didn't know it was you – why did you startle me so?' said she, somewhat testily, 'I hate anybody to come upon me so unexpectedly.'

'Why, what did you take me for?' said I, 'if I had known you were so nervous, I would have been more cautious; but – '

'Well, never mind. What did you come for? Are they all coming?'

'No; this little ledge could scarcely contain them all.'

'I'm glad, for I'm tired of talking.'

'Well then, I won't talk. I'll only sit and watch your drawing.'

'Oh, but you know I don't like that.'

'Then I'll content myself with admiring this magnificent prospect.'

She made no objection to this; and, for some time, sketched away in silence. But I could not help stealing a glance, now and then, from the splendid view at our feet to the elegant white hand that held the pencil, and the graceful neck and glossy raven curls that drooped over the paper.

'Now,' thought I, 'if I had but a pencil and a morsel of paper, I could make a lovelier sketch than hers, admitting I had the power to delineate faithfully what is before me.'

But though this satisfaction was denied me, I was very well content to sit beside her there, and say nothing.

'Are you there still, Mr Markham?' said she at length looking round upon me – for I was seated a little behind on a mossy projection of the cliff – 'Why don't you go and amuse yourself with your friends?'

'Because I am tired of them, like you; and I shall have enough of them tomorrow – or at any time hence; but you, I may not have the pleasure of seeing again for I know not how long.'

'What was Arthur doing when you came away?'

'He was with Miss Millward where you left him – all right, but hoping mamma would not be long away. You didn't entrust him to me, by the by,' I grumbled, 'though I had the honour of a much longer acquaintance; but Miss Millward has the art of conciliating and amusing children,' I carelessly added, 'if she is good for nothing else.'

'Miss Millward has many estimable qualities, which such as you cannot be expected to perceive or appreciate. Will you tell Arthur that I shall come in a few minutes?'

'If that be the case, I will wait, with your permission, till those few minutes are past; and then I can assist you to descend this difficult path.'

'Thank you – I always manage best, on such occasions, without assistance.'

'But, at least, I can carry your stool and sketchbook.'

She did not deny me this favour; but I was rather offended at her evident desire to be rid of me, and was beginning to repent of my pertinacity, when she somewhat appeased me by consulting my taste and judgement about some doubtful matter in her drawing. My opinion, happily, met her approbation, and the improvement I suggested was adopted without hesitation.

'I have often wished in vain,' said she, 'for another's judgement to appeal to when I could scarcely trust the direction of my own eye and head, they having been so long occupied with the contemplation of a single object, as to become almost incapable of forming a proper idea respecting it.'

'That,' replied I, 'is only one of many evils to which a solitary life exposes us.'

'True,' said she; and again we relapsed into silence.

About two minutes after, however, she declared her sketch completed and closed the book.

On returning to the scene of our repast, we found all the company had deserted it, with the exception of three – Mary Millward, Richard Wilson, and Arthur Graham. The younger gentleman lay fast asleep with his head pillowed on the lady's lap; the other was seated beside her with a pocket edition of some classic author in his hand. He never went anywhere without such a companion wherewith to improve his leisure moments: all time seemed lost that was not devoted to study, or exacted, by his physical nature, for the bare support of life. Even now, he could not abandon himself to the enjoyment of that pure air and balmy sunshine – that splendid prospect, and those soothing sounds, the music of the waves and of the soft wind in the sheltering trees above him – not even with a lady by his side (though not a very charming one, I will allow) – he must pull out his book, and make the most of his time while digesting his temperate meal, and reposing his weary limbs, unused to so much exercise.

Perhaps, however, he spared a moment to exchange a word or a glance with his companion now and then – at any rate, she did not appear at all resentful of his conduct; for her homely features wore an expression of unusual cheerfulness and serenity, and she was studying his pale, thoughtful face with great complacency when we arrived.

The journey homeward was by no means so agreeable, to me, as the former part of the day; for now Mrs Graham was in the carriage, and Eliza Millward was the companion of my walk. She had observed my preference for the young widow, and evidently felt herself neglected. She did not manifest her chagrin by keen reproaches, bitter sarcasms, or pouting sullen silence – any or all of these I could easily have endured, or lightly laughed away; but she showed it by a kind of gentle melancholy, a mild, reproachful sadness that cut me to the heart. I tried to cheer her up, and apparently succeeded in some degree, before the walk was over; but in the very act my conscience reproved me, knowing, as I did, that, sooner or later, the tie must be broken, and this was only nourishing false hopes, and putting off the evil day.

When the pony-carriage had approached as near Wildfell Hall as the road would permit – unless, indeed, it proceeded up the long rough lane, which Mrs Graham would not allow – the young widow and her son alighted, relinquishing the driver's seat to Rose; and I persuaded Eliza to take the latter's place. Having put her comfortably in, bid her take care of the evening air, and wished her a kind good-night, I felt considerably relieved, and hastened to offer my services to Mrs Graham to carry her apparatus up the fields, but she had already hung her camp stool on her arm and taken her sketchbook in her hand; and insisted upon bidding me adieu then and there, with the rest of the company. But this time, she declined my proffered aid in so kind and friendly a manner, that I almost forgave her.

## CHAPTER 8

## *The Present*

Six weeks had past away. It was a splendid morning about the close of June. Most of the hay was cut, but the last week had been very unfavourable; and now that fine weather was come at last, being determined to make the most of it, I had gathered all hands together into the hayfield, and was working away myself, in the midst of them, in my shirt sleeves, with a light, shady straw hat on my head, catching up armfuls of moist, reeking grass, and shaking it out to the four winds of Heaven, at the head of a goodly file of servants and hirelings – intending so to labour, from morning to night, with as much zeal and assiduity as I could look for from any of them, as well to prosper the work by my own exertion as to animate the workers by my example – when, lo! my resolutions were overthrown in a moment, by the simple fact of my brother's running up to me and putting into my hand a small parcel, just arrived from London, which I had been for some time expecting. I tore off the cover, and disclosed an elegant and portable edition of *Marmion*.

'I guess, I know who that's for,' said Fergus, who stood looking on while I complacently examined the volume. 'That's for Miss Eliza, now.'

He pronounced this with a tone and look so prodigiously knowing, that I was glad to contradict him.

'You're wrong my lad,' said I; and taking up my coat, I deposited the book in one of its pockets, and then put it on (i.e. the coat). 'Now come here you idle dog, and make yourself useful for once,' I continued – 'Pull off your coat, and take my place in the field till I come back.'

'Till you come back? – and where are you going, pray?'

'No matter – *where* – the *when* is all that concerns you; and I shall be back by dinner, at least.'

'Oh ho! and I'm to labour away till then, am I – and to keep all these fellows hard at it besides? – Well, well! I'll submit – for once in a way – Come my lads, you must look sharp: *I'm* coming to help you now; and woe be to that man, or woman either, that pauses for a moment amongst you – whether to stare about him, to scratch his head, or blow his nose – no pretext will serve – nothing, but work, work, work in the sweat of your face' – etc., etc.

Leaving him thus haranguing the people, more to their amusement than edification, I returned to the house, and having made some alteration in my toilet, hastened away to Wildfell Hall, with the book in my pocket; for it was destined for the shelves of Mrs Graham.

'What, then, had she and you got on so well together as to come to the giving and receiving of presents?' – Not precisely, old buck; this was my first experiment in that line; and I was very anxious to see the result of it.

We had met several times since the — Bay excursion, and I had found she was not averse to my company, provided, I confined my conversation to the discussion of abstract matters, or topics of common interest; the moment I touched upon the sentimental or the complimentary, or made the slightest approach to tenderness in word or look, I was not only punished by an immediate change in her manner at the time, but doomed to find her more cold and distant, if not entirely inaccessible, when next I sought her company. This circumstance did not greatly disconcert me however, because, I attributed it not so much to any dislike of my person, as to some absolute resolution against a second marriage formed prior to the time of our acquaintance, whether from excess of affection for her late husband, or because she had had enough of him and the matrimonial state together. At first, indeed, she had seemed to take a pleasure in mortifying my vanity and crushing my presumption – relentlessly nipping off bud by bud as they ventured to appear; and then, I confess, I was deeply wounded, though, at the same time, stimulated to seek revenge; but latterly, finding, beyond a doubt, that I was not that empty-headed coxcomb she had first supposed me, she had repulsed my modest advances in quite a different spirit. It was a kind of serious, almost sorrowful displeasure, which I soon learnt carefully to avoid awakening.

'Let me first establish my position as a friend,' thought I – 'the patron and playfellow of her son, the sober, solid, plain-dealing friend of herself, and then, when I have made myself fairly necessary to her comfort and enjoyment in life (as I believe I can), we'll see what next may be effected.'

So we talked about painting, poetry, and music, theology, geology, and philosophy: once or twice I lent her a book, and once she lent me one in return: I met her in her walks as often as I could; I came to her house as often as I dared. My first pretext for invading the sanctum, was to bring Arthur a little waddling puppy of which Sancho was the father, and which delighted the child beyond expression, and, consequently, could not fail to please his mamma. My second was to bring him a book, which, knowing his mother's particularity, I had carefully selected, and which I submitted for her approbation before presenting it to him. Then, I brought her some plants for her garden, in my sister's name – having previously persuaded Rose to send them. Each of these times I enquired after the picture she was painting from the sketch taken on the cliff, and was admitted into the studio, and asked my opinion or advice respecting its progress.

My last visit had been to return the book she had lent me; and then it was, that, in casually discussing the poetry of Sir Walter Scott, she had expressed a wish to see *Marmion*, and I had conceived the presumptuous idea of making her a present of it, and, on my return home, instantly sent for the smart little volume I had this morning received. But an apology for invading the hermitage was still necessary; so I had furnished myself with a blue morocco collar for Arthur's little dog; and that being given and received, with much more joy and gratitude, on the part of the receiver, than the worth of the gift, or the selfish motive of the giver deserved, I ventured to ask Mrs Graham for one more look at the picture, if it was still there.

'Oh yes! come in,' said she (for I had met them in the garden). 'It is finished and framed, all ready for sending away; but give me your last opinion, and, if you can suggest any further improvement, it shall be – duly considered, at least.'

The picture was strikingly beautiful: it was the very scene itself, transferred as if by magic to the canvas; but I expressed my approbation in guarded terms, and few words, for fear of displeasing her. She, however, attentively watched my looks, and her artist's pride was gratified, no doubt, to read my heart-felt admiration in my eyes. But, while I gazed, I thought upon the book, and wondered how it was to be presented. My heart failed me; but I determined not to be such a fool as to come away without having made the attempt. It was useless waiting for an opportunity, and useless trying to concoct a speech for the occasion. The more plainly and naturally the thing was done, the better, I thought; so I just looked out of the window to screw up my courage, and then pulled out the book, turned round, and put it into her hand, with this short explanation.

'You were wishing to see *Marmion*, Mrs Graham; and here it is, if you will be so kind as to take it.'

A momentary flush suffused her face – perhaps, a blush of sympathetic shame for such an awkward style of presentation: she gravely examined the volume on both sides; then silently turned over the leaves, knitting her brows the while, in serious cogitation; then closed the book, and turning from it to me, quietly asked the price of it – I felt the hot blood rush to my face.

'I'm sorry to offend you, Mr Markham,' said she, 'but unless I pay for the book, I cannot take it.' And she laid it on the table.

'Why cannot you?'

'Because – ' she paused, and looked at the carpet.

'Why cannot you?' I repeated with a degree of irascibility that roused her to lift her eyes, and look me steadily in the face.

'Because I don't like to put myself under obligations that I can never repay – I *am* obliged to you already for your kindness to my son; but his grateful affection, and your own good feelings must reward you for that.'

'Nonsense!' ejaculated I.

She turned her eyes on me again, with a look of quiet, grave surprise, that had the effect of a rebuke, whether intended for such or not.

'Then you won't take the book?' I asked, more mildly than I had yet spoken.

'I will gladly take it, if you will let me pay for it.'

I told her the exact price, and the cost of the carriage besides, in as calm a tone as I could command – for in fact, I was ready to weep with disappointment and vexation.

She produced her purse, and coolly counted out the money, but hesitated to put it into my hand. Attentively regarding me, in a tone of soothing softness she observed – 'You think yourself insulted Mr Markham – I wish I could make you understand that – that I – '

'I do understand you, perfectly,' I said. 'You think that if you were to accept that trifle from me now, I should presume upon it hereafter; but you are

mistaken – if you will only oblige me by taking it, believe me, I shall build no hopes upon it, and consider this no precedent for future favours – and it is nonsense to talk about putting yourself under obligations to *me* when you must know that in such a case the obligation is entirely on my side – the favour on yours.'

'Well then I'll take you at your word,' she answered with a most angelic smile, returning the odious money to her purse – 'but *remember*!'

'I will remember – what I have said; but do not you punish my presumption by withdrawing your friendship entirely from me – or expect me to atone for it by being *more* distant than before,' said I, extending my hand to take leave, for I was too much excited to remain.

'Well then! let us be as we were,' replied she, frankly placing her hand in mine; and while I held it there, I had much difficulty to refrain from pressing it to my lips; but that would be suicidal madness: I had been bold enough already, and this premature offering had wellnigh given the death-blow to my hopes.

It was with an agitated burning heart and brain that I hurried homewards, regardless of that scorching noonday sun – forgetful of everything but her I had just left – regretting nothing but her impenetrability, and my own precipitancy and want of tact – fearing nothing but her hateful resolution, and my inability to overcome it – hoping nothing – but halt – I will not bore you with my conflicting hopes and fears – my serious cogitations and resolves.

## CHAPTER 9

### *A Snake in the Grass*

Though my affections might now be said to be fairly weaned from Eliza Millward, I did not yet entirely relinquish my visits to the vicarage, because I wanted, as it were, to let her down easy; without raising much sorrow, or incurring much resentment – or making myself the talk of the parish; and besides, if I had wholly kept away, the vicar, who looked upon my visits as paid chiefly, if not entirely to himself, would have felt himself decidedly affronted by the neglect. But when I called there the day after my interview with Mrs Graham, he happened to be from home – a circumstance by no means so agreeable to me now as it had been on former occasions. Miss Millward was there, it is true, but she, of course, would be little better than a non-entity. However, I resolved to make my visit a short one, and to talk to Eliza in a brotherly, friendly sort of way, such as our long acquaintance might warrant me in assuming, and which, I thought, could neither give offence nor serve to encourage false hopes.

It was never my custom to talk about Mrs Graham either to her or anyone else; but I had not been seated three minutes, before she brought that lady on to the carpet herself, in a rather remarkable manner.

'Oh, Mr Markham!' said she, with a shocked expression and voice subdued almost to a whisper – 'what do you think of these shocking reports about Mrs Graham? – can you encourage us to disbelieve them?'

'What reports?'

'Ah, now! *you* know!' she slyly smiled and shook her head.

'I know nothing about them – what in the world do you mean, Eliza?'

'Oh, don't ask *me*! – *I* can't explain it.' She took up the cambric handkerchief which she had been beautifying with a deep lace border, and began to be very busy.

'What is it, Miss Millward? What does she mean?' said I, appealing to her sister, who seemed to be absorbed in the hemming of a large, coarse sheet.

'I don't know,' replied she – 'Some idle slander, somebody has been inventing, I suppose. I never heard it till Eliza told me, the other day – but if all the parish dinned it in my ears, I shouldn't believe a word of it – I know Mrs Graham too well!'

'Quite right, Miss Millward! – and so do I – whatever it may be.'

'Well!' observed Eliza, with a gentle sigh – 'It's well to have such a comfortable assurance regarding the worth of those we love – I only wish you may not find your confidence misplaced.'

And she raised her face, and gave me such a look of sorrowful tenderness as might have melted my heart, but within those eyes there lurked a something that I did not like; and I wondered how I ever could have admired them: her sister's honest face and small grey optics appeared far more agreeable; but I was out of temper with Eliza, at that moment, for her insinuations against Mrs Graham – which were false, I was certain, whether she knew it or not.

I said nothing more on the subject, however, at the time, and but little on any other; for, finding I could not well recover my equanimity, I presently rose and took leave, excusing myself under the plea of business at the farm; and to the farm I went – not troubling my mind one whit about the possible truth of these mysterious reports, but only wondering what they were, by whom originated, and on what foundations raised – and how they could the most effectually be silenced or disproved.

A few days after this, we had another of our quiet little parties, to which the usual company of friends and neighbours had been invited, and Mrs Graham among the number. She could not now absent herself under the plea of dark evenings or inclement weather, and, greatly to my relief, she came. Without her I should have found the whole affair an intolerable bore; but the moment of her arrival brought new life to the house; and though I must not neglect the other guests for her, or expect to engross much of her attention and conversation to myself alone, I anticipated an evening of no common enjoyment.

Mr Lawrence came too. He did not arrive till some time after the rest were assembled. I was curious to see how he would comport himself to Mrs Graham. A slight bow was all that passed between them on his entrance; and having politely greeted the other members of the company, he seated himself quite aloof from the young widow, between my mother and Rose.

'Did you ever see such art!' whispered Eliza, who was my nearest neighbour. 'Would you not say they were perfect strangers?'

'Almost; but what then?'

'What then! – why you can't pretend to be ignorant?'

'Ignorant of *what*?' demanded I, so sharply that she started and replied – 'Oh, hush! don't speak so loud.'

'Well, tell me then,' I answered in a lower tone; 'what is it you mean? I hate enigmas.'

'Well you know, I don't vouch for the truth of it – indeed, far from it – but haven't you heard – '

'I've heard *nothing*, except from you.'

'You must be wilfully deaf then; for anyone will tell you that – but I shall only anger you by repeating it, I see; so I had better hold my tongue.'

She closed her lips and folded her hands before her with an air of injured meekness.

'If you had wished not to anger me, you should have held your tongue from the beginning; or else spoken out plainly and honestly all you had to say.'

She turned aside her face, pulled out her handkerchief, rose, and went to the window, where she stood for same time, evidently dissolved in tears. I was astounded, provoked, ashamed – not so much of my harshness as for her childish weakness. However, no one seemed to notice her, and shortly after, we were summoned to the tea-table; in those parts it was customary to sit to the table at tea-time, on all occasions, and make a meal of it; for we dined early. On taking my seat, I had Rose on one side of me, and an empty chair on the other.

'May I sit by you?' said a soft voice at my elbow.

'If you like,' was the reply; and Eliza slipped into the vacant chair; then looking up in my face with a half sad, half playful smile, she whispered – 'You're so stern, Gilbert.'

I handed down her tea with a slightly contemptuous smile, and said nothing, for I had nothing to say.

'What have I done to offend you?' said she, more plaintively. 'I wish I knew.'

'Come, take your tea, Eliza, and don't be foolish,' responded I, handing her the sugar and cream.

Just then, there arose a slight commotion on the other side of me, occasioned by Miss Wilson's coming to negotiate an exchange of seats with Rose.

'Will you be so good as to exchange places with me, Miss Markham?' said she, 'for I don't like to sit by Mrs Graham. If your mamma thinks proper to invite such persons to her house, she cannot object to her daughter's keeping company with them.'

This latter clause was added in a sort of soliloquy when Rose was gone; but I was not polite enough to let it pass: 'Will you be so good as to tell me what you mean, Miss Wilson?' said I.

The question startled her a little, but not much.

'Why, Mr Markham,' replied she coolly, having quickly recovered her self-possession, 'it surprises me rather that Mrs Markham should invite such a

person as Mrs Graham to her house; but, perhaps, she is not aware that the lady's character is considered scarcely respectable.'

'She is not, nor am I; and therefore, you would oblige me by explaining your meaning a little further.'

'This is scarcely the time or the place for such explanations; but I think you can hardly be so ignorant as you pretend: you must know her as well as I do.'

'I think I do, perhaps a little better; and therefore, if you will inform me what you have heard, or imagined against her, I shall, perhaps, be able to set you right.'

'Can you tell me, then, who was her husband; or if she ever had any?'

Indignation kept me silent. At such a time and place I could not trust myself to answer.

'Have you never observed,' said Eliza, 'what a striking likeness there is between that child of hers and – '

'And whom?' demanded Miss Wilson, with an air of cold, but keen severity.

Eliza was startled: the timidly spoken suggestion had been intended for my ear alone.

'Oh, I beg your pardon!' pleaded she, 'I may be mistaken – perhaps I *was* mistaken.' But she accompanied the words with a sly glance of derision directed to me from the corner of her disingenuous eye.

'There's no need to ask *my* pardon,' replied her friend; 'but I see no one here that at all resembles that child, except his mother; and when you hear ill-natured reports, Miss Eliza, I will thank you – that is, I think you will do well to refrain from repeating them. I presume the person you allude to is Mr Lawrence; but I think I can assure you that your suspicions, in that respect, are utterly misplaced; and if he has any particular connection with the lady at all (which no one has a right to assert), at least, he has (what cannot be said of some others) sufficient sense of propriety to withhold him from acknowledging anything more than a bowing acquaintance in the presence of respectable persons – he was evidently both surprised and annoyed to find her here.'

'Go it!' cried Fergus, who sat on the other side of Eliza, and was the only individual who shared that side of the table with us; 'go it like bricks! Mind you don't leave her one stone upon another.'

Miss Wilson drew herself up with a look of freezing scorn, but said nothing. Eliza would have replied, but I interrupted her by saying as calmly as I could, though in a tone which betrayed, no doubt, some little of what I felt within – 'We have had enough of this subject: if we can only speak to slander our betters, let us hold our tongues.'

'I think you'd better,' observed Fergus; 'and so does our good parson: he has been addressing the company in his richest vein all the while, and eyeing you, from time to time, with looks of stern distaste, while you sat there, irreverently whispering and muttering together; and once he paused in the middle of a story – or a sermon, I don't know which, and fixed his eyes upon you, Gilbert, as much as to say – "When Mr Markham has done flirting with those two ladies I will proceed!" '

What more was said at the tea-table I cannot tell; nor how I found patience to sit till the meal was over. I remember, however, that I swallowed with difficulty the remainder of the tea that was in my cup, and ate nothing; and that the first thing I did was to stare at Arthur Graham, who sat beside his mother on the opposite side of the table, and the second to stare at Mr Lawrence, who sat below; and, first, it struck me that there *was* a likeness; but, on further contemplation, I concluded it was only in imagination. Both, it is true, had more delicate features and smaller bones than commonly fall to the lot of individuals of the rougher sex, and Lawrence's complexion was pale and clear, and Arthur's delicately fair; but Arthur's tiny, somewhat snubby nose could never become so long and straight as Mr Lawrence's, and the outline of his face, though not full enough to be round, and too finely converging to the small, dimpled chin to be square, could never be drawn out to the long oval of the other's; while the child's hair was evidently of a lighter, warmer tint than the elder gentleman's had ever been, and his large, clear, blue eyes, though prematurely serious at times, were utterly dissimilar to the shy hazel eyes of Mr Lawrence, whence the sensitive soul looked so distrustfully forth, as ever ready to retire within, from the offences of a too rude, too uncongenial world. Wretch that I was to harbour that detestable idea for a moment! Did I not know Mrs Graham? Had I not seen her, conversed with her time after time? Was I not certain that she, in intellect, in purity and elevation of soul, was immeasurably superior to any of her detractors; that she was, in fact, the noblest, the most adorable, of her sex I had ever beheld, or even imagined to exist? Yes, and I would say with Mary Millward (sensible girl as she was) that if all the parish, ay, or all the world should din these horrible lies in my ears, I would not believe them; for I knew her better than they.

Meantime, my brain was on fire with indignation, and my heart seemed ready to burst from its prison with conflicting passions. I regarded my two fair neighbours with a feeling of abhorrence and loathing I scarcely endeavoured to conceal: I was rallied from several quarters for my abstraction and ungallant neglect of the ladies; but I cared little for that: all I cared about, besides that one grand subject of my thoughts, was to see the cups travel up to the tea-tray, and not come down again. I thought Mr Millward never *would* cease telling us that he was no tea-drinker, and that it was highly injurious to keep loading the stomach with slops to the exclusion of more wholesome sustenance, and so give himself time to finish his fourth cup.

At length it was over; and I rose and left the table and the guests, without a word of apology – I could endure their company no longer. I rushed out to cool my brain in the balmy evening air, and to compose my mind, or indulge my passionate thoughts in the solitude of the garden.

To avoid being seen from the windows, I went down a quiet, little avenue, that skirted one side of the enclosure, at the bottom of which was a seat embowered in roses and honeysuckles. Here I sat down to think over the virtues and wrongs of the lady of Wildfell Hall; but I had not been so occupied two minutes before voices and laughter, and glimpses of moving objects through the

trees, informed me that the whole company had turned out to take an airing in the garden too. However, I nestled up in a corner of the bower, and hoped to retain possession of it, secure alike from observation and intrusion. But no – confound it – there was someone coming down the avenue! Why couldn't they enjoy the flowers and sunshine of the open garden, and leave that sunless nook to me, and the gnats and midges?

But peeping through my fragrant screen of interwoven branches to discover who the intruders were (for a murmur of voices told me it was more than one), my vexation instantly subsided, and far other feelings agitated my still unquiet soul; for there was Mrs Graham, slowly moving down the walk with Arthur by her side, and no one else. Why were they alone? Had the poison of detracting tongues already spread through all; and had they all turned their backs upon her? I now recollected having seen Mrs Wilson, in the early part of the evening, edging her chair close up to my mother, and bending forward, evidently in the delivery of some important, confidential intelligence; and from the incessant wagging of her head, the frequent distortions of her wrinkled physiognomy, and the winking and malicious twinkle of her little ugly eyes, I judged it was some spicy piece of scandal that engaged her powers; and from the cautious privacy of the communication, I supposed some person then present, was the luckless object of her calumnies; and from all these tokens, together with my mother's looks and gestures of mingled horror and incredulity, I now concluded that object to have been Mrs Graham. I did not emerge from my place of concealment, till she had nearly reached the bottom of the walk, lest my appearance should drive her away; and when I did step forward, she stood still and seemed inclined to turn back as it was.

'Oh, don't let us disturb you, Mr Markham!' said she. 'We came here to seek retirement ourselves; not to intrude on your seclusion.'

'I am no hermit, Mrs Graham – though I own it looks rather like it, to absent myself in this uncourteous fashion from my guests.'

'I feared you were unwell,' said she with a look of real concern.

'I was rather, but it's over now. Do sit here a little, and rest, and tell me how you like this arbour,' said I, and lifting Arthur by the shoulders, I planted him in the middle of the seat by way of securing his mamma, who, acknowledging it to be a tempting place of refuge, threw herself back in one corner, while I took possession of the other.

But that word refuge disturbed me. Had their unkindness then really driven her to seek for peace in solitude?

'Why have they left you alone?' I asked.

'It is I who have left them,' was the smiling rejoinder. 'I was wearied to death with small-talk – nothing wears me out like that. I cannot imagine how they *can* go on as they do.'

I could not help smiling at the serious depth of her wonderment.

'Is it that they think it a *duty* to be continually talking,' pursued she, 'and so never pause to think, but fill up with aimless trifles and vain repetitions, when subjects of real interest fail to present themselves? – or do they really take a pleasure in such discourse?'

'Very likely they do,' said I: 'their shallow minds can hold no great ideas, and their light heads are carried away by trivialities, that would not move a better furnished skull; and their only alternative to such discourse, is to plunge over head and ears into the slough of scandal – which is their chief delight.'

'Not all of them surely?' cried the lady, astonished at the bitterness of my remark.

'No, certainly; I exonerate my sister from such degraded tastes – and my mother too, if you included *her* in your animadversions.'

'I meant no animadversions against anyone and certainly intended no dis-respectful allusions to your mother. I have known some sensible persons great adepts in that style of conversation, when circumstances impelled them to it; but it is a gift I cannot boast the possession of. I kept up my attention, on this occasion, as long as I could, but when my powers were exhausted, I stole away, to seek a few minutes' repose in this quiet walk. I hate talking, where there is no exchange of ideas or sentiments, and no good given or received.'

'Well,' said I, 'if ever I trouble you with my loquacity, tell me so at once, and I promise not to be offended; for I possess the faculty of enjoying the company of those I – of my friends as well in silence as in conversation.'

'I don't quite believe you; but if it were so, you would exactly suit me for a companion.'

'I am all you wish, then, in other respects?'

'No, I don't mean that. How beautiful those little clusters of foliage look, where the sun comes through behind them!' said she, on purpose to change the subject.

And they did look beautiful, where at intervals the level rays of the sun penetrating the thickness of trees and shrubs on the opposite side of the path before us, relieved their dusky verdure by displaying patches of semi-transparent leaves of resplendent golden green.

'I almost wish I were not a painter,' observed my companion.

'Why so? One would think at such a time you would most exult in your privilege of being able to imitate the various brilliant and delightful touches of nature.'

'No; for instead of delivering myself up to the full enjoyment of them as others do, I am always troubling my head about how I could produce the same effect upon canvas; and as that can never be done, it is mere vanity and vexation of spirit.'

'Perhaps you cannot do it to satisfy yourself, but you may and do succeed in delighting others with the result of your endeavours.'

'Well, after all I should not complain: perhaps few people gain their livelihood with so much pleasure in their toil as I do. Here is someone coming.'

She seemed vexed at the interruption.

'It is only Mr Lawrence and Miss Wilson,' said I, 'coming to enjoy a quiet stroll. They will not disturb us.'

I could not quite decipher the expression of her face; but I was satisfied there was no jealousy therein. What business had I to look for it?

'What sort of a person is Miss Wilson?' she asked.

'She is elegant and accomplished above the generality of her birth and station; and some say she is ladylike and agreeable.'

'I thought her somewhat frigid, and rather supercilious in her manner today.'

'Very likely she might be so to you. She has possibly taken a prejudice against you, for I think she regards you in the light of a rival.'

'Me? Impossible, Mr Markham!' said she, evidently astonished and annoyed.

'Well, I know nothing about it,' returned I, rather doggedly; for I thought her annoyance was chiefly against myself.

The pair had now approached within a few paces of us. Our arbour was set snugly back in a corner, before which, the avenue at its termination, turned off into the more airy walk along the bottom of the garden. As they approached this, I saw, by the aspect of Jane Wilson, that she was directing her companion's attention to us; and, as well by her cold, sarcastic smile, as by the few isolated words of her discourse that reached me, I knew full well that she was impressing him with the idea that we were strongly attached to each other. I noticed that he coloured up to the temples, gave us one furtive glance in passing, and walked on, looking grave, but seemingly offering no reply to her remarks.

It was true, then, that he *had* some designs upon Mrs Graham; and, were they honourable, he would not be so anxious to conceal them. *She* was blameless, of course, but he was detestable beyond all count.

While these thoughts flashed through my mind, my companion abruptly rose, and calling her son, said they would now go in quest of the company, and departed up the avenue. Doubtless she had heard or guessed something of Miss Wilson's remarks, and therefore, it was natural enough she should choose to continue the tête-à-tête no longer, especially as at that moment my cheeks were burning with indignation against my former friend, the token of which she might mistake for a blush of stupid embarrassment. For this I owed Miss Wilson yet another grudge; and still the more I thought upon her conduct, the more I hated her.

It was late in the evening before I joined the company. I found Mrs Graham already equipped for departure, and taking leave of the rest, who were now returned to the house. I offered – nay, begged to accompany her home. Mr Lawrence was standing by at the time, conversing with someone else. He did not look at us, but, on hearing my earnest request, he paused in the middle of a sentence to listen for her reply, and went on, with a look of quiet satisfaction the moment he found it was to be a denial.

A denial it was, decided, though not unkind. She could not be persuaded to think there was danger for herself or her child in traversing those lonely lanes and fields without attendance. It was daylight still, and she should meet no one; or if she did, the people were quiet and harmless she was well assured. In fact, she would not hear of anyone's putting himself out of the way to accompany her, though Fergus vouchsafed to offer his services, in case they should be more acceptable than mine, and my mother begged she might send one of the farming-men to escort her.

When she was gone, the rest was all a blank, or worse. Lawrence attempted

to draw me into conversation, but I snubbed him, and went to another part of the room. Shortly after, the party broke up, and he himself took leave. When he came to me, I was blind to his extended hand, and deaf to his good-night till he repeated it a second time; and then, to get rid of him, I muttered an inarticulate reply accompanied by a sulky nod.

'What is the matter, Markham?' whispered he.

I replied by a wrathful and contemptuous stare.

'Are you angry because Mrs Graham would not let you go home with her?' he asked with a faint smile that nearly exasperated me beyond control.

But, swallowing down all fiercer answers, I merely demanded – 'What business is it of yours?'

'Why, none,' replied he, with provoking quietness; 'only,' and here he raised his eyes to my face, and spoke with unusual solemnity, 'only let me tell you, Markham, that if you have any designs in that quarter they will certainly fail; and it grieves me to see you cherishing false hopes, and wasting your strength in useless efforts, for – '

'Hypocrite!' I exclaimed, and he held his breath, and looked very blank, turned white about the gills, and went away without another word.

I had wounded him to the quick; and I was glad of it.

## CHAPTER 10

### *A Contract and a Quarrel*

When all were gone, I learnt that the vile slander had indeed been circulated throughout the company, in the very presence of the victim. Rose, however, vowed she did not and would not believe it, and my mother made the same declaration, though not, I fear, with the same amount of real, unwavering incredulity. It seemed to dwell continually on her mind, and she kept irritating me from time to time by such expressions as – 'Dear, dear, who would have thought it! – Well! I always thought there was something odd about her – You see what it is for women to affect to be different to other people.' And once it was – 'I misdoubted that appearance of mystery from the very first – I *thought* there would no good come of it; but this is a sad, sad business to be sure!'

'Why, mother, you said you didn't believe these tales,' said Fergus.

'No more I do, my dear; but then, you know, there must be some foundation.'

'The foundation is in the wickedness and falsehood of the world,' said I, 'and in the fact that Mr Lawrence has been seen to go that way once or twice of an evening – and the village gossips say he goes to pay his addresses to the strange lady, and the scandal mongers have greedily seized the rumour, to make it the basis of their own infernal structure.'

'Well, but Gilbert, there must be something in her *manner* to countenance such reports.'

'Did *you* see anything in her manner?'

'No, certainly; but then you know, I always said there was something strange about her.'

I believe it was on that very evening that I ventured on another invasion of Wildfell Hall. From the time of our party, which was upwards of a week ago, I had been making daily efforts to meet its mistress in her walks; and, always disappointed (she must have managed it so on purpose), had nightly kept revolving in my mind some pretext for another call. At length, I concluded that the separation could be endured no longer (by this time, you will see I was pretty far gone), and, taking from the bookcase an old volume that I thought she might be interested in, though, from its unsightly and somewhat dilapidated condition, I had not yet ventured to offer it for her perusal, I hastened away – but not without sundry misgivings as to how she would receive me, or how I could summon courage to present myself with so slight an excuse. But, perhaps, I might see her in the field or the garden, and then, there would be no great difficulty: it was the formal knocking at the door, with the prospect of being gravely ushered in, by Rachel, to the presence of a surprised, uncordial mistress, that so greatly disturbed me.

My wish, however, was not gratified. Mrs Graham, herself, was not to be seen; but there was Arthur playing with his frolicsome little dog in the garden. I looked over the gate and called him to me. He wanted me to come in; but I told him I could not without his mother's leave.

'I'll go and ask her,' said the child.

'No, no, Arthur, you mustn't do that – but if she's not engaged, just ask her to come here a minute: tell her I want to speak to her.'

He ran to perform my bidding, and quickly returned with his mother. How lovely she looked with her dark ringlets streaming in the light summer breeze, her fair cheek slightly flushed, and her countenance radiant with smiles! – Dear Arthur! What did I not owe to you for this and every other happy meeting? – Through him, I was at once delivered from all formality, and terror, and constraint. In love affairs, there is no mediator like a merry, simple-hearted child – ever ready to cement divided hearts, to span the unfriendly gulf of custom, to melt the ice of cold reserve, and overthrow the separating walls of dread formality and pride.

'Well, Mr Markham, what is it?' said the young mother, accosting me with a pleasant smile.

'I want you to look at this book, and, if you please, to take it, and peruse it at your leisure. I make no apology for calling you out on such a lovely evening though it be for a matter of no greater importance.'

'Tell him to come in, mamma,' said Arthur.

'Would you like to come in?' asked the lady.

'Yes; I should like to see your improvements in the garden.'

'And how your sister's roots have prospered in my charge,' added she, as she opened the gate.

And we sauntered through the garden, and talked of the flowers, the trees,

and the book – and then of other things. The evening was kind and genial, and so was my companion. By degrees, I waxed more warm and tender than, perhaps, I had ever been before; but still, I said nothing tangible, and she attempted no repulse; until, in passing a moss rose tree that I had brought her some weeks since, in my sister's name, she plucked a beautiful half-open bud and bade me give it to Rose.

'May I not keep it myself?' I asked.

'No; but here is another for you.'

Instead of taking it quietly, I likewise took the hand that offered it, and looked into her face She let me hold it for a moment, and I saw a flash of ecstatic brilliance in her eye, a glow of glad excitement on her face – I thought my hour of victory was come – but instantly, a painful recollection seemed to flash upon her; a cloud of anguish darkened her brow, a marble paleness blanched her cheek and lip; there seemed a moment of inward conflict – and with a sudden effort, she withdrew her hand, and retreated a step or two back.

'Now, Mr Markham,' said she, with a kind of desperate calmness, 'I must tell you plainly, that I cannot do with this. I like your company, because I am alone here, and your conversation pleases me more than that of any other person; but if you cannot be content to regard me as a friend – a plain, cold, motherly, or sisterly friend, I must beg you to leave me now, and let me alone hereafter – in fact, we must be strangers for the future.'

'I will, then – be your friend – or brother, or anything you wish, if you will only let me continue to see you; but tell me why I cannot be anything more?'

There was a perplexed and thoughtful pause. 'Is it in consequence of some rash vow?'

'It is something of the kind,' she answered – 'someday I may tell you, but, at present you had better leave me; and never, Gilbert, put me to the painful necessity of repeating what I have just now said to you!' – she earnestly added, giving me her hand in serious kindness. How sweet, how musical my own name sounded in her mouth!

'I will not,' I replied. 'But you pardon *this* offence?'

'On condition that you never repeat it.'

'And may I come to see you now and then?'

'Perhaps – occasionally; provided you never abuse the privilege.'

'I make no empty promises, but you shall see.'

'The moment you do, our intimacy is at an end, that's all.'

'And will you always call me Gilbert? – it sounds more sisterly, and it will serve to remind me of our contract.'

She smiled, and once more bid me go – and, at length, I judged it prudent to obey; and she re-entered the house, and I went down the hill. But as I went, the tramp of horses' hoofs fell on my ear, and broke the stillness of the dewy evening; and, looking towards the lane, I saw a solitary equestrian coming up. Inclining to dusk as it was, I knew him at a glance: it was Mr Lawrence on his grey pony. I flew across the field – leaped the stone fence – and then walked down the lane to meet him. On seeing me, he suddenly drew in his little steed,

and seemed inclined to turn back, but on second thought, apparently judged it better to continue his course as before. He accosted me with a slight bow, and, edging close to the wall, endeavoured to pass on – but I was not so minded: seizing his horse by the bridle, I exclaimed: 'Now, Lawrence, I will have this mystery explained! Tell me where you are going, and what you mean to do – at once, and distinctly!'

'Will you take your hand off the bridle?' said he, quietly – 'you're hurting my pony's mouth.'

'You and your pony be — '

'What makes you so coarse and brutal, Markham? I'm quite ashamed of you.'

'You answer my questions – before you leave this spot! I *will* know what you mean by this perfidious duplicity?'

'I shall answer *no* questions till you let go the bridle – if you stand till morning.'

'Now then,' said I, unclosing my hand, but still standing before him.

'Ask me some other time, when you can speak like a gentleman,' returned he, and he made an effort to pass me again; but I quickly recaptured the pony, scarce less astonished than its master at such uncivil usage.

'Really, Mr Markham, this is *too* much!' said the latter. 'Can I not go to see my tenant on matters of business, without being assaulted in this manner by – '

'This is no time for business, sir! – I'll tell you, now, what I think of your conduct.'

'You'd better defer your opinion to a more convenient season,' interrupted he in a low tone – 'here's the vicar.'

And in truth, the vicar was just behind me, plodding homeward from some remote corner of his parish. I immediately released the squire; and he went on his way, saluting Mr Millward as he passed.

'What, quarrelling, Markham?' cried the latter, addressing himself to me – 'and about that young widow I doubt,' he added, reproachfully shaking his head. 'But let me tell you young man' (here he put his face into mine with an important, confidential air), 'she's not worth it!' and he confirmed the assertion by a solemn nod.

'Mr Millward!' I exclaimed, in a tone of wrathful menace that made the reverend gentleman look round – aghast – astounded at such unwonted insolence, and stare me in the face, with a look that plainly said: 'What, this to me!' But I was too indignant to apologise or to speak another word to him; I turned away, and hastened homewards, descending with rapid strides the steep, rough lane, and leaving him to follow as he pleased.

## CHAPTER II

## *The Vicar Again*

You must suppose about three weeks past over. Mrs Graham and I were now established friends – or brother and sister as we rather chose to consider ourselves. She called me Gilbert, by my express desire, and I called her Helen, for I had seen that name written in her books. I seldom attempted to see her above twice a week; and still I made our meetings appear the result of accident as often as I could – for I found it necessary to be extremely careful – and, altogether, I behaved with such exceeding propriety that she never had occasion to reprove me once. Yet I could not but perceive that she was at times unhappy and dissatisfied with herself – or her position, and truly I myself was not quite contented with the latter: this assumption of brotherly nonchalance was very hard to sustain, and I often felt myself a most confounded hypocrite with it all; I saw too, or rather I felt, that, in spite of herself, "I was not indifferent to her," as the novel heroes modestly express it, and while I thankfully enjoyed my present good fortune, I could not fail to wish and hope for something better in future; but of course, I kept such dreams entirely to myself.

'Where are you going, Gilbert?' said Rose, one evening, shortly after tea, when I had been busy with the farm all day.

'To take a walk,' was the reply.

'Do you always brush your hat so carefully, and do your hair so nicely, and put on such smart new gloves when you take a walk?'

'Not always.'

'You're going to Wildfell Hall, aren't you?'

'What makes you think so?'

'Because you look as if you were – but I wish you wouldn't go so often.'

'Nonsense child! I don't go once in six weeks – what do you mean?'

'Well, but if I were you, I wouldn't have so much to do with Mrs Graham.'

'Why, Rose, are you, too, giving in to the prevailing opinion?'

'No,' returned she, hesitatingly – 'but I've heard so much about her lately, both at the Wilsons and the vicarage; and besides mamma says, if she were a proper person, she would not be living there by herself – and don't you remember last winter, Gilbert, all that about the false name to the picture; and how she explained it – saying she had friends or acquaintances from whom she wished her present residence to be concealed, and that she was afraid of their tracing her out; and then, how suddenly she started up and left the room when that person came – whom she took good care not to let us catch a glimpse of, and who Arthur, with such an air of mystery, told us was his mamma's friend?'

'Yes, Rose, I remember it all; and I can forgive your uncharitable conclusions; for perhaps, if I did not know her myself, I should put all these things together,

and believe the same as you do; but thank God, I do know her; and I should be unworthy the name of a man, if I could believe anything that was said against her, unless I heard it from her own lips – I should as soon believe such things of you, Rose.'

'Oh, Gilbert!'

'Well, do you think I *could* believe anything of the kind – whatever the Wilsons and Millwards dared to whisper?'

'I should hope *not* indeed!'

'And why not? – Because I know you – well, and I know her just as well.'

'Oh, no! you know nothing of her former life; and last year at this time, you did not know that such a person existed.'

'No matter. There is such a thing as looking through a person's eyes into the heart, and learning more of the height, and breadth, and depth of another's soul in one hour, than it might take you a life time to discover, if he or she were not disposed to reveal it – or if you had not the sense to understand it.'

'Then you *are* going to see her this evening?'

'To be sure I am!'

'But what would mamma say, Gilbert?'

'Mamma needn't know.'

'But she must know sometime, if you go on.'

'Go on! – there's no going on in the matter. Mrs Graham and I are two friends – and will be; and no man breathing shall hinder it – or has a right to interfere between us.'

'But if you knew how they talk, you would be more careful – for her sake as well as for your own. Jane Wilson thinks your visits to the old hall but another proof of her depravity – '

'Confound Jane Wilson!'

'And Eliza Millward is quite grieved about you.'

'I hope she is.'

'But I wouldn't if I were you.'

'Wouldn't what? – How do they know that I go there?'

'There's nothing hid from them: they spy out everything.'

'O, I never thought of this! – And so they dare to turn my friendship into food for further scandal against her! – That proves the falsehood of their other lies, at all events, if any proof were wanting – Mind you contradict them, Rose, whenever you can.'

'But they don't speak openly to me about such things: it is only by hints and innuendoes and by what I hear others say, that I know what they think.'

'Well then, I won't go today, as it's getting latish. But oh, deuce take their cursed envenomed tongues!' I muttered in the bitterness of my soul.

And just at that moment, the vicar entered the room: we had been too much absorbed in our conversation to observe his knock. After his customary, cheerful and fatherly greeting of Rose, who was rather a favourite with the old gentleman, he turned somewhat sternly to me – 'Well, sir!' said he, 'you're quite a stranger. It is – let – me – see,' he continued slowly, as he deposited his ponderous bulk in

the armchair that Rose officiously brought towards him, 'it is just – six – weeks – by my reckoning, since you darkened – my – door!' He spoke it with emphasis, and struck his stick on the floor.

'Is it, sir?' said I.

'Ay! It is so!' He added an affirmatory nod, and continued to gaze upon me with a kind of irate solemnity, holding his substantial stick between his knees, with his hands clasped upon its head.

'I have been busy,' I said, for an apology was evidently demanded.

'Busy!' repeated he derisively.

'Yes; you know I've been getting in my hay; and now the harvest is beginning.'

'Humph!'

Just then my mother came in, and created a diversion in my favour, by her loquacious and animated welcome of the reverend guest. She regretted deeply that he had not come a little earlier, in time for tea, but offered to have some immediately prepared, if he would do her the favour to partake of it.

'Not any for me, I thank you,' replied he; 'I shall be at home in a few minutes.'

'Oh, but do stay and take a little! It will be ready in five minutes.'

But he rejected the offer, with a majestic wave of the hand.

'I'll tell you what I'll take, Mrs Markham,' said he: 'I'll take a glass of your excellent ale.'

'With pleasure!' cried my mother, proceeding with alacrity to pull the bell and order the favoured beverage.

'I thought,' continued he, 'I'd just look in upon you as I passed, and taste your home-brewed ale. I've been to call on Mrs Graham.'

'Have you indeed?'

He nodded gravely, and added with awful emphasis – 'I thought it incumbent upon me to do so.'

'Really!' ejaculated my mother.

'Why so, Mr Millward?' asked I. He looked at me with some severity, and turning again to my mother, repeated – 'I thought it incumbent upon me!' and struck his stick on the floor again. My mother sat opposite, an awestruck but admiring auditor.

' "Mrs Graham," said I,' he continued, shaking his head as he spoke, ' "these are terrible reports!" "What sir?" says she, affecting to be ignorant of my meaning. "It is my – duty – as – your pastor," said I, "to tell you both everything that I myself see reprehensible in your conduct, and all I have reason to suspect, and what others tell me concerning you." – So I told her!'

'You did, sir?' cried I, starting from my seat, and striking my fist on the table. He merely glanced towards me, and continued – addressing his hostess: 'It was a painful duty, Mrs Markham – but I told her!'

'And how did she take it?' asked my mother.

'Hardened, I fear – hardened!' he replied, with a despondent shake of the head; 'and at the same time, there was a strong display of unchastened, misdirected passions. She turned white in the face, and drew her breath through her teeth in a

savage sort of way; but she offered no extenuation or defence; and with a kind of shameless calmness – shocking indeed to witness, in one so young – as good as told me that my remonstrance was unavailing, and my pastoral advice quite thrown away upon her – nay, that my very *presence* was displeasing while I spoke such things. And I withdrew at length, too plainly seeing that nothing could be done – and sadly grieved to find her case so hopeless. But I am fully determined, Mrs Markham, that *my* daughters – shall – not – consort with her. Do you adopt the same resolution with regard to yours! – As for your sons – as for *you*, young man,' he continued, sternly turning to me.

'As for me, sir' – I began, but checked by some impediment in my utterance, and finding that my whole frame trembled with fury, I said no more – but took the wiser part of snatching up my hat and bolting from the room, slamming the door behind me, with a bang that shook the house to its foundations, and made my mother scream – and gave a momentary relief to my excited feelings.

The next minute saw me hurrying with rapid strides in the direction of Wildfell Hall – to what intent or purpose I could scarcely tell, but I must be moving somewhere, and no other goal would do – I must see her too, and speak to her – that was certain, but what to say or how to act, I had no definite idea. Such stormy thoughts – so many different resolutions crowded in upon me, that my mind was little better than a chaos of conflicting passions.

## CHAPTER 12

### *A Tête-à-Tête and a Discovery*

In little more than twenty minutes, the journey was accomplished. I paused at the gate to wipe my streaming forehead, and recover my breath and some degree of composure. Already the rapid walking had somewhat mitigated my excitement; and with a firm and steady tread, I paced the garden walk. In passing the inhabited wing of the building, I caught a sight of Mrs Graham, through the open window, slowly pacing up and down her lonely room.

She seemed agitated, and even dismayed at my arrival, as if she thought, I too was coming to accuse her. I had entered her presence intending to condole with her upon the wickedness of the world, and help her to abuse the vicar and his vile informants, but now I felt positively ashamed to mention the subject and determined not to refer to it, unless she led the way.

'I am come at an unseasonable hour,' said I, assuming a cheerfulness I did not feel, in order to reassure her; 'but I won't stay many minutes.'

She smiled upon me, faintly it is true, but most kindly – I had almost said thankfully, as her apprehensions were removed.

'How dismal you are, Helen! Why have you no fire?' I said, looking round on the gloomy apartment.

'It is summer yet,' she replied.

'But we *always* have a fire in the evenings – if we can bear it; and you especially require one in this cold house and dreary room.'

'You should have come a little sooner, and I would have had one lighted for you; but it is not worth while now – you won't stay many minutes you say, and Arthur is gone to bed.'

'But I have a fancy for a fire nevertheless. Will you order one, if I ring?'

'Why, Gilbert, you don't *look* cold!' said she, smilingly regarding my face, which no doubt seemed warm enough.

'No,' replied I, 'but I want to see you comfortable before I go.'

'Me comfortable!' repeated she, with a bitter laugh, as if there were something amusingly absurd in the idea. 'It suits me better as it is,' she added in a tone of mournful resignation.

But determined to have my own way I pulled the bell.

'There now, Helen!' I said, as the approaching steps of Rachel were heard in answer to the summons. There was nothing for it but to turn round and desire the maid to light the fire.

I owe Rachel a grudge to this day for the look she cast upon me ere she departed on her mission – the sour, suspicious, inquisitorial look that plainly demanded, 'what are *you* here for, I wonder?' Her mistress did not fail to notice it, and a shade of uneasiness darkened her brow.

'You must not stay long, Gilbert,' said she, when the door was closed upon us.

'I'm not going to,' said I, somewhat testily, though without a grain of anger in my heart against anyone but the meddling old woman. 'But Helen, I've something to say to you before I go.'

'What is it?'

'No, not now – I don't know yet precisely what it is – or how to say it,' replied I, with more truth than wisdom; and then, fearing lest she should turn me out of the house, I began talking about indifferent matters in order to gain time. Meanwhile Rachel came in to kindle the fire, which was soon effected by thrusting a red-hot poker between the bars of the grate, where the fuel was already disposed for ignition. She honoured me with another of her hard, inhospitable looks in departing, but, little moved thereby, I went on talking; and setting a chair for Mrs Graham on one side of the hearth and one for myself on the other, I ventured to sit down, though half suspecting she would rather see me go.

In a little while we both relapsed into silence, and continued for several minutes gazing abstractedly into the fire – she intent upon her own sad thoughts, and I reflecting how delightful it would be to be seated thus beside her with no other presence to restrain our intercourse – not even that of Arthur, our mutual friend, without whom we had never met before – if only I could venture to speak my mind, and disburden my full heart of the feelings that had so long oppressed it, and which it now struggled to retain, with an effort that it seemed impossible to continue much longer – and revolving the pros and cons for opening my heart to her there and then, and imploring a return of affection, the permission to regard her thenceforth as my own, and the right and the power to defend her from the calumnies of malicious tongues. On the one hand, I felt a

newborn confidence in my powers of persuasion – a strong conviction that my own fervour of spirit would grant me eloquence – that my very determination – the absolute necessity for succeeding, that I felt – must win me what I sought; while on the other, I feared to lose the ground I had already gained with so much toil and skill, and destroy all future hope by one rash effort, when time and patience might have won success. It was like setting my life upon the cast of a die; and yet, I was ready to resolve upon the attempt. At any rate I would entreat the explanation she had half promised to give me before: I would demand the reason of this hateful barrier, this mysterious impediment to my happiness and, as I trusted, to her own.

But while I considered in what manner I could best frame my request, my companion wakened from her reverie with a scarcely audible sigh, and looking towards the window where the blood-red harvest moon, just rising over one of the grim, fantastic evergreens, was shining in upon us, said – 'Gilbert, it is getting late.'

'I see,' said I. 'You want me to go, I suppose.'

'I think you ought. If my kind neighbours get to know of this visit – as no doubt they will – they will not turn it much to my advantage.'

It was with what the Vicar would doubtless have called a savage sort of a smile that she said this.

'Let them turn it as they will,' said I. 'What are their thoughts to you or me, so long as we are satisfied with ourselves – and each other? Let them go to the deuce with their vile constructions, and their lying inventions!'

This outburst brought a flush of colour to her face.

'You have heard, then, what they say of me?'

'I heard some detestable falsehoods; but none but fools would credit them for a moment, Helen, so don't let them trouble you.'

'I did not think Mr Millward a fool, and he believes it all; but however little you may value the opinions of those about you – however little you may esteem them as individuals, it is not pleasant to be looked upon as a liar and a hypocrite, to be thought to practice what you abhor, and to encourage the vices you would discountenance, to find your good intentions frustrated, and your hands crippled by your supposed unworthiness, and to bring disgrace on the principles you profess.'

'True; and if I, by my thoughtlessness and selfish disregard to appearances, have at all assisted to expose you to these evils, let me entreat you not only to pardon me, but to enable me to make reparation; authorise me to clear your name from every imputation: give me the right to identify your honour with my own, and to defend your reputation as more precious than my life!'

'Are you hero enough to unite yourself to one whom you know to be suspected and despised by all around you, and identify your interests and your honour with hers? Think! It is a serious thing.'

'I should be proud to do it, Helen! – most happy – delighted beyond expression! – and if that be all the obstacle to our union, it is demolished, and you must – you shall be mine!'

And starting from my seat in a frenzy of ardour, I seized her hand and would have pressed it to my lips, but she as suddenly caught it away, exclaiming in the bitterness of intense affliction – 'No, no, it is not all!'

'What is it then? You promised I should know sometime, and – '

'You shall know sometime – but not now – my head aches terribly,' she said, pressing her hand to her forehead, 'and I must have some repose – and surely, I have had misery enough today!' she added, almost wildly.

'But it could not harm you to tell it,' I persisted: 'it would ease your mind; and I should then know how to comfort you.'

She shook her head despondingly. 'If you knew all, you, too, would blame me – perhaps even more than I deserve – though I have cruelly wronged you,' she added in a low murmur, as if she mused aloud.

'*You*, Helen? Impossible!'

'Yes, not willingly; for I did not know the strength and depth of your attachment – I thought – at least I endeavoured to think your regard for me was as cold and fraternal as you professed it to be.'

'Or as yours?'

'Or as mine – ought to have been – of such a light and selfish, superficial nature that – '

'*There*, indeed, you wronged me.'

'I know I did; and sometimes, I suspected it then; but I thought, upon the whole, there could be no great harm in leaving your fancies and your hopes to dream themselves to nothing – or flutter away to some more fitting object, while your friendly sympathies remained with me; but if I had known the depth of your regard, the generous disinterested affection you seem to feel – '

'*Seem*, Helen?'

'That you *do* feel, then, I would have acted differently.'

'How? You *could* not have given me less encouragement, or treated me with greater severity than you did! And if you think you have wronged me by giving me your friendship, and occasionally admitting me to the enjoyment of your company and conversation, when all hopes of closer intimacy were vain – as indeed you always gave me to understand – if you think you have wronged me by this, you are mistaken; for such favours, in themselves alone, are not only delightful to my heart, but purifying, exalting, ennobling to my soul; and I would rather have your friendship than the love of any other woman in the world!'

Little comforted by this, she clasped her hands upon her knee, and glancing upward, seemed, in silent anguish, to implore divine assistance; then turning to me, she calmly said – 'Tomorrow, if you meet me on the moor about midday, I will tell you all you seek to know; and perhaps you will then see the necessity of discontinuing our intimacy – if, indeed, you do not willingly resign me as one no longer worthy of regard.'

'I can safely answer no, to that: you cannot have such grave confessions to make – you must be trying my faith, Helen.'

'No, no, no,' she earnestly repeated – 'I wish it were so! Thank Heaven;' she

added, 'I have no great crime to confess; but I have more than you will like to hear, or, perhaps, can readily excuse – and more than I can tell you now; so let me entreat you to leave me!'

'I will; but answer me this one question first; do you love me?'

'I will not answer it!'

'Then I will conclude you do; and so good-night.'

She turned from me to hide the emotion she could not quite control; but I took her hand and fervently kissed it.

'Gilbert, *do* leave me!' she cried, in a tone of such thrilling anguish that I felt it would be cruel to disobey.

But I gave one look back before I closed the door, and saw her leaning forward on the table, with her hands pressed against her eyes, sobbing convulsively; yet I withdrew in silence. I felt that to obtrude my consolations on her then would only serve to aggravate her sufferings.

To tell you all the questionings and conjectures – the fears, and hopes, and wild emotions that jostled and chased each other through my mind as I descended the hill, would almost fill a volume in itself. But before I was half way down a sentiment of strong sympathy for her I had left behind me had displaced all other feelings, and seemed imperatively to draw me back: I began to think, 'Why am I hurrying so fast in this direction? Can I find comfort or consolation – peace, certainty, contentment, all – or anything that I want at home? and can I leave all perturbation, sorrow and anxiety behind me there?'

And I turned round to look at the old hall. There was little besides the chimneys visible above my contracted horizon. I walked back to get a better view of it. When it rose in sight, I stood still a moment to look, and then continued moving towards the gloomy object of attraction. Something called me nearer – nearer still – and why not, pray? Might I not find more benefit in the contemplation of that venerable pile with the full moon in the cloudless heaven shining so calmly above it – with that warm yellow lustre peculiar to an August night – and the mistress of my soul within, than in returning to my home where all comparatively was light, and life, and cheerfulness, and therefore inimical to me in my present frame of mind – and the more so that its inmates all were more or less imbued with that detestable belief the very *thought* of which made my blood boil in my veins – and how could I endure to hear it openly declared – or cautiously insinuated – which was worse? – I had had trouble enough already, with some babbling fiend that would keep whispering in my ear, 'It may be true,' till I had shouted aloud, 'It is false! I defy you to make me suppose it!'

I could see the red firelight dimly gleaming from her parlour window. I went up to the garden wall, and stood leaning over it, with my eyes fixed upon the lattice, wondering what she was doing, thinking, or suffering now, and wishing I could speak to her but one word, or even catch one glimpse of her, before I went.

I had not thus looked, and wished, and wondered long, before I vaulted over the barrier, unable to resist the temptation of taking one glance through the

window, just to see if she were more composed than when we parted; and if I found her still in deep distress, perhaps I might venture to attempt a word of comfort – to utter one of the many things I should have said before, instead of aggravating her sufferings by my stupid impetuosity. I looked. Her chair was vacant: so was the room. But at that moment someone opened the outer door, and a voice – *her* voice – said – 'Come out – I want to see the moon, and breathe the evening air: they will do me good – if anything will.'

Here, then, were she and Rachel coming to take a walk in the garden. I wished myself safe back over the wall. I stood, however, in the shadow of the tall holly bush, which, standing between the window and the porch, at present screened me from observation, but did not present me from seeing two figures come forth into the moonlight: Mrs Graham followed by another – *not* Rachel, but a young man, slender and rather tall. Oh Heavens, how my temples throbbed! Intense anxiety darkened my sight; but I thought – yes, and the voice confirmed it – it was Mr Lawrence.

'You should not let it worry you so much, Helen,' said he; 'I will be more cautious in future; and in time – '

I did not hear the rest of the sentence; for he walked close beside her and spoke so gently that I could not catch the words. My heart was splitting with hatred; but I listened intently for her reply. I heard it plainly enough. 'But I must leave this place, Frederick,' she said – 'I never can be happy here – nor anywhere else, indeed,' she added, with a mirthless laugh – 'but I cannot rest here.'

'But where could you find a better place?' replied he – 'so secluded – so near me, if you think anything of that.'

'Yes,' interrupted she, 'it is all I could wish, if they could only have left me alone.'

'But wherever you go, Helen, there will be the same sources of annoyance. I cannot consent to lose you: I must go with you, or come to you; and there are meddling fools elsewhere, as well as here.'

While thus conversing, they had sauntered slowly past me, down the walk, and I heard no more of their discourse; but I saw him put his arm round her waist, while she lovingly rested her hand on his shoulder; and then, a tremulous darkness obscured my sight, my heart sickened and my head burned like fire. I half rushed, half staggered from the spot where horror had kept me rooted, and leaped or tumbled over the wall – I hardly know which – but I know that, afterwards, like a passionate child, I dashed myself on the ground and lay there in a paroxysm of anger and despair – how long, I cannot undertake to say; but it must have been a considerable time; for when, having partially relieved myself by a torrent of tears, and looked up at the moon, shining so calmly and carelessly on, as little influenced by my misery as I was by its peaceful radiance, and earnestly prayed for death or forgetfulness, I had risen and journeyed home-wards – little regarding the way, but carried instinctively by my feet to the door, I found it bolted against me, and everyone in bed except my mother, who hastened to answer my impatient knocking, and received me with a shower of questions and rebukes.

'Oh, Gilbert, how *could* you do so? Where *have* you been? Do come in and take your supper – I've got it all ready, though you don't deserve it, for keeping me in such a fright, after the strange manner you left the house this evening. Mr Millward was quite – Bless the boy! How ill he looks! Oh, gracious! What is the matter?'

'Nothing, nothing – give me a candle.'

'But won't you take some supper?'

'No, I want to go to bed,' said I, taking a candle and lighting it at the one she held in her hand.

'Oh, Gilbert, how you tremble!' exclaimed my anxious parent. 'How white you look! – Do tell me what it is? Has anything happened?'

'It's nothing!' cried I, ready to stamp with vexation because the candle would not light. Then, suppressing my irritation, I added, 'I've been walking too fast, that's all. Good-night,' and marched off to bed, regardless of the 'Walking too fast! where have you been?' that was called after me from below.

My mother followed me to the very door of my room with her questionings and advice concerning my health and my conduct; but I implored her to let me alone till morning; and she withdrew, and at length, I had the satisfaction to hear her close her own door. There was no sleep for me however, that night, as I thought; and instead of attempting to solicit it, I employed myself in rapidly pacing the chamber – having first removed my boots lest my mother should hear me. But the boards creaked, and she was watchful. I had not walked above a quarter of an hour before she was at the door again.

'Gilbert, why are you not in bed – you said you wanted to go?'

'Confound it! I'm going,' said I.

'But why are you so long about it? you must have something on your mind –'

'For Heaven's sake, let me alone, and get to bed yourself!'

'Can it be that Mrs Graham that distresses you so?'

'No, no, I tell you – it's nothing!'

'I wish to goodness it mayn't!' murmured she with a sigh, as she returned to her own apartment, while I threw myself on the bed, feeling most undutifully disaffected towards her for having deprived me of what seemed the only shadow of a consolation that remained, and chained me to that wretched couch of thorns.

Never did I endure so long, so miserable a night as that. And yet, it was not wholly sleepless: towards morning my distracting thoughts began to lose all pretensions to coherency, and shape themselves into confused and feverish dreams, and, at length, there followed an interval of unconscious slumber. But then the dawn of bitter recollection that succeeded – the waking to find life a blank, and worse than a blank – teeming with torment and misery – not a mere barren wilderness, but full of thorns and briars – to find myself deceived, duped, hopeless, my affections trampled upon, my angel not an angel, and my friend a fiend incarnate – it was worse than if I had not slept at all.

It was a dull, gloomy morning, the weather had changed like my prospects, and the rain was pattering against the window. I rose nevertheless, and went out;

not to look after the farm, though that would serve as my excuse, but to cool my brain, and regain, if possible, a sufficient degree of composure to meet the family at the morning meal without exciting inconvenient remarks. If I got a wetting, that, in conjunction with a pretended over exertion before breakfast, might excuse my sudden loss of appetite; and if a cold ensued, the severer the better, it would help to account for the sullen moods and moping melancholy likely to cloud my brow for long enough.

<div align="center">CHAPTER 13</div>

# A Return to Duty

'My dear Gilbert! I wish you *would* try to be a little more amiable,' said my mother, one morning after some display of unjustifiable ill humour on my part. 'You say there is nothing the matter with you, and nothing has happened to grieve you, and yet, I never *saw* anyone so altered as you within these last few days: you haven't a good word for anybody – friends and strangers, equals and inferiors – it's all the same. I do wish you'd try to check it.'

'Check what?'

'Why, your strange temper. You don't know *how* it spoils you. I'm sure a finer disposition than yours, by nature, could not be, if you'd let it have fair play; so you've no excuse *that* way.'

While she thus remonstrated, I took up a book, and laying it open on the table before me, pretended to be deeply absorbed in its perusal; for I was equally unable to justify myself, and unwilling to acknowledge my errors; and I wished to have nothing to say on the matter. But my excellent parent went on lecturing, and then came to coaxing, and began to stroke my hair; and I was getting to feel quite a good boy, but my mischievous brother who was idling about the room, revived my corruption by suddenly calling out – 'Don't touch him, mother! He'll bite! He's a very tiger in human form. *I've* given him up, for my part – fairly disowned him – cast him off, root and branch. It's as much as my life is worth to come within six yards of him. The other day he nearly fractured my skull for singing a pretty, inoffensive love song, on purpose to amuse him.'

'Oh, Gilbert! how could you?' exclaimed my mother.

'I told you to hold your noise first, you know, Fergus,' said I.

'Yes, but when I assured you it was no trouble, and went on with the next verse, thinking you might like it better, you clutched me by the shoulder and dashed me away, right against the wall there, with such force, that I thought I had bitten my tongue in two, and expected to see the place plastered with my brains; and when I put my hand to my head and found my skull not broken, I thought it was a miracle and no mistake. But poor fellow!' added he, with a sentimental sigh – 'his heart's broken – that's the truth of it – and his head's –'

'Will you be silent now?' cried I, starting up, and eyeing the fellow so fiercely

that my mother, thinking I meant to inflict some grievous bodily injury, laid her hand on my arm, and besought me to let him alone, and he walked leisurely out, with his hands in his pockets, singing provokingly – 'Shall I because a woman's fair,' etc.

'I'm not going to defile my fingers with him,' said I, in answer to the maternal intercession. 'I wouldn't touch him with the tongs.'

I now recollected that I had business with Robert Wilson, concerning the purchase of a certain field adjoining my farm – a business I had been putting off from day to day; for I had no interest in anything now; and besides, I was misanthropically inclined, and, moreover, had a particular objection to meeting Jane Wilson or her mother; for though I had too good reason, now, to credit their reports concerning Mrs Graham, I did not like *them* a bit the better for it – or Eliza Millward either – and the thought of meeting them was the more repugnant to me, that I could not, now, defy their seeming calumnies and triumph in my own convictions as before. But today, I determined to make an effort to return to my duty. Though I found no pleasure in it, it would be less irksome than idleness – at all events it would be more profitable. If life promised no enjoyment within my vocation, at least it offered no allurements out of it; and henceforth, I would put my shoulder to the wheel and toil away, like any poor drudge of a cart-horse that was fairly broken in to its labour, and plod through life, not wholly useless if not agreeable, and uncomplaining if not contented with my lot.

Thus resolving, with a kind of sullen resignation, if such a term may be allowed, I wended my way to Ryecote Farm, scarcely expecting to find its owner within at this time of day, but hoping to learn in what part of the premises he was most likely to be found.

Absent he was, but expected home in a few minutes; and I was desired to step into the parlour and wait. Mrs Wilson was busy in the kitchen, but the room was not empty; and I scarcely checked an involuntary recoil as I entered it; for there sat Miss Wilson chattering with Eliza Millward. However, I determined to be cool and civil. Eliza seemed to have made the same resolution on her part. We had not met since the evening of the tea party; but there was no visible emotion either of pleasure or pain, no attempt at pathos, no display of injured pride: she was cool in temper, civil in demeanour. There was even an ease and cheerfulness about her air and manner that I made no pretension to; but there was a depth of malice in her too expressive eye, that plainly told me I was not forgiven; for, though she no longer hoped to win me to herself, she still hated her rival, and evidently delighted to wreak her spite on me. On the other hand, Miss Wilson was as affable and courteous as heart could wish, and though I was in no very conversable humour myself, the two ladies between them managed to keep up a pretty continuous fire of small talk. But Eliza took advantage of the first convenient pause to ask if I had lately seen Mrs Graham, in a tone of merely casual enquiry, but with a sidelong glance – intended to be playfully mischievous – really, brimful and running over with malice.

'Not lately,' I replied, in a careless tone, but sternly repelling her odious

glances with my eyes; for I was vexed to feel the colour mounting to my forehead, despite my strenuous efforts to appear unmoved.

'What! Are you beginning to tire already? I thought so noble a creature would have power to attach you for a year at least!'

'I would rather not speak of her now.'

'Ah! then you are convinced at last, of your mistake – you have at length discovered that your divinity is not quite the immaculate – '

'I desired you not to speak of her, Miss Eliza.'

'Oh, I beg your pardon! I perceive Cupid's arrows have been too sharp for you: the wounds being more than skin-deep, are not yet healed and bleed afresh at every mention of the loved one's name.'

'Say rather,' interposed Miss Wilson, 'that Mr Markham feels that name is unworthy to be mentioned in the presence of right-minded females. I wonder, Eliza, you should think of referring to that unfortunate person – you might know the mention of her would be anything but agreeable to anyone here present.'

How could this be borne? I rose and was about to clap my hat upon my head and burst away, in wrathful indignation, from the house; but recollecting – just in time to save my dignity – the folly of such a proceeding, and how it would only give my fair tormentors a merry laugh at my expense, for the sake of one I acknowledged in my own heart to be unworthy of the slightest sacrifice – though the ghost of my former reverence and love so hung about me still, that I could not bear to hear her name aspersed by others – I merely walked to the window, and having spent a few seconds in vengibly biting my lips, and sternly repressing the passionate heavings of my chest, I observed to Miss Wilson, that I could see nothing of her brother, and added that as my time was precious, it would perhaps be better to call again tomorrow, at some time when I should be sure to find him at home.

'Oh no!' said she, 'if you wait a minute, he will be sure to come; for he has business at L—' (that was our market town) 'and will require a little refreshment before he goes.'

I submitted accordingly, with the best grace I could; and happily, I had not long to wait. Mr Wilson soon arrived, and indisposed for business as I was at that moment, and little as I cared for the field or its owner, I forced my attention to the matter in hand, with very creditable determination, and quickly concluded the bargain – perhaps more to the thrifty farmer's satisfaction, than he cared to acknowledge. Then, leaving him to the discussion of his substantial 'refreshment', I gladly quitted the house, and went to look after my reapers.

Leaving them busy at work on the side of the valley, I ascended the hill, intending to visit a cornfield in the more elevated regions, and see when it would be ripe for the sickle. But I did *not* visit it that day; for, as I approached, I beheld at no great distance, Mrs Graham and her son coming down in the opposite direction. They saw me; and Arthur, already, was running to meet me; but I immediately turned back and walked steadily homeward; for I had fully determined never to encounter his mother again; and regardless of the shrill

voice in my ear, calling upon me to 'wait a moment', I pursued the even tenor of my way; and he soon relinquished the pursuit as hopeless, or was called away by his mother. At all events, when I looked back, five minutes after, not a trace of either was to be seen.

This incident agitated and disturbed me most unaccountably – unless you would account for it by saying that Cupid's arrows not only had been too sharp for me, but they were barbed and deeply rooted, and I had not yet been able to wrench them from my heart. However that be, I was rendered doubly miserable for the remainder of the day.

### CHAPTER 14

## *An Assault*

Next morning, I bethought me, I, too, had business at L—; so I mounted my horse and set forth on the expedition, soon after breakfast. It was a dull, drizzly day; but that was no matter: it was all the more suitable to my frame of mind. It was likely to be a lonely journey; for it was no market-day, and the road I traversed was little frequented at any other time; but that suited me all the better too.

As I trotted along, however, chewing the cud of – *bitter* fancies, I heard another horse at no great distance behind me; but I never conjectured who the rider might be – or troubled my head about him, till on slackening my pace to ascend a gentle acclivity – or rather suffering my horse to slacken its pace into a lazy walk; for lost in my own reflections, I was letting it jog on as leisurely as it thought proper – I lost ground, and my fellow traveller overtook me. He accosted me by name; for it was no stranger – it was Mr Lawrence! Instinctively the fingers of my whip-hand tingled, and grasped their charge with convulsive energy; but I restrained the impulse, and answering his salutation with a nod, attempted to push on; but he pushed on beside me and began to talk about the weather and the crops. I gave the briefest possible answers to his queries and observations, and fell back. He fell back too, and asked if my horse was lame. I replied, with a *look* – at which he placidly smiled.

I was as much astonished as exasperated at this singular pertinacity and imperturbable assurance on his part. I had thought the circumstances of our last meeting would have left such an impression on his mind as to render him cold and distant ever after: instead of that he appeared, not only to have forgotten all former offences, but to be impenetrable to all present incivilities. Formerly, the slightest hint, or mere fancied coldness in tone or glance, had sufficed to repulse him: now, positive rudeness could not drive him away. Had he heard of my disappointment; and was he come to witness the result, and triumph in my despair? I grasped my whip with more determined energy than before – but still forbore to raise it, and rode on in silence, waiting for some more tangible cause

of offence, before I opened the floodgates of my soul, and poured out the dammed up fury that was foaming and swelling within.

'Markham,' said he, in his usual quiet tone, 'why do you quarrel with your friends, because you have been disappointed in one quarter? You have found your hopes defeated; but how am *I* to blame for it? I warned you beforehand, you know, but you would not – '

He said no more; for, impelled by some fiend at my elbow, I had seized my whip by the small end, and – swift and sudden as a flash of lightning – brought the other down upon his head. It was not without a feeling of savage satisfaction that I beheld the instant, deadly pallor that overspread his face, and the few red drops that trickled down his forehead, while he reeled a moment in his saddle, and then fell backward to the ground. The pony, surprised to be so strangely relieved of its burden, started and capered, and kicked a little, and then made use of its freedom to go and crop the grass of the hedge bank; while its master lay as still and silent as a corpse. Had I killed him? – an icy hand seemed to grasp my heart and check its pulsation, as I bent over him, gazing with breathless intensity upon the ghastly, upturned face. But no; he moved his eyelids and uttered a slight groan. I breathed again – he was only stunned by the fall. It served him right – it would teach him better manners in future. Should I help him to his horse? No. For any other combination of offences I would; but his were too unpardonable. He might mount it himself, if he liked – in a while: already he was beginning to stir and look about him – and there it was for him, quietly browsing on the roadside.

So with a muttered execration, I left the fellow to his fate, and clapping spurs to my own horse, galloped away, excited by a combination of feelings it would not be easy to analyse; and perhaps, if I did so, the result would not be very creditable to my disposition; for I am not sure that a species of exultation in what I had done, was not one principal concomitant.

Shortly, however, the effervescence began to abate, and not many minutes elapsed before I had turned and gone back to look after the fate of my victim. It was no generous impulse – no kind relentings that led me to this – nor even the fear of what might be the consequences to myself, if I finished my assault upon the squire by leaving him thus neglected, and exposed to further injury; it was, simply, the voice of conscience; and I took great credit to myself for attending so promptly to its dictates – and judging the merit of the deed by the sacrifice it cost, I was not far wrong.

Mr Lawrence and his pony had both altered their positions, in some degree. The pony had wandered eight or ten yards farther away; and he had managed, somehow, to remove himself from the middle of the road: I found him seated in a recumbent position on the bank – looking very white and sickly still, and holding his cambric handkerchief (now more red than white) to his head. It must have been a powerful blow; but half the credit – or the blame of it (which you please) must be attributed to the whip, which was garnished with a massive horse's head of plated metal. The grass, being sodden with rain, afforded the young gentleman a rather inhospitable couch; his clothes were considerably

bemired; and his hat was rolling in the mud, on the other side of the road. But his thoughts seemed chiefly bent upon his pony, on which he was wistfully gazing – half in helpless anxiety, and half in hopeless abandonment to his fate.

I dismounted however, and having fastened my own animal to the nearest tree, first picked up his hat, intending to clap it on his head; but either he considered his head unfit for a hat, or the hat, in its present condition, unfit for his head; for shrinking away the one, he took the other from my hand, and scornfully cast it aside.

'It's good enough for *you*,' I muttered.

My next good office was to catch his pony and bring it to him, which was soon accomplished; for the beast was quiet enough in the main, and only winced and flirted a trifle, till I got a hold of the bridle – but then, I must see him in the saddle.

'Here, you fellow – scoundrel – dog – give me your hand, and I'll help you to mount.'

No; he turned from me in disgust. I attempted to take him by the arm. He shrank away as if there had been contamination in my touch.

'What, you won't? Well! you may sit there till doomsday, for what I care. But I suppose you don't want to lose all the blood in your body – I'll just condescend to bind that up for you.'

'Let me alone, if you please.'

'Humph! with all my heart. You may go to the devil if you choose – and say I sent you.'

But before I abandoned him to his fate, I flung his pony's bridle over a stake in the hedge, and threw him my handkerchief, as his own was now saturated with blood. He took it and cast it back to me, in abhorrence and contempt, with all the strength he could muster. It wanted but this to fill the measure of his offences. With execrations not loud but deep, I left him to live or die as he could, well satisfied that I had done *my* duty in attempting to save him – but forgetting how I had erred in bringing him into such a condition, and how insultingly my after services had been offered – and sullenly prepared to meet the consequences if he should choose to say I had attempted to murder him – which I thought not unlikely, as it seemed probable he was actuated by some such spiteful motives in so perseveringly refusing my assistance.

Having remounted my horse, I just looked back to see how he was getting on, before I rode away. He had risen from the ground, and grasping his pony's mane, was attempting to resume his seat in the saddle; but scarcely had he put his foot in the stirrup, when a sickness or dizziness seemed to overpower him: he leant forward a moment, with his head drooped on the animal's back, and then made one more effort, which proving ineffectual, he sank back on to the bank, where I left him, reposing his head on the oozy turf, and, to all appearance, as calmly reclining as if he had been taking his rest on the sofa at home.

I ought to have helped him in spite of himself – to have bound up the wound he was unable to stanch, and insisted upon getting him on to his horse and seeing him safe home; but, besides my bitter indignation against himself, there

was the question what to say to his servants – and what to my own family. Either I should have to acknowledge the deed, which would set me down as a madman, unless I acknowledged the motive too – and that seemed impossible – or I must get up a lie, which seemed equally out of the question – especially as Mr Lawrence would probably reveal the whole truth, and thereby bring me to tenfold disgrace – unless I were villain enough, presuming on the absence of witnesses, to persist in my own version of the case, and make him out a still greater scoundrel than he was. No; he had only received a cut above the temple, and perhaps, a few bruises from the fall, or the hoofs of his own pony: that could not kill him if he lay there half the day; and, if he could not help himself, surely someone would be coming by: it would be impossible that a whole day should pass and no one traverse the road but ourselves. As for what he might choose to say hereafter, I would take my chance about it: if he told lies, I would contradict him; if he told the truth, I would bear it as I best could. I was not *obliged* to enter into explanations, further than I thought proper. Perhaps, he might choose to be silent on the subject, for fear of raising enquiries as to the cause of the quarrel, and drawing the public attention to his connection with Mrs Graham, which, whether for her sake or his own, he seemed so very desirous to conceal.

Thus reasoning, I trotted away to the town, where I duly transacted my business, and performed various little commissions for my mother and Rose, with very laudable exactitude, considering the different circumstances of the case. In returning home, I was troubled with sundry misgivings about the unfortunate Lawrence. The question, what if I should find him lying still on the damp earth, fairly dying of cold and exhaustion – or already stark and chill? thrust itself most unpleasantly upon my mind, and the appalling possibility pictured itself with painful vividness to my imagination as I approached the spot where I had left him. But no; thank Heaven, both man and horse were gone, and nothing was left to witness against me but two objects – unpleasant enough in themselves, to be sure, and presenting a very ugly, not to say murderous, appearance – in one place, the hat saturated with rain and coated with mud, indented and broken above the brim by that villainous whip-handle; in another, the crimson handkerchief, soaking in a deeply tinctured pool of water – for much rain had fallen in the interim.

Bad news fly fast: it was hardly four o'clock when I got home, but my mother gravely accosted me with – 'Oh, Gilbert! – *Such* an accident! Rose has been shopping in the village, and she's heard that Mr Lawrence has been thrown from his horse and brought home dying!'

This shocked me a trifle, as you may suppose; but I was comforted to hear that he had frightfully fractured his skull and broken a leg; for, assured of the falsehood of this, I trusted the rest of the story was equally exaggerated; and when I heard my mother and sister so feelingly deploring his condition, I had considerable difficulty in preventing myself from telling them the real extent of the injuries, as far as I knew them.

'You must go and see him tomorrow,' said my mother.

'Or today,' suggested Rose: 'there's plenty of time; and you can have the

pony, if your horse is tired. Won't you, Gilbert – as soon as you've had something to eat?'

'No, no – how can we tell that it isn't all a false report? It's highly im – '

'Oh, I'm sure it isn't; for the village is all alive about it; and I saw two people that had seen others that had seen the man that found him. That sounds far fetched; but it isn't so, when you think of it.'

'Well, but Lawrence is a good rider; it is not likely he would fall from his horse at all; and if he did, it is highly improbable he should break his bones in that way. It must be a gross exaggeration at least.'

'No, but the horse kicked him – or something.'

'What, his quiet little pony?'

'How do you know it was that?'

'He seldom rides any other.'

'At any rate,' said my mother, 'you will call tomorrow. Whether it be true or false, exaggerated or otherwise we shall like to know how he is.'

'Fergus may go.'

'Why not you?'

'He has more time: I am busy just now.'

'Oh! but Gilbert, how can you be so composed about it? You won't mind business, for an hour or two, in a case of this sort – when your friend is at the point of death!'

'He is *not*, I tell you!'

'For anything you know, he *may* be: you can't tell till you have seen him – At all events, he must have met with some terrible accident, and you ought to see him: he'll take it very unkind of you if you don't.'

'Confound it! I can't. He and I have not been on good terms, of late.'

'O my *dear* boy! Surely, surely, you are not so unforgiving as to carry your little differences to such a length as – '

'Little differences, indeed!' I muttered.

'Well, but only remember the occasion! Think how – '

'Well, well, don't bother me now – I'll see about it,' I replied.

And my seeing about it, was to send Fergus next morning, with my mother's compliments, to make the requisite enquiries; for, of course, my going was out of the question – or sending a message, either. He brought back intelligence that the young squire was laid up with the complicated evils of a broken head and certain contusions (occasioned by a fall – of which he did not trouble himself to relate the particulars – and the subsequent misconduct of his horse), and a severe cold, the consequence of lying on the wet ground in the rain; but there were no broken bones, and no immediate prospects of dissolution.

It was evident then, that, for Mrs Graham's sake, it was not his intention to criminate me.

## CHAPTER 15

### *An Encounter and its Consequences*

That day was rainy like its predecessor; but towards evening it began to clear up a little, and the next morning was fair and promising. I was out on the hill with the reapers. A light wind swept over the corn; and all nature laughed in the sunshine. The lark was rejoicing among the silvery floating clouds. The late rain had so sweetly freshened and cleared the air, and washed the sky, and left such glittering gems on branch and blade, that not even the farmers could have the heart to blame it. But no ray of sunshine could reach my heart, no breeze could freshen it; nothing could fill the void my faith, and hope, and joy in Helen Graham had left, or drive away the keen regrets, and bitter dregs of lingering love that still oppressed it.

While I stood, with folded arms, abstractedly gazing on the undulating swell of the corn not yet disturbed by the reapers, something gently pulled my skirts, and a small voice, no longer welcome to my ears, aroused me with the startling words: 'Mr Markham, mamma wants you.'

'Wants *me*, Arthur?'

'Yes. Why do you look so queer?' said he, half laughing, half frightened at the unexpected aspect of my face in suddenly turning towards him – 'and why have you kept so long away? – Come! – Won't you come?'

'I'm busy just now,' I replied, scarce knowing what to answer.

He looked up in childish bewilderment; but before I could speak again, the lady herself was at my side.

'Gilbert, I *must* speak with you!' said she in a tone of suppressed vehemence.

I looked at her pale cheek and glittering eye, but answered nothing.

'Only for a moment,' pleaded she. 'Just step aside into this other field' – she glanced at the reapers, some of whom were directing looks of impertinent curiosity towards her – 'I won't keep you a minute.'

I accompanied her through the gap.

'Arthur, darling, run and gather those bluebells,' said she, pointing to some that were gleaming, at some distance, under the hedge along which we walked. The child hesitated, as if unwilling to quit my side. 'Go, love!' repeated she more urgently, and in a tone, which, though not unkind, demanded prompt obedience, and obtained it.

'Well, Mrs Graham?' said I, calmly and coldly; for, though I saw she was miserable, and pitied her, I felt glad to have it in my power to torment her.

She fixed her eyes upon me with a look that pierced me to the heart; and yet, it made me smile.

'I don't ask the reason of this change, Gilbert,' said she with bitter calmness – 'I know it too well; but though I could see myself suspected and condemned by

everyone else, and bear it with calmness, I cannot endure it from you – Why did you not come to hear my explanation on the day I appointed to give it?'

'Because, I happened, in the interim, to learn all you would have told me – and a trifle more I imagine.'

'Impossible, for I would have told you all!' cried she, passionately – 'But I won't now, for I see you are not worthy of it!'

And her pale lips quivered with agitation.

'Why not, may I ask?'

She repelled my mocking smile with a glance of scornful indignation.

'Because you never understood me, or you would not soon have listened to my traducers – my confidence would be misplaced in you – you are not the man I thought you – Go! I won't care *what* you think of me!'

She turned away, and I went; for I thought that would torment her as much as anything; and I believe I was right; for, looking back a minute after, I saw her turn half round, as if hoping or expecting to find me still beside her; and then she stood still, and cast one look behind. It was a look less expressive of anger than of bitter anguish and despair; but I immediately assumed an aspect of indifference, and affected to be gazing carelessly round me, and I suppose she went on; for after lingering awhile to see if she would come back or call, I ventured one more glance, and saw her a good way off, moving rapidly up the field with little Arthur running by her side and apparently talking as he went; but she kept her face averted from him, as if to hide some uncontrollable emotion. And I returned to my business.

But I soon began to regret my precipitancy in leaving her so soon. It was evident she loved me – probably, she was tired of Mr Lawrence, and wished to exchange him for me; and if I had loved and reverenced her less to begin with, the preference might have gratified and amused me; but now, the contrast between her outward seeming and her inward mind, as I supposed – between my former and my present opinion of her, was so harrowing – so distressing to my feelings, that it swallowed up every lighter consideration.

But still, I was curious to know what sort of an explanation she would have given me – or would give now, if I pressed her for it – how much she would confess, and how she would endeavour to excuse herself. I longed to know what to despise, and what to admire in her, how much to pity, and how much to hate; and, what was more, I *would* know. I would see her once more, and fairly satisfy myself in what light to regard her, before we parted. Lost to me she was, for ever, of course; but still, I could not bear to think that we had parted, for the last time, with so much unkindness and misery on both sides. That last look of hers had sunk into my heart; I could not forget it – But what a fool I was! – Had she not deceived me, injured me – blighted my happiness for life? – 'Well I'll see her, however,' was my concluding resolve – 'but not today: today and tonight, she may think upon her sins, and be as miserable as she will: tomorrow, I will see her once again, and know something more about her. The interview may be serviceable to her, or it may not – At any rate, it will give a breath of excitement to the life she has doomed to stagnation, and may calm with certainty some agitating thoughts.'

I did go on the morrow; but not till towards evening, after the business of the day was concluded, that is between six and seven; and the westering sun was gleaming redly on the old hall, and flaming in the latticed windows, as I reached it, imparting to the place a cheerfulness not its own. I need not dilate upon the feelings with which I approached the shrine of my former divinity – that spot teeming with a thousand delightful recollections and glorious dreams – all darkened now, by one disastrous truth.

Rachel admitted me into the parlour, and went to call her mistress, for she was not there; but there was her desk left open on the little round table beside the high-backed chair, with a book laid upon it. Her limited but choice collection of books was almost as familiar to me as my own; but this volume I had not seen before. I took it up. It was Sir Humphrey Davy's *Last Days of a Philosopher*, and on the first leaf was written – 'Frederick Lawrence'. I closed the book, but kept it in my hand, and stood facing the door, with my back to the fireplace, calmly waiting her arrival; for I did not doubt she would come. And soon I heard her step in the hall. My heart was beginning to throb, but I checked it with an internal rebuke, and maintained my composure – outwardly, at least. She entered, calm, pale, collected.

'To what am I indebted for this favour, Mr Markham?' said she, with such severe but quiet dignity as almost disconcerted me; but I answered with a smile, and impudently enough – 'Well, I am come to hear your explanation.'

'I told you I would not give it,' said she. 'I said you were unworthy of my confidence.'

'Oh, very well,' replied I, moving to the door.

'Stay a moment,' said she. 'This is the last time I shall see you: don't go just yet.'

I remained, awaiting her further commands.

'Tell me,' resumed she, 'on what grounds you believe these things against me; who told you; and what did they say?'

I paused a moment. She met my eye as unflinchingly as if her bosom had been steeled with conscious innocence. She was resolved to know the worst, and determined to dare it too. 'I can crush that bold spirit,' thought I. But while I secretly exulted in my power, I felt disposed to dally with my victim like a cat. Showing her the book that I still held in my hand, and pointing to the name on the fly leaf, but fixing my eye upon her face, I asked – 'Do you know that gentleman?'

'Of course I do,' replied she; and a sudden flush suffused her features – whether of shame or anger I could not tell: it rather resembled the latter. 'What next, sir?'

'How long is it since you saw him?'

'Who gave you the right to catechise me, on this or any other subject?'

'Oh, no one! – it's quite at your option whether to answer or not – and now, let me ask – have you heard what has lately befallen this friend of yours? – because, if you have not – '

'I will not be insulted, Mr Markham!' cried she almost infuriated at my

manner – 'So you had better leave the house at once, if you came only for that.'

'I did not come to insult you: I came to hear your explanation.'

'And I tell you I won't give it!' retorted she, pacing the room in a state of strong excitement, with her hands clasped tightly together, breathing short, and flashing fires of indignation from her eyes. 'I will not condescend to explain myself to one that can make a jest of such horrible suspicions, and be so easily led to entertain them.'

'I do not make a jest of them, Mrs Graham,' returned I, dropping at once, my tone of taunting sarcasm. 'I heartily wish I could find them a jesting matter! And as to being easily led to suspect, God only knows what a blind, incredulous fool I have hitherto been, perseveringly shutting my eyes and stopping my ears against everything that threatened to shake my confidence in you, till proof itself confounded my infatuation!'

'What proof, sir?'

'Well, I'll tell you. You remember that evening when I was here last?'

'I do.'

'Even then, you dropped some hints that might have opened the eyes of a wiser man; but they had no such effect upon me: I went on trusting and believing, hoping against hope, and adoring where I could not comprehend – It so happened, however, that after I had left you, I turned back – drawn by pure depth of sympathy, and ardour of affection – not daring to intrude my presence openly upon you, but unable to resist the temptation of catching one glimpse through the window, just to see how you were; for I had left you apparently in great affliction, and I partly blamed my own want of forbearance and discretion as the cause of it. If I did wrong, love alone was my incentive, and the punishment was severe enough; for it was just as I had reached that tree, that you came out into the garden with your friend. Not choosing to show myself, under the circumstances, I stood still, in the shadow, till you had both passed by.'

'And how much of our conversation did you hear?'

'I heard quite enough, Helen. And it was well for me that I did hear it; for nothing less could have cured my infatuation. I always said and thought, that I would never believe a word against you, unless I heard it from your own lips. All the hints and affirmations of others I treated as malignant, baseless slanders; your own self accusations I believed to be overstrained; and all that seemed unaccountable in your position, I trusted that you could account for if you chose.'

Mrs Graham had discontinued her walk. She leant against one end of the chimney-piece, opposite that near which I was standing, with her chin resting on her closed hand, her eyes – no longer burning with anger, but gleaming with restless excitement – sometimes glancing at me while I spoke, then coursing the opposite wall, or fixed upon the carpet.

'You should have come to me, after all,' said she, 'and heard what I had to say in my own justification. It was ungenerous and wrong to withdraw yourself so secretly and suddenly, immediately after such ardent protestations of attachment,

without ever assigning a reason for the change. You should have told me all – no matter *how* bitterly – it would have been better than this silence.'

'To what end should I have done so? – You could not have enlightened me farther, on the subject which alone concerned me; nor could you have made me discredit the evidence of my senses. I desired our intimacy to be discontinued at once, as you yourself had acknowledged would probably be the case if I knew all; but I did not wish to upbraid you – though (as you also acknowledged) you had deeply wronged me – Yes; you have done me an injury you can never repair – or any other either – you have blighted the freshness and promise of youth, and made my life a wilderness! I might live a hundred years, but I could never recover from the effects of this withering blow – and never forget it! Hereafter – You smile Mrs Graham,' said I, suddenly stopping short, checked in my passionate declamation by unutterable feelings to behold her actually *smiling* at the picture of the ruin she had wrought.

'Did I?' replied she, looking seriously up, 'I was not aware of it. If I did, it was not for pleasure at the thoughts of the harm I had done you – Heaven knows I have had torment enough at the bare possibility of that! – it was for joy to find that you had some depth of soul and feeling after all, and to hope that I had not been utterly mistaken in your worth. But smiles and tears are so alike with me; they are neither of them confined to any particular feelings: I often cry when I am happy, and smile when I am sad.'

She looked at me again, and seemed to expect a reply; but I continued silent. 'Would you be *very* glad,' resumed she, 'to find that you were mistaken in your conclusions?'

'How can you ask it, Helen?'

'I don't say I can clear myself altogether,' said she, speaking low and fast, while her heart beat visibly and her bosom heaved with excitement – 'but would you be glad to discover I was better than you think me?'

'Anything, that could, in the least degree, tend to restore my former opinion of you, to excuse the regard I still feel for you, and alleviate the pangs of unutterable regret that accompany it, would be only too gladly – too eagerly received!'

Her cheeks burned and her whole frame trembled, now, with excess of agitation. She did not speak, but flew to her desk, and snatching thence what seemed a thick album or manuscript volume, hastily tore away a few leaves from the end, and thrust the rest into my hand, saying, 'You needn't read it all; but take it home with you' – and hurried from the room. But when I had left the house, and was proceeding down the walk, she opened the window and called me back. It was only to say – 'Bring it back when you have read it; and don't breathe a word of what it tells you to any living being – I trust to your honour.'

Before I could answer, she had closed the casement and turned away. I saw her cast herself back in the old oak chair, and cover her face with her hands. Her feelings had been wrought to a pitch that rendered it necessary to seek relief in tears.

Panting with eagerness, and struggling to suppress my hopes, I hurried

home, and rushed upstairs to my room – having first provided myself with a candle, though it was scarcely twilight yet – then, shut and bolted the door, determined to tolerate no interruption, and sitting down before the table, opened out my prize and delivered myself up to its perusal – first, hastily turning over the leaves and snatching a sentence here and there, and then, setting myself steadily to read it through.

I have it now before me; and though you could not of course, peruse it with half the interest that I did, I know you would not be satisfied with an abbreviation of its contents, and you shall have the whole, save, perhaps, a few passages here and there of merely temporal interest to the writer, or such as would serve to encumber the story rather than elucidate it. It begins somewhat abruptly, thus – but we will reserve its commencement for another chapter, and call it:

### CHAPTER 16

## *The Warnings of Experience*

June 1st, 1821 – We have just returned to Staningley – that is, we returned some days ago, and I am not yet settled, and feel as if I never should be. We left town sooner than was intended, in consequence of my uncle's indisposition – I wonder what would have been the result if we had stayed the full time. I am quite ashamed of my new-sprung distaste for country life. All my former occupations seem so tedious and dull, my former amusements so insipid and unprofitable. I cannot enjoy my music, because there is no one to hear it. I cannot enjoy my walks, because there is no one to meet. I cannot enjoy my books, because they have not power to arrest my attention: my head is so haunted with the recollections of the last few weeks, that I cannot attend to them. My drawing suits me best, for I can draw and think at the same time; and if my productions cannot now be seen by anyone but myself and those who do not care about them, they, possibly, may be, hereafter. But then, there is one face I am always trying to paint or to sketch, and always without success; and that vexes me. As for the owner of that face, I cannot get him out of my mind – and, indeed, I never try. I wonder whether he ever thinks of me; and I wonder whether I shall ever see him again. And then might follow a train of other wonderments, questions for time and fate to answer, concluding with: supposing all the rest be answered in the affirmative, I wonder whether I shall ever repent it – as my aunt would tell me I should, if she knew what I was thinking about. How distinctly I remember our conversation that evening before our departure for town, when we were sitting together over the fire, my uncle having gone to bed with a slight attack of the gout.

'Helen,' said she, after a thoughtful silence, 'do you ever think about marriage?'

'Yes, aunt, often.'

'And do you ever contemplate the possibility of being married yourself, or engaged, before the season is over?'

'Sometimes; but I don't think it at all likely that I *ever* shall.'

'Why so?'

'Because, I imagine there must be only a very, very few men in the world, that I should like to marry; and of those few, it is ten to one I may never be acquainted with one; or if I should, it is twenty to one, he may not happen to be single, or to take a fancy to me.'

'That is no argument at all. It may be very true – and I hope *is* true, that there are very few men whom you would choose to marry, of yourself – It is not, indeed, to be supposed that you would *wish* to marry *any*one, till you were asked: a girl's affections should never be won unsought. But when they *are* sought – when the citadel of the heart is fairly besieged, it is apt to surrender sooner than the owner is aware of, and often against her better judgement, and in opposition to all her preconceived ideas of what she could have loved, unless she be extremely careful and discreet. Now I want to warn you, Helen, of these things, and to exhort you to be watchful and circumspect from the very commencement of your career, and not to suffer your heart to be stolen from you by the first foolish or unprincipled person that covets the possession of it – You know, my dear, you are only just eighteen; there is plenty of time before you, and neither your uncle nor I are in any hurry to get you off our hands; and, I may venture to say, there will be no lack of suitors; for you can boast a good family, pretty considerable fortune and expectations, and, I may as well tell you likewise – for if I don't others will – that you have a fair share of beauty, besides – and I hope you may never have cause to regret it! – '

'I hope not, aunt; but why should you fear it?'

'Because, my dear, beauty is that quality which, next to money, is generally the most attractive to the worst kinds of men; and, therefore, it is likely to entail a great deal of trouble on the possessor.'

'Have *you* been troubled in that way, aunt?'

'No, Helen,' said she, with reproachful gravity, 'but I know many that have; and some, through carelessness, have been the wretched victims of deceit; and some, through weakness, have fallen into snares and temptations terrible to relate.'

'Well, I shall be neither careless nor weak.'

'Remember Peter, Helen! Don't boast, but *watch*. Keep a guard over your eyes and ears as the inlets of your heart, and over your lips as the outlet, lest they betray you in a moment of unwariness. Receive, coldly and dispassionately, every attention, till you have ascertained and duly considered the worth of the aspirant; and let your affections be consequent upon approbation alone. First study; then approve; then love. Let your eyes be blind to all external attractions, your ears deaf to all the fascinations of flattery and light discourse – These are nothing – and worse than nothing – snares and wiles of the tempter, to lure the thoughtless to their own destruction. Principle is the first thing, after all; and next to that, good sense, respectability, and moderate wealth. If you should

marry the handsomest, and most accomplished and superficially agreeable man in the world, you little know the misery that would overwhelm you, if, after all, you should find him to be a worthless reprobate, or even an impracticable fool.'

'But what are all the poor fools and reprobates to do, aunt? If everybody followed your advice the world would soon come to an end.'

'Never fear, my dear! The male fools and reprobates will never want for partners while there are so many of the other sex to match them; but do *you* follow my advice. And this is no subject for jesting, Helen, I am sorry to see you treat the matter in that light way. Believe me, *matrimony is a serious thing*.' And she spoke it so seriously that one might have fancied she had known it to her cost; but I asked no more impertinent questions, and merely answered – 'I know it is; and I know there is truth and sense in what you say; but you need not fear me, for I not only should think it *wrong* to marry a man that was deficient in sense or in principle, but I should never be *tempted* to do it; for I could not like him, if he were ever so handsome and ever so charming in other respects; I should hate him – despise him – pity him – anything but love him. My affections not only *ought* to be founded on approbation, but they will and must be so: for without approving I cannot love. It is needless to say I ought to be able to respect and honour the man I marry as *well* as love him, for I cannot love him without. So set your mind at rest.'

'I hope it may be so,' answered she.

'I *know* it *is* so,' persisted I.

'You have not been tried yet, Helen: we can but hope,' said she, in her cold, cautious way.

I was vexed at her incredulity; but I am not sure her doubts were entirely without sagacity; I fear I have found it much easier to remember her advice than to profit by it – indeed, I have sometimes been led to question the soundness of her doctrines on those subjects. Her counsels may be good, as far as they go – in the main points, at least; but there are some things she has overlooked in her calculations. I wonder if *she* was ever in love.

I commenced my career – or my first campaign, as my uncle calls it – kindling with bright hopes and fancies – chiefly raised by this conversation – and full of confidence in my own discretion. At first, I was delighted with the novelty and excitement of our London life; but, soon, I began to weary of its mingled turbulence and constraint, and sigh for the freshness and freedom of home. My new acquaintances, both male and female, disappointed my expectations, and vexed and depressed me by turns; for I soon grew tired of studying their peculiarities, and laughing at their foibles – particularly as I was obliged to keep my criticisms to myself, for my aunt would not hear them – and they – the ladies especially – appeared so provokingly mindless, and heartless, and artificial. The gentlemen seemed better, but perhaps, it was because I knew them less, perhaps, because they flattered me; but I did not fall in love with any of them, and if their attentions pleased me one moment, they provoked me the next, because they put me out of humour with myself, by revealing my vanity and making me fear I was becoming like some of the ladies I so heartily despised.

There was one elderly gentleman that annoyed me very much; a rich old friend of my uncle's who, I believe, thought I could not do better than marry him; but, besides being old, he was ugly and disagreeable – and wicked, I am sure, though my aunt scolded me for saying so; but she allowed he was no saint. And there was another, less hateful, but still *more* tiresome, because she favoured him, and was always thrusting him upon me, and sounding his praises in my ears, Mr Boarham, by name, Bore 'em as I prefer spelling it, for a terrible bore he was: I shudder still, at the remembrance of his voice, drone, drone, drone, in my ear, while he sat beside me, prosing away by the half-hour together, and beguiling himself with the notion that he was improving my mind by useful information, or, impressing his dogmas upon me, and reforming my errors of judgement, or perhaps, that he was talking down to my level, and amusing me with entertaining discourse. Yet he was a decent man enough, in the main, I dare say; and if he had kept his distance, I never would have hated him. As it was, it was almost impossible to help it; for he not only bothered me with the infliction of his own presence, but he kept me from the enjoyment of more agreeable society.

One night, however, at a ball, he had been more than usually tormenting, and my patience was quite exhausted – It appeared as if the whole evening was fated to be insupportable: I had just had one dance with an empty-headed coxcomb, and then Mr Boarham had come upon me, and seemed determined to cling to me for the rest of the night. He never danced himself, and there he sat, poking his head in my face, and impressing all beholders with the idea that he was a confirmed, acknowledged lover; my aunt looking complacently on, all the time, and wishing him Godspeed. In vain I attempted to drive him away by giving a loose to my exasperated feelings, even to positive rudeness: nothing could convince him that his presence was disagreeable. Sullen silence was taken for rapt attention, and gave him greater room to talk; sharp answers were received as smart sallies of girlish vivacity, that only required an indulgent rebuke; and flat contradictions were but as oil to the flames, calling forth new strains of argument to support his dogmas, and bringing down upon me endless floods of reasoning to overwhelm me with conviction.

But there was one present who seemed to have a better appreciation of my frame of mind. A gentleman stood by, who had been watching our conference for some time, evidently much amused at my companion's remorseless pertinacity and my manifest annoyance, and laughing to himself at the asperity and un-compromising spirit of my replies. At length, however, he withdrew, and went to the lady of the house, apparently for the purpose of asking an introduction to me, for, shortly after, they both came up, and she introduced him as Mr Huntingdon, the son of a late friend of my uncle's. He asked me to dance. I gladly consented, of course; and he was my companion during the remainder of my stay, which was not long, for my aunt, as usual, insisted upon an early departure.

I was sorry to go, for I had found my new acquaintance a very lively and entertaining companion. There was a certain graceful ease and freedom about

all he said and did, that gave a sense of repose and expansion to the mind, after so much constraint and formality as I had been doomed to suffer. There might be, it is true, a little too much careless boldness in his manner and address, but I was in so good a humour, and so grateful for my late deliverance from Mr Boarham, that it did not anger me.

'Well, Helen, how do you like Mr Boarham now?' said my aunt, as we took our seats in the carriage and drove away.

'Worse than ever,' I replied.

She looked displeased but said no more on that subject.

'Who was the gentleman you danced with last,' resumed she, after a pause – 'that was so officious in helping you on with your shawl?'

'He was not officious at all, aunt: he never *attempted* to help me, till he saw Mr Boarham coming to do so; and then he stepped laughingly forward and said, "Come I'll preserve you from that infliction."'

'Who was it, I ask?' said she, with frigid gravity.

'It was Mr Huntingdon, the son of uncle's old friend.'

'I have heard your uncle speak of young Mr Huntingdon. I've heard him say, "He's a fine lad, that young Huntingdon, but a bit wildish I fancy." So I'd have you beware.'

'What does "a bit wildish" mean?' I enquired.

'It means destitute of principle, and prone to every vice that is common to youth.'

'But I've heard uncle say he was a sad wild fellow himself, when he was young.'

She sternly shook her head.

'He was jesting then, I suppose,' said I, 'and here he was speaking at random – at least, I cannot believe there is any harm in those laughing blue eyes.'

'False reasoning, Helen!' said she with a sigh.

'Well, we ought to be charitable, you know, aunt – besides, I don't think it *is* false: I am an excellent physiognomist, and I always judge of people's characters by their looks – not by whether they are handsome or ugly, but by the general cast of the countenance. For instance, I should know by your countenance that you were not of a cheerful, sanguine disposition; and I should know by Mr Wilmot's that he was a worthless old reprobate, and by Mr Boarham's that he was not an agreeable companion, and by Mr Huntingdon's that he was neither a fool nor a knave, though, possibly, neither a sage nor a saint – but that is no matter to me, as I am not likely to meet him again – unless as an occasional partner in the ballroom.'

It was not so, however, for I met him again next morning. He came to call upon my uncle, apologising for not having done so before, by saying he was only lately returned from the continent, and had not heard, till the previous night, of my uncle's arrival in town; and after that, I often met him; sometimes in public, sometimes at home; for he was very assiduous in paying his respects to his old friend, who did not, however, consider himself greatly obliged by the attention.

'I wonder what the deuce the lad means by coming so often,' he would say –

'can *you* tell, Helen? – Hey? He wants none o' my company, nor I his – that's certain.'

'I wish you'd tell him so, then,' said my aunt.

'Why, what for? If I don't want him, somebody does mayhap' (winking at me). 'Besides, he's a pretty tidy fortune, Peggy, you know – not such a catch as Wilmot, but then Helen won't hear of that match; for, somehow, these old chaps don't go down with the girls – with *all* their money – and their experience to boot. I'll bet anything she'd rather have this young fellow without a penny, than Wilmot with his house full of gold – Wouldn't you Nell?'

'Yes, uncle; but that's not saying much for Mr Huntingdon, for I'd rather be an old maid and a pauper, than Mrs Wilmot.'

'And Mrs Huntingdon? What would you rather be than Mrs Huntingdon? eh?'

'I'll tell you when I've considered the matter.'

'Ah! it needs consideration then – But come now – would you rather be an old maid – let alone the pauper?'

'I can't tell till I'm asked.'

And I left the room immediately, to escape further examination. But five minutes after, in looking from my window, I beheld Mr Boarham coming up to the door. I waited nearly half an hour in uncomfortable suspense, expecting every minute to be called, and vainly longing to hear him go. Then, footsteps were heard on the stairs, and my aunt entered the room with a solemn countenance, and closed the door behind her.

'Here is Mr Boarham, Helen,' said she. 'He wishes to see you.'

'Oh, aunt! Can't you tell him I'm indisposed? – I'm sure I am – to see *him*.'

'Nonsense, my dear! This is no trifling matter. He is come on a very important errand – to ask your hand in marriage, of your uncle and me.'

'I hope my uncle and you told him it was not in your power to give it. What right had he to ask *any*one before me?'

'Helen!'

'What did my uncle say?'

'He said he would not interfere in the matter; if you liked to accept Mr Boarham's obliging offer, you –'

'Did he say obliging offer?'

'No; he said if you liked to take him you might; and if not, you might please yourself.'

'He said right; and what did you say?'

'It is no matter what I said. What will *you* say? – that is the question. He is now waiting to ask you himself; but consider well before you go; and if you intend to refuse him, give me your reasons.'

'I *shall* refuse him, of course, but you must tell me how, for I want to be civil and yet decided and when I've got rid of him, I'll give you my reasons afterwards.'

'But stay, Helen; sit down a little, and compose yourself. Mr Boarham is in no particular hurry, for he has little doubt of your acceptance; and I want to speak

with you. Tell me, my dear, what are your objections to him? Do you deny that he is an upright, honourable man?'

'No.'

'Do you deny that he is sensible, sober, respectable?'

'No; he may be all this, but – '

'*But*, Helen! How many such men do you expect to meet with in the world? Upright, honourable, sensible, sober, respectable! – Is *this* such an everyday character, that you should reject the possessor of such noble qualities, without a moment's hesitation? – Yes, *noble* I may call them; for, think of the full meaning of each, and how many inestimable virtues they include (and I might add many more to the list), and consider that all this is laid at your feet: it is in your power to secure this inestimable blessing for life – a worthy and excellent husband, who loves you tenderly, but not too fondly so as to blind him to your faults, and will be your guide throughout life's pilgrimage, and your partner in eternal bliss! Think how – '

'But I hate him, aunt,' said I, interrupting this unusual flow of eloquence.

'Hate him, Helen! Is this a Christian spirit? – *you hate him*? – and he so good a man!'

'I don't hate him as a man, but as a husband. As a man, I love him so much, that I wish him a better wife than I – one as good as himself, or better – if you think that possible – provided, she could like him; but I never could, and therefore – '

'But why not? What objection do you find?'

'Firstly, he is, at least, forty years old – considerably more I should think, and I am but eighteen; secondly, he is narrow-minded and bigoted in the extreme; thirdly, his tastes and feelings are wholly dissimilar to mine; fourthly, his looks, voice, and manner are particularly displeasing to me; and finally, I have an aversion to his whole person that I never can surmount.'

'Then you ought to surmount it! And please to compare him for a moment with Mr Huntingdon, and, good looks apart (which contribute nothing to the merit of the man, or to the happiness of married life, and which you have so often professed to hold in light esteem), tell me which is the better man.'

'I have no doubt Mr Huntingdon is a much better man than you think him – but we are not talking about him, now, but about Mr Boarham; and as I would rather grow, live and die in single blessedness than be his wife, it is but right that I should tell him so at once, and put him out of suspense – so let me go.'

'But don't give him a flat denial; he has no idea of such a thing, and it would offend him greatly: say you have no thoughts of matrimony, at present – '

'But I *have* thoughts of it.'

'Or that you desire a further acquaintance.'

'But I don't desire a further acquaintance – quite the contrary.'

And without waiting for further admonitions, I left the room, and went to seek Mr Boarham. He was walking up and down the drawing-room, humming snatches of tunes, and nibbling the end of his cane.

'My dear young lady,' said he, bowing and smirking with great complacency. 'I have your kind guardian's permission – '

'I know, sir,' said I, wishing to shorten the scene as much as possible, 'and I am greatly obliged for your preference, but must beg to decline the honour you wish to confer; for, I think, we were not made for each other – as you yourself would shortly discover if the experiment were tried.'

My aunt was right: it was quite evident he had had little doubt of my acceptance, and no idea of a positive denial. He was amazed – astounded at such an answer, but too incredulous to be much offended; and after a little humming and hawing, he returned to the attack.

'I know, my dear, that there exists a considerable disparity between us in years, in temperament, and perhaps some other things, but let me assure you, I shall not be severe to mark the faults and foibles of a young and ardent nature such as yours, and while I acknowledge them to myself, and even rebuke them with all a father's care, believe me, no youthful lover could be more tenderly indulgent towards the object of his affections, than I to you; and, on the other hand, let me hope that my more experienced years and graver habits of reflection will be no disparagement in your eyes, as I shall endeavour to make them all conducive to your happiness. Come now! What do you say? – Let us have no young lady's affectations and caprices, but speak out at once!'

'I will, but only to repeat what I said before, that I am certain we were not made for each other.'

'You really think so?'

'I do.'

'But you don't know me – you wish for a further acquaintance – a longer time to – '

'No, I don't. I know you as well as I ever shall, and better than you know me, or you would never dream of uniting yourself to one so incongruous – so utterly unsuitable to you in every way.'

'But my dear young lady, I don't look for perfection, I can excuse – '

'Thank you, Mr Boarham, but I won't trespass upon your goodness. You may save your indulgence and consideration for some more worthy object, that won't tax them so heavily.'

'But let me beg you to consult your aunt; that excellent lady, I am sure, will – '

'I have consulted her; and I know her wishes coincide with yours; but in such important matters, I take the liberty of judging for myself; and no persuasion can alter my inclinations, or induce me to believe that such a step would be conducive to my happiness, or yours – and I wonder that a man of your experience and discretion should think of choosing such a wife.'

'Ah, well!' said he – 'I have sometimes wondered at that myself. I have sometimes said to myself, "Now Boarham, what is this you're after? Take care man – look before you leap! This is a sweet, bewitching creature, but remember, the brightest attractions to the lover, too often prove the husband's greatest torments!" – I assure you my choice has not been made without much reasoning and reflection. The seeming imprudence of the match has cost me many an anxious thought by day, and many a sleepless hour by night; but at length, I satisfied myself, that it was not, in very deed, imprudent. I saw my

sweet girl was not without her faults, but of these, her youth, I trusted, was not one, but rather an earnest of virtues yet unblown – a strong ground of presumption that her little defects of temper, and errors of judgement, opinion, or manner were not irremediable, but might easily be removed or mitigated by the patient efforts of a watchful and judicious adviser, and where I failed to enlighten and control, I thought I might safely undertake to pardon, for the sake of her many excellencies. Therefore, my dearest girl, since *I* am satisfied why should *you* object – on my account, at least?'

'But to tell you the truth, Mr Boarham, it is on my own account I principally object; so let us – drop the subject.' I would have said, 'for it is worse than useless to pursue it any further,' but he pertinaciously interrupted me with, 'But why so? I would love you, cherish you, protect you, etc., etc.'

I shall not trouble myself to put down all that passed between us. Suffice it to say, that I found him very troublesome, and very hard to convince that I really meant what I said, and really *was* so obstinate and blind to my own interests, that there was no shadow of a chance that either he or my aunt would ever be able to overcome my objections. Indeed, I am not sure that I succeeded after all, though wearied with his so pertinaciously returning to the same point and repeating the same arguments over and over again, forcing me to reiterate the same replies, I at length turned short and sharp upon him, and my last words were – 'I tell you plainly, that it cannot be. No consideration can induce me to marry against my inclinations. I respect you – at least, I would respect you, if you would behave like a sensible man – but I cannot love you, and never could – and the more you talk the further you repel me; so pray don't say any more about it.'

Whereupon, he wished me a good-morning and withdrew, disconcerted and offended, no doubt; but surely it was not my fault.

## CHAPTER 17

## *Further Warnings*

The next day, I accompanied my uncle and aunt to a dinner party at Mr Wilmot's. He had two ladies staying with him, his niece Annabella, a fine dashing girl, or rather young woman, of some five and twenty, too great a flirt to be married, according to her own assertion, but greatly admired by the gentlemen, who universally pronounced her a splendid woman – and her gentle cousin Milicent Hargrave, who had taken a violent fancy to me, mistaking me for something vastly better than I was. And I in return, was very fond of her – I should entirely exclude poor Milicent in my general animadversions against the ladies of my acquaintance. But it was not on her account, or her cousin's, that I have mentioned the party: it was for the sake of another of Mr Wilmot's guests, to wit Mr Huntingdon. I have good reason to remember his presence there, for this was the last time I saw him.

He did not sit near me at dinner; for it was his fate to hand in a capacious old dowager, and mine to be handed in by Mr Grimsby, a friend of his, but a man I very greatly disliked: there was a sinister cast in his countenance, and a mixture of lurking ferocity and fulsome insincerity in his demeanour, that I could not away with. What a tiresome custom that is, by the by – one among the many sources of factitious annoyance of this ultra civilised life. If the gentlemen *must* lead the ladies into the dining-room, why cannot they take those they like best?

I am not sure, however, that Mr Huntingdon would have taken me, if he *had* been at liberty to make his own selection. It is quite possible he might have chosen Miss Wilmot; for she seemed bent upon engrossing his attention to herself, and he seemed nothing loath to pay the homage she demanded. I thought so, at least, when I saw how they talked and laughed, and glanced across the table, to the neglect and evident umbrage of their respective neighbours – and afterwards, as the gentlemen joined us in the drawing-room, when she, immediately upon his entrance, loudly called upon him to be the arbiter of a dispute between herself and another lady, and he answered the summons with alacrity, and decided the question without a moment's hesitation in her favour – though, to my thinking, she was obviously in the wrong – and then stood chatting familiarly with her and a group of other ladies; while I sat with Milicent Hargrave, at the opposite end of the room, looking over the latter's drawings and aiding her with my critical observations and advice, at her particular desire. But in spite of my efforts to remain composed my attention wandered from the drawings to the merry group, and against my better judgement my wrath rose, and doubtless my countenance lowered; for Milicent, observing that I must be tired of her daubs and scratches, begged I would join the company now, and defer the examination of the remainder to another opportunity. But while I was assuring her that I had no wish to join them, and was not tired, Mr Huntingdon himself came up to the little round table at which we sat.

'Are these yours?' said he, carelessly taking up one of the drawings.

'No, they are Miss Hargrave's.'

'Oh! well, let's have a look at them.'

And, regardless of Miss Hargrave's protestations, that they were not worth looking at, he drew a chair to my side, and receiving the drawings, one by one from my hand, successively scanned them over, and threw them on the table, but said not a word about them, though he was talking all the time. I don't know what Milicent Hargrave thought of such conduct, but *I* found his conversation extremely interesting, though as I afterwards discovered, when I came to analyse it, it was chiefly confined to quizzing the different members of the company present; and albeit he made some clever remarks, and some excessively droll ones, I do not think the whole would appear anything very particular, if written here, without the adventitious aids of look, and tone, and gesture, and that ineffable but indefinite charm, which cast a halo over all he did and said, and which would have made it a delight to look in his face, and hear the music of his voice, if he had been talking positive nonsense – and which, moreover, made me feel so bitter against my aunt when she put a stop to this enjoyment, by coming

composedly forward, under pretence of wishing to see the drawings, that she cared and knew nothing about, and while making believe to examine them, addressing herself to Mr Huntingdon, with one of her coldest and most repellent aspects, and beginning a series of the most common place and formidably formal questions and observations, on purpose to wrest his attention from me – on purpose to vex me, as I thought: and having now looked through the portfolio, I left them to their tête-à-tête, and seated myself on a sofa, quite apart from the company – never thinking how strange such conduct would appear, but merely to indulge, at first, the vexation of the moment, and subsequently to enjoy my private thoughts.

But I was not left long alone, for Mr Wilmot, of all men the least welcome, took advantage of my isolated position to come and plant himself beside me. I had flattered myself that I had so effectually repulsed his advances on all former occasions, that I had nothing more to apprehend from his unfortunate predilection; but it seems I was mistaken: so great was his confidence, either in his wealth or his remaining powers of attraction, and so firm his conviction of feminine weakness, that he thought himself warranted to return to the siege, which he did with renovated ardour, enkindled by the quantity of wine he had drunk – a circumstance that rendered him infinitely the more disgusting; but greatly as I abhorred him at that moment, I did not like to treat him with rudeness, as I was now his guest and has just been enjoying his hospitality; and I was no hand at a polite but determined rejection, nor would it have greatly availed me if I had; for he was too coarse-minded to take any repulse that was not as plain and positive as his own effrontery. The consequence was, that he waxed more fulsomely tender, and more repulsively warm, and I was driven to the very verge of desperation, and about to say, I know not what, when I felt my hand that hung over the arm of the sofa, suddenly taken by another and gently but fervently pressed. Instinctively, I guessed who it was, and on looking up, was less surprised than delighted, to see Mr Huntingdon smiling upon me. It was like turning from some purgatorial fiend to an angel of light, come to announce that the season of torment was past.

'Helen,' said he (he frequently called me Helen, and I never resented the freedom), 'I want you to look at this picture: Mr Wilmot will excuse you a moment, I'm sure.'

I rose with alacrity. He drew my arm within his, and led me across the room to a splendid painting of Vandyke's that I had noticed before, but not sufficiently examined. After a moment of silent contemplation, I was beginning to comment on its beauties and peculiarities, when, playfully pressing the hand he still retained within his arm, he interrupted me with – 'Never mind the picture, it was not for that I brought you here; it was to get you away from that scoundrelly old profligate yonder, who is looking as if he would like to challenge me for the affront.'

'I am very much obliged to you,' said I. 'This is twice you have delivered me from such unpleasant companionship.'

'Don't be too thankful,' he answered: 'it is not all kindness to you; it is partly

from a feeling of spite to your tormentors that makes me delighted to do the old fellows a bad turn, though I don't think I have any great reason to dread them as rivals – have I, Helen?'

'You know I detest them both.'

'And me?'

'I have no reason to detest *you*.'

'But what are your sentiments towards me? – Helen – Speak! – How do you regard me?'

And again he pressed my hand; but I feared there was more of conscious power than tenderness in his demeanour, and I felt he had no right to extort a confession of attachment from me when he had made no correspondent avowal himself, and knew not what to answer. At last I said – 'How do *you* regard *me*?'

'Sweet angel, I adore you! I – '

'Helen, I want you a moment,' said the distinct, low voice of my aunt, close beside us. And I left him, muttering maledictions against his evil angel.

'Well, aunt, what is it? What do you want?' said I, following her to the embrasure of the window.

'I want you to join the company, when you are fit to be seen,' returned she, severely regarding me; 'but please to stay here a little till that shocking colour is somewhat abated, and your eyes have recovered something of their natural expression. I should be ashamed for anyone to see you in your present state.'

Of course, such a remark had no effect in reducing the 'shocking colour;' on the contrary, I felt my face glow with redoubled fires kindled by a complication of emotions, of which indignant, swelling anger was the chief. I offered no reply, however, but pushed aside the curtain and looked into the night – or rather, into the lamp-lit square.

'Was Mr Huntingdon proposing to you, Helen?' enquired my too watchful relative.

'No.'

'What was he saying then? I heard something very like it.'

'I don't know what he would have said, if you hadn't interrupted him.'

'And would you have accepted him, Helen, if he had proposed?'

'Of course not – without consulting uncle and you.'

'Oh! I'm glad, my dear, you have so much prudence left. Well now,' she added, after a moment's pause, 'you have made yourself conspicuous enough for one evening. The ladies are directing enquiring glances towards us at this moment I see. I shall join them. Do you come too, when you are sufficiently composed to appear as usual.'

'I am so now.'

'Speak gently then; and don't look so malicious,' said my calm, but provoking aunt. 'We shall return home shortly, and then,' she added with solemn significance, 'I have much to say to you.'

So I went home prepared for a formidable lecture. Little was said by either party in the carriage during our short transit homewards; but when I had entered my room and thrown myself into an easy-chair to reflect on the events

of the day, my aunt followed me thither, and having dismissed Rachel, who was carefully stowing away my ornaments, closed the door; and placing a chair beside me, or rather at right angles with mine, sat down. With due deference I offered her my more commodious seat. She declined it, and thus opened the conference: 'Do you remember, Helen, our conversation the night but one before we left Staningley?'

'Yes, aunt.'

'And do you remember how I warned you against letting your heart be stolen from you by those unworthy of its possession; and fixing your affections where approbation did not go before, and where reason and judgement withheld their sanction?'

'Yes, but *my* reason –'

'Pardon me – and do you remember assuring me that there was no occasion for uneasiness on your account; for you should never be *tempted* to marry a man who was deficient in sense or principle, however handsome or charming in other respects he might be, for you could not love him, you should hate – despise – pity – anything but love him – were not those your words?'

'Yes, but –'

'And did you not say that your affection *must* be founded on approbation; and that unless you could approve and honour and respect, you could not love?'

'Yes, but I do approve and honour, and respect –'

'How so, my dear? Is Mr Huntingdon a good man?'

'He is a much better man than you think him.'

'That is nothing to the purpose. Is he a *good* man?'

'Yes – in some respects. He has a good disposition.'

'Is he a man of *principle*?'

'Perhaps not, exactly; but it is only for want of thought: if he had someone to advise him, and remind him of what is right –'

'He would soon learn, you think – and you yourself would willingly undertake to be his teacher? But, my dear, he is, I believe, full ten years older than you – how is it that you are so beforehand in moral acquirements?'

'Thanks to you, aunt, I have been well brought up, and had good examples always before me, which he, most likely, has not; and besides, he is of a sanguine temperament, and a gay, thoughtless temper, and I am naturally inclined to reflection.'

'Well, now you have made him out to be deficient in both sense and principle, by your own confession –'

'Then, my sense and my principle are at his service!'

'That sounds presumptuous, Helen! Do you think you have enough for both; and do you imagine your merry, thoughtless profligate would allow himself to be guided by a young girl like you?'

'No; I should not wish to guide him; but I think I might have influence sufficient to save him from some errors, and I should think my life well spent in the effort to preserve so noble a nature from destruction. He always listens attentively now, when I speak seriously to him (and I often venture to reprove his

random way of talking), and sometimes he says that if he had me always by his side he should never do or say a wicked thing, and that a little daily talk with me would make him quite a saint. It may be partly jest and partly flattery, but still – '

'But still you think it may be truth?'

'If I do think there is any mixture of truth in it, it is not from confidence in my own powers, but in *his* natural goodness – And you have no right to call him a profligate, aunt; he is nothing of the kind.'

'Who told you so, my dear? What was that story about his intrigue with a married lady – Lady who was it – Miss Wilmot herself was telling you the other day?'

'It was false – false!' I cried. 'I don't believe a word of it.'

'You think, then, that he is a virtuous, well conducted young man?'

'I know nothing positive respecting his character. I only know that I have heard nothing definitive against it – nothing that could be proved, at least; and till people can prove their slanderous accusations, I will not believe them. And I know this, that if he has committed errors, they are only such as are common to youth, and such as nobody thinks anything about; for I see that everybody likes him, and all the mammas smile upon him, and their daughters – and Miss Wilmot – herself are only too glad to attract his attention.'

'Helen, the world *may* look upon such offences as venial; a few unprincipled mothers *may* be anxious to catch a young man of fortune without reference to his character; and thoughtless girls *may* be glad to win the smiles of so handsome a gentleman, without seeking to penetrate beyond the surface; but *you*, I trusted were better informed than to see with their eyes, and judge with their perverted judgement. I did not think *you* would call these venial errors!'

'Nor do I, aunt; but if I hate the sins I love the sinner, and would do much for his salvation, even supposing your suspicions to be mainly true – which I do not and will not believe.'

'Well my dear, ask your uncle what sort of company he keeps, and if he is not banded with a set of loose, profligate young men, whom he calls his friends – his jolly companions, and whose chief delight is to wallow in vice, and vie with each other who can run fastest and farthest down the headlong road, to the place prepared for the devil and his angels.'

'Then, I will save him from them.'

'Oh, Helen, Helen! you little know the misery of uniting your fortunes to such a man!'

'I have such confidence in him, aunt, notwithstanding all you say, that I would willingly risk my happiness for the chance of securing his. I will leave better men to those who only consider their own advantage. If he has done amiss, I shall consider my life well spent in saving him from the consequences of his early errors, and striving to recall him to the path of virtue – God grant me success!'

Here the conversation ended, for at this juncture, my uncle's voice was heard, from his chamber, loudly calling upon my aunt to come to bed. He was in a bad humour that night; for his gout was worse. It had been gradually increasing upon him ever since we came to town; and my aunt took advantage of the

circumstance, next morning, to persuade him to return to the country immediately, without waiting for the close of the season. His physician supported and enforced her arguments; and contrary to her usual habits, she so hurried the preparations for removal (as much for my sake as my uncle's, I think), that in a very few days we departed; and I saw no more of Mr Huntingdon. My aunt flatters herself I shall soon forget him – perhaps, she thinks I have forgotten him, already, for I never mention his name; and she may continue to think so, till we meet again – if ever that should be. I wonder if it will.

## CHAPTER 18

### The Miniature

August 25th– I am now quite settled down to my usual routine of steady occupations and quiet amusements – tolerably contented and cheerful, but still looking forward to spring with the hope of returning to town, not for its gaieties and dissipations, but for the chance of meeting Mr Huntingdon once again; for still, he is always in my thoughts and in my dreams. In all my employments, whatever I do, or see, or hear, has an ultimate reference to him; whatever skill or knowledge I acquire is someday to be turned to his advantage or amusement; whatever new beauties in nature or art I discover, are to be depicted to meet his eye, or stored in my memory to be told him at some future period. This, at least, is the hope that I cherish, the fancy that lights me on my lonely way. It may be only an *ignis fatuus*, after all, but it can do no harm to follow it with my eyes and rejoice in its lustre, as long as it does not lure me from the path I ought to keep; and I think it will not, for I have thought deeply on my aunt's advice, and I see clearly, now, the folly of throwing myself away on one that is unworthy of all the love I have to give, and incapable of responding to the best and deepest feelings of my inmost heart – *so* clearly that even if I should see him again, and if he should remember me and love me still (which, alas! is too little probable, considering how he is situated, and by whom surrounded), and if he should ask me to marry him – I am determined not to consent until I know for certain whether my aunt's opinion of him or mine is nearest the truth; for if mine is altogether wrong, it is not he that I love; it is a creature of my own imagination. But I think it is not wrong – no, no – there is a secret something – an inward instinct that assures me I am right. There *is* essential goodness in him; and what delight to unfold it! If he has wandered, what bliss to recall him! If he is now exposed to the baneful influence of corrupting and wicked companions, what glory to deliver him from them! – Oh! if I could but believe that Heaven has designed me for this!

Today is the first of September; but my uncle has ordered the gamekeeper to spare the partridges till the gentlemen come. 'What gentlemen?' I asked when I

heard it – a small party he had invited to shoot. His friend Mr Wilmot was one, and my aunt's friend Mr Boarham another. This struck me as terrible news, at the moment, but all regret and apprehension vanished like a dream when I heard that Mr Huntingdon was actually to be a third! My aunt is greatly against his coming, of course: she earnestly endeavoured to dissuade my uncle from asking him; but he, laughing at her objections, told her it was no use talking for the mischief was already done: he had invited Huntingdon and his friend Lord Lowborough before we left London, and nothing now remained but to fix the day for their coming. So he is safe, and I am sure of seeing him. I cannot express my joy – I find it very difficult to conceal it from my aunt; but I don't wish to trouble her with my feelings till I know whether I ought to indulge them or not. If I find it my absolute duty to suppress them, they shall trouble no one but myself; and if I can really feel myself justified in indulging this attachment, I can dare anything, even the anger and grief of my best friend, for its object – surely, I shall soon know. But they are not coming till about the middle of the month.

We are to have two lady visitors also: Mr Wilmot is to bring his niece and her cousin Milicent. I suppose, my aunt thinks the latter will benefit me by her society and the salutary example of her gentle deportment, and lowly and tractable spirit; and the former, I suspect she intends as a species of counter-attraction to win Mr Huntingdon's attention from me. I don't thank her for this; but I shall be glad of Milicent's company: she is a sweet, good girl, and I wish I were like her – *more* like her, at least, than I am.

19th – They are come. They came the day before yesterday. The gentlemen are all gone out to shoot, and the ladies are with my aunt, at work, in the drawing-room. I have retired to the library, for I am very unhappy, and I want to be alone. Books cannot divert me; so having opened my desk, I will try what may be done by detailing the cause of my uneasiness. This paper will serve instead of a confidential friend into whose ear I might pour forth the overflowings of my heart. It will not sympathise with my distresses, but then, it will not laugh at them, and, if I keep it close, it cannot tell again; so it is perhaps, the best friend I could have for the purpose.

First, let me speak of his arrival – how I sat at my window and watched for nearly two hours, before his carriage entered the park gates – for they all came before him – and how deeply I was disappointed at every arrival, because it was not his. First came Mr Wilmot and the ladies. When Milicent had got into her room, I quitted my post a few minutes, to look in upon her and have a little private conversation, for she was now my intimate friend, several long epistles having passed between us since our parting. On returning to my window, I beheld another carriage at the door. Was it his? No; it was Mr Boarham's plain, dark chariot; and there stood he upon the steps, carefully superintending the dislodging of his various boxes and packages. What a collection! one would have thought he projected a visit of six months at least. A considerable time after, came Lord Lowborough in his barouche. Is he one of the profligate friends, I wonder? I should think not; for no one could call *him* a jolly companion,

I'm sure – and besides, he appears too sober and gentlemanly in his demeanour, to merit such suspicions. He is a tall, thin, gloomy looking man, apparently between thirty and forty, and of a somewhat sickly, careworn aspect.

At last, Mr Huntingdon's light phaeton came bowling merrily up the lawn. I had but a transient glimpse of him, for the moment it stopped, he sprang out over the side on to the portico steps, and disappeared into the house.

I now submitted to be dressed for dinner – a duty which Rachel had been urging upon me for the last twenty minutes; and when that important business was completed, I repaired to the drawing-room where I found Mr and Miss Wilmot, and Milicent Hargrave already assembled. Shortly after, Lord Lowborough entered, and then Mr Boarham, who seemed quite willing to forget and forgive my former conduct, and to hope that a little conciliation and steady perseverance on his part might yet succeed in bringing me to reason. While I stood at the window, conversing with Milicent, he came up to me, and was beginning to talk in nearly his usual strain, when Mr Huntingdon entered the room.

'How will he greet me, I wonder?' said my bounding heart; and instead of advancing to meet him, I turned to the window to hide or subdue my emotion. But having saluted his host and hostess, and the rest of the company, he came to me, ardently squeezed my hand, and murmured he was glad to see me once again. At that moment dinner was announced, my aunt desired him to take Miss Hargrave into the dining-room, and odious Mr Wilmot, with unspeakable grimaces, offered his arm to me; and I was condemned to sit between himself and Mr Boarham. But afterwards, when we were all again assembled in the drawing-room, I was indemnified for so much suffering by a few delightful minutes of conversation with Mr Huntingdon.

In the course of the evening, Miss Wilmot was called upon to sing and play for the amusement of the company, and I to exhibit my drawings, and, though he likes music, and she is an accomplished musician, I think I am right in affirming that he paid more attention to my drawings than to her music.

So far, so good; but, hearing him pronounce, sotto voce, but with peculiar emphasis concerning one of the pieces, 'This is better than all!' – I looked up, curious to see which it was, and, to my horror, beheld him complacently gazing at the *back* of the picture – It was his own face that I had sketched there and forgotten to rub out! To make matters worse in the agony of the moment, I attempted to snatch it from his hand; but he prevented me, and exclaiming, 'No – by George, I'll keep it!' placed it against his waistcoat, and buttoned his coat upon it with a delighted chuckle.

Then, drawing a candle close to his elbow, he gathered all the drawings to himself, as well what he had seen as the others, and muttering, 'I must look at *both* sides now,' he eagerly commenced an examination which I watched, at first, with tolerable composure, in the confidence that his vanity would not be gratified by any further discoveries; for, though I must plead guilty to having disfigured the backs of several with abortive attempts to delineate that too fascinating physiognomy, I was sure that, with that one unfortunate exception, I

had carefully obliterated all such witnesses of my infatuation. But the pencil frequently leaves an impression upon cardboard that no amount of rubbing can efface. Such, it seems, was the case with most of these; and I confess I trembled when I saw him holding them so close to the candle, and poring so intently over the seeming blanks; but still, I trusted he would not be able to make out these dim traces to his own satisfaction. I was mistaken however – having ended his scrutiny, he quietly remarked – 'I perceive, the backs of young ladies' drawings, like the postscripts of their letters, are the most important and interesting part of the concern.'

Then, leaning back in his chair, he reflected a few minutes in silence, complacently smiling to himself, and, while I was concocting some cutting speech wherewith to check his gratification, he rose, and passing over to where Annabella Wilmot sat vehemently coquetting with Lord Lowborough, seated himself on the sofa beside her, and attached himself to her for the rest of the evening.

'So then!' thought I – 'he despises me, because he knows I love him.'

And the reflection made me so miserable I knew not what to do. Milicent came and began to admire my drawings and make remarks upon them; but I could not talk to her – I could talk to no one; and upon the introduction of tea, I took advantage of the open door and the slight diversion caused by its entrance, to slip out – for I was sure I could not take any – and take refuge in the library. My aunt sent Thomas in quest of me, to ask if I were not coming to tea; but I bade him say I should not take any tonight; and happily she was too much occupied with her guests to make any further enquiries at the time.

As most of the company had travelled far that day, they retired early to rest; and having heard them all, as I thought, go upstairs, I ventured out, to get my candlestick from the drawing-room sideboard. But Mr Huntingdon had lingered behind the rest: he was just at the foot of the stairs when I opened the door; and hearing my step in the hall – though I could hardly hear it myself – he instantly turned back.

'Helen, is that you?' said he, 'why did you run away from us?'

'Good-night, Mr Huntingdon, said I coldly, not choosing to answer the question. And I turned away to enter the drawing-room.

'But you'll shake hands, won't you?' said he, placing himself in the doorway before me. And he seized my hand, and held it much against my will.

'Let me go, Mr Huntingdon!' said I – 'I want to get a candle.'

'The candle will keep,' returned he.

I made a desperate effort to free my hand from his grasp.

'Why are you in such a hurry to leave me, Helen?' he said, with a smile of the most provoking self-sufficiency – 'you don't hate me, you *know*.'

'Yes, I do – at this moment.

'Not you! It is Annabella Wilmot you hate, not me.'

'I have nothing to do with Annabella Wilmot,' said I, burning with indignation.

'But *I* have, you know,' returned he, with peculiar emphasis.

'That is nothing to me sir!' I retorted.

'*Is* it nothing to you, Helen? – Will you swear it? – Will you?'

'No, I won't, Mr Huntingdon! And I *will* go!' cried I, not knowing whether to laugh or to cry, or to break out into a tempest of fury.

'Go then, you vixen!' he said; but the instant he released my hand, he had the audacity to put his arm round my neck and kiss me.

Trembling with anger and agitation – and I don't know what besides, I broke away, and got my candle and rushed upstairs to my room. He would not have done so but for that hateful picture! And there he had it still in his possession, an eternal monument to his pride and my humiliation!

It was but little sleep I got that night; and in the morning I rose perplexed and troubled with the thoughts of meeting him at breakfast. I knew not how it was to be done; an assumption of dignified, cold indifference would hardly do after what he knew of my devotion – to his face, at least. Yet something must be done to check his presumption – I should not submit to be tyrannised over by those bright, laughing eyes. And accordingly, I received his cheerful morning salutation as calmly and coldly as my aunt could have wished, and defeated with brief answers his one or two attempts to draw me into conversation; while I comported myself with unusual cheerfulness and complaisance towards every other member of the party, especially Annabella Wilmot, and even her uncle and Mr Boarham were treated with an extra amount of civility on the occasion, not from any motives of coquetry, but just to show him that my particular coolness and reserve arose from no general ill-humour or depression of spirits.

He was not, however, to be repelled by such acting as this. He did not talk much to me, but when he did speak, it was with a degree of freedom and openness – and *kindliness* too – that plainly seemed to intimate he knew his words were music to my ears; and when his looks met mine, it was with a smile – presumptuous it might be – but oh, so sweet, so bright, so genial, that I could not possibly retain my anger; every vestige of displeasure soon melted away beneath it, like morning clouds before the summer sun.

Soon after breakfast all the gentlemen save one, with boyish eagerness, set out on their expedition against the hapless partridges; my uncle and Mr Wilmot on their shooting ponies, Mr Huntingdon and Lord Lowborough on their legs; the one exception being Mr Boarham, who, in consideration of the rain that had fallen during the night, thought it prudent to remain behind a little, and join them in a while, when the sun had dried the grass. And he favoured us all with a long and minute disquisition upon the evils and dangers attendant upon damp feet, delivered with the most imperturbable gravity, amid the jeers and laughter of Mr Huntingdon and my uncle, who, leaving the prudent sportsman to entertain the ladies with his medical discussions, sallied forth with their guns, bending their steps to the stables first, to have a look at the horses, and let out the dogs.

Not desirous of sharing Mr Boarham's company for the whole of the morning, I betook myself to the library; and there brought forth my easel, and began to paint. The easel and the painting apparatus would serve as an excuse for abandoning the drawing-room, if my aunt should come to complain of the

desertion; and besides, I wanted to finish the picture. It was one I had taken great pains with, and I intended it to be my masterpiece, though it was somewhat presumptuous in the design. By the bright azure of the sky, and by the warm and brilliant lights, and deep, long shadows, I had endeavoured to convey the idea of a sunny morning. I had ventured to give more of the bright verdure of spring or early summer to the grass and foliage, than is commonly attempted in painting. The scene represented was an open glade in a wood. A group of dark Scotch firs was introduced in the middle distance to relieve the prevailing freshness of the rest; but in the foreground, were part of the gnarled trunk and of the spreading boughs of a large forest tree, whose foliage was of a brilliant golden green – not golden from autumnal mellowness, but from the sunshine, and the very immaturity of the scarce expanded leaves. Upon this bough, that stood out in bold relief against the sombre firs, were seated an amorous pair of turtle doves, whose soft sad coloured plumage afforded a contrast of another nature; and beneath it, a young girl was kneeling on the daisy-spangled turf, with head thrown back and masses of fair hair falling on her shoulders, her hands clasped, lips parted, and eyes intently gazing upward in pleased, yet earnest contemplation of those feathered lovers – too deeply absorbed in each other to notice her.

I had scarcely settled to my work – which, however, wanted but a few touches to the finishing – when the sportsmen passed the window on their return from the stables. It was partly open, and Mr Huntingdon must have seen me as he went by, for in half a minute he came back, and setting his gun against the wall, threw up the sash, and sprang in, and set himself before my picture.

'Very pretty, i'faith!' said he, after attentively regarding it for a few seconds – 'and a very fitting study for a young lady – Spring just opening into summer – morning just approaching noon – girlhood just ripening into womanhood – and hope just verging on fruition. She's a sweet creature! but why didn't you make her black hair?'

'I thought light hair would suit her better. You see I have made her blue-eyed, and plump, and fair and rosy.'

'Upon my word – a very Hebe! I should fall in love with her, if I hadn't the artist before me. Sweet innocent! she's thinking there will come a time when she will be wooed and won like that pretty hen-dove, by as fond and fervent a lover; and she's thinking how pleasant it will be, and how tender and faithful he will find her.'

'And perhaps,' suggested I, 'how tender and faithful she shall find him.'

'Perhaps – for there is no limit to the wild extravagance of hope's imaginings, at such an age.'

'Do you call *that*, then, one of her wild, extravagant delusions?'

'No; my heart tells me it is not. I might have thought so once, but now, I say, give me the girl I love, and I will swear eternal constancy to her and her alone, through summer and winter, through youth and age, and life and death! If age and death *must* come.'

He spoke this in such serious earnest that my heart bounded with delight; but

the minute after he changed his tone, and asked, with a significant smile, if I had 'any more portraits'.

'No,' replied I, reddening with confusion and wrath. But my portfolio was on the table; he took it up, and coolly sat down to examine its contents.

'Mr Huntingdon, those are my unfinished sketches,' cried I, 'and I never let anyone see them.'

And I placed my hand on the portfolio to wrest it from him; but he maintained his hold, assuring me that he 'liked unfinished sketches of all things.'

'But I hate them to be seen,' returned I. 'I can't let you have it, indeed!'

'Let me have its bowels then,' said he; and just as I wrenched the portfolio from his hand, he deftly abstracted the greater part of its contents, and after turning them over a moment, he cried out – 'Bless my stars, here's another!' and slipped a small oval of ivory paper into his waistcoat pocket – a complete miniature portrait, that I had sketched with such tolerable success, as to be induced to colour it with great pains and care. But I was determined he should not keep it.

'Mr Huntingdon,' cried I, 'I *insist* upon having that back! It is mine, and you have no *right* to take it. Give it me, directly – I'll never forgive you, if you don't!'

But the more vehemently I insisted, the more he aggravated my distress by his insulting, gleeful laugh. At length however, he restored it to me, saying – 'Well, well, since you value it so much, I'll not deprive you of it.'

To show him how I valued it, I tore it in two, and threw it into the fire. He was not prepared for this. His merriment suddenly ceasing, he stared in mute amazement at the consuming treasure; and then, with a careless 'Humph! I'll go and shoot now,' he turned on his heel, and vacated the apartment by the window as he came and setting on his hat with an air, took up his gun and walked away, whistling as he went – and leaving me not too much agitated to finish my picture; for I was glad, at the moment, that I had vexed him.

When I returned to the drawing-room, I found Mr Boarham had ventured to follow his comrades to the field; and shortly after lunch, to which they did not think of returning, I volunteered to accompany the ladies in a walk, and show Annabella and Milicent the beauties of the country. We took a long ramble and re-entered the park just as the sportsmen were returning from their expedition. Toil-spent and travel-stained, the main body of them crossed over the grass to avoid us; but Mr Huntingdon, all spattered and splashed as he was, and stained with the blood of his prey – to the no small offence of my aunt's strict sense of propriety – came out of his way to meet us, with cheerful smiles and words for all but me, and placing himself between Annabella Wilmot and myself, walked up the road and began to relate the various exploits and disasters of the day, in a manner that would have convulsed me with laughter, if I had been on good terms with him; but he addressed himself entirely to Annabella, and I, of course, left all the laughter and all the badinage to her, and affecting the utmost indifference to whatever passed between them, walked along a few paces apart, and looking every way but theirs; while my aunt and Milicent went before,

linked arm in arm, and gravely discoursing together. At length, Mr Huntingdon turned to me, and addressing me in a confidential whisper, said – 'Helen, why did you burn my picture?'

'Because, I wished to destroy it,' I answered, with an asperity it is useless now to lament.

'Oh, very good!' was the reply, 'if *you* don't value me, I must turn to somebody that will.'

I thought it was partly in jest – a half playful mixture of mock resignation and pretended indifference; but immediately he resumed his place beside Miss Wilmot, and from that hour to this – during all that evening, and all the next day, and the next, and the next, and all this morning (the 22nd), he has never given me one kind word or one pleasant look – never spoken to me, but from pure necessity – never glanced towards me, but with a cold, unfriendly look I thought him quite incapable of assuming.

My aunt observes the change, and though she has not enquired the cause or made any remark to me on the subject, I see it gives her pleasure. Miss Wilmot observes it too, and triumphantly ascribes it to her own superior charms and blandishments; but I am truly miserable – more so than I like to acknowledge to myself. Pride refuses to aid me. It has brought me into the scrape, and will not help me out of it.

He meant no harm – it was only his joyous, playful spirit; and I, by my acrimonious resentment – so serious, so disproportioned to the offence – have so wounded his feelings – so deeply offended him, that I fear he will never forgive me – and all for a mere jest! He thinks I dislike him – and he must continue to think so. I must lose him for ever; and Annabella may win him, and triumph as she will.

But it is not my loss, nor her triumph that I deplore so greatly as the wreck of my fond hopes for his advantage, and her unworthiness of his affection, and the injury he will do himself by trusting his happiness to her. *She* does not love him: she thinks only of herself. She cannot appreciate the good that is in him: she will neither see it, nor value it, nor cherish it. She will neither deplore his faults nor attempt the amendment, but rather aggravate them by her own. And I doubt whether she will not deceive him after all: I see she is playing double between him and Lord Lowborough, and while she amuses herself with the lively Huntingdon, she tries her utmost to enslave his moody friend; and should she succeed in bringing both to her feet, the fascinating commoner will have but little chance against the lordly peer. If he observes her artful by-play, it gives him no uneasiness, but rather adds new zest to his diversion by opposing a stimulating check to his otherwise too easy conquest.

Messrs Wilmot and Boarham have severally taken occasion by his neglect of me to renew their advances; and if I were like Annabella and some others, I should take advantage of their perseverance to endeavour to pique him into a revival of affection; but, justice and honesty apart, I could not *bear* to do it; I am annoyed enough by their present persecutions without encouraging them farther; and even if I did, it would have precious little effect upon him. He sees

me suffering under the condescending attentions and prosaic discourses of the one and the repulsive obtrusions of the other, without so much as a shadow of commiseration for me, or resentment against my tormentors. He never could have loved me, or he would not have resigned me so willingly, and he would not go on talking to everybody else so cheerfully as he does – laughing and jesting with Lord Lowborough and my uncle, teasing Milicent Hargrave, and flirting with Annabella Wilmot – as if nothing were on his mind. Oh, why can't I hate him? I must be infatuated, or I should *scorn* to regret him as I do! But I must rally all the powers I have remaining, and try to tear him from my heart. There goes the dinner bell – and here comes my aunt to scold me for sitting here at my desk all day, instead of staying with the company – I wish the company were – gone.

## CHAPTER 19

## *An Incident*

Twenty-second – Night – What have I done? and what will be the end of it? I cannot calmly reflect upon it; I cannot sleep. I must have recourse to my diary again; I will commit it to paper tonight, and see what I shall think of it tomorrow.

I went down to dinner resolving to be cheerful and well-conducted, and kept my resolution very creditably, considering how my head ached, and how internally wretched I felt – I don't know what is come over me of late; my very energies both mental and physical must be strangely impaired, or I should not have acted so weakly in many respects, as I have done; but I have not been well this last day or two: I suppose it is with sleeping and eating so little, and thinking so much, and being so continually out of humour. But to return: I was exerting myself to sing and play for the amusement, and at the request of my aunt and Milicent, before the gentlemen came into the drawing-room (Miss Wilmot never likes to waste her musical efforts on ladies' ears alone): Milicent had asked for a little Scotch song, and I was just in the middle of it when they entered. The first thing Mr Huntingdon did, was to walk up to Annabella – 'Now, Miss Wilmot, won't *you* give us some music tonight?' said he. 'Do now! I know you will, when I tell you that I have been hungering and thirsting all day, for the sound of your voice. Come! the piano's vacant.'

It was; for I had quitted it immediately upon hearing his petition. Had I been endowed with a proper degree of self-possession, I should have turned to the lady myself, and cheerfully joined my entreaties to his; whereby I should have disappointed his expectations, if the affront had been purposely given or made him sensible of the wrong, if it had only arisen from thoughtlessness; but I felt it too deeply to do anything but rise from the music-stool, and throw myself back on the sofa, suppressing with difficulty the audible expression of the bitterness I

felt within. I knew Annabella's musical talents were superior to mine, but that was no reason why I should be treated as a perfect nonentity. The time and the manner of his asking her, appeared like a gratuitous insult to me; and I could have wept with pure vexation.

Meantime, she exultantly seated herself at the piano, and favoured him with two of his favourite songs, in such superior style that even I soon lost my anger in admiration, and listened with a sort of gloomy pleasure to the skilful modulations of her full-toned and powerful voice, so judiciously aided by her rounded and spirited touch; and while my ears drank in the sound, my eyes rested on the face of her principal auditor, and derived an equal or superior delight from the contemplation of his speaking countenance, as he stood beside her – that eye and brow lighted up with keen enthusiasm, and that sweet smile passing and appearing like gleams of sunshine on an April day. No wonder he should hunger and thirst to hear her sing. I now forgave him, from my heart, his reckless slight of me, and I felt ashamed at my pettish resentment of such a trifle – ashamed too of those bitter envious pangs that gnawed my inmost heart, in spite of all this admiration and delight.

'There now!' said she, playfully running her fingers over the keys, when she had concluded the second song. 'What shall I give you next?'

But in saying this, she looked back at Lord Lowborough, who was standing a little behind leaning against the back of a chair – an attentive listener, too, experiencing, to judge by his countenance, much the same feelings of mingled pleasure and sadness as I did. But the look she gave him, plainly said, 'Do you choose for me now: I have done enough for him, and will gladly exert myself to gratify you;' and thus encouraged, his lordship came forward, and turning over the music, presently set before her a little song that I had noticed before, and read more than once, with an interest arising from the circumstance of my connecting it in my mind with the reigning tyrant of my thoughts. And now with my nerves already excited and half unstrung, I could not hear those words so sweetly warbled forth, without some symptoms of emotion I was not able to suppress. Tears rose unbidden to my eyes, and I buried my face in the sofa-pillow that they might flow unseen while I listened. The air was simple, sweet, and sad, it is still running in my head – and so are the words –

> 'Farewell to thee! but not farewell
>   To all my fondest thoughts of thee:
> Within my heart they still shall dwell;
>   And they shall cheer and comfort me.
>
> O, beautiful, and full of grace!
>   If thou hadst never met mine eye,
> I had not dreamed a living face
>   Could fancied charms so far outvie.
>
> If I may ne'er behold again
>   That form and face, so dear to me,

Nor hear thy voice, still would I fain
　Preserve, for aye, their memory.

That voice, the magic of whose tone
　Can wake an echo in my breast,
Creating feelings that, alone,
　Can make my tranced spirit blest.

That laughing eye, whose sunny beam
　My memory would not cherish less;
And oh, that smile! whose joyous gleam
　No mortal language can express.

Adieu! but let me cherish, still,
　The hope with which I cannot part.
Contempt may wound, and coldness chill,
　But still it lingers in my heart.

And who can tell but Heaven, at last,
　May answer all my thousand prayers,
And bid the future pay the past
　With joy for anguish, smiles for tears?'

When it ceased, I longed for nothing so much as to be out of the room. The sofa was not far from the door, but I did not dare to raise my head, for I knew Mr Huntingdon was standing near me, and I knew by the sound of his voice, as he spoke in answer to some remark of Lord Lowborough's, that his face was turned towards me. Perhaps, a half suppressed sob had caught his ear, and caused him to look round – Heaven forbid! But, with a violent effort, I checked all further signs of weakness, dried my tears, and, when I thought he had turned away again, rose, and instantly left the apartment, taking refuge in my favourite resort, the library.

There was no light there but the faint red glow of the neglected fire; but I did not want a light; I only wanted to indulge my thoughts, unnoticed and undisturbed; and sitting down on a low stool before the easy-chair, I sunk my head upon its cushioned seat, and thought, and thought, until the tears gushed out again, and I wept like any child. Presently, however, the door was gently opened and someone entered the room. I trusted it was only a servant, and did not stir. The door was closed again – but I was not alone: a hand gently touched my shoulder, and a voice said, softly – 'Helen, what is the matter?'

I could not answer at the moment.

'You must and shall tell me,' was added more vehemently, and the speaker threw himself on his knees, beside me on the rug, and forcibly possessed himself of my hand; but I hastily caught it away, and replied – 'It is nothing to you, Mr Huntingdon.'

'Are you sure it is nothing to me?' he returned, 'can you swear that you were not thinking of me while you wept?'

This was unendurable. I made an effort to rise, but he was kneeling on my dress.

'Tell me,' continued he – 'I want to know – because, if you were, I have something to say to you – and if not, I'll go.'

'Go then!' I cried; but, fearing he would obey too well, and never come again, I hastily added – 'Or say what you have to say, and have done with it!'

'But which?' said he – 'for I shall only say it if you really were thinking of me. So tell me, Helen.'

'You're excessively impertinent, Mr Huntingdon!'

'Not at all – too pertinent, you mean – so you won't tell me? – Well, I'll spare your woman's pride, and, construing your silence into, "Yes," I'll take it for granted that I *was* the subject of your thoughts, and the cause of your affliction –'

'Indeed, sir –'

'If you deny it, I won't tell you my secret,' threatened he; and I did not interrupt him again – or even attempt to repulse him, though he had taken my hand once more, and half embraced me with his other arm – I was scarcely conscious of it, at the time.

'It is this,' resumed he: 'that Annabella Wilmot, in comparison with you, is like a flaunting peony compared with a sweet, wild rosebud gemmed with dew – and I love you to distraction! – Now, tell me if that intelligence gives you any pleasure – Silence again? That means yes – Then let me add that I cannot live without you, and if you answer no to this last question, you will drive me mad – Will you bestow yourself upon me? – you will!' he cried, nearly squeezing me to death in his arms.

'No, no!' I exclaimed, struggling to free myself from him – 'you must ask my uncle and aunt.'

'They won't refuse me, if you don't.'

'I'm not so sure of that – my aunt dislikes you.'

'But *you* don't, Helen – say you love me, and I'll go.'

'I wish you *would* go!' I replied.

'I will, this instant – if you'll only say you love me.'

'You know I do,' I answered. And again he caught me in his arms, and smothered me with kisses.

At that moment, my aunt opened wide the door, and stood before us, candle in hand, in shocked and horrified amazement, gazing alternately at Mr Huntingdon and me – for we both started up, and now stood wide enough asunder. But *his* confusion was only for a moment. Rallying in an instant, with the most enviable assurance, he began – 'I beg ten thousand pardons, Mrs Maxwell! Don't be too severe upon me. I've been asking your sweet niece to take me for better, for worse; and she, like a good girl, informs me she cannot think of it without her uncle's and aunt's consent. So let me implore you not to condemn me to eternal wretchedness: if *you* favour my cause, I am safe; for Mr Maxwell, I am certain, can refuse you nothing.'

'We will talk of this tomorrow, sir,' said my aunt, coldly. 'It is a subject that

demands mature and serious deliberation. At present, you had better return to the drawing-room.'

'But meantime,' pleaded he, 'let me commend my cause to your most indulgent – '

'No indulgence for you, Mr Huntingdon, must come between me and the consideration of my niece's happiness.'

'Ah, true! I know she is an angel, and I am a presumptuous dog to dream of possessing such a treasure; but, nevertheless, I would sooner die than relinquish her in favour of the best man that ever went to Heaven – and as for her happiness, I would sacrifice my body and soul – '

'Body and *soul*, Mr Huntingdon – sacrifice your *soul*?'

'Well, I would lay down life – '

'You would not be required to lay it down.'

'I would spend it, then – devote my life – and all its powers to the promotion and preservation – '

'Another time, sir, we will talk of this – and I should have felt disposed to judge more favourably of your pretensions, if you too had chosen another time and place, and – let me add – another *manner* for your declaration.'

'Why, you see, Mrs Maxwell,' he began –

'Pardon me, sir,' said she, with dignity – 'The company are enquiring for you in the other room.' And she turned to me.

'Then you must plead for me, Helen,' said he, and at length withdrew.

'You had better retire to your room, Helen,' said my aunt, gravely. 'I will discuss this matter with you, too, tomorrow.'

'Don't be angry, aunt,' said I.

'My dear, I am not angry,' she replied: 'I am *surprised*. If it is true that you told him you could not accept his offer without our consent – '

'It is true,' interrupted I.

'Then how could you permit – '

'I couldn't help it, aunt,' I cried, bursting into tears. They were not altogether the tears of sorrow, or of fear for her displeasure, but rather the outbreak of the general tumultuous excitement of my feelings. But my good aunt was touched at my agitation. In a softer tone, she repeated her recommendation to retire, and gently kissing my forehead, bade me good-night, and put her candle in my hand; and I went; but my brain worked so, I could not think of sleeping. I feel calmer now, that I have written all this; and I will go to bed, and try to win tired nature's sweet restorer.

## CHAPTER 20

### *Persistence*

September 24th – In the morning I rose, light and cheerful, nay, intensely happy. The hovering cloud cast over me by my aunt's views, and by the fear of not obtaining her consent, was lost in the bright effulgence of my own hopes, and the too delightful consciousness of requited love. It was a splendid morning; and I went out to enjoy it, in a quiet ramble in company with my own blissful thoughts. The dew was on the grass, and ten thousand gossamers were waving in the breeze; the happy red-breast was pouring out its little soul in song, and my heart overflowed with silent hymns of gratitude and praise to Heaven.

But I had not wandered far before my solitude was interrupted by the only person that could have disturbed my musings, at that moment, without being looked upon as an unwelcome intruder: Mr Huntingdon came suddenly upon me. So unexpected was the apparition, that I might have thought it the creation of an over-excited imagination, had the sense of sight alone borne witness to his presence; but immediately I felt his strong arm round my waist and his warm kiss on my cheek, while his keen and gleeful salutation, 'My own Helen!' was ringing in my ear.

'Not yours yet,' said I, hastily swerving aside from this too presumptuous greeting – 'remember my guardians. You will not easily attain my aunt's consent. Don't you see she is prejudiced against you?'

'I do, dearest; and you must tell me why, that I may best know how to combat her objections. I suppose she thinks I am a prodigal,' pursued he, observing that I was unwilling to reply, 'and concludes that I shall have but little worldly goods wherewith to endow my better half? If so, you must tell her that my property is mostly entailed, and I cannot get rid of it. There may be a few mortgages on the rest – a few trifling debts and encumbrances here and there, but nothing to speak of; and though I acknowledge I am not so rich as I might be – or have been – still, I think, we could manage pretty comfortably on what's left. My father, you know, was something of a miser, and in his latter days especially, saw no pleasure in life but to amass riches; and so it is no wonder that his son should make it his chief delight to spend them, which was accordingly the case, until my acquaintance with you, dear Helen, taught me other views and nobler aims. And the very idea of having you to care for under my roof, would force me to moderate my expenses and live like a Christian – not to speak of all the prudence and virtue you would instil into my mind by your wise counsels and sweet, attractive goodness.'

'But it is not that,' said I, 'it is not money my aunt thinks about. She knows better than to value worldly wealth above its price.'

'What is it then?'

'She wishes me to – to marry none but a really good man.'

'What, a man of "decided piety"? – ahem! – Well, come, I'll manage that too! It's Sunday today, isn't it? I'll go to church morning, afternoon, and evening, and comport myself in such a godly sort that she shall regard me with admiration and sisterly love, as a brand plucked from the burning. I'll come home sighing like a furnace, and full of the savour and unction of dear Mr Blatant's discourse – '

'Mr Leighton,' said I, dryly.

'Is Mr Leighton a "sweet preacher", Helen – a "dear, delightful, heavenly-minded man"?'

'He is a *good* man, Mr Huntingdon. I wish I could say half as much for you.'

'Oh, I forgot, you are a saint, too. I crave your pardon, dearest – but don't call me Mr Huntingdon, my name is Arthur.'

'I'll call you nothing – for I'll have nothing at all to do with you, if you talk in that way any more. If you really mean to deceive my aunt as you say, you are very wicked; and if not, you are very wrong to jest on such a subject.'

'I stand corrected,' said he, concluding his laugh with a sorrowful sigh. 'Now,' resumed he, after a momentary pause, 'let us talk about something else. And come nearer to me, Helen, and take my arm; and then I'll let you alone. I can't be quiet while I see you walking there.'

I complied; but said we must soon return to the house.

'No one will be down to breakfast yet, for long enough,' he answered. 'You spoke of your guardians just now, Helen, but is not your father still living?'

'Yes, but I always look upon my uncle and aunt as my guardians, for they are so, in deed, though not in name. My father has entirely given me up to their care. I have never seen him since dear mamma died when I was a very little girl, and my aunt, at her request, offered to take charge of me, and took me away to Staningley, where I have remained ever since; and I don't think he would object to anything for me, that she thought proper to sanction.'

'But would he sanction anything to which she thought proper to object?'

'No, I don't think he cares enough about me.'

'He is very much to blame – but he doesn't know what an angel he has for his daughter – which is all the better for me, as, if he did, he would not be willing to part with such a treasure.'

'And, Mr Huntingdon,' said I, 'I suppose you *know* I am not an heiress?'

He protested he had never given it a thought, and begged I would not disturb his present enjoyment by the mention of such uninteresting subjects. I was glad of this proof of disinterested affection; for Annabella Wilmot is the probable heiress to all her uncle's wealth, in addition to her late father's property, which she has already in possession.

I now insisted upon retracing our steps to the house; but we walked slowly, and went on talking as we proceeded. I need not repeat all we said: let me rather refer to what passed between my aunt and me, after breakfast, when Mr Huntingdon called my uncle aside, no doubt to make his proposals, and she beckoned me into another room, where she once more commenced a solemn

remonstrance which, however, entirely failed to convince me that her view of the case was preferable to my own.

'You judge him uncharitably, aunt, I know,' said I. 'His very friends are not half so bad as you represent them. There is Walter Hargrave, Milicent's brother, for one: he is but a little lower than the angels, if half she says of him is true. She is continually talking to me about him, and lauding his many virtues to the skies.'

'You will form a very inadequate estimate of a man's character,' replied she, 'if you judge by what a fond sister says of him. The worst of them generally know how to hide their misdeeds from their sister's eyes, and their mother's too.'

'And there is Lord Lowborough,' continued I, 'quite a decent man.'

'Who told you so? Lord Lowborough is a *desperate* man. He has dissipated his fortune in gambling and other things, and is now seeking an heiress to retrieve it. I told Miss Wilmot so; but you're all alike: she haughtily answered she was very much obliged to me, but she believed *she* knew when a man was seeking her for her fortune, and when for herself; she flattered herself she had had experience enough in those matters, to be justified in trusting to her own judgement – and as for his lordship's lack of fortune, she cared nothing about that, as she hoped her own would suffice for both; and as for his wildness, she supposed he was no worse than others – besides he was reformed now – Yes, they can all play the hypocrite when they want to take in a fond, misguided woman!'

'Well, I think he's about as good as she is,' said I. 'But when Mr Huntingdon is married, he won't have many opportunities of consorting with his bachelor friends; and the worse they are, the more I long to deliver him from them.'

'To be sure, my dear; and the worse *he* is, I suppose, the more you long to deliver him from himself.'

'Yes, provided he is not incorrigible – that is, the more I long to deliver him from his faults – to give him an opportunity of shaking off the adventitious evil got from contact with others worse than himself, and shining out in the unclouded light of his own genuine goodness – to do my utmost to help his better self against his worse, and make him what he would have been if he had not, from the beginning, had a bad, selfish, miserly father, who to gratify his own sordid passions, restricted him in the most innocent enjoyments of childhood and youth, and so disgusted him with every kind of restraint; and a foolish mother who indulged him to the top of his bent, deceiving her husband for him, and doing her utmost to encourage those germs of folly and vice it was her duty to suppress – and then, such a set of companions as you represent his friends to be –'

'Poor man!' said she, sarcastically, 'his kind have greatly wronged him!'

'They have!' cried I – 'and they shall wrong him no more – his wife shall undo what his mother did!'

'Well!' said she, after a short pause. 'I must say, Helen, I thought better of your judgement than this – and your taste too. How you can love such a man I

cannot tell, or what pleasure you can find in his company; for "What fellowship hath light with darkness; or he that believeth with an infidel?" '

'He is not an infidel; and I am not light, and he is not darkness, his worst and only vice is thoughtlessness.'

'And thoughtlessness,' pursued my aunt, 'may lead to every crime, and will but poorly excuse our errors in the sight of God. Mr Huntingdon, I suppose, is not without the common faculties of men: he is not so light-headed as to be irresponsible: his Maker has endowed him with reason and conscience as well as the rest of us; the scriptures are open to him as well as to others; and, "If he hear not them, neither will he hear though one rose from the dead." And, remember, Helen,' continued she solemnly, ' "The wicked shall be turned into hell, and they that *forget* God!" And suppose, even, that he should continue to love you, and you him, and that you should pass through life together with tolerable comfort – how will it be in the end, when you see yourselves parted for ever; you, perhaps, taken into eternal bliss, and he cast into the lake that burneth with unquenchable fire – there for ever to – '

'Not for ever,' I exclaimed, ' "only till he has paid the uttermost farthing"; for, "If any man's work abide not the fire, he shall suffer loss, yet himself shall be saved, but so as by fire," and He that "is able to subdue all things to Himself, will have all men to be saved", and "will, in the fullness of time, gather together in one all things in Christ Jesus, who tasted death for every man, and in whom God will reconcile all things to Himself, whether they be things in earth or things in Heaven".'

'Oh, Helen! Where did you learn all this?'

'In the Bible, aunt. I have searched it through, and found nearly thirty passages, all tending to support the same theory.'

'And is *that* the use you make of your Bible? And did you find no passages tending to prove the danger and the falsity of such a belief?'

'No: I found, indeed some passages that taken by themselves, might seem to contradict that opinion; but they will all bear a different construction to that which is commonly given, and in most the only difficulty is in the word which we translate "everlasting" or "eternal": I don't know the Greek, but I believe it strictly means for ages, and might signify either endless or long-enduring. And as for the danger of the belief, I would not publish it abroad, if I thought any poor wretch would be likely to presume upon it to his own destruction, but it is a glorious thought to cherish in one's own heart, and I would not part with it for all the world can give!'

Here our conference ended, for it was now high time to prepare for church. Everyone attended the morning service, except my uncle, who hardly ever goes, and Mr Wilmot, who stayed at home with him to enjoy a quiet game of cribbage. In the afternoon Miss Wilmot and Lord Lowborough likewise excused themselves from attending; but Mr Huntingdon vouchsafed to accompany us again. Whether it was to ingratiate himself with my aunt I cannot tell, but, if so, he certainly should have behaved better. I must confess, I did not like his conduct during service at all. Holding his prayer-book upside down, or open at any place but the right, he did nothing but stare about him,

unless he happened to catch my aunt's eye or mine, and then he would drop his own on his book, with a puritanical air of mock solemnity that would have been ludicrous, if it had not been too provoking. Once, during the sermon, after attentively regarding Mr Leighton for a few minutes, he suddenly produced his gold pencil case and snatched up a Bible. Perceiving that I observed the movement, he whispered he was going to make a note of the sermon; but instead of that – as I sat next him I could not help seeing that he was making a caricature of the preacher, giving to the respectable, pious, elderly gentleman, the air and aspect of a most absurd old hypocrite. And yet, upon his return, he talked to my aunt about the sermon with a degree of modest, serious discrimination that tempted me to believe he had really attended and profited by the discourse.

Just before dinner my uncle called me into the library for the discussion of a very important matter, which was dismissed in few words.

'Now Nell,' said he, 'this young Huntingdon has been asking for you: what must I say about it? Your aunt would answer no – but what say you?'

'I say yes, uncle,' replied I, without a moment's hesitation; for I had thoroughly made up my mind on the subject.

'Very good!' cried he. 'Now that's a good honest answer – wonderful for a girl! – Well, I'll write to your father tomorrow. He's sure to give his consent; so you may look on the matter as settled. You'd have done a deal better if you'd taken Wilmot, I can tell you; but that you won't believe. At your time of life, it's love that rules the roast: at mine, it's solid, serviceable gold. I suppose now, you'd never dream of looking into the state of your husband's finances, or troubling your head about settlements, or anything of that sort?'

'I don't think I should.'

'Well, be thankful, then, that you've wiser heads to think for you. I haven't had time, yet, to examine thoroughly into this young rascal's affairs, but I see that a great part of his father's fine property has been squandered away; but still, I think there's a pretty fair share of it left, and a little careful nursing may make a handsome thing of it yet; and then we must persuade your father to give you a decent fortune, as he has only one besides yourself to care for; and, if you behave well, who knows but what I may be induced to remember you in my will?' continued he, putting his finger to his nose, with a knowing wink.

'Thanks, uncle, for that and all your kindness,' replied I.

'Well, and I questioned this young spark on the matter of settlements,' continued he; 'and he seemed disposed to be generous enough on that point – '

'I knew he would!' said I. 'But pray don't trouble your head – or his, or mine about that; for all I have will be his, and all he has will be mine; and what more could either of us require?' And I was about to make my exit, but he called me back.

'Stop, stop!' cried he – 'We haven't mentioned the time yet. When must it be? Your aunt would put it off till the Lord knows when, but he is anxious to be bound as soon as may be: he won't hear of waiting beyond next month; and you, I guess, will be of the same mind, so – '

'Not at all, uncle; on the contrary, I should like to wait till after Christmas, at least.'

'Oh! pooh, pooh! Never tell me that tale – I know better,' cried he; and he persisted in his incredulity. Nevertheless, it is quite true. I am in no hurry at all. How can I be, when I think of the momentous change that awaits me, and of all I have to leave? It is happiness enough, to know that we *are* to be united; and that he really loves me, and I may love *him* as devotedly, and think of him as often as I please. However, I insisted upon consulting my aunt about the *time* of the wedding, for I determined her counsels should not be utterly disregarded; and no conclusions on that particular are come to yet.

## CHAPTER 21

### *Opinions*

October 1st – All is settled now. My father has given his consent, and the time is fixed for Christmas, by a sort of compromise between the respective advocates for hurry and delay. Milicent Hargrave is to be one bridesmaid, and Annabella Wilmot the other – not that I am particularly fond of the latter, but she is an intimate of the family, and I have not another friend.

When I told Milicent of my engagement, she rather provoked me by her manner of taking it. After staring a moment in mute surprise, she said – 'Well Helen, I suppose I ought to congratulate you – and I *am* glad to see you so happy; but I did not think you would take him; and I can't help feeling surprised that you should like him so much.'

'Why so?'

'Because you are so superior to him in every way, and there's something so bold – and reckless about him – so, I don't know how – but I always feel a wish to get out of his way, when I see him approach.'

'You are timid, Milicent, but that's no fault of his.'

'And then his look,' continued she. 'People say he's handsome, and of course he is, but *I* don't *like* that kind of beauty; and I wonder that you should.'

'Why so, pray?'

'Well, you know, I think there's nothing noble or lofty in his appearance.'

'In fact, you wonder that I can like anyone so unlike the stilted heroes of romance? Well! give me my flesh and blood lover, and I'll leave all the Sir Herberts and Valentines to you – if you can find them.'

'I don't want them,' said she. 'I'll be satisfied with flesh and blood too – only the spirit must shine through and predominate. But don't you think Mr Huntingdon's face is too red?'

'No!' cried I, indignantly. 'It is not red at all. There is just a pleasant glow – a healthy freshness in his complexion, the warm, pinky tint of the whole harmonising with the deeper colour of the cheeks, exactly as it ought to do. I

hate a man to be red and white, like a painted doll – or all sickly white, or smoky black, or cadaverous yellow!'

'Well, tastes differ – but *I* like pale or dark,' replied she. 'But, to tell you the truth Helen, I had been deluding myself with the hope that you would one day be my sister. I expected Walter would be introduced to you next season; and I thought you would like him, and was certain he would like you; and I flattered myself I should thus have the felicity of seeing the two persons I like best in the world – except mamma – united in one. He mayn't be exactly what you would call handsome, but he's far more distinguished-looking, and nicer and better than Mr Huntingdon; and I'm sure you would say so, if you knew him.'

'Impossible, Milicent! You think so, because you're his sister; and, on that account, I'll forgive you; but nobody else should so disparage Arthur Huntingdon to me, with impunity.'

Miss Wilmot expressed her feelings on the subject, almost as openly.

'And so, Helen,' said she, coming up to me with a smile of no amiable import, 'you are to be Mrs Huntingdon, I suppose?'

'Yes,' replied I. 'Don't you envy me?'

'Oh, *dear*, no!' she exclaimed. 'I shall probably be Lady Lowborough some-day, and then you know, dear, I shall be in a capacity to enquire, "Don't you envy *me*?" '

'Henceforth, I shall envy no one,' returned I.

'Indeed! Are you so happy then?' said she thoughtfully; and something very like a cloud of disappointment shadowed her face. 'And does he love you – I mean, does he idolise you as much as you do him?' she added, fixing her eyes upon me with ill-disguised anxiety for the reply.

'I don't want to be idolised,' I answered, 'but I am well assured that he *loves* me more than anybody else in the world – as I do him.'

'Exactly,' said she with a nod. 'I wish – ' she paused.

'What do you wish?' asked I, annoyed at the vindictive expression of her countenance.

'I wish,' returned she, with a short laugh, 'that all the attractive points and desirable qualifications of the two gentlemen were united in one – that Lord Lowborough had Huntingdon's handsome face and good temper, and all his wit, and mirth and charm, or else that Huntingdon had Lowborough's pedigree, and title, and delightful old family seat, and I had him; and you might have the other and welcome.'

'Thank you, dear Annabella, I am better satisfied with things as they are, for my own part; and for you, I wish you were as well content with your intended, as I am with mine,' said I; and it was true enough; for, though vexed at first at her unamiable spirit, her frankness touched me, and the contrast between our situations was such, that I could well afford to pity her and wish her well.

Mr Huntingdon's acquaintances appear to be no better pleased with our approaching union than mine. This morning's post brought him letters from several of his friends, during the perusal of which, at the breakfast-table, he excited the attention of the company, by the singular variety of his grimaces. But

he crushed them all into his pocket, with a private laugh, and said nothing till the meal was concluded. Then, while the company were hanging over the fire or loitering through the room, previous to settling to their various morning's avocations, he came and leant over the back of my chair, with his face in contact with my curls, and commencing with a quiet little kiss, poured forth the following complaints into my ear – 'Helen, you witch, do you know that you've entailed upon me the curses of all my friends? I wrote to them the other day, to tell them of my happy prospects, and now, instead of a bundle of congratulations, I've got a pocket-full of bitter execrations and reproaches. There's not one kind wish for me, or one good word for you among them all. They say there'll be no more fun now, no more merry days and glorious nights – and all my fault – I am the first to break up the jovial band, and others in pure despair, will follow my example. I was the very life and prop of the community, they do me the honour to say, and I have shamefully betrayed my trust –'

'You may join them again, if you like,' said I, somewhat piqued at the sorrowful tone of his discourse. 'I should be sorry to stand between any man – or body of men and so much happiness; and perhaps I can manage to do without you, as well as your poor deserted friends.'

'Bless you! No,' murmured he. 'It's "all for love or the world well lost", with me. Let them go to — where they belong, to speak politely. But if you saw how they abuse me, Helen, you would love me all the more, for having ventured so much for your sake.'

He pulled out his crumpled letters. I thought he was going to show them to me, and told him I did not wish to see them.

'I'm not going to show them to you, love,' said he. 'They're hardly fit for a lady's eyes – the most part of them. But look here. This is Grimsby's scrawl – only three lines, the sulky dog! He doesn't say much, to be sure, but his very silence implies more than all the others' words, and the less he says, the more he thinks – God damn him! – I beg your pardon, dearest – and this is Hargrave's missive. He is particularly grieved at me, because, forsooth, he had fallen in love with you from his sister's reports, and meant to have married you himself, as soon as he had sown his wild oats.'

'I'm vastly obliged to him,' observed I.

'And so am I,' said he. 'And look at this. This is Hattersley's – every page stuffed full of railing accusations, bitter curses, and lamentable complaints, ending up with swearing that he'll get married himself in revenge: he'll throw himself away on the first old maid that chooses to set her cap at him – as if I cared what he did with himself.'

'Well,' said I, 'if you give up your intimacy with these men, I don't think you will have much cause to regret the loss of their society; for it's my belief they never did you much good.'

'Maybe not; but we'd a merry time of it, too, though mingled with sorrow and pain, as Lowborough knows to his cost – ha, ha!' and while he was laughing at the recollection of Lowborough's troubles, my uncle came and clapped him on the shoulder.

'Come my lad!' said he. 'Are you too busy making love to my niece, to make war with the pheasants? – First of October remember! – Sun shines out – rain ceased – even Boarham's not afraid to venture in his waterproof boots; and Wilmot and I are going to beat you all. I declare, we old 'uns are the keenest sportsmen of the lot!'

'I'll show you what I can do today, however,' said my companion. 'I'll murder your birds by wholesale, just for keeping me away from better company than either you or them.'

And so saying he departed; and I saw no more of him till dinner. It seemed a weary time: I wonder what I shall do without him.

It is very true that the three elder gentlemen have proved themselves much keener sportsmen than the two younger ones; for both Lord Lowborough and Arthur Huntingdon have of late, almost daily neglected the shooting excursions to accompany us in our various rides and rambles. But these merry times are fast drawing to a close. In less than a fortnight the party breaks up, much to my sorrow, for every day I enjoy it more and more – now that Messrs Boarham and Wilmot have ceased to tease me, and my aunt has ceased to lecture me, and I have ceased to be jealous of Annabella – and even to dislike her – and now that Mr Huntingdon is become *my* Arthur, and I may enjoy his society without restraint – What *shall* I do without him, I repeat?

## CHAPTER 22

### *Traits of Friendship*

October 5th – My cup of sweets is not unmingled: it is dashed with a bitterness that I cannot hide from myself, disguise it as I will. I may try to persuade myself that the sweetness overpowers it; I may call it a pleasant aromatic flavour; but, say what I will, it is still there, and I cannot but taste it. I cannot shut my eyes to Arthur's faults; and the more I love him the more they trouble me. His very heart, that I trusted so, is, I fear, less warm and generous than I thought it. At least, he gave me a specimen of his character today, that seemed to merit a harder name than thoughtlessness. He and Lord Lowborough were accompanying Annabella and me in a long, delightful ride; he was riding by my side, as usual, and Annabella and Lord Lowborough were a little before us, the latter bending towards his companion as if in tender and confidential discourse.

'Those two will get the start of us, Helen, if we don't look sharp,' observed Huntingdon. 'They'll make a match of it, as sure as can be. That Lowborough's fairly besotted. But he'll find himself in a fix when he's got her, I doubt.'

'And she'll find *her*self in a fix when she's got *him*,' said I, 'if what I have heard of him is true.'

'Not a bit of it. She knows what she's about; but he, poor fool, deludes himself with the notion that she'll make him a good wife, and because she has

amused him with some rodomontade about despising rank and wealth in matters of love and marriage, he flatters himself that she's devotedly attached to him; that she will not refuse him for his poverty, and does not court him for his rank, but loves him for himself alone.'

'But is not *he* courting *her* for her fortune?'

'No, not he. That was the first attraction, certainly; but now, he has quite lost sight of it: it never enters his calculations, except merely as an essential without which, for the lady's own sake, he could not think of marrying her. No; he's fairly in love. He thought he never could be again, but he's in for it once more. He was to have been married before, some two or three years ago; but he lost his bride by losing his fortune. He got into a bad way among us in London: he had an unfortunate taste for gambling; and surely the fellow was born under an unlucky star, for he always lost thrice where he gained once. That's a mode of self-torment I never was much addicted to, when I spend my money I like to enjoy the full value of it: I see no fun in wasting it on thieves and black-legs; and as for *gaining* money, hitherto I have always had sufficient; it's time enough to be clutching for more, I think, when you begin to see the end of what you have. But I have sometimes frequented the gaming-houses just to watch the on-goings of those mad votaries of chance – a very interesting study, I assure you, Helen, and sometimes very diverting: I've had many a laugh at the boobies and bedlamites. Lowborough was quite infatuated – not willingly, but of necessity – he was always resolving to give it up, and always breaking his resolutions. Every venture was the "just once more": if he gained a little, he hoped to gain a little more next time, and if he lost, it would not do to leave off at that juncture; he must go on till he had retrieved that last misfortune, at least: bad luck could not last for ever; and every lucky hit was looked upon as the dawn of better times, till experience proved the contrary. At length he grew desperate, and we were daily on the look out for a case of *felo-de-se* – no great matter, some of us whispered, as his existence had ceased to be an acquisition to our club. At last, however, he came to a check. He made a large stake which he determined should be the last, whether he lost or won. He had often so determined before, to be sure, and as often broken his determination; and so it was this time. He lost; and while his antagonist smilingly swept away the stakes, he, turning chalky white, drew back in silence and wiped his forehead. I was present at the time; and while he stood with folded arms and eyes fixed on the ground, I knew well enough what was passing in his mind.

' "Is it to be the last, Lowborough?" said I, stepping up to him.

' "The last but one," he answered, with a grim smile; and then, rushing back to the table, he struck his hand upon it, and raising his voice high above all the confusion of jingling coins and muttered oaths and curses in the room, he swore a deep and solemn oath that, come what would, this trial *should* be the last, and imprecated unspeakable curses on his head, if ever he should shuffle a card or rattle a dice-box again. He then doubled his former stake, and challenged anyone present to play against him. Grimsby instantly presented himself. Lowborough glared fiercely at him, for Grimsby was almost as celebrated for

his luck as *he* was for his ill-fortune. However, they fell to work. But Grimsby had much skill and little scruple, and whether he took advantage of the other's trembling, blinded eagerness to deal unfairly by him, I cannot undertake to say; but Lowborough lost again, and fell dead sick.

'You'd better try once more,' said Grimsby, leaning across the table. And then he winked at me.

' "I've nothing to try with," said the poor devil, with a ghastly smile.

' "Oh, Huntingdon will lend you what you want," said the other.

' "No; you heard my oath," answered Lowborough, turning away in quiet despair. And I took him by the arm and led him out.

' "Is it to be the last, Lowborough?" I asked, when I got him into the street.

' "The last," he answered, somewhat against my expectation. And I took him home – that is, to our club – for he was as submissive as a child, and plied him with brandy and water till he began to look rather brighter – rather more alive, at least.

' "Huntingdon, I'm ruined!" said he, taking the third glass from my hand – he had drunk the others in dead silence.

' "Not you!" said I. "You'll find a man can live without his money as merrily as a tortoise without its head, or a wasp without its body."

' "But I'm in debt," said he – "deep in debt! And I can never, *never* get out of it!"

' "Well, what of that? Many a better man than you, has lived and died in debt, and they can't put you in prison, you know, because you're a peer." And I handed him his fourth tumbler.

' "But I hate to be in debt!" he shouted. "I wasn't born for it, and I cannot *bear* it!"

' "What can't be cured must be endured," said I, beginning to mix the fifth.

' "And then, I've lost my Caroline." And he began to snivel then, for the brandy had softened his heart.

' "No matter," I answered, "there are more Carolines in the world than one."

' "There's only one for me," he replied, with a dolorous sigh. "And if there were fifty more, who's to get them, I wonder, without money?"

' "Oh, somebody will take you for your title; and then you've your family estate yet; that's entailed, you know."

' "I wish to God I could sell it to pay my debts," he muttered.

' "And then," said Grimsby, who had just come in, "you can *try again*, you know. I *would* have one more chance if I were you. I'd never stop here."

' "I *won't*, I tell you!" shouted he. And he started up and left the room – walking rather unsteadily, for the liquor had got into his head. He was not so much used to it then, but after that, he took to it kindly to solace his cares.

'He kept his oath about gambling (not a little to the surprise of us all), though Grimsby did his utmost to tempt him to break it; but now he had got hold of another habit that bothered him nearly as much, for he soon discovered that the demon of drink was as black as the demon of play, and nearly as hard to get rid of – especially as his kind friends did all they could to second the promptings of his own insatiable cravings.'

'Then, they were demons themselves,' cried I, unable to contain my indignation. 'And you, Mr Huntingdon, it seems, were the first to tempt him.'

'Well, what could we do?' replied he, deprecatingly – 'We meant it in kindness – we couldn't bear to see the poor fellow so miserable – and besides, he was such a damper upon us, sitting there, silent and glum, when he was under the threefold influence of the loss of his sweetheart, the loss of his fortune, and the reaction of the last night's debauch; whereas, when he had something in him, if he was not merry himself, he was an unfailing source of merriment to us. Even Grimsby could chuckle over his odd sayings: they delighted him far more than my merry jests or Hattersley's riotous mirth. But one evening, when we were sitting over our wine, after one of our club dinners, and had all been hearty together – Lowborough giving us mad toasts, and hearing our wild songs and bearing a hand in the applause, if he did not help us to sing them himself – he suddenly relapsed into silence, sinking his head on his hand, and never lifting his glass to his lips; but this was nothing new; so we let him alone, and went on with our jollification, till, suddenly raising his head, he interrupted us in the middle of a roar of laughter, by exclaiming – ' "Gentlemen, where is all this to end? – Will you just tell me *that* now? – Where is it all to end?"

' "In Hell fire," growled Grimsby.

' "You've hit it – I thought so!" cried he. "Well then, I'll tell you what" – he rose.

' "A speech, a speech!" shouted we. "Hear, hear! Lowborough's going to give us a speech!"

'He waited calmly till the thunders of applause and jingling of glasses had ceased, and then proceeded – "It's only this, gentlemen – that I think we'd better go no farther. We'd better stop while we can."

' "Just so!" cried Hattersley –

> "Stop, poor sinner, stop and think
> Before you farther go,
> No longer sport upon the brink
> Of everlasting woe."

' "Exactly!" replied his lordship, with the utmost gravity. "And if *you* choose to visit the bottomless pit, I won't go with you – we must part company, for I swear I'll not move another step towards it! – What's this?" he said, taking up his glass of wine.

' "Taste it," suggested I.

' "This is Hell broth!" he exclaimed. "I renounce it for ever!" And he threw it out into the middle of the table.

' "Fill again!" said I, handing him the bottle – "and let us drink to your renunciation."

' "It's rank poison," said he, grasping the bottle by the neck, "and I forswear it! I've given up gambling, and I'll give up this too." He was on the point of deliberately pouring the whole contents of the bottle on to the table, but Hargrave wrested it from him. "On you be the curse, then!" said he. And

backing from the room, he shouted, "Farewell, ye tempters!" and vanished amid shouts of laughter and applause.

'We expected him back among us the next day; but to our surprise, the place remained vacant: we saw nothing of him for a whole week; and we really began to think he was going to keep his word. At last, one evening, when we were most of us assembled together again, he entered, silent and grim as a ghost, and would have quietly slipped into his usual seat at my elbow, but we all rose to welcome him, and several voices were raised to ask what he would have, and several hands were busy with bottle and glass to serve him; but I knew a smoking tumbler of brandy and water would comfort him best, and had nearly prepared it, when he peevishly pushed it away, saying,

' "Do let me alone, Huntingdon! Do be quiet, all of you! I'm not come to join you: I'm only come to be with you awhile, because I can't bear my own thoughts." And he folded his arms and leant back in his chair; so we let him be. But I left the glass by him; and after a while, Grimsby directed my attention towards it, by a significant wink; and, on turning my head, I saw it was drained to the bottom. He made me a sign to replenish, and quietly pushed up the bottle. I willingly complied; but Lowborough detected the pantomime, and, nettled at the intelligent grins that were passing between us, snatched the glass from my hand, dashed the contents of it in Grimsby's face, threw the empty tumbler at me, and then bolted from the room.'

'I hope he broke your head,' said I.

'No, love,' replied he, laughing immoderately at the recollection of the whole affair, 'he would have done so – and perhaps spoilt my face, too, but providentially, this forest of curls' (taking off his hat and showing his luxuriant chestnut locks), 'saved my skull, and prevented the glass from breaking till it reached the table.'

'After that,' he continued, 'Lowborough kept aloof from us a week or two longer. I used to meet him occasionally in the town; and then, as I was too good natured to resent his unmannerly conduct, and he bore no malice against me – he was never unwilling to talk to me; on the contrary, he would cling to me and follow me anywhere – but to the club, and the gaming-houses, and suchlike dangerous places of resort – he was so weary of his own moping, melancholy mind. At last, I got him to come in with me to the club, on condition that I would not tempt him to drink; and for some time, he continued to look in upon us pretty regularly of an evening – still abstaining, with wonderful perseverance, from the "rank poison" he had so bravely forsworn. But some of our members protested against this conduct. They did not like to have him sitting there like a skeleton at a feast, instead of contributing his quota to the general amusement, casting a cloud over all, and watching, with greedy eyes, every drop they carried to their lips, they vowed it was not fair; and some of them maintained that he should either be compelled to do as others did or expelled from the society, and swore that, next time he showed himself, they would tell him as much, and, if he did not take the warning, proceed to active measures. However, I befriended him on this occasion, and recommended them to let him be for a while,

intimating that, with a little patience on our parts, he would soon come round again – But, to be sure, it *was* rather provoking; for though he refused to drink like an honest Christian, it was well known to me, that he kept a private bottle of laudanum about him, which he was continually soaking at – or rather, holding off and on with, abstaining one day and exceeding the next, just like the spirits.

'One night, however, during one of our orgies – one of our high festivals, I mean – he glided in, like the ghost in *Macbeth*, and seated himself, as usual, a little back from the table, in the chair we always placed for "the spectre", whether it chose to fill it or not. I saw by his face that he was suffering from the effects of an overdose of his insidious comforter; but nobody spoke to him, and he spoke to nobody. A few sidelong glances, and a whispered observation that "the ghost was come", was all the notice he drew by his appearance, and we went on with our merry carousals as before, till he startled us all by suddenly drawing in his chair and leaning forward with his elbows on the table, and exclaiming with portentous solemnity – "Well! it puzzles me what you can find to be so merry about. What *you* see in life I don't know – *I* see only the blackness of darkness and a fearful looking for of judgement and fiery indignation!"

'All the company simultaneously pushed up their glasses to him, and I set them before him in a semicircle, and, tenderly patting him on the back, bid him drink and he would soon see as bright a prospect as any of us; but he pushed them back, muttering – "Take them away! I won't taste it, I tell you – I won't – I won't!" So I handed them down again to the owners; but I saw that he followed them with a glare of hungry regret as they departed. Then, he clasped his hands before his eyes to shut out the sight, and two minutes after, lifted his head again, and said, in a hoarse, but vehement whisper – "And yet I must! Huntingdon, get me a glass!"

' "Take the bottle, man!" said I, thrusting the brandy-bottle into his hand – but stop, I'm telling too much,' muttered the narrator, startled at the look I turned upon him. 'But no matter,' he recklessly added, and thus continued his relation – 'In his desperate eagerness, he seized the bottle and sucked away, till he suddenly dropped from his chair, disappearing under the table amid a tempest of applause. The consequence of this imprudence was something like an apoplectic fit, followed by a rather severe brain fever – '

'And what did you think of *yourself*, sir?' said I, quickly.

'Of course, I was very penitent,' he replied. 'I went to see him once or twice – nay, twice or thrice – or, by'r lady, some four times – and when he got better, I tenderly brought him back to the fold.'

'What do you mean?'

'I mean, I restored him to the bosom of the club, and compassionating the feebleness of his health and extreme lowness of his spirits, I recommended him to "take a little wine for his stomach's sake", and, when he was sufficiently re-established, to embrace the *media via* – ni-jamais-ni-toujours plan – not to kill himself like a fool, and not to abstain like a ninny – in a word, to enjoy himself like a rational creature, and do as I did; for don't think, Helen, that I'm a tippler; I'm nothing at all of the kind, and never was, and never shall be. I value my

comfort far too much. I see that a man cannot give himself up to drinking without being miserable one half his days and mad the other; besides, I like to enjoy my life at all sides and ends, which cannot be done by one that suffers himself to be the slave of a single propensity – and moreover, drinking spoils one's good looks,' he concluded, with a most conceited smile that ought to have provoked me more than it did.

'And did Lord Lowborough profit by your advice?' I asked.

'Why, yes, in a manner. For a while, he managed very well; indeed, he was a model of moderation and prudence – something too much so for the tastes of our wild community; but, somehow, Lowborough had not the gift of moderation: if he stumbled a little to one side, he must go down before he could right himself: if he overshot the mark one night, the effects of it rendered him so miserable the next day that he must repeat the offence to mend it; and so on from day to day, till his clamorous conscience brought him to a stand – And then, in his sober moments, he so bothered his friends with his remorse, and his terrors and woes, that they were obliged, in self-defence, to get him to drown his sorrows in wine, or any more potent beverage that came to hand; and when his first scruples of conscience were overcome, he would need no more persuading, he would often grow desperate, and be as great a blackguard as any of them could desire – but only to lament his own unutterable wickedness and degradation the more when the fit was over.

'At last, one day when he and I were alone together, after pondering awhile in one of his gloomy, abstracted moods, with his arms folded and his head sunk on his breast – he suddenly woke up, and vehemently grasping my arm, said – "Huntingdon, this won't do! I'm resolved to have done with it."

' "What, are you going to shoot yourself?" said I.

' "No I'm going to reform."

' "Oh, *that's* nothing new! You've been going to reform these twelve months and more."

' "Yes, but you wouldn't let me; and I was such a fool I couldn't live without you. But now I see what it is that keeps me back, and what's wanted to save me; and I'd compass sea and land to get it – only I'm afraid there's no chance." And he sighed as if his heart would break.

' "What is it, Lowborough?" said I, thinking he was fairly cracked at last.

' "A wife," he answered; "for I can't live alone, because my own mind distracts me, and I can't live with you, because you take the devil's part against me."

' "Who – I?"

' "Yes – all of you do – and you more than any of them, you know. But if I could get a wife, with fortune enough to pay off my debts and set me straight in the world – "

' "To be sure," said I.

' "And sweetness and goodness enough," he continued, "to make home tolerable, and to reconcile me to myself – I think I should do, yet. I shall never be in love again, that's certain; but perhaps that would be no great matter, it would enable me to choose with my eyes open – and I should make a good

husband in spite of it; but could anyone be in love with *me*? – that's the question – With *your* good looks and powers of fascination" (he was pleased to say), "I might hope; but as it is, Huntingdon, do you think *any*body would take me – ruined and wretched as I am?"

' "Yes, certainly."

' "Who?"

' "Why, any neglected old maid, fast sinking in despair, would be delighted to – "

' "No, no," said he – "it must be somebody that I can love."

' "Why, you just said you never could be in love again."

' "Well, love is not the word – but somebody that I can like – I'll search all England through, at all events!" he cried, with a sudden burst of hope, or desperation. "Succeed or fail, it will be better than rushing headlong to destruction at that damned club: so farewell to it and you. Whenever I meet you on honest ground or under a Christian roof, I shall be glad to see you; but never more shall you entice me to that *devil's den*!"

'This was shameful language, but I shook hands with him, and we parted. He kept his word: and from that time forward, he has been a pattern of propriety, as far as I can tell; but, till lately, I have not had very much to do with him. He occasionally sought my company but as frequently shrunk from it, fearing lest I should wile him back to destruction, and I found him not very entertaining, especially, as he sometimes attempted to awaken my conscience and draw me from the perdition he considered himself to have escaped; but when I did happen to meet him, I seldom failed to ask after the progress of his matrimonial efforts and researches, and in general he could give me but a poor account. The mothers were repelled by his empty coffers and his reputation for gambling, and the daughters by his cloudy brow and melancholy temper – besides, he didn't understand them; he wanted the spirit and assurance to carry his point.

'I left him at it when I went to the continent; and on my return, at the year's end, I found him still a disconsolate bachelor – though, certainly, looking somewhat less like an unblest exile from the tomb than before. The young ladies had ceased to be afraid of him, and were beginning to think him quite interesting; but the mammas were still unrelenting. It was about this time, Helen, that my good angel brought me into conjunction with you; and then I had eyes and ears for nobody else. But meantime, Lowborough became acquainted with our charming friend, Miss Wilmot – through the intervention of *his* good angel, no doubt he would tell you, though he did not dare to fix his hopes on one so courted and admired, till after they were brought into closer contact here at Staningley, and she, in the absence of her other admirers, indubitably courted his notice and held out every encouragement to his timid advances. Then indeed, he began to hope for a dawn of brighter days; and if for a while, I darkened his prospects by standing between him and his sun – and so, nearly plunged him again into the abyss of despair – it only intensified his ardour and strengthened his hopes when I chose to abandon the field in the pursuit of a brighter treasure. In a word, as I told you, he is fairly besotted. At first, he could

dimly perceive her faults, and they gave him considerable uneasiness; but now his passion and her art together, have blinded him to everything but her perfections and his amazing good fortune. Last night, he came to me brim-full of his new-found felicity: "Huntingdon, I am not a castaway!" said he, seizing my hand and squeezing it like a vice. "There is happiness in store for me, yet – even in this life – she loves me!"

'"Indeed!" said I. "Has she told you so?"

'"No, but I can no longer doubt it. Do you not see how pointedly kind and affectionate she is? And she knows the utmost extent of my poverty, and cares nothing about it! She knows all the folly and all the wickedness of my former life, and is not afraid to trust me – and my rank and title are no allurements to her; for them, she utterly disregards. She is the most generous, high-minded being that can be conceived of. She will save me, body and soul, from destruction. Already, she has ennobled me in my own estimation, and made me three times better, wiser, greater than I was. Oh! if I had but known her before, how much degradation and misery I should have been spared! But what have I done to deserve so magnificent a creature?"

'And the cream of the jest,' continued Mr Huntingdon, laughing, 'is that the artful minx loves nothing about him, but his title and pedigree, and "that delightful old family seat".'

'How do you know?' said I.

'She told me so herself; she said, "As for the man himself, I thoroughly despise him; but then, I suppose, it is time to be making my choice, and if I waited for someone capable of eliciting my esteem and affection, I should have to pass my life in single blessedness, for I detest you all!" Ha, ha! I suspect she was wrong there; but however, it is evident she has no love for *him*, poor fellow.'

'Then you ought to tell him so.'

'What, and spoil all her plans and prospects, poor girl? No, no: that would be a breach of confidence, wouldn't it, Helen? Ha, ha! Besides, it would break his heart.' And he laughed again.

'Well, Mr Huntingdon, I don't know what you see so amazingly diverting in the matter; *I* see nothing to laugh at.'

'I'm laughing at *you*, just now, love,' said he, redoubling his cachinnations.

And leaving him to enjoy his merriment alone, I touched Ruby with the whip, and cantered on to rejoin our companions; for we had been walking our horses all this time, and were consequently a long way behind. Arthur was soon at my side again; but not disposed to talk to him, I broke into a gallop. He did the same: and we did not slacken our pace till we came up with Miss Wilmot and Lord Lowborough, which was within half a mile of the park gates. I avoided all further conversation with him, till we came to the end of our ride, when I meant to jump off my horse and vanish into the house, before he could offer his assistance; but while I was disengaging my habit from the crutch, he lifted me off, and held me by both hands, asserting that he would not let me go till I had forgiven him.

'I have nothing to forgive,' said I. 'You have not injured *me*.'

'No, darling – God forbid that I should! – but you are angry, because it was to me that Annabella confessed her lack of esteem for her lover.'

'No, Arthur, it is not *that* that displeases me: it is the whole system of your conduct towards your friend; and if you wish me to forget it, go, now, and tell him what sort of a woman it is, that he adores so madly, and on whom he has hung his hopes of future happiness.'

'I tell you, Helen, it would break his heart – it would be the death of him – besides being a scandalous trick to poor Annabella. There is no help for him now; he is past praying for. Besides, she may keep up the deception to the end of the chapter; and then he will be just as happy in the illusion as if it were reality; or perhaps, he will only discover his mistake when he has ceased to love her; and if not, it is much better that the truth should dawn gradually upon him. So now, my angel, I hope I have made out a clear case, and fully convinced you that I cannot make the atonement you require. What other requisition have you to make? Speak, and I will gladly obey.'

'I have none but this,' said I, as gravely as before; 'that, in future, you will never make a jest of the sufferings of others, and always use your influence with your friends for their own advantage against their evil propensities, instead of seconding their evil propensities against themselves.'

'I will do my utmost,' said he, 'to remember and perform the injunctions of my angel monitress,' and after kissing both my gloved hands, he let me go.

When I entered my room, I was surprised to see Annabella Wilmot standing before my toilet-table, composedly surveying her features in the glass, with one hand flirting her gold-mounted whip, and the other holding up her long habit.

'She certainly *is* a magnificent creature!' thought I, as I beheld that tall, finely developed figure, and the reflection of the handsome face in the mirror before me, with the glossy dark hair, slightly and not ungracefully disordered by the breezy ride, the rich brown complexion glowing with exercise, and the black eyes sparkling with unwonted brilliance. On perceiving me, she turned round exclaiming, with a laugh that savoured more of malice than of mirth – 'Why, Helen! what *have* you been doing so long? – I came to tell you my good fortune,' she continued, regardless of Rachel's presence. 'Lord Lowborough has proposed, and I have been graciously pleased to accept him. Don't you envy me, dear?'

'No, love,' said I – 'or him either,' I mentally added. 'And do you like him, Annabella?'

'Like him! Yes, to be sure – over head and ears in love!'

'Well, I hope you'll make him a good wife.'

'Thank you, my dear! And what besides do you hope?'

'I hope you will both love each other, and both be happy.'

'Thanks; and I hope you will make a *very* good wife to Mr Huntingdon!' said she, with a queenly bow, and retired.

'Oh, miss! how could you say so to her?' cried Rachel.

'Say what?' replied I.

'Why, that you hoped she would make him a good wife – I never heard such a thing!'

'Because, I do hope it – or rather, I wish it – she's almost past hope.'

'Well!' said she, 'I'm sure I hope he'll make *her* a good husband. They tell queer things about him downstairs. They were saying – '

'I know, Rachel – I've heard all about him; but he's reformed now. And they have no business to tell tales about their masters.'

'No, mum – or else, they *have* said some things about Mr Huntingdon too.'

'I won't hear them, Rachel; they tell lies.'

'Yes, mum,' said she, quietly, as she went on arranging my hair.

'Do *you* believe them, Rachel?' I asked, after a short pause.

'No, miss, not all. You know when a lot of servants gets together, they like to talk about their betters; and some, for a bit of swagger, likes to make it appear as though they knew more than they do, and to throw out hints and things, just to astonish the others. But I think, if I was you, Miss Helen, I'd look very well before I leaped. I do believe a young lady can't be too careful who she marries.'

'Of course not,' said I – 'but quick, will you, Rachel? I want to be dressed.'

And indeed, I was anxious to be rid of the good woman, for I was in such a melancholy frame I could hardly keep the tears out of my eyes while she dressed me. It was not for Lord Lowborough – it was not for Annabella – it was not for myself – it was for Arthur Huntingdon that they rose.

13th. They are gone – and he is gone. We are to be parted for more than two months – above ten weeks! A long, long time to live and not to see him. But he has promised to write often, and made me promise to write still oftener, because he will be busy settling his affairs, and I shall have nothing better to do. Well, I think I shall always have plenty to say – But O! for the time when we shall be always together, and can exchange our thoughts without the intervention of these cold go-betweens, pen, ink, and paper!

22nd. I have had several letters from Arthur, already. They are not long, but passing sweet, and just like himself – full of ardent affection, and playful, lively humour; but – there is always a *but* in this imperfect world – and I do wish he would *sometimes* be serious. I cannot get him to write or speak in real, solid earnest. I don't much mind it *now*; but if it be always so, what shall I do with the serious part of myself?

CHAPTER 23

## First Weeks of Matrimony

Feb. 18th, 1822. Early this morning, Arthur mounted his hunter and set off in high glee to meet the — hounds. He will be away all day; and so I will amuse myself with my neglected diary – if I can give that name to such an irregular composition. It is exactly four months since I opened it last.

I am married now, and settled down as Mrs Huntingdon of Grassdale Manor. I have had eight weeks' experience of matrimony. And do I regret the step I have taken? – No – though I must confess, in my secret heart, that Arthur is not what I thought him at first, and if I had known him in the beginning, as thoroughly as I do now, I probably never should have loved him, and if I had loved him first, and then made the discovery, I fear I should have thought it my duty not to have married him. To be sure, I might have known him, for everyone was willing enough to tell me about him, and he himself was no accomplished hypocrite, but I was wilfully blind, and now, instead of regretting that I did not discern his full character before I was indissolubly bound to him, I am *glad*; for it has saved me a great deal of battling with my conscience, and a great deal of consequent trouble and pain; and, whatever I *ought* to have done, my duty, now, is plainly to love him and to cleave to him; and this just tallies with my inclination.

He is very fond of me – almost *too* fond. I could do with less caressing and more rationality: I should like to be less of a pet and more of a friend, if I might choose – but I won't complain of that: I am only afraid his affection loses in depth where it gains in ardour. I sometimes liken it to a fire of dry twigs and branches compared with one of solid coal – very bright and hot, but if it should burn itself out and leave nothing but ashes behind, what shall I do? But it won't – it *shan't*, I am determined – and surely I have power to keep it alive. So let me dismiss *that* thought at once. But Arthur is selfish – I am constrained to acknowledge that; and, indeed, the admission gives me less pain than might be expected; for, since *I* love him so much, I can easily forgive him for loving himself: he likes to be pleased, and it is my delight to please him – and when I regret this tendency of his, it is for his own sake, not for mine.

The first instance he gave was on the occasion of our bridal tour. He wanted to hurry it over, for all the continental scenes were already familiar to him: many had lost their interest in his eyes, and others had never had anything to lose. The consequence was, that, after a flying transit through part of France and part of Italy, I came back nearly as ignorant as I went, having made no acquaintance with persons and manners, and very little with things – my head swarming with a motley confusion of objects and scenes – some, it is true, leaving a deeper and more pleasing impression than others, but these embittered by the recollection

that my emotions had not been shared by my companion, but that, on the contrary, when I had expressed a particular interest in anything that I saw or desired to see, it had been displeasing to him in as much as it proved that I could take delight in anything disconnected with himself.

As for Paris, we only just touched at that, and he would not give me time to see one tenth of the beauties and interesting objects of Rome. He wanted to get me home, he said, to have me all to himself, and to see me safely installed as the mistress of Grassdale Manor, just as single-minded, as naive, and piquante as I was; and, as if I had been some frail butterfly, he expressed himself fearful of rubbing the silver off my wings by bringing me into contact with society, especially that of Paris and Rome; and, moreover, he did not scruple to tell me that there were ladies in both places that would tear his eyes out if they happened to meet him with me.

Of course I was vexed at all this; but, still, it was less the disappointment to myself that annoyed me, than the disappointment *in him*, and the trouble I was at to frame excuses to my friends for having seen and observed so little, without imputing one particle of blame to my companion. But when we got home – to my new, delightful home – I was so happy and he was so kind that I freely forgave him all; and I was beginning to think my lot *too* happy, and my husband actually too good for me, if not too good for this world, when, on the second Sunday after our arrival, he shocked and horrified me by another instance of his unreasonable exaction. We were walking home from the morning service – for it was a fine frosty day, and, as we are so near the church, I had requested the carriage should not be used – 'Helen,' said he, with unusual gravity, 'I am not quite satisfied with you.'

I desired to know what was wrong.

'But will you promise to reform, if I tell you?'

'Yes, if I can – and without offending a higher authority.'

'Ah! there it is, you see – you don't love me with all your heart.'

'I don't understand you, Arthur (at least, I hope I don't): pray tell me what I have done or said amiss?'

'It is nothing you have done or said; it is something that you *are*: you are too religious. Now I like a woman to be religious, and I think your piety one of your greatest charms, but then, like all other good things, it may be carried too far. To my thinking, a woman's religion ought not to lessen her devotion to her earthly lord. She should have enough to purify and etherialise her soul, but not enough to refine away her heart, and raise her above all human sympathies.'

'And am *I* above all human sympathies?' said I

'No, darling; but you are making more progress towards that saintly condition than I like; for, all these two hours, I have been thinking of you and wanting to catch your eye, and you were so absorbed in your devotions that you had not even a glance to spare for me – I declare, it is enough to make one jealous of one's Maker – which is very wrong, you know; so don't excite such wicked passions again, for my soul's sake!'

'I will give my whole heart and soul to my Maker if I can,' I answered, 'and

not one atom more of it to you than He allows. What are *you*, sir, that you should set yourself up as a god, and presume to dispute possession of my heart with Him to whom I owe all I have and all I am, every blessing I ever did or ever can enjoy – and yourself among the rest – if you *are* a blessing, which I am half inclined to doubt.'

'Don't be so hard upon me, Helen; and don't pinch my arm so, you're squeezing your fingers into the bone.'

'Arthur,' continued I, relaxing my hold of his arm, 'you don't love me half as much as I do you; and yet, if you loved me far less than you do, I would not complain, provided you loved your Maker more. I should *rejoice* to see you at any time, so deeply absorbed in your devotions that you had not a single thought to spare for me. But, indeed, I should lose nothing by the change, for the more you loved your God the more deep and pure and true would be your love to me.'

At this he only laughed, and kissed my hand, calling me a sweet enthusiast. Then taking off his hat, he added – 'But look here, Helen – what can a man do with such a head as this?'

The head looked right enough, but when he placed my hand on the top of it, it sunk in a bed of curls, rather alarmingly low, especially in the middle.

'You see I was not made to be a saint,' said he, laughing. 'If God meant me to be religious, why didn't He give me a proper organ of veneration?'

'You are like the servant,' I replied, 'who instead of employing his one talent in his master's service, restored it to him unimproved, alleging, as an excuse, that he knew him "to be a hard man, reaping where he had not sown and gathering where he had not strawed". Of him, to whom less is given, less will be required; but our utmost exertions are required of us all. You are not without the capacity of veneration, and faith and hope, and conscience and reason, and every other requisite to a Christian's character, if you choose to employ them; but all our talents increase in the using, and every faculty, both good and bad, strengthens by exercise; therefore, if you choose to use the bad – or those which tend to evil till they become your masters – and neglect the good till they dwindle away, you have only yourself to blame. But you *have* talents, Arthur – natural endowments, both of heart and mind, and temper such as many a better Christian would be glad to possess – if you would only employ them in God's service. I should never expect to see you a devotee, but it is quite possible to be a good Christian without ceasing to be a happy, merry-hearted man.'

'You speak like an oracle, Helen, and all you say is indisputably true; but listen here: I am hungry, and I see before me a good substantial dinner; I am told that, if I abstain from this today, I shall have a sumptuous feast tomorrow, consisting of all manner of dainties and delicacies. Now in the first place, I should be loath to wait till tomorrow, when I have the means of appeasing my hunger already before me; in the second place, the solid viands of today are more to my taste than the dainties that are promised me; in the third place, I don't *see* tomorrow's banquet, and how can I tell that it is not all a fable, got up by the greasy-faced fellow that is advising me to abstain, in order that he may

have all the good victuals to himself? In the fourth place, this table must be spread for somebody, and, as Solomon says, "Who can eat, or who else can hasten hereunto more than I?" and finally, with your leave, I'll sit down and satisfy my cravings of today, and leave tomorrow to shift for itself – who knows but what I may secure both this and that?'

'But you are not required to abstain from the substantial dinner of today; you are only advised to partake of these coarser viands in such moderation as not to incapacitate you from enjoying the choicer banquet of tomorrow. If, regardless of that counsel, you choose to make a beast of yourself now, and over-eat and over-drink yourself till you turn the good victuals into poison, who is to blame if, hereafter, while you are suffering the torments of yesterday's gluttony and drunkenness, you see more temperate men sitting down to enjoy themselves at that splendid entertainment which you are unable to taste?'

'Most true my patron saint; but again, our friend Solomon says – "There is nothing better for a man than to eat and to drink, and to be merry."'

'And again,' returned I, 'he says, "Rejoice, O young man, in thy youth, and walk in the ways of thine heart and in the sight of thine eyes; but know thou that, for all these things, God will bring thee into judgement."'

'Well, but Helen, I'm sure I've been very good these last few weeks. What have you seen amiss in me; and what would you have me to do?'

'Nothing – more than you do, Arthur: your actions are all right, so far; but I would have your thoughts changed; I would have you to fortify yourself against temptation, and not to call evil good, and good, evil; I should wish you to think more deeply, to look farther, and aim higher than you do.'

We now stood before our own door, and I said no more; but, with an ardent and tearful embrace, I left him, and went into the house, and upstairs to take off my bonnet and mantle. I wished to say nothing more on that subject at the time, lest I should disgust him with both it and me.

## CHAPTER 24

### First Quarrel

March 25th. Arthur is getting tired – not of me, I trust, but of the idle, quiet life he leads – and no wonder, for he has so few sources of amusement; he never reads anything but newspapers and sporting magazines; and when he sees me occupied with a book, he won't let me rest till I close it. In fine weather he generally manages to get through the time pretty well; but on rainy days, of which we have had a good many of late, it is quite painful to witness his ennui. I do all I can to amuse him, but it is impossible to get him to feel interested in what I most like to talk about; while, on the other hand, he likes to talk about things that cannot interest me – or even that annoy me – and these please him the most of all; for his favourite amusement is to sit or loll beside me on the sofa and tell me stories of his former amours, always turning upon the ruin of some

confiding girl or the cozening of some unsuspecting husband; and when I express my horror and indignation, he lays it all to the charge of jealousy, and laughs till the tears run down his cheeks. I used to fly into passions or melt into tears at first, but seeing that his delight increased in proportion to my anger and agitation, I have since endeavoured to suppress my feelings and receive his revelations in the silence of calm contempt; but still, he reads the inward struggle in my face, and misconstrues my bitterness of soul for his unworthiness into the pangs of wounded jealousy; and when he has sufficiently diverted himself with that, or fears my displeasure will become too serious for his comfort, he tries to kiss and sooth me into smiles again – never were his caresses so little welcome as then! This is *double* selfishness, displayed to me and to the victims of his former love. There are times when, with a momentary pang – a flash of wild dismay, I ask myself, 'Helen, what have you done?' But I rebuke the inward questioner, and repel the obtrusive thoughts that crowd upon me; for, were he ten times as sensual and impenetrable to good and lofty thoughts, I well know I have no right to complain. And I don't and won't complain. I do and will love him still; and I do not and will not regret that I have linked my fate with his.

April 4th. We have had a downright quarrel. The particulars are as follows – Arthur had told me, at different intervals, the whole story of his intrigue with Lady F—, which I would not believe before. It was some consolation, however, to find that, in this instance, the lady had been more to blame than he; for he was very young at the time, and she had decidedly made the first advances, if what he said was true. I hated her for it, for it seemed as if she had chiefly contributed to his corruption, and when he was beginning to talk about her the other day, I begged he would not mention her, for I detested the very sound of her name.

'Not because you loved her, Arthur, mind, but because she injured you, and deceived her husband, and was altogether a very abominable woman, whom you ought to be ashamed to mention.'

But he defended her by saying that she had a doting old husband, whom it was impossible to love.

'Then why did she marry him?' said I.

'For his money,' was the reply.

'Then that was another crime, and her solemn promise to love and honour him was another, that only increased the enormity of the last.'

'You are too severe upon the poor lady,' laughed he. 'But never mind, Helen, I don't care for her now; and I never loved any of them half as much as I do you; so you needn't fear to be forsaken like them.'

'If you had told me these things before, Arthur, I never should have given you the chance.'

'*Wouldn't* you, my darling!'

'Most certainly not!'

He laughed incredulously.

'I wish I could convince you of it now!' cried I, starting up from beside him; and for the first time in my life, and I hope the last, I wished I had not married him.

'Helen,' said he, more gravely, 'do you know that if I believed you now, I should be very angry? – but thank Heaven I don't. Though you stand there with your white face and flashing eyes, looking at me like a very tigress, I know the heart within you, perhaps a trifle better than you know it yourself.'

Without another word, I left the room, and locked myself up in my own chamber. In about half an hour, he came to the door; and first he tried the handle, then he knocked.

'Won't you let me in, Helen?' said he.

'No; you have displeased me,' I replied, 'and I don't want to see your face or hear your voice again till the morning.'

He paused a moment, as if dumbfoundered or uncertain how to answer such a speech, and then turned and walked away. This was only an hour after dinner: I knew he would find it very dull to sit alone all the evening; and this considerably softened my resentment, though it did not make me relent. I was determined to show him that my heart was not his slave, and I could live without him if I chose; and I sat down and wrote a long letter to my aunt – of course telling her nothing of all this. Soon after ten o'clock, I heard him come up again; but he passed my door and went straight to his own dressing-room, where he shut himself in for the night.

I was rather anxious to see how he would meet me in the morning, and not a little disappointed to behold him enter the breakfast-room with a careless smile.

'Are you cross still, Helen?' said he, approaching as if to salute me. I coldly turned to the table, and began to pour out the coffee, observing that he was rather late.

He uttered a low whistle and sauntered away to the window, where he stood for some minutes looking out upon the pleasing prospect of sullen, grey clouds, streaming rain, soaking lawn, and dripping, leafless trees – and muttering execrations on the weather, and then sat down to breakfast. While taking his coffee, he muttered it was 'damned cold'.

'You should not have left it so long,' said I.

He made no answer, and the meal was concluded in silence. It was a relief to both when the letter-bag was brought in. It contained, upon examination, a newspaper and one or two letters for him, and a couple of letters for me, which he tossed across the table without a remark. One was from my brother, the other from Milicent Hargrave, who is now in London with her mother. His, I think, were business letters, and apparently not much to his mind, for he crushed them into his pocket with some muttered expletives, that I should have reproved him for at any other time. The paper, he set before him, and pretended to be deeply absorbed in its contents during the remainder of breakfast, and a considerable time after.

The reading and answering of my letters, and the direction of household concerns afforded me ample employment for the morning; after lunch, I got my drawing, and from dinner till bedtime, I read. Meanwhile, poor Arthur was sadly at a loss for something to amuse him or to occupy his time. He wanted to appear as busy and as unconcerned as I did: had the weather at all permitted,

he would doubtless have ordered his horse and set off to some distant region – no matter where – immediately after breakfast, and not returned till night; had there been a lady anywhere within reach, of any age between fifteen and forty-five, he would have sought revenge and found employment in getting up – or trying to get up a desperate flirtation with her; but being, to my private satisfaction, entirely cut off from both these sources of diversion, his sufferings were truly deplorable. When he had done yawning over his paper and scribbling short answers to his shorter letters, he spent the remainder of the morning and the whole of the afternoon in fidgeting about from room to room, watching the clouds, cursing the rain, alternately petting, and teasing, and abusing his dogs, sometimes lounging on the sofa with a book that he could not force himself to read, and very often fixedly gazing at me, when he thought I did not perceive it, with the vain hope of detecting some traces of tears, or some tokens of remorseful anguish in my face. But I managed to preserve an undisturbed, though grave serenity throughout the day. I was not really angry: I felt for him all the time, and longed to be reconciled; but I determined he should make the first advances, or at least show some signs of an humble and contrite spirit, first; for, if I began, it would only minister to his self-conceit, increase his arrogance, and quite destroy the lesson I wanted to give him.

He made a long stay in the dining-room after dinner, and, I fear, took an unusual quantity of wine, but not enough to loosen his tongue; for when he came in and found me quietly occupied with my book, too busy to lift my head on his entrance, he merely murmured an expression of suppressed disapprobation, and, shutting the door with a bang, went and stretched himself at full length on the sofa, and composed himself to sleep. But his favourite cocker, Dash, that had been lying at my feet, took the liberty of jumping upon him and beginning to lick his face. He struck it off with a smart blow; and the poor dog squeaked, and ran cowering back to me. When he woke up, about half an hour after, he called it to him again; but Dash only looked sheepish and wagged the tip of his tail. He called again, more sharply, but Dash only clung the closer to me, and licked my hand as if imploring protection. Enraged at this, his master snatched up a heavy book and hurled it at his head. The poor dog set up a piteous outcry and ran to the door. I let him out, and then quietly took up the book.

'Give that book to me,' said Arthur, in no very courteous tone. I gave it to him.

'Why did you let the dog out?' he asked. 'You knew I wanted him.'

'By what token?' I replied; 'by your throwing the book at him? But perhaps, it was intended for me?'

'No – but I see you've got a taste of it,' said he, looking at my hand, that had also been struck, and was rather severely grazed.

I returned to my reading; and he endeavoured to occupy himself in the same manner; but, in a little while, after several portentous yawns, he pronounced *his* book to be 'cursed trash,' and threw it on to the table. Then followed eight or ten minutes of silence, during the greater part of which, I believe, he was staring at me. At last his patience was tired out.

'What *is* that book, Helen?' he exclaimed. I told him.

'Is it interesting?'

'Yes, very.'

'Humph!'

I went on reading – or pretending to read, at least – I cannot say there was much communication between my eyes and my brain; for, while the former ran over the pages, the latter was earnestly wondering when Arthur would speak next, and what he would say, and what I should answer. But he did not speak again till I rose to make the tea, and then it was only to say he should not take any. He continued lounging on the sofa, and alternately closing his eyes and looking at his watch and at me, till bedtime, when I rose, and took my candle and retired.

'Helen!' cried he, the moment I had left the room. I turned back, and stood awaiting his commands.

'What do you want, Arthur?' I said at length.

'Nothing,' replied he. 'Go!'

I went, but hearing him mutter something as I was closing the door, I turned again. It sounded very like 'confounded slut,' but I was quite willing it should be something else.

'Were you speaking, Arthur?' I asked.

'No,' was the answer; and I shut the door and departed. I saw nothing more of him till the following morning at breakfast, when he came down a full hour after the usual time.

'You're very late,' was my morning's salutation.

'You needn't have waited for me,' was his; and he walked up to the window again. It was just such weather as yesterday.

'Oh, this confounded rain!' he muttered. But after studiously regarding it for a minute or two, a bright idea seemed to strike him, for he suddenly exclaimed, 'But I know what I'll do!' and then returned and took his seat at the table. The letter-bag was already there, waiting to be opened. He unlocked it and examined the contents, but said nothing about them.

'Is there anything for me?' I asked.

'No.'

He opened the newspaper and began to read.

'You'd better take your coffee,' suggested I; 'it will be cold again.'

'You may go,' said he, 'if you've done. I don't want you.'

I rose, and withdrew to the next room, wondering if we were to have another such miserable day as yesterday, and wishing intensely for an end of these mutually inflicted torments. Shortly after, I heard him ring the bell and give some orders about his wardrobe that sounded as if he meditated a long journey. He then sent for the coachman, and I heard something about the carriage and the horses, and London, and seven o'clock tomorrow morning, that startled and disturbed me not a little.

'I must not let him go to London, whatever comes of it,' said I to myself: 'he will run into all kinds of mischief, and I shall be the cause of it. But the question

is, how am I to alter his purpose? – Well, I will wait awhile, and see if he mentions it.'

I waited most anxiously, from hour to hour; but not a word was spoken, on that or any other subject, to me. He whistled, and talked to his dogs, and wandered from room to room, much the same as on the previous day. At last I began to think I must introduce the subject myself, and was pondering how to bring it about, when John unwittingly came to my relief with the following message from the coachman.

'Please, sir, Richard says one of the horses has got a very bad cold, and he thinks, sir, if you could make it convenient to go the day after tomorrow, instead of tomorrow, he could physic it today so as – '

'Confound his impudence!' interjected the master.

'Please, sir, he says it would be a deal better if you could,' persisted John, 'for he hopes there'll be a change in the weather shortly, and he says it's not *likely*, when a horse is so bad with a cold, and physicked and all – '

'Devil take the horse!' cried the gentleman – 'Well, tell him I'll think about it,' he added, after a moment's reflection. He cast a searching glance at me, as the servant withdrew, expecting to see some token of deep astonishment and alarm; but, being previously prepared, I preserved an aspect of stoical indifference. His countenance fell as he met my steady gaze, and he turned away in very obvious disappointment, and walked up to the fireplace, where he stood in an attitude of undisguised dejection, leaning against the chimney-piece with his forehead sunk upon his arm.

'Where do you want to go, Arthur?' said I.

'To London,' replied he, gravely.

'What for?' I asked.

'Because I cannot be happy here.'

'Why not?'

'Because my wife doesn't love me.'

'She would love you with all her heart, if you deserved it.'

'What must I do to deserve it?'

This seemed humble and earnest enough; and I was so much affected, between sorrow and joy, that I was obliged to pause a few seconds before I could steady my voice to reply.

'If she gives you her heart,' said I, 'you must take it thankfully, and use it well, and not pull it in pieces, and laugh in her face, because she cannot snatch it away.'

He now turned round and stood facing me, with his back to the fire.

'Come then, Helen, are you going to be a good girl?' said he.

This sounded rather too arrogant, and the smile that accompanied it did not please me. I therefore hesitated to reply. Perhaps, my former answer had implied too much: he had heard my voice falter, and might have seen me brush away a tear.

'Are you going to forgive me, Helen?' he resumed, more humbly.

'Are *you* penitent?' I replied, stepping up to him and smiling in his face.

'Heart-broken!' he answered, with a rueful countenance – yet with a merry smile just lurking within his eyes and about the corners of his mouth; but this could not repulse me, and I flew into his arms. He fervently embraced me and though I shed a torrent of tears, I think I never was happier in my life than at that moment.

'Then you won't go to London, Arthur?' I said, when the first transport of tears and kisses had subsided.

'No, love – unless you will go with me.'

'I will, gladly,' I answered, 'if you think the change will amuse you, and if you will put off the journey till next week.'

He readily consented, but said there was no need of much preparation, as he should not be for staying long, for he did not wish me to be Londonised, and to lose my country freshness and originality by too much intercourse with the ladies of the world. I thought this folly; but I did not wish to contradict him now: I merely said that I was of very domestic habits, as he well knew, and had no particular wish to mingle with the world.

So we are to go to London on Monday, the day after tomorrow. It is now four days since the termination of our quarrel, and I'm sure it has done us both good: it has made me like Arthur a great deal better and made him behave a great deal better to me. He has never once attempted to annoy me, since, by the most distant allusion to Lady F— or any of those disagreeable reminiscences of his former life – I wish I could blot them from my memory, or else get him to regard such matters in the same light as I do. Well! It is something, however, to have made him see that they are not fit subjects for a conjugal jest. He may see farther sometime – I will put no limits to my hopes; and, in spite of my aunt's forebodings and my own unspoken fears, I trust we shall be happy yet.

## CHAPTER 25

### *First Absence*

On the eighth of April, we went to London; on the eighth of May I returned, in obedience to Arthur's wish: very much against my own, because I left him behind. If he had come with me, I should have been very glad to get home again, for he led me such a round of restless dissipation, while there, that, in that short space of time, I was quite tired out. He seemed bent upon displaying me to his friends and acquaintances in particular, and the public in general, on every possible occasion and to the greatest possible advantage. It was something to feel that he considered me a worthy object of pride; but I paid dear for the gratification, for in the first place, to please him, I had to violate my cherished predilections – my almost rooted principles in favour of a plain, dark, sober style of dress; I must sparkle in costly jewels and deck myself out like a painted butterfly, just as I had, long since, determined I would never do – and this was

no trifling sacrifice; in the second place, I was continually straining to satisfy his sanguine expectations and do honour to his choice, by my general conduct and deportment, and fearing to disappoint him by some awkward misdemeanour, or some trait of inexperienced ignorance about the customs of society, especially when I acted the part of hostess, which I was not unfrequently called upon to do; and in the third place, as I intimated before, I was wearied of the throng and bustle, the restless hurry and ceaseless change of a life so alien to all my previous habits. At last, he suddenly discovered that the London air did not agree with me, and I was languishing for my country home and must immediately return to Grassdale.

I laughingly assured him that the case was not so urgent as he appeared to think it, but I was quite willing to go home if he was. He replied that he should be obliged to remain a week or two longer, as he had business that required his presence.

'Then I will stay with you,' said I.

'But I can't do with you, Helen,' was his answer: 'as long as you stay, I shall attend to you and neglect my business.'

'But I won't let you,' I returned: 'now that I know you have business to attend to, I shall insist upon your attending to it, and letting me alone – and, to tell you the truth, I shall be glad of a little rest. I can take my rides and walks in the park as usual; and your business cannot occupy all your time; I shall see you at mealtimes and in the evenings, at least, and that will be better than being leagues away and never seeing you at all.'

'But, my love, I cannot let you stay. How can I settle my affairs when I know that you are here, neglected – '

'I shall not feel myself neglected: while you are doing your duty, Arthur, I shall never complain of neglect. If you had told me, before, that you had anything to do, it would have been half done before this; and now you must make up for lost time by redoubled exertions. Tell me what it is; and I will be your taskmaster, instead of being a hindrance.'

'No, no,' persisted the impracticable creature; 'you *must* go home, Helen; I must have the satisfaction of knowing that you are safe and well, though far away. Don't I see that you are looking quite rakish? – Your bright eyes are faded, and that tender, delicate bloom has quite deserted your cheek.'

'That is only with too much gaiety and fatigue.'

'It is not, I tell you; it is the London air: you are pining for the fresh breezes of your country home – and you shall feel them, before you are two days older. And remember your situation, dearest Helen; on your health, you know, depends the health, if not the life of our future hope.'

'Then you really wish to get rid of me?'

'Positively, I do; and I will take you down myself to Grassdale, and then return. I shall not be absent above a week – or fortnight at most.'

'But if I must go, I will go alone: if you must stay, it is needless to waste your time in the journey there and back.'

But he did not like the idea of sending me alone.

'Why, what helpless creature do you take me for,' I replied, 'that you cannot trust me to go a hundred miles in our own carriage with our own footman and maid to attend me? If you come with me I shall assuredly keep you. But tell me, Arthur, what *is* this tiresome business; and why did you never mention it before?'

'It is only a little business with my lawyer,' said he; and he told me something about a piece of property he wanted to sell in order to pay off a part of the encumbrances on his estate; but either the account was a little confused or I was rather dull of comprehension, for I could not clearly understand how that should keep him in town a fortnight after me. Still less can I now comprehend how it should keep him a month – for it is nearly that time since I left him, and no signs of his return as yet. In every letter he promises to be with me in a few days, and every time deceives me – or deceives himself. His excuses are vague and insufficient. I cannot doubt that he is got among his former companions again – oh, why did I leave him? I wish – I do intensely wish he would return!

June 29th. No Arthur yet; and for many days I have been looking and longing in vain for a letter. His letters, when they come, are kind – if fair words and endearing epithets can give them a claim to the title – but very short, and full of trivial excuses and promises that I cannot trust; and yet how anxiously I look forward to them! How eagerly I open and devour one of those little, hastily scribbled returns for the three or four long letters, hitherto unanswered, he has had from me!

Oh, it is cruel to leave me so long alone! He knows I have no one but Rachel to speak to, for we have no neighbours here, except the Hargraves, whose residence I can dimly descry from these upper windows embosomed among those low, woody hills beyond the Dale. I was glad when I learnt that Milicent was so near us; and her company would be a soothing solace to me now, but she is still in town with her mother: there is no one at the Grove but little Esther and her French governess, for Walter is always away. I saw that paragon of manly perfections in London: he seemed scarcely to merit the eulogiums of his mother and sister, though he certainly appeared more conversable and agreeable than Lord Lowborough, more candid and high-minded than Mr Grimsby, and more polished and gentlemanly than Mr Hattersley, Arthur's only other friend whom he judged fit to introduce to me – O Arthur, why won't you come! Why won't you write to me at least! You talked about my health – how can you expect me to gather bloom and vigour here; pining in solitude and restless anxiety from day to day? – It would serve you right to come back and find my good looks entirely wasted away. I would beg my uncle and aunt, or my brother to come and see me, but I do not like to complain of my loneliness to them – and indeed, loneliness is the least of my sufferings; but what is he doing – what is it that keeps him away? It is this ever-recurring question and the horrible suggestions it raises that distract me.

July 3rd. My last bitter letter has wrung from him an answer at last – and a rather longer one than usual; but still, I don't know what to make of it. He

playfully abuses me for the gall and vinegar of my latest effusion, tells me I can have no conception of the multitudinous engagements that keep him away, but avers that, in spite of them all, he will assuredly be with me before the close of next week; though it is impossible for a man, so circumstanced as he is, to fix the precise day of his return: meantime, he exhorts me to the exercise of patience, 'that first of woman's virtues,' and desires me to remember the saying, 'Absence makes the heart grow fonder,' and comfort myself with the assurance that the longer he stays away, the better he shall love me when he returns; and till he does return, he begs I will continue to write to him constantly, for, though he is sometimes too idle and often too busy to answer my letters as they come, he likes to receive them daily, and if I fulfil my threat of punishing his seeming neglect by ceasing to write, he shall be so angry that he will do his utmost to forget me. He adds this piece of intelligence respecting poor Milicent Hargrave – 'Your little friend Milicent is likely, before long, to follow your example, and take upon her the yoke of matrimony in conjunction with a friend of mine. Hattersley, you know, has not yet fulfilled his direful threat of throwing his precious person away on the first old maid that chose to evince a tenderness for him; but he still preserves a resolute determination to see himself a married man before the year is out: "Only," said he to me, "I must have somebody that will let me have my own way in everything – not like *your* wife, Huntingdon, she is a charming creature, but she looks as if she had a will of her own, and could play the vixen upon occasion" (I thought "you're right there, man," but I didn't say so). "I must have some good, quiet soul that will let me just do what I like and go where I like, keep at home or stay away, without a word of reproach or complaint; for I can't do with being bothered." "Well," said I. "I know some-body that will suit you to a tee, if you don't care for money, and that's Hargrave's sister, Milicent." He desired to be introduced to her forthwith, for he said he had plenty of the needful himself – or should have, when his old governor chose to quit the stage. So you see, Helen, I have managed pretty well, both for your friend and mine.'

Poor Milicent! But I cannot imagine she will ever be led to accept such a suitor – one so repugnant to all her ideas of a man to be honoured and loved.

5th. Alas! I was mistaken. I have got a long letter from her this morning, telling me she is already engaged, and expects to be married before the close of the month.

'I hardly know what to say about it,' she writes, 'or what to think. To tell you the truth, Helen, I don't like the thoughts of it at all. If I *am* to be Mr Hattersley's wife, I must try to love him; and I do try with all my might; but I have made very little progress yet; and the worst symptom of the case is, that the further he is from me the better I like him: he frightens me with his abrupt manners and strange hectoring ways, and I dread the thoughts of marrying him. "Then why have you accepted him?" you will ask; and I didn't know I had accepted him; but mamma tells me I have, and he seems to think so too. I certainly didn't mean to do so; but I did not like to give him a flat refusal for fear

mamma should be grieved and angry (for I knew she wished me to marry him), and I wanted to talk to her first about it, so I gave him what *I* thought was an evasive, half negative answer; but she says it was as good as an acceptance, and be would think me very capricious if I were to attempt to draw back – and indeed, I was so confused and frightened at the moment, I can hardly tell what I said. And next time I saw him, he accosted me in all confidence as his affianced bride, and immediately began to settle matters with mamma. I had not courage to contradict them then, and how can I do it now? I cannot: they would think me mad. Besides, mamma is so delighted with the idea of the match; she thinks she has managed so well for me; and I cannot bear to disappoint her. I do object sometimes, and tell her what I feel, but you don't know *how* she talks. Mr Hattersley, you know, is the son of a rich banker, and as Esther and I have no fortunes and Walter very little, our dear mamma is very anxious to see us all well married, that is, united to rich partners – it is not *my* idea of being well married, but she means it all for the best. She says when I am safe off her hands it will be such a relief to her mind; and she assures me it will be a good thing for the family as well as for me. Even Walter is pleased at the prospect, and when I confessed my reluctance to him, be said it was all childish nonsense. Do *you* think it nonsense, Helen? I should not care if I could see any prospect of being able to love and admire him, but I can't. There is nothing about him to hang one's esteem and affection upon: he is so diametrically opposite to what I imagined my husband should be. Do write to me, and say all you can to encourage me. Don't attempt to dissuade me, for my fate is fixed: preparations for the important event are already going on around me; and don't say a word against Mr Hattersley, for I want to think well of him; and though I have spoken against him myself, it is for the last time: hereafter, I shall never permit myself to utter a word in his dispraise, however he may seem to deserve it; and whoever ventures to speak slightingly of the man I have promised to love, to honour, and obey, must expect my serious displeasure. After all, I think he is quite as good as Mr Huntingdon, if not better; and yet, you love *him*, and seem to be happy and contented; and perhaps I may manage as well. You must tell me, if you can, that Mr Hattersley is better than he seems – that he is upright, honourable, and open-hearted – in fact, a perfect diamond in the rough. He may be all this, but I don't know him – I know only the exterior and what I trust is the worst part of him.'

She concludes with, 'Goodbye, dear Helen, I am waiting anxiously for your advice – but mind you let it be all on the right side.'

Alas! poor Milicent, what encouragement can I give you? – or what advice – except that it is better to make a bold stand now, though at the expense of disappointing and angering both mother and brother, and lover, than to devote your whole life, hereafter, to misery and vain regret?

Saturday, 13th. The week is over, and he is not come. All the sweet summer is passing away without one breath of pleasure to me or benefit to him. And I had all along been looking forward to this season with the fond, delusive hope that

we should enjoy it so sweetly together; and that, with God's help and my exertions, it would be the means of elevating his mind, and refining his taste to a due appreciation of the salutary and pure delights of nature, and peace, and holy love. But now – at evening, when I see the round, red sun sink quietly down behind those woody hills, leaving them sleeping in a warm, red, golden haze, I only think another lovely day is lost to him and me – and at morning, when roused by the flutter and chirp of the sparrows, and the gleeful twitter of the swallows – all intent upon feeding their young, and full of life and joy in their own little frames – I open the window to inhale the balmy, soul-reviving air, and look out upon the lovely landscape, laughing in dew and sunshine – I too often shame that glorious scene with tears of thankless misery, because *he* cannot feel its freshening influence; and when I wander in the ancient woods, and meet the little wild-flowers smiling in my path, or sit in the shadow of our noble ash trees by the waterside, with their branches gently swaying in the light summer breeze that murmurs through their feathery foliage – my ears full of that low music mingled with the dreamy hum of insects, my eyes abstractedly gazing on the glassy surface of the little lake before me, with the trees that crowd about its bank, some gracefully bending to kiss its waters, some rearing their stately heads high above, but stretching their wide arms over its margin, all faithfully mirrored far, far down in its glassy depth – though sometimes the images are partially broken by the sport of aquatic insects, and sometimes, for a moment, the whole is shivered into trembling fragments by a transient breeze that swept the surface too roughly – still I have no pleasure; for the greater the happiness that nature sets before me, the more I lament that *he* is not here to taste it: the greater the bliss we might enjoy together, the more I feel our present wretchedness apart (yes, ours; he must be wretched, though he may not know it); and the more my senses are pleased, the more my heart is oppressed; for he keeps it with him confined amid the dust and smoke of London – perhaps, shut up within the walls of his own abominable club.

But most of all, at night, when I enter my lonely chamber, and look out upon the summer moon, 'sweet regent of the sky,' floating above me in the 'black blue vault of heaven,' shedding a flood of silver radiance over park, and wood, and water, so pure, so peaceful, so divine – and think, Where is he now? – what is he doing at this moment? – wholly unconscious of this heavenly scene – perhaps, revelling with his boon companions, perhaps – God help me, it is too – *too* much!

23rd. Thank heaven, he is come at last! But how altered! – flushed and feverish, listless and languid, his beauty strangely diminished, his vigour and vivacity quite departed. I have not upbraided him by word or look; I have not even asked him what he has been doing. I have not the heart to do it, for I think he is ashamed of himself – he must be so indeed – and such enquiries could not fail to be painful to both. My forbearance pleases him – touches him even, I am inclined to think. He says he is glad to be home again, and God knows how glad I am to get him back, even as he is. He lies on the sofa nearly all day long;

and I play and sing to him for hours together. I write his letters for him, and get him everything he wants; and sometimes I read to him, and sometimes I talk, and sometimes only sit by him and soothe him with silent caresses. I know he does not deserve it; and I fear I am spoiling him; but this once, I will forgive him, freely and entirely – I will shame him into virtue if I can, and I will never let him leave me again.

He is pleased with my attentions – it may be, grateful for them. He likes to have me near him; and though he is peevish and testy with his servants and his dogs, he is gentle and kind to me. What he would be, if I did not so watchfully anticipate his wants, and so carefully avoid, or immediately desist from doing anything that has a tendency to irritate or disturb him, with however little reason, I cannot tell. How intensely I wish he were worthy of all this care! Last night as I sat beside him, with his head in my lap, passing my fingers through his beautiful curls, this thought made my eyes overflow with sorrowful tears – as it often does – but this time, a tear fell on his face and made him look up. He smiled, but not insultingly.

'Dear Helen!' he said – 'why do you cry? You know that I love you' (and he pressed my hand to his feverish lips), 'and what more could you desire?'

'Only, Arthur, that you would love *yourself*, as truly and as faithfully as you are loved by me.'

'That would be hard indeed!' he replied, tenderly squeezing my hand.

I don't know whether he fully understood my meaning, but he smiled – thoughtfully and even sadly – a most unusual thing with him; and then he closed his eyes and fell asleep, looking as careless and sinless as a child. As I watched that placid slumber, my heart swelled fuller than ever, and my tears flowed unrestrained.

August 24th. Arthur is himself again, as lusty and reckless, as light of heart and head as ever, and as restless and hard to amuse as a spoilt child – and almost as full of mischief too, especially when wet weather keeps him within doors. I wish he had something to do, some useful trade, or profession, or employment – anything to occupy his head or his hands for a few hours a day, and give him something besides his own pleasure to think about. If he would play the country gentleman, and attend to the farm – but that he knows nothing about, and won't give his mind to consider – or if he would take up with some literary study, or learn to draw or to play – as he is so fond of music, I often try to persuade him to learn the piano, but he is far too idle for such an undertaking: he has no more idea of exerting himself to overcome obstacles than he has of restraining his natural appetites; and these two things are the ruin of him. I lay them both to the charge of his harsh yet careless father and his madly indulgent mother. If ever I am a mother I will zealously strive against this *crime* of over indulgence – I can hardly give it a milder name when I think of the evils it brings.

Happily, it will soon be the shooting season, and then, if the weather permit, he will find occupation enough in the pursuit and destruction of the partridges and pheasants: we have no grouse, or he might have been similarly occupied at

this moment, instead of lying under the acacia tree pulling poor Dash's ears. But he says it is dull work shooting alone; he must have a friend or two to help him.

'Let them be tolerably decent then, Arthur,' said I. The word 'friend', in his mouth makes me shudder: I know it was some of his 'friends' that induced him to stay behind me in London, and kept him away so long – indeed, from what he has unguardedly told me, or hinted from time to time, I cannot doubt that he frequently showed them my letters, to let them see how fondly his wife watched over his interests and how keenly she regretted his absence; and that they induced him to remain week after week, and to plunge into all manner of excesses to avoid being laughed at for a wife-ridden fool, and, perhaps, to show how far he could venture to go without danger of shaking the fond creature's devoted attachment. It is a hateful idea, but I cannot believe it is a false one.

'Well,' replied he, 'I thought of Lord Lowborough for one; but there is no possibility of getting him without his better half, our mutual friend Annabella; so we must ask them both. You're not afraid of her, are you, Helen?' he asked, with a mischievous twinkle in his eyes.

'Of course not,' I answered: 'why should I – And who besides?'

'Hargrave for one – he will be glad to come, though his own place is so near, for he has little enough land of his own to shoot over, and we can extend our depredations into it, if we like; and he is thoroughly respectable, you know, Helen, quite a lady's man – and I think, Grimsby for another: he's a decent, quiet fellow enough – you'll not object to Grimsby?'

'I hate him; but, however, if you wish it, I'll try to endure his presence for a while.'

'All a prejudice, Helen – a mere woman's antipathy.'

'No; I have solid grounds for my dislike. And is that all?'

'Why, yes, I think so. Hattersley will be too busy billing and cooing with his bride to have much time to spare for guns and dogs, at present,' he replied – And that reminds me that I have had several letters from Milicent since her marriage, and that she either is or pretends to be quite reconciled to her lot. She professes to have discovered numberless virtues and perfections in her husband, some of which, I fear, less partial eyes would fail to distinguish, though they sought them carefully with tears; and now that she is accustomed to his loud voice and abrupt, uncourteous manners, she affirms she finds no difficulty in loving him as a wife should do, and begs I will burn that letter wherein she spoke so unadvisedly against him. So that I trust she may yet be happy; but if she is, it will be entirely the reward of her own goodness of heart; for had she chosen to consider herself the victim of fate, or of her mother's wordly wisdom, she might have been thoroughly miserable; and, if, for duty's sake, she had not made every effort to love her husband, she would doubtless have hated him to the end of her days.

CHAPTER 26

*The Guests*

September 23rd. Our guests arrived about three weeks ago. Lord and Lady
Lowborough have now been married above eight months; and I will do the lady
the credit to say that her husband is quite an altered man: his looks, his spirits,
and his temper are all perceptibly changed for the better since I last saw him.
But there is room for improvement still. He is not always cheerful nor always
contented, and she often complains of his ill-humour, which, however, of all
persons, *she* ought to be the last to accuse him of, as he never displays it against
her, except for such conduct as would provoke a saint. He adores her still, and
would go to the world's end to please her. She knows her power, and she uses it
too; but well knowing that to wheedle and coax is safer than to command, she
judiciously tempers her despotism with flattery and blandishments enough to
make him deem himself a favoured and a happy man. And yet, at times, a
sombre shadow overclouds his brow even in her presence, but evidently the
result of despondency rather than of ill-humour, and generally occasioned by
some display of her ill-regulated temper or misguided mind – some wanton
trampling upon his most cherished opinions – some reckless disregard of princi-
ple that makes him bitterly regret that she is not as good as she is charming and
beloved. I pity him from my heart, for I know the misery of such regrets.

But she has another way of tormenting him, in which I am a fellow sufferer – or
might be, if I chose to regard myself as such. This is by openly but not too
glaringly coquetting with Mr Huntingdon, who is quite willing to be her partner
in the game; but I don't care for it, because with him, I know there is nothing but
personal vanity and a mischievous desire to excite my jealousy, and perhaps to
torment his friend; and she, no doubt, is actuated by much the same motives; only
there is more of malice and less of playfulness in *her* manoeuvres. It is obviously,
therefore, my interest to disappoint them both, as far as I am concerned, by
preserving a cheerful, undisturbed serenity throughout; and accordingly I endeav-
our to show the fullest confidence in my husband and the greatest indifference to
the arts of my attractive guest. I have never reproached the former but once, and
that was for laughing at Lord Lowborough's depressed and anxious countenance
one evening, when they had both been particularly provoking; and then, indeed, I
said a good deal on the subject, and rebuked him sternly enough; but he only
laughed, and said – 'You can feel for him, Helen – can't you?'

'I can feel for anyone that is unjustly treated,' I replied, 'and I can feel for
those that injure them too.'

'Why, Helen, you are as jealous as he is!' cried he, laughing still more; and I
found it impossible to convince him of his mistake. So from that time I have
carefully refrained from any notice of the subject whatever, and left Lord

Lowborough to take care of himself. He either has not the sense or the power to follow my example, though he does try to conceal his uneasiness as well as he can; but still, it will appear in his face, and his ill-humour will peep out at intervals, though not in the expression of open resentment – they never go far enough for that. But I confess I do feel jealous at times – most painfully, bitterly so – when she sings and plays to him, and he hangs over the instrument and dwells upon her voice with no affected interest; for then, I know he is really delighted, and I have no power to awaken similar fervour. I can amuse and please him with my simple songs, but not delight him thus.

I might retaliate if I chose, for Mr Hargrave is disposed to be very polite and attentive to me as his hostess – especially so when Arthur is the most neglectful, whether in mistaken compassion for me, or ambitious to show off his own good breeding by comparison with his friend's remissness, I cannot tell; but in either case, his civilities are highly distasteful to me. If Arthur is a little careless, of course it is unpleasant to have the fault exaggerated by contrast; and to be pitied as a neglected wife when I am not such, is an insult I can ill endure. But for hospitality's sake, I endeavour to suppress my impulse of scarcely reasonable resentment, and behave with decent civility to our guest, who, to give him his due, is by no means a disagreeable companion: he has good conversational powers and considerable information and taste, and talks about things that Arthur never could be brought to discuss, or to feel any interest in. But Arthur dislikes me to talk to him, and is visibly annoyed by his commonest acts of politeness; not that my husband has any unworthy suspicions of me – or of his friend either, as I believe – but he dislikes me to have any pleasure but in himself, any shadow of homage or kindness but such as he chooses to vouchsafe: he knows he is my sun, but when he chooses to withhold his light, he would have my sky to be all darkness; he cannot bear that I should have a moon to mitigate the deprivation. This is unjust; and I am sometimes tempted to tease him accordingly; but I won't yield to the temptation: if he should carry his trifling with my feelings too far, I shall find some other means of checking him.

28th. Yesterday we all went to the Grove, Mr Hargrave's much neglected home. His mother frequently asks us over that she may have the pleasure of her dear Walter's company; and this time she had invited us to a dinner party, and got together as many of the country gentry as were within reach to meet us. The entertainment was very well got up; but I could not help thinking about the cost of it all the time. I don't like Mrs Hargrave; she is a hard, pretentious, worldly-minded woman. She has money enough to live very comfortably, if she only knew how to use it judiciously, and had taught her son to do the same; but she is ever straining to keep up appearances, with that despicable pride that shuns the semblance of poverty as of a shameful crime. She grinds her dependants, pinches her servants, and deprives even her daughters and herself of the real comforts of life, because she will not consent to yield the palm in outward show to those who have three times her wealth, and, above all, because she is determined her cherished son shall be enabled to "hold up his head with the

highest gentleman in the land". This same son, I imagine, is a man of expensive habits – no reckless spendthrift, and no abandoned sensualist, but one who likes to have "everything handsome about him", and to go to a certain length in youthful indulgences – not so much to gratify his own tastes as to maintain his reputation as a man of fashion in the world, and a respectable fellow among his own lawless companions; while he is too selfish to consider how many comforts might be obtained for his fond mother and sisters with the money he thus wastes upon himself: as long as they can contrive to make a respectable appearance once a year when they come to town, he gives himself little concern about their private stintings and struggles at home. This is a harsh judgement to form of "dear, noble-minded, generous-hearted Walter", but I fear it is too just.

Mrs Hargrave's anxiety to make good matches for her daughters is partly the cause and partly the result of these errors: by making a figure in the world and showing them off to advantage, she hopes to obtain better chances for them; and by thus living beyond her legitimate means and lavishing so much on their brother, she renders them portionless, and makes them burdens on her hands. Poor Milicent, I fear, has already fallen a sacrifice to the manœuvrings of this mistaken mother, who congratulates herself on having so satisfactorily discharged her maternal duty, and hopes to do as well for Esther. But Esther is a child as yet – a little merry romp of fourteen: as honest-hearted, and as guileless and simple as her sister, but with a fearless spirit of her own, that I fancy, her mother will find some difficulty in bending to her purposes.

## CHAPTER 27

### *A Misdemeanour*

October 9th. While the gentlemen are ranging the woods and Lady Lowborough is busy writing her letters, I will return to my chronicle for the purpose of recording sayings and doings, the last of the kind I hope I shall ever have cause to describe.

It was on the night of the 4th, a little after tea, that Annabella had been singing and playing, with Arthur as usual at her side: she had ended her song, but still she sat at the instrument; and he stood leaning on the back of her chair, conversing in scarcely audible tones, with his face in very close proximity with hers. I looked at Lord Lowborough. He was at the other end of the room, talking with Messrs Hargrave and Grimsby; but I saw him dart towards his lady and his host, a quick, impatient glance, expressive of intense disquietude, at which Grimsby smiled. Determined to interrupt the tête-à-tête, I rose, and selecting a piece of music from the music-stand, stepped up to the piano, intending to ask the lady to play it; but I stood transfixed and speechless on seeing her seated there, listening with what seemed an exultant smile on her flushed face, to his soft murmurings, with her hand quietly surrendered to his

clasp. The blood rushed first to my heart and then to my head – for there was more than this; almost at the moment of my approach, he cast a hurried glance over his shoulder towards the other occupants of the room, and then ardently pressed the unresisting hand to his lips. On raising his eyes he beheld me and dropped them again, confounded and dismayed. She saw me too, and confronted me with a look of hard defiance. I laid the music on the piano, and retired. I felt ill; but I did not leave the room: happily, it was getting late and could not be long before the company dispersed. I went to the fire and leant my head against the chimney-piece. In a minute or two, someone asked me if I felt unwell. I did not answer – indeed, at the time I knew not what was said – but I mechanically looked up, and saw Mr Hargrave standing beside me on the rug.

'Shall I get you a glass of wine?' said he.

'No, thank you,' I replied; and turning from him, I looked round. Lady Lowborough was beside her husband, bending over him as he sat, with her hand on his shoulder, softly talking and smiling in his face; and Arthur was at the table turning over a book of engravings. I seated myself in the nearest chair; and Mr Hargrave, finding his services were not desired, judiciously withdrew. Shortly after, the company broke up, and as the guests were retiring to their rooms, Arthur approached me, smiling with the utmost assurance.

'Are you *very* angry, Helen?' murmured he.

'This is no jest, Arthur,' said I seriously, but as calmly as I could – 'unless you think it a jest to lose my affection for ever.'

'What! So bitter?' he exclaimed, laughingly clasping my hand between both his; but I snatched it away, in indignation – almost in disgust, for he was obviously affected with wine.

'Then I must go down on my knees,' said he; and kneeling before me with clasped hands uplifted in mock humiliation, he continued imploringly – 'Forgive me, Helen! – dear Helen, forgive me, and I'll *never* do it again!' and burying his face in his handkerchief, he affected to sob aloud.

Leaving him thus employed, I took my candle, and slipping quietly from the room, hastened upstairs as fast as I could. But he soon discovered that I had left him, and rushing up after me, caught me in his arms, just as I had entered the chamber, and was about to shut the door in his face.

'No, no, by Heaven, you shan't escape me so!' he cried. Then, alarmed at my agitation, he begged me not to put myself in such a passion, telling me I was white in the face, and should kill myself if I did so.

'Let me go then,' I murmured; and immediately he released me – and it was well he did, for I was really in a passion. I sunk into the easy-chair and endeavoured to compose myself, for I wanted to speak to him calmly. He stood beside me, but did not venture to touch me or to speak, for a few seconds; then approaching a little nearer, he dropped on one knee – not in mock humility, but to bring himself nearer my level, and leaning his hand on the arm of the chair, he began in a low voice – 'It is all nonsense, Helen – a jest, a mere nothing – not worth a thought. Will you *never* learn?' he continued more boldly, 'that you have nothing to fear from me? That I love you wholly and

entirely? – or if,' he added with a lurking smile, 'I ever give a thought to another you may well spare it, for those fancies are here and gone like a flash of lightning, while my love for you burns on steadily, and for ever like the sun. You little exorbitant tyrant, will not *that* – '

'Be quiet a moment, will you, Arthur,' said I, 'and listen to me – and don't think I'm in a jealous fury: I am perfectly calm. Feel my hand.' And I gravely extended it towards him – but closed it upon his with an energy that seemed to disprove the assertion, and made him smile. 'You needn't smile, sir,' said I, still tightening my grasp, and looking steadfastly on him till he almost quailed before me. 'You may think it all very fine, Mr Huntingdon, to amuse yourself with rousing my jealousy; but take care you don't rouse my hate instead. And when you have once extinguished my love, you will find it no easy matter to kindle it again.'

'Well, Helen, I won't repeat the offence. But I meant nothing by it, I assure you. I had taken too much wine, and I was scarcely myself, at the time.'

'You often take too much; and that is another practice I detest.' He looked up astonished at my warmth. 'Yes,' I continued. 'I never mentioned it before, because I was ashamed to do so; but now I'll tell you that it distresses me, and may disgust me, if you go on and suffer the habit to grow upon you, as it will, if you don't check it in time. But the whole system of your conduct to Lady Lowborough, is not referable to wine; and this night you knew perfectly well what you were doing.'

'Well, I'm sorry for it,' replied he, with more of sulkiness than contrition: 'what more would you have?'

'You are sorry that I saw you, no doubt,' I answered coldly.

'If you had not seen me,' he muttered, fixing his eyes on the carpet, 'it would have done no harm.'

My heart felt ready to burst; but I resolutely swallowed back my emotion, and answered calmly, 'You think not?'

'No,' replied he, boldly. 'After all, what have I done? It's nothing – except as you choose to make it a subject of accusation and distress.'

'What would Lord Lowborough, your *friend* think, if he knew all? Or what would you yourself think, if he or any other had acted the same part to me, throughout, as you have to Annabella?'

'I would blow his brains out.'

'Well then, Arthur, how can you call it nothing – an offence for which you would think yourself justified in blowing another man's brains out? Is it nothing to trifle with your friend's feelings and mine – to endeavour to steal a woman's affections from her husband – what he values more than his gold, and therefore what it is more dishonest to take? Are the marriage vows a jest; and is it nothing to make it your sport to break them, and to tempt another to do the same? Can I love a man that does such things, and coolly maintains it is nothing?'

'You are breaking your marriage vows yourself,' said he, indignantly rising and pacing to and fro. 'You promised to honour and obey me, and now you attempt to hector over me, and threaten and accuse me and call me worse than a

highwayman. If it were not for your situation Helen, I would not submit to it so tamely. I won't be dictated to by a woman, though she be my wife.'

'What will you do then? Will you go on till I hate you; and then accuse me of breaking my vows?'

He was silent a moment, and then replied,

'You never will hate me.' Returning and resuming his former position at my feet, he repeated more vehemently – 'You cannot hate me, as long as I love you.'

'But how can I believe that you love me, if you continue to act in this way? Just imagine yourself in my place: would *you* think I loved *you*, if *I* did so? Would you believe my protestations, and honour and trust me under such circumstances?'

'The cases are different,' he replied. 'It is a woman's nature to be constant – to love one and one only, blindly, tenderly, and for ever – bless them, dear creatures! and you above them all – but you must have some commiseration for us, Helen; you must give us a little more licence, for as Shakespeare has it –

> However we do praise ourselves,
> Our fancies are more giddy and unfirm,
> More longing, wavering, sooner lost and won
> Than women's are.'

'Do you mean by that, that your fancies are lost to me, and won by Lady Lowborough?'

'No; Heaven is my witness that I think her mere dust and ashes in comparison with you – and shall continue to think so, unless you drive me from you by too much severity. She is a daughter of earth; you are an angel of Heaven; only be not too austere in your divinity, and remember that I am a poor, fallible mortal. Come now, Helen; won't you forgive me?' he said, gently taking my hand, and looking up with an innocent smile.

'If I do, you will repeat the offence.'

'I swear by –'

'Don't swear; I'll believe your word as well as your oath. I wish I could have confidence in either.'

'Try me then, Helen: only trust and pardon me this once, and you shall see! Come, I am in Hell's torments till you speak the word.'

I did not speak it, but I put my hand on his shoulder and kissed his forehead, and then burst into tears. He embraced me tenderly; and we have been good friends ever since. He has been decently temperate at table, and well-conducted towards Lady Lowborough. The first day he held himself aloof from her, as far as he could without any flagrant breach of hospitality: since that, he has been friendly and civil but nothing more – in my presence, at least, nor, I think, at any other time; for she seems haughty and displeased, and Lord Lowborough is manifestly more cheerful, and more cordial towards his host than before. But I shall be glad when they are gone, for I have so little love for Annabella that it is quite a task to be civil to her, and as she is the only woman here besides myself, we are necessarily thrown so much together. Next time Mrs Hargrave calls, I shall hail her advent as quite a relief. I have a good mind to ask Arthur's leave to

invite the old lady to stay with us till our guests depart. I think I will. She will take it as a kind attention, and, though I have little relish for her society, she will be truly welcome as a third to stand between Lady Lowborough and me.

The first time the latter and I were alone together, after that unhappy evening, was an hour or two after breakfast on the following day, when the gentlemen were gone out after the usual time spent in the writing of letters, the reading of newspapers, and desultory conversation. We sat silent for two or three minutes. She was busy with her work and I was running over the columns of a paper from which I had extracted all the pith some twenty minutes before. It was a moment of painful embarrassment to me, and I thought it must be infinitely more so to her; but it seems I was mistaken. She was the first to speak; and, smiling with the coolest assurance, she began – 'Your husband was merry last night, Helen: is he often so?'

My blood boiled in my face; but it was better she should seem to attribute his conduct to this than to anything else.

'No,' replied I, 'and never will be so again I trust.'

'You gave him a curtain lecture, did you?'

'No; but I told him I disliked such conduct, and he promised me not to repeat it.'

'I *thought* he looked rather subdued this morning,' she continued; 'and you, Helen; you've been weeping I see – that's our grand resource, you know – but doesn't it make your eyes smart? – and do you always find it to answer?'

'I never cry for effect; nor can I conceive how anyone can.'

'Well, I don't know: I never had occasion to try it; but I think if Lowborough were to commit such improprieties, I'd make *him* cry. I don't wonder at your being angry, for I'm sure I'd give my husband a lesson he would not soon forget for a lighter offence than that. But then he never *will* do anything of the kind; for I keep him in too good order for that.'

'Are you sure you don't arrogate too much of the credit to yourself? Lord Lowborough was quite as remarkable for his abstemiousness for some time before you married him as he is now, I have heard.'

'Oh, about the *wine* you mean – yes, he's safe enough for that. And as to looking askance at another woman – he's safe enough for that too, while I live, for he worships the very ground I tread on.'

'Indeed! and are you sure you deserve it?'

'Why, as to that, I can't say: you know we're all fallible creatures, Helen; we none of us deserve to be worshipped. But are *you* sure your darling Huntingdon deserves all the love you give to *him*?'

I knew not what to answer to this. I was burning with anger; but I suppressed all outward manifestations of it, and only bit my lip and pretended to arrange my work.

'At any rate,' resumed she, pursuing her advantage, 'you can console yourself with the assurance that *you* are worthy of all the love he gives to you.'

'You flatter me,' said I; 'but at least, I can try to be worthy of it.' And then I turned the conversation.

## CHAPTER 28

### *Parental Feelings*

December 25th. Last Christmas I was a bride, with a heart overflowing with present bliss, and full of ardent hopes for the future – though not unmingled with foreboding fears. Now I am a wife: my bliss is sobered, but not destroyed; my hopes diminished, but not departed; my fears increased but not yet thoroughly confirmed; and, thank Heaven, I am a mother too. God has sent me a soul to educate for Heaven, and given me a new and calmer bliss, and stronger hopes to comfort me. But where hope rises fear *must* lurk behind, and when I clasp my little darling to my breast, or hang over his slumbers with unutterable delight, and a world of hope within my heart, one of two thoughts is ever at hand to check my swelling bliss; the one: He may be taken from me; the other: He may live to curse his own existence. In the first, I have this consolation: that the bud, though plucked, would not be withered, only transplanted to a fitter soil to ripen and blow beneath a brighter sun; and though I might not cherish and watch my child's unfolding intellect, he would be snatched away from all the suffering and sins of earth; and my understanding tells me this would be no great evil; but my heart shrinks from the contemplation of such a possibility, and whispers I could not bear to see him die, and relinquish to the cold and cruel grave this cherished form, now warm with tender life, flesh of my flesh and shrine of that pure spark which it should be my life's sweet labour to keep unsullied from the world – and ardently implores that Heaven would spare him still, to be my comfort and my joy, and me to be his shield, instructor, friend – to guide him along the perilous path of youth, and train him to be God's servant while on earth, a blessed and honoured saint in Heaven. But in the other case, if he should live to disappoint my hopes, and frustrate all my efforts – to be a slave of sin, the victim of vice and misery, a curse to others and himself – Eternal Father, if Thou beholdest such a life before him, tear him from me now in spite of all my anguish, and take him from my bosom to Thine own, while he is yet a guileless, unpolluted lamb!

My little Arthur! There you lie in sweet, unconscious slumber, the tiny epitome of your father, but stainless yet as that pure snow, new fallen from Heaven – God shield thee from his errors! How will I watch and toil to guard thee from them! He wakes; his tiny arms are stretched towards me; his eyes unclose; they meet my gaze, but will not answer it. Little angel! You do not know me; you cannot think of me or love me yet; and yet how fervently my heart is knit to yours; how grateful I am for all the joy you give me! Would that your father could share it with me – that he could feel my love, my hope, and take an equal part in my resolves and projects for the future – nay, if he could but sympathise in half my views, and share one half my feelings, it would be indeed a

blessing to both himself and me: it would elevate and purify his mind, and bind him closer to his home and me.

Perhaps, he will feel awakening interest and affection for his child as it grows older. At present, he is pleased with the acquisition, and hopes it will become a fine boy and a worthy heir; and that is nearly all I can say. At first, it was a thing to wonder and laugh at, not to touch: now, it is an object almost of indifference, except when his impatience is roused by its "utter helplessness" and "imperturbable stupidity" (as he calls it), or my too close attention to its wants. He frequently comes and sits beside me while I am busied with my maternal cares. I hoped at first it was for the pleasure of contemplating our priceless treasure; but I soon found it was only to enjoy my company, or escape the pains of solitude. He is kindly welcome of course, but the best compliment to a mother is to appreciate her little one. He shocked me very much on one occasion: it was about a fortnight after the birth of our son, and he was with me in the nursery. We had neither of us spoken for some time: I was lost in the contemplation of my nursling, and I thought he was similarly occupied – as far, at least, as I thought about him at all. But suddenly he startled me from my reverie by impatiently exclaiming – 'Helen, I shall positively hate that little wretch, if you worship it so madly! You are absolutely infatuated about it.'

I looked up in astonishment, to see if he could be in earnest.

'You have not a thought to spare for anything else,' he continued in the same strain: 'I may go or come, be present or absent, cheerful or sad; it's all the same to you. As long as you have that ugly little creature to dote upon, you care not a farthing what becomes of me.'

'It is false, Arthur; when you enter the room, it always doubles my happiness; when you are near me, the sense of your presence delights me, though I don't look at you; and when I think about our child, I please myself with the idea that you share my thoughts and feelings, though I don't speak them.'

'How the devil can I waste my thoughts and feelings on a little worthless idiot like that?'

'It is your own son, Arthur – or, if that consideration has no weight with you, it is mine; and you ought to respect my feelings.'

'Well, don't be cross; it was only a slip of the tongue,' pleaded he. 'The little fellow is well enough, only I can't worship him as you do.'

'You shall nurse him for me, as a punishment,' said I, rising to put my baby in its father's arms.

'No, don't, Helen – don't!' cried he, in real disquietude.

'I will: you'll love him better, when you feel the little creature in your arms.'

I deposited the precious burden in his hands, and retreated to the other side of the room, laughing at the ludicrous, half-embarrassed air with which he sat, holding it at arm's length, and looking upon it as if it were some curious being of quite a different species to himself.

'Come, take it, Helen; take it,' he cried at length. 'I shall drop it, if you don't.'

Compassionating his distress – or rather the child's unsafe position, I relieved him of the charge.

'Kiss it, Arthur; do – you've never kissed it yet!' said I, kneeling and present-ing it before him.

'I would rather kiss its mother,' replied he, embracing me. 'There now; won't that do as well?'

I resumed my seat in the easy-chair, and gave my little one a shower of gentle kisses to make up for its other parent's refusal.

'There goes!' cried the jealous father. 'That's more, in one minute, lavished on that little senseless, thankless, oyster, than you have given me these three weeks past.'

'Come here then, you insatiable monopolist, and you shall have as many as you like, incorrigible and undeserving as you are – There now, won't that suffice? I have a good mind never to give you another till you have learnt to love my baby as a father should.'

'I like the little devil – '

'Arthur!'

'Well, the little angel – well enough,' and he pinched its delicate little nose to prove his affection, 'only I can't *love* it – what is there to love? It can't love me – or you either; it can't understand a single word you say to it, or feel one spark of gratitude for all your kindness. Wait till it can show some little affection for me, and then I'll see about loving it. At present it is nothing more than a little selfish, senseless, sensualist, and if *you* see anything adorable in it, it's all very well – I only wonder how you can.'

'If you were less selfish yourself, Arthur, you would not regard it in that light.'

'Possibly not, love; but so it is: there's no help for it.'

## CHAPTER 29

### *The Neighbour*

December 25th, 1823 – Another year is gone. My little Arthur lives and thrives. He is healthy but not robust, full of gentle playfulness and vivacity, already affectionate, and susceptible of passions and emotions it will be long ere he can find words to express. He has won his father's heart at last; and now my constant terror is, lest he should be ruined by that father's thoughtless indulgence. But I must beware of my own weakness too, for I never knew till now how strong are a parent's temptations to spoil an only child.

I have need of consolation in my son, for (to this silent paper I may confess it) I have but little in my husband. I love him still; and he loves me, in his own way – but oh, how different from the love I could have given, and once had hoped to receive! How little real sympathy there exists between us; how many of my thoughts and feelings are gloomily cloistered within my own mind; how much of my higher and better self is indeed unmarried – doomed either to harden and sour in the sunless shade of solitude, or to quite degenerate and fall away for lack

of nutriment in this unwholesome soil! – But, I repeat, I have no right to complain: only let me state the truth – some of the truth at least – and see hereafter, if any darker truths will blot these pages. We have now been full two years united – the "romance" of our attachment must be worn away. Surely I have now got down to the lowest gradation in Arthur's affection, and discovered all the evils of his nature: if there be any further change, it must be for the better, as we become still more accustomed to each other: surely we shall find no lower depth than this. And, if so, I can bear it well – as well, at least, as I have borne it hitherto.

Arthur is not what is commonly called a *bad* man: he has many good qualities; but he is a man without self-restraint or lofty aspirations – a lover of pleasure, given up to animal enjoyments: he is not a bad husband, but his notions of matrimonial duties and comforts are not my notions. Judging from appearances, his idea of a wife, is a thing to love one devotedly and to stay at home – to wait upon her husband, and amuse him and minister to his comfort in every possible way, while he chooses to stay with her; and, when he is absent, to attend to his interests, domestic or otherwise, and patiently wait his return; no matter how he may be occupied in the meantime.

Early in spring, he announced his intention of going to London: his affairs there demanded his attendance, he said, and he could refuse it no longer. He expressed his regret at having to leave me, but hoped I would amuse myself with the baby till he returned.

'But why leave me?' I said. 'I can go with you: I can be ready at any time.'

'You would not take that child to town?'

'Yes – why not?'

The thing was absurd: the air of the town would be certain to disagree with him, and with me as a nurse: the late hours and London habits would not suit me under such circumstances; and altogether he assured me that it would be excessively troublesome, injurious, and unsafe. I overruled his objections as well as I could, for I trembled at the thoughts of his going alone, and would sacrifice almost anything for myself, much even for my child, to prevent it; but at length he told me, plainly, and somewhat testily, that he could not do with me: he was worn out with the baby's restless nights, and must have some repose. I proposed separate apartments; but it would not do.

'The truth is, Arthur,' I said at last, 'you are weary of my company, and determined not to have me with you. You might as well have said so at once.'

He denied it; but I immediately left the room, and flew to the nursery to hide my feelings if I could not soothe them, there.

I was too much hurt to express any further dissatisfaction with his plans, or at all to refer to the subject again, except for the necessary arrangements concerning his departure and the conduct of affairs during his absence – till the day before he went, when I earnestly exhorted him to take care of himself and keep out of the way of temptation. He laughed at my anxiety, but assured me there was no cause for it, and promised to attend to my advice.

'I suppose it is no use asking you to fix a day for your return?' said I.

'Why, no: I hardly can, under the circumstances; but be assured, love, I shall not be long away.'

'I don't wish to keep you a prisoner at home,' I replied: 'I should not grumble at your staying whole months away – if you can be happy so long without me – provided I knew you were safe; but I don't like the idea of your being there, among your friends, as you call them.'

'Pooh, pooh, you silly girl! Do you think I can't take care of myself?'

'You didn't last time – But this time, Arthur,' I added, earnestly, 'show me that you can, and teach me that I need not fear to trust you!'

He promised fair, but in such a manner as we seek to soothe a child. And did he keep his promise? No; and, henceforth, *I can never trust his word*. Bitter, bitter confession! Tears blind me while I write. It was early in March that he went, and he did not return till July. This time, he did not trouble himself to make excuses as before, and his letters were less frequent, and shorter and less affectionate, especially after the first few weeks: they came slower and slower, and more terse and careless every time. But still, when *I* omitted writing he complained of my neglect. When I wrote sternly and coldly, as I confess I frequently did at the last, he blamed my harshness, and said it was enough to scare him from his home: when I tried mild persuasion, he was a little more gentle in his replies, and promised to return; but I had learnt, at last, to disregard his promises.

Those were four miserable months, alternating between intense anxiety, despair, and indignation; pity for him, and pity for myself. And yet, through all, I was not wholly comfortless; I had my darling, sinless, inoffensive little one to console me, but even this consolation was embittered by the constantly recurring thought, 'How shall I teach him, hereafter, to respect his father, and yet to avoid his example?'

But I remembered that I had brought all these afflictions, in a manner wilfully, upon myself; and I determined to bear them without a murmur. At the same time I resolved not to give myself *up* to misery for the transgressions of another, and endeavoured to divert myself as much as I could; and besides the companionship of my child and my dear, faithful Rachel, who evidently guessed my sorrows and felt for them, though she was too discreet to allude to them – I had my books and pencil, my domestic affairs, and the welfare and comfort of Arthur's poor tenants and labourers to attend to; and I sometimes sought and obtained amusement in the company of my young friend Esther Hargrave: occasionally, I rode over to see her, and once or twice I had her to spend the day with me at the manor. Mrs Hargrave did not visit London that season: having no daughter to marry, she thought it as well to stay at home and economise; and, for a wonder, Walter came down to join her in the beginning of June and stayed till near the close of August.

The first time I saw him was on a sweet, warm evening, when I was sauntering in the park with little Arthur and Rachel, who is head-nurse and lady's-maid in one – for, with my secluded life and tolerably active habits, I require but little attendance, and as she had nursed me and coveted to nurse my child, and was moreover so very trustworthy, I preferred committing the important charge to

her, with a young nursery-maid under her directions, to engaging anyone else –
besides it saves money; and since I have made acquaintance with Arthur's affairs,
I have learnt to regard that as no trifling recommendation; for, by my own desire,
nearly the whole of the income of my fortune is devoted, for years to come, to
the paying off of his debts, and the money he contrives to squander away in
London is incomprehensible – But to return to Mr Hargrave – I was standing
with Rachel beside the water, amusing the laughing baby in her arms, with a twig
of willow laden with golden catkins, when greatly to my surprise, he entered the
park, mounted on his costly black hunter, and crossed over the grass to meet me.
He saluted me with a very fine compliment, delicately worded, and modestly
delivered withal, which he had doubtless concocted as he rode along. He told me
he had brought a message from his mother, who, as he was riding that way, had
desired him to call at the manor and beg the pleasure of my company to a
friendly, family dinner tomorrow.

'There is no one to meet but ourselves,' said he; 'but Esther is very anxious to
see you; and my mother fears you will feel solitary in this great house so much
alone, and wishes she could persuade you to give her the pleasure of your
company more frequently, and make yourself at home in our more humble
dwelling, till Mr Huntingdon's return shall render this a little more conducive
to your comfort.'

'She is very kind,' I answered, 'but I am not alone, you see; and those, whose
time is fully occupied, seldom complain of solitude.'

'Will you not come tomorrow, then? She will be sadly disappointed if you
refuse.'

I did not relish being thus compassionated for my loneliness; but however, I
promised to come.

'What a sweet evening this is!' observed he, looking round upon the sunny
park, with its imposing swell and slope, its placid water, and majestic clumps of
trees. 'And what a paradise you live in!'

'It is a lovely evening,' answered I; and I sighed to think how little I had felt its
loveliness, and how little of a paradise sweet Grassdale was to me – how still less
to the voluntary exile from its scenes. Whether Mr Hargrave divined my
thoughts, I cannot tell, but, with a half-hesitating, sympathising seriousness of
tone and manner, he asked if I had lately heard from Mr Huntingdon.

'Not lately,' I replied.

'I thought not,' he muttered, as if to himself, looking thoughtfully on the
ground.

'Are you not lately returned from London?' I asked.

'Only yesterday.'

'And did you see him there?'

'Yes – I saw him.'

'Was he well?'

'Yes – that is,' said he, with increasing hesitation and an appearance of
suppressed indignation, 'he was as well as – as he deserved to be, but under
circumstances I should have deemed incredible for a man so favoured as he is.'

He here looked up and pointed the sentence with a serious bow to me. I suppose my face was crimson.

'Pardon me, Mrs Huntingdon,' he continued, 'but I cannot suppress my indignation when I behold such infatuated blindness and perversion of taste; but, perhaps you are not aware – ' He paused.

'I am aware of nothing, sir – except that he delays his coming longer than I expected; and if at present, he prefers the society of his friends to that of his wife, and the dissipations of the town to the quiet of country life, I suppose I have those friends to thank for it. *Their* tastes and occupations are similar to his, and I don't see why his conduct should awaken either their indignation or surprise.'

'You wrong me cruelly,' answered he: 'I have shared but little of Mr Huntingdon's society, for the last few weeks; and as for his tastes and occupations, they are quite beyond me – lonely wanderer as I am. Where I have but sipped and tasted, he drains the cup to the dregs; and if ever for a moment I have sought to drown the voice of reflection in madness and folly, or if I have wasted too much of my time and talents among reckless and dissipated companions, God knows I would gladly renounce them entirely and for ever, if I had but *half* the blessings that man so thanklessly casts behind his back – but *half* the inducements to virtue and domestic orderly habits that he despises – but *such* a home, and *such* a partner to share it! – It is infamous!' he muttered between his teeth. 'And don't think, Mrs Huntingdon,' he added aloud, 'that I could be guilty of inciting him to persevere in his present pursuits: on the contrary, I have remonstrated with him again and again; I have frequently expressed my surprise at his conduct and reminded him of his duties and his privileges – but to no purpose; he only – '

'Enough, Mr Hargrave; you ought to be aware that whatever my husband's faults may be, it can only aggravate the evil for me to hear them from a stranger's lips.'

'*Am* I then a stranger?' said he in a sorrowful tone. 'I am your nearest neighbour, your son's godfather, and your husband's friend: may I not be yours also?'

'Intimate acquaintance must precede real friendship: I know but little of you, Mr Hargrave, except from report.'

'Have you then forgotten the six or seven weeks I spent under your roof last autumn? *I* have not forgotten them. And I know enough of *you*, Mrs Huntingdon, to think that your husband is the most enviable man in the world, and I should be the next if you would deem me worthy of your friendship.'

'If you knew more of me, you would not think it – or if you did, you would not say it, and expect me to be flattered by the compliment.'

I stepped backward as I spoke. He saw that I wished the conversation to end; and immediately taking the hint, he gravely bowed, wished me good-evening, and turned his horse towards the road. He appeared grieved and hurt at my unkind reception of his sympathising overtures. I was not sure that I had done right in speaking so harshly to him; but at the time, I had felt irritated – almost insulted by his conduct; it seemed as if he was presuming upon the absence and neglect of my husband, and insinuating even more than the truth against him.

Rachel had moved on, during our conversation, to some yards' distance. He rode up to her, and asked to see the child. He took it carefully into his arms, looked upon it with an almost paternal smile, and I heard him say, as I approached – 'And this, too, he has forsaken!'

He then tenderly kissed it, and restored it to the gratified nurse.

'Are you fond of children, Mr Hargrave?' said I, a little softened towards him.

'Not in general,' he replied; 'but that is such a *sweet* child – and so like its mother,' he added in a lower tone.

'You are mistaken there; it is its father it resembles.'

'Am I not right, nurse?' said he, appealing to Rachel.

'I think, sir, there's a bit of both,' she replied.

He departed; and Rachel pronounced him a very nice gentleman. I had still my doubts on the subject.

When I met him on the morrow, under his own roof, he did not offend me with any more of his virtuous indignation against Arthur or unwelcome sympathy for me; and, indeed, when his mother began, in guarded terms, to intimate her sorrow and surprise at my husband's conduct, he, perceiving my annoyance, instantly came to the rescue, and delicately turned the conversation, at the same time warning her, by a sidelong glance, not to recur to the subject again. He seemed bent upon doing the honours of his house in the most unexceptionable manner, and exerting all his powers for the entertainment of his guest, and the display of his own qualifications as a host, a gentleman, and a companion; and actually succeeded in making himself very agreeable – only that he was too polite – And yet, Mr Hargrave, I don't much like you; there is a certain want of openness about you that does not take my fancy, and a lurking selfishness, at the bottom of all your fine qualities, that I do not intend to lose sight of. No; for, instead of combating my slight prejudice against you as uncharitable, I mean to cherish it, until I am convinced that I have no reason to distrust this kind, insinuating friendship you are so anxious to push upon me.

In the course of the following six weeks, I met him several times, but always, save once, in company with his mother or his sister, or both. When I called on them, he always happened to be at home, and when they called on me, it was always he that drove them over in the phaeton. His mother, evidently, was quite delighted with his dutiful attentions and newly acquired domestic habits.

The time that I met him alone was on a bright but not oppressively hot day in the beginning of July: I had taken little Arthur into the wood that skirts the park, and there seated him on the moss-cushioned roots of an old oak; and, having gathered a handful of bluebells and wild roses, I was kneeling before him, and presenting them, one by one, to the grasp of his tiny fingers; enjoying the heavenly beauty of the flowers, through the medium of his smiling eyes; forgetting, for the moment, all my cares, laughing at his gleeful laughter, and delighting myself with his delight – when a shadow suddenly eclipsed the little space of sunshine on the grass before us; and, looking up, I beheld Walter Hargrave standing and gazing upon us.

'Excuse me, Mrs Huntingdon,' said he, 'but I was spellbound; I had neither

the power to come forward and interrupt you, nor to withdraw from the contemplation of such a scene – How vigorous my little godson grows! And how merry he is this morning.' He approached the child and stooped to take his hand; but, on seeing that his caresses were likely to produce tears and lamentations instead of a reciprocation of friendly demonstrations, he prudently drew back.

'What a pleasure and comfort that little creature must be to you, Mrs Huntingdon!' he observed with a touch of sadness in his intonation, as he admiringly contemplated the infant.

'It is,' replied I; and then I asked after his mother and sister.

He politely answered my enquiries, and then returned again to the subject I wished to avoid; though with a degree of timidity that witnessed his fear to offend.

'You have not heard from Huntingdon lately?' he said.

'Not this week,' I replied – Not these three weeks, I might have said.

'I had a letter from him this morning. I wish it were such a one as I could show to his lady.' He half drew from his waistcoat pocket a letter with Arthur's still beloved hand on the address, scowled at it, and put it back again, adding – 'But he tells me he is about to return next week.'

'He tells *me* so every time he writes.'

'Indeed! – Well, it is like him – But to *me* he always avowed it his intention to stay till the present month.'

It struck me like a blow, this proof of premeditated transgression and systematic disregard of truth.

'It is only of a piece with the rest of his conduct,' observed Mr Hargrave, thoughtfully regarding me, and reading, I suppose, my feelings in my face.

'Then he is really coming next week?' said I after a pause.

'You may rely upon it – if the assurance can give you any pleasure –And is it *possible*, Mrs Huntingdon, that you can rejoice at his return?' he exclaimed, attentively perusing my features again.

'Of course, Mr Hargrave; is he not my husband!'

'Oh, Huntingdon, you know not *what* you slight!' he passionately murmured.

I took up my baby and, wishing him good-morning, departed, to indulge my thoughts unscrutinised, within the sanctum of my home.

And *was* I glad? – Yes, delighted; though I was angered by Arthur's conduct, and though I felt that he had wronged me, and was determined he should feel it too.

## CHAPTER 30

## *Domestic Scenes*

On the following morning, I received a few lines from him myself, confirming Hargrave's intimations respecting his approaching return. And he did come next week, but in a condition of body and mind even worse than before. I did not however intend to pass over his derelictions this time without a remark; I found it would not do. But the first day, he was weary with his journey, and I was glad to get him back: I would not upbraid him then; I would wait till tomorrow. Next morning, he was weary still: I would wait a little longer. But at dinner, when, after breakfasting at twelve o'clock on a bottle of soda-water and a cup of strong coffee, and lunching at two on another bottle of soda-water mingled with brandy, he was finding fault with everything on the table and declaring we must change our cook – I thought the time was come.

'It is the same cook as we had before you went, Arthur,' said I. 'You were generally pretty well satisfied with her then.'

'You must have been letting her get into slovenly habits then, while I was away. It is enough to poison one – eating such a disgusting mess!' And he pettishly pushed away his plate, and leant back despairingly in his chair.

'I think it is you that are changed, not she,' said I, but with the utmost gentleness, for I did not wish to irritate him.

'It may be so,' he replied carelessly, as he seized a tumbler of wine and water, adding, when he had tossed it off – 'for I have an infernal fire in my veins, that all the waters of the ocean cannot quench!'

'What kindled it?' I was about to ask, but at that moment the butler entered and began to take away the things.

'Be quick, Benson – do have done with that infernal clatter!' cried his master – 'And *don't* bring the cheese! – unless you want to make me sick outright.'

Benson, in some surprise, removed the cheese, and did his best to effect a quiet and speedy clearance of the rest, but, unfortunately, there was a rumple in the carpet, caused by the hasty pushing back of his master's chair, at which he tripped and stumbled, causing a rather alarming concussion with the trayful of crockery in his hands, but no positive damage, save the fall and breaking of a sauce-tureen; but, to my unspeakable shame and dismay, Arthur turned furiously around upon him, and swore at him with savage coarseness. The poor man turned pale, and visibly trembled as he stooped to pick up the fragments.

'He couldn't help it, Arthur,' said I; 'the carpet caught his foot – and there's no great harm done. Never mind the pieces now, Benson, you can clear them away afterwards.'

Glad to be released, Benson expeditiously set out the dessert and withdrew.

'What *could* you mean, Helen, by taking the servant's part against me,' said Arthur, as soon as the door was closed, 'when you knew I was distracted?'

'I did not know you were distracted, Arthur, and the poor man was quite frightened and hurt at your sudden explosion.'

'Poor man indeed! and do you think I could stop to consider the feelings of an insensate brute like that, when my own nerves were racked and torn to pieces by his confounded blunders?'

'I never heard you complain of your nerves before.'

'And why shouldn't I have nerves as well as you?'

'Oh, I don't dispute your claim to their possession, but *I* never complain of mine.'

'No – how should you, when you never do anything to try them?'

'Then why do you try yours, Arthur?'

'Do you think I have nothing to do but to stay at home and take care of myself like a woman?'

'Is it impossible then, to take care of yourself like a man when you go abroad? You told me that you could – and would too; and you promised – '

'Come, come, Helen, don't begin with that nonsense now; I can't bear it.'

'Can't bear what? – to be reminded of the promises you have broken?'

'Helen, you are cruel. If you knew how my heart throbbed, and how every nerve thrilled through me while you spoke, you would spare me. You can pity a dolt of a servant for breaking a dish; but you have no compassion for *me*, when my head is split in two and all on fire with this consuming fever.'

He leant his head on his hand, and sighed. I went to him and put my hand on his forehead. It was burning indeed.

'Then come with me into the drawing-room, Arthur; and don't take any more wine; you have taken several glasses since dinner, and eaten next to nothing all the day. How can *that* make you better?'

With some coaxing and persuasion, I got him to leave the table. When the baby was brought I tried to amuse him with that; but poor little Arthur was cutting his teeth, and his father could not bear his complaints; sentence of immediate banishment was passed upon him on the first indication of fretfulness; and, because, in the course of the evening, I went to share his exile for a little while, I was reproached, on my return, for preferring my child to my husband. I found the latter reclining on the sofa just as I had left him.

'Well!' exclaimed the injured man, in a tone of pseudo-resignation. 'I thought I wouldn't send for you; I thought I'd just see – how long it would please you to leave me alone.'

'I have not been *very* long, have I, Arthur? I have not been an hour, I'm sure.'

'Oh, of course, an hour is nothing to you, so pleasantly employed; but to *me* – '

'It has not been pleasantly employed,' interrupted I. 'I have been nursing our poor little baby, who is very far from well, and I could not leave him till I got him to sleep.'

'Oh to be sure, you're overflowing with kindness and pity for everything but me.'

'And why should I pity *you*? What is the matter with you?'

'Well! that passes everything! After all the wear and tear that I've had, when I come home sick and weary, longing for comfort, and expecting to find attention and kindness, at least, from my wife – she calmly asks what is the matter with me!'

'There is *nothing* the matter with you,' returned I, 'except what you have wilfully brought upon yourself against my earnest exhortation and entreaty.'

'Now, Helen,' said he, emphatically, half rising from his recumbent posture, 'if you bother me with another word, I'll ring the bell and order six bottles of wine – and, by Heaven, I'll drink them dry before I stir from this place!'

I said no more but sat down before the table and drew a book towards me.

'Do let me have quietness at least!' continued he, 'if you deny me every other comfort,' and sinking back into his former position, with an impatient expiration between a sigh and a groan, he languidly closed his eyes as if to sleep.

What the book was, that lay open on the table before me, I cannot tell, for I never looked at it. With an elbow on each side of it, and my hands clasped before my eyes, I delivered myself up to silent weeping. But Arthur was not asleep: at the first slight sob, he raised his head and looked round, impatiently exclaiming – 'What are you crying for, Helen? What the deuce is the matter *now*?'

'I'm crying for you, Arthur,' I replied, speedily drying my tears; and starting up, I threw myself on my knees before him, and, clasping his nerveless hand between my own, continued: 'Don't you know that you are part of myself? And do you think you can injure and degrade yourself, and I not feel it?'

'*Degrade* myself, Helen?'

'Yes, degrade! What have you been doing all this time?'

'You'd better not ask,' said he with a faint smile.

'And you had better not tell – but you can't deny that you *have* degraded yourself miserably. You have shamefully wronged yourself, body and soul – and me too; and I can't endure it quietly – and I won't!'

'Well, don't squeeze my hand so frantically and don't agitate me so, for Heaven's sake! Oh, Hattersley! You were right; this woman will be the death of me, with her keen feelings and her interesting force of character – There, there, do spare me a little.'

'Arthur, you *must* repent!' cried I, in a frenzy of desperation, throwing my arms around him and burying my face in his bosom. 'You *shall* say you are sorry for what you have done!'

'Well, well, I am.'

'You are not! You'll do it again.'

'I shall never live to do it again, if you treat me so savagely,' replied he, pushing me from him. 'You've nearly squeezed the breath out of my body.' He pressed his hand to his heart, and looked really agitated and ill.

'Now get me a glass of wine,' said he, 'to remedy what you've done, you she tiger! I'm almost ready to faint.'

I flew to get the required remedy It seemed to revive him considerably.

'What a shame it is,' said I, as I took the empty glass from his hand, 'for a strong young man like you to reduce yourself to such a state!'

'If you knew all, my girl, you'd say rather, "What a wonder it is you can bear it so well as you do!" I've lived more in these four months, Helen, than you have in the whole course of your existence, or will to the end of your days, if they numbered a hundred years; so I must expect to pay for it in some shape.'

'You will have to pay a higher price than you anticipate, if you don't take care – there will be the total loss of your own health, and of my affection too – if *that* is of any value to you.'

'What, you're at that game of threatening me with the loss of your affection again, are you? I think it couldn't have been very genuine stuff to begin with, if it's so easily demolished. If you don't mind, my pretty tyrant, you'll make me regret my choice in good earnest, and envy my friend Hattersley, his meek little wife – she's quite a pattern to her sex, Helen: he had her with him in London all the season, and she was no trouble at all. He might amuse himself just as he pleased, in regular bachelor style, and she never complained of neglect; he might come home at any hour of the night or morning, or not come home at all; be sullen sober, or glorious drunk; and play the fool or the madman to his own heart's desire without any fear or botheration. She never gives him a word of reproach or complaint, do what he will. He says there's not such a jewel in all England, and swears he wouldn't take a kingdom for her.'

'But he makes her life a curse to her.'

'Not he! She has no will but his, and is always contented and happy as long as he is enjoying himself.'

'In that case, she is as great a fool as he is; but it is not so. I have several letters from her, expressing the greatest anxiety about his proceedings, and complaining that you incite him to commit those extravagances – one especially, in which she implores me to use my influence with you to get you away from London, and affirms that her husband never did such things before you came, and would certainly discontinue them as soon as you departed and left him to the guidance of his own good sense.'

'The detestable little traitor! Give me the letter, and he shall see it as sure as I'm a living man.'

'No, he shall not see it without her consent; but if he did, there is nothing there to anger him – nor in any of the others. She never speaks a word against him; it is only anxiety *for* him that she expresses. She only alludes to his conduct in the most delicate terms, and makes every excuse for him that she can possibly think of – and as for her own misery, I rather *feel* it than *see* it expressed in her letters.'

'But she abuses *me*; and no doubt you helped her.'

'No; I told her she over rated my influence with you, that I would gladly draw you away from the temptations of the town if I could, but had little hope of success, and that I thought she was wrong in supposing that you enticed Mr Hattersley or anyone else into error. I had, myself, held the *contrary* opinion at one time, but I now believed that you mutually corrupted each other; and, perhaps, if she used a little gentle, but serious remonstrance with her husband, it might be of some service, as though he was more rough hewn than mine, I believed he was of a less impenetrable material.'

'And so *that* is the way you go on – heartening each other up to mutiny, and abusing each other's partners, and throwing out implications against your own, to the mutual gratification of both!'

'According to your own account,' said I, 'my evil counsel has had but little effect upon *her*. And as to abuse and aspersions, we are both of us far too deeply ashamed of the errors and vices of our other halves, to make them the common subject of our correspondence. Friends as we are, we would willingly keep your failings to ourselves – even *from* ourselves if we could, unless by knowing them we could deliver you from them.'

'Well, well! Don't worry me about them: you'll never effect any good by that. Have patience with me, and bear with my languor and crossness a little while, till I get this cursed low fever out of my veins, and then you'll find me cheerful and kind as ever. Why can't you be gentle and good as you were last time? – I'm sure I was very grateful for it.'

'And what good did your gratitude do? I deluded myself with the idea that you were ashamed of your transgressions, and hoped you would never repeat them again; but now, you have left me nothing to hope!'

'My case is quite desperate, is it? A very blessed consideration, if it will only secure me from the pain and worry of my dear, anxious wife's efforts to convert me, and her from the toil and trouble of such exertions, and her sweet face and silver accents from the ruinous effects of the same. A burst of passion is a fine, rousing thing upon occasion, Helen, and a flood of tears is marvellously affecting, but, when indulged too often, they are both deuced plaguey things for spoiling one's beauty and tiring out one's friends.'

Thenceforth, I restrained my tears and passions as much as I could. I spared him my exhortations and fruitless efforts at conversion too, for I saw it was all in vain: God might awaken that heart supine and stupefied with self-indulgence, and remove the film of sensual darkness from his eyes, but I could not. His injustice and ill-humour towards his inferiors, who could not defend them-selves, I still resented and withstood; but when I alone was their object, as was frequently the case, I endured it with calm forbearance, except at times when my temper, worn out by repeated annoyances, or stung to distraction by some new instance of irrationality, gave way in spite of myself, and exposed me to the imputations of fierceness, cruelty, and impatience. I attended carefully to his wants and amusements, but not, I own, with the same devoted fondness as before, because, I could not feel it: besides, I had now another claimant on my time and care – my ailing infant, for whose sake I frequently braved and suffered the reproaches and complaints of his unreasonably exacting father.

But Arthur is not naturally a peevish or irritable man – so far from it that there was something almost ludicrous in the incongruity of this adventitious fretfulness and nervous irritability, rather calculated to excite laughter than anger, if it were not for the intensely painful considerations attendant upon those symptoms of a disordered frame – and his temper gradually improved as his bodily health was restored which was much sooner than would have been the case, but for my strenuous exertions; for there was still one thing about him that

I did not give up in despair, and one effort for his preservation that I would not remit. His appetite for the stimulus of wine had increased upon him, as I had too well foreseen. It was now something more to him than an accessory to social enjoyment: it was an important source of enjoyment in itself. In this time of weakness and depression he would have made it his medicine and support, his comforter, his recreation, and his friend – and thereby sunk deeper and deeper – and bound himself down for ever in the bathos whereinto he had fallen. But I determined this should never be, as long as I had any influence left; and though I could not prevent him from taking more than was good for him, still, by incessant perseverance, by kindness, and firmness, and vigilance, by coaxing, and daring, and determination – I succeeded in preserving him from absolute bondage to that detestable propensity, so insidious in its advances, so inexorable in its tyranny, so disastrous in its effects.

And here, I must not forget that I am not a little indebted to his friend Mr Hargrave. About that time he frequently called at Grassdale, and often dined with us, on which occasions, I fear, Arthur would willingly have cast prudence and decorum to the winds and made "a night of it", as often as his friend would have consented to join him in that exalted pastime; and if the latter had chosen to comply, he might in a night or two, have ruined the labour of weeks, and overthrown with a touch, the frail bulwark it had cost me such trouble and toil to construct. I was so fearful of this at first, that I humbled myself to intimate to him in private, my apprehensions of Arthur's proneness to these excesses and to express a hope that he would not encourage it. He was pleased with this mark of confidence, and certainly did not betray it. On that and every subsequent occasion, his presence served rather as a check upon his host, than an incitement to further acts of intemperance; and he always succeeded in bringing him from the dining-room in good time and in tolerably good condition; for if Arthur disregarded such intimations, as 'Well, I must not detain you from your lady,' or 'We must not forget that Mrs Huntingdon is alone,' he would insist upon leaving the table himself, to join me, and his host, however unwillingly, was obliged to follow.

Hence, I learnt to welcome Mr Hargrave, as a real friend to the family, a harmless companion for Arthur, to cheer his spirits and preserve him from the tedium of absolute idleness and a total isolation from all society but mine, and a useful ally to me. I could not but feel grateful to him under such circumstances; and I did not scruple to acknowledge my obligation on the first convenient opportunity; yet, as I did so, my heart whispered all was not right, and brought a glow to my face, which he heightened by his steady, serious gaze, while, by his manner of receiving those acknowledgements, he more than doubled my misgivings. His high delight at being able to serve me, was chastened by sympathy for me and commiseration for himself – about I know not what, for I would not stay to enquire or suffer him to unburden his sorrows to me. His sighs and intimations of suppressed affliction seemed to come from a full heart; but either he must contrive to retain them within it, or breathe them forth in other ears than mine: there was enough of confidence between us already. It

seemed wrong that there should exist a secret understanding between my husband's friend and me, unknown to him, of which he was the object. But my afterthought was, 'If it is wrong, surely Arthur's is the fault, not mine.'

And indeed, I know not whether at the time, it was not for *him* rather than myself that I blushed; for, since he and I are one, I so identify myself with him, that I feel his degradation, his failings, and transgressions as my own; I blush for him, I fear for him; I repent for him, weep, pray, and feel for him as for myself; but I cannot act for him; and hence, I must be and I am debased, contaminated by the union, both in my own eyes, and in the actual truth. I am so determined to love him – so intensely anxious to excuse his errors, that I am continually dwelling upon them, and labouring to extenuate the loosest of his principles and the worst of his practices, till I am familiarised with vice and almost a partaker in his sins. Things that formerly shocked and disgusted me, now seem only natural. I know them to be wrong, because reason and God's word declare them to be so; but I am gradually losing that instinctive horror and repulsion which was given me by nature, or instilled into me by the precepts and example of my aunt. Perhaps, then, I was too severe in my judgements, for I abhorred the sinner as well as the sin; now, I flatter myself I am more charitable and consider-ate; but am I not becoming more indifferent and insensate too? Fool that I was to dream that I had strength and purity enough to save myself and him! Such vain presumption would be rightly served, if I should perish with him in the gulf from which I sought to save him! Yet, God preserve me from it! – and him too. Yes, poor Arthur, I will still hope and pray for you; and though I write as if you were some abandoned wretch, past hope and past reprieve, it is only my anxious fears – my strong desires that make me do so; one who loved you less would be less bitter – less dissatisfied.

His conduct has of late, been what the world calls irreproachable; but then I know his heart is still unchanged; and I know that spring is approaching, and deeply dread the consequences.

As he began to recover the tone and vigour of his exhausted frame, and with it something of his former impatience of retirement and repose, I suggested a short residence by the seaside, for his recreation and further restoration, and for the benefit of our little one as well. But no; watering-places were so intolerably dull – besides, he had been invited by one of his friends to spend a month or two in Scotland for the better recreation of grouse-shooting and deer-stalking, and had promised to go.

'Then you will leave me again, Arthur?' said I.

'Yes, dearest, but only to love you the better when I come back, and make up for all past offences and shortcomings; and you needn't fear me this time; there are no temptations on the mountains. And during my absence you may pay a visit to Staningley, if you like: your uncle and aunt have long been wanting us to go there, you know; but somehow, there's such repulsion between the good lady and me, that I never could bring myself up to the scratch.'

I was perfectly willing to avail myself of this permission, though not a little apprehensive of my aunt's questions and comments concerning my matrimonial

experience, regarding which I had been very reserved in my letters, for I had not much that was pleasant to communicate.

About the third week in August, Arthur set out for Scotland, and Mr Hargrave accompanied him thither, to my private satisfaction. Shortly after, I, with little Arthur and Rachel, went to Staningley, my dear old home, which, as well as my dear old friends its inhabitants, I saw again with mingled feelings of pleasure and pain so intimately blended that I could scarcely distinguish the one from the other, or tell to which to attribute the various tears, and smiles, and sighs awakened by those old familiar scenes, and tones, and faces. Not quite two years had past since I had seen and heard them last; but it seemed a far, far longer time; and well it might, for how immeasurably changed was I! How many things had I not seen, and felt, and learnt since then! My uncle too appeared perceptibly more aged and infirm, my aunt more sad and grave. I believe she thought I had repented of my rashness; though she did not openly express her conviction, or triumphantly remind me of her slighted counsels, as I had partly feared she would; but she observed me narrowly – more narrowly than I liked to be observed – and seemed to mistrust my cheerfulness and unduly mark each little indication of sadness or serious thought, to notice all my casual observations, and silently draw her own inferences from them; while, by a system of quiet cross-questioning renewed from time to time, she drew from me many things I should not otherwise have told her, and laying this and that together, obtained, I fear, a pretty clear conception of my husband's faults and my afflictions, though not of my remaining sources of comfort and hope, for though I endeavoured to impress her strongly with the notion of Arthur's redeeming qualities, of our mutual affection, and the many causes I had for thankfulness and self-congratulation, she received all such intimations coldly and calmly as if mentally making her own deductions – which deductions, I am persuaded, were generally far beyond the truth; though I certainly did exaggerate a little in attempting to picture the bright side of my position. Was it pride that made me so extremely anxious to appear satisfied with my lot – or merely a just determination to bear my self-imposed burden alone, and preserve my best friend from the slightest participation in those sorrows from which she had striven so hard to save me? It might have been something of each, but I am sure the latter motive was predominant.

I did not much prolong my visit, for, not only did I feel my aunt's relentless watchfulness and incredulity to be a restraint upon me, and a silent reproach that oppressed me more than she could well imagine, but I was sensible that my little Arthur was an annoyance to his uncle, though the latter wished him well, and no great amusement to his aunt, though an object of her earnest affection and anxious solicitude.

Dear aunt! Have you so tenderly reared me from infancy, so carefully guided and instructed me in childhood and youth; and could I give you no return but this – to disappoint your hopes, oppose your wishes, scorn your warnings and advice, and darken your latter years with anxious fears and sorrow for the sufferings you cannot relieve? – It almost broke my heart to think of it; and

again and again I endeavoured to convince her that I was happy and contented with my lot; but her last words, as she embraced me and kissed the child in my arms, before I entered the carriage, were – 'Take care of your son, Helen, and there may be happy days in store for you, yet. How great a comfort and treasure he is to you now I can well imagine; but if you spoil him to gratify your present feelings, it will be too late to repent it when your heart is broken.'

Arthur did not come home till several weeks after my return to Grassdale; but I did not feel so anxious about him now: to think of him engaged in active sports among the wild hills of Scotland, was very different from knowing him to be immersed amid the corruptions and temptations of London. His letters, now, though neither long nor lover-like, were more regular than ever they had been before; and when he did return, to my great joy instead of being worse than when he went, he was more cheerful and vigorous, and better in every respect. Since that time, I have had little cause to complain. He still has an unfortunate predilection for the pleasures of the table, against which I have to struggle and watch; but he has begun to notice his boy, and that is an increasing source of amusement to him within doors; while his fox-hunting and coursing are a sufficient occupation for him without, when the ground is not hardened by frost; so that he is not wholly dependant on me for entertainment. But it is now January: spring is approaching; and, I repeat, I dread the consequences of its arrival. That sweet season, I once so joyously welcomed as the time of hope and gladness, awakens, now, far other anticipations by its return.

## CHAPTER 31

### Social Virtues

March 20th, 1824. The dreaded time is come, and Arthur is gone, as I expected. This time he announced it his intention to make but a short stay in London, and pass over to the continent, where he should probably stay a few weeks; but I shall not expect him till after the lapse of many weeks: I now know that, with him, days signify weeks, and weeks months.

I was to have accompanied him, but, a little before the time arranged for our departure, he allowed – and even urged me, with an appearance of wonderful self-sacrifice, to go and see my unfortunate father, who is very ill, and my brother, who is very unhappy in consequence of both the illness and its cause, and whom I had not seen since the day our child was christened, when he stood sponsor along with Mr Hargrave and my aunt. Not willing to impose upon my husband's good-nature in thus allowing me to leave him, I made but a very short stay; but when I returned to Grassdale – he was gone.

He left a note to explain his so hasty departure, pretending that some sudden emergency had demanded his immediate presence in London, and rendered it impossible to await my return; adding that I had better not trouble myself to

follow him, as he intended to make such a short stay, that it would hardly be worth while; and as, of course, he could travel alone at less than half the expense than if I accompanied him, it would perhaps be better to defer the excursion to another year, when he should have got our affairs into a rather more settled state, as he was now endeavouring to do.

Was it really so? – or was the whole a contrivance to ensure his going forth upon his pleasure-seeking excursion, without my presence to restrain him? It is painful to doubt the sincerity of those we love, but after so many proofs of falsity and utter disregard to principle how can I believe so improbable a story?

I have this one source of consolation left – he had told me sometime previously, that if ever he went to London or Paris again, he should observe more moderation in his indulgences than before, lest he should destroy his capacity for enjoyment altogether: he had no ambition to live to a prodigious old age, but he should like to have his share of life, and above all, to relish its pleasures to the last – to which end, he found it necessary to economise, for already, he feared, he was not so handsome a fellow as he had been, and young as he was, he had lately detected some grey hairs among his beloved chestnut locks; he suspected he was getting a trifle fatter too, than was quite desirable – but that was with good living and idleness; and for the rest, he trusted he was as strong and hearty as ever: only there was no saying what *another* such a season of unlimited madness and devilment, as the last, might not do towards bringing him down. Yes; he said this to *me* – with unblushing effrontery, and that same blythe, roguish twinkle of the eyes I once so loved to see, and that low, joyous laugh it used to warm my heart to hear.

Well! Such considerations will doubtless have more weight with him than any that I could urge. We shall see what *they* can do towards his preservation, since no better hope remains.

July 30th. He returned about three weeks ago, rather better in health, certainly, than before, but still worse in temper. And yet, perhaps, I am wrong: it is *I* that am less patient and forbearing. I am tired out with his injustice, his selfishness and hopeless *depravity* – I wish a milder word would do; I am no angel and my corruption rises against it. My poor father died last week: Arthur was vexed to hear of it, because he saw that I was shocked and grieved, and he feared the circumstance would mar his comfort. When I spoke of ordering my mourning, he exclaimed – 'Oh, I hate black! But however, I suppose you must wear it awhile, for form's sake; but I hope, Helen, you won't think it your bounden duty to compose your face and manners into conformity with your funereal garb. Why should you sigh and groan, and I be made uncomfortable because an old gentleman in —shire, a perfect stranger to us both, has thought proper to drink himself to death? – There now, I declare you're crying! Well, it must be affectation.'

He would not hear of my attending the funeral, or going for a day or two, to cheer poor Frederick's solitude. It was quite unnecessary, he said, and I was unreasonable to wish it. What was my father to me? I had never seen him, but

once since I was a baby, and I well knew he had never cared a stiver about me; and my brother too, was little better than a stranger. 'Besides, dear Helen,' said he, embracing me with flattering fondness, 'I cannot spare you for a single day.'

'Then how have you managed without me, these *many* days?' said I.

'Ah! then I was knocking about the world, now I am at home; and home without you, my household deity, would be intolerable.'

'Yes, as long as I am necessary to your comfort; but you did not say so before, when you urged me to leave you, in order that you might get away from your home without me,' retorted I; but before the words were well out of my mouth, I regretted having uttered them. It seemed so heavy a charge: if false, too gross an insult; if true, too humiliating a fact to be thus openly cast in his teeth. But I might have spared myself that momentary pang of self-reproach. The accusation awoke neither shame nor indignation in him: he attempted neither denial nor excuse, but only answered with a long, low, chuckling laugh as if he viewed the whole transaction as a clever, merry jest from beginning to end. Surely that man will make me dislike him at last!

> 'Sine as ye brew, my maiden fair,
> Keep mind that ye maun drink the yill.'

Yes; and I *will* drink it to the very dregs: and none but myself shall know how bitter I find it!

August 20th. We are shaken down again to about our usual position. Arthur has returned to nearly his former condition and habits; and I have found it my wisest plan to shut my eyes against the past and future, as far as *he* at least is concerned, and live only for the present; to love him when I can; to smile (if possible) when he smiles, be cheerful when he is cheerful, and pleased when he is agreeable; and when he is not, to try to make him so – and if that won't answer, to bear with him, to excuse him, and forgive him, as well as I can, and restrain my own evil passions from aggravating his; and yet, while I thus yield and minister to his more harmless propensities to self-indulgence, to do all in my power to save him from the worse.

But we shall not be long alone together. I shall shortly be called upon to entertain the same select body of friends as we had the autumn before last, with the addition of Mr Hattersley and, at my special request, his wife and child. I long to see Milicent – and her little girl too. The latter is now above a year old; she will be a charming playmate for my little Arthur.

September 30th. Our guests have been here a week or two; but I have had no leisure to pass any comments upon them till now. I cannot get over my dislike to Lady Lowborough. It is not founded on mere personal pique; it is the woman herself that I dislike, because I so thoroughly disapprove of her. I always avoid her company as much as I can without violating the laws of hospitality; but when we do speak or converse together, it is with the utmost civility – even apparent cordiality on her part; but preserve me from such cordiality! It is like handling

briar-roses and may-blossoms – bright enough to the eye, and outwardly soft to the touch, but you know there are thorns beneath, and every now and then you feel them too; and perhaps resent the injury by crushing them in till you have destroyed their power, though somewhat to the detriment of your own fingers.

Of late, however, I have seen nothing in her conduct towards Arthur to anger or alarm me. During the first few days I thought she seemed very solicitous to win his admiration. Her efforts were not unnoticed by him: I frequently saw him smiling to himself at her artful manoeuvres: but, to his praise be it spoken, her shafts fell powerless by his side. Her most bewitching smiles, her haughtiest frowns were ever received with the same immutable, careless good-humour; till, finding he was indeed impenetrable, she suddenly remitted her efforts, and became, to all appearance, as perfectly indifferent as himself. Nor have I since witnessed any symptom of pique on his part, or renewed attempts at conquest upon hers.

This is as it should be; but Arthur never will let me be satisfied with him. I have never, for a single hour since I married him, known what it is to realise that sweet idea, 'In quietness and confidence shall be your rest.' Those two detestable men Grimsby and Hattersley have destroyed all my labour against his love of wine. They encourage him daily to overstep the bounds of moderation, and, not unfrequently, to disgrace himself by positive excess. I shall not soon forget the second night after their arrival. Just as I had retired from the dining-room, with the ladies, before the door was closed upon us, Arthur exclaimed – 'Now then, my lads, what say you to a regular jollification?'

Milicent glanced at me with a half reproachful look, as if *I* could hinder it; but her countenance changed when she heard Hattersley's voice shouting through door and wall.

'*I'm* your man! Send for more wine: here isn't *half* enough!'

We had scarcely entered the drawing-room before we were joined by Lord Lowborough.

'What *can* induce you to come so soon?' exclaimed his lady, with a most ungracious air of dissatisfaction.

'You know I never drink, Annabella,' replied he, seriously.

'Well, but you might stay with them a little: it looks so silly to be always dangling after the women – I wonder you can!'

He reproached her with a look of mingled bitterness and surprise, and sinking into a chair, suppressed a heavy sigh, bit his pale lips, and fixed his eyes upon the floor.

'You did right to leave them, Lord Lowborough,' said I. 'I trust you will always continue to honour us so early with your company. And if Annabella knew the value of true wisdom, and the misery of folly and – and intemperance, she would not talk such nonsense – even in jest.'

He raised his eyes while I spoke, and gravely turned them upon me with a half-surprised, half-abstracted look, and then bent them on his wife.

'At least,' said she, 'I know the value of a warm heart and a bold, manly spirit!'

And she pointed her words with a glance of triumph at me, which seemed to

say, 'And that is more than *you* do,' and a look of scorn at her husband, that entered into his soul. I was intensely exasperated; but it was not for me to reprove her, or, as it seemed, to express my sympathy with her husband without insulting his feelings. All I could do, to obey my inward impulse, was to hand him a cup of coffee, bringing it to him myself, and before I served either of the ladies, by way of balancing her contempt by my exceeding deference. He took it mechanically from my hand, with a slight inclination, and, next minute, rose and placed it untasted on the table, looking, not at it, but at her.

'Well, Annabella,' said he, in a deep and hollow tone, 'since my presence is disagreeable to you, I will relieve you of it.'

'Are you going back to them, then?' said she, carelessly.

'No,' exclaimed he, with harsh and startling emphasis; 'I will not go back to them! And I will never stay with them one moment longer than I think right, for you or any other tempter! But you needn't mind that – I shall never trouble you again, by intruding my company upon you so unseasonably.'

He left the room, I heard the hall door open and shut, and immediately after, on putting aside the curtain, I saw him pacing down the park, in the comfortless gloom of the damp, cloudy twilight.

Such scenes as this are always disagreeable to witness. Our little party was completely silenced for a moment. Milicent played with her teaspoon, and looked confounded and uncomfortable. If Annabella felt any shame or uneasiness, she attempted to hide it by a short, reckless laugh, and calmly betook herself to her coffee.

'It would serve you right, Annabella,' said I at length, 'if Lord Lowborough were to return to his old habits, which had so nearly effected his ruin, and which it cost him such an effort to break. You would then see cause to repent such conduct as this.'

'Not at all, my dear! I should not mind if his Lordship were to see fit to intoxicate himself every day: I should only the sooner be rid of him.'

'Oh, Annabella!' cried Milicent. 'How *can* you say such wicked things! It would indeed be a just punishment, as far as you are concerned, if Providence should take you at your word, and make you feel what others feel that – ' She paused as a sudden burst of loud talking and laughter reached us from the dining-room, in which the voice of Hattersley was pre-eminently conspicuous, even to my unpractised ear.

'What *you* feel at this moment, I suppose?' said Lady Lowborough, with a malicious smile, fixing her eyes upon her cousin's distressed countenance.

The latter offered no reply, but averted her face and brushed away a tear. At that moment the door opened and admitted Mr Hargrave; just a little flushed, his dark eyes sparkling with unwonted vivacity.

'Oh, I'm glad you're come, Walter!' cried his sister – 'But I wish you could have got Ralph to come too.'

'Utterly impossible, dear Milicent,' replied he, gaily. 'I had much ado to get away myself. Ralph attempted to keep me by violence; Huntingdon threatened me with the eternal loss of his friendship; and Grimsby, worse than all,

endeavoured to make me ashamed of my virtue, by such galling sarcasms and innuendos as he knew would wound me the most. So you see, ladies, you ought to make me welcome when I have braved and suffered so much for the favour of your sweet society.' He smilingly turned to me and bowed as he finished the sentence.

'Isn't he *handsome* now, Helen?' whispered Milicent, her sisterly pride overcoming, for the moment, all other considerations.

'He would be,' I returned, 'if that brilliance of eye, and lip, and cheek were natural to him; but look again, a few hours hence.'

Here the gentleman took a seat near me at the table, and petitioned for a cup of coffee.

'I consider this an apt illustration of Heaven taken by storm,' said he, as I handed one to him. 'I am in paradise now; but I have fought my way through flood and fire to win it. Ralph Hattersley's last resource was to set his back against the door, and swear I should find no passage but through his body (a pretty substantial one too). Happily, however, that was not the only door, and I effected my escape by the side entrance, through the butler's pantry, to the infinite amazement of Benson, who was cleaning the plate.'

Mr Hargrave laughed, and so did his cousin; but his sister and I remained silent and grave.

'Pardon my levity, Mrs Huntingdon,' murmured he, more seriously, as he raised his eyes to my face. 'You are not used to these things: you suffer them to affect your delicate mind too sensibly. But I thought of you in the midst of those lawless roisterers; and I endeavoured to persuade Mr Huntingdon to think of you too; but to no purpose: I fear he is fully determined to enjoy himself this night; and it will be no use keeping the coffee waiting for him or his companions: it will be much if they join us at tea. Meantime, I earnestly wish I could banish the thoughts of them from your mind – and my own too, for I hate to think of them – yes – even of my dear friend Huntingdon, when I consider the power he possesses over the happiness of one so immeasurably superior to himself, and the use he makes of it – I positively *detest* the man!'

'You had better not say so to me, then,' said I; 'for, bad as he is, he is part of myself, and you cannot abuse him without offending me.'

'Pardon me, then, for I would sooner die than offend you – But let us say no more of him for the present if you please.'

He then entirely changed the subject of discourse, and exerting all his powers to entertain our little circle, conversed on different topics with more than his usual brilliance and fluency, addressing himself, sometimes, exclusively to me, sometimes to the whole trio of ladies. Annabella cheerfully bore her part in the conversation; but I was sick at heart – especially when loud bursts of laughter and incoherent songs, pealing through the triple doors of hall and ante-room, startled my ear and pierced my aching temples; and Milicent partly shared my feelings; so that, to us, the evening appeared a very long one, in spite of Hargrave's apparently good-natured exertions to give it a contrary effect.

At last, they came; but not till after ten, when tea, which had been delayed for

more than half an hour, was nearly over. Much as I had longed for their coming, my heart failed me at the riotous uproar of their approach; and Milicent turned pale and almost started from her seat as Mr Hattersley burst into the room with a clamorous volley of oaths in his mouth, which Hargrave endeavoured to check by entreating him to remember the ladies.

'Ah! You do well to remind me of the ladies, you dastardly deserter,' cried he, shaking his formidable fist at his brother-in-law; 'if it were not for them, you well know, I'd demolish you in the twinkling of an eye, and give your body to the fowls of Heaven and the lilies of the field!' Then, planting a chair by Lady Lowborough's side, he stationed himself in it, and began to talk to her, with a mixture of absurdity and rascally impudence that seemed rather to amuse than to offend her; though she affected to resent his insolence, and to keep him at bay with sallies of smart and spirited repartee.

Meantime, Mr Grimsby seated himself by me, in the chair vacated by Hargrave as they entered, and gravely stated that he would thank me for a cup of tea: and Arthur placed himself beside poor Milicent, confidentially pushing his head into her face, and drawing in closer to her as she shrunk away from him. He was not so noisy as Hattersley, but his face was exceedingly flushed, he laughed incessantly, and while I blushed for all I saw and heard of him, I was glad that he chose to talk to his companion in so low a tone that no one could hear what he said but herself. It must have been intolerable nonsense at best, for she looked excessively annoyed, and first went red in the face, then indignantly pushed back her chair, and finally took refuge beside me on the sofa. Arthur's sole intention seemed to have been to produce some such disagreeable effects: he laughed immoderately on finding he had driven her away – drawing in his chair to the table, he leant his folded arms upon it, and delivered himself up to a paroxysm of weak, low, foolish laughter. When he was tired of this exercise he lifted his head and called aloud to Hattersley, and there ensued a clamorous contest between them about I know not what.

'What fools they are!' drawled Mr Grimsby, who had been talking away, at my elbow, with sententious gravity all the time; but I had been too much absorbed in contemplating the deplorable state of the other two – especially Arthur – to attend to him.

'Did you ever hear such nonsense as they talk, Mrs Huntingdon?' he continued. 'I'm quite ashamed of them for my part: they can't take so much as a bottle between them without its getting into their heads – '

'You are pouring the cream into your saucer, Mr Grimsby.'

'Ah! yes, I see, but we're almost in darkness here. Hargrave, snuff those candles, will you?'

'They're wax; they don't require snuffing,' said I.

' "The light of the body is the eye," ' observed Hargrave, with a sarcastic smile. ' "If thine eye be *single* thy whole body shall be full of light." '

Grimsby repulsed him with a solemn wave of the hand, and then, turning to me, continued, with the same drawling tones, and strange uncertainty of utterance and heavy gravity of aspect as before, 'But as I was saying, Mrs Huntingdon –

they have no head at all: they can't take half a bottle without being affected some way; whereas I – well, I've taken three times as much as they have tonight, and you see I'm perfectly steady. Now that may strike you as very singular, but I think I can explain it – you see *their* brains – I mention no names, but you'll understand to whom I allude – *their* brains are light to begin with, and the fumes of the fermented liquor render them lighter still, and produce an entire light-headedness, or giddiness, resulting in intoxication; whereas *my* brains being com-posed of more solid materials will absorb a considerable quantity of this alcoholic vapour without the production of any sensible result – '

'I think you will find a sensible result produced on that tea,' interrupted Mr Hargrave, 'by the quantity of sugar you have put into it. Instead of your usual complement of one lump you have put in six.'

'Have I so?' replied the philosopher, diving with his spoon into the cup and bringing up several half-dissolved pieces in confirmation of the assertion. 'Um! I perceive. Thus, madam, you see the evil of absence of mind – of thinking too much while engaged in the common concerns of life. Now if I had had my wits about me, like ordinary men, instead of within me like a philosopher, I should not have spoiled this cup of tea, and been constrained to trouble you for another – With your permission, I'll turn this into the slop-basin.'

'That is the sugar basin, Mr Grimsby. Now you have spoiled the sugar too; and I'll thank you to ring for some more – for here is Lord Lowborough, at last; and I hope his lordship will condescend to sit down with us, such as we are, and allow me to give him some tea.'

His lordship gravely bowed in answer to my appeal, but said nothing. Meantime, Hargrave volunteered to ring for the sugar, while Grimsby lamented his mistake and attempted to prove that it was owing to the shadow of the urn and the badness of the lights.

Lord Lowborough had entered a minute or two before, unobserved by anyone but me, and been standing before the door, grimly surveying the company. He now stepped up to Annabella, who sat with her back towards him, with Hattersley still beside her, though not now attending to her, being occupied in vociferously abusing and bullying his host.

'Well, Annabella,' said her husband, as he leant over the back of her chair, 'which of these three "bold, manly spirits" would you have me to resemble?'

'By Heaven and earth, you shall resemble us all!' cried Hattersley, starting up and rudely seizing him by the arm. 'Hallo, Huntingdon!' he shouted – '*I've* got him! Come, man, and help me! And damn me body and soul if I don't make him blind drunk before I let him go! He shall make up for all past delinquencies as sure as I'm a living soul!'

There followed a disgraceful contest; Lord Lowborough, in desperate earnest, and pale with anger, silently struggling to release himself from the powerful madman that was striving to drag him from the room. I attempted to urge Arthur to interfere in behalf of his outraged guest, but he could do nothing but laugh.

'Huntingdon, you fool, come and help me, can't you!' cried Hattersley, himself somewhat weakened by his excesses.

'I'm wishing you Godspeed, Hattersley,' cried Arthur, 'and aiding you with my prayers: I can't do anything else if my life depended on it! I'm quite used up. Oh, ho!' and leaning back in his seat, he clapped his hands on his sides and groaned aloud.

'Annabella, give me a candle!' said Lowborough whose antagonist had now got him round the waist and was endeavouring to root him from the doorpost to which he madly clung with all the energy of desperation.

'*I* shall take no part in your rude sports!' replied the lady, coldly drawing back, 'I wonder you can expect it.'

But I snatched up a candle and brought it to him. He took it and held the flame to Hattersley's hands till, roaring like a wild beast, the latter unclasped them and let him go. He vanished, I suppose to his own apartment, for nothing more was seen of him till the morning. Swearing and cursing like a maniac, Hattersley threw himself on to the ottoman beside the window. The door being now free, Milicent attempted to make her escape from the scene of her husband's disgrace; but he called her back, and insisted upon her coming to him.

'What do you want, Ralph?' murmured she, reluctantly approaching him.

'I want to know what's the matter with you,' said he, pulling her on to his knee like a child. 'What are you crying for, Milicent? – Tell me!'

'I'm not crying.'

'You are,' persisted he, rudely pulling her hands from her face. 'How dare you tell such a lie?'

'I'm not crying now,' pleaded she.

'But you have been – and just this minute too; and I *will* know what for. Come now, you *shall* tell me!'

'Do let me alone, Ralph! Remember we are not at home.'

'No matter: you *shall* answer my question!' exclaimed her tormentor; and he attempted to extort the confession by shaking her and remorselessly crushing her slight arms in the grip of his powerful fingers.

'Don't let him treat your sister in that way,' said I to Mr Hargrave.

'Come now, Hattersley, I can't allow that,' said that gentleman, stepping up to the ill-assorted couple. 'You let my sister alone, if you please.' And he made an effort to unclasp the ruffian's fingers from her arm, but was suddenly driven backward and nearly laid upon the floor by a violent blow in the chest accompanied with the admonition, 'Take that for your insolence! – and learn not to interfere between me and mine again.'

'If you were not beastly drunk, I'd have satisfaction for that!' gasped Hargrave, white and breathless as much from passion as from the immediate effects of the blow.

'Go to the devil!' responded his brother-in-law. 'Now Milicent, tell me what you were crying for.'

'I'll tell you some other time,' murmured she, 'when we are alone.'

'Tell me now!' said he with another shake and a squeeze that made her draw in her breath and bite her lip to suppress a cry of pain.

'*I'll* tell you, Mr Hattersley,' said I. 'She was crying from pure shame and humiliation for you; because she could not bear to see you conduct yourself so disgracefully.'

'Confound you, madam!' muttered he, with a stare of stupid amazement at my 'impudence'. 'It was *not* that – was it Milicent?'

She was silent.

'Come, speak up child!'

'I can't tell now,' sobbed she.

'But you can say "yes" or "no" as well as "I can't tell" – come!'

'Yes,' she whispered, hanging her head and blushing at the awful acknowledgement.

'Curse you for an impertinent hussy then!' cried he, throwing her from him with such violence that she fell on her side; but she was up again before either I or her brother could come to her assistance, and made the best of her way out of the room and, I suppose, upstairs, without loss of time.

The next object of assault was Arthur, who sat opposite, and had no doubt richly enjoyed the whole scene.

'Now, Huntingdon,' exclaimed his irascible friend, 'I will not have you sitting there and laughing like an idiot!'

'Oh, Hattersley!' cried he, wiping his swimming eyes – 'you'll be the death of me.'

'Yes I will, but not as you suppose: I'll have the heart out of your body, man, if you irritate me with any more of that imbecile laughter! – What! are you at it yet? – There! see if that'll settle you!' cried Hattersley, snatching up a footstool and hurling it at the head of his host; but he missed his aim and the latter still sat collapsed and quaking with feeble laughter, with the tears running down his face; a deplorable spectacle indeed.

Hattersley tried cursing and swearing, but it would not do; he then took a number of books from the table beside him and threw them, one by one, at the object of his wrath, but Arthur only laughed the more; and, finally, Hattersley rushed upon him in a frenzy, and, seizing him by the shoulders, gave him a violent shaking, under which he laughed and shrieked alarmingly. But I saw no more: I thought I had witnessed enough of my husband's degradation; and, leaving Annabella and the rest to follow when they pleased, I withdrew – but not to bed. Dismissing Rachel to her rest, I walked up and down my room, in an agony of misery, for what had been done, and suspense, not knowing what might further happen or how or when that unhappy creature would come up to bed.

At last he came, slowly and stumblingly, ascending the stairs, supported by Grimsby and Hattersley, who neither of them walked quite steadily themselves, but were both laughing and joking at him, and making noise enough for all the servants to hear. He himself was no longer laughing now, but sick and stupid – I will write no more about *that*.

Such disgraceful scenes (or nearly such) have been repeated more than once. I don't say much to Arthur about it, for if I did, it would do more harm than good; but I let him know that I intensely dislike such exhibitions; and each time

he has promised they should never again be repeated; but I fear he is losing the little self-command and self-respect he once possessed: formerly, he would have been ashamed to act thus at least, before any other witnesses than his boon companions, or such as they. His friend, Hargrave, with a prudence and self-government that I envy for *him*, never disgraces himself by taking more than sufficient to render him a little "elevated", and is always the first to leave the table, after Lord Lowborough, who, wiser still, perseveres in vacating the dining-room immediately after us; but never once, since Annabella offended him so deeply, has he entered the drawing-room before the rest; always spending the interim in the library, which I take care to have lighted for his accommodation – or, on fine moonlight nights, in roaming about the grounds. But I think she regrets her misconduct, for she has never repeated it since, and of late she has comported herself with wonderful propriety towards him, treating him with more uniform kindness and consideration than ever I have observed her to do before. I date the time of this improvement from the period when she ceased to hope and strive for Arthur's admiration.

## CHAPTER 32

### *Comparisons: Information Rejected*

October 5th. Esther Hargrave is getting a fine girl. She is not out of the schoolroom yet, but her mother frequently brings her over to call in the mornings when the gentlemen are out, and sometimes she spends an hour or two in company with her sister, and me, and the children; and when we go to the Grove, I always contrive to see her, and talk more to her than to anyone else, for I am very much attached to my little friend, and so is she to me. I wonder what she can see to like in me though, for I am no longer the happy, lively girl I used to be; but she has no other society – save that of her uncongenial mother, and her governess (as artificial and conventional a person as that prudent mother could procure to rectify the pupil's natural qualities), and, now and then, her subdued, quiet sister. I often wonder what will be *her* lot in life – and so does she; but *her* speculations on the future are full of buoyant hope – so were mine once. I shudder to think of her being awakened like me to a sense of their delusive vanity. It seems as if I should feel her disappointment even more deeply than my own: I feel, almost, as if I were born for such a fate, but *she* is so joyous and fresh, so light of heart and free of spirit, and so guileless and unsuspecting too – oh, it would be cruel to make her feel as I feel now, and know what I have known!

Her sister trembles for her too. Yesterday morning, one of October's brightest, loveliest days, Milicent and I were in the garden enjoying a brief half hour together with our children, while Annabella was lying on the drawing-room sofa, deep in the last new novel. We had been romping with the little

creatures, almost as merry and wild as themselves, and now paused in the shade of the tall copper beech, to recover breath and rectify our hair, disordered by the rough play and the frolicsome breeze – while they toddled together along the broad, sunny walk; my Arthur supporting the feebler steps of her little Helen, and sagaciously pointing out to her the brightest beauties of the border as they passed, with semi-articulate prattle that did as well for her as any other mode of discourse. From laughing at the pretty sight, we began to talk of the children's future life; and that made us thoughtful. We both relapsed into silent musing as we slowly proceeded up the walk; and I suppose Milicent by a train of associations was led to think of her sister.

'Helen,' said she, 'you often see Esther, don't you?'

'Not very often.'

'But you have more frequent opportunities of meeting her than I have: and she loves you I know, and reverences you too: there is nobody's opinion she thinks so much of; and she says you have more sense than mamma.'

'That is because she is self-willed, and my opinions more generally coincide with her own than your mamma's. But what then, Milicent?'

'Well, since you have so much influence with her, I wish you would seriously impress it upon her, never, on any account, or for anybody's persuasion, to marry for the sake of money, or rank, or establishment, or any earthly thing, but true affection and well-grounded esteem.'

'There is no necessity for that,' said I: 'for we have had some discourse on that subject already, and I assure you her ideas of love and matrimony are as romantic as anyone could desire.'

'But romantic notions will not do: I want her to have true notions.'

'Very right, but in my judgement, what the world stigmatises as romantic, is often more nearly allied to the truth than is commonly supposed; for, if the generous ideas of youth are too often overclouded by the sordid views of afterlife, that scarcely proves them to be false.'

'Well, but if you think her ideas are what they ought to be, strengthen them, will you? And confirm them, as far as you can; for *I* had romantic notions once, and I don't mean to say that I regret my lot, for I am quite sure I don't – but –'

'I understand you,' said I; 'you are contented for yourself, but you would not have your sister to suffer the same as you.'

'No – or worse. She might have far worse to suffer than I – for I *am really* contented, Helen, though you mayn't think it: I speak the solemn truth in saying that I would not exchange my husband for any man on earth, if I might do it by the plucking of this leaf.'

'Well, I believe you: now that you have him, you would not exchange *him* for another; but then you would gladly exchange some of his qualities for those of better men.'

'Yes; just as I would gladly exchange some of my own qualities for those of better women; for neither he nor I are perfect, and I desire his improvement as earnestly as my own. And he will improve – don't you think so, Helen? – he's only six and twenty yet.'

'He may,' I answered.

'He will – he will!' repeated she.

'Excuse the faintness of my acquiescence, Milicent; I would not discourage your hopes for the world, but mine have been so often disappointed, that I am become as cold and doubtful in my expectations as the flattest of octogenarians.'

'And yet you do hope, still – even for Mr Huntingdon?'

'I do, I confess – "even" for *him*; for it seems as if life and hope must cease together. And is he so *much* worse, Milicent, than Mr Hattersley?'

'Well, to give you my candid opinion, I think there is no comparison between them. But you mustn't be offended, Helen, for you know I always speak my mind; and you may speak yours too; I shan't care.'

'I am not offended, love; and *my* opinion is that if there *be* a comparison made between the two, the difference, for the most part, is certainly in Hattersley's favour.'

Milicent's own heart told her how much it cost me to make this acknowledgement; and, with a childlike impulse, she expressed her sympathy by suddenly kissing my cheek, without a word of reply, and then turning quickly away caught up her baby, and hid her face in its frock. How odd it is that we so often weep for each other's distresses, when we shed not a tear for our own! Her heart had been full enough of her own sorrows, but it overflowed at the idea of mine; and I too, shed tears at the sight of her sympathetic emotion, though I had not wept for myself for many a week.

But Milicent's satisfaction in her choice is not entirely feigned: she really loves her husband; and it is too true that he loses nothing by comparison with mine. Either he is less unbridled in his excesses, or owing to his stronger, hardier frame, they produce a much less deleterious effect upon him; for he never reduces himself to a state in any degree bordering on imbecility, and with him the worst effect of a night's debauch is a slight increase of irascibility, or it may be a season of sullen ferocity on the following morning: there is nothing of that lost, depressing appearance – that peevish, ignoble fretfulness, that wears one out with very shame for the transgressor. But then, it was not formerly so with Arthur: he can bear less now than he could at Hattersley's age; and if the latter does not reform, his powers of endurance may be equally impaired when he has tried them as long. He has five years the advantage of his friend, and his vices have not mastered him yet: he has not folded them to him and made them a part of himself. They seem to sit loose upon him, like a cloak that he could throw aside at any moment if he would – but how long will that option be left him? – Though a creature of passion and sense, regardless of the duties and the higher privileges of intelligent beings, he is no voluptuary: he prefers the more active and invigorating animal enjoyments, to those of a more relaxing, enervating kind. He does not make a *science* of the gratification of his appetites either in the pleasures of the table or anything else; he eats heartily what is set before him, without demeaning himself by any of that abandonment to the palate and the eye – that unbecoming particularity in approval or disapproval which it is so hateful to witness in those we would esteem. Arthur, I fear, would give himself

up to luxury as the chief good, and might ultimately plunge into the grossest excesses, but for the fear of irremediably blunting his appetites, and destroying his powers of further enjoyment. For Hattersley, graceless ruffian as he is, I believe there is more reasonable ground of hope; and – far be it from me to blame poor Milicent for his delinquencies – but I do think that if she had the courage or the will to speak her mind about them, and maintain her point unflinchingly, there would be more chance of his reclamation, and he would be likely to treat her better, and love her more, in the end. I am partly led to think so by what he said to me himself, not many days ago – I purpose to give her a little advice on the subject sometime; but still, I hesitate from the consciousness that her ideas and disposition are both against it, and if my counsels failed to do good, they would do harm by making her more unhappy.

It was one rainy day last week: most of the company were killing time in the billiard-room, but Milicent and I were with little Arthur and Helen in the library, and between our books, our children, and each other, we expected to make out a very agreeable morning. We had not been thus secluded above two hours, however, when Mr Hattersley came in attracted, I suppose, by the voice of his child as he was crossing the hall, for he is prodigiously fond of her, and she of him.

He was redolent of the stables, where he had been regaling himself with the company of his fellow-creatures, the horses, ever since breakfast. But that was no matter to my little namesake: as soon as the colossal person of her father darkened the door, she uttered a shrill scream of delight, and, quitting her mother's side, ran crowing towards him – balancing her course with out-stretched arms – and, embracing his knee, threw back her head and laughed in his face. He might well look smilingly down upon those small, fair features radiant with innocent mirth, those clear, blue, shining eyes, and that soft flaxen hair cast back upon the little ivory neck and shoulders. Did he not think how unworthy he was of such a possession? I fear no such idea crossed his mind. He caught her up, and there followed some minutes of very rough play, during which it is difficult to say whether the father or the daughter laughed and shouted the loudest. At length, however, the boisterous pastime terminated – suddenly, as might be expected: the little one was hurt and began to cry; and its ungentle playfellow tossed it into its mother's lap, bidding her 'make all straight.' As happy to return to that gentle comforter as it had been to leave her, the child nestled in her arms and hushed its cries in a moment; and, sinking its little weary head on her bosom, soon dropped asleep.

Meantime, Mr Hattersley strode up to the fire, and, interposing his height and breadth between us and it, stood, with arms akimbo, expanding his chest, and gazing round him as if the house and all its appurtenances and contents were his own undisputed possessions.

'Deuced bad weather this!' he began. 'There'll be no shooting today, I guess.' Then, suddenly lifting up his voice, he regaled us with a few bars of a rollicking song, which abruptly ceasing, he finished the tune with a whistle, and then continued – 'I say, Mrs Huntingdon, what a fine stud your husband has! – Not

large but good – I've been looking at them a bit this morning; and upon my word, Black Bess, and Grey Tom, and that young Nimrod are the finest animals I've seen for many a day!' Then followed a particular discussion of their various merits, succeeded by a sketch of the great things *he* intended to do in the horse-jockey line when his old governor thought proper to quit the stage – 'Not that I wish him to close his accounts,' added he; 'the old Trojan is welcome to keep his books open as long as he pleases for me.'

'I hope so, *indeed*, Mr Hattersley!'

'Oh yes! It's only my way of talking. The event must come, sometime, and so I look to the bright side of it – that's the right plan, isn't it, Mrs H.? – What are you two doing here, by the by – where's Lady Lowborough?'

'In the billiard-room.'

'What a splendid creature she *is*!' continued he, fixing his eyes on his wife, who changed colour, and looked more and more disconcerted as he proceeded. 'What a noble figure she has! And what magnificent black eyes; and what a fine spirit of her own; and what a tongue of her own, too, when she likes to use it – I perfectly adore her! – But never mind, Milicent; I wouldn't have her for my wife – not if she'd a kingdom for her dowry! I'm better satisfied with the one I have – Now *then*! What do you look so sulky for? Don't you believe me?'

'Yes, I believe you,' murmured she, in a tone of half-sad, half-sullen resignation, as she turned away to stroke the hair of her sleeping infant, that she had laid on the sofa beside her.

'Well *then*, what makes you so cross? Come here Milly, and tell me why you can't be satisfied with my assurance.'

She went, and, putting her little hand within his arm, looked up in his face, and said softly – 'What does it amount to, Ralph? Only to this, that though you admire Annabella so much, and for qualities that I don't possess, you would still rather have me than her for your wife, which merely proves that you don't think it necessary to love your wife: you are satisfied if she can keep your house and take care of your child. But I'm not cross; I'm only sorry; for,' added she in a low, tremulous accent, withdrawing her hand from his arm, and bending her looks on the rug, 'if you don't love me, you don't, and it can't be helped.'

'Very true: but who told you I didn't? Did I say I loved Annabella?'

'You said you adored her.'

'True, but adoration isn't love. I adore Annabella, but I don't love her; and I love thee, Milicent, but I don't adore thee.' In proof of his affection, he clutched a handful of her light brown ringlets and appeared to twist them unmercifully.

'Do you really, Ralph?' murmured she, with a faint smile beaming through her tears, just putting up her hand to his, in token that he pulled *rather* too hard.

'To be sure I do,' responded he: 'only you bother me rather, sometimes.'

'*I* bother you!' cried she in very natural surprise.

'Yes, *you* – but only by your exceeding goodness – when a boy has been cramming raisins and sugar-plums all day, he longs for a squeeze of sour orange by way of a change. And did you never, Milly, observe the sands on the sea-shore; how nice and smooth they look, and how soft and easy they feel to the

foot? But if you plod along, for half an hour, over this soft, easy carpet – giving way at every step, yielding the more the harder you press – you'll find it rather wearisome work, and be glad enough to come to a bit of good, firm rock, that won't budge an inch whether you stand, walk, or stamp upon it; and, though it be hard as the nether millstone, you'll find it the easier footing after all.'

'I know what you mean, Ralph,' said she, nervously playing with her watch-guard and tracing the figure on the rug with the point of her tiny foot, 'I know what you mean, but I thought you always liked to be yielded to; and I can't alter now.'

'I do like it,' replied he, bringing her to him by another tug at her hair. 'You mustn't mind my talk Milly. A man must have something to grumble about; and if he can't complain that his wife harries him to death with her perversity and ill-humour, he must complain that she wears him out with her kindness and gentleness.'

'But why complain at all, unless, because you are tired and dissatisfied?'

'To excuse my own failings, to be sure. Do you think I'll bear all the burden of my sins on my own shoulders, as long as there's another ready to help me, with none of her own to carry?'

'There is no such one on earth,' said she seriously; and then, taking his hand from her head, she kissed it with an air of genuine devotion, and tripped away to the door.

'What now?' said he. 'Where are you going?'

'To tidy my hair,' she answered, smiling through her disordered locks: 'you've made it all come down.'

'Off with you then! – An excellent little woman,' he remarked when she was gone, 'but a thought too soft – she almost melts in one's hands. I positively think I ill-use her sometimes, when I've taken too much – but I can't help it, for she never complains, either at the time or after. I suppose she doesn't mind it.'

'I can enlighten you on that subject, Mr Hattersley,' said I: 'she *does* mind it; and some other things she minds still more, which, yet, you may never hear her complain of.'

'How do you know? – does she complain to you?' demanded he, with a sudden spark of fury ready to burst into a flame if I should answer, "Yes."

'No,' I replied; 'but I have known her longer and studied her more closely than you have done – And I can tell you, Mr Hattersley, that Milicent loves you more than you deserve, and that you have it in your power to make her very happy, instead of which you are her evil genius, and, I will venture to say, there is not a single day passes in which you do not inflict upon her some pang that you might spare her if you would.'

'Well – it's not *my* fault,' said he, gazing carelessly up at the ceiling and plunging his hands into his pockets: 'if my ongoings don't suit her, she should tell me so.'

'Is she not exactly the wife you wanted? Did you not tell Mr Huntingdon you must have one that would submit to anything without a murmur, and never blame you, whatever you did?'

'True, but we shouldn't always have what we want: it spoils the best of us, doesn't it? How can I help playing the deuce when I see it's all one to her whether I behave like a Christian or like a scoundrel such as nature made me? – and how can I help teasing her when she's so invitingly meek and mim – when she lies down like a spaniel at my feet and never so much as squeaks to tell me that's enough?'

'If you are a tyrant by nature, the temptation is strong, I allow; but no generous mind delights to oppress the weak, but rather to cherish and protect.'

'I *don't* oppress her; but it's so confounded flat to be always cherishing and protecting; and then how can I tell that I *am* oppressing her when she "melts away and makes no sign"? I sometimes think she has no feeling at all; and then I go on till she cries – and that satisfies me.'

'Then you *do* delight to oppress her.'

'I don't, I tell you! – Only when I'm in a bad humour – or a particularly good one, and want to afflict for the pleasure of comforting; or when she looks flat and wants shaking up a bit. And sometimes, she provokes me by crying for nothing, and won't tell me what it's for; and then, I allow, it enrages me past bearing – especially, when I'm not my own man.'

'As is no doubt generally the case on such occasions,' said I. 'But in future, Mr Hattersley, when you see her looking flat or crying for "nothing" (as you call it), ascribe it all to yourself: be assured it is something you have done amiss, or your general misconduct that distresses her.'

'I don't believe it. If it were, she should tell me so: I don't like that way of moping and fretting in silence, and saying nothing – it's not honest. How can she expect me to mend my ways at that rate?'

'Perhaps she gives you credit for having more sense than you possess, and deludes herself with the hope that you will one day see your own errors and repair them, if left to your own reflection.'

'None of your sneers, Mrs Huntingdon! I *have* the sense to see that I'm not always quite correct – but sometimes I think that's no great matter, as long as I injure nobody but myself – '

'It *is* a great matter,' interrupted I, 'both to yourself (as you will hereafter find to your cost) and to all connected with you – most especially your wife – but indeed, it is nonsense to talk about injuring no one but yourself; it is impossible to injure yourself – especially by such acts as we allude to – without injuring hundreds, if not thousands, besides, in a greater or less degree, either by the evil you do or the good you leave undone.'

'And as I was saying,' continued he – 'or would have said if you hadn't taken me up so short – I sometimes think I should do better if I were joined to one that would always remind me when I was wrong, and give me a motive for doing good and eschewing evil by decidedly showing her approval of the one, and disapproval of the other.'

'If you had no higher motive than the approval of your fellow mortal, it would do you little good.'

'Well, but if I had a mate that would not always be yielding, and always

equally kind, but that would have the spirit to stand at bay now and then, and honestly tell me her mind at all times – such a one as yourself for instance – now if I went on with you as I do with her when I'm in London, you'd make the house too hot to hold me at times, I'll be sworn.'

'You mistake me: I'm no termagant.'

'Well, all the better for that, for I can't stand contradiction – in a general way – and I'm as fond of my own will as another: only I think too much of it doesn't answer for any man.'

'Well, I would never contradict you without a cause, but certainly I would always let you know what I thought of your conduct; and if you oppressed me, in body, mind, or estate, you should at least have no reason to suppose "I didn't mind it." '

'I know that my lady; and I think if my little wife were to follow the same plan it would be better for us both.'

'I'll tell her.'

'No, no, let her be; there's much to be said on both sides – and, now I think upon it, Huntingdon often regrets that you are not more like her – scoundrelly dog that he is – and you see, after all, you can't reform *him*: he's *ten* times worse than I – He's afraid of you, to be sure – that is, he's always on his best behaviour in your presence – but –'

'I wonder what his worst behaviour is like, then?' I could not forbear observing.

'Why, to tell you the truth, it's very bad indeed – isn't it, Hargrave?' said he, addressing that gentleman, who had entered the room unperceived by me, for I was now standing near the fire with my back to the door. 'Isn't Huntingdon,' he continued, 'as great a reprobate as ever was damned?'

'His lady will not hear him censured with impunity,' replied Mr Hargrave, coming forward, 'but I must say, I thank God I am not such another.'

'Perhaps it would become you better,' said I, 'to look at what you are, and say, "God be merciful to me a sinner." '

'You are severe,' returned he, bowing slightly and drawing himself up with a proud yet injured air. Hattersley laughed, and clapped him on the shoulder. Moving from under his hand with a gesture of insulted dignity, Mr Hargrave took himself away to the other end of the rug.

'Isn't it a shame, Mrs Huntingdon?' cried his brother-in-law – 'I struck Walter Hargrave when I was drunk, the second night after we came, and he's turned a cold shoulder on me ever since; though I asked his pardon the very morning after it was done!'

'Your manner of asking it,' returned the other, 'and the clearness with which you remembered the whole transaction, showed you were not too drunk to be fully conscious of what you were about, and quite responsible for the deed.'

'You wanted to interfere between me and my wife,' grumbled Hattersley, 'and that is enough to provoke any man.'

'You justify it then?' said his opponent, darting upon him a most vindictive glance.

'No, I tell you I wouldn't have done it if I hadn't been under excitement; and

if you choose to bear malice for it, after all the handsome things I've said – do so and be damned!'

'I *would* refrain from such language in a *lady's* presence, at least,' said Mr Hargrave, hiding his anger under a mask of disgust.

'What have I said?' returned Hattersley. 'Nothing but Heaven's truth – he will be damned, won't he, Mrs Huntingdon, if he doesn't forgive his brother's trespasses?'

'You ought to forgive him, Mr Hargrave, since he asks you,' said I.

'Do you say so? Then I will!' And, smiling almost frankly, he stepped forward and offered his hand. It was immediately clasped in that of his relative, and the reconciliation was apparently cordial on both sides.

'The affront,' continued Hargrave, turning to me, 'owed half its bitterness to the fact of its being offered in your presence; and since you bid me forgive it, I will – and forget it too.'

'I guess the best return I can make, will be to take myself off,' muttered Hattersley, with a broad grin.

His companion smiled; and he left the room. This put me on my guard. Mr Hargrave turned seriously to me, and earnestly began – 'Dear Mrs Huntingdon, how I have longed for, yet dreaded this hour! Do not be alarmed,' he added, for my face was crimson with anger; 'I am not about to offend you with any useless entreaties or complaints. I am not going to presume to trouble you with the mention of my own feelings or your perfections, but I have something to reveal to you which you ought to know, and which, yet, it pains me inexpressibly – '

'Then don't trouble yourself to reveal it!'

'But it is of importance – '

'If so, I shall hear it soon enough – especially if it is bad news, as you seem to consider it. At present, I am going to take the children to the nursery.'

'But can't you ring, and send them?'

'No; I want the exercise of a run to the top of the house – Come Arthur.'

'But you will return?'

'Not yet; don't wait.'

'Then, when may I see you again?'

'At lunch,' said I, departing with little Helen in one arm, and leading Arthur by the hand.

He turned away, muttering some sentence of impatient censure or complaint, in which 'heartless' was the only distinguishable word.

'What nonsense is this, Mr Hargrave?' said I, pausing in the doorway. 'What do you mean?'

'Oh, nothing – I did not intend you should hear my soliloquy. But the fact is, Mrs Huntingdon, I have a disclosure to make – painful for me to offer as for you to hear – and I want you to give me a few minutes of your attention in private, at any time and place you like to appoint. It is from no selfish motive that I ask it, and not for any cause that could alarm your superhuman purity; therefore, you need not kill me with that look of cold and pitiless disdain. I know too well the feelings with which the bearers of bad tidings are commonly regarded, not to – '

'What *is* this wonderful piece of intelligence?' said I, impatiently interrupting him. 'If it is anything of real importance, speak it in three words before I go.'

'In three words I cannot. Send those children away, and stay with me.'

'No; keep your bad tidings to yourself. I know it is something I don't want to hear, and something you would displease me by telling.'

'You have divined too truly I fear; but still since I know it, I feel it my duty to disclose it to you.'

'Oh, spare us both the infliction – and I will exonerate you from the duty. You have offered to tell; I have refused to hear: my ignorance will not be charged on you.'

'Be it so – you shall not hear it from me. But if the blow fall too suddenly upon you when it comes, remember – I wished to soften it!'

I left him. I was determined his words should not alarm me. What could *he* of all men, have to reveal that was of importance for *me* to hear? It was no doubt some exaggerated tale about my unfortunate husband, that he wished to make the most of to serve his own bad purposes.

6th. He has not alluded to this momentous mystery since; and I have seen no reason to repent of my unwillingness to hear it. The threatened blow has not been struck yet; and I do not greatly fear it. At present I am pleased with Arthur: he has not positively disgraced himself for upwards of a fortnight, and all this last week, has been so very moderate in his indulgence at table, that I can perceive a marked difference in his general temper and appearance. Dare I hope this will continue?

## CHAPTER 33

### Two Evenings

Seventh. Yes, I *will* hope! Tonight, I heard Grimsby and Hattersley grumbling together, about the inhospitality of their host. They did not know I was near, for I happened to be standing behind the curtain, in the bow of the window, watching the moon rising over the clump of tall, dark elm trees below the lawn and wondering why Arthur was so sentimental as to stand without, leaning against the outer pillar of the portico, apparently watching it too.

'So, I suppose we've seen the last of our merry carousals in this house,' said Mr Hattersley. 'I *thought* his good-fellowship wouldn't last long – But,' added he, laughing, 'I didn't expect it would meet its end this way. I rather thought our pretty hostess would be setting up her porcupine quills, and threatening to turn us out of the house, if we didn't mind our manners.'

'You didn't foresee *this*, then?' answered Grimsby with a guttural chuckle. 'But he'll change again when he's sick of her. If we come here a year or two hence, we shall have all our own way, you'll see.'

'I don't know,' replied the other: 'she's not the style of woman you soon tire of – but be that as it may, it's devilish provoking now that we can't be jolly because he chooses to be on his good behaviour.'

'It's all these cursed women!' muttered Grimsby. 'They're the very bane of the world! They bring trouble and discomfort wherever they come, with their false, fair faces and their damned deceitful tongues.'

At this juncture, I issued from my retreat, and smiling on Mr Grimsby as I passed, left the room and went out in search of Arthur. Having seen him bend his course towards the shrubbery, I followed him thither, and found him just entering the shadowy walk. I was so light of heart, so overflowing with affection, that I sprang upon him and clasped him in my arms. This startling conduct had a singular effect upon him: first, he murmured, 'Bless you, darling!' and returned my close embrace with a fervour like old times, and *then* he started, and in a tone of absolute terror, exclaimed – 'Helen! – What the devil is this!' and I saw, by the faint light gleaming through the overshadowing tree, that he was positively pale with the shock.

How strange that the instinctive impulse of affection should come first, and then the shock of the surprise! It shows at least that the affection is genuine: he is not sick of me yet.

'I startled you, Arthur,' said I, laughing in my glee. 'How nervous you are!'

'What the deuce did you do it for?' cried he, quite testily, extricating himself from my arms, and wiping his forehead with his handkerchief. 'Go back, Helen – go back directly! You'll get your death of cold!'

'I won't – till I've told you what I came for. They are blaming you, Arthur, for your temperance and sobriety, and I'm come to thank you for it. They say it is all "these cursed women", and that we are the bane of the world; but don't let them laugh, or grumble you out of your good resolutions, or your affection for me.'

He laughed. I squeezed him in my arms again, and cried in tearful earnest – 'Do – do persevere! – and I'll love you better than ever I did before!'

'Well, well, I will!' said he, hastily kissing me. 'There now, go – You mad creature, how *could* you come out in your light evening dress, this chill autumn night?'

'It is a glorious night,' said I.

'It is a night that will give you your death, in another minute. Run away, do!'

'Do you see my death among those trees, Arthur?' said I, for he was gazing intently at the shrubs, as if he saw it coming, and I was reluctant to leave him, in my new-found happiness, and revival of hope and love. But he grew angry at my delay, so I kissed him and ran back to the house.

I was in such a good humour that night: Milicent told me I was the life of the party, and whispered she had never seen me so brilliant. Certainly, I talked enough for twenty, and smiled upon them all. Grimsby, Hattersley, Hargrave, Lady Lowborough – all shared my sisterly kindness. Grimsby stared and wondered; Hattersley laughed and jested (in spite of the little wine he had been suffered to imbibe), but still, behaved as well as he knew how; Hargrave and

Annabella, from different motives and in different ways emulated me, and doubtless both surpassed me, the former in his discursive versatility and eloquence, the latter in boldness and animation at least. Milicent, delighted to see her husband, her brother and her over-estimated friend acquitting themselves so well, was lively and gay too, in her quiet way. Even Lord Lowborough caught the general contagion: his dark, greenish eyes were lighted up beneath their moody brows; his sombre countenance was beautified by smiles; all traces of gloom, and proud or cold reserve had vanished for the time; and he astonished us all, not only by his general cheerfulness and animation, but by the positive flashes of true force and brilliance he emitted from time to time. Arthur did not talk much, but he laughed, and listened to the rest, and was in perfect good-humour, though not excited by wine. So that, altogether we made a very merry, innocent and entertaining party.

9th. Yesterday, when Rachel came to dress me for dinner, I saw that she had been crying. I wanted to know the cause of it, but she seemed reluctant to tell. Was she unwell? No. Had she heard bad news from her friends? No. Had any of the servants vexed her?

'Oh, no, ma'am!' she answered – 'It's not for myself.'

'What then, Rachel? Have you been reading novels?'

'Bless you, no!' said she with a sorrowful shake of the head; and then she sighed and continued, 'But to tell you the truth, ma'am, I don't like master's ways of going on.'

'What do you mean, Rachel? – He's going on very properly – at present.'

'Well, ma'am, if you think so, it's right.'

And she went on dressing my hair, in a hurried way, quite unlike her usual calm, collected manner – murmuring, half to herself, she was sure it was beautiful hair, she 'could like to see 'em match it'. When it was done, she fondly stroked it and gently patted my head.

'Is that affectionate ebullition intended for my hair, or myself, nurse?' said I, laughingly turning round upon her; but a tear was even now in her eye. 'What *do* you mean, Rachel?' I exclaimed.

'Well, ma'am, I don't know – but if –'

'If what?'

'Well, if I was you, I wouldn't have that Lady Lowborough in the house another minute – not another *minute* I wouldn't!'

I was thunderstruck; but before I could recover from the shock sufficiently to demand an explanation, Milicent entered my room – as she frequently does, when she is dressed before me; and she stayed with me till it was time to go down. She must have found me a very unsociable companion this time, for Rachel's last words rung in my ears. But still, I hoped – I trusted they had no foundation but in some idle rumour of the servants from what they had seen in Lady Lowborough's manner last month; or, perhaps, from something that had passed between their master and her during her former visit. At dinner, I narrowly observed both her and Arthur, and saw nothing extraordinary in the

conduct of either – nothing calculated to excite suspicion, except in distrustful minds – which mine was not, and therefore I would not suspect.

Almost immediately after dinner, Annabella went out with her husband to share his moonlight ramble, for it was a splendid evening like the last. Mr Hargrave entered the drawing-room a little before the others, and challenged me to a game of chess. He did it without any of that sad, but proud humility he usually assumes in addressing me, unless he is excited with wine. I looked at his face to see if that was the case now. His eye met mine keenly, but steadily: there was something about him I did not understand, but he seemed sober enough. Not choosing to engage with him, I referred him to Milicent.

'She plays badly,' said he: 'I want to match my skill with yours. Come now! – you can't pretend you are reluctant to lay down your work – I know you never take it up except to pass an idle hour, when there is nothing better you can do.'

'But chess players are so unsociable,' I objected; 'they are no company for any but themselves.'

'There is no one here – but Milicent, and she – '

'Oh, I shall be delighted to watch you!' cried our mutual friend – 'Two *such* players – it will be quite a treat! I wonder which will conquer.'

I consented.

'Now Mrs Huntingdon,' said Hargrave, as he arranged the men on the board, speaking distinctly, and with a peculiar emphasis as if he had a double meaning to all his words, 'you are a good player – but I am a better: we shall have a long game, and you will give me some trouble; but I can be as patient as you, and, in the end, I shall certainly win.' He fixed his eyes upon me with a glance I did not like – keen, crafty, bold, and almost impudent; already half triumphant in his anticipated success.

'I hope not, Mr Hargrave!' returned I, with vehemence that must have startled Milicent at least; but *he* only smiled and murmured,

'Time will show.'

We set to work; he, sufficiently interested in the game, but calm and fearless in the consciousness of superior skill; I, intensely eager to disappoint his expectations, for I considered this the type of a more serious contest – as I imagined he did – and I felt an almost superstitious dread of being beaten: at all events, I could ill endure that present success should add one tittle to his conscious power (his insolent self-confidence, I ought to say), or encourage, for a moment, his dream of future conquest. His play was cautious and deep, but I struggled hard against him. For some time the combat was doubtful; at length, to my joy, the victory seemed inclining to my side: I had taken several of his best pieces, and manifestly baffled his projects. He put his hand to his brow and paused, in evident perplexity. I rejoiced in my advantage, but dared not glory in it yet. At length, he lifted his head, and, quietly making his move, looked at me and said, calmly – 'Now you think you will win, don't you.'

'I hope so,' replied I, taking his pawn, that he had pushed into the way of my bishop with so careless an air that I thought it was an oversight, but was not generous enough, under the circumstances, to direct his attention

to it, and too heedless, at the moment, to foresee the after consequences of my move.

'It is those bishops that trouble me,' said he; 'but the bold knight can overleap the reverend gentleman,' taking my last bishop with his knight; 'and now, those sacred persons once removed, I shall carry all before me.'

'Oh, Walter, how you talk!' cried Milicent – 'She has far more pieces than you still.'

'I intend to give you some trouble yet,' said I; 'and perhaps, sir, you will find yourself checkmated before you are aware. Look to your queen.'

The combat deepened. The game was a long one, and I *did* give him some trouble: but he *was* a better player than I.

'What keen gamesters you are!' said Mr Hattersley, who had now entered, and been watching us for some time. 'Why, Mrs Huntingdon, your hand trembles as if you had staked your all upon it! and Walter – you dog – you look as deep and cool as if you were certain of success – and as keen and cruel as if you would drain her heart's blood! – But if I were you, I wouldn't beat her, for very fear: she'll hate you if you do – she will, by Heaven! – I see it in her eye.'

'Hold your tongue, will you?' said I – his talk distracted me, for I was driven to extremities. A few more moves and I was inextricably entangled in the snare of my antagonist.

'Check,' cried he: I sought in agony some means of escape – 'mate!' he added, quietly but with evident delight. He had suspended the utterance of that last fatal syllable the better to enjoy my dismay. I was foolishly disconcerted by the event. Hattersley laughed; Milicent was troubled to see me so disturbed. Hargrave placed his hand on mine that rested on the table, and squeezing it with a firm but gentle pressure, murmured 'Beaten – beaten!' and gazed into my face with a look where exultation was blended with an expression of ardour and tenderness yet more insulting.

'No, *never*, Mr Hargrave!' exclaimed I, quickly withdrawing my hand.

'Do you deny?' replied he, smilingly pointing to the board.

'No, no,' I answered, recollecting how strange my conduct must appear; 'you have beaten me in that game.'

'Will you try another, then?'

'No.'

'You acknowledge my superiority?'

'Yes – as a chess-player.'

I rose to resume my work.

'Where is Annabella?' said Hargrave, gravely, after glancing round the room.

'Gone out with Lord Lowborough,' answered I, for he looked at me for a reply.

'And not yet returned!' he said seriously.

'I suppose not.'

'Where is Huntingdon?' looking round again.

'Gone out with Grimsby – as you know,' said Hattersley suppressing a laugh, which broke forth as he concluded the sentence.

Why did he laugh? Why did Hargrave connect them thus together? Was it true, then? – And was this the dreadful secret he had wished to reveal to me ? I must know – and that quickly. I instantly rose and left the room to go in search of Rachel, and demand an explanation of her words; but Mr Hargrave followed me into the ante-room, and before I could open its outer door, gently laid his hand upon the lock.

'May I tell you something, Mrs Huntingdon?' said he, in a subdued tone, with serious, downcast eyes.

'If it be anything worth hearing,' replied I, struggling to be composed, for I trembled in every limb.

He quietly pushed a chair towards me. I merely leant my hand upon it, and bid him go on.

'Do not be alarmed,' said he: 'what I wish to say is nothing in itself; and I will leave you to draw your own inferences from it. You say that Annabella is not yet returned?'

'Yes, yes – go on!' said I, impatiently, for I feared my forced calmness would leave me before the end of his disclosure, whatever it might be.

'And you hear,' continued he, 'that Huntingdon is gone out with Grimsby?'

'Well?'

'I heard the latter say to your husband – or the man who calls himself so – '

'Go on, sir!'

He bowed submissively, and continued, 'I heard him say – "I shall manage it, you'll see! They're gone down by the water; I shall meet them there, and tell him I want a bit of talk with him about some things that we needn't trouble the lady with; and she'll say she can be walking back to the house; and then I shall apologise, you know, and all that, and tip her a wink to take the way of the shrubbery. I'll keep him talking there, about those matters I mentioned, and anything else I can think of, as long as I can, and then bring him round the other way, stopping to look at the trees, the fields, and anything else I can find to discourse of." ' Mr Hargrave paused, and looked at me.

Without a word of comment or further questioning, I rose, and darted from the room and out of the house. The torment of suspense was not to be endured: I would not suspect my husband falsely, on this man's accusation, and I would not trust him unworthily – I must know the truth at once. I flew to the shrubbery. Scarcely had I reached it, when a sound of voices arrested my breathless speed.

'We have lingered too long; he will be back,' said Lady Lowborough's voice.

'Surely not, dearest!' was *his* reply, 'but you can run across the lawn, and get in as quietly as you can: I'll follow in a while.'

My knees trembled under me; my brain swam round: I was ready to faint. She must not see me thus. I shrunk among the bushes, and leant against the trunk of a tree to let her pass.

'Ah, Huntingdon!' said she reproachfully, pausing where I had stood with him the night before – 'it was here you kissed that woman!' She looked back into the leafy shade. Advancing thence, he answered, with a careless laugh – 'Well,

dearest, I couldn't help it. You know I must keep straight with her as long as I can. Haven't I seen you kiss your dolt of a husband, scores of times? – and do *I* ever complain?'

'But tell me, don't you love her still – a *little*?' said she placing her hand on his arm and looking earnestly in his face – for I could see them plainly, the moon shining full upon them from between the branches of the tree that sheltered me.

'Not *one bit*, by all that's sacred!' he replied, kissing her glowing cheek.

'Good Heavens, I *must* be gone!' cried she, suddenly breaking from him, and away she flew.

There he stood before me; but I had not strength to confront him now; my tongue cleaved to the roof of my mouth, I was well nigh sinking to the earth, and I almost wondered he did not hear the beating of my heart above the low sighing of the wind, and the fitful rustle of the falling leaves. My senses seemed to fail me, but still I saw his shadowy form pass before me, and through the rushing sound in my ears, I distinctly heard him say, as he stood looking up the lawn – 'There goes the fool! Run, Annabella, run! There – in with you! Ah, he didn't see! That's right, Grimsby, keep him back!' And even his low laugh reached me as he walked away.

'God help me now!' I murmured, sinking on my knees among the damp weeds and brushwood that surrounded me, and looking up at the moonlit sky, through the scant foliage above. It seemed all dim and quivering now to my darkened sight. My burning, bursting heart strove to pour forth its agony to God, but could not frame its anguish into prayer; until a gust of wind swept over me, which, while it scattered the dead leaves, like blighted hopes, around, cooled my forehead, and seemed a little to revive my sinking frame. Then, while I lifted up my soul in speechless, earnest supplication, some heavenly influence seemed to strengthen me within: I breathed more freely; my vision cleared; I saw distinctly the pure moon shining on, and the light clouds skimming the clear, dark sky; and then, I saw the eternal stars twinkling down upon me; I knew their God was mine, and He was strong to save and swift to hear. 'I will never leave thee, nor forsake thee,' seemed whispered from above their myriad orbs. No, no; I felt He would not leave me comfortless: in spite of earth and Hell I should have strength for all my trials, and win a glorious rest at last!

Refreshed, invigorated if not composed, I rose and returned to the house. Much of my newborn strength and courage forsook me, I confess, as I entered it, and shut out the fresh wind and the glorious sky: everything I saw and heard seemed to sicken my heart – the hall, the lamp, the staircase, the doors of the different apartments, the social sound of talk and laughter from the drawing-room. How could I bear my future life? In this house, among those people – oh, how could I endure to live! John just then entered the hall, and seeing me told me he had been sent in search of me, adding that he had taken in the tea, and master wished to know if I were coming.

'Ask Mrs Hattersley to be so kind as to make the tea, John,' said I. 'Say I am not well tonight, and wish to be excused.'

I retired into the large, empty dining-room, where all was silence and darkness,

but for the soft sighing of the wind without, and the faint gleam of moonlight that pierced the blinds and curtains; and there I walked rapidly up and down, thinking my bitter thoughts alone. How different was this from the evening of yesterday! *That* it seems, was the last expiring flash of my life's happiness. Poor, blinded fool that I was, to be so happy! I could now see the reason of Arthur's strange reception of me in the shrubbery: the burst of kindness was for his paramour, the start of horror for his wife. Now, too, I could better understand the conversation between Hattersley and Grimsby: it was doubtless of his love for *her* they spoke, not for me.

I heard the drawing-room door open: a light quick step came out of the ante-room, crossed the hall, and ascended the stairs. It was Milicent, poor Milicent, gone to see how I was – no one else cared for me; but *she* still was kind. I shed no tears before, but now they came – fast and free. Thus she did me good, without approaching me. Disappointed in her search, I heard her come down – more slowly than she had ascended. Would she come in there, and find me out? No; she turned in the opposite direction and re-entered the drawing-room. I was glad, for I knew not how to meet her or what to say. I wanted no confidant in my distress. I deserved none – and I wanted none. I had taken the burden upon myself: let me bear it alone.

As the usual hour of retirement approached I dried my eyes, and tried to clear my voice and calm my mind. I must see Arthur tonight, and speak to him; but I would do it calmly: there should be no scene – nothing to complain or to boast of to his companions – nothing to laugh at with his lady love. When the company were retiring to their chambers, I gently opened the door, and just as he passed, I beckoned him in.

'What's to do with *you*, Helen?' said he. 'Why couldn't you come to make tea for us? And what the deuce are you here for, in the dark? What ails you, young woman – you look like a ghost?' he continued, surveying me by the light of his candle.

'No matter,' I answered – 'to you – you have no longer any regard for me, it appears; and I have no longer any for you.'

'Hal–low! what the devil is this?' he muttered.

'I would leave you tomorrow,' continued I, 'and never again come under this roof, but for my child' – and I paused a moment to steady my voice.

'What in the devil's name *is* this, Helen?' cried he. 'What can you be driving at?'

'You know, perfectly well. Let us waste no time in useless explanation, but tell me, will you – '

He vehemently swore he knew nothing about it, and insisted upon hearing what poisonous old woman had been blackening his name, and what infamous lies I had been fool enough to believe.

'Spare yourself the trouble of forswearing yourself and racking your brains to stifle truth with falsehood,' I coldly replied. 'I have trusted to the testimony of no third person. I was in the shrubbery this evening, and I saw and heard for myself.'

This was enough. He uttered a suppressed exclamation of consternation and

dismay and muttering, 'I *shall* catch it now!' set down his candle on the nearest chair, and, rearing his back against the wall, stood confronting me with folded arms.

'Well! – what then?' said he, with the calm insolence of mingled shameless-ness and desperation.

'Only this,' returned I: 'will you let me take our child and what remains of my fortune, and go?'

'Go where?'

'Anywhere, where he will be safe from your contaminating influence, and I shall be delivered from your presence – and you from mine.'

'No – by *Jove* I won't!'

'Will you let me have the child then, without the money?'

'No – nor yourself without the child. Do you think I'm going to be made the talk of the country, for your fastidious caprices?'

'Then I must stay here, to be hated and despised – But henceforth, we are husband and wife only in the name.'

'Very good.'

'I am your child's mother, and your housekeeper – nothing more. So you need not trouble yourself any longer, to feign the love you cannot feel: I will exact no more heartless caresses from you – nor offer – nor endure them either – I will not be mocked with the empty husk of conjugal endearments, when you have given the substance to another!'

'Very good – if *you* please. We shall see who will tire first, my lady.'

'If I tire, it will be of living in the world with you; not of living without your mockery of love. When *you* tire of your sinful ways, and show yourself truly repentant, I will forgive you – and, perhaps, try to love you again, though that will be hard indeed.'

'Humph! – and meantime, you will go and talk me over to Mrs Hargrave, and write long letters to Aunt Maxwell to complain of the wicked wretch you have married?'

'I shall complain to no one. Hitherto, I have struggled hard to hide your vices from every eye, and invest you with virtues you never possessed – but now you must look to yourself.'

I left him – muttering bad language to himself, and went upstairs.

'You are poorly, ma'am,' said Rachel, surveying me with deep anxiety.

'It is too true, Rachel!' said I, answering her sad looks rather than her words.

'I knew it – or I wouldn't have mentioned such a thing.'

'But don't *you* trouble yourself about it,' said I, kissing her pale, time-wasted cheek – 'I can bear it – better than you imagine.'

'Yes, you were always for "bearing" – But if I was you I wouldn't bear it – I'd give way to it, and cry right hard! – and I'd talk too, I just *would* – I'd let him know what it was to – '

'I have talked,' said I: 'I've said enough.'

'Then I'd cry,' persisted she. 'I wouldn't look so white and so calm, and burst my heart with keeping it in!'

'I *have* cried,' said I, smiling in spite of my misery; 'and I *am* calm now, really, so don't discompose me again, nurse: let us say no more about it – and *don't* mention it to the servants. There, you may go now. Good-night; and don't disturb your rest for me: I shall sleep well – if I can.'

Notwithstanding this resolution, I found my bed so intolerable that, before two o'clock, I rose, and, lighting my candle by the rushlight that was still burning, I got my desk and sat down in my dressing-gown to recount the events of the past evening. It was better to be so occupied than to be lying in bed torturing my brain with recollections of the far past and anticipations of the dreadful future. I have found relief in describing the very circumstances that have destroyed my peace, as well as the little trivial details attendant upon their discovery. No sleep I could have got this night would have done so much towards composing my mind, and preparing me to meet the trials of the day – I fancy so, at least; and yet, when I cease writing, I find my head aches terribly; and when I look into the glass I am startled at my haggard, worn appearance.

Rachel has been to dress me, and says I have had a sad night of it she can see. Milicent has just looked in to ask me how I was. I told her I was better, but to excuse my appearance admitted I had had a restless night – I wish this day were over! I shudder at the thoughts of going down to breakfast – how shall I encounter them all? – Yet let me remember it is not *I* that am guilty: *I* have no cause to fear; and if *they* scorn me as the victim of their guilt, I can pity their folly and despise their scorn.

## CHAPTER 34

### *Concealment*

Evening. Breakfast passed well over, I was calm and cool throughout. I answered composedly all enquiries respecting my health; and whatever was unusual in my look or manner, was generally attributed to the trifling indisposition that had occasioned my early retirement last night. But how am I to get over the ten or twelve days that must yet elapse before they go? Yet why so long for their departure? When they *are* gone how shall I get through the months or years of my future life, in company with that man – my greatest enemy – for none could injure me as he has done? Oh! when I think how fondly, how foolishly I have loved him, how madly I have trusted him, how constantly I have laboured, and studied, and prayed, and struggled for his advantage; and how cruelly he has trampled on my love, betrayed my trust, scorned my prayers and tears, and efforts for his preservation – crushed my hopes, destroyed my youth's best feelings, and doomed me to a life of hopeless misery – as far as man can do it – it is not enough to say that I no longer love my husband – I hate him! The word stares me in the face like a guilty confession, but it is true: I hate him – I hate him! – But God have mercy on his miserable soul! – and make him see and feel

his guilt – I ask no other vengeance! If he could but fully know and truly feel my wrongs, I should be well avenged; and I could freely pardon all; but he is so lost, so hardened in his heartless depravity that, in this life, I believe he never will. But it is useless dwelling on this theme: let me seek once more to dissipate reflection in the minor details of passing events.

Mr Hargrave has annoyed me all day long with his serious, sympathising, and (as *he* thinks) unobtrusive politeness – if it were more obtrusive it would trouble me less, for then I could snub him; but, as it is, he contrives to appear so really kind and thoughtful that I cannot do so without rudeness and seeming ingratitude. I sometimes think I ought to give him credit for the good feeling he simulates so well; and then again, I think it is my *duty* to suspect him under the peculiar circumstances in which I am placed. His kindness may not all be feigned, but still, let not the purest impulse of gratitude to him, induce me to forget myself; let me remember the game of chess, the expressions he used on the occasion, and those indescribable looks of his, that so justly roused my indignation, and I think I shall be safe enough. I have done well to record them so minutely.

I think he wishes to find an opportunity of speaking to me alone: he has seemed to be on the watch all day! But I have taken care to disappoint him; not that I fear anything he could say, but I have trouble enough without the addition of his insulting consolations, condolences, or whatever else he might attempt; and, for Milicent's sake, I do not wish to quarrel with him. He excused himself from going out to shoot with the other gentlemen in the morning, under the pretext of having letters to write; and instead of retiring for that purpose into the library, he sent for his desk into the morning-room where I was seated with Milicent and Lady Lowborough. They had betaken themselves to their work; I, less to divert my mind than to deprecate conversation, had provided myself with a book. Milicent saw that I wished to be quiet, and accordingly let me alone. Annabella, doubtless, saw it too; but that was no reason why she should restrain her tongue, or curb her cheerful spirits: *she* accordingly chatted away, addressing herself almost exclusively to me, and with the utmost assurance and familiarity, growing the more animated and friendly, the colder and briefer my answers became. Mr Hargrave saw that I could ill endure it; and, looking up from his desk, he answered her questions and observations for me, as far as he could, and attempted to transfer her social attentions from me to himself; but it would not do. Perhaps, she thought I had a headache and could not bear to talk – at any rate, she saw that her loquacious vivacity annoyed me as I could tell by the malicious pertinacity with which she persisted. But I checked it, effectually, by putting into her hand the book I had been trying to read, on the fly leaf of which I had hastily scribbled – 'I am too well acquainted with your character and conduct to feel any real friendship for you, and, as I am without your talent for dissimulation, I cannot assume the appearance of it. I must, therefore, beg that hereafter all familiar intercourse may cease between us; and if I still continue to treat you with civility, as if you were a woman worthy of consideration and respect, understand that it is out of regard for your cousin Milicent's feelings, not for yours.'

Upon perusing this, she turned scarlet and bit her lip. Covertly tearing away the leaf, she crumpled it up and put it in the fire, and then employed herself in turning over the pages of the book and, really or apparently, perusing its contents. In a little while Milicent announced it her intention to repair to the nursery, and asked if I would accompany her.

'Annabella will excuse us,' said she, 'she's busy reading.'

'No, I won't,' cried Annabella, suddenly looking up and throwing her book on the table. 'I want to speak to Helen a minute. You may go Milicent, and she'll follow in a while' (Milicent went). 'Will you oblige me, Helen?' continued she.

Her impudence astounded me; but I complied, and followed her into the library. She closed the door, and walked up to the fire.

'Who told you this?' said she.

'No one: I am not incapable of seeing for myself.'

'Ah, you are suspicious!' cried she, smiling with a gleam of hope – hitherto, there had been a kind of desperation in her hardihood; now she was evidently relieved.

'If I *were* suspicious,' I replied, 'I should have discovered your infamy long before. No, Lady Lowborough, I do not found my charge upon suspicion.'

'On what *do* you found it then? said she, throwing herself into an armchair, and stretching out her feet to the fender, with an obvious effort to appear composed.

'I enjoy a moonlight ramble as well as you,' I answered, steadily fixing my eyes upon her: 'and the shrubbery happens to be one of my favourite resorts.'

She coloured again, excessively, and remained silent, pressing her finger against her teeth, and gazing into the fire. I watched her a few moments with a feeling of malevolent gratification; then, moving towards the door, I calmly asked if she had anything more to say.

'Yes, yes!' cried she eagerly, starting up from her reclining posture. 'I want to know if you will tell Lord Lowborough?'

'Suppose I do?'

'Well, if you are disposed to publish the matter, *I* cannot dissuade you, of course – but there will be terrible work if you do – and if you don't, I shall think you the most generous of mortal beings – and if there is anything in the world I can do for you – anything short of – ' she hesitated.

'Short of renouncing your guilty connection with my husband, I suppose you mean,' said I.

She paused, in evident disconcertion and perplexity, mingled with anger she dared not show.

'I cannot renounce what is dearer than life,' she muttered in a low, hurried tone. Then, suddenly raising her head and fixing her gleaming eyes upon me, she continued earnestly, 'But Helen – or Mrs Huntingdon, or whatever you would have me call you – *will* you tell him? If you are generous, here is a fitting opportunity for the exercise of your magnanimity; if you are proud, here am I – your rival – ready to acknowledge myself your debtor for an act of the most noble forbearance.'

'I shall not tell him.'

'You will not!' cried she delightedly. 'Accept my sincere thanks, then!'

She sprang up, and offered me her hand. I drew back.

'Give me no thanks; it is not for *your* sake that I refrain. Neither is it an act of any forbearance: I have no wish to publish your shame. I should be sorry to distress your husband with the knowledge of it.'

'And Milicent? will you tell her?'

'No, on the contrary I shall do my utmost to conceal it from her. I would not for much that she should know the infamy and disgrace of her relation!'

'You use hard words, Mrs Huntingdon – but I can pardon you.'

'And now Lady Lowborough,' continued I, 'let me counsel you to leave this house as soon as *possible*. You must be aware that your continuance here is excessively disagreeable to me – not for Mr Huntingdon's sake,' said I, observing the dawn of a malicious smile of triumph on her face – 'You are welcome to him, if you like him, as far as *I* am concerned – but because it is painful to be always disguising my true sentiments respecting you, and straining to keep up an appearance of civility and respect towards one for whom I have not the most distant shadow of esteem; and because, if you stay, your conduct cannot possibly remain concealed much longer from the only two persons in the house who do not know it already. And, for your husband's sake, Annabella, and even for your own, I wish – I earnestly advise and *entreat* you to break off this unlawful connection at once, and return to your duty while you may, before the dreadful consequences – '

'Yes, yes, of course,' said she, interrupting me with a gesture of impatience – 'But I cannot go, Helen, before the time appointed for our departure. What possible pretext could I frame for such a thing? Whether I proposed going back alone – which Lowborough would not hear of – or taking him with me, the very circumstance itself, would be certain to excite suspicion – and when our visit is so *nearly* at an end too – little more than a week – surely, you can endure my presence *so* long! I will not annoy you with any more of my friendly impertinences.'

'Well! I have nothing more to say to you.'

'Have you mentioned this affair to Huntingdon?' asked she, as I was leaving the room.

'How dare you mention his name to me!' was the only answer I gave.

No words have passed between us since, but such as outward decency or pure necessity demanded.

## CHAPTER 35

## *Provocations*

Nineteenth. In proportion as Lady Lowborough finds she has nothing to fear from me, and as the time of departure draws nigh, the more audacious and insolent she becomes. She does not scruple to speak to my husband with affectionate familiarity in my presence, when no one else is by, and is particularly fond of displaying her interest in his health and welfare, or in anything that concerns him, as if for the purpose of contrasting her kind solicitude with my cold indifference. And he rewards her by such smiles and glances, such whispered words, or boldly spoken insinuations, indicative of his sense of her goodness and my neglect, as makes the blood rush into my face, in spite of myself – for I would be utterly regardless of it all – deaf and blind to everything that passes between them, since the more I show myself sensible of their wickedness, the more she triumphs in her victory, and the more he flatters himself that I love him devotedly still, in spite of my pretended indifference. On such occasions I have sometimes been startled by a subtle, fiendish suggestion inciting me to show him the contrary by a seeming encouragement of Hargrave's advances; but such ideas are banished in a moment with horror and self-abasement; and then I hate him tenfold more than ever, for having brought me to this! – God pardon me for it – and all my sinful thoughts! Instead of being humbled and purified by my afflictions, I feel that they are turning my nature into gall. This must be my fault as much as theirs that wrong me. No true Christian could cherish such bitter feelings as I do against him and her – especially the latter: him, I still feel that I could pardon – freely, gladly – on the slightest token of repentance; but *she* – words cannot utter my abhorrence. Reason forbids, but passion urges strongly; and I must pray and struggle long ere I subdue it.

It is well that she is leaving tomorrow, for I could not well endure her presence for another day. This morning, she rose earlier than usual. I found her in the room alone, when I went down to breakfast.

'Oh Helen! is it you?' said she, turning as I entered.

I gave an involuntary start back on seeing her, at which she uttered a short laugh, observing – 'I think we are *both* disappointed.'

I came forward and busied myself with the breakfast-things.

'This is the last day I shall burden your hospitality,' said she, as she seated herself at the table. 'Ah, here comes one that will not rejoice at it!' she murmured, half to herself, as Arthur entered the room.

He shook hands with her and wished her good-morning: then, looking lovingly in her face, and still retaining her hand in his, murmured pathetically – 'The last – last day!'

'Yes,' said she with some asperity; 'and I rose early to make the best of it – I have been here alone this half hour, and *you*, you lazy creature!'

'Well, I thought I was early too,' said he – 'but,' dropping his voice almost to a whisper, 'you see we are not alone.'

'We never are,' returned she. But they were almost as good as alone, for I was now standing at the window, watching the clouds, and struggling to suppress my wrath.

Some more words passed between them, which, happily, I did not overhear; but Annabella had the audacity to come and place herself beside me, and even to put her hand upon my shoulder and say softly – 'You need not grudge him to me, Helen, for I love him more than ever you could do.'

This put me beside myself. I took her hand and violently dashed it from me, with an expression of abhorrence and indignation that could not be suppressed. Startled, almost appalled, by this sudden outbreak, she recoiled in silence. I would have given way to my fury and said more, but Arthur's low laugh recalled me to myself. I checked the half-uttered invective, and scornfully turned away, regretting that I had given him so much amusement. He was still laughing when Mr Hargrave made his appearance. How much of the scene he had witnessed I do not know, for the door was ajar when he entered. He greeted his host and his cousin both coldly, and me with a glance intended to express the deepest sympathy mingled with high admiration and esteem.

'How much allegiance do you owe to that man?' he asked below his breath, as he stood beside me at the window, affecting to be making observations on the weather.

'None,' I answered. And immediately returning to the table, I employed myself in making the tea. He followed, and would have entered into some kind of conversation with me, but the other guests were now beginning to assemble and I took no more notice of him, except to give him his coffee.

After breakfast, determined to pass as little of the day as possible in company with Lady Lowborough, I quietly stole away from the company and retired to the library. Mr Hargrave followed me thither, under pretence of coming for a book; and first, turning to the shelves, he selected a volume; and then, quietly, but by no means timidly, approaching me, he stood beside me, resting his hand on the back of my chair, and said softly – 'And so you consider yourself free, at last?'

'Yes,' said I, without moving, or raising my eyes from my book – 'free to do anything but offend God and my conscience.'

There was a momentary pause.

'Very right,' said he; 'provided your conscience be not too morbidly tender, and your ideas of God not too erroneously severe; but can you suppose it would offend that benevolent Being to make the happiness of one who would die for yours? – To raise a devoted heart from purgatorial torments to a state of heavenly bliss when you could do it without the slightest injury to yourself or any other?'

This was spoken in a low, earnest, melting tone as he bent over me. I now

raised my head; and, steadily confronting his gaze, I answered calmly – 'Mr Hargrave, do you mean to insult me?'

He was not prepared for this. He paused a moment to recover the shock; then, drawing himself up and removing his hand from my chair, he answered, with proud sadness – 'That was not my intention.'

I just glanced towards the door, with a slight movement of the head, and then returned to my book. He immediately withdrew. This was better than if I had answered with more words, and in the passionate spirit to which my first impulse would have prompted. What a good thing it is to be able to command one's temper! I must labour to cultivate this inestimable quality: God, only, knows how often I shall need it in this rough, dark road that lies before me.

In the course of the morning, I drove over to the Grove with the two ladies, to give Milicent an opportunity for bidding farewell to her mother and sister. They persuaded her to stay with them the rest of the day, Mrs Hargrave promising to bring her back in the evening and remain till the party broke up on the morrow. Consequently, Lady Lowborough and I had the pleasure of returning tête-à-tête in the carriage together. For the first mile or two, we kept silence, I looking out of my window, and she leaning back in her corner. But I was not going to restrict myself to any particular position for her: when I was tired of leaning forward, with the cold, raw wind in my face; and surveying the russet hedges, and the damp, tangled grass of their banks, I gave it up, and leant back too. With her usual impudence, my companion then made some attempts to get up a conversation; but the monosyllables 'yes' or 'no' or 'humph' were the utmost her several remarks could elicit from me. At last, on her asking my opinion upon some immaterial point of discussion, I answered – 'Why do you wish to talk to me, Lady Lowborough? – you must know what I think of you.'

'Well, if you *will* be so bitter against me,' replied she, 'I can't help it; but *I'm* not going to sulk for anybody.'

Our short drive was now at an end. As soon as the carriage door was opened, she sprang out and went down the park to meet the gentlemen, who were just returning from the woods. Of course I did not follow.

But I had not done with her impudence yet – after dinner, I retired to the drawing-room, as usual, and she accompanied me, but I had the two children with me, and I gave them my whole attention, and determined to keep them till the gentlemen came, or till Milicent arrived with her mother. Little Helen, however, was soon tired of playing, and insisted upon going to sleep; and while I sat on the sofa with her on my knee, and Arthur seated beside me, gently playing with her soft, flaxen hair – Lady Lowborough composedly came and placed herself on the other side.

'Tomorrow, Mrs Huntingdon,' said she, 'you will be delivered from my presence, which, no doubt, you will be very glad of – it is natural you should; but do you know I have rendered you a great service? – Shall I tell you what it is?'

'I shall be glad to hear of any service you have rendered me,' said I, determined to be calm, for I knew by the tone of her voice she wanted to provoke me.

'Well,' resumed she, 'have you not observed this salutary change in Mr

Huntingdon? Don't you see what a sober, temperate man he is become? You saw with regret the sad habits he was contracting, I know; and I know you did your utmost to deliver him from them – but without success, until I came to your assistance. I told him, in few words, that I could not bear to see him degrade himself so, and that I should cease to – no matter what I told him – but you see the reformation I have wrought; and you ought to thank me for it.'

I rose, and rang for the nurse.

'But I desire no thanks,' she continued, 'all the return I ask is, that you will take care of him when I am gone, and not, by harshness and neglect, drive him back to his old courses.'

I was almost sick with passion, but Rachel was now at the door: I pointed to the children, for I could not trust myself to speak: she took them away, and I followed.

'Will you, Helen?' continued the speaker.

I gave her a look that blighted the malicious smile on her face – or checked it, at least for a moment – and departed. In the ante-room I met Mr Hargrave. He saw I was in no humour to be spoken to, and suffered me to pass without a word; but when, after a few minutes' seclusion in the library, I had regained my composure, and was returning, to join Mrs Hargrave and Milicent, whom I had just heard come downstairs and go into the drawing-room – I found him there still, lingering in the dimly lighted apartment, and evidently waiting for me.

'Mrs Huntingdon,' said he as I passed, 'will you allow me one word?'

'What is it then? – be quick if you please.'

'I offended you this morning; and I cannot live under your displeasure.'

'Then, go, and sin no more,' replied I, turning away.

'No, no!' said he hastily, setting himself before me – 'Pardon me, but I must have your forgiveness. I leave you tomorrow, and I may not have an opportunity of speaking to you again. I was wrong, to forget myself – and you, as I did; but let me implore you to forget and forgive my rash presumption, and think of me as if those words had never been spoken; for, believe me, I regret them deeply, and the loss of your esteem is too severe a penalty – I cannot bear it.'

'Forgetfulness is not to be purchased with a wish; and I cannot bestow my esteem on all who desire it, unless they deserve it too.'

'I shall think my life well spent in labouring to deserve it, if you will but pardon this offence – Will you?'

'Yes.'

'Yes? But that is coldly spoken. Give me your hand and I'll believe you – You won't? Then, Mrs Huntingdon, you do *not* forgive me!'

'Yes – here it is, and my forgiveness with it: only – *sin no more*.'

He pressed my cold hand with sentimental fervour, but said nothing, and stood aside to let me pass into the room, where all the company were now assembled. Mr Grimsby was seated near the door: on seeing me enter almost immediately followed by Hargrave, he leered at me, with a glance of intolerable significance, as I passed. I looked him in the face, till he sullenly turned away, if not *ashamed*, at least *confounded* for the moment. Meantime, Hattersley had

seized Hargrave by the arm, and was whispering something in his ear – some coarse joke, no doubt, for the latter neither laughed nor spoke in answer, but, turning from him with a slight curl of the lip, disengaged himself and went to his mother, who was telling Lord Lowborough how many reasons she had to be proud of her son.

Thank Heaven, they are all going tomorrow.

## CHAPTER 36

### Dual Solitude

December 20th, 1824. This is the third anniversary of our felicitous union. It is now two months since our guests left us to the enjoyment of each other's society; and I have had nine weeks' experience of this new phase of conjugal life – two persons living together, as master and mistress of the house, and father and mother of a winsome, merry little child, with the mutual understanding that there is no love, friendship, or sympathy between them. As far as in me lies, I endeavour to live peaceably with him: I treat him with unimpeachable civility, give up my convenience to his, wherever it may reasonably be done, and consult him in a businesslike way on household affairs, deferring to his pleasure and judgement, even when I know the latter to be inferior to my own.

As for him: for the first week or two, he was peevish and low – fretting, I suppose, over his dear Annabella's departure – and particularly ill-tempered to me: everything I did was wrong; I was cold-hearted, hard, insensate; my sour, pale face was perfectly repulsive; my voice made him shudder; he knew not how he could live through the winter with me; I should kill him by inches. Again I proposed a separation, but it would not do: he was not going to be the talk of all the old gossips in the neighbourhood: he would not have it said that he was such a brute his wife could not live with him; no; he must contrive to bear with me.

'I must contrive to bear with *you*, you mean,' said I, 'for as long as I discharge my functions of steward and housekeeper, so conscientiously and well, without pay and without thanks, you cannot afford to part with me. I shall therefore remit these duties when my bondage becomes intolerable.' This threat, I thought, would serve to keep him in check, if anything would.

I believe he was much disappointed that I did not feel his offensive sayings more acutely, for when he had said anything particularly well calculated to hurt my feelings, he would stare me searchingly in the face, and then grumble against my 'marble heart,' or my 'brutal insensibility.' If I had bitterly wept, and deplored his lost affection, he would, perhaps, have condescended to pity me, and taken me into favour for a while, just to comfort his solitude and console him for the absence of his beloved Annabella, until he could meet her again, or some more fitting substitute. Thank Heaven, I am not so weak as that! I was

infatuated once, with a foolish, besotted affection, that clung to him in spite of his unworthiness, but it is fairly gone now – wholly crushed and withered away; and he has none but himself and his vices to thank for it.

At first (in compliance with his sweet lady's injunctions, I suppose), he abstained wonderfully well from seeking to solace his cares in wine; but at length he began to relax his virtuous efforts, and now and then exceeded a little, and still continues to do so – nay, sometimes, *not* a little. When he is under the exciting influence of these excesses, he sometimes fires up and attempts to play the brute; and then I take little pains to suppress my scorn and disgust: when he is under the *depressing* influence of the after consequences, he bemoans his sufferings and his errors, and charges them both upon me; he knows such indulgence injures his health, and does him more harm than good; but he says I drive him to it by my unnatural, unwomanly conduct; it will be the ruin of him in the end, but it is all my fault; and *then*, I am roused to defend myself – sometimes, with bitter recrimination. This is a kind of injustice I cannot patiently endure. Have I not laboured long and hard to save him from this very vice? Would I not labour still, to deliver him from it, if I could? But could I do so by fawning upon him and caressing him when I know that he scorns me? Is it *my* fault that I have lost my influence with him, or that he has forfeited every claim to my regard? And should I seek a reconciliation with him, when I feel that I abhor him, and that he despises me? – and while he continues still to correspond with Lady Lowborough, as I know he does? No, never, never, never! – he may drink himself dead, but it is not my fault!

Yet I do my part to save him still: I give him to understand that drinking makes his eyes dull, and his face red and bloated; and that it tends to render him imbecile in body and mind; and if Annabella were to see him as often as I do, she would speedily be disenchanted; and that she certainly will withdraw her favour from him, if he continues such courses. Such a mode of admonition wins only coarse abuse for me – and indeed I almost feel as if I deserved it, for I hate to use such arguments, but they sink into his stupefied heart, and make him pause, and ponder, and abstain, more than anything else I could say.

At present, I am enjoying a temporary relief from his presence: he is gone with Hargrave to join a distant hunt, and will probably not be back before tomorrow evening. How differently I used to feel his absence!

Mr Hargrave is still at the Grove. He and Arthur frequently meet to pursue their rural sports together: he often calls upon us here, and Arthur not unfrequently rides over to him. I do not think either of these soi-disant friends is overflowing with love for the other; but such intercourse serves to get the time on, and I am very willing it should continue, as it saves me some hours of discomfort in Arthur's society, and gives him some better employment than the sottish indulgence of his sensual appetites. The only objection I have to Mr Hargrave's being in the neighbourhood, is that the fear of meeting him at the Grove prevents me from seeing his sister so often as I otherwise should; for, of late he has conducted himself towards me with such unerring propriety that I have almost forgotten his former conduct. I suppose he is striving to

'win my esteem'. If he continue to act in this way, he *may* win it; but what then? The moment he attempts to demand anything more, he will lose it again.

February 10th. It is a hard, embittering thing to have one's kind feelings and good intentions cast back in one's teeth. I was beginning to relent towards my wretched partner – to pity his forlorn, comfortless condition, unalleviated as it is by the consolations of intellectual resources and the answer of a good conscience towards God – and to think I ought to sacrifice my pride, and renew my efforts once again to make his home agreeable and lead him back to the path of virtue; not by false professions of love, and not by pretended remorse, but by mitigating my habitual coldness of manner, and commuting my frigid civility into kindness wherever an opportunity occurred; and not only was I beginning to think so, but I had already begun to act upon the thought – and what was the result? No answering spark of kindness – no awakening penitence, but an unappeasable ill-humour and a spirit of tyrannous exaction that increased with indulgence, and a lurking gleam of self-complacent triumph, at every detection of relenting softness in my manner, that congealed me to marble again as often as it recurred; and this morning he finished the business – I think the petrifaction is so completely effected at last, that nothing can melt me again. Among his letters was one which he perused with symptoms of unusual gratification, and then threw across the table to me, with the admonition – 'There! Read that, and take a lesson by it!'

It was in the free, dashing hand of Lady Lowborough. I glanced at the first page; it seemed full of extravagant protestations of affection; impetuous longings for a speedy reunion; and impious defiance of God's mandates, and railings against His Providence for having cast their lot asunder, and doomed them both to the hateful bondage of alliance with those they could not love. He gave a slight titter on seeing me change colour. I folded up the letter, rose, and returned it to him, with no remark but – 'Thank you – I *will* take a lesson by it!'

My little Arthur was standing between his knees, delightedly playing with the bright, ruby ring on his finger. Urged by a sudden, imperative impulse to deliver my son from that contaminating influence, I caught him up in my arms and carried him with me out of the room. Not liking this abrupt removal, the child began to pout and cry. This was a new stab to my already tortured heart. I would not let him go; but, taking him with me into the library, I shut the door, and, kneeling on the floor beside him, I embraced him, kissed him, wept over him with passionate fondness. Rather frightened than consoled by this, he turned struggling from me and cried out aloud for his papa. I released him from my arms, and never were more bitter tears than those that now concealed him from my blinded, burning eyes. Hearing his cries, the father came to the room. I instantly turned away lest he should see and misconstrue my emotion. He swore at me, and took the now pacified child away.

It is hard that my little darling should love him more than me; and that, when the well-being and culture of my son is all I have to live for, I should see my

influence destroyed by one whose selfish affection is more injurious than the coldest indifference or the harshest tyranny could be. If I, for his good, deny him some trifling indulgence, he goes to his father, and the latter, in spite of his selfish indolence, will even give himself some trouble to meet the child's desires: if I attempt to curb his will, or look gravely on him for some act of childish disobedience, he knows his other parent will smile and take his part against me. Thus, not only have I the father's spirit in the son to contend against, the germs of his evil tendencies to search out and eradicate, and his corrupting intercourse and example in after life to counteract, but already *he* counteracts my arduous labour for the child's advantage, destroys my influence over his tender mind, and robs me of his very love; I had no earthly hope but this, and he seems to take a diabolical delight in tearing it away.

But it is wrong to despair; I will remember the counsel of the inspired writer to him 'that feareth the Lord and obeyeth the voice of his servant, that *sitteth in darkness and hath no light*; let him trust in the name of the Lord, and stay upon his God!'

## CHAPTER 37

## *The Neighbour Again*

December 20th, 1825. Another year is past; and I am weary of this life. And yet, I cannot wish to leave it: whatever afflictions assail me here, I cannot wish to go and leave my darling in this dark and wicked world alone, without a friend to guide him through its weary mazes, to warn him of its thousand snares, and guard him from the perils that beset him on every hand. I am not well fitted to be his only companion, I know; but there is no other to supply my place. I am too grave to minister to his amusements and enter into his infantile sports as a nurse or a mother ought to do, and often his bursts of gleeful merriment trouble and alarm me; I see in them his father's spirit and temperament, and I tremble for the consequences; and, too often, damp the innocent mirth I ought to share. That father on the contrary has no weight of sadness on his mind – is troubled with no fears, no scruples concerning his son's future welfare; and at evenings especially, the times when the child sees him the most and the oftenest, he is always particularly jocund and open-hearted: ready to laugh and to jest with anything or anybody – but me – and I am particularly silent and sad: therefore, of course, the child dotes upon his seemingly joyous, amusing, ever indulgent papa, and will at any time gladly exchange my company for his. This disturbs me greatly; not so much for the sake of my son's affection (though I do prize that highly, and though I feel it is my right, and know I have done much to earn it), as for that influence over him which, for his own advantage, I would strive to purchase and retain, and which for very spite his father delights to rob me of, and, from motives of mere idle egotism, is pleased to win to himself; making no use of it but

to torment me, and ruin the child. My only consolation is, that he spends comparatively little of his time at home, and, during the months he passes in London or elsewhere, I have a chance of recovering the ground I had lost, and overcoming with good the evil he has wrought by his wilful mismanagement. But then it is a bitter trial to behold him, on his return, doing his utmost to subvert my labours and transform my innocent, affectionate, tractable darling into a selfish, disobedient, and mischievous boy; thereby preparing the soil for those vices he has so successfully cultivated in his own perverted nature.

Happily, there were none of Arthur's 'friends' invited to Grassdale last autumn: he took himself off to visit some of them instead. I wish he would always do so, and I wish his friends were numerous and loving enough to keep him amongst them all the year round. Mr Hargrave, considerably to my annoyance, did not go with him; but I think I have done with that gentleman at last.

For seven or eight months, he behaved so remarkably well, and managed so skilfully too, that I was almost completely off my guard, and was really beginning to look upon him as a friend, and even to treat him as such, with certain prudent restrictions (which I deemed scarcely necessary); when, presuming upon my unsuspecting kindness, he thought he might venture to overstep the bounds of decent moderation and propriety that had so long retained him. It was on a pleasant evening at the close of May: I was wandering in the park, and he, on seeing me there as he rode past, made bold to enter and approach me, dismounting and leaving his horse at the gate. This was the first time he had ventured to come within its enclosure since I had been left alone, without the sanction of his mother's or sister's company, or at least the excuse of a message from them. But he managed to appear so calm and easy, so respectful and self-possessed in his friendliness, that, though a little surprised, I was neither alarmed nor offended at the unusual liberty, and he walked with me under the ash trees and by the waterside, and talked, with considerable animation, good taste, and intelligence, on many subjects, before I began to think about getting rid of him. Then, after a pause, during which we both stood gazing on the calm, blue water, I revolving in my mind the best means of politely dismissing my companion, he, no doubt, pondering other matters equally alien to the sweet sights and sounds that alone were present to his senses – he suddenly electrified me by beginning, in a peculiar tone, low, soft, but perfectly distinct, to pour forth the most unequivocal expressions of earnest and passionate love; pleading his cause with all the bold yet artful eloquence he could summon to his aid. But I cut short his appeal, and repulsed him so determinately, so decidedly, and with such a mixture of scornful indignation tempered with cool, dispassionate sorrow and pity for his benighted mind, that he withdrew, astonished, mortified, and discomforted; and, a few days after, I heard that he had departed for London. He returned however in eight or nine weeks and did not entirely keep aloof from me, but comported himself in so remarkable a manner that his quicksighted sister could not fail to notice the change.

'What have you done to Walter, Mrs Huntingdon?' said she one morning, when I had called at the Grove, and he had just left the room after exchanging a

few words of the coldest civility. 'He has been so extremely ceremonious and stately of late, I can't imagine what it is all about, unless you have desperately offended him. Tell me what it is, that I may be your mediator, and make you friends again.'

'I have done nothing willingly to offend him,' said I. 'If he is offended, he can best tell you himself what it is about.'

'I'll ask him,' cried the giddy girl, springing up and putting her head out of the window; 'he's only in the garden – Walter!'

'No, no, Esther! You will seriously displease me if you do; and I shall leave you immediately, and not come again for months – perhaps years.'

'Did you call, Esther?' said her brother, approaching the window from without.

'Yes; I wanted to ask you – '

'Good-morning, Esther,' said I, taking her hand and giving it a severe squeeze.

'To ask you,' continued she, 'to get me a rose for Mrs Huntingdon.' He departed. 'Mrs Huntingdon,' she exclaimed, turning to me and still holding me fast by the hand, 'I'm quite shocked at you – you're just as angry, and distant, and cold as he is: and I'm determined you shall be as good friends as ever, before you go.'

'Esther, how can you be so rude!' cried Mrs Hargrave, who was seated gravely knitting in her easy-chair. 'Surely, you never *will* learn to conduct yourself like a lady!'

'Well, mamma, you said, yourself – ' But the young lady was silenced by the uplifted finger of her mamma, accompanied with a very stern shake of the head.

'Isn't she cross?' whispered she to me; but, before I could add my share of reproof, Mr Hargrave reappeared at the window with a beautiful moss rose in his hand.

'Here, Esther, I've brought you the rose,' said he, extending it towards her.

'Give it her yourself, you blockhead!' cried she, recoiling with a spring from between us.

'Mrs Huntingdon would rather receive it from you,' replied he in a very serious tone, but lowering his voice that his mother might not hear. His sister took the rose and gave it to me.

'My brother's compliments, Mrs Huntingdon, and he hopes you and he will come to a better understanding by and by – Will that do, Walter?' added the saucy girl, turning to him and putting her arm round his neck, as he stood leaning upon the sill of the window – 'or should I have said that you are sorry you were so touchy? Or that you hope she will pardon your offence?'

'You silly girl! You don't know what you are talking about,' replied he gravely.

'Indeed I don't; for I'm quite in the dark.'

'Now, Esther,' interposed Mrs Hargrave, who, if equally benighted on the subject of our estrangement, saw at least that her daughter was behaving very improperly, 'I must insist upon your leaving the room!'

'Pray don't, Mrs Hargrave, for I'm going to leave it myself,' said I, and immediately made my adieux.

About a week after, Mr Hargrave brought his sister to see me. He conducted himself, at first, with his usual cold, distant, half-stately, half-melancholy, altogether injured air; but Esther made no remark upon it this time; she had evidently been schooled into better manners. She talked to me, and laughed and romped with little Arthur, her loved and loving playmate. He, somewhat to my discomfort, enticed her from the room to have a run in the hall; and, thence, into the garden. I got up to stir the fire. Mr Hargrave asked if I felt cold, and shut the door – a very unseasonable piece of officiousness, for I had meditated following the noisy playfellows, if they did not speedily return. He then took the liberty of walking up to the fire himself, and asking me if I were aware that Mr Huntingdon was now at the seat of Lord Lowborough, and likely to continue there some time.

'No; but it's no matter,' I answered carelessly; and if my cheek glowed like fire, it was rather at the question than the information it conveyed.

'You don't object to it?' he said.

'Not at all, if Lord Lowborough likes his company.'

'You have no love left for him, then?'

'Not the least.'

'I knew that – I knew you were too high-minded and pure in your own nature to continue to regard one so utterly false and polluted, with any feelings but those of indignation and scornful abhorrence!'

'Is he not your friend?' said I, turning my eyes from the fire to his face, with perhaps a slight touch of those feelings he assigned to another.

'He *was*,' replied he, with the same calm gravity as before, 'but do not wrong me by supposing that I could continue my friendship and esteem to a man who could so infamously – so impiously forsake and injure one so transcendently – well, I won't speak of it. But tell me, do you never think of revenge?'

'Revenge! No – what good would that do? – It would make him no better, and me no happier.'

'I don't know how to talk to you, Mrs Huntingdon,' said he smiling; 'you are only half a woman – your nature must be half human, half angelic. Such goodness overawes me; I don't know what to make of it.'

'Then, sir, I fear you must be very much worse than you should be, if I, a mere ordinary mortal, am by your own confession, so vastly your superior; and since there exists so little sympathy between us, I think we had better each look out for some more congenial companion.' And forthwith moving to the window, I began to look out for my little son and his gay young friend.

'No, *I* am the ordinary mortal, I maintain,' replied Mr Hargrave. 'I will not allow myself to be worse than my fellows; but *you*, madame – I equally maintain there is nobody like you. But are you happy?' he asked in a serious tone.

'As happy as some others, I suppose.'

'Are you as happy as you desire to be?'

'No one is so blest as that comes to, on this side eternity.'

'One thing I know,' returned he, with a deep, sad sigh; 'you are immeasurably happier than I am.'

'I am very sorry for you, then,' I could not help replying.

'Are you *indeed*? – No – for if you were, you would be glad to relieve me.'

'And so I should, if I could do so, without injuring myself or any other.'

'And can you suppose that I should wish you to injure yourself? – No; on the contrary, it is your own happiness I long for more than mine. You are miserable now, Mrs Huntingdon,' continued he, looking me boldly in the face. 'You do not complain, but I see – and feel – and know that you are miserable – and must remain so, as long as you keep those walls of impenetrable ice about your still warm and palpitating heart; and I am miserable too. Deign to smile on me, and I am happy: trust me, and you shall be happy also, for if you *are* a woman, I can make you so – and I *will* do it in spite of yourself!' he muttered between his teeth, 'and as for others, the question is between ourselves alone: you cannot injure your husband, you know; and no one else has any concern in the matter.'

'I have a son, Mr Hargrave, and you have a mother,' said I, retiring from the window, whither he had followed me.

'They need not know,' he began, but before anything more could be said on either side, Esther and Arthur re-entered the room. The former glanced at Walter's flushed, excited countenance, and then at mine – a little flushed and excited too, I dare say, though from far different causes. She must have thought we had been quarrelling desperately, and was evidently perplexed and disturbed at the circumstance; but she was too polite, or too much afraid of her brother's anger to refer to it. She seated herself on the sofa, and putting back her bright, golden ringlets, that were scattered in wild profusion over her face, she immediately began to talk about the garden and her little playfellow, and continued to chatter away in her usual strain till her brother summoned her to depart.

'If I have spoken too warmly, forgive me,' he murmured on taking his leave, 'or I shall never forgive myself.'

Esther smiled and glanced at me: I merely bowed, and her countenance fell. She thought it a poor return for Walter's generous concession, and was disappointed in her friend. Poor child, she little knows the world she lives in!

Mr Hargrave had not an opportunity of meeting me again in private for several weeks after this; but when he did meet me, there was less of pride and more of touching melancholy in his manner than before. Oh, *how* he annoyed me! I was obliged, at last almost entirely to remit my visits to the Grove, at the expense of deeply offending Mrs Hargrave and seriously afflicting poor Esther, who really values my society – for want of better, and who ought not to suffer for the fault of her brother. But that indefatigable foe was not yet vanquished: he seemed to be always on the watch. I frequently saw him riding lingeringly past the premises, looking searchingly round him as he went – or if *I* did not, Rachel did. That sharp-sighted woman soon guessed how matters stood between us, and descrying the enemy's movements from her elevation at the nursery window, she would give me a quiet intimation, if she saw me preparing for a walk when she had reason to believe he was about, or to think it likely that he would meet or

overtake me in the way I meant to traverse. I would then defer my ramble, or confine myself for that day to the park and gardens – or if the proposed excursion was a matter of importance, such as a visit to the sick or afflicted, I would take Rachel with me, and then I was never molested.

But one mild, sunshiny day, early in November, I had ventured forth alone, to visit the village school and a few of the poor tenants, and on my return, I was alarmed at the clatter of a horse's feet behind me approaching at a rapid, steady trot. There was no stile or gap at hand, by which I could escape into the fields: so I walked quietly on, saying to myself – 'It may not be he after all; and if it is, and if he *do* annoy me – it shall be for the last time – I am determined, if there be power in words and looks against cool impudence and mawkish sentimentality so inexhaustible as his.'

The horse soon overtook me, and was reined up close beside me. It *was* Mr Hargrave. He greeted me with a smile intended to be soft and melancholy, but his triumphant satisfaction at having caught me at last, so shone through, that it was quite a failure. After briefly answering his salutation and enquiring after the ladies at the Grove, I turned away and walked on; but he followed, and kept his horse at my side: it was evident he intended to be my companion all the way.

'Well! I don't much care. If you want another rebuff, take it – and welcome,' was my inward remark. 'Now, sir, what next?'

This question, though unspoken, was not long unanswered: after a few passing observations upon indifferent subjects, he began, in solemn tones, the following appeal to my humanity – 'It will be four years next April since I first saw you, Mrs Huntingdon – *you* may have forgotten the circumstance, but *I* never can – I admired you then, most deeply, but I dared not love you: in the following autumn, I saw so much of your perfections that I could not fail to love you, though I dared not show it. For upwards of three years, I have endured a perfect martyrdom. From the anguish of suppressed emotions, intense and fruitless longings, silent sorrow, crushed hopes, and trampled affections – I have suffered more than I can tell, or you imagine – and you were the cause of it – and not, altogether, the innocent cause. My youth is wasting away; my prospects are darkened; my life is a desolate blank; I have no rest day or night: I am become a burden to myself and others; and you might save me by a word – a glance, and will not do it – Is this right?'

'In the first place, I don't believe you,' answered I: 'in the second, if you will be such a fool, I can't hinder it.'

'If you affect,' replied he earnestly, 'to regard as folly, the best, the strongest, the most godlike impulses of our nature – *I* don't believe *you* – I know you are not the heartless, icy being you pretend to be – you had a heart once, and you gave it to your husband. When you found him utterly unworthy of the treasure you reclaimed it; and you will not *pretend* that you loved that sensual, earthly minded profligate so deeply, so devotedly that you can never love another? – I know that there are feelings in your nature that have never yet been called forth – I know, too, that in your present neglected, lonely state you are, and *must* be miserable. You have it in your power to raise two human beings from a state

of actual suffering to such unspeakable beatitude as only generous, noble self-forgetting love can give (for you *can* love me if you will; you may tell me that you scorn and detest me, but – since you have set me the example of plain speaking – I will answer that *I do not believe you*!). But you will not do it! You choose rather to leave us miserable; and you coolly tell me it is the will of God that we should remain so. *You* may call this religion, but *I* call it wild fanaticism!'

'There is another life both for you and for me,' said I. 'If it be the will of God that we should sow in tears, now, it is only that we may reap in joy, hereafter. It is His will that we should not injure others by the gratification of our own earthly passions; and you have a mother, and sisters, and friends, who would be seriously injured by your disgrace; and I too have friends, whose peace of mind shall never be sacrificed to my enjoyment – or yours either, with my consent – and if I were alone in the world, I have still my God and my religion, and I would sooner die than disgrace my calling and break my faith with Heaven to obtain a few brief years of false and fleeting happiness – happiness sure to end in misery, even here – for myself or any other!'

'There need be no disgrace – no misery or sacrifice in any quarter,' persisted he. 'I do not ask you to leave your home or defy the world's opinion.' – But I need not repeat all his arguments. I refuted them to the best of my power; but that power was provokingly small, at the moment, for I was too much flurried with indignation – and even shame – that he should thus dare to address me, to retain sufficient command of thought and language to enable me adequately to contend against his powerful sophistries. Finding, however, that he could not be silenced by reason, and even covertly exulted in his seeming advantage, and ventured to deride those assertions I had not the coolness to prove, I changed my course and tried another plan.

'Do you really love me?' said I seriously, pausing and looking him calmly in the face.

'Do I love you!' cried he.

'*Truly?*' I demanded.

His countenance brightened; he thought his triumph was at hand. He commenced a passionate protestation of the truth and fervour of his attachment which I cut short by another question – 'But is it not a selfish love? – Have you enough disinterested affection to enable you to sacrifice your own pleasure to mine?'

'I would give my life to serve you.'

'I don't want your life – but have you enough real sympathy for my afflictions to induce you to make an effort to relieve them, at the risk of a little discomfort to yourself?'

'Try me, and see!'

'If you have – *never mention this subject again*. You cannot recur to it in any way, without doubling the weight of those sufferings you so feelingly deplore. I have nothing left me but the solace of a good conscience and a hopeful trust in Heaven, and you labour continually to rob me of these. If you persist, I must regard you as my deadliest foe.'

'But hear me a moment – '

'No, sir! You said you would give your life to serve me: I only ask your *silence* on one particular point. I have spoken plainly; and what I say I mean. If you torment me in this way any more, I must conclude that your protestations are entirely false, and that you hate me in your heart as fervently as you profess to love me!'

He bit his lip and bent his eyes upon the ground in silence for a while.

'Then I must leave you,' said he at length, looking steadily upon me, as if with the last hope of detecting some token of irrepressible anguish or dismay awakened by those solemn words. 'I must leave you. I cannot live here, and be for ever silent on the all-absorbing subject of my thoughts and wishes.'

'Formerly, I believe, you spent but little of your time at home,' I answered: 'it will do you no harm to absent yourself again, for a while – if that be really necessary.'

'If that be really *possible*,' he muttered – 'and can you bid me go so coolly? Do you really wish it?'

'Most certainly I do. If you cannot see me without tormenting me as you have lately done, I would gladly say farewell and never see you more.'

He made no answer, but, bending from his horse, held out his hand towards me. I looked up at his face, and saw, therein, such a look of genuine agony of soul that, whether bitter disappointment, or wounded pride, or lingering love, or burning wrath were uppermost, I could not hesitate to put my hand in his as frankly as if I bade a friend farewell. He grasped it very hard, and immediately put spurs to his horse and galloped away. Very soon after, I learned that he was gone to Paris, where he still is, and the longer he stays there the better for me.

I thank God for this deliverance!

## CHAPTER 38

## *The Injured Man*

December 20th, 1826. The fifth anniversary of my wedding day, and I trust, the last I shall spend under this roof. My resolution is formed, my plan concocted, and already partly put in execution. My conscience does not blame me, but while the purpose ripens, let me beguile a few of these long winter evenings in stating the case for my own satisfaction – a dreary amusement enough, but having the air of a useful occupation, and being pursued as a task, it will suit me better than a lighter one.

In September, quiet Grassdale was again alive with a party of ladies and gentlemen (so called) consisting of the same individuals as those invited the year before last, with the addition of two or three others, among whom were Mrs Hargrave and her younger daughter. The gentlemen and Lady Lowborough were invited for the pleasure and convenience of the host; the

other ladies, I suppose for the sake of appearances, and to keep me in check and make me discreet and civil in my demeanour. But the ladies stayed only three weeks, the gentlemen, with two exceptions, above two months, for their hospitable entertainer was loath to part with them and be left alone with his bright intellect, his stainless conscience, and his loved and loving wife.

On the day of Lady Lowborough's arrival, I followed her into her chamber, and plainly told her that, if I found reason to believe that she still continued her criminal connection with Mr Huntingdon, I should think it my absolute duty to inform her husband of the circumstance – or awaken his suspicions at least – however painful it might be, or however dreadful the consequences. She was startled at first, by the declaration, so unexpected, and so determinately yet calmly delivered; but rallying in a moment, she coolly replied that if I saw anything at all reprehensible or suspicious in her conduct, she would freely give me leave to tell his lordship all about it. Willing to be satisfied with this, I left her; and certainly I saw nothing thenceforth particularly reprehensible or suspicious in her demeanour towards her host; but then I had the other guests to attend to, and I did not watch them narrowly – for to confess the truth, I *feared* to see anything between them. I no longer regarded it as any concern of mine, and if it was my duty to enlighten Lord Lowborough, it was a painful duty, and I dreaded to be called to perform it.

But my fears were brought to an end, in a manner I had not anticipated. One evening, about a fortnight after the visitors' arrival, I had retired into the library to snatch a few minutes' respite from forced cheerfulness and wearisome discourse – for after so long a period of seclusion, dreary indeed, as I had often found it, I could not always bear to be doing violence to my feelings, and goading my powers to talk, and smile and listen, and play the attentive hostess – or even the cheerful friend – I had just ensconced myself within the bow of the window, and was looking out upon the west where the darkening hills rose sharply defined against the clear amber light of evening, that gradually blended and faded away into the pure, pale blue of the upper sky, where one bright star was shining through, as if to promise – 'When that dying light is gone, the world will not be left in darkness, and they who trust in God – whose minds are unbeclouded by the mists of unbelief and sin, are never wholly comfortless' – when I heard a hurried step approaching, and Lord Lowborough entered – this room was still his favourite resort. He flung the door to with unusual violence, and cast his hat aside regardless where it fell. What could be the matter with him? His face was ghastly pale, his eyes were fixed upon the ground; his teeth clenched; his forehead glistened with the dews of agony. It was plain he knew his wrongs at last!

Unconscious of my presence, he began to pace the room in a state of fearful agitation, violently wringing his hands and uttering low groans or incoherent ejaculations. I made a movement to let him know that he was not alone; but he was too preoccupied to notice it. Perhaps, while his back was towards me, I might cross the room and slip away unobserved; I rose to make the attempt, but then he perceived me. He started and stood still a moment; then wiped

his streaming forehead, and advancing towards me, with a kind of unnatural composure, said in a deep, almost sepulchral tone – 'Mrs Huntingdon, I must leave you tomorrow.'

'Tomorrow!' I repeated, 'I do not ask the cause.'

'You know it then – and you can be so calm!' said he, surveying me with profound astonishment, not unmingled with a kind of resentful bitterness, as it appeared to me.

'I have so long been aware of – ' I paused in time, and added, 'of my husband's character, that nothing shocks me.'

'But *this* – how long have you been aware of this?' demanded he, laying his clenched hand on the table beside him, and looking me keenly and fixedly in the face.

I felt like a criminal.

'Not long,' I answered.

'You knew it!' cried he with bitter vehemence – 'and you did not tell me! You helped to deceive me!'

'My lord, I did *not* help to deceive you.'

'Then why did you not tell me?'

'Because, I knew it would be painful to you – I hoped she would return to her duty, and then there would be no need to harrow your feelings with such – '

'O God! How long has this been going on? How long has it been, Mrs Huntingdon? – Tell me – I must know!' he exclaimed with intense and fearful eagerness.

'Two years, I believe.'

'Great Heaven! And she has duped me all this time!' He turned away with a suppressed groan of agony, and paced the room again, in a paroxysm of renewed agitation. My heart smote me; but I would try to console him, though I knew not how to attempt it.

'She is a wicked woman,' I said. 'She has basely deceived and betrayed you. She is as little worthy of your regret as she was of your affection. Let her injure you no farther: abstract yourself from her, and stand alone.'

'And you, madam,' said he sternly, arresting his walk and turning round upon me – 'you have injured me too, by this ungenerous concealment!'

There was a sudden revulsion in my feelings. Something rose within me, and urged me to resent this harsh return for my heartfelt sympathy, and defend myself with answering severity. Happily, I did not yield to the impulse. I saw his anguish as, suddenly smiting his forehead, he turned abruptly to the window, and, looking upward at the placid sky, murmured passionately, 'O God, that I might die!' – and felt that to add one drop of bitterness to that already overflowing cup, would be ungenerous indeed. And yet, I fear there was more coldness than gentleness in the quiet tone of my reply – 'I might offer many excuses that some would admit to be valid, but I will not attempt to enumerate them – '

'I know them,' said he hastily, 'you would say that it was no business of yours – that I ought to have taken care of myself – that if my own blindness has led me

into this pit of Hell, I have no right to blame another for giving me credit for a larger amount of sagacity than I possessed – '

'I confess I was wrong,' continued I, without regarding this bitter interruption; 'but whether want of courage or mistaken kindness was the cause of my error, I think you blame me too severely. I told Lady Lowborough two weeks ago, the very hour she came, that I should certainly think it my duty to inform you if she continued to deceive you: she gave me full liberty to do so if I should see anything reprehensible or suspicious in her conduct – I have seen nothing; and I trusted she had altered her course.'

He continued gazing from the window while I spoke, and did not answer, but, stung by the recollections my words awakened, stamped his foot upon the floor, ground his teeth, and corrugated his brow, like one under the influence of acute physical pain.

'It was wrong – it was wrong!' he muttered, at length. 'Nothing can excuse it – nothing can atone for it – for nothing can recall those years of cursed credulity – nothing obliterate them! – nothing, nothing!' he repeated in a whisper whose despairing bitterness precluded all resentment.

'When I put the case to myself, I own it *was* wrong,' I answered; 'but I can only now regret that I did not see it in this light before, and that, as you say, nothing can recall the past.'

Something in my voice or in the spirit of this answer seemed to alter his mood. Turning towards me and attentively surveying my face by the dim light, he said in a milder tone than he had yet employed – 'You too have suffered, I suppose.'

'I suffered much, at first.'

'When was that?'

'Two years ago; and two years hence you will be as calm as I am now – and far, far happier, I trust, for you are a man, and free to act as you please.'

Something like a smile, but a *very* bitter one, crossed his face for a moment.

'You have not been happy lately?' he said with a kind of effort to regain composure, and a determination to waive the further discussion of his own calamity.

'Happy!' I repeated, almost provoked at such a question – 'Could I be so, with such a husband?'

'I have noticed a change in your appearance since the first years of your marriage,' pursued he: 'I observed it to – to that infernal demon,' he muttered between his teeth – 'and he said it was your own sour temper that was eating away your bloom: it was making you old and ugly before your time, and had already made his fireside as comfortless as a convent cell – You smile, Mrs Huntingdon – nothing moves you. I wish my nature were as calm as yours!'

'My nature was not originally calm,' said I: 'I have learned to appear so by dint of hard lessons, and many repeated efforts.'

At this juncture Mr Hattersley burst into the room.

'Hallow, Lowborough!' he began – 'Oh! I beg your pardon,' he exclaimed on seeing me; 'I didn't know it was a tête-à-tête. Cheer up, man!' he continued,

giving Lord Lowborough a thump on the back, which caused the latter to recoil from him with looks of ineffable disgust and irritation. 'Come, I want to speak with you a bit.'

'Speak, then.'

'But I'm not sure it would be quite agreeable to the lady, what I have to say.'

'Then it would not be agreeable to me,' said his lordship, turning to leave the room.

'Yes, it would,' cried the other, following him into the hall. 'If you've the heart of a man it would be the very ticket for you. It's just this, my lad,' he continued, rather lowering his voice, but not enough to prevent me from hearing every word he said, though the half-closed door stood between us: 'I think you're an ill-used man – nay, now, don't flare up – I don't want to offend you: it's only my rough way of talking. I must speak right out, you *know*, or else not at all; and I'm come – stop now! Let me explain – I'm come to offer you my services, for though Huntingdon is my friend, he's a devilish scamp as we all know, and I'll be *your* friend for the nonce. I know what it is you want, to make matters straight: it's just to exchange a shot with him, and then you'll feel yourself all right again; and if an accident happens – why, that'll be all right too, I dare say, to a desperate fellow like you – Come now! Give me your hand, and don't look so black upon it. Name time and place, and I'll manage the rest.'

'That,' answered the more low, deliberate voice of Lord Lowborough, 'is just the remedy my own heart – or the devil within it – suggested: to meet him, and *not to sever without blood*. Whether I or he should fall – or both, it would be an *inexpressible* relief to me, if – '

'Just so! Well then – '

'No!' exclaimed his lordship with deep, determined emphasis. 'Though I hate him from my heart, and should rejoice at any calamity that could befall him – I'll leave him to God; and though I abhor my own life, I'll leave that too, to Him that gave it.'

'But you see in this case,' pleaded Hattersley – 'I'll not hear you!' exclaimed his companion, hastily turning away. 'Not another word! I've enough to do against the fiend within me.'

'Then you're a white-livered fool, and I wash my hands of you,' grumbled the tempter as he swung himself round and departed.

'Right, right, Lord Lowborough!' cried I, darting out and clasping his burning hand, as he was moving away to the stairs. 'I begin to think the world is not worthy of you!'

Not understanding this sudden ebullition, he turned upon me with a stare of gloomy, bewildered amazement that made me ashamed of the impulse to which I had yielded; but soon a more humanised expression dawned upon his countenance, and, before I could withdraw my hand, he pressed it kindly, while a gleam of genuine feeling flashed from his eyes as he murmured – 'God help us both!'

'Amen!' responded I; and we parted.

I returned to the drawing-room, where, doubtless, my presence would be

expected by most, desired by one or two. In the ante-room was Mr Hattersley, railing against Lord Lowborough's poltroonery before a select audience, viz. Mr Huntingdon, who was lounging against the table exulting in his own treacherous villainy and laughing his victim to scorn, and Mr Grimsby, standing by, quietly rubbing his hands and chuckling with fiendish satisfaction. At the glance I gave them in passing, Hattersley stopped short in his animadversions and stared like a bull calf, Grimsby glowered upon me with a leer of malignant ferocity, and my husband muttered a coarse and brutal malediction.

In the drawing-room I found Lady Lowborough, evidently in no very enviable state of mind, and struggling hard to conceal her discomposure by an overstrained affectation of unusual cheerfulness and vivacity, very uncalled for under the circumstances, for she had herself given the company to understand that her husband had received unpleasant intelligence from home, which necessitated his immediate departure, and that he had suffered it so to bother his mind that it had brought on a bilious headache, owing to which, and the preparations he judged necessary to hasten his departure, she believed they would not have the pleasure of seeing him tonight. However, she asserted, it was only a business concern, and so she did not intend it should trouble *her*. She was just saying this as I entered, and she darted upon me such a glance of hardihood and defiance as at once astonished and revolted me.

'But I *am* troubled,' continued she, 'and vexed too, for I think it my duty to accompany his lordship, and of course I am very sorry to part with all my kind friends, so unexpectedly and so soon.'

'And yet, Annabella,' said Esther, who was sitting beside her, 'I never saw you in better spirits in my life.'

'Precisely so, my love; because I wish to make the best of your society, since it appears thus is to be the last night I am to enjoy it, till Heaven knows when; and I wish to leave a good impression on you all,' – she glanced round, and seeing her aunt's eye fixed upon her, rather too scrutinisingly, as she probably thought, she started up and continued – 'to which end I'll give you a song – Shall I, aunt? Shall I, Mrs Huntingdon? Shall I, ladies and gentlemen – all? – Very well, I'll do my best to amuse you.'

She and Lord Lowborough occupied the apartments next to mine. I know not how *she* passed the night, but I lay awake the greater part of it listening to his heavy step pacing monotonously up and down his dressing-room, which was nearest my chamber. Once I heard him pause and throw something out of the window, with a passionate ejaculation; and in the morning, after they were gone, a keen-bladed clasp-knife was found on the grass-plot below; a razor, likewise was snapped in two and thrust deep into the cinders of the grate, but partially corroded by the decaying embers. So strong had been the temptation to end his miserable life, so determined his resolution to resist it.

My heart bled for him as I lay listening to that ceaseless tread. Hitherto, I had thought too much of myself, too little of him: now I forgot my own afflictions, and thought only of his – of the ardent affection so miserably wasted, the fond faith so cruelly betrayed, the – no, I will not attempt to enumerate his wrongs –

but I hated his wife and my husband more intensely than ever, and not for my sake, but for his.

'That man,' I thought, 'is an object of scorn to his friends and the nice-judging world. The false wife and the treacherous friend who have wronged him are not so despised and degraded as he; and his refusal to avenge his wrongs has removed him yet farther beyond the range of sympathy, and blackened his name with a deeper disgrace. He knows this; and it doubles his burden of woe. He sees the injustice of it, but he cannot bear up against it; he lacks that sustaining power of self-esteem which leads a man, exulting in his own integrity, to defy the malice of traducing foes and give them scorn for scorn – or, better still, which raises him above earth's foul and turbulent vapours, to repose in Heaven's eternal sunshine. He knows that God is just, but cannot see His justice now: he knows this life is short, and yet death seems insufferably far away; he believes there is a future state, but so absorbing is the agony of this that he cannot realise its rapturous repose. He can but bow his head to the storm, and cling, blindly, despairingly, to what he knows to be right. Like the shipwrecked mariner cleaving to a raft, blinded, deafened, bewildered, he feels the waves sweep over him, and sees no prospect of escape; and yet he knows he has no hope but this, and still, while life and sense remain, concentrates all his energies to keep it. Oh, that I had a friend's right to comfort him, and tell him that I never esteemed him so highly as I do this night!'

They departed early in the morning before anyone else was down, except myself, and just as I was leaving my room, Lord Lowborough was descending to take his place in the carriage where his lady was already ensconced; and Arthur (or Mr Huntingdon as I prefer calling him, for the other is my child's name) had the gratuitous insolence to come out in his dressing-gown to bid his 'friend' goodbye.

'What, going already, Lowborough?' said he. 'Well, good-morning.' He smilingly offered his hand.

I think the other would have knocked him down, had he not instinctively started back before that bony fist quivering with rage and clenched till the knuckles gleamed white and glistening through the skin. Looking upon him with a countenance livid with furious hate, Lord Lowborough muttered between his closed teeth, a deadly execration he would not have uttered had he been calm enough to choose his words, and departed.

'I call that an unchristian spirit now,' said the villain. 'But I'd never give up an old friend for the sake of a wife. You may have mine if you like, and I call that handsome – I *can* do no more than offer restitution, can I?'

But Lowborough had gained the bottom of the stairs, and was now crossing the hall; and Mr Huntingdon, leaning over the banisters, called out – 'Give my love to Annabella! – and I wish you both a happy journey,' and withdrew laughing to his chamber.

He subsequently expressed himself rather glad she was gone: 'She was so deuced imperious and exacting,' said he: 'now I shall be my own man again, and feel rather more at my ease.'

I know nothing more of Lord Lowborough's subsequent proceedings but what I have heard from Milicent, who, though she is ignorant of the cause of his separation from her cousin, has informed me that such is the case; that they keep entirely separate establishments; that she leads a gay, dashing life in town and country, while he lives in strict seclusion at his old castle in the north. There are two children, both of whom he keeps under his own protection. The son and heir is a promising child nearly the age of my Arthur, and no doubt a source of some hope and comfort to his father; but the other, a little girl between one and two, with blue eyes and light auburne hair, he probably keeps from conscientious motives alone, thinking it wrong to abandon her to the teaching and example of such a woman as her mother. That mother never loved children, and has so little natural affection for her own that I question whether she will not regard it as a relief to be thus entirely separated from them, and delivered from the trouble and responsibility of their charge.

Not many days after the departure of Lord and Lady Lowborough, the rest of the ladies withdrew the light of their presence from Grassdale. Perhaps they might have stayed longer, but neither host nor hostess pressed them to prolong their visit – in fact, the former showed too plainly that he should be glad to get rid of them; and Mrs Hargrave retired with her daughters and her grandchildren (there are three of them now) to the Grove. But the gentlemen remained: Mr Huntingdon, as I intimated before, was determined to keep them as long as he could; and, being thus delivered from restraint, they gave a loose to all their innate madness, folly, and brutality, and made the house night after night one scene of riot, uproar, and confusion. Who among them behaved the worst, or who the best, I can not distinctly say; for, from the moment I discovered how things would be, I formed the resolution of retreating upstairs or locking myself into the library the instant I withdrew from the dining-room, and not coming near them again till breakfast; but this I must say for Mr Hargrave, that from all I could see of him, he was a model of decency, sobriety, and gentlemanly manners *in comparison* with the rest.

He did not join the party till a week or ten days after the arrival of the other guests; for he was still on the continent when they came, and I cherished the hope that he would not accept the invitation. Accept it he did, however, but his conduct towards me, for the first few weeks, was exactly what I should had wished it to be – perfectly civil and respectful without any affectation of despondency or dejection, and sufficiently distant without haughtiness, or any of such remarkable stiffness or iciness of demeanour as might be calculated to disturb or puzzle his sister, or call forth the investigation of his mother.

CHAPTER 39

## *A Scheme of Escape*

My greatest source of uneasiness, in this time of trial, was my son, whom his father and his father's friends delighted to encourage in all the embryo vices a little child can show, and to instruct in all the evil habits he could acquire – in a word, to 'make a man of him' was one of their staple amusements; and I need say no more to justify my alarm on his account, and my determination to deliver him at any hazard from the hands of such instructors. I first attempted to keep him always with me or in the nursery, and gave Rachel particular injunctions never to let him come down to dessert as long as these 'gentlemen' stayed; but it was no use; these orders were immediately countermanded and overruled by his father: he was not going to have the little fellow moped to death between an old nurse and a cursed fool of a mother. So the little fellow came down every evening, in spite of his cross mamma, and learnt to tipple wine like papa, to swear like Mr Hattersley, and to have his own way like a man, and sent mamma to the devil when she tried to prevent him. To see such things done with the roguish naivete of that pretty little child and hear such things spoken by that small infantile voice, was as peculiarly piquant and irresistibly droll to them as it was inexpressibly distressing and painful to me; and when he had set the table in a roar, he would look round delightedly upon them all, and add his shrill laugh to theirs. But if that beaming blue eye rested on me, its light would vanish for a moment, and he would say, in some concern – 'Mamma, why don't *you* laugh? Make her laugh, papa – she never will.'

Hence, was I obliged to stay among these human brutes, watching an opportunity to get my child away from them, instead of leaving them immediately after the removal of the cloth, as I should always otherwise have done. He was never willing to go, and I frequently had to carry him away by force; for which he thought me very cruel and unjust; and sometimes his father would insist upon my letting him remain; and then, I would leave him to his kind friends, and retire to indulge my bitterness and despair alone or to rack my brains for a remedy to this great evil.

But here again, I must do Mr Hargrave the justice to acknowledge that I never saw *him* laugh at the child's misdemeanours, nor heard him utter a word of encouragement to his aspirations after manly accomplishments. But when anything very extraordinary was said or done by the infant profligate, I noticed, at times, a peculiar expression in his face, that I could neither interpret nor define – a slight twitching about the muscles of the mouth – a sudden flash in the eye, as he darted a sudden glance at the child and then at me; and then, I could fancy there arose a gleam of hard, keen, sombre satisfaction in his countenance at the look of impotent wrath and anguish he was too certain to behold in mine.

But on one occasion, when Arthur had been behaving particularly ill, and Mr Huntingdon and his guests had been particularly provoking and insulting to me in their encouragement of him, and I particularly anxious to get him out of the room, and on the very point of demeaning myself by a burst of uncontrollable passion – Mr Hargrave suddenly rose from his seat, with an aspect of stern determination, lifted the child from his father's knee, where he was sitting half tipsy, cocking his head and laughing at me, and execrating me with words he little knew the meaning of – handed him out of the room, and setting him down in the hall, held the door open for me, gravely bowed as I withdrew, and closed it after me. I heard high words exchanged between him and his already half-inebriated host as I departed, leading away my bewildered and disconcerted boy.

But this should not continue; my child must not be abandoned to this corruption: better far that he should live in poverty and obscurity with a fugitive mother, than in luxury and affluence with such a father. These guests might not be with us long, but they would return again; and he, the most injurious of the whole, his child's worst enemy, would still remain. I could endure it for myself, but for my son it must be borne no longer: the world's opinion and the feelings of my friends must be alike unheeded here, at least, alike unable to deter me from my duty. But where should I find an asylum, and how obtain subsistence for us both? Oh, I would take my precious charge at early dawn, take the coach to M—, flee to the port of —, cross the Atlantic, and seek a quiet, humble home in New England, where I would support myself and him by the labour of my hands. The palette and the easel, my darling playmates once, must be my sober toil-fellows now. But was I sufficiently skilful as an artist to obtain my livelihood in a strange land, without friends and without recommendation? No; I must wait a little; I must labour hard to improve my talent and to produce something worthwhile as a specimen of my powers, something to speak favourably for me, whether as an actual painter or a teacher. Brilliant success, of course, I did not look for, but some degree of security from positive failure was indispensable – I must not take my son to starve. And then I must have money for the journey, the passage, and some little to support us in our retreat in case I should be unsuccessful at first; and not too little either, for who could tell how long I might have to struggle with the indifference or neglect of others, or my own inexperience, or inability to suit their tastes?

What should I do then? Apply to my brother, and explain my circumstances and my resolves to him? No, no; even if I told him *all* my grievances, which I should be very reluctant to do, he would be certain to disapprove of the step: it would seem like madness to him, as it would to my uncle and aunt, or to Milicent. No; I must have patience and gather a hoard of my own. Rachel should be my only confidant – I thought I could persuade her into the scheme; and she should help me, first to find out a picture dealer in some distant town; then, through her means, I would privately sell what pictures I had on hand that would do for such a purpose, and some of those I should thereafter paint. Besides this, I would contrive to dispose of my jewels – not the family jewels, but the few I brought with me from home, and those my uncle gave me on my marriage. A few

months' arduous toil might well be borne by me, with such an end in view; and in the interim, my son could not be much more injured than he was already.

Having formed this resolution, I immediately set to work to accomplish it. I might possibly have been induced to wax cool upon it afterwards, or perhaps, to keep weighing the pros and cons in my mind till the latter overbalanced the former, and I was driven to relinquish the project altogether, or delay the execution of it to an indefinite period – had not something occurred to confirm me in that determination to which I still adhere, which I still think I did well to form, and shall do better to execute.

Since Lord Lowborough's departure, I had regarded the library as entirely my own, a secure retreat at all hours of the day. None of our gentlemen had the smallest pretensions to a literary taste, expect Mr Hargrave; and he, at present, was quite contented with the newspapers and periodicals of the day. And if, by any chance, he should look in here, I felt assured he would soon depart on seeing me, for, instead of becoming less cool and distant towards me, he had become decidedly more so since the departure of his mother and sisters, which was just what I wished. Here, then, I set up my easel, and here I worked at my canvas from daylight till dusk, with very little intermission saving when pure necessity, or my duties to little Arthur called me away – for I still thought proper to devote some portion of every day exclusively to his instruction and amusement. But contrary to my expectation, on the third morning, while I was thus employed, Mr Hargrave *did* look in, and did *not* immediately withdraw on seeing me. He apologised for his intrusion, and said he was only come for a book; but when he had got it, he condescended to cast a glance over my picture. Being a man of taste, he had something to say on this subject as well as another, and having modestly commented on it, without much encouragement from me, he proceeded to expatiate on the art in general. Receiving no encouragement in that either, he dropped it, but did not depart.

'You don't give us much of your company, Mrs Huntingdon,' observed he, after a brief pause, during which I went on coolly mixing and tempering my colours; 'and I cannot wonder at it, for you must be heartily sick of us all. I myself am so thoroughly ashamed of my companions, and so weary of their irrational conversation and pursuits – now that there is no one to humanise them and keep them in check, since you have justly abandoned us to our own devices – that I think I shall presently withdraw from amongst them – probably within this week – and I cannot suppose you will regret my departure.'

He paused. I did not answer.

'Probably,' he added, with a smile, 'your only regret on the subject will be, that I do not take all my companions along with me. I flatter myself, at times, that though among them, I am not of them; but it is natural that you should be glad to get rid of me. I may regret this, but I cannot blame you for it.'

'I shall not rejoice at *your* departure, for you *can* conduct yourself like a gentleman,' said I, thinking it but right to make some acknowledgement for his good behaviour, 'but I must confess I shall rejoice to bid adieu to the rest, inhospitable as it may appear.'

'No one can blame you for such an avowal,' replied he gravely; 'not even the gentlemen themselves, I imagine. I'll just tell you,' he continued, as if actuated by a sudden resolution, 'what was said last night in the dining-room, after you left us – perhaps you will not mind it as you're so *very* philosophical on certain points,' he added with a slight sneer. 'They were talking about Lord Lowborough and his delectable lady, the cause of whose sudden departure is no secret amongst them; and her character is so well known to them all that, nearly related to me as she is, I could not attempt to defend it – God curse me,' he muttered *par parenthèse*, 'if I don't have vengeance for this! If the villain *must* disgrace the family, must he blazon it abroad to every low-bred knave of his acquaintance? – I beg your pardon, Mrs Huntingdon. Well, they were talking of these things, and some of them remarked that, as she was separated from her husband, he might see her again when he pleased.'

' "Thank you," said he; "I've had enough of her for the present: I'll not trouble to see her, unless she comes to me."

' "Then what do you mean to do, Huntingdon, when we're gone?" said Ralph Hattersley. "Do you mean to turn from the error of your ways, and be a good husband, a good father, and so forth – as I do, when I get shut of you and all these rollicking devils you call your friends? I think it's time; and your wife is fifty times too good for you, you *know* – "

'And he added some praise of you, which you would not thank me for repeating – nor him for uttering; proclaiming it aloud, as he did, without delicacy or discrimination, in an audience where it seemed profanation to utter your name – himself utterly incapable of understanding or appreciating your real excellencies. Huntingdon meanwhile, sat quietly drinking his wine, or looking smilingly into his glass and offering no interruption or reply, till Hattersley shouted out – ' "Do you hear me, man?"

' "Yes, go on," said he.

' "Nay, I've done," replied the other: "I only want to know if you intend to take my advice."

' "What advice?"

' "To turn over a new leaf, you double-dyed scoundrel," shouted Ralph, "and beg your wife's pardon, and be a good boy for the future."

' "My wife! what wife? I have no wife," replied Huntingdon, looking innocently up from his glass – "or if I have, look you gentlemen, I value her so highly that anyone among you, that can fancy her, may have her and welcome – you may, by Jove and my blessing into the bargain!"

'I – hem – someone asked if he really meant what he said, upon which, he solemnly swore he did, and no mistake – What do you think of that, Mrs Huntingdon?' asked Mr Hargrave, after a short pause, during which I had felt he was keenly examining my half-averted face.

'I say,' replied I, calmly, 'that what he prizes so lightly, will not be long in his possession.'

'You cannot mean that you will break your heart and die for the detestable conduct of an infamous villain like that!'

'By no means: my heart is too thoroughly dried to be broken in a hurry, and I mean to live as long as I can.'

'Will you leave him then?'

'Yes.'

'When – and how?' asked he, eagerly.

'*When* I am ready, and *how* I can manage it most effectually.'

'But your child?'

'My child goes with me.'

'He will not allow it.'

'I shall not ask him.'

'Ah, then, it is a secret flight you meditate – but with whom, Mrs Huntingdon?'

'With my son – and, possibly, his nurse.'

'Alone – and unprotected! But where can you go? What can you do? He will follow you and bring you back.'

'I have laid my plans too well for that. Let me once get clear of Grassdale, and I shall consider myself safe.'

Mr Hargrave advanced one step towards me, looked me in the face, and drew in his breath to speak; but that look, that heightened colour, that sudden sparkle of the eye made my blood rise in wrath: I abruptly turned away, and, snatching up my brush, began to dash away at my canvas with rather too much energy for the good of the picture.

'Mrs Huntingdon,' said he with bitter solemnity, 'you are cruel – cruel to me – cruel to yourself.'

'Mr Hargrave, remember your promise.'

'I *must* speak – my heart will burst if I don't! I have been silent long enough – and you *must* hear me!' cried he boldly intercepting my retreat to the door. 'You tell me you owe no allegiance to your husband; he openly declares himself weary of you, and calmly gives you up to anybody that will take you; you are about to leave him; no one will believe that you go alone – all the world will say, "She has left him at last, and who can wonder at it? Few can blame her, fewer still can pity him; but who is the companion of her flight?" Thus you will have no credit for your virtue (if you call it such): even your best friends will not believe in it; because, it is monstrous, and not to be credited – but by those who suffer from the effects of it, such cruel torments that they know it to be indeed reality – But what can you do in the cold, rough world alone? You, a young and inexperienced woman, delicately nurtured, and utterly – '

'In a word, you would advise me to stay where I am,' interrupted I. 'Well, I'll see about it.'

'By *all means*, leave him!' cried he earnestly, 'but not alone! Helen! Let *me* protect you!'

'Never! – while Heaven spares my reason,' replied I, snatching away the hand he had presumed to seize and press between his own. But he was in for it now; he had fairly broken the barrier: he was completely roused, and determined to hazard all for victory.

'I must not be denied!' exclaimed he vehemently; and seizing both my hands, he held them very tight, but dropped upon his knee, and looked up in my face with a half-imploring, half-imperious gaze. 'You have no reason now: you are flying in the face of Heaven's decrees. God has designed me to be your comfort and protector – I feel it – I know it as certainly as if a voice from Heaven declared "Ye twain shall be one flesh" – and you spurn me from you –'

'Let me go, Mr Hargrave!' said I sternly. But he only tightened his grasp.

'Let me go!' I repeated, quivering with indignation.

His face was almost opposite the window as he knelt. With a slight start, I saw him glance towards it; and then a gleam of malicious triumph lit up his countenance. Looking over my shoulder, I beheld a shadow just retiring round the corner.

'That is Grimsby,' said he deliberately. 'He will report what he has seen to Huntingdon and all the rest, with such embellishments as he thinks proper. He has no love for you, Mrs Huntingdon – no reverence for your sex – no belief in virtue – no admiration for its image. He will give such a version of this story as will leave no doubt at all, about your character, in the minds of those who hear it. Your fair fame is gone; and nothing that I or you can say can ever retrieve it. But give me the power to protect you, and show me the villain that dares to insult!'

'No one has ever dared to insult me as you are doing now!' said I, at length releasing my hands, and recoiling from him.

'I do not insult you,' cried he: 'I worship you. You are my angel – my divinity! I lay my powers at your feet – and you must and shall accept them!' he exclaimed impetuously, starting to his feet – 'I *will* be your consoler and defender! And if your conscience upbraid you for it say I overcame you and you could not choose but yield!'

I never saw a man so terribly excited. He precipitated himself towards me. I snatched up my palette-knife and held it against him. This startled him: he stood and gazed at me in astonishment; I dare say I looked as fierce and resolute as he. I moved to the bell and put my hand upon the cord. This tamed him still more. With a half-authoritative, half-deprecating wave of the hand, he sought to deter me from ringing.

'Stand off, then!' said I. He stepped back – 'And listen to me – I don't like you,' I continued, as deliberately and emphatically as I could, to give the greater efficacy to my words; 'and if I were divorced from my husband – or if he were dead, I would not marry you. There now! I hope you're satisfied.'

His face grew blanched with anger.

'I *am* satisfied,' he replied with bitter emphasis, 'that you are the most cold-hearted, unnatural, ungrateful woman I ever yet beheld!'

'Ungrateful, sir?'

'Ungrateful.'

'No, Mr Hargrave; I am not. For all the good you ever did me, or ever wished to do, I most sincerely thank you: for all the evil you have done me, and all you would have done, I pray God to pardon you, and make you of a better mind.'

Here the door was thrown open, and Messrs Huntingdon and Hattersley appeared without. The latter remained in the hall, busy with his ram-rod and his gun; the former walked in, and stood with his back to the fire, surveying Mr Hargrave and me, particularly the former, with a smile of insupportable meaning, accompanied as it was, by the impudence of his brazen brow and the sly, malicious twinkle of his eye.

'Well, sir?' said Hargrave interrogatively, and with the air of one prepared to stand on the defensive.

'Well, sir,' returned his host.

'We want to know if you're at liberty to join us in a go at the pheasants, Walter,' interposed Hattersley from without. 'Come! there shall be nothing shot besides, except a puss or two; *I'll* vouch for that.'

Walter did not answer, but walked to the window to collect his faculties. Arthur uttered a low whistle, and followed him with his eyes. A slight flush of anger rose to Hargrave's cheek; but in a moment, he turned calmly round, and said carelessly – 'I came here to bid farewell to Mrs Huntingdon, and tell her I must go tomorrow.'

'Humph! You're mighty sudden in your resolution. What takes you off so soon, may I ask?'

'Business,' returned he, repelling the other's incredulous sneer with a glance of scornful defiance.

'Very good,' was the reply; and Hargrave walked away. Thereupon, Mr Huntingdon, gathering his coat laps under his arms, and setting his shoulder against the mantelpiece, turned to me, and, addressing me in a low voice, scarcely above his breath, poured forth a volley of the vilest and grossest abuse it was possible for the imagination to conceive or the tongue to utter. I did not attempt to interrupt him; but my spirit kindled within me, and when he had done, I replied – 'If your accusation were true, Mr Huntingdon, how *dare you* blame me?'

'She's hit it, by Jove!' cried Hattersley, rearing his gun against the wall and, stepping into the room, he took his precious friend by the arm, and attempted to drag him away. 'Come, my lad,' he muttered; 'true or false, *you've* no right to blame her, you *know* – nor him either; after what you said last night. So come along.'

There was something implied here that I could not endure.

'Dare you suspect me, Mr Hattersley?' said I, almost beside myself with fury.

'Nay, nay, I suspect nobody. It's all right – it's all right. So come along, Huntingdon, you blackguard.'

'She can't deny it!' cried the gentleman thus addressed, grinning in mingled rage and triumph. 'She can't deny it if her life depended on it!' and muttering some more abusive language, he walked into the hall, and took up his hat and gun from the table.

'I scorn to justify myself to you!' said I. 'But you,' turning to Hattersley, 'if you presume to have any doubts on the subject, ask Mr Hargrave.'

At this, they simultaneously burst into a rude laugh that made my whole frame tingle to the fingers' ends.

'Where is he? I'll ask him myself!' said I, advancing towards them.

Suppressing a new burst of merriment, Hattersley pointed to the outer door. It was half open. His brother-in-law was standing on the front without.

'Mr Hargrave, will you please to step this way?' said I.

He turned and looked at me in grave surprise.

'Step this way, if you please!' I repeated, in so determined a manner that he could not, or did not choose to resist its authority. Somewhat reluctantly he ascended the steps and advanced a pace or two into the hall.

'And tell those gentlemen,' I continued – 'these *men* whether or not I yielded to your solicitations.'

'I don't understand you, Mrs Huntingdon.'

'You *do* understand me, sir; and I charge you upon your honour as a gentleman (if you have any), to answer truly. Did I, or did I not?'

'No,' muttered he, turning away.

'Speak up sir; they can't hear you. Did I grant your request?'

'You did not.'

'No, I'll be sworn she didn't,' said Hattersley, 'or he'd never look so black.'

'I'm willing to grant you the satisfaction of a gentleman, Huntingdon,' said Mr Hargrave, calmly addressing his host, but with a bitter sneer upon his countenance.

'Go to the deuce!' replied the latter, with an impatient jerk of the head.

Hargrave withdrew with a look of cold disdain, saying – 'You know where to find me, should you feel disposed to send a friend.'

Muttered oaths and curses were all the anger this intimation obtained.

'Now Huntingdon, you see!' said Hattersley, 'clear as the day.'

'I don't care *what* he sees,' said I, 'or what he imagines; but you, Mr Hattersley, when you hear my name belied and slandered, will you defend it?'

'I will. Blast me if I don't!'

I instantly departed, and shut myself into the library. What could possess me to make such a request of such a man? I cannot tell, but drowning men catch at straws: they had driven me desperate between them; I hardly knew what I said. There was no other to preserve my name from being blackened and aspersed among this nest of boon companions, and through them, perhaps into the world; and beside my abandoned wretch of a husband, the base, malignant Grimsby, and the false villain Hargrave, this boarish ruffian, coarse and brutal as he was, shone like a glow-worm in the dark among its fellow worms.

What a scene was this! Could I ever have imagined that I should be doomed to bear such insults under my own roof – to hear such things spoken in my presence – nay spoken *to* me and *of* me – and by those who arrogated to themselves the name of gentlemen? And could I have imagined that I should have been able to endure it as calmly, and to repel their insults as firmly and as boldly as I had done? A hardness such as this, is taught by rough experience and despair alone.

Such thoughts as these, chased one another through my mind, as I paced to and fro the room, and longed – oh, *how* I longed to take my child and leave them

now, without an hour's delay! But it could not be: there was work before me – hard work, that must be done.

'Then let me do it,' said I, 'and lose not a moment in vain repinings, and idle chafings against my fate, and those who influence it.'

And conquering my agitation with a powerful effort, I immediately resumed my task and laboured hard all day.

Mr Hargrave did depart on the morrow; and I have never seen him since. The others stayed on for two or three weeks longer; but I kept aloof from them as much as possible, and still continued my labour, and have continued it, with almost unabated ardour, to the present day. I soon acquainted Rachel with my design, confiding all my motives and intentions to her ear, and much to my agreeable surprise, found little difficulty in persuading her to enter into my views. She is a sober, cautious woman, but she so hates her master, and so loves her mistress and her nursling, that after several ejaculations, a few faint objections, and many tears and lamentations that I should be brought to such a pass, she applauded my resolution and consented to aid me with all her might – on one condition, only – that she might share my exile: otherwise, she was utterly inexorable, regarding it as perfect madness for me and Arthur to go alone. With touching generosity, she modestly offered to aid me with her little hoard of savings, hoping I would 'excuse her for the liberty, but really if I would do her the favour to accept it as a loan, she should be very happy'. Of course I could not think of such a thing; but now, thank Heaven, I have gathered a little hoard of my own, and my preparations are so far advanced, that I am looking forward to a speedy emancipation. Only let the stormy severity of this winter weather be somewhat abated, and then, some morning Mr Huntingdon will come down to a solitary breakfast-table, and perhaps be clamouring through the house for his invisible wife and child, when they are some fifty miles on their way to the western world – or it may be more, for we shall leave him hours before the dawn, and it is not probable he will discover the loss of both, until the day is far advanced.

I am fully alive to the evils that may, and must result upon the step I am about to take; but I never waver in my resolution, because I never forget my son. It was only this morning – while I pursued my usual employment, he was sitting at my feet, quietly playing with the shreds of canvas I had thrown upon the carpet – but his mind was otherwise occupied, for, in a while, he looked up wistfully in my face, and gravely asked – 'Mamma, why are you wicked?'

'Who told you I was wicked, love?'

'Rachel.'

'No, Arthur, Rachel never said so, I am certain.'

'Well then, it was papa,' replied he thoughtfully. Then, after a reflective pause, he added, 'At least, I'll tell you how it was I got to know: when I'm with papa, if I say mamma wants me, or mamma says I'm not to do something that he tells me to do – he always says, "Mamma be damned" – and Rachel says it's only wicked people that are damned. So mamma, that's why I think you must be wicked – and I wish you wouldn't.'

'My dear child, I am not. Those are bad words, and wicked people often say them of others better than themselves. Those words cannot make people be damned, nor show that they deserve it. God will judge us by our own thoughts and deeds, not by what others say about us. And when you hear such words spoken, Arthur, remember never to repeat them: it is wicked to say such things of others, not to have them said against you.'

'Then it's papa that's wicked,' said he, ruefully.

'Papa is wrong to say such things, and you will be very wrong to imitate him, now that you know better.'

'What *is* imitate?'

'To do as he does.'

'Does *he* know better?'

'Perhaps he does; but that is nothing to you.'

'If he doesn't, you ought to tell him, mamma.'

'I *have* told him.'

The little moralist paused and pondered. I tried in vain to divert his mind from the subject.

'I'm sorry papa's wicked,' said he mournfully, at length, 'for I don't want him to go to Hell.' And so saying he burst into tears.

I consoled him with the hope that perhaps his papa would alter and become good before he died – but is it not time to deliver him from such a parent?

**CHAPTER 40**

## *A Misadventure*

January 10th, 1827. While writing the above, yesterday evening, I sat in the drawing-room. Mr Huntingdon was present, but, as I thought, asleep on the sofa behind me. He had risen however, unknown to me, and, actuated by some base spirit of curiosity, been looking over my shoulder for I know not how long; for when I had laid aside my pen, and was about to close the book, he suddenly placed his hand upon it, and saying – 'With your leave, my dear, I'll have a look at this,' forcibly wrested it from me, and, drawing a chair to the table, composedly sat down to examine it – turning back leaf after leaf to find an explanation of what he had read. Unluckily for me, he was more sober that night than he usually is at such an hour.

Of course I did not leave him to pursue this occupation in quiet: I made several attempts to snatch the book from his hands, but he held it too firmly for that; I upbraided him in bitterness and scorn for his mean and dishonourable conduct, but that had no effect upon him; I extinguished both the candles, but he only wheeled round to the fire, and raising a blaze sufficient for his purposes, calmly continued the investigation. I had serious thoughts of getting a pitcher of water and extinguishing that light too; but it was evident his curiosity was too

keenly excited to be quenched by that, and the more I manifested my anxiety to baffle his scrutiny, the greater would be his determination to persist in it – besides it was too late.

'It seems very interesting, love,' said he, lifting his head and turning to where I stood wringing my hands in silent rage and anguish; 'but it's rather long; I'll look at it some other time; and meanwhile, I'll trouble you for your keys, my dear.'

'What keys?'

'The keys of your cabinet, desk, drawers, and whatever else you possess,' said he, rising and holding out his hand.

'I've not got them,' I replied. The key of my desk, in fact, was, at that moment, in the lock, and the others were attached to it.

'Then you must send for them,' said he; 'and if that old bitch, Rachel, doesn't immediately deliver them up, she tramps bag and baggage tomorrow.'

'She doesn't know where they are,' I answered, quietly placing my hand upon them, and taking them from the desk, as I thought, unobserved. '*I* know, but I shall not give them up without a reason.'

'And *I* know, too,' said he, suddenly seizing my closed hand and rudely abstracting them from it. He then took up one of the candles and relighted it by thrusting it into the fire.

'Now then,' sneered he, 'we must have a confiscation of property. But first, let us take a peep into the studio.'

And putting the keys into his pocket, he walked into the library. I followed, whether with the dim idea of preventing mischief or only to know the worst I can hardly tell. My painting materials were laid together on the corner table, ready for tomorrow's use, and only covered with a cloth. He soon spied them out, and putting down the candle, deliberately proceeded to cast them into the fire – palette, paints, bladders, pencils, brushes, varnish – I saw them all consumed – the palette knives snapped in two – the oil and turpentine sent hissing and roaring up the chimney. He then rang the bell.

'Benson, take those things away,' said he, pointing to the easel, canvas, and stretcher; 'and tell the housemaid she may kindle the fire with them: your mistress won't want them any more.'

Benson paused aghast and looked at me.

'Take them away, Benson,' said I; and his master muttered an oath.

'And this and all, sir?' said the astonished servant referring to the half-finished picture.

'That and all,' replied the master; and the things were cleared away.

Mr Huntingdon then went upstairs. I did not attempt to follow him, but remained seated in the armchair, speechless, tearless, and almost motionless, till he returned about half an hour after, and walking up to me, held the candle in my face and peered into my eyes with looks and laughter too insulting to be borne. With a sudden stroke of my hand, I dashed the candle to the floor.

'Hal–lo!' muttered he, starting back – 'She's the very devil for spite! Did *ever* any mortal see such eyes? – they shine in the dark like a cat's. *Oh*, you're a sweet

one!' So saying, he gathered up the candle and the candlestick. The former being broken as well as extinguished, he rang for another.

'Benson, your mistress has broken the candle: bring another.'

'You expose yourself finely,' observed I as the man departed.

'I didn't say *I'd* broken it, did I?' returned he. He then threw my keys into my lap, saying – 'There! you'll find nothing gone but your money, and the jewels – and a few little trifles I thought it advisable to take into my own possession, lest your mercantile spirit should be tempted to turn them into gold. I've left you a few sovereigns in your purse, which I expect to last you through the month – at all events, when you want more you will be so good as to give me an account of how that's spent. I shall put you upon a small monthly allowance, in future, for your own private expenses; and you needn't trouble yourself any more about my concerns; I shall look out for a steward, my dear; I won't expose you to the temptation. And as for the household matters, Mrs Greaves must be very particular in keeping her accounts: we must go upon an entirely new plan – '

'What great discovery have you made *now*, Mr Huntingdon? Have I attempted to defraud you?'

'Not in money matters, exactly, it seems, but it's best to keep out of the way of temptation.'

Here Benson entered with the candles, and there followed a brief interval of silence – I sitting still in my chair, and he standing with his back to the fire, silently triumphing in my despair.

'And so,' said he at length, 'you thought to disgrace me, did you, by running away and turning artist, and supporting yourself by the labour of your hands, forsooth? And you thought to rob me of my son too, and bring him up to be a dirty Yankee tradesman, or a low, beggarly painter?'

'Yes, to obviate his becoming such a gentleman as his father.'

'It's well you couldn't keep your own secret – ha, ha! It's well these women must be blabbing – if they haven't a friend to talk to, they must whisper their secrets to the fishes, or write them on the sand or something; and it's well too I wasn't over full tonight, now I think of it, or I might have snoozed away and never dreamt of looking what my sweet lady was about – or I might have lacked the sense or the power to carry my point like a man, as I have done.'

Leaving him to his self-congratulations, I rose to secure my manuscript, for I now remembered it had been left upon the drawing-room table, and I determined, if possible, to save myself the humiliation of seeing it in his hands again. I could not bear the idea of his amusing himself over my secret thoughts and recollections; though, to be sure, he would find little good of himself therein indited, except in the former part – and oh, I would sooner burn it all than he should read what I had written when I was such a fool as to love him!

'And by the by,' cried he as I was leaving the room, 'you'd better tell that damned old sneak of a nurse to keep out of my way for a day or two – I'd pay her her wages and send her packing tomorrow, but I know she'd do more mischief out of the house than in it.'

And as I departed, he went on cursing and abusing my faithful friend and

servant with epithets I will not defile this paper with repeating. I went to her as soon as I had put away my book, and told her how our project was defeated. She was as much distressed and horrified as I was – and more so than I was that night, for I was partly stunned by the blow, and partly excited and supported against it by the bitterness of my wrath. But in the morning, when I woke without that cheering hope that had been my secret comfort and support so long, and all this day, when I have wandered about restless and objectless, shunning my husband, shrinking even from my child – knowing that I am unfit to be his teacher or companion, hoping nothing for his future life, and fervently wishing he had never been born – I felt the full extent of my calamity – and I feel it now. I know that day after day such feelings will return upon me: I am a slave, a prisoner – but that is nothing; if it were myself alone, I would not complain, but I am forbidden to rescue my son from ruin, and what was once my only consolation, is become the crowning source of my despair.

Have I no faith in God? I try to look to him and raise my heart to Heaven, but it will cleave to the dust: I can only say – 'He hath hedged me about, that I cannot get out: He hath made my chain heavy. He hath filled me with bitterness, He hath made me drunken with wormwood' – I forget to add – 'But though He cause grief, yet will He have compassion according to the multitude of His mercies. For He doth not afflict willingly nor grieve the children of men.' I ought to think of this; and if there be nothing but sorrow for me in this world, what is the longest life of misery to a whole eternity of peace? And for my little Arthur – has he no friend but me? Who was it said, 'It is not the will of your Father which is in Heaven that one of these little ones should perish'?

## CHAPTER 41

### 'Hope Springs Eternal in the Human Breast'

March 20th. Having now got rid of Mr Huntingdon for a season, my spirits begin to revive. He left me early in February; and the moment he was gone, I breathed again, and felt my vital energy return; not with the hope of escape – he has taken care to leave me no visible chance of that – but with a determination to make the best of existing circumstances. Here was Arthur left to me at last; and rousing from my despondent apathy, I exerted all my powers to eradicate the weeds that had been fostered in his infant mind, and sow again the good seed they had rendered unproductive. Thank Heaven, it is not a barren or a stony soil; if weeds spring fast there, so do better plants. His apprehensions are more quick, his heart more overflowing with affection than ever his father's could have been; and it is no hopeless task to bend him to obedience and win him to love and know his own true friend, as long as there is no one to counteract my efforts.

I had much trouble at first in breaking him of those evil habits his father had

taught him to acquire, but already that difficulty is nearly vanquished now: bad language seldom defiles his mouth, and I have succeeded in giving him an absolute disgust for all intoxicating liquors, which I hope not even his father or his father's friends will be able to overcome. He was inordinately fond of them for so young a creature, and, remembering my unfortunate father as well as his, I dreaded the consequences of such a taste. But if I had stinted him in his usual quantity of wine or forbidden him to taste it altogether, that would only have increased his partiality for it, and made him regard it as a greater treat than ever. I therefore gave him quite as much as his father was accustomed to allow him – as much indeed, as he desired to have, but into every glass I surreptitiously introduced a small quantity of tartar-emetic – just enough to produce inevitable nausea and depression without positive sickness. Finding such disagreeable consequences invariably to result from this indulgence, he soon grew weary of it, but the more he shrank from the daily treat the more I pressed it upon him, till his reluctance was strengthened to perfect abhorrence. When he was thoroughly disgusted with every kind of wine, I allowed him, at his own request, to try brandy and water and then gin and water; for the little toper was familiar with them all, and I was determined that all should be equally hateful to him. This I have now effected; and since he declares that the taste, the smell, the sight of any one of them is sufficient to make him sick, I have given up teasing him about them, except now and then as objects of terror in cases of misbehaviour: 'Arthur, if you're not a good boy I shall give you a glass of wine,' or 'Now Arthur, if you say that again you shall have some brandy and water,' is as good as any other threat; and, once or twice, when he was sick, I have obliged the poor child to swallow a little wine and water *without* the tartar-emetic, by way of medicine; and this practice I intend to continue for some time to come; not that I think it of any real service in a physical sense, but because I am determined to enlist all the powers of association in my service. I wish this aversion to be so deeply grounded in his nature that nothing in after life may be able to overcome it.

Thus, I flatter myself, I shall secure him from this one vice; and for the rest, if on his father's return I find reason to apprehend that my good lessons will be all destroyed – if Mr Huntingdon commence again the game of teaching the child to hate and despise his mother and emulate his father's wickedness, I will yet deliver my son from his hands. I have devised another scheme that might be resorted to in such a case, and if I could but obtain my brother's consent and assistance, I should not doubt of its success. The old hall where he and I were born and where our mother died, is not now inhabited, nor yet quite sunk into decay, as I believe. Now if I could persuade him to have one or two rooms made habitable and to let them to me as a stranger, I might live there, with my child, under an assumed name, and still support myself by my favourite art. He should lend me the money to begin with, and I would pay him back, and live in lowly independence and strict seclusion, for the house stands in a lonely place, and the neighbourhood is thinly inhabited, and he himself should negotiate the sale of my pictures for me. I have arranged the whole plan in my head; and all I want, is to persuade Frederick to be of the same mind as myself: He is coming to see me

soon, and then I will make the proposal to him, having first enlightened him upon my circumstances sufficiently to excuse the project.

Already, I believe, he knows much more of my situation than I have told him. I can tell this by the air of tender sadness pervading his letters; and by the fact of his so seldom mentioning my husband, and generally evincing a kind of covert bitterness when he does refer to him; as well as by the circumstances of his never coming to see me when Mr Huntingdon is at home. But he has never openly expressed any disapprobation of him or sympathy for me; he has never asked any questions, or said anything to invite my confidence. Had he done so, I should probably have had but few concealments from him. Perhaps, he feels hurt at my reserve. He is a strange being – I wish we knew each other better. He used to spend a month at Staningley every year, before I was married; but, since our father's death, I have only seen him once, when he came for a few days while Mr Huntingdon was away. He shall stay many days this time, and there shall be more candour and cordiality between us than ever there was before, since our early childhood: my heart clings to him more than ever; and my soul is sick of solitude.

April 16th. He is come and gone. He would not stay above a fortnight. The time passed quickly, but very, very happily, and it has done me good. I must have a bad disposition, for my misfortunes have soured and embittered me exceedingly: I was beginning insensibly to cherish very unamiable feelings against my fellow mortals – the male part of them especially; but it is a comfort to see there is at least one among them worthy to be trusted and esteemed; and doubtless there are more, though I have never known them – unless I except poor Lord Lowborough, and he was bad enough in his day; but what would Frederick have been, if he had lived in the world and mingled from his childhood with such men as these of my acquaintance? And what *will* Arthur be, with all his natural sweetness of disposition, if I do not save him from that world and those companions? I mentioned my fears to Frederick and introduced the subject of my plan of rescue on the evening after his arrival, when I presented my little son to his uncle.

'He is like you, Frederick,' said I, 'in some of his moods: I sometimes think he resembles you more than his father; and I am glad of it.'

'You flatter me, Helen,' replied he, stroking the child's soft, wavy locks.

'No – you will think it no compliment when I tell you I would rather have him to resemble *Benson* than his father.'

He slightly elevated his eyebrows, but said nothing.

'Do you know what sort of man Mr Huntingdon is?' said I.

'I think I have an idea.'

'Have you so clear an idea that you can hear, without surprise or disapproval, that I meditate escaping with that child to some secret asylum where we can live in peace and never see him again?'

'Is it really so?'

'If you have not,' continued I, 'I'll tell you something more about him' – and

I gave a sketch of his general conduct, and a more particular account of his behaviour with regard to his child, and explained my apprehensions on the latter's account, and my determination to deliver him from his father's influence.

Frederick was exceedingly indignant against Mr Huntingdon, and very much grieved for me; but still, he looked upon my project as wild and impracticable; he deemed my fears for Arthur disproportioned to the circumstances, and opposed so many objections to my plan, and devised so many milder methods for ameliorating my condition, that I was obliged to enter into further details to convince him that my husband was utterly incorrigible, and that nothing could persuade him to give up his son whatever became of me, he being as fully determined the child should not leave him, as I was not to leave the child; and that, in fact, nothing would answer but this, unless I fled the country as I had intended before. To obviate that, he at length consented to have one wing of the old Hall put into a habitable condition, as a place of refuge against a time of need; but hoped I would not take advantage of it, unless circumstances should render it really necessary, which I was ready enough to promise; for, though, for my own sake, such a hermitage appears like paradise itself compared with my present situation, yet for my friends' sakes – for Milicent and Esther, my sisters in heart and affection, for the poor tenants of Grassdale, and above all for my aunt – I will stay if I possibly can.

July 29th. Mrs Hargrave and her daughter are come back from London. Esther is full of her first season in town; but she is still heart-whole and unengaged. Her mother sought out an excellent match for her, and even brought the gentleman to lay his heart and fortune at her feet; but Esther had the audacity to refuse the noble gifts. He was a man of good family and large possessions, but the naughty girl maintained he was old as Adam, ugly as sin, and hateful as — one who shall be nameless.

'But indeed, I had a hard time of it,' said she: 'mamma was very greatly disappointed at the failure of her darling project, and very, very angry at my obstinate resistance to her will – and is so still; but I can't help it. And Walter, too, is so seriously displeased at my perversity and absurd caprice, as he calls it, that I fear he will never forgive me – I did not think he *could* be so unkind as he has lately shown himself. But Milicent begged me not to yield, and I'm sure, Mrs Huntingdon, if you had seen the man they wanted to palm upon me, you would have advised me not to take him too.'

'I should have done so whether I had seen him or not,' said I. 'It is enough that you dislike him.'

'I knew you would say so; though mamma affirmed you would be quite shocked at my undutiful conduct – you can't imagine how she lectures me – I am disobedient and ungrateful; I am thwarting her wishes, wronging my brother, and making myself a burden on her hands – I sometimes fear she'll overcome me after all. I have a strong will, but so has she, and when she says such bitter things, it provokes me to such a pass that I feel inclined to do as she bids me, and then break my heart and say "There, mamma, it's all your fault!" '

'Pray don't!' said I. 'Obedience from such a motive would be positive wicked-
ness, and certain to bring the punishment it deserved. Stand firm, and your
mamma will soon relinquish her persecution; and the gentleman himself will
cease to pester you with his addresses if he finds them steadily rejected.'

'Oh, no! mamma will weary all about her before she tires herself with her
exertions; and as for Mr Oldfield, she has given him to understand that I have
refused his offer, not from any dislike of his person, but merely because I am
giddy and young, and cannot at present reconcile myself to the thoughts of
marriage under any circumstances: but, by next season, she has no doubt, I shall
have more sense, and hopes my girlish fancies will be worn away. So she has
brought me home, to school me into a proper sense of my duty, against the time
comes round again – indeed, I believe she will not put herself to the expense of
taking me up to London again, unless I surrender: she cannot afford to take me
to town for pleasure and nonsense, she says, and it is not *every* rich gentleman
that will consent to take me without a fortune, whatever exalted ideas I may have
of my own attractions.'

'Well, Esther, I pity you; but still, I repeat, stand firm. You might as well sell
yourself to slavery at once, as marry a man you dislike. If your mother and
brother are unkind to you, you may leave them, but remember you are bound to
your husband for life.'

'But I cannot leave them unless I get married, and I cannot get married if
nobody sees me. I saw one or two gentlemen in London, that I might have liked,
but they were younger sons, and mamma would not let me get to know them –
one especially, who I believe rather liked me, but she threw every possible
obstacle in the way of our better acquaintance – wasn't it provoking?'

'I have no doubt you would feel it so, but it is possible that if you married
him, you might have more reason to regret it hereafter, than if you married Mr
Oldfield. When I tell you not to marry *without* love, I do not advise you to marry
for love alone – there are many, many other things to be considered. Keep both
heart and hand in your own possession, till you see good reason to part with
them; and if such an occasion should never present itself, comfort your mind
with this reflection: that, though in single life your joys may not be very many,
your sorrows, at least, will not be more than you can bear. Marriage *may* change
your circumstances for the better, but in my private opinion, it is far more likely
to produce a contrary result.'

'So thinks Milicent, but allow me to say, *I* think otherwise. If I thought
myself doomed to oldmaidenhood, I should cease to value my life. The
thought of living on, year after year at the Grove – a hanger-on upon mamma
and Walter – a mere cumberer of the ground (now that I know in what light
they would regard it), is perfectly intolerable – I would rather run away with
the butler.'

'Your circumstances are peculiar I allow; but have patience, love; do nothing
rashly. Remember you are not yet nineteen, and many years are yet to pass
before anyone can set you down as an old maid: you cannot tell what Providence
may have in store for you. And meantime, remember you have a *right* to the

protection and support of your mother and brother, however they may seem to grudge it.'

'You are so grave, Mrs Huntingdon,' said Esther after a pause. 'When Milicent uttered the same discouraging sentiments concerning marriage, I asked if she was happy: she said she was; but I only half believed her; and now I must put the same question to you.'

'It is a very impertinent question,' laughed I, 'from a young girl to a married woman so many years her senior – and I shall not answer it.'

'Pardon me, dear *madam*,' said she, laughingly throwing herself into my arms, and kissing me with playful affection; but I felt a tear on my neck, as she dropped her head on my bosom and continued, with an odd mixture of sadness and levity, timidity and audacity – 'I know you are not so happy as I mean to be, for you spend half your life alone at Grassdale, while Mr Huntingdon goes about enjoying himself where, and how he pleases – I shall expect *my* husband to have no pleasures but what he shares with me; and if his greatest pleasure of all is not the enjoyment of my company – why – it will be the worse for him – that's all.'

'If such are your expectations of matrimony, Esther, you must indeed be careful whom you marry – or rather you must avoid it altogether.'

## CHAPTER 42

### *A Reformation*

September 1st. No Mr Huntingdon yet. Perhaps he will stay among his friends till Christmas; and then, next spring, he will be off again. If he continue this plan, I shall be able to stay at Grassdale well enough – that is, I *shall* be able to stay, and that is enough; even an occasional bevy of friends at the shooting season, may be borne if Arthur get so firmly attached to me – so well established in good sense and principles, before they come, that I shall be able, by reason and affection, to keep him pure from their contaminations. Vain hope, I fear! But still, till such a time of trial comes, I will forbear to think of my quiet asylum in the beloved old hall.

Mr and Mrs Hattersley have been staying at the Grove a fortnight; and as Mr Hargrave is still absent, and the weather was remarkably fine, I never passed a day without seeing my two friends, Milicent and Esther, either there or here. On one occasion, when Mr Hattersley had driven them over to Grassdale in the phaeton, with little Helen and Ralph, and we were all enjoying ourselves in the garden – I had a few minutes' conversation with that gentleman, while the ladies were amusing themselves with the children.

'Do you want to hear anything of your husband, Mrs Huntingdon?' said he.

'No, unless you can tell me when to expect him home.'

'I can't – You don't want him, do you?' said he with a broad grin.

'No.'

'Well, I think you're better without him, sure enough – for my part, I'm downright weary of him. I told him I'd leave him if he didn't mend his manners – and he wouldn't; so I left him – you see I'm a better man than you think me; and what's more, I have serious thoughts of washing my hands of him entirely, and the whole set of 'em, and comporting myself from this day forward, with all decency and sobriety as a Christian and the father of a family should do – What do you think of that?'

'It is a resolution you ought to have formed long ago.'

'Well, I'm not thirty yet: it isn't too late, is it?'

'No; it is never too late to reform, as long as you have the sense to desire it, and the strength to execute your purpose.'

'Well, to tell you the truth, I've thought of it often and often before, but he's such devilish good company is Huntingdon, after all – you can't imagine what a jovial good-fellow he is when he's not fairly drunk, only just primed or half-seas-over – we all have a bit of a liking for him at the bottom of our hearts, though we can't respect him.'

'But should you wish yourself to be like him?'

'No, I'd rather be like myself, bad as I am.'

'You can't continue as bad as you are without getting worse – and more brutalised every day – and therefore more like him.'

I could not help smiling at the comical, half-angry, half-confounded look he put on at this rather unusual mode of address.

'Never mind my plain speaking,' said I; 'it is from the best of motives. But tell me, should you wish your sons to be like Mr Huntingdon – or even like yourself?'

'Hang it, no.'

'Should you wish your daughter to despise you – or, at least, to feel no vestige of respect for you, and no affection but what is mingled with the bitterest regret?'

'Oh, blast it, no! I couldn't stand that.'

'And finally, should you wish your wife to be ready to sink into the earth when she hears you mentioned; and to loathe the very sound of your voice, and shudder at your approach?'

'She never will; she likes me all the same, whatever I do.'

'Impossible, Mr Hattersley! You mistake her quiet submission for affection.'

'Fire and fury –'

'Now don't burst into a tempest at that – I don't mean to say she does not love you – she does, I know, a great deal better than you deserve – but I am quite sure, that if you behave better, she will love you more, and if you behave worse, she will love you less and less till all is lost in fear, aversion, and bitterness of soul, if not in secret hatred and contempt. But, dropping the subject of affection, should you wish to be the tyrant of her life – to take away all the sunshine from her existence, and make her thoroughly miserable?'

'Of course not; and I don't, and I'm not going to.'

'You have done more towards it than you suppose.'

'Pooh, pooh! She's not the susceptible, anxious, worriting creature you imagine: she's a little meek, peaceable, affectionate body; apt to be rather sulky at times, but quiet and cool in the main, and ready to take things as they come.'

'Think of what she was five years ago, when you married her, and what she is now.'

'I know – she was a little plump lassie then, with a pretty pink and white face: now, she's a poor little bit of a creature, fading and melting away like a snow-wreath – but hang it! – by Jupiter, that's not my fault!'

'What is the cause of it then? Not years, for she's only five and twenty.'

'It's her own delicate health, and – confound it, madam! What would you make of me? – and the children, to be sure, that worry her to death between them.'

'No, Mr Hattersley, the children give her more pleasure than pain: they are fine well-dispositioned children – '

'I know they are – bless 'em!'

'Then why lay the blame on them? – I'll tell you what it is: it's silent fretting and constant anxiety on your account, mingled, I suspect, with something of bodily fear on her own. When you behave well, she can only rejoice with trembling; she has no security, no confidence in your judgement or principles; but is continually dreading the close of such short-lived felicity: when you behave ill, her causes of terror and misery are more than anyone can tell but herself. In patient endurance of evil, she forgets it is our duty to admonish our neighbours of their transgressions – Since you *will* mistake her silence for indifference, come with me, and I'll show you one or two of her letters – no breach of confidence, I hope, since you are her other half.'

He followed me into the library. I sought out and put into his hand two of Milicent's letters; one dated from London and written during one of his wildest seasons of reckless dissipation; the other in the country during a lucid interval. The former was full of trouble and anguish; not accusing *him*, but deeply regretting his connection with his profligate companions, abusing Mr Grimsby and others, insinuating bitter things against Mr Huntingdon, and most ingeniously throwing the blame of her husband's misconduct on to other men's shoulders. The latter was full of hope and joy, yet with a trembling consciousness that this happiness would not last; praising his goodness to the skies, but with an evident, though but half-expressed wish that it were based on a surer foundation than the natural impulses of the heart, and a half prophetic dread of the fall of that house so founded on the sand – which fall had shortly after taken place, as Hattersley must have been conscious while he read.

Almost at the commencement of the first letter, I had the unexpected pleasure of seeing him blush; but he immediately turned his back to me and finished the perusal at the window. At the second, I saw him, once or twice, raise his hand and hurriedly pass it across his face. Could it be to dash away a tear? When he had done, there was an interval spent in clearing his throat and staring out of the window, and then, after whistling a few bars of a favourite air, he turned round, gave me back the letters and silently shook me by the hand.

'I've been a cursed rascal, God knows,' said he as he gave it a hearty squeeze, 'but you see if I don't make amends for it – God damn me if I don't!'

'Don't curse yourself, Mr Hattersley; if God had heard half your invocations of that kind, you would have been in Hell long before now – and you *cannot* make amends for the past by doing your duty for the future, in as much as your duty is only what you *owe* to your Maker, and you cannot do *more* than fulfil it – another must make amends for your past delinquencies. If you intend to reform, invoke God's blessing, His mercy, and His aid; not His curse.'

'God help me, then – for I'm sure I need it – Where's Milicent?'

'She's there, just coming in with her sister.'

He stepped out at the glass door, and went to meet them. I followed at a little distance. Somewhat to his wife's astonishment, he lifted her off from the ground and saluted her with a hearty kiss and a strong embrace; then, placing his two hands on her shoulders, he gave her, I suppose, a sketch of the great things he meant to do, for she suddenly threw her arms round him and burst into tears, exclaiming – 'Do, do, Ralph – we shall be so happy! How very, very good you are!'

'Nay, not I,' said he, turning her round and pushing her towards me. 'Thank *her*; it's her doing.'

Milicent flew to thank me, overflowing with gratitude. I disclaimed all title to it, telling her her husband was predisposed to amendment before I added my mite of exhortation and encouragement, and that I had only done what she might – and ought to – have done herself.

'Oh, no!' cried she, 'I couldn't have influenced him, I'm sure, by anything that I could have said. I should only have bothered him by my clumsy efforts at persuasion, if I had made the attempt.'

'You never tried me, Milly,' said he.

Shortly after, they took their leave They are now gone on a visit to Hattersley's father. After that, they will repair to their country home. I hope his good resolutions will not fall through, and poor Milicent will not be again disappointed. Her last letter was full of present bliss and pleasing anticipations for the future; but no particular temptation has yet occurred to put his virtue to the test. Henceforth, however, she will doubtless be somewhat less timid and reserved, and he more kind and thoughtful – Surely, then, her hopes are not unfounded; and I have one bright spot, at least, whereon to rest my thoughts.

## CHAPTER 43

### *The Boundary Past*

October 10th. Mr Huntingdon returned about three weeks ago. His appearance, his demeanour and conversation, and my feelings with regard to him, I shall not trouble myself to describe. The day after his arrival, however, he surprised me by the announcement of an intention to procure a governess for little Arthur: I told him it was quite unnecessary, not to say ridiculous, at the present season: I thought I was fully competent to the task of teaching him myself – for some years to come, at least: the child's education was the only pleasure and business of my life; and since he had deprived me of every other occupation, he might surely leave me that.

He said I was not fit to teach children, or to be with them: I had already reduced the boy to little better than an automaton, I had broken his fine spirit with my rigid severity; and I should freeze all the sunshine out of his heart, and make him as gloomy an ascetic as myself, if I had the handling of him much longer. And poor Rachel, too, came in for her share of abuse, as usual; he cannot endure Rachel, because he knows she has a proper appreciation of him.

I calmly defended our several qualifications as nurse and governess, and still resisted the proposed addition to our family; but he cut me short by saying, it was no use bothering about the matter, for he had engaged a governess already, and she was coming next week; so that all I had to do was to get things ready for her reception. This was a rather startling piece of intelligence. I ventured to enquire her name and address, by whom she had been recommended, or how he had been led to make choice of her.

'She is a very estimable, pious young person,' said he; 'you needn't be afraid. Her name is Myers, I believe; and she was recommended to me by a respectable old dowager – a lady of high repute in the religious world. I have not seen her myself, and therefore cannot give you a particular account of her person and conversation and so forth; but, if the old lady's eulogies are correct, you will find her to possess all desirable qualifications for her position – an inordinate love of children among the rest.'

All this was gravely and quietly spoken, but there was a laughing demon in his half-averted eye that boded no good I imagined. However, I thought of my asylum in —shire, and made no further objections.

When Miss Myers arrived, I was not prepared to give her a very cordial reception. Her appearance was not particularly calculated to produce a favourable impression at first sight, nor did her manners and subsequent conduct, in any degree, remove the prejudice I had already conceived against her. Her attainments were limited, her intellect noways above mediocrity. She had a fine voice, and could sing like a nightingale, and accompany herself sufficiently well on the

piano; but these were her only accomplishments. There was a look of guile and subtlety in her face, a sound of it in her voice. She seemed afraid of me, and would start if I suddenly approached her. In her behaviour, she was respectful and complaisant even to servility: she attempted to flatter and fawn upon me at first, but I soon checked that. Her fondness for her little pupil was overstrained, and I was obliged to remonstrate with her on the subject of over-indulgence and injudicious praise; but she could not gain his heart. Her piety consisted in an occasional heaving of sighs and uplifting of eyes to the ceiling, and the utterance of a few cant phrases. She told me she was a clergyman's daughter, and had been left an orphan from her childhood, but had had the good fortune to obtain a situation in a very pious family; and then spoke so gratefully of the kindness she had experienced from its different members that I reproached myself for my uncharitable thoughts and unfriendly conduct, and relented for a time – but not for long; my causes of dislike were too rational, my suspicions too well founded for that; and I knew it was my duty to watch and scrutinise till those suspicions were either satisfactorily removed or confirmed.

I asked the name and residence of the kind and pious family. She mentioned a common name, and an unknown and distant place of abode, but told me they were now on the continent, and their present address was unknown to her. I never saw her speak much to Mr Huntingdon; but he would frequently look into the schoolroom to see how little Arthur got on with his new companion, when I was not there. In the evening, she sat with us in the drawing-room, and would sing and play to amuse him – or *us*, as she pretended – and was very attentive to his wants, and watchful to anticipate them, though she only talked to me – indeed, he was seldom in a condition to be talked to. Had she been other than she was, I should have felt her presence a great relief to come between us thus, except, indeed, that I should have been thoroughly ashamed for any decent person to see him as he often was.

I did not mention my suspicions to Rachel; but she, having sojourned for half a century in this land of sin and sorrow, has learned to be suspicious herself. She told me from the first she was 'down of that new governess', and I soon found she watched her quite as narrowly as I did; and I was glad of it, for I longed to know the truth: the atmosphere of Grassdale seemed to stifle me, and I could only live by thinking of Wildfell Hall.

At last, one morning, she entered my chamber with such intelligence that my resolution was taken before she had ceased to speak. While she dressed me, I explained to her my intentions and what assistance I should require from her, and told her which of my things she was to pack up, and what she was to leave behind for herself, as I had no other means of recompensing her for this sudden dismissal, after her long and faithful service – a circumstance I most deeply regretted but could not avoid.

'And what will you do, Rachel?' said I – 'will you go home, or seek another place?'

'I have no home, ma'am, but with you,' she replied; 'and if I leave you, I'll never go into place again as long as I live.'

'But I can't afford to live like a lady, now,' returned I: 'I must be my own maid and my child's nurse.'

'What *signifies*?' replied she in some excitement. 'You'll want somebody to clean and wash, and cook, won't you? I can do all that; and never mind the wages – I've my bits o' savings yet, and if you wouldn't take me, I should have to find my own board and lodging out of 'em somewhere, or else work among strangers – and it's what I'm not used to – so you can please yourself, ma'am.' Her voice quavered as she spoke, and the tears stood in her eyes.

'I should like it above all things, Rachel, and I'd give you such wages as I could afford – such as I should give to any servant of all work I might employ; but don't you see I should be dragging you down with me, when you have done nothing to deserve it?'

'Oh, fiddle!' ejaculated she.

'And besides, my future way of living will be so widely different to the past – so different to all you have been accustomed to – '

'Do you think, ma'am, I can't bear what my missis can? – surely I'm not so proud and so dainty as that comes to – and my little master too, God bless him.'

'But I'm young, Rachel; I shan't mind it; and Arthur is young too – it will be nothing to him.'

'Nor me either: I'm not so old but what I can stand hard fare and hard work, if it's only to help and comfort them as I've loved like my own barns – for all I'm too old to bide the thoughts o' leaving 'em in trouble and danger, and going amongst strangers myself.'

'Then you shan't, Rachel!' cried I, embracing my faithful friend. 'We'll all go together, and you shall see how the new life suits you.'

'Bless you, honey!' cried she affectionately returning my embrace. 'Only let us get shut of this wicked house and we'll do right enough, you'll see.'

'So think I,' was my answer; and so that point was settled.

By that morning's post, I despatched a few hasty lines to Frederick, beseeching him to prepare my asylum for my immediate reception– for I should probably come to claim it within a day after the receipt of that note – and telling him in few words, the cause of my sudden resolution. I then wrote three letters of adieu: the first to Esther Hargrave, in which I told her that I found it impossible to stay any longer at Grassdale, or to leave my son under his father's protection; and, as it was of the last importance that our future abode should be unknown to him and his acquaintance, I should disclose it to no one but my brother, through the medium of whom I hoped still to correspond with my friends. I then gave her his address, exhorted her to write frequently, reiterated some of my former admonitions regarding her own concerns, and bade her a fond farewell.

The second was to Milicent; much to the same effect, but a little more confidential, as befitted our longer intimacy, and her greater experience and better acquaintance with my circumstances.

The third was to my aunt – a much more difficult and painful undertaking, and therefore I had left it to the last; but I must give her some explanation of that

extraordinary step I had taken – and that quickly, for she and my uncle would no doubt hear of it within a day or two after my disappearance, as it was probable that Mr Huntingdon would speedily apply to them to know what was become of me. At last, however, I told her I was sensible of my error: I did not complain of its punishment, and I was sorry to trouble my friends with its consequences; but in duty to my son, I must submit no longer; it was absolutely necessary that he should be delivered from his father's corrupting influence. I should not disclose my place of refuge even to her, in order that she and my uncle might be able, with truth, to deny all knowledge concerning it; but any communications addressed to me under cover to my brother, would be certain to reach me. I hoped she and my uncle would pardon the step I had taken, for if they knew all, I was sure they would not blame me; and I trusted they would not afflict themselves on my account, for if I could only reach my retreat in safety and keep it unmolested, I should be very happy, but for the thoughts of them; and should be quite contented to spend my life in obscurity, devoting myself to the training up of my child, and teaching him to avoid the errors of both his parents.

These things were done yesterday: I have given two whole days to the preparation for our departure, that Frederick may have more time to prepare the rooms, and Rachel to pack up the things – for the latter task must be done with the utmost caution and secrecy, and there is no one but me to assist her: I can help to get the articles together, but I do not understand the art of stowing them into the boxes, so as to take up the smallest possible space; and there are her own things to do, as well as mine and Arthur's. I can ill afford to leave anything behind, since I have no money, except a few guineas in my purse; and besides, as Rachel observed, whatever I left would most likely become the property of Miss Myers, and I should not relish that.

But what trouble I have had throughout these two days struggling to appear calm and collected – to meet him and her as usual, when I was obliged to meet them, and forcing myself to leave my little Arthur in her hands for hours together! But I trust these trials are over now: I have laid him in my bed for better security, and never more, I trust, shall his innocent lips be defiled by their contaminating kisses, or his young ears polluted by their words. But shall I escape in safety? Oh, that the morning were come, and we were on our way at least! This evening, when I had given Rachel all the assistance I could, and had nothing left me but to wait, and wish and tremble, I became so greatly agitated, that I knew not what to do. I went down to dinner, but I could not force myself to eat. Mr Huntingdon remarked the circumstance.

'What's to do with you *now*?' said he, when the removal of the second course gave him time to look about him.

'I am not well,' I replied: 'I think I must lie down a little – you won't miss me much?'

'Not the least; if you leave your chair, it'll do just as well – better a trifle,' he muttered as I left the room, 'for I can fancy somebody else fills it.'

'Somebody else *may* fill it tomorrow,' I thought – but did not say. 'There! I've seen the last of *you*, I hope,' I muttered as I closed the door upon him.

Rachel urged me to seek repose, at once, to recruit my strength for tomorrow's journey, as we must be gone before the dawn, but in my present state of nervous excitement, that was entirely out of the question. It was equally out of the question to sit, or wander about my room, counting the hours and the minutes between me and the appointed time of action, straining my ears and trembling at every sound lest someone should discover and betray us after all. I took up a book and tried to read. My eyes wandered over the pages, but it was impossible to bind my thoughts to their contents. Why not have recourse to the old expedient, and add this last event to my chronicle? I opened its pages once more, and wrote the above account – with difficulty, at first, but gradually my mind became more calm and steady. Thus several hours have past away: the time is drawing near; and now my eyes feel heavy, and my frame exhausted: I will commend my cause to God, and then lie down and gain an hour or two of sleep; and *then*! – Little Arthur sleeps soundly. All the house is still: there can be no one watching. The boxes were all corded by Benson, and quietly conveyed down the back stairs after dusk, and sent away in a cart to the M— coach-office. The name upon the cards was Mrs Graham, which appellation I mean henceforth to adopt. My mother's maiden name was Graham, and therefore I fancy I have some claim to it, and prefer it to any other, except my own, which I dare not resume.

## CHAPTER 44

### *The Retreat*

October 24th. Thank Heaven, I am free and safe at last! – Early we rose, swiftly and quietly dressed, slowly and stealthily descended to the hall, where Benson stood ready with a light to open the door and fasten it after us. We were obliged to let one man into our secret on account of the boxes, etc. All the servants were but too well acquainted with their master's conduct, and either Benson or John would have been willing to serve me, but as the former was more staid and elderly, and a crony of Rachel's besides, I of course directed her to make choice of him as her assistant and confidant on the occasion, as far as necessity demanded. I only hope he may not be brought into trouble thereby, and only wish I could reward him for the perilous service he was so ready to undertake. I slipped two guineas into his hand, by way of remembrance, as he stood in the doorway, holding the candle to light our departure, with a tear in his honest grey eye and a host of good wishes depicted on his solemn countenance. Alas! I could offer no more: I had barely sufficient remaining for the probable expenses of the journey.

What trembling joy it was when the little wicket closed behind us, as we issued from the park! Then, for one moment, I paused, to inhale one draught of that cool, bracing air, and venture one look back upon the house. All was dark and still; no light glimmered in the windows; no wreath of smoke obscured the

stars that sparkled above it in the frosty sky. As I bade farewell for ever to that place, the scene of so much guilt and misery, I felt glad that I had not left it before, for now there was no doubt about the propriety of such a step – no shadow of remorse for him I left behind: there was nothing to disturb my joy but the fear of detection; and every step removed us farther from the chance of that.

We had left Grassdale many miles behind us before the round, red sun arose to welcome our deliverance, and if any inhabitant of its vicinity had chanced to see us then, as we bowled along on the top of the coach, I scarcely think they would have suspected our identity. As I intend to be taken for a widow I thought it advisable to enter my new abode in mourning: I was therefore attired in a plain black silk dress and mantle, a black veil (which I kept carefully over my face for the first twenty or thirty miles of the journey), and a black silk bonnet, which I had been constrained to borrow of Rachel for want of such an article myself – it was not in the newest fashion, of course; but none the worse for that, under present circumstances. Arthur was clad in his plainest clothes, and wrapped in a coarse woollen shawl; and Rachel was muffled in a grey cloak and hood that had seen better days, and gave her more the appearance of an ordinary, though decent old woman, than of a lady's maid.

Oh, what delight it was to be thus seated aloft, rumbling along the broad, sunshiny road, with the fresh morning breeze in my face, surrounded by an unknown country all smiling – cheerfully, gloriously, smiling in the yellow lustre of those early beams – with my darling child in my arms, almost as happy as myself and my faithful friend beside me; a prison and despair behind me, receding farther, farther back at every clatter of the horses' feet – and liberty and hope before! I could hardly refrain from praising God aloud for my deliverance or astonishing my fellow passengers by some surprising outburst of hilarity.

But the journey was a very long one, and we were all weary enough before the close of it. It was far into the night when we reached the town of L—, and still we were seven miles from our journey's end; and there was no more coaching – nor any conveyance to be had, except a common cart – and that with the greatest difficulty, for half the town was in bed. And a dreary ride we had of it that last stage of the journey, cold and weary as we were; sitting on our boxes, with nothing to cling to, nothing to lean against, slowly dragged and crudely shaken over the rough, hilly roads. But Arthur was asleep in Rachel's lap, and between us we managed pretty well to shield him from the cold night air.

At last we began to ascend a terribly steep and stony lane which, in spite of the darkness, Rachel said she remembered well: she had often walked there with me in her arms, and little thought to come again so many years after, under such circumstances as the present. Arthur being now awakened by the jolting and the stoppages, we all got out and walked. We had not far to go; but what if Frederick should not have received my letter? Or if he should not have had time to prepare the rooms for our reception; and we should find them all dark, damp, and comfortless; destitute of food, fire, and furniture, after all our toil?

At length the grim, dark pile appeared before us. The lane conducted us round by the back way. We entered the desolate court, and in breathless

anxiety surveyed the ruinous mass. Was it all blackness and desolation? No; one faint red glimmer cheered us from a window where the lattice was in good repair. The door was fastened, but after due knocking and waiting, and some parleying with a voice from an upper window, we were admitted, by an old woman who had been commissioned to air and keep the house till our arrival – into a tolerably snug little apartment, formerly the scullery of the mansion, which Frederick had now fitted up as a kitchen. Here she procured us a light, roused the fire to a cheerful blaze, and soon prepared a simple repast for our refreshment; while we disencumbered ourselves of our travelling gear, and took a hasty survey of our new abode. Besides the kitchen there were two bedrooms, a good-sized parlour, and another smaller one, which I destined for my studio, all well aired and seemingly in good repair, but only partly furnished with a few old articles chiefly of ponderous black oak – the veritable ones that had been there before, and which had been kept as antiquarian relics in my brother's present residence, and now in all haste, transported back again.

The old woman brought my supper and Arthur's into the parlour, and told me, with all due formality, that, 'The master desired his compliments to Mrs Graham, and he had prepared the rooms as well as he could upon so short a notice, but he would do himself the pleasure of calling upon her tomorrow, to receive her further commands.'

I was glad to ascend the stern-looking stone staircase, and lie down in the gloomy old-fashioned bed, beside my little Arthur. He was asleep in a minute; but, weary as I was, my excited feelings and restless cogitations kept me awake till dawn began to struggle with the darkness; but sleep was sweet and refreshing when it came, and the waking was delightful beyond expression. It was little Arthur that roused me, with his gentle kisses – he was here, then – safely clasped in my arms, and many leagues away from his unworthy father! – Broad daylight illumined the apartment, for the sun was high in Heaven, though obscured by rolling masses of autumnal vapour.

The scene, indeed, was not remarkably cheerful in itself, either within or without. The large bare room with its grim old furniture, the narrow, latticed windows, revealing the dull, grey sky above and the desolate wilderness below, where the dark stone walls and iron gate, the rank growth of grass and weeds, and the hardy evergreens of preternatural forms, alone remained to tell that there had been once a garden – and the bleak and barren fields beyond might have struck me as gloomy enough at another time, but now, each separate object seemed to echo back my own exhilarating sense of hope and freedom: indefinite dreams of the far past and bright anticipations of the future seemed to greet me at every turn. I should rejoice with more security, to be sure, had the broad sea rolled between my present and my former homes, but surely in this lonely spot I might remain unknown; and then, I had my brother here to cheer my solitude with his occasional visits.

He came that morning; and I have had several interviews with him since; but he is obliged to be very cautious when and how he comes: not even his servants, or his best friends must know of his visits to Wildfell – except on such occasions

as a landlord might be expected to call upon a stranger tenant – lest suspicion should be excited against me, whether of the truth or of some slanderous falsehood.

I have now been here nearly a fortnight, and but for one disturbing care, the haunting dread of discovery, I am comfortably settled in my new home: Frederick has supplied me with all requisite furniture and painting materials: Rachel has sold most of my clothes for me, in a distant town, and procured me a wardrobe more suitable to my present position: I have a second-hand piano, and a tolerably well-stocked bookcase in my parlour; and my other room has assumed quite a professional, businesslike appearance already. I am working hard to repay my brother for all his expenses on my account; not that there is the slightest necessity for anything of the kind, but it pleases me to do so: I shall have so much more pleasure in my labour, my earnings, my frugal fare, and household economy, when I know that I am paying my way honestly, and that what little I possess is legitimately all my own; and that no one suffers for my folly – in a pecuniary way at least – I shall make him take the last penny I owe him, if I can possibly effect it without offending him too deeply. I have a few pictures already done, for I told Rachel to pack up all I had; and she executed her commission but too well, for among the rest, she put up a portrait of Mr Huntingdon that I had painted in the first year of my marriage. It struck me with dismay, at the moment, when I took it from the box and beheld those eyes fixed upon me in their mocking mirth, as if exulting, still, in his power to control my fate, and deriding my efforts to escape.

How widely different had been my feelings in painting that portrait to what they now were in looking upon it! How I had studied and toiled to produce something, as I thought, worthy of the original! What mingled pleasure and dissatisfaction I had had in the result of my labours! – pleasure for the likeness I had caught; dissatisfaction, because I had not made it handsome enough. Now, I see no beauty in it – nothing pleasing in any part of its expression; and yet it is far handsomer and far more agreeable – far less repulsive I should rather say – than he is now; for these six years have wrought almost as great a change upon himself as on my feelings regarding him. The frame, however, is handsome enough; it will serve for another painting. The picture itself I have not destroyed, as I had first intended; I have put it aside; not, I think, from any lurking tenderness for the memory of past affection, nor yet to remind me of my former folly, but chiefly that I may compare my son's features and countenance with this, as he grows up, and thus be enabled to judge how much or how little he resembles his father – if I may be allowed to keep him with me still, and never to behold that father's face again – a blessing I hardly dare reckon upon.

It seems Mr Huntingdon is making every exertion to discover the place of my retreat. He has been in person to Staningley, seeking redress for his grievances – expecting to hear of his victims, if not to find them there – and has told so many lies, and with such unblushing coolness, that my uncle more than half believes him, and strongly advocates my going back to him and being friends again; but my aunt knows better: she is too cool and cautious, and too well acquainted with

both my husband's character and my own to be imposed upon by any specious falsehoods the former could invent. But he does not *want* me back; he wants my child; and gives my friends to understand that if I prefer living apart from him, he will indulge the whim and let me do so unmolested, and even settle a reasonable allowance on me, provided I will immediately deliver up his son. But, Heaven help me! I am not going to sell my child for gold, though it were to save both him and me from starving: it would be better that he should die with me, than that he should live with his father.

Frederick showed me a letter he had received from that gentleman, full of cool impudence such as would astonish anyone who did not know him, but such as, I am convinced, none would know better how to answer than my brother. He gave me no account of his reply, except to tell me that he had not acknowledged his acquaintance with my place of refuge, but rather left it to be inferred that it was quite unknown to him, by saying it was useless to apply to him or any other of my relations for information on the subject, as it appeared I had been driven to such extremity that I had concealed my retreat even from my best friends; but that if he *had* known it, or should at any time be made aware of it, most certainly Mr Huntingdon would be the last person to whom he should communicate the intelligence; and that he need not trouble himself to bargain for the child, for he (Frederick) fancied he knew enough of his sister to enable him to declare, that wherever she might be, or however situated, no consideration would induce her to deliver him up.

30th. Alas! my kind neighbours will not let me alone. By some means they have ferreted me out, and I have had to sustain visits from three different families, all more or less bent upon discovering who and what I am, whence I came, and why I have chosen such a home as this. Their society is unnecessary to me, to say the least, and their curiosity annoys and alarms me: if I gratify it, it may lead to the ruin of my son, and if I am too mysterious, it will only excite their suspicions, invite conjecture, and rouse them to greater exertions – and perhaps be the means of spreading my fame from parish to parish, till it reach the ears of someone who will carry it to the lord of Grassdale Manor.

I shall be expected to return their calls, but if, upon enquiry, I find that any of them live too far away for Arthur to accompany me, they must expect in vain for a while, for I cannot bear to leave him, unless it be to go to church; and I have not attempted *that* yet, for – it may be foolish weakness, but I am under such constant dread of his being snatched away that I am never easy when he is not by my side; and I fear these nervous terrors would so entirely disturb my devotions, that I should obtain no benefit from the attendance. I mean, however, to make the experiment next Sunday, and oblige myself to leave him in charge of Rachel for a few hours. It will be a hard task, but surely no imprudence; and the vicar has been to scold me for my neglect of the ordinances of religion. I had no sufficient excuse to offer, and I promised, if all were well, he should see me in my pew next Sunday; for I do not wish to be set down as an infidel; and besides, I know I should derive great comfort and benefit from an occasional attendance at

public worship, if I could only have faith and fortitude to compose my thoughts in conformity with the solemn occasion, and forbid them to be for ever dwelling on my absent child, and on the dreadful possibility of finding him gone when I return; and surely God in His mercy will preserve me from so severe a trial: for my child's own sake, if not for mine, He will not suffer him to be torn away.

November 3rd. I have made some further acquaintance with my neighbours. The fine gentleman and beau of the parish and its vicinity (in his own estimation, at least) is a young . . .

* * *

Here it ended. The rest was torn away. How cruel – just when she was going to mention me! For I could not doubt it *was* your humble servant she was about to mention, though not very favourably of course – I could tell that, as well by those few words as by the recollection of her whole aspect and demeanour towards me in the commencement of our acquaintance. Well! I could readily forgive her prejudice against me, and her hard thoughts of our sex in general, when I saw to what brilliant specimens her experience had been limited.

Respecting me, however, she had long since seen her error, and perhaps fallen into another in the opposite extreme; for if, at first, her opinion of me had been lower that I deserved I was convinced that now my deserts were lower than her opinion; and if the former part of this continuation had been torn away to avoid wounding my feelings, perhaps the latter portion had been removed for fear of ministering too much to my self-conceit. At any rate, I would have given much to have seen it all – to have witnessed the gradual change, and watched the progress of her esteem and friendship for me – and whatever warmer feeling she might have – to have seen how much of love there was in her regard, and how it had grown upon her in spite of her virtuous resolutions and strenuous exertions to – but no, I had no right to see it: all this was too sacred for any eyes but her own, and she had done well to keep it from me.

## CHAPTER 45

### *Reconciliation*

Well, Halford, what do you think of all this? And while you read it, did you ever picture to yourself what my feelings would probably be during its perusal? Most likely not; but I am not going to descant upon them now: I will only make this acknowledgement, little honourable as it may be to human nature, and especially to myself – that the former half of the narrative was, to me, more painful than the latter; not that I was at all insensible to Mrs Huntingdon's wrongs or unmoved by her sufferings, but, I must confess, I felt a kind of selfish gratification in watching her husband's gradual decline in her good graces, and seeing how

completely he extinguished all her affection at last. The effect of the whole, however, in spite of all my sympathy for her and my fury against him, was to relieve my mind of an intolerable burden and fill my heart with joy, as if some friend had roused me from a dreadful nightmare.

It was now near eight o'clock in the morning, for my candle had expired in the midst of my perusal, leaving me no alternative but to get another, at the expense of alarming the house, or to go to bed and wait the return of daylight. On my mother's account, I chose the latter; but how *willingly* I sought my pillow, and how much sleep it brought me, I leave you to imagine.

At the first appearance of dawn I rose, and brought the manuscript to the window, but it was impossible to read it yet. I devoted half an hour to dressing, and then returned to it again. Now, with a little difficulty, I could manage; and with intense and eager interest, I devoured the remainder of its contents. When it was ended, and my transient regret at its abrupt conclusion was over, I opened the window and put out my head to catch the cooling breeze, and imbibe deep draughts of the pure morning air. A splendid morning it was; the half-frozen dew lay thick on the grass, the swallows were twittering round me, the rooks cawing and cows lowing in the distance; and early frost and summer sunshine mingled their sweetness in the air. But I did not think of that: a confusion of countless thoughts and varied emotions crowded upon me while I gazed abstractedly on the lovely face of nature. Soon, however, this chaos of thoughts and passions cleared away, giving place to two distinct emotions: joy unspeakable that my adored Helen was all I wished to think her – that through the noisome vapours of the world's aspersions and my own fancied convictions, her character shone bright, and clear, and stainless as that sun I could not bear to look on; and shame and deep remorse for my own conduct.

Immediately after breakfast, I hurried over to Wildfell Hall. Rachel had risen many degrees in my estimation since yesterday. I was ready to greet her quite as an old friend; but every kindly impulse was checked by the look of cold distrust she cast upon me on opening the door. The old virgin had constituted herself the guardian of her lady's honour, I suppose, and doubtless she saw in me another Mr Hargrave, only the more dangerous in being more esteemed and trusted by her mistress.

'Missis can't see anyone today, sir – she's poorly,' said she in answer to my enquiry for Mrs Graham.

'But I must see her, Rachel,' said I, placing my hand on the door to prevent its being shut against me.

'Indeed, sir, you can't,' replied she, settling her countenance in still more iron frigidity than before.

'Be so good as to announce me.'

'It's no manner of use, Mr Markham; she's poorly, I tell you.'

Just in time to prevent me from committing the impropriety of taking the citadel by storm, and pushing forward unannounced, an inner door opened, and little Arthur appeared with his frolicsome playfellow the dog. He seized my hand between both his, and smilingly drew me forward.

'Mamma says you're to come in, Mr Markham,' said he, 'and I'm to go out and play with Rover.'

Rachel retired with a sigh, and I stepped into the parlour and shut the door. There, before the fireplace, stood the tall, graceful figure wasted with many sorrows. I cast the manuscript on the table, and looked in her face. Anxious and pale, it was turned towards me; her clear, dark eyes were fixed on mine with a gaze so intensely earnest that they bound me like a spell.

'Have you looked it over?' she murmured. The spell was broken.

'I've read it through,' said I, advancing into the room – 'and I want to know if you'll forgive me – if you *can* forgive me?'

She did not answer, but her eyes glistened, and a faint red mantled on her lip and cheek. As I approached, she abruptly turned away, and went to the window. It was not in anger, I was well assured, but only to conceal or control her emotion. I therefore ventured to follow and stand beside her there – but not to speak. She gave me her hand, without turning her head, and murmured, in a voice she strove in vain to steady – 'Can *you* forgive *me*?'

It might be deemed a breach of trust, I thought, to convey that lily hand to my lips, so I only gently pressed it between my own, and smilingly replied – 'I hardly can. You should have told me this before. It shows a want of confidence – '

'Oh, no,' cried she, eagerly interrupting me, 'it was not that! It was no want of confidence in you; but if I had told you anything of my history, I must have told you all, in order to excuse my conduct; and I might well shrink from such a disclosure, till necessity obliged me to make it. But you forgive me? – I have done very, very wrong, I know; but, as usual, I have reaped the bitter fruits of my own error – and must reap them to the end.'

Bitter indeed, was the tone of anguish, repressed by resolute firmness, in which this was spoken. Now, I raised her hand to my lips, and fervently kissed it again and again; for tears prevented any other reply. She suffered these wild caresses without resistance or resentment; then, suddenly turning from me, she paced twice or thrice through the room. I knew by the contraction of her brow, the tight compression of her lips, and wringing of her hands, that meantime a violent conflict between reason and passion, was silently passing within. At length she paused before the empty fireplace, and turning to me, said calmly – if that might be called calmness, which was so evidently the result of a violent effort – 'Now, Gilbert, you must leave me – not this moment, but soon – and you must *never come again.*'

'Never again, Helen? Just when I love you more than ever!'

'For that very reason, if it be so, we should not meet again. I thought *this* interview was necessary – at least, I persuaded myself it was so – that we might severally ask and receive each other's pardon for the past; but there can be no excuse for another. I shall leave this place, as soon as I have means to seek another asylum; but our intercourse must end here.'

'End here!' echoed I; and approaching the high, carved chimney-piece, I leant my hand against its heavy mouldings, and dropped my forehead upon it in silent, sullen despondency.

'You must not come again,' continued she. There was a slight tremor in her voice, but I thought her whole manner was provokingly composed, considering the dreadful sentence she pronounced. 'You must know why I tell you so,' she resumed; 'and you must see that it is better to part at once – if it be hard to say adieu for ever, you ought to help me.' She paused. I did not answer. 'Will you promise not to come? – If you won't, and if you do come here again, you will drive me away before I know where to find another place of refuge – or how to seek it.'

'Helen,' said I, turning impatiently towards her, 'I cannot discuss the matter of eternal separation, calmly and dispassionately as you can do. It is no question of mere expedience with *me*; it is a question of life and death!'

She was silent. Her pale lips quivered, and her fingers trembled with agitation, as she nervously entwined them in the hair chain to which was appended her small gold watch – the only thing of value she had permitted herself to keep. I had said an unjust and cruel thing; but I must needs follow it up with something worse.

'But, Helen!' I began in a soft, low tone, not daring to raise my eyes to her face – 'that man is *not* your husband: in the sight of Heaven he has forfeited all claim to – ' She seized my arm with a grasp of startling energy.

'*Gilbert, don't!*' she cried, in a tone that would have pierced a heart of adamant. 'For God's sake, don't *you* attempt these arguments! No *fiend* could torture me like this!'

'I won't, I won't!' said I, gently laying my hand on hers; almost as much alarmed at her vehemence, as ashamed of my own misconduct.

'Instead of acting like a true friend,' continued she, breaking from me and throwing herself into the old armchair – 'and helping me with all your might – or rather taking your own part in the struggle of right against passion – you leave all the burden to me; and not satisfied with that, you do your utmost to fight against me – when you know that I – ' She paused, and hid her face in her handkerchief.

'Forgive me, Helen!' pleaded I, 'I will never utter another word on the subject. But may we not still meet as friends?'

'It will not do,' she replied, mournfully shaking her head; and then she raised her eyes to mine, with a mildly reproachful look that seemed to say, 'You must know that as well as I.'

'Then what *must* we do?' cried I, passionately. But immediately I added in a quieter tone – 'I'll do whatever you desire; only *don't* say that this meeting is to be our last.'

'And why not? Don't you know that every time we meet, the thoughts of the final parting will become more painful? Don't you *feel* that every interview makes us dearer to each other than the last?'

The utterance of this last question was hurried and low, and the downcast eyes and burning blush too plainly showed that *she*, at least, had felt it. It was scarcely prudent to make such an admission, or to add – as she presently did – 'I have power to bid you go, now: another time it might be different' – but I was not base enough to attempt to take advantage of her candour.

'But we may write,' I timidly suggested – 'You will not deny me that consolation?'

'We can hear of each other through my brother.'

'Your brother!' A pang of remorse and shame shot through me. She had not heard of the injury he had sustained at my hands; and I had not the courage to tell her. 'Your brother will not help us,' I said: 'he would have all communion between us to be entirely at an end.'

'And he would be right, I suppose. As a friend of both, he would wish us both well; and every friend would tell us it was our interest, as well as our duty, to forget each other, though we might not see it ourselves. But don't be afraid, Gilbert,' she added, smiling sadly at my manifest discomposure, 'there is little chance of my forgetting you. But I did not mean that Frederick should be the means of transmitting messages between us, only that each might know, through him, of the other's welfare; and more than this ought not to be; for you are young, Gilbert, and you ought to marry – and will sometime, though you may think it impossible now – and though I hardly can say I wish you to forget me, I know it is right that you should, both for your own happiness and that of your future wife; and therefore I must and will wish it,' she added resolutely.

'And you are young too, Helen,' I boldly replied, 'and when that profligate scoundrel has run through his career, you will give your hand to me – I'll wait till then.'

But she would not leave me this support. Independently of the moral evil of basing our hopes upon the death of another, who, if unfit for this world, was at least no less so for the next, and whose amelioration would thus become our bane and his greatest transgression our greatest benefit – she maintained it to be madness: many men of Mr Huntingdon's habits had lived to a ripe though miserable old age; 'and if I,' said she, 'am young in years I am old in sorrow; but even if trouble should fail to kill me before vice destroys him, think, if he reached but fifty years or so, would you wait twenty or fifteen – in vague uncertainty and suspense – through all the prime of youth and manhood – and marry at last a woman faded and worn as I shall be – without ever having seen me from this day to that? – You would not,' she continued, interrupting my earnest protestations of unfailing constancy – 'or if you would you should not. Trust me, Gilbert; in this matter I know better than you. You think me cold and stony hearted, and you may, but – '

'I don't, Helen.'

'Well, never mind; you might if you would – but I have not spent my solitude in utter idleness, and I am not speaking now from the impulse of the moment as you do: I have thought of all these matters again and again; I have argued these questions with myself, and pondered well our past, and present, and future career; and believe me, I have come to the right conclusion at last. Trust my words rather than your own feelings, now, and in a few years you will see that I was right – though at present I hardly can see it myself,' she murmured with a sigh as she rested her head on her hand – 'And don't argue against me any more:

all you can say had been already said by my own heart and refuted by my reason. It was hard enough to combat those suggestions as they were whispered within me; in your mouth they are ten times worse, and if you knew how much they pain me you would cease at once, I know. If you knew my present feelings, you would even try to relieve them at the expense of your own.'

'I will go – in a minute, if *that* can relieve you – and never return!' said I with bitter emphasis – 'But, if we may never meet, and never hope to meet again, is it a crime to exchange our thought by letter? May not kindred spirits meet, and mingle in communion whatever be the fate and circumstances of their earthly tenements?'

'They may, they may!' cried she with a momentary burst of glad enthusiasm. 'I thought of that too, Gilbert, but I feared to mention it, because I feared you would not understand my views upon the subject – I fear it even now – I fear any kind friend would tell us we are *both* deluding ourselves with the idea of keeping up a spiritual intercourse without hope or prospect of anything further – without fostering vain regrets and hurtful aspirations, and feeding thoughts that should be sternly and pitilessly left to perish of inanition – '

'Never mind our kind friends: if they can part our bodies, it is enough; in God's name, let them not sunder our souls!' cried I, in terror lest she should deem it her duty to deny us this last remaining consolation.

'But no letters can pass between us here,' said she, 'without giving fresh food for scandal; and when I departed, I had intended that my new abode should be unknown to you as to the rest of the world; not that I should doubt your word if you promised not to visit me, but I thought you would be more tranquil in your own mind if you knew you could not do it; and likely to find less difficulty in abstracting yourself from me if you could not picture my situation to your mind. But listen,' said she, smilingly putting her finger to check my impatient reply: 'in six months you shall hear from Frederick precisely where I am; and if you still retain your wish to write to me, and think you can maintain a correspondence all thought, all spirit – such as disembodied souls or unimpassioned friends, at least, might hold – write, and I will answer you.'

'Six months!'

'Yes, to give your present ardour time to cool and try the truth and constancy of your soul's love for mine. And now, enough has been said between us – Why can't we part at once!' exclaimed she almost wildly, after a moment's pause, as she suddenly rose from her chair with her hands resolutely clasped together. I thought it was my duty to go without delay; and I approached and half extended my hand as if to take leave; she grasped it in silence. But this thought of final separation was too intolerable: it seemed to squeeze the blood out of my heart; and my feet were glued to the floor.

'And must we never meet again?' I murmured in the anguish of my soul.

'We shall meet in Heaven. Let us think of that,' said she in a tone of desperate calmness; but her eyes glittered wildly, and her face was deadly pale.

'But not as we are now,' I could not help replying. 'It gives me little consolation to think I shall next behold you as a disembodied spirit, or an

altered being, with a frame perfect and glorious, but not like this! – and a heart, perhaps, entirely estranged from me.'

'No, Gilbert, there is perfect love in Heaven!'

'*So* perfect, I suppose, that it soars above distinctions, and you will have no closer sympathy with me than with any one of the ten thousand angels and the innumerable multitude of happy spirits round us.'

'Whatever I am, you will be the same, and therefore, cannot possibly regret it; and whatever that change may be, we know it must be for the better.'

'But if I am to be so changed that I shall cease to adore you with my whole heart and soul, and love you beyond every other creature, I shall not be myself; and, though, if ever I win Heaven at all, I must, I know, be infinitely better and happier than I am now, my earthly nature cannot rejoice in the anticipation of such beautitude, from which itself and its chief joy must be excluded.'

'Is your love *all* earthly then?'

'No, but I am supposing we shall have no more intimate communion with each other, than with the rest.'

'If so, it will be because we love them more and not each other less. Increase of love brings increase of happiness, when it is mutual, and pure as that will be.'

'But can *you*, Helen, contemplate with delight this prospect of losing me in a sea of glory?'

'I own I cannot; but we know not that it will be so; and I do know that to regret the exchange of earthly pleasures for the joys of Heaven, is as if the grovelling caterpillar should lament that it must one day quit the nibbled leaf to soar aloft and flutter through the air, roving at will from flower to flower, sipping sweet honey from their cups or basking in their sunny petals. If these little creatures knew how great a change awaited them, no doubt they would regret it; but would not all such sorrow be misplaced? And if that illustration will not move you, here is another – We are children now; we feel as children, and we understand as children; and when we are told that men and women do not play with toys, and that our companions will one day weary of the trivial sports and occupations that interest them and us so deeply now, we cannot help being saddened at the thoughts of such an alteration, because we cannot conceive that as we grow up, our own minds will become so enlarged and elevated that we ourselves shall then regard as trifling those objects and pursuits we now so fondly cherish, and that, though our companions will no longer join us in those childish pastimes, they will drink with us at other fountains of delight, and mingle their souls with ours in higher aims and nobler occupations beyond our present comprehension, but not less deeply relished or less truly good for that – while yet both we and they remain essentially the same individuals as before. But, Gilbert, can you really derive no consolation from the thought that we may meet together where there is no more pain and sorrow, no more striving against sin, and struggling of the spirit against the flesh; where both will behold the same glorious truths, and drink exalted and supreme felicity from the same fountain of light and goodness – that Being whom both will worship with the same intensity of holy ardour, and whose

pure and happy creatures both will love with the same divine affection? If you cannot, never write to me!'

'Helen, I can, if faith would never fail.'

'Now, then,' exclaimed she, 'while this hope is strong within us – '

'We will part,' I cried. 'You shall not have the pain of another effort to dismiss me: I will go at once; but – '

I did not put my request in words: she understood it instinctively and *this* time she yielded too – or rather, there was nothing so deliberate as requesting or yielding in the matter: there was a sudden impulse that neither could resist. One moment I stood and looked into her face, the next I held her to my heart, and we seemed to grow together in a close embrace from which no physical or mental force could rend us. A whispered 'God bless you!' and 'Go – go!' was all she said; but while she spoke, she held me so fast that, without violence, I could not have obeyed her. At length, however, by some heroic effort, we tore ourselves apart, and I rushed from the house.

I have a confused remembrance of seeing little Arthur running up the garden walk to meet me, and of bolting over the wall to avoid him – and subsequently running down the steep fields, clearing the stone fences and hedges as they came in my way, till I got completely out of sight of the old hall and down to the bottom of the hill; and then of long hours spent in bitter tears and lamentations, and melancholy musings in the lonely valley, with the eternal music in my ears, of the west wind rushing through the overshadowing trees, and the brook babbling and gurgling along its stony bed – my eyes, for the most part, vacantly fixed on the deep, checkered shades restlessly playing over the bright sunny grass at my feet, where now and then a withered leaf or two would come dancing to share the revelry, but my heart was away up the hill in that dark room where she was weeping desolate and alone – she whom I was not to comfort, not to see again, till years or suffering had overcome us both, and torn our spirits from their perishing abodes of clay.

There was little business done that day, you may be sure. The farm was abandoned to the labourers, and the labourers were left to their own devices. But one duty must be attended to: I had not forgotten my assault upon Frederick Lawrence; and I must see him to apologise for the unhappy deed. I would fain have put it off till the morrow; but what if he should denounce me to his sister in the meantime? No, no, I must ask his pardon today, and entreat him to be lenient in his accusation, if the revelation must be made. I deferred it however, till the evening, when my spirits were more composed and when – oh, wonderful perversity of human nature! – some faint germs of indefinite hopes were beginning to rise in my mind; not that I intended to cherish them after all that had been said on the subject, but there they must lie for a while, uncrushed though not encouraged, till I had learnt to live without them.

Arrived at Woodford, the young squire's abode, I found no little difficulty in obtaining admission to his presence. The servant that opened the door told me his master was very ill, and seemed to think it doubtful whether he would be able to see me. I was not going to be balked however. I waited calmly in the hall to be

announced, but inwardly determined to take no denial. The message was such as I expected – a polite intimation that Mr Lawrence could see no one; he was feverish and must not be disturbed.

'I shall not disturb him long,' said I; 'but I must see him for a moment: it is on business of importance that I wish to speak to him.'

'I'll tell him sir,' said the man. And I advanced farther into the hall and followed him nearly to the door of the apartment where his master was – for it seemed he was not in bed. The answer returned, was that Mr Lawrence hoped I would be so good as to leave a message or a note with the servant, as he could attend to no business at present.

'He may as well see me as you,' said I; and, stepping past the astonished footman, I boldly rapped at the door, entered, and closed it behind me. The room was spacious and handsomely furnished – very comfortably, too, for a bachelor. A clear, red fire was burning in the polished grate: a superannuated greyhound, given up to idleness and good living lay basking before it on the thick, soft rug, on one corner of which, beside the sofa, sat a smart young springer, looking wistfully up in its master's face; perhaps, asking permission to share his couch, or, it might be, only soliciting a caress from his hand or a kind word from his lips. The invalid himself looked very interesting as he lay reclining there, in his elegant dressing-gown, with a silk handkerchief bound across his temples. His usually pale face was flushed and feverish; his eyes were half closed, until he became sensible of my presence – and then he opened them wide enough; one hand was thrown listlessly over the back of the sofa, and held a small volume with which, apparently, he had been vainly attempting to beguile the weary hours. He dropped it, in his start of indignant surprise as I advanced into the room and stood before him on the rug. He raised himself on his pillows and gazed upon me with equal degrees of nervous horror, anger, and amazement depicted on his countenance.

'Mr Markham, I scarcely expected this!' he said; and the blood left his cheek as he spoke.

'I know you didn't,' answered I; 'but be quiet a minute, and I'll tell you what I came for.' Unthinkingly I advanced a step or two nearer. He winced at my approach, with an expression of aversion and instinctive physical fear anything but conciliatory to my feelings. I stepped back however.

'Make your story a short one,' said he, putting his hand on the small silver bell that stood on the table beside him – 'or I shall be obliged to call for assistance. I am in no state to bear your brutalities now, or your presence either.' And in truth the moisture started from his pores and stood on his pale forehead like dew.

Such a reception was hardly calculated to diminish the difficulties of my unenviable task. It must be performed, however, in some fashion: and so I plunged into it at once, and floundered through it as I could.

'The truth is, Lawrence,' said I, 'I have not acted quite correctly towards you of late – especially on this last occasion; and I'm come to – in short, to express my regret for what has been done, and to beg your pardon – If you don't choose

to grant it,' I added hastily, not liking the aspect of his face, 'it's no matter – only, *I've* done *my* duty – that's all.'

'It's easily done,' replied he, with a faint smile bordering on a sneer: 'to abuse your friend and knock him on the head, without any assignable cause, and then tell him the deed was not quite correct, but it's no matter whether he pardons it or not.'

'I forgot to tell you that it was in consequence of a mistake,' muttered I. 'I should have made a very handsome apology, but you provoked me so confoundedly with your – Well, I suppose it's my fault. The fact is, I didn't know that you were Mrs Graham's brother, and I saw and heard some things respecting your conduct towards her, which were calculated to awaken unpleasant suspicions, that allow me to say, a little candour and confidence on your part might have removed; and at last, I chanced to overhear a part of a conversation between you and her that made me think I had a right to hate you.'

'And how came you to know that I was her brother?' asked he in some anxiety.

'She told me herself. She told me all. *She* knew I might be trusted. But you needn't disturb yourself about *that*, Mr Lawrence, for I've seen the last of her!'

'The last! is she gone then?'

'No, but she has bid adieu to me; and I have promised never to go near that house again while she inhabits it.' I could have groaned aloud at the bitter thoughts awakened by this turn in the discourse. But I only clenched my hands, and stamped my foot upon the rug. My companion however, was evidently relieved.

'You have done right!' he said in a tone of unqualified approbation, while his face brightened into almost a sunny expression.

'And as for the mistake, I am sorry for both our sakes that it should have occurred. Perhaps you can forgive my want of candour, and remember, as some partial mitigation of the offence, how little encouragement to friendly confidence you have given me of late.'

'Yes, yes, I remember it all: nobody can blame me more than I blame myself in my own heart – at any rate, nobody can regret more sincerely than I do the result of my *brutality* as you rightly term it.'

'Never mind that,' said he, faintly smiling; 'let us forget all unpleasant words on both sides, as well as deeds, and consign to oblivion everything that we have cause to regret. Have you any objection to take my hand – or you'd rather not?' It trembled through weakness, as he held it out, and dropped before I had time to catch it and give it a hearty squeeze, which he had not the strength to return.

'How dry and burning your hand is, Lawrence,' said I. 'You are really ill, and I have made you worse by all this talk.'

'Oh, it is nothing: only a cold got by the rain.'

'My doing, too.'

'Never mind that – but tell me, did you mention this affair to my sister?'

'To confess the truth, I had not the courage to do so; but when you tell her, will you just say that I deeply regret it, and – '

'Oh, never fear! I shall say nothing against you, as long as you keep your good resolution of remaining aloof from her. She has not heard of my illness then, that you are aware of?'

'I think not.'

'I'm glad of that, for I have been all this time tormenting myself with the fear that somebody would tell her I was dying, or desperately ill, and she would be either distressing herself on account of her inability to hear from me or do me any good, or perhaps committing the madness of coming to see me. I must contrive to let her know something about it, if I can,' continued he reflectively, 'or she will be hearing some such story. Many would be glad to tell her such news, just to see how she would take it; and then she might expose herself to fresh scandal.'

'I wish I had told her,' said I. 'If it were not for my promise, I would tell her now.'

'By no means! I am not dreaming of that; but if I were to write a short note, now – not mentioning you, Markham, but just giving a slight account of my illness, by way of excuse for my not coming to see her, and to put her on her guard against any exaggerated reports she may hear – and address it in a disguised hand – would you do me the favour to slip it into the post-office as you pass? For I dare not trust any of the servants in such a case.'

Most willingly I consented, and immediately brought him his desk. There was little need to disguise his hand, for the poor fellow seemed to have considerable difficulty in writing at all, so as to be legible. When the note was done, I thought it time to retire, and took leave after asking if there was anything in the world I could do for him, little or great, in the way of alleviating his sufferings, and repairing the injury I had done.

'No,' said he; 'you have already done much towards it; you have done more for me than the most skilful physician could do; for you have relieved my mind of two great burdens – anxiety on my sister's account, and deep regret upon your own, for I do believe these two sources of torment have had more effect in working me up into a fever, than anything else; and I am persuaded I shall soon recover now. There is one more thing you can do for me, and that is, come and see me now and then – for you see I am very lonely here, and I promise your entrance shall not be disputed again.'

I engaged to do so, and departed with a cordial pressure of the hand. I posted the letter on my way home, most manfully resisting the temptation of dropping in a word from myself at the same time.

## CHAPTER 46

### *Friendly Counsels*

I felt strongly tempted, at times, to enlighten my mother and sister on the real character and circumstances of the persecuted tenant of Wildfell Hall; and at first I greatly regretted having omitted to ask that lady's permission to do so; but, on due reflection, I considered that if it were known to them, it could not long remain a secret to the Millwards and Wilsons, and such was my present appreciation of Eliza Millward's disposition, that, if once she got a clue to the story, I should fear she would soon find means to enlighten Mr Huntingdon upon the place of his wife's retreat. I would therefore wait patiently till these weary six months were over, and then, when the fugitive had found another home, and I was permitted to write to her, I would beg to be allowed to clear her name from these vile calumnies: at present I must content myself with simply asserting that I knew them to be false, and would prove it some day, to the shame of those who slandered her. I don't think anybody believed me: but everybody soon learned to avoid insinuating a word against her, or even mentioning her name in my presence. They thought I was so madly infatuated by the seductions of that unhappy lady that I was determined to support her in the very face of reason; and meantime I grew insupportably morose and misanthropical from the idea that everyone I met was harbouring unworthy thoughts of the supposed Mrs Graham, and would express them if he dared. My poor mother was quite distressed about me; but I couldn't help it – at least I thought I could not; though sometimes I felt a pang of remorse for my undutiful conduct to her, and made an effort to amend, attended with some partial success – and indeed I was generally more humanised in my demeanour to her than to anyone else, Mr Lawrence excepted. Rose and Fergus usually shunned my presence; and it was well they did, for I was not fit company for them, nor they for me, under the present circumstances.

Mrs Huntingdon did not leave Wildfell Hall till above two months after our farewell interview. During that time she never appeared at church, and I never went near the house: I only knew she was still there by her brother's brief answers to my many and varied enquiries respecting her. I was a very constant and attentive visitor to him throughout the whole period of his illness and convalescence; not only from the interest I took in his recovery, and my desire to cheer him up and make the utmost possible amends for my former 'brutality', but from my growing attachment to himself, and the increasing pleasure I found in his society – partly, from his increased cordiality to me, but chiefly on account of his close connection – both in blood and affection – with my adored Helen. I loved him for it better than I liked to express; and I took a secret delight in pressing those slender, white fingers, so marvellously like her own, considering

he was not a woman, and in watching the passing changes in his fair, pale features, and observing the intonations of his voice – detecting resemblances which I wondered had never struck me before. He provoked me at times, indeed, by his evident reluctance to talk to me about his sister, though I did not question the friendliness of his motives in wishing to discourage my remembrance of her.

His recovery was not quite so rapid as he had expected it to be: he was not able to mount his pony till a fortnight after the date of our reconciliation; and the first use he made of his returning strength, was to ride over by night to Wildfell Hall, to see his sister. It was a hazardous enterprise both for him and for her, but he thought it necessary to consult with her on the subject of her projected departure, if not to calm her apprehensions respecting his health, and the worst result was a slight relapse of his illness; for no one knew of the visit, but the inmates of the old hall – except myself; and I believe it had not been his intention to mention it to me, for when I came to see him the next day, and observed he was not so well as he ought to have been, he merely said he had caught cold by being out too late in the evening.

'You'll *never* be able to see your sister, if you don't take care of yourself,' said I, a little provoked at the circumstance on her account, instead of commiserating him.

'I've seen her already,' said he, quietly.

'You've seen her!' cried I, in astonishment.

'Yes.' And then he told me what considerations had impelled him to make the venture, and with what precautions he had made it.

'And how was she?' I eagerly asked.

'As usual,' was the brief though sad reply.

'As usual – that is, far from happy and far from strong.'

'She is not positively ill,' returned he; 'and she will recover her spirits in a while I have no doubt –but so many trials have been almost too much for her. How threatening those clouds look!' continued he, tuning towards the window. 'We shall have thunder showers before night, I imagine; and they are just in the midst of stacking my corn. Have you got yours all in yet?'

'No – And, Lawrence, did she – did your sister mention me?'

'She asked if I had seen you lately.'

'And what else did she say?'

'I cannot tell you all she said,' replied he with a slight smile, 'for we talked a good deal, though my stay was but short; but our conversation was chiefly on the subject of her intended departure, which I begged her to delay till I was better able to assist her in her search after another home.'

'But did she say no more about me?'

'She did not say much about you, Markham. I should not have encouraged her to do so, had she been inclined; but happily she was not: she only asked a few questions concerning you, and seemed satisfied with my brief answers; wherein she showed herself wiser than her friend – and I may tell you too that she seemed to be far more anxious lest you should think too much of her, than lest you should forget her.'

'She was right.'

'But I fear *your* anxiety is quite the other way, respecting her.'

'No, it is not: I wish her to be happy; but I don't wish her to forget me altogether. She knows it is impossible that I should forget her; and she is right to wish me not to remember her too well. I should not desire her to regret me *too* deeply; but I can scarcely imagine she will make herself very unhappy about me, because I know I am not worthy of it, except in my appreciation of her.'

'You are neither of you worthy of a broken heart – nor of all the sighs, and tears, and sorrowful thoughts that have been, and I fear will be wasted upon you both; but at present, each has a more exalted opinion of the other than, I fear, he or she deserves; and my sister's feeling are naturally full as keen as yours, and I believe *more* constant; but she has the good sense and fortitude to strive against them in this particular; and I trust she will not rest till she has entirely weaned her thoughts – ' he hesitated.

'From me,' said I.

'And I wish you would make the like exertions,' continued he.

'Did she *tell* you that that was her intention?'

'No; the question was not broached between us: there was no necessity for it, for I had no doubt that such was her determination.'

'To forget me?'

'Yes, Markham! Why not?'

'Oh! well,' was my only audible reply; but I internally answered – 'No, Lawrence, you're wrong there, she is *not* determined to forget me. It would be *wrong* to forget one so deeply and fondly devoted to her, who can so thoroughly appreciate her excellencies and sympathise with all her thoughts as I can do, and it would be wrong in me to forget so excellent and divine a piece of God's creation as she, when I have once so truly loved and known her.' But I said no more to him on that subject. I instantly started a new topic of conversation, and soon took leave of my companion, with a feeling of less cordiality towards him than usual. Perhaps I had no right to be annoyed at him, but I was so nevertheless.

In little more than a week after this, I met him returning from a visit to the Wilsons; and I now resolved to do *him* a good turn, though at the expense of his feelings, and, perhaps, at the risk of incurring that displeasure which is so commonly the reward of those who give disagreeable information or tender their advice unasked. In this, believe me, I was actuated by no motives of revenge for the occasional annoyances I had lately sustained from him – nor yet by any feeling of malevolent enmity towards Miss Wilson, but purely by the fact that I could not endure that such a woman should be Mrs Huntingdon's sister, and that, as well for his own sake as for hers, I could not bear to think of his being deceived into a union with one so unworthy of him, and so utterly unfitted to be the partner of his quiet home, and the companion of his life. He had had uncomfortable suspicions on that head himself, I imagined, but such was his inexperience, and such were the lady's powers of attraction and her skill in bringing them to bear upon his young imagination, that they had not disturbed him long, and I believe the only effectual cause of the vacillating indecision that

had preserved him hitherto from making an actual declaration of love, was the consideration of her connections, and especially of her mother, whom he could not abide. Had they lived at a distance, he might have surmounted the objection, but within two or three miles of Woodford, it was really no light matter.

'You've been to call on the Wilsons, Lawrence,' said I as I walked beside his pony.

'Yes,' replied he, slightly averting his face: 'I thought it but civil to take the first opportunity of returning their kind attentions, since they have been so very particular and constant in their enquiries, throughout the whole course of my illness.'

'It's all Miss Wilson's doing.'

'And if it is,' returned he, with a very perceptible blush, 'is that any reason why I should not make a suitable acknowledgement?'

'It is reason why you should not make the acknowledgement she looks for.'

'Let us drop that subject if you please,' said he in evident displeasure.

'No, Lawrence, with your leave we'll continue it a while longer; and I'll tell you something, now we're about it, which you may believe or not as you choose – only please to remember that it is not my custom to speak falsely, and that in this case, I can have no motive for misrepresenting the truth – '

'Well, Markham! what now?'

'*Miss Wilson hates your sister*. It may be natural enough that, in her ignorance of the relationship, she should feel some degree of enmity against her, but no good or amiable woman would be capable of evincing that bitter, cold-blooded, designing malice towards a fancied rival that I have observed in her.'

'Markham!!'

'Yes – and it is my belief that Eliza Millward and she, if not the very originators of the slanderous reports that have been propagated, were designedly the encouragers and chief disseminators of them. She was not desirous to mix up *your* name in the matter, of course, but her delight was, and still is, to blacken your sister's character to the utmost of her power without risking too greatly the exposure of her own malevolence!'

'I cannot believe it,' interrupted my companion, his face burning with indignation.

'Well, as I cannot prove it, I must content myself with asserting that it *is* so to the best of my belief; but as you would not willingly marry Miss Wilson if it *were* so, you will do well to be cautious, till you have proved it to be otherwise.'

'I never told you, Markham, that I *intended* to marry Miss Wilson,' said he proudly.

'No, but whether you do or not, she intends to marry you.'

'Did she tell you so?'

'No, but – '

'Then you have no right to make such an assertion respecting her.' He slightly quickened his pony's pace, but I laid my hand on its mane, determined he should not leave me yet.

'Wait a moment, Lawrence, and let me explain myself; and don't be so very –
I don't know what to call it – *inaccessible* as you are – I know what you think of
Jane Wilson; and I believe I know how far you are mistaken in your opinion: you
think she is singularly charming, elegant, sensible, and refined: you are not
aware that she is selfish, cold-hearted, ambitious, artful, shallow-minded – '

'Enough, Markham, enough.'

'No; let me finish – You don't know that, if you married her, your home
would be rayless and comfortless; and it would break your heart at last to find
yourself united to one so wholly incapable of sharing your tastes, feelings, and
ideas – so utterly destitute of sensibility, good feeling, and true nobility of soul.'

'Have you done?' asked my companion quietly.

'Yes; I know you hate me for my impertinence, but I don't care if it only
conduces to preserve you from that fatal mistake.'

'Well!' returned he, with a rather wintry smile – 'I'm glad you have over-
come, or forgotten your own afflictions so far as to be able to study so deeply the
affairs of others, and trouble your head, so unnecessarily, about the fancied or
possible calamities of their future life.'

We parted – somewhat coldly again; but still we did not cease to be friends;
and my well-meant warning, though it might have been more judiciously
delivered, as well as more thankfully received, was not wholly unproductive of
the desired effect: his visit to the Wilsons was not repeated, and, though, in our
subsequent interviews, he never mentioned her name to me, nor I to him – I
have reason to believe he pondered my words in his mind, eagerly though
covertly sought information respecting the fair lady from other quarters,
secretly compared my character of her with what he had himself observed and
what he heard from others, and finally came to the conclusion that, all things
considered, she had much better remain Miss Wilson of Ryecote Farm, than be
transmuted into Mrs Lawrence of Woodford Hall. I believe, too, that he soon
learned to contemplate with secret amazement his former predilection, and to
congratulate himself on the lucky escape he had made; but he never confessed it
to me, or hinted one word of acknowledgement for the part I had had in his
deliverance – but this was not surprising to anyone that knew him as I did.

As for Jane Wilson, she, of course, was disappointed and embittered by the
sudden cold neglect, and ultimate desertion of her former admirer. Had I done
wrong to blight her cherished hopes? I think not, and certainly my conscience
has never accused me, from that day to this, of any evil design in the matter.

## CHAPTER 47

### *Startling Intelligence*

One morning, about the beginning of November, while I was inditing some business letters, shortly after breakfast, Eliza Millward came to call upon my sister. Rose had neither the discrimination nor the virulence to regard the little demon as I did, and they still preserved their former intimacy. At the moment of her arrival, however, there was no one in the room but Fergus and myself, my mother and sister being both of them absent, 'on household cares intent;' but *I* was not going to lay myself out for her amusement, whoever else might so incline: I merely honoured her with a careless salutation and a few words of course, and then went on with my writing, leaving my brother to be more polite if he chose. But she wanted to tease me.

'What a pleasure it is to find you at home, Mr Markham!' said she, with a disingenuously malicious smile. 'I so seldom see you now, for you never come to the vicarage. Papa is quite offended I can tell you,' she added playfully, looking into my face with an impertinent laugh, as she seated herself, half beside and half before my desk, off the corner of the table.

'I have had a good deal to do of late,' said I, without looking up from my letter.

'Have you indeed! Somebody said you had been strangely neglecting your business these last few months.'

'Somebody said wrong, for, these last *two* months – especially, I have been particularly plodding and diligent.'

'Ah! Well, there's nothing like active employment, I suppose, to console the afflicted; and, excuse me, Mr Markham, but you look so very far from well, and have been, by all accounts, so moody and thoughtful of late – I could almost think you have some secret care preying on your spirits. *Formerly*,' said she timidly, 'I could have ventured to ask you what it was, and what I could do to comfort you: I dare not do it now.'

'You're very kind, Miss Eliza. When I think you can do anything to comfort me, I'll make bold to tell you.'

'Pray do! – I suppose I mayn't guess what it is that troubles you?'

'There's no necessity, for I'll tell you plainly. The thing that troubles me the most at present, is a young lady sitting at my elbow, and preventing me from finishing my letter, and thereafter, repairing to my daily business.'

Before she could reply to this ungallant speech, Rose entered the room; and Miss Eliza rising to greet her, they both seated themselves near the fire, where that idle lad, Fergus, was standing, leaning his shoulder against the corner of the chimney-piece, with his legs crossed and his hands in his breeches pockets.

'Now, Rose, I'll tell you a piece of news – I hope you've not heard it before,

for good, bad or indifferent, one always likes to be the first to tell – It's about that sad Mrs Graham – '

'Hush – sh – sh!' whispered Fergus, in a tone of solemn import. ' "We never mention her: her name is never heard." ' And glancing up, I caught him with his eye askance on me, and his finger pointed to his forehead: then, winking at the young lady with a doleful shake of the head, he whispered – 'a monomania – but don't mention it – all right but that.'

'I should be sorry to injure anyone's feelings,' returned she, speaking below her breath, 'another time, perhaps.'

'Speak out, Miss Eliza!' said I, not deigning to notice the other's buffooneries, 'you needn't fear to say anything in my presence – that is *true*.'

'Well,' answered she, 'perhaps you know already that Mrs Graham's husband is not really dead, and that she had run away from him?' I started, and felt my face glow; but I bent it over my letter, and went on folding it up as she proceeded, 'but perhaps you did *not* know that she is now gone back to him again, and that a perfect reconciliation has taken place between them? Only think,' she continued, turning to the confounded Rose, 'what a fool the man must be!'

'And who gave you this piece of intelligence, Miss Eliza?' said I, interrupting my sister's exclamations.

'I had it from a very authentic source, sir.'

'From whom, may I ask?'

'From one of the servants at Woodford.'

'Oh! I was not aware that you were on such intimate terms with Mr Lawrence's household.'

'It was not from the man himself, that I heard it; but he told it in confidence to our maid Sarah, and Sarah told it to me.'

'In confidence, I suppose; and you tell it in confidence to us; but *I* can tell *you* that it is but a lame story after all, and scarcely one half of it true.'

While I spoke, I completed the sealing and direction of my letters, with a somewhat unsteady hand, in spite of all my efforts to retain composure, and in spite of my firm conviction that the story *was* a lame one – that the supposed Mrs Graham, most certainly, had not *voluntarily* gone back to her husband, or dreamt of a reconciliation. Most likely, she was gone away, and the tale-bearing servant, not knowing what was become of her, had *conjectured* that such was the case, and our fair visitor had detailed it as a certainty, delighted with such an opportunity of tormenting me. But it was possible – barely possible, that someone might have betrayed her, and she had been taken away by force. Determined to know the worst, I hastily pocketed my two letters, and muttering something about being too late for the post, left the room, rushed into the yard and vociferously called for my horse. No one being there, I dragged him out of the stable myself, strapped the saddle on to his back and the bridle on to his head, mounted, and speedily galloped away to Woodford. I found its owner pensively strolling in the grounds.

'Is your sister gone?' were my first words as I grasped his hand, instead of the usual enquiry after his health.

'Yes; she's gone,' was his answer, so calmly spoken, that my terror was at once removed.

'I suppose I mayn't know where she is?' said I, as I dismounted and relinquished my horse to the gardener, who, being the only servant within call, had been summoned by his master, from his employment of raking up the dead leaves on the lawn, to take him to the stables.

My companion gravely took my arm, and leading me away to the garden, thus answered my question – 'She is at Grassdale Manor, in —shire.'

'Where?' cried I, with a convulsive start.

'At Grassdale Manor.'

'How was it?' I gasped. 'Who betrayed her?'

'She went of her own accord.'

'Impossible, Lawrence!! She *could* not be so frantic!' exclaimed I, vehemently grasping his arm, as if to force him to unsay those hateful words.

'She did,' persisted he in the same grave, collected manner as before – 'and not without reason,' he continued, gently disengaging himself from my grasp: 'Mr Huntingdon is ill.'

'And so she went to nurse him?'

'Yes.'

'Fool!' I could not help exclaiming – and Lawrence looked up with a rather reproachful glance. 'Is he dying then?'

'I think not, Markham.'

'And how many more nurses has he? – How many ladies are there besides, to take care of him?'

'None: he was alone, or she would not have gone.'

'Oh, confound it! This is intolerable!'

'What is? That he should be alone?'

I attempted no reply, for I was not sure that this circumstance did not partly conduce to my distraction. I therefore continued to pace the walk in silent anguish, with my hand pressed to my forehead; then suddenly pausing and turning to my companion, I impatiently exclaimed,

'Why did she take this infatuated step? What fiend persuaded her to it?'

'Nothing persuaded her but her own sense of duty.'

'Humbug!'

'I was half inclined to say so myself, Markham, at first. I assure you it was not by my advice that she went, for I detest that man as fervently as you can do – except, indeed, that his reformation would give me much greater pleasure than his death – but all I did was to inform her of the circumstance of his illness (the consequence of a fall from his horse in hunting), and to tell her that that unhappy person, Miss Myers, had left him some time ago.'

'It was ill done! Now, when he finds the convenience of her presence, he will make all manner of lying speeches and false, fair promises for the future, and she will believe him, and then her condition will be ten times worse and ten times more irremediable than before.'

'There does not appear to be much ground for such apprehensions at

present,' said he, producing a letter from his pocket: 'from the account I received this morning, I should say – '

It was *her* writing! By an irresistible impulse, I held out my hand, and the words – 'Let me see it,' involuntarily passed my lips. He was evidently reluctant to grant the request, but while he hesitated, I snatched it from his hand. Recollecting myself, however, the minute after, I offered to restore it.

'Here, take it,' said I, 'if you don't want me to read it.'

'No,' replied he, 'you may read it if you like.'

I read it and so may you.

*Grassdale, Nov. 4th.*

DEAR FREDERICK – I know you will be anxious to hear from me: and I will tell you all I can. Mr Huntingdon is very ill, but not dying, or in any immediate danger; and he is rather better at present than he was when I came. I found the house in sad confusion: Mrs Greaves, Benson, every decent servant had left, and those that were come to supply their places were a negligent, disorderly set, to say no worse – I must change them again if I stay. A professional nurse, a grim, hard old woman, had been hired to attend the wretched invalid. He suffers much, and has no fortitude to bear him through. The immediate injuries he sustained from the accident, however, were not very severe, and would, as the doctor says, have been but trifling to a man of temperate habits; but with *him* it is very different. On the night of my arrival, when I first entered his room, he was lying in a kind of half delirium. He did not notice me till I spoke; and then, he mistook me for another.

'Is it you, Alice, come again?' he murmured. 'What did you leave me for?'

'It is I, Arthur – it is Helen, your wife,' I replied.

'My wife!' said he, with a start. 'For Heaven's sake, don't mention her! – I have none – Devil take her,' he cried, a moment after – 'and you too! What did you do it for?'

I said no more; but observing that he kept gazing towards the foot of the bed, I went and sat there, placing the light so as to shine full upon me; for I thought he might be dying and I wanted him to know me. For a long time, he lay silently looking upon me, first with a vacant stare, then with a fixed gaze of strange, growing intensity. At last he startled me by suddenly raising himself on his elbow and demanding in a horrified whisper, with his eyes still fixed upon me – 'Who is it?'

'It is Helen Huntingdon,' said I, quietly rising, at the same time, and removing to a less conspicuous position.

'I must be going mad,' cried he – 'or something – delirious perhaps – but leave me, whoever you are – I can't bear that white face, and those eyes – for God's sake go, and send me somebody else, that doesn't look like that!'

I went, at once, and sent the hired nurse. But next morning, I ventured to enter his chamber again; and, taking the nurse's place by his bedside, I watched him and waited on him for several hours, showing myself as little as possible, and only speaking when necessary, and then not above my breath. At first he

addressed me as the nurse, but, on my crossing the room to draw up the window-blinds, in obedience to his directions, he said – 'No, it isn't nurse; it's Alice. Stay with me do! That old hag will be the death of me.'

'I mean to stay with you,' said I. And after that, he would call me Alice – or some other name almost equally repugnant to my feelings. I forced myself to endure it for a while, fearing a contradiction might disturb him too much: but when, having asked for a glass of water, while I held it to his lips, he murmured, 'Thanks, dearest!' – I could not help distinctly observing – 'You would not say so if you knew me,' intending to follow that up with another declaration of my identity, but he merely muttered an incoherent reply, so I dropped it again, till some time after, when, as I was bathing his forehead and temples with vinegar and water to relieve the heat and pain in his head, he observed, after looking earnestly upon me for some minutes – 'I have such strange fancies – I can't get rid of them, and they won't let me rest; and the most singular and pertinacious of them all, is your face and voice; they seem just like hers. I could swear at this moment, that she was by my side.'

'She is,' said I.

'That seems comfortable,' continued he, without noticing my words; 'and while you do it, the other fancies fade away – but *this* only strengthens. Go on – go on, till it vanishes too. I can't stand such a mania as this; it would kill me!'

'It never will vanish,' said I distinctly, 'for it is the truth.'

'The truth!' he cried, starting as if an asp had stung him. 'You don't mean to say that you are really she!'

'I do; but you needn't shrink away from me, as if I were your greatest enemy: I am come to take care of you, and do what none of *them* would do.'

'For God's sake, don't torment me now!' cried he in pitiable agitation; and then he began to mutter bitter curses against me, or the evil fortune that had brought me there; while I put down the sponge and basin, and resumed my seat at the bedside.

'Where are they?' said he – 'have they all left me – servants and all?'

'There are servants within call, if you want them; but you had better lie down now and be quiet: none of them could or would attend you as carefully as I shall do.'

'I can't understand it at all,' said he, in bewildered perplexity. 'Was it a dream that – ' and he covered his eyes with his hand, as if trying to unravel the mystery.

'No, Arthur, it was not a dream, that your conduct was such as to oblige me to leave you; but I heard that you were ill and alone, and I am come back to nurse you. You need not fear to trust me: tell me all your wants, and I will try to satisfy them. There is no one else to care for you; and I shall not upbraid you now.'

'Oh! I see,' said he with a bitter smile, 'it's an act of Christian charity, whereby you hope to gain a higher seat in Heaven for yourself, and scoop a deeper pit in Hell for me.'

'No; I came to offer you that comfort and assistance your situation required; and if I could benefit your soul as well as your body, and awaken some sense of contrition and – '

'Oh, yes; if you could overwhelm me with remorse and confusion of face, now's the time. What have you done with my son?'

'He is well, and you may see him sometime, if you will compose yourself, but not now.'

'Where is he?'

'He is safe.'

'Is he here?'

'Wherever he is, you will not see him till you have promised to leave him entirely under my care and protection, and to let me take him away whenever and wherever I please, if I should hereafter judge it necessary to remove him again. But we will talk of that tomorrow: you must be quiet now.'

'No, let me see him now. I promise, if it *must* be so.'

'No –'

'I swear it, as God is in Heaven! Now then, let me see him.'

'But I cannot trust your oaths and promises: I must have a written agreement, and you must sign it in presence of a witness – but not today, tomorrow.'

'No, today – now,' persisted he: and he was in such a state of feverish excitement, and so bent upon the immediate gratification of his wish, that I thought it better to grant it at once, as I saw he would not rest till I did. But I was determined my son's interest should not be forgotten; and having clearly written out the promise I wished Mr Huntingdon to give upon a slip of paper, I deliberately read it over to him, and made him sign it in the presence of Rachel. He begged I would not insist upon this: it was a useless exposure of my want of faith in his word, to the servant. I told him I was sorry, but since he had forfeited my confidence, he must take the consequence. He next pleaded inability to hold the pen. 'Then we must wait until you can hold it,' said I. Upon which, he said he would try; but then, he could not see to write. I placed my finger where the signature was to be, and told him he might write his name in the dark, if he only knew where to put it. But he had not power to form the letters. 'In that case, you must be too ill to see the child,' said I; and finding me inexorable, he at length managed to ratify the agreement; and I bade Rachel send the boy.

All this may strike you as harsh, but I felt I must not lose my present advantage, and my son's future welfare should not be sacrificed to any mistaken tenderness for this man's feelings. Little Arthur had not forgotten his father, but thirteen months of absence, during which he had seldom been permitted to hear a word about him, or hardly to whisper his name, had rendered him somewhat shy; and when he was ushered into the darkened room where the sick man lay, so altered from his former self, with fiercely flushed face and wildly gleaming eyes – he instinctively clung to me, and stood looking on his father with a countenance expressive of far more awe than pleasure.

'Come here, Arthur,' said the latter, extending his hand towards him. The child went, and timidly touched that burning hand, but almost started in alarm, when his father suddenly clutched his arm and drew him nearer to his side.

'Do you know me?' asked Mr Huntingdon, intently perusing his features.

'Yes.'

'Who am I?'

'Papa.'

'Are you glad to see me?'

'Yes.'

'You're *not!*' replied the disappointed parent, relaxing his hold, and darting a vindictive glance at me.

Arthur, thus released, crept back to me and put his hand in mine. His father swore I had made the child hate him, and abused and cursed me bitterly. The instant he began I sent our son out of the room; and when he paused to breathe, I calmly assured him that he was entirely mistaken; I had never once attempted to prejudice his child against him.

'I did indeed desire him to *forget* you,' I said, 'and especially to forget the lessons you taught him; and for that cause, and to lessen the danger of discovery, I own I have generally discouraged his inclination to talk about you; but no one can blame me for that, I think.'

The invalid only replied by groaning aloud and rolling his head on the pillow in a paroxysm of impatience.

'I am in Hell already! cried he. 'This cursed thirst is burning my heart to ashes! Will *nobody* – '

Before he could finish the sentence, I had poured out a glass of some acidulated, cooling drink that was on the table, and brought it to him. He drank it greedily, but muttered, as I took away the glass – 'I suppose you're heaping coals of fire on my head – you think.'

Not noticing this speech, I asked if there was anything else I could do for him.

'Yes; I'll give you another opportunity of showing your Christian magnanimity,' sneered he – 'set my pillow straight – and these confounded bed-clothes.' I did so. 'There – now, get me another glass of that slop.' I complied. 'This is delightful! isn't it?' said he with a malicious grin, as I held it to his lips – 'You never hoped for such a glorious opportunity?'

'Now, shall I stay with you?' said I, as I replaced the glass on the table – 'or will you be more quiet if I go, and send the nurse?'

'Oh, yes, you're wondrous gentle and obliging! – But you've driven me mad with it all!' responded he, with an impatient toss.

'I'll leave you then,' said I, and I withdrew, and did not trouble him with my presence again that day, except for a minute or two at a time, just to see how he was and what he wanted.

Next morning, the doctor ordered him to be bled; and after that, he was more subdued and tranquil. I passed half the day in his room at different intervals. My presence did not appear to agitate or irritate him as before, and he accepted my services quietly, without any bitter remarks – indeed he scarcely spoke at all, except to make known his wants, and hardly then. But on the morrow – that is, today – in proportion as he recovered from the state of exhaustion and stupefaction – his ill-nature appeared to revive.

'Oh, this sweet revenge!' cried he, when I had been doing all I could to make

him comfortable and to remedy the carelessness of his nurse. 'And you can enjoy it with such a quiet conscience too, because it's all in the way of duty.'

'It is well for me that I *am* doing my duty,' said I, with a bitterness I could not repress, 'for it is the only comfort I have; and the satisfaction of my own conscience, it seems, is the only reward I need look for!'

He looked rather surprised at the earnestness of my manner.

'What reward *did* you look for?' he asked.

'You will think me a liar if I tell you – but I *did* hope to benefit you: as well to better your mind, as to alleviate your present sufferings; but it appears I am to do neither – your own bad spirit will not let me. As far as *you* are concerned, I have sacrificed my own feelings, and all the little earthly comfort that was left me, to no purpose; and every little thing I do for you is ascribed to self-righteous malice and refined revenge!'

'It's all very fine, I dare say,' said he, eyeing me with stupid amazement; 'and of course I ought to be melted to tears of penitence and admiration at the sight of so much generosity and superhuman goodness – but you see I can't manage it. However, pray do me all the good you can, if you do really find any pleasure in it; for you perceive I am almost as miserable just now as you need wish to see me. Since you came, I confess, I have had better attendance than before, for these wretches neglected me shamefully, and all my old friends seem to have fairly forsaken me. I've had a dreadful time of it, I assure you: I sometimes thought I should have died – do you think there's any chance?'

'There's always a chance of death; and it is always well to live with such a chance in view.'

'Yes, yes – but do you think there's any likelihood that this illness will have a fatal termination?'

'I cannot tell; but, supposing it should, how are you prepared to meet the event?'

'Why, the doctor told me I wasn't to think about it, for I was sure to get better, if I stuck to his regimen and prescriptions.'

'I hope you may, Arthur, but neither the doctor nor I can speak with certainty in such a case: there is internal injury, and it is difficult to know to what extent.'

'There now! You want to scare me to death.'

'No; but I don't want to lull you to false security. If a consciousness of the uncertainty of life can dispose you to serious and useful thoughts, I would not deprive you of the benefit of such reflections, whether you do eventually recover or not. Does the idea of death appal you *very* much?'

'It's just the only thing I can't bear to think of; so if you've any –'

'But it must come sometime,' interrupted I; 'and if it be years hence, it will as certainly overtake you as if it came today – and no doubt be as unwelcome then as now, unless you –'

'Oh, hang it! don't torment me with your preachments now, unless you want to kill me outright – I can't stand it, I tell you – I've sufferings enough without that. If you think there's danger, save me from it; and then, in gratitude, I'll hear whatever you like to say.'

I accordingly dropped the unwelcome topic. And now, Frederick, I think I may bring my letter to a close. From these details, you may form your own judgement of the state of my patient, and of my own position and future prospects. Let me hear from you soon, and I will write again to tell you how we get on; but now that my presence is tolerated – and even required in the sick-room, I shall have but little time to spare between my husband and my son – for I must not entirely neglect the latter: it would not do to keep him always with Rachel, and I dare not leave him for a moment with any of the other servants, or suffer him to be alone, lest he should meet them. If his father get worse, I shall ask Esther Hargrave to take charge of him for a time, till I have re-organised the household at least; but I greatly prefer keeping him under my own eye.

I find myself in rather a singular position: I am exerting my utmost endeavours to promote the recovery and reformation of my husband, and if I succeed what shall I do? My duty of course – but how? – No matter; I can perform the task that is before me now, and God will give me strength to do whatever He requires hereafter – Goodbye, dear Frederick.

HELEN HUNTINGDON

'What do you think of it?' said Lawrence as I silently refolded the letter.

'It seems to me,' returned I, 'that she is casting her pearls before swine. May they be satisfied with trampling them under their feet, and not turn again and rend her! But I shall say no more against her: I see that she was actuated by the best and noblest motives in what she has done; and if the act is not a wise one, may Heaven protect her from its consequences! May I keep this letter, Lawrence? – you see she has never once mentioned me throughout – or made the most distant allusion to me; therefore, there can be no impropriety or harm in it.'

'And, therefore, why should you wish to keep it?'

'Were not these characters written by her hand? And were not these words conceived in her mind, and many of them spoken by her lips?'

'Well,' said he. And so I kept it; otherwise, Halford, you could never have become so thoroughly acquainted with its contents.

'And when you write,' said I, 'will you have the goodness to ask her if I may be permitted to enlighten my mother and sister on her real history and circumstance, just so far as is necessary to make the neighbourhood sensible of the shameful injustice they have done her? I want no tender messages, but just ask her that, and tell her it is the greatest favour she could do me; and tell her – no, nothing more – You see I know the address, and I might write to her myself, but I am so virtuous as to refrain.'

'Well, I'll do this for you, Markham.'

'And as soon as you receive an answer, you'll let me know?'

'If all be well, I'll come myself and tell you, immediately.'

CHAPTER 48

## Further Intelligence

Five or six days after this, Mr Lawrence paid us the honour of a call; and when he and I were alone together – which I contrived as soon as possible, by bringing him out to look at my cornstacks – he showed me another letter from his sister. This one he was quite willing to submit to my longing gaze: he thought, I suppose, it would do me good. The only answer it gave to my message was this – 'Mr Markham is at liberty to make such revelations concerning me as he judges necessary. He will know that I should wish but little to be said on the subject. I hope he is well; but tell him he must not think of me.'

I can give you a few extracts from the rest of the letter, for I was permitted to keep this also – perhaps, as an antidote to all pernicious hopes and fancies.

* * *

He is decidedly better, but very low from the depressing effects of his severe illness and the strict regimen he is obliged to observe – so opposite to all his previous habits. It is deplorable to see how completely his past life has degenerated his once noble constitution, and vitiated the whole system of his organisation. But the doctor says he may now be considered out of danger, if he will only continue to observe the necessary restrictions. Some stimulating cordials he must have, but they should be judiciously diluted and sparingly used; and I find it very difficult to keep him to this. At first, his extreme dread of death rendered the task an easy one; but in proportion as he feels his acute suffering abating and sees the danger receding, the more intractable he becomes. Now also, his appetite for food is beginning to return; and here too, his long habits of self-indulgence are greatly against him. I watch and restrain him as well as I can, and often get bitterly abused for my rigid severity; and sometimes he contrives to elude my vigilance, and sometimes acts in open opposition to my will. But he is now so completely reconciled to my attendance in general that he is never satisfied when I am not by his side. I am obliged to be a little stiff with him sometimes, or he would make a complete slave of me; and I know it would be unpardonable weakness to give up all other interests for him. I have the servants to overlook and my little Arthur to attend to – and my own health too, all of which would be entirely neglected were I to satisfy his exorbitant demands. I do not generally sit up at nights, for I think the nurse who has made it her business, is better qualified for such undertakings than I am; but still, an unbroken night's rest is what I but seldom enjoy, and never can venture to reckon upon; for my patient makes no scruple of calling me up at any hour when his wants or his fancies require my presence. But he is manifestly afraid of my displeasure; and if at one time he tries my patience by his unreasonable exactions, and fretful

complaints and reproaches, at another, he depresses me by his abject submission and deprecatory self-abasement when he fears he has gone too far. But all this I can readily pardon; I know it is chiefly the result of his enfeebled frame and disordered nerves – what annoys me the most, is his occasional attempts at affectionate fondness that I can neither credit nor return; not that I hate him: his sufferings and my own laborious care have given him some claim to my regard – to my affection even, if he would only be quiet and sincere, and content to let things remain as they are, but the more he tries to conciliate me the more I shrink from him and from the future.

'Helen, what do you mean to do when I get well?' he asked this morning. 'Will you run away again?'

'It entirely depends upon your own conduct.'

'Oh, I'll be very good.'

'But if I find it necessary to leave you, Arthur, I shall not "run away": you know I have your own promise that I may go whenever I please, and take my son with me.'

'Oh, but you shall have no cause.' And then followed a variety of professions, which I rather coldly checked.

'Will you not forgive me then?' said he.

'Yes – I *have* forgiven you; but I know you cannot love me as you once did – and I should be very sorry if you were to, for I could not pretend to return it: so let us drop the subject, and never recur to it again. By what I *have* done for you, you may judge of what I *will* do – if it be not incompatible with the higher duty I owe to my son (higher, because he never forfeited his claims, and because I hope to do more good to him than I can ever do to you): and if you wish me to feel kindly towards you, it is *deeds* not *words* that must purchase my affection and esteem.'

His sole reply to this was a slight grimace, and a scarcely perceptible shrug. Alas unhappy man! Words, with him, are so much cheaper than deeds; it was as if I had said, 'Pounds, not pence, must buy the article you want.' And then he sighed a querulous, self-commiserating sigh, as if in pure regret that he, the loved and courted of so many worshippers, should be now abandoned to the mercy of a harsh, exacting, cold-hearted woman like that, and even glad of what kindness she chose to bestow.

'It's a pity, isn't it?' said I; and whether I rightly divined his musings or not, the observation chimed in with his thoughts, for he answered – 'It can't be helped,' with a rueful smile at my penetration.

I have seen Esther Hargrave twice. She is a charming creature, but her blithe spirit is almost broken, and her sweet temper almost spoiled, by the still unremitting persecutions of her mother, in behalf of her rejected suitor – not violent, but wearisome and unremitting like a continual dropping. The unnatural parent seems determined to make her daughter's life a burden if she will not yield to her desires.

'Mamma does all she can,' said she, 'to make me feel myself a burden and

encumbrance to the family, and the most ungrateful, selfish, and undutiful daughter that ever was born; and Walter, too, is as stern and cold, and haughty as if he hated me outright. I believe I should have yielded at once if I had known, from the beginning, how much resistance would have cost me; but now, for very obstinacy's sake, I *will* stand out!'

'A bad motive for a good resolve,' I answered. 'But, however, I know you have better motives, really, for your perseverance: and I counsel you to keep them still in view.'

'Trust me, I will. I threaten mamma sometimes, that I'll run away, and disgrace the family by earning my own livelihood, if she torments me any more; and then that frightens her a little. But I *will* do it, in good earnest, if they don't mind.'

'Be quiet and patient awhile,' said I, 'and better times will come.'

Poor girl! I wish somebody that was worthy to possess her would come and take her away – don't you, Frederick?

\* \* \*

If the perusal of this letter filled me with dismay for Helen's future life and mine, there was one great source of consolation: it was now in my power to clear her name from every foul aspersion. The Millwards and the Wilsons should see with their own eyes, the bright sun bursting from the cloud – and they should be scorched and dazzled by its beams; and my own friends too should see it – they whose suspicions had been such a gall and wormwood to my soul. To effect this, I had only to drop the seed into the ground, and it would soon become a stately, branching herb: a few words to my mother and sister, I knew, would suffice to spread the news throughout the whole neighbourhood, without any further exertion on my part.

Rose was delighted; and as soon as I had told her all I thought proper which was all I affected to know – she flew with alacrity to put on her bonnet and shawl, and hasten to carry the glad tidings to the Millwards and Wilsons – glad tidings I suspect, to none but herself and Mary Millward – that steady, sensible girl, whose sterling worth had been so quickly perceived and duly valued by the supposed Mrs Graham, in spite of her plain outside; and who, on her part, had been better able to see and appreciate the lady's true character and qualities than the brightest genius among them.

As I may never have occasion to mention her again, I may as well tell you here, that she was at this time privately engaged to Richard Wilson – a secret, I believe to everyone but their two selves. That worthy student was now at Cambridge, where his most exemplary conduct and his diligent perseverance in the pursuit of learning carried him safely through, and eventually brought him with hard-earned honours and an untarnished reputation, to the close of his collegiate career. In due time, he became Mr Millward's first and only curate – for that gentleman's declining years forced him at last to acknowledge that the duties of his extensive parish were a little too much for those vaunted energies which he was wont to boast over his younger and less active brethren of the cloth. This was

what the patient, faithful lovers had privately planned, and quietly waited for years ago; and in due time they were united, to the astonishment of the little world they lived in, that had long since declared them both born of single blessedness; affirming it impossible that the pale, retiring bookworm should ever summon courage to seek a wife, or be able to obtain one if he did, and equally impossible that the plain-looking, plain-dealing, unattractive, unconciliating Miss Millward should ever find a husband.

They still continued to live at the vicarage, the lady dividing her time between her father, her husband, and their poor parishioners – and subsequently, her rising family; and now that the Reverend Michael Millward has been gathered to his fathers, full of years and honours, the Reverend Richard Wilson has succeeded him to the vicarage of Lindenhope, greatly to the satisfaction of its inhabitants, who had so long tried and fully proved his merits, and those of his excellent and well-loved partner.

If you are interested in the after fate of that lady's sister, I can only tell you – what perhaps you have heard from another quarter – that some twelve or thirteen years ago, she relieved the happy couple of her presence by marrying a wealthy tradesman of L—; and I don't envy him his bargain. I fear she leads him a rather uncomfortable life, though, happily he is too dull to perceive the extent of his misfortune. I have little enough to do with her myself: we have not met for many years; but, I am well assured, she has not yet forgotten or forgiven either her former lover or the lady whose superior qualities first opened his eyes to the folly of his boyish attachment.

As for Richard Wilson's sister, she, having been wholly unable to recapture Mr Lawrence or obtain any partner rich and elegant enough to suit her ideas of what the husband of Jane Wilson ought to be, is yet in single blessedness. Shortly after the death of her mother, she withdrew the light of her presence from Ryecote Farm, finding it impossible any longer to endure the rough manners and unsophisticated habits of her honest brother Robert and his worthy wife, or the idea of being identified with such vulgar people in the eyes of the world – and took lodgings in — the county town, where she lived, and still lives, I suppose, in a kind of close-fisted, cold, uncomfortable gentility, doing no good to others and but little to herself; spending her days in fancy-work and scandal; referring frequently to her 'brother the vicar' and her 'sister the vicar's lady', but never to her brother the farmer and her sister the farmer's wife; seeing as much company as she can without too much expense, but loving no one and beloved by none – a cold-hearted, supercilious, keenly, insidiously censorious old maid.

## CHAPTER 49

### 'The rain descended, and the floods came, and the winds blew, and beat upon the house; and it fell: and great was the fall of it.'

Though Mr Lawrence's health was now quite re-established, my visits to Woodford were as unremitting as ever; though often less protracted than before. We seldom *talked* about Mrs Huntingdon; but yet we never met without mentioning her, for I never sought his company but with the hope of hearing something about her, and he never sought mine at all, because he saw me often enough without. But I always began to talk of other things, and waited first to see if *he* would introduce the subject. If he did not, I would casually ask, 'Have you heard from your sister lately?' If he said, 'No,' the matter was dropped: if he said 'Yes,' I would venture to enquire, 'How is she?' but never 'How is her husband?' though I might be burning to know; because, I had not the hypocrisy to profess any anxiety for his recovery, and I had not the face to express any desire for a contrary result. Had I any such desire? – I fear I must plead guilty: but since you have heard my confession, you must hear my justification as well – a few of the excuses, at least, wherewith I sought to pacify my own accusing conscience – In the first place, you see, his life did harm to others, and evidently no good to himself; and though I wished it to terminate, I would not have hastened its close if, by the lifting of a finger, I could have done so, or if a spirit had whispered in my ear that a single effort of the will would be enough – unless, indeed, I had the power to exchange him for some other victim of the grave, whose life might be of service to his race, and whose death would be lamented by his friends. But was there any harm in wishing that, among the many thousands whose souls would certainly be required of them before the year was over, this wretched mortal might be one? I thought not; and therefore I wished with all my heart that it might please Heaven to remove him to a better world, or if that might not be, still, to take him out of this, for if he were unfit to answer the summons now, after a warning sickness, and with such an angel by his side, it seemed but too certain that he never would be – that, on the contrary, returning health would bring returning lust and villainy, and as he grew more certain of recovery, more accustomed to her generous goodness, his feelings would become more callous, his heart more flinty and impervious to her persuasive arguments – but God knew best. Meantime, however, I could not but be anxious for the result of His decrees; knowing, as I did, that (leaving myself entirely out of the question) however Helen might feel interested in her husband's welfare, however she might deplore his fate, still, while he lived, she *must* be miserable.

A fortnight passed away, and my enquiries were always answered in the negative. At length a welcome 'yes' drew from me the second question. Lawrence

divined my anxious thoughts, and appreciated my reserve. I feared at first, he was going to torture me by unsatisfactory replies, and either leave me quite in the dark concerning what I wanted to know, or force me to drag the information out of him, morsel by morsel, by direct enquiries – 'and serve you right,' you will say; but he was more merciful; and in a little while, he put his sister's letter into my hand. I silently read it, and restored it to him without comment or remark. This mode of procedure suited him so well that thereafter he always pursued the plan of showing me her letters at once, when I enquired after her, if there were any to show: it was so much less trouble than to tell me their contents; and I received such confidences so quietly and discreetly that he was never induced to discontinue them.

But I devoured those precious letters with my eyes, and never let them go till their contents were stamped upon my mind; and when I got home, the most important passages were entered in my diary among the remarkable events of the day.

The first of these communications brought intelligence of a serious relapse in Mr Huntingdon's illness, entirely the result of his own infatuation in persisting in the indulgence of his appetite for stimulating drink. In vain had she remonstrated, in vain she had mingled his wine with water: her arguments and entreaties were a nuisance, her interference was an insult so intolerable that at length, on finding she had covertly diluted the pale port that was brought him, he threw the bottle out of the window, swearing he would not be cheated like a baby, ordered the butler, on pain of instant dismissal, to bring a bottle of the strongest wine in the cellar, and affirming that he should have been well long ago if he had been let to have his own way, but she wanted to keep him weak in order that she might have him under her thumb – but by the Lord Harry, he would have no more humbug – seized a glass in one hand and the bottle in the other, and never rested till he had drunk it dry. Alarming symptoms were the immediate result of this 'imprudence' as she mildly termed it – symptoms which had rather increased than diminished since; and this was the cause of her delay in writing to her brother. Every former feature of his malady had returned with augmented virulence: the slight external wound, half-healed, had broken out afresh; internal inflammation had taken place, which might terminate fatally if not soon removed. Of course, the wretched sufferer's temper was not improved by this calamity – in fact, I suspect it was wellnigh insupportable, though his kind nurse did not complain; but she said she had been obliged, at last, to give her son in charge to Esther Hargrave, as her presence was so constantly required in the sick-room that she could not possibly attend to him herself; and though the child had begged to be allowed to continue with her there, and to help her to nurse his papa, and though she had no doubt he would have been very good and quiet – she could not think of subjecting his young and tender feelings to the sight of so much suffering, or of allowing him to witness his father's impatience, or hear the dreadful language he was wont to use in his paroxysms of pain or irritation.

'The latter,' continued she, 'most deeply regrets the step that has occasioned his relapse – but, as usual, he throws the blame upon me. If I had reasoned with him like a rational creature, he says, it never would have happened; but to be

treated like a baby or a fool, was enough to put any man past his patience, and drive him to assert his independence even at the sacrifice of his own interest – he forgets how often I had *reasoned* him "past his patience" before. He appears to be sensible of his danger; but nothing can induce him to behold it in the proper light. The other night while I was waiting on him, and just as I had brought him a draught to assuage his burning thirst – he observed, with a return of his former sarcastic bitterness – ' "Yes, you're mighty attentive *now*! – I suppose there's *nothing* you wouldn't do for me now?"

' "You know," said I, a little surprised at his manner, " 'that I am willing to do anything I can to relieve you."

' "Yes, *now*, my immaculate angel; but when once you have secured your regard, and find yourself safe in Heaven, and me howling in Hell-fire, catch you lifting a finger to serve me *then*! – No, you'll look complacently on, and not so much as dip the tip of your finger in water to cool my tongue!"

' "If so, it will be because of the great gulf over which I cannot pass; and if I *could* look complacently on in such a case, it would be only from the assurance that you were being purified from your sins, and fitted to enjoy the happiness I felt. But are you *determined*, Arthur, that I shall not meet you in Heaven?"

' "Humph! What should I do there, I should like to know?"

' "Indeed, I cannot tell; and I fear it is too certain that your tastes and feelings must be widely altered before you can have any enjoyment there. But do you prefer sinking, without an effort, into the state of torment you picture to yourself?"

' "Oh, it's all a fable," said he, contemptuously,

' "Are you sure, Arthur? are you *quite* sure? Because if there is any doubt, and if you *should* find yourself mistaken after all, when it is too late to turn – "

' "It would be rather awkward, to be sure," said he; "but don't bother me now – I'm not going to die yet – I can't and won't," he added vehemently, as if suddenly struck with the appalling aspect of that terrible event, "Helen, you must save me!" And he earnestly seized my hand, and looked into my face with such imploring eagerness that my heart bled for him, and I could not speak for tears.'

The next letter brought intelligence that the malady was fast increasing; and the poor sufferer's horror of death was still more distressing than his impatience of bodily pain. *All* his friends had not forsaken him, for Mr Hattersley, hearing of his danger, had come to see him from his distant home in the north. His wife had accompanied him, as much for the pleasure of seeing her dear friend, from whom she had been parted *so* long, as to visit her mother and sister.

Mrs Huntingdon expressed herself glad to see Milicent once more, and pleased to behold her so happy and well. 'She is now at the Grove,' continued the letter, 'but she often calls to see me. Mr Hattersley spends much of his time at Arthur's bedside. With more good feeling than I gave him credit for, he evinces considerable sympathy for his unhappy friend, and is far more willing than able to comfort him. Sometimes he tries to joke and laugh with him, but that will not do; sometimes he endeavours to cheer him with talk about old

times: and this, at one time, may serve to divert the sufferer from his own sad thoughts; at another it will only plunge him into deeper melancholy than before; and then Hattersley is confounded, and knows not what to say – unless it be a timid suggestion that the clergyman might be sent for. But Arthur will never consent to that: he knows he has rejected the clergyman's well-meant admonitions with scoffing levity at other times, and cannot dream of turning to him for consolation now.

'Mr Hattersley sometimes offers his services instead of mine, but Arthur will not let me go: that strange whim still increases, as his strength declines – the fancy to have me always by his side. I hardly ever leave him except to go into the next room, where I sometimes snatch an hour or so of sleep when he is quiet; but even then, the door is left ajar that he may know me to be within call. I am with him now, while I write; and I fear my occupation annoys him; though I frequently break off to attend to him, and though Mr Hattersley is also by his side. That gentleman came, as he said, to beg a holiday for me, that I might have a run in the park, this fine, frosty morning, with Milicent, and Esther, and little Arthur, whom he had driven over to see me. Our poor invalid evidently felt it a heartless proposition, and would have felt it still more heartless in me to accede to it. I therefore said I would only go and speak to them a minute, and then come back. I did but exchange a few words with them, just outside the portico – inhaling the fresh, bracing air as I stood – and then, resisting the earnest and eloquent entreaties of all three to stay a little longer, and join them in a walk round the garden – I tore myself away and returned to my patient. I had not been absent five minutes, but he reproached me bitterly for my levity and neglect. His friend espoused my cause – ' "Nay, nay, Huntingdon," said he, "you're too hard upon her – she must have food and sleep, and a mouthful of fresh air now and then, or she can't stand it, I tell you. Look at her, man, she's worn to a shadow already."

' "What are her sufferings to mine?" said the poor invalid. "You don't grudge me these attentions, do you, Helen?"

' "No, Arthur, if I could really serve you by them. I would give my life to save you, if I might."

' "Would you *indeed*? – No!"

' "Most willingly, I would."

' "Ah! that's because you think yourself more fit to die!"

'There was a painful pause. He was evidently plunged in gloomy reflections, but while I pondered for something to say, that might benefit without alarming him, Hattersley, whose mind had been pursuing almost the same course, broke silence with – ' "I say, Huntingdon, I *would* send for a parson, of some sort – If you didn't like the vicar, you know, you could have his curate, or somebody else."

' "No; none of them can benefit me if *she* can't," was the answer. And the tears gushed from his eyes as he earnestly exclaimed – "Oh, Helen, if I had listened to you, it never would have come to this! And if I had heard you long ago – oh, God! how different it would have been!"

' "Hear me now, then, Arthur," said I, gently pressing his hand.

' "It's too late now," said he despondently. And after that another paroxysm of pain came on; and then his mind began to wander, and we feared his death was approaching; but an opiate was administered, his sufferings began to abate, he gradually became more composed, and at length sank into a kind of slumber. He has been quieter since; and now Hattersley has left him, expressing a hope that he shall find him better when he calls tomorrow.

' "Perhaps, I *may* recover," he replied, "who knows? – This may have been the crisis. What do *you* think, Helen?"

'Unwilling to depress him, I gave the most cheering answer I could, but still recommended him to prepare for the possibility of what I inly feared was but too certain. But he was determined to hope. Shortly after, he relapsed into a kind of doze – but now he groans again.

'There is a change. Suddenly he called me to his side, with such a strange, excited manner that I feared he was delirious – but he was not. "That *was* the crisis, Helen!" said he delightedly – "I had an infernal pain here – it is quite gone now; I never was so easy since the fall – Quite gone, by Heaven!" and he clasped and kissed my hand in the very fullness of his heart; but, finding I did not participate his joy, he quickly flung it from him, and bitterly cursed my coldness and insensibility. How could I reply? Kneeling beside him, I took his hand and fondly pressed it to my lips – for the first time since our separation – and told him as well as tears would let me speak, that it was not *that* that kept me silent; it was the fear that this sudden cessation of pain was not so favourable a symptom as he supposed – I immediately sent for the doctor. We are now anxiously awaiting him: I will tell you what he says. There is still the same freedom from pain – the same deadness to all sensation where the suffering was most acute.

'My worst fears are realised – mortification has commenced. The doctor has told him there is no hope – no words can describe his anguish – I can write no more.'

The next was still more distressing in the tenor of its contents. The sufferer was fast approaching dissolution – dragged almost to the verge of that awful chasm he trembled to contemplate, from which no agony of prayers or tears could save him. Nothing could comfort him now: Hattersley's rough attempts at consolation were utterly in vain. The world was nothing to him: life and all its interests, its petty cares and transient pleasures were a cruel mockery. To talk of the past, was to torture him with vain remorse; to refer to the future, was to increase his anguish; and yet to be silent, was to leave him a prey to his own regrets and apprehensions. Often he dwelt with shuddering minuteness on the fate of his perishing clay – the slow, piecemeal dissolution already invading his frame; the shroud, the coffin, the dark, lonely grave, and all the horrors of corruption.

'If I try,' said his afflicted wife, 'to divert him from these things – to raise his thoughts to higher themes, it is no better – "Worse and worse!" he groans. "If there be really life beyond the tomb, and judgement after death how *can* I face it?" – I cannot do him any good; he will neither be enlightened, nor roused,

nor comforted by anything I say; and yet he clings to me with unrelenting pertinacity – with a kind of childish desperation, as if *I* could save him from the fate he dreads. He keeps me night and day beside him. He is holding my left hand now, while I write; he has held it thus for hours: sometimes quietly, with his pale face upturned to mine: sometimes clutching my arm with violence – the big drops starting from his forehead, at the thoughts of what he sees, or thinks he sees before him. If I withdraw my hand for a moment, it distresses him – ' "Stay with me, Helen," he says; "let me hold you so: it seems as if harm could not reach me while you are here. But death *will* come – it is coming now – fast, fast! – and – oh, if I *could* believe there was nothing after!"

' "Don't try to believe it, Arthur; there is joy and glory after, if you will but try to reach it!"

' "What, for *me*?" he said, with something like a laugh. "Are we not to be judged according to the deeds done in the body? Where's the use of a prob-ationary existence, if a man may spend it as he pleases, just contrary to God's decrees, and then go to Heaven with the best – if the vilest sinner may win the reward of the holiest saint, by merely saying, "I repent – "

' "But if you *sincerely* repent – "

' "I *can't* repent; I only fear."

' "You only regret the past for its consequences to yourself?"

' "Just so – except that I'm sorry to have wronged you Nell, because you're so good to me."

' "Think of the goodness of God, and you cannot but be grieved to have offended Him."

' "What *is* God – I cannot see Him or hear Him? – God is only an idea."

' "God is Infinite Wisdom, and Power, and Goodness – and LOVE; but if this idea is too vast for your human faculties – if your mind loses itself in its overwhelming infinitude, fix it on Him who condescended to take our nature upon Him, who was raised to Heaven even in His glorified human body, in whom the fullness of the godhead shines." '

'But he only shook his head and sighed. Then, in another paroxysm of shuddering horror, he tightened his grasp on my hand and arm, and groaning and lamenting, still clung to me with that wild, desperate earnestness so harrowing to my soul, because I know I cannot help him. I did my best to sooth and comfort him.

' "Death is so terrible," he cried, "I cannot bear it! *You* don't know, Helen – you can't imagine what it is, because you haven't it before you; and when I'm buried, you'll return to your old ways and be as happy as ever, and all the world will go on just as busy and merry as if I had never been; while I – " He burst into tears.

' "You needn't let *that* distress you," I said; "we shall all follow you soon enough."

' "I wish to God I could take you with me now!" he exclaimed, "you should plead for me."

' "No man can deliver his brother, nor make agreement unto God for him," I

replied: "it cost more to redeem their souls – it cost the blood of an incarnate God, perfect and sinless in Himself, to redeem us from the bondage of the evil one; let *Him* plead for you."

'But I seem to speak in vain. He does not now, as formerly, laugh these blessed truths to scorn: but still he cannot trust, or will not comprehend them. He cannot linger long. He suffers dreadfully, and so do those that wait upon him – but I will not harass you with further details: I have said enough, I think, to convince you that I did well to go to him.'

\* \* \*

Poor, poor Helen! Dreadful indeed her trials must have been! And I could do nothing to lessen them – nay, it almost seemed as if I had brought them upon her myself, by my own secret desires; and whether I looked at her husband's sufferings or her own, it seemed almost like a judgement upon myself for having cherished such a wish.

The next day but one, there came another letter. That too was put into my hands without a remark, and these are its contents –

*December 5th*

He is gone at last. I sat beside him all night, with my hand fast locked in his, watching the changes of his features and listening to his failing breath. He had been silent a long time, and I thought he would never speak again, when he murmured, faintly but distinctly – 'Pray for me, Helen!'

'I do pray for you – every hour and every minute, Arthur; but you must pray for yourself.'

His lips moved, but emitted no sound; then his looks became unsettled; and, from the incoherent, half-uttered words that escaped him from time to time, supposing him to be now unconscious, I gently disengaged my hand from his, intending to steal away for a breath of fresh air, for I was almost ready to faint; but a convulsive movement of his fingers, and a faintly whispered "Don't leave me!" immediately recalled me: I took his hand again, and held it till he was no more – and then I fainted: it was not grief; it was exhaustion that, till then, I had been enabled successfully to combat. Oh, Frederick! None can imagine the miseries, bodily and mental, of that deathbed! How could I endure to think that that poor trembling soul was hurried away to everlasting torment? It would drive me mad! But thank God I have hope – not only from a vague dependence on the possibility that penitence and pardon might have reached him at the last, but from the blessed confidence that, through whatever purging fires the erring spirit may be doomed to pass – whatever fate awaits it, still, it is not lost, and God, who hateth nothing that He hath made, *will* bless it in the end!

His body will be consigned on Thursday to that dark grave he so much dreaded; but the coffin must be closed as soon as possible. If you will attend the funeral come quickly, for I need help.

HELEN HUNTINGDON

## CHAPTER 50

### *Doubts and Disappointments*

On reading this, I had no reason to disguise my joy and hope from Frederick Lawrence, for I had none to be ashamed of. I felt no joy but that his sister was at length released from her afflictive, overwhelming toil – no hope but that she would in time recover from the effects of it, and be suffered to rest in peace and quietness, at least, for the remainder of her life. I experienced a painful commiseration for her unhappy husband (though fully aware that he had brought every particle of his sufferings upon himself, and but too well deserved them all), and a profound sympathy for her own afflictions, and deep anxiety for the consequences of those harassing cares, those dreadful vigils, that incessant and deleterious confinement beside a living corpse – for I was persuaded she had not hinted half the sufferings she had had to endure.

'You will go to her, Lawrence?' said I, as I put the letter into his hand.

'Yes, immediately.'

'That's right! I'll leave you, then, to prepare for your departure.

'I've done that, already, while you were reading the letter, and before you came; and the carriage is now coming round to the door.'

Inly approving his promptitude, I bade him good-morning, and withdrew. He gave me a searching glance as we pressed each other's hands at parting; but whatever he sought in my countenance, he saw there nothing but the most becoming gravity, it might be, mingled with a little sternness in momentary resentment at what I suspected to be passing in his mind.

Had I forgotten my own prospects, my ardent love, my pertinacious hopes? It seemed like sacrilege to revert to them now, but I had not forgotten them. It was, however, with a gloomy sense of the darkness of those prospects, the fallacy of those hopes, and the vanity of that affection, that I reflected on those things as I remounted my horse and slowly journeyed homewards. Mrs Huntingdon was free now; it was no longer a crime to think of her – but did she ever think of *me*? – Not *now* – of course it was not to be expected – but would she when this shock was over? – In all the course of her correspondence with her brother (our mutual friend, as she herself had called him), she had never mentioned me but once – and that was from necessity. This, alone, afforded strong presumption that I was already forgotten; yet this was not the worst: it might have been her sense of duty that had kept her silent, she might be only *trying* to forget; but in addition to this, I had a gloomy conviction that the awful realities she had seen and felt, her reconciliation with the man she had once loved, his dreadful sufferings and death, must eventually efface from her mind all traces of her passing love for me. She might recover from these horrors so far as to be restored to her former health, her tranquillity, her cheerfulness

even – but never to those feelings which would appear to her, henceforth, as a fleeting fancy, a vain, illusive dream; especially as there was no one to remind her of my existence – no means of assuring her of my fervent constancy now that we were so far apart, and delicacy forbade me to see her or to write to her, for months to come at least. And how could I engage her brother in my behalf? How could I break that icy crust of shy reserve? Perhaps he would disapprove of my attachment now, as highly as before; perhaps he would think me too poor – too lowly born, to match with his sister. Yes, there was another barrier: doubtless there was a wide distinction between the rank and circumstances of Mrs Huntingdon, the lady of Grassdale Manor, and those of Mrs Graham the artist, the tenant of Wildfell Hall; and it might be deemed presumption in me to offer my hand to the former – by the world, by her friends – if not by herself – a penalty I might brave, if I were certain she loved me; but otherwise, how could I? And finally, her deceased husband, with his usual selfishness, might have so constructed his will as to place restrictions upon her marrying again. So that you see I had reasons enough for despair if I chose to indulge it.

Nevertheless, it was with no small degree of impatience that I looked forward to Mr Lawrence's return from Grassdale – impatience that increased in proportion as his absence was prolonged. He stayed away some ten or twelve days. All very right that he should remain to comfort and help his sister, but he might have written to tell me how she was – or at least to tell me when to expect his return; for he might have known I was suffering tortures of anxiety for her, and uncertainty for my own future prospects. And when he did return, all he told me about her, was that she had been greatly exhausted and worn by her unremitting exertions in behalf of that man who had been the scourge of her life, and had dragged her with him nearly to the portals of the grave – and was still much shaken and depressed by his melancholy end and the circumstances attendant upon it; but no word in reference to me – no intimation that my name had ever passed her lips, or even been spoken in her presence. To be sure, I asked no questions on the subject: I could not bring my mind to do so, believing, as I did, that Lawrence was indeed averse to the idea of my union with his sister.

I saw that he expected to be further questioned concerning his visit, and I saw too, with the keen perception of awakened jealousy, or alarmed self-esteem – or by whatever name I ought to call it – that he rather shrank from that impending scrutiny, and was no less pleased than surprised to find it did not come. Of course, I was burning with anger, but pride obliged me to suppress my feelings, and preserve a smooth face – or at least, a stoic calmness throughout the interview. It was well it did, for, reviewing the matter in my sober judgement, I must say it would have been highly absurd and improper to have quarrelled with him on such an occasion: I must confess too that I wronged him in my heart: the truth was, he liked me very well, but he was fully aware that a union between Mrs Huntingdon and me would be what the world calls a *mésalliance*; and it was not in his nature to set the world at defiance; especially in such a case as this, for its dread laugh, or ill opinion, would be far more terrible to him directed against

his sister than himself. Had he believed that a union was necessary to the happiness of both, or of either, or had he known how fervently I loved her, he would have acted differently; but seeing me so calm and cool, he would not for the world disturb my philosophy; and though refraining entirely from any active opposition to the match he would yet do nothing to bring it about, and would much rather take the part of prudence, in aiding us to overcome our mutual predilections, than that of feeling, to encourage them. 'And he was in the right of it,' you will say. Perhaps he was – at any rate, I had no business to feel so bitterly against him as I did; but I could not then regard the matter in such a moderate light; and, after a brief conversation upon indifferent topics, I went away, suffering all the pangs of wounded pride and injured friendship, in addition to those resulting from the fear that I was indeed forgotten, and the knowledge that she I loved was alone and afflicted, suffering from injured health and dejected spirits, and I was forbidden to console or assist her – forbidden even to assure her of my sympathy, for the transmission of any such message through Mr Lawrence was now completely out of the question.

But what should I do? I would wait, and see if she would notice me – which of course she would not, unless by some kind message entrusted to her brother, that, in all probability, he would not deliver, and then – dreadful thought! – she would think me cooled and changed for not returning it – or perhaps, he had already given her to understand that I had ceased to think of her! I would wait, however, till the six months after our parting were fairly passed (which would be about the close of February), and then I would send her a letter modestly reminding her of her former permission to write to her at the close of that period and hoping I might avail myself of it at least to express my heart-felt sorrow for her late afflictions, my just appreciation of her generous conduct, and my hope that her health was now completely re-established, and that she would, sometime, be permitted to enjoy those blessings of a peaceful, happy life, which had been denied her so long, but which none could more truly be said to merit than herself – adding a few words of kind remembrance to my little friend Arthur, with a hope that he had not forgotten me, and, perhaps, a few more in reference to bygone times – to the delightful hours I had passed in her society, and my unfading recollection of them, which was the salt and solace of my life – and a hope that her recent troubles had not entirely banished me from her mind. If she did not answer this, of course I should write no more: if she did (as surely she would, in *some* fashion) my future proceedings should be regulated by her reply.

Ten weeks was long to wait in such a miserable state of uncertainty, but courage! It must be endured; and meantime I would continue to see Lawrence now and then, though not so often as before, and I would still pursue my habitual enquiries after his sister – if he had lately heard from her, and how she was, but nothing more.

I did so, and the answers I received were always provokingly limited to the letter of the enquiry: She was much as usual: She made no complaints, but the tone of her last letter evinced great depression of mind: She said she was better:

and, finally: She said she was well, and very busy with her son's education, and with the management of her late husband's property and the regulation of his affairs. The rascal had never told me how that property was disposed, or whether Mr Huntingdon had died intestate or not; and I would sooner die than ask him, lest he should misconstrue into covetousness my desire to know. He never offered to show me his sister's letters now; and I never hinted a wish to see them. February, however, was approaching; December was past, January, at length, was almost over – a few more weeks, and then, certain despair or renewal of hope would put an end to this long agony of suspense.

But alas! it was just about that time she was called to sustain another blow in the death of her uncle – a worthless old fellow enough, in himself, I dare say, but he had always shown more kindness and affection to her than to any other creature, and she had always been accustomed to regard him as a parent. She was with him when he died, and had assisted her aunt to nurse him during the last stage of his illness. Her brother went to Staningley to attend the funeral, and told me, upon his return, that she was still there, endeavouring to cheer her aunt with her presence, and likely to remain some time. This was bad news for me, for while she continued there, I could not write to her, as I did not know the address, and would not ask it of him. But week followed week, and every time I enquired about her she was still at Staningley.

'Where *is* Staningley?' I asked at last.

'In —shire,' was the brief reply: and there was something so cold and dry in the manner of it, that I was effectually deterred from requesting a more definite account.

'When will she return to Grassdale?' was my next question.

'I don't know.'

'Confound it!' I muttered.

'Why, Markham?' asked my companion, with an air of innocent surprise. But I did not deign to answer him, save by a look of silent, sullen contempt, at which he turned away, and contemplated the carpet with a slight smile, half pensive, half amused; but quickly looking up, he began to talk of other subjects, trying to draw me into a cheerful and friendly conversation; but I was too much irritated to discourse with him, and soon took leave.

You see Lawrence and I somehow could not manage to get on very well together. The fact is, I believe, we were both of us a little too touchy. It is a troublesome thing, Halford, this susceptibility to affronts where none are intended. I am no martyr to it now, as you can bear me witness: I have learned to be merry and wise, to be more easy with myself and more indulgent to my neighbours, and I can afford to laugh at both Lawrence and you.

Partly from accident, partly from wilful negligence on my part (for I was really beginning to dislike him), several weeks elapsed before I saw my friend again. When we did meet, it was *he* that sought *me* out. One bright morning early in June, he came into the field where I was just commencing my hay harvest.

'It is long since I saw you, Markham,' said he after the first few words had passed between us. 'Do you never mean to come to Woodford again?'

'I called once, and you were out.'

'I was sorry: but that was long since; I hoped you would call again; and now, *I* have called, and *you* were out – which you generally are, or I would do myself the pleasure of calling more frequently – but being determined to see you this time, I have left my pony in the lane, and come over hedge and ditch to join you; for I am about to leave Woodford for a while, and may not have the pleasure of seeing you again for a month or two.'

'Where are you going?'

'To Grassdale first,' said he, with a half-smile he would willingly have suppressed if he could.

'To Grassdale! Is she there, then?'

'Yes, but in a day or two she will leave it to accompany Mrs Maxwell to F— for the benefit of the sea air; and I shall go with them.' (F— was at that time a quiet but respectable watering place: it is considerably more frequented now.)

Lawrence seemed to expect me to take advantage of this circumstance to entrust him with some sort of a message to his sister; and I believe he would have undertaken to deliver it without any material objections, if I had had the sense to ask him, though of course he would not *offer* to do so, if I was content to let it alone. But I could not bring myself to make the request; and it was not till after he was gone, that I saw how fair an opportunity I had lost; and then, indeed, I deeply regretted my stupidity and my foolish pride; but it was now too late to remedy the evil.

He did not return till towards the latter end of August. He wrote to me twice or thrice from F—; but his letters were most provokingly unsatisfactory, dealing in generalities or in trifles that I cared nothing about, or replete with fancies and reflections equally unwelcome to me at the time – saying next to nothing about his sister, and little more about himself. I would wait, however, till he came back: perhaps I could get something more out of him then. At all events, I would not write to her now, while she was with him and her aunt, who doubtless would be still more hostile to my presumptuous aspirations than himself. When she was returned to the silence and solitude of her own home it would be my fittest opportunity.

When Lawrence came, however, he was as reserved as ever on the subject of my keen anxiety. He told me that his sister had derived considerable benefit from her stay at F—, that her son was quite well, and – alas! that both of them were gone, with Mrs Maxwell, back to Staningley; and there they stayed at least three months But instead of boring you with my chagrin, my expectations and disappointments, my fluctuations of dull despondency and flickering hope, my varying resolutions, now to drop it, and now to persevere – now to make a bold push and now to let things pass and patiently abide my time – I will employ myself in settling the business of one or two of the characters, introduced in the course of this narrative, whom I may not have occasion to mention again.

Sometime before Mr Huntingdon's death, Lady Lowborough eloped with another gallant to the continent, where, having lived awhile in reckless gaiety and dissipation, they quarrelled and parted. She went dashing on for a season,

but years came and money went: she sunk, at length, in difficulty and debt, disgrace and misery; and died at last, as I have heard, in penury, neglect, and utter wretchedness. But this might be only a report: she may be living yet for anything I, or any of her relatives or former acquaintance, can tell; for they have all lost sight of her long years ago, and would as thoroughly forget her if they could. Her husband, however, upon this second misdemeanour, immediately sought and obtained a divorce, and, not long after, married again. It was well he did, for Lord Lowborough, morose and moody as he seemed, was not the man for a bachelor's life. No public interests, no ambitious projects, or active pursuits – or ties of friendship even (if he had had any friends), could compensate to him for the absence of domestic comforts and endearments. He had a son and a nominal daughter, it is true, but they too painfully reminded him of their mother, and the unfortunate little Annabella was a source of perpetual bitterness to his soul. He had obliged himself to treat her with paternal kindness: he had forced himself not to hate her and even, perhaps, to feel some degree of kindly regard for her, at last, in return for her artless and unsuspecting attachment to himself; but the bitterness of his self-condemnation for his inward feelings towards that innocent being, his constant struggles to subdue the evil promptings of his nature (for it was not a generous one), though partly guessed at by those who knew him, could be known to God and his own heart alone; so also was the hardness of his conflicts with the temptation to return to the vice of his youth, and seek oblivion for past calamities, and deadness to the present misery of a blighted heart, a joyless, friendless life, and a morbidly disconsolate mind, by yielding again to that insidious foe to health, and sense, and virtue, which had so deplorably enslaved and degraded him before.

The second object of his choice was widely different from the first. Some wondered at his taste; some even ridiculed it – but in this their folly was more apparent than his. The lady was about his own age – i.e. between thirty and forty – remarkable neither for the beauty nor wealth, nor brilliant accomplishments; nor any other thing that I ever heard of, except genuine good sense, unswerving integrity, active piety, warm-hearted benevolence, and a fund of cheerful spirits. These qualities however, as you may readily imagine, combined to render her an excellent mother to the children, and an invaluable wife to his lordship. *He*, with his usual self-deprecation (or *ap*preciation?) thought her a world too good for him, and while he wondered at the kindness of Providence in conferring such a gift upon him, and even at her taste in preferring him to other men, he did his best to reciprocate the good she did him, and so far succeeded that she was, and I believe still is, one of the happiest and fondest wives in England; and all who question the good taste of either partner, may be thankful if *their* respective selections afford them half the genuine satisfaction in the end, or repay their preference with affection half as lasting and sincere.

If you are at all interested in the fate of that low scoundrel, Grimsby, I can only tell you that he went from bad to worse, sinking from bathos to bathos of vice and villainy, consorting only with the worst members of his club and the lowest dregs of society – happily for the rest of the world – and at last met his

end in a drunken brawl from the hands, it is said, of some brother scoundrel he had cheated at play.

As for Mr Hattersley, he had never wholly forgotten his resolution to "come out from among them", and behave like a man and a Christian, and the last illness and death of his once jolly friend Huntingdon, so deeply and seriously impressed him with the evil of their former practices, that he never needed another lesson of the kind. Avoiding the temptations of the town, he continued to pass his life in the country immersed in the usual pursuits of a hearty, active country gentleman; his occupations being those of farming and breeding horses and cattle, diversified with a little hunting and shooting, and enlivened by the occasional companion- ship of his friends (better friends than those of his youth), and the society of his happy little wife (now cheerful and confiding as heart could wish), and his fine family of stalwart sons and blooming daughters. His father, the banker, having died some years ago and left him all his riches, he has now full scope for the exercise of his prevailing tastes, and I need not tell you that Ralph Hattersley, Esq. is celebrated throughout the country for his noble breed of horses.

## CHAPTER 51

### An Unexpected Occurrence

We will now turn to a certain still, cold, cloudy afternoon about the com- mencement of December, when the first fall of snow lay thinly scattered over the blighted fields and frozen roads, or stored more thickly in the hollows of the deep cart ruts and footsteps of men and horses, impressed in the now petrified mire of last month's drenching rains. I remember it well, for I was walking home from the vicarage, with no less remarkable a personage than Miss Eliza Millward by my side. I had been to call upon her father – a sacrifice of civility undertaken entirely to please my mother, not myself, for I hated to go near the house; not merely on account of my antipathy to the once so bewitching Eliza, but because I had not half forgiven the old gentleman himself for his ill opinion of Mrs Huntingdon; for though now constrained to acknowledge himself mistaken in his former judgement, he still maintained that she had done wrong to leave her husband; it was a violation of her sacred duties as a wife, and a tempting of Providence by laying herself open to temptation; and nothing short of bodily ill-usage (and that of no trifling nature) could excuse such a step – nor even that, for in such a case she ought to appeal to the laws for protection. But it was not of him I intended to speak; it was of his daughter Eliza. Just as I was taking leave of the vicar, she entered the room, ready equipped for a walk.

'I was just coming to see your sister, Mr Markham,' said she; 'and so if you have no objection, I'll accompany you home. I like company when I'm walking out – don't you?'

'Yes, when it's agreeable.'

'That of course,' rejoined the young lady, smiling archly. So we proceeded together.

'Shall I find Rose at home do you think?' said she, as we closed the garden gate, and set our faces towards Linden-car.

'I believe so.'

'I trust I shall, for I've a little bit of news for her – if you haven't forestalled me.'

'I?'

'Yes: do you know what Mr Lawrence is gone for?' She looked up anxiously for my reply.

'*Is* he gone?' said I, and her face brightened.

'Ah! then he hasn't told you about his sister?'

'What of *her*?' I demanded, in terror lest some evil should have befallen her.

'Oh, Mr Markham, how you blush!' cried she with a tormenting laugh. 'Ha, ha, you have not forgotten her yet! But you had better be quick about it, I can tell you, for – alas, alas! – she's going to be married next Thursday!'

'No, Miss Eliza! that's false.'

'Do you charge me with a falsehood, sir?'

'You are misinformed.'

'Am I? Do you know better then?'

'I think I do.'

'What makes you look so pale then?' said she, smiling with delight at my emotion. 'Is it anger at poor me for telling such a fib? Well, I only "tell the tale as 'twas told to me": I don't vouch for the truth of it; but at the same time, I don't see what reason Sarah should have for deceiving me, or her informant for deceiving her; and that was what she told me the footman told her – that Mrs Huntingdon was going to be married on Thursday, and Mr Lawrence was gone to the wedding. She did tell me the name of the gentleman, but I've forgotten that. Perhaps you can assist me to remember it. Is there not someone that lives near – or frequently visits the neighbourhood, that has long been attached to her? a Mr – oh dear! – Mr –'

'Hargrave?' suggested I, with a bitter smile.

'You're right!' cried she, 'that was the very name.'

'Impossible, Miss Eliza!' I exclaimed in a tone that made her start.

'Well, you know, that's what they told me,' said she, composedly staring me in the face. And then she broke out into a long shrill laugh that put me to my wits' end with fury.

'Really, you must excuse me,' cried she: 'I know it's very rude, but ha, ha, ha! – Did you think to marry her yourself? Dear, dear, what a pity! Ha, ha, ha! – Gracious, Mr Markham! Are you going to faint? O mercy! Shall I call this man? Here, Jacob –' But checking the word on her lips, I seized her arm and gave it, I think, a pretty severe squeeze, for she shrank into herself with a faint cry of pain or terror; but the spirit within her was not subdued: instantly rallying, she continued, with well-feigned concern – 'What can I do for you? Will you have

some water – some brandy? – I dare say they have some in the public house down there, if you'll let me run.'

'Have done with this nonsense!' cried I sternly. She looked confounded – almost frightened again, for a moment. 'You know I hate such jests,' I continued.

'*Jests* indeed! I wasn't *jesting*!'

'You were laughing, at all events; and I don't like to be laughed at,' returned I, making violent efforts to speak with proper dignity and composure, and to say nothing but what was coherent and sensible. 'And since you are in such a merry mood, Miss Eliza, you must be good enough company for yourself; and therefore I shall leave you to finish your walk alone – for, now I think of it, I have business elsewhere; so good-evening.'

With that I left her (smothering her malicious laughter) and turned aside into the fields, springing up the bank, and pushing through the nearest gap in the hedge. Determined at once to prove the truth – or rather the falsehood of her story, I hastened to Woodford as fast as my legs could carry me – first, veering round by a circuitous course, but the moment I was out of sight of my fair tormentor, cutting away across the country, just as a bird might fly – over pasture-land and fallow, and stubble, and lane – clearing hedges and ditches and hurdles, till I came to the young squire's gates. Never till now had I known the full fervour of my love – the full strength of my hopes, not wholly crushed even in my hours of deepest despondency, always tenaciously clinging to the thought that one day she might be mine – or if not that, at least that something of my memory, some slight remembrance of our friendship and our love would be for ever cherished in her heart. I marched up to the door, determined if I saw the master, to question him boldly concerning his sister, to wait and hesitate no longer, but cast false delicacy and stupid pride behind my back, and know my fate at once.

'Is Mr Lawrence at home?' I eagerly asked of the servant that opened the door.

'No, sir, master went yesterday,' replied he, looking very alert.

'Went where?'

'To Grassdale, sir – wasn't you aware, sir? He's very close, is master,' said the fellow with a foolish, simpering grin. 'I suppose, sir – '

But I turned and left him, without waiting to hear what he supposed. I was not going to stand there to expose my tortured feelings to the insolent laughter and impertinent curiosity of a fellow like that.

But what was to be done now? Could it be possible that she had left me for *that* man? I could not believe it. Me she might forsake, but *not* to give herself to him! Well, I would know the truth – to no concerns of daily life could I attend, while this tempest of doubt and dread, of jealousy and rage distracted me. I would take the morning coach from L— (the evening one would be already gone), and fly to Grassdale; I *must* be there before the marriage. And why? Because a thought struck me, that *perhaps* I might prevent it – that if I did not, she and I might both lament it to the latest moment of our lives. It struck me that someone might have belied me to her: perhaps her brother – yes, no doubt

her brother had persuaded her that I was false and faithless, and taking advantage of her natural indignation, and perhaps her desponding carelessness about her future life, had urged her, artfully, cruelly on, to this other marriage in order to secure her from me. If this *was* the case, and if she should only discover her mistake when too late to repair it – to what a life of misery and vain regret might she be doomed as well as me! And what remorse for me, to think my foolish scruples had induced it all! Oh, I *must* see her – she must know the truth even if I told it at the church door! I might pass for a madman or an impertinent fool – even she might be offended at such an interruption, or at least might tell me it was now too late – but if I *could* save her! if she *might* be mine – it was too rapturous a thought!

Winged by this hope, and goaded by these fears, I hurried homewards to prepare for my departure on the morrow. I told my mother that urgent business which admitted no delay, but which I could not then explain, called me away to — (the last large town through which I had to pass). My deep anxiety and serious preoccupation, could not be concealed from her maternal eyes; and I had much ado to calm her apprehensions of some disastrous mystery.

That night there came a heavy fall of snow which so retarded the progress of the coaches on the following day, that I was almost driven to distraction. I travelled all night, of course, for this was Wednesday: tomorrow morning, doubtless, the marriage would take place. But the night was long and dark; the snow heavily clogged the wheels and balled the horses' feet; the animals were consumedly lazy, the coachmen most execrably cautious, the passengers confoundedly apathetic in their supine indifference to the rate of our progression. Instead of assisting me to bully the several coachmen and urge them forward, they merely stared and grinned at my impatience: one fellow even ventured to rally me upon it – but I silenced him with a look that quelled him for the rest of the journey; and when, at the last stage, I would have taken the reins into my own hand they all with one accord opposed it.

It was broad daylight when we entered M— and drew up at the Rose and Crown. I alighted and called aloud for a post-chaise to Grassdale. There was none to be had: the only one in the town was under repair. 'A gig then – a fly – car – anything – only be quick!' There was a gig but not a horse to spare. I sent into the town to seek one; but they were such an intolerable time about it that I could wait no longer: I thought my own feet would carry me sooner, and bidding them send the confounded conveyance after me, if it were ready within an hour, I set off as fast as I could walk. The distance was little more than six miles, but the road was strange, and I had to keep stopping to enquire my way – hallooing to carters and clodhoppers, and frequently invading the cottages, for there were few abroad that winter's morning – sometimes knocking up the lazy people from their beds, for where so little work was to be done – perhaps so little food and fire to be had, they cared not to curtail their slumbers. I had no time to think of *them*, however: aching with wearied desperation, I hurried on. The gig did not overtake me: it was well I had not waited for it – vexatious, rather, that I had been fool enough to wait so long.

At length, however, I entered the neighbourhood of Grassdale. I approached

the little rural church – but lo! There stood a train of carriages before it – it needed not the white favours bedecking the servants and horses, nor the merry voices of the village idlers assembled to witness the show, to apprise me that there was a wedding within. I ran in among them, demanding, with breathless eagerness, had the ceremony long commenced? They only gaped and stared. In my desperation I pushed past them, and was about to enter the churchyard gate, when a group of ragged urchins, that had been hanging like bees to the windows, suddenly dropped off and made a rush for the porch, vociferating in the uncouth dialect of their county, something which signified, 'It's over – they're coming out!'

If Eliza Millward had seen me then, she might indeed have been delighted. I grasped the gatepost for support, and stood intently gazing towards the door to take my last look on my soul's delight, my first on that detested mortal who had torn her from my heart, and doomed her, I was certain, to a life of misery and hollow, vain repining – for what happiness could she enjoy with him? I did not wish to shock her with my presence now, but I had not power to move away. Forth came the bride and bridegroom. Him I saw not; I had eyes for none but her. A long veil shrouded half her graceful form, but did not hide it; I could see that while she carried her head erect, her eyes were bent upon the ground, and her face and neck were suffused with a crimson blush; but every feature was radiant with smiles, and, gleaming through the misty whiteness of her veil, were clusters of golden ringlets! O Heavens! It was *not* my Helen! The first glimpse made me start – but my eyes were darkened with exhaustion and despair – dare I trust them? Yes – it *is* not she! It was a younger, slighter, rosier beauty – lovely, indeed, but with far less dignity and depth of soul – without that indefinable grace, that keenly *spirituel* yet gentle charm, that ineffable power to attract and subjugate the heart – *my* heart at least. I looked at the bridegroom – it was Frederick Lawrence! I wiped away the cold drops that were trickling down my forehead, and stepped back as he approached; but his eye fell upon me, and he knew me, altered as my appearance must have been.

'Is that you, Markham?' said he, startled and confounded at the apparition – perhaps, too, at the wildness of my looks.

'Yes, Lawrence – is that you?' I mustered the presence of mind to reply.

He smiled and coloured, as if half-proud and half-ashamed of his identity; and if he had reason to be proud of the sweet lady on his arm, he had no less cause to be ashamed of having concealed his good fortune so long.

'Allow me to introduce you to my bride,' said he, endeavouring to hide his embarrassment by an assumption of careless gaiety. 'Esther, this is Mr Markham; my friend Markham, Mrs Lawrence, late Miss Hargrave.'

I bowed to the bride, and vehemently wrung the bridegroom's hand.

'Why did you not tell me of this?' I said reproachfully, pretending a resentment I did not feel (for in truth I was almost wild with joy to find myself so happily mistaken, and overflowing with affection to him for this and for the base injustice I felt that I had done him in my mind – he might have wronged me, but not to *that* extent; and as I had hated him like a demon for the last forty hours,

the reaction from such a feeling was so great, that I could pardon all offences for the moment – and love him in spite of them too).

'I did tell you,' said he, with an air of guilty confusion; 'you received my letter?'

'What letter?'

'The one announcing my intended marriage.'

'I never received the most distant hint of such an intention.'

'It must have crossed you on your way then – it should have reached you yesterday morning – it was rather late, I acknowledge. But what brought you here then, if you received no information?'

It was now *my* turn to be confounded; but the young lady, who had been busily patting the snow with her foot during our short, *sotto voce* colloquy, very opportunely came to my assistance by pinching her companion's arm and whispering a suggestion that his friend should be invited to step into the carriage and go with them; it being scarcely agreeable to stand there among so many gazers, and keeping their friends waiting, into the bargain.

'And so cold as it is too!' said he, glancing with dismay at her slight drapery, and immediately handing her into the carriage. 'Markham, will you come? We are going to Paris, but we can drop you anywhere between this and Dover.'

'No, thank you. Goodbye – I needn't wish you a pleasant journey; but I shall expect a very handsome apology, sometime, mind, and scores of letters, before we meet again.'

He shook my hand and hastened to take his place beside his lady. This was no time or place for explanation or discourse: we had already stood long enough to excite the wonder of the village sightseers, and perhaps the wrath of the attendant bridal party; though, of course, all this passed in a much shorter time than I have taken to relate or even than you will take to read it. I stood beside the carriage, and, the window being down, I saw my happy friend fondly encircle his companion's waist with his arm, while she rested her glowing cheek on his shoulder, looking the very impersonation of loving, trusting bliss. In the interval between the footman's closing the door and taking his place behind, she raised her smiling brown eyes to his face, observing playfully – 'I fear you must think me very insensible, Frederick: I know it is the custom for ladies to cry on these occasions, but I couldn't squeeze a tear for my life.'

He only answered with a kiss, and pressed her still closer to his bosom.

'But what is this?' he murmured. 'Why, Esther, you're crying now!'

'Oh, it's nothing – it's only too much happiness – and the wish,' sobbed she, 'that our dear Helen were as happy as ourselves.'

'Bless you for that wish!' I inwardly responded as the carriage rolled away – 'and Heaven grant it be not wholly vain!'

I thought a cloud had suddenly darkened her husband's face as she spoke. What did *he* think? Could he grudge such happiness to his dear sister and his friend as he now felt himself? At *such* a moment it was impossible. The contrast between her fate and his *must* darken his bliss for a time. Perhaps too he thought of me: perhaps he regretted the part he had had in preventing our union, by

omitting to help us, if not by actually plotting against us – I exonerated him from *that* charge, now, and deeply lamented my former ungenerous suspicions; but he *had* wronged us, still – I hoped, I trusted that he had. He had not attempted to check the course of our love by actually damming up the streams in their passage, but he had passively watched the two currents wandering through life's arid wilderness, declining to clear away the obstructions that divided them, and secretly hoping that both would lose themselves in the sand before they could be joined in one. And meantime, he had been quietly proceeding with his own affairs: perhaps his heart and head had been so full of his fair lady that he had had but little thought to spare for others. Doubtless he had made his first acquaintance with her – his first intimate acquaintance at least – during his three months' sojourn at F—, for I now recollected that he had once casually let fall an intimation that his aunt and sister had a young friend staying with them at the time, and this accounted for at least one half his silence about all transactions there. Now too I saw a reason for many little things that had slightly puzzled me before; among the rest, for sundry departures from Woodford, and absences more or less prolonged, for which he never satisfactorily accounted, and concerning which he hated to be questioned on his return. Well might the servant say his master was 'very close'. But why this strange reserve to *me*? Partly, from that remarkable idiosyncrasy to which I have before alluded; partly, perhaps, from tenderness to my feelings, or fear to disturb my philosophy by touching upon the infectious theme of love.

### CHAPTER 52

## *Fluctuations*

The tardy gig had overtaken me at last. I entered it, and bade the man who brought it drive to Grassdale Manor – I was too busy with my own thoughts to care to drive it myself. I would see Mrs Huntingdon – there could be no impropriety in that now that her husband had been dead above a year – and by her indifference or her joy at my unexpected arrival, I could soon tell whether her heart was truly mine. But my companion, a loquacious, forward fellow, was not disposed to leave me to the indulgence of my private cogitations.

'There they go!' said he as the carriages filed away before us. 'There'll be brave doings on yonder *today*, as what come tomorra – Know anything of that family, sir? Or you're a stranger in these parts?'

'I know them by report.'

'Humph! – There's the best of 'em gone anyhow. And I suppose the old missis is a-going to leave after this stir's gotten overed, and take herself off, somewhere, to live on her bit of a jointure; and the young 'un – at least the new 'un (she's none so very young) is coming down to live at the Grove.'

'Is Mr Hargrave married, then?'

'Ay sir, a few months since. He should a been wed afore, to a widow lady, but they couldn't agree over the money: she'd a rare long purse, and Mr Hargrave wanted it all to his-self; but she wouldn't let it go, and so then they fell out. This one isn't quite as rich – nor as handsome either, but she hasn't been married before. She's very plain, they say, and getting on to forty or past, and so, you know, if she didn't jump at this hopportunity, she thought she'd never get a better. I guess she thought such a handsome young husband was worth all 'at ever she had, and he might take it and welcome; but I lay she'll rue her bargain afore long. They say she begins already to see 'at he isn't not altogether that nice, generous, perlite, delightful gentleman 'at she thought him afore marriage – he begins a being careless, and masterful already. Ay, and she'll find him harder and carelesser nor she thinks on.'

'You seem to be well acquainted with him,' I observed.

'I am, sir; I've known him since he was quite a young gentleman; and a proud 'un he was, and a wilful. I was servant yonder for several years; but I couldn't stand their niggardly ways – she got ever longer and worse, did missis, with her nipping and screwing, and watching and grudging; so I thought I'd find another place as *what* came.'

And then he discoursed upon his present position as ostler at the Rose and Crown, and how greatly superior it was to his former one, in comfort and freedom, though inferior in outward respectability; and entered into various details respecting the domestic economy at the Grove, and the characters of Mrs Hargrave and her son – to which I gave no heed, being too much occupied with my own anxious, fluttering anticipations and with the character of the country through which we passed, that, in spite of the leafless trees and snowy ground, had for some time begun to manifest unequivocal signs of the approach to a gentleman's country seat.

'Are we not near the house?' said I, interrupting him in the middle of his discourse.

'Yes, sir; yond's the park.'

My heart sank within me to behold that stately mansion in the midst of its expansive grounds – the park as beautiful now, in its wintry garb, as it could be in its summer glory; the majestic sweep, the undulating swell and fall, displayed to full advantage in that robe of dazzling purity, stainless and printless – save one long, winding track left by the trooping deer – the stately timber trees with their heavy laden branches gleaming white against the dull, grey sky; the deep, encircling woods; the broad expanse of water sleeping in frozen quiet; and the weeping ash and willow drooping their snowclad boughs above it – all presented a picture, striking, indeed, and pleasing to an unemcumbered mind, but by no means encouraging to me. There was one comfort however – all this was entailed upon little Arthur, and could not under any circumstances, strictly speaking, be his mother's. But how was she situated? Overcoming with a sudden effort my repugnance to mention her name to my garrulous companion, I asked him if he knew whether her late husband had left a will, and how the property had been disposed of. Oh yes, he knew all about it; and I was quickly informed

that to her had been left the full control and management of the estate during her son's minority, besides the absolute, unconditional possession of her own fortune (but I knew her father had not given her much), and the small additional sum that had been settled upon her before marriage.

Before the close of the explanation, we drew up at the park gates. Now for the trial – if I should find her within – but alas! she might be still at Staningley: her brother had given me no intimation to the contrary. I enquired at the porter's lodge if Mrs Huntingdon were at home. No, she was with her aunt in —shire, but was expected to return before Christmas. She usually spent most of her time at Staningley, only coming to Grassdale occasionally, when the management of affairs, or the interest of her tenants and dependants required her presence.

'Near what town is Staningley situated?' I asked. The requisite information was soon obtained. 'Now then, my man, give me the reins, and we'll return to M—. I must have some breakfast at the Rose and Crown, and then away to Staningley by the first coach for —'

'You'll not get there today, sir.'

'No matter, I don't want to get there today; I want to get there tomorrow, and pass the night on the road.'

'At an inn, sir? You'd better by half stay at *our* house; and then start fresh tomorrow, and have the whole day for your journey.'

'What, and lose twelve hours? Not I.'

'Perhaps, sir, you're *related* to Mrs Huntingdon?' said he, seeking to indulge his curiosity since his cupidity was not to be gratified.

'I have not that honour.'

'Ah! well,' returned he with a dubious, sidelong glance at my splashed, grey trousers and rough pea jacket. 'But,' he added, encouragingly, 'there's many a fine lady like that 'at has kinsfolks poorer nor what you are, sir, I should think.'

'No doubt – and there's many a fine gentleman would esteem himself vastly honoured to be able to claim kindred with the lady you mention.'

He now cunningly glanced at my face. 'Perhaps, sir, you *mean* to –'

I guessed what was coming, and checked the impertinent conjecture with – 'Perhaps you'll be so good as to be quiet a moment. I'm busy.'

'Busy, sir?'

'Yes, in my mind, and don't want to have my cogitations disturbed.'

'Indeed, sir!'

You will see that my disappointment had not *very* greatly affected me, or I should not have been able so quietly to bear with the fellow's impertinence. The fact is I thought it as well – nay better, all things considered, that I should not see her today – that I should have time to compose my mind for the interview – to prepare it for a heavier disappointment, after the intoxicating delight experienced by this sudden removal of my former apprehensions; not to mention that, after travelling a night and a day without intermission, and rushing in hot haste through six miles of new-fallen snow, I could not possibly be in a very presentable condition.

At M— I had time before the coach started to replenish my forces with a

hearty breakfast, and to obtain the refreshment of my usual morning's ablutions, and the amelioration of some slight change in my toilet – and also to dispatch a short note to my mother (excellent son that I was) to assure her that I was still in existence and to excuse my nonappearance at the expected time. It was a long journey to Staningley for those slow travelling days; but I did not deny myself needful refreshment on the road, nor even a night's rest at a wayside inn; choosing rather to brook a little delay than to present myself worn, wild, and weather-beaten before my mistress and her aunt, who would be astonished enough to see me without that. Next morning, therefore, I not only fortified myself with as substantial a breakfast as my excited feelings would allow me to swallow, but I bestowed a little more than usual time and care upon my toilet; and, furnished with a change of linen from my small carpet-bag, well-brushed clothes, well-polished boots, and neat new gloves – I mounted 'the Lightning,' and resumed my journey. I had nearly two stages yet before me, but the coach, I was informed, passed through the neighbourhood of Staningley, and, having desired to be set down as near the Hall as possible, I had nothing to do but to sit with folded arms and speculate upon the coming hour.

It was a clear, frosty morning. The very fact of sitting exalted aloft, surveying the snowy landscape and sweet, sunny sky, inhaling the pure, bracing air, and crunching away over the crisp, frozen snow, was exhilarating enough in itself; but add to this the idea of to what goal I was hastening, and whom I expected to meet, and you may have some faint conception of my frame of mind at the time – only a *faint* one though, for my heart swelled with unspeakable delight, and my spirits rose almost to madness – in spite of my prudent endeavours to bind them down to a reasonable platitude by thinking of the undeniable difference between Helen's rank and mine; of all that she had passed through since our parting; of her long, unbroken silence; and, above all, of her cool, cautious aunt, whose counsels she would doubtless be careful not to slight again. These considerations made my heart flutter with anxiety, and my chest heave with impatience to get the crisis over, but they could not dim her image in my mind, or mar the vivid recollection of what had been said and felt between us – or destroy the keen anticipation of what was to be – in fact, I could not realise their terrors now. Towards the close of the journey, however, a couple of my fellow passengers kindly came to my assistance, and brought me low enough.

'Fine land this,' said one of them, pointing with his umbrella to the wide fields on the right, conspicuous for their compact hedgerows, deep, well-cut ditches, and fine timber trees, growing sometimes on the borders, sometimes in the midst of the enclosure; '*very* fine land, if you saw it in the summer or spring.'

'Ay,' responded the other – a gruff elderly man, with a drab great coat buttoned up to the chin and a cotton umbrella between his knees. 'It's old Maxwell's I suppose.'

'It *was* his, sir, but he's dead now, you're aware, and has left it all to his niece.'

'All!'

'Every rood of it – and the mansion-house and all – every hatom of his

worldly goods! – except just a trifle, by way of remembrance to his nephew down in —shire and an annuity to his wife.'

'It's strange, sir!'

'It is, sir. And she wasn't his own niece neither; but he had no near relations of his own – none but a nephew he'd quarrelled with – and he always had a partiality for this one. And then his wife advised him to it, they say: she'd brought most of the property and it was her wish that this lady should have it.'

'Humph! – She'll be a fine catch for somebody.'

'She will so. She's a widow, but quite young yet, and uncommon handsome – a fortune of her own, besides, and only one child – and she's nursing a fine estate for him in —. There'll be lots to speak for her! – 'fraid there's no chance for uz' – (facetiously jogging me with his elbow, as well as his companion) – 'ha, ha, ha! No offence, sir, I hope?' (to me). 'Ahem! – I should think she'll marry none but a nobleman, myself. Look ye sir,' resumed he, turning to his other neighbour, and pointing past me with his umbrella, 'that's the Hall – grand park, you see – and all them woods – plenty of timber there, and lots of game – hallo! what now?'

This exclamation was occasioned by the sudden stoppage of the coach at the park gates.

'Gen'leman for Staningley Hall?' cried the coachman; and I rose and threw my carpet-bag on to the ground, preparatory to dropping myself down after it.

'Sickly, sir?' asked my talkative neighbour, staring me in the face (I dare say it was white enough).

'No. Here, coachman.'

'Thank 'ee, sir – All right!'

The coachman pocketed his fee and drove away, leaving me not walking up the park, but pacing to and fro before its gates, with folded arms and eyes fixed upon the ground – an overwhelming force of images, thoughts, impressions crowding on my mind, and nothing tangibly distinct but this – My love had been cherished in vain; my hope was gone for ever; I must tear myself away at once, and banish or suppress all thoughts of her like the remembrance of a wild, mad dream. Gladly would I have lingered round the place for hours, in the hope of catching, at least one distant glimpse of her before I went, but it must not be: I must not suffer her to see me; for what could have brought me hither but the hope of reviving her attachment, with a view, hereafter to obtain her hand? And could I bear that she should think me capable of such a thing? – of presuming upon the acquaintance – the *love* if you will – accidentally contracted, or rather forced upon her against her will, when she was an unknown fugitive, toiling for her own support, apparently without fortune, family or connections – to come upon her now, when she was reinstated in her proper sphere, and claim a share in her prosperity, which, had it never failed her, would most certainly have kept her unknown to me for ever? And this too, when we had parted sixteen months ago, and she had expressly forbidden me to hope for a reunion in this world – and never sent me a line or a message from that day to this? No! The very idea was intolerable.

And even if she should have a lingering affection for me still, ought I to disturb her peace by awakening those feelings? to subject her to the struggles of conflicting duty and inclination – to whichsoever side the latter might allure, or the former imperatively call her – whether she should deem it her duty to risk the slights and censures of the world, the sorrow and displeasure of those she loved, for a romantic idea of truth and constancy to me, or to sacrifice her individual wishes to the feelings of her friends and her own sense of prudence and the fitness of things? No – and I would not! I would go at once, and she should never know that I had approached the place of her abode; for though I might disclaim all idea of ever aspiring to her hand, or even of soliciting a place in her friendly regard, her peace should not be broken by my presence, nor her heart afflicted by the sight of my fidelity.

'Adieu then, dear Helen, for ever! – For ever adieu!'

So said I – and yet I could not tear myself away. I moved a few paces, and then looked back, for one last view of her stately home, that I might have its outward form, at least impressed upon my mind as indelibly as her own image, which alas! I must not see again – then, walked a few steps farther; and then lost in melancholy musings, paused again and leant my back against a rough old tree that grew beside the road.

## CHAPTER 53

### Conclusion

While standing thus, absorbed in my gloomy reverie, a gentleman's carriage came round the corner of the road. I did not look at it; and had it rolled quietly by me, I should not have remembered the fact of its appearance at all; but a tiny voice from within it roused me by exclaiming – 'Mamma, mamma, here's Mr Markham!'

I did not hear the reply, but presently the same voice answered – 'It is indeed, mamma – look for yourself.'

I did not raise my eyes, but I suppose mamma looked, for a clear, melodious voice, whose tones thrilled through my nerves, exclaimed – 'Oh, aunt! Here's Mr Markham – Arthur's friend! – Stop, Richard!'

There was such evidence of joyous though suppressed excitement in the utterance of those few words – especially that tremulous, 'Oh, aunt – ' that it threw me almost off my guard. The carriage stopped immediately, and I looked up and met the eye of a pale, grave, elderly lady surveying me from the open window. She bowed and so did I, and then she withdrew her head, while Arthur screamed to the footman to let him out; but before that functionary could descend from his box, a hand was silently put forth from the carriage window. I knew that hand, though a black glove concealed its delicate whiteness and half its fair proportions, and quickly seizing it, I pressed it in my own – ardently for a moment, but instantly

recollecting myself, I dropped it, and it was immediately withdrawn.

'Were you coming to see us, or only passing by?' asked the low voice of its owner, who, I felt, was attentively surveying my countenance from behind the thick, black veil which, with the shadowing panels, entirely concealed her own from me.

'I – I came to see the place,' faltered I.

'The *place*,' repeated she, in a tone which betokened more displeasure or disappointment than surprise.

'Will you not enter it then?'

'If you wish it.'

'Can you doubt?'

'Yes, yes! He *must* enter,' cried Arthur running round from the other door; and seizing my hand in both his, he shook it heartily.

'Do you remember me, sir?' said he.

'Yes, full well, my little man, altered though you are,' replied I, surveying the comparatively tall, slim young gentleman with his mother's image visibly stamped upon his fair, intelligent features, in spite of the blue eyes beaming with gladness, and the bright locks clustering beneath his cap.

'Am I not grown?' said he, stretching himself up to his full height.

'Grown! Three inches upon my word!'

'I was *seven* last birthday,' was the proud rejoinder. 'In seven years more, I shall be as tall as you, nearly.'

'Arthur,' said his mother, 'tell him to come in. Go on Richard.'

There was a touch of sadness as well as coldness in her voice, but I knew not to what to ascribe it. The carriage drove on and entered the gates before us. My little companion led me up the park, discoursing merrily all the way. Arrived at the Hall door, I paused on the steps and looked round me, waiting to recover my composure, if possible – or at any rate, to remember my new formed resolutions and the principles on which they were founded; and it was not till Arthur had been for some time gently pulling my coat, and repeating his invitations to enter, that I at length consented to accompany him into the apartment where the ladies awaited us.

Helen eyed me as I entered with a kind of gentle, serious scrutiny and politely asked after Mrs Markham and Rose. I respectfully answered her enquiries. Mrs Maxwell begged me to be seated, observing it was rather cold, but she supposed I had not travelled far that morning.

'Not quite twenty miles,' I answered.

'Not on foot!'

'No, madam, by coach.'

'Here's Rachel, sir,' said Arthur, the only truly happy one amongst us, directing my attention to that worthy individual, who had just entered to take her mistress's things. She vouchsafed me an almost friendly smile of recognition – a favour that demanded, at least, a civil salutation on my part, which was accordingly given and respectively returned – she had seen the error of her former estimation of my character.

When Helen was divested of her lugubrious bonnet and veil, her heavy winter cloak etc. she looked so like herself that I knew not how to bear it. I was particularly glad to see her beautiful black hair unstinted still and unconcealed in its glossy luxuriance.

'Mamma has left off her widow's cap in honour of uncle's marriage,' observed Arthur, reading my looks with a child's mingled simplicity and quickness of observation. Mamma looked grave and Mrs Maxwell shook her head. 'And Aunt Maxwell is never going to leave off hers,' persisted the naughty boy; but when he saw that his pertness was seriously displeasing and painful to his aunt, he went and silently put his arm round her neck, kissed her cheek, and withdrew to the recess of one of the great bay windows, where he quietly amused himself with his dog while Mrs Maxwell gravely discussed with me the interesting topics of the weather, the season, and the roads. I considered her presence very useful as a check upon my natural impulses – an antidote to those emotions of tumultuous excitement which would otherwise have carried me away against my reason and my will, but *just then* I felt the restraint almost intolerable, and I had the greatest difficulty in forcing myself to attend to her remarks and answer them with ordinary politeness; for I was sensible that Helen was standing within a few feet of me beside the fire. I dared not look at her, but I felt her eye was upon me, and from one hasty, furtive glance, I thought her cheek was slightly flushed and that her fingers, as she played with her watch chain, were agitated with that restless, trembling motion which betokens high excitement.

'Tell me,' said she, availing herself of the first pause in the attempted conversation between her aunt and me, and speaking fast and low with her eyes bent on the gold chain – for I now ventured another glance – 'Tell me how you all are at Lindenhope? – has nothing happened since I left you?'

'I believe not.'

'Nobody dead? Nobody married?'

'No.'

'Or – or expecting to marry? – No old ties dissolved or new ones formed? No old friends forgotten or supplanted?'

She dropped her voice so low in the last sentence that no one could have caught the concluding words but myself, and at the same time turned her eyes upon me with a dawning smile, most sweetly melancholy, and a look of timid though keen enquiry that made my cheeks tingle with inexpressible emotions.

'I believe not,' I answered – 'Certainly not, if others are as little changed as I.' Her face glowed in sympathy with mine.

'And you really did not mean to call?' she exclaimed.

'I feared to intrude.'

'To intrude!' cried she with an impatient gesture – 'What' – But as if suddenly recollecting her aunt's presence, she checked herself and turning to that lady continued – 'Why aunt, this man is my brother's close friend and was my own intimate acquaintance (for a few short months at least) and professed a great attachment to my boy – and when he passes the house, so many scores of miles from his home, he declines to look in for fear of intruding!'

'Mr Markham is over modest,' observed Mrs Maxwell.

'Over ceremonious rather,' said her niece – 'over – well it's no matter.' And turning from me, she seated herself in a chair beside the table, and pulling a book to her by the cover, began to turn over the leaves in an energetic kind of abstraction.

'If I had known,' said I, 'that you would have honoured me by remembering me as an intimate acquaintance, I most likely should not have denied myself the pleasure of calling upon you, but I thought you had forgotten me long ago.'

'You judged of others by yourself,' muttered she without raising her eyes from the book, but reddening as she spoke and hastily turning over a dozen leaves at once.

There was a pause of which Arthur thought he might venture to avail himself to introduce his handsome young setter and show me how wonderfully it was grown and improved, and to ask after the welfare of its father Sancho. Mrs Maxwell then withdrew to take off her things. Helen immediately pushed the book from her and after silently surveying her son, his friend, and his dog for a few moments, she dismissed the former from the room under pretence of wishing him to fetch his last new book to show me. The child obeyed with alacrity; but I continued caressing the dog. The silence might have lasted till its master's return had it depended on me to break it, but, in half a minute or less, my hostess impatiently rose, and taking her former station on the rug between me and the chimney corner, earnestly exclaimed – 'Gilbert, what *is* the matter with you? – Why are you so changed? – It is a very indiscreet question I know,' she hastened to add: 'perhaps, a very rude one – don't answer it if you think so – but I hate mysteries and concealments.'

'I am not changed, Helen – unfortunately I am as keen and passionate as ever – it is not I, it is circumstances that are changed.'

'What circumstances? *Do* tell me!' Her cheek was blanched with the very anguish of anxiety – could it be with the fear that I had rashly pledged my faith to another?

'I'll tell you at once,' said I. 'I will confess that I came here for the purpose of seeing you (not without some monitory misgivings at my own presumption, and fears that I should be as little welcome as expected when I came), but I did not know that this estate was yours, until enlightened on the subject of your inheritance by the conversation of two fellow passengers in the last stage of my journey; and then, I saw at once the folly of the hopes I had cherished and the madness of retaining them a moment longer; and though I alighted at your gates, I determined not to enter within them; I lingered a few minutes to see the place, but was fully resolved to return to M— without seeing its mistress.'

'And if my aunt and I had not been just returning from our morning drive, I should have seen and heard no more of you?'

'I thought it would be better for both that we should not meet,' replied I as calmly as I could, but not daring to speak above my breath from conscious inability to steady my voice, and not daring to look in her face lest my firmness should forsake me altogether: 'I thought an interview would only disturb your

peace and madden me. But I am glad, now, of this opportunity of seeing you once more and knowing that you have not forgotten me, and of assuring you that I shall never cease to remember you.'

There was a moment's pause. Mrs Huntingdon moved away, and stood in the recess of the window. Did she regard this as an intimation that modesty alone prevented me from asking her hand? And was she considering how to repulse me with the smallest injury to my feelings? Before I could speak to relieve her from such a perplexity, she broke the silence herself by suddenly turning towards me and observing – 'You might have had such an opportunity before – as far I mean as regards assuring me of your kindly recollections, and yourself of mine, if you had written to me.'

'I would have done so, but I did not know your address, and did not like to ask your brother, because I thought he would object to my writing – but this would not have deterred me for a moment, if I could have ventured to believe that you expected to hear from me, or even wasted a thought upon your unhappy friend; but your silence naturally led me to conclude myself forgotten.'

'Did you expect me to write to *you* then?'

'No, Helen – Mrs Huntingdon,' said I, blushing at the implied imputation, 'certainly not; but if you had sent me a message through your brother, or even asked him about me now and then – '

'I did ask about you, frequently. I was not going to do more,' continued she, smiling, 'so long as you continued to restrict yourself to a few polite enquiries about my health.'

'Your brother never told me that you had mentioned my name.'

'Did you ever ask him?'

'No; for I saw he did not wish to be questioned about you, or to afford the slightest encouragement or assistance to my too obstinate attachment.' Helen did not reply. 'And he was perfectly right,' added I. But she remained in silence looking out upon the snowy lawn. 'Oh, I will relieve her of my presence!' thought I; and immediately I rose and advanced to take leave, with a most heroic resolution – but pride was at the bottom of it, or it could not have carried me through.

'Are you going already?' said she, taking the hand I offered, and not immediately letting it go.

'Why should I stay any longer?'

'Wait till Arthur comes, at least.'

Only too glad to obey, I stood and leant against the opposite side of the window.

'You told me you were not changed,' said my companion: 'you *are* – very much so.'

'No, Mrs Huntingdon, I only *ought* to be.'

'Do you mean to maintain that you have the same regard for me that you had when last we met?'

'I have, but it would be wrong to talk of it now.'

'It was wrong to talk of it *then*, Gilbert; it would *not* now – unless to do so would be to violate the truth.'

I was too much agitated to speak; but, without waiting for an answer, she turned away her glistening eye and crimson cheek, and threw up the window and looked out, whether to calm her own excited feelings or to relieve her embarrassment – or only to pluck that beautiful half-blown Christmas rose that grew upon the little shrub without, just peeping from the snow, that had hitherto, no doubt, defended it from the frost, and was now melting away in the sun. Pluck it, however, she did, and having gently dashed the glittering powder from its leaves, approached it to her lips and said – 'This rose is not so fragrant as a summer flower, but it has stood through hardships none of *them* could bear: the cold rain of winter has sufficed to nourish it, and its faint sun to warm it; the bleak winds have not blanched it, or broken its stem, and the keen frost has not blighted it. Look, Gilbert, it is still fresh and blooming as a flower can be, with the cold snow even now on its petals – Will you have it?'

I held out my hand: I dared not speak lest my emotion should over-master me. She laid the rose across my palm, but I scarcely closed my fingers upon it, so deeply was I absorbed in thinking what might be the meaning of her words, and what I ought to do or say upon the occasion; whether to give way to my feelings or restrain them still. Misconstruing this hesitation into indifference – or reluctance even – to accept her gift, Helen suddenly snatched it from my hand, threw it out on to the snow, shut down the window with an emphasis, and withdrew to the fire.

'Helen! what means this?' I cried, electrified at this startling change in her demeanour.

'You did not understand my gift,' said she – 'or, what is worse, you despised it. I'm sorry I gave it you; but since I did make such a mistake, the only remedy I could think of, was to take it away.'

'You misunderstood me, cruelly,' I replied, and in a minute I had opened the window again, leaped out, picked up the flower, brought it in, and presented it to her, imploring her to give it me again, and I would keep it for ever for her sake, and prize it more highly than anything in the world I possessed.

'And will this content you?' said she as she took it in her hand.

'It shall,' I answered.

'There, then; take it.'

I pressed it earnestly to my lips, and put it in my bosom, Mrs Huntingdon looking on with a half sarcastic smile.

'Now, are you going?' said she.

'I will if – if I must.'

'You *are* changed,' persisted she – 'you are grown either very proud or very indifferent.'

'I am neither, Helen – Mrs Huntingdon. If you could see my heart –'

'You *must* be one – if not both. And why Mrs Huntingdon? – Why not Helen, as before?'

'Helen, then – dear Helen!' I murmured. I was in an agony of mingled love, hope, delight, uncertainty, and suspense.

'The rose I gave you was an emblem of my heart,' said she; 'would you take it away and leave me here alone?'

'Would you give me your hand too, if I asked it?'

'Have I not said enough?' she answered with a most enchanting smile. I snatched her hand and would have fervently kissed it, but suddenly checked myself and said – 'But have you considered the consequences?'

'Hardly, I think, or I should not have offered myself to one too proud to take me, or too indifferent to make his affection outweigh my worldly goods.'

Stupid blockhead that I was! – I trembled to clasp her in my arms, but dared not believe in so much joy, and yet restrained myself to say – 'But if you *should* repent!'

'It would be your fault,' she replied: 'I never shall, unless you bitterly disappoint me. If you have not sufficient confidence in my affection to believe this, let me alone.'

'My darling angel – my *own* Helen,' cried I, now passionately kissing the hand I still retained, and throwing my left arm around her, 'you never shall repent, if it depend on me alone – But have you thought of your aunt?' I trembled for the answer and clasped her closer to my heart in the instinctive dread of losing my new-found treasure.

'My aunt must not know of it yet,' said she. 'She would think it a rash, wild step, because she could not imagine how well I know you; but she must know you herself, and learn to like you. You must leave us now, after lunch, and come again in spring, and make a longer stay, and cultivate her acquaintance; and I know you will like each other.'

'And then you will be mine,' said I printing a kiss upon her lips, and another, and another – for I was as daring and impetuous now as I had been backward and constrained before.

'No – in another year,' replied she, gently disengaging herself from my embrace, but still fondly clasping my hand.

'Another year! Oh. Helen, I could not wait so long!'

'Where is your fidelity?'

'I mean I could not endure the misery of so long a separation.'

'It would not be a separation: we will write every day; my spirit shall be always with you; and sometimes you shall see me with your bodily eye. I will not be such a hypocrite as to pretend that I desire to wait so long myself; but as my marriage is to please myself alone, I ought to consult my friends about the time of it.'

'Your friends will disapprove.'

'They will not greatly disapprove, dear Gilbert,' said she, earnestly kissing my hand – 'they cannot, when they know you – or if they could, they would not be true friends; I should not care for their estrangement. – Now are you satisfied?' She looked up in my face with a smile of ineffable tenderness.

'Can I be otherwise, with your love? And you *do* love me, Helen?' said I, not doubting the fact, but wishing to hear it confirmed by her own acknowledgement.

'If you loved as *I* do,' she earnestly replied, 'you would not have so nearly lost me – these scruples of false delicacy and pride would never thus have troubled you – you would have seen that the greatest worldly distinctions and

discrepancies of rank, birth, and fortune are as dust in the balance compared with the unity of accordant thoughts and feelings, and truly loving, sympathising hearts and souls.'

'But this is too much happiness,' said I, embracing her again; 'I have not deserved it, Helen – I dare not believe in such felicity: and the longer I have to wait, the greater will be my dread that something will intervene to snatch you from me – and think, a thousand things may happen in a year! – I shall be in one long fever of restless terror and impatience all the time. And besides, winter is such a dreary season.'

'I thought so too,' replied she gravely: 'I would not be married in winter – in December, at least,' she added with a shudder – for in that month had occurred both the ill-starred marriage that had bound her to her former husband and the terrible death that released her – 'and therefore, I said another year in spring.'

'*Next* spring.'

'No, no – next autumn, perhaps.'

'Summer, then.'

'Well, the close of summer. There now! be satisfied.'

While she was speaking, Arthur re-entered the room – good boy for keeping out so long.

'Mamma, I couldn't find the book in either of the places you told me to look for it' (there was a conscious something in mamma's smile that seemed to say, 'No, dear, I knew you could not'), 'but Rachel got it for me at last. Look, Mr Markham, a natural history with all kinds of birds and beasts in it, and the reading as nice as the pictures!'

In great good humour, I sat down to examine the book and drew the little fellow between my knees. Had he come a minute before, I should have received him less graciously, but now I affectionately stroked his curling locks, and even kissed his ivory forehead: he was my own Helen's son, and therefore mine; and as such I have ever since regarded him. That pretty child is now a fine young man: he has realised his mother's brightest expectations, and is at present residing in Grassdale Manor with his young wife, the merry little Helen Hattersley, of yore.

I had not looked through half the book, before Mrs Maxwell appeared to invite me into the other room to lunch. That lady's cool, distant manners rather chilled me at first; but I did my best to propitiate her, and not entirely without success I think, even in that first short visit; for when I talked cheerfully to her, she gradually became more kind and cordial, and when I departed she bade me a gracious adieu, hoping ere long to have the pleasure of seeing me again.

'But you must not go till you have seen the conservatory, my aunt's winter garden,' said Helen, as I advanced to take leave of her, with as much philosophy and self-command as I could summon to my aid.

I gladly availed myself of such a respite, and followed her into a large and beautiful conservatory, plentifully furnished with flowers considering the season – but of course, I had little attention to spare for *them*. It was not however for any tender colloquy that my companion had brought me there – 'My aunt

is particularly fond of flowers,' she observed, 'and she is fond of Staningley too: I brought you here to offer a petition in her behalf that this may be her home as long as she lives, and – if it be not our home likewise – that I may often see her and be with her; for I fear she will be sorry to lose me; and, though she leads a retired and contemplative life, she is apt to get low-spirited if left too much alone.'

'By all means, dearest Helen! – Do what you will with your own. I should not dream of wishing your aunt to leave the place under any circumstances; and we will live either here or elsewhere as you and she may determine, and you shall see her as often as you like. I know she must be pained to part with you, and I am willing to make any reparation in my power. I love her for your sake, and her happiness shall be as dear to me as that of my own mother.'

'Thank you, darling! You shall have a kiss for that. Goodbye. There now – there Gilbert – let me go – here's Arthur, don't astonish his infantile brain with your madness.'

But it is time to bring my narrative to a close – anyone but you would say I had made it too long already; but for *your* satisfaction, I will add a few words more; because I know you will have a fellow-feeling for the old lady, and will wish to know the last of her history. I did come again in spring, and agreeably to Helen's injunctions, did my best to cultivate her acquaintance. She received me very kindly, having been doubtless, already prepared to think highly of my character, by her niece's too favourable report. I turned my best side out, of course, and we got along marvellously well together. When my ambitious intentions were made known to her, she took it more sensibly than I had ventured to hope. Her only remark on the subject, in my hearing, was – 'And so Mr Markham, you are going to rob me of my niece I understand. Well! I hope God will prosper your union, and make my dear girl happy at last. Could she have been contented to remain single, I own I should have been better satisfied; but if she must marry again, I know of no one, now living, and of a suitable age, to whom I would more willingly resign her than yourself, or who would be more likely to appreciate her worth and make her truly happy, as far as I can tell.'

Of course I was delighted with the compliment, and hoped to show her she was not mistaken in her favourable judgement.

'I have, however, one request to offer,' continued she. 'It seems I am still to look on Staningley as my home: I wish you to make it yours likewise, for Helen is attached to the place and to me – as I am to her. There are painful associations connected with Grassdale, which she cannot easily overcome; and I shall not molest you with my company or interference here: I am a very quiet person, and shall keep my own apartments and attend to my own concerns, and only see you now and then.'

Of course I most readily consented to this; and we lived in the greatest harmony with our dear aunt until the day of her death, which melancholy event took place a few years after – melancholy, not to herself (for it came quietly

upon her, and she was glad to reach her journey's end), but only to the few loving friends and grateful dependants she left behind.

To return, however, to my own affairs: I was married in summer, on a glorious August morning. It took the whole eight months, and all Helen's kindness and goodness to boot, to overcome my mother's prejudices against my bride elect, and to reconcile her to the idea of my leaving Linden-car and living so far away. Yet she was gratified at her son's good fortune after all, and proudly attributed it all to his own superior merits and endowments. I bequeathed the farm to Fergus, with better hopes of its prosperity than I should have had a year ago under similar circumstances; for he had lately fallen in love with the vicar of L——'s eldest daughter, a lady whose superiority had roused his latent virtues and stimulated him to the most surprising exertions, not only to gain her affection and esteem, and to obtain a fortune sufficient to enable him to aspire to her hand, but to render himself worthy of her, in his own eyes, as well as in those of her parents; and in the end he was successful, as you already know. As for myself? I need not tell you how happily my Helen and I have lived and loved together, and how blessed we still are in each other's society, and in the promising young scions that are growing up about us. We are just now looking forward to the advent of you and Rose, for the time of your annual visit draws nigh, when you must leave your dusty, smoky, noisy, toiling, striving city for a season of invigorating relaxation and social retirement with us.

Till then, farewell,

GILBERT MARKHAM

Staningley, June 10th, 1847